COMICS VALUES ANNUAL

2005 EDITION
THE COMIC BOOK PRICE GUIDE

by Alex G. Malloy

edited by Stuart W. Wells III

Preface: Robert J. Sodaro

©2005 By Alex G. Malloy & Stuart W. Wells III

Published by

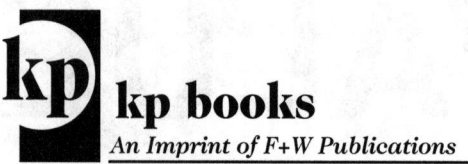

kp books

An Imprint of F+W Publications

700 East State Street • Iola, WI 54990-0001
715-445-2214 • 888-457-2873

Our toll-free number to place an order or obtain
a free catalog is (800) 258-0929.

Library of Congress Catalog Number: 1062-4503

ISBN: 0-87349-963-8

Designed by Stuart W. Wells III

Edited by Karen O'Brien

Printed in United States of America

CONTENTS

Preface 2005

By Alex G. Malloy, with Bob Sodaro

As we open this year's remarks, we can't help but feel that last year's improved economic conditions have significantly heated up the market for Golden Age comics, and increased demand for the middle-priced *Four-Color* and various TV-related comics. At the same time, the market is improving for 20-year-old comics that have been previously overlooked. Further, Golden- and Silver-related non-DC and Marvel books are also finding an audience and commanding higher prices.

This renewed interest in the Golden Age of comics has got to be at least partially inspired by Michael Chabon's award-winning book, *The Amazing Adventures of Kavalier and Clay* (Picador, 2001) which is now due to become a movie in the near future. In addition to Chabon's fabulous book, an article ran in *Heritage* about the nice Jewish boys (Jerry Siegel and Joe Schuster) who created Superman, as well as a wonderful series of articles that ran in *Reform Judaism* about the beginnings of our industry. The inspired multi-part article by Arie Kaplan goes into great details about how the comic-book industry was essentially invented by Jews who emigrated to the U.S. from Europe and Israel. We briefly met Kaplan who indicated that there was so much left out of the articles that he is considering writing a book. We wish him well in this endeavor, for—as our dear friend John "T.H.U.N.D.E.R. Agents" Carbonaro recently said to us, "We are losing guys like him nowadays," and these guys are a link to our collective past. Having said that, we can only note that as we write this article we have lost both Kelly Freas and, just the other day, Will Eisner. Documenting and collecting their past works can only benefit us all as an industry.

DC Highlights

Many of our readers feel that the DC event of the year is *Identity Crisis*. This seven-issue mini-series illustrates the vulnerability of super-heroes regarding their loved ones, and that super-heroes can make mistakes, too.

Readers were absorbed into this world through DC's ever-popular and always stellar cast. The Justice League of America must make real-world decisions, all of which turn DC's brightly lit world just a little darker. The death of a beloved spouse, Sue Dibny (wife of Elongated Man), is the driving force behind the story and sets the heroes a course of action to find the murderer while protecting their families.

I'm willing to admit that DC missed some opportunities to reflect on things. To me, the series feels like the company was trying to press everything possible plus a ham sandwich and a bag of chips into a seven-issue mini-series. Good, bad, or indifferent, they accomplished this and changed our views of the series' heroes and their world. They made us think about how Superman goes out to save the world while his wife, Lois Lane, is left vulnerable without his protection. (In his own comic book, Superman messes up on that but more on that later.) He and each hero must make hard choices and leave a loved one vulnerable. And in this Crisis series, when a second victim goes down, it ripples throughout the DC universe. Again, not a hero, but a loved family member is caught up in the story's crossfire.

Interestingly, the writers don't resolve the subplot of how to handle certain villains and even dissenting heroes. A fracture exists within the Justice League of America and has become a time bomb in the storylines of its major characters, individually and as a whole.

Speaking of major characters, Batman enjoyed an epic run for about two to three months in a saga in the "War Games" storyline. There was a great set-up, strong middle story, and action straight on through until the very loose (and unfortunately) unsatisfying end. It's like watching a good movie with solid plot, story, dialogue, and actors, and then asking yourself, "what on earth just happened?" at the conclusion. Still, it was a good story arc even though the writers negated much of its importance. *Identity Crisis* looms much larger on that scale.

A good deal of DC's success this year may be attributed to the "Jim Lee factor." Jim's a friend and an artist who almost became a doctor but went into comics. He used to do *X-Men*, watched those guys become a top-selling team, and then helped found the WildStorm area of Image Comics, before he transferred ownership over to DC. Jim was brought in to work on the "Hush" story arc for *Batman*. The story was solidly drawn and well written. Emotions ran high between villains and lovers, and comics fans seemed united in singing its praises. I'm sure this story line brought wandering readers back into the fold, as the high sales numbers for both *Batman* and comics overall would appear to indicate.

DC then gave Lee the assignment of drawing another of its icons—its biggest icon—The Man of Steel. Lee added fine artwork to a storyline revolving around an emotional rift in Superman's life. I doubt any were disappointed by this blend of Lee and Superman's attack of human frailty. His talks with a priest (who is battling cancer) bring in emotional questions on Superman's limits to help people, without resorting to the old "who's stronger?" routine. Here, Superman must confront his inability to help people—even his own wife. In this story arc, Lois goes missing along with a whole lot of other people, and Superman is struggling to discover what happened. But still, he is seemingly helpless and needs an outlet, his own priest, to vent/talk things out.

Again, Lee and writer Brian Azzarello brought Superman's sales to the top and brought in new readers. DC will put this, as it's already done with "Hush," into trade paperbacks to perpetuate his endeavors for many "new" readers ... and that is what the industry needed.

DC (along with Marvel) continued serving the high end of the market by reprinting the *Avengers/JLA* crossover in a hardback. The *DC Archives* series continued giving us fine collected works, including Steve Ditko on Captain Atom (*Action Hero Archives*), Jack Kirby and Wally Wood on Challengers of the Unknown, and brought Wally Wood's *T.H.U.N.D.E.R. Agents* (plus *Dynamo* and *Noman*) series closer to its conclusion of the complete series. Most of this material has not been reprinted for over 30 years. Thank you so much, Paul Levitz.

While many people overlook it, it remains strong and maintained by DC, a great fun book called *Mad* (originally a comic book, and now a magazine that just recently began to include ads in its pages). In DC's hands, the darn book may wind up outlasting us all.

Marvel Highlights

From the "House that Jack Built," Marvel's foray into the Ultimate universe is what this long-time Stan Lee fan can only call a bold move. Heroes and characters that have been set in stone for a generation are suddenly in flux. Nick Fury is a black man; Tony Stark needs a phalanx of technos to run the IT systems that power him as Iron Man; Thor is an arrogant jerk (who doesn't speak in Shakespearian English); and all super-heroes (not just mutants) are tracked by a very suspicious government (headed up by the aforementioned General Fury and his still high-tech S.H.I.E.L.D. forces).

Then, there's the matter of the company's very visible—and one could argue, most visible icon and corporate symbol—Spider-Man, that populist management would tell us must remain static, and never change because of licensing issues. Well that's another idea that should find its way into the circular file. Currently, Marvel is delivering at least five distinct versions (not merely variant flavors) of their company icon.

Classic Spidey: This is the version that was first introduced to us in *Amazing Fantasy #15*. We grew up with him and he currently appears primarily in *Amazing Spider-Man* and *Spectacular Spider-Man*, with side trips to many of the secondary and limited series starring our favorite arachnid.

Movie Spidey: We all saw this version in the theaters. (Bob Sodaro interviewed a 20-something woman in the theater before a showing of *Spider-Man 2* and asked why she was there. She replied that she loved Spidey, but acknowledged that she had never read a Spidey comic.)

Media Spidey: A subset of this group includes the stage show of Spidey as performed at Rockefeller Center and had Norman Osborn become the first Goblin. It also includes the 1970s television Spidey starring Nicholas Hammond, and the various animated Spideys—including the MTV CGI version that gave us an unusual melding of the Classic and Ultimate Spidey characters.

Ultimate Spidey: We talked about this earlier. This is the next (current?) generation's "With great power ..." mantra.

Spider-Girl: The daughter of the original Spider-Man in an on-going comic book picking up on a divergent point from a storyline in an alternate timeline as marvelously and entertainingly written by former Marvel editor-in-chief, and Spider-scribe Tom DeFalco (who wrote the original tale). This book naturally features dear old Spider-dad in a supporting (read: retired) role.

Marvel Age/Adventures Spidey: Classic Lee/Ditko Spider stories re-interpreted by today's top talent wherein the characters exist in some sort of limbo where they are drawn equally between Classic and modern-day molds.

Licensing Spidey: This is the one we hate the most (even Bob). It is Spider-Man boiled down to what the Marvel Marketing Dept. thinks that Joe Public is willing to digest, and then Spidey's mug is pasted on everything from videogames to toddler-friendly "Action Buddies," to plush pillow figures that include "Spider-Man's cousin Spider-Girl" (please let's move on here, and not get Bob started up again, shall we? Thanks so much.)

At any rate, there are currently so many separate and distinct versions of Spider-Man that this ought to finally prove that there are some concepts that are larger and more universal than their perceived image.

Comics Gone "Hollywood"

Finally, in an area that we always find interesting, there has been more Hollywood interest in comics this past year prompted by the phenomenal success of *Spider-Man 2* (which was hailed as the greatest comic-book movie of all times). As we all know, each successful comic-book film generates more interest in comics (both media and general population) and (hopefully) brings more people into comic-book shops around the country.

Anyway, other comic-book films of note (both good and bad) this past year included *Hellboy* (Dark Horse), *The Punisher* (Marvel), and *Catwoman* (DC); while comic-strip films brought us the inimitable *Garfield*. Even animated films are still enjoying a huge success with films like *Shrek 2*, *Shark Tale*, and *Yu-Gi-Oh! The Movie*. (Some of which were not only better received than others, but better made.) Still, the best of the bunch was Pixar's *The Incredibles*—which resident movie reviewer Bob Sodaro claims is not only the best of the bunch, but perhaps the second-best super-hero movie ever made. (Which falls into place right after *Spider-Man 2*, but knowing what a Spider-geek he is, we think that he's just a touch prejudiced.) And of course we can't pass up related films like the Dark Horse-inspired film *Alien vs. Predator*, as well as the beautifully rendered *Sky Captain and the World of Tomorrow*. In 2005, we are eagerly looking forward to both *Fantastic Four*, and *Batman Begins* among other comic-book fare.

Getting back to comic books, the independent market is really only OK, but mainstream super-heroes are still all the rage as both Marvel and DC continue to issue trade paperback collections of recent story arcs of popular series. This is good for the industry (if bad for the back-issue market) as it allows publishers to distribute their product to chain bookstore outlets like Borders, Barnes and Noble, and Amazon that don't normally carry regular comics. It also is a boon to casual readers who may have heard some good buzz about a series, but aren't interested (or simply can't) make weekly trips to their local comic shops (or perhaps even don't have a nearby local shop).

Still, as always, we are fans of comic books, and feel that anything that promotes the industry is ultimately good for us all. Once again we thank all our readers and publisher for keeping us in print, as well as all of the hard-working professionals that bring us the ongoing adventures of our favorite characters in our favorite medium.

Well, that's about it for us this time around. See you all in the funny papers!

....

*with a nod and a tip of the cowl to our good ol' bud John C.!

The fearless creators of this book have also written others. Among them are:
American Games by Alex G. Malloy (Krause, May 2000, ISBN 0-930615-60-9);
Kiddy Meal Collectibles by Robert J. Sodaro (Krause, ISBN 0-930625-16-1);
A Universe of Star Wars Collectibles, Identification and Price Guide, 2nd Edition,
by Stuart W. Wells III (Krause, July 2002, ISBN 0-87349-415-6),
all available from Krause (see the copyright page for website and catalog information).

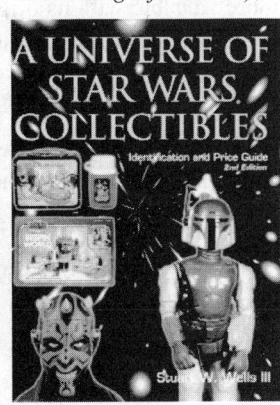

CVA GRADING GUIDE

In David Brin's science fiction–fantasy novel, *The Practice Effect*, things improve with use. You start with a crudely made tool and keep using it until it becomes a fine instrument. If our world worked that way, you could read your golden age comics as often as you liked and they would just get better looking each time. Unfortunately, our world does not work that way, and reading your comics (along with just about everything else) causes comics to deteriorate.

Even if you could protect your comics from external light, heat, cold, moisture, pressure and everything else, you couldn't protect them from their own paper. Most comic books were printed on pulp paper, which has a high acid content. This means that the paper slowly turns brittle with age, no matter what you do to it, short of special museum-style preservation.

Very old, well-preserved comics are coveted collector's items. In most cases, people did not save their comic books for future generations. They read them and discarded them. Comic books were considered harmless ephemera for children. When these children outgrew their comics, their parents often threw them away. If everybody kept all of their comics, comics would not be valuable because everybody would have them scattered about the house!

The value of any comic depends on scarcity, popularity and condition. Scarcity increases with age and popularity depends on the whim of the public — only condition automatically decreases with age. Newer comics are generally available in near-mint condition, so newer comics in lesser condition have little collector potential. However, older comics are scarce, so they are still collectible in less than near-mint condition, but the value is obviously less. This is a basic tenet of all collectibles. A car is more valuable with its original paint. A baseball card is more valuable if it has not been marred by bicycle spokes. Coke bottles, stamps, coins, and toys in good condition are all more valuable than their abused counterparts. Comic books are no exception.

New comic book collectors should learn how to assess the prospective value of a comic in order to protect themselves from being fleeced by unscrupulous dealers or hucksters. Yet, a majority of dealers, especially store owners, can be considered reliable judges of comic grade. Because comic retail may be their primary source of income, certain dealers are particularly adept at noticing comic book imperfections, especially in issues they intend to purchase. As such, hobbyists and collectors must understand that dealers need to make a minimum profit on their investments. Buying collectible comics entails certain risks. Therefore, dealers must scrutinize a comic to determine if the particular book will stand a chance of resale. Well-preserved comics are invariably more desirable to dealers because they are more desirable to collectors.

There are eight standard comic grades: mint, near mint, very fine, fine, very good, good, fair, and poor. Clearly, these eight grades could be split into even finer categories when haggling over an exceptionally rare or coveted Golden Age comic. In most cases, however, comic books can be evaluated using these eight standard grades. The values listed in *Comics Values Annual* are all for comics in "Near Mint" condition. The grading/price chart given at the back of this book should be used to adjust this price for comics in different grades.

Mint

Finding new comics in true mint condition can be difficult. Finding old comics in mint condition is almost impossible. Mint condition comics usually fetch prices higher than price guide listings. Mint comics can sell for 120% or more of *Comics Values Annual* listed prices. The reason for this is the strict criteria reserved for mint comics.

Mint comics are perfect comics and allow no room for imperfections. Pages and covers must be free of discoloration, wear, and wrinkles. A mint comic is one that looks like it just rolled off the press. Staples and spine must meet perfectly without cover "rollover." The cover must be crisp, bright, and trimmed perfectly. The staples must not be rusted and the cover should not have any visible creases.

The interior pages of a mint comic are equally crisp and new. A mint comic must not show any signs of age or decay. Because of the paper stock used on many older comics, acid and oxygen cause interior pages to yellow and flake. It is much harder to find pre-1970 mint comics because of inferior storage techniques and materials. In the early days of collecting, few people anticipated that the very boxes and bags in which they stored their comics were contributing to decay. Acid from bags, backing boards, and boxes ate away at many comics.

Near Mint

A near mint comic and a mint comic are close siblings, with their differences slight, even to an experienced eye. Most of the new comics on the shelf of the local comic shop are in near mint condition. These are comics that have been handled gingerly to preserve the original luster of the book.

Near mint comics are bright, clean copies with no major or minor defects. Slight stress lines near the staples and perhaps a very minor printing defect are permissible. Corners must still be sharp and devoid of creases. Interior pages of newsprint stock should show almost no discernible yellowing. Near mint comics usually trade for 100% of the suggested *Comics Values Annual* listed prices.

Very Fine

A very fine comic is one that is routinely found on the shelves and back issue bins of most good direct market comic shops. This grade comic has few defects, none of them major. Stress around the staples of a very fine comic are visible but not yet radical enough to create wrinkles. Both the cover and interior pages should still be crisp and sharp, devoid of flaking and creases. Interior pages may be slightly yellowed from age.

Most high-quality older comics graded as very fine can obtain 80-90% of *Comics Values Annual* listed prices. Newer comics graded as very fine get about 70-85% because many near mint copies probably exist. Despite that, very fine comics are desirable for most collectors.

Fine

Fine comics are often issues that may have been stored carefully under a bed or on a shelf by a meticulous collector. This grade of comic is also very desirable because it shows little wear and retains much of its original sharpness. The cover may be slightly off center from rollover. The cover retains less of its original gloss and may even possess a chip or wrinkle. The corners should be sharp but may also have a slight crease. Yellowing begins to creep into the interior pages of a comic graded as fine.

Fine comics are respectable additions to collections and sell for about 40-60% of the listed prices.

Very Good

A very good comic may have been an issue passed around or read frequently. This grade is the common condition of older books. Its cover will probably have lost some luster and may have two or three creases around the staples or edges. The corners of the book may begin to show the beginnings of minor rounding and chipping, but it is by no means a damaged or defaced comic. Comics in very good condition sell for about 30-40% of *Comics Values Annual* listed prices.

Good

A good comic is one that has been well read and is beginning to show its age. Although both front and back covers are still attached, a good grade comic may have a number of serious wrinkles and chips. The corners and edges of this grade comic may show clear signs of rounding and flaking. There should be no major tears in a good comic nor should any pages be clipped out or missing. Interior pages may be fairly yellowed and brittle. Good comics sell for about 15-25% of the *Comics Values Annual* listed prices.

Fair

A fair comic is one that has definitely seen better days and has considerably limited resale value for most collectors. This comic may be soiled and damaged on the cover and interior. Fair comics should be completely intact and may only be useful as a comic to lend to friends. Fair comics sell for about 10-20% of the *Comics Values Annual* listed prices.

Poor

Comics in poor condition are generally unsuitable for collecting or reading because they range from damaged to unrecognizable. Poor comics may have been water damaged, attacked by a small child, or worse, perhaps, gnawed on by the family pet! Interior and exterior pages may be cut apart or missing entirely. A poor comic sells for about 5-15% of the *Comics Values Annual* listed price.

Sniffing Out Grades

Despite everything that is mentioned about comic grading, the process remains relative to the situation. A comic that seems to be in very good condition may actually be a restored copy. A restored copy is generally considered to be in between the grade it was previous to restoration and the grade it has become. Many collectors avoid restored comics entirely.

Each collector builds his collection around what he believes is important. Some want every issue of a particular series or company. Others want every issue of a favorite artist or writer. Because of this, many collectors will purchase lower-grade comics to fill out a series or to try out a new series. Mint and near mint comics are usually much more desirable to hard-core collectors. Hobbyists and readers may find the effort and cost of collecting only high-grade comics financially prohibitive.

Getting artists or writers to autograph comics has also become a source of major dispute. Some collectors enjoy signed comics and others consider those very comics defaced! The current trends indicate that most collectors do enjoy signed comics. A signature does not usually change the grade of the comic.

As mentioned, comic grading is a subjective process that must be agreed upon by the buyer and seller. Buyers will often be quick to note minor defects in order to negotiate a better price. Sellers are sometimes selectively blind to their comic's defects. *Comics Values Annual:200*5 provides this grading guide as a protection for both parties.

Name	Abbreviation
Abel, Jack	JA
Abell, Dusty	DAb
Abnett, Dan.	DAn
Abrams, Paul	PlA
Adams, Art	AAd
Adams, Neal	NA
Addeo, Stephen	StA
Adkins, Dan	DA
Adlard, Charlie	CAd
Albano, John	JAo
Albrecht, Jeff	JAl
Alcala, Alfredo	AA
Alcazar, Vincent	VAz
Alexander, Chris	CAx
Alibaster, Jo	JoA
Allred, Michael	MiA
Alstaetter, Karl	KlA
Althorp, Brian	BAp
Amaro, Gary	GyA
Amendola, Sal	Sal
Ammerman, David	DvA
Anderson, Bill	BAn
Anderson, Brent	BA
Anderson, Murphy	MA
Andriola, Alfred	AlA
Andru, Ross	RA
Aparo, Jim	JAp
Aragones, Sergio	SA
Arcudi, John	JAr
Artis, Tom	TAr
Ashe, Edd	EA
Asamiya	KiA
Augustyn, Brian	BAu
Austin, Terry	TA
Avison, Al	AAv
Ayers, Dick	DAy
Bachalo, Chris	**CBa**
Badger, Mark	MBg
Bagley, Mark	MBa
Baikie, Jim	JBa
Bailey, Bernard	BBa
Bair, Michael	MlB
Baker, Kyle	KB
Baker, Matt	MB
Balent, Jim	JBa
Banks, Darryl	DBk
Barks, Carl	CB
Baron, Mike	MBn
Barr, Mike	MiB
Barras, John	DBs
Barreiro, Mike	MkB
Barreto, Ed	EB
Barry, Dan	DBa
Batista, Chris	CsB
Battlefield, D.	DB
Beatty, John	JhB
Beatty, Terry	TBe
Beauvais, Denis	DB
Beeston, John	JBe
Belardinelli, M.	MBe
Bell, Bob Boze	BBB
Bell, George	GBl
Bell, Julie	JuB
Benefiel, Scott	ScB
Benes, Ed	EBe
Benitez, Joe	JBz
Benjamin, Ryan	RBn
Bennett, Joe	JoB
Bennett, Richard	RiB
Benson, Scott	StB
Berger, Charles	ChB
Bernado, Ramon	RBe
Bernstein, Robert	RbB
Bierbaum, Mary	MBm
Bierbaum, Tom	TBm
Biggs, Geoffrey	GB
Binder, Jack	JaB
Bingham, Jerry	JBi
Birch, JJ	JJB
Biro, Charles	CBi
Bisley, Simon	SBs
Bissette, Stephen	SBi
Blaisdell, Tex	TeB
Blasco, Jesus	JBl
Blevins, Bret	BBl
Blum, Alex	AB
Bode, Vaughn	VB
Bogdanove, Jon	JBg
Bolland, Brian	BB
Bolle, Frank	FBe
Boller, David	DdB
Bolton, John	JBo
Bond, Philip	PBd
Booth, Brett	BBh
Boring, Wayne	WB
Bossart, William	WmB
Boxell, Tim	TB
Bradstreet, Tim	TBd
Braithwaite, Doug.	DBw
Brasfield, Craig	CrB
Braun, Russell	RsB
Breeding, Brett	BBr
Brereton, Daniel	DlB
Brewster, Ann	ABr
Breyfogle, Norm	NBy
Bridwell, E. Nelson	ENB
Briefer, Dick	DBr
Bright, Mark	MBr
Brigman, June	JBr
Broderick, Pat	PB
Brodsky, Allyn	AyB
Broom, John	JBm
Broome, Matt	MtB
Brothers, Hernandez	HB
Brown, Bob	BbB
Browne, Dick	DkB
Brunner, Frank	FB
Bryant, Rick	RkB
Buckingham, Mark	MBu
Buckler, Rich	RB
Budget, Greg	GBu
Bugro, Carl	CBu
Bulanadi, Danny	DBl
Burchett, Rick	RBr
Burgard, Tim	TmB
Burke, Fred	FBk
Burns, John	JBn
Burns, Robert	RBu
Burroughs, W.	WBu
Buscema, John	JB
Buscema, Sal	SB
Busiek, Kurt	KBk
Butler, Jeff	JBt
Butler, Steve	SBt
Buzz	Buzz
Byrd, Mitch	MBy
Byrne, John	JBy
Calafiore, Jim	**JCf**
Caldes, Charles	CCa
Callahan, Jim	JiC
Calnan, John	JCa
Cameron, Don	DCn
Cameron, Lou	LC
Campbell, Eddie	ECa
Campbell, J. Scott	JSC
Campbell, Stan	StC
Campenella, Robert	RbC
Campos, Marc	MCa
Capullo, Greg	GCa
Cardy, Nick	NC
Carey, Mike	MCy
Cariello, Sergio	SCi
Carlin, Mike	MCr
Carpenter, Brent D.	BDC
Carralero, Ricky	RCl
Carrasco, Dario	DoC
Carter, Joe	JCt
Case, Richard	RCa
Casey, Joe	JoC
Castellaneta, Dan.	DaC
Castellini, Claudio	CCt
Castrillo, Anthony	ACa
Chadwick, Paul	PC
Chan, Ernie	ECh
Chang, Bernard	BCh
Charest, Travis	TC
Chase, Bobbie	BCe
Chaykin, Howard	HC
Check, Sid	SC
Chen, Mike	MCh
Chen, Sean	SCh
Chestney, Lillian	LCh
Chiarello, Mark	MCo
Chichester, D.G.	DGC
Chiodo, Joe	JCh
Choi, Brandon	BCi
Chriscross	Ccs
Christopher, Tom	TmC
Chua, Ernie	Chu
Chun, Anthony	ACh
Churchhill, Ian	IaC
Cirocco, Frank	FC
Citron, Sam	SmC
Claremont, Chris	CCl
Clark, Mike	MCl
Clark, Scott	ScC
Cockrum, Dave	DC
Cohn, Gary	GCh
Coker, Tomm	TCk
Colan, Gene	GC
Colby, Simon	SCy
Cole, Jack	JCo
Cole, Leonard B.	LbC
Colletta, Vince	ViC
Collins, Max Allan.	MCn
Collins, Mike	MC
Collins, Nancy	NyC
Colon, Ernie	EC
Conner, Amanda	ACo
Conway, Gerry	GyC
Cooper, Dave	DvC
Cooper, John	JCp
Corben, Richard	RCo
Costanza, Peter	PrC
Cowan, Denys	DCw
Cox, Jeromy	JCx
Craig, Johnny	JCr
Crandall, Reed	RC
Crespo, Steve	SCr
Crilley, Mark	MCi
Crumb, Robert	RCr
Cruz, E. R.	ERC
Cruz, Jerry	JCz
Cruz, Roger	RCz
Culdera, Chuck	CCu
Cullins, Paris	PCu
Currie, Andrew	ACe
Damaggio, Rodolfo	**RDm**
Daniel, Tony	TnD
Danner, Paul	PuD
Darrow, Geof	GfD
David, Peter	PDd
Davis, Alan	AD
Davis, Dan	DDv
Davis, Guy	GyD
Davis, Jack	JDa
Davis, Malcolm.	MDa
Davison, Al	ADv
Day, Dan	Day
Day, Gene	GD
DeFalco, Tom	TDF
Deitch, Kim	KDe
Delano, Jamie	JaD
DeLaRosa, Sam.	SDR
Delgado, Richard	RdD
Dell, John	JhD
DeMatteis, J. M.	JMD
DeMulder, Kim.	KDM
Deodato, Jr., Mike	MD2
Derenick, Tom	TDr
DeZago, Todd	TDz
DeZuniga, M.	MDb
DeZuniga, Tony	TD
Diaz, Paco	PaD
Dillin, Dick	DD
Dillon, Glyn	GlD
Dillon, Steve	SDi
Dini, Paul	PDi
Ditko, Steve	SD
Dixon, Chuck	CDi
Dixon, John	JDx
Dobbyn, Nigel	ND
Dodson, Terry	TyD
Doherty, Peter	PD
Dominguez, Luis	LDz
Doran, Colleen	CDo
Dorey, Mike	MDo
Dorkin, Evan	EDo
Dorman, Dave	DvD
Doucet, Julie	JDo
Drake, Stan	SDr
Dresser, Larry	LDr
Dringenberg, Mike	MDr
Drucker, Mort	MD
DuBerkr, Randy	RDB
Duffy, Jo	JDy
Dumm, Gary	GDu
Dunn, Ben	BDn
Duranona, Leo	LDu
Duursema, Jan	JD
Dwyer, Kieron	KD
Eastman, Kevin	**KEa**
Eaton, Scott	SEa
Edginton, Ian	IEd
Edlund, Ben	BEd
Egeland, Marty	MEg
Eisner, Will	WE
Elder, Bill	BE
Eldred, Tim	TEl
Elias, Lee	LE
Elliot, D.	DE
Ellis, Warren	WEl
Ellison, Harlan	HaE
Emberlin, Randy	RyE

Name	Abbr.	Name	Abbr.	Name	Abbr.	Name	Abbr.
Englehart, Steve	SEt	Goodman, Till	TGo	Hobbs, Bill	BlH	Kolins, Scott	ScK
Ennis, Garth	GEn	Goodwin, Archie	AGw	Hoberg, Rick	RHo	Krause, Peter	PKr
Epting, Steve	SEp	Gordon, Al	AG	Hoffer, Mike	MkH	Krenkel, Roy	RKu
Erskine, Gary	GEr	Gottfredson, Floyd	FG	Hogarth, Burne	BHg	Krigstein, Bernie	BK
Erwin, Steve	StE	Gould, Chester	ChG	Holcomb, Art	AHo	Kristiansen, Teddy H.	TKr
Esposito, Mike	ME	Grant, Alan	AlG	Holdredge, John	JHo	Kruse, Brandon	BKr
Estes, John	JEs	Grant, Steve	StG	Hoover, Dave	DHv	Kubert, Adam	AKu
Estrada, Ric	RE	Grau, Peter	PGr	Hopgood, Kevin	KHd	Kubert, Andy	NKu
Evans, George	GE	Gray, Mick	MGy	Horie, Richard	RHe	Kubert, Joe	JKu
Everett, Bill	BEv	Green, Dan	DGr	Hotz, Kyle	KHt	Kupperberg, Paul	PuK
Ewins, Brett	BEw	Green, Randy	RGr	Howarth, Matt.	MHo	Kurtzman, Harvey.	HK
Ezquerra, Carlos	CE	Greene, Sid	SGe	Howell, Rich	RHo	Kwitney, Alisa	AaK
Fabry, Glenn	**GF**	Grell, Mike	MGr	Hudnall, James	JHl	**LaBan, Terry**	**TLa**
Fago, Al	AFa	Griffith, Bill	BG	Hughes, Adam	AH	Lago, Ray	RyL
Farmer, Mark	MFm	Griffiths, Martin	MGs	Hund, Dave	DeH	Laird, Peter	PLa
Fegredo, Duncan	DFg	Grindberg, Tom	TGb	Hunt, Chad	CH	Lanning, Andy	ALa
Feldstein, Al	AF	Gross, Daerick	DkG	**Immonen, Stuart**	**SI**	Lansdale, Joe	JLd
Ferry, Pascual	PFe	Gross, Peter	PrG	Infantino, Carmine	CI	Lapham, Dave	DL
Fine, Lou	LF	Grossman, R.	RGs	Ingles, Graham	GrI	Lark, Michael	MLr
Fingeroth, Danny	DFr	Gruenwald, Mark	MGu	Iorio, Medio	MI	Larkin, Bob	BLr
Finnocchiaro, Sal	SF	Grummett, Tom	TG	Isherwood, Geoff	GI	LaRocque, Greg	GrL
Fleisher, Michael	MFl	Guardineer, Frank.	FG	Ivie, Larry	LI	Larroca, Salvador	SvL
Fleming, Robert	RFl	Guay, Rebecca	RGu	Ivy, Chris.	CIv	Larsen, Erik	EL
Flemming, Homer	HFl	Guice, Jackson	JG	**Jackson, Julius**	**JJn**	Lash, Batton	BLs
Foreman, Dick	DiF	Guichet, Yvel	YG	Jaffee, Al	AJ	Lashley, Ken	KeL
Forte, John	JF	Guinan, Paul	PGn	Janke, Dennis	DJa	Lavery, Jim	JLv
Forton, Gerald	GFo	Gulacy, Paul	PG	Janson, Klaus	KJ	Lawlis, Dan	DLw
Fosco, Frank	FFo	Gustovich, Mike	MG	Javinen, Kirk	KJa	Lawrence, Terral	TLw
Foster, Alan Dean	ADF	**Ha, Gene**	**GeH**	Jenkins, Paul	PJe	Lawson, Jim	JmL
Fox, Gardner	GaF	Haley, Matt	MHy	Jenney, Robert	RJ	Layton, Bob	BL
Fox, Gill	GFx	Hall, Bob	BH	Jensen, Dennis	DJ	Leach, Garry	GL
Fox, Matt	MF	Halsted, Ted	TeH	Jimenez, Leonardo	LJi	Leach, Rick	RkL
Fraga, Dan	DaF	Hama, Larry	LHa	Jimminiz, Phil	PJ	Lee, Elaine	ELe
Franchesco	Fso	Hamilton, Tim	TH	Johnson, Dave	DvJ	Lee, Jae	JaL
Frank, Gary	GFr	Hamner, Cully	CHm	Johnson, Jeff	JJ	Lee, Jim	JLe
Frazetta, Frank	FF	Hampton, Bo	BHa	Johnson, Paul	PuJ	Lee, Patrick	PtL
Freeman, John	JFr	Hampton, Scott	SHp	Johnson, Todd	TJn	Lee, Scott	ScL
Freeman, Simon	SFr	Hanna, Scott	SHa	Jones, Casey	CJ	Lee, Stan	StL
Frenz, Ron	RF	Hannigan, Ed	EH	Jones, Gerard	GJ	Leeke, Mike	MLe
Friedman, Michael Jan	MFr	Hanson, Neil	NHa	Jones, J.B.	JJo	Leialoha, Steve	SL
Friedrich, Mike	MkF	Harras, Bob	BHs	Jones, Jeff	JeJ	Leon, John Paul	JPL
Frolechlich, A.	AgF	Harris, N. Steven	NSH	Jones, Kelley	KJo	Leonardi, Rick	RL
Fry III, James	JFy	Harris, Tim	THa	Jones, Malcolm.	MJ	Levins, Rik	RLe
Fujitani(Fuje), Bob	BF	Harris, Tony	TyH	Jones, R.A.	RAJ	Lieber, Larry	LLi
Furman, Simon	SFu	Harrison, Lou	LuH	Jones, Robert	RJn	Liefeld, Rob	RLd
Gaiman, Neil	**NGa**	Harrison, Simon	SHn	Jurgens, Dan	DJu	Lightle, Steve	SLi
Galan, Manny	MaG	Hart, Ernest	EhH	Jusko, Joe	JJu	Lim, Ron	RLm
Gallant, Shannon	ShG	Hartsoe, Everette	EHr	**Kaluta, Mike**	**MK**	Linsner, Joseph M.	JLi
Gammill, Kerry	KGa	Hathaway, Kurt	KtH	Kamen, Jack	JKa	Livingstone, R.	RLv
Garcia, Dave	DaG	Hawkins, Matt	MHw	Kaminski, Len	LKa	Lloyd, David	DvL
Garner, Alex	AGo	Hayes, Drew	DHa	Kane & Romita	K&R	Lobdell, Scott	SLo
Garney, Ron	RG	Haynes, Hugh	HH	Kane, Bob	Bka	Locke, Vince	VcL
Garzon, Carlos	CG	Hazlewood, Douglas.	DHz	Kane, Gil	GK	Loeb, Jeph	JLb
Gascoine, Phil	PGa	Heath, Russ	RH	Kanigher, Bob	BbK	Lopez, Jose	JL
Gaudino, Stefano	SGa	Hebbard, Robert	RtH	Kaniuga, Trent	TKn	Lopresti, Aaron	AaL
Gaughan, Jack	JGa	Heck, Don	DH	Karounos, Paris T.	PaK	Louapre, Dave	DLp
Gecko, Gabe	GG	Heisler, Mike	MHs	Katz, Jack	JKz	Lowe, John	Low
Geggan	Ggn	Hempel, Mark	MaH	Kavanagh, Terry	TKa	Lubbers, Bob	BLb
Gerard, Ruben	RGd	Henry, Flint	FH	Kelly, Walt	WK	Lustbader, Eric Van	ELu
Gerber, Steve	SvG	Herman, Jack	JH	Kennedy, Cam	CK	Luzniak, Greg	GLz
Giacoia, Frank	FrG	Hernandez, Gilbert	GHe	Keown, Dale	DK	Luzniak, Tom	TL
Giarrano, Vince	VGi	Hernandez, Jaime	JHr	Kerschl, Karl	KlK	**Macchio, Ralph**	**RMc**
Gibbons, Dave	DGb	Herrera,Ben	BHr	Kesel, Babara	BKs	Mack, David	DMk
Gibson, Ian	IG	Hester, Phil	PhH	Kesel, Karl	KK	Mackie, Howard	HMe
Giella, Joe	JoG	Hewlett, Jamie	JHw	Kieth, Sam	SK	Madan, Dev	DeM
Giffen, Keith	KG	Hibbard, E.E.	EHi	King, Hannibal	HbK	Madureira, Joe	JMd
Gilbert, Michael T.	MGi	Hicklenton, John	JHk	Kinsler, Everett R.	EK	Maggin, Elliot S.	ESM
Giordano, Dick	DG	Higgins, Graham	GHi	Kirby, Jack	JK	Maguire, Kevin	KM
Glanzman, Sam	SG	Higgins, John	JHi	Kisnino, Yukito	YuK	Magyar, Rick	RM
Golden, Michael	MGo	Higgins, Michael	MHi	Kitson, Barry	BKi	Mahlstedt, Larry	LMa
Gonzalez, Jorge	JGz	Hitch, Bryan	BHi	Kobasic, Kevin	KoK	Mahnke, Doug	DoM

Name	Abbr.
Mandrake, Tom	TMd
Maneely, Joe	JMn
Manley, Mike	MM
Mann, Roland	RMn
Mann, Roland	Man
Manning, Russ	RsM
Marais, Raymond	RdM
Mariotte, Jeff	JMi
Maroto, Esteban	EM
Marrinan, Chris	ChM
Marrs, Lee	LMr
Martin, Gary	GyM
Martin, Joe	JMt
Martinbrough, Shawn	SMa
Martinez, Henry	HMz
Martinez, Roy Allan	RMr
Marz, Ron	RMz
Marzan, Jose	JMz
Mason, Tom	TMs
Massengill, Nathan	NMa
Matsuda, Jeff	JMs
Mattsson, Steve	SMt
Maus, Bill	BMs
Mayer, Sheldon	ShM
Mayerik, Val	VMk
Mazzucchelli, David	DM
McCarthy, Brendon	BMy
McCloud, Scott	SMl
McCorkindale, B	BMC
McCraw, Tom	TMw
McCrea, John	JMC
McDaniel, Scott	SMc
McDaniel, Walter	WMc
McDonnell, Luke	LMc
McDuffie, Dwayne	DMD
McFarlane, Todd	TM
McGregor, Don	DMG
McKean, Dave	DMc
McKeever, Ted	TMK
McKenna, Mike	MkK
McKie, Angus	AMK
McKone, Mike	MMK
McLaughlin, Frank	FMc
McLaughlin, Sean	SML
McLeod, Bob	BMc
McMahon, M.	MMc
McManus, Shawn	SwM
McWilliams, Al	AMc
Medina, Angel	AMe
Medley, Linda	LiM
Mercadoocasio, H.	HMo
Meskin, Mort	MMe
Messmer, Otto	OM
Messner-Loebs, Bill	BML
Michelinie, David	DvM
Miehm, Grant	GtM
Mighten, Duke	DMn
Mignola, Michael	MMi
Miki, Danny	DaM
Milgrom, Al	AM
Millar, Mark	MMr
Miller, Frank	FM
Miller, Mike S.	MsM
Miller, Steve	SM
Milligan, Peter	PrM
Mills, Pat	PMs
Minor, Jason	JnM
Mitchel, Barry	BM
Moder, Lee	LMd
Moebius	Moe
Moeller, Chris	CsM
Moench, Doug	DgM
Montano, Steve	SeM
Mooney, Jim	JM
Moore, Alan	AMo
Moore, Jeff	JMr
Moore, Jerome	JeM
Moore, John Francis	JFM
Moore, Terry	TMr
Morales, Rags	RgM
Moretti, Mark	MMo
Morgan, Tom	TMo
Morisi, Pete	PMo
Morosco, Vincent	VMo
Morrison, Grant	GMo
Morrow, Gray	GM
Mortimer, Win	WMo
Motter, Dean	DMt
Moy, Jeffrey	JMy
Murray, Brian	BrM
Musial, Joe	JoM
Muth, Jon J.	JMu
Mychaels, Marat	MMy
Naifeh, Ted	**TNa**
Napolitano, Nick	NNa
Napton, Bob	BNa
Nauck, Todd	TNu
Neary, Paul	PNe
Nebres, Rudy	RN
Nelson	Nel
Netzer, Mike	MN
Newton, Don	DN
Nguyen, Hoang	HNg
Nichols, Art	ANi
Nicieza, Fabian	FaN
Nino, Alex	AN
Nocenti, Ann	ANo
Nocon, Cedric	CNn
Nodell, Martin	MnN
Nolan, Graham	GN
Nord, Cary	CNr
Norem, Earl	EN
Nostrand, Howard	HN
Novick, Irv	IN
Nowlan, Kevin	KN
Nutman, Philip	PNu
O'Barr, James	**JOb**
O'Neil, Denny	DON
O'Neill, Kevin	KON
Olbrich, Dave	DO
Olivetti, Ariel	AOl
Olliffe, Patrick	PO
One, Dark	DOe
Ordway, Jerry	JOy
Orlando, Joe	JO
Ortiz, Jose	JOt
Oskner, Bob	BO
Ostrander, John	JOs
Owen, James	JOn
Ozkan, Tayyar	TOz
Pace, Richard	**RPc**
Pacella, Mark	MPa
Pacheco, Carlos	CPa
Palais, Rudy	RP
Palmer, Tom	TP
Palmiotti, Jimmy	JP
Pamai, Gene	GPi
Panalign, Noly	NPl
Paniccia, Mark	MPc
Panosian, Dan	DPs
Parkhouse, Annie	APh
Parkhouse, Steve	SvP
Parobeck, Mike	MeP
Pascoe, James	JmP
Pasko, Martin	MPk
Patterson, Bruce	BrP
Pearson, Jason	JPn
Pelletier, Paul	PaP
Pence, Eric	ErP
Pennington, Mark	MPn
Pensa, Shea Anton	SAP
Perez, George	GP
Perham, James	JPh
Perlin, Don	DP
Perryman, Edmund	EP
Peterson, Brandon	BPe
Peterson, Jonathan	JPe
Petrucha, Stefan	SPr
Peyer, Tom	TPe
Phillips, Joe	JoP
Phillips, Scott	SPl
Phillips, Sean	SeP
Pini, Richard	RPi
Pini, Wendy	WP
Platt, Stephen	SPa
Pleece, Warren	WaP
Ploog, Mike	MP
Plunkett, Kilian	KPl
Pollack, Rachel	RaP
Pollard, Keith	KP
Pollina, Adam	AdP
Pope, Paul	PPo
Porch, David	DPo
Portacio, Whilce	WPo
Porter, Howard	HPo
Post, Howard	HwP
Potts, Carl	CP
Powell, Bob	BP
Power, Dermot	DPw
Pratt, George	GgP
Priest, Christopher	CPr
Prosser, Jerry	JeP
Pugh, Steve	StP
Pulido, Brian	BnP
Queen, Randy	**RQu**
Quesada, Joe	JQ
Quinn, David	DQ
Quinones, Peter	PQ
Raab, Ben	**BRa**
Raboy, Mac	MRa
Ramos, Humberto	HuR
Ramos, Rodney	RyR
Randall, Ron	RoR
Raney, Tom	TR
Rankin, Rich	RRa
Rapmund, Norm	NRd
Raymond, Alex	AR
Redondo, Nestor	NR
Reed, David	DvR
Reeves-Stevens, Judith	JRv
Reinhold, Bill	BR
Richards, Ted	TR
Richardson, Mike	MRi
Ricketts, Mark	MRc
Rico, Don	DRi
Ridgeway, John	JRy
Rieber, John Ney	JNR
Riley, John	JnR
Riply	Rip
Robbins, Frank	FR
Robbins, Trina	TrR
Robertson, Darrick	DaR
Robinson, James	JeR
Rodier, Denis	DRo
Rogers, Marshall	MR
Romita, John	JR
Romita, John Jr.	JR2
Rosenberger, J.	JRo
Ross, Alex	AxR
Ross, David	DR
Ross, John	JRs
Ross, Luke	LRs
Roth, Werner	WR
Royle, Jim	JRl
Royle, John	JRe
Rozum, John	JRz
Rubi, Melvin	MvR
Rubinstein, Joe	JRu
Rude, Steve	SR
Ruffner, Sean	SRf
Russell, P. Craig	CR
Russell, Vince	VRu
Ryan, Matt	MRy
Ryan, Paul	PR
Ryder, Tom	TmR
Sakakibara, Mizuki	MiS
Sakai, Stan	SS
Sale, Tim	TSe
Salmons, Tony	TSa
Saltares, Javier	JS
Sanders, Jim III	JS3
Sasso, Mark	MSo
Saviuk, Alex	AS
Schaffenberger, Kurt	KS
Schane, Tristan	TnS
Schiller, Fred	FdS
Schmitz, Mark	MaS
Schultz, Mark	MSh
Scoffield, Sean	SSc
Scott, Jeffery	JSc
Scott, Trevor	TvS
Seagle, Steven T.	SSe
Sears, Bart	BS
Sekowsky, Mike	MSy
Semeiks, Val	VS
Senior, Geoff	GSr
Serpe, Jerry	JyS
Severin, John	JSe
Shamray, Gerry	GSh
Shanower, Eric	EiS
Sharp, Liam	LSh
Shaw, Sean	SSh
Sherman, Jim	JSh
Shoemaker, Terry	TSr
Shooter, Jim	JiS
Shum, Howard	HSm
Shuster, Joe	JoS
Sibal, Jonathan	JSb
Siegel & Shuster	S&S
Sienkiewicz, Bill	BSz
Silvestri, Eric	EcS
Silvestri, Mark	MS
Sim, Dave	DS
Simon & Kirby	S&K
Simon, Joe	JSm
Simonson, Louise	LSi
Simonson, Walt	WS
Simpson, Don	DSs
Simpson, Howard	HSn
Simpson, Will	WSm
Sinnott, Joe	JSt
Skroce, Steve	SSr
Smith, Andy	ASm
Smith, Barry W.	BWS

Smith, Beau . . . . BSt	Sweetman, Dan . . . . . DSw	Vance, Steve . . . . SVa	Williams, David . . . . . DdW
Smith, Cam. . . . . CaS	**Taggart, Tom . . . . TTg**	VanHook, Kevin . . . . . KVH	Williams, J.H. . . . . JWi
Smith, Jeff. . . . . JSi	Takenaga, Francis . . . . FTa	Vargas, Vagner VV	Williams, Keith . . . . . . KWi
Smith, John . . . . JnS	Takezaki, Tony . . . . ToT	Veitch, Rick. . . . . RV	Williams, Kent . . . . KW
Smith, Kevin. . . . . . . KSm	Talbot, Bryan. . . . . BT	Velez, Ivan, Jr. IV	Williams, Scott . . . . . . SW
Smith, Malcolm . . . . . MSt	Tallarico, Tony . . . . TyT	Velluto, Sal . . . . SaV	Williamson, Al. . . . . . . AW
Smith, Paul . . . . PS	Tan, Billy . . . . BTn	Vess, Charles CV	Williamson, Skip . . . . SWi
Smith, Robin . . . . . . RSm	Tanaka, Masashi. . . . . MTk	Vey, Al . . . . AV	Willingham, Bill . . . . . BWg
Smith, Ron . . . . RS	Tanghal, Romeo . . . . . RT	Vigil, Tim . . . . TV	Willis, Damon. . . . . . . DaW
Snejbjerg, Peter . . . . . . PSj	Tappin, Steve . . . . SeT	Vokes, Neil . . . . NV	Wilshire, Mary . . . . . . MW
Sniegoski, Tom . . . . . . TSg	Taylor, David . . . . DTy	Von Eeden, Trevor . . . TVE	Wilson, Colin. . . . . . . CWi
Spark . . . . Spk	Taylor, R.G. . . . . RGT	Vosburg, Mike . . . . MV	Wilson, Gahan. . . . . . . GW
Sparling, Jack . . . . . . JkS	Templeton, Ty . . . . . . TTn	**Wagner, Matt . . . . . . MWg**	Wilson, Keith S. . . . . . KSW
Spiegelman, Art. . . . . . ASp	Teney, Tom . . . . TmT	Wagner,Ron. . . . . RoW	Woch, Stan. . . . . SnW
Spiegle, Dan . . . . DSp	Tenney, Mark . . . . MaT	Waid, Mark . . . . MWa	Woggin, Bill . . . . BWo
Spinks, Frank. . . . . FrS	Texeira, Mark . . . . MT	Walker, Kevin. . . . . . . KeW	Wojtkiewicz, Chuck . . . Woj
Springer, Frank . . . . . . FS	Thibert, Art . . . . ATi	Waltrip, Jason. . . . . . . JWp	Wolf, Chance . . . . CWf
Sprouse, Chris . . . . . CSp	Thomas, Dann. . . . . . . DTs	Waltrip, John . . . . JWt	Wolfe, Joseph . . . . . . JWf
St.Pierre, Joe . . . . JPi	Thomas, Roy. . . . . RTs	Ward, Bill . . . . BWa	Wolfman, Marv . . . . . MWn
Starlin, Jim. . . . . JSn	Thomason, Derek . . . . DeT	Warner, Chris. . . . . CW	Wolverton, Basil. . . . . . BW
Starr, Leonard. . . . . . . LSt	Thompson, Jill. . . . . JlT	Warren, Adam . . . . . . AWa	Wood, Bob. . . . . BoW
Staton, Joe . . . . JSon	Thorne, Frank . . . . FT	Washington 3, Robert 3RW	Wood, Teri Sue. . . . . . TWo
Steacy, Ken . . . . KSy	Tinker, Ron . . . . RnT	Watkiss, John . . . . JWk	Wood, Wally . . . . WW
Steffan, Dan . . . . DnS	Torres, Angelo . . . . AT	Weeks, Lee. . . . . LW	Woodring, Jim. . . . . . . JWo
Stelfreeze, Brian . . . . BSf	Toth, Alex. . . . . ATh	Wein, Len . . . . LWn	Wormer, Kirk Van. . . . KWo
Stephenson, Eric . . . . ErS	Totleben, John . . . . JTo	Weinstein, Howard. . . HWe	Wright, Greg. . . . . GWt
Steranko, Jim. . . . . . . JSo	Trimpe, Herb. . . . . HT	Welch, Larry . . . . LyW	Wrightson, Berni . . . . . BWr
Stern, Roger. . . . . RSt	Truman, Timothy . . . . . TT	Wendel, Andrew. . . . . AdW	Wyman, M.C. . . . . . . MCW
Stern, Steve . . . . SSt	Truog, Chas . . . . ChT	Wenzel, David . . . . . . DWe	**Yaep, Chap . . . . CYp**
Stevens, Dave . . . . . . DSt	Tucci, Bill . . . . BiT	Weringo, Mike . . . . . . MeW	Yeates, Tom . . . . TY
Stiles, Steve . . . . SvS	Turner, Dwayne. . . . . . . DT	West, Kevin . . . . KWe	Yeowell, Steve. . . . . . . SY
Story, Karl. . . . . KlS	Tuska, George . . . . GT	Weston, Chris . . . . . CWn	**Zabel, Joe. . . . . JZe**
Stout, William . . . . . . WiS	**Ulm, Chris . . . . CU**	Wheatley, Mark . . . . . MkW	Zachary, Dean. . . . . . . DZ
Stradley, Randy. . . . . RSd	**Vachss, Andrew . . . . AVs**	Whitney, Ogden. . . . . . OW	Zaffino, Jorge. . . . . JZ
Strazewski, Len. . . . . LeS	Vado, Dan . . . . DVa	Wiacek, Bob . . . . BWi	Zeck, Mike . . . . MZ
Stroman, Larry. . . . . . LSn	Valentino, Jim . . . . JV	Wiesenfeld, Aron . . . . AWs	Zick, Bruce . . . . BZ
Sullivan, Lee . . . . LS	Vallejo, Boris . . . . BV	Wildey, Doug. . . . . DW	Zulli, Michael . . . . MZi
Sutton, Tom. . . . . TS	Van Fleet, John . . . . . . JVF	Wildman, Andrew . . . . Wld	Zyskowski, Joseph. . . . JZy
Swan, Curt . . . . CS	Vancata, Brad . . . . BVa	Williams, Anthony . . . . AWi	Zyskowski, Steven . . . . SZ

GENERAL ABBREVIATIONS FOR COMICS LISTINGS

Adaptation . . . . Adapt.	Giant Size . . . . G-Size	Prestige Format . . . . PF
Appearance of. . . . . A:	Golden Age . . . . G.A.	Preview. . . . . Prev.
Anniversary. . . . . Anniv.	Graphic Album . . . . GAm	Reprinted issue . . . . rep.
Annual . . . . Ann.#	Graphic Novel. . . . . GN or GNv	Retold . . . . rtd.
Art & Cover . . . . (a&c)	Hardcover . . . . HC	Return/Revival of. . . . . R:
Art & Plot. . . . . (a&pl)	Identity Revealed . . . . IR:	Scripted/Written by . . . . (s)
Art & Script. . . . . (a&s)	Inks by . . . . (i)	Scripts & inks . . . . (s&i)
Artist. . . . . (a)	Introduction of. . . . . I:	Silver Age. . . . . S.A.
Back-Up Story. . . . . BU:	Joins of. . . . . J:	Softcover . . . . SC
Beginning of . . . . B:	King Size . . . . K-Size	Special . . . . Spec.
Birth of . . . . b:	Leaving of . . . . L:	Team-up . . . . T.U.
Cameo Appearance . . . . . . C:	New Costume . . . . N:	Trade Paperback . . . . TPB
Cover . . . . (c)	No Issue Number. . . . . N#	Versus . . . . V: or vs.
Cover and Script . . . . (c&s)	Origin of . . . . O:	Wedding of . . . . W:
Crossover with . . . . x-over	Painted Cover . . . . P(c)	With . . . . w/
Death/Destruction of . . . . . . D:	Part . . . . pt. or Pt.	Without . . . . w/o
Edition . . . . Ed.	Pencils by . . . . (p)	
Ending of . . . . E:	Photographic cover . . . . . Ph(c)	
Features . . . . F:	Plotted by. . . . . (pl)	

3RW. Robert Washington 3	BDn . . . . Ben Dunn	CE . . . . . Carlos Ezquerra	DHz . . Douglas Hazlewood
AA . . . . Alfredo Alcala	BE . . . . Bill Elder	CG . . . . . . Carlos Garzon	DiF. . . . . . . Dick Foreman
AAd . . . . Art Adams	BEd . . . . Ben Edlund	CH . . . . Chad Hunt	DJ . . . . Dennis Jensen
AaK . . . . . Alisa Kwitney	BEv. . . . . Bill Everett	ChB . . . . . Charles Berger	DJa . . . . . . Dennis Janke
AaL. . . . . . Aaron Lopresti	BEw . . . . Brett Ewins	ChG . . . Chester Gould	DJu . . . . Dan Jurgens
AAv . . . . Al Avison	BF . . Bob Fujitani(Fuje)	ChM . . . Chris Marrinan	DK . . . . Dale Keown
AB . . . . Alex Blum	BG. . . . . Bill Griffith	CHm . . . . . Cully Hamner	DkB . . . . . . Dick Browne
ABr. . . . . . . Ann Brewster	BH . . . . Bob Hall	ChT . . . . Chas Truog	DkG. . . . . . Daerick Gross
ACa . . . . Anthony Castrillo	BHa . . . . . . Bo Hampton	Chu . . . . Ernie Chua	DL . . . . Dave Lapham
ACe. . . . . Andrew Currie	BHg . . . . . Burne Hogarth	CI. . . . . Carmine Infantino	DlB . . . . . Daniel Brereton
ACh. . . . . . Anthony Chun	BHi . . . . Bryan Hitch	CIv . . . . Chris Ivy	DLp . . . . . Dave Louapre
ACo . . . . . Amanda Conner	BHr. . . . . . . Ben Herrera	CJ . . . . Casey Jones	DLw . . . . . . Dan Lawlis
AD . . . . Alan Davis	BHs . . . . . . Bob Harras	CK . . . . . Cam Kennedy	DM . . . David Mazzucchelli
ADF . . . . Alan Dean Foster	BiT . . . . Bill Tucci	CNn . . . . . . Cedric Nocon	DMc. . . . . Dave McKean
AdP. . . . . . Adam Pollina	BK . . . . . Bernie Krigstein	CNr . . . . Cary Nord	DMD . . Dwayne McDuffie
ADv. . . . . Al Davison	Bka. . . . . Bob Kane	CP . . . . Carl Potts	DMG . . . . Don McGregor
AdW . . . . . Andrew Wendel	BKi . . . . Barry Kitson	CPa . . . Carlos Pacheco	DMk. . . . . David Mack
AF . . . . Al Feldstein	BKr. . . . . Brandon Kruse	CPr . . . Christopher Priest	DMn. . . . . Duke Mighten
AFa . . . . Al Fago	BKs . . . . . Babara Kesel	CR . . . . . P. Craig Russell	DMt . . . . . . Dean Motter
AG . . . . Al Gordon	BL . . . . Bob Layton	CrB. . . . Craig Brasfield	DN . . . . Don Newton
AgF . . . . . . A. Frolechlich	BLb . . . . Bob Lubbers	CS. . . . . Curt Swan	DnS . . . . . . Dan Steffan
AGo . . . . . . Alex Garner	BlH. . . . . Bill Hobbs	CsB . . . . . . Chris Batista	DO . . . . . . Dave Olbrich
AGw . . . . . Archie Goodwin	BLr . . . . Bob Larkin	CsM . . . . . Chris Moeller	DoC . . . . Dario Carrasco
AH . . . . Adam Hughes	BLs . . . . . . Batton Lash	CSp . . . . . Chris Sprouse	DOe . . . . Dark One
AHo . . . . Art Holcomb	BM . . . . . . Barry Mitchel	CU . . . . Chris Ulm	DoM. . . . . Doug Mahnke
AIA . . . . . Alfred Andriola	BMc . . . . . Bob McLeod	CV . . . . Charles Vess	DON. . . . . O'Neil, Denny
AJ. . . . . Al Jaffee	BMC . . . B. McCorkindale	CW . . . . . . Chris Warner	DP . . . . Don Perlin
AKu. . . . . . Adam Kubert	BML. . Bill Messner-Loebs	CWf . . . . . . Chance Wolf	DPo . . . . . . Porch, David
ALa . . . . . . Andy Lanning	BMs. . . . . . . Bill Maus	CWi . . . . . Colin Wilson	DPs . . . Dan Panosian
AlG . . . . Alan Grant	BMy . . Brendon McCarthy	CWn . . . . . Chris Weston	DPw . . . . . Power, Dermot
AM . . . . Al Milgrom	BNa. . . . . . Bob Napton	CYp . . . . Chap Yaep	DQ . . . . . . David Quinn
AMc. . . . . . . Al McWilliams	BnP . . . . . Brian Pulido	**DA . . . . Dan Adkins**	DR . . . . Ross, David
AMe . . . . . Angel Medina	BO . . . . . . Bob Oskner	DAb . . . . . Dusty Abell	Rd . . . . . Richard Delgado
AMK . . . . . Angus McKie	BoW . . . . . Bob Wood	DaC . . Dan Castellaneta	DRi . . . . Don Rico
AMo. . . . . . . Alan Moore	BP . . . . Bob Powell	DaF. . . . . Dan Fraga	DRo. . . . . . Denis Rodier
AN . . . . Alex Nino	BPe. . . Brandon Peterson	DaG . . . . . Dave Garcia	DS . . . . Dave Sim
ANi . . . . Art Nichols	BR . . . . Bill Reinhold	DaM. . . . . Danny Miki	DSp . . . . . Dan Spiegle
ANo . . . . . Ann Nocenti	BRa . . . . . . Ben Raab	DAn. . . . . Dan Abnett	DSs . . . . . . Don Simpson
AOl . . . . . . Ariel Olivetti	BrM . . . . Brian Murray	DaR. . . . Darrick Robertson	DSt. . . . . . Dave Stevens
APh . . . . Annie Parkhouse	BrP. . . . . Bruce Patterson	DaW . . . Damon Willis	DSw . . . . Dan Sweetman
AR . . . . Alex Raymond	BS. . . . . Bart Sears	Day . . . . Dan Day	DT . . . . Dwayne Turner
AS. . . . . Alex Saviuk	BSf . . . . . Brian Stelfreeze	DAy. . . . . . . Dick Ayers	DTs . . . . . . Dann Thomas
ASm . . . . Andy Smith	BSt . . . . Beau Smith	DB. . . . . . . D. Battlefield	DTy. . . . . . . David Taylor
ASp . . . . . Art Spiegelman	BSz . . . . . Bill Sienkiewicz	DB. . . . . . Denis Beauvais	DvA . . . . David Ammerman
AT . . . . . . Angelo Torres	BT . . . . . . Bryan Talbot	DBa . . . . . . Dan Barry	DVa . . . . Dan Vado
ATh . . . . Alex Toth	BTn. . . . . Billy Tan	DBk . . . . . Darryl Banks	DvC . . . . . . Dave Cooper
ATi. . . . . Art Thibert	Buzz. . . . . Buzz	DBl . . . . . Danny Bulanadi	DvD . . . . . . Dave Dorman
AV . . . . Al Vey	BV . . . . Boris Vallejo	DBr . . . . . Dick Briefer	DvJ . . . . . Dave Johnson
AVs . . . . . Andrew Vachss	BVa. . . . . . . Brad Vancata	DBs . . . . . John Barras	DvL . . . . David Lloyd
AW . . . . Al Williamson	BW . . . . . Basil Wolverton	DBw . . . Doug Braithwaite	DvM . . . David Michelinie
AWa . . . . . . Adam Warren	BWa. . . . . Bill Ward	DC . . . . . . Dave Cockrum	DvR. . . . . . . David Reed
AWi . . . . Anthony Williams	BWg . . . . . Bill Willingham	DCn . . . Don Cameron	DW . . . . Doug Wildey
AWs . . . . Aron Wiesenfeld	BWi. . . . . . . Bob Wiacek	DCw . . . Denys Cowan	DWe. . . . . David Wenzel
AxR . . . . Alex Ross	BWo . . . . Bill Woggin	DD . . . . . . Dick Dillin	DZ . . . . . . Dean Zachary
AyB . . . . Allyn Brodsky	BWr . . . . Berni Wrightson	DdB . . . . . . David Boller	**EA. . . . . Edd Ashe**
BA . . . . . Brent Anderson	BWS. Barry Windsor-Smith	DDv. . . . . . . Dan Davis	EB. . . . . Ed Barreto
BAn . . . . . . Bill Anderson	BZ . . . . Bruce Zick	DdW . . . David Williams	EBe . . . . Ed Benes
BAp . . . . Brian Althorp	**CAd. . . . . . Charlie Adlard**	DE . . . . D. Elliot	EC. . . . . Ernie Colon
BAu . . . . . Brian Augustyn	CaS . . . . Cam Smith	DeH . . . . Dave Hund	ECa . . . . . Eddie Campbell
BB . . . . . . Brian Bolland	CAx . . . . Chris Alexander	DeM . . . . Dev Madan	ECh . . . . . . Ernie Chan
BBa . . . . . . Bernard Bailey	CB. . . . . Carl Barks	DeT . . . . . Derek Thomason	EcS . . . . Eric Silvestri
BbB . . . . Bob Brown	CBa . . . . . . Chris Bachalo	DFg . . . . Duncan Fegredo	EDo . . . . Evan Dorkin
BBB. . . . . . Bob Boze Bell	CBi. . . . . . Charles Biro	DFr . . . . Danny Fingeroth	EH. . . . . Ed Hannigan
BBh . . . . . Brett Booth	CBu . . . . Carl Bugro	DG . . . . . . Dick Giordano	EhH . . . . . . Ernest Hart
BbK . . . . . . Bob Kanigher	CCa . . . . . Charles Caldes	DGb . . . . Dave Gibbons	EHi . . . . . . E.E. Hibbard
BBl . . . . Bret Blevins	CCl. . . . . . Chris Claremont	DGC . . . . D.G. Chichester	EHr . . . . Everette Hartsoe
BBr . . . . . Brett Breeding	Ccs . . . . Chriscross	DgM . . . . Doug Moench	EiS . . . . . . Eric Shanower
BCe . . . . . Bobbie Chase	CCt. . . . . Claudio Castellini	DGr . . . . . Dan Green	EK . . . . Everett R. Kinsler
BCh . . . . . Bernard Chang	CCu . . . . . Chuck Culdera	DH . . . . Don Heck	EL . . . . Erik Larsen
BCi. . . . . . . Brandon Choi	CDi . . . . Chuck Dixon	DHa . . . . . . Drew Hayes	ELe . . . . Elaine Lee
BDC . . Brent D Carpenter	CDo . . . . . Colleen Doran	DHv. . . . . . . Dave Hoover	ELu . . . Eric Van Lustbader

Abbr.	Name
EM	Esteban Maroto
EN	Earl Norem
ENB	E. Nelson Bridwell
EP	Edmund Perryman
ERC	E.R. Cruz
ErP	Eric Pence
ErS	Eric Stephenson
ESM	Elliot S. Maggin
FaN	**Fabian Nicieza**
FB	Frank Brunner
FBe	Frank Bolle
FBk	Fred Burke
FC	Frank Cirocco
FdS	Fred Schiller
FF	Frank Frazetta
FFo	Frank Fosco
FG	Frank Guardineer
FG	Floyd Gottfredson
FH	Flint Henry
FM	Frank Miller
FMc	Frank McLaughlin
FR	Frank Robbins
FrG	Frank Giacoia
FrS	Frank Spinks
FS	Frank Springer
Fso	Francesco
FT	Frank Thorne
FTa	Francis Takenaga
GaF	**Gardner Fox**
GB	Geoffrey Biggs
GBl	George Bell
GBu	Greg Budget
GC	Gene Colan
GCa	Greg Capullo
GCh	Gary Cohn
GD	Gene Day
GDu	Gary Dumm
GE	George Evans
GeH	Gene Ha
GEn	Garth Ennis
GEr	Gary Erskine
GF	Glenn Fabry
GfD	Geof Darrow
GFo	Gerald Forton
GFr	Gary Frank
GFx	Gill Fox
GG	Gabe Gecko
Ggn	Geggan
GgP	George Pratt
GHe	Gilbert Hernandez
GHi	Graham Higgins
GI	Geoff Isherwood
GJ	Gerard Jones
GK	Gil Kane
GL	Garry Leach
GlD	Glyn Dillon
GLz	Greg Luzniak
GM	Gray Morrow
GMo	Grant Morrison
GN	Graham Nolan
GP	George Perez
GPi	Gene Pamai
GrI	Graham Ingles
GrL	Greg LaRocque
GSh	Gerry Shamray
GSr	Geoff Senior
GT	George Tuska
GtM	Grant Miehm
GW	Gahan Wilson
GWt	Greg Wright
GyA	Gary Amaro
GyC	Gerry Conway
GyD	Guy Davis
GyM	Gary Martin
HaE	**Harlan Ellison**
HB	Hernandez Brothers
HbK	Hannibal King
HC	Howard Chaykin
HFl	Homer Flemming
HH	Hugh Haynes
HK	Harvey Kurtzman
HMe	Howard Mackie
HMo	H. Mercadoocasio
HMz	Henry Martinez
HN	Howard Nostrand
HNg	Hoang Nguyen
HPo	Howard Porter
HSm	Howard Shum
HSn	Howard Simpson
HT	Herb Trimpe
HuR	Humberto Ramos
HWe	Howard Weinstein
HwP	Howard Post
IaC	**Ian Churchhill**
IEd	Ian Edginton
IG	Ian Gibson
IN	Irv Novick
IV	Ivan Velez, Jr.
JA	**Jack Abel**
JaB	Jack Binder
JaD	Jamie Delano
JaL	Jae Lee
JAl	Jeff Albrecht
JAo	John Albano
JAp	Jim Aparo
JAr	John Arcudi
JB	John Buscema
JBa	Jim Baikie
JBa	Jim Balent
JBe	John Beeston
JBg	Jon Bogdanove
JBi	Jerry Bingham
JBl	Jesus Blasco
JBm	John Broom
JBn	John Burns
JBo	John Bolton
JBr	June Brigman
JBt	Jeff Butler
JBy	John Byrne
JBz	Joe Benitez
JCa	John Calnan
JCf	Jim Calafiore
JCh	Joe Chiodo
JCo	Jack Cole
JCp	John Cooper
JCr	Johnny Craig
JCt	Joe Carter
JCx	Jeromy Cox
JCz	Jerry Cruz
JD	Jan Duursema
JDa	Jack Davis
JDo	Julie Doucet
JDx	John Dixon
JDy	Jo Duffy
JeJ	Jeff Jones
JeM	Jerome Moore
JeP	Jerry Prosser
JeR	James Robinson
JEs	John Estes
JF	John Forte
JFM	John Francis Moore
JFr	John Freeman
JFy	James Fry III
JG	Jackson Guice
JGa	Jack Gaughan
JGz	Jorge Gonzalez
JH	Jack Herman
JhB	John Beatty
JhD	John Dell
JHi	John Higgins
JHk	John Hicklenton
JHl	James Hudnall
JHo	John Holdredge
JHr	Jaime Hernandez
JHw	Jamie Hewlett
JiC	Jim Callahan
JiS	Jim Shooter
JJ	Jeff Johnson
JJB	JJ Birch
JJn	Julius Jackson
JJo	J.B. Jones
JJu	Joe Jusko
JK	Jack Kirby
JKa	Jack Kamen
JkS	Jack Sparling
JKu	Joe Kubert
JKz	Jack Katz
JL	Jose Lopez
JLb	Jeph Loeb
JLd	Joe Lansdale
JLe	Jim Lee
JLi	Joseph M. Linsner
JIT	Jill Thompson
JLv	Jim Lavery
JM	Jim Mooney
JMC	John McCrea
JMd	Joe Madureira
JMD	J.M. DeMatteis
JMi	Jeff Mariotte
JmL	Jim Lawson
JMn	Joe Maneely
JmP	James Pascoe
JMr	Jeff Moore
JMs	Jeff Matsuda
JMt	Joe Martin
JMu	Jon J. Muth
JMy	Jeffrey Moy
JMz	Jose Marzan
JnM	Jason Minor
JnR	John Riley
JNR	John Ney Rieber
JnS	John Smith
JO	Joe Orlando
JoA	Jo Alibaster
JoB	Joe Bennett
JoC	Joe Casey
JOb	James O'Barr
JoG	Joe Giella
JoM	Joe Musial
JOn	James Owen
JoP	Joe Phillips
JoS	Joe Shuster
JOs	John Ostrander
JOt	Jose Ortiz
JOy	Jerry Ordway
JP	Jimmy Palmiotti
JPe	Jonathan Peterson
JPh	James Perham
JPi	Joe St.Pierre
JPL	John Paul Leon
JPn	Jason Pearson
JQ	Joe Quesada
JR	John Romita
JR2	John Romita, Jr.
JRe	John Royle
JRl	Jim Royle
JRo	J. Rosenberger
JRs	John Ross
JRu	Joe Rubinstein
JRv	Judith Reeves-Stevens
JRy	John Ridgeway
JRz	John Rozum
JS	Javier Saltares
JS3	Jim Sanders III
JSb	Jonathan Sibal
JSc	Jeffery Scott
JSC	J. Scott Campbell
JSe	John Severin
JSh	Jim Sherman
JSi	Jeff Smith
JSm	Joe Simon
JSn	Jim Starlin
JSo	Jim Steranko
JSon	Joe Staton
JSt	Joe Sinnott
JTo	John Totleben
JuB	Julie Bell
JV	Jim Valentino
JVF	John Van Fleet
JWf	Joseph Wolfe
JWi	J.H. Williams
JWk	John Watkiss
JWo	Jim Woodring
JWp	Jason Waltrip
JWt	John Waltrip
JyS	Jerry Serpe
JZ	Jorge Zaffino
JZe	Joe Zabel
JZy	Joseph Zyskowski
K&R	**Kane & Romita**
KB	Kyle Baker
KBk	Kurt Busiek
KD	Kieron Dwyer
KDe	Kim Deitch
KDM	Kim DeMulder
KEa	Kevin Eastman
KeL	Ken Lashley
KeW	Kevin Walker
KG	Keith Giffen
KGa	Kerry Gammill
KHd	Kevin Hopgood
KHt	Kyle Hotz
KiA	Kia Asamiya
KJ	Klaus Janson
KJa	Kirk Javinen
KJo	Kelley Jones
KK	Karl Kesel
KlA	Karl Alstaetter
KlK	Karl Kerschl
KlS	Karl Story
KM	Kevin Maguire
KN	Kevin Nowlan
KoK	Kevin Kobasic
KON	Kevin O'Neill
KP	Keith Pollard
KPl	Kilian Plunkett
KS	Kurt Schaffenberger
KSm	Kevin Smith
KSW	Keith S. Wilson
KSy	Ken Steacy
KtH	Kurt Hathaway
KVH	Kevin VanHook
KW	Kent Williams
KWe	Kevin West

Abbreviation	Name
KWi	Keith Williams
KWo	Kirk Van Wormer
LbC	**Leonard B. Cole**
LC	Lou Cameron
LCh	Lillian Chestney
LDr	Larry Dresser
LDu	Leo Duranona
LDz	Luis Dominguez
LE	Lee Elias
LeS	Len Strazewski
LF	Lou Fine
LHa	Larry Hama
LI	Larry Ivie
LiM	Linda Medley
LJi	Leonardo Jimenez
LKa	Len Kaminski
LLi	Larry Lieber
LMa	Larry Mahlstedt
LMc	Luke McDonnell
LMd	Lee Moder
LMr	Lee Marrs
Low	John Lowe
LRs	Luke Ross
LS	Lee Sullivan
LSh	Liam Sharp
LSi	Louise Simonson
LSn	Larry Stroman
LSt	Leonard Starr
LuH	Lou Harrison
LW	Lee Weeks
LWn	Len Wein
LyW	Larry Welch
MA	**Murphy Anderson**
MaG	Manny Galan
MaH	Mark Hempel
Man	Roland Mann
MaS	Mark Schmitz
MaT	Mark Tenney
MB	Matt Baker
MBa	Mark Bagley
MBe	M. Belardinelli
MBg	Mark Badger
MBm	Mary Bierbaum
MBn	Mike Baron
MBr	Mark Bright
MBu	Mark Buckingham
MBy	Mitch Byrd
MC	Mike Collins
MCa	Marc Campos
MCh	Mike Chen
MCi	Mark Crilley
MCl	Mike Clark
MCn	Max Allan Collins
MCo	Mark Chiarello
MCr	Mike Carlin
MCW	M.C. Wyman
MCy	Mike Carey
MD	Mort Drucker
MD2	Mike Deodato, Jr.
MDa	Malcolm Davis
MDb	M. DeZuniga
MDo	Mike Dorey
MDr	Mike Dringenberg
ME	Mike Esposito
MEg	Marty Egeland
MeP	Mike Parobeck
MeW	Mike Weringo
MF	Matt Fox
MFl	Michael Fleisher
MFm	Mark Farmer
MFr	Michael Jan Friedman
MG	Mike Gustovich
MGi	Michael T. Gilbert
MGo	Michael Golden
MGr	Mike Grell
MGs	Martin Griffiths
MGu	Mark Gruenwald
MGy	Mick Gray
MHi	Michael Higgins
MHo	Matt Howarth
MHs	Mike Heisler
MHw	Matt Hawkins
MHy	Matt Haley
MI	Medio Iorio
MiA	Michael Allred
MiB	Mike Barr
MiS	Mizuki Sakakibara
MK	Mike Kaluta
MkB	Mike Barreiro
MkF	Mike Friedrich
MkH	Mike Hoffer
MkK	Mike McKenna
MkW	Mark Wheatley
MlB	Michael Bair
MLe	Mike Leeke
MLr	Michael Lark
MM	Mike Manley
MMc	M. McMahon
MMe	Mort Meskin
MMi	Michael Mignola
MMK	Mike McKone
MMo	Mark Moretti
MMr	Mark Millar
MMy	Marat Mychaels
MN	Mike Netzer
MnN	Martin Nodell
Moe	Moebius
MP	Mike Ploog
MPa	Mark Pacella
MPc	Mark Paniccia
MPk	Martin Pasko
MPn	Mark Pennington
MR	Marshall Rogers
MRa	Mac Raboy
MRc	Mark Ricketts
MRi	Mike Richardson
MRy	Matt Ryan
MS	Mark Silvestri
MSh	Mark Schultz
MsM	Mike S. Miller
MSo	Mark Sasso
MSt	Malcolm Smith
MSy	Mike Sekowsky
MT	Mark Texeira
MtB	Matt Broome
MTk	Masashi Tanaka
MV	Mike Vosburg
MvR	Melvin Rubi
MW	Mary Wilshire
MWa	Mark Waid
MWg	Matt Wagner
MWn	Marv Wolfman
MZ	Mike Zeck
MZi	Michael Zulli
NKu	Andy Kubert
NMa	Nathan Massengill
NNa	Nick Napolitano
NPl	Noly Panalign
NR	Nestor Redondo
NRd	Norm Rapmund
NSH	N. Steven Harris
NV	Neil Vokes
NyC	Nancy Collins
OW	**Ogden Whitney**
OM	Otto Messmer
PaD	**Paco Diaz**
PaK	Paris T. Karounos
PaP	Paul Pelletier
PB	Pat Broderick
PBd	Philip Bond
PC	Paul Chadwick
PCu	Paris Cullins
PD	Peter Doherty
PDd	Peter David
PDi	Paul Dini
PFe	Pascual Ferry
PG	Paul Gulacy
PGa	Phil Gascoine
PGn	Paul Guinan
PGr	Peter Grau
PhH	Phil Hester
PJ	Phil Jimminiz
PJe	Paul Jenkins
PKr	Peter Krause
PlA	Paul Abrams
PLa	Peter Laird
PMo	Pete Morisi
PMs	Pat Mills
PNe	Paul Neary
PNu	Philip Nutman
PO	Patrick Olliffe
PPo	Paul Pope
PQ	Peter Quinones
PR	Paul Ryan
PrC	Peter Costanza
PrG	Peter Gross
PrM	Peter Milligan
PS	Paul Smith
PSj	Peter Snejberg
PtL	Patrick Lee
PuD	Paul Danner
PuJ	Paul Johnson
PuK	Paul Kupperberg
RA	**Ross Andru**
RAJ	R.A. Jones
RaP	Rachel Pollack
RB	Rich Buckler
RbB	Robert Bernstein
RbC	Robert Campenella
RBe	Ramon Bernado
RBn	Ryan Benjamin
RBr	Rick Burchett
RBu	Robert Burns
RC	Reed Crandall
RCa	Richard Case
RCl	Ricky Carralero
RCo	Richard Corben
RCr	Robert Crumb
RCz	Roger Cruz
RDB	Randy DuBerkr
RdM	Raymond Marais
RDm	Rodolfo Damaggio
RdD	Richard Delgado
RE	Ric Estrada
RF	Ron Frenz
RFl	Robert Fleming
RG	Ron Garney
RGd	Ruben Gerard
RgM	Rags Morales
RGr	Randy Green
RGs	R. Grossman
RGT	R.G. Taylor
RGu	Rebecca Guay
RH	Russ Heath
RHe	Richard Horie
RHo	Rick Hoberg
RHo	Rich Howell
RiB	Richard Bennett
Rip	Riply
RJ	Robert Jenney
RJn	Robert Jones
RkB	Rick Bryant
RkL	Rick Leach
RKu	Roy Krenkel
RL	Rick Leonardi
RLd	Rob Liefeld
RLe	Rik Levins
RLm	Ron Lim
RLv	R. Livingstone
RM	Rick Magyar
RMc	Ralph Macchio
RMn	Roland Mann
RMr	Roy Allan Martinez
RMz	Ron Marz
RN	Rudy Nebres
RnT	Ron Tinker
RoR	Ron Randall
RoW	on Wagner
RP	Rudy Palais
RPc	Richard Pace
RPi	Richard Pini
RQu	Randy Queen
RRa	Rich Rankin
RS	Ron Smith
RsB	Russell Braun
RSd	Randy Stradley
RsM	Russ Manning
RSm	Robin Smith
RSt	Roger Stern
RT	Romeo Tanghal
RtH	Robert Hebbard
RTs	Roy Thomas
RV	Rick Veitch
RyE	Randy Emberlin
RyL	Ray Lago
RyR	Rodney Ramos
S&K	**Simon & Kirby**
S&S	Siegel & Shuster
SA	Sergio Aragones
Sal	Sal Amendola
SAP	Shea Anton Pensa
SaV	Sal Velluto
SB	Sal Buscema
SBi	Stephen Bissette
SBs	Simon Bisley
SBt	Steve Butler
SC	Sid Check
ScB	Scott Benefiel
ScC	Scott Clark
SCh	Sean Chen
SCi	Sergio Cariello
ScK	Scott Kolins
ScL	Scott Lee
SCr	Steve Crespo
SCy	Simon Colby
SD	Steve Ditko

SDi . . . . Steve Dillon	SSc . . . . . . Sean Scoffield	TH . . . . Tim Hamilton	TVE . . . . Trevor Von Eeden
SDr. . . . . Stan Drake	SSe . . . . . Steven T. Seagle	THa . . . . Tim Harris	TvS . . . . Trevor Scott
SDR . . . . . Sam DeLaRosa	SSh . . . . Sean Shaw	TJn . . . . Todd Johnson	TWo . . . . . . Teri Sue Wood
SEa . . . . Scott Eaton	SSr . . . . Steve Skroce	TKa . . . . . Terry Kavanagh	TY . . . . Tom Yeates
SeM . . . . . Steve Montano	SSt. . . . . Steve Stern	TKn . . . . . . Trent Kaniuga	TyD . . . . Terry Dodson
SeP . . . . Sean Phillips	StA . . . . . . Stephen Addeo	TKr . . Teddy H. Kristiansen	TyH . . . . Tony Harris
SEp . . . . Steve Epting	StB . . . . Scott Benson	TL . . . . Tom Lyle	TyT . . . . Tony Tallarico
SeT . . . . Steve Tappin	StC . . . . . . Stan Campbell	TLa . . . . Terry LaBan	**VAz . . . . . Vincent Alcazar**
SEt . . . . . . Steve Englehart	StE . . . . Steve Erwin	TLw . . . . . Terral Lawrence	VB . . . . Vaughn Bode
SF . . . . . Sal Finnocchiaro	StG . . . . Steve Grant	TM . . . . . Todd McFarlane	VcL. . . . . Vince Locke
SFr. . . . . . Simon Freeman	StL . . . . Stan Lee	TmB . . . . Tim Burgard	VGi. . . . . . . Vince Giarrano
SFu . . . . . Simon Furman	StP . . . . Steve Pugh	TmC . . . . Tom Christopher	ViC. . . . . . . Vince Colletta
SG. . . . . . Sam Glanzman	SVa . . . . Steve Vance	TMd . . . . . . Tom Mandrake	VMk. . . . . Val Mayerik
SGa. . . . Stefano Gaudino	SvG . . . . . . Steve Gerber	TMK . . . . . . Ted McKeever	VMo. . . . . Vincent Morosco
SGe . . . . Sid Greene	SvL . . . . . Salvador Larroca	TMo . . . . Tom Morgan	VRu . . . . Vince Russell
SHa . . . . Scott Hanna	SvP . . . . Steve Parkhouse	TmR . . . . Tom Ryder	VS . . . . Val Semeiks
ShG. . . . Shannon Gallant	SvS . . . . Steve Stiles	TMr. . . . . Terry Moore	VV . . . . . . Vagner Vargas
ShM. . . . . Sheldon Mayer	SW . . . . . . Scott Williams	TMs . . . . Tom Mason	**WaP . . . . . Warren Pleece**
SHn. . . . . Simon Harrison	SWi. . . . . Skip Williamson	TmT . . . . Tom Teney	WB . . . . . . Wayne Boring
SHp . . . . . Scott Hampton	SwM. . . . Shawn McManus	TMw . . . . . . Tom McCraw	WBu. . . . . . . W. Burroughs
SI . . . . . . Stuart Immonen	SY . . . . Steve Yeowell	TNa. . . . . Ted Naifeh	WE . . . . Will Eisner
SK . . . . Sam Kieth	SZ . . . . Steven Zyskowski	TnD . . . . Tony Daniel	WEl. . . . . Warren Ellis
SL. . . . . . . Steve Leialoha	**TA . . . . Terry Austin**	TnS . . . . . . Tristan Schane	WiS . . . . William Stout
SLi. . . . . Steve Lightle	TAr . . . . Tom Artis	TNu. . . . . Todd Nauck	WK. . . . . Walt Kelly
SLo . . . . Scott Lobdell	TB . . . . Tim Boxell	ToT . . . . . . Tony Takezaki	Wld . . . . Andrew Wildman
SM. . . . . Steve Miller	TBd. . . . . . Tim Bradstreet	TOz . . . . . . Tayyar Ozkan	WmB . . . . William Bossart
SMa . Shawn Martinbrough	TBe. . . . . Terry Beatty	TP . . . . Tom Palmer	WMc . . . . Walter McDaniel
SmC. . . . . Sam Citron	TBm . . . . . Tom Bierbaum	TPe. . . . . Tom Peyer	WMo. . . . . . Win Mortimer
SMc . . . . . Scott McDaniel	TC. . . . . . . Travis Charest	TR . . . . Tom Raney	Woj. . . . Chuck Wojtkiewicz
SMl . . . . . . Scott McCloud	TCk . . . . Tomm Coker	TR. . . . . Ted Richards	WP. . . . . Wendy Pini
SML . . . . Sean McLaughlin	TD . . . . Tony DeZuniga	TrR. . . . . Trina Robbins	WPo . . . . . Whilce Portacio
SMt . . . . . Steve Mattsson	TDF . . . . . . Tom DeFalco	TS . . . . Tom Sutton	WR . . . . Werner Roth
SnW . . . . Stan Woch	TDr. . . . . . . Tom Derenick	TSa . . . . . Tony Salmons	WS. . . . . . Walt Simonson
SPa . . . . . . Stephen Platt	TDz . . . . . Todd DeZago	TSe . . . . Tim Sale	WSm . . . . . Will Simpson
Spk . . . . Spark	TeB . . . . Tex Blaisdell	TSg. . . . . Tom Sniegoski	WW. . . . . Wally Wood
SPl. . . . . . . Scott Phillips	TeH . . . . Ted Halsted	TSr . . . . Terry Shoemaker	**YG . . . . Yvel Guichet**
SPr. . . . . Stefan Petrucha	TEl . . . . Tim Eldred	TT . . . . . Timothy Truman	YuK . . . . . . Yukito Kisniro
SR . . . . Steve Rude	TG . . . . . . Tom Grummett	TTg. . . . . . . Tom Taggart	
SRf . . . . Sean Ruffner	TGb . . . . . Tom Grindberg	TTn. . . . . . . Ty Templeton	
SS. . . . . Stan Sakai	TGo . . . . . . Till Goodman	TV . . . . Tim Vigil	

GENERAL ABBREVIATIONS FOR COMICS LISTINGS

A: . . . . Appearance of	GAm . . . . Graphic Album	pt. or Pt. . . . . Part
(a). . . . . Artist	GN or GNv . . . . . . Graphic Novel	rep. . . . . Reprinted issue
Adapt. . . . . Adaptation	G-Size . . . . Giant Size	R:. . . . . Return/Revival of
Anniv. . . . . Anniversary	HC . . . . Hardcover	rtd. . . . . Retold
Ann.# . . . . Annual	I: . . . . Introduction of	(s) . . . . Scripted/Written by
(a&c) . . . . Art & Cover	(i) . . . . Inks by	S.A. . . . . Silver Age
(a&pl) . . . . Art & Plot	IR: . . . . Identity Revealed	SC . . . . Softcover
(a&s) . . . . Art & Script	J:. . . . . Joins of	(s&i) . . . . Scripts & inks
B: . . . . Beginning of	K-Size . . . . King Size	Spec. . . . . Special
b: . . . . Birth of	L: . . . . Leaving of	TPB . . . . Trade Paperback
BU: . . . . Back-Up Story	N: . . . . New Costume	T.U. . . . . Team-up
C: . . . . . . Cameo Appearance	N# . . . . No Issue Number	V: or vs. . . . . Versus
(c) . . . . Cover	O: . . . . Origin of	W: . . . . Wedding of
(c&s) . . . . . Cover and Script	P(c) . . . . Painted Cover	w/ . . . . With
D: . . . . Death/Destruction of	(p). . . . . Pencils by	w/o . . . . Without
Ed. . . . . Edition	PF . . . . . Prestige Format	x-over . . . . . . Crossover with
E: . . . . Ending of	Ph(c) . . . . . Photographic cover	
F: . . . . Features	(pl) . . . . Plotted by	
G.A. . . . . Golden Age	Prev. . . . . Preview	

BIBLIOGRAPHY

Daniels, Les. *Comix: A History of Comic Books in America.* New York, NY: Bonanza Books, 1971.

Gerber, Ernst. *The Photo Journal Guide to Comic Books.* Minden, NV: Gerber Publishing, 1989. Vols. 1 & 2.

Gerber, Ernst. *The Photo Journal Guide to Marvel Comics.* Minden, NV: Gerber Publishing, 1991. Vols. 3 & 4.

Goulart, Ron. *The Adventurous Decade.* New Rochelle, NY: Arlington House, 1975.

Goulart, Ron. *Comic Book Culture, An Illustrated History.* Portland, OR: Collectors Press, 2000

Goulart, Ron. *The Encyclopedia of American Comics.* New York, NY. Facts on File Publications, 1990.

Goulart, Ron. *Over 50 Years of American Comic Books.* Lincolnwood, IL: Mallard Press, 1991.

Hegenburger, John. *Collectors Guide to Comic Books.* Radnor, PA: Wallace Homestead Book Company, 1990.

Kennedy, Jay. *The Official Underground and Newave Price Guide.* Cambridge, MA: Boatner Norton Press, 1982.

Malan, Dan. *The Complete Guide to Classics Collectibles.* St. Louis, MO: Malan Classical Enterprises, 1991.

Miller, John Jackson et al. *The Standard Catalog of Comic Books.* Iola, WI: Krause Publications, 2002.

O'Neil, Dennis. *Secret Origins of DC Super Heroes.* New York, NY: Warner Books, 1976.

Overstreet, Robert. *The Overstreet Comic Book Price Guide (28th Edition).* New York, NY. Avon Books, 1998

Rovin, Jeff. *The Encyclopedia of Super Heroes.* New York, NY: Facts on File Publications, 1985.

Rovin, Jeff. *The Encyclopedia of Super Villians.* New York, NY: Facts on File Publications, 1987.

Thompson, Don & Maggie. *The Golden Age of Comics, Summer 1982.* Tainpa, FL: New Media Publishing, 1982.

DC COMICS

A. BIZARRO

1999

1 (of 4) SvG,MBr,F:Al Bizarro 2.50
2 SvG,MBr,A:Superman 2.50
3 SvG,MBr, ... 2.50
4 SvG,MBr, Viva Bizarro 2.50

ACCELERATE

DC/Vertigo, June, 2000

1 (of 4) Great Escape 3.00
2 Great Escape,pt.2 . . . . 3.00
3 Great Escape,pt.3 . . . . 3.00
4 Great Escape,pt.4,concl. 3.00

Action Comics #14 © DC Comics, Inc.

ACTION

June, 1938

1 JoS,I&O:Superman;Rescues Evelyn
 Curry from electric chair. 450,000.00
2 JoS,V:Emil Norvell 50,000.00
3 JoS,V:Thorton Blakely 30,000.00
4 JoS,V:Coach Randall 18,000.00
5 JoS,Emergency of
 Vallegho Dam 18,000.00
6 JoS,I:Jimmy Olsen,
 V:Nick Williams 18,000.00
7 JoS,V:Derek Niles 37,000.00
8 JoS,V:Gimpy 12,000.00
9 JoS,A:Det.Captain Reilly . . 12,000.00
10 JoS,Superman fights
 for prison reform 25,000.00
11 JoS,Disguised as
 Homer Ramsey 6,500.00
12 JoS,Crusade against
 reckless drivers 7,000.00
13 JoS,I:Ultra Humanite 12,000.00
14 JoS,BKa,V:Ultra Humanite,
 B:Clip Carson 6,500.00
15 JoS,BKa,Superman in
 Kidtown. 10,000.00
16 JoS,BKa,Crusade against
 Gambling 4,500.00
17 JoS,BKa,V:Ultra Humanite. . 7,500.00
18 JoS,BKa,V:Mr.Hamilton
 O:Three Aces 4,500.00
19 JoS,BKa,V:Ultra Humanite
 B:Superman (c) 7,500.00
20 JoS,BKa,V:Ultra Humanite. . 6,500.00
21 JoS,BKa,V:Ultra Humanite. . 4,000.00
22 JoS,BKa,War between Toran
 and Galonia 4,000.00

23 JoS,BKa,SMo,I:Lex Luthor. 11,000.00
24 JoS,BKa,BBa,SMo,FG,Meets
 Peter Carnahan 4,000.00
25 JoS,BKa,BBa,SMo,V:Medini 4,000.00
26 JoS,BKa,V:Clarence Cobalt. 4,000.00
27 JoS,BKa,V:Mr & Mrs.Tweed 3,200.00
28 JoS,BKa,JBu,V:Strongarm
 Bandit 3,200.00
29 JoS,BKa,V:Martin 3,800.00
30 JoS,BKa,V:Zolar 3,200.00
31 JoS,BKa,JBu,V:Baron
 Munsdorf 2,200.00
32 JoS,BKa,JBu,I:Krypto Ray Gun
 V:Mr.Preston. 2,200.00
33 JoS,BKa,V:Brett Hall,
 O:Mr. America. 2,200.00
34 JoS,BKa,V:Jim Laurg. 2,200.00
35 JoS,BKa,V:Brock Walter . . . 2,200.00
36 JoS,BKa,V:StuartPemberton 2,200.00
37 JoS,BKa,V:Commissioner
 Kennedy, O:Congo Bill 2,100.00
38 JoS,BKa,V:Harold Morton . . 2,000.00
39 JoS,BKa,Meets Britt Bryson 2,000.00
40 JoS,BKa,Meets Nancy
 Thorgenson 2,000.00
41 JoS,BKa,V:Ralph Cowan,
 E:Clip Carson 1,700.00
42 V:Lex Luthor,I&O:Vigilante. . 2,300.00
43 V:Dutch O'Leary,Nazi(c) . . . 1,700.00
44 V:Prof. Steffens,Nazi(c) 1,700.00
45 V:Count Von Henzel,
 I:Stuff,Nazi(c) 1,700.00
46 V:The Domino 1,700.00
47 V:Lex Luthor—1st app. w/super
 powers,I:Powerstone 2,500.00
48 V:The Top. 1,600.00
49 I:Puzzler. 1,650.00
50 Meets Stan Doborak 1,600.00
51 I:Prankster. 1,900.00
52 V:Emperor of America 2,100.00
53 JBu,V:Night-Owl. 1,600.00
54 JBu,Meets Stanley
 Finchcomb 1,500.00
55 JBu,V:Cartoonist Al Hatt . . . 1,500.00
56 V:Emil Loring 1,500.00
57 V:Prankster 1,500.00
58 JBu,V:Adonis 1,500.00
59 I:Susie Thompkins,Lois
 Lane's niece 1,400.00
60 JBu,Lois Lane-Superwoman 1,500.00
61 JBu,Meets Craig Shaw 1,500.00
62 JBu,V:Admiral Von Storff . . . 1,500.00
63 JBu,V:Professor Praline. . . . 1,500.00
64 I:Toyman 1,600.00
65 JBu,V:Truman Treadwell . . . 1,200.00
66 JBu,V:Mr.Annister 1,200.00
67 JBu,Superman School for
 Officer's Training 1,200.00
68 A:Susie Thompkins 1,200.00
69 V:Prankster 1,200.00
70 JBu,V:Thinker 1,200.00
71 Superman Valentine's
 Day Special 1,000.00
72 V:Mr. Sniggle 1,000.00
73 V:Lucius Spruce. 1,000.00
74 Meets Adelbert Dribble 1,000.00
75 V:Johnny Aesop. 1,000.00
76 A Voyage with Destiny 1,000.00
77 V:Prankster 1,000.00
78 The Chef of Bohemia. 1,000.00
79 JBu,A:J. Wilbur Wolfingham 1,000.00
80 A:Mr. Mxyzptlk (2nd App). . . 1,400.00
81 Meets John Nicholas 1,000.00
82 JBu,V:Water Sprite 950.00
83 I:Hocus and Pocus 950.00

84 JBu,V:Dapper Gang 950.00
85 JBu,V:Toyman. 950.00
86 JBu,V:Wizard of Wokit 950.00
87 V:Truck Hijackers 950.00
88 A:Hocus and Pocus 950.00
89 V:Slippery Andy. 950.00
90 JBu,V:Horace Rikker and the
 Amphi-Bandits 950.00
91 JBu,V:Davey Jones. 900.00
92 JBu,V:Nowmie Norman. 900.00
93 Superman Christmas story . . . 900.00
94 JBu,V:Bullwer `Bull' Rylie . . . 900.00
95 V:Prankster 900.00
96 V:Mr. Twister 900.00
97 A:Hocus and Pocus 900.00
98 V:Mr. Mxyzptlk, A:Susie
 Thompkins 900.00
99 V:Keith Langwell 900.00
100 I:InspectorErskineHawkins. 1,300.00
101 V:Specs Dour,A-Bomb(c) . . 1,900.00
102 V:Mr. Mxyzptlk. 800.00
103 V:Emperor Quexo 800.00
104 V:Prankster 800.00
105 Superman Christmas story . . 800.00
106 Clark Kent becomes Baron
 Edgestream 800.00
107 JBu,A:J.Wilbur Wolfingham . 800.00
108 JBu,V:Vince Vincent 900.00
109 V:Prankster 800.00
110 A:Susie Thompkins 800.00
111 Cameras in the Clouds 800.00
112 V:Mr. Mxyzptlk. 800.00
113 Just an Ordinary Guy 800.00
114 V:Mike Chesney 800.00
115 Meets Arthur Parrish 800.00
116 A:J. Wilbur Wolfingham. . . . 800.00
117 Superman Christmas story . . 800.00
118 The Execution of Clark Kent. 800.00
119 Meets Jim Banning 800.00
120 V:Mike Foss 800.00
121 V:William Sharp 800.00
122 V:Charley Carson 800.00
123 V:Skid Russell. 800.00
124 Superman becomes
 radioactive. 750.00
125 V:Lex Luthor 750.00
126 V:Chameleon 750.00
127 JKu,Superman on Truth or
 Consequences. 800.00
128 V:`Aces' Deucey 750.00
129 Meets Gob-Gob 750.00

Action Comics #36 © DC Comics, Inc.

All comics prices listed are for *Near Mint* condition.

Action Comics #75 © DC Comics, Inc.

130 V:Captain Kidder......... 750.00
131 V:Lex Luthor............. 750.00
132 Superman meets George
    Washington............. 750.00
133 V:Emma Blotz............ 750.00
134 V:Paul Strong............ 750.00
135 V:John Morton........... 750.00
136 Superman Show-Off!...... 750.00
137 Meets Percival Winter...... 750.00
138 Meets Herbert Hinkle...... 750.00
139 Clark Kent...Daredevil!..... 750.00
140 Superman becomes Hermit. 750.00
141 V:Lex Luthor............. 750.00
142 V:Dan the Dip........... 750.00
143 Dates Nikki Larve........ 750.00
144 O:Clark Kent reporting for
    Daily Planet............. 750.00
145 Meets Merton Gloop...... 700.00
146 V:Luthor................ 700.00
147 V:`Cheeks' Ross......... 700.00
148 Superman, Indian Chief.... 700.00
149 The Courtship on Krypton!.. 700.00
150 V:Morko................ 700.00
151 V:Mr.Mxyzptlk,Lex Luthor
    and Prankster........... 700.00
152 I:Metropolis Shutterbug
    Society................ 700.00
153 V:Kingpin............... 700.00
154 V:Harry Reed............ 700.00
155 V:Andrew Arvin.......... 700.00
156 Lois Lane becomes Super-
    woman,V:Lex Luthor....... 700.00
157 V:Joe Striker............ 700.00
158 V:Kane Korrell
    O:Superman (retold)...... 1,600.00
159 Meets Oswald Whimple.... 700.00
160 V:Minerva Kent.......... 700.00
161 Meets Antara............ 700.00
162 V:`IT!'................. 650.00
163 Meets Susan Semple...... 650.00
164 Meets Stefan Andriessen... 650.00
165 V:Crime Czar............ 650.00
166 V:Lex Luthor............ 650.00
167 V:Prof. Nero............ 650.00
168 O:Olaf................. 650.00
169 Caveman Clark Kent!...... 650.00
170 V:Mad Artist of Metropolis... 650.00
171 The Secrets of Superman... 650.00
172 Lois Lane...Witch!........ 650.00
173 V:Dragon Lang........... 650.00
174 V:Miracle Twine Gang..... 650.00
175 V:John Vinden........... 650.00
176 V:Billion Dollar Gang...... 650.00
177 V:General.............. 650.00
178 V:Prof. Sands........... 650.00
179 Superman in Mapleville.... 650.00
180 V:Syndicate of Five....... 650.00

181 V:Diamond Dave Delaney .. 600.00
182 Return from Planet Krypton . 600.00
183 V:Lex Luthor............. 600.00
184 Meets Donald Whitmore.... 600.00
185 V:Issah Pendleton........ 600.00
186 The Haunted Superman.... 600.00
187 V:Silver................ 600.00
188 V:Cushions Raymond gang . 600.00
189 Meets Mr.& Mrs. Vandeveir.. 600.00
190 V:Mr. Mxyzptlk........... 600.00
191 V:Vic Vordan............ 600.00
192 Meets Vic Vordan......... 600.00
193 V:Beetles Brogan......... 600.00
194 V:Maln................. 600.00
195 V:Tiger Woman........... 600.00
196 Superman becomes Mental
    Man.................. 600.00
197 V:Stanley Stark........... 600.00
198 The Six Lives of Lois Lane .. 600.00
199 V:Lex Luthor............. 600.00
200 V:Morwatha............. 600.00
201 V:Benny the Brute......... 600.00
202 Lois Lane's X-Ray Vision ... 500.00
203 Meets Pietro Paresca...... 500.00
204 Meets Sam Spulby........ 500.00
205 Sergeant Superman....... 500.00
206 Imaginary story F:L.Lane ... 500.00
207 Four Superman Medals!.... 500.00
208 V:Mr. Mxyzptlk........... 500.00
209 V:`Doc' Winters.......... 500.00
210 V:Lex,I:Superman Land 500.00
211 Superman Spectaculars 500.00
212 V:Thorne Varden......... 500.00
213 V:Paul Paxton............ 500.00
214 Superman,Sup.Destroyer! . 500.00
215 I:Superman of 2956 ...... 500.00
216 A:Jor-El................ 500.00
217 Meets Mr&Mrs.Roger Bliss.. 500.00
218 I:Super-Ape from Krypton... 500.00
219 V:Art Shaler............. 500.00
220 Interplanetary Olympics 500.00
221 V:Jay Vorrell............ 400.00
222 The Duplicate Superman ... 400.00
223 A:Jor-El................ 400.00
224 I:Superman Island........ 400.00
225 The Death of Superman.... 400.00
226 V:Lex Luthor............ 400.00
227 Man with Triple X-Ray Eyes . 400.00
228 A:Superman Museum...... 400.00
229 V:Dr. John Haley......... 400.00
230 V:Bart Wellins........... 400.00
231 Sir Jimmy Olsen, Knight of
    Metropolis.............. 400.00
232 Meets Johnny Kirk........ 400.00
233 V:Torm................ 400.00
234 Meets Golto 400.00
235 B:Congo Bill,
    B:Tommy Tomorrow........ 400.00
236 A:Lex Luthor............ 400.00
237 V:Nebula Gang........... 400.00
238 I:King Krypton,the Gorilla ... 400.00
239 Superman's New Face...... 400.00
240 V:Superman Sphinx 400.00
241 WB,A:Batman,Fortress of
    Solitude (Fort Superman) ... 350.00
242 I&O:Brainiac........... 2,500.00
243 Lady and the Lion......... 350.00
244 CS,A:Vul-Kor,Lya-La....... 350.00
245 WB,V:Kak-Kul........... 350.00
246 WB,A:Krypton Island....... 350.00
247 WB,Superman Lost Parents . 350.00
248 B&I:Congorilla........... 350.00
249 AP,A:Lex Luthor.......... 350.00
250 WB,The Eye of Metropolis .. 350.00
251 AP,E:Tommy Tomorrow..... 350.00
252 I&O:Supergirl.......... 2,500.00
253 B:Supergirl 650.00
254 I:Adult Supergirl......... 500.00
255 I:Bizarro Lois............ 400.00
256 Superman of the Future 250.00
257 WB,JM,V:Lex Luthor....... 250.00

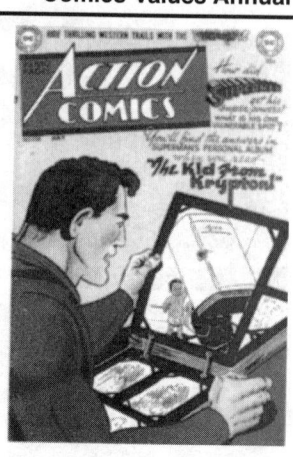

Action Comics #158 © DC Comics, Inc.

258 A:Cosmic Man........... 250.00
259 A:Lex Luthor,Superboy..... 250.00
260 A:Mighty Maid........... 250.00
261 I:Streaky,E:Congorilla...... 250.00
262 A:Bizarro............... 250.00
263 O:Bizarro World 300.00
264 V:Bizarro............... 250.00
265 A:Hyper-Man............ 250.00
266 A:Streaky,Krypto 250.00
267 JM,3rd A:Legion,I:Invisible
    Kid................... 650.00
268 WB,A:Hercules........... 225.00
269 A:Jerro................ 225.00
270 CS,JM,A:Batman 250.00
271 A:Lex Luthor 225.00
272 A:Aquaman............. 225.00
273 A:Mr.Mxyzptlk 225.00
274 A:Superwoman.......... 225.00
275 WB,JM,V:Braimiac 225.00
276 JM,6th A:Legion,I:Brainiac 5,
    Triplicate Girl,Bouncing Boy . 350.00
277 CS,JM,V:Lex Luthor....... 175.00
278 CS,Perry White Becomes
    Master Man............. 175.00
279 JM,V:Hercules,Samson 175.00
280 CS,JM,V:Braniac,
    A:Congorilla............. 175.00
281 JM,A:Krypto 175.00
282 JM,V:Mxyzptlk........... 175.00
283 CS,JM,A:Legion of Super
    Outlaws 200.00
284 A:Krypto,Jerro.......... 175.00
285 JM,Supergirl Existence Revealed,
    C:Legion (12th app.)...... 200.00
286 CS,JM,V:Lex Luthor....... 150.00
287 JM,A:Legion............ 150.00
288 JM,A:Mon-El............ 150.00
289 JM,A:Adult Legion........ 150.00
290 JM,C:Phantom Girl....... 150.00
291 JM,V:Mxyzptlk........... 150.00
292 JM,I:Superhorse......... 150.00
293 JM,O:Comet-Superhorse ... 200.00
294 JM,V:Lex Luthor......... 150.00
295 CS,JM,O:Lex Luthor....... 150.00
296 V:Super Ants............ 150.00
297 CS,JM,A:Mon-El 150.00
298 CS,JM,V:Lex Luthor....... 150.00
299 O:Superman Robots....... 150.00
300 JM,A:Mxyzptlk........... 175.00
301 CS(c),JM,O:Superhorse 100.00
302 CS(c),JM,O:Superhorse.... 100.00
303 CS(c),Red Kryptonite story... 100.00
304 CS,JM,I&O:Black Flame.... 125.00
305 CS(c),O:Supergirl........ 100.00
306 JM,C:Mon-El,Brainiac 5 .... 100.00
307 CS,JM,A:Saturn Girl....... 100.00

308 CS(c),V:Hercules	100.00
309 CS,A:Batman,JFK,Legion	125.00
310 CS,JM,I:Jewel Kryptonite	90.00
311 CS,JM,O:Superhorse	90.00
312 CS,JM,V:Metallo-Superman	90.00
313 JM,A:Supergirl,Lex,Batman	90.00
314 JM,A:Justice League	90.00
315 JM,V:Zigi,Zag	90.00
316 JM,A:Zigi,Zag,Zyra	90.00
317 JM,V:Lex Luthor	90.00
318 CS,JM,A:Brainiac	90.00
319 CS,JM,A:Legion,V:L.Luthor	90.00
320 CS,JM,V:Atlas,Hercules	90.00
321 CS,JM,A:Superhorse	90.00
322 JM,Coward of Steel	90.00
323 JM,A:Superhorse	90.00
324 JM,A:Abdul	90.00
325 CS,JM,SkyscraperSuperman	90.00
326 CS,JM,V:Legion of Super	
Creatures	90.00
327 CS,JM,C:Brainiac	90.00
328 JM,Hands of Doom	90.00
329 JM,V:Drang	90.00
330 JM,V:Krypto	90.00
331 CS,V:Dr.Supernatural	90.00
332 CS,A:Brainiac	90.00
333 CS(c),A:Lex Luthor	90.00
334 JM(c),A:Lex Luthor,80pgs	150.00
335 CS,V:Lex Luthor	85.00
336 CS,O:Akvar	85.00
337 CS,V:Tiger Gang	85.00
338 CS,JM,V:Muto	85.00
339 CS,V:Muto,Brainiac	85.00
340 JM,I:Parasite	85.00
341 CS,V:Vakox,A:Batman	65.00
342 WB,JM,V:Brainiac	65.00
343 WB,V:Eterno	65.00
344 WB,JM,A:Batman	65.00
345 CS(c),A:Allen Funt	65.00
346 WB,JM	65.00
347 CS(c),A:Supergirl,80pgs	100.00
348 WB,JM,V:Acid Master	50.00
349 WB,JM,V:Dr.Kryptonite	50.00
350 A:JLA	50.00
351 WB,I:Zha-Vam	50.00
352 WB,V:Zha-Vam	50.00
353 WB,JM,V:Zha-Vam	50.00
354 JM,A:Captain Incredible	50.00
355 WB,JM,V:Lex Luthor	50.00
356 WB,JM,V:Jr. Annihilitor	50.00
357 WB,JM,V:Annihilitor	50.00
358 NA(c),CS,JM,A:Superboy	50.00
359 NA(c),CS,KS,C:Batman	50.00
360 CS(c),A:Supergirl,80pgs	100.00
361 NA(c),A:Parasite	45.00
362 RA,KS,V:Lex Luthor	45.00
363 RA,KS,V:Lex Luthor	45.00
364 RA,KS,V:Lex Luthor	45.00
365 A:Legion & J.L.A.	45.00
366 RA,KS,A:J.L.A.	45.00
367 NA(c),CS,KS,A:Supergirl	45.00
368 CS,KS,V:Mxyzptlk	45.00
369 CS,KS,Superman's Greatest	
Blunder	45.00
370 NA(c),CS,KS	45.00
371 NA(c),CS,KS	45.00
372 NA(c),CS,KS	45.00
373 A:Supergirl,(giant size)	90.00
374 NA(c),CS,KS,V:Super Thief	40.00
375 CS,KS,The Big Forget	40.00
376 CS,KS,E:Supergirl	40.00
377 CS,KS,B:Legion	40.00
378 CS,KS,V:Marauder	40.00
379 CS,JA,MA,V:Eliminator	40.00
380 KS,Confessions of Superman	40.00
381 CS,Dictators of Earth	40.00
382 CS,Clark Kent-Magician	35.00
383 CS,The Killer Costume	35.00
384 CS,The Forbidden Costume	35.00
385 CS,The Mortal Superman	35.00
386 CS,Home For Old Supermen	35.00

387 CS,A:Legion,Even	
Supermen Die	35.00
388 CS,A:Legion,Puzzle of	
The Wild Word	35.00
389 A:Legion,The Kid Who	
Struck Out Superman	35.00
390 CS,Self-Destruct Superman	35.00
391 CS,Punishment of	
Superman's Son	35.00
392 CS,E:Legion	35.00
393 CS,MA,RA,A:Super Houdini	35.00
394 CS,MA	35.00
395 CS,MA,A:Althea	35.00
396 CS,MA	35.00
397 CS,MA,Imaginary Story	35.00
398 NA(c),CS,MA,I:Morgan Edge	35.00
399 NA(c),CS,MA,A:Superbaby	35.00
400 NA(c),CS,MA,Kandor Story	50.00
401 CS,MA,V:Indians	35.00
402 NA(c),CS,MA,V:Indians	40.00
403 CS,MA,Vigilante rep.	40.00
404 CS,MA,Aquaman rep	40.00
405 CS,MA,Vigilante rep.	40.00
406 CS,MA,Atom & Flash rep.	40.00

Action Comics #250 © DC Comics Inc.

407 CS,MA,V:Lex Luthor	40.00
408 CS,MA,Atom rep.	40.00
409 CS,MA,T.Tommorrow rep.	40.00
410 CS,MA,T.Tommorrow rep.	40.00
411 CS,MA,O:Eclipso rep.	40.00
412 CS,MA,Eclipso rep.	40.00
413 CS,MA,V:Brainiac	40.00
414 CS,MA,B:Metamorpho	20.00
415 CS,MA,V:Metropolis Monster	20.00
416 CS,MA	20.00
417 CS,MA,V:Luthor	20.00
418 CS,MA,V:Luthor,	
E:Metamorpho	20.00
419 CS,MA,Cl,DG,I:HumanTarget	22.00
420 CS,MA,DG,V:Towbee	18.00
421 CS,MA,B:Green Arrow	20.00
422 CS,DG,O:Human Target	18.00
423 CS,MA,DG,A:Lex Luthor	18.00
424 CS,MA,Green Arrow	20.00
425 CS,DD,NA,DG,B:Atom	35.00
426 CS,MA,Green Arrow	15.00
427 CS,MA,DD,DG,Atom	15.00
428 CS,MA,DG,Luthor	15.00
429 CS,BO,DG,C:JLA	15.00
430 CS,MA,DD,DG,Atom	15.00
431 CS,MA,Green Arrow	15.00
432 CS,MA,DG,Toyman	18.00
433 CS,BO,DD,DG,A:Atom	15.00
434 CS,DD,Green Arrow	15.00
435 FM(c),CS,DD,DG,Atom	15.00

436 CS,DD,Green Arrow	15.00
437 CS,DG,Green Arrow,100-pg	50.00
438 CS,BO,DD,Atom	15.00
439 CS,BO,DD,Atom	15.00
440 1st MGr Green Arrow	22.00
441 CS,BO,MGr,A:Green Arrow,	
Flash,R:Krypto	15.00
442 CS,MS,MGr,Atom	15.00
443 CS,A:JLA(100 pg.giant)	50.00
444 MGr,Green Arrow	15.00
445 MGr,Green Arrow	15.00
446 MGr,Green Arrow	15.00
447 CS,BO,RB,KJ,Atom	15.00
448 CS,BO,DD,JL,Atom	15.00
449 CS,BO	20.00
450 MGr,Green Arrow	10.00
451 MGr,Green Arrow	8.00
452 CS,MGr,Green Arrow	8.00
453 CS,Atom	8.00
454 CS,E:Atom	8.00
455 CS,Green Arrow	8.00
456 CS,MGr,Green Arrow	8.00
457 CS,MGr,Green Arrow	8.00
458 CS,MGr,I:Black Rock	8.00
459 CS,BO,Blackrock	8.00
460 CS,I:Karb-Brak	8.00
461 CS,V:Karb-Brak	8.00
462 CS,V:Karb-Brak	8.00
463 CS,V:Karb-Brak	8.00
464 CS,KS,V:Pile-Driver	8.00
465 CS,FMc,Luthor	8.00
466 NA(c),CS,V:Luthor	8.00
467 CS,V:Mzyzptlk	8.00
468 NA(c),CS,FMc,V:Terra-Man	8.00
469 CS,TerraMan	8.00
470 CS,Flash Green Lantern	8.00
471 CS,V:Phantom Zone Female	8.00
472 CS,V:Faora Hu-Ul	8.00
473 NA(c),CS,Phantom Zone	
Villians	8.00
474 KS,V:Doctor Light	8.00
475 KS,V:Karb-Brak,A:Vartox	8.00
476 KS,V:Vartox	8.00
477 CS,DD,Land Lords of Earth	8.00
478 CS,Earth's Last	8.00
479 CS	8.00
480 CS,A:JLA,V:Amazo	8.00
481 CS,A:JLA,V:Amazo	8.00
482 CS,Amazo	8.00
483 CS,Amazo,JLA	8.00
484 CS,W:Earth 2 Superman	
& Lois Lane	15.00
485 NA(c),CS,rep.Superman#233	10.00
486 GT,KS,V:Lex Luthor	8.00
487 CS,AS,O:Atom	8.00
488 CS,AS,A:Air Wave	8.00
489 CS,AS,A:JLA,Atom	8.00
490 CS,Brainiac	8.00
491 CS,A:Hawkman	8.00
492 CS,Superman's After Life	8.00
493 CS,A:UFO	8.00
494 CS	8.00
495 CS	8.00
496 CS,A:Kandor	8.00
497 CS	8.00
498 CS,Vartox	8.00
499 CS,Vartox	8.00
500 CS,Superman's Life Story	
A:Legion	14.00
501 KS	4.00
502 CS,A:Supergirl,Gal.Golem	4.00
503 CS,A Save in Time	4.00
504 CS,The Power and Choice	4.00
505 CS	4.00
506 CS	4.00
507 CS,A:Jonathan Kent	4.00
508 CS,A:Jonathan Kent	4.00
509 CS,JSn,DG	4.00
510 CS,Luthor	4.00
511 CS,AS,V:Terraman,	
A:Air Wave	4.00

All comics prices listed are for *Near Mint* condition.   CVA Page 23

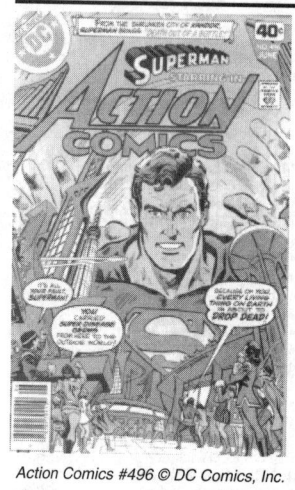

Action Comics #496 © DC Comics, Inc.

512 CS,RT,V:Luthor,A:Air Wave . . . 4.00
513 CS,RT,V:Krell,A:Air Wave 4.00
514 CS,RT,V:Brainiac,A:Atom 4.00
515 CS,AS,A:Atom 4.00
516 CS,AS,V:Luthor,A:Atom 4.00
517 CS,DH,A:Aquaman 4.00
518 CS,DH,A:Aquaman 4.00
519 CS,DH,A:Aquaman 4.00
520 CS,DH,A:Aquaman 4.00
521 CS,AS,I:Vixen,A:Atom 4.00
522 CS,AS,A:Atom 4.00
523 CS,AS,A:Atom 4.00
524 CS,AS,A:Atom 4.00
525 JSon,FMc,AS,I:Neutron
     A:Air Wave. 4.00
526 JSon,AS,V:Neutron. 4.00
527 CS,AS,I:Satanis,A:Aquaman . . 4.50
528 CS,AS,V:Brainiac,A:Aquaman . 4.00
529 GP(c),CS,DA,AS,A:Aquaman,
     V:Brainiac 4.00
530 CS,DA,Brainiac. 4.00
531 JSon,FMc,AS,A:Atom. 4.00
532 CS,C:New Teen Titans 4.00
533 CS,V:The. 4.00
534 CS,AS,V:Satanis,A:Air Wave . 4.00
535 GK(c),JSon,AS,
     A:Omega Men 4.00
536 JSon,AS,FMc,A:Omega Men . . 4.00
537 IN,CS,AS,V:Satanis
     A:Aquaman 4.00
538 IN,AS,FMc,V:Satanis,
     A:Aquaman 4.00
539 KG(c),GK,AS,DA,A:Flash,
     Atom,Aquaman 4.00
540 GK,AS,V:Satanis. 4.00
541 GK,V:Satanis. 4.00
542 AS,V:Vandal Savage 4.00
543 CS,V:Vandal Savage 4.00
544 CS,MA,GK,GP,45th Anniv.
     D:Ardora,Lexor 6.00
545 GK,Brainiac. 4.00
546 GK,A:JLA,New Teen Titans . . 4.00
547 GK(c),CS. 4.00
548 GK(c),AS,Phantom Zone 4.00
549 GK(c),AS. 4.00
550 AS(c),GT 4.00
551 GK,Starfire becomes
     Red Star 4.00
552 GK,Forgotten Heroes
     (inc.Animal Man) 9.00
553 GK,Forgotten Heroes(inc.
     Animal Man) 9.00
554 GK(a&c) 4.00
555 CS,A:Parasite (X-over
     Supergirl #20) 4.00

556 CS,KS,C:Batman 4.00
557 CS,Terra-man 4.00
558 KS 4.00
559 KS,AS 4.00
560 AS,KG,BO,A:Ambush Bug 4.00
561 KS,WB,Toyman. 4.00
562 KS,Queen Bee 4.00
563 AS,KG,BO,A:Ambush Bug 4.00
564 AS,V:Master Jailer 4.00
565 KG,KS,BO,A:Ambush Bug 4.00
566 BO(i),MR 4.00
567 KS,AS,PB 4.00
568 CS,AW,AN 4.00
569 IN,The Force of Revenge 4.00
570 KS, Jimmy Olsen's Alter-Ego . . 4.00
571 BB(c),AS,A:Thresh 222 . . . . . . 4.00
572 WB,BO 4.00
573 KS,BO,AS 4.00
574 KS 4.00
575 KS,V:Intellax 4.00
576 KS,Earth's Sister Planet 4.00
577 KG,BO,V:Caitiff 4.00
578 KS,Parasite. 4.00
579 KG,BO,Asterix Parody 4.00
580 GK(c),KS,Superman's Failure . 4.00
581 DCw(c),KS,Superman
     Requires Legal aid 4.00
582 AS,KS,Superman's Parents
     Alive. 4.00
583 CS,KS,AMo(s),Last Pre
     Crisis Superman 12.00
584 JBy,DG,A:NewTeenTitans,
     I:Modern Age Superman. 6.00
585 JBy,DG,Phantom Stranger 4.50
586 JBy,DG,Legends,V:New
     Gods,Darkseid. 4.50
587 JBy,DG,Demon 4.50
588 JBy,DG,Hawkman 4.50
589 JBy,DG,Gr.Lant.Corp. 4.50
590 JBy,DG,Metal Men 4.50
591 JBy,V:Superboy,A:Legion 4.50
592 JBy,Big Barda 4.50
593 JBy,Mr. Miracle 4.50
594 JBy,A:Booster Gold. 4.50
595 JBy,A:M.Manhunter,
     I:Silver Banshee 4.50
596 JBy,A:Spectre,Millenium 4.50
597 JBy,L.Starr(i),Lois V:Lana 4.50
598 JBy,TyT,I:Checkmate 6.00
599 RA,JBy(i),A:MetalMen,
     BonusBook 4.50
600 JBy,GP,KS,JOy,DG,CS,MA,
     MMi,A:Wonder Woman;
     Man-Bat,V:Darkseid 7.00
Becomes:

ACTION WEEKLY
1988–89
601 GK,DSp,CS,DJu,TD,
     B:Superman,Gr.Lantern,
     Blackhawk,Deadman,Secret
     Six,Wilddog 3.50
602 GP(c),GK,DSp,CS,DJu,TD . . . 3.50
603 GK,CS,DsP,DJu,TD 3.50
604 GK,DSp,CS,DJu,TD 3.50
605 NKu/AKu(c),GK,DSp,CS,
     DJu,TD 3.50
606 DSp,CS,DJu,TD 3.50
607 SLi(c),TD,DSp,CS,DJu 3.50
608 DSp,CS,DJu,TD,E:Blackhawk . 3.50
609 BB(c),DSp,DJu,TD,CS,
     E:Wild Dog,B:Black Canary. . . 3.50
610 KB,DJu,CS,DSp,TD,CS
     A:Phantom Stranger 3.50
611 AN(c),DJu,DSp,CS,BKi,TD,
     BKi,B:Catwoman 3.75
612 PG(c),DSp,CS,BKi,TD,
     E:Secret Six,Deadman 3.50
613 MK(c),BKi,CS,MA,TGr,
     Nightwing,B:Phantom Stranger . 3.50

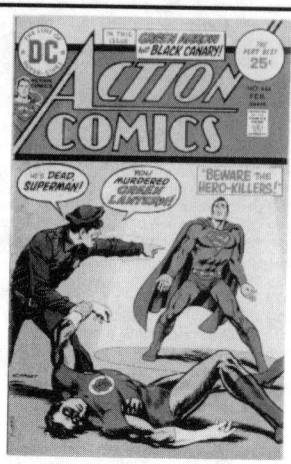

Action Comics #606 © DC Comics, Inc.

614 TG,CS,Phantom Stranger
     E:Catwoman 3.50
615 MMi(c),CS,MA,BKi,TGr,
     Blackhawk,B:Wild Dog 3.50
616 ATh(c),CS,MA,E:Bl.Canary. . . . 3.50
617 CS,MA,JO,A:Ph.Stranger 3.50
618 JBg(c),CS,MA,JKo,TD,
     B:Deadman,E:Nightwing 3.50
619 CS,MA,FS,FMc,KJo,TD,FMc,
     B:Sinister Six. 3.50
620 CS,MA,FS,FMc,KJo,TD 3.50
621 JO(c),CS,MA,FS,FMc,KJo,
     TD,MBr,E:Deadman 3.50
622 RF(c),MBr,TL,CS,MA,FS,
     FMc,A:Starman,E:Wild
     Dog,Blackhawk 3.50
623 MBr,TD,CS,MA,FS,FMc,JL,
     JKo,A:Ph.Stranger,
     B:Deadman,Shazam 3.50
624 AD(c),MBr,FS,FMc,CS,MA,
     TD,B:Black Canary 3.50
625 MBr,FS,FMc,CS,MA,
     TD,FMc 3.50
626 MBr,FS,FMc,CS,MA,JKo,TD,
     E:Shazam,Deadman 3.50
627 GK(c),MBr,RT,FS,FMc,CS,
     MA,TMd,B:Nightwing,Speedy . . 3.50
628 TY(c),MBr,RT,TMd,CS,MA,
     FS,FMc,B:Blackhawk 3.50
629 CS,MA,MBr,RT,FS,FMc,TMd . . 3.50
630 CS,MA,MBr,RT,FS,FMc,TMd,
     E:Secret Six. 3.50
631 JS(c),CS,MA,MBr,RT,TMd,
     B:Phantom Stranger 3.50
632 TGr(c),CS,MA,MBr,RT,TMd . . . 3.50
633 CS,MA,MBr,RT,TMd 3.50
634 CS,MA,MBr,RT,TMd,E:Ph.Strangr,
     Nightwing/Speedy,Bl.hawk . . . 3.50
635 CS,MA,MBr,RT,EB,E:Black
     Canary,Green Lantern. 3.50
636 DG(c),CS,MA,NKu,MPa,FMc,
     B:Demon,Wild Dog,Ph.Lady,
     Speedy,A:Phantom Stranger . . . 3.50
637 CS,MA,KS,FMc,MPa,
     B:Hero Hotline 3.50
638 JK(c),CS,MA,KS,FMc,MPa 3.50
639 CS,MA,KS,FMc,MPa 3.50
640 CS,KS,MA,FS,FMc,MPa,
     E:Speedy,Hero Hotline 3.50
641 CS,MA,JL,DG,MPa,E:Demon,
     Phant.Lady,Superman,Wild Dog,
     A:Ph.Stranger,Hum.Target. 3.50
642 GK,SD,ATi,CS,JAp,JM,CI,KN,
     Green Lantern,Superman 3.50
Becomes:

DC COMICS

ACTION COMICS
1989–2002

643 B:RSt(s),GP,BBr,V:Intergang . . 4.50
644 GP,BBr,V:Matrix 3.50
645 GP,BBr,I:Maxima. 3.50
646 KG,V:Alien Creature,
    A:Brainiac 4.00
647 GP,KGa,BBr,V:Brainiac. 3.50
648 GP,KGa,BBr,V:Brainiac. 3.50
649 GP,KGa,BBr,V:Brainiac. 3.50
650 JOy,BBr,CS,BMc,GP,KGa,
    ATi,DJu,A:JLA,C:Lobo. 5.50
651 GP,KGa,BBr,Day of Krypton
    Man #3,V:Maxima 3.50
652 GP,KGa,BBr,Day of Krypton
    Man #6,V:Eradicator 5.00
653 BMc,BBr,D:Amanda 3.50
654 BMc,BBr,A:Batman Pt.3 . . . . . . 3.50
655 BMc,BBr,V:Morrisson,Ma
    Kent's Photo Album. 3.50
656 BMc,BBr,Soul Search #1,
    V:Blaze 3.50
657 KGa,BBr,V:Toyman 3.50
658 CS,Sinbad Contract #3 . . . . . . 3.50
659 BMc,BBr,K.Krimson
    Kryptonite #3 . . . . 5.00
660 BMc,BBr,D:Lex Luthor 4.50
661 BMc,BBr,A:Plastic Man. 3.50
662 JOy,JM,TG,BMc,V:Silver
    Banshee,Clark tells
    Lois his identity 5.50
662a 2nd printing 5.00
663 BMc,Time & Time Again,pt.2,
    A:JSA,Legion. 3.50
664 BMc,Time & Time Again,pt.5 . . 3.50
665 TG,V:Baron Sunday 3.50
666 EH,Red Glass Trilogy,pt.3. . . . . 3.50
667 JOy,JM,TG,ATi,DJu,Revenge
    of the Krypton Man,pt.4 . . . . . . 3.75
668 BMc,Luthor confirmed dead . . . 3.50
669 BMc,V:Intergang,A:Thorn 3.50
670 BMc,A:Waverider,JLA,JLE 3.50
671 KD,Blackout,pt.2 . . . . 3.50
672 BMc,Superman Meets Lex
    Luthor II 3.50
673 BMc,V:Hellgramite 3.50
674 BMc,Panic in the Sky (Prologue)
    R:Supergirl(Matrix) 6.00
675 BMc,Panic in the Sky #4,
    V:Brainiac 3.50
676 B:KK(s),JG,A:Supergirl,Lex
    Luthor II 3.50
677 JG,Supergirl V:Superman 3.50
678 JG,O:Lex Luthor II. 3.50
679 JG,I:Shellshock 3.50
680 JG,Blaze/Satanus War,pt.2 . . . . 3.50
681 JG,V:Hellgramite 3.50
682 DAb,TA,V:Hi-Tech 3.50
683 JG,I:Jackal,C:Doomsday. 3.50
683a 2nd printing 3.00
684 JG,Doomsday Pt.4. . . . . 4.00
684a 2nd printing 3.00
685 JG,Funeral for a Friend#2. . . . . 3.50
686 JG,Funeral for a Friend#6. . . . . 3.50
687 JG,Reign of Superman #1,Direct
    Sales,Die-Cut(c),Mini-Poster,
    F:Last Son of Krypton 3.00
687a newsstand Ed. 3.00
688 JG,V:Guy Gardner. 3.00
689 JG,V:Man of Steel,A:Superboy,
    Supergirl,R:Real Superman . . . 3.50
690 JG,Cyborg Vs. Superboy 3.00
691 JG,A:All Supermen,V:Cyborg
    Superman,Mongul. 3.00
692 JG,A:Superboy,Man of Steel. . . 3.00
693 JG,A:Last Son of Krypton 3.00
694 JG,Spilled Blood#2,V:Hi-Tech . . 3.00
695 JG,Foil(c),I:Cauldron,A:Lobo. . . 3.50
695a Newsstand Ed. 3.00
696 JG,V:Alien,C:Doomsday 3.00

697 JG,Bizarro's World #3,
    V:Bizarro 3.00
698 JG,A:Lex Luthor 3.00
699 JG,A:Project Cadmus 3.00
700 JG,Fall of Metropolis#1 . . . . . . 4.00
700a Platinum Edition 15.00
701 JG,Fall of Metropolis#5,
    V:Luthor. 3.00
702 JG,DvM,B:DyM(s),R:Bloodsport 3.00
703 JG,DvM,Zero Hour 3.00
704 JG,DvM,Eradicator 3.00
705 JG,DvM,Supes real? 3.00
706 JG,DvM,A:Supergirl. 3.00
707 JG,DvM,V:Shado Dragon 3.00
708 JG,DvM,R:Deathtrap 3.00
709 JG,DvM,A:Guy Gardner,
    Warrior. 3.00
710 JG,DvM,Death of Clark Kent,pt.3
    [new Miraweb format begins] . . 3.00
711 JG,DvM,Death of Clark
    Kent,pt.7 . . . . 3.00
712 Rescue Jimmy Olsen 3.00
713 Scarlet Salvation. 3.00
714 R:The Joker 3.00
715 DvM,DaR,V:Parasite. 3.00
716 DvM,DaR,Trial of Superman. . . . 3.00
717 DvM,DaR,Trial of Superman. . . . 3.00
718 DvM,DRo,mystery of Demolitia . 3.00
719 DvM,DRo 3.00
720 DvM,DRo,Lois ends
    engagement 3.50
721 DvM,DRo,lottery fever 3.00
722 DvM,DaR,Tornados in
    Smallville 3.00
723 V:Brainiac 3.00
724 V:S.T.A.R.labs monster. 3.00
725 Tolos 3.00
726 DvM(s),TMo,DRo,Krisis of the
    Krimson Kryptonite follow-up. . . 3.00
727 DvM(s),TMo,DRo,brutal weather
    in Metropolis, Final Night tie-in . 3.00
728 DvM(s),TG,DRo, Some
    Honeymoon! 3.00
729 DvM(s),TG,DRo, in Fortress of
    Solitude 3.00
730 DvM(s),TG,Ro, ... 3.00
731 DvM(s),TG,DRo, R:Cauldron . . 3.00
732 DvM(s),TG,DRo, Atomic Skull
    rampages through Metropolis . . 3.00
733 DvM(s),TG,DRo, V:Matallo,
    A:Ray. 3.00
734 DvM(s),TG,DRo, Superman &
    Atom in Kandor. 3.00
735 DvM(s),TG,DRo, V:Savior. 3.00
736 DvM(s),TG,DRo. 3.00

Action Comics #687 © DC Comics Inc.

737 MWa(s),TG,DRo, Luthor gets
    day in court 3.00
738 SI,JMz,Lois sent to Australia . . 3.00
739 SI,JMz,Superman imprisoned. . 3.00
740 SI,JMz,Lucy Lane disappears. . 3.00
741 SI,JMz,V:C.O.M.P.U.T.O. 3.00
742 SI,JMz. 3.00
743 SI,JMz,F:Slam Bradley 3.00
744 SI,JMz,Millennium Giants
    x-over. 3.00
745 SI,JMz,The Prankster. 2.50
746 SI,JMz,The Prankster,pt.2 . . . . 2.50
747 SI,JMz,The Prankster,pt.3 . . . . 2.50
748 SI,JMz,Dominus Theory 2.50
749 RMz(s),TGb,TP,City of the
    Future, pt.1 x-over. 2.50
750 SI,JMz,I:Crazytop, 48-page . . . 3.50
751 SI,JMz,A:Geo-Force 2.50
752 SI,JMz,Supermen of
    America x-over 2.50
753 SI,JMz,A:JLA 2.50
754 SI,JMz,R:Dominus,
    A:Wonder Woman 2.50
755 SI&MMr(s),King of the
    World aftermath. 2.50
756 VGi,old villain is back 2.50
757 TPe(s),TGb,Hawkworld,pt.3 . . 2.50
758 SI,JMz,V:Boss Moxie 2.50
759 RF,SB,Strange Visitor,pt.3 . . . . 2.50
760 JRu,F:Encantadora 2.50
761 JRu 2.50
762 JRu,V:Demon Etrigan 2.50
763 JRu,V:Brainiac 13 . . . . 2.50
764 JRu,marital troubles 2.50
765 JRu,V:Joker & Harley Quinn. . . 2.50
766 F:Batman 2.50
767 CriticalCondition,pt.4,x-over . . . 2.50
768 F:Marvel Family 3.00
769 Superman:Arkham,concl. 3.00
770 Superman:Emperor,48-pg. 4.50
771 CDi(s),F:Nightwing 2.50
772 V:Ra's al Ghul,pt.1 . . . . 2.50
773 V:Ra's al Ghul,pt.2 . . . . 2.50
774 A:Martian Manhunter 2.50
775 48-page. 18.00
775a 2nd printing (2004) 4.50
776 Return to Krypton,pt.4. . . . . 2.50
777 Kancer. 2.50
778 MWm,Infestation x-over,pt.4 . . . 2.50
779 V:Killer,pt.1 . . . . 2.50
780 V:Killer,pt.2 . . . . 2.50
781 Our Worlds at War,All-OutWar . 2.50
782 Our Worlds at War,Casualties . . 2.50
783 V:Ocean Master,Scorch 2.50
784 Joker:Last Laugh tie-in 2.50
785 R:Bizarro. 2.50
786 PFe,kidnapped by aliens 2.50
787 PFe,Byakko, Gunshin, Sakki . . 2.50
788 PFe,Jikei Ketsuki,pt.1 . . . . 2.50
789 Evil from the Gorge. 2.50
790 Krypto vs. Kancer 2.50
791 Smallville, flash-back tale 2.50
792 Superman, detective. 2.50
793 PFe,Return to KryptonII,concl. . 2.50
794 F:Quintessence 2.50
795 Ending Battle,pt.4 . . . . 2.50
796 Ending Battle,pt.8 . . . . 2.50
797 New General Zod 2.50
798 Lost Hearts, pt.4 x-over 2.50
799 TR,SHa,F:Girl 13 . . . . 2.50
800 64-page, life re-examined. 4.50
801 metahumans 2.50
802 PFe,CaS,The Harvest,pt.1 . . . . 2.50
803 PFe,CaS,The Harvest,pt.2 . . . . 2.50
804 PFe,CaS,The Harvest,pt.3 . . . . 2.50
805 PFe,CaS,The Harvest,pt.4 . . . . 2.50
806 PFe,CaS,The Harvest,pt.5 . . . . 2.50
807 PFe,CaS,Supergirl 2.50
808 PFe,CaS,Supergirls 2.50
809 PFe,CaS,murder suspect 2.50
810 PFe,CaS,New Year's 2.25

All comics prices listed are for *Near Mint* condition.

811 KIK,Strange New Visitor 3.00
812 Godfall,pt.1 . . . . 7.00
812a 2nd printing 5.00
813 Godfall,pt.4 . . . . 2.50
814 MCa,Job in jeopardy. 2.50
815 MCa,V:Gog. 2.50
816 MCa,F:Teen Titans 2.50
817 MCa,F:W.Woman & Superboy . 2.50
818 MCa,F:W.Woman & Superboy . 2.50
819 MCa,I:Sodom & Gomorrah. . . . 2.50
820 V:Silver Banshee 2.50
Ann.#1 AAd,DG,A:Batman 8.00
Ann.#2 MMi,CS,GP,JOy,DJu,BBr,
    V:Mongul 4.00
Ann.#3 TG,Armageddon X-over. . . 3.50
Ann.#4 Eclipso,A:Captain Marvel . 3.50
Ann.#5 MZ(c),Bloodlines, I:Loose
    Cannon 3.50
Ann.#6 Elseworlds,JBy(a&S) 3.50
Ann.#7 Year One Annual 4.50
Ann.#8 DvM,Legends of the Dead
    Earth 3.50
Ann.#9 DvM,VGi,BBr,Pulp Heroes . 4.50
Gold.Ann.rep.#1 . . . . 2.50
#0 Peer Pressure,pt.4 (1994) 2.50
Spec.#1,000,000 MSh(s),RLm,JMz. 2.50

ADAM STRANGE
1990
1 NKu,A.Strange on Rann 5.00
2 NKu,Wanted:Adam Strange. 4.00
3 NKu,final issue. 4.00
TPB Man of Two Worlds (2003) . . 19.95
2nd Series, Sept. 2004
1 (of 8) PFe,R:Adam Strange 2.95
2 PFe 2.95

Advanced Dungeons & Dragons #25
© DC Comics, Inc.

ADVANCED
DUNGEONS & DRAGONS
1988–91
1 JD,I:Onyx,Priam,Timoth,
    Cybriana,Vajra,Luna 5.00
2 JD,V:Imgig Zu,I:Conner. 4.00
3 JD,V:Imgig Zu 4.00
4 JD,V:Imgig Zu,I:Kyriani 3.00
5 JD,Spirit of Myrrth I 3.00
6 JD,Spirit of Myrrth II. 3.00
7 JD,Spirit of Myrrth III 2.50
8 JD,Spirit of Myrrth IV 2.50
9 JD,Catspawn Quartet I 2.50
10 JD,Catspawn Quartet II 2.50

11 JD,Catspawn Quartet III 2.50
12 JD,Catspawn Quartet IV 2.50
13 JD,Spell Games I 2.50
14 JD,Spell Games II. 2.50
15 JD,Spell Games III 2.50
16 JD,Spell Games IV 2.50
17 JD,RM,Kyriani's Story I. 2.50
18 JD,RM,Kyriani's Story II 2.50
19 JD,RM,Luna I 2.50
20 JD,RM,Luna II. 2.50
21 JD,RM,Luna III 2.50
22 JD,RM,Luna IV 2.50
23 TMd,RM,Siege Dragons I 2.50
24 Scavengers. 2.50
25 JD,RM,Centaur Village 2.25
26 JD,Timoth the Centaur 2.25
27 JD,Kyriani,Dragons Eye #1. . . . 2.25
28 JD,Dragons Eye #2. . . . . 2.25
29 JD,RM,Dragons Eye #3 . . . . . . 2.25
30 JD,RM,Carril's Killer Revealed . . 2.25
31 TMd,Onyx Father,pt.1 . . . . 2.25
32 TMd,Onyx Father,pt.2 . . . . 2.25
33 JD,Waterdeep,pt.1 . . . . 2.25
34 JD,Waterdeep,pt.2 . . . . 2.25
35 JD,RM,Waterdeep,pt.3 . . . . 2.25
36 JD,RM,final issue 2.25
Ann.#1 JD,RM,Tmd 4.00

ADVENTURE COMICS
Nov., 1938–83
[Prev: New Comics]
32 CF(c) 4,000.00
33 . . . . 2,000.00
34 FG(c) 2,000.00
35 FG(c) 2,000.00
36 Giant Snake(c). 2,000.00
37 Rampaging Elephant(c) 2,000.00
38 Tiger(c). 2,000.00
39 Male Bondage(c) 2,100.00
40 CF(c),1st app. Sandman . . 65,000.00
41 Killer Shark(c) 8,000.00
42 CF,Sandman(c) 10,000.00
43 CF(c) 4,500.00
44 CF,Sandman(c) 10,000.00
45 FG(c) 4,500.00
46 CF,Sandman(c) 7,000.00
47 Sandman (c) 7,000.00
48 1st app.& B:Hourman 37,000.00
49 . . . . 3,000.00
50 Hourman(c) 3,000.00
51 BBa(c),Sandman(c) 4,800.00
52 BBa(c),Hourman(c) 2,800.00
53 BBa(c),1st app. Minuteman . 2,800.00
54 BBa(c),Hourman(c) 2,800.00
55 BBa(c),same 2,800.00
56 BBa(c),same 2,800.00
57 BBa(c),same 2,800.00
58 BBa(c),same 2,800.00
59 BBa(c),same 2,800.00
60 Sandman(c) 4,800.00
61 CF(c),JBu,Starman(c) . . . 18,000.00
62 JBu(c),JBu,Starman(c). . . . 2,400.00
63 JBu(c),JBu,same 2,400.00
64 JBu(c),JBu,same 2,400.00
65 JBu(c),JBu,same 2,400.00
66 JBu(c),JBu,O:Shining Knight,
    Starman(c) 2,900.00
67 JBu(c),JBu,O:Mist 2,400.00
68 JBu(c),JBu,same 2,400.00
69 JBu(c),JBu,1st app. Sandy,
    Starman(c) 2,700.00
70 JBu(c),JBu,Starman(c). . . . 2,200.00
71 JBu(c),JBu,same 2,200.00
72 JBu(c),S&K,JBu,Sandman. 18,000.00
73 S&K(c),S&K,I:Manhunter . 19,000.00
74 S&K(c),S&K,You can't Escape
    your Fate-The Sandman . . 2,400.00
75 S&K(c),S&K,Sandman and
    Sandy Battle Thor. 2,400.00
76 S&K(c),Sandman(c),S&K. . 2,400.00

Adventure Comics #42
© DC Comics, Inc.

77 S&K,(c),S&K,same. 2,400.00
78 S&K(c),S&K,same 2,400.00
79 S&K(c),S&K,Manhunter . . . 3,000.00
80 S&K(c),Sandman(c),S&K. . 2,400.00
81 S&K(c),MMe,S&K,same. . . 1,500.00
82 S&K(c),S&K,Sandman
    X-Mas story 1,500.00
83 S&K(c),S&K,Sandman
    Boxing(c),E:Hourman 1,500.00
84 S&K(c),S&K,same 1,500.00
85 S&K(c),S&K,Sandman in
    The Amazing Dreams of
    Gentleman Jack 1,500.00
86 S&K(c),Sandman(c). 1,500.00
87 S&K(c),same 1,500.00
88 S&K(c),same 1,500.00
89 S&K(c),same 1,500.00
90 S&K(c),same 1,500.00
91 S&K(c),JK 1,400.00
92 S&K(c) 1,300.00
93 S&K(c),Sandman in Sleep
    for Sale. 1,300.00
94 S&K(c),Sandman(c). 1,300.00
95 S&K(c),same 1,300.00
96 S&K(c),same 1,300.00
97 S&K(c),same 1,300.00
98 JK(c),Sandman in Hero
    of Dreams. 1,300.00
99 JK(c). 1,300.00
100 . . . . 1,700.00
101 S&K(c) 1,300.00
102 S&K(c) 1,300.00
103 B:Superboy stories,(c),BU:
    Johnny Quick,Aquaman,Shining
    Knight,Green Arrow 4,000.00
104 S&S,ToyTown USA 1,400.00
105 S&S,Palace of Fantasy . . . 1,000.00
106 S&S,Weather Hurricane . . 1,000.00
107 S&S,The Sky is the Limit. . 1,000.00
108 S&S,Proof of the Proverbs 1,000.00
109 S&S,You Can't Lose 1,000.00
110 S&S,The Farmer Takes
    it Easy. 1,000.00
111 S&S,The Whiz Quiz Club . . 1,000.00
112 S&S,Super Safety First . . . 1,000.00
113 S&S,The 33rd Christmas . . . 900.00
114 S&S,Superboy SpellsDanger 900.00
115 S&S,The Adventure of
    Jaguar Boy 900.00
116 S&S,JBu,Superboy Toy
    Tester. 900.00
117 S&S,JBu,Miracle Plane. 900.00
118 S&S,JBu,The Quiz Biz
    Broadcast 900.00
119 WMo,JBu,Superboy
    Meets Girls 900.00

120 S&S,JBu,A:Perry White;
I:Ringmaster 950.00
121 S&S,Great Hobby Contest . . 800.00
122 S&S,Superboy-Super-
Magician 800.00
123 S&S,Lesson For a Bully 800.00
124 S&S,Barbed Wire Boys
Town 800.00
125 S&S,The Weight Before
Christmas 800.00
126 S&S,Superboy:Crime
Fighting Poet 800.00
127 MMe,O:Shining Knight;
Super Bellboy 800.00
128 WMo,How Clark Kent Met
Lois Lane 800.00
129 WMo,Pupils of the Past 800.00
130 WMo,Superboy Super
Salesman 800.00
131 WMo,The Million Dollar
Athlete 700.00
132 WMo,Superboy Super
Cowboy 700.00
133 WMo,Superboy's Report
Card 700.00
134 WMo,Silver Gloves Sellout . . 700.00
135 WMo,The Most Amazing
of All Boys 700.00
136 WMo,My Pal Superboy 700.00
137 WMo,Treasure of Tondimo . . 700.00
138 WMo,Around the World in
Eighty Minutes 700.00
139 WMo,Telegraph Boy 700.00
140 Journey to the Moon 700.00
141 WMo,When Superboy Lost
His Powers 700.00
142 WMo,The Man Who Walked
With Trouble 700.00
143 WMo,The Superboy Savings
Bank,A:Wooden Head Jones 700.00
144 WMo,The Way to Stop
Superboy 700.00
145 WMo,Holiday Hijackers 700.00
146 The Substitute Superboy . . . 700.00
147 Clark Kent,Orphan 700.00
148 Superboy Meets Mummies . . 700.00
149 Fake Superboys 700.00
150 FF,Superboy's Initiation 850.00
151 FF,No Hunting(c) 850.00
152 Superboy Hunts For a Job . . 800.00
153 FF,Clark Kent,Boy Hobo 850.00
154 The Carnival Boat Crimes . . 600.00
155 FF,Superboy-Hollywood
Actor 850.00
156 The Flying Peril 600.00
157 FF,The Worst Boy in
Smallville 850.00
158 The Impossible Task 600.00
159 FF,Superboy Millionaire? . . . 875.00
160 Superboy's Phoney Father . . 600.00
161 FF 850.00
162 Super-Coach of
Smallville High! 600.00
163 FF,Superboy's Phoney
Father 850.00
164 Discovers the Secret of
a Lost Indian Tribe! 600.00
165 Superboy's School for
Stunt Men! 600.00
166 Town That Stole Superboy . . 600.00
167 Lana Lang, Super-Girl! 600.00
168 The Boy Who Out Smarted
Superboy 600.00
169 Clark Kent's Private Butler . . 600.00
170 Lana Lang's Big Crush 600.00
171 Superboy's Toughest Tasks . . 550.00
172 Laws that Backfired 550.00
173 Superboy's School of
Hard Knocks 550.00
174 The New Lana Lang! 550.00
175 Duel of the Superboys 550.00

176 Superboy's New Parents! . . . 550.00
177 Hot-Rod Chariot Race! 550.00
178 Boy in the Lead Mask 550.00
179 World's Whackiest
Inventors 550.00
180 Grand Prize o/t Underworld . 550.00
181 Mask for a Hero 550.00
182 Super Hick from Smallville . . 500.00
183 Superboy and Cleopatra 500.00
184 Shutterbugs of Smallville . . . 500.00
185 The Mythical Monster 500.00
186 . . . . 500.00
187 25th Century Superboy 500.00
188 Bull Fighter from
Smallville 500.00
189 Girl of Steel(Lana Lang) 500.00
190 The Two Clark Kents 500.00
191 . . . . 500.00
192 Coronation of Queen
Lana Lang 500.00
193 Superboy's Lost Costume . . . 500.00
194 Super-Charged Superboy . . . 500.00
195 Lana Lang's Romance
on Mars! 500.00
196 Superboy vs. King Gorilla . . . 500.00
197 V:Juvenile Gangs 500.00
198 Super-Carnival from Space . . 500.00
199 Superboy meets Superlad . . . 500.00
200 Superboy and the Apes! 700.00
201 Safari in Smallville! 450.00
202 Superboy City, U.S.A. 450.00
203 Uncle Superboy! 475.00
204 Super-Brat of Smallville 450.00
205 Journey of the Second
Superboy! 450.00
206 The Impossible Creatures . . . 450.00
207 Smallville's Worst Athlete . . . 450.00
208 Rip Van Winkle of
Smallville? 450.00
209 Superboy Week! 450.00
210 I:Krypto,The Superdog
from Krypton 5,000.00
211 Superboy's Amazing Dream! . 400.00
212 Superboy's Robot Twin 400.00
213 Junior Jury of Smallville! 400.00
214 A:Krypto 700.00
215 Super-Hobby of Superboy . . 400.00
216 The Wizard City 400.00
217 Farewell to Smallville 400.00
218 Two World's of Superboy . . . 400.00
219 Rip Van Wrinkle of
Smallville 400.00
220 Greatest Show on Earth
A:Krypto 475.00

Adventure Comics #170
© DC Comics Inc.

221 The Babe of Steel 350.00
222 Superboy's Repeat
Performance 350.00
223 Hercules Junior 350.00
224 Pa Kent Superman 350.00
225 Bird with Super-Powers 350.00
226 Superboy's Super Rival! 350.00
227 Good Samaritan of
Smallville 350.00
228 Clark Kent's Body Guard . . . 350.00
229 . . . . 350.00
230 Secret o/t Flying Horse 325.00
231 Super-Feats of Super-Baby . 325.00
232 House where Superboy
was Born 325.00
233 Joe Smith, Man of Steel 325.00
234 1,001 Rides of Superboy . . . 325.00
235 Confessions of Superboy . . . 325.00
236 Clark Kent's Super-Dad 325.00
237 Robot War of Smallville 325.00
238 Secret Past of
Superboy's Father 325.00
239 Super-Tricks of
the Dog of Steel 325.00
240 Super Teacher from Krypton . 325.00
241 Super-Outlaw of Smallville . . 325.00
242 The Kid From Krypton 325.00
243 Super Toys from Krypton . . . 325.00
244 Poorest Family in Smallville . 325.00
245 The Mystery of Monster X . . 325.00
246 Girl Who Trapped Superboy . 325.00
247 I&O:Legion 7,700.00
248 Green Arrow 300.00
249 CS,Green Arrow 300.00
250 JK,Green Arrow 300.00
251 JK,Green Arrow 300.00
252 JK,Green Arrow 300.00
253 JK,1st Superboy &
Robin T.U. 400.00
254 JK,Green Arrow 300.00
255 JK,Green Arrow 300.00
256 JK,O:Green Arrow 850.00
257 CS,LE,A:Hercules,Samson . . 250.00
258 LE,Aquaman,Superboy 250.00
259 I:Crimson Archer 250.00
260 1st S.A. O:Aquaman 1,000.00
261 GA,A:Lois Lane 200.00
262 O:Speedy 200.00
263 GA,Aquaman,Superboy 200.00
264 GA,A:Robin Hood 200.00
265 GA,Aquaman,Superboy 200.00
266 GA,I:Aquagirl 200.00
267 N:Legion(2nd app.) 1,200.00
268 I:Aquaboy 200.00
269 I:Aqualad,E:Green Arrow . . . 350.00
270 2nd A:Aqualad,B:Congorilla . 200.00
271 O:Lex Luthor rtd 350.00
272 I:Human Flying Fish 200.00
273 Aquaman,Superboy 200.00
274 Aquaman,Superboy 200.00
275 O:Superman/Batman
T.U. rtd 300.00
276 Superboy,3rd A:Metallo 200.00
277 Aquaman,Superboy 200.00
278 Aquaman,Superboy 200.00
279 CS,Aquaman,Superboy 200.00
280 CS,A:Lori Lemaris 200.00
281 Aquaman,Superboy
E:Congorilla 200.00
282 5th A:Legion,I:Starboy 300.00
283 I:Phantom Zone 275.00
284 CS,JM,Aquaman,Superboy . 150.00
285 WB,B:Bizarro World 250.00
286 I:Bizarro Mxyzptlk 250.00
287 I:Dev-Em,Bizarro Perry White,
Jimmy Olsen 150.00
288 A:Dev-Em 150.00
289 Superboy 150.00
290 8th A:Legion,O&J:Sunboy,
I:Brainiac 5 . . . . 275.00
291 A:Lex Luthor 150.00

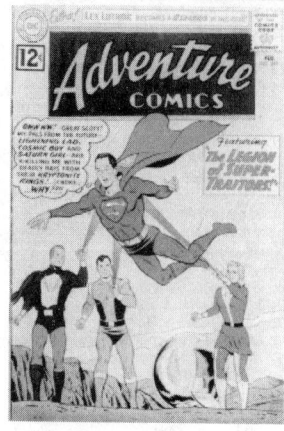

Adventure Comics #293
© DC Comics, Inc.

292 Superboy,I:Bizarro Lucy Lane,
   Lana Lang 150.00
293 CS,O&I:Marv-El,I:Bizarro
   Luthor 250.00
294 I:Bizarro M.Monroe,JFK . . . 200.00
295 I:Bizarro Titano 150.00
296 A:Ben Franklin,George
   Washington 150.00
297 Lana Lang Superboy Sister . 150.00
298 The Fat Superboy 150.00
299 I:Gold Kryptonite 150.00
300 B:Legion,J:Mon-El,
   E:Bizarro World 650.00
301 CS,O:Bouncing Boy 225.00
302 CS,Legion 150.00
303 I:Matter Eater Lad 150.00
304 D:Lightning Lad 150.00
305 A:Chameleon Boy 150.00
306 I:Legion of Sub.Heroes 150.00
307 I:Element Lad 150.00
308 I:Light Lass 150.00
309 I:Legion of Super Monsters . 150.00
310 A:Mxyzptlk 150.00
311 CS,V:Legion of Substitue
   Heroes 125.00
312 R:Lightning Lad 150.00
313 CS,J:Supergirl 125.00
314 A:Hitler 125.00
315 A:Legion of Substitute
   Heroes 125.00
316 O:Legion 100.00
317 I&J:Dreamgirl 100.00
318 Legion 100.00
319 Legion 100.00
320 A:Dev-Em 100.00
321 I:Time Trapper 100.00
322 JF,A:Legion of Super Pets . . . 90.00
323 JF,BU:Kypto 90.00
324 JF,I:Legion of Super Outlaws . 90.00
325 JF,V:Lex Luthor 90.00
326 BU:Superboy 90.00
327 I&J:Timber Wolf 90.00
328 Legion 90.00
329 I:Legion of Super Bizarros . . . 90.00
330 Legion 90.00
331 Legion 75.00
332 Legion 75.00
333 Legion 75.00
334 Legion 75.00
335 Legion 75.00
336 Legion 75.00
337 Legion 75.00
338 Legion 75.00
339 Legion 75.00
340 I:Computo 75.00

341 CS,D:Triplicate Girl (becomes
   Duo Damsel) 65.00
342 CS,Star Boy expelled 60.00
343 CS,V:Lords of Luck 60.00
344 CS,Super Stalag,pt.1 . . . . 60.00
345 CS,Super Stalag,pt.2 . . . . 60.00
346 CS,I&J:Karate Kid,Princess
   Projectra,I:Nemesis Kid 75.00
347 CS,Legion 60.00
348 I:Dr.Regulus 75.00
349 CS,I:Rond Vidar 60.00
350 CS,I:White Witch 75.00
351 CS,R:Star Boy 60.00
352 CS,I:Fatal Fire 60.00
353 CS,D:Ferro Lad 75.00
354 CS,Adult Legion 60.00
355 CS,J:Insect Queen 50.00
356 CS,Five Legion Orphans 50.00
357 CS,I:Controller 50.00
358 I:Hunter 50.00
359 CS,Outlawed Legion,pt.1 . . . . 50.00
360 CS,Outlawed Legion,pt.2 . . . . 50.00
361 I:Dominators (30th century) . . 50.00
362 I:Dr.Mantis Morto 50.00
363 V:Dr.Mantis Morlo 50.00
364 A:Legion of Super Pets 50.00
365 CS,I:Shadow Lass,
   V:Fatal Five 50.00
366 CS,J:Shadow Lass 50.00
367 N:Legion H.Q.,I:Dark Circle . . 50.00
368 CS 50.00
369 CS,JAb,I:Mordru 50.00
370 CS,JAb,V:Mordru 50.00
371 CS,JAb,I:Chemical King 55.00
372 CS,JAb,J:Timber Wolf,
   Chemical King 55.00
373 I:Tornado Twins 45.00
374 WM,I:Black Mace 45.00
375 I:Wanderers 45.00
376 Execution of Cham.Boy 45.00
377 Heroes for Hire 45.00
378 Twelve Hours to Live 45.00
379 Burial In Space 45.00
380 The Amazing Space Odyssey
   of the Legion,E:Legion 45.00
381 The Supergirl Gang
   C:Batgirl,B:Supergirl 125.00
382 NA(c),The Superteams Split
   Up,A:Superman 40.00
383 NA(c),Please Stop my Funeral,
   A:Superman,Comet,Streaky . . 40.00
384 KS,The Heroine Haters,
   A:Superman 40.00
385 Supergirl's Big Sister 40.00
386 The Beast That Loved
   Supergirl 40.00
387 Wolfgirl of Stanhope;
   A:Superman;V:Lex Luthor 40.00
388 Kindergarten Criminal;
   V:Luthor,Brainiac 40.00
389 A:Supergirl's Parents,
   V:Brainiac 40.00
390 Linda Danvers Superstar
   (80 page giant) 75.00
391 The Super Cheat;A:Comet . . 40.00
392 Supergirls Lost Costume 40.00
393 KS,Unwanted Supergirl 40.00
394 KS,Heartbreak Prison 40.00
395 Heroine in Haunted House . . . 40.00
396 Mystery o/t Super Orphan . . . 40.00
397 Now Comes Zod,N:Supergirl,
   V:Luthor 40.00
398 Maid of Doom,A:Superman,
   Streaky,Krypto,Comet 40.00
399 CI,Johnny Dee,Hero Bum . . . 50.00
400 MSy,35th Anniv.,Return of the
   Black Flame 30.00
401 MSy,JAb,The Frightened
   Supergirl,V:Lex Luthor 30.00
402 MSy,JAb,TD,I:Starfire,
   Dr.Kangle 40.00

403 68 page giant 75.00
404 MSy,JAb,V:Starfire 25.00
405 V:Starfire,Dr.Kangle 25.00
406 MSy,JAb,Suspicion 25.00
407 MSy,JAb,Suspicion Confirmed
   N:Supergirl 25.00
408 The Face at the Window 25.00
409 MSy,DG,Legion rep. 40.00
410 N:Supergirl 40.00
411 CI,N:Supergirl 40.00
412 rep.Strange Adventures #180
   (I:Animal Man) 45.00
413 GM,JKu,rep.Hawkman 40.00
414 Animal Man rep. 40.00
415 BO,GM,CI,Animal Man rep. . . 40.00
416 CI,All women issue,giantsize . 40.00
417 GM,inc.rep.Adventure #161,
   Frazetta art. 35.00
418 ATh,Black Canary 35.00
419 ATh,Black Canary 40.00
420 Animal Man rep. 35.00
421 MSy,Supergirl 20.00
422 MSy,Supergirl 20.00
423 MSy,Supergirl 20.00
424 MSy,E:Supergirl,A:JLA 20.00
425 AN,ATh,I:Captain Fear 35.00
426 MSy,DG,JAp,Vigilante 20.00
427 TD 20.00
428 TD,I:Black Orchid 75.00
429 TD,AN,Black Orchid 35.00
430 A:Black Orchid 35.00
431 JAp,ATh,B:Spectre 75.00
432 JAp,AN,A:Spectre,Capt.Fear . 35.00
433 JAp,AN 35.00
434 JAp 35.00
435 MGr(1st work),JAp,Aquaman . 35.00
436 JAp,MGr,Aquaman 35.00
437 JAp,MGr,Aquaman 35.00
438 JAp,HC,DD,7 Soldiers 35.00
439 JAp 35.00
440 JAp,O:New Spectre 55.00
441 JAp,B:Aquaman 15.00
442 JAp,A:Aquaman 15.00
443 JAp 15.00
444 JAp 15.00
445 JAp,RE,JSon,Creeper 18.00
446 JAp,RE,JSon,Creeper 18.00
447 JAp,RE,JSon,Creeper 18.00
448 JAp,Aquaman 15.00
449 JAp,MN,TA,J'onn J'onz. 15.00
450 JAp,MN,TA,Supergirl 15.00
451 JAp,MN,TA,Hawkman 15.00
452 JAp,Aquaman 15.00
453 MA,CP,JRu,B:Superboy
   & Aqualad 15.00
454 CP,DG,A:Kryptonite Kid 15.00
455 CP,DG,A:Kryptonite Kid
   E:Aqualad 15.00
456 JSon,JA. 15.00
457 JSon,JA,JO,B:Eclipso 15.00
458 JSon,JAp,JO,BL,E:Superboy
   & Eclipso 15.00
459 IN,FMc,JAp,JSon,DN,JA,A:Wond.
   Woman,New Gods,Green Lantern,
   Flash,Deadman,(giant size) . . 25.00
460 IN,FMc,JAp,DN,DA,JSon,JA,
   D:Darkseid. 25.00
461 IN,FMc,JAp,JSon,DN,JA,
   B:JSA & Aquaman 25.00
462 IN,FMc,DH,JL,DG,JA,
   D:Earth 2,Batman 25.00
463 DH,JL,JSon,FMc. 20.00
464 DH,JAp,JSon,DN,DA,
   Deadman 20.00
465 DN,JSon,DG,JL. 20.00
466 MN,JL,JSon,DN,DA 20.00
467 JSon,SD,RT,I:Starman
   B:Plastic Man 25.00
468 SD,JSon 8.00
469 SD,JSon,O:Starman 8.00
470 SD,JSon,O:Starman 8.00

Adventure Comics #426
© DC Comics, Inc.

471 SD,JSon,I:Brickface 8.00
472 SD,RT,JSon 8.00
473 SD,RT,JSon 8.00
474 SD,RT,JSon 8.00
475 BB(c),SD,RT,JSon,DG,
    B:Aquaman 8.00
476 SD,RT,JSon,DG 8.00
477 SD,RT,JSon,DG 8.00
478 SD,RT,JSon,DG 8.00
479 CI,DG,JSon,Dial H For Hero,
    E:Starman and Aquaman 8.00
480 CI,DJ,B:Dial H for Hero 8.00
481 CI,DJ 8.00
482 CI,DJ,DH. 8.00
483 CI,DJ,DH. 8.00
484 GP(c),CI,DJ,DH 8.00
485 GP(c),CI,DJ. 8.00
486 GP(c),DH,RT,TVE 8.00
487 CI,DJ,DH. 8.00
488 CI,DJ,TVE. 8.00
489 CI,FMc,TVE 8.00
490 GP(c),CI,E:Dial H for Hero 8.00
491 KG(c),DigestSize,DN,
    Shazam,rep.other material . . . 20.00
492 KG(c),DN,E:Shazam. 20.00
493 KG(c),GT,B:Challengers of
    the Unknown,reprints 20.00
494 KG(c),GT,Challengers,
    reprints. 20.00
495 ATh,reprints,Challengers. 20.00
496 GK(c),ATh,reprints,
    Challengers 20.00
497 ATh,DA,reps.,E:Challengers . . 20.00
498 GK(c),reprints,Rep.Legion . . . 20.00
499 GK(c),reprints,Rep 20.00
500 KG(c),Legion reprints,Rep . . . 20.00
501 reprints,Rep 20.00
502 reprints,Rep 20.00
503 reprints,final issue 20.00
Giant #1, 80 page, 7 tales (1998) . 15.00

ADVENTURE COMICS
1999
1 JeR,PSj,F:Starman & The Atom . 2.00

ADVENTURES IN
THE DC UNIVERSE
1997–98
1 F:New JLA 6.00
2 F:The Flash,Catwoman 4.00
3 Wonder Woman vs. Cheetah;
    Poison Ivy vs. Batman. 4.00

4 F:Green Lantern vs. Glorious
    Godfrey; Mister Miracle 4.00
5 F:Martian Manhunter, all alien
    issue 4.00
6 F:Ocean Master, Power Girl 4.00
7 SVa(s),F:Shazam Family 4.00
8 SVa(s),F:Blue Beetle &
    Booster Gold 4.00
9 SVa(s),F:Flash,V:Grodd,Cipher . . 4.00
10 SVa(s),Legion month 4.00
11 SVa(s),F:Gr.Lantern & W.Woman 4.00
12 SVa(s) 4.50
13 SVa(s),A:Martian Manhunter . . . 4.00
14 SVa(s),Flash races Superboy . . . 4.00
15 SVa(s),Shazam,Aquaman. 4.00
16 SVa(s),F:Green Lantern 4.00
17 SVa(s),F:Batman, Creeper 4.00
18 SVa(s),F:JLA. 4.50
19 F:Catwoman, Wonder Woman . . 4.00
Ann.#1 magic amulets,5 stories. . . . 5.00

ADVENTURES IN THE
RIFLE BRIGADE
DC/Vertigo, Aug., 2000
1 (of 3) GEn, ... 2.50
2 F:Gerta Gash 2.50
3 GEn,Up Yours Fritz, concl. 2.50

ADVENTURES IN THE
RIFLE BRIGADE:
OPERATION BOLLOCK
DC/Vertigo, Aug., 2001
1 GEn,find Hitler's testicle! 2.50
2 GEn,still looking. 2.50
3 GEn,concl. 2.50

ADVENTURES OF
ALAN LADD
1949–51
1 Ph(c) 1,200.00
2 Ph(c) 600.00
3 Ph(c) 450.00
4 Ph(c) 450.00
5 Ph(c),inc.Destination Danger. . 400.00
6 Ph(c) 400.00
7 . . . . 400.00
8 Grand Duchess takes over . . . 400.00
9 Deadlien in Rapula 400.00

ADVENTURES OF
BOB HOPE
1951–68
1 Ph(c) 2,500.00
2 Ph(c) 1,100.00
3 Ph(c) 650.00
4 Ph(c) 650.00
5 thru 10 . . . . @500.00
11 thru 20 . . . . @300.00
21 thru 40 . . . . @200.00
41 thru 60 . . . . @150.00
61 thru 90 . . . . @75.00
91 thru 93 . . . . @60.00
94 C:Aquaman. 75.00
95 1st Superhip 75.00
96 thru 105 . . . . @60.00
106 thru 109 NA . . . . @85.00

ADVENTURES OF
DEAN MARTIN AND
JERRY LEWIS
1952–57
1 . . . . 1,350.00
2 . . . . 650.00
3 thru 10 . . . . @350.00
11 thru 20 . . . . @250.00

Adventures in the DC Universe #15
© DC Comics Inc.

21 thru 40 . . . . @150.00
Becomes:

ADVENTURES OF
JERRY LEWIS
1957–71
41 thru 55 . . . . @125.00
56 thru 69 . . . . @100.00
70 thru 87 . . . . @75.00
88 A:Bob Hope. 75.00
89 thru 91 . . . . @50.00
92 C:Superman 70.00
93 Beatles 65.00
94 thru 96 . . . . @60.00
97 A:Batman & Joker. 125.00
98 thru 101 . . . . @55.00
102 NA,Beatles 125.00
103 and 104 NA . . . . @75.00
105 A:Superman 80.00
106 thru 111 . . . . @45.00
112 A:Flash 55.00
113 thru 116 . . . . @40.00
117 A:Wonder Woman 80.00
118 thru 124 . . . . @35.00

ADVENTURES OF
FORD FAIRLANE
1990
1 thru 4 DH . . . . @2.00

ADVENTURES OF
THE OUTSIDERS
(see BATMAN & THE OUT-
SIDERS)

ADVENTURES OF OZZIE
AND HARRIET
1949–50
1 Ph(c) 1,200.00
2 . . . . 650.00
3 thru 5 . . . . @500.00

ADVENTURES OF REX,
THE WONDERDOG
1952–59
1 ATh 1,600.00
2 ATh. 750.00
3 ATh. 600.00
4 . . . . 450.00
5 . . . . 450.00

DC COMICS

6 thru 10 . . . . @350.00
11 Atom Bomb 400.00
12 thru 20. . . . . @200.00
21 thru 46. . . . . @150.00

ADVENTURES OF SUPERBOY
See: SUPERBOY

ADVENTURES OF SUPERMAN
See: SUPERMAN

AGENT LIBERTY
1992
Spec. 1 DAb,O:Agent Liberty. 2.00

ALIEN NATION
1988
1 JBi,movie adaption 2.50

ALL-AMERICAN COMICS
1939–48
1 B:Hop Harrigan,Scribbly,Mutt&Jeff,
  Red,White&Blue,Bobby Thatcher,
  Skippy,Daiseybelle,Mystery Men
  of Mars,Tooonerville 7,500.00
2 B:Ripley's Believe It or Not . . 2,500.00
3 Hop Harrigan (c) 1,700.00
4 Flag(c). 1,700.00
5 B:The American Way 1,700.00
6 ShM(c),Fredric Marchin in
  The American Way. 1,500.00
7 E:Bobby Thatcher,C.H.
  Claudy's A Thousand Years
  in a Minute 1,500.00
8 B:Ultra Man. 3,000.00
9 A:Ultra Man. 1,500.00
10 ShM(c),E:The American Way,
  Santa-X-Mas(c) 1,400.00
11 Ultra Man(c) 1,500.00
12 E:Toonerville Folks. 1,200.00
13 The Infra Red Des'Royers . . 1,200.00
14 Ultra Man 1,200.00
15 E:Tippie and Reg'lar Fellars 1,500.00
16 O&1st App:Green Lantern,
  B:Lantern(c) 170,000.00
17 SMo(c) 24,000.00
18 SMo(c) 15,000.00
19 SMo(c),O&I: Atom, E:Ultra
  Man. 24,000.00
20 I:Atom's costume,Hunkle
  becomes Red Tornado 6,500.00
21 E:Wiley of West Point
  & Skippy 3,700.00
22 . . . . 3,500.00
23 E:Daieybelle. 3,700.00
24 E:Ripley's Believe It or Not . 4,500.00
25 O&I:Dr. Mid-Nite. 14,000.00
26 O&I:Sargon the Sorcerer . . . 5,000.00
27 I:Doiby Dickles. 5,000.00
28 . . . . 2,400.00
29 ShM(c) 2,400.00
30 ShM(c) 2,400.00
31 Adventures of the underfed
  orphans. 2,400.00
32 . . . . 1,800.00
33 . . . . 1,800.00
34 . . . . 1,800.00
35 Doiby discovers Lantern's ID 1,800.00
36 . . . . 1,800.00
37 . . . . 1,800.00
38 . . . . 1,800.00
39 . . . . 1,800.00
40 . . . . 1,800.00
41 . . . . 1,500.00

42 . . . . 1,500.00
43 . . . . 1,500.00
44 I Accuse the Green Lantern! 1,500.00
45 . . . . 1,500.00
46 . . . . 1,500.00
47 Hop Harrigan meets the
  Enemy,(c) 1,500.00
48 . . . . 1,500.00
49 . . . . 1,500.00
50 E:Sargon 1,500.00
51 Murder Under the Stars 1,200.00
52 . . . . 1,200.00
53 Green Lantern delivers
  the Mail. 1,200.00
54 . . . . 1,200.00
55 The Riddle of the
  Runaway Trolley. 1,200.00
56 V:Elegant Esmond. 1,200.00
57 V:The Melancholy Men 1,200.00
58 . . . . 1,200.00
59 The Story of the Man Who
  Couldn't Tell The Truth 1,200.00
60 . . . . 1,200.00
61 O:Soloman Grundy,Fighters
  Never Quit 7,500.00
62 Da Distrik Attorney. 1,100.00
63 . . . . 1,100.00
64 A Bag of Assorted Nuts!. . . . 1,100.00
65 The Man Who Lost
  Wednesday. 1,100.00
66 The Soles of Manhattan! . . . 1,100.00
67 V:King Shark 1,100.00
68 F:Napolean & Joe Safeen . . 1,100.00
69 Backwards Man! 1,100.00
70 JKu,I:Maximillian O'Leary,
  V:Colley, the Leprechaun . . 1,100.00
71 E:Red,White&Blue,The
  Human Bomb 1,000.00
72 B:Black Pirate 1,000.00
73 B:Winkey,Blinky&Noddy,
  Mountain Music Mayhem . . 1,000.00
74 . . . . 1,000.00
75 . . . . 1,000.00
76 Spring Time for Doiby 1,000.00
77 Hop Harrigan(c) 1,000.00
78 . . . . 1,000.00
79 Mutt & Jeff 1,000.00
80 . . . . 1,000.00
81 . . . . 1,000.00
82 . . . . 1,000.00
83 Mutt & Jeff 1,000.00
84 The Adventure of the Man
  with Two Faces. 1,000.00
85 . . . . 1,000.00
86 V:Crime of the Month Club . 1,000.00

All-American Comics #26
© DC Comics, Inc.

87 The Strange Case of
  Professor Nobody. 1,000.00
88 Canvas of Crime 1,000.00
89 O:Harlequin 1,500.00
90 O:Icicle. 1,500.00
91 Wedding of the Harlequin . 1,500.00
92 The Icicle goes South 1,500.00
93 Double Crossing Decoy. . . 1,500.00
94 A:Harlequin 1,500.00
95 The Unmasking of the
  Harlequin 1,500.00
96 ATh(c),Solve the Mystery
  of the Emerald Necklaces! . 1,500.00
97 ATh(c),The Country Fair
  Crimes 1,500.00
98 ATh,ATh(c),End of Sports! . 1,500.00
99 ATh,ATh(c),E:Hop Harrigan . 1,500.00
100 ATh,I:Johnny Thunder 2,500.00
101 ATh,ATh(c),E:Mutt & Jeff . . 1,800.00
102 ATh,ATh(c),E:GrnLantern. . 5,000.00
Becomes:

ALL-AMERICAN WESTERN
1948–52
103 A:Johnny Thunder,The City
  Without Guns, All Johnny
  Thunder stories 700.00
104 ATh(c),Unseen Allies. 450.00
105 ATh(c),Hidden Guns 400.00
106 ATh(c),Snow Mountain
  Ambush 350.00
107 ATh(c),Cheyenne Justice . . 400.00
108 ATh(c),Vengeance of
  the Silver Bullet 350.00
109 ATh(c),Secret of
  Crazy River 350.00
110 ATh(c),Ambush at
  Scarecrow Hills 350.00
111 ATh(c),Gun-Shy Sheriff 350.00
112 ATh(c),Double Danger. 350.00
113 ATh(c),Johnny Thunder
  Indian Chief. 375.00
114 ATh(c),The End of
  Johnny Thunder. 350.00
115 ATh(c),Cheyenne Mystery. . 350.00
116 ATh(c),Buffalo Raiders
  of the Mesa 350.00
117 ATh(c),V:Black Lightnin 250.00
118 ATh(c),Challenge of
  the Aztecs 250.00
119 GK(c),The Vanishing
  Gold Mine 250.00
120 GK(c),Ambush at
  Painted Mountain 250.00
121 ATh(c),The Unmasking of
  Johnny Thunder. 250.00
122 ATh(c),The Real
  Johnny Thunder. 250.00
123 GK(c),Johnny Thunder's
  Strange Rival. 250.00
124 ATh(c),The Iron Horse's
  Last Run 250.00
125 ATh(c),Johnny Thunder's
  Last Roundup 250.00
126 ATh(c),Phantoms of the
  Desert 250.00
Becomes:

ALL-AMERICAN MEN OF WAR
1952–66
127 (0). 1,500.00
128 (1) 900.00
2 JGr(c),Killer Bait. 750.00
3 Pied Piper of Pyong-Yang 700.00
4 JGr(c),The Hills of Hate. 700.00
5 One Second to Zero 700.00
6 IN(c),Jungle Killers. 600.00
7 IN(c),Beach to Hold 600.00
8 IN(c),Sgt. Storm Cloud. 600.00

DC COMICS

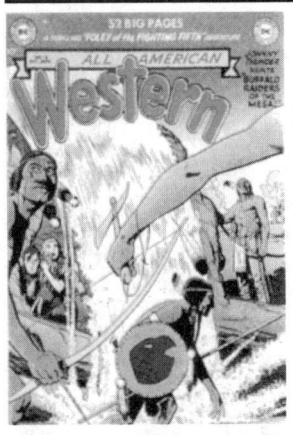

All-American Western #116
© DC Comics, Inc.

9 . . . . 600.00
10 . . . . 600.00
11 JGr(c),Dragon's Teeth. 600.00
12 . . . . 500.00
13 JGr(c),Lost Patrol 500.00
14 IN(c),Pigeon Boss. 500.00
15 JGr(c),Flying Roadblock 500.00
16 JGr(c),The Flying Jeep 500.00
17 JGr(c),Booby Trap Ridge 500.00
18 JKu(c),The Ballad of
   Battling Bells 500.00
19 JGr(c),IN,Torpedo Track 350.00
20 JGr(c),JKu,Lifenet to
   Beach Road. 350.00
21 JGr(c),IN,RH,The
   Coldest War. 350.00
22 JGr(c),IN,JKu,Snipers Nest . . 350.00
23 JGr(c),The Silent War. 350.00
24 JGr(c),The Thin Line. 350.00
25 JGr(c),IN,For Rent-One
   Foxhole 350.00
26 . . . . 350.00
27 JGr(c),RH,Fighting Pigeon . . . 350.00
28 JGr(c),RA,JKu,Medal
   for A Dog 350.00
29 IN(c),JKu,Battle Bridges 350.00
30 JGr(c),RH,Frogman Hunt 350.00
31 JGr(c),Battle Seat 275.00
32 JGr(c),RH,Battle Station 275.00
33 JGr(c),IN,Sky Ambush 275.00
34 JGr(c),JKu,No Man's Alley . . . 250.00
35 JGr(c),IN, Battle Call. 250.00
36 JGr(c),JKu,Battle Window. . . . 250.00
37 JGr(c),JKu,The Big Stretch. . . 250.00
38 JGr(c),RH,JKu,The
   Floating Sentinel 250.00
39 JGr(c),JKu,The Four Faces
   of Sgt. Fay. 250.00
40 JGr(c),IN,Walking Helmet. . . . 250.00
41 JKu(c),RH,JKu,The 50-50 War 225.00
42 JGr(c),JKu,Battle Arm. 225.00
43 JGr(c),JKu,Command Post. . . 225.00
44 JKu(c),The Flying Frogman . . 225.00
45 JGr(c),RH,Combat Waterboy . 225.00
46 JGr(c),IN,RH,Tank Busters . . 225.00
47 JGr(c),JKu,MD,Battle Freight . 225.00
48 JGr(c),JKu,MD,Roadblock . . 225.00
49 JGr(c),Walking Target 225.00
50 IN,RH,Bodyguard For A Sub. . 225.00
51 JGr(c),RH,Bomber's Moon . . 175.00
52 JKu(c),RH,MD,Back
   Seat Driver 175.00
53 JGr(c),JKu,Night Attack 175.00
54 JKu(c),IN,Diary of a
   Fighter Pilot 175.00

55 JKu(c),RH,Split-Second Target 175.00
56 JKu,IN,RH,Frogman Jinx 175.00
57 Pick-Up for Easy Co. 175.00
58 JKu(c),RH,MD,A Piece of Sky 175.00
59 JGr(c),JKu,The Hand of War . 175.00
60 JGr(c),The Time Table 175.00
61 JGr(c),IN,MD,Blind Target. . . . 175.00
62 JGr(c),RH,RA,No(c) 175.00
63 JGr(c),JKu,Frogman Carrier. . 175.00
64 JKu(c),JKu,RH,The Other
   Man's War 175.00
65 JGr(c),JKu,MD,Same
   Old Sarge 175.00
66 JGr(c),The Walking Fort 175.00
67 JGr(c),RH,A:Gunner&Sarge,
   The Cover Man 500.00
68 JKu(c),Gunner&Sarge,
   The Man & The Gun 225.00
69 JKu(c),A:Tank Killer,
   Bazooka Hill 225.00
70 JKu(c),IN,Pigeon
   Without Wings 175.00
71 JGr(c),A:Tank Killer,Target
   For An Ammo Boy 125.00
72 JGr(c),A:Tank Killer,T.N.T.
   Broom 125.00
73 JGr(c),JKu,No Detour 125.00
74 The Minute Commandos 125.00
75 JKu(c),Sink That Flattop 125.00
76 JKu(c),A:Tank Killer,
   Just One More Tank 125.00
77 JKu(c),IN,MD,Big Fish-
   little Fish 125.00
78 JGr(c),Tin Hat for an
   Iron Man 125.00
79 JKu(c),RA,Showdown Soldier. 125.00
80 JGr(c),RA,The Medal Men . . . 125.00
81 JGr(c),IN,Ghost Ship of
   Two Wars. 100.00
82 IN(c),B:Johnny Cloud,
   The Flying Chief 200.00
83 IN(c),Fighting Blind 125.00
84 IN(c),Death Dive 100.00
85 RH(c),Battle Eagle 100.00
86 JGr(c),Top-Gun Ace 100.00
87 JGr(c),Broken Ace 100.00
88 JGr(c),The Ace of Vengeance 100.00
89 JGr(c),The Star Jockey. 100.00
90 JGr(c),Wingmate of Doom . . . 75.00
91 RH(c),Two Missions To Doom . 75.00
92 JGr(c),The Battle Hawk 75.00
93 RH(c),The Silent Rider 75.00
94 RH(c),Be Brave-Be Silent. . . . 75.00
95 RH(c),Second Sight
   For a Pilot 75.00
96 RH(c),The Last Flight
   of Lt. Moon 75.00
97 IN(c),A Target Called
   Johnny 75.00
98 The Time-Bomb Ace 75.00
99 IN(c),The Empty Cockpit. 75.00
100 RH(c),Battle o/t Sky Chiefs. . 75.00
101 RH(c),Death Ship of
   Three Wars 55.00
102 JKu(c),Blind Eagle-Hungry
   Hawk 55.00
103 IN(c),Battle Ship-
   Battle Heart 55.00
104 JKu(c),The Last Target 55.00
105 IN(c),Killer Horse-Ship 55.00
106 IN(c),Death Song For
   A Battle Hawk 55.00
107 IN(c),Flame in the Sky 55.00
108 IN(c),Death-Dive of the Aces . 55.00
109 IN(c),The Killer Slot. 55.00
110 RH(c),The Co-Pilot was
   Death. 55.00
111 RH(c),E:Johnny Cloud, Tag-
   You're Dead. 55.00
112 RH(c),B:Balloon Buster,Lt.
   Steve Savage-Balloon Buster . 55.00

113 JKu(c),The Ace of
   Sudden Death 55.00
114 JKu(c),The Ace Who
   Died Twice. 55.00
115 IN(c),A:Johnny Cloud,
   Deliver One Enemy Ace-
   Handle With Care 55.00
116 JKu(c),A:Baloon Buster,
   Circle of Death. 55.00
117 Sept.–Oct., 1966. . . . . 55.00

ALL-AMERICAN COMICS
1999
1 RMz(s),F:Green Lantern &
   Johnny Thunder. 2.00

ALL-FLASH
1941–47
1 EHi,O:Flash,I:The Monocle. 22,000.00
2 EHi,The Adventure of Roy
   Revenge. 4,800.00
3 EHi,The Adventure of
   Misplaced Faces 2,400.00
4 EHi,Tale of the Time
   Capsule 2,400.00
5 EHi,The Case of the Patsy
   Colt! Last Quarterly 1,700.00
6 EHi,The Ray that Changed
   Men's Souls 1,400.00
7 EHi,Adventures of a Writers
   Fantasy, House of Horrors . 1,400.00
8 EHi,Formula to Fairyland!. . . 1,400.00
9 EHi,Adventure of the Stolen
   Telescope 1,400.00
10 EHi,Case of the Curious Cat 1,400.00
11 EHi,Troubles come
   in Doubles 1,200.00
12 EHi,Tumble INN to Trouble,
   Becomes Quarterly on orders
   from War Production Board
   O:The Thinker. 1,200.00
13 EHi,I:The King 1,200.00
14 EHi,I:Winky,Blinky & Noddy
   Green Lantern (c). 1,400.00
15 EHi,Secrets of a Stranger . . 1,200.00
16 EHi,A:The Sinister 1,200.00
17 Tales of the Three Wishes . 1,200.00
18 A:Winlky,Blinky&Noddy
   B:Mutt & Jeff reprints 1,200.00
19 No Rest at the Rest Home . 1,200.00
20 A:Winky, Blinky & Noddy . . . 1,200.00
21 I:Turtle. 900.00
22 The Money Doubler,E:Mutt
   & Jeff reprints 900.00

All-Flash Quarterly #2
© DC Comics Inc.

DC COMICS

23 The Bad Men of Bar Nothing . 900.00
24 I:Worry Wart,3 Court
   Clowns Get Caught 900.00
25 I:Slapsy Simmons,
   Flash Jitterbugs 900.00
26 I:The Chef,The Boss,Shrimp
   Coogan,A:Winky, Blinky &
   Noddy 900.00
27 A:The Thinker,Gangplank
   Gus story 900.00
28 A:Shrimp Coogan,Winky,
   Blinky & Noddy 900.00
29 The Thousand-Year Old Terror,
   A:Winky,Blinky & Noddy 900.00
30 The Vanishing Snowman 900.00
31 A:Black Hat,Planet of Sport . . 900.00
32 I:Fiddler,A:Thinker 1,500.00

ALL FUNNY COMICS
1943–48

1 Genius Jones. 600.00
2 same 250.00
3 same 175.00
4 same 175.00
5 thru 10 . . . . @175.00
11 Genius Jones 175.00
12 same 175.00
13 same 100.00
14 . . . . 100.00
15 . . . . 100.00
16 A:DC Superheroes 350.00
17 thru 23 . . . . @100.00

ALL-STAR COMICS
Summer, 1940–51

1 B:Flash,Hawkman,Hourman,
   Sandman,Spectre,Red White
   & Blue 19,000.00
2 B:Green Lantern and Johnny
   Thunder 7,500.00
3 First meeting of Justice Society
   with Flash as Chairman . . 58,000.00
4 First mission of JSA 8,000.00
5 V:Mr. X,I:Hawkgirl 6,500.00
6 Flash leaves 4,000.00
7 Green Lantern becomes Chairman,
   L:Hourman, C:Superman,
   Batman & Flash 4,500.00
8 I:Wonder Women;Starman and
   Dr. Mid-Nite join,Hawkman
   becomes chairman. 45,000.00
9 JSA in Latin America. 4,500.00
10 C:Flash & Green Lantern,
   JSA Time Travel story 4,500.00

WINTER ISSUE   NO.3

All-Star Comics #3 © DC Comics, Inc.

11 Wonder Women joins;
   I:Justice Battalion 6,000.00
12 V:Black Dragon society 3,500.00
13 V:Hitler 3,500.00
14 JSA in occupied Europe . . . 3,500.00
15 I:Brain Wave,A:JSA's
   Girl Friends 3,500.00
16 Propaganda/relevance issue 2,400.00
17 V:Brain Wave 2,400.00
18 I:King Bee 2,500.00
19 Hunt for Hawkman 2,400.00
20 I:Monster 2,400.00
21 Time travel story 2,000.00
22 Sandman and Dr. Fate leave,
   I:Conscience, Good Fairy. . 2,000.00
23 I:Psycho-Pirate. 2,000.00
24 Propaganda/relevance issue,
   A:Conscience&Wildcat,Mr.Terrific;
   L:Starman & Spectre; Flash
   & Green Lantern return . . . 2,000.00
25 JSA whodunit issue 1,800.00
26 V:Metal Men from Jupiter. . . 1,800.00
27 Handicap issue,A:Wildcat . . 1,800.00
28 Ancient curse comes to life . 1,600.00
29 I:Landor from 25th century . 1,600.00
30 V:Brain Wave 1,600.00
31 V:Zor 1,600.00
32 V:Psycho-Pirate 1,600.00
33 V:Soloman Grundy,A:Doiby
   Dickles, Last appearance
   Thunderbolt 4,800.00
34 I:Wizard 1,500.00
35 I:Per Degaton. 1,500.00
36 A:Superman and Batman. . . 4,000.00
37 I:Injustice Society of
   the World 2,000.00
38 V:Villains of History,
   A:Black Canary. 2,400.00
39 JSA in magic world,
   Johnny Thunder leaves . . . 1,500.00
40 A:Black Canary,Junior Justice
   Society of America 1,500.00
41 Black Canary joins,A:Harlequin,
   V:Injustice Society
   of the World 1,500.00
42 I:Alchemist 1,400.00
43 V:Interdimensional gold men 1,400.00
44 I:Evil Star 1,400.00
45 Crooks develop stellar
   JSA powers 1,400.00
46 Comedy issue 1,400.00
47 V:Billy the Kid. 1,400.00
48 Time Travel story 1,400.00
49 V:Comet-being invaders . . . 1,400.00
50 V:Flash's Classmate 1,500.00
51 V:Diamond men from center
   of the Earth. 1,400.00
52 JSA disappears from
   Earth for years 1,400.00
53 Time Travel issue. 1,400.00
54 Circus issue 1,400.00
55 JSA fly to Jupiter 1,400.00
56 V:Chameleons from
   31st Century 1,400.00
57 I:Key. 2,100.00
Becomes:

ALL STAR WESTERN
April-May, 1951

58 Trigger Twins 600.00
59 . . . . 300.00
60 . . . . 300.00
61 thru 64 ATh 250.00
65 . . . . 250.00
66 . . . . 275.00
67 GK,B:Johnny Thunder 300.00
68 thru 81 . . . . @125.00
82 thru 98 . . . . @125.00
99 FF 150.00
100 . . . . 125.00
101 thru 104 . . . . @100.00

105 O:JSA, March, 1987 . . . . . . 100.00
106 and 107 . . . . @100.00
108 O:Johnny Thunder 235.00
109 thru 116 . . . . @100.00
117 CI,O:Super-Chief. 125.00
118 . . . . 100.00
119 . . . . 100.00

ALL-STAR COMICS
1976–78

58 RE,WW,R:JSA,I:Power Girl . . . 65.00
59 RE,WW,Brain Wave 40.00
60 KG,WW,I:Vulcan 40.00
61 KG,WW,V:Vulcan 40.00
62 KG,WW,A:E-2 Superman 40.00
63 KG,WW,A:E-2 Superman,
   Solomon Grundy 40.00
64 WW,Shining Knight 40.00
65 KG,WW,E-2 Superman,
   Vandal Savage 40.00
66 JSon,BL,Injustice Society 40.00
67 JSon,BL 40.00
68 JSon,BL 40.00
69 JSon,BL,A:E-2 Superman,
   Starman,Dr.Mid-Nite 60.00
70 JSon,BL,Huntress 40.00
71 JSon,BL 40.00
72 JSon,A:Golden Age Huntress. . 40.00
73 JSon 40.00
74 JSon 40.00

ALL STAR COMICS
1999

1 JeR(s),F:Justice Society
   of America, V:Stalker's Seven . . 3.00
2 JeR(s) conclusion 3.00
Giant #1 80-page 5.00

ALL STAR SQUADRON
1981–87

1 RB,JOy,JSa,I:Degaton. 8.00
2 RB,JOy,Robotman 5.00
3 RB,JOy,Robotman 5.00
4 RB,JOy,Robotman 5.00
5 RB/JOy,I:Firebrand(Dannette) . . . 5.00
6 JOy,Hawkgirl 5.00
7 JOy,Hawkgirl 5.00
8 DH/JOy,A:Steel 5.00
9 DH/JOy,A:Steel 5.00
10 JOy,V:Binary Brotherhood 5.00
11 JOy,V:Binary Brotherhood. . . . 5.00
12 JOy,R:Dr.Hastor O:Hawkman . . 5.00
13 JOy,photo(c) 5.00
14 JOy,JLA crossover 5.00
15 JOy,JLA crossover 5.00
16 I&D:Nuclear. 5.00
17 Trial of Robotman 5.00
18 V:Thor 5.00
19 V:Brainwave 5.00
20 JOy,V:Brainwave 5.00
21 JOy,I:Cyclotron (1st JOy
   Superman) 7.00
22 JOy,V:Deathbolt,Cyclotron . . . 5.00
23 JOy,I:Amazing-Man. 5.00
24 JOy,I:Brainwave,Jr. 7.00
25 JOy,I:Infinity Inc. 5.00
26 JOy,Infinity Inc. 7.00
27 Spectre 5.00
28 JOy,Spectre. 5.00
29 JOy,retold story. 5.00
30 V:Black Dragons 5.00
31 All-Star gathering 5.00
32 O:Freedom Fighters 5.00
33 Freedom Fighters,I:Tsunami . . . 5.00
34 Freedom Fighters 5.00
35 RB,Shazam family 5.00
36 Shazam family 5.00
37 A:Shazam Family 5.00
38 V:The Real American 5.00

All Star Squadron #29
© DC Comics Inc.

39 V:The Real American 5.00
40 D:The Real American 5.00
41 O:Starman. 5.00
42 V:Tsunami,Kung 5.00
43 V:Tsunami,Kung 5.00
44 I:Night & Fog. 5.00
45 I:Zyklon 5.00
46 V:Baron Blitzkrieg 5.00
47 TM,O:Dr.Fate 10.00
48 A:Blackhawk 5.00
49 A:Dr.Occult 5.00
50 Crisis 7.00
51 AA,Crisis 5.00
52 Crisis 5.00
53 Crisis,A:The Dummy 5.00
54 Crisis,V:The Dummy 5.00
55 Crisis,V:Anti-Monitor 5.00
56 Crisis 5.00
57 A:Dr.Occult 5.00
58 I:Mekanique 5.00
59 A:Mekanique,Spectre 5.00
60 Crisis 1942, conclusion. 5.00
61 O:Liberty Belle 5.00
62 O:The Shining Knight 5.00
63 O:Robotman 5.00
64 WB/TD,V:Funny Face. 5.00
65 DH/TD,O:Johnny Quick 5.00
66 TD,O:Tarantula 5.00
67 TD,Last Issue,O:JSA 5.00
Ann.#1 JOy,O:G.A.,Atom 5.00
Ann.#2 JOy,Infinity Inc. 5.00
Ann.#3 WB,JOy,KG,GP,DN 5.00

ALL STAR WESTERN
(see WEIRD WESTERN TALES)

ALPHA CENTURION
1996
Spec.#1 . . . . 3.00

AMBER:
THE GUNS OF AVALON
Aug., 1996
1 (of 3) adapt. of Roger Zelazny
   classic 7.00
2 and 3 conclusion . . . . @7.00

AMBUSH BUG
1985
1 KG,I:Cheeks. 3.00

---

2 KG thru 4 . . . . @3.00
Spec.#1 Stocking Stuffer,
   KG,R:Cheeks (1986) 3.00
Spec.#1 Nothing Special
   KG,A:Sandman,Death (1992) . . 3.50

AMERICA vs.
JUSTICE SOCIETY
Jan.–April, 1985
1 AA,R,Thomas Script 7.00
2 AA 5.00
3 AA 5.00
4 AA, ... 5.00

AMERICAN CENTURY
DC/Vertigo, March, 2001
1 HC,vet hijacks plane 5.00
2 HC,Hell hotter for Harry. 3.00
3 HC,Guatemalan Revolution. 3.00
4 HC,Bananarama 3.00
5 HC,The Protector,pt.1 . . . . 3.00
6 HC,The Protector,pt.2 . . . . 3.00
7 HC,The Protector,pt.3 . . . . 3.00
8 HC,The Protector,pt.4 . . . . 3.00
9 HC,Route 66 . . . . 3.00
10 HC,White Lightning,pt.1 . . . . . . 3.00
11 HC,White Lightning,pt.2 . . . . . . 3.00
12 HC,White Lightning,pt.3 . . . . . . 3.00
13 HC,White Lightning,pt.4 . . . . . . 3.00
14 HC,An American in Paris,pt.1 . . 3.00
15 HC,An American in Paris,pt.2. . 3.00
16 HC,An American in Paris,pt.3 . . 3.00
17 HC,Coming Home,pt.1 . . . . 3.00
18 HC,Coming Home,pt.2 . . . . 3.00
19 HC,Coming Home,pt.3 . . . . 3.00
20 HC,Coming Home,Pt.4 . . . . 3.00
21 HC,Coming Home,pt.5 . . . . 3.00
22 HC,Tramps,pt.1. . . . . 3.00
23 HC,Tramps,pt.2. . . . . 3.00
24 HC,one-shot. 3.00
25 HC,Bite the Big Apple,pt.1 . . . . 3.00
26 HC,Bite the Big Apple,pt.2 . . . . 3.00
27 HC,Bite the Big Apple,pt.3 . . . . 3.00
TPB Scars and Stripes, HC 8.95
TPB Hollywood Babylon 12.95

AMERICAN FREAK: A
TALE OF THE UN-MEN
DC/Vertigo, 1994
1 B:DLp,(s),VcL,R:Un-Men 2.25
2 VcL,A:Crassus 2.25
3 VcL,A:Scylla. 2.25
4 VcL,A:Scylla. 2.25
5 VcL,Final Issue 2.25

AMETHYST
[Limited Series], 1983–84
[PRINCESS OF GEMWORLD]
1 Origin 2.50
2 thru 7 EC . . . . @2.50
8 EC,O:Gemworld. 2.50
9 thru 12 EC . . . . @2.50
Spec.#1 KG 2.50
[Regular Series], 1985–86
1 thru 12 EC . . . . @2.50
13 EC,Crisis,A:Dr.Fate. 2.50
14 EC. 2.50
15 EC,Castle Amethyst Destroyed . 2.50
16 EC. 2.50
Spec.#1 EM 2.50
[Mini-Series], 1987–88
1 EM 2.00
2 EM 2.00
3 EM 2.00
4 EM,O:Mordru 2.00

ANARKY
March, 1997
1 AIG(s),NBy,JRu,Anarky vs.
   Etrigan 4.00
2 AIG(s),NBy,JRu,V:Darkseid 2.50
3 AIG(s),NBy,JRu,A:Batman 2.50
4 AIG(s),NBy,JRu,A:Batman,concl.. 2.50
2nd Series,1999
1 AIG(s),NBy,JRu,F:JLA 2.50
2 AIG(s),NBy,JRu,F:GreenLantern . 2.50
3 AIG(s),NBy,JRu,F:GreenLantern . 2.50
4 AIG(s),NBy,JRu,V:Ra's al Ghul . . 2.50
5 AIG(s),NBy,JRu,V:Ra's
   al Ghul,pt.2 . . . . 2.50
6 AIG(s),NBy,JRu,F:Ra's
   al Ghul,pt.3 . . . . 2.50
7 AIG,NBy,JRu,Day of Judgment . . 2.50
8 AIG(s),NBy,JRu, final issue 2.50

ANGEL & THE APE
1991
1 Apes of Wrath,pt.1 . . . . 3.00
2 Wrath pt.2,A:G.Gardner. 3.00
3 Wrath,pt.3,A:InferiorFive 3.00
4 Wrath,pt.4,A:InferiorFive 3.00

ANGEL AND THE APE
DC/Vertigo, Aug., 2001
1 (of 4) HC,F:Angel O'Day 3.00
2 thru 4 HC . . . . @3.00

ANIMA
DC/Vertigo, 1994–95
1 R:Anima. 2.50
2 V:Scarecrow. 2.50
3 V:Scarecrow. 2.50
4 A:Nameless one. 2.50
5 CI,V:Arkana 2.50
6 CI,V:Arkana 2.50
7 Zero Hour. 2.50
8 Nameless One. 2.50
9 Superboy & Nameless One. . . . 2.50
10 A:Superboy 2.50
11 V:Nameless One 2.50
12 A:Hawkman,V:Shrike 2.50
13 A:Hawkman,Shrike 2.50
14 Return to Gotham City 2.50
15 V:Psychic Vampire, final issue . . 3.00

ANIMAL ANTICS
1946–49
1 . . . . 450.00
2 . . . . 250.00
3 thru 10 . . . . @150.00
11 thru 23 . . . . @100.00

ANIMAL-MAN
1988–95
1 BB(c),B:GMo(s),ChT,DHz,
   B:Animal Rights,I:Dr.Myers . . . 12.00
2 BB(c),ChT,DHz,A:Superman 6.00
3 BB(c),ChT,DHz,A:B'wana Beast . 3.00
4 BB(c),ChT,DHz,V:B'wana Beast,
   E:Animal Rights. 3.00
5 BB(c),ChT,DHz,
   I&D:Crafty Coyote 3.50
6 BB(c),ChT,DHz,A:Hawkman 3.00
7 BB(c),ChT,DHz,D:Red Mask 3.00
8 BB(c),ChT,DHz,V:Mirror Master. . 3.00
9 BB(c),DHz,TG,A:Martian
   Manhunter 3.00
10 BB(c),ChT,DHz,A:Vixen,
   B:O:Animal Man 3.00
11 BB(c),ChT,DHz,I:Hamed Ali,
   Tabu,A:Vixen 3.00
12 BB(c),D:Hamed Ali,A:Vixen,
   B'wanaBeast 3.00

Animal Man #6 © DC Comics, Inc.

13 BB(c),I:Dominic Mndawe,R:B'wana
   Beast,Apartheid. 3.00
14 BB(c),TG,SeM,A:Future Animal
   Man,I:Lennox. 3.00
15 BB(c),ChT,DHz,A:Dolphin. 3.00
16 BB(c),ChT,DHz,A:JLA. 3.00
17 BB(c),ChT,DHz,A:Mirr.Master. . . 3.00
18 BB(c),ChT,DHz,A:Lennox 3.00
19 BB(c),ChT,DHz,D:Ellen,
   Cliff,Maxine 3.00
20 BB(c),ChT,DHz,I:Bug-Man 3.00
21 BB(c),ChT,DHz,N&V:Bug-Man . . 3.00
22 BB(c),PCu,SeM,A:Rip Hunter. . . 3.00
23 BB(c),A:Phantom Stranger 3.00
24 BB(c),V:Psycho Pirate 3.00
25 BB(c),ChT,MFm,I:Comic
   Book Limbo 3.00
26 BB(c),E:GMo(s),ChT,MFm,
   A:Grant Morrison. 3.00
27 BB(c),B:PMi(s),ChT,MFm 3.00
28 BB(c),ChT,MFm,I:Nowhere Man,
   I&D:Front Page 3.00
29 ChT,SDi,V:National Man 3.00
30 BB(c),ChT,MFm,V:Angel Mob. . . 3.00
31 BB(c),ChT,MFm 3.00
32 BB(c),E:PMi(s),ChT,MFm 3.00
33 BB(c),B:TV(s),SDi,A:Travis
   Cody 3.00
34 BB(c),SDi,Requiem. 3.00
35 BB(c),SDi,V:Radioactive Dogs . . 3.00
36 BB(c),SDi,A:Mr.Rainbow. 3.00
37 BB(c),SDi,Animal/Lizard Man . . . 3.00
38 BB(c),SDi,A:Mr.Rainbow. 3.00
39 BB(c),TMd,SDi,Wolfpack in
   San Diego 3.00
40 BB(c),SDi,War of the Gods
   x-over. 3.00
41 BB(c),SDi,V:Star Labs
   Renegades,I:Winky 3.00
42 BB(c),SDi,V:Star Labs
   Renegades 3.00
43 BB(c),SDi,I:Tristess,A:Vixen . . . 3.00
44 BB(c),SDi,A:Vixen. 3.00
45 BB(c),StP,SDi,I:L.Decker. 3.00
46 BB(c),SDi,I:Frank Baker 3.00
47 BB(c),SDi,I:Shining Man,
   (B'wana Beast) 3.00
48 BB(c),SDi,V:Antagon. 3.00
49 BB(c),SDi,V:Antagon. 3.00
50 BB(c),E:TV(s),SDi,I:Metaman. . . 5.00
51 BB(c),B:JaD(s),StP,B:Flesh
   and Blood 3.00
52 BB(c),StP,Homecoming. 3.00
53 BB(c),StP,Flesh and Blood 3.00
54 BB(c),StP,Flesh and Blood 3.00

55 BB(c),StP,Flesh and Blood 3.00
56 BB(c),StP,E:Flesh and Blood,
   Double-sized 6.00

DC/Vertigo, 1993
57 BB(c),StP,B:Recreation,
   Ellen in NY. 3.00
58 BB(c),StP,Wild Side 3.00
59 BB(c),RsB,GHi(i),Wild Town . . . 3.00
60 RsB,GHi(i),Wild life 3.00
61 BB(c),StP,Tooth and Claw#1. . . 3.00
62 BB(c),StP,Tooth and Claw#2. . . 3.00
63 BB(c),V:Leviathan. 3.00
64 DIB(c),WSm,DnS(i),
   Breath of God 3.00
65 RDB(c),WSm,
   Perfumed Garden 3.00
66 A:Kindred Spirit. 3.00
67 StP,Mysterious Ways #1 . . . . . . 3.00
68 StP,Mysterious Ways #2 . . . . . . 3.00
69 Animal Man's Family. 3.00
70 GgP(c),StP 3.00
71 GgP(c),StP,Maxine Alive? 3.00
72 StP 3.00
73 StP,Power Life Church 3.00
74 StP,Power Life Church 3.00
75 StP,Power Life Church 3.00
76 StP,Pilgrimage problems. 3.00
77 Cliff shot 3.00
78 StP,Animal Man poisoned. 3.00
79 New Direction 3.00
80 New Direction 3.00
81 Wild Type,pt.1 . . . . 3.00
82 Wild Type,pt.2 . . . . 3.00
83 Wild Type,pt.3 . . . . 3.00
84 F:Maxine,SupernaturalDreams. . 3.00
85 Animal Mundi,pt.1 . . . . 3.00
86 Animal Mundi,pt.2 . . . . 3.00
87 Animal Mundi,pt.3 . . . . 3.00
88 Morphogenetic Fields 3.00
89 final issue 3.00
Ann.#1 BB(c),JaD,TS(i),RIB(i),
   Children Crusade,F:Maxine. . . . 4.25
TPB Rep.#1 thru #10. . . . . 19.95
TPB Animal Man, 2nd pr. 19.95
TPB Origin of the Species 19.95
TPB Deus Ex Machina (2003) 19.95

ANIMANIACS
Warner Bros./DC May, 1995
1 F:Yakko,Wakko,Dot 8.00
2 thru 20 . . . . @4.00
21 thru 59 . . . . @3.00
Christmas Spec. 4.00

ANTHRO
1968–69
1 HwP 75.00
2 HwP. 45.00
3 thru 5 HwP . . . . @50.00
6 HwP,WW(c&a) 50.00

AQUAMAN
[1st Regular Series], 1962–78
1 NC,I:Quisp 1,300.00
2 NC,V:Captain Sykes 500.00
3 NC,Aquaman from Atlantis . . . 250.00
4 NC,A:Quisp 200.00
5 NC,The Haunted Sea 200.00
6 NC,A:Quisp 175.00
7 NC,Sea Beasts of Atlantis 175.00
8 NC,Plot to Steal the Seas 175.00
9 NC,V:King Neptune 175.00
10 NC,A:Quisp. 175.00
11 I: Mera. 150.00
12 NC,The Cosmic Gladiators. . . 150.00
13 NC,Invasion of the Giant
   Reptiles. 150.00
14 NC,AquamanSecretPowers. . . 150.00
15 NC,Menace of the Man-Fish. . 150.00

Aquaman 1st Series #60
© DC Comics, Inc.

16 NC,Duel of the Sea Queens. . 150.00
17 NC,Man Who Vanquished
   Aquaman. 150.00
18 W:Aquaman & Mera 150.00
19 NC,Atlanteans for Sale 150.00
20 NC,Sea King's DoubleDoom . 150.00
21 NC,I:Fisherman. 80.00
22 NC,The Trap of the Sinister
   Sea Nymphs 80.00
23 NC,I:Aquababy 80.00
24 NC,O:Black Manta 80.00
25 NC,Revolt of Aquaboy 80.00
26 NC,I:O.G.R.E. 80.00
27 NC,Battle of the Rival
   Aquamen. 80.00
28 NC,Hail Aquababy,King of
   Atlantis. 80.00
29 I:Ocean Master 75.00
30 NC,C:JLA 75.00
31 NC,V:O.G.R.E. 75.00
32 NC,V:Tryton 75.00
33 NC,I:Aquagirl. 100.00
34 NC,I:Aquabeast. 60.00
35 I:Black Manta 60.00
36 NC,What Seeks the
   Awesome Threesome? 60.00
37 I:Scavenger. 60.00
38 NC,I:Liquidator 60.00
39 NC,How to Kill a Sea King . . . 60.00
40 JAp,Sorcerers from the Sea . . 60.00
41 JAp,Quest for Mera,pt.1 . . . . . 50.00
42 JAp,Quest for Mera,pt.2 . . . . . 50.00
43 JAp,Quest for Mera,pt.3 . . . . . 50.00
44 JAp,Quest for Mera,pt.4 . . . . . 50.00
45 JAp,Quest for Mera,pt.5 . . . . . 50.00
46 JAp,Quest for Mera concl. . . . 50.00
47 JAp,Revolution in Atlantis #1
   rep.Adventure #268. . . . . 50.00
48 JAp,Revolution in Atlantis #2
   rep.Adventure #260. . . . . 65.00
49 JAp,As the Seas Die. 50.00
50 JAp,NA,A:Deadman 90.00
51 JAp,NA,A:Deadman 90.00
52 JAp,NA,A:Deadman 90.00
53 JAp,Is California Sinking?. . . . 20.00
54 JAp,Crime Wave. 20.00
55 JAp,Return of the Alien. 20.00
56 JAp,I&O:Crusader (1970) 20.00
57 JAp,V:Black Manta (1977) 20.00
58 JAp,O:Aquaman rtd 25.00
59 JAp,V:Scavenger 20.00
60 DN,V:Scavenger. 20.00
61 DN,BMc,A:Batman 20.00

62 DN,A:Ocean Master 15.00
63 DN,V:Ocean Master,
    final issue 15.00

[2nd Regular Series], 1991–92
1 Poseidonis Under Attack,
    C:J'onn J'onzz,Blue Beetle 3.00
2 V:Oumland. 2.50
3 I:Iqula. 2.50
4 V:Iqula,A:Queequeg. 2.50
5 A:Aqualad,Titans,M.Manhunter,
    R:Manta. 2.50
6 V: Manta. 2.50
7 R:Mera. 2.50
8 A:Batman,V:NKV Demon. 2.50
9 Eco-Wars#1,A:Sea Devils. 2.50
10 Eco-Wars#2,A:Sea Devils. . . . 2.50
11 V:Gigantic Dinosaur 2.50
12 A:Iaula. 2.50
13 V:The Scavenger 2.50
14 V:The Scavenger 2.50

[3rd Regular Series], 1994–97
0 B:PDd(s),Paternal secret. 7.00
1 PDd(s),R:Aqualad,I:Charybdis. . . 6.00
2 V:Charybdis 7.00
3 B:PDd(s),Superboy 4.00
4 B:PDd(s),Lobo 4.00
5 New Costume 4.00
6 V:The Deep Six 4.00
7 Kako's Metamorphosis 4.00
8 V:Corona and Naiad 4.00
9 JPi(c&a),V:Deadline,A:Koryak . . 3.00
10 A:Green Lantern,Koryak 3.00
11 R:Mera 3.00
12 F:Mera. 3.00
13 V:Thanatos 3.00
14 PDd,V:Major Disaster,Underworld
    Unleashed tie-in 3.00
15 PDd,V:Tiamat. 3.00
16 PDd,A:Justice League 3.00
17 PDd,V:underwater gargoyles . . . 3.00
18 . . . . 3.00
19 PDd,V:Ocean Master 3.00
20 PDd,V:Ocean Master 3.00
21 PDd,JCf,A:Dolphin,
    V:ThiernaNaOge 3.00
22 PDd(s). 3.00
23 PDd(s),I:Deep Blue (Neptune
    Perkins) 3.00
24 PDd(s),A:Neptune Perkins 3.00
25 PDd(s),MEg,HSm,Atlantis united,
    Aquaman king? 3.00
26 PDd(s),MEg,HSm,Oceans
    threatened, Final Night tie-in . . . 3.00
27 PDd(s),MEg,HSm,V:Demon
    Gate, dolphin killer. 3.00
28 PDd(s),JCf,JP,A:J'onn J'onzz . . . 3.00
29 PDd(s),MEg,HSm, ... 3.00
30 PDd(s),MEg,HSm,The Pit. 3.00
31 PDd(s),V:The Shark, mind-
    controlled aquatic army 3.00
32 PDd(s),A:Swamp Thing 3.00
33 PDd(s),Aquaman's dark powers
    affect him physically 3.00
34 PDd(s),V:Triton 3.00
35 PDd(s),JCf,I:Gamesman,
    A:Animal Man 3.00
36 PDd(s),JCf,R:Poseidonis,
    Tempest,Vulko. 3.00
37 PDd,JCf,Genesis,V:Darkseid . . . 3.00
38 PDd,JCf,capitalism 3.00
39 PDd,JCf,Perkins Family Reunion . 3.00
40 PDd,JCf,Dr. Polaris. 3.00
41 PDd,JCf,BSf,F:Power Girl. 2.50
42 PDd,JCf. 2.50
43 PDd,JCf,Millennium Giants,
    pt.2 x-over, A:Superman Red . . 2.50
44 PDd,JCf,F:Golden Age Flash,
    Sentinel 2.50
45 PDd,JCf,V:Triton 2.50
46 PDd,JCf,news of Mera 2.50

47 DAn,Shadows on Water,pt.1. . . . 2.50
48 DAn,Shadows on Water,pt.2. . . . 2.50
49 DAn,ALa,JCf,V:Tempest 2.50
50 EL,NRd,New Costume 2.50
51 EL,NRd,V:King Noble 2.50
52 EL,V:Fire Trolls 2.50
53 EL,A:Superman. 2.50
54 EL,A:Landlovers 2.50
55 EL,wooing Mera 2.50
56 EL,V:Piranha Man,pt.1 . . . . 2.50
57 EL,V:Piranha Man,pt.2 . . . . 2.50
58 EL,V:DemonGate & BlackManta. 2.50
59 EL,drugs in Atlantis 2.50
60 NRd,W:Tempest & Dolphin. . . . 2.50
61 NRd,Day of Judgment x-over . . . 2.50
62 EL(s),NRd 2.50
63 NRd. 2.50
64 DJu,SEp,NRd 2.50

Aquaman 3rd Series #7
© DC Comics Inc.

65 DJu,SEp,NRd 2.50
66 DJu,PR,NRd,F:JLA 2.50
67 DJu,SEp,NRd 2.50
68 DJu,SEp,NRd,V:Cerdia. 2.50
69 DJu,SEp,NRd,. 2.50
70 DJu,new alliance. 3.00
71 DJu,SEp,NRd,A:Warlord. 3.00
72 DJu,SEp,NRd,V:Ch'Rinn 3.00
73 DJu,SEp,NRd,V:Valgos. 3.00
74 DJu,SEp,NRd,death of friend . . . 3.00
75 DJu,SEp,NRd,final issue 3.00
Ann.#1 Year One Annual, V:Triton,
    A:Superman,Mera 4.00
Ann.#2 Legends o/t Dead Earth . . . 3.50
Ann.#3 Pulp Heroes (Hard Boiled) . 5.00
Ann.#4 PDa, Ghosts 3.50
Ann.#5 JOs(s),MBr,DG, JLApe
    Gorilla Warfare 3.50
Spec.#1,000,000 DAn&ALa(s),TGb,
    BAn, King of Waterworld 3.00
Secret Files #1 EL 5.00
TPB Time and Tide 10.00

AQUAMAN
[1st Limited Series] 1986
1 V:Ocean Master. 6.00
2 V:Ocean Master. 4.00
3 V:Ocean Master. 4.00
4 V:Ocean Master. 4.00

[2nd Limited Series], 1989
1 CS,Atlantis Under Siege 3.50
2 CS,V:Invaders 3.00
3 CS,Mera turned Psychotic. 3.00
4 CS,Poseidonis Under Siege 3.00

5 CS,Last Stand,final issue. 3.00
Spec#1 MPa,Legend o/Aquaman . . 3.00

AQUAMAN
Dec. 2002
1 Obsidian Age aftermath. 3.00
2 F:Martian Manhunter 3.00
3 New look and costume 3.00
4 F:Tempest 3.00
5 V:The Thirst 3.00
6 V:The Thirst 3.00
7 undead pirates 3.00
8 V:Black Mantra 3.00
9 V:Black Mantra 3.00
10 V:The Thirst 3.00
11 V:The Thirst. 3.00
12 V:The Thirst 3.00
13 Perfect storm 2.50
14 Octo-Man 2.50
15 American Tidal,pt.1. . . . . 2.50
16 American Tidal,pt.2 . . . . 2.50
17 American Tidal,pt.3 . . . . 2.50
18 American Tidal,pt.4 . . . . 2.50
19 F:Lorena 2.50
20 American Tidal,concl. 2.50
21 With the Fishes,pt.1 . . . . 2.50
22 With the Fishes,pt.2 . . . . 2.50
23 With the Fishes,pt.3 . . . . 2.50
TPB Aquaman: The Water Bearer. 12.95
Spec. Secret Files 2003. . . . . 4.95

AQUAMAN: TIME & TIDE
1993–94
1 PDd(s),O:Aquaman 3.00
2 and 3 PDd(s),O:Aquaman
    contd. . . . . @3.00
4 PDd(s),O:Aquaman,final issue. . . 3.00
TPB rep.#1–4. . . . . 10.00

ARAK
1981–85
1 EC,O:Ara 3.00
2 EC 2.50
3 EC,I:Valda 2.50
4 thru 10 EC . . . . @2.50
11 EC,AA 2.50
12 EC,AA,I:Satyricus 2.50
13 thru 19 AA . . . . @2.50
20 AA,O:Angelica. 2.50
21 thru 23 AA. 2.50
24 Double size 2.50
25 thru 30. . . . . @2.50
31 D Arak,becomes shaman 2.50
32 thru 48. . . . . @2.50
49 CI/TD. 2.50
50 TD 2.50
Ann.#1 . . . . 2.50

ARCANA: THE BOOKS OF MAGIC
DC/Vertigo, 1994
Ann.#1 JBo(c),JNR(s),PrG,Children's
    Crusade,R:Tim Hunter,
    A:Free Country 4.00

ARGUS
[Mini-Series], 1995
1 R:Argus,I:Raver 2.00
2 Blinded by metahuman hitmen . . . 2.00
3 Spy Satellite 2.00
4 The Watcher 2.00
5 Data Highways 2.00
6 Restored Sight. 2.00

Arion, Lord of Atlantis #7
© DC Comics, Inc.

ARION, LORD OF ATLANTIS
1982–85
1 JDu,Star Spawn Sun Death	3.00
2 JDu,I:Mara	2.50
3 JDu	2.50
4 JDu,O:Arion	2.50
5 JDu	2.50
6 JDu	2.50
7 thru 12	@2.50
13 thru 15 JDu	@2.50
16 thru 35	@2.50
Spec.	2.50

ARION THE IMMORTAL
1992
1 RWi,R:Arion	3.00
2 RWi,V:Garffon	2.25
3 RWi,V:Garn Daanuth	2.25
4 RWi,V:Garn Daanuth	2.25
5 RWi,Darkworlet	2.25
6 RWi,MG,A:Power Girl	2.25

ARKHAM ASYLUM: LIVING HELL
May 2003
1 (of 6) F:Warren White	3.00
2 Food Fight	3.00
3 Humphry Dumpler	3.00
4 F:Killer Croc	3.00
5 F:Jason Blood	3.00
6 Concl.	3.00
TPB	12.95

ARMAGEDDON 2001
May, 1991
1 DJu,DG,I&O:Waverider	4.00
1a 2nd printing	2.50
1b 3rd printing (silver)	2.50
2 DJu,ATi,Monarch revealed as Hawk, D:Dove,L:Capt Atom(JLE)	3.00
Spec.#1 MR	3.00

ARMAGEDDON 2001 ARMAGEDDON: THE ALIEN AGENDA
1991–92
1 DJu,JOy,A:Monarch,Capt.Atom	2.50

2 V:Ancient Romans	2.50
3 JRu(i),The Old West	2.50
4 DG,GP,V:Nazi's,last issue	2.50

ARMAGEDDON: INFERNO
1992
1 TMd,LMc,A:Creeper,Batman, Firestorm	2.50
2 AAd,LMc,WS,I:Abraxis,A:Lobo	2.50
3 AAd,WS,LMc,TMd,MN,R:Justice Society	2.50
4 AAd,WS,LMc,TMd,MN,DG, V:Abraxis,A:Justice Society	2.50

ARSENAL
Aug., 1998
1 (of 4) F:Black Canary	2.50
2 F:Green Arrow	2.50
3 F:Vandal Savage	2.50
4 conclusion	2.50

ARTEMIS: REQUIEM
1996
1 BML(s) (of 6).	3.00
2 thru 6 BML(s),EBe,	@3.00

ATARI FORCE
1984–85
1 JL,I:TempestDart	5.00
2 JL	3.00
3 JL	3.00
4 RA/JL/JO	3.00
5 RA/JL/JO	3.00
6 thru 12 JL	@3.00
13 KG	3.00
14 thru 21 EB	@3.00

ATLANTIS CHRONICLES
1990
1 EM,Atlantis 50,000 years ago	3.50
2 EM,Atlantis Sunk	3.25
3 EM,Twin Cities of Poseidonis & Tritonis	3.25
4 EM,King Orin's Daughter Cora Assumes Throne.	3.25
5 EM,Orin vs. Shalako	3.25
6 EM,Contact with Surface Dwellers.	3.25
7 EM,Queen Atlanna gives Birth to son(Aquaman)48 pg.final issue.	3.25

ATOM, THE
1962–68
1 MA,GK,I:Plant Master	1,300.00
2 MA,GK,V:Plant Master	500.00
3 MA,GK,I:Chronos.	325.00
4 MA,GK,Snapper Carr.	250.00
5 MA,GK	250.00
6 MA,GK	250.00
7 MA,GK,1st Atom & Hawkman team-up	450.00
8 MA,GK,A:JLA,V:Doctor Light.	200.00
9 MA,GK	200.00
10 MA,GK	200.00
11 MA,GK.	125.00
12 MA,GK	125.00
13 MA,GK	125.00
14 MA,GK	125.00
15 MA,GK	125.00
16 MA,GK	100.00
17 MA,GK	100.00
18 MA,GK	100.00
19 MA,GK,A:Zatanna.	100.00
20 MA,GK	100.00
21 MA,GK	80.00

22 MA,GK	80.00
23 MA,GK	80.00
24 MA,GK,V:Jason Woodrue.	80.00
25 MA,GK	80.00
26 GK.	75.00
27 GK.	75.00
28 GK.	75.00
29 GK,A:E-2 Atom,Thinker.	250.00
30 GK.	75.00
31 GK,A:Hawkman	70.00
32 GK.	70.00
33 GK.	70.00
34 GK,V:Big Head	70.00
35 GK.	70.00
36 GK,A:Golden Age Atom	100.00
37 GK,I:Major Mynah.	70.00
38 Sinister stopover Earth	70.00

Becomes:

ATOM & HAWKMAN
1968–69
39 MA, V:Tekla.	75.00
40 DD,JKu,MA.	65.00
41 DD,JKu,MA.	65.00
42 MA,V:Brama	65.00
43 MA,I:Gentleman Ghost	65.00
44 DD.	65.00
45 DD.	65.00

ATOM SPECIAL
1 SDi,V:Chronos (1993)	3.00
2 Zero Hour Atom (1994)	3.00

AVATAR
1991
1 A:Midnight & Allies.	7.00
2 Search for Tablets	6.00
3 V:Cyric, Myrkul, final issue	6.00

AVENGERS/JLA
DC/Marvel 2003
2 (of 4) KBk,GP(c), 48-pg.	5.95
4 KBk,GP,48-pg.	5.95

AZRAEL
1994
1 I:New Azreal,Brian Bryan.	5.00
2 A:Batman,New Azreal	3.50
3 V:Order of St. Dumas	3.50
4 The System	3.00
5 BKi(c&a),R:Ra's al Ghul,Talia [new Miraweb format begins]	3.00
6 BKi(c&a),Ra's al Ghul,Talia	3.00
7 Sister Lily's Transformation	3.00
8 System Secret	2.50
9 Jean Paul Vanishes	2.50
10 DON,BKi,JmP,F:Neron, Underworld Unleashed tie-in	2.50
11 DON,BKi,JmP,A:Batman	2.50
12 DON,BKi,JmP,Azreal looks for Shondra	2.50
13 DON,BKi,Demon Time,pt.1	2.50
14 DON,BKi,Demon Time,pt.2	2.50
15 DON,BKi,Contagion,pt.5	3.00
16 DON,BKi,Contagion,pt.10	2.50
17 DON,BKi,JmP,A:Dr.Orchid	2.50
18 DON,BKi,JmP,A:Dr.Orchid	2.50
19 DON(s)	2.50
20 DON(s)	2.50
21 DON(s)	2.50
22 DON(s),BKi,JmP,Angel in Hiding, pt.2 (of 3).	2.50
23 DON(s),BKi,JmP,Angel in Hiding, pt.3	2.50
24 DON(s),BKi,JmP,The Order's return	2.50
25 DON(s),BKi,JmP,V:Brother Rollo	2.50
26	2.50

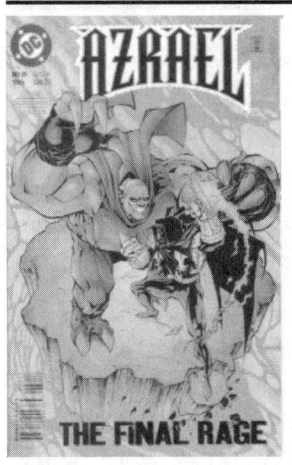

Azrael #20 © DC Comics Inc.

27 DON(s),BKi,JmP,Angel Insane,
    pt.1 . . . . 2.50
28 DON(s),BKi,JmP,Joker, Riddler
    & Two-Face escape from
    Arkham Asylum 2.50
29 DON(s),DBw,JmP, F:Ra's Al
    Ghul, pt.1 . . . . 2.50
30 DON(s),DBw,JmP, F:Ra's Al
    Ghul, pt.2 . . . . 2.50
31 DON(s),JmP Angel and the
    Monster Maker, pt.1 (of 3) 2.50
32 DON(s),JmP Angel and the
    Monster Maker, pt.2 . . . . 2.50
33 DON(s),JmP Angel and the
    Monster Maker, pt.3 concl. 2.50
34 DON(s),JmP,Genesis,
    a parademon 2.50
35 DON(s),JmP,F:Hitman 2.50
36 DON,JmP,Return of Bane,pt.1 . . 2.50
37 DON,JmP,Return of Bane,pt.2 . . 2.50
38 DON,JmP,Return of Bane,pt.3 . . 2.50
39 DON,JmP 2.50
40 DON,JmP,Cataclysm,pt.4,x-over 4.50
41 DON,JmP,A:Devil Latour 2.50
42 DON,JmP,Madame Kalypso 2.50
43 DON,JmP,Lilhy,Brian Bryan 2.50
44 DON,JmP,Luc & Lilhy disappear 2.50
45 DON,JmP,V:Deathstroke,
    A:Calibax 2.50
46 DON(s),JmP,V:Calibax 2.50
47 Road to No Man's Land, flip-book
    Batman:Shadow of the Bat 5.00
48 DON(s),JmP,No Man's Land. . . . 2.50
49 DON(s),JmP,New Costume 2.50
50 DON(s),JmP,New Costume 2.50
51 DON(s),JmP,V:Demonic Trio . . . 2.50
52 DON(s),JmP,No Man's Land. . . . 2.50
53 DON(s),JmP,V:Joker. 2.50
54 DON(s),JmP,V:Death Dancer . . . 2.50
55 DON(s),JmP,V:Death Dancer . . . 2.50
56 DON(s),JmP,A:Batgirl 2.50
57 DON(s),JmP,No Man's Land. . . . 2.50
58 DON(s),JmP,Day of
    Judgment x-over 2.50
59 DON(s),JmP,F:Catwoman. 2.50
60 DON(s) 2.50
61 DON(s),F:Batgirl,V:Joker 2.50
62 DON(s) 2.50
63 DON(s),F:Huntress 2.50
64 DON(s),F:Huntress 2.50
65 DON(s),Nicholas Scratch 2.50
66 DON(s),F:Lilhi 2.50
67 DON(s),JmP,to Africa 2.50
68 DON(s),JmP, ... 2.50

69 DON(s),JmP,stranded 2.50
70 DON(s),SCi,JmP,Prophet,pt.1. . . 2.50
71 DON(s),SCi,JmP,Prophet,pt.2. . . 2.50
72 DON(s),SCi,JmP,Prophet,pt.3. . . 2.50
73 DON(s),SCi,JmP,Batman,pt.1 . . . 2.50
74 DON(s),SCi,JmP,Batman,pt.2. . . 2.50
75 DON(s),SCi,JmP,N:Azrael,
    F:Batman. 4.50
76 DON(s),SCi,JmP,A:Batman 2.50
77 DON(s),SCi,V:Mr. Prymm 2.50
78 DON(s),SCi,Captain Death. 2.50
79 DON(s),SCi,F:Jean Paul. 2.50
80 DON(s),SCi,JmP,F:Jean Paul. . . 2.50
81 DON(s),SCi,JmP,imprisoned. . . . 2.50
82 DON(s),SCi,JmP,escape. 2.50
83 DON(s),SCi,JmP,Jokerized. 2.50
84 DON(s),SCi,JmP,madman 2.50
85 DON(s),SCi,JmP,new villain 2.50
86 DON(s),SCi,JmP,Spartan 2.50
87 DON(s),SCi,new foe 2.50
88 DON(s),JmP,SCi,F:Nightwing . . . 2.50
89 DON(s),F:Nightwing 2.50
90 DON(s),F:Nightwing 2.50
91 Bruce Wayne:Fugitive,pt.15 . . . . 2.50
92 DON(s),SCi,F:Batman 2.50
93 DON(s),SCi,war on crime 2.95
94 DON(s),SCi,Demon Biis 2.95
95 DON(s),SCi,Biis,Two-face. 2.95
96 DON(s),SCi,A:Batman,
    V:Two-Face 2.95
97 DON(s),MZ,JOy,New costume . . 2.95
98 DON(s),MZ,JOy,on the brink . . . 2.95
99 DON(s),MZ,JOy, ... 2.95
100 DON(s),MZ,JOy,final issue . . . 2.95
Ann.#1 Year One Annual 3.00
Ann.#2 Legends o/t Dead Earth . . . 4.00
Ann.#3 Pulp Heroes (Hard Boiled) . 5.00
Spec.#1,000,000 DON(s),VGi,JmP
    F:Green Arrow,Robin,Hawkman 3.00
GN Azrael/Ash 5.00

AZRAEL/ASH

March, 1997

1 one-shot DON(s),JQ,V:Surtr,
    A:Batman, x-over. 5.00

AZRAEL PLUS

Oct., 1996

1 one-shot, DON(s),VGi,F:Vic
    Sage, The Question 3.00

AZTEK:
THE ULTIMATE MAN

1996–97

1 GMo&MMr(s),NSH,I:Aztek &
    Synth 6.00
2 GMo&MMr(s),NSH,A:Green
    Lantern 4.00
3 GMo&MMr(s),NSH,V:Doll-Face. . 4.00
4 GMo&MMr(s),NSH,I:Lizard King,
    Vanity. 4.00
5 GMo&MMr(s),NSH,O:Aztek,
    V:Lizard King 4.00
6 GMo&MMr(s),NSH,V:Vanity,
    A: Joker 4.00
7 GMo&MMr(s),NSH,A:Batman . . . 4.00
8 GMo&MMr(s),NSH,return to Brother-
    hood of Zuetzatcoatl,A:Raptor. . 4.00
9 GMo&MMr(s),NSH,V:Parasite,
    A:Superman. 4.00
10 GMo&MMr(s),NSH,A:Justice
    League, final issue 12.00

BABYLON 5

1995

1 From TV series 14.00
2 From TV series 8.00
3 Mysterious Assassin 8.00

4 V:Mysterious Assassin. 8.00
5 Shadows of the Present,pt.1 . . . . 8.00
6 Shadows of the Present,pt.2 . . . . 8.00
7 Shadows of the Present,pt.3 . . . . 7.00
8 Laser-Mirror Starweb,pt.1 . . . . . 7.00
9 Laser-Mirror Starweb,pt.2 . . . . . 7.00
10 Laser-Mirror-Starweb,pt.3 . . . . . 7.00
11 final issue 7.00
TPB The Price of Peace 10.00

Babylon 5: In Valen's Name #1
© DC Comics, Inc.

BABYLON 5:
IN VALEN'S NAME

Jan., 1998

1 (of 3) PDd, from TV series. 4.00
2 PDd 4.00
3 PDd 4.00

BAD GIRLS

Aug. 2003

1 (of 6) F:Lauren. 2.50
2 thru 6 . . . . @2.50

BALL AND CHAIN

Homage/DC Sept., 1999

1 (of 4) SLo. 2.50
2 thru 4 SLo . . . . @2.50

BATGIRL

Feb., 2000

1 No Man's Land follow-up 10.00
1a 2nd printing 2.50
2 saves dying man 7.00
3 A:Batman 4.00
4 A:Batman 4.00
5 V:Ezra 4.00
6 A:Batman 4.00
7 A:Batman 4.00
8 V:Lady Shiva 4.00
9 Batgirl questions her motives . . . 3.50
10 Too slow to stop a killer 3.50
11 This Issue: Batman Dies! 3.50
12 Officer Down tie-in 3.50
13 Government trained killers 3.50
14 A:Batman 3.50
15 RbC,ghastly murders 3.50
16 RbC,young boy's father 3.50
17 RbC,A:Oracle,Cassandra 3.50
18 RbC,A:Robin,V:Deadeye 3.50
19 RbC,Nobody dies tonight 3.50
20 CDi,F:The Spoiler 3.50

21 CDi,Joker:Last Laugh 3.50
22 RbC,F:Cain 3.50
23 RbC,F:Lady Shiva. 3.50
24 RbC,BruceWayne:Murderer,pt.2. 3.50
25 RbC,V:Lady Shiva,40-pg. 4.00
26 VGi,Spoiler 3.00
27 RbC,Bruce Wayne:Fugitive,pt.4 . 3.00
28 RbC,I:Sensor 3.00
29 RbC,Bruce Wayne:Fugitive,pt.13 3.00
30 CDi,KJ,Roman military cult. 3.00
31 CDi,F:Robin, Spoiler 3.00
32 CDi,all-star issue. 3.00
33 RbC,A:Batman,metahunt 3.00
34 RbC,A:Batman,detective skills . . 3.00
35 RbC,V:Alpha,A:Batman 3.00
36 RbC,V:Alpha 3.00
37 RbC,save the child 3.00
38 RbC,F:Spoiler 3.00
39 V:Black Wind. 3.00
40 V:Black Wind. 3.00
41 First date,A:Superboy 3.00
42 I:New Dr. Death 3.00
43 V:Dr. Death 3.00
44 V:Dr. Death 3.00
45 RL,drug Soul 3.00
46 RL,F:Oracle. 3.00
47 RL,V:Doll Man. 2.50
48 missing girl 2.50
49 V:The Lost Girls 2.50
50 RL,V:Batman. 3.25
51 RL,V:Poison Ivy 2.50
52 RL,V:Poison Ivy 2.50
53 F:Girl Wonder,V:Penguin 2.50
54 RL,vs. cyborg 2.50
55 War Games,Act 1,pt.6 . . . . 2.50
56 War Games,Act 2,pt.6 . . . . 2.50
57 War Games,Act 3,pt.6 . . . . 2.50
Ann.#1 Planet DC,A:Batman 3.50
Spec.#1 V: Cormorant,
   I:Slash (1988) 10.00
Spec. Secret Files #1, 48-pg. 5.00
TPB A Knight Alone, 160-page . . . 12.95
TPB Silent Running, 144-page . . . 12.95
TPB Death Wish 14.95
TPB Batgirl: Fists of Fury. 14.95

BATGIRL ADVENTURES
Dec., 1997
1-shot RBr,V:Poison Ivy,A:Harley
  Quinn. 4.00

BATGIRL: YEAR ONE
Dec. 2002
1 CDi(s),F:Barbara Gordon. 3.00
2 CDi(s),meets JSA 3.00
3 CDi(s),Dynamic Duo 3.00
4 CDi(s),Dynamic Duo 3.00
5 CDi(s),Killer Moth. 3.00
6 CDi(s),F:Black Canary. 3.00
7 CDi(s),A:Robin. 3.00
8 CDi(s),V:Blockbuster 3.00
9 CDi(s),Origin concl. 3.00
TPB O:Barbara Gordon 17.95

BATMAN
Spring, 1940
1 I:Joker,Cat(Catwoman),
  V:Hugo Strange . . . 135,000.00
2 V:Joker/Catwoman team . . 20,000.00
3 V:Catwoman 14,000.00
4 V:Joker 10,000.00
5 V:Joker 7,000.00
6 V:Clock Maker 6,500.00
7 V:Joker 6,200.00
8 V:Joker 5,000.00
9 V:Joker 5,000.00
10 V:Catwoman 5,000.00
11 V:Joker,Penguin 10,000.00
12 V:Joker. 4,000.00

Batman #41 © DC Comics, Inc.

13 V:Joker. 4,200.00
14 V:Penguin;Propaganda sty . 4,000.00
15 V:Catwoman 4,000.00
16 I:Alfred,V:Joker 7,500.00
17 V:Penguin 3,000.00
18 V:Tweedledum &
  Tweedledee 3,800.00
19 V:Joker. 3,000.00
20 V:Joker. 3,000.00
21 V:Penguin 2,000.00
22 V:Catwoman,Cavalier 2,000.00
23 V:Joker. 3,000.00
24 I:Carter Nichols, V:Tweedledum
  & Tweedledee. 2,000.00
25 V:Joker/Penguin team 3,200.00
26 V:Cavalier 2,000.00
27 V:Penguin 4,000.00
28 V:Joker. 2,000.00
29 V:Scuttler 2,000.00
30 V:Penguin,I:Ally Babble 2,000.00
31 I:Punch and Judy. 1,500.00
32 O:Robin,V:Joker. 1,500.00
33 V:Penguin,Jackall 1,700.00
34 A:Ally Babble 1,500.00
35 V:Catwoman 1,500.00
36 V:Penguin,A:King Arthur . . . 1,500.00
37 V:Joker. 2,000.00
38 V:Penguin 1,700.00
39 V:Catwoman,Xmas Story. . . 1,500.00
40 V:Joker. 2,000.00
41 V:Penguin 1,100.00
42 V:Catwoman 1,100.00
43 V:Penguin 1,100.00
44 V:Joker,A:Carter Nichols,Meets
  ancester Silas Wayne. 2,000.00
45 V:Catwoman 1,100.00
46 V:Joker,A:Carter Nichols,
  Leonardo Da Vinci 1,100.00
47 O:Batman,V:Catwoman 4,500.00
48 V:Penguin, Bat-Cave story . 1,500.00
49 I:Mad Hatter & Vicki Vale . . 2,200.00
50 V:Two-Face,A:Vicki Vale . . . 1,200.00
51 V:Penguin 1,000.00
52 V:Joker. 1,300.00
53 V:Joker. 1,300.00
54 V:The Treasure Hunter 1,000.00
55 V:Joker. 1,300.00
56 V:Penguin 1,000.00
57 V:Joker. 1,000.00
58 V:Penguin 1,000.00
59 I:Deadshot 1,000.00
60 V:`Shark' Marlin 1,000.00
61 V:Penguin 1,100.00
62 O:Catwoman,I:Knight
  & Squire 1,700.00

63 V:Joker. 1,000.00
64 V:Killer Moth 850.00
65 I:Wingman,V:Catwoman . . . 1,000.00
66 V:Joker. 1,000.00
67 V:Joker. 1,000.00
68 V:Two-Face,Alfred story 850.00
69 I:King of the Cats,
  A:Catwoman. 1,000.00
70 V:Penguin 850.00
71 V:Mr. Cipher 850.00
72 The Jungle Batman. 850.00
73 V:Joker,A:Vicki Vale. 1,100.00
74 V:Joker 850.00
75 I:The Gorilla Boss 850.00
76 V:Penguin 850.00
77 The Crime Predictor 850.00
78 The Manhunter from Mars . . 1,100.00
79 A:Vicki Vale 850.00
80 V:Joker 850.00
81 V:Two-Face. 850.00
82 The Flying Batman 750.00
83 V:`Fish' Frye 1,000.00
84 V:Catwoman 1,000.00
85 V:Joker 750.00
86 V:Joker 750.00
87 V:Joker 750.00
88 V:Mr. Mystery 750.00
89 I:Aunt Agatha 750.00
90 I:Batboy. 750.00
91 V:Blinky Grosset 750.00
92 I:Ace, the Bat-Hound 750.00
93 The Caveman Batman 700.00
94 Alfred has Amnesia. 600.00
95 The Bat-Train 600.00
96 Batman's College Days 600.00
97 V:Joker 600.00
98 A:Carter Nichols,Jules Verne . 600.00
99 V:Penguin,A:Carter Nichols,
  Bat Masterson 600.00
100 Great Batman Contest. . . . 3,300.00
101 The Great Bat-Cape Hunt. . . 600.00
102 V:Mayne Mallok 550.00
103 A:Ace, the Bat-Hound 550.00
104 V:Devoe 550.00
105 A:Batwoman 750.00
106 V:Keene Harper gang. 600.00
107 V:Daredevils 600.00
108 Bat-cave story 600.00
109 1,000 Inventions of Batman . 600.00
110 V:Joker 550.00
111 . . . . 450.00
112 I:Signalman 450.00
113 I:Fatman 450.00
114 I:Bat Ape 450.00
115 . . . . 450.00
116 . . . . 450.00
117 . . . . 450.00
118 . . . . 450.00
119 . . . . 450.00
120 . . . . 450.00
121 I:Mr.Zero (Mr.Freeze) 600.00
122 . . . . 300.00
123 A:Joker 325.00
124 Mystery Seed from Space . . 300.00
125 . . . . 300.00
126 . . . . 300.00
127 A:Superman & Joker. 325.00
128 . . . . 300.00
129 O:Robin (Retold) 350.00
130 . . . . 300.00
131 I:2nd Batman 250.00
132 Lair of the Sea-Fox. 250.00
133 . . . . 250.00
134 . . . . 250.00
135 . . . . 250.00
136 A:Joker,Bat-Mite 300.00
137 V:Mr.Marvel,The Brand. 250.00
138 A:Bat-Mite. 250.00
139 I:Old Batgirl 250.00
140 A:Joker 250.00
141 V:Clockmaster. 250.00

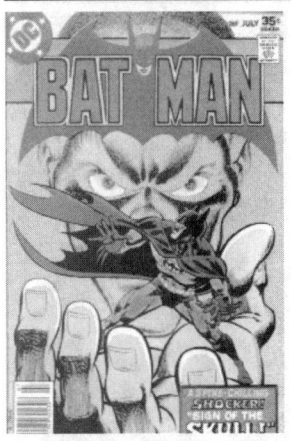

Batman #289 © DC Comics, Inc.

142 Batman robot story	250.00
143 A:Bathound	250.00
144 A:Joker,Bat-Mite,Bat-Girl.	250.00
145 V:Mr.50,Joker	300.00
146 A:Bat-Mite,Joker	300.00
147 Batman becomes Bat-Baby	200.00
148 A:Joker	250.00
149 V:Maestro	200.00
150 V:Biff Warner,Jack Pine	200.00
151 V:Harris Boys	150.00
152 A:Joker	165.00
153 Other Dimension story	150.00
154 V:Dr. Dorn	150.00
155 1st S.A. Penguin	500.00
156 V:Gorilla Gang	165.00
157 V:Mirror Man	165.00
158 A:Bathound,Bat-Mite	165.00
159 A:Joker,Clayface	175.00
160 V:Bart Cullen	165.00
161 A:Bat-Mite	165.00
162 F:Robin	165.00
163 A:Joker	165.00
164 CI,A:Mystery Analysts,new Batmobile.	150.00
165 V:The Mutated Man	150.00
166 Escape story	150.00
167 V:Karabi & Hydra, the Crime Cartel	150.00
168 V:Mr. Mammoth.	150.00
169 A:Penguin	175.00
170 V:Getaway Genius	150.00
171 CI,1st S.A. Riddler	650.00
172 V:Flower Gang	125.00
173 V:Elwood Pearson	125.00
174 V:Big Game Hunter.	125.00
175 V:Eddie Repp	125.00
176 Giant rep.A:Joker,Catwom.	150.00
177 BK,A:Elongated Man,Atom.	125.00
178 CI	125.00
179 CI,2nd Riddler(Silver)	250.00
180 BK,A:Death-Man.	125.00
181 CI,I:Poison Ivy.	300.00
182 A:Joker,(giant size rep).	150.00
183 CI,A:Poison Ivy	150.00
184 CI,Mystery of the Missing Manhunters	125.00
185 Giant rep.	125.00
186 A:Joker	125.00
187 Giant rep.A:Joker	125.00
188 CI,A:Eraser	75.00
189 CI,A:Scarecrow	150.00
190 CI,A:Penguin	100.00
191 CI,The Day Batman Soldout.	75.00
192 CI,The Crystal ball that betrayed Batman	75.00
193 Giant rep.	125.00

194 MSy,BK,A:Blockbuster,Mystery Analysts of Gotham City	75.00
195 CI	75.00
196 BK,Psychic Super-Sleuth	75.00
197 MSy,A:Bat Girl,Catwoman	125.00
198 A:Joker,Penguin,Catwoman, O:Batman rtd,(G-Size rep)	125.00
199 CI,Peril o/t Poison Rings.	75.00
200 NA(c),O:rtd,A:Joker,Pengiun, Scarecrow	225.00
201 A:Batman Villians	75.00
202 BU:Robin.	65.00
203 NA(c),(giant size)	100.00
204 FR(s),IN,JG.	65.00
205 FR(s),IN,JG.	65.00
206 FR(s),IN,JG.	65.00
207 FR(s),IN,JG.	65.00
208 GK,new O:Batman, A:Catwoman	100.00
209 FR(s),IN,JG.	100.00
210 A:Catwoman	100.00
211 FR(s),IN,JG.	65.00
212 FR(s),IN,JG.	65.00
213 RA,30th Anniv.Batman,new O: Robin,rep.O:Alfred,Joker.	125.00
214 IN,A:Batgirl	65.00
215 IN,DG	65.00
216 IN,DG,I:DaphnePennyworth	65.00
217 NA(c).	65.00
218 NA(c),giant	75.00
219 NA,IN,DG,Batman Xmas.	75.00
220 NA(c),IN	50.00
221 IN,DG	50.00
222 IN,Rock'n Roll story	65.00
223 NA(c),giant	65.00
224 NA(c).	50.00
225 NA(c),IN,DG	50.00
226 IN,DG I:10-Eyed Man	50.00
227 IN,DG,A:Daphne Pennyworth	50.00
228 giant Deadly Traps rep.	75.00
229 IN	50.00
230 NA(c),Robin	50.00
231 F:Ten-Eyed Man	50.00
232 DON(s),NA,DG, I:Ras al Ghul	175.00
233 giant Bruce Wayne iss.	75.00
234 NA,DG,IN,1stS.A.Two-Face	225.00
235 CI,V:Spook	50.00
236 NA.	50.00
237 NA,I:The Reaper.	100.00
238 NA,JC,JKu,giant	75.00
239 NA,RB.	50.00
240 NA(c),RB,giant,R-Ghul	50.00
241 IN,DG,RB,A:Kid Flash	50.00
242 RB,MK.	50.00
243 NA,DG,Ras al Ghul	75.00
244 NA,Ras al Ghul	75.00
245 NA,IN,DG,FMc,Ras al Ghul	75.00
246	40.00
247 Deadly New Year	40.00
248	40.00
249 Citidel of Crime	40.00
250 IN,DG	40.00
251 NA,V:Joker	100.00
252	40.00
253 AN,DG,A:Shadow	40.00
254 NA,GK,B:100 page issues	75.00
255 GK,CI,NA,DG,I:CrazyQuilt	75.00
256 Catwoman.	75.00
257 IN,DG,V:Penguin.	75.00
258 IN,DG	75.00
259 GK,IN,DG,A:Shadow.	75.00
260 IN,DG,Joker.	100.00
261 CI,GK,E:100 page issues	75.00
262 A:Scarecrow	50.00
263 DG(i),A:Riddler	20.00
264 DON(s),DG,A:Devil Dayre.	20.00
265 RB,BWr.	25.00
266 DG,Catwoman(old Costume)	22.00
267 DG.	20.00

268 DON(s),IN,TeB,V:Sheikh.	20.00
269 A:Riddler	20.00
270 B:DvR(s)	20.00
271 IN,FMc	20.00
272 JL	20.00
273 V:Underworld Olympics/76	20.00
274	20.00
275	20.00
276	20.00
277	20.00
278	20.00
279 A:Riddler	22.00
280	20.00
281	20.00
282	20.00
283 V:Camouflage	20.00
284 JA,R:Dr.Tzin Tzin	20.00
285	20.00
286 V:Joker	30.00
287 BWi,MGr,Penguin	25.00
288 BWi,MGr,Penguin	25.00
289 MGr, V:Skull	20.00
290 MGr,V:Skull Dagger	20.00
291 B:Underworld Olympics #1, A:Catwoman	30.00
292 A:Riddler	20.00
293 A:Superman & Luthor	20.00
294 E:DvR(s),E:Underworld Olympics,A:Joker.	30.00
295 GyC(s),MGo,JyS,V:Hamton	20.00
296 B:DvR(s),V:Scarecrow	20.00
297 RB,Mad Hatter	20.00
298 JCA,DG,V:Baxter Bains	20.00
299 DG.	20.00
300 WS,DG,A:Batman E-2, Robin E-2	35.00
301 JCa,TeB	15.00
302 JCa,DG,V:Human Dynamo	15.00
303 JCa,DG.	15.00
304 E:DvR(s),V:Spook	15.00
305 GyC,JCa,DeH,V:Thanatos	16.00
306 JCa,DeH,DN,V:Black Spider.	20.00
307 B:LWn(s),JCa,DG, I:Limehouse Jack	20.00
308 JCa,DG,V:Mr.Freeze	16.00
309 E:LWn(s),JCa,FMc, V:Blockbuster	16.00
310 IN,DG,A:Gentleman Ghost	16.00
311 SEt,FMc,IN,Batgirl, V:Dr.Phosphorus	16.00
312 WS,DG,Calenderman	16.00
313 IN,FMc,VTwo-Face	16.00
314 IN,FMc,V:Two-Face	16.00
315 IN,FMc,V:Kiteman.	16.00

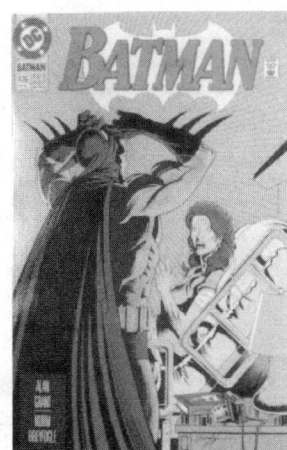

Batman #476 © DC Comics Inc.

Batman #480 © DC Comics, Inc.

316 IN,FMc,F:Robin,
  V:Crazy Quilt 16.00
317 IN,FMc,V:Riddler. 17.00
318 IN,I:Fire Bug 16.00
319 JKu(c),IN,DG,A:Gentleman
  Ghost,E:Catwoman 16.00
320 BWr(c). 17.00
321 DG,WS,A:Joker,Catwoman . . . 20.00
322 V:Cap.Boomerang,Catwoman 16.00
323 IN,A:Catwoman. 16.00
324 IN,A:Catwoman. 16.00
325 . . . . 16.00
326 A:Catwoman 16.00
327 IN,A:Proffessor.Milo 16.00
328 A:Two-Face 16.00
329 IN,A:Two-Face 16.00
330 . . . . 16.00
331 DN,FMc,V:Electrocutioner . . . 16.00
332 IN,DN,Ras al Ghul.1st solo
  Catwoman story 20.00
333 IN,DN,A:Catwoman,
  Ras al Ghul 15.00
334 FMc,Ras al Ghul,Catwoman. . 15.00
335 IN,FMc,Catwoman,Ras al
  Ghul. 15.00
336 JL,FMc,Loser Villains 15.00
337 DN,V:Snow Man 15.00
338 DN,Deathsport 15.00
339 A:Poison Ivy 15.00
340 GC,A:Mole 15.00
341 A:Man Bat 15.00
342 V:Man Bat 15.00
343 GC,KJ,I:The Dagger 15.00
344 GC,KJ,Poison Ivy 15.00
345 I:New Dr.Death,A:Catwoman . 15.00
346 DN,V:Two Face 15.00
347 A:Alfred 15.00
348 GC,KJ,Man-Bat,A:Catwoman . 15.00
349 GC,AA,A:Catwoman 15.00
350 GC,TD,A:Catwoman 15.00
351 GC,TD,A:Catwoman 15.00
352 Col Blimp 15.00
353 JL,DN,DA,A:Joker. 22.00
354 DN,AA,V:HugoStrange,A:
  Catwoman 15.00
355 DN,AA:A:Catwoman 15.00
356 DG,DN,Hugo Strange 15.00
357 DN,AA,I:Jason Todd 16.00
358 A:King Croc. 15.00
359 DG,O:King Croc,Joker 20.00
360 I:Savage Skull. 15.00
361 DN,Man-Bat,I:Harvey Bullock . 15.00
362 V:Riddler 15.00
363 V:Nocturna 15.00

364 DN,AA,J.Todd 1st full solo
  story (cont'd Detective #531) . 15.00
365 DN,AA,C:Joker 15.00
366 DN,AA,Joker,J.Todd in
  Robin Costume 20.00
367 DN,AA,PoisonIvy 14.00
368 DN,AA,I:2nd Robin
  (Jason Todd) 15.00
369 DN,AA,I:Dr.Fang,V:Deadshot . 12.00
370 DN,AA. 12.00
371 DN,AA,V:Catman 10.00
372 DN,AA,A:Dr.Fang 7.00
373 DN,AA,V:Scarecrow 7.00
374 GC,AA,V:Penguin 8.00
375 GC,AA,V:Dr.Freeze. 7.00
376 DN,Halloween issue 7.00
377 DN,AA,V:Nocturna 7.00
378 V:Mad Hatter. 7.00
379 V:Mad Hatter. 7.00
380 AA,V:Nocturna 7.00
381 V:Batman 7.00
382 A:Catwoman 8.00
383 GC. 7.00
384 V:Calender Man 7.00
385 V:Calender Man 7.00
386 I:Black Mask 7.00
387 V:Black Mask 7.00
388 V:Capt.Boomerang & Mirror
  Master 7.00
389 V:Nocturna,Catwoman 7.00
390 V:Nocturna,Catwoman 7.00
391 V:Nocturna,Catwoman 7.00
392 A:Catwoman 7.00
393 PG,V:Cossack 6.00
394 PG,V:Cossack 6.00
395 V:Film Freak 6.00
396 V:Film Freak 6.00
397 V:Two-Face,Catwoman. 7.00
398 V:Two-Face,Catwoman. 7.00
399 HaE(s),Two-Face 6.00
400 BSz,AAd,GP,BB,A:Joker. 25.00
401 JBy(c),TVE,Legends,
  A:Magpie 6.00
402 JSn,Fake Batman 6.00
403 DCw,Batcave discovered 6.00
404 DM,FM(s),B:Year 1,I:Modern
  Age Catwoman 22.00
405 FM,DM,Year 1 . . . . 16.00
406 FM,DM,Year 1 . . . . 16.00
407 FM,DM,E:Year 1 . . . . 16.00
408 CW,V:Joker,
  new O:Jason Todd. 10.00
408a 2nd printing 3.00
409 DG,RA,V:Crime School 10.00
409a 2nd printing 3.00
410 DC,Jason Todd 10.00
411 DC,DH,V:Two Face 6.00
412 DC,DH,I:Mime. 6.00
413 DC,DH. 6.00
414 JAp,Slasher. 6.00
415 JAp,Millenium Week #2 . . . . . . 6.00
416 JAp,1st Batman/Nightwing
  T.U. 6.00
417 JAp,B:10 Nights,I:KGBeast. . . 12.00
418 JAp,V:KGBeast. 12.00
419 JAp,V:KGBeast. 12.00
420 JAp,E:10 Nights,D:KGBeast . . 12.00
421 DG. 7.00
422 MBr,V:Dumpster Slayer 6.00
423 TM(c),DC,Who is Batman. 7.00
424 MBr,Robin 6.00
425 MBr,Gordon Kidnapped 6.00
426 JAp,B:Death in the Family,
  V:Joker 20.00
427 JAp,V:Joker. 18.00
428 JAp,D:2nd Robin. 18.00
429 JAp,A:Superman,
  E:Death in the Family 15.00
430 JAp,JSn,V:Madman 5.00
431 JAp,Murder Investigation 4.00
432 JAp 4.00

Batman #500 © DC Comics, Inc.

433 JBy,JAp,Many Deaths of the
  Batman #1 . . . . 5.00
434 JBy,JAp,Many Deaths #2 . . . . 4.50
435 JBy,Many Deaths #3. . . . . 4.50
436 PB,B:Year#3,A:Nightwing,I:Tim
  Drake as child 5.00
436a 2ndPrint(green DC logo). 3.00
437 PB,year#3. . . . . 4.00
438 PB,year#3 . . . . 3.50
439 PB,year#3 . . . . 3.50
440 JAp,Lonely Place of Dying #1,
  A:Tim Drake (face not shown). . 4.00
441 JAp,Lonely Place Dying 4.00
442 JAp,I:3rd Robin(Tim Drake) . . . 5.00
443 JAp,I:Crimesmith. 3.00
444 JAp,V:Crimesmith 3.00
445 JAp,I:K.G.Beast Demon 3.00
446 JAp,V:K.G.Beast Demon 3.00
447 JAp,D:K.G.Beast Demon 3.00
448 JAp,A:Penguin#1 . . . . 3.50
449 MBr,A:Penguin#3 . . . . 3.50
450 JAp,I:Joker II. 3.00
451 JAp,V:Joker II 3.00
452 KD,Dark Knight Dark City#1 . . 3.00
453 KD,Dark Knight Dark City#2. . 3.00
454 KD,Dark Knight Dark City#3 . . 3.00
455 Identity Crisis#1,
  A:Scarecrow 3.00
456 IdentityCrisis#2 . . . . 4.00
457 V:Scarecrow,A:Robin,
  New Costume 6.00
457a 2nd printing. 3.00
458 R:Sarah Essen 3.00
459 A:Sarah Essen 3.00
460 Sisters in Arms,pt.1
  A:Catwoman 3.50
461 Sisters in Arms,pt.2
  Catwoman V:Sarah.Essen 3.50
462 Batman in San Francisco 3.00
463 Death Valley 3.00
464 V:Two-Hearts 3.00
465 Batman/Robin T.U. 3.50
466 Robin Trapped 3.00
467 Shadowbox #1(sequel to
  Robin Mini-Series) 3.50
468 Shadowbox #2 . . . . 3.00
469 Shadowbox #3 . . . . 3.00
470 War of the Gods x-over 3.00
471 V:Killer Croc 3.00
472 The Idiot Root,pt.1 . . . . 3.00
473 The Idiot Root,pt.3 . . . . 3.00
474 Destroyer,pt.1 (LOTDK#27) . . . 3.50
475 R:Scarface,A:VickiVale 3.00
476 A:Scarface. 3.00
477 Ph(c),Gotham Tale,pt.1 . . . . . . 3.00

478 Ph(c),Gotham Tale,pt.2 . . . . . . 3.00
479 TMd,I:Pagan 3.00
480 JAp,To the father I never
     knew 3.00
481 JAp,V:Maxie Zeus 3.00
482 JAp,V:Maxie Zeus 3.00
483 JAp,I:Crash & Burn 3.00
484 JAp,R:Black Mask 3.00
485 TGr,V:Black Mask 3.00
486 JAp,I:Metalhead 3.00
487 JAp,V:Headhunter 3.00
488 JAp,N:Azrael 10.00
489 JAp,Bane vs Killer Croc,
     I:Azrael as Batman 6.00
489a 2nd Printing 3.00
490 JAp,Bane vs.Riddler 7.00
490a 2nd Printing 2.50
490b 3rd Printing 2.00
491 JAp,V:Joker,A:Bane 4.50
491a 2nd Printing 2.00
492 B:DgM(s),NB,Knightfall#1,
     V:Mad Hatter,A:Bane 5.00
492a Platinum Ed. 10.00
492b 2nd Printing 2.00
493 NB,Knightfall,#3,Mr.Zsasz 4.00
494 JAp,TMd,Knightfall #5,A:Bane,
     V:Cornelius,Stirk,Joker 3.50
495 NB,Knightfall#7,V:Poison
     Ivy,A:Bane 3.50
496 JAp,JRu,Knightfall#9,V:Joker,
     Scarecrow,A:Bane 3.50
497 JAp,DG,Knightfall#11,V:Bane,
     Batman gets back broken 5.50
497a 2nd Printing 2.50
498 JAp,JRu,Knightfall#15,A:Bane,
     Catwoman,Azrael Becomes
     Batman 3.00
499 JAp,SHa,Knightfall#17,
     A:Bane,Catwoman 3.00
500 JQ(c),JAp,MM,Die Cut(c),
     Direct Market,Knightfall#19,
     V:Bane,N:Batman 6.00
500a KJo(c),Newstand Ed. 3.50
501 MM,I:Mekros 3.00
502 MM,V:Mekros 3.00
503 MM,V:Catwoman 3.00
504 MM,V:Catwoman 3.00
505 MM,V:Canibal 3.00
506 KJo(c),MM,A:Ballistic 3.00
507 KJo(c),MM,A:Ballistic 3.00
508 KJo(c),MM,V:Abattior 3.00
509 KJo(c),MM,KnightsEnd#1,
     A:Shiva 3.50
510 KJo(c),MM,Knights End #7,
     V:Azrael 3.00
511 Zero Hour, A:Batgirl 3.00
512 Killer Croc sewer battles 3.00
513 Two-Face and convicts 3.00
514 Identity Crisis 3.00
515 KJo,Return of Bruce Wayne,
     Troika,pt.1 . . . . 3.00
515 Collector's Edition 3.50
516 V:The Sleeper 3.00
517 V:The Sleeper 3.00
518 V:The Black Spider 3.00
519 KJo,V:The Black Spider
     [new Miraweb format begins] . . 3.00
520 EB,A:James Gordon 3.00
521 R:Killer Croc 3.00
522 R:Scarecrow 3.00
523 V:Scarecrow 3.00
524 DgM,KJo,V:Scarecrow 3.00
525 DgM,KJo,Underworld
     Unleashed tie-in 3.00
526 DgM,A:Alfred,Nightwing,Robin . 3.00
527 DgM,V:Two-Face,I:Schism 3.00
528 . . . . 3.00
529 DgM,KJo,Contagion,pt.6 . . . . . 3.50
530 DgM,KJo,The Aztec
     Connection,pt.1 . . . . 3.50
530a collector's edition 3.50

531 DgM,KJo,The Aztec
     Connection,pt.2 . . . . 3.00
531a collectors edition 3.50
532 DgM(s),KJo,The Aztec Connec-
     tion, pt.3, A:Deadman 3.00
532a card stock cover 3.50
533 DgM(s),KJo,Legacy prelude . . . 3.00
534 DgM(s),KJo,Legacy, pt.5 . . . . . 3.00
535 DgM(s),KJo,JhB,I:The Ogre,
     double size 4.00
535a Collector's edition,
     gatefold cover 5.00
536 DgM(s),KJo,JhB,V:Man-Bat,
     Final Night tie-in 3.00
537 DgM(s),KJo,JhB,A:Man-Bat,
     pt.2 . . . . 3.00
538 DgM(s),KJo,JhB,A:Man-Bat,
     pt.3 . . . . 3.00
539 . . . . 3.00
540 DgM(s),KJo,JhB,Spectre,pt.1 . . 3.00
541 DgM(s),KJo,JhB,Spectre,pt.2 . . 3.00
542 DgM(s),KJo,JhB,V:Faceless,
     pt. 1 . . . . 3.00
543 DgM(s),KJo,JhB,pt. 2 . . . . 3.00
544 DgM(s),KJo,JhB, F:Joker,pt.1 . . 3.00
545 DgM(s),KJo, F:Joker, Demon,
     pt.2 . . . . 3.00
546 DgM(s),KJo,JhB,F:Joker,
     Demon, pt.3 concl. 3.00
547 DgM,KJo,JhB,Genesis tie-in . . . 3.00
548 DgM,KJo,JhB,V:Penguin,pt.1 . 3.00
549 DgM,KJo,JhB,V:Penguin, pt.2 . 3.00
550 DgM,KJo,JhB,I:Chase 3.50
550a deluxe, with file card inserts . 3.50
551 DgM,KJo,JhB,F:Ragman 2.50
552 DgM, ... 2.50
553 DgM,KJo,SB,Cataclysm
     x-over, pt.3 . . . . 4.50
554 DgM,KJo,SB,Cataclysm, ... 3.00
555 DGm,JhB,SB,BSf,Aftershock . . 2.50
556 DGm,NBy,BSf,Aftershock 2.50
557 DGm,VGi,SB,BSf,F:Ballistic . . 2.50
558 DGm,JAp,SB,doubts 2.50
559 DgM(s),BH,SB,Aftershock 2.50
560 CDi,SB,A:Nightwing & Robin . . 2.50
561 CDi(s),JAp, No Man's Land . . . 2.50
562 CDi(s),JAp, No Man's Land . . . 2.50
563 No Law and A New Order, pt.3 . 6.00
564 F:Batgirl, Mosaic,pt.1 . . . . 2.50
565 F:Batgirl, Mosaic,pt.3 . . . . 2.50
566 JBg,A:Superman 2.50
567 SCi,F:Batgirl, pt.1,x-over 2.50
568 DJu,BSz,Fruit of the
     Earth, pt.2 . . . . 2.50

Batman #558 © DC Comics Inc.

569 F:Batgirl. 2.50
570 MD2,No Man's Land, The
     Code, pt.1 . . . . 2.50
571 CDi,MtB,Goin'Downtown,pt.1 . . 2.50
572 Jurisprudence,pt.1 . . . . 2.50
573 . . . . 2.50
574 Endgame, pt.2 x-over 2.50
575 LHa,SMc,KIS. 2.50
576 LHa,SMc,KIS,kidnapping 2.50
577 LHa,SMc,KIS,rodents 2.50
578 LHa,SMc,MPn,serial killer. 2.50
579 LHa,SMc,KIS,V:Orca,pt.1 . . . . . 2.50
580 LHa,SMc,KIS,V:Orca,pt.2 . . . . . 2.50
581 LHa,SMc,KIS,V:Orca,pt.3 . . . . . 2.50
582 SMc,KIS,Fearless,pt.1 . . . . 2.50
583 SMc,KIs,Fearless,pt.2 . . . . 2.50
584 SMc,KIS,A:Penguin. 2.50
585 SMc,KIS,V:Penguin. 2.50
586 SMc,KIS,V:Penguin, This issue:
     Batman Dies!. 2.50
587 RBr,RyR,Officer Down,pt.1 . . . . 2.50
588 SMc,KIS,Close Before Striking . 2.50
589 SMc,KIS,Close Before Striking . 2.50
590 SMc,KIS,Close Before Striking . 2.50
591 SMc,KIS,Shot thru the Heart . . 2.50
592 SMc,KIS,Shot thru the Heart . . 2.50
593 SMc,KIS,Worlds at War tie-in . . 2.50
594 SMc,KIS,Worlds at War tie-in . . 2.50
595 SMc,F:Lew Moxon 2.50
596 SMc,Joker:Last Laugh 2.50
597 SMc,V:Zeiss 2.50
598 SMc,Christmas in Gotham 2.50
599 Bruce Wayne:Murderer,pt.7 . . . 2.50
600 Bruce Wayne:Fugitive,pt.1 . . . . 6.00
600a 2nd printing 4.00
601 Bruce Wayne:Fugitive,pt.3 . . . . 2.50
602 SMc,V:Nicodemus 2.50
603 Bruce Wayne:Fugitive,pt.11 . . . 2.50
604 SMc,Crime Alley 2.50
605 Bruce Wayne:Fugitive,concl. . . 3.50
606 SMc,F:Deadshot 2.50
607 SMc,F:Deadshot,pt.2 . . . . 2.50
608 JLb,JLe,SW,Hush,pt.1 . . . . 12.00
608a 2nd printing, new cover 40.00
609 JLb,JLe,SW,Hush,pt.2 . . . . 7.00
610 JLb,JLe,SW,Hush,pt.3 . . . . 6.00
611 JLb,JLe,SW,Hush,pt.4 . . . . 6.00
612 JLb,JLe,SW,Hush,pt.5 . . . . 20.00
612a 2nd printing, B&W(c). 25.00
613 JLb,JLe,SW,Hush,pt.6 . . . . 7.00
614 JLb,JLe,SW,Hush,pt.7 . . . . 4.00
615 JLb,JLe,SW,Hush,pt.8 . . . . 18.00
616 JLb,JLe,SW,Hush,pt.9 . . . . 4.00
617 JLb,JLe,SW,Hush,pt.10 . . . . . . 4.00
618 JLb,JLe,SW,Hush,pt.11. . . . . . 4.00
619 JLb,JLe,SW,Hush,pt.12 . . . . . . 3.00
619a newsstand cover. 3.00
620 Broken City, pt.1 . . . . 2.50
621 Broken City, pt.2 . . . . 2.50
622 Broken City, pt.3 . . . . 2.25
623 Broken City, pt.4 . . . . 2.25
624 Broken City, pt.5 . . . . 2.25
625 Broken City, pt.6 . . . . 2.25
626 As the Crow Flies,pt.1 . . . . 2.25
627 As the Crow Flies,pt.2. . . . . 2.25
628 As the Crow Flies,pt.3. . . . . 2.25
629 As the Crow Flies,pt.4. . . . . 2.25
630 As the Crow Flies,pt.5. . . . . 2.25
631 War Games,Act 1,pt.8 . . . . 2.25
632 War Games,Act 2,pt.8 . . . . 2.25
633 War Games,Act 3,pt.8,40-pg . . 2.95
Ann.#1 CS,O:BatCave 1,100.00
Ann.#2 . . . . 450.00
Ann.#3 A:Joker. 450.00
Ann.#4 . . . . 200.00
Ann.#5 . . . . 200.00
Ann.#6 . . . . 150.00
Ann.#7 . . . . 150.00
Ann.#8 TVE,A:Ras al Ghul 10.00
Ann.#9 JOy,AN,PS. 9.00
Ann.#10 DCw,DG,V:HugoStrange . . 9.00

Batman/Harley Quinn Graphic Novel
© DC Comics, Inc.

Ann.#11 JBy(c),AMo(s),V:Penguin. 10.00
Ann.#12 RA,V:Killer 7.00
Ann.#13 A:Two-Face 8.00
Ann.#14 O:Two-Face 6.00
Ann.#15 Armageddon,pt.3 . . . . 8.00
Ann.#15a 2nd printing(silver) 4.00
Ann.#16 SK(c),Eclipso,V:Joker 4.00
Ann.#17 EB,Bloodline#8,
  I:Decimator 4.00
Ann.#18 Elseworld Story 5.00
Ann.#19 Year One, O:Scarecrow. . 6.00
Ann.#20 Legends o/t Dead Earth . 5.00
Ann.#21 Pulp Heroes (Weird
  Mystery) DgM(s) 6.00
Ann.#22 BWr(c) Ghosts 5.00
Ann.#23 CDi(s),GN,MPn, JLApe
  Gorilla Warfare 5.00
Ann.#24 Planet DC 5.00
Specials & 1-shots
Giant Ann.#1 Facsimile edition 6.00
Spec.#0 (1994) 4.00
Spec.#1 MGo,I:Wrath 5.00
Spec.#1,000,000 DgM(s),SB,
  F:Toy Wonder 3.00
Spec.#1 Our Worlds at War (2001) . 4.00
Giant #1, 7 tales, 80-page (1998) . . 6.00
Giant #2, 80-page (1999). 6.00
Giant #3 CDi(s) 80-page (2000) . . . 7.00
Batman: Arkham Asylum — Tales
  of Madness, AIG, Cataclysm
  tie-in (1998) 4.00
Batman: Batgirl, JBa,RBr,
  Girlfrenzy (1998) 3.00
Batman: Blackgate, CDi(s), JSon,
  in Blackgate prison (1996) 4.50
Batman: Blackgate — Isle of Men,
  DgM, JAp,BSf,BSz,
  Cataclysm (1998) 3.00
Batman Dark Knight Gallery (1995). 3.50
Batman: Day of Judgment 4.00
Batman: Death of Innocents, DON(s),
  JSt, BSz, Land mine victims
  (1996) 4.00
Batman Gallery,collection of past
  (c),posters,pin-ups,JQ(c) (1992) 4.00
Batman: Gotham By Gaslight,MMi,
  V:Jack the Ripper 6.00
Gotham City Secret Files #1 . . . . . . 5.00
Batman: The Hill (2000) 3.00
Batman: Joker's Apprentice 4.00
Batman: The Killing Joke,BB,AMo(s),
  O:Joker,Batgirl paralyzed
  (1988) 15.00

2nd thru 6th printings . . . . . . @5.00
Batman: Mitefall, V:Bane
  Mite (1995) 5.00
Batman: Penguin Triumphant
  (1992) 5.00
Batman: Plus (1997) 3.00
Batman Record Comic (1996) 2.00
Batman/Riddler: The Riddle
  Factory (1995) 5.00
Secret Files #1 SMc(c) inc.
  O:Batman (1997) 6.00
Batman: Seduction of the Gun,
  V:Illegal Gun Control (1992) . . . 3.00
Spec. The 10-Cent Adventure 0.10
3-D Batman:Scarecrow 4.00
Batman 12-cent Adventure,
  War Games,pt.1 . . . . 0.12
Batman/Two-Face: Crime and
  Punishment (1995) 5.00
  2nd printing (1998) 5.00
Two-Face Strikes Twice #1 . . . . . . 5.25
Two-Face Strikes Twice #2 . . . . . . 5.25
Batman: Vengeance of Bane,
  GN,I:Bane (1992) 30.00
  2nd Printing 5.00
Batman: Vengeance of Bane II
  (1995) 4.00
Batman Villains Secret Files,
  AIG,CDi,RMz,BB,F:Greatest Foes
  (1998) 5.00
Elseworld 1-shots
Batman of Arkham (2000) 6.00
Batman: The Blue, The Grey, and
  The Bat, JL (1992) 6.00
Batman: Brotherhood of the Bat
  (1995) 6.00
Batman: Castle of the Bat 6.00
Batman: Dark Allegiances (1996) . . 6.00
Batman: Holy Terror (1991) 6.50
Batman: I, Joker, BH, in
  2083 (1998) 5.00
Batman: In Darkest Knight
  MiB(s),JBi (1994). 5.50
Batman Knightgallery (1995) 3.50
Batman: Masque, MGr, in turn of
  the century Gotham 7.00
Batman: Master of the Future,EB,
  Sequel to Goth.by Gaslight
  (1991) 6.00
Batman: Scar of the Bat (1996). . . . 5.00
Batman: Two Faces (1998) 5.00
Batman: Master of the Future(1998) 6.00
Graphic Novels
The Abduction 6.00
Batman A Lonely Place of Dying
  (1990) rep. Batman #440–442
  & New Titans #60–61 . . . . 4.00
Batman: Blind Justice, rep. Detective
  Comics #598–#600 (1992) 7.50
Batman: Bloodstorm 13.00
Batman: Bullock's Law. 5.00
The Book of Shadows 6.00
Child of Dreams, manga 25.00
Crimson Mist, Elseworlds (2001). . 15.00
Batman: Dark Joker, KJo 12.00
Many Deaths of the Batman;
  rep. #433-#435 (1992). 4.00
Batman: Dreamland (2000) 6.00
Batman: Ego (2000). 7.00
Batman: Full Circle AD,
  A:Reaper (1992) 7.00
Batman/Joker: Switch 7.00
Golden Steets of Gotham 7.00
Gotham Noir, 64-page (2001) 7.00
Batman: Harley Quinn (1998) 6.00
Batman: Mr. Freeze 5.00
Batman/Nightwing: Bloodborne
  48-pg. (2002) 6.00
No Man's Land, 48-page No Law
  and a New Order, pt.1 . . . . 3.00
No Man's Land, lenticular (c) 4.00

No Man's Land Gallery 4.00
Nosferatu 6.00
The Order of Beasts (2004) 6.00
Batman: Poison Ivy 5.00
Batman/Poison Ivy:
  Cast Shadows (2004) 7.00
Reign of Terror 5.00
Roomful of Strangers (2004) 6.00
Batman: Scar of the Bat 5.00
Scarface—A Psychodrama (2001) . 6.00
The Scottish Connection 6.00
Batman: Ten Knights of the Beast,
  rep. #417–#420 (1994) 6.00
Batman: Two Faces 5.00
Batman: The Ultimate Evil:
  1 Novel adaptation (of 2). 6.00
  2 Novel adaptation, finale 6.00
Trade Paperbacks
Batman: Absolution 18.00
The Batman Adventures 8.00
Batman: Anarky 13.00
Batman: Arkham Asylum,DMc . . . 15.00
As the Crow Flies (2004) 13.00
The Arrow, The Ring & The Bat. . . 20.00
Birth of the Demon, O:Ras al
  Ghul (1993) 13.00
Batman: Black and White 20.00
Black and White, Vol.2. . . . . 20.00
Batman: Bloodstorm,KJo,V:Joker,
  Vampires 13.00
Bride of the Demon, TGr, V:Ra's
  al Ghul 13.00
Bruce Wayne-Fugitive, Vol. 1 . . . . 13.00
Bruce Wayne-Fugitive, Vol. 2 . . . . 13.00
Bruce Wayne-Fugitive, Vol. 3 . . . . 13.00
Bruce Wayne-Murderer? 13.00
Batman: Cataclysm 18.00
Batman: The Chalice (2000) 15.00
Batman: Contagion 13.00
Contagion. 20.00
Batman: The Cult. 20.00
The Dark Knight Adventures 8.00
Batman: Dark Knight Dynasty, three
  elseworlds stories (1999) 15.00
Dark Knight Strikes Again (2004). . 20.00
Batman: Dark Victory (2002) 20.00
Death and the Maidens (2004) . . . 20.00
Batman: A Death in the Family,
  rep. Batman #426-429 (1988)
  TPB 8.00
  2nd printing 5.00
  3rd printing 4.00
Batman/Deathblow: After the Fire . 13.00
Batman: Detective No. 27 (2004) . 13.00
Batman: Evolution (2001) 13.00
Batman: Faces (1995) 10.00
Batman: Fortunate Son (1999) . . . 15.00
Batman: Gothic, rept. Legends of
  the Dark Knight #6–#10 (1992) 13.00
Greatest Batman Stories 16.00
Greatest Batman Stories, Vol. 2 . . 17.00
Harvest Breed 18.00
Batman: Hong Kong (2004) 18.00
Batman/Huntress: Cry For Blood. . 13.00
Batman: Hush, Vol. 1 (2004) 13.00
Batman: Hush, Vol. 2 (2004) 13.00
Batman in the Forties. 20.00
Batman in the Fifties 20.00
Batman in the Sixties 20.00
Batman in the Seventies 20.00
Batman in the Eighties 20.00
Greatest Joker Stories 15.00
Batman/Judge Dredd Files (2004). 15.00
Batman: Knight's End, rep. 15.00
Knightfall rep. #1–#11 . . . . 13.00
Knightfall rep. #12–#19 . . . . 13.00
Batman: The Last Angel, F:Catwoman
  V:Aztec bat-god (1994) 13.00
Batman: The Last Arkham 13.00
Batman: Legacy, seq.to Contagion . 18.00
Batman: Night Cries,SHa. 13.00

Batman: Nine Lives 18.00
Batman: Officer Down (2001) 13.00
Batman: Prodigal, rep, ... 15.00
Batman: Son of the Demon,JBi . . . 17.00
  2nd thru 4th printings. . . . . . . @9.00
Batman: Strange Apparitions
  (1999) 13.00
Batman/Superman: World'sFinest . 20.00
Batman: Tales of the Demon (1991)
  TPB 20.00
  TPB (1999) 18.00
Batman: Terror 13.00
Batman: Thrillkiller 13.00
Batman: War Drums (2004) 18.00
Batman: Year One Rep. Batman
  #404-#407 (1998) 14.00
  Later Printings 10.00
Batman: Four of a Kind, from
  Year One annuals (1998) 15.00
Year Two (1990) rep. Detective
  Comics #575–#578 . . . . 10.00
Year Two: Fear the Reaper(2002) . 18.00
Movies
TPB The Movies, (all 4) (1997) . . . 20.00
Batman, JOy, Movie adaptation 3.00
  Perfect Bound 6.00
Batman Returns, SE,JL Movie
  Adaption, ... 6.00
  Newsstand Format 4.00
Batman: Mask of the Phantasm,
  animated movie adapt. 6.00
  Newstand Ed. 3.50
Batman Forever, Movie Adaptation . 6.00
  Newsstand version 4.00
Batman and Robin, DON(s), Movie
  Adaptation (1997) 4.00
  Collector's edition, ... 6.00
GN Batman: Bane, BSz(c) movie
  tie-in (1997) 5.00
GN Batman: Batgirl, BSz(c) movie
  tie-in (1997) 5.00
GN Batman: Mr. Freeze, BSz(c)
  movie tie-in (1997). 5.00
GN Batman: Poison Ivy, BSz(c)
  movie tie-in (1997). 5.00
X-overs
Batman & Superman Adventures:
  World's Finest (1997) adaptation
  of animated adventures, 64pg. . 7.00
Batman/Captain America (DC/Marvel
  1996) Elseworlds 6.00
Batman/Deadman, Death and
  Glory, JeR(s),JEs (1996) 13.00
Batman/Demon (1996) 5.00
Batman/Demon: A Tragedy (2000) . 6.00
Batman/Dracula: Red Rain KJo,MJ,
  Batman becomes Vampire,
  SC (1992) 12.00
  TPB Elseworlds (1999) 13.00
Batman/Green Arrow: The Poison
  Tomorrow,MN,JRu,V:Poison
  Ivy (1992) 6.25
  GN rep. (2000) 6.00
Batman/Houdini: The Devil's
  Workshop (1993) 6.50
Batman: Huntress/Spoiler—Blunt
  Trauma, CDi,Cataclysm (1988) . 3.00
Batman/Judge Dredd: Judgement on
  Gotham,SBs,V:Scarecrow, Judge
  Death (1991) 9.00
Batman/Judge Dredd: Vendetta in
  Gotham, AIG(s),V:Ventriliquist
  (1993) 5.25
Batman/Judge Dredd: The Ultimate
  Riddle (1995) 5.00
Batman/Lobo, Elseworlds (2000) . . . 6.00
Batman/Phantom Stranger, AIG(s),
  Lemurian artifact (1997) 5.00
Batman/Punisher: Lake of Fire,
  DON(s),BKi,A:Punisher,V:Jigsaw
  (DC/Marvel 1994) 5.25

Batman/Spawn: War Devil, DgM,CDi,
  AIG(s), KJ,V:Croatoan (1994) . . 6.00
Batman/Spawn: War Devil (1999) . . 5.00
Batman/Spider-Man JMD,GN,KK,
  V:Kingpin&Ra's al Ghul(1997). . 5.00
Batman vs. The Incredible Hulk
  (DC/Marvel 1995) 4.00

Batman Adventures #30
© DC Comics Inc.

BATMAN ADVENTURES
1992–95
(Based on cartoon series)
1 MeP,V:Penguin 5.00
2 MeP,V:Catwoman 4.00
3 MeP,V:Joker 3.00
4 MeP,V:Scarecrow 3.00
5 MeP,V:Scarecrow 3.00
6 MeP,A:Robin 3.00
7 MeP,V:Killer Croc,w/card 6.00
8 MeP,Larceny my Sweet 3.00
9 MeP,V:Two Face 3.00
10 thru 24 MeP . . . . @3.00
25 MeP,dbl.size,Superman 3.50
26 thru 32 . . . . @3.00
33 thru 36 . . . . @2.50
Ann.#1 Roxy Rocket 3.00
Ann.#2 JBa,BBI,DG,TG,SHa,BKi,MM,
  GN,JRu,V:Demon,Ra's al
  Ghul,Etrigan. 3.50
Holiday Special 2.95
Spec. Mad Love 3.95
TPB Collected Adventures #1 . . . . 6.00
TPB Collected Adventures #2 . . . . 6.00

BATMAN ADVENTURES:
THE LOST YEARS
Nov., 1997
1 (of 5) BHa,TBe,Batgirl 2.50
2 BHa,TBe,Dick Grayson quits. . . . 2.50
3 . . . . 2.50
4 BHa,TBe,F:Tim Drake 2.50
5 BHa,TBe,Tim Drake new Robin . 2.50

BATMAN ADVENTURES:
THE LOST YEARS
1999
1 (of 6) TBe. 2.50
2 thru 6 . . . . @2.50
TPB series rep. 5.95

BATMAN ADVENTURES
May 2003
1 TTn 2.25
1a newsstand edition 2.25
2 TTn,F:Riddler. 2.25
3 F:Joker & Harley 2.25
4 TTn,RBr,V:Ra's al Ghul 2.25
5 TTn,V:Deadshot. 2.25
6 TTn,TBe,V:Black Mask 2.25
7 RBr,TBe,V:Phantasm. 2.25
8 RBr,TBe,V:Black Mask 2.25
9 death trap. 2.25
10 thru 14 RBr,TBe . . . . @2.25
15 TBe,Mr.Freeze 2.25
16 TBe,Joker & Harley wedding . . . 2.25
17 TBe,RBr 2.25
TPB Dangerous Dames & Demons 14.95
TPB Rogues' Gallery 6.95
TPB Shadows & Masks 6.95

BATMAN/ALIENS II
DC/Dark Horse Dec. 2002
GN #1 (of 3) IEd(s) 5.95
GN #2 IEd(s) 5.95
GN #3 IEd(s) 5.95
TPB Batman/Aliens II. 14.95

BATMAN AND
THE OUTSIDERS
Aug., 1983
1 B:MiB(s),JAp,O:Outsiders,
  O:Geo Force 4.50
2 JAp,V:Baron Bedlam 3.00
3 JAp,V:Agent Orange 2.50
4 JAp,V:Fearsome Five 2.50
5 JAp,A:New Teen Titans 3.00
6 JAp,V:Cryonic Man 2.50
7 JAp,V:Cryonic Man 2.50
8 JAp,A:Phantom Stranger 2.50
9 JAp,I:Master of Disaster 2.50
10 JAp,A:Master of Disaster 2.50
11 JAp,V:Takeo 2.50
12 JAp,DG,O:Katana 2.50
13 JAp,Day,O:Batman 2.50
14 BWg,Olympics,V:Maxi Zeus . . . 2.50
15 TVE,Olympics,V:Maxi Zeus . . . 2.50
16 JAp,L:Halo 2.50
17 JAp,V:Ahk-Ton 2.50
18 JAp,V:Ahk-Ton 2.50
19 JAp,A:Superman. 2.50
20 JAp,V:Syonide,R:Halo 2.50
21 TVE,JeM,Solo Stories. 2.50
22 AD,O:Halo,I:Aurakles 2.50
23 AD,O:Halo,V:Aurakles. 2.50
24 AD,C:Kobra 2.50
25 AD,V:Kobra 2.50
26 AD 2.50
27 AD,V:Kobra 2.50
28 AD,I:Lia Briggs(Looker). 2.50
29 AD,V:Metamorpho. 2.50
30 AD,C:Looker 2.50
31 AD,I&J:Looker. 2.50
32 AD,L:Batman. 2.50
Ann.#1 JA N:Geo-Force,
  I:Force of July 3.00
Ann.#2 V:Tremayne,W:Metamorpho
  & Sapphire Stagg 3.00
Becomes:

ADVENTURES OF
THE OUTSIDERS
May, 1986
33 AD,V:Baron Bedlam 2.25
34 AD,Masters of Disaster. 2.25
35 AD,V:Adolph Hitler 2.25
36 AD,A:Masters of Disaster 2.25
37 . . . . 2.25
38 . . . . 2.25

All comics prices listed are for *Near Mint* condition.

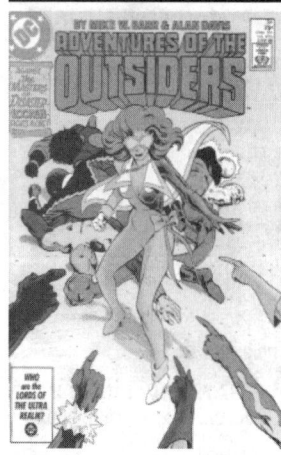

Adventures of the Outsiders #34
© DC Comics Inc.

39 thru 47 JAp, reprints
Outsiders #1-#9 . . . . @2.25

BATMAN AND ROBIN ADVENTURES, THE
Nov., 1995
1 TTn 3.00
2 TTn,V:Two-Face 3.00
3 TTn,V:The Riddler 3.00
4 TTn,V:The Penguin 3.00
5 TTn 3.00
6 TTn,Robin Fired? 2.50
7 TTn,V:Scarface 2.50
8 TTn(s) 2.50
9 TTn(s),F:Batgirl & Talia 2.50
10 TTn(s),F:Ra's Al Ghul 2.50
11 TTn(s),Alfred & Robin look
for monster in Batcave 2.50
12 TTn(s),BKr,RBr, sequel to
Bane TV episode 2.50
13 TTn(s),BKr,RBr,V:Scarecrow . . . 2.50
14 TTn(s),BKr,RBr, young criminal
turns to Batman for help 2.50
15 TTn(s) 2.50
16 TTn(s),V:Catman,A:Catwoman . . 2.50
17 PDi&TTn(s),JSon,RBr,Mad
Hatter dies in Arkham 2.50
18 TTn(s),BKr,TBe,A:Joker,
Harley Quinn 2.50
19 TTn(s),BKr,TBe,The Huntress . . 2.50
20 TTn(s),BKr,TBe, office pool 2.50
21 TTn(s),JSon,Riddler kidnaps
Commissioner Gordon 2.50
22 TTn(s),BKr,TBe,V:Two-Face . . . 2.50
23 TTn(s),TBe,V:Killer Croc 2.50
24 TTn(c),F:Poison Ivy 2.50
25 TTn,TBe,final issue, 48pg. 3.50
Ann.#1 PDi(s),TTn, sequel to
Batman: Mask of the Phantasm 3.00
Ann.#2 JSon,TBe,V:Hypnotist 4.00
Sub-Zero one-shot, F:Mr. Freeze,
Nora, 64pg. 3.95

BATMAN & SUPERMAN: WORLD'S FINEST
1999
1 (of 10) KK(s),DTy,RbC,48-page. . 7.00
2 KK(s),DTy,RbC. 3.50
3 KK(s),DTy,RbC,Arkham Asylum . 3.00
4 KK(s),DTy,RbC,Metropolis 3.00
5 KK(s),DTy,RbC,Batgirl 3.00

6 KK(s),DTy,RbC,trade identities . . 3.00
7 KK(s),PD,RbC 3.00
8 KK(s),PD,RbC 3.00
9 KK(s),RbC,split issue. 3.00
10 concl.. . . . . 3.00
GN 6.95

BATMAN: THE ANKH
Nov., 2001
1 (of 2) CDi,JVF,ancient Egypt . . . 5.95
2 CDi,JVF,V:Khatera, concl. 5.95

BATMAN: BANE OF THE DEMON
Feb., 1998
1 (of 4) CDi,GN,TP, Bane &
Ra's al Ghul. 2.50
2 CDi,GN,TP,Talia 2.50
3 CDi,GN,TP,the Lazarus Pit 2.50
4 CDi,GN,TP,Bane imprisoned 2.50

BATMAN BEYOND
Mini-series 1999
1 (of 6) RBr,TBe,Rebirth 2.50
2 RBr,TBe,Rebirth,pt.2 . . . . 2.50
3 RBr,TBe,V:Blight 2.50
4 JSon,TBe,F:Demon Etrigan. 2.50
5 JSon,TBe,V:Mummy 2.50
6 JSon,TBe,V:Inque 2.50
TPB rep. mini-series 10.00

BATMAN BEYOND
1999
1 Batman: Classic vs. Future 3.00
2 V:Inque. 2.50
3 . . . . 2.50
4 V:Royal Flush Gang. 2.50
5 V:Shriek 2.50
6 V:Stalker. 2.50
7 V:Jokerz. 2.50
8 V:Vendetta 2.50
9 V:Curare. 2.50
10 V:Golem 2.50
11 nanotechnology. 2.50
12 F:Terminal. 2.50
13 Commissioner Barbara Gordon . 2.50
14 F:Etrigan the Demon. 2.50
15 thru 20 BSf(c) . . . . @2.50
21 I:Justice League Unlimited 2.50
22 In Blackest Day, concl. 2.50
23 New Royal Flush Gang. 2.50
24 final issue 2.50
Spec. Return of the Joker 3.00

BATMAN BLACK & WHITE
1996
1 JLe(c) numerous artists 5.00
2 thru 4 . . . . @4.00

BATMAN: BOOK OF THE DEAD
1999
1 (of 2) DgM(s),BKi,Elsewords . . 5.00
2 DgM(s),BKi,Conclusion 5.00

BATMAN/CATWOMAN: TRAIL OF THE GUN
Aug. 2004
1 & 2 48-pg. . . . . @5.95

BATMAN CHRONICLES
1995
1 CDi,LW,BSz, multiple stories. . . . 5.00
2 V:Feedback 4.00

Batman Beyond #1
© DC Comics, Inc.

3 All villains issue 4.00
4 F:Hitman 15.00
5 Oracle, Year One story 3.50
6 Ra's Al Ghul 3.50
7 JOy,LW, woman on death row . . . 3.50
8 Talia goes to Gotham to
eliminate Batman. 3.50
9 CDi(s),F:Batgirl, Mr. Freeze,
Poison Ivy 3.50
10 BSn, anthology 3.50
11 CDi,JFM, Elsewords stories 3.00
12 Cataclysm x-over 3.00
13 F:GCPD 3.00
14 SB(c),F:Alfred,Huntress 3.00
15 Road to No Man's Land 3.00
16 F:Batgirl,No Man's Land tie-in . . 3.00
17 V:Penguin,No Man's Land 3.00
18 No Man's Land 3.00
19 . . . . 3.00
20 SBe(s)&IEd(s),48-pg. 3.00
21 DG,JRu,3 Elsewords tales 3.00
22 F:Lady Shiva,48-pg. 3.00
23 BSf(c) final issue. 3.00
Gallery #1, Pin-ups 3.50
GN The Gauntlet 5.00

BATMAN: CITY OF LIGHT
Oct. 2003
1 (of 8) Gotham transformed 2.95
2 thru 8 . . . . @2.95

BATMAN: THE CULT
1988
1 JSn,BWr,V:Deacon Blackfire 8.00
2 thru 4 JSn,BWr. . . . . @6.00
TPB Rep.#1-#4 . . . . 14.95

BATMAN: CYBER REVOLUTION
May 2004
1 (of 5) Joker's robot army 2.95
2 thru 5 . . . . @2.95

BATMAN: DARK KNIGHT OF THE ROUND TABLE
1998
1 (of 2) BL,DG,Elsewords,48pg . . 5.00
2 BL,DG, conclusion 5.00

BATMAN: THE DARK KNIGHT RETURNS
1986

1 FM,KJ,V:Two-Face	30.00
1a 2nd printing	5.00
1b 3rd printing	3.00
2 FM,KJ,V:Sons of the Batman	10.00
2a 2nd printing	3.00
2b 3rd printing	2.50
3 FM,KJ,D:Joker	7.00
3a 2nd printing	3.00
4 FM,KJ,Batman vs.Superman, A:Green Arrow,D:Alfred	7.00
Paperback book	20.00
Warner paperback	17.00
2nd-8th printing	13.00
TPB 10th Anniv. Spec, 224 pg.	15.00

BATMAN: THE DARK KNIGHT STRIKES AGAIN
Dec., 2001

1 (of 3) FM,80-pg.	8.00
2 FM, 80-pg.	8.00
3 FM, 80-pg. concl.	8.00

BATMAN: DARK VICTORY
Oct., 1999

1 (of 13) JLb,TSe,48-pg.	6.00
2 JLb,TSe	5.00
3 JLb,TSe,V:Scarecrow	3.00
4 JLb,TSe,V:Two-Face	3.00
5 JLb,TSe,F:Catwoman	3.00
6 JLb,TSe,F:Penguin	3.00
7 JLb,TSe,V:Calendar Man	3.00
8 JLb,TSe,V:Hang Man	3.00
9 JLb,TSe,F:Bruce & Dick	3.00
10 JLb,TSe,V:Two-Face	3.00
11 JLb,TSe,V:Poison Ivy	3.00
12 JLb,TSe,Revenge	3.00
13 JLb,TSe, conclusion	5.00

BATMAN: DEATH AND THE MAIDENS
Aug. 2003

1 (of 9) KJ,V:Ra's al Ghul	3.00
2 KJ,F:Nyssa	3.00
3 KJ,Ra's al Ghul, Nyssa	3.00
4 KJ,Ra's al Ghul	3.00
5 thru 9 KJ.	@3.00

BATMAN/DEATHBLOW: AFTER THE FIRE
DC/Wildstorm March, 2002

1 (of 3)TBd,x-over,48-pg.	6.00
2 TBd, 48-pg.	6.00
3 TBd, 48-pg., concl.	6.00

BATMAN: THE DOOM THAT CAME TO GOTHAM
Sept., 2000

1 (of 3) Elseworlds	5.00
2 MMi,DJa, return from the Arctic	5.00
3 Elseworlds, concl.	5.00

BATMAN FAMILY
Sept.–Oct., 1975

1 MGr,NA(rep.) Batgirl & Robin begins,giant	35.00
2 V:Clue Master	20.00
3 Batgirl & Robin reveal ID	20.00
4 I:Fatman	20.00
5 I:Bat Hound	20.00
6 Joker Daughter	25.00

Batman GCPD #4
© DC Comics, Inc.

7 CS,A:Sportsmaster, G.A.Huntress	13.00
8 First solo Robin story, C:Joker's Daughter	13.00
9 Joker's Daughter	25.00
10 R:B'woman,1st solo Batgirl sty.	27.00
11 MR,Man-Bat begins	25.00
12 MR	25.00
13 MR,DN,BWi.	25.00
14 HC/JRu,Man-Bat.	22.00
15 MGo,Man-Bat	22.00
16 MGo,Man-Bat	22.00
17 JA,DH,MG,Batman, B:Huntress A:Demon,MK(c),A:Catwoman	25.00
18 MGo,JSon,BL,Huntress,BM	25.00
19 MGo,JSon,BL,Huntress,BM	25.00
20 MGo,JSon,DH,A:Elongatedman, RagMan, Oct.–Nov.,1978	25.00

BATMAN: FAMILY
Oct., 2002

1 (of 8) JFM,SFa,RHo,The Tracker	3.50
2 JFM,SFa,RHo,Athena	2.25
3 JFM,SFa,RHo,Bugg & Dr.Excess	2.25
4 JFM,SFa,RHo,Suicide King	2.25
5 JFM,SFa,RHo,Freeway	2.25
6 JFM,RHo,The Technician	2.25
7 JFM,Mr. Fun.	2.25
8 JFM,RHo,Blackout, 48-pg.	3.50

BATMAN: GCPD
Mini-Series Aug., 1996

1 thru 4 CDi(s),JAp,BSz	@2.50

BATMAN: GORDON'S LAW
October, 1996

1 CDi(s),KJ,Gordon looks for bad cops	2.50
2 CDi(s),KJ,Gordon vs. corruption	2.50
3 CDi(s),KJ,	2.50
4 (of 4) CDi(s),KJ, concl.	2.50

BATMAN: GORDON OF GOTHAM
April, 1998

1 (of 4) DON,DG,KJ,F:Jim Gordon	2.50
2 DON,DG,KJ,Cuchulain.	2.50
3 DON,DG,KJ,break-in	2.50
4 DON,DG,KJ,past revealed	2.50

Batman: Gordon of Gotham #4
© DC Comics Inc.

BATMAN: GOTHAM ADVENTURES
April, 1998

1 TTn,RBr,TBe,F:Joker	3.50
2 TTn,RBr,TBe,F:Two-Face	2.50
3 TTn,RBr,TBe,V:Scarecrow.	2.50
4 TTn,RBr,TBe,A:Catwoman	2.50
5 RBr,TBe,TTn,A:Mr.Freeze	2.50
6 TTn,RBr,TBe,O:Deadman	2.50
7 TTn,RBe,TBe,V:Danger Dixon.	2.50
8 TTn,RBe,TBe,Batgirl	2.50
9 TTn,RBe,TBe,V:League of Assassins	2.50
10 TTn,RBe,TBe,V:Nightwing & Robin, A:Harley Quinn	2.50
11 TTn,RBe,TBe,V:Riddler.	2.50
12 TTn,RBe,TBe,V:Two-Face	2.50
13 RBe,TBe,V:Mastermind	2.50
14 TTn(s),TBe,V:Harley Quinn	2.50
15 V:Bane	2.50
16 TBe,Alfred Kidnapped.	2.50
17 TBe	2.50
18 TBe,R:Man-Bat.	2.50
19 TBe,Eden's Own,Poison Ivy	2.50
20 TBe,	2.50
21 TBe,	2.50
22 TBe,F:Comm.Gordon & Batgirl.	2.50
23 TBe,V:Ra's al Ghul	2.50
24 TBe,F:Killer Croc	2.50
25 TBe,A:Flash	2.50
26 TBe,F:Kristov	2.50
27 TBe,	2.50
28 TBe,V:Riddler	2.50
29 CDi(s),TBe,Batman poisoned	2.50
30 TBe,F:Clayface	2.50
31 TTn,TBe,Blackout in Gotham	2.50
32 TBe,V:Scarecrow	2.50
33 A:Phantom Stranger	2.50
34 V:Maxie Zeus	2.50
35 TBe,On the jury.	2.50
36 TBe,A:Superman	2.50
37 TBe,V:Joker, Penguin	2.50
38 TBe,F:Robin, Batgirl	2.50
39 TBe,V:Clayface	2.50
40 TBe,V:Mr. Freeze	2.50
41 TBe,The Man called Joe	2.50
42 Tuesday Night.	2.50
43 TBe,F:Harley Quinn	2.50
44 TBe,F:Two-Face	2.50
45 TBe,Running the Asylum	2.50
46 TBe,Saving Face	2.50
47 TBe,Gotham's Underworld	2.50

48 TBe,RBr,F:Dick Grayson	2.50
49 TBe,Facade	2.50
50 TBe,Catwoman returns	2.50
51 TA,Mr. Freeze	2.50
52 TBe,Bane	2.50
53 TBe,Poison Ivy superplant	2.50
54 TBe,crime spree	2.50
55 TBe,RBr,mobsters	2.50
56 TBe,V:Riddler?	2.50
57 TBe,V:Riddler	2.50
58 TTn,V:Ventriloquist	2.50
59 TBe,financial scandal	2.50
60 TBe,final issue	2.50
TPB Batman: Gotham Adventures	9.95

BATMAN: GOTHAM KNIGHTS
Feb., 2000

1 WEl,JLe	5.00
2 JBy,BB(c),F:Batgirl	3.00
3 PPo,PR,BB(c),Samsara,pt.1	3.00
4 PR,BB(c),Samsara,pt.2	3.00
5 BB(c)V:The Key	3.00
6 WS,PR,JPL,F:Oracle	3.00
7 SD,PR,	3.00
8 Transference,pt.1	3.00
9 Transference,pt.2	3.00
10 Transference,pt.3,	3.00
11 BB(c),Transference,pt.4,48-pg.	3.50
12 This issue: Batman dies!	3.00
13 Officer Down,x-over,concl.	3.00
14 V:Double Dare	3.00
15 TPe,GC,V:Poison Ivy	3.00
16 Matatoa,pt.1	3.00
17 Matatoa,pt.2	3.00
18 Cavernous,F:Aquaman	3.00
19 CDi,MSh,DG,F:Titus	3.00
20 A:Superman	3.00
21 TA,Retribution, pt.2	3.00
22 TA,Chemical attack	3.00
23 BB(c),F:Scarecrow	3.00
24 TDz,Kls,F:Bruce Wayne	3.00
25 Bruce Wayne:Murderer,pt.4	4.00
26 Bruce Wayne:Murderer,pt.10	4.00
27 DCw,A:Man of Steel	3.00
28 Bruce Wayne:Fugitive,pt.7	3.00
29 Mortician,pt.2	3.00
30 Bruce Wayne:Fugitive,pt.14	3.00
31 Bruce Wayne:Fugitive,pt.17	3.00
32 MK,lives Batman impacts	3.00
33 SBe(s),BSz,F:Bane	3.00
34 SBe(s),Tabula Rasa,pt.1	3.00

Batman/Grendel #1
© DC Comics, Inc.

35 SBe(s),Tabula Rasa,pt.2	3.50
36 SBe(s),F:Robin,Nightwing	3.00
37 SBe(s),F:Spoiler	3.00
38 SBe(s),V:Checkmate	3.00
39 SBe(s),V:Checkmate	3.00
40 SBe(s),Knight Moves	3.00
41 SBe(s),V:Elongated Man	3.00
42 SBe(s),Alfred's illness	3.00
43 SBe(s),F:Batgirl,Robin	3.00
44 SBe(s),death of Jason Todd	3.00
45 SBe(s),Knights Passed	3.00
46 SBe(s),F:Nightwing,Robin	3.00
47 WPo,F:Bane,Nightwing	3.00
48 F:Bane,Nightwing	2.75
49 F:Bane	2.75
50 V:Hush	3.00
51 V:Hush,Riddler,Joker	2.75
52 F:Tailor,Hush,40-pg.	3.00
53 F:Hush,Green Arrow,40-pg.	3.00
54 F:Joker,40-pg.	3.00
55 Hush vs. Joker, 48-pg.	3.75
56 War Games,Act 1,pt.4	2.50
57 War Games,Act 2,pt.4	2.50
58 War Games,Act 3,pt.5	2.50

(BATMAN:) GOTHAM NIGHTS
[Mini-Series] 1992

1 Gotham City	2.50
2 thru 4 Gotham Citizens Lives.	@2.50

BATMAN: GOTHAM NIGHTS II
1995

1 Sequel to Gotham Nights	2.50
2 F:Carmine Sansone.	2.50
3 Fire	2.50
4 JQ(c) Decisions	2.50

BATMAN/GRENDEL
[First Series]
DC/Comico, 1993

1 MWg,Devil's Riddle	5.25
2 MWg,Devil's Masque	5.25

[Second Series]
DC/Dark Horse, 1996

1 MWg,Devil's Bones	5.00
2 MWg,Devil's Dance	5.00

BATMAN: HARLEY & IVY
April 2004

1 (of 3) PDi	2.50
2 PDi,Zombie Root	2.50
3 PDi, finale	2.50

BATMAN: HAUNTED GOTHAM
Dec., 1999

1 (of 4) DgM,KJo,JhB,Elseworlds.	5.00
2 thru 4 DgM,KJo,JhB	@5.00

BATMAN/HELLBOY/ STARMAN
DC/Dark Horse 1998

1 JeR(s),MMi, x-over	2.50
2 JeR(s),MMi, conclusion	2.50

BATMAN: HOLLYWOOD KNIGHT
Feb., 2001

1 (of 3) DG,Elseworlds	2.50
2 DG,F:Byron Wyatt	2.50
3 DG, concl.	2.50

BATMAN/HUNTRESS: CRY FOR BLOOD
April, 2000

1 (of 6) RBr,O:Huntress	2.50
2 thru 6 RBr	@2.50

BATMAN: IT'S JOKER TIME
May, 2000

1 (of 3) BH	4.95
2 BH	4.95
3 BH, concl.	4.95

BATMAN: JAZZ
Mini-Series 1995

1 I:Blue Byrd	2.50
2 V:Brotherhood of Bop	2.50
3 F:Blue Byrd	2.50

BATMAN/JUDGE DREDD: DIE LAUGHING
1998

1 (of 2) AlG(s),GF 48-pg.	5.00
2 AlG(s),GF conclusion	5.00

BATMAN: LEAGUE OF BATMEN
April, 2001

1 MBr,RT,48-page, Elseworlds	5.95
2 MBr,RT,48-page, concl.	5.95

BATMAN: LEGENDS OF THE DARK KNIGHT
1989

1 EH,Shaman of Gotham,pt.1, Yellow(c)	5.00
1a Blue,Orange or Pink(c)	4.00
2 EH,Shaman of Gotham,pt.2	3.00
3 EH,Shaman of Gotham,pt.3	3.00
4 EH,Shaman of Gotham,pt.4	3.00
5 EH,Shaman of Gotham,pt.5	3.00
6 KJ,Gothic,pt.1	3.00
7 KJ,Gothic,pt.2	3.00
8 KJ,Gothic,pt.3	3.00
9 KJ,Gothic,pt.4	3.00
10 KJ,Gothic,pt.5	3.00
11 PG,TA,Prey,pt.1	6.00
12 PG,TA,Prey,pt.2	5.00
13 PG,TA,Prey,pt.3	5.00
14 PG,TA,Prey,pt.4	5.00
15 PG,TA,Prey,pt.5	4.00
16 TVE,Venom,pt.1	5.00
17 TVE,JL,Venom,pt.2	5.00
18 TVE,JL,Venom,pt.3	5.00
19 TVE,JL,Venom,pt.4	5.00
20 TVE,JL,Venom,pt.5	5.00
21 BS,Faith,pt.1	3.00
22 BS,Faith,pt.2	3.00
23 BS,Faith,pt.3	3.00
24 GK,Flyer,pt.1	3.00
25 GK,Flyer,pt.2	3.00
26 GK,Flyer,pt.3	3.00
27 Destroyer,pt.2 (Batman#474)	3.50
28 MWg,Faces,pt.1,V:Two-Face	4.00
29 MWg,Faces,pt.2,V:Two-Face	4.00
30 MWg,Faces,pt.3,V:Two-Face	4.00
31 BA,Family	3.00
32 Blades,pt.1	3.00
33 Blades,pt.2	3.00
34 Blades,pt.3	3.00
35 BHa,Destiny Pt.1	3.00
36 BHa,Destiny Pt.2	3.00
37 I:Mercy,V:The Cossack	3.00
38 KON,R:Bat-Mite	3.00
39 BT,Mask#1	3.00

Batman Legends of the Dark Knight #113 © DC Comics, Inc.

40 BT,Mask#2 . . . . 3.00
41 Sunset. 3.00
42 CR,Hothouse #1 . . . . 3.00
43 CR,Hothouse #2,V:Poison Ivy . . 3.00
44 SMc,Turf #1 . . . . 3.00
45 Turf#2 . . . . 3.00
46 RH,A:Catwoman,V:Catman 3.00
47 RH,A:Catwoman,V:Catman 3.00
48 RH,A:Catwoman,V:Catman 3.00
49 RH,A:Catwoman,V:Catman 3.00
50 BBl,JLe,KN,KM,WS,MZ,BB,
    V:Joker 6.00
51 JKu,A:Ragman 3.00
52 Tao #1,V:Dragon 3.00
53 Tao #2,V:Dragon 3.00
54 MMi 3.50
55 B:Watchtower 3.00
56 CDi(s),V:Battle Guards 3.00
57 CDi(s),E:Watchtower 3.00
58 Storm. 3.00
59 DON(s),RoW,B:Qarry 3.00
60 RoW,V:Asp 3.00
61 RoW,V:Asp 3.00
62 RoW,KnightsEnd#4,A:Shiva,
    Nightwing. 4.50
63 Knights End #10,V:Azrael. 3.00
64 CBa. 3.00
65 Joker. 3.00
66 Joker. 3.00
67 Going Sane,pt.3 . . . . 3.00
68 Going Sane,pt.4 . . . . 3.50
69 Criminals,pt.1 . . . . 3.50
70 Criminals,pt.2 . . . . 3.50
71 Werewolf,pt.1 . . . . 3.00
72 JWk(c&a),Werewolf,pt.2
    [new Miraweb format begins] . . 3.00
73 JWk(c&a),Werewolf,pt.3 . . . . 3.00
74 Engins,pt.1 . . . . 3.00
75 Engins,pt.2 . . . . 3.00
76 The Sleeping,pt.1 . . . . 3.00
77 The Sleeping,pt.2 . . . . 3.00
78 The Sleeping,pt.3 . . . . 3.00
79 Favorite Things 3.00
80 Idols,pt.1 . . . . 3.00
81 Idols,pt.2 . . . . 3.00
82 Idols, climax 3.00
83 new villain 3.00
84 WEl(s) 3.00
85 JeR(s) 3.00
86 RH,A:Catwoman,V:Catman 3.00
86 DgM,JWi,MGy,Conspiracy,pt.1 . . 3.00
87 DgM,JWi,MGy,Conspiracy,pt.2 . . 3.00
88 DgM,JWi,MGy,Conspiracy,pt.3 . . 3.00
89 AlG(s),Clay,pt. 1 . . . . 3.00

90 AlG(s),Clay,pt. 2 . . . . 3.00
91 Freakout, pt.1 . . . . 3.50
92 GEn(s),WSm,Freakout, pt.2 . . . . 3.50
93 GEn(s),WSm,Freakout, pt.3 . . . . 3.50
94 MGi(s),Saul Fisher's story 3.00
95 DAn&ALa(s),AWi,ALa,Dirty
    Tricks,pt.1 . . . . 3.00
96 DAn&ALa(s),AWi,ALa,Dirty
    Tricks, pt.2 . . . . 3.00
97 DAn&ALa(s),AWi,ALa,,Dirty
    Tricks, concl. 3.00
98 PJe(s),SeP,Steps, pt.1 . . . . 3.00
99 PJe(s),SeP,Steps, pt.2 . . . . 3.00
100 DON,JRo,F:Robin, 64pg. 6.00
101 CE,KN(c)100 years in future. . . 3.00
102 JRo,PuJ,Spook, pt.1 . . . . 3.00
103 JRo,PuJ,Spook, pt.2 . . . . 3.00
104 JRo,PuJ,Spook, pt.3 . . . . 3.00
105 TVE,JRu,Duty, pt.1 . . . . 3.00
106 TVE,JRu,Duty, pt.2 . . . . 3.00
107 LMr,Stalking, pt.1 . . . . 3.00
108 LMr,Stalking, pt.2 . . . . 3.00
109 SEt,DAb,Primal Riddle,pt.1. . . . 3.00
110 SEt,DAb,Primal Riddle,pt.2 . . . 3.00
111 SEt,DAb,Primal Riddle,pt.3 . . . 3.00
112 DVa,FC,V:Lord Demise,pt.1 . . . 3.00
113 DVa,FC,V:Lord Demise,pt.2 . . . 3.00
114 JeR(s),DIB,TBd 3.00
115 LMc,DIB(c) 3.00
116 IEd,Bread and Circuses,pt.1. . . 5.00
117 IEd,Bread and Circuses,pt.2. . . 2.50
118 JPn,Alfred in No Man's Land . . 2.50
119 MD2,Claim Jumping,pt.1. . . . . . 5.00
120 MD2,Assembly 5.00
121 RBr,V:Mr.Freeze 3.50
122 LHa(s),PG, Low Road to Golden
    Mountain,pt.1. . . . . 3.50
123 PR,ALa,Underground
    Railroad,pt.1 . . . . 3.50
124 CDi(s),MkK,No Man's Land . . . 3.50
125 No Man's Land 3.00
126 Endgame, pt.1 x-over 3.00
127 MRy,F:Green Arrow,pt.1 . . . . . . 2.50
128 MRy,F:Green Arrow,pt.2 . . . . . . 2.50
129 MRy,F:Green Arrow,pt.3 . . . . . . 2.50
130 MRy,F:Green Arrow,pt.4 . . . . . . 2.50
131 MRy,F:Green Arrow,pt.5 . . . . . . 2.50
132 AGw,JeR,MR,BWi,Siege,pt.1 . . 2.50
133 AGw,JeR,MR,BWi,Siege,pt.2 . . 2.50
134 AGw,JeR,MR,BWi,Siege,pt.3 . . 2.50
135 AGw,JeR,MR,BWi,Siege,pt.4 . . 2.50
136 AGw,JeR,MR,BWi,Siege,pt.5 . . 2.50
137 DgM,PG,JP,Terror,pt.1. . . . . . . 2.50
138 DgM,PG,JP,Terror,pt.2. . . . . . . 2.50
139 DgM,PG,JP,Terror,pt.3. . . . . . . 2.50
140 DgM,PG,JP,Terror,pt.4. . . . . . . 2.50
141 DgM,PG,JP,Terror,pt.5. . . . . . . 2.50
142 CDi,JAp,Demon Laughs,pt.1 . . 2.50
143 CDi,JAp,Demon Laughs,pt.2 . . 2.50
144 CDi,JAp,Demon Laughs,pt.3 . . 2.50
145 CDi,JaP,Demon Laughs,pt.4. . . 2.50
146 DgM,BKi,Bad,pt.1 . . . . 2.50
147 DgM,BKi,Bad,pt.2 . . . . 2.50
148 DgM,BKi,Bad,pt.3 . . . . 2.50
149 JMD,TVE, Grimm, pt.1 . . . . 2.50
150 JMD,TVE, Grimm, pt.2 . . . . 2.50
151 JMD,TVE, Grimm, pt.3 . . . . 2.50
152 JMD,TVE, Grimm, pt.4 . . . . 2.50
153 JMD,TVE, Grimm, pt.5 . . . . 2.50
154 MBn,BR,Colossus,pt.1 . . . . 2.50
155 MBn,BR,Colossus,pt.2 . . . . 2.50
156 DGr,Blink,pt.1 . . . . 2.50
157 DGr,Blink,pt.2 . . . . 2.50
158 DGr,Blink,pt.3 . . . . 2.50
159 JOs,DGr,Loyalties,pt.1 . . . . 2.50
160 JOs,DGr,Loyalties,pt.2 . . . . 2.50
161 JOs,DGr,Loyalties,pt.3 . . . . 2.50
162 JAr(s),Auteurism,pt.1 . . . . 2.50
163 JAr(s),Auteurism,pt.2 . . . . 2.50
164 DMD,DGr,Don't Blink,pt.1 . . . . 2.50
165 DMD,DGr,Don't Blink,pt.2 . . . . 2.50

166 DMD,DGr,Don't Blink,pt.3 . . . . 2.50
167 DMD,DGr,Don't Blink,pt.4 . . . . 2.50
168 Urban Legend 2.50
169 TyH,Irresistible,pt.1 . . . . 2.50
170 TyH,Irresistible,pt.2 . . . . 2.50
171 TyH,Irresistible,pt.3 . . . . 2.50
172 V:Rough Justice 2.50
173 V:Rough Justice 2.50
174 O:Rough Justice 2.50
175 Testament,pt.6 . . . . 2.50
176 Testament,pt.5 . . . . 2.50
177 Lost Cargo,pt.1 . . . . 2.50
178 Lost Cargo,pt.2 . . . . 2.50
179 O:Fat Man & Little Boy 2.50
180 Virtual Gotham City. 2.50
181 Cyber-world. 2.50
182 War Games,Act 1,pt.2 . . . . 2.50
183 War Games,Act 2,pt.2 . . . . 2.50
184 War Games,Act 3,pt.2 . . . . 2.50
Ann.#1 JAp,KG,DSp,TL,JRu,
    MGo,JQ,`Duel',C:Joker. 5.50
Ann.#2 MN,LMc,W:Gordn&Essen . 5.00
Ann.#3 MM,I:Cardinal Sin 5.00
Ann.#4 JSon(c),Elseworlds Story . . 5.00
Ann.#5 CDi(s)Year One Annuals,
    O:Man-Bat 5.50
Ann.#6 Legends o/t Dead Earth . . . 4.00
Ann.#7 Pulp Heroes (War). 7.00
Halloween Spec.I 8.00
Halloween Spec.II 5.00
Ghosts, Halloween Special 5.00
TPB Shaman rep.#1-#5 (1993) . . . 13.00
TPB Batman: Gothic, rep. #6-#10
    (1992) 13.00
TPB Prey, rep.Legends of the Dark
    Knight #11–#15 (1992) 13.00
TPB Batman: Venom, TVE, rep.
    #16–#20 (1993) 10.00
TPB Collected Legends of the Dark
    Knight,BB(c),rep.#32-#34,#38,
    #42-#43 (1994) 13.00
TPB Other Realms. 13.00

BATMAN: THE LONG HALLOWEEN
Oct., 1996
1 (of 13) JLb,TSe,Who is Holiday?
    F: usual suspects. 11.00
2 JLb(s),TSe,V:Holiday,A:Solomon
    Grundy. 8.00
3 JLb,TSe, ... 9.00
4 JLb(s),TSe,New Year's Eve 9.00
5 JLb(s),TSe,F:Poison Ivy, Search
    for Holiday 6.00
6 JLb(s),TSe,F:Poison Ivy,
    Catwoman 6.00
7 JLb(s),TSe,V:The Riddler 5.00
8 JLb(s),TSe,V:Scarecrow 5.00
9 JLb(s),TSe,A:Holiday,Scarecrow. 5.00
10 JLb(s),TSe,V:Scarecrow,Mad
    Hatter. 5.00
11 JLb(s),TSe,V:Holiday 5.00
12 JLb(s),TSe,Harvey Dent. 5.00
13 JLb(s),TSe,concl.,48pg. 7.00
TPB Haunted Knight, rep. Fears,
    Madness & Ghosts 12.95
TPB The Long Halloween 19.95

BATMAN: MAN-BAT
1995
1 R:Man-Bat, painted series 5.00
2 F:Marilyn Muno 5.00
3 JBo,Elseworlds story, concl. 5.00
TPB rep. mini-series 14.95

BATMAN: NEVERMORE
April 2003
1 (of 5) Elseworlds,BWr(c) 2.50
2 GyD,BWr(c),Raven Murders 2.50

DC COMICS

3 GyD,BWr(c),Raven Murders 2.50
4 GyD,BWr(c),Raven Murders 2.50
5 GyD,BWr(c),concl............. 2.50

BATMAN: NO MAN'S LAND
Sept., 1999

0 F:Huntress................. 4.95
Secret Files #1.............. 4.95
TPB Vol. 1 thru Vol. 5, x-over
reps. .... @12.95

BATMAN: ORPHEUS RISING
Aug., 2001

1 (of 5) DT,DaM 2.50
2 DT,DaM,caught in cross-fire 2.50
3 DT,DaM,who's behind it........ 2.50
4 DT,DaM,The Deacons 2.50
5 DT,DaM,concl 2.50

BATMAN: OUTLAWS
July, 2000

1 (of 3) DgM,PG 5.00
2 DgM,PG,V:Bloodhawks 5.00
3 DgM,PG,concl............... 5.00

BATMAN: RUN, RIDDLER RUN
1992

1 MBg,Batman V:Riddler 5.50
2 MBg,Batman V:Riddler 5.25
3 MBg,V:Perfect Securities...... 5.25

BATMAN: SHADOW OF THE BAT
1992–97

1 NB,Last Arkham Pt.1 .... 5.00
1a Collector set,w/posters,pop-up . 6.00
2 NB,Last Arkham Pt.2.......... 4.00
3 NB,Last Arkham Pt.3.......... 4.00
4 NB,Last Arkham Pt.4.......... 4.00
5 NB,A:Black Spider 3.00
6 NB,I:Chancer 3.00
7 Misfits Pt.1................. 3.00
8 Misfits Pt.2................. 3.00
9 Misfits Pt.3................. 3.00
10 MC,V:Mad Thane of Gotham ... 3.00

Batman: Shadow of the Bat #51
© DC Comics, Inc.

11 V:Kadaver 2.50
12 V:Kadaver,A:Human Flea 2.50
13 NB,The Nobody 2.50
14 NB,Gotham Freaks#1 .... 2.50
15 NB,Gotham Freaks#2 .... 2.50
16 BBl,MM,A:Anarchy,Scarecrow .. 2.50
17 BBl,V:Scarecrow 2.50
18 BBl,A:Anarchy,Scarecrow 2.50
19 BBl,Knightquest:The Crusade,pt.2,
V:Gotham criminals 2.50
20 VGi,Knightquest:The Crusade,
V:Tally Man 2.50
21 BBl,Knightquest:The Search,
V:Mr.Asp 2.50
22 BBl,Knightquest:The Search,
In London 2.50
23 BBl,Knightquest:The Search. ... 2.50
24 BBl,Knightquest:The Crusade .. 2.50
25 BSf(c),BBl,Knightquest: Crusade,
A:Joe Public,V:Corrosive Man. . 2.50
26 BSf(c),BBl,Knightquest: Crusade,
V:Clayface 2.50
27 BSf(c),BBl,Knightquest: Crusade,
I:Clayface Baby 2.50
28 BSf(c),BBl 2.50
29 BSf(c),BBl,KnightsEnd#2,
A:Nightwing 4.00
30 BSf(c),BBl,KnightsEnd#8,
V:Azrael 2.50
31 Zero Hour, V:Butler.......... 2.50
32 Ventriloquist,Two-Face 2.50
33 Two-Face 2.50
34 V:Tally Man 2.50
35 BKi,Return of Bruce Wayne,
Troika,pt.2 .... 2.50
35a Collectors Edition 3.50
36 Black Canary 2.50
37 Joker Hunt 2.50
38 V:The Joker. 2.50
39 BSf(c),R:Solomon Grundy
[new Miraweb format begins] .. 2.50
40 BSf(c), F:Anarky 2.50
41 Explosive Dirigible 2.50
42 .... 2.50
43 Secret of the Universe,pt1 ..... 2.50
44 AIG,BSz(c) Secret of the
Universe,pt.3 .... 2.50
45 AIG,BSz(c) 100 year old corpse . 2.50
46 AIG,BSz(c) V:Cornelius Stirk 2.50
47 AIG,BSz(c) V:Cornelius Stirk 2.50
48 AIG 2.50
49 AIG,Contagion,pt.7 .... 2.50
50 AIG,Nightmare on Gotham,pt.1 .. 2.50
51 AIG,DTy, Nightmare on
Gotham,pt.2 (of 3) 2.50
52 AIG(s),Nightmare on Gotham,
pt.3....................... 2.50
53 AIG(s),Legacy, prelude 2.50
54 AIG(s),Legacy, pt. 4, x-over 2.50
55 AIG(s),RBr,KJ,Bruce Wayne a
murderer? A:Nightwing 2.50
56 AIG(s),DTy,SnW,Leaves of
Grass,pt.1,V:Poison Ivy 2.50
57 AIG(s),DTy,SnW,Grass,pt.2. .... 2.50
58 AIG(s),DTy,SnW,Grass,pt.3. .... 2.50
59 AIG(s),DTy,SnW,Killer,
Killer, pt.1................ 2.50
60 AIG(s),DTy,SnW,Killer, pt.2 ..... 2.50
61 AIG(s),JAp,SnW,night of
second chances 2.50
62 AIG(s),DTy,SnW,Two-Face,pt.1 . 2.50
63 AIG(s),DTy,SnW,Two-Face,pt.2 . 2.50
64 AIG(s),DTy,SnW,A:Jason Blood . 2.50
65 AIG(s),NBy,JRu, A:Oracle, pt.1 .. 2.50
66 AIG(s),NBy,JRu, V:Thinker,
Cheat, pt.2. .... 2.50
67 AIG(s),NBy,SnW,CsM,V:Thinker,
Cheat, pt.3, concl. 2.50
68 AIG(s),JAp,SnW,annual killer ... 2.50
69 AIG(s),MBu,WF,CsM,
The Spirit of 2000, pt. 1 ...... 2.50

70 AIG(s),MBu,WF,CsM, pt.2 ...... 2.50
71 AIG(s),MBu,WF,CsM,detective .. 2.50
72 AIG(s),MBu,WF 2.50
73 AIG(s),MBu,WF,Cataclysm
x-over,pt.1 .... 3.50
74 AIG(s),MBu,WF,Cataclysm
cont.................... 2.50
75 AIG(s),MBu,WF,Aftershock 3.50
76 AIG(s),MBu,WF,Aftershock 2.50
77 AIG(s),MBu,WF,quake-torn 2.50
78 AIG(s),MBu,Aftershock 2.50
79 AIG(s),MBu,V:Mad Hatter,
Narcosis. 2.50
80 Road to No Man's Land, flip-book
Azrael:Agent of the Bat #47 ... 5.00
81 AIG(s),MBu,No Man's Land 2.50
82 AIG(s),MBu,No Man's Land 2.50
83 No Law and a New Order, pt.2. 14.00
84 IEd,Bread and Circuses, pt.2 ... 5.00
85 IEd(s),Bread & Circuses,concl... 5.00
86 GyD,No Man's Land 3.00
87 MD2, Claim Jumping, pt.2 ...... 3.00
88 DJu,BSz,Fruit of
the Earth,pt.1.............. 3.00
89 IEd(s),SB,No Man's Land 3.00
90 LHa(s),PG,No Man's Land 3.00
91 PR,ALa,Underground
Railroad,pt.2 .... 3.00
92 No Man's Land,A:Superman. ... 3.00
93 No Man's Land 3.00
94 final issue 3.00
Ann.#1 TVE,DG,Bloodlines#3,
I:Joe Public............... 4.00
Ann.#2 Elseworlds story 4.00
Ann.#3 Year One Annual 4.00
Ann.#4 Legends of the Dead
Earth 3.00
Ann.#5 AIG(s), Pulp Heroes....... 4.00
Spec.#1,000,000 AIG(s),MBu, Origin of
853rd-century Dark Knight 2.00

BATMAN/SUPERMAN/ WONDER WOMAN: TRINITY
June 2003

1 (of 3) MWg, first meeting....... 6.95
2 MWg,V:Bizarro.............. 6.95
3 MWg,concl................. 6.95

BATMAN: SWORD OF AZRAEL
1992–93

1 JQ,KN,I:Azrael.............. 12.00
2 JQ,KN,A:Azrael 9.00
3 JQ,KN,V:Biis,A:Azrael 8.00
4 JQ,KN,V:Biis,A:Azrael 8.00
TPB rep.#1-#4 .... 11.00
TPB Platinum................. 25.00

BATMAN: TENSES
Aug. 2003

1 & 2 JoC(s) .... @6.95

BATMAN: TOYMAN
1998

1 (of 4) LHa(s),AWi,KJ 2.50
2 thru 4 LHa(s),AWi,KJ .... @2.50

BATMAN: TURNING POINTS
Nov., 2000

1 (of 5) F:Gordon & Batman...... 2.50
2 TTn(c),Robin arrives 2.50
3 DG,JKu(c),Batgirl dead 2.50
4 CDi,BA,HC(c),Azrael 2.50
5 No Man's Land 2.50

BATMAN vs. PREDATOR
DC/Dark Horse 1991–92
1 NKu,AKu,inc.8 trading cards
  bound in (Prestige) 5.00
1a Newsstand 4.00
2 NKu,AKu,Inc. pinups (prestige) . . 4.00
2a Newsstand 3.00
3 NKu,AKu,conclusion,inc.
  8 trading cards (Prestige) 4.00
3a Newsstand 3.00
TPB,rep.#1-#3 . . . . 5.95

BATMAN vs. PREDATOR II BLOODMATCH
1994–95
1 R:Predators 3.00
2 A:Huntress 3.00
3 Assassins 3.00
4 V:Head Hunters 3.00
TPB Rep.#1-#4 . . . . 6.95

BATMAN/PREDATOR III: BLOOD TIES
DC/Dark Horse 1997
1 (of 4) CDi,RDm,RbC, vs. pair
  of Predators 2.50
2 CDi,RDm,RbC, pt.2 . . . . 2.50
3 CDi,RDm,RbC, pt.3 . . . . 2.50
4 CDi,RDm,RbC, concl. 2.50
TPB rep 8.00

BATMAN STRIKES, THE
Sept. 2004
1 V:Penguin 2.25
2 F:Man-Bat 2.25

BATMAN/WILDCAT
Feb., 1997
1 (of 3) CDi&BSt(s),SCi,ATi,
  Batman and Robin discover
  Secret Ring of combat 2.50
2 CDi&BSt(s),SCi,V:KGBeast,
  Willis Danko 2.50
3 CDi&BSt(s),SCi, Batman vs.
  Wildcat, concl. 2.50

BEAST BOY
Nov., 1999
1 (of 4)BRa,Clv 3.00
2 BRa,Clv,A:Nightwing 3.00
3 BRa,Clv,V:Nightwing 3.00
4 BRa,Clv,F:Flamebird 3.00

BATTLEAXES
DC/Vertigo, March, 2000
1 (of 4) female sword & sorcery . . . 2.50
2 . . . . 2.50
3 . . . . 2.50
4 conclusion 2.50

BATTLE CLASSICS
Sept.–Oct., 1978
1 JKu, reprints 15.00

BEAUTIFUL STORIES FOR UGLY CHILDREN
Piranha Press 1989–91
1 thru 11 . . . . @3.00
12 thru 14 . . . . @3.00
15 Blood Day 3.50
16 thru 20 . . . . @3.00
21 thru 30 . . . . @4.00

BEOWOLF
April-May, 1975
1 . . . . 25.00
2 thru 3 . . . . @10.00
4 Dracula 15.00
5 . . . . 10.00
6 Flying Saucer,Feb.–Mar.1976 . . 12.00

BEST OF THE BRAVE & THE BOLD
1988
1 JL(c),NA,rep.B&B #85. . . . . 5.00
2 thru 6 JL(c),NA,rep.B&B . . . . . @5.00

Beware the Creeper #2
© DC Comics Inc.

BEWARE THE CREEPER
1968–69
1 . . . . 150.00
2 thru 6 . . . . 75.00

BEWARE THE CREEPER
DC/Vertigo April 2003
1 thru 5 . . . . @3.00

BIG ALL-AMERICAN COMIC BOOK
Dec., 1944
1 JKu 20,000.00

BIG BOOK OF FUN COMICS
Spring, 1936
1 . . . . 20,000.00

THE BIG BOOK OF ...:
DC/Paradox Press (B&W)
1994–2001
TPB Conspiracies (1995) 13.00
TPB Death (1994) 13.00
TPB Hoaxes (1996) 15.00
TPB Little Criminals (1996) 15.00
TPB Losers 15.00
TPB Martyrs (1997) 15.00
TPB Scandal (1997) 15.00
TPB Thugs (1996) 15.00
TPB Unexplained DgM(s) (1997). . 15.00
TPB Urban Legends (1994) 13.00
TPB Weirdos (1995) 13.00

TPB Weird Wild West (1998) 15.00
TPB Big Book of the '70s (2000) . . 15.00
TPB Wild Women,192-pg.(2001) . 15.00

BIG DADDY DANGER
Aug., 2002
1 (of 9) AdP,masked wrestler 3.00
2 AdP,Danny Danger 3.00
3 AdP,Diablo X 3.00
4 AdP,Diablo X 3.00
5 AdP,home dimension 3.00
6 AdP,V:Danny Danger 3.00
7 AdP,Diablo X 3.00
8 AdP,Daddy's soul 3.00
9 AdP,concl. 3.00

BIGG TIME
DC/Vertigo, Aug., 2002
TPB TTn, 128-pg. (b&w) 15.00

BIRDS OF PREY: MANHUNT
1996
1 CDi(s),MHy,F:Black Canary,
  Oracle 10.00
2 CDi(s),MHy,V,Archer Braun,
  A:Catwoman 7.00
3 CDi(s),MHy,V:Catwoman,
  Huntress 7.00
4 CDi(s),MHy,V:Lady Shiva 7.00
1-shot Birds of Prey: Batgirl CDi,
  Batgirl & Black Canary (1997). . 3.00
1-shot Birds of Prey: Revolution
  CDi(s),BMc 3.00
1-shot Birds of Prey: The Ravens,
  CDi, Girlfrenzy (1998) 3.00
1-shot Birds of Prey: Wolves
  CDi,DG (1997) 3.00

BIRDS OF PREY
1998
1 CDi(s),Black Canary & Oracle . . . 8.00
2 CDi(s),V:Jackie Pajamas 5.00
3 CDi(s),V:Hellbound 5.00
4 CDi(s),V:Ravens 5.00
5 CDi(s),V:Ravens,pt.2 . . . . 3.00
6 CDi(s),V:Ravens,pt.3 . . . . 3.00
7 CDi(s),PKr, ... 3.00
8 CDi(s),F:Nightwing. 30.00
9 CDi(s),V:Iron Brigade. 3.00
10 CDi(s),DG,V:Dr.Pop 3.00
11 CDi(s),DG 3.00
12 CDi(s),DG,F:Catwoman 3.00
13 CDi(s),DG 3.00
14 CDi(s),DG,V:Lashina 3.00
15 CDi(s),JG 3.00
16 CDi(s),JG,V:maniac. 2.50
17 CDi(s),JG,V:Joker. 2.50
18 CDi(s),JG,Transbelvia 2.50
19 CDi(s),JG,A:Nightwing,Robin . . . 2.50
20 CDi(s),Hunt for Oracle,pt.2 . . . . 2.50
21 CDi(s),Hunt for Oracle,concl. . . . 2.50
22 CDi(s),Gorilla City 2.50
23 CDi(s),Gorilla City 2.50
24 CDi,search for heart donor 3.00
25 CDi,Deathstroke,Blue Beetle . . 2.50
26 CDi,This issue Batman dies! . . . 2.50
27 Officer Down x-over,pt.3 . . . . . . 2.50
28 CDi,History Lession,pt.1 . . . . . . 2.50
29 CDi,History Lession,pt.2 . . . . . . 2.50
30 CDi,History Lession,pt.3 . . . . . . 2.50
31 CDi,star-crossed love 2.50
32 CDi,love, and marriage? 2.50
33 CDi,Black Canary,Ra's Al Ghul . . 2.50
34 CDi,A:Power Girl,Blue Beetle . . 2.50
35 CDi,rescue Black Canary 2.50
36 CDi,Joker: Last Laugh 2.50
37 CDi,Last Laugh aftermath 2.50

DC COMICS

DC COMICS

38 CDi,F:Dinah 2.50
39 CDi,BruceWayne:Murderer,pt.5 . 6.00
40 CDi,BruceWayne:Murderer,pt.12 6.50
41 CDi,BruceWayne:Fugitive,pt.2 . . 6.50
42 CDi,GF,F:Power Girl 2.50
43 CDi,BruceWayne:Fugitive,pt.10 . 2.50
44 CDi,Deathstroke 2.50
45 CDi,Deathstroke, dinosaurs 2.50
46 CDi,Deathstroke 2.50
47 TMr(s),JP,Heartache,pt.1 . . . . . . 2.50
48 TMr(s),JP,Heartache,pt.2 . . . . . . 2.50
49 TMr(s),JP,Heartache,pt.3 . . . . . . 2.50
50 GHe,CJ 2.50
51 GHe,CJ 2.50
52 GHe,CJ 2.50
53 GHe,CJ 2.50
54 GHe,CJ 2.50
55 GHe,CJ 2.50
56 EBe,V:Savant 6.00
57 EBe,V:Savant 4.00
58 EBe,V:Savant 3.00
59 EBe,V:Savant 3.50
60 EBe,R:Huntress 2.50
61 EBe,consequences 2.50
62 EBe,F:Lady Shiva 2.50
63 EBe,F:Lady Shiva 2.50
64 EBe,V:Cheshire 2.50
65 EBe,F:Cheshire 2.50
66 MGo,MM,ATh(c) 2.50
67 EBe,Sensei and Student 2.50
68 Date for Huntress 2.50
69 Between Dark and Dawn,pt.1 . . . 2.50
70 Between Dark and Dawn,pt.2 . . . 2.50
71 Between Dark and Dawn,pt.3 . . . 2.50
72 Between Dark and Dawn,pt.4 . . . 2.50
73 Between Dark and Dawn,pt.5 . . . 2.50
74 Between Dark and Dawn,pt.6 . . . 2.50
75 EBe,40-pg. BU: EB 2.95
TPB Birds of Prey 18.00
  New edition (2002) 17.95
TPB Old Friends, New Enemies . . 17.95
TPB Of Like Minds 14.95
Spec. Secret Files 2003 . . . . 4.95

BIRDS OF PREY:
CATWOMAN/BATGIRL
Feb. 2003
1 JFM,JP,DaR 6.00
2 . . . . 6.00
GN Catwoman/Oracle 6.00

BITE CLUB
DC/Vertigo April 2004
1 (of 6) HC(s),vampire,mafia 5.00
2 Bikinis 4.00
3 HC(s),Leto Del Toro 3.00
4 HC(s),plot for revenge 3.00
5 HC(s),Leto learns truth 3.00
6 HC(s),concl. 3.00

BIZARRO COMICS
March 2003
TPB 20.00

BLACK CANARY
[Limited Series], 1991–92
1 TVE/DG,New Wings,pt.1 . . . . 2.50
2 TVE/DG,New Wings,pt.2 . . . . 2.50
3 TVE/DG,New Wings,pt.3 . . . . 2.50
4 TVE/DG,New Wings,pt.4,Conc . . 2.50
[Regular Series], 1993
1 TVE,Hero Worship,pt.1 . . . . 3.00
2 TVE,Hero Worship,pt.2 . . . . 3.00
3 TVE,Hero Worship,pt.3 . . . . 3.00
4 TVE,V:Whorrsman 3.00
5 . . . . 3.00
6 Blynde Woman's Bluff 3.00

7 TVE,V:Maniacal Killer 3.00
8 . . . . 3.00
9 A:Huntress 3.00
10 TVE,A:Nightwing,Huntress 3.00
11 TVE,A:Nightwing 3.00
12 final issue 3.00

BLACK CANARY/ORACLE:
BIRDS OF PREY
1996
1-shot DDi, double size 10.00

BLACK CONDOR
1992–93
1 I&O:Black Condor 3.00
2 V:Sky Pirate 3.00
3 V:Sky Pirate 3.00
4 V:The Shark 3.00
35 V:Mind Force 3.00
6 V:Mind Force 3.00
7 Forest Fire 3.00
8 MG,In Jail 3.00
9 A:The Ray 3.00
10 . . . . 3.00
11 O:Black Condor 3.00

BLACKHAWK
Prev: Golden Age
1957–1984
108 DD,CCu,DD&CCu(c),The
  Threat from the Abyss
  A:Blaisie 650.00
109 DD,CCu,DD&CCu(c),The
  Avalance Kid 250.00
110 DD,CCu,DD&CCu(c),Mystery
  of Tigress Island 250.00
111 DD,CCu,DD&CCu(c),Menace
  of the Machines 250.00
112 DD,CCu,DD(c),The Doomed
  Dog Fight 250.00
113 DD,CCu,CCu(c),Volunteers
  of Doom 250.00
114 DD,CCu,DD&CCu(c),Gladiators
  of Blackhawk Island 250.00
115 DD,CCu,DD&CCu(c),The
  Tyrant's Return 250.00
116 DD,CCu,DD&CCu(c),Prisoners
  of the Black Island 250.00
117 DD,CCu,DD&CCu(c),Menace
  of the Dragon Boat 250.00
118 DD,CCu,DD&SMo(c),FF,The
  Bandit With 1,000 Nets 260.00
119 DD,CCu,DD&SMo(c),
  V:Chief Blackhawk 200.00
120 DD,CCu,DD&SMo(c),The
  Challenge of the Wizard 200.00
121 DD,CCu,DD&CCu(c),Secret
  Weapon of the Archer 200.00
122 DD,CCu,DD&CCu(c),The
  Movie That Backfired 200.00
123 DD,CCu,DD&CCu(c),The
  Underseas Gold Fort 200.00
124 DD,CCu,DD&CCu(c),Thieves
  With A Thousand Faces 200.00
125 DD,CCu,DD&CCu(c),Secrets
  o/t Blackhawk Time Capsule . 200.00
126 DD,CCu,DD&CCu(c),Secret
  of the Glass Fort 200.00
127 DD,CCu,DD&CCu(c),Blackie-
  The Winged Sky Fighter 200.00
128 DD,CCu,DD&CCu(c),The
  Vengeful Bowman 200.00
129 DD,CCu,DD&CCu(c),The
  Cavemen From 3,000 B.C. . . . 200.00
130 DD,CCu,DD&SMo(c),The
  Mystery Missle From Space . 200.00
131 DD,CCu,DD&CCu(c),The
  Return of the Rocketeers . . . 150.00

132 DD,CCu,DD&CCu(c),Raid
  of the Rocketeers 150.00
133 DD,CCu,DD&CCu(c),Human
  Dynamo 150.00
134 DD,CC,DD&CC(c),The
  Sinister Snowman 150.00
135 DD,CCu,DD&CCu(c),The
  Underworld Supermarket . . . 150.00
136 DD,CCu,DD&CCu(c),The
  Menace of the Smoke-Master 150.00
137 DD,CCu,DD&CCu(c),The
  Weapons That Backfired 150.00
138 DD,CCu,DD&CCu(c),The
  Menace of the Blob 150.00
139 DD,CCu,DD&CCu(c),The
  Secret Blackhawk 150.00
140 DD,CCu,DD&CCu(c),The
  Space Age Marauders 150.00
141 DD,CCu,DD&CCu(c),Crimes
  of the Captive Masterminds . 100.00
142 DD,CCu,DD&CCu(c),Alien
  Blackhawk Chief 100.00
143 DD,SMo,DD&CCu(c),Lady
  Blackhawk's Rival 100.00
144 DD,CCu,DD&CCu(c),The
  Underworld Sportsmen 100.00
145 DD,CCu,DD&CCu(c),The
  Deadly Lensman 100.00
146 DD,CCu,DD&CCu(c),Black-
  hawk's Fantastic Fables 100.00
147 DD,SMo,DD&CCu(c),The
  Blackhawk Movie Queen 100.00
148 DD,CCu,DD&CCu(c),Four
  Dooms For The Blackhawks . 100.00
149 DD,CCu,DD&CCu(c),Masks
  of Doom 100.00
150 DD,CCu,DD&SMo(c), Black-
  hawk Mascot from Space . . . 100.00
151 DD,CCu,Lost City 125.00
152 DD,CCu,DD&SMo(c),Noah's
  Ark From Space 100.00
153 DD,CCu,DD&SMo(c),
  Boomerang Master 100.00
154 DD,CCu,DD&CCu(c),The
  Beast Time Forgot 100.00
155 DD,CCu,DD&CCu(c),Killer
  Shark's Land Armada 100.00
156 DD,CCu,DD&SMo(c),Peril of
  the Plutonian Raider 100.00
157 DD,CCu,DD&SMo(c),Secret
  of the Blackhawk Sphinx 100.00
158 DD,CCu,DD&SMo(c),Bandit
  Birds From Space 100.00

Blackhawk #225
© DC Comics, Inc.

159 DD,CCu,DD&SMo(c),Master
of the Puppet Men. 100.00
160 DD,CCu,DD&CCu(c),The
Phantom Spy 100.00
161 DD,SMo,DD&SMo(c),Lady
Blackhawk's Crime Chief. . . . 100.00
162 DD,CCu,DD&CCu(c),The
Invisible Blackhawk 100.00
163 DD,CCu,DD&SMo(c),
Fisherman of Crime. 100.00
164 DD,O:Blackhawk retold. 125.00
165 DD,V:League of Anti
Blackhawks 100.00
166 DD,A:Lady Blackhawk 100.00
167 DD,The Blackhawk Bandits . . 75.00
168 DD,Blackhawk Time
Travelers 60.00
169 DD,Sinister Hunts of Mr.
Safari. 60.00
170 DD,A:Lady Blackhawk,V:Killer
Shark. 60.00
171 DD,Secret of Alien Island 60.00
172 DD,Challenge of the
GasMaster. 60.00
173 DD,The Super Jungle Man. . . 60.00
174 DD,Andre's Impossible
World 60.00
175 DD,The Creature with
Blackhawk's Brain 60.00
176 DD,Stone Age Blackhawks . . . 55.00
177 DD,Town that time Forgot. . . . 55.00
178 DD,Return of the Scorpions . . 55.00
179 DD,Invisible Dr.Dunbar 55.00
180 DD,Son of Blackhawk. 55.00
181 DD,I:Tom Thumb Blackhawk . 60.00
182 DD,A:Lady Blackhawk 60.00
183 DD,V:Killer Shark 60.00
184 DD,Island of Super
Monkeys 60.00
185 DD,Last 7 days of the
Blackhawks 60.00
186 DD,A:Lady Blackhawk 60.00
187 DD,V:Porcupine 60.00
188 DD,A:Lady Blackhawk 60.00
189 DD:O:rtd 60.00
190 DD,FantasticHumanStarfish . . 60.00
191 DD,A:Lady Blackhawk 60.00
192 DD,V:King Condor 35.00
193 DD,The Jailer's Revenge 35.00
194 DD,The Outlaw Blackhawk. . . 35.00
195 DD,A:Tom Thumb Blackhawk. 35.00
196 DD,Blackhawk WWII Combat
Diary story 35.00
197 DD:new look 35.00
198 DD:O:rtd 40.00
199 DD,Attack with the Mummy
Insects 40.00
200 DD,A:Lady Blackhawk,
I:Queen Killer Shark 40.00
201 DD,Blackhawk Detached Diary
Story,F:Hendrickson 40.00
202 DD,Combat Diary,F:Andre . . . 40.00
203 DD:O:Chop-Chop 40.00
204 DD,A:Queen Killer Shark 40.00
205 DD,Combat Diary story. 40.00
206 DD,Combat Diary, F:Olaf 40.00
207 DD,Blackhawk Devil Dolls . . . 40.00
208 DD,Detached service diary
F:Chuck. 40.00
209 DD,V:King Condor 40.00
210 DD,Danger..Blackhawk Bait
rep.Blackhawk #139. . . . . 35.00
211 DD,GC,Detached service
diary. 30.00
212 DD,Combat Diary,
F:Chop-Chop. 30.00
213 DD,Blackhawk goes
Hollywood 30.00
214 DD,Team of Traitors 30.00
215 DD,Detached service diary
F:Olaf. 30.00

Blackhawk 3rd Series #11
© DC Comics, Inc.

216 DD,A:Queen Killer Shark 30.00
217 DD,Detached service diary
F:Stanislaus. 30.00
218 DD,7 against Planet Peril 30.00
219 DD,El Blackhawk Peligroso . 30.00
220 DD,The Revolt of the
Assembled Man. 30.00
221 DD,Detach service diary
F:Hendrickson 30.00
222 DD,The Man from E=MC2 . . . 30.00
223 DD,V:Mr.Quick CHange 30.00
224 DD,Combat Diary,
F:Stanislaus. 30.00
225 DD,A:Queen Killer Shark 30.00
226 DD,Secret Monster of
Blackhawk Island. 30.00
227 DD,Detached Service diary
F:Chop-Chop. 30.00
228 DD (1st art on JLA characters)
Blackhawks become super-heroes,
Junk-Heap heroes #1(C:JLA) . 35.00
229 DD,Junk-Heap Heroes #2
(C:JLA) 30.00
230 DD,Junk-Heap Heroes concl.
(C:JLA) 30.00
231 DD,A:Lady Blackhawk 30.00
232 DD,A:Lady Blackhawk 30.00
233 DD,Too Late,The Leaper 30.00
234 DD,The Terrible Twins 30.00
235 DD,A Coffin for
a Blackhawk 30.00
236 DD,Melt,Mutant, Melt 30.00
237 DD,Magnificent 7 Assassins . . 30.00
238 DD,Walking Booby-Traps 30.00
239 DD,The Killer That Time
Forgot 30.00
240 DD,He Who Must Die 30.00
241 DD,A Blackhawk a Day 30.00
242 Blackhawks back in blue &
black costumes 30.00
243 Mission Incredible (1968) . . . 30.00
244 GE,new costumes,Blackhawks
become mercenaries (1976) . . 10.00
245 GE,Death's Double Deal. 10.00
246 RE,GE,Death's Deadly Dawn. 10.00
247 RE,AM,Operation:Over Kill . . . 10.00
248 JSh,Vengeance is Mine!..
Sayeth the Cyborg. 10.00
249 RE,GE,V:Sky-Skull 10.00
250 RE,GE,FS,D:Chuck(1977) . . . 10.00
251 DSp,Back to WWII(1982) 10.00
252 thru 258 DSp. . . . . @10.00
259 . . . . 10.00

260 HC,ATh 10.00
261 thru 271 DSp. . . . . @10.00
272. . . . . 10.00
273 DSp 10.00
274 DSp 10.00

[2nd Series], 1988
1 HC Mini-series,Blackhawk accused
of communism. 5.00
2 HC,visits Soviet Union. 4.00
3 HC,Atom Bomb threat to N.Y. . . . 4.00

[3rd Series], 1989
1 All in color for a Crime,pt.1
I:The Real Lady Blackhawk. . . . 4.00
2 All in color for a Crime,pt.2 . . . . 2.50
3 Agent Rescue Attempt in Rome . 2.50
4 Blackhawk's girlfriend murdered . 2.50
5 I:Circus Organization. 2.50
6 Blackhawks on false mission. . . . 2.50
7 V:Circus,A:Suicide Squad, rep.
1st Blackhawk story. 3.00
8 Project: Assimilation. 2.50
9 V:Grundfest 2.50
10 Blackhawks Attacked 2.50
11 Master plan revealed 2.50
12 Raid on BlackhawkAirwaysHQ . . 2.50
13 Team Member Accused of 2.50
14 Blackhawk test pilots 2.50
15 Plans for independence 2.50
16 Independence, final issue. 2.50
Ann.#1 Hawks in Albania. 2.95
Spec.#1 Assassination of JFK
to Saigon,1975 . . . . 3.50

Black Hood Ann. #1
© DC Comics Inc.

BLACK HOOD
Impact, 1991–92
1 O:Black Hood. 4.00
2 Nick Cray becomes Black Hood . 3.00
3 New Year's Eve,A:Creeptures . . . 3.00
4 Nate Cray become Black Hood,
Dr.M.Harvey becomes Ozone . . 3.00
5 E:Nate Cray as Black Hood
V:Ozone. 3.00
6 New Black Hood 3.00
7 History of Seaside City 3.00
8 V:Hit Coffee 3.00
9 V:Hit Coffee 3.00
10 Slime of Your Life #1. . . . . 3.00
11 Slime of Your Life #2. . . . . 3.00
12 Final Issue 3.00
Ann#1 Earthquest,w/trading card . . 3.00

BLACK LAMB, THE
DC/Helix, Sept., 1996
1 TT,Vampire saga 2.50
2 thru 6 TT . . . . @2.50

BLACK LIGHTNING
1977–78
1 TVE/FS,I&O:Black Lightning . . . 15.00
2 TVE/FS,A:Talia 7.00
3 TVE,I:Tobias Whale 7.00
4 TVE,A:Jimmy Olsen. 8.00
5 TVE,A:Superman. 8.00
6 TVE,I:Syonide 7.00
7 TVE,V:Syonide. 7.00
8 TVE,V:Tobias Whale 7.00
9 TVE,V:Annihilist 7.00
10 TVE,V:Trickster. 7.00
11 TVE,BU:The Ray. 10.00

[2nd Series], 1995–96
1 He's Back. 3.00
2 V:Painkiller. 3.00
3 V:Painkiller. 3.00
4 V:Painkiller,Royal Family 3.00
5 Flashbacks of Past 3.00
6 V:Gangbuster. 3.00
7 V:Gangbuster. 3.00
8 V:Tobias Whale 3.00
9 I&V:Demolition 3.00
10 Jefferson Pierce becomes Black
    Lightning full time 3.00
11 Hunt for Sick Nick 3.00
12 V:Sick Nick's death squad 3.00
13 final issue 3.00

BLACK MASK
1993–94
1 I:Black Mask 5.00
2 V:Underworld 5.00
3 V:Valentine. 5.00

BLACK ORCHID
1993–95
1 DMc,O:Black Orchid,
    A:Batman,Luthor,Poison Ivy . . . 6.00
2 DMc,O:cont,Arkham Asylum 7.00
3 DMc,A:SwampThing,conc. 6.00
TPB rep. #1 thru #3 . . . . 20.00

DC/Vertigo
1 DMc(c),B:DiF(s),JIT,SnW,I:Sherilyn
    Somers,I:Logos,F:Walt Brody . . 2.50
1a Platinum Ed. 12.00
2 JIT,SnW,Uprooting,V:Logos 2.50
3 JIT,SnW,Tainted Zone,
    V:Fungus 2.50
4 JIT,SnW,I:Nick & Orthia 2.50
5 DMc(c),JIT,SnW,
    A:Swamp Thing 2.50
6 JIT,BMc(i),God in the Cage 2.50
7 JIT,RGu,SnW,
    Upon the Threshold. 2.50
8 DMc(c),RGu,A:Silent People 2.50
9 DMc(c),RGu. 2.50
10 DMc(c),RGu 2.50
11 DMc(c),RGu,In Tennessee 2.50
12 DMc(c),RGu 2.50
13 DMc(c),RGu,F:Walt Brody 2.50
14 DMc(c),RGu,Black Annis 2.50
15 DMc(c),RGu,Kobolds 2.50
16 DMc(c),RGu,Suzy,Junkin 2.50
17 Twisted Season,pt.1 . . . . 2.50
18 Twisted Season,pt.2 . . . . 2.50
19 Twisted Season,pt.3 . . . . 2.50
20 Twisted Season,pt.4 . . . . 2.50
21 Twisted Season,pt.5 . . . . 2.50
22 Twisted Season,pt.6, final iss. . . 2.50
Ann.#1 DMc(c),DiF(s),GyA,JnM,F:Suzy,
    Childrens Crusade,BU:retells
    Adventure Comics#430 . . . . . . 4.25

BLASTERS SPECIAL
1989
1 A:Snapper Carr, Spider Guild . . . 2.00

BLOOD: A TALE
DC/Vertigo, Sept., 1996
[Mini-series,
re-release of Marvel Epic]
1 JMD(s),KW, quest for truth
    begins 3.00
2 JMD(s),KW, Blood falls in love . . 3.00
3 JMD(s),KW, companion dies 3.00
4 JMD(s),KW, finale 3.00

BLOOD & SHADOWS
DC/Vertigo, 1996
1 . . . . 6.00
2 Journal of Justice Jones 6.00
3 Chet Daley flung into
    21st century. 6.00
4 V:God of the Razor, finale 6.00

BLOOD AND WATER
DC/Vertigo March 2003
1 (of 5) F:Adam Heller 3.00
2 vampire 3.00
3 sex for Adam 3.00
4 past, present, future. 3.00
5 concl. 3.00

BLOODBATH
1993
1 A:Superman 4.00
2 A:New Heroes, Hitman 8.00

BLOODPACK
[Mini-Series], 1995
1 I:Blood Pack, V:Demolition 2.25
2 A:Superboy 2.25
3 Loira's Corpse 2.25
4 Real Heroes Final Issue 2.25

BLOODHOUND
July 2004
1 F:Travis Clevenger 3.00
2 thru 4 Concl.. . . . . @3.00

BLOOD SYNDICATE
DC/Milestone, 1993–96
1 I:Blood Syndicate,Rob Chaplick,
    Dir.Mark.Ed.,w/B puzzle piece,
    Skybox card,Poster 3.50
1a Newstand Ed. 2.50
2 I:Boogieman,Tech-9 Vs.
    Holocaust. 2.50
3 V:S.Y.S.T.E.M.,I:Mom,D:Tech-9 . . 2.50
4 V:S.Y.S.T.E.M. 2.50
5 I:John Wing,Kwai,Demon Fox . . . 2.50
6 V:John Wing 2.50
7 I:Edmund,Cornelia 2.50
8 V:Demon Fox. 2.50
9 O:Blood Syndicate,I:Templo 2.50
10 WS(c),Ccs,Shadow War,I:Iota,
    Sideshow,Rainsaw,Slag,Ash,
    Bad Betty,Oro 2.75
11 IV(s),Ccs,A:Aquamaria 2.50
12 IV(s),Ccs,V:Dinosaur 2.50
13 IV(s),Ccs,B:Roach War. 2.50
14 IV(s),Ccs,V:Roaches. 2.50
15 IV(s),Ccs,E:Roach War. 2.50
16 IV(s),Ccs,Worlds Collide#6,
    A:Superman. 2.50
17 Ccs,Worlds Collide#13,V:Rift . . . 2.50
18 Ccs,V:S.Y.S.T.E.M. 2.50
19 . . . . 2.50
20 . . . . 2.50

BloodSyndicate #8
© DC Comics, Inc.

21 . . . . 2.50
22 . . . . 2.50
23 F:Boogieman. 2.50
24 L:Third Rail,Brickhouse. 2.50
25 R:Tech-9 . . . . 3.50
26 Return of the Dead 2.50
27 R:Masquerade 2.50
28 Tech-9 takes control 2.75
29 Reader's Choice. 2.50
30 Long Hot Summer. 2.50
31 V:New Threat 2.50
32 MC(c),V:Soulbreaker 2.50
33 Kwai returns to paris Island 2.50
34 Visit to Kwen Lun 2.50
35 final issue 3.50

BLOODY MARY
DC/Helix, Aug., 1996
1 (of 4) GEn(s),CE, near-
    future war 3.00
2 thru 4 GEn(s),CE, near-future
    war, concl. . . . . @3.00

BLOODY MARY:
LADY LIBERTY
DC/Helix, July, 1996
1 (of 4) GEn(s),CE,. 4.00
2 GEn(s),CE,V:Achilles Seagal . . . 4.00
3 GEn(s),CE,V:Vatman 4.00
4 GEn(s),CE,V:Vatman, concl. 4.00

BLUE BEETLE
1986–88
1 O:Blue Beetle. 4.00
2 V:Fire Fist 2.50
3 V:Madmen 2.50
4 V:Doctor Alchemy 2.50
5 A:Question 2.50
6 V:Question 2.50
7 A:Question 2.50
8 A:Chronos 2.50
9 A:Chronos 2.50
10 Legends, V:Chronos 2.50
11 A:New Teen Titans 2.50
12 A:New Teen Titans 2.50
13 A:New Teen Titans 2.50
14 Pago Island,I:Catalyst. 2.50
15 RA:V:Carapax 2.50
16 RA,Chicago Murders 2.50
17 R:Dan Garrett/Blue Beetle 2.50
18 D:Dan Garrett 2.50

19 RA,R:Dr. Cyber 2.50
20 RA,Millennium,A:JLI 3.00
21 RA,A:Mr.Miracle,
   Millennium tie in. 2.25
22 RA,Prehistoric Chicago. 2.25
23 DH,V:The Madmen 2.25
24 DH,final issue 2.25

BLUE DEVIL
1984–86
1 O:Blue Devil 4.00
2 thru 16 . . . . @2.50
17 Crisis 3.00
18 Crisis 3.00
19 thru 31 . . . . @2.50
Ann.#1 . . . . 2.50

BOB, THE GALACTIC BUM
[Mini-Series], 1995
1 A:Lobo 2.50
2 Planet Gnulp,A:Lobo 2.50
3 V:Khunds 2.50
4 Rando's Coronation 2.50

BODY DOUBLES
Aug., 1999
1 (of 4) DAn,ALa,JoP 2.50
2 thru 3 DAn,ALa,JoP . . . . @2.50

BOMBA,
THE JUNGLE BOY
1967–68
1 CI,MA,I:Bomba 50.00
2 thru 7 . . . . @35.00

BOOK OF FATE, THE
1997–98
1 KG(s),RoW,BR, ... 3.00
2 KG(s),RoW,BR,The Chaos-
   Order War, pt.1 (of 4) 3.00
3 KG(s),RoW,BR,The Chaos-
   Order War, pt.2 . . . . 3.00
4 KG(s),RoW,BR,The Chaos-
   Order War, pt.3, A:Two-Face . . . 3.00
5 KG(s),RoW,BR,The Chaos-
   Order War, pt.4 . . . . 3.00
6 KG(s),RoW,BR,Convergence,
   pt.1 x-over 3.00
7 KG(s),RoW,BR, Signs, pt.1 . . . . . 3.00
8 KG(s),RoW,BR, Signs, pt.2 . . . . . 3.00
9 KG,AIG,BR,Signs, pt.3 . . . . 3.00
10 KG,AIG,BR,Signs,pt.4 . . . . 3.00
11 KG,AIG, in a Swiss Jail 3.00
12 AIG,KG,F:Lobo, final issue 3.00

BOOKS OF FAERIE, THE
DC/Vertigo, Jan., 1997
1 PrG,F:Titania and Auberon 3.00
2 thru 3 PrG, ... @3.00
TPB 15.00

BOOKS OF FAERIE, THE:
AUBERON'S TALE
DC/Vertigo, June, 1998
1 (of 3) PrG,VcL,F:Early life of
   King Auberon 3.00
2 thru 3 PrG,VcL, early life . . . . . @3.00
TPB Books of Faerie 15.00

BOOKS OF FAERIE, THE:
MOLLY'S STORY
DC/Vertigo, 1999
1 (of 4) JNR(s) 3.00
2 thru 4 CV(c) . . . . @3.00

Books of Magic #57
© DC Comics Inc.

BOOKS OF MAGIC
[Limited Series], 1990–91
1 B:NGa(s),JBo,F:Phantom Stranger,
   A:J.Constantine,Tim Hunter,
   Doctor Occult,Mister E. 11.00
2 SHp,F:J.Constantine,A:Spectre,
   Dr.Fate,Demon,Zatanna 11.00
3 CV,F:Doctor Occult,
   A:Sandman 8.00
4 E:NGa(s),PuJ,F:Mr.E,A:Death . . . 9.00
TPB rep.#1-#4 . . . . 20.00
[Regular Series]
DC/Vertigo, 1994–97
1 MkB,B:Bindings,R:Tim Hunter . . 13.00
1a Platinum Edition 25.00
2 CV(c),MkB,V:Manticore 6.00
3 CV(c),MkB,E:Bindings 6.00
4 CV(c),MkB,A:Death 7.00
5 CV(c),I:Khara 4.00
6 Sacrifices,pt.I 4.00
7 Sacrifices,pt.II 4.00
8 Tim vs. evil Tim 4.00
9 Artificial Heart,pt.1 . . . . 4.00
10 Artificial Heart,pt.2 . . . . 4.00
11 Artificial Heart,pt.3 . . . . 4.00
12 Small Glass Worlds,pt.1 . . . . 4.00
13 Small Glass Worlds,pt.2 . . . . 4.00
14 CV(c),A:The Wobbly 4.00
15 Hell and Back,pt.1 . . . . 4.00
16 Hall and Back,pt.2 . . . . 3.50
17 Playgrounds,pt.1 . . . . 3.50
18 JNR,PrG,Playgrounds,cont. 3.50
19 JNR,PrG,Playgrounds,concl. 3.50
20 Barabatos gives the orders 3.50
21 JNR,PrG,Molly seeks Mayra 3.50
22 . . . . 3.50
23 JNR,V:Margraves Strafenkinder . 3.50
24 JNR,PrG,F:Molly vs. Amadan . . . 3.50
25 JNR,PrG,Death and the Endless . 3.50
26 JNR,PrG,Rites of Passage, pt.1 . 3.00
27 JNR,PrG,Rites of Passage, pt.2 . 3.00
28 JNR,PrG,Rites of Passage, pt.3,
   Cupid & Psyche 3.00
29 JNR,PrG,Rite of Passage 3.00
30 JNR,PrG,Rite of Passage 3.00
31 JNR,PrG,Rite of Passage 3.00
32 JNR(s),PSj,Rites of Passage . . . 3.00
33 JNR(s),PSj,Rites of Passage . . . 3.00
34 JNR(s),PSj,Rites of Passage . . . 3.00
35 JNR(s),PrG,Rites of Passage . . . 3.00
36 JNR,Rites of Passage, cont 3.00
37 JNR,Rites of Passage, concl. . . . 3.00

38 JNR,Rites of Passage, concl. . . . 3.00
39 PrG, at Sphinx casino 3.00
40 JNR(s),F:Tim & Molly 3.00
41 JNR(s),V:Gargoyles 3.00
42 JNR(s),JIT,magical havok 3.00
43 JNR(s),PrG,F:The Wobbly 3.00
44 JNR(s),goodbye to Zatanna 3.00
45 JNR(s) Slave of Heavens, pt.1 . . 3.00
46 JNR(s) Slave of Heavens, pt.2 . . 3.00
47 JNR(s) Slave of Heavens, pt.3 . . 3.00
48 JNR(s) Slave of Heavens, pt.4 . . 3.00
49 JNR(s) Slave of Heavens, pt.5 . . 3.00
50 JNR(s) Slave of Heavens, pt.6 . . 3.00
51 PrG,MK,an Opener 2.50
52 PrG,MK,Homecoming 2.50
54 PrG,MK,V:Thomas 2.50
55 PrG,MK,Coming of the Other . . . 2.50
56 PrG,MK,Last Molly Story 2.50
57 PrG,MK,after car crash 2.50
58 PrG,MK,The Other 2.50
59 PrG,MK,The Other 2.50
60 PrG,MK,The Other 2.50
61 PrG,MK(c),The Other, concl. . . . 2.50
62 PrG,MK(c),crossroads 2.50
63 GyA,MK(c), ... 2.50
64 PrG,MK(c),Wild Hunt 2.50
65 PrG,MK,new life cont. 2.50
66 PrG,A Day,A Night &
   A Dream,pt.1 . . . . 2.50
67 PrG,A Day, A Night &
   A Dream,concl. 2.50
68 PrG 2.50
69 PrG 2.50
70 PrG 2.50
71 PrG,MK(c) 2.50
72 PrG,MK(c),F:Timothy Hunter. . . . 2.50
73 PrG,MK(c),V:Other self 2.50
74 PrG,MK(c),V:Other self 2.50
75 PrG,MK(c), final issue 2.50
Ann.#2 JNR(s) Minotaur 4.00
Ann.#3 PrG 4.00
TPB Rep. #5–#13 & Rave #1 . . . . 12.95
TPB Reckonings, rep. #14–#20. . . 12.95
TPB Reckonings, new printing. . . . 14.95
TPB Bindings, GyA,PrG,WK 13.00
TPB Transformations PrG,MK 13.00
TPB The Books of Magic 20.00
TPB Girl in the Box 15.00
TPB The Burning Girl 17.95
TPB Death After Death 19.95

BOOKS OF MAGICK, THE:
LIFE DURING WARTIME
DC/Vertigo July 2004
1 NGa(s),F:Timothy Hunter 2.50
2 thru 4 NGa(s) . . . . @2.50

BOOSTER GOLD
1986–88
1 DJ,V:Blackguard 3.00
2 DJ,V:Minddancer 2.50
3 DJ,V:Minddancer 2.50
4 DJ,V:Minddancer 2.50
5 DJ,V:Fascinator 2.50
6 DJ,A:Superman 2.50
7 DJ,A:Superman 2.50
8 DJ,A:Braniac 5,Cham.Boy,
   Ultra Boy,pt.1 . . . . 2.50
9 DJ,A:Braniac 5,Cham.Boy,
   Ultra Boy,pt.2 . . . . 2.50
10 DJ,V:1000 . . . . 2.50
11 DJ,V:Shockwave 2.50
12 DJ,Booster Weakening 2.50
13 DJ,I:Rip Hunter(modern) 2.50
14 DJ,Rip Hunter 2.50
15 DJ,Rip Hunter 2.50
16 DJ,Boosters new company 2.50
17 DJ,A:Cheshire & Hawk 2.50
18 DJ,V:Broderick 2.50

19 DJ,V:Rainbow Raider 2.50
20 DJ,V:Rainbow Raider 2.50
21 DJ,Goldstar captured by aliens . 2.50
22 DJ,A:J.L.I.,D:Goldstar 2.50
23 DJ,A:Superman & Luthor 2.50
24 DJ,Millenium 2.50
25 DJ,last issue 2.50

BOY COMMANDOS
Winter, 1942–43
1 S&K,O:Liberty Belle;Sandman
& Newsboy Legion 8,000.00
2 S&K,Hitler(c) 3,000.00
3 S&K,WWII(c). 1,500.00
4 WWII(c). 1,200.00
5 WWII(c). 1,200.00
6 S&K,WWII(c). 1,200.00
7 S&K,WWII(c) 750.00
8 S&K,WWII(c) 750.00
9 WWII(c) 750.00
10 S&K,WWII(c). 750.00
11 WWII(c) 650.00
12 WWII(c). 450.00
13 WWII(c). 450.00
14 . . . . 350.00
15 1st Crazy Quilt 500.00
16 . . . . 350.00
17 Science Fiction(c) 400.00
18 S&K. 350.00
19 S&K. 375.00
20 Science Fiction (c) 400.00
21 . . . . 250.00
22 Judy Canova. 250.00
23 S&K,S&K,(c) 350.00
24 Superhero. 350.00
25 superhero(c) 275.00
26 Science Fiction(c) 300.00
27 . . . . 250.00
28 . . . . 250.00
29 S&K story 275.00
30 Baseball Story. 275.00
31 . . . . 250.00
32 A:Dale Evans(c) 260.00
33 . . . . 250.00
34 I:Wolf. 250.00
35 . . . . 250.00
36 Sci-Fi(c),Nov.–Dec., 1949. . . . 450.00

BRAINBANX
DC/Helix, Jan., 1997
1 ELe(s),Down Upon the
Darkness 2.50
2 ELe(s),Anna flees to the Sheol . . 2.50
3 Ele(s),Anna stranded 2.50
4 ELe(s),Anna & Logan 2.50
5 ELe(s),To Enter the Kingdom . . . 2.50
6 (of 6) 2.50

BRAVE AND THE BOLD
Aug.–Sept., 1955
1 JKu,RH,IN,I:VikingPrince,Golden
Gladiator,Silent Knight 5,000.00
2 F:Viking Prince 2,000.00
3 F:Viking Prince 1,200.00
4 F:Viking Prince 1,200.00
5 B:Robin Hood 1,100.00
6 JKu,F:Robin Hood,E:Golden
Gladiator 750.00
7 JKu,F:Robin Hood 750.00
8 JKu,F:Robin Hood 750.00
9 JKu,F:Robin Hood 750.00
10 JKu,F:Robin Hood 750.00
11 JKu,F:Viking Prince. 550.00
12 JKu,F:Viking Prince 550.00
13 JKu,F:Viking Prince 550.00
14 JKu,F:Viking Prince 525.00
15 JKu,F:Viking Prince 525.00
16 JKu,F:Viking Prince 525.00
17 JKu,F:Viking Prince 525.00

The Brave and the Bold #28
© DC Comics, Inc.

18 JKu,F:Viking Prince 525.00
19 JKu,F:Viking Prince 525.00
20 JKu,F:Viking Prince 525.00
21 JKu,F:Viking Prince 525.00
22 JKu,F:Viking Prince 525.00
23 JKu,O:Viking Prince 750.00
24 JKu,E:Viking Prince,Silent
Knight 550.00
25 RA,I&B:Suicide Squad 700.00
26 F:Suicide Squad 450.00
27 Creature of Ghost Lake 450.00
28 I:Justice League of
America,O:Snapper Carr . . 8,500.00
29 F:Justice League 3,500.00
30 F:Justice League 2,500.00
31 F:Cave Carson 600.00
32 F:Cave Carson 350.00
33 F:Cave Carson 350.00
34 JKu,I&O:S.A. Hawkman. . . . 3,500.00
35 JKu:F:Hawkman 800.00
36 JKu:F:Hawkman 750.00
37 F:Suicide Squad 400.00
38 F:Suicide Squad 300.00
39 F:Suicide Squad 300.00
40 JKu,F:Cave Carson 250.00
41 F:Cave Carson 250.00
42 JKu,F:Hawkman 450.00
43 JKu,O:Hawkman 550.00
44 JKu,F:Hawkman 400.00
45 CI,F:Strange Sports 125.00
46 CI,F:Strange Sports 125.00
47 CI,F:Strange Sports 125.00
48 CI,F:Strange Sports 125.00
49 CI,F:Strange Sports 125.00
50 F:GreenArrow & J'onnJ'onzz 275.00
51 F:Aquaman & Hawkman 350.00
52 JKu,F:Sgt.Rock 275.00
53 ATh,F:Atom & Flash 125.00
54 I&O:Teen Titans 450.00
55 F:Metal Man & Atom 100.00
56 F:Flash & J'onn J'onzz 100.00
57 I&O:Metamorpho. 275.00
58 F:Metamorpho. 135.00
59 F:Batman & Green Lantern . . 150.00
60 A:Teen Titans,I:Wonder Girl . . 150.00
61 MA,O:Starman,BlackCanary. . 200.00
62 MA,O:Starman,BlackCanary. . 200.00
63 F:Supergirl&WonderWoman . 100.00
64 F:Batman,V:Eclipso. 125.00
65 DG,FMc,F:Flash & Doom
Patrol 75.00
66 F:Metamorpho & Metal Men . . 75.00
67 CI,F:Batman & Flash 90.00

68 F:Batman,Metamorpho,Joker,
Riddler,Penguin 125.00
69 F:Batman & Green Lantern . . . 75.00
70 F:Batman & Hawkman 75.00
71 F:Batman & Green Arrow 75.00
72 CI,F:Spectre & Flash 85.00
73 F:Aquaman & Atom. 75.00
74 B:Batman T.U.,A:Metal Men . . . 75.00
75 F:Spectre 75.00
76 F:Plastic Man 75.00
77 F:Atom 75.00
78 F:Wonder Woman. 75.00
79 NA,F:Deadman 125.00
80 NA,DG,F:Creeper 100.00
81 NA,F:Flash 100.00
82 NA,F:Aquaman,O:Ocean
Master 100.00
83 NA,F:Teen Titans 100.00
84 NA,F:Sgt.Rock 100.00
85 NA,F:Green Arrow 100.00
86 NA,F:Deadman 100.00
87 F:Wonder Woman. 50.00
88 F:Wildcat. 50.00
89 RA,F:Phantom Stranger 50.00
90 F:Adam Strange 50.00
91 F:Black Canary 50.00
92 F:Bat Squad 50.00
93 NA,House of Mystery 75.00
94 NC,F:Teen Titans 65.00
95 F:Plastic Man 65.00
96 F:Sgt.Rock 50.00
97 NC(i),F:Wildcat 50.00
98 JAp,F:Phantom Stranger 50.00
99 NC,F:Flash 50.00
100 NA,F:Green Arrow 75.00
101 JA,F:Metamorpho 40.00
102 NA,JA,F:Teen Titans 40.00
103 FMc,F:Metal Men 25.00
104 JAp,F:Deadman 25.00
105 JAp,F:Wonder Woman 25.00
106 JAp,F:Green Arrow 25.00
107 JAp,F:Black Canary 25.00
108 JAp,F:Sgt.Rock 25.00
109 JAp,F:Demon 25.00
110 JAp,F:Wildcat 25.00
111 JAp,F:Joker 30.00
112 JAp,F:Mr.Miracle 50.00
113 JAp,F:Metal Men 50.00
114 JAp,F:Aquaman 50.00
115 JAp,O:Viking Prince 50.00
116 JAp,F:Spectre 50.00
117 JAp,F:Sgt.Rock 50.00
118 JAp,F:Wildcat,V:Joker. 50.00
119 JAp,F:Man-Bat 20.00
120 JAp,F:Kamandi 20.00

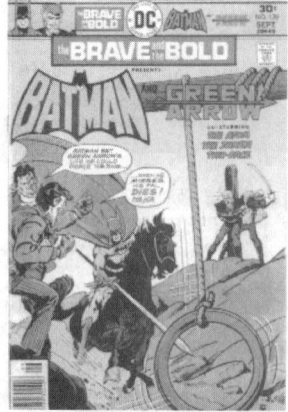

The Brave and the Bold #129
© DC Comics, Inc.

121 JAp,F:Metal Men. 20.00	
122 JAp,F:Swamp Thing 20.00	
123 JAp,F:Plastic Man. 20.00	
124 JAp,F:Sgt.Rock. 20.00	
125 JAp,F:Flash. 20.00	
126 JAp,F:Aquaman 20.00	
127 JAp,F:Wildcat 20.00	
128 JAp,F:Mr.Miracle. 20.00	
129 F:Green Arrow,V:Joker 22.00	
130 F:Green Arrow,V:Joker 22.00	
131 JAp,F:WonderWoman,	
A:Catwoman 20.00	
132 JAp,F:King Fu Foom. 18.00	
133 JAp,F:Deadman 18.00	
134 JAp,F:Green Lantern 18.00	
135 JAp,F:Metal Men. 18.00	
136 JAp,F:Metal Men,Green Arr. . 18.00	
137 F:Demon. 18.00	
138 JAp,F:Mr.Miracle 18.00	
139 JAp,F:Hawkman 18.00	
140 JAp,F:Wonder Woman. 18.00	
141 JAp,F:Bl.Canary,A:Joker. . . . 25.00	
142 JAp,F:Aquaman 10.00	
143 O:Human Target 10.00	
144 JAp,F:Green Arrow 10.00	
145 JAp,F:Phantom Stranger 10.00	
146 JAp,F:E-2 Batman 10.00	
147 JAp,A:Supergirl. 10.00	
148 JSon,JAp,F:Plastic Man 10.00	
149 JAp,F:Teen Titans 12.00	
150 JAp,F:Superman. 10.00	
151 JAp,F:Flash. 12.00	
152 JAp,F:Atom 10.00	
153 DN,F:Red Tornado 10.00	
154 JAp,F:Metamorpho 10.00	
155 JAp,F:Green Lantern 10.00	
156 DN,F:Dr.Fate. 10.00	
157 JAp,F:Kamandi. 10.00	
158 JAp,F:Wonder Woman 10.00	
159 JAp,A:Ras al Ghul 10.00	
160 JAp,F:Supergirl. 10.00	
161 JAp,F:Adam Strange. 10.00	
162 JAp,F:Sgt.Rock. 10.00	
163 DG,F:Black Lightning 10.00	
164 JL,F:Hawkman 10.00	
165 DN,F:Man-bat 10.00	
166 DG,TA,DSp,F:Black Canary	
A:Penguin,I:Nemesis. 10.00	
167 DC,DA,F:Blackhawk 10.00	
168 JAp,DSp,F:Green Arrow 7.00	
169 JAp,DSp,F:Zatanna. 7.00	
170 JA,F:Nemesis 7.00	
171 JL,DSp,V:Scalphunter. 7.00	
172 CI,F:Firestorm. 7.00	
173 JAp,F:Guardians. 7.00	
174 JAp,F:Green Lantern 7.00	
175 JAp,A:Lois Lane 7.00	
176 JAp,F:Swamp Thing 7.00	
177 JAp,F:Elongated Man 7.00	
178 JAp,F:Creeper. 7.00	
179 EC,F:Legion o/Superheroes. . 7.00	
180 JAp,F:Spectre,Nemesis 7.00	
181 JAp,F:Hawk & Dove 7.00	
182 JAp,F:E-2 Robin 7.00	
183 CI,V:Riddler. 8.00	
184 JAp,A:Catwoman 8.00	
185 F:Green Arrow 7.00	
186 JAp,F:Hawkman 7.00	
187 JAp,F:Metal Men. 7.00	
188 JAp,F:Rose & Thorn 7.00	
189 JAp,A:Thorn 7.00	
190 JAp,F:Adam Strange. 7.00	
191 JAp,V:Joker,Penguin. 10.00	
192 JAp,F:Superboy 7.00	
193 JAp,D:Nemesis 7.00	
194 CI,F:Flash 7.00	
195 JA,I:Vampire 7.00	
196 JAp,F:Ragman 7.00	
197 JSon,W:Earth II Batman &	
Catwoman 7.00	
198 F:Karate Kid 7.00	

199 RA,F:Spectre 7.00	
200 DGb,JAp,A:Earth-2 Batman,I:	
Outsiders (GeoForce,Katana,Halo),	
E:Batman T.U.,final issue 15.00	
Ann. #1-1969 80-page giant (2001). 6.00	

[Limited Series]

1 SAP,Green Arrow/Butcher T.U. . . 2.50	
2 SAP,A:Black Canary,Question. . . 2.50	
3 SAP,Green Arrow/Butcher 2.50	
4 SAP,GA on Trial;A:Black	
Canary 2.50	
5 SAP,V:Native Canadians,I.R.A. . . 2.50	

BRAVE OLD WORLD
DC/Vertigo, Dec., 1999

1 (of 4) BML,GyD,PhH,Y2K story. . 2.50	
2 thru 4 BML,GyD,PhH . . . . @2.50	

BREATHTAKER
1990

1 I:Breathtaker(Chase Darrow). . . . 6.00	
2 Chase Darrow captured. 6.00	
3 O:Breathtaker. 6.00	
4 V:The Man, final issue 5.00	
TPB Breathtaker 15.00	

BROTHER POWER,
THE GEEK
Sept.–Oct., 1968

1. . . . . 75.00	
2 Nov.–Dec., 1968 . . . . 50.00	

BUGS BUNNY
1990

1 Search for Fudd Statues 3.50	
2 V:WitchHazel. 3.50	
3 Bugs&Co.in outer space, final. . . 3.50	
TPB Bugs & Friends Celebration	
Celebration (2000). 14.95	

BUTCHER, THE
[Limited Series], 1990

1 MB,I:John Butcher. 3.50	
2 MB,in San Francisco 3.00	
3 MB,V:Corporation 3.00	
4 MB,A:Green Arrow. 2.50	
5 MB,A:Corvus,final issue. 2.25	

BUZZY
1944–58

1. . . . . 350.00	
2 . . . . 175.00	
3 thru 5 . . . . @125.00	
6 thru 10 . . . . @75.00	
11 thru 15 . . . . @65.00	
16 thru 25 . . . . @65.00	
26 thru 35 . . . . @50.00	
36 thru 45 . . . . @45.00	
46 thru 77 . . . . @42.00	

CAMELOT 3000
Dec., 1982

1 BB,O:Arthur,Merlin. 3.50	
2 BB,A:Morgan LeFay 3.00	
3 BB,J:New Knights 3.00	
4 BB,V:McAllister 3.00	
5 BB,O:Morgan Le Fay. 3.00	
6 BB,TA,W:Arthur 3.00	
7 BB,TA,R:Isolde 3.00	
8 BB,TA,D:Sir Kay 3.00	
9 BB,TA,L:Sir Percival 3.00	
10 BB,TA,V:Morgan Le Fay 3.00	
11 BB,TA,V:Morgan Le Fay 3.00	
12 BB,TA,D:Arthur 3.00	

Buzzy #1 © DC Comics Inc.

CAPER
Oct. 2003

1 (of 12) organized crime 3.00	
2 . . . . 3.00	
3 Jewish Mafia hitmen 3.00	
4 Jacob & Isadore Weiss 3.00	
5 thru 8 JSe. . . . . @3.00	
9 thru 12 . . . . @3.00	

CAPTAIN ACTION
[Based on toy] Oct.–Nov., 1968

1 WW,I:Captain Action,Action	
Boy,A:Superman 175.00	
2 GK,WW, V:Krellik. 125.00	
3 GK,I:Dr.Evil 125.00	
4 GK,A:Dr.Evil. 125.00	
5 GK,WW,A:Matthew Blackwell . . 75.00	

CAPTAIN ATOM
March, 1987

1 PB,O:Captain Atom 4.50	
2 PB,C:Batman. 2.50	
3 PB,O:Captain Atom 2.50	
4 PB,A:Firestorm 2.50	
5 PB,A:Firestorm 2.50	
6 PB,Dr.Spectro 2.50	
7 R:Plastique 2.50	
8 PB,Capt.Atom/Plastique 2.50	
9 V:Bolt. 2.50	
10 PB,A:JLI 2.50	
11 PB,A:Firestorm 2.50	
12 PB,I:Major Force 2.50	
13 PB,Christmas issue 2.50	
14 PB,A:Nightshade. 2.50	
15 PB,Dr.Spectro, Major Force 2.50	
16 PB,A:JLI,V:Red Tornado. 2.50	
17 V:Red Tornado;A:Swamp	
Thing,JLI. 2.50	
18 PB,A:Major Force 2.50	
19 PB,Drug War. 2.50	
20 FMc,BlueBeetle. 2.50	
21 PB,A:Plastique,Nightshade. 2.50	
22 PB,A:MaxLord,Nightshade,	
Plastique 2.50	
23 PB,V:The Ghost 2.50	
24 PB,Invasion X-over. 2.50	
25 PB,Invvasion X-over 2.50	
26 A:JLA,Top Secret,pt.1 . . . . 2.50	
27 A:JLA,Top Secret,pt.2 . . . . 2.50	
28 V:Ghost, Top Secret,pt.3. . . . . . 2.50	

All comics prices listed are for *Near Mint* condition.

DC COMICS

29 RT,Captain Atom cleared
   (new direction). 2.50
30 Janus Directive #11,V:Black
   Manta. 2.50
31 RT,Capt.Atom's Powers,
   A:Rocket Red 2.50
32 Loses Powers 2.50
33 A:Batman 3.00
34 C:JLE 2.50
35 RT,Secret o/t Silver Shield,
   A:Major Force. 2.50
36 RT,Las Vegas Battle,A:Major
   Force 2.50
37 I:New Atomic Skull 2.50
38 RT,A:Red Tornado,
   Black Racer. 2.50
39 RT,A:Red Tornado. 2.50
40 RT,V:Kobra 2.50
41 RT,A:Black Racer,
   Red Tornado 2.50
42 RT,A:Phantom Stranger,Red
   Tornado,Black Racer,
   Death from Sandman 2.50
43 RT,V:Nekron. 2.50
44 RT,V:Plastique. 2.50
45 RT,A:The Ghost,I:Ironfire 2.50
46 RT,A:Superman. 2.50
47 RT,A:SupermanV:Ghost 2.50
48 RT,R:Red Tornado 2.50
49 RT,Plastique on trial 2.50
50 RT,V:The Ghost,DoubleSize. . . . 3.00
51 RT 2.50
52 RT,Terror on RTE.91. . . . . . . 2.50
53 RT,A:Aquaman 2.50
54 RT,A:Rasputin,Shadowstorm . . . 2.50
55 RT,Inside Quantum Field 2.50
56 RT,Quantum Field cont. 2.50
57 RT,V:ShadowStorm,
   Quantum.Field. 2.50
Ann.#1 I:Maj.Force. 3.50
Ann.#2 A:RocketRed,Maj.Force. . . . 3.50

CAPTAIN CARROT
1982–83
1 RA,A:Superman,Starro 2.50
2 AA 2.50
3 thru 19 . . . . @2.50
20 A:Changeling. 2.50

CAPTAIN STORM
May-June, 1964
1 IN(c),Killer Hunt 75.00
2 IN(c),First Shot-Last Shot 50.00
3 JKu,Death of a PT Boat. 50.00
4 IN(c),First Command-Last
   Command 50.00
5 IN(c), Killer Torpedo 50.00
6 JKu,IN(c),Medals for an Ocean . 50.00
7 IN(c),A Bullet For The General . 50.00
8 IN(c),Death of A Sub 60.00
9 IN(c),Sink That Flattop. 50.00
10 IN(c),Only The Last Man Lives. 50.00
11 IN(c),Ride a Hot Torpedo 50.00
12 JKu(c),T.N.T. Tea Party Abroad
   PT 47. . . . . 50.00
13 JKu,Yankee Banzai. 50.00
14 RH(c),Sink Capt. Storm 50.00
15 IN(c),My Enemy-My Friend. . . 50.00
16 IN(c),Battle of the Stinging
   Mosquito 50.00
17 IN(c),First Shot for a
   Dead Man 50.00
18 March-April, 1967 . . . . 50.00

CARTOON CARTOONS
Jan., 2001
1 thru 33 From TV shows . . . . . @2.25
TPB Vol. 1 Name That Toon 7.00
TPB Vol. 2 The Gang's All Here . . . 7.00

CARTOON NETWORK BLOCK PARTY
Sept. 2004
1 thru 2 . . . . @2.25
Spec. Jam-Packed Action 8.00

CARTOON NETWORK PRESENTS
Warner Bros./DC June, 1997
1 Dexter's Laboratory 4.50
2 thru 24 from TV shows. . . . . . @2.50

CARTOON NETWORK STARRING
Warner Bros./DC, 1999
1 F:Powerpuff Girls 4.00
2 thru 18 From TV shows . . . . . @2.50

Catwoman #9 © DC Comics, Inc.

CATWOMAN
[Limited Series], 1989
1 O:Catwoman 11.00
2 Catwoman'sSister kidnapped . . 10.00
3 Battle 9.00
4 Final,V:Batman 9.00

[Regular Series], 1993
0 JBa,O:Catwoman. 3.50
1 B:JDy(s),JBa,DG,A:Bane 5.00
2 JBa,DG,A:Bane 3.50
3 JBa,DG,at Santa Prisca 3.50
4 JBa,DG,Bane's Secret 3.00
5 JBa,V:Ninjas 3.00
6 JBa,A:Batman 3.00
7 JBa,A:Batman 3.00
8 JBa,V:Zephyr 3.00
9 JBa,V:Zephyr 3.00
10 JBa,V:Arms Dealer 3.00
11 JBa 3.00
12 JBa,Knights End #6,A:Batman . 5.00
13 JBa,Knights End,Aftermath#2. . 3.00
14 JBa,Zero Hour 3.00
15 JBa,new path 3.00
16 JBa,Island forterss 3.00
17 . . . . 3.00
18 . . . . 3.00
19 Amazonia 3.00
20 Hollywood 3.00
21 JBa(c&a)V:Movie Monster
   [new Miraweb format begins] . . 2.50
22 JBa(c&a) Family Ties,pt.1. . . . . 2.50
23 Family Ties,pt.2. . . . . 2.50
24 . . . . 2.50

25 A:Robin,Psyba-Rats 3.00
26 AIG,JBa,The Secret of the
   Universe,pt.2 (of 3) 2.50
27 CDi,Underworld Unleashed tie-in 2.50
28 CDi,Catwoman enlists help. 2.50
29 CDi,A:Penguin 2.50
30 . . . . 2.50
31 . . . . 3.00
32 CDi,JBa,Contagion,pt.9 . . . . . . 3.00
33 CDi,JBa,Hellhound,pt.1. . . . . . . 2.50
34 CDi,JBa,Hellbound,pt.2 (of 3). . . 2.50
35 CDi,JBa. 2.75
36 CDi,JBa, Legacy, pt.2 x-over . . . 3.00
37 CDi,JBa, Panara, the Leopard
   Woman 2.50
38 DgM(s),JBa,MPn,Catwoman,
   Year One,pt.1 (of 3) 2.50
39 DgM(s),JBa,MPn,Catwoman,
   Year One,pt. 2 . . . . 2.50
40 DgM(s),JBa,MPn,Catwoman,
   Year One, pt. 3 . . . . 2.50
41 DgM(s),JBa,I:MorelandMcShane 2.50
42 DgM(s),JBa,RedFangClaw,pt.1 . 2.50
43 DgM(s),JBa,RedFangClaw,pt.2 . 2.50
44 DgM(s),JBa,Red FangClaw,pt.3 . 2.50
45 DgM(s),JBa,Nine Deaths of
   the Cat. 2.50
46 DgM(s),JBa,F:Two Face,pt.1 . . . 2.50
47 DgM(s),JBa,F:Two Face,pt.2 . . . 2.50
48 DgM(s),JBa,V:Morella,pt.1 . . . . . 2.50
49 DgM(s),JBa,V:Morella,pt. 2. . . . . 2.50
50 DgM(s),JBa,V:Cybercat 3.00
50a metallic cover, collectors ed. . . . 3.00
51 DgM(s),JBa,F:Huntress,pt.1 . . . 2.50
52 DgM(s),JBa,F:Huntress,pt.2 . . . . 2.50
53 DgM(s),JBa,F:identity learned . . 2.50
54 JBa,improving security 2.50
55 JBa, ... 2.50
56 JBa,Cataclysm x-over,pt.6 . . . . 4.00
57 JBa,Cataclysm, V:Poison Ivy . . . 3.00
58 JBa,F:Scarecrow, pt.1. . . . . 2.50
59 JBa,F:Scarecrow, pt.2. . . . . 2.50
60 JBa,F:Scarecrow, pt.3. . . . . 2.50
61 JBa,Bank robbery 2.50
62 JBa,A:Nemesis 2.50
63 JBa,A:Batman & Joker, pt.1 . . . . 2.50
64 JBa,A:Batman & Joker, pt.2 . . . . 2.50
65 JBa,A:Batman & Joker, pt.3 . . . . 2.50
66 JBa,I'll Take Manhattan,pt.1 . . . . 2.50
67 JBa,I'll Take Manhattan,pt.2 . . . . 2.50
68 JBa,I'll Take Manhattan,pt.3 . . . . 2.50
69 JBa,I'll Take Manhattan,pt.4 . . . . 2.50
70 JBa,I'll Take Manhattan,pt.5 . . . . 2.50
71 JBa,I'll Take Manhattan,pt.6 . . . . 2.50
72 JOs(s),JBa,A:Batman 2.50
73 JOs(s),JBa,No Man's Land. 2.50
74 JOs(s),JBa,No Man's Land. 2.50
75 JOs(s),JBa,No Man's Land. 2.50
76 JOs(s),JBa,No Man's Land. 2.50
77 JOs(s),JBa,No Man's Land. 2.50
78 . . . . 2.50
79 A:Batman 2.50
80 going to jail 2.50
81 solitary confinement 2.50
82 payback time. 2.50
83 A:Batman,CommissionerGordon 2.25
84 F:Harley Quinn 2.25
85 anger & revenge 2.25
86 V:Banner. 2.25
87 NSH, from Catwoman's past . . . 2.25
88 V:Banner. 2.25
89 This issue: Batman dies! 2.25
90 Officer Down x-over,pt.4 . . . . . . 2.25
91 Second Catwoman 2.25
92 JFM(s), V:Scarecrow,pt.1 . . . . . 2.25
93 JFM(s),V:Scarecrow,pt.2 . . . . . . 2.25
94 JFM(s), final issue. 2.25
Ann.#1 Elseworlds Story,A:Ra's Al
   Ghul. 3.50
Ann.#2 JBa(c&a) Year One Annuals,
   Young Selina Kyle 4.50

Ann.#3 Legends of the Dead Earth . 4.00
Ann.#4 Pulp Heroes (Macabre) . . . 4.50
Spec. Catwoman Defiant,TGr,DG,
    V:Mr.Handsome. 6.00
Spec. Catwoman Plus, LKa,AWi,
    ALa, F:Screamqueen (1997). . . 3.00
Spec.#1,000,000 JBa, on prison
    planet of Pluto 2.00
TPB The Catfile, rep.#15–#19 . . . . 10.00

CATWOMAN
Nov., 2001
1 MiA,R:Selina Kyle 7.00
2 MiA,serial murders. 4.00
3 MiA,Selina undercover. 3.00
4 MiA,V:Serial killer. 3.00
5 Selina & Holly 2.50
6 F:Holly 2.50
7 Holly in danger. 2.50
8 RBr,East End's Crooked Cops . . 2.50
9 RBr,Disguises 2.50
10 RBr,Death's Row killer 2.50
11 F:Slam Bradley 2.50
12 F:Slam Bradley, Bruce Wayne . . 2.50
13 F:Slam Bradley, Holly 2.50
14 Holly 2.50
15 V:Black Mask 2.50
16 V:Black Mask 2.50
17 No Easy Way Down,pt.1 . . . . 2.50
18 No Easy Way Down,pt.2. . . . . . . 2.50
19 No Easy Way Down,pt.3. . . . . . . 2.50
20 A: Wildcat 2.50
21 V:Captain Cold 2.50
22 V:Captain Cold 2.50
23 Opal City 2.50
24 Wild Ride, concl. 2.50
25 JP,PG,back to Gotham 2.50
26 JP,PG,kidnapping 2.50
27 JP,PG,F:Batman 2.50
28 JP,PG,V:Penguin 2.50
29 JP,PG 2.50
30 JP,PG,V:Zeiss 2.50
31 JP,PG,Selina Kyle missing 2.50
32 SeP,East End 2.50
33 PG,JP,V:Galante 2.50
34 War Games,Act 1,pt.7,PG,JP . . . 2.50
35 War Games,Act 2,pt.7,PG,JP . . . 2.50
36 War Games,Act 3,pt.7,PG,JP . . . 2.50
TPB The Dark End of the Street . . 13.00
TPB Crooked Little Town 15.00
TPB Selina's Big Score 18.00
TPB Movie & Other Cat Tales 10.00
TPB 9 Lives of Feline Fatale 15.00
TPB The Dark End of the Street . . 15.00
GN Catwoman: The Movie 5.00
Spec. Secret Files #1. . . . . 5.00

CATWOMAN: GUARDIAN OF GOTHAM
1999
1 (of 2) Elseworlds,V:Bat-Man 6.00
2 DgM,JBa 6.00

CATWOMAN: WHEN IN ROME
Sept. 2004
1 (of 6) JLb(s),TSe 3.50
2 JLb(s),TSe 3.50

CATWOMAN/WILDCAT
June, 1998
1 (of 4) CDi,TP,SCi,BSf,
    V:Claw Hammer 3.00
2 CDi,BSt,TP,SCi,BSf 3.00
3 CDi,BSt,TP,SCi,BSf, ... 3.00
4 CDi,BSt,TP,SCi,BSf 3.00

CENTURIONS
June, 1987
1 DH,V:Doc Terror. 2.50
2 DH,O:Centurions 2.50
3 DH,V:Doc Terror. 2.50
4 DH,Sept., 1987 . . . . 2.50

Chain Gang War #1 © DC Comics Inc.

CHAIN GANG WAR
1993–94
1 I:Chain Gang 3.00
2 V:8-Ball 2.50
3 C:Deathstroke 2.50
4 C:Deathstroke 2.50
5 Embossed(c),A:Deathstroke . . . 3.00
6 A:Deathstroke,Batman. 2.50
7 V:Crooked Man 2.50
8 B:Crooked Man 2.50
9 V:Crooked Man 2.50
10 A:Deathstroke,C:Batman 2.50
11 A:Batman. 2.50
12 E:Crooked Man,D:Chain Gang,
    Final Issue. 2.50

CHALLENGERS OF THE UNKNOWN
1958–78
1 JK&JK(c),The Man Who
    Tampered With Infinity 3,800.00
2 JK&JK(c),The Monster
    Maker 1,200.00
3 JK&JK(c),The Secret of the
    Sorcerer's Mirror. 1,000.00
4 JK,WW,JK(c),The Wizard of
    Time 750.00
5 JK,WW&JK(c),The Riddle of
    the Star-Stone 750.00
6 JK,WW,JK(c),Captives of
    the Space Circus 750.00
7 JK,WW,JK(c),The Isle of
    No Return. 750.00
8 JK,WW,JK&WW(c),The
    Prisoners of the Robot Planet 750.00
9 The Plot To Destroy Earth 450.00
10 The Four Faces of Doom 450.00
11 The Creatures From The
    Forbidden World 275.00
12 The Three Clues To Sorcery. . 275.00
13 The Prisoner of the
    Tiny Space Ball 275.00
14 O: Multi Man 275.00

15 Lady Giant and the Beast. . . . 275.00
16 Prisoners of the Mirage World 200.00
17 The Secret of the
    Space Capsules. 200.00
18 Menace of Mystery Island. . . . 200.00
19 The Alien Who Stole a Planet. 200.00
20 Multi-Man Strikes Back 200.00
21 Weird World That Didn't Exist. 200.00
22 The Thing In
    Challenger Mountain. 200.00
23 The Island In The Sky. 100.00
24 The Challengers Die At Dawn 100.00
25 Captives of the Alien Hunter. . 100.00
26 Death Crowns The
    Challenge King 100.00
27 Master of the Volcano Men. . . 100.00
28 The Riddle of the
    Faceless Man 100.00
29 Four Roads to Doomsday. . . . 100.00
30 Multi-Man...Villain Turned
    Hero. 100.00
31 O:Challengers. 125.00
32 One Challenger Must Die 60.00
33 Challengers Meet Their Master 60.00
34 Beachhead, USA 60.00
35 War Against The Moon Beast. . 60.00
36 Giant In Challenger Mountain. . 60.00
37 Triple Terror of Mr. Dimension . 60.00
38 Menace the Challengers Made. 60.00
39 Phantom of the Fair 60.00
40 Super-Powers of the
    Challengers 60.00
41 The Challenger Who Quit. 50.00
42 The League of
    Challenger-Haters 50.00
43 New look begins 50.00
44 The Curse of the Evil Eye. 50.00
45 Queen of the
    Challenger-Haters 50.00
46 Strange Schemes of the
    Gargoyle 50.00
47 The Sinister Sponge 50.00
48 A:Doom Patrol. 50.00
49 Tyrant Who Owned the World . 50.00
50 Final Hours for the
    Challengers 50.00
51 A:Sea Devil 50.00
52 Two Are Dead - Two To Go. . . . 50.00
53 Who is the Traitor Among Us? . 50.00
54 War of the Sub-Humans 50.00
55 D:Red Ryan 50.00
56 License To Kill. 50.00
57 Kook And The Kilowatt Killer . . 50.00
58 Live Till Tomorrow. 50.00

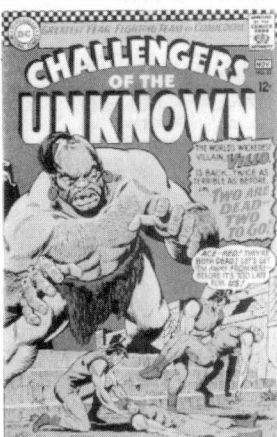

*Challengers of the Unknown #52
© DC Comics Inc.*

59 Seekeenakee - The Petrified
   Giant 50.00
60 R:Red Ryan 50.00
61 Robot Hounds of Chang 50.00
62 Legion of the Weird 50.00
63 None Shall Escape the
   Walking Evil 50.00
64 JKu(c),Invitation to a Hanging . 50.00
65 The Devil's Circus 28.00
66 JKu(c),Rendezvous With
   Revenge 28.00
67 NA(c),The Dream Killers 28.00
68 NA(c),One of Us is a Madman . 28.00
69 JKu(c),I:Corinna 28.00
70 NA(c),Scream of Yesterdays . . . 28.00
71 NC(c),When Evil Calls 28.00
72 NA(c),A Plague of Darkness . . . 28.00
73 NC(c),Curse of the Killer
   Time Forgot 28.00
74 GT&NA(c),A:Deadman 50.00
75 JK(c),Ultivac Is Loose 20.00
76 JKu(c),The Traitorous
   Challenger 20.00
77 JK(c),Menace of the
   Ancient Vials 20.00
78 JK(c),The Island of No Return . 20.00
79 JKu(c),The Monster Maker 20.00
80 NC(c),The Day The Earth
   Blew Up 20.00
81 MN&NA(c),Multi-Man's
   Master Plan 12.00
82 MN&NA(c),Swamp Thing 12.00
83 Seven Doorways to Destiny . . . 12.00
84 To Save A Monster 12.00
85 The Creature From The End
   Of Time 12.00
86 The War At Time's End 12.00
87 final issue, July, 1978 . . . . 12.00

CHALLENGERS OF
THE UNKNOWN
[Mini-Series], 1991

1 BB(c) In The Spotlight 2.50
2 thru 8 . . . . @2.50

CHALLENGERS OF
THE UNKNOWN
1997

1 StG(s),JPL 3.00
2 StG(s),LKa,JPL,SMa,Zombies . . . 2.50
3 StG(s),JPL,death of Challenger . . 2.50
4 StG&LKa(s),JPL,SMa,
   O:Challengers 2.50
5 StG&LKa(s)JPL,SMa, V:The
   Fearslayer 2.50
6 StG(s),JPL,SMa,Convergence
   pt. 3 x-over 2.50
7 StG(s),JPL,PastPerfect,pt.1 . . . . . 2.50
8 StG(s),JPL,PastPerfect,pt.2 . . . . . 2.50
9 StG(s),JPL,PastPerfect,pt.3 . . . . . 2.50
10 StG(s),JIT,F:Brenda Ruskin 2.50
11 StG(s),JPL,in Gothan, pt.1 . . . . . 2.50
12 StG(s),JPL,in Gothan, pt.2 . . . . . 2.50
13 StG(s),F:Marlon Corbett 2.50
14 . . . . 2.50
15 StG(s),JPL,Millennium Giants
   pt. 3, x-over 2.75
16 StG(s),JPL,MZ, original Chalis . . 2.75
17 StG(s),JPL,disappearances 2.75
18 StG(s),DRo,MZ, final issue 2.75

CHALLENGERS OF
THE UNKNOWN
June 2004

1 (of 6) HC 3.00
2 thru 5 HC . . . . @3.00
TPB Challengers Must Die 20.00

CHASE
Dec., 1997

1 JWi,MGy,from Batman #550 . . . . 2.50
2 JWi,MGy 2.50
3 JWi,MGy,Rocket Reds 2.50
4 JWi,MGy,F:Teen Titans 2.50
5 JWi,MGy,flashback story 2.50
6 JWi,MGy,Chase's past 2.50
7 JWi,Shadowing the Bat,pt.1 . . . . 2.50
8 JWi,Shadowing the Bat,pt.2 . . . . 2.50
9 JWi,MBr,MGy,A:Green Lantern . . 2.50
Spec.#1,000,000 Final Issue 2.50

CHECKMATE
April, 1988

1 From Vigilante & Action Comics . 3.00
2 Chicago Bombings cont. 2.50
3 V:Terrorist Right 2.50
4 V:Crime Lords Abroad,B.U.Story
   `Training of a Knight' begins . . . 2.50
5 Renegade nation of Quarac 2.50
6 Secret Arms Deal 2.50
7 Checkmate Invades Quarac 2.50
8 Consequences-Quarac Invasion . 2.50
9 Checkmate's security in doubt . . . 2.50
10 V:Counterfeiting Ring 2.50
11 Invasion X-over 2.50
12 Invasion Aftermath extra 2.50
13 CommanderH.Stein's vacation . . 2.50
14 R:Blackthorn 2.50
15 Janus Directive #1 . . . . 2.50
16 Janus Directive #3 . . . . 2.50
17 Janus Directive #6 . . . . 2.50
18 Janus Directive #9 . . . . 2.50
19 Reorganization of Group 2.50
20 Shadow of Bishop
   A:Peacemaker,pt.1 . . . . 2.50
21 Peacemaker behind Iron
   Curtain,pt.2 . . . . 2.50
22 Mystery of Bishop Cont.,pt.3 . . . 2.50
23 European Scientists
   Suicides,pt.4 . . . . 2.50
24 Bishop Mystery cont.,pt.5 . . . . . . 2.50
25 Bishop's Identity Revealed 2.50
26 Mazarin kidnaps H.Stein's kids . . 2.50
27 Stein rescue attempt,I:Cypher . . 2.50
28 A:Cypher, Bishop-Robots 2.50
29 A:Cypher,Blackthorn 2.50
30 Irish Knight W.O'Donnell/British
   Knight L.Hawkins team-up 2.50
31 thru 32 . . . . @2.50

CHIAROSCURO: THE
PRIVATE LIVES OF
LEONARDO DaVINCI
DC/Vertigo, 1995–96

1 Biographical, Adult 2.50
2 Two of Da Vinci Sisters 2.50
3 . . . . 2.50
4 thru 10 . . . . @3.00

CHILDREN'S CRUSADE
DC/Vertigo, 1993–94

1 NGa(s),CBa,MkB(i),F:Rowland,
   Payne (From Sandman) 4.75
2 NGa(s),AaK(s),JaD(s),PSj,A:Tim
   Hunter,Suzy,Maxine,final issue . 4.50

CHRISTMAS WITH
THE SUPER-HEROES
1988–89

1 JBy(c) 5.00
2 PC,GM,JBy,NKu,DG A:Batman
   Superman,Deadman,(last
   Supergirl appearance) 4.00

Chronos #1 © DC Comics, Inc.

CHRONOS
Jan., 1998

1 JFM,PGn,SL,Time Travel 2.50
2 JFM,PGn,SL 2.50
3 JFM,PGn,SL, in 1873 . . . . 2.50
4 JFM,PGn,SL,in Chronopolis 2.50
5 JFM,PGn,DHz,SL,WalkerGabriel . 2.50
6 JFM,PGn,Tattooed man 2.50
7 JFM,PGn,DRo,SL,Star City 2.50
8 JFM,PGn,DRo,SL,
   V:Metrognomes 2.50
9 JFM(s),PGn,SL, The Man
   Who Chose Not to Exist 2.50
10 JFM(s),PGn,SL,Forever Engin . . 2.50
11 JFM(s),PGn,SL final issue 2.50
Spec.#1,000,000 JFM(s) Steals
   time gauntlets 2.50

CINDER & ASHE
March, 1988

1 JL,I:Cinder & Ashe 2.50
2 JL,Viet Nam Flashbacks 2.50
3 JL,Truth About Lacey revealed . . 2.50
4 JL,final issue, June, 1988 . . . . . . 2.50

CINNAMON: EL CICLO
Aug. 2003

1 (of 5) RbC, New West 2.50
2 thru 5 RbC,HC(c) . . . . @2.50

CLASH
1991

1 AKu,I:Joe McLash(b/w) 5.00
2 AKu,Panja-Rise to Power 5.00
3 AKu,V:Archons,conclusion 5.00

CLAW THE
UNCONQUERED
May-June, 1975

1 . . . . 15.00
2 . . . . 8.00
3 Nudity panel 10.00
4 . . . . 8.00
5 . . . . 8.00
6 . . . . 8.00
7 . . . . 8.00
8 KG 8.00
9 KG/BL,Origin 8.00
10 KG 8.00
11 KG 8.00
12 KG/BL,Aug.–Sept., 1978 . . . . . . 8.00

COMET, THE
Impact, 1991–92
1 TL,I&O:Comet I:Applejack, Victoria
  Johnson, Ben Lee 3.00
2 TL,A:Applejack,Lance Perry 2.50
3 TL,V:Anti-nuclear terrorists 2.50
4 TL,I&V:Black Hood,I:Inferno 2.50
5 V:Cyborg Soldier 2.50
6 TL,I:The Hangman. 2.50
7 Press Problems 2.50
8 TL,Comet ID discovered 2.50
9 TL,Bad Judgment 2.50
10 Fly/Comet T.U.,V:Dolphus. 2.50
11 V:Inferno 2.50
12 V:Inferno 2.50
13 O:Comet's Powers 2.50
14 O:Comet's Powers Pt.2 . . . . 2.50
15 Rob finds his mother. 2.50
16 V:Aliens. 2.50
17 Shocking Truth 2.50
18 Last Issue 2.50
Ann.#1 Earthquest,w/trading card . . 2.50

CODENAME: KNOCKOUT
DC/Vertigo, April, 2001
0 sexy spy thriller satire 3.00
1 MFm,JCh,Devil You Say,pt.1 . . . . 3.00
1a variant JCh(c) (1:2) 3.00
2 MFm,JCh,Devil You Say,pt.2 . . . . 2.50
3 MFm,Little Orphan Angela. 2.50
4 MFm,St. Grace Under Fire 2.50
5 MFm,Arms & Legs for Hostages . 2.50
6 MFm,Arms & Legs for Hostages . 2.50
7 MFm,Go-Go-A-Go-Go 2.50
8 MFm,A is for Anarchy 2.50
9 JP,ACo,Enigma Variations 2.50
10 Undressed to Kill,pt.1 . . . . 2.50
11 Undressed to Kill,pt.2 . . . . 2.50
12 Undressed to Kill,pt.3 . . . . 2.50
13 Fleshback 1932:Roma 2.50
14a JP,JLe(c) 2.50
14b variant JSC(c) 2.50
15 EBe,F:Whole cast. 2.50
16 EBe,Amok in America,pt.1 . . . . . 2.75
17 EBe,Amok in America,pt.2 . . . . . 2.75
18 EBe,Amok in America,pt.3 . . . . . 2.75
19 Fleshback '69 . . . . 2.75
20 Rebel Yell 2.75
21 Secrets & Thighs,pt.1 . . . . 2.75
22 Secrets & Thighs,pt.2 . . . . 2.75
23 final issue 2.75

COMIC CAVALCADE
1942–43
1 Green Lantern, Flash,
  Wildcat, Wonder Woman,
  Black Pirate 14,000.00
2 ShM,B:Mutt & Jeff. 3,200.00
3 ShM,B:HotHarrigan,Sorcerer 2,200.00
4 Gay Ghost, A:Scribby,
  A:Red Tornado 2,000.00
5 Gr.Lantern,Flash,W.Woman . 1,900.00
6 Flash,W.Woman,Gr.Lantern . 1,500.00
7 A:Red Tornado, E:Scribby . . 1,500.00
8 Flash,W.Woman,Gr.Lantern . 1,500.00
9 Flash,W.Woman,Gr.Lantern . 1,500.00
10 Flash,W.Woman,Gr.Lantern . 1,500.00
11 Flash,W.Woman,Gr.Lantern . 1,300.00
12 E:Red, White & Blue 1,300.00
13 A:Solomon Grundy. 2,000.00
14 Flash,W.Woman,Gr.Lantern . 1,300.00
15 B:Johnny Peril 1,400.00
16 Flash,W.Woman,Gr.Lantern . 1,200.00
17 Flash,W.Woman,Gr.Lantern . 1,200.00
18 Flash,W.Woman,Gr.Lantern . 1,200.00
19 Flash,W.Woman,Gr.Lantern . 1,200.00
20 Flash,W.Woman,Gr.Lantern . 1,200.00
21 Flash,W.Woman,Gr.Lantern . 1,200.00
22 A:Atom 1,200.00

Comic Cavalcade #6
© DC Comics Inc.

23 A:Atom 1,200.00
24 A:Solomon Grundy. 1,500.00
25 A:Black Canary 1,000.00
26 ATh, E:Mutt & Jeff 1,000.00
27 ATh,ATh(c) 1,000.00
28 ATh E:Flash, Wonder Woman
  Green Lantern 1,000.00
29 E:Johnny Peril 1,200.00
30 RG,B:Fox & Crow 500.00
31 thru 39 RG . . . . @300.00
40 RG,ShM. 200.00
41 thru 49 RG,ShM . . . . @175.00
50 thru 62 RG,ShM . . . . @225.00
63 RG,ShM, July, 1954 . . . . 400.00

CONGO BILL
1954–56
1 . . . . 2,000.00
2 thru 7 . . . . @1,500.00

CONGO BILL
DC/Vertigo, 1999
1 (of 4) RCo(c) 3.00
2 thru 4 . . . . @3.00

CONGORILLA
1992–93
1 R:Congo Bill. 2.50
2 thru 4 BB(c),V:Congo Bill. . . . . @2.50

CONJURORS
1999
1 (of 3) CDi(s),EB, Elseworlds 3.00
2 thru 3 CDi(s),EB. . . . . @3.00

CONQUEROR OF
THE BARREN EARTH
1985
1 thru 4 . . . . @3.00

COOL WORLD
1992
1 Prequel to Movie 2.25
2 Movie Adapt. 2.25
3 Movie Adapt. 2.25
4 . . . . 2.25

COPS
1988–89
1 PB,O:Cops,double-size 3.50

2 PB,V:Big Boss 2.50
3 PB,RT,V:Dr.Bad Vibes 2.50
4 BS,A:Sheriff Sundown 2.50
5 PB,Blitz the Robo-Dog. 2.50
6 PB,A:Ms.Demeaner 2.50
7 PB,A:Tramplor 2.50
8 PB,V:BigBoss & Ally 2.50
9 PB,Cops Trapped 2.50
10 PB,Dr.Bad Vibes becomes
  Dr.Goodvibes. 2.50
11 PB,V:Big Boss. 2.50
12 PB,V:Dr.Badvibe's T.H.U.G.S . . . 2.50
13 Berserko/Ms.Demeanor
  marriage proposal 2.50
14 A:Buttons McBoom-Boom. 2.50
15 Cops vs. Crooks, final issue 2.50

COSMIC BOY
Dec., 1986
1 KG,EC,Legends tie-in 2.50
2 KG,EC,Is History Destiny. 2.50
3 KG,EC,Past,Present,Future. 2.50
4 KG,EC,Legends 2.50

COSMIC ODYSSEY
1988
1 MMi,A:Superman,Batman,John
  Stewart,Starfire,J'onn J'onzz,
  NewGods,Demon,JSn story . . . 6.00
2 MMi,Disaster'(low dist) 6.00
3 MMi,Return to New Genesis 6.00
4 MMi,A:Dr.Fate, final. 6.00
TPB Cosmic Odyssey (2003) 20.00

Creature Commandos #5
© DC Comics Inc.

CREATURE COMMANDOS
March, 2000
1 (of 8) TT,SEa, ... 2.50
2 TT,SEa,V:Saturna 2.50
3 TT,SEa, ... 2.50
4 TT,SEa, ... 2.50
5 TT,SEa,F:Claw. 2.50
6 TT,SEa,V:Saturna 2.50
7 TT,SEa,V:Claw. 2.50
8 TT,SEa,War Movie, concl. 2.50

CREEPER, THE
Oct., 1997
1 LKa,SMa,SB,R:Creeper. 3.00
2 LKa,SMa,SB,A:Dr. Skolos 3.00
3 LKa,SMa,SB,V:Proteus 3.00

4 LKa,SMa,SB 3.00
5 LKa,SMa,SB, new job 3.00
6 LKa,SMa,SB, strange meals 3.00
7 LKa,SMa,SB,F:Joker, pt.1 . . . . . . 3.00
8 LKa,SMa,SB,F:Joker, pt.2 . . . . . . 3.00
9 DAn,ALa,All-star issue 3.00
10 LKa,SB,Jack Ryder 3.00
11 LKa,SB,SMa,Creeper splits
    again 3.00
Spec.#1,000,000 LKa,SB,final issue 3.00

CRIMSON AVENGER
1988
1 Mini-series 2.50
2 V:Black Cross 2.50
3 V:Killers of the Dark Cross 2.50
4 V:Dark Cross,final issue 2.50

CRISIS ON
INFINITE EARTHS
April, 1985
1 B:MWn(s),GP,DG,I:Pariah,I&O:Alex
    Luthor,D:Crime Syndicate 18.00
2 GP,DG,V:Psycho Pirate,
    A:Joker,Batman 12.00
3 GP,DG,D:Losers 10.00
4 GP,D:Monitor,I:2nd Dr.Light 10.00
5 GP,JOy,I:Anti-Monitor 10.00
6 GP,JOy,I:2nd Wildcat,A:Fawcett,
    Quality & Charlton heroes 10.00
7 GP,JOy,DG,D:Supergirl 25.00
8 GP,JOy,D:1st Flash 22.00
9 GP,JOy,D:Aquagirl 10.00
10 GP,JOy,D:Psimon,A:Spectre . . . 10.00
11 GP,JOy,D:Angle Man 12.00
12 E:MWn(s),GP,JOy,D:Huntress,Kole,
    Kid Flash becomes 2nd Flash,
    D:Earth 2 . . . . 15.00
TPB MWn,GP,DG,JOy,(2001) 30.00

CRISIS ON MULTIPLE
EARTHS
July, 2002
TPB Justice League rep. 15.00
TPB Vol. 2 . . . . 15.00
TPB Vol. 3 . . . . 15.00

CRUCIBLE
Impact, 1993
1 JQ,F:The Comet 2.50
2 JQ,A:Black Hood,Comet 2.50

Crucible #4 © DC Comics, Inc.

3 JQ,Comet Vs.Black Hood 2.50
4 JQ,V:Tomorrow Men 2.50
5 JQ,Black Hod vs Shield 2.50
6 JQ,V:The Crucible 2.50

CRUEL AND UNUSUAL
DC/Vertigo, 1999
1 (of 4) JaD&TPe(s),JMC,satire . . . 3.00
2 thru 4 JaD&TPe(s),JMC . . . . . . @3.00

CRUSADERS
Impact, May, 1992
1 DJu(c),I:Crusaders,inc Trading
    cards 2.50
2 V:Kalathar 2.50
3 V:Kalathar 2.50
4 Crusaders form as group 2.50
5 V:Cyber-Punks 2.50
6 V:Cyborg Villains 2.50
7 Woj,Low,F:Fireball 2.50
8 Last Issue 2.50

CRUSADES, THE
DC/Vertigo, March, 2001
1 KJo,F:Venus 5.00
2 KJo,V:Dark Ages Knight 3.50
3 KJo,MBu,in San Francisco 3.50
4 KJo,MBu,Anton Marx 3.00
5 KJo,Marx eats crow 3.00
6 KJo,second Crusade 3.00
7 KJo,V:The Knight 3.00
8 KJo,Knight's lair 3.00
9 KJo,Godfrey 3.00
10 KJo,sex, sin, subjugation 3.00
11 KJo,origin of the Knight? 3.00
12 KJo,Knight's hidden enclave. . . . 3.00
13 KJo,Third Crusade begins 3.00
14 KJo,Ash Wednesday Killer 3.00
15 KJo,Ash Wednesday Killer 3.00
16 KJo,Ash Wednesday Killings . . . 3.00
17 KJo,Venus Kostopikas 3.00
18 KJo,Shockjock Anton 3.00
19 KJo,back to Medieval times 3.00
20 KJo,final issue 3.00
Spec. Urban Decree, KJo,48-page . 3.95

CYBERELLA
DC/Helix, Sept., 1996
1 HC(s),DCn, ... 2.25
2 HC(s),DCn,Secret history
    revealed 2.25
3 HC(s),DCn,Sunny goes on
    rampage 2.25
4 HC(s),DCn,Attack on MacroCorp 2.25
5 HC(s),DCn,V:Army of
    Necronauts 2.25
6 HC(s),DCn, ... 2.25
7 HC(s),DCn,Trip to Hell 2.25
8 HC(s),DCn,V:BTIII, concl. 2.50
9 DCn, The Informers 2.25
10 HC(s),DCn,Wuvzums,pt.1 . . . . . 2.25
11 HC(s),DCn,Wuvzums,pt.2 . . . . . 2.25
12 HC(s),final issue 2.50

DALE EVANS COMICS
1948–52
1 Ph(c),ATh,B:Sierra Smith . . . 1,400.00
2 Ph(c),ATh 650.00
3 ATh 400.00
4 thru 11 . . . . @350.00
12 thru 20 . . . . @200.00
21 thru 24 . . . . @225.00

DAMAGE
1994–96
1 I:Damage,V:Metallo 4.00
2 V:Symbolix 3.00

Damage #6
© DC Comics, Inc.

3 V:Troll 3.00
4 V:Troll 3.00
5 A:New Titans,V:Baron 3.00
6 Zero Hour,A:New Titans 3.00
7 Trial 3.00
8 Fragments,pt.1 . . . . 3.00
9 Fragments,pt.2 . . . . 3.00
10 Fragments,pt.3 . . . . 3.00
11 Fragments,pt.4 . . . . 3.00
12 Fragments,pt.5 . . . . 3.00
13 Picking Up The Pieces,pt.1 . . . . 3.00
14 Picking Up The Pieces,pt.2
    A:The Ray 3.00
15 Picking Up the Pieces,pt.3 . . . . . 3.00
16 . . . . 3.00
17 V:Bounty 3.00
18 Underworld Unleashed tie-in . . . 3.00
19 Underworld Unleashed tie-in . . . 3.00
20 final issue 3.00

DANGER TRAIL
July-Aug., 1950
1 CI,Ath,I:King For A Day 1,700.00
2 ATh 1,200.00
3 ATh 1,400.00
4 ATh 900.00
5 March-April, 1951 . . . . 900.00

DANGER TRAIL
[Mini-Series], 1993
1 thru 4 CI,FMc,F:King Faraday
    V:Cobra 2.25

DARK MANSION OF
FORBIDDEN LOVE, THE
Sept.–Oct., 1971
1 . . . . 250.00
2 and 4 March-April, 1972 . . . @100.00

DARKSEID VS.
GALACTUS THE HUNGER
1995
1-shot Orion vs. Silver Surfer 5.00
GN JBy,in Apokolips 6.00

DARKSTARS
1992–96
0 History 2.00
1 TC(c),LSn,I:Darkstars 3.50

DC COMICS

2 TC(c),LSn,F:Ferin Colos 2.50
3 LSn,J:Mo,Flint,V:Evil Star 2.50
4 TC,V:Evilstar 3.00
5 TC,A:Hawkman,Hawkwoman . . . 3.00
6 TC,A:Hawkman 2.50
7 TC,V:K'llash 2.50
8 F:Ferris Colos 2.50
9 Colos vs K'lassh 2.50
10 V:Con Artists 2.50
11 TC,Trinity#4,A:Green Lantern,
    L.E.G.I.O.N. 2.50
12 TC(c),Trinity#7,A:Green Lantern,
    L.E.G.I.O.N. 2.50
13 TC(c),V:Alien Underworld 2.50
14 I:Annihilator 2.50
15 V:Annihilator 2.50
16 V:Annihilator 2.50
17 Murders 2.50
18 B:Eve of Destruction 2.50
19 A:Flash 2.50
20 E:Eve of Destruction 2.50
21 A:John Stewart,Donna Troy 2.50
22 A:Controllers 2.50
23 Donna Troy is new Darkstar 2.50
24 Zero Hour,V:HalJordan,Entropy . 2.50
25 Stewart 2.50
26 Alien criminals 2.50
27 and 28 . . . . @2.50
29 V:Alien Syndicate 2.50
30 A:Green Lantern 2.50
31 V:Darkseid 2.50
32 Crimelord/Syndicate War,pt.3,
    A:New Titans,Supergirl,
    Deathstroke 2.50
33 V:Jeddigan 2.50
34 . . . . 2.50
35 A:Flash 2.50
36 MkF,MC,A:Flash 2.50
37 MkF,MC,Colos vs. Warrior 2.50
38 final issue 2.50

DAY OF JUDGMENT
Sept., 1999
1 (of 5) Spectre x-over 4.00
2 F:Wonder Woman, Supergirl 3.00
3 F:Superman & Green Lantern . . . 3.00
4 F:Superman's team 3.00
5 conclusion 3.00
Spec. Secret Files #1 . . . . 5.00

DC CHALLENGE
Nov., 1985
1 GC,Batman 3.00
2 Superman 2.50
3 CI,Adam Strange 2.50
4 GK/KJ,Aquaman 2.50
5 DGb,Dr.Fate,Capt.Marvel 2.50
6 Dr. 13 . . . . 2.50
7 Gorilla Grodd 2.50
8 DG,Outsiders, New Gods 2.50
9 New Teen Titans,JLA 2.50
10 CS,New Teen Titans,JLA 2.50
11 KG,Outsiders 2.50
12 DCw,TMd,DSp,New Teen Titans,
    Oct., 1986 . . . . 2.50

DC COMICS PRESENTS
July-Aug., 1978
[all have Superman]
1 JL,DA,F:Flash 25.00
2 JL,DA,F:Flash 16.00
3 JL,F:Adam Strange 16.00
4 JL,F:Metal Men,A:Mr.IQ 16.00
5 MA,F:Aquaman 8.00
6 CS,F:Green Lantern 8.00
7 DD,F:Red Tornado 8.00
8 MA,F:Swamp Thing 8.00
9 JSon,JA,RH,F:Wonder Woman . . 8.00
10 JSon,JA,F:Sgt.Rock 8.00

DC Comics Presents #71
© DC Comics Inc.

11 JSon,F:Hawkman 7.00
12 RB,DG,F:Mr.Miracle 7.00
13 DD,DG,F:Legion 8.00
14 DD,DG,F:Superboy 7.00
15 JSon,F:Atom,C:Batman 7.00
16 JSon,F:Black Lightning 7.00
17 JL,F:Firestorm 7.00
18 DD,F:Zatanna 7.00
19 JSon,F:Batgirl 7.00
20 JL,F:Green Arrow 6.00
21 JSon,JSa,F:Elongated Man 6.00
22 DD,FMc,F:Captain Comet 6.00
23 JSon,F:Dr.Fate 6.00
24 JL,F:Deadman 6.00
25 DD,FMc,F:Phantom Stranger . . . 6.00
26 GP,DG,JSn,I:New Teen Titans,
    Cyborg,Raven,Starfire
    A:Green Lantern 30.00
27 JSn,RT,I:Mongul 7.00
28 JSn,RT,GK,F:Mongul 6.00
29 JSn,RT,AS,F:Spectre 6.00
30 CS,AS,F:Black Canary 6.00
31 JL,DG,AS,F:Robin 6.00
32 KS,AS,F:Wonder Woman 6.00
33 RB,DG,AS,F:Captain Marvel 6.00
34 RB,DG,F:Marvel Family 6.00
35 CS,GK,F:Man-bat 6.00
36 JSn,F:Starman 7.00
37 JSn,AS,F:Hawkgirl 6.00
38 GP(c),DH,AS,DG,D:Crimson
    Avenger,F:Flash 6.00
39 JSon,AS,F:PlasticMan,Toyman . . 6.00
40 IN,FMc,AS,F:Metamorpho 6.00
41 JL,FMc,GC,RT,I:New Wonder
    Woman,A:Joker 8.00
42 IN,FMc,F:Unknown Soldier 6.00
43 BB(c),CS,F:Legion 6.00
44 IN,FMc,F:Dial H for Hero 7.00
45 RB,F:Firestorm 6.00
46 AS,I:Global Guardians 6.00
47 CS,I:Masters of Universe 15.00
48 GK(c),AA,IN,FMc,F:Aquaman . . . 5.00
49 RB,F:Shazam!,V:Black Adam . . . 5.00
50 KS,CS,F:Clark Kent 5.00
51 AS,FMc,CS,F:Atom,Masters
    of the Universe 7.00
52 KG,F:Doom Patrol,
    I:Ambush Bug 5.00
53 CS,TD,RA,DG,I:Atari Force 5.00
54 DN,DA,F:Gr.Arrow,Bl.Canary . . . 5.00
55 AS,F:Air Wave,A:Superboy 5.00
56 GK(c),F:Power Girl 5.00
57 AS,FMc,F:Atomic Knights 5.00

58 GK(c),AS,F:Robin,Elongated
    Man 5.00
59 KG,KS,F:Ambush Bug 5.00
60 GK(c),IN,TD,F:Guardians 5.00
61 GP,F:Omac 5.00
62 GK(c),IN,F:Freedom Fighters . . . 5.00
63 AS,EC,F:Amethyst 5.00
64 GK(c),AS,FMc,F:Kamandi 5.00
65 GM,F:Madame Xanadu 5.00
66 JKu,F:Demon 5.00
67 CS,MA,F:Santa Claus 5.00
68 GK(c),CS,MA,F:Vixen 5.00
69 IN,DJ,F:Blackhawk 5.00
70 AS,TD,F:Metal Men 5.00
71 CS,F:Bizarro 5.00
72 AS,DG,F:Phant.Stranger,Joker . . 6.00
73 CI,F:Flash 5.00
74 AS,RT,F:Hawkman 5.00
75 TMd,F:Arion 5.00
76 EB,F:Wonder Woman 5.00
77 CS,F:Forgotten Heroes 5.00
78 CS,F:Forgotten Villains 6.00
79 CS,AW,F:Legion 6.00
80 CS,F:Clark Kent 5.00
81 KG,BO,F:Ambush Bug 5.00
82 KJ,F:Adam Strange 5.00
83 IN,F:Batman/Outsiders 5.00
84 JK,ATh,MA,F:Challengers 7.00
85 RV,AW,AMo(s),
    F:Swamp Thing 7.00
86 Crisis,F:Supergirl 5.00
87 CS,AW,Crisis,I:Earth Prime
    Superboy 5.00
88 KG,Crisis,F:Creeper 5.00
89 MMi(c),AS,F:Omega Men 5.00
90 DCw,F:Firestorm,Capt.Atom 5.00
91 CS,F:Captain Comet 5.00
92 CS,F:Vigilante 5.00
93 JSn(c),AS,KS,F:Elastic Four 5.00
94 GP(c),TMd,DH,Crisis,F:Lady
    Quark,Pariah,Harbinger 5.00
95 MA(i),F:Hawkman 5.00
96 JSon,KS,F:Blue Devil 5.00
97 RV,F:Phantom Zone Villians,
    final issue,double-sized 5.00
Ann.#1,RB,F:Earth 2 Superman . . . 5.00
Ann.#2 GK(c),KP,I:Superwoman . . 5.00
Ann.#3 GK,F:Captain Marvel 5.00
Ann.#4 EB,JOy,F:Superwoman 5.00

DC COMICS PRESENTS
July 2004
The Atom #1 . . . . 2.50
Batman #1 . . . . 2.50
The Flash #1 . . . . 2.50
Green Lantern #1 . . . . 2.50
Hawkman #1 . . . . 2.50
Justice League of America #1 . . . . . 2.50
Mystery in Space #1 . . . . 2.50
Superman #1 . . . . 2.50

DC/MARVEL:
ALL ACCESS
October 1996
sequel to DC Versus Marvel
1 (of 4) RMz(s),JG,JRu, crossover
    crisis again, 48pg 4.00
2 RMz(s),JG,JRu,F:Jubilee,Robin,
    Daredevil,Two-Face 3.00
3 RMz(s),JG,JRu,F:Doctor
    Strange, X-Men 3.00
4 RMz(s),JG,JRu,48pg 3.50

DC/MARVEL
CROSSOVER CLASSICS
TPB rep. all x-overs 18.00
TPB Vol. 2 (1998) 15.00
TPB Vol. 4 . . . . 15.00

DC COMICS

DC FIRST
May, 2002
Superman/Lobo, 48-pg. 3.50
The Flash/Superman, 48-pg. 3.50
Batgirl/The Joker, 48-pg. 3.50
Green Lantern/Green Lantern 3.50

DC GRAPHIC NOVEL
Nov., 1983
1 JL,Star Raiders 16.00
2 Warlords. 16.00
3 EC,Medusa Chain 16.00
4 JK,Hunger Dogs 50.00
5 Me and Joe Priest 16.00
6 Space Clusters. 16.00

DC MILLENNIUM EDITIONS
Dec., 1999–2000
Action Comics #1. . . . . 4.00
Action Comics #252. . . . . 2.50
Adventure Comics #247 . . . . 2.50
Adventure Comics #761 . . . . 4.00
All-Star Comics #3 . . . . 4.00
All-Star Comics #3, chromium 5.00
All Star Comics #8 . . . . 4.00
All-Star Western #10 . . . . 3.00
Batman #1 . . . . 4.00
Batman #1 chromium. 5.00
Batman: Dark Knight Returns #1. . . 6.00
The Brave and the Bold #28 . . . . . 2.50
The Brave and the Bold #85 . . . . . 2.50
Crisis on Infinte Earths #1 . . . . 2.50
Detective Comics #27 . . . . 4.00
Detective Comics #38 . . . . 4.00
Detective Comics #327 . . . . 2.50
Detective Comics #359 . . . . 2.50
Detective Comics #395 . . . . 2.50
Flash Comics #1 . . . . 4.00
Flash #123 . . . . 2.50
Gen 13 #1 . . . . 2.50
Green Lantern/Green Arrow #76 . . . 2.50
Hellblazer #1 . . . . 3.00
House of Mystery #1 . . . . 2.50
House of Secrets #92 . . . . 2.50
JLA #1 . . . . 2.50
Justice League #1 . . . . 2.50
Justice League #1, chromium 5.00
Kingdom Come #1 . . . . 6.00
The Man of Steel #1 . . . . 2.50
Military Comics #1 . . . . 4.00
More Fun Comics #101 . . . . 3.00
Mysterious Suspense #1 . . . . 2.50
New Gods #1 . . . . 2.50
New Teen Titans #1 . . . . 2.50
Our Army at War #81. . . . . 2.50
Plop! #1 . . . . 2.50
Police Comics #1 . . . . 4.00
Preacher #1 . . . . 3.00
Saga of the Swamp Thing #21 . . . . 2.50
Sandman #1. . . . . 3.00
Sensation Comics #1. . . . . 4.00
The Shadow #1 . . . . 2.50
Showcase #22 . . . . 2.50
Showcase #4 . . . . 2.50
Spirit #1 . . . . 4.00
Superboy #1. . . . . 3.00
Superman #1 . . . . 4.00
Superman #1 Chromium edition . . . 5.00
Superman #76 . . . . 3.00
Superman #75 Death of Superman. 2.50
Superman's Pal Jimmy Olsen #1 . . 2.50
Watchmen #1. . . . . 2.50
Whiz Comics #2. . . . . 4.00
WildC.A.T.S #1. . . . . 2.50
Wonder Woman 1st.Series #1. . . . . 4.00
Wonder Woman #1 . . . . 2.50
World's Finest Comics #71 . . . . 2.50
Young Romance #1, JK, JSm 3.00

DC: THE NEW FRONTIER
Jan. 2004
1 (of 6) Silver age universe 8.00
2 thru 6 . . . . @7.00

DC 100-PAGE SUPERSPECTACULAR
May 2004
Spec. Facsimile edition (2004) 7.00

DC ONE MILLION
1998
1 GMo(s),VS,in 853rd-century 3.00
2 GMo(s),VS,V:Hourman Virus. . . . 2.50
3 GMo(s),VS,V:Solaris 2.50
4 GMo(s),VS,finale 2.50
TPB series rep. 15.00

DC REPLICA EDITIONS
1999–2000
DC 100-Page Super-Spectacular:
   Love Stories 7.00
Justice Society of America
   100-page Super Spectacular #1 7.00
Teen Titans Annual #1 (1967) 5.00
Sgt. Rock's Prize Battle Tales
   80-pg. Giant. 6.00

DC SCIENCE FICTION GRAPHIC NOVEL
1985–87
1 KG,Hell on Earth 15.00
2 Nightwings. 15.00
3 Frost and Fire 15.00
4 Merchants of Venus 15.00
5 Metalzoic 15.00
6 MR,Demon-Glass Hand. 15.00
7 Sandkings 15.00

DC SPECIAL
Oct.–Dec., 1968
[All reprint]
1 CI,F:Flash,Batman,Adam Strange,
   (#1 thru #21 reps) 100.00
2 F:Teen Titans 125.00
3 GA,F:Black Canary 100.00
4 Mystery 50.00
5 JKu,F:Viking Prince/Sgt.Rock . . 50.00

DC Super-Stars #2
© *DC Comics, Inc.*

6 Wild Frontier 50.00
7 F:Strange Sports 50.00
8 Wanted. 50.00
9 . . . . 50.00
10 LAW 50.00
11 NA,BWr,F:Monsters 50.00
12 JKu,F:Viking Prince 50.00
13 F:Strange Sports 50.00
14 Wanted,F:Penguin/Joker 60.00
15 GA,F:Plastic Man 60.00
16 F:Super Heroes & Gorillas 25.00
17 F:Green Lantern 25.00
18 Earth Shaking Stories 25.00
19 F:War Against Gianta 25.00
20 Green Lantern. 25.00
21 F:War Against Monsters 25.00
22 Three Musketeers. 25.00
23 Three Musketeers. 25.00
24 Three Musketeers. 25.00
25 Three Musketeers. 25.00
26 F:Enemy Ace(rep). 25.00
27 RB,JR,F:Captain Comet 25.00
28 DN,DA,Earth disasters 25.00
29 JSon,BL,O:JSA 25.00

DC SPECIAL SERIES
Sept., 1977
1 MN,DD,IN,FMc,JSon,JA,BMc,
   JRu,F:Batman,Flash,Green
   Lantern,Atom,Aquaman. 30.00
2 BWr(c),BWr,F:Swamp
   Thing rep. 15.00
3 JKu(c),F:Sgt.Rock 18.00
4 AN,RT,Unexpected Annual 18.00
5 CS,F:Superman 24.00
6 BMc(i),Secret Society Vs.JLA . . 18.00
7 AN,F:Ghosts 18.00
8 RE,DG,F:Brave&Bold,Deadman 18.00
9 SD,RH,DAy,F:Wonder Woman . 25.00
10 JSon,MN,DN,TA,Secret Origins,
   O:Dr.Fate. 18.00
11 JL,KS,MA,IN,WW,AS,F:Flash . . 18.00
12 MK(c),RT,RH,TS,Secrets of
   Haunted House 20.00
13 JKu(c),RT,SBi,RE,F:Sgt.Rock. . 20.00
14 BWr(c),F:Swamp Thing rep. . . . 18.00
15 MN,JRu,MR,DG,MGo,
   F:Batman. 25.00
16 RH,D:Jonah Hex. 75.00
17 F:Swamp Thing rep. 12.00
18 JK(c),digest,F:Sgt.Rock rep. . . 18.00
19 digest,Secret Origins
   O:Wonder Woman. 18.00
20 BWr(c),F:Swamp Thing rep. . . . 12.00
21 FM,JL,DG,RT,DA,F:Batman,
   Legion 35.00
22 JKu(c),F:G.I.Combat 18.00
23 digest size,F:Flash 18.00
24 F:Worlds Finest. 18.00
25 F:Superman II,Photo Album . . . 18.00
26 RA,F:Superman's Fortress 22.00
27 JL,DG,F:Batman vs.Hulk. 35.00

DC SUPER-STARS
1976–78
1 F:Teen Titans rep. 25.00
2 F:DC Super-Stars of Space 12.00
3 CS,F:Superman,Legion 12.00
4 DC,MA,F:Super-Stars of Space. 12.00
5 CI,F:Flash rep. 12.00
6 MA,F:Super-Stars of Space 12.00
7 F:Aquaman rep. 12.00
8 CI,MA,F:Adam Strange 15.00
9 F:Superman rep. 12.00
10 DD,FMc,F:Superhero Baseball
   Special,A:Joker 15.00
11 GM,Super-Stars of Magic 12.00
12 CS,MA,F:Superboy. 12.00
13 SA 25.00
14 RB,BL,JA,JRu,Secret Origins. . 12.00

15 JKu(c),RB,RT(i),War Heroes . . 12.00
16 DN,BL,I:Star Hunters 12.00
17 JSon,MGr,BL,I&O:Huntress,O:Gr.
   Arrow,D:EarthII Catwoman . . . 50.00
18 RT,DG,BL,F:Deadman,Phantom
   Stranger. 20.00

DC TWO THOUSAND
July, 2000

1 (of 2) TPe,VS. 7.00
2 TPe,VS,JLA & Golden age JSA . 7.00

DC UNIVERSE
1997–2003

Heroes, Secret Files #1 . . . . 5.00
Villains, Secret Files #1 . . . . 5.00
TPB Christmas, Tyt(c) (2000) 20.00
GN Holiday Bash #1 (1997). 4.00
GN Holiday Bash #2 (1998). 4.00
GN Holiday Bash #3 (1999). 5.00
TPB The DC Universe Stories
   of Alan Moore (2003). 20.00

DC UNIVERSE: TRINITY
1993

1 TC,GeH,BKi,F:Darkstars,Green
   Lantern,L.E.G.I.O.N.,V:Triarch. . 4.00
2 BKi,SHa,F:Darkstars,Green Lantern,
   L.E.G.I.O.N.,V:Triarch 4.00

DC VS. MARVEL
1996

1 RMz. 5.50
1 2nd printing 4.00
2 & 3 see Marvel
4 PDa 5.00

DEAD CORPS(E)
DC/Helix, July, 1998

1 StP, C.J.Rataan 2.50
2 StP, CJ becomes an expired 2.50
3 StP,Death is not the end 2.50
4 StP, conclusion. 2.50

DEADENDERS
DC/Vertigo, Jan., 2000

1 WaP,Stealing the Sun,pt.1 . . . . . 2.50
2 WaP,Stealing the Sun,pt.2 . . . . . 2.50
3 WaP,Stealing the Sun,pt.3 . . . . . 2.50
4 WaP,Stealing the Sun,pt.4 . . . . . 2.50
5 WaP,Now and Then,pt.1 . . . . . . 2.50
6 WaP,Now and Then,pt.2 . . . . . . 2.50
7 WaP,Now and Then,pt.3 . . . . . . 2.50
8 WaP,scooter races. 2.50
9 More Fun in New World,pt.1 . . . . 2.50
10 More Fun in New World,pt.2. . . . 2.50
11 Sector 9. . . . . 2.50
12 V:Science Corp. 2.50
13 Scooter race 2.50
14 Behind the Wheel, pt.1 . . . . 2.50
15 Behind the Wheel, pt.2. . . . . . . 2.50
16 Behind the Wheel, pt.3 . . . . 2.50
TPB Stealing the Sun 10.00

DEADMAN
May, 1985

1 CI,NA,rep. 4.00
2 thru 7 NA,rep. . . . . @3.00

[Mini-Series], 1986

1 JL,A:Batman 3.00
2 JL,V:Sensei,A:Batman. 3.00
3 JL,D:Sensei 3.00
4 JL,V:Jonah, final issue. 3.00

Deadman #3
© DC Comics Inc.

DEADMAN
Dec., 2001

1 SVa(s) F:Boston Brand 2.50
2 SVa(s),Sirna. 2.50
3 SVa(s),F:Duroc, drugs 2.50
4 SVa(s),nuclear submarine 2.50
5 SVa(s),Death & the Maiden,pt.1 . 2.50
6 SVa(s),Death & the Maiden,pt.2 . 2.50
7 SVa(s),children of Nanda Parbat . 2.50
8 SVa(s),Nanda Parbat,Onyx 2.50
9 SVa(s),final issue. 2.50

DEADMAN: DEAD AGAIN
Aug., 2001

1 SVa,RBr,A:Flash 2.50
2 SVa,RBr,JAp,A:Robin 2.50
3 SVa,RBr,A:Superman,Doomsday 2.50
4 SVa,RBr,MBr,A:Green Lantern . . 2.50
5 SVa,RBr,concl., ... 2.50

DEADMAN: EXORCISM
[Limited-Series], 1992

1 KJo,A:Phantom Stranger. 5.25
2 KJo,A:Phantom Stranger. 5.25

DEADMAN: LOST SOULS
TPB MBn, KJo, rep. Exorcism
   and Love After Death 20.00

DEADMAN: LOVE AFTER DEATH
1989–90

1 KJo,Circus of Monsters 4.25
2 KJo,Circus of Monsters 4.25

DEADSHOT
1988–89

1 LMc,From Suicide Squad 2.50
2 LMc,Search for Son. 2.50
3 LMc,V:Pantha 2.50
4 LMc,final issue. 2.50

DEATH GALLERY
DC/Vertigo

1 DMc(c),NGa Death Sketch
   Various Pinups. 3.50

DEATH: THE HIGH COST OF LIVING
DC/Vertigo, 1993

1 B:NGa(s),CBa,MBu(i),Death
   becomes Human,A:Hettie 6.00
1a Platinum Ed. 18.00
2 CBa,MBu(i),V:Eremite,A:Hettie . 4.00
3 E:NGa(s),CBa,MBu(i),V:Eremite,
   A:Hettie 3.50
3a Error Copy 7.00
TPB w/Tori Amos Intro. 13.00

DEATH: THE TIME OF YOUR LIFE
DC/Vertigo, 1995

1 NGa,MBu,four-issue miniseries. . 3.00
2 NGa,MBu,F:Foxglove 3.00
3 NGa,MBu,conclusion. 3.00
TPB NGa(s),rep. 13.00

DEATHSTROKE: THE TERMINATOR
1991–94

1 MZ(c),(from New Teen Titans)
   SE,I:2nd Ravager 4.00
1a Second Printing,Gold. 3.00
2 MZ(c),SE,Quraci Agents 4.00
3 SE,V:Ravager 4.00
4 SE,D:2ndRavager(Jackel) 3.00
5 Winter Green Rescue Attempt. . . 3.00
6 MZ(c),SE,B:City of Assassins,
   A:Batman. 3.00
7 MZ(c),SE,A:Batman. 2.50
8 MZ(c),SE,A:Batman. 2.50
9 MZ(c),SE,E:City of Assassins,
   A:Batman;I:2nd Vigilante. 2.50
10 MZ(c),ANi,GP,A:2nd Vigilante. . 2.50
11 MZ(c),ANi,GP,A:2nd Vigilante . . 2.50
12 MGo,Short Stories re:Slade 2.50
13 SE,V:Gr.Lant.,Flash,Aquaman . . 2.50
14 ANi,Total Chaos#1,A:New Titans,
   Team Titans,V:Nightwing 2.50
15 ANi,Total Chaos#4,A:New Titans,
   Team Titans,I:Sweet Lili. 2.50
16 ANi,Total Chaos#7 . . . . 2.50
17 SE,Titans Sell-Out #2
   A:Brotherhood of Evil 2.50
18 SE,V:Cheshire,R:Speedy 2.50
19 SE,V:Broth.of Evil,A:Speedy. . . . 2.50
20 SE,MZ(c),V:Checkmate 2.50

Deathstroke The Terminator #17
© DC Comics, Inc.

21 SE,MZ(c),A:Checkmate 2.50
22 MZ(c),Quality of Mercy#1 . . . . . 2.50
23 MZ(c),Quality of Mercy#2 . . . . . 2.50
24 MZ(c),V:The Black Dome 2.50
25 MZ(c),V:The Black Dome 2.50
26 MZ(c),SE,in Kenya 2.50
27 MZ(c),SE,B:World Tour,
  in Germany 2.50
28 MZ(c),SE,in France. 2.50
29 KM(c),SE,in Hong Kong 2.50
30 SE,A:Vigilante 2.50
31 SE,in Milwaukie 2.50
32 SE,in Africa 2.50
33 SE,I:Fleur de Lis 2.50
34 SE,E:World Tour 2.50
35 V:Mercenaries. 2.50
36 V:British General. 2.50
37 V:Assassin 2.50
38 A:Vigilante 2.50
39 A:Vigilante 2.50
40 Wedding in Red 2.50
Ann.#1 Eclipso,A:Vigilante 4.00
Ann.#2 SE,I:Gunfire. 4.00
Ann.#3 Elseworlds Story 4.25
TPB Full Circle rep#1-#4,
  New Titans#70. . . . . 12.95
Becomes:

DEATHSTROKE: THE HUNTED
1994–95
0 Slade 2.50
41 Bronze Tiger 2.50
42 Wounded. 2.50
43 . . . . 2.50
44 . . . . 2.50
45 A:New Titans. 2.50
Becomes:

DEATHSTROKE
1995–96
46 Checkmate,Wintergreen 2.50
47 I:New Vigilante 2.50
48 Crimelord/Syndicate War,pt.1 . . 2.50
49 Crimelord/Syndicate War,pt.4
  A:Supergirl, New Titans,
  Hawkman, Blood Pack 2.50
50 A:Titans,Outsiders,Steel 3.50
51 No Fate or Future,pt.1 . . . . 2.50
52 No Fate or Future,pt.2 . . . . 2.50
53 The Borgia Plague,pt.1 . . . . 2.50
54 The Borgia Plague,pt.2 . . . . 2.50
55 MWn,Rebirth?. 2.50
56 MWn,Night of the Karrion,pt.2 . . 2.50
57 . . . . 2.50
58 MWn,V:The Joker. 2.50
59 MWn,F:Hellriders 2.50
60 MWn,final issue 2.50

DEATHWISH
1994–95
1 New mini-series. 2.50
2 F:Rahme 2.50
3 . . . . 2.50
4 V:Boots 2.50

DEMOLITION MAN
1993–94
1 thru 4 Movie Adapt. 2.50

DEMON
[1st Regular Series], 1972–74
1 JK,I:Demon 65.00
2 JK. 35.00
3 JK. 30.00
4 JK. 30.00
5 JK. 30.00
6 thru 16 JK. . . . . @20.00

Demon #31
© DC Comics Inc.

[Limited Series], 1987
1 MWg,B:Jason Blood's Case 3.00
2 MWg,Fight to Save Gotham 3.00
3 MWg,Fight to Save Gotham 3.00
4 MWg,final issue 3.00
[2nd Regular Series], 1990–95
0 Relationships 2.50
1 VS,A:Etrigan (32 pages) 4.00
2 VS,V:TheCrone 3.00
3 VS,A:Batman 3.00
4 VS,A:Batman 3.00
5 VS,ThePit. 3.00
6 VS,In Hell. 3.00
7 VS,Etrigan-King of Hell 3.00
8 VS,Klarion the Witch Boy 3.00
9 VS,Jason Leaves Gotham. 3.00
10 VS,A:PhantomStranger. 3.00
11 VS,A:Klarion,C:Lobo 3.00
12 VS,Etrigan Vs. Lobo 3.00
13 VS,Etrigan Vs. Lobo 3.00
14 VS,V:Odd Squad,A:Lobo 3.00
15 VS,Etrigan Vs.Lobo 3.00
16 VS,Etrigan & Jason Blood
  switch bodies. 3.00
17 VS, War of the Gods x-over 3.00
18 VS,V:Wotan,A:Scape Goat. 3.00
19 VS,O:Demon,Demon/Lobo
  pin-up. 3.50
20 VS,V:Golden Knight 2.50
21 VS,Etrigan/Jason,
  A:Lobo,Glenda. 2.50
22 MWg,V:Mojo & Hayden 2.50
23 VS,A:Robin 2.50
24 VS,A:Robin 2.50
25 VS,V:Gideon Ryme. 2.50
26 VS,B:America Rules 2.50
27 VS,A:Superman 2.50
28 VS,A:Superman 2.50
29 VS,E:America Rules 2.50
30 R:Asteroth. 2.50
31 VS(c),A:Lobo. 2.50
32 VS(c),A:Lobo,W.Woman. 2.50
33 VS(c),A:Lobo,V:Asteroth. 2.50
34 A:Lobo. 2.50
35 A:Lobo,V:Belial 2.50
36 A:Lobo,V:Belial 2.50
37 A:Lobo,Morax 2.50
38 A:Lobo,Morax 2.50
39 A:Lobo. 2.50
40 New Direction,B:GEn(s) 3.50
41 V:Mad Bishop 3.00
42 V:Demons 3.00
43 A:Hitman 10.00
44 V:Gotho-Demon,A:Hitman 15.00

45 V:Gotho-Demon,A:Hitman 15.00
46 R:Haunted Tank 5.00
47 V:Zombie Nazis. 5.00
48 A:Haunted Tank,V:Zombie
  Nazis 5.00
49 b:Demon's Son,A:Joe Gun 2.50
50 GEn(s). 3.00
51 GEn(s),Son & Lovers 2.50
52 Etrigan & son–Hitman. 4.00
53 Glenda & child–Hitman. 4.00
54 Suffer the Children 4.00
55 Rebellion. 2.50
56 F:Etrigan 2.50
57 Last Stand. 2.50
58 Last issue 2.50
Ann.#1 Eclipso,V:Klarion 3.25
Ann.#2 I:Hitman 15.00

DEMON, THE: DRIVEN OUT
Sept. 2003
1 (of 6) ATi,F:Etrigan. 2.50
2 thru 6 ATi . . . . @2.50

DESPERADOES: QUIET OF THE GRAVE
Homage/DC May, 2001
1 (of 5) JMi,JSe 3.00
2 JMi,JSe 3.00
3 JMi,JSe 3.00
4 JMi,JSe 3.00
5 JMi,JSe, concl.. . . . . 3.00
TPB JMi,JSe series rep. 15.00

DESTINY: A CHRONICLE OF DEATHS FORETOLD
DC/Vertigo, Sept., 1997
1 (of 3) F:Destiny of the Endless . . 6.00
2 Destiny of the Endless, pt.2. . . . . 6.00
3 Destiny of the Endless, pt.3. . . . . 6.00
TPB series rep. 14.95

DETECTIVE COMICS
March, 1937
1 I:Slam Bradley 75,000.00
2 JoS 25,000.00
3 JoS 15,000.00
4 JoS 8,500.00
5 JoS 8,000.00
6 JoS 6,500.00
7 JoS 6,000.00
8 JoS,Mr. Chang(c) 9,000.00
9 JoS 6,000.00
10 . . . . 6,000.00
11 . . . . 4,800.00
12 . . . . 4,800.00
13 . . . . 4,800.00
14 . . . . 4,800.00
15 . . . . 4,800.00
16 . . . . 4,800.00
17 I:Fu Manchu. 4,800.00
18 Fu Manchu(c). 7,500.00
19 . . . . 4,500.00
20 I:Crimson Avenger 7,000.00
21 . . . . 3,500.00
22 . . . . 4,800.00
23 . . . . 3,500.00
24 . . . . 3,500.00
25 . . . . 3,500.00
26 . . . . 3,500.00
27 BK,I:Batman. 385,000.00
28 BK,V:Frenchy Blake. 30,000.00
29 BK,I:Doctor Death 50,000.00
30 BK,V:Dr. Death. 12,000.00
31 BK,I:Monk 50,000.00
32 BK,V:Monk. 9,000.00
33 O:Batman,V:Scarlet Horde 65,000.00

Detective Comics #4
© *DC Comics, Inc.*

34 V:Due D'Orterre	7,500.00
35 V:Sheldon Lenox	18,000.00
36 I:Hugo Strange	12,000.00
37 V:Count Grutt, last	
Batman solo	11,000.00
38 I:Robin, the Boy Wonder	60,000.00
39 V:Green Dragon	9,000.00
40 I:Clayface (Basil Karlo)	10,000.00
41 V:Graves	5,000.00
42 V:Pierre Antal	3,500.00
43 V:Harliss Greer	3,500.00
44 Robin Dream Story	3,500.00
45 V:Joker	5,000.00
46 V:Hugo Strange	3,000.00
47 Meets Harvey Midas	3,000.00
48 Meets Henry Lewis	3,000.00
49 V:Clayface	3,000.00
50 V:Three Devils	3,000.00
51 V:Mindy Gang	2,000.00
52 V:Loo Chung	2,000.00
53 V:Toothy Hare gang	2,000.00
54 V:Hook Morgan	2,000.00
55 V:Dr. Death	2,000.00
56 V:Mad Mack	2,000.00
57 Meet Richard Sneed	2,000.00
58 I:Penguin	6,000.00
59 V:Penguin	2,200.00
60 V:Joker,I:Air Wave	2,200.00
61 The Three Racketeers	2,000.00
62 V:Joker	3,500.00
63 I:Mr. Baffle	2,000.00
64 I:Boy Commandos,V:Joker	5,500.00
65 Meet Tom Bolton	4,500.00
66 I:Two-Face	5,500.00
67 V:Penguin	3,200.00
68 V:Two-Face	2,300.00
69 V:Joker	2,300.00
70 Meet the Amazing Carlo	1,700.00
71 V:Joker	2,000.00
72 V:Larry the Judge	1,500.00
73 V:Scarecrow	1,900.00
74 I:Tweedledum&Tweedledee	1,500.00
75 V:Robber Baron	1,500.00
76 V:Joker	2,300.00
77 V:Dr. Matthew Thorne	1,700.00
78 V:Baron Von Luger	1,700.00
79 Destiny's Auction	1,700.00
80 V:Two-Face	1,800.00
81 I:Cavalier	1,200.00
82 V:Blackee Blondeen	1,200.00
83 V:Dr. Goodwin	1,400.00
84 V:Ivan Krafft	1,200.00
85 V:Joker	1,700.00
86 V:Gentleman Jim Jewell	1,200.00

87 V:Penguin	1,300.00
88 V:Big Hearted John	1,200.00
89 V:Cavalier	1,200.00
90 V:Capt. Ben	1,200.00
91 V:Joker	1,500.00
92 V:Braing Bulow	1,000.00
93 V:Tiger Ragland	1,000.00
94 V:Lefty Goran	1,000.00
95 V:The Blaze	1,000.00
96 F:Alfred	1,000.00
97 V:Nick Petri	1,000.00
98 Meets Casper Thurbridge	1,000.00
99 V:Penguin	1,500.00
100 V:Digger	1,600.00
101 V:Joe Bart	1,000.00
102 V:Joker	1,500.00
103 Meet Dean Gray	1,000.00
104 V:Fat Frank gang	1,000.00
105 V:Simon Gurlan	1,000.00
106 V:Todd Torrey	1,000.00
107 V:Bugs Scarpis	1,000.00
108 Meet Ed Gregory	1,000.00
109 V:Joker	1,000.00
110 V:Prof. Moriarty	1,000.00
111 Coaltown, USA	1,000.00
112 Case Without A Crime	1,000.00
113 V:Blackhand	1,000.00
114 V:Joker	1,000.00
115 V:Basil Grimes	1,000.00
116 A:Carter Nichols,	
Robin Hood	1,000.00
117 Steeplejack's Slowdown	1,000.00
118 V:Joker	1,300.00
119 V:Wiley Derek	1,000.00
120 V:Penguin	2,200.00
121 F:Commissioner Gordon	1,000.00
122 V:Catwoman	2,000.00
123 V:Shiner	950.00
124 V:Joker	1,200.00
125 V:Thinker	900.00
126 V:Penguin	900.00
127 V:Dr. Agar	900.00
128 V:Joker	1,200.00
129 V:Diamond Dan mob	900.00
130	900.00
131 V:Trigger Joe	800.00
132 V:Human Key	800.00
133 Meets Arthur Loom	800.00
134 V:Penguin	800.00
135 A:Baron Frankenstein,	
Carter Nichols	800.00
136 A:Carter Nichols	800.00
137 V:Joker	1,100.00
138 V:Joker,O:Robotman	1,500.00
139 V:Nick Bailey	800.00
140 I:Riddler	6,500.00
141 V:Blackie Nason	800.00
142 V:Riddler	1,600.00
143 V:Pied Piper	800.00
144 A:Kay Kyser (radio	
personality)	800.00
145 V:Yellow Mask mob	800.00
146 V:J.J. Jason	800.00
147 V:Tiger Shark	800.00
148 V:Prof. Zero	800.00
149 V:Joker	1,200.00
150 V:Dr. Paul Visio	800.00
151 I&O:Pow Wow Smith	1,000.00
152 V:Goblin	800.00
153 V:Slits Danton	1,000.00
154 V:Hatch Marlin	800.00
155 A:Vicki Vale	800.00
156 The Batmobile of 1950	800.00
157 V:Bart Gillis	800.00
158 V:Dr. Doom	800.00
159 V:T. Worthington Chubb	800.00
160 V:Globe-Trotter	800.00
161 V:Bill Waters	800.00
162 Batman on railroad	800.00
163 V:Slippery Jim Elgin	800.00
164 Bat-signal story	800.00

165 The Strange Costumes	
of Batman	800.00
166 Meets John Gillen	800.00
167 A:Carter Nichols, Cleopatra	800.00
168 O:Joker	5,000.00
169 V:Squint Tolmar	800.00
170 Batman teams with Navy	
and Coast Guard	800.00
171 V:Penguin	1,200.00
172 V:Paul Gregorian	750.00
173 V:Killer Moth	750.00
174 V:Dagger	750.00
175 V:Kangaroo Kiley	750.00
176 V:Mr. Velvet	750.00
177 Bat-Cave story	650.00
178 V:Baron Swane	650.00
179 Mayor Bruce Wayne	650.00
180 V:Joker	650.00
181 V:Human Magnet	650.00
182 V:Maestro Dorn	650.00
183 V:John Cook	650.00
184 I:Firefly(Garfield Lynns)	650.00
185 Secrets of Batman's	
Utility Belt	650.00
186 The Flying Bat-Cave	650.00
187 V:Two-Face	650.00
188 V:William Milden	650.00
189 V:Styx	650.00
190 Meets Dr. Sampson,	
O:Batman	1,000.00
191 V:Executioner	650.00
192 V: Nails Riley	650.00
193 V:Joker	650.00
194 V:Sammy Sabre	650.00
195 Meets Hugo Marmon	650.00
196 V:Frank Lumardi	650.00
197 V:Wrecker	650.00
198 Batman in Scotland	650.00
199 V:Jack Baker	650.00
200 V:Brand Keldon	900.00
201 Meet Human Target	650.00
202 V:Jolly Roger	650.00
203 V:Catwoman	650.00
204 V:Odo Neral	650.00
205 O:Bat-Cave	900.00
206 V:Trapper	650.00
207 Meets Merko the Great	650.00
208 V:Groff	650.00
209 V:Inventor	650.00
210 V:Brain Hobson	650.00
211 V:Catwoman	650.00
212 Meets Jonathan Bard	650.00
213 O:Mirror-Man	800.00
214 The Batman Encyclopedia	650.00
215 I:Ranger, Legionairy, Gaucho &	
Musketeer,A:Knight & Squire	
(See: World's Finest 89)	600.00

Detective Comics #81
© *DC Comics, Inc.*

All comics prices listed are for *Near Mint* condition.   **CVA Page 65**

216 A:Brane Taylor 600.00
217 Meets Barney Barrows 600.00
218 V:Dr. Richard Marston 600.00
219 V:Marty Mantee. 600.00
220 A:Roger Bacon, historical
   scientist/philosopher 600.00
221 V:Paul King 600.00
222 V:`Big Jim' Jarrell 600.00
223 V:`Blast' Varner 600.00
224 . . . . 600.00
225 I&O:Martian Manhunter
   (J'onn J'onzz) 8,000.00
226 O:Robin's costume,
   A:J'onn J'onzz 2,000.00
227 A:Roy Raymond,J'onnJ'onzz 700.00
228 A:Roy Raymond,J'onnJ'onzz 700.00
229 A:Roy Raymond,J'onnJ'onzz 700.00
230 A:Martian Manhunter,
   I:Mad Hatter. 750.00
231 A:Batman,Jr.,Roy Raymond
   J'onn J'onzz. 500.00
232 A:J'onn J'onzz. 500.00
233 I&O:Batwoman 1,900.00
234 V:Jay Caird 500.00
235 O:Batman's Costume 900.00
236 V:Wallace Walby 650.00
237 F:Robin 500.00
238 V:Checkmate(villain) 500.00
239 Batman robot story 500.00
240 V:Burt Weaver. 500.00
241 The Rainbow Batman 500.00
242 Batcave story 400.00
243 V:Jay Vanney 400.00
244 O:Batarang 400.00
245 F:Comm.Gordon 400.00
246 . . . . 400.00
247 I:Professor Milo. 400.00
248 . . . . 400.00
249 V:Collector 400.00
250 V:John Stannor 400.00
251 V:Brand Ballard. 400.00
252 Batman in a movie 400.00
253 I:Terrible Trio 400.00
254 A:Bathound 400.00
255 V:Fingers Nolan 400.00
256 Batman outer-space story. . . 400.00
257 Batman sci-fi story 400.00
258 Batman robot story 400.00
259 I:Calendar Man 400.00
260 Batman outer space story. . . 400.00
261 I:Dr. Double X 300.00
262 V:Jackal-Head. 300.00
263 V:The Professor 300.00
264 . . . . 300.00
265 O:Batman retold 500.00
266 V:Astro 300.00

Detective Comics #140
© DC Comics, Inc.

267 I&O:Bat-Mite 500.00
268 V:'Big Joe' Foster 300.00
269 V:Director 300.00
270 Batman sci-fi story 300.00
271 V:Crimson Knight,O:Martian
   Manhunter(retold) 300.00
272 V:Crystal Creature 300.00
273 A:Dragon Society 250.00
274 V:Nails Lewin 250.00
275 A:Zebra-Man 250.00
276 A:Batmite. 250.00
277 Batman Monster story. 250.00
278 A:Professor Simms 250.00
279 Batman robot story 250.00
280 A:Atomic Man 250.00
281 Batman robot story 200.00
282 Batman sci-fi story 200.00
283 V:Phantom of Gotham City . . 200.00
284 V:Hal Durgan 200.00
285 V:Harbin 200.00
286 A:Batwoman 200.00
287 A:Bathound 200.00
288 V:Multicreature 200.00
289 A:Bat-Mite 200.00
290 Batman's robot story 200.00
291 Batman sci-fi story 200.00
292 Last Roy Raymond 200.00
293 A:Aquaman,J'onn J'onzz . . . 200.00
294 V:Elemental Men,
   A:Aquaman 200.00
295 A:Aquaman 200.00
296 A:Aquaman 200.00
297 A:Aquaman 200.00
298 I:Clayface(Matt Hagen) 400.00
299 Batman sci-fi stories 200.00
300 I:Mr.Polka-dot,E:Aquaman . . 175.00
301 A:J'onn J'onzz. 150.00
302 A:J'onn J'onzz. 135.00
303 A:J'onn J'onzz. 135.00
304 A:Clayface,J'onnJ'onz. 135.00
305 Batman sci-fi story 135.00
306 A:J'onn J'onzz. 135.00
307 A:J'onn J'onzz. 135.00
308 A:J'onn J'onzz. 135.00
309 A:J'onn J'onzz. 135.00
310 A:Bat-Mite, J'onn J'onzz 135.00
311 I:Cat-Man,Zook 150.00
312 A:Clayface,J'onn J'onzz . . . 125.00
313 A:J'onn J'onzz. 125.00
314 A:J'onn J'onzz. 125.00
315 I:Jungle Man 125.00
316 A:Dr.Double X,J'onn J'onzz . 125.00
317 A:J'onn J'onzz. 125.00
318 A:Cat-Man,J'onn J'onzz . . . 125.00
319 A:J'onn J'onzz. 125.00
320 A:Vicki Vale 125.00
321 I:Terrible Trio 135.00
322 A:J'onn J'onzz. 130.00
323 I:Zodiac Master,
   A:J'onn J'onzz 130.00
324 A:Mad Hatter,J'onn J'onzz . . 130.00
325 A:Cat-Man,J'onn J'onzz . . . 130.00
326 Batman sci-fi story 130.00
327 Cl,25th ann,symbol change . 200.00
328 D:Alfred,I:WayneFoundation . 200.00
329 A:Elongated Man 130.00
330 "Fallen Idol of Gotham". 130.00
331 A:Elongated Man 130.00
332 A:Joker 100.00
333 A:Gorla 100.00
334 . . . . 100.00
335 . . . . 100.00
336 . . . . 100.00
337 Deep Freeze Menace 100.00
338 . . . . 100.00
339 . . . . 100.00
340 . . . . 100.00
341 A:Joker 100.00
342 . . . . 100.00
343 BK,Cl,Elongated Man 100.00
344 . . . . 100.00

Detective Comics #291
© DC Comics, Inc.

345 Cl,I:Blockbuster. 100.00
346 . . . . 100.00
347 Cl,Elongated Man. 100.00
348 Elongated Man 100.00
349 BK(c),Cl,Blockbuster. 100.00
350 Elongated Man 100.00
351 Cl,A:Elongated Man,
   I:Cluemaster 100.00
352 BK,Elongated Man 100.00
353 . . . . 100.00
354 BK,Elongated Man,I:Dr.
   Tzin-Tzin 100.00
355 Cl,Elongated Man 100.00
356 BK,Outsider,Alfred 100.00
357 . . . . 100.00
358 BK,Elongated Man 100.00
359 I:new Batgirl 200.00
360 . . . . 80.00
361 Cl 80.00
362 Cl,Elongated Man 80.00
363 Cl,Elongated Man 80.00
364 BK,Elongated Man 80.00
365 A:Joker 80.00
366 Elongated Man 80.00
367 Elongated Man 80.00
368 BK,Elongated Man 80.00
369 CA,Elongated Man,
   Catwoman 125.00
370 BK,Elongated Man 80.00
371 BK,Elongated Man 125.00
372 BK,Elongated Man 75.00
373 BK,Elongated Man 75.00
374 BK,Elongated Man 75.00
375 Cl,Elongated Man 75.00
376 . . . . 75.00
377 MA,Elongated Man,
   V:Riddler 75.00
378 Elongated Man 75.00
379 Cl,Elongated Man 75.00
380 Elongated Man 75.00
381 GaF,Marital Bliss Miss 75.00
382 FR(s),BbB,JoG,GaF(s),SGe . . 75.00
383 FR(s),BbB,JoG,GaF(s),SGe . . 75.00
384 FR(s),BbB,JoG,GaF(s),SGe,
   BU:Batgirl 75.00
385 E:FR(s),BbB,JoG,NA(c),GK,MA,
   MkF,BU:Batgirl. 75.00
386 BbK,MkF,BbB,JoG,
   BU:Batgirl 75.00
387 RA,rep.Detective #27 . . . . . . 90.00
388 JBr(s),BbB,JoG,
   GK,MA,FR(s). 85.00
389 FR(s),BbB,JoG,GK,MA 75.00
390 FR(s),BbB,JoG,GK,MA,
   A:Masquerader 75.00

391 FR(s),NA(c),BbB,
  JoG,GK,MA 50.00
392 FR(s),BbB,JoG,I:Jason Bard . . 50.00
393 FR(s),BbB,JoG,GK,MA 50.00
394 FR(s),BbB,JoG,GK,MA 50.00
395 FR(s),NA,DG,GK,MA 75.00
396 FR(s),BbB,JoG,GK,MA 50.00
397 DON(s),NA,DG,GK,MA 75.00
398 FR(s),BbB,JoG,GK,ViC 50.00
399 NA(c),DON(s),BbB,JoG,
  GK,ViC,Robin 75.00
400 FR(s),NA,DG,GK,I:Man-Bat . 150.00
401 NA(c),FR(s),JoG,
  BbB,JoG,GK,ViC 50.00
402 FR(s),NA,DG,V:Man-Bat 75.00
403 FR(s),BbB,JoG,NA(c),GK,ViC,
  BU:Robin 75.00
404 NA,GC,GK,A:Enemy Ace 80.00
405 IN,GK,I:League of Assassins . 75.00
406 DON(s),BbB,FrG 75.00
407 FR(s),NA,DG,V:Man-bat 80.00
408 MWn(s),LWn(s),NA,DG,
  V:DrTzin Tzin 80.00
409 B:FR(s),BbB,FrG,DH,DG . . . 55.00
410 DON(s),FR(s),NA,DG,DH . . . 55.00
411 NA(c),DON(s),BbB,DG,DH . . . 45.00
412 NA(c),BbB,DG,DH 45.00
413 NA(c),BbB,DG,DH 45.00
414 DON(s),IN,DG,DH 50.00
415 BbB,DG,DH 50.00
416 DH 50.00
417 BbB,DG,DH,BU:Batgirl 50.00
418 DON(s),DH,IN,DG,A:Creeper . 50.00
419 DON(s),DH 50.00
420 DH 50.00
421 DON(s),BbB,DG,DH,A:Batgirl . 45.00
422 BbB,DG,DH,Batgirl 45.00
423 BbB,DG,DH 45.00
424 BbB,DG,DH,Batgirl 45.00
425 BWr(c),DON(s),IN,DG,DH . . . 45.00
426 LWn(s),DG,A:Elongated Man . 35.00
427 IN,DG,DH,BU:Batgirl 35.00
428 BbB,DG,ENB(s),DD,JoG,
  BU:Hawkman 35.00
429 DG,JoG,V:Man-Bat 35.00
430 BbB,NC,ENS(s),DG,
  A:Elongated Man 35.00
431 DON(s),IN,MA 35.00
432 MA,A:Atom 35.00
433 DD,DG,MA 35.00
434 IN,DG,ENB(s),RB,DG 35.00
435 E:FR(s),DG,IN 35.00
436 MA,(i),DG,A:Elongated Man . 35.00
437 JA,WS,I:Manhunter 55.00
438 JA,WS,Manhunter 75.00
439 DG,WS,O:Manhunter,Kid
  Eternity rep 75.00
440 JAp,WS 75.00
441 HC,WS 75.00
442 ATh,WS 75.00
443 WS,D:Manhunter 75.00
444 JAp,B:Bat-Murderer,
  A:Ra's Al Ghul 75.00
445 JAp,MGr,A:Talia 75.00
446 JAp,last giant 22.00
447 DG(i),A:Creeper 22.00
448 DG(i),E:Bat-Murderer,
  A:Creeper,Ra's Al Ghul 22.00
449 Midnight Rustler in Gotham . . 22.00
450 WS 25.00
451 . . . . 22.00
452 . . . . 22.00
453 . . . . 22.00
454 . . . . 22.00
455 MGr,A:Hawkman,V:Vampire . 22.00
456 V:Ulysses Vulcan 22.00
457 O:Batman rtd 25.00
458 A:Man Bat 22.00
459 A:Man Bat 22.00
460 . . . . 22.00
461 V:Capt.Stingaree 18.00

462 V:Capt.Stingaree,A:Flash 18.00
463 MGr,Atom,I:Calc.,Bl.Spider . . . 18.00
464 MGr,TA,BlackCanary 18.00
465 TA,Elongated Man 18.00
466 MR,TA,V:Signalman 35.00
467 MR,TA 35.00
468 MR,TA,A:JLA 35.00
469 WS,I:Dr.Phosphorus 18.00
470 WS,AM,V:Dr.Phosphorus 18.00
471 MR,TA,A:Hugo Strange 35.00
472 MR,TA,A:Hugo Strange 35.00
473 MR,TA,R:Deadshot 35.00
474 MR,TA,A:Penguin,
  N:Deadshot 35.00
475 MR,TA,A:Joker 75.00
476 MR,TA,A:Joker 75.00
477 MR,DG,rep.NA 35.00
478 MR,DG,I:3rd Clayface 35.00
479 MR,DG,A:3rd Clayface 35.00
480 DN,MA 18.00
481 JSt,CR,DN,DA,MR,
  A:ManBat 24.00
482 HC,MGo,DG,A:Demon 20.00
483 DN,DA,SD,A:Demon,
  40 Anniv 22.00
484 DN,DA,Demon,O:1st Robin . . 18.00
485 DN,DA,D:Batwoman,A:Demon
  A:Ras al Ghul 18.00
486 DN,DA,DG,I:Odd Man,
  V:Scarecrow 18.00
487 DN,DA,A:Ras Al Ghul 18.00
488 DN,V:Spook,Catwoman 18.00
489 IN,DH,DN,DA,Ras Al Ghul . . . 18.00
490 DN,DA,PB,FMc,A:Black
  Lightning;A:Ras Al Ghul 18.00
491 DN,DA,PB,FMc,A:Black
  Lightning;V:Maxie Zeus 18.00
492 DN,DA,A:Penguin 18.00
493 DN,DA,A:Riddler 18.00
494 DN,DA,V:Crime Doctor 18.00
495 DN,DA,V:Crime Doctor 18.00
496 DN,DA,A:Clayface I 10.00
497 DN,DA 10.00
498 DN,DA,V:Blockbuster 10.00
499 DN,DA,V:Blockbuster 10.00
500 DG,CI,WS,TY,JKu,Deadman,
  Hawkman,Robin 20.00
501 DN,DA 10.00
502 DN,DA 10.00
503 DN,DA,Batgirl,Robin,
  V:Scarecrow 10.00
504 DN,DA,Joker 12.00
505 DN,DA 10.00

Detective Comics #468
© DC Comics Inc.

506 DN,DA 10.00
507 DN,DA 10.00
508 DN,DA,V:Catwoman 11.00
509 DN,DA,V:Catman,Catwoman . 11.00
510 DN,DA,V:Madhatter 10.00
511 DN,DA,I:Mirage 10.00
512 GC,45th Anniv 10.00
513 V:Two-Face 11.00
514 . . . . 10.00
515 . . . . 10.00
516 . . . . 10.00
517 . . . . 10.00
518 V:Deadshot 10.00
519 . . . . 10.00
520 A:Hugo Strange,
  Catwoman 11.00
521 IN,TVE,A:Catwoman,B:
  BU:Green Arrow 12.00
522 D:Snowman 10.00
523 V:Solomon Grundy 10.00
524 2nd A:J.Todd 11.00
525 J.Todd 10.00
526 DN,AA,A:Joker,Catwoman
  500th A:Batman 20.00
527 V:Man Bat 6.00
528 Green Arrow,Ozone 6.00
529 I:Night Slayer,Nocturna 6.00
530 V:Nocturna 6.00
531 GC,AA,Chimera,J.Todd (see
  Batman #364) 6.00
532 GC,Joker 8.00
533 . . . . 6.00
534 GC,A:Gr.Arrow,V:PoisonIvy . . 6.00
535 GC,A:Gr.Arrow,V:Crazy Quitt
  2nd A:New Robin 7.00
536 GC,A:Gr.Arrow,V:Deadshot . . 6.00
537 GC,A:Gr.Arrow 6.00
538 GC,A:Gr.Arrow,V:Catman 6.00
539 GC,A:Gr.Arrow 6.00
540 GC,A:Gr.Arrow,V:Scarecrow . . 6.00
541 GC,A:Gr.Arrow,V:Penguin 7.00
542 GC,A:Gr.Arrow 6.00
543 GC,A:Gr.Arrow,V:Nightslayer . 6.00
544 GC,A:Gr.Arrow,V:Nightslayer . 6.00
545 . . . . 6.00
546 . . . . 6.00
547 . . . . 6.00
548 PB 6.00
549 PB,KJ,AMo(s),Gr.Arrow 7.00
550 KJ,AMo(s),Gr.Arrow 7.00
551 PB,V:Calendar Man 6.00
552 V:Black Mask 6.00
553 V:Black Mask 6.00
554 KJ,N:Black Canary 6.00
555 GC,DD,GreenArrow 6.00
556 GC,Gr.Arrow,V:Nightslayer . . . 6.00
557 V:Nightslayer 6.00
558 GC,Green Arrow 6.00
559 GC,Green Arrow 6.00
560 GC,A:Green Arrow 6.00
561 . . . . 6.00
562 GC,V:Film Freak 6.00
563 V:Two Face 6.00
564 V:Two Face 6.00
565 GC,A:Catwoman 7.00
566 GC,Joker 8.00
567 GC,HarlanEllison 6.00
568 KJ,Legends tie-in,A:Penguin . . 7.00
569 AD,V:Joker 7.00
570 AD,EvilCatwoman,A:Joker 7.00
571 AD,V:Scarecrow 6.00
572 AD,CI,A:Elongated Man,Sherlock
  Holmes,SlamBradley,50thAnn . . 7.50
573 AD,V:Mad Hatter 6.00
574 AD,End old J.Todd/Robin sty . . 6.00
575 AD,Year 2,pt.1,I:Reaper 18.00
576 TM,AA,Year 2,pt.2,
  R:Joe Chill 17.00
577 TM,AA,Year 2,pt.3,V:Reaper . . 17.00
578 TM,AA,Year 2,pt.4,
  D:Joe Chill 17.00

579 I:NewCrimeDoctor. 4.00
580 V:Two Face. 4.00
581 V:Two Face. 4.00
582 Millennium X-over. 4.00
583 I:Ventriloquist. 4.00
584 V:Ventriloquist. 4.00
585 I:Rat Catcher. 4.00
586 V:Rat Catcher. 4.00
587 NB,V:Corrosive Man 4.00
588 NB,V:Corrosive Man 4.00
589 Bonus Book #5 . . . . 5.00
590 NB,V:Hassan 4.00
591 NB,V:Rollo 4.00
592 V:Psychic Vampire 4.00
593 NB,V:Stirh 4.00
594 NB,A:Mr.Potato 4.00
595 IN,bonus book #11 . . . . 4.00
596 V:Sladek 4.00
597 V:Sladek 4.00
598 DCw,BSz,Blind Justice #1 . . . . 5.00
599 DCw,BSz,Blind Justice #2 . . . . 5.00
600 DCw,BSz,Blind Justice #3,
    50th Anniv.(double size) 6.00
601 NB,I:Tulpa 4.00
602 NB,A:Jason Blood. 3.00
603 NB,A:Demon. 3.00
604 NB,MudPack #1,V:Clayface,
    poster insert. 3.00
605 NB,MudPack #2,V:Clayface . . . 3.00
606 NB,MudPack #3,V:Clayface . . . 3.00
607 NB,MudPack #4,V:Clayface,
    poster insert. 3.00
608 NB,I:Anarky. 3.00
609 NB,V:Anarky. 3.00
610 NB,V:Penguin. 4.00
611 NB,V:Catwoman,Catman 4.00
612 NB,A:Vicki Vale. 3.00
613 Search for Poisoner 3.00
614 V:Street Demons. 3.00
615 NB,Return Penguin #2 (see
    Batman #448-#449). 3.50
616 NB. 3.00
617 A:Joker 3.00
618 NB,DG,A:Tim Drake 3.00
619 NB,V:Moneyspider 3.00
620 NB,V:Obeah,Man 3.00
621,NB,SM,Obeah,Man. 3.00
622 Demon Within,pt.1 . . . . 3.00
623 Demon Within,pt.2 . . . . 3.00
624 Demon Within,pt.3 . . . . 3.00
625 JAp,I:Abattior 3.00
626 JAp,A:Electrocutioner 3.00
627 600th issue w/Batman,rep.
    Detective #27 . . . . 5.00
628 JAp,A:Abattoir. 3.00
629 JAp,The Hungry Grass. 3.00
630 JAp,I:Stiletto 3.00
631 JAp,V:Neo-Nazi Gangs. 3.00
632 JAp,V:Creature 3.00
633 TMd,Fake Batman? 3.00
634 The Third Man 3.00
635 Video Game,pt.1. . . . . 3.00
636 Video Game,pt.2. . . . . 3.00
637 Video Game,pt.3. . . . . 3.00
638 JAp,Walking Time Bomb. 3.00
639 JAp,The Idiot Root,pt.2. . . . . . . 3.00
640 JAp,The Idiot Root,pt.4. . . . . . . 3.00
641 JAp,Destroyer,pt.3
    (see LOTDK#27) 3.00
642 JAp,Faces,pt.2 . . . . 3.00
643 JAp,Librarian of Souls. 3.00
644 TL,Electric City,pt.1
    A:Electrocutioner 3.00
645 TL,Electric City,pt.2. . . . . 3.00
646 TL,Electric City,pt.3. . . . . 3.00
647 TL,V:Cluemaster,I:Spoiler 15.00
648 MWg(c),TL,V:Cluemaster 10.00
649 MWg(c),TL,V:Cluemaster 10.00
650 TL,A:Harold,Ace 3.00
651 TL,A Bullet for Bullock 3.00
652 GN,R:Huntress 3.00

653 GN,A:Huntress 3.00
654 MN,The General,pt.1 . . . . 3.00
655 MN,The General,pt.2 . . . . 3.00
656 MN,The General,pt.3,C:Bane . . 4.00
657 MN,A:Azrael,I:Cypher 5.00
658 MN,A:Azrael 3.50
659 MN,Knightfall#2,
    V:Ventriloquist,A:Bane. 3.50
660 Knightfall#4,Bane Vs.
    Killer Croc 3.00
661 GN,Knightfall#6,V:Firefly,
    Joker,A:Bane. 3.00
662 GN,Knightfall#8,V:Firefly,
    Joker,A:Huntress,Bane 3.00
663 GN,Knightfall#10,V:Trogg,
    Zombie,Bird,A:Bane 3.00

Detective Comics #636
© DC Comics, Inc.

664 GN,Knightfall#12,A:Azrael 3.00
665 GN,Knightfall#16,A:Azrael 3.00
666 GN,SHa,A:Azrael,Trogg,
    Zombie,Bird. 3.00
667 GN,SHa,Knightquest:Crusade,
    V:Trigger Twins 3.00
668 GN,SHa,Knightquest:Crusade,
    Robin locked out of Batcave . . . 3.00
669 GN,SHa,Knightquest:Crusade,
    V:Trigger Twins 3.00
670 GN,SHa,Knightquest:Crusade,
    F:Rene Montoya 3.00
671 GN,SHa,V:Joker 3.00
672 KJ(c),GN,SHa,Knightquest:
    Crusade,V:Joker 3.00
673 KJ(c),GN,SHa,Knightquest:
    Crusade,V:Joker 3.00
674 KJ(c),GN,SHa,Knightquest:
    Crusade. 3.00
675 Foil(c),KJ(c),GN,SHa,Knightquest:
    Crusade,V:Gunhawk,foil(c) 4.00
675a Newsstand ed. 3.00
675b Platinum edition 5.00
676 KJ(c),GN,SHa,Knights End #3,
    A:Nightwing 4.00
677 KJ(c),GN,SHa,Knights End #9
    V:Azrael. 3.00
678 GN,SHa,Zero Hour 3.00
679 Ratcatcher. 3.00
680 Batman,Two-Face. 3.00
681 CDi,GN,KJ,Jean-Paul Valley . . 3.00
682 CDi,GN,SHa,Return of Bruce
    Wayne,Troika,pt.3 . . . . 3.00
682a Collector's Edition. 3.50
683 R:Penguin,I:Actuary 3.00
684 Daylight Heist 3.00
685 Chinatown War 3.00

686 V:King Snake,Lynx 3.00
687 CDi,SHa,V:River Pirate. 3.00
688 V:Captian Fear 3.00
689 F:Black Mask,Firefly 3.00
690 F:Black Mask,Firefly 3.00
691 V:Spellbinder 3.00
692 CDi,SHa,Underworld
    Unleashed tie-in 3.00
693 CDi,SHa,V:Poison Ivy
    & Agent Orange. 3.00
694 CDi,find plant-killer 3.00
695 CDi 3.00
696 CDi,GN,SHa,Contagion,pt.8 . . . 3.00
697 CDi,GN,SHa,pt.1 (of 3)
    V:Lock-up 3.00
698 CDi(s),A:Two-Face 3.00
699 CDi(s), ... 3.00
700 double size, Legacy, pt.1
    x-over, R:Bane. 3.50
700a cardstock cover. 6.00
701 Legacy, pt. 6 x-over, V:Bane. . . 3.00
702 CDi(s),GN,SHa,Legacy
    aftermath 3.00
703 CDi(s),GN,SHa, riots in Gotham
    City, Final Night tie-in 3.00
704 CDi(s),GN,TP,V:Al Gabone. . . . 3.00
705 CDi(s),GN,Riddler & Cluemaster
    clash 3.00
706 CDi(s),GN 3.00
707 CDi(s),GN,Riddler/Cluemaster
    concl. 3.00
708 CDi(s),GN,BSz,F:Deathstroke,
    R:Gunhawk, pt.1 (of 3) 3.00
709 CDi(s),GN,BSz,F:Deathstroke,
    Gunhawk,pt.2 . . . . 3.00
710 CDi(s),GN,BSz,F:Deathstroke,
    Gunhawk,pt.3 . . . . 3.00
711 CDi(s),GN,CaS,Bruce Wayne
    fights crime 3.00
712 CDi(s),GN,I:Gearhead 3.00
713 CDi(s),GN,V:Gearhead,pt.2 . . . 3.00
714 CDi(s),GN,F:MartianManhunter . 3.00
715 CDi(s),GN,F:MartianManhunter 3.00
716 CDi,JAp,SNw,BSf 3.00
717 CDi,GN,BSf,V:Gearhead,pt.1 . . 3.00
718 CDi,GN,BSf,V:Gearhead,pt.2 . . 3.00
719 . . . . 3.00
720 CDi,GN,KJ,Cataclysm
    x-over,pt.5 . . . . 4.00
721 CDi,GN,KJ,Cataclysm. 3.00
722 CDi,JAp,BSf,Aftershock 3.00
723 CDi,BSz,Brotherhood of
    the Fist x-over, pt.2 . . . . 3.00
724 CDi,JAp,BSf,F:Nightwing 3.00
725 CDi,TP,BSf,Aftershock 3.00
726 CDi(s),BSf,V:Joker 3.00
727 . . . . 3.00
728 CDi(s),BSf,SB,No Man's Land . 3.00
729 CDi(s),SB,No Man's Land. 3.00
730 No Law and a New Order,
    concl. 5.00
731 F:Batgirl, Mosaic, pt.2 . . . . 3.00
732 F:Batgirl, Mosaic, pt.4 . . . . 3.00
733 SB,Alfreds advice 3.00
734 F:Batgirl,pt.2 x-over 3.00
735 DJu,BSz,Fruit of
    the Earth,pt.3. . . . . 3.00
736 LHa(s),MD2,V:Bane 3.00
737 TMo, No Man's Land,
    The Code, concl. 3.00
738 CDi,MtB,Goin'Downtown,pt.2 . . 3.00
739 Jurisprudence,concl. 3.00
740 . . . . 3.00
741 Endgame, pt.3,40-pg.x-over . . . 3.00
742 SMa,40-pg. 3.00
743 SMa,40-pg,new logo 3.00
744 SMa,40-pg. 3.00
745 SMa,V:Whisperer 3.00
746 SMa,B.U.:The Jacobian 3.00
747 JJ,F:Renee Montoya. 3.00
748 JJ,Urban Renewal,pt.1 . . . . . . 3.00

DC COMICS

749 JJ,PhH,Urban Renewal,pt.2 . . . 3.00
750 V:Ra's Al Ghul,64-pg. 6.00
751 SMa,JJ,DPS,F:Poison Ivy 3.00
752 SMa,JJ,DPs,F:Poison Ivy 3.00
753 SMa,JJ,DPs,This issue:
      Batman dies! 3.00
754 Officer Down x-over,pt.6 . . . . . 3.00
755 SMa,DPs,V:Two-Face. 3.00
756 Lord of the Ring x-over pt.2 . . . 3.00
757 RBr,RyR,DPs,Air Time 3.00
758 SMa,Crooked Cops in Gotham. 3.00
759 SMa,BU:Catwoman,pt.1 . . . . . . 3.00
760 SMa,V:Mad Hatter,BU:pt.2 . . . 3.00
761 SMa,BU:Catwoman,pt.3 . . . . . . 3.00
762 RBr,BU:Catwoman,concl. 3.00
763 SMa,F:Sasha,V:Cucilla 3.00
764 SMa,F:Vesper 3.00
765 RBr,James Gordon 3.00
766 Bruce Wayne:Murderer,pt.1 . . 3.00
767 Bruce Wayne:Murderer,pt.8 . . . 5.00
768 MGy,shipment of heroin 3.00
769 Bruce Wayne:Fugitive,pt.5 . . . 3.00
770 Bruce Wayne:Fugitive,pt.8 . . . 3.00
771 BruceWayne:Fugitive,pt.12. . . 3.00
772 BruceWayne:Fugitive,pt.16. . . 2.75
773 F:Sasha Bordeaux in prison . . . 2.75
774 BSz(c),Checkmate 2.75
775 BSz(c),V:Checkmate 48-pg. . . 3.50
776 BWi,A cop's vendetta 2.75
777 Dead Reckoning,pt.1 . . . . 2.75
778 Dead Reckoning,pt.2 . . . . 2.75
779 Dead Reckoning,pt.3 . . . . 2.75
780 Dead Reckoning,pt.4 . . . . 2.75
781 Dead Reckoning,pt.5 . . . . 2.75
782 Dead Reckoning,pt.6 . . . . 2.75
783 SMa,KJ,More Perfect 2.75
784 Made of Wood,pt.1 . . . . 2.75
785 Made of Wood,pt.2 . . . . 2.75
786 Made of Wood,pt.3 . . . . 2.75
787 RBr,Low,Mad Hatter,Man-Bat . 2.75
788 Randori Stone, pt.1 . . . . 2.75
789 Randori Stone, pt.2 . . . . 2.75
790 CaS,Scarification 2.75
791 CaS,The Surrogate,pt.1 . . . . . . 2.75
792 CaS,The Surrogate,pt.2 . . . . . . 2.75
793 CaS,The Surrogate,pt.3 . . . . . 2.95
794 CaS,The Rotting,pt.1 . . . . 2.95
795 CaS,The Rotting,pt.2 . . . . 2.95
796 CaS,Mr.Zsasz 2.95
797 War Games,Act 1,pt.1,40-pg. . 2.95
798 War Games,Act 2,pt.1,40-pg. . 2.95
799 War Games,Act 3,pt.1,40-pg. . 2.95
Ann.#1 KJ,TD,A:Question,Talia,
      V:Penguin 6.00
Ann.#2 VS,A:Harvey Harris 6.00
Ann.#3 DJu,DG,Batman in Japan . . 2.50
Ann.#4 Armageddon,pt.10 . . . . 3.00
Ann.#5 SK(c),TMd,Eclipso,V:The
      Ventriloquist,Joker. 3.00
Ann.#6 JBa,I:Geist. 2.75
Ann.#7 CDi,Elseworlds Story. 3.25
Ann.#8 CDi,KD(c) Year One Annual
      O:The Riddler 3.95
Ann.#9 Legends o/t Dead Earth . . 2.95
Ann.#10 Pulp Heroes (War) CDi(s),
      SB,KJ. 3.95
Spec.#1,000,000 CDi(s). 2.00
TPB Manhunter AGw,WS 10.00

DETENTION COMICS
Aug., 1996
one-shot DON(s) 64pg, 3 stories. . . 3.50

DEXTER'S LABORATORY
Warner Bros./DC, 1999
1 Kirbytron 6000 . . . . 5.00
2 Let's Save the World, You Jerk . . 4.00
3 thru 10 . . . . @3.00
11 thru 24 . . . . @2.50
25 thru 34 . . . . @2.25

DISAVOWED
Homage/DC Jan., 2000
1 BCi 2.50
2 thru 6 BCi(s). . . . . @2.50

DOC SAVAGE
1987–88
1 AKu/NKu,D:Orig. Doc Savage . . . 3.00
2 AKu/NKu,V:Nazi's 3.00
3 AKu/NKu,V:Nazi's 3.00
4 AKu/NKu,V:Heinz. 3.00

[2nd Series], 1988–90
1 Five in the Sky'(painted cov.) . . . 3.00
2 Chip Lost in Himalayas 3.00
3 Doc declares war on USSR. 3.00
4 Doc Savage/Russian team-up . . . 3.00
5 V:The Erisians 3.00
6 U.S.,USSR,China Alliance
      vs. Erisians 3.00
7 Mind Molder,pt.1, I:Pat Savage . . 3.00
8 . . . . 3.00
9 In Hidalgo. 3.00
10 V:Forces of the Golden God. . . . 3.00
11 Sunlight Rising,pt.1 . . . . 3.00
12 Sunlight Rising,pt.2. . . . . 3.00
13 Sunlight Rising,pt.3. . . . . 3.00
14 Sunlight Rising,pt.4. . . . . 3.00
15 SeaBaron #1 . . . . 3.00
16 EB,Shadow & Doc Savage 3.50
17 EB,Shadow & Doc Savage 4.00
18 EB,Shadow/Doc Savage conc. . 4.00
19 All new 1930's story 3.00
20 V:Airlord & his Black Zepplin . . . 3.00
21 Airlord (30's story conc.) 3.00
22 Doc Savages Past,pt.1 . . . . 3.00
23 Doc Savages Past,pt.2. . . . . . . 3.00
24 Doc Savages Past,pt.3 (final). . . 3.00
Ann.#1 1956 Olympic Games. 4.50

DOCTOR FATE
July, 1987
1 KG,V:Lords of Chaos 3.00
2 KG,New Dr. Fate 3.00
3 KG,A:JLI 3.00
4 KG,V:Lords of Chaos Champion . 3.00

[2nd Series], 1988–92
1 New Dr.Fate,V:Demons 4.00
2 A:Andrew Bennett(I),Vampire) . . 3.00
3 A:Andrew Bennett(I),Vampire) . . . 3.00
4 V:I,Vampire 3.00
5 Dr.Fate & I,Vampire in Europe. . . 3.00
6 A:Petey 3.00
7 Petey returns home dimension . . 3.00
8 Linda become Dr.Fate again 3.00
9 Eric's Mother's Ghost,
      A:Deadman 3.00
10 Death of Innocence,pt.1 . . . . . . 3.00
11 Return of Darkseid, Death of
      Innocence,pt.2. . . . . 3.00
12 Two Dr.Fates Vs.Darkseid,
      Death of Innocence,pt.3 . . . . . 3.00
13 Linda in the Astral Realm,
      Death of Innocence,pt.4 . . . . . 3.00
14 Kent & Petey vs. Wotan 3.00
15 V:Wotan,A:JLI 3.50
16 Flashback-novice Dr.Fate 2.50
17 Eric's Journey thru afterlife 2.50
18 Search for Eric 2.50
19 A:Dr.Benjamine Stoner, Lords of
      Chaos, Phantom Stranger,
      Search for Eric continued 2.50
20 V:Lords of Chaos,Dr.Stoner,
      A:Phantom Stranger 2.50
21 V:Chaos,A:PhantomStranger . . 2.50
22 A:Chaos and Order. 2.50
23 Spirits of Kent & Inza Nelson . . . 2.50
24 L:Dr.Fate Characters 2.50
25 I:New Dr. Fate. 2.50

Doc Savage #3
© DC Comics, Inc.

26 Dr.Fate vs. Orig.Dr.Fate 2.50
27 New York Crime 2.50
28 Diabolism 2.50
29 Kent Nelson 2.50
30 Resurrection 2.50
31 Resurrection' contd. 2.50
32 War of the Gods x-over 2.50
33 War of the Gods x-over 2.50
34 A:T'Gilian. 2.50
35 Kent Nelson in N.Y. 2.50
36 Search For Inza,A:Shat-Ru. 2.50
37 Fate Helmet Powers revealed . . 2.50
38 The Spirit Motor,'Flashback 2.50
39 U.S.Senate Hearing 2.50
40 A:Wonder Woman. 2.50
41 O:Chaos and Order,last issue . . 2.50
Ann.#1 TS,R:Eric's dead mother . . . 3.00

DR. FATE
Aug. 2003
1 (of 5) Hector Hall 2.50
2 Salem mystics 2.50
3 Nabu disappeared 2.50
4 The Curse 2.50
5 Concl.. . . . . 2.50

DOCTOR MID-NITE
1999
1 (of 3) MWg,F:Dr. Piter Cross 6.00
2 MWg 6.00
3 MWg, conclusion 6.00
TPB 19.95

DOME, THE:
GROUND ZERO
DC/Helix, July, 1998
1-shot DGb,AMK 8.00

DOOM FORCE
1992
Spec.#1 MMi(c),RCa,WS,PCu,KSy,
      I:Doom Force. 3.00

DOOM PATROL
[1st series]
See: MY GREATEST
ADVENTURE

Doom Patrol #14 © DC Comics Inc.

DOOM PATROL
[2nd Regular Series], 1987

1 SLi,R:Doom Patrol,plus Who's Who background of team, I:Kalki.... 5.00
2 SLi,V:Kalki 3.50
3 SLi,I:Lodestone 3.50
4 SLi,I:Karma 3.50
5 SLi,R:Chief................. 3.50
6 B:PuK(s),EL,GyM(i), I:Scott Fischer 4.50
7 EL,GyM(i),V:Shrapnel 3.50
8 EL,GyM(i),V:Shrapnel 3.50
9 E:PuK(s),EL,GyM(i),V:Garguax, & Bonus Book 3.50
10 EL,A:Superman............. 3.50
11 EL,R:Garguax 3.00
12 EL,A:Garguax 3.00
13 EL,A:Power Girl 3.00
14 EL,A:Power Girl 3.00
15 EL,Animal-Veg.-Mineral Man .. 3.00
16 V:GenImmotus,Animal-Veg.-Mineral Man 3.00
17 D:Celsius,A:Aquaman & Sea Devils, Invasion tie-in 4.00
18 Invasion................... 3.00
19 B:GMo(s),New Direction, I:Crazy Jane 18.00
20 I:Rebis(new Negative-Being), A:CrazyJane,Scissormen 10.00
21 V:Scissormen 10.00
22 City of Bone,V:Scissormen.... 10.00
23 A:RedJack,Lodestone kidnap .. 5.00
24 V:Red Jack 5.00
25 Secrets of New Doom Patrol ... 5.00
26 I:Brotherhood of Dada 4.00
27 V:Brotherhood of Dada 4.00
28 Trapped in nightmare,V:Dada... 4.00
29 Trapped in painting, A:Superman............... 4.00
30 SBs(c),V:Brotherhood of Dada . 4.00
31 SBs(c),A:The Pale Police 4.00
32 SBs(c),V:Cult of Unwritten Book 4.00
33 SBs(c),V:Cult,A:Anti-God the DeCreator 4.00
34 SBs(c),Robotman vs. his brain, R:The Brain & Mr.Mallah...... 4.00
35 SBs(c),A:Men from N.O.W.H.E.R.E.............. 9.00
36 SBs(c),V:Men from N.O.W.H.E.R.E. 17.00
37 SBs(c),Rhea Jones Story 4.00
38 SBs(c),V:Aliens 4.00
39 SBs(c),V:Aliens.............. 4.00

40 SBs(c),Aliens 4.00
41 SBS(c),Aliens 4.00
42 O:Flex Mentallo.............. 18.00
43 SBs(c),V:N.O.W.H.E.R.E....... 6.00
44 SBs(c),V:N.O.W.H.E.R.E....... 6.00
45...................... 4.00
46 SBs(c),RCa,MkK,A:Crazy Jane, Dr.Silence 5.00
47 Scarlet Harlot (Crazy Jane) ... 4.00
48 V:Mr.Evans................. 4.00
49 TTg(c),RCa,MGb,I:Mr.Nobody .. 4.00
50 SBs(c),V:Brotherhood of Dada & bonus artists portfolio. ... 4.00
51 SBs(c),Mr.Nobody Runs for President 4.00
52 SBs(c),Mr.Nobody saga conc... 4.00
53 SBs(c),Parody Issue,A:Phantom Stranger,Hellbalzer,Mr.E 4.00
54 Rebis Transformation 4.00
55 SBs(c),V:Crazy Jane, Candle Maker 4.00
56 SBs(c),RCa,V:Candle Maker ... 4.00
57 SBs(c),RCa,V:Candle Maker, O:Team,Double-sized 4.00
58 SBs(c),V:Candle Maker 4.00
59 TTg(c),RCa,SnW(i),A:Candlemaker D:Larry Trainor 4.00
60 JHw(c),RCa,SnW(i), V:Candlemaker,A:Magnus..... 4.00
61 TTg(c),RCa,SnW(i),A:Magnus D:Candlemaker 4.00
62 DFg(c),RCa,SnW(i), V:Nanomachines 4.00
63 E:GMo(s),RCa,R:Crazy Jane, V:Keysmiths,BU:Sliding from the Wreckage 4.00

DC/Vertigo, 1993

64 BB(c),B:RaP(s),RCa,SnW(i), B:Sliding from the Wreckage, R:Niles Caulder 3.00
65 TTg(c),RCa,SnW(i),Nannos 3.00
66 RCa,E:Sliding from the Wreckage 3.00
67 TTg(c),RCa,GHi(i),New HQ,I:Charlie, George,Marion,V:Wild Girl..... 3.00
68 TTg(c),LiM,GHi(i),I:Indentity Addict..................... 3.00
69 TTg(c),LiM,GHi(i),V:Identity Addict..................... 3.00
70 TTg(c),SEa,TS(i),I:Coagula, V:Codpiece 3.00
71 TTg(c),LiM,TS(i),Fox & Crow ... 3.00
72 TTg(c),LiM,TS(i),Fox vs Crow... 3.00
73 LiM,GPi(i),Head's Nightmare ... 3.00
74 LiM,TS(i),Bootleg Steele 3.00
75 BB(c),TMK,Teiresias Wars#1, Double size 3.00
76 Teiresias Wars#2 .... 3.00
77 BB(c),TMK,N:Cliff 3.00
78 BB(c),V:Tower of Babel........ 3.00
79 BB(c),E:Teiresias Wars 3.00
80 V:Yapping Dogs 3.00
81 B:Masquerade............... 3.00
82 E:Masquerade............... 3.00
83 False Memory............... 3.00
84 The Healers 3.00
85 Charlie the Doll 3.00
86 Imagine Ari's Friends 3.00
87 KB(c),final issue 3.00
Ann.#1 A:Lex Luthor 3.00
Ann.#2 RaP(s),MkW,Children's Crusade,F:Dorothy,A:Maxine .. 4.25
Doom Patrol/Suicide Squad #1 EL, D:Mr.104,Thinker,Psi,Weasel .. 2.50
TPB SBs(c),rep.#19-#25 .... 19.95

DOOM PATROL
Oct., 2001

1 JAr,R:Doom Patrol............ 3.00
2 JAr,F:Robotman, Thayer 3.75

3 JAr,V:Gomz 2.50
4 JAr,new Doom Patrol?......... 2.50
5 JAr,Doom Force.............. 2.50
6 JAr,Robotman gone........... 2.50
7 JAr,search for Robotman....... 2.50
8 JAr,new Robotman 2.50
9 JAr,Cliff Steele, Robotman...... 2.50
10 JAr,Black Vulture,Amazo 2.50
11 JAr,in Hell 2.50
12 JAr,V:Demon Raum 2.50
13 JAr(s),Monsters,pt.1 .... 2.50
14 JAr(s),Monsters,pt.2 .... 2.50
15 JAr(s),F:Robotman 2.50
16 JAr(s),V:Purple Purposeless.... 2.50
17 JAr(s),R:Tycho 2.50
18 JAr(s),ancient China 2.50
19 JAr(s),R:Tycho 2.50
20 television studios 2.50
21 O:Tycho................... 2.50
22 final issue 2.50

DOOM PATROL
July 2004

1 JBy,DHz,V:Crucifer 2.50
2 JBy,DHz,escaped specimens ... 2.50
3 JBy,DHz,Cold Night's Death 2.50
4 JBy,DHz,Waters Under World ... 2.50
5 JBy,DHz 2.50
TPB Crawling From the Wreckage 19.95
TPB Painting That Ate Paris 19.95

DOOMSDAY
1995
Ann.#1 Year One annuals 4.00

DOORWAY TO NIGHTMARE
1978
1 I:Madame Xanadu 20.00
2 thru 5 .... @15.00

DOUBLE ACTION COMICS
Jan., 1940
2 Pre-Hero DC........... 18,000.00

DRAGONLANCE
1988–91

1 Krynn's Companion's advent. ... 4.00
2 Vandar&Riva vs.Riba's brother .. 3.50
3 V:Takhesis,Queen of Darkness .. 3.50
4 V:Lord Soth & Kitiara 3.50
5 V:Queen of Darkness 3.50
6 Gnatch vs. Kalthanan 3.50
7 Raistlin's Evil contd............ 3.50
8 Raistlin's Evil concl............ 3.00
9 Journey to land o/t Minotaurs A:Tanis, Kitiara 3.00
10 Blood Sea,Arena of Istar 3.00
11 Cataclysm of Krynn Revealed Arena of Istar' contd........ 3.00
12 Horak vs.Koraf, Arena contd. ... 3.00
13 Test of High Sorcery #1 .... 3.00
14 Test of High Sorcery #2 .... 3.00
15 Test of High Sorcery #3 .... 3.00
16 Test of High Sorcery #4 .... 3.00
17 Winter'sKnight:DragonkillPt.1 ... 3.00
18 Winter'sKnight:DragonkillPt.1 ... 3.00
19 Winter'sKnight:DragonkillPt.1 ... 3.00
20 Winter'sKnight:DragonkillPt.1 ... 3.00
21 Move to New World 3.00
22 Taladas,pt.1,A:Myrella......... 3.00
23 Taladas,pt.2,Riva vs. Dragon ... 3.00
24 Taladas,pt.3,V:Minotaur Lord ... 3.00
25 Taladas,pt.4,V:Axantheas 3.00
26 Rune Discovery,V:Agents of Eristem 3.00

27 V:Agents of Eristem 3.00
28 Riva continued. 3.00
29 Riva continued 3.00
30 Dwarf War,pt.1 . . . . 3.00
31 Dwarf War,pt.2 . . . . 3.00
32 Dwarf War,pt.3 . . . . 3.00
33 Dwarf War,pt.4 . . . . 3.00
34 conc., last issue 3.00
Ann.#1 Myrella of the Robed
    Wizards 2.95

The Dreaming #44 © DC Comics Inc.

DREAMING, THE
DC/Vertigo, June, 1996

1 TLa(s),PSj,GoldieFactor,pt.1 . . . . 4.50
2 TLa(s),PSj,GoldieFactor,pt.2 . . . . 4.00
3 TLa(s),PSj,GoldieFactor,pt.3 . . . . 4.00
4 SvP,The Lost Boy,pt.1 . . . . 3.50
5 SvP,The Lost Boy,pt.2 . . . . 2.50
6 SvP,The Lost Boy,pt.3 . . . . 2.50
7 SvP,The Lost Boy,pt.4 . . . . 2.50
8 AaK(s),MZi,visitor from past 2.50
9 BT(s),PD,TOz,Weird Romance,
    pt.1. . . . . 2.50
10 BT(s),PD,TOz,Romance,pt.2 . . . 2.50
11 BT(s),PD,TOz,Romance,pt.3 . . . 2.50
12 BT(s),PD,TOz,Romance,pt.4 . . . 2.50
13 TLa,JIT,Coyote's Kiss,pt.1. . . . . 2.50
14 TLa,JIT,Coyote's Kiss,pt.2. . . . . 2.50
15 . . . . 2.50
16 GyA,F:Nuala 2.50
17 PD,DMc,Souvenirs, pt.1 . . . . 2.50
18 PD,DMc,Souvenirs, pt.2 . . . . 2.50
19 PD,DMc,Souvenirs, pt.3 . . . . 2.50
20 ADv, The Dark Rose, pt.1. . . . . . 2.50
21 ADv, The Dark Rose, pt.2. . . . . . 2.50
22 The Unkindness of One, pt.1 . . . 2.50
23 The Unkindness of One, pt.2 . . . 2.50
24 The Unkindness of One, pt.3 . . . 2.50
25 My Life as a Man 2.50
26 Restitution. 2.50
27 Caretaker Cain 2.50
28 Victims of famous fires 2.50
29 PSj,DMc,Abel'sHouse ofSecrets. 2.50
30 DMc(c),Lucien's mysteries 2.50
31 House of Secrets, 48-pg. 4.00
32 DG,SvP 2.50
33 The Little Mermaid 2.50
34 MaH, Cave of Nightmares 2.50
35 DMc(c),Kaleidoscope 2.50
36 DMc(c),The Gyres, pt.1 . . . . 2.50
37 DMc(c),The Gyres, pt.2 . . . . 2.50
38 DMc(c),The Gyres, pt.3 . . . . 2.50
39 DMc(c),Lost Language
    of Flowers 2.50

40 DMc(c),Foxes & Hounds,pt.1 . . 2.50
41 DMc(c),Foxes & Hounds,pt.2 . . 2.50
42 DMc(c),Foxes & Hounds,pt.3 . . 2.50
43 DMc(c),Foxes & Hounds,pt.4 . . 2.50
44 Trinket,pt.1 . . . . 2.50
45 Trinket,pt.2 . . . . 2.50
46 Trinket,pt.3 . . . . 2.50
47 CV,RoR 2.50
48 . . . . 2.50
49 DMc(c),The Dawn Stone 2.50
50 DMc(c),rebuilding 2.50
51 DMc(c),in Manhattan 2.50
52 Exiles,pt.1 . . . . 2.50
53 Exiles,pt.2 . . . . 2.50
54 Exiles,pt.3 . . . . 2.50
55 F:Danny Nod. 2.50
56 1stAdventure of CatterinaPoe.. . 2.50
57 Rise,pt.1 . . . . 2.50
58 Rise,pt.2 . . . . 2.50
59 Rise,pt.3 . . . . 2.50
60 Rise,pt.4 . . . . 2.50
TPB Beyond the Shores of Night. . 20.00
TPB Through the Gates of
    Horn & Ivory 20.00
GN Trial and Error 6.00

DYNAMIC CLASSICS
Sept-Oct., 1978

1 NA,WS,rep.Detective 395&438 . 15.00

ECLIPSO
1992–94

1 BS,MPn,V:South American
    Drug Dealers 2.50
2 BS,MPn,A:Bruce Gordon. 2.25
3 BS,MPn,R:Amanda Waller 2.25
4 BS,A:Creeper,Cave Carson. 2.25
5 A:Creeper,Cave Carson. 2.25
6 LMc,V:Bruce Gordon 2.25
7 London,1891 . . . . 2.25
8 A:Sherlock Holmes 2.25
9 I:Johnny Peril. 2.25
10 CDo,V:Darkseid 2.25
11 A:Creeper,Peacemaker,Steel . . 2.25
12 V:Shadow Fighters 2.25
13 D:Manhunter,Commander Steel,
    Major Victory,Peacemaker,
    Wildcat,Dr.Midnight,Creeper . . . 2.25
14 A:JLA. 2.25
15 A:Amanda Waller 2.25
16 V:US Army 2.25
17 A:Amanda Waller,Martian
    Manhunter,Wonder Woman,Flash,
    Bloodwynd,Booster Gold. 2.25
18 A:Spectre,JLA,final issue 2.25
Ann.#1 I:Prism 2.50

ECLIPSO: THE DARKNESS WITHIN
1992

1 BS,Direct w/purple diamond,
    A:Superman,Creeper. 4.00
1a BS,Newstand w/out diamond . . 3.00
2 BS,MPn,DC heroes V:Eclipso,
    D:Starman 3.00

EGYPT
1995–96

1 College Experiments 3.50
2 College Experiments 3.00
3 New York Haunt. 3.00
4 V:Seth,Isis 3.00
5 V: The Priests 3.00
6 . . . . 3.00
7 finale 3.00

80 PAGE GIANTS
Aug., 1964

1 Superman 750.00
2 Jimmy Olsen 400.00
3 Lois Lane 300.00
4 Golden Age-Flash 300.00
5 Batman 300.00
6 Superman 250.00
7 JKu&JKu(c),Sgt. Rock's Prize
    Battle Tales 250.00
8 Secret Origins,O:JLA,Aquaman,
    Robin,Atom, Superman 600.00
9 Flash 250.00
10 Superboy. 250.00
11 Superman,A:Lex Luthor 250.00
12 Batman 250.00
13 Jimmy Olsen. 250.00
14 Lois Lane 250.00
15 Superman & Batman 250.00
16 thru 89 in regular series runs

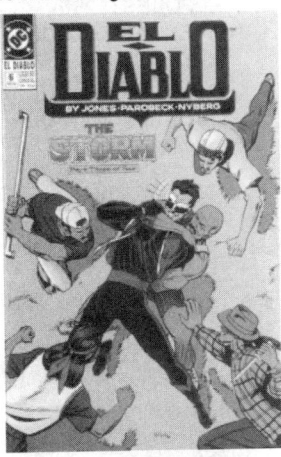

El Diablo #6 © DC Comics, Inc.

EL DIABLO
1989–91

1 I:El Diablo, double-size 3.00
2 V:Crime Lord Benny Contreras . . 2.50
3 Day of the Dead' Celebration . . . 2.50
4 Storm #1 . . . . 2.50
5 Storm #2 . . . . 2.50
6 Storm #3 . . . . 2.50
7 Storm #4 . . . . 2.50
8 V:Car-Theft Ring 2.50
9 V:Crime Lord of Dos Rios 2.50
10 The Franchise #1 . . . . 2.50
11 The Franchise #2 . . . . 2.50
12 A:Greg Sanders (golden age). . . 2.50
13 The River #1 . . . . 2.50
14 The River #2. . . . . 2.50
15 The River #3. . . . . 2.50
16 Final Issue 2.50

EL DIABLO
DC/Vertigo, Jan., 2001

1 (of 4) Weird Western Tales 2.50
2 thru 4 . . . . @2.50

ELECTRIC WARRIOR
1986–87

1 SF series,I:Electric Warriors 2.50
2 Bloodstalker Mode. 2.25
3 Rogue Warrior vs. Z-Primes 2.25
4 Primmies vs. Electric Warriors. . . 2.25
5 Lek 0-03 Rebels 2.25

6 Lek 0-03 vs. Masters 2.25
7 Lek'sFate,Derek Two-Shadows . . 2.25
8 Derek Two-Shadows Betrayed . . 2.25
9 Fate of Derek Two-Shadows 2.25
10 Two-Shadows as one 2.25
11 Rebellion 2.25
12 Rebellion continued 2.25
13 V:Prime One 2.25
14 Mutants Join Rebellion 2.25
15 Invaders Arrival 2.25
16 Unified Warriors vs. Invaders . . . 2.25
17 V:Terrans, O:Electric Warriors . . 2.25
18 Origin continued, final issue . . . 2.25

ELFQUEST: THE GRAND QUEST
Jan. 2004
TPB Vol. 1 thru Vol. 5 WP . . . . . @10.00

ELFQUEST: 25th ANNIVERSARY EDITION
DC 2003
Spec. WP,RPi, rep. Elfquest #1 . . . . 3.00

ELFQUEST: WOLFRIDER
Sept. 2003
TPB Vol. 1 . . . . 10.00
TPB Vol. 2 . . . . 10.00

*Elongated Man #1
© DC Comics, Inc.*

ELONGATED MAN
1992
1 A:Copperhead 2.25
2 Modora,A:Flash,I:Sonar 2.25
3 A:Flash,V:Wurst Gang 2.25

ELRIC: THE MAKING OF A SORCERER
Sept. 2004
1 (of 4) WS, from M.Moorcock 5.95
2 WS 5.95

ELSEWORLD'S FINEST
DC/Elseworlds 1998
1 (of 2) JFM,KD,F:Bruce Wayne
    and Clark Kent, ... 5.00
2 JFM,KD,concl. 5.00
GN Supergirl & Batgirl 6.00

ELVIRA
1986–87
1 DSp,BB(c) 5.00
2 thru 9 . . . . @4.00
10 . . . . 4.00
11 DSt(c)Find Cain. 5.00

EMPIRE
June 2003
0 JmP,from Gorilla Comics 4.95
1 (of 6) JmP,V:Golgoth 2.50
2 thru 5 BKi,JmP . . . . @2.50
6 concl. 2.50
TPB 15.00

ENEMY ACE: WAR IN HEAVEN
March, 2001
1 (of 2) GEn, 48-page 6.00
2 GEn,48-page 6.00
TPB Enemy Ace:War in Heaven . . 15.00

ENGINEHEAD
April 2004
1 (of 8) TMK,six heroes in one 2.50
2 TMK,why am I here? 2.50
3 TMK,cosmic mechanic. 2.50
4 TMK,V:Metallo 2.50
5 TMk,band of terrorists 2.50
6 TMk,Metal Men 2.50

ENIGMA
DC/Vertigo, 1993
1 B:PrM(s),DFg,I:Enigma,Michael
    Smith,V:The Head 3.00
2 DFg,I:The Truth 3.00
3 DFg,V:The Truth,I:Envelope Girl,
    Titus Bird 3.00
4 DFg,D:The Truth,I:Interior
    League. 3.00
5 DFg,I:Enigma's Mother 3.00
6 DFg,V:Envelope Girl 3.00
7 DFg,V:Enigma's Mother,D:Envelope
    Girl,O:Enigma 3.00
8 E:PrM(s),DFg,final issue 3.00
TPB Rep. #1-#8 . . . . 20.00

ERADICATOR
1996
1 IV,Low, ... 2.50
2 IV,Low, ... 2.50
3 IV,Low,Reign of the Superman
    concl.,A:Superboy 2.50

ESSENTIAL VERTIGO: SWAMP THING
DC/Vertigo, Sept., 1996
B&W reprints
1 AMo(s), rep. Saga of
    the Swamp Thing #21. . . . . 3.00
2 thru 11 AMo(s), rep. Saga of
    the Swamp Thing #22–#31. . @3.00
12 AMo(s) rep. Saga Ann. #2 . . . . 3.00
13 AMo(s) rep. Saga #32–#42 . . @3.00
24 AMo,Windfall, final issue 3.00

ESSENTIAL VERTIGO: THE SANDMAN
DC/Vertigo, 1996
3 NGa(s),SK,MDr,rep. 3.00
4 NGa(s),SK,MDr,rep. F:Etrigan . 3.00
5 NGa(s),SK,MJ,F:Morpheus,
    John Dee 3.00
6 NGa(s),SK,MJ,V:Dr. Destiny . . . 3.00

7 . . . . 3.00
8 NGa(s),MDr,MJ,The Sound
    of Her Wings 3.00
9 NGa(s),MDr,MJ,The Doll's
    House, F:Nada 3.00
10 NGa(s),MDr,MJ,Doll's House . . . 3.00
11 NGa(s),MDr,RT 3.00
12 NGa(s),CBa,MJ,Doll'sHouse . . 3.00
13 NGa,rep.Doll's House,pt.4 . . . . 3.00
14 NGa,rep.Doll's House,pt.5 . . . . 3.00
15 NGa,rep.Doll's House,pt.6 . . . . 3.50
16 NGa,rep.Lost Hearts. 3.00
17 NGa,rep.Dream Country. 3.00
18 NGa,Dream of Thousand Cats . . 3.00
19 NGa,rep.Sandman #19. . . . . . . 3.00
20 NGa,rep.Sandman #20. . . . . . . 3.00
21 NGa,rep.Sandman #21. . . . . . . 3.00
22 NGa,rep.Season of Mists pt.1 . . 3.00
23 NGa,rep.Season of Mists pt.2 . . 3.00
24 NGa,rep.Season of Mists pt.3 . . 3.00
25 NGa,rep.Season of Mists pt.4 . . 3.00
26 NGa,rep.Season of Mists pt.5 . . 3.00
27 NGa,rep.Season of Mists pt.6. . 3.00
28 NGa,rep.Season of Mists,epilog . 3.00
29 NGa,rep.Thermidor. 3.00
30 NGa,rep.August 3.00
31 NGa,rep.Three Septembers
    and a January 3.00
32 NGa,rep. Sandman Special #1
    final issue 4.50

EXTREME JUSTICE
1995–96
O New Group 3.50
1 V:Captain Atom 3.00
2 V:War Cyborgs. 3.00
3 V:Synge 3.00
4 R:Firestorm the Nuclear Man . . 3.00
5 Firestorm & Elementals 3.00
6 Monarch,Captain Atom, Booster
    Gold, Maxima 3.00
7 F:Monarch,Captain Atom 3.00
8 . . . . 3.00
9 F:Firestorm 3.00
10 Underworld Unleashed tie-in . . . 3.00
11 Underworld Unleashed tie-in. . . 3.00
12 Monarch's scheme revealed. . . 3.00
13 Monarch vs. Captain Atom 3.00
14 . . . . 3.00
15 TMo,V:The Slavemaster from
    the Stars 3.00
16 TMo,V:Legion of Doom 3.00
17 TMo,V:Legion of Doom 3.00

EXTREMIST
DC/Vertigo, 1993
1 B:PrM(s),TMK,I:The Order,
    Extremist(Judy Tanner) 2.50
1a Platinum Ed. 5.00
2 TMK,D:Extremist(Jack Tanner) . . 2.25
3 TMK,V:Patrick 2.25
4 E:PrM(s),TMK,D:Tony Murphy . . 2.25

FABLES
DC/Vertigo, May, 2002
1 SL, Legends in Exile,pt.1 . . . . . 20.00
1a variant (c). 20.00
2 SL, Legends in Exile,pt.2 . . . . 12.00
3 SL, Legends in Exile,pt.3 . . . . . 7.00
4 BWg,Legends in Exile,pt.4 . . . . 6.00
5 SL, Legends in Exile,pt.5 . . . . . 6.00
6 MBu,SL,Animal Farm,pt.1 . . . . . 6.00
7 MBu,SL,Animal Farm,pt.2 . . . . . 4.00
8 MBu,SL,Animal Farm,pt.3 . . . . . 4.00
9 MBu,SL,Animal Farm,pt.4 . . . . . 4.00
10 MBu,SL,Animal Farm,pt.5. . . . . 4.00
11 Jack of the Tales 4.00
12 Fables caper,pt.1 . . . . 4.00
13 Fables caper,pt.2 . . . . 3.00

14 Storybook Love,pt.1 . . . . 3.00
15 Storybook Love,pt.2 . . . . 3.00
16 Storybook Love,pt.3 . . . . 3.00
17 Storybook Love,pt.4 . . . . 3.00
18 The Barley Corn Brides 2.50
19 MBu,SL 2.50
20 MBu,SL 2.50
21 MBu,SL 2.50
22 JP,Ex-wives Club 2.50
23 MBu,SL 2.50
24 MBu,SL,Boy Blue missing 2.50
25 MBu,SL,Wooden Soldiers 2.50
26 MBu,SL,Wooden Soldiers 2.50
27 MBu,SL,Wooden Soldiers 2.50
28 JP,War Stories,pt.1 . . . . 2.50
29 JP,War Stories,pt.2 . . . . 2.50
30 MBu,SL,The Year After,pt.1 . . . 2.50
TPB March of Wooden Soldiers . . 18.00
TPB Storybook Love 15.00
TPB Fables: Legends in Exile 15.00
TPB Fables: Animal Farm 13.00
Spec. The Last Castle 6.00

FAITH
DC/Vertigo, Sept., 1999
1 (of 5) TMK 2.50
2 thru 5 TMK . . . . @2.50

FALLEN ANGEL
July 2003
1 PDd(s),Bete Noire 2.50
2 PDd(s),Asia Minor 2.50
3 PDd(s),Little Better,pt.1 . . . . 2.50
4 PDd(s),Little Better,pt.2 . . . . 2.50
5 PDd(s),Little Better,pt.3 . . . . 2.50
6 PDd(s),Little Better,pt.4 . . . . 2.50
7 PDd(s),F:Black Mariah. 2.50
8 PDd(s),F:Black Mariah. 2.50
9 PDd(s),F:Black Mariah. 2.50
10 PDd(s),F:Black Mariah 2.95
11 PDd(s),F:Black Mariah 2.50
12 PDd(s),Doctor Juris 2.50
13 PDd(s),V:Asia Minor 2.50
14 PDd(s),Bete Noire. 2.50
15 PDd(s). 2.50
16 PDd(s). 2.50
TPB 12.95

FAMILY MAN
Paradox 1995
1 I:Family Man 5.50
2 V:Brother Charles 5.50
3 Escape. 5.50

Fate #4 © DC Comics, Inc.

FANBOY
1999
1 (of 6) SA, various artists 2.50
2 . . . . 2.50
3 A:JLA 2.50
4 SA, A:Sgt. Rock. 2.50
5 SA, A:Batman 2.50
6 SA, A:Wonder Woman, concl. . . . 2.50
TPB F:Finster, 144-page(2001) . . . 12.95

FATE
1994–96
1 Dr. Fate 2.50
2 Nabu,Astral plane 2.25
3 Bloodstain 2.25
4 Decisions 2.25
5 Judged by Enclave 2.25
6 V:Grimoire 2.25
7 V:Dark Agent 2.25
8 V:Dark Agent 2.25
9 Tries to change his destiny 2.25
10 A:Zatanna 2.25
11 . . . . 2.25
12 A:Sentinel 2.25
13 V:Blaze 2.25
14 LKa,ALa,AWi,Underworld
    Unleashed tie-in 2.25
15 LKa,ALa,AWi,V:Charnelle. 2.25
16 LKa,ALa,AWi,canibal drug-cult . . 2.25
17 LKa,ALa,AWi. 2.25
18 LKa,ALa,AWi,V:Charnelle. 2.25
19 LKa,ALa,AWi,V:men in black . . . 2.25

FAULT LINES
DC/Vertigo, March, 1997
Mini-series
1 LMr(s),F:Tracey Farrand 2.50
2 LMr(s) 2.50
3 LMr(s) 2.50
4 LMr(s) 2.50
5 (of 6) LMr(s) 2.50
6 LMrs(s) concl. 2.50

FIGHT FOR TOMORROW
DC/Vertigo, Sept., 2002
1 (of 6) DCw,JLe(c) kung-fu 2.50
2 DCw,KW, more kung-fu 2.50
3 thru 6 DCw. . . . . @2.50

FIGHTING AMERICAN
1994
1 GrL,R:Fighting American 2.50
2 GrL,Media Circus. 2.50
3 GrL,I&V:Gross Nation Product,
    Def Iffit. 2.50
4 GrL,V:Gross Nation Product,
    Def Iffit. 2.50
5 GrL,PhorOptor 2.50
6 Final Issue 2.50

FILTH, THE
DC/Vertigo, June, 2002
1 (of 13) GMo 3.00
2 GMo, Perfect Victim. 3.00
3 GMo, unexpected guest 3.00
4 GMo, Otto Von Vermun 3.00
5 GMo, Pornomancer 3.00
6 GMo,World of Anders Klimaaks. . 3.00
7 GMo,Libertania 3.00
8 GMo,Libertania 3.00
9 GMo,Answers 3.00
10 GMo,Mother Dirt 3.00
11 GMo,Greg Feely 3.00
12 GMo,Mother Dirt 3.00
13 GMo,concl. 3.00
TPB 19.95

FINAL NIGHT, THE
Sept., 1996
[Cross-Over Series]
1 KK(s),SI,JMz, Alien crash lands
    on Earth. 4.00
2 KK(s),SI,JMz, Earth's sun
    extinguished 2.50
3 KK(s),SI,JMz, Attempts to stave
    off inevitable 2.50
4 KK(s),SI,JMz, Can they save the
    world, and at what price? 2.50
TPB rep. 13.00

Finals #1 © DC Comics, Inc.

FINALS
DC/Vertigo, 1999
1 (of 4) College satire 3.00
2 thru 4 JIT . . . . @3.00

FIREBRAND
1995
1 SaV,Alex Sanchez becomes
    Firebrand 2.25
2 SaV 2.25
3 SaV,Generation Prime case
    climax 2.25
4 SaV,Young gang member 2.25
5 SaV,V;serial killer(s). 2.25
6 thru 9 . . . . @2.25

FIRESTORM
March, 1978
1 AM,JRu,I&O:Firestorm. 12.00
2 AM,BMc,A:Superman 7.00
3 AM,I:Killer Froat. 7.00
4 AM,BMc,I:Hyena 7.00
5 AM,BMc,Hyena 7.00

FIRESTORM
May 2004
1 Ccs,F:Jason Rusch 2.50
2 Ccs,Eye Contact,pt.2 . . . . 2.50
3 Ccs,power's price 2.50
4 Ccs,Everybody Wants You 2.50
5 Ccs,Everybody Wants You 2.50
6 CsB,DGr,x-over 2.50

FIRESTORM, THE NUCLEAR MAN
(see FURY OF FIRESTORM)

DC COMICS

FIRST ISSUE SPECIAL
April, 1975

1 JK,Atlas 20.00
2 Green Team 15.00
3 Metamorpho 15.00
4 Lady Cop 10.00
5 JK,Manhunter 20.00
6 JK,Dingbats 20.00
7 SD,Creeper 20.00
8 MGr,Warlord 30.00
9 WS,Dr.Fate 15.00
10 Outsiders(not Batman team) . . . 12.00
11 NR,AM Code:Assassin 12.00
12 new Starman 12.00
13 return of New Gods 30.00

FLASH COMICS
Jan., 1940

1 SMo,SMo(c),O:Flash,Hawkman,The
  Whip & Johnny Thunder,B:Cliff
  Cornwall,Minute Movies . 100,000.00
2 B:Rod Rain 12,000.00
3 SMo,SMo(c),B:The King 7,500.00
4 SMo,SMo(c),F:The Whip . . . 6,000.00
5 SMo,SMo(c),F:The King 5,000.00
6 F:Flash 7,000.00
7 Hawkman(c) 6,500.00
8 Male bondage(c) 4,200.00
9 Hawkman(c) 4,500.00
10 SMo,SMo(c),Flash(c) 4,500.00
11 SMo,SMo(c) 2,800.00
12 SMo,SMo(c),B:Les Watts . . . 2,800.00
13 SMo,SMo(c) 2,800.00
14 SMo,SMo(c) 3,500.00
15 SMo,SMo(c) 2,800.00
16 SMo,SMo(c) 2,800.00
17 SMo,SMo(c),E:CliffCornwall 2,800.00
18 SMo,SMo(c) 2,800.00
19 SMo,SMo(c) 2,800.00
20 SMo,SMo(c) 2,800.00
21 SMo(c) 2,700.00
22 SMo,SMo(c) 2,400.00
23 SMo,SMo(c) 2,400.00
24 SMo,SMo(c),Flash V:Spider-
  Men of Mars,A:Hawkgirl . . . 3,000.00
25 SMo,SMo(c) 1,600.00
26 SMo,SMo(c) 1,600.00
27 SMo,SMo(c) 1,600.00
28 SMo,SMo(c),Flash goes
  to Hollywood 1,600.00
29 SMo,SMo(c) 1,700.00
30 SMo,SMo(c),Flash inAdventure
  of the Curiosity Ray! 1,600.00

31 SMo,SMo(c),Hawkman(c) . . 1,600.00
32 SMo,SMo(c),Flash inAdventure
  of the Fictious Villians 1,600.00
33 SMo,SMo(c) 1,600.00
34 SMo,SMo(c),Flash In The Robbers
  of the Round Table 1,600.00
35 SMo,SMo(c) 1,600.00
36 SMo,SMo(c),F:Flash,Mystery of
  Doll Who Walks Like a Man 1,600.00
37 SMo,SMo(c) 1,600.00
38 SMo,SMo(c) 1,600.00
39 SMo,SMo(c) 1,600.00
40 SMo,SMo(c),F:Flash, Man Who
  Could Read Man's Souls! . . 1,600.00
41 SMo,SMo(c) 1,300.00
42 SMo,SMo(c),Flash V:The
  Gangsters Baby! 1,300.00
43 SMo,SMo(c) 1,300.00
44 SMo,SMo(c),Flash V:The
  Liars Club 1,300.00
45 SMo,SMo(c),F:Hawkman,Big
  Butch Makes Hall of Fame . 1,300.00
46 SMo,SMo(c) 1,300.00
47 SMo,SMo(c),Hawkman in Crime
  Canned for the Duration . . . 1,300.00
48 SMo,SMo(c) 1,300.00
49 SMo,SMo(c) 1,300.00
50 SMo,SMo(c),Hawkman, Tale
  of the 1,000 Dollar Bill 1,300.00
51 SMo,SMo(c) 1,200.00
52 SMo,SMo(c),Flash, Machine
  that Thinks Like a Man 1,200.00
53 SMo,SMo(c),Hawkman, Simple
  Simon Met the Hawkman . . 1,200.00
54 SMo,SMo(c),Flash, Mysterious
  Bottle from the Sea 1,200.00
55 SMo,SMo(c),Hawkman, Riddle of
  the Stolen Statuette! 1,200.00
56 SMo,SMo(c) 1,200.00
57 SMo,SMo(c),Hawkman,
  Adventure of the Gangster
  & the Ghost 1,200.00
58 SMo,SMo(c),Merman meets
  the Flash 1,200.00
59 SMo,SMo(c),Hawkman
  V:Pied Piper 1,200.00
60 SMo,SMo(c),Flash
  V:The Wind Master 1,200.00
61 SMo,SMo(c),Hawkman
  V:The Beanstalk 1,200.00
62 JKu,Flash in High Jinks
  on the Rinks 1,600.00
63 JKu(c),Hawkman in The
  Tale of the Mystic Urn 1,100.00
64 . . . . 1,100.00
65 JKu(c),Hawkman in Return
  of the Simple Simon 1,100.00
66 . . . . 1,100.00
67 JKu(c) 1,100.00
68 Flash in The Radio that
  Ran Wild 1,100.00
69 . . . . 1,100.00
70 JKu(c) 1,100.00
71 JKu(c),Hawkman in Battle
  of the Birdmen 1,100.00
72 JKu 1,100.00
73 JKu(c) 1,100.00
74 JKu(c) 1,100.00
75 JKu(c),Hawkman in Magic
  at the Mardi Gras 1,100.00
76 A:Worry Wart 1,100.00
77 Hawkman in The Case of
  the Curious Casket 1,100.00
78 . . . . 1,100.00
79 Hawkman in The Battle
  of the Birds 1,100.00
80 Flash in The Story of
  the Boy Genius 1,100.00
81 JKu(c),Hawkman's Voyage
  to Venus 1,100.00
82 A:Walter Jordan 1,100.00

83 JKu,JKu(c),Hawkman in
  Destined for Disaster 1,100.00
84 Flash V:The Changeling . . . 1,100.00
85 JKu,JKu(c),Hawkman in
  Hollywood 1,100.00
86 JKu,1st Black Canary,Flash
  V:Stone Age Menace 4,000.00
87 Hawkman meets the Foil . . . 1,600.00
88 JKu,Flash in The Case
  of the Vanished Year! 1,600.00
89 I:The Thorn 2,200.00
90 Flash in Nine Empty
  Uniforms 1,600.00
91 Hawkman V:The Phantom
  Menace 1,700.00
92 1st full-length Black
  Canary story 5,000.00
93 Flash V:Violin of Villainy . . . 1,700.00
94 JKu(c) 1,700.00
95 . . . . 1,700.00
96 . . . . 1,700.00
97 Flash in The Dream
  that Didn't Vanish 1,700.00
98 JKu(c),Hawkman in
  Crime Costume! 1,700.00
99 Flash in The Star Prize
  of the Year 1,700.00
100 Hawkman in The Human
  -Fly Bandits! 4,200.00
101 . . . . 3,500.00
102 Hawkman in The Flying
  Darkness 3,500.00
103 . . . . 4,200.00
104 JKu,Hawkman in Flaming
  Darkness' Feb., 1949 . . . . 10,000.00

FLASH
Feb.–March, 1959

105 CI,O:Flash,I:Mirror
  Master 9,000.00
106 CI,I&O:Gorilla Grodd,
  O:Pied Piper 3,000.00
107 CI,A:Grodd 1,500.00
108 CI,A:Grodd 1,200.00
109 CI,A:Mirror Master 1,000.00
110 CI,MA,I:Kid Flash,
  Weather Wizard 2,500.00
111 CI,A:Kid Flash,The Invasion
  Of the Cloud Creatures 700.00
112 CI,I&O:Elongated Man,
  A:Kid Flash 800.00
113 CI,I&O:Trickster 700.00
114 CI,A:Captain Cold 500.00
115 CI,A:Grodd 400.00

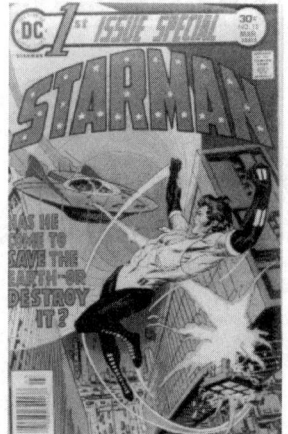

First Issue Special #12
© DC Comics, Inc.

Flash Comics #1
© DC Comics, Inc.

116 Cl,A:Kid Flash,The Man
Who Stole Central City 400.00
117 Cl,MA,I:Capt.Boomerang . . . 475.00
118 Cl,MA 375.00
119 Cl,W:Elongated Man 375.00
120 Cl,A:Kid Flash,Land of
Golden Giants 375.00
121 Cl,A:Trickster 300.00
122 Cl,I&O:The Top 300.00
123 I:Earth 2,R:G.A.Flash 2,200.00
124 Cl,A:Capt.Boomerang 225.00
125 Cl,A:Kid Flash,The
Conquerors of Time 225.00
126 Cl,A:Mirror Master 225.00
127 Cl,A:Grodd 225.00
128 Cl,O:Abra Kadabra 225.00
129 Cl,A:Capt.Cold,Trickster,A:Gold.
Age Flash,C:JLA (flashback) . 450.00
130 Cl,A:Mirror Master,
Weather Wizard 225.00
131 Cl,A:Green Lantern 200.00
132 Cl,A:Daphne Dean 200.00
133 Cl,A:Abra Kadabra 200.00
134 Cl,A:Captain Cold 200.00
135 Cl,N:Kid Flash 200.00
136 Cl,A:Mirror Master 200.00
137 Cl,Vandal Savage,R:JSA,
A:G.A.Flash 675.00
138 Cl,A:Pied Piper 225.00
139 Cl,I&O:Prof.Zoom(Reverse
Flash) 225.00
140 Cl,O:Heat Wave 225.00
141 Cl,A:Top 175.00
142 Cl,A:Trickster 175.00
143 Cl,A:Green Lantern 175.00
144 Cl,A:Man Missile,Kid Flash . . 175.00
145 Cl,A:Weather Wizard 175.00
146 Cl,A:Mirror Master 175.00
147 Cl,A:Mr.Element,A:Reverse
Flash 175.00
148 Cl,A:Capt.Boomerang 175.00
149 Cl,A:Abra Kadabra 175.00
150 Cl,A:Captain Cold 175.00
151 Cl,A:Earth II Flash,
The Shade 200.00
152 Cl,V:Trickster 150.00
153 Cl,A:Mr.Element,Rev.Flash . . 150.00
154 Cl,The Day Flash Ran Away
with Himself 150.00
155 Cl,A:MirrorMaster,Capt.Cold,Top
Capt. Boomerang,Grodd 150.00
156 Cl,A:Kid Flash,The Super Hero
who Betrayed the World 150.00
157 Cl,A:Doralla Kon,The Top . . . 150.00
158 Cl,V:The Breakaway Bandit
A:The Justice League 150.00
159 Cl,A:Kid Flash 150.00
160 Cl,giant 200.00
161 Cl,A:Mirror Master 125.00
162 Cl,Who Haunts the Corridor
of Chills 125.00
163 Cl,A:Abra kadabra 125.00
164 Cl,V:Pied Piper,A:Kid Flash . 125.00
165 Cl,W:Flash,Iris West 135.00
166 Cl,A:Captain Cold 125.00
167 Cl,O:Flash,I:Mopee 125.00
168 Cl,A:Green Lantern 125.00
169 Cl,O:Flash rtd,giant 175.00
170 Cl,A:Abra Kadabra,
G.A.Flash 125.00
171 Cl,A:Dexter Myles,Justice
League,Atom;V:Dr Light 125.00
172 Cl,A:Grodd 125.00
173 Cl,A:Kid Flash,EarthII Flash
V:Golden Man 125.00
174 Cl,A:Mirror Master,Top
Captain Cold 125.00
175 2nd Superman/Flash race,
C:Justice League o/America . 300.00
176 giant-size 125.00
177 RA,V:The Trickster 125.00

Flash #192 © DC Comics Inc.

178 Cl,(giant size) 150.00
179 RA,Fact or Fiction 125.00
180 RA,V:Baron Katana 125.00
181 RA,V:Baron Katana 100.00
182 A:Abra Kadabra 100.00
183 RA,V:The Frog 100.00
184 RA,V:Dr Yom 100.00
185 RA,Threat of the High Rise
Buildings 100.00
186 RA,A:Sargon 100.00
187 Cl,AbraKadabra,giant 125.00
188 A:Mirror Master 100.00
189 JKu(c),RA,A:Kid Flash 100.00
190 JKu(c),RA,A:Dexter Myles . . 100.00
191 JKu(c),RA,A:Green Lantern . 100.00
192 RA;V:Captain Vulcan 100.00
193 A:Captain Cold 100.00
194 . . . . 100.00
195 GK,MA 100.00
196 Cl,giant 125.00
197 GK 100.00
198 GK 100.00
199 GK 100.00
200 IN,MA 100.00
201 IN,MA,A:G.A. Flash 50.00
202 IN,MA,A:Kid Flash 50.00
203 IN 50.00
204 . . . . 50.00
205 giant 100.00
206 A:Mirror Master 50.00
207 . . . . 50.00
208 . . . . 50.00
209 A:Capt.Boomerang,Grodd
Trickster 50.00
210 Cl 50.00
211 O:Flash 50.00
212 A:Abra Kadabra 50.00
213 Cl 50.00
214 Cl,rep.Showcase #37
(O:Metal Men),giant size 60.00
215 IN,FMc,rep.Showcase #14 . . . 60.00
216 A:Mr.Element 35.00
217 NA,A:Gr.Lant,Gr.Arrow 60.00
218 NA,A:Gr.Lant,Gr.Arrow 60.00
219 NA,L:Greeen Arrow 60.00
220 IN,DG,A:KidFlash,Gr.Lantern . 40.00
221 IN 25.00
222 IN 25.00
223 DG,Green Lantern 25.00
224 IN,DG,A:Green Lantern 25.00
225 IN,DG,A:Gr.Lant,Rev.Flash . . 22.00
226 NA,A:Capt. Cold 30.00
227 IN,FMc,DG,Capt.Boomerang,
Green Lantern 22.00

228 IN 22.00
229 IN,FMc,A:Green Arrow,
V:Rag Doll (giant size) 60.00
230 A:VandalSavage,Dr.Alchemy . 22.00
231 FMc 22.00
232 giant 60.00
233 giant 60.00
234 V:Reverse Flash 18.00
235 . . . . 16.00
236 MGr 16.00
237 IN,FMc,MGr,A:Prof Zoom,
Green Lantern 18.00
238 MGr 16.00
239 . . . . 16.00
240 MGr 16.00
241 A:Mirror Master 16.00
242 MGr,D:Top 16.00
243 IN,FMc,MGr,TA,O:Top,
A:Green Lantern 16.00
244 IN,FMc,A:Rogue's Gallery . . . 16.00
245 IN,FMc,DD,TA,I:PlantMaster . . 16.00
246 IN,FMc,DD,TA,I:PlantMaster . 16.00
247 . . . . 16.00
248 FMc,IN,I:Master 16.00
249 FMc,IN,V:Master 16.00
250 IN,FMc,I:Golden Glider 16.00
251 FMc,IN,V:Golden Glider 12.00
252 FMc,IN,I:Molder 12.00
253 FMc,IN,V:Molder 12.00
254 FMc 12.00
255 FMc,A:MirrorMaster 12.00
256 FMc,V:Top 12.00
257 FMc,A:Green Glider 12.00
258 FMc,A:Black Hand 12.00
259 FMc,IN 12.00
260 FMc,IN 12.00
261 FMc,IN,V:Golden Glider 12.00
262 FMc,IN,V:Golden Glider 12.00
263 FMc,IN,V:Golden Glider 12.00
264 FMc,IN,V:Golden Glider 12.00
265 FMc,IN 12.00
266 FMc,IN,V:Heat Wave 12.00
267 FMc,IN,V:Heat Wave 12.00
268 FMc,IN,A:E2 Flash 12.00
269 FMc,IN,A:Kid Flash 12.00
270 FMc,IN,V:Clown 12.00
271 RB,V:Clown 12.00
272 RB,V:Clown 12.00
273 RB 12.00
274 RB 12.00
275 AS,D:Iris West,PCP story 14.00
276 AS,A:JLA 12.00
277 AS,FMc,A:JLA,
V:MirrorMaster 12.00
278 A:Captain.Boomerang
& Heatwave 12.00
279 A:Captain.Boomerang
& Heatwave 12.00
280 DH 12.00
281 DH,V:Reverse Flash 14.00
282 DH,V:Reverse Flash 14.00
283 DH,V:Reverse Flash 14.00
284 DH,Flash's life story
I:Limbo Lord 12.00
285 DH,V:Trickster 12.00
286 DH,I:Rainbow Raider 12.00
287 DH,V:Dr.Alchemy 12.00
288 DH,V:Dr.Alchemy 12.00
289 DH,GP,1st GP DC art; V:Dr.
Alchemy;B:B.U.Firestorm . . . 15.00
290 GP 8.00
291 GP,DH,V:Sabretooth 8.00
292 GP,DH,V:Mirror Master 8.00
293 GP,DH,V:Pied Piper 8.00
294 GP,DH,V:Grodd 8.00
295 Cl,JSn,V:Grodd 8.00
296 JSn,A:Elongated Man 8.00
297 Cl,A:Captain Cold 8.00
298 Cl,V:Shade,Rainbowraider 8.00
299 Cl,V:Shade,Rainbowraider 8.00
300 A:New Teen Titans 10.00

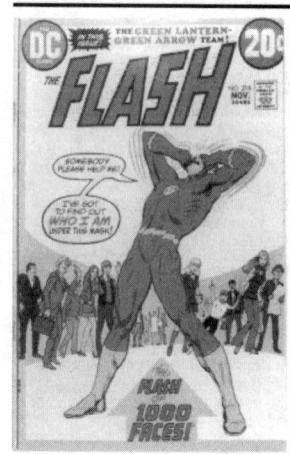

Flash #218 © DC Comics, Inc.

FLASH

[2nd Series] Oct., 1985

1 JG,Legends,C:Vandal Savage . . 12.00
2 JG,V:Vandal Savage 5.00
3 JG,I:Kilgore 4.00
4 JG,A:Cyborg 4.00
5 JG,V:Speed Demon 4.00
6 JG,V:Speed Demon 4.00
7 JG,V:Red Trinity 4.00
8 JG,V:BlueTrinity,Millennium 4.00
9 JG,I:Chunk,Millennium 4.00
10 V:Chunk,Chunks World 3.00
11 Return to Earth 3.00
12 Velocity 9 . . . . 3.00
13 Vandal Savage,V:Velocity 9
    Adicts 3.00
14 V:Vandal Savage 3.00
15 A:Velocity 9 Junkies 3.00
16 C:V.Savage,SpeedMcGeePt.1 . 3.00
17 GLa,Speed McGee,pt.2 . . . . . . 3.00
18 GLa,SpeedMcGeePt.3,
    V:V.Savage 3.00
19 JM:+bonus book,R:Rogue
    Gallery,O:Blue/Red Trinity 3.00
20 A:Durlan 3.00
21 A:Manhunter,Invasion x-over . . . 3.00
22 A:Manhunter,Invasion x-over . . . 3.00
23 V:Abrakadabra 3.00
24 GLa,FlashRegainsSpeed,
    A:L.Lane 3.00
25 GLa,Search for Flash 3.00
26 GLa,I:Porcupine Man 3.00
27 GLa,Porcupine Man as Flash . . . 3.00
28 GLa,A:Golden Glider,
    Capt.Cold 3.00
29 A:New Phantom Lady 3.00
30 GLa,Turtle Saga,pt.1 . . . . 3.00
31 GLa,Turtle Saga,pt.2 . . . . 3.00
32 GLa,Turtle Saga,pt.3,
    R:G.A.Turtle 3.00
33 GLa,Turtle Saga,pt.4 . . . . 3.00
34 GLa,Turtle Saga,pt.5 . . . . 3.00
35 GLa,Turtle Saga,pt.6,
    D:G.A.Turtle 3.00
36 GLa,V:Cult 3.00
37 GLa,V:Cult 3.00
38 GLa,V:Cult 3.00
39 GLa,V:Cult 3.00
40 GLa,A:Dr.Alchemy 3.00
41 GLa,A:Dr.Alchemy 3.00
42 GLa,MechanicalTroubles 3.00
43 GLa,V:Kilgore 3.00
44 GLa,V:Velocity 3.00
45 V:Rogues Gallery 3.00
46 V:Gorilla Grod 3.00
47 V:Gorilla Grod 3.00
48 . . . . 3.00
49 A:Vandal Savage 3.00
50 N:Flash (double sz)V:Savage . . . 5.00
51 I:Proletariat 3.00
52 I.R.S. Mission 3.00
53 A:Superman,Race to Save
    Jimmy Olsen 3.00
54 Terrorist Airline Attack 3.00
55 War of the Gods x-over 3.00
56 The Way of a Will,pt.1 . . . . 3.00
57 The Way of a Will,pt.2 . . . . 3.00
58 Meta Gene-activated Homeless . 3.00
59 The Last Resort 3.00
60 Love Song of the Chunk 3.00
61 Wally's Mother's Wedding Day . . 3.00
62 GLa,Year 1,pt.1 . . . . 4.00
63 GLa,Year 1,pt.2 . . . . 4.00
64 GLa,Year 1,pt.3 . . . . 4.00
65 GLa,Year 1,pt.4 . . . . 4.00
66 A:Aq'man,V:Marine Marauder . . . 4.00
67 GLa,V:Abra Kadabra 4.00
68 GLa,V:Abra Kadabra 4.00
69 GLa,Gorilla Warfare#2 . . . . 4.00
70 Gorilla Warfare#4 . . . . 4.00
71 GLa,V:Dr.Alchemy 4.00

301 CI,A:Firestorm 8.00
302 CI,V:Golden Glider 8.00
303 CI,V:Golden Glider 8.00
304 CI,PB,I:Col.Computron;E:B.U.
    Firestorm 8.00
305 KG,CI,A:G.A.Flash,B:Dr.Fate . . 8.00
306 CI,KG,V:Mirror Master 8.00
307 CI,KG,V:Pied Piper 8.00
308 CI,KG 8.00
309 CI,KG 8.00
310 CI,KG,V:Capt.Boomerang 6.00
311 CI,KG,V:Capt.Boomerang 6.00
312 CI,A:Heatwave 6.00
313 KG,A:Psylon,E:Dr.Fate 6.00
314 CI,I:Eradicator 6.00
315 CI,V:Gold Face 6.00
316 CI,V:Gold Face 6.00
317 CI,V:Gold Face 6.00
318 CI,DGb,V:Eradicator;B:
    B.U.Creeper 6.00
319 CI,DGb,V:Eradicator 6.00
320 CI,V:Eradicator 6.00
321 CI,D:Eradicator 5.00
322 CI,V:Reverse Flash 5.00
323 CI,V:Reverse Flash;E:
    B.U.Creeper 5.00
324 CI,D:Reverse Flash 5.50
325 CI,A:Rogues Gallery 5.00
326 CI,A:Weather Wizard 5.00
327 CI,A:JLA,G.Grodd 5.00
328 CI 5.00
329 CI,A:J.L.A.,G.Grodd 5.00
330 CI,FMc,V:G.Grodd 5.00
331 CI,FMc,V:G.Grodd 5.00
332 CI,FMc,V:Rainbow Raider 5.00
333 CI,FMc,V:Pied Piper 5.00
334 CI,FMc,V:Pied Piper 5.00
335 CI,FMc,V:Pied Piper 5.00
336 CI,FMc,V:Pied Piper 5.00
337 CI,FMc,V:Pied Piper 5.00
338 CI,FMc,I:Big Sir 5.00
339 CI,FMc,A:Big Sir 5.00
340 CI,FMc,Trial,A:Big Sir 5.00
341 CI,FMc,Trial,A:Big Sir 5.00
342 CI,FMc,Trial,V:RogueGallery . . 5.00
343 CI,FMc,Trial,A:GoldFace 5.00
344 CI,O:Kid Flash,Trial 5.00
345 CI,A:Kid Flash 5.00
346 CI,FMc,Trial,V:AbraKadabra . . . 5.00
347 CI,FMc,Trial,V:AbraKadabra . . . 5.00
348 CI,FMc,Trial,V:AbraKadabra . . . 5.00
349 CI,FMc,Trial,V:AbraKadabra . . . 5.00
350 CI,FMc,Trial,V:AbraKadabra . . . 7.00
Ann.#1 O:ElongatedMan,
    G.Grodd 600.00

Flash 2nd Series #12
© DC Comics, Inc.

72 GLa,V:Dr.Alchemy,C:Barry
    Allen 4.00
73 GLa,Xmas Issue,R:Barry Allen . . 5.00
74 GLa,A:Barry Allen? 4.50
75 GLa,A:Reverse Flash,V:Mob
    Violence 4.50
76 GLa,A:Reverse Flash 4.00
77 GLa,G.A.Flash vs
    Reverse Flash 4.00
78 GLa,V:Reverse Flash 4.00
79 GLa,V:Reverse Flash,48 pgs . . . 5.00
80 AD(c),V:Frances Kane 5.00
80a Newstand Ed 3.00
81 AD(c) 4.00
82 AD(c),A:Nightwing 4.00
83 AD(c),A:Nightwing,Starfire 4.00
84 AD(c),I:Razer 4.00
85 AD(c),V:Razer 4.00
86 AD(c),A:Argus 4.00
86 V:Santa Claus 4.00
87 Christmas issue 4.00
88 . . . . 4.00
89 On Trial 4.00
90 On Trial#2 . . . . 4.00
91 Out of Time 5.00
92 I:3rd Flash 12.00
93 A:Impulse 5.00
94 Zero Hour 5.00
95 Terminal Velocity,pt.1 . . . . 4.00
96 Terminal Velocity,pt.2 . . . . 5.00
97 Terminal Velocity,pt.3 . . . . 4.00
98 Terminal Velocity,pt.4 . . . . 4.00
99 Terminal Velocity,pt.5 . . . . 4.00
100 I:New Flash 5.00
100a Collector's Edition 3.00
101 Velocity Aftermath 4.00
102 V:Mongul 3.00
103 Supernatural threat from
    Linda's Past Secret 3.00
104 Exorcise Demons 3.00
105 . . . . 3.00
106 R:Magenta 3.00
107 MWa,Underworld Unleashed
    tie-in 3.00
108 MWa,Dead Heat,pt.1 . . . . 3.00
109 MWa,Dead Heat,pt.2 . . . . 3.00
110 MWa,Dead Heat,pt.4 . . . . 3.00
111 MWa,Dead Heat,pt.6 . . . . 3.00
112 MWa,New Flash in town 3.00
113 MWa,F:Linda 3.00
114 MWa,V:Chillblaine 3.00
115 thru 117 . . . . @3.00
118 MWa&BAu(s),Flash returns
    from the future 3.00

119 MWa&BAu(s),PR,Final Night
   tie-in 3.00
120 MWa&BAu(s),PR,Presidential
   Race,pt.1 . . . . 3.00
121 MWa&BAu(s),PR,Presidential
   Race,pt.2 . . . . 3.00
122 MWa&BAu(s),PR, ... 3.00
123 MWa&BAu(s),PR,Flash moves
   to Santa Marta 3.00
124 MWa&BAu(s),PR,Wally doesn't
   know reality from illusion 3.00
125 MWa&BAu(s),PR,California,
   V:Major Disaster 3.00
126 MWa&BAu(s),PR,V:Major
   Disaster 3.00
127 MWa&Bau(s),PR,Hell to Pay,
   pt.1 . . . . 3.00
128 MWa&BAu(s),PR,Hell to Pay
   pt.2, A:JLA 3.00
129 MWa&BAu(s),PR,HellPay,pt.3 . 3.00
130 GMo&MMr(s),PR,new menace . 3.00
131 GMo&MMr(s),PR,V:The Suit. . . 3.50
132 GMo&MMr(s),PR,V:The Suit. . . 3.50
133 GMo&MMr(s),PR,V:Mirror
   Master 3.00
134 GMo&MMr(s),PR,V:Weather
   Wizard & Captain Cold 3.00
135 GMo&MMr(s), ... 3.00
136 GMo&MMr(s),PR,Human
   Race,pt.1 . . . . 3.00
137 GMo&MMr(s),PR,Human
   Race,pt.2 . . . . 3.00
138 GMo&MMr(s),PR,Human
   Race,pt.3 . . . . 3.00
139 MMr(s),Clv,Black Flash,pt.1 . . 3.00
140 MMr(s),Clv,Black Flash,pt.2 . . 3.00
141 MMr(s),Clv,Black Flash,pt.3 . . . 3.00
142 MWa&BAu(s),Clv,SLi,wedding of
   Wally West & Linda Park 3.00
143 MWa&BAu(s),Clv,V:CobaltBlue 3.00
144 MWa&BAu(s),Clv,O:CobaltBlue 3.00
145 MWa&BAu(s),PaP,VRu,
   Chain Lightning, pt.1 . . . . 3.00
146 MWa&BAu(s),PaP,VRu,
   Chain Lightning, pt.2 . . . . 3.00
147 MWa&BAu(s),PaP,VRu,
   Chain Lightning, pt.3 . . . . 3.00
148 MWa&BAu(s),PaP,VRu,
   Chain Lightning, pt.4 . . . . 3.00
149 MWa&BAu(s),PaP,VRu,
   Chain Lightning, pt.5 . . . . 3.00
150 MWa&BAu(s),PaP,VRu, Chain
   Lightning, pt.6, 48-page. 4.00
151 MWa&BAu(s),PaP,A:Robin
   & Aqualad, flashback issue 2.50
152 MWa&BAu(s),PaP,VRu,
   new costume 2.50
153 MWa&BAu(s),PaP,JMz,
   V:Folded Man 2.50
154 MWa&BAu(s),PaP,JMz, ... 2.50
155 MWa&BAu(s),PaP,JMz,
   V:Replicant 2.50
156 MWa&BAu(s),PaP,JMz 2.50
157 MWa&BAu(s),PaP,JMz,fate of
   Linda Park 2.50
158 MWa&BAu(s),PaP,DHz 2.50
159 MWa&BAu(s),PaP,Dark Flash . 2.50
160 BAu(s),Honeymoon on the Run 2.50
161 PaP,DHz,F:Original JSA 2.50
162 PaP,DHz,R:Felix Faust 2.50
163 RLm,DHz,A:JLA 2.50
164 DHz,BBo(c),Wonderland,pt.1 . . 5.00
165 DHz,Wonderland,pt.2 . . . . 2.50
166 DHz,Wonderland,pt.3 . . . . 2.50
167 DHz,Wonderland,pt.4 . . . . 2.50
168 DHz,Wonderland,pt.5 . . . . 2.50
169 DHz,Wonderland,pt.6 . . . . 2.50
170 DHz,Blood Will Run,pt.1 . . . . . . 2.50
171 DHz,Blood Will Run,pt.2 . . . . . . 2.50
172 DHz,Blood Will Run,pt.3 . . . . . . 2.50
173 DHz,Blood Will Run,pt.4 . . . . . . 2.50

174 DHz,Moving Right Along 2.50
175 DHz,Deadly storm. 2.50
176 DHz,The Rainmaker 2.50
177 DHz,interdimensional menace . 2.50
178 DHz,Caged,V:Gorilla Grodd . . . 2.50
179 DHz,Joker:Last Laugh 2.50
180 DHz,V:Peekaboo 2.50
181 DHz,BB(c),V:Fallout 2.50
182 DPs,Absolute Zero 2.50
183 DHz,BB(c),new Trickster. 2.50
184 DHz,BB(c),Crossfire,pt.1 . . . . . 2.50
185 DHz,BB(c),Crossfire,pt.2 . . . . . 2.50
186 DHz,BB(c),Crossfire,pt.3 . . . . . 2.50
187 DHz,BB(c),Crossfire,pt.4 . . . . . 2.50
188 DHz,BB(c),Crossfire,pt.5 . . . . . 3.00
189 RBr,DPs,F:Cyborg, ... 2.50
190 Rogues spotlight,Pied Piper . . . 2.50
191 ScK,DHz,F:Hawkman 2.50
192 ScK,DHz,Run Riot,pt.1 . . . . 2.50
193 ScK,DHz,Run Riot,pt.2 . . . . 2.50
194 ScK,DHz,Run Riot,pt.3 . . . . 2.50
195 ScK,DHz,The Top 2.50
196 V:Peek-a-Boo 2.50
197 ScK,Blitz,pt.1. . . . . 10.00
198 ScK,Blitz,pt.2. . . . . 5.00
199 ScK,Blitz,pt.3. . . . . 3.00
200 ScK,DHz,Blitz,concl.48-pg. 3.50
201 Ignition,pt.1 . . . . 2.25
202 Ignition,pt.2 . . . . 2.25
203 Ignition,pt.3 . . . . 2.25
204 Ignition,pt.4 . . . . 2.25
205 Ignition,pt.5 . . . . 2.25
206 Ignition,pt.6,concl. 2.25
207 Kid Flash & Jay Garrick 7.00
208 Kid Flash & Jay Garrick 3.00
209 Fastest Hero Alive. 2.50
210 F:New Teen Titans 2.50
211 F:Nightwing 2.50
212 F:Mirror Master 2.50
213 Sins of the Father,pro. 2.50
214 Sins of the Father,pt.1 . . . . 2.50
215 Sins of the Father,pt.2 . . . . 2.50
Ann.#1 JG,The Deathtouch 4.00
Ann.#2 A:Wally's Father. 3.00
Ann.#3 Roots 3.00
Ann.#4 Armageddon,pt7 . . . . 3.00
Ann.#5 TC(1st Full Work),Eclipso,
   V:Rogue's Gallery 8.00
Ann.#6 Bloodlines#4,I:Argus 3.00
Ann.#7 Elseworlds story 3.50
Ann.#8 Year One story. 4.00
Ann.#9 Legends o/t Dead Earth . . . 3.50
Ann.#10 Pulp Heroes (Romance) . . 4.50
Ann.#11 BAu, BWr, Ghosts 3.50
Ann.#12 DBw,AAd(c),JLApe: Gorilla
   Warfare 3.50
Ann.#13 Planet DC 4.00
Ann.#1 (1963) replica ed.(2001) . . . 7.50
Spec #1,IN,DG,CI,50th Anniv.,
   Three Flash's. 5.00
Spec.#1,000,000 MWa(s),JMz,
   A:Capt.Marvel of 853rd-cent. . . 2.50
Spec.#1 Our Worlds at War,48-pg . 3.50
T.V. Spec.#1,JS,w/episode guide. . 4.25
TPB Terminal Velocity 12.95
TPB The Life Story of the Flash . . 13.00
TPB The Return of Barry Allen . . . 13.00
TPB Born to Run 13.00
TPB Dead Heat 15.00
TPB Race Against Time, 168-pg. . 15.00
TPB Blood will Run (2002) 18.00
TPB Return of Barry Allen 13.00
TPB Rogues. 15.00
TPB Terminal Velocity 15.00
TPB Crossfire. 18.00
TPB Return of Barry Allen 13.00
TPB The Flash: Blitz 20.00
GN Iron Heights, 48-page 6.00
GN Time Flies, 48-pg. (2002) 6.00
Secret Files #1 MWa,BAu,PRy,
   O:Flash family 5.00

Secret Files #2 (1999) 5.00
Secret Files #3, 48-page (2001) . . . 5.00
Giant #1 MWa,80-page (1998) 5.00
Giant #2 80-page 5.00

FLASH & GREEN LANTERN: THE BRAVE & THE BOLD

1999

1 (of 6) MWa&TPe(s),BKi 2.50
2 MWa&TPe(s),BKi. 2.50
3 MWa&TPe(s),BKi. 2.50
4 MWa&TPe(s),BKi. 2.50
5 MWa&TPe(s),BKi. 2.50
6 MWa&TPe(s),BKi,concl. 2.50
TPB Flash & Green Lantern,
   Brave and the Bold, 144-page 13.00

THE FLASH PLUS

Nov., 1996

1 MWa(s),F:Wally West, Dick
   Grayson 3.50

Flash Gordon #9
© DC Comics Inc.

FLASH GORDON

1988

1 DJu,I:New Flash Gordon 3.00
2 DJu,A:Lion-Men,Shark-Men 3.00
3 DJu,V:Shark-Men. 3.00
4 DJu,Dale Kidnapped by Voltan . . 3.00
5 DJu,Alliance Against Ming 3.00
6 DJu,Arctic City 3.00
7 DJu,Alliance vs. Ming 3.00
8 DJu,Alliance vs. Ming 3.00
9 DJu,V:Ming, final issue 3.00

FLASHPOINT

Oct., 1999

1 (of 3) NBy,Elseworlds 3.00
2 NBy,Flash in wheelchair 3.00
3 NBy 3.00

FLINCH

DC/Vertigo, 1999

1 JLe,RCo,horror anthology 2.50
2 BSz,RCo(c),3 horror tales 2.50
3 KJo,3 horror tales 2.50
4 TTn,PGu,3 horror tales 2.50
5 JLd(s),RBr,3 horror tales 2.50

DC COMICS

6 WML(s) 2.50
7 WML(s) 2.50
8 . . . . 2.50
9 3 Tales of horror. 2.50
10 . . . . 2.50
11 JLd(s) 2.50
12 . . . . 2.50
13 Hubris & dark whimsy 2.50
14 . . . . 2.50
15 3 grim tales 2.50
16 RCo(c) final issue 2.50

FLINTSTONES AND THE JETSONS, THE
Warner Bros./DC, 1997
1 Ancestors & Descendents meet . 3.00
2 thru 21 . . . . @3.00

FLY, THE
Impact, 1991–92
1 I&O:Fly I:Arachnus,Chromium . . . 3.00
2 V:Chromium 2.50
3 O:Arachnus, I:Lt.Walker Odell . . . 2.50
4 A:Black Hood, V:Arachnus 2.50
5 V:Arachnus 2.50
6 I:Blackjack 2.50
7 Oceanworld,V:Dolphus 2.50
8 A:Comet,Dolphus 2.50
9 F:Fireball, with trading card 2.50
10 V:General Mechanix 2.50
11 Suicide Issue 2.50
12 V:Agent from WEB 2.50
13 I:Tremor 2.50
14 and 15 V:Domino . . . . @2.50
16 V:Arachnus 2.50
17 Final Issue 2.50
Ann.#1 Earthquest,pt.4,w/card. 3.00

FORBIDDEN TALES OF DARK MANSION
May-June, 1972
5 DH 65.00
6 JK 30.00
7 MK(c&a 25.00
8 MK(c&a). 25.00
9 NA(c),MK,AA 30.00
10 thru 15 Feb.–March, 1974 . . . . 25.00

FOREVER MAELSTROM
Nov., 2002
1 (of 6) HC,EB,time-jumping. 3.00
2 HC,EB,time past 3.00
3 HC,EB,V:Praetor 3.00
4 HC,EB,V:Ragnarok 3.00
5 HC,EB,robots. 3.00
6 HC,EB,concl. 3.00

FOREVER PEOPLE, THE
1971–72
1 JK,I:Forever People,A:Superman,
 A:Darkseid 100.00
2 JK,A:Darkseid 50.00
3 JK,A:Darkseid 50.00
4 JK,A:Darkseid 50.00
5 JK. 40.00
6 thru 11 JK. . . . . @35.00

FOREVER PEOPLE
1988
1 Return of Forever People 3.00
2 Return of Earth of Yesterday 3.00
3 A:Mark Moonrider 3.00
4 The Dark controlls M.Moonrider . 3.00
5 R:MotherBox,Infinity Man 3.00
6 Donny's Fate, final issue 3.00

FORGOTTEN REALMS
1989–91
1 A:RealmsMaster,PriamAgrivar. . . 4.00
2 Mystic Hand of Vaprak,
 A:Ogre Mage 3.00
3 Mystic Hand of Vaprak contd. . . . 2.75
4 Ogre Mage vs.Omen the Wizard. 2.75
5 Dragon Reach #1 . . . . 2.75
6 Dragon Reach #2 . . . . 2.50
7 Dragon Reach #3 . . . . 2.50
8 Dragon Reach #4 . . . . 2.50
9 V:Giant Squid. 2.50
10 Head Cheese 2.50
11 Triangles #1 . . . . 2.50
12 Triangles #2 . . . . 2.50
13 Triangles #3 . . . . 2.50
14 A:Lich Viranton the Mage 2.25
15 Avatar Comics tie-in 2.25
16 Mad Gods and Paladins,pt.1 . . . 2.25
17 Mad Gods and Paladins,pt.2 . . . 2.25
18 Mad Gods and Paladins,pt.3 . . . 2.25
19 Mad Gods and Paladins,pt.4 . . . 2.25
20 Realms Master Crew captured. . 2.25
21 Catewere Tribe 2.25
22 V:The Akri 2.25
23 A:Sandusk the Leprechaun. . . . 2.25
24 Everybody wants to rule
 the realms 2.25
25 The Wake, final issue 2.25
Ann.#1 V:Advanced D&D crew 3.50

FORMERLY KNOWN AS THE JUSTICE LEAGUE
July 2003
1 (of 6) F:Maxwell Lord. 2.50
2 JRu,KM 2.50
3 JRu,KM,V:Roulette 2.50
4 JRu,KM,F:Mary Marvel 2.50
5 JRu,R:G'nort 2.50
6 JRu,concl. 2.50
TPB 12.50

FOUR HORSEMEN
DC/Vertigo, Dec., 1999
1 (of 4) F:Famine 2.50
2 F:War. 2.50
3 F:Pestilence 2.50
4 F:Death, concl.. . . . . 2.50

FOUR STAR BATTLE TALES
1973
1 MD 40.00
2 RH 25.00
3 MD 25.00
4 MD,JKo 25.00
5 MD,RH,BK 25.00

FOUR STAR SPECTACULAR
March-April, 1976
1 . . . . 25.00
2 thru 6 . . . . @12.00

FOURTH WORLD GALLERY
1-shot pin-up collection (1996) 3.50

FOUR WOMEN
Homage/DC Oct., 2001
1 (of 5) SK 3.00
2 SK 3.00
3 thru 5 SK . . . . @3.00
TPB SK rep. #1-#5. . . . . 17.95

Fox and the Crow #4
© DC Comics, Inc.

FOX AND THE CROW
Dec.–Jan., 1951
1 . . . . 1,450.00
2 . . . . 675.00
3 . . . . 400.00
4 . . . . 400.00
5 . . . . 400.00
6 thru 10 . . . . @300.00
11 thru 20 . . . . @225.00
21 thru 40 . . . . @150.00
41 thru 60 . . . . @100.00
61 thru 80 . . . . @75.00
81 thru 94 . . . . @50.00
95 . . . . 65.00
96 thru 99. . . . . @35.00
100 . . . . 40.00
101 thru 108 . . . . @35.00
Becomes:

STANLEY & HIS MONSTER
109 thru 112 Oct.Nov.,1968 . . . . @50.00

FRACTION
DC Focus, April 2004
1 Philly guys 2.50
2 thru 5 . . . . @2.50

FREEDOM FIGHTERS
March-April, 1976
1 Freedom Fighters go to Earth-1 25.00
2 . . . . 12.00
3 . . . . 12.00
4 . . . . 12.00
5 A:Wonder Woman 15.00
6 . . . . 12.00
7 . . . . 12.00
8 . . . . 12.00
9 . . . . 12.00
10 O:Doll Man 12.00
11 O:Ray 12.00
12 O:Firebrand. 12.00
13 O:Black Condor 15.00
14 A:Batgirl. 15.00
15 O:Phantom Lady. 15.00

FROM BEYOND THE UNKNOWN
Oct.–Nov., 1969
1 JKu,CI 70.00
2 MA(c),CI,ATh 40.00

From Beyond The Unknown #10
© DC Comics Inc.

3 NA(c),CI	30.00
4 MA(c),CI	30.00
5 MA(c),CI	30.00
6 NA(c),I:Glen Merrit.	35.00
7 CI,JKu(c)	40.00
8 NA(c),CI	40.00
9 NA(c),CI	40.00
10 MA(c),CI	40.00
11 MA(c),CI	40.00
12 JKu(c),CI	40.00
13 JKu(c),CI,WW	40.00
14 JKu(c),CI	40.00
15 MA(c),CI	40.00
16 MA(c),CI	40.00
17 MA(c),CI	40.00
18 MK(c),CI,Star Rovers	30.00
19 MK(c),CI,Star Rovers	30.00
20	30.00
21	30.00
22 MA(c)	32.00
23 CI,Space Museum	30.00
24 CI	30.00

FUNNY STOCKING STUFFER
March, 1985

1	5.00

FUNNY STUFF
Summer, 1944

1 B:3 Mousketeer Terrific Whatzit	1,200.00
2	600.00
3	350.00
4	350.00
5	350.00
6 thru 10	@225.00
11 thru 20	@175.00
21	125.00
22 C:Superman	450.00
23 thru 30	@125.00
31 thru 78	@100.00
79 July-Aug., 1954.	100.00

FURY OF FIRESTORM
June, 1982

1 PB,I:Black Bison	7.00
2 PB,V:Black Bison.	3.00
3 PB,V:Pied Piper, Killer Frost	2.50
4 PB,A:JLA,Killer Frost	2.50
5 PB,V:Pied Piper	2.50
6 V:Pied Piper	2.50

7 I:Plastique	2.50
8 V:Typhoon	2.50
9 V:Typhoon	2.50
10 V:Hyena	2.50
11 V:Hyena.	2.50
12 PB,V:Hyena	2.50
13	2.50
14 PB,I:Enforcer,A:Multiplex	2.50
15 V:Multiplex	2.50
16 V:Multiplex	2.50
17 I:2000 Committee,Firehawk	2.50
18 I:Tokamak,A:Multiplex	2.50
19 GC,V:Goldenrod	2.50
20 A:Killer Frost	2.50
21 D:Killer Frost.	3.00
22 O:Firestorm.	3.00
23 I:Bug & Byte	2.50
24 I:Blue Devil,Bug & Byte	2.75
25 I:Silver Deer	2.50
26 V:Black Bison	2.50
27 V:Black Bison	2.50
28 I:Slipknot	2.50
29 I:2000 C'tee,I:Breathtaker.	2.50
30 V:2000 Committee	2.50
31 V:2000 Committee	2.50
32 Phantom Stranger.	2.50
33 A:Plastique	2.50
34 I:Killer Frost 2	2.50
35 V:K.Frost/Plastique,I:Weasel	2.50
36 V:Killer Frost & Plastique	2.50
37	2.50
38 V:Weasel.	2.50
39 V:Weasel.	2.50
40	2.50
41 Crisis.	2.50
42 Crisis,A:Firehawk	2.50
43 V:Typhoon.	2.50
44 V:Typhoon.	2.50
45 V:Multiplex	2.50
46 A:Blue Devil	2.50
47 A:Blue Devil	2.50
48 I:Moonbow	2.50
49 V:Moonbow	2.50
50 W:Ed Raymond.	2.50
51 A:King Crusher	2.50
52 A:King Crusher	2.50
53 V:Steel Shadow.	2.50
54 I:Lava	2.50
55 Legends,V:World's Luckiest Man	2.50
56 Legends,A:Hawk.	2.50
57	2.50
58 I:Parasite II	2.50
59	2.50
60 Secret behind Hugo's accident.	2.50
61 V:Typhoon.	2.50
61a Superman Logo	40.00
62 A:Russian Firestorm	2.50
63 A:Capt.Atom	2.50
64 A:Suicide Squad	2.50
Ann.#1 EC,A:Firehawk, V:Tokamak.	2.50
Ann.#2	2.50
Ann.#3	2.50
Ann.#4 KG,CS,GC,DG	2.50

Becomes:

FIRESTORM, THE NUCLEAR MAN
Nov., 1987

65 A:New Firestorm	2.00
66 A:Green Lantern	2.00
67 Millenium, Week 1	2.00
68 Millenium.	2.00
69 V:Zuggernaut,Stalnivolk USA	2.00
70 V:Flying Dutchman	2.00
71 Trapped in the Timestream.	2.00
72 V:Zuggernaut	2.00
73 V:Stalnivolk & Zuggernaut	2.00
74 Quest for Martin Stein.	2.00
75 Return of Martin Stein.	2.00

Firestorm The Nuclear Man #93
© DC Comics, Inc.

76 Firestorm & Firehawk vs Brimstone	2.00
77 Firestorm & Firehawk in Africa	2.00
78 Exile From Eden,pt.1	2.00
79 Exile From Eden,pt.2	2.00
80 A:Power Girl,Starman,Invasion x-over.	2.00
81 A:Soyuz,Invasion aftermath	2.00
82 Invasion Aftermath	2.00
83 V:Svarozhich	2.00
84	2.00
85 Soul of Fire,N:Firestorm	2.00
86 TMd,Janus Directive #7	2.00
87 TMd.	2.00
88 TMd,E:Air Wave B:Maser	2.00
89 TMd,V:Firehawk,Vandermeer Steel.	2.00
90 TMd,Elemental War #1	2.00
91 TMd,Elemental War #2	2.00
92 TMd,Elemental War #3	2.00
93 TMd,Elemental War concl.	2.00
94 TMd,A:Killer Frost	2.00
95 TMd,V:Captains of Industry	2.00
96 TMd,A:Shango,African God & Obatala,Lord o/t White Cloth.	2.00
97 TMd,A:Obatala,V:Shango	2.00
98 TMd,A:Masar	2.00
99 TMd,A:Brimstone,PlasmaGiant.	2.00
100 TMd,AM,V:Brimstone (Firestorm back-up story) final issue	3.00
Ann.#5 JLI,Suicide Squad I:New Firestorm	2.50

GAMMARAUDERS
1989

1 I:Animal-Warrior Bioborgs	2.25
2 thru 10	@2.25

GANG BUSTERS
1947–58

1	1,200.00
2	500.00
3	400.00
4	400.00
5	400.00
6	400.00
7	400.00
8	400.00
9 Ph(c)	275.00
10 Ph(c)	275.00
11 Ph(c)	225.00
12 Ph(c)	225.00

13 Ph(c) 225.00	
14 Ph(c),FF 500.00	
15 . . . . 200.00	
16 . . . . 200.00	
17 . . . . 500.00	
18 . . . . 175.00	
19 . . . . 175.00	
20 . . . . 175.00	
21 thru 25 . . . . @150.00	
26 JK 150.00	
27 thru 40 . . . . @150.00	
41 thru 44 . . . . @125.00	
45 Comics Code 125.00	
46 thru 50 . . . . @125.00	
51 MD 125.00	
52 thru 67 . . . . @125.00	

GANGLAND
April, 1998
1 (of 4) crime anthology 3.00
2 Platinum Nights 3.00
3 Gang Buff. 3.00
4 conclusion 3.00
TPB series rep. 12.95

GEMINI BLOOD
DC/Helix, 1996–97
1 Species: Paratwa, pt.1 . . . . 2.25
2 Species: Paratwa, pt.2 . . . . 2.25
3 Species: Paratwa, pt.3 . . . . 2.50
4 Species: Paratwa, pt.4 . . . . 2.25
5 WSi(c),Species: Paratwa,pt.5 . . 2.25
6 Species: Paratwa, pt.6 . . . . 2.50
7 BSz, Gillian's secret revealed . . . 2.50
8 Loothka BI-Modal,pt.1 . . . . 2.50
9 Loothka BI-Modal,pt.2
   final issue 2.50

GENESIS
Aug., 1997
1 (of 4) JBy,RoW,JRu,AD,MFm,
   Marvel x-over. 3.00
2 JBy,RoW,JRu,AD,MFm,x-over. . . 3.00
3 JBy,RoW,JRu,AD,MFm,x-over. . . 3.00
4 JBy,RoW,JRu,AD,MFm,concl. . . . 3.00

GHOSTDANCING
DC/Vertigo, 1995
[Mini-Series]
1 I:Snake,Ghost Dancing 2.50
2 Secrets. 2.50
3 I:Father Craft 2.50
4 Coyote prisoner 2.50
5 F:Snot Boy 2.50

GHOSTS
Sept.–Oct., 1971
1 JAp,NC(c),Death's Bride-
   groom! 200.00
2 WW,NC(c),Mission
   Supernatural 100.00
3 TD,NC(c),Death is my Mother . . 75.00
4 GT,NC(c),The Crimson Claw . . . 75.00
5 NC(c),Death, The Pale
   Horseman 75.00
6 NC(c),A Specter Poured
   The Potion 40.00
7 MK(c),Death's Finger Points . . . 40.00
8 NC(c),The Cadaver In
   The Clock 40.00
9 AA,NC(c),The Last Ride
   Of Rosie The Wrecker 40.00
10 NC(c),A Specter Stalks Saigon . 40.00
11 NC(c),The Devils Lake 25.00
12 NC(c),The Macabre Mummy
   Of Takhem-Ahtem 25.00
13 NC(c),Hell Is One Mile High . . . 25.00

14 NC(c),The Bride Wore
   A Shroud 25.00
15 AA,NC(c),The Ghost That
   Wouldn't Die 25.00
16 NC(c),Death's Grinning Face . . 25.00
17 NC(c),Death Held the
   Lantern High 25.00
18 AA,NC(c),Graveyard of
   Vengeance. 25.00
19 AA,NC(c),The Dead Live On . . 25.00
20 NC(c),The Haunting Hussar
   Of West Point 25.00
21 NC(c),The Ghost In The
   Devil's Chair 15.00
22 NC(c),The Haunted Horns
   Of Death 15.00
23 NC(c),Dead Is My Darling! 15.00
24 AA,NC(c),You Too, Will Die. . . . 15.00
25 AA,NC(c),Three Skulls On
   The Zambezi 15.00
26 DP,NC(c),The Freaky Phantom
   Of Watkins Glen 15.00
27 NC(c),Conversation With
   A Corpse 15.00
28 DP,NC(c),Flight Of The
   Lost Phantom 15.00
29 NC(c),The Haunted Lady
   Of Death 15.00
30 NC(c),The Fangs of
   the Phantom 15.00
31 NC(c),Blood On The Moon 15.00
32 NC(c),Phantom Laughed Last . 15.00
33 NC(c),The Hangman of
   Haunted Island 15.00

Ghosts #97 © DC Comics, Inc.

34 NC(c),Wrath of the Ghost Apes 15.00
35 NC(c),Feud with a Phantom . . . 15.00
36 NC(c),The Boy Who Returned
   From The Gave 15.00
37 LD(c),Fear On Ice 15.00
38 LD(c),Specter In The Surf. 15.00
39 LD(c),The Haunting Hitchhiker 15.00
40 LD(c),The Nightmare That
   Haunted The World 30.00
41 LD(c),Ship of Specters 20.00
42 LD(c),The Spectral Sentries . . . 20.00
43 LD(c),3 Corpses On A Rope . . . 20.00
44 LD(c),The Case of the
   Murdering Specters 20.00
45 LD(c),Bray of the
   Phantom Beast 20.00
46 LD(c),The World's Most
   Famous Phantom 20.00
47 LD(c),Wrath of the
   Restless Specters 20.00

48 DP,LD(c),The Phantom Head . . 20.00
49 The Ghost in the Cellar. 20.00
50 Home Is Where The Grave Is. . 20.00
51 The Ghost Who Would Not Die 20.00
52 LD(c),Thunderhead Phantom . . 20.00
53 LD(c),Whose Spirit Invades Me 20.00
54 LD(c),The Deadly Dreams
   Of Ernie Caruso. 20.00
55 LD(c),The House That Was
   Built For Haunting 20.00
56 LD(c),The Triumph Of The
   Teen-Age Phantom 20.00
57 LD(c),The Flaming Phantoms
   of Oradour 20.00
58 LD(c),The Corpse in the Closet 20.00
59 LD(c),That Demon Within Me . . 20.00
60 LD(c),The Spectral Smile
   of Death. 10.00
61 LD(c),When Will I Die Again . . 10.00
62 LD(c),The Phantom Hoaxer!. . . 10.00
63 LD(c),The Burning Bride 10.00
64 LD(c),Dead Men Do Tell Tales . 10.00
65 LD(c),The Imprisoned Phantom 10.00
66 LD(c),Conversation With A
   Corpse. 10.00
67 LD(c),The Spectral Sword 10.00
68 LD(c),The Phantom of the
   Class of '76 . . . . 8.00
69 LD(c),The Haunted Gondola. . . 8.00
70 LD(c),Haunted Honeymoon . . . 8.00
71 LD(c),The Ghost Nobody Knew . 8.00
72 LD(c),The Ghost of
   Washington Monument 8.00
73 LD(c),The Specter Of The
   Haunted Highway 8.00
74 LD(c),The Gem That Haunted
   the World! 8.00
75 LD(c),The Legend Of The
   Lottie Lowry 8.00
76 LD(c),Two Ghosts of
   Death Row. 8.00
77 LD(c),Ghost, Where Do
   You Hide? 8.00
78 LD(c),The World's Most
   Famous Phantom 8.00
79 LD(c),Lure of the Specter 8.00
80 JO(c),The Winged Specter 8.00
81 LD(c),Unburied Phantom 8.00
82 LD(c),The Ghost Who
   Wouldn't Die 8.00
83 LD(c),Escape From the Haunt
   of the Amazon Specter 8.00
84 LD(c),Torment of the
   Phantom Face. 8.00
85 LD(c),The Fiery Phantom
   of Faracutin 8.00
86 LD(c),The Ghostly Garden 8.00
87 LD(c),The Phantom Freak 8.00
88 LD(c),Harem In Hell 8.00
89 JKu(c),Came The Specter
   Shrouded In Seaweed. 8.00
90 The Ghost Galleon 8.00
91 LD(c),The Haunted Wheelchair . 8.00
92 DH(c),Double Vision 8.00
93 MK(c),The Flaming Phantoms
   of Nightmare Alley 8.00
94 LD(c),Great Caesar's Ghost . . . 8.00
95 All The Stage Is A Haunt 8.00
96 DH(c),Dread of the
   Deadly Domestic 8.00
97 JAp(c),A Very Special Spirit
   A:Spectre 15.00
98 JAp(c),The Death of a Ghost
   A:Spectre 15.00
99 EC(c),Till Death Do Us Join
   A:Spectre 15.00
100 EC&DG(c),The Phantom's
   Final Debt 10.00
101 MK(c),The Haunted Hospital . . 5.00
102 RB&DG(c),The Fine Art
   Of Haunting 5.00

103 RB&DG(c),Visions and
  Vengeance. 5.00
104 LD(c),The First Ghost 5.00
105 JKu(c) 5.00
106 JKu(c) 5.00
107 JKu(c) 5.00
108 JKu(c) 5.00
109 EC(c) 5.00
110 EC&DG(c) 5.00
111 JKu(c) 5.00
112 May, 1982 . . . . 5.00

GIANTKILLER
1999
1 (of 6) 2.50
2 DIB 2.50
3 DIB 2.50
4 DIB,O:Jill 2.50
5 DIB,V:Nox 2.50
6 . . . . 2.50

G.I. COMBAT
Jan., 1957
Prev: Golden Age
44 RH,JKu,The Eagle and
  the Wolves. 900.00
45 RH,JKu,Fireworks Hill 400.00
46 RH,The Long Walk
  To Wansan. 350.00
47 RH, The Walking Weapon . . . 350.00
48 No Fence For A Jet. 350.00
49 Frying Pan Seat 350.00
50 Foxhole Pilot. 350.00
51 RH,The Walking Grenade. . . . 350.00
52 Jku,JKu(c),Call For A Tank . . . 250.00
53 JKu,The Paper Trap 250.00
54 RH,JKu,Sky Tank 250.00
55 Call For A Gunner. 250.00
56 JKu,JKu(c),The D.I.-And the
  Sand Fleas 350.00
57 RH,Live Wire For Easy 300.00
58 JKu(c),Flying Saddle. 300.00
59 JKu,Hot Corner. 250.00
60 RH,Bazooka Crossroads 250.00
61 JKu(c),The Big Run 225.00
62 RH,JKu,Drop An Inch 225.00
63 MD,JKu(c),Last Stand. 225.00
64 MD,RH,JKu,JKu(c),The
  Silent Jet 225.00
65 JKu,Battle Parade. 225.00
66 MD,The Eagle of Easy
  Company 300.00
67 JKu(c),I:Tank Killer 300.00
68 JKu,RH,The Rock 1,000.00
69 JKu,RH,The Steel Ribbon. . . . 200.00
70 JKu,Bull's-Eye Bridge 200.00
71 MD,JKu(c),Last Stand. 200.00
72 MD,JKu(c),Ground Fire. 200.00
73 RH,JKu(c),Window War 200.00
74 RH,A Flag For Joey 200.00
75 RH,Dogtag Hill 250.00
76 MD,RH,JKu,Bazooka For
  A Mouse 250.00
77 RH,JKu,H-Hour For A Gunner 250.00
78 MD,RH,JKu(c),Who Cares
  About The Infantry. 250.00
79 JKu,RH,Big Gun-Little Gun. . . 250.00
80 JKu,RH(c),Flying Horsemen. . 250.00
81 Jump For Glory. 200.00
82 IN,Get Off My Back. 200.00
83 Too Tired To Fight 200.00
84 JKu(c),Dog Company
  Is Holding 180.00
85 IN,JKu(c),The T.N.T. Trio 180.00
86 JKu,RH(c),Not Return. 180.00
87 RH(c),I:Haunted Tank. 900.00
88 RH,JKu(c),Haunted Tank Vs.
  Ghost Tank 325.00
89 JA,RH,IN,Tank With Wings. . . 200.00

90 JA,IN,RH,Tank Raiders. 200.00
91 IN,RH,Tank and the Turtle . . . 200.00
92 JA,IN,The Tank of Doom 200.00
93 RH(c),JA,No-Return Mission . 200.00
94 IN,RH(c),Haunted Tank Vs.
  The Killer Tank. 200.00
95 JA,RH(c),The Ghost of
  the Haunted Tank 200.00
96 JA,RH(c),The Lonesome Tank 200.00
97 IN,RH(c),The Decoy Tank. . . . 200.00
98 JA,RH(c),Trap of Dragon's
  Teeth 200.00
99 JA,JKu,RH(c),Battle of the
  Thirsty Tanks 200.00
100 JA,JKu,Return of the
  Ghost Tank 200.00
101 JA,The Haunted Tank Vs.
  Attila's Battle Tiger. 125.00
102 JKu(c),Haunted Tank
  Battle Window 125.00
103 JKu,JA,RH(c),Rabbit Punch
  For A Tiger. 125.00
104 JA,JKu,RH(c),Blind
  Man's Radar 125.00
105 JA,JKu(c),Time Bomb Tank . 125.00
106 JA,JKu(c),Two-Sided War. . . 125.00
107 JKu(c),The Ghost Pipers . . . 125.00
108 JKu(c),The Wounded
  Won't Wait,I:Sgt.Rock 125.00
109 JKu(c),Battle of the Tank
  Graveyard 125.00
110 IN,JKu(c),Choose Your War . 125.00
111 JA,JKu(c),Death Trap 125.00
112 JA,JKu(c),Ghost Ace. 90.00
113 JKu,RH(c),Tank Fight In
  Death Town 90.00
114 JA,RH(c),O:Haunted Tank. . . 200.00
115 JA,RH(c),MedalsForMayhem . 90.00
116 IN,JA,JKu(c),Battle Cry
  For A Dead Man 90.00
117 JA,RH,JKu(c),Tank In
  The Ice Box. 90.00
118 IN,JA,RH(c),My Buddy-
  My Enemy 90.00
119 IN,RH(c),Target For
  A Firing Squad. 90.00
120 IN,JA,RH(c),Pull a Tiger'sTail . 90.00
121 RH(c),Battle of Two Wars 75.00
122 JA,JKu(c),Who Dies Next? . . . 75.00
123 IN,RH(c),The Target of Terro . 75.00
124 IN,RH(c),Scratch That Tank . . 75.00
125 RH(c),Stay Alive-Until Dark. . . 75.00
126 JA,RH(c),Tank Umbrella 75.00
127 JA,JKu(c),Mission-Sudden
  Death. 75.00

G.I. Combat #190 © DC Comics Inc.

128 RH(c),The Ghost of
  the Haunted Tank 75.00
129 JA,RH(c),Hold That Town
  For A Dead Man 75.00
130 RH(c),Battle of the Generals . 75.00
131 JKu&RH(c),Devil For Dinner. . 75.00
132 JA,JKu(c),The Executioner. . . 75.00
133 JKu(c),Operation:Death Trap . 75.00
134 MD,JKu(c),Desert Holocaust . 75.00
135 GE,JKu(c),Death is the Joker . 75.00
136 JKu(c),Kill Now-Pay Later. . . . 75.00
137 JKu(c),We Can't See 75.00
138 JKu(c),I:The Losers 135.00
139 JKu(c),Corner of Hell 60.00
140 RH,MD,JKu(c),The LastTank . 60.00
141 MD,JKu(c),Let Me Live..
  Let Me Die. 30.00
142 RH,JKu(c),Checkpoint-Death . 30.00
143 RH,JKu(c),Iron Horseman . . . 30.00
144 RH,MD,JKu(c),Every
  Man A Fort. 40.00
145 MD,JKu(c),Sand,Sun
  and Death 40.00
146 JKu(c),Move the World 40.00
147 JKu(c),Rebel Tank 40.00
148 IN,JKu(c),The Gold-Plated
  General 40.00
149 JKu(c),Leave The
  Fighting To Us 30.00
150 JKu(c),The Death of the
  Haunted Tank 30.00
151 JKu(c),A Strong Right Arm . . . 30.00
152 JKu(c),Decoy Tank 30.00
153 JKu(c),The Armored Ark 30.00
154 JKu(c),Battle Prize 30.00
155 JKu(c),The Long Journey . . . 15.00
156 JKu(c),Beyond Hell 15.00
157 JKu(c),The Fountain 15.00
158 What Price War. 15.00
159 JKu(c),Mission Dead End . . . 15.00
160 JKu(c),Battle Ghost. 15.00
161 JKu(c),The Day of the Goth . 15.00
162 JKu(c),The Final Victor 15.00
163 A Crew Divided 15.00
164 Siren Song 15.00
165 JKu(c),Truce,Pathfinder 15.00
166 Enemy From Yesterday 15.00
167 JKu(c),The Finish Line 15.00
168 NA(c),The Breaking Point. . . . 25.00
169 WS(c),The Death of the
  Haunted Tank 15.00
170 Chain of Vengeance 15.00
171 JKu(c),The Man Who
  Killed Jeb Stuart 14.00
172 RH(c),At The Mercy of
  My Foes. 14.00
173 JKu(c),The Final Crash. 14.00
174 JKu(c),Vow To A Dead Foe. . 14.00
175 JKu(c),The Captive Tank . . . 14.00
176 JKu(c),A Star Can Cry 14.00
177 JKu(c),The Tank That
  Missed D-Day 14.00
178 JKu(c),A Tank Is Born 14.00
179 JKu(c),One Last Charge. . . . 14.00
180 JKu(c),The Saints Go
  Riding On 14.00
181 JKu(c),The Kidnapped Tank . 14.00
182 JKu(c),Combat Clock 14.00
183 JKu(c),6 Stallions To
  Hell- And Back. 14.00
184 JKu(c),Battlefield Bundle 14.00
185 JKu(c),No Taps For A Tank . . . 14.00
186 JKu(c),Souvenir
  From A Headhunter 14.00
187 JKu(c),The General
  Died Twice. 14.00
188 The Devil's Pipers. 14.00
189 The Gunner is a Gorilla 14.00
190 The Tiger and The Terrier 14.00
191 Decoy For Death. 14.00
192 The General Has Two Faces . 14.00

G. I. Combat #288 © DC Comics, Inc.

193 JKu(c),The War That
Had To Wait 14.00
194 GE(c),Blitzkrieg Brain 14.00
195 JKu(c),The War That
Time Forgot 14.00
196 JKu(c),Dead Men Patrol 14.00
197 JKu(c),Battle Ark 14.00
198 JKu(c),The Devil
Rides A Panzer 14.00
199 JKu(c),A Medal From A Ghost 14.00
200 JKu(c),The Tank That Died . . . 15.00
201 NA&RH(c),The Rocking
Chair Soldiers 20.00
202 NA&RH(c),Walking Wounded
Don't Cry 20.00
203 JKu(c),To Trap A Tiger 15.00
204 JKu(c),A Winter In Hell 15.00
205 JKu(c),A Gift From
The Emperor 15.00
206 JKu(c),A Tomb For A Tank . . . 15.00
207 JKu(c),Foxhole for a Sherman 15.00
208 JKu(c),Sink That Tank. 15.00
209 JKu(c),Ring Of Blood 15.00
210 JKu(c),Tankers Also Bleed . . . 15.00
211 JKu(c),A Nice Day For Killing . 15.00
212 JKu(c),Clay Pigeon Crew 12.00
213 JKu(c),Back Door To War 12.00
214 JKu(c),The Tanker Who
Couldn't Die. 12.00
215 JKu(c),Last Stand For Losers . 12.00
216 JKu(c),Ghost Squadron 12.00
217 JKu(c), The Pigeon Spies 12.00
218 JKu(c), 48 Hours to Die 12.00
219 thru 230 . . . . @12.00
231 thru 288 . . . . @10.00

GIFTS OF THE NIGHT
DC/Vertigo, 1999
1 (of 4) PC,JBo 3.00
2 thru 4 PC,JBo. . . . . @3.00

GILGAMESH II
1989
1 JSn,O:Gilgamesh. 5.00
2 JSn,V:Nightshadow 4.50
3 JSn,V:Robotic Ninja. 4.50
4 JSn,final issue 4.00

GIRL WHO WOULD
BE DEATH, THE
DC/Vertigo, 1998
1 thru 4 F:Plath . . . . @2.50

GODDESS
DC/Vertigo, 1995–96
[Mini-Series]
1 I:Rosie Nolan 4.00
2 Rosie arrested 4.00
3 I:Jenny 4.00
4 CIA Chase 4.00
5 V:Agent Hooks 4.00
6 V:Harry Hooks 4.00
7 Mudhawks Past 4.00
8 finale 4.00
TPB Goddess, GEn, 256-page . . . 19.95

GOLDEN AGE
Elseworld 1993–94
1 PS,F:JSA,All-Star Squadron 8.00
2 PS,I:Dynaman 7.00
3 PS,IR:Mr. Terrific is
Ultra-Humanite 7.00
4 PS,D:Dynaman,Mr. Terrific 6.00
1 Secret Files,48-page(2000) 4.95

GON
DC/Paradox 1996
Book 1 . . . . 7.00
Book 2 Gon Again! 7.00
Book 3 Here Today, Gon Tomorrow . 7.00
Book 4 Going, Going, Gon 7.00
TPB Gon Swimmin' 7.00
TPB Color Spectacular 6.00
TPB Gon Wild rep. books 3 & 4 . . 10.00
TPB 224-page (2001) 9.95

GOTHAM CENTRAL
Dec. 2002
1 MLr,F:Gotham Detectives 3.50
2 MLr,cop murdered 3.00
3 MLr,V:Firebug 3.00
4 MLr,V:Firebug 2.50
5 MLr,two cases 2.50
6 MLr,Half a Life,pt.1 . . . . 2.50
7 MLr,Half a Life,pt.2 . . . . 2.50
8 MLr,Half a Life,pt.3 . . . . 2.50
9 MLr,Half a Life,pt.4 . . . . 2.50
10 MLr,Half a Life,pt.5 . . . . 2.50
11 F:Stacy 2.50
12 A sniper strikes 2.50
13 shadow of the Joker 2.50
14 Joker's reign of terror 2.50
15 Joker sniper spree 2.50
16 Sarge and Crowe 2.50
17 Murder of businesswoman 2.50
18 Hot homicide case 2.50
19 Harvey Bullock 2.50
20 Mad Hatter, Penguin 2.50
21 Mad Hatter, Penguin, Harvey . . 2.50
22 High School BB Massacre 2.50
23 War Games tie-in 2.50
24 War Games tie-in 2.50
TPB Batman: Gotham Central 10.00

GOTHAM GIRLS
Aug., 2002
1 (of 5) F:Catwoman. 2.25
2 Catwoman,Batgirl,P.Ivy,H.Quinn . 2.25
3 Poison Ivy, Harley Quinn 2.25
4 Batgirl. 2.25
5 Renee Montoya, concl. 2.25

GREATEST STORIES
EVER TOLD
TPB Superman (1989) 16.00
TPB Batman (1989) 16.00
TPB Vol.#2 Catwoman & Penguin . 17.00
TPB Joker (1989) BBo(c). 15.00
TPB Flash (1991). 15.00
TPB Golden Age (1990). 15.00
TPB Fifties 15.00
TPB Team-Up (1990). 15.00

GREEN ARROW
[Limited Series], 1983
1 TVE,DG,O:Green Arrow. 5.00
2 TVE,DG,A:Vertigo 4.00
3 TVE,DG,A:Vertigo 4.00
4 TVE,DG,A:Black Canary 4.00
[Regular Series], 1988–97
1 EH,DG,V:Muncie 5.00
2 EH,DG,V:Muncie 4.00
3 EH,DG,FMc,V:Fyres. 4.00
4 EH,DG,FMc,V:Fryes. 4.00
5 EH,DG,FMc,Gauntlet 4.00
6 EH,DG,FMc,Gauntlet 4.00
7 EB,DG,A:Black Canary 4.00
8 DG,Alaska 3.50
9 EH,DG,FMc,R:Shado. 3.50
10 EH,DG,FMc,A:Shado 3.50
11 EH,DG,FMc,A:Shado 3.50
12 EH,DG,FMc,A:Shado 3.00
13 DJu,DG,FMc,Moving Target . . . 3.00
14 EH,DG,FMc. 3.00
15 EH,DG,FMc,Seattle And Die. . . 3.00
16 EH,DG,FMc,Seattle And Die. . . 3.00
17 DJu,DG,FMc,The Horse Man . . 2.50
18 DJu,DG,FMc,The Horse Man . . 2.50
19 EH,DG,FMc,A:Hal Jordan 2.50
20 EH,DG,FMc,A:Hal Jordan 2.50
21 DJu,DG,B:Blood of Dragon,
A:Shado. 4.00
22 DJu,DG,A:Shado. 2.50
23 DJu,DG,A:Shado. 2.50
24 DJu,DG,E:Blood of Dragon . . . 2.50
25 TVE,Witch Hunt #1 . . . . 2.50
26 Witch Hunt #2 . . . . 2.50
27 DJu,DG,FMc,R:Warlord 2.50
28 DJu,DG,FMc,A:Warlord 2.50
29 DJu,DG,FMc,Coyote Tears 2.50
30 DJu,DG,FMc,Coyote Tears 2.50
31 FMc,V:Drug Dealers 2.50
32 FMc,V:Drug Dealers 2.50
33 DJu,FMc,Psychology Issue . . . 2.50
34 DJu,DG,A:Fryes,Arrested 2.50
35 B:Black Arrow Saga,A:Shade . . 2.50
36 Black Arrow Saga,A:Shade. . . . 2.50
37 Black Arrow Saga,A:Shade. . . . 2.50
38 E:Black Arrow Saga,A:Shade . . 2.50
39 DCw,Leaves Seattle 2.50
40 MGr,Spirit Quest,A:
Indian Shaman 2.50
41 DCw,I.R.A. 2.50
42 DCw,I.R.A. 2.50
43 DCw,I.R.A. 2.50
44 DCw,Rock'n'Runes,pt.1 . . . . . . 2.50
45 Rock'n'Runes,pt.2. . . . . 2.50
46 DCw,Africa 2.50
47 DCw,V:Trappers 2.50
48 DCw,V:Trappers 2.50
49 V:Trappers 2.50
50 MGr(c),50th Anniv.,R:Seattle . . 3.00
51 Tanetti's Murder,pt.1 . . . . 2.50
52 Tanetti's Murder,pt.2 . . . . 2.50
53 The List,pt.1,A:Fyres. 2.50
54 The List,pt.2,A:Fyres. 2.50
55 Longbow Hunters tie-in. 2.50
56 A:Lt. Cameron. 2.50
57 And Not A Drop to Drink,pt.1 . . 2.50
58 And Not A Drop to Drink,pt.2 . . 2.50
59 Predator,pt.1 . . . . 2.50
60 Predator,pt.2 . . . . 2.50
61 FS,F:Draft Dodgers 2.50
62 FS 2.50
63 FS,B:Hunt for Red Dragon 2.50
64 FS,Hunt for Red Dragon. 2.50
65 MGr(c),Hunt for Red Dragon . . . 2.50
66 MGr(c),E:Hunt for Red Dragon . . 2.50
67 MGr(c),FS,V:Rockband Killer . . . 2.50
68 MGr(c),FS,BumRap 2.50

All comics prices listed are for *Near Mint* condition.

Green Arrow #73
© DC Comics, Inc.

69 MGr(c),Reunion Tour #1 . . . . 2.50
70 Reunion Tour #2 . . . . 2.50
71 Wild in the Streets #1 . . . . 2.50
72 MGr(c),Wild in the Streets#2 . . . 2.50
73 MGr(c),F:Vietnam Vet 2.50
74 SAP,MGr(c),V:Sniper 2.50
75 MGr(c),A:Speedy Shado,
    Black Canary 3.00
76 MGr(c),R:Eddie Fyers 2.50
77 MGr(c),A:Eddie Fyers 2.50
78 MGr(c),V:CIA 2.50
79 MGr(c),V:CIA 2.50
80 MGr(c),E:MGr(s),V:CIA 2.50
81 B:CDi(s),JAp,V:Shrapnel,
    Nuklon 2.50
82 JAp,I:Rival 2.50
83 JAp,V:Yakuza 2.50
84 E:CDi(s),JAp,In Las Vegas 2.50
85 AIG(s),JAp,A:Deathstroke 2.50
86 DgM(s),JAp,A:Catwoman 2.50
87 JAp,V:Factory Owner 2.50
88 JAp,A:M.Manhunter,Bl.Beetle . . . 2.50
89 JAp,A:Anarky 2.50
90 Zero Hour 2.50
91 Hitman 2.50
92 Partner attacked 2.50
93 Secrets of Red File 2.50
94 I:Camo Rouge 2.50
95 V:Camo Rouge 2.50
96 I:Slyfox,A:Hal Jordan 2.50
97 Where Angels Fear to Tread 2.50
98 Where Angels Fear to
    Tread,pt.3, A:Arsenal 2.50
99 Where Angels Fear to Tread 2.50
100 . . . . 12.00
101 A:Superman,Black Canary . . 35.00
102 CDi,RbC,Underworld
     Unleashed tie-in 3.00
103 CDi,RbC,Underworld
     Unleashed tie-in 3.00
104 CDi,RbC,A:Green Lantern 3.00
105 CDi,RbC,A:Robin 3.00
106 . . . . 2.50
107 CDi,RbC,protects child-king . . . 2.50
108 CDi,A:Thorn 2.50
109 CDi,JAp,BSz,in Metropolis 2.50
110 CDi(s),RbC,I:Hatchet, Green
     Lantern x-over 3.50
111 CDi(s),RbC,I:Hatchet, Green
     Lantern x-over 3.50
112 CDi(s),RbC, ... 2.50
113 CDi(s),RbC,In the Mongolian
     wastes 2.50

114 CDi(s) RbC,airplane downed,
     Final Night tie-in 2.50
115 CDi(s),RbC,IronDeath,pt.1 . . . 2.50
116 CDi(s),RbC,IronDeath,pt.2 . . . . 2.50
117 CDi(s),RbC,IronDeath,pt.3 . . . . 2.50
118 CDi(s),DBw,RbC,Endangered
     Species, pt.1 . . . . 2.50
119 CDi(s),DBw,RbC,Endangered
     Species, pt.2 . . . . 2.50
120 CDi(s),RbC,at grandfather's
     ranch 2.50
121 CDi(s),RbC,V:The Silver
     Monkey 2.50
122 CDi(s),RbC, at Idaho ranch . . . 2.50
123 CDi(s),JAp,KJ,The
     Stormbringers, concl. 2.50
124 CDi(s),RbC,V:Milo Armitage . . 2.50
125 CDi(s),DBw,Green Lantern
     x-over,pt.1, 48pg 3.50
126 CDi(s),DBw,x-over, pt.3 . . . . . . 3.00
127 CDi(s),DBw,to San Francisco . . 3.00
128 CDi(s),DWb,Russian Mob. 3.00
129 CDi,DBw,Jansen prisoner,pt.2 . 3.00
130 CDi,DBw, ... 3.00
131 CDi,DBw,F:Crackshot 3.00
132 CDi,DBw,Eddie Fyers returns . . 3.00
133 CDi,DBw,Eddie Fyers pt.2 . . . . 3.00
134 CDi,DBw,Brotherhood of
     the Fist x-over,pt.1 . . . . 3.00
135 CDi,DBw,Brotherhood of the
     Fist x-over, concl. 3.00
136 CDi,DBw,Green Pastures,pt.1 . 3.00
137 CDi(s),A:Superman 15.00
Ann.#1 A:Question,FablesII 4.00
Ann.#2 EH,DG,FMc,A:Question 3.50
Ann.#3 A:Question 3.50
Ann.#4 The Black Alchemist 3.50
Ann.#5 TVE,FS,Eclipso,Batman . . . 3.50
Ann.#6 JBa(c),I:Hook 3.50
Ann.#7 CDi, Year One 4.25
Spec. #0 Return 2.50
Spec.#1,000,000 CDi(s), A:Superman
     final issue 2.50

GREEN ARROW
Feb., 2001
1 PhH,Quiver,pt.1 . . . . 15.00
1a 2nd printing 3.00
2 PhH,Quiver,pt.2 . . . . 8.00
3 PhH,Quiver,pt.3 . . . . 6.00
4 PhH,Quiver,pt.4,A:JLA 6.00
5 PhH,Quiver,pt.5,A:Batman 6.00
6 PhH,Quiver,pt.6,F:Arsenal 4.00
7 PhH,Quiver,pt.7 . . . . 4.00
8 PhH,Quiver,pt.8 . . . . 4.00
9 PhH,Quiver,pt.9 . . . . 4.00
10 PhH,Quiver,concl. 4.00
11 KSm(s),PhH,rediscovery 3.50
12 KSm(s),PhH,Ollie,Connor 3.50
13 KSm(s),PhH,Oliver & Connor . . . 3.00
14 KSm(s),PhH,Onomatopoeia 3.00
15 KSm(s),PhH,last Smith issue . . . 3.00
16 PhH,Archers Quest,pt.1 . . . . 5.00
17 PhH,Archers Quest,pt.2 . . . . 3.50
18 PhH,Archers Quest,pt.3 . . . . 3.50
19 PhH,Archers Quest,pt.4,F:JLA . . 3.50
20 PhH,Archers Quest,pt.5 . . . . 3.50
21 PhH,Archers Quest,pt.6 . . . . 3.50
22 PhH,V:Count Vertigo 3.00
23 CAd,Urban Knights,pt.1 x-over . . 3.00
24 CAd,Urban Knights,pt.3 x-over . . 3.00
25 CAd,Urban Knights,pt.5 x-over . . 3.00
26 PhH,Straight Shooter,pt.1 . . . . . 2.50
27 PhH,Straight Shooter,pt.2 . . . . . 2.50
28 PhH,Straight Shooter,pt.3 . . . . . 2.50
29 PhH,Straight Shooter,pt.4 . . . . . 2.50
30 PhH,Straight Shooter,pt.5 . . . . . 2.50
31 PhH,Straight Shooter,pt.6 . . . . . 2.50
32 F:Arsenal,Green Arrow II 2.50
33 SMa,F:Superman,Plastic Man . . 2.50

34 PhH,City Walls,pt.1 . . . . 2.50
35 PhH,City Walls,pt.2 . . . . 2.50
36 PhH,City Walls,pt.3 . . . . 2.50
37 PhH,City Walls,pt.4 . . . . 2.50
38 PhH,City Walls,pt.5 . . . . 2.50
39 PhH,City Walls,pt.6 . . . . 2.50
40 PhH,New Blood,pt.1 . . . . 2.50
41 PhH,New Blood,pt.2 . . . . 2.50
42 PhH,New Blood,pt.3 . . . . 2.50
Spec. Secret Files #1,64-pg. 5.00
GN Green Arrow by Jack Kirby 6.00
TPB Traitor, 144-page 13.00
TPB Quiver 18.00
TPB The Sounds of Violence 13.00
TPB Straight Shooter 13.00
TPB Archer's Quest 15.00

GREEN ARROW
LONGBOW HUNTERS
Aug., 1987
1 MGr,N:GreenArrow,I:Shado 7.00
1a 2nd printing 3.00
2 MGr,Shadow Revealed 5.00
2a 2nd printing 3.00
3 MGr,Tracking Snow 5.00
TPB, rep. #1-#3 . . . . 13.00
TPB Longbow Hunters, new pr. . . . 15.00

GREEN ARROW:
THE WONDER YEARS
1993
1 MGr,GM,B:New O:Green Arrow . 2.50
2 MGr,GM,I:Brianna Stone 2.50
3 MGr,GM,A:Brianna Stone 2.50
4 MGr,GM,Conclusion 2.50

GREEN CANDLES
1995
1 Paradox Mystery,F:John Halting . 6.00
2 F:John Halting 6.00
3 finale 6.00
TPB B&W rep. #1—#3 . . . . 10.00

GREEN LANTERN
Autumn, 1941
1 O:Green Lantern, V:Master of
    Light, Arson in the Slums . 55,000.00
2 V:Baldy,Tycoon's Legacy . . 10,000.00
3 War cover 7,500.00
4 Doiby and Green Lantern
    join the Army. 6,000.00

Green Lantern #8 © DC Comics Inc.

Green Lantern #12
© DC Comics, Inc.

5 V:Nazis and Black
Prophet,A:General Prophet 4,000.00
6 V:Nordo & Hordes of War Hungry
Henchmen,Exhile of Exiles,
A:Shiloh 3,000.00
7 The Wizard of Odds 3,100.00
8 The Lady and Her Jewels,
A:Hop Harrigan. 3,000.00
9 V:The Whistler, The School
for Vandals 2,500.00
10 V:Vandal Savage,The Man Who
Wanted the World,O:Vandal
Savage 2,500.00
11 The Distardly Designs of
Doiby Dickles' Pals 1,900.00
12 O:The Gambler 1,900.00
13 A:Angela Van Enters 1,900.00
14 Case of the Crooked Cook . 1,900.00
15 V:Albert Zero, One...Two...
Three...Stop Thinking 1,900.00
16 V:The Lizard. 1,900.00
17 V:Kid Triangle, Reward for
Green Lantern 1,900.00
18 V:The Dandy,The Connoisseur
of Crime, X-mas(c) 2,200.00
19 V:Harpies, Sing a Song of
Disaster A:Fate 1,800.00
20 A:Gambler 1,800.00
21 V:The Woodman,The Good
Humor Man 1,500.00
22 A:Dapper Dan Crocker. 1,500.00
23 Doiby Dickles Movie
Ajax Pictures 1,500.00
24 A:Mike Mattson,OnceA Cop. 1,500.00
25 The Diamond Magnet 1,500.00
26 The Scourge of the Sea. . . . 1,500.00
27 V:Sky Pirate 1,500.00
28 The Tricks of the
Sports Master 1,500.00
29 Meets the Challange of
the Harlequin 1,500.00
30 I:Streak the Wonder Dog . . . 1,500.00
31 The Terror of the Talismans . 1,300.00
32 The Case of the
Astonishing Juggler 1,300.00
33 Crime goes West 1,300.00
34 Streak meets the Princess . . 1,300.00
35 V:Three-in-One Criminal . . . 1,300.00
36 The Mystery of the
Missing Messanger 1,700.00
37 A:Sargon 1,700.00
38 DoublePlay,May-June,1949 . 1,700.00

GREEN LANTERN
1960–72, 1976–86

1 GK,O:Green Lantern. 7,000.00
2 GK,I:Qward,Pieface 1,500.00
3 GK,V:Qward. 800.00
4 GK,Secret of GL Mask. 600.00
5 GK,I:Hector Hammond 600.00
6 GK,I:Tomar-Re. 600.00
7 GK,I&O:Sinestro 500.00
8 GK,1st Story in 5700 A.D. 450.00
9 GK,A:Sinestro 450.00
10 GK,O:Green Lantern's Oath . . 450.00
11 GK,V:Sinestro 300.00
12 GK,Sinestro,I:Dr.Polaris 300.00
13 GK,A:Flash,Sinestro 450.00
14 GK,I&O:Sonar,1st Jordan
Brothers story 250.00
15 GK,Zero Hour story. 250.00
16 GK,MA,I:Star Saphire,
O:Abin Sur. 250.00
17 GK,V:Sinestro 250.00
18 GK. 250.00
19 GK,A:Sonar. 250.00
20 GK,A:Flash 250.00
21 GK,O:Dr.Polaris 200.00
22 GK,A:Hector Hammond,Jordan
Brothers story 200.00
23 GK,I:Tattooed Man 200.00
24 GK,O:Shark. 200.00
25 GK,V:Sonar,HectorHammond. 200.00
26 GK,A:Star Sapphire 200.00
27 GK. 200.00
28 GK,I:Goldface 200.00
29 GK,I:Black Hand 220.00
30 GK,I:Katma Tui 200.00
31 GK,Jordan brothers story . . . 175.00
32 GK. 175.00
33 GK,V:Dr. Light. 175.00
34 GK,V:Hector Hammond 175.00
35 GK,I:Aerialist. 175.00
36 GK. 175.00
37 GK,I:Evil Star. 175.00
38 GK,A:Tomar-Re. 175.00
39 GK,V:Black Hand 175.00
40 GK,O:Guardians,A:Golden
Age Green Lantern 800.00
41 GK,A:Star Sapphire 150.00
42 GK,A:Zatanna 150.00
43 GK,A:Major Disaster. 150.00
44 GK,A:Evil Star. 150.00
45 GK,I:Prince Peril,A:Golden
Age Green Lantern 225.00
46 GK,V:Dr.Polaris. 150.00
47 GK,5700 A.D. V:Dr.Polaris . . 150.00
48 GK,I:Goldface 150.00
49 GK,I:Dazzler 150.00
50 GK,V:Thraxon the Powerful . . 150.00
51 GK,Green Lantern's Evil
Alter-ego 125.00
52 GK,A:Golden Age Green
Lantern Sinestro 150.00
53 GK,CI,Jordon brothers story . . 125.00
54 GK,Menace in the Iron Lung . . 125.00
55 GK,Cosmic Enemy #1 . . . . . 125.00
56 GK. 125.00
57 GK,V:Major Disaster 125.00
58 GK,Perils of the Powerless
Green Lantern 125.00
59 GK,I:Guy Gardner(imaginary
story) 325.00
60 GK,I:Lamplighter. 80.00
61 GK,A:Gold.Age Gr.Lantern . . . 80.00
62 Steel Small,Rob Big 80.00
63 NA(c),This is the Way the
World Ends 80.00
64 MSy,We Vow Death to Green
Lantern 80.00
65 MSy,Dry up and Die 80.00
66 MSy,5700 AD story 80.00
67 DD,The First Green Lantern . . . 80.00

Green Lantern #76
© DC Comics, Inc.

68 GK,I Wonder Where The
Yellow Went? 80.00
69 GK,WW,If Earth Fails the
Test.. It Means War 80.00
70 GK,A Funny Thing Happened
on the way to Earth 80.00
71 GK,DD,MA,Jordan brothers . . . 65.00
72 GK,Phantom o/t SpaceOpera . . 65.00
73 GK,MA,A:Star Sapphire,
Sinestro 65.00
74 GK,MA,A:Star Sapphire,
Sinestro 65.00
75 GK,Qward. 65.00
76 NA,Gr.Lantern & Gr.Arrow
team-up begins 450.00
77 NA,Journey to Desolation 125.00
78 NA,A:Black Canary,A Kind of
Loving..A Way to Death. 100.00
79 NA,DA,A:Black Canary,Ulysses
Star is Still Alive 100.00
80 NA,DG,Even an Immortal
can die. 100.00
81 NA,DG,A:Black Canary,Death
be my Destiny 100.00
82 NA,DG,A:Black Canary,
V:Sinestro,(BWr 1 page) 100.00
83 NA,DG,A:BlackCanary,Gr.Lantern
reveals I.D. to Carol Ferris . . 100.00
84 NA,BWr,V:Black Hand 100.00
85 NA,Speedy on Drugs,pt.1,
rep.Green Lantern #1 . . . . . . 125.00
86 NA,DG,Speedy on Drugs,pt.2,
ATh(rep)Golden Age G.L. . . . 125.00
87 NA,DG,I:John Stewart,
2nd Guy Gardner app. 100.00
88 all reprints. 45.00
89 NA,And Through Him Save
the World 75.00
90 MGr,New Gr.Lantern rings 25.00
91 MGr,V:Sinestro 15.00
92 MGr,V:Sinestro 15.00
93 MGr,TA,War Against the
World Builders 15.00
94 MGr,TA,DG,Green Arrow
Assassin,pt.1 . . . . 15.00
95 MGr,Gr.Arrow Assassin,pt.2 . . 15.00
96 MGr,A:Katma Tui 15.00
97 MGr,V:Mocker. 15.00
98 MGr,V:Mocker. 15.00
99 MGr,V:Mocker. 15.00
100 MGr,AS,I:Air Wave 25.00
101 MGr,A:Green Arrow 15.00
102 AS,A:Green Arrow. 10.00
103 AS,Earth-Asylum for an Alien . 10.00
104 AS,A:Air Wave 10.00

DC COMICS

105 AS,Thunder Doom 10.00
106 MGr,Panic..In High Places
   & Low 10.00
107 AS,Green Lantern Corp.story . 10.00
108 MGr,BU:G.A.Green Lantern,
   V:Replikon 15.00
109 MGr,Replicon#2,GA.GL.#2 . . . 10.00
110 MGr,GA.GL.#3 . . . . 10.00
111 AS,O:Green Lantern,
   A:G.A.Green Lantern 15.00
112 AS,O&A:G.A. Green Lantern. . 20.00
113 AS,Christmas story 10.00
114 AS,I:Crumbler. 10.00
115 AS,V:Crumbler. 10.00
116 Guy Gardner as Gr.Lantern . . 50.00
117 JSon,I:KariLimbo,V:Prof.Ojo . . 12.00
118 JSon,V:Prof.Ojo 12.00
119 AS,G.L.& G.A.solo storys. 12.00
120 DH,A:Kari,V:El Espectro 6.00
121 DH,V:El Espectro 6.00
122 DH,A:Guy Gardner,Superman 10.00
123 JSon,DG,E:Green Lantern/Green
   Arrow T.U.,A:G.Gardner,
   V:Sinestro 12.00
124 JSon,V:Sinestro 6.00
125 JSon,FMc,V:Sinestro 6.00
126 JSon,FMc,V:Shark 6.00
127 JSon,FMc,V:Goldface 6.00
128 JSon,V:Goldface 6.00
129 JSon,V:Star Sapphire 6.00
130 JSon,FMc,A:Sonar,B:Tales of the
   Green Lantern Corps. 6.00
131 JSon,AS,V:Evil Star 6.00
132 JSon,AS,E:Tales of GL Corps
   B:B.U.Adam Strange 6.00
133 JSon,V:Dr.Polaris 5.00
134 JSon,V:Dr.Polaris 5.00
135 JSon,V:Dr.Polaris 5.00
136 JSon,A:Space Ranger,
   Adam Strange 5.00
137 JSon,CI,MA,I:Citadel,A:Space
   Ranger,A.Strange 5.00
138 JSon,A&O:Eclipso. 6.00
139 JSon,V:Eclipso 5.00
140 JSon,I:Congressman Block
   Adam Strange 5.00
141 JSon,I:OmegaMen 7.00
142 JSon,A:OmegaMen. 6.00
143 JSon,A:OmegaMen. 6.00
144 JSon,D:Tattooed Man,Adam
   Strange 5.00
145 JSon,V:Goldface 5.00
146 JSon,CI,V:Goldface
   E:B.U.Adam Strange 5.00
147 JSon,CI,V:Goldface 5.00
148 JSon,DN,DA,V:Quardians. 5.00
149 JSon,A:GL.Corps 5.00
150 JSon,anniversary 6.00
151 JSon,GL.Exiled in space. 5.00
152 JSon,CI,GL Exile #2 . . . . 5.00
153 JSon,CI,Gr.Lantern Exile #3 . . . 5.00
154 JSon,Gr.Lantern Exile #4 . . . . . 5.00
155 JSon,Gr.Lantern Exile #5 . . . . . 5.00
156 GK,Gr.Lantern Exile #6. . . . . . . 5.00
157 KP,IN,Gr.Lantern Exile #7. . . . . 5.00
158 KP,IN,Gr.Lantern Exile #8. . . . . 5.00
159 KP,Gr.Lantern Exile #9 . . . . . . 5.00
160 KP,Gr.Lantern Exile #10 . . . . . 5.00
161 KP,A:Omega Men,Exile #11 . . . 5.00
162 KP,Gr.Lantern Exile #12 . . . . . . 6.00
163 KP,Gr.Lantern Exile #13 . . . . . . 5.00
164 KP,A:Myrwhidden,Exile #14 . . . 5.00
165 KP,A:John Stewart & Gr.Arrow
   Green Lantern Exile #15 . . . . . 5.00
166 GT,FMc,DGi,Exile #16 . . . . 5.00
167 GT,FMc,G.L.Exile #17 . . . . 5.00
168 GT,FMc,G.L. Exile #18 . . . . 5.00
169 Green Lantern Exile #19. . . . . . 5.00
170 GT,MSy,GreenLanternCorps. . . 5.00
171 ATh,TA,DGb,Green Lantern
   Exile #20 . . . . 5.00

172 DGb,E:Gr.Lant.Exile 5.00
173 DGb,I:Javelin,A:Congressman
   Bloch 5.00
174 DGb,V:Javelin 4.50
175 DGb,A:Flash 4.50
176 DGb,V:The Shark 4.50
177 DGb,rep. Gr.Lant #128 . . . . . . 4.50
178 DGb,A:Monitor,V:Demolition
   Team 4.50
179 DGb,I:Predator 4.50
180 DGb,A:JLA 4.50
181 DGi,Hal Jordan quits as Green
   Lantern 5.00
182 DGi,John Stewart takes over
   V:Major Disaster 10.00
183 DGi,V:Major Disaster 3.50
184 DGb,Rep. Gr.Lant. #59. . . . . . 4.00
185 DGi,DH,V:Eclipso 4.00
186 DGi,V:Eclipso 4.00
187 BWi,John Stewart meets
   Katma Tui 3.50
188 JSon,C:GrArrow,V:Sonar,John
   Stewart reveals I.D. to world . . . 6.00
189 JSon,V:Sonar 3.50
190 JSon,A:Green Arrow/Black
   Canary,Guy Gardner 3.50
191 JSon,IR:Predator is Star
   Sapphire 3.50
192 JSon,O:Star Sapphire 3.50
193 JSon,V:Replikon,
   A:G.Gardner. 3.50
194 JSon,Crisis,R:G.Gardner. 5.00
195 JSon,Guy Gardner as Green
   Lantern,develops attitude 10.00
196 JSon,V:Shark,Hal Jordan
   regains ring 4.00
197 JSon,V:Shark,Sonar,
   Goldface 4.00
198 JSon,D:Tomar-Re,Hal returns as
   Green Lantern,(double size) . . . 5.00
199 JSon,V:Star Sapphire 3.50
200 JSon,final Gr.Lantern issue. . . . 5.00
Becomes:

GREEN LANTERN
CORPS
1986–88

201 JSon,I:NewGr.LantCorps,V:Star
   Sapphire, Sonar, Dr.Polaris. . . . 3.50
202 JSon,set up headquarters. 3.50
203 JSon,tribute to Disney. 3.50
204 JSon,Arisia reaches puberty. . . . 3.50
205 JSon,V:Black Hand. 3.50

Green Lantern Corps #220
© DC Comics Inc.

206 JSon,V:Black Hand. 3.00
207 JSon, Legends crossover 3.00
208 JSon,I:Rocket Red Brigade,
   Green Lanterns in Russia#1 . . . 3.00
209 JSon,In Russia #2. . . . . 3.00
210 JSon,In Russia #3. . . . . 3.00
211 JSon,John Stewart proposes
   to Katma Tui 3.00
212 JSon,W:J.Stewart&KatmaTui . . 3.00
213 JSon,For Want of a Male 3.00
214 IG,5700 A.D. Story 3.00
215 IG,Salaak and Chip quit 3.00
216 IG,V:Carl 3.00
217 JSon,V:Sinestro 3.00
218 BWg,V:Sinestro. 3.00
219 BWg,V:Sinestro. 3.00
220 JSon,Millennium,pt.3. . . . . 3.00
221 JSon,Millennium 3.00
222 JSon,V:Sinestro 3.00
223 GK,V:Sinestro 3.00
224 GK,V:Sinestro 3.00
Ann.#1 GK 3.00
Ann.#2 JSa,BWg,S:AnM 3.50
Ann.#3 JBy,JL,JR. 3.00
Spec.#1 A:Superman 3.00
Spec.#2 MBr,RT,V:Seeker 3.00
TPB rep.#84-#87,#89,Flash
   #217-#219 . . . . 12.95
TPB rep. reprints of #1-#7 . . . . 8.95

GREEN LANTERN
[2nd Regular Series], 1990
1 PB,A:Hal Jordan,John Stuart,
   Guy Gardner 5.00
2 PB,A:Tattooed Man 4.50
3 PB,Jordan vs.Gardner. 4.50
4 PB,Vanishing Cities 4.00
5 PB Return to OA 4.00
6 PB 3GL'sCaptive 4.00
7 PB R:Guardians. 4.00
8 PB R:Guardians. 4.00
9 JSon,G.Gardner,pt.1 . . . . 4.00
10 JSon,G.Gardner,pt.2 . . . . 4.00
11 JSon,G.Gardner,pt.3 . . . . 4.00
12 JSon,G.Gardner,pt.4 . . . . 4.00
13 Jordan,Gardner,Stuart(giant) . . 4.00
14 PB,Mosaic,pt.1 . . . . 4.00
15 RT,Mosaic,pt.2 . . . . 4.00
16 MBr,RT,Mosaic,pt.3. . . . . 4.00
17 MBr,RT,Mosaic,pt.4. . . . . 4.00
18 JSon,JRu,G.Gardner,
   A:Goldface 4.00
19 MBr,PB,JSon,A:All Four G.L.'s,
   O:Alan Scott,A:Doiby Dickles
   (D.Size-50th Ann.Iss.) 5.00
20 PB,RT,Hal Jordan G.L. Corp
   story begins, A:Flicker 3.00
21 PB,RT,G.L. Corp.,pt.2,
   V:Flicker. 3.00
22 PB,RT,G.L. Corp.,pt.3,
   R:Star Sapphire 3.00
23 PB,RT,V:Star Sapphire,
   A:John Stuart. 3.00
24 PB,RT,V:Star Sapphire 3.00
25 MBr,JSon,RT,Hal Vs.Guy,
   A:JLA 3.00
26 MBr,V:Evil Star,Starlings 3.00
27 MBr,V:Evil Star,Starlings 3.00
28 MBr,V:Evil Star.Starlings 3.00
29 MBr,RT,R:Olivia Reynolds 3.00
30 MBr,RT,Gorilla Warfare#1 . . . . . 3.00
31 MBr,RT,Gorilla Warfare#3 . . . . . 3.00
32 RT(i),A:Floro,Arisia 3.00
33 MBr,RT,Third Law#1,
   A;New Guardians 3.00
34 MBr,RT,Third Law#2,I:Entropy . . 3.00
35 MBr,RT,Third Law#3,V:Entropy. . 3.00
36 V:Dr.Light 3.00
37 MBg,RT,A:Guy Gardner 3.00
38 MBr,RT,A:Adam Strange 3.00

Green Lantern 2nd Series #3
© DC Comics, Inc.

39 MBr,RT,A:Adam Strange 3.00
40 RT(i),A:Darkstar,
    V:Reverse Flash 3.00
41 MBr,RT,V:Predator,
    C:Deathstroke 3.00
42 MBr,RT,V:Predator,
    Deathstroke 3.00
43 RT(i),A:Itty 3.00
44 RT(i),Trinity#2,A:L.E.G.I.O.N. . . . 3.00
45 GeH,Trinity#5,A:L.E.G.I.O.N.,
    Darkstars 3.00
46 MBr,A:All Supermen,
    V:Mongul 8.00
47 A:Green Arrow 6.00
48 KM(c),B:Emerald Twilight,I:Kyle
    Rayner (Last Green Lantern) . . 7.00
49 KM(c),GJ(s),A:Sinestro 6.00
50 KM(c),GJ(s),D:Sinestro,Kiliwog,
    Guardians,I:Last Green
    Lantern (in Costume). 8.00
51 V:Ohm,A:Mongul 5.00
52 V:Mongul 4.00
53 A:Superman,V:Mongul 4.00
54 D:Alex,V:Major Force 4.00
55 Zero Hour,A:Alan Scott,
    V:Major Force 4.00
56 Green Lantern and ring 3.50
57 Psimon 3.50
58 Donna Troy,Felix Faust. 3.50
59 V:Dr. Polaris 3.50
60 Capital Punishment,pt.3 . . . . 3.50
61 V:Kalibak,A:Darkstar 3.50
62 V:Duality,R:Ganthet. 3.50
63 Parallax View: The Resurrection
    of Hal Jordan,pt.1 . . . . 3.00
64 Parallax View,pt.2,A:Superman,
    Flash,V:Parallax 3.00
65 Siege of ZiCharan,pt.2 . . . . 3.00
66 V:Sonar 3.00
67 A:Flash,V:Sonar 3.00
68 RMz,RT,Underworld
    Unleashed tie-in 3.00
69 RMz,RT,Underworld
    Unleashed tie-in 3.00
70 RMz,RT,A:Supergirl 3.00
71 RMz,RT,Hero Quest,pt.1 . . . . 3.00
72 RMz,RT,Hero Quest,pt.2 . . . . 3.00
73 RMz,RT,Hero Quest,pt.3 . . . . 3.00
74 RMz,RT,A:Adam Strange,
    V:Grayven 3.00
75 A:Adam Strange 3.00
76 Green Arrow x-over. 3.00
77 Green Arrow x-over. 3.00

78 . . . . 3.00
79 V:Sonar 3.00
80 RMz(s),JWi,MGy,V:Dr. Light,
    Final Night tie-in 3.00
81 RMz(s),DBk,RT,Memorial for
    Hal Jordan 6.00
81a deluxe edition + extra stories,
    foil cover on cardstock 9.00
82 RMz(s),TGb,RT,F:Kyle Rayner,
    Alan Scott, Guy Gardner &
    John Stewart 3.00
83 . . . . 3.00
84 Retribution, pt.2 . . . . 3.00
85 Retribution, concl. 3.00
86 RMz,JJ,RT,A:Jade, V:Obsidian . . 3.00
87 RMz,TGb,RT,A:Martian
    Manhunter, vs. Alien Invasion . . 3.00
88 RMz(s),DBk,TA,A:Donna Troy,
    Visit Kyle's Mom 3.00
89 RM(s),TA,V:Machine Messiah . . 3.00
90 RM(s),Why did Kyle Rayner
    become Green Lantern 3.00
91 RMz(s),DBk,TA,V:Desaad. 3.00
92 RMz(s),DBk,TA,A:Green Arrow,
    x-over. 3.00
93 RMz(s),DBk,TA,F:Deadman 3.00
94 RMz(s),PaP,TA,F:Superboy 3.00
95 RMz(s),JSn,TA, deep space 3.00
96 RMz(s) 3.00
97 RMz(s),MMK,TA,V:Grayven 3.00
98 RMz,DBk,TA,Future Shock,pt.1 . 3.00
99 RMz,DBk,TA,Future Shock,pt.2 . 3.00
100 RMz,DBk,AT,Kyle Rayner and
    Hal Jordan,V:Sinestro, 48pg . . . 6.00
100a deluxe edition 4.00
101 RMz(s),JJ,BWi,Emerald
    Knights,pt.1, bi-weekly 4.00
102 RMz(s),PaP,TA,Emerald
    Knights,pt.2, bi-weekly 4.00
103 RMz(s),JJ,BWi,Emerald
    Knights,pt.3, bi-weekly 4.00
104 RMz(s),JJ,BWi,Greener Pastures
    x-over, concl., Emerald
    Knights,pt.4, bi-weekly 4.00
105 RMz(s),JJ,SEa,BWi,Emerald
    Knights,pt.5, bi-weekly 4.00
106 RMz(s),PaP,TA,Emerald
    Knights,concl. 4.00
107 RMz(s),TA,Emerald Knights
    aftermath 2.50
108 DBk,TA,A:Wonder Woman 2.50
109 RMz(s),PaP,TA 2.50
110 RMz(s),TA,A:Green Arrow. 2.50
111 RMz(s),TA,DBk,V:Fatality 2.50
112 RMz(s),TA,DBk,back to Earth . . 2.50
113 RMz(s),TA,DBk,Burning
    in Effigy,pt.1 . . . . 2.50
114 RMz(s),TA,DBk,Burning
    in Effigy,pt.2 . . . . 2.50
115 DJu(s),A:Plastic Man &
    Booster Gold, pt.1 . . . . 2.50
116 DJu(s),A:Plastic Man &
    Booster Gold, pt.1 . . . . 2.50
117 RMz(s),DBk,TA,R:Donna Troy . 2.50
118 RMz(s),DBk,TA,Day of
    Judgment x-over 2.50
119 RMz,DBk,CaS,Day of
    Judgment aftermath 2.50
120 RMz,DBk,CaS. 2.50
121 RMz,DBk,CaS. 2.50
122 RMz,DBk,CaS. 2.50
123 RMz,DBk,V:Controllers 2.50
124 RMz,DBk,V:Controllers 2.50
125 RMz,Unmooning secrets 2.50
126 Goes undercover 2.50
127 F:Effigy & Killer Frost 2.50
128 F:Arsenal. 2.50
129 DBk,ASm,V:Manhuters 2.50
130 DBk,ASm,V:Manhunters 2.50
131 DBk,ASm,V:Manhunters 2.50
132 DBk,While Rome Burned,pt.1 . . 2.50

133 DBk,MBr,Rome Burned,pt.2 . . 2.50
134 DBk,While Rome Burned,pt.3 . . 2.50
135 DBk,While Rome Burned,pt.4 . . 2.50
136 DBk,While Rome Burned,pt.5 . . 2.50
137 DBk,Friends & Lovers. 2.50
138 DBk,Away From Home,pt.1 . . . 2.50
139 DBk,Away From Home,pt.2 . . . 2.50
140 DBk,A:Alan Scott 2.50
141 DBk,A:Jade,V:arsonist 2.50
142 V:Inferno 2.50
143 JLe,Joker:Last Laugh,tie-in. . . . 2.50
144 Battle to control his powers . . . 2.50
145 V:Nero 2.50
146 incredible metamorphosis 2.50
147 F:John Stewart 2.50
148 A:Superman,R:Jade 2.50
149 F:JLA. 2.50
150 End of Ion,48-pg. 5.00
151 JLe(c) Hand of God,aftermath . 2.50
152 RbC,uncontrollable madness . . 2.50
153 JLe(c),high school reunion 2.50
154 JLe&SW(c),attacked 2.50
155 JLe&SW(c),A:Flash,JLA 2.50
156 John Stewart back,A:Sentinel . . 2.50
157 Girl Talk 2.50
158 industrialist nomads 2.50
159 Boar Beasts 2.50
160 Child Guardians 2.50
161 V:Amazon 2.50
162 CAd,Urban Knights,pt.2 x-over. 2.50
163 CAd,Urban Knights,pt.4 x-over. 2.50
164 CAd,Urban Knights,pt.6 x-over. 2.50
165 RBr,A Tiny Spark. 2.50
166 RBr,The Blind,pt.1. . . . . 2.50
167 RBr,The Blind,pt.2. . . . . 2.50
168 RBr 2.50
169 RBr,Kilowog's soul 2.50
170 RBr 2.50
171 Wanted, pt.1 . . . . 2.50
172 kidnappers 2.50
173 V:Weaponers of Qward. 2.50
174 V:Black Circle 2.50
175 Qwardians,48-pg. 3.50
176 LRs,RyR,Homecoming,pt.1 . . . 2.25
177 LRs,RyR,Homecoming,pt.2 . . . 2.25
178 LRs,RyR,Homecoming,pt.3 . . . 2.25
179 LRs,RyR,Homecoming,pt.4 . . . 2.25
180 LRs,RyR,Homecoming,pt.5 . . . 2.25
181 LRs,RyR,Homecoming,pt.6 . . . 2.25
Ann.#1 Eclipso,V:Star Sapphire. . . . 4.00
Ann.#1 80pg, rep. 5.00
Ann.#2 Bloodlines#7,I:Nightblade . . 4.00
Ann.#3 Elseworlds Story 3.50
Ann.#4 Year One story. 4.00
Ann.#5 Legends o/t Dead Earth . . . 3.50
Ann.#6 RMz(s),JJ,Low,Pulp
    Heroes, 64pg. 4.50
Ann.#7 SV,RLm,Clv,BWr,Ghosts . . 3.50
Ann.#8 MCa,AAd(c),JLApe:Gorilla
    Warfare 3.50
Ann.#9 Planet DC 4.00
Spec.#1,000,000 RMz(s),BHi,PNe . 2.50
Spec. 3-D #1 V:Dr. Light 4.00
Spec.#1 Our Worlds at War(2001). . 2.95
Secret Files #1. . . . . 5.00
Secret Files Spec.#2 . . . . 5.00
Secret Files #3, 48-pg. 4.95
Green Lantern Plus, 1-shot RMz(s),
    F:The Ray,V:Dr. Polaris. 3.00
Green Lantern/Silver Surfer, 1-shot
    DC/Marvel RMz,TA A:Thanos
    vs. Parallax 5.00
Green Lantern Gallery, 1 one-shot . 3.50
Green Lantern: Ganthet's Tale,
    1-shot, JBy,O:Guardians 7.00
Giant #1 80-page. 5.50
Giant #2 80-page. 5.50
Giant #3 80-page. 5.95
GN Ganthet's Tale, JBy 6.00
GN Green Lantern/Superman:
    Legends of the Green Flame . . 5.95

GN 1001 Emerald Nights(2001) . . . 6.95
GN Brightest Day/Blackest Night. . . 5.95
TPB A New Dawn 10.00
TPB Emerald Twilight 6.25
TPB Emerald Knights 13.00
TPB A New Dawn 10.00
TPB Baptism of Fire. 13.00
TPB Fear Itself. 15.00
TPB Emerald Allies, rep. 15.00
TPB New Journey, Old Path 13.00
TPB Circle of Fire 18.00
TPB Emerald Dawn (rep. 2003) . . 15.00
TPB The Power of Ion (2003) . . . 15.00
TPB Emerald Dawn II (2003). 13.00
TPB Brother's Keeper 13.00
TPB The Road Back 15.00
TPB Emerald Twilight/New Dawn . 20.00
TPB Willworld. 18.00
TPB Gr.Lantern/Gr.Arrow,Vol.1 . . . 13.00
TPB Gr.Lantern/Gr.Arrow,Vol.2 . . . 13.00
TPB Passing the Torch 13.00

GREEN LANTERN & SENTINEL: HEART OF DARKNESS
Feb., 1998
1 (of 3) RMz(s),PaP,DDv 3.00
2 RMz(s),PaP,DDv 3.00
3 RMz(s),PaP,DDv 3.00

GREEN LANTERN: CIRCLE OF FIRE
Aug., 2000
1 (of 2) NBy,64-pg. x-over 5.00
2 48-pg.x-over concl. 5.00
Spec.Gr.Lant.: Adam Strange #1 . . . 2.50
Spec.Gr.Lant.: The Atom #1 . . . . . . 2.50
Spec.Gr.Lant.: Firestorm #1 . . . . . . 2.50
Spec.Gr.Lant.: Green Lantern #1 . . . 2.50
Spec.Gr.Lant.: Power Girl #1 . . . . . . 2.50

GREEN LANTERN CORPS QUARTERLY
1992–94
1 DAb,JSon,FH,PG,MBr,F:Alan
    Scott G'nort 3.00
2 DAb,JSon,PG,AG,Alan Scott . . . 2.75
3 DAb,RT,F:Alan Scott,G'Nort 2.75
4 TA,AG(i),F:H.Jordan,G'Nort. 2.75

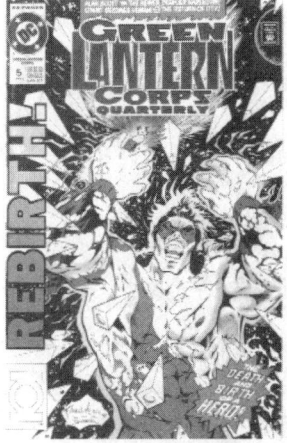

Green Lantern Corps Quarterly #5
© DC Comics, Inc.

5 F:Alan Scott,I:Adam. 2.75
6 JBa,TC,F:Alan Scott 3.25
7 Halloween Issue 3.25
8 GeH,SHa,final issue 3.25

GREEN LANTERN: DRAGON LORD
April, 2001
1 (of 3) PG, 48-page 5.00
2 PG, 48-page. 5.00
3 PG, 48-page. 5.00

GREEN LANTERN: EMERALD DAWN
[1st Limited Series], 1989–90
1 MBr,RT,I:Mod.Age.Gr.Lantern . . . 5.00
2 MBr,RT,I:Legion (not group) 4.00
3 MBr,RT,V:Legion 3.00
4 MBr,RT,A:Green Lantern Corps. . 3.00
5 MBr,RT,V:Legion 3.00
6 MBr,RT,V:Legion 3.00
TPB rep#1-#6. . . . . 5.50

[2nd Limited Series], 1991
1 MBr,A:Sinestro,Guy Gardner. . . . 2.00
2 MBr,RT,V:Alien Aliance 2.00
3 MBr,RT,Sinestro's Home Planet . 2.00
4 MBr,RT,Korugar Revolt 2.00
5 MBr,RT,A:G.Gardner 2.00
6 MBr,RT,Trial of Sinestro. 2.00

GREEN LANTERN: EVIL'S MIGHT
Aug., 2002
1 (of 3) HC, Elseworlds, 48-pg. . . . 5.95
2 HC,F:Kyle Rayner 5.95
3 HC,concl. 5.95

GREEN LANTERN/ GREEN ARROW
1983–84
1 NA rep. 5.00
2 thru 7 NA,DG rep. . . . . @4.00
TPB Roadback. 9.00
TPB Traveling Heroes, Vol.1 . . . . 12.95
TPB Traveling Heroes, Vol.2 . . . . 12.95

GREEN LANTERN: MOSAIC
1992–93
1 F:John Stewart. 2.25
2 D:Ch'p 2.25
3 V:Sinestro 2.25
4 F:The Children on Oa 2.25
5 V:Hal Jordan 2.25
6 A:Kilowog. 2.25
7 V:Alien Faction. 2.25
8 V:Ethereal Creatures 2.25
9 Christmas issue 2.25
10 V:Guardians 2.25
11 R:Ch'p 2.25
12 V:KKK 2.25
13 V:KKK,Racism 2.25
14 A:Salaak,Ch'p 2.25
15 A:Katma Tui,Ch'p 2.25
16 LMc,A:JLA,Green Lantern 2.25
17 A:JLA. 2.25
18 final issue 2.25

GREEN LANTERN: THE NEW CORPS
1999
1 (of 2) CDi(s),SEa 5.00
2 CDi(s),SEa, concl. 5.00

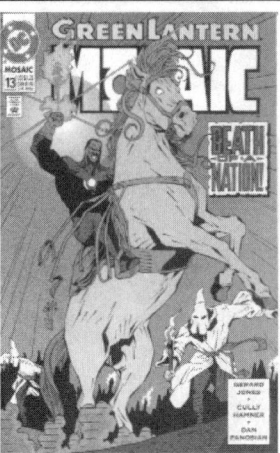

Green Lantern Mosaic #13
© DC Comics Inc.

GREEN LANTERN: REBIRTH
Oct. 2004
1 (of 6) 40-pg. 2.95

GREGORY
DC/Piranha
1 MaH, b&w 8.00
2 MaH 5.00
3 MaH Bookshelf Ed. 5.00
3a Platinum Ed. 8.00
4 MaH, b&w 5.00
TPB #1 Gregory Treasury,MaH . . . 10.00
TPB #2 Gregory Treasury,MaH . . . 10.00

GRIFFIN
1991–92
1 I:Matt Williams as Griffin 5.50
2 V:Carson 5.25
3 A:Mary Wayne 5.25
4 A:Mary Wayne 5.25
5 Face to Face with Himself 5.25
6 Final Issue 5.25

GRIP: THE STRANGE WORLD OF MEN
DC/Vertigo, Nov., 2001
1 (of 5) GHe 2.50
2 GHe 2.50
3 GHe 2.50
4 GHe 2.50
5 GHe, concl. 2.50

GROSS POINT
July, 1997
1 MWa&BAu(s) parody. 2.50
2 Independence Day picnic 2.50
3 Ed Gein High School 2.50
4 paranoid driving instructor 2.50
5 Halloween 2.50
6 Trip to Chicago 2.50
7 Stuck in Gross Point 2.50
8 Dru Hardly & Nancy Boys 2.50
9 . . . . 2.50
10 Businessman of the Year 2.50
11 Mystery Meat 2.50
12 Cold Hands, Still Heart 2.50
13 Terminal illness 2.50
14 The Aisle of Doctor Morose 2.50

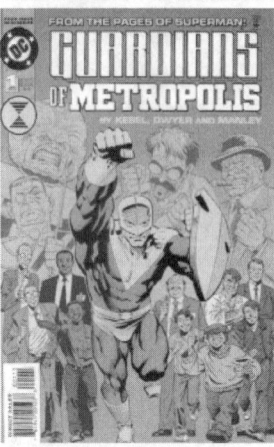

Guardians of Metropolis #1
© DC Comics, Inc.

GUARDIANS
OF METROPOLIS
Nov., 1994

1 Kirby characters. 2.25
2 Donovan's creations 2.25
3 . . . . 2.25
4 Female Furies 2.25

GUNFIRE
1994–95

1 B:LWn(s),StE,I:Ricochet 2.25
2 StE,V:Ricochet 2.25
3 StE,I:Purge. 2.25
4 StE,V:Maraud 3 . . . . 2.25
5 StE,I:Exomorphic Man. 2.25
6 New costume. 2.25
7 Ragnarok 2.25
8 V:Tattoo 2.25
9 V:Ragnarock 2.25
10 V:Yakuza 2.25
11 V:Yakuza. 2.25
12 I:New Weapon 2.25
13 A:JLA,V:Ragnarok, final issue . . 2.25

GUNS OF THE DRAGON
Aug., 1998

1 (of 4) TT, set in 1920s 2.50
2 TT. 2.50
3 TT. 2.50
4 TT conclusion 2.50

GUY GARDNER
1992–94

1 JSon,A:JLA,JLE. 2.50
2 JSon,A:Kilowog 2.50
3 JSon,V:Big,Ugly Alien 2.50
4 JSon,G.Gardner vs Ice 2.50
5 JSon,A:Hal Jordan,V:Goldface . 2.50
6 JSon,A:Hal Jordan,V:Goldface . . 2.50
7 JSon,V:Goldface 2.50
8 JSon,V:Lobo 2.50
9 JSon,Boodikka. 2.50
10 JSon,V:Boodikka. 2.50
11 JSon,B:Year One 2.50
12 JSon,V:Batman,Flash,Green
Lantern 2.50
13 JSon,Year One#3 . . . . 2.50
14 JSon,E:Year One 2.50
15 V:Bad Guy Gardner 2.50
16 B:CDi(s),MaT,V:Guy's Brother . . 2.50
Becomes:

GUY GARDNER:
WARRIOR
1994–96

17 V:Militia 2.50
18 B:Emerald Fallout,N:Guy Gardner,
V:Militia 4.00
19 A:G.A.Green Lantern,V:Militia . . 4.00
20 A:JLA,Darkstars. 2.50
21 E:Emerald Fallout,V:H.Jordan . 2.50
22 I:Dementor 2.50
23 A:Buck Wargo 2.50
24 Zero Hour 2.50
25 A:Buck Wargo 3.00
26 Zero Hour 2.50
27 Capital Punishment. 2.50
28 Capital Punishment,pt.2 . . . . . . 2.50
29 I:Warriors Bar 2.50
29a Collector's Edition. 3.25
30 V:Superman,Supergirl. 2.50
31 A:Sentinel,Supergirl,
V:Dementor 2.50
32 Way of the Warrior,pt.1,A:JLA . 2.50
33 Way of the Warrior,pt.4 . . . . 2.50
34 . . . . 2.50
35 Return of an Old Foe 2.50
36 Underworld Unleashed tie-in . . . 2.50
37 Underworld Unleashed tie-in . . . 2.50
38 A new woman 2.50
39 Guest stars galore 2.50
40 . . . . 2.50
41 V:Dungeon 2.50
42 Martika revealed as Seductress . 2.50
43 V:5 Foes 2.50
Ann.#1 Year One Annual, Leechun
vs. Vuldarians 4.00
Ann.#2 Dead Earth 3.50

GUY GARDNER: REBORN
1992

1 JSon,JRu,V:Goldface,C:Lobo . . . 6.00
2 JSon,JRu,A:Lobo,V:Weaponers
of Qward 5.50
3 JSon,JRu,A:Lobo,N:G.Gardner
V:Qwardians 5.50

HACKER FILES
1992–93

1 TS,Soft Wars#1,I:Jack Marshall . 2.25
2 TS,Soft Wars#2 . . . . 2.25
3 TS,Soft Wars#3 . . . . 2.25
4 TS,Soft Wars#4 . . . . 2.25
5 TS,A:Oracle(Batgirl). 2.25
6 TS,A:Oracle,Green Lantern. 2.25
7 TS,V:Digitronix 2.25
8 TS,V:Digitronix 2.25
9 TS,V:Digitronix 2.25
10 V:Digitronix 2.25
11 TS,A:JLE 2.25
12 TS,V:Digitronix,final issue 2.25

HAMMER LOCKE
1992–93

1 I:Hammerlocke. 3.00
2 V:Tharn the Iron Spider 2.25
3 V:Tharn the Iron Spider 2.25
4 O:Hammerlocke. 2.25
5 V:Sahara Skyhawk 2.25
6 V:Tharn the Iron Spider 2.25
7 V:Tharn 2.25
8 CSp,V:Iron Spider 2.25

HARDCORE STATION
May, 1998

1 (of 6) JSn,JRu,F:Maximillian 2.50
2 JSn,JRu,V:Synnar 2.50
3 JSn,JRu,F:Kyle Rayner 2.50
4 JSn,JRu,V:Synnar 2.50

5 JSn,JRu,F:JLA. 2.50
6 JSn,JRu,conclusion 2.50

HARD TIME
DC Focus Feb. 2004

1 F:Ethan Harrow 2.50
2 Day One. 2.50
3 Skinhead beaten to pulp 2.50
4 Mysterious power. 2.50
5 Pandemonium at the pen 2.50
6 V:Gantry. 2.50
7 B-block. 2.50
8 Escape. 2.50
9 . . . . 2.50
TPB rep, #1-#6 . . . . 9.95

HARDWARE
DC/Milestone, 1993–96

1 DCw,I:Hardware,Edwin Alva,Reprise,
Dir.Mark.Ed.,w/A puzzle piece,
Skybox Card,Poster 4.00
1a NewsstandEd. 2.50
1b Platinum Ed. 6.00
2 DCw,V:Repirise,I:Barraki Young . 2.50
3 DCw,O:Edwin Alva,
I:S.Y.S.T.E.M. 2.50
4 DCw,V:S.Y.S.T.E.M. 2.50
5 DCw,I:Deathwish 2.50
6 DCw,V:Deathwish 2.50
7 DCw,O:Deathwish 2.50
8 DCw(c),O:Hardware 2.50
9 DCw(c),I:Technique 2.50
10 DCw(c),I:Harm,Transit 2.50
11 WS(c),DCw,Shadow War,
I:Iron Butterfly,Dharma. 2.50
12 RB,V:Harm 2.50
13 DCw,A:Reprise 2.50
14 DCw 2.50
15 DCw(c),HuR,V:Alva 2.50
16 Die-Cut(c),JBy(c),DCw,
N:Hardware 4.25
16a Newsstand ED. 2.50
17 Worlds Collide,pt.2,A:Steel 2.50
18 Worlds Collide,pt.9,V:Rift 2.50
19 I:Evan,Tetras. 2.50
20 . . . . 2.50
21 Arcana,Helga 2.50
22 Curt & Assistant 2.50
23 . . . . 2.50
24 . . . . 2.50
25 V:Death Row, Sanction. 3.00
26 Hunt For Deathwish,pt.1 . . . . . . 2.50

Hardware #41
© DC Comics, Inc.

27 Hunt For Deathwish,pt.2	2.50
28 Hunt For Deathwish,pt.3	2.50
29 Long Hot Summer, A:The Blood Syndicate, spec.low price	2.50
30 Long Hot Summer	2.50
31	2.50
32 Control of Alva	2.50
33 HC(c), Cyborg	2.50
34 V:Huaca Aires	2.50
35 A:Sanction	2.50
36 A:Sanction	2.50
37	2.50
38 V:Malleus, without armor	2.50
39 F:Sabrina Alva	2.50
40 V:Top Dog	2.50
41	2.50
42	2.50
43	2.50
44 A:Heroes	2.50
45 DGC(s),Hardware & Hard Company go back to basics	2.50
46 DGC(s),Discovery of Edwin Alva's artificial intelligence	2.50
47 DGC(s),The truth behind a brutal murder	2.50
48	2.50
49 DGC(s),Moe(c),V:Tyrant	2.50
50 DGC(s), 48pg. anniversary issue	3.95
51 DMc(s) final issue	2.50

HARLEY QUINN
October, 2000

1 KK,TyD,A:Batman,48 pg.	3.00
2 KK,TyD,A:Two-Face,Poison Ivy.	2.50
3 KK,TyD,A:Catwoman	2.50
4 KK,TyD,I:Quinntettes	2.50
5 KK,TyD,F:Quinntettes	2.50
6 KK,TyD,A:Oracle	2.50
7 KK,TyD,F:Big Barda	2.50
8 KK,TyD,Harley's Past	2.50
9 KK,TyD,V:Quinntettes	2.50
10 KK,TyD,F:Barbara Gordon	2.50
11 KK,TyD,F:Nightwing	2.50
12 KK,TyD,40-page	3.50
13 KK,Joker:Last Laugh	2.50
14 KK,TyD,to Metropolis	2.50
15 KK,TyD,Lovers advice	2.50
16 KK,TyD,City of Tomorrow	2.50
17 KK,TyD,F:Bizarro	2.50
18 KK,TyD,F:Bizarro	2.50
19 KK,TyD,A:Superman	2.50
20 KK,Harley pays price for evil	2.50
21 KK,ultimate prison	2.50
22 KK,TyD,Highwater	2.50
23 KK,TyD,World Without Harley.	2.50
24 KK,DDv,back from Hell	2.50
25 KK,DDv,F:Batman,A:Joker	2.50
26 wanted for murder	2.50
27 Harley a psychiatrist	2.50
28 new patient	2.50
29 a stalker	2.50
30 Who framed Harley?	2.50
31 Harley and Doc	2.50
32 A:Joker	2.50
33 Behind Blue Eyes,pt.1	2.50
34 Behind Blue Eyes,pt.2	2.50
35 Behind Blue Eyes,pt.3	2.50
36 Behind Blue Eyes,pt.4	2.50
37 Behind Blue Eyes,pt.5	2.50
38 CAd,final issue	2.50
Spec.#1 Our Worlds at War,48-pg.	3.25
GN Harley & Ivy, Love on the Lam	6.50

HAVEN:
THE BROKEN CITY
Dec., 2001

1 (of 9) AOI,F:JLA	2.50
2 AOI,A:JLA	2.50
3 AOI,A:Superman,I:HankVelveeda	2.50

4 AOI,F:Nia	2.50
5 AOI,Eater of Filth	2.50
6 AOI,search for crash survivors.	2.50
7 AOI,V:Ivas the ultra-powerful	2.50
8 AOI,Anathema	2.50
9 AOI,Valadin	2.50

HAWK & DOVE
[1st Regular Series], 1968–69

1 SD	125.00
2 SD	75.00
3 GK	75.00
4 GK	75.00
5 GK,C:Teen Titans	75.00
6 GK	75.00

[Limited Series], 1988–89

1 RLd,I:New Dove	4.00
2 RLd,V:Kestrel	3.50
3 RLd,V:Kestrel	3.50
4 RLd,V:Kestrel	3.50
5 RLd,V:Kestrel,O:New Dove	3.50
TPB rep. #1-#5	10.50

[2nd Regular Series], 1989–91

1 A:Superman,Green Lantern Hawkman	2.50
2 V:Aztec Goddess	2.50
3 V:Aztec Goddess	2.50
4 I:The Untouchables	2.50
5 I:Sudden Death, A:1st Dove's Ghost	2.50
6 A:Barter,Secrets o/Hawk&Dove	2.50
7 A:Barter,V:Count St.Germain	2.50
8 V:Count St.Germain	2.50
9 A:Copperhead	2.50
10 V:Gauntlet & Andromeda	2.50
11 A:New Titans,V:M.A.C., Andromeda Gauntlet	2.50
12 A:New Titans,V:Scarab	2.50
13 1960's,I:Shellshock	2.50
14 Prelue to O:Hawk & Dove, V:Kestrel	2.50
15 O:Hawk & Dove begins	2.50
16 HawkV:Dove,V:Lord of Chaos	2.50
17 V:Lords-Order & Chaos	2.50
18 The Creeper #1	2.50
19 The Creeper #2	2.50
20 KM,DG,Christmas Story	2.50
21 Dove	2.50
22 V:Sudden Death	2.50
23 A:Velv.Tiger,SuddenDeath	2.50
24 A:Velv.Tiger,SuddenDeath	2.50
25 Recap 1st 2 yrs.(48 pg)	2.50
26 Dove's past	2.50
27 The Hunt for Hawk	2.50
28 War of the Gods,A:Wildebeest A:Uncle Sam,final issue, double size	3.00
Ann.#1 In Hell	3.00
Ann.#2 CS,KGa,ArmageddonPt.5	3.00
TPB RLd	9.95

HAWK & DOVE
Sept., 1997

1 (of 5) MBn,DZ,DG,Sasha Martens & Wiley Wolverman	2.50
2 MBn,DZ,DG,Vixen & Vigilante	2.50
3 MBn,DZ,DG,grave desecrations	2.50
4 MBn,DZ,DG,V:Suicide Squad	2.50

HAWKMAN
[1st Regular Series], 1964–68

1 MA,V:Chac	1,000.00
2 MA,V:Tralls	300.00
3 MA,V:Sky Raiders	250.00
4 MA,I&O:Zatanna	225.00
5 MA	175.00
6 MA	175.00
7 MA,V:I.Q.	175.00

Hawkman #15 © DC Comics Inc.

8 MA	175.00
9 MA,V:Matter Master	175.00
10 MA,V:Caw	175.00
11 MA	125.00
12 MA	125.00
13 MA	125.00
14 GaF,MA,V:Caw	125.00
15 GaF,MA,V:Makkar	125.00
16 GaF,MA,V:Ruthvol	125.00
17 GaF,MA,V:Raven	125.00
18 GaF,MA,A:Adam Strange	100.00
19 GaF,MA,A:Adam Strange	100.00
20 GaF,MA,V:Lionmane	70.00
21 GaF,MA,V:Lionmane	70.00
22 V:Falcon	70.00
23 V:Dr.Malevolo	70.00
24 Robot Raiders from Planet Midnight	70.00
25 DD,V:Medusa,G.A.Hawkman	70.00
26 RdM,CCu,DD	70.00
27 DD,JKu(c),V:Yeti	70.00

[2nd Regular Series], 1986–87

1 DH,A:Shadow Thief	3.00
2 DH,V:Shadow Thief	2.50
3 DH,V:Shadow Thief	2.50
4 DH A:Zatanna	2.50
5 DH,V:Lionmane	2.50
6 DH,V:Gentleman Ghost, Lionmane	2.50
7 DH,Honor Wings	2.50
8 DH,Shadow War contd.	2.50
9 DH,Shadow War contd.	2.50
10 JBy(c),D:Hyatis Corp	2.50
11 End of Shadow War	2.50
12 Hawks on Thanagar	2.50
13 DH,Murder Case	2.50
14 DH,Mystery o/Haunted Masks	2.50
15 DH,Murderer Revealed	2.50
16 DH,Hawkwoman lost	2.50
17 EH,DH,final issue	2.50
TPB rep.Brave & Bold apps.	19.95

[3rd Regular Series], 1993–96

1 B:JOs(s),JD,R:Hawkman, V:Deadline	5.00
2 JD,A:Gr.Lantern,V:Meta-Tech	3.00
3 JD,I:Airstryke	2.75
4 JD,RM	2.50
5 JD(c),V:Count Viper	2.50
6 JD(c),A:Eradicator	2.50
7 JD(c),PuK(s),LMc,B:King of the Netherworld	2.50
8 LMc,E:King of the Netherworld	2.50
9 BML(s)	2.50
10 I:Badblood	2.50

11 V:Badblood 2.50
12 V:Hawkgod 2.75
13 V:Hawkgod 2.75
14 New abilities,pt.1 . . . . 2.50
15 New abilities,pt.2 . . . . 2.50
16 Eyes of the Hawk,pt.3 . . . . 2.50
17 Eyes of the Hawk,pt.4 . . . . 2.50
18 Seagle,Ellis, Pepoy 2.50
19 F:Hawkman 2.50
21 RLm,V:Shadow Thief,
　 Gentleman Ghost 2.75
22 Way of the Warrior,pt.3
　 A:Warrior,JLA 2.75
23 Way of the Warrior,pt.6 . . . . 2.75
24 . . . . 2.75
25 V:Lionmane,painted(c) 2.75
26 WML,Underworld
　 Unleashed tie-in 2.75
27 WML,Underworld
　 Unleashed tie-in 2.75
28 WML,V:Doctor Polaris 2.75
29 HC(c),V:Vandal Savage 2.75
30 . . . . 2.75
31 serial killer has Tangarian
　 technology 2.75
32 MC,Search for serial killer 2.75
Ann.#1 JD,I:Mongrel 3.75
Ann.#2 Year One Annual 3.95

[4th Regular Series], 2002
1 RgM,MiB,Hawkman & Hawkgirl . . 2.50
2 RgM,MiB,F:Hawkgirl 2.50
3 RgM,MiB,inter-dimensional portal 2.50
4 RgM,MiB,trapped in Battlelands . 2.50
5 RgM,MiB,Slings and Arrows,pt.1 . 2.50
6 RgM,MiB,Slings and Arrows,pt.2 . 2.50
7 RgM,TT,Lives past 2.50
8 RgM,MiB,F:Atom 2.50
9 RgM,F:Dr.Fate 2.50
10 RgM,find Speed Saunders 2.50
11 RgM,V:Hath-Set 2.50
12 RgM,V:Darkraven 2.50
13 Hawk vs. Hawk 2.50
14 Hawkgirl's parents' murderer . . . 2.50
15 Shayera Thai 2.50
16 RgM,The Thanagarian,pt.1 . . . . 2.50
17 RgM,The Thanagarian,pt.2 . . . . 2.50
18 RgM,The Thanagarian,pt.3 . . . . 2.50
19 F:Black Adam 2.50
20 RgM,MIB,V:Headhunter,pt.1 . . . 2.50
21 RgM,MIB,V:Headhunter,pt.2 . . . 2.50
22 RgM,MIB,V:Headhunter,pt.3 . . . 2.50
23 Black Reign,pt.2,x-over 2.50
24 Black Reign,pt.4,x-over 2.50
25 Black Reign,pt.6,x-over 2.50
26 Rabid vampires 2.50
27 SeP,Past Lives 2.50
28 Fate's Warning,pt.1 . . . . 2.50
29 Fate's Warning,pt.2 . . . . 2.50
30 Fate's Warning,pt.3 . . . . 2.50
31 Fate's Warning,pt.4 . . . . 2.50
32 JoB,F:The Atom 2.50
33 ASm,MGy,F:Monolith 2.50
Spec. Secret Files #1, 48-pg. 4.95
TPB Endless Flight 12.95
TPB Enemies & Allies 14.95

HAWKWORLD
1989
1 TT,Hawkman, Origin retold 5.00
2 TT,Katar tried for treason 4.00
3 TT,Hawkgirl's debut 4.00

[1st Regular Series], 1990–93
1 GN,Byth on Earth,R:Kanjar Ro . . 3.00
2 GN,Katar & Shayera in Chicago . 2.50
3 GN,V:Chicago Crime 2.50
4 GN,Byth's Control Tightens 2.50
5 GN,Return of Shadow Thief 2.50
6 GN,Stolen Thanagarian Ship 2.50
7 GN,V:Byth 2.50
8 GN,Hawkman vs. Hawkwoman . . 2.50

Hawkworld #19 © DC Comics, Inc.

9 GN,Hawkwoman in Prison 2.50
10 Shayera returns to Thanagar . . . 2.50
11 GN,Blackhawk,Express 2.50
12 GN,Princess Treska 2.50
13 TMd,A:Firehawk,V:Marauder . . . 2.50
14 GN,Shayera's Father 2.50
15 GN,War of the Gods X-over . . . 2.50
16 GN War of the Gods X-over 2.50
17 GN,Train Terrorists 2.50
18 GN,V:Atilla 2.50
19 GN,V:Atilla 2.50
20 V:Smir'Beau 2.50
21 GN,Thanagar Pt.1,
　 A:J.S.A. Hawkman 2.50
22 GN,Thanagar Pt.2 . . . . 2.50
23 GN,Thanagar Pt.3 . . . . 2.50
24 GN,Thanagar Pt.4 . . . . 2.50
25 GN,Thanagar Pt.5 . . . . 2.50
26 GN,V:Attilla battle armor 2.50
27 JD,B:Flight's End 2.50
28 JD,Flight's End #2 . . . . 2.50
29 TT(c),JDu,Flight's End #3 . . . . . 2.50
30 TT,Flight's End #4 . . . . 2.50
31 TT,Flight's End #5 . . . . 2.50
32 TT,V:Count Viper,final issue 3.00
Ann.#1 A:Flash 4.50
Ann.#2 Armageddon,pt.6 . . . . 4.00
Ann.#2a reprint (Silver) 3.50
Ann.#3 Eclipso tie-in 3.25

HAYWIRE
1988–89
1 . . . . 2.25
2 thru 13 . . . . 2.25

HEARTLAND
DC/Vertigo, Jan., 1997
1 GEn(s),SDi,Kit faces childhood
　 memories 4.95

HEART THROBS
DC/Vertigo, 1998
1 (of 4) anthology 3.00
2 modern romance 3.00
3 . . . . 3.00
4 . . . . 3.00

HEAVY LIQUID
DC/Vertigo, 1999
1 PPo,pt 1 of 5 . . . . 6.00
2 thru 5 PPo,pt.2 thru pt.5 . . . . . @6.00
TPB PPo, 240-page 29.95

HECKLER, THE
1992–93
1 KG,MJ,I:The Heckler 2.25
2 KG,MJ,V:The Generic Man 2.25
3 KG,MJ,V:Cosmic Clown 2.25
4 KG,V:Bushwacker 2.25
5 KG,Theater Date 2.25
6 KG,I:Lex Concord 2.25
7 KG,V:Cuttin'Edge 2.25

HELLBLAZER
Jan., 1988
1 B:JaD(s),JRy,F:John
　 Constantine 20.00
2 JRy,I:Papa Midnight 10.00
3 JRy,I:Blathoxi 8.00
4 JRy,I:Resurrection Crusade,
　 Gemma 8.00
5 JRy,F:Pyramid of Fear 8.00
6 JRy,V:Resurrection Crusade,
　 I:Nergal 6.00
7 JRy,V:Resurrection Crusade,
　 I:Richie Simpson 6.00
8 JRy,AA,Constantine receives
　 demon blood,V:Nergal 6.00
9 JRy,A:Swamp Thing 6.00
10 JRy,V:Nergal 6.00
11 MBu,Newcastle Incident,pt.1 . . . 5.00
12 JRy,D:Nergal 5.00
13 JRy,John has a Nightmare 5.00
14 JRy,B:The Fear Machine,
　 I:Mercury,Marj,Eddie 5.00
15 JRy,Shepard's Warning 5.00
16 JRy,Rough Justice 5.00
17 MkH,I:Mr. Wester 5.00
18 JRy,R:Zed 5.00
19 JRy,I:Simon Hughes,Sandman . 10.00
20 JRy,F:Mr.Webster 6.00
21 JRy,I:Jallakuntiliokan 6.00
22 JRy,E:The Fear Machine 6.00
23 I&D:Jerry O'Flynn 5.00
24 E:JaD(s),I:Sammy Morris 5.00
25 GMo(s),DvL,Early Warning 5.00
26 GMo(s) 5.00
27 NGa(s),DMc,Hold Me 17.00
28 B:JaD(s),RnT,KeW,F:S.Morris . . 5.00
29 RnT,KeW,V:Sammy Morris 5.00
30 RnT,KeW,D:Sammy Morris 5.00
31 E:JaD(s),SeP,Constantine's
　 Father's Funeral 5.00
32 DiF(s),StP,I&D:Drummond 4.50
33 B:JaD(s),MPn,I:Pat McDonell . . 4.50
34 SeP,R:Mercury,Marj 4.50
35 SeP,Constantine's Past 4.50
36 Future Death,(preview of
　 World Without End) 4.50
37 Journey to England's Secret
　 Mystics 4.50
38 Constantine's Journey contd. . . . 4.50
39 Journey to Discovery 4.50
40 DMc,I:2nd Kid Eternity 5.00
41 B:GEn(s),WSm,MPn,Dangerous
　 Habits 9.00
42 Dangerous Habits 4.50
43 I:Chantinelle 4.50
44 Dangerous Habits 4.50
45 Dangerous Habits 4.50
46 Dangerous Habits epilogue,
　 I:Kit(John's girlfriend) 4.50
47 SnW(i),Pub Where I Was Born . . 4.00
48 Love Kills 4.00
49 X-mas issue,Lord o/t Dance 4.00
50 WSm,Remarkable Lives,A:Lord
　 of Vampires (48pgs) 6.00
51 JnS,SeP,Laundromat-
　 Possession 5.00
52 GF(c),WSm, Royal Blood 5.00
53 GF(c),WSm, Royal Blood 5.00
54 GF(c),WSm, Royal Blood 5.00
55 GF(c),WSm, Royal Blood 5.00

Hellblazer #2 © DC Comics, Inc.

56 GF(c),B:GEn(s),DvL,
  V:Danny Drake 5.00
57 GF(c),SDi,Mortal Clay#1,
  V:Dr. Amis 5.00
58 GF(c),SDi,Mortal Clay#2,
  V:Dr. Amis 5.00
59 GF(c),WSm,MkB(i),KDM,B:Guys
  & Dolls 5.00
60 GF(c),WSm,MkB(i),F:Tali,
  Chantinelle 5.00
61 GF(c),WSm,MkB(i),E:Guys &
  Dolls, V:First of the Fallen 5.00
62 GF(c),SDi,End of the Line,I:Gemma,
  AIDS storyline insert w/Death . . 6.00

DC/Vertigo, 1993

63 GF(c),SDi,C:Swamp Thing,Zatanna
  Phantom Stranger 5.00
64 GF(c),SDi,B:Fear & Loathing,
  A:Gabriel (Racism) 4.00
65 GF(c),SDi,D:Dez 4.00
66 GF(c),SDi,E:Fear and Loathing . 4.00
67 GF(c),SDi,Kit leaves John 4.00
68 GF(c),SDi,F:Lord of Vampires,
  Darius,Mary 4.00
69 GF(c),SDi,D:Lord of Vampires . . 4.00
70 GF(c),SDi,Kit in Ireland 4.00
71 GF(c),SDi,A:WWII Fighter Pilot . 4.00
72 GF(c),SDi,B:Damnation's
  Flame,A:Papa Midnight 4.00
73 GF(c),SDi,Nightmare NY,
  A:JFK 4.00
74 GF(c),SDi,I:Cedella,A:JFK 4.00
75 GF(c),SDi,E:Damnation'sFlame . 4.00
76 GF(c),SDi,R:Brendan 4.00
77 Returns to England 4.00
78 GF(c),SDi,B:Rake at the
  Gates of Hell 4.00
79 GF(c),SDi,In Hell 4.00
80 GF(c),SDi,In London 4.00
81 GF(c),SDi 4.00
82 Kit 4.00
83 Rake,Gates of Hell 4.00
84 John's past 4.00
85 Warped Notions,pt.1 . . . . 4.00
86 Warped Notions,pt.2 . . . . 4.00
87 Warped Notions,pt.3 . . . . 4.00
88 Warped Notions,pt.4 . . . . 4.00
89 Dreamtime 4.00
90 Dreamtime,pt.2 . . . . 4.00
91 Visits Battlefield 4.00
92 Critical Mass,pt.1 . . . . 4.00
93 Critical Mass,pt.2 . . . . 4.00
94 Critical Mass,pt.3 . . . . 4.00
95 SeP,Critical Mass,pt.4 . . . . 4.00

96 SeP,Critical Mass,pt.5 . . . . 4.00
97 SeP,Critical Mass epilogue 4.00
98 SeP, helps neighbor 4.00
99 SeP 4.00
100 SeP, In a coma 5.00
101 SeP,deal with a demon 3.50
102 SeP,DifficultBeginnings,pt.1 . . . 3.50
103 SeP,DifficultBeginnings,pt.2 . . . 3.50
104 SeP,DifficultBeginnings,pt.3 . . . 3.50
105 . . . . 3.50
106 PJe(s),SEp,In the Line of
  Fire, pt.1 (of 2) 3.50
107 PJe(s),SEp,Line of Fire,pt.2 . . . 3.50
108 PJe(s),SeP,a Bacchic
  celebration 3.50
109 PJe(s),SeP,cattle mutilations
  in Northern England 3.50
110 PJe(s),SeP,Last Man
  Standing,pt.1 . . . . 3.50
111 PJe(s),SeP,Last Man,pt.2 . . . . . 3.50
112 PJe(s),SeP,Last Man,pt.3 . . . . . 3.50
113 PJe(s),SeP,Last Man,pt.4 . . . . . 3.50
114 PJe(s),SeP,Last Man,pt.5 . . . . . 3.50
115 PJe(s),SeP(s),Dani's ex-
  boyfriend 3.50
116 SeP,Widdershins,pt.1 (of 2) . . . 3.50
117 SeP,Widdershins,pt.2 . . . . 3.50
118 PJe(s),SeP,John's a Godfather. 4.00
119 PJe(s),SeP,disasters 3.50
120 PJe(s),SeP,10th anniv. 48pg. . . 3.00
121 PJe(s),SeP, Up the Down
  Staircase pt.1 . . . . 3.00
122 PJe(s),SeP, Up the Down
  Staircase pt.2 . . . . 3.00
123 PJe(s),SeP, Up the Down
  Staircase pt.3 . . . . 3.00
124 PJe(s),SeP, Up the Down
  Staircase pt.4 . . . . 3.00
125 PJe(s),SeP, How to Play
  with Fire, pt.1 . . . . 3.00
126 PJe(s),SeP,Play/Fire,pt.2 . . . . . 3.00
127 PJe(s),SeP,Play/Fire,pt.3 . . . . . 3.00
128 PJe(s),SeP,Play/Fire,pt.4 . . . . . 3.00
129 . . . . 3.00
130 GEn,JHi,GF,Son of Man,pt.2 . . 3.00
131 GEn,JHi,GF,Son of Man,pt.3 . . 2.75
132 GEn,JHi,GF,Son of Man,pt.4 . . 2.75
133 GEn,JHi,GF,Son of Man,pt.5 . . 2.75
134 WEl(s),JHi,Haunted,pt.1 . . . . . . 2.75
135 WEl(s),JHi,Haunted,pt.2 . . . . . . 2.75
136 WEl(s),JHi,Haunted,pt.3 . . . . . . 2.75
137 WEl(s),JHi,Haunted,pt.4 . . . . . . 2.75
138 WEl(s),JHi,Haunted,pt.5 . . . . . . 2.75
139 WEl(s),JHi,Haunted,pt.6 . . . . . . 2.75
140 WEl(s),Locked. 2.75
141 WEl(s),ALa 2.75
142 WEl,TBd,Setting Sun 2.75
143 WEl,TBd,Telling Tales 2.75
144 GEr,ALa,Ashes & Honey,pt.1 . . 2.75
145 GEr,ALa,Ashes & Honey,pt.2 . . 2.75
146 RC,Hard Time 2.75
147 RC,Hard Time,pt.2 . . . . 2.75
148 RC,Hard Time,pt.3 . . . . 2.75
149 RC,Hard Time,pt.4 . . . . 2.75
150 RC,Hard Time,concl. 2.75
151 Good Intentions,pt.1 . . . . 2.75
152 Good Intentions,pt.2 . . . . 2.75
153 Good Intentions,pt.3 . . . . 2.75
154 Good Intentions,pt.4 . . . . 2.75
155 Good Intentions,pt.5 . . . . 2.75
156 Good Intentions,pt.6 . . . . 2.75
157 SDi,"...and buried?". 2.75
158 Freezes Over,pt.1 . . . . 2.75
159 Freezes Over,pt.2 . . . . 2.75
160 Freezes Over,pt.3 . . . . 2.75
161 Freezes Over,pt.4 . . . . 2.75
162 Lapdogs and Englishmen 2.75
163 Lapdogs and Englishmen 2.75
164 Highwater, pt.1 . . . . 2.75
165 Highwater, pt.2 . . . . 2.75
166 Highwater, pt.3 . . . . 2.75

167 Highwater, pt.4 . . . . 2.75
168 A Fresh Coat of Red Paint 2.75
169 Constantine in LA 2.75
170 Ashes and Dust,pt.1 . . . . 2.75
171 Ashes and Dust,pt.2 . . . . 2.75
172 Ashes and Dust,pt.3 . . . . 2.75
173 Ashes and Dust,pt.4 . . . . 2.75
174 Ashes and Dust,pt.5 . . . . 2.75
175 SDi,JP,High on Life,pt.1 . . . . . . 2.75
176 SDi,JP,High on Life, pt.2 . . . . . . 2.75
177 Red Sepulchre,pt.1 . . . . 2.75
178 Red Sepulchre,pt.2 . . . . 2.75
179 Red Sepulchre,pt.3 . . . . 2.75
180 Red Sepulchre,pt.4 . . . . 2.75
181 Red Sepulchre,concl. 2.75
182 MCy(s),Black Flowers,pt.1 . . . . 2.75
183 MCy(s),Black Flowers,pt.2 . . . . 2.75
184 MCy(s),Wild Card 2.75
185 MCy(s),Ordeal. 2.75
186 MCy(s),The Pit 2.75
187 MCy(s),Bred in Bone,pt.1 . . . . . 2.75
188 MCy(s),Bred in Bone,pt.2 . . . . . 2.75
189 MCy(s),Staring at Wall,pt.1 . . . . 2.75
190 MCy(s),Staring at Wall,pt.2 . . . . 2.75
191 MCy(s),Staring at Wall,pt.3 . . . . 2.75
192 MCy(s),Staring at Wall,pt.4 . . . . 2.75
193 MCy(s),Staring at Wall,pt.5 . . . . 2.75
194 MCy(s) 2.75
195 MCy(s),Out of Season,pt.1 . . . . 2.75
196 MCy(s),Out of Season,pt.2 . . . . 2.75
197 Stations of the Cross,pt.1 . . . . . 2.75
198 Stations of the Cross,pt.2 . . . . . 2.75
199 Stations of the Cross,pt.3 . . . . . 2.75
200 Married life 4.50
201 Thieves 2.75
Ann.#1 JaD(s),BT,Raven Scar. 7.00
Spec.#1 GF(c),GEn(s),SDi,John
  Constantine's teenage years . . . 4.50
Secret Files #1 . . . . 5.00
TPB Original Sins,rep.#1–#9 . . . . . 20.00
TPB Dangerous Habits 15.00
TPB Fear and Loathing 15.00
TPB Damnation's Flame 17.00
TPB Hard Time, 128-page 10.00
TPB Good Intentions (2002) 13.00
TPB Haunted (2003) 13.00
TPB Hellblazer: Freezes Over 15.00
TPB Rake at the Gates of Hell 20.00
TPB Son of Man (2004) 13.00
TPB Highwater (2004) 20.00
TPB Setting Sun (2004) 13.00

HELLBLAZER/
THE BOOKS OF MAGIC
Oct., 1997

1 (of 2) PJe,JNR 2.50
2 PJe,JNR 2.50

HELLBLAZER SPECIAL:
BAD BLOOD
DC/Vertigo, July, 2000

1 (of 4) JaD,PBd 3.50
2 JaD,PBd, ... 3.50
3 JaD,PBd. 3.50
4 JaD,PBd,concl. 3.50

HELLBLAZER SPECIAL:
LADY CONSTANTINE
DC/Vertigo Dec. 2002

1 (of 4) F:Johanna Constantine . . . 3.00
2 thru 4 . . . . @3.00

HERCULES UNBOUND
Oct.–Nov., 1975

1 WW 20.00
2 thru 8 . . . . @12.00
9 thru 12 WS,Aug.–Sept.,1977 . . . 10.00

H-E-R-O
Feb. 2003
1 Jerry Feldon	9.00
2 life-saving mission	5.00
3 F:Molly	5.00
4 Powers and Abilities	5.00
5 F:Matt Allen	3.00
6 F:Andrea Allen	3.00
7 Chaos, Inc.	3.00
8 Chaos, Inc.,pt.2	3.00
9 World Made of Glass,pt.1	3.00
10 World Made of Glass,pt.2	2.50
11 Prehistoric superhero?	2.50
12 Ch-Ch-Ch-Changes,pt.1	2.50
13 Ch-Ch-Ch-Changes,pt.2	2.50
14 Ch-Ch-Ch-Changes,pt.3	2.50
15 Good Guys & Bad Guys,pt.1	2.50
16 Good Guys & Bad Guys,pt.2	2.50
17 Good Guys & Bad Guys,pt.3	2.50
18 Good Guys & Bad Guys,pt.4	2.50
19 Picking Up the Pieces,pt.1	2.50
20 Picking Up the Pieces,pt.2	2.50
21 Picking Up the Pieces,pt.3	2.50
Spec. Double Feature,rep.#1&#2	5.00
TPB Powers and Abilities	10.00

HEROES
DC/Milestone, 1996
1 Six heroes join	3.50
2 battle royale	2.50
3	2.50
4	2.50
5	2.50
6 final issue	2.50

HEROES AGAINST HUNGER
1986
1 NA,DG,JBy,CS,AA,BWr,BS, Superman,Batman	4.00

HERO HOTLINE
1989
1 thru 6, Mini-series	@2.00

HEX
Sept., 1985
1 MT,I:Hex	7.00
2 MT	5.00
3 MT,V:Conglomerate	5.00
4 MT,V:Conglomerate	5.00
5 MT,A:Chainsaw Killer	5.00
6 MT,V:Conglomerate	5.00
7 MT,Tries to Return to own era	5.00
8 MT,The Future	6.00
9 MT,Future Killer Cyborgs	5.00
10 MT,V:Death Cult	5.00
11 MT,V:The Batman	6.00
12 MT,A:Batman,V:Terminators	6.00
13 MT,I:New Supergroup	5.00
14 MT,A:The Dogs of War	5.00
15 KG,V:Chainsaw Killer	5.00
16 KG,V:Dogs of War	5.00
17 KG,Hex/Dogs of War T.U. V:XXGG	5.00
18 KGr,Confronting the Past, final issue	5.00

HISTORY OF DC UNIVERSE
Sept., 1986
1 GP, From start to WWII	5.00
2 GP, From WWII to present	5.00
TPB MWn(s),GP,KK,AxR(c)(2002)	10.00

A HISTORY OF VIOLENCE
DC/Paradox Press March, 1997
GN B&W	10.00

HITCHHIKER'S GUIDE TO THE GALAXY
1993
1 Based on Douglas Adams book	7.00
2 Based on the book	6.50
3 Based on the book	6.50
GN from Douglas Adams book	15.00

HITMAN
1996–2001
1 GEn, F:Tommy Monaghan	10.00
2 GEn, Attempt to kill Joker	7.00
3 GEn(s),JMC, Mawzin & The Arkanonne	5.00
4 GEn(s),JMC,	4.00
5 GEn(s),JMC,	4.00
6 GEn(s),JMC,A:Johnny Navarone, Natt the Hatt	3.00
7 GEn(s),JMC, Pat's dead, Hitman wants revenge	3.00
8 GEn(s),JMC,barricaded in Noonan's Bar, Final Night tie-in.	3.00
9 GEn(s),JMC,A:Six-Pack	3.00
10 GEn(s),JMC,A:Green Lantern	3.00
11	3.00
12 GEn(s),JMC,Local Heroes, A:Green Lantern	3.00
13	3.00
14 GEn(s),JMC, Zombie Night at the Aquarium, concl.	3.00
15 GEn(s),JMC, Ace of Killers, pt.1, V:Mawzir	3.00
16 GEn(s),JMC,Ace of Killers,pt.2	3.00
17 GEn(s),JMC,Ace of Killers,pt.3, A:Catwoman, Demon Etrigan	3.00
18 GEn(s),JMC,Ace of Killers,pt.4, A:Demon Etrigan, Baytor	3.00
19 GEn(s),JMC,Ace/Killers,pt.5,	3.00
20 GEn(s),JMC,Ace/Killers,concl.	3.00
21 GEn(s),JMC,Romeo & Juliet	2.50
22 GEn(s),JMC,holiday special	2.50
23 GEn(s),JMc,Who Dares Wins,pt.1	2.50
24 GEn(s),JMc,Dares/Wins,pt.2	2.50
25 GEn(s),JMc,Dares/Wins,pt.3	2.50
26 GEn(s),JMc,Dares/Wins,pt.4	2.50
27 GEn(s),JMc,Dares/Wins,pt.5	2.50
28 GEn(s),JMC,aftermath	2.50
29 GEn(s),JMC,Tommy's Heroes, pt.1	2.50
30 GEn(s),JMC,Heroes, pt.2	2.50
31 GEn(s),JMC,Heroes, pt.3	2.50
32 GEn(s),JMC,Heroes, pt.4	2.50
33 GEn(s),JMC,Heroes, pt.5	2.50
34 GEn(s),A:Superman	2.50
35 GEn(s),Frances Monaghan	2.50
36 GEn(s),	2.50
37 GEn(s),	2.50
38 GEn(s),Dead Man's Land, concl.	2.50
39 GEn(s),JMC,A:RingoChen,pt.1	2.50
40 GEn(s),JMC,A:RingoChen,pt.2	2.50
41 GEn(s),JMC,A:RingoChen,pt.3	2.50
42 GEn(s),JMC,A:RingoChen,pt.4	2.50
43 GEn(s),JMC,	2.50
44 GEn(s),JMC	2.50
45 GEn(s),JMC	2.50
46 GEn(s),JMC	2.50
47 GEn(s),JMC,Old Dog	2.50
48 GEn(s),JMC,Old Dog,pt.2	2.50
49 GEn(s),JMC,Old Dog,pt.3	2.50
50 GEn(s),JMC,Hitman's future	2.50
51 GEn(s),JMC,Superguy,pt.1	2.50
52 GEn(s),JMc,Superguy,pt.2	2.50
53 GEn(s),JMc,ClosingTime,pt.1	2.50
54 GEn(s),JMc,ClosingTime,pt.2	2.50
55 GEn(s),JMc,ClosingTime,pt.3	2.50
56 GEn,JMC,GL,O:Tommy Monaghan	2.50
57 GEn,JMC,GL,O:Natt	2.50
58 GEn,JMC,GL,Closing time	2.50
59 GEn,JMC,GL,Closing time	2.50
60 GEn,JMC,GL,Closing time,final	2.50
Ann.#1 Pulp Heroes (Western)	3.95
Spec.#1,000,000 GEn(s),JMC	2.50
Spec. Hitman/Lobo: That Stupid Bastich!	3.95
TPB rep. Demon Annual #2, Batman Chronicles #4, Hitman #1–#3	10.00
TPB Hitman,rep.#1–#3,+other	9.95
TPB Ten Thousand Bullets, rep. #4–#8	9.95
TPB Hitman: Ten Thousand Bullets	10.00
TPB Hitman: Local Heroes	18.00
TPB Hitman GEn(s),JMC	9.95
TPB Ace of Killers	17.95
TPB Who Dares Wins, GEn,JMC	12.95

Hopalong Cassidy #108
© DC Comics, Inc.

HOPALONG CASSIDY
Feb., 1954
86 GC,Ph(c):William Boyd & Topper, Secret o/t Tattooed Burro	500.00
87 GC,Ph(c),Tenderfoot Outlaw.	250.00
88 Ph(c),GC,15 Robbers of Rimfire Ridge	175.00
89 GC,Ph(c),One-Day Boom Town	175.00
90 GC,Ph(c),Cowboy Clown Robberies	175.00
91 GC,Ph(c),The Riddle of the Roaring R Ranch	175.00
92 GC,Ph(c),Sky-RidingOutlaws	150.00
93 GC,Ph(c),Silver Badge of Courage	150.00
94 GC,Ph(c),Mystery of the Masquerading Lion	150.00
95 GC,Ph(c),Showdown at the Post-Hole Bank	150.00
96 GC,Ph(c),Knights of the Range	150.00
97 GC,Ph(c),The Mystery of the Three-Eyed Cowboy	150.00
98 GC,Ph(c),Hopalong's Unlucky Day	150.00
99 GC,Ph(c),Partners in Peril	150.00
100 GC,Ph(c),The Secrets of a Sheriff	175.00
101 GC,Ph(c),Way Out West Where The East Begins	125.00
102 GC,Ph(c),Secret of the Buffalo Hat	125.00

103 GC,Ph(c),The Train-Rustlers
of Avalance Valley 125.00
104 GC,Ph(c),Secret of the
Surrendering Outlaws 125.00
105 GC,Ph(c),Three Signs
to Danger. 125.00
106 GC,Ph(c),The Secret of
the Stolen Signature 125.00
107 GC,Ph(c),The Mystery Trail
to Stagecoach Town 125.00
108 GC,Ph(c),The Mystery
Stage From Burro Bend 125.00
109 GC,The Big Gun on Saddletop
Mountain 125.00
110 GC,The Dangerous Stunts
of Hopalong Cassidy 100.00
111 GC,Sheriff Cassidy's
Mystery Clue 100.00
112 GC,Treasure Trail to
Thunderbolt Ridge. 100.00
113 GC,The Shadow of the
Toy Soldier. 100.00
114 GC,Ambush at Natural
Bridge 100.00
115 GC,The Empty-Handed
Robberies 100.00
116 GC,Mystery of the
Vanishing Cabin. 100.00
117 GC,School for Sheriffs 100.00
118 GC,The Hero of
Comanche Ridge. 100.00
119 GC,The Dream Sheriff of
Twin Rivers 100.00
120 GC,Salute to a Star-Wearer . 100.00
121 GC,The Secret of the
Golden Caravan 100.00
122 GC,The Rocking
Horse Bandits 100.00
123 GK,Mystery of the
One-Dollar Bank Robbery . . . 100.00
124 GK,Mystery of the
Double-X Brand. 100.00
125 GK,Hopalong Cassidy's
Secret Brother 100.00
126 GK,Trail of the
Telltale Clues. 100.00
127 GK,Hopalong Cassidy's
Golden Riddle 100.00
128 GK,The House That
Hated Outlaws. 100.00
129 GK,Hopalong Cassidy's
Indian Sign 100.00
130 GK,The Return of the
Canine Sheriff 100.00
131 GK&GK(c),The Amazing
Sheriff of Double Creek. 100.00
132 GK,Track of the
Invisible Indians. 100.00
133 GK,Golden Trail to Danger . . 100.00
134 GK,Case of the
Three Crack-Shots 100.00
135 GK,May-June, 1959 . . . . 100.00

HORRORIST
DC/Vertigo, 1995
1 I:Horrorist. 6.50
2 conclusion 6.50

HOT WHEELS
March-April, 1970
1 ATh. 125.00
2 thru 5 ATh. . . . . @75.00
6 NA(c) 80.00

HOURMAN
1999
1 TPe,RgM,A:JLA 2.50
2 TPe(s),RgM,F:Tomorrow Woman 2.50
3 TPe(s),RgM,Timepoint,pt.1 . . . . . 2.50

4 TPe(s),RgM,Timepoint,pt.2 . . . . . 2.50
5 TPe(s),RgM,Rex Tyler's life 2.50
6 TPe,RgM,JLAndroids,pt.1 . . . . . . 2.50
7 TPe,RgM,JLAndroids,pt.2 . . . . . . 2.50
8 TPe,RgM,Day of Judgment
x-over. 2.50
9 TPe,RgM,F:Rick Tyler 2.50
10 TPe,RgM. 2.50
11 TPe,RgM,One Million,pt.1 . . . . . 2.50
12 TPe,RgM,One Million,pt.2 . . . . . 2.50
13 TPe,RgM,One Million,pt.3 . . . . . 2.50
14 TPe,RgM,V:Undersoul 2.50
15 TPe,RgM,human secrets 2.50
16 TPe,RgM,F:Snapper. 2.50
17 TPe,100 Years of Solitude 2.50
18 TPe,RgM,High Society,pt.1 . . . . 2.50
19 TPe,RgM,High Society,pt.2 . . . . 2.50
20 TPe,RgM,F:Snapper. 2.50
21 TPe,RgM,reduced to nothing . . 2.50
22 TPe,TyH 2.50
23 TPe,RgM,Unbelievable
Truth,pt.1 . . . . 2.50
24 TPE,RgM,Unbel.Truth,pt.2 . . . . . 2.50
25 TPE,RgM,final issue 2.50

HOUSE OF MYSTERY
Dec.–Jan., 1952
1 I Fell In Love With
a Monster 3,000.00
2 The Mark of X 1,300.00
3 The Dummy of Death 1,000.00
4 The Man With the Evil Eye . . 650.00
5 The Man With the Strangler
Hands! 650.00
6 The Monster in Clay! 550.00
7 Nine Lives of Alger Denham! . . 550.00
8 Tattoos of Doom 550.00
9 Secret of the Little Black Bag . 550.00
10 The Wishes of Doom 550.00
11 Deadly Game of G-H-O-S-T . . 450.00
12 The Devil's Chessboard 450.00
13 The Theater Of A
Thousand Thrills! 450.00
14 The Deadly Dolls 450.00
15 The Man Who Could Change
the World 450.00
16 Dead Men Tell No Tales! 350.00
17 Man With the X-Ray Eyes . . . 275.00
18 Dance of Doom. 275.00
19 The Strange Faces of Death. . 275.00
20 The Beast Of Bristol 275.00
21 Man Who Could See Death . . 275.00
22 The Phantom's Return 275.00
23 Stamps of Doom 275.00
24 Kill The Black Cat 275.00
25 The Man With Three Eyes! . . . 275.00
26 The Man with Magic Ears . . . 250.00
27 Fate Held Four Aces! 250.00
28 The Wings Of Mr. Milo! 250.00
29 . . . . 250.00
30 . . . . 250.00
31 The Incredible Illusions! 250.00
32 Pied Piper of the Sea 250.00
33 Mr. Misfortune! 250.00
34 The Hundred Year Duel 250.00
35 . . . . 250.00
36 The Treasure of Montezuma! . 200.00
37 MD,The Statue That
Came to Life 200.00
38 The Voyage Of No Return . . . 200.00
39 . . . . 200.00
40 The Coins That Came To Life. 200.00
41 The Impossible Tricks! 200.00
42 The Stranger From Out There 200.00
43 . . . . 200.00
44 The Secret Of Hill 14 . . . . 200.00
45 . . . . 200.00
46 The Bird of Fate 200.00
47 The Robot Named Think. 200.00
48 The Man Marooned On Earth. 200.00

49 The Mysterious Mr. Omen . . . 200.00
50 . . . . 225.00
51 Man Who Stole Teardrops . . . 175.00
52 The Man With The Golden
Shoes 175.00
53 The Man Who Hated Mirrors . 175.00
54 The Woman Who Lived Twice 175.00
55 I Turned Back Time. 175.00
56 The Thing In The Black Box . . 175.00
57 The Untamed 175.00
58 . . . . 175.00
59 The Tomb Of Ramfis. 175.00
60 The Prisoner On Canvas 175.00
61 JK,Superstition Day 175.00
62 The Haunting Scarecrow 135.00
63 JK,The Lady & The Creature . 175.00
64 The Golden Doom 135.00
65 JK,The Magic Lantern. 200.00
66 JK,Sinister Shadow. 200.00
67 The Wizard of Water. 135.00
68 The Book That Bewitched. . . . 135.00
69 The Miniature Disasters 135.00
70 JK,The Man With Nine Lives . 140.00
71 Menace of the Mole Man 140.00
72 JK,Dark Journey 140.00
73 Museum That Came to Life . 135.00
74 Museum That Came To Life . . 135.00
75 Assignment Unknown! 135.00
76 JK,Prisoners Of The Tiny
Universe 135.00
77 The Eyes That Went Berserk . 125.00
78 JK(c),The 13th Hour 135.00
79 JK(c),The Fantastic Sky
Puzzle 135.00
80 Man With Countless Faces! . . 125.00
81 The Man Who Made Utopia . . 125.00
82 The Riddle of the Earth's
Second Moon 125.00
83 The Mystery of the
Martian Eye 125.00
84 JK,BK,100-Century Doom . . . 200.00
85 JK(c),Earth's Strangest
Salesman. 175.00
86 The Baffling Bargains 150.00
87 The Human Diamond 150.00
88 Return of the Animal Man. . . . 165.00
89 The Cosmic Plant! 165.00
90 The Invasion Of the Energy
Creatures! 165.00
91 DD&SMo(c),The Riddle of the
Alien Satellite. 165.00
92 DD(c),Menace of the
Golden Globule 165.00

House of Mystery #178
© DC Comics Inc.

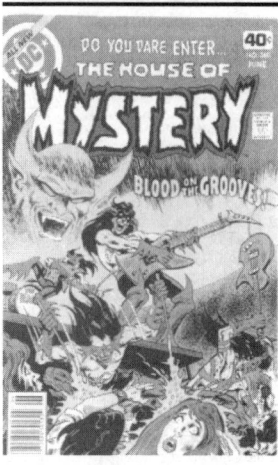

House of Mystery #269
© DC Comics, Inc.

93 NC(c),I Fought The
   Molten Monster 165.00
94 DD&SMo(c),The Creature
   In Echo Lake 165.00
95 The Wizard's Gift 165.00
96 The Amazing 70-Ton Man. . . . 165.00
97 The Alien Who Change
   History 165.00
98 DD&SMo(c),The Midnight
   Creature. 165.00
99 The Secret of the
   Leopard God 165.00
100 The Beast Beneath Earth . . . 175.00
101 The Magnificent Monster . . . 125.00
102 Cellmate to a Monster 125.00
103 Hail the Conquering Aliens . . 125.00
104 I was the Seeing-Eye Man . . 125.00
105 Case of the Creature X-14 . . 125.00
106 Invaders from the Doomed
   Dimension 125.00
107 Captives o/t Alien
   Fisherman 125.00
108 RMo,Four Faces of Frank
   Forbes 125.00
109 ATh,JKu,Secret of the Hybrid
   Creatures. 125.00
110 Beast Who Stalked Through
   Time. 125.00
111 Operation Beast Slayer. 125.00
112 Menace of Craven's
   Creatures. 125.00
113 RMo,Prisoners of Beast
   Asteroid. 125.00
114 The Movies from Nowhere . . 125.00
115 Prisoner o/t Golden Mask . . . 125.00
116 RMo,Return of the
   Barsfo Beast 125.00
117 Menace of the Fire Furies. . . 110.00
118 RMo,Secret of/SuperGorillas . 110.00
119 Deadly Gift from the Stars . . . 110.00
120 ATh,Catman of KarynPeale. . 110.00
121 RMo,Beam that Transformed
   Men 110.00
122 Menace fo the Alien Hero . . . 110.00
123 RMo,Lure o/t Decoy
   Creature. 110.00
124 Secret of Mr. Doom. 110.00
125 Fantastic Camera Creature. . 110.00
126 The Human Totem Poles . . . 110.00
127 RMo,Cosmic Game o/Doom. 110.00
128 NC,The Sorcerer's Snares . . 110.00
129 Man in the Nuclear Trap 110.00
130 The Alien Creature Hunt 110.00

131 Vengeance o/t GeyserGod . . 100.00
132 MMe,Beware My Invisible
   Master 100.00
133 MMe,Captive Queen of
   Beast Island. 100.00
134 MMe,Secret Prisoner of
   Darkmore Dungeon 100.00
135 MMe,Alien Body Thief. 100.00
136 MMe,Secret o/t StolenFace . 100.00
137 MMe,Tunnel to Disaster 100.00
138 MMe,Creature Must Die 100.00
139 MMe,Creatures of
   Vengeful Eye 100.00
140 I&Only app.:Astro 100.00
141 MMe,The Alien Gladiator . . . 100.00
142 MMe,The Wax Demons 100.00
143 J'onn J'onzz begins 350.00
144 J'onn J'onzz on Weird
   World of Gilgana 150.00
145 J'onn J'onzz app. 100.00
146 BP,J'onn J'onzz. 100.00
147 J'onn J'onzz 100.00
148 J'onn J'onzz 100.00
149 ATh,J'onn J'onzz. 100.00
150 MMe,J'onn J'onzz. 100.00
151 J'onn J'onzz 100.00
152 MMe,J'onn J'onzz. 100.00
153 J'onn J'onzz 100.00
154 J'onn J'onzz 100.00
155 J'onn J'onzz 100.00
156 JM,I:Dial H for Hero (Giantboy
   Cometeer,Mole)J.J'onzz sty . 125.00
157 JM,Dial H for Hero (Human
   Bullet,Super Charge,Radar
   Sonar Man) J.J'onzz sty 100.00
158 JM,Dial H for Hero (Quake
   MasterSquid)J'onn J'onzz sty . 90.00
159 JM,Dial H for Hero (Human
   Starfish,Hypno Man,Mighty
   Moppet) J'onn J'onzz sty. 90.00
160 JM,Dial H for Hero (King Kandy
   A:Plastic Man,I:Marco Xavier (J'onn
   J'onzz new secret I.D.) 165.00
161 JM,Dial H for Hero (Magneto,
   Hornet Man,Shadow Man) . . . 75.00
162 JM,Dial H for Hero (Mr.Echo,
   Future Man) J'onnJ'onzz sty . . 75.00
163 JM,Dial H for Hero(Castor&Pollux,
   King Coil) J'onnJ'onzz sty 75.00
164 JM,Dial H for Hero (Super Nova
   Zip Tide) J'onnJ'onzz sty. 75.00
165 JM,Dial H for Hero (Whoozis,
   Whatsis,Howzis) J'onn J'onzz
   story. 75.00
166 JM,Dial H for Hero (Yankee
   Doodle Kid,Chief Mighty Arrow)
   J'onn J'onzz sty. 75.00
167 JM,Dial H for Hero (Balloon Boy,
   Muscle Man,Radar Sonar Man)
   J'onn J'onzz sty. 75.00
168 JM,Dial H for Hero (Thunderbolt,
   Mole,Cometeer,Hoopster)
   J'onn J'onzz sty. 75.00
169 JM,I:Gem Girl in Dial H for
   Hero,J'onn J'onzz sty 75.00
170 JM,Dial H for Hero (Baron
   BuzzSaw,Don Juan,Sphinx
   Man) J'onn J'onzz sty 75.00
171 JM,Dial H for Hero (King Viking
   Whirl-I-Gig)J'onn J'onzz sty. . . 65.00
172 JM,Dial H for Hero 65.00
173 E:Dial H for Hero,F:J'onn
   J'onzz 65.00
174 New direction,SA pg.13 . . . . 125.00
175 I:Cain. 75.00
176 SA,Cain's Game Room. 65.00
177 Curse of the Car. 65.00
178 NA,The Game. 85.00
179 BWr,NA,JO,Widow'sWalk . . . 125.00
180 GK,WW,BWr,SA,Room 13 . . . 75.00
181 BWr,The Siren of Satan 75.00

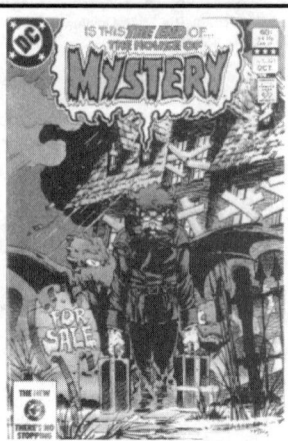

House of Mystery #321
© DC Comics, Inc.

182 ATh,The Devil's Doorway 50.00
183 BWr,WW(i),DeadCanKill 75.00
184 ATh,GK,WW,Eye o/Basilisk . . 50.00
185 AW,The Beautiful Beast 50.00
186 BWr,NA,Nightmare 50.00
187 ATh,Mask of the Red Fox 45.00
188 TD,BWr,NA(c),House of
   Madness 50.00
189 WW(i),NA(c),Eyes of the Cat . 40.00
190 ATh,Fright 40.00
191 BWr,TD,NA(c),Christmas
   Story 60.00
192 JAp,GM,DH,NA(c),Garnener
   of Eden 40.00
193 BWr(c). 40.00
194 ATh,NR,RH(rep),JK(rep)
   Born Loser. 60.00
195 NR,BWr,ThingsOld..Things
   Forgotten. 75.00
196 GM,GK,ATh(rep)A Girl &
   Her Dog. 40.00
197 DD,NR,NA(c),House of
   Horrors. 45.00
198 MSy,NC,Day of the Demon . . 50.00
199 WW,RB,NA(c),Sno'Fun. 60.00
200 MK,TD,The Beast's Revenge . 60.00
201 JAp,The Demon Within. 45.00
202 MSy,GC(rep),SA,The Poster
   Plague,John Prentice? 45.00
203 NR,Tower of Prey 45.00
204 BWr,AN,All in the Family 50.00
205 The Coffin Creature 25.00
206 MSy,TP,The Burning 25.00
207 JSn,The Spell 30.00
208 Creator of Evil. 25.00
209 AA,JAp,Tomorrow I Hang 30.00
210 The Immortal. 25.00
211 NR,Deliver Us From Evil. 30.00
212 MA,AN,Ever After 25.00
213 AN,Back from the Realm of
   the Damned. 30.00
214 NR,The Shaggy Dog. 30.00
215 The Man Who Wanted Power
   over Women 25.00
216 TD,Look into My Eyes & Kill . . 25.00
217 NR,AA,Swamp God 35.00
218 FT,An Ice Place to Visit. 25.00
219 AA,NR,BWr(c),Pledge to
   Satan 35.00
220 AA,AN,They Hunt Butterflies
   Don't They?. 25.00
221 FT,BWr,MK,He Who Laughs
   Last 35.00
222 AA,Night of the Teddy Bear . . 20.00

223 Demon From the Deep 20.00
224 FR,AA,SheerFear,B:100pg . . . 65.00
225 AA,FT,AN,See No Evil 65.00
226 AA,FR,NR,SA,Monster in House
     Tour of House of Mystery 65.00
227 NR,AA,The Carriage Man 65.00
228 FR,NA(i),The Rebel 65.00
229 NR,Nightmare Castle,
     last 100 page 65.00
230 Experiment In Fear 15.00
231 Cold,Cold Heart 15.00
232 Last Tango in Hell 15.00
233 FR,Cake! 15.00
234 AM,Lafferty's Luck 15.00
235 NR,Wings of Black Death 15.00
236 SD,NA(i),BWr(c),Death
     Played a Sideshow 25.00
237 FT,Night of the Chameleon . . . 15.00
238 . . . . 15.00
239 Day of the Witch 15.00
240 The Murderer 15.00
241 FR,NR,DeathPulls theStrings . 15.00
242 FR,The Balloon Vendor 15.00
243 Brother Bear 15.00
244 FT,Kronos..Zagros-Eborak . . . 15.00
245 AN,Check the J.C.Demon
     Catalogue Under...Death 15.00
246 DeathVault of Eskimo Kings . . 15.00
247 SD,Death Rides the Waves . . 15.00
248 NightJamieGaveUp theGhost . 15.00
249 Hit Parade of Death 15.00
250 AN,Voyage to Hell 15.00
251 WW,AA,NA(c),The Collector,
     68-pages 25.00
252 DP,RT,AA,FR,AN,NA(c),
     ManKillers 25.00
253 TD,AN,GK,KJ,NA(c),Beware
     the Demon Child 25.00
254 SD,AN,MR,NA(c),The
     Devil's Place 25.00
255 RE,GM,BWr(c),Sometimes
     Leopards 25.00
256 DAy,AN,BWr(c),Museum of
     Murders 25.00
257 RE,MGo,TD(i),MBr,Xmas iss . 24.00
258 SD,RB,BMc,DG(i),The Demon
     and His Boy 24.00
259 RE,RT,MGo,DN,BL,Hair Today,
     Gone Tomorrow, last giant 24.00
260 Go to Hades 10.00
261 The Husker 10.00
262 FreedFrom Infernos of Hell . . . 10.00
263 JCr,Is There Vengeance
     After Death? 10.00
264 Halloween Issue 10.00
265 The Perfect Host 10.00
266 The Demon Blade 10.00
267 A Strange Way to Die 10.00
269 Blood on the Grooves 10.00
270 JSh,JRu,JBi,Black Moss 10.00
271 TS,HellHound of
     Brackenmoor 10.00
272 DN,DA,theSorcerer's Castle . . 10.00
273 The Rites of Inheritance 10.00
274 MR,JBi,Hell Park 10.00
275 JCr,Final Installment 10.00
276 SD,MN,Epode 10.00
277 HC,AMi,Limited Engagement . 10.00
278 TV or Not TV 10.00
279 AS,Trial by Fury 10.00
280 VMK,DAy,Hungry Jaws
     of Death 10.00
281 Now Dying in this Corner 10.00
282 JSw,DG,Superman/Radio
     Shack ins 10.00
283 RT,AN,Kill Me Gently 10.00
284 KG,King and the Dragon 10.00
285 Cold Storage 10.00
286 Long Arm of the Law 10.00
287 NR,AS,BL,Legend o/t Lost . . . 10.00
288 DSp,Piper at Gates of Hell . . . 10.00

289 Brother Bobby's Home for
     Wayward Girls & Boys 10.00
290 TS,I:I..Vampire 20.00
291 TS,DAy,I..Vampire #2 . . . . 10.00
292 TS,MS,TD,RE,DSp,Wendigo . 10.00
293 GT,TS,A:I..Vampire #3 . . . . . . 10.00
294 CI,TY,GT,TD,The Darkness . . 10.00
295 TS,TVE,JCr,I..Vampire #4 . . . 10.00
296 CI,BH,Night Women 10.00
297 TS,DCw,TD,I..Vampire #5 . . . 10.00
298 TS,Stalker on a StarlessNight . 10.00
299 TS,DSp,I..Vampire #6 . . . . . . 10.00
300 GK,DA,JSon,JCr,DSp,Anniv . . 15.00
301 JDu,TVE,KG,TY `...Virginia' . . 12.00
302 TS,NR,DSp,I..Vampire #7 . . . 12.00
303 TS,DSp,I..Vampire #8 . . . . . . 12.00
304 EC,RE,I..Vampire #9 . . . . 12.00
305 TVE,EC,I..Vampire #10 . . . . . 12.00
306 TS,TD,I..Vampire #11,
     A:Jack the Ripper 12.00
307 TS,I..Vampire #12 . . . . 12.00
308 TS,MT,NR,I..Vampire #13 . . . . 12.00
309 TS,I..Vampire #14 . . . . 12.00
310 TS(i),I..Vampire #15 . . . . 12.00
311 I..Vampire #16 . . . . 12.00
312 TS(i),I..Vampire #17 . . . . 12.00
313 TS(i),CI,I..Vampire #18 . . . . . . 12.00
314 TS,I..Vampire #19 . . . . 12.00
315 TS(i),TY,I..Vampire #20 . . . . . 12.00
316 TS(i),GT,TVE,I..Vampire #21 . 12.00
317 TS(i),I..Vampire #22 . . . . 12.00
318 TS(i),I..Vampire #23 . . . . 12.00
319 TS,JOy,I..Vampire conc 15.00
320 GM,Project: Inferior 15.00
321 final issue 15.00
Welcome Back to the House of Mystery
     GN BWr(c) horror stories rep . . 15.00

HOUSE OF SECRETS
Nov.–Dec., 1956

1 MD,JM,The Hand of Doom . . 2,100.00
2 JPr,RMo,NC,Mask of Fear 700.00
3 JM,JK,MMe,The Three
     Prophecies 600.00
4 JM,JK,MMe,Master of
     Unknown 500.00
5 MMe,The Man Who
     Hated Fear 325.00
6 NC,MMe,Experiment 1000 . . . 325.00
7 RMo,Island o/t Enchantress . . 325.00
8 JK,RMo,The Electrified Man . . 350.00
9 JM,JSt,The Jigsaw Creatures . 275.00
10 JSt,NC,I was a Prisoner
     of the Sea 275.00

House of Secrets #13
© *DC Comics Inc.*

11 KJ(c),NC,The Man who
     couldn't stop growing 275.00
12 JK,The Hole in the Sky 300.00
13 The Face in the Mist 200.00
14 MMe,The Man who Stole Air . 200.00
15 The Creature in the Camera . . 200.00
16 NC,We matched wits with a
     Gorilla genius 175.00
17 DW,Lady in the Moon 175.00
18 MMe,The Fantastic
     Typewriter 175.00
19 MMe,NC,Lair of the
     Dragonfly 175.00
20 Incredible Fireball Creatures . . 175.00
21 Girl from 50,000 Fathoms 175.00
22 MMe,Thing from Beyond 175.00
23 MMe,I&O:Mark Merlin 200.00
24 NC,Mark Merlin story 175.00
25 MMe,Mark Merlin story 150.00
26 NC,MMe, Mark Merlin story . . 150.00
27 MMe,Mark Merlin 150.00
28 MME,Mark Merlin 150.00
29 NC,MMe,Mark Merlin 150.00
30 JKu,MMe,Mark Merlin 150.00
31 DD,MMe,RH,Mark Merlin 140.00
32 MMe,Mark Merlin 140.00
33 MMe,Mark Merlin 140.00
34 MMe,Mark Merlin 140.00
35 MMe,Mark Merlin 140.00
36 MMe,Mark Merlin 140.00
37 MMe,Mark Merlin 140.00
38 MMe,Mark Merlin 140.00
39 JKu,MMe,Mark Merlin 140.00
40 NC,MMe,Mark Merlin 140.00
41 MMe,Mark Merlin 140.00
42 MMe,Mark Merlin 140.00
43 RMo,MMe,CI,Mark Merlin 140.00
44 MMe,Mark Merlin 140.00
45 MMe,Mark Merlin 140.00
46 MMe,Mark Merlin 140.00
47 MMe,Mark Merlin 140.00
48 ATh,MMe,Mark Merlin 140.00
49 MMe,Mark Merlin 140.00
50 MMe,Mark Merlin 140.00
51 MMe,Mark Merlin 140.00
52 MMe,Mark Merlin 140.00
53 CI,Mark Merlin 140.00
54 RMo,MMe,Mark Merlin 140.00
55 MMe,Mark Merlin 140.00
56 MMe,Mark Merlin 140.00
57 MMe,Mark Merlin 140.00
58 MMe,O:Mark Merlin 140.00
59 MMe,Mark Merlin 140.00
60 MMe,Mark Merlin 140.00
61 I:Eclipso,A:Mark Merlin 250.00
62 MMe,Eclipso,Mark Merlin 140.00
63 GC,ATh,Eclipso,Mark Merlin . . 125.00
64 MMe,ATh,M Merlin,Eclipso . . . 125.00
65 MMe,ATh,M Merlin,Eclipso . . . 125.00
66 MMe,ATh,M Merlin,Eclipso . . . 150.00
67 MMe,ATh,M Merlin,Eclipso . . . 125.00
68 MMe,Mark Merlin,Eclipso 125.00
69 MMe,Mark Merlin,Eclipso 125.00
70 MMe,Mark Merlin,Eclipso 125.00
71 MMe,Mark Merlin,Eclipso 125.00
72 MMe,Mark Merlin,Eclipso 125.00
73 MMe,D:Mark Merlin,I:Prince
     Ra-Man; Eclipso 125.00
74 MMe,Prince Ra-Man,Eclipso . 125.00
75 MMe,Prince Ra-Man,Eclipso . 125.00
76 MMe,Prince Ra-Man,Eclipso . 125.00
77 MMe,Prince Ra-Man,Eclipso . 125.00
78 MMe,Prince Ra-Man,Eclipso . 125.00
79 MMe,Prince Ra-Man,Eclipso . 125.00
80 MMe,Prince Ra-Man,Eclipso . 125.00
81 I:Abel, new mystery format
     Don't Move It 100.00
82 DD,NA,One & only, fully guaran–
     teed super-permanent 100% . . 50.00
83 ATh,The Stuff that Dreams
     are Made of 50.00

84 DD,If I had but world enough
   and time. 50.00
85 DH,GK,NA,Second Chance . . . 60.00
86 GT,GM,Strain 60.00
87 DD,DG,RA,MK,BWr,The Coming
   of Ghaqlan. 65.00
88 DD,The Morning Ghost. 60.00
89 GM,DH,Where Dead MenWalk. 60.00
90 GT,RB,NA,GM,The Symbionts . 65.00
91 WW,MA,The Eagle's Talon 60.00
92 BWr,TD(i),I:Swamp Thing
   (Alex Olson). 900.00
93 JAp,TD,ATh(rep.)Lonely in
   Death. 50.00
94 TD,ATh(rep.)Hyde.and
   go Seek. 50.00
95 DH,NR,The Bride of Death. . . . 50.00
96 DD,JAb,WW,BWr,the Monster . 50.00
97 JAp,Divide and Murder. 50.00
98 MK,ATh(rep),Born Losers 50.00
99 NR,TD(i),BWr,,Beyond His
   Imagination 40.00
100 TP,TD,AA,BWr,Rest in Peace. 60.00
101 AN,MK,Small Invasion 25.00
102 NR,MK,A Lonely Monstrosity . 25.00
103 AN,BWr,Village on Edge
   of Forever 20.00
104 NR,AA,GT,Ghosts Don't
   Bother Me...But... . . . . 20.00
105 JAp,AA,MK,An Axe to Grind . 20.00
106 AN,AA,BWr,This Will Kill You . 25.00
107 AA,BWr(c),The Night of
   the Nebbish 25.00
108 A New Kid on the Block 20.00
109 AA,AN...And in Death, there
   is no Escape 20.00
110 Safes Have Secrets, Too 20.00
111 TD,Hair-I-Kari 20.00
112 Case of the Demon Spawn . . . 20.00
113 MSy,NC,NR,Spawns
   of Satan 20.00
114 FBe,Night Game 20.00
115 AA,AN,Nobody Hurts My
   Brother. 20.00
116 NR,Like Father,Like Son. 20.00
117 AA,AN,Revenge for the Deadly
   Dummy 20.00
118 GE,Very Last Picture Show . . 20.00
119 A Carnival of Dwarves. 20.00
120 TD,AA,The Lion's Share 20.00
121 Ms.Vampire Killer 20.00
122 AA,Requiem for Igor 15.00
123 ATh,A Connecticut Ice Cream
   Man in King Arthur's Court . . . 15.00
124 Last of the Frankensteins 15.00
125 AA,FR,Instant Re-Kill 15.00
126 AN,On Borrowed Time 15.00
127 MSy,A Test of Innocence 15.00
128 AN,Freak Out! 15.00
129 Almost Human 15.00
130 All Dolled Up! 15.00
131 AN,Point of No Return 15.00
132 Killer Instinct 15.00
133 Portraits of Death 15.00
134 NR,Inheritance of Blood 15.00
135 BWr,The Vegitable Garden . . . 15.00
136 BWr,NR,Last Voyage of
   Lady Luck 15.00
137 BWr,The Harder They Fall . . . 15.00
138 Where Dreams are Born. 20.00
139 SD,NR,A Real Crazy Kid 20.00
140 NR,O:Patchwork Man. 25.00
141 You Can't Beat the Devil. 10.00
142 Playmate. 10.00
143 The Evil Side. 10.00
144 The Vampire of Broadway . . . 10.00
145 Operation was Successful,But 10.00
146 GM,Snake's Alive 10.00
147 AN,GM,See-Through Thief . . . 10.00
148 GM,SD,Sorcerer's Apprentice. 10.00
149 MK,The Evil One. 10.00

150 JSN(c),A:Phantom Stranger
   and Dr.13. . . . . 10.00
151 MGo,MK,Nightmare 10.00
152 Sister Witch. 10.00
153 VM,AN,Don't Look Now 10.00
154 TS,MK,JL,Last issue. 10.00

HOUSE OF SECRETS
DC/Vertigo, Aug., 1996
1 SSe(s),TKr, judgments on your
   darkest secrets 4.00
2 SSe(s),TKr, F:Rain. 3.00
3 SSe(s),TKr,Seattle's citizens
   secrets. 3.00
4 SSe(s),TKr,Eric's secrets
   exposed. 3.00
5 . . . . 3.00
6 SSe(s),DFg,Other rooms:
   Meeting 3.00
7 SSe(s),TKr,Blueprint:
   Elevation A 3.00
8 SSe(s),TKr,Road to You,pt.1 . . . 3.00
9 SSe(s),TKr,Road to You,pt.2 . . . 3.00
10 SSe(s),TKr,Road to You,pt.3 . . . 3.00
11 The Book of Law, pt.1 (of 5) . . . 3.00
12 The Book of Law, pt.2. . . . . 3.00
13 SSe,The Book of Law, pt.3 . . . . 3.00
14 SSe,The Book of Law, pt.4 . . . . 3.00
15 SSe,The Book of Law, pt.5 . . . . 3.00
16 SSe,Book of Law, epilogue. . . . 3.00
17 SSe,The Road to You, pt.1 . . . . 3.00
18 SSe,The Road to You, pt.2 . . . . 3.00
19 SSe,The Road to You, pt.3 . . . . 3.00
20 SSe,Other Rooms story 3.00
21 SSe,Basement, pt.1 . . . . 3.00
22 SSe,Basement, pt.2 . . . . 3.00
23 SSe,Basement, pt.3 . . . . 3.00
24 SSe,TKr,Attic. 3.00
25 SSe,TKr, final issue 3.00
TPB Foundation, rep.#1–#5. . . . . 15.00

HOUSE OF SECRETS:
FACADE
DC/Vertigo, March, 2001
1 (of 2) TKr, 48-page 6.00
2 TKr,48-page 6.00

HUMAN DEFENSE CORPS
May 2003
1 (of 6) TTn. 2.50
2 TTn,Parasitic aliens 2.50
3 TTn,What dreams may come . . . 2.50
4 TTn,Seance 2.50
5 TTn,War is Hell 2.50
6 TTn,concl. 2.50

HUMAN TARGET
SPECIAL
1991
1 DG(i),Prequel to T.V. Series. 3.00

HUMAN TARGET
DC/Vertigo, 1999
1 (of 4) PrM(s) 3.50
2 PrM(s) 3.00
3 PrM(s) 3.00
4 PrM(s), concl. 3.00
TPB 13.00

HUMAN TARGET
DC/Vertigo Aug. 2003
1 PrM(s),40-pg. 3.00
2 PrM(s),Unshredded Man,pt.1 . . . 3.00
3 PrM(s),Unshredded Man,pt.2 . . . 3.00
4 PrM(s),Ball Game, pt.1 . . . . 3.00
5 PrM(s),Ball Game, pt.2 . . . . 3.00

6 PrM(s) 3.00
7 Wind Blows,pt.1. . . . . 3.00
8 Wind Blows,pt.2. . . . . 3.00
9 Wind Blows,pt.3. . . . . 3.00
10 Sex and violence 3.00
11 PrM(s),F:Mary 3.00
12 PrM(s),Crossing the Border 3.00
13 PrM(s),Crossing the Border 3.00
14 PrM(s),Second Coming,pt.1 . . . . 3.00
15 The Second Coming,pt.2 . . . . . . 3.00
TPB Human Target: Final Cut 20.00
TPB Strike Zones. 10.00

HUNTER:
THE AGE OF MAGIC
DC/Vertigo, July, 2001
1 R:The Hunter. 3.50
2 F:Kalesh. 3.00
3 The Worlds of The White School. 3.00
4 The Sardonyx Warriors 3.00
5 The Red Man's Devastation 3.00
6 Whose funeral is it. 3.00
7 Welcome Home Timothy Hunter . 3.00
8 The Evil Gene,pt.1. . . . . 3.00
9 The Evil Gene,pt.2. . . . . 3.00
10 The Evil Gene,pt.3 . . . . 3.00
11 The Evil Gene,pt.4 . . . . 3.00
12 F:Tim. 3.00
13 A Declaration of War. 3.00
14 War begins 3.00
15 Tim vs. Arawn Kruder. 3.00
16 Tim vs. Arawn Kruder 3.00
17 Ash Walker 3.00
18 Mr. Lily 3.00
19 Sefer Raziel 3.00
20 Janosh-el 3.00
21 art and magic 3.00
22 art and magic 3.00
23 Art of Magic. 3.00
24 Stone of Albion 3.00
25 final issue 3.00

HUNTER'S HEART
1995
1 Cops vs. Serial Killer 4.95
2 thru 3 . . . . @4.95

HUNTRESS, THE
1989–90
1 JSon/DG 2.50
2 JSon,Search for Family's
   Murderer 2.50

Huntress #6 © DC Comics, Inc.

3 JSon,A:La Bruja. 2.50
4 JSon,Little Italy/Chinatown
  Gangs 2.50
5 JSon,V:Doctor Mandragora 2.50
6 JSon,Huntress'secrets revealed . 2.50
7 JSon,V:Serial Killer 2.50
8 JSon,V:Serial Killer 2.50
9 JSon,V:Serial Killer 2.50
10 JSon,Nuclear Terrorists in NY. . . 2.50
11 JSon,V:Wyvern,Nuclear
  Terrorists contd.. . . . . 2.50
12 JSon,V:Nuclear Terrorists cont . . 2.50
13 JSon,Violence in NY 2.50
14 JSon,Violence contd.,New
  Mob boss. 2.50
15 JSon,I:Waterfront Warrior 2.50
16 JSon,Secret of Waterfront
  Warrior revealed 2.50
17 JSon,Batman+Huntress#1 . . . . . 2.50
18 JSon,Batman+Huntress#2 . . . . . 2.50
19 JSon,Batman+Huntress#3,final
  issue 2.50

HUNTRESS
[Limited Series], 1994
1 CDi(s),MN,V:Redzone 2.25
2 MN,V:Redzone. 2.25
3 MN,V:Redzone. 2.25
4 MN,V:Spano,Redzone 2.25

iCANDY
Sept. 2003
1 DAn&ALa(s). 2.50
2 DAn&ALa(s) thru 6. . . . . @2.50

ICON
DC/Milestone, 1993–96
1 Direct Market Ed.,MBr,MG,I:Icon,
  Rocket,S.H.R.E.D.,w/poster,
  card,C puzzle piece. 3.50
1a Newsstand Ed.. . . . . 2.00
2 MBr,MG,I:Payback 2.50
3 MBr,MG,V:Payback 2.50
4 MBr,MG,Teen Pregnancy Issue . . 2.50
5 MBr,MG,V:Blood Syndicate 2.50
6 MBr,MG,V:Blood Syndicate 2.50
7 MBr,MG 2.50
8 MBr,MG,O:Icon 2.50
9 WS(c),MBr,MG,Shadow War,
  I:Donner,Blitzen 2.50
10 MBr,MG,V:Holocaust. 2.50
11 MBr,Hero Worship. 2.50

Icon #4 © DC Comics, Inc.

12 Sanctimony 2.50
13 MBr,Rocket & Static T.U.. . . . . . . 2.50
14 JBy(c) 2.50
15 Worlds Collide,pt.4,A:Superboy . 2.50
16 Worlds Collide,pt.11,
  V:Superman,Rift 2.50
17 Mothership Connection. 2.50
18 Mothership Connection,pt.2 . . . . 2.50
19 Mothership Connection,pt.3 . . . . 2.50
20 Rocket. 2.50
21 . . . . 2.50
22 . . . . 2.50
23 New Rocket 2.50
24 F:Buck Wild. 2.50
25 V:Oblivion 3.00
26 V:Oblivion 2.50
27 Move to Paris Island projects . . . 2.50
28 Long Hot Summer. 2.50
29 Long Hot Summer. 2.50
30 Icon Leaves Earth. 2.50
31 HC(c) Readers Choice comic . . . 2.50
32 Rocket, Galactic Corporate. 2.50
33 V:Rocket 2.50
34 V:Cooperative 2.50
35 . . . . 2.50
36 Rocket returns to Earth. 2.50
37 MBr,RT,F:Rocket. 2.50
38 DMD(s),RT 2.50
39 DMD(s),RT,V:Holocaust & Blood
  Syndicate 2.50
40 DMD(s),RT, V:Holocaust. 2.50
41 DMD(s),RT, V:Blood Syndicate. . 2.50
42 DMD(s),RT 2.50
43 DMD(s),RT,Blood Reign, concl. . 2.50
44 DMD(s),RT,V:Smurphs 2.50
45 DMD(s),RT, final issue 2.50
TPB A Hero's Welcome 12.95

IDENTITY CRISIS
June 2004
1 (of 7) RgM,MIB,48-pg. 7.50
2 thru 5 RgM,MIB,40-pg. . . . . . . @5.00

IMMORTAL DR. FATE
1995
1 WS,KG,rep. 2.25
2 and 3 KG,rep. . . . . @2.25

IMPACT WINTER
SPECIAL
Impact, 1991
1 CI/MR/TL,A:All Impact Heros,
  President Kidnapped. 2.50

IMPULSE
1995–2002
1 Young Flash Adventures 6.00
2 V:Terrorists. 3.50
3 In School 3.00
4 V:White Lightning. 3.00
5 V:White Lightning. 3.00
6 . . . . 3.00
7 V:Gridlock 3.00
8 MWa,Underworld
  Unleashed tie-in 3.00
9 MWa,F:XS,. 3.00
10 MWa,Dead Heat,pt.3 . . . . 3.00
11 MWa,Dead Heat,pt.5. . . . . 3.00
12 . . . . 3.00
13 MWa,new daredevil in town 2.50
14 AWi,A:White Lightning 2.50
15 . . . . 2.50
16 . . . . 2.50
17 . . . . 2.50
18 MPk(s),AWi,Virtual reality
  nightmare. 2.50
19 MWa(s),HuR, Bart's dreams. . . . 2.50
20 MWa(s),HuR, baseball 2.50

Impulse #36 © DC Comics Inc.

21 MWa(s),F:Legion of Super-
  Heroes. 2.50
22 MWa(s) 2.50
23 MWa(s),HuR,Mercury at a
  crossroads. 2.50
24 MWa(s),HuR,Impulse's mother
  comes from the future 2.50
25 MWa(s),HuR,Impulse & his mom
  in 30th century. 2.50
26 MWa(s),Bart Allen back in the
  20th century. 2.50
27 MWa(s) 2.50
28 . . . . 2.50
29 BML,Bart searches for Max
  Mercury 2.50
30 BML, pt.2, Genesis tie-in 2.50
31 BML, pt.3,V:Dr. Morlo 2.50
32 BML,Max is home. 2.50
33 BML,White Lightning. 2.50
34 BML,Devonian Age, pt.1 . . . . . . 2.50
35 BML. 2.50
36 BML,Court Dates 2.50
37 BML,Dr. Morlo. 2.50
38 BML,freak snow storm 2.50
39 BML,V:Trickster. 2.50
40 BML,WF, kid picnic 2.50
41 Return of Arrowette. 2.50
42 BML(s),virtual monsters 2.50
43 BML(s),F:Jamal. 2.50
44 BML(s),V:Evil Eye 2.50
45 BML(s),Christmas. 2.50
46 BML(s),Chain Lightning x-over . . 2.50
47 BML(s),A:Superman 2.50
48 BML(s),A:Riddler. 2.50
49 BML(s),C:Flash 2.50
50 TDz(s),A:Batman, Joker 2.50
51 TDz(s),V:Frog Prince 2.50
52 TDz(s),WS,F:Kalibak,pt.1 . . . . . . 2.50
53 TDz(s),WS,F:Kalibak,pt.2 . . . . . . 2.50
54 TDz(s),Day of Judgment x-over . 2.50
55 V:Sir Real 2.50
56 . . . . 2.50
57 TDz(s),F:Plastic Man 2.50
58 TDz(s),F:Max Mercury 2.50
59 TDz(s),F:Arrowette 2.50
60 DMD(s),V:Alabama 2.50
61 F:Max Mercury,S.T.R.I.P.E. 2.50
62 TDz(s),Mercury Falling,pt.1 . . . . 2.50
63 TDz(s),Mercury Falling,pt.2 . . . . 2.50
64 TDz(s),Mercury Falling,pt.3 . . . . 2.50
65 TDz(s),Mercury Falling,pt.4 . . . . 2.50
66 TDz(s),Mercury Falling,pt.5 . . . . 2.50
67 TDz,RyR,Mercury Falling
  epilogue. 2.50

68 TDz,F:Green Lantern,pt.1 . . . . . . 2.50
69 TDz,F:Green Lantern,pt.2 . . . . . . 2.50
70 TDz, ... 2.50
71 TDz,V:Lucius Keller 2.50
72 TDz,Carol kidnapped 2.50
73 TDz,The Dark Tomorrow 2.50
74 TDz,The Dark Tomorrow,pt.2 . . . . 2.50
75 TDz,The Dark Tomorrow,pt.2 . . . . 2.50
76 TDz,V:White Lightning 2.50
77 TDz,Our Worlds at War tie-in 2.50
78 ImpulseNoMore,F:YoungJustice . 2.50
79 TDz,Joker:Last Laugh 2.50
80 TDz,V:White Lightning 2.50
81 TDz,V:Captain Saturn 2.50
82 TDz,Double Visions 2.50
83 TDz,fearsome monsters 2.50
84 TDz,F:Jay Garrick 2.50
85 World WithoutYoungJustice,pt.2 . 2.50
86 TDz,Bedlam's Abilities 2.50
87 TDz,The power of Impulse 2.50
88 TDz,TA,rescue Carol 2.50
89 TDz,TA,final issue 2.50
Ann.#2 Pulp Heroes (Western) 3.95
Spec.#1,000,000 BML(s) 2.25
GN Bart Saves the Universe 6.00
TPB Reckless Youth MWa(s) rep.
    Flash #92–#94. . . . . 15.00
Spec. Impulse/Atom Double-Shot
    DJu, x-over concl. (1997) 3.00
Spec. Impulse Plus 48pg.
    with Grossout (1997) 3.00

INDUSTRIAL GOTHIC
DC/Vertigo, 1995

1 Jail Break Plans 2.50
2 thru 5 Jail Break Plans . . . . . . @2.50

INFERIOR FIVE
March-April, 1967

1 MSy 75.00
2 MSy,A:Plastic Man 45.00
3 . . . . 40.00
4 . . . . 40.00
5 . . . . 40.00
6 . . . . 25.00
7 . . . . 25.00
8 . . . . 25.00
9 . . . . 25.00
10 A:Superman 35.00
11 JO(c&a) 25.00
12 JO(c&a) 25.00

INFERNO
Aug., 1997

1 (of 4) SI, from Legion 4.00
2 SI,mall grrls 3.00
3 SI,Legion Month tie-in 3.00
4 SI, concl. 3.00

INFINITY, INC.
March, 1984

1 JOy,O:Infinity Inc. 5.00
2 JOy,End of Origin 4.00
3 JOy,O:Jade 3.00
4 JOy,V:JSA 3.00
5 JOy,V:JSA 3.00
6 JOy,V:JSA 3.00
7 JOy,V:JSA 3.00
8 JOy,V:Ultra Humanite 3.00
9 JOy,V:Ultra Humanite 3.00
10 JOy,V:Ultra Humanite 3.00
11 DN,GT,O:Infinity Inc. 3.00
12 Infinity Unmasks,I:Yolanda
    Montez (New Wildcat) 3.00
13 DN,V:Rose & Thorn 3.00
14 1st TM DC art,V:Chroma 10.00
15 TM,V:Chroma 4.00
16 TM,I:Helix (Mr. Bones) 4.00

Infinity Inc. #47 © DC Comics, Inc.

17 TM,V:Helix 4.00
18 TM,Crisis 4.00
19 TM,JSA,JLA x-over,
    I:Mekanique 4.00
20 TM,Crisis 4.00
21 TM,Crisis,I:HourmanII,
    Dr.Midnight 4.00
22 TM,Crisis 4.00
23 TM,Crisis 4.00
24 TM,Crisis 4.00
25 TM,Crisis,JSA 4.00
26 TM,V:Carcharo 4.00
27 TM,V:Carcharo 4.00
28 TM,V:Carcharo 4.00
29 TM,V:Helix 4.00
30 TM,Mourning of JSA 4.00
31 TM,V:Psycho Pirate 4.00
32 TM,V:Psycho Pirate 4.00
33 TM,O:Obsidian 4.00
34 TM,A: Global Guardians 4.00
35 TM,V:Infinitors 4.00
36 TM,V:Injustice Unl. 4.00
37 TM,TD,O:Northwind 4.00
38 Helix on Trial 3.00
39 O:Solomon Grundy 3.00
40 V:Thunderbolt 3.00
41 Jonni Thunder 3.00
42 TD,V:Hastor,L:Fury 3.00
43 TD,V:Hastor,Silver Scarab 3.00
44 TD,D:Silver Scarab 3.00
45 MGu,A:New Teen Titans,
    V:Ultra-Humanite 3.00
46 TD,Millennium,V:Floronic Man . 3.00
47 TD,Millennium,V:Harlequin 3.00
48 TD,O:Nuklon 3.00
49 Silver Scarab becomes
    Sandman 3.00
50 TD,V:The Wizard,O:Sandman . 3.50
51 W:Fury & Sandman,D:Skyman . 3.00
52 V:Helix 3.00
53 V:Justice Unlimited,last issue . . . 3.00
Ann.#1 TM,V:Thorn 4.00
Ann.#2 V:Degaton,x-over Young
    All-Stars Annual #1 . . . . 3.00
Spec.#1 TD,A:Outsiders,V:Psycho
    Pirate 3.00

INVASION!
1988–89

1 TM,I:Vril Dox,Dominators
    (20th century) 4.00
2 TM,KG,DG,I:L.E.G.I.O.N. 3.00
3 BS,DG,I:Blasters 3.00
Daily Planet-Invasion! 16p 2.00

INVISIBLES
DC/Vertigo, 1994–96

1 GMo(s) 7.00
2 GMo(s),Down & Out,pt.1 . . . . . . 4.00
3 GMo(s),Down & Out,pt.2 . . . . . . 4.00
4 GMo(s),Down & Out,pt.3 . . . . . . 4.00
5 Arcadia,pt.1 . . . . 4.00
6 Arcadia,pt.2 . . . . 4.00
7 Arcadia,pt.3 . . . . 4.00
8 Arcadia,pt.4 . . . . 4.00
9 SeP(c),L:Dane 3.00
10 SeP(c),CWn,Jim Crow v. 3
    Zombies 3.00
11 V:New Breed of Hunter 3.00
12 . . . . 3.00
13 GMO,Sheman,pt.1 . . . . 3.00
14 GMo,SeP,Sheman,pt.2 . . . . 3.00
15 GMo,Sheman,pt.3 . . . . 3.00
16 GMo,An offer from Sir Miles . . . 3.00
17 GMo,Entropy in the U.K.,pt.1 . . 3.00
18 GMo,Entropy in the U.K.,pt.2 . . 3.00
19 GMo,Entropy in the U.K.,pt.3 . . 3.00
20 GMo,F:RaggedRobin,Dane,Boy . 4.00
21 GMo,PuJ,F:Dane 4.00
22 GMo(s),MBu,MPn 4.00
23 GMo(s),MBu,MPn 4.00
24 GMo(s),MBu,MPn 4.00
25 GMo(s),MBu,MPn,final issue
    Aug., 1996 . . . . 5.00

[Volume 2] DC/Vertigo, 1996

1 GMo(s),PJ,Black Science,pt.1 . . 4.00
2 GMo(s),PJ,Black Science,pt.2 . . 3.00
3 GMo(s),PJ,Black Science,pt.3 . . 3.00
4 GMo(s),PJ,Black Science,pt.4 . . 3.00
5 GMo(s),PJ,In SanFrancisco,pt.1 . 3.00
6 GMo(s),PJ,In SanFrancisco,pt.2 . 3.00
7 GMo(s),PJ,BB(c),Time Machine
    Go, concl. 3.00
8 GMo(s),PJ,BB(c),Sensitive
    Criminals,pt.1 . . . . 3.00
9 GMo(s),PJ,BB(c),Criminals,pt.2 . . 3.00
10 GMo(s),PJ,Criminals,pt.3 . . . . . 3.00
11 GMo(s),PJ,BB(c),Hand of Glory
    pt.1 . . . . 3.00
12 GMo(s),PJ,BB(c),Glory,pt.2 . . 3.00
13 GMo(s),PJ,BB(c),Glory,concl. . . 3.00
14 GMo(s),BB(c),Archons aftermath 3.00
15 GMo(s),BB(c), The Philadelphia
    Experiment, pt.1 . . . . 3.00
16 GMo(s),BB(c),Experiment,pt.2 . . 3.00
17 GMo,CWn,BB,Black Science II
    pt.1 . . . . 3.00
18 GMo,CWn,BB,Science,pt.2 . . . . 3.00
19 GMo,CWn,BB,Science,pt.3 . . . . 3.00
20 GMo,CWn,BB(c),Science,pt.4 . . 2.50
21 GMo,CWn,BB(c),King Mob 2.50
22 GMo,CWn,BB(c) The Tower . . . 2.50
TPB Counting to None 20.00
TPB Say You Want a Revolution . . 20.00
TPB Bloody Hell in America 13.00
TPB Kissing Mister 19.95
TPB Apocalipstick, 208-page 19.95
TPB Entropy in the U.K. 19.95

[Volume 3] DC/Vertigo, 1999

12 GMo,Satanstorm,pt.1 . . . . 3.00
11 GMo,Satanstorm,pt.2 . . . . 3.00
10 GMo,Satanstorm,pt.3 . . . . 3.00
9 GMo,Satanstorm,pt.4 . . . . 3.00
8 GMo,Karmageddon,pt.1 . . . . 3.00
7 GMo,Karmageddon,pt.2 . . . . 3.00
6 GMo,Karmageddon,pt.3 . . . . 3.00
5 GMo 3.00
4 GMo,Invisible Kingdom,pt.1 . . . . 3.00
3 GMo,Invisible Kingdom,pt.2 . . . . . 3.00
2 GMo,Invisible Kingdom,pt.3 . . . . . 3.00
1 GMo,conclusion 3.00
GN The Mystery Play 10.00
TPB The Invisible Kingdom 20.00
TPB Kissing Mister Quimper 20.00

DC COMICS

IRONWOLF
1986
1 HC,rep. 2.25

ISIS
Oct.–Nov., 1976
1 RE/WW 20.00
2 thru 6 . . . . @10.00
7 O:Isis 12.00
8 Dec.–Jan., 1977–78. . . . . 10.00

IT'S GAMETIME
Sept.–Oct., 1955
1 . . . . 1,000.00
2 Dodo and the Frog. 700.00
3 . . . . 700.00
4 March-April, 1956 . . . . 700.00

JACKIE GLEASON AND THE HONEYMOONERS
June-July, 1956
1 Based on TV show 1,300.00
2 . . . . 700.00
3 . . . . 500.00
4 . . . . 500.00
5 . . . . 500.00
6 . . . . 500.00
7 . . . . 500.00
8 . . . . 500.00
9 . . . . 500.00
10 . . . . 500.00
11 . . . . 500.00
12 April-May, 1958. . . . . 850.00

JACK KIRBY'S FOURTH WORLD
Jan., 1997
1 JBy,Worlds of New Genesis &
   Apokolips become one 2.25
2 JBy,F:Big Barda vs. Thor 2.25
3 JBy,at Wall of the Source 2.25
4 JBy,Can Highfather save his son 2.25
5 JBy,conflict between the gods . . . 2.25
6 JBy,Cause of Orion's
   transformation 2.25
7 JBy,Orion taught lesson. 2.25
8 JBy,WS,Genesis tie-in 2.25
9 JBy,WS(c),Genesis aftermath . . . 2.25
10 JBy,WS, ... 2.25
11 JBy,WS,F:Orion. 2.25
12 JBy, WS, F:Mister Miracle. 2.25
13 JBy,WS 2.25
14 JBy,WS,Promethean Giant 2.25
15 JBy,WS,Armaghetto 2.25
16 JBy,WS,Kalibak vs. Darkseid . . . 2.25
17 JBy,WS,Darkseid 2.25
18 JBy,WS,Darkseid freed. 2.25
19 JBy,WS,two stories 2.25
20 JBy,WS,A:Superman,final issue . 2.25
TPB JK. 13.00

JAGUAR
Impact, 1991
1 I&O:Jaguar I: Timon De Guzman,
   Maxx 13,Prof.Ruiz, Luiza
   Timmerman 2.25
2 Development of Powers 2.25
3 A:Maxx-13 . . . . 2.25
4 A:Black Hood. 2.25
5 V:Void,The Living Black Hole . . . 2.25
6 The Doomster,A:Maxx-13 . . . . . 2.25
7 Jaguar Secret Discovered,
   V:Void 2.25
8 V:Aryan League 2.25
9 I:Moonlighter(w/trading cards) . . . 2.25
10 V:Invisible Terror 2.25

Jaguar #6
© DC Comics, Inc.

11 Defending Comedienne 2.25
12 V:The Bodyguard 2.25
13 V:Purge 2.25
14 'Frightmare in Rio',last iss. 2.25
Ann.#1 Earthquest,w/trading card . . 2.50

JEMM, SON OF SATURN
Sept., 1984
1 GC/KJ mini-series 2.50
2 GC 2.50
3 GC,Origin. 2.50
4 A:Superman 2.50
5 Kin 2.50
6 thru 12 GC, Aug., 1985 . . . . . @2.50

JIMMY OLSEN: ADVENTURES
July 2003
TPB JK. 20.00
TPB Vol. 2 JK. 20.00

JIMMY WAKELY
Sept.–Oct., 1949
1 Ph(c),ATh,The Cowboy
   Swordsman. 1,500.00
2 Ph(c),ATh,The Prize Pony 600.00
3 Ph(c),ATh,The Return of
   Tulsa Tom 600.00
4 Ph(c),ATh,FF,HK,Where There's
   Smoke There's Gunfire 625.00
5 ATh,The Return of the
   Conquistadores 475.00
6 ATh,Two Lives of
   Jimmy Wakely 475.00
7 The Secret of Hairpin Canyon . 475.00
8 ATh,The Lost City of
   Blue Valley 475.00
9 ATh,The Return of the
   Western Firebrands. 350.00
10 ATh,Secret of Lantikin'sLight . 350.00
11 ATh,Trail o/a Thousand Hoofs. 350.00
12 ATh,JKU,The King of Sierra
   Valley 350.00
13 ATh,The Raiders of Treasure
   Mountain 350.00
14 ATh(c),JKu,The Badmen
   of Roaring Flame Valley 350.00
15 GK(c),Tommyguns on the
   Range 350.00

16 GK(c),The Bad Luck Boots. . . 300.00
17 GK(c),Terror atThunderBasin . 300.00
18 July-Aug., 1952. . . . . 350.00

JLA
Nov., 1996
1 GMo(s),HPo,JhD,V:Hyperclan . . 16.00
2 . . . . 12.00
3 GMo(s),HPo,JhD,War of the
   Worlds 10.00
4 GMo(s),HPo,JhD,battle of the
   super-heroes, conc. 10.00
5 GMo(s),HPo,JhD Woman of
   Tomorrow 7.00
6 GMo(s),HPo,JhD,Fire in theSky . 6.00
7 GMo(s),HPo,JhD,Heaven on
   Earth 6.00
8 GMo(s),HPo,JhD,Imaginary
   Stories, F:Green Arrow 6.00
9 GMo(s),V:The Key 6.00
10 GMo(s),HPo,JhD,R:Injustice
   Gang, pt.1 (of 6) 6.00
11 GMo(s),HPo,JhD,Rock of Ages,
   pt.2. 6.00
12 GMo(s),HPo,JhD,Rock of Ages,
   pt.3, A:Hourman 6.00
13 GMo(s),HPo,JhD,Rock of Ages,
   pt.4. 6.00
14 GMo(s),HPo,JhD,Rock of Ages,
   pt.5. 6.00
15 GMo(s),HPo,JhD,Rock of Ages
   pt.6, concl, 48 pg. 6.00
16 GMo(s),HPo,JhD, new member . 6.00
17 GMo(s),HPo,JhD,V:Prometheus. 6.00
18 MWa,Engine of Chance, pt.1 . . . 6.00
19 MWa,Engine of Chance, pt.2 . . . 6.00
20 MWa,F:Adam Strange,pt.1 . . . . 6.00
21 MWa,F:Adam Strange,pt.2 . . . . 6.00
22 GMo(s),The Star Conquerer . . . 2.50
23 GMo,V:Star Conquerer,
   A:Sandman 2.50
24 GMo,HPo,Ultra-Marines,pt.1 . . . 2.50
25 GMo,HPo,Ultra-Marines,pt.2 . . . 2.50
26 GMo,HPo,Ultra-Marines,pt.3. . . 2.50
27 GMo,HPo,CrisisTimesFive,pt.1 . 2.50
28 GMo,HPo,CrisisTimesFive,pt.2 . 2.50
29 GMo,HPo,CrisisTimesFive,pt.3 . 2.50
30 GMo,HPo,CrisisTimesFive,pt.4 . 2.50
31 GMo,HPo,CrisisTimes
   Five,concl. 2.50
32 MWa(s),No Man's Land 2.50
33 MWa(s),No Man's Land 2.50
34 GMo,Super-villains riot 2.50
35 JMD(s),F:New Spectre 2.50
36 GMo,HPo,World War 3,pt.1 . . . . 2.50
37 GMo,HPo,World War 3,pt.2 . . . . 2.50
38 GMo,HPo,World War 3,pt.3 . . . . 2.50
39 GMo,HPo,World War 3,pt.4 . . . . 2.50
40 GMo,HPo,World War 3,pt.5 . . . . 2.50
41 GMo,HPo,World War 3,
   concl.48-pg. 3.00
42 Miniscule civilization 2.50
43 MWa(s),HPo,V:Ra's al Ghul 2.25
44 HPo,Tower of Babel,pt.2 . . . . . . 2.25
45 HPo,Tower of Babel,pt.3. . . . . . 2.25
46 HPo,Tower of Babel,concl. 2.25
47 MWa,BHi,PNe,Queen ofFables . 2.25
48 MWa,BHi,PNe,Queen ofFables . 2.25
49 MWa,BHi,PNe,Queen ofFables . 2.25
50 MWa,BHi,PNe,48-page. 5.00
51 MWa,MsM,Man and Superman . 2.25
52 MWa,BHi,PNe. 2.25
53 MWa,BHi,PNe. 2.25
54 MWa,BHi,PNe,Man & Superman 2.25
55 MWa,Terror Incognita,pt.1 . . . . . 2.25
56 MWa,Terror Incongita,pt.2 . . . . . 2.25
57 MWa,Terror Incongita,pt.3. . . . . 2.25
58 MWa,Terror Incongita,pt.4 . . . . . 2.25
59 CDi,DBk,Joker:Last Laugh 2.25
60 MWa,F:Santa Claus 2.25

61 DoM,TG,+16-pg.PowerCompany 2.25
62 DoM,Golden Perfect,pt.1 . . . . . . 2.25
63 DoM,Golden Perfect,pt.2 . . . . . . 2.25
64 DoM,Golden Perfect,pt.3 . . . . . . 2.25
65 DoM,Batman & Plastic Man 2.25
66 DoM,warrior priests. 2.25
67 DoM,human sacrifice 2.25
68 DoM,Obsidian Age prologue. . . . 2.25
69 Hunt for Aquaman,pt.1 . . . . 2.25
70 DoM,Hunt for Aquaman,pt.2 . . . . 2.25
71 DoM,Hunt for Aquaman,pt.3 . . . . 2.25
72 DoM,Hunt for Aquaman,pt.4 . . . . 2.25
73 DoM,Hunt for Aquaman,pt.5 . . . . 2.25
74 DoM,Hunt for Aquaman,pt.6 . . . . 2.25
75 DoM,Hunt for Aquaman,64-pg. . . 5.00
76 DoM,after Obsidian Age 2.25
77 RV(s),memories stolen 2.25
78 DoM, ... 2.25
79 DoM,F:Faith 2.25
80 White Rage,pt.1 . . . . 2.25
81 White Rage,pt.2 . . . . 2.25
82 White Rage,pt.3 . . . . 2.25
83 Qurac 2.25
84 Trial by Fire,pt.1 . . . . 2.25
85 Trial by Fire,pt.2 . . . . 2.25
86 Trial by Fire,pt.3 . . . . 2.25
87 Trial by Fire,pt.4 . . . . 2.25
88 Trial by Fire,pt.5 . . . . 2.25
89 Trial by Fire,pt.6 . . . . 2.25
90 F:Batman,Wonder Woman 2.25
91 DON(s),Extinction,pt.1 . . . . 2.25
92 DON(s),Extinction,pt.2 . . . . 2.25
93 DON(s),Extinction,pt.3 . . . . 2.25
94 JBy,JOy,10th Circle,pt.1 . . . . 2.25
95 JBy,JOy,10th Circle,pt.2 . . . . 2.25
96 JBy,JOy,10th Circle,pt.3 . . . . 2.25
97 JBy,JOy,10th Circle,pt.4 . . . . 2.25
98 JBy,JOy,10th Circle,pt.5 . . . . 2.25
99 JBy,JOy,10th Circle,pt.6 . . . . 2.25
100 R:The Elite,48-pg. 3.50
101 RG,Pain of the Gods,pt.1 . . . . . 2.25
102 RG,Pain of the Gods,pt.2 . . . . . 2.25
103 RG,Pain of the Gods,pt.3 . . . . . 2.25
104 RG,Pain of the Gods,pt.4 . . . . . 2.25
105 RG,Pain of the Gods,pt.5 . . . . . 2.25
106 RG,Pain of the Gods,pt.6 . . . . . 2.25
107 KBk(s),RG,DGr,space egg 2.25
Ann.#1 Pulp Heroes (Hard Boiled) . 4.50
Ann.#2 TTn,BWr,Ghosts 3.50
Ann.#3 JLApe Gorilla Warfare 3.50
Ann.#4 Planet DC 4.00
Spec.#1,000,000 GMo(s),HPo,
   V:Justice Legion A. 2.50
SuperSpec.#1 Justice League
   of America 6.00
Spec.#1 Our Worlds at War,48-pg. . 3.00
Giant #1, 7 new stories, 80-pg. 5.00
Giant #2, 80-page. 5.00
Giant #3, 80-page 6.00
SC Secret Origins, oversize. 8.00
JLA: Tomorrow Woman, 1-shot
   TPe,Girlfrenzy (1998) 2.00
GN New World Order GMo(s),HPo,
   JhD, rep. #1–#4. . . . . 6.00
GN American Dreams rep.#5–#9. . . 8.00
GN Secret Files 4.00
GN Secret Files deluxe 5.00
GN Secret Files #2 . . . . 4.00
GN Secret Files #3 How Talia stole
   Batman's Secret Files 5.00
GN Foreign Bodies 6.00
GN JLA/WildC.A.T.S, GMo(s),
   VS,x-over. 6.00
GN JLA/Haven: Arrival (2001) 6.00
GN JLA: Earth 2,96-page,
   F:Crime Syndicate (2000) 15.00
GN Gods and Monsters. 7.00
GN Seven Caskets,DIB, 48-page . . 6.00
GN JLA: Superpower. 6.00
GN JLA Primeval 6.00
GN Shogun of Steel,Elseworlds . . . 7.00

GN JLA:Haven:Anathema (2002) . . 6.00
GN The Island of Dr. Moreau,GP
   Elseworlds (2002) 7.00
GN JLA: Liberty and Justice 10.00
JLA/Witchblade, x-over 6.00
TPB Heaven's Ladder 10.00

JLA Ann. #3 © DC Comics, Inc.

TPB JLA:Rock of Ages 10.00
TPB Strength in Numbers 13.00
TPB Justice League of America:
   The Nail, Elseworlds 13.00
TPB Secret Origins Featuring JLA 15.00
TPB JLA:World War III,208-page. . 13.00
TPB JLA vs. Predator x-over. 6.00
TPB Tower of Babel, 160-page . . . 13.00
TPB Divided We Fall (2002) 18.00
TPB A League of One, CsM (2002) 15.00
TPB Terra Incognita (2002) 13.00
JLA Showcase 80-pg Giant #1 . . . . 5.00
TPB The Golden Perfect 13.00
TPB Riddle of the Beast 15.00
TPB The Obsidian Age, Vol.1 . . . 13.00
TPB The Obsidian Age, Vol.2 . . . 13.00
TPB Zatanna's Search. 13.00
TPB Rules of Engagement 13.00
TPB Vol.14 Trial by Fire. 13.00
Spec. JLA: Workweek 7.00
Spec. Secret Files 2004. . . . . 5.00

JLA: ACT OF GOD
Nov., 2000
1 (of 3) Elseworlds,48-page 5.00
2 powers gone,48-page 5.00
3 concl.,48-page 5.00

JLA: AGE OF WONDER
April 2003
1 (of 2) Elseworlds 6.00
2 concl. 6.00

JLA: BLACK BAPTISM
March, 2001
1 (of 4) F:Faust. 2.50
2 F:Faust. 2.50
3 V:Daiblos 2.50
4 concl. 2.50

JLA: CREATED EQUAL
Feb., 2000
1 FaN,KM,JRu,Elseworlds 6.00
2 FaN,KM,JRu 6.00

JLA: DESTINY
June, 2002
1 (of 4) TMd,48-pg 6.00
2 JAr(s),TMd, Elseworlds 6.00
3 JAr(s),TMd,Luthor,Mongul 6.00
4 JAr(s),TMc,concl. 6.00

JLA: GATEKEEPER
Oct., 2001
1 (of 3) TT, 48-page 5.00
2 TT, 48-page 5.00
3 TT,48-page, concl. 5.00

JLA: INCARNATIONS
May, 2001
1 (of 7) JOs,VS,V:Wotan 3.50
2 JOs,VS,Batman joins. 3.50
3 JOs,VS,V:Lex Luthor, Kobra 3.50
4 JOs,VS,F:Aquaman. 3.50
5 JOs,VS,F:Aquaman. 3.50
6 JOs,VS,two tales 3.50
7 JOs,VS,concl. 3.50

JLA/JSA
Nov., 2002
1 Secret files, Team-up,
   prelude,64-pg. 5.00
TPB Virtue and Vice 18.00

JLA: PARADISE LOST
Nov., 1997
1 (of 3) MMr,AOI,F:Zauriel 2.25
2 MMr,AOI,F:Zauriel,Martian
   Manhunter 2.25

JLA: SCARY MONSTERS
Mar. 2003
1 (of 6) CCI,V:Ancient spirits. 2.50
2 CCI. 2.50
3 CCI,ancient evil 2.50
4 CCI,Kishana secret 2.50
5 CCI,Kishana's origin 2.50
6 CCI,concl. 2.50

JLA/THE SPECTRE: SOUL WAR
Jan. 2003
1 (of 2) DBk,PNe 6.00
2 DBk,PNe 6.00

JLA/TITANS
1998
1 (of 3) JLA vs. Teen Titans 3.00
2 . . . . 3.00
3 conclusion, New Titans 3.00
TPB The Technis Imperative 13.00

JLA: WORLD WITHOUT GROWN-UPS
June, 1998
1 (of 2) I:Young Justice 48pg 5.00
2 Young Justice, concl. 5.00
TPB World Without Grown-Ups. . . 10.00

JLA: YEAR ONE
Nov., 1997
1 (of 12) MWa,BAu,BKi,48pg.. . . . . 6.00
2 MWa,BAu,BKi,V:Vandal Savage . 4.00
3 MWa,BAu,BKi 4.00
4 MWa,BAu,BKi,V:Locus 4.00
5 MWa,BAu,BKi,F:Doom Patrol . . . 4.00
6 MWa,BAu,BKi,V:Doom Patrol . . . 4.00
7 MWa,BAu,BKi,V:Weapon Master 4.00

8 MWa,BAu,BKi,MIB,V:Locus 4.00
9 MWa,BAu,BKi,MIB,V:Locus 3.00
10 MWa,BAu,BKi,MIB,V:Locus 3.00
11 MWa,BAu,BKi,MIB 3.00
12 MWa,BAu,BKi,MIB, concl.. . . . . . 3.50
TPB Year One 20.00

JLA-Z
Sept. 2003
1 (of 3) handbook 2.50
2 . . . . 2.50
3 conclusion 2.50

Johnny Thunder #1 © DC Comics Inc.

JOHNNY THUNDER
Feb.–March, 1973
1 ATh. 25.00
2 GK,MD. 15.00
3 ATh,GK,MD,July-Aug., 1973 . . . 15.00

JOKER, THE
1975–76
1 IN,DG,A:TwoFace 60.00
2 IN,JL WillieTheWeeper 30.00
3 JL,A:Creeper 30.00
4 JL,A:GreenArrow 25.00
5 . . . . 25.00
6 V:Sherlock Holmes 25.00
7 IN,A:Luthor. 25.00
8 . . . . 25.00
9 A:Catwoman 30.00
The Devil's Advocate HC GN 25.00
GN 13.00

JOKER, THE: LAST LAUGH
Oct., 2001
1 (of 6) CDi,Oracle vs. villains 3.00
2 CDi,Batman,Riot in the Slab 3.00
3 CDi,F:JLA vs. Joker army 3.00
4 CDi,F:Mr. Mind, Lex Luthor 3.00
5 CDi,Harley Quinn is last hope . . . 3.00
6 CDi,Joker's final stand. 3.00
Secret Files #1 64-page. 6.00

JONAH HEX
1977–85
1 Vengeance For A Fallen
   Gladiator 150.00
2 The Lair of the Parrot 75.00
3 The Fugitive. 50.00

4 The Day of Chameleon 50.00
5 Welcome to Paradise 50.00
6 The Lawman 40.00
7 Son of the Apache 50.00
8 O:Jonah Hex 50.00
9 BWr(c) 40.00
10 GM(c),Violence at Vera Cruz . . 40.00
11 The Holdout. 30.00
12 JS(c) 30.00
13 The Railroad Blaster. 30.00
14 The Sin Killer 30.00
15 Saw Dust and Slow Death 30.00
16 The Wyandott Verdict! 25.00
17 . . . . 25.00
18 . . . . 25.00
19 The Duke of Zarkania! 25.00
20 Phantom Stage to William
   Bend 25.00
21 The Buryin'!. 25.00
22 Requiem For A Pack Rat 25.00
23 Massacre of the Celestials 25.00
24 Minister of the Lord. 25.00
25 The Widow Maker. 25.00
26 Death Race to Cholera Bend!. . 15.00
27 The Wooden Six Gun! 15.00
28 Night of the Savage 15.00
29 The Innocent. 15.00
30 O:Jonah Hex. 15.00
31 A:Arbee Stoneham 15.00
32 A:Arbee Stoneham 15.00
33 The Crusader 15.00
34 Christmas in an Outlaw Town . . 15.00
35 The Fort Charlotte Brigade 15.00
36 Return to Fort Charlotte 15.00
37 DAy,A:Stonewall Jackson 15.00
38 . . . . 15.00
39 The Vow of a Samurai! 15.00
40 DAy 15.00
41 DAy,Two for the Hangman!. . . . 15.00
42 Wanted for Murder 15.00
43 JKu(c) 15.00
44 JKu(c),DAy 15.00
45 DAy,Jonah gets married 15.00
46 JKu(c),DAy 15.00
47 DAy,Doom Rides the Sundown
   Town 15.00
48 DAy,A:El Diablo. 15.00
49 DAy 15.00
50 DAy,The Hunter 15.00
51 DAy,The Comforter. 6.00
52 DAy,Rescue! 6.00
53 DAy 6.00
54 . . . . 6.00
55 Trail of Blood. 6.00
56 DAy,The Asylum 6.00
57 B:El Diablo backup story 6.00
58 DAy,The Treasure of Catfish
   Pond 6.00
59 DAy,Night of the White Lotus . . . 6.00
60 DAy,Domain of the Warlord 6.00
61 DAy,In the Lair of
   the Manchus 6.00
62 DAy,Belly of the Malay Tiger. . . . 6.00
63 DAy 6.00
64 DAy,The Pearl! 6.00
65 DAy,The Vendetta! 6.00
66 DAy,Requiem for a Coward 6.00
67 DAy,Deadman's Hand! 6.00
68 DAy,Gunfight at Gravesboro! . . . 6.00
69 DAy,The Gauntlet!. 6.00
70 DAy 6.00
71 DAy,The Masquerades 6.00
72 DAy,Tarantula 6.00
73 DAy,Jonah in a wheel chair 6.00
74 DAy,A:Railroad Bill 6.00
75 DAy,JAp,A:Railroad Bill. 6.00
76 DAy,Jonah goes to Jail 5.00
77 DAy,Over the Wall. 5.00
78 DAy,Me Ling returns 5.00
79 DAy,Duel in the Sand 5.00
80 A:Turnbull 5.00

81 thru 89 DAy . . . . @7.00
90 thru 91 . . . . @7.00
92 . . . . 20.00

JONAH HEX AND OTHER WESTERN TALES
Sept.–Oct., 1979
1 . . . . 15.00
2 NA,ATh,SA,GK 18.00
3 Jan.–Feb., 1980. . . . . 15.00

Jonah Hex, Riders of the Worm
and Such #4 © DC Comics, Inc.

JONAH HEX: RIDERS OF THE WORM AND SUCH
[Mini-Series] DC/Vertigo, 1995
1 R:Ronah Hex. 4.00
2 At Wildes West Ranch. 4.00
3 History Lesson. 4.00
4 I:Autumn Brothers 4.00
5 V:Big worm, final issue 4.00

JONAH HEX: SHADOWS WEST
DC/Vertigo, 1998
1 (of 3) JLd(s),TTn 4.00
2 JLd(s),TTn 4.00
3 JLd(s),TTn concl. 4.00

JONAH HEX: TWO-GUN MOJO
DC/Vertigo, 1993
1 B:JLd(s),TT,SG(i),R:Jonah Hex,
   I:Slow Go Smith. 7.00
1a Platinum Ed. 17.00
2 TT,SG(i),D:Slow Go Smith,I:Doc
   Williams,Wild Bill Hickok 4.00
3 TT,SG(i),Jonah captured 4.00
4 TT,SG(i),O:Doc Williams 4.00
5 TT,SG(i),V::Doc Williams 4.00

JONNI THUNDER
Feb., 1985
1 DG,origin issue. 2.25
2 DG 2.25
3 DG 2.25

DC COMICS

JONNY DOUBLE
DC/Vertigo, July, 1998
1	3.00
2 MCo(c) detective	3.00
3	3.00
4	3.00
TPB series rep.	12.95

JSA
1999
1 JeR,V:Dark Lord	12.00
2 JeR,AD&Mfm(c),A:Hawkgirl.	6.00
3 JeR,AD&MFm(c),V:Dark Lord	5.00
4 JeR,AD&MFm(c),V:Mordru	5.00
5 JeR,AD&MFm(c),	5.00
6	4.00
7 Darkness Falls, pt.1	4.00
8 Darkness Falls, pt.2	4.00
9 Darkness Falls, pt.3	4.00
10 V:Injustice Society.	4.00
11 V:Kobra	4.00
12 V:Kobra,Whitehorse project	4.00
13 Hunt for Extant,pt.1	4.00
14 Hunt for Extant,pt.2.	4.00
15 Hunt for Extant,concl.	4.00
16 Injustice be Done, pt.1	4.00
17 Injustice be Done, pt.2	4.00
18 Injustice be Done, pt.3	4.00
19 Injustice be Done, pt.4	4.00
20 Injustice be Done, pt.5	4.00
21 Hawkman prologue.	4.00
22 Hawkman prologue.	4.00
23 Return of Hawkman,pt.1	4.00
24 Return of Hawkman,pt.2.	6.00
25 Return of Hawkman,pt.3,48-pg.	6.50
26 Return of Hawkman,pt.4.	4.00
27 F:Captain Marvel,V:Black Adam.	3.00
28 V:Roulette	3.00
29 PSj,Joker:Last Laugh,tie-in.	3.00
30 V:Roulette	3.00
31 RgM(c),MakingWaves,A:Batman	3.00
32 RgM(c),Stealing Thunder,prev.	3.00
33 RgM(c),Stealing Thunder,pt.1	3.00
34 RgM(c),Stealing Thunder,pt.2	3.00
35 RgM(c),Stealing Thunder,pt.3	3.00
36 RgM(c),Stealing Thunder,pt.4	3.00
37 RgM(c),Thunder,pt.5,40-pg.	4.00
38 RgM(c),F:Rick Tyler	3.00
39 RgM(c),F:Power Girl	3.00
40 RgM(c),Shadower's grandson	3.00
41 RgM(c),V:Black Barax.	3.00
42 V:Black Barax	3.00
43 F:JSA B.C.	3.00
44 F:Vandal Savage	3.00
45 F:Doctor Fate	3.00
46 Princes of Darkness,pt.1.	3.00
47 Princes of Darkness,pt.2.	3.00
48 Princes of Darkness,pt.3.	3.00
49 Princes of Darkness,pt.4.	3.00
50 Princes of Darkness,concl.	4.50
51 Dr. Fate.	3.00
52 F:Black Adam	3.00
53 V:Crimson Avenger.	3.00
54 F:Superman,Batman.	3.00
55 F:Original members	2.50
56 Black Reign,pt.1,x-over.	2.50
57 Black Reign,pt.3,x-over.	2.50
58 Black Reign,pt.5,x-over.	2.50
59 SeP,F:Degaton	2.50
60 Redemption Lost,pt.1	2.50
61 TMd,Redemption Lost,pt.2	2.50
62 TMc,Redemption Lost,pt.3	2.50
63 JOy,Wake of Sandman,pt.1	2.50
64 JOy,Wake of Sandman,pt.2	2.50
65 Out of Time,pt.1	2.50
66 Out of Time,pt.2	2.50
Ann.#1 Planet DC	4.50
Spec.#1 Our Worlds at War,48-pg.	3.50
Secret Files #1.	5.00
Secret Files #2, 64-page	5.00

TPB Darkness Falls, 232-page	20.00
TPB Justice be Done.	15.00
TPB The Return of Hawkman	20.00
TPB Fair Play.	15.00
TPB Stealing Thunder	15.00
TPB Savage Times	15.00
TPB The Liberty Files	20.00

JSA: ALL-STARS
May 2003
1 (of 8) SaV,past and present.	2.50
2 JLb,TSe,F:Hawkgirl	2.50
3 Salem Mass.	2.50
4 F:Stargirl	2.50
5 F:Hourman	2.50
6 F:Dr. Mid-Nite.	2.50
7 40 pg.,BU: Mr. Terrific	3.50
8 F:Spectre	2.50
TPB	15.00

JSA: THE LIBERTY FILES
Dec., 1999
1 (of 2) Elseworlds	7.00
2 TyH, concl.	7.00

JSA: STRANGE ADVENTURES #3
Aug. 2004
1 (of 6) BKi,GEr,V:Dynamo.	3.50
2 thru 3 BKi,GEr	@3.50

JSA: THE UNHOLY THREE
Feb. 2003
1 (of 2) Elseworlds	7.00
2 concl.	7.00

JUDGE DREDD
1994–96
1 R:Judge Dredd.	3.00
2 Silicon Dreams.	2.50
3 Terrorists	2.75
4 Mega-City One crisis	2.50
5 Solitary Dredd	2.50
6 V:Richard Magg.	2.50
7	2.50
8 V:Ministry of Fear.	2.50
9 V:Mister Synn	2.50
10 D:Judge Dredd	2.50
11 Mega-City One Chaos	2.50
12 V:Wally Squad	2.50
13 Block Wars,pt.1.	2.50
14 Block Wars,pt.2.	2.50
15 Block Wars,pt.3.	2.50
16 R:Judge with a Grudge.	2.50
17 F:Judge Cadet Lewis, Nova Scotia.	2.50
18 final issue	2.50
Movie Adaptation	5.95

JUDGE DREDD: LEGENDS OF THE LAW
1994–95
1 Organ Donor,pt.1	3.00
2 Organ Donor,pt.2.	2.50
3 Organ Donor,pt.3	2.50
4 Organ Donor,pt.4.	2.50
5 Trial By Gunfire,pt.1.	2.50
6 Trial By Gunfire,pt.2.	2.50
7 JHi(c),Trial By Gunfire,pt.3	2.50
8 JBy(s),Fall From Grace,pt.1	2.50
9 Fall From Grace,pt.2	2.50
10 Fall From Grace,pt.3.	2.50
11 Dredd of Night,pt.1	2.50
12 Dredd of Night,pt.2.	2.50
13 Dredd of Night,pt.3,final issue	2.50

JUNK CULTURE
DC/Vertigo, May, 1997
1 (of 2) TMK	2.50
2 (of 2) TMK, Deuces Wild	2.50

JUST IMAGINE...
July 2001
TPB DC Universe, by StL,Vol.2	20.00
TPB DC Universe, by StL,Vol.3	20.00

Justice #1 © DC Comics, Inc.

JUSTICE, INC.
May-June, 1975
1 AMc,JKu(c),O:Avenger	20.00
2 JK.	15.00
3 JK.	15.00
4 JK,JKu(c),Nov.–Dec., 1975.	15.00

[Mini-Series], 1989
1 PerfectBound `Trust & Betrayal'	4.00
2 PerfectBound.	4.00

JUSTICE LEAGUE ADVENTURES
Nov., 2001
1 TTn,based on Cartoon show	2.50
2 magical cult	2.25
3 travelers from Daxam	2.25
4 World War of the Sexes.	2.25
5 Starro Wars	2.25
6 Super-Heroes for sale	2.25
7 JSon,RBr,Fastest Fax Alive.	2.25
8 Moon used as monster incubator	2.25
9 Stepping Out	2.25
10 Superman v. Martian Manhunter	2.25
11 back from the future,F:Atom	2.25
12 F:Mr. Freeze	2.25
13 I:All-Star	2.25
14 F:Aquaman	2.25
15 V:Kanjar-Ro	2.25
16 Hide and Seek	2.25
17 renegade Amazon.	2.25
18 F:The Atom	2.25
19 F:Green Lantern	2.25
20 Psycho-Pirates	2.25
21 JOs,Dominators	2.25
22 Shayol.	2.25
23 V:Kobra	2.25
24 boy or super-villain	2.25
25 F:Adam Strange	2.25
26 concl.	2.25
27 F:Hawkgirl & Green Lantern	2.25

28 F:Legion of Super-Heroes 2.25
29 Mysterious menace........... 2.25
30 F:Flash & Kamandi........... 2.25
31 F:The Phantom Stranger 2.25
32 V:The Construct 2.25
33 New danger................. 2.25
34 Final issue.................. 2.25
TPB Justice League Adventures ... 9.95
TPB Vol. 1 Magnificent Seven..... 6.95
TPB Vol. 2 Friends and Foes...... 6.95

JUSTICE LEAGUE AMERICA
(see JUSTICE LEAGUE INTERNATIONAL)

JUSTICE LEAGUE ELITE
July 2004
1 (of 12) DoM 2.50
2 thru 4 DoM................ @2.50

JUSTICE LEAGUE EUROPE
1989–93
1 BS,A:Wonder Woman 4.00
2 BS,Search for Nazi-Killer....... 3.00
3 BS,A:Jack O'Lantern,
   Queen Bee 2.50
4 BS,V:Queen Bee 2.50
5 JRu,BS,Metamorpho's Baby,
   A:Sapphire Starr 2.50
6 BS,V:Injustice League 2.50
7 BS,Teasdale Imperative#2,
   A:JLA 2.50
8 BS,Teasdale Imperative#4,
   A:JLA 2.50
9 BS,ANi,A:Superman 2.50
10 BS,V:Crimson Fox 2.50
11 BS,C:DocMagnus&Metal Men .. 2.50
12 BS,A:Metal Men 2.50
13 BS,V:One-Eyed Cat, contd
   from JLA #37 .... 2.50
14 I:VCR 2.50
15 BS,B:Extremists Vector saga,
   V:One-Eyed Cat,A:BlueJay ... 2.50
16 BS,A:Rocket Reds, Blue Jay .. 2.50
17 BS,JLI in Another Dimension ... 2.50
18 BS,Extremists Homeworld 2.50
19 BS,E:Extremist Vector Saga.... 2.50
20 MR,I:Beefeater,V:Kilowog...... 2.50
21 MR,JRu,New JLE embassy in
   London,A:Kilowog 2.50

Justice League Europe #44
© DC Comics, Inc.

22 MR,JLE's Cat stolen 2.50
23 BS,O:Crimson Fox 2.50
24 BS,Worms in London 2.50
25 BS,V:Worms 2.50
26 BS,V:Starro 2.50
27 BS,JLE V:JLE,A:JLA,V:Starro .. 2.50
28 BS, JLE V:JLE,A:J'onn J'onzz,
   V:Starro 2.50
29 BS,Breakdowns #2,V:Global
   Guardians 2.50
30 Breakdowns#4,V:J.O'Lantern ... 2.50
31 Breakdowns #6,War of the
   Gods tie-in 2.50
32 Breakdowns #8,A:Chief(Doom
   Patrol) 2.50
33 Breakdowns #10,Lobo vs.
   Despero.................. 2.50
34 Breakdowns #12,Lobo
   vs.Despero 2.50
35 Breakdowns #14,V:Extremists,
   D:Silver Sorceress.......... 2.50
36 Breakdowns #16,All Quit 2.50
37 B:New JLE,I:Deconstructo ... 2.50
38 V:Deconstructo,A:Batman...... 2.50
39 V:Deconstructo,A:Batman...... 2.50
40 J:Hal Jordan,A:Metamorpho ... 2.50
41 A:Metamorpho,Wond.Woman... 2.50
42 A:Wonder Woman,V:Echidna ... 2.50
43 V:Amos Fortune 2.50
44 V:Amos Fortune 2.50
45 Red Winter#1,V:Rocket Reds... 2.50
46 Red Winter#2 .... 2.50
47 Red Winter#3,V:Sonar 2.50
48 Red Winter#4,V:Sonar 2.50
49 Red Winter #5,V:Sonar....... 2.50
50 Red Winter#6,Double-sized,
   V:Sonar,J:Metamorpho 3.50
Ann.#1 A:Global Guardians 2.50
Ann.#2 MR,CS,ArmageddonPt.7 ... 3.00
Ann.#3 RT(i),Eclipso tie-in 2.75
Justice League Spectacular JLE(c)
   New Direction 2.50
Becomes:

JUSTICE LEAGUE INTERNATIONAL
[2nd Series]

JUSTICE LEAGUE [INTERNATIONAL]
[1st Series], 1987
1 KM,TA,New Team,I:Max. Lord... 8.00
2 KM,AG,A:BlueJay & Silver
   Sorceress 6.00
3 KM,AG,J:Booster Gold, V:Rocket
   Lords 5.00
3a Superman Logo 60.00
4 KM,AG,V:Royal Flush 3.00
5 KM,AG,A:The Creeper........ 3.00
6 KM,AG,A:The Creeper........ 3.00
Becomes:

JUSTICE LEAGUE INTERNATIONAL
1988–89
7 KM,AG,L:Dr.Fate,Capt.Marvel,
   J:Rocket Red,Capt.Atom
   (Double size).............. 4.00
8 KM,AG,KG,Move to Paris Embassy,
   I:C.Cobert,B.U.Glob.Guardians. 3.50
9 KM,AG,KG,Millennium,Rocket
   Red-Traitor 3.50
10 KG,KM,AG,A:G.L.Corps,
   Superman,I:G'Nort.......... 3.50
11 KM,AG,V:Construct,C:Metron ... 3.50
12 KG,KM,AG,O:Max Lord....... 3.50
13 KG,AG,A:Suicide Squad 3.50
14 SL,AG,J:Fire&Ice,L:Ron,
   I:Manga Kahn 3.50
15 SL,AG,V:Magna Kahn........ 3.50

Justice League International #11
© DC Comics Inc.

16 KM,AG,I:Queen Bee 3.50
17 KM,AG,V:Queen Bee 3.50
18 KM,AG,MPn,A:Lobo,Guy Gardner
   (bonus book) 3.50
19 KM,JRu,A:Lobo vs.Guy Gardner,
   J:Hawkman & Hawkwoman... 3.50
20 KM,JRu(i),A:Lobo,G.Gardner ... 3.50
21 KM,JRu(i),A:Lobo vs.Guy
   Gardner 3.50
22 KM,JRu,Imskian Soldiers 3.50
23 KM,JRu,I:Injustice League 3.50
24 KM,JRu,DoubleSize + Bonus
   Bk#13,I:JusticeLeagueEurope.. 4.00
25 KM(c),JRu(i),Vampire story..... 2.50
Ann.#1 BWg,DG,CR............. 2.50
Ann.#2 BWg,JRu,A:Joker 3.00
Ann.#3 KM(c),JRu,JLI Embassies .. 2.50
Spec.#1 Mr.Miracle 2.00
Spec.#2,The Huntress 3.00
TPB new beginning,rep.#1-#7 .... 13.00
TPB The Secret Gospel of Maxwell
   Lord Rep. #8-#12, Ann.#1.... 13.00
Becomes:

JUSTICE LEAGUE AMERICA
1989–96
26 KM(c),JRu(i),Possessed Blue
   Beetle 3.00
27 KM(c),JRu,DG(i),'Exorcist',
   (c)tribute 2.50
28 KM(c),JRu(i), A:Black Hand 2.50
29 KM(c),JRu(i),V:Mega-Death 2.50
30 KM(c),BWg,JRu,J:Huntress,
   D:Mega-Death............. 2.50
31 ANi,AH,JRu,Teasdale Imperative
   #1,N:Fire,Ice,A:JLE 3.00
32 ANi,AH,Teasdale Imperative
   #3, A:JLE 3.00
33 ANi,AH,GuyGardner vs.Kilowog . 2.50
34 ANi,AH,'Club JLI,'A:Aquaman .. 2.50
35 ANi,JRu,AH,A:Aquaman 2.50
36 Gnort vs. Scarlet Skier 2.50
37 ANi,AH,L:Booster Gold 2.50
38 JRu,AH,R:Desparo,D:Steel..... 2.50
39 JRu,AH,V:Desparo,D:Mr.Miracle,
   Robot.................... 2.50
40 AH,Mr.Miracle Funeral 2.50
41 MMc,MaxForce 2.50
42 MMc,J:L-Ron................ 2.50
43 AH,KG,The Man Who Knew Too
   Much #1.................. 2.50

DC COMICS

44 AH,Man Knew Too Much #2 . . . . 2.50	78 MC,V:The Extremists 2.50	54 RoR,I:Creator 2.25
45 AH,MJ,JRu,Guy & Ice's 2nd	79 MC,V:The Extremists 2.50	55 RoR,A:Creator 2.25
date 2.50	80 KWe,N:Booster Gold 2.50	56 RoR,V:Terrorists 2.25
46 Glory Bound #1,I:Gen.Glory 2.50	81 KWe,A:Captain Atom 2.50	57 RoR,V:Terrorists 2.25
47 Glory Bound #2,J:Gen.Glory. . . . 2.50	82 KWe,A:Captain Atom 2.50	58 RoR,V:Aliens. 2.25
48 Glory Bound #3,V:DosUberbot . . 2.50	83 KWe,V:Guy Gardner 2.50	59 RoR,A:Guy Gardner 2.25
49 Glory Bound #4. . . . . 2.50	84 KWe,A:Ice. 2.50	60 GJ(s),RoR. 2.25
50 Glory Bound #5 (double size). . . 3.00	85 KWe,V:Frost Giants 2.50	61 GJ(s),V:Godfrey 2.25
51 JRu,AH,V:BlackHand,	86 B:Cults of the Machine 2.50	62 GJ(s),N:Metamorpho,V:Godfrey . 2.25
R:Booster Gold 2.50	87 N:Booster Gold 2.50	63 GJ(s),In Africa 2.25
52 TVE,Blue Beetle Vs. Guy Gardner	88 E:Cults of the Machine 2.50	64 GJ(s),V:Cadre 2.25
A:Batman. 2.50	89 Judgement Day#1,	65 JudgmentDay#3,V:Overmaster. . 2.25
53 Breakdowns #1, A:JLE 2.50	V:Overmaster 2.50	66 JudgmentDay#6,V:Overmaster. . 2.25
54 Breakdowns #3, A:JLE 2.50	90 Judgement Day#4. . . . . 2.50	67 Aftershock #3 . . . . 2.25
55 Breakdowns #5,V:Global	91 Aftershocks #1 . . . . 2.50	68 Zero Hour, Final Issue 2.25
Guardians 2.50	92 Zero Hour,I:Triumph 2.50	Ann.#4 Bloodlines#9,I:Lionheart . . . 2.75
56 Breakdowns #7, U.N. revokes	93 Power Girl and child 2.50	Ann.#5 . . . . 3.25
JLA charter 2.50	94 Scarabus. 2.50	Ann.#6 Elseworlds Story 3.00
57 Breakdowns #9,A:Lobo,	95 . . . . 2.50	
V:Despero 2.50	96 Funeral 2.50	**JUSTICE LEAGUE**
58 BS,Breakdowns #11,Lobo	97 I:Judgment 2.50	**[INTERNATIONAL]**
Vs.Despero 2.50	98 J:Blue Devil, Ice Maiden. 2.50	**QUARTERLY**
59 BS,Breakdowns #13,	99 V:New Metahumes 2.50	**1990–94**
V:Extremists. 2.50	100 GJ,Woj,V:Lord Havok,dbl.size . 4.50	1 I:Conglomerate 4.00
60 KM,TA,Breakdowns #15,	100a Collector's Edition. 4.50	2 MJ(i),R:Mr.Nebula 3.50
End of J.L.A... . . . . 2.50	101 GJ,Woj,Way of the	3 V:Extremists,C:Original JLA. 3.50
61 DJu,I:Weapons Master,B:New	Warrior,pt.2 . . . . 2.50	4 KM(c),MR,CR,A:Injustice
JLA Line-up,I:Bloodwynd. 3.00	102 Way of the Warrior,pt.5 . . . . 2.50	League. 3.00
62 DJu,V:Weapons Master 2.50	103 . . . . 2.50	5 KM(c),Superhero Attacks. 3.00
63 DJu,V:Starbreaker. 2.50	104 F:Metamorpho. 2.50	6 EB,Elongated Man,B.U.Global
64 DJu,V:Starbreaker. 2.50	105 GJ,Woj,Underworld	Guardians,Powergirl,B.Beetle . . 3.00
65 DJu,V:Starbreaker. 2.50	Unleashed tie-in 2.50	7 EB,DH,MR.Global Guardians . . . 3.00
66 DJu,Superman V:Guy Gardner. . 2.50	106 GJ,Woj,Underworld	8 . . . . 3.00
67 DJu,Bloodwynd mystery 2.50	Unleashed tie-in 2.50	9 DC,F:Power Girl,Booster Gold . . 3.50
68 DJu,V:Alien Land Baron 2.50	107 GJ,Woj,secret of Power	10 F:Flash,Fire & Ice 3.50
69 DJu, Doomsday Pt.1-A 10.00	Girl's son 2.50	11 F:JL Women 3.50
69a 2nd printing. 2.50	108 GJ,Woj,The Arcana revealed . . 2.50	12 F:Conglomerate 3.50
70 DJu,Funeral for a Friend#1. . . . . 6.00	109 . . . . 2.50	13 V:Ultraa 7.00
70a 2nd printing. 2.50	110 GJ,Woj,V:El Diablo 2.50	14 MMi(c),PuK(s),F:Captain Atom,Blue
71 DJu,J:Agent Liberty,Black Condor,	111 GJ,Woj,The Purge,pt.1 (of 3) . . 2.50	Beetle,Nightshade,Thunderbolt. 3.75
The Ray,Wonder Woman 5.00	112 GJ,Woj,The Purge,pt.2 (of 3) . . 2.50	15 F:Praxis. 3.50
71a Newsstand ed. 2.50	113 GJ,Woj,The Purge,pt.3 (of 3) . . 2.50	16 F:Gen Glory 3.50
71b 2nd Printing. 2.50	Ann.#4 KM(c),I:JL Antartica 3.50	17 Final Issue 3.50
72 DJu,A:Green Arrow,Black	Ann.#5 MR,KM,DJu,Armageddon . 3.50	
Canary,Atom,B:Destiny's Hand . 4.00	Ann.#5a 2nd Printing,silver 2.50	**JUSTICE LEAGUE:**
73 DJu,Destiny's Hand #2 . . . . 3.00	Ann.#6 DC,Eclipso. 3.00	**A MIDSUMMER'S**
74 DJu,Destiny's Hand #3 . . . . 2.50	Ann.#7 I:Terrorsmith. 3.00	**NIGHTMARE**
75 DJu,E:Destiny's Hand #4,Martian	Ann.#8 Elseworlds Story 3.50	**1996**
Manhunter as Bloodwynd 2.50	Ann.#9 Year One Annual 4.00	1 (of 3) MWa(s),FaN,JJ,DaR, ... 5.00
76 DJu,Blood Secrets#1,	Ann.#10 CPr(s),SCi,NNa,Legends	2 MWa(s),FaN,JJ,DaR,Batman &
V:Weaponmaster 2.50	of the Dead Earth 3.50	Superman attempt to free
77 DJu,Blood Secrets#2,	Justice League Spectacular DJu,	other heroes 4.00
V:Weaponmaster. 2.50	JLA(c) New Direction. 2.50	3 MWa&FaN(s), Know-Man's plot
	Archives Vol. 4 . . . . 50.00	revealed, finale 4.00
		TPB Rep. 3 issues. 9.00

Justice League America #65
© DC Comics, Inc.

JUSTICE LEAGUE OF AMERICA: ANOTHER NAIL
May 2004

1 AD,MFm,F:Superman 6.00	
2 AD,MFm,Darkseid's secrets 6.00	
3 AD,MFm,concl. 6.00	

JUSTICE LEAGUE OF AMERICA: THE NAIL
June, 1998
Elseworlds

1 World without a Superman 5.00	
2 AID,MFm,Robin & Batgirl dead . . 5.00	
3 AID,MFm,concl. 5.00	

JUSTICE LEAGUE INTERNATIONAL
[2nd Regular Series], 1993–94
Prev: Justice League Europe

51 Aztec Cult 2.25	
52 V:Aztec Cult 2.25	
53 R:Fox's Husband 2.25	

JUSTICE LEAGUE OF AMERICA
Oct.–Nov., 1960

1 MSy,I&O:Despero 7,500.00	
2 MSy,A:Merlin. 2,000.00	
3 MSy,I&O:Kanjar Ro. 1,500.00	
4 MSy,J:Green Arrow 800.00	
5 MSy,I&O:Dr.Destiny 750.00	
6 MSy,Prof. Fortune 550.00	
7 MSy,Cosmic Fun-House 550.00	
8 MSy,For Sale-Justice League . 550.00	
9 MSy,O:JLA. 750.00	
10 MSy,I:Felix Faust 550.00	
11 MSy,A:Felix Faust 350.00	
12 MSy,I&O:Dr Light 350.00	
13 MSy,A:Speedy. 350.00	
14 MSy,I:Atom. 350.00	
15 MSy,V:Untouchable Aliens . . . 350.00	
16 MSy,I:Maestro. 300.00	
17 MSy,A:Tornado Tyrant. 300.00	
18 MSy,V:Terrane,Ocana. 300.00	

19 MSy,A:Dr.Destiny 300.00
20 MSy,V:Metal Being 300.00
21 MSy,R:JSA,1st S.A Hourman,
    Dr.Fate. 550.00
22 MSy,R:JSA 500.00
23 MSy,I:Queen Bee 250.00
24 MSy,A:Adam Strange 250.00
25 MSy,I:Draad,the Conqueror . . 250.00
26 MSy,A:Despero. 250.00
27 MSy,V:I,A:Amazo 250.00
28 MSy,I:Headmaster Mind,
    A:Robin 250.00
29 MSy,I:Crime Syndicate,A:JSA,
    1st S.A. Starman 300.00
30 MSy,V:Crime Syndicate,
    A:JSA. 250.00
31 MSy,J:Hawkman 200.00
32 MSy,I&O:Brain Storm 150.00
33 MSy,I:Endless One 125.00
34 MSy,A:Dr.Destiny,Joker 150.00
35 MSy,A:Three Demons. 125.00
36 MSy,A:Brain Storm,
    Handicap story 125.00
37 MSy,A:JSA,x-over,
    1st S.A.Mr.Terrific 200.00
38 MSy,A:JSA,Mr.Terrific 200.00
39 Giant 200.00
40 MSy,A:Shark,Penguin. 125.00
41 MSy,I:Key 125.00
42 MSy,A:Metamorpho 100.00
43 MSy,I:Royal Flush Gang. 100.00
44 MSy,A:Unimaginable. 100.00
45 MSy,I:Shaggy Man 100.00
46 MSy,A:JSA,Blockbuster,Solomon
    Grundy,1st S.A.Sandman . . . 200.00
47 MSy,A:JSA,Blockbuster,
    Solomon Grundy 125.00
48 Giant 135.00
49 MSy,A:Felix Faust. 100.00
50 MSy,A:Robin 100.00
51 MSy,A:Zatanna,Elong.Man . . 100.00
52 MSy,A:Robin,Lord of Time . . 100.00
53 MSy,A:Hawkgirl. 100.00
54 MSy,A:Royal Flush Gang 100.00
55 MSy,A:JSA,E-2 Robin 125.00
56 MSy,A:JSA,E-2 Robin 100.00
57 MSy,Brotherhood 100.00
58 Reprint(giant size). 110.00
59 MSy,V:Impossibles 100.00
60 MSy,A:Queen Bee,Batgirl 100.00
61 MSy,A:Lex Luthor,Penguin . . . 75.00
62 MSy,V:Bulleters. 75.00
63 MSy,A:Key 75.00
64 DD,I:Red Tornado,A:JSA 85.00
65 DD,A:JSA 85.00
66 DD,A:Demmy Gog 75.00
67 MSy,Giant reprints 85.00
68 DD,V:Choas Maker. 75.00
69 DD,L:Wonder Woman. 75.00
70 DD,A:Creeper. 75.00
71 DD,L:J'onn J'onzz. 75.00
72 DD,A:Hawkgirl. 75.00
73 DD,A:JSA 75.00
74 DD,D:Larry Lance,A:JSA 75.00
75 DD,J:Black Canary. 75.00
76 Giant,MA,two page pin-up 75.00
77 DD,A:Joker,L:Snapper Carr . . . 50.00
78 DD,R:Vigilante. 50.00
79 DD,A:Vigilante. 50.00
80 DD,A:Tomar-Re,Guardians. . . . 50.00
81 DD,V:Jest-Master 50.00
82 DD,A:JSA 45.00
83 DD,A:JSA,Spectre 60.00
84 DD,Devil in Paradise. 40.00
85 Giant reprint 65.00
86 DD,V:Zapper. 45.00
87 DD,A:Zatanna,I:Silver
    Sorceress,Blue Jay 50.00
88 DD,A:Mera 50.00
89 DD,A:Harlequin Ellis,
    (i.e. Harlan Ellison) 50.00

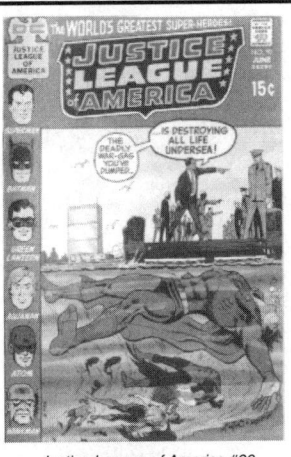

Justice League of America #90
© DC Comics Inc.

90 CI(c),MA(ci),DD,V:Pale People. 50.00
91 DD,A:JSA,V:Solomon Grundy . 50.00
92 DD,A:JSA,V:Solomon Grundy . 50.00
93 DD:A:JSA,(giant size) 50.00
94 DD,NA,O:Sandman,rep.
    Adventure #40 . . . . 125.00
95 DD,rep.More Fun Comics #67,
    All American Comics #25 . . . 65.00
96 DD,I:Starbreaker. 55.00
97 DD,MS,O:JLA 50.00
98 DD,A:Sargon,Gold.Age reps. . . 50.00
99 DD,G.A. reps.. . . . . 50.00
100 DD,A:JSA,Metamorpho,
    R:7 Soldiers of Victory. 60.00
101 DD,A:JSA,7 Soldiers. 40.00
102 DD,DG,A:JSA,7 Soldiers
    D:Red Tornado 40.00
103 DD,DG,Halloween issue,
    A:Phantom Stranger 25.00
104 DD,DG,A:Shaggy Man,
    Hector Hammond 25.00
105 DD,DG,J:ElongatedMan 25.00
106 DD,DG,J:RedTornado 25.00
107 DD,DG,I:Freedom Fighters,
    A:JSA. 30.00
108 DD,DG,A:JSA,
    Freedom Fighters 30.00
109 DD,DG,L:Hawkman. 30.00
110 DD,DG,A:John Stewart,
    Phantom Stranger 55.00
111 DD,DG,I:Injustice Gang 55.00
112 DD,DG,A:Amazo 55.00
113 DD,DG,A:JSA 55.00
114 DD,DG,A:SnapperCarr 55.00
115 DD,FMc,A:J'onn J'onzz. 55.00
116 DD,FMc,I:Golden Eagle 55.00
117 DD,FMc,R:Hawkman 20.00
118 DD,FMc. 20.00
119 DD,FMc,A:Hawkgirl. 20.00
120 DD,FMc,A:Adam Strange 20.00
121 DD,FMc,W:Adam Strange . . . 20.00
122 DD,FMc,JLA casebook story
    V:Dr.Light. 20.00
123 DD,FMc,A:JSA 22.00
124 DD,FMc,A: JSA. 22.00
125 DD,FMc,A:Two-Face. 20.00
126 DD,FMc,A:Two-Face. 20.00
127 DD,FMc,V:Anarchist 20.00
128 DD,FMc,J:W.Woman. 20.00
129 DD,FMC,D:RedTornado 20.00
130 DD,FMc,O:JLASatellite. 20.00
131 DD,FMc,V:Queen Bee,Sonar . 20.00
132 DD,FMc,A:Supergirl 20.00
133 DD,FMc,A:Supergirl 20.00

134 DD,FMc,A:Supergirl 20.00
135 DD,FMc,A:Squad.of Justice . . 20.00
136 DD,FMc,A:E-2Joker 22.00
137 DD,FMc,Superman vs.
    Capt. Marvel 25.00
138 NA(c),DD,FMc,A:Adam
    Strange 20.00
139 NA(c),DD,FMc,A:AdamStrange,
    Phantom Stranger,doub.size . . 16.00
140 DD,FMc,Manhunters. 16.00
141 DD,FMc,Manhunters. 16.00
142 DD,FMc,F:Aquaman,Atom,
    Elongated Man 16.00
143 DD,FMc,V:Injustice Gang 16.00
144 DD,FMc,O:JLA 16.00
145 DD,FMc,A:Phant.Stranger 16.00
146 J:Red Tornado,Hawkgirl 16.00
147 DD,FMc,A:Legion 16.00
148 DD,FMc,A:Legion 16.00
149 DD,FMc,A:Dr.Light 16.00
150 DD,FMc,A:Dr.Light 16.00
151 DD,FMc,A:Amos Fortune 15.00
152 DD,FMc. 15.00
153 GT,FMc,I:Ultraa. 15.00
154 MK(c),DD,FMc 15.00
155 DD,FMc. 15.00
156 DD,FMc. 15.00
157 DD,FMc,W:Atom. 15.00
158 DD,FMc,A:Ultraa. 15.00
159 DD,FMc,A:JSA,Jonah Hex,
    Enemy Ace 14.00
160 DD,FMc,A:JSA,Jonah Hex,
    Enemy Ace 14.00
161 DD,FMc,J:Zatanna 14.00
162 DD,FMc. 14.00
163 DD,FMc,V:Mad Maestro 14.00
164 DD,FMc,V:Mad Maestro 14.00
165 DD,FMc. 14.00
166 DD,FMc,V:Secret Society 14.00
167 DD,FMc,V:Secret Society 14.00
168 DD,FMc,V:Secret Society 14.00
169 DD,FMc,A:Ultraa. 14.00
170 DD,FMc,A:Ultraa. 14.00
171 DD,FMc,A:JSA,D:Mr.Terrific . . 14.00
172 DD,FMc,A:JSA,D:Mr.Terrific . . 14.00
173 DD,FMc,A:Black Lightning . . . 14.00
174 DD,FMc,A:Black Lightning . . . 14.00
175 DD,FMc,V:Dr.Destiny 14.00
176 DD,FMc,V:Dr.Destiny 12.00
177 DD,FMc,V:Desparo 7.00
178 JSn(c),DD,FMc,V:Desparo 7.00
179 JSn(c),DD,FMc,J:Firestorm 7.00
180 JSn(c),DD,FMc,V:Satin Satan . 7.00
181 DD,FMc,L:Gr.Arrow,V:Star 8.00
182 DD,FMc,A:Green Arrow,
    V:Felix Faust 8.00
183 JSn(c),DD,FMc,A:JSA,
    NewGods. 8.00
184 GP,FMc,A:JSA,NewGods 8.00
185 JSn(c),GP,FMc,A:JSA,
    New Gods 7.00
186 FMc,GP,V:Shaggy Man. 6.00
187 DH,FMc,N:Zatanna 6.00
188 DH,FMc,V:Proteus 6.00
189 BB(c),RB,FMc,V:Starro 6.00
190 BB(c),RB,LMa,V:Starro 6.00
191 RB,V:Amazo 6.00
192 GP,O:Red Tornado 6.00
193 GP,RB,JOy,I:AllStarSquad 6.00
194 GP,V:Amos Fortune 6.00
195 GP,A:JSA,V:Secret Society. . . . 6.00
196 GP,RT,A:JSA,V:Secret Soc. . . . 6.00
197 GP,RT,KP,A:JSA,V:Secret
    Society. 6.00
198 DH,BBr,A:J.Hex,BatLash 6.00
199 GP(c),DH,BBr,A:Jonah Hex,
    BatLash. 6.00
200 GP,DG,BB (1st Batman),PB,TA,
    BBr,GK,CI,JAp,JKu,Anniv.,A:Adam
    Strange,Phantom Stranger,
    J:Green Arrow 8.00

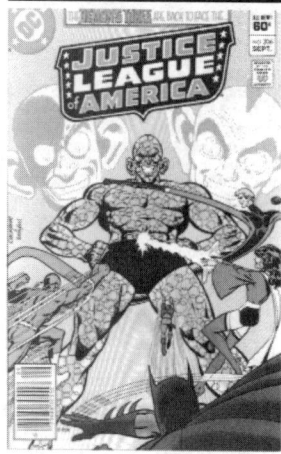

Justice League of America #206
© DC Comics, Inc.

201 GP(c),DH,A:Ultraa 3.00
202 GP(c),DH,BBr,JLA in Space . . . 3.00
203 GP(c),DH,RT,V:Royal
    Flush Gang 3.00
204 GP(c),DH,RT,V:R.FlushGang . . 3.00
205 GP(c),DH,RT,V:R.FlushGang . . 3.00
206 DH,RT,A:Demons 3 . . . . 3.00
207 GP(c),DH,RT,A:All Star
    Squadron,JSA 4.00
208 GP(c),DH,RT,A:All Star
    Squadron,JSA 4.00
209 GP(c),DH,RT,A:All Star
    Squadron,JSA 3.00
210 RB,RT,JLA casebook #1 . . . . . . 3.00
211 RB,RT,JLA casebook #2 . . . . . . 3.00
212 GP(c),RB,PCu,RT,c.book #3 . 3.00
213 GP(c),DH,RT. 3.00
214 GP(c),DH,RT,I:Siren Sist.h'd. . . 3.00
215 GP(c),DH,RT. 3.00
216 DH 3.00
217 GP(c),RT(i) 3.00
218 RT(i),A:Prof.Ivo 3.00
219 GP(c),RT(i),A:JSA 4.00
220 GP(c),RT,O:Bl.Canary,A:JSA . . 4.00
221 Beasts #1 . . . . 3.00
222 RT(i),Beasts #2 . . . . 3.00
223 RT(i),Beasts #3 . . . . 3.00
224 DG(i),V:Paragon 3.00
225 V:Hellrazor 3.00
226 FMc(i),V:Hellrazor 3.00
227 V:Hellrazor,I:Lord Claw 3.00
228 GT,AN,R:J'onn J'onzz,War of
    the Worlds,pt.1 . . . . 3.00
229 War of the Worlds,pt.2 . . . . 3.00
230 War of the Worlds conc. 3.00
231 RB(i),A:JSA,Supergirl 3.00
232 A:JSA Supergirl 3.00
233 New JLA takes over book,
    B:Rebirth,F:Vibe 3.00
234 F:Vixen 3.00
235 F:Steel. 3.00
236 E:Rebirth,F:Gypsy. 3.00
237 A:Superman,Flash,WWoman . . 3.00
238 A:Superman,Flash,WWoman . . 3.00
239 V:Ox 3.00
240 MSy,TMd. 3.00
241 GT,V:Amazo 3.00
242 GT,V:Amazo,Mask(Toy tie-in)
    insert 3.00
243 GT,L:Aquaman,V:Amazo 3.00
244 JSon,Crisis,A:InfinityInc,JSA. . . 4.00
245 LMc,Crisis,N:Steel. 4.00
246 LMc,JLA leaves Detroit 3.00

247 LMc,JLA returns to old HQ 3.00
248 LMc,F:J'onn J'onzz 3.00
249 LMc,Lead-in to Anniv. 3.00
250 LMc,Anniv.,A:Superman,
    Green Lantern,Green Arrow,
    Black Canary,R:Batman 3.00
251 LMc,V:Despero 3.00
252 LMc,V:Despero,N:Elongated
    Man 3.00
253 LMc,V:Despero 3.00
254 LMc,V:Despero 3.00
255 LMc,O:Gypsy 3.00
256 LMc,Gypsy 3.00
257 LMc,A:Adam,L:Zatanna 3.00
258 LMc,Legends x-over,D:Vibe . . 3.00
259 LMc,Legends x-over 3.00
260 LMc,Legends x-over,D:Steel. . . 6.00
261 LMc,Legends,final issue 8.00
Ann.#1 DG(i),A:Sandman 3.50
Ann.#2 I:NewJLA 3.00
Ann.#3 MG(i),Crisis 3.00

JUSTICE LEAGUES
Jan., 2001
Pt.1 Justice Leagues #1,GP(c) 2.50
Pt.2 Just.League of Amazons #1. . . 2.50
Pt.3 Just.League of Atlantis #1 . . . . 2.50
Pt.4 Just.League of Arkham #1 . . . . 2.50
Pt.5 Just.League of Aliens #1 . . . . 2.50
Pt.6 Just.League of America #1. . . . 2.50

Justice League Task Force #5
© DC Comics, Inc.

JUSTICE LEAGUE
TASK FORCE
1993–96
1 F:Mart.Manhunter,Nightwing,
    Aquaman,Flash,Gr.Lantern 2.25
2 V:Count Glass,Blitz 2.25
3 V:Blitz,Count Glass 2.25
4 DG,F:Gypsy,A:Lady Shiva 2.25
5 JAl,Knightquest:Crusade,F:Bronze
    Tiger,Green Arrow,Gypsy 2.25
6 JAl,Knightquest:Search,F:Bronze
    Tiger,Green Arrow,Gypsy 2.25
7 PDd(s),F:Maxima,Wonder Woman,
    Dolphin,Gypsy,Vixen,V:Luta . . . 2.25
8 PDd(s),SaV,V:Amazons. 2.25
9 GrL,V:Wildman. 2.25
10 Purification Plague #1. . . . . 2.25
11 Purification Plague #2. . . . . 2.25
12 Purification Plague #3. . . . . 2.25
13 Judgement Day #2, ... 2.25

14 Jugdement Day#5,
    V:Overmaster 2.25
15 Aftershocks #2 . . . . 2.25
16 Zero Hour,A:Triumph 2.25
17 Savage 2.25
18 Savage 2.25
19 Martian Manhunter 2.25
20 thru 35 . . . . @2.25

JUSTICE LEAGUE
UNLIMITED
Sept. 2004
1 From animated series 2.25
2 F:Booster Gold, Steel 2.25

JUSTICE RIDERS
1999
1-shot, Elseworlds 7.00

JUSTICE SOCIETY
OF AMERICA
[Limited Series]
April–Nov., 1991
1 B:Veng.From Stars,A:Flash 3.00
2 A:BlackCanary,V:Solomon Grundy,
    C:G.A.Green Lantern. 2.50
3 A:G.A.Green Lantern,Black Canary,
    V:Sol.Grundy 2.50
4 A:G.A.Hawkman,C:G.A.Flash. . . . 2.50
5 A:G.A.Hawkman,Flash 2.50
6 FMc(i),A:Bl.Canary,G.A.Gr.Lantern,
    V:Sol.Grundy,V.Savage 2.50
7 JSA united,V:Vandal Savage 2.50
8 E:Veng.FromStar,V:V.Savage,
    Solomon Grundy 2.50
Spec.#1 DR,MG,End of JSA 2.50
[Regular Series], 1992–93
1 V:The New Order. 2.50
2 V:Ultra Gen 2.50
3 R:Ultra-Humanite 2.50
4 V:Ultra-Humanite 2.50
5 V:Ultra-Humanite 2.50
6 F:Johnny Thunderbolt 2.50
7 ..Or give me Liberty 2.50
8 Pyramid Scheme 2.50
9 V:Kulak. 2.50
10 V:Kulak,final issue. 2.50
TPB Justice Society
    Returns (2003) 19.95

JUST IMAGINE...
July, 2001
GN Aquaman, by StL & SMc 6.00
GN Batman, by StL & JKu 6.00
GN Catwoman, by StL & CBa 6.00
GN Crisis, by StL 6.00
GN The Flash, by StL & KM 6.00
GN Green Lantern, by StL & DGb . . 6.00
GN The JLA, by StL & JOy 6.00
GN Robin, by StL & JBy 6.00
GN Sandman, by StL & WS 6.00
GN Shazam!, by StL & GFr 6.00
GN Superman, by StL & JB 6.00
GN Wonder Woman, by StL & JLe . 6.00
GN Just Imagine Secret Files 5.00
TPB The DC Universe, by StL 20.00

KAMANDI, THE LAST
BOY ON EARTH
Oct.–Nov., 1972
1 JK,O:Kamandi 90.00
2 JK. 50.00
3 JK. 50.00
4 JK,I:Prince Tuftan 40.00
5 JK. 40.00

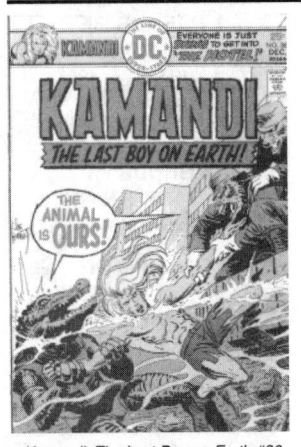

Kamandi, The Last Boy on Earth #36
© DC Comics, Inc.

6 JK	35.00
7 JK	35.00
8 JK	35.00
9 JK	35.00
10 JK	35.00
11 JK	20.00
12 JK	20.00
13 thru 24 JK	@20.00
25 thru 28 JK	@15.00
29 A:Superman	20.00
30 JK	15.00
31	15.00
32 Double size	20.00
33 thru 57	@15.00
58 A:Karate Kid	18.00
59 JSn,A:Omac, Sept.–Oct,1978	20.00

KAMANDI: AT EARTH'S END
[Mini-Series], 1993

1 R:Kamandi	2.50
2 V:Kingpin,Big Q	2.50
3 A:Sleeper Zom,Saphira	2.50
4 A:Superman	2.50
5 A:Superman,V:Ben Boxer	2.50
6 final issue	2.50

KARATE KID
March-April, 1976

1 I:Iris Jacobs,A:Legion	15.00
2 A:Major Disaster	8.00
3 thru 10	@8.00
11 A:Superboy/Legion	8.00
12 A:Superboy/Legion	8.00
13 A:Superboy/Legion	8.00
14 A:Robin	8.00
15 July-Aug., 1978	8.00

KENTS, THE
1997

1 (of 12) JOs(s),TT,MiB	3.00
2 JOs(s),TT,MiB, tragedy strikes	3.00
3 JOs,TT,MiB,Jed & Nate Kent	3.00
4 JOs,TT,MiB,Bleeding Kansas, concl.	3.00
5 JOs,TT,Brother vs.Brother pt.1	3.00
6 JOs,TT,Brother vs.Brother pt.2	3.00
7 JOs,TT,MiB,Quantrill, Wild Bill Hickcock	3.00
8 JOs,	3.00
9 JOs,TMd,To the Stars by Hard Ways,pt.1	3.00

10 JOs,TMd,To the Stars,pt.2	3.00
11 JOs,TMd,To the Stars,pt.3	3.00
12 JOs,TMd,To the Stars,pt.4	3.00
TPB The Kents, rep.	19.95

KID ETERNITY
1991

1 GMo(s),DFg,O:Kid Eternity	5.50
2 GMo(s),DFg,A:Mr.Keeper	5.50
3 GMo(s),DFg,True Origin revealed, final issue	5.50

KID ETERNITY
DC/Vertigo, 1993–94

1 B:ANo(s),SeP,R:Kid Eternity, A:Mdm.Blavatsky,Hemlock	2.75
2 SeP,A:Sigmund Freud,Carl Jung, A:Malocchio	2.50
3 SeP,A:Malocchio,I:Dr.Pathos	2.25
4 SeP,A:Neal Cassady	2.25
5 SeP,In Cyberspace	2.25
6 SeP,A:Dr.Pathos,Marilyn Monroe	2.25
7 SeP,I:Infinity	2.25
8 SeP,In Insane Asylum	2.25
9 SeP,Asylum,A:Dr.Pathos	2.25
10 SeP,Small Wages	2.25
11 ANi(s),I:Slap	2.25
12 SeP,A:Slap	2.25
13 SeP,Date in Hell,pt.1	2.25
14 SeP,Date in Hell,pt.2	2.25
15 SeP,Date in Hell,pt.3	2.25
16 SeP,The Zone	2.25

KILL YOUR BOYFRIEND
DC/Vertigo, 1995, 1999

GNv PBd(c) (1995)	4.95
1-shot GMo (1999)	6.00

KINETIC
DC Focus, March 2004

1 WaP,F:Tom Morell	2.50
2 WaP,newfound super-powers	2.50
3 thru 8 WaP	@2.50

KINGDOM, THE
1998

1 (of 2) MWa,AOl	5.00
2 MWa,MZ,JhB,V:Gog	4.00
Spec.#1 Kid Flash	2.25
Spec.#1 Offspring	2.25
Spec.#1 Nightstar	2.25
Spec.#1 Planet Krypton	2.25
Spec.#1 Son of the Bat	2.25
DirectCurrents Spec.	free
TPB	14.95

KINGDOM COME
Elseworlds 1996

1 MWa,AxR	8.00
2 MWa,AxR,R:JLA	7.00
3 MWa,AxR,A:Capt. Marvel	7.00
4 MWa,AxR, final issue	7.00
TPB MWa,AxR, rep.	15.00

KOBALT
DC/Milestone, 1994–95

1 JBy(c),I:Kobalt,Richard Page	3.00
2	2.50
3 I:Slick,Volt,Red Light	2.50
4 I:Slick,Volt,Red Light Richard Page	2.50
5 Richard Page	2.50
6 Volt	2.50
7 Static	2.50
8 A:Hardward	2.50
9	2.50

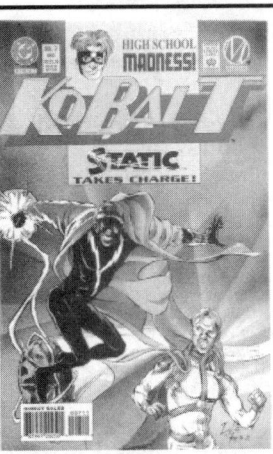

Kobalt #7 © DC Comics Inc.

10 A:Harvest	2.50
11 V:St.Cloud	2.50
12 V:Rabid	2.50
13 V:Harvester	2.50
14 Long Hot Summer, V:Harvester	3.00
15 Long Hot Summer	3.00

KOBRA
1976–77

1 JK,I:Kobra & Jason Burr	15.00
2 I:Solaris	8.00
3 KG/DG,TA,V:Solaris	8.00
4 V:Servitor	8.00
5 RB/FMc,A:Jonny Double	8.00
6 MN/JRu,A:Jonny Double	8.00
7 MN/JRu,A:Jonny Double last iss	8.00

KONG THE UNTAMED
June-July, 1975

1 AA,BWr(c)	15.00
2 AA,BWr(c)	12.00
3 AA	10.00
4	10.00
5 Feb.–March, 1976	10.00

KORAK, SON OF TARZAN
1975
(Prev. published by Gold Key)

46 JKu(c),B:Carson of Venus	25.00
47 JKu(c)	10.00
48 JKu(c)	10.00
49 JKu(c),Origin of Korak	15.00
50 thru 59 JKu(c),1975	10.00

Becomes:

TARZAN FAMILY

KRYPTON CHRONICLES
1981

1 CS,A:Superman	5.00
2 CS,A:Black Flame	4.00
3 CS,O:Name of Kal-El	4.00

LAB RATS
April, 2002

1 by the one and only JBy	7.00
1a 2nd printing	4.50
2 JBy, amusement park	6.00
2a 2nd printing	4.50
3 JBy,	2.50
4 JBy,time travel,pt.1	2.50

All comics prices listed are for *Near Mint* condition.

5 JBy,time travel,pt.2 . . . . 2.50
6 JBy,time travel,pt.3,A:Superman . 2.50
7 JBy,interplanetary adventure 2.50
8 JBy, final issue 2.50

LAST DAYS OF THE JUSTICE SOCIETY
1986
1 . . . . 5.00

LAST ONE
DC/Vertigo, 1993
1 B:JMD(s),DSw,I:Myrwann,Patrick
  Maguire's Story 3.25
2 DSw,Pat's Addiction to Drugs . . . 3.00
3 DSw,Pat goes into Coma. 3.00
4 DSw,In Victorian age 3.00
5 DSw,Myrwann Memories. 3.00
6 E:JMD(s),DSw,final Issue 3.00

L.A.W.
1999
1 (of 6) BL,DG,Living Assault
  Weapons 2.50
2 thru 6 BL,DG . . . . @2.50

LAZARUS FIVE
May, 2000
1 (of 5) THy,F:Inquisitors 2.50
2 thru 5 THy . . . . @2.50

LEADING COMICS
Winter, 1941–42
1 O:Seven Soldiers of Victory,
  B:Crimson Avenger,Green Arrow
  & Speedy,Shining Knight,
  A:The Dummy 6,500.00
2 MMe,V:Black Star 2,100.00
3 V:Dr. Doome 1,600.00
4 Seven Steps to Conquest,
  V:The Sixth Sense 1,200.00
5 The Miracles that Money
  Couldn't Buy. 1,200.00
6 Treasure that Time Forgot . . 1,000.00
7 The Wizard of Wisstark 1,000.00
8 Seven Soldiers Go back
  through the Centuries. 1,000.00
9 V:Mr. X,Chameleon of Crime 1,000.00
10 King of the Hundred Isles . . 1,000.00
11 The Hard Luck Hat!. 700.00
12 The Million Dollar
  Challenge! 700.00

Leading #12 © DC Comics, Inc.

13 The Trophies of Crime 700.00
14 Bandits from the Book 700.00
15 (fa). 250.00
16 thru 22 (fa) . . . . @100.00
23 (fa),I:Peter Porkchops. 250.00
24 thru 30 (fa) . . . . @100.00
31 (fa). 75.00
32 (fa). 75.00
33 (fa). 75.00
34 thru 40 (fa) . . . . @75.00
41 (fa),Feb.–March, 1950 . . . . . . 75.00

LEAGUE OF JUSTICE
1996
1 (of 2) Elseworlds 5.95
2 (of 2) Elseworlds 5.95

LEAVE IT TO BINKY
Feb.–March, 1948
1 Teen-age stories 300.00
2 . . . . 150.00
3 . . . . 75.00
4 . . . . 75.00
5 thru 14 . . . . @50.00
15 SM,Scribbly. 55.00
16 thru 60 . . . . @40.00
61 thru 71 . . . . @35.00

LEGEND OF THE HAWKMAN
July, 2000
1 BRa,Hawkman & Hawkgirl 4.95
2 BRa,V:Thanagarian zealots. . . . 4.95
3 BRa,concl. 4.95

LEGEND OF THE SHIELD
DC/Impact, 1991–92
1 I:Shield,V:Mann-X,I:Big Daddy,
  Lt.Devon Hall,Arvell Hauser,Mary
  Masterson-Higgins. 2.50
2 Shield in Middle East. 2.50
3 Shield Goes A.W.O.L. 2.50
4 Hunt for Shield. 2.50
5 A:Shield's Partner Dusty 2.50
6 O:Shield, V:The Jewels 2.50
7 Shield/Fly team-up. 2.50
8 V:Weapon 2.50
9 Father Vs. Son. 2.50
10 Arvell Hauser 2.50
11 inc,Trading cards. 2.50
12 . . . . 2.50
13 Shield court martialed. 2.50
14 Mike Barnes becomes Shield . . 2.50
15 Shield becomes a Crusader . . . 2.50
16 V:Soviets,final issue 2.50
Ann.#1 Earthquest,w/trading card . . 2.25

LEGEND OF WONDER WOMAN
1986
1 Return of Atomia 4.00
2 A:Queens Solalia & Leila 3.50
3 Escape from Atomia 3.50
4 conclusion 3.50

LEGENDS
1986–87
1 JBy,V:Darkseid. 5.00
2 JBy,A:Superman 4.00
3 JBy,I:Suicide Squad. 4.00
4 JBy,V:Darkseid. 4.00
5 JBy,A:Dr. Fate 4.00
6 JBy,I:Justice League 5.00
TPB rep.#1-#6 JBy(c) 9.95

LEGENDS OF DANIEL BOONE, THE
Oct., 1955–Jan., 1957
1 . . . . 750.00
2 . . . . 550.00
3 thru 8 . . . . 450.00

LEGENDS OF THE DARK KNIGHT
(see BATMAN)

LEGENDS OF THE DC UNIVERSE
Dec., 1997
1 JeR,VS,PNe,A:Superman, pt.1 . . 3.50
2 JeR,VS,PNe,A:Superman, pt.2 . . 4.00
3 JeR,VS,PNe,A:Superman, pt.3 . . 2.50
4 BML,MD2,VRu,Moments, pt.1 . . 2.50
5 BML,MD2,VRu,Moments, pt.2 . . 2.50
6 DTy,KN,Robin meets Superman . 2.50
7 DON,DG,Peacemakers, pt.1 . . . 2.50
8 DON,DG,Peacemakers, pt.2 . . . 2.50
9 DON,DG,Peacemakers, pt.3 . . . 2.50
10 TyD,KN,F:Batman & Batgirl,pt.1 2.50
11 KN,TyD,F:Batman & Batgirl,pt.2 . 2.50
12 CPr(s),Critical Mass,pt.1 . . . . . 2.50
13 CPr(s),Critical Mass,pt.2 . . . . . 2.50
14 JK,BR,SR,64-page 5.00
15 RCa,Dark Matters, pt.1 . . . . 2.50
16 RCa,Dark Matters, pt.2 . . . . 2.50
17 RCa,Dark Matters, pt.3 . . . . 2.50
18 MWn(s),JG,F:New Teen Titans . . 2.50
19 RT,F:Impulse. 2.50
20 StG(s),MZ,KJ,Trail of the
  Traitor, pt.1 . . . . 2.50
21 StG(s),MZ,KJ,Trail of the
  Traitor, pt.2 . . . . 2.50
22 Transilvane,pt.1. . . . . 2.50
23 Transilvane,pt.2. . . . . 2.50
24 StP,The Jump,pt.1. . . . . 2.50
25 StP,The Jump,pt.2. . . . . 2.50
26 TVE,JRu,Aquaman&Joker,pt.1 . 2.50
27 TVE,JRu,Aquaman&Joker,pt.2 . 2.50
28 GK,KJ,pt.1. . . . . 2.50
29 GK,KJ,pt.2,F:Traitor 2.50
30 CPr(s),Wonder Woman,pt.1 . . . 2.50
31 CPr(s),Wonder Woman,pt.2 . . . 2.50
32 CPr(s),Wonder Woman,pt.3 . . . 2.50
33 JMD,MZi,VcL,F:Spectre,pt.1 . . . 2.50
34 JMD,MZi,VcL,F:Spectre,pt.2 . . . 2.50
35 JMD,MZi,VcL,F:Spectre,pt.3 . . . 2.50
36 JMD,MZi,VcL,F:Spectre,pt.4 . . . 2.50
37 ScK,KJ,Traitor Trilogy,pt.1 . . . . 2.50
38 ScK,KJ,V:Traitor,pt.2. . . . . 2.50
39 RGr,Sole Survivor of Earth 2.50
40 RGr,Lessons in Time,pt.1 . . . . . 2.50
41 RGr,Lessons in Time,pt.2 . . . . . 2.50
Giant #1 JKu(c), 80 pg. 5.00
Spec 3-D Gallery #1 . . . . 3.00
GN Crisis on Infinite Earths 5.00

LEGENDS OF THE LEGION
Dec., 1997
1 (of 4) BKi,TPe,TNu,O:Ultra Boy. . 2.75
2 thru 4 BKi,TPe . . . . @2.50

LEGENDS OF THE WORLD FINEST
1994
1 WS(s),DIB,V:Silver Banshee,
  Blaze,Tullus,Foil(c) 6.00
2 WS(s),DIB,V:Silver Banshee,
  Blaze,Tullus,Foil(c) 6.00

3 WS(s),DIB,V:Silver Banshee,
  Blaze,Tullus,Foil(c) 6.00
TPB 14.95

L.E.G.I.O.N. '89-94
1989–94

1 BKi,V:Computer Tyrants 6.00
2 BKi,V:Computer Tyrants 3.50
3 BKi,V:Computer Tyrants,
  A:Lobo 3.50
4 BKi,V: Lobo 3.50
5 BKi,J:Lobo(in the rest of the
  series),V:Konis-Biz 3.50
6 BKi,V:Konis-Biz 3.50
7 BKi,Stealth vs. Dox 3.50
8 BKi,R:Dox 3.50
9 BKi,J:Phase (Phantom Girl) 3.00
10 BKi,Stealth vs Lobo 3.00
11 BKi,V:Mr.Stoorr 3.00
12 BKi,V:Emerald Eye 3.00

L.E.G.I.O.N. '91 #30
© DC Comics, Inc.

13 BKi,V:Emerald Eye 3.00
14 BKi,V:Pirates. 3.00
15 BKi,V:Emerald Eye 3.00
16 BKi,J:LarGand. 3.00
17 BKi,V:Dragon-Ro 3.00
18 BKi,V:Dragon-Ro 3.00
19 V:Lydea,L:Stealth 3.00
20 Aftermath. 3.00
21 D:Lyrissa Mallor,V:Mr.Starr 3.00
22 V:Mr.Starr 3.00
23 O:R.J.Brande(double sized) 3.50
24 BKi,V:Khunds 3.00
25 BKi,V:Khunds 3.00
26 BKi,V:Khunds 3.00
27 BKi,J:Lydea Mallor 3.00
28 KG,Birth of Stealth's Babies 3.00
29 BKi,J:Capt.Comet,Marij'n Bek . . 3.00
30 BKi,R:Stealth. 3.00
31 Lobo vs.Capt.Marvel 4.00
32 V:Space Biker Gang 3.00
33 A:Ice-Man 3.00
34 MPn,V:Ice Man 3.00
35 Legion Disbanded. 3.00
36 Dox proposes to Ignea 3.00
37 V:Intergalactic Ninjas 3.00
38 BKi,Lobo V:Ice Man 3.00
39 BKi,D:G'odd,V:G'oddSquad 3.00
40 BKi,V:Kyaltic Space Station 3.00
41 BKi,A:Stealth'sBaby 3.00
42 BKi,V:Yeltsin-Beta. 3.00
43 BKi,V:Yeltsin-Beta 3.00
44 V:Yeltsin-Beta,C:Gr.Lantern 3.00

45 . . . . 3.00
46 BKi,A:Hal Jordan 3.00
47 BKi,Lobo vs Hal Jordan 3.00
48 BKi,R:Ig'nea 3.00
49 BKi,V:Ig'nea 3.00
50 BKi,V:Ig'nea,A:Legion'67 . . . . . . 4.00
51 F:Lobo,Telepath 3.00
52 BKi,V:Cyborg Skull of Darius . . . 3.00
53 BKi,V:Shadow Creature 3.00
54 BKi,V:Shadow Creature 3.00
55 BKi,V:Shadow Beast. 3.00
56 BKi,A:Masked Avenger 3.00
57 BKi,Trinity,V:Green Lantern 3.00
58 BKi,Trinity#6,A:Green Lantern,
   Darkstar. 3.00
59 F:Phase. 3.00
60 V:Phantom Riders. 3.00
61 Little Party 3.00
62 A:R.E.C.R.U.I.T.S. 3.00
63 A:Superman 3.00
64 BKi(c),V:Mr.B 3.00
65 BKi(c),V:Brain Bandit 3.00
66 Stealth and Dox name child 3.00
67 F:Telepath 3.00
68 . . . . 3.00
69 . . . . 3.00
70 Zero Hour, last issue. 3.00
Ann.#1 A:Superman,V:Brainiac . . 5.50
Ann.#2 Armageddon 2001 . . . . 3.50
Ann.#3 Eclipso tie-in 3.25
Ann.#4 SHa(i),I:Pax 3.75
Ann.#5 Elseworlds story 3.50

LEGION, THE
Oct., 2001

1 DAn,ALa, New era dawns 5.00
2 DAn,ALa,F:Oversight Watch 4.00
3 DAn,ALa,new headquarters. 4.00
4 DAn,ALa,Footstep Drive Tech. . . 3.50
5 DAn,ALa,Return to Lost Galaxy . 3.00
6 DAn,ALa,Moon & Inhabitants . . . 3.00
7 DAn,ALa,V:Ra's Al Ghul 3.00
8 DAn,ALa,V:Ra's Al Ghul 3.00
9 DAn,ALa,Apparition,Ultra-Boy . . 3.00
10 DAn,ALa,Robotica to Earth. 3.00
11 DAn,ALa,F:Robotica 2.75
12 DAn,ALa,F:JLA 2.75
13 DAn,ALa,V:Robotica 2.75
14 DAn,ALa,V:Robotica 2.75
15 DAn,ALa,F:Timber Wolf 2.75
16 DAn,ALa,F:Lone Wolf 2.75
17 DAn,ALa,The Fittest,pt.1 . . . . . . 2.75
18 DAn,ALa,The Fittest,pt.2 . . . . . . 2.50
19 DAn,MFm,Dream Crime,pt.1 . . . 2.50
20 DAn,MFm,Dream Crime,pt.2 . . . 2.50
21 DAn,MFm,Dream Crime,pt.3 . . . 2.50
22 DAn,MFm,Dream Crime,pt.4 . . . 2.50
23 DAn,MFm,Dream Crime,pt.5 . . . 2.50
24 DAn,ALa,F:Umbra. 2.50
25 Foundations,pt.1,48-pg. 4.00
26 DAn,ALa,Foundations,pt.2 . . . . . 2.50
27 DAn,ALa,Foundations,pt.3 . . . . . 2.50
28 DAn,ALa,Foundations,pt.4 . . . . . 2.50
29 DAn,ALa,Foundations,pt.5 . . . . . 2.50
30 DAn,ALa,Foundations,pt.6 . . . . . 2.50
31 KG,AM,deadly virus 2.50
32 DAn,ALa,V:Credo 2.50
33 DAn,ALa,F:Livewire 2.50
34 SLi,Wildfire,Qward 2.50
35 DJu,ASm,No Better Reason 2.50
36 DJu,ASm,No Better Reason. 2.50
37 DJu,ASm,No Better Reason. 2.50
38 DJu,ASm,No Better Reason. 2.50
GN Legion Secret Files 3003 . . . . . 4.95
TPB The Legion: Foundations. . . . 19.95

LEGION LOST
March, 2000

1 (of 12) DAn,ALa. 8.00
2 DAn,ALa,V:Progeny. 4.00

3 DAn,ALa,V:Progeny. 4.00
4 DAn,ALa, ... 4.00
5 DAn,ALa,Brainiac 5.1 . . . . 4.00
6 DAn,ALa,F:Umbra 3.00
7 DAn,ALa,F:Ultra Boy 3.00
8 DAn,ALa, ... 3.00
9 DAn,ALa 3.00
10 DAn,ALa 3.00
11 DAn,ALA 3.00
12 DAn,ALA conclusion 3.00

LEGIONNAIRES
1992

1 CSp,V:Mano and the Hand,Bagged
  w/SkyBox promo card 4.00
1a w/out card 3.00
2 CSp,V:Mano. 3.00
3 CSp,I:2nd Emerald Empress 3.00
4 CSp,R:Fatal Five 3.00
5 CSp,V:Fatal Five 3.00
6 CSp,V:Fatal Five 2.50
7 AH,V:Devil Fish 2.50
8 CDo,F:Brainiac 5 . . . . 2.50
9 CSp,A:Kid Quantum 2.50
10 CSp,A:Kono,I:2nd Kid Pyscho . . 2.50
11 CSp,J:2nd Kid Pyscho 2.50
12 CSp,A:2nd Kid Pyscho 2.50
13 FFo,V:Grimbor 2.50
14 V:Grimbor 2.50
15 V:Grimbor 2.50
16 In Time 2.50
17 End of An Era #1 . . . . 2.50
18 Zero Hour, LSH. 3.00
19 Problems. 2.50
20 Moon Battle. 2.50
21 and 22 . . . . @2.50
23 Saturday Night 2.50
24 F:Triad. 2.50
25 F:Chameleon 2.50
26 F:Apparition, Ultra Boy 2.50
27 V:The Daxamites 2.50
28 V:Daxamites 2.50
29 . . . . 2.50
30 Silbing Rivalry,pt.2 . . . . 2.50
31 Future Tense,pt.3 . . . . 2.50
32 Two Timer, pt.2 . . . . 2.50
33 deadly new villain 2.50
34 Shrinking Violet killed? 2.50
35 . . . . 2.50
36 RSt,V:Fatal Five 2.50
37 RSt,A:Kinetix,The Empress 2.50
38 . . . . 2.50
39. . . . . 2.50

Legionnairs #22 © DC Comics Inc.

Legionnaires #25 © DC Comics, Inc.

40 . . . . 2.50
41 RSt&TMw(s),JMy,Legion of
   Super-Heroes #84 aftermath. . . 2.50
42 RSt&TMw(s),JMy,Mysa vs.
   Kinetix 2.50
43 RSt&TMw(s),JMy,Legionnaire
   try-outs 2.50
44 TPe&TMw(s),JMy,revenge by
   rejected applicants 2.50
45 . . . . 2.50
46 RSt&TMw(s),JMy,M'Onel's life
   hangs by a thread 2.50
47 TPe&TMw(s),JMy,Brainiac 5 has
   plan to return Legionnaires to
   the future 2.50
48 RSt&TMw(s),JMy,Dawn of the
   Dark Lord,pt.1 . . . . 2.50
49 RSt&TMw(s),JMy,Dawn of the
   Dark Lord,pt.2 . . . . 2.50
50 RSt&TMw(s),JMy,The Bride of
   Mordru, 48pg, with poster 5.00
51 Picking Up the Pieces. 2.50
52 RSt&TMw(s),JMy,LeVlathan 2.50
53 RSt&TMw(s),JMy,F:Monstress . . 2.50
54 TPe&TMw(s),JMy,F:G.A. Legion. 2.50
55 RSt&TMw(s),JMy,V:Composite
   Man 2.50
56 RSt&TMw(s),JMy,F:M'Onel. . . . 2.50
57 RSt&TMw(s),JMy,V:Khunds 2.50
58 . . . . 2.50
59 RSt&TMw(s),JMy,date night 2.50
60 RSt&TMw(s),JMy,2 join, 2 leave. 2.50
61 RSt&TMw(s),JMy,Adventures
   in Action x-over 2.50
62 RSt&TMw(s),JMy,Dark
   Circle Rising x-over, pt.1 . . . . . 2.50
63 RSt&TMw(s),JMy,Dark Circle
   Rising, x-over,pt.3. . . . . 2.50
64 RSt&TMw(s),JMy, Dark Circle
   Rising, x-over pt.5 . . . . 2.50
65 RSt&TMw(s),JMy,aftermath 2.50
66 F:Invisible Kid 2.50
67 RSt&TMw(s),JMy,Star Boy 2.50
68 RSt&TMw(s),JMy,Cosmic Boy . . 2.50
69 RSt&TMw(s),JMy,Lori Morning . . 2.50
70 RSt&TMw(s),JMy,Alux Cuspin . . 2.50
71 RSt&TMw(s),JMy,Dragonmage. . 2.50
72 RSt&TMw(s),JMy,V:Mordru. 2.50
73 RSt&TMw(s),JMy,V:Mordru. 2.50
74 RSt&TMw(s),JMy,V:Elements
   of Disaster 2.50
75 TPe(s),JMy, ... 2.50
76 RSt&TMw(s),JMy 2.50
77 RSt, TMw(s),JMy 2.50
78 DAn&ALa(s),rescue mission. . . . 2.50

79 ALa,Legion of the Damned,pt.2 . 2.50
80 ALa,Legion of the Damned,pt.4 . 2.50
81 DAn&ALa(s),final issue 2.50
Ann.#1 Elseworlds Story 3.50
Ann.#2 Year One Story 3.50
Ann.#3 RSt&TMw(s) 4.00
Spec.#1,000,000 TPe(s),SeP, Justice
   Legion L. 2.50

LEGIONNAIRES THREE
1986
1 EC,Saturn Girl,Cosmic Boy 4.00
2 EC,V:Time Trapper,pt.1 . . . . 3.00
3 EC,V:Time Trapper,pt.2 . . . . 3.00
4 EC,V:Time Trapper,pt.3 . . . . 3.00

LEGION OF
SUBSTITUTE HEROES
1985
Spec.#1 KG 3.00

LEGION OF
SUPER-HEROES
[Reprint Series], 1973
1 rep. Tommy Tomorrow 25.00
2 rep. Tommy Tomorrow 15.00
3 rep. Tommy Tomorrow 15.00
4 rep. Tommy Tomorrow 15.00

[1st Regular Series], 1980–84
Prev: SUPERBOY (& LEGION)
259 JSon,L:Superboy 15.00
260 RE,I:Circus of Death 8.00
261 RE,V:Circus of Death 8.00
262 JSh,V:Engineer. 8.00
263 V:Dagon the Avenger 8.00
264 V:Dagon the Avenger 8.00
265 JSn,DG,Superman/Radio Shack
   insert 8.00
266 R:Bouncing Boy,Duo Damsel . . 8.00
267 SD,V:Kantuu 8.00
268 SD,BWi,V:Dr.Mayavale 8.00
269 V:Fatal Five. 8.00
270 V:Fatal Five. 8.00
271 V:Tharok (Dark Man) 6.00
272 CI,SD,O:J:Blok, I:New
   Dial 'H' for Hero. 6.00
273 V:Stargrave 6.00
274 SD,V:Captain Frake 6.00
275 V:Captain Frake 6.00
276 SD,V:Mordru 6.00
277 A:Reflecto(Superboy) 6.00
278 A:Reflecto(Superboy) 6.00
279 A:Reflecto(Superboy) 6.00
280 R:Superboy. 6.00
281 SD,V:Time Trapper 6.00
282 V:Time Trapper 6.00
283 O:Wildfire 6.00
284 PB,V:Organleggor. 6.00
285 PB,KG(1st Legion)V:Khunds . 8.00
286 PB,KG,V:Khunds. 8.00
287 KG,V:Kharlak. 8.00
288 KG,V:Kharlak. 8.00
289 KG,Stranded 8.00
290 KG,B:Great Darkness Saga,
   J:Invisible Kid II 8.00
291 KG,V:Darkseid's Minions. 6.00
292 KG,V:Darkseid's Minions. 6.00
293 KG,Daxam destroyed 6.00
294 KG,E:Great Darkness Saga,
   V:Darkseid,A:Auron,Superboy. . 8.00
295 KG,A:Green Lantern Corps. . . . 3.50
296 KG,D:Cosmic Boys family 3.50
297 KG,O:Legion,A:Cosmic Boy . . 3.50
298 KG,EC,I:Amethyst. 3.50
299 KG,R:Invisible Kid I 3.50
300 KG,CS,JSon,DC,KS,DG 6.00
301 KG,R:Chameleon Boy. 3.50

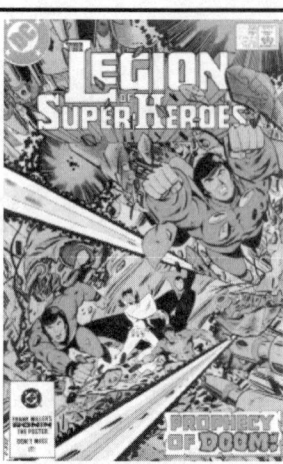

Legion of Super-Heroes #308
© DC Comics, Inc.

302 KG,A:Chameleon Boy. 3.50
303 KG,V:Fatal Five. 3.50
304 KG,V:Fatal Five. 3.50
305 KG,V:Micro Lad 3.50
306 KG,CS,RT,O:Star Boy 3.50
307 KG,GT,Omen 3.50
308 KG,V:Omen. 3.50
309 KG,V:Omen 3.50
310 KG,V:Omen 3.50
311 KG,GC,New Headquarters 3.50
312 KG,V:Khunds. 3.50
313 KG,V:Khunds. 3.50
Ann.#1 IT,KG,I:Invisible Kid 4.00
Ann.#2 DGb,W:Karate Kid and
   Princess Projectra 3.00
Ann.#3 CS,RT,A:Darkseid 3.00
Ann.#4 reprint 3.00
Ann.#5 reprint 3.00
Becomes:

TALES OF LEGION OF
SUPER HEROES

LEGION OF
SUPER-HEROES
[3rd Regular Series], 1984–89
1 KG,V:Legion of Super-Villains . . . 5.00
2 KG,V:Legion of Super-Villians . . . 4.00
3 KG,V:Legion of Super-Villians . . . 4.00
4 KG,D:Karate Kid. 4.00
5 KG,D:Nemesis Kid 4.00
6 JO,F:Lightning Lass. 3.00
7 SLi,A:Controller 3.00
8 SLi,V:Controller 3.00
9 Sli,V:Sklarians 3.00
10 V:Khunds 3.00
11 EC,KG,L:Orig 3 members 3.00
12 SLi,EC,A:Superboy 3.00
13 SLi,V:Lythyls,F:TimberWolf. . . . 3.00
14 SLi,J:Sensor Girl (Princess
   Projectra),Quislet,Tellus,Polar
   Boy,Magnetic Kid. 3.00
15 GLa,V:Dr. Regulus 3.00
16 SLi,Crisis tie-in,F:Braniac5 . . . . 3.00
17 GLa,O:Legion 3.00
18 GLa,Crisis tie-in,V:InfiniteMan . . 3.00
19 GLa,V:Controller 3.00
20 GLa,V:Tyr 3.00
21 GLa,V:Emerald Empress 4.00
22 GLa,V:Restorer,A:Universo. . . . 4.00
23 SLi,GLa,A:Superboy,
   Jonah Hex 4.00

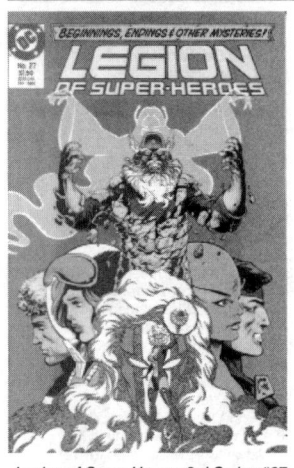

Legion of Super-Heroes 3rd Series #27
© DC Comics Inc.

24 GLa,NBi,A:Fatal Five 4.00
25 GLa,V:FatalFive 4.00
26 GLa,V:FatalFive,O:SensorGirl . . 3.00
27 GLa,GC,A:Mordru. 3.00
28 GLa,L:StarBoy. 3.00
29 GLa,V:Starfinger 3.00
30 GLa,A:Universo. 3.00
31 GLa,A:Ferro Lad,Karate Kid . . . 3.00
32 GLa,V:Universo,I:Atmos 3.00
33 GLa,V:Universo. 3.00
34 GLa,V:Universo. 3.00
35 GLa,V:Universo,R:Saturn Girl . . 3.00
36 GLa,R:Cosmic Boy 3.00
37 GLa,V:Universo,I:Superboy
   (Earth Prime) 12.00
38 GLa,V:TimeTrapper,
   D:Superboy 14.00
39 CS,RT,O:Colossal Boy 3.00
40 GLa,I:New Starfinger 3.00
41 GLa,V:Starfinger 3.00
42 GLa,Millennium,V:Laurel Kent . 3.00
43 GLa,Millennium,V:Laurel Kent . 3.00
44 GLa,O:Quislet 3.00
45 GLa,CS,MGr,DC,30th Ann. 4.00
46 GLa,Conspiracy 3.00
47 GLa,PB,V:Starfinger 3.00
48 GLa,Conspiracy,A:Starfinger. . . 3.00
49 PB,Conspiracy,A:Starfinger. . . . 3.00
50 KG,V:Time Trapper,A:Infinite
   Man,E:Conspiracy 4.00
51 KG,V:Gorak,L:Braniac5 . . . . . . 3.00
52 KG,V:Gil'Dishpan. 3.00
53 KG,V:Gil'Dishpan. 3.00
54 KG,V:Gorak. 3.00
55 KG,EC,JL,EL,N:Legion 3.00
56 EB,V:Inquisitor 3.00
57 KG,V:Emerald Empress 3.00
58 KG,V:Emerald Empress 3.00
59 KG,MBr,F:Invisible Kid 3.00
60 KG,B:Magic Wars 3.00
61 KG,Magic Wars 3.00
62 KG,D:Magnetic Lad. 3.00
63 KG,E:Magic Wars #4,final iss. . . 3.00
Ann.#1 KG,Murder Mystery 3.00
Ann.#2 KG,CS,O:Validus,
   A:Darkseid. 3.50
Ann.#3 GLa,I:2nd Karate Kid. 3.00
Ann.#4 BKi,V:Starfinger 3.00
Ann #5 I:2nd Legion Sub.Heroes . . 3.50

[4th Regular Series], 1989–97
1 KG,R:Cosmic Boy, Chameleon . . 5.00
2 KG,R:Ultra Boy,I:Kono 3.50
3 KG,D:Block,V:Roxxas 3.50

4 KG,V:Time Trapper 3.50
5 KG,V:Mordru,A:Glorith 3.50
6 KG,I:Laurel Gand 3.50
7 KG,V:Mordru 3.00
8 KG,O:Legion 3.00
9 KG,O:Laurel Gand 3.00
10 KG,V:Roxxas. 3.00
11 KG,V:Roxxas 3.00
12 KG,I:Kent Shakespeare 3.00
13 KG,V:Dominators,posters 3.00
14 KG,J:Tenzil Kem 3.00
15 KG,Khund Invasion 3.00
16 KG,V:Khunds. 3.00
17 KG,V:Khunds. 3.00
18 KG,V:Khunds. 3.00
19 KG,cont.from Adv.of Superman
   #478,A:Original Dr. Fate 3.00
20 KG,V:Dominators 3.00
21 KG,B:Quiet Darkness,
   A:Lobo,Darkseid 3.50
22 KG,A:Lobo,Darkseid 3.00
23 KG,A:Lobo,Darkseid 3.00
24 KG,E:Quiet Darkness,A:Lobo,
   Darkseid,C:Legionairres 3.00
25 DAb,I:Legionairres 3.50
26 JPn,B:Terra Mosaic,V:B.I.O.N. . . 2.50
27 JPn,V:B.I.O.N. 2.50
28 JPn,O:Sun Boy 2.50
29 JPn,I:Monica Sade 2.50
30 JPn,V:Dominators 2.50
31 CS,AG,F:Shvaughn as man . . . 2.50
32 JPn,D:Karate Kid,Prin.Projectra,
   Chameleon Boy(Legionaires) . . 2.50
33 R:Kid Quantum 2.50
34 R:Sun Boy. 2.50
35 JPN,V:Dominators 2.50
36 JPn,E:Terra Mosaic. 2.50
37 JBr,R:Star Boy,Dream Girl 2.50
38 JPn,Earth is destroyed 5.00
39 SI,A:Legionnaires 2.50
40 SI,Legion meets Legionnaires . 2.50
41 SI,F:The Legionnaires 2.50
42 SI,V:Glorith 2.50
43 SI,B:Mordru Arises 2.50
44 SI,R:Karate Kid 2.50
45 SI,R:Roxxas 2.50
46 SI, ... 2.50
47 SI, ... 2.50
48 SI,E:Mordru Arises 2.50
49 F:Matter Eater Lad 2.50
50 W:Tenzil & Saturn Queen,
   R:Wlidfire,V:B.I.O.N 4.00
51 F:Kent,Celeste,Ivy,V:Grimbor. . 2.50
52 F:Timber Wolf 2.50
53 SI,V:Glorith 2.50
54 SI,Foil,Die-Cut(c),
   N:L.E.G.I.O.N. 5.00
55 SI,On Rimbor 2.50
56 SI,R:Espionage Squad 2.50
57 SI,R:Khund Legionnaires 2.50
58 SI,D:Laurel Gand 2.50
59 SI,R:Valor,Dawnstar 2.50
60 SI,End of an Era#3 . . . . 2.50
61 SI,End of an Era#6 . . . . 2.50
62 I:New Team 2.50
63 Alien Attack 2.50
64 . . . . 2.50
65 . . . . 2.50
66 I:New Team Members 2.50
67 F:Leviathan 2.50
68 F:Leviathan 2.50
69 V:Durlan 2.50
70 A:Andromeda, Brainiac 5 . . . . . 2.50
71 Planet Trom 2.50
72 . . . . 2.50
73 Sibling Rivalry,pt.1 . . . . 2.50
74 Future Tense,pt2 . . . . 2.50
75 Two Timer,pt.1 (of 2) 2.50
76 F:Valor & Triad 2.50
77 F:Brainiac 5. . . . . 2.50
78 . . . . 2.50

79 Fatal Five attacks 2.50
80 V:Fatal Five. 2.50
81 R:Dirk Morgna. 2.50
82 . . . . 2.50
83 . . . . 2.50
84 . . . . 2.50
85 TPe&TMw(s),LMd,A:Superman,
   back in 20th century 2.50
86 TPe&TMw(s),LMd,Final Night
   tie-in. 2.50
87 TPe&TMw(s),LMd,F:Deadman . . 2.50
88 TPe&TMw(s),LMd,A:Impulse . . . 2.50
89 TPe&TMw(s),LMd, ... 2.50
90 TPe&TMw(s),LMd,V:Dr. Psycho . 2.50
91 TPe&TMw(s),LMd,Legion back
   together, but trapped in
   timestream. 2.50
92 TPe&TMs(s),LMd,Displaced
   in Time. 2.50
93 TPe&TMw(s),MC, All-tragedy
   issue 2.50
94 TPe&TMw(s),LMd,22 short
   pages about the Legion of
   Super-Heroes 2.50
95 MFm,F:Brainiac 5 . . . . 2.50
96 MFm,wedding 2.50
97 TPe,LMd,Genesis tie-in 2.50
98 TPe&TMC,LMd,C.O.M.P.U.TO.
   the Conqueror, pt.1 . . . . 2.50
99 TPe&TMw(s),LMd,Computo, pt.2 . 2.50
100 TPe&TMw,LMd,Computo, pt.3 . 7.50
101 TPe&TMw(s),AD&MFm(c),
   F:Sparks 2.50
102 . . . . 2.50
103 TPe&TMw,AD&MFm(c),Star
   Boy 2.50
104 TPe&TMw,AD&MFm(c),
   changes. 2.50
105 TPe&TMw,AD&MFm(c),
   Adventures in Action x-over . . . 2.50
106 TPe&TMw,AD&MFm(c),Dark
   Circle Rising, x-over pt.2 . . . . . 2.50
107 TPe&TMw,AD&MFm(c),Dark
   Circle Rising, x-over pt.4 . . . . . 2.50
108 TPe&TMw,AD&MFm(c),Dark
   Circle Rising, x-over pt.6 . . . . . 2.50
109 DDv,AD,MFm,F:Violet. 2.50
110 TPe,V:Thunder 2.50
111 TPe&TMw(s),V:Daxamite 2.50
112 TPe&TMw(s),In Space 2.50
113 TPe&TMw(s),Kinetix 2.50
114 TPe&TMw(s),Bizarro
   Legion,pt.1 . . . . 2.50
115 TPe&TMw(s),Bizarro
   Legion, pt.2 . . . . 2.50
116 TPe&TMw(s),V:Pernisius,pt.1 . 2.50
117 TPe&TMw(s),V:Pernisius,pt.2 . . 2.50
118 TPe&TMw(s),V:Pernisius,pt.3 . . 2.50
119 TPe&TMw(s),A:Valor & Phase . 2.50
120 TPe,TMw,V:Fatal Four,pt.1 . . . 2.50
121 TPe,TMw,V:Fatal Five,pt.2 . . . 2.50
122 DAn,ALa,Legion of
   the Damned,pt.1 . . . . 2.50
123 DAn,ALa,Legion of
   the Damned,pt.3 . . . . 2.50
124 DAn,ALa,Legion of the Damned,
   aftermath 2.50
125 DAn,ALa,final issue 2.50
Ann.#1 O:Ultra Boy,V:Glorith 3.50
Ann.#2 O:Valor. 3.50
Ann.#3 N:Timberwolf 4.00
Ann.#4 I:Jamm. 3.50
Ann.#5 SI(c),CDo,MFm,TMc,
   Elseworlds Story 3.75
Ann.#6 Year One Annual + pin-ups . 3.95
Ann.#7 TPe(s),MC,MFm,Legends
   of the Dead Earth 3.50
Spec.#1,000,000 TPe(s),KG,AG . . . 2.50
TPB Great Darkness Saga 17.95
TPB DarknessSaga,no poster 14.95
TPB Legion Archives, rep.#1-#3 . . 39.95

Right margin vertical text: DC COMICS

TPB Legion Archives, rep.#4 . . . . . 49.95
TPB The Beginnings of Tomorrow. 17.95
GN Secret Files, inc.O:Legion 5.00
GN Secret Files #2 . . . . 4.95

LEGION: SCIENCE POLICE
June, 1998

1 (of 4) DvM,PR,JRu,set in
  30th century. 2.50
2 DvM,PR,JRu,Jarik Shadder. 2.50
3 DvM,PR,JRu, ... 2.50
4 DvM,PR,JRu 2.25

LEGION WORLDS
April, 2001

1 (of 6) DAn,ALa. 3.95
2 DAn,ALa 3.95
3 DAn,ALa, On Braal 3.95
4 DAn,ALa, heading for Xanthu . . . 3.95
5 DAn,ALa, SDi, on Steele 3.95
6 DAn,ALa, concl 3.95

Life, The Universe and Everything #1
© DC Comics, Inc.

LIFE, THE UNIVERSE AND EVERYTHING
1996

1 thru 3 Doug Adams adapt. . . . . @6.95

LIGHT BRIGADE, THE
Feb. 2004

1 thru 4 PSj. . . . . @5.95

LIMITED COLLECTORS EDITION
Summer, 1973

21 Shazam. 40.00
22 Tarzan. 30.00
23 House of Mystery 45.00
24 Rudolph, the Red-nosed
  Reindeer 125.00
25 NA,NA(c),Batman 60.00
27 Shazam. 30.00
29 Tarzan. 30.00
31 NA,O:Superman 30.00
32 Ghosts. 50.00
33 Rudolph. 100.00
34 X-Mas with Superheroes 30.00
35 Shazam. 25.00
36 The Bible. 25.00

---

37 Batman 35.00
38 Superman 25.00
39 Secret Origins 25.00
40 Dick Tracy 25.00
41 ATh,Super Friends 25.00
42 Rudolph. 65.00
43 X-mas with Super-Heroes. 25.00
44 NA,Batman 25.00
45 Secret Origins-Super Villians . . 25.00
46 ATh,JLA. 25.00
47 Superman 25.00
48 Superman-Flash Race 25.00
49 Superboy & Legion of
  Super-Heroes 25.00
50 Rudolph. 60.00
51 NA,NA(c),Batman 35.00
52 NA,NA(c),The Best of DC 30.00
57 Welcome Back Kotter 30.00
59 NA,BWr,Batman,1978. . . . . 35.00

LITTLE SHOP OF HORRORS
Feb., 1987

1 GC 2.50

LOBO
[1st Limited Series], 1990–91

1 SBs,Last Czarnian #1 . . . . 4.00
1a 2nd Printing 2.00
2 SBs,Last Czarnian #2 . . . . 3.00
3 SBs,Last Czarnian #3 . . . . 3.00
4 SBs,Last Czarnian #4 . . . . 3.00
Ann.#1 Bloodlines#1,I:Layla 3.75
Lobo Paramilitary X-Mas SBs 5.50
Lobo:Blazing Chain of Love,DCw . . 2.00
TPB Last Czarnian,rep.#1-#4 . . . 9.95
TPB Lobo's Greatest Hits 12.95

[Regular Series], 1993–97

1 VS,Foil(c),V:Dead Boys 3.25
2 VS 3.00
3 VS 2.75
4 VS,Quigly Affair 2.75
5 V:Bludhound 2.50
6 I:Bim Simms. 2.50
7 A:Losers. 2.50
8 A:Losers. 2.50
9 V:Lobo 2.50
10 Preacher 2.50
11 Goldstar vs. Rev.Bo 2.50
12 . . . . 2.50
13 . . . . 2.50
14 Lobo, P.I. 2.50
15 Lobo, P.I.,pt.2 . . . . 2.50
16 Lobo, P.I.,pt.3 . . . . 2.50
17 Lobo, P.I.,pt.4 . . . . 2.50
18 Lobo, P.I.,pt.5 . . . . 2.50
19 . . . . 2.50
20 Toilot Fight 2.50
21 AIG,KON,R:Space Cabby 2.50
22 AIG,UnderworldUnleashed tie-in . 2.50
23 AIG,Stargaze Rally,pt.1 . . . . 2.50
24 AIG,Stargaze Rally,pt.2 . . . . 2.50
25 AIG 2.50
26 AIG,V:Erik the Khund 2.50
27 AIG,V:Billy Krono 2.50
28 AIG,A:Great Big Fat Bastiches . . 2.50
29 . . . . 2.50
30 . . . . 2.50
31 . . . . 2.50
32 AIG(s),Lobo attends a seance,
  frags himself 2.50
33 AIG(s),Lobo returns from spirit
  world 2.50
34 AIG(s),vs. Japan, whaling, ... 2.50
35 AIG(s), Deathtrek 2.50
36 . . . . 2.50
37 AIG(s),BKi,Lobo's Guide to Girls 2.50
38 AIG(s),Bomandi The Last Boy
  on Earth. 2.50

---

39 AIG(s),In the Belly of the
  Behemoth,pt. 1 . . . . 2.50
40 AIG(s),Belly of Behemoth,pt.2. . 2.50
41 AIG(s),roommates 2.50
42 AIG(s),A:Perfidia 2.50
43 AIG(s),A:Jonas 2.50
44 AIG(s),Genesis tie-in 2.50
45 AIG(s),battle royale 2.50
46 AIG(s),Jackie Chin 2.50
47 AIG(s),V:Kiljoy Riggs. 2.50
48 AIG(s),F:the penguins 2.50
49 AIG(s) 2.50
50 AIG(s),war on DC universe 2.50
51 AIG(s),Slater and Candy. 2.50
52 AIG(s),Goldstar funeral 2.50
53 AIG(s),disrupted ceremony 2.50
54 AIG(s),Good Vibes machine . . . 2.50
55 AIG(s),Sheepworld 2.50
56 AIG(s),MPn,GLz,the wedding . . 2.50
57 AIG(s),MPn, GLz, Intergalactic
  Police convention 2.50
58 KG&AIG(s) 2.50
59 AIG(s),V:Bad Wee Bastards . . . 2.50
60 AIG(s),All-New, Nonviolent
  Adventures of Superbo, pt.1 . . . 2.50
61 AIG(s),Superbo, pt.2 . . . . 2.50
62 AIG(s),Superbo, pt.3 . . . . 2.50
63 AIG(s),Soul Brothers,pt.1 . . . . . 2.50
64 AIG(s),Soul Brothers,pt.2 . . . . . 2.50
Ann.#1 Bloodlines 4.00
Ann.#2 Elseworlds Story 3.50
Ann.#3 AIG Year One. 4.95
Spec.#1,000,000 AIG(s),GLz 2.50
Spec. Lobo's Big Babe Spring Break,
  Miss Voluptuous Contest. 2.50
Spec. Blazing Chains of Love 2.00
Spec. Bounty Hunting for Fun
  and Profit, F:Fanboy 4.95
Spec. Lobo: Chained AIG(s),
  Lobo in prison 2.50
Spec. Lobo/Demon: Hellowe'en,
  AIG(s),VGi 2.25
Spec. Lobo In the Chair, AIG(s) . . . 2.25
Spec. Lobo:I Quit,AIG,
  nicotine withdrawal 2.25
Spec. Lobo/Judge Dredd: Psycho
  Bikers vs. Mutants From Hell . . 5.00
Spec. Lobo: Portrait of a Victim
  VS,I:John Doe 2.25
GN Fragtastic Voyage AGr,
  miniaturized 6.00
TPB Lobo's Back's Back 10.00
TPB Lobo's Greatest Hits 13.00
Convention Special, comic con 2.00

Lobo #4 © DC Comics, Inc.

LOBO: A CONTRACT ON GAWD
1994
1 AlG(s),KD. 2.50
2 AlG(s),KD,A:Dave 2.50
3 AlG(s),KD. 2.50
4 AlG(s),KD,Final Issue 2.50

LOBO'S BACK
1992
1 SBs,w/3(c) inside,V:Loo. 2.50
1a 2nd printing 2.00
2 SBs,Lobo becomes a woman . . . 2.50
3 SBs,V:Heaven 2.50
4 SBs,V:Heaven 2.50
TPB GF(c),rep.#1-#4 . . . . 10.00

LOBO: DEATH & TAXES
[Mini-Series], Aug., 1996
1 (of 4) KG&AlG(s) 2.25
2 KG&AlG(s),Interstellar Revenue
  learns Lobo doesn't pay taxes . 2.25
3 KG&AlG(s),Lobo walks into
  IRS trap 2.25
4 KG&AlG(s),Lobo destroys IRS . . 2.25

LOBO: INFANTICIDE
1992–93
1 KG,V:Su,Lobo Bastards. 2.50
2 Lobo at Boot Camp 2.50
3 KG,Lobo Vs.his offspring 2.50
4 KG,V:Lobo Bastards. 2.50

LOBO/MASK
1 AlG&JAr(s),DoM,Kwi, humorous
  x-over. 6.00
2 AlG&JAr(s),DoM,Kwi, concl. 6.00

LOBO: UNAMERICAN GLADIATORS
1993
1 CK,V:Satan's Brothers. 2.50
2 CK,V:Jonny Caesar 2.50
3 CK,MMi(c),V:Satan Brothers 2.50
4 CK,MMi(c),V:Jonny Caeser 2.50

LOBO UNBOUND
June 2003
1 (of 6) mass-murder 3.00
2 thru 6 . . . . @3.00

LOBOCOP
1 StG(s). 2.25

LOIS AND CLARK: THE NEW ADVENTURES OF SUPERMAN
TPB 10.00
TPB stories that became episodes 10.00

LOIS LANE
Aug., 1986
1 and 2 GM. . . . . @3.00

LONG HOT SUMMER, THE
Milestone, 1995
[Mini-Series]
1 Blood Syndicate v. G.R.I.N.D. . . . 3.00
2 A:Icon,Xombi,Hardware. 2.50

LOONEY TUNES MAG.
1 thru 6 . . . . @2.00

LOONEY TUNES
1994
1 thru 6 Warner Bros. cartoons. . @3.00
7 thru 11 Warner Bros. . . . . @3.00
12 thru 25. . . . . @2.50
26 thru 119 . . . . @2.25
Spec. Back in Action: Movie . . . 4.00

Loose Cannon #1 © DC Comics Inc.

LOOSE CANNON
[Mini-Series], 1995
1 AdP,V:Bounty Hunters 2.50
2 V:Bounty Hunters & The
  Eradicator 2.25
3 A:Eradicator. 2.25

LORDS OF THE ULTRAREALM
1986
1 PB 3.50
2 PB 2.25
3 thru 6 PB . . . . @2.25
Spec.#1 PB,DG,Oneshot 2.25

LOSERS
DC/Vertigo June 2003
1 crime espionage 4.00
2 thru 6 Goliath,pt.1–pt.5 . . . . . . @3.50
7 SMa,Downtime,pt.1 . . . . 3.00
8 SMa,Downtime,pt.2 . . . . 3.00
9 Island Life,pt.1 . . . . 3.00
10 Island Life,pt.2 . . . . 3.00
11 Island Life,pt.3. . . . . 3.00
12 Island Life,pt.4 . . . . 3.00
13 Sheikdown,pt.1 . . . . 3.00
14 Sheikdown,pt.2 . . . . 3.00
15 F:Aisha 3.00
16 The Pass,pt.1 . . . . 3.00
17 The Pass,pt.2 . . . . 3.00
TPB Ante Up 10.00

LOSERS SPECIAL
1985
1 Crisis,D:Losers 4.00

LUCIFER
DC/Vertigo, Apr., 2000
1 Lucifer strugles to regain power . 6.00
2 Living Tarot Deck. 4.00
3 V:Jill Presto 4.00
4 WaP,F:Elaine Belloc. 4.00

5 PrG,House of Windowless
  Rooms,pt.1 . . . . 3.00
6 PrG,Windowless Rooms,pt.2 . . . 3.00
7 PrG,Windowless Rooms,pt.3 . . . 3.00
8 PrG,Windowless Rooms,pt.4 . . . 3.00
9 Immortality 3.00
10 Children & Monsters,pt.1 . . . . . 3.00
11 Children & Monsters,pt.2 . . . . . 2.50
12 Children & Monsters,pt.3 . . . . . 2.50
13 Children & Monsters,pt.4 . . . . . 2.50
14 Triptych 2.50
15 Triptych,Two Edge Sword 2.50
16 Triptych,Ancestral Deed 2.50
17 Dalliance with the Dead,pt.1. . . . 2.50
18 Dalliance with the Dead,pt.2. . . . 2.50
19 Dalliance with the Dead,pt.3. . . . 2.50
20 The Thunder Sermon 2.50
21 Paradiso,pt.1. . . . . 2.50
22 Paradiso,pt.2. . . . . 2.50
23 Paradiso,pt.3. . . . . 2.50
24 The Writing on the Wall 2.50
25 Purgatorio,pt.1. . . . . 2.50
26 Purgatorio,pt.2 . . . . 2.50
27 Purgatorio,pt.3 . . . . 2.50
28 F:Gaudium 2.50
29 MCy,Inferno,pt.1 . . . . 2.50
30 MCy,Inferno,pt.2 . . . . 2.50
31 MCy,Inferno,pt.3 . . . . 2.50
32 MCy,Inferno,pt.4 . . . . 2.50
33 MCy,robbery 2.50
34 MCy,Come to Judgment,pt.1 . . . 2.50
35 MCy,Come to Judgment,pt.2 . . . 2.50
36 MCy,Naglfar,pt.1 . . . . 2.50
37 MCy,Naglfar,pt.2 . . . . 2.50
38 MCy,Naglfar,pt.3 . . . . 2.50
39 MCy,Naglfar,pt.4 . . . . 2.50
40 MCy,Naglfar,pt.5 . . . . 2.50
41 MCy,Sisters of Mercy 2.50
42 MCy,Brothers in Arms,pt.1 . . . . 2.50
43 MCy,Brothers in Arms,pt.2 . . . . 2.50
44 MCy,Brothers in Arms,pt.3 . . . . 2.50
45 MCy(s)F:John Sewell 2.50
46 Stitchglass Slide,pt.1. . . . . 2.50
47 Stitchglass Slide,pt.2. . . . . 2.50
48 Stitchglass Slide,pt.3. . . . . 2.50
49 Stitchflass Slide,pt.4 . . . . 2.50
50 CR,48-pg. 3.50
51 Wolf Beneath the Tree,pt.1 . . . . . 2.50
52 Wolf Beneath the Tree,pt.2. . . . . 2.50
53 Wolf Beneath the Tree,pt.3. . . . . 2.50
54 Wolf Beneath the Tree,pt.4. . . . . 2.50
55 MCy,MaH,new religion 2.50
TPB Devil in the Gateway 15.00
TPB Children and Monsters. 18.00
TPB A Dalliance with the Damned. 15.00
TPB The Divine Comedy 18.00
TPB Lucifer: Inferno. 15.00
TPB Mansions of the Silence 15.00
GN Nirvana, 48-pg. 6.00

MADAME XANADU
1981
1 MR/BB 5.00

MAJESTIC
Aug. 2004
1 (of 4) KIK,F:Mr.Majestic. 3.00
2 KIK 3.00
3 KIK. 3.00

MAJOR BUMMER
June, 1997
1 JAr(s),DoM,I:Major Bummer 2.50
2 JAr(s),DoM,Major Bummer gets
  new costume 2.50
3 JAr(s),DoM,bad guys arrive. 2.50
4 JAr(s),DoM,alien germs. 2.50
5 JAr(s),DoM,dinosaurs, Nazis. . . . 2.50
6 JAr(s),DoM,Mutant bully 2.50

DC COMICS

7 JAr(s),DoM. 2.50	16 V:Outlaw 2.25	8 JOs(s),TMd,A:JLA,pt.3 . . . . 2.50
8 . . . . 2.50	17 In Gotham,A:Batman 2.25	9 JOs(s),TMd,A:JLA,pt.4 . . . . 2.50
9 JAr(s),DoM,epic fight 2.50	18 Saints & Sinners,pt.1,R:Dumas . 2.25	10 JOs(s),A:Fire. 2.50
10 JAr(s),DoM,Nunzio dead? 2.50	19 Saints & Sinners,pt.2,V:Dumas. . 2.25	11 JOs,PNe,BHi, ... 2.50
11 JAr(s),DoM,everyone dies? 2.50	20 Saints & Sinners,pt.3,V:Dumas. . 2.25	12 JOs,TMd,Day of Judgment
12 JAr(s),DoM,Lou Martin dead. . . . 2.50	21 Saints & Sinners,pt.4,	x-over. 2.50
13 JAr(s),DoM,Lauren 2.50	A:Manhunter Grandmaster 2.25	13 JOs,TMd,Rings of Saturn,pt.1 . 2.50
14 JAr(s),DoM,tells the future off. . . 2.50	22 Saints & Sinners,pt.5,	14 JOs,TMd,Rings of Saturn,pt.2 . 2.50
15 JAr(s),DoM, final issue 2.50	A:Manhunter Grandmaster 2.25	15 JOs,TMd,Rings of Saturn,pt.3 . 2.50
	23 Saints & Sinners,pt.6,V:Dumas. . 2.25	16 JOs,TMd,Rings of Saturn,pt.4 . 2.50
### MAN-BAT	24 DG,Showdown, final issue 2.25	17 JOs,TMd,Rings of Saturn,pt.5 . 2.50
1975–76	**[2nd Series], 1994–95**	18 JOs,TMd,V:Kanto 2.50
1 SD,AM,A:Batman. 30.00	0 . . . . 2.50	19 JOs,TMd,defeated, captured . . . 2.50
2 V:The Ten-Eyed Man 25.00	1 . . . . 2.50	20 JOs,TMd,year one on earth 2.50
Reprint NA(c) 15.00	2 N:Wild Huntsman. 2.50	21 JOs,TT,A:Abin Sur 2.50
	3 V:Malig. 2.50	22 JOs,TMd,A:Batman. 2.50
### MAN-BAT	4 Necrodyne 2.50	23 JOs,TMd,F:Spectre. 2.50
1996	5 V:Skin Walker 2.50	24 JOs,TMd,F:Just.Leag.Int. 2.50
1 CDi,terrorizes city 2.25	6 V:Barbarian,Incarnate 2.50	25 JOs,TMd,F:Gypsy 2.50
2 . . . . 2.25	7 V:Incarnate,A:White Lotus	26 JOs,TMd,Renegades of Mars. . 2.50
3 CDi,V:Steeljacket, finale 2.25	& Capt. Atom. 2.25	27 JOs,TMd,Renegades of Mars. . . 2.50
	8 V:Butcher Boys 2.25	28 JOs,TMd,at Stonehenge 2.50
### MAN-BAT vs. BATMAN	9 V:Butcher Boys 2.25	29 JOs,TMd,telepath 2.50
1 NA,DG,reprint. 4.00	10 V:Necrodyne 2.25	30 JOs,TMd,Altered Egos,pt.1. . . . . 2.50
	11 Return of Old Enemy 2.25	31 JOs,TMd,Altered Egos,pt.2. . . . . 2.50
### A MAN CALLED	12 Underworld Unleashed, finale. . . 2.25	32 TMd,V:Bloodworms of Mars . . . 2.50
### AX		33 TMd,J'onn J'onzz hidden life . . . 2.50
Aug., 1997	### MANHUNTER	34 JOs,V:Darkseid. 2.50
1 MWn(s),SwM, part rep. 2.50	**Aug. 2004**	35 JOs,V:Malefic 2.50
2 thru 8 MWn(s),SwM, ... @2.50	1 JP,JLe(c),Identity Crisis 2.50	36 JOs,final issue 2.50
	2 thru 3 JP,JLe(c) . . . . @2.50	Ann.#1 TT,AOI,BWr,Ghosts x-over . 3.00
### MANHUNTER		Ann.#2 AAd(c),JLApe:Gorilla
1988–90	### MAN OF STEEL	Warfare 3.00
1 from Millennium-Suicide Squad. . 2.50	**1986**	Spec.#1,000,000 JOs,TMd 2.00
2 in Tokyo,A:Dumas 2.25	1 JBy,DG,I:Modern Superman 7.00	
3 The Yakuza,V:Dumas 2.25	1a 2nd edition 7.00	
4 Secrets Revealed-Manhunter,	2 JBy,DG,R:Lois Lane. 5.00	
Dumas & Olivia 2.25	3 JBy,DG,A:Batman 5.00	
5 A:Silvia Kandery. 2.25	4 JBy,DG,V:Lex Luther 5.00	
6 A:Argent,contd.Suicide Squad	5 JBy,DG,I:Modern Bizarro 5.00	
Annual #1 . . . . 2.25	6 JBy,DG,A:Lana Lang 5.00	
7 Vlatavia, V:Count Vertigo. 2.25	TPB rep. Man of Steel #1–#6 . . . . 20.00	
8 FS,A:Flash,Invasion x-over 2.25	TPBa 2nd printing 8.00	
9 FS,Invasion Aftermath extra		
(contd from Flash #22) 2.25	### MANY LOVES OF	
10 Salvage,pt.1 . . . . 2.25	### DOBIE GILLIS	
11 Salvage,pt.2 . . . . 2.25	**May-June, 1960**	
12. . . . . 2.25	1 . . . . 300.00	
13 V:Catman 2.25	2 . . . . 150.00	
14 Janus Directive #5 . . . . 2.25	3 . . . . 100.00	
15 I:Mirage. 2.25	4 . . . . 100.00	
	5 thru 9 . . . . @75.00	
	10 thru 25 . . . . @75.00	
	26 Oct., 1964 . . . . 75.00	

Mask #6 © DC Comics, Inc.

MARTIAN MANHUNTER
1988

1 A:JLI. 3.00
2 A:JLI,V:Death God 2.50
3 V:Death God,A:Dr.Erdel. 2.50
4 A:JLI,final issue 2.50

MASK
Dec., 1985

1 HC(c),TV tie-in,I:Mask Team 2.50
2 HC(c),In Egypt,V:Venom 2.50
3 HC(c),Anarchy in the U.K. 2.50
4 HC(c),V:Venom, final issue,
March, 1986 . . . . 2.50

[Mini-Series]

1 EB,American Secrets #1 . . . . 5.25
2 EB,American Secrets #2 . . . . 5.25
3 EB,American Secrets #3 . . . . 5.25

[2nd Series], Feb.–Oct., 1987

1 CS/KS,reg.series 2.50
2 CS/KS,V:Venom. 2.50
3 CS/KS,V:Venom. 2.50
4 CS/KS,V:Venom. 2.50
5 CS/KS,Mask operatives hostage . 2.50
6 CS/KS,I:Jacana 2.50
7 CS/KS,Mask gone bad? 2.50
8 CS/KS,Matt Trakker,V:Venom . . . 2.50
9 CS/KS,V:Venom, last issue 2.50

MARTIAN MANHUNTER
Aug., 1998

0 JOs,TMd,A:Batman,Superman . . 3.00
1 JOs,TMd,V:Headman 2.50
2 JOs,TMd,V:Antares 2.50
3 JOs,TMd,V:Bette Noir 2.50
4 JOs,TMd,J'emm, Son of Saturn . 2.50
5 JAr,JD,A:Chase 2.50
6 JOs,TMd,A:JLA,pt.1. . . . . 2.50
7 JOs(s),TMd,A:JLA,pt.2 . . . . 2.50

Manhunter #21 © DC Comics, Inc.

MASTERS OF THE UNIVERSE
May, 1986
1 GT,AA,O:He-Man. 6.00
2 GT,AA,V:Skeletor. 5.00
3 GT,V:Skeletor. 5.00

MASTERWORKS SERIES OF GREAT COMIC BOOK ARTISTS
May, 1983
1 . . . . 5.00
2 . . . . 4.00
3 Dec., 1983. . . . . 4.00

'MAZING MAN
Jan., 1986
1 I:Maze 3.00
2 . . . . 2.50
3 . . . . 2.50
4 . . . . 2.50
5 . . . . 2.50
6 Shea Stadium 2.50
7 Shea Stadium 2.50
8 Cat-Sitting 2.50
9 Bank Hold-up. 2.50
10. . . . . 2.50
11 Jones Beach 2.50
12 FM(c),last issue, Dec., 1986. . . . 3.00
Spec.#1 . . . . 2.25
Spec.#2 . . . . 2.25
Spec.#3 KB/TM 2.25

MEN OF WAR
Aug., 1977
1 I:Gravedigger,Code Name:
  Gravedigger,I:Enemy Ace 20.00
2 JKu(c),The Five-Walled War . . . 10.00
3 JKu(c),The Suicide Strategem. . 10.00
4 JKu(c),Trail by Fire 10.00
5 JKu(c),Valley of the Shadow . . . 10.00
6 JKu(c),A Choice of Deaths 10.00
7 JKu(c),Milkrun 10.00
8 JKu(c),Death-Stroke 10.00
9 JKu(c),Gravedigger-R.I.P. 10.00
10 JKu(c),Crossroads 10.00
11 JKu(c),Berkstaten 8.00
12 JKu(c),Where Is Gravedigger?. . 8.00
13 JKu(c),Project Gravedigger -
   Plus One 8.00
14 JKu(c),The Swirling
   Sands of Death 8.00
15 JKu(c),The Man With the
   Opened Eye 8.00
16 JKu(c),Hide and Seek The Spy . 8.00
17 JKu(c),The River of Death 8.00
18 JKu(c),The Amiens Assault. . . . 8.00
19 JKu(c),An Angel Named Marie . . 8.00
20 JKu(c),Cry:Jerico 8.00
21 JKu(c),Home-Is Where
   The Hell Is 8.00
22 JKu(c),Blackout On
   The Boardwalk 8.00
23 JKu(c),Mission: Six Feet Under . 8.00
24 JKu&DG(c),The Presidential
   Peril 8.00
25 GE(c),Save the President. 8.00
26 March, 1980 . . . . 8.00

MENZ INSANA
DC/Vertigo, 1998
GN JBo 8.00

MERCY
DC/Vertigo, 1993
Graphic Novel I:Mercy. 8.00

Metal Men #42 © DC Comics Inc.

METAL MEN
1965–78
[1st Regular Series]
1 RA,I:Missile Men 900.00
2 RA,Robot of Terror. 300.00
3 RA,Moon's Invisible Army 200.00
4 RA,Bracelet of Doomed Hero . 200.00
5 RA,Menace of the Mammoth
  Robots 200.00
6 RA,I:Gas Gang 150.00
7 RA,V:Solar Brain 125.00
8 RA,Playground of Terror 125.00
9 RA,A:Billy. 125.00
10 RA,A:Gas Gang 125.00
11 RA,The Floating Furies. 125.00
12 RA,A:Missle Men 100.00
13 RA,I:Nameless 100.00
14 RA,A:Chemo. 100.00
15 RA,V:B.O.L.T.S. 100.00
16 RA,Robots for Sale 100.00
17 JKu(c),RA,V:Bl.Widow Robot . 100.00
18 JKu(c),RA 100.00
19 RA,V:Man-Horse of Hades . . . 100.00
20 RA,V:Dr.Yes 100.00
21 RA,C:Batman & Robin,Flash
   Wonder Woman. 75.00
22 RA,A:Chemo 75.00
23 RA,A:Sizzler 75.00
24 RA,V:Balloonman 75.00
25 RA,V:Chemo 75.00
26 RA,V:Metal Mods 75.00
27 RA,O:Metal Men,rtd 100.00
28 RA. 75.00
29 RA,V:Robot Eater 75.00
30 RA,GK,in the Forbidden Zone . 75.00
31 RA,GK. 50.00
32 RA,Robot Amazon Blues 50.00
33 MS,The Hunted Metal Men. . . . 50.00
34 MS. 50.00
35 MS. 50.00
36 MS,The Cruel Clowns. 50.00
37 MS,To walk among Men 50.00
38 MS. 50.00
39 MS,Beauty of the Beast 50.00
40 MS. 50.00
41 MS. 50.00
42 RA,reprint 20.00
43 RA,reprint 20.00
44 RA,reprint,V:Missile Men 20.00
45 WS 20.00
46 WS,V:Chemo 20.00
47 WS,V:Plutonium Man 20.00
48 WS,A:Eclipso 22.00
49 WS,A:Eclipso 22.00
50 WS,JSa. 15.00
51 JSn,V:Vox 15.00
52 JSn,V:Brain Children. 15.00
53 JA(c),V:Brain Children 15.00
54 JSn,A:Green Lantern 15.00
55 JSn,A:Green Lantern 15.00
56 JSn,V:Inheritor 15.00
[Limited Series], 1993–94
1 DJu,BBr,Foil(c). 5.00
2 DJu,BBr,O:Metal Men 3.00
3 DJu,BBr,V:Missile Men 3.00
4 DJu,BBr,final issue. 3.00

METAMORPHO
July-Aug., 1965
[Regular Series]
1 A:Kurt Vornok. 200.00
2 Terror from the Telstar 100.00
3 Who stole the USA 100.00
4 V:Cha-Cha Chaves 75.00
5 V:Bulark 75.00
6 . . . . 75.00
7 thru 9 . . . . @50.00
10 I:Element Girl 70.00
11 thru 17 March-April, 1968 . . . @45.00
[Mini-Series], 1993
1 GN,V:The Orb of Ra 2.50
2 GN,A:Metamorpho's Son. 2.50
3 GN,V:Elemental Man. 2.50
4 GN,final Issue 2.50

METROPOLIS S.C.U.
Nov., 1994
1 Special Police unit 2.25
2 Eco-terror in Metropolis 2.25
3 Superman 2.25
4 final issue. 2.25

MICHAEL MOORCOCK'S MULTIVERSE
DC/Helix, Sept., 1997
1 WS,three stories, inc. Eternal
  Champion adapt. 2.50
2 WS,Eternal Champion 2.50
3 WS,Moonbeams & Roses 2.50
4 WS,Moonbeams & Roses 2.50
5 . . . . 2.50
6 Duke Elric 2.50
7 Metatemporal Detective. 2.50
8 Castle Silverskin 2.50
9 Duke Elric 2.50
10 Eternal Champion. 2.50
11 WS, Silverskin. 2.50
12 WS, concl. 2.50
TPB rep. #1–#12 . . . . 20.00

MIDNIGHT, MASS
DC/Vertigo, April, 2002
1 JRz,F:Adam & Julia. 2.50
2 JRz,a lone farmhouse 2.50
3 JRz,JP 2.50
4 JRz,JP,The Four Sisters,pt.1 . . . 2.50
5 JRz,JP,The Four Sisters,pt.2 . . . 2.50
6 JRz,JP,The Four Sisters,pt.3 . . . 2.50
7 JRz,JP,3 uninvited visitors 2.50
8 JRz,Secrets 2.50

MIDNIGHT, MASS: HERE THERE BE MONSTERS
DC/Vertigo Jan. 2004
1 (of 6) 3.00
2 thru 6 . . . . @3.00

All comics prices listed are for *Near Mint* condition.

MILLENNIUM
Jan., 1988
1 JSa,SEt, The Plan 3.00
2 JSa,SEt, The Chosen 2.50
3 JSa,SEt, Reagen/Manhunters . . . 2.50
4 JSa,SEt, Mark Shaw/Batman . . . 2.50
5 JSa,SEt, The Chosen 2.50
6 JSa,SEt, Superman 2.50
7 JSa,SEt, Boster Gold. 2.50
8 JSa,SEt,I:New Guardians 2.50

MILLENNIUM FEVER
1995–96
1 Young Love 2.50
2 Nightmares Worsen 2.50
3 Worst Nightmare 2.50
4 . . . . 2.50

MINX, THE
DC/Vertigo, Aug., 1998
1 PrM,SeP,The Chosen, pt.1 . . . . . 3.00
2 PrM,SeP,The Chosen, pt.2 . . . . . 2.50
3 PrM,SeP,The Chosen, pt.3 . . . . . 2.50
4 PrM,SeP,Monkey Quartet,pt.1 . . . 2.50
5 PrM,SeP,Monkey Quartet,pt.2 . . . 2.50
6 PrM,SeP,Monkey Quartet,pt.3 . . . 2.50
7 PrM,SeP,Monkey Quartet,pt.4 . . . 2.50
8 PrM,SeP,final issue 2.50

MISTER E
1991
1 (From Books of Magic) 2.50
2 A:The Shadower 2.50
3 A:The Shadower 2.50
4 A:Tim Hunter, Dr. Fate, Phantom
   Stranger, final issue 2.50

MISTER MIRACLE
1971–78
1 JK,I:Mr.Miracle 100.00
2 JK,I:Granny Goodness 50.00
3 JK,Paraniod Pill 50.00
4 JK,I:Barda 55.00
5 JK,I:Vermin Vundabar 55.00
6 JK,I:Female Furies. 55.00
7 JK,V:Kanto 55.00
8 JK,V:Lump 55.00
9 JK,O:Mr.Miracle,C:Darkseid . . . 25.00
10 JK,A:Female Furies 25.00
11 JK,V:Doctor Bedlum 25.00
12 JK,Mystivac 25.00
13 JK,The Dictator's Dungeon 25.00

Mister Miracle #17 © DC Comics, Inc.

14 JK,I:Madame Evil Eye 25.00
15 JK,O:Shilo Norman 25.00
16 JK,F:Shilo Norman 25.00
17 JK,Murder Lodge 25.00
18 JK,W:Mr.Miracle & Barda 25.00
19 MR,NA,DG,TA,JRu,AM 25.00
20 MR 10.00
21 MR 10.00
22 MR 10.00
23 MG 10.00
24 MG,RH 10.00
25 MG,RH 10.00
Spec.#1 SR 3.50

[2nd Series], 1989–91
1 IG,O:Mister Miracle 3.00
2 IG. 2.50
3 IG,A:Highfather,Forever People . 2.50
4 IG,A:The Dark,Forever People . . 2.50
5 IG,V:TheDark,A:Forever People . 2.50
6 A:G.L. Gnort 2.50
7 A:Blue Beetle,Booster Gold 2.50
8 RM,A:Blue Beetle,Booster Gold . 2.50
9 I:Maxi-Man 2.50
10 V:Maxi-Man 2.50
11 . . . . 2.50
12 . . . . 2.50
13 Manga Khan Saga begins,
   A:L-Ron,A:Lobo 3.00
14 A:Lobo. 2.50
15 Manga Khan cont. 2.50
16 MangaKhan cont.,JLA#39tie-in. . 2.50
17 On Apokolips,A:Darkseid 2.50
18 On Apokolips 2.50
19 Return to Earth, contd
   from JLA#42 . . . . 2.50
20 IG,Oberon 2.50
21 Return of Shilo 2.50
22 New Mr.Miracle revealed 2.50
23 Secrets of the 2 Mr. Miracles
   revealed, A:Mother Box 2.50
24 . . . . 2.50
25 . . . . 2.50
26 Monster Party,pt.1 . . . . 2.50
27 Monster Party,pt.2,
   A:Justice League. 2.50
28 final issue 2.50

[3rd Series], 1996
1 JK, new mythology 2.25
2 V:Justice League 2.25
2 How can Scott Free save
   Big Barda. 2.25
3 accepts his powers 2.25
4 corruption throughout
   the cosmos 2.25
5 SCr. 2.25
6 SCr. 2.25
7 SCr,final issue 2.25
TPB Jack Kirby's Mister Miracle . . 13.00

MR. DISTRICT ATTORNEY
Jan.–Feb., 1948
1 The Innocent Forger. 1,400.00
2 The Richest Man In Prison . . . 600.00
3 The Honest Convicts 400.00
4 The Merchant of Death 400.00
5 The Booby-Trap Killer 400.00
6 The D.A. Meets Scotland Yard 350.00
7 The People vs. Killer Kane . . . 350.00
8 The Rise and Fall of 'Lucky'
   Lynn. 350.00
9 The Case of the Living
   Counterfeit. 350.00
10 The D.A. Takes a Vacation . . 250.00
11 The Game That Has
   No Winners 250.00
12 Fake Accident Racket. 250.00
13 The Execution of Caesar
   Larsen 250.00

14 The Innocent Man In
   Murderers' Row 250.00
15 Prison Train. 250.00
16 The Wire Tap Crimes 250.00
17 The Bachelor of Crime 250.00
18 The Case of the Twelve
   O'Clock Killer. 250.00
19 The Four King's Of Crime . . . 250.00
20 You Catch a Killer 250.00
21 I Was A Killer's Bodyguard . . 175.00
22 The Marksman of Crime 175.00
23 Diary of a Criminal 175.00
24 The Killer In The Iron Mask . . 175.00
25 I Hired My Killer 175.00
26 The Case of the Wanted
   Criminals 175.00
27 The Case of the Secret Six . . 175.00
28 Beware the Bogus Beggars . . 175.00
29 The Crimes of Mr. Jumbo . . . 175.00
30 Man of a Thousand Faces . . . 175.00
31 The Hot Money Gang 175.00
32 The Case o/t Bad Luck Clues. 175.00
33 A Crime Is Born. 175.00
34 The Amazing Crimes of Mr. X. 175.00
35 This Crime For Hire 175.00
36 The Chameleon of Crime 175.00
37 Miss Miller's Big Case 175.00
38 The Puzzle Shop For Crime . . 175.00
39 Man Who Killed Daredevils . . 175.00
40 The Human Vultures. 175.00
41 The Great Token Take 175.00
42 Super-Market Sleuth. 175.00
43 Hotel Detective 175.00
44 S.S. Justice,B:Comics Code. . 150.00
45 Miss Miller, Widow 150.00
46 Mr. District Attorney,
   Public Defender. 150.00
47 The Missing Persons Racket . 150.00
48 Manhunt With the Mounties . . 150.00
49 The TV Dragnet 150.00
50 The Case of Frank Bragan,
   Little Shot 150.00
51 The Big Heist 150.00
52 Crooked Wheels of Fortune . . 150.00
53 The Courtroom Patrol. 150.00
54 The Underworld Spy Squad . . 150.00
55 The Flying Saucer Mystery . . . 150.00
56 The Underworld Oracle. 150.00
57 The Underworld Employment
   Agency. 150.00
58 The Great Bomb Scare. 150.00
59 Great Underworld Spy Plot . . . 150.00
60 The D.A.'s TV Rival 150.00
61 SMo(c),Architect of Crime. . . . 150.00
62 A-Bombs For Sale. 150.00
63 The Flying Prison 150.00
64 SMo(c),The Underworld
   Treasure Hunt 150.00
65 SMo(c),World Wide Dragnet. . 150.00
66 SMo(c),The Secret of the
   D.A.'s Diary 150.00
67 Jan.–Feb., 1959 . . . . 150.00

MOBFIRE
1994–95
1 WaP,Gangsters in London 2.50
2 WaP,. 2.50
3 WaP,The Bocor 2.50
4 WaP,V:Bocor 2.50
5 WaP,Voice in My Head 2.50
6 WaP,Genetic Babies, final issue . 2.50

MODESTY BLAISE
1 DG,V:Gabriel 5.00
2 DG,V:Gabriel 5.00
GN Spy Thriller 20.00

MONOLITH, THE
Feb. 2004
1 JP(s),56-pg. 3.50
2 JP(s) 3.00
3 JP(s),Heart of Stone 3.00
4 JP(s),Last Rites,pt.1 . . . . 3.00
5 JP(s),Last Rites,pt.2 . . . . 3.00
6 JP(s),Friendly Fire,pt.1 . . . . 3.00
7 JP(s),Friendly Fire,pt.2 . . . . 3.00
8 JP(s),Friendly Fire,pt.3 . . . . 3.00
9 JP(s),gangsters retaliate 3.00

MOONSHADOW
DC/Vertigo, 1994–95
1 JMD(s),JMu,rep. 2.50
2 thru 4 JMD . . . . @2.50
5 fully painted 2.50
6 . . . . 2.50
7 F:Shady Lady. 2.50
8 Rep. Search for Ira 2.50
9 JMD,JMu,A:Tittletat Twins 2.50
10 JMD,JMu,Interplanetary
   Prostitutes 2.50
11 JMu,Ira's life story 2.50
12 Rep. w/6pg new material 3.50

MORE FUN COMICS
See: NEW FUN COMICS

MOVIE COMICS
1939
1 Gunga Din. 4,500.00
2 Stagecoach. 3,000.00
3 East Side of Heaven. 2,500.00
4 Captain Fury,B:Oregon Trail . 1,800.00
5 Man in the Iron Mask 1,800.00
6 Phantom Creeps. 2,500.00

Ms. Tree Quarterly #2
© DC Comics, Inc.

MS. TREE QUARTERLY
1990
1 MGr,A:Batman 5.00
2 A:Butcher 4.00
3 A:Butcher 4.00
4 Paper Midnight. 4.50
5 Murder/Rape Investigation. 4.50
6 Gothic House. 4.50
7 The Family Way 4.50
8 CI,FMc,Ms Tree Pregnant(c),
   B.U. King Faraday 4.50
9 Child Kidnapped 4.50
10 V:International Mob. 4.00

MUCHA LUCHA
April 2003
1 (of 3) 2.25
2 It's All Buena 2.25
3 Flea loses match 2.25

MUKTUK WOLFSBREATH:
HARD-BOILED SHAMAN
DC/Vertigo, June, 1998
1 (of 3) TLa,SvP,Lady Shaman. . . . 2.50
2 . . . . 2.50
3 TLa,SvP, concl. 2.50

MUTT AND JEFF
1939
1 . . . . 1,500.00
2 . . . . 750.00
3 Bucking Broncos 550.00
4 and 5 . . . . @500.00
6 thru 10 . . . . @250.00
11 thru 20 . . . . @175.00
21 thru 30 . . . . @125.00
31 thru 50 . . . . @100.00
51 thru 70 . . . . @75.00
71 thru 80 . . . . @65.00
81 thru 99 . . . . @50.00
100 . . . . 65.00
101 thru 103 . . . . @50.00
104 thru 148 . . . . @45.00

MY FAITH IN FRANKIE
DC/Vertigo Jan. 2004
1 (of 4) MaH 3.00
2 thru 4 MaH . . . . @3.00
TPB 7.00

MY GREATEST
ADVENTURE
Jan.–Feb., 1955
1 LSt,I Was King Of
   Danger Island 2,200.00
2 My Million Dollar Dive 900.00
3 I Found Captain
   Kidd's Treasure 600.00
4 I Had A Date With Doom 600.00
5 I Escaped From Castle Morte . 500.00
6 I Had To Spend A Million 500.00
7 I Was A Prisoner On Island X . 475.00
8 The Day They Stole My Face . 475.00
9 I Walked Through The Doors
   of Destiny 475.00
10 We Found A World Of
   Tiny Cavemen 475.00
11 LSt(c),My Friend, Madcap
   Manning. 350.00
12 MMe(c),I Hunted Big Game
   in Outer Space. 350.00
13 LSt(c),I Hunted Goliath
   The Robot 350.00
14 LSt,I Had the Midas
   Touch of Gold 350.00
15 JK, I Hunted the Worlds
   Wildest Animals 350.00
16 JK,I Died a Thousand Times . 350.00
17 JK,I Doomed the World 350.00
18 JK(c),We Discovered The
   Edge of the World 450.00
19 I Caught Earth's
   Strangest Criminal 350.00
20 JK,I Was Big-Game
   on Neptune 350.00
21 JK,We Were Doomed By
   The Metal-Eating Monster . . . 350.00
22 I Was Trapped In The
   Magic Mountains 325.00
23 I Was A Captive In
   Space Prison 325.00

24 NC(c),I Was The Robinson
   Crusoe of Space 325.00
25 I Led Earth's Strangest
   Safari! 325.00
26 NC(c),We Battled The
   Sand Creature. 325.00
27 I Was the Earth's First Exile . . 325.00
28 I Stalked the Camouflage
   Creatures. 325.00
29 I Tracked the
   Forbidden Powers 200.00
30 We Cruised Into the
   Supernatural! 200.00
31 I Was A Modern Hercules . . . 175.00
32 We Were Trapped In A Freak
   Valley! 175.00
33 I Was Pursued by
   the Elements 175.00
34 DD,We Unleashed The Cloud
   Creatures. 175.00
35 I Solved the Mystery of
   Volcano Valley 175.00
36 I Was Bewitched
   By Lady Doom. 175.00
37 DD&SMo(c),I Hunted the
   Legendary Creatures! 175.00
38 DD&SMo(c),I Was the Slave
   of the Dream-Master 175.00
39 DD&SMo(c),We were Trapped
   in the Valley of no Return . . . 175.00
40 We Battled the Storm
   Creature. 175.00
41 DD&SMo(c),I Was Tried
   by a Robot Court. 150.00
42 DD&SMo(c),My Brother
   Was a Robot 150.00
43 DD&SMo(c),I Fought the
   Sonar Creatures 150.00
44 DD&SMo(c),We Fought the
   Beasts of Petrified Island . . . 150.00
45 DD&SMo(c),We Battled the
   Black Narwahl 150.00
46 DD&SMo(c),We Were Prisoners
   of the Sundial of Doom 150.00
47 We Became Partners of the
   Beast Brigade 150.00
48 DD&SMo(c),I Was Marooned
   On Earth 150.00
49 DD&SMo(c),I Was An Ally
   Of A Criminal Creature 150.00
50 DD&SMo(c),I Fought the
   Idol King 150.00
51 DD&SMo(c),We Unleashed
   the Demon of the Dungeon. . 135.00

My Greatest Adventure #40
© DC Comics Inc.

DC COMICS

My Greatest Adventure #57
© DC Comics, Inc.

52 DD&SMo(c),I Was A
   Stand-In For an Alien. 135.00
53 DD&SMo(c),I, Creature Slayer 135.00
54 I Was Cursed With
   an Alien Pal 135.00
55 DD&SMo(c),I Beacame The
   Wonder-Man of Space. 135.00
56 DD&SMo(c),My Brother-The
   Alien. 135.00
57 DD&SMo(c),Don't Touch Me
   Or You'll Die. 135.00
58 DD&SMo(c),ATh,I was Trapped
   in the Land of L'Oz 150.00
59 DD&SMo(c),Listen Earth-I
   Am Still Alive 150.00
60 DD&SMo(c),ATh,I Lived in
   Two Worlds 150.00
61 DD&SMo(c),ATh,I Battled For
   the Doom-Stone 150.00
62 DD&SMo(c),I Fought For
   An Alien Enemy. 100.00
63 DD&SMo(c),We Braved the
   Trail of the Ancient Warrior . . 100.00
64 DD&SMo(c),They Crowned My
   Fiance Their King! 100.00
65 DD&SMo(c),I Lost the Life
   or Death Secret. 100.00
66 DD&SMo(c),I Dueled with
   the Super Spirits 100.00
67 I Protected the Idols
   of Idoro! 100.00
68 DD&SMo(c),My Deadly Island
   of Space 100.00
69 DD&SMo(c),I Was A Courier
   From the Past 100.00
70 DD&SMo(c),We Tracked the
   Fabled Fish-Man! 100.00
71 We Dared to open the Door
   of Danger Dungeon. 100.00
72 The Haunted Beach 100.00
73 I Defeiller Mountain. 100.00
74 GC(c),We Were Challenged
   By The River Spirit 100.00
75 GC(c),Castaway Cave-Men
   of 1950 . . . . 100.00
76 MMe(c),We Battled the
   Micro-Monster 100.00
77 ATh,We Found the Super-
   Tribes of Tomorrow 125.00
78 Destination-'Dead Man's Alley' 100.00
79 Countdown in Dinosaur Valley 100.00
80 BP,I:Doom Patrol 750.00
81 BP,ATh,I:Dr. Janus 250.00
82 BP,F:Doom Patrol. 225.00
83 BP,F:Doom Patrol. 225.00

84 BP,V:General Immortus 225.00
85 BP,ATh,F:Doom Patrol 225.00
Becomes:

DOOM PATROL
March, 1964
86 BP,I:Brogherhood of Evil. 150.00
87 BP,O:Negative Man 125.00
88 BP,O:Chief 125.00
89 BP,I:Animal-Veg.-MineralMan . 125.00
90 BP,A:Brotherhood of Evil 125.00
91 BP,I:Manto, Gargvax. 125.00
92 BP,I:Dr.Tyme, A:Mento 125.00
93 BP,A:Brotherhood of Evil 125.00
94 BP,I:Dr.Radich, The Claw 125.00
95 BP,A:Animal-Vegetable
   -Mineral Man 125.00
96 BP,A:General Immortus,
   Brotherhood of Evil 125.00
97 BP,A:General Immortus,
   Brotherhood of Evil 125.00
98 BP,I:Mr.103 . . . . 125.00
99 I:Beast Boy 120.00
100 BP,O:Beast Boy,Robotman. . 130.00
101 BP,A:Beast Boy. 75.00
102 BP,A:Beast Boy,Challengers
   of the Unknown 70.00
103 BP,A:Beast Boy. 70.00
104 BP,W:Elasti-Girl,Mento,
   C:JLA,Teen Titans 70.00
105 BP,A:Beast Boy. 70.00
106 BP,O:Negative Man 70.00
107 BP,A:Beast Boy, I:Dr.Death. . 70.00
108 BP,A:Brotherhood of Evil . . . 70.00
109 BP,I:Mandred 70.00
110 BP,A:Garguax,Mandred,
   Brotherhood of Evil 50.00
111 BP,I:Zarox-13,A:Brotherhood
   of Evil. 50.00
112 BP,O:Beast Boy,Madame
   Rouge 50.00
113 BP,A:Beast Boy,Mento 50.00
114 BP,A:Beast Boy. 50.00
115 BP,A:Beast Boy. 50.00
116 BP,A:Madame Rouge 50.00
117 BP,I:Black Vulture 50.00
118 BP,A:Beast Boy. 50.00
119 BP,A:Madam Rouge 50.00
120 I:Wrecker. 50.00
121 JO,D:Doom Patrol. 150.00
122 rep.Doom Patrol #89. . . . . . . 15.00
123 rep.Doom Patrol #95. . . . . . . 15.00
124 rep.Doom Patrol #90. . . . . . . 15.00

[2nd Series]
See: DOOM PATROL

MY NAME IS CHAOS
1992
1 JRy,Song Laid Waste to Earth. . . 5.00
2 JRy,Colonization of Mars. 5.00
3 JRy,Search for Eternal Beings. . . 5.00
4 JRy,final issue 5.00

MY NAME IS HOLOCAUST
DC/Milestone, 1995
[Mini-Series]
1 F:Holocaust (Blood Syndicate) . . 2.50
2 V:Cantano 2.50
3 A:Blood Syndicate 2.50

MYSTERY IN SPACE
April-May, 1951
1 CI&FrG(c),FF,B:Knights of the
   Galaxy,Nine Worlds to
   Conquer 4,600.00
2 CI(c),MA,A:Knights of the
   Galaxy, Jesse James-
   Highwayman of Space 1,700.00

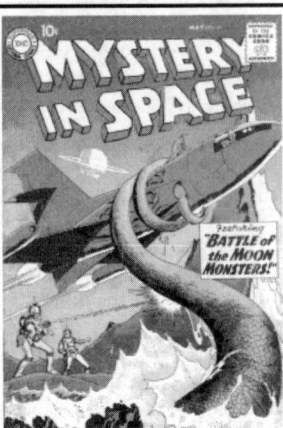

Mystery in Space #51
© DC Comics, Inc.

3 CI(c),A:Knights of the
   Galaxy, Duel of the Planets 1,300.00
4 CI(c),S&K,MA,A:Knights of the
   Galaxy, Master of Doom. . . 1,100.00
5 CI(c),A:Knights of the Galaxy,
   Outcast of the Lost World. . 1,100.00
6 CI(c),A:Knights of the Galaxy,
   The Day the World Melted . . 800.00
7 GK(c),ATh,A:Knights of the Galaxy,
   Challenge o/t Robot Knight . . 800.00
8 MA,It's a Women's World 800.00
9 MA(c),The Seven Wonders
   of Space 800.00
10 MA(c),The Last Time I
   Saw Earth 800.00
11 GK(c),Unknown Spaceman. . . 600.00
12 MA,The Sword in the Sky 600.00
13 MA(c),MD,Signboard
   in Space. 600.00
14 MA,GK(c),Hollywood
   in Space. 600.00
15 MA(c),Doom from Station X . . 600.00
16 MA(c),Honeymoon in Space. . 600.00
17 MA(c),The Last Mile of Space 600.00
18 MA(c),GK,Chain Gang
   of Space 600.00
19 MA(c),The Great
   Space-Train Robbery. 600.00
20 MA(c),The Man in the
   Martian Mask. 500.00
21 MA(c),Interplanetary
   Merry- Go-Round 500.00
22 MA(c),The Square Earth. 500.00
23 MA(c),Monkey-Rocket
   to Mars 500.00
24 MA(c),A:Space Cabby,
   Hitchhiker of Space 500.00
25 MA(c),Station Mars on the Air. 425.00
26 GK(c),Earth is the Target 425.00
27 The Human Fishbowl 425.00
28 The Radio Planet 425.00
29 GK(c),Space-Enemy
   Number One 425.00
30 GK(c),The Impossible
   World Named Earth. 425.00
31 GK(c),The Day the Earth
   Split in Two 400.00
32 GK(c),Riddle of the
   Vanishing Earthmen 400.00
33 The Wooden World War 400.00
34 GK(c),The Man Who
   Moved the World 400.00
35 The Counterfeit Earth 400.00

36 GK(c),Secret of the
   Moon Sphinx 400.00
37 GK(c),Secret of the
   Masked Martians 400.00
38 GK(c),The Canals of Earth . . . 400.00
39 GK(c),Sorcerers of Space 400.00
40 GK(c),Riddle of the
   Runaway Earth 400.00
41 GK(c),The Miser of Space . . . 325.00
42 GK(c),The Secret of the
   Skyscraper Spaceship 325.00
43 GK(c),Invaders From the
   Space Satellites 325.00
44 GK(c),Amazing Space Flight
   of North America 325.00
45 GK(c),MA,Flying Saucers
   Over Mars 325.00
46 GK(c),MA,Mystery of the
   Moon Sniper 325.00
47 GK(c),MA,Interplanetary Tug
   of War 325.00
48 GK(c),MA,Secret of the
   Scarecrow World 325.00
49 GK(c),The Sky-High Man 325.00
50 GK(c),The Runaway
   Space-Train 325.00
51 GK(c),MA,Battle of the
   Moon Monsters 325.00
52 GK(c),MSy,Mirror Menace
   of Mars 325.00
53 GK(c),B:Adam Strange stories,
   Menace o/t Robot Raiders . 3,000.00
54 GK(c),Invaders of the
   Underground World 750.00
55 GK(c),The Beast From
   the Runaway World 600.00
56 GK(c),The Menace of
   the Super-Atom 325.00
57 GK(c),Mystery of the
   Giant Footsteps 325.00
58 GK(c),Chariot in in the Sky . . . 325.00
59 GK(c),The Duel of the
   Two Adam Stranges 325.00
60 GK(c),The Attack of the
   Tentacle World 325.00
61 CI&MA(c),Threat of the
   Tornado Tyrant 250.00
62 CI&MA(c),The Beast with
   the Sizzling Blue Eyes 250.00
63 The Weapon that
   Swallowed Men 250.00
64 The Radioactive Menace 250.00
65 Mechanical Masters of Rann . 250.00
66 Space-Island of Peril 250.00
67 Challenge of the
   Giant Fireflies 250.00
68 CI&MA(c),Fadeaway Doom . . 250.00
69 CI&MA(c),Menace of the
   Aqua-Ray Weapon 250.00
70 CI&MA(c),Vengeance of
   the Dust Devil 250.00
71 CI&MA(c),The Challenge of
   the Crystal Conquerors 250.00
72 The Multiple Menace Weapon 200.00
73 CI&MA(c),The Invisible
   Invaders of Rann 200.00
74 CI&MA(c),The Spaceman
   Who Fought Himself 200.00
75 CI&MA(c),The Planet That
   Came to a Standstill 400.00
76 CI&MA(c),Challenge of
   the Rival Starman 200.00
77 CI&MA(c),Ray-Gun in the Sky 200.00
78 CI&MA(c),Shadow People
   of the Eclipse 200.00
79 CI&MA(c),The Metal
   Conqueror of Rann 200.00
80 CI&MA(c),The Deadly
   Shadows of Adam Strange . . 200.00
81 CI&MA(c),The Cloud-Creature
   That Menaced Two Worlds . . 150.00

Mystery in Space #107
© *DC Comics Inc.*

82 CI&MA(c),World War on
   Earth and Rann 150.00
83 CI&MA(c),The Emotion-Master
   of Space 150.00
84 CI&MA(c),The Powerless
   Weapons of Adam Strange . . 150.00
85 CI&MA(c),Riddle of the
   Runaway Rockets 150.00
86 CI&MA(c),Attack of the
   Underworld Giants 150.00
87 MA(c),The Super-Brain of
   Adam Strange,B:Hawkman . . 300.00
88 CI&MA(c),The Robot Wraith
   of Rann 250.00
89 MA(c),Siren o/t Space Ark . . . 225.00
90 CI&MA(c),Planets and
   Peril, E:Hawkman 225.00
91 CI&MA(c),Puzzle of
   the Perilous Prisons 100.00
92 DD&SMo(c),The Alien Invasion
   From Earth,B:Space Ranger . 100.00
93 DD&SMo(c),The Convict
   Twins of Space 100.00
94 DD&SMo(c),The Adam
   Strange Story 100.00
95 The Hydra-Head From
   Outer Space 100.00
96 The Coins That Doomed
   Two Planets 100.00
97 The Day Adam Strange
   Vanished 100.00
98 The Wizard of the Cosmos . . . 100.00
99 DD&SMo(c),The World-
   Destroyer From Space 100.00
100 DD&SMo(c),GK,The Death
   of Alanna 100.00
101 GK(c),The Valley of
   1,000 Dooms 100.00
102 GK,The Robot World of Rann 100.00
103 The Billion-Dollar Time-
   Capsule(Space Ranger),I:Ultra
   the Multi-Agent 100.00
104 thru 109 . . . . @60.00
110 Series ends, Sept., 1966 . . . . 60.00

[Series Revived], Sept., 1980
111 JAp,SD,MR,DSp, ... 10.00
112 JAp,TS,JKu(c) 10.00
113 JKu(c),MGo 10.00
114 JKu(c),JCr,SD,DSp 10.00
115 JKu(c),SD,GT,BB 10.00
116 JSn(c),JCr,SD 10.00
117 DN,GT,March, 1981 . . . . 10.00

MYTHOS:
THE FINAL TOUR
DC/Vertigo, Oct., 1996
1 JNR(s),GyA,PrG,F:Rock Star
   Adam Case 6.00
2 JNR(s),PSj,F:Rock Star Adam
   Case 6.00
3 JNR(s), finale 6.00

NAMES OF MAGIC, THE
DC/Vertigo, Dec., 2000
1 (of 5) JBo(c),F:Tim Hunter 10.00
2 thru 5 JBo(c) . . . . @10.00
TPB rep 15.00

NATHANIEL DUSK
Feb., 1984
1 GC(p) 2.25
2 thru 4 GC(p) . . . . @2.25

NATHANIEL DUSK II
Oct., 1985
1 thru 4 GC,Jan., 1986 . . . . @2.25

NATIONAL COMICS
1999
1 MWa(s),AAl,F:Flash &
   Mr. Terrific 2.25

NAZZ, THE
1990–91
1 Michael'sBook 5.50
2 Johnny'sBook 5.00
3 Search for Michael Nazareth 5.00
4 V:Retaliators,final issue 5.00

NEVADA
DC/Vertigo, March, 1998
1 (of 6) SvG,SL,show girl 2.50
2 thru 6 SvG,SL . . . . @2.50
TPB Nevada, rep. 15.00

NEW ADVENTURES
OF SUPERBOY
See: SUPERBOY

NEW BOOK OF COMICS
1937
1 Dr.Occult 20,000.00
2 Dr.Occult 10,000.00

NEW COMICS
1935
1 . . . . 25,000.00
2 . . . . 10,000.00
3 thru 6 . . . . @7,500.00
7 thru 11 . . . . @6,000.00
Becomes:

NEW ADVENTURE
COMICS
Jan., 1937
12 S&S 6,000.00
13 thru 20 . . . . @5,000.00
21 . . . . 4,000.00
22 thru 31 . . . . @3,000.00
Becomes:

ADVENTURE COMICS

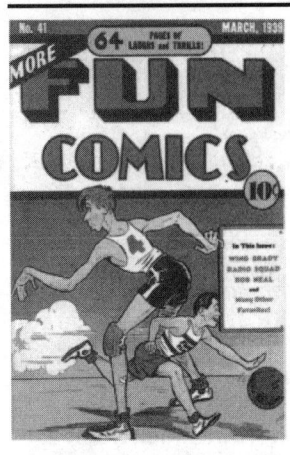

More Fun #41 © DC Comics, Inc.

NEW FUN COMICS
Feb., 1935

1 B:Oswald the Rabbit, Jack Woods	60,000.00
2	30,000.00
3	15,000.00
4	15,000.00
5	15,000.00
6 S&S,B:Dr.Occult, Henri Duval	30,000.00

Becomes:

MORE FUN COMICS
Jan., 1936

7 S&S,WK	8,000.00
8 S&S,WK	7,500.00
9 S&S,E:Henri Duval	9,000.00
10 S&S	5,000.00
11 S&S,B:Calling all Girls	4,800.00
12 S&S	4,000.00
13 S&S	3,800.00
14 S&S,Color,Dr.Occult.	16,000.00
15 S&S	8,000.00
16 S&S,Christmas(c)	8,000.00
17 S&S	7,500.00
18 S&S	3,000.00
19 S&S	3,000.00
20 HcK,S&S	3,000.00
21 S&S	3,500.00
22 S&S	3,500.00
23 S&S	3,500.00
24 S&S	3,500.00
25 S&S	2,700.00
26 S&S	2,500.00
27 S&S	2,500.00
28 S&S	2,400.00
29 S&S	2,400.00
30 S&S	2,400.00
31 S&S	2,500.00
32 S&S,E:Dr. Occult	2,400.00
33	2,400.00
34	2,400.00
35	2,400.00
36 B:Masked Ranger	2,400.00
37 thru 40	@3,000.00
41 E:Masked Ranger	2,000.00
42 thru 50	@2,000.00
51 I:The Spectre	7,000.00
52 O:The Spectre,pt.1, E:Wing Brady	85,000.00
53 O:The Spectre,pt.2, B:Capt.Desmo	45,000.00
54 E:King Carter,Spectre(c)	18,000.00
55 I:Dr.Fate,E:Bulldog Martin, Spectre(c)	22,000.00

56 B:Congo Bill,Dr.Fate(c)	9,000.00
57 Spectre(c)	7,000.00
58 Spectre(c)	7,000.00
59 A:Spectre	7,000.00
60 Spectre(c)	7,000.00
61 Spectre(c)	7,000.00
62 Spectre(c)	4,000.00
63 Spectre(c),E:St.Bob Neal	4,000.00
64 Spectre(c),B:Lance Larkin	4,000.00
65 Spectre(c)	4,000.00
66 Spectre(c)	4,000.00
67 Spectre(c),O:Dr. Fate, E:Congo Bill,Biff Bronson	9,500.00
68 Dr.Fate(c),B:Clip Carson	3,000.00
69 Dr.Fate(c)	3,000.00
70 Dr.Fate(c),E:Lance Larkin	3,000.00
71 Dr.Fate(c),I:Johnny Quick	7,500.00
72 Dr. Fate has Smaller Helmet, E:Sgt. Carey,Sgt.O'Malley	3,000.00
73 Dr.Fate(c),I:Aquaman,Green Arrow,Speedy	20,000.00
74 Dr.Fate(c),A:Aquaman	3,800.00
75 Dr.Fate(c)	3,000.00
76 Dr.Fate(c),MMe,E:Clip Carson, B:Johnny Quick	3,000.00
77 MMe,Green Arrow(c)	3,000.00
78 MMe,Green Arrow(c)	3,000.00
79 MMe,Green Arrow(c)	3,000.00
80 MMe,Green Arrow(c)	3,000.00
81 MMe,Green Arrow(c)	1,800.00
82 MMe,Green Arrow(c)	1,800.00
83 MMe,Green Arrow(c)	1,800.00
84 MMe,Green Arrow(c)	1,800.00
85 MMe,Green Arrow(c)	1,800.00
86 MMe	1,800.00
87 MMe,E:Radio Squad	1,800.00
88 MMe,Green Arrow(c)	1,800.00
89 MMe,O:Gr.Arrow&Speedy	1,900.00
90 MMe,Green Arrow(c)	1,800.00
91 MMe,Green Arrow(c)	1,000.00
92 MMe,Green Arrow(c)	1,000.00
93 MMe,B:Dover & Clover	1,000.00
94 MMe,Green Arrow(c)	1,000.00
95 MMe,Green Arrow(c)	1,000.00
96 MMe,Green Arrow(c)	1,000.00
97 MMe,JKu,E:Johnny Quick	1,000.00
98 E:Dr. Fate	1,400.00
99 Green Arrow(c)	1,000.00
100 Anniversary Issue	1,600.00
101 O&I:Superboy, E:The Spectre	13,000.00
102 A:Superboy	1,800.00
103 A:Superboy	1,300.00
104 Superboy(c)	1,100.00
105 Superboy(c)	1,100.00
106	1,100.00
107 E:Superboy	1,100.00
108 A:Genius Jones,Genius Meets Genius	300.00
109 A:Genius Jones, The Disappearing Deposits	300.00
110 A:Genius Jones, Birds, Brains and Burglary	300.00
111 A:Genius Jones, Jeepers Creepers	300.00
112 A:Genius Jones, The Tell-Tale Tornado	300.00
113 A:Genius Jones, Clocks and Shocks	300.00
114 A:Genius Jones, The Milky Way	300.00
115 A:Genius Jones,Foolish Questions	300.00
116 A:Genius Jones,Palette For Plunder	300.00
117 A:Genius Jones,Battle of the Pretzel Benders	300.00
118 A:Genius Jones,The Sinister Siren	300.00
119 A:Genius Jones,A Perpetual Jackpot	300.00

120 A:Genius Jones,The Man in the Moon	300.00
121 A:Genius Jones,The Mayor Goes Haywire	250.00
122 A:Genius Jones,When Thug-Hood Was In Floor	250.00
123 A:Genius Jones,Hi Diddle Diddle, the Cat and the Fiddle	250.00
124 A:Genius Jones, The Zany Zoo	250.00
125 Genius Jones, Impossible But True	1,100.00
126 A:Genius Jones,The Case of the Gravy Spots	250.00
127 Nov.–Dec., 1947	400.00

NEW GODS, THE
Feb.–March, 1971

1 JK,I:Orion	125.00
2 JK	70.00
3 JK	50.00
4 JK,O:Manhunter, rep.	40.00
5 JK,I:Fastbak & Black Racer	40.00
6 JK	40.00
7 JK,O:Orion	40.00
8 JK	40.00
9 JK,I:Forager	40.00
10 JK	40.00
11 JK	40.00
12 DN,DA,R:New Gods	10.00
13 DN,DA	10.00
14 DN,DA	10.00
15 RB,BMc	10.00
16 DN,DA	10.00
17 DN,DA	10.00
18 DN,DA	10.00
19 DN,DA	10.00

NEW GODS
(Reprints) 1984

1 JK reprint	4.00
2 thru 5 JK reprint	@3.50
6 JK rep.+NewMaterial	3.50

NEW GODS
[2nd Series], 1989

1 From Cosmic Odyssey	3.00
2 A:Orion of New Genesis	2.50
3 A:Orion	2.50
4 Renegade Apokolyptian Insect Colony	2.50
5 Orion vs. Forager	2.50
6 A:Eve Donner, Darkseid	2.50
7 Bloodline #1	2.50
8 Bloodline #2	2.50
9 Bloodline #3	2.50
10 Bloodline #4	2.50
11 Bloodline #5	2.50
12 Bloodlines #6	2.50
13 Back on Earth	2.50
14 I:Reflektor	2.50
15 V:Serial Killer	2.50
16 A:Fastbak & Metron	2.50
17 A:Darkseid, Metron	2.50
18 A:YugaKhan,Darkseid, Moniters	2.50
19 V:Yuga Khan	2.50
20 Darkseid Dethroned, V:Yuga Khan	2.50
21 A:Orion	2.50
22 A:Metron	2.50
23 A:Forever People	2.50
24 A:Forever People	2.50
25 The Pact #1,R:Infinity Man	2.50
26 The Pact #2	2.50
27 Asault on Apokolips,Pact#3	2.50
28 Pact #4, final issue	2.50

[3rd Series], 1995–97

1 F:Orion vs. Darkseid	2.50

DC COMICS

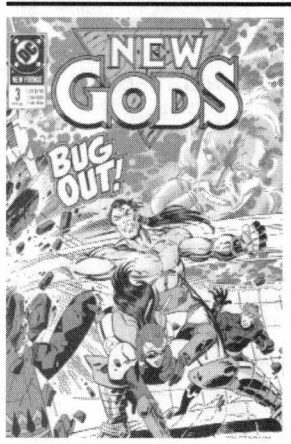

New Gods, 2nd Series #3
© DC Comics Inc.

2 RaP,UnderworldUnleashed tie-in. 2.50
3 RaP,Darkseid destroyed 2.50
4 RaP,F:Lightray 2.50
5 RaP,F:Orion 2.50
6 . . . . 2.50
7 RaP,R:Darkseid 2.50
8 RaP,DZ,F:Highfather,Darkseid. . . 2.50
9 thru 11 . . . . @2.50
12 JBy,BWi,F:Metron 2.50
13 JBy,BWi,Orion reappears
   on Earth 2.50
14 JBy,BWi,A:Forever People,
   Lightray 2.50
TPB rep. #1–#11,b&w 12.00
Secret Files #1 KK,JBy 5.00

NEW GUARDIANS
1988–89
1 JSon,from Millennium series 3.00
2 JSon,Colombian Drug Cartel. . . . 2.25
3 JSon,in South Africa,
   V:Janwillem's Army 2.25
4 JSon,V:Neo-Nazi Skinheads
   in California 2.25
5 JSon,Tegra Kidnapped 2.25
6 JSon, In China, Invasion x-over . 2.25
7 JSon, Guardians Return Home . . 2.25
8 JSon, V:Janwillem 2.25
9 JSon, A:Tome Kalmaku,
   V:Janwillem 2.25
10 JSon, A:Tome Kalmaku. 2.25
11 PB,Janwillem's secret 2.25
12 PB,New Guardians Future
   revealed, final issue. 2.25

NEW TEEN TITANS
Nov., 1980
1 GP,RT,V:Gordanians (see DC
   Comics Presents #26 . . . . 17.00
2 GP,RT,I:Deathstroke the
   Terminator, I&D:Ravager. 12.00
3 GP,I:Fearsome Five 6.00
4 GP,RT,A:JLA,O:Starfire 6.00
5 CS,RT,O:Raven,I:Trigon 6.00
6 GP,V:Trigon,O:Raven. 6.00
7 GP,RT,O:Cyborg 6.00
8 GP,RT,A Day in the Life 6.00
9 GP,RT,A:Terminator,
   V:Puppeteer. 6.00
10 GP,RT,A:Terminator 6.00
11 GP,RT,V:Hyperion 3.50
12 GP,RT,V:Titans of Myth 3.50
13 GP,RT,R:Robotman. 3.50

14 GP,RT,I:New Brotherhood of
   Evil,V:Zahl and Rouge. 3.50
15 GP,RT,D:Madame Rouge 3.50
16 GP,RT,I:Captain Carrot 3.50
17 GP,RT,I:Frances Kane 3.00
18 GP,RT,A:Orig.Starfire 3.00
19 GP,RT,A:Hawkman 3.00
20 GP,RT,V:Disruptor. 3.00
21 GP,RT,GC,I:Brother Blood,
   Night Force 3.00
22 GP,RT,V:Brother Blood 3.00
23 GP,RT,I:Blackfire 3.00
24 GP,RT,A:Omega Men,I:X-hal . . . 3.00
25 GP,RT,A:Omega Men 3.00
26 GP,RT,I:Terra,Runaway #1 . . . . 3.00
27 GP,RT,A:Speedy,Runaway #2. . . 3.00
28 GP,RT,V:Terra 4.00
29 GP,RT,V:Broth.of Evil 3.00
30 GP,RT,V:Broth.of Evil,J:Terra . . . 3.00
31 GP,RT,V:Broth.of Evil 3.00
32 GP,RT,I:Thunder & Lightning . . . 3.00
33 GP,I:Trident. 3.00
34 GP,V:The Terminator. 3.00
35 KP,RT,V:Mark Wright. 3.00
36 KP,RT,A:Thunder & Lightning . . . 3.00
37 GP,RT,A:Batman/Outsiders(x-over
   BATO#5),V:Fearsome Five 3.00
38 GP,O:Wonder Girl 3.00
39 GP,Grayson quits as Robin. 5.00
40 GP,A:Brother Blood. 3.00
Ann.#1 GP,RT,Blackfire 3.50
Ann.#2 GP,I:Vigilante. 3.00
Ann.#3 GP,DG,D:Terra,A:Deathstroke
   V:The H.I.V.E. 3.50
Ann.#4 rep.Direct Ann.#1. . . . . 2.50
TPB Judas Contract rep.#39–#44,
   Ann.#3,new GP(c) 14.95
TPB The Terror of Trigon 17.95

[Special Issues]
Keebler:GP,DG,Drugs 2.50
Beverage:Drugs,RA 2.50
IBM:Drugs 3.00
Becomes:

TALES OF THE
TEEN TITANS
1984–88
41 GP,A:Brother Blood. 3.00
42 GP,DG,V:Deathstroke 5.00
43 GP,DG,V:Deathstroke 5.00
44 GP,DG,I:Nightwing,O:Deathstroke
   Joe Wilson becomes Jericho . . 8.00
45 GP,A:Aqualad,V:The H.I.V.E. . . . 3.00
46 GP,A:Aqualad,V:The H.I.V.E. . . . 3.00
47 GP,A:Aqualad,V:The H.I.V.E. . . . 3.00
48 SR,V:The Recombatants 3.00
49 GP,CI,V:Dr.Light,A:Flash. 3.00
50 GP/DG W:Wonder Girl &
   Terry Long,C:Batman,
   Wonder Woman. 4.00
51 RB,A:Cheshire 2.50
52 RB,A:Cheshire 2.50
53 RB,I:Ariel,A:Terminator 2.50
54 RB,A:Terminator 2.50
55 A:Terminator 2.50
56 A:Fearsome Five. 2.50
57 A:Fearsome Five. 2.50
58 thru 91 rep. . . . . @2.50

NEW TEEN TITANS
[Direct sales series]
Aug., 1984
1 B:MWn(s),GP,L:Raven. 6.00
2 GP,D:Azareth,A:Trigon. 4.00
3 GP,V:Raven 4.00
4 GP,V:Trigon,Raven 4.00
5 GP,D:Trigon,Raven disappears . . 4.00
6 GP,A:Superman,Batman 3.00
7 JL,V:Titans of Myth 3.00

New Teen Titans #19
© DC Comics, Inc.

8 JL,V:Titans of Myth 3.00
9 JL,V:Titans of Myth,I:Kole 3.00
10 JL,O:Kole 3.00
11 JL,O:Kole 2.50
12 JL,Ghost story. 2.50
13 EB,Crisis. 2.50
14 EB,Crisis. 2.50
15 EB,A:Raven 2.50
16 EB,A:OmegaMen 2.50
17 EB,V:Blackfire 2.50
18 E:MWn(s),EB,V:Blackfire 2.50
19 EB,V:Mento. 2.50
20 GP(c),EB,V:Cheshire,J.Todd . . . 2.50
21 GP(c),EB,V:Cheshire,J.Todd . . . 2.50
22 GP(c),EB,V:Blackfire,Mento,
   Brother Blood 2.50
23 GP(c),V:Blackfire 2.50
24 CB,V:Hybrid 2.50
25 EB,RT,V:Hybrid,Mento,A:Flash. . 2.50
26 KGa,V:Mento 2.50
27 KGa,Church of Br.Blood 2.50
28 EB,RT,V:BrotherBlood,A:Flash . . 2.50
29 EB,RT,V:Brother Blood,
   A:Flash,Robin 2.50
30 EB,Batman,Superman 2.50
31 EB,RT,V:Brother Blood,A:Flash
   Batman,Robin,Gr.Lantern Corps
   Superman 2.50
32 EB,RT,Murder Weekend 2.50
33 EB,V:Terrorists 2.50
34 EB,RT,V:Mento,Hybird 2.50
35 PB,RT,V:Arthur & Eve. 2.50
36 EB,RT,I:Wildebeest. 2.50
37 EB,RT,V:Wildebeest. 2.50
38 EB,RT,A:Infinity. 2.50
39 EB,RT,F:Raven 2.50
40 EB,RT,V:Gentleman Ghost 2.50
41 EB,V:Wildebeest,A:Puppeteer,
   Trident,Wildebeest. 2.50
42 EB,RT,V:Puppeteer,Gizmo,
   Trident,Wildebeest. 2.50
43 CS,RT,V:Phobia 2.50
44 RT,V:Godiva 2.50
45 EB,RT,A:Dial H for Hero 2.50
46 EB,RT,A:Dial H for Hero 2.50
47 O:Titans,C:Wildebeest 2.50
48 EB,V:Wildebeest 2.50
49 EB,RT,A:Red Star 2.50
Ann.#1 A:Superman,V:Brainiac 2.50
Ann.#2 JBy,JL,O:Brother Blood 3.00
Ann.#3 I:Danny Chase 2.50
Ann.#4 V:Godiva 2.50
Becomes:

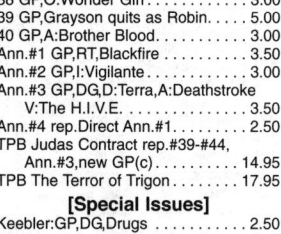

NEW TITANS
1988–96

50 B:MWn(s),GP,BMc,B:Who is
   Wonder Girl? 7.00
51 GP,BMc 3.00
52 GP,BMc 3.00
53 GP,RT 3.00
54 GP,RT,E:Who is Wonder Girl? . . 3.00
55 GP,RT,I:Troia 3.00
56 MBr,RT,Tale of Middle Titans . . . 3.00
57 GP,BMc,V:Wildebeast 3.00
58 GP,TG,BMc,V:Wildebeast 3.00
59 GP,TG,BMc,V:Wildebeast 3.00
60 GP,TG,BMc,3rd A:Tim Drake
   (Face Revealed),Batman 5.00
61 GP,TG,BMc,A:Tim Drake,
   Batman 5.00
62 TG,AV,A:Deathstroke 3.00
63 TG,AV,A:Deathstroke 3.00
64 TG,AV,A:Deathstroke 3.00
65 TG,AV,A:Deathstroke,Tim Drake,
   Batman 3.00
66 TG,AV,V:Eric Forrester 2.50
67 TG,AV,V:Eric Forrester 2.50
68 SE,V:Royal Flush Gang 2.50
69 SE,V:Royal Flush Gang 2.50
70 SE,A:Deathstroke 3.00
71 TG,AV,B:Deathstroke,
   B:Titans Hunt 5.00
72 TG,AV,D:Golden Eagle 4.00
73 TG,AV,I:Phantasm 4.00
74 TG,AV,I:Pantha 3.00
75 TG,AV,IR:Jericho/Wildebeest . . . 3.00
76 TG,AV,V:Wildebeests 2.50
77 TG,AV,A:Red Star,N:Cyborg . . . 2.50
78 TG,AV,V:Cyborg 2.50
79 TG,AV,I:Team Titans 3.00
80 KGa,PC,A:Team Titans 2.50
81 CS,AV,War of the Gods 2.50
82 TG,AV,V:Wildebeests 2.50
83 TG,AV,D:Jericho 3.00
84 TG,AV,E:Titans Hunt 2.50
85 TG,AV,I:Baby Wildebeest 2.50
86 CS,AV,E:Deathstroke 2.50
87 TG,AV,A:Team Titans 2.50
88 TG,AV,CS,V:Team Titans 2.50
89 JBr,I:Lord Chaos 2.50
90 TG,AV,Total Chaos#2,A:Team
   Titans,D'stroke,V:Lord Chaos . . 2.50
91 TG,AV,Total Chaos#5,A:Team
   Titans,D'stroke,V:Lord Chaos . . 2.50
92 E:MWn(s),TG,AV,Total Chaos#8,
   A:Team Titans,V:Lord Chaos . . . 2.50
93 TG,AV,Titans Sell-Out#3 . . . . . . 2.50
94 PJ,F:Red Star & Cyborg 2.50
95 PJ,Red Star gains new powers. . 2.50
96 PJ,I:Solar Flare,
   V:Konstantine 2.50
97 TG,AV,B:The Darkening,R:Speedy
   V:Brotherhood of Evil 2.50
98 TG,AV,V:Brotherhood of Evil 2.50
99 TG,AV,I:Arsenal (Speedy) 2.50
100 TG,AV,W:Nightwing&Starfire,
   V:Deathwing,Raven,A:Flash,Team
   Titans,Hologram(c) 4.00
101 AV(i),L:Nightwing. 2.50
102 AV(i),A:Prester John 2.50
103 AV(i),V:Bro. of Evil. 2.50
104 Terminus #1 . . . . 2.50
105 Terminus #2 . . . . 2.50
106 Terminus #3 . . . . 2.50
107 Terminus #4 . . . . 2.50
108 A:Supergirl,Flash. 2.50
109 F:Starfire 2.50
110 A:Flash,Serg.Steele. 2.50
111 A:Checkmate 2.50
112 A:Checkmate. 2.50
113 F:Nightwing 2.75
114 L:Starfire, Nightwing,Panthra,
   Wildebeest. 2.50
115 A:Trigon. 2.50

New Titans #97 © DC Comics, Inc.

116 Changling 2.50
117 V:Psimon 2.50
118 V:Raven + Brotherhood 2.50
119 Suffer the Children,pt.1 . . . . 2.50
120 Forever Evil,pt.2 . . . . 2.50
121 Forever Evil,pt.3 . . . . 2.50
122 Crimelord/Syndicate War,pt.2
   J:Supergirl 2.50
123 MWn(s),RRa,O:Minion 2.50
124 The Siege of Zi Charan 2.50
125 The Siege of Zi Charan 3.00
126 Meltdown,pt.1 . . . . 2.50
127 MWn,Meltdown, cont. 2.50
128 MWn,Meltdown, cont. 2.50
129 MWn,Meltdown, cont. 2.50
130 MWn,Meltdown,final issue 2.50
Ann.#5 V:Children of the Sun 3.00
Ann.#6 CS,F:Starfire 3.00
Ann.#7 Armageddon 2001,I:Future
   Teen Titans 4.00
Ann.#8 PJ,Eclipso,V:Deathstroke . . 3.75
Ann.#9 Bloodlines#5,I:Anima. 3.75
Ann.#10 Elseworlds story 3.75
Ann.#11 Year One Annual 4.00
#0 Spec. Zero Hour,new team 2.50

NEW T.H.U.N.D.E.R. AGENTS, THE
July, 2003

1 JP. 3.00

NEW YEAR'S EVIL:
Dec., 1997

Body Doubles #1 DAn,ALa,JoP,
   JPn(c) 2.00
Dark Nemesis #1 DJu,Ccs,JPn(c) . . 2.00
Darkseid #1 JBy,SB,JPn(c) 2.00
Gog #1 MWa,JOy,DJa,JPn(c) 2.00
Mr. Mxyzptlk #1 AlG,TMo,JPn(c) . . . 2.00
Prometheus #1 GMo,JPn(c) 2.00
Scarecrow #1 PrM,DFg,JPn(c) 2.00
The Rogues #1 BAu,RoW,JPn(c) . . 2.00

NEW YORK WORLD'S FAIR

1 1939 . . . . 30,000.00
2 1940 . . . . 17,000.00

NIGHTFALL:
THE BLACK CHRONICLES
Homage/DC, Oct., 1999

1 monsters living among us 3.00

2 . . . . 3.00
3 . . . . 3.00

NIGHT FORCE
Aug., 1982

1 GC,1:Night Force. 5.00
2 thru 13 GC . . . . @3.00
14 GC,Sept.,1983 . . . . 3.00

NIGHT FORCE
Oct., 1996

1 MWn(s),BA,Baron Winters leads. 2.50
2 MWn(s) 2.25
3 MWn(s) 2.25
4 MWn(s),EB,HellSeemsHeaven . . 2.25
5 MWn(s),Low,SMa,Dreamers of
   Dreams,pt.1 . . . . 2.25
6 MWn(s),Low,SMa,Dreamers,pt.2 . 2.25
7 MWn(s),Low,SMa,Dreamers,pt.3. 2.25
8 MWn(s),Convergence, x-over . . . 2.25
9 MWn(s),Low,Sma,The Eleventh
   Man pt.1 (of 3). 2.25
10 MWn(s),Eleventh Man, pt.2 . . . . 2.50
11 MWn(s),Eleventh Man, pt.3 . . . . 2.50
12 MWn(s),Lady of the Leopard
   final issue,Sept., 1997. . . . . . . 2.50

NIGHTWING
1995

1 R:Nightwing 5.00
2 N:Nightwing 4.00
3 visit to Kravia 4.00
4 conclusion 4.00
1-shot Alfred's Return, DG. 5.00

NIGHTWING
Aug., 1996

1 CDi(s),SMc,KIS,Nightwing goes
   to Bluhaven 18.00
2 CDi(s),SMc,KIS,V:smugglers. . . . 8.00
3 CDi(s),SMc,KIS,run-down bank
   iheld up 8.00
4 CDi(s),SMc,KIS,V:Lady Vick 5.00
5 CDi(s),SMc,KIS,. 5.00
6 CDi(s),SMc,KIS,A:Tim Drake. . . . 5.00
7 CDi(s),SMc,KIS,Rough Justice . . 5.00
8 CDi(s),SMc,KIS,V: the kingpin
   of Bluhaven 5.00
9 CDi(s),SMc,KIS,kidnapping, pt.1 . 5.00
10 CDi(s),SMc,KIS,nightmare
   or dream? 5.00
11 CDi(s),SMc,V:Soames,
   Blockbuster 5.00
12 CDi(s),SMc,Mutt 4.00
13 CDi(s),SMc,KIS,A:Batman 3.50
14 CDi(s),SMc,KIS,A:Batman,pt.2 . . 3.50
15 CDi(s),SMc,KIS,A:Batman,pt.3 . . 3.00
16 CDi(s),SMc,KIS,Nightwingmobile 3.00
17 CDi(s),SMc,KIS,V:Man-Bat 3.00
18 CDi(s),SMc,KIS. 3.00
19 CDi(s),SMc,KIS,Cataclysm
   x-over, pt.2. . . . . 4.00
20 CDi(s),SMc,KIS,Cataclysm 3.00
21 CDi(s),SMc,KIS,post Cataclysm 2.50
22 CDi(s),SMc,KIS,V:Lady Vic. 2.50
23 Brotherhood of
   the Fist x-over, pt.4 . . . . 2.50
24 CDi(s),SMc,KIS,cop story 2.50
25 CDi(s),SMc,KIS,A:Robin 2.50
26 CDi(s),SMc,KIS,A;Huntress 2.50
27 CDi(s),SMc,KIS,V:Torque 2.50
28 CDi(s),SMc,KIS,V:Torque 2.50
29 CDi(s),SMc,KIS,A:Huntress 2.50
30 CDi(s),SMc,KIS,A:Superman . . . 2.50
31 CDi(s),SMc,KIS,A:Nite-Wing. . . . 3.00
32 CDi(s),SMc,KIS,V:DoubleDare . . 2.50
33 CDi(s),SMc,KIS,
   V:Electrocutioner 2.50

34 CDi(s),SMc,KIS,x-over 2.50
35 CDi(s),SMc,KIS,No
   Man's Land,pt.1 . . . . 2.50
36 CDi(s),SMc,No
   Man's Land,pt.2 . . . . 2.50
37 CDi(s),SMc,KIS,No Man's
   Land, concl. 2.50
38 CDi(s),SMc,KIS,F:Oracle 2.50
39 CDi(s),SMc,KIS 2.50
40 CDi(s),SMc,KIS,R:Tarantula 2.50
41 CDi(s),Police Academy grad. . . . 2.50
42 CDi(s),V:Nite-wing 2.50
43 CDi(s),V:Torque 2.50
44 CDi(s),F:Nite-wing. 2.50
45 CDi(s),Hunt for Oracle,pt.1 . . . . . 2.50
46 CDi(s),Hunt for Oracle,pt.3 . . . . . 2.50
47 CDi(s),showdown 2.50
48 CDi(s),JMz,F:Slyph 2.50
49 CDi(s),JMz,F:Torque 2.50
50 CDi,JMz,at crossroads,48-pg. . . 4.00
51 CDi,KD,O:Nite-wing 2.50
52 CDi,This issue: Batman dies! . . . 2.50
53 Officer Down x-over,pt.5 . . . . 2.50
54 CDi,life-threatening accident. . . . 2.50
55 CDi,A:Blockbuster,Shrike 2.50
56 CDi,V:Blockbuster,Shrike 2.50
57 CDi,RL,MFm,V:Shrike. 2.50
58 CDi,V:Shrike 2.50
59 CDi,RL,Where's Freddy Minh . . . 2.50
60 CDi,Low,V:Transbelvan mob . . . 2.50
61 CDi,V:Bank Robbers. 2.50
62 CDi,Joker:Last Laugh 2.50
63 CDi,Last Laugh, aftermath 2.50
64 CDi,On a Christmas Evening . . . 2.50
65 CDi,BruceWayne:Murderer,pt.3 . . 2.50
66 CDi,BruceWayne:Murderer,pt.9 . . 2.50
67 CDi,V:Amygdala 2.50
68 CDi,BruceWayne:Fugitive,pt.6 . . . 2.50
69 CDi,BruceWayne:Fugitive,pt.9 . . . 2.50
70 CDi,in Arizona 2.50
71 RL,Something About Mary,pt.1 . . 2.50
72 RL,Something About Mary,pt.2 . . 2.50
73 RL,Something About Mary,pt.3 . . 2.50
74 RL,Something About Mary,pt.4 . . 2.50
75 RL,MGo,40-pg 3.50
76 MGo(c) 2.50
77 cops go bad 2.50
78 V:new Tarantula 2.50
79 Source of madness. 2.50
80 Venn Diagram,pt.1 . . . . 2.50
81 Venn Diagram,pt.2 . . . . 2.50
82 Venn Diagram,pt.3 . . . . 2.50
83 Murder of Chief Redhorn 2.50
84 RL,Chief Redhorn case 2.50
85 Tarantula or Nite-Wing 2.50
86 Cyber-punks 2.50
87 V:Blockbuster 2.25
88 V:Blockbuster 2.25
89 V:Blockbuster 2.25
90 V:Blockbuster 2.25
91 V:Shrike 2.25
92 V:Blockbuster 2.25
93 V:Blockbuster showdown 2.25
94 F:Tarantula 2.25
95 Tarantula vs. Copperhead. 2.25
96 War Games,Act 1,pt.3 . . . . 2.25
97 War Games,Act 2,pt.3 . . . . 2.25
98 War Games,Act 3,pt.3 . . . . 2.25
Ann.#1 Pulp Heroes (Romance) . . . 4.50
Spec.#1,000,000 CDi(s),SMc,KIS . . 2.50
Secret Files #1 64-page. 5.50
Spec.#1 Our Worlds at War,48-pg . . 3.50
Giant #1 80-pg.CDi,I:Hella. 5.95
GN The Target,CDi,SMc,48-page . . 5.95
TPB A Knight in Bludhaven,CDi,
   SMc,KIS, rep. #1–#8 . . . . 15.00
TPB Ties That Bind, DON,AIG,
   DG,KIS,rep. 13.00
TPB Rough Justice 18.00
TPB Love and Bullets,rep. 18.00
TPB A Darker Shade of Justice . . . 20.00

TPB Love and Bullets 18.00
TPB The Hunt for Oracle 15.00
TPB Nightwing/Huntress 10.00
TPB Nightwing: Big Guns 15.00

NIGHTWING
AND HUNTRESS
March, 1998

1 (of 4) BSz,conflict 2.50
2 BSz,good cop, bad cop 2.50
3 BSz,Malfatti 2.50
4 BSz,concl. 2.50

NUTSY SQUIRREL
Sept.–Oct., 1954

61 SM. 100.00
62 thru 71. . . . . @50.00
72 Nov., 1957. . . . . 50.00

OMAC
Sept.–Oct., 1974

1 JK,I&O:Omac. 50.00
2 JK,I:Mr.Big 22.00
3 JK,100,000 foes. 22.00
4 JK,V:Kafka 22.00
5 JK,New Bodies for Old 22.00
6 JK,The Body Bank. 22.00
7 JK,The Ocean Stealers 22.00
8 JK,Last issue 22.00

[2nd Series], 1991

1 JBy,B&W prestige 5.00
2 JBy,The Great Depression era . . 4.50
3 JBy,To Kill Adolf Hitler 4.50
4 JBy,D:Mr.Big 4.50

OMEGA MEN
Dec., 1982

1 KG,V:Citadel. 3.50
2 KG,O:Broot. 2.50
3 KG,I:Lobo. 8.00
4 KG,D:Demonia,I:Felicity. 2.50
5 KG,V:Lobo 3.00
6 KG,V:Citadel,D:Gepsen 2.50
7 O:Citadel,L:Auron 2.50
8 R:Nimbus,I:H.Hokum 2.50
9 V:HarryHokum,A:Lobo 2.50
10 A:Lobo (First Full Story) 6.00
11 V:Blackfire 2.50
12 R:Broots Wife 2.50
13 A:Broots Wife 2.50

Omega Men #13 © DC Comics Inc.

14 Karna 2.50
15 Primus Goes Mad. 2.50
16 Spotlight Issue 2.50
17 V:Psions 2.50
18 V:Psions 2.50
19 V:Psions,C:Lobo 2.50
20 V:Psions,A:Lobo 2.50
21 Spotlight Issue 2.50
22 Nimbus 2.50
23 Nimbus 2.50
24 Okaara 2.50
25 Kalista 2.50
26 V:Spiderguild 2.50
27 V:Psions 2.50
28 V:Psions 2.50
29 V:Psions 2.50
30 R:Primus,I:Artin. 2.50
31 Crisis tie-in 2.50
32 Felicity. 2.50
33 Regufe World 2.50
34 A:New Teen Titans 2.50
35 A:New Teen Titans 2.50
36 Last Days of Broot 2.50
37 V:Spiderguild,A:Lobo 5.00
38 A:Tweener Network. 2.50
Ann.#1 KG,R:Harpis. 2.50
Ann.#2 KG,O:Primus 2.50

100 BULLETS
DC/Vertigo, 1999

1 F:Dizzy Cordova & AgentGraves 12.00
2 . . . . 7.00
3 F:Mr.Shepard 5.00
4 Shot, Water Back,pt.1 . . . . 5.00
5 Shot, Water Back,pt.2 . . . . 5.00
6 Short Con, Long Odds,pt.1 . . . . . 4.00
7 Short Con, Long Odds,pt.2 . . . . . 4.00
8 F:Agent Graves 4.00
9 Right Ear,Left in the Cold,pt.1 . . . 4.00
10 Right Ear,Left in the Cold,pt.2. . . 4.00
11 F:Lilly Roach 3.50
12 Parlez Kung Vous,pt.1 . . . . 3.50
13 Parlez Kung Vous,pt.2 . . . . 3.50
14 Parlez Kung Vous,concl. 3.50
15 Hang Up on Hang Low,pt.1 . . . . 3.50
16 Hang Up on Hang Low,pt.2 . . . . 3.50
17 Hang Up on Hang Low,pt.3 . . . . 3.00
18 Hang Up on Hang Low,pt.4 . . . . 3.00
19 Hang Up on Hang Low,pt.5 . . . . 3.00
20 Hot House. 3.00
21 Sell Fish & Out to Sea,pt.1 . . . . 3.00
22 Sell Fish & Out to Sea,pt.2 . . . . 3.00
23 Red Prince Blues,pt.1. . . . . 3.00
24 Red Prince Blues,pt.2. . . . . 3.50
25 Red Prince Blues,pt.3. . . . . 2.50
26 Mr. Branch & the Family Tree. . . 2.50
27 Idol Chatter 2.50
28 Contrabandolero,pt.1 . . . . 2.50
29 Contrabandolero,pt.2 . . . . 2.50
30 Contrabandolero,pt.3 . . . . 2.50
31 Counterfeit Detective,pt.1 . . . . . 2.50
32 Counterfeit Detective,pt.2 . . . . . 2.50
33 Counterfeit Detective,pt.3 . . . . . 2.50
34 Counterfeit Detective,pt.4 . . . . . 2.50
35 Counterfeit Detective,pt.5 . . . . . 2.50
36 Counterfeit Detective,pt.6 . . . . . 2.50
37 On Accidental Purpose 2.50
38 Cole Burns Slow Hand 2.50
39 Ambition's Audition 2.50
40 Night of the Payday 2.50
41 A Crash 2.50
42 V:Wylie Times 2.50
43 Chill in the Oven,pt.1 . . . . 2.50
44 Chill in the Oven,pt.2 . . . . 2.50
45 Chill in the Oven,pt.3 . . . . 2.50
46 Chill in the Oven,pt.4 . . . . 2.50
47 In Stinked,pt.1. . . . . 2.50
48 In Stinked,pt.2. . . . . 2.50
49 In Stinked,pt.3. . . . . 2.50
50 Agent Graves,40-pg. 3.50

51 Wylie Runs the Voodoo Down	2.50
52 Wylie Runs the Voodoo Down	2.50
53 Wylie Runs the Voodoo Down	2.50
54	2.50
TPB First Shot,Last Call	10.00
TPB Split Second Chance	15.00
TPB Hang Up on the Hang Low	10.00
TPB A Foregone Tomorrow	18.00
TPB The Counterfifth Detective	13.00
TPB Six Feet Under The Gun	13.00
TPB Samurai	13.00

100%

DC/Vertigo, June, 2002

1 (of 5) PPo, 48-pg. b&w	6.00
2 thru 5 PPo, Sci-fi, 48-pg. b&w	@6.00

100% TRUE?

DC/Paradox Press, (B&W) 1996

1 rep. from Paradox Press books	5.00

ORION

April, 2000

1 WS,Darkseid	2.50
2 WS,V:Darkseid	2.50
3 WS,FM,V:Suicide Jockeys	2.50
4 WS,DGb,V:Darkseid	2.50
5 WS,V:Darkseid	2.50
6 WS,EL,AG,F:Mortalla	2.50
7 WS,HC,V:Kalibak	2.50
8 WS,RLe,JLb,V:Kalibak	2.50
9 WS,V:Desaad	2.50
10 WS,AAd,V:Desaad	2.50
11 WS,New Genesis,Anti-Life	2.50
12 WS,JLe,return to Apokolips	2.50
13 WS,TA,JBy,F:Captain Marvel	2.50
14 WS,TA,JBy,F:Captain Marvel	2.50
15 WS,JPL,48-page	4.50
16 WS,Abysmal Plane,V:Clockwerx	2.50
17 WS,Abysmal Plane,V:Clockwerx	2.50
18 WS,AM,F:Rakar	2.50
19 WS,ECa,Joker-crazed Deep Six.	2.50
20 WS,fall from Grace	2.50
21 WS,V:Arnicus Wolfram	2.50
22 WS,young teen	2.50
23 WS,BWi,young teen	2.50
24 WS,BWi,Tactical nuke.	2.50
25 WS,BWi,48-pg.final issue	4.25
TPB The Gates of Apokolips	12.95

OUR ARMY AT WAR

Aug., 1952

1 CI(c),Dig Your FoxholeDeep.	2,800.00
2 CI(c),Champ	1,200.00
3 GK(c),No Exit.	850.00
4 IN(c),Last Man	700.00
5 IN(c),T.N.T. Bouquet	650.00
6 IN(c),Battle Flag	650.00
7 IN(c),Dive Bomber	650.00
8 IN(c),One Man Army	650.00
9 GC(c),Undersea Raider	650.00
10 IN(c),Soldiers on the High Wire	650.00
11 IN(c),Scratch One Meatball	650.00
12 IN(c),The Big Drop	500.00
13 BK(c),Ghost Ace	650.00
14 BK(c),Drummer of Waterloo	650.00
15 IN(c),Thunder in the Skies	500.00
16 IN(c),A Million To One Shot	500.00
17 IN(c),The White Death	500.00
18 IN(c),Frontier Fighter	500.00
19 IN(c),The Big Ditch	500.00
20 IN(c),Abandon Ship	500.00
21 IN(c),Dairy of a Flattop	350.00
22 JGr(c),Ranger Raid.	350.00
23 IN(c),Jungle Navy	350.00
24 IN(c),Suprise Landing.	350.00
25 JGr(c),Take 'Er Down	350.00

*Our Army at War #7 ©
DC Comics, Inc.*

26 JGr(c),Sky Duel	350.00
27 IN(c),MD,Diary of a Frogman	350.00
28 JGr(c),Detour-War	350.00
29 IN(c),Grounded Fighter	350.00
30 JGr(c),Torpedo Raft	350.00
31 IN(c),Howitzer Hill	350.00
32 JGr(c),Battle Mirror	350.00
33 JGr(c),Fighting Gunner	350.00
34 JGr(c),Point-Blank War	350.00
35 JGr(c),Frontline Tackle	350.00
36 JGr(c),Foxhole Mascot	350.00
37 JGr(c),Walking Battle Pin	350.00
38 JGr(c),Floating Pillbox	350.00
39 JGr(c),Trench Trap	350.00
40 RH(c),Tank Hunter	350.00
41 JGr(c),Jungle Target	350.00
42 IN(c),Shadow Targets	250.00
43 JGr(c),A Bridge For Billy	250.00
44 JGr(c),Thunder In The Desert	250.00
45 JGr(c),Diary of a Fighter Pilot.	250.00
46 JGr(c),Prize Package	250.00
47 JGr(c),Flying Jeep	250.00
48 JGr(c),Front Seat	250.00
49 JKu(c),Landing Postponed	250.00
50 JGr(c),RH,Mop-Up Squad	250.00
51 JGr(c),Battle Tag	250.00
52 JGr(c),Pony Express Pilot.	250.00
53 JGr(c),One Ringside-For War.	250.00
54 JKu(c),No-Man Secret	250.00
55 JGr(c),No Rest For A Raider.	250.00
56 JKu(c),You're Next	250.00
57 JGr(c),Ten-Minute Break.	250.00
58 JKu(c),The Fighting SnowBird	250.00
59 JGr(c),The Mustang Had My Number	250.00
60 JGr(c),Ranger Raid.	250.00
61 JGr(c),A Pigeon For Easy Co.	225.00
62 JKu(c),Trigger Man	225.00
63 JGr(c),The Big Toss	225.00
64 JKu(c),Tank Rider	225.00
65 JGr(c),Scramble-War Upstairs	225.00
66 RH(c),Gunner Wanted	225.00
67 JKu(c),MD,Boiling Point	225.00
68 JKu(c),MD,End of the Line	225.00
69 JGr(c),Combat Cage.	225.00
70 JGr(c),Torpedo Tank	225.00
71 JGr(c),Flying Mosquitoes	225.00
72 JGr(c),No. 1 Pigeon	225.00
73 JKu(c),Shooting Gallery	225.00
74 JGr(c),Ace Without Guns	225.00
75 JGr(c),Blind Night Fighter	225.00
76 JKu(c),Clipped Hellcat	225.00
77 JGr(c),Jets Don't Dream	225.00
78 IN(c),Battle Nurse	225.00

79 JGr(c),MD,What's the Price of a B-17?	225.00
80 JGr(c),The Sparrow And The...Hawk	225.00
81 JGr(c),Sgt. Rock in The Rock of Easy Co.	4,000.00
82 JGr(c),MD,Gun Jockey	900.00
83 JGr(c),MD,B:Sgt.Rock Stories, The Rock and the Wall.	3,000.00
84 JKu(c),Laughter On Snakehead Hill	450.00
85 JGr(c),Ice Cream Soldier	600.00
86 RH(c),Tank 711	400.00
87 RH(c),Calling Easy Co.	400.00
88 JKu(c),The Hard Way	400.00
89 RH(c),No Shoot From Easy	400.00
90 JKu(c),3 Stripes Hill	400.00
91 JGr(c),No Answer from Sarge	1,200.00
92 JGr(c),Luck of Easy	250.00
93 JGr(c),Deliver One Airfield	250.00
94 JKu(c),Target-Easy Company.	250.00
95 JKu(c),Battle of the Stripes.	250.00
96 JGr(c),MD,Last Stand For Easy	250.00
97 JKu(c),What Makes A Sergeant Run?	250.00
98 JKu(c),Soldiers Never Die	250.00
99 JKu(c),Easy's Hardest Battle	250.00
100 JKu(c),No Exit For Easy	250.00
101 JKu(c),End Of Easy	200.00
102 JKu(c),The Big Star.	200.00
103 RH(c),Easy's Had It	200.00
104 JKu(c),A New Kind Of War	200.00
105 JKu(c),T.N.T. Birthday.	200.00
106 JKu(c),Meet Lt. Rock	200.00
107 JKu(c),Doom Over Easy	200.00
108 JGr(c),Unknown Sergeant	200.00
109 JKu(c),Roll Call For Heroes	200.00
110 JKu(c),That's An Order	200.00
111 JKu(c),What's The Price Of A Dog Tag	200.00
112 JKu(c),Battle Shadow	200.00
113 JKu(c),Eyes Of A Blind Gunner	200.00
114 JKu(c),Killer Sergeant	200.00
115 JKu(c),Rock's Battle Family	200.00
116 JKu(c),S.O.S. Sgt. Rock	200.00
117 JKu(c),Snafu Squad	200.00
118 RH(c),The Tank Vs. The Tin Soldier	200.00
119 JKu(c),A Bazooka For Babyface	200.00
120 JGr(c),Battle Tags For Easy Co.	150.00
121 JKu(c),New Boy In Easy.	125.00
122 JKu(c),Battle of the Pajama Commandoes.	125.00
123 JGr(c),Battle Brass Ring.	125.00
124 JKu(c),Target-Sgt. Rock	125.00
125 JKu(c),Hold-At All Costs	125.00
126 RH(c),The End Of Easy Company	125.00
127 JKu(c),4 Faces of Sgt. Rock.	125.00
128 JKu(c),O:Sgt. Rock.	350.00
129 JKu(c),Heroes Need Cowards	125.00
130 JKu(c),No Hill For Easy	125.00
131 JKu(c),One Pair of Dogtags For Sale	125.00
132 JKu(c),Young Soldiers Never Cry	125.00
133 JKu(c),Yesterday's Hero	125.00
134 JKu(c),The T.N.T. Book.	125.00
135 JKu(c),Battlefield Double	125.00
136 JKu(c),Make Me A Hero	125.00
137 JKu(c),Too Many Sergeants	125.00
138 JKu(c),Easy's Lost Sparrow	125.00
139 JKu(c),A Firing Squad For Easy	125.00
140 JKu(c),Brass Sergeant	125.00

141 JKu(c),Dead Man's Trigger . . 125.00
142 JKu(c),Easy's New Topkick . . 125.00
143 JKu(c),Easy's T.N.T. Crop . . . 125.00
144 JKu(c),The Sparrow And
   The Tiger 125.00
145 JKu(c),A Feather For
   Little Sure Shot 125.00
146 JKu(c),The Fighting Guns
   For Easy 125.00
147 JKu(c),Book One:Generals
   Don't Die 125.00
148 JKu(c),Book Two:Generals
   Don't Die:Generals Are
   Sergeants With Stars. 125.00
149 JKu(c),Surrender Ticket 125.00
150 JKu(c),Flytrap Hill 125.00
151 JKu(c),War Party,
   I:Enemy Ace 600.00
152 Jku(c),Last Man-Last Shot . . 125.00
153 JKu(c),Easy's Last Stand . . . 300.00
154 JKu(c),Boobytrap Mascot . . . 100.00
155 JKu(c),No Stripes For Me . . . 200.00
156 JKu(c),The Human Tank Trap 100.00
157 JKu(c),Nothin's Ever
   Lost In War 100.00
158 JKu(c),Iron Major-Rock
   Sergeant 100.00
159 JKu(c),The Blind Gun 100.00
160 JKu(c),What's The Color
   Of Your Blood 100.00
161 JKu(c),Dead End
   For A Dogface 100.00
162 JKu(c),The Price and
   The Sergeant. 100.00
163 JKu(c),MD,RE,Kill Me-Kill Me 100.00
164 JKu(c),CE,No Exit For Easy,
   reprint from #100 . . . . 200.00
165 GE,JKu(c),The Return of the
   Iron Major 100.00
166 GE,JKu(c),Half A Sergeant . . 100.00
167 GE,JKu(c),Kill One-
   Save One 100.00
168 GE,JKu(c),I Knew The
   Unknown Soldier 200.00
169 GE,JKu(c),Nazi On My Back . 90.00
170 GE,JKu(c),Buzzard Bait Hill . . 90.00
171 GE,JKu(c),The Sergeant
   Must Die 80.00
172 GE,JKu(c),A Slug for a
   Sergeant 80.00
173 GE,JKu(c),Easy's Hardest
   Battle, reprint from #99 . . . . . 80.00
174 GE,JKu(c),One Kill Too
   Many 80.00
175 JKu(c),T.N.T. Letter 80.00
176 MD,JKu(c),Give Me Your
   Stripes 80.00
177 RH,JKu(c),Target-Easy Company,
   reprint from #94, giant-size . . 125.00
178 RH,JKu(c),Only One Medal
   For Easy 80.00
179 RH,JKu(c),A Penny Jackie
   Johnson 80.00
180 RH,JKu(c),You Can't
   Kill A General. 80.00
181 RH,Monday's Coward-
   Tuesday's Hero 80.00
182 NA,RH,The Desert Rats
   of Easy 90.00
183 RH,NA,JKu(c),Sergeants
   Don't Stay Dead 100.00
184 RH,JKu(c),Candidate For A
   Firing Squad 75.00
185 RH,JKu(c),Battle Flag For
   A G.I. 75.00
186 RH,NA,JKu(c),3 Stripes Hill
   reprint from #90, Origin 75.00
187 RH,JKu(c),Shadow of a
   Sergeant 65.00
188 RH,JKu(c),Death Comes for
   Easy. 65.00

189 RH,JKu(c),The Mission Was
   Murder 65.00
190 RH,JKu(c),What Make's A
   Sergeant Run?, reprint
   from #97, giant-size 100.00
191 RH,JKu(c),Death Flies High,
   A:Johnny Cloud 100.00
192 RH,JKu(c),A Firing Squad
   For A Sergeant 100.00
193 RH,JKu(c),Blood In
   the Desert 100.00
194 RH,JKu(c),Time For
   Vengeance. 100.00
195 RH,JKu(c),Dead Town 100.00
196 RH,JKu(c),Stop The War-
   I Want To Get Off. 100.00
197 RH,JKu(c),Last Exit For Easy 100.00
198 RH,JKu(c),Plugged Nickel . . 100.00
199 RH,JKu(c),Nazi Ghost Wolf . 100.00
200 RH,GE,JKu(c),The
   Troubadour 75.00
201 RH,JKu(c),The Graffiti Writer . 50.00
202 RH,JKu(c),The Sarge Is Dead 50.00
203 RH,MD,JKu(c),Easy's Had It,
   reprint from # 103, giant-size . 90.00
204 RH,JKu(c) 50.00
205 RH,JKu(c) 50.00
206 RH,JKu(c),There's A War On . 45.00
207 RH,JKu(c),A Sparrow's
   Prayer 45.00
208 RH,JKu(c),A Piece of Rag...
   And A Hank of Hair 45.00
209 RH,JKu(c),I'm Still Alive 45.00
210 RH,JKu(c),I'm Kilroy 45.00
211 RH,JKu(c),The Treasure of
   St. Daniel. 45.00
212 RH,MD,JKu(c),The Quiet War 45.00
213 RH,JKu(c),A Letter For
   Bulldozer 45.00
214 RH,JKu(c),Where Are You? . . 45.00
215 RH,JKu(c),Pied Piper of Peril . 45.00
216 RH,JKu(c),Doom Over Easy,
   reprint from # 107, Giant-size . 75.00
217 RH,JKu(c),Surprise Party 35.00
218 RH,JKu(c),Medic! 35.00
219 RH,JKu(c),Yesterday's Hero . 35.00
220 RH,JKu(c),Stone-Age War . . . 35.00
221 RH,JKu(c),Hang-Up 35.00
222 RH,JKu(c),Dig In, Easy. 35.00
223 RH,JKu(c),On Time. 35.00
224 RH,JKu(c),One For The
   Money 35.00
225 RH,JKu(c),Face Front. 35.00
226 RH,JKu(c),Death Stop 35.00
227 RH,JKu(c),Traitor's Blood 35.00
228 RH,JKu(c),It's A Dirty War. . . . 35.00
229 RH,JKu(c),The Battle of the
   Sergeants, reprint #128,
   Giant-size 50.00
230 RH,JKu(c),Home Is The
   Hunter 25.00
231 RH,JKu(c),My Brother's
   Keeper. 25.00
232 RH,JKu(c),3 Men In A Tub . . . 25.00
233 RH,JKu(c),Head Count. 25.00
234 RH,JKu(c),Summer In Salerno 25.00
235 RH,ATh,JKu(c),Pressure
   Point, giant-size. 35.00
236 RH,JKu(c),Face The Devil,
   giant-size. 35.00
237 RH,JKu(c),Nobody Cares,
   giant-size. 35.00
238 RH,JKu(c),I Kid You Not,
   giant-size 35.00
239 RH,JKu(c),The Soldier,
   giant-size 35.00
240 RH,JKu(c),NA, giant-size 50.00
241 RH,ATh,JKu(c),War Story,
   giant-size 35.00
242 RH,JKu(c),Infantry 35.00
243 RH,MD,JKu(c),24 Hour Pass . 30.00

Our Army at War #219
© DC Comics Inc.

244 RH,MD,JKu(c),Easy's First
   Tiger 30.00
245 RH,JKu(c),The Prisoner 30.00
246 RH,JKu(c),Naked Combat . . . 30.00
247 RH,JKu(c),The Vision 20.00
248 RH,JKu(c),The Firing Squad. . 20.00
249 RH,JKu(c),The Luck of
   Easy,WW 22.00
250 RH,JKu(c),90 Day Wonder . . . 20.00
251 RH,JKu(c),The Iron Major. . . . 20.00
252 RH,JKu(c),The Iron Hand 20.00
253 RH,JKu(c),Rock and Iron 20.00
254 RH,ATh,JKu(c),The Town 20.00
255 RH,JKu(c),What's It Like. 20.00
256 RH,JKu(c),School For
   Sergeants 20.00
257 RH,JKu(c),The Castaway 20.00
258 RH,JKu(c),The Survivors 20.00
259 RH,JKu(c),Lost Paradise 20.00
260 RH,JKu(c),Hell's Island. 20.00
261 RH,JKu(c),The Medal That
   Nobody Wanted. 20.00
262 RH,JKu(c),The Return 20.00
263 RH,JKu(c),The Cage 20.00
264 RH,JKu(c),The Hunt 20.00
265 RH,JKu(c),The Brother. 20.00
266 RH,GE,JKu(c),The Evacuees. 20.00
267 RH,JKu(c),A Bakers Dozen . . 20.00
268 RH,JKu(c),The Elite 20.00
269 RH,MD,GE,JKu(c), giant-size. 50.00
270 RH,JKu(c),Spawn of the
   Devil. 20.00
271 RH,JKu(c),Brittle Harvest . . . 18.00
272 RH,JKu(c),The Bloody Flag . . 17.00
273 RH,JKu(c),The Arena 17.00
274 RH,GE,JKu(c),Home Is The
   Hero. 17.00
275 RH,MD,JKu(c),Graveyard
   Battlefield, giant-size 50.00
276 RH,GE,JKu(c),A Bullet For
   Rock 16.00
277 RH,JKu(c),Gashouse Gang . . 16.00
278 RH,GE,JKu(c),Rearguard
   Action. 16.00
279 JKu(c),Mined City 16.00
280 RH,GE,MD,JKu(c),Mercy
   Mission 30.00
281 RH,JKu(c),Dead Man's Eyes . 14.00
282 JKu(c),Pieces of Time. 14.00
283 JKu(c),Dropouts 14.00
284 JKu(c),Linkup 14.00
285 JKu(c),Bring Him Back 14.00
286 JKu(c),Firebird 12.00
287 MGr,JKu(c),The Fifth
   Dimension 12.00

288 JKu(c),Defend-Or Destroy . . . 12.00
289 JKu(c),The Line 12.00
290 JKu(c),Super-Soldiers. 12.00
291 JKu(c),Death Squad 12.00
292 JKu(c),A Lesson In Blood 12.00
293 JKu(c),It Figures 12.00
294 JKu(c),Coffin For Easy 12.00
295 JKu(c),The Devil in Paradise . 12.00
296 JKu(c),Combat Soldier 12.00
297 JKu(c),Percentages 12.00
298 JKu(c),Return to Chartres. . . . 12.00
299 JKu(c),Three Soldiers 12.00
300 JKu(c),300th Hill 16.00
301 JKu(c),The Farm. 12.00

Becomes:

SGT. ROCK
1977–88

302 JKu(c),Anzio-The Bloodbath,
    part I 40.00
303 JKu(c),Anzio, part II 20.00
304 JKu(c),Anzio, part III 20.00
305 JKu(c),Dead Man's Trigger,
    reprint from #141. . . . . 20.00
306 JKu(c),The Last Soldier 20.00
307 JKu(c),I'm Easy. 20.00
308 JKu(c),One Short Step 20.00
309 JKu(c),Battle Clowns 20.00
310 JKu(c),Hitler's Wolf Children. . 20.00
311 JKu(c),The Sergeant and
    the Lady. 15.00
312 JKu(c),No Name Hill 15.00
313 JKu(c),A Jeep For Joey 15.00
314 JKu(c),Gimme Sky 15.00
315 JKu(c),Combat Antenna 15.00
316 JKu(c),Another Hill. 15.00
317 JKu(c),Hell's Oven 15.00
318 JKu(c),Stone-Age War 15.00
319 JKu(c),To Kill a Sergeant 15.00
320 JKu(c),Never Salute a
    Sergeant 15.00
321 JKu(c),It's Murder Out Here . . 10.00
322 JKu(c),The Killer 10.00
323 JKu(c),Monday's Hero 10.00
324 JKu(c),Ghost of a Tank 10.00
325 JKu(c),Future Kill, part I 10.00
326 JKu(c),Future Kill, part II 10.00
327 JKu(c),Death Express. 10.00
328 JKu(c),Waiting For Rock. 10.00
329 JKu(c),Dead Heat 10.00
330 JKu(c),G.I. Trophy 10.00
331 JKu(c),The Sons of War 10.00
332 JKu(c),Pyramid of Death. 10.00
333 JKu(c),Ask The Dead 10.00

Our Army at War #282
© DC Comics, Inc.

334 JKu(c),What's Holding Up
    The War. 10.00
335 JKu(c),Killer Compass 10.00
336 JKu(c),The Red Maple Leaf . . 10.00
337 JKu(c),A Bridge Called Charlie 10.00
338 JKu(c),No Escape From
    the Front 10.00
339 JKu(c),I Was Here Before. . . . 10.00
340 JKu(c),How To Win A War. . . . 10.00
341 JKu(c),High-Flyer 10.00
342 JKu(c),The 6 sides of
    Sgt. Rock. 10.00
343 thru 350. . . . . @10.00
351 thru 422. . . . . @7.00

OUR FIGHTING FORCES
Oct.–Nov., 1954

1 IN,JGr(c),Human Booby Trap 1,800.00
2 RH,IN,IN(c),Mile-Long Step . . . 700.00
3 RA,JKu(c),Winter Ambush. . . . 550.00
4 RA,JGr(c),The Hot Seat 450.00
5 IN,RA,JGr(c),The Iron Punch . 450.00
6 IN,RA,JGr(c),The Sitting Tank . 375.00
7 RA,JKu,JGr(c),Battle Fist. . . . 375.00
8 IN,RA,JGr(c),No War
    For A Gunner. 375.00
9 JKu,RH,JGr(c),Crash-
    Landing At Dawn 375.00
10 WW,RA,JGr(c),Grenade
    Pitcher 375.00
11 JKu,JGr(c),Diary of a Sub. . . 300.00
12 IN,JKu,JGr(c),Jump Seat . . . 300.00
13 RA,JGr(c),Beach Party 300.00
14 JA,RA,IN,JGr(c),Unseen War . 300.00
15 RH,JKu,JGr(c),Target For
    A Lame Duck. 300.00
16 RH,JGr(c),Night Fighter 300.00
17 RA,JGr(c),Anchored Frogman 300.00
18 RH,JKu,JGr(c),Cockpit Seat . . 300.00
19 RA,JKu(c),StraightenThatLine 300.00
20 RA,MD,JGr(c),The
    Floating Pilot 350.00
21 RA,JKu(c),The Bouncing
    Baby of Company B 200.00
22 JKu,RA,JGr(c),3 Doorways
    To War 200.00
23 RA,IN,JA,JGr(c),Tin Fish Pilot 200.00
24 RA,RH,JGr(c),Frogman Duel . 200.00
25 RA,JKu(c),Dead End 200.00
26 IN,RH,JKu(c),Tag Day 200.00
27 MD,RA,JKu(c),TNT Escort . . . 200.00
28 RH,MD,JKu(c),AllQuiet atC.P. 200.00
29 JKu,JKu(c),Listen To A Jet . . . 200.00
30 IN,RA,JKu(c),Fort
    For A Gunner. 200.00
31 MD,RA,JKu(c),Silent Sub 200.00
32 RH,MD,RH(c),PaperWorkWar 200.00
33 RH,JKu,JKu(c),Frogman
    In A Net 200.00
34 JA,JGr,JKu(c),Calling U-217. . 200.00
35 JA,JGr,JKu(c),Mask of
    a Frogman. 200.00
36 MD,JA,JKu(c),Steel Soldier . . 200.00
37 JA,JGr,JGr(c),Frogman
    In A Bottle 200.00
38 RH,RA,JA,JGr(c),Sub Sinker . 200.00
39 JA,RH,RH(c),Last Torpedo . . . 200.00
40 JGr,JA,JKu,JKu(c),The
    Silent Ones 200.00
41 JGr,RH,JA,JKu(c),Battle
    Mustang. 250.00
42 RH,MD,JGr(c),Sorry-
    Wrong Hill 175.00
43 MD,JKu,JGr(c),Inside Battle . . 175.00
44 MD,RH,RA,JGr(c),Big Job
    For Baker. 175.00
45 RH,RA,JGr(c),B:Gunner and
    Sarge, Mop-Up Squad. 600.00
46 RH,RA,JGr(c),Gunner'sSquad 250.00
47 RH,JKu(c),TNT Birthday 175.00

Our Fighting Forces #8
© DC Comics, Inc.

48 JA,RH,JGr(c),A Statue
    For Sarge 175.00
49 MD,RH,JGr(c),Blind Gunner . . 225.00
50 JA,RH,JGr(c),I:Pooch,My
    Pal, The Pooch 175.00
51 RA,JA,RH(c),Underwater
    Gunner. 150.00
52 MD,JKu,JKu(c),The Gunner
    and the Nurse 125.00
53 JA,RA,JGr(c),An Egg
    For Sarge 125.00
54 . . . . 125.00
55 MD,RH,JGr(c),The Last Patrol 125.00
56 RH,RA,JGr(c),Bridge of
    Bullets 125.00
57 JA,IN,JGr(c),A Tank For Sarge 125.00
58 JA,JGr(c),Return of the Pooch 125.00
59 RH,JA,JGr(c),Pooch-Patrol
    Leader 125.00
60 RH,JA,JGr(c),Tank Target. . . . 125.00
61 JA,JGr(c),Pass to Peril 125.00
62 JA,JGr(c),The Flying Pooch . . 125.00
63 JA,RH,JGr(c),Pooch-Tank
    Hunter 125.00
64 JK,RH,JGr(c),A Lifeline
    For Sarge 125.00
65 IN,JA,JGr(c),Dogtag Patrol . . . 125.00
66 JKu,JA,JGr(c),Trail of the
    Ghost Bomber 125.00
67 IN,JA,JGr(c),Purple Heart
    For Pooch 125.00
68 JA,JGr(c),Col. Hakawa's
    Birthday Party 125.00
69 JA,JKu,JGr(c),
    Destination Doom 125.00
70 JA,JKu(c),The Last Holdout . . 125.00
71 JA,JGr(c),End of the Marines . 100.00
72 JA,JGr(c),Four-Footed Spy. . . 100.00
73 IN,JGr(c),The Hero Maker . . . 100.00
74 IN,JGr(c),Three On A T.N.T.
    Bull's-Eye. 100.00
75 JKu(c),Purple Heart Patrol . . . 100.00
76 JKu(c),The T.N.T. Seat 100.00
77 JKu(c),No Foxhole-No Home . 100.00
78 JGr(c),The Last Medal 100.00
79 JA,JGr(c),Backs to the Sea . . 100.00
80 JA,JGr(c),Don't Come Back . . 100.00
81 JA,JGr(c),Battle of
    the Mud Marines 100.00
82 JA,JGr(c),Battle of the
    Empty Helmets 100.00
83 RA,JKu(c),Any Marine
    Can Do It. 100.00
84 JA,JKu(c),The Gun of Shame. 100.00
85 Ja,JKu(c),The TNT Pin-Points 100.00

86 JKu(c),3 Faces of Combat . . . 100.00
87 JKu(c),Battle of the
   Boobytraps 100.00
88 GC,JKu(c),Devil Dog Patrol . . 100.00
89 JKu(c),TNT Toothache 100.00
90 JKu(c),Stop the War 100.00
91 JKu(c),The Human Shooting
   Gallery 50.00
92 JA,JKu(c),The Bomb That
   Stopped The War. 50.00
93 IN,JKu(c),The Human Sharks. . 50.00
94 RH(c),E:Gunner,Sarge & Pooch,
   The Human Blockbusters 50.00
95 GC,RH(c),B:The Fighting Devil
   Dog, Lt. Rock, The
   Fighting Devil Dog. 50.00
96 JA,RH(c),Battle of Fire 50.00
97 IN(c),Invitation To A
   Firing Squad 50.00
98 IN(c),E:The Fighting Devil
   Dog, Death Wore A Grin 50.00
99 JA,JKu(c),B:Capt. Hunter,
   No Mercy in Vietnam. 50.00
100 GC,IN(c),Death Also
   Stalks the Hunter. 50.00
101 JA,RH(c),Killer of Vietnam . . . 35.00
102 RH,JKu(c),Cold Steel
   For A Hot War 35.00
103 JKu(c),The Tunnels of Death . 35.00
104 JKu(c),Night Raid In Vietnam . 35.00
105 JKu(c),Blood Loyality 35.00
106 IN(c),Trail By Fury. 35.00
107 IN(c),Raid Of The Hellcats . . . 35.00
108 IN(c),Kill The Wolf Pack 35.00
109 IN(c),Burn, Raiders, Burn 35.00
110 IN(c),Mountains Full of Death . 35.00
111 IN(c),Train of Terror. 35.00
112 IN(c),What's In It For
   The Hellcats? 35.00
113 IN(c),Operation-Survival 35.00
114 JKu(c),No Loot For The
   Hellcats 35.00
115 JKu(c),Death In The Desert . . 35.00
116 JKu(c),Peril From the Casbah 35.00
117 JKu(c),Colder Than Death . . . 35.00
118 JKu(c),Hell Underwater. 35.00
119 JKu(c),Bedlam In Berlin 35.00
120 JKu(c),Devil In The Dark 35.00
121 JKu(c),Take My Place. 35.00
122 JKu(c),24 Hours To Die 35.00
123 JKu(c),B:Born Losers,No
   Medals No Graves. 75.00
124 JKu(c),Losers Take All 25.00
125 Daughters of Death. 25.00
126 JKu(c),Lost Town 25.00
127 JKu(c),Angels Over Hell's
   Corner 25.00
128 JKu(c),7 11 War 25.00
129 JKu(c),Ride The Nightmare . . 25.00
130 JKu(c),Nameless Target 25.00
131 JKu(c),Half A Man. 25.00
132 JKu(c),Pooch, The Winner . . . 25.00
133 JKu(c),Heads or Tails,
   giant-size 35.00
134 JKu(c),The Real Losers,
   giant-size 35.00
135 JKu(c),Death Picks A Loser,
   giant-size 35.00
136 JKu(c),Decoy For Death,
   giant-size 35.00
137 JKu(c),God Of The Losers,
   giant-size 35.00
138 JKu(c),The Targets 18.00
139 JKu(c),The Pirate 18.00
140 JKu(c),Lost...One Loser 18.00
141 JKu(c),Bad Penny, The. 18.00
142 JKu(c), 1/2 A Man 18.00
143 JKu(c),Diamonds Are
   For Never 18.00
144 JKu(c),The Lost Mission 18.00
145 JKu(c),A Flag For Losers 18.00

Our Fighting Forces #166
© *DC Comics Inc.*

146 JKu(c),The Forever Walk 18.00
147 NA(c),The Glory Road 22.00
148 JKu(c),The Last Charge 18.00
149 FT(c),A Bullet For
   A Traitor. 18.00
150 JKu(c),Mark Our Graves. 18.00
151 JKu(c),Kill Me With Wagner . . 20.00
152 JK(c),A Small Place In Hell. . . 20.00
153 JK(c),Big Max 20.00
154 JK(c),Bushido,Live By The
   Code, Die By The Code 20.00
155 JK(c),The Partisans 20.00
156 JK(c),Good-Bye Broadway . . . 20.00
157 JK(c),Panama Fattie. 20.00
158 JK(c),Bombing Out On
   The Panama Canal 20.00
159 JK(c),Mile-A-Minute Jones . . . 20.00
160 JKu(c),Ivan 20.00
161 JKu(c),The Major's Dream . . . 20.00
162 Gung-Ho 20.00
163 JKu(c),The Unmarked Graves 12.00
164 JKu(c),A Town Full Of Losers. 12.00
165 LD(c),The Rowboat Fleet 12.00
166 LD(c),Sword of Flame. 12.00
167 LD(c),A Front Seat In Hell. . . . 12.00
168 LD(c),A Cold Day To Die. 12.00
169 JKu(c),Welcome Home-And
   Die. 12.00
170 JKu(c),A Bullet For
   The General 12.00
171 JKu(c),A Long Day...
   A Long War 12.00
172 JKu(c),The Two-Headed Spy . 12.00
173 JKu(c),An Appointment
   With A Direct Hit 12.00
174 JKu(c),Winner Takes-Death . . 12.00
175 JKu(c),Death Warrant. 12.00
176 JKu(c),The Loser Is A
   Teen-Ager 12.00
177 JKu(c),This Loser Must Die . . 12.00
178 JKu(c),Last Drop For Losers . 12.00
179 JKu(c),The Last Loser 12.00
180 JKu(c),Hot Seat In A
   Cold War 12.00
181 JKu(c),Sept.–Oct., 1978 . . . . 18.00

OUTCASTS
Oct., 1987

1 . . . . 2.25
2 thru 11 . . . . @2.25

OUTLAW NATION
DC/Vertigo, Aug., 2000

1 JaD(s),F:pulp-fiction writer. 2.50
2 JaD(s),Southern bayou 2.50
3 JaD,F:Devil Kid 2.50
4 JaD,F:Kid Gloves. 2.50
5 JaD,F:Kid Gloves. 2.50
6 JaD, ... 2.50
7 JaD, ... 2.50
8 JaD,Women,tequila & guns 2.50
9 JaD,Hell Holes. 2.50
10 JaD,V:Gloves 2.50
11 JaD,Hate, Murder and Revenge . 2.50
12 JaD,Temptation. 2.50
13 JaD,Desperado. 2.50
14 JaD,The Devil Kid 2.50
15 JaD,The Devil Kid 2.50
16 JaD,Under siege 2.50
17 JaD,Quicksand 2.50
18 JaD,Old Asa 2.50
19 JaD,final issue 2.50

OUTLAWS
1991

1 LMc,I:Hood 2.25
2 LMc,O:Hood. 2.25
3 LMc,V:Evil King 2.25
4 LMc,V:Lord Conductor. 2.25
5 LMc,Archery contest 2.25
6 LMc,Raid on King's Castle 2.25
7 LMc,Refuge, V:Lord Conductor . . 2.25

OUTSIDERS, THE
Nov., 1985
[1st Regular Series]

1 JAp,I:Looker. 3.00
2 JAp,V:Nuclear Family 2.50
3 JAp,V:Force of July 2.50
4 JAp,V:Force of July 2.50
5 JAp,Christmas Issue 2.50
6 JAp,V:Duke of Oil 2.50
7 JAp,V:Duke of Oil 2.50
8 JAp,Japan 2.50
9 JAp/SD/JOp,Bik Lightning 2.50
10 JAp,I:Peoples Heroes. 2.50
11 JAp,Imprisoned in death camp . 2.50
12 JAp,Imprisoned in death camp . 2.50
13 JAp,Desert island 2.50
14 JAp,Looker/murder story 2.50
15 DJu,V:Bio-hazard 2.50
16 Halo vs.Firefly 2.50
17 JAp,J:Batman 2.50
18 JAp,BB,V:Eclipso 2.50
19 JAp,V:Windfall. 2.50
20 JAp,Masters of Disaster 2.50
21 JAp,V:Kobra,I:Clayface IV 2.50
22 JAp,V:Strike Force Kobra 2.50
23 Return of People's Heroes 2.50
24 TVE,JAp,V:Skull,A:Duke of Oil . . 2.50
25 JAp,V:Skull 2.50
26 JAp,in Markovia 2.50
27 EL,Millennium 2.50
28 EL,Millennium,final issue 2.50
Ann.#1,KN,V:Skull,A:Batman. 2.50
Spec.#1,A:Infinity,Inc 2.50

[2nd Regular Series], 1993–95

1 Alpha,TC(c),B:MiB(s),PaP,
   I:Technocrat,Faust,Wylde 3.00
1a Omega,TC(c),PaP,V:Vampires . 3.00
2 PaP,V:Sanction 2.25
3 PaP,V:Eradicator 2.25
4 PaP,A:Eradicator 2.25
5 PaP,V:Atomic Knight,A:Jihad . . . 2.25
6 PaP,V:Jihad 2.25
7 PaP,C:Batman 2.25
8 PaP,V:Batman,I:Halo 2.25
9 PaP,V:Batman 2.25
10 PaP,B:Final Blood, R:Looker . . . 2.50

11 PaP,Zero Hour,E:Final Blood . . . 2.25	
12 PaP 2.25	
13 New base 2.25	
14 Martial Arts Spectacular 2.25	
15 V:New Year's Evil 2.25	
16 R:Windfall 2.25	
17 A:Green Lantern 2.25	
18 Sins of the Father 2.25	
19 Sins of the Father, pt.2 . . . . 2.25	
20 DvA,V:Metamorpho. 2.25	
21 A:Apokolips 2.25	
22 Alien Assassin 2.25	
23 V:Defilers 2.25	
24 finale 2.25	

OUTSIDERS
June 2003

1 TR,SHa 6.00
1a 2nd printing 3.00
2 TR,SHa,F:Jade 4.00
3 TR,SHa,Gorilla Grodd 3.00
4 Ccs,V:Brother Blood 3.00
5 CCs,V:Brother Blood 3.00
6 CCs,V:Brother Blood 2.50
7 TR,SHa,two Metamorphos 2.50
8 TR,F:Huntress 2.50
9 TR,F:Black Lightning 2.50
10 TR,F:Captain Marvel Jr. 2.50
11 F:Arsenal. 2.50
12 V:Psimon. 2.50
13 TR,Five by Five,pt.1 . . . . 2.50
14 TR,Five by Five,pt.2 . . . . 2.50
15 TR,Five by Five,pt.3 . . . . 2.50
16 V:Arsenal 2.50
17 TR,Most Wanted 2.50
TPB Looking For Trouble 13.00

PARALLAX:
EMERALD NIGHT
Nov., 1996

1 RMz(s),MMK,MkK, pivotal tie-in
   to Final Night 4.50

PEACEMAKER
Jan., 1988

1 A:Dr.Tzin-Tzin 2.50
2 The Wages of Tzin 2.50
3 and 4 . . . . @2.50

PENGUIN
TRIUMPHANT

1 JSon,A:Batman,Wall Street 6.00

PETER CANNON:
THUNDERBOLT
1992–93

1 thru 6 MC . . . . @2.25
7 MC,Battleground 2.25
8 MC,Cairo Kidnapped 2.25
9 MC 2.25
10 MC,A:JLA 2.25
11 MC,V:Havoc,A:Checkmate 2.25
12 MC,final Issue 2.25

PETER PANDA
Aug.–Sept., 1953

1 . . . . 500.00
2 . . . . 200.00
3 thru 9 . . . . @200.00
10 Aug.–Sept., 1958 . . . . 200.00

PETER PORKCHOPS
Nov.–Dec., 1949

1 . . . . 350.00
2 . . . . 175.00

---

3 thru 10 . . . . @125.00
11 thru 30 . . . . @100.00
31 thru 61 . . . . @75.00
62 Oct.–Dec., 1960 . . . . 75.00

PHANTOM, THE
Oct., 1987

1 JO,A:Modern Phantom,13th
   Phantom 3.00
2 JO,Murder Trial in Manhattan . . . 3.00
3 JO,A:Chessman. 3.00
4 JO,V:Chessman,final issue 3.00

PHANTOM, THE
1989–90

1 LMc,V:Gun Runners 3.00
2 LMc,V:Gun Runners 2.50
3 LMc,V:Drug Smugglers 2.50
4 LMc,In America,A:Diana Palner. . 2.50
5 LMc,Racial Riots 2.50
6 LMc,in Africa,Toxic Waste
   Problem 2.50
7 LMc,Gold Rush 2.50
8 LMc,Train Surfing 2.50
9 LMc,The Slave Trade 2.50
10 LMc,Famine in Khagana. 2.50
11 LMc,Phantom/Diana Wedding
   proposal. 2.50
12 LMc,Phantom framed for
   murder 2.50
13 W:Phantom & Diana Palner
   C:Mandrake last issue. 2.50

PHANTOM STRANGER
Aug.–Sept., 1952

1 . . . . 2,500.00
2 . . . . 1,500.00
3 . . . . 1,200.00
4 . . . . 1,200.00
5 . . . . 1,200.00
6, June-July, 1953 . . . . 1,200.00

PHANTOM STRANGER
May-June, 1969

1 CI rep.&new material 150.00
2 CI rep.&new material 75.00
3 CI rep.&new material 75.00
4 NA,I:Tala,1st All-new issue 80.00
5 MSy,MA,A:Dr.13 . . . . 50.00
6 MSy,A:Dr.13 . . . . 50.00
7 JAp,V:Tala 50.00

Phantom Stranger #37
© DC Comics, Inc.

---

8 JAp,A:Dr.13 . . . . 50.00
9 JAp,A:Dr.13 . . . . 50.00
10 JAp,I:Tannarak 50.00
11 JAp,V:Tannarak 30.00
12 JAp,TD,Dr.13 solo story 30.00
13 JAp,TD,Dr.13 solo. 30.00
14 JAp,TD,Dr.13 solo. 30.00
15 JAp,ATh(rep),TD,Iron Messiah,
   giant-size 35.00
16 JAp,TD,MMes(rep)Dr.13 solo
   giant-size 35.00
17 JAp,I:Cassandra Craft,
   giant-size 35.00
18 TD,Dr.13 solo, giant-size 35.00
19 JAp,TD,Dr.13 solo, giant-size . . 35.00
20 JAp,Child Shall Lead Them 25.00
21 JAp,TD,Dr.13 solo. 20.00
22 JAp,TD,I:Dark Circle 20.00
23 JAp,MK,I:Spawn-Frankenstein . 20.00
24 JAp,MA,Spawn Frankenstein . . 30.00
25 JAp,MA,Spawn Frankenstein . . 30.00
26 JAp,A:Frankenstein. 35.00
27 V:Dr. Zorn 30.00
28 BU:Spawn of Frankenstein 30.00
29 V:Dr.Zorn,BU:Frankenstein 30.00
30 E:Spawn of Frankenstein 30.00
31 B:BU:Black Orchid 35.00
32 NR,BU:Black Orchid 20.00
33 MGr,A:Deadman 25.00
34 BU:Black Orchid 20.00
35 BU:Black Orchid 20.00
36 BU:Black Orchid 20.00
37 Crimson Gold,BU:BlackOrchid . 20.00
38 Images of the Dead 20.00
39 A:Deadman 25.00
40 A:Deadman 25.00
41 A:Deadman 25.00

PHANTOM STRANGER
Oct., 1987–Jan., 1988

1 MMi,CR,V:Eclipso 3.00
2 and 4 MMi,CR,V:Eclipso . . . . . @3.00

PHANTOM ZONE, THE
Jan., 1982

1 GD/TD,A:Jax-Ur. 2.50
2 GC/TD,A:JLA 2.50
3 GC/TD,A:Mon-El 2.50
4 GC/TD 2.50

PICTURE STORIES
FROM THE BIBLE
Autumn, 1942–43

1 thru 4 Old Testament . . . . . . @275.00
1 thru 3 New Testament 250.00

PINKY AND THE BRAIN
Warner Bros./DC, 1996

1 from animated TV series 3.00
2 thru 27 . . . . @3.00

PLASTIC MAN
[1st Series]
Nov.–Dec., 1966

1 GK,I:Dr.Drome (1966 series
   begins). 140.00
2 V:The Spider 60.00
3 V:Whed 60.00
4 V:Dr.Dome 60.00
5 1,001 Plassassins 60.00
6 V:Dr.Dome 50.00
7 O:Plastic Man Jr.,A:Original
   Plastic Man,Woozy Winks 50.00
8 V:The Weasel 50.00
9 V:Joe the Killer Pro 50.00
10 V:Doll Maker(series ends) 50.00
11 (1976 series begins) 10.00

12 I:Carrot-Man 10.00
13 A:Robby Reed. 10.00
14 V:Meat By-Product & Sludge . . 10.00
15 I:Snuffer,V:Carrot-Man 10.00
16 V:Kolonel Kool 10.00
17 O:Plastic Man 10.00
18 V:Professor Klean. 10.00
19 I&Only App.Marty Meeker. 10.00
20 V:Snooping Sneetches
    Oct.–Nov., 1977. . . . . 10.00

PLASTIC MAN
1988–89
1 Mini-series,Origin retold. 2.25
2 V:The Ooze Brothers. 2.25
3 In Los Angeles. 2.25
4 End-series,A:Superman. 2.25

PLASTIC MAN
1999
Spec.#1 TTn(s),ALo,RBr,48-page . . 4.00

PLASTIC MAN
DC Dec. 2003
1 KB,O:Plastic Man. 2.50
2 KB,Eel O'Brien on the Lam 3.00
3 KB,Eel O'Brien on the Lam 3.00
4 KB,Eel O'Brien on the Lam 3.00
5 KB,ghosts of his past. 3.00
6 KB,Eel O'Brien,concl. 3.00
7 Love Makes a Fella Woozy 3.00
8 Continuity Bandit,pt.1. . . . . 3.00
9 Continuity Bandit,pt.2. . . . . 3.00
10 Halloween issue 3.00
11 Homeland Security 3.00
GN The Lost Annual, rep. 7.00
TPB On the Lam 15.00

PLOP!
Sept.–Oct., 1973
1 SA-AA,GE,ShM 40.00
2 AA,SA 20.00
3 AA,SA 20.00
4 BW,SA 25.00
5 MA,MSy,SA,BWr 22.00
6 MSy,SA 20.00
7 SA 20.00
8 SA 20.00
9 SA 20.00
10 SA 20.00
11 ATh,SA 20.00
12 SA 20.00
13 WW(c),SA 22.00
14 WW,SA 22.00
15 WW(c),SA 22.00
16 SD,WW,SA 22.00
17 SA 22.00
18 SD,WW,SA 22.00
19 WW,SA 22.00
20 SA,WW 22.00
21 JO,WW 25.00
22 JO,WW,BW. 25.00
23 BW,WW. 25.00
24 SA,WW,Nov.–Dec., 1976 . . . . . 25.00

POWER COMPANY, THE
Jan., 2002
1 KBk,TG,V:Doctor Cyber. 2.50
2 KBk,TG,V:Dragoneer. 2.50
3 KBk,TG,V:Dragoneer, Godstone . 2.50
4 KBk,TG,offices under attack 2.50
5 KBk,TG,F:Manhunter. 2.50
6 KBk,TG,F:Green Arrow 2.50
7 KBk,F:Striker Z. 2.75
8 KBk,TG,Power Loss,pt.1 . . . . . . 2.75
9 KBk,TG,Power Loss,pt.2 . . . . . . 2.75
10 KBk,TG,anger aside 2.75
11 KBk,new member 2.75

Power of Shazam #2
© DC Comics Inc.

12 KBk,F:Witchfire 2.75
13 KBk,TG,V:Dr. Polaris. 2.75
14 KBk,TG,V:Dr.Polaris,Cadre 2.75
15 KBk,TG,V:Dark Knight. 2.75
16 KBk,TG,Witchfire. 2.75
17 KBk,TG,barbaric world 2.75
18 KBk,TG,final issue. 2.75
Spec. Josiah Power,A:Superman . . 2.50
Spec. Striker Z,A:Superboy 2.50
Spec. Witchfire,A:Wonder Woman. . 2.50
Spec. Skyrocket, A:Hal Jordan 2.50
Spec. Bork, A:Batman & Flash 2.50
Spec. Sapphire,A:JLA 2.50
Spec. Manhunter,A:Nightwing 2.50

POWER GIRL
[Mini-Series], 1988
1 . . . . 3.00
2 A:The Weaver, mongo Krebs. . . . 3.00
3 V:The Weaver 3.00
4 V:Weaver, final issue 3.00

POWER OF SHAZAM!
1995–97
1 R:Captain Marvel. 4.00
2 V:Arson Fiend 3.00
3 V:Ibac. 3.00
4 JOy,R:Mary Marvel,Tawky,
    Tawny 3.00
5 JOy(c&a),F:Mary Marvel,
    V:Black Adam 3.00
6 R:Captain Marvel 3.00
7 V:Captain Nazi 3.00
8 R:Captain Marvel,Jr. 3.00
9 JOy,MM,V:Black Adam 3.00
10 JOy,MM,V:Seven Deadly
    Enemies of Man 3.00
11 JOy,MM,R:Ibis as Capt.Marvel . . 3.00
12 JOy,MM,How Billy Batson's
    father met Shazam 3.00
13 JOy,MM 3.00
14 JOy,GK,MM,F:CaptainMarvelJr . 3.00
15 JOy,MM,V:Mr.Mind 3.00
16 thru 18 . . . . @3.00
19 JOy(s),GK,MM,Captain Marvel
    Jr. V:Captain Nazi 3.00
20 JOy(s),PKr,MM,A:Superman. . . 3.00
21 JOy(s),PKr,MM,V:Liquidator . . . 2.50
22 JOy(s),PKr,MM,A:Batman. 2.50
23 JOy(s),PKr,MM,. 2.50
24 JOy(s),PKr,MM,V:Baron Blitz-
    krieg, prelude to new family . . . 2.50

25 JOy(s),PKr,MM,The Marvel
    Family '97 . . . . 2.50
26 JOy(s),PKr,MM,new Capt.
    Marvel framed for murder 2.50
27 JOy(s),PKr,MM,D:Captain
    Marvel 2.50
28 JOy(s),DG, V:Patty Patty
    Bang Bang. 2.50
29 JOy(c),DG,F:Hoppy. 2.50
30 JOy(c),PKr,DG,V:Mr. Finish. . . 2.50
31 JOy,PKr,DG,Genesis x-over . . . 2.50
32 JOy,PKr,DG,Genesis aftermath. . 2.50
33 JOy,PKr,DG,Madam M, Sin. . . . 2.50
34 JOy,PKr,DG,F:Gangbuster 2.50
35 JOy,PKr,DG,Lightning &
    Stars, pt.2 x-over 2.50
36 JOy 2.50
37 JOy,MM,DG,F:Capt.Marvel Jr. . . 2.50
38 JOy,PKr,DG,Monster Society
    of Evil, pt.1 . . . . 2.50
39 JOy,PKr,DG,Monster, pt.2 . . . . 2.50
40 JOy,PKr,DG,Monster, pt.3 . . . . 2.50
41 JOy,PKr,DG,Monster, pt.4 . . . . 2.50
42 JOy,DG,new logo & design 2.50
43 JOy,DG,I:Bulletgirl. 2.50
44 JOy,DG,V:Chain Lightning 2.50
45 JOy,DG,A:JLA 2.50
46 JOy,DG,A:Superman. 2.50
47 JOy,V:Black Adam, final issue . . 2.50
Ann.#1 JOy(s),MM,Legends of
    the Dead Earth 3.00
Spec.#1,000,000 JOy,DG 2.50
GN Power of Shazam 7.50
GNv JOy(a&s),O:Captain Marvel. . 10.00
TPB JOy, reoffer 7.50

POWER OF THE ATOM
1988–89
1 1st Issue, Origin retold. 2.25
2 Return of Powers. 2.25
3 I:Strobe 2.25
4 A:Hawkman+bonus book #8 . . . . 2.25
5 DT,A:Elongated Man 2.25
6 JBy,V:Chronos 2.25
7 GN,Invasion,V:Khunds,Chronos . 2.25
8 GN,Invasion,V:Chronos 2.25
9 GN,A:Justice League. 2.25
10 GN,I:Humbug 2.25
11 GN,V:Paul Hoben 2.25
12 GN,V:Edg the Destroyer. 2.25
13 GN,Blood Stream Journey 2.25
14 GN,V:Humbug. 2.25
15 GN,V:Humbug. 2.25
16 GN,V:The CIA. 2.25
17 GN,V:The Sting 2.25
18 GN,V:The CIA, last issue 2.25

POWERPUFF GIRLS
Warner Bros./DC March, 2000
1 . . . . 3.50
2 DaF, ... 2.25
3 Mysterious meteor 2.25
4 Video game 2.00
5 thru 55 . . . . @2.25
Double Whammy, rep. #1 & #2 . . . 4.00
Spec.Powerpuff Girls movie comic . 3.00
TPB Titans of Townsville 7.00
TPB Go, Girls, Go 7.00

PREACHER
DC/Vertigo, 1995
1 I:Jesse Custer, Genesis. 22.00
2 Saint of Killers 18.00
3 GF(c),I:Angels 15.00
4 GF(c),V:Saint of Killers 10.00
5 Naked City,pt.1 . . . . 10.00
6 Naked City,pt.2 . . . . 10.00
7 Naked City,pt.3 . . . . 8.00
8 GEn,SDi,All in the Family,pt.1 . . . 5.00

9 GEn,SDi,All in the Family,pt.2 . . . 5.00
10 GEn,SDi,All in the Family,pt.3 . . 5.00
11 GEn,SDi,All in the Family,pt.4. . . 5.00
12 GEn,SDi,All in the Family,pt.5 . . 6.00
13 GEn,SDi,Hunters,pt.1 . . . . 5.00
14 GEn,SDi,Hunters,pt.2 (of 4) 4.00
15 and 16 . . . . @4.00
17 Star captures Cassidy. 3.00
18 GEn(s),SDi,secret of Jesse
  Custer's cigarette lighter 3.00
19 GEn(s),SDi,Crusaders, pt.1 . . . 3.00
20 GEn(s),SDi,Crusaders, pt.2 . . . 3.00
21 GEn(s),SDi,Crusaders, pt. 3 . . . 3.00
22 GEn(s),SDi,Crusaders, pt.4 . . . 3.00
23 GEn(s),SDi,Crusaders, pt.5 . . . 3.00
24 GEn(s),SDi,Crusaders, concl. . . . 3.00
25 GEn(s),SDi,Cry Blood, Cry
  Erin 3.00
26 GEn(s),SDi,To the Streets of
  Manhattan I Wandered Away . . 2.50
27 GEn(s),SDi, Jessie & Tulip in
  New York, pt.1 . . . . 2.50
28 GEn(s),SDi, Jessie & Tulip in
  New York, pt.2 . . . . 2.50
29 GEn(s),SDi, south to New
  Orleans 2.50
30 GEn,SDi,in New Orleans 2.50
31 GEn,SDi,in New Orleans 2.50
32 GEn,SDi,in New Orleans 2.50
33 GEn,SDi,in New Orleans,concl. . . 2.50
34 GEn,SDi,War in the Sun,pt.1 . . 2.50
35 GEn,SDi,War in the Sun,pt.2 . . 2.50
36 GEn,SDi,War in the Sun,pt.3 . . 2.50
37 GEn,SDi,War in the Sun,pt.4 . . 2.50
38 GEn,SDi,GF,Utah radioactive . . 2.50
39 GEn,SDi,GF,out of the desert . . 2.50
40 GEn,SDi,GF,Arsefaced World. . . 2.50
41 . . . . 2.50
42 GEn(s),SDi,GF,V:Meatman . . . 2.50
43 GEn(s),SDi,GF,V:Meat Man 2.50
44 GEn(s),SDi,GF,Gunther Hahn . . 2.50
45 GEn(s),SDi,GF,V:Meat Man . . . 2.50
46 GEn(s),SDi,GF,Miss Oatlash . . . 2.50
47 GEn(s),SDi,GF,Salvation 2.50
48 GEn(s),SDi,GF,Salvation 2.50
49 GEn(s),SDi,GF,First Contact. . . . 2.50
50 GEn(s),SDi,GF,48-page
  I:100 Bullets. 4.00
51 GEn(s),SDi,GF,Tulip's past,pt.1 . 4.00
52 GEn(s),SDi,GF,Tulip's past,pt.2 . . 2.50
53 GEn(s),SDi,GF,road trip story . . . 2.50
54 GEn(s),SDi,GF,Jesse & Tulip . . 2.50
55 GEn(s),SKi,GF 2.50
56 GEn(s),GF. 2.50
57 GEn(s), ... 2.50
58 GEn(s),SDi,. 2.50
59 GEn(s),SDi,Alamo,pt.1 . . . . 2.50
60 GEn(s),SDi,Alamo,pt.2 . . . . 2.50
61 GEn(s),SDi,Alamo,pt.3 . . . . 2.50
62 GEn(s),SDi,Alamo,pt.4 . . . . 2.50
63 GEn(s),SDi,Alamo,pt.5 . . . . 2.50
64 GEn(s),SDi,Alamo,pt.6 . . . . 2.50
65 GEn(s),SDi,Alamo,pt.7 . . . . 5.00
66 GEn(s),SDi,Alamo,pt.8,
  final issue 5.00
TPB Gone to Texas, rep.#1–#7 . . 15.00
TPB Proud Americans GEn(s). . . . 15.00
TPB Until the End of the World . . . 15.00
TPB Ancient History. 15.00
TPB War in the Sun. 15.00
TPB All Hell's A-Coming 18.00
TPB Alamo, GEn,SDi. 18.00
TPB Dead or Alive 20.00
GN Preacher Spec. Cassidy: Blood
  and Whisky, GEn(s) (1997) . . . 6.00
GN Tall in the Saddle. 6.00
Spec. The Good Old Boys, parody . 5.50
Spec. The Story of You-Know-Who
  GEn(s),RCa,O:Arseface (1996) 5.00
Spec. One Man's War 5.00

PREACHER SPECIAL: SAINT OF KILLERS
DC/Vertigo, 1996
1 GEn(s),StP. 5.00
2 GEn(s),StP. 4.50
3 GEn(s),StP. 3.50
4 GEn(s),StP. 3.00

PREZ
Aug.–Sept., 1973
1 I:Prez (from Sandman #54) 35.00
2 thru 4 F:Prez 20.00

PRIDE & JOY
DC/Vertigo, May, 1997
[Mini-series]
1 (of 4) GEn(s),JHi,. 2.50
2 GEn(s),JHi 2.50
3 GEn(s),JHi 2.50
4 GEn(s),JHi,concl. 2.50
TPB (2004). 15.00

Primal Force #0 © DC Comics, Inc.

PRIMAL FORCE
1994–95
O New Team. 2.25
1 Claw. 2.25
2 Cataclysm 2.25
3 . . . . 2.25
4 Claw. 2.25
5 thru 14 . . . . @2.25

PRINCE
DC/Piranha Press 1991
1 DCw,KW,based on rock star . . . 10.00
1a Second printing 2.50
1b 3rd printing. 2.00

PRISONER, THE
1988–89
1 Based on TV series 4.00
2 By Hook or by Crook 4.00
3 Confrontation 4.00
4 Departure, final issue 4.00

PROPOSITION PLAYER
DC/Vertigo, Oct., 2000
1 (of 6) PGn,BWg, ... 2.50
2 thru 6 PGn,BWg, ... @2.50
TPB 14.95

PSYBA-RATS, THE
[Mini-Series], 1995
1 CDi,A:Robin 2.50
2 CDi,A:Robin 2.00
3 CDi,F:Razorsharp,final issue 2.00

PSYCHO, THE
1991
1 I:Psycho 12.00
2 Sonya Rescue 10.00
3 Psycho against the World 7.00

PULP FANTASTIC
DC/Vertigo, Dec., 1999
1 (of 3) HC,RBr,detective 2.50
2 HC,RBr 2.50
3 HC,RBr,conclusion. 2.50

QUEST FOR CAMELOT
June, 1998
1-shot movie adaptation 5.00

QUESTION, THE
Feb., 1987
1 DCw,R:Question,I:Myra,A:Shiva . 3.00
2 DCw,A:Batman,Shiva 2.50
3 DCw,I:Mayor Firman 2.50
4 DCw,V:Hatch 2.50
5 DCw,Hub City fall Apart 2.50
6 DCw,Abuse story 2.50
7 DCw,V:Mr.Volk 2.50
8 DCw,I:Mikado. 2.50
9 DCw,O:Rodor. 2.50
10 DCw,O:Rodor cont. 2.50
11 DCw,Transformation 2.50
12 DCw,Poisoned Ground 2.50
13 DCw,V:The Spartans 2.50
14 DCw,V:The Spartans. 2.50
15 DCw,The Klan in Hub City 2.50
16 DCw,Butch Cassidy &
  Sundance Kid 2.50
17 DCw,A:Green Arrow 2.50
18 DCw,A:Green Arrow 2.50
19 DCw,V:Terrorists 2.50
20 DCw,Travelling Circus. 2.50
21 DCw,V:Junior Musto 2.50
22 DCw,Election Night 2.50
23 DCw,Election Night contd 2.50
24 DCw,Election Night contd 2.50
25 DCw,Myra Critically Ill 2.50
26 A:Riddler 2.50
27 DCw 2.50
28 DCw,A:Lady Shiva 2.50
29 DCw,V:Lady Shiva 2.50
30 DCw,A:Lady Shiva 2.50
31 DCw,Hub City Chaos contd 2.50
32 DCw,Identity Crisis 2.50
33 DCw,Identity Crisis contd 2.50
34 DCw,Identity Crisis contd 2.50
35 DCw,Fate of Hub City 2.50
36 DCw,final issue (contd.G.A.Ann#3
  Question Quarterly #1) 2.50
Ann.#1 DCw,A:Batman,G.A. 3.00
Ann.#2 A:Green Arrow 4.00

QUESTION QUARTERLY
1 DCw. 4.50
2 DCw 4.00
3 DCw(c) Film. 3.00
4 DCw,MM,Waiting for Phil 3.00
5 DCw,MMi,MM,last issue 3.00

RAGMAN
[1st Limited Series], 1976–77
1 I&O:Ragman 20.00
2 I:Opal 12.00
3 V:Mr. Big 10.00

4 JKu(1st interior on character) . . 10.00
5 JKu,O:Ragman,final issue 10.00

[2nd Limited Series], 1991–92
1 PB,O:Ragman 3.00
2 PB,O:Ragman Powers 3.00
3 PB,Original Ragman 3.00
4 PB,Gang War 3.00
5 PB,V:Golem 3.00
6 PB,V:Golem,A:Batman 3.00
7 PB,V:Golem,A:Batman 3.00
8 PB,V:Golem,A:Batman 3.00

RAGMAN:
CRY OF THE DEAD
1993–94
1 JKu(c),R:Ragman 3.50
2 JKu(c),A:Marinette 3.00
3 JKu(c),V:Marinette 3.00
4 JKu(c),Exorcism 3.00
5 JKu(c),V:Marinette 3.00
6 JKu(c),final issue 3.00

THE RAY
[Limited Series], 1992
1 JQ,ANi,I&O:Ray(Ray Torril) 5.00
2 JQ,ANi,I:G.A. Ray 3.00
3 JQ,ANi,A:G.A. Ray 3.00
4 JQ,ANi,V:Dr.Polaris 4.00
5 JQ,ANi,V:Dr.Polaris 3.00
6 JQ,ANi,C:Lobo,final issue 3.00
TPB In A Blaze of Power 10.00

[Regular Series], 1994–96
1 JQ(c),RPr,V:Brinestone,
  A:Superboy 3.00
1a Newsstand Ed 2.25
2 RPr,V:Brinestone,A:Superboy . . . 2.25
3 RPr,I:Death Masque 2.25
4 JQ(c),RPr,I:Death Masque,
  Dr. Polaris 2.25
5 JQ(c),RPr,V:G.A.Ray 2.25
6 JQ(c),RPr,V:Black Canary 2.25
7 JQ(c),RPr,V:Canary/Ray 2.25
8 V:Lobo,Black Canary 2.25
9 Ray Undoes the past 2.25
10 F:Happy Terril 2.25
11 30 years in future 2.25
12 V:Mystech 2.25
13 V:Death Masque 2.25
14 The Ray needs help, V:Death
  Masque 2.25
15 F:Vandal Savage 2.25
16 D:Happy Terrill 2.25

The Ray #13 © DC Comics, Inc.

17 I:Josh Terrill,V:Atomic Skull 2.25
18 Underworld Unleashed tie-in . . 2.25
19 Underworld Unleashed tie-in . . . 2.25
20 F:Black Condor 2.25
21 Black Condor captured 2.25
22 . . . . 2.25
23 V:Death Masque 2.25
24 . . . . 2.25
25 double size 3.50
26 . . . . 2.25
27 . . . . 2.25
28 CPr,final issue 2.25
Ann.#1 Year One Annual 3.95

REAL FACT COMICS
March-April, 1946
1 S&K,Harry Houdini story 800.00
2 S&K, Rin-Tin-Tin story 500.00
3 H.G. Wells story 450.00
4 Jimmy Stewart story,B:Just
  Imagine 475.00
5 Batman & Robin(c) 2,500.00
6 O:Tommy Tomorrow 1,800.00
7 The Flying White House 225.00
8 VF,A:Tommy Tomorrow 800.00
9 S&K,Glen Miller story 350.00
10 MMe(s),The Vigilante 350.00
11 EK,How the G-Men Capture
  Public Enemies! 200.00
12 How G-Men are Trained 200.00
13 Dale Evans story 650.00
14 Will Rogers story,Diary of
  Death 200.00
15 A:The Master Magician-
  Thurston,A-Bomb 225.00
16 A:Four Reno Brothers,
  T.Tommorrow 650.00
17 I Guard an Armored Car 200.00
18 The Mystery Man of
  Tombstone 200.00
19 Weapon that Won the West . . 200.00
20 JKu,Daniel Boone 225.00
21 JKu,KitCarson,July-Aug.,1949 200.00

REAL SCREEN COMICS
Spring, 1945
1 B:Fox & the Crow,Flippity
  & Flop 1,400.00
2 (fa) 650.00
3 (fa) 400.00
4 thru 7 (fa) . . . . @250.00
8 thru 11 (fa) . . . . @200.00
12 thru 20 (fa) . . . . @175.00
21 thru 30 (fa) . . . . @150.00
31 thru 40 (fa) . . . . @125.00
41 thru 128 (fa) . . . . @100.00
Becomes:
TV SCREEN CARTOONS
129 thru 137 . . . . @100.00
138 Jan.–Feb., 1961 . . . . 100.00

REALWORLDS
March, 2000
GN Batman, 48-pg. 6.00
GN Wonder Woman, 48-pg. 6.00
GN JLA, 48-pg. 6.00
GN Superman 6.00

R.E.B.E.L.S '94–'96
0 New team 2.50
1 L.E.G.I.O.N.,Green Lantern 2.50
2 Dissent 2.50
3 . . . . 2.50
4 Ship goes Insane 2.50
5 F:Dox 2.25
6 Dox Defeated 2.25
7 John Sin 2.25
8 V:Galactic Bank 2.25

Rebels '95 #5 © DC Comics Inc.

9 F:Dox,Ignea,Garv,Strata 2.25
10 V:World Bank 2.25
11 . . . . 2.25
12 F:Iceman Assassin 2.25
13 Underworld Unleashed tie-in . . . 2.25
14 F:Lyrl Dox 2.25
15 V:Lyrl Dox 2.25
16 V:Lyrl Dox's satellite 2.25

RED TORNADO
1985
1 CI/FMc 3.00
2 CI/FMc,A:Superman 3.00
3 CI/FMc 3.00
4 CI/FMc 3.00

REIGN OF THE ZODIAC
Aug. 2003
1 BWi,CDo 2.75
2 thru 6 BWi,CDo . . . . @2.75
7 KG(s) 2.75
8 KG(s),CDo,BWi 2.75

RELATIVE HEROES
Feb., 2000
1 (of 6) Olympian super-teens 2.50
2 Things to Do in Olympus
  When Your're Dead 2.50
3 F:Impulse 2.50
4 F:Blindside 2.50
5 O:Omni 2.50
6 Concl 2.50

REMARKABLE WORLDS
OF PHINEAS B. FUDDLE
DC/Paradox, 1999
1 (of 4) F:Angus & McKee 6.00
2 . . . . 6.00
3 ancient India 6.00
4 concl 6.00
TPB 192-page 20.00

RESTAURANT AT THE
END OF THE UNIVERSE
1994
1 Adapt. 2nd book in Hitchhikers'
  Guide to the Galaxy,
  I:The Restaurant 7.00
2 V:The Meal 7.00
3 Final issue 7.00

RESURRECTION MAN
March, 1997
1 DAn(s),JG,lenticular death's
　head cover. 6.00
2 DAn(s),JG,V:Amazo 5.00
3 DAn(s),JG,Scorpion Memories
　pt.1 (of 3) 4.00
4 DAn(s),JG,Scorpion,pt.2 . . . . . . 4.00
5 DAn(s),JG,Scorpion,pt.3 . . . . . . 4.00
6 DAn&ALa(s),JoP,Genesis tie-in . . 3.00
7 DAn&ALa(s),TGb,BG,A:Batman . . 3.00
8 DAn&ALa(s),BG,Big Howler 3.00
9 DAn&ALa(s),F:Hitman, pt.1 . . . . 3.00
10 DAn&ALa(s),F:Hitman, pt.2 . . . 3.00
11 DAn&ALa(s), Origin of the
　Species, pt.1 . . . . 2.50
12 DAn&ALa(s), Origin of the
　Species, pt.2 . . . . 2.50
13 DAn&ALa(s),Candy Man 2.50
14 DAn&ALa(s),really dead? 2.50
15 DAn&ALa(s),JG,V:Rider 2.50
16 DAn&ALa(s),BG,Avenging
　Angels x-over.pt.1 . . . . 2.50
17 DAn&ALa(s),BG,Avenging
　Angels x-over pt.3 . . . . 2.50
18 DAn&ALa(s),A:Phantom Stranger,
　Deadman. 2.50
19 DAn&ALa(s),Cape Fear, pt.1 . . 2.50
20 DAn&ALa(s),Cape Fear, pt.2 . . 2.50
21 DAn&ALa(s),Cape Fear, pt.3 . . 2.50
22 DAn&ALa(s) 2.50
23 DAn&ALa(s),Resurrection
　Woman 2.50
24 DAn&ALa(s) 2.50
25 DAn&ALa(s)Millennium
　Meteor,pt.1 . . . . 2.50
26 DAn&ALa(s)Millennium Meteor,
　pt.2,A:Superman, Titans 2.50
27 DAn&ALa(s)Millennium Meteor,
　pt.3,final issue 2.50
Spec.#1,000,000 DAn&ALa(s). . . . 2.50

RICHARD DRAGON,
KUNG FU FIGHTER
April-May, 1975
1 O:Richard Dragon 20.00
2 JSn/AM 15.00
3 JK. 12.00
4 thru 8 RE/WW . . . . @10.00
9 thru 17 RE . . . . @8.00
18 Nov.–Dec., 1977 . . . . 8.00

RICHARD DRAGON
May 2004
1 CDi(s),SMc 2.50
2 thru 6 CDi(s),SMc . . . . @2.50

RIMA,
THE JUNGLE GIRL
April-May, 1974
1 NR,I:Rima,O:Pt. 1 . . . . 20.00
2 NR,O:Pt.2 . . . . 10.00
3 NR,O:Pt.3 . . . . 10.00
4 NR,O:Pt.4 . . . . 10.00
5 NR 10.00
6 NR 10.00
7 April-May, 1975 . . . . 10.00

RING, THE
[OF THE NIEBLUNG]
1989
1 GK,Opera Adaption 12.00
2 GK,Sigfried's Father's Sword . . . 7.00
3 GK,to save Brunhilde. 6.00
4 GK, final issue 6.00
TPB rep.#1 thru #4 . . . . 20.00

Rip Hunter, Time Master #15
© DC Comics, Inc.

RIP HUNTER,
TIME MASTER
March-April, 1961
1 . . . . 900.00
2 . . . . 450.00
3 thru 5 . . . . @250.00
6 and 7 Ath . . . . @150.00
8 thru 15 . . . . @125.00
16 thru 20 . . . . @125.00
21 thru 28 . . . . @100.00
29 Nov.–Dec., 1965 . . . . 100.00

ROAD TO PERDITION
DC/Paradox/Pocket, 1998
TPB 6"x8" 304pg., b&w 25.00
TPB b&w,new edition (2002) 15.00
TPB Vol. 2 Sanctuary. 8.00

ROBIN
[1st Limited Series], 1991
1 TL,BB(c),Trial,pt.1(&Poster). . . . 5.00
1a 2nd printing 2.50
1b 3rd printing. 2.25
2 TL,BB(c) Trial,pt.2 . . . . 2.50
2a 2nd printing 2.25
3 TL,BB(c) Trial,pt.3 . . . . 2.50
4 TL,Trial,pt.4 . . . . 2.50
5 TL,Final issue,A:Batman 2.50
TPB BB(c),rep 8.00

[2nd Limited Series], 1991
[ROBIN II: THE JOKER'S WILD]
1 Direct,Hologram(c)Joker face . . . 3.00
1a (c)Joker straightjacket 2.25
1b (c)Joker standing 2.25
1c (c)Batman 2.25
1d Newsstand(no hologram) 2.25
1e collectors set,extra holo. 10.00
2 Direct,Hologram(c) Robin/Joker
　Knife 2.25
2a (c)Joker/Robin-Dartboard 2.25
2b (c)Robin/Joker-Hammer 2.25
2c Newsstand(no hologram) 2.25
2d collectors set,extra holo. 9.00
3 Direct,Holo(c)Robin standing . . . 2.25
3a (c)Robin swinging 2.25
3b Newsstand(no hologram) 2.25
3c collectors set,extra holo. 7.00
4 Direct,Hologram. 2.25
4a Newsstand (no hologram) 2.25
4b collectors set,extra holo. 7.00
Collectors set (#1 thru #4) 30.00

[3rd Limited Series], 1992–93
[ROBIN III: CRY OF THE HUNTRESS]
1 TL,A:Huntress,Collector's Ed.
　movable(c),poster 3.00
1a MZ(c),Newsstand Ed. 2.25
2 TL,V:KGBeast,A:Huntress 2.75
2a MZ(c),Newsstand Ed 2.25
3 TL,V:KGBeast,A:Huntress 2.75
3a MZ(c),newsstand Ed. 2.25
4 TL,V:KGBeast,A:Huntress 2.75
4a MZ(c),newsstand Ed. 2.25
5 TL,V:KGBeast,A:Huntress 2.75
5a MZ(c),newsstand Ed. 2.25
6 TL,V:KGBeast,King Snake,
　A:Huntress. 2.75
6a MZ(c),Newsstand Ed. 2.25

[Regular Series], 1993–2002
1 B:CDi(s),TG,SHa,V:Speedboyz . . 4.00
1a Newsstand Ed. 2.25
2 TG,V:Speedboyz 2.50
3 TG,V:Cluemaster,
　Electrocutioner. 2.50
4 TG,V:Cluemaster,Czonk,
　Electrocutioner. 2.50
5 TG,V:Cluemaster,Czonk,
　Electrocutioner. 2.50
6 TG,A:Huntress 2.50
7 TG,R:Robin's Father 2.50
8 TG,KnightsEnd#5,A:Shiva 3.00
9 TG,Knights End:Aftermath 2.50
10 TG,Zero Hour,V:Weasel 2.50
11 New Batman 2.50
12 Robin vs. thugs. 2.50
13 V:Steeljacket 2.50
14 CDi(s),TG,Return of Bruce
　Wayne,Troika,pt.4 . . . . 3.00
14a Collector's edition 3.00
15 Cluemaster Mystery 2.50
16 F:Spoiler 2.50
17 I:Silver Monkey,V:King Snake,Lynx
　[New Miraweb format begins] . . 2.50
18 Gotham City sabotaged 2.50
19 V:The General. 2.50
20 F:Robin 2.50
21 Ninja Camp,pt.1 . . . . 2.50
22 CDi,TG,Ninja Camp,pt.2 . . . . . . 2.50
23 CDi,Underworld Unleashed tie-in 2.50
24 CDi,V:Charaxes 2.50
25 CDi,F:Green Arrow 2.50
26 . . . . 2.50
27 . . . . 2.50
28 CDi,Contagion: conclusion 2.50
29 CDi,FFo,SnW,A:Maxie Zeus. . . . 2.50
30 CDi,FFo,SnW,A:Maxie Zeus. . . . 2.50
31 CDi(s),A:Wildcat 2.50
32 CDi(s),Legacy, pt. 3 x-over. . . . 2.50
33 CDi(s),Legacy, pt. 7 x-over 2.50
34 CDi(s),JhD,action at a
　Shakespear play 2.50
35 CDi(s),Robin & Spoiler, Final
　Night tie-in 2.50
36 CDi(s),V:Toyman, The General. . 2.50
37 CDi(s),V:The General, Toyman. . 2.50
38 CDi(s), ... 2.50
39 CDi(s), pt.2 . . . . 2.50
40 CDi(s), ... 2.50
41 CDi(s),F:Tim and Ariana 2.50
42 CDi(s),F:Crocky the Crocodile . . 2.50
43 CDi(s),A:Spoiler 2.50
44 CDi(s) Pt.2 (of 2). 2.50
45 CDi(s) Tim Drake grounded 2.50
46 CDi(s) Genesis tie-in. 2.50
47 CDi,V:General, pt.1. . . . . 2.50
48 CDi,V:General, pt.2. . . . . 2.50
49 CDi,to Paris. 2.50
50 CDi(s),F:Lady Shiva & King
　Snake, 48pg 3.50
51 CDi(s) 2.50
52 CDi(s) Cataclysm x-over,pt.7 . . . 3.00

DC COMICS

53 CDi(s),SnW,Cataclysm concl.... 3.00
54 CDi(s),SnW,Aftershock......... 2.50
55 CDi(s),SnW, Brotherhood of
    the Fist x-over, pt.3.......... 2.50
56 CDi(s),SnW,tearful turning point. 2.50
57 CDi(s),SnW,A:Spoiler......... 2.50
58 CDi(s),SnW,A:Spoiler......... 2.50
59 CDi(s),SnW,V:Steeljacket...... 2.50
60 CDi(s),SnW,Alvin Draper....... 2.50
61 CDi(s),SnW,V:Phil Delinger.... 2.50
62 CDi(s),SnW,A:Flash, pt.1...... 2.50
63 CDi(s),SnW,A:Flash, pt.2...... 2.50
64 CDi(s),SnW,A:Flash, pt.3...... 2.50
65 CDi(s),SnW,A:Spoiler......... 2.50
66 CDi(s),SnW,V:demons........ 2.50
67 CDi(s),SnW,No Man's Land.... 2.50
68 CDi(s),No Man's Land........ 2.50
69 CDi(s),No Man's Land........ 2.50
70 CDi(s),No Man's Land........ 2.50
71 CDi(s),V:Killer Croc.......... 2.50
72 CDi(s)................... 2.50
73 CDi(s),F:Batgirl............ 2.50
74 CDi(s),F:Batman & Nightwing... 2.50
75 CDi(s),48-pg.............. 3.50
76 CDi(s),R:Man-Bat.......... 2.50
77 CDi(s),I:Jaeger............ 2.50
78 CDi(s),V:Arrakhat.......... 2.50
79 CDi(s),F:Green Arrow........ 2.50
80 CDi(s),A:Star............. 2.50
81 CDi(s),MPn,.............. 2.50
82 CDi(s),Spoiler,Star.......... 2.50
83 CDi,Vacation time.......... 2.50
84 CDi,A:Lagoon Boy.......... 2.50
85 CDi,This issue: Batman dies!... 2.50
86 Officer Down x-over,pt.2...... 5.00
87 CDi,A:Spoiler............. 2.50
88 CDi,Road trip............. 2.50
89 CDi,to Himalayas.......... 2.50
90 CDi,V:mini-yeti............ 2.50
91 CDi,F:Danny Temple......... 2.50
92 CDi,SBe,A:Batman,Spoiler..... 2.50
93 CDi,F:Spoiler.............. 2.50
94 CDi,F:Spoiler,Wesley......... 2.50
95 CDi,Joker:Last Laugh tie-in.... 2.50
96 CDi,Last Laugh aftermath...... 2.50
97 CDi,F:Normandy............ 2.50
98 Bruce Wayne:Murderer,pt.8.... 5.00
99 Bruce Wayne:Murderer,pt.11... 5.00
100 CDi,Spoiler,48-pg........... 5.00
101 WorldWithoutYoungJustice,pt.3 2.25
102 Spoiler................. 2.25
103 Nocturna's secret.......... 2.25
104 Astrology Lady............ 2.25
105 riddle of Natalia........... 2.25
106 A:Batman............... 2.25
107 F:Charaxis............... 2.25
108 F:Charaxis............... 2.25
109 V:Charaxis............... 2.25
110 F:Nightwing.............. 2.25
111 F:Spoiler................ 2.25
112 to Pennsylvania........... 2.25
113 V:The Riddler............. 2.25
114 The Wrong Town.......... 2.25
115 The Wrong Town........... 2.25
116 Identity compromised....... 2.25
117 Identity compromised....... 2.25
118 Traitor's identity.......... 2.25
119 Traitor's identity.......... 2.25
120 Hell in a handbasket........ 2.25
121 BWg(s),Johnny Got His Gun.. 4.00
122 BWg(s),Bad to the Bone..... 3.00
123 BWg(s),Nemesis........... 3.00
124 F:Spoiler................ 3.00
125 BWg(s),secret itentity....... 3.00
126 BWg(s),search for new Robin.. 4.00
127 BWg(s),Girl Wonder,Batman.. 3.00
128 BWg(s),V:Scarab.......... 2.25
129 War Games,Act 1,pt.5....... 2.25
130 War Games,Act 2,pt.5....... 2.25
131 War Games,Act 3,pt.4....... 2.25
Ann.#1 TL,Eclipso tie-in,V:Anarky.. 3.00

Ann.#2 KD,JL,Bloodlines#10,
    I:Razorsharp.............. 2.75
Ann.#3 Elseworlds Story......... 3.25
Ann.#4 Year One Annual........ 3.00
Ann.#5 CDi,Legends of the Dead
    Earth................... 3.00
Ann.#5 Legends o/t Dead Earth... 3.00
Ann.#6 Pulp Heroes (Western),
    CDi(s).................. 4.00
Spec.#1,000,000 CDi(s),SnW..... 2.00
Spec. Robin/Argent Double Shot
    DJu,CDi,V:Spoiler x-over (1997) 2.00
TPB A Hero Reborn,JAp,TL...... 5.00
TPB Tragedy and Triumph,
    TL,NBy.................. 10.00
TPB Robin: Flying Solo........ 13.00
TPB Robin: Unmasked......... 13.00
80-page Giant #1 CDi.......... 6.00

ROBIN PLUS
1996
1 MWa&BAu(s), F:Bart Allen, skiing
    rips, V:Mystral.............. 3.00
2 LKa,CDi,AWi,ALa,F:Fang...... 3.00

ROBIN 3000
1992
1 CR,Elseworlds,V:Skulpt....... 5.25
2 CR,Elseworlds,V:Skulpt....... 5.25

ROBIN: YEAR ONE
October, 2000
1 CDi,SBe,F:Dick Grayson...... 5.00
2 CDi,SBe,F:Dick Grayson...... 5.00
3 CDi,SBe,RbC,F:Dick Grayson... 5.00
4 CDi,SBe,concl.............. 5.00
TPB series rep.............. 14.95

ROBIN HOOD TALES
1957–58
7....................... 450.00
8 thru 14................. @400.00

ROBOTECH DEFENDERS
1985
1 MA,mini-series.............. 3.50
2 MA................... 3.00

ROGAN GOSH
DC/Vertigo, 1994
1 PF PrM(s) (From Revolver)..... 7.25

RONIN
July, 1983
1 FM,1:Billy................ 6.00
2 FM,I:Casey............... 5.00
3 FM,V:Agat................ 5.00
4 FM,V:Agat................ 5.00
5 FM,V:Agat................ 6.00
6 FM,D:Billy................ 8.00
Paperback, FM inc. Gatefold..... 12.00

ROOTS OF THE SWAMP THING
July, 1986
1 BWr,rep.SwampThing#1&#2.... 3.50
2 BWr,rep.SwampThing#3&#4.... 3.50
3 BWr,rep.SwampThing#5&#6.... 3.50
4 BWr,rep.SwampThing#7&#8.... 3.50
5 BWr,rep.SwampThing#9&#10,
    H.O.S. #92, final issue....... 3.50

ROSE & THORN
Dec. 2003
1 (of 6) DGr................. 3.00
2 thru 6 DGr................ @3.00

RUDOLPH THE RED–NOSED REINDEER
Dec., 1950
1950................... 250.00
1951 thru 1954............. @125.00
1955 thru 1962 Winter...... @100.00

RUSSIAN ROULETTE
DC/Vertigo, 1999
1 (of 3)................... 3.00

Saga of Ras Al Ghul #1
© *DC Comics Inc.*

SAGA OF RAS AL GHUL
1988
1 NA,DG,reprints.............. 6.00
2 rep................... 5.00
3 rep.Batman #242&#243....... 5.00
4 rep.Batman #244&#245....... 5.00
TPB reps................. 17.95

SAGA OF THE SWAMP THING
1982–85
1 JmP(s),TY,DSp,O:Swamp Thing,
    BU:PhantomStranger......... 7.00
2 Ph(c),TY,DSp,I:Grasp......... 4.00
3 TY,DSp,V:Vampires........... 4.00
4 TY,TD,V:Demon............. 4.00
5 TY................... 4.00
6 TY,I:General Sunderland....... 4.00
7 TY................... 4.00
8 TY................... 4.00
9 TY................... 4.00
10 TY................... 4.00
11 TY,I:Golem.............. 4.00
12 LWn(s),TY.............. 4.00
13 TY,D:Grasp............. 4.00
14 A:Phantom Stranger....... 4.00
15................... 4.00
16 SBi,JTo................ 5.00
17 I:Matthew Cable......... 5.00
18 JmP(s),LWn(s),SBi,JTo,BWr,
    R:Arcane................ 5.00

19 JmP(s),SBi,JTo,V:Arcane 5.00
20 B:AMo(s),Day,JTo(i),D:Arcane
   (Original incarnation) 22.00
21 SBi,JTo,O:Swamp Thing,I:Floronic
   Man,D:General Sunderland. . . 20.00
22 SBi,JTo,O:Floronic Man 13.00
23 SBi,JTo,V:Floronic Man. 13.00
24 SBi,JTo,V:Floronic Man,A:JLA,
   In Arkham 13.00
25 SBi,A:Jason Blood,I:Kamara . . 10.00
26 SBi,A:Demon,
   D:Matthew Cable. 10.00
27 SBi,D:Kamara,A:Demon 7.00
28 SwM,Burial of Alec Holland 7.00
29 SBi,JTo,R:Arcane 7.00
30 SBi,AA,D:Abby,C:Joker,
   V:Arcane 9.00
31 RV,JTo,D:Arcane. 7.00
32 SwM,Tribute to WK Pogo strip . . 7.00
33 rep.H.O.S.#92,A:Cain & Abel . . . 7.00
34 SBi,JTo,Swamp Thing & Abby
   Fall in Love 8.00
35 SBi,JTo,Nukeface,pt.1. . . . . 6.00
36 SBi,JTo,Nukeface,pt.2. . . . . 7.00
37 RV,JTo,I:John Constantine,
   American Gothic,pt.1 . . . . 22.00
38 SnW,JTo,V:Water-Vampires
   (Pt.1) A:J.Constantine. 9.00
39 SBi,JTo,V:Water-Vampires
   (Pt.2) A:J.Constantine 9.00
40 SBi,JTo,C:J.Constantine,
   The Curse 9.00
41 SBi,AA,Voodoo Zombies #1 . . . . 4.00
42 SBi,JTo,RoR,
   Voodoo Zombies #2 . . . . 4.00
43 SnW,RoR,Windfall,
   I:Chester Williams 4.00
44 SBi,JTo,RoR,V:Serial Killer,
   C:Batman,Constantine,Mento . . 5.00
45 SnW,AA,Ghost Dance 4.00
Ann.#1 MT,TD,Movie Adaption 4.00
Ann.#2 AMo(s),E:Arcane,A:Deadman,
   Phantom Stranger,Spectre,
   Demon,Resurrection of Abby . . 8.00
TPB rep.#21–#27 . . . . 13.00
TPB rep.#28–#34,Ann.#2 . . . . 15.00
TPB Love and Death 20.00
Becomes:

SWAMP THING

SAMURAI JACK
Warner Bros./DC July, 2002
Spec. #1 64-pg. 3.95

SANDMAN
[1st Regular Series], 1974–75
1 JK,I&O:Sandman,I:General
   Electric. 60.00
2 V:Dr.Spider. 25.00
3 Brain that Blanked
   out the Bronx. 25.00
4 JK,Panic in the Dream Stream . 25.00
5 JK,Invasion of the Frog Men . . . 25.00
6 JK,WW,V:Dr.Spider 32.00

[2nd Regular Series], 1989–93
1 B:NGa(s),SK,I:2nd Sandman. . 35.00
2 SK,A:Cain,Abel 20.00
3 SK,A:John Constantine 15.00
4 SK,A:Demon 15.00
5 SK,A:Mr.Miracle,J'onn J'onzz . . 15.00
6 V:Doctor Destiny 10.00
7 V:Doctor Destiny 10.00
8 Sound of her wings,F:Death . . . 25.00
8a Guest Ed.Pin-Up Cover. 50.00
9 Tales in the Sand,Doll's House
   prologue. 10.00
10 B:Doll's House,A:Desire
   & Despair,I:Brut & Glob 10.00
11 MovingIn,A:2ndS-man. 10.00

Sandman #1 © DC Comics Inc.

12 Play House,D;2ndS'man. 10.00
13 Men of Good Fortune,A:Death,
   Lady Constantine 10.00
14 Collectors,D:Corinthian. 10.00
15 Into' Night,DreamVortex 10.00
16 E:Doll's House,Lost Hearts. . . . 10.00
17 Calliope. 10.00
18 Dream of a 1000 Cats 10.00
18a error pg.1 . . . . 20.00
19 Midsummer Nights Dream 6.00
19a error copy 15.00
20 Strange Death Element Girl,
   A:Death 7.00
21 Family Reunion,B:Season
   of Mists 8.00
22 Season of Mists,I:Daniel Hall . . 13.00
23 Season of Mists 7.00
24 Season of Mists 7.00
25 Season of Mists 7.00
26 Season of Mists 6.00
27 E:Season of Mists. 6.00
28 Ownership of Hell 6.00
29 A:Lady J.Constantine 5.00
30 Ancient Rome;A:Death,Desire . . 5.00
31 Ancient Rome,pt.2 . . . . 5.00
32 B:The Game of You 5.00
33 The Game of You 5.00
34 The Game of You 4.00
35 The Game of You 4.00
36 The Game of You,48pgs. 5.00
37 The Game of You,Epilogue. . . . 4.00
38 Convergence. 4.00
39 Convergence,A:Marco Polo . . . 4.00
40 Convergence,A:Cain,Abel,Eve,
   Matthew the Raven 4.00
41 JIT,VcL,(i),B:Brief Lives,
   F:Endless. 4.00
42 JIT,VcL,(i),F:Delirium,Dream. . . 4.00
43 JIT,VcL,(i),A:Death,Etain. 4.00
44 JIT,VcL,(i),R:Corinthian,
   Destruction 4.00
45 JIT,VcL,(i),F:Tiffany,
   Ishtar(Belli) 4.00
46 JIT,VcL,(i),F:Morpheus/Bast,
   A:Aids insert story,F:Death . . . 4.00

DC/Vertigo, 1994–96
47 JIT,VcL,(i),A:Endless. 4.00
48 JIT,VcL,(i),L:Destruction 4.00
49 JIT,VcL,(i),E:Brief Lives,
   F:Orpheus 4.00
50 DMc(c),CR,Tales of Baghdad,
   pin-upsby TM,DMc,MK 5.00
50a Gold Ed. 22.00
51 BT,MBu(i),B:Inn at the end of
   the World,Gaheris' tale 4.00

52 BT,MBu(i),JWk,Cluracan's
   Story 4.00
53 BT,DG,MBu(i),MZi,Hob's
   Leviathan. 4.00
54 BT,MiA,MBu(i),R:Prez. 4.00
55 SAp,VcL,BT,MBu(i),F:Klaproth
   Cerements's Story 4.00
56 BT,MBu(i),DG(i),SLi(i),GyA,TyH(i),
   E:Inn at the end of the World,
   C:Endless 4.00
57 MaH,B:Kindly Ones,Inc.American
   Freak Preview 5.00
58 MaH,Kindly Ones,pt.2,
   A:Lucifer 5.00
59 MaH,Kindly Ones,pt.3,R:Fury . . . 5.00
60 MaH,Kindly Ones,pt.4. . . . . 5.00
61 MaH,Kindly Ones,pt.5. . . . . 5.00
62 Kindly Ones,pt.6,Murder. 5.00
63 MaH,Kindly Ones,pt.7,
   A:Rose Walker. 5.00
64 Kindly Ones,pt.8 . . . . 5.00
65 MaH,Kindly Ones,pt.9,Dream
   Kingdom 5.00
66 MaH,Kindly Ones,pt.10. . . . . . . 5.00
67 MaH,Kindly Ones,pt.11 . . . . 5.00
68 MaH,Kindly Ones,pt.12. . . . . . . 5.00
69 MaH,Kindly Ones finale 6.00
70 The Wake,pt.1. . . . . 4.00
71 The Wake,pt.2. . . . . 4.00
72 NGa,DMc,The Wake,pt.3 . . . . . 4.00
73 NGa,Sunday Mourning 4.00
74 NGa,V:Lord of Dreams 4.00
75 NGa,last issue 5.00
TPB Preludes & Nocturnes,
   rep. #1–#8 . . . . 20.00
TPB Doll's House, rep #8–#16 . . 18.00
TPB Dream Country,Rep.#17–#20. 15.00
TPB Fables & Reflections,rep.. . . 20.00
TPB Season of Mists,rep.#21–#28. 20.00
TPB A Game of You,rep.#32–#37 . 20.00
TPB Brief Lives 20.00
TPB The Wake, rep #70–#75 . . . 20.00
TPB World's End DMc(c). 20.00
Sandman Covers, 1989–96 . . . . . 40.00
Spec.BT,Glow in the Dark(c),The
   Legend of Orpheus
   (inc. Portrait Gallery) 6.00

SANDMAN MYSTERY THEATRE
DC/Vertigo, 1993–99
1 B:MWg(s),GyD,R:G.A.Sandman,
   B:Tarantula,I:Mr.Belmont,
   Dian Belmont. 5.00
2 GyD,V:Tarantula. 3.00
3 GyD,V:Tarantula. 3.00
4 GyD,E:Tarantula 3.00
5 JWk,B:The Face 3.00
6 JWk,The Face #2 . . . . 3.00
7 JWk,The Face #3 . . . . 3.00
8 JWk,E:The Face 3.00
9 RGT,B:The Brute,I:Rocket
   Ramsey 3.00
10 RGT,The Brute#2 . . . . 3.00
11 RGT,The Brute#3 . . . . 3.00
12 RGT,E:The Brute 3.00
13 GyD,B:The Vamp 3.00
14 GyD,The Vamp#2 . . . . 3.00
15 GyD,The Vamp#3 . . . . 3.00
16 GyD,E:The Vamp 3.00
17 GyD,B:The Scorpion 3.00
18 GyD,The Scorpion,pt.2 . . . . 3.00
19 GyD,The Scorpion,pt.3 . . . . 3.00
20 GyD,The Scorpion,pt.4 . . . . 3.00
21 Dr. Death. 3.00
22 Dr. Death,pt.2 . . . . 3.00
23 Dr. Death,pt.3 . . . . 3.00
24 Dr. Death,pt.4 . . . . 3.00
25 The Butcher,pt.1 . . . . 3.00
26 The Butcher,pt.2 . . . . 3.00

27 The Butcher,pt.3 . . . . 3.00
28 The Butcher,pt.4 . . . . 3.00
29 The Hourman,pt.1 . . . . 3.00
30 The Hourman,pt.2 . . . . 3.00
31 The Hourman,pt.3 . . . . 3.00
32 The Hourman,pt.4 . . . . 3.00
33 The Python,pt.1 . . . . 3.00
34 The Python,pt.2 . . . . 3.00
35 The Python,pt.3 . . . . 3.00
36 The Python,pt.4 . . . . 3.00
37 The Mist,pt.1 . . . . 3.00
38 The Mist,pt.2 . . . . 3.00
39 The Mist,pt.3 . . . . 3.00
40 The Mist,pt.4 . . . . 3.00
41 MWg&SSe(s),GyD,Phantom of
the Fair,pt.1 . . . . 2.50
42 MWg&SSe(s),GyD,Phantom of
the Fair,pt.2 . . . . 2.50
43 MWg&SSe(s),GyD,Phantom of
the Fair, pt. 3 . . . . 2.50
44 MWg&SSe(s),GyD,Phantom of
the Fair, pt. 4 . . . . 2.50
45 MWg&SSe(s),Blackhawk,pt.1 . . 2.50
46 MWg&SSe(s),Blackhawk,pt.2 . . 2.50
47 MWg&SSe(s),Blackhawk,pt.3 . . 2.50
48 MWg&SSe(s),RCa,Blackhawk . . 2.50
49 MWg&SSe(s),ScarletGhost,pt.1 . 2.50
50 MWg&SSe(s),The Scarlet
Ghost,pt.2, 48pg. 4.50
51 MWg&SSe(s),ScarletGhost,pt.3 . 2.50
52 MWg&SSe(s),ScarletGhost,pt.4 . 2.50
53 MWg&SSe(s),The Crone,pt.1 . . 2.50
53 MWg&SSe(s),The Crone,pt.2 . . 2.50
54 SSe&MWg(s),The Crone,pt.3 . . 2.50
55 SSe&MWg(s),The Crone,pt.4 . . 2.50
56 SSe&MWg(s),The Crone, concl. . 2.50
57 SSe&MWg(s),The Cannon,pt.1 . 2.50
58 SSe&MWg(s),The Cannon,pt.2 . 2.50
59 SSe&MWg(s),The Cannon,pt.3 . 2.50
60 SSe&MWg(s),The Cannon,pt.4 . 2.50
61 SSe(s),GyD,The City, pt.1 . . . . . 2.50
62 SSe(s),GyD,The City, pt.2 . . . . . 2.50
63 SSe(s),GyD,The City, pt.3 . . . . . 2.50
64 SSe(s),GyD,The City, pt.4 . . . . . 2.50
65 SSe,GyD,The Goblin, pt.1 . . . . . 2.50
66 SSe,GyD,The Goblin, pt.2 . . . . . 2.50
67 SSe,GyD,The Goblin, pt.3 . . . . . 2.50
68 SSe,GyD,The Goblin, pt.4 . . . . . 2.50
69 SSe,GyD 2.50
70 SSe,GyD,final issue 2.50
Ann.#1 . . . . 4.00
TPB The Tarantula 15.00
TPB Vol 1 The Tarantula (2004) . . 10.00
TPB The Dream Hunters 20.00
TPB Season of the Mists 20.00
TPB Sandman Companion 15.00
TPB Vol 2 Face & the Brute (2004) 20.00

SANDMAN PRESENTS:
LOVE STREET
DC/Vertigo, 1999
1 (of 3) MZi,VcL, ... 3.00
2 MZi,VcL,F:John Constantine 3.00
3 MZi,VcL,Concl. 3.00

LUCIFER
DC/Vertigo, 1999
1 (of 3) SHp, Morningstar Option . . 3.00
2 SHp 3.00
3 SHp, conclusion. 3.00

PETREFAX
DC/Vertigo, 2000
1 (of 4) SL 3.00
2 thru 4 SL . . . . @3.00

DEAD BOY DETECTIVES
DC/Vertigo, 2001
1 (of 4) 2.50
2 thru 4 SL . . . . @2.50

CORINTHIAN, THE
DC/Vertigo, 2001
1 (of 3) 2.50
2 thru 3 . . . . @2.50

THESSALIAD, THE
DC/Vertigo, 2002
1 (of 4) 2.50
2 thru 4 DMc(c) . . . . @2.50

BAST
DC/Vertigo, 2003
1 (of 3) F:Lady Bast 3.00
2 thru 3 . . . . @3.00
Spec.1-Shot, Merv Pumpkinhead
Agent of Dream,MBu. 6.00
Spec. Everything You've Ever
Wanted to Know About Dreams
But Were Afraid to Ask 4.50
TPB The Furies (2003) 18.00
TPB Taller Tales (2003) 20.00

THESSALY
DC Vertigo Feb. 2004
1 (of 4) Witch for Hire 3.00
2 thru 4 . . . . @3.00

SCARAB
DC/Vertigo, 1993–94
1 GF(c),B:JnS(s),SEa,MkB(i),
R&O:Scarab,V:Halaku-umid . . . 2.25
2 thru 8 GF(c),SEa,MkB(i) . . . . @2.25

SCARE TACTICS
Oct., 1996
1 LKa(s),AWi,ALa,monsters of
the MTV age 2.25
2 LKa(s),AWi,ALa,I:Scaremobile . . 2.25
3 LKa(s),AWi,ALa, ... 2.25
4 LKa(s),AWi,ALa, Big For His
Age, O:Grossout 2.25
5 LKa(s),AWi,ALa, Valentine's Day
issue 2.25
6 LKa(s),AWi,Ala, F:Fang 2.25
7 LKa(s),AWi,ALa, F:The Children
of the Beast 2.25
8 LKa(s),AWi,ALa, Convergence,
x-over, concl. 2.25
9 LKa(s),AWi,ALa,Snake Oil,
concl. 2.25
10 LKa(s),AWi,ALa,in Gotham. . . . 2.25
11 LKa(s),AWi,ALa,A:Batman 2.25

Scarlett #14 © DC Comics, Inc.

SCARLETT
1993–94
1 I:Scarlett,Blood of the Innocent . . 3.50
2 Blood of the Innocent cont. 2.25
3 Blood of the Innocent cont. 2.25
4 thru 14 . . . . @2.25

SCENE OF THE CRIME
DC/Vertigo, 1999
1 (of 4) 2.50
2 thru 4 . . . . @2.50
TPB A Little Piece of Goodnight . . 12.95

S.C.I.-SPY
DC/Vertigo, Feb., 2002
1 (of 6) DgM,PG,JP,F:Sebastian
Starchild secret agent 2.50
2 thru 6 DgM,PG,JP . . . . @2.50

SCRATCH
June 2004
1 (of 5) SK,werewolf v.Batman 2.50
2 thru 5 SK . . . . @2.50

SCRIBBLY
Aug., 1948–Dec.–Jan., 1951–52
1 SM 1,000.00
2 . . . . 650.00
3 . . . . 500.00
4 . . . . 500.00
5 . . . . 500.00
6 thru 10 . . . . @350.00
11 thru 15 . . . . @300.00

SCOOBY-DOO
Warner Bros./DC June, 1997
1 . . . . 5.00
2 thru 50 . . . . @2.50
51 thru 89 . . . . @2.25
Spooky Spectacular 2000 . . . . 3.95
Spooky Summer Special #1 . . . . . 3.95
Spec. Super Scarefest #1 . . . . 3.95
Spec. Dollar Comic, rep.#1 . . . . . . 1.00
TPB Vol. 1,You Meddling Kids 6.95
TPB Vol. 2,Ruh Roh! 6.95

SEA DEVILS
Sept.–Oct., 1961
1 RH 900.00
2 RH 450.00
3 RH 275.00
4 RH 250.00
5 RH 250.00
6 thru 10 RH . . . . @150.00
11 . . . . 125.00
12 . . . . 125.00
13 JKu,GC,RA 125.00
14 thru 20 . . . . @125.00
21 I:Capt X,Man Fish 75.00
22 thru 35, May-June, 1967 . . . @75.00

SEAGUY
DC/Vertigo May 2004
1 (of 3) GMo(s) 3.00
2 thru 3 GMo(s). . . . . @3.00

SEBASTIAN O
DC/Vertigo, 1993
1 GMo(s),SY,I:Sebastian O,A:Lord
Lavender,Roaring Boys 2.50
2 GMo(s),SY,V:Roaring Boys,
Assassins,A:Abbe 2.50
3 GMo(s),SY,D:Lord Lavender 2.50

DC COMICS

SECRET FILES & ORIGINS
2000
TPB DAn,ALa,guide to DCU 7.00
GN Secret Files Guide to DCU
  2001-2002 . . . . 5.00

SECRET HEARTS
Sept.–Oct., 1949–July, 1971
1 Make Believe Sweetheart 700.00
2 ATh,Love Is Not A Dream 350.00
3 Sing Me A Love Song 275.00
4 ATh 275.00
5 ATh 275.00
6 . . . . 275.00
7 . . . . 500.00
8 thru 20 . . . . @175.00
21 thru 26 . . . . @150.00
27 B:Comics Code 125.00
28 thru 30 . . . . @125.00
31 thru 70 . . . . @100.00
71 thru 110 . . . . @50.00
111 thru 120 . . . . @30.00
121 thru 150 . . . . @25.00
151 thru 153 . . . . @20.00

SECRET ORIGINS
Feb., 1973–Oct., 1974
1 O:Superman,Batman,Ghost,
  Flash 65.00
2 O:Green Lantern,Atom,
  Supergirl 30.00
3 O:Wonder Woman,Wildcat 30.00
4 O:Vigilante by MMe 30.00
5 O:The Spectre 30.00
6 O:Blackhawk,Legion of Super
  Heroes 30.00
7 O:Robin, Aquaman 30.00

SECRET ORIGINS
April, 1986
1 JOy,WB,F:Superman 7.00
2 GK,F:Blue Beetle 4.00
3 JBi,F:Captain Marvel 4.00
4 GT,F:Firestorm 4.00
5 GC,F:Crimson Avenger 4.00
6 DG,MR,F:Batman 5.00
7 F:Sandman,Guy Gardner 3.50
8 MA,F:Shadow Lass,Dollman . . . 2.50
9 GT,F:Skyman,Flash 2.50
10 JL,JO,JA,F:Phantom Stranger . . 2.50
11 LMc,TD,F:Hawkman,Powergirl . . 2.50
12 F:Challengers of the Unknown
  I:G.A. Fury 2.50
13 EL,F:Nightwing 3.00
14 F:Suicide Squad 2.50
15 KMo,DG,F:Deadman,Spectre . . . 2.50
16 AKu,F:Hourman,Warlord 2.50
17 KGi,F:Green Lantern 2.75
18 . . . . 2.50
19 JM(c),MA 2.50
20 RL,DG,F:Batgirl 3.00
21 GM,MA,F:Jonah Hex 2.50
22 F:Manhunter,Millennium tie-in . . 2.50
23 F:Manhunter,Millennium tie-in . . . 2.50
24 F:Dr.Fate,Blue Devil 2.50
25 F:The Legion 2.50
26 F:Black Lightning 2.50
27 F:Zatanna,Zatara 2.50
28 RLd,GK,F:Nightshade,Midnight . 2.50
29 F:Atom,Red Tornado 2.50
30 F:Elongated Man 2.50
31 F:Justice Society of America 2.50
32 F:Justice League America 3.00
33 F:Justice League Inter. 2.50
34 F:Justice League Inter. 2.50
35 KSu,F:Justice League Inter. 2.50
36 F:Green Lantern 3.00
37 F:Legion of Subst. Heroes 2.50

Secret Origins #29 © DC Comics, Inc.

38 F:Green Arrow,Speedy 2.50
39 F:Batman,Animal Man 3.50
40 F:Gorilla City 2.50
41 F:Flash Villains 2.75
42 DC,F:Phantom Girl 2.50
43 TVE,TT,F:Hawk & Dove 2.50
44 F:Batman,Clayface tie-in 3.00
45 F:Blackhawk,El Diablo 2.50
46 CS,F:All Headquarters 2.50
47 CS,F:The Legion 2.50
48 KG,F:Ambush Bug 2.50
49 F: The Cadmus Project 2.50
50 GP,CI,DG,F:Batman,Robin,
  Flash,Black Canary 4.00
Ann.#1 JBy,F:Doom Patrol 3.00
Ann.#2 CI,MA,F:Flash 2.50
Ann.#3 F:The Teen Titans 3.00
Spec.#1 SK,PB,DG,F:Batman's worst
  Villians,A:Penguin 4.00
TPB DG,New Origin Batman 4.50
GN rep of 1961 Annual 5.00
Replica Edition 80-page. 5.00
Vol.3 Even More Secret Origins . . . 7.00

SECRET ORIGINS OF SUPER-VILLAINS
2000
1 80-pg. Giant 5.00

SECRET SOCIETY OF SUPER-HEROES
Aug., 2000
1 (of 2) HC,MMK,JP,Elseworlds . . . 6.00
2 HC,MMK,JP,concl. 6.00

SECRET SOCIETY OF SUPER-VILLAINS
May-June, 1976
1 A:Capt.Boomerang, Grodd,
  Sinestro 30.00
2 R:Capt.Comet,A:Green Lantern 15.00
3 A:Mantis, Darkseid 12.00
4 A:Kalibak,Darkseid,Gr.Lantern . 12.00
5 RB,D:Manhunter,A:JLA 12.00
6 RB/BL,A:Black Canary 12.00
7 RB/BL,A:Hawkgirl,Lex Luthor . . 12.00
8 RB/BL,A:Kid Flash 12.00
9 RB/BMc,A:Kid Flash, Creeper . . 12.00
10 DAy/JAb,A:Creeper 12.00
11 JO,N:Wizard 12.00
12 BMc,A:Blockbuster 12.00
13 A:Crime Syndicate of America . 12.00

14 A:Crime Syndicate of America . 12.00
15 A:G.A.Atom, Dr. Mid Nite 12.00

SECRETS OF HAUNTED HOUSE
April-May, 1975
1 LD(c),Dead Heat 60.00
2 ECh(c),A Dead Man 25.00
3 ECh(c),Pathway To Purgatory . . 25.00
4 LD(c),The Face of Death 25.00
5 BWr(c),Gunslinger! 30.00
6 JAp(c),Deadly Allegiance 20.00
7 JAp(c),It'll Grow On You 20.00
8 MK(c),Raising The Devil 20.00
9 LD(c),The Man Who Didn't
  Believe in Ghosts 20.00
10 MK(c),Ask Me No Questions . . 20.00
11 MK(c),Picasso Fever! 20.00
12 JO&DG(c),Yorick's Skull 20.00
13 JO&DG(c),The Cry of the
  Warewolf 20.00
14 MK(c),Selina 20.00
15 LD(c),Over Your Own Dead
  Body 15.00
16 MK(c),Water, Water Every Fear 15.00
17 LD(c),Papa Don 15.00
18 LD(c),No Sleep For The Dying . 15.00
19 LD(c),The Manner of Execution 15.00
20 JO(c),The Talisman of the
  Serpent 15.00
21 LD(c),The Death's Head
  Scorpion 15.00
22 LD(c),See How They Die 15.00
23 LD(c),The Creeping Red Death 15.00
24 LD(c),Second Chance To Die . . 15.00
25 LD(c),The Man Who Cheated
  Destiny 15.00
26 MR(c),Elevator to Eternity 15.00
27 DH(c),Souls For the Master . . . 15.00
28 DH(c),Demon Rum 15.00
29 MK(c),Duel of Darkness 15.00
30 JO(c),For the Love of Arlo 15.00
31 I:Mister E. 20.00
32 The Legend of the Tiger's Paw. 10.00
33 In The Attic Dwells Dark Seth . . 10.00
34 Double Your Pleasure 10.00
35 Deathwing, Lord of Darkness . . 10.00
36 RB&DG(c),Sister Sinister 10.00
37 RB&DG(c),The Third Wish Is
  Death 10.00
38 RB&DG(c),Slaves of Satan. . . . 10.00
39 RB&DG(c),The Witch-Hounds
  of Salem 10.00
40 RB&DG(c),The Were-Witch
  of Boston 10.00
41 JKu(c),House at Devil's Tail . . . 10.00
42 JKu(c),Mystic Murder 10.00
43 JO(c),Mother of Invention 10.00
44 BWr(c),Halloween God 10.00
45 EC&JO(c),Star-Trakker 10.00
46 March, 1982 . . . . 10.00

SINISTER HOUSE OF SECRET LOVE
Oct.–Nov., 1971
1 . . . . 250.00
2 JJ(c) 100.00
3 ATh 125.00
4 April-May, 1972 . . . . 100.00
Becomes:

SECRETS OF SINISTER HOUSE
June-July, 1972
5 . . . . 60.00
6 . . . . 30.00
7 NR 30.00
8 . . . . 30.00
9 . . . . 30.00

DC COMICS

10 NA(i) 35.00
11 thru 16 . . . . @20.00
17 DBa. 20.00
18 June-July, 1974. . . . . 20.00

SECRETS OF THE LEGION OF SUPER-HEROES
Jan., 1981
1 O:Legion 3.50
2 O:Brainiac 5. . . . . 3.50
3 March, 1981,O:Karate Kid 3.50

SEEKERS
DC/Vertigo
1 & 2 . . . . @2.50

SEEKERS INTO THE MYSTERY
1996
1 Pilgrimage of Lucas Hart,pt.1 . . . 2.50
2 Pilgrimage of Lucas Hart,pt.2 . . . 2.50
3 Pilgrimage of Lucas Hart,pt.3 . . . 2.50
4 Pilgrimage of Lucas Hart,pt.4 . . . 2.50
5 Pilgrimage of Lucas Heaven,pt.5 . . . 2.50
6 Falling Down to Heaven,pt.1 . . . . 2.50
7 Falling Down to Heaven,pt.2 . . . . 2.50
8 Falling Down to Heaven,pt.3 . . . . 2.50
9 JMD(s),MZi,Falling Down from
     Heaven,pt.4 concl. 2.50
10 JMD(s),JMu,F:Charlie Limbo . . . 2.50
11 JMD(s),JIT,God's Shadow,pt.1 . . 2.50
12 JMD(s),JIT,God's Shadow,pt.2 . . 2.50
13 JMD(s),JIT,God's Shadow,pt.3 . . 2.50
14 JMD(s),JIT,God's Shadow,pt.4 . . 2.50
15 JMD(s),JMu,Hart meets
     Magician, final issue 3.00

SENSATION COMICS
1942–52
1 I:Wonder Woman,Wildcat . . 44,000.00
2 I:Etta Candy & the Holiday
     Girls, Dr. Poison 6,500.00
3 Diana Price joins Military
     Intelligence 3,500.00
4 I:Baroness PaulaVonGunther 2,500.00
5 V:Axis Spies 2,000.00
6 Wonder Woman receives magic
     lasso,V:Baroness Gunther . 2,000.00
7 V:Baroness Gunther 1,400.00

Sensation #22 © DC Comics Inc.

8 Meets Gloria Bullfinch. 1,400.00
9 A:The Real Diana Prince . . . 1,400.00
10 V:Ishti 1,400.00
11 I:Queen Desira 1,400.00
12 V:Baroness Gunther 1,300.00
13 V:Olga,Hitler(c) 1,800.00
14 . . . . 1,300.00
15 V:Simon Slikery 1,300.00
16 V:Karl Schultz 1,300.00
17 V:Princess Yasmini 1,300.00
18 V:Quito 1,300.00
19 Wonder Woman goes
     berserk 1,300.00
20 V:Stoffer 1,300.00
21 V:American Adolf 1,000.00
22 V:Cheetah 1,000.00
23 'War Laugh Mania' 1,000.00
24 I:Wonder Woman's
     mental radio 1,000.00
25 . . . . 1,000.00
26 A:Queen Hippolyte 1,000.00
27 V:Ely Close 1,000.00
28 V:Mayor Prude 1,000.00
29 V:Mimi Mendez 1,000.00
30 V:Anton Unreal. 1,000.00
31 Grow Down Land 750.00
32 V:Crime Chief 750.00
33 Meets Percy Pringle 750.00
34 I:Sargon 800.00
35 V:Sontag Henya in Atlantis . . 650.00
36 V:Bedwin Footh. 650.00
37 A:Mala((1st app. All-Star #8) . 650.00
38 V:The Gyp. 650.00
39 V:Nero 650.00
40 I:Countess Draska Nishki 650.00
41 V:Creeper Jackson 600.00
42 V:Countess Nishki. 600.00
43 Meets Joel Heyday 600.00
44 V:Lt. Sturm 600.00
45 V:Jose Perez. 600.00
46 V:Lawbreakers Protective
     League. 600.00
47 V:Unknown 600.00
48 V:Topso and Teena 600.00
49 V:Zavia 600.00
50 V:`Ears' Fellock. 600.00
51 V:Boss Brekel 550.00
52 Meets Prof. Toxino 550.00
53 V:Wanta Wynn 550.00
54 V:Dr. Fiendo 550.00
55 V:Bughumans 550.00
56 V:Dr. Novel 550.00
57 V:Syonide 550.00
58 Meets Olive Norton 550.00
59 V:Snow Man 550.00
60 V:Bifton Jones. 550.00
61 V:Bluff Robust. 550.00
62 V:Black Robert of Dogwood . 550.00
63 V:Prof. Vibrate. 550.00
64 V:Cloudmen 550.00
65 V:Lim Slait. 550.00
66 V:Slick Skeener. 550.00
67 V:Daredevil Dix 550.00
68 Secret of the Menacing
     Octopus 550.00
69 V:Darcy Wells 450.00
70 Unconquerable Woman of
     Cocha Bamba 450.00
71 V:Queen Flaming 450.00
72 V:Blue Seal Gang 450.00
73 Wonder Woman time
     travel story. 450.00
74 V:Spug Spangle 450.00
75 V:Shark 450.00
76 V:King Diamond 450.00
77 V:Boss Brekel 450.00
78 V:Furiosa. 450.00
79 Meets Leila and Solala 450.00
80 V:Don Enrago 450.00
81 V:Dr. Frenzi. 550.00
82 V:King Lunar 400.00

83 V:Prowd 400.00
84 V:Duke Daxo. 400.00
85 Meets Leslie M. Gresham. . . . 400.00
86 Secret of the Amazing
     Bracelets 400.00
87 In Twin Peaks(in Old West) . . 400.00
88 Wonder Woman in Holywood . 400.00
89 V:Abacus Rackeett gang 400.00
90 The Secret of the Modern
     Sphinx 400.00
91 . . . . 400.00
92 V:Duke of Deceptions 400.00
93 V:Talbot 400.00
94 Girl Isue 600.00
95 . . . . 550.00
96 . . . . 550.00
97 . . . . 550.00
98 Strange Mission 550.00
99 I:Astra 550.00
100 . . . . 700.00
101 Battle for the Atom World . . . 550.00
102 Queen of the South Seas . . . 550.00
103 V:Robot Archers 550.00
104 The End of Paradise
     Island. 550.00
105 Secret of the Giant Forest . . 550.00
106 E:Wonder Woman. 550.00
107 ATh,Mystery issue. 950.00
108 ATh,GK,I:Johnny Peril. 750.00
109 Ath,GK,A:Johnny Peril 1,000.00
Becomes:

SENSATION MYSTERY
1952–53
110 MA(c),B:Johnny Peril 600.00
111 GK,Spectre in the Flame. . . . 550.00
112 GK,Death has 5 Guesses . . . 550.00
113 GK, ... 550.00
114 GK,GC,The Haunted
     Diamond 550.00
115 GK,The Phantom Castle 550.00
116 The Toy Assassins 550.00

SENSATION COMICS
1999
1 JeR(s),ScB, F:Wonder Woman &
     Hawkgirl. 2.25

SERGEANT BILKO
May-June, 1957
1 Based on TV show 1,000.00
2 . . . . 500.00
3 . . . . 400.00
4 . . . . 350.00
5 . . . . 350.00
6 thru 17 . . . . @300.00
18 March-April, 1960 . . . . 300.00

SERGEANT BILKO'S PVT. DOBERMAN
June-July, 1958
1 . . . . 550.00
2 . . . . 300.00
3 . . . . 225.00
4 . . . . 225.00
5 photo (c). 225.00
6 thru 10 . . . . @150.00
11 Feb.–March, 1960 . . . . 150.00

SGT. ROCK
See: OUR ARMY AT WAR

SGT. ROCK SPECIAL
Oct., 1988
#1 rep.Our Army at War#162-#63 . 12.00
#2 rep.Brave & Bold #52 . . . . 7.00
#3 rep.Showcase #45 . . . . 7.00

#4 rep.Our Army at War#147-#48 . . 7.00
#5 rep.Our Army at War#81&#103 . 7.00
#6 rep.Our Army at War #160 . . . . . 7.00
#7 rep.Our Army at War #85 . . . . . . 7.00
#8 rep. 7.00
#9 thru #20 reprints. . . . . @7.00
Spec. #1 TT,MGo,JKu,CR,(new
    stories). 5.00

SGT. ROCK'S PRIZE BATTLE TALES
Winter, 1964
1 . . . . 500.00

SHADE
June-July, 1977
[1st Regular Series]
1 SD,I&O: Shade 20.00
2 SD,V:Form 15.00
3 SD,V:The Cloak 12.00
4 SD,Return to Meta-Zone 12.00
5 SD,V:Supreme Decider 12.00
6 SD,V:Khaos 12.00
7 SD,V:Dr.Z.Z. 12.00
8 SD,last issue 12.00

SHADE, THE
Feb., 1997
1 (of 4) JeR(s),GeH,A:Ludlows. . . . 3.00
2 JeR(s),JWi,MGy,poisoned by love
    of his life 3.00
3 JeR(s),BBI,Golden Age Flash Jay
    Garrick retiring. 3.00
4 JeR(s),MZi,V:last of the Ludlows. 3.00

SHADE, THE CHANGING MAN
July, 1990
1 B:PrM(s),CBa,MPn,I:Kathy George,
    I&D:Troy Grezer 5.00
2 CBa,MPn,Who Shot JFK#1 . . . . . 4.00
3 CBa,MPn,Who Shot JFK#2 . . . . . 3.00
4 CBa,MPn,V:American Scream . . 3.00
5 CBa,MPn,V:Hollywood
    Monsters 3.00
6 CBa,MPn,V:Ed Loot. 3.00
7 CBa,MPn,I:Arnold Major 3.00
8 CBa,Mpn,I:Lenny 3.00
9 CBa,MPn,V:Arnold Major. 3.00
10 CBa,MPn,Paranoia 2.75

Shade, The Changing Man 3
© DC Comics, Inc.

11 CBa,MPn,R:Troy Grezer. 2.50
12 CBa,MPn,V:Troy Grezer. 2.50
13 CBa,MPn,I:Fish Priest 2.50
14 CBa,MPn,V:Godfather of Guilt . 2.50
15 CBa,MPn,I:Spirit 2.50
16 CBa,MPn,V:American Scream . . 2.50
17 RkB(i),V:Rohug. 2.50
18 MPn,E:American Scream 2.50
19 MPn,V:Dave Messiah Seeker. . . 2.50
20 JD,CBa,MPn,RkB,R:Roger. 2.50
21 MPn,The Road,A:Stringer. 2.25
22 The Road,Childhood. 2.25
23 The Road 2.25
24 The Road 2.25
25 The Road 2.25
26 MPn(i),F:Lenny 2.25
27 MPn(i),Shade becomes female . 2.25
28 MPn(i),Changing Woman #2 . . . 2.25
29 MPn(i),Changing Woman #3 . . . 2.25
30 Another Life. 2.25
31 Ernest & Jim #1 . . . . 2.25
32 Ernest & Jim #2 . . . . 2.25

DC/Vertigo, 1993
33 CBa,B:Birth Pains. 2.25
34 CBa,RkB(i),GID(i),A:Brian Juno,
    Garden of Pain 2.25
35 CBa,RkB(i),E:Birth Pains,
    V:Juno 2.25
36 CBa,PrG(i),RkB(i),B:Passion child,
    I:Miles Laimling 2.25
37 CBa,RkB(i),Shade/Kathy 2.25
38 CBa,RkB(i),Great American
    Novel 2.25
39 CBa,SEa,RkB(i),Pond Life 2.25
40 PBd,at Hotel Shade 2.25
41 GID,Pandora's Story,Kathy is
    pregnant 2.25
42 CBa,RkB(i),SY,B:History Lesson,
    A:John Constantine 2.50
43 CBa,RkB(i),PBd,Trial of William
    Matthieson,A:J.Constantine. . . . 2.50
44 CBa,RkB(i),E:History Lesson,
    D:William Matthieson,A:John
    Constantine 2.50
45 CBa,B:A Season in Hell 2.25
46 CBa(c),GID,Season in Hell#2 . . 2.25
47 CBa(c),GID,A:Lenny 2.25
48 CBa(c),GID 2.25
49 CBa(c),GID,Kathy's Past 2.25
50 GID,BBI,MiA,pin-up gallery 3.25
51 GID,BBI,MiA,Masks,pt.1 . . . . . . 2.00
52 GID,BBI,MiA,Masks,pt.2 . . . . . . 2.00
53 GID,BBI,MiA,Masks,pt.3 . . . . . . 2.00
54 Meeting 2.00
55 . . . . 2.00
56 . . . . 2.00
57 MBu,PrM,F:George. 2.00
58 PrM,Michael Lark 2.00
59 MBu,PrM,Nasty Infections,pt.1 . 2.00
60 MBu,PrM,Nasty Infections,pt.2 . 2.25
61 MBu,PrM,Nasty Infections,pt.3 . 2.25
62 Nasty Infections,pt.4 . . . . 2.25
63 Nasty Infections,finale. 2.25
64 The Madness 2.25
65 The Roots of Madness,pt.1 . . . . 2.25
66 The Roots of Madness,pt.2. . . . . 2.25
67 The Roots of Madness,pt.3. . . . . 2.25
68 After Kathy,pt.1 . . . . 2.25
69 After Kathy,pt.2 . . . . 2.25
70 After Kathy,pt.3, final issue . . . 2.25
TPB The American Scream 17.95

SHADO, SONG OF THE DRAGON
1992
1 GM(i),From G.A. Longbow
    Hunters 5.50
2 GM(i),V:Yakuza 5.00
3 GM(i),V:Yakuza 5.00
4 GM(i),V:Yakuza 5.00

SHADOW, THE
[1st Regular Series], 1973–75
1 MK,The Doom Puzzle 50.00
2 MK,V:Freak Show Killer. 25.00
3 MK,BWr 30.00
4 MK,HC,BWr,Ninja Story. 25.00
5 FR 20.00
6 MK 22.00
7 FR 12.00
8 FR 12.00
9 FR 12.00
10 JCr 15.00
11 A:Avenger 12.00
12 . . . . 12.00

[Limited Series], 1986
1 HC,R:Shadow 5.00
2 HC,O:Shadow 4.00
3 HC,V:Preston Mayrock 3.00
4 HC,V:Preston Mayrock 3.00
TPB rep. #1 thru #4 . . . . 12.95

[2nd Regular Series], 1987–89
1 BSz,Shadows & Light,pt.1 . . . . . 3.50
2 BSz,Shadows & Light,pt.2 . . . . . 3.50
3 BSz,Shadows & Light,pt.3 . . . . . 3.50
4 BSz,Shadows & Light,pt.4 . . . . . 3.50
5 BSz,Shadows & Light,pt.5 . . . . . 3.50
6 BSz,Shadows & Light,pt.6 . . . . . 3.50
7 MR,KB,Harold Goes to
    Washington 3.00
8 KB,Seven Deadly Finns,pt.1 . . . 3.00
9 KB,Seven Deadly Finns,pt.2 . . . 3.00
10 KB,Seven Deadly Finns,pt.3. . . 3.00
11 KB,Seven Deadly Finns,pt.4. . . 3.00
12 KB,Seven Deadly Finns,pt.5. . . 3.00
13 KB,Seven Deadly Finns,pt.6. . . 3.00
14 KB,Body And Soul,pt.1 . . . . . . 3.00
15 KB,Body And Soul,pt.2 . . . . . . 3.00
16 KB,Body And Soul,pt.3 . . . . . . 3.00
17 KB,Body And Soul,pt.4 . . . . . . 3.00
18 KB,Body And Soul,pt.5 . . . . . . 3.00
19 KB,Body And Soul,pt.6 . . . . . . 3.00
Ann.#1 JO,AA,Shadows & Light
    prologue. 4.00
Ann.#2 KB,Agents 3.50

SHADOW CABINET
Milestone, 1994–95
0 WS(c),3RL,Shadow War,Foil(c),A:All
    Milestone characters 3.00
1 JBy(c),3RW,I&D:Corpsickle 2.50
2 3RW,V:Arcadian League 2.50
3 3RW,F:Sideshow 2.50

Shadow Cabinet #11
© DC Comics Inc.

4 3RW,F:Sideshow 2.50
5 . . . . 2.50
6 . . . . 2.50
7 . . . . 2.50
8 New Cabinet 2.50
9 R:Old Cabinet 2.50
10 V:Red Dog 2.50
11 Death Issue 2.50
12 SYSTEM 2.50
13 A:Hardware,Starlight 2.50
14 Long Hot Summer, Iron Butterfly
    Starlight 2.50
15 Long Hot Summer. 2.50
16 Changing of the Guard 2.50
17 V:Dharma,final issue 2.50

SHADOWDRAGON ANNUAL
1995
Ann.#1 Year One Annual 3.50

SHADOW OF BATMAN
1 reprints of Detective Comics . . . 10.00
2 thru 4 . . . . @7.50

SHADOW OF THE BATMAN
1985–86
1 WS,AM,MR,rep. 7.00
2 MR,TA,rep.A:Hugo Strange 5.00
3 MR,TA,rep.A:Penguin 5.00
4 MR,TA,rep.A:Joker 6.00
5 MR,DG,rep. 5.00

SHADOW'S FALL
1994–95
1 JVF,Voyage of self-discovery. . . . 3.00
2 JVF,More of tale. 3.00
3 JVF,Shen confronts shadow 3.00
4 JVF,Gale wounded. 3.00
5 JVF,Shadow goes Berserk 3.00
6 JVF,F:Warren Gale,final issue . . . 3.00

SHADOW STRIKES!, THE
1989–92
1 EB,Death's Head 3.00
2 EB,EB,PoliticalKiller,V:Rasputin . . 2.50
3 EB,V:Mad Monk,V:Rasputin 2.50
4 EB,D:Mad Monk,V:Rasputin 4.00
5 EB,Shadow & Doc Savage#1 . . . 4.00
6 Shadow & Doc Savage #3 . . . . . 2.50
7 RM,A:Wunderkind,O:Shadow's
    Radio Show 2.50
8 EB,A:Shiwan Khan 2.50
9 Fireworks#2 . . . . 2.50
10 EB,Fireworks#3. . . . . 2.50
11 EB,O:Margo Lane 2.50
12 EB,V:Chicago Mob 2.50
13 EB,V:Chicago Mob 2.50
14 EB,V:Chicago Mob 2.50
15 EB,V:Chicago Mob 2.50
16 Assassins,pt.1 . . . . 2.50
17 Assassins,pt.2 . . . . 2.50
18 Shrevvie 2.50
19 NY,NJ Tunnel 2.50
20 Shadow+Margo Vs.Nazis 2.50
21 V:Shiwan Khan 2.50
22 V:Shiwan Khan 2.50
23 V:Shiwan Khan 2.50
24 Search for Margo Lane. 2.50
25 In China 2.50
26 V:Shiwan Khan 2.50
27 V:Shiwan Khan,Margo
    Rescued 2.50
28 SL,In Hawaii 2.50
29 DSp,Valhalla,V:Nazis 2.50
30 The Shadow Year One,pt.1 . . . . 2.50

31 The Shadow Year One,pt.2 . . . . 2.50
Ann.#1 DSp, Crimson Dreams 4.00

SHADOW WAR OF HAWKMAN
May, 1985
1 AA,V:Thangarians 2.50
2 AA,V:Thangarians 2.50
3 AA,V:Thangarians,A:Aquaman,
    Elong.Man 2.50
4 AA,V:Thangarians 2.50
Spec.#1 V:Thangarians 2.50

SHAZAM!
1973–78
[1st Regular Series]
1 B:DON(s),CCB,O:Capt.Marvel . 45.00
2 CCB,A:Mr.Mind 15.00
3 CCB,V:Shagg Naste 15.00
4 E:DON(s),CCB,V:Ibac 15.00
5 B:ESM(s),CCB,A:Leprechaun . 15.00
6 B:DON(s),CCB,Dr,Sivana 10.00
7 CCB,A:Capt Marvel Jr. 10.00
8 CCB,O:Marvel Family 65.00
9 E:DON(S)DC,CCB,A:Mr.Mind,
    Captain Marvel Jr. 10.00
10 ESM(s)CCB,BO 10.00
11 ViCKS,BO,rep. 10.00
12 BO,DG 55.00
13 BO,KS,A:Luthor 55.00
14 KS,A:Monster Society. 55.00
15 KS,BO,Luther 55.00
16 KS,BO. 55.00
17 KS,BO. 55.00
18 KS,BO. 10.00
19 KS,BO,Mary Marvel 10.00
20 KS,A:Marvel Family 10.00
21 reprint 10.00
22 reprint 10.00
23 reprint 10.00
24 reprint 10.00
25 KS,DG,I&O:Isis 15.00
26 KS 10.00
27 KS,A:Kid Eternity 15.00
28 KS 10.00
29 KS 10.00
30 KS 10.00
31 KS,A:Minute Man 10.00
32 KS 10.00
33 KS 10.00
34 O:Capt.Marvel Jr. 10.00
35 DN,KS,A:Marvel Family 10.00
GN Power of Hope,64-page 10.00

Shazam #18 © DC Comics Inc.

SHAZAM! FAMILY
July, 2002
Annual #1 (1953, rep.) 80-pg. 6.00

SHAZAM, THE NEW BEGINNING
April, 1987
1 O:Shazam & Capt.Marvel 2.50
2 V:Black Adam 2.50
3 V:Black Adam 2.50
4 V:Black Adam 2.50

SHERLOCK HOLMES
Sept.–Oct., 1975
1 ERc,WS 35.00

SHEVA'S WAR
DC/Helix, Aug., 1998
1 (of 5) CsM,Iron Empires 3.00
2 CsM,Iron Empires 3.00
3 CsM,Iron Empires 3.00
4 CsM, ... 3.00
5 CsM 3.00

SHOWCASE
1956–70, 1977–78
1 F:Fire Fighters 5,500.00
2 JKu,F:Kings of Wild 1,600.00
3 F:Frogmen 1,500.00
4 CI,JKu,I&O:S.A. Flash
    (Barry Allen) 42,000.00
5 F:Manhunters 1,400.00
6 JK,I&O:Challengers of the
    Unknown. 6,000.00
7 JK,F:Challengers 2,800.00
8 CI,F:Flash,I:Capt.Cold 17,500.00
9 F:Lois Lane 12,000.00
10 F:Lois Lane 4,600.00
11 JK(c),F:Challengers 2,500.00
12 JK(c),F:Challengers 2,500.00
13 CI,F:Flash,Mr.Element 6,500.00
14 CI,F:Flash,Mr.Element. 6,800.00
15 I:Space Ranger 3,000.00
16 F:Space Ranger. 1,400.00
17 GK(c),I:Adam Strange 3,700.00
18 GK(c),F:Adam Strange 1,800.00
19 GK(c),F:Adam Strange 2,000.00
20 I:Rip Hunter 1,500.00
21 F:Rip Hunter 750.00
22 GK,I&O:S.A. Green Lantern
    (Hal Jordan) 7,200.00
23 GK,F:Green Lantern 2,400.00
24 GK,F:Green Lantern 2,400.00
25 JKu,F:Rip Hunter 500.00
26 JKu,F:Rip Hunter 500.00
27 RH,I:Sea Devils 1,300.00
28 RH,F:Sea Devils 600.00
29 RH,F:Sea Devils 600.00
30 O:Aquaman 1,200.00
31 GK(c),F:Aquaman. 600.00
32 F:Aquaman 600.00
33 F:Aquaman 650.00
34 GK,MA,I&O:S.A. Atom 2,400.00
35 GK,MA,F:Atom 1,200.00
36 GK,MA,F:Atom 900.00
37 RA,I:Metal Man 1,000.00
38 RA,F:Metal Man 650.00
39 RA,F:Metal Man 500.00
40 RA,F:Metal Man 425.00
41 F:Tommy Tomorrow 275.00
42 F:Tommy Tomorrow 275.00
43 F:Dr.No(James Bond 007) . . 675.00
44 F:Tommy Tomorrow 200.00
45 JKu,O:Sgt.Rock 450.00
46 F:Tommy Tomorrow 150.00
47 F:Tommy Tomorrow 150.00
48 F:Cave Carson 150.00

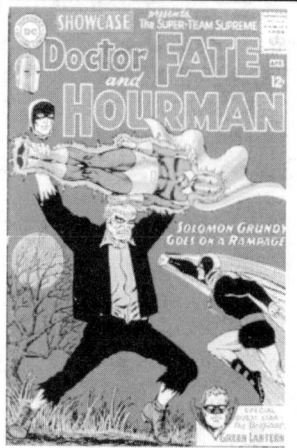

Showcase #55 © DC Comics, Inc.

49 F:Cave Carson	150.00
50 MA,CI,F:I Spy	125.00
51 MA,CI,F:I Spy	125.00
52 F:Cave Carson	100.00
53 JKu(c),RH,F:G.I.Joe	175.00
54 JKu(c),RH,F:G.I.Joe	175.00
55 MA,F:Dr.Fate,Spectre,1st S.A.	
Gr. Lantern,Solomon Grundy	375.00
56 MA,F:Dr.Fate.	225.00
57 JKu,F:Enemy Ace	325.00
58 JKu,F:Enemy Ace	175.00
59 F:Teen Titans	175.00
60 MA,F:Spectre	450.00
61 MA,F:Spectre	225.00
62 JO,I:Inferior 5	150.00
63 JO,F:Inferior 5.	90.00
64 MA,F:Spectre	235.00
65 F:Inferior 5	75.00
66 I:B'wana Beast	65.00
67 F:B'wana Beast.	65.00
68 I:Maniaks	65.00
69 F:Maniaks	65.00
70 I:Binky.	65.00
71 F:Maniaks	65.00
72 JKu,ATh,F:Top Gun	75.00
73 SD,I&O:Creeper	250.00
74 I:Anthro.	150.00
75 SD,I:Hawk & Dove	200.00
76 NC,I:Bat Lash	100.00
77 BO,I:Angel & Ape	100.00
78 I:Jonny Double	65.00
79 I:Dolphin	90.00
80 NA(c),F:Phantom Stranger . . .	125.00
81 I:Windy & Willy	75.00
82 I:Nightmaster.	125.00
83 BWr,MK,F:Nightmaster	100.00
84 BWr,MK,F:Nightmaster	100.00
85 JKu,F:Firehair	35.00
86 JKu,F:Firehair.	35.00
87 JKu,F:Firehair	35.00
88 F:Jason's Quest	25.00
89 F:Jason's Quest	25.00
90 F:Manhunter	25.00
91 F:Manhunter	25.00
92 F:Manhunter	25.00
93 F:Manhunter (1970)	25.00

[Series Resumes], 1977

94 JA,JSon,I&O:2nd	
Doom Patrol	20.00
95 JA,JSon,F:2nd Doom Patrol . .	12.00
96 JA,JSon,F:2nd Doom Patrol . .	12.00
97 JO,JSon,O:Power Girl	12.00
98 JSon,DG,Power Girl	12.00
99 JSon,DG,Power Girl	12.00

100 JSon,all star issue.	20.00
101 JKu(c),AM,MA,Hawkman	12.00
102 JKu(c),AM,MA,Hawkman	12.00
103 JKu(c),AM,MA,Hawkman	12.00
104 RE,OSS Spies	12.00
TPB Rep.1956–59	20.00

SHOWCASE '93

1 AAd(c),EH,AV,F:Catwoman,	
Blue Devil,Cyborg	4.00
2 KM(c),EH,AV,F:Catwoman,	
Blue Devil,Cyborg	3.50
3 KM(c),EH,TC,F:Catwoman,	
Blue Devil,Flash	3.00
4 F:Catwoman,Blue Devil,	
Geo-Force	3.00
5 F:KD,DG,BHi,F:Robin,Blue	
Devil,Geo-Force	3.00
6 MZ(c),KD,DG,F:Robin,Blue	
Devil,Deathstroke	3.00
7 BSz(c),KJ,Knightfall#13,F:Two-	
Face,Jade&Obsidian	5.00
8 KJ,Knightfall#14,F:Two-Face,	
Peacemaker,Fire and Ice	4.00
9 F:Huntress,Peacemaker,Shining	
Knight	3.00
10 BWg,SI,F:Huntress,Batman,	
Dr.Light,Peacemaker,Deathstroke,	
Katana,M.Manhunter	3.00
11 GP(c),F:Robin,Nightwing,	
Peacemaker,Deathstroke,Deadshot,	
Katana,Dr.Light,Won.Woman . .	3.00
12 AD(c),BMc,F:Robin,Nightwing,	
Green Lantern,Creeper	3.00

SHOWCASE '94

1 KN,F:Joker,Gunfire,Orion,Metro	3.00
2 KON(c),E:Joker,B:Blue Beetle. .	3.00
3 MMi(c),B:Razorsharpe.	3.00
4 AIG(s),DG,F:Arkham Asylum inmates	
E:Razorsharpe,Blue Bettle	3.00
5 WS(s),CDi(s),PJ,B:Robin&Huntress,	
F:Bloodwynd,Loose Cannon . . .	3.00
6 PJ,KK(s),F:Robin & Huntress . .	3.00
7 JaL(c),PDd(s),F:Comm. Gordon .	3.00
8 AIG(s),O:Scarface,Ventriloquist,	
F:Monarch,1st Wildcat.	3.25
9 AIG(s),DJ,O:Scarface,Ventriloquist,	
F:Monarch,Waverider	3.00
10 JQ(c),AIG(s),F:Azrael,Zero Hour,	
B:Black Condor	3.25
11 Black Condor, Man-Bat.	3.00
12 Barbara Gordon	3.00

SHOWCASE '95

1 Supergirl	3.00
2	3.00
3 F:Eradicator,Claw	3.00
4 A:Catwoman,Hawke	3.00
5 F:Thorne,Firehawk.	3.00
6 thru 12	@3.00

SHOWCASE '96

1 F:Steel & Warrior	3.00
2 F:Steel and Warrior	3.00
3 thru 7	@3.00
8 F:Superman, Superboy &	
Supergirl	5.00
9 F:Lady Shiva & Shadowdragon,	
Martian Manhunter	3.00
10 F:Ultra Boy, Captain Comet . . .	3.00
11 Legion of Super-Heroes	3.00
12 10,000 Brainiacs	3.00

SILVER AGE
DC CLASSICS

Action #252(rep)	3.00
Adventure #247(rep)	3.00
Brave and Bold #28 (rep)	3.00

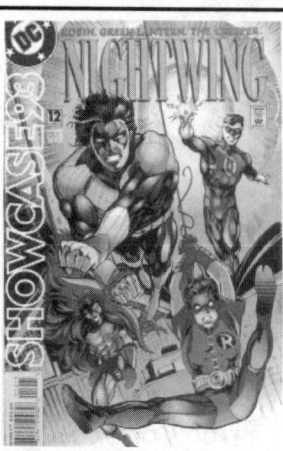

Showcase '93 #12 © DC Comics Inc.

Detective #225 (rep)	3.00
Detective #327 (rep)	3.00
Green Lantern #76 (rep)	3.00
House of Secrets #92 (rep)	3.00
Showcase #4 (rep).	3.00
Showcase #22 (rep).	3.00
Sugar & Spike #99(1st printing). .	3.00

SILVER AGE
May, 2000

Secret Files #1.	5.00
Justice League of America #1	2.50
Challengers of the Unknown #1 . .	2.50
Teen Titans #1	2.50
Doom Patrol #1	2.50
Dial "H" For Hero #1	2.50
The Flash #1	2.50
Green Lantern #1.	2.50
The Brave and the Bold #1	2.50
Showcase #1	2.50
80-Page Giant #1, 80-pg	6.50
Silver Age #1, 48-pg	3.95

SILVERBLADE
Sept., 1987

1 KJ,GC,maxi-series.	2.25
2 thru 12 GC	@2.25

SINS OF YOUTH
March, 2000

Aquaboy/Lagoon Man #1 x-over . .	2.50
Batboy & Robin #1 x-over	2.50
JLA/Jr. #1 x-over	2.50
Kid Flash/Impulse #1 x-over	2.50
Secret/Deadboy #1 x-over	2.50
Starwoman & JSA #1 x-over	2.50
Superman,Jr./Superboy,Sr.#1	
x-over.	2.50
Wonder Girls #1 x-over	2.50

SKIN GRAFT
DC/Vertigo, 1993

1 B:JeP(s),WaP,I:John Oakes,	
A:Tattooed Man(Tarrant)	3.25
2 WaP,V:Assassins	3.00
3 WaP,In Kyoto,I:Mizoguchi Kenji .	3.00
4 E:JeP(s),WaP,V:Tarrant,Kenji . .	3.00

SKREEMER
May, 1989

1 thru 6	@2.25
TPB (2002).	20.00

DC COMICS

SKULL AND BONES
1992
1 EH,I&O:Skull & Bones 5.00
2 EH,V:KGB 5.00
3 EH,V:KGB 5.00

SLASH MARAUD
Nov., 1987
1 PG 2.25
2 PG 2.25
3 thru 10 PG . . . . @2.25

SMALLVILLE
Sept., 2002
Spec. TV series 4.00

SMALLVILLE
March 2003
1 camping trip 5.00
2 Miss Smallville Pageant 4.00
3 F:Lex Luthor 4.00
4 F:Lex Luthor 4.00
5 . . . . 4.00
6 Lex & Clark,48-pg 4.00
7 TG,Television x-over,pt.1 . . . . . . 4.00
8 TG,Television x-over,pt.2 . . . . . . 4.00
9 Mysterious men 4.00
10 Who shot Lionel Luthor 4.00
TPB Rep 10.00

SMASH COMICS
1999
1 TPe(s),F:Doctor Mid-Nite
   & Hourman 2.25

SMAX
DC/Vertigo 2003
1 (of 5) AMo(s) 3.00
2 thru 4 AMo(s) 3.00

SOLO
2004
1 TSe,48-pg. 4.00

SONIC DISRUPTORS
1987–88
1 thru 10 . . . . @3.00

SON OF AMBUSH BUG
July, 1986
1 thru 6 KG . . . . @2.25

SOVEREIGN SEVEN
1995–98
1 CCl(s),DT,I:Sovereign Seven,
   V:Female Furies,A:Darkseid . . 3.00
2 I:Nike,Kratos,Zelus,Bia 2.50
3 V:Nike,Kratos,Zelus,Bia 2.50
4 I:Skin Dance 2.50
5 CCl,DT,V:Skin Dance 2.50
6 CCl,DT,V:Force Majeure 2.50
7 CCl,DT,Wild Hunt,pt.2 . . . . 2.50
8 CCl,DT,Clv,Wild Hunt,pt.3 . . . . . 2.50
9 CCl,DT,Clv 2.50
10 CCl,DT,Clv,Road Trip,pt.1 . . . . . 2.50
11 CCl,DT,Clv,Road Trip,pt.2 (of 3) . 2.50
12 CCl(s) 2.25
13 CCl(s) 2.25
14 CCl(s) 2.25
15 CCl,DT,Clv,Sovereign team
   betrayed 2.25
16 CCl,DT,Clv,Network betrays
   Sovereigns, Final Night tie-in . . 2.25
17 CCl(s),RLm,Clv,V:Network 2.25

18 CCl(s),RLm,Clv,V:Network and
   Kim 2.25
19 CCl(s) 2.25
20 CCl(s),VGi,Finale trapped in
   Forest Fire 2.25
21 CCl(s),RLm,DC,Clv,Danae's
   secret 2.25
22 CCl(s),RLm,DC,Clv,Indigo &
   Rampart fall 2.25
23 CCl(s),RLm,DC,Clv,Finale
   hallucinates 2.25
24 CCl(s),RLm,Clv,A:Superman . . . 2.25
25 CCl(s),RLm,Clv,V:Power Girl . . . 2.25
26 CCl(s),RLm,Clv,A:Hitman 2.25
27 CCl(s),RLm,Clv,Genesis tie-in . 2.25
28 CCl(s),RLm,Clv,A:Impulse 2.25
29 CCl(s),RLm,Clv,Sovereign dies . 2.25
30 CCl(s),RLm,Clv,revenge 2.25
31 CCl(s),RLm,Clv,F:Power Girl . . . 2.25
32 CCl(s),RLm,Clv,F:Power Girl . . . 2.25
33 CCl(s),RLm,Clv,F:Power Girl . . . 2.25
34 CCl(s),RLm,Clv,in Kuristan 2.25
35 CCl(s),RLm,Clv,The Rapture . . . 2.25
36 CCl(s),RLm,Clv,final issue 2.25
Ann.#1 CCl, Year One Annual 4.00
Ann.#2 CCl(s),RL,KJ,Legends of
   the Dead Earth 3.00
1-shot Sovereign Seven Plus
   (1977) 2.95
TPB CCl(s),DT, rep.#1–#5 . . . . . . 12.95

SPACE JAM
Warner Bros./DC, Oct., 1996
one-shot comic adaptation of movie 5.95

SPANNER'S GALAXY
Dec., 1984
1 mini-series 2.25
2 thru 6 . . . . @2.25

SPECTRE, THE
1967–69
1 MA,V:Captain Skull 200.00
2 NA,V:Dirk Rawley 125.00
3 NA,A:Wildcat 125.00
4 NA 125.00
5 NA 125.00
6 MA 75.00
7 MA,BU:Hourman 75.00
8 MA,Parchment of Power
   Perilous 75.00
9 BWr(2nd BWr Art) 100.00
10 MA 75.00

[2nd Regular Series], 1987–89
1 GC,O:Spectre 5.00
2 GC,Cult of BRM 4.00
3 GC,Fashion Model Murders 3.00
4 GC 3.00
5 GC,Spectre's Murderer 3.00
6 GC,Spectre/Corrigan separated . 3.00
7 A:Zatanna,Wotan 3.00
8 A:Zatanna,Wotan 3.00
9 GM,Spectre's Revenge 3.00
10 GM,A:Batman,Millennium 3.00
11 GM,Millennium 3.00
12 GM,The Talisman,pt.1 . . . . 3.00
13 GM,The Talisman,pt.2 . . . . 3.00
14 GM,The Talisman,pt.3 . . . . 3.00
15 GM,The Talisman,pt.4 . . . . 3.00
16 Jim Corrigan Accused 3.00
17 New Direction,Final Destiny 3.00
18 Search for Host Body 3.00
19 Dead Again 3.00
20 Corrigan Detective Agency 3.00
21 A:Zoran 3.00
22 BS,Sea of Darkness,A:Zoran . . . 3.00
23 A:Lords of Order,
   Invasion x-over 3.00

24 BWg,Ghosts i/t Machine#1 . . . . . 3.00
25 Ghosts in the Machine #2 . . . . . . 3.00
26 Ghosts in the Machine #3 . . . . . . 3.00
27 Ghosts in the Machine #4 . . . . . . 3.00
28 Ghosts in the Machine #5 . . . . . . 3.00
29 Ghosts in the Machine #6 . . . . . . 3.00
30 Possession 3.00
31 Spectre possessed, final issue . . 3.00
Ann.#1, A:Deadman 3.00

Spectre, 3rd Series #6
© DC Comics Inc.

[3rd Regular Series], 1992–97
1 B:JOs(s),TMd,R:Spectre,
   Glow in the dark(c) 7.00
2 TMd,Murder Mystery 6.00
3 TMd,O:Spectre 4.00
4 TMd,O:Spectre 4.00
5 TMd,BB(c),V:Kidnappers 3.50
6 TMd,Spectre prevents evil 3.50
7 TMd 3.50
8 TMd,Glow in the dark(c) 5.00
9 TMd,MWg(c),V:The Reaver 3.00
10 TMd,V:Michael 3.00
11 TMd,V:Azmodeus 3.00
12 V:Reaver 3.00
13 TMd,V:Count Vertigo,
   Glow in the dark(c) 4.00
14 JoP,A:Phantom Stranger 2.50
15 TMd,A:Phantom Stranger,Demon,
   Doctor Fate,John Constantine . . 2.50
16 JAp,V:I.R.A. 2.50
17 TT(c),TMd,V:Eclipso 2.50
18 TMd,D:Eclipso 2.50
19 TMd,V:Hate 2.50
20 A:Lucien 2.50
21 V:Naiad,C:Superman 3.00
22 A:Superman 2.50
23 Book of Judgment, pt.1 . . . . 2.50
24 Book of Judgment, pt.2 . . . . 2.50
25 Book of Judgment, pt.3 . . . . 2.50
26 . . . . 2.50
27 R:Azmodus 2.50
28 V:Azmodus 2.50
29 V:Azmodus 2.50
30 V:Azmodus 2.50
31 Descent into Pandemonium 2.50
32 V:Killo 2.50
33 . . . . 2.50
34 Power of the Undead 2.50
35 JOs,TMd,Underworld
   Unleashed tie-in 2.50
36 JOs,TMd,Underworld
   Unleashed tie-in 2.50
37 JOs,TMd,The Haunting of
   America,pt.1 . . . . 2.50

38 JOs,TMd,The Haunting of
   America,pt.2 . . . . 2.50
39 JOs,TMd,The Haunting of
   America,pt.3 . . . . 2.50
40 JOs,TMd,The Haunting of
   America,pt.4 . . . . 2.50
41 JOs,TMd,The Haunting of
   America,pt.5 . . . . 2.50
42 JOs,TMd,The Haunting of
   America,pt.6 . . . . 2.50
43 Witchcraft 2.50
44 Madame Xanadu 2.50
45. . . . . 2.50
46 JOs(s),TMd,discovery of the
   Spear of Destiny 2.50
47 JOs(s),TMd,The Haunting of
   America, Final Night tie-in 2.50
48 JOs(s),TMd,The Haunting of
   America 2.50
49 JOs(s),TMd,The Haunting of
   America 2.50
50 JOs(s),TMd, ... 2.50
51 JOs(s),TMd,A:Batman,Joker. . . . 2.50
52 JOs(s),TMd,Nate Kane discovers
   murder evidence 2.50
53 JOs(s),TMd,Haunting of Jim
   Corrigan, cont. 2.50
54 JOs(s),TMd,hunt for murderer of
   Mister Terrific 2.50
55 JOs(s),TMd,Corrigan implicated
   in murder. 2.50
56 JOs(s),TMd,JTo, Haunting of Jim
   Corrigan. 2.50
57 JOs(s),TMd,Spectre & Jim
   Corrigan in Heaven 2.50
58 JOs,TMd,Genesis tie-in 2.50
59 JOs,TMd,BWr(c), alien pod 2.50
60 JOs,TMd,Quest for God, cont. . . 2.50
61 JOs,TMd,Quest for God, concl. . 2.50
62 JOs,TMd,final issue 2.50
Ann.#1 JOs,TMd,Year One 4.00
TPB Punishment and Crimes 10.00
TPB Crimes & Punishments 10.00

SPECTRE, THE
Jan., 2001
1 JMD,F:Hal Jordan 3.00
2 JMD,Redeeming the Demon,pt.1 2.50
3 JMD,Redeeming the Demon,pt.2 2.50
4 JMD,Redeeming the Demon,pt.3 2.50
5 JMD,F:Two-Face/Harvey Dent . . 2.50
6 JMD,The Redeemer,pt.1 . . . . . . 2.50
7 JMD,The Redeemer,pt.2 . . . . . . 2.50
8 JMD,The Redeemer,pt.3 . . . . . . 2.50
9 JMD,stolen soul 2.50
10 JMD,Joker:Last Laugh 2.50
11 JMD,F:Phantom Stranger 2.50
12 JMD,Spectre of Christmas 2.50
13 JMD,Eternity in an Hour 2.50
14 JMD,vampire-lord 2.50
15 JMD,NBy,Mystery in Space,pt.1 . 2.50
16 JMD,NBy,Mystery in Space,pt.2 . 2.50
17 JMD,NBy,Mystery in Space,pt.3 . 2.50
18 JMD,NBy,Abin Sur, Materna. . . . 2.50
19 NBy,DJa,V:Darkseid 2.50
20 NBy,DJa,magazine publisher . . . 2.75
21 NBy,DJa,Stigmonus,C.Ferris . . . 2.75
22 NBy,DJa,A:G.Arrow,
   M.Manhunter 2.75
23 JMD,NBy,DJa,Return of
   Sinestro,pt.3 . . . . 2.75
24 JMD,DJa,F:DCU characters 2.75
25 JMD,DJa,F:Rabid 2.75
26 JMD,DJa,terrorist 2.75
27 JMD,DJa,final issue 2.75

SPEED FORCE
Sept., 1997
1 MWa,BAu,JBy,BML,JAp,BSn,
   Flash stories, 64pg. 4.00

Spelljammer #14 © DC Comics, Inc.

SPELLJAMMER
Sept., 1990
1 RogueShip#1 . . . . 3.00
2 RogueShip#2 . . . . 2.50
3 RogueShip#3 . . . . 2.25
4 RogueShip#4 . . . . 2.25
5 New Planet 2.25
6 Tember, Planet contd 2.25
7 Planet contd. 2.25
8 conclusion 2.25
9 Meredith Possessed 2.25
10 Tie-in w/Dragonlance #33&34. . 2.25
11 Dwarf Citidel 2.25
12 Kirstig Vs. Meredith. 2.25
13 Tember to the Rescue 2.25
14 Meredith's Son #1. . . . . 2.25
15 Meredith's Son #2. . . . . 2.25

STALKER
1975–1976
1 SD,WW,O&I:Stalker. 25.00
2 thru 4 SD,WW . . . . @15.00

STANLEY & HIS MONSTER
(see FOX AND THE CROW)

STANLEY & HIS MONSTER
1993
1 R:Stanley 2.25
2 I:Demon Hunter 2.25
3 A:Ambrose Bierce 2.25
4 final issue. 2.25

S.T.A.R. CORPS
1993
1 A:Superman 2.25
2 I:Fusion,A:Rampage 2.25
3 thru 6 . . . . @2.25

STAR CROSSED
DC/Helix, April, 1997
1 (of 3) MHo,Dyltah's romance
   with Saa. 2.50
2 MHo,Love During Wartime 2.50
3 concl. 2.50

[NEIL GAIMAN & CHARLES VESS'] STARDUST
DC/Vertigo, Oct., 1997
1 (of 4) NGa(s),CV 6.00
2 NGa(s),CV adult faerie tale 6.00
3 NGa(s),CV. 6.00
4 NGa(s),CV. 6.00

STARFIRE
1976–77
1 . . . . 20.00
2 thru 8 . . . . @12.00

STAR HUNTERS
Oct.–Nov., 1977
1 DN&BL. 20.00
2 LH&BL 12.00
3 MN&BL,D:Donovan Flint 12.00
4 thru 7 . . . . @12.00

STARMAN
1988–92
1 TL,I&O:New Starman. 4.00
2 TL,V:Serial Killer,C:Bolt 3.00
3 TL,V:Bolt 3.00
4 TL,V:Power Elite 2.50
5 TL,Invasion,A:PowerGirl,
   Firestorm 2.50
6 TL,Invasion,A:G.L.,Atom 2.50
7 TL,Soul Searching Issue 2.50
8 TL,V:LadyQuark. 2.50
9 TL,A:Batman,V:Blockbuster 2.50
10 TL,A:Batman,V:Blockbuster 2.50
11 TL,V:Power Elite 2.50
12 TL,V:Power Elite,A:Superman . . 2.50
13 TL,V:Rampage 2.50
14 TL,A:A:Superman,V:Parasite . . . 2.50
15 TL,V:Deadline 2.50
16 TL,O:Starman 2.50
17 TL,V:Dr.Polaris,A:PowerGirl 2.50
18 TL,V:Dr.Polaris,A:PowerGirl 2.50
19 TL,V:Artillery 2.50
20 TL,FireFighting 2.50
21 TL,Starman Quits 2.50
22 TL,V:Khunds 2.50
23 TL,A:Deadline 2.50
24 TL,A:Deadline 2.50
25 TL,V:Deadline 2.50
26 V:The Mist. 6.00
27 V:The Mist. 5.00
28 A:Superman 7.00
29 V:Plasmax 2.50
30 Seduction of Starman #1 . . . . . 2.50
31 Seduction of Starman #2 . . . . . 2.50
32 Seduction of Starman #3 . . . . . 2.50
33 Seduction of Starman #4 . . . . . 2.50
34 A:Batman 2.50
35 A:Valor,Mr.Nebula,ScarletSkier. . 2.50
36 A:Les Mille Yeux 2.50
37 A:Les Mille Yeux 2.50
38 War of the Gods X-over 2.50
39 V:Plasmax. 2.50
40 V:Las Vegas 2.50
41 V:Maaldor 2.50
42 Star Shadows,pt.1,A:Eclipso . . . 3.00
43 Star Shadows,pt.2,A:Lobo,
   Eclipso. 2.50
44 Star Shadows,pt.3,A:Eclipso
   V:Lobo 2.50
45 Star Shadows,pt.4, V:Eclipso . . . 2.50

[2nd Series], 1994
0 New Starman 8.00
1 Threat of the Mist. 8.00
2 . . . . 7.00
3 V:Son of the Mist. 6.00
4 . . . . 6.00

Starman #71 © DC Comics, Inc.

5 V:Starman	6.00
6 Times Past Features	6.00
7 Sinister Circus	6.00
8 TyH(c),Sinister Circus	5.00
9 TyH(c),Mist's daughter breaks out of prison	5.00
10 Sins of the Chile,prelude	5.00
11	5.00
12 JeR,TyH,Sins of the Child,pt.1	5.00
13 JeR,TyH,Sins of the Child,pt.2	5.00
14 JeR,TyH,Sins of the Child,pt.3	5.00
15 JeR,TyH,Sins of the Child,pt.4	5.00
16 JeR,TyH,Sins of the Child,pt.5	5.00
17 JeR,TyH	5.00
18 JeR,TyH,Orig.Starman vs.The Mist	4.00
19 JeR,TyH,Talking with David 2	4.00
20 JeR(s),TyH,GyD,Sand and Stars,pt.1	4.00
21 JeR,TyH,GyD,Sand/Stars,pt.2	3.00
22 JeR,TyH,GyD,Sand/Stars,pt.3	3.00
23 JeR,TyH,GyD,Sand/Stars,pt.4	3.00
24 JeR(s),TyH,Hell & Back,pt.1	3.00
25 JeR(s),TyH,Hell & Back,pt.2	3.00
26 JeR(s),TyH,Hell & Back,pt.3	3.00
27	3.00
28 JeR(s)Superfreaks and Backstabbers	3.00
29 JeR(s),TyH,GyD,V:The Shade, Starman history	3.00
30 JeR(s),TyH,Infernal Devices pt.1 (of 6)	3.00
31 JeR(s),TyH,Devices,pt.2	3.00
32 JeR(s),TyH,Devices,pt.3	3.00
33 JeR(s),TyH,Infernal Devices pt.4,A:Batman, Sentinel	3.00
34 JeR(s),TyH,A:Batman, Sentinel, Floronic Man	3.00
35 JeR(s),TyH,A:Batman, Floronic Man, Sentinel	3.00
36 JeR(s),TyH,F:Will Payton	3.00
37 JeR(s),TyH,F:GoldenAgeHeroes	3.00
38 JeR(s),TyH,new JLE	2.50
39 JeR(s),TyH,Lightning & Stars, pt.1 x-over	2.50
40 JeR(s),TyH	2.50
41 JeR(s),GEr,TyH	2.50
42 JeR(s),MS,Nazis,Demon	2.50
43 JeR(s),TyH,help from JLA	2.50
44 JeR(s),times past story	2.50
45 JeR(s),search for Will Payton	2.50
46 JeR(s),TyH,Bobo	2.50
47 JeR,SY,TyH	2.50
48 JeR,SY,A:Swamp Thing	2.50

49 JeR,SY,Talking with David	2.50
50 JeR(s),PSj,48-page	5.00
51 JeR(s),PSj,to Krypton	2.50
52 JeR(s),PSj,A:Adam Strange	2.50
53 JeR(s),PSj,A:Adam Strange	2.50
54 JeR(s),Times Past tale	2.50
55 JeR(s),PSj,A:Space Cabby	2.50
56 JeR(s),PSj,A:ElongatedMan	2.50
57 JeR(s),PSj,TyH,AxR,A:Tigorr & Fastbak, pt.1	2.50
58 JeR,TyH,AxR, pt.2	2.50
59 JeR,TyH,AxR, pt.3	2.50
60 JeR,TyH,AxR, concl.	2.50
61 JeR,TyH,AxR	2.50
62 JeR,PSj,Grand Guignol,pt.1	2.50
63 JeR,PSj,Grand Guignol,pt.2	2.50
64 JeR,PSj,Grand Guignol,pt.3	2.50
65 JeR,PSj,Grand Guignol,pt.4	2.50
66 JeR,PSj,Grand Guignol,pt.5	2.50
67 JeR,PSj,Grand Guignol,pt.6	2.50
68 JeR,PSj,Grand Guignol,pt.7	2.50
69 JeR,PSj,flashback	2.50
70 JeR,PSj,Grand Guignol,pt.8	2.50
71 JeR,PSj,Grand Guignol,pt.9	2.50
72 JeR,PSj,Grand Guignol, concl.	2.50
73 JeR,PSj,Grand Guignol,Eulogy	2.50
74 JeR,RH,Times Past	2.50
75 JeR,A:Superman	2.50
76 JeR,Talking With David:2001	2.50
77 JeR,1951,pt.1	2.50
78 JeR,1951,pt.2	2.50
79 JeR,1951,pt.3	2.50
80 JeR,48-page final issue	4.50
Ann.#1 Legends o/t Dead Earth	4.00
Ann.#2 Pulp Heroes (Romance)	4.50
Spec.#1,000,000 JeR(s),PSj	2.50
Secret Files #1,O:Starmen	5.00
Giant #1 80-page	5.00
Spec. Starman: The Mist, F:Mary Marvel, Girlfrenzy (1998)	2.50
TPB Sins of the Father,rep.#0–#5	12.95
TPB Night and Day, rep. stories from #7–#16	14.95
TPB A Wicked Inclination, rep.	18.00
TPB Times Past	18.00
TPB Infernal Devices	17.95
TPB To Reach the Stars	17.95
TPB A Starry Knight (2002)	17.95
TPB Stars My Destination	14.95
TPB Grand Guignol	19.95

STARS AND S.T.R.I.P.E.
1999

0 LMd,DDv,I:Courtney Whitman	3.00
1 LMd,DDv,O:Star-Spangled Kid	2.50
2 LMd,DDv,V:Paintball	2.50
3 LMd,DDv,V:Skeeter	2.50
4 LMd,DDv,Day of Judgment x-over	2.50
5 LMd,DDv,F:Young Justice,pt.1	2.50
6	2.50
7 LMd,DDv,F:Mike Dugan	2.50
8 LMd,DDv	2.50
9 LMd,DDv,R:Nebula Man	2.50
10 LMd,DDv,cheating	2.50
11 DDv,V:Dr. Graft	2.50
12 DDv,V:Dragon King	2.50
13 DDv,V:Dragon King	2.50
14 LMd,DDv,final issue	2.50

STAR SPANGLED COMICS
Oct., 1941

1 O:Tarantula,B:Captain X of the R.A.F.,Star Spangled Kid, Armstrong of the Army	7,500.00
2 V:Dr. Weerd	2,200.00
3	1,400.00
4 V:The Needle	1,400.00

5 V:Dr. Weerd	1,400.00
6 E:Armstrong	850.00
7 S&K,O&1st app:The Guardian, B:Robotman,The Newsboy Legion, TNT	9,500.00
8 O:TNT & Dan the Dyna-Mite	3,000.00
9	2,200.00
10	2,200.00
11	1,600.00
12 Newsboy Legion stories, Prevue of Peril!	1,600.00
13 Kill Dat Story!	1,600.00
14 Meanest Man on Earth	1,600.00
15 Playmates of Peril	1,600.00
16 Playboy of Suicide Slum!	1,600.00
17 V:Rafferty Mob	1,600.00
18 O:Star Spangled Kid	2,200.00
19 E:Tarantula	1,600.00
20 B:Liberty Belle	1,600.00
21	1,400.00
22 Brains for Sale	1,400.00
23 Art for Scrapper's Sake	1,400.00
24	1,400.00
25 Victuals for Victory	1,400.00
26 Louie the Lug goes Literary	1,400.00
27 Turn on the Heat!	1,400.00
28 Poor Man's Rich Man	1,400.00
29 Cabbages and Comics	1,400.00
30	750.00
31 Questions Please!	750.00
32	750.00
33	750.00
34 From Rags to Run!	750.00
35 The Proud Poppas	750.00
36 Cowboy of Suicide Slum.	750.00
37	750.00
38	750.00
39 Two Guardians are a Crowd.	750.00
40	750.00
41 Back the 6th War Loan(c)	650.00
42	650.00
43 American Red Cross(c)	650.00
44	650.00
45 7th War Loan (c)	650.00
46	650.00
47	650.00
48	650.00
49	650.00
50	650.00
51 A:Robot Robber	650.00
52 Rehearsal for Crime	650.00
53 The Poet of Suicide Slum.	650.00
54 Dead-Shot Dade's Revenge.	650.00
55 Gabby Strikes a Gusher	650.00
56 The Treasuer of Araby	650.00

Star Spangled Comics #63 © DC Comics Inc.

57 Recruit for the Legion 650.00	
58 Matadors of Suicide Slum. . . . 650.00	
59 . . . . 650.00	
60 . . . . 650.00	
61 . . . . 650.00	
62 Prevue of Tomorrow 650.00	
63 . . . . 650.00	
64 Criminal Cruise 650.00	
65 B:Robin,(c) & stories 2,000.00	
66 V:No Face 1,200.00	
67 The Castle of Doom 900.00	
68 . . . . 900.00	
69 The Stolen Atom Bomb 1,400.00	
70 V:The Clock 900.00	
71 Perils of the Stone Age 900.00	
72 Robin Crusoe 900.00	
73 V:The Black Magician 900.00	
74 V:The Clock 900.00	
75 The State vs. Robin 900.00	
76 V:The Fence 900.00	
77 The Boy who Wanted Robin	
for Christmas 900.00	
78 Rajah Robin 900.00	
79 V:The Clock,The Tick-Tock	
Crimes 900.00	
80 The Boy Disc Jockey 900.00	
81 The Seeing-Eye Dog Crimes . 700.00	
82 The Boy who Hated Robin . . . 650.00	
83 Who is Mr. Mystery,B:Captain	
Compass backup story 650.00	
84 How can we Fight Juvenile	
Delinquency? 1,100.00	
85 Peril at the Pole 650.00	
86 . . . . 700.00	
87 V:Sinister Knight 1,100.00	
88 Robin Declares War on	
Batman, B:Batman app. 750.00	
89 Batman's Utility Belt? 750.00	
90 Rancho Fear! 750.00	
91 Cops 'n' Robbers? 750.00	
92 Movie Hero No. 1? 750.00	
93 . . . . 750.00	
94 Underworld Playhouse 800.00	
95 The Man with the Midas Touch,	
E:Robin(c),Batman story 800.00	
96 B:Tomahawk(c) & stories 500.00	
97 The 4 Bold Warriors 400.00	
98 . . . . 400.00	
99 The Second Pocahontas 400.00	
100 The Frontier Phantom 500.00	
101 Peril on the High Seas 400.00	
102 . . . . 400.00	
103 Tomahawk's Death Duel! . . . 400.00	
104 Race with Death! 400.00	

105 The Unhappy Hunting
Grounds. 400.00
106 Traitor in the War Paint. 400.00
107 The Brave who Hunted
Tomahawk 400.00
108 The Ghost called Moccasin
Foot!' 400.00
109 The Land Pirates of
Jolly Roger Hill! 400.00
110 Sally Raines Frontier Girl . . 400.00
111 The Death Map of Thunder
Hill 400.00
112 . . . . 400.00
113 FF,V:The Black Cougar 550.00
114 Return of the Black Cougar . 550.00
115 Journey of a Thousand
Deaths 400.00
116 The Battle of Junction Fort . . 400.00
117 Siege? 400.00
118 V:Outlaw Indians 375.00
119 The Doomed Stockade? 375.00
120 Revenge of Raven Heart! . . . 400.00
121 Adventure in New York! 375.00
122 I:Ghost Breaker,(c)& stories . 500.00
123 The Dolls of Doom 350.00
124 Suicide Tower 350.00
125 The Hermit's Ghost Dog! . . . 350.00
126 The Phantom of Paris! 350.00
127 The Supernatural Alibi! 350.00
128 C:Batman,The Girl who
lived 5,000 Years! 350.00
129 The Human Orchids 375.00
130 The Haunted Town,
. July, 1952 . . . . 400.00

Becomes:

STAR SPANGLED
WAR STORIES
Aug., 1952

131 CS&StK(c),I Was A Jap
Prisoner of War 1,300.00
132 CS&StK(c),The G.I. With
The Million-Dollar Arm. 850.00
133 CS&StK(c),Mission-San
Marino 700.00
3 CS&StK(c),Hundred-Mission
Mitchell 450.00
4 CS&StK(c),The Hot Rod Tank . 450.00
5 LSt(c),Jet Pilot 450.00
6 CS(c),Operation Davy Jones . . 450.00
7 CS(c),Rookie Ranger,The 400.00
8 CS(c),I Was A
Holywood Soldier 400.00
9 CS&StK(c),Sad Sack Squad . . 400.00
10 CS,The G.I. & The Gambler . . 400.00
11 LSt(c),The Lucky Squad 400.00
12 CS(c),The Four Horseman of
Barricade Hill 400.00
13 No Escape 400.00
14 LSt(c),Pitchfork Army 400.00
15 The Big Fish 400.00
16 The Yellow Ribbon 400.00
17 IN(c),Prize Target 400.00
18 IN(c),The Gladiator 400.00
19 IN(c),The Big Lift. 400.00
20 JGr(c),The Battle of
the Frogmen 400.00
21 JGr(c),Dead Man's Bridge . . . 300.00
22 JGr(c),Death Hurdle 300.00
23 JGr(c),The Silent Frogman . . . 300.00
24 JGr(c),Death Slide 300.00
25 JGr(c),S.S. Liferaft 300.00
26 JGr(c),Bazooka Man 300.00
27 JGr(c),Taps for a Tail Gunner . 300.00
28 JGr(c),Tank Duel 300.00
29 JGr(c),A Gun Called Slugger . 300.00
30 JGr(c),The Thunderbolt Tank . 300.00
31 IN(c),Tank Block 200.00
32 JGr(c),Bridge to Battle 200.00
33 JGr(c),Pocket War 200.00

Star Spangled War Stories #8
© DC Comics, Inc.

34 JGr(c),Fighting...Snowbirds . . 200.00
35 JGr(c),Zero Hour. 200.00
36 JGr(c),A G.I. Passed Here . . . 200.00
37 JGr(c),A Handful of T.N.T. . . . 200.00
38 RH(c),One-Man Army 200.00
39 JGr(c),Flying Cowboy 200.00
40 JGr(c),Desert Duel 200.00
41 IN(c),A Gunner's Hands 175.00
42 JGr(c),Sniper Alley 175.00
43 JGr(c),Top Kick Brother 175.00
44 JGr(c),Tank 711
Doesn't Answer 175.00
45 JGr(c),Flying Heels 175.00
46 JGr(c),Gunner's Seat 175.00
47 JGr(c),Sidekick 175.00
48 JGr(c),Battle Hills 175.00
49 JGr(c),Payload 175.00
50 JGr(c),Combat Dust 175.00
51 JGr(c),Battle Pigeon 125.00
52 JGr(c),Cannon-Man 125.00
53 JGr(c),Combat Close-Ups . . . 125.00
54 JGr(c),Flying Exit 125.00
55 JKu(c),The Burning Desert . . 125.00
56 JKu(c),The Walking Sub 125.00
57 JGr(c),Call For a Frogman . . . 125.00
58 JGr(c),MD,Waist Punch 125.00
59 JGr(c),Kick In The Door 125.00
60 JGr(c),Hotbox 125.00
61 JGr(c),MD,Tow Pilot 125.00
62 JGr(c),The Three GIs 125.00
63 JGr(c),Flying Range Rider . . . 125.00
64 JGr(c),MD,Frogman Ambush . 125.00
65 JGr(c),JSe,Frogman Block . . . 125.00
66 JGr(c),Flattop Pigeon 125.00
67 RH(c),MD,Ashcan Alley 125.00
68 JGr(c),The Long Step 125.00
69 JKu(c),Floating Tank, The. . . . 125.00
70 JKu(c),No Medal For
Frogman 125.00
71 JKu(c),Shooting Star. 125.00
72 JGr(c),Silent Fish 125.00
73 JGr(c),MD,The Mouse &
the Tiger 125.00
74 JGr(c),MD,Frogman Bait. 125.00
75 JGr(c),MD,Paratroop
Mousketeers 125.00
76 MD,JKu(c),Odd Man 125.00
77 MD,JKu(c),Room to Fight 125.00
78 MD,JGr(c),Fighting Wingman . 125.00
79 MD,JKu(c),Zero Box 125.00
80 MD,JGr(c),Top Gunner 125.00
81 MD,RH(c),Khaki Mosquito . . 125.00
82 MD,JKu(c),Ground Flier 125.00
83 MD,JGr(c),Jet On
My Shoulder 125.00

Star Spangled Comics #65
© DC Comics, Inc.

84 MD,IN(c),O:Mademoiselle
Marie 250.00
85 IN(c),A Medal For Marie 150.00
86 JGr(c),A Medal For Marie 150.00
87 JGr(c),T.N.T. Spotlight. 150.00
88 JGr(c),The Steel Trap 150.00
89 IN(c),Trail of the Terror 150.00
90 RA(c),Island of
Armored Giants 550.00
91 JGr(c),The Train of Terror . . . 125.00
92 Last Battle of the
Dinosaur Age. 200.00
93 Goliath of the Western Front . 125.00
94 JKu(c),The Frogman and
the Dinosaur 275.00
95 Guinea Pig Patrol,Dinosaurs . 200.00
96 Mission X,Dinosaur. 200.00
97 The Sub-Crusher, Dinosaur . . 200.00
98 Island of Thunder, Dinosaur . . 200.00
99 The Circus of Monsters,
Dinosaur 200.00
100 The Volcano of Monsters,
Dinosaur 225.00
101 The Robot and the Dinosaur 150.00
102 Punchboard War,Dinosaur . . 150.00
103 Doom at Dinosaur Island,
Dinosaur 150.00
104 The Tree of Terror,
Dinosaurs 150.00
105 The War of Dinosaur Island . 150.00
106 The Nightmare War,
Dinosaurs 150.00
107 Battle of the Dinosaur
Aquarium 150.00
108 Dinosaur D-Day 150.00
109 The Last Soldiers 150.00
110 thru 133 . . . . @150.00
134 NA. 160.00
135 . . . . 150.00
136. . . . . 150.00
137 Dinosaur 150.00
138 Enemy Ace 175.00
139 O:Enemy Ace 125.00
140 . . . . 100.00
141 . . . . 100.00
142 . . . . 100.00
143 . . . . 100.00
144 NA,JKu 125.00
145 . . . . 100.00
146 Enemy Ace(c) 75.00
147 New Enemy Ace 75.00
148 New Enemy Ace 75.00
149 . . . . 75.00
150 JKu,Viking Prince 75.00
151 I:Unknown Soldier. 225.00
152 Rep. New Enemy Ace. 75.00
153 . . . . 75.00
154 O:Unknown Soldier. 175.00
155 Rep. New Enemy Ace. 50.00
156 I:Battle Album 50.00
157 thru 160. . . . . 40.00
161 E:Enemy Ace 40.00
162 thru 170 . . . . @35.00
171 thru 200 . . . . @15.00
201 thru 204 . . . . @12.00
Becomes:

UNKNOWN SOLDIER
April-May, 1977
205 thru 247. . . . . @17.00
248 and 249 O:Unknown Soldier @12.00
250 . . . . 12.00
251 B:Enemy Ace 12.00
252 thru 268. . . . . @12.00

STAR SPANGLED COMICS
1999
1 CWn, F:Sandman & Star
Spangled Kid 2.25

Star Trek #56 © DC Comics, Inc.

STAR TREK
1984–88
[1st Regular Series]
1 TS,The Wormhole Connection . . 15.00
2 TS,The Only Good Klingon 8.00
3 TS,Errand of War. 7.00
4 TS,Deadly Allies. 7.00
5 TS,Mortal Gods 7.00
6 TS,Who is Enigma? 6.00
7 EB,O:Saavik 6.00
8 TS,Blood Fever 6.00
9 TS,Mirror Universe Saga #1 . . . . 6.00
10 TS,Mirror Universe Saga #2 . . . . 6.00
11 TS,Mirror Universe Saga #3 . . . . 6.00
12 TS,Mirror Universe Saga #4 . . . . 6.00
13 TS,Mirror Universe Saga #5 . . . . 5.00
14 TS,Mirror Universe Saga #6 . . . . 5.00
15 TS,Mirror Universe Saga #7 . . . . 5.00
16 TS,Mirror Universe Saga end . . . 5.00
17 TS,The D'Artagnan Three. 5.00
18 TS,Rest & Recreation 5.00
19 DSp,W.Koenig story 5.00
20 TS,Girl. 5.00
21 TS,Dreamworld. 5.00
22 TS,The Wolf #1. . . . . 5.00
23 TS,The Wolf #2. . . . . 4.00
24 TS,Double Blind #1. . . . . 4.00
25 TS,Double Blind #2. . . . . 4.00
26 TSV:Romulans 4.00
27 TS,Day in the Life 4.00
28 GM,The Last Word 4.00
29 Trouble with Bearclaw. 4.00
30 CI,F:Uhura 4.00
31 TS,Maggie's World 4.00
32 TS,Judgment Day 4.00
33 TS,20th Anniv. 5.00
34 V:Romulans 3.00
35 GM,Excelsior. 3.00
36 GM,StarTrek IV tie-in 3.00
37 StarTrek IV tie-in. 3.00
38 AKu,The Argon Affair 3.00
39 TS,A:Harry Mudd 3.00
40 TS,A:Harry Mudd 3.00
41 TS,V:Orions. 3.00
42 TS,The Corbomite Effect 3.00
43 TS,Paradise Lost #1 . . . . 3.00
44 TS,Paradise Lost #2 . . . . 3.00
45 TS,Paradise Lost #3 . . . . 3.00
46 TS,Getaway 3.00
47 TS,Idol Threats 3.00
48 TS,The Stars in Secret
Influence 3.00
49 TS,Aspiring to be Angels 3.00
50 TS,Anniv. 4.00
51 TS,Haunted Honeymoon 3.00

52 TS,'Hell in a Hand Basket. 3.00
53 You're Dead,Jim 3.00
54 Old Loyalties. 3.00
55 TS,Finnegan's Wake. 3.00
56 GM,Took place during 5 year
Mission 3.00
Ann.#1 All Those Years Ago 4.00
Ann.#2 DJw,The Final Voyage. . . . 3.00
Ann.#3 CS,F:Scotty 3.00
Star Trek III Adapt.TS. 2.50
Star Trek IV Adapt. TS. 2.50
StarTrek V Adapt. 2.50

[2nd Regular Series], 1989–96
1 The Return. 9.00
2 The Sentence 5.00
3 Death Before Dishonor 4.00
4 Reprocussions 4.00
5 Fast Friends. 4.00
6 Cure All 4.00
7 Not Sweeney! 4.00
8 Going,Going. 3.50
9 ...Gone 3.50
10 Trial of James Kirk #1. . . . . 3.50
11 Trial of James Kirk #2 . . . . 3.50
12 Trial of James Kirk #3. . . . . 3.50
13 Return of Worthy #1 . . . . 3.50
14 Return of Worthy #2 . . . . 3.50
15 Return of Worthy #3 . . . . 3.50
16 Worldsinger. 3.00
17 Partners? #1 . . . . 3.00
18 Partners? #2 . . . . 3.00
19 Once A Hero 3.00
20 . . . . 3.00
21 Kirk Trapped 3.00
22 A:Harry Mudd 3.00
23 The Nasgul,A:Harry Mudd 3.00
24 25th Anniv.,A:Harry Mudd. 4.00
25 Starfleet Officers Reunion. 2.50
26 Pilkor 3 . . . . 2.50
27 Kirk Betrayed 2.50
28 V:Romulans 2.50
29 Mediators 2.50
30 Veritas #1 . . . . 2.50
31 Veritas #2 . . . . 2.50
32 Veritas #3 . . . . 2.50
33 Veritas #4 . . . . 2.50
34 JD,F:Kirk,Spock,McCoy 2.50
35 Tabukan Syndrome#1 . . . . 2.50
36 Tabukan Syndrome#2 . . . . 2.50
37 Tabukan Syndrome#3 . . . . 2.50
38 Tabukan Syndrome#4 . . . . 2.50
39 Tabukan Syndrome#5 . . . . 2.50
40 Tabukan Syndrome#6 . . . . 2.50
41 Runaway 2.50
42 Helping Hand 2.50
43 V:Binzalans 2.50
44 Acceptable Risk 2.50
45 V:Trelane. 2.50
46 V:Captain Klaa 2.50
47 F:Spock & Saavik 2.50
48 The Neutral Zone 2.50
49 Weapon from Genesis 2.50
50 "The Peacemaker" 4.00
51 "The Price" 2.50
52 V:Klingons. 2.50
53 Timecrime #1 . . . . 2.50
54 Timecrime #2 . . . . 2.50
55 Timecrime #3 . . . . 2.50
56 Timecrime #4 . . . . 2.50
57 Timecrime #5 . . . . 2.50
58 F:Chekov. 2.50
59 Uprising. 2.50
60 Hostages. 2.50
61 On Talos IV 2.50
62 Alone,pt.1, V:aliens 2.50
63 Alone,pt.2 . . . . 2.50
64 Kirk 2.50
65 Kirk in Space. 2.50
66 Spock 2.50
67 Ambassador Stonn 2.50
68 . . . . 2.50

69 Wolf in Cheap Clothing,pt.1 . . . . 2.50
70 Wolf in Cheap Clothing,pt.2 . . . . 2.50
71 Wolf in Cheap Clothing,pt.3 . . . . 2.75
72 Wolf in Cheap Clothing,pt.4 . . . . 2.75
73 Star-crossed,pt.1 . . . . 2.75
74 Star-crossed,pt.2 . . . . 2.50
75 Star-crossed,pt.3 . . . . 4.50
76 Tendar 2.50
77 to the Romulan Neutral Zone . . . 2.50
78 The Chosen,pt.1 (of 3) 2.50
79 The Chosen,pt.2 . . . . 2.50
80 The Chosen,pt.3 . . . . 2.50
Ann.#1 GM,sty by G.Takei(Sulu) . . . 4.00
Ann.#2 Kirks 1st Yr At Star
    Fleet Academy 4.00
Ann #3 KD,F:Ambassador Sarek. . . 4.00
Ann.#4 F:Spock on Pike's ship 4.00
Ann.#6 Convergence,pt.1 . . . . 4.50
Spec.#1 PDd(s),BSz 4.00
Spec.#2 The Defiant 4.50
Spec.#3 V:Orion pirates 4.50
Debt of Honor,AH,CCl(s),HC 27.00
Debt of Honor SC 15.00
Spec. 25th Anniv.. . . . . 7.00
Star Trek VI,movie adapt(direct) . . . 6.00
Star Trek VI,movie(newsstand) 3.00
TPB Best of Star Trek reps. 20.00
TPB Star Trek: Revisitations
    rep. #22–#24,F:Gary Seven,
    #49–#50,F:Harry Mudd, 176pg 20.00
TPB Who Killed Captain Kirk?,
    rep.Star Trek#49–#55. . . . . . . 17.00
TPB The Ashes of Eden, Shatner
    novel adapt. 15.00

STAR TREK: THE
MODALA IMPERATIVE
1991

1 Planet Modula 6.00
2 Modula's Rebels 4.50
3 Spock/McCoy rescue Attempt . . . 4.00
4 Rebel Victory 4.00
TPB reprints both minis 20.00

STAR TREK: THE
NEXT GENERATION
Feb., 1988
[1st Regular Series]

1 based on TV series,Where No
    Man Has Gone Before 10.00
2 Spirit in the Sky 8.00
3 Factor Q. 5.00
4 Q's Day 5.00
5 Q's Effects 5.00
6 Here Today 5.00

[2nd Regular Series], 1989–95

1 Return to Raimon 15.00
2 Murder Most Foul 9.00
3 Derelict. 7.50
4 The Hero Factor 7.50
5 Serafin's Survivors. 6.00
6 Shadows in the Garden. 6.00
7 The Pilot. 5.00
8 The Battle Within 5.00
9 The Pay Off 5.00
10 The Noise of Justice. 5.00
11 The Imposter 4.00
12 Whoever Fights Monsters. 4.00
13 The Hand of the Assassin. 4.00
14 Holiday on Ice. 4.00
15 Prisoners of the Ferengi 3.50
16 I Have Heard the Mermaids
    Singing. 3.50
17 The Weapon 3.50
18 MM,Forbidden Fruit 3.50
19 The Lesson. 3.50
20 Lost Shuttle. 3.50

21 Lost Shuttle cont. 3.50
22 Lost Shuttle cont. 3.50
23 Lost Shuttle cont. 3.50
24 Lost Shuttle conc. 3.50
25 Okona S.O.S. 3.50
26 Search for Okona 3.50
27 Worf,Data,Troi,Okona trapped
    on world. 3.50
28 Worf/K'Ehleyr story 3.50
29 Rift,pt.1 . . . . 3.50
30 Rift,pt.2 . . . . 3.50
31 Rift conclusion 3.50
32 . . . . 3.50
33 R:Mischievous Q. 3.50
34 V:Aliens,F:Mischievous Q 3.50
35 Way of the Warrior 3.50
36 Shore Leave in Shanzibar#1 . . 3.25
37 Shore Leave in Shanzibar#2 . . 3.25
38 Shore Leave in Shanzibar#3 . . 3.25
39 Divergence #1. . . . . 3.25
40 Divergence #2. . . . . 3.25
41 V:Strazzan Warships. 3.25
42 V:Strazzans. 3.25
43 V:Strazzans. 3.25
44 Disrupted Lives. 3.25
45 F:Enterprise Surgical Team 3.25
46 Deadly Labyrinth. 3.25
47 Worst of Both World's#1 . . . . 3.00
48 Worst of Both World's#2 . . . . 3.00
49 Worst of Both World's#3 . . . . 3.00
50 Double Sized,V:Borg. 4.00
51 V:Energy Beings 3.00
52 in the 1940's 3.00
53 F:Picard. 3.00
54 F:Picard. 3.00
55 Data on Trial 3.00
56 Abduction 3.00
57 Body Switch 3.00
58 Body Switch 3.00
59 B:Children in Chaos 3.00
60 Children in Chaos#2 . . . . 3.00
61 E:Children in Chaos 3.00
62 V:Stalker 3.00
63 A:Romulans. 3.00
64 Geordie 3.00
65 Geordie 3.00
66 . . . . 3.00
67 Friends/Strangers 3.00
68 Friends/Strangers,pt.2 . . . . 3.00
69 Friends/Strangers,pt.3 . . . . 3.00
70 Friends/Strangers,pt.4 . . . . 3.00
71 War of Madness,pt.1. . . . . 3.00
72 War of Madness,pt.2. . . . . 3.00
73 War of Madness,pt.3. . . . . 3.00
74 War of Madness,pt.4. . . . . 3.00
75 War of Madness,pt.5. . . . . 4.50
76 F:Geordi 3.00
77 Gateway, pt.1 . . . . 3.00
78 Gateway, pt.2 . . . . 3.00
79 Crew transformed into androids . 3.00
80 Mysterious illness 3.00
Ann.#1 A:Mischievous Q 4.50
Ann.#2 BP,V:Parasitic Creatures . . . 4.00
Ann.#3 . . . . 4.00
Ann.#4 MiB(s),F:Dr.Crusher. 4.00
Ann.#6 Convergence,pt.2 . . . . 4.50
Series Finale 4.25
Spec.#1 . . . . 3.75
Spec.#2 CCl(s). 4.00
Star Trek N.G.:Sparticus. 5.00
TPB Beginnings, BSz(c) rep. 20.00

STAR TREK:
THE NEXT GENERATION
DEEP SPACE NINE
1994–95

1 Crossover with Malibu 2.50
2 . . . . 2.50

STAR TREK:
THE NEXT GENERATION
ILL WIND
1995–96

1 Solar-sailing race. 2.50
2 Explosion Investigated. 2.50
3 A bomb aboard ship. 2.50
4 finale 2.50

STAR TREK
THE NEXT GENERATION
MODALA IMPERATIVE
1991

1 A:Spock,McCoy 6.00
2 Modula Overrun by Ferengi. 5.00
3 Picard,Spock,McCoy & Troi
    trapped 4.00
4 final issue. 4.00

STAR TREK
THE NEXT GENERATION
SHADOWHEART
1994–95

1 thru 3 . . . . @2.50
4 Worf Confront Nikolai 2.50

STATIC
Milestone, 1993–96

1 JPL,I:Static,Hotstreak,Frieda Goren,
    w/poster,card,D puzzle piece . . 4.00
1a Newstand Ed. 2.50
1b Platinum Ed. 8.00
2 JPL,V:Hotstreak,I:Tarmack 2.50
3 JPL,V:Tarmack. 2.50
4 JPL,A:Holocaust,I:Don Cornelius 2.50
5 JPL,I:Commando X 2.50
6 JPL,V:Commando X 2.50
7 3RW,V:Commando X. 2.50
8 WS(c),3RW,Shadow War,I:Plus. . 2.50
9 3RW,I:Virus 2.50
10 3RW,I:Puff,Coil 2.50
11 3RW,V:Puff,Coil. 2.50
12 3RW,I:Joyride 2.50
13 I:Shape Changer. 2.50
14 Worlds Collide,V:Rift. 3.00
15 V:Paris Bloods 2.50
16 Revelations. 2.50
17 Palisade 2.50
18 Princess Nightmare 2.50

Static #13
© DC Comics, Inc.

19	2.50
20	2.50
21 A:Blood Syndicate	2.50
22 V:Rabis	2.50
23 A:Boogieman	2.50
24 A:Dusk	2.50
25 Long Hot Summer, V:Dusk, 48pgs	3.95
26 Long Hot Summer	2.50
27	2.50
28 Drug Raid	2.50
29 HC(c), Friend Drug Dealer	2.50
30 Deals with Friend's Death	2.50
31 GK	2.50
32 V:Swarm	2.50
33	2.50
34 V:Ruberband Man	2.50
35 new Prometheus	2.50
36 JP,V:Sinister Botanist	2.50
37	2.50
38	2.50
39	2.50
40 JMr	2.50
41 Virgil's relationship with Daisy	2.50
42 V:six enemies	2.50
43 A:Brickhouse, V:Frieda Goren	2.50
44	2.50
45 MBr(s),JMr,Static lays a trap for Laserjet	2.50
46 MBr(s),JMr	2.50
47 DMD(s),JMr, final issue	2.50

STATIC SHOCK!: REBIRTH OF THE COOL
DC/Milestone, Nov., 2001

1 (of 4) DMD	2.50
2 DMD,F:Hardware	2.50
3 DMD,A:Hardware,Iron Butterfly	2.50
4 DMD,V:Power Junkie	2.50

STEEL
1994–98

1 JBg(c),B:LSi(s),CsB,N:Steel	3.00
2 JBg(c),CsB,V:Toastmaster	2.50
3 JBg(c),CsB,V:Amertek	2.50
4 JBg(c),CsB	2.50
5 JBg(c),CsB,V:Sister's Attacker	2.50
6 JBg(c),CsB,Worlds Collide,pt.5	2.50
7 Worlds Collide,pt.6	2.50
8 Zero Hour,I:Hazard	2.50
9 F:Steel	2.50
10 F:Steel	2.50
11	2.50
12	2.50
13 A:Maxima	2.50
14 A:Superman	2.50
15 R:White Rabbit	2.50
16 V:White Rabbit [new Miraweb format begins]	2.50
17 Steel controls armor powers	2.50
18 Abduction	2.50
19	2.50
20 Body Rejects Armor	2.50
21 LSi,Underworld Unleashed tie-in	2.50
22 Steel separated from Superboy	2.50
23 Steel attacked	2.50
24 V:Hazard's	2.50
25	2.50
26 Natasha gains superpowers	2.50
27 LSi,V:Hazard	2.50
28	2.50
29	2.50
30	2.50
31 LSi(s),V:Armorbeast	2.50
32 V:Blockbuster	2.50
33 JAp,DG,Natasha's drug abuse	2.50
34 CPr(s),DCw,TP,A:Natasha, in Jersey City	2.50
35 CPr(s),DCw,TP	2.50

Steel #7 © DC Comics Inc.

36 CPr(s),DCw,TP,Combing the sewers of Jersey City	2.50
37 CPr(s),DCw,TP,John Irons, Amanda Quick & Skorpio a romantic triangle	2.50
38 CPr(s),DCw,TP,A:The Question	2.50
39 CPr(s),DCw,TP,V:Crash	2.50
40 CPr(s),VGi,Steel tries out new hammer	2.50
41 CPr(s),DCw,TMo, John Irons guilty of murder?	2.50
42 CPr(s),DCw,TP,Irons and Amanda assaulted	2.50
43 CPr(s),DCw,TP,to Metropolis	2.50
44 CPr(s),DCw,TP,Genesis tie-in	2.50
45 CPr(s),DCw,TP,seek policeman	2.50
46 CPr(s),DCw,TP,F:Superboy	2.50
47 CPr(s),DCw,TP,F:Amanda	2.50
48	2.50
49 CPr(s),DCw,TP,V:Deadline	2.50
50 CPr(s),DCw,TP,Millennium Giants	2.50
51 CPr(s),DCw,TP,bounty hunter	2.50
52 CPr(s),final issue	2.50
1-shot, movie adaptation	5.00
Ann.#1 Elseworlds story	3.00
TPB THe Forging of a Hero LSi(s)	20.00

STEEL, THE INDESTRUCTIBLE MAN
March, 1978

1 DH,I:Steel	12.00
2 DH	8.00
3 DH	8.00
4 DH	8.00
5 Oct.–Nov., 1978	12.00

STRANGE ADVENTURES
1950–74

1 The Menace of the Green Nebula	4,700.00
2 S&K,JM(c),Doom From Planet X	2,200.00
3 The Metal World	1,500.00
4 BP,The Invaders From the Nth Dimension	1,500.00
5 The World Inside the Atom	1,200.00
6 Confessions of a Martian	1,200.00
7 The World of Giant Ants	1,200.00
8 MA,ATh,Evolution Plus	1,200.00
9 MA,B:Captain Comet,The Origin of Captain Comet	2,800.00
10 MA,CI,The Air Bandits From Space	1,200.00
11 MA,CI,Day the Past Came Back	800.00
12 MA,CI,GK(c),The Girl From the Diamond Planet	800.00
13 MA,CI,GK(c),When the Earth was Kidnapped	800.00
14 MA,CI,GK(c),Destination Doom	800.00
15 MA,CI,GK(c),Captain Comet-Enemy of Earth	750.00
16 MA,CI,GK(c),The Ghost of Captain Comet	750.00
17 MA,CI,GK(c),Beware the Synthetic Men	750.00
18 CI,MA(c),World of Flying Men	750.00
19 CI,MA(c),Secret of the Twelve Eternals	750.00
20 CI,Slaves of the Sea Master	750.00
21 CI,MA(c),Eyes of the Other Worlds	600.00
22 CI,The Guardians of the Clockwork Universe	600.00
23 CI,MA(c),The Brain Pirates of Planet X	600.00
24 CI,MA(c),Doomsday on Earth	600.00
25 CI,GK(c),The Day That Vanished	600.00
26 CI,Captain Vs. Miss Universe	600.00
27 CI,MA(c),The Counterfeit Captain Comet	600.00
28 CI,Devil's Island in Space	600.00
29 CI,The Time Capsule From 1,000,000 B.C.	600.00
30 CI,MA(c),Menace From the World of Make-Believe	550.00
31 CI,Lights Camera Action	550.00
32 CI,MA(c),The Challenge of Man-Ape the Mighty	550.00
33 CI,MA(c),The Human Beehive	550.00
34 CI,MA(c)	550.00
35 CI,MA(c),Cosmic Chessboard	550.00
36 CI,MA(c),The Grab-Bag Planet	550.00
37 CI,MA(c),The Invaders From the Golden Atom	550.00
38 CI,MA(c),Seeing-Eye Humans	550.00
39 CI,MA(c),The Guilty Gorilla	550.00
40 CI,MA(c),The Mind Monster	550.00
41 CI,MA(c),The Beast From Out of Time	550.00
42 CI,MD,MA(c),The Planet of Ancient Children	550.00
43 CI,MD,MA(c),The Phantom Prize Fighter	550.00
44 CI,MA(c),The Planet That Plotted Murder	550.00
45 CI,MD,MA(c),Gorilla World	550.00
46 CI,MA(c),E:Captain Comet Interplanetary War Base	550.00
47 CI,MA(c),The Man Who Sold the Earth	550.00
48 CI,MA(c),Human Phantom	550.00
49 CI,MA(c),The Invasion from Indiana	550.00
50 CI,MA(c),The World Wrecker	400.00
51 CI,MA(c),The Man Who Stole Air	400.00
52 CI,MA(c),Prisoner of the Parakeets	400.00
53 CI,MA(c),The Human Icicle	400.00
54 CI,MA(c),The Electric Man	300.00
55 CI,MA(c),The Gorilla Who Challanged the World,pt.I	300.00
56 CI,The Jungle Emperor,pt.II	300.00
57 CI,The Spy from Saturn	300.00
58 CI,I Hunted the Radium Man	300.00
59 CI,The Ark From Planet X	300.00
60 CI,Across the Ages	300.00
61 CI,The Mirages From Space	300.00

Strange Adventures #9
© DC Comics, Inc.

62 CI,The Fireproof Man 300.00
63 CI,I Was the Man in the Moon 300.00
64 CI,GK(c),Gorillas In Space . . . 300.00
65 CI,GK(c),Prisoner From Pluto. 300.00
66 CI,GK(c),The Human Battery . 300.00
67 CI,GK(c),Martian Masquerader300.00
68 CI,The Man Who Couldn't
    Drown 300.00
69 CI,Gorilla Conquest of Earth. . 300.00
70 CI,Triple Life of Dr. Pluto 300.00
71 CI,MSy,Zero Hour For Earth . . 250.00
72 CI,The Skyscraper That Came
    to Life. 250.00
73 CI,Amazing Rain of Gems . . . 250.00
74 CI,The Invisible Invader
    From Dimension X. 250.00
75 CI,Secret of the Man-Ape 250.00
76 CI,B:Darwin Jones,The Robot
    From Atlantis 250.00
77 CI,A:Darwin Jones,The World
    That Slipped Out of Space . . 250.00
78 CI,The Secret of the Tom
    Thumb Spaceman 250.00
79 CI,A:Darwin Jones,Invaders
    from the Ice World. 250.00
80 CI,Mind Robbers of Venus . . . 250.00
81 CI,The Secret of the
    Shrinking Twins 250.00
82 CI,Giants of the Cosmic Ray . 225.00
83 CI,Assignment in Eternity 225.00
84 CI,Prisoners of the Atom
    Universe 225.00
85 CI,The Amazing Human Race 225.00
86 CI,The Dog That Saved the
    Earth 225.00
87 CI,New Faces For Old 225.00
88 CI,A:Darwin Jones,The Gorilla
    War Against Earth 225.00
89 CI,Earth For Sale 225.00
90 CI,The Day I Became a
    Martian 225.00
91 CI,Midget Earthmen of Jupiter 225.00
92 CI,GK(c),The Amazing Ray
    of Knowledge. 225.00
93 CI,GK(c),A:Darwin Jones,
    Space-Rescue By Proxy 225.00
94 MA,CI,GK(c),Fisherman of
    Space. 225.00
95 CI,The World at my Doorstep. 225.00
96 CI,MA(c),The Menace of
    Saturn's Rings 225.00
97 CI,MA(c),MSy,Secret of the
    Space-Giant. 225.00

98 CI,GK(c),MSy,Attack on Fort
    Satellite 225.00
99 CI,MSy,GK(c),Big Jump Into
    Space. 225.00
100 CI,MSy,The Amazing Trial
    of John (Gorilla) Doe 250.00
101 CI,MSy,GK(c),Giant From
    Beyond 150.00
102 MSy,GK(c),The Three Faces
    of Barry Morrell 150.00
103 GK(c),The Man Who
    Harpooned Worlds. 150.00
104 MSy,GK(c),World of Doomed
    Spacemen 150.00
105 MSy,GK(c),Fisherman From
    the Sea 150.00
106 MSy,CI,GK(c),Genie in the
    Flying Saucer 150.00
107 MSy,CI,GK(c),War of the
    Jovian Bubble-Men 150.00
108 MSy,CI,GK(c),The Human
    Pet of Gorilla Land 150.00
109 MSy,CI,GK(c),The Man Who
    Weighted 100 Tons 150.00
110 MSy,CI,GK(c),Hand From
    Beyond 150.00
111 MSy,CI,GK(c),Secret of
    the Last Earth-Man 150.00
112 MSy,CI,GK(c),Menace of
    the Size-Changing Spaceman150.00
113 MSy,CI,GK(c),Deluge From
    Space. 150.00
114 MSy,CI,GK(c),Secret of the
    Flying Buzz Saw 150.00
115 MSy,CI,GK(c),The Great
    Space-Tiger Hunt. 150.00
116 MSy,CI,RH,GK(c),Invasion
    of the Water Warriors 150.00
117 MSy,CI,MA(c),I:Atomic
    Knights. 850.00
118 MSy,CI,The Turtle-Men of
    Space. 175.00
119 MSy,CI,MA(c),Raiders
    From the Giant World 150.00
120 MSy,CI,MA,Attack of the Oil
    Demons 350.00
121 MSy,CI,MA(c),Invasion of the
    Flying Reptiles. 125.00
122 MSy,CI,MA(c),David and the
    Space-Goliath 125.00
123 MSy,CI,MA(c),Secret of the
    Rocket-Destroyer. 225.00
124 MSy,CI,MA(c),The Face-Hunter
    From Saturn 150.00
125 MSy,CI,The Flying Gorilla
    Menace 125.00
126 MSy,CI,MA(c),Return of the
    Neanderthal Man. 200.00
127 MSy,CI,MA(c),Menace
    From the Earth-Globe 125.00
128 MSy,CI,MA(c),The Man
    With the Electronic Brain. . . . 125.00
129 MSy,CI,MA(c),The Giant
    Who Stole Mountains 150.00
130 MSy,CI,MA.War With the
    Giant Frogs 125.00
131 MSy,CI,MA(c),Emperor
    of the Earth 125.00
132 MSy,CI,MA(c),The Dreams
    of Doom. 150.00
133 MSy,CI,MA(c),The Invisible
    Dinosaur 125.00
134 MSy,CI,MA(c), The Aliens
    Who Raided New York 150.00
135 MSy,CI,MA(c),Fishing Hole
    in the Sky. 125.00
136 MSy,CI,MA(c),The Robot
    Who Lost Its Head. 100.00
137 MSy,CI,MA(c),Parade of the
    Space-Toys 100.00

138 MSy,CI,MA(c),Secret of the
    Dinosaur Skeleton 125.00
139 MSy,CI,MA(c),Space-Roots
    of Evil. 100.00
140 MSy,CI,MA(c),Prisoner of
    the Space-Patch 100.00
141 MSy,CI,MA(c),Battle Between
    the Two Earths 125.00
142 MSy,CI,MA(c),The Return of
    the Faceless Creature. 100.00
143 MSy,CI,MA(c),The Face in
    the Atom-Bomb Cloud 100.00
144 MSy,CI,MA(c),A:Atomic
    Knights, When the Earth
    Blacked Out. 175.00
145 MSy,CI,MA,The Man Who
    Lived Forever 100.00
146 MSy,CI,MA(c),Perilous Pet
    of Space 100.00
147 MSy,CI,MA(c),The Dawn-
    World Menace 125.00
148 MSy,CI,MA(c),Earth Hero,
    Number One 100.00
149 MSy,CI,MA(c),Raid of
    the Rogue Star 100.00
150 MSy,CI,MA(c),When Earth
    Turned into a Comet 125.00
151 MSy,CI,MA(c),Invasion Via
    Radio-Telescope 100.00
152 MSy,MA(c),The Martian
    Emperor of Earth 100.00
153 MSy,MA(c),Threat of the
    Faceless Creature 100.00
154 CI,MSy,MA,GK(c),Earth's
    Friendly Invaders. 100.00
155 MSy,MA,GK(c),Prisoner
    of the Undersea World 100.00
156 MSy,CI,MA(c),The Man
    With the Head of Saturn 100.00
157 MSy,CI,MA(c),Plight of
    the Human Cocoons 100.00
158 MSy,CI,MA(c),The Mind
    Masters of Space. 100.00
159 MSy,CI,MA(c),The Maze
    of Time. 100.00
160 MSy,CI,MA(c),A:Atomic
    Knights, Here Comes the
    Wild Ones 100.00
161 MSy,CI,MA(c),Earth's Frozen
    Heat Wave,E:Space Museum . 75.00
162 CI,MA(c),Mystery of the
    12 O'Clock Man. 75.00
163 MA(c),The Creature in
    the Black Light. 75.00

Strange Adventures #243
© DC Comics Inc.

164 DD&SMo(c),I Became
    a Robot 75.00
165 DD&SMo(c),I Broke the
    Supernatural Barrier 75.00
166 DD&SMo(c),I Lived in
    Two Bodies 75.00
167 JkS(c),The Team That
    Conqured Time 75.00
168 JkS(c),I Hunted Toki
    the Terrible. 75.00
169 DD&SMo(c),The Prisoner
    of the Hour Glass 75.00
170 DD&SMo(c),The Creature
    From Strange Adventures 75.00
171 The Diary of the
    9-Planet Man? 75.00
172 DD&SMo(c),I Became
    the Juggernaut Man 75.00
173 The Secret of the
    Fantasy Films 75.00
174 JkS(c),The Ten Ton Man. 75.00
175 Danger: This Town is
    Shrinking 75.00
176 DD&SMo(c),The Case of
    the Cosmonik Quartet 75.00
177 I Lived a Hundred Lives,
    O:Immortal Man. 75.00
178 JkS(c),The Runaway Comet. . 75.00
179 JkS(c),I Buried Myself Alive . . 75.00
180 CI,I:Animal Man,I Was the
    Man With Animal Powers . . . 300.00
181 The Man of Two Worlds 50.00
182 JkS(c),The Case of the
    Blonde Bombshell 50.00
183 JM(c),The Plot to Destroy
    the Earth 50.00
184 GK(c),A:Animal Man,The
    Return of the Man With
    Animal Powers 175.00
185 JkS(c),Ilda-Gangsters Inc. . . . 50.00
186 Beware the Gorilla Witch 50.00
187 JkS(c),O:The Enchantress . . . 60.00
188 SD,JkS(c),I Was the
    Four Seasons 50.00
189 SD,JkS(c),The Way-Out
    Worlds of Bertram Tilley 50.00
190 CI,A:Animal Man,A-Man-the
    Hero with Animal Powers . . . 225.00
191 JkS(c),Beauty vs. the Beast . . 50.00
192 Freak Island 50.00
193 The Villian Maker 50.00
194 JkS(c),The Menace of the
    Super- Gloves 50.00
195 JkS(c),Secret of the Three
    Earth Dooms,A:Animal Man . 125.00
196 JkS(c),Mystery of the
    Orbit Creatures 50.00
197 The Hostile Hamlet 40.00
198 JkS(c),Danger! Earth
    is Doomed 40.00
199 Robots of the Round Table . . . 40.00
200 . . . . 40.00
201 JkS,Animal Man 75.00
202 . . . . 40.00
203 . . . . 40.00
204 . . . . 40.00
205 CI,I&O:Deadman. 175.00
206 NA,MSy. 125.00
207 NA 100.00
208 NA 100.00
209 NA 100.00
210 NA 100.00
211 NA 100.00
212 NA 100.00
213 NA 100.00
214 NA 100.00
215 NA 100.00
216 NA 100.00
217 MA,MSy,A:Adam Strange . . . 25.00
218 MA,CI,MSy 25.00
219 CI,JKu 25.00

220 CI,JKu 25.00
221 CI 25.00
222 MA,New Adam Strange 40.00
223 MA,CI 25.00
224 MA,CI 25.00
225 MA,JKu 25.00
226 MA,JKu,New Adam Strange . 40.00
227 JKu 25.00
228 NA(c). 35.00
229 . . . . 30.00
230 GM(c) 25.00
231 E:Atomic Knights 25.00
232 JKu 25.00
233 JKu 25.00
234 JKu 25.00
235 NA(c). 30.00
236 . . . . 20.00
237 . . . . 15.00
238 MK(c) 15.00
239 . . . . 15.00
240 MK(c) 15.00
241 . . . . 15.00
242 MA. 15.00
243 F:Adam Strange 15.00
244 Oct.–Nov., 1974 . . . . 15.00

STRANGE ADVENTURES
DC/Vertigo, Sept., 1999
1 (of 4) BB,DGb 2.50
2 KJ,Expiration Date 2.50
3 . . . . 2.50
4 concl. 2.50

STRANGE SPORTS STORIES
Sept.–Oct., 1973
1 CS,DG 40.00
2 thru 6 . . . . @ 25.00

STRAY
Homage/DC March, 2001
1 SLo,AdP,Stray dog, 48-page 6.00

STREETS
1993
1 Tenderloin 5.00
2 Procurement 5.00
3 . . . . 5.00

Sugar & Spike #69
© DC Comics, Inc.

SUGAR & SPIKE
April-May, 1956
1 SM 3,000.00
2 SM 1,000.00
3 SM 750.00
4 SM 750.00
5 SM 750.00
6 thru 10 SM . . . . @ 450.00
11 thru 20 SM . . . . @ 350.00
21 thru 29 SM . . . . @ 250.00
30 SM,A:Scribbly 250.00
31 thru 50 SM . . . . @ 200.00
51 thru 70 SM . . . . @ 125.00
71 thru 79 SM . . . . @ 100.00
80 SM,I:Bernie the Brain 100.00
81 thru 97 SM . . . . @ 75.00
98 SM,Oct.–Nov., 1971 . . . . 75.00
1 Facsimile Edition,rep.(2002) 2.95

SUICIDE SQUAD
1987–91
1 LMc,Legends,I:Jihad 2.50
2 LMc,V:The Jihad 2.25
3 LMc,V:Female Furies. 2.25
4 LMc,V:William Hell. 2.25
5 LM,A:Penguin 2.50
6 LM,A:Penguin 2.50
7 LMc,V:Peoples Hero 2.25
8 LMc,O:SquadMembers 2.25
9 LMc,Millennium 2.25
10 LMc,A:Batman 2.25
11 LMc,A:Vixen,Speedy. 2.25
12 LMc,Enchantress,
    V:Nightshade 2.25
13 LMc,X-over,JLI#13 . . . . 2.25
14 Nightshade Odyssey #1 . . . . . 2.25
15 Nightshade Odyssey #2 . . . . . 2.25
16 R:Shade 3.25
17 LMc,V:The Jihad 2.25
18 LMc,V:Jihad 2.25
19 LMc,Personal Files 1988 . . . . . 2.25
20 LMc,V:Mirror Master 2.25
21 LMc,bonus book #10 . . . . 2.25
22 LMc,D:Senator Cray 2.25
23 LMc,Invasion. 2.25
24 LMc,V:Guerillas. 2.25
25 L:Nightshade. 2.25
26 D:Rick Flag,Jihad 2.25
27 Janus Directive #2 . . . . 2.25
28 Janus Directive #4 . . . . 2.25
29 Janus Directive #8 . . . . 2.25
30 Janus Directive #10 . . . . 2.25
31 Personal Files 1989 . . . . 2.25
32 V:Female Furies 2.25
33 GI,V:Female Furies. 2.25
34 GI,V:Granny Goodness. 2.25
35 LMc,GI,V:Female Furies. 2.25
36 GI,D:Original Dr.Light 2.25
37 GI,A:Shade,The Changing
    Man,V:Loa 2.25
38 LMc,GI,O:Bronze Tiger. 2.25
39 GI,D:Loa 2.25
40 Phoenix Gambit #1,A:Batman
    Int. Poster 2.25
41 Phoenix Gambit #2. . . . . 2.25
42 Phoenix Gambit,A:Batman 2.25
43 Phoenix Gambit,A:Batman 2.25
44 I:New Atom,O:Captain
    Boomerang 2.25
45 A:Kobra 2.25
46 A:Kobra 2.25
47 GI,A:Kobra,D:Ravan 2.25
48 GI,New Thinker 2.25
49 GI,New Thinker. 2.25
50 GI,50 Years of S.Squad 2.25
51 A:Deadshot 2.25
52 R:Docter Light. 2.25
53 GI,The Dragon's Horde #1 . . . . 2.25
54 GI,The Dragon's Horde #2 . . . . 2.25
55 GI,The Dragon's Horde #3 . . . . 2.25

Suicide Squad #47
© DC Comics, Inc.

56 GI,The Dragon's Horde #4 . . . . . 2.25
57 GI,The Dragon's Horde conc. 2.25
58 GI,War of the Gods x-over 2.25
59 GI,A:Superman, Batman,
    Aquaman,A:Jihad, Hayoth. 2.25
60 GI,A:Superman,Batman,
    Aquaman,Jihad,The Hayoth . . . 2.25
61 GI,A:Superman,Batman,
    Aquaman,V:Jihad 2.25
62 GI,R:Ray Palmer,A:Batman
    Superman,Aquaman 2.25
63 GI,I:Gvede, Lord of Death 2.25
64 GI,A:Task Force X. 2.25
65 GI,Bronze Tiger. 2.25
66 GI,Final Iss.E:Suicide Squad . . . 2.25
Ann.#1 GN,V:Argent,A:Manhunter. . 2.25

SUICIDE SQUAD
Sept., 2001

1 KG,R:Suicide Squad 2.50
2 KG,F:Sgt. Rock 2.50
3 KG,Ants 2.50
4 KG,Need to Know 2.50
5 KG,Deadshot 2.50
6 KG,new squad 2.50
7 KG,near KooeyKkooeykooey. . . . 2.50
8 KG,Casualties of War. 2.50
9 KG,Havana vs. the Wall. 2.50
10 KG,JSe,back in time 2.50
11 KG,JSe,old foe 2.50
12 KG, F:JSA,final issue 2.50

SUPERBOY
1949–76

1 Superman (c) 15,000.00
2 Superboy Day. 3,000.00
3 . . . . 2,000.00
4 The Oracle of Smallville . . . 1,500.00
5 Superboy meets Supergirl,
    Pre-Adventure #252 . . . . . . 1,300.00
6 I:Humpty Dumpty,the Hobby
    Robber 1,200.00
7 WB,V:Humpty Dumpty 1,200.00
8 CS,I:Superbaby,V:Humpty
    Dumpty. 1,000.00
9 V:Humpty Dumpty. 1,000.00
10 CS,I:Lana Lang 1,000.00
11 CS,2nd Lang,V:Humpty
    Dumpty. 900.00
12 CS,The Heroes Club. 900.00
13 CS,Scout of Smallville 900.00
14 CS,I:Marsboy 900.00

15 CS,A:Superman 900.00
16 CS,A:Marsboy. 600.00
17 CS,Superboy's Double 600.00
18 CS,Lana Lang-Hollywood
    Star 600.00
19 CS,The Death of Young
    Clark Kent 600.00
20 CS,The Ghost that Haunted
    Smallville 600.00
21 CS,Lana Lang-Magician 450.00
22 CS,The New Clark Kent 450.00
23 CS,The Super Superboy. . . . 450.00
24 CS,The Super Fat Boy of
    Steel. 450.00
25 CS,Cinderella of Smallville . . 450.00
26 CS,A:Superbaby. 450.00
27 CS,Clark Kent-Runaway. . . . 450.00
28 CS,The Man Who Defeated
    Superboy 450.00
29 CS,The Puppet Superboy. . . 450.00
30 CS,I:Tommy Tuttle 400.00
31 CS,The Amazing Elephant
    Boy From Smallville. 400.00
32 CS,His Majesty King
    Superboy 400.00
33 CS,The Crazy Costumes of
    the Boy of Steel 400.00
34 CS,Hep Cats o/Smallville . . . 400.00
35 CS,The Five Superboys 400.00
36 . . . . 400.00
37 CS,I:Thaddeus Lang. 400.00
38 CS,Public Chimp #1 . . . . 400.00
39 CS,Boy w/Superboy Powers. . 400.00
40 CS,The Magic Necklace 350.00
41 CS,Superboy Meets
    Superbrave 350.00
42 CS,Gaucho of Smallville 350.00
43 CS,Super-Farmer o/Smallville 350.00
44 The Amazing Adventure of
    Superboy's Costume 350.00
45 A Trap For Superboy. 350.00
46 The Battle of Fort Smallville . . 350.00
47 CS,A:Superman 350.00
48 CS,Boy Without Super-Suit . . 350.00
49 I:Metallo (Jor-El's Robot) . . . 350.00
50 The Super-Giant of Smallville. 350.00
51 I:Krypto 250.00
52 CS,The Powerboy from Earth. 250.00
53 CS,A:Superman 250.00
54 CS,The Silent Superboy 250.00
55 CS,A:Jimmy Olson 250.00
56 CS,A:Krypto 250.00
57 CS,One-Man Baseball Team . 250.00
58 CS,The Great Kryptonite
    Mystery 250.00
59 CS,A:Superbaby. 250.00
60 The 100,000 Cowboy 250.00
61 The School For Superboys. . . 200.00
62 I:Gloria Kent 200.00
63 CS,The Two Boys of Steel . . . 200.00
64 CS,A:Krypto 200.00
65 Superboy's Moonlight Spell . . 200.00
66 The Family with X-Ray Eyes . 200.00
67 I:Klax-Ar 200.00
68 O&I:Bizarro 700.00
69 How Superboy Learned
    To Fly 150.00
70 O:Superboy's Glasses 150.00
71 A:Superbaby 150.00
72 The Flying Girl of Smallville . . 150.00
73 CS,A:Superbaby. 150.00
74 A:Jor-El & Lara 150.00
75 A:Superbaby 150.00
76 I:Super Monkey. 150.00
77 Superboy's Best Friend 150.00
78 O:Mr.Mzyzptik 250.00
79 A:Jar-El & Lara 150.00
80 Superboy meets Supergirl . . . 200.00
81 The Weakling From Earth. . . . 135.00
82 A:Bizarro Krypto 135.00
83 I:Kryptonite Kid 135.00

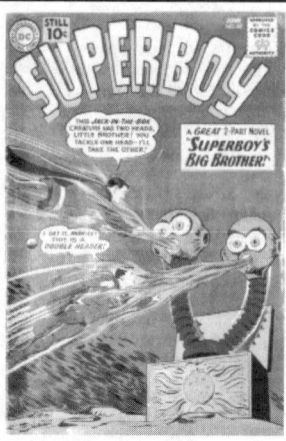

Superboy #89
© DC Comics, Inc.

84 A:William Tell. 135.00
85 Secret of Mighty Boy 135.00
86 I:PeteRoss,A:Legion 275.00
87 I:Scarlet Jungle of Krypton . . 135.00
88 The Invader from Earth. 135.00
89 I:Mon-El. 400.00
90 A:Pete Ross 135.00
91 CS,Superboy in Civil War. . . . 135.00
92 CS,I:Destructo,A:Lex Luthor . 135.00
93 A:Legion 135.00
94 I:Superboy Revenge Squad,
    A:Pete Ross 100.00
95 Imaginary Story,The Super
    Family From Krypton. 100.00
96 A:Pete Ross,Lex Luthor 100.00
97 Krypto Story 100.00
98 Legion,I&O:Ultraboy 150.00
99 O: The Kryptonite Kid 100.00
100 I:Phantom Zone 275.00
101 The Handsome Hound
    of Steel 90.00
102 O:Scarlet Jungle of Krypton . . 90.00
103 CS,A:King Arthur,Jesse James
    Red Kryptonite. 90.00
104 O:Phantom Zone 90.00
105 CS,The Simpleton of Steel . . 90.00
106 CS,A:Brainiac 90.00
107 CS,I:Superboy Club of
    Smallville 100.00
108 The Kent's First Super Son . . 90.00
109 The Super Youth of Bronze . . 90.00
110 A:Jor-El 90.00
111 Red Kryptonite Story 90.00
112 CS,A:Superbaby 90.00
113 The Boyhood of Dad Kent . . . 90.00
114 A:Phantom Zone,
    Mr.Mxyzptlk 90.00
115 A:Phantom Zone,Lex Luthor . . 90.00
116 The Wolfboy of Smallville 90.00
117 A:Legion 90.00
118 CS,The War Between
    Superboy and Krypto. 90.00
119 V:Android Double 90.00
120 A:Mr.Mxyzptlk 90.00
121 CS,A:Jor-El,Lex Luthor 90.00
122 Red Kryptonite Story. 90.00
123 CS,The Curse of the
    Superboy Mummy 90.00
124 I:Insect Queen 90.00
125 O:Kid Psycho 90.00
126 O:Krypto 90.00
127 A:Insect Queen 75.00
128 A:Phantom Zone,Kryptonite
    Kid,Dev En 75.00

129 rep.A:Mon-El,SuperBaby . . . 125.00	
130 . . . . 75.00	
131 A;Lex Luthor,Mr.Mxyzptlk,I:	
Space Canine Patrol Agents . . 75.00	
132, CS,A:Space Canine	
Patrol Agents 75.00	
133 A:Robin, repr. 75.00	
134 The Scoundrel of Steel 75.00	
135 A:Lex Luthor 75.00	
136 A:Space Canine Agents 75.00	
137 Mysterious Mighty Mites 75.00	
138 giant, Superboy's Most	
Terrific Battles 90.00	
139 The Samson of Smallville 75.00	
140 V:The Gambler 50.00	
141 No Mercy for a Hero 50.00	
142 A:Super Monkey 50.00	
143 NA(c),The Big Fall 50.00	
144 Superboy's Stolen Identity . . . 50.00	
145 NA(c)Kents become young . . . 50.00	
146 NA(c),CS,The Runaway 50.00	
147 giant O:Legion 55.00	
148 NA(c),CS,C:PolarBoy 50.00	
149 NA(c),A:Bonnie & Clyde 50.00	
150 JAb,V:Mr.Cipher 50.00	
151 NA(c),A:Kryptonite Kid 50.00	
152 NA(c),WW 50.00	
153 NA(c),WW,A;Prof Mesmer . . 50.00	
154 WW(i),A:Jor-El & Lara	
Blackout For Superboy 50.00	
155 NA(c),WW,Revolt of the	
Teenage Robots 50.00	
156 giant 50.00	
157 WW 50.00	
158 WW,A:Jor-El & Lara 50.00	
159 WW(i),A:Lex Luthor 50.00	
160 WW,I Chose Eternal Exile . . . 50.00	
161 WW,The Strange Death of	
Superboy 50.00	
162 A:Phantom Zone 50.00	
163 NA(c),Reform School Rebel . . 50.00	
164 NA(c),Your Death Will	
Destroy Me 50.00	
165 giant 50.00	
166 NA(c),A:Lex Luthor 30.00	
167 NA(c),MA,A:Superbaby 30.00	
168 NA(c),MA,Hitler 30.00	
169 MA,A:Lex Luthor 30.00	
170 MA,A:Genghis Khan 30.00	
171 MA,A:Aquaboy 30.00	
172 MA(i),GT,A:Legion,	
O:Lightning Lad,Yango 35.00	
173 NA(c),GT,DG,O:CosmicBoy . . 30.00	
174 giant 50.00	
175 NA(c),MA,Rejuvenation of	
Ma & Pa Kent 30.00	
176 NA(c),MA,GT,WW,A:Legion . 30.00	
177 MA,A:Lex Luthor 35.00	
178 NA(c),MA,Legion Reprint 35.00	
179 MA,A:Lex Luthor 35.00	
180 MA,O:Bouncing Boy 35.00	
181 MA 35.00	
182 MA,A:Bruce Wayne 35.00	
183 MA,GT,CS(rep),A:Legion . . . 35.00	
184 MA,WW,O:Dial H rep. 35.00	
185 A:Legion 20.00	
186 MA 20.00	
187 MA 20.00	
188 MA,DC,O:Karkan,A:Legn . . . 20.00	
189 MA 20.00	
190 MA,WW 20.00	
191 MA,DC,O:SunBoy retold 20.00	
192 MA 20.00	
193 MA,WW,N:Chameleon Boy,	
Shrinking Violet 20.00	
194 MA 20.00	
195 MA,WW,I:Wildfire,	
N:Phantom Girl 20.00	
196 last Superboy solo 30.00	
197 DC,Legion begins, New	
Costumes,I:Tyr 30.00	

198 DC,N:Element Lad,	
Princess Projects. 20.00	
199 DC,A:Tyr, Otto Orion. 20.00	
200 DC,M:Bouncing Boy	
& Duo Damsel 25.00	
201 DC,Wildfire returns 18.00	
202 N:Light Lass 60.00	
203 MGr,D:Invisible Kid 25.00	
204 MGr,A:Supergirl 15.00	
205 MGr,CG,100 pages 50.00	
206 MGr,A:Ferro Lad 25.00	
207 MGr,O:Lightning Lad. 25.00	
208 MGr,CS,68pp,Legion of	
Super Villains 28.00	
209 MGr,N:Karate Kid 20.00	
210 MGr,O:Karate Kid 25.00	
211 MGr. 15.00	
212 MGr,L:Matter Eater Lad 15.00	
213 MGr,V:Benn Pares 15.00	
214 MGr,V:Overseer 15.00	
215 MGr,A:Emerald Empress . . . 15.00	
216 MGr,I:Tyroc 15.00	
217 MGr,I:Laurel Kent 15.00	
218 J:Tyroc,A:Fatal Five 15.00	
219 MGr,A:Fatal Five. 15.00	
220 MGi,BWi 15.00	
221 MGr,BWi,I:Grimbor 10.00	
222 MGr,BWi,MN,BL,A:Tyroc . . . 10.00	
223 MGr,BWi 10.00	
224 MGr,BWi,V:Pulsar Stargrave. . 10.00	
225 MGr(c),BWi,JSh,MN 10.00	
226 MGr(c),MN,JSh,JA,	
I:Dawnstar 10.00	
227 MGr(c),JSon,JA,V:Stargrave. . 10.00	
228 MGr(c),JSh,JA,	
D:Chemical King 10.00	
229 MGr(c),JSh,JA,V:Deregon . . . 10.00	
230 MGr(c),JSh,V:Sden. 10.00	
Spec. #147 facsimile (2003) 6.95	

Becomes:

SUPERBOY & THE LEGION OF SUPER-HEROES
1976–79

231 MGr(c),JSh,MN,JA,doub.size	
begins,V:Fatal Five 18.00	
232 MGr(c),JSh,RE,JA,V:	
Dr.Regulus 18.00	
233 MGr(c),JSh,BWi,MN,BL,	
I:Infinite Man 18.00	
234 MGr(c),RE,JA,V:Composite	
Creature. 18.00	
235 MGr,GT 18.00	

Superboy #209 © DC Comics Inc.

236 MGr(c),BMc,JSh,MN,JRu,	
V:Khunds. 18.00	
237 MGr(c),WS,JA. 18.00	
238 JSn(c),reprint 18.00	
239 MGR(c),JSn,JRu,Ultra Boy	
accused 18.00	
240 MGr(c),HC,BWi,JSh,BMc,	
O:Dawnstar;V:Grimbor 18.00	
241 JSh,BMc,A:Ontir. 18.00	
242 JSh,BMc,E:Double Size 18.00	
243 MGr(c),JA,JSon 18.00	
244 JSon,V:Dark Circle 18.00	
245 MA,JSon,V:Mordu. 15.00	
246 MGr(c),JSon,DG,MA,	
V:Fatal Five 15.00	
247 JSon,JA,anniv.issue. 15.00	
248 JSon 15.00	
249 JSon,JA. 15.00	
250 JSn,V:Omega 15.00	
251 JSn,Brainiac 5 goes insane . . 15.00	
252 JSon,V:Starburst bandits 12.00	
253 JSon,I:Blok,League of	
Super Assassins 12.00	
254 JSon,V:League of Super	
Assassins 12.00	
255 JSon,A:Jor-El 12.00	
256 JSon 12.00	
257 SD,JSon,DA,V:Psycho	
Warrior 12.00	
258 JSon,V:Psycho Warrior. 12.00	

Becomes:

LEGION OF SUPER HEROES
[2nd Series]

[NEW ADVENTURES OF] SUPERBOY
Jan., 1980

1 KS 6.00	
2 KS 3.00	
3 KS 3.00	
4 KS 3.00	
5 KS 3.00	
6 KS 3.00	
7 KS,JSa 3.00	
8 thru 33 KS . . . . @3.00	
34 KS,I:Yellow Peri 3.00	
35 thru 44 KS . . . . @3.00	
45 KS,I:Sunburst 3.00	
46 KS,A:Sunburst 3.00	
47 KS,A:Sunburst 3.00	
48 KS 3.00	
49 KS,A:Zatara 3.00	
50 KS,KG,A:Legion 3.00	
51 KS,FM(c)In Between Years. . . . 3.00	
52 KS 3.00	
53 KS 3.00	
54 KS 3.00	

SUPERBOY
1990–91

1 TV Tie-in,JM,photo(c) 5.00	
2 JM,T.J.White Abducted 3.00	
3 JM,Fountain of Youth. 3.00	
4 JM,Big Man on Campus 3.00	
5 JM,Legion Homage 3.00	
6 JM,Luthor. 3.00	
7 JM,Super Boy Arrested 3.00	
8 JM,AAd(i),Bizarro. 3.00	
9 JM/CS,PhantomZone#1 . . . . . . 3.00	
10 JM/CS,PhantomZone#2 . . . . . 3.00	
11 CS 3.00	
12 CS,X-Mas in Smallville 3.00	

Becomes:

ADVENTURES OF SUPERBOY
1991

13 A:Mr.Mxyzptlk 3.50	

DC COMICS

Superboy 2nd Series #11
© DC Comics, Inc.

14 CS,A:Brimstone	3.00
15 CS,Legion Homage	3.00
16 CS,Into the Future	3.00
17 CS,A:Luthor	3.00
18 JM,At the Movies	3.00
19 JM,Blood Transfusion	3.00
20 JM,O:Nicknack,(G.Gottfried script)	3.00
21 V:Frost Monster	3.00
22	3.00
Spec.#1 CS,A:Ma Kent	2.50

SUPERBOY
[2nd Series], 1994

1 B:KK(s),TG,DHz,V:Sidearm	4.00
2 TG,DHz,I:Knockout	2.50
3 TG,DHz,I:Scavenger	2.50
4 TG,DHz,MeP,I:Lock n' Load	2.50
5 TG,DHz,I:Silver Sword	2.50
6 TG,DHz,Worlds Collide,pt.3 C:Rocket	2.50
7 Worlds Collide, pt.8,V:Rift	2.50
8 Zero Hour,A:Superboy	2.50
9 Silican Dragon	2.50
10 Monster	2.50
11 Techno	2.50
12 Copperhead	2.50
13 Watery Grave,pt.1	2.50
14 Watery Grave,pt.2	2.50
15 Watery Grave,pt.3	2.50
16 TG,DHz,KK,V:Loose Cannon [New Miraweb format begins]	2.50
17 TG,DHz,KK Looking for Roxy Leech	2.50
18 V:Valor	2.50
19	2.50
20 R:Scavenger	2.50
21 KK,TG,DHz,Future Tense,Pt.1	2.50
22 KK,TG,DHz,Underworld Unleashed x-over	2.50
23 KK,TG,DHz,V:Technician	2.50
24 KK,TG,DHz,V:Silversword	2.50
25 New Gods	3.00
26 KK,DHz,Losin'it,pt.2	2.25
27 KK,DHz,Losin'it,pt.3	2.25
28 KK,DHz,Losin'it,pt.4 (of 6)	2.25
29	2.25
30	2.25
31	2.25
32 RMz(s),RBe,DHz,V:King Shark	2.25
33 RMz(s),RBe,DHz, survivors flee to Hawaii, Final Night tie-in	2.25
34 RMz(s),RBe,DHz, V:Dubbilex	2.25

35 RMz(s),RBe,DHz, Superboy abducted	2.25
36 RMz(s),RBe,DHz,V:King SHark	2.25
37 RMz(s),SB,V:Sledge	2.25
38 RMz,RBe,DHz,Meltdown,pt.1	2.25
39 RMz,RBe,DHz,Meltdown,pt.2	2.25
40 RMz,RBe,DHz,Meltdown,pt.2, x-over	2.25
41 RMz,RBe,DHz,Meltdown,pt.3	2.25
42 SB,	2.25
43 SB,Lanie & Ken	2.25
44 SB,island of teenagers	2.25
45 RMz,DHz,TGu,A:Legion	2.25
46 RMz,DHz,TGu,V:Silver Sword	2.25
47 RMz,DHz,TGu,F:Green Lantern	2.25
48 BKs,DHz,TGu,theme park	2.25
49 DHz	2.25
50 KK,TGu,Last Boy on Earth pt.1	2.25
51 KK,TGu,Last Boy on Earth pt.2	2.25
52 KK,TGu,Last Boy on Earth pt.3	2.25
53 KK,TGu,Last Boy on Earth pt.4	2.25
54 KK,TGu,A:Wild Men	2.25
55 KK,TGu,V:Grokk, Hex	2.25
56 KK,TGu,Project Cadmus	2.25
57 KK,TGu,Demolition Run,pt.1	2.25
58 KK,TGu,Demolition Run,pt.2	2.25
59 KK,DAb,A:Superman	2.25
60 KK,TGu,A:JLA,Hyper-Tension	2.25
61 KK,TGu,Hyper-Tension,pt.2	2.25
62 KK,TGu,Hyper-Tension,pt.3	2.25
63 KK,TGu,Hyper-Tension,pt.4	2.25
64 KK,TGu,Hyper-Tension,pt.5	2.25
65 KK,TGu,guest-star packed	2.25
66 KK,TGu,Wild Lands	2.25
67 KK,AaL, in Wild Lands	2.25
68 KK,TG,MM,Day of Judgment x-over, F:Demon	2.25
69 KK,TG,return to Hawaii	2.25
70 KK,TG,Evil Factory,pt.1	2.25
71 KK,TG,Evil Factory,pt.2	2.25
72 KK,TG,Evil Factory,pt.3	2.25
73 KK,TG,Evil Factory,pt.4	2.25
74 KK,TG,Sins of Youth	2.25
75 KK,TG,as normal teenager	2.25
76 KK,TG,still Superboy	2.25
77 KK,TG,MBa,V:Kossak	2.25
78 KK,TG,prisoners	2.25
79 KK,TG,V:Kossak the Slaver	2.25
80 BHr,F:The Titans,pt.1	2.25
81 BHr,F:The Titans,pt.2	2.25
82 JMz,V:Negative G.	2.25
83 PFe,F:Young Justice	2.25
84 PFe,off to L.A.	2.25
85 PFe,A:Batman,Batgirl	2.25
86 PFe,shotgun wedding	2.25
87 V:Shrapnel,Deadman	2.25
88 PFe,V:DNAngels	2.25
89 PFe,Our Worlds at War, tie-in	2.25
90 PFe,Our Worlds at War, tie-in	2.25
91 PFe,Our Worlds at War, tie-in	2.25
92 PFe,R:Doctor Sin	2.25
93 PFe,Joker:Last Laugh, tie-in	2.25
94 JMC,finding an apartment	2.25
95 JP,JMC,Slaughterhouse Six	2.25
96 JP,Trixie & Wipeout	2.25
97 JP,JMC,F:Wipeout	2.25
98 JP,JMC,F:Jimmy Olsen	2.25
99 WorldWithoutYoungJustice,pt.4	2.25
100 JP,KK,TG,48-pg.	3.50
Ann.#1 Elseworlds Story	3.50
Ann.#2 KK,BKs, Year One	4.50
Ann.#3 Legends o/t Dead Earth	3.50
Ann.#4 Pulp Heroes (High-Adventure)	4.50
Spec.#1,000,000 KK,TGu	2.50

SUPERBOY
& THE RAVERS
1996–98

1 KK&SMt(s),PaP,DDv,	2.50

2 KK&SMt(s),PaP,DDv,InterC.E.P.T. pursues Superboy and Kaliber	2.50
3 KK&SMT(s),PaP,DDv,teleported to Rann,V:Half-Life	2.50
4 KK&SMt(s),PaP,DDv,A:Adam Strange	2.50
5 KK&SMt(s),PaP,DDv,O:Hero	2.50
6 KK&SMt(s),PaP,DDv,	2.50
7 KK&SMt(s),PaP,DDv, Road Trip, pt.1,A:Impulse	2.50
8 KK&SMt(s),PaP,DDv, Road Trip, pt.2,A:Guy Gardner	2.50
9 KK&SMt(s),PaP,DDv, Road Trip, pt.3,A:Aura	2.50
10 KK&SMt(s),DDv,Meltdown,pt.4	2.50
11 KK&SMt(s),PaP,DDv, Superboy presumed dead	2.50
12 KK(s),AaL,	2.50
13 KK(s),SMt,F:Hero,Sparx	2.50
14 KK&SMt(s),Genesis tie-in	2.50
15 KK&SMt(s),new Rave	2.50
16 KK&SMt(s),Half-Life	2.50
17 KK&SMt(s),Kaliber	2.50
18 KK&SMt(s),V:Qward	2.50
19	2.50

SUPERBOY PLUS
Nov., 1996

1 RMz(s),ASm,F:Captain Marvel Jr.	3.50
2 LKa,AWi,ALa,F:Slither	3.00

SUPERBOY/RISK
DOUBLE-SHOT
Dec., 1997

1 DJu,JoP,x-over	2.50

SUPERBOY'S LEGION
Feb., 2001

1 (of 2) Elseworlds, 48-page	5.95
2 MFm,AD, concl.	5.95

SUPER DC GIANT
1970–71, 1976

S-13 Binky	150.00
S-14 JKu,GK,Top Guns of the West	75.00
S-15 JKu,GK,Western Comics	65.00
S-16 JKu,Best of the Brave & the Bold	50.00

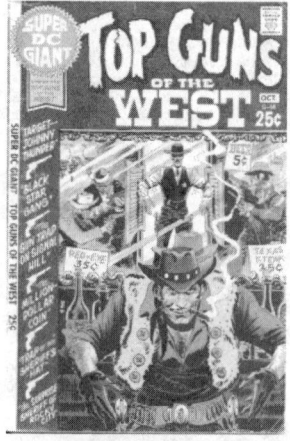

Super DC Giant #S-14
© DC Comics Inc.

S-17 Love 1970 . . . . 375.00
S-18 Three Mouseketeers 150.00
S-19 NA,Jerry Lewis 175.00
S-20 NA,JK,House of Mystery . . . 100.00
S-21 Love 1971 . . . . 450.00
S-22 JKu,Top Guns of the West . . 40.00
S-23 The Unexpected 50.00
S-24 Supergirl 50.00
S-25 Challengers of the Unknown. 50.00
S-26 Aquaman 40.00
S-27 GK,Strange Flying Saucer
   Adventures (1976) 35.00

SUPER FRIENDS
Nov., 1976

1 ECh(c),JO,RE,Fury of the
   Superfoes,A:Penguin 50.00
2 RE,A:Penguin 20.00
3 RF(c),RF,A:JLA 15.00
4 RF,V:Riddler,I:Skyrocket 15.00
5 RF(c),RF,V:Greenback 15.00
6 RF(c),RF,A:Atom 12.00
7 RF(c),RF,I:Zan & Jana,
   A:Seraph 12.00
8 RF(c),RF,A:JLA 12.00
9 RF(c),RF,A:JLA,I:Iron Maiden . . 12.00
10 RF(c),RFTheMonkeyMenace . . 12.00
11 RF(c),RF 10.00
12 RF(c),RF,A:TNT 10.00
13 RF(c),RF 10.00
14 RF(c),RF 10.00
15 RF(c),RF, A:The Elementals . . . 10.00
16 RF(c),RF,V:The Cvags 10.00
17 RF(c),RF,A:Queen Hippolyte . . 10.00
18 KS(c),V:Tuantra,Time Trapper . 10.00
19 RF(c),RF,V:Menagerie Man . . . 10.00
20 KS(c),KS,V:Frownin' Fritz 10.00
21 RF(c),RF,V:Evil Superfriends
   Doubles 9.00
22 RF(c),RF,V:Matador Mob 9.00
23 FR(c),RF,V:Mirror Master 9.00
24 RF(c),RF,V:Exorians 9.00
25 RF(c),RF,V:Overlord,
   A:Green Lantern, Mera 9.00
26 RF(c),RF,A:Johnny Jones 9.00
27 RF(c),RF,The Spaceman Who
   Stole the Stars 9.00
28 RF(c),RF,A:Felix Faust 9.00
29 RF(c),RF,B.U.KS,Scholar From
   the Stars 9.00
30 RF(c),RF,V:Grodd & Giganta . . 9.00
31 RF(c),RF,A:Black Orchid 10.00
32 KS(c),KS,A:Scarecrow 8.00
33 RF(c),RF,V:Menagerie Man 8.00
34 RF(c)RF,The Creature That
   Slept a Million Years 8.00
35 RT,Circus o/t Super Stars 8.00
36 RF(c),RF,A:Plastic Man
   & Woozy 8.00
37 RF(c),RF,A:Supergirl;
   B.U. A:Jack O'Lantern 8.00
38 RF(c),RF,V:Grax;
   B.U. A:Serpah 8.00
39 RF(c),RF,A:Overlord;
   B.U. A:Wonder Twins 8.00
40 RF(c),RF,V:The Monacle;
   B.U. Jack O'Lantern 8.00
41 RF(c),RF,V:Toyman;
   B.U. A:Seraph 8.00
42 RT,A:Flora,V:Flame; B.U.Wonder
   Twins' Christmas Special 8.00
43 KS(c),RT,V:Futuro; B.U.JSon
   A:Plastic Man 8.00
44 KS(c),RT,Peril o/t Forgotten
   Identities'; B.U.Jack O'Lantern . 8.00
45 KS(c),RT,A:Bushmaster,
   Godiva, Rising Sun, Olympian,
   Little Mermaid, Wild Huntsman;
   B.U. Plastic Man,V: Sinestro . . . 8.00

46 RT,V:The Conqueror;
   B.U. BO,Seraph 8.00
47 KS(c),RT,A:Green Fury
   Aug., 1981 . . . . 8.00
TPB Super Friends, 176-page 14.95
TPB Truth,Justice&Peace(2003) . . 14.95

SUPERGIRL
[1st Regular Series]
Nov., 1972—Sept., 1974

1 Trail of the Madman';
   Superfashions From Fans;
   B:B.U. DG,Zatanna 75.00
2 BO(c)A:Prof.Allan,Bottle
   City of Kandor 30.00
3 BO(c),The Garden of Death . . . 25.00
4 V:Super Scavanger 30.00
5 BO(c),A:Superman,V:Dax; B.U.
   MA:Rep.Hawkman #4 . . . . 35.00
6 BO(c),Love & War 30.00
7 BO(c),A:Zatanna 30.00
8 BO(c),A:Superman,Green
   Lantern, Hawkman 35.00
9 BO(c),V:Sharkman 30.00
10 A:Prey,V:Master Killer 30.00

[DARING NEW ADVENTURES OF] SUPERGIRL
[2nd Regular Series]
Nov., 1982

1 CI,BO,I:Psi; B:B.U.Lois Lane 3.00
2 CI,BO,C:Decay 3.00
3 CI,BO,V:Decay,Decay Day 3.00
4 CI,BO,V:The Gang 3.00
5 CI,BO,V:The Gang 3.00
6 CI,BO,V:The Gang 3.00
7 CI,BO,V:The Gang 3.00
8 CI,BO,A:Doom Patrol 3.00
9 CI,BO,V:Reactron
   A:Doom Patrol 3.00
10 CI,BO,Radiation Fever 3.00
11 CI,BO,V:Chairman 3.00
12 CI,BO,V:Chairman 3.00
13 CI,BO,N:Supergirl,A:Superman
   V:Blackstarr 3.00
Becomes:

SUPERGIRL
Dec., 1983–Sept., 1984

14 GK(c),CI,BO,V:Blackstarr
   A:Rabbi Nathan Zuber. 3.00
15 CI,BO,V:Blackstarr,
   A:Blackstarr's Mom 3.00
16 KG/BO(c),CI,BO,
   A:Ambush Bug 3.00
17 CI/DG(c),CI,BO,V:Matrix
   Prime 3.00
18 DG(c),CI,BO, V:Kraken 3.00
19 EB/BO(c),CI,BO,Who Stole
   Supergirl's Life 3.00
20 CI,BO,C:JLA,Teen Titans:
   Teh Parasite 3.00
21 EB/BO(c),EB,Kryptonite Man . . . 3.00
22 EB(c),CI,BO,I Have Seen the
   Future & it is Me 3.00
23 EB(c),CI,BO,The Future
   Begins Today 3.00
Spec.#1 JL/DG(c),GM,MovieAdapt . 3.00
Spec.#1 AT,Honda give-away 3.00

[Limited Series], 1994

1 KGa(c),B:RSt(s),JBr,O:Supergirl . 5.00
2 KGa(c),JBr 4.00
3 KGa(c),JBr,D:Clones 3.00
4 KGa(c),RSt(s),JBr,final Issue . . . 3.00

Supergirl #17
© DC Comics, Inc.

SUPERGIRL
Sept., 1996

1 PDd(s),GFr,CaS, ... 11.00
1a 2nd printing 3.00
2 PDd(s),GFr,CaS,V:Chakat 5.00
3 PDd(s),GFr,CaS,V:Grodd, Final
   Night tie-in 5.00
4 PDd(s),GFr,CaS,transformed into
   savage 4.00
5 PDd(s),GFr,CaS,Supergirl visits
   the Kents,V:Chemo 4.00
6 PDd(s),GFr,CaS, ... 4.00
7 PDd(s),GFr,CaS,Supergirl learns
   about Linda Danvers 4.00
8 PDd(s),GFr,CaS,Buzz gets date
   with Supergirl. 4.00
9 PDd(s),GFr,CaS,V:Tempus 4.00
10 PDd(s),Linda tries to relax 4.00
11 PDd(s),CaS,V:Silver Banshee . . 4.00
12 PDd(s),Mattie possessed by
   Silver Banshee 4.00
13 CaS, 3 girls dreams invaded by
   incubus 3.00
14 PDa,CaS,Genesis tie-in 3.00
15 PDa,CaS,V:Extremists 3.00
16 PDa,CaS,F:Power Girl 3.00
17 PDa,CaS,L-Ron, Despero 3.00
18 PDa,CaS,V:Despero 3.00
19 . . . . 3.00
20 PDa,CaS,Millennium Giants 3.00
21 PDa,CaS,Comet 3.00
22 PDa, ... 3.00
23 PDa,A:Steel 3.00
24 PDa,Avenging Angels x-over . . . 3.00
25 PDa,truth about Comet 3.00
26 PDd,truth discovered 3.00
27 PDd(s),V:Female Furies,pt.1 . . . 3.00
28 PDd(s),V:Female Furies,pt.2 . . . 3.00
29 PDd(s),V:Female Furies,pt.3 . . . 3.00
30 PDd(s),V:Matrix 3.00
31 PDd(s),A:Superman 3.00
32 PDd(s),SeP,V:Mr.Carnivean . . . 3.00
33 PDd(s),V:Mr.Carnivean 3.00
34 PDd(s),V:Parasite 3.00
35 PDd(s),V:Parasite, concl. 3.00
36 PDd(s),Hell's Angel's,pt.2 . . . . . 2.50
37 PDd(s),Hell's Angels,pt.4 . . . . . 2.50
38 PDd(s),Day of Judgment x-over . 2.50
39 PDd(s),F:Comet 2.50
40 PDd(s) 2.50
41 PDd(s),F:Ember,V:Satan Girl . . . 2.50
42 PDd(s),dates Dick Malverne 2.50
43 PDd(s),date become nightmare . 2.50

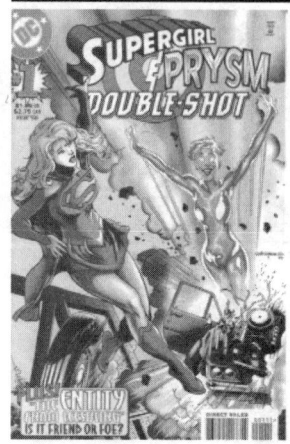

Supergirl/Prysm Double-Shot Special
© DC Comics, Inc.

44 PDd(s),F:Dick Malverne,dying . . 2.50
45 PDd(s),F:Comet,V:Carnivore . . . 2.50
46 PDd(s),V:Comet,Carnivore 2.50
47 PDd(s),V:Carnivore. 2.50
48 PDd(s), ... 2.50
49 PDd(s),V:Carnivore. 2.50
50 PDd(s),48-pg. 4.00
51 PDd(s),to Metropolis, minus
    powers. 2.50
52 PDd(s),V:Riot & Prankster 2.50
53 PDd(s),F:Green Lantern 2.50
54 PDd(s),F:Green Lantern 2.50
55 PDd(s),A:Lex Luthor. 2.50
56 PDd(s),Buzz's daughter 2.50
57 PDd(s),Daddy's Little Girl 2.50
58 PDd(s),Buzz close to death 2.50
59 PDd(s),Our Worlds at War,tie-in . 2.50
60 PDd(s),Our Worlds at War,tie-in . 2.50
61 PDd(s),Our Worlds at War,tie-in . 2.50
62 PDd(s),A:Two-Face. 2.50
63 PDd(s),Joker:Last Laugh,tie-in . . 2.50
64 PDd(s),A:Lagoon Boy 2.50
65 PDd(s),hearing-impaired kids . . . 2.25
66 PDd(s),F:Demon Etrigan 2.25
67 PDd(s),F:Demon Etrigan 2.25
68 PDd(s),F:Mary Marvel. 2.25
69 PDd(s),F:Capt.Marvel,Jr. 2.25
70 PDd(s),F:Mary Marvel. 2.25
71 PDd(s),V:Tara 2.50
72 PDd(s),V:Quetzlcoatl 2.50
73 PDd(s),Garden of Eden 2.50
74 PDd(s),Linda,Supergirl re-merge 2.50
75 PDd(s),EBe,spacecraft crashes 12.00
76 PDd(s),F:Superboy,Kara Zor-El 12.00
77 PDd(s),V:Fatalist. 5.00
78 PDd(s),V:Fatalist. 5.00
79 PDd(s),S.A.Supergirl. 5.00
80 PDd(s),V:Kara & Xenon 5.00
Ann.#1 Legends o/t Dead Earth . . . 3.00
Ann.#2 TPe,CDi,ACa, Pulp Heroes . 4.00
Spec.#1,000,000 PDd(s),DAb 2.00
GN Wings, Elseworlds, 48-page . . . 5.95
TPB PDd(s),GFr,rep.#1-#9 . . . . . . 15.00
TPB Many Happy Returns. 15.00
Spec. Supergirl/Lex Luthor JBr,
    F:Lex Luthor (1993). 4.00
Spec. Supergirl/Prysm Double-Shot
    DJu,TGb,Clv, x-over (1997) . . . 2.00

SUPER HEROES
BATTLE SUPER GORILLA
Winter, 1976
1 Superman Flash rep. 15.00

SUPERMAN
1939–86
1 JoS,O:Superman,reprints Action
    Comics #1-#4 . . . . 280,000.00
2 JoS,I:George Taylor 18,000.00
3 JoS,V:Superintendent
    Lyman 11,000.00
4 JoS,V:Lex Luthor. 11,000.00
5 JoS,V:Lex Luthor 8,000.00
6 JoS,V:Brute' Bashby. 4,500.00
7 JoS,I:Perry White 3,800.00
8 JoS,V:Jackal. 3,600.00
9 JoS,V:Joe Gatson. 3,600.00
10 JoS,V:Lex Luthor 3,500.00
11 JoS,V:Rolf Zimba 2,800.00
12 JoS,V:Lex Luthor 2,800.00
13 JoS,I:Jimmy Olsen,V:Lex
    Luthor,The Archer. 2,800.00
14 JoS,I:Lightning Master. 4,500.00
15 JoS,V:The Evolution King . . 2,800.00
16 JoS,V:Mr. Sinus 2,300.00
17 JoS,V:Lex Luthor,Lois Lane
    first suspects Clark
    is Superman 2,300.00
18 JoS,V:Lex Luthor 2,200.00
19 JoS,V:Funnyface,
    1st Imaginary story. 2,200.00
20 JoS,V:Puzzler,Leopard 2,200.00
21 JoS,V:Sir Gauntlet 1,800.00
22 JoS,V:Prankster. 1,800.00
23 JoS,Propaganda story 1,800.00
24 V:Cobra King 2,500.00
25 Propaganda story 1,700.00
26 I:J.Wilbur Wolfingham,
    A:Mercury. 1,700.00
27 V:Toyman 1,700.00
28 V:J.Wilbur Wolfingham,
    A:Hercules. 1,700.00
29 V:Prankster 1,700.00
30 I&O:Mr. Mxyztplk 3,000.00
31 V:Lex Luthor. 1,400.00
32 V:Toyman 1,400.00
33 V:Mr. Mxyzptlk. 1,400.00
34 V:Lex Luthor. 1,400.00
35 V:J.Wilbur Wolfingham. 1,400.00
36 V:Mr. Mxyzptlk. 1,400.00
37 V:Prankster,A:Sinbad. 1,400.00
38 V:Lex Luthor. 1,400.00
39 V:J.Wilbur Wolfingham. 1,400.00
40 V:Mr. Mxyzptlk,A:Susie
    Thompkins 1,400.00
41 V:Prankster 1,100.00
42 V:J.Wilbur Wolfingham. 1,100.00
43 V:Lex Luthor. 1,100.00
44 V:Toyman,A:Shakespeare . . 1,100.00
45 A:Hocus & Pocus,Lois Lane
    as Superwoman 1,100.00
46 V:Mr. Mxyzptlk,Lex Luthor,
    Superboy flashback 1,100.00
47 V:Toyman 1,100.00
48 V:Lex Luthor. 1,100.00
49 V:Toyman 1,100.00
50 V:Prankster 1,100.00
51 V:Mr. Mxyzptlk. 900.00
52 V:Prankster 900.00
53 WB,O:Superman 3,800.00
54 V:Wrecker 900.00
55 V:Prankster 900.00
56 V:Prankster 900.00
57 V:Lex Luthor 900.00
58 V:Tiny Trix 900.00
59 V:Mr.Mxyztplk 900.00
60 V:Toyman 900.00
61 I:Kryptonite,V:Prankster. . . . 1,800.00
62 V:Mr.Mxyzptlk,A:Orson
    Welles 900.00
63 V:Toyman 900.00
64 V:Prankster 900.00
65 V:Mala,Kizo and U-Ban 900.00
66 V:Prankster 900.00

67 A:Perry Como,I:Brane
    Taylor. 900.00
68 V:Lex Luthor 900.00
69 V:Prankster,A:Inspector
    Erskine Hawkins 900.00
70 V:Prankster. 900.00
71 V:Lex Luthor 800.00
72 V:Prankster. 800.00
72a giveaway 1,000.00
73 Flashback story. 800.00
74 V:Lex Luthor 800.00
75 V:Prankster 800.00
76 A:Batman, Superman & Batman
    revel eachother's identities. 2,200.00
77 A:Pocahontas 750.00
78 V:Kryptonian snagriff,
    A:Lana Lang 750.00
79 V:Lex Luthor,A:Inspector
    Erskine Hawkins 750.00
80 A:Halk Kar. 750.00
81 V:Lex Luthor 750.00
82 V:Mr. Mxyzptlk. 650.00
83 V:The Brain. 650.00
84 Time-travel story 650.00
85 V:Lex Luthor 650.00
86 V:Mr.Mxyzptlk 650.00
87 WB,V:The Thing from
    40,000 AD 650.00
88 WB,V:Lex Luthor,Toyman,
    Prankster team 750.00
89 V:Lex Luthor 650.00
90 V:Lex Luthor 700.00
91 The Superman Stamp. 650.00
92 Goes back to 12th Century
    England 650.00
93 V:The Thinker 650.00
94 Clark Kent's Hillbilly Bride. . . 650.00
95 A:Susie Thompkins. 650.00
96 V:Mr. Mxyzptlk. 475.00
97 Superboy's Last Day In
    Smallville. 475.00
98 Clark Kent, Outlaw!. 475.00
99 V:Midnite gang 475.00
100 F:Superman-Substitute
    Schoolteacher. 2,800.00
101 A:Lex Luthor 475.00
102 I:Superman Stock
    Company 475.00
103 A:Mr.Mxyzptlk 475.00
104 F:Clark Kent,Jailbird 475.00
105 A:Mr.Mxyzptlk 475.00
106 A:Lex Luthor 500.00
107 F:Superman In 30th century
    (pre-Legion) 475.00
108 I:Perry White Jr. 475.00

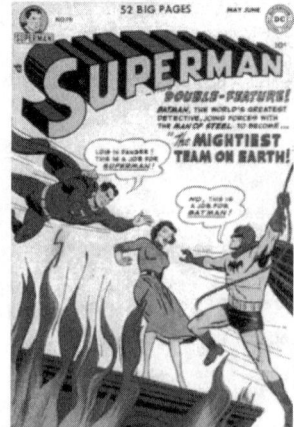

Superman #76 © DC Comics, Inc.

DC COMICS

109 I:Abner Hokum 475.00	
110 A:Lex Luthor 475.00	
111 Becomes Mysto the Great. . . 400.00	
112 A:Lex Luthor 400.00	
113 A:Jor-El 400.00	
114 V:The Great Mento 400.00	
115 V:The Organizer 400.00	
116 Return to Smallville. 400.00	
117 A:Lex Luthor 400.00	
118 F:Jimmy Olsen 400.00	
119 A:Zoll Orr. 400.00	
120 V:Gadget Grim 400.00	
121 I:XL-49 (Futureman) 350.00	
122 In the White House. 350.00	
123 CS,pre-Supergirl tryout	
A:Jor-El & Lara 375.00	
124 F:Lois Lane 350.00	
125 F:Superman College Story . 350.00	
126 F:Lois Lane 350.00	
127 WB,I&O:Titano 375.00	
128 V:Vard & Boka. 350.00	
129 WB,I&O:Lori Lemaris 375.00	
130 A:Krypto,the Superdog 350.00	
131 A:Mr. Mxyzptlk. 275.00	
132 A:Batman & Robin 275.00	
133 F:Superman Joins Army 275.00	
134 A:Supergirl & Krypto 275.00	
135 A:Lori Lemaris,Mr.Mxyzptlk. . 275.00	
136 O:Discovery Kryptonite 275.00	
137 CS,I:Super-Menace 275.00	
138 A:Titano,Lori Lemaris 275.00	
139 CS,O:Red Kryptonite 275.00	
140 WB,I:Bizarro Jr,Bizarro	
Supergirl,Blue Kryptonite. . . . 275.00	
141 I:Lyla Lerrol,A:Jor-EL	
& Lara 225.00	
142 WB,CS,A:Al Capone. 225.00	
143 WB,F:Bizarro meets	
Frankenstein 225.00	
144 O:Superboy's 1st Public	
Appearance. 225.00	
145 F:April Fool's Issue 225.00	
146 F:Superman's life story 275.00	
147 CS,I:Adult Legion 275.00	
148 CS,V:Mxyzptlk. 225.00	
149 CS:A:Luthor,C:JLA 225.00	
150 CS,KS,V:Mxyzptlk. 150.00	
151 CS. 150.00	
152 A:Legion 150.00	
153 CS. 150.00	
154 CS,V:Mzyzptlk. 150.00	
155 WB,CS,V:Cosmic Man 150.00	
156 CS,A:Legion,Batman 150.00	
157 CS,I:Gold kryptonite 165.00	
158 CS,I:Nightwing&Flamebird . . 150.00	
159 CS,Imaginary Tale	
F:Lois Lane 150.00	
160 CS,F:Perry White 150.00	
161 D:Ma & Pa Kent 165.00	
162 A:Legion 165.00	
163 CS. 150.00	
164 CS,Luthor,I:Lexor 150.00	
165 CS,A:Saturn Woman 150.00	
166 CS. 150.00	
167 CS,I:Ardora,Brainiac. 165.00	
168 CS. 125.00	
169 Great DC Contest 125.00	
170 CS,A:J.F.Kennedy,Luthor . . . 125.00	
171 CS,Mxyzptlk 125.00	
172 CS,Luthor,Brainiac 125.00	
173 CS,A:Batman 125.00	
174 Mxyzptlk 125.00	
175 CS,Luthor 125.00	
176 CS,Green Kryptonite. 125.00	
177 Fortress of Solitude. 125.00	
178 CS, Red Kryptonite 125.00	
179 CS,Clark Kent in Marines . . . 125.00	
180 CS. 125.00	
181 Superman 2965 . . . . 125.00	
182 CS,Toyman 125.00	
183 giant 125.00	

184 Secrets of the Fortress 100.00
185 JM,Superman's Achilles
Heel. 100.00
186 CS,The Two Ghosts of
Superman. 100.00
187 giant 100.00
188 V:Zunial,The Murder Man . . . 100.00
189 WB,The Mystery of Krypton's
Second Doom. 100.00
190 WB,I:Amalak 100.00
191 The Prisoner of Demon 100.00
192 CS,Imaginary Story,
I:Superman Jr.. . . . . 100.00
193 giant 100.00
194 CS,Imaginary,A:Supes Jr.. . . 100.00
195 CS,V:Amalak 100.00
196 WB,reprint. 100.00
197 giant 100.00
198 CS,F:The Real Clark Kent . . 100.00
199 CS,F:Superman/Flash race,
A:JLA. 400.00
200 WB,A:Brainiac. 125.00
201 CS,F:Clark Kent Abandons
Superman. 75.00
202 A:Bizarro,(giant size). 90.00
203 F:When Superman Killed His
Friends 75.00
204 NA(c),RA,A:Lori Lemaris . . . 75.00
205 NA(c),I:Black Zero 75.00
206 NA(c),F:The Day Superman
Became An Assistant 75.00
207 CS,F:The Case Of the
Collared Crimefighter 90.00
208 NA(c),CS. 75.00
209 CS,F:The Clark Kent Monster 75.00
210 CS,F:Clark Kent's Last Rites . 75.00
211 CS,RA 75.00
212 giant 90.00
213 CS,JA,V:Luthor,C:Brainiac 5. . 75.00
214 NA(c),CS,JA,F:The Ghosts
That Haunted Superman. 75.00
215 NA(c),CS,JA,V:Luthor,
Imaginary Story 75.00
216 JKu(c),RA,Superman in Nam . 75.00
217 CS,A:Mr.Mxyzptlk 80.00
218 CS,JA,A:Mr.Mxyzptlk 75.00
219 CS,F:Clark Kent-Hero,
Superman Public Enemy. 75.00
220 CS,A:Flash 75.00
221 CS,F:The Two Ton Superman 75.00
222 giant 90.00
223 CS,A:Supergirl 50.00
224 CS,Imaginary Story. 50.00
225 CS,F:The Secret of the
Super Imposter 50.00

Superman #237 © DC Comics Inc.

226 CS,F:When Superman Became
King Kong 50.00
227 Krypton,(giant) 75.00
228 CS,DA. 50.00
229 WB,CS 50.00
230 CS,DA,Luthor 50.00
231 CS,DA,Luthor 50.00
232 F:Krypton,(giant) 75.00
233 CS,MA,I:Quarrum 50.00
234 NA(c),CS,MA 50.00
235 CS,MA. 50.00
236 CS,MA,DG,A:Green Arrow . . . 50.00
237 NA(c),CS,MA 50.00
238 CS,MA,GM 50.00
239 giant 75.00
240 CS,DG,MK,A:I-Ching. 35.00
241 CS,MA,A:Wonder Woman . . . 40.00
242 CS,MA,A:Wonder Woman . . . 40.00
243 CS,MA. 40.00
244 CS,MA. 40.00
245 100 pg reprints 45.00
246 CS,MA,RB,I:S.T.A.R. Labs . . 35.00
247 CS,MA,Guardians o/Universe. 35.00
248 CS,MA,A:Luthor,I:Galactic
Golem 35.00
249 CS,MA,DD,NA,I:Terra-Man. . . 50.00
250 CS,MA,Terraman 35.00
251 CS,MA,RB. 35.00
252 NA(c),rep.100pgs 45.00
253 CS,MA. 35.00
254 CS,MA,NA. 50.00
255 CS,MA,DG 20.00
256 CS,MA. 20.00
257 CS,MA,DD,DG,A:Tomar-Re . . 20.00
258 CS,MA,DC 20.00
259 CS,MA,A:Terra-Man 20.00
260 CS,DC,I:Valdemar. 20.00
261 CS,MA,V:Star Sapphire 20.00
262 CS,MA. 20.00
263 CS,MA,DD,FMc 20.00
264 DC,CS,I:Steve Lombard 20.00
265 CS,MA. 20.00
266 CS,MA,DD,V:Snowman 20.00
267 CS,MA,BO 20.00
268 CS,BO,DD,MA,A:Batgirl 20.00
269 CS,MA. 20.00
270 CS,MA,V:Valdemar 20.00
271 CS,BO,DG,V:Brainiac 20.00
272 100pg.reprints. 50.00
273 CS,DG. 20.00
274 CS 20.00
275 CS,DG,FMc. 20.00
276 CS,BO,I&O:Captain Thunder . 20.00
277 CS 20.00
278 CS,BO,Terraman,100page . . 50.00
279 CS,Batgirl,Batman 20.00
280 CS,BO. 20.00
281 CS,BO,I:Vartox 20.00
282 CS,KS,N:Luthor 20.00
283 CS,BO,Mxyzptlk 20.00
284 CS,BO,100p reprint 50.00
285 CS,BO. 20.00
286 CS,BO. 20.00
287 CS,BO,R:Krypto 20.00
288 CS,BO. 20.00
289 CS,BO,JL 20.00
290 CS,V:Mxyzptlk. 20.00
291 CS,BO. 20.00
292 CS,BO,AM,O:Luthor 20.00
293 CS,BO. 20.00
294 CS,JL,A:Brain Storm. 20.00
295 CS,BO. 20.00
296 CS,BO,Identity Crisis #1 . . . . 20.00
297 CS,BO,Identity Crisis #2. . . . 20.00
298 CS,BO,Identity Crisis #3 . . . . 20.00
299 CS,BO,Identity Crisis #4
A:Luthor,Brainiac,Bizarro. . . . 20.00
300 CS,BO,2001,anniversary 30.00
301 BO,JL,V:Solomon Grundy. . . 10.00
302 JL,BO,V:Luthor,A:Atom. 10.00

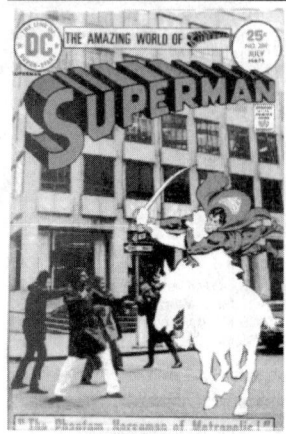

Superman #289 © DC Comics, Inc.

303 CS,BO,I:Thunder&Lightning . . 10.00
304 CS,BO,V:Parasite 10.00
305 CS,BO,V:Toyman 10.00
306 CS,BO,V:Bizarro 10.00
307 NA(c),JL,FS,A:Supergirl 10.00
308 NA(c),JL,FS,A:Supergirl 10.00
309 JL,FS,A:Supergirl 10.00
310 CS,V:Metallo 10.00
311 CS,FS,A:Flash 10.00
312 CS,FS,A:Supergirl. 10.00
313 NA(c),CS,DA,A:Supergirl 10.00
314 NA(c),CS,DA,A:Gr.Lantern . . . 10.00
315 CS,DA,V:Blackrock 10.00
316 CS,DA,V:Metallo 10.00
317 NA(c),CS,DA,V:Metallo 10.00
318 CS 10.00
319 CS,V:Solomon Grundy 10.00
320 CS,V:Solomon Grundy 10.00
321 CS,V:Parasite 9.00
322 CS,V:Solomon Grundy 9.00
323 CS,DA,I:Atomic Skull 9.00
324 CS,A:Atomic Skull. 9.00
325 CS 9.00
326 CS,V:Blackrock 9.00
327 CS,KS,V:Kobra,C:JLA 9.00
328 CS,KS,V:Kobra 9.00
329 KS,CS 9.00
330 CS,F:glasses explained 9.00
331 CS,I:Master Jailer 9.00
332 CS,V:Master Jailer 9.00
333 CS,V:Bizarro 9.00
334 CS 7.00
335 CS,W:Mxyzptlk 7.00
336 CS,V:Rose And Thorn. 7.00
337 CS,A:Brainiac,Bizarro 7.00
338 CS,F:Kandor enlarged 7.00
339 CS,I:N.R.G.X. 7.00
340 CS,V:N.R.G.X 7.00
341 CS,F:Major Disaster 7.00
342 CS,V:Chemo 7.00
343 CS 7.00
344 CS,A:Phantom Stranger 7.00
345 CS,When time ran backward . . 7.00
346 CS,Streak of Bad Luck 7.00
347 JL 7.00
348 CS 7.00
349 CS,V:Mxyzptlk. 7.00
350 CS,Clark Kent's Vanishing
    Classmate 6.00
351 CS,JL,A:Mxyzptlk 6.00
352 CS,RB 6.00
353 CS,origin 6.00
354 CS,JSon,I:Superman 2020 . . . 6.00
355 CS,JSon,F:Superman 2020 . . . 6.00
356 CS,V:Vartox. 6.00
357 CS,DCw,F:Superman 2020 . . . 6.00

358 CS,DG,DCw 6.00
359 CS 6.00
360 CS,AS,F:World of Krypton 6.00
361 CS,AS 6.00
362 CS,KS,DA 6.00
363 CS,RB,C:Luthor 6.00
364 GP(c),RB,AS. 6.00
365 CS,KS 6.00
366 CS,KS 6.00
367 CS,GK,F:World of Krypton 6.00
368 CS,AS 6.00
369 RB,FMc,V:Parasite 6.00
370 CS,KS,FMc,A:Chemo 6.00
371 CS 6.00
372 CS,GK,F:Superman 2021. . . . . 6.00
373 CS,V:Vartox. 6.00
374 GK(c),CS,DA,KS,V:Vartox 6.00
375 CS,DA,GK,V:Vartox 6.00
376 CS,DA,CI,BO,SupergirlPrev... . 5.00
377 GK(c),CS,V:Terra-Man 5.00
378 CS. 5.00
379 CS,V:Bizarro 5.00
380 CS. 5.00
381 GK(c),CS. 5.00
382 GK(c),CS. 5.00
383 CS. 5.00
384 GK(c),CS. 5.00
385 GK(c),CS,V:Luthor 5.00
386 GK(c),CS,V:Luthor 5.00
387 GK(c),CS. 5.00
388 GK(c),CS. 5.00
389 GK(c),CS. 5.00
390 GK(c),CS,V:Vartox 5.00
391 GK(c),CS,V:Vartox 5.00
392 GK(c),CS,V:Vartox 5.00
393 IN,DG,V:Master Jailer 5.00
394 CS,V:Valdemar 5.00
395 CS,V:Valdemar 5.00
396 CS. 5.00
397 EB,V:Kryptonite Man. 5.00
398 CS,AS,DJ 5.00
399 CS,BO,EB. 5.00
400 HC(c),FM,AW,JO,JSo,MR,
    TA,WP,MK,KJ,giant 8.00
401 CS,BO,V:Luthor 5.00
402 CS,BO,WB 5.00
403 CS,BO,AS 5.00
404 CI,BO,V:Luthor 5.00
405 KS,KK,AS,F:Super-Batman . . . 5.00
406 IN,AS,KK. 5.00
407 IN,V:Mxyzptlk 5.00
408 CS,AW,JRu,F:Nuclear
    Holocaust. 5.00
409 CS,AW,KS. 5.00
410 CS,AW,V:Luthor 5.00
411 CS,MA,F:End Earth-Prime 5.00
412 CS,AW,V:Luthor 5.00
413 CS,AW,V:Luthor 5.00
414 CS,AW,Crisis tie-in 6.00
415 CS,AW,Crisis,W:Super Girl.... 6.00
416 CS,AW,Luthor 5.00
417 CS,V:Martians 5.00
418 CS,V:Metallo 5.00
419 CS,V:Iago 5.00
420 CS,F:Nightmares 5.00
421 CS,V:Mxyzptlk. 5.00
422 BB(c),CS,TY,LMa,V:Werewolf. . 5.00
423 AMo(s),CS,GP,F:Last
    Superman 12.00
Ann.#1 I:Supergirl Rep 1,700.00
Ann.#2 I&O:Titano 650.00
Ann.#3 I:Legion 450.00
Ann.#4 O:Legion 350.00
Ann.#5 A:Krypton 275.00
Ann.#6 A:Legion. 275.00
Ann.#7 O:Superman,Silver Anniv. 200.00
Ann.#8 F:Secret origins 175.00
Ann.#9 GK(c),ATh,TA,CS,
    A:Batman. 7.00
Ann.#10 CS,MA,F:Sword of
    Superman. 5.00

Ann.#11 AMo(s),DGb,A:Batman,
    Robin,Wonder Woman 6.00
Ann.#12 BB(c),AS,A:Lex Luthor,
    Last War Suit. 4.00
Game Give-away 10.00
Giveaway CS,AT 2.25
Pizza Hut 1977 . . . . 6.00
Radio Shack 1980 JSw,DG 5.00
Radio Shack 1981 CS 5.00
Radio Shack 1982 CS 5.00
Spec.#1 GK 3.50
Spec.#2 GK,V:Brainiac 3.50
Spec.#3 IN,V:Amazo 3.50
Superman III Movie,CS 2.50
Superman IV Movie,DH,DG,FMc . . 2.50
Becomes:

ADVENTURES OF
SUPERMAN
1987

424 JOy,I:Man O'War. 4.00
425 JOy,Man O'War. 3.00
426 JOy,Legends,V:Apokolips 3.00
427 JOy,V:Qurac 3.00
428 JOy,V:Qurac,I:JerryWhite 3.00
429 JOy,V:Concussion. 3.00
430 JOy,V:Fearsome Five 3.00
431 JOy,A:Combattor. 3.00
432 JOy,I:Jose Delgado. 3.00
433 JOy,V:Lex Luthor 3.00
434 JOy,I:Gang Buster 3.00
435 JOy,A:Charger 3.00
436 JOy,Millennium x-over 5.00
437 JOy,Millennium X-over 3.50
438 JOy,N:Brainiac 3.00
439 JOy,R:Superman Robot 3.00
440 JOy,A:Batman,Wond.Woman . . 3.00
441 JOy,V:Mr.Mxyzptlk. 3.00
442 JOy,V:Dreadnaught,A:JLI 3.00
443 JOy,DHz,I:Husque 3.00
444 JOy,Supergirl SagaPt.2 . . . . . . 3.00
445 JOy,V:Brainiac. 3.00
446 JOy,A:Gangbuster,
    A:Luthor's Old Costume 3.00
447 JOy,A:Gangbuster. 3.00
448 JOy,I:Dubbilex,A:Gangbuster . . 3.00
449 JOy,Invasion X-over 3.00
450 JOy,Invasion X-over 3.00
451 JOy,Superman in Space 3.00
452 DJu,V:Wordbringer 3.00
453 JOy,DJu,A:Gangbuster 3.00
454 JOy,DJu,I:New Mongul 4.00
455 DJu,ATb,A:Eradicator 3.50
456 DJu,ATb,V:Turmoil 3.50

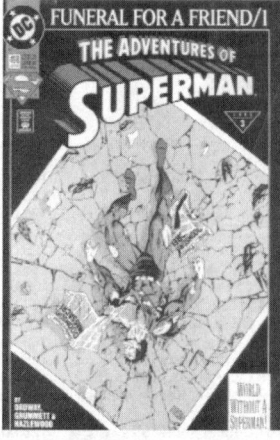

The Adventures of Superman #498
© DC Comics, Inc.

457 DJu,V:Intergang 3.50
458 DJu,KJ,R:Elastic Lad
(Jimmy Olsen) 3.50
459 DJu,V:Eradicator 3.50
460 DJu,NKu,V:Eradicator 3.50
461 DJu,GP,V:Eradicator 3.50
462 DJu,ATb,Homeless
Christmas Story 3.50
463 DJu,ATb,Superman Races
Flash 3.50
464 DJu,ATb,Day of Krypton
Man #2,A:Lobo 6.00
465 DJu,ATb,Day of Krypton
Man #5,V:Draaga 3.00
466 DJu,DG,V:Team Excalibur
Astronauts,I:Hank Henshaw
(becomes Cyborg Superman) . . 4.50
467 DJu,ATb,A:Batman 3.00
468 DJu,ATb,Man Of Steel's
Journal,V:Hank Henshaw 3.00
469 DJu,ATb,V:Dreadnaught 3.00
470 DJu,ATb,Soul Search #3,
D:Jerry White. 3.00
471 CS,Sinbad Contract #2 . . . . 3.00
472 DJu,ATb,Krisis of Krimson
Kryptonite #2 . . . . 3.00
473 DJu,ATb,A:Green Lantern,
Guy Gardner 3.00
474 DJu,ATb,Drunk Driving issue . . 3.00
475 DJu,ATb,V:Kilgrave,Sleez 3.00
476 DJu,BBr,Time & Time Again,pt.1,
A:Booster Gold,Legion 3.00
477 DJu,BBr,T & T Again,pt.4,
A:Legion 3.00
478 DJu,BBr,T & T Again,pt.7,
A:Legion,Linear Man 3.00
479 EH,Red Glass Trilogy#2 . . . . . . 3.00
480 JOy,DJu,BMc,TG,BBr,CS,
Revenge of the Krypton
Man,pt.3. . . . . 3.00
481 1st TG Supes,DHz,V:Parasite . 3.00
482 TG,DHz,V:Parasite 3.00
483 TG,DHz,V:Blindspot 3.00
484 TG,Blackout #1,V:Mr.Z 3.00
485 TG,DHz,Blackout #5,A:Mr.Z . . . 3.00
486 TG,V:Purge 3.00
487 TG,DHz,X-mas,A:Agent
Liberty 3.00
488 TG,Panic in the Sky,pt.3,
V:Brainiac. 3.00
489 TG,Panic in the Sky,Epiloge . . . 2.75
490 TG,A:Agent Liberty,Husque. . . . 3.00
491 TG,DHz,V:Cerberus,Metallo . . . 3.00

492 WS(c),V:Sons of Liberty,
A:Agent Liberty 3.00
493 TG,Blaze/Satanus War,pt.1 . . . . 3.00
494 TG,DHz,I:Kismet 3.00
495 TG,DHz,A:Forever People,
Darkseid 3.00
496 V:Mr.Mxyzptlk,C:Doomsday . . . 3.00
496a 2nd printing 2.50
497 TG,Doomsday Pt.3,A:Maxima,
Bloodwynd 5.00
497a 2nd printing 2.50
498 TG,Funeral for a Friend#1 . . . . 4.00
498a 2nd Printing. 2.50
499 TG,DHz,Funeral for a
Friend#5 . . . . 3.50
500 JOy(c),B:KK(s),TG,DJu,JBg,JG,
BBr,Bagged,Superman in limbo,
I:Four Supermen,Direct Sales . . 3.50
500a Newsstand Ed. 3.00
500b Platinum Ed. 20.00
501 TG,Reign of Supermen#2,Direct
Sales,Die-Cut(c),Mini-poster
F:Superboy 3.00
501a Newstand Ed. 2.25
502 TG,A:Supergirl,V:Stinger 2.25
503 TG,Cyborg Superman Vs.
Superboy 2.50
504 TG,DHz,A:All Supermen,
V:Mongul 2.50
505 TG,DHz,Superman returns to
Metropolis,Holografx(c) 3.00
505a Newstand Ed. 2.25
506 TG,DHz,A:Guardian 2.50
507 Spilled Blood#1,V:Bloodsport . . 2.50
508 BKi,A:Challengers of the
Unknown 2.50
509 BKi,A:Auron 2.50
510 BKi,Bizarro's World #2,
V:Bizarro 2.50
511 BKi,A:Guardian 2.50
512 BKi,V:Parasite. 2.50
513 BKi,Battle for Metropolis #4 . . . 2.50
514 BKi,Fall of Metropolis #4. . . . . . 2.50
515 BKi,Massacre in Metropolis . . . 2.50
516 BKi,Zero Hour,I:Alpha
Centurion 2.50
517 BKi,deathtrap 2.50
518 BKi 2.50
519 KK,BKi,Secret of Superman's
Tomb 2.50
520 SI,KK,JMz,100 crimes at
midnight. 2.50
521 SI,KK,R:Thorn. 2.50
522 SI,KKIdentity known 2.50
523 SI,KK,Death of C.Kent,pt.2 . . . . 2.50
524 SI,KK,Death of C.Kent,pt.6
[New Miraweb format begins] . . 2.50
525 SI,KK. 2.50
526 Bloodsport vs. Bloodsport. 2.50
527 . . . . 2.50
528 Trial of Superman,prelude 2.50
529 Trial of Superman 2.50
530 KK,SI,JMz,Trial of Superman . . 2.50
531 KK,SI,JMz,Trial of Superman,
concl. 2.50
532 KK,SI,JMz, return of Lori
Lemaris 2.50
533 KK,SI,JMz 2.50
534 KK,SI,JMz,V:Lord Satannus . . . 2.50
535 KK,SI,JMz,Lois & LoriLemaris . . 2.50
536 . . . . 2.50
537 . . . . 2.50
538 . . . . 2.50
539 F:Guardian and the Newsboy
Legion 2.50
540 KK(s),TyD,KIS,A:Ferro, Final
Night tie-in 2.50
541 KK(s),SI,JMz,on Honeymoon,
A:Superboy,Tana Moon,Kekona 2.50
542 KK&JOy(s),PR,JMz,V:Misa . . 2.50
543 . . . . 2.50

544 KK(s),SI,JMz,Who Killed Clark
Kent in broad daylight? 2.50
545 KK(s),SEa,JMz,Return of the
Atomic Skull,new blue costume 2.50
546 KK(s),SI,JMz,V:Metallo, uses
new powers. 2.50
547 KK(s),SI,JMz,Superman goes
to Kandor,A:The Atom 2.50
548 KK(s),SI,JMz,V:Lex Luthor 2.50
549 KK(s),SI,JMz,F:Jimmy Olsen . . 2.50
550 KK(s),SI,TGu,JMz,DRo, 48pg. . 3.50
551 DJu,TGu,DRo,Genesis,
V:Cyborg 2.25
552 KK,TGu,DRo,V:Parasite. 2.25
553 KK,TGu,DRo,disappearances. . 2.25
554 KK,TGu,DRo,disappearances. . 2.25
555 KK,TRu,DRo,Red/Blue x-over . . 2.25
556 KK,TRu,DRo,Red & Blue 2.25
557 KK,VS,DRo,Millennium Giants
x-over 2.25
558 KK,JOy,DRo,silver age?,pt.1 . . 2.25
559 KK,JOy,DRo,silver age?,pt.2 . . 2.25
560 KK,JOy,DRo,silver age?,pt.3 . . 2.25
561 KK,JOy,TGu,DRo,Waverider. . . 2.25
562 KK(s),JOy,TGu,DRo,Lexcom . . 2.25
563 RMz,TGb,TP,City of the
Future, pt.4 x-over. 2.25
564 KK&JOy(s),TGu,DRo,
A:Geo-Force 2.25
565 KK&JOy(s),TGu,DRo,A:JLA . . . 2.25
566 KK&JOy(s),TGu,DRo,V:Lex
Luthor 2.25
567 KK&JOy(s),DRo,PR,. 2.25
568 LSi(s),TMo,DRo,V:Metallo 2.25
569 LSi(s),TMo,DRo,V:S.C.U. 2.25
570 RMz&TPe(s),TGb,TP,
A:JLA,pt.2 x-over. 2.25
571 LSi(s),DRo,V:Atomic Skull 2.25
572 RF,SB,Strange Visitor,pt.2 . . . . 2.25
573 SI,SEp,DRo,flashbacks. 2.25
574 SI. 2.25
575 SI,F:Lex Luthor 2.25
576 SI,V:Brainiac 13 . . . . 2.25
577 SI,JMz,A:Luthor 2.25
578 JMD(s),JMz,alien utopia 2.25
579 JMD(s),Lois has vanished 2.25
580 JMD(s),CriticalCondition,pt.2 . . 2.25
581 JMD(s),V:Adversary,Lex Luthor 2.25
582 JMD(s),Arkham,pt.2 . . . . 2.25
583 JMD,JMz,Superman:Emperor. . 2.25
584 JMD(s),JMz,V:Devouris 2.25
585 JMD,JMz,V:LexLuthor,Satanus. 2.25
586 JMD,JMz,V:Satanus 2.25
587 JMD,JMz,V:Satanus 2.25
588 JoC,JMz,V:Satanus. 2.25
589 JoC,JMz,Return toKrypton,pt.1 . 2.25
590 JoC,JMz,Luthor's Lackey? 2.25
591 MWm,Infestation x-over,pt.2 . . . 2.25
592 JoC,JMz,F:Jimmy Olson 2.25
593 JoC,JMz,V:Manchester Black . . 2.25
594 JoC,MeW,All-Out War,x-over . . 2.25
595 JoC,MeW,Casualties of War . . . 2.25
596 JoC,MeW,No Superman's Job . 5.00
597 JoC,Joker:Last Laugh tie-in . . . 2.25
598 JoC,JMz,F:Perry White. 2.25
599 JoC,JMz,Russian submarine . . 2.25
600 JoC,Lex Luthor, 64-pg. 5.00
601 JoC,Cult of Persuasion,pt.1 . . . 2.25
602 JoC,Cult of Persuasion,pt.2 . . . 2.25
603 JoC,F:Superbaby 2.25
604 JoC,V:Ultra-Man 2.25
605 JoC,F:Superbaby, concl. 2.25
606 JoC,Return to KryptonII,pt.2 . . . 2.25
607 F:Argent 2.25
608 JoC,Ending Battle,pt.2 . . . . 2.25
609 JoC,Ending Battle,pt.6 . . . . 2.25
610 JoC,in Guatemala 2.25
611 Lost Hearts,pt.2 x-over 2.25
612 JoC,Hollow Man 2.25
613 JoC,Captain Cold 2.25
614 JoC,Hollow Men 2.25

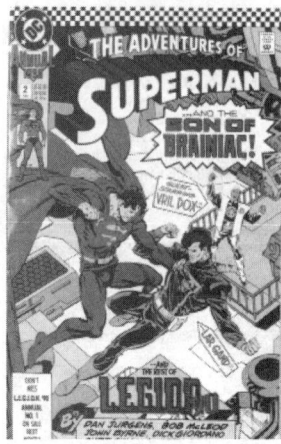

Adventures of Superman Ann. #2
© DC Comics, Inc.

615 JoC,Hollow Men 2.25
616 JoC,Hollow Men 2.25
617 JoC,V:two Mr.Mxyzptlks 2.25
618 JoC,CAd,Mxy Twins 2.25
619 JoC,Lois and Clark 2.25
620 JoC,the Candidate 2.25
621 JoC,Minuteman 2.25
622 prophecy of the Minuteman . . . 2.25
623 Superman & Lois 2.50
624 KIK,Strange New Visitor 2.50
625 Godfall,pt.2 . . . . 2.50
626 Godfall,pt.5 . . . . 2.50
627 Special Crimes Unit 2.50
628 F:Wond.Woman & Gr.Lantern . 2.50
629 Lois,Replikon 2.50
630 Hostage situation 2.50
631 Lois behind enemy lines 2.50
632 V:Propaganda 2.50
633 ALa, New Parasites 2.50
Ann.#1 JSn(c),DJu,I:Word Bringer . 3.00
Ann.#2 CS/JBy,KGa/DG,BMc,
   A:L.E.G.I.O.N.'90 (Lobo) 4.00
Ann.#3 BHi,JRu,DG,
   Armageddon 2001. . . . . 3.00
Ann.#4 BMc,A:Lobo,Guy Gardner,
   Eclipso tie-in 3.00
Ann.#5 TG,I:Sparx 2.75
Ann.#6 MMi(c),Elseworlds Story . . . 3.00
Ann.#7 Year One Story 4.00
Ann.#8 Legends o/t Dead Earth . . . 2.95
Ann.#9 Pulp Heroes (Western) 3.95
Spec.#1,000,000 ALa&DAn(s)LMa,
   A:Teen Titans, V:Solaris 3.00
GN Vol. 1 Up, Up and Away 6.95
GN Vol. 2 Never-Ending Battle 6.95

SUPERMAN'S BUDDY
1954
1 w/costume, giveaway 1,800.00
1 w/out costume, giveaway 800.00

SUPERMAN'S
CHRISTMAS ADVENTURE
1 (1940) giveaway 6,000.00
2 (1944) giveaway 1,500.00

SUPERMAN AND THE
GREAT CLEVELAND FIRE
1948
1 for Hospital Fund, giveaway . . 800.00

SUPERMAN (miniature)
1942
1 Py-Co-Pay Tooth Powder
   Give- Away 900.00
2 CS,Superman Time Capsule . . 500.00
3 CS,Duel in Space 450.00
4 CS,Super Show in Metropolis . 450.00

SUPERMAN RECORD
COMIC
1966
1 w/record 200.00
1 w/out record 100.00

SUPERMAN
SPECTACULAR
1982
1 A:Luthor & Terra-Man 2.50

SUPERMAN-TIM
STORE PAMPHLETS
1942
Superman-Tim store Monthly Membership Pamphlets, stories, games
  (1942), each 1,500.00
  (1943), each 500.00
  (1944), each 475.00
  (1945), each 450.00
  (1946), color(c) each 550.00
  (1947), color(c) each 350.00
  (1948), color(c) each 300.00
  (1949), color(c) each 300.00
  (1950), color(c) each 350.00
Superman-Tim stamp albums,
  (1946) 400.00
  (1947) Superman story 500.00
  (1948) 400.00

SUPERMAN WORKBOOK
1945
1 rep. Superman #14 . . . . 1,300.00

SUPERMAN
[2nd Regular Series], 1987
1 JBy,TA,I:Metallo 5.00
2 JBy,TA,V:Luthor 3.00
3 JBy,TA,Legends tie-in 3.00
4 JBy,KK,V:Bloodsport 3.00
5 JBy,KK,V:Host 3.00
6 JBy,KK,V:Host 3.00
7 JBy,KK,V:Rampage 3.00
8 JBy,KK,A:Superboy,Legion 3.00
9 JBy,KK,V:Joker 5.00
10 JBy,KK,V:Rampage 3.00
11 JBy,KK,V:Mr.Mxyzptlk 2.50
12 JBy,KK,A:Lori Lemerias 2.50
13 JBy,KK,Millennium 2.50
14 JBy,KK,A:Green Lantern 2.50
15 JBy,KK,I:New Prankster 2.50
16 JBy,KK,A:Prankster 4.00
17 JBy,KK,O:Silver Banshee 2.50
18 MMi,KK,A:Hawkman 2.50
19 JBy,V:Skyhook 2.50
20 JBy,KK,A:Doom Patrol 3.00
21 JBy,A:Supergirl 4.00
22 JBy,A:Supergirl 2.50
23 MMi,CR,O:Silver Banshee 2.50
24 KGa,V:Rampage 2.50
25 KGa,V:Brainiac 2.50
26 KGa,BBr,V:Baron Sunday 2.50
27 KGa,BBr,V:Guardian 2.50
28 KGa,BBr,Supes Leaves Earth . . 2.50
29 DJu,BBr,V:Word Bringer 2.50
30 KGa,DJu,A:Lex Luthor 2.50
31 DJu,PCu,V:Mxyzptlk 2.50
32 KGa,V:Mongul. 2.50

33 KGa,A:Cleric 2.50
34 KGa,V:Skyhook. 2.50
35 CS,KGa,A:Brainiac 2.50
36 JOy,V:Prankster 2.50
37 JOy,A:Guardian. 2.50
38 JOy,Jimmy Olsen Vanished . . . 2.50
39 JOy,KGa,V:Husque. 2.50
40 JOy,V:Four Armed Terror 2.50
41 JOy,Day of Krypton Man #1,
   A:Lobo 3.50
42 JOy,Day of Krypton Man #4,
   V:Draaga 3.50
43 JOy,V:Krypton Man 2.50
44 JOy,A:Batman 2.50
45 JOy,F:Jimmy Olsen's Dairy 2.50
46 DJu,JOy,A:Jade,Obsidian,
   I:New Terra-Man 2.50
47 JOy,Soul Search #2,V:Blaze 2.50
48 CS,Sinbad Contract #1 . . . . 2.50
49 JOy,Krisis of K.Kryptonite#1 . . . 3.00
50 JBy,KGa,DJu,JOy,BBr,CS,Krisis
   of Krimson Kryptonite #4,
   Clark Proposes To Lois 6.00
50a 2nd printing 2.50
51 JOy,I:Mr.Z 2.50
52 KGa,V:Terra-Man 2.50
53 JOy,Superman reveals i.d. 3.50
53a 2nd Printing. 2.50
54 JOy,KK,Time & Time Again#3. . 2.50
55 JOy,KK,Time & Time Again#6. . 2.50
56 EH,KK,Red Glass Trilogy#1 . . . 2.50
57 JOy,DJu,BBr,ATi,JBg,BMc,TG,
   Revenge o/t Krypton Man #2 . 3.50
58 DJu,BBr,I:Bloodhounds. 2.50
59 DJu,BBr,A:Linear Men 2.50
60 DJu,EB,I:Agent Liberty,
   V:Intergang 2.50
61 DJu,BBr,A:Waverider,
   V:Linear Men 2.50
62 DJu,BBr,Blackout #4,A:Mr.Z . . . 2.50
63 DJu,A:Aquaman 2.50
64 JG,Christmas issue 2.50
65 DJu,Panic in the Sky#2,
   I:New Justice League 3.50
66 DJu,Panic in the Sky#6,
   V:Brainiac 8.00
67 DJu,Aftermath 2.50
68 DJu,V:Deathstroke 2.50
69 WS(c),DJu,A:Agent Liberty 2.50
70 DJu,BBr,A:Robin,V:Vampires . . . 2.50
71 DJu,Blaze/Satanus War 2.50
72 DJu,Crisis at Hand#2 . . . . 2.50
73 DJu,A:Waverider,V:Linear
   Men,C:Doomsday 5.00

Superman 2nd Series #39
© DC Comics, Inc.

Superman, 2nd Series #136
© DC Comics Inc.

73a 2nd printing 2.50
74 DJu,V:Doomsday,A:JLA 7.00
74a 2nd printing 2.00
75 DJu,V:Doomsday,D:Superman,
　　Collectors Ed. 20.00
75a newstand Ed. 9.00
75b 2nd printing 4.00
75c 3rd printing 2.50
75d 4th Printing 2.50
75e Platinum Ed. 45.00
76 DJu,BBr,Funeral for Friend#4 . . . 3.00
77 DJu,BBr,Funeral for Friend#8 . . . 3.00
78 DJu,BBr,Reign of Supermen#3,
　　Die-Cut(c),Mini poster,F:Cyborg
　　Supes,A:Doomsday 3.00
78a Newsstand Ed. 2.50
79 DJu,BBr,Memorial Service for
　　Clark 3.00
80 DJu,O:Cyborg Superman,
　　V:Mongul 4.00
81 DJu,O:Cyborg Superman 3.50
82 DJu,Chromium(c),A:All Supermen,
　　V:Cyborg Superman 5.00
82a Newstand Ed. 2.50
83 DJu,A:Batman 3.00
84 DJu,V:Toyman 3.00
85 DJu,V:Toyman 3.00
86 DJu,A:Sun Devils 3.00
87 DJu(c&s),SI,JRu,Bizzaro's
　　World#1, R:Bizarro 3.00
88 DJu(c&s),SI,JRu,Bizzaro's
　　World#5, D:Bizarro 3.00
89 DJu(c&s),V:Cadmus Project 3.00
90 DJu(c&s),Battle for
　　Metropolis#3 . . . . 3.00
91 DJu(c&s),Fall of Metropolis#3. . . 3.00
92 Massacre in Metropolis 3.00
93 Zero Hour,A:Batman 3.00
94 Conduit 3.00
95 Brainiac 3.00
96 Virtual Reality 3.00
97 Shadow Dragon 3.00
98 R:Shadow Strike 3.00
99 R:Agent Liberty 3.00
100 BBr,DJu,Death of C.Kent,pt.1 . . 3.50
100a Collectors Edition 4.00
101 Death of Clark Kent,pt.5
　　[New Miraweb format begins] . . 3.00
102 DJu,A:Captain Marvel 3.00
103 O:Arclight 3.00
104 . . . . 3.00
105 A:Green Lantern 3.00
106 DJu,RF,The Trial of Superman . 3.00

107 DJu,RF,The Trial of Superman . 3.00
108 DJu,RF,The Trial of Superman . 3.00
109 DJu,RF,V:Kill Fee 3.00
110 . . . . 3.00
111 DJu,RF,Cat Grant in charge . . . 3.00
112 DJu,RF,Lois & Clark 3.00
113 DJu(s),RF,JRu, ... 3.00
114 DJu(s),RF,JRu,A:Brainiac 3.00
115 DJu(s),RF,JRu,Lois leaves
　　Metropolis 3.00
116 DJu(s),RF,JRu,battle city siga
　　concl., V:Daxamite,B.U. Teen
　　Titans preview 3.00
117 DJu(s),RF,JRu,V: his own
　　robots, Final Night tie-in 3.00
118 DJu(s),RF,JRu,F:time-lost
　　Legion of Super Heroes 3.00
119 DJu(s),RF,JRu,A:Legion of
　　Super Heroes 3.00
120 DJu(s),RF,JRu, ... 3.00
121 DJu(s),RF,JRu,They Call it
　　Suicide Slum 3.00
122 DJu(s),RF,JRu,Lois visits
　　Fortress of Solitude 3.00
123 DJu(s),RF,Jru,Superman gets
　　New Costume 4.00
123a collector's edition, glow-in-
　　the-dark cover, ... 5.00
124 DJu(s),RF,JRu,A:Scorn, prince
　　of Kandor 2.50
125 DJu(s),RF,JRu,Kandor and
　　Metropolis,A:Atom 2.50
126 DJu(s),RF,JRu,A:Batman 2.50
127 DJu(s),RF,JRu,F:Jimmy Olsen . 2.50
128 DJu(s),RF,JRu, Genesis tie-in . . 2.50
129 DJu(s),PR,JRu,A:Scorn 2.50
130 DJu(s),RF,JRu,dragon's tooth. . 2.50
131 DJu(s),RF,JRu,Luthor &
　　Contessa's kid 2.50
132 DJu,RF,JRu,Red/Blue x-over . . 2.50
133 . . . . 2.50
134 DJu,RF,JRu,Millennium Giants . 2.50
135 DJu,RF,JRu,aftermath. 3.50
136 DJu,PR,JRu,The Superman
　　of 2999 A.D., pt.1 . . . . 2.50
137 DJu,PR,JRu,2999 AD,pt.2 . . . . 2.50
138 DJu,PR,JRu,2999 AD,pt.3 . . . . 2.50
139 DJu(s),JSn,JRu,V:Dominus 2.50
140 RMz(s),TGb,TP,City of the
　　Future, pt.3 x-over 2.50
141 DJu(s),SEa,JRu,I:Outburst 2.50
142 DJu(s),JRu,F:Outburst 2.50
143 DJu(s),SEp,JRu, ... 2.50
144 DJu(s),SEp,JRu,V:Lex Luthor . . 2.50
145 DJu(s),SEp,JRu,hate mail 2.50
146 DJu(s),SEp,JRu,V:Toyman 2.50
147 RMz(s),TGb,BAn,A:JLA,pt.1 . . 2.50
148 DJu(s),SEp,JRu, ... 2.50
149 RF,SB,Strange Visitor,pt.1 . . . . 2.50
150 DJu(s),SEp,JRu,48-pg. 3.50
150a foil cover 4.50
151 JLb,MMK,Faster than a
　　speeding bullet 3.00
152 JLb,MMK. 2.50
153 JLb,MMK,V:Imperiex. 3.00
154 JLb,CaS,V:Brainiac 13 . . . . 3.00
155 JLb,CaS,F:Superboy. 3.00
156 JLb,CaS,V:Parasite. 3.00
157 JLb,CaS,Lois vs. Superman? . . 3.00
158 JLb,CaS,CriticalCondition,pt.1 . 3.00
159 JLb,CaS,F:Green Lantern. 3.00
160 JLb,CaS,Arkham,pt.1 . . . . 3.00
161 JLb,CaS,Superman:Emperor? . 3.50
162 JLb,CaS,A:Aquaman,pt.1 . . . . . 3.00
163 JLb,PaP,CaS,F:Aquaman,pt.2 . 2.50
164 JLb,CaS,V:Bizarro 2.50
165 JLb,AAd,A:Linear Man 2.50
166 JLb,CaS,O:Superman(new) . . . 4.00
166a holofoil(c) 7.00
167 JLb,CaS,Return toKrypton,pt.1 . 2.50
168 JLb,CaS,Lord of the Ring,pt.1 . 5.00

169 MWm,Infestation x-over,pt.1 . . . 2.50
170 JLb,CaS,DK,V:Mogul 2.50
171 JLb,OurWorlds atWar,prelude. . 2.50
172 JLb,All-Out War. 2.50
173 JLb,Casualties of War. 2.50
174 JLb,CaS,War aftermath 2.50
175 JLb,CaS,Last Laugh,48-pg. . . . 3.50
176 JLb,IaC,NRd,F:Dr. Foster 2.25
177 JLb,CaS,F:Toyman,Metallo. . . . 2.25
178 JLb,CaS,F:Uncle Sam 2.25
179 JLb,African-American hero 2.25
180 JLb,IaC,NRd,V:Dracula. 3.50
181 JLb,CaS,F:Bizarro. 3.50
182 JLb,CaS,F:Suicide Squad. 2.25
183 JLb,CaS,Clarke fired from job . 2.25
184 PFe,CaS,Return to Krypton II. . 2.25
185 BA,PFe(c),baseball game. 2.25
186 PFe,CaS,Ending Battle,pt.1 . . . 2.25
187 PFe,CaS,Ending Battle,pt.5 . . . 2.25
188 F:Lois Lane. 2.25
189 PFe,Lost Hearts,pt.1 x-over . . . 2.25
190 SSe(c),SMc,rogue robot 2.25
190a spec.newsstand ed.,56-pg. . . 4.25
191 F:The Flash. 2.25
192 Supergirl vs. Radion 4.00
193 Supergirl vs. Radion 2.25
194 SMc,I:Ed 2.25
195 SMc,Futuresmiths. 2.25
196 SMc,new adversary 2.25
197 SMc,deaf Superman,Krypto . . . 2.25
198 SMc,V:Bizarro. 2.25
199 SMc,Supergirl origins 2.25
200 SMc,Futuresmiths, 48-pg. 3.50
201 KIK,Strange New Visitor 3.50
202 Godfall,pt.3 . . . . 5.00
203 Godfall,pt.6 . . . . 4.00
204 JLe,SW,I:FatherLeone,40-pg. . . 3.00
205 JLe,SW,For Tomorrow,pt.2 . . . . 3.00
206 JLe,SW,For Tomorrow,pt.3 . . . . 2.50
207 JLe,SW,For Tomorrow,pt.4 . . . . 2.50
208 JLe,SW,For Tomorrow,pt.5 . . . . 2.50
209 JLe,SW,For Tomorrow,pt.6 . . . . 2.50
210 JLe,SW,For Tomorrow,pt.7 . . . . 2.50
Ann.#1 RF,BBr,A:Titano 4.00
Ann.#2 RF,BBr,R:Newsboy Legion
　　& Guardian 4.00
Ann.#3 DAb(1st Work),TA,DG,
　　Armageddon 2001. . . . . 9.00
Ann.#3a 2nd printing(silver). 3.00
Ann.#4 Eclipso 3.00
Ann.#5 Bloodlines#6,DL,I:Myriad. . 3.00
Ann.#6 Elseworlds Story 3.50

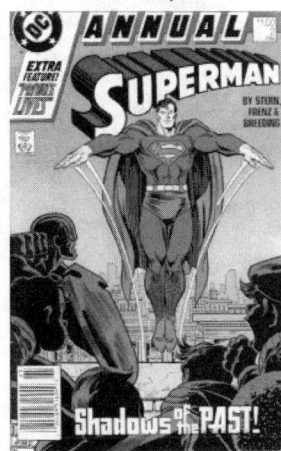

Superman 2nd Series Annual #2
© DC Comics Inc.

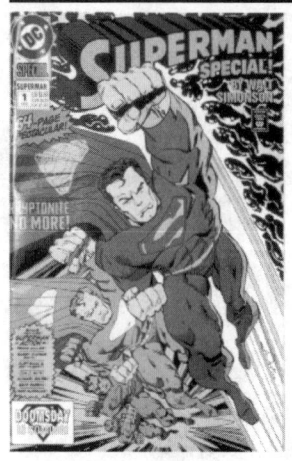

Superman Special #1
© *DC Comics, Inc.*

Ann.#7 WS(c),Year One Annual
  A:Dr. Occult 4.50
Ann.#8 Legends o/t Dead Earth . . . 3.00
Ann.#9 Pulp Heroes (High-
  Adventure) DJu 4.50
Ann.#10 DJu(s),PR,Clv,BWr,
  Ghosts 3.00
Ann.#11 JoP,AAd(c),JLApe:Gorilla
  Warfare 3.50
Ann.#12 Planet DC 2.50
Spec.#1,000,000 DAn&ALa(s),NBy . 2.50
Giant Ann.#1 Replica edition 5.00
Giant #1 80-page 5.00
Giant #2 80-page 5.00
Giant #3 80-page 5.95
Spec.#0 PeerPressure,pt.3 (1994) . 2.00
Spec.King of the World, foil 5.00
Spec.King of the World, reg. 4.00
Spec. Superman: Lois Lane,
  Girlfrenzy (1998) 2.00
Spec.#1 WS,V:L.Luthor,Sandman . . 6.00
Spec. Superman Plus One (1997) . . 3.00
Spec.#1 Superman: The Earth
  Stealers, JBy,CS,JOy (1988) . . . 3.50
  2nd printing 3.00
Spec. Superman:Emperor?(2000) . . 3.50
Spec. Superman Forever, KK,DJu,LSi,
  JBy,SI,DG, Luthor's kidnapped
  daughter (1998) 5.00
  Deluxe ed.,AxR(c), lenticular. . . 6.00
Spec.#1 Superman: The Legacy of
  Superman,WS,JG,F:Guardian,
  Waverider,Sinbad (1993) 4.00
Spec. Superman & Savage Dragon:
  Metropolis, KK,JBg,x-over 4.95
Spec. Superman/Toyman (1996) . . . 2.00
Spec. Team Superman, MMr(s),
  DHz,48-page,F:Superboy,
  Supergirl & Steel 3.00
Spec. 3-D #1 LSi,V:Mainframe 4.00
Spec. Whatever Happened to the
  Man of Tomorrow. 6.00
Spec. Superman Y2K,JBg (1999) . . 5.00
Newstime-The Life and Death of
  the Man of Steel-Magazine,
  DJu,BBr,JOy,JG,JBg 3.25
Spec.#1 Superman Gallery (1993) . 3.00
Superman Secret Files, DJu,JOy,
  etc.,inc. O:Superman (1997) . . . 5.00
Secret Files #1 Superman Villains. . 5.00
Secret Files #2. . . . . 5.00
Secret Files #1 Our Worlds at War . 6.00
Secret Files #1 President Luthor . . . 5.00

Secret Files 2004. . . . . 5.00
Spec. Metropolis Secret Files #1. . . 5.00
Spec. Team Superman Secret Files 5.00
Spec. 1-shot,Superman:Lex 2000,
  JLb,TyH,DoM,Vote for Lex . . . 3.50
Spec. 10-Cent Adventure,SMc. . . . 0.10
Spec. Superman vs. Darkseid:
  Apokolips Now, MSh(s),48-pg. . 3.00
Spec. Blood of my Ancestors. 7.00
GN Death of Superman rep.(1993) . 6.00
  Later printings 6.00
  Platinum Edition 15.00
GN Superman At Earth's End
  (Elseworlds 1995) 5.00
GN Superman: Distant Fires, HC,GK,
  nuclear winter (1997). 6.00
GN Superman: Earth Day 1991, KGa
  Metropolis Clean-Up 5.50
GN Superman For Earth (1991) . . . 5.00
GN Superman: Kal, Medieval
  Superman (Elseworlds 1995) . . 6.00
GN Superman: Last God of Krypton 5.00
GN Last Stand on Krypton (2003) . . 7.00
GN Superman's Metropolis, RLo &
  RTs(s),TMK, in Fritz Lang's
  Metropolis (Elseworlds 1996) . . 6.00
GN The Superman Monster. 7.00
GN A Nation Divided 5.00
GN Superman: The Odyssey. 5.00
GN Peace on Earth, oversized . . . 10.00
GN Superman Red/Superman Blue,
  V:Toyman, Cyborg, Superman
  split into two entities (1997). . . . 4.00
  Deluxe, 3-D cover 5.00
GN Superman: Silver Banshee, 48pg,
  prestige format (1998) 5.00
GN Superman: Speeding Bullets,
  EB (Elseworlds 1993) 6.00
GN Superman, Under a Yellow Sun
  by Clark Kent,KGa,EB (1994) . . 6.00
GN Superman: The Wedding Album,
  collector's edition, 96 pg.,
  cardstock cover 5.00
GN War of the Worlds,Elseworlds . . 6.00
GN Superman, Inc. 7.00
GN Superman: Mann & Superman . 6.00
GN Superman:Where is thy Sting? . 7.00
GN Superman & Savage Dragon:
  Chicago, x-over, EL (2002) 6.00
  Metropolis, x-over,KK,JBg 5.00
TPB Superman: Bizarro's World . . 10.00
TPB Tales of the Bizarro World . . . 15.00
TPB Critical Condition (2003) 15.00
TPB Day of Doom (2003) 10.00
TPB Superman: The Death of Clark
  Kent, rep. (1997) 20.00
TPB End of the Century (2003) . . . 18.00
TPB Eradication. 13.00
TPB Exile 15.00
TPB Superman/Fantastic Four . . . 10.00
TPB Krisis of the Krimson Kryptonite
  rep. 13.00
TPB Panic in the Sky rep. 10.00
TPB President Lex (2003) 18.00
TPB Return of Superman rep. Reign
  of Superman 15.00
TPB The Revenge Squad (2000) . 13.00
TPB Son of Superman (2000) 15.00
TPB Superman Vs. Revenge
  Squad 13.00
TPB They Saved Luthor's Brain . . 15.00
TPB Time and Time Again (1994) . . 7.50
TPB The Wedding and
  Beyond rep. 15.00
TPB World Without Superman. 7.50
TPB Superman in the fifties 20.00
TPB Superman in the sixties 20.00
TPB Superman in the seventies . . 20.00
TPB Sunday Classics 1939–1943. 20.00
TPB The Dailies,Vol.1 . . . . 15.00
TPB The Dailies,Vol.2 . . . . 15.00

TPB The Dailies,Vol.3 . . . . 15.00
TPB No Limits, 208-page. 15.00
TPB Endgame, 176-page 15.00
TPB Superman/Gen 13, 80-page . 10.00
TPB Superman Vs. Predator. 15.00
TPB Superman for All Seasons . . . 15.00
TPB Til Deat Do Us Part (2001) . . 18.00
TPB Our Worlds at War, Vol.1 . . . 20.00
TPB Our Worlds at War, Vol.2 . . . . 20.00
TPB Greatest Superman Stories
  Ever Told 16.00
TPB Return to Krypton. 18.00

SUPERMAN ADVENTURES
Sept., 1996

1 PDi(s),RBr,TA, from animated
  TV show 3.00
2 SMI,RBr,TA,V:Metallo 2.50
3 SMI(s),RBr,TA,V:Brainiac. 2.50
4 SMI(s), ... 2.50
5 SMI(s),BBI,TA,V:Livewire 2.50
6 SMI(s),RBr,TA,Metropolis
  in ruins 2.50
7 SMI(s),RBr,TA,V:Jax-Ur, Mala . . 2.50
8 SMI(s),RBr,TA,V:Jax-Ur 2.50
9 SMI(s),MM,TA,Return of
  the Hero. 2.50
10 SMI(s),RBr,TA,V:Toyman 2.50
11 SMI(s),RBr,TA,struck down
  by strange malady. 2.50
12 SMI(s),RBr,TA,BB, Kryptonian
  virus, concl. 2.50
13 SMI(s),RBr,TA,BB, alien races . . 2.50
14 TA,Angela Chen 2.50
15 RBr,TA,Superman's pal Bibbo . 2.50
16 MMr(s),TA, meets Man of Steel . 2.50
17 . . . . 2.50
18 TA,should Clark quit? 2.50
19 TA,V:Multi-Face. 2.50
20 RBr,TA,V:MasterTrax 2.50
21 Supergirl Adventures, 64pg. 5.50
22 MMr,TA,RBr,War Games, pt.1 . . 2.50
23 MMr,TA,RBr,War Games, pt.2 . . 2.50
24 MMr,TA,RBr,V:Parasite 2.50
25 MMr,TA,RBr,F:Batgirl,C:Batman,
  Robin, Nightwing 2.50
26 MMr,TA,V:Mr.Mxyzptlk 2.50
27 MMr,TA,F:Lex Luthor 2.50
28 MMr,MM,TA,F:Jimmy Olsen . . . 2.50
29 MMr,TA,A:Lobo, Bizarro 2.50
30 MMr,TA,A:Lara, pt.1 . . . . 2.50
31 MMr,TA,A:Lara, pt.2 . . . . 2.50
32 DvM(s),Lois Hypnotized 2.50
33 DvM(s),TA,Secret Identity. 2.50
34 MMr(s),TA,MM,A:Dr.Fate 2.50
35 MMr(s),TA,A:Toyman 2.50
36 MMr(s),TA, many emergencies. . 2.50
37 MMr(s),TA,Clark Kent,Public
  Enemy Number One 2.50
38 MMr(s),TA,V:Parasite 2.50
39 TA 2.50
40 TTn(s),TA,F:Mxyzptlk 2.50
41 TTn,RBr,22 stories 2.50
42 TA,F:Mr. Miracle 2.50
43 TA,MM(c),Mother Box 2.50
44 TA,MM(c),F:The Commander . . . 2.50
45 TA,MM(c),Three young sisters . . 2.50
46 TA,MM(c),Smallville 2.50
47 TA,MM(c),shrinking ray 2.50
48 TA,MM(c),alien abduction 2.50
49 TA,MM(c),powers lost 2.50
50 TA,MM(c),accused of murder . . 2.50
51 TA,MM(c),Lois & Lana 2.50
52 TA,MM(c),Death in the Family . . 2.50
53 TA,MM(c),F:Mister Miracle 2.50
54 TA,MM(c),Kryptonite No More . . 2.50
55 TA,MM(c),Kryptonite No More . . 2.50
56 TA,MM(c),Poker Face 2.50
57 TA,MM(c),Four-PointPerspective 2.50

58 TA,AxR(c),What Lurks Below . . . 2.50
59 TA,MM(c),Ghost Flowers 2.50
60 TA,MM(c),F:Jimmy Olsen 2.50
61 TA,MM(c),V:Parasite 2.50
62 TA,MM(c),Heart of Stone 2.50
63 TA,MM(c),Magic Wand 2.50
64 TA,MM(c),F:Batman Beyond. . . . 2.50
65 TA,MM(c),Power Play,pt.1 . . . . . 2.50
66 TA,MM(c),Power Play,pt.2,
  final issue 2.50
Ann.#1 JoS,DDv,V:Akamin 4.50
TPB rep.#1–#6. . . . . 8.00
Spec. #1 Superman vs. Lobo –
  Misery in Space, DvM,MM,
  A:Man of Tomorrow 4.00

SUPERMAN/BATMAN
Aug., 2003
1 JLb,V:Metallo 4.00
2 JLb,both injured 4.00
3 JLb,V:Gorilla Grodd 2.95
4 F:Captain Atom,Luthor. 2.95
5 JLb(s),V:Luthor 2.95
6 JLb(s),V:Luthor 2.95
7 JLb(s),F:Robin,Superboy. 2.95
8 Supergirl from Krypton,pt.1 . . . . 2.95
9 Supergirl from Krypton,pt.2 . . . . 2.95
10 Supergirl from Krypton,pt.3. . . . 2.95
11 Supergirl from Krypton,pt.4 . . . . 2.95
12 Supergirl from Krypton,pt.5. . . . 2.95
13 JLb(s) V:Darkseid 2.95
14 JLb(s),CPa,Absolute Power 2.95
15 JLb(s),CPa,Absolute Power 2.95
Spec. Secret Files (2003) 4.95
TPB Superman: Greatest Stories . 20.00

SUPERMAN & BATMAN: GENERATIONS — AN IMAGINARY TALE
1998
1 (of 4) JBy, Elseworlds 5.00
2 JBy,V:Bat-Mite 5.00
3 JBy. 5.00
4 JBy, conclusion 5.00
TPB, rep. 14.95

SUPERMAN & BATMAN: GENERATIONS II
Aug., 2001
1 (of 4) JBy,Elseworlds,48-page. . . 5.95
2 JBy,48-page. 5.95
3 JBy,48-page. 5.95
4 JBy,48-page, concl. 5.95
TPB JBy. 20.00

SUPERMAN & BATMAN: GENERATIONS III
Jan., 2003
1 (of 12) JBy,Elseworlds 3.00
2 JBy,Super Twins 3.00
3 JBy,22nd Century 3.00
4 JBy,23rd Century 3.00
5 JBy,24th Century 3.00
6 JBy,25th Century 3.00
7 JBy,26th Century 3.00
8 JBy,26th Century 3.00
9 JBy,27th Century 3.00
10 JBy,28th Century 3.00
11 JBy,29th century Superboy. . . . 3.00
12 JBy,earth destroyed 2.95

SUPERMAN & BATMAN: WORLD'S FUNNEST
Nov., 2000
1-shot, Elseworlds,. 6.95

Superman Doomsday Huntr/Prey #3
© DC Comics, Inc.

SUPERMAN & BUGS BUNNY
1999
1 (of 4) JSon,TP 2.50
2 thru 4 TP,JSon . . . . @2.50

SUPERMAN: BIRTHRIGHT
July 2003
1 (of 12) F:Jor-El,40-pg. 4.00
2 South Africa,40-pg. 3.50
3 O:retold 3.50
4 Job interview 3.50
5 anti-terrorism weapons 3.50
6 Lex & Clark 2.95
7 Inhuman alien 2.95
8 Lex Luthor 2.95
9 Lex's Plans; Krypton 2.95
10 Threat to Krypton 2.95
11 Krypton Invades Earth 2.95
12 conclusion 2.95

SUPERMAN: THE DARK SIDE
Elseworlds, Aug., 1998
1 JFM,KD,First Son of Apokolips . . 5.00
2 . . . . 5.00
3 KD, conclusion. 5.00
TPB Superman: The Dark Side . . . 13.00

SUPERMAN: DAY OF DOOM
Nov., 2002
1 (of 4) DJu,BSz,F:Ty Duffy 2.95
2 DJu,BSz. 2.95
3 DJu,BSz. 2.95
4 DJu,BSz,concl. 2.95

SUPERMAN/DOOMSDAY: HUNTER/PREY
1994
1 DJu(a&s),BBr,R:Doomsday,R:Cyborg
  Superman,A:Darkseid 5.50
2 DJu(a&s),BBr,V:Doomsday,Cyborg
  Superman,A:Darkseid 5.25
3 DJu(a&s),BBr,V:Doomsday 5.25
TPB Rep. #1-#3. . . . . 14.95

SUPERMAN: THE DOOMSDAY WARS
1998
1 (of 3) DJu,BBr,R:Doomsday 5.00
2 DJu,V:Doomsday. 5.00
3 DJu, conclusion 5.00

SUPERMAN FAMILY
Prev: Superman's Pal, Jimmy Olsen
1974–82
164 KS,NC(c),Jimmy Olsen:Death
  Bites with Fangs of Stone 60.00
165 KS,NC(c),Supergirl:Princess
  of the Golden Sun 40.00
166 KS,NC(c),Lois Lane:The
  Murdering Arm of Metropolis. . 35.00
167 KS,NC(c),Jimmy Olsen:A
  Deep Death for Mr. Action 35.00
168 NC(c),Supergirl:The Girl
  with the See-Through Mind . . . 35.00
169 NC(c),Lois Lane:Target of
  the Tarantula 35.00
170 KS(c),Jimmy Olsen:The Kid
  Who Adopted Jimmy Olsen. . . 25.00
171 ECh(c),Supergirl:Cleopatra-
  Queen of America 25.00
172 KS(c),Lois Lane:The Cheat
  the Whole World Cheered. . . . 25.00
173 KS(c),Jimmy Olsen:Menace
  of the Micro-Monster 25.00
174 KS(c),Supergirl:Eyes of
  the Serpent 25.00
175 KS(c),Lois Lane:Fadeout
  For Lois 25.00
176 KS(c),Jimmy
  Olsen:Nashville, Super-Star . . 25.00
177 KS(c),Supergirl:Bride
  of the Stars 20.00
178 KS(c),Lois Lane:The Girl
  With the Heart of Steel 20.00
179 KS(c),Jimmy Olsen:I Scared
  Superman to Death 20.00
180 KS,Supergirl:The Secret of
  the Spell-Bound Supergirl 20.00
181 ECh(c),Lois Lane:The Secret
  Lois Lane Could Never Tell . . . 20.00
182 CS&NA(c),Jimmy Olsen:
  Death on Ice 20.00
183 NA(c),Supergirl:Shadows
  of Phantoms 20.00
184 NA(c),Supergirl:The
  Visitors From The Void 20.00
185 NA(c),Jimmy Olsen: The
  Fantastic Fists and Fury
  Feet of Jimmy Olsen 20.00
186 JL&DG(c),Jimmy Olsen:
  The Bug Lady 20.00
187 JL(c),Jimmy Olsen:The
  Dealers of Death 20.00
188 JL&DG(c),Jimmy Olsen:
  Crisis in Kandor. 20.00
189 JL(c),Jimmy Olsen:The
  Night of the Looter. 20.00
190 Jimmy Olsen:Somebody
  Stole My Town 20.00
191 Superboy:The Incredible
  Shrinking Town 20.00
192 RA&DG(c),Superboy:This
  Town For Plunder 20.00
193 RA&DG(c),Superboy:Menace
  of the Mechanical Monster . . . 20.00
194 MR,Superboy:When
  the Sorcerer Strikes. 20.00
195 RA&DG(c),Superboy:The Curse
  of the Un-Secret Identity 20.00
196 JL&DG(c),Superboy:The
  Shadow of Jor-El. 20.00

197 JL(c),Superboy:Superboy's
   Split Personality. 20.00
198 JL(c),Superboy:Challenge
   of the Green K-Tastrophe 20.00
199 RA&DG(c),Supergirl:The
   Case of Cape Caper 20.00
200 RA&DG(c),Lois Lane:
   Unhappy Anniversary 22.00
201 RA&DG(c),Supergirl:The
   Face on Cloud 9 . . . . 8.00
202 RA&DG(c),Supergirl:The
   Dynamic Duel 8.00
203 RA&DG(c),Supergirl:The
   Supergirl From Planet Earth . . . 8.00
204 RA&DG(c),Supergirl:The
   Earth-quake Enchantment. 8.00
205 RA&DG(c),Supergirl:Magic
   Over Miami 8.00
206 RA&DG(c),Supergirl:Strangers
   at the Heart's Core 8.00
207 RA&DG(c),Supergirl:Look
   Homeward, Argonian. 8.00
208 RA&DG(c),Supergirl:The
   Super-Switch to New York. 8.00
209 Supergirl:Strike Three-
   You're Out 8.00
210 Supergirl:The Spoil Sport
   of New York 8.00
211 RA&DG(c):Supergirl:The Man
   With the Explosive Mind 8.00
212 RA&DG(c):Supergirl:Payment
   on Demand 8.00
213 thru 222 . . . . @8.00

SUPERMAN FOR ALL SEASONS
June, 1998

1 (of 4) JLb,TSe, from farmboy
   to superhero 7.00
2 JLb,TSe,V:Lex Luthor 5.00
3 JLb,TSe,V:Lex Luthor 5.00
4 JLb,TSe, conclusion 5.00

SUPERMAN/GEN13
DC/Wildstorm April, 2000

1 (of 3) AH, x-over 2.50
1a variant cover (1:4) 2.50
2 AH,x-over. 2.50
2a variant cover (1:4) 2.50
3 AH, 40-pg. 3.50

SUPERMAN: LAST SON OF EARTH
July, 2000

1 (of 2) Elseworlds 5.95
2 Green Lantern's powers 5.95

SUPERMAN: METROPOLIS
Feb. 2003

1 (of 12) F:Jimmy Olsen 2.95
2 Mystery of the Tech 2.95
3 Rebecca. 2.95
4 The Tech or the Devil. 2.95
5 Jimmy and Lena 2.95
6 Jimmy and Lena 2.95
7 thru 12 . . . . @2.95

SUPERMAN: THE MAN OF STEEL
1991–2003

1 B:LSi(s),DJu,BMc,JOy,BBr,TG,
   Revenge o/t Krypton Man#1 . . 5.00
2 JBg,V:Cerberus 4.00
3 JBg,War of the Gods X-over . . . 3.00
4 JBg,V:Angstrom. 3.00

5 JBg,CS,V:Atomic Skull 3.00
6 JBg,Blackout#3,A:Mr.Z 3.00
7 JBg,V:Cerberus 3.00
8 KD,V:Jolt,Blockhouse 3.00
9 JBg,Panic in the Sky#1,
   V:Brainiac. 3.50
10 JBg,Panic in the Sky#5,
   D:Draaga 3.00
11 JBg,V:Flashpoint. 3.00
12 JBg,V:Warwolves 3.00
13 JBg,V:Cerberus 3.00
14 JBg,A:Robin,V:Vampires. 3.00
15 KG,KGa,Blaze/Satanus War . . . 3.00
16 JBg,Crisis at Hand#1 . . . . 3.00
17 JBg,V:Underworld,
   C:Doomsday 8.00
17a 2nd printing. 2.50
18 JBg,I:Doomsday,V:Underworld. 10.00
18a 2nd printing. 4.00
18b 3rd printing 2.50
19 JBg,Doomsday,pt.5. . . . . 7.00
19a 2nd printing. 2.50
20 JBg,Funeral for a Friend#3. . . . 3.00
21 JBg,Funeral for a Friend#7. . . . 3.00
22 JBg,Reign of Supermen#4,Direct
   Sales,Die-Cut(c),mini-poster,
   F:Man of Steel 2.50
22a Newsstand Ed. 2.50
23 JBg,V:Superboy 2.50
24 JBg,V:White Rabbit,A:Mongul. . 2.50
25 JBg,A:Real Superman 3.00
26 JBg,A:All Supermen,V:Mongul,
   Cyborg Superman 2.75
27 JBg,A:Superboy,Lex Luthor . . . 2.50
28 JBg(c),A:Steel. 2.50
29 LSi(s),JBg,Spilled Blood#3,
   V:Hi-Tech,Blood Thirst. 2.50
30 LSi(s),JBg,V:Lobo,Vinyl(c) 3.50
30a Newstand Ed. 2.50
31 MBr,A:Guardian 2.50
32 MBr,Bizarro's World#4,
   V:Bizarro 2.50
33 MBr,V:Parasite 2.50
34 JBg,A:Lex Men,Dubbile Men . . . 2.50
35 JBg,Worlds Collide#1,
   I:Fred Bentson 2.50
36 JBf,Worlds Collide,pt.10,V:Rift
   A:Icon 2.50
37 JBg,Zero Hour,A:Batman 2.50
38 Mystery 2.50
39 JBg,Luthor. 2.50
40 . . . . 2.50
41 Locke 2.50

Superman: The Man of Steel #12
© DC Comics, Inc.

42 F:Locke. 2.50
43 V:Deathtrap. 2.50
44 Prologue to Death. 2.50
45 JGb,DJa,Death of Clark Kent,pt.4
   [New Miraweb format begins] . . 2.50
46 JBg,DJa,A:Shadowdragon 2.50
47 O:Bloodsport. 2.50
48 . . . . 2.50
49 Skyhook 2.50
50 JBg,DJa,The Trial of
   Superman, 48pg 4.00
51 JBg,DJa,The Trial of Superman . 2.50
52 JBg,The Trial of Superman. . . . 2.50
53 JBg,DRo,A:Lex Luthor,Contessa 2.50
54 JBg 2.50
55 JBg,DJa, Clark dates Lori
   Lemaris 2.50
56 JBg,DJa, manipulator revealed. . 2.50
57 RSt,JBg,DJa, more twisters . . . 2.50
58 LSi(s),JBg,DJa,A:Supergirl 2.50
59 LSi(s),JBg,DJa,Parasite, Steel . 2.50
60 LSi(s),JBg,DJa,R:Bottled City
   of Kandor. 2.50
61 LSi(s),JBg,DJa,V:Riot 2.50
62 LSi(s),JBg,DJa, Superman
   looses powers, Final Night tie-in 2.50
63 LSi(s),JBg,DJa,Clark is
   kidnapped & revealed identity . . 2.50
64 LSi(s),JBg,DJa,Superman tries to
   restore his powers. 2.50
65 LSi(s),SB,DJa,V:Superman
   Revenge Squad. 2.50
66 LSi(s),JBg,DJa,V:Metallo 2.50
67 LSi(s),JBg,DJa,New powers
   prequel. 3.00
68 LSi(s),JBg,DJa,V:Metallo 3.00
69 KK&LSi(s),SEa,DJa,A:Atom,
   in Kandor. 2.50
70 LSi(s),SEa,DJa,V:Saviour. 2.50
71 LSi(s),SEa,DJa,V:Mainframe,
   Superman Revenge Squad. . . . 2.50
72 LSi(s),SEa,JP,DJa,JBg,Genesis
   V:Mainframe 2.50
73 LSi&MWa(s),SEa,DJa,V:Revenge
   Squad 2.50
74 LSi(s),SEa,DJa,dragon's tooth . . 2.50
75 LSi(s),DJa,JBg,Mr.Mxyzptlk dies
   parody of Superman #75. . . . . 2.50
76 LSi(s),JBb,DJa,V:Mokkari. 2.50
77 . . . . 2.50
78 JBg, Millennium Giants, pt.1
   x-over. 2.50
79 JBg, Millennium Giants. 2.50
80 LSi,JBg,DJa,golden age?,pt.1 . . 2.50
81 LSi,JBg,DJa,golden age?,pt.2 . . 2.50
82 LSi,JBg,DJa,golden age?,pt.3 . . 2.50
83 LSi,SEa,DJa,Dominus 2.50
84 RMz(s),TGb,TP,City of the
   Future, pt.2 x-over. 2.50
85 JBg,DJa,V:Simyan & Mokkari. . . 2.50
86 LSi(s),SEa,DJa,dreams
   of disasters 2.50
87 MSh(s),DoM,DJa,A:Steel,
   Superboy, Supergirl. 2.50
88 MSh(s),DoM,DJa 2.50
89 MSh(s),DoM,V:Dominus 2.50
90 MSh(s),V:Superman's Robot . . . 2.50
91 MSh(s),DoM,paranoia. 2.50
92 TPe(s),TGb,TP,Secret
   origins,concl. 2.50
93 MSh,DoM 2.50
94 RF,SB,Strange Visitor,concl. . . . 2.50
95 MSh,DoM,Fortress of Solitude . . 2.50
96 MSh,DoM, ... 2.50
97 MSh,DoM,F:Eradicator 2.50
98 MSh,DoM,V:Brainiac 13 . . . . . . 2.50
99 MSh,DoM,new armor 2.50
100 MSh,DoM,new Fortress of
   Solitude, 48-pg. 4.00
100a Collectors edition 4.25
101 MSh,DoM,growing sicker 2.50

102 MSh,DoM,Crit.Condition,pt.3 . . 2.50
103 MSh,DoM,A:Supergirl 2.25
104 MSh,DoM,Arkham,pt.3 . . . . . . 2.25
105 MSh,DoM,Superman:Emperor . 2.25
106 MSh,HuR,V:Kosnor,Netkon . . . 2.25
107 MSh,DoM, to Phantom Zone . . 2.25
108 MSh,DoM, from Phantom Zone . 2.25
109 MSh,A:Linear Man 2.25
110 MSh,DoM,A:Star-SpangledKid . 2.25
111 MSh,DoM,Return-Krypton,pt.3 . 2.25
112 MSh,A:Superdog. 2.25
113 MWm,Infestation x-over,pt.3 . . 2.25
114 MSh,DoM,R:Eradicator 2.25
115 MSh,DoM,Metropolis abducted. 2.25
116 MSh,DoM,JMz,All-out War . . . 2.25
117 MSh,DoM,Casualties of War. . 2.25
118 MSh,DoM,F:Spectre 2.25
119 MSh,Joker:Last Laugh,tie-in . . 4.50
120 MSh,V:LexCorp. 2.25
121 TNu,Royal Flush Gang 2.25
122 MSh(s),Entropy Aegis Armor . . 2.25
123 MSh(s),Metropolis Gangs,pt.1 . 2.25
124 MSh(s),Metropolis Gangs,pt.2 . 2.25
125 MSh(s),Metropolis Gangs,pt.3 . 2.25
126 MSh(s),The Pantheon,pt.1 . . . . 2.25
127 MSh(s),The Pantheon,pt.2 . . . . 2.25
128 MSh(s),ReturntoKryptonII,pt.3 . 2.25
129 Bloodsport. 2.25
130 MSh(s),Ending Battle,pt.3 . . . . . 2.25
131 MSh(s),Ending Battle,pt.7 . . . . . 2.25
132 MSh,Parade, A:Mr.Mxyzptlk . . . 2.25
133 Lost Hearts,pt.3 x-over 2.25
134 MSh,40-pg.,final issue 3.00
Ann.#1 Eclipso tie-in,A:Starman . . . 3.00
Ann.#2 Bloodlines#2,I:Edge. 3.00
Ann.#3 MBr,Elseworlds Story 3.50
Ann.#4 Year One Annual 3.50
Ann.#5 Legends o/t Dead Earth . . . 3.50
Ann.#6 Pulp Heroes (Hard Boiled)
   LSi(s),DJa 4.50
Spec.#1,000,000 KK&JOy(s),
   AWi,DJa 3.00
Gallery 1. . . . . 3.50
TPB 7.50
TPB The Man of Steel,Vol.1 . . . . . . 9.95
TPB The Man of Steel,Vol.2 . . . . . . 9.95
TPB The Man of Steel,Vol.3 . . . . . 20.00

SUPERMAN:
THE MAN OF TOMORROW
1995–96
1 TGu,BBr,RSt(s),V:Lex Luthor. . . . 2.50

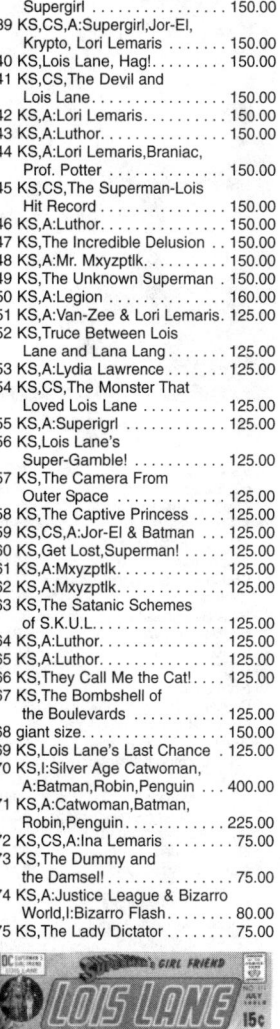

Superman The Man of Tomorrow #11
© DC Comics, Inc.

2 V:Parasite 2.50
3 TG,BBr, The Trial of Superman . . 2.50
4 RSt(s),PR,BBr,A:Shazam 2.50
5 RSt(s),PR,BBr,Wedding of Lex
   Luthor 2.50
6 RSt(s),PR,BBr,Superman V:
   Jackal again 2.50
7 RSt(s),PR,BBr,. 2.50
8 RSt(s),PR,BBr,V:Carbide 2.50
9 RSt(s),PR,BBr,Ma and Pa Kent
   open their album 2.50
10 . . . . 2.50
11 LSi(s),PR,DJa,BBr 2.50
12 LSi(s),PR,DJa, ... 2.50
13 LSi(s),PR,DJa,A:JLA. 2.50
14 LSi(s),PR,DJa,V:Riot 2.50
15 Day of Judgment x-over,48-pg. . 3.00
Spec.#1,000,000 MSh(s),DRo 2.00

SUPERMAN: RED SON
April 2003
1 (of 3) Elseworlds,MMr(s) 5.95
2 MMr(s) 5.95
3 MMr(s),concl. 5.95
TPB series rep. 17.95

SUPERMAN: SECRET
IDENTITY
Jan. 2004
1 (of 4) SI 5.95
2 SI Clark Kent gains powers. 5.95
3 SI 5.95
4 SI concl. 5.95

SUPERMAN'S GIRL
FRIEND, LOIS LANE
1958–74
1 CS,KS 6,000.00
2 CS,KS 1,500.00
3 CS,KS,spanking panel 1,000.00
4 CS,KS 750.00
5 CS,KS 750.00
6 CS,KS 550.00
7 CS,KS 550.00
8 CS,KS 450.00
9 CS,KS, A:Pat Boone 450.00
10 CS,KS 450.00
11 CS,KS 300.00
12 CS,KS 300.00
13 CS,KS 300.00
14 KS,Three Nights in the
   Fortress of Solitude 300.00
15 KS,I:Van-Zee. 300.00
16 KS, Lois' Signal-Watch 300.00
17 KS,CS,A:Brainiac 300.00
18 KS,A:Astounding Man. 300.00
19 KS,Superman of the Past 300.00
20 KS,A:Superman 325.00
21 KS,A:Van-Zee 225.00
22 KS,A:Robin Hood 225.00
23 KS,A:Elastic Lass, Supergirl . 225.00
24 KS,A:Van-Zee, Bizarro 225.00
25 KS,Lois Lane's
   Darkest Secret. 225.00
26 KS,A:Jor-El 225.00
27 KS,CS,A:Bizarro 225.00
28 KS,A:Luthor. 225.00
29 CS,A:Aquaman,Batman,Green
   Arrow 225.00
30 KS,A:Krypto,Aquaman 150.00
31 KS,A:Lori Lemaris 150.00
32 KS,CS,A:Bizarro 150.00
33 KS,CS,A:Phantom Zone,Lori
   Lemaris, Mon-El 150.00
34 KS,A:Luthor,Supergirl 150.00
35 KS,CS,A:Supergirl 150.00
36 KS,CS,Red Kryptonite Story . . 150.00
37 KS,CS,The Forbidden Box . . . 150.00

38 KS,CS,A:Prof.Potter,
   Supergirl 150.00
39 KS,CS,A:Supergirl,Jor-El,
   Krypto, Lori Lemaris 150.00
40 KS,Lois Lane, Hag!. 150.00
41 KS,CS,The Devil and
   Lois Lane. 150.00
42 KS,A:Lori Lemaris. 150.00
43 KS,A:Luthor. 150.00
44 KS,A:Lori Lemaris,Braniac,
   Prof. Potter 150.00
45 KS,CS,The Superman-Lois
   Hit Record 150.00
46 KS,A:Luthor. 150.00
47 KS,The Incredible Delusion . . 150.00
48 KS,A:Mr. Mxyzptlk. 150.00
49 KS,The Unknown Superman . 150.00
50 KS,A:Legion 160.00
51 KS,A:Van-Zee & Lori Lemaris. 125.00
52 KS,Truce Between Lois
   Lane and Lana Lang 125.00
53 KS,A:Lydia Lawrence 125.00
54 KS,CS,The Monster That
   Loved Lois Lane 125.00
55 KS,A:Superigrl 125.00
56 KS,Lois Lane's
   Super-Gamble! 125.00
57 KS,The Camera From
   Outer Space 125.00
58 KS,The Captive Princess 125.00
59 KS,CS,A:Jor-El & Batman . . . 125.00
60 KS,Get Lost,Superman! 125.00
61 KS,A:Mxyzptlk. 125.00
62 KS,A:Mxyzptlk. 125.00
63 KS,The Satanic Schemes
   of S.K.U.L. 125.00
64 KS,A:Luthor. 125.00
65 KS,A:Luthor. 125.00
66 KS,They Call Me the Cat!. . . . 125.00
67 KS,The Bombshell of
   the Boulevards 125.00
68 giant size. 150.00
69 KS,Lois Lane's Last Chance . 125.00
70 KS,I:Silver Age Catwoman,
   A:Batman,Robin,Penguin . . . 400.00
71 KS,A:Catwoman,Batman,
   Robin,Penguin 225.00
72 KS,CS,A:Ina Lemaris 75.00
73 KS,The Dummy and
   the Damsel! 75.00
74 KS,A:Justice League & Bizarro
   World,I:Bizarro Flash. 80.00
75 KS,The Lady Dictator 75.00

Superman's Girl Friend Lois Lane #111
© DC Comics Inc.

Superman's Girl Friend Lois Lane #119
© DC Comics, Inc.

76 KS,A:Hap-El 75.00
77 giant size. 125.00
78 KS,Courtship,Kryptonian Style . 75.00
79 KS,B:NA(c) 75.00
80 KS,Get Out of My Life,
  Superman 75.00
81 KS,No Witnesses in
  Outerspace 75.00
82 GT,A:Brainiac&Justice League . 50.00
83 GT,Witch on Wheels 50.00
84 GT,KS,Who is Lois Lane?. 50.00
85 GT,KS,A:Kandorians. 50.00
86 giant size. 75.00
87 GT,KS,A:Cor-Lar. 50.00
88 GT,KS,Through a Murderer's
  Eyes. 50.00
89 CS,A:Batman & Batman Jr. . . . 55.00
90 GT,A:Dahr-nel 50.00
91 GT,A:Superlass. 50.00
92 GT,A:Superhorse 50.00
93 GT,A:Wonder Woman 50.00
94 GT,KS,A:Jor 50.00
95 giant size. 100.00
96 GT,A:Jor 40.00
97 GT,KS,A:Lori Lemaris,
  Luma Lynai,Lyla Lerrol 40.00
98 GT,A:Phantom Zone 40.00
99 GT,KS,A:Batman. 40.00
100 GT,A:Batman. 40.00
101 GT,KS,The Super-Reckless
  Lois Lane. 40.00
102 GT,KS,When You're Dead,
  You're Dead. 40.00
103 GT,KS,A:Supergirl. 40.00
104 giant size. 75.00
105 RA,I&O:Rose & Thorn 75.00
106 WR,I am Curious Black! 50.00
107 WR,The Snow-Woman Wept . 40.00
108 WR,The Spectre Suitor. 40.00
109 WR,I'll Never Fall
  in Love Again. 40.00
110 WR,Indian Death Charge!. . . . 40.00
111 WR,A:Justice League 40.00
112 WR,KS,A:Lori Lemaris 50.00
113 giant size. 75.00
114 WR,KS,A:Rose & Thorn 40.00
115 WR,A:The Black Racer. 40.00
116 WR,A:Darkseid & Desaad. . . . 40.00
117 WR,S.O.S From Tomorrow! . . 40.00
118 WR,A:Darkseid & Desaad. . . . 40.00
119 WR,A:Darkseid & Lucy Lane . 40.00
120 WR,Who Killed Lucy Lane? . . 40.00
121 WR,A:The Thorn. 40.00
122 WR,A:The Thorn 40.00

123 JRo,Ten Deadly Division
  of the 100 . . . . 40.00
124 JRo,The Hunters. 25.00
125 JRo,Death Rides Wheels!. . . . 25.00
126 JRo,The Brain Busters 25.00
127 JRo,Curse of the Flame 25.00
128 JRo,A:Batman & Aquaman. . . 25.00
129 JRo,Serpent in Paradise 25.00
130 JRo,The Mental Murster 25.00
131 JRo,Superman–Marry Me! . . . 25.00
132 JRo,Zatanna B.U. 25.00
133 JRo,The Lady is a Bomb 25.00
134 JRo,A:Kandor. 25.00
135 JRo,Amazing After-Life
  of Lois Lane. 25.00
136 JRo,A:Wonder Woman 25.00
137 JRo,The Stolen Subway 30.00
Ann.#1 . . . . 325.00
Ann.#2 . . . . 225.00

SUPERMAN:
SILVER BANSHEE
1998
1 (of 2) DIB(s),ALa 2.25
2 DIB(s),ALa, conclusion 2.25

SUPERMAN'S NEMESIS,
LEX LUTHOR
1999
1 (of 4) VS,DJa, ... 2.50
2 VS,DJa. 2.50
3 VS,DJa. 2.50
4 VS,DJa, conclusion 2.50

SUPERMAN'S PAL,
JIMMY OLSEN
1954–74
1 CS,The Boy of 100 Faces! . . 8,500.00
2 CS,The Flying Jimmy Olsen. 2,500.00
3 CS,The Man Who Collected
  Excitement 1,300.00
4 CS,King For A Day! 900.00
5 CS,The Story of Superman's
  Souvenirs. 900.00
6 CS,Kryptonite story 650.00
7 CS,The King of Marbles 650.00
8 CS,Jimmy Olsen, Crooner. . . . 600.00
9 CS,The Missile of Steel 600.00
10 CS,Jungle Jimmy Olsen 600.00
11 CS,TNT.Olsen,The Champ . . . 400.00
12 CS,Invisible Jimmy Olsen. . . . 400.00
13 CS,Jimmy Olsen's
  Super Issue 400.00
14 CS,The Boy Superman 400.00
15 CS,Jimmy Olsen,Speed
  Demon. 400.00
16 CS,The Boy Superman. 400.00
17 CS,J.Olsen as cartoonist 400.00
18 CS,A:Superboy. 400.00
19 CS,Supermam's Kid Brother. . 400.00
20 CS,Merman of Metropolis. . . . 400.00
21 CS,The Wedding of Jimmy
  Olsen. 250.00
22 CS,The Super Brain of
  Jimmy Olsen 250.00
23 CS,The Adventure of
  Private Olsen. 250.00
24 CS,The Gorilla Reporter 250.00
25 CS,The Day There Was
  No Jimmy Olsen 250.00
26 CS,Bird Boy of Metropolis . . . 250.00
27 CS,The Outlaw Jimmy Olsen . 250.00
28 CS,The Boy Who Killed
  Superman 250.00
29 CS,A:Krypto 250.00
30 CS,The Son of Superman 250.00
31 CS,I:Elastic Lad 225.00
32 CS,A:Prof.Potter. 200.00

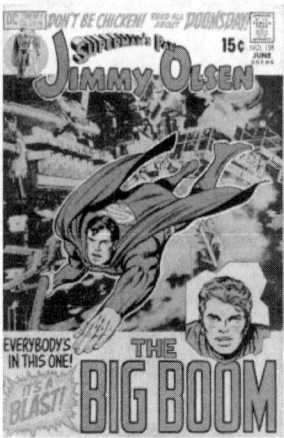

Superman's Pal Jimmy Olsen #138
© DC Comics Inc.

33 CS,Human Flame Thrower. . . 200.00
34 CS,Superman's Pal of Steel . . 200.00
35 CS,Superman's Enemy 200.00
36 CS,I:Lois Lane,O:Jimmy Olsen
  as Superman's Pal 200.00
37 CS,O:Jimmy Olsen's SignalWatch,
  A:Elastic Lad(Jimmy Olsen) . 200.00
38 CS,Olsen's Super-Supper . . . 200.00
39 CS,The Super-Lad of Space. . 200.00
40 CS,A:Supergirl,Hank White
  (Perry White's son) 200.00
41 CS,The Human Octopus. 150.00
42 CS,Jimmy The Genie 150.00
43 WB,CS,Jimmy Olsen's Private
  Monster 150.00
44 CS,Miss Jimmy Olsen. 150.00
45 CS,A:Kandor. 150.00
46 CS,A:Supergirl,Elastic Lad . . 150.00
47 CS,Monsters From Earth!. . . . 150.00
48 CS,I:Superman Emergency
  Squad 150.00
49 CS,A:Congorilla & Congo Bill . 150.00
50 CS,A:Supergirl,Krypto,Bizarro 150.00
51 CS,A:Supergirl 125.00
52 CS,A:Mr. Mxyzptlk,
  Miss Gzptlsnz 125.00
53 CS,A:Kandor,Lori Lemaris,
  Mr.Mxyztlk 125.00
54 CS,A:Elastic Lad. 125.00
55 CS,A:Aquaman,Thor. 125.00
56 KS,Imaginary story 125.00
57 KS,A:Supergirl,Imaginary story100.00
58 CS,C:Batman 100.00
59 CS,A:Titano. 100.00
60 CS,The Fantastic Army of
  General Olsen 100.00
61 CS,Prof. Potter 100.00
62 CS,A:Elastic Lad,Phantom
  Zone 100.00
63 CS,A:Supergirl,Kandor 125.00
64 CS,Jimmy Olsen's
  Super-Romance 100.00
65 CS,A:Miss Gzptlsnz 100.00
66 CS,KS,A:Mr. Mxyzptlk. 100.00
67 CS,The Dummy That Haunted
  Jimmy Olsen 100.00
68 CS,The Helmet of Hate 100.00
69 CS,A:Nightwing,Flamebird . . . 100.00
70 A:Supergirl,Lori Lemaris,
  Element Lad 100.00
71 CS,A:Mr. Mxyzptlk. 75.00
72 CS,A:Legion of Super-Heroes,
  Jimmy Olsen becomes honorary
  member 75.00

Superman's Pal Jimmy Olsen #148
© DC Comics Inc.

73 A:Kandor 75.00
74 CS,A:Mr. Mxyzptlk,Lex Luthor . 70.00
75 CS,A:Supergirl 70.00
76 CS,A:Legion of Super-Heroes . 70.00
77 CS,Jimmy Olsen becomes
    Colossal Boy, A:Titano. 70.00
78 CS,A:Aqualad 70.00
79 CS,The Red-Headed Beetle
    of 1,000 B.C. 70.00
80 CS,A:Bizarro. 70.00
81 CS,KS,A:Lori Lemaris,I&O
    only A:Mighty Eagle. 70.00
82 CS,The Unbeatable Jimmy
    Olsen 70.00
83 CS,A:Kandor. 70.00
84 CS,A:Titano. 70.00
85 CS,C:Legion of Super-Heroes . 75.00
86 CS,A:Congorilla,Braniac 70.00
87 A:Lex Luthor,Brainiac,Legion
    of Super-Villians 75.00
88 C:Legion of Super-Heroes 70.00
89 I:Agent Double-Five,C:John F.
    Kennedy 70.00
90 CS,A:Mr. Mxyzptlk 70.00
91 CS,C:Batman & Robin 70.00
92 JM,A:Batman,Robin,Supergirl. . 70.00
93 The Batman-Superman of
    Earth-X! 70.00
94 O:Insect Queen retold. 70.00
95 Giant 100.00
96 I:Tempus 60.00
97 A:Fortress of Solitude 60.00
98 The Bride of Jungle Jimmy 60.00
99 A:Legion of Super-Heroes 60.00
100 A:Legion of Super-Heroes . . . 75.00
101 A:Jor-El and Lara 40.00
102 Superman's Greatest Double
    Cross! 40.00
103 The Murder of Clark Kent! 40.00
104 Giant 50.00
105 V:Tempus 40.00
106 CS,A:Legion of Super-Heroes 40.00
107 A:Krypto 40.00
108 CS,The Midas of Metropolis . . 40.00
109 A:Lex Luthor 40.00
110 CS,Jimmy Olsen's Blackest
    Deeds! 40.00
111 . . . . 40.00
112 . . . . 40.00
113 V:Magnaman 75.00
114 The Wrong Superman! 40.00
115 A:Aquaman 40.00
116 A:Brainiac 40.00

117 Planet of the Capes 40.00
118 A:Lex Luthor 40.00
119 Nine Lives Like a Cat!. 40.00
120 V:Climate King 40.00
121 . . . . 40.00
122 . . . . 40.00
123 . . . . 40.00
124 . . . . 40.00
125 Superman's Saddest Day. . . . 40.00
126 CS,Riddle of Kryptonite Plus . 40.00
127 CS,Jimmy in Revolutionary
    War. 40.00
128 I:Mark Olsen(Jimmy'sFather) . 40.00
129 MA,A:Mark Olsen 40.00
130 MA,A:Robin,Brainiac. 40.00
131 . . . . 75.00
132 MA,When Olsen Sold out
    Superman 40.00
133 JK,B:New Newsboy Legion,
    I:Morgan Edge 100.00
134 JK,I:Darkseid. 125.00
135 JK,I:New Guardian 75.00
136 JK,O:New Guardian,
    I:Dubbilex. 60.00
137 JK,I:Four Armed Terror 50.00
138 JK,V:Four Armed Terror 50.00
139 JK,A:Don Rickles,I:Ugly
    Mannheim 50.00
140 Rep. Jimmy Olsen #69, #72
    and Superman #158 . . . . 50.00
141 JK,A:Don Rickles,Lightray
    B:Newsboy Legion rep 50.00
142 JK,I:Count Dragorian 50.00
143 JK,V:Count Dragorian. 50.00
144 JK,A Big Thing in a Deep
    Scottish Lake. 50.00
145 JK,Brigadoon 50.00
146 JK,Homo Disastrous. 50.00
147 JK,Superman on New
    Genesis,A:High Father,
    I:Victor Volcanium 50.00
148 JK,V:Victor Volcanium,
    E:Newsboy Legion rep 50.00
149 BO(i),The Unseen Enemy,
    B:Plastic Man rep 50.00
150 BO(i) A Bad Act to Follow 50.00
151 BO(i),A:Green Lantern 25.00
152 MSy,BO,I:Real Morgan Edge . 25.00
153 MSy,Murder in Metropolis. . . . 25.00
154 KS,The Girl Who Was Made
    of Money 25.00
155 KS,Downfall of Judas Olsen . . 25.00
156 KS,Last Jump for
    a Skyjacker 25.00
157 KS,Jimmy as Marco Polo 25.00
158 KS,A:Lena Lawrence
    (Lucy Lane) 25.00
159 KS,Jimmy as Spartacus 25.00
160 KS,A:Lena Lawrence
    (Lucy Lane) 25.00
161 KS,V:Lucy Lane 25.00
162 KS,A:Lex Luthor 25.00
163 KS,Jimmy as Marco Polo 25.00

SUPERMAN:
SAVE THE PLANET
Aug., 1998
1 LSi,SEa,DRo,JP,KN, last
    front page 3.00
1 collector's edition 4.00

SUPERMAN:
THE KANSAS SIGHTING
Nov. 2003
GN #1 F:Jor-El 7.00
GN #2 F:Jor-El 7.00

SUPERMAN,
THE SECRET YEARS
Feb., 1985
1 CS,KS,FM(c) 3.00
2 CS,KS,FM(c) 2.50
3 CS,KS,FM(c) 2.50
4 CS,KS,FM(c), May, 1985. . . . . . 2.50

SUPERMAN VS.
AMAZING SPIDER-MAN
DC/Marvel April, 1976
1 RA/DG,oversized 100.00
1a 2nd printing, signed 175.00

SUPERMAN
VS. PREDATOR
DC/Dark Horse May, 2000
1 (of 3) weakened by virus 5.00
2 . . . . 5.00
3 conclusion 5.00

SUPERMAN/
WONDER WOMAN:
WHOM GODS DESTROY
Elseworlds Oct., 1996
Mini-series
1 CCI(s),DAb, Lois becomes the
    immortal Wonder Woman 5.00
2 CCI(s),DAb, search for Lana
    Lang. 5.00
3 . . . . 5.00
4 CCI(s),DAb, romance of the
    century, concl. 5.00

SUPERMEN OF AMERICA
1999
GN with membership kit. 5.00
GN standard edition. 4.00
1 (of 6) FaN,DBw,. 2.50
2 FaN,DBw,V:Lex Luthor 2.50
3 FaN,DBw,F:Brahma. 2.50
4 FaN,DBw,F:White Lotus 2.50
5 FaN,F:The Loser 2.50
6 FaN,A:Superman,concl. 2.50

SUPER POWERS
1984
[Kenner Action Figures]
1 A:Batman & Joker 5.50
2 A:Batman & Joker 5.50
3 A:Batman & Joker 5.50
4 A:Batman & Joker 5.50
5 JK(c),JK,A:Batman & Joker 5.50
[2nd Series], 1985–86
1 JK,Seeds of Doom. 4.00
2 JK,When Past & Present Meet . . 4.00
3 JK,Time Upon Time 4.00
4 JK,There's No Place Like Rome . 4.00
5 JK,Once Upon a Tomorrow 4.00
6 JK,Darkkseid o/t Moon 4.00
[3rd Series], 1986
1 CI,Threshold 3.50
2 CI,Escape 3.50
3 CI,Machinations. 3.50
4 CI,A World Divided 3.50

SUPER-TEAM FAMILY
1975–78
1 rep. 30.00
2 Creeper/Wildcat. 15.00
3 RE/WW,Flash & Hawkman 15.00
4 . . . . 18.00

5	18.00
6	18.00
7	18.00
8 JSh,Challengers	20.00
9 JSh,Challengers	20.00
10 JSh,Challengers	20.00
11 Supergirl,Flash,Atom.	20.00
12 Green Lantern,Hawkman	20.00
13 Aquaman, Capt. Comet	20.00
14 Wonder Woman,Atom.	20.00
15 Flash & New Gods	22.00

Swamp Thing #1 © DC Comics, Inc.

SWAMP THING
[1st Regular Series]
Oct.–Nov., 1972

1 B:LWn(s),BWr,O:Swamp Thing	200.00
2 BWr,I:Arcane	90.00
3 BWr,I:Patchwork Man	60.00
4 BWr	50.00
5 BWr	50.00
6 BWr	50.00
7 BWr,A:Batman	55.00
8 BWr,Lurker in Tunnel 13	50.00
9 BWr	50.00
10 E:BWr,A:Arcane	50.00
11 thru 24 NR	@20.00
TPB rep.#1-#10,House of Secrets #92, Dark Genesis Saga	20.00

SWAMP THING
1986–96
Previously:
SAGA OF THE SWAMP THING

46 B:AMo(s) cont'd,SBi,JTo,Crisis, A:John Constantine,Phantom Stranger	4.00
47 SBi,Parliment of Trees,Full origin,A:Constantine	4.00
48 SBi,JTo,V:Brujeria, A:Constantine	4.00
49 SBi,AA,A:Constantine,Demon,Ph. Stranger,Spectre,Deadman	4.00
50 SBi,RV,JTo,concl.American Gothic,D:Zatara&Sargon, Double Size	6.00
51 RV,AA,L:Constantine	4.00
52 RV,AA,Arkham Asylum,A:Flor. Man,Lex Luthor,C:Joker, 2-Face,Batman	4.00
53 JTo,V:Batman,Swamp Thing Banished to Space	5.00
54 JTo script,RV,AA,C:Batman	4.00

55 RV,AA,JTo,A:Batman,	4.00
56 RV,AA,My Blue Heaven	4.00
57 RV,AA,A:Adam Strange	4.00
58 RV,AA,A:Adam Strange,GC, Spectre preview	4.00
59 JTo,RV,AA,D:Patchwork Man	4.00

Direct Sales Only

60 JTo,Loving the Alien	4.00
61 RV,AA,All Flesh is Grass G.L.Corps X-over	4.00
62 RV(&script),AA,Wavelength, A:Metron,Darkseid	4.00
63 RV,AA,Loose Ends(reprise)	4.00
64 E:AMo(s),SBi,TY,RV,AA, Return of the Good Gumbo	4.00
65 RV,JTo,A:Constantine	3.50
66 RV,Elemental Energy	3.00
67 RV,V:Solomon Grundy, Hellblazer preview	4.00
68 RV,O:Swamp Thing	3.00
69 RV,O:Swamp Thing	3.00
70 RV,AA,Quest for SwampThing	3.00
71 RV,AA,Fear of Flying	3.00
72 RV,AA,Creation	3.00
73 RV,AA,A:John Constantine	3.50
74 RV,AA,Abbys Secret	3.00
75 RV,AA,Plant Elementals	3.00
76 RV,AA,A:John Constantine	3.50
77 TMd,AA,A:John Constantine	3.50
78 TMd,AA,Phantom Pregnancy	3.00
79 RV,AA,A:Superman,Luthor	3.00
80 RV,AA,V:Aliends	3.00
81 RV,AA,Invasion x-over	3.00
82 RV,AA,A:Sgt.Rock & Easy Co.	3.00
83 RV,AA,A:Enemy Ace	3.00
84 RV,AA,A:Sandman	8.00
85 RV,TY,Time Travel contd.	3.00
86 RV,TY,A:Tomahawk.	3.00
87 RV,TY,Camelot,A:Demon	3.00
88 RV,TY,A:Demon,Golden Gladiator	3.00
89 MM,AA,The Dinosaur Age	3.00
90 BP,AA,Birth of Abbys Child (Tefe)	3.25
91 PB,AA,Abbys Child (New Elemental)	3.00
92 PB,AA,Ghosts of the Bayou	3.00
93 PB,AA,New Power	3.00
94 PB,AA,Ax-Murderer	3.00
95 PB,AA,Toxic Waste Dumpers	3.00
96 PB,AA,Tefes Powers.	3.00
97 PB,AA,Tefe,V:Nergal, A:Arcane	3.00
98 PB,AA,Tefe,in Hell	3.00
99 PB,AA,Tefe,A:Mantago, John Constantine	3.50
100 PB,AA,V:Angels of Eden, (48 pages)	4.00
101 AA,A:Tefe	3.00
102 V:Mantagos Zombies,inc. prev. of Worlds Without End.	3.00
103 Green vs. Grey	3.00
104 Quest for Elementals,pt.1	3.00
105 Quest for Elementals,pt.2	3.00
106 Quest for Elementals,pt.3	3.00
107 Quest for Elementals,pt.4	3.00
108 Quest for Elementals,pt.5	3.00
109 Quest for Elementals,pt.6	3.00
110 TMd,A:Father Tocsin	3.00
111 V:Ghostly Zydeco Musician	3.00
112 TMd,B:Swamp Thing for Governor	3.00
113 E:Swamp Thing for Governor	3.00
114 TMd,Hellblazer	3.25
115 TMd,A:Hellblazer,V:Dark Conrad	3.25
116 From Body of Swamp Thing	3.00
117 JD,The Lord of Misrule, Mardi Gras.	3.00
118 A Childs Garden,A:Matthew the Raven	3.00

119 A:Les Perdu	3.00
120 F:Lady Jane	3.00
121 V:Sunderland Corporation	3.00
122 I:The Needleman	3.00
123 V:The Needleman	3.00
124 In Central America	3.00
125 V:Anton Arcane,20th Anniv.	4.00
126 Mescalito.	3.00
127 Project Proteus #1	3.00
128 Project proteus #2.	3.00

DC/Vertigo, 1993

129 CV(c),B:NyC(s),SEa,KDM(i), Sw.Thing's Deterioration	3.00
130 CV(c),SEa,KDM(i),A:John Constantine,V:Doctor Polygon	3.00
131 CV(c),SEa,KDM(i),I:Swamp Thing's,Doppleganger, F:The Folk	3.50
132 CV(c),SEa,KDM(i), V:Doppleganger.	3.50
133 CV(c),SEa,KDM(i),R:General Sunderland,V:Thunder Petal	3.50
134 CV(c),SEa,KDM(i),Abby Leaves, C:John Constantine	3.50
135 CV(c),SEa,KDM(i),A:J.Constantine, Swamp Thing Lady Jane meld	3.50
136 CV(c),RsB,KDM(i),A:Lady Jane, Dr.Polygon,John Constantine	3.50
137 CV(c),E:NyC(s),RsB,KDM(i), IR:Sunderland is Anton Arcane, A:J.Constantine	3.50
138 CV(c),DiF(s),RGu,KDM,B:Mind Fields	3.50
139 CV(c),DiF(s),RGu,KDM,A:Black Orchid,In Swamp Thing's mind, cont'd fr.Black Orchid #5	3.50
140 B:Bad Gumbo	3.50
140a Platinum Ed.	10.00
141 A:Abigail Arcane	3.00
142 Bad Gumbo#3.	3.00
143 E:Bad Gumbo	3.00
144 In New York City	3.00
145 In Amsterdam	3.00
146 V:Nelson Strong	3.00
147 Hunter	3.00
148 Sargon	3.00
149 Sargon	3.00
150 V:Sargon	3.50
151	3.00
152 River Run,pt.1	3.00
153 River Run	3.00
154 River Run	3.00
155 River Run	3.00
156 PJ,River Run.	3.00
157	3.00

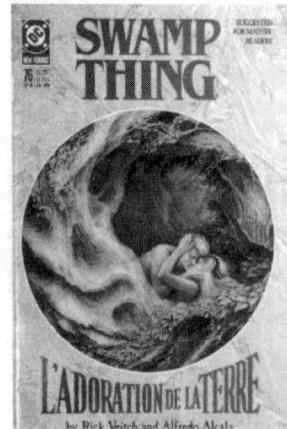

Swamp Thing #76 © DC Comics, Inc.

158 . . . . 3.00
159 Swamp Dog 3.00
160 PhH,KDM,Atmospheres 3.00
161 Atmospheres. 2.50
162 Atmospheres. 2.50
163 Atmospheres. 2.50
164 . . . . 2.50
165 CS,KDM,F:Chester Williams. . . 2.50
166 PhH,KDM,Trial by Fire,pt.1. . . . 2.50
167 PhH,KDM,Trial by Fire,pt.2. . . . 2.50
168 MMr(s),PhH,KDM,Trial,pt.3. . . . 2.50
169 MMr(s),PhH,KDM,Trial,pt.4. . . . 2.50
170 MMr(s),PhH,KDM,Trial,pt.5. . . . 2.50
171 MMr(s),PhH,KDM,Trial by Fire,
    pt.6, last issue 2.50
Ann.#3 AMo(s),Ape issue 4.00
Ann.#4 PB/AA,A:Batman 4.00
Ann.#5 A:BrotherPower Geek 4.00
Ann.#6 Houma. 4.00
Ann.#7 CV(c),NyC(s),MBu(i),Childrens
    Crusade,F:Tefe,A:Maxine,BU:
    Beautyand the Beast. 7.00

SWAMP THING
DC/Vertigo, March, 2000
1 JRu,F:Tefe Holland 4.00
2 JRu,new secrets 3.00
3 JRu, ... 3.00
4 Killing Time,pt.1 . . . . 3.00
5 Killing Time,pt.2 . . . . 3.00
6 Killing Time,pt.3 . . . . 3.00
7 RM 3.00
8 RM 3.00
9 RM 3.00
10 RM 3.00
11 RM,Red Harvest, pt.1 . . . . 3.00
12 RM,Red Harvest, pt.2 . . . . 3.00
13 RM,Red Harvest, pt.3 . . . . 3.00
14 RM,Red Harvest, pt.4 . . . . 3.00
15 RM,Red Harvest, pt.5 . . . . 3.00
16 RM,Red Harvest, pt.6 . . . . 3.00
17 Red Harvest, pt.7 . . . . 3.00
18 R:Original Swamp Thing. 3.00
19 The Tree of Knowledge 3.00
20 final issue 3.00
Secret Files #1, 64-pg. 5.00
TPB The Curse, AMo(s). 20.00
TPB A Murder of Crows 20.00
TPB Earth to Earth. 18.00
TPB Dark Genesis (2003) 20.00
TPB Reunion (2003) 20.00

SWAMP THING
DC/Vertigo March 2004
1 classic Swamp Thing. 3.00
2 Bad Seed,pt.2 . . . . 3.00
3 Bad Seed,pt.3 . . . . 3.00
4 Bad Seed,pt.4 . . . . 3.00
5 Bad Seed,pt.5,40-pg. 3.00
6 Bad Seed,pt.6 . . . . 3.00
7 RCo,Missing Links,pt.1 . . . . 3.00
8 RCo,Missing Links,pt.2 . . . . 3.00
TPB Swamp Thing: Regenesis . . . 18.00

SWEATSHOP
April 2003
1 F:Mel Bowling 3.00
2 A Traitor in Our Midst. 3.00
3 Peerless Penciller 3.00
4 Freddy Ferret. 3.00
5 comic-book convention 3.00
6 I Have No Son 3.00

SWORD OF SORCERY
Feb.–March, 1973
1 MK(c),HC. 25.00
2 BWv,NA,Hc 30.00
3 BWv,HC,MK,WS 25.00

4 HC,WS. 10.00
5 Nov.–Dec., 1973 . . . . 10.50

SWORD OF THE ATOM
Sept., 1983
1 GK 3.00
2 thru 4 GK . . . . @3.00
Spec.#1 GK 2.50
Spec.#2 GK 2.50
Spec.#3 PB 2.50

TAILGUNNER JO
Sept., 1988
1 . . . . 2.50
2 thru 6 . . . . @2.50

TAKION
1996
1 PuK,AaL,Josh Sanders
    becomes Takion. 2.50
2 thru 4 . . . . @2.50
5 PuK,AaL,Adventures of Source
    Elemental, cont. 2.50
6 PuK,AaL,Final Night tie-in 2.50
7 PuK,AaL,Arzaz trains Takion,
    final issue 2.50

TALES OF THE GREEN
LANTERN CORPS
May, 1981
1 JSon,FMc,O:Green Lantern. 2.50
2 JSon,FMc. 2.50
3 JSon,FMc. 2.50

TALES OF THE LEGION
OF SUPER HEROES
Aug., 1984
(Previously:
Legion of Super Heroes)
314 KG,V:Ontiir 2.50
315 KG(i),V:Dark Circle 2.50
316 KG(i),O:White Witch 2.50
317 KG(i),V:Dream Demon 2.50
318 KG(i),V:Persuader. 2.50
319 KG(i),V:Persuader,
    A:Superboy 2.50
320 DJu,V:Magpie 2.50
321 DJu,Exile,V:Kol 2.50
322 DJu,Exile,V:Kol 2.50

Tales of the Legion of Super-Heroes
#334 © DC Comics Inc.

323 DJu,Exile,V:Kol 2.50
324 DJu,EC,V:Dev-Em 2.50
325 DJu,V:Dark Circle 2.50
326 thru 354 rep. of Legion of Super
    Heroes, 3rd Series #1–#29 . . . . 2.50
Ann.#4 rep. Baxter Ann.#1. . . . . . . 2.50
Ann.#5 rep. Baxter Ann.#2. . . . . . . 2.50

TALES OF THE
NEW TEEN TITANS
June, 1982
1 GP, O:Cyborg. 3.50
2 GP, O:Raven 3.50
3 GD, O:Changling 3.50
4 GP/EC,O:Starfire 3.50

TALES OF THE
TEEN TITANS
(see NEW TEEN TITANS)

TALES OF THE
UNEXPECTED
1956–68
1 The Out-Of-The-World Club . 1,700.00
2 . . . . 750.00
3 . . . . 500.00
4 Seven Steps to the Unknown . 500.00
5 . . . . 500.00
6 The Girl in the Bottle 400.00
7 NC(c),Pen That Never Lied. . . 400.00
8 . . . . 400.00
9 LSt(c),The Amazing Cube 400.00
10 MMe(c),The Strangest Show
    On Earth 400.00
11 LSt(c),Who Am I? 250.00
12 JK,Four Threads of Doom . . . 350.00
13 JK(c),Weapons of Destiny . . . 350.00
14 SMo(c),The Forbidden Game . 250.00
15 JK,MMe,Three Wishes
    to Doom. 350.00
16 JK,The Magic Hammer 350.00
17 JK,Who Is Mr. Ashtar? 350.00
18 JK(c),MMe,A Man Without A
    World 350.00
19 NC,Man From Two Worlds . . . 325.00
20 NC(c),The Earth Gladiator . . . 325.00
21 JK,The Living Phantoms. 325.00
22 JK(c),The Man From Robot
    Island. 325.00
23 JK,The Invitation From Mars! . 325.00
24 LC,The Secret Of Planetoid
    Zero! 325.00
25 The Sorcerer's Asteroid! 225.00
26 MMe,The Frozem City 225.00
27 MMe,The Prison In Space . . . 225.00
28 The Melting Planet 225.00
29 The Phantom Raider. 225.00
30 The Jinxed Planet. 225.00
31 RH,Keep Off Our Planet 200.00
32 Great Space Cruise Mystery. . 200.00
33 The Man Of 1,000 Planets . . . 200.00
34 Ambush In Outer Space 200.00
35 MMe,I was a Space Refugee . 200.00
36 The Curse Of The
    Galactic Goodess 200.00
37 The Secret Prisoners
    Of Planet 13 . . . . 200.00
38 The Stunt Man Of Space 200.00
39 The Creatures From The
    Space Globe 200.00
40 B:Space Ranger,The Last
    Days Of Planet Mars! 1,600.00
41 SMo(c),The Destroyers From
    The Stars! 550.00
42 The Secret Of The
    Martian Helmet 550.00
43 The Riddle Of The Burning
    Treasures,I:Space Ranger . 1,200.00

DC COMICS

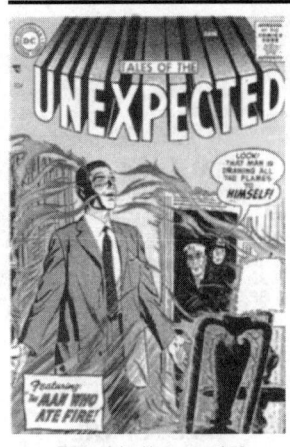

Tales of the Unexpected #9
© DC Comics, Inc.

44 DD&SMo(c),The Menace Of
The Indian Aliens.......... 375.00
45 DD&SMo(c),The Sheriff
From Jupiter 375.00
46 DD&SMo(c),The
Duplicate Doom! 375.00
47 DD(c),The Man Who Stole
The Solar System 275.00
48 Bring 'Em Back Alive-
From Space 275.00
49 RH,The Fantastic Lunar-Land 275.00
50 MA,King Barney The Ape 275.00
51 Planet Earth For Sale 275.00
52 Prisoner On Pluto 275.00
53 InterplanetaryTroubleShooter . 275.00
54 The Ugly Sleeper Of Klanth,
Dinosaur 275.00
55 The Interplanetary
Creature Trainer 275.00
56 B:Spaceman At Work,Invaders
From Earth 275.00
57 The Jungle Beasts Of Jupiter . 275.00
58 The Boss Of The
Saturnian Legion 275.00
59 The Man Who Won A World . . 275.00
60 School For Space Sleuths ... 275.00
61 The Mystery Of The
Mythical Monsters 225.00
62 The Menace Of The Red
Snow Crystals 225.00
63 Death To Planet Earth 225.00
64 Boy Usurper Of Planet Zonn . 225.00
65 The Creature That
Couldn't Exist 225.00
66 MMe,Trap Of The Space
Convict. 225.00
67 The Giant That
Devoured A Village 225.00
68 Braggart From Planet Brax. . . 125.00
69 Doom On Holiday Asteroid . . . 125.00
70 The Hermit Of Planetoid X . . . 125.00
71 Manhunt In Galaxy G-2! 125.00
72 The Creature Of 1,000 Dooms 125.00
73 The Convict Defenders
Of Space!. 125.00
74 Prison Camp On Asteroid X-3! 125.00
75 The Hobo Jungle Of Space . . 125.00
76 The Warrior Of Two Worlds!. . 125.00
77 Dateline-Outer Space 125.00
78 The Siren Of Space 125.00
79 Big Show On Planet Earth!. . . 125.00
80 The Creature Tamer!. 125.00
81 His Alien Master!. 125.00
82 Give Us Back Our Earth!,
E:Space Ranger 125.00

83 DD&SMo(c),The Anti-Hex
Merchant!. 90.00
84 DD&SMo(c),The Menace Of
The 50-Fathom Men 90.00
85 JkS(c),The Man Who Stole My
Powers,B:Green Glob 90.00
86 DD&SMo(c),They'll Never
Take Me Alive! 75.00
87 JkS(c),The Manhunt Through
Two Worlds 75.00
88 DD&SMo(c),GK,The Fear
Master 75.00
89 DD,SMo(c),Nightmare on Mars 75.00
90 JkS(c),The Hero Of 5,000 BC. . 75.00
91 JkS(c),The Prophetic Mirages,
I:Automan 90.00
92 The Man Who Dared To Die! . . 75.00
93 JkS(c),Prisoners Of Hate
Island 75.00
94 The Monster Mayor - USA 75.00
95 The Secret Of Chameleo-Man . 75.00
96 Wanted For Murder...1966...
6966. .... 75.00
97 One Month To Die. 75.00
98 Half-Man/Half Machine 75.00
99 JkS(c),Nuclear Super-Hero! . . . 75.00
100 Judy Blonde, Secret Agent! . . 90.00
101 The Man in The Liquid Mask!. 60.00
102 Bang!Bang! You're Dead 60.00
103 JA,ABC To Disaster 60.00
104 NA(c),Master Of The
Voodoo Machine 60.00
Becomes:

UNEXPECTED, THE
1968–82
105 The Night I Watched
Myself Die 75.00
106 B:Johnny Peril,The Doorway
Into Time 50.00
107 MD,JkS(c),The Whip Of Fear! 50.00
108 JkS(c),Journey To
A Nightmare. 50.00
109 JkS(c),Baptism By Starfire!. . . 50.00
110 NA(c),Death Town, U.S.A.! . . . 50.00
111 NC(c),Mission Into Eternity . . . 50.00
112 NA(c),The Brain Robbers!. . . . 50.00
113 NA(c),The Shriek Of
Vengeance. 50.00
114 NA(c),My Self-My Enemy!. . . . 40.00
115 BWr,NA(c),Diary Of
A Madman 40.00
116 NC(c),Express Train
To Nowhere! 35.00
117 NC(c),Midnight Summons
The Executioner! 30.00
118 NA(c),A:Judge Gallows,Play
A Tune For Treachery 30.00
119 BWr,NC(c),Mirror,Mirror
On The Wall. 55.00
120 NC(c),Rambeau's Revenge . . 35.00
121 BWr,NA(c),Daddy's
Gone-A-Hunting. 35.00
122 WW,DG(c),The Phantom
Of The Woodstock Festival . . . 35.00
123 NC(c),Death Watch! 35.00
124 NA(c),These Walls Shall
Be Your Grave............. 35.00
125 NC(c),Screech Of Guilt! 35.00
126 ATh,NC(c),You Are Cordially
Invited To Die! 35.00
127 GT,JK,ATh,NC(c),Follow The
Piper To Your Grave 35.00
128 DW,BWr,NC(c),Where Only
The Dead Are Free!. 50.00
129 NC(c),Farewell To A
Fading Star 35.00
130 NC(c),One False Step 35.00
131 NC(c),Run For Your Death! . . 35.00
132 MD,GT,NC(c),The Edge Of
Madness 40.00

133 WW,JkS(c),A:Judge Gallows,
Agnes Doesn't Haunt Here
Anymore!. 35.00
134 GT,NC(c),The Restless Dead . 35.00
135 NC(c),Death, Come
Walk With Me! 35.00
136 SMo,GT,NC(c),An Incident
of Violence. 35.00
137 WW,NC(c),Dark Vengeance! . . 20.00
138 WW,NC(c),Strange Secret of
the Huan Shan Idol 25.00
139 GT,NC(c),The 2 Brains of
Beast Bracken! 20.00
140 JkS(c),The Anatomy of Hate. . 20.00
141 NC(c),Just What Did Eric
See? 20.00
142 NC(c),Let The Dead Sleep! . . 20.00
143 NC(c),Fear is a Nameless
Voice 20.00
144 NC(c),The Dark Pit of
Dr. Hanley 20.00
145 NC(c),Grave of Glass 20.00
146 NC(c),The Monstrosity!. 20.00
147 NC(c),The Daughter of
Dr. Jekyll 20.00
148 NC(c),Baby Wants Me Dead! . 20.00
149 NC(c),To Wake the Dead 20.00
150 NC(c),No One Escapes From
Gallows Island 20.00
151 NC(c),Sorry, I'm Not Ready
To Die! 20.00
152 GT,NC(c),Death Wears Many
Faces. 20.00
153 NC(c),Who's That Sleeping
In My Grave?. 20.00
154 NC(c),Murder By Madness . . . 20.00
155 NC(c),Non-Stop Journey
Into Fear 20.00
156 NC(c),A Lunatic Is Loose
Among Us!. 20.00
157 NC(c),The House of
the Executioner 50.00
158 NC(c),Reserved for Madmen
Only. 50.00
159 NC(c),A Cry in the Night 50.00
160 NC(c),Death of an Exorcist. . . 50.00
161 BWr,NC(c),Has Anyone
Seen My Killer............. 50.00
162 JK,NC(c),I'll Bug You
To Your Grave 50.00
163 DD,LD(c),Room For Dying . . . 15.00
164 House of the Sinister Sands. . 15.00
165 LD(c),Slayride in July 15.00
166 LD(c),The Evil Eyes of Night . 15.00
167 LD(c),Scared Stiff 15.00
168 LD(c),Freak Accident 15.00
169 LD(c),What Can Be Worse
Than Dying? 15.00
170 LD(c),Flee To Your Grave 15.00
171 LD(c),I.O.U. One Corpse 15.00
172 LD(c),Strangler in Paradise . . 15.00
173 LD(c),What Scared Sally? . . . 15.00
174 LD(c),Gauntlet of Fear 15.00
175 LD(c),The Haunted Mountain . 15.00
176 JkS(c),Having A
Wonderful Crime 15.00
177 ECh(c),Reward for the Wicked 15.00
178 LD(c),Fit To Kill! 15.00
179 LD(c),My Son, The Mortician . 15.00
180 GT,LD(c),The Loathsome
Lodger of Nightmare Inn 18.00
181 LD(c),Hum of the Haunted . . . 15.00
182 LD(c),Sorry, This Coffin
is Occupied 15.00
183 LD(c),The Dead Don't
Always Die. 15.00
184 LD(c),Wheel of Misfortune!. . . 15.00
185 LD(c),Monsters from a
Thousand Fathoms 15.00
186 LD(c),To Catch a Corpse . . . 15.00
187 LD(c),Mangled in Madness. . . 15.00

188 LD(c),Verdict From The Grave 15.00
189 SD,LD(c),Escape From The
Grave.................... 16.00
190 LD(c),The Jigsaw Corpse 16.00
191 MR,JO(c),Night of the Voodoo
Curse................... 18.00
192 LD(c),A Killer Cold & Clammy. 15.00
193 DW,LD(c),Don't Monkey the
Murder.................. 15.00
194 LD(c),Have I Got a Ghoul
For You 15.00
195 JCr,LD(c),Whose Face is at
My Window 15.00
196 LD(c),The Fear of Number 13 10.00
197 LD(c),Last Laugh of a Corpse 10.00
198 JSn(c),Rage of the
Phantom Brain............ 10.00
199 LD(c),Dracula's Daughter 10.00
200 GT,RA&DG(c),A:Johnny Peril,
House on the Edge of Eternity 11.00
201 Do Unto Others............. 10.00
202 JO,LD(c),Death Trap........ 10.00
203 MK(c),Hang Down Your
Head, Joe Mundy 10.00
204 DN,JKu(c),Twinkle, Twinkle
Little Star................ 10.00
205 JkS,A:Johnny Peril,The Second
Possession of Angela Lake... 10.00
206 JkS,A:Johnny Peril,The
Ultimate Assassin 10.00
207 JkS,A:Johnny Peril,Secret of
the Second Star........... 10.00
208 JkS,A:Johnny Peril,Factory
of Fear 10.00
209 JkS,Game for the Ghastly ... 10.00
210 Vampire of the Apes,Time
Warp 10.00
211 A:Johnny Peril,The Temple
of the 7 Stars............. 10.00
212 JkS,MK(c),A:Johnny Peril,The
Adventure of the Angel's Smile 10.00
213 A:Johnny Peril,The Woman
Who Died Forever......... 10.00
214 JKu(c),Slaughterhouse Arena. 10.00
215 JKu(c),Is Someone
Stalking Sandra 10.00
216 GP,JKu(c),Samurai Nightmare 10.00
217 ShM,DSp,EC(c),Dear Senator 10.00
218 KG,ECh&DG(c),I'll Remember
You Yesterday 10.00
219 JKu(c),A Wild Tale.......... 10.00
220 ShM,JKu(c),The Strange
Guide................... 10.00
221 SD,ShM,JKu(c),Em the
Energy Monster........... 10.00
222 KG,SD(c).................. 10.00

TALOS OF THE
WILDERNESS SEA
Aug., 1987
1-shot GK 2.25

TANGENT COMICS
(All Oct., 1997)
The Atom #1 DJu,PR,V:Fatal Five.. 3.00
The Flash #1, TDz,GFr,CaS 3.00
Doom Patrol #1 DJu,SCh, ... 3.00
Green Lantern #1 JeR,JWi,MGy ... 3.00
The Joker #1 KK,MHy,.......... 3.00
Metal Men #1 MRz,MkK 3.00
Nightwing #1 JOs,JD 3.00
Sea Devils #1 KBk,VGi,TP 3.00
The Secret Six #1 CDi,TG, ... 3.00

TANGENT '98
(All June, 1998)
The Batman #1 DJu,KJ 2.25
JLA #1 DJu,DBk,V:UltraHumanites . 2.25
Joker's Wild #1 KK 2.25

Tangent: The Joker #1
© DC Comics, Inc.

Nightwing: Night Force #1 JOs 2.25
Powergirl #1 RMz 2.25
The Superman #1 Harvey Dent.... 2.25
Tales of the Green Lantern #1 ..... 2.25
The Trials of the Flash #1,
V:Plastic Man................ 2.25
Wonder Woman #1 PDa,......... 2.25

TANK GIRL
1995
1 Movie Adaptation 6.00

TANK GIRL:
APOCALYPSE
1995–96
1 AIG,BBo(c) 3.00
2 AIG,BBo(c)Tank Girl Pregnant ... 3.00
3 AIG,BBo(c) 3.00
4 AIG, finale.................. 3.00

TANK GIRL:
THE ODYSSEY
DC/Vertigo, 1995
1 New Limited Series 3.00
2 BBo(c),Land of Milk & Honey ... 3.00
3 I:The Sirens 3.00

TARZAN
April, 1972
(Prev. published by Gold Key)
207 JKu,O:Tarzan,pt.1 .... 75.00
208 thru 210 JKu,O:Tarzan,pt.2–4. 30.00
211 thru 229 .... @20.00
230 RH...................... 40.00
231 thru 235 .... @38.00
236 and 237 .... @15.00
238 giant-size................ 25.00
239 thru 258 Feb., 1977....... @15.00

TARZAN FAMILY
Nov.–Dec., 1975
(Prev. published by Korak, Son of Tarzan)
60 B:Korak................... 20.00
61 thru 66 Nov.–Dec.,1976 .... @15.00

TATTERED BANNERS
1998
1 (of 4) AIG(s),MMc 3.00
2 AIG&KG(s),MMc 3.00

3 AIG(s),MMc 3.00
4 AIG(s),MMc, conclusion........ 3.00

TEAM TITANS
1992–94
1 KM,Total Chaos#3,A:New Titans,
Deathstroke,V:Lord Chaos,
BU:KGa,Killowat 4.00
1a BU:AV(i),Mirage............ 2.50
1b BU:MN,GP,Nightrider......... 2.50
1c BU:AH,Redwing............. 2.50
1d BU:GP(i),Terra............. 2.50
2 KM,Total Chaos#6,A:New
Titans, V:Chaos,C:Battalion.... 2.50
3 KM,Total Chaos#9,V:Lord
Chaos, A:New Titans......... 2.50
4 KM,Titans Sell-Out#4,
J:Battalion, Troia 2.50
5 KM,A:Battalion.............. 2.50
6 ANi,A:Battalion.............. 2.50
7 PJ,I:Nightwing of 2001........ 2.50
8 PJ,A:Raven 2.50
9 PJ,V:Bloodwing 2.50
10 PJ,V:Vampiric Creatures...... 2.50
11 PJ,F:Battalion 2.50
12 PJ,F:Battalion 2.50
13 PJ,New Direction 2.50
14 PJ,V:Clock King,Chronos,Calander
Man,Time Commander 2.50
15 PJ 2.50
16 PJ,F:Nightrider............. 2.50
17 PJ,A:Deathwing 2.50
18 IR:Leader 2.50
19 V:Leader 2.50
20 PJ,V:Lazarium............. 2.50
21 PJ,V:US Government 2.50
22 PJ,A:Chimera 2.50
23 PJ,I:Warhawk(Redwing) 2.50
24 PJ,Zero Hour,R.Kole,last issue. . 2.50
Ann.#1 I:Chimera............. 3.50
Ann.#2 PJ,Elseworlds Story...... 3.75

TEEN BEAT
Nov.–Dec., 1967
1 Monkees photo 125.00
Becomes:

TEEN BEAM
2 Monkees 125.00

TEEN TITANS
[1st Series]
Jan., 1966
1 NC,Titans join Peace Corps .. 400.00
2 NC,I:Garn Akaru 175.00
3 NC,I:Ding Dong Daddy 125.00
4 NC,A:Speedy.............. 125.00
5 NC,I:Ant.................. 125.00
6 NC,A:Beast Boy............ 100.00
7 NC,I:Mad Mod 100.00
8 IN/JAb,I:Titans Copter 100.00
9 NC,A:Teen Titan Sweatshirts . 100.00
10 NC,I:Bat-Bike 100.00
11 IN/NC A:Speedy 75.00
12 NC,in Spaceville 100.00
13 NC,Christmas story......... 75.00
14 NC,I:Gargoyle............. 75.00
15 NC,I:Capt. Rumble 75.00
16 NC,I:Dimension X 75.00
17 NC,A:Mad Mod 75.00
18 NC,1:Starfire (Russian)...... 75.00
19 GK,WW,J:Speedy 75.00
20 NA,NC J:Joshua 100.00
21 NA,NC,A:Hawk,Dove 100.00
22 NA,NC,O:Wondergirl........ 100.00
23 GK,NC,N:Wondergirl........ 50.00
24 GK,NC................... 50.00
25 NC,I:Lilith,A:J.L.A 50.00
26 NC,I:Mal 50.00

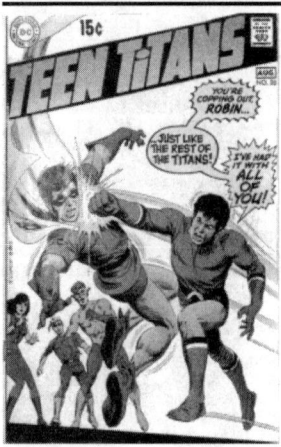

Teen Titans #28 © DC Comics, Inc.

27 NC	50.00
28 NC,A:Ocean Master	50.00
29 NC,A:Ocean Master	50.00
30 NC,A:Aquagirl	50.00
31 NC,GT,A:Hawk,Dove	50.00
32 NC,I:Gnarrk	25.00
33 GT,NS,A:Gnarrk	25.00
34 GT,NC	25.00
35 GT,NC,O:Mal.	25.00
36 GT,NC,JAp,V:Hunchback	25.00
37 GT,NC	25.00
38 GT,NC	25.00
39 GT,NC,Rep.Hawk & Dove.	25.00
40 NC,A:Aqualad	25.00
41 NC,DC,Lilith Mystery	25.00
42 NC.	25.00
43 NC,Inherit the Howling Night	25.00
44 C:Flash	25.00
45 IN,V:Fiddler	25.00
46 IN,A:Fiddler	25.00
47 C:Two-Face	15.00
48 I:Bumblebee,Harlequin, A:Two-Face	25.00
49 R:Mal As Guardian	15.00
50 DH,I:Teen Titans West	20.00
51 DH,A:Teen Titans West.	15.00
52 DH,A:Teen Titans West.	15.00
53 O:Teen Titans, A:JLA	15.00

TEEN TITANS, THE
Aug., 1996

1 DJu(s),GP,Titan's Children, pt.1 (of 3)	5.00
2 DJu(s),GP,Titan's Children, pt.2,V:Prysm	4.00
3 DJu(s),GP,Titan's Children, pt.3	4.00
4 DJu(s),GP,Coming Out,pt.1, A:Robin	4.00
5 DJu(s),GP,Coming Out,pt.2	3.00
6 DJu(s),DJu,GP,F:Risk	3.00
7 DJu(s),DJu,GP,The Atom quits team.	3.00
8 DJu(s),DJu,GP,J:Atom,V:Dark Nemesis.	3.00
9 DJu(s),DJu,GP,Lost World of Skartaris, pt.1	3.00
10 DJu(s),DJu,GP,Lost World of Skartaris, pt.2	3.00
11 DJu(s),DJu,GP,Lost World of Skartaris, concl.,A:Warlord,	3.00
12 DJu(s),DJu,GP,Original Titans, pt.1 (of 4) 48pg	4.00

13 DJu,GP,Original Titans, pt.2 Genesis tie-in	3.00
14 DJu,GP,Original Titans, pt.3	3.00
15 DJu,GP,Original Titans, pt.4	3.00
16 DJu,GP,aftermath	3.00
17 DJu,PJ,team reunites	3.00
18 DJu,PR	3.00
19 DJu,PJ,Millennium Giants, A:Superman Red.	3.00
20 DJu, night with the Titans	3.00
21 DJu,Titans Hunt,pt.1	3.00
22 DJu,Titans Hunt,pt.2	3.00
23 DJu,Titans Hunt,pt.3	3.00
24 DJu,Titans Hunt,pt.4	3.00
Ann.#1 Pulp Heroes (High-Adventure)	4.50
Ann.#1 (1967) 80-page, rep.	5.00

TEEN TITANS
July 2003

1 MMK	8.00
1a 2nd printing	3.50
2 MMK,Cyborg	2.50
3 MMK,	2.50
4 MMK,disobey order	2.50
5 MMk,Infighting	2.50
6 MMk,	2.50
7 MMk,F:Superman	2.50
8 TG,F:Raven	2.50
9 Raven Rising,pt.1	2.50
10 Raven Rising,pt.2	2.50
11 Raven Rising,pt.3	2.50
12 Raven Rising,pt.4	2.50
13 Raven Rising,pt.5	2.50
14 Beast Boys and Girls,pt.1	2.50
15 Beast Boys and Girls,pt.2	2.50
16 MMk,Lost to the Legion,pt.1	2.50
17 MMk,Titans Tomorrow,pt.1	2.50
TPB Family Lost	10.00
TPB A Kid's Game	10.00
Spec. Swingin' Elseworlds Spec.	6.00
Spec. Teen Titans/Legion.	3.50
Spec. Teen Titans Outsiders, Secret Files	6.00

TEEN TITANS GO!
Nov. 2003

1 F:Robin,Cyborg,Beast Boy	2.50
2 thru 12	@2.25
TPB Digest No. 1	7.00
TPB Digest No. 2	7.00

TEEN TITANS SPOTLIGHT
Aug., 1986

1 DCw,DG,Starfire Apartheid.	4.00
2 DCw,DG,Starfire Apartheid#2.	3.00
3 RA,Jericho	3.00
4 RA,Jericho	3.00
5 RA,Jericho	3.00
6 RA,Jericho	3.00
7 JG,Hawk.	4.00
8 JG,Hawk.	3.00
9 Changeling.	3.00
10 EL,Aqualad And Mento.	3.00
11 JO,Brotherhood of Evil	3.00
12 EC,Wondergirl.	3.00
13 Cyborg	3.00
14 1st Nightwing/BatmanTeam-up.	4.00
15 EL,Omega Men.	3.00
16 Thunder And Lightning	3.00
17 DH,Magennta	3.00
18 ATi,Aqualad,A:Aquaman	3.00
19 Starfire,A:Harbinger,Millennium X-over	3.00
20 RT(i),Cyborg	3.00
21 DSp,Flashback sty w/orig.Teen Titans.	3.00

Teen Titans Spotlight #10 © DC Comics, Inc.

TEMPEST
Mini-series Sept., 1996

1 (of 4) from Aquaman	2.25
2 new costume	2.25
3 O:Tempest	2.25
4 finale	2.25

TEMPUS FUGITIVE
1990

1 KSy,Time Travel,I:Ray 27	6.00
2 KSy,Viet Nam.	6.00
3 KSy,World War I.	6.00
4 KSy,final issue	6.00

TERMINAL CITY
DC/Vertigo, 1996–97

1 thru 3 DMt(s),MLr,	@2.50
4 DMt(s),MLr,I:Kid Gloves.	2.50
5 DMt(s),MLr,Missing link on the loose	2.50
6 DMt(s),MLr,	2.50
7 DMt(s),MLr,A:Lady in Red	2.50
8 DMt(s),MLr,	2.50
9 (of 9) DMt(s),MLr,finale	2.50
TPB rep. mini-series	20.00

TERMINAL CITY: AERIAL GRAFFITI
DC/Vertigo, Sept., 1997

1 (of 5) DMt,MLr,MCo(c)	2.50
2 DMt,MLr,MCo(c),F:Cosmo Quinn	2.50
3 DMt,MLr,MCo(c),	2.50
4 DMt,MLr,MCo(c)	2.50

3-D BATMAN
1953, 1966

1 rep.Batman #42 & #48	1,500.00
1a A:Tommy Tomorrow (1966)	500.00

THRILLER
Nov., 1983

1 TVE	2.25
2 TVE,O:Thriller	2.25
3 TVE	2.25
4 TVE	2.25
5 TVE,DG,Elvis satire	2.25
6 TVE,Elvis satire	2.25
7 thru 10 TVE	@2.25
11 & 12 AN	@2.25

THRILLING COMICS
1999
1 CDi(s),RH,F:Hawkman &
Wildcat. 2.25

THRILLKILLER
Elseworlds 1997
1 HC(s),DIB,F:Robin and Batgirl. . . 3.50
2 HC(s),DIB, ... 3.00
3 HC(s),DIB,conl. 3.00

THRILLKILLERS '62
Feb., 1998
GN HC,DIB. 5.00

TIMBER WOLF
1992–93
1 AG(i),V:Thrust 2.25
2 V:Captain Flag. 2.25
3 AG(i),V:Creeper 2.25
4 AG(i),V:Captain Flag 2.25
5 AG(i),V:Dominators,Capt.Flag . . . 2.25

TIME BREAKERS
DC/Helix, 1997
1 (of 5) RaP(s),CWn,time
paradoxes created. 2.50
2 RaP(s),CWn, ... 2.50
3 RaP(s),CWn,expedition to 20th
century England 2.50
4 RaP(s),CWn,Angela travels back
in time 2.50
5 RaP(s),CWn,final issue 2.50

TIME MASTERS
Feb., 1990
1 ATi,O:Rip Hunter,A:JLA 2.50
2 ATi,A:Superman 2.25
3 ATi,A:Jonah Hex, Cave Carson. . 2.25
4 thru 8 ATi, ... @2.25

TIME WARP
Oct.–Nov., 1979
1 JAp,RB,SD,MK(c),DN,TS 18.00
2 DN,JO,TS,HC,SD,MK(c),GK . . . 12.00
3 DN,SD,MK(c),TS 12.00
4 MN,SD,MK(c),DN 12.00
5 DN,MK(c),July, 1980 . . . . 10.00

TITANS
1999
1 MBu, new team, two covers 3.50
2 MBu,A:Superman 3.00
3 MBu 3.00
4 MBu,V:Goth 3.00
5 MBu,A:Siren. 3.00
6 MBu,A:Green Lantern 3.00
7 MBu,Velocity 10, pt.1 . . . . 3.00
8 MBu,Velocity 10, pt.2. . . . . 3.00
9 Day of Judgment x-over 3.00
10 MBu,F:Changeling
& Deathstroke 3.00
11 MBu. 3.00
12 MBu,This Immortal Coil,pt.3 . . . . 3.50
13 internal fight 3.00
14 to Scotland 3.00
15 MBu,pt.1 . . . . 3.00
16 MBu,V:Gargoyle 3.00
17 ALa,into space 3.00
18 ALa,into space,pt.2 . . . . 3.00
19 ALa,into space,pt.3 . . . . 3.00
20 ALa,end of Cyborg 3.00
21 PaP,Hangmen. 3.00
22 PaP,Arsenal vs. Deathstroke . . . 3.00
23 PaP,Who's Troia?,pt.1. . . . . 3.00
24 PaP,Who's Troia?,pt.2. . . . . 3.00

Titans #31
© DC Comics Inc.

25 MWn,GP,48-page 4.00
26 PaP,V:Shockwave. 3.00
27 PaP,F:Cheshire,Epsilon 3.00
28 PaP,The All-Nighter. 3.00
29 PaP,tower of troublemakers 3.00
30 JP,Sins of the Past 3.00
31 JP,V:Theta. 3.00
32 V:Dakota Jameson 3.00
33 V:Theta 3.00
34 Cheshire Smile,Last Laugh. 3.00
35 F:Beast Boy & Flamebird 3.00
36 V:Wildebeests 3.00
37 BKi,in the Orphanage 3.00
38 BKi,V:Epsilon,final stand. 3.00
39 BKi,V:Dark Nemesis 3.00
40 BKi,F:The Favored 3.00
41 PGr,F:Nikki 3.00
42 BKi,Chemical World,pt.1 . . . . . . 3.00
43 BKi,Chemical World,pt.2. . . . . . . 3.00
44 BKi,JmP,Chemical World,pt.3 . . . 3.00
45 BKi,JmP,F:Damage. 3.00
46 BKi,JmP,F:Damag,Jesse 3.00
47 TPe,BKi,PGr,JmP 3.00
48 TPe,BKi,JmP,Murder,pt.1 . . . . . 3.00
49 TPe,BKi,JmP,Murder,pt.2 . . . . . 3.00
50 TPe,BKi,JmP,final issue 3.00
Ann.#1 Planet DC 4.00
Spec. Secret Files #1. . . . . 5.50
Spec. Secret Files #2. . . . . 5.50
GN Scissors, Paper, Stone, manga
style (1997) 5.50

TITANS SELL-OUT SPECIAL
1 SE,AV,I:Teeny Titans,
w/Nightwing poster 3.75

TITANS, THE/LEGION OF SUPER-HEROES: UNIVERSE ABLAZE
Jan., 2000
1 (of 4) DJu,PJ 5.00
2 thru 4 DJu,PJ . . . . @5.00

TITANS, THE/ YOUNG JUSTICE: GRADUATION DAY
May 2003
1 (of 3) 14.00
2 Indigo. 8.00
3 Concl.. 8.00

TOE TAGS FEATURING GEORGE ROMERO
2004
1 . . . . 2.95

TOMAHAWK
1950–72
1 Prisoner Called Tomahawk. . 2,200.00
2 FF(4pgs),Four Boys
Against the Frontier. 850.00
3 Warpath 450.00
4 Tomahawk Wanted: Dead
or Alive. 450.00
5 The Girl Who Was Chief 450.00
6 Tomahawk-King of the Aztecs . 350.00
7 Punishment of Tomahawk 350.00
8 The King's Messenger. 350.00
9 The Five Doomed Men 350.00
10 Frontied Sabotage 350.00
11 Girl Who Hated Tomahawk . . . 250.00
12 Man From Magic Mountain. . . 250.00
13 Dan Hunter's Rival 250.00
14 The Frontier Tinker 250.00
15 The Wild Men of
Wigwam Mountain. 250.00
16 Treasure of the Angelique. . . . 250.00
17 Short-Cut to Danger 250.00
18 Bring In M'Sieur Pierre 250.00
19 The Lafayette Volunteers 250.00
20 NC(c),The Retreat of
Tomahawk 250.00
21 NC(c),The Terror of the
Wrathful Spirit 200.00
22 CS(c),Admiral Tomahawk 200.00
23 CS(c),The Indian Chief
from Oxford 200.00
24 NC(c),Adventure In the
Everglades. 200.00
25 NC(c),The Star-Gazer of
Freemont. 200.00
26 NC(c),Ten Wagons For
Tomahawk 200.00
27 NC(c),Frontier Outcast 200.00
28 I:Lord Shilling 225.00
29 Conspiracy of Wounded Bear. 250.00
30 The King of the Thieves 200.00
31 NC(c),The Buffalo Brave
From Misty Mountain. 200.00
32 NC(c),The Clocks That
Went to War. 200.00
33 The Paleface Tribe 200.00
34 The Capture of General
Washington 200.00
35 Frontier Feud 200.00
36 NC(c),A Cannon for Fort
Reckless 200.00
37 NC(c),Feathered Warriors. . . . 200.00
38 The Frontier Zoo. 200.00
39 The Redcoat Trickster. 200.00
40 Fearless Fettle-Daredevil 200.00
41 The Captured Chieftain. 200.00
42 The Prisoner Tribe 200.00
43 Tomahawk's Little Brother. . . . 200.00
44 The Brave Named Tomahawk 200.00
45 The Last Days of Chief Tory . . 200.00
46 The Chief With 1,000 Faces. . 125.00
47 The Frontier Rain-Maker. 125.00
48 Indian Twin Trouble. 125.00
49 The Unknown Warrior. 125.00
50 The Brave Who Was Jinxed . . 125.00
51 General Tomahawk. 125.00
52 Tom Thumb of the Frontier . . . 125.00
53 The Four-Footed Renegade . . 125.00
54 Mystery of the 13th Arrows. . . 125.00
55 Prisoners of the Choctaw 125.00
56 The Riddle of the
Five Little Indians 125.00
57 The Strange Fight
at Fort Bravo 150.00

DC COMICS

58 Track of the Mask	100.00
59 The Mystery Prisoner of Lost Island	100.00
60 The Amazing Walking Fort	100.00
61 Tomahawk's Secret Weapons	75.00
62 Strongest Man in the World	75.00
63 The Frontier Super Men	75.00
64 The Outcast Brave	75.00
65 Boy Who Wouldn't Be Chief	75.00
66 DD&SMo(c),A Trap For Tomahawk	75.00
67 DD&SMo(c),Frontier Sorcerer	75.00
68 DD&SMo(c),Tomahawk's Strange Ally	75.00
69 DD&SMo(c),Tracker-King of the Wolves	75.00
70 DD&SMo(c),Three Tasks for Tomahawk	75.00
71 DD&SMo(c),The Boy Who Betrayed His Country	75.00
72 DD&SMo(c),The Frontier Pupil	75.00
73 DD&SMo(c),The Secret of the Indian Sorceress	75.00
74 DD&SMo(c),The Great Paleface Masquerade	75.00
75 DD&SMo(c),The Ghost of Lord Shilling	75.00
76 DD&SMo(c),The Totem-Pole Trail	75.00
77 DD&SMo(c),The Raids of the One-Man Tribe	75.00
78 DD&SMo(c),The Menace of the Mask	75.00
79 DD&SMo(c),Eagle Eye's Debt of Honor	75.00
80 DD&SMo(c),The Adventures of Tracker	60.00
81 The Strange Omens of the Indian Seer	60.00
82 The Son of the Tracker	60.00
83 B:Tomahawk Rangers, Against the Tribe	60.00
84 There's a Coward Among the Rangers	60.00
85 The Wispering War	60.00
86 Rangers vs. King Colossus	40.00
87 The Secrets of Sgt. Witch Doctor	40.00
88 The Rangers Who Held Back the Earth	40.00
89 The Terrible Tree-Man	40.00
90 The Prisoner In The Pit	40.00
91 The Tribe Below the Earth	40.00
92 The Petrified Sentry of Peaceful Valley	40.00
93 The Return of King Colosso	40.00
94 Rip Van Ranger	40.00
95 The Tribe Beneath the Sea	40.00
96 The Ranger Killers	40.00
97 The Prisoner Behind the Bull's-Eye	40.00
98 The Pied Piper Rangers	40.00
99 The Rangers vs.ChiefCobweb	40.00
100 The Weird Water-Tomahawk	50.00
101 Tomahawk, Enemy Spy	35.00
102 The Dragon Killers	35.00
103 The Frontier Frankenstein	35.00
104 The Fearful Freak of Dunham's Dungeon	35.00
105 The Attack of the Gator God	35.00
106 The Ghost of Tomahawk	35.00
107 Double-Cross of the Gorilla Ranger	35.00
108 New Boss For the Rangers	35.00
109 The Caveman Ranger	35.00
110 Tomahawk Must Die	35.00
111 Vengeance of the Devil-Dogs	35.00
112 The Rangers vs. Tomahawk	35.00
113 The Mad Miser of Carlisle Castle	35.00

114 The Terrible Power of Chief Iron Hands	35.00
115 The Deadly Flaming Ranger	35.00
116 NA(c),The Last Mile of Massacre Trail	35.00
117 NA(c),Rangers'Last Stand	35.00
118 NA(c),Tomahawk, Guilty of Murder	35.00
119 NA(c),Bait For a Buzzard	35.00
120 NC(c),The Coward Who Lived Forever	35.00
121 NA(c),To Kill a Ranger	35.00
122 IN(c),Must the Brave Die	35.00
123 NA(c),The Stallions of Death	35.00
124 NA(c),The Valley of No Return	35.00
125 NA(c),A Chief's Feather For Little Bear	35.00
126 NA(c),The Baron of Gallows Hill	35.00
127 NA(c),The Devil is Waiting	35.00
128 NA(c),Rangers-Your 9 Lives For Mine	35.00
129 NA(c),Treachery at Thunder Ridge	35.00
130 NA(c),Deathwatch at Desolation Valley	35.00
131 JKu(c),B:Son of Tomahawk, Hang Him High	35.00
132 JKu(c),Small Eagle...Brother Hawk	25.00
133 JKu(c),Scalp Hunter	25.00
134 JKu(c),The Rusty Ranger	25.00
135 JKu(c),Death on Ghost Mountain	25.00
136 JKu(c),A Piece of Sky	30.00
137 JKu(c),Night of the Knife	30.00
138 JKu(c),A Different Kind of Christmas	30.00
139 JKu(c),Death Council	35.00
140 Jku(c),The Rescue	30.00

TOR
May-June, 1975

1 JKu,O:Tor	15.00
2 thru 6, Tor reprints	@10.00

TOTAL JUSTICE
Sept., 1996

1 thru 3 CPr(s),RBe,DG, toy line tie-in	@2.25

TOTAL RECALL
1990

1 Movie Adaption	3.00

TOTEMS
DC/Vertigo, Dec., 1999

GN TPe,DFg	6.00

TOUCH
DC Focus Apr. 2004

1 Rory Goodman, Las Vegas	2.50
2 thru 6	@2.50

TOXIC GUMBO
DC/Vertigo, March, 1998

1-shot GN	6.00

TRANSMETROPOLITAN
DC/Helix, July, 1997

1 WEI,DaR,JeM, gonzo journalism in 21st century	10.00
2 WEI,DaR,Angels 8 district	6.00
3 WEI,DaR, riot in Angels 8	5.00
4 WEI,DaR, Vs President of US	4.00

5 WEI,DaR, Watches TV	4.00
6 WEI,DaR,evangelicals	4.00
7 WEI,DaR	4.00
8 WEI,DaR,AnotherColdMorning	4.00
9 WEI,DaR,Wild in the Country	3.00
10 WEI,DaR,Freeze Me with Your Kiss, pt.1	3.00
11 WEI,DaR,Freeze Me, pt.2	3.00
12 WEI,DaR,Freeze Me, pt.3	3.00
13 WEI,DaR,JaL(c),Year of the Bastard, pt.1	3.00
14 WEI,DaR,JaL(c),Bastard,pt.2	3.00
15 WEI,DaR,JaL(c),Bastard,pt.3	3.00
16 WEI,DaR,Bastard,pt.4	3.00
17 WEI,DaR,Bastard,pt.5	3.00
18 WEI,DaR,Bastard, concl.	3.00
19 WEI,DaR,New Scum,pt.1	3.00
20 WEI,DaR,New Scum,pt.2	3.00
21 WEI,DaR,New Scum,pt.3	2.50
22 WEI,DaR,New Scum,pt.4	2.50
23 WEI,DaR,New Scum,pt.5	2.50
24 WEI,DaR,New Scum,pt.6	2.50
25 WEI,DaR,JLe(c),Days in the City #1	2.50
26 WEI,DaR,RyR,JLe(c),Days in the City #2	2.50
27 WEI,DaR,RyR,JLe(c)	2.50
28 WEI,DaR,RyR,LonelyCity,pt.1	2.50
29 WEI,DaR,RyR,LonelyCity,pt.2	2.50
30 WEI,DaR,RyR,LonelyCity,pt.3	2.50
31 WEI,DaR,RyR,F:Spider	2.50
32 WEI,DaR,RyR,	2.50
33 WEI,DaR,RyR	2.50
34 WEI,DaR,RyR,Gouge Away,pt.1	2.50
35 WEI,DaR,RyR,Gouge Away,pt.2	2.50
36 WEI,DaR,RyR,Gouge Away,pt.3	2.50
37 WEI,DaR,Back to Basics,pt.1	2.50
38 WEI,DaR,Back to Basics,pt.2	2.50
39 WEI,DaR,Back to Basics,pt.3	2.50
40 WEI,DaR,Streets atNight,pt.1	2.50
41 WEI,DaR,Streets atNight,pt.2	2.50
42 WEI,DaR,Streets atNight,pt.3	2.50
43 WEI,DaR,Dirge,pt.1	2.50
44 WEI,DaR,Dirge,pt.2	2.50
45 WEI,DaR,Dirge,pt.3	2.50
46 WEI,DaR,Dirge aftermath	2.50
47 WEI,DaR,A Disaster Zone	2.50
48 WEI,DaR,Year Four begins	2.50
49 WEI,DaR,rebuild Spider's case	2.50
50 WEI,DaR,Filthy Assistants	2.50
51 WEI,DaR,F:Mitchell Royce	2.50
52 WEI,DaR,The Cure,pt.1	2.50
53 WEI,DaR,The Cure,pt.2	2.50
54 WEI,DaR,The Cure,pt.3	2.50

Transmetropolitan #8
© *DC Comics, Inc.*

All comics prices listed are for *Near Mint* condition.

55 WEI,DaR,Vita Severn Zone 2.50
56 WEI,DaR,Martial law......... 2.50
57 WEI,DaR,White House siege ... 2.50
58 WEI,DaR,martial law......... 2.50
59 WEI,DaR,final meeting 2.50
60 WEI,DaR,final issue 2.50
GN I Hate it Here.............. 6.00
GN Filth of the City 6.00
TPB Lust For Life.............. 15.00
TPB Year of the Bastard 13.00
TPB Back on the Street......... 8.00
TPB New Scum, rep.#19–#24 .... 13.00
TPB Lonely City............... 15.00
TPB Gouge Away (2002)........ 15.00
TPB Spider's Thrash (2002) 15.00
TPB The Cure (2003) 15.00
TPB Dirge (2003).............. 15.00
TPB One More Time (2004) 15.00
TPB Tales of Human Waste (2004) 10.00

TRENCHCOAT BRIGADE
DC/Vertigo, 1999
1 (of 4) JNR(s),F:John Constantine,
  Mister E, Dr.Occult, Phantom
  Stranger 2.50
2 JNR 2.50
3 JNR 2.50
4 JNR, conclusion............. 2.50

TRIUMPH
[Mini-Series], 1995
1 From Zero Hour.............. 2.25
2 Teamates Peril 2.25
3 V:Mind Readers............. 2.25

TROUBLE MAGNET
Dec., 1999
1 (of 4) KPI, F:robot whose mind
  has been stolen............. 2.50
2 KPI 2.50
3 KPI 2.50
4 KPI,concl.................. 2.50

TRUE FAITH
DC/Vertigo, Aug., 1997
TPB GEn,WaP, series rep....... 25.00

TSR WORLDS
TSR 1990
1 I:SpellJammer 4.50

TV SCREEN CARTOONS
(see REAL SCREEN COMICS)

2020 VISIONS
DC/Vertigo, April, 1997
1 (of 12) the Disunited States
  of America 2.25
2 JaD(s),.................... 2.25
3 JaD(s),.................... 2.25
4 JaD(s),WaP,La Tormenta,pt.1 .. 2.25
5 JaD(s),WaP,La Tormenta,pt.2 .. 2.25
6 JaD(s),WaP,La Tormenta,pt.3 .. 2.25
7 JaD(s),Renegade,pt.1 .... 2.25
8 JaD(s),Renegade,pt.2 .... 2.25
9 JaD(s),Renegade,pt.3 .... 2.25
10 JaD(s),Repro-Man,pt.1 ...... 2.25
11 JaD(s),Repro-Man,pt.2 ...... 2.25
12 JaD(s),Repro-Man,pt.3 ...... 2.25

TWILIGHT
1990–91
1 JL,Last Frontier 5.50
2 JL,K.SorensenVs.T.Tomorrow ... 5.00
3 JL,K.SorensenVs.T.Tomorrow ... 5.00

UNAUTHORIZED BIO OF LEX LUTHOR
1 EB 4.00

UNCLE SAM
DC/Vertigo, Nov, 1997
GN 1 (of 2) AxR............... 5.00
GN 2 AxR.................... 5.00
TPB 10.00

UNDERCOVER GENIE
DC/Vertigo June 2003
TPB 14.95

UNDERWORLD
Dec., 1987
1 EC,New Yorks Finest......... 2.50
2 EC,A:Black Racer 2.50
3 EC,V:Black Racer 2.50
4 EC,final issue............... 2.50

UNDERWORLD UNLEASHED
1995–96
1 PWa,F:Neron 5.00
2 PWa,Neron Vs.Green Lantern... 4.00
3 PWa,conclusion............ 4.00
Abyss—Hell's Nest 1-shot 3.00
Apokolips-Dark Uprising 1-shot .. 3.00
Batman—Devil's Asylum 1-shot
  AIG,BSz 3.00
Patterns of Fear 1-shot 3.00

UNEXPECTED, THE
(see TALES OF THE UNEXPECTED)

UNKNOWN SOLDIER
(see STAR SPANGLED)

UNKNOWN SOLDIER
April, 1988
1 True Origin revealed,Viet
  Nam 1970 .... 4.00
2 Origin contd.,Iran 1977 ...... 3.00
3 Origin contd.Afghanistan1982 ... 3.00
4 Nicaragua 3.00
5 Nicaragua contd............. 3.00
6 .... 3.00
7 Libia 3.00
8 Siberia, U.S.S.R............. 3.00
9 North Korea 1952 .... 3.00
10 C.I.A..................... 3.00
11 C.I.A., Army Intelligence 3.00
12 final issue,1989............. 3.00

UNKNOWN SOLDIER
DC/Vertigo, Feb., 1997
1 (of 4) GEn(s),KPI,F:maverick
  CIA agent................. 7.00
2 GEn(s),KPI,search for Unknown
  Soldier continues........... 5.00
3 GEn(s),KPI,search for Unknown
  Soldier continues........... 5.00
4 GEn(s),KPI,intrigue, finale 5.00
TPB series rep. 13.00

UNTOLD LEGEND OF BATMAN
July, 1980
1 JA,JBy,(1st DC work)O:Batman . 6.00
2 JA,O:Joker&Robin 4.50
3 JA,O:Batgirl 4.50

Untold Legend of Batman #1
© DC Comics Inc.

USER
DC/Vertigo, Jan., 2001
1 (of 3) 48-page 6.00
2 JBo,SeP,48-page 6.00
3 JBo,SeP,48-page 6.00

V
(TV Adaptation)
Feb., 1985
1 CI/TD..................... 3.00
2 thru 5 CI/TD .... @2.25
6 thru 16 CI/TD .... @2.25
17 & 18 DG .... @2.25

VALOR
1992–94
1 N:Valor,A:Lex Luthor Jr 3.00
2 MBr,AG,V:Supergirl 2.50
3 MBr,AG,V:Lobo 2.50
4 MBr,AG,V:Lobo 2.50
5 MBr,A:Blasters.............. 2.50
6 A:Blasters,V:Kanjar Ru 2.50
7 A:Blasters................. 2.50
8 AH(c),V:The Unimaginable 2.50
9 AH(c),PCu,A:Darkstar 2.50
10 AH(c),V:Unimaginable........ 2.50
11 A:Legionnaires 2.50
12 AH(c),B:D.O.A. 3.00
13 AH(c),D:Valor's Mom 3.00
14 AH(c),A:JLA,Legionnaires...... 2.50
15 SI(c),D.O.A #4. .... 2.50
16 CDo,D.O.A #5.............. 2.50
17 CDo,LMc,D:Valor........... 2.50
18 A:Legionnaires 2.50
19 CDo,A:Legionnaires,V:Glorith .. 2.50
20 CDo,A:Wave Rider 2.50
21 .... 2.50
22 End of an Era,pt.2........... 2.50
23 Zero Hour 2.50

VAMPS
DC/Vertigo, 1994–95
1 BB(c) 3.00
2 BB(c) 3.00
3 BB(c) 3.00
4 BB(c) 3.00
5 BB(c) 3.00
6 BB(c),last issue............. 3.00
TPB 10.00

VAMPS:
HOLLYWOOD & VEIN
DC/Vertigo, 1996
1 F:Mink 2.50
2 . . . . 2.50
3 I:Maggot 2.50
4 F:Mink,Screech 2.50
5 off to rescue Hugh Evans (of 6) . 2.50
6 . . . . 2.50

VAMPS: PUMPKIN TIME
DC/Vertigo, 1998
1 (of 3) Halloween mini-series 2.50
2 thru 3 . . . . @2.50

VERMILLION
DC/Helix, Aug., 1996
1 ADv,MKu(c) Lucius Shepard
   story 2.50
2 ADv,MKu(c) Jonathan Cave's
   cover blown 2.50
3 ADv,riot aboard space ship,
   Ildiko's tale 2.50
4 ADv,Starship's engines run wild. . 2.50
5 ADv 2.50
6 ADv,Creation of Vermillion 2.50
7 ADv,Jonathan Cave discovers
   hiding place of enemy 2.50
8 ADv,Joyland 2.50
9 GEr, the library in Kaia Mortai . . . 2.50
10 GEr, Lord Iron and Lady
   Manganese, pt.2 . . . . 2.50
11 GEr,Lord Iron and Lady
   Manganese, concl. 2.50
12 final issue 2.50

VERTICAL
DC/Vertigo Dec. 2003
Spec. MiA,64-pg. 5.00

VERTIGO GALLERY:
DREAMS AND
NIGHTMARES
1995
1 Various artists 3.50

VERTIGO JAM
1993
1 GF(c),NGa(s),ANo(s),PrM(s),GEn(s),
   JaD(s),KN,SDi,SEa,NyC(s),EiS,PhH,
   KDM(i),SeP,MiA,RaP(s),MPn(i),
   Vertigo Short Stories 4.50

VERTIGO POP!
TOKYO
DC/Vertigo, July, 2002
1 (of 4) by Seth Fisher 3.00
2 thru 4 . . . . @3.00

LONDON
DC/Vertigo, Nov., 2002
1 (of 4) PrM,PBd 3.00
2 thru 4 PrM,PBd . . . . @3.00

BANGKOK
DC Vertigo May 2003
1 (of 4) 3.00
2 thru 4 . . . . @3.00

VERTIGO PREVIEW
1992
Preview of new Vertigo titles,
   new Sandman story 2.25

VERTIGO VERITE:
HELL ETERNAL
Feb., 1998
1-shot JaD,SeP 7.00

THE SYSTEM
1 thru 3 . . . . @3.00
GN Seven Miles a Second 8.00

THE UNSEEN HAND
DC/Vertigo, 1996
1 thru 3 TLa. . . . . @2.50
4 TLa, final issue 2.50

DR. OCCULT
1 F:Dr. Occult 4.00

DR. THIRTEEN
DC/Vertigo, July, 1998
GN evil artificial intelligence 6.00

VERTIGO VISIONS:
THE GEEK
1993
1 RaP(s),MiA,V:Dr.Abuse 4.25

PHANTOM STRANGER
1993
1 AaK(s),GyD,The Infernal House . 3.75

THE EATERS
1995
1 I:The Quills. 5.00

TOMAHAWK
DC/Vertigo, May, 1998
GN RaP,TY 5.00

VERTIGO:
WINTER'S EDGE
DC/Vertigo, 1998
TPB BB(c) rep. 8.00
GN Winter's Edge II 7.00
GN Winter's Edge III 6.95

VEXT
1999
1 KG,MMK,MkM 2.50
2 KG,MMK,MkM 2.50
3 KG,MMK,MkM 2.50
4 KG,MMK,MkM 2.50
5 KG,MMK,MkM 2.50
6 KG,MMK,MkM, final issue 2.50

V FOR VENDETTA
Sept., 1988
1 Reps.Warrior Mag(U.K.),I:V,
   A:M.Storm (Moore scripts) 5.00
2 Murder Spree 3.50
3 Govt. Investigators close in 3.00
4 T.V. Broadcast take-over 3.00
5 Govt.Corruption Expose 3.00
6 Evey in Prison 3.00
7 Evey released 3.00
8 Search for V,A:Finch 3.00
9 V:Finch 3.00
10 D:V 3.00
TPB 1990 . . . . 15.00

VIGILANTE
Oct., 1983
1 KP,DG,F:Adrian Chase 3.50
2 KP 3.00
3 KP,Cyborg 2.50
4 DN,V:Exterminator 2.50
5 KP 2.50
6 O:Vigilante 3.00
7 O:Vigilante 3.00
8 RA,V:Electrocutioner 2.50

Vigilante #1 © DC Comics, Inc.

9 RA,V:Electrocutioner 2.50
10 RA,DG,avenges J.J. 2.50
11 RA,V:Controller 2.50
12 GK,"Journal" 2.50
13 GK,"Locke Room Murder". 2.50
14 RA,V:Hammer. 2.50
15 RA,V:Electrocutioner. 2.50
16 RA 2.50
17 Moore 4.00
18 Moore 4.00
19 RA 2.50
20 A:Nightwing 2.50
21 A:Nightwing 2.50
22 . . . . 2.50
23 V:Electrocutioner 2.50
24 "Mother's Day" 2.50
25 RM,V:Police Torturers 2.50
26 V:Electrocutioner. 2.50
27 V:Electrocutioner. 2.50
28 New Vigilante 2.50
29 RM,New Vigilante 2.50
30 RM,D:Glitz Jefferson. 2.50
31 RM,New York Violence 2.50
32 RM,New York Violence 2.50
33 RM,V:Rapist 2.50
34 . . . . 2.50
35 JBy(c),O:MadBomber 2.50
36 MGr(c),V:Peacemaker 2.50
37 MGr,RM,V:Peacemaker 2.50
38 MGr,PeaceMaker 2.50
39 White Slavery 2.50
40 HC(c),White Slavery 2.50
41 . . . . 2.50
42 A:Peacemaker,V:Terrorists 2.50
43 V:PeaceMaker 2.50
44 DC,V:Qurac. 2.50
45 I:Black Thorn. 2.50
46 Viigilante in Jail. 2.50
47 A:Batman 2.50
48 I:Homeless Avenger 2.50
49 . . . . 2.50
50 KSy(c)D:Vigilante 3.00
Ann.#1 . . . . 3.00
Ann.#2 V:Cannon. 2.50

VIGILANTE:
CITY LIGHTS,
PRAIRIE JUSTICE
1995–96
1 JeR,MCo,(of 4) 2.50
2 JeR,V:Bugsy Siegel 2.50
3 JeR 2.50
4 finale 2.50

VIPER
1994
1 Based on the TV Show	2.25
2	2.25
3	2.25
4 final issue	2.25

WANDERERS
June, 1988
1 I:New Team	3.00
2 V:The Performer	3.00
3 A:Legion of Superheroes	3.00
4 V:Controller Hunters	3.00
5 O:Wanderers	3.00
6 V:Terrorists	3.00
7 V:Medtorians	3.00
8 O:Psyche	3.00
9 O:Psyche	3.00
10 F:Quantum Queen	3.00
11 F:Quantum Queen	3.00
12 V:Aliens	3.00
13 V:Dinosaurs	3.00

WANTED: THE WORLD'S MOST DANGEROUS VILLIANS
July-Aug., 1972
1 GK,rep. Batman,Green Lantern.	50.00
2 CI,Batman/Joker/Penguin	35.00
3 JK,MMe,Dr. Fate	30.00
4 Green Lantern	30.00
5 GK,Dollman/Green Lantern	30.00
6 JK,Starman	30.00
7 JK,MMe,Hawkman/Flash	30.00
8 Dr. Fate/Flash	30.00
9 Sandman/Superman	30.00

WARLORD
Jan., 1976
1 MGr,O:Warlord	30.00
2 MGr,I:Machiste	15.00
3 MGr,War Gods of Skartaris	10.00
4 MGr,Duel of the Titans	10.00
5 MGr,The Secret of Skartaris	10.00
6 MGr,I:Mariah,Stryker	7.00
7 MGr,O:Machiste	7.00
8 MGr,A:Skyra	7.00
9 MGr,N:Warlord	7.00
10 MGr,I:Ashiya	7.00
11 MGr,rep.1st Issue special #8	5.00
12 MGr,I:Aton	5.00
13 MGr,D:Stryker	5.00
14 MGr,V:Death	5.00
15 MGr,I:Joshua	5.00
16 MGr,I:Saaba	5.00
17 MGr,Citadel of Death	5.00
18 MGr,I:Shadow	5.00
19 MGr,Wolves of the Steppes	5.00
20 MGr,I:Joshua clone	7.00
21 MGr,D:Joshua clone,Shadow	4.00
22 MGrBeast in the Tower	4.00
23 MGr,Children of Ba'al	4.00
24 MGr,I:Iigia	4.00
25 MGr,I:Ahir	4.00
26 MGr,The Challenge	4.00
27 MGr,Atlantis Dying	4.00
28 MGr,I:Wizard World	4.00
29 MGr,I:Mongo Ironhand	4.00
30 MGr,C:Joshua	4.00
31 MGr,Wing over Shamballah	4.00
32 MGr,I:Shakira	4.00
33 MGr,Birds of Prey,A:Shakira	4.00
34 MGr,Sword of the Sorceror, I:Hellfire	4.00
35 MGr,C:Mike Grell	4.00
36 MGr,Interlude	4.00
37 MGr,JSn,I:Firewing,B:Omac	6.00

Warlord #87 © DC Comics, Inc.

38 MGr,I:Jennifer,A:Omac	4.00
39 MGr,JSn,Feast of Agravar	4.00
40 MGr,N:Warlord	4.00
41 MGr,A:Askir	4.00
42 MGr,JSn,A:Tara,Omac	4.00
43 MGr,JSn,Berserk'A:Omac	4.00
44 MGr,The Gamble	4.00
45 MGr,Nightmare in Vista Vision,A:Omac	4.00
46 MGr,D:Shakira	4.00
47 MGr,I:Mikola,E:Omac	4.00
48 MGr,EC,TY,I:Arak,Claw(B)	4.00
49 MGr,TY,A:Shakira,E:Claw	3.00
50 MGr,By Fire and Ice	3.00
51 MGr,TY,rep.#1, I(B):Dragonsword	3.00
52 MGr,TY,Back in the U.S.S.R.	3.00
53 MT,TY,Sorcerer's Apprentice	3.00
54 MT,Sorceress Supreme, E:Dragonsword	3.00
55 MT,Have a Nice Day	3.00
56 MT,JD,I:Gregmore,(B:)Arion	3.00
57 MT,The Two Faces of Travis Morgan	3.00
58 MT,O:Greamore	3.00
59 MGr,A:Joshua	3.00
60 JD,Death Dual	3.00
61 JD,A:Greamore	3.00
62 JD,TMd,A:Mikola,E:Arion	3.00
63 JD,RR,I(B):Barren Earth	4.00
64 DJu,RREIsewhere	3.00
65 DJu,RR,A:Wizard World, No Barren Earth	3.00
66 DJuWizard World, No Barren Earth	3.00
67 DJu,RR,The Mark	3.00
68 DJu,RR	3.00
69 DJu,RR	3.00
70 DJu,Outback	3.00
71 DJu/DA,The Journey Back No Barren Earth	3.00
72 DJu,DA,I:Scarhart,No Barren Earth	3.00
73 DJ,DA,Cry Plague	3.00
74 DJu,No Barren Earth	3.00
75 DJu,All Dreams Must Pass No Barren Earth	3.00
76 DJu,DA,RR,A:Sarga	3.00
77 DJu,DA,RR,Let My People Go	3.00
78 DJu,RR,Doom's Mouth	3.00
79 PB,RM,Paradox,No Barren Earth	3.00
80 DJu,DA,RR,Future Trek	3.00
81 DJu,DA,RR,Thief's Magic	3.00

82 DJu,DA,RR,Revolution	3.00
83 DJu,RR,All the President's Men	3.00
84 DJu,DA,RR,Hail to the Chief	3.00
85 DJu,RR,The Price of Change	3.00
86 DJ,DA,No Barren Earth	3.00
87 DJu,RB,RR,I:Hawk	3.00
88 DJu,RB,RR,I:Patch,E:Barren Earth	3.00
89 RB,I:Sabertooth	3.00
90 RB,Demon's of the Past	3.00
91 DJu,DA,I:Maddox,O:Warlord O:Jennifer	3.00
92 NKu,Evil in Ebony	3.00
93 RR,A:Sabertooth	3.00
94 Assassin's Prey	3.00
95 AKu,Dragon's Doom	3.00
96 Nightmare Prelude	3.00
97 RB,A:Saaba,D:Scarhart	3.00
98 NKu,Crisis tie-in	3.00
99 NKuFire and Sword	3.00
100 AKu,D:Greamore,Sabertooth	4.00
101 MGr,Temple of Demi-god	3.00
102 I:Zuppara,Error-Machiste with two hands.	3.00
103 JBi,Moon Beast	3.00
104 RR,Dragon Skinner	3.00
105 RR,Stalilers of Skinner	3.00
106 RR,I:Daimon	3.00
107 RR,Bride of Yano	3.00
108 RR,I:Mortella	3.00
109 RR,A:Mortella	3.00
110 RR,A:Skyra III	3.00
111 RR,Tearing o/t Island Sea	3.00
112 RR,Obsession	3.00
113 RR,Through Fiends Destroy Me	3.00
114 RR,Phenalegeno Dies	3.00
115 RR,Citadel of Fear	3.00
116 RR,Revenge of the Warlord	3.00
117 RR,A:Power Girl	3.00
118 RR,A:Power Girl	3.00
119 RR,A:Power Girl	3.00
120 ATb,A:Power Girl	3.00
121 ATb,A:Power Girl	3.00
122 ATb,A:Power Girl	3.00
123 JD,TMd,N:Warlord	3.00
124 JD,TMd,I:Scavenger	3.00
125 JD,TMd,D:Tara	3.00
126 JD,TMd,A:Machiste	3.00
127 JD,The Last Dragon	3.00
128 JD,I:Agife	3.00
129 JD,Vision of Quest	3.00
130 JD,A:Maddox	3.00

Warlord #124 © DC Comics Inc.

All comics prices listed are for *Near Mint* condition.

DC COMICS

131 JD,RLd,Vengeful Legacies 5.00
132 A New Beginning. 3.00
133 JD,final issue (44pg) 4.00
Ann.#1 MGr,A:Shakira 4.00
Ann.#2 I:Krystovar 3.00
Ann.#3 DJu,Full Circle 3.00
Ann.#4 A:New Gods,
  Legends tie-in 3.00
Ann.#5 AKu,Hellfire 3.00
Ann.#6 F:New Gods 3.00
TPB Warlord:Savage Empire,
  Rep.#1-#10,#12,Special #8 . . . 20.00

[Limited Series], 1992

1 Travis Morgan retrospective . . . 2.25
2 Fate of T. Morgan revealed 2.25
3 Return of Deimos. 2.25
4 V:Deimos 2.25
5 MGr(c),Skartaros at War 2.25
6 finale 2.25

WAR OF THE GODS
1991

1 GP,A:Lobo,Misc.Heroes,Circe
  (direct) 2.25
2 GP,A:Misc.Heroes,V:Circe,
  w/poster 2.25
2a (Newsstand). 2.25
3 GP,A:Misc.Heroes,V:Circe,
  w/poster 2.25
3a Newsstand 2.25
4 GP,A:Misc.Heroes,V:Circe,
  w/poster 2.25
4a Newsstand 2.25

WAR STORY
DC/Vertigo, Sept., 2001

Spec. Johann's Tiger,GEn 5.00
Spec. D-Day Dodgers,GEn 5.00
Spec. Screaming Eagles,GEn 5.00
Spec. The Reivers 5.00
Spec. Nightingale,GEn. 5.00
Spec. J for Jenny 5.00
Spec. Condors 5.00
Spec. Archangel. 5.00
Spec. Johann's Tiger 5.00
TPB 20.00

WASTELAND
Dec., 1987

1 Selection of Horror stories. 2.25
2 . . . . 2.25
3 . . . . 2.25

Wasteland #11 © DC Comics, Inc.

4 . . . . 2.25
5 The big crossover story 2.25
6 . . . . 2.25
7 Great St.Louis Electrical
  Giraffe Caper. 2.25
8 Dead Detective 2.25
9 . . . . 2.25
10 TT,African Folk Tale 2.25
11 Revenge o/t Swamp Creature . . 2.25
12 JO,After the Dead Detective. . . . 2.25
13 TT(c),JO 2.25
14 JO,RM,Whistling Past the
  Graveyard 2.25
15 JO,RM. 2.25
16 JO 2.25
17 JO 2.25
18 JO,RM,final issue 2.25

WATCHMEN
Sept., 1986

1 B:AMo,DGb,D:Comedian. 10.00
2 DGb,Funeral for Comedian 6.00
3 DGb,F:Dr.Manhattan 5.00
4 DGb,O:Dr.Manhattan 5.00
5 DGb,F:Rorschach 5.00
6 DGb,O:Rorschach 5.00
7 DGb,F:Nite Owl 5.00
8 DGb,F:Silk Spectre 5.00
9 DGb,O:Silk Spectre 5.00
10 DGb,A:Rorschach 5.00
11 DGb,O:Ozymandius 5.00
12 DGb,D:Rorsharch 5.00
TPB rep.#1-#12 . . . . 15.00
TPB 20.00

WEB, THE
DC/Impact, 1991–92

1 I:Gunny, Bill Grady, Templar 2.25
2 O:The Web, I:Brew, Jump,
  Sunshine Kid 2.25
3 Minions of Meridian, I:St.James . 2.25
4 Agent Jump vs. UFO 2.25
5 Agent Buster/Fly team-up
  V:Meridian 2.25
6 I:Posse,A:Templar 2.25
7 V:Meridian's Forces 2.25
8 R: Studs 2.25
9 Earthquest,pt.1 . . . . 2.50
10 V:Templar 2.25
11 V:Templar 2.25
12 "The Gauntlet",A:Shield 2.25
13 Frenzy#1 . . . . 2.25
14 Frenzy#2 . . . . 2.25
Ann.#1 Earthquest,w/trading card . . 2.50

WEIRD, THE
April, 1988

1 BWr,A:JLI 4.00
2 BWr,A:JLI 3.00
3 BWr,V:Jason 3.00
4 final issue 3.00

WEIRD
DC/Paradox Press, 1997

1 B&W magazine 3.00
2 . . . . 3.00
3 . . . . 3.00

WEIRD SECRET ORIGINS
Aug. 2004

Spec. 80-page giant 6.00

WEIRD WAR TALES
Sept.–Oct., 1971

1 JKu(c),JKu,RH,Fort which
  Did Not Return. 350.00
2 JKu,MD,Military Madness 125.00

Weird War Tales #42
© DC Comics, Inc.

3 JKu(c),RA,The Pool. 100.00
4 JKu(c),Ghost of Two Wars. 75.00
5 JKu(c),RH,Slave 75.00
6 JKu(c),Pawns, The Sounds
  of War 65.00
7 JKu(c),JKu,RH,Flying Blind 65.00
8 NA(c),The Avenging Grave 75.00
9 NC(c),The Promise 65.00
10 NC(c),Who is Haunting
  the Haunted Chateau 65.00
11 NC(c),ShM,Oct. 30, 1918:
  The German Trenches, WWI . 30.00
12 MK(c),God of Vengeance 30.00
13 LD(c),The Die-Hards. 30.00
14 LD(c),ShM,The Ghost of
  McBride's Woman 30.00
15 LD(c),Ace King Just Flew
  In From Hell. 30.00
16 LD(c),More Dead Than Alive . . 30.00
17 GE(c),Dead Man's Hands. 30.00
18 GE(c),Captain Dracula 30.00
19 LD(c),The Platoon That
  Wouldn't Die 30.00
20 LD(c),Operation Voodoo. 30.00
21 LD(c),One Hour To Kill 25.00
22 LD(c),Wings of Death 25.00
23 LD(c),The Bird of Death 25.00
24 LD(c),The Invisible Enemy 25.00
25 LD(c),Black Magic...White
  Death 25.00
26 LD(c),Jump Into Hell. 25.00
27 LD(c),Survival of the
  Fittest. 25.00
28 LD(c),Isle of Forgotten
  Warriors. 25.00
29 LD(c),Breaking Point. 25.00
30 LD(c),The Elements of Death . . 25.00
31 LD(c),Death Waits Twice 25.00
32 LD(c),The Enemy, The Stars . . 25.00
33 LD(c),Pride of the Master
  Race 25.00
34 LD(c),The Common Enemy . . . 25.00
35 LD(c),The Invaders. 25.00
36 JKu(c),Escape. 30.00
37 LD(c),The Three Wars of
  Don Q 12.00
38 JKu(c),Born To Die 12.00
39 JKu(c),The Spoils of War 12.00
40 ECh(c),Back From The Dead . . 12.00
41 JL(c),The Dead Draftees of
  Regiment Six. 12.00
42 JKu(c),Old Soldiers Never
  Die 12.00

43 ECh(c),Bulletproof. 12.00
44 JKu(c),ShM,The Emperor
   Weehawken. 12.00
45 JKu(c),The Battle of Bloody
   Valley 12.00
46 Kill Or Be Killed. 12.00
47 JKu(c),Bloodbath of the Toy
   Soldiers 12.00
48 JL(c),Ultimate Destiny. 12.00
49 The Face Of The Enemy 12.00
50 ECh(c),-An Appointment With
   Destiny. 12.00
51 JKu(c),Secret Weapon 12.00
52 JKu(c),The Devil Is A
   Souvenir Hunter 12.00
53 JAp(c), Deadly Demons. 12.00
54 GM(c),Soldier of Satan 12.00
55 JKu(c),A Rebel Shall Rise
   From The Grave 12.00
56 AM(c),The Headless Courier . . 12.00
57 RT(c),Trial By Combat 12.00
58 JKu(c),Death Has A Hundred
   Eyes. 12.00
59 The Old One 12.00
60 JKu(c),Night Flight 12.00
61 HC(c),Mind War 10.00
62 JKu(c),The Grubbers 10.00
63 JKu(c),Battleground 10.00
64 JKu(c),FM(1st DC),D-Day. 25.00
65 JKu(c),The Last Cavalry
   Charge 10.00
66 JKu(c),The Iron Star 10.00
67 JKu(c),The Attack of the
   Undead 10.00
68 FM,JKu(c),The Life and Death of
   Charlie Golem 22.00
69 JKu(c),The Day After Doomsday 7.00
70 LD(c),The Blood Boat 7.00
71 LD(c),False Prophet 7.00
72 JKu(c),Death Camp 7.00
73 GE(c),The Curse of Zopyrus . . . 7.00
74 GE(c),March of the Mammoth . . 7.00
75 JKu(c),The Forgery. 7.00
76 JKu(c),The Fire Bug 7.00
77 JKu(c),Triad 7.00
78 JKu(c),Indian War In Space 7.00
79 JKu(c),The Gods Themselves . . 7.00
80 JKu(c),An Old Man's Profession. 7.00
81 JKu(c),It Takes Brains To
   Be A Killer 7.00
82 GE(c),Funeral Fire 7.00
83 GE(c),Prison of the Mind 7.00
84 JKu(c),Devil's Due 7.00
85 thru 124 June, 1983 . . . . . @7.00

WEIRD WAR TALES
DC/Vertigo, April, 1997
1 (of 4) anthology 3.00
2 MK(c) 3.00
3 . . . . 3.00
4 final issue. 3.00
Spec.#1 GEn (2000) 5.00

ALL-STAR WESTERN
Aug.–Sept., 1970
1 NA(c),CI 75.00
2 NA(c),GM,B:Outlaw 50.00
3 NA(c),GK,O:El Diablo 50.00
4 NA(c),GK,JKu,GM 50.00
5 NA(c),JAp,E:Outlaw. 50.00
6 GK,B:Billy the Kid 50.00
7 JKu. 40.00
8 E:Billy the Kid 40.00
9 FF 40.00
10 GM,I:Jonah Hex 550.00
11 GM,A:Jonah Hex. 250.00
Becomes:

All-Star Western #3
© DC Comics Inc.

WEIRD WESTERN TALES
June–July, 1972
12 NA,BWr,JKu 175.00
13 . . . . 125.00
14 ATh 75.00
15 NA(c),GK. 50.00
16 thru 28 . . . . @35.00
29 O:Jonah Hex. 50.00
30 . . . . 25.00
31 thru 38 . . . . @25.00
39 I&O:Scalphunter 25.00
40 thru 70 . . . . @15.00

WEIRD WESTERN TALES
DC/Vertigo, Feb., 2001
1 (of 4) 2.50
2 thru 4 . . . . @2.50

WEIRD WORLDS
Aug.–Sept., 1971
1 JO,MA,John Carter 50.00
2 NA,JO(c),MA,BWr 40.00
3 MA,NA 25.00
4 MK(c),MK. 20.00
5 MK(c),MK. 20.00
6 MK(c),MK. 20.00
7 John Carter ends 20.00
8 HC,I:Iron Wolf 20.00
9 and 10 HC . . . . @20.00

WESTERN COMICS
Jan.–Feb., 1948
1 MMe,B:Vigilante,Rodeo Rick,
   Wyoming Kid, Cowboy
   Marshal. 1,100.00
2 MMe,Vigilante vs. Dirk Bigger . 450.00
3 MMe,Vigilante vs. Pecos Kid . . 400.00
4 MMe,Vigilante as Pecos Kid . . . 400.00
5 I:Nighthawk 350.00
6 Wyoming Kid vs. The
   Murder Mustang 250.00
7 Wyoming Kid in The Town
   That Was Never Robbed. . . . 250.00
8 O:Wyoming Kid 400.00
9 Wyoming Kid vs. Jack
   Slaughter. 250.00
10 Nighthawk in Tunnel ofTerror . 250.00
11 Wyoming Kid vs. Mayor Brock 225.00
12 Wyoming Kid vs. Baldy Ryan . 225.00
13 I:Running Eagle 225.00

14 Wyoming Kid in The Siege
   of Prairie City. 225.00
15 Nighthawk in Silver, Salt
   and Pepper 225.00
16 Wyoming Kid vs. Smilin' Jim. . 225.00
17 BP,Wyoming Kid vs. Prof.
   Penny 225.00
18 LSt on Nighthawk,Wyoming Kid
   in Challenge of the Chiefs. . . 225.00
19 LSt,Nighthawk in The
   Invisible Rustlers 225.00
20 LSt,Nighthawk in The Mystery
   Mail From Defender Dip 175.00
21 LSt,Nighthawk in Rattlesnake
   Hollow 175.00
22 LSt,I:Jim Pegton 175.00
23 LSt,Nighthawk reveals
   ID to Jim 175.00
24 The $100,000 Impersonation . 175.00
25 V:Souix Invaders. 175.00
26 The Storming of the Sante
   Fe Trail 175.00
27 The Looters of Lost Valley . . . 175.00
28 The Thunder Creek Rebellion. 175.00
29 Six Guns of the Wyoming Kid. 175.00
30 V:Green Haired Killer 175.00
31 The Sky Riding Lawman. 175.00
32 Death Rides the Stage Coach 175.00
33 . . . . 175.00
34 Prescription For Killers 175.00
35 The River of Rogues. 175.00
36 Nighthawk(c),Duel in the Dark 150.00
37 The Death Dancer 150.00
38 Warpath in the Sky 150.00
39 Death to Fort Danger 150.00
40 Blind Man's Bluff 150.00
41 thru 60 . . . . @125.00
61 thru 85. . . . . @100.00

WE3
DC/Vertigo Aug. 2004
1 (of 3) GMo,Animal assassins. . . . 3.00
2 GMo. 3.00

WHERE IN THE WORLD
IS CARMEN SANDIEGO?
DC/Helix, 1996
1 thru 3 . . . . @2.25
4 . . . . 2.25

WILL EISNER LIBRARY
April, 2000
TPB The Building. 10.00
TPB City People Notebook 10.00
TPB A Contract with God. 13.00
GN The Dreamer 8.00
TPB Dropsie Avenue 16.00
TPB A Family Matter 16.00
TPB Invisible People 13.00
TPB Life on Another Planet 13.00
TPB Minor Miracles 13.00
TPB New York: The Big City 13.00
TPB To the Heart of the Storm . . . 15.00
TPB Will Eisner Reader. 10.00

WHO'S WHO
1985–87
1 . . . . 5.00
2 thru 9 . . . . @4.00
10 inc. 4.00
11 inc. Infinity Inc. 4.00
12 inc. Kamandi. 4.00
13 inc. Legion of Super Heroes/
   Villains 4.00
14 inc. 4.00
15 inc. Metal Men 4.00
16 inc. New Gods 4.00
17 inc. Outsiders 4.00

DC COMICS

18 inc. Power Girl 4.00
19 inc. Robin 4.00
20 inc. 4.00
21 inc. The Spectre 4.00
22 inc. Superman. 4.00
23 inc. Teen Titans. 4.00
24 inc. Unknown Soldier 4.00
25 inc. 4.00
26 inc. 4.00

WHO'S WHO IN
THE DC UNIVERSE
1990–92
1 inc. Superman 6.00
1a 2nd printing 5.50
2 inc. Flash 5.50
2a 2nd printing 5.00
3 inc. Green Lantern. 5.50
4 inc. Wonder Woman 5.50
5 inc. Batman. 5.50
6 inc. Hawkman 5.50
7 inc. Shade 5.50
8 inc. Lobo 6.00
9 inc. Legion of Super-Heroes 5.50
10 inc. Robin 5.50
11 inc. L.E.G.I.O.N. '91 . . . . 5.50
12 inc. Aquaman 5.50
13 Villains issue, inc. Joker 6.00
14 inc. New Titans 5.50
15 inc. Doom Patrol 5.50
16 inc. Catwoman,final issue. 5.00

WHO'S WHO
IN IMPACT
1991
1 Shield. 5.00
2 Black Hood 5.00

WHO'S WHO
IN THE LEGION
1987–88
1 History/Bio of Legionnaires 3.50
2 inc. Dream Girl. 3.50
3 inc. Karate Kid 3.50
4 inc. Lightning Lad 3.50
5 inc. Phantom Girl 3.50
6 inc. Timber Wolf. 3.50
7 wraparound(c) 3.50

WHO'S WHO
IN STAR TREK
1987
1 HC(c) 6.00
2 HC(c) 6.00

WHO'S WHO
UPDATE '87
1 inc. Blue Beetle 3.00
2 inc. Catwoman. 3.00
3 inc. Justice League 3.00
4 . . . . 3.00
5 inc. Superboy. 3.00

WHO'S WHO
UPDATE '88
1 inc. Brainiac. 3.00
2 inc. JusticeLeagueInternational . . 3.00
3 inc. Shado 3.00
4 inc. Zatanna 3.00
WHO'S WHO UPDATE '93
1 F:Eclipso,Azrael. 5.25

WILD DOG
Sept., 1987
1 mini series DG(i),I:Wild Dog 3.00
2 DG(i),V:Terrorists 2.50
3 DG(i) 2.50
4 DG(i),O:Wild Dog, final issue. . . . 2.50
Spec.#1 . . . . 2.50

WILD WILD WEST
1999
1-shot movie adaptation 5.00

WINDY & WILLY
May-June, 1969
1 . . . . 50.00
2 thru 4 . . . . @30.00

WISE SON:
THE WHITE WOLF
DC/Milestone, Sept., 1996
1 by Ho Che Anderson 2.50
2 thru 4 . . . . @2.50

WITCHCRAFT
DC/Vertigo, 1994
1 CV(c),Three Witches from
    Sandman 4.00
2 F:Mildred 3.50
3 Final issue 3.25
TPB rep. mini-series 15.00

WITCHCRAFT:
LA TERREUR
Feb., 1998
1 (of 3) JeR, sequel 2.50
2 & 3 JeR . . . . @2.50

WITCHING, THE
DC/Vertigo June 2004
1 Triple Goddess. 3.00
2 thru 4 . . . . @3.00
5 MBu 3.00

WITCHING HOUR
1969–78
1 NA,ATh 200.00
2 ATh. 75.00
3 ATh,BWr. 85.00

Witching Hour #47 © DC Comics, Inc.

4 ATh. 50.00
5 ATh,BWr. 75.00
6 ATh. 75.00
7 ATh. 45.00
8 NA,ATh 45.00
9 ATh. 45.00
10 ATh 45.00
11 ATh 45.00
12 ATh 45.00
13 NA 50.00
14 AW,CG,NA(c) 65.00
15 thru 20 . . . . @25.00
21 thru 30 . . . . @20.00
31 thru 37 . . . . @20.00
38 100-pg. 75.00
39 thru 60 . . . . @15.00
61 thru 85 . . . . @12.00

THE WITCHING HOUR
DC/Vertigo, Dec., 1999
1 (of 3) JLb,CBa,ATi 6.00
2 JLb,CBa,ATi. 6.00
3 JLb,CBa,ATi, concl. 6.00
TPB 20.00

WONDER WOMAN
1942–86
1 O:Wonder Woman,A:Paula
    Von Gunther 35,000.00
2 I:Earl of Greed,Duke of Deception
    and Lord Conquest. 6,000.00
3 Paula Von Gunther reforms . 3,000.00
4 A:Paula Von Gunther 2,200.00
5 I:Dr. Psycho,A:Mars 2,200.00
6 I:Cheetah 1,700.00
7 . . . . 1,700.00
8 I:Queen Clea. 1,700.00
9 I:Giganto 1,700.00
10 I:Duke Mephisto Saturno . . . 2,000.00
11 I:Hypnoto 1,400.00
12 I:Queen Desira. 1,400.00
13 V:King Rigor & the Seal Men 1,400.00
14 I:Gentleman Killer 1,400.00
15 I:Solo 1,400.00
16 I:King Pluto 1,400.00
17 Wonder Woman goes to
    Ancient Rome. 1,400.00
18 V:Dr. Psycho 1,400.00
19 V:Blitz. 1,400.00
20 V:Nifty and the Air Pirates . . 1,400.00
21 I:Queen Atomia 1,200.00
22 V:Saturno 1,200.00
23 V:Odin and the Valkyries . . . 1,200.00
24 I:Mask 1,200.00
25 V:Purple Priestess 1,200.00
26 I:Queen Celerita. 1,200.00
27 V:Pik Socket. 1,200.00
28 V:Cheetah,Clea,Dr. Poison,
    Giganta,Hypnata,Snowman,
    Zara (Villainy,Inc.). 1,100.00
29 V:Paddy Gypso 1,100.00
30 The Secret of the
    Limestone Caves 1,100.00
31 V:Solo 800.00
32 V:Uvo 800.00
33 V:Inventa 800.00
34 V:Duke of Deception. 800.00
35 Jaxo,Master of Thoughts 800.00
36 V:Lord Cruello 800.00
37 A:Circe 800.00
38 V:Brutex 800.00
39 The Unmasking of Wonder
    Woman 800.00
40 Hollywood Goes To Paradise
    Island. 800.00
41 Wonder Woman,Romance
    Editor. 700.00
42 V:General Vertigo 700.00
43 The Amazing Spy Ring
    Mystery 700.00

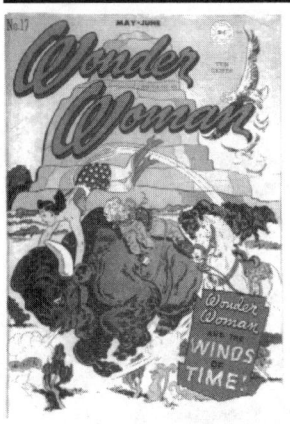

Wonder Woman #17
© DC Comics, Inc.

44 V:Master Destroyer......... 700.00
45 The Amazon and the
    Leprachaun............. 1,200.00
46 V:Prof. Turgo.............. 625.00
47 V:Duke of Deception........ 625.00
48 V:Robot Woman............. 625.00
49 V:Boss................... 625.00
50 V:Gen. Voro 625.00
51 V:Garo................... 450.00
52 V:Stroggo 450.00
53 V:Crime Master of Time 450.00
54 A:Merlin................. 450.00
55 The Chessmen of Doom..... 450.00
56 V:Plotter Gang 450.00
57 V:Mole Men............... 450.00
58 V:Brain 450.00
59 V:Duke Dozan............. 450.00
60 A:Paula Von Gunther 450.00
61 Earth's Last Hour 400.00
62 V:Angles Andrews.......... 400.00
63 V:Duke of Deception........ 400.00
64 V:Thought Master.......... 400.00
65 V:Duke of Deception........ 400.00
66 V:Duke of Deception........ 400.00
67 Confessions of a Spy 400.00
68 Landing of the Flying
    Saucers 400.00
69 A:Johann Gutenberg,Chris.
    Columbus, Paul Revere
    and the Wright Brothers 400.00
70 I:Angle Man............... 400.00
71 One-Woman Circus 400.00
72 V:Mole Goldings 400.00
73 V:Prairie Pirates 400.00
74 The Carnival of Peril........ 350.00
75 V:Angler 350.00
76 .... 350.00
77 V:Smokescreen gang 350.00
78 V:Angle Man 350.00
79 V:Spider 350.00
80 V:Machino 350.00
81 V:Duke of Deception,
    Angle Man 350.00
82 A:Robin Hood 350.00
83 The Boy From Nowhere 350.00
84 V:Duke of Deception,
    Angle Man 350.00
85 V:Capt. Virago............. 350.00
86 V:Snatcher 350.00
87 The Day the Clocks Stopped . 350.00
88 V:Duke of Deception........ 350.00
89 The Triple Heroine 350.00
90 Wonder Woman on Jupiter... 350.00
91 The Interplanetary Olympics.. 275.00

92 V:Angle Man 275.00
93 V:Duke of Deception........ 275.00
94 V:Duke of Deception,
    A:Robin Hood 275.00
95 O:Wonder Woman's tiara 275.00
96 V:Angle Man 275.00
97 The Runaway Time Express.. 275.00
98 .... 275.00
99 V:Silicons 275.00
100 Anniversary Issue 350.00
101 V:Time Master............. 250.00
102 F:Steve Trevor 250.00
103 V:Gadget-Maker........... 250.00
104 A:Duke of Deception 250.00
105 O,I:Wonder Woman...... 1,200.00
106 W.Woman space adventure . 250.00
107 Battles space cowboys 250.00
108 Honored by U.S. Post Off. .. 250.00
109 V:Slicker 250.00
110 I:Princess 1003 .... 200.00
111 I:Prof. Menace............ 200.00
112 V:Chest of Monsters 200.00
113 A:Queen Mikra 200.00
114 V:Flying Saucers 200.00
115 A:Angle Man 200.00
116 A:Professor Andro 200.00
117 A:Etta Candy............. 200.00
118 A:Merman 200.00
119 A:Mer Boy 200.00
120 A:Hot & Cold Alien 200.00
121 A:Wonder Woman Family ... 150.00
122 I:Wonder Tot 150.00
123 A:Wonder Girl,Wonder Tot . 150.00
124 A:Wonder Girl,Wonder Tot . 150.00
125 WW-Battle Prize 150.00
126 I:Mr.Genie 150.00
127 Suprise Honeymoon 125.00
128 O:InvisiblePlane 125.00
129 A:WonderGirl,WonderTot ... 125.00
130 A:Angle Man 125.00
131 .... 125.00
132 V:Flying Saucer........... 125.00
133 A:Miss X 125.00
134 V:Image-Maker 125.00
135 V:Multiple Man 125.00
136 V:Machine Men........... 125.00
137 V:Robot Wonder Woman ... 125.00
138 V:Multiple Man 125.00
139 Amnesia revels Identity.... 125.00
140 A:Morpheus,Mr.Genie 125.00
141 A:Angle Man 125.00
142 A:Mirage Giants 125.00
143 A:Queen Hippolyte 125.00
144 I:Bird Boy 125.00
145 V:Phantom Sea Beast 125.00
146 $1,000 Dollar Stories 125.00
147 Wonder Girl becomes Bird Girl
    and Fish Girl 125.00
148 A:Duke of Deception....... 125.00
149 Last Day of the Amazons ... 125.00
150 V:Phantome Fish Bird...... 125.00
151 F:1st Full Wonder Girl story .. 75.00
152 F:Wonder Girl 75.00
153 V:Duke of Deception....... 75.00
154 V:Boiling Man 75.00
155 I married a monster 75.00
156 V:Brain Pirate 75.00
157 A:Egg Fu,the First......... 75.00
158 A:Egg Fu,the First......... 75.00
159 Origin 125.00
160 A:Cheetah,Dr. Psycho...... 75.00
161 A:Angle Man 75.00
162 O:Diana Prince 75.00
163 A:Giganta 75.00
164 A:Angle Man 75.00
165 A:Paper Man,Dr.Psycho..... 75.00
166 A:Egg Fu,The Fifth 75.00
167 A:Crimson Centipede 75.00
168 RA,ME,V:Giganta 75.00
169 RA,ME,Crimson Centipede... 75.00
170 RA,ME,V:Dr.Pyscho 75.00

Wonder Woman #122
© DC Comics Inc.

171 A:Mouse Man 60.00
172 IN,A:Android Wonder Woman 60.00
173 A:Tonia 60.00
174 A:Angle Man 60.00
175 V:Evil Twin 60.00
176 A:Star Brothers 60.00
177 A:Super Girl 100.00
178 MSy,DG,I:New Wonder
    Woman 100.00
179 D:Steve Trevor,I:Ching 75.00
180 MSy,DG,wears no costume
    I:Tim Trench............ 50.00
181 MSy,DG,A:Dr.Cyber 50.00
182 MSy,DG................. 50.00
183 MSy,DG,V:War 50.00
184 MSy,DG,A:Queen Hippolyte .. 50.00
185 MSy,DG,V:Them 50.00
186 MSy,DG,I:Morgana 50.00
187 MSy,DG,A:Dr.Cyber 50.00
188 MSy,DG,A:Dr.Cyber 50.00
189 MSy,DG................. 50.00
190 MSy,DG................. 50.00
191 MSy,DG................. 50.00
192 MSy,DG................. 50.00
193 MSy,DG................. 50.00
194 MSy,DG................. 50.00
195 MSy,WW 50.00
196 MSy,DG,giant,Origin rep. 55.00
197 MSy,DG................. 55.00
198 MSy,DG................. 55.00
199 JJ(c),DG 75.00
200 JJ(c),DG 90.00
201 DG,A:Catwoman 35.00
202 DG,A:Catwoman,I:Fafhrd
    & the Gray Mouser 35.00
203 DG,Womens lib............ 25.00
204 DH,BO,rewears costume ... 50.00
205 DH,BO.................. 25.00
206 DH,O:Wonder Woman 25.00
207 RE..................... 25.00
208 RE..................... 25.00
209 RE..................... 25.00
210 RE..................... 25.00
211 RE,giant 75.00
212 CS,A:Superman,tries to
    rejoin JLA 22.00
213 IN,A:Flash 22.00
214 CS,giant,A:Green Lantern ... 75.00
215 A:Aquaman.............. 20.00
216 A:Black Canary 20.00
217 DD,A:Green Arrow,giant 32.00
218 KS,Red Tornado 20.00
219 CS,A:Elongated Man 20.00
220 DG,NA,A:Atom 20.00
221 CS,A:Hawkman........... 20.00

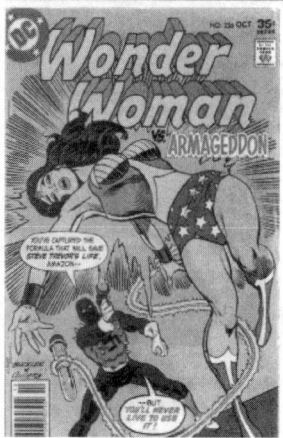

Wonder Woman #236
© DC Comics, Inc.

Wonder Woman 2nd Series #3
© DC Comics, Inc.

222 A:Batman	20.00
223 R:Steve Trevor	20.00
224	20.00
225	20.00
226	20.00
227	20.00
228 B:War stories	20.00
229	20.00
230 V:Cheetah	20.00
231	20.00
232 MN,A:JSA	20.00
233 GM	20.00
234	20.00
235	20.00
236	20.00
237 RB(c),O:Wonder Woman	22.00
238 RB(c)	15.00
239 RB(c)	15.00
240	15.00
241 JSon,DG,A:Spectre	18.00
242	12.00
243	12.00
244	12.00
245	12.00
246	12.00
247	12.00
248 D:Steve Trevor	15.00
249 A:Hawkgirl	12.00
250 I:Orana	12.00
251 O:Orana	12.00
252	15.00
253	12.00
254	12.00
255 V:Bushmaster	12.00
256 V:Royal Flush Gang	12.00
257	12.00
258	12.00
259	12.00
260	12.00
261	12.00
262 RE,A:Bushmaster	12.00
263	12.00
264	12.00
265	12.00
266	12.00
267 R:Animal Man	15.00
268 A:Animal Man	15.00
269 WW(i),Rebirth of Wonder Woman,pt.1	10.00
270 Rebirth,pt.2	10.00
271 JSon,B:Huntress,Rebirth,pt.3	10.00
272 JSon	10.00
273 JSon,A:Angle Man	10.00
274 JSon,I:Cheetah II	10.00

275 JSon,V:Cheetah II	10.00
276 JSon,V:Kobra	10.00
277 JSon,V:Kobra	10.00
278 JSon,V:Kobra	10.00
279 JSon,A:Demon,Catwoman	10.00
280 JSon,A:Demon,Catwoman	10.00
281 JSon,Earth 2 Joker	9.00
282 JSon,Earth 2 Joker	9.00
283 Earth 2 Joker	9.00
284	6.00
285 JSon,V:Red Dragon	6.00
286	6.00
287 DH,RT,JSon,Teen Titans	7.00
288 GC,RT,New Wonder Woman	7.00
289 GC,RT,JSon,New W.Woman	6.00
290 GC,RT,JSon,New W.Woman	6.00
291 GC,FMc,A:Zatanna	7.00
292 GC,FMc,RT,Supergirl	7.00
293 GC,FMc,Starfire,Raven	7.00
294 GC,FMc,JSon,V:Blockbuster	6.00
295 GC,FMc,JSon,Huntress	6.00
296 GC,Fmc,JSon	6.00
297 MK(c),GC,FMc,JSon	6.00
298 GC,FMc,JSon	6.00
299 GC,FMc,JSon	6.00
300 GC,FMc,RA,DG,KP,RB,KG C:New Teen Titans	8.00
301 GC,FMc	6.00
302 GC,FMc,V:Artemis	6.00
303 GC,FMc,Huntress	6.00
304 GC,FMc,Huntress	6.00
305 GC,Huntress,I:Circe	7.00
306 DH,Huntress	6.00
307 DH,Huntress,Black Canary	6.00
308 DH,Huntress,Black Canary	6.00
309 DH,Huntress	6.00
310 DH,Huntress	6.00
311 DH,Huntress	6.00
312 DH,DSp,A:Gremlins	6.00
313 DH,V:Circe	6.00
314 DH,Huntress	6.00
315 DH,Huntress	6.00
316 DH,Huntress	6.00
317 DH,V:Cereberus	6.00
318 DH,V:Space Aliens	6.00
319 DH,V:Dr.Cyber	6.00
320 DH	6.00
321 DH,Huntress	6.00
322 IN	6.00
323 DH,A:Cheetah, Angle Man	6.00
324 DH	6.00
325 DH	6.00
326 DH	6.00
327 DH,Crisis	6.00
328 DH,Crisis	6.00
329 DH,Crisis, giant	12.00

WONDER WOMAN
[2nd Regular Series], 1987

1 GP,O:Amazons,Wonder Woman	8.00
2 GP,I:Steve Trevor	6.00
3 GP,I:Julia Vanessa	6.00
4 GP,V:Decay	6.00
5 GP,V:Deimos,Phobos	6.00
6 GP,V:Ares	5.00
7 GP,I:Myndi Mayer	5.00
8 GP,O:Legends,A:JLA,Flash	5.00
9 GP,I:New Cheetah	5.00
10 GP,V:Seven Headed Hydra, Challenge of the Gods,pt.1, gatefold(c)	4.00
10a regular(c)	3.00
11 GP,V:Echidna,Challenge of the Gods,pt.3	4.00
12 GP,Millennium,V:Pan, Challenge of the Gods,pt.3, Millennium x-over	4.00
13 GP,Millennium,A:Ares,Challenge of the Gods,pt.4	4.00
14 GP,A:Hercules	4.00

15 GP,I:New Silver Swan	4.00
16 GP,V:Silver Swan	4.00
17 GP,DG,V:Circe	4.00
18 GP,DG,V:Circe,+Bonus bk#4	4.00
19 GP,FMc,V:Circe	4.00
20 GP,BMc,D:Myndi Mayer	4.00
21 GP,BMc,L:Greek Gods, Destruction of Olympus	3.00
22 GP,BMc,F:Julia, Vanessa	3.00
23 GP,R:Hermes,V:Phobos, Prelude to New Titans #50	3.00
24 GP,V:Ixion, Phobos	3.00
25 CMa,Invasion,A:JLA	3.00
26 CMa,Invasion,V:Capt.Atom	3.00
27 CMa,V:Khunds,A:Cheetah	3.00
28 CMa,V:Cheetah	3.00
29 CMa,V:Cheetah	3.00
30 CMa,V:Cheetah	3.00
31 CMa,V:Cheetah	3.00
32 TG,V:Amazons,A:Hermes	3.00
33 CMa,V:Amazons,Cheetah	3.00
34 CMa,I:Shim'Tar	3.00
35 CMa,V:Shim'Tar	3.00
36 CMa,A:Hermes	3.00
37 CMa,V:Discord,A:Superman	3.00
38 CMa,V:Eris	3.00
39 CMa,V:Eris,A:Lois Lane	3.00
40 CMa,V:Eris,A:Lois Lane	3.00
41 CMa,RT,F:Julia,Ties that Bind	3.00
42 CMa,RT,V:Silver Swan	3.00
43 CMA,RT,V:Silver Swan	3.00
44 CMa,RT,V:SilverSwan	3.00
45 CM,RT,Pandora's Box	3.00
46 RT,Suicide Issue,D:Lucy	3.00
47 RT,A:Troia	3.00
48 RTP,A:Troia	3.00
49 recap of 1st four years	3.00
50 RT,SA,BB,AH,CM,KN,PCR,MW A:JLA,Superman	4.00
51 RT,V:Mercury	3.00
52 CM,KN,Shards,V:Dr.Psycho	3.00
53 RT,A:Pariah	3.00
54 RT,V:Dr.Psycho	3.00
55 RT,V:Dr.Psycho	3.00
56 RT,A:Comm.Gordon	3.00
57 RT,A:Clark Kent,Bruce Wayne	3.00
58 RT,War of the Gods,V:Atlas	3.50
59 RT,War of the Gods, A:Batman Robin	3.50
60 RT,War of the Gods, A:Batman, Lobo	3.50
61 RT,War of the Gods,V:Circe	3.50
62 War o/t Gods,Epilogue	3.00
63 BB(c)A:Deathstroke,Cheetah	5.00

64 BB(c),Kidnapped Child 2.50
65 BB(c),PCu,V:Dr.Psycho 2.50
66 BB(c),PCu,Exodus In Space#1 . . 2.50
67 BB(c),PCu,Exodus In Space#2 . . 2.50
68 BB(c),PCu,Exodus In Space#3 . . 2.50
69 PCu, Exodus In Space#4 . . . . . . 2.50
70 PCu,Exodus In Space#5 . . . . . . 2.50
71 BB(c),DC,RT,Return fr.space . . . 2.50
72 BB(c),O:retold 2.50
73 BB(c),Diana gets a job 2.50
74 BB(c),V:White Magician 2.50
75 BB(c),A:The White Magician. . . 2.50
76 BB(c),A:Doctor Fate 2.50
77 BB(c). 2.50
78 BB(c),A:Flash 2.50
79 BB(c),V:Mayfly,A:Flash 2.50
80 BB(c),V:Ares Buchanan 2.50
81 BB(c),V:Ares Buchanan 2.50
82 BB(c),V:Ares Buchanan 2.50
83 BB(c),V:Ares Buchanan 2.50
84 BB(c),V:Ares Buchanan 2.50
85 BB(c). 13.00
86 BB(c),Turning Point. 6.00
87 BB(c),No Quarter,NoSanctuary . 6.00
88 BB(c),A:Superman 7.00
89 BB(c),A:Circle 6.00
90 New Direction 7.00
91 Choosing Wonder Woman 4.00
92 New Wonder Woman 4.00
93 New Wonder Woman 4.00
94 . . . . 5.00
95 V:Cheetah. 5.00
96 V:The Joker. 5.00
97 V:The Joker. 5.00
98 BB(c),F:Artemis. 3.00
99 BB(c),A:White Magician 3.00
100 BB(c) White Magician defeats
    Artemis 5.00
100a Collector's ed., holo(c) 6.00
101 V:White Magician 3.00
102 V:Metron,Darkseid 2.50
103 JBy,A:Darkseid 2.50
104 JBy,Diana takes crown? 2.50
105 JBy,Grecian artifact comes
    to life 2.50
106 JBy,A:The Demon,Phantom
    Stranger. 2.50
107 . . . . 2.50
108 JBy,F:The Demon,Arion,The
    Phantom Stranger 2.50
109 JBy,V:The Flash,I:Champion . . 2.50
110 JBy,V:Sinestro. 2.50
111 JBy,I:New Wonder Girl,
    V:Doomsday 2.50
112 JBy,V:Doomsday,A:Superman . 3.00
113 JBy,Wonder Girl vs. Decay 2.50
114 JBy,V:Doctor Psycho 2.50
115 JBy,beneath the Arctic ice. 2.50
116 JBy,beneath the Arctic ice. 2.50
117 JBy,V:Earth Moovers. 2.50
118 JBy 2.50
119 JBy,fight to regain Cheetah's
    humanity, cont. 2.50
120 JBy,48pg., pin-ups 4.00
121 JBy,Wonder Woman reverting
    to clay 2.50
122 JBy,Gods of Olympus are back 2.50
123 JBy,R:Artemis. 2.50
124 JBy,A:Demon 2.50
125 JBy,A:Donna Troy & JLA 2.50
126 JBy,JL,Genesis tie-in 2.50
127 JBy,JL(c),new era 2.50
128 JBy,JL,V:Egg Fu 2.50
129 JBy,JL,Hippolyta debuts as
    replacement Wonder Woman . . 2.50
130 JBy,JL,pt.1,A:Golden-age
    Flash 2.50
131 JBy,pt.2 . . . . 2.50
132 JBy,pt.3,A:Justice Society. 2.50
133 . . . . 2.50
134 JBy,Who is Donna Troy? 2.50

Wonder Woman 2nd Series #99
© DC Comics Inc.

135 JBy,secret revealed 2.50
136 JBy,back to Earth 2.50
137 CPr,V:Circe, pt.1 . . . . 2.50
138 MBr,F:Hippolyta,V:Circe,pt.2 . . 2.50
139 MBr,. 2.50
140 BMc,A:Superman & Batman. . . 2.50
141 BMc,A:Superman & Batman. . . 2.50
142 BMc,The Wonder Dome 2.50
143 BMc,Devastation,pt.1 . . . . 2.50
144 BMc,Devastation,pt.2 . . . . 2.50
145 BMc,Devastation,pt.3 . . . . 2.50
146 BMc,Devastation,pt.4 . . . . 2.50
147 BMc,GodWar begins. 2.50
148 BMc, GodWar, pt.2. . . . . 2.50
149 RBr,BMc,GodWar,pt.3. . . . . 2.50
150 GodWar, 48-pg. 4.00
151 AH(c),V:Dr. Poison 2.50
152 . . . . 2.50
153 MMr,F:Wonder Girl 2.50
154 Three Hearts,pt.1 . . . . 2.50
155 Three Hearts,pt.2 . . . . 2.50
156 Devastation Returns,pt.1 . . . . . 2.50
157 Devastation Returns,pt.2 . . . . . 2.50
158 Devastation Returns,concl. 2.50
159 WonderDome comes to Earth . 2.50
160 A Piece of You,pt.1 . . . . 2.50
161 A Piece of You,pt.2 . . . . 2.50
162 GodComplex,pt.1,A:Aquaman . 2.50
163 GodComplex,pt.2,A:Aquaman . 2.50
164 Gods of Gotham,pt.1 . . . . 6.00
165 Gods of Gotham,pt.2 . . . . 3.00
166 Gods of Gotham,pt.3 . . . . 3.00
167 Gods of Gotham,pt.4 . . . . 3.00
168 GP,Paradise Island Lost,pt.1 . . 2.25
169 GP,Paradise Island Lost,pt.2 . . 2.25
170 PJ,ALa,Lois & Diana 2.25
171 Our Worlds at War, tie-in 2.25
172 Our Worlds at War, tie-in 2.25
173 Our Worlds at War, tie-in 2.25
174 PJ,ALa,Witch & Warrior,pt.1 . . 2.25
175 PJ,ALa,Witch & Warrior,pt.2 . . 3.50
176 PJ,ALa,Witch & Warrior,pt.3 . . 2.25
177 PJ,ALa,Our Worlds at War 2.25
178 PJ,ALa,date with Trevor 2.25
179 PJ,ALa,V:Villainy,Inc. 2.25
180 PJ,ALa,O:new Villainy, Inc. . . . 2.25
181 PJ,ALa,prisoners of Skartaris . . 2.25
182 PJ,ALa,Shamballa 2.25
183 PJ,ALa,Skartaris mastermind . . 2.25
184 PJ,ALa,Diana,pt.1. . . . . 2.25
185 PJ,ALa,Diana in '40s,pt.2 . . . . 2.25
186 PJ,ALa,V:Barbara Minerva . . . 2.25
187 PJ,ALa,Cat fight 2.25
188 PJ,ALa,Day in the Life 2.25

189 WS,JOy,CR,Game Gods,pt.1 . . 2.25
190 WS,JOy,CR,Game Gods,pt.2 . . 4.00
191 WS,JOy,CR,Game Gods,pt.3 . . 2.25
192 WS,JOy,CR,Game Gods,pt.4 . . 2.25
193 WS,JOy,CR,Game Gods,pt.5 . . 2.25
194 WS,JOy,CR,Game Gods,pt.6 . . 2.50
195 AH. 3.00
196 Down to Earth,pt.1 . . . . 2.50
197 Down to Earth,pt.2 . . . . 2.50
198 Down to Earth,pt.3 . . . . 2.25
199 Down to Earth,pt.4 . . . . 2.25
200 Down to Earth, 64-pg. 4.00
201 Themyscira 2.25
202 V:Veronica Cale 2.25
203 Bitter Pills,pt.1 . . . . 2.25
204 Bitter Pills,pt.2. . . . . 2.25
205 Bitter Pills,pt.3. . . . . 2.25
206 Stoned,pt.1 . . . . 2.25
207 Stoned,pt.2 . . . . 2.25
208 Stoned,pt.3 . . . . 2.25
209 Stoned,pt.4 . . . . 2.25
Ann.#1,GP,AAd,RA,BB,JBo,JL,CS
    Tales of Paradise Island 4.00
Ann.#2 CM,F:Mayer Agency 4.00
Ann.#3 Eclipso tie-in 3.00
Ann.#4 Year One Annual 4.00
Ann.#5 JBy,DC,NBy,Legends of the
    Dead Earth 3.50
Ann.#6 Pulp Heroes (Macabre) 4.50
Ann.#7 Ghosts 3.50
Ann.#8 JLApe Gorilla Warfare 3.50
Annual #1 (1967) (rep.2003) 5.00
Spec.#1,000,000 CPr(s),MC,BMc . . 2.50
Spec #1 A:Deathstroke,Cheetah . . . 2.25
Spec.#0 History of Amazons 7.00
Spec.#1 Our Worlds at War,48-pg . . 3.00
GN Amazonia, BML 8.00
GN The Once and Future Story 5.00
GN Amazonia, Elseworlds 8.00
GN The Gods of Gotham, rep. 6.00
Secret Files #2. . . . . 5.00
Secret Files #3, 48-pg. 5.00
Spec. Wonder Woman: Donna Troy
    Girlfrenzy (1998) 2.00
Spec. Wonder Woman Plus CPr(s),
    MC, TP,Jesse Quick & Wonder
    Woman (1996). 3.00
Spec. The Blue Amazon (2003). . . . 7.00
TPB The Contest, rep. #90,#0
    #91-#93 . . . . 10.00
TPB The Challenge of Artemas . . 10.00
TPB Second Genesis JBy, rep.
    #101–#105. . . . . 10.00
TPB Spirit of Truth, over-size 10.00
TPB Paradise Lost, rep. 15.00
TPB Paradist Found (2003) 15.00
TPB The Hiketeia (2003) 18.00
TPB Gods and Mortals (2004). . . . 20.00
TPB Down to Earth (2004) 15.00
TPB Challenge of the Gods(2004) 20.00

WORLD OF KRYPTON

July, 1979

1 HC/MA.O:Jor-El. 10.00
2 HC/MA,A:Superman 6.00
3 HC 6.00

[2nd Series], 1987–88

1 MMi,John Byrne script. 3.00
2 MMi,John Byrne script. 3.00
3 MMi,John Byrne script. 3.00
4 MMi,A:Superman. 3.00

WORLD OF METROPOLIS

1988

1 DG(i),O:Perry White. 2.50
2 DG(i),O:Lois Lane 2.50
3 DG(i),O:Clark Kent 2.50
4 DG(i),O:Jimmy Olsen. 2.50

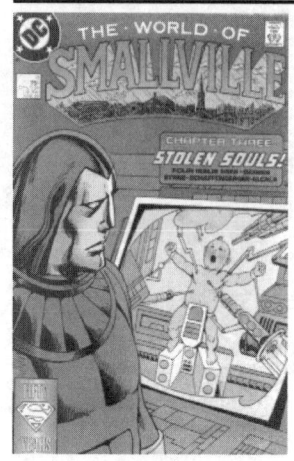

World of Smallville #3
© DC Comics, Inc.

WORLD OF SMALLVILLE
1988
1 KS/AA,Secrets of Ma&Pa Kent . . 3.00
2 KS/AA,Stolen Moments 3.00
3 KS/AA,Lana Lang/Manhunter . . . 3.00
4 KS/AA,final issue 3.00

WORLDS COLLIDE
1994
1 MBr(c),3RW,CsB,Ccs,DCw,
 TG,A:Blood Syndicate,Icon,
 Hardware,Static,Superboy,
 Superman,Steel,Vinyl Cling(c). . 4.25
1a Newsstand Ed. 2.75

WORLD'S BEST COMICS
Oct. 2003
Spec. G.A. DC Archives Sampler. . . 1.00
Spec. S.A. DC Archives Sampler. . . 1.00

WORLD'S BEST COMICS
Spring, 1941
1 Superman vs. the Rainmaker,
 Batman vs. Wright 22,000.00
Becomes:

WORLD'S FINEST COMICS
1941–86
2 Superman V:The Unknown X,
 Batman V:Ambrose Taylor . 6,500.00
3 I&O:Scarecrow 4,800.00
4 Superman V:Dan Brandon,
 Batman V:Ghost Gang 3,500.00
5 Superman V:Lemuel P.Potts,
 Batman V:Brains Kelly . . . 3,500.00
6 Superman V:Metalo,Batman
 meets Scoop Scanlon 2,600.00
7 Superman V:Jenkins,Batman
 V:Snow Man Bandits 2,600.00
8 Superman:Talent Unlimited
 Batman V:Little Nap Boyd,
 B:Boy Commandos 2,400.00
9 Superman:One Second to
 Live,Batman V:Bramwell B.
 Bramwell. 2,600.00
10 Superman V:The Insect Master,
 Batman reforms OliverHunt 2,300.00
11 Superman V:Charlie Frost,
 Batman V:Rob Calendar . . 1,800.00

12 Superman V:Lynx,Batman:
 Alfred Gets His Man 1,800.00
13 Superman V:Dice Dimant,
 Batman,V:Swami Pravhoz . 1,800.00
14 Superman V:Al Bandar,Batman
 V:Jib Buckler. 1,800.00
15 Superman V:Derby Bowser,
 Batman V:Mennekin 1,800.00
16 Superman:Music for the Masses,
 Batman V:Nocky Johnson . 1,800.00
17 Superman:The Great Godini,
 Batman V:Dr.Dreemo 1,800.00
18 Superman:The Junior Reporters,
 Batman V:Prof.Brane 1,700.00
19 A:The Joker 1,700.00
20 A:Toyman 1,700.00
21 Superman:Swindle in
 Sweethearts!. 1,100.00
22 Batman V:Nails Finney 1,100.00
23 Superman:The Colossus
 of Metropolis. 1,100.00
24 . . . . 1,100.00
25 Superman V:Ed Rook,Batman:
 The Famous First Crimes. . 1,100.00
26 Confessions of Superman . . 1,100.00
27 The Man Who Out-Supered
 Superman. 1,100.00
28 A:Lex Luther,Batman V:Glass
 Man. 1,100.00
29 Superman:The Books that
 couldn't be Bound. 1,100.00
30 Superman:Sheriff Clark Kent,
 Batman V:Joe Coyne 1,100.00
31 Superman's Super-Rival,Batman:
 Man with the X-Ray Eyes. . 1,000.00
32 Superman visits
 Ancient Egypt. 1,000.00
33 Superman Press, Inc.,
 Batman V:James Harmon . 1,000.00
34 The Un-Super Superman. . . 1,000.00
35 Daddy Superman,A:Penguin 1,000.00
36 Lois Lane,Sleeping Beauty . 1,000.00
37 The Superman Story,Batman
 V:T-Gun Jones 1,000.00
38 If There were No Superman 1,000.00
39 Superman V:Big Jim Martin,
 Batman V:J.J.Jason 1,000.00
40 Superman V:Check,Batman:4
 Killers Against Fate! 1,000.00
41 I:Supermanium,
 E:Boy Commandos 800.00
42 Superman goes to Uranus,
 A:Marco Polo & Kubla Khan . 800.00
43 A:J.Wilbur Wolfingham 800.00
44 Superman:The Revolt of the
 Thought Machine. 800.00
45 Superman:Lois Lane and Clark
 Kent,Private Detectives. . . . 800.00
46 Superman V:Mr. 7. . . . . 800.00
47 Superman:The Girl Who
 Hated Reporters 800.00
48 A:Joker 800.00
49 Superman meets the
 Metropolis Shutterbug
 Society, A:Penguin. 800.00
50 Superman Super Wrecker . . . 800.00
51 Superman:The Amazing
 Talents of Lois Lane 800.00
52 A:J.Wilbur Wolfingham 800.00
53 Superman V:Elias Toomey . . . 800.00
54 The Superman Who Avoided
 Danger! 800.00
55 A:Penguin 800.00
56 Superman V:Dr.Vallin,Batman
 V:Big Dan Hooker 800.00
57 The Artificial Superman. 800.00
58 Superman V:Mr.Fenton. 800.00
59 A:Lex Luthor,Joker 800.00
60 A:J.Wilbur Wolfingham 800.00
61 A:Joker,Superman's
 Blackout. 700.00

World's Finest #144
© DC Comics, Inc.

62 A:Lex Luthor 700.00
63 Superman:Clark Kent,
 Gangster 700.00
64 Superman:The Death of Lois
 Lane,Batman:Bruce Wayne...
 Amateur Detective. 700.00
65 The Confessions of Superman,
 Batman V:The Blaster 1,000.00
66 Superman,Ex-Crimebuster;
 Batman V:Brass Haley 700.00
67 Superman:Metropolis-Crime
 Center!. 700.00
68 Batman V:The Crimesmith . . . 700.00
69 A:Jor-El,Batman
 V:Tom Becket 700.00
70 The Two Faces of Superman,
 Batman:Crime Consultant . . . 700.00
71 B:Superman/Batman
 team-ups. 1,500.00
72 V:Heavy Weapon gang 1,000.00
73 V:Fang 1,000.00
74 The Contest of Heroes 800.00
75 V:The Purple Mask Mob 750.00
76 When Gotham City
 Challenged Metropolis. 700.00
77 V:Prof.Pender 600.00
78 V:Varrel mob 600.00
79 A:Aladdin. 600.00
80 V:Mole. 600.00
81 Meet Ka Thar from future 450.00
82 A:Three Musketeers 450.00
83 The Case of the Mother
 Goose Mystery 450.00
84 V:Thad Linnis gang. 450.00
85 Meet Princess Varina 450.00
86 V:Henry Bartle. 450.00
87 V:Elton Craig. 450.00
88 1st team-up Luthor & Joker . . . 475.00
89 I:Club of Heroes 450.00
90 A:Batwoman 450.00
91 V:Rohtul,descendent of Lex
 Luthor 350.00
92 lst & only A:Skyboy. 350.00
93 V:Victor Danning. 350.00
94 O:Superman/Batman team,
 A:Lex Luthor 900.00
95 Battle o/t Super Heroes 350.00
96 Super-Foes from Planet X . . . 350.00
97 V:Condor Gang. 350.00
98 I:Moonman 350.00
99 JK,V:Carl Verril 350.00
100 A:Kandor, Lex Luthor 600.00
101 A:Atom Master 225.00
102 V:Jo-Jo Groff gang,
 B:Tommy Tomorrow. 225.00

103 The Secrets of the
Sorcerer's Treasure 225.00
104 A:Lex Luthor 225.00
105 V:Khalex 225.00
106 V:Duplicate Man 225.00
107 The Secret of the Time
Creature 225.00
108 The Star Creatures 225.00
109 V:Fangan 225.00
110 The Alien Who Doomed
Robin! 225.00
111 V:Floyd Frisby 225.00
112 . . . . 225.00
113 1st Bat-Mite/Mr.Mxyzptlk
team-up 225.00
114 Captives o/t Space Globes . . 225.00
115 The Curse That Doomed
Superman 175.00
116 V:Vance Collins 175.00
117 A:Batwoman,Lex Luthor 175.00
118 V:Vath-Gar 175.00
119 V:General Grambly 175.00
120 V:Faceless Creature 175.00
121 I:Miss Arrowette 175.00
122 V:Klor 175.00
123 A:Bat-Mite & Mr. Mxyzptlk . . . 125.00
124 V:Hroguth,E:Tommy
Tomorrow 125.00
125 V:Jundy,B:Aquaman 125.00
126 A:Lex Luthor 125.00
127 V:Zerno 125.00
128 V:Moose Morans 125.00
129 Joker/Luthor T.U. 150.00
130 . . . . 125.00
131 V:Octopus 125.00
132 V:Denny Kale,Shorty Biggs . 125.00
133 . . . . 125.00
134 V:Band of Super-Villians 125.00
135 V:The Future Man 125.00
136 The Batman Nobody
Remembered 125.00
137 A:Lex Luthor 125.00
138 V:General Grote 125.00
139 V:Sphinx Gang,E:Aquaman . 125.00
140 CS,V:Clayface 125.00
141 CS,A:Jimmy Olsen 125.00
142 CS,O:Composite Man 125.00
143 CS,A:Kandor,I:Mailbag 75.00
144 CS,A:Clayface,Braniac 75.00
145 CS,Prison for Heroes 75.00
146 CS,Batman,Son of Krypton . . 75.00
147 CS,A:Jimmy Olsen 75.00
148 CS,A:Lex Luthor,Clayface . . . 75.00
149 CS,The Game of the
Secret Identities 75.00
150 CS,V:Rokk and Sorban 65.00
151 CS,A:Krypto,BU:Congorilla . . . 65.00
152 CS,A:The Colossal Kids,Bat-
mite,V:Mr.Mxyzptlk 65.00
153 CS,V:Lex Luthor 65.00
154 CS,The Sons of Batman &
Superman(Imaginary) 65.00
155 CS,The 1000th Exploit of
Batman & Superman 65.00
156 CS,I:BizarroBatman,V:Joker . 150.00
157 CS,The Abominable Brats
(Imaginary story) 65.00
158 CS,V:Brainiac 65.00
159 CS,A:Many Major villians,I:Jim
Gordon as Anti-Batman & Perry
White as Anti-Superman 65.00
160 V:Dr Zodiac 65.00
161 CS,80 page giant 90.00
162 V:The Jousting Master 50.00
163 CS,The Court of No Hope . . . 50.00
164 CS,I:Genia,V:Brainiac 50.00
165 CS,The Crown of Crime 50.00
166 CS,V:Muto & Joker 60.00
167 CS,The New Superman &
Batman(Imaginary) V:Luthor . . 50.00
168 CS,R:Composite Superman . . 50.00

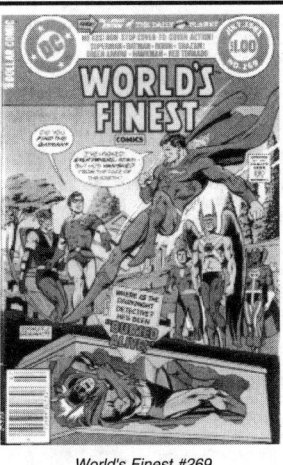

World's Finest #269
© DC Comics Inc.

169 The Supergirl/Batgirl Plot;
V:Batmite,Mr.Mxyzptlk 50.00
170 80 page giant,reprint 90.00
171 CS,V:The Executioners 50.00
172 CS,Superman & Batman
Brothers (Imaginary) 50.00
173 CS,The Jekyll-Hyde
Heroes 125.00
174 CS,Secrets of the Double
Death Wish 60.00
175 NA(1st Batman),C:Flash 65.00
176 NA,A:Supergirl & Batgirl 65.00
177 V:Joker & Luthor 60.00
178 CS,The Has-Been Superman . 50.00
179 CS,giant 75.00
180 RA,ME,Supermans Perfect
Crime 50.00
181 RA,ME 50.00
182 RA,ME,The Mad Manhunter . . 50.00
183 RA,ME,Superman's Crimes
of the Ages 50.00
184 RA,ME,A:JLA,Robin 50.00
185 CS,The Galactic Gamblers . . . 50.00
186 RA,ME,The Bat Witch 50.00
187 RA,ME,Demon Superman . . . 50.00
188 giant,reprint 75.00
189 RA,ME,V:Lex Luthor 40.00
190 RA,V:Lex Luthor 30.00
191 RA,A:Jor-El,Lara 30.00
192 RA,The Prison of No Escape . 30.00
193 The Breaking of Batman
and Superman 30.00
194 RA,ME,Inside the Mafia 30.00
195 RA,ME,Dig Now-Die Later . . . 30.00
196 CS,The Kryptonite Express,
E:Batman 30.00
197 giant 75.00
198 DD,B:Superman T.U.,
A:Flash 125.00
199 DD,Superman & Flash race . 125.00
200 NA(c),DD,Prisoners of the
Immortal World; A:Robin 40.00
201 NA(c),DD,A Prize of Peril,
A:Green Lantern,Dr. Fate 25.00
202 NA(c),DD,Vengeance of the
Tomb Thing,A:Batman 25.00
203 NA(c),DD,Who's Minding the
Earth,A:Quamar 25.00
204 NA(c),DD,Journey to the End
of Hope,A:Wonder Woman . . . 25.00
205 NA(c),DD,The Computer that
Captured a Town,Frazetta Ad,
A:Teen Titans 30.00
206 DD,giant reprint 65.00

207 DD,Superman,A:Batman,
V:Dr.Light 35.00
208 NA(c),DD,A:Dr Fate 35.00
209 NA(c),DD,A:Green Arrow,
Hawkman,I&V:The Temper . . . 35.00
210 NA(c),DD,A:Batman 35.00
211 NA(c),DD,A:Batman 35.00
212 CS(c),And So My World
Begins,A:Martian Manhunter . . 35.00
213 DD,Peril in a Very Small
Place,A:The Atom 35.00
214 DD,A:Vigilante 35.00
215 DD,Saga of the Super Sons
(Imaginary story) 40.00
216 DD,R:Super Sons,Little Town
with a Big Secret 20.00
217 DD,MA,Heroes with
Dirty Hands 20.00
218 DD,DC,A:Batman,
BU:Metamorpho 20.00
219 DD,Prisoner of Rogues Rock;
A:Batman 20.00
220 DD,MA,Let No Man Write My
Epitaph,BU:Metamorpho 20.00
221 DD,Cry Not For My Forsaken
Son; R:Super Sons 20.00
222 DD,Evil In Paradise 20.00
223 DD,giant,A:Deadman,Aquaman
Robotman 60.00
224 DD,giant,A:Super Sons,
Metamorpho,Johnny Quick . . . 60.00
225 giant,A:Rip Hunter,Vigilante,
Black Canary,Robin 60.00
226 A:Sandman,Metamorpho,
Deadman,Martian Manhunter . 60.00
227 MGr,BWi,A:The Demonic Duo,
Vigilante,Rip Hunter,Deadman,
I:Stargrave 60.00
228 ATh,A:Super Sons,Aquaman,
Robin,Vigilante 60.00
229 I:Powerman,A:Metamorpho . . 30.00
230 A:Super-Sons,Deadman,
Aquaman, giant-size 50.00
231 A:Green Arrow,Flash 18.00
232 DD,The Dream Bomb 18.00
233 A:Super-Sons 18.00
234 CS,Family That Fled Earth . . . 18.00
235 DD,V:Sagitaurus 18.00
236 DD,A:The Atom 18.00
237 Intruder from a Dead World . . 18.00
238 DD,V:Luthor,A:Super-Sons . . . 18.00
239 CS,A:Gold(from Metal Men) . . 18.00
240 DD,A:Kandor 15.00
241 Make Way For a New World . . 15.00
242 EC,A:Super-Sons 15.00
243 CS,AM,A:Robin 15.00
244 NA(c),JL,MA,MN,TA,giant
B:Green Arrow 22.00
245 NA(C),CS,MA,MN,TA,
GM,JSh,BWi,giant 22.00
246 NA(c),KS,MA,MN,TA,GM,
DH,A:JLA 22.00
247 KS,GM,giant 22.00
248 KS,GM,DG,TVE,A:Sgt.Rock . . 18.00
249 KS,SD,TVE,A:Phantom
Stranger,B:Creeper 18.00
250 GT,SD,Superman,Batman,
Wonder Woman,Green Arrow,
Black Canary,team-up 20.00
251 GT,SD,JBi,BL,TVE,RE,
JA,A:Poison Ivy,Speedy,
I:CountVertigo 20.00
252 GT,TVE,SD,JA,giant 20.00
253 KS,DN,TVE,SD,B:Shazam . . . 14.00
254 GT,DN,TVE,SD,giant 14.00
255 JL,DA,TVE,SD,DN,KS,
E:Creeper 14.00
256 MA,DN,KS,DD,Hawkman,Black
Lightning,giant 14.00
257 DD,FMc,DN,KS,GT,RB,
RT,giant 14.00

All comics prices listed are for *Near Mint* condition.

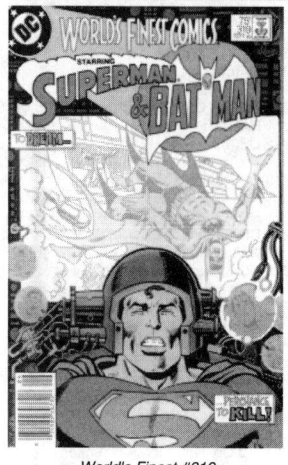

World's Finest #319
© DC Comics, Inc.

258 NA(c),RB,JL,DG,DN,KS,RT,
　　giant.................... 15.00
259 RB,DG,MR,MN,DN,KS 14.00
260 RB,DG,MN,DN 14.00
261 RB,DG,AS,RT,EB,DN,
　　A:Penguin, Terra Man 14.00
262 DG,DN,DA,JSon,RT,
　　Aquaman.................. 14.00
263 RB,DG,DN,TVE,JSh,Aquaman,
　　Adam Strange 14.00
264 RB,DG,TVE,DN,Aquaman ... 14.00
265 RB,DN,RE,TVE............. 14.00
266 RB,TVE,DN............... 14.00
267 RB,DG,TVE,AS,DN,
　　A:Challengers of the Unknown 14.00
268 DN,TVE,BBr,RT,AS......... 14.00
269 RB,FMc,TVE,BBr,AS,DN,DA . 14.00
270 NA(c),RB,RT,TVE,AS,
　　DN,LMa.................. 14.00
271 GP(c),RB,FMc,O:Superman/
　　Batman T.U............... 14.00
272 RB,DN,TVE,BBr,AS 12.00
273 TVE,LMa,JSon,AS,DN,DA,
　　A:Plastic Man 12.00
274 TVE,LMa,BBr,GC,AS,DN,
　　Green Arrow 12.00
275 RB,FMc,TVE,LMa,DSp,AS,
　　DN,DA,A:Mr.Freeze........ 12.00
276 GP(c),RB,TVE,LMa,DSp,CI,
　　DN,DA 12.00
277 GP(c),RT,TVE,DSp,AS,DN,
　　DH,V:Dr.Double X 12.00
278 GP(c),RB,TVE,LMa,DSp,DN . 12.00
279 KP,TVE,LMa,AS,DN,
　　B:Kid Eternity............. 12.00
280 RB,TVE,LMa,AS,DN 12.00
281 GK(c),IN,TVE,LMa,AS,DN ... 12.00
282 IN,FMc,GK,CI,last giant
　　E:Kid Eternity............. 12.00
283 GT,FMc,GK.............. 12.00
284 GT,DSp,A:Legion,E:G.Arrow . 12.00
285 FM(c),RB,A:Zatanna....... 12.00
286 RB,A:Flash 12.00
287 TVE,A:Flash 12.00
288 A:JLA.................. 12.00
289 GK(c),Kryll way of Dying..... 12.00
290 TD(i),I:Stalagron 12.00
291 WS(c),TD(i),V:Stalagron 12.00
292 .... 12.00
293 .... 12.00
294 .... 12.00
295 FMc(i) 12.00
296 RA.................... 12.00

297 GC,V:Pantheon........... 12.00
298 V:Pantheon.............. 12.00
299 GC,V:Pantheon........... 12.00
300 RA,GP,KJ,MT,FMc,A:JLA 12.00
301 Rampage 5.00
302 DM,NA(rep)............... 5.00
303 Plague.................. 5.00
304 SLi,O:Null&Void 5.00
305 TVE,V:Null&Void 5.00
306 SLi,I:Swordfish & Barracuda... 5.00
307 TVE,V:Null&Void........... 5.00
308 GT,Night and Day 5.00
309 MT,AA,V:Quantum 5.00
310 I:Sonik.................. 5.00
311 A:Monitor................ 5.00
312 AA,I:Network............. 5.00
313 AA(i),V:Network........... 5.00
314 AA(i),V:Executrix.......... 5.00
315 V:Cathode 5.00
316 LSn,I:Cheapjack 5.00
317 LSn,V:Cheapjack 5.00
318 AA(i),A:Sonik............. 5.00
319 AA(i),I:REM 5.00
320 AA(i),V:REM 5.00
321 AA,V:Chronos............ 5.00
322 KG,The Search 5.00
323 AA(i),final issue........... 5.00
Spec.#1 Our Worlds at War,48-pg.. 4.00

WORLD'S FINEST
[Limited Series], 1990
1 SR,KK,Worlds Apart 8.00
2 SR,KK,Worlds Collide 6.00
3 SR,KK,Worlds At War 6.00
TPB rep.#1-#3 .... 20.00

WORLD'S FINEST:
SUPERBOY/ROBIN
Oct., 1996
1 (of 2) CDi&KK(s),TG,SHa,
　　V:Poison Ivy, Metallo 5.00
2 CDi&KK(s),TG,SHa, V:Poison
　　Ivy, Metallo............... 5.00

WORLD'S GREATEST
SUPER-HEROES
1977
1 A:Batman,Robin............. 35.00

WORLD WITHOUT END
1990
1 The Host, I:Brother Bones...... 5.00
2 A:Brother Bones............. 3.50
3 .... 3.50
4 House of Fams 2.50
5 Female Fury................ 2.50
6 conclusion 2.50

WRATH OF THE
SPECTRE
May, 1988
1 JAp,rep.Adventure #431-#433... 4.00
2 JAp,rep.Adventure #434-#436... 4.00
3 JAp,rep.Adventure #437-#440... 4.00
4 JAp,reps.,final issue.......... 5.00

XENOBROOD
1994–95
0 New team.................. 2.25
1 Battles 2.25
2 Bestiary 2.25
3 A:Superman................ 2.25
4 V:Bestiary................. 2.25
5 V:Vimian.................. 2.25
6 final issue................. 2.25

XERO
March, 1997
1 Cpr(s),Ccs,Trane Walker/Xero .. 3.00
2 CPr(s),Ccs,The Rookie 2.50
3 Cpr(s),Ccs,The Beast 2.50
4 CPr(s) 2.50
6 CPr, Genesis tie-in.......... 2.50
7 CPr(s),O:Zero, pt.1 .... 2.50
8 CPr,O:Zero................ 2.25
9 CPr(s),.................. 2.25
10 CPr,a matter of ethics........ 2.25
11 .... 2.25
12 CPr, final issue, Xero dead..... 2.25

XOMBI
Milestone, 1994–96
0 WS(c),DCw,Shadow War,Foil(c),
　　I:Xombi,Twilight 2.50
1 JBy(c),B:Silent Cathedrals...... 2.00
1a Platinum ed................ 7.00
2 I:Rabbi Simmowitz,Golms,Liam
　　Knight of the Spoken Fire 2.50
3 A:Liam 2.00
4 Silent Cathedrals 2.00
5 Silent Cathedrals 2.50
6 Silent Cathedrals 2.50
7 School of Anguish 2.50
8 School of Anguish,pt.2......... 2.50
9 School of Anguish,pt.3......... 2.50
10 School of Anguish,pt.4 .... 2.50
11 School of Anguish,pt.5 .... 2.50
12 Truth and Surprises 2.50
13 V:Kinderessen.............. 2.50
14 Long Hot Summer, A:Cheryl
　　Saltz..................... 2.50
15 Long Hot Summer............ 2.50
16 Long Hot Summer............ 2.50
17 Reader's Choice 2.50
18 Serpent's Tail 2.50
19 Mister Missy, Bellhop 2.50
20 .... 2.50
21 final issue 3.50

Y: THE LAST MAN
DC/Vertigo, July, 2002
1 JMz,UnManned,pt.1,40-pg...... 30.00
2 JMz,UnManned,pt.2........... 25.00
3 JMz,UnManned,pt.3........... 20.00
4 JMz,UnManned,pt.4........... 15.00
5 JMz,UnManned,pt.5........... 10.00
6 JMz,Cycles,pt.1 .... 7.00
7 JMz,Cycles,pt.2 .... 6.00
8 JMz,Cycles,pt.3 .... 6.00
9 JMz,Cycles,pt.4 .... 6.00
10 JMz,Cycles,pt.5............. 4.00
11 JMz,One Small Step,pt.1 ...... 4.00
12 JMz,One Small Step,pt.2 ...... 4.00
13 JMz,One Small Step,pt.3 ...... 4.00
14 JMz,One Small Step,pt.4 ..... 3.50
15 JMz,One Small Step,pt.5 ..... 3.50
16 JMz,Comedy&Tragedy,pt.1..... 3.50
17 JMz,Comedy&Tragedy,pt.2..... 3.00
18 JMz,Safeword,pt.1 .... 3.00
19 JMz,Safeword,pt.2 .... 3.00
20 JMz,Safeword,pt.3 .... 3.00
21 JMz,Widow's Pass,pt.1........ 3.00
22 JMz,Widow's Pass,pt.2........ 3.00
23 JMz,Widow's Pass,pt.3........ 3.00
24 JMz,Tongues of Flame,pt.1..... 3.00
25 JMz,Tongues of Flame,pt.2..... 3.00
26 JMz,Hero's Journey 3.00
27 JMz,Ring of Truth,pt.1......... 3.00
TPB Unmanned 13.00
TPB Cycles 13.00
TPB One Small Step 13.00

YEAH!
Homage/DC, 1999

1 GHe	3.00
2 GHe	3.00
3 GHe	3.00
4 GHe,Origins of Yeah,pt.1	3.00
5 GHe,Origins of Yeah,pt.2	3.00
6 GHe,	3.00
7 GHe,	3.00
8 GHe,	3.00
9 GHe,final issue	3.00

YOUNG ALL STARS
June, 1987

1 I:IronMunro&FlyingFox,D:TNT	4.50
2 V:Axis Amerika	2.50
3 V:Axis Amerika	2.25
4 I:The Tigress	2.25
5 I:Dyna-mite,O:Iron Munro	2.25
6	2.25
7 Baseball Game,A:Tigress	2.25
8 Millennium	2.25
9 Millennium	2.25
10 Hugo Danner	2.25
11 Birth of Iron Munro	2.25
12 Secret of Hugo Danner	2.25
13 V:Deathbolt,Ultra-Humanite	2.25
14 Fury+Ultra Humanite	2.25
15 IronMunro At high school	2.25
16 Ozyan Inheritance	2.25
17 Ozyan Inheritance	2.25
18 Ozyan Inheritance	2.25
19 Ozyan	2.25
20 O:Flying Fox	2.25
21 Atom & Evil#1	2.25
22 Atom & Evil#2	2.25
23 Atom & Evil#3	2.25
24 Atom & Evil#4	2.25
25	2.25
26 End of the All Stars?	2.25
27 Sons of Dawn' begins	2.25
28 Search for Hugo Danner	2.25
29 A:Hugo Danner	2.25
30 V:Sons of Dawn	2.25
31 V:Sons of Dawn,last issue	2.25
Ann.#1 MG,V:Mekanique	2.50

YOUNG HEROES IN LOVE
April, 1997

1 DeM,F:Hard Drive	3.00
2 DeM,sex, lies and superheroics	2.50
3 A:Superman	2.50
4 F:Hard Drive	2.50
5 Genesis tie-in	2.50
6 The Rat Pack	2.50
7 Secret Identity Issue	2.50
8 V:Scarecrow	2.50
9 F:Frostbite & Bonfire	2.50
10 V:Grundo'mu	2.50
11 V:Grundo'mu	2.50
12 Hard Drive dead?	2.50
13 New leader picked	2.50
14 Man of Inches vs. Man of Candles	2.50
15 Junior vs. Birthday Boy	2.50
16 DeM,Zip-Kid	2.50
17 DeM,Monstergirl's Uncle	2.50
Spec.#1,000,000 DeM final issue	3.00

YOUNG JUSTICE
July, 1998

1 PDd,TNu,Robin,Superboy, Impulse	4.50
2 PDd,TNu,V:Super-Cycle	3.00
3 PDd(s),TNu,V:Mr.Mxyzptlk	3.00

4 PDd(s),TNu,Girls join team	3.00
5 PDd(s),TNu,V:Harm	3.00
6 PDd(s),TNu,F:JLA	3.00
7 PDd(s),TNu,A:Nightwing	3.00
8 CDi(s),TNu,A:Razorsharp	3.00
9 PDd(s),V:Huggathugees	3.00
10 PDd(s),V:The Acolyte	3.00
11 PDd(s),Rescue Red Tornado	3.00
12 PDd(s),TNu,Supergirl x-over Hell's Angels,pt.1	3.00
13 PDd(s), Hell's Angels,pt.3	3.00
14 PDd(s),Day of Judgment x-over	3.00
15 PDd(s),F:Arrowette	3.00
16 PDd(s)	3.00
17 PDd(s),A:A.P.E.S.	3.00
18 PDd(s),Young Injustice	3.00
19 PDd(s),I:Empress	3.00
20 PDd(s),new team	3.00
21 PDd(s),all new?	2.75
22 Day in the life	2.75
23 PDd,TNu,AustraliaGames,pt.1	2.75
24 PDd,TNu,AustraliaGames,pt.2	2.75
25 PDd,TNu,Into space,pt.1	2.75
26 PDd,TNu,Into space,pt.2	2.75
27 PDd,TNu,Into space,pt.3	2.75
28 PDd,TNu,New Genesis	2.75
29 PDd,TNu,F:Forever People	2.75
30 PDd,TNu,Secret vs. Spoiler	2.75
31 PDd,TNu,F:Empress	2.75
32 PDd,TNu,F:Empress	2.75
33 PDd,TNu,WendyWerewolfHunter	2.75
34 PDd,TNu,wolf bites	2.75
35 PDd,TNu,Worlds at War,tie-in	2.75
36 PDd,TNu,Worlds at War,tie-in	2.75
37 PDd,TNu,stuck in Hell	2.75
38 PDd,TNu,jokerized Match	2.75
39 PDd,TNu,V:New Genesis	2.75
40 PDd(s),Christmas Past	2.75
41 PDd(s),TNu,F:Ray	2.75
42 PDd(s),TNu,F:Hal Jordan	2.75
43 PDd(s),TNu,F:Traya	2.75
44 PDd(s),TNu,WorldWithoutYJ,pt.1	2.75
45 PDd(s),TNu,WorldWithoutYJ,pt.5	2.75
46 PDd(s),TNu,election day at HQ	2.75
47 PDd(s),TNu,Fighting MAAD,pt.1	2.75
48 PDd(s),TNu,Fighting MAAD,pt.2	2.75
49 PDd(s),TNu,Fighting MAAD,pt.3	2.75
50 PDd(s),TNu,F.MAAD,pg.4,48-pg	3.95
51 PDd(s),TNu, on Zandia	2.75
52 PDd(s),TNu,Real World	2.75
53 PDd(s),TNu,V:Secret	2.75
54 PDd(s),TNu,V:Secret	2.75
55 PDd(s),TNu,final issue	2.75
Spec.#1,000,000 PDd(s),TNu	3.00
Giant#1 Secret Origins, 80-page	5.00
Giant#1 80-page	5.00
Secret Files #1	5.00
Spec.#1 Young Justice in No Man's Land, CDi(s)	4.00
Spec.#1 Young Justice: The Secret Impulse,Superboy,Robin (1998)	2.50
Spec.#1 Our Worlds at War	2.95
TPB A League of Their Own	14.95

YOUNG JUSTICE: SINS OF YOUTH
March, 2000

1 (of 2) PDd,x-over	4.00
2 PDd,x-over	4.00
Secret Files #1	5.00
TPB Sins of Youth	20.00

YOUNG LOVE
Sept.–Oct., 1963

39	75.00
40 thru 50	@50.00

51 thru 60	@40.00
61 thru 68	@40.00
69 giant size	75.00
70 thru 80	@40.00
81 thru 99 giants, 52-page	@30.00
100	35.00
101 thru 106	@25.00
107 GC, Giant, 100-page	125.00
108 thru 114 Giant, 100-page	@100.00
115 thru 126 52-page	@50.00

Zatanna #3 © DC Comics Inc.

ZATANNA
1987

1 R:Zatanna	2.25
2 N:Zatanna	2.25
3 Come Together	2.25
4 V:Xaos	2.25

ZERO GIRL
DC/Homage Dec., 2000

1 (of 5) SK,F:Amy Snooster	3.00
2 SK,	3.00
3 SK,Vice Principal Hooly	3.00
4 SK,Mr. Foster	3.00
5 SK, concl.	3.00
TPB series rep. 144-page	13.00

ZERO GIRL: FULL CIRCLE
DC/Vertigo, Nov., 2002

1 (of 5) SK	3.00

ZERO HOUR: CRISIS IN TIME
1994

4 DJu(a&s),JOy,A:All DC Heroes, D;2nd Flash	4.50
3 DJu(a&s),JOy,D:G.A.Sandman, G:A.Atom,Dr.Fate,1st Wildcat IR:Time Trapper is Rokk Krinn, Hawkmen merged	2.50
2 DJu(a&s),Joy	2.50
1 DJu(a&s),JOy,b:Power Gir's Child	2.50
0 DJu(A&s),JOy,Gatefold(c),Extant vs. Spectre	2.50

AMAZON
DC, 1996–97
1 JBy,TA 3.00
1 one-shot JBy,Princess Ororo
   is Wonder Woman 2.25

ASSASSINS
DC, 1996–97
1 DGC,SMc. 3.00
1 one-shot DGC(s),SMc,F:Dare
   and Catsai 2.25

BAT-THING
DC, 1997
1 one-shot LHa(s),RDm,BSz,
   V:motorcycle gang 2.25

BRUCE WAYNE:
AGENT OF S.H.I.E.L.D.
Marvel, 1996
1 CDi, ... 3.00

BULLETS & BRACELETS
Marvel, 1996
1 JOs,GFr,CaS 3.00

CHALLENGERS OF
THE FANTASTIC
Marvel, 1997
1 KK,TGu,AV 2.25

DARK CLAW
ADVENTURES, THE
DC, 1997
1 one-shot TTy,RBr,V:Ladia Talia . . 2.25

DC VERSUS MARVEL
MARVEL VERSUS DC
1 (DC)DJu. 6.00
1a 2nd printing 4.00
2 (Marvel)PDd,DJu 5.00
2a 2nd printing 4.00
3 (Marvel)DJu 4.00
4 (DC)PDd,DJu 4.00
TPB rep. mini series #1–#4 . . . . . 13.00

DOCTOR STRANGEFATE
DC, 1996–97
1 RMz,KN 3.00
1 one-shot RMz(s),JL,KN,Supreme
   Lord of Order 2.25

EXCITING X-PATROL
Marvel, 1997
1 BKs,BHi 2.25

GENERATION HEX
DC, 1997
1 one-shot,PrM(s),AdP,F:Jono Hex,
   Madam Banshee 2.25

IRON LANTERN
Marvel, 1997
1 KB,PSm,AW. 2.25

JLX
DC Comics 1996–97
1 MWa,GJ, ... 3.00
1 one-shot,MWa(s),GJ,HPo,JhD . . 2.25

JLX UNLEASHED
DC, 1997
1 one-shot, CPr,The Inextinguish-
   able Flame. 2.25

LEGENDS OF
THE DARK CLAW
DC, 1996–97
1 LHa,JBa, ... 3.00
1 one-shot LHa(s),JBa, ... 2.25
1 2nd printing 2.25

LOBO THE DUCK
DC, 1997
1 one-shot, AlG,VS, ... 2.25

MAGNETO &
THE MAGNETIC MEN
Marvel, 1996
1 MWa,GJ,JMs,ATi 3.00

MAGNETIC MEN
FEATURING MAGNETO
Marvel, 1997
1 TPe,BKi,DPs 2.25

SPEED DEMON
Marvel, 1996
1 HMe,SvL,AM 3.00

SPIDER-BOY
Marvel, 1996
1 KK,MeW. 3.00

SPIDER-BOY TEAM-UP
Marvel, 1997
1 KK,RSt 2.25

SUPER-SOLDIER
DC, 1996–97
1 MWa,DGb 3.00
1-shot MWa(s),DGb,V:Ultra-
   Metallo, Green Skull, Hydra . . . 2.25

SUPER SOLDIER:
MAN OF WAR
DC, 1997
1 one-shot MWa(s),DGb,JP,
   V:Nazis 2.25

THORION OF
THE NEW ASGODS
Marvel, 1997
1 KG,JR2. 2.25

X-PATROL
Marvel, 1996
1 KK,BKs, ... 3.00
The Amalgam Age of Comics: The DC
Comics Collection TPBs 13.00
The Amalgam Age of Comics: The
Marvel Comics Collection TPBs . . 13.00

Return to the Amalgam Age of Comics:
The DC Comics Collection TPB . . 13.00

Assassins #1 © DC/Marvel

Lobo The Duck #1 © DC/Marvel

Super Soldier #1 © DC/Marvel

MARVEL

MARVEL

ABOMINATIONS
1996
1 (of 3) IV,AMe, Future Imperfect
spin-off 2.25
2 IV,AMe, ... 2.25
3 IV,AMe, ... 2.25

ABRAHAM STONE
1995
1 JKu, Early 20th century 7.00
2 Wandering Man in the 20s. 7.00

ACTION FORCE
March, 1987
1 U.K. G.I. Joe Series 2.25
2 thru 40 . . . . @2.25

ACTUAL CONFESSIONS
See: LOVE ADVENTURES

ACTUAL ROMANCES
Oct., 1949
1 . . . . 125.00
2 Photo Cover. 75.00

ADVENTURE INTO FEAR
See: FEAR

ADVENTURE INTO MYSTERY
Atlas, 1956–57
1 BP,BEv(c),Future Tense 400.00
2 Man on the 13th Floor 200.00
3 Next Stop Eternity 175.00
4 BP,AW, The Hex 200.00
5 JO,BEv,The People Who
Weren't 175.00
6 The Wax Man 175.00
7 AT,BEv(c) 175.00
8 AT,JWo,TSe 175.00

ADVENTURES INTO TERROR
See: JOKER COMICS

ADVENTURES INTO WEIRD WORLDS
Jan., 1952–June, 1954
1 RH,GT,The Walking Death . . . 800.00
2 GT,JMe,Thing in the Bottle . . . 450.00
3 JMe,The Thing That Waited . . 300.00
4 BEv,RH,TheVillageGraveyard . 300.00
5 BEv,I Crawl Thru Graves 300.00
6 The Ghost Still Walks 300.00
7 OW,Monsters In Disguise 300.00
8 DAy,Nightmares. 300.00
9 Do Not Feed 300.00
10 BEv,Down In The Cellar 300.00
11 JMe,Phantom 250.00
12 GT,Lost In the Graveyard 250.00
13 JeR,DRi,Where Dead Men
Walk. 250.00
14 A Shriek In the Night. 250.00
15 GT,Terror In Our Town 250.00
16 The Kiss of Death. 250.00
17 RH,He Walks With A Ghost . . 250.00

Adventures Into Weird Worlds #6
© Marvel Entertainment Group

18 Ivan & Petroff 250.00
19 It Happened One Night. 250.00
20 JMe,The Doubting Thomas . . 250.00
21 JF,What Happened In
the Cave,Hitler. 300.00
22 JMe,RH,Vampire's Partner . . . 250.00
23 JMe,The Kiss of Death 225.00
24 JF,Halfway Home 225.00
25 BEv,JSt,The Mad Mamba 225.00
26 DAy,Good-Bye Earth. 250.00
27 The Dwarf of Horror Moor. . . . 450.00
28 DW,Monsters From the Grave 250.00
29 Bone Dry. 175.00
30 JSt,The Impatient Ghost 175.00

ADVENTURES OF CAPTAIN AMERICA
Sept., 1991
1 KM,JRu,O:Capt. America. 5.75
2 KM,KWe,TA,O:Capt.America. . . . 5.50
3 KM,KWe,JRu,D:Lt.Col.Fletcher . . 5.50
4 KWe,JRu,V:Red Skull 5.50

ADVENTURES OF CYCLOPS & PHOENIX
1994
1 SLo(s),GeH,AV,O:Cable 5.00
2 SLo(s),GeH,AV,O:Cable 4.00
3 SLo(s),GeH,AV,O:Cable 4.00
4 SLo(s),GeH,AV,O:Cable 4.00
TPB rep. #1-#4 . . . . 14.95

ADVENTURES OF HOMER GHOST
Atlas, June–Aug., 1957
1 . . . . 100.00
2 . . . . 100.00

ADVENTURES OF PINKY LEE
Atlas, July, 1955
1 . . . . 300.00
2 . . . . 200.00
3 thru 5 . . . . @175.00

ADVENTURES OF SNAKE PLISSKIN
1997
1-shot LKa, Escape From L.A.
movie adapt. 3.00

ADVENTURES OF SPIDER-MAN
1996
1 from animated TV show. 3.00
2 V:Hammerhead 3.00
3 thru 8 . . . . 3.00
8 AS,V:Kingpin 3.00
9 MHi,A:Dr. Strange,. 3.00
10 AS,V:The Beetle 3.00
11 AS,V:Doctor Octopus, Venom. . . 3.00
12 AS,V:Doctor Octopus, Venom. . . 3.00

ADVENTURES OF THE THING
April–July, 1992
1 rep. Marvel 2 in 1 #50 . . . . 2.50
2 rep. Marvel 2 in 1 #80 . . . . 2.25
3 rep. Marvel 2 in 1 #51 . . . . 2.25
4 rep. Marvel 2 in 1 #77 . . . . 2.25

ADVENTURES OF THE UNCANNY X-MEN
1995
1 Rep. 2.50

ADVENTURES OF THE X-MEN
1996–97
1 from animated TV show. 3.00
2 X-Factor vs. X-Men 3.00
3 thru 12 . . . . @3.00

ADVENTURES ON THE PLANET OF THE APES
Oct., 1975
1 GT,Planet of the Apes Movie
Adaptation 30.00
2 GT,Humans Captured 15.00
3 GT,Man Hunt 15.00
4 GT,Trial By Fear. 15.00
5 GT, Fury in the Forbidden Zone 15.00
6 GT,The Forbidden Zone,Cont'd . 30.00
7 AA,Man Hunt Cont'd 30.00
8 AA,Brent & Nova Enslaved 15.00
9 AA,Mankind's Demise 15.00
10 AA,When Falls the Lawgiver. . . 15.00
11 AA,Final Chapter,Dec.,1976 . . . 20.00

AGENT X
July, 2002
1 Taskmaster trainee,40-pg. 3.50
2 Hunts the Punisher 3.00
3 V:Taskmaster. 3.00
4 Who is Mary Zero 3.00
5 . . . . 2.50
6 . . . . 2.50
7 . . . . 2.50
8 MkK,pt.1. . . . . 2.50
9 MkK,pt.2. . . . . 2.50
10 EDo(s). 3.00
11 EDo(s). 3.00

12 BSf(c)	3.00
13 Deedpool Walkin,pt.1	3.00
14 Deedpool Walkin,pt.2	3.00
15 Deedpool Walkin,pt.3	3.00

AGE OF INNOCENCE
1995
1-shot Timeslid aftermath 2.50

AIRTIGHT GARAGE
Epic, July–Oct., 1993
1 thru 4 rep.Moebius GNv. . . . . @3.50

AKIRA
Epic, Sept., 1988

1 The Highway,I:Kaneda,Tetsuo, Koy,Ryu,Colonel,Takaski	30.00
1a 2nd printing	4.00
2 Pursuit,I:Number27,(Masaru)	17.00
2a 2nd printing	3.50
3 Number 41,V:Clown Gang	12.00
4 King of Clowns,V:Colonel	12.00
5 Cycle Wars,V:Clown Gang	12.00
6 D:Yamagota	10.00
7 Prisoners and Players,I:Miyo	10.00
8 Weapon of Vengeance	10.00
9 Stalkers	10.00
10 The Awakening	10.00
11 Akira Rising	7.00
12 Enter Sakaki	7.00
13 Desperation	7.00
14 Caught in the Middle	7.00
15 Psychic Duel	7.00
16 Akira Unleashed	7.00
17 Emperor of Chaos	7.00
18 Amid the Ruins	6.00
19 To Save the Children	6.00
20 Revelations	6.00
21	6.00
22	6.00
23	6.00
24 Clown Gang	6.00
25 Search For Kay	6.00
26 Juvenile A Project	6.00
27 Kay and Kaneda	6.00
28 Tetsuo	6.00
29 Tetsuo	6.00
30 Tetsuo,Kay,Kaneda	6.00
31 D:Kaori,Kaneda,Vs.Tetsuo	6.00
32 Tetsuo'sForces vs.U.S.Forces	6.00
33 Tetsuo V:Kaneda	6.00
34 64pt. R:Otomo	14.00
35 Leads toward final battle	14.00
36 Lady Miyako	14.00
37 ghost of Tetsuo	14.00
38 conclusion	14.00
TPB Akira:Reprints#1–#3	14.00
TPB Akira:Reprints#4–#6	14.00
TPB Akira:Reprints#7–#9	14.00
TPB Akira:Reprints#10–#12	15.00
TPB Akira:Reprints#13–#15	15.00
TPB Akira:Reprints#16–#18	15.00
TPB Akira:Reprints#19–#21	17.00
TPB Akira:Reprints#22–#24	17.00
TPB Akira:Reprints#25–#27	17.00
TPB Akira:Reprints#28–#30	18.00

ALADDIN
1994

1 Aladdin's Quest	2.25
2 thru 12	@2.25

ALF
Star, March, 1988

1 Photo Cover	4.00
1a 2nd printing	2.50
2 Alf Causes trouble	2.50
3 More adventures	2.50

4 Willie on Melmac	2.50
5 I:Alf's evil twin	2.50
6 Photo Cover	2.50
7 Pygm-Alien	2.50
8 Ochmoneks' Garage	2.50
9 Alf's Independence Day	2.50
10 Alf goes to College	2.50
11 Halloween special	2.50
12 Alf loses memory	2.50
13 Racetrack of my Tears	2.50
14 Night of the Living Bread	2.50
15 Alf on the Road	2.50
16 More Adventures	2.50
17 Future vision	2.50
18 More Adventures	2.50
19 The Alf-strologer	2.50
20 Alf the Baby Sitter,pt.1	3.00
21 Alf the Baby Sitter,pt.2	3.00
22 X-Men parody	3.00
23 Alf visits Australia	2.50
24 Rhonda visits Earth.	2.50
25 More Adventures	2.50
26 Alf gets a job	2.50
27 Alf lost	2.50
28 Alf's Amnesia	2.50
29 Alf/Brian reporters	2.50
30 Shakespeare Baby	2.50
31 Alf's Summer Camp	3.00
32 Arnold Schwarzemeimac	3.00
33 Dungeons & Dragons Spoof	3.00
34 Alf-Red & Alf-Blue(2 Alfs)	3.00
35 Gone with the Wind	3.00
36 More Adventures	3.00
37 Melmacian Gothic	3.00
38 Boundtree Hunters	3.00
39 Pizarro Alf	3.00
40 A:Zoreo	3.00
41 TV	3.00
42 V:Alf	3.00
43 House Break-in	3.00
44 A:Fantastic Fur	4.00
45 Melmenopaus	4.00
46 Goes to Center of Earth	3.00
47 Meteor Bye-Products,pt.1	3.00
48 Meteor Bye-Products,pt.2	3.00
49 1st Rhonda solo story	3.00
50 Final Issue, giant size	4.00
Ann.#1 Evol.War	3.00
Ann.#2	3.00
Spring Spec.#1	3.00
Holiday Spec.#2	3.00

ALIAS
Marvel Max, Sept., 2001

1 BMB(s)	10.00
2 BMB(s), F:Jessica Jones	6.00
3 BMB(s)	6.00
4 BMB(s),DMk(c)	6.00
5 BMB(s),DMk(c)	4.00
6 BMB(s),DMk(c),	4.00
7 BMB(s),BSz	4.00
8 BMB(s),BSz	4.00
9 BMB(s),2nd story, concl.	4.00
10 BMB(s),J.J.Jameson,Jessica	3.50
11 BMB(s),to small town	3.50
12 BMB(s),in small town	3.50
13 BMB(s)	3.50
14 BMB(s),DMk(c),case concludes	3.50
15 BMB(s),DMk(c),Cage again	3.50
16 BMB(s),DMk(c),Underneath	3.50
17 BMB(s),DMk(c),Underneath	3.50
18 BMB(s),DMk(c),Underneath	3.50
19 BMB(s),DMk(c),Underneath	3.50
20 BMB(s),DMk(c),Underneath	3.50
21 BMB(s),DMk(c),Underneath	3.50
22 BMB(s),DMk(c),Jessica Jones	3.25
23 BMB(s),DMk(c),Jessica Jones	3.25
24 BMB(s),DMk(c),Purple,pt.1	3.25
25 BMB(s),DMk(c),Purple,pt.2	3.25
26 BMB(s),DMk(c),Purple,pt.3	3.25

27 BMB(s),DMk(c),Purple,pt.4	3.25
28 BMB(s),DMk(c),Purple,pt.5	4.00
TPB Vol. 1	20.00
TPB Vol. 2: Come Home	14.00
TPB Vol. 3: Underneath	17.00
TPB Vol. 4: Secret Origins	18.00

Alien Legion #2
© Marvel Entertainment Group

ALIEN LEGION
Epic, April, 1984

1 FC,TA,I:Sarigar,Montroc	4.00
2 FC,TA,CP,V:Harkilons	3.50
3 FC,TA,CW,V:Kroyzo	3.00
4 FC,TA,CW,F:Skob	3.00
5 FC,CW,D:Skob	3.00
6 FC,CW,WPo,V:Harkilons	3.00
7 CW,WPo,I:Lora	3.00
8 CW,WPo,V:Harkilons	3.00
9 CW,V:Harkilons	3.00
10 CW,LSn,V:Harkilons	3.00
11 CW,LSn,V:Harkilons	3.00
12 LSn,A:Aob-Sin	3.00
13 LSn,F:Montroc	3.00
14 LSn,V:Cordar	3.00
15 LSn,V:Alphor,Betro,&Gamoid	3.00
16 LSn,J:Tomaro	3.00
17 LSn,Durge on Drugs	3.00
18 LSn,V:Dun	3.00
19 LSn,A:GalarcyScientist	3.00
20 LSn,L:Skilene	3.00

[2nd Series], Aug., 1987

1 LSn,I:Guy Montroc	3.00
2 LSn,V:Quallians	2.50
3 LSn,Hellscope	2.50
4 LSn,V:Harkillons	2.50
5 LSn,F:JuggerGrimrod	2.50
6 LSn,F:JuggerGrimrod	2.50
7 LSn,A:Guy Montroc	2.50
8 LSn,I:Nakhira	2.50
9 LSn,V:Harkilons	2.50
10 LSn,V:Harkilons	2.50
11 LSn,V:Harkilons	2.50
12 LSn,Tamara Pregnant	2.50
13 LSn,V:MomojianKndrel	2.50
14 LSn,J:Saravil	2.50
15 LSn,J:Spellik	2.50
16 LSn,D:Jugger's Father	2.50
17 LSn,O:JuggerGrimrod	2.50
18 LSn,O:JuggerGrimrod	2.50
GN Grimrod	5.95
1-shot Alien Legion: Binary Deep with trading card (1993)	3.50

ALIEN LEGION: JUGGER GRIMROD

Epic, Aug., 1992

Book One 6.00

ALIEN LEGION: ONE PLANET AT A TIME

Epic, Heavy Hitters May, 1993

1 HNg,CDi,One Planet at a Time . . 5.00
2 HNg,CDi.................... 5.00
3 HNg,CDi.................... 5.00

ALIEN LEGION: ON THE EDGE

Epic, Nov., 1990

1 LSn,V:B'Be No N'ngth 5.00
2 LSn,V:B'Be No N'ngth 5.00
3 LSn,V:B'Be No N'ngth 5.00
4 LSn,V:B'Be No N'ngth 5.00

ALIEN LEGION: TENANTS OF HELL

Epic, 1991

1 LSn,Nomad Squad On
   Combine IV 5.00
2 LSn,L:Torie Montroc,I:Stagg 5.00
TPB Alien Legion:Slaughterworld . 10.00

ALL-SELECT COMICS

Timely, (Daring Comics)
Fall, 1943

1 B:Capt.America,Sub-Mariner,
   Human Torch;WWII 18,000.00
2 A:Red Skull,V:Axis Powers.. 6,000.00
3 B:Whizzer,V:Axis........... 3,500.00
4 V: Axis.................... 2,400.00
5 E:Sub-Mariner,V:Axis 2,400.00
6 A:The Destroyer,V:Axis..... 1,800.00
7 MSu,E:Whizzer,V:Axis 1,800.00
8 MSu,V:Axis Powers 1,800.00
9 V:Axis Powers............. 1,800.00
10 E:Capt.America,Human Torch;
   A:The Destroyer......... 1,800.00
11 I:Blonde Phantom,A:Miss
   America 3,500.00
Becomes:

BLONDE PHANTOM

1946

12 B:Miss America;The Devil's
   Playground 2,200.00
13 B:Sub-Mariner;Horror In
   Hollywood.............. 1,400.00
14 E:Miss America;Horror At
   Haunted Castle.......... 1,200.00
15 The Man Who Deserved
   To Die 1,200.00
16 A:Capt.America,Bucky;
   Modeled For Murder...... 1,700.00
17 Torture & Rescue 1,000.00
18 Jealously,Hate & Cruelty .. 1,000.00
19 Killer In the Hospital....... 1,000.00
20 Blonde Phantom's Big Fall . 1,000.00
21 Murder At the Carnival..... 1,000.00
22 V: Crime Bosses 1,000.00
Becomes:

LOVERS

1949

23 Love Stories 175.00
24 My Dearly Beloved 100.00
25 The Man I Love 100.00
26 thru 29.................. @75.00
30 MK...................... 100.00
31 thru 36 .... @75.00
37 .... 100.00

All-Select Comics #1
© Marvel Entertainment Group

38 BK..................... 100.00
39 .... 75.00
40 .... 75.00
41BEv.................... 100.00
42 thru 65 .... @75.00
66 .... 60.00
67 ATh 75.00
68 thru 86 Aug., 1957........ @60.00

ALL SURPRISE

Timely, Fall, 1943

1 (fa),F:Super Rabbit,Gandy,
   Sourpuss 300.00
2 .... 150.00
3 .... 125.00
4 thru 10 .... @125.00
11 HK 135.00
12 Winter, 1946 .... 100.00

ALL-TRUE CRIME
See: OFFICIAL TRUE CRIME CASES

ALL WINNERS COMICS

Summer, 1941

1 S&K,BEv,B:Capt.America & Bucky,
   Human Torch & Toro,Sub-Mariner
   A:The Angel,Black Marvel 33,000.00
2 S&K,B:Destroyer,Whizzer... 7,500.00
3 BEv,Bucky & Toro Captured . 4,500.00
4 BEv,Battle For Victory
   For America 5,000.00
5 V:Nazi Invasion Fleet 3,000.00
6 V:Axis Powers,A:
   Black Avenger.......... 3,500.00
7 V:Axis Powers............ 2,700.00
8 V:Axis Powers............ 2,500.00
9 V:Nazi Submarine Fleet 2,500.00
10 V:Nazi Submarine Fleet.... 2,700.00
11 V: Nazis 1,900.00
12 A:Red Skull,E:Destroyer;
   Jap P.O.W. Camp........ 2,000.00
13 V:Japanese Fleet......... 1,900.00
14 V:Japanese Fleet......... 1,900.00
15 Japanese Supply Train 1,900.00
16 In Alaska V:Gangsters..... 1,900.00
17 V:Gansters;Atomic
   Research Department 1,900.00
18 V:Robbers;Internal Revenue
   Department............. 2,100.00

19 I:All Winners Squad,
   Fall, 1946 .... 6,500.00
21 A:All-Winners Squad;Riddle
   of the Demented Dwarf ... 5,500.00
Becomes:

ALL TEEN COMICS

1947

20 F:Georgie,Willie,
   Mitzi,Patsy Walker........ 150.00
Becomes:

TEEN COMICS

1947

21 HK,A:George,Willie,Mitzi,
   Patsy Walker, Hey Look 175.00
22 A:George,Willie,Margie,
   Patsy Walker 125.00
23 A:Patsy Walker,Cindy,George. 125.00
24 .... 150.00
25 thru 27................. @125.00
28 .... 150.00
29 .... 125.00
30 HK,Hey Look............. 150.00
31 thru 34................. @125.00
35 May, 1950 .... 125.00
Becomes:

JOURNEY INTO UNKNOWN WORLDS

Atlas, Sept., 1950

36(1) RH,End of the Earth.... 3,200.00
37(2) BEv,GC,When Worlds
   Collide................ 1,400.00
38(3) GT,Land of Missing Men 1,100.00
4 MS,RH,Train to Nowhere..... 700.00
5 MS,Trapped in Space 700.00
6 GC,RH,World Below
   the Atlantic............. 700.00
7 BW,RH,JMn,House That
   Wasn't............... 1,200.00
8 RH,JMn,The Stone Thing 700.00
9 MS,JSt,The People Who
   Couldn't Exist 750.00
10 THe Undertaker 700.00
11 BEv,Frankie Was Afraid 500.00
12 BK,Last Voice You Hear 500.00
13 The Witch Woman 400.00
14 BW,BEv,CondemnedBuilding . 900.00
15 JMn,They Crawl By Night 900.00
16 JMn,Scared to Death 400.00
17 BEv,GC,RH,The Ice
   Monster Cometh 450.00
18 The Broth Needs Somebody . 450.00
19 MF,GC,The Long Wait 450.00

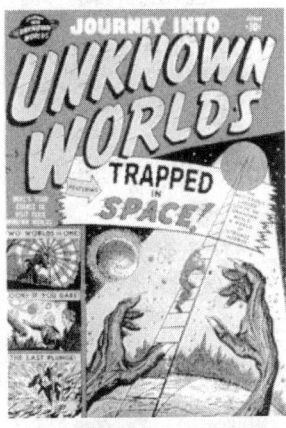

Journey Into Unknown Worlds #5
© Marvel Entertainment Group

Journey Into Unknown Worlds #38
© Marvel Entertainment Group

20 GC,RH,The Race That
 Vanished 400.00
21 MF,JMn,JSt,Decapitation 300.00
22 thru 32 . . . . @300.00
33 LO 300.00
34 MK,AT,DAy 250.00
35 AT,MD 250.00
36 thru 44 . . . . @200.00
45 AW,SD 225.00
46 & 47. . . . . @200.00
48 GW,GM 200.00
49 JF,JMn. 200.00
50 JDa,RC 200.00
51 WW,SD,JSe 200.00
52 . . . . 200.00
53 RC,BP 200.00
54 AT,BP 200.00
55 AW,RC,BEv. 200.00
56 BEv 200.00
57 JO 175.00
58 MO,MD,JMn 175.00
59 AW,Aug., 1957 . . . . 200.00

ALL WINNERS COMICS
[2nd Series], Aug., 1948
1 F:Blonde Phantom,A:Capt.America
Sub-Mariner,Human Torch 4,000.00
Becomes:

ALL WESTERN WINNERS
1948–49
2 B,I&O:Black Rider,B:Two-Gun
 Kid, Kid-Colt. 1,000.00
3 Black Rider V: Satan 450.00
4 Black Rider Unmasked 450.00
Becomes:

WESTERN WINNERS
1949
5 I Challenge the Army. 400.00
6 The Mountain Mystery 350.00
7 Ph(c) Randolph Scott 350.00
Becomes:

BLACK RIDER
1950–55
8 Ph(c),B:Black Rider;Valley
 of Giants 550.00
9 Wrath of the Redskin. 275.00
10 O:Black Rider 325.00
11 Redmen on the Warpath. 200.00
12 GT,The Town That Vanished. . 200.00
13 The Terrified Tribe. 200.00
14 The Tyrant of Texas 200.00

---

15 Revolt of the Redskins 175.00
16 . . . . 175.00
17 . . . . 175.00
18 . . . . 175.00
19 SSh,GT,A:Two-Gun Kid 175.00
20 GT. 200.00
21 SSh,GT,A:Two-Gun Kid 175.00
22 SSh,DAy(c),A:Two-Gun Kid . . 175.00
23 SSh,A:Two-Gun Kid 175.00
24 SSh,JSt. 175.00
25 SSh,JSt,A:Arrowhead 175.00
26 SSh,A:Kid-Colt 175.00
27 SSh,A:Kid-Colt 200.00
Becomes:

WESTERN TALES OF BLACK RIDER
1955
28 JSe,D:Spider. 225.00
29 . . . . 150.00
30 . . . . 150.00
31 . . . . 150.00
Becomes:

GUNSMOKE WESTERN
1955–63
32 MD,MB,F:Kid Colt,Billy
 Buckskin 200.00
33 MD 150.00
34 MB. 125.00
35 GC. 150.00
36 AW,GC 150.00
37 JDa 125.00
38 . . . . 100.00
39 GC. 100.00
40 AW 125.00
41 thru 43. . . . . @75.00
44 AT 75.00
45 & 46. . . . . @75.00
47 JK 100.00
48 & 49. . . . . @75.00
50 JK,RC 125.00
51 JK 100.00
52 thru 54. . . . . @75.00
55 & 56 MB . . . . @75.00
57 Two Gun Kid 60.00
58 & 59. . . . . @60.00
60 Sam Hawk (Kid Colt) 75.00
61 RC. 90.00
62 thru 67 JK . . . . @80.00
68 . . . . 60.00
69 JK 80.00
70 . . . . 60.00
71 JK 80.00
72 O:Kid Colt 75.00
73 JK 80.00
74 thru 76. . . . . @60.00
77 JK,July, 1963 . . . . 125.00

(TIMELY PRESENTS:) ALL-WINNERS
Oct., 1999
Spec. 48-pg. 4.00

ALPHA FLIGHT
Aug., 1983
1 JBy,I:Puck,Marrina,Tundra. 4.00
2 JBy,I:Master,Vindicator Becomes
 Guardian,B:O:Marrina 2.50
3 JBy,O:Master,A:Namor,Invisible
 Girl, ... 2.50
4 JBy,A:Namor,Invisible Girl,
 E:O:Marrina,A:Master 2.50
5 JBy,B:O:Shaman,F:Puck 2.50
6 JBy,E:O:Shaman,I:Kolomag . . . 2.50
7 JBy,B:O:Snowbird,I:Delphine
 Courtney & Deadly Ernest. 2.50
8 JBy,E:O:Snowbird,O:Deadly
 Ernest,I:Nemesis 2.50

---

9 JBy,O:Aurora,A:Wolverine,
 Super Skrull. 2.50
10 JBy,O:Northstar,V:SuperSkrull . . 2.50
11 JBy,I:Omega Flight,Wild Child
 O:Sasquatch 2.50
12 JBy,D:Guardian,V:Omega
 Flight 2.50
13 JBy,C:Wolverine,Nightmare . . . 3.00
14 JBy,V:Genocide. 2.50
15 JBy,R:Master. 2.50
16 JBy,BWi,V:Master,C:Wolverine
 I:Madison Jeffries 2.75
17 JBy,BWi,A:Wolverine,X-Men. . . 3.00
18 JBy,BWi,J:Heather,I:Ranaq. . . . 2.50
19 JBy,I:Talisman,V:Ranaq 2.50
20 JBy,I:Gilded Lily,N:Aurora 2.50
21 JBy,BWi,O:Gilded Lily,Diablo . . 2.50
22 JBy,BWi,I:Pink Pearl 2.50
23 JBy,BWi,D:Sasquatch,
 I:Tanaraq 2.50
24 JBy,BWi,V:Great Beasts,J:Box . . 2.50
25 JBy,BWi,V:Omega Flight
 I:Dark Guardian. 2.50
26 JBy,BWi,A:Omega Flight,Dark
 Guardian 2.50
27 JBy,V:Omega Flight 2.50
28 JBy,Secret Wars II,V:Omega
 Flight,D:Dark Guardian 2.50
29 MMi,V:Hulk,A:Box 2.50
30 MMi,I&O:Scramble,R:Deadly
 Ernest 2.50
31 MMi,D:Deadly Ernest,
 O:Nemesis 2.50
32 MMi(c),JBg,O:Puck,I:2nd
 Vindicator. 2.50
33 MMi(c),SB,X-Men,I:Deathstrike . 4.00
34 MMi(c),SB,Wolverine,V:
 Deathstrike 3.00
35 DR,R:Shaman. 2.50
36 MMi(c),DR,A:Dr.Strange 2.50
37 DR,O:Pestilence,N:Aurora 2.50
38 DR,A:Namor,V:Pestilence. 2.50
39 MMi(c),DR,WPo,A:Avengers . . 2.75
40 DR,WPo,W:Namor & Marrina . . . 2.75
41 DR,WPo,I:Purple Girl,
 J:Madison Jeffries 2.75
42 DR,WPo,I:Auctioneer,J:Purple
 Girl,A: Beta Flight 2.75
43 DR,WPo,V:Mesmero,Sentinels. . 2.75
44 DR,WPo,D:Snowbird,
 A:Pestilence. 2.75
45 JBr,WPo,R:Sasquatch,
 L:Shaman 2.75
46 JBr,WPo,I:2nd Box 2.75
47 MMi,WPo,TA,Vindicator solo . . 2.75
48 SL(i),I:Omega 2.75
49 JBr,WPo,I:Manikin,D:Omega . . 2.75
50 WS(c),JBr,WPo,L:Northstar,Puck,
 Aurora,A:Loki,Double size 3.00
51 JLe(1st Marv),WPo(i),V:Cody . . . 7.00
52 JBr,WPo(i),I:Bedlam,
 A:Wolverine 3.00
53 JLe,WPo(i),I:Derangers,Goblin
 D&V:Bedlam,A:Wolverine 4.00
54 WPo(i),O&J:Goblyn. 2.50
55 JLe,TD,V:Tundra. 3.50
56 JLe,TD,V:Bedlamites 3.50
57 JLe,TD,V:Crystals,
 C:Dreamqueen 3.50
58 JLe,AM,V:Dreamqueen. 3.50
59 JLe,AM,I:Jade Dragon,R:Puck . . 3.50
60 JLe,AM,V:J.Dragon,D.Queen . . . 3.50
61 JLe,AM,on Trial
 (1st JLe X-Men). 3.50
62 JLe,AM,V:Purple Man. 3.50
63 MG,V:U.S.Air Force. 2.50
64 JLe,AM,V:Great Beasts 3.50
65 JLe(c),AM(i),Dream Issue. 3.00
66 JLe(c),I:China Force 3.00
67 JLe(c),O:Dream Queen 3.00
68 JLe(c),V:Dream Queen 3.00

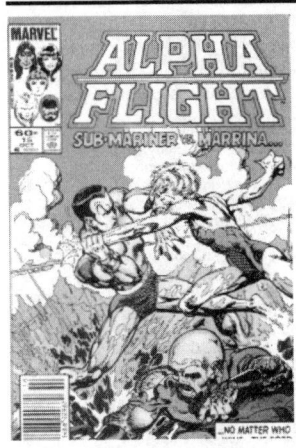

Alpha Flight #15
© Marvel Entertainment Group

69 JLe(c),V:Dream Queen 3.00
70 MM(i),V:Dream Queen 2.50
71 MM(i),I:Sorcerer 2.50
72 V:Sorcerer 2.50
73 MM(i),V:Sorcerer 3.00
74 MM(i),Alternate Earth 3.00
75 JLe(c),MMi(i),Double Size 3.00
76 MM(i),V:Sorcerer 2.25
77 MM(i),V:Kingpin 2.25
78 MM(i),A:Dr.Strange,Master 2.25
79 MM(i),AofV,V:Scorpion,Nekra . . . 2.25
80 MM(i),AofV,V:Scorpion,Nekra . . . 2.25
81 JBy(c),MM(i),B:R:Northstar 2.25
82 JBy(c),MM(i),E:R:Northstar 2.25
83 JSh 2.25
84 MM(i),Northstar 2.25
85 MM(i) 2.25
86 MBa,MM,V:Sorcerer 2.25
87 JLe(c),MM(i),A:Wolverine 3.00
88 JLe(c),MM(i),A:Wolverine 3.00
89 JLe(c),MM(i),R:Guardian,A:
    Wolverine 3.00
90 JLe(c),MM(i),A:Wolverine 3.00
91 MM(i),A:Dr.Doom 2.25
92 Guardian vs.Vindicator 2.25
93 MM(i),A:Fant.Four,I:Headlok 2.25
94 MM(i),V:Fant.Four,Headlok 2.25
95 MM(i),Lifelines 2.25
96 MM(i),A:Master 2.25
97 B:Final Option,A:Her 2.25
98 A:Avengers 2.25
99 A:Avengers 2.25
100 JBr,TMo,DR,LMa,E:Final Option
    A:Galactus,Avengers,D:
    Guardian,G-Size 2.50
101 TMo,Final Option Epilogue,
    A:Dr.Strange,Avengers 2.25
102 TMo,I:Weapon Omega, ... 2.25
103 TMo,V:Diablo,U.S.Agent 2.25
104 TMo,N:Alpha Flight,Weapon
    Omega is Wild Child 2.25
105 TMo,V:Pink Pearl 2.25
106 MPa,Aids issue,Northstar
    acknowledges homosexuality . . 3.00
106a 2nd printing 2.50
107 A:X-Factor,V:Autopsy 2.25
108 A:Soviet Super Soldiers 2.25
109 V:Peoples Protectorate 2.25
110 PB,Infinity War,I:2nd Omega
    Flight,A:Wolverine 2.25
111 PB,Infinity War,V:Omega
    Flight,A:Wolverine 2.25
112 PB,Infinity War,V:Master 2.25
113 V:Mauler 2.25

114 A:Weapon X 2.25
115 PB,I:Wyre,A:Weapon X 2.25
116 PB,I:Rok,V:Wyre 2.25
117 PB,V:Wyre 2.25
118 PB,V:Thunderball 2.25
119 PB,V:Wrecking Crew 2.25
120 PB,10th Anniv.,V:Hardliners,
    w/poster 3.00
121 PCu,V:Brass Bishop,A:Spider-
    Man,Wolverine,C:X-Men 2.50
122 PB,BKi,Inf.Crusade 2.50
123 PB,BKi,Infinity Crusade 2.50
124 PB,BKi,Infinity Crusade 2.50
125 PB,V:Carcass 2.50
126 V:Carcass 2.50
127 SFu(s),Infinity Crusade 2.50
128 B:No Future 2.50
129 C:Omega Flight 2.50
130 E:No Future,last issue,
    Double Sized 3.00
Ann.#1 LSn,V:Diablo,Gilded Lily . . 3.00
Ann.#2 JBr,BMc 2.50
Spec.#1 PB,A:Wolverine,
    O:First Team,V:Egghead 3.75
Spec.#1–#3 Newsstand versions
    of #97–#99 . . . . @2.50
Spec.#4 Newsstand ver.of #100 . . . 2.50

ALPHA FLIGHT
1997

1 SSe,ScC, former team kidnapped,
    I:Murmur, Radius,Flex,Guardian 5.00
2 SSe,ScC 4.00
2 variant cover 3.50
3 SSe,ScC, ... 3.50
4 SSe,ScC,V:Mesmero 3.00
5 SSe,ScC,A:Mesmero 3.00
6 SSe,What's up with Sasquatch? . 3.00
7 SSe,Evils explode 3.00
8 SSe,ScC,North & South prelude . 3.00
9 SSe,ScC,North & South pt.1,
    X-men x-over 3.00
10 SSe,Flung into Prometheus Pit . 3.00
11 SSe,race to save 2 worlds 3.00
12 SSe,Alphan dies,48pg. 3.50
13 SSe,F:Basil Killbrew 2.50
14 SSe,I:Brass Bishop 2.50
15 SSe 2.50
16 SSe,V:Brass Bishop 2.50
17 SSe,V:X the Unknown 2.50
18 SSe,Alpha:Omega,pt.1 . . . . 2.50
19 SSe,Alpha:Omega,pt.2 . . . . 2.50
20 SSe,Alpha:Omega,pt.3 . . . . 2.50
Spec. #1 SSe,In the Beginning,
    Flashback, A:Wolverine 2.50
Ann.1998 Alpha Flight/Inhumans . . 3.50

ALPHA FLIGHT
March, 2004

1 SLo,You Gotta Be Kiddin,pt.1 . . . 3.00
2 SLo,You Gotta Be Kiddin,pt.2 . . . 3.00
3 SLo,You Gotta Be Kiddin,pt.3 . . . 3.00
4 SLo,You Gotta Be Kiddin,pt.4 . . . 3.00
5 SLo,You Gotta Be Kiddin,pt.5 . . . 3.00
6 SLo,You Gotta Be Kiddin,pt.6 . . . 3.00
7 Waxing Poetic,pt.1 . . . . 3.00
8 Waxing Poetic,pt.2 . . . . 3.00

ALPHA FLIGHT SPECIAL
1991

1 thru 4 reprints . . . . @2.25

AMAZING ADVENTURES
June, 1961

1 JK,SD,O&B:Dr.Droom;Torr . 2,100.00
2 JK,SD,This is Manoo 850.00
3 JK,SD,Trapped in the
    Twilight World 700.00

4 JK,SD, I Am X 650.00
5 JK,SD, Monsteroso 650.00
6 JK,SD,E:Dr.Droom; Sserpo . . . 650.00
Becomes:

AMAZING ADULT
FANTASY
Dec., 1961

7 SD,Last Man on Earth 900.00
8 SD,The Coming of the Krills . . 700.00
9 SD,The Terror of Tim Boo Ba . 650.00
10 SD,Those Who Change 650.00
11 SD,In Human Form 650.00
12 SD,Living Statues 650.00
13 SD,At the Stroke of Midnight . 650.00
14 SD,Beware of the Giants 675.00
Becomes:

AMAZING FANTASY
Aug., 1962

15 JK(c),SD,I&O:Spider-Man,I:Aunt
    May, Flash Thompson, Burglar,
    I&D:Uncle Ben 50,000.00
Marvel Milestone rep.#15 (1992) . . . 3.00
[Second Series], 1995
15a gold Rep. (1995) 25.00
16 KBk, O:Spider-Man,painted 4.00
17 KBk, More early adventures 4.00
18 KBk,conclusion 4.00

AMAZING ADVENTURES
Aug., 1970
[1st Regular Series]

1 JK,JB,B:Inhumans,Bl.Widow . . . 75.00
2 JK,JB,A:Fantastic Four 35.00
3 JK,GC,BEv,V:Mandarin 35.00
4 JK,GC,BEv,V:Mandarin 35.00
5 NA,TP,DH,BEv,V:Astrologer . . . 50.00
6 NA,DH,SB,V:Maximus 50.00
7 NA,DH,BEv 50.00
8 NA,DH,BEv,E:Black Widow,
    A:Thor,(see Avengers #95) . . . 50.00
9 MSy,BEv,V:Magneto 30.00
10 GK(c),MSy,V:Magneto,
    E:Inhumans 30.00
11 GK(c),TS,B:O:New Beast,
    A:X-Men 175.00
12 GK(c),TS,MP,A:Iron Man 50.00
13 JR(c),TS,V:New Br'hood
    Evil Mutants,I:Buzz Baxter
    (Mad Dog) 50.00
14 GK(c),TS,JM,V:Quasimodo . . . 50.00

Amazing Adventures #21
© Marvel Entertainment Group

MARVEL

15 JSn(c),TS,A:X-Men,V:Griffin . . . 50.00
16 JSn(c),FMc(i),V:Juggernaut . . . 50.00
17 JSn,A:X-Men,E:Beast 50.00
18 HC,NA,B:Killraven. 50.00
19 HC,Sirens on 7th Avenues 12.00
20 Coming of the Warlords 12.00
21 Cry Killraven 12.00
22 Killraven 12.00
23 Killraven 12.00
24 New Year Nightmare-2019AD. . 12.00
25 RB,V:Skar 12.00
26 GC,V:Ptson-Rage Vigilante . . . 12.00
27 CR,JSn,V:Death Breeders 12.00
28 JSn,CR,V:Death Breeders 12.00
29 CR,Killraven 12.00
30 CR,Killraven 12.00
31 CR,Killraven 12.00
32 CR,Killraven 12.00
33 CR,Killraven 12.00
34 CR,D:Hawk 12.00
35 KG,Killraven Continued 12.00
36 CR,Killraven Continued 12.00
37 CR,O:Old Skull 12.00
38 CR,Killraven Continued 12.00
39 CR,E:Killraven. 12.00

[2nd Regular Series], 1979
1 rep.X-Men#1,38,Professor X . . . 10.00
2 thru 14 reps . . . . @8.00

AMAZING COMICS
Timely, Fall, 1944
1 F:Young Allies,Destroyer,
   Whizzer, Sergeant Dix 2,800.00
Becomes:

COMPLETE COMICS
2 F:Young Allies,Destroyer,Whizzer
   Sergeant Dix;Winter'44-45 . 2,000.00

AMAZING DETECTIVE CASES
Atlas, Nov., 1950
3 Detective/Horror Stories 350.00
4 Death of a Big Shot 200.00
5 . . . . 200.00
6 Danger in the City 200.00
7 . . . . 175.00
8 . . . . 175.00
9 GC, The Man Who Wasn't . . . 175.00
10 GT 175.00
11 The Black Shadow 350.00
12 MS,BK, Harrigan's Wake 350.00
13 BEv,JSt, ... 400.00
14 Hands Off; Sept., 1952 . . . . . 350.00

AMAZING FANTASY
June, 2004
1 (of 6) 4.00
2 thru 5 . . . . @4.00

AMAZING HIGH ADVENTURE
Aug., 1984
1 BSz,JSo,JS 4.00
2 PS,AW,BSz,TA,MMi,BBl,CP,CW . 3.00
3 MMi,VM,JS 3.00
4 JBo,JS,SBi 3.00
5 JBo; Oct., 1986 . . . . 3.00

AMAZING SCARLET SPIDER
1995
1 MBa,LMa,VirtualMortality,pt.2 . . 2.50
2 TDF,MBa,CyberWar,pt.2 . . . . . . 2.50

Amazing Spider-Man #4
© *Marvel Entertainment Group*

AMAZING SPIDER-MAN
March, 1963
1 JK(c),SED,I:Chameleon,J.Jonah &
   John Jameson,A:F.Four . . 35,000.00
2 SD,I:Vulture,Tinkerer
   C:Mysterio(disguised) 6,500.00
3 SD,I&O:Dr.Octopus 5,000.00
4 SD,I&O:Sandman,I:Betty
   Brant,Liz Allen 4,000.00
5 SD,V:Dr.Doom,C:Fant.Four . 3,200.00
6 SD,I&O:Lizard,The Connors . 3,000.00
7 SD,V:Vulture 2,000.00
8 SD,JK,I:Big Brain,V:Human
   Torch,A:Fantastic Four 1,900.00
9 SD,I&O:Electro 2,000.00
10 SD,I:Enforcers,Big Man . . . 1,900.00
11 SD,V:Dr.Octopus,
   D:Bennett Brant 1,300.00
12 SD,V:Dr.Octopus 1,300.00
13 SD,I:Mysterio 1,700.00
14 SD,I:Green Goblin,
   V:Enforcers, Hulk 3,500.00
15 SD,I:Kraven,A:Chameleon . . 1,500.00
16 SD,A:Daredevil,
   V:Ringmaster 1,200.00
17 SD,2nd A:Green Goblin,
   A:Human Torch 1,500.00
18 SD,V:Sandman,Enforcers,
   C:Avengers,F.F.,Daredevil . . 900.00
19 SD,V:Sandman,I:Ned Leeds
   A:Human Torch 750.00
20 SD,I&O:Scorpion 1,000.00
21 SD,A:Beetle,Human Torch . . 650.00
22 SD,V:The Clown,Masters of
   Menace 600.00
23 SD,V:GreenGoblin(3rd App.) . 800.00
24 SD,V:Mysterio 500.00
25 SD,I:Spider Slayer,Spencer
   Smythe,C:Mary Jane 600.00
26 SD,I:CrimeMaster,V:Green
   Goblin 650.00
27 SD,V:CrimeMaster,
   Green Goblin 600.00
28 SD,I:Molten Man,Peter Parker
   Graduates High School,rare
   in near-mint condition 1,200.00
29 SD,V:Scorpion 400.00
30 SD,I:Cat Burglar 400.00
31 SD,I:Gwen Stacy,Harry Osborn
   Prof.Warren,V:Dr.Octopus . . 400.00
32 SD,V:Dr.Octopus 350.00
33 SD,V:Dr.Octopus 350.00
34 SD,V:Kraven 350.00
35 SD,V:Molten Man 350.00

36 SD,I:The Looter 350.00
37 SD,V:Professor Stromm,
   I:Norman Osborn 350.00
38 SD,V:Joe Smith(Boxer) 350.00
39 JR,IR:Green Goblin is Norman
   Osborn 500.00
40 JR,O:Green Goblin 650.00
41 JR,I:Rhino,C:Mary Jane 450.00
42 JR,V:John Jameson,I:Mary
   Jane (Face Revealed) 325.00
43 JR,O:Rhino 225.00
44 JR,V:Lizard(2nd App.) 225.00
45 JR,V:Lizard 225.00
46 JR,I&O:Shocker 250.00
47 JR,V:Kraven 225.00
48 JR,I:Fake Vulture,A:Vulture . . 225.00
49 JR,V:Fake Vulture,Kraven . . . 225.00
50 JR,I:Kingpin,Spidey Quits,
   C:Johnny Carson 1,000.00
51 JR,V:Kingpin 350.00
52 JR,V:Kingpin,I:Robbie
   Robertson,D:Fred Foswell . . . 200.00
53 JR,V:Dr.Octopus 175.00
54 JR,V:Dr.Octopus 175.00
55 JR,V:Dr.Octopus 175.00
56 JR,V:Dr.Octopus,I:Capt.Stacy . 175.00
57 JR,DH,A:Ka-Zar 175.00
58 JR,DH,V:Spencer Smythe,
   Spider Slayer 175.00
59 JR,DH,V:Kingpin 175.00
60 JR,DH,V:Kingpin 175.00
61 JR,DH,V:Kingpin 175.00
62 JR,DH,V:Medusa 125.00
63 JR,DH,V:1st & 2nd
   Vulture 125.00
64 JR,DH,V:Vulture 125.00
65 JR,JM,V:Prisoners 125.00
66 JR,DH,V:Mysterio 125.00
67 JR,JM,V:Mysterio,I:Randy
   Robertson 125.00
68 JR,JM,V:Kingpin 135.00
69 JR,JM,V:Kingpin 135.00
70 JR,JM,V:Kingpin 135.00
71 JR,JM,V:Quicksilver,C:Scarlet
   Witch,Toad,A:Kingpin 125.00
72 JR,JB,JM,V:Shocker 125.00
73 JR,JB,JM,I:Man Mountain Marko,
   Silvermane 125.00
74 JR,JM,V:Silvermane 125.00
75 JR,JM,V:Silvermane,A:Lizard . 100.00
76 JR,JM,V:Lizard,A:H.Torch . . . 100.00
77 JR,JM,V:Lizard,A:H.Torch . . . 100.00
78 JR,JM,I&O:Prowler 125.00
79 JR,JM,V:Prowler 100.00
80 JR,JB,JM,V:Chameleon 100.00
81 JR,JB,JM,I:Kangaroo 100.00
82 JR,JM,V:Electro 100.00
83 JR,I:Richard Fisk(as Schemer),
   Vanessa(Kingpin's wife) 100.00
84 JR,JB,JM,V:Schemer,Kingpin . 100.00
85 JR,JB,JM,V:Schemer,Kingpin . 100.00
86 JR,JM,V:Black Widow, C:Iron
   Man, Hawkeye. 100.00
87 JR,JM,Reveals ID to his
   friends,changes mind 100.00
88 JR,JM,V:Dr.Octopus 100.00
89 GK,JR,V:Dr.Octopus 100.00
90 GK,JR,V:Dr.Octopus
   D:Capt.Stacy 150.00
91 GK,JR,I:Bullit. 125.00
92 GK,JR,V:Bullit,A:Iceman 125.00
93 JR,V:Prowler 125.00
94 JR,SB,V:Beetle,O:Spider-Man 150.00
95 JR,SB,London,V:Terrorists . . . 100.00
96 GK,JR,A:Green Goblin,Drug
   Mention,No Comic Code 175.00
97 GK,V:Green Goblin,Drugs . . . 175.00
98 GK,V:Green Goblin,Drugs . . . 175.00
99 GK,Prison Riot,A:Carson 125.00
100 JR(c),GK,Spidey gets four
   arms from serum 325.00

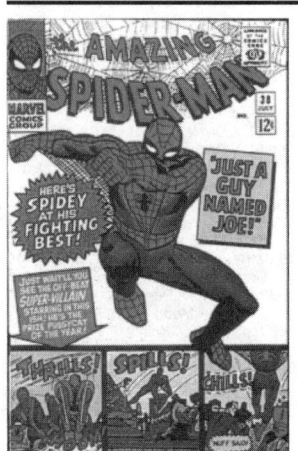

Amazing Spider-Man #38
© Marvel Entertainment Group

101 JR(c),GK,I:Morbius,the
Living Vampire,A:Lizard..... 250.00
101a Reprint,Metallic ink......... 5.00
102 JR(c),GK,O:Morbius,
V:Lizard.................. 175.00
103 GK,V:Kraven,A:Ka-Zar...... 75.00
104 GK,V:Kraven,A:Ka-Zar...... 75.00
105 GK,V:Spenser Smythe,
Spider Slayer.............. 75.00
106 JR,V:Spenser Smythe,
Spider Slayer.............. 75.00
107 JR,V:Spenser Smythe,
Spider Slayer.............. 75.00
108 JR,R:Flash Thompson,
I:Sha-Shan,V:Vietnamese.... 75.00
109 JR,A:Dr.Strange,
V:Vietnamese.............. 75.00
110 JR,I:The Gibbon........... 75.00
111 JR,V:The Gibbon,Kraven.... 75.00
112 JR,Spidey gets an Ulcer..... 75.00
113 JSn,JR,I:Hammerhead
V:Dr.Octopus............. 75.00
114 JSn,JR,V:Hammerhead,Dr.
Octopus,I:Jonas Harrow..... 75.00
115 JR,V:Hammerhead,
Dr.Octopus................ 75.00
116 JR,JM,V:The Smasher...... 75.00
117 JR,JM,V:Smasher,Disruptor.. 75.00
118 JR,JM,V:Smasher,Disruptor.. 75.00
119 JR,A:Hulk................ 80.00
120 GK,JR,V:Hulk............. 80.00
121 GK,JR,V:Green Goblin
D:Gwen Stacy,Drugs....... 300.00
122 GK,JR,D:Green Goblin..... 275.00
123 GK,JR,A:Powerman........ 75.00
124 GK,JR,I:Man-Wolf.......... 90.00
125 RA,JR,O:Man-Wolf......... 75.00
126 JM(c),RA,JM,V:Kangaroo,
A: Human Torch............ 75.00
127 JR(c),RA,V:3rd Vulture,
A:Human Torch............. 75.00
128 JR(c),RA,V:3rd Vulture..... 75.00
129 K&R(c),RA,I:Punisher,Jackal 450.00
130 JR(c),RA,V:Hammerhead,
Dr.Octopus,I:Spider-Mobile... 50.00
131 GK(c),RA,V:Hammerhead,
Dr.Octopus................ 50.00
132 GK(c),JR,V:Molten Man..... 50.00
133 JR(c),RA,V:Molten Man..... 50.00
134 JR(c),RA,I:Tarantula,C:
Punisher(2nd App.)......... 60.00
135 JR(c),RA,V:Tarantula,
A:Punisher................ 100.00

136 JR(c),RA,I:2nd GreenGoblin. 100.00
137 GK(c),RA,V:Green Goblin.... 90.00
138 K&R(c),RA,I:Mindworm...... 50.00
139 K&R(c),RA,I:Grizzly,V:Jackal. 50.00
140 GK(c),RA,I:Gloria Grant,
V:Grizzly,Jackal............ 50.00
141 JR(c),RA,V:Mysterio........ 50.00
142 JR(c),RA,V:Mysterio........ 50.00
143 K&R(c),RA,I:Cyclone....... 50.00
144 K&R(c),RA,V:Cyclone....... 50.00
145 K&R(c),RA,V:Scorpion...... 50.00
146 RA,JR,V:Scorpion.......... 50.00
147 JR(c),RA,V:Tarantula....... 50.00
148 GK(c),RA,V:Tarantula,IR:Jackal
is Prof.Warren............. 60.00
149 K&R(c),RA,D:Jackal....... 100.00
150 GK(c),RA,V:Spenser Smythe. 60.00
151 RA,JR,V:Shocker.......... 50.00
152 K&R(c),RA,V:Shocker...... 30.00
153 K&R(c),RA,V:Paine........ 30.00
154 JR(c),SB,V:Sandman....... 30.00
155 JR(c),SB,V:Computer...... 30.00
156 JR(c),RA,I:Mirage,W:Ned
Leeds & Betty Brant........ 30.00
157 JR(c),RA,V:Dr.Octopus..... 30.00
158 JR(c),RA,V:Dr.Octopus..... 30.00
159 JR(c),RA,V:Dr.Octopus..... 30.00
160 K&R(c),RA,V:Tinkerer...... 30.00
161 K&R(c),RA,A:Nightcrawler,
C:Punisher................ 40.00
162 JR(c),RA,Nightcrawler,
Punisher,I:Jigsaw.......... 40.00
163 JR(c),RA,V:Kingpin........ 20.00
164 JR(c),RA,V:Kingpin........ 20.00
165 JR(c),RA,V:Lizard......... 20.00
166 JR(c),RA,V:Lizard......... 20.00
167 JR(c),RA,V:Spiderslayer,
I:Will-o-the Wisp........... 20.00
168 JR(c),KP,V:Will-o-the Wisp... 22.00
169 RA,V:Dr.Faustas........... 20.00
170 RA,V:Dr.Faustas........... 20.00
171 RA,A:Nova............... 22.00
172 RA,V:Molten Man.......... 20.00
173 JR(c),RA,JM,V:Molten Man.. 20.00
174 RA,TD,JM,A:Punisher...... 25.00
175 RA,JM,A:Punisher,D:Hitman.. 25.00
176 RA,TD,V:Green Goblin...... 30.00
177 RA,V:Green Goblin......... 30.00
178 RA,JM,V:Green Goblin...... 30.00
179 RA,V:Green Goblin......... 30.00
180 RA,IR&V:Green Goblin is Bart
Hamilton)................. 30.00
181 GK(c),SB,O:Spider-Man..... 22.00
182 RA,A:Rocket Racer......... 20.00
183 RA,BMc,V:Rocket Racer..... 20.00
184 RA,V:White Tiger.......... 20.00
185 RA,V:White Tiger.......... 20.00
186 KP,A:Chameleon,Spidey
cleared by police of charges.. 20.00
187 JSn,BMc,A:Captain
America,V:Electro.......... 20.00
188 KP,A:Jigsaw.............. 20.00
189 JBy,JM,A:Man-Wolf........ 25.00
190 JBy,JM,A:Man-Wolf........ 25.00
191 KP,V:Spiderslayer......... 25.00
192 KP,JM,V:The Fly.......... 25.00
193 KP,JM,V:The Fly.......... 25.00
194 KP,I:Black Cat............ 40.00
195 KP,AM,JM,O:Black Cat..... 20.00
196 AM,JM,D:Aunt May,A:Kingpin. 15.00
197 KP,JM,V:Kingpin.......... 15.00
198 SB,JM,V:Mysterio......... 15.00
199 SB,JM,V:Mysterio......... 15.00
200 JR(c),KP,JM,D:Burglar,Aunt May
alive,O:Spider-Man......... 40.00
201 KP,JM,A:Punisher......... 18.00
202 KP,JM,A:Punisher......... 18.00
203 FM(c),KP,A:Dazzler........ 15.00
204 JR2(c),KP,V:Black Cat...... 15.00
205 KP,JM,V:Black Cat........ 15.00
206 JBy,GD,V:Jonas Harrow..... 15.00

Amazing Spider-Man #201
© Marvel Entertainment Group

207 JM,V:Mesmero............ 15.00
208 JR2,AM,BBr,V:Fusion(1stJR2
SpM art),I:Lance Bannon..... 15.00
209 KJ,BMc,JRu,BWi,AM,
I:Calypso, V:Kraven........ 20.00
210 JR2,JSt,I:Madame Web..... 15.00
211 JR2,JM,A:Sub-mariner...... 15.00
212 JR2,JM,I:Hydro-Man....... 15.00
213 JR2,JM,V:Wizard.......... 15.00
214 JR2,JM,V:Frightful Four,
A: Namor,Llyra............ 15.00
215 JR2,JM,V:Frightful Four,
A: Namor,Llyra............ 15.00
216 JR2,JM,A:Madame Web..... 15.00
217 JR2,JM,V:Sandman,
Hydro-Man................ 15.00
218 FM(c),JR2,JM,AM,V:Sandman
Hydro-Man................ 15.00
219 FM(c),LMc,JM,V:Grey
Gargoyle,A:Matt Murdock.... 15.00
220 BMc,A:Moon Knight........ 12.00
221 JM(i),A:Ramrod........... 12.00
222 WS(c),BH,JM,I:SpeedDemon. 12.00
223 JR2,AM,A:Red Ghost....... 12.00
224 JR2,V:Vulture............. 12.00
225 JR2,BWi,V:Foolkiller....... 12.00
226 JR2,JM,A:Black Cat........ 12.00
227 JR2,JM,A:Black Cat........ 12.00
228 RL,Murder Mystery........ 12.00
229 JR2,JM,V:Juggernaut....... 12.00
230 JR2,JM,V:Juggernaut....... 12.00
231 JR2,AM,V:Cobra........... 12.00
232 JR2,JM,V:Mr.Hyde........ 12.00
233 JR2,JM,V:Tarantula....... 12.00
234 JR2,DGr,V:Tarantula....... 12.00
235 JR2,V:Tarantula,C:Deathlok
O:Will-o-the Wisp.......... 12.00
236 JR2,D:Tarantula.......... 12.00
237 BH,A:Stilt Man........... 12.00
238 JR2,JR,I:Hobgoblin (inc.
Tattoo transfer)........... 100.00
238a w/out Tattoo........... 12.00
239 JR2,V:Hobgoblin.......... 60.00
240 JR2,BL,Vulture............ 12.00
241 JR2,O:Vulture............ 12.00
242 JR2,Mad Thinker......... 12.00
243 JR2,Peter Quits School..... 12.00
244 JR2,KJ,V:Hobgoblin....... 18.00
245 JR2,V:Hobgoblin.......... 20.00
246 JR2,DGr,Daydreams issue... 12.00
247 JR2,JR,V:Thunderball...... 12.00
248 JR2,BBr,RF,TA,V:Thunderball,
Kid who Collects Spider-Man. 12.00

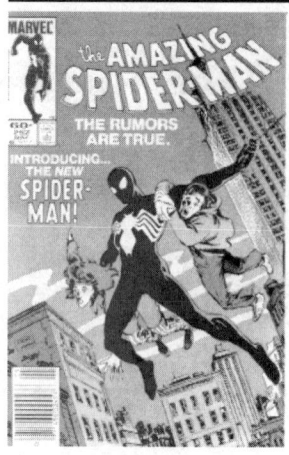

Amazing Spider-Man #252
© Marvel Entertainment Group

249 JR2,DGr,V:Hobgoblin,
A:Kingpin 20.00
250 JR2,KJ,V:Hobgoblin 20.00
251 RF,KJ,V:Hobgoblin,Spidey
Leaves for Secret Wars 20.00
252 RF,BBr,returns from Secret
Wars,N:Spider-Man 50.00
253 RL,I:Rose 12.00
254 RL,JRu,V:Jack O'Lantern 10.00
255 RF,JRu,Red Ghost 10.00
256 RF,JRu,I:Puma,A:Black Cat . . . 10.00
257 RF,JRu,V:Puma,
A:Hobgoblin 10.00
258 RF,JRu,A:Black Cat,Fant.Four,
Hobgoblin,V:Black Costume . . 15.00
259 RF,JRu,A:Hobgoblin,O:
Mary Jane 15.00
260 RF,JRu,BBr,V:Hobgoblin 12.00
261 CV(c),RF,JRu,V:Hobgoblin 12.00
262 Ph(c),BL,Spidey Unmasked . . . 13.00
263 RF,BBr,I:Spider-Kid 10.00
264 Paty,V:Red Nine 10.00
265 RF,JRu,V:Black Fox,
I:Silver Sable 15.00
265a 2nd printing 3.00
266 RF,JRu,I:Misfits,Toad 10.00
267 BMc,PDd(s),A:Human Torch . . 10.00
268 JBy(c),RF,JRu,Secret WarsII . . 10.00
269 RF,JRu,V:Firelord 10.00
270 RF,BMc,V:Firelord,
A:Avengers,I:Kate Cushing . . . 10.00
271 RF,JRu,A:Crusher Hogan,
V:Manslaughter 10.00
272 SB,KB,I&O:Slyde 10.00
273 RF,JRu,Secret Wars II,
A:Puma 10.00
274 TMo,JR,Secret Wars II,
Beyonder V:Mephisto,A:1st
Ghost Rider 10.00
275 RF,JRu,V:Hobgoblin,O:Spidey
(From Amaz.Fantasy#15) 20.00
276 RF,BBr,V:Hobgoblin 15.00
277 RF,BL,CV,A:Daredevil,Kingpin 10.00
278 A:Hobgoblin,V:Scourge,
D:Wraith 10.00
279 RL,A:Jack O'Lantern,
2nd A:Silver Sable 10.00
280 RF,BBr,V:Sinister Syndicate,
A:Silver Sable,Hobgoblin,
Jack O'Lantern 10.00
281 RF,BBr,V:Sinister Syndicate,
A:Silver Sable,Hobgoblin,
Jack O'Lantern 15.00
282 RL,BL,A:X-Factor 10.00

283 RF,BL,V:Titania,Absorbing
Man,C:Mongoose 10.00
284 RF,BBr,JRu,B:Gang War,
A: Punisher,Hobgoblin 15.00
285 MZ(c),A:Punisher,Hobgoblin . . 15.00
286 ANi(i),V:Hobgoblin,A:Rose . . . 15.00
287 EL,ANi,A:Daredevl,Hobgoblin. 15.00
288 E:Gang War,A:Punisher,
Falcon,Hobgoblin,Daredevil,
Black Cat, Kingpin 15.00
289 TMo,IR:Hobgoblin is Ned Leeds,
I:2nd Hobgoblin (Jack O'
Lantern) 25.00
290 JR2,Peter Proposes 10.00
291 JR2,V:Spiderslayer 10.00
292 AS,V:Spiderslayer,Mary
Jane Accepts proposal 10.00
293 MZ,BMc,V:Kraven 12.00
294 MZ,BMc,D:Kraven 12.00
295 BSz(c),KB(i),Mad Dog,pt.#2 . . 10.00
296 JBy(c),AS,V:Dr.Octopus 10.00
297 AS,V:Dr.Octopus 10.00
298 TM,BMc,V:Chance,C:Venom
(not in costume). 50.00
299 TM,BMc,V:Chance,I:Venom . . 30.00
300 TM,O:Venom. 100.00
301 TM,A:Silver Sable 20.00
302 TM,V:Nero,A:Silver Sable 20.00
303 TM,A:Silver Sable,Sandman. . 20.00
304 TM,JRu,V:Black Fox,Prowler
I:Jonathan Caesar 18.00
305 TM,JRu,V:BlackFox,Prowler. . 18.00
306 TM,V:Humbug,Chameleon . . . 15.00
307 TM,O:Chameleon 15.00
308 TM,V:Taskmaster,J.Caesar. . . 15.00
309 TM,I:Styx & Stone 15.00
310 TM,V:Killershrike 15.00
311 TM,Inferno,V:Mysterio 15.00
312 TM,Inferno,Hobgoblin V:
Green Goblin 20.00
313 TM,Inferno,V:Lizard. 15.00
314 TM,X-mas issue,V:J.Caesar . . 15.00
315 TM,V:Venom,Hydro-Man. 20.00
316 TM,V:Venom 20.00
317 TM,V:Venom,A:Thing 20.00
318 TM,V:Scorpion 20.00
319 TM,V:Scorpion,Rhino 15.00
320 TM,B:Assassin Nation Plot
A:Paladin,Silver Sable 15.00
321 TM,A:Paladin,Silver Sable . . . 12.00
322 TM,A:Silver Sable,Paladin . . . 12.00
323 TM,A:Silver Sable,Paladin,
Captain America 12.00
324 TM(c),EL,AG,V:Sabretooth,A:
Capt.America,Silver Sable . . . 12.00
325 TM,E:Assassin Nation Plot,
V:Red Skull,Captain America,
Silver Sable 12.00
326 V:Graviton,A of V. 7.00
327 EL,AG,V:Magneto,A of V. 7.00
328 TM,V:Hulk,A of V. 12.00
329 EL,V:Tri-Sentinel 7.00
330 EL,A:Punisher,Black Cat. 7.00
331 EL,A:Punisher,C:Venom 6.00
332 EL,V:Venom,Styx & Stone 7.00
333 EL,V:Venom,Styx & Stone 7.00
334 EL,B:Sinister Six,A:Iron Man . . 5.00
335 EL,TA,A:Captain America 5.00
336 EL,D:Nathan Lubensky,
A:Dr.Strange,Chance. 5.00
337 WS(c),EL,TA,A:Nova 5.00
338 EL,A:Jonathan Caesar 5.00
339 EL,JR,E:Sinister Six,A:Thor
D:Jonathan Caesar 5.00
340 EL,V:Femme Fatales 5.00
341 EL,V:Tarantula,Powers Lost . . . 5.00
342 EL,A:Blackcat,V:Scorpion 5.00
343 EL,Powers Restored,
C:Cardiac,V:Chameleon 5.00
344 EL,V:Rhino,I:Cardiac,Cletus
Kassady(Carnage),A:Venom. . 15.00

345 MBa,V:Boomerang,C:Venom,
A:Cletus Kassady(infected
with Venom-Spawn). 15.00
346 EL,V:Venom 10.00
347 EL,V:Venom 10.00
348 EL,A:Avengers 4.00
349 EL,A:Black Fox 4.00
350 EL,V:Doctor Doom,Black Fox . . 6.00
351 MBa,A:Nova,V:Tri-Sentinel . . . 6.00
352 MBa,A:Nova,V:Tri-Sentinel 4.00
353 MBa,B:Round Robin:The Side
Kick's Revenge,A:Punisher,
Nova,Moon Knight,Darkhawk . . 4.00
354 MBa,A:Nova,Punisher,
Darkhawk,Moon Knight 4.00
355 MBa,A:Nova,Punisher,
Darkhawk,Moon Knight 4.00
356 MBa,A:Moon Knight,
Punisher,Nova 4.00
357 MBa,A:Moon Knight,
Punisher,Darkhawk,Nova 4.00
358 MBa,E:Round Robin:The Side
Kick's Revenge,A:Darkhawk,
Moon Knight,Punisher,Nova,
Gatefold(c). 4.00
359 CMa,A:Cardiac,C:Cletus
Kasady (Carnage) 5.00
360 CMa,V:Cardiac,C:Carnage 6.00
361 MBa,I:Carnage 9.00
361a 2nd printing 3.00
362 MBa,V:Carnage,Venom 6.00
362a 2nd printing 3.00
363 MBa,V:Carnage,Venom, ... 6.00
364 MBa,V:Shocker 3.00
365 MBa,JR,V:Lizard,30th Anniv.,
Hologram(c),w/poster,Prev.of
Spider-Man 2099 by RL 6.00
366 JBi,A:Red Skull,Taskmaster . . . 3.00
367 JBi,A:Red Skull,Taskmaster . . . 3.00
368 MBa,B:Invasion of the Spider
Slayers #1,BU:Jonah Jameson. 3.00
369 MBa,V:Electro,BU:Green
Goblin 3.00
370 MBa,V:Scorpion,BU:A.May. . . . 3.00
371 MBa,V:Spider-Slayer,
BU:Black Cat 3.00
372 MBa,V:Spider-Slayer. 3.00
373 MBa,V:Sp.-Slayer,BU:Venom . . 4.00
374 MBa,V:Venom 5.00
375 MBa,V:Venom,30th Anniv.,Holo
graphx(c) 6.00
376 V:Styx&Stone,A:Cardiac 3.00
377 V:Cardiac,O:Styx&Stone 3.00

Amazing Spider-Man #266
© Marvel Entertainment Group

378 MBa,Total Carnage#3,V:Shriek,
 Carnage,A:Venom,Cloak 3.00
379 MBa,Total Carnage#7,
 V:Carnage,A:Venom 3.00
380 MBa,Maximum Carnage#11 . . . 3.00
381 MBa,V:Dr.Samson,A:Hulk 3.00
382 MBa,V:Hulk,A:Dr.Samson 3.00
383 MBa,V:Jury 3.00
384 MBa,AM,V:Jury 3.00
385 B:DvM(s),MBa,RyE,V:Jury 3.00
386 MBa,RyE,B:Lifetheft,V:Vulture . 3.00
387 MBa,RyE,V:Vulture 3.00
388 Blue Foil(c),MBa,Rlm,TP,
 E:Lifetheft,D:Peter's Synthetic
 Parents,BU:Venom,Cardiac,
 Chance,. 5.00
388a Newsstand Ed. 3.00
389 MBa,RyE,E:Pursuit,
 V:Chameleon, ... 3.00
390 MBa,RyE,B:Shrieking,
 A:Shriek,w/cel 4.00
390a Newsstand Ed. 3.00
391 MBa,RyE,V:Shriek,Carrion 3.00
392 MBa,RyE,V:Shriek,Carrion 3.00
393 MBa,RyE,E:Shrieking,
 V:Shriek,Carrion 3.00
394 MBa,RyE,Power & Responsibility,
 pt.2,V:Judas Traveller,. 4.00
394a w/flip book,2 covers 3.00
395 MBa,RyE,R:Puma. 3.00
396 MBa,RyE,A:Daredevil,
 V:Vulture, Owl 3.00
397 MBa,Web of Death,pt.1,
 V:Stunner,Doc Ock 3.50
398 MBa,Web of Death,pt.3 . . . . . . 4.00
399 MBa,Smoke and Mirrors,pt.2 . . 2.50
400 MBa,Death of a Parker. 6.00
400a die-cut cover 10.00
401 MBa,The Mark of Kaine,pt.2. . . 3.00
402 MBa,R:Judas Travellor 3.00
403 MBa,JMD,LMa The Trial of
 Peter Parker, pt.2 . . . . 3.00
404 Maximum Clonage 3.00
405 JMD,DaR,LMa,Exiled,pt.2, ... 3.00
406 I:New Doc Ock 3.00
407 TDF,MBa,LMa,Return of
 Spider-Man,pt.2 . . . . 3.00
408 TDF,MBa,LMa,Media
 Blizzard,pt.2. . . . . 3.00
409 . . . . 3.00
410 . . . . 3.00
411 TDF,MBa,LMa,Blood
 Brothers,pt.2 . . . . 3.00
412 . . . . 3.00
413 . . . . 3.00
414 A:The Rose. 3.00
415 Onslaught saga,V:Sentinels . . . 3.00
416 Onslaught epilogue. 3.00
417 TDF,RG,secrets of Scrier &
 Judas Traveler. 3.00
418 Revelations,pt.3, R:Norman
 Osborn. 3.00
419 TDF,SSr,V:Black Tarantula . . . 3.00
420 TDF,SSr,X-Man x-over,pt.1 . . . 3.00
421 TDF,SSr,I:Dragonfly; Electro
 Kidnapped 3.00
422 TDF,SSr,V:Electro,Tarantula . . 3.00
423 TDF,V:Electro 3.00
424 TDF,JoB,V:Black Tarantula, The
 Hand, Dragonfly, Delilah,
 The Rose, Elektra 3.00
425 TDF,SSr, V:Electro,double size. 4.00
426 TDF,SSr,V:Doctor Octopus . . . 3.00
427 TDF,SSr,JR gatefold cover,
 V:Doctor Octopus 4.00
428 TDF,SSr,V:Doctor Octopus . . . 3.00
429 TDF,A:Daredevil, X-Man,
 Absorbing Man, Titania 3.00
430 TDF,SSr,V:Carnage,A:Silver
 Surfer. 3.00

Amazing Spider-Man #400
© Marvel Entertainment Group

431 TDF,SSr,V:Carnage (with Silver
 Surfer's powers) 3.00
432 SSr,JR2,Spider-Hunt,pt.2
 x-over. 4.00
432a variant cover 4.00
433 TDF,TL,Identity Crisis prelude,
 good-bye to Joe Robertson. . . . 3.00
434 TDF,JoB,Identity Crisis, as
 Ricochet vs. Black Tarantula . . . 3.00
435 TDF,MD2,Ricochet,A:Delilah . . 3.00
436 TDF,JoB,V:Black Tarantula . . . 3.00
437 TDF,JoB,V:Plant Man 3.00
Bi-weekly
438 TDF,V:Daredevil 3.00
439 TDF,future history chronicle . . . 3.00
440 JBy,The Gathering of the Five,
 Pt.2 (of 5) x-over 3.00
441 JBy,V:Green Goblin, The
 Final Chapter, pt.1 . . . . 5.00
Minus 1 Spec., TDF,JBe, flashback,
 early Kingpin 2.50
Ann.#1 SD,I:Sinister Six 1,500.00
Ann.#2 SD,A:Dr.Strange 600.00
Ann.#3 JR,DH,A:Avengers 225.00
Ann.#4 A:H.Torch,V:Mysterio,
 Wizard 200.00
Ann.#5 JR(c),A:Red Skull,I:Peter
 Parker's Parents 200.00
Ann.#6 JR(c),Rep.Ann.#1,Fant.
 Four Ann.#1,SpM #8 . . . . 65.00
Ann.#7 JR(c),Rep.#1,#2,#38 . . . . . 65.00
Ann.#8 Rep.#46,#50 . . . . 65.00
Ann.#9 JR(c),Rep.Spec.SpM #2 . . 65.00
Ann.#10 JR(c),GK,V:Human Fly . . 30.00
Ann.#11 GK(c),DP,JM,JR2,AM, . . . 20.00
Ann.#12 JBy(c),KP,Rep.#119,
 #120. . . . . 25.00
Ann.#13 JBy,TA,V:Dr.Octopus 25.00
Ann.#14 FM,TP,A:Dr.Strange,
 V:Dr.Doom,Dormammu 25.00
Ann.#15 FM,KJ,BL,Punisher 25.00
Ann.#16 JR2,JR,I:New Captain
 Marvel,A:Thing 10.00
Ann.#17 EH,JM,V:Kingpin 10.00
Ann.#18 RF,BL,JG,V:Scorpion 10.00
Ann.#19 JR(c),MW,V:Spiderslayer. 10.00
Ann.#20 BWi(i),V:Iron Man 2020 . . 10.00
Ann.#21 JR(c),PR,W:SpM,direct . . 20.00
Ann.#21a W:SpM,news stand 15.00
Ann.#22 JR(c),MBa(1stSpM),SD,
 JG,RLm,TD,Evolutionary War,
 I:Speedball,New Men 8.00
Ann.#23 JBy(c),RLd,MBa,RF,
 AtlantisAttacks#4,A:She-Hulk . . 7.00

Ann.#24 GK,SD,MZ,DGr,
 A:Ant Man 4.00
Ann.#25 EL(c),SB,PCu,SD,
 Vibranium Vendetta#1,Venom . . 6.00
Ann.#26 Hero Killers#1,A:New
 Warriors,BU:Venom,Solo. 6.00
Ann.#27 TL,I:Annex,w/card 4.00
Ann.#28 SBt(s),V:Carnage,BU:Cloak
 & Dagger,Rhino. 4.00
Ann. '96 two new stories, 48pg,. . . . 3.50
Ann. '97 RSt,TL,RJn, 48pg,. 3.50
Ann. '98 TL,TDF,F:Spider-Man &
 Devil Dinosaur, 48pg. 3.00
G-Size Superheroes #1 GK,
 A:Morbius,Man-Wolf 75.00
G-Size #1 JR(c),RA,DH,
 A:Dracula. 40.00
G-Size #2 K&R(c),RA,AM,
 A:Master of Kung Fu 40.00
G-Size #3 GK(c),RA,DocSavage. . 40.00
G-Size #4 GK(c),RA,Punisher 75.00
G-Size #5 GK(c),RA,V:Magnum . . 30.00
G-Size #6 Rep.Ann.#4. . . . . 30.00
G-Size Spec.#1 O:Symbiotes 5.00
Marvel Milestone rep. #1 (1993) . . . 3.00
Marvel Milestone rep. #3 (1995) . . . 3.00
Marvel Milestone rep. #129 (1992) . 3.00
Marvel Milestone rep. #149 (1994) . 3.00
GN Fear Itself RA,A:S.Sable 13.00
GN Spirits of the Earth CV,Scotland,
 V:Hellfire Club 25.00
TPB Assassination Plot, rep. 15.00
TPB Carnage, rep. 7.00
TPB Cosmic Adventures, rep. 20.00
TPB Kraven's Last Hunt, rep. 16.00
TPB Origin of the Hobgoblin, rep. . 15.00
TPB Saga of the Alien Costume . . . 10.00
TPB Spider-Man Vs. Venom, rep. . 10.00
TPB Venom Returns rep. 13.00
TPB The Wedding, rep. 13.00
Nothing Can Stop the Juggernaut . . 4.00
Sensational Spider-Man,reps. 5.00
Skating on Thin Ice(Canadian) . . . 15.00
Skating on Thin Ice(US). 2.00
Soul of the Hunter MZ,BMc,
 R:Kraven 7.00
Unicef:Trial of Venom,
 A:Daredevil,V:Venom 50.00
See Also:
PETER PARKER;
SPECTACULAR SPIDER-MAN;
WEB OF SPIDER-MAN

AMAZING SPIDER-MAN
Jan., 1999

1 HMe,JBy,DHz,V:Scorpion,48-page
 prismatic etched (c). 7.00
1a Dynamic Forces JR2 . . . . 15.00
2 HMe,JBy,DHz,I:Shadrac 5.00
2a variant BiT cover 6.00
3 HMe,JBy,DHz,V:Shadrac,
 A:Iceman. 3.00
4 HMe,JBy,SHa,A:Fantastic Four. . 3.00
5 HMe,JBy,SHa,I:new
 Spider-Woman. 3.00
6 JBy,HMe,SHa,F:Spider-Woman. . 3.00
7 JBy,HMe,SHa,Reality Bent 3.00
8 JMy,HMe,SHa,JR2(c),
 Reality Bent x-over 3.00
9 JMy,HMe,SHa,JR2(c),V:Scorpion 3.00
10 JMy,HMe,SHa,JR2(c),MaryJane. 3.00
11 HMe,SHa,JBy,marital problems . 3.00
12 HMe,SHa,JBy,48-pg. 4.00
13 HMe,JBy 3.00
14 HMe,JBy,A:Sp.-Woman,x-over . . 3.00
15 HMe,JBy,DGr,x-over. 3.00
16 HMe,JBy,DGr,Mary Jane gone . . 3.00
17 HMe,JBy,DGr,A:Sandman 3.00
18 HMe,JBy,JR,V:Green Goblin . . . 3.00
19 HMe,EL,DGr,Eddie Brock 3.00

MARVEL

20 HMe,EL,JBy,100-pg	3.50
21 HMe,EL,JhB,AlistairSmythe	3.00
22 HMe,JR2,SHa,Senator Ward	3.00
23 HMe,JR2,SHa,Ranger	3.00
24 HMe,JR2,SHa,Max.Security	3.00
25 HMe,JR2,SHa,A:Green Goblin	3.00
25a holographic foil(c)	7.00
26 HMe,JR2,SHa,F:Spidey's dad	3.00
27 HMe,JR2,SHa,V:A.I.M.	3.00
28 HMe,JR2,SHa,Enforcers.	7.00
29 HMe,JR2,SHa,x-over	3.00
30 B:MSz(s),JR2,JSC(c)	21.00
31 MSz(s),JR2,JSC(c)	10.00
32 MSz(s),JR2,SHa,Ezekiel.	10.00
33 MSz(s),JR2,SHa,Morlun	10.00
34 MSz(s),JR2,SHa,V:Morlun	8.00
35 MSz(s),JR2,SHa,pt.1	8.00
36 MSz(s),JR2,SHa	15.00
37 MSz(s),JR2,SHa	5.00
38 MSz(s),JR2,SHa,'Nuff Said	3.00
39 MSz(s),JR2,SHa,Aunt May	3.00
40 MSz(s),JR2,SHa,Aunt May	3.00
41 MSz(s),JR2,SHa	3.00
42 MSz(s),JR2,SHa,	3.00
43 MSz(s),JR2,SHa	3.00
44 MSz(s),JR2,SHa	3.00
45 MSz(s),JR2,SHa	3.00
46 MSz(s),JR2,SHa	3.00
47 MSz(s),JR2,SHa	3.00
48 MSz(s),JR2,SHa	3.00
49 MSz(s),JR2,SHa	3.00
50 MSz(s),JR2,SHa,F:Mary Jane	4.50
51 MSz(s),JR2,SHa,F:Mary Jane	2.25
52 MSz(s),JR2,SHa,F:Mary Jane	2.25
53 MSz(s),JR2,SHa,F:Mary Jane	2.25
54 MSz(s),JR2,Digger	2.25
55 MSz(s),JR2,Consequences,pt.1	2.25
56 MSz(s),JR2,Consequences,pt.2	2.25
57 MSz(s),JR2,pt.1	2.25
58 MSz(s),JR2,pt.2	2.25
500 MSz(s),JR2,48-pg	4.00
501 MSz(s),JR2	2.25
502 MSz(s),JR2	2.25
503 JR2,A Dark Shadow,pt.1	2.25
504 JR2,A Dark Shadow,pt.2	2.25
505 MSz(s),JR2,Ezekiel,pt.1	2.25
506 MSz(s),JR2,Ezekiel,pt.2	2.25
507 MSz(s),JR2,Ezekiel,pt.3	2.25
508 MSz(s),JR2,Ezekiel,pt.4	2.25
509 MSz(s),MD2,Sins Past,pt.1	2.25
510 MSz(s),MD2,Sins Past,pt.2	2.25
511 MSz(s),MD2,Sins Past,pt.3	2.25
512 MSz(s),MD2,Sins Past,pt.4	2.25
513 MSz(s),MD2,Sins Past,pt.5	2.25
TPB Vol. 3	13.00
TPB Vol. 4	12.00
TPB Vol. 5	13.00
TPB Vol. 6 Happy Birthday	13.00
TPB Vol. 7 Book of Ezekiel	13.00
Spec. Must Have,Rep. #30–#32	4.00
Ann.1999 JB,HMe, 48-page	4.00
Ann.2000 HMe,48-pg.	4.00
Ann.2001 48-page	4.00
Giant Sized 80-pg.	4.50
Spec.Spider-Man/Sentry,PJe,RL,TA	3.00
Spec.Spider-Man/Marrow,SLo	3.00
Spec.Coll. ed.,rep #30–#32	4.00
Coll.Classics rep. #300	2.50
Coll.Classics rep. #300 signed	30.00
Coll.Classics rep. Sp-M #1.	2.50
Coll.Classics rep. Sp-M #1 signed.	30.00
TPB Revelations, 96-pg.	9.00

AMAZING SPIDER-MAN INDEX
See: OFFICIAL MARVEL INDEX TO THE AMAZING SPIDER-MAN

AMAZING SPIDER-MAN COLLECTION

1 Mark Bagley card set.	3.00
2 and 3 MBa, from card set	@3.00

AMAZING X-MEN, THE
March–June, 1995

1 X-Men after Xavier.	4.00
2 Exodus,Dazzler,V:Abyss	3.00
3 F:Bishop.	3.00
4 V:Apocalypse	2.50
TPB Rep. #1-#4.	9.00

AMERICAN TAIL II
Dec., 1991

1 & 2 movie adaption	@2.25

A-NEXT
Aug., 1998

1 TDF,RF,BBr,Next Generation of Avengers	3.00
2 TDF,RF,BBr,V:Kree & Sentry	2.25
2a variant cover	2.25
3 TDF,RF,BBr,Orig.Defenders vs. New Avengers	2.25
4 TDF,RF,BBr,turning points	2.25
5 TDF,RF,BBr,SB,Ghosts of the Past	2.25
6 TDF,RF,BBr,Majority Rules	2.25
7 TDF,RF,BBr,Last Days of the Avengers	2.25
8 TDF,RF,BBr,A:Ant-Man,Uneasy Allies	2.25
9 TDF,RF,BBr,Critical Choices	2.25
10 TDF,RF,BBr,Incredible Journeys.	2.25
11 TDF,RF,BBr,A:Captain America & Doctor Doom	2.25
12 TDF,RF,BBr,I:Revengers.	2.25

ANIMAX
Star, 1986–87

1 Based on Toy Line	3.00
2 thru 4	@3.00

ANNEX
Aug.–Nov., 1994

1 WMc,I:Brace, Crucible of Power	2.25
2 WMc,V:Brace, Crucible, pt.2	2.25
3 Crucible of Power, pt.3	2.25
4 Crucible of Power, pt.4	2.25

Annex #1
© Marvel Entertainment Group

ANNIE
(Treasury Edition)
Oct., 1982

1 Movie Adaptation	3.00
2 Nov., 1982	3.00

ANNIE OAKLEY
Atlas, Spring, 1948

1 A:Hedy Devine	550.00
2 CCB,I:Lana, A:Hedy Devine	300.00
3	250.00
4	250.00
5	175.00
6 thru 8	@150.00
9 AW,	165.00
10	125.00
11 June, 1956	125.00

ANT-MAN
Dec., 2003

1 (of 5) Size does matter	3.00
2 thru 5	@3.00

ANT-MAN'S BIG CHRISTMAS
Dec., 1999

GN 48-pg.	6.00

A-1
1993

1 The Edge.	8.00
2 Cheeky,Wee Budgie Boy.	8.00
3 King Leon.	8.00
4 King Leon.	8.00

APACHE SKIES
July, 2002

1 (of 4) JOs,Apache Kid,wild west	3.00
2 thru 4 JOs	@3.00
TPB	13.00

APOCALYPSE STRIKEFILES

1 After Xavier special	2.50

ARCHANGEL
1996

1-shot B&W	2.50

ARIZONA KID
Atlas, March, 1951

1 RH,Coming of the Arizons Kid.	300.00
2 RH,Code of the Gunman	150.00
3 RH(c)	125.00
4 PMo	125.00
5 PMo	125.00
6 PMo,JSt,Jan., 1952	125.00

ARRGH!
Dec., 1974
Satire

1 MSy,TS,Vampire Rats	35.00
2 AA,TS.	25.00
3 TS,AA(c),Beauty and the Big Foot	25.00
4 The Night Gawker	25.00
5 Sept., 1975	25.00

ARROWHEAD
April, 1954

1 JSt,Indian Warrior Stories	200.00
2 JSt	125.00

3 JSt 125.00
4 JSt,Nov., 1954 . . . . 125.00

ASTONISHING
See: MARVEL BOY

Astonishing Tales #19
© Marvel Entertainment Group

ASTONISHING TALES
Aug., 1970
1 BEv(c),JK,WW,Ka-Zar,Dr.Doom 75.00
2 JK,WW,Ka-Zar,Dr.Doom 40.00
3 BWS,WW,Ka-Zar,Dr.Doom 50.00
4 BWS,WW,Ka-Zar,Dr.Doom 50.00
5 BWS,GT,Ka-Zar,Dr.Doom 50.00
6 BWS,BEv,GT,I:Bobbi Morse . . . 50.00
7 HT,GC,Ka-Zar,Dr.Doom 25.00
8 HT,TS,GT,GC,TP,Ka-Zar 25.00
9 GK(c),JB,Ka-Zar,Dr.Doom 20.00
10 GK(c),BWS,SB,Ka-Zar 25.00
11 GK,O:Ka-Zar 25.00
12 JB,DA,NA,V:Man Thing 40.00
13 JB,RB,DA,V:Man Thing 30.00
14 GK(c),rep. Ka-Zar 15.00
15 GK,TS,Ka-Zar 15.00
16 RB,AM,A:Ka-Zar 15.00
17 DA,V:Gemini 15.00
18 JR(c),DA,A:Ka-Zar 15.00
19 JR(c),DA,JSn,JA,I:Victorious . . 15.00
20 JR(c),A:Ka-Zar 15.00
21 RTs(s),DAy,B:It 35.00
22 RTs(s),DAy,V:Granitor 25.00
23 RTs(s),DAy,A:Fin Fang Foom . . 25.00
24 RTs(s),DAy,E:It 25.00
25 RB(a&s),B:I&O:Deathlok,
    GP(1st art) 60.00
26 RB(a&s),I:Warwolf 20.00
27 RB(a&s),V:Warwolf 20.00
28 RB(a&s),V:Warwolf 20.00
29 rep.Marv.Super Heroes #18 . . . 15.00
30 RB(a&s),KP, ... 15.00
31 RB(a&s),BW,KP,V:Ryker. 18.00
32 RB(a&s),KP,V:Ryker 18.00
33 RB(a&s),KJ,I:Hellinger 18.00
34 RB(a&s),KJ,V:Ryker 18.00
35 RB(a&s),KJ,I:Doomsday-Mech. 18.00
36 RB(a&s),KP,E:Deathlok,
    I:Godwulf 25.00

ASTONISHING X-MEN
March–June, 1995
1 Uncanny X-Men 5.00
2 V:Holocaust 3.50

3 V:Abyss 3.00
4 V:Beast,Infinities 3.00
TPB Rep. #1-#4 . . . . 9.00

ASTONISHING X-MEN
July, 1999
1 (of 3) BPe,HMe,new X-Men team 2.50
2 BPe,HMe,The Shattering x-over . 2.50
3 BPe,HMe,Shattering,concl. 2.50
TPB 160-pg. 15.95

ASTONISHING X-MEN
May, 2004
1 Gifted,pt.1 . . . . 3.00
1a Director's Cut 4.00
2 thru 6 Gifted,pt.2 thru pt.6 . . . . @3.00

A-TEAM
March, 1984
1 . . . . 5.00
2 . . . . 5.00
3 May, 1984 . . . . 5.00

ATOMIC AGE
Epic, Nov., 1990
1 AW 4.50
2 AW 4.50
3 AW,Feb., 1991 . . . . 4.50

AVATAARS: COVENANT OF THE SHIELD
July, 2000
1 (of 3) LKa,Capt.Avalon 3.00
2 LKa,Dreadlord 3.00

AVENGERS
Sept., 1963
1 JK,O:Avengers,V:Loki 5,000.00
2 JK,V:Space Phantom 1,100.00
3 JK,V:Hulk,Sub-Mariner 700.00
4 JK,R&J:Captain America . . . 3,200.00
5 JK,L:Hulk,V:Lava Men 450.00
6 JK,I:Masters of Evil 450.00
7 JK,V:BaronZemo,Enchantress. 450.00
8 JK,I:Kang 325.00
9 JK(c),DH,I&D:Wonder Man . . . 325.00
10 JK(c),DH,I:Immortus 300.00
11 JK(c),DH,A:Spider-Man,
    V:Kang. 400.00
12 JK(c),DH,V:Moleman,
    Red Ghost 300.00
13 JK(c),DH,I:Count Nefaria 300.00
14 JK,DH,V:Count Nefaria 300.00
15 JK,DH,D:Baron Zemo 250.00
16 JK,J:Hawkeye,Scarlet Witch,
    Quicksilver. 300.00
17 JK(c),DH,V:Mole Man,A:Hulk . 200.00
18 JK(c),DH,V:The Commisar . . . 200.00
19 JK(c),DH,I&O:Swordsman,
    O:Hawkeye 200.00
20 JK(c),DH,WW,V:Swordsman,
    Mandarin 125.00
21 JK(c),DH,WW,V:Power Man
    (not L.Cage),Enchantress . . . 125.00
22 JK(c),DH,WW,V:Power Man . . 125.00
23 JK(c),DH,JR,V:Kang 100.00
24 JK(c),DH,JR,V:Kang. 100.00
25 JK(c),DH,V:Dr.Doom 100.00
26 DH,V:Attuma 100.00
27 DH,V:Attuma,Beetle 100.00
28 JK(c),DH,I:1st Goliath,
    I:Collector 100.00
29 DH,V:Power Man,Swordsman 100.00
30 JK(c),DH,V:Swordsman 100.00
31 DH,V:Keeper of the Flame . . . 100.00
32 DH,I:Bill Foster 75.00

33 DH,V:Sons of the Serpent
    A:Bill Foster. 75.00
34 DH,V:Living Laser. 75.00
35 DH,V:Mandarin 75.00
36 DH,V:The Ultroids 75.00
37 GK(c),DH,V:Ultroids 75.00
38 GK(c),DH,V:Enchantress,
    Ares,J:Hercules 75.00
39 DH,V:Mad Thinker 75.00
40 DH,V:Sub-Mariner. 75.00
41 JB,V:Dragon Man,Diablo 65.00
42 JB,V:Dragon Man,Diablo 65.00
43 JB,V:Red Guardian. 65.00
44 JB,V:Red Guardian,
    O:Black.Widow 65.00
45 JB,V:Super Adoptoid. 65.00
46 JB,V:Whirlwind 65.00
47 JB,GT,V:Magneto 75.00
48 GT,I&O:New Black Knight. 75.00
49 JB,V:Magneto 65.00
50 JB,V:Typhon 65.00
51 JB,GT,R:Iron Man,Thor,
    V:Collector 65.00
52 JB,J:Black Panther,
    I:Grim Reaper 65.00
53 JB,GT,A:X-Men; x-over
    X-Men #45 . . . . 100.00
54 JB,GT,V:Masters of Evil
    I:Crimson Cowl(Ultron) 75.00
55 JB,I:Ultron,V:Masters of Evil . . . 75.00
56 JB,D:Bucky retold,
    V:Baron Zemo 75.00
57 JB,I:Vision,V:Ultron 200.00
58 JB,O&J:Vision 100.00
59 JB,I:Yellowjacket 65.00
60 JB,W:Yellowjacket & Wasp 65.00
61 JB,A:Dr.Strange,x-over
    Dr. Strange #178 . . . . 65.00
62 JB,I:Man-Ape,A:Dr.Strange. . . . 65.00
63 GC,I&O:2nd Goliath(Hawkeye)
    V:Egghead. 65.00
64 GC,V:Egghead,O:Hawkeye 65.00
65 GC,V:Swordsman,Egghead 65.00
66 BWS,I:Ultron 6,Adamantium . . . 70.00
67 BWS,V:Ultron 6. . . . . 70.00
68 SB,V:Ultron 60.00
69 SB,I:Nighthawk,Grandmaster,
    Squadron Supreme, V:Kang . . 60.00
70 SB,O:Squadron Supreme
    V:Kang. 60.00
71 SB,I:Invaders,V:Kang 85.00
72 SB,A:Captain Marvel,
    I:Zodiac 50.00
73 HT(i),V:Sons of Serpent 50.00

Avengers #58
© Marvel Entertainment Group

74 JB,TP,V:Sons of Serpent,
    IR:Black Panther on TV 50.00
75 JB,TP,I:Arkon 50.00
76 JB,TP,V:Arkon 50.00
77 JB,TP,V:Split-Second Squad . . . 50.00
78 SB,TP,V:Lethal Legion 50.00
79 JB,TP,V:Lethal Legion 50.00
80 JB,TP,I&O:Red Wolf 55.00
81 JB,TP,A:Red Wolf 50.00
82 JB,TP,V:Ares,A:Daredevil 50.00
83 JB,TP,I:Valkyrie,
    V:Masters of Evil 55.00
84 JB,TP,V:Enchantress,Arkon . . . 50.00
85 JB,V:Squadron Supreme 50.00
86 JB,JM,A:Squad Supreme 50.00
87 SB(i),O:Black Panther,
    V: A.I.M. 65.00
88 SB,JM,V:Psyklop,A:Hulk,
    Professor.X 55.00
88a 2nd Printing 10.00
89 SB,B:Kree/Skrull War 45.00
90 SB,V:Sentry #459,Ronan,
    Skrulls 45.00
91 SB,V:Sentry #459,Ronan,
    Skrulls 45.00
92 SB,V:Super Skrull,Ronan, ... 55.00
93 NA,TP,V:Super-Skrull,G-Size . 125.00
94 NA,JB,TP,V:Super-Skrull,
    I:Mandroids 75.00
95 NA,TP,V:Maximus,Skrulls,
    A:Inhumans,O:Black Bolt 70.00
96 NA,TP,V:Skrulls,Ronan 70.00
97 GK&BEv(c),JB,TP,E:Kree-Skrull
    War,V:Annihilus,Ronan,Skrulls,
    A:Golden Age Heroes 60.00
98 BWS,SB,V:Ares,R:Hercules,
    R&N:Hawkeye 60.00
99 BWS,TS,V:Ares 60.00
100 BWS,JSr,V:Ares & Kratos . . 150.00
101 RB,DA,A:Watcher 40.00
102 RB,JSt,V:Grim Reaper,
    Sentinels 40.00
103 RB,JSt,V:Sentinels 40.00
104 RB,JSt,V:Sentinels 40.00
105 JB,JM,V:Savage Land
    Mutates; A:Black Panther 40.00
106 GT,DC,RB,V:Space Phantom . 40.00
107 GT,DC,JSn,V:Space
    Phantom, Grim Reaper 35.00
108 DH,DC,JSt,V:Space
    Phantom,Grim Reaper 40.00
109 DH,FMc,V:Champion,
    L:Hawkeye 40.00
110 DH,V:Magneto,A:X-Men 50.00

Avengers #130
© Marvel Entertainment Group

111 DH,J:Bl.Widow,A:Daredevil,
    X-Men,V:Magneto 45.00
112 DH,I:Mantis,V:Lion-God,
    L:Black Widow 40.00
113 FBe(i),V:The Living Bombs . . . 25.00
114 JR(c),V:Lion-God,J:Mantis,
    Swordsman 25.00
115 JR(c),A:Defenders,V:Loki,
    Dormammu 25.00
116 JR(c),A:Defenders,S.Surfer
    V:Loki,Dormammu 25.00
117 JR(c),FMc(i),A:Defenders,Silv.
    Surfer,V:Loki,Dormammu 25.00
118 JR(c),A:Defenders,S.Surfer
    V:Loki,Dormammu 25.00
119 JR(c),DH(i),V:Collector 25.00
120 JSn(c),DH(i),V:Zodiac 25.00
121 JR&JSn(c),JB,DH,V:Zodiac . . 25.00
122 K&R(c),V:Zodiac 25.00
123 JR(c),DH(i),O:Mantis. 25.00
124 JR(c),JB,DC,V:Kree,O:Mantis. 25.00
125 JR(c),JB,DC,V:Thanos 22.00
126 DC(i),V:Klaw,Solarr 22.00
127 GK(c),SB,JSon,A:Inhumans,
    V:Ultron,Maximus 22.00
128 K&R(c),SB,JSon,V:Kang. 20.00
129 SB,JSon,V:Kang 20.00
130 GK(c),SB,JSon,V:Slasher,
    Titanic Three 20.00
131 GK(c),SB,JSon,V:Kang,
    Legion of the Unliving 20.00
132 SB,JSon,Kang,Legion
    of the Unliving 20.00
133 GK(c),SB,JSon,O:Vision 20.00
134 K&R(c),SB,JSon,O:Vision . . . 20.00
135 JSn&JR(c),GT,O:Mantis,
    Vision,C:Thanos 25.00
136 K&R(c),rep Amazing Adv#12 . 20.00
137 JR(c),GT,J:Beast,
    Moondragon 20.00
138 GK(c),GT,V:Toad 20.00
139 K&R(c),GT,V:Whirlwind 18.00
140 K&R(c),GT,V:Whirlwind 18.00
141 GK(c),GP,V:Squad.Sinister . . . 12.00
142 K&R(c),GP,V:Squadron
    Sinister,Kang 12.00
143 GK(c),GP,V:Squadron
    Sinister,Kang 12.00
144 GP,GK(c),V:Squad.Sinister,
    O&J:Hellcat,O:Buzz Baxter . . . 25.00
145 GK(c),DH,V:Assassin 12.00
146 GK(c),DH,KP,V:Assassin 12.00
147 GP,V:Squadron Supreme 12.00
148 JK(c),GP,V:Squad.Supreme . . 12.00
149 GP,V:Orka 15.00
150 GP,JK,rep.Avengers #16. . . . . 12.00
151 GP,new line-up,
    R:Wonder Man 15.00
152 JB,JSt,I:New Black Talon 15.00
153 JB,JSt,V.L.Laser,Whizzer 12.00
154 GP,V:Attuma 12.00
155 SB,V:Dr.Doom,Attuma 12.00
156 SB,I:Tyrak,V:Attuma 12.00
157 DH,V:Stone Black Knight 12.00
158 JK(c),SB,I&O:Graviton, ... 12.00
159 JK(c),SB,V:Graviton, ... 12.00
160 GP,V:Grim Reaper 12.00
161 GP,V:Ultron,A:Ant-Man 12.00
162 GP,V:Ultron,I:Jocasta 12.00
163 GT,A:Champions,V:Typhon. . . 15.00
164 JBy,V:Lethal Legion 15.00
165 JBy,V:Count Nefario 12.00
166 JBy,V:Count Nefario 12.00
167 GP,A:Guardians,A:Nighthawk,
    Korvac,V:Porcupine 8.00
168 GP,A:Guardians,V:Korvac,
    I:Gyrich 8.00
169 SB,I:Eternity Man 8.00
170 GP,R:Jocasta,C:Ultron,
    A:Guardians 8.00

171 GP,V:Ultron,A:Guardians,
    Ms Marvel 8.00
172 SB,KJ,V:Tyrak 8.00
173 SB,V:Collector. 8.00
174 GP(c),V:Collector 8.00
175 V&O:Korvac,A:Guardians 8.00
176 V:Korvac,A:Guardians 8.00
177 DC(c),D:Korvac,A:Guardians . . 8.00
178 CI,V:Manipulator 8.00
179 JM,AG,V:Stinger,Bloodhawk . . 8.00
180 JM,V:Monolith,Stinger,
    D:Bloodhawk 8.00
181 JBy,GD,I:Scott Lang 10.00
182 JBy,KJ,V:Maximoff 10.00
183 JBy,KJ,J:Ms.Marvel. 10.00
184 JBy,KJ,J:Falcon,
    V:Absorbing Man 10.00
185 JBy,DGr,O:Quicksilver & Scarlet
    Witch,I:Bova,V:Modred 10.00
186 JBy,DGr,V:Modred,Chthon . . . 10.00
187 JBy,DGr,V:Chthon,Modred . . . 10.00
188 JBy,DGr,V:The Elements 10.00
189 JBy,DGr,V:Deathbird 10.00
190 JBy,DGr,V:Grey Gargoyle,
    A:Daredevil 10.00
191 JBy,DGr,V:Grey Gargoyle,
    A:Daredevil 10.00
192 I:Inferno 8.00
193 FM(c),SB,DGr,O:Inferno 10.00
194 GP,JRu,J:Wonder Man 10.00
195 GP,JRu,A:Antman,
    I&C:Taskmaster 10.00
196 GP,JA,A:Antman,
    V:Taskmaster, ... 10.00
197 CI,JAb,V:Red Ronin 10.00
198 GP,DGr,V:Red Ronan 10.00
199 GP,DGr,V:Red Ronan 10.00
200 GP,DGr,V:Marcus,
    L:Ms.Marvel 11.00
201 GP,DGr,F:Jarvis 4.00
202 GP,V:Ultron 4.00
203 CI,V:Crawlers,F:Wonderman . . 4.00
204 DN,DGr,V:Yellow Claw 4.00
205 DGr,V:Yellow Claw 4.00
206 GC,DGr,V:Pyron 4.00
207 GC,DGr,V:Shadowlord 4.00
208 GC,DGr,V:Berserker 4.00
209 DGr,A:Mr.Fantastic,V:Skrull . . . 4.00
210 GC,DGr,V:Weathermen 4.00
211 GC,DGr,Moon Knight,J:Tigra . . 4.00
212 DGr,V:Elfqueen 4.00
213 BH,DGr,L:Yellowjacket 4.00
214 BH,DGr,V:Gh.Rider,A:Angel . . . 7.00
215 DGr,A:Silver Surfer,
    V:Molecule Man 5.00
216 DGr,A:Silver Surfer,
    V:Molecule Man 5.00
217 BH,DGr,V:Egghead,
    R:Yellowjacket,Wasp3 . . . . 5.00
218 DP,V:M.Hardy 5.00
219 BH,A:Moondragon,Drax 5.00
220 BH,DGr,D:Drax,V:MnDragon . . 5.00
221 J:She Hulk 5.00
222 V:Masters of Evil 5.00
223 A:Antman 5.00
224 AM,A:Antman 5.00
225 A:Black Knight. 5.00
226 A:Black Knight. 5.00
227 J:2nd Captain Marvel,
    O:Avengers 5.00
228 V:Masters of Evil. 5.00
229 JSt,V:Masters of Evil. 5.00
230 A:Cap.Marvel,L:Yellowjacket . . 5.00
231 AM,JSi,J:2nd Captain Marvel,
    Starfox 5.00
232 AM,JSi. 5.00
233 JBy,V:Annihilus 5.00
234 AM,JSi,O:ScarletWitch 5.00
235 AM,JSi,V:Wizard 5.00
236 AM,JSi,A:SpM,V:Lava Men. . . . 4.50
237 AM,JSi,A:SpM,V:Lava Men . . . 4.50

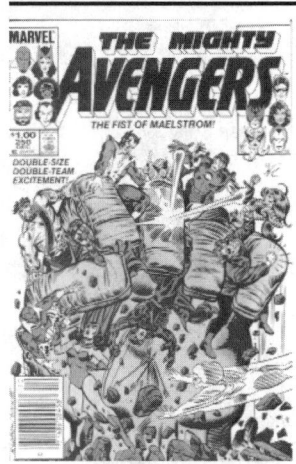

Avengers #250
© Marvel Entertainment Group

238 AM,JSi,V:Moonstone,
    O:Blackout 4.00
239 AM,JSi,A:David Letterman 4.00
240 AM,JSi,A:Dr.Strange 4.00
241 AM,JSi,V:Morgan LeFey 4.00
242 AM,JSi,Secret Wars 4.00
243 AM,JSi,Secret Wars 4.00
244 AM,JSi,V:Dire Wraiths. 4.00
245 AM,JSi,V:Dire Wraiths. 4.00
246 AM,JSi,V:Eternals 4.00
247 AM,JSi,A:Eternals,V:Deviants. . 4.00
248 AM,JSi,A:Eternals,V:Deviants. . 4.00
249 AM,JSi,A:Maelstrom 4.00
250 AM,JSi,A:W.C.A.
    V:Maelstrom 5.00
251 BH,JSi,A:Paladin. 4.00
252 BH,JSi,J:Hercules
    V:Blood Brothers 4.00
253 BH,JSi,J:Black Knight 4.00
254 BH,JSi,A:W.C.A. 4.00
255 TP,p(c),JB,Legacy of
    Thanos/Santuary II 4.00
256 JB,TP,A:Ka-Zar. 4.00
257 JB,TP,D:Savage Land,
    I:Nebula 4.00
258 JB,TP,A:SpM,Firelord,Nebula . . 4.00
259 JB,TP,V:Nebula 4.00
260 JB,TP,SecretWarsII, IR:Nebula
    is Thanos' Granddaughter. 4.00
261 JB,TP,Secret Wars II. 4.00
262 JB,TP,J:Submariner 4.00
263 JB,TP,X-Factor tie-in,
    Rebirth,Marvel Girl,pt.1 . . . . . . 6.00
264 JB,TP,I:2nd Yellow Jacket. 4.00
265 JB,TP,Secret Wars II. 3.50
266 JB,TP,Secret Wars II,A:
    Silver Surfer. 3.50
267 JB,TP,V:Kang 3.50
268 JB,TP,V:Kang 3.50
269 JB,TP,V:Kang,A:Immortus. 3.50
270 JB,TP,V:Moonstone. 3.50
271 JB,TP,V:Masters of Evil. 3.50
272 JB,TP,A:Alpha Flight. 3.50
273 JB,TP,V:Masters of Evil. 3.50
274 JB,TP,V:Masters of Evil. 3.50
275 JB,TP,V:Masters of Evil. 3.50
276 JB,TP,V:Masters of Evil. 3.50
277 JB,TP,V:Masters of Evil. 3.50
278 JB,TP,V:Tyrok,J:Dr.Druid. 3.50
279 JB,TP,new leader 3.50
280 BH,KB,O:Jarvis. 3.50
281 JB,TP,V:Olympian Gods 3.50
282 JB,TP,V:Cerberus 3.50

283 JB,TP,V:Olympian Gods 3.50
284 JB,TP,V:Olympian Gods 3.50
285 JB,TP,V:Zeus 3.50
286 JB,TP,V:Fixer 3.50
287 JB,TP,V:Fixer 3.50
288 JB,TP,V:Sentry 459. . . . . 3.50
289 JB,TP,J:Marrina. 3.50
290 JB,TP,V:Adaptoid 3.50
291 JB,TP,V:Marrina 3.50
292 JB,TP,V:Leviathon. 3.50
293 JB,TP,V:Leviathon. 3.50
294 JB,TP,V:Nebula. 3.50
295 JB,TP,V:Nebula. 3.50
296 JB,TP,V:Nebula. 3.50
297 JB,TP,V:Nebula. 3.50
298 JB,TP,Inferno,Edwin Jarvis 3.50
299 JB,TP,Inferno,V:Orphan
    Maker,R:Gilgemesh 3.50
300 JB,TP,WS,Inferno,V:Kang,
    O:Avengers,J:Gilgemesh,
    Mr.Fantastic,Invis.Woman 5.00
301 BH,DH,A:SuperNova 3.50
302 RB,TP,V:SuperNova,
    A:Quasar 3.50
303 RB,TP,V:SuperNova,A:FF. 3.50
304 RB,TP,V:U-Foes,Puma 3.50
305 PR,TP,V:Lava Men 5.00
306 PR,TP,O:Lava Men 3.50
307 PR,TP,V:Lava Men 3.50
308 PR,TP,A:Eternals,J:Sersi 3.50
309 PR,TP,V:Blastaar 3.50
310 PR,TP,V:Blastaar 3.50
311 PR,TP,Acts of Veng.,V:Loki. . . . 3.50
312 PR,TP,Acts of Vengeance,
    V:Freedom Force. 3.50
313 PR,TP,Acts of Vengeance,
    V:Mandarin,Wizard 3.50
314 PR,TP,J:Sersi,A:Spider-Man,
    V:Nebula 4.00
315 PR,TP,A:SpM,V:Nebula 4.00
316 PR,TP,J:Spider-Man 4.00
317 PR,TP,A:SpM,V:Nebula 4.00
318 PR,TP,A:SpM,V:Nebula 4.00
319 PR,B:Crossing Line 3.00
320 PR,TP,A:Alpha Flight 3.00
321 PR,Crossing Line#3 . . . . 3.00
322 PR,TP,Crossing Line#4. . . . . . . 3.00
323 PR,TP,Crossing Line#5. . . . . . . 3.00
324 PR,TP,E:Crossing Line 3.00
325 V:MotherSuperior,3
    Machinesmith 3.00
326 TP,I:Rage 5.00
327 TP,V:Monsters. 3.00
328 TP,O:Rage 4.00
329 TP,J:Sandman,Rage 3.00
330 TP,V:Tetrarch of Entropy 3.00
331 TP,J:Rage,Sandman 3.00
332 TP,V:Dr.Doom 3.00
333 HT,V:Dr.Doom 3.00
334 NKu,TP,B:Collector,
    A:Inhumans 3.00
335 RLm(c),SEp,TP,V:Thane
    Ector,A:Collector, ... 3.00
336 RLm(c),SEp,TP. 3.00
337 RLm(c),SEp,TP,V:ThaneEctor . 3.00
338 RLm(c),SEp,TP,A:Beast,. 3.00
339 RLm(c),SEp,TP,E:Collector. . . . 3.00
340 RLm(c),F:Capt.Amer.,Wasp . . . 3.00
341 SEp,TP,A:New Warriors,V:Sons
    of Serpents 3.00
342 SEP,TP,A:New Warriors,
    V:Hatemonger 3.00
343 SEp,TP,J:Crystal,C&I:2nd
    Swordsman,Magdalene. 3.00
344 SEp,TP,I:Proctor 3.00
345 SEp,TP,Oper. Galactic Storm
    Pt.5,V:Kree,Shiar. 3.00
346 SEp,TP,Oper. Galactic Storm
    Pt.12,I:Star Force 3.00
347 SEp,TP,Oper. Galactic Storm
    Pt.19,D:Kree Race,Conclusion . 3.00

Avengers #393
© Marvel Entertainment Group

348 SEp,TP,F:Vision 3.00
349 SEp,TP,V:Ares 3.00
350 SEp,TP,rep.Avengers#53,A:Prof.
    X,Cyclops,V:StarJammers. 4.00
351 KWe,V:Star Jammers 3.00
352 V:Grim Reaper 3.00
353 V:Grim Reaper 3.00
354 V:Grim Reaper 3.00
355 BHs(s),SEp,I:Gatherers,
    Coal Tiger 3.00
356 B:BHs(s),SEp,TP,A:Bl.Panther
    D:Coal Tiger 3.00
357 SEp,TP,A:Watcher 3.00
358 SEp,TP,V:Arkon 3.00
359 SEp,TP,V:Arkon 3.00
360 SEp,TP,V:Proctor,double-size,
    bronze foil(c) 4.50
361 SEp,I:Alternate Vision. 2.50
362 SEp,TP,V:Proctor 3.00
363 SEp,TP,V:Proctor,D:Alternate
    Vision,C:Deathcry,Silver Foil(c),
    30th Anniv., ... 4.00
364 SEp,TP,I:Deathcry,V:Kree 3.00
365 SEp,TP,V:Kree 3.00
366 SEp,TP,V:Kree,N:Dr.Pym,Gold
    Foil(c). 5.00
367 F:Vision. 3.00
368 SEp,TP,Bloodties#1,
    A:X-Men. 4.00
369 SEp,TP,E:BHs(s),Bloodties#5,
    D:Cortez,V:Exodus,Platinum
    Foil(c). 4.00
370 SEp(c),TP(c),GI,V:Deviants,
    A:Kro,I:Delta Force 3.00
371 GM,TP,V:Deviants,A:Kro. 3.00
372 B:BHs(s),SEp,TP,I:2nd
    Gatherers,A:Proctor. 3.00
373 SEp,TP,I:Alternate Jocasta,
    V:Sersi 3.00
374 SEp,TP,O&IR:Proctor is Alternate
    Black Knight 3.00
375 SEp,TP,Double Sized,D:Proctor,
    L:Sersi,Black Knight 3.50
376 F:Crystal,I:Terrigen 3.00
377 F:Quicksilver. 3.00
378 TP,I:Butcher 3.00
379 TP,Hercules,V:Hera. 3.00
379a Avengers Double Feature #1
    flip-book with Giant-Man #1 . . . 3.50
380 Hera 6.00
380a Avengers Double Feature #2
    flip-book with Giant Man #2. . . . 5.00
381 Quicksilvr, Scarlet Witch 4.00
381a Avengers Double Feature #3
    flip-book with Giant Man #3. . . . 3.00

MARVEL

382 Wundagore 2.50
382a Avengers Double Feature #4
    flip-book with Giant Man #4. . . 3.00
383 A:Fantastic Force,V:Arides 3.00
384 Hercules Vs. Stepmom 4.00
385 V:Red Skull 3.00
386 F:Black Widow 3.00
387 Taking A.I.M.,pt.2 . . . . 3.00
388 Taking A.I.M.,pt.4 . . . . 3.00
389 B:Mike Deodato 3.00
390 BHs,TP,The Crossing, prelude . 3.00
391 BHs,Cont. From Avg. Crossing. 3.00
392 BHs,TP,The Crossing 3.00
393 BHs,TP,The Crossing 3.00
394 BHs,TP,The Crossing 3.00
395 BHs,TP,Timeslide concludes . . 3.00
396 . . . . 3.00
397 TP,Incred.Hulk #440 x-over . . 3.00
398 TP,V:Unknown foe 3.00
399 . . . . 3.00
400 MeW,MWa,double size 4.50
401 MeW,MWa,Onslaught saga . . . 3.00
402 MWa,MD2,Onslaught, finale. . . 3.00
Ann.#1 DH,V:Mandarin,
    Masters of Evil 125.00
Ann.#2 DH,JB,V:Scar.Centurion . . 75.00
Ann.#3 rep.#4,T.ofSusp.#66-68 . . . 50.00
Ann.#4 rep.#5,#6 . . . . 30.00
Ann.#5 JK(c),rep.#8,#11 . . . . 25.00
Ann.#6 GP,HT,V:Laser,Nuklo,
    Whirlwind 20.00
Ann.#7 JSn,JRu,V:Thanos,A:Captain
    Marvel,D:Warlock(2nd) 40.00
Ann.#8 GP,V:Dr.Spectrum 15.00
Ann.#9 DN,V:Arsenal. 10.00
Ann.#10 MGo,A:X-Men,Spid.Woman,
    I:Rogue,V:Br.o/Evil Mutants. . . 40.00
Ann.#11 DP,V:Defenders 6.00
Ann.#12 JG,V:Inhumans,Maximus. . 5.00
Ann.#13 JBy,V:Armin Zola 5.00
Ann.#14 JBy,KB,V:Skrulls 5.00
Ann.#15 SD,KJ,V:Freedom Force . . 5.00
Ann.#16 RF,BH,TP,JR2,BSz,KP,AW,
    MR,BL,BWi,JG,KN,A:Silver
    Surfer,Rebirth Grandmaster . . . 5.00
Ann.#17 MBr,MG,Evol.Wars,J:2nd
    Yellow Jacket. 5.00
Ann.#18 MBa,MG,Atlan.Attack#8,
    J:Quasar 4.00
Ann.#19 HT,Terminus Factor 4.00
Ann.#20 Subterran.Odyssey#1 . . . . 4.00
Ann.#21 Citizen Kang#4 . . . . 4.00
Ann.#22 I:Bloodwraith,w/card 4.00
Ann.#23 JB 4.00
G-Size#1 JR(c),RB,DA,I:Nuklo . . . 35.00
G-Size#2 JR(c),DC,O:Kang,
    D:Swordsman,O:Rama-Tut . . . 20.00
G-Size#3 GK(c),DC,V:Kang,Legion
    of the Unliving 20.00
G-Size#4 K&R(c),DH,W:Scarlet Witch
    &Vision,O:Mantis,Moondragon 25.00
G-Size#5 rep,Annual #1. . . . . 15.00
GNv Death Trap:The Vault RLm,
    A:Venom 20.00
Marvel Milestone rep. #1 (1993) . . 2.95
Marvel Milestone rep. #4 (1995) . . . 2.95
Marvel Milestone rep. #16 (1993) . . 2.95
TPB Greatest Battles of the
    Avengers 15.95
TPB Korvac Saga, rep. 12.95
TPB Yesterday Quest, rep. 6.95

AVENGERS
Nov., 1996

1 RLd,JV,CYp,JSb,Heroes Reborn,
    F:Thor, Captain America,
    V:Loki. 6.00
1A Variant cover 8.00
1 gold signature edition, bagged . 20.00
2 RLd,JV,CYp,JSb,V:Kang 4.00

Avengers Vol. 2, #4
© *Marvel Entertainment Group*

3 RLd,JV,CYp,JSb,V:Kang,A:Nick
    Fury 4.00
4 RLd,JLb,CYp,JSb, ... 4.00
4A variant cover 4.00
5 RLd,CYp,JSb,V:Hulk,concl. 5.00
6 RLd,JLb,CYp,JSb,Industrial
    Revolution,pt.1 x-over 5.00
7 RLd,JLb,IaC,JSb, ... 3.50
8 RLd,JLb,IaC,JSb,F:Simon
    Williams (Wonder Man),V:Ultron,
    Lethal Legion. 3.50
9 JLb,RLd,IaC,F:Vision, Wonder
    Man 5.00
10 WS, ... 3.50
11 . . . . 3.50
12 WS,Galactus Saga, x-over 3.50
13 JeR, Wildstorm x-over 3.50
Minus 1 Spec., JLb,RLd,IaC,JSb,
    flashback 2.50

AVENGERS
Dec., 1997

1 GP,KBk,AV,F:Everyone,48 pg. . . . 5.00
1a Variant (c) 10.00
2 KBk,GP,AV,A:Scarlet Witch 5.00
3 KBk,GP,AV,trapped in midieval
    present. 4.00
4 KBk,GP,AV,who makes the
    team?. 5.00
5 KBk,GP,AV,Squadron Supreme. . 5.00
6 KBk,GP,AV,V:SquadronSupreme. 5.00
7 KBk,GP,AV,Live Kree or Die,pt.4 . 2.50
8 KBk,GP,AV,I:Triathlon 2.50
9 KBk,GP,AV,V:Moses Magnum . . 2.50
10 KBk,GP,AV,V:Grim Reaper 2.50
11 KBk,GP,AV,V:Grim Reaper 2.50
12 KBk,GP,AV,V:Thunderbolts,
    48-page 35.00
12a Variant, white background 3.00
13 KBk,GP,AV,R:New Warriors . . . 2.50
14 KBk,GP,AV,R:Beast. 2.50
15 KBk,GP,AV,A:Iron Man 2.50
16 JOy,AG,R:Photon 5.00
16a variant JOy,GP cover 2.50
17 JOy,AG,A:Warbird &
    Black Knight 2.50
18 JOy,AG,V:Wrecking Crew 2.50
19 KBk,GP,AV,Ultron,pt.1 . . . . 2.50
19a signed 30.00
20 KBk,GP,AV,Ultron,pt.2. . . . . . . 2.50
21 KBk,GP,AV,Ultron,pt.3. . . . . . . 2.50
22 KBk,GP,AV,Ultron,pt.4. . . . . . . 2.50
23 KBk,GP,AV,V:Wonder Man 2.50
24 KBk,GP,AV 2.50

25 KBk,GP,AV, 48-pg. 3.50
26 KBk,GP,AV,SI,V:Triune 2.50
27 KBk,GP,AV,100-pg. 3.50
28 KBk,GP,AV,Kulan Gath,pt.1 . . . . 2.50
29 KBk,GP,AV,Kulan Gath,pt.2 . . . 2.50
30 KBk,GP,AV,Kulan Gath,pt.3 . . . 2.50
31 KBk,GP,AV,F:Vision 2.50
32 KBk,GP,AV,F:Black Widow 2.50
33 KBk,GP,AV,Thunderbolts 2.50
34 KBk,GP,AV,Thunderbolts 3.50
35 KBk,JR2,AV,MaximumSecurity . . 2.50
36 KBk,SEp,AV,A:Capt.Am.+poster. 2.50
37 KBk,SEp,AV,F:Capt.Am. 2.50
38 KBk,AD,MFm 2.50
39 KBk,AD,MFm,F:Silverclaw 2.50
40 KBk,AD,MFm,F:Hulk,Silverclaw . 2.50
41 KBk,AD,MFm,A:Kang 2.50
42 KBk,AD,MFm,A:Kang 2.50
43 KBk,AD,MFm,V:Kang. 2.50
44 KBk,KK,V:Kang,Thor berserk . . 2.50
45 KBk,KK,V:Conqueror 2.50
46 KBk,Kang Dynasty 2.50
47 KBk,Kang Dynasty 2.50
48 KBk,KD,100-page. 4.00
49 KBk,KD,F:Kang,'Nuff Said 2.50
50 KBk,KD,V:Kang, 48-pg. 4.00
51 KBk,KD,F:Wonder Man,
    Scarlet Witch 2.25
52 KBk,KD,Kang War 2.25
53 KBk,KD,Avengers Avenge 2.25
54 KBk,KD,Kang War,concl. 2.25
55 KBk,KD,Kang War,aftermath . . . 2.25
56 KBk,F:Beast,She-Hulk,USAgent. 2.25
57 KD,World Trust, pt.1 . . . . 2.75
58 KD,World Trust, pt.2 . . . . 2.25
59 KD,World Trust, pt.3 . . . . 2.25
60 KD,World Trust, concl.,40-pg . . . 4.00
61 GFr, ... 2.25
62 GFr 2.25
63 AD,MFm,Standoff,pt.3,x-over . . . 3.00
64 F:Falcon 2.25
65 ALa,Red Zone,pt.1 . . . . 2.25
66 ALa,Red Zone,pt.2 . . . . 2.25
67 ALa,Red Zone,pt.3 . . . . 2.25
68 ALa,Red Zone,pt.4 . . . . 2.25
69 ALa,Red Zone,pt.5 . . . . 2.25
70 ALa,Red Zone,pt.6 . . . . 2.25
71 V:Wasp, Yellowjacket 3.00
72 ScK,Search for She-Hulk,pt.1. . 2.25
73 ScK,Search for She-Hulk,pt.2. . . 2.25
74 ScK,Search for She-Hulk,pt.3. . . 2.25
75 ScK,Search for She-Hulk,pt.4. . . 2.25
76 JaL(c),an Avenger falls 2.25
77 Lionheart of Avalon,pt.1 . . . . . . 0.50
78 Lionheart of Avalon,pt.2 . . . . . . 2.25
79 Lionheart of Avalon,pt.3 . . . . . . 2.25
80 Lionheart of Avalon,pt.4 . . . . . . 2.25
81 Lionheart of Avalon, concl. 2.25
82 Once an Invader,pt.1 . . . . 2.25
83 Once an Invader,pt.2 . . . . 2.25
84 Once an Invader,pt.3 . . . . 2.25
500 BMB,Disassembled,pt.1,48-pg. 5.00
500a Director's Cut,64-pg. 5.00
501 BMB,Disassembled,pt.2,48-pg. 3.50
502 BMB,Disassembled,pt.3,48-pg. 3.50
503 BMB,Disassembled,pt.4,48-pg. 3.50
Ann. '98 Avengers/Squadron Supreme
    KBk,CPa,GP, 48pg 2.50
Ann.1999 KBk,JFM, Why Avengers
    disbanded, 48-page. 3.50
Ann.2000 KBk,NBy,48-pg 3.50
Ann.2001 KBk,IaC,NRd 3.00
Rough Cut Edition KBk,GP, 48pg,
    original pencils of #1, b&w 3.00
Spec. 1-1/2, 32-pg.RSt. 2.50
Spec. Avengers: Year in Review . . 3.00
GN Ultron Imperative,BWS(c) 6.00
TPB Avengers: Under Siege 16.95
TPB Avengers Visionaries:
    George Perez, 176-page. 16.95
TPB The Morgan Conquest 14.95

MARVEL

TPB The Kree/Skrull War 24.95
TPB Ultron Unlimited,112-page . . . 14.95
TPB Supreme Justice,304-page . . 17.95
TPB Clear & Present Danger 19.95
TPB Celestial Madonna, 224-pg . . . 19.95
TPB Avengers/Defenders War 17.95
TPB The Korvac Saga (2002) 19.95
TPB The Kang Dynasty (2002) . . . 30.00
TPB Vol.1: World Trust (2003) 15.00
TPB Vol.2: Red Zone (2003) 15.00
TPB Vol. 3: Search for She-Hulk . . 13.00
TPB Vol. 4: Lionheart of Avalon . . . 12.00
TPB Vol. 5: Once an Invader 15.00
TPB Living Legends 20.00

AVENGERS: CELESTIAL QUEST
Sept., 2001
1 (of 8) SEt,SHa 2.50
2 SEt,SHa,F:Mantis 3.00
3 SEt,SHa,F:Quoi,Mantis 3.00
4 SEt,SHa,F:Quoi,Thanos 2.50
5 SEt,SHa,F:Thanos 2.50
6 SEt,SHa,F:Mantis & Vision 2.50
7 SEt,SHa,F:Mantis,Quoi,Vision . . . 2.50
8 SEt,SHa,finale,48-pg. 3.50

AVENGERS FOREVER
Oct., 1998
1 (of 12) GP,KBk,CPa,Rick Jones
 radiation poisoning 4.00
2 GP,KBk,CPa,new Avengers 3.00
3 GP,KBk,CPa,Kang/Immortus 3.00
4 KBk,different eras 3.00
4a, b & c variant covers . . . . @3.00
5 KBk,RSt,A:1950s Avengers 3.00
6 KBk,RSt,V:Immortus 3.00
7 KBk,RSt,reunited 3.00
8 KBk,Immortus' plan 3.00
9 KBk,RSt,Kang the Conqueror . . . 3.00
10 KBk,RSt,V:Immortus 3.00
11 KBk,RSt,V:Avengers Battalion . . 3.00
12 KBk,RSt,concl. 3.00
TPB Avengers Forever,288-page . . 24.95

AVENGERS ICONS: TIGRA
March, 2002
1 (of 4) MD2, ... 3.00
2 MD2,Brethren of the Blue Fist . . . 3.00
3 MD2,Brethren of the Blue Fist . . . 3.00
4 MD2,concl. 3.00

AVENGERS ICONS: THE VISION
Aug., 2002
1 (of 4) 3.00
2 thru 4 . . . . @3.00

AVENGERS INDEX
See: OFFICIAL MARVEL INDEX TO THE AVENGERS

AVENGERS INFINITY
July, 2000
1 (of 4) RSt,SCh,SHa 3.00
2 RSt,SCh,SHa,Servitors 3.00
3 RSt,SCh,SHa,Infinites 3.00
4 RSt,SCh,SHa,concl 3.00

AVENGERS LOG
1994
1 GP(c),History of the Avengers . . . 2.25

AVENGERS SPOTLIGHT
Aug., 1989
Formerly: Solo Avengers
21 AM,DH,TMo,JRu,Hawkeye,
 Starfox 3.00
22 AM,DH,Hawkeye,O:Swordsman . 2.50
23 AM,DH,KD,Hawkeye,Vision 2.50
24 AM,DH,Hawkeye,O:Espirita 2.50
25 AM,TMo,Hawkeye,Rick Jones . . 2.50
26 A of V,Hawkeye,Iron Man 2.50
27 A of V,AM,DH,DT,Hawkeye
 Avengers 2.50
28 A of V,AM,DH,DT,Hawkeye,
 Wonder Man,Wasp 2.50
29 A of V,DT,Hawkeye,Iron Man . . . 2.50
30 AM,DH,Hawkeye,New Costume . 2.50
31 AM,DH,KW,Hawkeye,US.Agent . 2.50
32 AM,KW,Hawkeye,U.S.Agent 2.50
33 AM,DH,KW,Hawkeye,US.Agent . 2.50
34 AM,DH,KW,SLi(c),Hawkeye
 U.S.Agent 2.50
35 JV,Gilgamesh 2.50
36 AM,DH,Hawkeye 2.50
37 BH,Dr.Druid 2.50
38 JBr,Tigra 2.50
39 GCo,Black Knight 2.50
40 Vision,Last Issue 2.50

AVENGERS STRIKEFILE
1994
1 BHa(s),Avengers Pin-ups 2.25

AVENGERS: THE CROSSING
1995
1 BHs,Death of an Avenger,
 chromium cover,48pg 6.00

AVENGERS: THE TERMINATRIX OBJECTIVE
1993
1 B:MGu(s),MG,Holografx(c),
 V:Terminatrix 2.75
2 MG,V:Terminatrix,A:Kangs 2.25
3 MG,V:Terminatrix,A:Kangs 2.25
4 MG,Last issue 2.25

AVENGERS/ THUNDERBOLTS
March, 2004
1 (of 6) FaN&KBk(s),BKi 3.00
2 FaN&KBk(s),BKi 3.00
3 thru 6 FaN&KBk(s),TG . . . . @3.00
TPB Vol. 1: Nefaria Protocols . . . 20.00
TPB Vol. 2: Best Intentions 15.00

AVENGERS: TIMESLIDE
1996
1 BHs,TKa,End of the Crossing
 Megallic chrome cover 5.00

AVENGERS TWO: WONDER MAN & THE BEAST
Mar., 2000
1 (of 3) RSt,MBa, ... 3.00
2 RSt,MBa, ... 3.00
3 RSt,MBa,concl. 3.00

AVENGERS/ULTRAFORCE
1995
1 V:Malibu's Ultraforce 4.00

AVENGERS: UNITED THEY STAND
Sept., 1999
1 TTn,RCa, Cartoon tie-in 3.00
2 TTn, ... 2.25
3 TTn, ... 2.25
4 TTn, ... 2.25
5 TTn,Hawkeye&Black Widow 2.25
6 TTn,A:Capt.America 2.25
7 TTn,F:Devil Dinosaur,Moonboy . . 3.25

AVENGERS UNIVERSE
June, 2000
1 rep. 3 stories, 80-pg. 5.00
2 rep. 3 stories, 80-pg. 5.00
3 rep. 3 stories, 80-pg. 5.00
4 rep. 3 stories, 80-pg. 4.25
5 rep. 3 stories, 80-pg. 4.25

AVENGERS UNLEASHED
1995
1 V:Count Nefarious 2.25
Becomes:

AVENGERS UNPLUGGED
1996
2 Crushed by Graviton 2.25
3 x-over with FF Unplugged 2.25
4 The Old Ball and Chain 2.25
5 A:Captain Marvel 2.25
6 final issue 2.25

AVENGERS WEST COAST
Sept., 1989
Prev: West Coast Avengers
47 JBy,V:J.Random 3.00
48 JBy,V:J.Random 3.00
49 JBy,V:J.Random,W.Man 3.00
50 JBy,R:G.A.Human Torch 4.00
51 JBy,R:Iron Man 2.50
52 JBy,V:MasterPandmonum. 2.50
53 JBy,Acts ofVeng.,V:U-Foes 2.50
54 JBy,Acts ofVeng.,V:MoleMan . . . 2.50
55 JBy,Acts ofVeng.finale,V:Loki
 Magneto kidnaps Sc.Witch 2.50
56 JBy,V:Magneto 2.50
57 JBy,V:Magneto 2.50
58 V:Vibro, ... 2.50
59 TMo,V:Hydro-Man,A:Immortus . . 2.50
60 PR,V:Immortus, ... 2.50
61 PR,V:Immortus 2.50

Avengers West Coast #96
© Marvel Entertainment Group

MARVEL

62 V:Immortus 2.50
63 PR,I:Living Lightning. 2.50
64 F:G.A.Human Torch 2.50
65 PR,V:Ultron,Grim Reaper 2.50
66 PR,V:Ultron,Grim Reaper 2.50
67 PR,V:Ultron,Grim Reaper 2.50
68 PR,V:Ultron. 2.50
69 PR,USAgent vs Hawkeye,
   I:Pacific Overlords 2.50
70 DR,V:Pacific Overlords 3.00
71 DR,V:Pacific Overlords 3.00
72 DR,V:Pacific Overlords 3.00
73 DR,V:Pacific Overlords 3.00
74 DR,J:Living Lightning,Spider
   Woman,V:Pacific Overlords. . . . 3.00
75 HT,A:F.F,V:Arkon,double 3.00
76 DR,Night Shift,I:Man-Demon . . . 2.50
77 DR,A:Satannish & Nightshift. . . . 2.50
78 DR,V:Satannish & Nightshift. . . . 2.50
79 DR,A:Dr.Strange,V:Satannish . . 2.50
80 DR,Galactic Storm,pt.2 . . . . 2.50
81 DR,Galactic Storm,pt.9 . . . . 2.50
82 DR,Galactic Storm,pt.16
   A:Lilandra 2.50
83 V:Hyena 2.50
84 DR,I:Deathweb,A:SpM,
   O:Spider-Woman. 3.00
85 DR,A:SpM,V:Death Web. 2.50
86 DR,A:SpM,V:Death Web. 2.50
87 DR,A:Wolverine,V:Bogatyri 3.00
88 DR,A:Wolverine,V:Bogatyri 2.50
89 DR,V:Ultron. 2.50
90 DR,A:Vision,V:Ultron. 2.50
91 DR,V:Ultron,I:War Toy. 2.50
92 DR,V:Goliath(Power Man) 2.50
93 DR,V:Doctor Demonicus. 2.50
94 DR,J:War Machine 2.50
95 DR,A:Darkhawk,V:Doctor
   Demonicus. 2.50
96 DR,Inf.Crusade x-over 2.50
97 ACe,Inf.Crusade,V:Power
   Platoon 2.50
98 DR,I:4th Lethal Legion 2.50
99 DR,V:4th Lethal Legion. 2.50
100 DR,D:Mockingbird,V:4th Lethal
   Legion,Red Foil(c) 4.50
101 DR,Bloodties#3,V:Exodus. 4.00
102 DR,L:Iron Man,Spider-Woman,
   US Agent,Scarlet Witch,War
   Machine,last issue. 4.00
Ann.#4 JBy,TA,MBa,Atlan.Attacks
   #12,V:Seven Brides of Set 4.00
Ann.#5 Terminus Factor. 3.50
Ann.#6 Subterranean Odyssey#5 . . 2.50
Ann.#7 Assault on Armor City#4 . . 2.25
Ann.#8 DR,I:Raptor w/card 3.25

BACKPACK MARVELS:

Avengers (2001) 7.25
Spider-Man Vol. 1 (2001). 7.25
X-Men Vol.1 (2000) 7.25
X-Men Vol.2 (2000) 7.25

BALDER THE BRAVE
Nov., 1985

1 WS,SB,V:Frost Giants 3.00
2 WS,SB,V:Frost Giants 3.00
3 WS,SB,V:Frost Giants 3.00
4 WS,SB,V:Frost Giants;Feb,1986 . 3.00

BANNER
Startling Stories, July, 2001

1 (of 4) RCo, F:Hulk 3.00
2 RCo,. 3.00
3 RCo,. 3.00
4 RCo, concl. 3.00
TPB RCo(c) 96-page 12.95

BARBIE
Jan., 1991

1 polybagged with Credit Card . . . 15.00
2 . . . . 10.00
3 thru 49 . . . . @8.00
50 Anniv. issue, Disney World(c) . . 12.00
51 thru 66 . . . . @7.00

Barbie Fashion #49
© Marvel Entertainment Group

BARBIE FASHION
Jan., 1991

1 bagged with doorknob hanger. . 12.00
2 thru 63 . . . . @7.00

BATTLE
Atlas, March, 1951

1 They called Him a Coward . . . 350.00
2 The War Department Secrets . 175.00
3 The Beast of the Bataan 125.00
4 JMn,I:Buck Private O'Toole . . . 125.00
5 Death Trap Of Gen. Wu. 125.00
6 RH, JMn. 125.00
7 Enemy Sniper 125.00
8 A Time to Die 125.00
9 RH 100.00
10 . . . . 100.00
11 SC 100.00
12 thru 20 . . . . @110.00
21 . . . . 110.00
22 . . . . 75.00
23 BK 75.00
24 . . . . 75.00
25 . . . . 75.00
26 JR 75.00
27 . . . . 75.00
28 JSe 75.00
29 . . . . 75.00
30 . . . . 75.00
31 RH,JMn. 75.00
32 JSe,GT 75.00
33 GC,JSe,JSt 75.00
34 JSe 75.00
35 . . . . 75.00
36 BEv 75.00
37 RA,JSt. 90.00
38 thru 46. . . . . @75.00
47 JO 75.00
48 . . . . 75.00
49 JDa 85.00
50 BEv 75.00
51 . . . . 75.00
52 GWb 75.00

53 BP 75.00
54 . . . . 75.00
55 GC,AS,BP,AW,GWb 90.00
56 . . . . 65.00
57 . . . . 65.00
58 . . . . 65.00
59 AT 65.00
60 A:Combat Kelly 65.00
61 JMn,A:Combat Kelly 65.00
62 A:Combat Kelly 65.00
63 SD 125.00
64 JK 125.00
65 JK 125.00
66 JSe,JK,JDa 125.00
67 JSe,JK,AS,JDa 125.00
68 JSe,JK,AW,SD 125.00
69 RH,JSe,JK,SW 135.00
70 BEv,SD; June, 1960 . . . . 135.00

BATTLE ACTION
Atlas, Feb., 1952

1 . . . . 300.00
2 . . . . 150.00
3 JSt,RH 75.00
4 . . . . 75.00
5 . . . . 75.00
6 JeR 75.00
7 JeR 75.00
8 RH 90.00
9 thru 15 . . . . @75.00
16 thru 27. . . . . @70.00
28 GWb 70.00
29 . . . . 70.00
30 GWb,Aug., 1957 . . . . 70.00

BATTLEBOOKS
Nov., 1998

Captain America, BiT(c) 4.00
Citizen V, BiT(c) 4.00
Colossus, BiT(c). 4.00
Elektra, BiT(c) 4.00
Gambit, BiT(c) 4.00
Iron Man, BiT(c) 4.00
Rogue, BiT(c). 4.00
Spider-Girl, BiT(c) 4.00
Spider-Man, BiT(c). 4.00
Storm, BiT(c) 4.00
Thor, BiT(c) 4.00
Wolverine, BiT(c) 4.00

BATTLE BRADY
See: MEN IN ACTION

BATTLEFIELD
Atlas, April, 1952

1 RH, Slaughter on Suicide
   Ridge 250.00
2 RH 125.00
3 Ambush Patrol 125.00
4 . . . . 125.00
5 Into the Jaws of Death 125.00
6 thru 10 . . . . @90.00
11 GC,May, 1953. . . . . 90.00

BATTLEFRONT
Atlas, June, 1952

1 JeR,RH(c),Operation Killer . . . 325.00
2 JeR 200.00
3 JeR,Spearhead 125.00
4 JeR,Death Trap of General
   Chun 125.00
5 JeR,Terror of the Tank Men . . . 125.00
6 A:Combat Kelly 125.00
7 A:Combat Kelly 125.00
8 A:Combat Kelly 125.00
9 A:Combat Kelly 125.00
10 A:Combat Kelly 125.00

11 thru 20 . . . . @100.00
21 thru 39 . . . . @75.00
40 AW 100.00
41 . . . . 75.00
42 AW 90.00
43 thru 48 Aug.,1957 . . . . @95.00

BATTLEGROUND
Atlas, Sept., 1954
1 . . . . 250.00
2 JKz. 125.00
3 thru 8 . . . . @100.00
9 BK 100.00
10 . . . . 100.00
11 AW,GC,GT. 125.00
12 MD,JSe. 75.00
13 AW 75.00
14 JD 125.00
15 thru 17. . . . . @75.00
18 AS 125.00
19 JMn,JSe 75.00
20 Aug., 1957. . . . . 75.00

Battlestar Galactica #3
© Marvel Entertainment Group

BATTLESTAR GALACTICA
March, 1979
1 EC,B:TV Adaptation;
  Annihalation 10.00
2 EC,Exodus 8.00
3 EC,Deathtrap 8.00
4 WS,Dogfight 8.00
5 WS,E:TV Adaptation;Ambush . . . 8.00
6 Nightmare 7.00
7 Commander Adama Trapped . . . 7.00
8 Last Stand 7.00
9 Space Mimic 7.00
10 This Planet Hungers. 7.00
11 WS,Starbuck's Dilemma 7.00
12 WS,Memory Ends. 7.00
13 WS,All Out Attack 7.00
14 Radiation Threat 7.00
15 Ship of Crawling Death. 7.00
16 . . . . 7.00
17 Animal on the Loose 7.00
18 Battle For the Forbidden Fruit. . . 7.00
19 Starbuck's Back 7.00
20 Duel to the Death 7.00
21 To Slay a Monster..To Deatroy
  a World 7.00
22 WS,A Love Story?. 7.00
23 Dec., 1981 . . . . 7.00

BATTLETIDE
1990
1 thru 4 F: Death's Head II and
  Killpower . . . . @2.25

BATTLETIDE II
1993
1 Foil embossed cover 3.25
2 thru 8 F: Death's Head II and
  Killpower . . . . @2.25

BEAST
March, 1997
1 (of 3) KG,CNn,F:Karma, Cannonball, V:Viper & Spiral 3.00
2 KG,CNn,V:Spiral. 3.00
3 KG,CNn, concl. 3.00

BEAUTY AND THE BEAST
Jan., 1985
1 DP,Beast & Dazzler,direct 3.00
1a DP,Beast & Dazzler,UPC. 3.00
2 DP,Beast & Dazzler 3.00
3 DP,Beast & Dazzler 3.00
4 DP,Beast & Dazzler 3.00

BEAVIS & BUTT-HEAD
March, 1994
1 Based on the MTV Show. 5.00
1a 2nd Printing 2.50
2 Dead from the Neck up 3.50
3 Break out at Burger World 3.00
4 Tattoo Parlor 2.50
5 Field Day 2.50
6 Revulsion 2.50
7 Oldies bot. 2.50
8 Be a clown 2.50
9 Makin' movies 2.50
10 Halloween. 2.50
11 . . . . 2.50
12 . . . . 2.50
13 . . . . 2.50
14 Join Biker Gang 2.50
15 Spring Break 2.50
16 Capture The Flag 2.50
17 with video camera. 2.50
18 Woodsuck 2.50
19 thru 28 . . . . @2.50
TPB Greatest Hits, rep.#1–#4 . . . . 12.95
TPB Holidazed and Confused 12.95

Beavis & Butt-Head #12
© Marvel Entertainment Group

BEFORE THE FANTASTIC 4: GRIMM AND LOGAN
May, 2000
1 (of 3) LHa,Wolverine&Thing 3.25
2 LHa,A:Carol Danvers. 3.25
3 LHa,concl. 3.25

BEFORE THE FANTASTIC 4: REED RICHARDS
July, 2000
1 (of 3) PDa,DFg,V:Dr.Doom 3.25
2 PDa,DFg. 3.25
3 PDa,DFg,concl. 3.25

BEFORE THE FANTASTIC 4: THE STORMS
Oct., 2000
1 (of 3) TKa,CAd,F:Sue &
  Johnny Storm 3.25
2 V:St. Germaine 3.25
3 TKa,CaD,concl. 3.25

BEST OF MARVEL '96
TPB 224pg. 20.00

BEST WESTERN
June, 1949
58 A:KidColt,BlackRider,Two-Gun
  Kid; Million Dollar Train
  Robbery 250.00
59 A:BlackRider,KidColt,Two-Gun
  Kid;The Black Rider Strikes. . 225.00
Becomes:

WESTERN OUTLAWS & SHERIFFS
1949
60 PH(c),Hawk Gaither 250.00
61 Ph(c),Pepper Lawson 200.00
62 Murder at Roaring
  House Bridge. 200.00
63 thru 65 . . . . @200.00
66 Hanging. 200.00
67 Cannibalism 200.00
68 thru 72 . . . . @175.00
73 June, 1952 . . . . 175.00

BEWARE
March, 1973
1 Reprints 25.00
2 thru 8 . . . . @20.00
Becomes:

TOMB OF DARKNESS
1974
9 Reprints 30.00
10 thru 22 . . . . @20.00
23 November, 1976 . . . . 25.00

BIKER MICE FROM MARS
1993
1 I:Biker Mice 2.25
2 thru 3 . . . . 2.25

BILL & TED'S BOGUS JOURNEY
Nov., 1991
1 Movie Adaption 3.25

BILL & TED'S EXCELLENT COMICS
Dec., 1991
1 From Movie; Wedding Reception 2.25

MARVEL

MARVEL

2 Death Takes a Vacation 2.25
3 `Daze in the Lives' 2.25
4 Station Plague 2.25
5 Bill & Ted on Trial 2.25
6 Time Trial 2.25
7 Time Trial, Concl 2.25
8 History Final 2.25
9 I:Morty(new Death) 2.25
10 'Hyperworld' 2.25
11 Lincoln assassination 2.25
12 Last issue 2.25

BILLY BUCKSKIN WESTERN
Atlas, Nov., 1955
1 MD,Tales of the Wild Frontier . 175.00
2 MD,Ambush 100.00
3 MD,AW, Thieves in the Night . 125.00
Becomes:

2-GUN KID
1956
4 SD,A: Apache Kid 125.00
Becomes:

TWO-GUN WESTERN
1956
5 B:Apache Kid,Doc Holiday,
  Kid Colt Outlaw 200.00
6 . . . . 125.00
7 . . . . 125.00
8 RC 150.00
9 AW 150.00
10 . . . . 150.00
11 AW 165.00
12 Sept., 1957,RC 150.00

BISHOP
1994
1 Mountjoy, foil cover 4.00
2 foil stamped cover 4.00
3 JOs 3.50
4 V:Mountjoy 3.50

BISHOP: THE LAST X-MAN
Aug., 1999
1 R:Bishop, 48-page debut 4.00
2A I:Nom,Link,Jinx & Scorch 2.50
2B variant (c) 2.50
3 V:Chronomancer 2.50
4 . . . . 2.50
5 V:The Kith 2.50
6 V:Chronomancer 2.50
7 ATi,A:Hellfire Club 2.50
8 ATi,V:GOL-19 . . . . 2.50
9 ATi,A:Trevor Fitzroy 2.50
10 ATi,Morlocks 2.50
11 ATi,A:Trevor Fitzroy 2.50
12 ATi,Chronowar,pt.1 . . . . 2.50
13 ATi,Chronowar,pt.2 . . . . 2.50
14 ATi,Chronowar,pt.3 . . . . 2.50
15 ATi,Maximum Security 2.50
16 NMa,Dream'sEnd,pt.3,x-over . . 2.50

BISHOP: XAVIER'S SECURITY ENFORCER
Nov., 1997
1 (of 3) JOs,SEp 3.00
2 JOs,SEp,hunted by X.S.E. 3.00
3 JOs,SEp,Bishop v. Rook, concl. . 3.00

BIZARRE ADVENTURES
See: MARVEL PREVIEW

BLACK AXE
1993
1 JR2(c),A:Death's Head II 3.00
2 JR2(2),A:Sunfire,V:The Hand . . . 3.00
3 A:Death's Head II,V:Mesphisto . . 3.00
4 in ancient Egypt 3.00
5 KJ(c),In Wakanda 3.00
6 KJ(c),A:Black Panther 3.00
7 KJ(c),A:Black Panther 3.00
8 thru 13 . . . . @3.00

BLACK CAT
[Limited Series]
1 Wld,A:Spider-Man,V:Cardiac,
  I:Faze 2.25
2 Wld,V:Faze 2.25
3 Wld,Cardiac 2.25
4 Wld,V:Scar 2.25

BLACK DRAGON
Epic, May, 1985
1 JBo 4.00
2 thru 6 JBo . . . . @3.00

Black Goliath #1
© Marvel Entertainment Group

BLACK GOLIATH
Feb., 1976—Nov., 1976
1 GT,O:Black Goliath,Cont's
  From Powerman #24 . . . . 30.00
2 GT,V:Warhawk 15.00
3 GT,D:Atom-Smasher 15.00
4 KP,V:Stilt-Man 15.00
5 D:Mortag 15.00

BLACK KNIGHT, THE
Atlas, May, 1955—April, 1956
1 JMn,O: Crusader;The Black
  Knight Rides 1,200.00
2 JMn,Siege on Camelot 750.00
3 JMn,Black Knight Unmasked . 600.00
4 JMn,Betrayed 600.00
5 JMn,SSh,The Invincible Tartar. 600.00

BLACK KNIGHT
June, 1990—Sept., 1990
1 TD,R:Original Black Knight 2.00
2 TD,A:Dreadknight 2.00
3 RB,A:Dr.Strange 2.00
4 RB,TD,A:Dr Strange, Valkyrie . . . 2.00

BLACK KNIGHT: EXODUS
1996
1-shot R:Black Knight,A:Sersi,
  O:Exodus 2.50

BLACK PANTHER
[1st Series]
Jan., 1977—May, 1979
1 JK,V:Collectors 30.00
2 JK,V:Six Million Year Man 20.00
3 JK,V:Ogar 20.00
4 JK,V:Collectors 20.00
5 JK,V:Yeti 20.00
6 JK,V:Ronin 20.00
7 JK,V:Mister Little 20.00
8 JK,D:Black Panther 20.00
9 JK,V:Jakarra 20.00
10 JK,V:Jakarra 20.00
11 JK,V:Kilber the Cruel 20.00
12 JK,V:Kilber the Cruel 20.00
13 JK,V:Kilber the Cruel 20.00
14 JK,A:Avengers,V:Klaw 25.00
15 JK,A:Avengers,V:Klaw 25.00

BLACK PANTHER
July, 1988—Oct., 1988
[1st Mini-Series]
1 I:Panther Spirit 2.50
2 V:Supremacists 2.50
3 A:Malaika 2.50
4 V:Panther Spirit 2.50

[2nd Mini-Series]
PANTHER'S PREY
May, 1991
1 DT,A:W'Kabi,V:Solomon Prey . . . 5.00
2 thru 4 DT,V:Solomon Prey . . . . @5.00

BLACK PANTHER
Sept., 1998
1 CPr,MT,A:T'Challa 5.00
2 CPr,MT,A:Mephisto 3.00
2a variant cover 3.00
3 CPr,MT,JQ,I:Achebe 3.00
4 CPr,MT,JQ,V:Mephisto 3.00
5 CPr,V:Mephisto 3.00
6 CPr,JJu,V:Kraven the Hunter 2.50
7 CPr,JJu,V:Kraven, round 2 . . . . . 2.50
8 CPr,JJu,A:Avengers 2.50
9 CPr,MM,A:Avengers 2.50
10 CPr,MM,political counter-attack . 2.50
11 CPr,MBr,Enemy o/t State,pt.3 . . 2.50
12 CPr,MBr,Enemy o/t State,pt.4 . . 2.50
13 CPr,A:T'Challa 2.50
14 CPr, ... 2.50
15 CPr,A:Hulk 2.50
16 CPr,V:Killmonger. 2.50
17 CPr,V:Killmonger. 2.50
18 CPr,V:Killmonger,A:Nakia 2.50
19 CPr,F:Queen Divine 2.50
20 CPr,F:Moon Knight 2.50
21 CPr,F:Moon Knight 2.50
22 CPr,A:T'Challa 2.50
23 CPr,Cat Trap,pt.2,x-over 2.50
24 CPr,MBr,Malice 2.50
25 CPr,Maximum Security 2.50
26 CPr,A:Storm 2.50
27 CPr,A:Storm,Avengers 2.50
28 CPr,A:Lord Ghaur,Dr.Doom 2.50
29 CPr,V:Klaw 2.50
30 CPr,NBy,A:Capt.America 2.50
31 CPr,SaV,A:Dakota North 2.50
32 CPr,SaV,V:Malice 2.50
33 CPr,SaV,V:Malice 2.50
34 CPr,JCf,A:Man-Ape 2.50
35 CPr,JCf,Gorilla Warfare 2.50
36 CPr,SaV,100-page 3.50
37 CPr,SaV,Once & Future King . . . 2.50

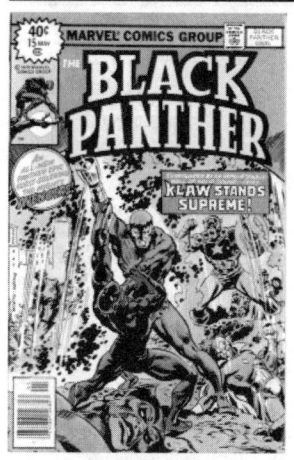

Black Panther #15
© Marvel Entertainment Group

38 CPr,SaV,Return of the Dragon . . 2.50
39 CPr,SaV,V:Iron Fist,'Nuff Said . . 2.50
40 CPr,SaV,Return of the Dragon . . 2.50
41 CPr,SaV,Enemy of the State II . . 2.50
42 CPr,SaV,Enemy of the State II . . 2.50
43 CPr,SaV,Enemy of the State II . . 2.50
44 CPr,SaV,Enemy of the State II . . 2.50
45 CPr,SaV,Enemy of the State II . . 2.50
46 CPr,in Texas, in the past. 2.50
47 CPr,trapped in the old west 2.50
48 CPr,Death of the Black Panther . 2.50
49 CPr,Death of the Black Panther . 2.50
50 CPr,NKu(c),T'Challa gone 2.50
51 CPr,DaF,Black & White,pt.1 . . . . 2.50
52 CPr,Black & White,pt.2 . . . . 2.50
53 CPr,Black & White,pt.3 . . . . 2.50
54 NKu,Black & White,pt.4 . . . . . . 2.50
55 NKu,Black & White,pt.5 . . . . . . 2.50
56 NKu,Black & White,pt.6 . . . . . . 2.50
57 F:T'Challa,pt.1. . . . . 3.00
58 F:T'Challa,pt.2. . . . . 3.00
59 NRd,Ascension,pt.1 . . . . 3.00
60 NRd,Ascension,pt.2 . . . . 3.00
61 NRd,Ascension,pt.3 . . . . 3.00
62 NRd,Ascension,pt.4 . . . . 3.00
63 NRd,Ascension,pt.5 . . . . 3.00
TPB The Client, 128-page 14.95
TPB Enemy of the State, 224-pg. . 16.95

BLACK RIDER
See: ALL WINNERS
COMICS

BLACK RIDER
RIDES AGAIN
Atlas, Sept., 1957
1 JK,Treachery at Hangman's
Ridge 275.00

BLACKSTONE, THE
MAGICIAN
May, 1948—Sept., 1948
2 B:Blonde Phantom. 800.00
3 . . . . 500.00
4 Bondage(c) 550.00

BLACK WIDOW
Apr. 1999
1 (of 3) Black Widow replaced? . . . 6.00

1a variant cover (1:4) 7.00
2 A:Daredevil 4.00
3 conclusion 4.00
TPB Web of Intrigue, rep. 4.00

BLACK WIDOW
Nov., 2000
1 (of 3) SHp,Natasha vs.Yelena . . . 3.00
2 SHp,. 3.00
3 SHp,concl. 3.00
TPB rep. 2 series, 144-page 16.00

BLACK WIDOW
Sept., 2004
1 (of 6) BSz,F:Natasha Romanova. 3.00
2 BSz 3.00

BLACK WIDOW:
PALE LITTLE SPIDER
Marvel Max, April, 2002
1 (of 3) F:Belova 3.25
2 . . . . 3.25
3 concl. 3.25

BLACKWULF
1994–95
1 AMe,Embossied(c),I:Mammoth,
Touchstone,Toxin,D:Pelops,
V:Tantalus, ... 3.00
2 AMe,I:Sparrow,Wildwind 2.25
3 AMe,I:Scratch 2.25
4 AMe,I:Giant-man 2.25
5 AMe 2.25
6 AMe,Tantalus 2.25
7 AMe,V:Tantalus 2.25
8 AMe 2.25
9 Seven Worlds of Tantalus,pt.1
A:Daredevil 2.25
10 Seven Worlds of Tantalus,pt.2,
last issue 2.25

BLADE,
THE VAMPIRE HUNTER
1994–95
1 Foil(c),Clv(i),R:Dracula 3.50
2 Clv(i),V:Dracula 2.50
3 Clv(i) 2.50
4 Clv(i) 2.50
5 Clv(i) 2.50
6 Clv(i) 2.50
7 Clv(i) 2.50
8 Bible John, Morbius 2.50
9 . . . . 2.50
10 R:Dracula 2.50
11 Dracula Untombed,pt.2 . . . . 2.50

BLADE
Sept., 1998
1 (of 6) DMG,40-page, photo(c) . . . 3.50
1a variant cover (1:4) 3.50
2 DMG,A:Morbius,Dominique 3.00
2a variant cover 3.00
3 DMG, ... 3.00
4 DMG,F:Morbius 3.00
1-shot Blade: Crescent City Blues,
MPe,V:Deacon Frost (1998) . . 3.50
1-shot DMG, movie tie-in (1998) . . 3.00
1-shot movie adaptation,48 pg . . . 6.00
TPB Duel with Dracula (2002) 17.95

BLADE:
VAMPIRE HUNTER
Oct., 1999
1 (of 6) BS, 48-pg. 4.00
2 BS 3.00

3 BS,V:Reaper 3.00
4 BS,V:Hrolf 3.00
5 BS,V:Reaper 3.00
6 BS,V:Reaper, concl. 3.00

BLADE
Marvel Max, March, 2002
1 StP,V:Tryks. 3.25
2 StP,F:Tryks,Seven 3.25
3 StP,date with Susan. 3.25
4 StP,Fofo's missing fingers 3.25
5 StP,V:Rowks. 3.25
6 horror hits home 3.25
GN Bloodhunt, movie adapt. 5.95

Blade Runner #2
© Marvel Entertainment Group

BLADE RUNNER
Oct., 1982
1 AW, Movie Adaption. 4.00
2 AW,. 4.00

BLAZE
[Limited Series], 1993–94
1 HMe(s),RoW,A:Clara Menninger . 2.50
2 HMe(s),RoW,I:Initiate. 2.50
3 HMe(s),RoW, ... 2.50
4 HMe(s),RoW,D:Initiate 2.50
[Regular Series], Aug., 1994
1 HMz,LHa,foil (c) 3.50
2 HMz,LHa,I:Man-Thing 2.50
3 HMz,LHa,V:Ice Box Bob 2.50
4 HMz,LHa,Apache Autumn,pt.1 . . 2.50
5 HMz,LHa,Apache Autumn,pt.2 . . 2.50
6 Apache Autumn,pt.3. . . . . 2.50
7 Carnivale Quintano 2.50
8 A:Arcae 2.50
9 Clara's Eyeballs 2.50
10 Undead M.C. 2.50
11 A:Punisher. 2.50
12 reunited with children 2.50

BLAZE CARSON
Sept., 1948
1 SSh(c),Fight,Lawman
or Crawl 300.00
2 Guns Roar on Boot Hill 225.00
3 A:Tex Morgan 225.00
4 A:Two-Gun Kid 225.00
5 A:Tex Taylor 250.00

MARVEL

Becomes:

REX HART
1949
6 CCB,Ph(c),B:Rex Hart,
A:Black Rider 300.00
7 Ph(c),Mystery at Bar-2 Ranch 200.00
8 Ph(c),The Hombre Who
Killed His Friends 200.00
Becomes:

WHIP WILSON
1950
9 Ph(c),B:Whip Wilson,O:Bullet;
Duel to the Death 800.00
10 Ph(c),Wanted for Murder . . 400.00
11 Ph(c) 400.00
Becomes:

GUNHAWK, THE
1950
12 The Redskin's Revenge 250.00
13 GT,The Man Who Murdered
Gunhawk 175.00
14 . . . . 150.00
15 . . . . 150.00
16 EC 150.00
17 . . . . 150.00
18 JMn,Dec., 1951 . . . . 150.00

BLAZE OF GLORY
Dec., 1999
1 (of 4) JOs,F:John Woo 3.00
2 JOs, ... 3.00
3 JOs, ... 3.00
4 JOs,concl. 3.00
TPB westerns, 96-pg. (2002) 11.50

BLAZE,
THE WONDER COLLIE
Oct., 1949
2 Ph(c),Blaze-Son of Fury 300.00
3 Ph(c), Lonely Boy;Feb.,1950. . 300.00

BLINK
Dec., 2000
1 (of 4) SLo,AKu(c) 3.25
2 SLo,Age of Apocalypse story 3.25
3 SLo,AKu(c),in love 3.25
4 SLo,AKu(c),V:Blastaar 3.25

BLONDE PHANTOM
See: ALL-SELECT
COMICS

BLOOD
Feb., 1988 — April, 1988
1 . . . . 6.00
2 thru 4 . . . . @5.00

BLOOD & GLORY
1993
1 KJ Cap & the Punisher 6.00
2 KJ Cap & the Punisher 6.00
3 KJ Cap & the Punisher 6.00

BLOODLINES
Epic, 1992
1 F:Kathy Grant-Peace Corps 6.00

BLOODSEED
1993
1 LSh,I:Bloodseed 2.25
2 LSh,V:Female Bloodseed 2.25

BLOODSTONE
Oct., 2001
1 DAn,ALa,SHa,F:Elsa Bloodstone 3.25
2 DAn,ALa,SHa,F:Dracula 3.25
3 DAn,ALa,SHa,Living Mummy . . . 3.25
4 DAn,ALa,SHa, concl. 3.25

BOOK OF THE DEAD
1993–94
1 thru 4 Horror rep . . . . @4.00
5 . . . . @4.00

BORN
June, 2003
1 (of 4) GEn(s),O:Punisher 6.00
2 GEn(s),Capt. Frank Castle 4.00
3 GEn(s),attacked 4.00
4 GEn(s),concl. 4.00

BOZZ CHRONICLES, THE
Epic, Dec., 1985
1 thru 5 . . . . @3.00
6 May, 1986 . . . . 3.00

BRATS BIZARRE
Epic, *Heavy Hitters* 1994
1 with trading card 3.25
2 thru 4 with trading card . . . . . . @2.75

BREAK THE CHAIN
1 KB,KRS-One,w/audio tape 7.00

BROTHERHOOD, THE
May, 2001
1 BSz(c),F:Magneto 2.75
2A BSz(c), ... 2.50
2B variant cover 2.50
3 BSz(c) 2.50
4 JP,BWS(c) 2.50
5 JP,GF(c) 2.50
6 JP,GF(c) message to daddy 2.50
7 SeP,KW, X speaks out 2.50
8 SeP,KW, ... 2.50
9 SeP,KW, final issue 2.50

BRUTE FORCE
Aug., 1990
1 JD/JSt 2.50

Brute Force #1
© Marvel Entertainment Group

2 . . . . 2.50
3 . . . . 2.50
4 November, 1990 . . . . 2.50

B-SIDES
Sept., 2002
1 SK, super-team from New Jersey 3.00
2 SK, F:Fantastic Four 3.00
3 SK, F:Fantastic Four 3.00

BUCK DUCK
Atlas, June, 1953
1 (fa)stories 150.00
2 and 3 . . . . @75.00
4 Dec., 1953 . . . . 75.00

BUCKAROO BANZAI
Dec., 1984
1 Movie Adaption 3.00
2 Conclusion, Feb., 1985 . . . . 2.50

BUG
1997
1-shot 48pg. 3.25

BULLSEYE:
GREATEST HITS
Sept., 2004
1 (of 5) SDi,O:Bullseye 3.00
2 SDi,F:Punisher 3.00

BULLWINKLE & ROCKY
Star, Nov., 1987
1 EC&AM,Based on 1960's TV
Series 4.00
2 thru 9 EC&AM . . . . @3.00
TPB, Bullwinkle & Rocky Collection
AM,early stories 4.95

CABLE
[Limited Series], 1992
1 JR2,DGr,V:Mutant Liberation
Front,A:Weapon X 4.00
2 JR2,DGr,V:Stryfe,O:Weapon X . . 3.00
[Regular Series], 1993
1 B:FaN(s),ATi,O:Cable,V:New
Canaanites,A:Stryfe,foil(c) 5.00
2 ATi,V:Stryfe 4.00
3 ATi,A:Six Pack 4.00
4 ATi,A:Six Pack 4.00
5 DaR,V:Sinsear 4.00
6 DT,A:Tyler,Zero,Askani,
Mr.Sinister,C:X-Men 4.00
7 V:Tyler,A:Askani,X-Men,Domino . 4.00
8 O:Cable,V:Tyler,A:X-Men,Cable is
Nathan Summers 4.00
9 MCW,B:Killing Field,A:Excalibur,
V:Omega Red 4.00
10 MCW,A:Acolytes,Omega Red . . 4.00
11 MCW,E:Killing Field,D:Katu 4.00
12 SLo(s),B:Fear & Loathing,
V:Senyaka 4.00
13 V:D'Spayre 4.00
14 V:S'yM 4.00
15 A:Thorn 4.00
16 Foil(c),Dbl-size,A:Jean,Scott
Logan,V:Phalanx 9.00
16a Newsstand ed. 3.00
17 Deluxe ed. 3.00
17a Newsstand ed. 2.25
18 Deluxe ed. 3.00
18a Newsstand ed. 2.25
19 Deluxe ed. 3.00
19a Newsstand ed. 3.00
20 V:Legion, Deluxe ed. w/card . . . 5.00

MARVEL

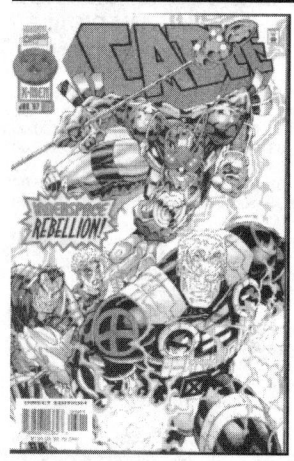

Cable #39
© *Marvel Entertainment Group*

20a Newsstand ed. 2.25
21 Cable makes tough decisions,
    A:Domino. 3.00
22 V:Fortress 3.00
23 IaC,A:Domino 3.00
24 F:Blaquesmith. 3.00
25 IaC,SHa,F:Cable's Wife,foil(c) . . 5.00
26 Tries to return to X-Mansion 3.00
27 IaC, A:Domino. 3.00
28 IaC,SHa,concl. war in Genosha . 3.00
29 . . . . 3.00
30 . . . . 3.00
31 IaC, cont.X-Men/Cable war. 3.00
32 Onslaught saga. 3.50
33 Onslaught saga. 3.00
34 Onslaught saga. 3.00
35 Onslaught saga. 3.00
36 . . . . 3.00
37 JLb,IaC,SHa,V:Askani'son,Kane. 3.00
38 JLb,IaC,SHa,V:PSycho-Man,
    A:Kane. 3.00
39 JLb,IaC,SHa,V:Psycho-Man . . . 3.00
40 TDz,IaC,SHa,A:Renee Majcomb 3.00
41 TDz,SHa,F:Bishop 3.00
42 TDz,RGr,SHa,The Prophecy
    of the Twelve 3.00
43 TDz,RGr,Images of Nathan's
    past 3.00
44 TDz,RGr,SHa,A:Madelyne Pryor
    (Cable's mom) 3.00
45 JeR,RGr,Zero Tolerance,
    No Escape,pt.2 . . . . 3.00
46 JeR,RGr,SHa,Zero Tolerance,
    No Escape, pt.2 (of 3) 3.00
47 JeR,RGr,SHa, Operation Zero
    Tolerance,V:Batsion 3.00
48 JeR,SHa,V:Hellfire Club 3.00
49 JeR,SHa,V:Hellfire Club 3.00
50 JeR,SHa,A:Cyclops, Phoenix,
    Union Jack, 48pg. 4.00
51 JeR,Hellfire Hunt. 2.50
52 JeR,Hellfire Hunt, pt.5. . . . . 2.50
53 JoC,Hellfire Hunt, concl. 2.50
54 JoC,A:Black Panther,V:Klaw. . . . 2.50
55 JoC,A:Irene Merryweather,
    Domino 2.50
56 JoC,V:Stilt-Man & Hydro-Man. . . 2.50
57 JoC,Cable powers altered by
    EMP wave 2.50
58 JoC,Persecution, pt.1 . . . . 2.50
59 JoC,I:Agent 18,V:Zzaxx 2.50
60 JoC,Nemesis Contract,pt.2 . . . . . 2.50
61 JoC,Nemesis Contract,pt.3 . . . . . 2.50

62 JoC,Nemesis Contract,pt.4 . . . . . 2.50
63 JoC,Blood Brothers,pt.2,x-over. . 2.50
64 JoC,O:Cable 2.50
65 JoC,Millennium countdown. 2.50
66 JoC,Sign of the End Times,pt.1 . 2.50
67 JoC,Sign of the End Times,pt.2 . 2.50
68 JoC,Sign of the End Times,pt.3 . 2.50
69 JoC,A:Blaquesmith,Archangel . . 2.50
70 JoC,A:Archangel 2.50
71 RLd,abandons his destiny,
    with RLd poster 2.50
72 RLd,reunited with X-force 2.50
73 RLd,reunited 2.50
74 V:Caliban 2.50
75 RLd,Apocalypse 3.50
76 Apocalypse The 12:pt.6 . . . . 3.00
77 Ages of Apocalypse,pt.2 . . . . . . 3.00
78 mutant no more. 3.00
79 X-Men: Revolution 3.00
79a variant (c) 3.50
80 Apocalypse gone 2.50
81 The Undying 2.50
82 Nathan Summers, murderer? . . . 2.50
83 R:Domino 2.50
84 Phoenix & Beast 2.50
85 Mother Askani, Gaunt. 2.50
86 Gaunt 2.50
87 Dream'sEnd,pt.2,x-over 2.50
88 F:Nightcrawler. 2.50
89 in Washington DC. 2.50
90 Dark Sisterhood 2.50
91 Dark Sisterhood 2.50
92 Cable quits X-Men? 2.50
93 V:Dark Sisterhood. 2.50
94 V:Dark Sisterhood. 2.50
95 V:Dark Sisterhood,concl. 2.50
96 Old Man Coll. 2.50
97 Path of Most Resistance. 2.50
98 Shining Path 2.50
99 V:Shining Path 2.50
100 V:Techno-OrganicVirus,64-pg. . 4.50
101 Macedonian Plot. 2.50
102 Albanians' deadly plan 2.50
103 shot in the head 2.50
104 on the wrong side? 2.50
105 in Rio. 2.50
106 In Kazakhstan 2.50
107 final issue 2.50
Ann. '98 AOI(c) F:Cable vs. Machine
    Man, O:Bastion 3.00
Ann.1999 48-page 3.50
Minus 1 Spec., TDz,JeR, flashback. 2.00
GN Cable/Wolverine Guts 'N' Glory. 6.00
Cable: Second Genesis 4.00

Cage #5
© *Marvel Entertainment Group*

TPB Cable,rep.New Mutants 16.00
TPB The Shining Path, 144-pg. . . . 16.00
TPB Vol.2 The End (2002). 15.00

CABLE & DEADPOOL
Nov., 2003
1 RLd(c),Looks Could Kill,pt.1 . . . . 3.50
2 RLd(c),Looks Could Kill,pt.2 . . . . 3.50
3 RLd(c),Looks Could Kill,pt.3 . . . . 3.00
4 RLd(c),Looks Could Kill,pt.4 . . . . 3.00
5 RLd(c),Looks Could Kill,pt.5 . . . . 3.00
6 Looks Could Kill,pt.6 . . . . 3.00
7 Passion of the Cable,pt.1 . . . . . . 3.00
8 Passion of the Cable,pt.2 . . . . . . 3.00
TPB If Looks Could Kill 15.00

CABLE & X-FORCE
1995–97
Cable & X-Force '95 Spec. 4.00
Cable & X-Force '96 Spec.48pg. . . 3.50
Cable & X-Force '97 Spec.#1
    JFM,CJ,V:Malekith,48pg. 3.50

CADILLACS &
DINOSAURS
Epic, Nov., 1990
1 Rep.Xenozoic Tales. 5.00
2 thru 6 Rep.Xenozoic Tales. . . . @3.00

CAGE
1992–93
1 DT,R:Luke Cage,I:Hardcore, ... 3.00
2 DT,V:Hammer 2.50
3 DT,A:Punisher,V:Untouchables . . 2.50
4 DT,A:Punisher,V:Untouchables . . 2.50
5 DT,I:New Power Man. 2.50
6 DT,V:New Power Man 2.50
7 DT,A:Avengers West Coast 2.50
8 DT,V:Steele,Wonder Man 2.50
9 V:Rhino,A:Hulk. 2.50
10 DT,V:Hulk,Rhino 2.50
11 DT,V:Rapidfire 2.50
12 A:Iron Fist,double size 2.50
13 V:The Thinker 2.50
14 PCu,I:Coldfire 2.50
15 DT,For Love Nor Money#2,
    A:Silver Sable,Terror 2.50
16 DT,For Love Nor Money#5,
    A:Silver Sable,Terror 2.50
17 DT,Infinty Crusade 2.50
18 A:Dred,V:Creed. 2.50
19 A:Dakota North 2.50
20 Last issue 2.50

CAGE
Marvel Max, Feb., 2002
1 (of 5) RCo,Justice isn't cheap . . . 5.00
2 RCo,teen-age girl murdered 4.00
3 RCo,. 4.00
4 RCo,secret shame. 4.00
5 RCo,Hammerhead. 4.00
TPB RCo 20.00
TPB 13.00

CALL, THE
April, 2003
1 PO, everyday heroes. 2.25
2 thru 4 PO . . . . @2.25
TPB Vol. 1, series rep. 9.00

CALL OF DUTY, THE:
THE BROTHER HOOD
June, 2002
1 (of 6) ATi,F:FDNY,48-pg. 4.00
2 thru 6 ATi,F:FDNY . . . . @2.50

All comics prices listed are for *Near Mint* condition.

The Call of Duty, Must Have ed. . . . 3.00
TPB Vol. I. 15.00
TPB Vol. II: Precinct & Wagon. . . . 15.00

THE CALL OF DUTY: THE PRECINCT
July, 2002
1 (of 5) TMd,F:NYPD 3.00
2 thru 5 TMd . . . . @2.50

THE CALL OF DUTY: THE WAGON
Marvel Aug., 2002
1 (of 4) F:NYC EMS 2.50
2 thru 4 . . . . @2.50

CAMP CANDY
May, 1990
1 thru 6, Oct., 1990 . . . . @4.00

CAPTAIN AMERICA COMICS
Timely/Atlas, 1941–54
1 S&K,Hitler(c),I&O:Capt.America &
  Bucky,A:Red Skull,B:Hurricane,
  Tuk the Caveboy 135,000.00
2 S&K,RC,AAv,Hitler(c),
  I:Circular Shield;Trapped
  in the Nazi Stronghold . . . 21,000.00
3 S&K,RC,AAv,Stan Lee's 1st Text,
  A:Red Skull,Bondage(c) . 17,000.00
4 S&K,AAv,Horror Hospital . . 12,000.00
5 S&K,AAv,Ringmaster's
  Wheel of Death 10,000.00
6 S&K,AAv,O:Father Time,
  E:Tuk 8,200.00
7 S&K,A: Red Skull 10,000.00
8 S&K, The Tomb 6,500.00
9 S&K,RC,V:Black Talon 6,500.00
10 S&K,RC,Chamber
  of Horrors 6,500.00
11 AAv,E:Hurricane;Feuding
  Mountaneers. 5,500.00
12 AAv,B:Imp,E:Father Time;
  Pygmie's Terror. 5,000.00
13 AAv,O:Secret Stamp;All Out
  For America 5,000.00
14 AAv,V:Japs;Pearl Harbor
  Symbol cover 5,500.00
15 AAv,Den of Doom 5,500.00
16 AAv,A:R.Skull;CapA
  Unmasked 6,500.00
17 AAv,I:Fighting Fool;
  Graveyard. 4,400.00
18 AAv,V:Japanese 4,400.00
19 AAv,V:Ghouls,
  B:Human Torch. 3,500.00
20 AAv,A:Sub-Mariner,V:Nazis . 3,500.00
21 SSh(c),Bucky Captured . . . 3,200.00
22 SSh(c),V:Japanese 3,200.00
23 SSh(c),V:Nazis. 3,200.00
24 SSh(c),V:Black
  Dragon Society. 3,200.00
25 SSh(c),V:Japs;Drug Story . . 3,200.00
26 ASh(c),V:Nazi Fleet 3,100.00
27 ASh(c)CapA&Russians
  V:Nazis, E:Secret Stamp . 3,100.00
28 ASh(c),NaziTortureChamber 3,100.00
29 ASh(c),V:Nazis;French
  Underground. 3,100.00
30 SSh(c),Bucky Captured . . . 3,100.00
31 ASh(c),Bondage(c). 2,800.00
32 SSh(c),V: Japanese Airforce 2,800.00
33 ASh(c),V:Nazis;BrennerPass 2,800.00
34 SSh(c),Bondage(c) 2,800.00
35 SSh(c),CapA in Japan 2,800.00
36 SSh(c),V:Nazis;Hitler(c) 4,000.00

Captain America #18
© Marvel Entertainment Group

37 ASh(c),CapA in Berlin,
  A:Red Skull. 3,300.00
38 ASh(c),V:Japs;Bondage(c). . 2,700.00
39 ASh(c),V:Japs;Boulder Dam 2,700.00
40 SSh(c),V:Japs;Ammo Depot 2,700.00
41 ASh(c),FinalJapaneseWar(c) 2,300.00
42 ASh(c),V:Bank Robbers. . . . 2,300.00
43 ASh(c),V:Gangsters 2,300.00
44 ASh(c),V:Gangsters 2,300.00
45 ASh(c),V:Bank Robbers. . . . 2,300.00
46 ASh(c),Holocaust(c) 3,000.00
47 ASh(c),Final Nazi War(c) . . . 2,300.00
48 ASh(c),V:Robbers 1,800.00
49 ASh(c),V:Sabatuers 1,800.00
50 ASh(c),V:Gorilla Gang 1,800.00
51 ASh(c),V:Gangsters 1,800.00
52 ASh(c),V:AtomBombThieves 1,800.00
53 ASh(c),V:Burglars 1,800.00
54 ASh(c),TV Studio,
  V:Gangsters 1,800.00
55 V:Counterfeiters. 1,800.00
56 SSh(c),V:Art Theives 1,800.00
57 Symbolic CapA(c) 1,800.00
58 ASh(c),V:Bank Robbers. . . . 1,800.00
59 SSh(c)O:CapA Retold;Private
  Life of Captain America . . . 4,500.00
60 V:The Human Fly. 1,800.00
61 SSh(c),V:Red Skull;
  Bondage(c). 4,000.00
62 SSh(c),Kingdom of Terror . . 2,200.00
63 SSh(c),I&O:Asbestos Lady;
  The Parrot Strikes. 2,300.00
64 Diamonds Spell Doom. 2,400.00
65 When Friends Turn Foes . . . 2,400.00
66 O:Golden Girl;Bucky Shot . . 2,500.00
67 E:Toro(in Human Torch);
  Golden Girl Team-Up 2,400.00
68 A:Golden Girl;Riddle of
  the Living Dolls. 2,400.00
69 Weird Tales of the Wee
  Males, A:Sun Girl 2,400.00
70 A:Golden Girl,Sub-Mariner,
  Namora;Worlds at War . . . 2,400.00
71 A:Golden Girl; Trapped 2,400.00
72 Murder in the Mind. 2,400.00
73 The Outcast of Time 2,400.00
74 A:Red Skull;Capt.America's
  Weird Tales. 8,000.00
75 Thing in the Chest 2,400.00
76 JR(c),Capt.America,Commie
  Smasher. 2,400.00
77 Capt.A,Commie Smasher . . 1,300.00
78 JR(c),V:Communists 1,300.00
Marvel Milestone rep. #1 (1995) . . . 3.95

CAPTAIN AMERICA
Prev: Tales of Suspense
April, 1968
100 JK,A:Avengers 600.00
101 JK,I:4th Sleeper 150.00
102 JK,V:Red Skull,4th Sleeper . 100.00
103 JK,V:Red Skull 100.00
104 JK,DA,JSo,V:Red Skull. 100.00
105 JK,DA,A:Batroc. 75.00
106 JK,Cap.Goes Wild 75.00
107 JK,Red Skull 75.00
108 JK,Trapster 75.00
109 JK,O:Captain America 125.00
110 JSo,JSt,A:Hulk,Rick Jones
  in Bucky Costume 125.00
111 JSo,JSt,I:Man Killer 125.00
112 JK,GT,Album 60.00
113 JSo,TP,Avengers,
  D:Madame Hydra 125.00
114 JR,SB,C:Avengers 40.00
115 JB,SB,A:Red Skull 40.00
116 GC,JSt,A:Avengers 40.00
117 JR(c),GC,JSt,I:Falcon 100.00
118 JR(c),GC,JSt,A:Falcon 30.00
119 GC,JSt,O:Falcon 30.00
120 GC,JSt,A:Falcon 30.00
121 GC,JSt,V:Man Brute 25.00
122 GC,JSt,Scorpion 22.00
123 GC,JSt,A:NickFury,
  V:Suprema. 22.00
124 GC,JSt,I:Cyborg 22.00
125 GC,Mandarin. 22.00
126 JK&BEv(c),GC,A:Falcon 22.00
127 GC,WW,A:Nick Fury 22.00
128 GC,V:Satan's Angels 22.00
129 GC,Red Skull 22.00
130 GC,I:Batroc 22.00
131 GC,V:Hood 22.00
132 GC,A:Bucky Barnes 22.00
133 GC,O:Modok,B:Capt.America/
  Falcon Partnership 22.00
134 GC,V:Stone Face 22.00
135 JR(c),GC,TP,A:Nick Fury 22.00
136 GC,BEv,V:Tyrannus 22.00
137 GC,BEv,A:Spider-Man 30.00
138 JR,A:Spider-Man. 28.00
139 JR,Falcon solo 22.00
140 JR,O:Grey Gargoyle 22.00
141 JR,JSt,V:Grey Gargoyle 20.00
142 JR,JSt,Nick Fury 20.00
143 JR,Red Skull 22.00
144 GM,JR,N:Falcon,V:Hydra . . . 20.00
145 GK,JR,V:Hydra 20.00
146 JR(c),SB,V:Hydra 18.00
147 GK(c),SB,V:Hydra. 18.00
148 SB,JR,Red Skull 18.00
149 GK(c),SB,JM,V:Batroc 18.00
150 K&R(c),SB,V:The Stranger . . 18.00
151 SB,V:Mr.Hyde 18.00
152 SB,V:Scorpion,Mr.Hyde 18.00
153 SB,JM,V:50's Cap 18.00
154 SB,V:50's Cap. 18.00
155 SB,FMc,O:50's Cap 18.00
156 SB,FMc,V:50's Cap 18.00
157 SB,I:The Viper 18.00
158 SB,V:The Viper 18.00
159 SB,V:PlantMan,Porcupine . . . 18.00
160 SB,FMc,V:Solarr. 18.00
161 SB,V:Dr.Faustus 18.00
162 JSn(c),SB,V:Dr.Faustus 18.00
163 SB,I:Serpent Squad 18.00
164 JR(c),I:Nightshade 18.00
165 SB,FMc,V:Yellow Claw 18.00
166 SB,FMc,V:Yellow Claw 18.00
167 SB,V:Yellow Claw 18.00
168 SB,I&O:Phoenix
  (2nd Baron Zemo) 18.00
169 SB,FMc,C:Black Panther . . . 18.00
170 K&R(c),SB,C:Black Panther . . 18.00
171 JR(c),SB,A:Black Panther. . . . 18.00

MARVEL

Captain America #132
© *Marvel Entertainment Group*

172 GK(c),SB,C:X-Men 22.00
173 GK(c),SB,A:X-Men 25.00
174 GK(c),SB,A:X-Men 25.00
175 SB,A:X-Men 25.00
176 JR(c),SB,O:Capt.America. . . . 18.00
177 JR(c),SB,A:Lucifer,Beast 15.00
178 SB,A:Lucifer 15.00
179 SB,A:Hawkeye 15.00
180 GK(c),SB,I:1st Nomad(Cap) . . 25.00
181 GK(c),SB,I&O:New Cap 20.00
182 FR,Madam Hydra 10.00
183 GK(c),FR,R:Cap,D:New Cap . 15.00
184 K&R(c),HT,A:Red Skull 10.00
185 GK(c),SB,FR,V:Red Skull 10.00
186 GK(c),FR,O:Falcon 15.00
187 K&R(c),FR,V:Druid 10.00
188 GK(c),SB,V:Druid 10.00
189 GK(c),FR,V:Nightshade 10.00
190 GK(c),FR,A:Nightshade 10.00
191 FR,A:Stilt Man,N.Fury 10.00
192 JR(c),FR,A:Dr.Faustus 10.00
193 JR(c),JK,`Mad Bomb' 20.00
194 JK,I:Gen.Heshin 22.00
195 JK,1984 . . . . 22.00
196 JK,Madbomb 22.00
197 JK,Madbomb 22.00
198 JK,Madbomb 22.00
199 JK,Madbomb 22.00
200 JK,Madbomb 20.00
201 JK,Epilogue 15.00
202 JK,Night People 15.00
203 JK,Night People 15.00
204 JK,I:Argon 15.00
205 JK,V:Argon 15.00
206 JK,I:Swine 15.00
207 JK,V:Swine 15.00
208 JK,I:Arnim Zola,D:Swine 15.00
209 JK,O:Arnim Zola,I:Primus 15.00
210 JK,A:Red Skull 15.00
211 JK,A:Red Skull 15.00
212 JK,A:Red Skull 15.00
213 JK,I:Night Flyer 15.00
214 JK,D:Night Flyer 15.00
215 GT,Redwing 10.00
216 Reprint,JK 10.00
217 JB, I:Quasar(Marvel Boy)
　　I:Vamp 10.00
218 SB,A:Iron Man 6.00
219 SB,JSt,V:TheCorporation 6.00
220 SB,D:L.Dekker 6.00
221 SB,Ameridroid 6.00
222 SB,I:Animus(Vamp) 6.00
223 SB,Animus 6.00
224 MZ,V:Animus 6.00

225 SB,A:Nick Fury 6.00
226 SB,A:Nick Fury 6.00
227 SB,A:Nick Fury 6.00
228 SB,Constrictor 6.00
229 SB,R:SuperAgents of Shield . . 6.00
230 SB,A:Hulk 8.00
231 SB,DP,A:Grand Director 6.00
232 SB,DP,V:Grand Director 6.00
233 SB,DP,D:Sharon Carter 6.00
234 SB,DP,A:Daredevil 6.00
235 SB,FM,A:Daredevil 8.00
236 SB,V:Dr.Faustus 6.00
237 SB,`From the Ashes' 6.00
238 SB,V:Hawk Riders 6.00
239 JBy(c),SB,V:Hawk Riders 6.00
240 SB,V:A Guy Named Joe 6.00
241 A:Punisher 16.00
242 JSt,A:Avengers 6.00
243 GP(c),RB,V:Adonis 6.00
244 TS,`A Monster Berserk' 6.00
245 CI,JRn,Nazi Hunter 6.00
246 GP(c),JBi,V:Joe 6.00
247 JBy,V:BaronStrucker 8.00
248 JBy,JRu,Dragon Man 8.00
249 JBy,O:Machinesmith,
　　A:Air-Walker 8.00
250 JBy,Cap for Pres 8.00
251 JBy,V:Mr.Hyde 8.00
252 JBy,V:Batrok 8.00
253 JBy,V:Baron Blood 8.00
254 JBy,D:B.Blood,UnionJack,I:3rd
　　Union Jack 8.00
255 JBy,40th Anniv.,O:Cap 8.00
256 GC,V:Demon Druid 3.50
257 A:Hulk 3.50
258 MZ,V:Blockbuster 3.50
259 MZ,V:Dr. Octopus 3.50
260 AM,In Jail 3.50
261 MZ,A:Nomad 4.00
262 MZ,V:Ameridroid 3.50
263 MZ,V:Red Skull 3.50
264 MZ,X-Men 4.00
265 MZ,A:Spider-Man,N.Fury 3.50
266 MZ,A:Spider-Man 3.50
267 MZ,V:Everyman 3.00
268 MZ,A:Defenders(x-over from
　　Def.#106) 3.00
269 MZ,A:Team America 3.00
270 MZ,V:Tess-One 3.00
271 MZ,V:Mr.X 3.00
272 MZ,I:Vermin 3.50
273 MZ,A:Nick Fury 3.00
274 MZ,D:SamSawyer 3.00
275 MZ,V:Neo-Nazis 3.00
276 MZ,V:Baron Zemo 3.00
277 MZ,V:Baron Zemo 3.00
278 MZ,V:Baron Zemo 3.00
279 MZ,V:Primus 3.00
280 MZ,V:Scarecrow 3.00
281 MZ,A:Spider Woman,
　　R:'50's Bucky 3.00
282 MZ,I:2nd Nomad 6.00
282a (second primting) 2.50
283 MZ,A:Viper 4.00
284 SB,Nomad 3.00
285 MZ,V:Porcupine 3.00
286 MZ,V:Deathlok 5.00
287 MZ,V:Deathlok 5.00
288 MZ,V:Deathlok,D:Hellinger 5.00
289 MZ,A:Red Skull 3.00
290 JBy(c),RF,A:Falcon 3.00
291 JBy(c),HT,V:Tumbler 3.00
292 I&O:Black Crow 3.00
293 V:Mother Superior 3.00
294 R:Nomad 3.00
295 V:Sisters of Sin 3.00
296 V:Baron Zemo 3.00
297 O:Red Skull 3.00
298 V:Red Skull 3.00
299 V:Red Skull 3.00
300 D:Red Skull 4.00

Captain America #237
© *Marvel Entertainment Group*

301 PNe,A:Avengers 3.00
302 PNe,I:Machete,V:Batroc 3.00
303 PNe,V:Batroc 3.00
304 PNe,V:Stane Armor 3.00
305 PNe,A:Capt.Britain,V:Modred . . 3.00
306 PNe,A:Capt.Britain,V:Modred . . 3.00
307 PNe,I:Madcap 3.00
308 PNe,I:Armadillo,
　　Secret WarsII 3.00
309 PNe,V:Madcap 3.00
310 PNe,V:Serpent Society,I:Cotton
　　Mouth,Diamondback 3.00
311 PNe,V:Awesome Android 3.00
312 PNe,I:Flag Smasher 3.00
313 PNe,D:Modok 3.00
314 PNe,A:Nighthawk 3.00
315 PNe,V:Serpent Society 3.00
316 PNe,A:Hawkeye 3.00
317 PNe,I:Death-Throws 3.00
318 PNe,V&D:Blue Streak 3.00
319 PNe,V:Scourge,D:Vamp 3.00
320 PNe,V:Scourge 3.00
321 PNe,V:Flagsmasher,
　　I:Ultimatum 3.00
322 PNe,V:Flagsmasher 3.00
323 PNe,I:Super Patriot
　　(US Agent) 5.00
324 PNe,V:Whirlwind,Trapster 3.00
325 I:Slug,A:Nomad 3.00
326 V:Dr.Faustus 3.00
327 MZ(c)V:SuperPatriot 4.00
328 MZ(c),I:Demolition Man 3.00
329 MZ(c),A:Demolition Man 3.00
330 A:Night Shift,Shroud 3.00
331 A:Night Shift,Shroud 3.00
332 BMc,Rogers resigns 7.00
333 B:John Walker Becomes
　　6th Captain America 5.00
334 I:4th Bucky 5.00
335 V:Watchdogs 4.00
336 A:Falcon 3.00
337 TMo,I:The Captain 3.00
338 KD,AM,V:Professor Power 3.00
339 KD,TD,Fall of Mutants,
　　V:Famine 3.00
340 KD,AM,A:Iron Man, ... 3.00
341 KD,AM,I:Battlestar,A:Viper 3.00
342 KD,AM,A:D-Man,Falcon,
　　Nomad,Viper 3.00
343 KD,AM,A:D-Man,Falcon,
　　Nomad 3.00
344 KD,AM,A:D-Man,Nomad 4.00
345 KD,AM,V:Watchdogs 4.00

346 KD,AM,V:Resistants 4.00
347 KD,AM,V:RWinger&LWinger. . . 4.00
348 KD,AM,V:Flag Smasher 4.00
349 KD,AM,V:Flag Smasher 4.00
350 KD,AM,doub-size,Rogers Ret.
   as Captain Am,V:Red Skull,
   E:6th Cap 5.00
351 KD,AM,V:Nick Fury. 3.00
352 KD,AM,I:Supreme Soviets 3.00
353 KD,AM,V:Supreme Soviets. . . . 3.00
354 KD,AM,I:USAgent,
   V:Machinesmith 3.50
355 RB,AM,A:Falcon,Battlestar . . . 3.00
356 AM,V:Sisters of Sin 3.00
357 KD,AM,V:Sisters of Sin
   Baron Zemo,Batroc 3.00
358 KD,B:Blood Stone Hunt 3.00
359 KD,V:Zemo,C:Crossbones 3.00
360 KD,I:Crossbones. 3.00
361 KD,V:Zemo,Batroc 3.00
362 KD,V:Zemo,Crossbones 3.00
363 KD,E:Blood Stone Hunt,
   V:Crossbones,C:Wolverine . . . 3.00
364 KD,V:Crossbones 3.00
365 KD,Acts of Vengeance,
   V:SubMariner,Red Skull 3.00
366 1st RLm Capt.Amer.,Acts of
   Vengeance,V:Controller. 3.00
367 KD,Acts of Vengeance,
   Magneto Vs. Red Skull 3.00
368 RLm,V:Machinesmith 3.00
369 RLm,I:Skeleton Crew 3.00
370 RLm,V:Skeleton Crew. 3.00
371 KD,V:Trump,Poundcakes. 3.00
372 RLm,B:Streets of Poison,
   Cap on Drugs,C:Bullseye 3.00
373 RLm,V:Bullseye,A:Bl.Widow . . . 3.00
374 RLm,V:Bullseye,A:Daredevil. . . 3.00
375 RLm,V:Daredevil. 3.00
376 RLm,A:Daredevil. 3.00
377 RLm,V:Crossbones,Bullseye . . . 3.00
378 RLm,E:Streets of Poison,Red
   Skull vs Kingpin,V:Crossbones . 3.00
379 RLm(c),V:Serpent Society 3.00
380 RLm,V:Serpent Society. 3.00
381 RLm,V:Serpent Society. 3.00
382 RLm,V:Serpent Society. 3.00
383 RLm(c),RLm,50th Anniv.
   64Pages 5.00
384 RLm,A:Jack Frost. 2.50
385 RLm,A:USAgent 2.50
386 RLm,Cap./USAgent T.U. 2.50
387 B:Superia Strategem 2.50
388 A:Paladin. 2.50
389 Superia Strategem #3. . . . . . . 2.50
390 Superia Strategem #4 . . . . . . 2.50
391 Superia Strategem #5. . . . . . . 2.50
392 E:Superia Strategem. 2.50
393 V:Captain Germany 2.50
394 A:Red Skull,Diamondback 2.50
395 A:Red Skull,Crossbones 2.50
396 I:2nd Jack O'Lantern. 2.50
397 V:Red Skull,X-Bones,Viper 2.50
398 Operation:Galactic Storm
   Pt.1,V:Warstar 2.50
399 Operation Galactic Storm
   Pt.8,V:Kree Empire 2.50
400 Operation Galactic Storm
   Pt.15,BU:rep.Avengers #4. . . . . 4.00
401 R:D-Man,A:Avengers 2.50
402 RLe,B:Man & Wolf,
   A:Wolverine. 2.50
403 RLe,A:Wolverine. 2.50
404 RLe,A:Wolverine. 2.50
405 RLe,A:Wolverine. 2.50
406 RLe,A:Wolverine. 2.50
407 RLe,A:Wolverine,Cable. 2.50
408 RLe,E:Man & Wolf 2.50
409 RLe,V:Skeleton Crew 2.50
410 RLe,V:Crossbones,Skel.Crew . 2.50
411 RLe,V:Snapdragon 2.50

412 RLe,V:Batroc,A:Shang-Chi 2.50
413 A:Shang-Chi,V:Superia. 2.50
414 RLe,A:Ka-Zar,Black Panther. . . 2.50
415 Rle,A:Black Panther,Ka-Zar . . . 2.50
416 RLe,Savage Land Mutates,
   A:Black.Panther,Ka-Zar. 2.50
417 RLe,A:Black Panther,Ka-Zar,
   V:AIM. 2.50
418 RLe,V:Night People 2.50
419 RLe,V:Viper. 2.50
420 RLe,I:2nd Blazing Skull,
   A:Nightshift 3.00
421 RLe,V:Nomad 2.50
422 RLe,I:Blistik. 2.50
423 RTs(s),MCW,V:Namor. 2.50
424 MGv(s),A:Sidewinder 2.50
425 B:MGu(s),DHv,Embossed(c),
   I:2nd SuperPatriot,DeadRinger . 4.00
426 DHv,A:Super Patriot,Dead
   Ringer,V:Resistants 2.50
427 DHv,V:Super Patriot,Dead
   Ringer 2.50
428 DHv,I:Americop. 2.50
429 DHv,V:Kono. 2.50
430 Daemon Dran, Americop 2.50
431 DHv,I:Free Spirit 2.50
432 DHv,Fighting Chance 2.50
433 DHv,Baron Zemo 2.50
434 DHv,A:Fighting Spirit,
   V:King Cobra 2.50
435 DHv,Fighting Chance 2.50
436 V:King Cobra, Mister Hyde,
   Fighting Chance conclusion . . . 2.50
437 Cap in a Coma 2.50
438 I:New Body Armor. 2.50
439 Dawn's Early Light,pt.2 . . . . . . 2.50
440 Taking A.I.M.,pt.1 . . . . 2.50
441 Taking A.I.M.,pt.3 . . . . 2.50
442 Batroc, Cap,V:Zeitgeist. 2.50
443 MGu,24 hours to live 2.50
444 MWa,RG,President Kidnapped . 6.00
445 MWa,RG,R:Captain America. . . 4.00
446 MWa,RG,Operation
   Rebirth,pt.2 . . . . 4.00
447 MWa,RG,Op.Rebirth,pt.3 . . . . . 4.00
448 MWa,RG,Operation
   Rebirth,pt.4,double size. 6.00
449 MWa,RG,A:Thor 4.00
450 MWa,RG,Man Without a
   Country, pt,1 . . . . 4.00
450a alternate cover 4.00
451 MWa,RG,DRo,Man Without
   A Country,pt.2,new costume . . . 3.50

Captain America #436
© Marvel Entertainment Group

452 MWa,RG,Man Without a
   Country, pt.3 . . . . 3.50
453 MWa,RG Man Without a
   Country, concl.,old costume . . . 3.50
454 MWa,RG,A:Avengers 3.50
Ann.#1 rep. 50.00
Ann.#2 rep. 35.00
Ann.#3 JK, ... 25.00
Ann.#4 JK,V:Magneto,I:Mutant
   Force 25.00
Ann.#5 `Deathwatcher' 6.00
Ann.#6 A:Contemplator 6.00
Ann.#7 O:Shaper of Worlds. 6.00
Ann.#8 MZ,A:Wolverine 35.00
Ann.#9 MBa,SD,Terminus Factor
   #1,N:Nomad 4.50
Ann.#10 MM,Baron Strucker,pt.3
   (see Punisher Ann.#4). 4.00
Ann.#11 Citizen Kang#1 . . . . 4.00
Ann.#12 I:Bantam,w/card. 4.00
Ann.#13 RTs(s),MCW, ... 4.00
Drug Wars PDd(s),SaV,A:New
   Warriors 3.00
G-Size#1 GK(c),rep.O:Cap.Amer. . . 7.00
Medusa Effect RTs(s),MCW,RB,
   V:Master Man 3.50
Movie Adapt 3.00
Spec.#1 Rep.Cap.A #110,#111 . . . . 2.00
Spec.#2 Rep.Cap.A.#113
   & Strange Tales #169 . . . . 2.00
TPB Bloodstone Hunt, rep. 15.95
TPB Captain America: Man Without
   a Country, MWa,RG,SK, rep. . . 15.00
TPB Streets of Poison, rep. 12.95
TPB War and Remembrance, rep. 12.95
Collector's Preview 1.95
Ashcan. 75

[2nd Series], Nov., 1996
1 RLd,CDi,JSb, Heroes Reborn,
   I:Nick Fury,48pg. 7.00
1A Stars and stripes background
   variant cover 7.50
1b gold signature edition,
   cardstock cover. 18.00
1c San Diego Con edition. 25.00
2 RLd,JLb,JSb,Falcon & Red Skull 3.00
3 RLd,JLb,JSb,A:Hulk,V:Red Skull
   & Master Man 3.00
4 RLd,JLb,JSb,F:Prince Namor, . . . 3.00
5 RLd,JLb,JSb,V:Crossbones. 3.00
6 RLd,JLb,JSb,Industrial
   Revolution, epilogue,A:Cable . . 3.00
7 RLd,JLb,DaF, ... 3.00
8 RLd,JLb,SPa,A:Nick Fury,
   WWII story 3.00
9 JLb,RLd,SPa,WWII story. 3.00
10 JLb,RLd,SPa,WWII story, concl.. 3.00
11 JeR,JoB,Odyssey across
   America, pt.4, concl. 3.00
12 JeR,JoB,Heroes Reborn, Galactus
   concl. 4.00
13 JeR,RLm,Wildstorm x-over. 3.00
Ashcan, ComicCon 5.00

[3rd Series], Nov., 1997
1 MWa,RG,BWi,A:Lady Deathstrike,
   Red Skull, Sharon Carter, 48pg 4.00
1a variant cover 10.00
2 MWa,RG,BWi,A devastating loss. 5.00
2a variant cover 4.00
3 MWa,RG,BWi,V:Hydra 4.00
4 MWa,RG,BWi,F:Batroc 3.00
5 MWa,RG,BWi,V:Hordes of Hydra 3.00
6 MWa,RG,V:Skrulls 3.00
7 MWa,NKu,Power & Glory concl. . 3.00
8 MWa,Nku,Live Kree or Die, pt.2
   x-over. 3.50
9 MWa,NKu,American Nightmare,
   pt.1. . . . . 3.00
10 MWa,NKu,American Nightmare,
   pt.2. . . . . 3.00

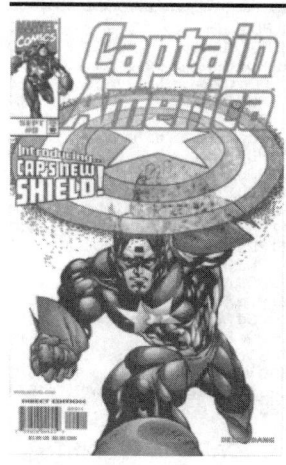

Captain America, 3rd Series #9
© Marvel Entertainment Group

11 MWa,NKu,American
Nightmare, pt.3 . . . . 3.00
12 MWa,NKu,American Night-
mare, pt.4, 48-page. 4.00
13 MWa,MFm,R:Red Skull 2.50
14 MWa,MFm,R:Red Skull 2.50
15 MWa,NKu,V:Red Skull 2.50
16 MWa,NKu,V:Red Skull 2.50
17 MWa,NKu,V:Red Skull 2.50
18 MWa,LW,RbC,V:Cosmic Cube
double-size 3.50
19 MWa,NKu,V:2 foes 2.50
20 MWa,NKu,Shield secrets 2.50
21 MWa,NKu,A:Black Panther. . . . 2.50
22 MWa,NKu,A:Black Panther. . . . 2.50
23 MWa,Capt.America convict?. . . 2.50
24 TDF,RF,V:Hydra 2.50
25 DJu,NKu,DGr,Twisted
Tomorrows,pt.1 . . . . 4.00
26 DJu,NKu,DGr,Twisted,pt.2 . . . . 2.50
27 DJu,NKu,DGr,Twisted,pt.3 . . . . 2.50
28 DJu,NKu,DGr,V:CountNefaria. . . 2.50
29 DJu,DGr,A:Ka-Zar. 2.50
30 DJu,DGr,NKu,Savage Land 2.50
31 DJu,NKu,DGr,F:Sharon Carter. . 2.50
32 DJu,JO,kidnapped 2.50
33 DJu,ATi,Protocide 2.50
34 DJu,ATi,Cache 2.50
35 DJu,ATi,Protocide 2.50
36 DJu,ATi,Maximum Security. . . . 2.50
37 DJu,ATi,V:Protocide 2.50
38 DJu,ATi,Capt.Am. unleashed . . . 2.50
39 DJu,V:A.I.M. 2.50
40 DJu,V:A.I.M. 2.50
41 DJu,Batroc the Leaper 2.50
42 DJu,BL,V:Crimson Dynamo . . . 2.50
43 DJu,DR,BL,A:David Ferrari. . . . 2.50
44 DJu,BL,A:Taskmaster 2.50
45 DJu,BL,America Lost,pt.1 . . . . . 2.50
46 DJu,BL,America Lost,pt.2. . . . . 2.50
47 DJu,BL,America Lost,pt.3. . . . . 2.50
48 DJu,BL,America Lost,pt.4. . . . . 2.50
49 DJu,BL,F:Sam Wilson. 2.50
50 96-page, last issue 6.50
Ann.1998 Captain America/
Citizen V,KBk,KK, 48-page 4.00
Ann. 1999 JoC,V:Flag Smasher . . . 4.00
Ann.2000 DJu,DGr,48-pg. 4.00
Ann.2001 DJu,48-page 3.50
Spec.#1 Captain America (2000). . . 2.50
Spec.Cap: A Universe X Special . . . 4.00
GN Captain America/Nick Fury:
The Otherworld War (2001). . . . 6.95

TPB The Classic Years,Vol.2 . . . . 24.95
TPB To Serve and Protect 17.95

CAPTAIN AMERICA
April, 2002
1 JNR(s), terrorism, 48-pg. 4.00
2 JNR(s), terrorism,pt.2 . . . . 3.50
3 JNR(s), terrorism,pt.3 . . . . 3.50
4 JNR(s), terrorism,pt.4 . . . . 3.50
5 JNR(s), terrorism,pt.5 . . . . 3.50
6 JNR(s), terrorism,concl. 3.50
7 JNR(s) 3.50
8 JNR(s),Extremists,pt.2 . . . . 3.50
9 JNR(s),Extremists,pt.3 . . . . 3.50
10 JNR(s),Extremists,pt.4 . . . . 3.50
11 JNR(s),Extremists,pt.5 . . . . 3.50
12 JNR(s),JaL,Ice,pt.1 . . . . 3.50
13 JNR(s),JaL,Ice,pt.2 . . . . 3.50
14 JNR(s),JaL,Ice,pt.3 . . . . 3.50
15 JNR(s),JaL,Ice,pt.4 . . . . 3.50
16 JNR(s),JaL,Ice,pt.5 . . . . 3.50
17 LW,Cap.Am Lives Again,pt.1 . . 3.50
18 LW,Cap.Am Lives Again,pt.2 . . 3.50
19 LW,Cap.Am Lives Again,pt.3 . . 3.50
20 LW,Cap.Am Lives Again,pt.4 . . 3.50
21 CBa,Homeland,pt.1. . . . . 3.00
22 CBa,Homeland,pt.2. . . . . 3.00
23 CBa,Homeland,pt.3. . . . . 3.00
24 CBa,Homeland,pt.4. . . . . 3.00
25 CBa,Homeland,pt.5. . . . . 3.00
26 CBa,F:Bucky Barnes 3.00
27 ECa 3.00
28 ECa 3.00
29 Avengers Disassembled tie-in . . 3.00
30 Avengers Disassembled,pt.2 . . . 3.00
31 Avengers Disassembled,pt.3 . . . 3.00
32 SEa,Disassembled,tie-in,pt.4 . . . 3.00
TPB The New Deal 17.00
TPB Vol. 2: Extremists. 14.00
TPB Vol. 3: Ice. 13.00
TPB Vol. 4: Lives Again 13.00
TPB Vol. 5: Homeland 20.00

CAPTAIN AMERICA & THE FALCON
March, 2004
1 BS,Two Americas,pt.1 . . . . 3.00
2 BS,Two Americas,pt.2 . . . . 3.00
3 BS,Two Americas,pt.3 . . . . 3.00
4 BS,Two Americas,pt.4 . . . . 3.00
5 Avengers Disassembled tie-in . . . 3.00
6 Avengers Disassembled,pt.2 . . . . 3.00
7 Avengers Disassembled,pt.3 . . . . 3.00
8 JoB,Brothers & Keepers,pt.1 . . . . 3.00
TPB Madbomb 17.00
TPB Vol. 1: Two Americas 10.00

CAPTAIN AMERICA: DEAD MAN RUNNING
Jan., 2002
1 (of 3) distress call 3.25
2 . . . . 3.25
3 concl. 3.25

CAPTAIN AMERICA: SENTINEL OF LIBERTY
July, 1998
1 MWa,RG,new foe, in future 2.50
1 signed by MWa & RG 5.00
2A MWa,RG(c&a) F:Invaders,
V:Nazis 2.25
2B variant JSm(c). 2.25
3 MWa,RG,DGr,A:Sub-Mariner. . . . 2.25
4 MWa,RG,DGr,A:Human Torch . . . 2.25
5 MWa,RG,MFm,Tales of
Suspense pt.1 . . . . 2.25

6 MWa,RG,MFm,Tales of
Suspense pt.2 . . . . 3.50
7 RSt,RF,civil war tale concl. 2.25
8 MWa,R:Falcon 2.25
9 MWa,A:Falcon 2.25
10 psychedelic look back. 2.25
11 MWa,A:Human Torch 2.25
12 MWa,DGr,F:Bucky,48-page 3.50
Spec.RoughCut #1,MWa,RG,48-pg . 3.00

CAPTAIN AMERICA: WHAT PRICE GLORY
March, 2003
1 (of 4) SR 3.25
2 thru 4 SR . . . . @3.25

CAPTAIN BRITAIN
Jan., 2002
TPB 208-pg.. . . . . 19.95

CAPTAIN BRITAIN CLASSICS
1 AD rep. 2.50

CAPTAIN CONFEDERACY
Epic, Nov., 1991
1 I:Capt.Confederacy,Kid Dixie. . . . 2.25
2 Meeting of Superhero Reps. 2.25
3 Framed for Murder. 2.25
4 Superhero conference,final iss. . . 2.25

CAPTAIN JUSTICE
March, 1988
1 Based on TV Series 2.25
2 April, 1988 . . . . 2.25

CAPTAIN MARVEL
May, 1968
1 GC,O:retold,V:Sentry#459. . . . 200.00
2 GC,V:Super Skrull 75.00
3 GC,V:Super Skrull 45.00
4 GC,Sub-Mariner. 45.00
5 DH,I:Metazoid 45.00
6 DH,I:Solam 30.00
7 JR(c),DH,V:Quasimodo 30.00
8 DH,I:Cuberex 30.00
9 DH,D:Cuberex 30.00
10 DH,V:Number 1. . . . . 30.00
11 BWS(c),I:Z0. . . . . 30.00

Captain Marvel #30
© Marvel Entertainment Group

MARVEL

12 K&R(c),I:Man-Slayer 22.00
13 FS,V:Man-Slayer 22.00
14 FS,Iron Man 22.00
15 TS,DA,Z0 . . . . 20.00
16 DH,Ronan 20.00
17 GK,DA,O:R.Jones ret,N:Capt.
   Marvel 22.00
18 GK,JB,DA,I:Mandroid 20.00
19 GK,DA,Master.of.MM 20.00
20 GK,DA,I:Rat Pack 20.00
21 GK,DA,Hulk 20.00
22 GK(c),WB,V:Megaton 20.00
23 GK(c),WB,FMc,V:Megaton 20.00
24 GK(c),WB,ECh,I:L.Mynde 20.00
25 1st JSn,Cap.Marvel,Cosmic
   Cube Saga Begins 35.00
26 JSn,DC,Thanos(2ndApp.)
   A:Thing 40.00
27 JSn,V:Thanos,A:Mentor,
   Starfox, I:Death 30.00
28 JSn,DGr,Thanos Vs.Drax,
   A:Avengers 30.00
29 JSn,AM,O:Zeus,C:Thanos
   I:Eon,O:Mentor 22.00
30 JSn,AM,Controller,C:Thanos . . 22.00
31 JSn,AM,Avengers,
   Thanos,Drax,Mentor 22.00
32 JSn,AM,DGr,O:Drax,
   Moondragon,A:Thanos 22.00
33 JSn,KJ,E:Cosmic Cube Saga
   1st D:Thanos 30.00
34 JSn,JA,V:Nitro(leads to
   his Death) 20.00
35 GK(c),AA,Ant Man 10.00
36 AM,Watcher,Rep.CM#1 . . . . . . 10.00
37 AM,KJ,Nimrod 10.00
38 AM,KJ,Watcher 10.00
39 AM,KJ,Watcher 10.00
40 AM,AMc,Watcher 10.00
41 AM,BWr,CR,BMc,TA,Kree 12.00
42 AM,V:Stranger,C:Drax 8.00
43 AM,V:Drax 8.00
44 GK(c),AM,V:Drax 12.00
45 AM,I:Rambu 12.00
46 AM,TA,D:Fawn 8.00
47 AM,TA,A:Human Torch 8.00
48 AM,TA,I:Chetah 8.00
49 AM,V:Ronan,A:Cheetah 8.00
50 AM,TA,Avengers,
   V:Super Adaptiod 9.00
51 AM,TA,V:Mercurio,4-D Man . . . 12.00
52 AM,TA,V:Phae-dor 12.00
53 AM,TA,A:Inhumans 8.00
54 PB,V:Nitro 8.00

55 PB,V:Death-grip 8.00
56 PB,V:Death-grip 8.00
57 PB,V:Thor,A;Thanos 12.00
58 PB,Drax/Titan 8.00
59 PB,Drax/Titan,I:Stellarax 8.00
60 PB,Drax/Titan 8.00
61 PB,V:Chaos 8.00
62 PB,V:Stellarax 8.00
G-Size #1 reprints 10.00

CAPTAIN MARVEL
1989

1 MBr,I:Powerkeg,V:Moonstone . . . 3.00
1 DyM(s),MBr,V:Skinhead(1993) . . 2.50
PF Death of Captain Marvel 8.00
TPB Life of Captain Marvel,JSn . . 15.00

CAPTAIN MARVEL
1995

1 FaN,R:Captain Marvel(son of) . . . 4.00
2 FaN,V:X-Treme,Erik the Red 3.00
3 FaN,V:X-treme 3.00
4 thru 6 FaN . . . . @3.00

CAPTAIN MARVEL
Jan., 2000

1A PDd,Ccs,A:Rick Jones 5.00
1B variant JOy (c) 5.50
2 PDd,Ccs 7.00
3 PDd,Ccs,V:Wendigo 3.00
4 PDd,Ccs,A:Moondragon 3.00
5 PDd,Ccs,V:Drax 3.00
6 PDd,Ccs,V:Marlo 3.00
7 PDd,Ccs,A:Comet Man 3.00
8 PDd,Ccs,V:Super-Skrull 3.00
9 PDd,Ccs,V:Hyssta 3.00
10 PDd,Ccs,V:Genis 3.00
11 PDd,JSn 3.00
12 PDd,Ccs,Maximum Security . . . 3.00
13 PDd,Ccs,V:kids of Yon-Rogg . . . 3.00
14 PDd,Ccs,F:Psycho-Man 3.00
15 PDd,Ccs,F:Psycho-Man 3.00
16 PDd,Ccs,V:Psycho-Man 3.00
17 PDd,JSn,AM,V:Thanos 3.00
18 PDd,JSn,AM,A:Thor,Thanos . . . 3.00
19 PDd,Ccs,A:Thor,Thanos 3.00
20 PDd,Ccs, ... 3.00
21 PDd,Ccs, ... 3.00
22 PDd,Ccs,Supreme Intelligence . . 3.00
23 PDd,Ccs, ... 3.00
24 PDd,Ccs,Negative Zone 3.00
25 PDd,Ccs,V:Quasar, ... 3.00
26 PDd,F:Rick Jones,'Nuff Said . . . 3.00
27 PDd,CCs,Time Flies,pt.1 . . . . . . 3.00
28 PDd,Time Flies, pt.2 . . . . 3.00
29 PDd,Time Flies, pt.3 . . . . 3.00
30 PDd,Time Flies, pt.4 . . . . 3.00
31 PDd,Ccs,F:Marlo,V:Mephisto . . . 3.00
32 PDd,Ccs,F:Moondragon 3.00
33 PDd,Ccs,V:Magus 3.50
34 PDd,Ccs,V:Magus,Rick Jones . . 3.00
35 PDd, last issue 3.00
TPB The Life and Death of
   Captain Marvel, 304-pg. 24.95
TPB First Contact (2002) 16.95

CAPTAIN MARVEL
Sept., 2002

1 PDd,Ccs, U-Decide 3.00
1b Variant JJu(c) 2.25
1c Variant AxR(c) 2.25
2 PDd,Ccs,F:Punisher 2.25
3 PDd,Ccs,AxR 2.25
3a Director's Cut, AxR, 40-pg. 3.50
4 PDd,CCs 2.25
5 PDd,CCs 2.25
6 PDd,CCs 2.25
7 PDd,A:Thor,pt.1 . . . . 2.25

8 PDd,A:Thor,pt.2 . . . . 3.00
9 PDd,Coven,pt.1 . . . . 3.00
10 PDd,Coven,pt.2 . . . . 3.00
11 PDd,Coven,pt.3 . . . . 3.00
12 PDd,Coven,pt.4 . . . . 3.00
13 PDd,Pop,V:Badoon 3.00
14 PDd,accidents do happen 3.00
15 PDd,NA(c),V:Kree 3.00
16 PDd,Crazy Like a Fox,pt.2 . . . . 3.00
17 PDd,Crazy Like a Fox,pt.3 . . . . 3.00
18 PDd,Crazy Like a Fox,pt.4 . . . . 3.00
19 PDd,Odyssey,pt.1 . . . . 3.00
20 PDd,Odyssey,pt.2 . . . . 3.00
21 PDd,Odyssey,pt.3 . . . . 3.00
22 PDd,AsL,Odyssey,pt.4 . . . . 3.00
23 PDd,AsL,Odyssey,pt.5 . . . . 3.00
24 PDd,Odyssey,pt.6 . . . . 3.00
25 PDd,Exit Strategy 3.00
TPB Vol. 1: Nothing to Lose 13.00
TPB Vol. 2: Coven 15.00
TPB Vol. 3: Crazy Like a Fox 15.00
TPB Vol. 4: Odyssey 17.00

CAPTAIN PLANET
Oct., 1991

1 I&O:Captain Planet 5.00
2 thru 12 . . . . @3.00

CAPT. SAVAGE & HIS
LEATHERNECK RAIDERS
Jan., 1968

1 SSh(c),C:Sgt Fury;The Last
   Bansai 60.00
2 SSh(c),O:Hydra;Return of Baron
   Strucker 25.00
3 SSh,Two Against Hydra 25.00
4 SSh,V:Hydra;The Fateful Finale 25.00
5 SSh,The Invincible Enemy 25.00
6 Mission:Save a Howler 25.00
7 SSh,Objective:Ben Grimm 28.00
8 Mission:Foul Ball 25.00
Becomes:

CAPT. SAVAGE & HIS
BATTLEFIELD RAIDERS
1968

9 . . . . 25.00
10 To the Last Man 25.00
11 A:Sergeant Fury 25.00
12 V:The Japanese 25.00
13 The Junk Heap Juggernauts . . . 25.00
14 Savage's First Mission 25.00
15 Within the Temple Waits Death. 22.00
16 V:The Axis Powers 22.00
17 V:The Axis Powers 22.00
18 V:The Axis Powers 22.00
19 March, 1970 . . . . 22.00

CARE BEARS
Star, Nov., 1985

1 . . . . 3.00
2 thru 14 . . . . @3.00

Marvel 1988

15 thru 20 . . . . @3.00

CARNAGE

1-shot Carnage: Its a Wonderful
   Life (1996) 3.00
1-shot Carnage: Mindbomb
   foil cover (1996) 3.50

CARTOON KIDS
Atlas, 1957

1 JMn,A:Dexter the Demon, Little
   Zelda,Willie,Wise Guy 100.00

Captain Marvel Vol. 2 #1
© Marvel Entertainment Group

All comics prices listed are for *Near Mint* condition.

CAR WARRIORS
Epic, 1990
1 Based on Roll Playing Game . . . 2.50
2 Big Race Preparations. 2.50
3 Ft.Delorean-Lansing Race begin. 2.50
4 Race End, Final issue 2.50

CASEY–CRIME PHOTOGRAPHER
Aug., 1949
1 Ph(c),Girl on the Docks 275.00
2 Ph(c),Staats Cotsworth 200.00
3 Ph(c),He Walked With Danger 200.00
4 Ph(c),Lend Me Your Life 200.00
Becomes:

TWO GUN WESTERN
[1st Series], 1950
5 JB,B,I&O:Apache Kid 300.00
6 JMn,The Outcast 225.00
7 Human Sacrifice 225.00
8 JR,DW,A:Kid Colt,Texas Kid,
  Doc Holiday 225.00
9 JMn,GM,A:Kid Colt,Marshall
  `Frosty' Bennet Texas Kid . . 225.00
10. . . . . 225.00
11 thru 14 JMn,June, 1952 . . . @150.00

CASPER
1996
1 From Animated TV show 2.25
2 visit to Harvey Castle. 2.25
3 and 4 . . . . @2.25

CAT, THE
Nov., 1972—June, 1973
1 JM,I&O:The Cat 50.00
2 JM,V:The Owl 25.00
3 BEv,V:Kraken 25.00
4 JSn,V:Man-Bull 30.00

CENTURY: DISTANT SONS
1996
1-shot DAn,48pg. 3.25

CHAMBER OF CHILLS
Nov., 1972
1 SSh,A Dragon Stalks By
  Night,(H.Ellison Adapt.) 40.00
2 FB,BEv,SD,Monster From the
  Mound,(RE Howard Adapt.) . . 20.00
3 FB,BEv,SD, Thing on the Roof . 20.00
4 FB,BEv,SD, Opener of the
  Crypt,(J.Jakes,E.A.Poe Adapt) 20.00
5 FB,BEv,SD, Devils Dowry 20.00
6 FB,BEv,SD, Mud Monster 20.00
7 thru 24 FB,BEv,SD . . . . @20.00
25 FB,BEv,SD Nov., 1976 . . . . . . 20.00

CHAMBER OF DARKNESS
Oct., 1969
1 JB, Tales of Maddening Magic . 75.00
2 NA(script),Enter the Red Death. 50.00
3 JK,BWS,JB, Something Lurks
  on Shadow Mountain. 40.00
4 JK Monster Man Came Walking,
  BU:BWS 100.00
5 JCr,JK,SD, And Fear Shall
  Follow, plus Lovecraft adapt.. 25.00
6 SD 25.00
7 SD,JK,BWr, Night of the
  Gargoyle 55.00
8 BWr(c),DA,BEv, Beast that Walks
  Like a Man Special, 5 Tales of
  Maddening Magic, Jan.,1972 100.00

Chamber of Darkness #2
© Marvel Entertainment Group

Becomes:

MONSTERS ON THE PROWL
1971
9 SAD,BWS,Monster Stories
  Inc,Gorgilla 40.00
10 JK,Roc 25.00
11 JK,A Titan Walks the Land 25.00
12 HT,JK,Gomdulla The Living
  Pharoah 25.00
13 HT,JK,Tragg 30.00
14 JK,SD,Return of the Titan. 30.00
15 FrG,JK,The Thing Called It 25.00
16 JSe,SD,JK, Serpent God of
  Lost Swamp,A:King Kull 25.00
17 JK,SD,Coming of Colossus . . . 25.00
18 JK,SD,Bruttu 25.00
19 JK,SD,Creature From the
  Black Bog 25.00
20 JK,SD,Oog Lives Again 25.00
21 JK,SD,A Martian Stalks
  the City 25.00
22 JK,SD,Monster Runs Amok . . . 18.00
23 JK,The Return of Grogg 18.00
24 JK,SD, Magnetor 18.00
25 JK,Colossus Lives Again 18.00
26 JK,SD,The Two Headed Thing . 18.00
27 JK,Sserpo 18.00
28 JK,The Coming of Monsteroso. 18.00
29 JK,SD Monster at my Window . 18.00
30 JK,Diablo Demon from the 5th
  Dimension, Oct., 1974. . . . . . 18.00

CHAMPIONS
Oct., 1975
1 GK(c),DH,I&O:Champions. 35.00
2 DH,O:Champions. 15.00
3 GT,Assault on Olympus 13.00
4 GT,`Murder at Malibu' 12.00
5 DH,I:Rampage 15.00
6 JK(c),GT,V:Rampage 15.00
7 GT,O:Black Widow,I:Darkstar . 15.00
8 BH,O:Black Widow 12.00
9 BH,BL,V:Crimson Dynamo 12.00
10 BH,BL,V:Crimson Dynamo 12.00
11 JBy,A:Black Goliath,Hawkeye. . 16.00
12 JBy,BL,V:Stranger. 16.00
13 JBy,BL,V:Kamo Tharn. 16.00
14 JBy,I:Swarm 16.00
15 JBy,V:Swarm. 16.00
16 BH,A:Magneto,Dr.Doom,
  Beast. 12.00

17 GT,JBy,V:Sentinels,last issue . . 13.00

CHILDREN OF THE VOYAGE
Frontier 1993
1 F:Sam Wantling 3.25
2 Counterfeit Man 2.25
3 V:Voyager 2.25
4 Last Issue 2.25

CHILI
May, 1969
1 Millie's Rival. 90.00
2 . . . . 50.00
3 . . . . 50.00
4 . . . . 50.00
5 . . . . 50.00
6 thru 15 . . . . @30.00

Chili #8
© Marvel Entertainment Group

16 thru 20 . . . . @25.00
21 thru 25 . . . . @22.00
26 Dec., 1973. . . . . 22.00
Spec.#1, 1971. . . . . 45.00

CHUCK NORRIS
Star, Jan.–Sept., 1987
1 SD 4.00
2 thru 5 . . . . @5.00

CINDY COMICS
See: KRAZY COMICS

CITIZEN V
April, 2001
1 (of 3) FaN,F:V-Battalion. 3.25
2 FaN,. 3.25
3 FaN,F:Iron Cross. 3.25

CITIZEN V & THE V BATTALION: THE EVERLASTING
Feb., 2002
1 (of 4) FaN,. 3.25
2 FaN,Marduk. 3.25
3 FaN,. 3.25
4 FaN, concl.. . . . . 3.25

Clandestine #3
© *Marvel Entertainment Group*

CLANDESTINE
Oct., 1994–Sept., 1995
Preview issue, Intro (1994) 2.00
1 MFm,AD,foil(c) 3.25
2 Wraparound (c),A:Silver Surfer . . 2.75
3 I:Argent,Kimera,A:SilverSurfer. . . 2.75
4 R:Adam 2.75
5 MFm,AD,O:Adam Destine 2.75
6 A:Spider-Man 2.75
7 A:Spider-Man 2.75
8 A:Dr.Strange. 2.75
9 thru 14 . . . . @2.75
TPB AD,MFm (1997) 12.00

CLASSIC CONAN
See: CONAN SAGA

CLASSIC X-MEN
See: X-MEN

CLIVE BARKER'S
BOOK OF THE DAMNED
Epic, Nov., 1991
1 JBo,Hellraiser companion 5.00
2 MPa,Hellraiser Companion 5.00

CLIVE BARKER'S
HELLRAISER
Epic, 1989–93
1 BWr,DSp 7.00
2 . . . . 6.00
3 . . . . 6.50
4 . . . . 4.50
5 . . . . 4.50
6 . . . . 7.00
7 The Devil's Brigade #1 . . . . 7.00
8 The Devil's Brigade #2&3 . . . . . . 7.00
9 The Devil's Brigade #4&5 . . . . . . 7.00
10 The Devil's Brigade #6&7
   foil Cover 5.00
11 The Devil's Brigade #8&9 . . . . . . 4.50
12 The Devil's Brigade #10-12 . . . . 4.50
13 MMi,RH,Devil's Brigade #13. . . . 4.50
14 The Devil's Brigade #14 . . . . 5.00
15 The Devil's Brigade #15 . . . . 5.00
16 E:Devil's Brigade 5.00
17 BHa,DR,The Harrowing 10.00
18 O:Harrowers 5.00

19 A:Harrowers 5.00
20 NGa(s),DMc,Last Laugh 9.00
Dark Holiday Spec.#1 (1992). 5.00
Spring Slaughter Spec.#1 (1994). . . 7.00
Summer Spec.#1 (1992 . . . . 6.00

CLOAK & DAGGER
(Limited Series) Oct., 1983
1 RL,TA,I:Det.O'Reilly,
   Father Delgado 3.00
2 RL,TA,V:Duane Hellman 3.00
3 RL,TA,V:Street Gang 3.00
4 RL,TA,O:Cloak & Dagger, ... 3.00

CLOAK & DAGGER
[1st Regular Series], July, 1985
1 RL,Pornography. 3.00
2 RL,Dagger's mother 2.50
3 RL,A:Spider-Man 2.50
4 RL,Secret Wars II 2.50
5 RL,I:Mayhem 2.50
6 RL,A:Mayhem 2.50
7 RL,A:Mayhem 2.50
8 TA, Drugs. 2.50
9 AAd,TA,A:Mayhem. 2.75
10 BBI,TA,V:Dr. Doom 2.50
11 BBI,TA,Last Issue 2.50

[Mutant Misadventures of]
CLOAK & DAGGER
[2nd Regular Series]
Oct., 1988
1 CR(i),A:X-Factor 3.00
2 CR(i),C:X-Factor,V:Gromitz 2.50
3 SW(i),JLe(c),A:Gromitz 2.50
4 TA(i),Inferno,R:Mayhem 2.50
5 TA(i),R:Mayhem. 2.50
6 TA(i),A:Mayhem 2.50
7 A:Crimson Daffodil,V:Ecstacy . . . 2.50
8 Acts of Vengeance prelude 2.50
9 Acts of Vengeance. 2.50
10 Acts of Vengeance,X-Force
   name used,Dr.Doom 2.50
11 . . . . 2.50
12 A:Dr.Doom. 2.50
13 A:Dr.Doom. 2.50
14 & 15 RL . . . . @2.50
16 RL,A:Spider-Man 2.50
17 A:Spider-Man, ... 2.50
18 Inf.Gauntlet X-over,
   A:Spider-Man, Ghost Rider 2.50
19 O:Cloak & Dagger,final issue . . . 2.50
GN Predator and Prey 15.00

A CLUELESS VALENTINE
1 characters from movie, 48pg. . . . 2.50

CODENAME: GENETIX
1993
1 PGa,A:Wolverine 3.00
2 PGa,V:Prime EvilA:Wolverine . . . 3.00
3 . . . . 3.00
4 A:Wolverine,Ka-Zar 3.00

CODE OF HONOR
1996
1 (of 4) CDi,TnS,I:Jeff Piper,
   fully painted 6.00
2 thru 4 CDi, ... @6.00

CODE NAME: SPITFIRE
See: SPITFIRE AND
THE TROUBLESHOOTERS

COLOSSUS
Aug., 1997
1-shot BRa,Colossus & Meggan
   V:Arcade, 48pg 3.50

COLOSSUS:
GOD'S COUNTRY
PF V:Cold Warriors 7.00

COMBAT
Atlas, June, 1952
1 JMn,War Stories, Bare
   Bayonets 275.00
2 RH, Break Thru,(Dedicated to
   US Infantry) 150.00
3 JMn(c) 100.00
4 BK 125.00
5 thru 10 . . . . @100.00
11 April, 1953 . . . . 120.00

COMBAT CASEY
See: WAR COMBAT

COMBAT KELLY AND
THE DEADLY DOZEN
Atlas, Nov., 1951
1 RH,Korean war stories 350.00
2 Big Push 175.00
3 The Volunteer 125.00
4 JMn,V:Communists 125.00
5 JMn,OW,V:Communists. 125.00
6 V:Communists 125.00
7 JMn,V:Communists 125.00
8 JMn,Death to the Reds 125.00
9 . . . . 125.00
10 JMn(c) 125.00
11 . . . . 100.00
12 thru 16. . . . . @100.00
17 A:Combat Casey 125.00
18 A:Battle Brady 65.00
19 V:Communists. 65.00
20 V:Communists 65.00
21 Transvestite Cover 75.00
22 thru 40 . . . . @65.00
41 thru 44 Aug., 1957 . . . . @65.00

COMBAT KELLY
June, 1972
1 JM, Stop the Luftwaffe 30.00
2 The Big Breakout. 15.00
3 O:Combat Kelly 20.00
4 Mutiny,A:Sgt.Fury and the
   Howling Commandoes 20.00
5 Escape or Die 15.00
6 The Fortress of Doom 15.00
7 Nun Hostage,V:Nazis 15.00
8 V:Nazis. 15.00
9 Oct., 1973 . . . . 15.00

COMET MAN
Feb., 1987
1 BSz(c),I:Comet Man 2.50
2 BSz(c),A:Mr.Fantastic 2.50
3 BSz(c),A:Hulk 2.50
4 BSz(c),A:Fantistic Four 2.50
5 BSz(c),A:Fantastic Four. 2.50
6 BSz(c),Last issue, July,1987 . . . . 2.50

COMIX BOOK
(black & white magazine) 1974
1 BW 65.00
2 BW 50.00
3 . . . . 35.00
4 & 5 . . . . @30.00

COMIX ZONE
1 video game tie-in 2.50
2 video game tie-in 2.50

Commando Adventures #2
© Marvel Entertainment Group

COMMANDO ADVENTURES
Atlas, June, 1957
1 Seek, Find and Destroy 150.00
2 MD, Hit 'em and Hit 'em
   Hard, Aug.,1957 . . . . 100.00

COMPLETE COMICS
See: AMAZING COMICS

COMPLETE MYSTERY
Aug., 1948
1 Seven Dead Men 600.00
2 Jigsaw of Doom 450.00
3 Fear in the Night 450.00
4 A Squealer Dies Fast 450.00
Becomes:

TRUE COMPLETE MYSTERY
1949
5 Rice Mancini,
   The Deadly Dude 300.00
6 Ph(c),Frame-up that Failed . . 250.00
7 Ph(c),Caught 250.00
8 Ph(c),The Downfall of Mr.
   Anderson, Oct., 1949 . . . . . 250.00

CONAN
1995–96
1 Pit Fighter 3.00
2 LHa,Hyborean tortue factory . . . 3.00
3 V:Cannibals 3.00
4 LHa,JP,Rune Conan Prelude . . . 3.00
5 LHa,V:yeti 3.00
6 LHa, the plague 3.00
7 LHa,BBI,V:The Iron Man 3.00
8 thru 11 . . . . @3.00

CONAN: DEATH COVERED IN GOLD
July, 1999
1 (of 3) RTs 3.00
2 RTs 3.00
3 RTs,JB,concl. 3.00

CONAN THE ADVENTURER
1994–95
1 RT(s),RK,Red Foil(c) 3.00
2 RT(s),RK 2.50
3 RT(s),RK 2.50
4 thru 14 . . . . @2.50

CONAN THE BARBARIAN
Oct., 1970
1 BWS/DA,O:Conan,A:Kull 350.00
2 BWS/SB,Lair o/t Beast-Men . . 125.00
3 BWS,SB,Grey God Passes . . . 225.00
4 BWS,SB,Tower o/t Elephant . . 100.00
5 BWS,Zukala's Daughter 100.00
6 BWS,SB,Devil Wings Over
   Shadizar 75.00
7 BWS,SB,DA,C:Thoth-Amon,
   I:Set 75.00
8 BWS,TS,TP,Keepers o/t Crypt . . 75.00
9 BWS,SB,Garden of Fear 75.00
10 BWS,SB,JSe,Beware Wrath of
   Anu;BU:Kull 100.00
11 BWS,SB,Talons of Thak 100.00
12 BWS,GK,Dweller in the Dark,
   Blood of the Dragon B.U. 75.00
13 BWS,SB,Web o/t Spider-God . . 75.00
14 BWS,SB,Green Empress of
   Melnibone 75.00
15 BWS,SB 75.00
16 BWS,Frost Giant's Daughter . . 60.00
17 GK,Gods of Bal-Sagoth,
   A:Fafnir 35.00
18 GK,DA,Thing in the Temple,
   A:Fafnir 35.00
19 BWS,DA,Hawks from
   the Sea 60.00
20 BWS,DA,Black Hound of
   Vengeance,A:Fafnir 60.00
21 BWS,CR,VM,DA,SB, Monster
   of the Monoliths 45.00
22 BWS,DA,rep.Conan #1 . . . . . . 50.00
23 BWS,DA,Shadow of the
   Vulture,I:Red Sonja 75.00
24 BWS,Song of Red Sonja 75.00
25 JB,SB,JSe,Mirrors of Kharam
   Akkad,A:Kull 25.00
26 JB,Hour of the Griffin 20.00
27 JB,Blood of Bel-Hissar 20.00
28 JB,Moon of Zembabwei 20.00
29 JB,Two Against Turan 20.00
30 JB,The Hand of Nergal 20.00
31 JB,Shadow in the Tomb 12.00
32 JB,Flame Winds of Lost Khitai . 12.00
33 JB,Death & 7 Wizards 12.00
34 JB,Temptress in the Tower
   of Flame 12.00
35 JB,Hell-Spawn of Kara-Shehr . . 12.00
36 JB,Beware of Hyrkanians
   bearing Gifts 12.00
37 NA,Curse of the Golden Skull . . 25.00
38 JB,Warrior & Were-Woman . . . 12.00
39 JB,Dragon from the
   Inland Sea 12.00
40 RB,Fiend from Forgotten City . . 12.00
41 JB,Garden of Death & Life 15.00
42 JB,Night of the Gargoyle 15.00
43 JB,Tower o/Blood,A:RedSonja . 15.00
44 JB,Flame&Fiend,A:RedSonja . . 15.00
45 JB,NA,Last Ballad of
   Laza-Lanti 12.00
46 JB,NA,JSt,Curse of the
   Conjurer 12.00
47 JB,DA,Goblins in the
   Moonlight 12.00
48 JB,DG,DA,Rats Dance at Raven
   gard,BU:Red Sonja 12.00
49 JB,DG,Wolf-Woman 12.00
50 JB,DG,Dweller in the Pool 12.00

51 JB,DG,Man Born of Demon 8.00
52 JB,TP,Altar and the Scorpion . . . 8.00
53 JB,FS,Brothers of the Blade 8.00
54 JB,TP,Oracle of Ophir 8.00
55 JB,TP,Shadow on the Land 8.00
56 JB,High Tower in the Mist 8.00
57 MP,Incident in Argos 8.00
58 JB,Queen o/tBlackCoast,
   2nd A:Belit 10.00
59 JB,Ballad of Belit,O:Belit. 7.00
60 JB,Riders o/t River Dragons 7.00
61 JB,She-Pirate,I:Amra 7.00
62 JB,Lord of the Lions,O:Amra . . . 7.00
63 JB,Death Among Ruins,
   V&D:Amra 7.00
64 JSon,AM,rep.Savage Tales#5 . . 7.00
65 JB,Fiend o/tFeatheredSerpent . . 7.00
66 JB,Daggers & Death Gods,
   C:Red Sonja 6.00
67 JB,Talons of the Man-Tiger,
   A:Red Sonja 6.00
68 JB,Of Once & Future Kings,
   V:KingKull,A:Belit,Red Sonja . . 6.00
69 VM,Demon Out of the Deep 6.00
70 JB,City in the Storm 6.00
71 JB,Secret of Ashtoreth 6.00
72 JB,Vengeance in Asgalun 6.00
73 JB,..In the Well of Skelos 6.00
74 JB,Battle at the Black Walls
   C:Thoth-Amon 6.00
75 JB,Hawk-Riders of Harakht 7.00
76 JB,Swordless in Stygia 7.00
77 JB,When Giants Walk
   the Earth 7.00
78 JB,rep.Savage Sword #1,
   A:Red Sonja 7.00
79 HC,Lost Valley of Iskander 7.00
80 HC,Trial By Combat 6.00
81 HC,The Eye of the Serpent 5.00
82 HC,The Sorceress o/t Swamp . . 5.00
83 HC,The Dance of the Skull 5.00
84 JB,Two Against the Hawk-City,
   I:Zula 5.00
85 JB,Of Swordsmen & Sorcerers,
   O:Zulu 5.00
86 JB,Devourer of the Dead 5.00
87 TD, rep. Savage Sword #3 . . . . . 5.00
88 JB,Queen and the Corsairs 5.00
89 JB,Sword & the Serpent,
   A:Thoth-Amon 5.00
90 JB,Diadem of the Giant-Kings . . 5.00
91 JB,Savage Doings in Shem 5.00
92 JB,The Thing in the Crypt 5.00
93 JB,Of Rage & Revenge 5.00

Conan the Barbarian #39
© Marvel Entertainment Group

94 JB,BeastKing ofAbombi,L:Zulu . . 5.00	160 Veil of Darkness 3.00	209 VS,GI,Heku epilogue 2.50
95 JB,The Return of Amra 5.00	161 JB,House of Skulls,A:Fafnir . . . 3.00	210 VS,GI,V:Sevante 2.50
96 JB,Long Night of Fang	162 JB,Destroyer in the Flame,	211 VS,GI,V:Sevante 2.50
& Talon,pt.1 . . . . 5.00	A:Fafnir 3.00	212 EC,GI 2.50
97 JB,Long Night of Fang	163 JB,Cavern of the Vines of	213 V:Ghamud Assassins 2.50
& Talon,pt.2 . . . . 5.00	Doom,A:Fafnir 3.00	214 AA 2.50
98 JB,Sea-Woman 5.00	164 The Jeweled Sword of Tem . . . 3.00	215 VS,AA,Conan Enslaved 2.50
99 JB,Devil Crabs o/t Dark Cliffs . . 5.00	165 JB,V:Nadine 3.00	216 V:Blade of Zed 2.50
100 JB,Death on the Black Coast,	166 JB,GI,Blood o/t Titan,A:Fafnir . . 3.00	217 JLe(c),V:Blade of Zed 2.50
D:Belit (double size) 7.00	167 JB,Creature From Time's	218 JLe(c),V:Picts 2.50
101 JB,The Devil has many Legs . . 3.00	Dawn,A:Fafnir 3.00	219 JLe(c),V:Forgotten Beasts 2.50
102 JB,The Men Who	168 JB,Bird Woman & the Beast . . . 3.00	220 Conan the Pirate. 2.50
Drink Blood. 3.00	169 JB,Tomb of the Scarlet Mage . . 3.00	221 Conan the Pirate. 2.50
103 JB,Bride of the Vampire 3.00	170 JB,Dominion of the Dead,	222 AA,DP,Revenge 2.50
104 JB,The Vale of Lost Women . . . 3.00	A&D:Fafnir 3.00	223 AA,Religious Cult 2.50
105 JB,Whispering Shadows 3.00	171 JB,Barbarian Death Song 3.00	224 AA,Cannibalism. 2.50
106 JB,Chaos in Kush 3.00	172 JB,Reavers in Borderland. 3.00	225 AA,Conan Blinded. 2.50
107 JB,Demon of the Night 3.00	173 JB,Honor Among Thieves 3.00	226 AA,Quest for Mystic Jewel 2.50
108 JB,Moon-Eaters of Darfar 3.00	174 JB,V:Tetra 3.00	227 AA,Mystic Jewel,pt.2 . . . . 2.50
109 JB,Sons of the Bear God 3.00	175 JB,V:Spectre ofDeath 3.00	228 AA,Cannibalism,pt.1 . . . . 2.50
110 JB,Beward the Bear of Heaven 3.00	176 JB,Argos Rain. 2.50	229 AA,Cannibalism,pt.2 . . . . 2.50
111 JB,Cimmerian Against a City. . . 3.00	177 JB,V:Nostume 2.50	230 FS,SDr,Citadel,pt.1 . . . . 2.50
112 JB,Buryat Besieged 3.00	178 JB,A:Tetra,Well of Souls 2.50	231 FS,DP,Citadel,pt.2. . . . . 2.50
113 JB,A Devil in the Family 3.00	179 JB,End of all there is,A:Kiev . . . 2.50	232 RLm,Birth of Conan 3.00
114 JB,The Shadow of the Beast . . 3.00	180 JBV:AnitRenrut 2.50	233 RLm,DA,B:Conan as youth . . . 2.50
115 JB,A War of Wizards, A:Red	181 JB,V:KingMaddoc II 2.50	234 RLm,DA 2.50
Sonja double size 10th Anniv.	182 JB,V:King of Shem 2.50	235 RLm,DA 2.50
(L:Roy Thomas script) 4.00	183 JB,V:Imhotep 2.50	236 RLm,DA 2.50
116 JB,NA,Crawler in the Mist. 5.00	184 JB,V:Madoc. 2.50	237 DA,V:Jormma 2.50
117 JB,Corridor of Mullah-Kajar. . . . 3.00	185 JB,R:Tetra 2.50	238 DA,D:Conan 2.50
118 JB,Valley of Forever Night 3.00	186 JB,The Crimson Brotherhood . . 2.50	239 Conan Possessed. 2.50
119 JB,Voice of One Long Gone . . . 3.00	187 JB,V:Council of Seven 2.50	240 Conan Possessed. 2.50
120 JB,The Hand of Erlik. 3.00	188 JB,V:Devourer-Souls 2.50	241 TM(c),R:RoyThomasScript 3.50
121 JB,BMc,Price of Perfection. . . . 3.00	189 JB,V:Devourer-Souls 2.50	242 JLe(c),A:Red Sonja 2.50
122 JB,BMc,The City Where Time	190 JB,Devourer-Souls 2.50	243 WPo(c),V:Zukala. 2.50
Stood Still. 3.00	191 Deliverance. 2.50	244 A:Red Sonja,Zula 2.50
123 JB,BMc,Horror Beneath the	192 JB,V:TheKeeper 2.50	245 A:Red Sonja,V:King
Hills 3.00	193 Devourer-Souls. 2.50	of Vampires 2.50
124 JB,BMc,the Eternity War. 3.00	194 V:Devourer-Souls 2.50	246 A:Red Sonja,V:MistMonster . . . 2.50
125 JB,BMc,the Witches ofNexxx . . 3.00	195 Blood of Ages 2.50	247 A:Red Sonja,Zula 2.50
126 JB,BMc,Blood Red Eye	196 V:Beast 2.50	248 V:Zulu 2.50
of Truth 3.00	197 A:Red Sonja 2.50	249 A:Red Sonja,Zula 2.50
127 GK,Snow Haired Woman	198 A:Red Sonja 2.50	250 A:RedSonja,Zula,V:Zug
of the Wastes 3.00	199 O:Kaleb. 2.50	double size. 5.00
128 GK,And Life Sprang Forth	200 JB,D.sizeV:Dev-Souls 5.00	251 Cimmeria,V:Shumu Gorath. . . . 3.00
From These 3.00	201 NKu,GI,Thulsa Doom 2.50	252 ECh. 3.00
129 GK,The Creation Quest 3.00	202 . . . . 2.50	253 ECh,V:Kulan-Goth(X-Men
130 GK,The Quest Ends 3.00	203 V:Thulsa Doom 2.50	Villain) 3.00
131 GK,The Ring of Rhax 3.00	204 VS,GI,A:Red Sonja,I:Strakkus . 2.50	254 ECh,V:Shuma-Gorath (Dr.
132 GK,Games of Gharn 3.00	205 A:Red Sonja 2.50	Strange Villain) 3.00
133 GK,The Witch of Windsor 3.00	206 VS,GI,Heku trilogy,pt.1 . . . . . . 2.50	255 ECh,V:Shuma-Gorath 3.00
134 GK,A Hitch in Time 3.00	207 VS,GI,Heku,pt.2,O:Kote 2.50	256 ECh,D:Nemedia's King 3.00
135 MS,JRu,Forest of the Night . . . 3.00	208 VS,GI,Heku,pt.3 . . . . 2.50	257 ECh,V:Queen Vammator 3.00
136 JB,The River of Death 3.00		258 AA(i),A:Kulan Gath 3.00
137 AA,Titans Gambit 3.00		259 V:Shuma-Gorath 3.00
138 VM,Isle of the Dead 3.00		260 AA(i),V:Queen Vammatar 3.00
139 VM,In the Lair of		261 V:Cult of the Death Goddess . . 3.00
the Damned. 3.00		262 V:The Panther. 3.00
140 JB,Spider Isle 3.00		263 V:Malaq. 3.00
141 JB,The Web Tightens 3.00		264 V:Kralic 3.00
142 JB,The Maze,the Man,		265 V:Karlik 3.00
the Monster 3.00		266 Conan the Renegade (adapt.) . 3.00
143 JB,Life Among the Dead. 3.00		267 adapt.,pt.2 . . . . 3.00
144 JB,The Blade & the Beast 3.00		268 adapt.,pt.3 . . . . 3.00
145 Son of Cimmeria. 3.00		269 V:Agohoth,Prince Borin. 3.00
146 JB,Night o/t Three Sisters. 3.00		270 Devourer of the Dead 3.00
147 JB,Tower of Mitra 3.00		271 V:Devourer of Souls 3.00
148 JB,The Plague of Forlek. 3.00		272 V:Devourer 3.00
149 JB,Deathmark. 3.00		273 V:Purple Lotus 3.00
150 JB,Tower of Flame 3.00		274 V:She-Bat 3.00
151 JB,Vale of Death. 3.00		275 RTs(s),Last Issue cont. in
152 JB,Dark Blade of		Savage Sword of Conan 5.00
Jergal Zadh 3.00		G-Size#1 GK,TS,Hour of the
153 JB,Bird Men of Akah Ma'at . . . 3.00		Dragon, inc.rep.Conan#3,
154 JB,the Man-Bats of		I:Belit 25.00
Ur-Xanarrh. 3.00		G-Size#2 GK,TS,Conan Bound,
155 JB,SL,The Anger of Conan . . . 3.00		inc. rep Conan #5 . . . . 12.00
156 JB,The Curse 3.00		G-Size#3 GK,TS,To Tarantia
157 JB,The Wizard 3.00		& the Tower,inc.rep.Conan#6 . . 8.00
158 JB,Night of the Wolf 3.00	*Conan The Barbarian #169*	G-Size#4,GK,FS,Swords of the
159 JB,Cauldron of the Doomed . . . 3.00	*© Marvel Entertainment Group*	South,inc.rep.Conan #7. . . . . . 8.00

Conan The Barbarian #169
© Marvel Entertainment Group

Conan The Destroyer Movie Special #2
© Marvel Entertainment Group

G-Size#5 rep.Conan #14,#15
  & Back-up story #12 . . . . 8.00
KingSz.#1 rep.Conan #2,#4. . . . . . 13.00
Ann.#2 BWS,Phoenix on the Sword
  A:Thoth-Amon 10.00
Ann.#3 JB,HC,Mountain of
  the Moon God, B.U.Kull story . . 8.00
Ann.#4 JB,Return of the
  Conqueror,A:Zenobia 8.00
Ann.#5 JB,W:Conan/Zenobia 5.00
Ann.#6 GK,King of the
  Forgotten People. 5.00
Ann.#7 JB,Red Shadows
  & Black Kraken 4.00
Ann.#8 VM,Dark Night of the
  White Queen 4.00
Ann.#9 . . . . 4.00
Ann.#10 Scorched Earth
  (Conan #176 x-over) 4.00
Ann.#11 . . . . 4.00
Conan-Barbarian Movie Spec.#1. . . 3.00
Conan-Barbarian Movie Spec.#2. . . 3.00
Conan-Destroyer Movie Spec.#1. . . 3.00
Conan-Destroyer Movie Spec.#2. . . 3.00
Red Nails Special Ed.BWS 4.00
TPB Conan & Ravagers Out
  of Time. 10.00
TPB Conan the Reaver 10.00
TPB Conan the Rogue,JB 10.00
TPB Horn of Azroth 10.00
TPB Skull of Set. 10.00

CONAN: THE FLAME AND THE FIEND
June, 2000
1 (of 3) RTs,GI,V:Kulan Gath 3.00
2 RTs,GI,Bone Dragon 3.00
3 RTs,GI,concl. 3.00

CLASSIC CONAN
June, 1987
1 BWS,rep. 7.00
2 BWS,rep. 5.00
3 BWS,rep. 5.00
Becomes:

CONAN SAGA
1987
4 thru 10 rep. . . . . @3.50
11 thru 98 rep. . . . . @3.00

CONAN CLASSICS
1994–95
1 rep. Conan #1 . . . . 2.25
2 rep. Conan #2 . . . . 2.25
3 rep. Conan #3 . . . . 2.25
2 thru 11 rep. . . . . @2.25

CONAN/RUNE
1995
1 BWS,Conan Vs. Rune 3.50

CONAN
1997
1 CCt, ... 2.00
2 CCt,V:Sorcerer. 2.00
3 (of 3) CCt, ... 2.00

CONAN: RIVER OF BLOOD
April, 1998
1 (of 3) Valeria, vs. giant crocs. . . . 2.50
2 Caught in the middle of a war . . . 2.50
3 Lord of the Crocodiles, concl. . . . 2.50

CONAN THE BARBARIAN VS. THE LORD OF THE SPIDERS
Jan., 1998
1 (of 3) RTs,V:Harpagus 2.50
2 RTs, ... 2.50
3 RTs,V:Harpagus. 2.50

CONAN: THE RETURN OF STYRM
July, 1998
1 (of 3) V:Mecora 2.50
2 (of 3) V:Mecora 3.00
3 conclusion 3.00

CONAN: THE SCARLET SWORD
Oct., 1998
1 (of 3) RTs,V:Thun'da 3.00
2 RTs,A:Helliana 3.00
3 RTs,conclusion. 3.00

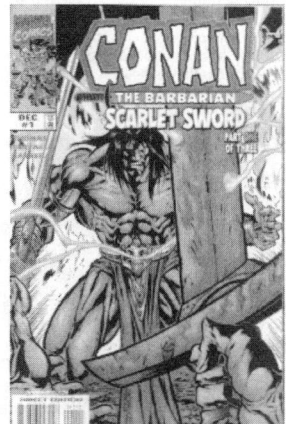

Conan: The Scarlet Sword #1
© Marvel Entertainment Group

CONAN: THE USURPER
Oct., 1997
1 (of 3) CDi,KJ,Conan attacks
  Cimmeria? 2.50
2 CDi,KJ, ... 2.50
3 CDi,KJ, concl. 2.50

KING CONAN
March, 1980
1 JB/ECh,I:Conn,V:Thoth-Amon . . . 7.00
2 JB,Black Sphinx of Nebthu 4.00
3 JB,Dragon Wings Over
  Zembabwei 4.00
4 JB,V:Thoth-Amon. 4.00
5 JB,The Sorcerer in the Realm
  of Madness 4.00
6 JB,The Lady's Name Is..Trouble . 4.00
7 PS,JB. 4.00
8 A:Queen Reclaimed. 4.00
9 JB,V:Medusa Monster 4.00
10 V:Sea Monster 4.00
11 V:Giant Totem Monster 4.00
12 V:Monster 4.00
13 V:Monster 4.00
14 V:Demon 4.00
15 V:Sea Monster 4.00
16 Conan Into Battle 4.00
17 A:Conn 4.00
18 King of the Freaks? 4.00
19 MK(c),Skull & X-Bones cover . . . 4.00
Becomes:

CONAN THE KING
1984
20 MS,The Prince is Dead. 4.00
21 MS,Shadows. 3.00
22 GI/MS,The Black Dragons,Prince
  Conan II back-up story begins . 3.00
23 MS/GI,Ordeal 3.00
24 GI/MS,Fragments:AWitch'sTale . 3.00
25 MS/GI,Daggers 3.00
26 MS/GI,PrinceConanII B.U.ends . 3.00
27 MS/GI,A Death in Stygia 3.00
28 MS/GI,Call of the Wild,
  A:Red Sonja 3.00
29 MS,The Sleeping Lion 3.00
30 GI,Revenge on the Black River . 3.00
31 GI,Force of Arms. 3.00
32 GI,Juggernaut 3.00
33 . . . . 3.00
34 . . . . 3.00
35 . . . . 3.00
36 . . . . 3.00
37 AW,Sack of Belverus 3.00
38 MM,A:Taurus,Leora. 3.00
39 The Tower 3.00
40 . . . . 3.00
41 V:Leora 3.00
42 Thee Armada,A:Conn 3.00
43 . . . . 3.00
44 . . . . 3.00
45 V:Caliastros. 3.00
46 V:Caliastros. 3.00
47 TD,V:Caliastros. 3.00
48 . . . . 3.00
49 . . . . 3.00
50 GI,50th Anniversary issue. 3.00
51 thru 55 GI . . . . @3.00

CONAN THE SAVAGE
1995–96
(Black & White Magazine)
1 New Series 3.00
2 CDi,Conan a gladiator 3.00
3 V:Monster. 3.00
4 CDi,Conan vs. Rune 3.00
5 MBn,VMk,Ice age tale 3.00
6 Bros.Hildebrandt(c),V:FallenIdol . 3.00
7 CDi,F:Iron Maidens 3.00

MARVEL

MARVEL

8 & 9 . . . . @3.00
10 JB story, 48pg. 3.00

CONEHEADS
1994
1 Based Saturday Night Live 2.25
2 There Goes the Neighborhood . . 2.25
3 In Paris. 2.25

CONSPIRACY
Dec., 1997
1 (of 2) DAn,Were the origins of
  Marvel's superheroes really a
  conspiracy, not an accident? . . . 3.00
2 DAn,concl. 3.00

CONTEST OF CHAMPIONS
June, 1982
1 JR2,Grandmaster vs. Mistress
  Death, A:Alpha Flight. 8.00
2 JR2,Grandmaster vs. Mistress
  Death, A:X-Men. 7.00
3 JR2,D:Grandmaster, Rebirth
  Collector, A:X-Men. 7.00

CONTEST OF CHAMPIONS II
July, 1999
1 (of 5) CCI,Marvel vs. Marvel 3.00
2 CCI,Atlas vs. Storm 3.00
3 CCI,super hero slugfest 3.00
4 CCI 3.00
5 CCI, conclusion 3.00
TPB Contest of Champions,
  '70s rep.. . . . . 18.00

COPS: THE JOB
1992
1 MGo(c),V:Serial killer. 2.25
2 MGo(c). 2.25
3 MGo(c),V:Eviscerator. 2.25
4 MGo(c),D:Eviscerator,Nick 2.25

COSMIC POWERS
1994
1 RMz(s),RLm,JP,F:Thanos 2.75
2 RMz(s),JMr,F:Terrax 2.75
3 RMz(s),F:Jack of Hearts 2.75
4 RMz(s),RLm,F:Legacy. 2.75
5 RMz(s),F&O:Morg 2.75
6 RMz(s),F&O:Tyrant 2.75

COSMIC POWERS UNLIMITED
1995–96
1 Surfer vs. Thanos 4.25
2 Jack of Hearts vs. Jakar 4.25
3 GWt,JB,F:Lunatik,64pg. 4.25
4 GWt,SEa,cont.StarMasters#3 . . 4.25
5 GWt,SEa,R:Captain Universe . . . 4.25

COUNT DUCKULA
Star, Nov., 1988
1 O:CountDuckula,B:DangerMouse 4.00
2 A:Danger Mouse 3.00
3 thru 15 . . . . @3.00

COWBOY ACTION
See: WESTERN THRILLERS

COWBOY ROMANCES
Oct., 1949
1 Ph(c),Outlaw and the Lady . . . 275.00
2 Ph(c),William Holden/Mona
  Freeman,Streets of Laredo . . 250.00
3 Phc,Romance in
  Roaring Valley 150.00
Becomes:

YOUNG MEN
1950
4 A Kid Names Shorty. 225.00
5 Jaws of Death 150.00
6 Man-Size 150.00
7 The Last Laugh 150.00
8 Adventure stories continued . . 150.00

Young Men #25
© Marvel Entertainment Group

9 Draft Dodging story 150.00
10 JMn,US Draft Story. 150.00
11 Adventure stories continued . . 150.00
12 JMn,B:On the Battlefield,
  inc.Spearhead 150.00
13 RH,Break-through 150.00
14 GC,RH,Fox Hole. 150.00
15 GC,JMn,Battlefield stories
  cont. 150.00
16 Sniper Patrol 150.00
17 Battlefield stories cont, ... 150.00
18 BEv,Warlord 150.00
19 BEv 150.00
20 BEv,E:On the Battlefield 150.00
21 B:Flash Foster and his High
  Gear Hot Shots 150.00
22 Screaming Tires 150.00
23 E:Flash Foster and his High
  Gear Hot Shots 150.00
24 BEv,B:Capt. America,Human
  Torch,Sub-Mariner,O:Capt.
  America,Red Skull 3,600.00
25 BEv,JR, Human Torch,Capt.
  America,Sub-Mariner 1,500.00
26 BEv,Human Torch, Capt.
  America,Sub Mariner 1,500.00
27 Bev, Human Torch/Toro
  V:Hypnotist 1,400.00
28 E:Human Torch, Capt.America,
  Sub Mariner,June, 1954 . . . 1,400.00

COWGIRL ROMANCES
See: DARING MYSTERY

COYOTE
Epic, June, 1983
1 SL 3.00
2 SL 2.50
3 BG 2.50
4 thru 6 SL . . . . @2.50
7 SL,SD 2.50
8 SL 2.50
9 SL,SD 2.50
10 SL 2.50
11 FS,1st TM art,O:Slash 7.00
12 TM. 4.00
13 TM. 4.00
14 FS,TM,A:Badger 4.00
15 SL 3.00
16 SL,A:Reagan,Gorbachev 3.00

CRASH RYAN
Epic, Oct., 1984
1 War Story 2.25
2 Doomsday 2.25
3 Fortress Japan. 2.25
4 Jan., 1985 . . . . 2.25

CRAZY
Atlas, Dec., 1953
1 JMn,BEv,satire, Frank N.
  Steins Castle 325.00
2 JMn,BEv,Beast from 1000
  Fathoms. 225.00
3 JMn,BEv,RH,Madame Knock-
  wurst's Whacks Museum. . . . 175.00
4 JMn,BEv,DAv,I Love Lucy
  satire 175.00
5 JMn,BEv,Censorship satire . . . 175.00
6 JMn,BEv,MD,satire 200.00
7 JMn,BEv,RH,satire,July, 1954 175.00

Crazy #1
© Marvel Entertainment Group

CRAZY
Feb., 1973–June, 1973
1 Not Brand Echh reps,
  Forbushman 30.00
2 Big,Batty Love & Hisses issue . 25.00
3 Stupor-Man,A:FantasticalFour . . 25.00

CREATURES ON THE LOOSE
See: TOWER OF SHADOWS

CREW
May, 2003
1 JoB,DaM,Big Trouble,pt.1 . . . . . 2.50
2 thru 7 JoB,Big Trouble,pt.2–7 . @2.50

CRIME CAN'T WIN
See: KRAZY COMICS

CRIME FIGHTERS
April, 1948–Nov., 1949
1 Police Stories. 275.00
2 Jewelry robbery 150.00
3 The Nine who were Doomed,
   addiction 165.00
4 Human Beast at Bay 125.00
5 V:Gangsters. 125.00
6 Pickpockets 125.00
7 True Cases, Crime Can't Win . 125.00
8 True Cases, Crime Can't Win . 125.00
9 Ph(c),It Happened at Night . . . 125.00
10 Ph(c),Killer at Large 125.00
Atlas, Sept., 1954–Jan., 1955
11 JMn,V:Gangsters. 135.00
12 V:Gangsters 125.00
13 Clay Pidgeon 125.00

CRIMSON DYNAMO
Marvel Epic, June, 2003
1 high tech weapon 3.00
2 new cold war? 2.50
3 Dynamo's armor 2.50
4 Going Up 2.50
5 F:Iron Man 2.50
6 Motherland,concl. 2.50

CRITICAL MASS
Epic, Jan.–July, 1990
1 KS,GM,BSzF:ShadowlineSaga . . 5.00
2 . . . . 5.00
3 GM,SDr,JRy. 5.00
4 . . . . 5.00
5 JZ 5.00
6 . . . . 5.00
7 July, 1990. . . . . 5.00

CROSSOVER CLASSICS
TPB Marvel and D.C. GP(c),reprints
   both Spider-Man/Superman,the
   Batman/Hulk and the X-Men/New
   Teen Titans Battles 18.00
TPB Vol.1 320-pg. (2001) 25.00

CRYPT OF SHADOWS
Jan., 1973
1 BW,RH,GK,Midnight on Black
   Mountain 50.00
2 GT,BEv,JMn,Monster at
   the Door. 35.00
3 Dead Man's Hand 25.00
4 CI,Secret in the Vault. 25.00
5 JM,The Graveyard Ghoul 25.00
6 BEv,GK,Don't Bury Me Deep. . . 35.00
7 JSt,The Haunting of Bluebeard . 35.00
8 How Deep my Grave 25.00
9 Beyond Death 25.00
10 A Scream in the Dark 25.00
11 The Ghouls in my Grave. 20.00
12 BP,Behind the Locked Door . . 25.00
13 BEv,SD,Back From the Dead . . 25.00
14 The Thing that Creeps 20.00
15 My Coffin is Crowded 20.00
16 . . . . 20.00
17 In the Hands of Shandu 20.00
18 SD,Face of Fear 25.00
19 SD,Colossus that Challenged
   the World. 25.00

20 A Monster walks Among Us . . . 20.00
21 SD,Death Will Be Mine,
   Nov., 1975 . . . . 25.00

CUPID
Dec., 1949–March, 1950
1 Ph(c),Cora Dod's Amazing
   Decision. 175.00
2 Ph(c),BP,Betty Page 400.00

CURSE OF THE WEIRD
1993–94
1 thru 4 SD,rep. 50's Sci-Fi 2.25

CUTTING EDGE
1995
1 WML,F:Hulk,Ghosts of the
   Future tie-in 3.25

CYBERSPACE 3000
1993
1 A:Dark Angel,Galactus,V:Badoon,
   Glow in the dark(c) 3.25
2 SeT,A:Galactus,Dark Angel 2.25
3 SeT,A:Galactus,Keeper 2.25
4 SeT,A:Keeper. 2.25
5 SeT,A:Keeper. 2.25
6 SeT,A:Warlock 2.25
7 SeT,I:Gamble. 2.25
8 SeT,A:Warlock 2.25
9 SeT 2.25
10 SeT 2.25
11 SeT 2.25

CYCLOPS
Aug., 2001
1 (of 4) MT,JP 2.75
2 MT,JP,I:Ulysses 2.75
3 MT,JP,in a savage land 2.75
4 MT,JP,V:Ulysses 2.75
TPB X-Men Icons: Cyclops 13.00

DAILY BUGLE
B&W 1996
1 (of 3) KIK,GA 2.75
2 KIK,GA. 2.75
3 KIK,GA. 2.75

Dakota North #1
© *Marvel Entertainment Group*

DAKOTA NORTH
1986–87
1 (Now in Cage) 2.25
2 thru 5 . . . . @2.25

DAMAGE CONTROL
May, 1989
1 EC/BWi;A:Spider-Man 3.00
2 EC/BWi;A:Fant.Four 2.50
3 EC/BWi;A:Iron Man 2.50
4 EC/BWi;A:X-Men 2.50
[2nd Series], 1989–90
1 EC,A:Capt.America&Thor 3.00
2 EC,A:Punisher 2.50
3 EC 2.50
4 EC,Punisher. 2.50
[3rd Series], 1991
1 Clean-up Crew Returns. 2.50
2 A:Hulk,New Warriors 2.50
3 A:Avengers W.C.,Wonder Man,
   Silver Surfer. 2.50
4 A:SilverSurfer & others 2.50

DANCES WITH DEMONS
Frontier 1993
1 CAd 3.50
2 CAd,V:Manitou. 2.50
3 CAd,V:Manitou. 2.50
4 CAd,last issue 2.50
5 Okay, there's more! 2.50
6 . . . . 2.50

DAREDEVIL
April, 1964
1 B:StL(s),JK(c),BEv,I&O:Daredevil,
   I:Karen Page,Foggy Nelson 5,000.00
2 JK(c),JO,V:Electro 1,200.00
3 JK(c),JO,I&O:The Owl 800.00
4 JK(c),JO,I&O:Killgrave. 700.00
5 JK(c),WW,V:Masked Matador . 400.00
6 WW,I&O Original Mr. Fear. . . . 300.00
7 WW,I:Red Costume,V:Namor . 900.00
8 WW,I&O:Stiltman 250.00
9 WW(i),Killers Castle. 250.00
10 WW(i),V:Catman 250.00
11 WW(i),R:Cat 200.00
12 JK,JR,2nd A:Ka-Zar 200.00
13 JK,JR,O:Ka-Zar. 200.00
14 JR,If This Be Justice. 200.00
15 JR,A:Ox. 200.00
16 JR,A:Spider-Man,
   I:Masked Marauder 300.00
17 JR,A:Spider-Man. 300.00
18 DON(s),JR,I:Gladiator. 200.00
19 JR,V:Gladiator. 100.00
20 JR(c),GC,V:Owl 100.00
21 GC,BEv,V:Owl 100.00
22 GC,V:Tri-man 100.00
23 GC,V:Tri-man 90.00
24 GC,A:Ka-Zar 125.00
25 GC,V:Leapfrog 100.00
26 GC,V:Stiltman 100.00
27 GC,Spider-Man 100.00
28 GC,V:Aliens 100.00
29 GC,V:The Boss 100.00
30 BEv(c),GC,A:Thor 100.00
31 GC,V:Cobra 75.00
32 GC,V:Cobra 75.00
33 GC,V:Beetle 75.00
34 BEv(c),GC,O:Beetle 75.00
35 BEv(c),GC,A:Susan Richards. . 75.00
36 GC,A:FF 75.00
37 GC,V:Dr.Doom 75.00
38 GC,A:FF 75.00
39 GC,GT,V:Unholy Three. 75.00
40 GC,V:Unholy Three. 75.00
41 GC,D:Mike Murdock 60.00
42 GC,DA,I:Jester 60.00

MARVEL

43 JK(c),GC,A:Capt.America 60.00	121 GK(c),A:Shield 15.00	173 FM,KJ,V:Gliadator. 18.00
44 JSo(c),GC,V:Jester 50.00	122 GK(c),V:Blackwing 15.00	174 FM,KJ,A:Gladiator. 18.00
45 GC,V:Jester 50.00	123 V:Silvermane,I:Jackhammer. . 15.00	175 FM,KJ,A:Elektra,V:Hand 20.00
46 GC,V:Jester 50.00	124 B:MWn(s),GK(c),GC,KJ,	176 FM,KJ,A:Elektra 18.00
47 GC,`Brother Take My Hand' . . 50.00	I:Copperhead. 15.00	177 FM,KJ,A:Stick 20.00
48 GC,V:Stiltman 50.00	125 GK(c),KJ(i),V:Copperhead . . . 15.00	178 FM,KJ,A:PowerMan&I.Fist . . . 18.00
49 GC,V:Robot,I:Starr Saxon. . . . 50.00	126 GK(c),KJ(i),D: 2nd Torpedo . . 15.00	179 FM,KJ,V:Elektra 18.00
50 JR(c),BWS,JCr,V:Robot 65.00	127 GK(c),KJ(i),V:3rd Torpedo. . . 15.00	180 FM,KJ,V:Kingpin 18.00
51 B:RTs(s),BWS,V:Robot 65.00	128 GK(c),KJ(i),V:Death Stalker . . 15.00	181 FM,KJ,V:Bullseye,D:Elektra,
52 BWS,JCr,A:Black Panther . . . 65.00	129 KJ(i),V:Man Bull 15.00	A:Punisher. 35.00
53 GC,O:Daredevil. 55.00	130 KJ(i),V:Brother Zed 15.00	182 FM,KJ,A:Punisher. 15.00
54 GC,V:Mr.Fear,A:Spidey. 50.00	131 KJ(i),I&O:2nd Bullseye 65.00	183 FM,KJ,V:PunisherDrug 15.00
55 GC,V:Mr.Fear 40.00	132 KJ(i),V:Bullseye. 35.00	184 FM,KJ,V:PunisherDrug 15.00
56 GC,V:Death Head. 40.00	133 JM(i),GK(c),V:Jester 12.00	185 FM,KJ,V:King Pin 10.00
57 GC,V:Death Head. 40.00	134 JM(i),V:Chamelon 12.00	186 FM,KJ,V:Stiltman 10.00
58 GC,V:Stunt Master 40.00	135 JM(i),V:Jester 12.00	187 FM,KJ,A:Stick 10.00
59 GC,V:Torpedo 40.00	136 JB,JM,V:Jester 12.00	188 FM,KJ,A:Black Widow 10.00
60 GC,V:Crime Wave 40.00	137 JB,V:Jester 12.00	189 FM,KJ,A:Stick,A:BlackWidow . 10.00
61 GC,V:Cobra 40.00	138 JBy,A:Ghost Rider 18.00	190 FM,KJ,R:Elektra 10.00
62 GC,O:Night Hawk. 40.00	139 SB,V:A Bomber. 12.00	191 FM,TA,A:Bullseye 10.00
63 GC,V:Gladiator 40.00	140 SB,V:Gladiator 12.00	192 KJ,V:Kingpin 5.00
64 GC,A:Stuntmaster. 40.00	141 GC,Bullseye 25.00	193 KJ,Betsy 5.00
65 GC,V:BrotherBrimstone 40.00	142 GC,V:Cobra 12.00	194 KJ,V:Kingpin 5.00
66 GC,V:BrotherBrimstone 40.00	143 E:MWn(s),GC,V:Cobra 12.00	195 KJ,Tarkington Brown. 5.00
67 BEv(c),GC,Stiltman. 40.00	144 GT,V:Manbull 12.00	196 KJ,A:Wolverine 15.00
68 AC,V:Kragg Blackmailer,	145 GT,V:Owl. 12.00	197 V:Bullseye. 5.00
a:Bl.Panther,DD'sID Rev. . . 40.00	146 GC,V:Bullseye. 35.00	198 V:Dark Wind 5.00
69 E:RTs(s),GC,V:Thunderbolts,	147 GC,V:Killgrave 12.00	199 V:Dark Wind 5.00
A:Bl.Panther(DD's ID Rev) . . . 40.00	148 GC,V:Deathstalker 12.00	200 JBy(c),V:Bullseye 7.00
70 GC,V:Terrorists 40.00	149 KI,V:Smasher 12.00	201 JBy(c),A:Black Widow. 5.00
71 RTs(s),GC,V:Terrorists 40.00	150 GC,KJ,I:Paladin 12.00	202 I:Micah Synn 5.00
72 GyC(s),GC,Tagak,V:Quother . . 40.00	151 GC,Daredevil Unmasked 12.00	203 JBy(c),I:Trump 5.00
73 GC,V:Zodiac 40.00	152 KJ,V:Paladin 12.00	204 BSz(c),V:Micah Synn 5.00
74 B:GyC(s),GC,I:Smasher 40.00	153 GC,V:Cobra 12.00	205 I:Gael 5.00
75 GC,V:El Condor 40.00	154 GC,V:Mr. Hyde 12.00	206 V:Micah Synn 5.00
76 GC,TP,V:El Condor 40.00	155 V:Avengers 12.00	207 BSz(c),A:Black Widow 5.00
77 GC,TP,V:Manbull. 40.00	156 GC,V:Death Stalker. 12.00	208 Harlan Ellison 6.00
78 GC,TP,V:Manbull. 40.00	157 GC,V:Death Stalker. 12.00	209 Harlan Ellison 6.00
79 GC,TP,V:Manbull. 40.00	158 FM,V:Death Stalker. 90.00	210 DM,V:Micah Synn 5.00
80 GK(c),GC,TP,V:Owl. 40.00	159 FM,V:Bullseye. 45.00	211 DM,V:Micah Synn 5.00
81 GK(c),GC,JA,A:Black Widow . . 50.00	160 FM,Bullseye 35.00	212 DM,V:Micah Synn 5.00
82 GK(c),GC,JA,V:Scorpion 25.00	161 FM,V:Bullseye. 35.00	213 DM,V:Micah Synn 5.00
83 JR(c),BWS,BEv,V:Mr.Hyde . . . 28.00	162 SD,JRu,`Requiem' 12.00	214 DM,V:Micah Synn 5.00
84 GK(c),GC,Assassin. 25.00	163 FM,V:Hulk,I:Ben Urich 25.00	215 DM,A:Two-Gun Kid 5.00
85 GK(c),GC,A:Black Widow 25.00	164 FM,KJ,A:Avengers 25.00	216 DM,V:Gael 5.00
86 GC,TP,V:Ox. 25.00	165 FM,KJ,V:Dr.Octopus 25.00	217 BS(c),V:Gael 5.00
87 GC,TP,V:Electro 25.00	166 FM,KJ,V:Gladiator. 25.00	218 KP,V:Jester 5.00
88 GK(c),GC,TP,O:Black Widow . . 25.00	167 FM,KJ,V:Mauler 25.00	219 FM,JB 6.00
89 GC,TP,A:Black Widow 25.00	168 FM,KJ,I&O:Elektra 125.00	220 DM,D:Heather Glenn 5.00
90 E:StL(s),GK(c),GC,TP,V:Ox . . 25.00	169 FM,KJ,V:Bullseye 45.00	221 DM,Venice. 5.00
91 GK(c),GC,TP,I:Mr. Fear III . . . 25.00	170 FM,KJ,V:Bullseye 20.00	222 DM,A:Black Widow 5.00
92 GK(c),GC,TP,A:BlackPanther . 25.00	171 FM,KJ,V:Kingpin 18.00	223 DM,Secret Wars II 5.00
93 GK(c),GC,TP,A:Black Widow . 25.00	172 FM,KJ,V:Bullseye 18.00	224 DM,V:Sunturion. 5.00
94 GK(c),GC,TP,V:Damon Dran . . 25.00		225 DM,V:Vulture. 5.00
95 GK(c),GC,TP,V:Manbull 25.00		226 FM(plot),V:Gladiator 5.00
96 GK(c),GC,ECh,V:Manbull 25.00		227 FM,Kingpin,Kar.Page 12.00
97 GK(c),V:Dark Messiah 25.00		228 FM,DM,V:Kingpin 10.00
98 E:GyC(s),GC,ECh,V:Dark		229 FM,Kingpin,Turk 10.00
Messiah. 25.00		230 R:Matt's Mother 10.00
99 B:SvG(s),JR(c),V:Hawkeye. . . 25.00		231 FM,DM,V:Kingpin 10.00
100 GC,V:Angar the Screamer . . 40.00		232 FM,V:Kingpin,Nuke 10.00
101 RB,A:Angar the Screamer . . 20.00		233 FM,Kingpin,Nuke,Capt.Am. . . 10.00
102 A:Black Widow 20.00		234 SD,KJ,V:Madcap. 5.00
103 JR(c),DH,A:Spider-Man 20.00		235 SD,KJ,V:Mr. Hyde 5.00
104 GK(c),DH,V:Kraven. 20.00		236 BWS,A:Black Widow. 6.00
105 DH,JSn,DP,C:Thanos 25.00		237 AW(i),V:Klaw 5.00
106 JR(c),DH,A:Black Widow . . . 18.00		238 SB,SL,AAd(c)V:Sabretooth. . . 7.00
107 JSn(c),JB(i),A:Capt.Marvel . . . 18.00		239 AAd(c),AW,Gl(i),V:Rotgut 5.00
108 K&R(c),PG(i),V:Beetle 18.00		240 AW,V:Rotgut 5.00
109 GK(c),DH(i),V:Beetle 18.00		241 MZ(c),TM,V:Trixter 6.00
110 JR(c),GC,A:Thing,O:Nekra . . 18.00		242 KP,V:Caviar Killer 5.00
111 JM(i),I:Silver Samurai 20.00		243 AW,V:Nameless One 5.00
112 GK(c),GC,V:Mandrill 18.00		244 TD(i),V:Nameless One 5.00
113 JR(c),V:Gladiator. 18.00		245 TD(i),A:Black Panther. 5.00
114 GK(c),I:Death Stalker 18.00		246 TD(i),V:Chance 5.00
115 V:Death Stalker 18.00		247 KG,A:Black Widow 5.00
116 GK(c),GC,V:Owl 18.00		248 RL,AW,A:Wolverine,
117 E:SvG(s),K&R(c),V:Owl. 18.00		V:Bushwhacker. 7.00
118 JR(c),DH,I:Blackwing 18.00		249 RL,AW,V:Wolverine,
119 GK(c),DH(i),V:Crusher 18.00		Bushwhacker. 7.00
120 GK(c),V:Hydra,I:El Jaguar . . . 18.00		250 JR2,AW,I:Bullet 5.00

Daredevil #100
© Marvel Entertainment Group

Daredevil #225
© Marvel Entertainment Group

251 JR2,AW,V:Bullet 5.00
252 JR2,AW,Fall o/Mutants 6.00
253 JR2,AW,V:Kingpin. 5.00
254 JR2,AW,I:Typhoid Mary 13.00
255 JR2,AW,A:Kingpin,TMary 6.00
256 JR2,AW,A:Kingpin,TMary 6.00
257 JR2,AW,A:Punisher 10.00
258 RLm,V:Bengal. 6.00
259 JR2,AW,V:TyphoidMary 5.00
260 JR2,AW,V:T.Mary,K.pin 5.00
261 JR2,AW,HumanTorch 5.00
262 JR2,AW,Inferno. 5.00
263 JR2,AW,Inferno. 5.00
264 SD,AW,MM,V:The Owl 5.00
265 JR2,AW,Inferno. 5.00
266 JR2,AW,V:Mephisto 5.00
267 JR2,AW,V:Bullet 5.00
268 JR2,AW,V:TheMob 5.00
269 JR2,AW,V:Pyro&Blob 5.00
270 JR2,AW,A:Spider-Man,
    I:Blackheart 5.00
271 JR2,AW,I:Number9 . . . . 5.00
272 JR2,AW,I:Shotgun. 5.50
273 JR2,AW,V:Shotgun 5.00
274 JR2,AW,V:Inhumans 5.00
275 JR2,AW,ActsOfVen.,V:Ultron . . 5.00
276 JR2,AW,ActsOfVen.,V:Ultorn . . 5.00
277 RL,AW,Vivian's Story 5.00
278 JR2,AW,V:Blackheart,
    A:Inhumans 5.00
279 JR2,AW,V:Mephisto,
    A:Inhumans 5.00
280 JR2,AW,V:Mephisto,
    A:Inhumans 5.00
281 JR2,AW,V:Mephisto,
    A:Inhumans 5.00
282 JR2,AW,V:Mephisto,
    A:Silver Surfer, Inhumans 5.00
283 MBa,AW,A:Captain America 5.00
284 LW,AW,R:Bullseye 5.00
285 LW,AW,B:Bullseye
    become DD#1 . . . . 5.00
286 LW,AW,GCa,Fake
    Daredevil #2 . . . . 5.00
287 LW,AW,Fake Daredevil #3 . . . . 5.00
288 LW,AW,A:Kingpin 5.00
289 LW,AW,A:Kingpin 5.00
290 LW,AW,E:Fake Daredevil 5.00
291 LW,AW,V:Bullet 5.00
292 LW,A:Punisher,V:Tombstone. . . 5.00
293 LW,A:Punisher,V:Tombstone. . . 5.00
294 LW,V:The Hand. 5.00
295 LW,V:The Hand,A:GhostRider. . 5.00

296 LW,AW,V:The Hand 5.00
297 B:DGC(s),LW,AW,B:Last Rites,
    V:Typhoid Mary,A:Kingpin 5.00
298 LW,AW,A:Nick Fury,Kingpin . . . 5.00
299 LW,AW,A:Nick Fury,Kingpin . . . 5.00
300 LW,AW,E:Last Rites,. 8.00
301 V:The Owl. 5.00
302 V:The Owl 5.00
303 V:The Owl. 5.00
304 AW,Non-action issue. 5.00
305 AW,A:Spider-Man 5.00
306 AW,A:Spider-Man 5.00
307 1st SMc DD,Dead Man's
    Hand #1,A:Nomad. 6.00
308 SMc,Dead Man's Hand #5,
    A:Punisher,V:Silvermane. . . 5.00
309 SMc,Dead Man's Hand#7,
    A:Nomad,Punisher 5.00
310 SMc,Inf.War,V:Calipso 5.00
311 SMc,V:Calypso 5.00
312 Firefighting issue. 5.00
313 SMc,V:Pyromaniac 5.00
314 SMc,V:Mr.Fear,I:Shock 5.00
315 SMc,V:Mr.Fear 5.00
316 Goes Underground 5.00
317 SMc,Comedy Issue. 5.00
318 SMc,V:Taskmaster 5.00
319 SMc,Fall from Grace Prologue,
    A:Silver Sable,Garrett,Hand . . . 7.00
319a 2nd Printing. 3.00
320 SMc,B:Fall from Grace,
    V:Crippler,S.Sable,A:Stone 7.00
321 SMc,N:Daredevil,A:Venom,
    Garret, V:Hellspawn,Glow
    in the Dark(c). 6.00
321a Newsstand Ed. 5.00
322 SMc,A:Venom,Garret,Siege . . . 4.00
323 SMc,V:Venom,A:Siege,Garret,
    I:Erynys 4.00
324 SMc,A:Garret,R:Elektra,
    A:Stone, Morbius. 4.00
325 SMc,E:Fall from Grace, A:Garret,
    Siege,Elektra,Morbius,V:Hand,
    D:Hellspawn,Double size 4.00
326 SMc,B:Tree of Knowledge,
    I:Killobyte,A:Capt.America. 3.00
327 E:DGC(s),SMc,A:Capt.Amer. . . 3.00
328 GtW(s),V:Wirehead,A:Captain
    America,S.Sable,Wild Pack. . . . 3.00
329 B:DGC(s),SMc,A:Captain
    America, S.Sable,Iron Fist. 3.00
330 SMc,A:Gambit. 3.00
331 SMc,A:Captain America,
    V:Hydra. 3.00
332 A:Captain America,Gambit 3.00
333 TGb,GWt. 3.00
334 TGb,GWt. 3.00
335 . . . . 3.00
336 . . . . 3.00
337 V:Kingpin,A:Blackwulf 3.00
338 Wages of Sin,pt.1 . . . . 3.00
339 Wages of Sin,pt.2 . . . . 3.00
340 R:Kingpin 3.00
341 Kingpin 3.00
342 DGc,KP,V:Kingpin. 3.00
343 Without Costume 3.00
344 Identity Crisis,pt.1 . . . . 3.00
345 Identity Crisis,pt.2 . . . . 3.00
346 V:Sir 3.00
347 V:mystery man 3.00
348 In NY City 3.50
349 Retreats to the Chaste 3.50
350 Double size 4.00
351 . . . . 3.00
352 Return of Matt Murdock 3.00
353 KK,CNr,A:Mr. Hyde. 3.00
354 KK,CNr,A:Spider-Man 3.00
355 KK,CNr,A:Pyro 3.00
356 KK,CNr,. 3.00
357 KK,CNr,. 3.00
358 KK,CNr,MRy,A:Mysterio 3.00

Daredevil #358
© Marvel Entertainment Group

359 KK,CNr,A:Absorbing Man 3.00
360 KK,CNr,MRy,V:Onslaught. 3.00
361 KK,CNr,MRy,A:Black Widow. . . 3.00
362 KK,CNr,Romance 3.00
363 KK,GC,CaS,V:Insomnia 3.00
364 KK,CNr,MRy,V:Insomnia. 3.00
365 CNr,MRy,V:Mr. Fear,
    A:Molten Man 3.00
366 GC,V:Gladiator 3.00
367 GC,V:Gladiator, concl. 3.00
368 GC,A:Black Widow and Omega
    Red 3.00
369 AOI,V:Soviet Super Soldiers. . . 3.00
370 GC,Black Widow, concl. 3.00
371 AOI,Matt Murdock & Karen
    Page's relationship 3.00
372 AOI,Killers after Karen Page. . . 3.00
373 AOI,V:The 3. . . . . 3.00
374 AOI:V:Mr. Fear 3.00
375 AOI,RL,V:Mr. Fear,double size . 4.00
376 SLo,CHm,Daredevil deep
    undercover. 3.00
377 SLo,TMo,SHa,Flying Blind,pt.2 3.00
378 SLo,TMo,SHa,Flying Blind,pt.3. 3.00
379 SLo,CHm,Flying Blind,concl. . . 3.00
380 DGC,LW,RbC, V:Bullseye,Bush-
    wacker,Kingpin, double size . . . 5.00
Minus 1 Spec., GC, flashback 3.00
Ann.#1 GC 60.00
Ann.#2 reprints. 25.00
Ann.#3 reprints. 25.00
Ann.#4 (1976)GT,A:Black
    Panther,Namor 7.00
Ann.#5 (1989)MBa,JLe,JR2,KJ,
    WPo,AM,Atlantis Attacks,
    A:Spider-Man. 5.00
Ann.#6 TS,Lifeform#2,A:Typhoid
    Mary. 5.00
Ann.#7 JG,JBr,Von Strucker
    Gambit,pt.1,A:Nick Fury 5.00
Ann.#8 Sys.Bytes#2,A:Deathlok . . . 5.00
Ann.#9 MPa,I:Devourer,w/card,tie-in
    to Fall From Grace 5.00
Ann.#10 I:Ghostmaker,A:Shang
    Chi, Elektra 4.00
G-Size #1 GK(c),reprints 12.00
TPB Born Again,rep.#227-#233. . . 10.95
TPB Fall of the Kingpin, rep. 15.95
TPB Gangwar, rep. 12.95
TPB Marked for Death, rep. 9.95
Daredevil/Punisher:Child's Play rep. 7.00
TPB Daredevil: Man Without Fear. 15.95

DAREDEVIL
Sept., 1998

1 JP,JQ,F:Matt Murdock 32.00
1a Deluxe edition 7.50
2 JP,JQ,blind faith dilemma 18.00
2a variant JSC cover 15.00
3 JP,JQ,Guardian Devil,pt.3 . . . . . 12.00
4 JP,JQ,Guardian Devil,pt.4 . . . . . 12.00
5 JP,JQ,Guardian Devil,pt.5 . . . . . 20.00
5a Variant (c) 18.00
6 JP,JQ,Guardian Devil,pt.6 . . . . . 11.00
7 JP,JQ,Guardian Devil,pt.7 . . . . . 11.00
8 JP,JQ,Guardian Devil,concl. . . . 11.00
8a signed 25.00
9 JP,JQ,DMk,V:Kingpin. 5.00
9a signed 25.00
10 JP,JQ,DMk,I:Echo 5.00
11 JP,JQ,DMk,A:Kingpin 5.00
12 JP,JQ,DMk,V:Kingpin 5.00
13 JP,JQ,DMk,V:Kingpin 5.00
14 JQ,DMk,V:Kingpin. 6.00
15 JQ,DMk,V:Echo 5.00
16 BMB,DMk,. 6.00
17 BMB,DMk,F:Ben Urich 6.00
18 BMB,DMk,F:Ben, Timmy 5.00
19 BMB,DMk,F:Ben, Timmy 5.00
20 40-page,BU:F:Spider-Man 6.00
21 A:Jester. 5.00
22 Matt Murdock vs. Daredevil 5.00
23 Matt Murdock vs. Daredevil 5.00
24 MPn,the trial begins 5.00
25 Playing to the Camera 5.00
26 BMB,V:Nitro 12.00
27 BMB,V:Silke,Kingpin. 7.00
28 BMB,Elektra x-over,'Nuff Said . . 7.00
29 BMB,Kingpin's Empire 7.00
30 BMB,Kingpin's Secrets 7.00
31 BMB,plot twist. 7.00
32 BMB,Kingpin's Empire 10.00
33 BMB,F:Matt Murdock 6.00
34 BMB, anger's terms 5.00
35 BMB,V:Mr. Hyde 5.00
36 BMB,F:Luke Cage 5.00
37 BMB,F:Elektra. 5.00
38 BMB,Trial of White Tiger,pt.1 . . 5.00
39 BMB,Trial of White Tiger,pt.2 . . 5.00
40 BMB,Trial of the Century 5.00
41 BMB,Lowlife,pt.1. . . . . 0.50
42 BMB,Lowlife,pt.2. . . . . 3.00
43 BMB,Lowlife,pt.3. . . . . 3.00
44 BMB,Lowlife,pt.4. . . . . 3.00
45 BMB,Lowlife,concl. 3.00
46 BMB,Hardcore,pt.1 . . . . 3.00
47 BMB,Hardcore,pt.2 . . . . 3.00
48 BMB,Hardcore,pt.3 . . . . 3.00
49 BMB,Hardcore,pt.4 . . . . 3.00
50 BMB,Hardcore,pt.5 . . . . 3.00
51 DMk,R:Echo,pt.1. . . . . 3.00
52 DMk,V:Echo,pt.2 . . . . 3.00
53 DMk,V:Echo,pt.3 . . . . 3.00
54 DMk,V:Echo,pt.4,F:Wolverine. . . 3.00
55 DMk,Echo's vision quest. 3.00
56 BMB,New Kingpin. 3.00
57 BMB,A:Spider-Man 3.00
58 BMB,King of Hell's Kitchen,pt.3 . 3.00
59 BMB,King of Hell's Kitchen,pt.4 . 3.00
60 BMB,King of Hell's Kitchen,pt.5 . 3.00
61 BMB,The Widow,pt.1 . . . . 3.00
62 BMB,The Widow,pt.2 . . . . 3.00
63 BMB,The Widow,pt.3 . . . . 3.00
64 BMB,The Widow,pt.4 . . . . 3.00
65 BMB,Anniversary Spec.,48-pg. . . 4.00
66 BMB,Golden Age,pt.1 . . . . 3.00
Spec.Daredevil vs. Punisher 3.50
Spec. Daredevil/Deadpool, BCh, JHo,
　Two annuals in one,48pg.(1997) 5.00
Spec. Daredevil/Batman, DGC,
　SMc, 48pg. (1997). 6.00
Spec.#1 Daredevil (2000) 2.25
Spec. Daredevil Movie adapt. 3.50

TPB rep. #1–#3 . . . . 10.00
TPB Gang War,FM,KJ 16.00
TPB Daredevil: Born Again 18.00
TPB Visionaries: Frank Miller . . . 25.00
TPB Visionaries: Kevin Smith . . . 20.00
TPB Parts of a Hole, 160-pg.. . . . 17.00
TPB Wake Up (2002). 10.00
TPB Underboss, 144-pg. (2002) . . 15.00
TPB Love's Labor Lost (2002). . . . 20.00
TPB Daredevil Movie adapt. 13.00
TPB Legends Vol.4:Typhoid Mary . 20.00
TPB Vol.4:Hardcore 14.00
TPB Vol.5:Out 20.00
TPB Vol.6:Lowlife. 14.00
TPB Vol.7:Hardcore 14.00
TPB Vol.8:Echo–Vision Quest . . . 14.00
TPB Vol.9:King of Hell's Kitchen . . 14.00

DAREDEVIL: FATHER
April, 2004

1 (of 5) JQ,DaM 3.50
2 JQ 3.50

Daredevil: The Man Without Fear #4
© Marvel Entertainment Group

3 JQ 3.50

DAREDEVIL: THE MAN WITHOUT FEAR
1993–94

1 B:FM(s),JR2,AW,O:Daredevil,
　A:Stick,D:Daredevil's Father . . . 7.00
2 JR2,AW,A:Stick,Stone,Elektra . . . 6.00
3 JR2,AW,A:Elektra,Kingpin 6.00
4 JR2,AW,A:Kingpin,I:Mickey 6.00
5 JR2,AW,A:Mickey,Last Issue. . . . 6.00
TPB rep.#1#5. . . . . 16.00

DAREDEVIL: NINJA
Oct., 2000

1 (of 3) BMB,Stick. 5.00
2 BMB,V:Hand 5.00
3 BMB,concl. 5.00
TPB rep. 80-page 9.00

DAREDEVIL/SHI
SHI/DAREDEVIL
Marvel/Crusade 1996

1 (Daredevil/Shi) TSg,AW,
　x-over,pt.1 . . . . 5.00
1 (Shi/Daredevil) x-over, pt.2 . . . . . 5.00

DAREDEVIL/SPIDER-MAN
Nov., 2000

1 (of 4) AxR,PJe, ... 4.00
2 AxR,PJe,Gladiator,Stilt-Man. 4.00
3 AxR,PJe,Owl,Copperhead 4.00
4 AxR,PJe,TP,concl. 4.00

DAREDEVIL: THE TARGET
Nov., 2002

1 (of 4) KSm,GF,V:Bullseye 3.50

DAREDEVIL: YELLOW
March, 2001

1 (of 6) JLb,TSe,O:Daredevil 10.00
2 JLb,TSe,Vengeance 7.00
3 JLb,TSe,F:Fantastic Four 7.00
4 JLb,TSe,V:Electro 7.00
5 JLb,TSe,V:Owl. 7.00
6 JLb,TSe,last yellow costume 7.00
TPB series rep. 15.00

DARING MYSTERY COMICS
Timely, Jan., 1940

1 ASh(c),JSm,O:Fiery Mask,
　A:Monako John Steele,Doc Doyle,
　Flash FosterBarney Mullen,
　Sea Rover, Bondage (c). . 30,000.00
2 ASh(c),JSm,O:Phantom Bullet
　A:Zephyr Jones & K4,Laughing
　Mask Mr.E,B:Trojak 15,000.00
3 ASh(c),JSm,A:Phantom
　Reporter,Marvex,Breeze
　Barton, B:Purple Mask . . . 8,000.00
4 ASh(c),A:G-Man Ace,K4,
　Monako,Marvex,E:Purple
　Mask,B:Whirlwind Carter . . 5,000.00
5 JSm,B:Falcon,A:Fiery Mask,K4,
　Little Hercules,Bondage(c) 5,000.00
6 S&K,O:Marvel Boy,A:Fiery
　Mask, Flying Fame,Dynaman,
　Stuporman,E:Trojak 6,000.00
7 S&K,O:Blue Diamond,A:The Fin,
　Challenger,Captain Daring,
　Silver Scorpion,Thunderer . 5,000.00
8 S&K,O:Citizen V,A:Thunderer,
　Fin Silver Scorpion,Captain
　Daring Blue Diamond. 4,000.00
Becomes:

DARING COMICS
1944

9 ASh(c),B:Human Torch,Toro,
　Sub Mariner 1,600.00
10 ASh(c),A;The Angel 1,300.00
11 ASh(c),A:The Destroyer. . . . 1,300.00
12 E:Human Torch,Toro,Sub-
　Mariner, Fall, 1945 . . . . 1,300.00
Becomes:

JEANIE COMICS
1947

13 B:Jeanie,Queen of the
　Teens Mitzi,Willie. 200.00
14 Baseball(c) 150.00
15 Schoolbus(c). 150.00
16 Swimsuit(c) 165.00
17 HK,Fancy dress party(c),
　Hey Look 125.00
18 HK,Jeanie'sDate(c),Hey Look. 100.00
19 Ice-Boat(c),Hey Look 125.00
20 Jukebox(c) 100.00
21 . . . . 100.00
22 HK,Hey Look. 125.00
23 . . . . 100.00
24 . . . . 100.00
25 . . . . 100.00
26 . . . . 100.00

27 E:Jeanie,Queen of Teens 100.00
Becomes:

COWGIRL ROMANCES
1950
28 Ph(c),Mona Freeman/MacDonald
    Carey,Copper Canyon...... 225.00

DARK ANGEL
See: HELL'S ANGEL

DARK CRYSTAL
April, 1983
1 movie adaption 3.00
2 movie adaption,May, 1983...... 3.00

Dark Guard #3
© Marvel Entertainment Group

DARK GUARD
1993–94
1 A:All UK Heroes............. 3.00
2 A:All UK Heroes............. 2.25
3 V:Leader,MyS-Tech 2.25
4 V:MyS-Tech 2.25
5 .... 2.25
6 and 7 .... @2.25

DARKHAWK
March, 1991
1 MM,I&O:Darkhawk,
    A:Hobgoblin................. 5.00
2 MM,A:Spider-Man,V:Hobgoblin . 3.00
3 MM,A:Spider-Man,V:Hobgoblin . 3.00
4 MM,I:Savage Steel 3.00
5 MM,I:Portal 3.00
6 MM,A:Cap.Am,D.D.,Portal,
    V:U-Foes................... 3.00
7 MM,I:Lodestone 2.50
8 MM,V:Lodestone 2.50
9 MM,A:Punisher,V:Savage Steel. . 2.50
10 MM,A&N:Tombstone.......... 2.50
11 MM,V:Tombstone............ 2.50
12 MM,V:Tombstone,R:Dark
    Hawks'Father............... 2.50
13 MM,V:Venom 3.00
14 MM,V:Venom,D:Dark
    Hawks Father 3.00
15 MM,Heart of the Hawk,concl ... 2.25
16 MM,V:Terrorists............. 2.25
17 MM,I:Peristrike Force 2.25
18 MM,V:Mindwolf............. 2.25

19 MM,R:Portal,A:Spider-Man,V:The
    Brotherhood of Evil Mutants ... 2.25
20 MM,A:Spider-Man,Sleepwalker,
    V:Brotherhood of Evil Mutants. . 2.25
21 MM,B:Return to Forever....... 2.25
22 MM,A:Ghost Rider 2.25
23 MM,I:Evilhawk............... 2.25
24 V:Evilhawk 2.25
25 MM,O:Darkhawk,V:Evilhawk,
    Holo-graphx(c).............. 3.50
26 A:New Warriors............. 2.25
27 A:New Warriors,V:Zarrko 2.25
28 A:New Warriors,Zarrko 2.25
29 A:New Warriors 2.25
30 I:Purity................... 2.25
31 Infinity Crusade............. 2.25
32 R:Savage Steel............. 2.25
33 I:Cuda................... 2.25
34 V:Cuda 2.25
35 DFr(s),V:Venom 2.25
36 DFr(s),V:Scokers,A:Venom..... 2.25
37 DFr(s),V:Venom 2.25
38 DFr(s),N:Darkhawk.......... 2.25
39 DFr(s) 2.25
40 DFr(s) 2.25
41 DFr(s) 2.25
42 DFr(s), V:Portal,I:Shaper 2.25
43 DFr(s) 2.25
44 DFr(s) 2.25
45 DFr(s),A:Portal 2.25
46 DFr(s) 2.25
47 .... 2.25
48 R:Darkhawk,V:Mahari......... 2.25
49 V:Overhawk 2.25
50 V:Overhawk 3.00
Ann.#1 MM,Assault on ArmorCity . . 3.00
Ann.#2 GC,AW,I:Dreamkiller,
    w/Trading card.............. 3.00
Ann.#3 I:Damek............... 3.00

DARKHOLD
1992–94
1 RCa,I:Redeemers,Polybagged
    w/poster,A:Gh.Rider,Blaze..... 3.00
2 RCa,R:Modred............... 2.50
3 A:Modred,Scarlet Witch........ 2.25
4 V:Sabretooth,N'Garai.......... 2.25
5 A:Punisher, Ghost Rider 2.25
6 RCa,V:Dr.Strange 2.25
7 A:Dr.Strange,V:Japanese Army . . 2.25
8 Betrayal #1................. 2.25
9 Diabolique 2.25
10 V:Darkholders 2.25

Darkhold #7
© Marvel Entertainment Group

11 Midnight Massacre#3,D:Modred,
    Vicki..................... 2.50
12 V:Chthon................. 2.25
13 V:Missing Link.............. 2.25
14 Vicki's Secret revealed 2.25
15 Siege of Darkness,pt.#4 ...... 2.25
16 Siege of Darkness,pt.#12...... 2.25

DARK MAN
MOVIE ADAPTION
Sept., 1990
1 BH/MT/TD 3.00
2 BH/TD 2.50
3 BH/TD,final issue............ 2.50

DARKMAN
Sept., 1990
1 JS,R:Darkman 4.50
2 JS,V:Witchfinder 3.00
3 JS,Witchfinder 3.00
4 JS,V:Dr.West 3.00
5 JS,Durant................. 3.00
6 JS,V:Durant 3.00

DATE WITH MILLIE
Atlas, Oct., 1956
[1st Series]
1 .... 300.00
2 .... 150.00
3 thru 7 .... @100.00
[2nd Series], Oct., 1959
1 .... 150.00
2 thru 7 .... @100.00
Becomes:

LIFE WITH MILLIE
1960
8 .... 125.00
9 & 10 .... @75.00
11 thru 20 .... @65.00
Becomes:

MODELING WITH MILLIE
1963
21 .... 125.00
22 thru 54 June, 1967 .... @65.00

DATE WITH PATSY
Sept., 1957
1 A:Patsy Walker............. 125.00

DAYDREAMERS
Aug., 1997
1 (of 3) JMD,MEg,HSm 2.75
2 JMD,MEg,HSm............. 2.75
3 JMD,TDz,MEg,HSm,concl. 2.75

DAZZLER
March, 1981
1 AA,JR2,A:X-Men,Spm,
    O:Dazzler.................. 5.00
2 WS,JR2,AA,X-Men,A:SpM...... 3.00
3 JR2,Dr.Doom 3.00
4 FS,Dr.Doom............... 3.00
5 FS,I:Blue Shield 3.00
6 FS,Hulk 3.00
7 FS,Hulk 3.00
8 FS,Quasar 3.00
9 FS,D:Klaw 3.00
10 FS,Galactus 3.00
11 FS,Galactus 3.00
12 FS,The Light That Failed 3.00
13 FS,V:Grapplers............ 3.00
14 FS,She Hulk 3.00
15 FS,BSz,Spider Women........ 3.00
16 FS,BSz,Enchantress.......... 3.00

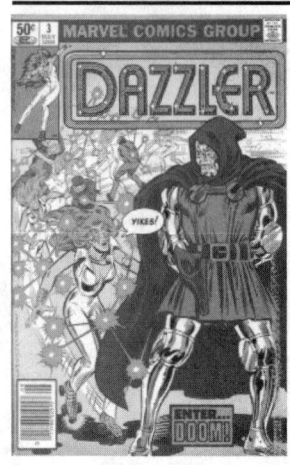

Dazzler #3
© Marvel Entertainment Group

17 FS,Angel,V:Doc Octopus 3.00
18 FS,BSz,A:Fantastic Four,Angel,
　V:Absorbing Man 3.00
19 FS,Blue Bolt,V:Absorbing Man . . 3.00
20 FS,V:Jazz and Horn 3.00
21 FS,A:Avengers,F.F.,C:X-Men,
　(double size) 3.00
22 FS,V:Rogue,Mystique 4.00
23 FS,V:Rogue,A:Powerman,
　Iron Fist 3.00
24 FS,V:Rogue,A:Powerman,
　Iron Fist 4.00
25 FS,`The Jagged Edge' 3.00
26 FS,Lois London. 3.00
27 FS,Fugitive 3.50
28 FS,V:Rogue 4.00
29 FS,Roman Nekoboh 3.00
30 FS,Moves to California 3.00
31 FS,The Last Wave 3.00
32 FS,A:Inhumans 3.00
33 Chiller 3.50
34 FS,Disappearance 3.00
35 FS,V:Racine Ramjets 3.00
36 JBy(c),FS,V:Tatterdemalion 3.00
37 JBy(c),FS 3.00
38 PC,JG,X-Men 5.00
39 PC,JG,Caught in the grip of
　death 3.00
40 PC,JG,Secret Wars II 3.50
41 PC,JG,A:Beast 3.50
42 PC,JG,A:Beast,last issue 3.50

DEADLIEST HEROES
OF KUNG FU
Summer, 1975
1 Magazine size 30.00

DEADLINE
April, 2002
1 (of 4) GyD, F:Katherine Farrell
　Daily Bugle reporter. 3.25
2 GyD,The Judge 3.25
3 GyD,The Judge 3.25
4 GyD,finale 3.25
TPB series rep. 10.00

DEADLY FOES
OF SPIDER-MAN
May, 1991
1 AM,KGa,V:Sinister Syndicate . . . 4.00

2 AM,Boomerang on Trial 3.00
3 AM,Deadly Foes Split 3.00
4 AM,Conclusion. 3.00
TPB rep. #1–#4 . . . . 13.00

DEADLY HANDS
OF KUNG FU
April, 1974
1 NA(c),JSa,JSon,O:Sons of
　the Tiger, B:Shang-Chi,
　Bruce Lee Pin-up 50.00
2 NA(c),JSa 40.00
3 NA(c),JSon,A:Sons of the Tiger. 30.00
4 NA(Bruce Lee)(c),JSon,Bruce
　Lee biography 30.00
5 BWS,PG 25.00
6 GP,JSon,A:Sons of the Tiger . . 25.00
7 GP,JSon,A:Sons of the Tiger . . 30.00
8 GP,JSon,A:Sons of the Tiger . . 22.00
9 GP,JSon,A:Sons of the Tiger. . 22.00
10 GP,JSon,A:Sons of the Tiger . . 30.00
11 NA(c),GP,JSon,A:Sons
　of the Tiger 22.00
12 NA(c),GP,JSon,A:Sons
　of the Tiger 22.00
13 GP,JSon,A:Sons of the Tiger . . 22.00
14 NA(c),GP,HC,JSon,A:Sons
　of the Tiger 65.00
15 JS.PG,JSn,,Annual #1 . . . . 22.00
16 JSn,A:Sons of the Tiger 20.00
17 NA(c),JSn,KG,A:Sons
　of the Tiger 20.00
18 JSn,A:Sons of the Tiger 20.00
19 JSn,I:White Tiger 22.00
20 GP,O:White Tiger 20.00
21 . . . . 20.00
22 KG,C:Jack of Hearts 20.00
23 GK,Jack of Hearts. 25.00
24 KG,Ironfist 25.00
25 I:Shimaru. 25.00
26 . . . . 25.00
27 . . . . 20.00
28 Bruce Lee Special. 75.00
29 Ironfist vs. Shang Chi 25.00
30 Swordquest. 20.00
31 JSon, Jack of Hearts 20.00
32 MR,JSon,Daughters of the
　Dragon. 20.00
33 MR,Feb., 1977 . . . . 22.00
Spec. Album Ed.,NA, Sum.,1974 . . 25.00

DEAD OF NIGHT
Dec., 1973–Aug., 1975
1 JSt,Horror reprints,A Haunted
　House is not a Home. 30.00
2 BEv(c),House that Fear Built . . 15.00
3 They Lurk Below 15.00
4 Warewolf Beware. 15.00
5 Deep Down 15.00
6 Jack the Ripper 15.00
7 SD,The Thirteenth Floor 15.00
8 Midnight Brings Dark Madness . 15.00
9 Deathride 15.00
10 SD,I Dream of Doom 15.00
11 GK/BWr(c),I:Scarecrow, Fires
　of Rebirth,Fires of Death 35.00

DEADPOOL
1993
1 B:FaN(s),JMd,MFm(i),
　V:Slayback,Nyko 5.00
2 JMd,MFm(i),V:Black Tom
　Cassidy,Juggernaut. 4.00
3 JMd,MFm(i),I:Comcast,
　Makeshift,Rive,A:Slayback 4.00
4 E:FaN(s),JMd,MFm(i),
　A:Slayback,Kane. 4.00

[2nd Limited Series], 1994
1 A:Banshee,Syrin,Juggernaut
　Black Tom 4.00
2 A:Banshee,Syrin,V:Juggernaut . . 4.00
3 A:Syrin,Juggernaut 4.00
4 Final issue 4.00

DEADPOOL
1996
1 NMa,V:Sasquatch,48pg, ... 7.00
2 NMa,A:Copycat 4.00
3 NMa,A:Siryn. 3.00
4 NMa,Will Hulk cure him? 3.00
5 NMa,A:Siryn,T-Ray 3.00
6 NMa,I: 3.00
7 AaL,A:Typhoid Mary. 3.00
8 NMa, cont. from Daredevil/
　Deadpool '97,A:Gerry 3.00
9 NMa, new villain 3.00
10 NMa,A:Great Lake Avengers . . 3.00
11 NMa,Fall through time, A:Alfred . 5.00
12 NMa,Typhoid Mary, Zoe
　Cullodon & Siryn return 3.00
13 NMa,V:T-Ray 3.00
14 WMc,Deal of a Lifetime 3.00
15 WMc,A:Landau, Luckman
　& Lake 3.00
16 WMc, in middle east 3.00
17 WMc, Landau, Luckman
　& Lake's plan. 3.00
18 WMc,V:Ajax 3.00
19 WMc,more secrets of blind Al. . . 3.00
20 Cosmic Messiah 3.00
21 . . . . 3.00
22 WMc,A:Cable 3.00
23 WMc,Dead Reckoning,pt.1
　48-page 3.00
24 WMc,Dead Reckoning,pt.2 . . . . 3.00
25 WMc,Dead Reckoning,pt.3 . . . . 3.00
26 Dead Reckoning,aftermath 3.00
27 V:A.I.M. concl. 3.00
28 R:Weasel 3.00
29 V:Bullseye 3.00
30 A:Mercedes,T-Ray 3.00
31 V:T-Ray. 3.00
32 V:T-Ray,A:Mercedes. 3.00
33 V:T-Ray 3.00
34 CPr,Chapter Pt.1. . . . . 3.00
35 CPr 3.00
36 CPr 3.00
37 CPr,Chapter X,Addendum 3.00
38 CPr,F:Taskmaster 3.00
39 CPr,F:Taskmaster 3.00
40 CPr,space station 3.00
41 CPr,V:Dirty Wolf 2.50
42 V:Humbug. 2.50
43 CPr,JCf,V:Rasputin 2.50
44 CPr,JCf,CatTrap,pt.1,x-over . . 2.50
45 CPr,JCf,Constrictor 2.50
46 JJu,JP,PC,CruelSummer,pt.1 . . 2.50
47 JP,PC,CruelSummer,pt.2 . . . . 2.50
48 JP,PC,CruelSummer,pt.3 . . . . . 2.50
49 JP,dating? 2.50
50 AAd,JP,DaR,I:Kid Deadpool . . 2.50
51 JP,DaR,F:Kid Deadpool 2.50
52 JP,AWi,ALa,V:Mercy Sisters 2.50
53 JP,AWi,ALa,V:Mercy Sisters . . . 2.50
54 JP,V:Punisher 2.50
55 JP,V:Punisher, round two 2.50
56 F:Siryn. 2.50
57 JHo,BWS(c),Agent of Weapon X 3.00
58 JHo,BWS(c),Agent of Weapon X 3.00
59 JHo,BWS(c),Agent of Weapon X 3.00
60 JHo,BWS(s),Agent of Weapon X 3.00
61 Funeral For a Freak 1. . . . . 2.50
62 Funeral For a Freak 2. . . . . 2.50
63 Funeral For a Freak 3. . . . . 2.50
64 Funeral For a Freak 4. . . . . 2.50
65 Did Deadpool survive 3.50
66 steal from Rhino? 3.50

MARVEL

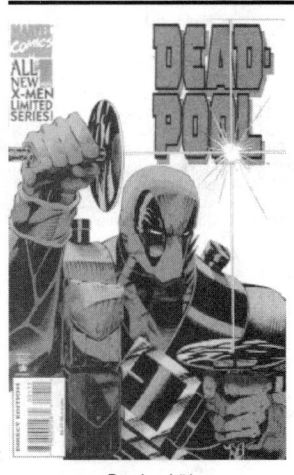

Deadpool #1
© Marvel Entertainment Group

67 R:Dazzler 3.50
68 V:Black Swan, insanity 3.50
69 V:Black Swan 3.50
Ann. '98 BCh(c) F:Deadpool & Death,
    48pg. 3.00
Minus 1 Spec., ALo, flashback,
    O:Deadpool 2.00
Spec. Deadpool Team-Up,2
    Deadpools,F:Widdle Wade 3.00
Spec. Baby's First Deadpool Book . 3.00
Spec. Encyclopedia Deadpoolica . . 3.00
TPB Circle Chase,FaN,JMd,MFm, 13.00
TPB Mission Improbable 15.00
TPB MWa,IaC,Sins of the Past,rep. 6.00

DEATH3
1993
1 I:Death Metal,Death Wreck 3.00
2 V:Ghost Rider 2.50
3 A:Hulk,Cable,Storm,Thing 2.50
4 Last issue. 2.50

DEATHLOK
[Limited Series], July, 1990
1 JC,SW,I:Michael Colins
    (2nd Deathlok). 4.00
2 JC,SW,V:Wajler 3.50
3 DCw,SW,V:Cyberants 3.50
4 DCw,SW,V:Sunfire,final issue . . . 3.50
[Regular Series], 1991–94
1 DCw,MM,V:Warwolf 2.50
2 DCw,MM,A:Dr.Doom,Machine
    Man,Forge. 2.50
3 DCw,MM,V:Dr.Doom,
    A:Mr.Fantastic 2.50
4 DCw,MM,A:X-Men,F.F.,Vision,
    O:Mechadoom 2.50
5 DCw,MM,V:Mechadoom,
    A:X-Men,Fantastic Four. 2.50
6 DCw,MM,A:Punisher,
    V:Silvermane 2.50
7 DCw,MM,A:Punisher,
    V:Silvermane 2.50
8 A:Main Frame,Ben Jacobs 2.00
9 DCw,MM,A:Ghost Rider,
    V:Nightmare. 2.50
10 DCw,MM,A:GhR,V:Nightmare. . . 2.50
11 DCw,MM,V:Moses Magnum 2.50
12 DCw,MM,Biohazard Agenda. . . . 2.50
13 DCw,MM,Biohazard Agenda. . . . 2.50
14 DCw,MM,Biohazard Agenda. . . . 2.50

15 DCw,MM,Biohazard Agenda. . . . 2.50
16 DCw,MM,Inf.War,V:Evilok 2.50
17 WMc,MM,B:Cyberwar. 2.50
18 WMc,A:Silver Sable 2.50
18a Newstand Ed. 2.50
19 SMc,Cyberwar#3 . . . . 3.50
20 SMc,Cyberwar#4 . . . . 2.50
21 E:Cyberwar,A:Cold Blood
    Nick Fury. 2.50
22 V:MosesMagnum,A:Bl.Panther. . 2.50
23 A:Bl.Panther,V:Phreak,Stroke . . . 2.50
24 V:MosesMagnum,A:Bl.Panther. . 2.50
25 WMc,V:MosesMagnum,A:Black
    Panther,holo-grafx(c). 3.50
26 V:Hobogoblin 2.50
27 R:Siege 2.50
28 Infinty Crusade 2.50
29 Inner Fears 2.50
30 KHd,V:Hydra 2.50
31 GWt(s),KoK,B:Cyberstrike,
    R:1st Deathlok. 2.50
32 GWt(s),KoK,A:Siege. 2.50
33 GWt(s),KoK,V:Justice Peace . . . 2.50
34 GWt(s),KoK,E:Cyberstrike,V:Justice
    Peace,final issue 2.50
Ann.#1 JG,I:Timestream 3.00
Ann.#2 I:Tracer,w/card. 3.25

DEATHLOK
July, 1999
1 JoC,JQ&JaL(c),Marvel Tech 2.50
2 JoC,A:Nick Fury. 2.25
2a variant cover 2.25
3 JoC,I:Billy Bailey 2.25
4 JoC,R:Clown 2.25
5 JoC,I:Jack Truman. 2.25
6 JoC, ... 2.25
7 JoC,V:Serpent Society. 2.25
8 JoC,Nick Fury 2.50
9 JoC,V:Ringmaster 2.50
10 JoC,V:Clown 2.50
11 JoC,V:Clown 2.50

DEATHLOK: DETOUR
Jan., 2004
1 (of 4) DaR 3.00
2 thru 4 DaR . . . . @3.00

DEATHLOK SPECIAL
1991
1 Rep.Mini Series 2.50
2 Rep.Mini Series 2.50
3 Rep.Mini Series 2.50
4 Rep.Mini Series, final issue 2.50

DEATH METAL
Marvel UK, 1994
1 JRe,I:Argon,C:Alpha Flight 2.25
2 JRe,V:Alpha Flight 2.25
3 JRe,I:Soulslug 2.25
4 Re,Last Issue. 2.25

DEATH METAL
VS. GENETIX
Marvel UK, 1993–94
1 PaD,w/card 3.00
2 PaD,w/card 3.00

DEATH'S HEAD
Marvel UK, Dec., 1988
1 V:Backbreaker 5.00
2 A:Dragons Claws 4.00
3 . . . . 4.00
4 V:Plague Dog. 3.00
5 V:Big Shot 3.00
6 V:Big Shot 3.00

Death's Head II #9
© Marvel Entertainment Group

7 & 8 . . . . @3.00
9 A:Fantastic Four. 3.50
10 A:Iron Man 3.50
TPB Reprints#1-#10 . . . . 12.95

DEATH'S HEAD
[Limited Series]
1 A:`Old' Death's Head 2.00

DEATH'S HEAD II
Marvel UK, March, 1992
[Limited Series]
1 LSh,I:2nd Death's Head,
    D:1st Death's Head. 4.00
1a 2nd printing,Silver 2.50
2 LSh,A:Fantastic Four. 3.00
2a 2nd printing,Silver 3.00
3 LSh,I:Tuck 3.50
4 LSh,A:Wolverine,Spider-Man,
    Punisher 3.50
[Regular Series], 1992
1 LSh,A:X-Men,I:Wraithchilde. 3.00
2 LSh,A:X-Men. 2.25
3 LSh,A:X-Men,V:Raptors. 2.25
4 LSh,A:X-Men,V:Wraithchilde 2.25
5 V:UnDeath's Head II,
    A:Warheads. 2.25
6 R:Tuck,V:Major Oak. 2.25
7 V:Major Oak. 2.25
8 V:Wizard Methinx. 2.25
9 BHi,V:Cybernetic Centaurs 2.25
10 DBw,A:Necker. 2.25
11 SCy,R:Charnel 2.25
12 DAn(s),SvL,V:Charnel. 2.25
13 SvL,A:Liger. 2.25
14 SvL,Brain Dead Cold,Blue
    Foil(c). 3.25
15 SvL,V:Duplicates. 2.25
16 SvL,DAn 2.25
17 SvL,DAn 2.00
18 SvL,DAn 2.00
Spec. Gold Ed. LSh(a&s). 4.00

DEATH'S HEAD II/DIE CUT
Marvel UK, 1993
1 I:Die Cut. 3.25
2 O:Die Cut. 2.25

MARVEL

DEATH'S HEAD II/
KILLPOWER: BATTLETIDE

[1st Limited Series]

1 GSr,A:Wolverine	2.50
2 thru 4 GSr,A:Wolverine	@2.25

[2nd Limited Series]

1 A:Hulk	3.25
2 V:Hulk	2.25
3 A:Hulk	2.25
4 last issue	2.25

DEATH-WRECK

Marvel UK, 1994

1 A:Death's Head II	2.25
2 V:Gangsters	2.25
3 A:Dr.Necker	2.25
4 last issue	2.25

DEEP, THE

Nov., 1977

1 CI,Movie Adaption	8.00

DEFENDERS

Aug., 1972

1 SB,I&D:Necrodames	150.00
2 SB,V:Calizuma	75.00
3 GK(c),SB,JM,V:UndyingOne	50.00
4 SB,FMc,Bl.Knight,V:Valkyrie	50.00
5 SB,FMc,D:Omegatron	50.00
6 SB,FMc,V:Cyrus Black	40.00
7 SB,FBe,A:Hawkeye	35.00
8 SB,FBe,Avengers,SilverSurfer	45.00
9 SB,FMc,Avengers	45.00
10 SB,FBe,Thor vs. Hulk	60.00
11 SB,FBe,A:Avengers	35.00
12 SB,JA,Xemnu	20.00
13 GK(c),SB,KJ,J:Night Hawk	20.00
14 SB,DGr,O:Hyperion	20.00
15 SB,KJ,A:Professor X,V:Magneto, Savage Land Mutates	25.00
16 GK(c),SB,Professor X,V:Magneto, Savage Land Mutates	25.00
17 SB,DGr,Power Man	12.00
18 GK(c),SB,DGr,A:Power Man	12.00
19 GK(c),SB,KJ,A:Power Man	12.00
20 K&R(c),SB,A:Thing	12.00
21 GK(c),SB,O:Valkyrie	7.00
22 GK(c),SB,V:Sons o/t Serpent	7.00
23 GK(c),SB,A:Yellow Jacket	7.00
24 GK(c),SB,BMc,A:Daredevil	7.00
25 GK(c),SB,JA,A:Daredevil	7.00
26 K&R(c),SB,A:Guardians	10.00
27 K&R(c),SB,A:Guardians C:Starhawk	10.00
28 K&R(c),SB,A:Guardians I:Starhawk	8.00
29 K&R(c),SB,A:Guardians	8.00
30 JA(i),A:Wong	6.00
31 GK(c),SB,JM,Nighthawk	6.00
32 GK(c),SB,JM,O:Nighthawk	6.00
33 GK(c),SB,JM,V:Headmen	6.00
34 SB,JM,V:Nebulon	6.00
35 GK(c),SB,KJ,I:Red Guardian	6.00
36 GK(c),SB,KJ,A:Red Guardian	12.00
37 GK(c),SB,KJ,J:Luke Cage	7.00
38 SB,KJ,V:Nebulon	12.00
39 SB,KJ,V:Felicia	5.00
40 SB,KJ,V:Assassin	5.00
41 KG,KJ,Nighthawk	5.00
42 KG,KJ,V:Rhino	5.00
43 KG,KJ,Cobalt Man,Egghead	5.00
44 KG,KJ,J:Hellcat,V:Red Rajah	5.00
45 KG,KJ,Valkyrie II	5.00
46 KG,KJ,L:DrStrange,LukeCage	5.00
47 KG,KJ,Moon Knight	5.00
48 KG,A:Wonder Man	5.00
49 KG,O:Scorpio	5.00
50 KG,Zodiac,D:Scorpio	5.00

51 KG,Moon Knight	5.00
52 KG,Hulk,V:Sub Mariner	5.00
53 KG,DC,MG,TA,C&I:Lunatik	4.00
54 MG,Nigh Fury	4.00
55 CI,O:Red Guardian	4.00
56 CI,KJ,Hellcat,V:Lunatik	4.00
57 DC,Ms.Marvel	4.00
58 Return of Dr.Strange	4.00
59 I:Belathauzer	4.00
60 V:Vera Gemini	4.00
61 Spider-Man,A:Lunatik	5.00
62 Hercules,C:Polaris	3.00
63 Mutli Heroes	3.00
64 Mutli Heroes	3.00
65 Red Guardian	3.00
66 JB,Valkyrie I	3.00
67 Valkryie II	3.00
68 HT,When Falls the Mountain	3.00
69 HT,A:The Anything Man	3.00
70 HT,A:Lunatik	3.00
71 HT,O:Lunatik	3.00

Defenders #51
© *Marvel Entertainment Group*

72 HT,V:Lunatik	3.00
73 HT,Foolkiller,V:WizardKing	5.00
74 HT,Foolkiller,L:Nighthawk	5.00
75 HT,Foolkiller	4.00
76 HT,O:Omega	2.50
77 HT,Moon Dragon	2.50
78 HT,Yellow Jacket	2.50
79 HT,Tunnel World	2.50
80 HT,DGr,Nighthawk	2.50
81 HT,Tunnel World	2.50
82 DP,JSt,Tunnel World	2.50
83 DP,JSt,Tunnel World	2.50
84 DP,JSt,Black Panther	2.50
85 DP,JSt,Black Panther	2.50
86 DP,JSt,Black Panther	2.50
87 DP,JSt,V:Mutant Force	2.50
88 DP,JSt,Matt Mardock	2.50
89 DP,JSt,D:Hellcat's Mother, O:Mad-Dog	2.50
90 DP,JSt,Daredevil	2.50
91 DP,JSt,Daredevil	2.50
92 DP,JSt,A:Eternity, Son of Satan	3.00
93 DP,JSt,Son of Satan	3.00
94 DP,JSt,I:Gargoyle	2.50
95 DP,JSt,V:Dracula,O:Gargoyle	2.50
96 DP,JSt,Ghost Rider	3.00
97 DP,JSt,False Messiah	2.50
98 DP,JSt,A:Man Thing	2.50
99 DP,JSt,Conflict	2.50
100 DP,JSt,DoubleSize,V:Satan	6.00
101 DP,JSt,Silver Surfer	2.50

102 DP,JSt,Nighthawk	2.50
103 DP,JSt,I:Null	2.50
104 DP,JSt,Devilslayer,J:Beast	2.50
105 DP,JSt,V:Satan	2.50
106 DP,Daredevil,D:Nighthawk	2.50
107 DP,JSt,Enchantress,A:D.D.	2.50
108 DP,A:Enchantress	2.50
109 DP,A:Spider-Man	3.00
110 DP,A:Devilslayer	2.50
111 DP,A:Hellcat	2.50
112 DP,A:SquadronSupreme	2.50
113 DP,A:SquadronSupreme	2.50
114 DP,A:SquadronSupreme	2.50
115 DP,A:Submariner	2.50
116 DP,Gargoyle	2.50
117 DP,Valkyrie	2.50
118 DP,V:Miracleman	2.50
119 DP,V:Miracleman	2.50
120 DP,V:Miracleman	2.50
121 DP,V:Miracleman	2.50
122 DP,A:Iceman	2.50
123 DP,I:Cloud,V:Secret Empire	2.50
124 DP,V:Elf	2.50
125 DP,New Line-up:Gargoyle,Moon dragon,Valkyrie,Iceman,Beast, Angel,W:Son of Satan & Hellcat I:Mad Dog	5.00
126 DP,A:Nick Fury	2.50
127 DP,V:Professor Power	2.50
128 DP,V:Professor Power	2.50
129 DP,V:Professor Power,New Mutants X-over	2.50
130 DP,V:Professor Power	2.50
131 DP,V:Walrus,A:Frogman	2.50
132 DP,V:Spore Monster	2.50
133 DP,V:Spore Monster	2.50
134 DP,I:Manslaughter	2.50
135 DP,V:Blowtorch Brand	2.50
136 DP,V:Gargoyle	2.50
137 DP,V:Gargoyle	2.50
138 DP,O:Moondragon	2.50
139 DP,A:Red Wolf,V:Trolls	2.50
140 DP,V:Asgardian Trolls	2.50
141 DP,All Flesh is Grass	2.50
142 DP,V:M.O.N.S.T.E.R.	2.50
143 DP,I:Andromeda,Runner	2.50
144 DP,V:Moondragon	2.50
145 DP,V:Moondragon	2.50
146 DP,Cloud	2.50
147 DP,A:Andromeda,I:Interloper	2.50
148 DP,A:Nick Fury	2.50
149 DP,V:Manslaughter,O:Cloud	2.50
150 DP,O:Cloud,double-size	5.00
151 DP,A:Interloper	2.50
152 DP,Secret Wars II,D:Moon-dragon,Valkyrie,Gargoyle	5.00
G-Size#1 GK(c),JSn,AM,O:Hulk	22.00
G-Size#2 GK,KJ,Son of Satan	15.00
G-Size#3 JSn,DA,JM,DN,A:D.D.	10.00
G-Size#4 GK(c),DH,A:YellowJack	20.00
G-Size#5 K&R(c),DH,A:Guardians	25.00
Ann.#1 SB,KJ	7.00

DEFENDERS

Jan., 2001

1 EL,KBk,KJ,48-page	6.00
2A EL,KBk,KJ,	3.00
2B variant AAd(c)	3.50
3 EL,KBk,KJ,V:Pluto	2.50
4 EL,KBk,KJ,V:Pluto	2.50
5 EL,KBk,KJ,A:Dr.Strange	2.50
6 EL,KBk,KJ,A:Red Raven	2.50
7 EL,KBk,KJ,A:Red Raven	2.50
8 EL,KBk,AG,V:Headmen	2.50
9 EL,KBk,RF,V:Headmen	2.50
10 EL,KBk,SB,V:Headmen	2.50
11 EL,KBk,SB,V:Attuma,DeepSix	2.50
12 EL,KBk,'Nuff Said,48-pg.	3.50
Spec.Day of the Defenders, mag.	3.50

DEFENDERS OF DYNATRON CITY
1992
1 FC,I:Defenders of Dynatron City
 (from video game & TV ser.) . . . 3.00
2 FC,O:Defender of D.City 3.00
3 FC,A:Dr Mayhem. 3.00
4 FC 3.00
5 FC,V:Intelligent Fleas 3.00
6 FC,V:Dr.Mayhem 3.00

DEFENDERS OF THE EARTH
Jan., 1987–Sept., 1984
1 AS,Flash Gordon & Mandrake. . . 5.00
2 AS,Flash Gordon & Mandrake. . . 4.00
3 AS,O:Phantom. 4.00
4 AS,O:Mandrake 4.00

DELLA VISION
Atlas, April, 1955
1 The Television Queen 175.00
2 . . . . 125.00
3 . . . . 125.00
Becomes:
PATTY POWERS
1955
4 . . . . 100.00
5 . . . . 50.00
6 . . . . 50.00
7 Oct., 1956 . . . . 50.00

Dennis The Menace #7
© Marvel Entertainment Group

DENNIS THE MENACE
Nov., 1981–Nov., 1982
1 . . . . 12.00
2 thru 13 . . . . @7.00

DESTROYER, THE
1989–90
1 Black & White Mag. 3.50
2 thru 10 . . . . @2.50
TPB rep. B/w mag(color) 9.95

THE DESTROYER: TERROR
Dec., 1991
1 V:Nuihc 2.50

2 V:Nuihc 2.25
3 GM,V:Nuihc 2.25
4 DC,`The Last Dinosaur' 2.25

DEVIL DINOSAUR
April, 1978–Dec., 1978
1 JK,I:Devil Dinosaur,Moon Boy . 25.00
2 JK,War With the Spider God . . . 15.00
3 JK,Giant 15.00
4 JK,Objects From the Sky 15.00
5 JK,The Kingdom of the Ants . . . 15.00
6 JK,The Fall 15.00
7 JK,Prisoner of the Demon Tree 15.00
8 JK,V:Dino Riders 15.00
9 JK,Lizards That Stand 15.00

DEVIL DINOSAUR SPRING FLING
1997
Spec. F:Devil Dinosaur,Moon-Boy . . 3.00

DEVIL-DOG DUGAN
Atlas, July, 1956
1 War Stories 150.00
2 JSe(c) 90.00
3 . . . . 75.00
Becomes:
TALE OF THE MARINES
4 BP,War Stories 75.00
Becomes:
MARINES AT WAR
5 War Stories 75.00
6 . . . . 75.00
7 The Big Push, Aug., 1957 . . . . . 75.00

DEXTER THE DEMON
See: MELVIN THE MONSTER

DIE-CUT
Marvel UK, 1993–94
1 A:Beast 2.50
2 V:X-Beast. 2.25
3 A:Beast,Prof.X 2.25
4 V:Red Skull 2.25

DIE-CUT VS. G-FORCE
Marvel UK, 1993
1 SFr(s),LSh(c),I:G-Force 3.00
2 SFr(s),LSh(c),Last issue 3.00

DIGITEK
Marvel UK, 1992–93
1 DPw,I:Digitek,C:Deathlok. 2.25
2 DPw,A:Deathlok,V:Bacillicons . . 2.25
3 DPw,A:Deathlok,V:Bacillicons . . 2.25
4 DPw,V:Bacillicons 2.25

DINO RIDERS
Feb., 1989
1 Based on Toys 3.00
2 . . . . 3.00
3 May, 1989 . . . . 3.00

DINOSAURS: A CELEBRATION
Epic, 1992
Horns and Heavy Armor 5.00
Bone-Heads and Duck-Bills. 5.00
Terrible Claws and Tyrants 5.00
Egg Stealers and Earth Shakers . . 5.00
TPB 192pg. 12.95

DISNEY AFTERNOON
1994–95
1 DarkwingDuck vs.FearsomeFive. 3.50
2 thru 10 . . . . @3.00

DISNEY COMIC HITS
1995
1 . . . . 5.00
2 thru 9 . . . . @4.00
10 Hunchback of Notre Dame 5.00
11 thru 17 . . . . @4.00

DISNEY PRESENTS
1 F:Aladdin 2.50
2 F:Timon & Pummba. 2.50
3 . . . . 2.50

DISTRICT X
May, 2004
1 Mr.M,pt.1,F:Bishop,Ismael 3.00
2 thru 6 Mr.M,pt.2 thru pt.6 . . . . @3.00

Doc Samson #4
© Marvel Entertainment Group

DOC SAMSON
1996
1 From The Incredible Hulk 2.25
2 A:She-Hulk. 2.25
3 . . . . 2.25
4 . . . . 2.25

DOC SAVAGE
Oct., 1972
1 JM,Pulp Adapts,Death Eighty
 Stories High 30.00
2 JSo(c),The Feathered Serpent
 Strikes 20.00
3 JSo(c),Silver Death's Head 20.00
4 JSo(c),The Hell Diver 15.00
5 GK(c),Night of the Monsters . . . 15.00
6 JSo(c),Where Giants Walk 15.00
7 JSo(c),Brand of the Werewolfs . 15.00
8 In the Lair of the Werewolf
 Jan., 1974 . . . . 15.00
G-Size#1 thru #2 Reprints 12.00

DOC SAVAGE
Aug., 1975
(black & white magazine)
1 JB,Ph(c),Ron Ely 20.00

2 JB 15.00
3 JB 15.00
4 thru 7 . . . . @15.00
8 Spring 1977 . . . . 15.00

DOCTOR OCTOPUS: NEGATIVE EXPOSURE
Oct., 2003
1 (of 5) 2.50
2 V:Vulture 2.50
3 thru 5 . . . . @3.00
TPB 14.00

DOCTOR SPECTRUM
Aug., 2004
1 (of 6) F:Corporal Joe Ledger 3.00
2 . . . . 3.00
3 . . . . 3.00

DR. STRANGE
[1st Series], June, 1968
Prev: Strange Tales
169 DA,O:Dr.Strange 225.00
170 DA,A:Ancient One. 75.00
171 TP,DA,V:Dormammu. 65.00
172 GC,TP,V:Dormammu 65.00
173 GC,TP,V:Dormammu 65.00
174 GC,TP,I:Satannish 65.00
175 GC,TP,I:Asmodeus 65.00
176 GC,TP,V:Asmodeus 65.00
177 GC,TP,D:Asmodeus,
    N:Dr.Strange 65.00
178 GC,TP,A:Black Knight. 65.00
179 BWS(c),rep.Amazing Spider-
    Man #2 . . . . 65.00
180 GC,TP,V:Nightmare. 65.00
181 FB(c),GC,TP,I:Demons of
    Despair 65.00
182 GC,TP,V:Juggernaut. 60.00
183 BEv(c),GC,TP,
    I:Undying Ones 60.00

[2nd Regular Series], 1974–87
1 FB,DG,I:Silver Dagger 75.00
2 FB,DG,I:Soul Eater 35.00
3 FB,A:Dormammu 20.00
4 FB,DG,V:Death 20.00
5 FB,DG,A:Silver Dagger 20.00
6 FB(c),GC,KJ,A:Gaea,I:Gaea . . . 12.00
7 GC,JR,A:Dormammu. 12.00
8 GK(c),GC,TP,O:Clea 12.00
9 GK(c),GC,A:Dormammu,O:Clea 12.00
10 B:MWn(s),GK(c),GC,A:Eternity. 12.00
11 JR(c),GC,TP,A:Eternity 7.00
12 GC,TP,A:Eternity. 7.00
13 GC,TP,A:Eternity. 7.00
14 GC,TP,A:Dracula. 7.00
15 GC,TP,A:Devil 7.00
16 GC,TP,A:Devil 7.00
17 GC,TP,A:Styggro. 7.00
18 GC,A:Styggro 7.00
19 GC,AA,I:Xander 7.00
20 A:Xander 7.00
21 DA,O:Dr.Strange 8.00
22 I:Apalla 8.00
23 E:MWn(s),JSn,A:Wormworld . . 8.00
24 JSn,A:Apalla,I:Visamajoris 8.00
25 AM,V:Dr.Strange Yet 8.00
26 JSn,A:The Ancient One 8.00
27 TS,A:Stygyro,Sphinx 8.00
28 TS,A:Ghost Rider,
    V:In-Betweener 5.00
29 TS,A:Nighthawk 4.00
30 I:Dweller 4.00
31 TS,A:Sub Mariner 4.00
32 A:Sub Mariner 4.00
33 TS,A:The Dreamweaver 4.00
34 TS,A:Nightmare,D:CyrusBlack . . 4.00
35 TS,V:Dweller,I:Ludi 4.00

Doctor Strange 2nd Series, #34
© Marvel Entertainment Group

36 Thunder of the Soul 4.00
37 Fear,the Final Victor 4.00
38 GC,DG,A:Baron Mordo 4.00
39 GC,DG,A:Baron Mordo 4.00
40 GC,A:Asrael 4.00
41 GC,A:Man Thing 3.50
42 GC,A:Black Mirror. 3.50
43 V:Shadow Queen 3.50
44 GC,A:Princess Shialmar 3.50
45 GC,A:Demon in the Dark 3.50
46 FM,A:Sibylis 3.50
47 MR,TA,I:Ikonn 3.50
48 MR,TA,Brother Voodoo 3.50
49 MR,TA,A:Baron Mordo 3.50
50 MR,TA,A:Baron Mordo 3.50
51 MR,TA,A:Sgt. Fury,
    V:Baron Mordo 3.50
52 MR,TA,A:Nightmare 4.00
53 MR,TA,A:Nightmare,Fantastic
    Four,V:Rama-Tut 4.00
54 PS,V:Tiboro. 4.00
55 MGo,TA,V:Madness 4.00
56 PS,TA,O:Dr.Strange 5.00
57 KN,TA,A:Dr.Doom. 4.00
58 DGr,TA,V:Dracula 5.00
59 DGr,TA,V:Dracula 5.00
60 DGr,TA,Scarlet Witch 5.00
61 DGr,TA,V:Dracula 5.00
62 SL,V:Dracula 5.00
63 CP,V:Topaz 4.00
64 TSa,`Art Rage' 4.00
65 PS,Charlatan. 4.00
66 PS,`The Cosen One'. 4.00
67 SL,A:Jessica Drew,Shroud 4.00
68 PS,A:Black Knight. 4.00
69 PS,A:Black Knight. 4.00
70 BBl,V:Umar. 4.00
71 DGr,O:Dormammu 4.00
72 PS,V:Umar 4.00
73 PS,V:Umar 4.00
74 MBg,Secret Wars II. 4.00
75 A:Fantastic Four 4.00
76 A:Fantastic Four 4.00
77 A:Topaz 4.00
78 A:Cloak,I:Ecstacy 3.50
79 A:Morganna 3.00
80 A:Morganna,C:Rintah 3.00
81 V:Urthona,I:Rintah. 3.00
Ann.#1 CR,`Doomworld' 15.00
GN Dr.Strange: What is it that
    Distrubs you, Stephen?, CR,
    revised from Dr.Strange Ann.#1,
    48pg bookshelf (Aug., 1997) . . 10.00

G-Size#1 K&R(c),reps Strange
    Tales#164-#168. . . . . 10.00

[3rd Regular Series], 1988–96
1 V:Dorammu 4.00
2 V:Dorammu 3.00
3 I:Dragon Force. 3.00
4 EL(c),A:Dragon Force 3.00
5 JG,V:Baron Mordo 3.50
6 JG,I:Mephista 3.00
7 JG,V:Agamotto,Mephista 3.00
8 JG,V:Mephisto & Satanish 3.00
9 JG,O:Dr.Strange. 3.00
10 JG,V:Morbius. 3.50
11 JG,A of V,V:Hobgoblin,
    C:Morbius 4.00
12 JG,A of V,V:Enchantress 2.75
13 JG,A of V,V:Arkon 2.75
14 JG,B:Vampiric Verses,
    A:Morbius 3.50
15 JG,A:Morbius,Amy Grant(C) . . . 5.00
16 JG,A:Morbius,Brother Voodoo . 3.50
17 JV,TD,A:Morbius,Br.Voodoo . . . 3.50
18 JG,E:Vampiric Verses,A:Morbius,
    Brother Voodoo,R:Varnae 3.50
19 GC,A:Azrael 2.50
20 JG,TD,A:Morbius,V:Zom 3.50
21 JG,TD,B:Dark Wars,
    R:Dormammu 2.50
22 JG,TD,LW,V:Dormammu. 2.50
23 JG,LW,V:Dormammu. 2.50
24 JG,E:Dark Wars,V:Dormammu . 2.50
25 RLm,A:Red Wolf, Black Crow. . 2.50
26 GI,V:Werewolf By Night 2.50
27 GI,V:Werewolf By Night 2.50
28 X-over Ghost Rider #12,
    V:Zodiac 3.00
29 A:Baron Blood. 2.50
30 Topaz' Fate 2.50
31 TD,Inf.Gauntlet,A:Silver Surfer . . 3.00
32 Inf.Gauntlet,A:Warlock,Silver
    Surfer,V:Silver Dagger. 2.50
33 Inf.Gauntlet,V:Thanos,
    Zota,A:Pip 2.50
34 Inf.Gauntlet,V:Dr.Doom,
    A:Pip,Scarlet Witch. 2.50
35 Inf.Gauntlet,A:Thor,Pip,
    Scarlet Witch 2.50
36 Inf.Gauntlet,A:Warlock(leads
    into Warlock&Inf.Watch#1) 3.00
37 GI,V:Frankensurfer 2.50
38 GI,Great Fear #1. . . . . 2.50
39 GI,Great Fear #2. . . . . 2.50
40 GI,Great Fear #3,A:Daredevil. . . 2.50
41 GI,A:Wolverine 3.00
42 GI,Infinity War,V:Galactus,A:
    Silver Surfer. 2.50
43 GI,Infinity War,Galactus Vs.
    Agamotto,A:Silver Surfer. 2.50
44 GI,Infinity War,V:Juggernaut . . . 2.50
45 GI,Inf.War,O:Doctor Strange . . . 2.50
46 GI,Inf.War,R:old costume 2.50
47 GI,Inf.War,V:doppleganger 2.50
48 GI,V:The Vishanti 2.50
49 GI,R:Dormammu. 2.50
50 GI,A:Hulk,Ghost Rider,Silver
    Surfer,V:Dormammu(leads into
    Secret Defenders)holo-grafx(c) . 3.50
51 GI,V:Religious Cult 2.50
52 GI,A:Morbius. 2.50
53 GI,Closes Mansion,L:Wong . . . 2.50
54 GI,Infinity Crusade 2.50
55 GI,Inf.Crusade. 2.50
56 GI,Inf.Crusade. 2.50
57 A:Kyllian,Urthona 2.50
58 V:Urthona 2.50
59 GI,V:Iskelior 2.50
60 B:DQ(s),Siege of
    Darkness,pt.#7 . . . . 4.00
61 Siege of Darkness,pt.#15 . . . . . 3.25
62 V:Dr.Doom 2.50
63 JJ(c),V:Morbius 2.50

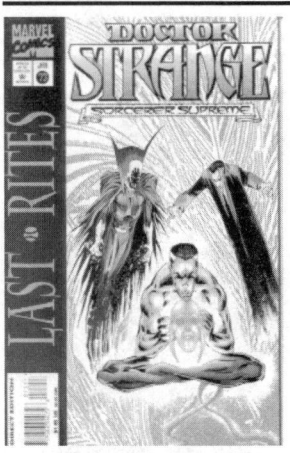

Doctor Strange, 3rd Series, #73
© Marvel Entertainment Group

64 MvR,V:Namor 2.50
65 MvR,V:Namor,Vengeance 2.75
66 A:Wong 2.75
67 R:Clea 2.75
68 MvR 2.50
69 MvR 2.50
70 A:Hulk 2.50
71 V:Hulk 2.50
72 Metallic(c),Last Rites,pt.1 . . . . 2.50
73 Last Rites,pt.2 . . . . 2.50
74 SY,DQ,Last Rites,pt.3 . . . . 2.50
75 Prismatic cover 4.00
76 I:New Costume 2.50
77 Mob Clean-up 2.50
78 R:Chton 2.50
79 Doc's new Asylum 2.50
80 Missing for four months? 2.50
81 A:Nick Fury 2.50
82 A:Hellstorm 2.50
83 V:Tempo Mob,Dormammu 2.50
84 The Homecoming,pt.1 . . . . 2.50
85 The Homecoming,pt.2 . . . . 2.50
86 The Homecoming,pt.3 . . . . 2.50
87 The Homecoming,pt.4 . . . . 2.50
88 The Fall of the Tempo,pt.1 . . . . 2.50
89 The Fall of the Tempo,pt.2 . . . . 2.50
90 final issue 2.50
Ann #2 Return of Defenders,Pt4 . . . 5.00
Ann #3 GI,I:Killiam,w/card 3.50
Ann.#4 V:Salome 3.50
Spec. Dr. Strange/Ghost Rider#1
  Newsstand vers. of Dr.
  Strange #28 (1991) 6.00
Spec.#1 Dr. Strange vs. Dracula
  rep. MWn(s),GC (1994) 2.50
GNv Triumph and Torment MBg,
  F:Dr. Strange & Dr.Doom 9.95
  HC 14.95
Ashcan 75
TPB A Separate Reality, 224-pg. . . 19.95

DOCTOR STRANGE
Dec., 1998
1 (of 4) TyH,killer pursued 3.00
2 TyH,secrets in Topaz 3.00
3 TyH,magic in Manhattan 3.00
4 TyH,PC,conclusion 3.00

DR. STRANGE CLASSICS
March, 1984
1 SD,Reprints 3.50
2 thru 4 . . . . @3.50

DOCTOR WHO
1984–86
1 BBC TV Series,UK reprints,
  Return of the Daleks 7.00
2 Star Beast 6.00
3 Transformation 5.00
4 A:K-9,Daleks 5.00
5 V:Time Witch,Colin Baker
  interview 5.00
6 B:Ancient Claw saga 5.00
7 . . . . 5.00
8 The Collector 5.00
9 The Life Bringer 5.00
10 This is your Life 5.00
11 The Deal 5.00
12 End of the Line 5.00
13 V:The Cybermen 5.00
14 Clash of the Neutron Knight . . . 5.00
15 B:Peter Davison-Dr. Who 5.00
16 Into the Realm of Satan, ... 5.00
17 Peter Davison Interview 5.00
18 A:Four Dr.Who's 5.00
19 A:The Sontarans 5.00
20 The Stockbridge Horror 5.00
21 The Stockbridge Horror 5.00
22 The Stockbridge Horror 5.00
23 The Unearthly Child 5.00

DR. ZERO
Epic, April, 1988
1 BSz,DCw,I:Dr.Zero 2.50
2 BSz,DCw 2.25
3 BSz,DCw 2.25
4 thru 6 . . . . @2.25
7 DSp 2.25
8 End series, Aug., 1989 . . . . 2.25

DOLLY DILL
1945
1 Newsstand 165.00

DOMINATION FACTOR
Sept., 1999
1.1 Fantastic Four (of 4) DJu,
  JOy,BMc,x-over 2.50
1.2 Avengers, DJu,JO,
  DJa, x-over 2.50
2.3 Fantastic Four, DJu,BMc 2.50
2.4 Avengers, DJu,JOy,DJa 2.50
3.5 Fantastic Four, DJu,BMc 2.50
3.6 Avengers, JOy,DJa 2.50
4.7 Fantastic Four, DJu,BMc 2.50
4.8 Avengers, DJa,JOy,concl 2.50

DOMINO
1996
1 thru 3 . . . . @2.25

DOMINO
May, 2003
1 (of 4) BSf 2.50
2 thru 4 BSf . . . . @2.50

DOOM 2099
1993–96
1 PB,I:Doom 2099,V:Tiger Wylde,
  foil(c) 3.00
2 I:Rook Seven 2.50
3 PB,V:Tiger Wylde 2.50
4 PB,V:Tiger Wylde 2.50
5 PB,I:Fever 2.50
6 I:Duke Stratosphear 2.50
7 PB,I:Paloma,V:Duke,Fever Haze 2.50
8 PB,C:Ravage 2.50
9 EC,V:Jack the Ripper 2.50
10 PB,w/Poster 2.50

11 PB,I:Thandaza 2.50
12 PB,V:Thandaza 2.50
13 PB(c),JFm(s),V:Necrotek 2.50
14 RLm(c),PB,Fall o/t Hammer#4 . . 2.50
15 PB,I:Radian 2.50
16 EC(a&s), ... 2.50
17 PB,V:Radian,w/card 2.50
18 PB, ... 2.50
19 PB,C:Bloodhawk 2.50
20 PB,A:Bloodhawk 2.50
21 PB,Shadow King 2.50
22 PB,R:Duke Stratosphere 2.50
23 PB,R:Tyger Wylde 2.50
24 PB 2.50
25 PB 3.50
25a foil cover 4.00
26 . . . . 2.50
27 Revolution 2.50
28 Prologue to D-Day 2.50

Doom 2099 #25
© Marvel Entertainment Group

Becomes:

DOOM 2099 A.D.
1995
29 Doom Invades America 4.00
29a Chromium Cover 4.00
30 D:Corporate Head 2.50
31 PB,One Nation Under Doom . . . 2.50
32 Ravage Aftermath 2.50
33 . . . . 2.50
34 I:Anthony Herod 2.50
35 E:One Nation Under Doom 2.50
36 . . . . 2.50
37 thru 39 . . . . @2.50
40 Rage Against Time,pt.1 . . . . 2.50
41 Rage Against Time,pt.2 . . . . 2.50
TPB Villainy of Doctor Doom 18.00

DOOM
Aug., 2000
1 (of 3) CDi,F:Dr.Doom 3.00
2 CDi,Al Khalad 3.00
3 CDi,concl. 3.00

DOOM:
THE EMPEROR RETURNS
Nov., 2001
1 CDi,F:Dr. Doom 2.50
2 CDi,center of Counter-Earth 2.50
3 CDi, ... 2.50
TPB Doom, rep. 144-pg. 16.00

DOPEY DUCK COMICS
Timely, Fall, 1945
1 A:Casper Cat,Krazy Krow 250.00
2 A:Casper Cat,Krazy Krow 225.00
Becomes:

WACKY DUCK
1946
3 Paperchase(c) 225.00
4 Wacky Duck(c) 200.00
5 Duck & Devil(c) 175.00
6 Cliffhanger(c) 175.00
1 Baketball(c) 125.00
2 Traffic Light(c) 125.00
Becomes:

JUSTICE COMICS

DOUBLE DRAGON
July, 1991
1 I:Billy&Jimmy Lee 2.50
2 Dragon Statue Stolen,V:Stelth . . . 2.50
3 Billy Vs. Jimmy 2.50
4 Dragon Force out of control. 2.50
5 V:Stealth. 2.50
6 V:Nightfall, final issue 2.50

DOUBLE EDGE
1995
Alpha Punisher vs. Nick Fury 5.00
Omega D:Major Character. 5.00

D.P. 7
Nov., 1986
1 O:DP7 .... 2.50
2 V:Headhunter. 2.50
3 RT,Headhunters. 2.50
4 RT,V:Wompus 2.50
5 RT,Exorcist. 2.50
6 RT,I:The Sweat Shop. 2.50
7 RT,V:Clinic 2.50
8 RT,V:Clinic 2.50
9 RT,AW,I:New Paranormals 2.50
10 RT,I:Mysterious People........ 2.50
11 AW(i)V:Regulator. 2.50
12 O:Randy 2.50
13 O:Charly 2.50
14 AW 2.50
15 .... 2.50
16 V:BlackPower 2.50
17 .... 2.50
18 Pitt tie-in 2.50
19 .... 2.50
20 Spitfire.................... 2.50
21 .... 3.00
22 .... 3.00
23 A:PsiForce. 3.00
24 A:Mastodon. 3.00
25 V:Famileech 3.00
26 V:Famileech 3.00
27 The Pitt 3.00
28 V:The Candidate. 3.00
29 Deadweight. 3.00
30 V:Para-troop 3.00
31 A:Chrome 3.00
32 I:The Cure,last issue,
    June, 1989. .... 3.00
Ann.#1,I:Witness 3.00

DRACULA LIVES
B&W Magazine, 1973—75
1 GC 75.00
2 NA,GC,JSn,O:Dracula........ 50.00
3 NA,JB, ... 40.00
4 MP 30.00
5 GC 30.00
6 JB,GC 30.00
7 GE 30.00

8 GC 30.00
9 AA,RG 30.00
10 .... 40.00
11 thru 13 .... @35.00

DRACULA:
LORD OF THE UNDEAD
Oct., 1998
1 (of 3) PO,TP,R:Dracula 3.00
2 PO,TP,V:Seward 3.00
3 PO,TP,conclusion 3.00

DRAFT, THE
1988
1 Sequel to The Pit............. 3.75

DRAGON LINES
Epic, *Heavy Hitters* 1993
[1st Limited Series]
1 RLm,V:Terrorist on Moon,
    Embossed(c) 3.00
2 RLm,V:Kuei Emperor.......... 2.25
3 RLm,V:Spirit Boxer 2.25
4 RLm,K:Kuei Emperor. 2.25
[Regular Series]
1 B:PQ(s),RLm,I:Tao............ 2.50
2 RLm, ... 2.50

DRAGONSLAYER
Oct.–Nov., 1981
1 Movie adapt. 3.00
2 Movie adapt. 3.00

DRAGON STRIKE
1994
1 Based on TSR Game 2.25

DRAGON'S TEETH/
DRAGON'S CLAWS
July, 1988
1 GSr,I:Mercy Dragon,
    Scavenger,Digit Steel 2.25
2 GSr,V:Evil Dead.............. 2.25
3 GSr,Go Home 2.25
4 GSr 2.25
5 GSr,I:Death's Head 18.00
6 thru 10 GSr .... @2.00

DREADLANDS
Epic, 1992
1 Post-Apocalyptic Mini-series 4.00
2 Trapped in Prehistoric Past..... 4.00
3 V:Alien Time Travelers......... 4.00
4 Final Issue 4.00

DREADSTAR
Epic, Nov., 1982
1 JSn,I:Lord Papal 5.00
2 JSn,O:Willow 3.50
3 JSn,V:Lord Papal. 3.50
4 JSn,I:Z 3.50
5 JSn,V:Teutun 3.50
6 JSn,BWr,Interstellar Toybox.... 4.00
7 JSn,BWr,V:Dr.Mezlo 4.00
8 JSn,V:Z 3.00
9 JSn,V:Z 3.00
10 JSn,V:Z 3.00
11 JSn,O:Lord Papal 3.00
12 JSn,I:Dr.Delphi 3.00
13 JSn,V:Infra Red & Ultra Violet . . 3.00
14 JSn,V:Lord Papal 3.00
15 JSn,new powers 3.00
16 JSn,V:Lord Papal 3.00
17 JSn,V:Willows father........ 3.00

Dreadstar #23
© Marvel Entertainment Group

18 JSn,V:Dr.Mezlo 3.00
19 JSn,V:Dr Mezlo. 3.00
20 JSn,D:Oedi 3.00
21 JSn,D:Dr.Delphi 3.00
22 JSn,V:Lord Papal 3.00
23 JSn,V:Lord Papal 3.00
24 JSn,JS,V:Lord Papal. 3.00
25 JSn,V:Lord Papal 3.00
26 JSn,R:Oedi 3.00
Ann.#1 JSn,The Price 3.00
See COLOR COMICS section

DREADSTAR & COMPANY
July, 1985
1 JSo,reprint 2.25
2 thru 5 JSo,rep.............. @2.25

DROIDS
Star, April, 1986
1 JR 25.00
2 AW 15.00
3 JR/AW 15.00
4 AW 15.00
5 AW 15.00
6 EC/AW,A:Luke Skywalker 15.00
7 EC/AW,A:Luke Skywalker 15.00
8 EC/AW,A:Luke Skywalker 15.00

DRUID
1995
1 R:Dr. Druid Surprise!!! 3.50
2 F:Nekra 3.00
3 deranged canibal wisemen 3.00
4 Why Must He Die?. 3.00

DUNE
April–June, 1985
1 Movie Adapt,Rep. Marvel
    Super Spec,BSz 3.50
2 Movie Adapt,BSz 3.50
3 Movie Adapt,BSz, ... 3.50

DYNOMUTT
Nov., 1977
1 Based on TV series 50.00
2 thru 5 .... @30.00
6 Sept., 1978 .... 30.00

EARTHWORM JIM
1995–96
1 I:Earthworm Jim. 3.00

2 Cow tipping 3.00
3 V:Lawyers,conclusion 3.00

EARTH X
Jan., 1999
0 (of 14) AxR,JPL,Machine Man
  & Watcher 6.00
0a signed 25.00
1 AxR,JPL,V:Inhumans,32-page. . . 8.00
1a signed 30.00
2 AxR,JPL,fate of Fant.Four 4.00
3 AxR,JPL,World Super Powers. . . . 4.00
4 JPL,AxR(c),A:new Hulk 4.00
5 JPL,AxR(c),V:Doombots 4.00
6 JPL,AxR(c),different X-Men 4.00
7 JPL,AxR(c),A:Hulk. 4.00
8 JPL,AxR(c),A:Venom. 4.00
9 JPL,AxR(c),Revelations. 4.00
10 JPL,AxR(c) 4.00
11 JPL,AxR(c),V:Skull 4.00
12 JPL,AxR(c),concl 4.00
Spec.X AxR(c) concl.,48-pg 6.00
Sketchbook 6.00
TPB 464-page, rep. 24.95

Ectokid #4
© Marvel Entertainment Group

ECTOKID
Razorline 1993–94
1 I:Dex Mungo,BU:Hokum & Hex. . 3.50
2 O:Dex. 2.50
3 I:Ectosphere. 2.50
4 I:Brothers Augustine 2.50
5 A:Saint Sinner 2.50
6 Highway 61 Revisited 2.50
7 . . . . 2.50
8 V:Ice Augustine 2.50
9 Love is like a Bullet 2.50
10 . . . . 2.50
Ectokid Unleashed. 3.25

EDEN'S TRAIL
Nov., 2002
1 (of 6) western. 3.00
2 thru 5 . . . . @3.00

ELECTRIC UNDERTOW
Dec., 1989
1 MBa,Strike Force 4.00
2 thru 5 MBa . . . . @4.00

ELEKTRA
Nov., 1996
1 PrM,MD2,. 3.50
1A variant (c). 4.50
2 PrM,MD2,V:Bullseye, round two . 3.00
3 PrM,MD2,. 3.00
4 PrM,MD2 . . . . 3.00
5 PrM,MD2,. 3.00
6 PrM,MD2 . . . . 3.00
7 PrM,MD2,A:Konrad,The Architect 3.00
8 PrM,MD2,V:The Architect 3.00
9 PrM,MD2,V:The Four Winds . . . 3.00
10 PrM,MD2,V:Daredevil,American
  Samurai, pt.1 . . . . 3.00
11 PrM,MD2,F:Daredevil 3.00
12 PrM,MD2,F:Daredevil,V:American
  Samuri 3.00
13 PrM,MD2,F:Daredevil, concl. . . . 3.00
14 LHa,MD2,A:Wolverine 3.00
15 LHa,MD2,A:Silver Samurai. 3.00
16 LHa,MD2,A Hole in the Soul. . . . 3.00
17 LHa,MD2,V:The Hand. 3.00
18 LHa,MD2,A:Shang-Chi&Kingpin . 3.00
19 LHa,MD2,last issue. 3.00
Minus 1 Spec.,PMg,MD2,flashback . 3.00

ELEKTRA
July, 2001
1 BMB,non-comics code series . . . 5.00
2A BMB,A:S.H.I.E.L.D. 3.00
2B variant BSz(c) 3.00
3 BMB,A:Hydra. 3.50
4 BMB,A:Nick Fury 3.50
5 BMB,concl 3.50
6 BMB,F:Daredevil,'Nuff Said. . . . 3.50
7 Hubris, pt.1 . . . . 3.50
8 Hubris, pt.2 . . . . 3.50
9 Hubris, pt.3 . . . . 3.00
10 Hubris, concl. 3.00
11 Elektra between jobs. 3.00
12 F:Mr. Locke. 3.00
13 DaM 3.00
14 DaM,Elektra fights back 3.00
15 DaM 3.00
16 DaM 3.00
17 DaM 3.00
18 DaM 3.00
19 DaM 3.00
20 DaM,V:The Hand 3.00
21 V:The Hand. 3.00
22 V:The Hand, concl. 3.00
23 BSz(c),pt.1 . . . . 3.00
24 BSz(c),pt.2 . . . . 3.00
25 BSz(c),How to,pt.1 . . . . 3.00
26 How to,pt.2 . . . . 3.00
27 How to,pt.3,concl. 3.00
28 . . . . 3.00
29 Assassination 3.00
30 Prophet & Loss,pt.2 . . . . 3.00
31 Prophet & Loss,pt.3 . . . . 3.00
32 Fever,pt.1 . . . . 3.00
33 Fever,pt.2 . . . . 3.00
34 Fever,pt.3 . . . . 3.00
35 Visits grave 3.00
36 JoB,pt.1. . . . . 3.00
TPB Vol. 1: Introspect 17.00
TPB Vol. 2: Everything Old 17.00
TPB Vol. 3: Relentless. 15.00
TPB Vol. 4: Frenzy. 15.00
TPB Elektra Lives Again, FM. 25.00

ELEKTRA: ASSASSIN
Aug., 1986
1 FM,BSz,V:Shield 8.00
2 FM,BSz,I:Garrett 5.00
3 FM,BSz,V:Shield,A:Garrett 5.00
4 FM,BSz,V:Shield,A:Garrett 5.00
5 FM,BSz,I:Chastity,A:Garrett. 5.00
6 FM,BSz,A:Nick Fury,Garrett 5.00

Elektra: Assassin #3
© Marvel Entertainment Group

7 FM,BSz,V:Ken Wind,A:Garrett . . 5.00
8 FM,BSz,V:Ken Wind,A:Garrett . . 6.00
TPB Rep #1-8 . . . . 13.00

ELEKTRA:
GLIMPSE & ECHO
July, 2002
1 (of 4) F:The Hand 3.50
2 thru 4 . . . . @3.50

ELEKTRA: THE HAND
Sept., 2004
1 (of 5) The First Impression 3.00
2 & 3 . . . . @3.00

ELEKTRA LIVES AGAIN
1991
Graphic Novel FM,R:Elektra,A:Matt
  Murdock,V:The Hand. 30.00
TPB FM, rep. of HC, 80pg. 7.00

ELEKTRA: ROOT OF EVIL
1 V:Snakeroot. 3.00
2 V:Snakeroot. 3.00
3 Elektra's Brother 3.00
4 V:The Hand 3.00

ELEKTRA: SAGA
Feb., 1984
1 FM,rep.Daredevil 7.00
2 FM,rep.Daredevil 7.00
3 FM,rep.Daredevil 7.00
4 FM,rep.Daredevil 7.00
TPB Reprints#1-#4 . . . . 17.00
GN Book One FM,KJ, rep. from
  Daredevil, 96pg. 4.00
GN Book Two FM,KJ, rep. from
  Daredevil, 96pg. 4.00

ELEKTRA & WOLVERINE:
THE REDEEMER
Nov., 2001
GN#1 painted, 48-page 6.50
GN#2 48-page 6.50
GN#3 concl., 48-page 6.50

ELEKTRA/WITCHBLADE
1-shot Devil's Reign,
  pt.6, x-over 3.00

Elfquest #1
© *Marvel Entertainment Group*

ELFQUEST
Aug., 1985
1 WP,reprints. 4.00
2 WP. 2.50
3 WP. 2.50
4 WP. 2.50
5 WP. 2.50
6 WP,Young Cutter V:Mad Coil. . . . 2.50
7 WP,Young Cutter V:Mad Coil. . . . 2.50
8 WP. 2.50
9 WP. 2.50
10 WP,A:Cutter, Skywise. 2.50
11 WP,I:Two Edge 2.50
12 WP,The Mysterious Forest 2.50
13 WP,The Forest, A:Leetah 2.50
14 WP,A:The Bone Woman. 2.50
15 WP,The Forest, continued 2.50
16 WP,Forbidden Grove 2.50
17 WP,Blue Mountain. 2.50
18 WP,Secrets 2.50
19 WP,Twisted Gifts. 2.50
20 WP,Twisted Gifts. 2.50
21 WP 2.50
22 WP,A:Winnowill 2.50
23 WP,Blue Mountain,A:Winnowill . . 2.50
24 WP,The Quest Usurped 2.50
25 WP,Northern Wastelands 2.50
26 WP,Rayeks Story 2.50
27 WP,Battle Preparations. 2.50
28 WP,Elves vs. Trolls. 2.50
29 WP,Battle Beneath Blue
   Mountain 2.50
30 and 31 WP . . . . @2.50
32 WP,Conclusion, March, 1988 . . . 2.50

ELSEWHERE PRINCE
Epic, May–Oct., 1990
1 thru 6 . . . . @3.00

ELVIRA
Oct., 1988
Spec.B&W, Movie Adapt. 3.00

EMMA FROST
July, 2003
1 RGr,Higher Learning,pt.1. . . . . . . 7.00
2 RGr,Higher Learning,pt.2. . . . . . . 4.00
3 RGr,Higher Learning,pt.3. . . . . . . 4.00
4 RGr,Higher Learning,pt.4. . . . . . . 4.00
5 RGr,Higher Learning,pt.5. . . . . . . 4.00
6 RGr,White Queen 4.00

7 Mind Games,pt.1 . . . . 2.50
8 Mind Games,pt.2 . . . . 2.50
9 Mind Games,pt.3 . . . . 3.00
10 Mind Games,pt.4 . . . . 3.00
11 Mind Games,pt.5. . . . . 3.00
12 Mind Games,pt.6 . . . . 3.00
13 Bloom,pt.1. . . . . 3.00
14 Bloom,pt.2. . . . . 3.00
15 Bloom,pt.3. . . . . 3.00
16 Bloom,pt.4. . . . . 3.00
Digest Vol. 1: Higher Learning. 8.00

EPIC
1992
1 Wildcards,Hellraiser. 6.00
2 Nightbreed,Wildcards 6.00
3 DBw,MFm,Alien Legion. 6.00
4 Stalkers,Metropol,Wildcards 6.00

EPIC ANTHOLOGY
April, 2004
1 . . . . 6.00

EPIC, GRAPHIC NOVEL
Moebius 1: Upon a Star. 10.00
Moebius 2: Arzach 10.00
Moebius 3: Airtight Garage 10.00
Moebius 4: Long Tomorrow 10.00
Moebius 5: 10.00
Moebius 6: Pharadonesia 10.00
Last of Dragons 7.00
The Incal 1 Moebius. 11.00
The Incal 2 Moebius. 11.00
The Incal 3 Moebius. 11.00
JBo,Someplace Strange 7.00
MZ,Punisher. 17.00

EPIC, ILLUSTRATED
Spring, 1980
1 Black and White/Color Mag. . . . 14.00
2 thru 10 . . . . @8.00
11 thru 20 . . . . @10.00
21 thru 25 . . . . @12.00
26 thru 34, March, 1986. . . . . . @14.00

EPIC, LITE
Epic, Nov., 1991
One-shot short stories 4.00

ESSENTIALS
1999–2004
(528 pages, B&W reprints)
TPB Ant-Man, 576-pg. (2002) 16.00
TPB Avengers,Vol.1 . . . . 16.00
TPB Avengers,Vol.2, ... 16.00
TPB Avengers,Vol.3,rep.#47–#68 . 16.00
TPB Avengers,Vol.4 (2004) 17.00
TPB Avengers (2003) 17.00
TPB Captain America,Vol.1 . . . . . . 16.00
TPB Captain America,Vol.2 (2002) 16.00
TPB Conan,Vol.1 . . . . 17.00
TPB Daredevil, Vol.1 (2002) 17.00
TPB Daredevil Vol. 2 (2004) 17.00
TPB Fantastic Four,Vol.1 . . . . 16.00
TPB Fantastic Four,Vol.2(2000). . . 16.00
TPB Fantastic Four,Vol.3(2001). . . 16.00
TPB Howard the Duck (2002) 16.00
TPB Hulk, Vol.1 (2002) 17.00
TPB Human Torch, Vol. 1 . . . . 17.00
TPB Incredible Hulk,Vol.1 . . . . 16.00
TPB Incredible Hulk,Vol.2(2001) . . 16.00
TPB Iron Fist, Vol. 1 (2004) 17.00
TPB Iron Man, Vol.1 (2002) 17.00
TPB Marvel Team-Up (2002) 16.00
TPB Monster of Frankenstein 17.00
TPB Punisher,Vol.1 (2004) 15.00
TPB Silver Surfer,Vol.1 . . . . 16.00

TPB Spider-Man,Vol.1 (1997) 17.00
TPB Spider-Man,Vol.2 (1997) 17.00
TPB Spider-Man,Vol.3 . . . . 16.00
TPB Spider-Man,Vol.4 . . . . 16.00
TPB Spider-Man,Vol.5 (2002) 16.00
TPB Spider-Man,Vol.6 (2004) 17.00
TPB Super-VillainTeam-up(2004) . 17.00
TPB Thor,Vol.1 . . . . 16.00
TPB Tomb of Dracula (2002). 17.00
TPB Tomb of Dracula,#2 (2004) . . 17.00
TPB Tomb of Dracula,#3 (2004 . . . 17.00
TPB Wolverine,Vol.1 . . . . 16.00
TPB Wolverine,Vol.2 . . . . 16.00
TPB Wolverine,Vol.3 (1998) 17.00
TPB Uncanny X-Men, Vol.1 (2002) 17.00
TPB X-Men,Vol.1 . . . . 16.00
TPB X-Men,Vol.2 . . . . 16.00
TPB X-Men,Vol.3 . . . . 16.00
TPB X-Men,Vol.4 . . . . 16.00
TPB X-Men Vol. 5 (2004). 17.00

ETERNAL
Marvel Max, June, 2003
1 Gift of the Gods,pt.1 . . . . 3.00
2 thru 6 Gift of the Gods,pt.2–6 . @3.00

ETERNALS
[1st Series], July, 1976
1 JK,I:Ikaris,25 cent edition 25.00
2 JK,I:Ajak,25 cent edition 15.00
3 JK,I:Sersi 10.00
4 JK,Night of the Demons. 10.00
5 JK,I:Makarri,Zuras Thena,Domo 10.00
6 JK,Gods & Men at City College. . 10.00
7 JK,V:Celestials. 10.00
8 JK,I:Karkas, Reject 10.00
9 JK,I:Sprite,Reject vs. Karkas . . . 10.00
10 JK,V:Celestials 10.00
11 JK,I:Kingo Sunen 10.00
12 JK,I:Uni-Mind 15.00
13 JK,I:ForgottenOne(Gilgamesh). 15.00
14 JK,V:Hulk 15.00
15 JK,V:Hulk 15.00
16 JK,I:Dromedan 15.00
17 JK,I:Sigmar. 10.00
18 JK,I:Nerve Beast. 10.00
19 JK,Secret o/t Pyramid. 10.00
Ann.#1 JK,V:Timekillers 12.00

[2nd Series], Oct., 1985
1 SB,I:Cybele 3.00
2 thru 7 SB,V:Deviants . . . . @2.50
8 thru 10 WS,SB,V:Deviants. . . . @2.50
11 &12 WS,KP,V:Deviants . . . . . . @2.50

ETERNALS:
HEROD FACTOR
Nov., 1991
1 MT/BMc,A:Sersi (giant size) 2.50

EVERYMAN
Epic, 1991
1-shot Supernatural Story 8.00

EWOKS
Star, June, 1985—Sept., 1987
1 Based on TV Series. 18.00
2 . . . . 15.00
3 . . . . 15.00
4 A:Foonars 15.00
5 Wicket vs. Ice Demon. 15.00
6 Mount Sorrow, A:Teebo 15.00
7 A:Logray,V:Morag 15.00
8 . . . . 15.00
9 Lost in Time 15.00
10 AW,Lost in Time 18.00
11 thru 15 . . . . @15.00

Excalibur #1
© Marvel Entertainment Group

EXCALIBUR
April, 1988
1 AD,Special,O:Excalibur,
V:Technet............. 5.00
1a 2nd Printing.............. 2.50
1b 3rd Printing.............. 2.00
2 AAd,Mojo Mayhem,A:X-Babies .. 4.00
3 Air Apparent Spec.RLm,KJ,JG,TP,
RL,EL,JRu,A:Coldblood....... 4.00

[Regular Series]
1 B:CCl(s),AD,V:Warwolves,
I:Widget................. 6.00
2 AD,V:Warwolves,I:Kylun....... 5.00
3 AD,V:Juggernaut............ 4.00
4 AD,V:Arcade,Crazy Gang...... 4.00
5 AD,V:Arcade.............. 3.00
6 AD,Inferno,I:Alistaire Stuart..... 3.00
7 AD,Inferno............... 3.00
8 RLm,JRu,A:New Mutants...... 3.00
9 AD,I:Nazi-Excalibur........... 3.00
10 MR,V:Nazi-Excalibur.......... 3.00
11 MR,V:Nazi-Excalibur.......... 3.00
12 AD,Fairy Tale Dimension...... 3.00
13 AD,The Prince,N:Capt.Britian... 3.00
14 AD,Too Many Heroes........ 2.50
15 AD,I:US James Braddock...... 2.50
16 AD,V:Anjulie............. 2.50
17 AD,C:Prof.X,Starjammers...... 2.50
18 DJ,DA,V:Jamie Braddock...... 2.50
19 RL,TA,AM,V:Jamie Braddock ... 2.50
20 RLm,JRu,V:Demon Druid...... 2.50
21 I:Crusader X.............. 2.50
22 V:Crusader X............. 2.50
23 AD,V:Magik.............. 2.50
24 AD,Return Home,C:Galactus ... 2.50
25 E:CCl(s),AM,A:Galactus,Death,
Watcher.................. 2.50
26 RLm,JRu,V:Mastermind....... 2.50
27 BWS,BSz,A:Nth Man......... 3.00
28 BBl,Night at Bar............ 2.50
29 JRu,V:Nightmare,A:PowerPack . 2.50
30 DR,AM,A:Doctor Strange...... 2.50
31 DR,AM,V:Son of Krakoa....... 2.50
32 V:Mesmero.............. 2.50
33 V:Mesmero.............. 2.50
34 V:Mesmero.............. 2.50
35 AM,Missing Child........... 2.50
36 AM,V:Silv.Sable,Sandman..... 2.50
37 A:Avengers W.C.,Dr.Doom..... 2.50
38 A:Avengers W.C.,Dr.Doom..... 2.50
39 A:Avengers W.C.,Dr.Doom..... 2.50
40 O:Excalibur,Trial-Lockheed..... 2.50

41 V:Warwolves,C:Cable........ 3.00
42 AD,Team Broken Up........ 3.50
43 AD,Nightcrawler,V:Capt.Brit... 3.00
44 AD,Capt.Britain On Trial...... 3.00
45 AD,I:N-Men.............. 3.00
46 AD,Return of Kylun,C:Cerise ... 3.00
47 AD,I:Cerise.............. 3.00
48 AD,A:Anti-Phoenix.......... 3.00
49 AD,MFm,V:Necrom,R:Merlyn ... 3.00
50 AD,Phoenix,V:Necrom,Merlyn .. 5.00
51 V:Giant Dinosaurs........... 2.50
52 O:Phoenix,A:Prof X,MarvGirl... 2.50
53 A:Spider-Man,V:The Litter...... 2.50
54 AD,MFm,V:Crazy Gang....... 2.50
55 AD,MFm,A:Psylocke......... 2.50
56 AD,MFm,A:Psylocke,
V:Saturyne,Jamie Braddock ... 2.50
57 A:X-Men,Alchemy,V:Trolls..... 2.75
58 A:X-Men,Alchemy,V:Trolls..... 2.75
59 A:Avengers.............. 2.50
60 A:Avengers.............. 2.50
61 AD,MFm,Phoenix Vs.Galactus .. 2.50
62 AD,MFm,A:Galactus......... 2.50
63 AD,MFm,V:Warpies.......... 2.50
64 AD,MFm,V:RCX,R:Rachel..... 2.50
65 AD,MFm,R:Dark Phoenix...... 2.50
66 AD,MFm,V:Ahab,Sentinels,
O:Widget................ 2.50
67 AD,MFm,V:Ahab,Sentinels..... 2.50
68 V:Starjammers............. 2.50
69 A:Starjammers............. 2.50
70 A:Starjammers............. 2.50
71 DaR,Hologram(c),N:Excalibur... 5.00
72 KeL,V:Siena Blaze.......... 2.50
73 TSr,V:Siena Blaze........... 2.50
74 InC,A:Mr.Sinster,Siena Blaze ... 2.50
75 SLo(s),KeL,I:Daytripper(Amanda
Sefton),Britannic(Capt.Britain),
BU:Nightcrawler............ 4.00
75a Newstand Ed.............. 2.25
76 KeL,V:D'spayre............ 2.50
77 KeL,R:Doug Ramsey......... 2.50
78 A:Zero,Doug Ramsey........ 2.50
79 A:Zero,Doug Ramsey........ 2.50
80 A:Zero,Doug Ramsey........ 2.50
81 Doug Ramsey............. 2.50
82................... 3.00
82a foil(c)................ 3.50
83 regular ed............... 2.25
83a Deluxe ed. Kitty,Nightcrawler .. 2.50
84 regular ed............... 2.25
84a Deluxe ed............. 2.50
85 regular ed............... 2.25
85a Deluxe ed............. 2.50
86 regular ed............... 2.25
86a Deluxe ed............. 2.50
87 KeL,Secrets of the Genoshan
Mutate Technology.......... 2.50
88 Dream Nails,pt.1........... 2.50
89 Dream Nails,pt.2........... 2.50
90 Between Uncreated,Phalanx ... 4.00
91 F:Colossus.............. 2.50
92 F:Colossus.............. 2.50
93 F:Wolfsbane............. 2.50
94 A:Karma & Psylocke........ 2.50
95................. 2.50
96................. 2.50
97 BWi,B.Braddock's secrets told .. 2.50
98................. 2.50
99 European Hellfire Club,
Onslaught................ 2.50
100 Onslaught saga, double size ... 4.00
101................. 2.50
102................. 2.50
103 WEl,F:Colossus,Kitty &
Nichtcrawler.............. 2.50
104 JAr,BHi,PNe,Douglock's
dark side................ 2.50
105 JAr,BHi,PNe,V:Moonstar,..... 2.50
106................. 2.50
107 SvL,New direction.......... 2.50

Excalibur #99
© Marvel Entertainment Group

108 Dragons of the Crimson Dawn . 2.50
109 V:Spiral,A:Captain Britain..... 2.50
110 V:The Dragons of the
Crimson Dawn.............. 2.50
111 F:Shadowcat,R:Rory Cambell
(Ahab?)................ 2.50
112 Quicksilver tie-in............ 2.50
113 BRa,Colossus & Meggan..... 2.50
114 BRa,Vanisher............ 2.50
115 BRa,Quarantine,F:GenerationX 2.50
116 BRa,Legacy Virus, cont....... 2.50
117 BRa,F:Kitty Pryde, Colossus &
Nightcrawler.............. 2.50
118 BRa,V:Creatures from the
Shadows................ 2.50
119 BRa,V:Nightmare.......... 2.50
120 BRa,F:Kitty Pryde & Pete
Wisdom................ 2.50
121 BRa,to Egypt............. 2.50
122 BRa,V:Original X-Men?....... 2.50
123 BRa,V:Mimic............. 2.50
124 BBr,Captain Britain's bachelor
party................. 2.50
125 TvS,SHa, W:Captain Britain &
Meggan, final issue.......... 4.00
Minus 1 Spec., flashback,
F:Nightcrawler.............. 2.50
Ann.#1 I:Khaos,w/card......... 3.25
Spec #1 The Possession......... 4.00
Spec #2 RLm,DT,JG,RL,
A:Original X-Men........... 3.00
PF Cold Blood............. 5.00
GN Weird War III............. 10.00
TPB Wild, Wild Life........... 6.00

EXCALIBUR
May, 2004
1 CCl,Forging the Sword,pt.1..... 3.00
2 CCl,Forging the Sword,pt.2..... 3.00
3 CCl,Forging the Sword,pt.3..... 3.00
4 CCl,Forging the Sword,pt.4..... 3.00
5 CCl,Food Fight,pt.1......... 3.00
6 CCl,Food Fight,pt.2.......... 3.00
TPB Forging the Sword......... 10.00

EXCALIBUR:
SWORD OF POWER
Dec., 2000
1 (of 4) IaC,BRa,F:Capt.Britain.... 3.00
2 BRa,................. 3.00
3 BRa,V:Roma.............. 3.00
4 BRa, concl................ 3.00

MARVEL

EXILES
June, 2001

1 MkK,F:Blink, 48-page	11.00
2A MkK,	6.00
2B variant JWi(c)	6.00
3 MkK,trial of Phoenix	4.00
4 MkK,trial of Phoenix	4.00
5 MkK,JCf,F:Hulk	4.00
6 MkK,JCf,F:Alpha Flight	4.00
7 MkK,'Nuff Said (no words)	4.00
8 MkK,A World Apart,pt.1	4.00
9 MkK,A World Apart,pt.2	4.00
10 MkK,A World Apart,pt.3	4.00
11 MkK,F:Morph	3.50
12 MkK,New team	3.50
13 MkK,team must kill	3.50
14 MkK,V:Dr. Doom	3.50
15 MkK,Mimic vs. Namor	3.50
16 MkK,	3.50
17 world gone reptile	3.50
18 MkK,F:Morph	3.50
19 MkK,JHo	3.50
20 JCf,V:Legacy Virus,pt.1	3.00
21 JCf,V:Legacy Virus,pt.2	3.00
22 JCf,One goew down	3.00
23 With an Iron Fist,pt.1	3.00
24 With an Iron Fist,pt.2	3.00
25 With an Iron Fist,pt.3	3.50
26 Hard Choices,pt.1	3.00
27 Hard Choices,pt.2	3.00
28 Unnatural Selection,pt.1	3.00
29 Unnatural Selection,pt.2	3.00
30 Unnatural Selection,pt.3	3.00
31 Avengers Forever,pt.1	3.00
32 Avengers Forever,pt.2	3.00
33 A Second Farewell,pt.1	3.00
34 A Second Farewell,pt.2	3.00
35 Fantastic Voyage,pt.1	3.00
36 Fantastic Voyage,pt.2	3.00
37 Fantastic Voyage,pt.3	3.50
38 King Hyperion,pt.1	3.50
39 King Hyperion,pt.2	3.50
40 King Hyperion,pt.3	3.50
41 A Nocturne's Tale,pt.1	3.00
42 A Nocturne's Tale,pt.2	3.00
43 Blink in Time,pt.1	3.00
44 Blink in Time,pt.2	3.00
45 Blink in Time,pt.3	3.00
46 Earn Your Wings,pt.1	3.00
47 Earn Your Wings,pt.2	3.00
48 Earn Your Wings,pt.3	3.00
49 Capitol dome dump.	3.00
50 The Big M,pt.1	3.00
51 The Big M,pt.2	3.00
52 Living Planet,pt.1	3.00
53 Living Planet,pt.2	3.00
TPB rep. #1–#4	13.00
TPB Vol.1 A World Apart	15.00
TPB Vol. 3: Out of Time	18.00
TPB Vol. 4: Legacy	13.00
TPB Vol. 5: Unnatural Instinct	15.00
TPB Vol. 6: Fantastic Voyage	18.00
TPB Vol. 7: A Blink in Time	20.00
TPB Vol. 8: Earn Your Wings	15.00

FACTOR X
1995

1 After Xavier	4.00
2 Scott vs. Alex Summers	3.00
3 Cyclops vs. Havok	3.00
4 Jean & Scott	3.00
TPB Rep. #1–#4	8.95

FAFHRD AND THE GRAY MOUSER
Epic, Oct., 1990

1 MMi,Fritz Leiber adapt.	5.00
2 & 3 MMi	@5.00
4 MMi, Feb., 1991	5.00

FAITHFUL
Nov., 1949

1 Ph(c),I Take This Man	100.00
2 Ph(c),Love Thief,Feb.,1950	100.00

FALCON
Nov., 1983

1 PS,V:Nemesis	3.00
2 V:Sentinels	3.00
3 V:Electro	3.00
4 A:Capt.America, Feb., 1984	3.00

FALLEN ANGELS
April, 1987

1 KGa,TP,A:Sunspot,Warlock	3.00
2 KGa,TP,I:Gomi,Fallen Angels	2.50
3 KGa,TP,A:X-Factor	2.50
4 KGa,TP,A:Moon Boy, Devil Dinosaur	2.50
5 JSon,D:Angel,Don	2.50
6 JSon,Coconut Grove	2.50
7 KGa,Captured in CoconutGrove	2.50
8 KGa,L:Sunspot,Warlock	2.50

FANTASTIC FIRSTS
Marvel Dec., 2001

TPB Superhero origins, 428-pg.	29.95

FANTASTIC FIVE
Aug., 1999

1 TDF,PR,AM,New Team:Human Torch Thing,Ms.Fantastic,Psilord & Big Brain	2.25
2A TDF,PR,AM,Bloody Reunions x-over	2.25
2B variant MSh(c)	2.25
3 TDF,PR,AM,A:Spider-Girl	2.25
4 TDF,PR,AM	2.25
5 TDF,PR,AM,A:Kristoff	2.25

FANTASTIC FORCE
1994–96

1 Foil stamped cover	3.00
2 thru 18	@2.25

FANTASTIC FOUR
Nov., 1961

1 JK,I&O:Mr.Fantastic,Thing Invisible Girl,Human Torch Mole Man	36,000.00
2 JK,I:Skrulls	7,000.00
3 JK,I:Miracleman	4,500.00
4 JK,R:Submariner	5,000.00
5 JK,JSt,I&O:Doctor Doom	6,800.00
6 JK,V:Doctor Doom	2,800.00
7 JK,I:Kurrgo	2,000.00
8 JK,I:Alicia Masters,I&O: Puppet Master	2,000.00
9 JK,V:Submariner	2,000.00
10 JK,V:Doctor Doom,I:Ovoids	2,000.00
11 JK,I:Impossible Man	1,500.00
12 JK,V:Hulk	3,200.00
13 JK,SD,I&O:Red Ghost, I:Watcher	1,000.00
14 JK,SD,V:Submariner	750.00
15 JK,I:Mad Thinker	750.00
16 JK,V:Doctor Doom	750.00
17 JK,V:Doctor Doom	750.00
18 JK,I:Super Skrull	750.00
19 JK,I&O:Rama Tut	750.00
20 JK,I:Molecule Man	800.00
21 JK,I:Hate Monger	550.00
22 JK,V:Mole Man	350.00
23 JK,V:Doctor Doom	350.00
24 JK,I:Infant Terrible	350.00
25 JK,Thing vs.Hulk	900.00

26 JK,V:Hulk,A:Avengers	900.00
27 JK,A:Doctor Strange	500.00
28 JK,1st X-Men x-over	650.00
29 JK,V:Red Ghost	350.00
30 JK,I&O:Diablo	350.00
31 JK,V:Mole Man	300.00
32 JK,V:Superskrull	300.00
33 JK,I:Attuma	300.00
34 JK,I:Gideon	300.00
35 JK,I:Dragon Man,A:Diablo	300.00
36 JK,I:Medusa,Frightful Four	300.00
37 JK,V:Skrulls	275.00
38 JK,V:Frightful Four,I:Trapster	275.00
39 JK,WW,A:Daredevil	275.00
40 JK,A:Daredevil,Dr.Doom	275.00
41 JK,V:Fright.Four,A:Medusa	200.00
42 JK,V:Frightful Four	200.00
43 JK,V:Frightful Four	200.00
44 JK,JSt,I:Gorgon, V:Dragon Man	135.00
45 JK,JSt,I:Inhumans(Black Bolt, Triton,Lockjaw,Crystal, Karnak)	275.00
46 JK,JSt,V:Seeker	175.00
47 JK,JSt,I:Maximus,Attilan, Alpha Primitives.	175.00
48 JK,JSt,I:Silver Surfer, C:Galactus	1,500.00
49 JK,JSt,A:Silver Surfer, V:Galactus	550.00
50 JK,JSt,V:Galactus,Silver Surfer,I:Wyatt Wingfoot	700.00
51 JK,JSt,I:Negative Zone	175.00
52 JK,JSt,I:Black Panther	400.00
53 JK,JSt,I:Klaw,Vibranium	200.00
54 JK,JSt,I:Prester John	125.00
55 JK,JSt,A:Silver Surfer	250.00
56 JK,JSt,O:Klaw,A:Inhumans, C:Silver Surfer	150.00
57 JK,JSt,V:DocDoom,A:S.Surfer	150.00
58 JK,JSt,V:DocDoom,A:S.Surfer	150.00
59 JK,JSt,V:DocDoom,A:S.Surfer	150.00
60 JK,JSt,V:DocDoom,A:S.Surfer	150.00
61 JK,JSt,V:Sandman,A:S.Surfer	150.00
62 JK,JSt,I:Blastaar	100.00
63 JK,JSt,V:Blastaar	100.00
64 JK,JSt,I:The Kree,Sentry	100.00
65 JK,JSt,I:Ronan,Supreme Intelligence	100.00
66 JK,JSt,O:Him,A:Crystal	200.00
67 JK,JSt,I:Him	200.00
68 JK,JSt,V:Mad Thinker	100.00
69 JK,JSt,V:Mad Thinker	125.00
70 JK,JSt,V:Mad Thinker	125.00

Fantastic Four #27
© Marvel Entertainment Group

All comics prices listed are for *Near Mint* condition.

71 JK,JSt,V:Mad Thinker 125.00
72 JK,JSt,A:Watcher,S.Surfer . . . 150.00
73 JK,JSt,A:SpM,DD,Thor 125.00
74 JK,JSt,A:Silver Surfer 120.00
75 JK,JSt,A:Silver Surfer 120.00
76 JK,JSt,V:Psycho Man,S.Surf. . . 80.00
77 JK,JSt,V:Galactus,S.Surfer 80.00
78 JK,JSt,V:Wizard 80.00
79 JK,JSt,A:Crystall,V:MadThinker 80.00
80 JK,JSt,A:Crystal 80.00
81 JK,JSt,J:Crystal,V:Wizard 80.00
82 JK,JSt,V:Maximus 80.00
83 JK,JSt,V:Maximus 80.00
84 JK,JSt,V:Doctor Doom 80.00
85 JK,JSt,V:Doctor Doom 70.00
86 JK,JSt,V:Doctor Doom 70.00
87 JK,JSt,V:Doctor Doom 70.00
88 JK,JSt,V:Mole Man 70.00
89 JK,JSt,V:Mole Man 70.00
90 JK,JSt,V:Skrulls 55.00
91 JK,JSt,V:Skrulls,I:Torgo. 55.00
92 JK,JSt,V:Torgo,Skrulls. 55.00
93 JK,V:Torgo,Skrulls. 55.00
94 JK,JSt,I:Agatha Harkness 55.00
95 JK,JSt,I:Monocle 55.00
96 JK,JSt,V:Mad Thinker 55.00
97 JK,JSt,V:Monster from
    Lost Lagoon. 55.00
98 JK,JSt,V:Kree Sentry 55.00
99 JK,JSt,A:Inhumans 55.00
100 JK,JSt,V:Puppetmaster 150.00
101 JK,JSt,V:Maggia 60.00
102 JK,JSt,V:Magneto 60.00
103 JR,V:Magneto 60.00
104 JR,V:Magneto 60.00
105 JR,L:Crystal 60.00
106 JR,JSt,`Monster's Secret' 60.00
107 JB,JSt,V:Annihilus. 60.00
108 JK,JB,JR,JSt, V:Annihilus 60.00
109 JB,JSt,V:Annihilus 60.00
110 JB,JSt,V:Annihilus 60.00
111 JB,JSt,A:Hulk. 45.00
112 JB,JSt,Thing vs. Hulk 160.00
113 JB,JSt,I:Overmind 40.00
114 JR(c),JB,V:Overmind. 40.00
115 JR(c),JB,JSt,I:Eternals 40.00
116 JB,JSt,O:Stranger 50.00
117 JB,JSt,V:Diablo 35.00
118 JR(c),JB,JM,V:Diablo 35.00
119 JB,JSt,V:Klaw 35.00
120 JB,JSt,I:Gabriel(Airwalker)
    (Robot). 35.00
121 JB,JSt,V:Silver Surfer,D:
    Gabriel Destroyer 40.00

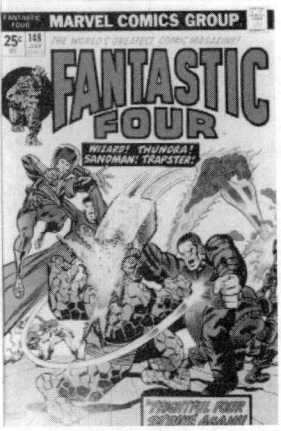
Fantastic Four #148
© *Marvel Entertainment Group*

122 JR(c),JB,JSt,V:Galactus,
    A:Silver Surfer 40.00
123 JB,JSt,V:Galactus,
    A:Silver Surfer 40.00
124 JB,JSt,V:Monster 30.00
125 E:StL(s),JB,JSt,V:Monster. . . . 30.00
126 B:RTs(s),JB,JSt,
    O:FF,MoleMan 30.00
127 JB,JSt,V:Mole Man 30.00
128 JB,JSt,V:Mole Man 30.00
129 JB,JSt,I:Thundra,
    V:Frightful Four 30.00
130 JSo(c),JB,JSt,V:Frightful Four. 30.00
131 JSo(c),JB,JSt,V:QuickSilver . . 30.00
132 JB,JSt,J:Medusa 30.00
133 JSt(i),V:Thundra 30.00
134 JB,JSt,V:Dragon Man 30.00
135 JB,JSt,V:Gideon 30.00
136 JB,JSt,A:Shaper 30.00
137 JB,JSt,A:Shaper 30.00
138 JB,JSt,O:Miracle Man 30.00
139 JB,V:Miracle Man 30.00
140 JB,JSt,O:Annihilus 30.00
141 JR(c),JB,JSt,V:Annihilus 30.00
142 RB,JSt,A:Doc Doom 30.00
143 GK(c),RB,V:Doc Doom 30.00
144 RB,JSt,V:Doc Doom 30.00
145 JSt&GK(c),RA,I:Ternak 30.00
146 RA,JSt,V:Ternak 30.00
147 RB,JSt,V:Subby 30.00
148 RB,JSt,V:Frightful Four. 30.00
149 RB,JSt,V:Sub-Mariner. 30.00
150 GK(c),RB,JSt,W:Crystal &
    Quicksilver,V:Ultron 35.00
151 RB,JSt,O:Thundra 15.00
152 JR(c),RB,JM,A:Thundra 15.00
153 GK(c),RB,JSt,A:Thundra 15.00
154 GK(c),rep.Str.Tales #127. . . . 15.00
155 RB,JSt,A:Surfer. 20.00
156 RB,JSt,A:Surfer,V:Doom. 20.00
157 RB,JSt,A:Surfer. 20.00
158 RB,JSt,V:Xemu 15.00
159 RB,JSt,V:Xemu 15.00
160 K&R(c),JB,V:Arkon 15.00
161 RB,JSt,V:Arkon 10.00
162 RB,DA,JSt,V:Arkon 10.00
163 RB,JSt,V:Arkon 10.00
164 JK(c),GP,JSt,V:Crusader,R:
    Marvel Boy,I:Frankie Raye . . . 10.00
165 GP,JSt,O:Crusader,
    O&D:Marvel Boy 10.00
166 GP,V:Hulk 18.00
167 JK(c),GP,JSt,V:Hulk 18.00
168 RB,JSt,J:Luke Cage 10.00
169 RB,JSt,V:Puppetmaster 10.00
170 GP,JSt,L:Luke Cage 10.00
171 JK(c),RB,GP,JSt,I:Gor. 10.00
172 JK(c),GP,JSt,V:Destroyer 10.00
173 JB,JSt,V:Galactus,O:Heralds . 10.00
174 JB,V:Galactus 10.00
175 JB,A:High Evolutionary 10.00
176 GP,JSt,V:Impossible Man . . . 10.00
177 JP,JS,A:Frightful Four
    I:Texas Twister,Capt.Ultra . . . 10.00
178 GP,V:Frightful Four,Brute 10.00
179 JSt,V:Annihilus 10.00
180 reprint #101 . . . . 10.00
181 E:RTs(s),JSt,V:Brute,
    Annihilus 10.00
182 SB,JSt,V:Brute,Annihilus. . . . 10.00
183 SB,JSt,V:Brute,Annihilus. . . . 10.00
184 GP,JSt,V:Eliminator 10.00
185 GP,JSt,V:Nich.Scratch 10.00
186 GP,JSi,I:Salem's Seven 10.00
187 GP,JSt,V:Klaw,Molecule Man . 10.00
188 GP,JSt,V:Molecule Man 10.00
189 reprint FF Annual #4 . . . . . . 10.00
190 SB,O:Fantastic Four 11.00
191 GP,JSt,V:Plunderer,
    Team Breaks Up 10.00
192 GP,JSt,V:Texas Twister 10.00

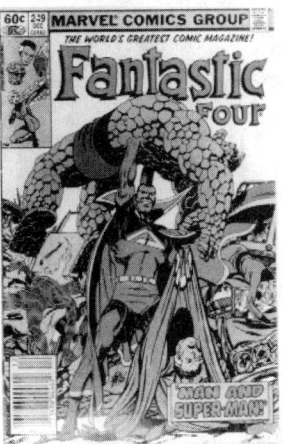
Fantastic Four #249
© *Marvel Entertainment Group*

193 KP,JSt,V:Darkoth,Diablo 10.00
194 KP,V:Darkoth,Diablo 10.00
195 KP,A:Sub-Mariner 10.00
196 KP,V:Invincible Man (Reed),
    A:Dr.Doom,Team Reunited . . . 10.00
197 KP,JSt,Red Ghost 10.00
198 KP,JSt,V:Doc Doom 10.00
199 KP,JSt,V:Doc Doom 10.00
200 KP,JSt,V:Doc Doom 15.00
201 KP,JSt,FF's Machinery 7.00
202 KP,JSt,V:Quasimodo. 7.00
203 KP,JSt,V:Mutant 7.00
204 KP,JSt,V:Skrulls 7.00
205 KP,JSt,V:Skrulls 7.00
206 KP,JSt,V:Skrulls,A:Nova 7.00
207 SB,JSt,V:Monocle,A:SpM 7.00
208 SB,V:Sphinx,A:Nova 7.00
209 JBy,JSt,I:Herbie,A:Nova 8.00
210 JBy,JS,A:Galactus 7.00
211 JBy,JS,I:Terrax,A:Galactus . . . 8.00
212 JBy,JSt,V:Galactus,Sphinx . . . 7.00
213 JBy,JSt,V:Terrax,Galactus
    Sphinx 7.00
214 JBy,JSt,V:Skrull 7.00
215 JBy,JSt,V:Blastaar. 7.00
216 JBy,V:Blastaar. 7.00
217 JBy,JSt,A:Dazzler 7.00
218 JBy,JSt,V:FrightfulFour,
    A:Spider-Man. 7.00
219 BSz,JSt,A:Sub-Mariner. 6.00
220 JBy,JSt,A:Vindicator 6.00
221 JBy,JSt,V:Vindicator 6.00
222 BSz,JSt,V:Nicholas Scratch . . 6.00
223 BSz,JSt,V:Salem's Seven 6.00
224 BSz,A:Thor 6.00
225 BSz,A:Thor 6.00
226 BSz,A:Shogun. 6.00
227 BSz,JSt,V:Ego-Spawn. 6.00
228 BSz,JSt,V:Ego-Spawn. 6.00
229 BSz,JSt,I:Firefrost,Ebon
    Seeker 6.00
230 BSz,JSt,A:Avengers,
    O:Firefrost & Ebon Seeker 6.00
231 BSz,JSt,V:Stygorr 6.00
232 JBy,New Direction,V:Diablo . . 7.00
233 JBy,V:Hammerhead 6.00
234 JBy,V:Ego 6.00
235 JBy,O:Ego. 6.00
236 JBy,V:Dr.Doom,A:Puppet
    Master, 20th Anniv. 6.00
237 JBy,V:Solons. 5.00
238 JBy,O:Frankie Raye,
    new Torch 5.00

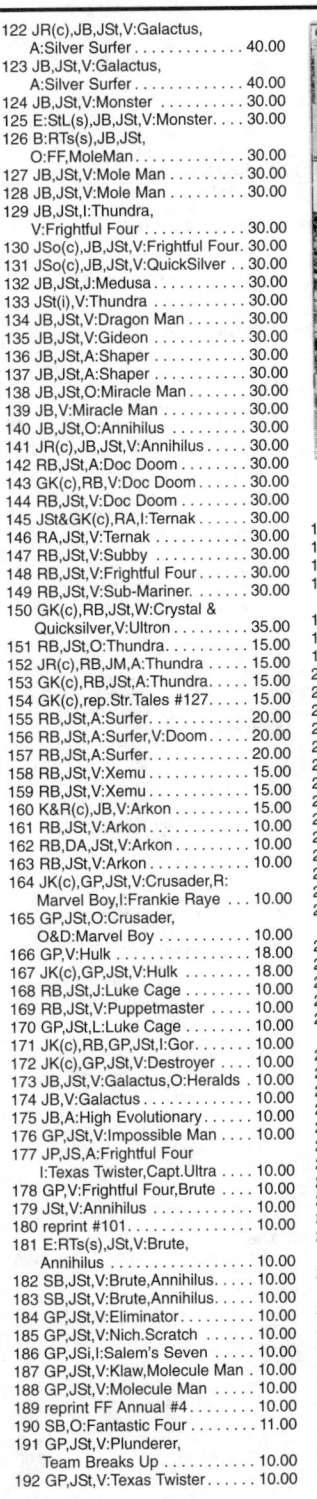

239 JBy,I:Aunt Petunia,
Uncle Jake. 6.00
240 JBy,A:Inhumans,b:Luna 5.00
241 JBy,A:Black Panther. 5.00
242 JBy,A:Daredevil,Thor,Iron Man
Spider-Man,V:Terrax 5.00
243 JBy,A:Daredevil,Dr.Strange,
Spider-Man,Avengers,V:Galactus,
Terrax. 5.00
244 JBy,A:Avengers,Dr.Strange,
Galactus, Becomes Nova 5.00
245 JBy,V:Franklin Richards 5.00
246 JBy,V:Dr.Doom,
A:Puppet Master 5.00
247 JBy,A:Dr.Doom,I:Kristoff,
D:Zorba. 5.00
248 JBy,A:Inhumans 5.00
249 JBy,V:Gladiator. 5.00
250 JBy,A:Capt.Am.,SpM,
V:Gladiator. 5.00
251 JBy,A:Annihilus 5.00
252 JBy,1st sideways issue,V:
Ootah,A:Annihilus,w/tattoo . . . 5.00
252a w/o tattoo 5.00
253 JBy,V:Kestorans,A:Annihilus. . . 5.00
254 JBy,V:Mantracora,
A:She-Hulk,Wasp 5.00
255 JBy,A:Daredevil,Annihilus,
V:Mantracora. 5.00
256 JBy,A:Avengers,Galactus,
V:Annihilus,New Costumes . . . 5.00
257 JBy,A:Galactus,Death,Nova,
Scarlet Witch 4.50
258 JBy,A:Dr.Doom,D:Hauptmann . 4.50
259 JBy,V:Terrax,Dr.Doom,
C:Silver Silver 4.50
260 JBy,V:Terrax, Dr.Doom,
A:Silver Surfer,Sub-Mariner. . . 5.00
261 JBy,A:Sub-Mariner,Marrina,
Silver Surfer,Sc.Witch,Lilandra . 5.00
262 JBy,O:Galactus,A:Odin,
(J.Byrne in story) 4.00
263 JBy,V:Messiah,A:Mole Man . . 4.00
264 JBy,V:Messiah,A:Mole Man . . 4.00
265 JBy,A:Trapster,Avengers,
J:She-Hulk,Secret Wars 4.00
266 KGa,JBy,A:Hulk,Sasquatch,
V:Karisma 4.00
267 JBy,A:Hulk,Sasquatch,Morbius,
V:Dr.Octopus,Sue miscarries . . 4.00
268 JBy,V:Doom's Mask 4.00
269 JBy,R:Wyatt Wingfoot,
I:Terminus 4.00

Fantastic Four #394
© Marvel Entertainment Group

270 JBy,V:Terminus 4.00
271 JBy,V:Gormuu. 4.00
272 JBy,I:Warlord (Nathaniel
Richards). 4.00
273 JBy,V:Warlord 4.00
274 JBy,AG,cont.from Thing#19,
A:Spider-Man's Black Costume. 4.00
275 JBy,AG,V:T.J.Vance. 4.00
276 JBy,JOy,V:Mephisto,
A:Dr.Strange 4.00
277 JBy,JOy,V:Mephisto,
A:Dr.Strange,R:Thing. 4.00
278 JBy,JOy,O:Dr.Doom,A:Kristoff
(as Doom) 4.00
279 JBy,V:Dr.Doom(Kristoff),
I:New Hate-Monger 4.00
280 JBy,JOy,I:Malice,
V:Hate-Monger 4.00
281 JBy,JOy,A:Daredevil,V:Hate
Monger,Malice 4.00
282 JBy,JOy,A:Power Pack,Psycho
Man,Secret Wars II 4.00
283 JBy,JOy,V:Psycho-Man. 4.00
284 JBy,JOy,V:Psycho-Man. 4.00
285 JBy,JOy,Secret Wars II
A:Beyonder 4.00
286 JBy,TA,R:Jean Grey,
A:Hercules Capt.America 5.00
287 JBy,JSt,A:Wasp,V:Dr.Doom . . 4.00
288 JBy,JSt,V:Dr.Doom,Secret
Wars II 5.00
289 JBy,AG,D:Basilisk,V:Blastaar,
R:Annihilus 4.00
290 JBy,AG,V:Annihilus 4.00
291 JBy,CR,A:Nick Fury 4.00
292 JBy,AG,A:Nick Fury,V:Hitler . . 4.00
293 JBy,AG,A:Avengers.W.C. 4.00
294 JOy,AG,V:FutureCentralCity . . . 3.00
295 JOy,AG,V:Fut.Central City. . . . 3.00
296 BWS,KGa,RF,BWi,AM,KJ,JB,
SL,MS,JRu,JOy,JSt,25th
Anniv.,V:MoleMan 5.00
297 JB,SB,V:Umbra-Sprite 3.00
298 JB,SB,V:Umbra-Sprite 2.50
299 JB,SB,She-Hulk,V:Thing,
A:Spider-Man,L:She-Hulk 3.00
300 JB,SB,W:Torch & Fake Alicia
(Lyja),A:Puppet-Master,Wizard,
Mad Thinker,Dr.Doom 4.00
301 JB,SB,V:Wizard,MadThinker . . 3.00
302 JB,SB,V:Project Survival. 3.00
303 JB,RT,A:Thundra,V:Machus . . 3.00
304 JB,JSt,V:Quicksilver,
A:Kristoff 3.00
305 JB,JSt,V:Quicksilver,
J:Crystal,A:Dr.Doom 3.00
306 JB,JSt,A:Capt.America,
J:Ms.Marvel,V:Diablo. 3.00
307 JB,JSt,L:Reed&Sue,V:Diablo . . 3.00
308 JB,JSt,I:Fasaud. 3.00
309 JB,JSt,V:Fasaud 3.00
310 KP,JSt,V:Fasaud,N:Thing
& Ms.Marvel 3.00
311 KP,JSt,A:Black Panther,
Dr.Doom,V:THRob. 3.00
312 KP,JSt,A:Black Panther,
Dr.Doom,X-Factor 3.00
313 SB,JSt,V:Lava Men,
A:Moleman 3.00
314 KP,JSt,V:Belasco 3.00
315 KP,JSt,V:Mast.Pandem. 3.00
316 KP,JSt,A:CometMan 3.00
317 KP,JSt,L:Crystal 3.00
318 KP,JSt,V:Dr.Doom 3.00
319 KP,JSt,G-Size,O:Beyonder . . . 3.00
320 KP,JSt,Hulk vs Thing. 3.00
321 RLm,RT,A:She-Hulk 3.00
322 KP,JSt,Inferno,V:Graviton 3.00
323 KP,JSt,RT,Inferno A:Mantis . . . 3.00
324 KP,JSt,RT,A:Mantis 3.00

325 RB,RT,A:Silver Surfer,
D:Mantis 3.00
326 KP,RT,I:New Frightful Four 3.00
327 KP,RT,V:Frightful Four. 3.00
328 KP,RT,V:Frightful Four. 3.00
329 RB,RT,V:Mole Man 3.00
330 RB,RT,V:Dr.Doom 3.00
331 RB,RT,V:Ultron 3.00
332 RB,RT,V:Aron 3.00
333 RB,RT,V:Aron,Frightful Four . . . 3.00
334 RB,Acts of Vengeance 3.00
335 RB,RT,Acts of Vengeance 3.00
336 RLm,Acts of Vengeance, ... 3.00
337 WS,A:Thor,Iron Man,
B:Timestream saga 4.00
338 WS,V:Deathshead,A:Thor,
Iron Man 3.00
339 WS,V:Gladiator 3.00
340 WS,V:Black Celestial 3.00
341 WS,A:Thor,Iron Man 3.00
342 A:Rusty,C:Spider-Man 3.00
343 WS,V:Stalin 3.00
344 WS,V:Stalin 3.00
345 WS,V:Dinosaurs 3.00
346 WS,V:Dinosaurs 3.00
347 AAd,ATi(i)A:Spider-Man,
GhostRider,Wolverine,Hulk 4.00
347a 2nd printing 3.00
348 AAd,ATi(i)A:Spider-Man,
GhostRider,Wolverine,Hulk 4.00
348a 2nd printing 3.00
349 AAd,ATi(i),AM(i)A:Spider-Man,
Wolverine,GhostRider,Hulk,
C:Punisher. 3.50
350 WS,Am(i),R:Ben Grimm as
Thing,(48p) 3.50
351 MBa,Kubic. 3.00
352 WS,Reed Vs.Dr.Doom 3.00
353 WS,E:Timestream Saga,
A:Avengers. 3.00
354 WS,Secrets of the Time
Variance Authority 3.00
355 AM,V:Wrecking Crew 3.00
356 B:TDF(s),PR,A:New Warriors,
V:Puppet Master 3.00
357 PR,V:Mad Thinker,
Puppetmaster. 3.00
358 PR,AAd,30th Anniv.,1st Marv.
Die Cut(c),D:Lyja,V:Paibok,
BU:Dr.Doom 3.50
359 PR,I:Devos the Devastator 3.00
360 PR,V:Dreadface 3.00
361 PR,V:Dr.Doom,X-masIssue . . . 3.00
362 PR,A:Spider-Man,
I:WildBlood 3.00
363 PR,I:Occulus,A:Devos 3.00
364 PR,V:Occulus 3.00
365 PR,V:Occulus 3.00
366 PR,Infinity War,R:Lyja 3.00
367 PR,Inf.War,A:Wolverine 3.00
368 PR,V:Infinity War X-Men 3.00
369 PR,Inf.War,R:Malice,
A:Thanos 3.00
370 PR,Inf.War,V:Mr.Fantastic
Doppleganger 3.00
371 PR,V:Lyja,foil(c) 4.00
371a 2nd Printing. 3.00
372 PR,A:Spider-Man,Silver
Sable 3.00
373 PR,V:Aron,Silver sable 3.00
374 PR,V:Secret Defenders. 3.00
375 V:Dr.Doom,A:Inhumans,Lyja,
Holo-Grafix(c) 3.50
376 PR,A:Nathan Richards,V:Paibok,
Devos,w/Dirt Magazine 3.50
376a w/out Dirt Magazine 2.50
377 PR,V:Paibok,Devos,Klaw,
I:Huntara 2.50
378 PR,A:Sandman,SpM,DD. 2.50
379 PR,V:Ms.Marvel 2.50
380 PR,A:Dr.Doom,V:Hunger 2.50

Fantastic Four #414
© Marvel Entertainment Group

381 PR,D:Dr.Doom,Mr.Fantastic,
　　V:Hunger 5.00
382 PR,V:Paibok,Devos,Huntara. . . 3.00
383 PR,V:Paibok,Devos,Huntara. . . 2.50
384 PR,A:Ant-Man,V:Franklin
　　Richards 2.50
385 PR,A:Triton,Tiger Shark,
　　Starblast#7. . . . . 2.50
386 PR,Starblast#11,A:Namor,Triton,
　　b:Johnny & Lyja child 2.50
387 Die-Cut & Foil (c),PR,N:Invisible
　　Woman,J:Ant-Man,A:Namor . . . 4.00
387a Newsstand Ed. 2.50
388 PR,I:Dark Raider,V:FF,
　　Avengers,w/cards 2.50
389 PR,I:Raphael Suarez,A:Watcher,
　　V:Collector. 2.50
390 PR,A:Galactus 2.50
391 PR,I:Vibraxas 2.50
392 Dark Raider. 2.50
393 . . . . 2.50
394 Neon(c) w/insert print 3.00
394a Newsstand ed.,no bag/inserts 2.50
395 Thing V:Wolverine. 2.50
396 . . . . 2.50
397 Resurrection,pt.1. . . . . 2.50
398 regular edition 2.50
398a Enhanced cover 3.00
399 Watcher's Lie 3.00
399a Foil stamped cover 3.00
400 Watcher's Lie,pt.3 . . . . 5.00
401 V:Tantalus 2.50
402 Atlantis Rising,Namor
　　vs. Black Bolt. 2.50
403 TDF,PR,DBi,F:Thing,Medusa . . 2.50
404 R:Namor,I:New Villian. 2.50
405 J:Namor 2.50
406 TDF,PR,DBI,R:Dr. Doom,
　　I:Hyperstorm. 2.50
407 TDF,PR,DBi,Return of
　　Reed Richards. 2.50
408 TDF,PR,DBi,Original FF unite. . 2.50
409 TDF,PR,DBi,All new line-up . . . 2.50
410 . . . . 2.50
411 . . . . 2.50
412 TDF,PR,DBi,Mr.Fantastic
　　vs. Sub-Mariner. 2.50
413 . . . . 2.50
414 Galactus vs. Hyperstorm 4.00
415 Onslaught saga, A:X-Men. 4.00
416 Onslaught saga, A:Dr. Doom,
　　double size, finale 5.00
Ann.#1 JK,SD,I:Atlantis,Dorma,
　　Krang,V:Namor,O:FF 1,200.00

Ann.#2 JK,JSt,O:Dr.Doom 600.00
Ann.#3 JK,W:Reed and Sue 250.00
Ann.#4 JK,JSt,I:Quasimodo. 150.00
Ann.#5 JK,JSt,A:Inhumans,Silver
　　Surfer,Black Panther,
　　I:Psycho Man. 160.00
Ann.#6 JK,JSt,I:Annihilus,
　　Franklin Richards 100.00
Ann.#7 JK(c),reprints 50.00
Ann.#8 JR(c),reprints 30.00
Ann.#9 JK(c),reprints. 30.00
Ann.#10 reprints Ann.#3 . . . . 30.00
Ann.#11 JK(c),JB,A:The Invaders . 12.00
Ann.#12 A:The Invaders 12.00
Ann.#13 V:The Mole Man 12.00
Ann.#14 GP,V:Salem's Seven 12.00
Ann.#15 GP,V:Dr.Doom,Skrulls . . . 10.00
Ann.#16 V:Dragonlord 10.00
Ann.#17 JBy,V:Skrulls 10.00
Ann.#18 KGa,V:Skrulls,W:Black
　　Bolt and Medusa,A:Inhumans. 10.00
Ann.#19 JBy,V:Skrulls 10.00
Ann.#20 TD(i),V:Dr.Doom 4.00
Ann.#21 JG,JSt,Evol.Wars. 4.00
Ann.#22 RB,Atlantis Attacks,
　　A:Avengers 4.00
Ann.#23 JG,GCa,Days of Future
　　Present #1. . . . . 5.00
Ann.#24 JG,AM,Korvac Quest #1,
　　A:Guardians of the Galaxy 3.00
Ann.#25 Citizen Kang #3. . . . . 3.00
Ann.#26 HT,I:Wildstreak,
　　V:Dreadface,w/card 3.50
Ann.#27 MGu,V:Justice Peace 3.50
G-Size#1 RB,Thing/Hulk 17.00
G-Size#2 K&R(c),JB,Time to Kill . . 15.00
G-Size#3 RB,JSt,Four Horseman . 15.00
G-Size#4 JB,JSt,I:Madrox 15.00
G-Size#5 JK(c),V:Psycho Man,
　　Molecule Man 12.00
G-Size#6 V:Annihilus. 12.00
Spec.#1 Rep.Ann.#1 JBy(c). 2.50
TPB Rep.#347-349 . . . . 5.95
TPB Nobody Gets Out Alive, rep. . 15.95
TPB Trial of Galactus, rep. 9.95
Marvel Milestone rep. #1 (1991) . . 2.95
Marvel Milestone rep. #5 (1992) . . 2.95
Ashcan. 75
Spec. The Origin of Galactus. 2.50

[2nd Series], Nov., 1996
1 JLe,BCi,SW, 48pg 5.00
1A Mole Man cover. 12.00
1B Gold signature, bagged,
　　limited 25.00
2 JLe,BCi,V:Namor. 5.00
3 JLe,BCi,SW,A:Avengers 4.00
4 JLe,BCi,SW,I:Black Panther 4.00
4A x-mas cover. 5.00
5 JLe,BCi,SW,V:Dr. Doom 4.00
6 JLe,BCi,SW,Industrial Revolution
　　prologue. 3.00
7 JLe,BCi,BBh,V:Blastaar. 3.00
8 JLe,BCi,BBh,V:Inhumans. 3.00
9 JLe,BCi,BBh,V:Inhumans 3.00
10 JLe,BCi,BBh,A:Silver Surfer,
　　Tyrax 3.00
11 JLe,BCi,BBh,A:Silver Surfer,
　　Firelord, Terrax 3.00
12 JLe,BCi,BBh,GalactusSaga,pt.1,
　　reunited 5.00
13 JeR,Wildstorm x-over 3.00
Ashcan, signed, numbered 10.00

[3rd Series], Nov., 1997
1 SLo,AD,MFm, The Ruined, 48pg
　　debut 5.00
2 SLo,AD,MFm,A:Iconoclast. 4.00
3 SLo,AD,MFm,V:Red Ghost 4.00
4 SLo,SvL,ATi,A:Silver Surfer,
　　double size 4.00
4 signed by SLo, (500 copies) . . . 20.00

Fantastic Four 2nd Series #5
© Marvel Entertainment Group

5 SLo,SvL,ATi,V:The Crucible 3.00
6 CCi,SvL, new villains. 3.00
7 CCi,SvL,ATi,V:Technet. 3.00
8 CCi,SvL,V:Captain Britain corp. . . 3.00
9 CCi,SvL,A:Spider-Man. 3.00
10 CCi,SvL,ATi. 3.00
11 CCi,SvL,ATi,Crucible—unleashed
　　in Genosha 3.00
12 CCi,SvL,ATi,V:Fantastic Four
　　double-size 4.50
13 CCi,SvL,A:Ronan the Accuser . . 2.50
14 CCi,SvL,V:Ronan 2.50
15 CCi,SvL,ATi,Iron Man x-over . . . 2.50
16 CCi,SvL,ATi,V:Kree Avengers. . . 2.50
17 CCi,SvL,ATi,I:Lockdown 2.50
18 CCi,SvL,ATi,Jail Break 2.50
19 CCi,SvL,ATi,V:Annihilus 2.50
20 CCi,SvL,ATi,V:Ruined 2.50
21 CCi,SvL,ATi,V:Hades 2.50
22 CCi,SvL,ATi,V:Valeria
　　Von Doom 2.50
23 CCi,SvL,ATi,A:She-Hulk 2.50
24 CCi,SvL,ATi,F:FranklinRichards . 2.50
25 CCi,SvL,ATi,V:Dr.Doom 3.50
26 CCi,SvL,ATi,F:ValeriaVonDoom . 3.00
27 CCi,SvL,F:Invisible Woman 3.00
28 CCi,SvL,ATi,Planet Doom. 3.00
29 CCi,SvL,ATi,Frightful Four 2.50
30 CCi,SvL,ATi,Castle Doom. 2.25
31 CCi,SvL,ATi,InvisibleWoman . . . 2.25
32 CCi,SvL,ATi,InvisibleWoman . . . 2.25
33 JFM,SvL,ATi,Kid Colt 2.25
34 JFM,SvL,ATi,aliens 2.25
35A CPa,Diablo,foil (c). 5.00
35B painted (c) 2.25
36 CPa,Diablo triumphant 2.25
37 CPa,F:Johnny Storm. 2.25
38 CPa,JLb,V:Grey Gargoyle 2.25
39 CPa,JLb,V:Grey Gargoyle 2.25
40 CPa,JLb,Negative Zone 2.25
41 CPa,JLb,Hellscout 2.25
42 CPa,JLb,SI,V:Namor. 2.25
43 CPa,JLb,JoB,new Fant.Four. . . . 2.25
44 CPa,JLb,Negative Zone,concl. . . 2.25
45 CPa,JLb,one new costume. 2.25
46 CPa,JLb,Abraxas Saga 2.25
47 CPa,JLb,Abraxas,pt.3. . . . . 2.25
48 CPa,JLb,Abraxas,pt.4. . . . . 2.25
49 CPa,JLb,Abraxas,pt.5. . . . . 2.25
50 Four new stories,BWS(c),64-pg. . 5.00
51 MBa,KK,F:Inhumans. 3.50
52 MBa,KK,F:Dr. Doom 2.25
53 MBa,KK,Inhumans 2.25

Fantastic Four 3rd Series #1
© Marvel Entertainment Group

54 MBa,KK,Inhumans, 100-pg. 4.00
55 KK,SI,Thing,Human Torch 2.25
56 F:Thing 2.25
57 AWa,F:Thing,pt.1 . . . . 2.25
58 AWa,F:Thing,pt.2 . . . . 2.25
59 AWa,F:Thing,pt.3 . . . . 2.25
60 MWa,KK 2.25
61 MWa,KK 3.00
62 MWa,KK,Sentient,pt.1, 48-pg . . 3.00
63 MWa,KK,Sentient,pt.2. . . . . 3.00
64 MWa,KK,Sentient,pt.3. . . . . 3.00
65 MWa,MBu,Small Stuff/Big Stuff. . 3.00
66 MWa,MBu,Small Stuff/Big Stuff. . 3.00
67 MWa,KK,Unthinkable 5.00
68 MWa,KK,Unthinkable 3.50
69 MWa,KK,Unthinkable 3.50
70 MWa,Unthinkable 3.50
500 MWa,Unthinkable,48-pg. 5.00
500a Director's Cut, foil 5.00
501 MWa,CJ,Fifth Wheel,pt.1 . . . . . 2.25
502 MWa,CJ,Fifth Wheel,pt.2 . . . . . 2.25
503 MWa,Authoritative Action,pt.1. . 2.25
504 MWa,Authoritative Action,pt.2. . 2.25
505 MWa,Authoritative Action,pt.3. . 2.25
506 MWa,Authoritative Action,pt.4. . 2.25
507 MWa,Authoritative Action,pt.5. . 2.25
508 MWa,Authoritative Action,pt.6. . 2.25
509 MWa,Hereafter,pt.1 . . . . 2.25
510 MWa,Hereafter,pt.2 . . . . 2.25
511 MWa,Hereafter,pt.3 . . . . 2.25
512 MWa,Spider Sense,pt.1 . . . . 2.25
513 MWa,Spider Sense,pt.2 . . . . 2.25
514 MWa&KK(s),Dysfunctional,pt.1. 2.25
515 MWa&KK(s),Dysfunctional,pt.2. 2.25
516 MWa,KK(s),Dysfunctional,pt.3 . 2.25
517 MWa(s),Fourtitude,pt.1 . . . . 3.00
518 Fourtitude,pt.2. . . . . 3.00
519 Fourtitude,pt.3. . . . . 3.00
Ann.1998 Fant.Four & Fant.Four. . . 4.00
Ann.1999 CCI,I:Mechamage 4.00
Ann.2000 LSi,SvL,48-pg. 4.00
Ann.2001 Galactus,48-page 3.50
Spec.#1 KIK FantasticFour (2000). . 2.25
Spec. Fantastic Four/Sentry 3.00
Spec. Fantastic Fourth Voyage
      of Sinbad, 48-page (2001) 6.00
TPB Heroes Return, 96-page 11.00
TPB Heroes Reborn, 176-pg. 18.00
TPB Into the Breach, 144-pg. 16.00
TPB (Vol.3) Flesh & Stone (2002). 13.00
TPB (Vol.1) Visionaries (2002) . . . 20.00
TPB Vol. 1: Imaginauts (2003). . . . 18.00
TPB Legends, Vol. 1 (2003) 14.00
TPB Vol. 2: Unthinkable (2003) . . . 18.00

TPB Vol. 3: Authoritative Action . . . 13.00
TPB Vol. 4: Hereafter. 12.00

FANTASTIC FOUR: ATLANTIS RISING
1995
1 B:Atlantis Rising. 5.00
2 TDF,MCW,finale, acetate(c). 5.00

FANTASTIC FOUR INDEX
See: OFFICIAL MARVEL INDEX TO THE FANTASTIC FOUR

FANTASTIC FOUR: 1 2 3 4
June, 2001
1 (of 4) GMo,JaL,F:Thing 3.00
2 GMo,JaL,F:Invisible Woman 3.00
3 GMo,JaL,F:Human Torch. 3.00
4 GMo,JaL,F:Mr. Fantastic 3.00
TPB JaL,GMo 10.00

FANTASTIC FOUR ROAST
May, 1982
1 FH/MG/FM/JB/MA/TA 5.00

FANTASTIC FOUR'S BIG TOWN
Nov., 2000
1 (of 4) SEt,MMK,MkK,48-page . . . 3.50
2 SEt,MMK,MkK 3.00
3 SEt,MMK,MkK 3.00
4 SEt,MMK,MkK,48-page 3.50

FANTASTIC FOUR 2099
1996
1 Cont. from 2099 Genesis. 4.00
2 thru 5 . . . . @2.25

FANTASTIC FOUR UNLIMITED
1993–96
1 HT,A:Bl.Panther,V:Klaw 4.50
2 HT,JQ(c),A:Inhumans 4.25
3 HT,V:Blastaar,Annihilus 4.25
4 RTs(s),HT,V:Mole Man,A:Hulk . . . 4.25
5 RTs(s),HT,V:Frightful Four 4.25
6 RTs(s),HT,V:Namor 4.00
7 HT,V:Monsters 4.00
8 . . . . 4.00
9 A:Antman 4.00
10 RTs,HT,V:Maelstrom,A:Eternals . 4.00
11 RTs,HT,Atlantis Rising fallout . . . 4.00
12 RTs,TDF,V:Hyperstorm 4.00
13 . . . . 4.00

FANTASTIC FOUR UNPLUGGED
1995–96
1 comic for a buck 2.25
2 Reed Richard's Will 2.25
3 F:Mr. Fantastic. 2.25
4 . . . . 2.25
5 Back in NY,V:Blastaar 2.25

FANTASTIC FOUR: UNSTABLE MOLECULES
Jan., 2003
1 (of 4) GyD 3.00
2 GyD 3.00
3 GyD 3.00

FANTASTIC FOUR VS. X-MEN
Feb., 1987
1 JBg,TA,V:Dr.Doom. 5.00
2 JBg,TA,V:Dr.Doom. 4.00
3 JBg,TA,V:Dr.Doom. 4.00
4 JBg,TA,V:Dr.Doom, June, 1987. . 4.00
TPB Reprints Mini-series. 12.95

FANTASTIC FOUR THE WORLD'S GREATEST COMIC MAGAZINE
Dec., 2000
1 (of 12) EL,ErS,V:Dr.Doom 3.00
2 F:Dr.Doom,Crystal 3.00
3 A:X-Men,Spider-Man 3.00
4 A:X-Men,Capt.America 3.00
5 EL(c),Hulk vs. Thing 3.00
6 MGo(c),A:Silver Surfer. 3.00
7 KG(c),A:Dr.Doom,Inhumans 3.00
8 KG(c),F:Avengers 3.00
9 EL,KG,A:Dr.Doom 3.00
10 EL,KG,Cosmic Cube. 3.00
11 RF,Planet Doom 3.00
12 StL,EL,JSt, concl. 3.00

FANTASTIC WORLD OF HANNA-BARBERA
Dec., 1977
1 . . . . 30.00
2 . . . . 20.00
3 June, 1978 . . . . 20.00

FANTASY MASTERPIECES
Feb., 1966
1 JK/DH/SD,reprints. 85.00
2 JK,SD,DH,Fin Fang Foom. 50.00
3 GC,DH,JK,SD,Capt.A rep. 60.00
4 JK,Capt.America rep. 60.00
5 JK,Capt.America rep. 60.00
6 JK,Capt.America rep. 60.00
7 SD,Sub Mariner rep. 60.00
8 H.Torch & Sub M.rep. 60.00
9 SD,MF,O:Human Torch Rep . . . 65.00
10 rep.All Winners #19 . . . . 60.00
11 JK,(rep),O:Toro 50.00
Becomes:

MARVEL SUPER-HEROES

FANTASY MASTERPIECES
[Volume 2], Dec., 1979
1 JB,JSt,Silver Surfer rep. 5.00
2 thru 7 JB,JSt,Silver Surfer rep. @5.00
8 thru 11 JB/JSn,.Strange Tales . @4.00
12 thru 14 JB,JSn,rep.Warlock . . @4.00

FAREWELL TO WEAPONS
1 DirtBag,W/Nirvana Tape 3.50

FEAR
Nov., 1970
1 JK,1950's Monster rep.B:I
    Found Monstrum,The Dweller
    in the Black Swamp. 60.00
2 JK,X The Thing That Lived 35.00
3 JK,Zzutak, The Thing That
    Shouldn't Exist. 35.00
4 JK,I Turned Into a Martian. 35.00
5 JK,I Am the Gorilla Man. 35.00
6 JK,SD,The Midnight Monster. . . 35.00
7 JK,SD,I Dream of Doom 20.00
8 JK,SD,It Crawls By Night! 20.00
9 JK,Dead Man's Escape 20.00
Becomes:

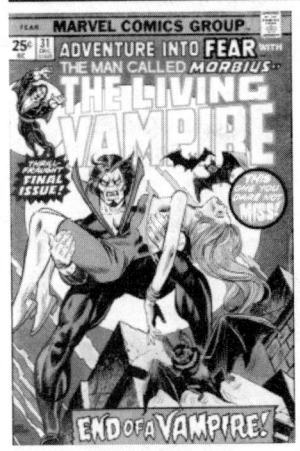

Adventure Into Fear #31
© Marvel Entertainment Group

ADVENTURE INTO FEAR
1972
10 HC,GM,B:Man-Thing 50.00
11 RB,I:Jennifer Kale,Thog 22.00
12 JSn,RB 22.00
13 VM,Where World's Collide 18.00
14 VM,Plague o/t Demon Cult 18.00
15 VM,Lord o/t Dark Domain..... 18.00
16 VM,ManThing in Everglades.. 18.00
17 VM,I:Wundarr(Aquarian)...... 18.00
18 VM........................ 18.00
19 VM,FMc,I:Howard the Duck,
    E:Man-Thing 50.00
20 PG,GK,B:Morbius 50.00
21 GK,V:Uncanny Caretaker 18.00
22 RB,V:Cat-Demond 18.00
23 GC,GK,1st CR art,A World He
    Never Made.............. 18.00
24 CR,SMn,V:Blade, The Vampire
    Slayer 35.00
25 FR,GK,You Always Kill the
    One You Love 15.00
26 FR,GK,V:Uncanny Caretaker .. 15.00
27 FR,GK,V:Simon Stroud....... 15.00
28 GK,Doorway Down into Hell... 15.00
29 Death has a Thousand Eyes .. 15.00
30 Bloody Sacrifice 15.00
31 FR,GK,last issue,Dec., 1975 .. 15.00

FEUD
Epic, 1993
1 I:Skids,Stokes,Kite........... 3.00
2 thru 4 .... @2.25

FIGHT MAN
1993
1 I:Fight Man.................. 2.25

FIRESTAR
March, 1986
1 MW,SL,O:Firestar,A:X-Men,
    New Mutants 5.00
2 MW,BWI,A:New Mutants 4.00
3 AAd&BSz(c),MW,SL,
    A:White Queen 4.00
4 MW,SL,V:White Queen 4.00

FISH POLICE
1992–93
1 V:S.Q.U.I.D,Hook............ 2.50
2 thru 6 .... @2.50

FLASH GORDON
1995
1 R:Flash Gordon 3.00
2 AW,V:Ming, final issue 3.00

FLINTSTONE KIDS
Star, Aug., 1987
1 thru 10 .... @5.00
11 April, 1989................. 5.00

FLINTSTONES
Oct., 1977–Feb., 1979
1 From TV Series 50.00
2 .... 50.00
3 .... 30.00
4 A:Jetsons 30.00
5 thru 7 .... @35.00

FLYING HERO BARBIE
1 Super Hero Barbie........... 2.25

FOOFUR
Star, Aug., 1987
1 thru 6 .... @3.00

FOOLKILLER
Oct., 1990
1 I:Kurt Gerhardt
    (Foolkiller III) 3.50
2 O:Foolkiller I & II 3.00
3 Old Costume 3.00
4 N:Foolkiller................ 2.50
5 Body Count 2.50
6 thru 10 .... @2.25

FORCE WORKS
1994–96
1 TmT,Pop-up(c),I:Century,V:Kree,
    N:US Agent 4.00
2 TmT,V:Scatter 2.25
3 TmT,V:Scatter 2.25
4 Civil War 2.25
5 regular cover 2.25
5a Neon(c),bagged w/print 3.25
6 Hands of the Mandarin,pt.1 ... 2.25
7 Hands of the Mandarin,pt.2 ... 2.25
8 DAn,ALa,Christmas Party 2.25
9 I:Dream Guard.............. 2.25
10 V:Dream Guard............. 2.25
11 F:War Machine 2.25
12 V:Recorder 3.00
13 DAn,ALa,A:Avengers 2.25
14 .... 2.25
15 DAn,ALa,O:Century 2.25
16 .... 2.25
17 DAn,ALa,The Crossing....... 2.25
18 DAn,ALa,The Crossing 2.25
19 DAn,ALa,The Crossing 2.25
20 DAn,cont.Avengers:Timeslide... 2.25

411
April, 2003
1 thru 3 .... @3.50

FOR YOUR EYES ONLY
1 HC,James Bond rep........... 3.00
2 HC,James Bond rep........... 3.00

FRAGGLE ROCK
1985
1 thru 8 .... @5.00
[Volume 2], April, 1988
1 thru 5 rep.................. @2.50
6 Sept., 1988 .... 2.50

FRANCIS, BROTHER
OF THE UNIVERSE
1980
1-shot SB.................... 5.00

FRANKENSTEIN
See: MONSTER OF
FRANKENSTEIN

Foolkiller #4
© Marvel Entertainment Group

FRED HEMBECK
1-shot Destroys the Marvel
    Universe, parody (1989) 2.25
1-shot Sells the Marvel Universe
    parody (1990) 2.25

FRIGHT
June, 1975
1 Son of Dracula............. 15.00

FRONTIER WESTERN
Feb., 1956
1 RH,...................... 225.00
2 AW,GT,GC,JMn 150.00
3 MD 150.00
4 MD,Ringo Kid............. 100.00
5 RC,DW,JDa 150.00
6 AW,GC................... 125.00
7 JR,JMn.................. 100.00
8 RC,DW................... 100.00
9 JMn 100.00
10 SC,Aug., 1957 .... 100.00

FUNNY FROLICS
Summer, 1945
1 Shardy Fox,KrazyKroid,(fa) ... 250.00
2 .... 150.00
3 .... 100.00
4 .... 100.00
5 HK 125.00

FURTHER ADVENTURES
OF CYCLOPS
AND PHOENIX
1996
1 thru 4 .... @3.00
TPB PrM,JPL, O:Mr. Sinister, ... 12.00

All comics prices listed are for *Near Mint* condition.

FURY
1994
1 MCW,O:Fury,A:S.A. Heroes 3.25

FURY
Marvel Max, Sept., 2001
1 (of 6) GEn,DaR,JP,F:Nick Fury .. 6.00
2 GEn,DaR,JP,F:Rudi Gagarin 4.00
3 GEn,DaR,JP, ... 4.00
4 GEn,DaR,JP 4.00
5 GEn,DaR,JP 4.00
6 GEn,DaR,JP 4.00
TPB GEn,DaR, 144-pg. 16.00

FURY/AGENT 13
March, 1998
1 (of 2) TKa,is Nick Fury alive? ... 3.00
2 TKa,MZ(c),Sharon Carter's searches
   for Nick 3.00

FURY OF S.H.I.E.L.D.
1995
1 Foil etched cover 3.00
2 A:Iron Man 2.50
3 J:Hydra 2.50
4 w/decoder card 3.00

GALACTIC GUARDIANS
1994
1 KWe,C:Woden 2.25
2 KWe,I:Hazmat,Savant,Ganglia .. 2.25
3 KWe 2.25
4 KWe,final issue 2.25

GALACTUS
THE DEVOURER
April, 1999
1 (of 6) JMu,LSi,A:Silver Surfer,
   Fant.Four & Avengers,48-page . 4.00
2 LSi,JB,BSz 2.50
3 LSi,JB,BSz 2.50
4 LSi,JB,BSz,A:Silver Surfer...... 2.50
5 LSi,JB,BSz 2.50
6 LSi,JB,BSz,concl 3.50

GAMBIT
1997
1 HMe(c),LW,KJ,V:Assassin'sGuild,
   D:Henri LeBeau,Embossed(c).. 5.00
1a Gold Ed. 15.00
2 LW,KJ,C:Gideon,A:Rogue 3.00
3 LW,KJ,A:Candra,Rogue,
   D:Gambit's Father 3.00
4 LW,KJ,A:Candra,Rogue,D:Tithe
   Collector 3.00
TPB Rep.#1-#4 .... 9.00

GAMBIT
1997
1 (of 4) HMe,KJ,In Miami 3.50
2 HMe,KJ, ... 3.00
3 HMe,KJ,in the Vatican 3.00
4 HMe V:Stoker, concl. 3.00

GAMBIT
Dec., 1998
1 FaN,SSr,O:Gambit,48-page..... 4.00
1a signed 25.00
2 FaN,SSr,V:Storm 3.00
2a variant cover 3.00
3 FaN,SSr,V:Mengo Brothers 2.50
4 FaN,SSr,A:Blade 2.50
5 FaN,SSr,F:Rogue 2.50
6 FaN,SSr,I:The Pig 2.50

7 FaN,SSr, ... 2.50
8 FaN,A:Sinister,Sabretooth 2.50
9 FaN,The Shattering,x-over 2.50
10 FaN,V:Candra & Fenris 2.50
11 FaN,A:Daredevil 2.50
12 FaN 2.50
13 FaN,Black Womb 2.50
14 FaN,ALa,A:Mr. Sinister 2.50
15 FaN,F:Rogue 2.50
16 FaN,X-Men: Revolution 2.50
16a variant (c) 2.50
17 FaN,AssassinationGame,pt.1 ... 2.25
18 FaN,AssassinationGame,pt.2 ... 2.25
19 FaN,AssassinationGame,pt.3 ... 2.25
20 FaN,Fontanelle 2.25
21 FaN,Remy LeBeau 2.25
22 FaN,Neo,Remy LeBeau,Rax ... 2.25
23 FaN,X-Cutioner 2.25
24 FaN,V:New Son 2.25
25 SLo, 48-page 3.50
Ann.1999 48-page 3.50
Ann.2000 FaN,F:X-Men 3.50
Giant Sized Gambit, 96-page, rep. . 4.00

GAMBIT
Sept., 2004
1 House of Cards,pt.1 .... 3.00
2 House of Cards,pt.2 .... 3.00
3 House of Cards,pt.3 .... 3.00

GAMBIT & BISHOP:
SONS OF THE ATOM
Jan., 2001
1 SLo,Bishop captured 2.25
2 SLo,on the run 2.25
3 SLo,common enemy 2.25
4 SLo, ... 2.25
5 SLo,Ultimate sacrifice 2.25
6 SLo,finale 2.25
Spec. Alpha, SLo,CNr 2.25
Spec. Genesis,CCl 3.50

GAMBIT AND
THE X-TERNALS
1995
1 X-Force after Xavier 3.50
2 V:Deathbird,Starjammers 2.50
3 V:Imperial Guard 2.50
4 Charles Kidnapped 2.50

Gargoyles #3
© Marvel Entertainment Group

GARGOYLE
June, 1985
1 BWr(c),from `Defenders' 4.00
2 thru 4 .... @3.00

GARGOYLES
1995–96
1 TV Series 4.00
2 TV Series 3.00
3 F:Broadway 3.00
4 V:Statues 3.00
5 Humanoid Gargoyles 3.00
6 Medusa Project concl. 3.00
7 Demona & Triad 3.00
8 I:The Pack 3.00
9 V:Demonia,Triad 3.00
10 Demonia gains magical powers . 3.00
11 Elisa turns to Xanatos 3.00
12 Sorceress traps Gargoyles 3.00
13 Behind Enemy Lines. 3.00
14 .... 3.00
15 .... 3.00
16 Hammer of Fear 3.00

GENE DOGS
Marvel UK, 1993–94
1 I:Gene DOGS,w/cards 3.00
2 V:Genetix 2.25
3 V:Hurricane 2.25
4 last issue 2.25

GENERATION NEXT
1995
1 Generation X AX 3.50
2 Genetic Slave Pens 2.50
3 V:Sugar Man 2.50
4 V:Sugar Man 2.50

GENERATION X
Oct., 1994
1 CBa,Banshee & White Queen... 7.00
2 CBa,SLo 4.00
2a Deluxe edition 4.00
3 CBa 3.00
3a Deluxe edition 4.00
4 CBa,V:Nanny,Orphanmaker 3.00
4a Deluxe edition 4.00
5 SLo,CBa,MBu,two new young
   mutants at the Academy 3.50
6 A:Wolverine 3.50
7 SLo,F:Banshee,A:White Queen. . 3.50
8 F:Banshee 3.50
9 SLo,TG,Chamber in a kilt. 3.50
10 SLo,TG,MBu,Banshee vs.
   OmegaRed 3.50
11 SLo,TG,V:Omega Red 3.00
12 SLo,TG,V:Emplate 3.00
13 .... 3.00
14 .... 3.00
15 SLo,MBu,Synch goes psycho... 3.00
16 .... 3.00
17 SLo,CBa,Onslaught saga,
   X-Cutioner vs. Skin 3.00
18 SLo,CBa,Onslaught saga 3.00
19 SLo,CBa, ... 3.00
20 SLo,CBa, ... 3.00
21 SLo,CBa,MBu,F:Skin & Chamber,
   A:Beverly Switzer, Howard
   the Duck 3.00
22 SLo,CBa, ... 3.00
23 SLo,CBa,V:Black Tom Cassidy.. 3.00
24 SLo,MBy,F:Monet,Emplate 3.00
25 SLo,CBa,double size 4.00
26 SLo,CBa,Shot down over the
   Atlantic. 3.00
27 SLo,CBa,on nuclear sub. 3.00
28 SLo,CBa,No Exit prelude 3.00
29 JeR,CBa, V:Sentinels 3.00

30 JeR,CBa, V:Zero Tolerance 3.00
31 JeR,CBa, ... 3.00
32 TDF,MBu,F:Banshee, Moira
   McTaggert 3.00
33 LHa,MBu,new direction....... 3.00
34 LHa,Truth behind M 3.00
35 LHa,Jubilee,V:Emplate 3.00
36 LHa,Final Fate of M 3.00
37 LHa,Final Fate of M 3.00
38 LHa,TyD,kids save universe.... 2.50
39 LHa,TyD, multi-dimensional trip . 2.50
40 LHa,TyD,Penance mystery
   revealed................. 2.50
41 LHa,TyD,Jubilee,V:Bastion,
   Omega Red, Sabretooth 2.50
42 LHa,TyD,results of EMP wave ... 2.50
43 LHa,TyD,V:Bianca LaNiege 2.50
44 LHa,TyD,V:White Queen....... 2.50
45 LHa,TyD,F:Banshee 2.50
46 LHa,TyD,F:Forge 2.50
47 LHa,TyD,Danger Room 2.50
48 TyD,Jubilee vs. M........... 2.50
49 TyD,V:Maggott 2.50
50 TyD,War of the Mutants,pt.1 ... 3.50
50a signed.................. 20.00
51 V:Hunter Brawn............. 2.50
52 TyD,blackmail.............. 2.50
53 TyD,V:Rising Sons,A:Paladin ... 2.50
54 TyD,A:Paladin.............. 2.50
55 TyD,in bodies of Hellions 2.50
56 TyD,A:X-Men of past........ 2.50
57 TyD, double sized........... 3.50
58 TyD, new Penance 2.50
59 TyD,.................... 2.50
60 TyD,F:Siryn............... 2.50
61 TyD,ATi,R:Mondo 2.50
62 TyD,F:Monet St. Croix....... 2.50
63a variant (c) 2.50
64 WEI,Correction,pt.2.......... 2.25
65 WEI,Correction,pt.3.......... 2.25
66 WEI,Correction,pt.4.......... 2.25
67 WEI,Come On Die Young,pt.1 .. 2.25
68 WEI,Come On Die Young,pt.2 .. 2.25
69 WEI,Come On Die Young,pt.3 .. 2.25
70 WEI,Come On Die Young,pt.4 .. 2.25
71 WEI,Four Days,pt.1.......... 2.25
72 AAd(c),StP,Four Days,pt.2 .... 2.25
73 AAd(c),StP,Four Days,pt.3 .... 2.25
74 AAd(c),StP,Four Days,pt.4 .... 2.25
75 AAd(c),StP,final issue 3.50
Minus 1 Spec., JeR,CBa, flashback,
   F:Banshee................. 2.50
Ann. '95 SLo,J:Mondo,
   V:Hellfire Club 4.50
Ann. '96 GN MGo,JJ,DPs,V:Fenris . 3.50
Ann. '97, Haunted by Ghosts
   of Hellions 3.50
Ann.1998 Generation X/Dracula ... 4.00
Ann.1999 48-pg. 4.00
Holliday Spec. 48-page 1-shot..... 4.00

GENERATION X/GEN 13
Dec., 1997
1-shot JeR,SvL,V:Mr. Pretorious ... 4.00
1a variant cover CBa (1:4)........ 4.00

GENERATION X: UNDERGROUND
March, 1998
1-shot by Jim Mahfood, b&w 2.50

GENERIC COMIC
1 .... 2.25

GENETIX
Marvel UK, 1993–94
1 B:ALa(s),w/cards 3.00

Generation X/Gen13 Special
© Marvel Entertainment Group

2 I:Tektos 2.25
3 V:Tektos 2.25
4 PGa,V:MyS-Tech............. 2.25
5 PGa,V:MyS-Tech............. 2.25
6 V:Tektos 2.25

GEORGIE COMICS
Spring, 1945
1 Georgie stories begin 275.00
2 Pet Shop (c) 150.00
3 Georgie/Judy(c) 125.00
4 Wedding Dress(c) 125.00
5 Monty/Policeman(c) 125.00
6 Classroom(c) 125.00
7 Fishing(c) 135.00
8 Soda Jerk(c) 135.00
9 Georgie/Judy(c),HK,Hey Look 135.00
10 Georgie/Girls(c),HK,Hey Look 135.00
11 Table Tennis(c),A:Margie,Millie . 75.00
12 Camping(c)................ 75.00
13 Life Guard(c),HK,Hey Look. . 100.00
14 Classroom(c),HK,Hey Look . 100.00
15 Winter Sports(c) 75.00
16 .... 75.00
17 HK,Hey Look............... 75.00
18 .... 75.00
19 Baseball(c) 75.00
Becomes:

GEORGIE & JUDY COMICS
20 .... 75.00
21 .... 60.00
Becomes:

GEORGIE COMICS
22 Georgie comics 60.00
23 .... 60.00
24 .... 60.00
25 Driben painted (c)......... 100.00
26 thru 28.................. @60.00
29 .... 75.00
30 thru 38.................. @60.00
39 Oct., 1952............... 60.00

GETALONG GANG
May, 1985–March, 1986
1 thru 6 .... @3.50

GHOST RIDER
1967
1 O&I:Ghost Rider (western) ... 125.00
2 V:Tarantula................ 75.00
3 Cougar's Circus of Fear 50.00

4 Sting Ray................. 50.00
5 Tarantula Strikes Back........ 50.00
6 Behold a Falling Star 50.00
7 Mystery of Massacre Mountain . 50.00

GHOST RIDER
[1st Regular Series], Sept., 1973
1 GK,JSt,C:Son of Satan 100.00
2 GK,I:Son of Satan,A:Witch
   Woman 50.00
3 JR,D:Big Daddy Dawson,
   new Cycle 35.00
4 GK,A:Dude Jensen 35.00
5 GK,JR,I:Roulette 35.00
6 JR,O:Ghost Rider 25.00
7 JR,A:Stunt Master 25.00
8 GK,A:Satan,I:Inferno 25.00
9 GK,TP,O:Johnny Blaze 25.00
10 JSt,A:Hulk 25.00
11 GK,KJ,SB,A:Hulk 25.00
12 GK,KJ,FR,A:Phantom Eagle. . 15.00
13 GK,JS,GT,A:Trapster 15.00
14 GT,A:The Orb 15.00
15 SB,O:The Orb 15.00
16 DC,GT,Blood in the Water 15.00
17 RB,FR,I:Challenger.......... 15.00
18 RB,FR,A:Challenger,
   Spider-Man 15.00
19 GK,FR,A:Challenger 15.00
20 GK,KJ,JBy,A:Daredevil 22.00
21 A:Gladiator,D:Eel. 10.00
22 AM,DH,KP,JR,A:Enforcer 10.00
23 JK,DH,DN,I:Water Wiz....... 10.00
24 GK,DC,DH,A:Enforcer 10.00
25 GK,DH,A:Stunt Master 10.00
26 GK,DP,A:Dr. Druid 10.00
27 SB,DP,A:Hawkeye 10.00
28 DP,A:The Orb 10.00
29 RB,DP,A:Dormammu 10.00
30 DP,A:Dr.Strange 10.00
31 FR,DP,BL,A:Bounty Hunt..... 10.00
32 KP,BL,DP,A:Bounty Hunt..... 10.00
33 DP,I:Dark Riders 10.00
34 DP,C:Cyclops 10.00
35 JSn,AM,A:Death 15.00
36 DP,Drug Mention........... 10.00
37 DP,I:Dick Varden........... 10.00
38 DP,A:Death Cult 10.00
39 DP,A:Death Cult 10.00
40 DP,I:Nuclear Man 10.00
41 DP,A:Jackal Gang........... 10.00

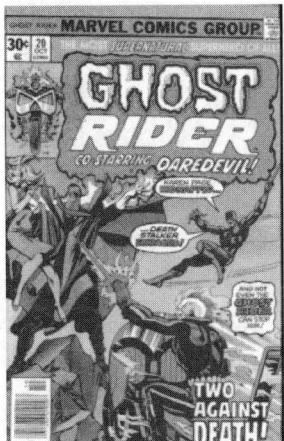

Ghost Rider #20
© Marvel Entertainment Group

MARVEL

42 DP,A:Jackal Gang 10.00	9 JS,MT,A:Morlocks,X-Factor 2.50	74 A:Blaze, Vengeance 2.50
43 CI:Crimson Mage 10.00	10 JS,MT,V:Zodiac. 2.50	75 . . . . 2.50
44 JAb,CI,A:Crimson Mage 10.00	11 LSn,MT,V:Nightmare,	76 V:Vengeance. 2.50
45 DP,I:Flagg Fargo. 10.00	A:Dr.Strange 2.50	77 A:Dr. Strange. 2.50
46 DP,A:Flagg Fargo 10.00	12 JS,MT,A:Dr.Strange 2.50	78 new costume, A:Dr. Strange . . 2.50
47 AM,DP. 10.00	13 MT,V:Snow Blind,R:J.Blaze . . . 2.50	79 IV,New costume, A:Valkyrie, . . 2.50
48 BMc,DP. 10.00	14 MT,Blaze Vs.Ghost Rider. 2.50	80 IV,V:Furies,Valkyrie
49 DP,I:The Manitou 10.00	15 MT,A:Blaze,V:Blackout	A:Black Rose. 2.50
50 DP,A:Night Rider. 15.00	Glow in Dark(c) 3.00	81 IV,A:Howard the Duck,
51 AM,PD,A:Cycle Gang 6.00	15a 2nd printing (gold). 2.50	Devil Dinosaur 2.25
52 AM,DP. 6.00	16 MT,A:Blaze,Spider-Man,	82 IV,A:Devil Dinosaur, ... 2.25
53 DP,I:Lord Asmodeus 6.00	V:Hobgoblin. 2.50	83 IV,A:Scarecrow,Lilith 2.25
54 DP,A:The Orb 6.00	17 MT,A:Spider-Man,Blaze,	84 IV,A:Scarecrow, Lilith 2.25
55 DP,A:Werewolf By Night 6.00	V:Hobgoblin. 2.50	85 IV,V:Lilith, Scarecrow 2.25
56 DP,A:Moondark,I:Night Rider . . . 6.00	18 MT,V:Reverend Styge 2.50	86 IV,rampage through the Bronx . . 2.25
57 AM,DP,I:The Apparition. 6.00	19 MT,A:Mephisto 2.50	87 IV,KIK,AM, ... 2.25
58 DP,FM,A:Water Wizard. 6.00	20 MT(i),O:Zodiac 2.50	88 IV, V:Pao Fu,Blackheart 2.25
59 V:Water Wizard,Moon Dark 6.00	21 MT(i),V:Snowblind,	89 IV,JS, ... 2.25
60 DP,HT,A:Black Juju 6.00	A:Deathwatch 2.50	90 IV,JS,Last Temptation, pt.1 . . . . 2.25
61 A:Arabian Knight. 6.00	22 MT,A:Deathwatch,Ninjas. 2.50	91 IV,JS,A:Blackheart 2.25
62 KJ,A:Arabian Knight 6.00	23 MT,I:Hag & Troll,A:Deathwatch. . 2.50	92 IV,JS,Journey into the past 2.25
63 LMc,A:The Orb 6.00	24 MT,V:Deathwatch,D:Snowblind,	93 IV,JS,MT,Last Temptation concl.,
64 BA,V:Azmodeus 6.00	C:Johnny Blaze 2.50	double sized 3.00
65 A:Fowler 6.00	25 V:Blackout (w/Center spread	94 IV,JS,MT,Becomes Lord of the
66 BL,A:Clothilde 6.00	pop-up) 3.00	Underworld, last issue 2.00
67 DP,A:Sally Stantop 6.00	26 A:X-Men,V:The Brood 3.00	Ann.#1 I:Night Terror,w/card 3.25
68 O:Ghost Rider. 6.00	27 A:X-Men,V:The Brood 3.00	Ann.#2 F:Scarecrow 3.00
69 . . . . 6.00	28 NKu,JKu,Rise of the Midnight	GN Ghost Rider/Captain America:
70 I:Jeremy 6.00	Sons#1,V:Lilith,w/poster 3.00	Fear, AW, V:Scarecrow (1992) . 6.25
71 DP,I:Adam Henderson 6.00	29 NKu,JKu,A:Wolverine,Beast . . . 2.50	GN Ghost Rider/Wolverine/Punisher:
72 A:Circus of Crime 6.00	30 NKu,JKu,V:Nightmare 2.50	Dark Design (1994) 6.00
73 A:Circus of Crime 6.00	31 NKu,JKu,Rise o/t Midnight	GN Ghost Rider/Wolverine/Punisher:
74 A:Centurions 6.00	Sons#6, A:Dr.Strange,Morbius,	Hearts of Darkness, JR2/KJ,V:
75 I:Steel Wind. 6.00	Nightstalkers,Redeemers,	Blackheart, gatefold(c) (1991). . 5.50
76 DP,A:Mephisto,I:Saturnine 6.00	V:Lilith,w/poster 3.00	TPB Midnight Sons, rep. 20.00
77 O:Ghost Rider's Dream 6.00	32 BBi,A:Dr.Strange 2.50	TPB Resurrected rep.#1-#7 . . . . . 13.00
78 A:Nightmare 6.00	33 BBI,AW,V:Madcap (inc.Superman	TPB Resurrected (2000) 13.00
79 A:Man Cycles 6.00	tribute on letters page) 2.50	Poster Book. 5.00
80 A:Centurions 6.00	34 BBI,V:Deathwatchs' ninja 2.50	Spec. Crossroads 4.00
81 D:Ghost Rider. 15.00	35 BBI,AW,A:Heart Attack 2.50	Minus 1 Spec., IV,JS, flashback. . . . 2.00
	36 BBI,V:Mr.Hyde,A:Daredevil 2.50	
[2nd Regular Series], 1990–98	37 BBI,A:Archangel,V:HeartAttack. . 2.50	
1 JS,MT,I:2nd Ghost Rider,	38 MM,V:Scarecrow. 2.50	**GHOST RIDER/**
Deathwatch 6.00	39 V:Vengeance. 2.50	**BALLISTIC/CYBLADE**
1a 2nd printing 3.00	40 Midnight Massacre#2,	**Marvel/Top Cow 1996**
2 JS,MT,I:Blackout 3.00	D:Demogblin 3.00	1-shot IV,ACh,Devil's Reign,
3 JS,MT,A:Kingpin,V:Blackout,	41 Road to Vengeance#1 . . . . 2.50	pt.2, x-over 3.25
Deathwatch 3.00	42 Road to Vengeance#2 . . . . 2.50	1-shot WEI,BTn,Devil's
4 JS,MT,V:Mr.Hyde 3.00	43 Road to Vengeance#3 . . . . 2.50	Reign, pt.3, x-over. 3.00
5 JLe(c),JS,MT,A:Punisher 3.00	44 Siege of Darkness,pt.#2 . . . . . . 2.50	
5a rep.Gold. 2.50	45 Siege of Darkness,pt.#10 . . . . . 2.50	**GHOST RIDER/BLAZE**
6 JS,MT,A:Punisher 3.00	46 HMe(s),New Beginning 2.50	**SPIRITS OF VENGEANCE**
7 MT,V:Scarecrow. 3.00	47 HMe(s),RG, ... 2.50	**1992–94**
8 JS,MT,V:H.E.A.R.T 3.00	48 HMe(s),RG,A:Spider-Man 2.50	1 AKu,polybagged w/poster,V:Lilith,
	49 HMe(s),RG,A:Hulk,w/card 2.50	Rise of the Midnight Sons#2 . . . 3.50
	50 Red Foil(c),AKu,SMc,A:Blaze,	2 AKu,V:Steel Wind. 3.00
	R:2nd Ghost Rider. 3.25	3 AKu,CW,V:The Lilin 3.00
	50a Newsstand Ed. 2.75	4 AKu,V:Hag & Troll,C:Venom 3.00
	51 SvL 2.50	5 AKu,BR,Spirits of Venom#2,
	52 SvL 2.50	A:Venom,Spidey,Hobgoblin 5.00
	53 SvL,V:Blackout 2.50	6 AKu,Spirits of Venom#4,A:Venom,
	54 SvL,V:Blackout 2.50	Spider-Man,Hobgoblin. 3.50
	55 V:Mr. Hyde 2.50	7 AKu,V:Steel Vengeance. 2.25
	56 The Next Wave 2.50	8 V:Mephisto 2.25
	57 A:Wolverine 2.50	9 I:Brimstone. 2.25
	58 HMe,SvL,Betrayal,pt.1 . . . . 2.50	10 AKu,V:Vengeance 2.25
	59 Betrayal,pt.2 . . . . 2.50	11 V:Human Spider Creature 2.25
	60 Betrayal,pt.3 . . . . 2.50	12 AKu,BR,Vengeance,glow in the
	61 Betrayal,pt.4 . . . . 3.00	dark(c) 3.25
	62 EventInChains,pt.1,A:Fury 2.50	13 AKu,Midnight Massacre#5 . . . . . 2.50
	63 EventInChains,pt.2 . . . . 2.50	14 Missing Link#2 . . . . 2.25
	64 EventInChains,pt.3 . . . . 2.50	15 Missing Link#3 . . . . 2.25
	65 EventInChains,pt.4,R:Blackout . . 2.50	16 V:Zarathos,Lilith 2.25
	66 V:Blackout. 2.50	17 HMe(s),Siege/Darkness,pt.8 . . . . 2.25
	67 A:Gambit,V:Brood 2.50	18 HMe(s),Siege/Darkness,pt.13. . . . 2.25
	68 A:Gambit,Wolverine,V:Brood . . . 2.50	19 HMe(s),HMz,V:Vampire 2.25
	69 Domestic Violence 2.50	20 HMe(s),A:Steel Wind 2.25
	70 New Home in Bronx 2.50	21 HMe(s),HMz,V:Werewolves 2.25
	71 . . . . 2.50	22 HMe(s),HMz,V:Cardiac. 2.25
	72 . . . . 2.50	23 HMe(s),HMz,A:Steel Wind 2.25
	73 John Blaze is back 2.50	

Ghost Rider 2nd Series Annual #1
© Marvel Entertainment Group

GHOST RIDER: THE HAMMER LANE
June, 2001
1 (of 6) TKn. 3.00
2 TKn,DaM 3.00
3 TKn,DaM,Gunmetal Gray 3.00
4 TKn,DaM,Gunmetal Gray 3.00
5 TKn,DaM,Gunmetal Gray 3.00
6 TKn,DaM,Gunmetal Gray 3.00
TPB series rep. 144-pg. 15.95

GHOST RIDER: HIGHWAY TO HELL
June, 2001
Spec. 64-pages 3.50

GHOST RIDER 2099
1994–96
1 Holografx(c),LKa,CBa,MBu,I:Ghost
  Rider 2099,w/card 3.00
1a Newsstand Ed. 2.25
2 LKa,CBa,MBu, ... 2.25
3 LKa,CBa,MBu,I:Warewolf 2.25
4 LKa,CBa,MBu,V:Warewolf. 2.25
5 LKa,CBa,MBu 2.25
6 LKa,CBa,MBu 2.25
7 LKa,CBa,MBu 2.25
8 LKa,CBa,MBu 2.25
9 . . . . 2.25
10 . . . . 2.25
11 V:Bloodsport Society. 2.25
12 I:Coda 2.25

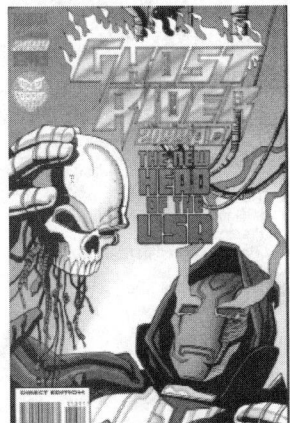

Ghost Rider 2099 A.D. #13
© Marvel Entertainment Group

Becomes:

GHOST RIDER 2099 A.D.
1995
13 F:Doom. 2.25
14 Deputized by Doom 2.25
15 One Nation Under Doom 2.25
16 V:Max Synergy 2.25
17 . . . . 2.25
18 V:L-Cipher. 2.25
19 V:L-Cipher. 2.25
20 . . . . 2.25
21 V:Vengeance 2099 . . . . 2.25
22 V:Vengeance 2099 . . . . 2.25
23 . . . . 2.25
24 . . . . 2.25
25 Double size final issue 3.50

GIANT-SIZE CHILLERS
1975
1 AA, ... 35.00
2 . . . . 25.00
3 BWr,Night of the Gargoyle. . . . 30.00

GIANT-SIZE CHILLERS
1974
1 I&O:Lilith,F:Curse of Dracula. . . 60.00
Becomes:

GIANT-SIZE DRACULA
2 Vengeance of the Elder Gods . . 30.00
3 rep. Uncanny Tales #6. . . . . . . 20.00
4 SD,Demon of Devil's Lake. 20.00
5 JBy, 1st Marvel art. 50.00

GIANT-SIZE MINI-MARVELS: STARRING SPIDEY
Dec., 2001
1 F:Hawkeye, 48-pg. 3.50

G.I. JOE: A REAL AMERICAN HERO
June, 1982
1 HT,BMc,Baxter paper. 25.00
2 DP,JAb,North Pole. 20.00
3 HT,JAb,Trojan Robot 15.00
4 HT,JAb,Wingfield 15.00
5 DP,Central Park. 15.00
6 HT,V:Cobra 15.00
7 HT,Walls of Death 15.00
8 HT,Sea Strike. 15.00
9 The Diplomat 15.00
10 Springfield. 15.00
11 Alaska Pipeline 12.00
12 V:Snake Eyes 12.00
13 Rio Lindo. 12.00
14 V:Destro 12.00
15 A:Red Eye. 12.00
16 V:Cobra. 12.00
17 Loose Ends. 12.00
18 V:Destro 12.00
19 D:General Kwinn. 12.00
20 JBy(c),GI,Clutch 12.00
21 SL(i),Silent Interlude 35.00
22 V:Destro 7.00
23 I:Duke 7.00
24 RH,I:Storm Shadow 7.00
25 FS,I:Zartan 7.00
26 SL(i),O:Snake Eyes 9.00
27 FS,O:Snake Eyes 9.00
28 Swampfire. 7.00
29 FS,V:Destro 7.00
30 JBy(c),FS,V:Dreddnoks 7.00
31 V:Destro 3.00
32 FS,V:Dreddnoks 3.00
33 FS,Celebration 3.00
34 Shakedown. 3.00
35 JBy(c),MBr,V:Dreddnoks. 3.00
36 MBr,Shipwar 3.00
2a to 36a 2nd printings . . . . . . @2.00
37 FS,Twin Brothers,I:Flint 3.00
38 V:Destro 3.00
39 Jungle 3.00
40 Hydrofoil 3.00
41 . . . . 3.00
42 A:Stormshadow 3.00
43 Death Issue,New Joe 3.00
44 V:Cobra. 3.00
45 V:Cobra. 3.00
46 V:Cobra. 3.00
47 V:Cobra,D:Stormshadow 3.00
48 V:Cobra. 3.00
49 V:Cobra,I:Serpentor 3.00
50 I:G.I.Joe Missions,R:S'shadow . . 3.00
51 V:Cobra Emperor 3.00

G.I. Joe #54
© Marvel Entertainment Group

52 V:Stormshadow. 3.00
53 Hawk V:Cobra. 3.00
54 V:Destro 3.00
55 The Pit 3.00
56 V:Serpentor 3.00
57 V:Destro 3.00
58 V:Cobra. 3.00
59 Armor 3.00
60 TM,I:Zanzibar 6.00
61 MR,D:Cobra Commander. 3.00
62 Trial 3.00
63 A:GI Joe Snow Job. 3.00
64 V:Baroness 3.00
65 V:Cobra. 3.00
66 Stalker Rescued 3.00
67 . . . . 3.00
68 I:Battleforce 2000 . . . . 3.00
69 TSa 3.00
70 V:Destro 3.00
71 . . . . 3.00
72 . . . . 3.00
73 . . . . 3.00
74 . . . . 3.00
75 MR 3.00
76 D:Serpentor. 3.00
77 MR,V:Cobra 3.00
78 V:Cobra. 3.00
79 MR,V:Dreadnoks. 3.00
80 V:Cobra. 3.00
81 MR,V:Dreadnoks. 3.00
82 MR,V:Cobra 3.00
83 I:RoadPig 3.00
84 MR,O:Zartan 3.00
85 Storm Shadow,Vs.Zartan 3.00
86 MR,25th Anniv. 3.00
87 TSa,V:Cobra 3.00
88 TSa,V:Python Patrol 3.00
89 MBr,V:Road Pig 3.00
90 MBr,R:Red Ninjas 3.00
91 TSa,V:Red Ninjas,D:Blind
   Masters 4.00
92 MBr,V:Cobra Condor. 4.00
93 MBr,V:Baroness 15.00
94 MBr,A:Snake Eyes 6.00
95 MBr,A:Snake Eyes 6.00
96 MBr,A:Snake Eyes 6.00
97 . . . . 4.00
98 MBr,R:Cobra Commander 4.00
99 HT 4.00
100 MBr 4.00
101 MBr 4.00
102 MBr 4.00
103 MBr,A:Snake Eyes 4.00

All comics prices listed are for *Near Mint* condition.

MARVEL

104 MBr,A:Snake Eyes	4.00
105 MBr,A:Snake Eyes	4.00
106 MBr,StormShadowStalker	4.00
107	4.00
108 I:G.I.Joe Dossiers	4.00
109 Death Issue	4.00
110 Mid-East Crisis	5.00
111 A:Team Ninjas	4.00
112 A:Team Ninjas	4.00
113 V:Cobra	4.00
114 V:Cobra	4.00
115 Story Concl.Dusty Dossier	4.00
116 Destro:Search&Destroy #1	4.00
117 Destro:Search&Destroy #2	4.00
118 Destro:Search&Destroy #3	4.00
119 HT,Android Dopplegangers	4.00
120 V:Red Ninjas,Slice & Dice	6.00
121 V:Slice & Dice	4.00
122 V:Slice & Dice	4.00
123 I:Eco-Warriors,A:Big Man	4.00
124 V:Headman	4.00
125 V:Headhunters	4.00
126 R:Firefly	4.00
127 R:Original G.I.Joe	4.00
128 V:Firefly	4.00
129 V:Cobra Commander	4.00
130 V:Cobra Commander	4.00
131 V:Cobra Commander	4.00
132 V:Cobra	4.00
133 V:Cobra	4.00
134 V:Red Ninjas, Firefly, Hostilities	4.00
135 V:Cobra Ninja w/card	5.00
136 w/Trading Card	5.00
137 V:Night Creepers,w/card	5.00
138 V:Night Creepers,w/card	5.00
139 R:Transformers,V:Cobra	5.00
140 A:Transformers	5.00
141 A:Transformers	5.00
142 A:Transformers	5.00
143 F:Scarlet	5.00
144 O:Snake Eyes	5.00
145 V:Cobra	5.00
146 F:Star Brigade	5.00
147 F:Star Brigade	5.00
148 F:Star Brigade	5.00
149	5.00
150 Cobra Commander vs. Snake Eyes	15.00
151 V:Cobra	10.00
152 First G.I. Joe	10.00
153 V:Cobra	10.00
154	20.00
155 final issue	25.00
SC GI Joe and the Transformers	4.95
Spec. TM rep.#61	4.00
Ann.#1	4.00
Ann.#2	4.00
Ann.#3	4.00
Ann.#4	4.00
Ann.#5	4.00
Yearbook #1 (1985)	4.00
Yearbook #2 (1986)	4.00
Yearbook #3 (1987)	4.00
Yearbook #4 (1988)	4.00
TPB Vol.1, 240-pg. (2002)	24.95
TPB Vol.2, 240-pg. (2002)	24.95
TPB Vol.3, 240-pg. (2002)	24.95
TPB Vol.4 (2002)	26.00
TPB Vol 5 (2003)	25.00

G.I. JOE
EUROPEAN MISSIONS
June, 1988

1 British rep.	7.00
2	5.00
3	7.00
4	5.00
5 thru 15	@5.00

G.I. JOE
SPECIAL MISSIONS
Oct., 1986

1 HT,New G.I. Joe	4.00
2 HT	4.00
3 HT	4.00
4 HT	4.00
5 HT	4.00
6 HT,Iron Curtain	4.00
7 HT	4.00
8 HT	4.00
9 HT	4.00
10 thru 20 HT	@4.00
21 & 22	@5.00
23 HT	5.00
24	5.00
25 HT	5.00
26 HT	5.00
27	5.00
28 HT,final	5.00

G.I. JOE AND
THE TRANSFORMERS
1987

1 HT,mini-series	3.00
2 HT,Cobra	3.00
3 HT,Cobra,Deceptions	3.00
4 HT,Cobra,Deceptions	3.00

G.I. JOE UNIVERSE

1 Biographies rep.#1	3.50
2	2.50
3 MZ(c)	2.50
4	2.50

G.I. TALES
See: SERGEANT BARNEY
BARKER

GIRL COMICS
Atlas, Nov., 1949

1 Ph(c),True love stories,I Could Escape From Love	250.00
2 Ph(c),JKu,Blind Date	135.00
3 BEv,Ph(c),Liz Taylor	250.00
4 PH(c),Borrowed Love	100.00
5 Love stories	100.00
6 same	100.00
7 same	100.00
8 same	100.00
9 same	100.00
10 The Deadly Double-Cross	100.00
11 Love stories	100.00
12 BK,The Dark Hallway	125.00

Becomes:

GIRL CONFESSIONS
1952

13	135.00
14	90.00
15	90.00
16 BEv	120.00
17 BEv	120.00
18 BEv	120.00
19	75.00
20	75.00
21 thru 34	@60.00
35 Aug., 1954	60.00

GIRLS' LIFE
Atlas, Jan., 1954

1	125.00
2	75.00
3	60.00
4	60.00
5	60.00

Godzilla #15
© Marvel Entertainment Group

6 November, 1954	60.00

GLADIATOR/SUPREME
1997

1 KG,ASm,x-over	5.00

GODZILLA
Aug., 1977

1 HT,JM,Based on Movie Series	30.00
2 HT,FrG,GT,Seattle Under Seige	12.00
3 HT,TD,A;Champions	20.00
4 TS,TD,V;Batragon	10.00
5 TS,KJ,Isle of the Living Demons	10.00
6 HT,A Monster Enslaved	10.00
7 V:Red Ronin	10.00
8 V:Red Ronin	10.00
9 Las Gamble in Las Vegas	10.00
10 V:Yetrigar	10.00
11 V;Red Ronin,Yetrigar	8.00
12 Star Sinister	8.00
13 V:Mega-Monster	8.00
14 V:Super-Beasts	8.00
15 Stampede	8.00
16 Jaws of Fear	8.00
17 Godzilla Shrunk	8.00
18 Battle Beneath Eighth Avenue	8.00
19 Panic on the Pier	8.00
20 A;Fantastic Four	10.00
21 V;Devil Dinosaur	8.00
22 V:Devil Dinosaur	8.00
23 A;Avengers	10.00
24 July, 1979	8.00

GOLDEN AGE
OF MARVEL

TPB RyL	10.00
Vol.1, 176-page	20.00
Vol.2, 176-page	20.00

GREATEST SPIDER-MAN
& DAREDEVIL TEAM-UPS

TPB 175pg	10.00

GREEN GOBLIN
1995–96

1 I:New Green Goblin	4.00
2 TDF,SMc,V:Rhino	2.25
3 TDF,SMc,CyberWar tie-in	2.25
4 TDF,SMc,V:Hobgoblin	2.25

All comics prices listed are for *Near Mint* condition.

5 TDF,V:Hobgoblin	2.25
6	2.25
7	2.25
8 TDF,SMc,I:Angelface	2.25
9	2.25
10	2.25
11	2.25
12 Onslaught saga.	2.25
13 Onslaught saga.	2.25

GROO CHRONICLES
Epic, 1989

1 SA	5.00
2 thru 6 SA	@4.00

[SERGIO ARAGONE'S] GROO, THE WANDERER
(see Pacific, Eclipse)
Epic, 1985–95

1 SA,I:Minstrel	17.00
2 SA,A:Minstrel	9.00
3 SA,Medallions	8.00
4 SA,Airship	8.00
5 SA,Slavers	8.00
6 SA,The Eye of the Kabala	8.00
7 SA,A:Sage	8.00
8 SA,A:Taranto	8.00
9 SA,A:Sage	8.00
10 SA,I:Arcadio	8.00
11 SA,A:Arcadio	6.00
12 SA,Groo Meets the Thespians	6.00
13 SA,A:Sage	6.00
14 SA	6.00
15 SA,Monks	6.00
16 SA,A:Taranto	6.00
17 SA,Pirannas	6.00
18 SA,I:Groo Ella	6.00
19 SA,A:Groo Ella	4.00
20 SA,A:Groo Ella	4.00
21 SA,I:Arba,Dakarba	4.00
22 SA,Ambassador	4.00
23 SA,I:Pal,Drumm	4.00
24 SA,Arcadio's	4.00
25 SA,Taranto	4.00
26 SA,A:Arba,Taranto	4.00
27 SA,A:Minstrel,Sage	4.00
28 SA	4.00
29 SA,I:Ruferto	5.00
30 SA,A:Ruferto	4.00
31 SA,A:Pal,Drumm	4.00
32 SA,C:Sage	4.00

Groo, The Wanderer #18
© Marvel Entertainment Group

33 SA,Pirates	4.00
34 SA,Wizard's amulet	4.00
35 SA,A:Everybody	4.00
36 SA,A:Everybody	4.00
37 SA,A:Ruferto	4.00
38 SA,Dognappers.	4.00
39 SA,A:Pal,Drumm	4.00
40 SA	4.00
41 SA,I:Granny Groo	4.00
42 SA,A:Granny Groo	4.00
43 SA,A:Granny Groo	4.00
44 SA,A:Ruferto	4.00
45 SA	4.00
46 SA,New Clothes	4.00
47 SA,A:Everybody	4.00
48 SA,A:Ruferto	4.00
49 SA,C:Chakaal	4.00
50 SA,double size	4.00
51 SA,A:Chakaal	3.00
52 SA,A:Chakaal	3.00
53 SA,A:Chakaal	3.00
54 SA,A:Ahak.	3.00
55 SA,A:Ruferto	3.00
56 SA,A:Minstrael	3.00
57 SA,A:Ruferto	3.00
58 SA,A:Idol	3.00
59 SA	3.00
60 SA,A:Ruferto	3.00
61 SA,A:Horse	3.00
62 SA,A:Horse	3.00
63 SA,A:Drumm	3.00
64 SA,A:Artist.	3.00
65 SA	3.00
66 SA	3.00
67 SA	3.00
68 SA	3.00
69 SA	3.00
70 SA	3.00
71 SA	3.00
72 SA	3.00
73 SA,Amnesia,pt1	3.00
74 SA,Amnesia,pt2	3.00
75 SA,Memory Returns	3.00
76 SA	3.00
77 SA	3.00
78 SA,R:Weaver,Scribe	3.00
79 SA,Groo the Assassin.	3.00
80 SA,I:Thaiis,pt.1	3.00
81 SA,Thaiis,pt.2	3.00
82 SA,Thaiis,pt.3	3.00
83 SA,Thaiis,pt.4	3.00
84 SA,Thaiis Conclusion	3.00
85 SA,Groo turns invisible	3.00
86 SA,Invisible Groo	3.00
87 SA,Groo's Army	3.00
88 SA,V:Cattlemen,B.U. Sage	4.00
89 SA,New Deluxe Format	3.00
90 SA,Worlds 1st Lawyers.	3.00
91 SA,Bonus Pages.	3.00
92 SA,Groo Becomes Kid Groo.	3.00
93 SA,Groo destroys glacier	3.00
94 SA	3.00
95 SA,Endangered Species.	3.00
96 SA,Wager of the Gods#1	3.00
97 SA,Wager of the Gods#2	3.00
98 SA,Wager of the Gods#3	3.00
99 SA,E:Wager of the Gods	3.00
100 SA,Groo gets extra IQ points	8.00
101 SA,Groo loses intelligence	4.00
102 SA,F:Newly literate Groo	4.00
103 SA,General Monk	4.00
104 SA,F:Oso,Ruferto	4.00
105 SA,V:Minotaurs	4.00
106 SA,B:Man of the People	4.00
107 SA,Man of the People#2.	4.00
108 SA,Man of the People#3.	4.00
109 SA,E:Man of the People	4.00
110 SA,Mummies.	4.00
111 SA,The Man who Killed Groo	4.00
112 SA,Rufferto Avenged.	4.00
113 SA	4.00

114 SA,V:Vultures	4.00
115 SA	4.00
116 SA,Early unto Morning	4.00
117 SA	4.00
118 SA	4.00
119 SA	4.00
120 Groo hangs up swords	4.00
GNv Death of Groo	15.00
GNv 2nd print.	8.00
TPB Groo Adventures	9.00
TPB Groo Carnival.	9.00
TPB Groo Expose	9.00
TPB GRoo Festival	9.00
TPB Groo Garden	11.00

GROOVY
March, 1968–July, 1968

1 Monkeys,Ringo Starr,Photos	125.00
2 Cartoons,Gags,Jokes	75.00
3	75.00

GUARDIANS
2004

1 (of 5) Reach for the Stars	3.00
2 thru 5 Reach for the Stars	@3.00

GUARDIANS OF THE GALAXY
June, 1990

1 B:JV(a&s),I:Taserface,R:Aleta	4.00
2 MZ(c),JV,V:Stark,C:Firelord	3.00
3 JV,V:Stark,I:Force,C:Firelord	3.00
4 JV,V:Stark,A:Force,Firelord	3.00
5 JV,TM(c),V:Force,I:Mainframe (Vision)	3.00
6 JV,V:Force,Vance Possesses Capt.America Shield	3.00
7 GP(c),JV,I:Malevolence, O:Starhawk	3.00
8 SLi(c),JV,V:Yondu,C:Rancor	3.00
9 RLd(c),JV,I:Replica,Rancor	3.00
10 JLe(c),JV,V:Rancor,The Nine I&C:Overkill(Taserface)	3.00
11 BWi(c),JV,V:Rancor,I:Phoenix	3.00
12 ATb(c),JV,V:Overkill A:Firelord	3.00
13 JV,A:Ghost Rider,Force, Malevolence	3.00
14 JS(c),JV,A:Ghost Rider,Force, Malevolence	3.00
15 JSn(c),JV,I:Protege,V:Force	3.00

Guardians of the Galaxy #20
© Marvel Entertainment Group

16 JV,V:Force,A:Protege,
　　Malevolence,L:Vance Astro 3.00
17 JV,V:Punishers(Street Army),
　　L:Martinex,N:Charlie-27, ... 2.50
18 JV,V:Punishers,I&C:Talon,A:
　　Crazy Nate 3.00
19 JV,V:Punishers,A:Talon. 2.50
20 JV,I:Major Victory (Vance Astro)
　　J:Talon & Krugarr. 2.50
21 JV,V:Rancor 2.50
22 JV,V:Rancor 2.50
23 MT,V:Rancor,C:Silver Surfer 2.50
24 JV,A:Silver Surfer 3.00
25 JV, Prismatic Foil(c)
　　V:Galactus,A:SilverSurfer 3.50
25a 2nd printing,Silver. 2.50
26 JV,O:Guardians(retold) 2.25
27 JV,Infinity War,O:Talon,
　　A:Inhumans 2.25
28 JV,Inf.War,V:Various Villians 2.25
29 HT,Inf.War,V:Various Villians. . . . 2.25
30 KWe,A:Captain America 2.25
31 KWe,V:Badoon,A:Capt.A. 2.25
32 KWe,V:Badoon Gladiator 2.25
33 KWe,A:Dr.Strange,R:Aleta 2.25
34 KWe,J:Yellowjacket II 2.25
35 KWe,A:Galatic Guardians,
　　V:Bubonicus 2.25
36 KWe,A:Galatic Guardians,
　　V:Dormammu 2.25
37 KWe,V:Dormammu,A:Galatic
　　Guardians 2.25
38 KWe,N:Y.jacket,A:Beyonder 2.25
39 KWe,Rancor Vs. Dr.Doom,Holo-
　　grafx(c) 3.25
40 KWe,V:Loki,Composite 2.25
41 KWe,V:Loki,A:Thor 2.25
42 KWe,I:Woden 2.25
43 KWe,A:Woden,V:Loki 2.25
44 KWe,R:Yondu 2.25
45 KWe,O:Starhawk. 2.25
46 KWe,N:Major Victory. 2.25
47 KWe,A:Beyonder,Protoge,
　　Overkill. 2.25
48 KWe,V:Overkill 2.25
49 KWe,A:Celestial 2.25
50 Foil(c),R:Yondu,Starhawk sep-
　　arated,BU:O:Guardians 3.25
51 KWe,A:Irish Wolfhound. 2.25
52 KWe,A:Drax 2.25
53 KWe,V:Drax 2.25
54 KWe,V:Sentinels 2.25
55 KWe,Ripjack 2.25
56 Ripjack 2.25
57 R:Keeper. 2.25
58 . . . . 2.25
59 A:Keeper. 2.25
60 F:Starhawk 2.25
61 F:Starhawk 2.25
62 Guardians Stop War of the Worlds
　　last issue 2.25
Ann.#1 Korvac Quest #4,I:Krugarr. . 3.25
Ann.#2 HT,I:Galactic Guardians,
　　System Bytes #4 . . . . 3.25
Ann.#3 CDo,I:Irish Wolfhound,
　　w/Trading card. 3.25
Ann.#4 V:Nine 3.25
TPB rep #1 thru #6 . . . . 12.95

GUNHAWK, THE
See: BLAZE CARSON

GUNHAWKS
Oct., 1972
1 SSh,B:Reno Jones & Kid
　Cassidy Two Rode Together . . 30.00
2 Ride out for Revenge. 25.00
3 Indian Massacre 25.00
4 Trial by Ordeal 25.00

5 The Reverend Mr. Graves 25.00
6 E:Reno Jones & Kid Cassidy
　D:Kid Cassidy 25.00
7 A Gunhawks Last Stand
　A;Reno Jones, Oct., 1973　. . . 25.00

GUNRUNNER
Marvel UK, 1993–94
1 I:Gunrunner,w/trading cards 3.00
2 A:Ghost Rider 2.25
3 V:Cynodd 2.25
4 . . . . 2.25
5 A:Enhanced 2.25
6 final issue. 2.25

GUNSLINGERS
Dec., 1999
1-shot 64-pg. 3.00

GUNSLINGER
See: TEX DAWSON,
GUNSLINGER

GUNSMOKE WESTERN
See: ALL WINNERS
COMICS

GUN THEORY
Marvel Epic, Aug., 2003
1 (of 4) 2.50
2 & 3 . . . . @2.50
4 concl. 2.50

HARROWERS
1993–94
1 MSt(s),GC,F:Pinhead. 3.50
2 GC,AW(i), ... 3.00
3 GC,AW(i), ... 3.00
4 GC,AW(i), ... 3.00
5 GC,AW(i),Devil's Pawn#1 . . . . . . 3.00
6 GC,AW(i),Devil's Pawn#2 . . . . . . 3.00

HARVEY
Oct., 1970–Dec., 1972
1 . . . . 125.00
2 thru 6 . . . . @75.00

HARVEY PRESENTS:
CASPER
1 . . . . 2.25

HAVOK & WOLVERINE
Epic, March, 1988
1 JMu,KW,V:KGB,Dr.Neutron. 5.00
2 JMu,KW,V:KGB,Dr.Neutron 4.00
3 JMu,KW,V:Meltdown 4.00
4 JMu,KW,V:Meltdown,Oct.1989 . . 4.00
TPB rep.#1-4 . . . . 16.95

HAWKEYE
[1st Limited Series], Sept., 1983
1 A:Mockingbird 3.00
2 I:Silencer 3.00
3 I:Bombshell,Oddball. 3.00
4 V:Crossfire,W:Hawkeye &
　Mockingbird, Dec., 1983 . . . . . 3.00
[2nd Limited Series], 1994
1 B:CDi(s),ScK,V:Trickshot,
　I:Javelynn,Rover 2.25
2 ScK,V:Viper 2.25
3 ScK,A:War Machine,N:Hawkeye,
　V:Secret Empire 2.25

Hawkeye Vol. 2 #1
© *Marvel Entertainment Group*

4 E:CDi(s),ScK,V:Trickshot,Viper,
　Javelynn 2.25

HAWKEYE
Oct., 2003
1 FaN(s),High,Hard Shaft,pt.1 . . . . 3.00
2 FaN(s),High,Hard Shaft,pt.2 . . . . 3.00
3 FaN(s),High,Hard Shaft,pt.3 . . . . 3.00
4 FaN(s),High,Hard Shaft,pt.4 . . . . 3.00
5 FaN(s),High,Hard Shaft,pt.5 . . . . 3.00
6 FaN(s),High,Hard Shaft,pt.6 . . . . 3.00
7 FaN(s),A Little Murder,pt.1. . . . . . 3.00
8 FaN(s),A Little Murder,pt.2. . . . . . 3.00

HAWKEYE: EARTH'S
MIGHTIEST MARKSMAN
Aug., 1998
1-shot TDF,MBa,JJ,DR,AM 48pg. . . 3.00

HEADMASTERS
Star, July, 1987
1 FS,Transformers 2.25
2 and 3 . . . . @2.25
4 Jan., 1988 . . . . 2.25

HEATHCLIFF
Star, April, 1985
1 . . . . 7.00
2 thru 10 . . . . @4.00
11 thru 16 . . . . @3.00
17 Masked Moocher 5.00
18 thru 49 . . . . @3.00
50 Double-size. 3.00
51 thru 55 . . . . @3.00

HEATHCLIFF'S
FUNHOUSE
Star, May, 1987
1 thru 9 . . . . @3.00
10 1988 . . . . 3.00

HEAVY HITTERS
Ann.#1 (1993) 4.00

HEDY DEVINE COMICS
Aug., 1947—Sept., 1952
22 I:Hedy Devine 275.00

23 BW,Beauty and the Beach,
   HK,Hey Look 200.00
24 High Jinx in Hollywood,
   HK, Hey Look 200.00
25 Hedy/Bull(c),HK,Hey Look . . . 200.00
26 Skating(c),HK,Giggles&Grins . 175.00
27 Hedy at Show(c),HK,HeyLook 125.00
28 Hedy/Charlie(c),HK,HeyLook . 125.00
29 Tennis(c),HK,Hey Look 125.00
30 . . . . 125.00
31 thru 50 . . . . @125.00

HEDY WOLFE
Atlas, Aug., 1957
1 Patsy Walker's Rival 125.00

HELLCAT
July, 2000
1 (of 3) SEt,NBy,F:PatsyWalker . . . 3.00
2 SEt,NBy, ... 3.00
3 SEt,NBy,Concl. 3.00

HELLHOUND
1993–94
1 Hellhound on my Trial 3.00
2 Love in Vain 3.00
3 Last Fair Deal Gone Down 3.00

HELLRAISER
See: CLIVE BARKER'S
HELLRAISER

HELLRAISER III
HELL ON EARTH
1 Movie Adaptation,(prestige) 5.00
1a Movie Adapt.(magazine) 3.00

HELLSTORM,
PRINCE OF LIES
1993
1 R:Daimon Hellstrom,
   Parchment(c) 3.50
2 A:Dr.Strange,Gargoyle 3.00
3 O:Hellstorm 2.75
4 V:Ghost Rider 2.75
5 MB, ... 2.50
6 MB,V:Dead Daughter 2.50
7 A:Armaziel 2.50

Hell's Angel #2
© Marvel Entertainment Group

8 Hell is where the heart is 2.50
9 LKa(s),Highway to Heaven 2.50
10 LKa(s),Heaven's Gate 2.50
11 LKa(s),PrG,Life in Hell. 2.50
12 Red Miracles 2.50
13 Red Miracles Sidewalking. 2.50
14 Red Miracles Murder is Easy . . . 2.50
15 Cigarette Dawn 3.00
16 Down Here 2.50
17 The Saint of the Pit 2.50
18 . . . . 2.50
19 . . . . 2.50
20 . . . . 2.50
21 final issue 2.50

HELL'S ANGEL
1992
1 GSr,A:X-Men,O:Hell's Angel 3.00
2 GSr,A:X-Men,V:Psycho Warriors . 2.50
3 GSr,A:X-Men,V:MyS-Tech 2.25
4 GSr,A:X-Men,V:MyS-Tech 2.25
5 GSr,A:X-Men,V:MyS-Tech 2.25
6 Gfr,A:X-Men,V:MyS-Tech 2.25
Becomes:

DARK ANGEL
1992
7 DMn,A:Psylocke,V:MyS-Tech . . . 2.25
8 DMn,A:Psylocke 2.25
9 A:Punisher 2.25
10 MyS-Tech Wars tie-in 2.25
11 A:X-Men,MyS-Tech wars tie-in . . 2.25
12 A:X-Men 2.25
13 A:X-Men,Death's Head II 2.25
14 Aftermath#2. . . . . 2.25
15 Aftermath#3. . . . . 2.25
16 SvL,E:Aftermath,last issue 2.25

HERCULES AND THE
HEART OF CHAOS
Limited Series Aug., 1997
1 (of 3) TDF,RF,PO, ... 2.50
2 TDF,RF,PO, ... 2.50
3 TDF,RF,PO,V:Ares, concl. 2.50

HERCULES PRINCE
OF POWER
Sept., 1982
1 BL,I:Recorder. 5.00
2 BL,I:Layana Sweetwater 3.00
3 BL,V:The Brothers,C:Galactus . . 3.00
4 BL,A:Galactus 3.00
[2nd Series], March, 1984
1 BL,I:Skyypi. 3.00
2 BL,A:Red Wolf 2.50
3 BL,A:Starfox 2.50
4 BL,D:Zeus, June, 1984 . . . . 2.50
TPB BL rep. Vol.1 and Vol.2 . . . . . 6.00

HERO
May, 1990
1 . . . . 2.50
2 thru 6 . . . . @2.25

HERO FOR HIRE
June, 1972
1 GT,JR,I&O:Power Man 75.00
2 GT,A:Diamond Back 35.00
3 GT,I:Mace 25.00
4 V:Phantom of 42nd St. 25.00
5 GT,A:Black Mariah 25.00
6 V:Assassin 15.00
7 GT,Nuclear Bomb issue 15.00
8 GT,A:Dr.Doom 15.00
9 GT,A:Dr.Doom,Fant.Four 15.00
10 GT,A:Dr.Death,Fant.Four 15.00
11 GT,A:Dr.Death 12.00

12 GT,C:Spider-Man 12.00
13 A:Lion Fang 12.00
14 V:Big Ben 12.00
15 Cage Goes Wild 12.00
16 O:Stilletto,D:Rackham 12.00
Becomes:

POWER MAN

HEROES FOR HIRE
July, 1997
1 JOs,PFe,F:Iron Fist 5.00
2 JOs,PFe,V:Nitro 3.00
2A Variant PFe cover 3.00
3 JOs,PFe,V:Nitro 3.00
4 JOs,Power Man vs. Iron Fist 3.00
5 JOs,V:Sersi, Diabolical Deviants . 3.00
6 JOs,PFe, Deviants 3.00
7 JOs V:Thunderbolts 3.00
8 JOs,Iron Fist's agenda revealed . 3.00
9 JOs,Search for Punisher 3.00
10 JOs,Deadpool hired 3.00
11 JOs,PFe,A:Deadpool, V:Silver
   Sable and Wild Pack 3.00
12 JOs,PFe,Traitor revealed, 48pg . 3.50
13 JOs,PFe,V:Master. 3.00
14 JOs,F:Black Knight 3.00
15 JOs,PFe,Siege of Wundagore,
   pt.1 (of 5) 3.00
16 JOs,PFe,Siege of Wundagore,
   pt.3 . . . . 3.00
17 JOs,DBw,F:Luke Cage
   & She-Hulk 3.00
18 JOs,PFe,A:Wolverine 3.00
19 JOs,PFe,F:Wolverine 3.00
Ann.'98 JOs,BWi,PFe,Heroes For
   Hire/Quicksilver, The Siege of
   Wundagore, pt.5 (of 5) 48pg . . . 3.00

Heroes For Hope #1
© Marvel Entertainment Group

HEROES FOR HOPE
1985
1 TA/JBy/HC/RCo/BWr,A:XMen . . . 7.00

HEROES REBORN:
THE RETURN
Oct., 1997
? Heroes Reborn prequel, (Marvel/
   Wizard 1996) 7.50
1 (of 4) PDd,ATi,SvL,F:Franklin
   Richards 4.00
2 PDd,ATi,SvL, F:Spider-Man,
   Thunderbolts & Doctor Strange . 4.00

MARVEL

3 PDd,SvL,ATi,A UniverseMayDie . 4.00
4 PDd,SvL,ATi, crossover to Marvel
  Universe? 4.00
TPB Return of the Heroes 14.95

Hokum & Hex #4
© Marvel Entertainment Group

HOKUM & HEX
Razorline 1993–94
1 BU:Saint Sinner 3.00
2 I:Analyzer 2.25
3 I:Wrath 2.25
4 I:Z-Man 2.25
5 V:Hyperkind 2.25
6 B:Bloodshed 2.25
7 V:Bloodshed 2.25
8 V:Bloodshed 2.25
9 E:Bloodshed,final issue 2.25

HOLIDAY COMICS
Jan., 1951
1 LbC(c),Christmas(c) 450.00
2 LbC(c),Easter Parade(c) 450.00
3 LbC(c),4th of July(c) 300.00
4 LbC(c),Summer Vacation 275.00
5 LbC(c),Christmas(c) 275.00
6 LbC(c),Birthday(c) 275.00
7 LbC(c),Rodeo (c) 275.00
8 LbC(c),Xmas(c) Oct., 1952 . . . 275.00

HOLLYWOOD SUPERSTARS
Epic, Nov., 1990
1 DSp 3.00
2 thru 5 DSp, March, 1991 . . . . . @2.50

HOMER, THE HAPPY GHOST
March, 1955
1 . . . . 250.00
2 . . . . 150.00
3 . . . . 125.00
4 thru 15 . . . . @125.00
16 thru 22 . . . . @75.00

[2nd Series], Nov., 1969
1 . . . . 150.00
2 thru 5 . . . . @100.00

HOOD, THE
Marvel Max, May, 2002
1 (of 6) F:Parker Robbins,40-pg. . . 3.00
2 FBI attention 3.00

3 diamond heist 3.00
4 . . . . 3.00
5 . . . . 3.00
6 concl. 3.00
TPB Vol. 1: Blood From Stones . . . 15.00

HOOK
1992
1 JRy,GM,movie adaption 2.25
2 JRy,Return to Never Land 2.25
3 Peter Pans Magic 2.25
4 conclusion 2.25
Hook Super Spec.#1 . . . . 3.00

HORRORS, THE
Jan., 1953—April, 1954
11 LbC(c),The Spirit of War 350.00
12 LbC(c),Under Fire 325.00
13 LbC(c),Terror Castle 325.00
14 LbC(c),Underworld Terror 325.00
15 LbC(c),The Mad Bandit 325.00

HOT SHOTS
AVENGERS
1 Painted Pin-ups (1995) 3.00
SPIDER-MAN
1 Painted pin-ups 3.00
X-MEN
1 Painted pin-ups 3.00

HOUSE II
1 1987, Movie Adapt. 2.00

HOWARD THE DUCK
Jan., 1976
1 FB,SL,A:Spider-Man,I:Beverly . . 30.00
2 FB,V:TurnipMan&Kidney Lady . . 10.00
3 JB,Learns Quack Fu 10.00
4 GC,V:Winky Man 10.00
5 GC,Becomes Wrestler 9.00
6 GC,V:Gingerbread Man 6.00
7 GC,V:Gingerbread Man 6.00
8 GC,A:Dr.Strange,ran for Pres. . . . 6.00
9 GC,V:Le Beaver 6.00
10 GC,A:Spider-Man 6.00
11 GC,V:Kidney Lady 6.00
12 GC,I:Kiss 25.00
13 GC,A:Kiss 30.00
14 GC,Howard as Son of Satan . . . 4.00
15 GC,A:Dr.Strange,A:Dr.Bong 4.00
16 GC,DC,JB,DG,TA,
  V:Incredible Creator 4.00
17 GC,D:Dr.Bong 4.00
18 GC,Howard the Human #1 . . . . 4.00
19 GC,Howard the Human #2 . . . . 4.00
20 GC,V:Sudd 4.00
21 GC,V:Soofi 4.00
22 A:ManThing,StarWars Parody . . 4.00
23 A:ManThing,StarWars Parody . . 4.00
24 GC,NightAfter..SavedUniverse . . 4.00
25 GC,V:Circus of Crime 4.00
26 GC,V:Circus of Crime 4.00
27 GC,V:Circus of Crime 4.00
28 GC,Cooking With Gas 4.00
29 Duck-Itis Poster Child 1978 . . . 4.00
30 Iron Duck,V:Dr. Bong 4.00
31 Iron Duck,V:Dr. Bong 4.00
32 V:Gopher 4.00
33 BB(c),The Material Duck 6.00
Ann.#1, V:Caliph of Bagmom 3.00
Holiday Spec. LHa,ATi,PFe (1996) . 3.50

HOWARD THE DUCK
Marvel Max, Jan., 2002
1 (of 6) SvG,Making the Band 4.00
2 SvG,Beverly's ex 3.00

3 SvG,GF,The former Duck 3.00
4 SvG,GF,House of Mystery 3.00
5 SvG,GF,House of Mystery,pt.2 . . 3.00
6 SvG,GF,Duck or Mouse 3.00
TPB series rep. 15.00

HOWARD THE DUCK MAGAZINE
(B&W) Oct., 1979–March, 1981
1 . . . . 6.00
2 & 3 . . . . @5.00
4 Beatles,Elvis,Kiss 6.00
5 thru 9 . . . . @5.00

HUGGA BUNCH
Star, Oct., 1986—Aug., 1987
1 . . . . 4.00
2 thru 6 . . . . @3.00

HULK, THE
Feb., 1999
1 JBy,RG,DGr,48-page 4.00
1a signed 20.00
1b gold foil cover 10.00
2 JBy,RG,DGr,Hulk unleashed 3.00
2a variant AdP cover 3.00
3 JBy,RG,DGr,Hulk berserk 3.00
4 JBy,RG,DGr,old foe 3.00
5 JBy,RG,DGr,V:Man-Thing 3.00
6 JBy,RG,DGr,V:Man-Thing 3.00
7 JBy,RG,DGr,A:Avengers 3.00
8 JBy,RG,DGr,V:Wolverine 20.00
9 RG,V:Thing 3.00
10 RG 3.00
11 PJe,RG,SB,A:DocSamson 3.00
Becomes:

INCREDIBLE HULK
2000
12 PJe,RG,SB,48-pg 3.00
13 PJe,RG,SB,new Hulk 2.50
14 PJe,RG,SB,V:Ryker 2.50
15 PJe,RG,SB,Dogs of War,pt.2 . . 2.50
16 PJe,RG,SB,Dogs of War,pt.3 . . 2.50
17 PJe,RG,SB,Dogs of War,pt.4 . . 2.50
18 PJe,RG,SB,Dogs of War,pt.5 . . 2.50
19 PJe,RG,SB,Dogs of War,pt.6 . . 2.50
20 PJe,RG,SB,Dogs of War,pt.7 . . 2.50
21 PJe,Maximum Security 2.50
22 PJe,Joe Fixit's Money 2.50
23 PJe,Nobby Stiles 2.50
24 PJe,JR2,V:Abomination 2.50
25 PJe,JR2,V:Abomination 3.50
26 Psyche of child-like Hulk 2.50
27 PJe,JR2,TP 2.50
28 PJe,JR2,TP,V:Devil Hulk 2.50
29 FaN,A:Angela,Doc Samson . . . 2.50
30 PJe,JoB,TP 2.50
31 PJe,JoB,TP,Banner gone 2.50
32 PJe,JoB,TP,Ant-Man inside . . . 2.50
33 CPr,JBg,100-page 4.00
34 JR2,TP,The beast within 2.50
35 JR2,TP,crosses the line? 2.50
36 JR2,TP,Gangs All Here,pt.1 . . . 2.50
37 JR2,TP,Remember This,pt.2 . . . 2.50
38 JR2,TP 2.50
39 JR2,TP,Tag-You're Dead 2.50
40 LW,TP,madman with gun 2.50
41 JR2,TP,madman with gun 2.50
42 LW,TP,hostage crisis 2.50
43 JR2,TP,hostage crisis,concl. . . . 2.50
44 SI 2.50
45 SI,dream lover 2.50
46 SI 2.50
47 SI 2.50
48 SI 2.50
49 SI 2.50
50 MD2,R:Abomination,pt.1 . . . . . 4.00
51 MD2,R:Abomination,pt.2 . . . . . 2.50

52 MD2,R:Abomination,pt.3	2.50
53 MD2,R:Abomination,pt.4	2.50
54 MD2,R:Abomination,pt.5	2.50
55 Hide in Plain Sight,pt.1	0.50
56 Hide in Plain Sight,pt.2	2.50
57 Hide in Plain Sight,pt.3	2.50
58 Hide in Plain Sight,pt.4	2.50
59 Hide in Plain Sight,pt.5	2.50
60 MD2,Split Decisions,pt.1	2.50
61 MD2,Split Decisions,pt.2	2.50
62 MD2,Split Decisions,pt.3	2.50
63 MD2,Split Decisions,pt.4	2.50
64 MD2,Split Decisions,pt.5	2.25
65 MD2,Split Decisions,concl.	2.25
66 MD2,Bury Me Not,pt.1	2.25
67 DBw,MD2(c),Bury Me Not,pt.2	2.25
68 DBw,MD2(c),Bury Me Not,pt.3	2.25
69 DBw,MD2(c),Bury Me Not,pt.4	2.25
70 MD2	2.25
71 MD2,Big Things,pt.1	2.25
72 MD2,Big Things,pt.2	2.25
73 MD2,Big Things,pt.3	2.25
74 DBw,Big Things,pt.4	2.25
75 DaR,Wake to Nightmare,48-pg.	3.50
76 DBw,Shattered,48-pg.	3.50
Ann. 1999 JBy,DGr,48-page	4.00
Ann. 2001 EL,V:Thor	3.50
Spec. Hulk/Sentry	3.50
GN The End, DK,	5.95
TPB Transformations	17.95
TPB Ground Zero	17.95
TPB The Dogs of War,224-page	19.95
TPB Vol.1,Return of the Monster.	13.00
TPB Vol.2, The Morning After	9.00
TPB Vol. 3: Transfer of Power	13.00
TPB Vol. 4: Abominable	12.00
TPB Vol. 5: Hide in Plain Sight	12.00
TPB Vol. 6: Split Decisions	13.00
TPB Vol. 7: Dead Like Me	13.00
TPB Vol. 8: Big Things	18.00
Spec. Must Have, rep. #34–#36	4.00

HULK: GRAY
Oct., 2003
1 JLb,TSe	3.50
2 thru 6 JLb,TSe	@3.50

HULK: THE MOVIE ADAPTATION
June, 2003
Spec. 48-pg.	3.50
TPB Movie	13.00

HULK: NIGHTMERICA
June, 2003
1 (of 6)	3.00
2 thru 6	@3.00

HULK SMASH
Jan., 2001
1 (of 2) GEn,JMC	3.00
2 GEn,JMC	3.00

HULK & THING: HARD KNOCKS
Sept., 2004
1 (of 4) JaL	3.50
2 JaL	3.50

HULK 2099
1994–95
1 GJ,Foil(c),V:Draco	3.00
2 GJ,V:Draco	2.25
3 I:Golden Boy	2.25
4	2.25
5 Ultra Hulk	2.25

Hulk 2099 #1
© Marvel Entertainment Group

Becomes:

HULK 2099 A.D.
1995
6 Gamma Ray Scientist	2.25
7 A:Doom,Dr.Apollo	2.25
8 One Nation Under Doom	2.25
9 California Quake	2.25

HULK/WOLVERINE: 6 HOURS
Jan., 2003
1 (of 4) ScK,SBs(c),rescue	3.00
2 ScK,SBs(c)	3.00
3 ScK,SBs(c)	3.00
4 ScK,SBs(c),concl.	3.00
TPB Hulk Legends, Vol. 1, rep.	14.00

HUMAN FLY
July, 1987
1 I&O:Human Fly,A:Spider-Man	12.00
2 A:Ghost Rider	15.00
3 DC,JSt(c),DP,Fortress of Fear	5.00
4 JB/TA(c),David Drier	5.00
5 V:Makik	5.00
6 Fear in Funland	5.00
7 ME,Fury in the Wind	5.00
8 V:White Tiger	5.00
9 JB/TA(c),ME,V:Copperhead,A:White Tiger,Daredevil	7.00
10 ME,Dark as a Dungeon	5.00
11 ME,A:Daredevil	5.00
12 ME,Suicide Sky-Dive	5.00
13 BLb/BMc(c),FS,V:Carl Braden	5.00
14 BLb/BMc(c),SL,Fear Over Fifth Avenue.	5.00
15 BLb/BMc(c),War in the Washington Monument	5.00
16 BLb/BMc(c),V:Blaze Kendall.	5.00
17 BLb,DP,Murder on the Midway	5.00
18 V:Harmony Whyte.	5.00
19 BL(c),V:Jacopo Belbo March, 1979	10.00

RED RAVEN COMICS
Timely Comics Aug., 1940
1 JK,O:Red Raven,I:Magar,A:Comet Pierce & Mercury,Human Top, Eternal Brain	19,000.00

Becomes:

HUMAN TORCH
Fall, 1940–Aug., 1954
2 (#1)ASh(c),BEv,B:Sub-Mariner A:Fiery Mask,Falcon,Mantor, Microman	45,000.00
3 (#2)Ash(c),BEv,V:Sub-Mariner,Bondage(c)	7,500.00
4 (#3)ASh(c),BEv,O:Patriot	5,800.00
5 (#4)V:Nazis,A:Patriot,Angel crossover	4,500.00
5a(#5)ASh(c),V:Sub-Mariner	7,200.00
6 ASh(c),Doom Dungeon	3,000.00
7 ASh(c),V:Japanese	3,200.00
8 ASh(c),BW,V:Sub-Mariner	4,500.00
9 ASh(c),V:General Rommel	3,500.00
10 ASh(c),BW,V:Sub-Mariner	3,600.00
11 ASh(c),Nazi Oil Refinery	2,300.00
12 ASh(c),V:Japanese, Bondage(c)	4,000.00
13 ASh(c),V:Japanese, Bondage(c)	2,300.00
14 ASh(c),V:Nazis	2,300.00
15 ASh(c),Toro Trapped	2,300.00
16 ASh(c),V:Japanese	1,700.00
17 ASh(c),V:Japanese	1,700.00
18 ASh(c),V:Japanese, MacArthurs HQ.	1,700.00
19 ASh(c),Bondage(c).	1,700.00
20 ASh(c),Last War Issue	1,700.00
21 ASh(c),V:Organized Crime.	1,700.00
22 ASh(c),V:Smugglers.	1,700.00
23 ASh(c),V:Giant Robot.	1,800.00
24 V:Mobsters	1,500.00
25 The Masked Monster.	1,500.00
26 Her Diary of Terror.	1,500.00
27 SSh(c),BEv,V:The Asbestos Lady.	1,500.00
28 BEv,The Twins Who Weren't	1,500.00
29 You'll Die Laughing	1,500.00
30 BEv,The Stranger, A:Namora	1,400.00
31 A:Namora.	1,300.00
32 A:Sungirl,Namora.	1,300.00
33 Capt.America crossover	1,400.00
34 The Flat of the Land	1,300.00
35 A;Captain America,Sungirl	1,400.00
36 A:Submariner	1,300.00
37 BEv,A:Submariner	1,300.00
38 BEv,A:Submariner	1,300.00

HUMAN TORCH
Sept., 1974
1 JK,rep.StrangeTales #101	25.00

The Human Torch #3
© Marvel Entertainment Group

2 rep.Strange Tales #102 . . . . 15.00
3 rep.Strange Tales #103 . . . . 15.00
4 rep.Strange Tales #104 . . . . 15.00
5 rep.Strange Tales #105 . . . . 15.00
6 rep.Strange Tales #106 . . . . 15.00
7 rep.Strange Tales #107 . . . . 15.00
8 rep.Strange Tales #108 . . . . 15.00

HUMAN TORCH
April, 2003
1 KK(s),Burn,pt.1 . . . . 2.50
2 KK(s),Burn,pt.2 . . . . 2.50
3 KK(s),Burn,pt.3 . . . . 2.50
4 KK(s),Burn,pt.4 . . . . 2.50
5 KK(s),Burn,pt.5 . . . . 2.50
6 KK(s),Burn,concl. 2.50
7 KK(s),Plague of Locusts,pt.1 . . . . 2.50
8 KK(s),Plague of Locusts,pt.2 . . . 3.00
9 KK(s),Plague of Locusts,pt.3 . . . 3.00
10 KK(s),Plague of Locusts,pt.4 . . . 3.00
11 KK(s),F:Namorita 3.00
12 KK(s),series finale. 3.00
TPB Human Torch: Burn, Vol.1 . . . 15.00

HUMAN TORCH COMICS
Feb., 1999
1-shot V:Sub-Mariner, 48-page 4.00

HYPERKIND
Marvel/Razorline 1993
1 I:Hyperkind,BU:EctoKid 3.00
2 thru 9 . . . . @2.25

HYPERKIND UNLEASHED
1994
1 BU,V:Thermakk 3.25

Iceman #1
© Marvel Entertainment Group

ICEMAN
Dec., 1984
1 DP,mini-series 3.00
2 DP,V:Kali 3.00
3 DP,A;Original X-Men,Defenders
  Champions 3.00
4 DP,Oblivion,June, 1985 . . . . 4.00

ICEMAN
Oct., 2001
1 (of 4) DAn,ALa,KIK 3.00
2 DAn,ALa,KIK,A:Augmen 3.00

3 DAn,ALa,KIK,F:Foe-Dog,Augmen 3.00
4 DAn,ALa, concl. 3.00

IDEAL
Timely, July, 1948
1 Antony and Cleopatra 400.00
2 The Corpses of Dr.Sacotti . . . 350.00
3 Joan of Arc 325.00
4 Richard the Lionhearted
  A:The Witness 500.00
5 Phc,Love and Romance 225.00
Becomes:

LOVE ROMANCES
6 Ph(c),I Loved a Scoundrel . . . 175.00
7 Ph(c) 120.00
8 Ph(c) 135.00
9 thru 12 Ph(c) . . . . @120.00
13 thru 20 . . . . @120.00
21 BK 100.00
22 . . . . 80.00
23 . . . . 80.00
24 BK 100.00
25 . . . . 80.00
26 thru 35 . . . . @80.00
36 BK 80.00
37 . . . . 75.00
38 BK 90.00
39 thru 44 . . . . @75.00
45 MB. 100.00
46 . . . . 75.00
47 . . . . 75.00
48 . . . . 60.00
49 ATh 75.00
50 . . . . 65.00
51 . . . . 65.00
52 . . . . 65.00
53 ATh 90.00
54 . . . . 75.00
55 . . . . 75.00
56 . . . . 75.00
57 MB. 80.00
58 thru 74 . . . . @75.00
75 MB. 80.00
76 . . . . 75.00
77 MB. 80.00
78 . . . . 75.00
79 . . . . 75.00
80 RH(c). 75.00
81 . . . . 75.00
82 MB,JK(c). 90.00
83 JSe,JK(c) 90.00
84 JK 90.00
85 JK 90.00
86 thru 95 . . . . @60.00
96 JK 120.00
97 . . . . 100.00
98 JK 120.00
99 JK 120.00
100 thru 104. . . . . @120.00
105 JK 120.00
106 JK,July, 1963 . . . . 120.00

IDEAL COMICS
Timely, Fall, 1944
1 B:Super Rabbit,Giant Super
  Rabbit V:Axis(c) 275.00
2 Super Rabbit at Fair(c) 150.00
3 Beach Party(c). 135.00
4 How to Catch Robbers 135.00
Becomes:

WILLIE COMICS
1946
5 B:Willie,George,Margie,Nellie
  Football(c) 225.00
6 Record Player(c) 135.00
7 Soda Fountain(c),HK 135.00
8 Fancy Dress(c) 125.00
9 . . . . 125.00
10 HK,Hey Look. 125.00

11 HK,Hey Look. 125.00
12 . . . . 100.00
13 . . . . 100.00
14 thru 18. . . . . @100.00
19 . . . . 125.00
20 Li'L Willie Comics 100.00
21 Li'L Willie Comics 100.00
22 . . . . 100.00
23 May, 1950 . . . . 100.00

IDENTITY DISK
June, 2004
1 (of 5) JP. 3.00
2 thru 5 . . . . @3.00

IDOL
Epic, 1992
1 I:Idol. 3.25
2 Phantom of the Set 3.25
3 Conclusion 3.25

ILLUMINATOR
1993
1 . . . . 5.50
2 . . . . 5.50
3 . . . . 3.25
4 . . . . 3.25

IMMORTALIS
1 A:Dr.Strange. 2.25
2 A:Dr.Strange. 2.25
3 A:Dr.Strange,V:Vampires 2.25
4 Mephisto, final issue 2.25

IMPERIAL GUARD
[Limited Series], 1997
1 (of 3) BAu,Woj. 2.25
2 and 3 BAu,Woj. . . . . @2.25

IMPOSSIBLE MAN
SUMMER VACATION
1990–91
1 GCa,DP 2.50
2 . . . . 2.50
Summer Fun Spec. TPe, Vacation
  on Earth. 2.50

INCAL, THE
Epic, Nov., 1988
1 Moebius,Adult 12.00
2 Moebius,Adult 12.00
3 Moebius,Adult, Jan., 1989 . . . 12.00

INCOMPLETE
DEATH'S HEAD
1993
1 . . . . 3.50
2 thru 11 rep.Death's Head #1
  thru #11 . . . . @2.25

INCREDIBLE HULK
May, 1962
1 JK,I:Hulk(Grey Skin),Rick Jones,
  Thunderbolt Ross,Betty Ross,
  Gremlin,Gamma Base . . . 25,000.00
2 JK,SD,O:Hulk,(Green skin). . 4,800.00
3 JK,O:rtd.,I:Ring Master,
  Circus of Crime. 2,800.00
4 JK,V:Mongu 2,600.00
5 JK,I:General Fang. 2,600.00
6 SD,I:Metal Master 3,500.00
See: Tales to Astonish #59-#101
April, 1968
102 MSe,GT,O:Retold 350.00

Incredible Hulke #129
© Marvel Entertainment Group

154 HT,JSe,A:Ant Man,
  V:Chameleon. 22.00
155 HT,JSe,I:Shaper of Worlds . . . 22.00
156 HT,V:Hulk 22.00
157 HT,I:Omnivac,Rhino 22.00
158 HT,C:Warlock,V:Rhino 22.00
159 HT,V:Abomination,Rhino. . . . 22.00
160 HT,V:Tiger Shark. 22.00
161 HT,V:Beast 35.00
162 HT,I:Wendigo I 40.00
163 HT,I:Gremlin 20.00
164 HT,I:Capt.Omen 20.00
165 HT,I:Aquon 20.00
166 HT,I:Zzzax. 20.00
167 HT,JAb,V:Modok 20.00
168 HT,JAb,I:Harpy 20.00
169 HT,JAb,I:Bi-Beast 20.00
170 HT,JAb,V:Volcano 20.00
171 HT,JAb,A:Abomination,Rhino . 20.00
172 HT,JAb,X:X-Men 50.00
173 HT,V:Cobolt Man. 18.00
174 HT,V:Cobolt Man. 18.00
175 JAb,V:Inhumans 18.00
176 HT,JAb,A:Man-Beast,C:Warlock
  Crisis on Counter-Earth. 20.00
177 HT,JAb,D:Warlock. 20.00
178 HT,JAb,Warlock Lives. 20.00
179 HT,JAb 18.00
180 HT,JAb,I:Wolverine
  V:Wendigo I. 200.00
181 HT,JAb,A:Wolverine (1st
  Full Story),V:Wendigo II . . . 1,300.00
182 HT,JAb,I&D:Crackajack
  Jackson,C:Wolverine. 150.00
183 HT,V:Zzzax 18.00
184 HT,V:Living Shadow 18.00
185 HT,V:General Ross 18.00
186 HT,I:Devastator 18.00
187 HT,JSt,V:Gremlin. 18.00
188 HT,JSt,I:Droog. 18.00
189 HT,JSt,I:Datrine 18.00
190 HT,MSe,Toadman 18.00
191 HT,JSt,Toadman,I:Glorian 18.00
192 HT,V:The Lurker 18.00
193 HT,JSt,Doc.Samson regains
  Powers. 18.00
194 SB,JSt,V:Locust 18.00
195 SB,JSt,V:Abomination. 18.00
196 SB,JSt,V:Army 18.00
197 BWr(c),SB,JSt,A:Man-Thing . . 18.00
198 SB,JSt,A:Man-Thing 18.00
199 SB,JSt,V:Shield,Doc.Samson . 18.00
200 SB,JSt,Multi,Hulk in Glenn
  Talbots Brain 30.00
201 SB,JSt,V:Fake Conan 7.00
202 SB,JSt,A:Jarella 7.00
203 SB,JSt,A:Jarella 7.00
204 SB,JStI:Kronus 7.00
205 SB,JSt,D:Jarella 7.00
206 SB,JSt,C:Dr.Strange 7.00
207 SB,JSt,A:Dr.Strange 7.00
208 SB,JSt,V:Absorbing Man. 7.00
209 SB,JSt,V:Absorbing Man. 7.00
210 SB,A:Dr.Druid,O:Merlin II . . . 7.00
211 SB,A:Dr.Druid 7.00
212 SB,I:Constrictor. 8.00
213 SB,TP,I:Quintronic Man 7.00
214 SB,Jack of Hearts 7.00
215 SB,V:Bi-Beast 6.00
216 SB,Gen.Ross 6.00
217 SB,I:Stilts,A:Ringmaster 6.00
218 SB,KP,Doc.Samson versus
  Rhino. 6.00
219 SB,V:Capt.Barravuda 6.00
220 SB,Robinson Crusoe 6.00
221 SB,AA,A:Sting Ray 6.00
222 JSn,AA,Cavern of Bones 6.00
223 SB,V:Leader 6.00
224 SB,V:The Leader 6.00
225 SB,V:Leader,A:Doc.Samson . . 6.00
226 SB,JSt,A:Doc.Samson 6.00

103 MSe,I:Space Parasite 200.00
104 MSe,O&N:Rhino 175.00
105 MSe,GT,I:Missing Link 125.00
106 MSe,HT,GT 125.00
107 HT,V:Mandarin 125.00
108 HT,JMe,A:Nick Fury 125.00
109 HT,JMe,A:Ka-Zar 100.00
110 HT,JMe,A:Ka-Zar. 100.00
111 HT,DA,I:Galaxy Master 80.00
112 HT,DA,O:Galaxy Master 60.00
113 HT,DA,V:Sandman 60.00
114 HT,DA 60.00
115 HT,DA,A:Leader 60.00
116 HT,DA,V:Super Humanoid . . 60.00
117 HT,DA,A:Leader 60.00
118 HT,V:Sub-Mariner 60.00
119 HT,V:Maximus. 50.00
120 HT,V:Maximus. 50.00
121 HT,I:The Glob 50.00
122 HT,V:Thing 100.00
123 HT,V:Leader 50.00
124 HT,SB,V:Rhino,Leader 50.00
125 HT,V:Absorbing Man. 50.00
126 HT,A:Dr.Strange 50.00
127 HT,Moleman vs.Tyrannus
  I:Mogol. 35.00
128 HT,A:Avengers 35.00
129 HT,V:Glob 35.00
130 HT,Banner vs. Hulk. 35.00
131 HT,A:Iron Man. 35.00
132 HT,JSe,V:Hydra 35.00
133 HT,JSe,I:Draxon 35.00
134 HT,SB,I:Golem 35.00
135 HT,SB,V:Kang 35.00
136 HT,SB,I:Xeron 35.00
137 HT,V:Abomination 35.00
138 HT,V:Sandman 35.00
139 HT,V:Leader 35.00
140 HT,V:Psyklop. 35.00
141 HT,JSe,I&O:Doc.Samson 80.00
142 HT,JSe,V:Valkyrie,A:Doc
  Samson 40.00
143 DA,JSe,V:Dr.Doom 40.00
144 DA,JSe,V:Dr.Doom 40.00
145 HT,JSe,O:Retold 45.00
146 HT,JSe,Leader 22.00
147 HT,JSe,Doc.Samson loses
  Powers. 22.00
148 HT,JSe,I:Fialan 22.00
149 HT,JSe,I:Inheritor 22.00
150 HT,JSe,I:Viking,A:Havoc. . . . 22.00
151 HT,JSe,C:Ant Man 22.00
152 HT,DA,Many Cameos 22.00
153 HT,JSe,C:Capt.America 22.00

Incredible Hulk #278
© Marvel Entertainment Group

227 SB,JK,A:Doc.Samson 6.00
228 SB,BMc,I:Moonstone,V:Doc
  Samson 8.00
229 SB,O:Moonstone,V:Doc
  Samson 6.00
230 JM,BL,A:Bug Thing. 6.00
231 SB,I:Fred Sloan 6.00
232 SB,A:Capt.America. 6.00
233 SB,A:Marvel Man 6.00
234 SB,Marvel Man Changes name
  to Quasar. 6.00
235 SB,A:Machine Man 6.00
236 SB,A:Machine Man 6.00
237 SB,A:Machine Man 6.00
238 SB,JAb,Jimmy Carter 6.00
239 SB,I:Gold Bug 6.00
240 SB,Eldorado 6.00
241 SB,A:Tyrannus 6.00
242 SB,Eldorado 6.00
243 SB,A:Gammernon. 6.00
244 SB,A:It. 6.00
245 SB,A:Super Mandroid 6.00
246 SB,V:Capt.Marvel 6.00
247 SB,A:Bat Dragon 6.00
248 SB,V:Gardener 6.00
249 SD,R:Jack Frost 6.00
250 SB,A:Silver Surfer. 12.00
251 MG,A:3-D Man 5.00
252 SB,A:Woodgod 5.00
253 SB,A:Woodgod 5.00
254 SB,I:U-Foes 5.00
255 SB,V:Thor 5.00
256 SB,I&O:Sabra 5.00
257 SB,I&O:Arabian Knight 5.00
258 I:Soviet Super Soldiers 5.00
259 SB,A:Soviet Super-Soldiers,
  O:Darkstar 5.00
260 SB,Sugata. 5.00
261 SB,V:Absorbing Man. 5.00
262 SB,I:Glazer 5.00
263 SB,Avalanche 5.00
264 SB,A:Corruptor 5.00
265 SB,I:Rangers. 5.00
266 SB,V:High Evolutionary. 5.00
267 SB,V:Rainbow,O:Glorian. 5.00
268 SB,I:Pariah 5.00
269 SB,I:Bereet 5.00
270 SB,A:Abomination. 5.00
271 SB,I:Rocket Raccoon,
  20th Anniv. 5.00
272 SB,C:X-Men,I:Wendigo III. . . . 6.00
273 SB,A:Alpha Flight 5.00
274 SB,Beroct 5.00

MARVEL

275 SB,JSt,I:Megalith 5.00
276 SB,JSt,V:U-Foes 5.00
277 SB,JSt,U-Foes 5.00
278 SB,JSt,C:X-Men,
    Avengers,Fantastic Four 6.00
279 SB,JSt,C:X-Men,
    Avengers,Fantastic Four 6.00
280 SB,JSt,Jack Daw 5.00
281 SB,JSt,Trapped in Space 5.00
282 SB,JSt,A:She Hulk 5.00
283 SB,JSt,A:Avengers 5.00
284 SB,JSt,A:Avengers 5.00
285 SB,JSt,Northwind,V:Zzzax 5.00
286 SB,JSt,V:Soldier 5.00
287 SB,JSt,V:Soldier 5.00
288 SB,JSt,V:Abomination 5.00
289 SB,JSt,V:Modok 5.00
290 SB,JSt,V:Modok 5.00
291 SB,JSt,V:Thunderbolt Ross 5.00
292 SB,JSt,V:Dragon Man 5.00
293 SB,V:Nightmare 5.00
294 SB,V:Boomerang 5.00
295 SB,V:Boomerang 5.00
296 SB,A:Rom 5.00
297 SB,V:Nightmare 5.00
298 KN(c),SB,V:Nightmare 5.00
299 SB,A:Shield 5.00
300 SB,A:Spider-Man,Avengers
    Doctor Strange 8.00
301 SB,Crossroads 4.00
302 SB,Crossroads 4.00
303 SB,V:The Knights 4.00
304 SB,V:U-Foes 4.00
305 SB,V:U-Foes 4.00
306 SB,V:Klaatu 4.00
307 SB,V:Klaatu 4.00
308 SB,V:Puffball Collective 4.00
309 SB,V:Goblin & Glow 4.00
310 Crossroads 4.00
311 Crossroads 4.00
312 Secret Wars II,O:Bruce 4.50
313 A:Alpha Flight 4.00
314 JBy,V:Doc.Samson 6.00
315 JBy,A:Doc.Samson,Banner
    & Hulk Separated 4.00
316 JBy,A:Avengers,N:Doc
    Samson 4.00
317 JBy,I:Hulkbusters,A:Doc
    Samson 4.00
318 JBy,A:Doc.Samson 4.00
319 JBy,W:Bruce & Betty 6.00
320 AM,A:Doc.Samson 3.00
321 AM,A:Avengers 3.00
322 AM,A:Avengers 3.00
323 AM,A:Avengers 3.00
324 AM,R:Grey Hulk(1st since #1),
    A:Doc.Samson 15.00
325 AM,Rick Jones as Hulk 6.00
326 A:Rick Jones,New Hulk 7.00
327 AM,F:General Ross 3.00
328 AM,1st PDd(s),Outcasts 7.00
329 AM,V:Enigma 5.00
330 1st TM Hulk,D:T-bolt Ross . . 22.00
331 TM,V:Leader 20.00
332 TM,V:Leader 20.00
333 TM,V:Leader 20.00
334 TM,I:Half-life 20.00
335 Horror Issue 5.00
336 TM,A:X-Factor 20.00
337 TM,A:X-Factor, A:DocSamson 20.00
338 TM,I:Mercy,V:Shield 20.00
339 TM,A:RickJones 20.00
340 TM,Hulk vs Wolverine 45.00
341 TM,V:Man Bull 8.00
342 TM,V:Leader 8.00
343 TM,V:Leader 8.00
344 TM,V:Leader 8.00
345 TM,V:Leader,Double-Size 9.00
346 TM,EL,L:Rick Jones 8.00
347 In Las Vegas,I:Marlo Chandler,
    V:Absorbing Man 5.00

348 V:Absorbing Man 4.00
349 A:Spider-Man 4.00
350 Hulk vs Thing,A:Beast
    V:Dr.Doom 5.00
351 R:Jarella's World 3.00
352 V:Inquisitor 3.00
353 R:Bruce Banner 3.00
354 V:Maggia 3.00
355 V:Glorian 3.00
356 V:Glorian,Cloot 3.00
357 V:Glorian,Cloot 3.00
358 V:Glorian,Cloot 3.00
359 JBy(c),C:Wolverine(illusion) . . . 4.00
360 V:Nightmare & Dyspare 3.00
361 A:Iron Man,V:Maggia 3.00
362 V:Werewolf By Night 3.00
363 Acts of Vengeance 3.00
364 A:Abomination,B:Countdown . . 3.00
365 A:Fantastic Four 3.00
366 A:Leader,I:Riot Squad 3.00
367 1st DK Hulk,I:Madman(Leader's
    brother),E:Countdown 10.00
368 SK,V:Mr.Hyde 5.00
369 DK,V:Freedom Force 3.00
370 DK,R:Original Defenders 3.00
371 DK,BMc,A:Orig.Defenders 3.00
372 DK,R:Green Hulk 10.00

Incredible Hulk #425
© Marvel Entertainment Group

373 DK,Green Hulk & Grey Hulk . . . 4.00
374 DK,BMc,Skrulls,
    R:Rick Jones 4.00
375 DK,BMc,V:Super Skrull 4.00
376 DK,BMc,Green Hulk,Grey
    Hulk & Banner fight 5.00
377 DK,BMc,New Green Hulk,
    combination of green, grey, and
    Bruce Banner,A:Ringmaster . . 11.00
377a 2nd printing (gold) 5.00
378 V:Rhino,Christmas Issue 3.00
379 DK,MFm,I:Pantheon 4.00
380 A:Nick Fury,D:Crazy-8 . . . . . . 3.00
381 DK,MFm,Hulk,J:Pantheon 4.00
382 DK,MFm,A:Pantheon 4.00
383 DK,MFm,Infinity Gauntlet 4.00
384 DK,MFm,Infinity Gauntlet 4.00
385 DK,MFm,Infinity Gauntlet 4.00
386 DK,MFm,V:Sabra,A:Achilles . . . 4.00
387 DK,MFm,V:Sabra,A:Achilles . . . 4.00
388 DK,MFm,I:Speed Freak,Jim
    Wilson,revealed to have AIDS. . 5.00
389 1st Comic art By Gary Barker
    (Garfield),A:Man-Thing,Glob . . 4.00
390 DK,MFm,B:War & Pieces,
    C:X-Factor 4.00
391 DK,MFm,V:X-Factor 4.00

392 DK,MFm,E:War & Pieces,
    A:X-Factor 4.00
393 DK,MFm,R:Igor,A:Soviet Super
    Soldiers,30th Ann.,Green foil(c) 6.00
393a 2nd printing,Silver 2.50
394 MFm(i),F:Atalanta,I:Trauma . . . 3.00
395 DK,MFm,A:Punisher,
    I:Mr.Frost 3.00
396 DK,MFm,A:Punisher,
    V:Mr.Frost 3.00
397 DK,MFm,B:Ghost of the
    Past,V:U-Foes,A:Leader 3.00
398 DK,MFm,D:Marlo,V:Leader. . . . 3.00
399 JD,A:FF,Dr.Strange 3.00
400 JD,MFm,E:Ghost of the Past,
    V:Leader,1st Holo-grafx(c),1st
    GFr Hulk(pin-up) 3.50
400a 2nd Printing. 3.00
401 JDu,O:Agememnon 3.00
402 JDu,V:Juggernaut 3.00
403 GFr,V:Red Skull,A:Avengers. . . 3.00
404 GFr,V:Red Skull,Juggernaut,
    A:Avengers 3.50
405 GFr,Ajax vs. Achilles 3.00
406 GFr,V:Captain America 3.00
407 GFr,I:Piecemeal,A:Madman
    B:O:Ulysses 3.00
408 GFr,V:Madman,Piecemeal,
    D:Perseus,A:Motormouth,
    Killpower 3.00
409 GFr,A:Motormouth,Killpower,
    V:Madman 3.00
410 GFr,A:Nick Fury,S.H.I.E.L.D.,
    Margo agrees to marry Rick . . . 3.00
411 GFr,V:Nick Fury,S.H.I.E.L.D. . . . 3.00
412 PaP,V:Bi-Beast,A:She-Hulk. . . . 3.00
413 GFr,CaS,B:Troyjan War,
    I:Cassiopea,Armageddon,
    V:Trauma 3.00
414 GFr,CaS,V:Trauma,C:S.Surfer . 3.00
415 GFr,CaS,V:Trauma,A:Silver
    Surfer,Starjammers 3.00
416 GFr,CaS,E:Troyjan War,D:Trauma,
    A:S.Surfer,Starjammers 3.00
417 GFr,CaS,Rick's/Marlo's Bachelor/
    Bachelorette Party 5.00
418 GFr,CaS,W:Rick & Marlo,
    A:Various Marvel persons,
    Die Cut(c) 5.00
418a Newsstand ed. 3.00
419 CaS,V:Talos 3.00
420 GFr,CaS,AIDS Story,
    D:Jim Wilson 3.50
421 CaS,B:Myth Conceptions 3.00
422 GFr,Myth Conceptions,pt.2 . . . . 3.00
423 GFr,CaS,Myth Concept.,pt.3 . . . 3.00
424 B:Fall of the Hammer 3.00
425 Regular edition 3.00
425a Enhanced cover 4.00
426 PDa,LSh,R:Mercy 3.00
426a Deluxe edition. 3.00
427 A:Man-Thing 3.00
427a Deluxe edition 3.00
428 Suffer The Children. 3.00
429 Abortion Issue 3.00
430 A:Speed Freak 3.00
431 PDa,LSh R:Abomination 3.00
432 V:Abomination. 3.00
433 PDd,V:Abomination 3.00
434 Funeral of the Year 3.00
435 Hulk vs. Rhino baseball 4.00
436 PDd,AMe,Ghosts of the
    Future,pt.1 . . . . 3.00
437 PDd,AMe,Ghosts of the
    Future,pt.2 . . . . 3.00
438 PDd,AMe,Ghosts of the
    Future,pt.3 . . . . 3.00
439 PDd,AMe,Ghosts of the
    Future,pt.4 . . . . 3.00
440 PDd,AMe. 3.00
441 PDd,AMe,A:She-Hulk 3.00

442 A:Molecule Man, She-Hulk 3.00
443 Janis 3.00
444 Onslaught saga, V:Cable 4.50
445 Onslaught saga. 4.00
446 Blamed for loss of Fantastic
     Four and Avengers 3.50
447 PDd,MD2,F:Unleashed Hulk. . . 4.00
447a Variant Tank Smashing cover . 7.50
448 PDd,MD2,V:The Pantheon 3.00
449 PDd,MD2,I:Thunderbolts 10.00
450 PDd,MD2,F:Doctor Strange,
     56pg. 6.00
451 PDd,MD2, ... 3.00
452 PDd,MD2, ... 3.00
453 PDd,MD2,V:Future Hulk 3.00
454 PDd,AKu,MFm,A God,
     In Savage Land 3.00
455 PDd,AKu,MFm,in X-Mansion . . 3.00
456 PDd,AKu,MFm,A:Apocalypse . . 3.00
457 PDd,Hulk vs. Juggernaut 3.00
458 PDd,AKu,MFm,V:Mercy 3.00
459 PDd,AKu,MFm,V:Abomination . 3.00
460 PDa,AKu,MFm, Return of Bruce
     Banner. 3.00
461 PDa,V:Thunderbolt Ross 3.00
462 PDa,AKu,MFm,V:Thunderbolt
     Ross 3.00
463 PDa,AKu,MFm,V:Thunderbolt
     Ross 3.00
464 PDa,AKu,MFm,V:Troygens &
     Silver Surfer. 3.00
465 PDa,MFm,Poker game 3.00
466 PDa,AKu,MFm,tragic loss. 6.00
467 PDa,AKu,MFm,Hulk attempts
     suicide 6.00
468 JoC,new direction 2.50
469 JoC,LMa,F:Super-Adaptoid . . . 3.00
470 JoC,NMa,V:Ringmaster
     & Circus of Crime 2.50
471 JoC,NMa,Circus of
     Crime,concl.. . . . . 2.50
472 JoC,Great Astonishment,pt.1 . . 2.50
473 JoC,Great Astonishment,pt.2 . . 2.50
474 JoC,Great Astonishment,pt.3 . . 4.00
Spec.#1 A:Inhumans (1968) . . . 125.00
Spec.#2 rep.O:Hulk,A:Leader
     (1969) 75.00
Spec.#3 rep.A:Leader (1971). 25.00
Spec.#4 IR:Hulk/Banner (1972) . . . 25.00
Ann.#5 V:Xemnu,Diablo (1976) . . . 18.00
Ann.#6 HT,A:Dr.Strange,I:Paragon
     (Her) (1977). 12.00
Ann.#7 JBy,BL,A:Angel,Iceman
     A:Doc.Samson (1978) 12.00

Incredible Hulk Annual #19
© Marvel Entertainment Group

Ann.#8 Alpha Flight (1979) 12.00
Ann.#9 Checkmate (1980). 6.00
Ann.#10 A:Captain Universe (1981) 6.00
Ann.#11 RB,JSt,A:Spider-Man,
     Avengers,V:Unis (1982) 5.00
Ann.#12 (1983) 4.00
Ann.#13 (1984) 4.00
Ann.#14 JBy,SB (1985) 4.00
Ann.#15 V:Abomitation (1986). . . . 4.00
Ann.#16 HT,Life Form #3,
     A:Mercy (1990) 4.00
Ann.#17 Subterran.Odyssey #2
     (1991) 4.00
Ann #18 KM,TA,TC(1st Work),Return
     of the Defenders,Pt.1 (1992). . . 7.00
Ann.#19 I:Lazarus,w/card (1993). . . 4.00
Ann.#20 SvL,SI (1994) 4.00
Ann.'98 F:Hulk&Sub-Mariner, 48pg . 3.00
Ann. Hulk 1999 . . . . 3.50
Marvel Milestone rep. #1 (1991) . . 3.00
G-Size#1 rep. Greatest Foes. 10.00
Minus 1 Spec., PDd,AKu,MFm,
     flashback. 3.00
Spec. '97 Onslaught aftermath 3.00
Spec. Incredible Hulk
     vs. Superman, 48-pg. 6.00
Spec. Hulk vs. Superman, signed . 20.00
Milestone #181, F:Wolverine 3.00
Hulk vs. Thing, rep. 4.00
TPB Ground Zero rep. 12.95
TPB Future Imperfect, PDd,GP . . . 12.00
TPB Ghosts of the Past, rep.. . . . . 12.00
TPB Transformations, 176pg. 12.00
TPB Beauty and the Beast 17.00

INCREDIBLE HULK: FUTURE IMPERFECT
1993
1 GP,V:Maestro 10.00
2 GP,V:Maestro. 8.00
TPB Rep. 12.95

INCREDIBLE HULK MEGAZINE
TPB six stories, 96pg. 4.00

INCREDIBLE HULK/PITT
1997
Spec. PDd,DK,x-over 6.00

INCREDIBLE HULK VS. WOLVERINE
Oct., 1986
1 HT,rep. #181 B:,V:Wolverine. . . 12.00
1a 2nd printing 4.00

INDEPENDENCE DAY
1996
0 . . . . 5.00
1 . . . . 2.50
2 . . . . 2.50
TPB rep. #0–#2, 96pg 6.95

[Further Adventures of] INDIANA JONES
Jan., 1983–Mar., 1986
1 JBy/TA 3.00
2 JBy/TA 2.50
3 . . . . 2.50
4 KGa 2.50
5 KGa 2.50
6 HC/TA 2.50
7 thru 24 KGa . . . . @2.50
25 thru 34 SD . . . . @2.50

Indiana Jones #5
© Marvel Entertainment Group

INDIANA JONES AND THE LAST CRUSADE
1 B&W,Mag.,movie adapt, 1989. . . 3.00

[Mini-Series], 1989
1 Rep., Movie adapt., 1989. . . . . . . 3.50
2 Rep., Movie adapt. 3.50
3 Rep., Movie adapt. 3.50
4 Rep., Movie adapt. 3.50

INDIANA JONES AND THE TEMPLE OF DOOM
1984
1 Movie adapt. 3.00
2 Movie adapt. 3.00
3 Movie adapt. 3.00

INFINITY ABYSS
June, 2002
1 (of 6) JSn,AM,V:Thanos 3.00
2 JSn,AM,F:Adam Warlock. 3.00
3 JSn,AM,Spider-Man,Capt.Marvel 3.00
4 JSn,AM,Eternity & Infinity 3.00
5 JSn,AM 3.00
6 48-pg. 3.50
TPB JSn, rep. 18.00

INFINITY CRUSADE
1993
1 RLm,AM,I:Goddess,A:Marvel
     Heroes,foil(c) 4.00
2 RLm,AM,V:Goddess 3.00
3 RLm,AM,V:Goddess,Mephisto. . . 3.00
4 RLm,AM,V:Goddess,A:Magnus . . 3.00
5 RLm,AM,V:Goddess 3.00
6 RLm,AM,V:Goddess 3.00

INFINITY GAUNTLET
July, 1991
1 GP,O:Infinity Gauntlet 5.00
2 GP,JRu,2nd Rebirth:Warlock 4.00
3 GP,JRu,I:Terraxia. 4.00
4 GP,JRu,RLm,V:Thanos 4.00
5 JRu,RLm,V:Thanos,D:Terraxia . . 4.00
6 RLm,JRu,V:Nebula 4.00
TPB rep. #1 thru #6 . . . . 25.00
TPB GP,rep. #1-#6 (2002) 25.00

MARVEL

INFINITY WAR
1992
1 RLm,AM,R:Magus,Thanos 5.00
2 RLm,AM,V:Magus,A:Everyone . . 3.00
3 RLm,AM,V:Magus,A:Everyone . . 2.50
4 RLm,AM,Magus gets Gauntlet . . 2.50
5 RLm,AM,V:Magus 2.50
6 RLm,AM,V:Magus 2.50

INHUMANOIDS
Star, Jan.–July, 1987
1 Hasbro Toy. 3.00
2 O:Inhumanoids 3.00
3 V:D'Compose. 3.00
4 A:Sandra Shore 3.00

INHUMANS
Oct., 1975
1 GP,V:Blastaar. 25.00
2 GP,V:Blastaar. 10.00
3 GP,I:Kree S 15.00
4 GK,Maximus 15.00
5 GK,V:Maximus 15.00
6 GK,Maximus 15.00
7 GK,DP,I:Skornn 15.00
8 GP,DP,Skornn 15.00
9 rep., V:Mor-Tog 15.00
10 KP,D:Warkon. 15.00
11 KP,JM,I:Pursuer 15.00
12 KP,Hulk 15.00
Spec.#1(The Untold Saga),
   O:Inhumans 4.00
Spec. Atlantis Rising story 3.00

INHUMANS
Sept., 1998
1 (of 12) PJe,JaL,F:Black Bolt,
   Medusa, Karnak, Triton, Gorgon,
   Crystal, Lockjaw 9.00
2 PJe,JaL,F:Tonaje 4.00
2a Variant cover 3.00
3 PJe,JaL,Attilan's dark side 3.00
4 PJe,JaL,War against Attilan. 3.00
5 PJe,JaL,Earth vs. Attilan 3.00
6 PJe,JaL,V:Maximus 3.00
7 PJe,JaL,F:Black Bolt 3.00
8 PJe,JaL,F:Lockjaw. 3.00
9 PJe,JaL,F:Triton. 3.00
10 PJe,JaL,F:Woz & Medusa 3.00
11 PJe,JaL,F:Black Bolt. 3.00
12 PJe,JaL,concl. 3.00
TPB 264pg. 25.00

INHUMANS
Apr. 2000
1 (of 4) V:Ronan the Accuser 3.00
2 A:Kree 3.00
3 Maximus the Mad 3.00
4 concl. 3.00

INHUMANS
May, 2003
1 Lunar,pt.1 . . . . 2.50
2 Lunar,pt.2 . . . . 2.50
3 Lunar,pt.3 . . . . 2.50
4 Culture Shock,pt.1 . . . . 2.50
5 Culture Shock,pt.2 . . . . 2.50
6 Culture Shock,pt.3 . . . . 2.50
7 San finds love 3.00
8 Alaris 3.00
9 No Matter the Cost,pt.1 . . . . 3.00
10 No Matter the Cost,pt.2 . . . . . . 3.00
11 No Matter the Cost,pt.3. . . . . . . 3.00
12 No Matter the Cost,pt.4 . . . . . . 3.00
TPB Vol. 1 Lunar 15.00

INTERFACE
Epic, Dec., 1989
1 ESP 2.50
2 thru 7 . . . . @2.25
8 . . . . 2.25

INVADERS
Aug., 1975
1 FR,JR(c),A:Invaders,
   A:Mastermind 60.00
2 FR,JR(c),I:Brain Drain 25.00
3 FR,JR(c),I:U-Man. 25.00
4 FR,O&V:U-Man. 25.00
5 RB,JM,V:Red Skull 25.00
6 FR,V:Liberty Legion 15.00
7 FR,I:Baron Blood,
   1st Union Jack. 15.00
8 FR,FS,J:Union Jack. 15.00
9 FR,FS,O:Baron Blood 15.00
10 FR,FS,rep.Captain
   America Comics #22 . . . . 15.00
11 FR,FS,I:Blue Bullet 10.00
12 FR,FS,I:Spitfire 10.00
13 FR,FS,GK(c),I:Golem,
   Half Face. 10.00
14 FR,FS,JK(c),I:Crusaders. 10.00
15 FR,FS,JK(c),V:Crusaders 10.00
16 FR,JK(c),V:Master Man 10.00
17 FR,FS,GK(c),I:Warrior Woman. 10.00
18 FR,FS,GK(c),R:1st Destroyer . 10.00
19 FR,FS,V:Adolph Hitler. 10.00
20 FR,FS,GK(c),I&J:2nd Union Jack,
   BU:rep.Marvel Comics #1 . . . . 15.00
21 FR,FS,GK(c),BU:rep.Marvel
   Mystery #10. . . . . 10.00
22 FR,FS,GK(c),O:Toro 8.00
23 FR,FS,GK(c),I:Scarlet Scarab . 8.00
24 FR,FS,GK(c),rep.Marvel
   Mystery #17. . . . . 10.00
25 FR,FS,GK(c),V:Scarlet Scarab . . 8.00
26 FR,FS,GK(c),V:Axis Agent 8.00
27 FR,FS,GK(c),V:Axis Agent 8.00
28 FR,FS,I:2nd Human Top,
   Golden Girl,Kid Commandos. . . 8.00
29 FR,FS,I:Teutonic Knight 8.00
30 FR,FS,V:Teutonic Knight. 8.00
31 FR,FS,V:Frankenstein 8.00
32 FR,FS,JK(c),A:Thor 10.00
33 FR,FS,JK(c),A:Thor 10.00
34 FR,FS,V:Master Man 8.00
35 FR,FS,I:Iron Cross 8.00
36 FR,FS,O:Iron Cross 8.00

Invaders #38
© *Marvel Entertainment Group*

37 FR,FS,V:Iron Cross. 8.00
38 FR,FS,V:Lady Lotus 8.00
39 FR,FS,O:Lady Lotus 8.00
40 FR,FS,V:Baron Blood 8.00
41 E:RTs(s)FR,FS,V:Super Axis,
   double-size 15.00
Ann.#1 A:Avengers,R:Shark 10.00
G-Size#1 FR,rep.Submariner #1 . . 10.00

[Limited Series], 1993
1 R:Invaders 2.50
2 V:Battle Axis. 2.50
3 R:Original Vison (1950's). 2.50
4 V:The Axis 2.50

INVADERS
June, 2004
0 Once an Invader,pt.4 . . . . 3.00
1 To End All Wars,pt.1 . . . . 3.00
2 To End All Wars,pt.2 . . . . 3.00
3 To End All Wars,pt.3 . . . . 3.00

IRON FIST
Nov., 1975
1 JBy,A:Iron Man 75.00
2 JBy,V:H'rythl. 35.00
3 JBy,KP,KJ,V:Ravager. 25.00
4 JBy,V:Radion 25.00
5 JBy,V:Scimitar 25.00
6 JBy,O:Misty Knight. 25.00
7 JBy,V:Khimbala Bey. 25.00
8 JBy,V:Chaka 25.00
9 JBy,V:Chaka 25.00
10 JBy,DGr,A:Chaka 25.00
11 JBy,V:Wrecking Crew 25.00
12 JBy,DGr,V:Captain America . . . 25.00
13 JBy,A:Boomerang 25.00
14 JBy,I:Sabretooth 165.00
15 JBy,A&N:Wolverine,A:X-Men
   Sept., 1977 . . . . 70.00
Marvel Milestone rep. #14 (1992) . . 4.00

IRON FIST
May, 1998
1 (of 3) DJu,JG, from Heroes For
   Hire 3.00
2 DJu,JG,search for Scorpio Key,
   V:S.H.I.E.L.D. 3.00
3 DJu,JG,concl. 3.00

IRON FIST
March, 2004
1 Breathless,pt.1 . . . . 3.00
2 Breathless,pt.2 . . . . 3.00
3 Breathless,pt.3 . . . . 3.00
4 Breathless,pt.4 . . . . 3.00
5 Breathless,pt.5 . . . . 3.00
6 Breathless,pt.6 . . . . 3.00

IRON FIST/WOLVERINE
Sept., 2000
1 (of 4) F:DannyRand,Junzo Moto . 3.00
2 K'un L'un 3.00
3 A:Capt.America,Dragon Kings. . . 3.00
4 concl. 3.00

IRON MAN
May, 1968
1 B:StL,AGw(s),JCr,GC,
   I:Mordius 600.00
2 JCr,I:Demolisher 200.00
3 JCr,V:The Freak. 125.00
4 JCr,A:Unicorn. 100.00
5 JCr,GT,I:Cerebos 90.00
6 JCr,GT,V:Crusher. 85.00
7 JCr,GT,V:Gladiator. 85.00
8 JCr,GT,O:Whitney Frost. 85.00
9 JCr,GT,A:Mandarin 85.00

Iron Man #5
© Marvel Entertainment Group

10 JCr,GT,V:Mandarin 85.00
11 JCr,GT,V:Mandarin 65.00
12 JCr,GT,I:Controller 65.00
13 JCr,GT,A:Nick Fury 65.00
14 JCr,V:Night Phantom 65.00
15 JCr,GT,A:Red Ghost 65.00
16 JCr,GT,V:Unicorn 50.00
17 JCr,GT,I:Madam Masque,
    Midas 50.00
18 JCr,GT,V:Madame Masque . . . 50.00
19 JCr,GT,V:Madame Masque . . . 50.00
20 JCr,I:Charlie Gray 50.00
21 JCr,I:Eddie 35.00
22 JCr,D:Janice Cord 35.00
23 JCr,I:Mercenary 38.00
24 JCr,GT,V:Madame Masque . . . 35.00
25 JCr,A:Sub-Mariner 38.00
26 JCr,DH,J:Val-Larr 35.00
27 JCr,DH,I:Firebrand 35.00
28 E:AGw(s),JCr,DH,
    V:Controller 35.00
29 B:StL,AyB(s),DH,V:Myrmidon . . 35.00
30 DH,I:Monster Master 35.00
31 DH,I:Mastermind 35.00
32 GT,I:Mechanoid 35.00
33 DH,I:Spy Master 35.00
34 DH,A:Spy Master 35.00
35 DH,A:Daredevil,Spy Master . . . 35.00
36 E:AyB(s),DH,I:Ramrod 35.00
37 DH,A:Ramrod 35.00
38 GT,Jonah 35.00
39 HT,I:White Dragon 30.00
40 GT,A:White Dragon 30.00
41 GT,JM,I:Slasher 30.00
42 GT,I:Mikas 30.00
43 GT,JM,A:Mikas,I:Guardsmen . . 30.00
44 GT,A:Capt.America 30.00
45 GT,A:Guardsman 30.00
46 GT,D:Guardsman 30.00
47 BS,JM,O:Iron Man 35.00
48 GT,V:Firebrand 22.00
49 GT,V:Adaptoid 22.00
50 B:RTs(s),GT,V:Prin.Python . . . 22.00
51 GT,C:Capt.America 22.00
52 GT,I:Raga 22.00
53 GT,JSn,I:Black Lama 22.00
54 GT,BEv,Sub-Mariner,I:Madame
    MacEvil (Moondragon) 40.00
55 JSn,I:Destroyer,Thanos,Mentor
    Starfox(Eros),Blood Bros. . . . 125.00
56 JSn,I:Fangor 30.00
57 GT,R:Mandarin 20.00
58 GT,V:Mandarin 20.00

59 GT,A:Firebrand 20.00
60 GT,C:Daredevil 20.00
61 GT,Marauder 20.00
62 whiplash 20.00
63 GT,A:Dr.Spectrum 20.00
64 GT,I:Rokk 20.00
65 GT,O:Dr.Spectrum 20.00
66 GT,V:Thor 25.00
67 GT,V:Freak 20.00
68 GT,O:Iron Man 16.00
69 GT,V:Mandarin 15.00
70 GT,A:Sunfire 15.00
71 GT,V:Yellow Claw 12.00
72 E:RTs(s),GT,V:Black Lama 12.00
73 B:LWn(s),KP,JM,V:Titanic
    Three 12.00
74 KP,V:Modok. 12.00
75 V:Black Lama 12.00
76 Rep., A:Hulk 12.00
77 V:Thinker. 12.00
78 GT,V:Viet Cong 12.00
79 GT,I:Quasar(not Current one) . . 12.00
80 JK(c),O:Black Lama 12.00
81 A:Black Lama 11.00
82 MSe,A:Red Ghost 11.00
83 E:LWn(s),HT,MSe,Red Ghost . . 11.00
84 HT,A:Dr.Ritter 11.00
85 HT,MSe,A:Freak 11.00
86 B:MWn(s),GT,I:Blizzard. 11.00
87 GT,V:Blizzard. 11.00
88 E:MWn(s),GT,
    V:Blood Brothers 11.00
89 GT,A:D.D.,Blood Bros. 11.00
90 JK(c),GT,Controller,A:Thanos . 12.00
91 GT,BL,A:Controller 10.00
92 JK(c),GT,V:Melter 10.00
93 JK(c),HT,V:Kraken 10.00
94 JK(c),HT,V:Kraken 10.00
95 JK(c),GT,PP,V:Ultimo 10.00
96 GT,DP,V:Ultimo 10.00
97 GT,DP,I:Guardsman II 10.00
98 GT,DP,A:Sunfire 10.00
99 GT,V:Mandarin 10.00
100 JSn(c),GT,V:Mandarin. 28.00
101 GT,I:Dread Knight 14.00
102 GT,O:Dread Knight 14.00
103 GT,V:Jack of Hearts 14.00
104 GT,V:Midas 9.00
105 GT,V:Midas 9.00
106 GT,V:Midas 9.00
107 KP,V:Midas 9.00
108 CI,A:Growing Man 9.00
109 JBy(c),CI,V:Van Guard 9.00
110 KP,I:C.Arcturus 9.00
111 KP,O:Rigellians 9.00
112 AA,KP,V:Punisher from
    Beyond 9.00
113 KP,HT,V:Unicorn,Spy Master. . 10.00
114 KG,I:Arsenal 9.00
115 JR2,O:Unicorn,V:Ani-men 9.00
116 JR2,BL,V:Madame Masque . . . 9.00
117 BL,JR2,1st Romita Jr 10.00
118 JBy,BL,A:Nick Fury 10.00
119 BL,JR2,Alcoholic Plot 10.00
120 JR2,BL,A:Sub-Mariner,
    I:Rhodey(becomes War Machine),
    Justin Hammer 10.00
121 BL,JR2,A:Submariner 9.00
122 DC,CI,BL,O:Iron Man 9.00
123 BL,JR2,V:Blizzard 9.00
124 BL,JR2,A:Capt.America 7.00
125 BL,JR2,A:Ant-Man 7.00
126 BL,JR2,V:Hammer 7.00
127 BL,JR2,Battlefield 7.00
128 BL,JR2,Alcohol 9.00
129 SB,A:Dread Night 7.00
130 BL,V:Digital Devil 7.00
131 BL,V:Hulk 7.00
132 BL,V:Hulk 7.00
133 BL,A:Hulk,Ant-Man 7.00
134 BL,V:Titanium Man 7.00

Iron Man #129
© Marvel Entertainment Group

135 BL,V:Titanium Man 7.00
136 V:Endotherm 7.00
137 BL,Fights oil rig fire 7.00
138 BL,Dreadnought,Spymaster . . . 7.00
139 BL,Dreadnought,Spymaster . . . 7.00
140 BL,V:Force 7.00
141 BL,JR2,V:Force. 7.00
142 BL,JR2,Space Armor 7.00
143 BL,JR2,V:Sunturion 7.00
144 BL,JR2,Sunturion,O:Rhodey. . . 7.00
145 BL,JR2,A:Raiders 7.00
146 BL,JR2,I:Black Lash 7.00
147 BL,JR2,V:Black Lash 6.00
148 BL,JR2,V:Terrorists 6.00
149 BL,JR2,V:Dr.Doom 6.00
150 BL,JR2,V:Dr.Doom,Dble 8.00
151 TA,BL,A:Ant-Man 4.00
152 BL,JR2,New Armor 4.00
153 BL,JR2,V:Living Laser 4.00
154 BL,JR2,V:Unicorn 4.00
155 JR2,V:Back-Getters 4.00
156 JR2,I:Mauler 4.00
157 V:Spores 4.00
158 CI,AM,Iron Man Drowning 4.00
159 PS,V:Diablo. 4.00
160 SD,V:Serpent'sSquad 4.00
161 A:Moon Knight 4.00
162 V:Space Ships 4.00
163 V:Chessmen 4.00
164 LMc,A:Bishop 4.00
165 LMc,Meltdown. 4.00
166 LMc,V:Melter. 4.00
167 LMc,Alcoholic Issue 4.00
168 LMc,A:Machine Man 4.00
169 LMc,B:Rhodey as 2nd
    Iron Man 10.00
170 LMc,2nd Iron Man 8.00
171 LMc,2nd Iron Man. 3.00
172 LMc,V:Firebrand 3.00
173 LMc,Stane International 3.00
174 LMc,Alcoholism. 3.50
175 LMc,Alcoholism 3.50
176 LMc,Alcoholism 3.50
177 LMc,Alcoholism 3.00
178 LMc,V:Wizard 3.00
179 LMc,V:Mandarin 3.00
180 LMc,V:Mandarin 3.00
181 LMc,V:Mandarin 3.00
182 LMc,Secret Wars 3.00
183 LMc,Turning Point. 3.00
184 LMc,Moves to California 3.00
185 LMc,V:Zodiac Field 3.00
186 LMc,I:Vibro 3.00

187 LMc,V:Vibro. 3.00
188 LMc,I:New Brother's Grimm . . 3.00
189 LMc,I:Termite. 3.00
190 LMc,O:Termite,A:Scar.Witch. . . 3.00
191 LMc,New Grey Armor. 5.00
192 LMc,V:Iron Man(Tony Stark) . . 5.00
193 LMc,V:Dr.Demonicus 3.00
194 LMc,I:Scourge,A:West Coast
   Avengers. 3.00
195 LMc,A:Shaman 3.00
196 LMc,V:Dr.Demonicus 3.00
197 LMc,Secret Wars II 3.00
198 SB,V:Circuit Breaker. 3.00
199 LMc,E:Rhodey as 2nd Iron Man,
   V:Obadiah Stone 3.00
200 LMc,D:Obadiah Stone. 6.00
201 MBr,V:Madam Masque 3.00
202 A:Ka-Zar 3.00
203 MBr,A:Hank Pym 3.00
204 MBr,V:Madame Masque 3.00
205 MBr,V:A.I.M. 3.00
206 MBr,V:Goliath 3.00
207 MBr,When the Sky Rains Fire . 3.00
208 MBr,V:A.I.M. 3.00
209 V:Living Laser 3.00
210 MBr,V:Morgan LeFey 3.00
211 AS,V:Living Laser 3.00
212 DT,V:Iron Monger 3.00
213 A:Dominic Fortune 3.00
214 A:Spider-Woman 4.00
215 BL,A.I.M. 4.00
216 BL,MBr,D:Clymenstra 3.00
217 BL,MBr,V:Hammer 3.00
218 BL,MBr,Titanic. 3.00
219 BL,V:The Ghost 3.00
220 BL,MBr,V:The Ghost,
   D:Spymaster 3.00
221 BL,MBr,V:The Ghost. 3.00
222 BL,MBr,R:Abrogast 3.00
223 BL,MBr,V:Blizzard,Beetle 3.00
224 BL,V:Justin Hammer,Force. . . . 3.00
225 BL,MBr,B:Armor Wars. 5.00
226 BL,MBr,V:Stingray. 4.50
227 BL,MBr,V:Mandroids. 4.00
228 BL,MBr,V:Guardsmen. 4.00
229 BL,D:Titanium Man 4.00
230 V:Firepower, ... 4.00
231 V:Firepower,N:Iron Man 4.00
232 BWS,Nightmares,E:Armor
   Wars 4.50
233 JG,BL,A:Ant-Man 2.50
234 JG,BL,A:Spider-Man 4.00
235 JG,BL,V:Grey Gargoyle. 3.00
236 JG,BL,V:Grey Gargoyle. 3.00
237 JG,BL,V:SDI Monster 3.00
238 JG,BL,V:Rhino,D:M.Masque . . . 2.50
239 JG,BL,R:Ghost 2.50
240 JG,BL,V:Ghost 2.50
241 BL,V:Mandarin 2.50
242 BL,BWS,V:Mandarin. 3.00
243 BL,BWS,Stark Paralyzed 2.50
244 BL,V:Fixer,A:Force,double-size . 5.00
245 BL(c),V:Dreadnaughts. 2.50
246 BL,HT,V:A.I.M.,Maggia 2.50
247 BL,A:Hulk 4.00
248 BL,Tony Stark Cured. 2.50
249 BL,V:Dr.Doom 2.50
250 BL,V:Dr.Doom,A of V 3.00
251 HT,AM,V:Wrecker,A of V 2.50
252 HT,AM,V:Chemistro,A of V . . . 2.50
253 BL,V:Slagmire. 2.50
254 BL,V:Spymaster 2.50
255 HT,V:Devestator
   I:2nd Spymaster 2.50
256 JR2,V:Space Station 2.50
257 V:Samurai Steel 2.50
258 JR2,BWi,B:Armor Wars II,V:
   Titanium Man. 2.50
259 JR2,BWi,V:Titanium Man 2.50
260 JR2,BWi,V:Living Laser 2.50
261 JR2,BWi,A:Mandarin. 2.50

Iron Man #218
© Marvel Entertainment Group

262 JR2,BWi,A:Mandarin. 2.50
263 JR2,BWi,A:Wonderman,
   V:Living Laser 2.50
264 JR2,BWi,A:Mandarin. 2.50
265 JR2,BWi,V:Dewitt 2.50
266 JR2,BWi,E:Armor Wars II 2.50
267 PR,BWi,B:New O:Iron Man,
   Mandarin,V:Vibro. 2.50
268 PR,BWi,E:New O:Iron Man. . . . 2.50
269 PR,BWi,A:Black Widow 2.50
270 PR,BWi,V:Fin Fang Foom 2.50
271 PR,BWi,V:Fin Fang Foom 2.50
272 PR,BWi,O:Mandarin 2.50
273 PR,BWi,V:Mandarin 2.50
274 MBr,BWi,V:Mandarin. 2.50
275 PR,BWi,A:Mandarin,Fin Fang
   Foom, double-size. 4.00
276 PR,BWi,A:Black Widow 2.50
277 PR,BWi,A:Black Widow 2.50
278 BWi,Galactic Storm,pt.6
   A:Capt.America,V:Shatterax . . 2.50
279 BWi,Galactic Storm,pt.13,
   V:Ronan,A:Avengers. 2.50
280 KHd,V:The Stark 2.50
281 KHd,I&V:Masters of Silence,
   C:War Machine Armor. 5.00
282 KHd,I:War Machine Armor,
   V:Masters of Silence 4.00
283 KHd,V:Masters of Silence. 2.50
284 KHd,Stark put under Cryogenic
   Freeze,B:Rhodey as Iron Man . 3.50
285 KHd,BWi(i),Tony's Funeral 2.50
286 KHd,V:Avengers West Coast . . 2.50
287 KHd,I:New Atom Smasher 2.50
288 KHd,30th Anniv.,V:Atom
   Smasher,foil(c). 4.50
289 KHd,V:Living Laser,
   R:Tony Stark 2.50
290 KHd,30th Anniv.,N:Iron Man,
   Gold foil(c) 5.00
291 KHd,E:Rhodey as Iron Man,
   Becomes War Machine 2.50
292 KHd,Tony reveals he is alive . . 2.50
293 KHd,V:Controller. 2.50
294 KHd,Infinity Crusade. 2.50
295 KHd,Infinity Crusade. 2.50
296 KHd,V:Modam,A:Omega Red. . 2.50
297 KHd,V:Modam,Omega Red . . . 2.50
298 KHd(c),I:Earth Mover 2.50
299 KHd(c),R:Ultimo 2.50
300 KHd,TMo,N:Iron Man,I:Iron
   Legion,A:War Machine,V:Ultimo
   Foil(c). 5.00

300a Newsstand ed. 2.75
301 KHd,B:Crash and Burn,
   A:Deathlok,C:Venom 2.50
302 KHd,V:Venom 2.50
303 KHd,V:New Warriors,
   C:Thundrstrike. 2.50
304 KHd,C:Hulk,V:New Warriors,
   Thundrstrike,N:Iron Man 2.50
305 KHd,V:Hulk. 2.50
306 KHd,E:Stark Enterprise. 2.50
307 TMo,I:Vor/Tex,R:Mandarin 2.50
308 TMo,Vor/Tex 2.50
309 TMo,Vor/Tex 2.50
310 regular. 3.00
310a Neon(c),with insert print 3.50
311 V:Mandarin 2.50
312 double-size 3.00
313 LKa,TMo,AA Meeting 2.50
314 LKa,TMo,new villain 2.50
315 A:Black Widow 2.50
316 I:Slag,A:Crimson Dynamo 2.50
317 In Dynamos Armor 3.00
318 LKa,TMo,V:Slag 2.50
319 LKa,TMo,New Space Armor . . . 2.50
320 F:Hawkeye 2.50
321 Cont. From Avg. Crossing 2.50
322 TKa,TheCrossing,V:JackFrost . 2.50
323 TKa,V:Avengers 2.50
324 TKa,The Crossing. 2.50
325 TKa,Avengers:Timeslide after. . 3.50
326 First Sign,pt.3 . . . . 2.50
327 Frostbite 2.50
328 TKa,Tony Stark at ColumbiaU. . 2.50
329 Stark Enterprises taken over . . 2.50
330 . . . . 2.50
331 . . . . 2.50
332 final issue 4.00
Ann.#1 rep.Iron Man #25. . . . . . . 45.00
Ann.#2 rep.Iron Man #6. . . . . 25.00
Ann.#3 SB,Manthing 15.00
Ann.#4 DP,GT,V:Modok,
   A:Champions. 10.00
Ann.#5 JBr,A:Black Panther 6.00
Ann.#6 A:Eternals,V:Brother
   Tode. 6.00
Ann.#7 LMc,A:West Coast
   Avengers, I:New Goliath 6.00
Ann.#8 A:X-Factor 6.00
Ann.#9 V:Stratosfire,A:Sunturion . . . 5.00
Ann.#10 PS,BL,Atlantis Attacks #2
   A:Sub-Mariner 4.00
Ann.#11 SD,Terminus Factor #2 . . 4.00
Ann.#12 Subterran.Odyssey #4. . . 4.00
Ann.#13 GC,AW,Assault on Armor
   City,A:Darkhawk 4.00
Ann.#14 TMo,I:Face Theif,w/card,
   BU:War Machine 4.00
Ann.#15 GC,V:Controller. 4.00
Spec.#1 rep.Sub-Mariner x-over . . 40.00
Spec.#2 rep.(1971) 20.00
Marvel Milestone rep. #55 (1992) . . 2.95
G-Size#1 Reprints 15.00
1-shot Iron Man/Force Works Collec-
   tors' Preview, Neon wrap-around
   cover, double size, X-over. 2.50
1-shot Iron Manual, BSz(c),Guide
   to Iron Man's technology. 2.50
GN Iron Man 2020 . . . . 5.95
TPB Armor Wars rep. 12.95
TPB Many Armors of Iron Man . . 15.95
TPB Power of Iron Man 9.95
TPB Iron Man vs. Dr. Doom, rep. . 12.95

[2nd Series], Nov., 1996
1 JLe,SLo,WPo,SW,A:Bruce
   Banner, New O:Hulk,48pg. 4.00
1A variant Hulk showing cover 5.00
1 gold signature ed., bagged 18.00
2 JLe,SLo,WPo,SW 4.00
3 JLe,SLo,WPo,SW,Heroes brawl . 3.00
4 JLe,SLo,WPo,SW,V:Laser. 3.00
4A X-mas cover 5.00

Iron Man Vol. 2 #7
© Marvel Entertainment Group

5 JLe,SLo,WPo,SW, Whirlwind. . . . 3.00
6 JLe,SLo,WPo,SW,Industrial
 Revolution, pt.2 x-over 3.00
7 JLe,SLo,WPo,SW,A:Pepper
 Potts,Villain revealed. 3.00
8 JLe,SLo,RBn,fate of Rebel 3.00
9 JLe,SLo,RBn,V:Mandarin 3.00
10 JLe,SLo,RBn,F:The Hulk 3.00
11 JLb,RBn,V:Dr. Doom,A:Hydra. . . 3.00
12 WPo,JLe,JLb,F:Dr. Doom,
 Galactus 3.00
13 JeR,LSn,Wildstorm x-over 3.00

[3rd Series], 1997
1 SCh,KBk,V:Mastermind,48-pg. . . 5.00
2 KBk,SCh,in Switzerland. 3.50
3 KBk,SCh,V:Hydra Dreadnought
 Robot. 3.00
4 KBk,SCh,R:Firebrand 3.00
5 KBk,SCh,V:Firebrand. 3.00
6 KBk,F:Black Widow 3.00
7 KBk,SCh,Live Kree or Die,pt.1
 x-over. 3.00
8 KBk,SCh,secret identity out. 3.00
9 KBk,SCh,A:Black Widow 3.00
10 KBk,SCh,A:Avengers 3.00
11 KBk,SCh,A:Warbird &
 War Machine 3.00
12 KBk,V:War Machine 3.00
13 KBk,SCh,V:Controller,48-pg. . . . 4.00
13a signed 20.00
14 KBk,SCh,Fant.Four x-over 3.00
15 KBk,SCh,V:Nitro 3.00
16 KBk,RSt,V:Dragon Lord 3.00
17 KBk,RSt,SCh,V:Fin Fang Foom . 3.00
18 KBk,RSt,SCh,V:War Machine . . . 3.00
19 KBk,RSt,SCh,V:War Machine . . . 3.00
20 KBk,RSt,SCh,V:War Machine . . . 3.00
21 KBk,RSt,TGu,MBa,
 Eighth Day prologue 3.00
22 KBk,RSt,Eighth Day,pt.2,
 I:Carnivore. 3.00
23 KBk,RSt,UltimateDanger,pt.1 . . . 3.00
24 KBk,RSt,UltimateDanger,pt.2 . . . 3.25
25 KBk,RSt,Ultimate
 Danger,pt.3, 48-pg. 3.50
26 JQ,Mask of Iron Man,pt.1 . . . . . . 2.50
27 JQ,Mask of Iron Man,pt.2 . . . . . . 2.50
28 JQ,Mask of Iron Man,pt.3 . . . . . . 2.50
29 JQ,Mask of Iron Man,pt.4 . . . . . . 2.50
30 JQ,Mask of Iron Man,pt.5 . . . . . . 2.50
31 JQ,Sons of Yinsen,pt.1 . . . . 2.50
32 JQ,Sons of Yinsen,pt.2 . . . . 2.50
33 JQ,Sons of Yinsen,pt.3 . . . . 2.50
34 JQ,Dr. Power 2.50

35 JQ,Maximum Security. 2.50
36 CDi,PR 2.50
37 JQ,F:Tyberius Stone 2.50
38 R:classic foe 2.50
39 MPn,Remote Control 2.50
40 MPn,Remote Control 2.50
41 new art team. 2.50
42 Big Bang Theory,pt.1 . . . . 2.50
43 Big Bang Theory,pt.2 . . . . 2.50
44 Big Bang,pt.3,new armor 2.50
45 Big Bang Theory,pt.4 . . . . 2.50
46 Frankenstein Syndrome,pt.1
 100-pages 4.00
47 IaC,Frankenstein Syndrome. . . . 2.25
48 IaC,Frankenstein Syndrome 2.25
49 CsB,V:Titanium Man 2.25
50 MGr,48-pg. 4.00
51 MGr,Jane Doe,pt.1 . . . . 2.25
52 MGr,Jane Doe,pt.2 . . . . 2.25
53 MGr,Book of Ten Rings. 2.25
54 MGr,Temugin. 2.25
55 MGr,would be #400 issue,54-pg. 4.00
56 MGr,fall-out begins 2.25
57 MGr,fight on, fight on 2.25
58 MGr. 2.25
59 MGr,In Shining Armor 2.25
60 MGr,In Shining Armor,pt.2. . . . . 2.25
61 MGr,In Shining Armor,pt.3. . . . . 2.25
62 MGr,You Can't Always Get,pt.1 . 2.25
63 MGr,You Can't Always Get,pt.2 . 2.25
64 AD,MFm,MGr,Standoff,pt.1. . . . 2.25
65 MGr,Manhunt,pt.1 . . . . 2.25
66 MGr,Manhunt,pt.2 . . . . 2.25
67 MGr,Manhunt,pt.3 . . . . 3.00
68 MGr,Manhunt,pt.4 . . . . 3.00
69 MGr,Manhunt,pt.5 . . . . 3.00
70 Vegal Bleeds Neon,pt.1. . . . . . . 3.00
71 Vegas Bleeds Neon,pt.2 . . . . . . 3.00
72 Vegas Bleeds Neon,pt.3 . . . . . . 3.00
73 The Best Defense,pt.1 . . . . 3.00
74 The Best Defense,pt.2 . . . . 3.00
75 Secretary of Defense? 3.00
76 The Best Defense,pt.4 . . . . 3.00
77 The Best Defense,pt.5 . . . . 3.00
78 The Best Defense,pt.6 . . . . 3.00
79 The Deep End,pt.1 . . . . 3.00
80 The Deep End,pt.2 . . . . 3.00
81 The Deep End,pt.3 . . . . 3.00
82 The Deep End,pt.4 . . . . 3.00
83 F:Titanium Man 3.00
84 Top-secret materials 3.00
85 Top-secret materials 3.00
86 Singularity,pt.1 . . . . 3.00
87 Singularity,pt.2 . . . . 3.00
88 Singularity,pt.3 . . . . 3.00
89 Singularity,pt.4 . . . . 3.00
Ann.1998 Iron Man/Captain
 America, KBk,MWa, 48-pg. 3.00
Ann.1999 KBk,JoC,48-pg. 3.50
Ann.2000 Sons of Yin-Sen,pt.3 . . . . 3.50
Ann.2001 CCl,48-pg. 3.00
Spec.#1 Age of Innocence, Avengers:
 Timeslide 2.50
TPB The Mask in the Iron Man . . . 14.95

IRON MAN &
SUBMARINER
April, 1968
1 GC, 2 stories 225.00

IRON MAN: BAD BLOOD
July, 2000
1 (of 4) BL,DvM,V:JustinHammer. . 3.00
2 BL,DvM,Spymaster 3.00
3 BL,DvM,James Rhodes. 3.00
4 BL,DvM,Justin Hammer. 3.00

IRON MAN:
THE IRON AGE
June, 1998
1 (of 2) KBk,48pg bookshelf 6.00
2 KBk,48pg bookshelf, concl. 6.00

ISLAND OF DR. MOREAU
Oct., 1977
1 GK(c),movie adapt. 8.00

IT'S A DUCK'S LIFE
Feb., 1950
1 F;Buck Duck,Super Rabbit . . . 150.00
2 . . . . 80.00
3 thru 11 . . . . @75.00

JACK OF HEARTS
Jan., 1984
1 thru 4 . . . . @2.50

JAMES BOND JR.
1992
1 I&O:JamesBondJr.(TVseries) . . . 3.00
2 thru 12 . . . . @2.25

JANN OF THE JUNGLE
See: JUNGLE TALES

JEANIE COMICS
See: DARING MYSTERY

JIHAD
Epic
1 Cenobites vs. Nightbreed 4.50
2 E:Cenobites vs. Nightbreed. 4.50

JLA/AVENGERS
Marvel/DC, Sept., 2003
1 KBk,GP(c),x-over,48-pg. 6.00
3 KBk,GP,x-over,48-pg. 6.00

JOHN CARTER,
WARLORD OF MARS
June, 1977
1 GK,DC,O:John Carter,Created
 by Edgar Rice Burroughs 15.00

John Carter, Warlord of Mars #21
© Marvel Entertainment Group

MARVEL

2 GK/DC(c),GK,RN, White Apes	
of Mars 7.00	
3 GK,RN,Requiem for a Warlord .. 7.00	
4 GK,RN, Raiding Party 7.00	
5 GK,RN,Giant Battle Issue 7.00	
6 GK/DC(c),GK,Alone Against a	
World 7.00	
7 GK,TS,Showdown 7.00	
8 GK,RN,Beast With Touch of	
Stone 7.00	
9 GK,RN,Giant Battle Issue 7.00	
10 GK,The Death of Barsoom? 7.00	
11 RN,O:Dejah Thoris 7.00	
12 RN,City of the Dead 7.00	
13 RN,March of the Dead 7.00	
14 RN,The Day Helium Died 7.00	
15 RN,GK,Prince of Helium	
Returns 7.00	
16 RN,John Carters Dilemna 7.00	
17 BL,What Price Victory 10.00	
18 FM,Tars Tarkas Battles Alone ... 7.00	
19 RN(c),War With the Wing Men ... 7.00	
20 RN(c),Battle at the Bottom	
of the World 7.00	
21 RN(c),The Claws of the Banth .. 7.00	
22 RN(c),The Canyon of Death 7.00	
23 Murder on Mars 7.00	
24 GP/TA(c),Betrayal 7.00	
25 Inferno.................... 7.00	
26 Death Cries the Guild of	
Assassins 7.00	
27 Death Marathon 7.00	
28 Guardians of the Lost	
City Oct., 1979 .... 7.00	
Ann.#1 RN(c),GK,Battle story 7.00	
Ann.#2 RN(c),GK,Outnumbered 7.00	
Ann.#3 RN(c),GK,Battle story 7.00	

JOKER COMICS
Timely, April, 1942

1 BW,I&B:Powerhouse Pepper,	
A:Stuporman 3,500.00	
2 BW,I:Tessie the Typist 1,200.00	
3 BW,A:Tessie the Typist,	
Squat Car Squad 700.00	
4 BW,Squat Car (c) 675.00	
5 BW,same 675.00	
6 BW, ... 500.00	
7 BW 500.00	
8 BW 500.00	
9 BW 500.00	
10 BW,Shooting Gallery (c) 500.00	
11 BW 400.00	
12 BW 400.00	
13 BW 400.00	
14 BW 400.00	
15 BW 400.00	
16 BW 400.00	
17 BW 400.00	
18 BW 400.00	
19 BW 400.00	
20 BW 400.00	
21 BW 350.00	
22 BW 350.00	
23 BW,HK,Hey Look 350.00	
24 BW,HK,Laff Favorites 350.00	
25 BW,HK,same. 350.00	
26 BW,HK,same. 350.00	
27 BW 350.00	
28 .... 125.00	
29 BW 350.00	
30 BW 350.00	
31 BW 350.00	
32 B:Millie, Hedy. 125.00	
33 HK...................... 150.00	
34 .... 125.00	
35 HK 150.00	
36 HK 125.00	
37 .... 125.00	
38 .... 125.00	

39 .... 125.00	
40 .... 125.00	
41 A:Nellie the Nurse. 125.00	
42 I:Patty Pin-up 150.00	

Becomes:

ADVENTURES INTO TERROR
1950

43(1)AH,B:Horror Stories 900.00	
44(2)AH,Won't You Step Into	
My Palor 600.00	
3 GC,I Stalk By Night 350.00	
4 DR,The Torture Room 350.00	
5 GC,DR,The Hitchhiker 375.00	
6 RH,The Dark Room 325.00	
7 GT(c),BW,JMn,Where Monsters	
Dwell 750.00	
8 JSt,Enter... the Lizard 325.00	
9 RH(c),JSt,The Dark	
Dungeon 300.00	
10 JMn,When the Vampire Calls . 300.00	
11 JMn,JSt,Dead Man's Escape . 250.00	
12 BK,Man Who Cried Ghost ... 265.00	
13 BEv(c),The Hands of Death .. 265.00	
14 GC,GT,The Hands 250.00	
15 Trapped by the Tarantula ... 250.00	
16 RH(c),Her Name Is Death ... 250.00	
17 I Die Too Often,Bondage(c) .. 250.00	
18 He's Trying To Kill Me 250.00	
19 The Girl Who Couldn't Die ... 240.00	
20 .... 240.00	
21 GC,JMn. 225.00	
22 JMn 225.00	
23 .... 225.00	
24 MF,GC. 225.00	
25 MF. 275.00	
26 GC. 225.00	
27 .... 225.00	
28 GC. 225.00	
29 GC,JMn. 225.00	
30 .... 225.00	
31 May, 1954 .... 225.00	

JOURNEY INTO MYSTERY
June, 1952

1 RH(c),B:Mystery/Horror	
stories 4,500.00	
2 Don't Look 1,500.00	
3 I Didn't See Anything 1,000.00	
4 RH,BEv(c),I'm Drowning,	
severed hand (c) 1,000.00	
5 RH,BEv(c),Fright 700.00	

Journey Into Mystery #96
© Marvel Entertainment Group

6 BEv(c),Till Death Do	
Us Part 700.00	
7 BEv(c),Ghost Guard 700.00	
8 He Who Hesitates 700.00	
9 BEv(c),I Made A Monster 700.00	
10 The Assassin of Paris 700.00	
11 RH,GT,Meet the Dead. 675.00	
12 A Night At Dragmoor Castle . . 550.00	
13 The Living and the Dead 550.00	
14 DAy,RH,The Man Who	
Owned A World 550.00	
15 RH(c),Till Death Do Us Part . . 550.00	
16 DW,Vampire Tale 550.00	
17 SC,Midnight On Black	
Mountain 550.00	
18 He Wouldn't Stay Dead. 550.00	
19 JF,The Little Things. 550.00	
20 BEv,BP,After Man, What 550.00	
21 JKu,The Man With No Past . . 550.00	
22 Haunted House. 550.00	
23 GC,Gone, But Not Forgotten . 350.00	
24 The Locked Drawer 350.00	
25 The Man Who Lost Himself . . 350.00	
26 The Man From Out There. ... 350.00	
27 BP,JSe,Masterpiece 350.00	
28 The Survivor 350.00	
29 Three Frightened People 350.00	
30 JO,The Lady Who Vanished. . 350.00	
31 The Man Who Had No Fear . . 350.00	
32 Elevator In The Sky 350.00	
33 SD,AW,There'll Be Some	
Changes Made 400.00	
34 BP,BK,The Of The	
Mystic Ring 350.00	
35 LC,JF,Turn Back The Clock . . 350.00	
36 I, The Pharaoh 350.00	
37 BEv(c),The Volcano 350.00	
38 SD,Those Who Vanish 350.00	
39 BEv(c),DAy,WW,The	
Forbidden Room 350.00	
40 BEv(c),JF,The Strange	
Secret Of Henry Hill 350.00	
41 BEv(c),GM,RC,I Switched	
Bodies 300.00	
42 BEv(c),GM,What Was	
Farley's Other Face. 300.00	
43 AW,Ghost Ship 300.00	
44 SD,JK,BEv 300.00	
45 BEv,JO 275.00	
46 .... 275.00	
47 BEv 275.00	
48 .... 275.00	
49 .... 275.00	
50 SD 275.00	
51 SD,JK 300.00	
52 JK 275.00	
53 DH. 275.00	
54 AW 300.00	
55 .... 300.00	
56 thru 61 SD,JK .... @275.00	
62 SD,JK,I:Xemnu 450.00	
63 SD,JK 275.00	
64 SD,JK 275.00	
65 SD,JK 275.00	
66 Hulk Type 450.00	
67 SD,JK 275.00	
68 SD,JK 275.00	
69 SD,JK 275.00	
70 Sandman Type 375.00	
71 JK,SD 275.00	
72 JK,SD 275.00	
73 JK,DH,Spider-Man type 575.00	
74 .... 275.00	
75 JK,DH 275.00	
76 JK,DH 250.00	
77 DH,SD,JK 225.00	
78 DH,Dr.Strange Type 375.00	
79 JK,DH,SD 350.00	
80 JK,DH,SD 225.00	
81 JK,DH,SD 225.00	
82 JK,DH,SD 225.00	

83 JK,SD,I&O:Thor 9,500.00
84 JK,SD,DH,I:Executioner. . . . 2,500.00
85 JK,SD,I:Loki,Heimdall,Balder,
   Tyr,Odin,Asgard 1,500.00
86 JK,SD,DH,V:Tomorrow Man 1,000.00
87 JK,SD,V:Communists 650.00
88 JK,SD,V:Loki 650.00
89 JK,SD,O:Thor(rep) 650.00
90 SD,I:Carbon Copy 500.00
91 JSt,SD,I:Sandu 450.00
92 JSt,SD,V:Loki,I:Frigga 450.00
93 DAy,JK,SD,I:Radioactive Man 500.00
94 JSt,SD,V:Loki 450.00
95 JSt,SD,I:Duplicator 450.00
96 JSt,SD,I:Merlin II 450.00
97 JK,I:Lava Man,O:Odin 500.00
98 DH,JK,I&O:Cobra 350.00
99 DH,JK,I:Mr.Hyde,Surtur 350.00
100 DH,JK,V:Mr.Hyde 350.00
101 JK,V:Tomorrow Man 250.00
102 JK,I:Sif,Hela 250.00
103 JK,I:Enchantress,
   Executioner 250.00
104 JK,Giants 250.00
105 JK,V:Hyde,Cobra 250.00
106 JK,O:Balder. 250.00
107 JK,I:Grey Gargoyle,Karnilla . 250.00
108 JK,A:Dr.Strange 250.00
109 JK,V:Magneto 550.00
110 JK,V:Hyde,Cobra,Loki 250.00
111 JK,V:Hyde,Cobra,Loki 250.00
112 JK,V:Hulk,O:Loki 600.00
113 JK,V:Grey Gargoyle 200.00
114 JK,I&O:Absorbing Man 200.00
115 JK,O:Loki,V:Absorbing Man . 275.00
116 JK,V:Loki,C:Daredevil 200.00
117 JK,V:Loki 200.00
118 JK,I:Destroyer 200.00
119 JK,V:Destroyer,I:Hogun,
   Fandrall,Volstagg. 200.00
120 JK,A:Avengers,Absorbing
   Man 200.00
121 JK,V:Absorbing Man 200.00
122 JK,V:Absorbing Man 200.00
123 JK,V:Absorbing Man 200.00
124 JK,A:Hercules 225.00
125 JK,A:Hercules 225.00
Annual #1, JK,I:Hercules 350.00
Becomes:

THOR

JOURNEY INTO MYSTERY

[2nd series], Oct., 1972
1 GK,TP,MP,Dig Me No Grave . . 35.00
2 GK,Jack the Ripper 25.00
3 JSn,TP,Shambler From
   the Stars 25.00
4 GC,DA,Haunter of the Dark,
   H.P. Lovecraft adaptation 25.00
5 RB,FrG,Shadow From the
   Steeple,R. Bloch adaptation . . 25.00
6 Mystery Stories 20.00
7 thru 19 . . . . @20.00

JOURNEY INTO UNKNOWN WORLDS
See: ALL WINNERS COMICS

JUBILEE
Sept., 2004
1 In Los Angeles 3.00
2 F:Meg Devereaux 3.00

Journey Into Mystery 2nd Series #2
© Marvel Entertainment Group

J-2
Aug., 1998
1 TDF,RLm,AM,F:J2 with the powers
   of Juggernaut 2.25
2 TDF,RLm,AM,V:Buffer Zone,
   Enthralla & Uncanny X-People . 2.25
2a variant cover 2.25
3 TDF,RLm,AM,V:Hulk 2.25
4 TDF,RLm,AM,turning points. . . . 2.25
5 TDF,RLm,AM,Ghosts of the Past 2.25
6 TDF,RLm,AM,Majority Rules . . . 2.25
7 TDF,RLm,AM,Last Days of
   the Original Juggernaut. 2.25
8 TDF,RLm,AM,Uneasy Allies. . . . 2.25
9 TDF,RLm,AM,Critical Choices . . . 2.25
10 TDF,RLm,AM,Incredible
   Journeys 2.25
11 TDF,RLm,AM,Master of Jug-Fu . 2.25
12 TDF,RLm,AM,A:Juggernaut,
   last issue 2.25

JUGGERNAUT
1997
1-shot 48pg. 3.00

JUGGERNAUT: THE EIGHTH DAY
Sept., 1999
1-shot JoC,TSr,AKu(c),x-over,pt.4 . . 3.00

JUNGLE ACTION
Atlas, Oct., 1954
1 JMn,JMn(c),B:Leopard Girl . . . 450.00
2 JMn,JMn(c) 475.00
3 JMn,JMn(c) 300.00
4 JMn,JMn(c) 300.00
5 JMn,JMn(c) 300.00
6 JMn,JMn(c),Aug., 1955 . . . . . 300.00

JUNGLE ACTION
Oct., 1972–Nov., 1976
1 JB(c),Lorna,Tharn,Jann
   reprints 25.00
2 GK(c),same 15.00
3 JSn(c),same 15.00
4 GK(c),same 15.00
5 JR(c),JB,B:Black Panther,
   V:Man-Ape 30.00
6 RB/FrG(c),RB,V:Kill-Monger . . 25.00
7 RB/KJ(c),RB,V:Venomn 15.00

Jungle Action #19
© Marvel Entertainment Group

8 RB/KJ(c),RB,GK,
   O:Black Panther 20.00
9 GK/KJ(c),RB,V:Baron Macabre 15.00
10 GK/FrG(c),V:King Cadaver 15.00
11 GK(c),V:Baron Macabre,Lord
   Karnaj 15.00
12 RB/KJ(c),V:Kill Monger 10.00
13 GK/JK(c),V:White Gorilla,
   Sombre 10.00
14 GK(c),V:Prehistoric Monsters . . 10.00
15 GK(c),V:Prehistoric Monsters . 10.00
16 GK(c),V:Venomm 10.00
17 GK(c),V:Kill Monger 10.00
18 JKu(c),V:Madame Slay 10.00
19 GK(c),V:KKK,Sacrifice of Blood 10.00
20 V:KKK,Slaughter In The
   Streets 10.00
21 V:KKK,Cross Of Fire, Cross
   Of Death 9.00
22 JB(c),V:KKK,Soul Stranger 9.00
23 JBy(c),V:KKK 9.00
24 GK(c),I:Wind Eagle 9.00

JUNGLE TALES
Atlas, Sept., 1954
1 B:Jann of the Jungle,Cliff
   Mason,Waku 450.00
2 GT,Jann Stories cont. 300.00
3 Cliff Mason,White Hunter,
   Waku Unknown Jungle 300.00
4 Cliff Mason,Waku,Unknown
   Jungle 300.00
5 RH(c),SSh,Cliff Mason,Waku,
   Unknown Jungle 300.00
6 DH,SSh,Cliff Mason,Waku,
   Unknown Jungle 300.00
7 DH,SSh,Cliff Mason,Waku,
   Unknown Jungle 300.00
Becomes:

JANN OF THE JUNGLE
1955
8 SH,SSh,The Jungle Outlaw . . . 400.00
9 With Fang and Talons 250.00
10 AW,The Jackal's Lair. 250.00
11 Bottonless Pit 250.00
12 The Lost Safari 250.00
13 When the Trap Closed 250.00
14 V:Hunters 250.00
15 BEv(c),DH,V:Hunters 250.00
16 BEv(c),AW,JungleVengeance . 275.00
17 BEv(c),DH,AW,June, 1957 . . . 275.00

MARVEL

JUSTICE
Nov., 1986
1 I:Justice 2.25
2 . . . . 2.25
3 Yakuza Assassin 2.25
4 thru 31 . . . . @2.25
32 Last issue,A:Joker 2.25

JUSTICE COMICS
Atlas, Fall, 1947
7(1) B:FBI in Action,Mystery of
  White Death. 350.00
8(2),HK,Crime is For Suckers . . . 250.00
9(3),FBI Raid 200.00
4 Bank Robbery 200.00
5 Subway(c) 175.00
6 E:FBI In Action 175.00
7 Symbolic(c) 175.00
8 Funeral(c) 175.00
9 B:True Cases Proving Crime
  Can't Win 175.00
10 Ph(c),Bank Hold Up 175.00
11 Ph(c),Behind Bars. 175.00
12 Ph(c),The Crime of
  Martin Blaine 135.00
13 Ph(c),The Cautiouc Crook . . . 135.00
14 Ph(c) 135.00
15 Ph(c) 135.00
16 F:"Ears"Karpik-Mobster. 125.00
17 The Ragged Stranger 125.00
18 Criss-Cross 125.00
19 Death Of A Spy 125.00
20 Miami Mob 125.00
21 Trap. 125.00
22 The Big Break. 125.00
23 thru 40 . . . . @100.00
41 Electrocution cover 200.00
42 thru 51 . . . . @100.00
52 Flare Up 100.00
Becomes:

TALES OF JUSTICE
May, 1955—Aug., 1957
53 BEv,Keeper Of The Keys 200.00
54 thru 57 . . . . @175.00
58 BK 150.00
59 BK 150.00
60 thru 63 . . . . @100.00
64 RC,DW,JSe. 125.00
65 RC. 125.00
66 JO,AT 125.00
67 DW 125.00

JUSTICE: FOUR BALANCE
1994
1 A:Thing, Yancy Street Gang 2.25
2 V:Hate Monger. 2.25
3 the story continues... . . . . 2.25
4 ...to its conclusion 2.25

KABUKI
July, 2004
1 DMk,The Alchemy,pt.1 . . . . 3.00
2 DMk,The Alchemy,pt.2 . . . . 3.00

KATHY
Atlas, Oct., 1959—Feb., 1964
1 Teenage Tornado 125.00
2 . . . . 100.00
3 thru 15 . . . . @75.00
16 thru 27 . . . . @60.00

KA-ZAR
[Reprint Series], Aug., 1970
1 X-Men ID 45.00
2 Daredevil 12, 13 . . . . 30.00

---

3 DDH,Spider-Man,March, 1971 . 30.00
[1st Series], Jan., 1974
1 O:Savage Land 20.00
2 DH,JA,A:Shanna The She-Devil 10.00
3 DH,V:Man-God,A:El Tigre 10.00
4 DH,V:Man-God 10.00
5 DH,D:El-Tigre. 6.00
6 JB/AA,V:Bahemoth 6.00
7 JB/BMcRevenge of the
  River-Gods 6.00
8 JB/AA,Volcano of
  Molten Death. 6.00
9 JB,Man Who Hunted Dinosaur . . 6.00
10 JB,Dark City of Death 6.00
11 DH/FS,Devil-God of Sylitha . . . 5.00
12 RH,Wizard of Forgotten
  Death. 5.00
13 V:Lizard Men. 5.00
14 JAb,V:Klaw 5.00
15 VM,V:Klaw,Hellbird 5.00
16 VM,V:Klaw 5.00
17 VM,V:Klaw 5.00
18 VM,V:Klaw,Makrum. 5.00
19 VM,V:Klaw,Raknor the Slayer. . . 5.00
20 VM,V:Klaw,Fortress of Fear . . . 5.00
[2nd Series], Apr. 1981
1 BA,O:Ka-Zar 4.00
2 thru 7 BA . . . . @3.00
8 BA,Ka-Zar Father. 2.50
9 BA 2.50
10 BA,Direct D 2.50
11 BA/GK,Zabu 2.50
12 BA,Panel Missing 2.50
12a Scarce Reprint 2.50
13 BA 2.50
14 BA/GK,Zabu 2.50
15 BA 2.50
16 . . . . 2.50
17 Detective. 2.50
18 . . . . 2.50
19 . . . . 2.50
20 A:Spider-Man 3.00
21 . . . . 3.00
22 A:Spider-Man 3.00
23 A:Spider-Man 3.00
24 A:Spider-Man 3.00
25 A:Spider-Man 3.00
26 A:Spider-Man 3.00
27 A:Buth 3.00
28 Pangea 3.00
29 W:Ka-Zar & Shanna, Doub.Size . 3.00
30 V:Pterons 3.00
31 PangeaWarII 3.00

Kazar 2nd Series #22
© Marvel Entertainment Group

---

32 V:Plunderer 3.00
33 V:Plunderer 3.00
34 Last Issue Doub.Size 3.00
[3rd Series], 1997
1 MWa,NKu,Ka-Zar, Shanna, Zabu,
  V:Gregor, 40pg 5.00
1a 2nd printing 2.50
2 MWa,NKu,V:Gregor 4.00
2A NKu variant cover 3.00
3 MWa,NKu,Ka-Zar's son dead? . . 3.00
4 MWa,NKu,in New York City 3.00
5 MWa,NKu, ... 2.50
6 MWa,V:Rampaging Rhino 2.25
7 MWa,NKu,F:Shanna the
  She-Devil. 2.25
8 MWa,NKu, Urban Jungle, pt.1 . . 2.25
9 MWa,NKu, Urban Jungle, pt.2 . . 2.25
10 MWa,NKu, Urban Jungle, pt.3 . . 2.25
11 MWa,NKu, Urban Jungle, pt.4,
  concl. 2.25
12 MWa,A:High Evolutionary 2.25
13 MWa,A:High Evolutionary 2.25
14 MWa,NKu,end old & begin new
  storyline, double size 3.50
15 A:Punisher. 3.00
16 A:Punisher. 2.25
17 Ka-Zar clears his name,
  A:Jameka. 2.25
18 People of the Savage Land
  revolt 2.25
19 V:Gregor 2.25
20 A:Gregor,Zira, final issue 2.25
Ann. '97 V:Garrok, Petrified Man . . . 2.50
Ann. '98 Ka-Zar/Daredevil heroes
  unite. 3.00
1-shot Ka-Zar of the Savage Land,
  CDi,V:Sauron, 48-pg., prelude to
  3rd series (1996) 3.00
1-shot Ka-Zar: Sibling Rivalry,
  MWa,TDz,Flashback (1997) . . . 2.00

KELLYS, THE
See: KID KOMICS

KENT BLAKE OF THE SECRET SERVICE
May, 1951—July, 1953
1 U.S. Govt. Secret Agent
  stories,Bondage cover 250.00
2 JSt,Drug issue,Man with
  out A Face 175.00
3 JMn,Trapped By The Chinese
  Reds. 125.00
4 Secret Service Stories 125.00
5 RH(c),Condemned To Death . . 125.00
6 Cases from Kent Blake files . . 125.00
7 RH(c),Behind Enemy Lines . . 125.00
8 GT,V:Communists 125.00
9 thru 14 . . . . @125.00

KICKERS INC.
Nov., 1986
1 SB,O:Kickers 2.50
2 SB 2.50
3 RF,Witches. 2.50
4 RF,FIST 2.50
5 RF,A:D.P.7 . . . . 2.50
6 thru 12 . . . . @2.50

KID & PLAY
1 Based on Rap Group. 2.25
2 thru 9 . . . . @2.25

KID COLT OUTLAW
Atlas, Aug., 1948
1 B:Kid Colt,A:Two-Gun Kid . . 1,400.00
2 Gun-Fighter and the Girl 700.00

3 Colt-Quick Killers
   For Hire 550.00
4 Wanted,A:Tex Taylor 550.00
5 Mystery of the Misssing
   Mine,A:Blaze Carson. 550.00
6 A:Tex Taylor,Valley of
   the Warewolf 350.00
7 B:Nimo the Lion 350.00
8 . . . . 350.00
9 . . . . 350.00
10 The Whip Strikes,E:Nimo
   the Lion. 350.00
11 O:Kid Colt 400.00
12 . . . . 225.00
13 DRi 225.00
14 . . . . 225.00
15 Gun Whipped in ShotgunCity . 225.00
16 . . . . 225.00
17 . . . . 225.00
18 DRi 225.00
19 . . . . 200.00
20 The Outlaw 200.00
21 thru 30. . . . . @200.00
31 . . . . 200.00
32 . . . . 200.00
33 thru 45 A:Black Rider . . . . . @150.00
46 RH(c). 125.00
47 DW 125.00
48 RH(c),JKu 125.00
49 . . . . 125.00
50 . . . . 125.00
51 thru 56. . . . . @100.00
57 AW 100.00
58 AW 100.00
59 AW 100.00
60 AW 100.00
61 . . . . 75.00
62 . . . . 75.00
63 . . . . 75.00
64 RC. 80.00
65 RC. 80.00
66 AW 125.00
67 thru 78. . . . . @75.00
79 Origin Retold. 80.00
80 thru 86. . . . . @75.00
87 JDa(reprint). 80.00
88 AW 90.00
89 AW,Matt Slade 90.00
90 thru 99 . . . . @60.00
100 JK 65.00
101 JK 60.00
102 JK 60.00
103 JK,The Great Train Robbery. . 60.00
104 JKu(c),DH,Trail of
   Kid Colt. 60.00
105 DH,V:Dakota Dixon 60.00
106 JKu(c),The Circus
   of Crime. 60.00
107 JK,SciFi(c). 75.00
108 BEv 60.00
109 DAy,V:The Barracuda 60.00
110 GC,V:Iron Mask 75.00
111 JKu(c),V:Sam Hawk, The
   Man Hunter 55.00
112 JKu(c),V:Mr. Brown 55.00
113 JKu(c),GC,V:Bull Barton 55.00
114 JKu(c),Return of Iron Mask. . . 55.00
115 JKu(c),V:The Scorpion 55.00
116 JKu(c),GC,V:Dr. Danger &
   Invisible Gunman. 55.00
117 JKu(c),GC,V:The Fatman &
   His Boomerang 55.00
118 V:Scorpion,Bull Barton,
   Dr. Danger. 55.00
119 DAy(c),JK,V:Bassett The
   Badman 55.00
120 Cragsons Ride Again 55.00
121 A:Rawhide Kid,Iron Mask . . . 35.00
122 V:Rattler Ruxton 35.00
123 V:Ringo Barker 35.00
124 A:Phantom Raider. 35.00

Kid Colt Outlaw #103
© Marvel Entertainment Group

125 A:Two-Gun Kid 35.00
126 V:Wes Hardin 35.00
127 thru 129. . . . . @35.00
130 O:Kid Colt 45.00
131 thru 150. . . . . @30.00
151 thru 200 reprints . . . . @25.00
201 thru 228 reprints . . . . @20.00
229 April, 1979. . . . . 20.00

KID FROM DODGE CITY
Atlas, July, 1957—Sept., 1957
1 . . . . 125.00
2 . . . . 65.00

KID FROM TEXAS
Atlas, June, 1957—Aug., 1957
1 . . . . 100.00
2 . . . . 65.00

KID KOMICS
Timely, Feb., 1943
1 SSh(c),BW,O:Captain Wonder
   & Tim Mulrooney I:Whitewash,
   Knuckles,Trixie Trouble,
   Pinto Pete Subbie. 6,000.00
2 AsH(c),F:Captain Wonder
   Subbie, B:Young Allies,
   B:Red Hawk,Tommy Tyme 2,500.00
3 ASh(c),A:The Vision &
   Daredevils 2,000.00
4 ASh(c),B:Destroyer,A:Sub-Mariner,
   E:Red Hawk,Tommy Tyme 1,600.00
5 ASh(c),V:Nazis 1,200.00
6 ASh(c),V:Japanese 1,200.00
7 ASh(c),B;Whizzer 1,100.00
8 ASh(c),V:Train Robbers 1,100.00
9 ASh(c),V:Elves 1,100.00
10 ASh(c),E:Young Allies,
   The Destoyer,The Whizzer 1,100.00
Becomes:

KID MOVIE KOMICS
1946
11 F:Silly Seal,Ziggy Pig
   HK,Hey Look 300.00
Becomes:

RUSTY COMICS
1947
12 F:Rusty,A:Mitzi 225.00
13 Do not Disturb(c). 125.00
14 Beach(c),BW,HK,Hey Look. . . 250.00

15 Picnic(c),HK,Hey Look 175.00
16 Juniors Grades,HK,HeyLook . 175.00
17 John in Trouble,HK,HeyLook . 175.00
18 John Fired. 125.00
19 Fridge raid(c),HK 125.00
20 And Her Family,HK 200.00
21 And Her Family,HK 250.00
22 HK. 250.00
Becomes:

KELLYS, THE
1950
23 F:The Kelly Family(Pop,
   Mom,Mike,Pat & Goliath) . . . 125.00
24 Mike's Date,A;Margie 75.00
25 Wrestling(c). 75.00
Becomes:

SPY CASES
1950
26(#1) Spy stories 275.00
27(#2) BEv,Bondage(c) 175.00
28(#3) Sabotage,A:Douglas
   Grant Secret Agent. 175.00
4 The Secret Invasion 150.00
5 The Vengeance of Comrade
   de Casto 150.00
6 A:Secret Agent Doug Grant . . 150.00
7 GT,A:Doug Grant 150.00
8 Atom Bomb(c),Frozen
   Horror 150.00
9 Undeclared War 125.00
10 Battlefield Adventures. 125.00
11 Battlefield Adventures 125.00
12 Battlefield Adventures 125.00
13 Battlefield Adventures 125.00
14 Battlefield Adventures 125.00
15 Doug Grant 125.00
16 Doug Grant 125.00
17 Doug Grant 125.00
18 Contact in Ankara 125.00
19 Final Issue,Oct., 1953. . . . . . 125.00

KID SLADE GUNFIGHTER
See: MATT SLADE

KILLFRENZY
1 . . . . 2.25
2 Castle Madspike 2.25

KILLPOWER:
THE EARLY YEARS
1993
1 B:MiB,Goes on Rampage 3.25
2 thru 3 O:Killpower . . . . @2.25
4 E:MiB,last issue 2.25

KILLRAVEN
Dec., 2000
Spec. JLi,R:Killraven 3.00

KILLRAVEN
Oct., 2002
1 (of 6) AD,MFm,V:Martians 3.00
2 AD,MFm. 3.00
3 AD,MFm. 3.00
4 AD,MFm. 3.00
5 AD,MFm. 3.00
6 AD,MFm. 3.00

KING ARTHUR & THE
KNIGHTS OF JUSTICE
1993–94
1 Based on Cartoon 2.25
2 Based on Cartoon 2.25
3 Based on Cartoon 2.25

KING CONAN:
See: CONAN THE KING

KINGPIN
Nov., 1997
1-shot StL,JR, bookshelf 48pg. 6.00

KINGPIN
June, 2003
1 SeP,KJ,Wilson Fixk 2.50
2 thru 7 SeP,KJ . . . . @2.50

KISSNATION
1997
1 Rock & Roll, A:X-Men 10.00

KITTY PRYDE:
AGENT OF S.H.I.E.L.D.
Oct., 1997
1 (of 3) LHa,V:Ogun 2.50
2 LHa,V:Ogun 2.50
3 LHa,Ogun's Slave? 2.50

KITTY PRYDE
& WOLVERINE
Nov., 1984
1 AM,V:Ogun. 6.00
2 AM,V:Ogun. 5.00
3 thru 5 AM,V:Ogun. . . . . @5.00
6 AM,D:Ogun, April, 1985. . . . . . . 5.00

Knights of Pendragon #11
© Marvel Entertainment Group

KNIGHTS OF
PENDRAGON
[1st Regular Series], July, 1990
1 GEr 2.75
2 thru 7 . . . . @2.25
8 inc.SBi Poster 2.25
9 V:Bane Fisherman 2.25
10 Cap.Britain/Union Jack 2.25
11 A:Iron Man. 2.25
12 A:Iron Man,Union Jack 2.25
13 O:Pendragon. 2.25
14 A:Mr.Fantastic,Invisible Woman
   Black Panther 2.25
15 BlackPanther/Union Jack T.U. . . 2.25
16 A:Black Panther 2.25

17 D:Albion, Union Jack,
   A:Black Panther. 2.25
18 A:Iron Man,Black Panther. 2.25
[2nd Regular Series], 1992
1 GEr,A:Iron Man,R:Knights of
   Pendragon,V:MyS-TECH 2.25
2 A:Iron Man,Black Knight 2.25
3 PGa,A:Iron Man,Black Knight . . . 2.25
4 Gawain Vs. Bane. 2.25
5 JRe,V:Magpie 2.25
6 A:Spider-Man 2.25
7 A:Spider-Man,V:Warheads. 2.25
8 JRe,A:Spider-Man 2.25
9 A:Spider-Man,Warheads 2.25
10 V:Baron Blood. 2.25
11 . . . . 2.25
12 MyS-TECH Wars,V:Skire 2.25
13 A:Death's Head II 2.25
14 A:Death's Head II 2.25
15 D:Adam,A:Death's Head II 2.25

KRAZY KOMICS
Timely, July, 1942
1 B:Ziggy Pig,Silly Seal 750.00
2 Toughy Tomcat(c) 325.00
3 Toughy Tomcat/Bunny(c) 250.00
4 Toughy Tomcat/Ziggy(c) 250.00
5 Ziggy/Buzz Saw(c) 250.00
6 Toughy/Cannon(c) 250.00
7 Cigar Store Indian(c) 250.00
8 Toughy/Hammock(c) 250.00
9 Hitler(c) 275.00
10 Newspaper(c) 225.00
11 Canoe(c) 225.00
12 Circus(c) 300.00
13 Pirate Treasure(c) 200.00
14 Fishing(c) 200.00
15 Ski-Jump(c) 175.00
16 Airplane(c). 125.00
17 Street corner(c) 125.00
18 Mallet/Bell(c) 125.00
19 Bicycle(c) 125.00
20 Ziggy(c) 125.00
21 Toughy's date(c) 125.00
22 Crystal Ball(c) 125.00
23 Sharks in bathtub(c) 150.00
24 Baseball(c) 125.00
25 HK,Krazy Krow(c) 150.00
26 Super Rabbit(c). 125.00
Becomes:
CINDY COMICS
1947
27 HK,B:Margie,Oscar. 250.00
28 HK,Snow sled(c) 150.00
29 . . . . 150.00
30 . . . . 150.00
31 HK. 150.00
32 . . . . 100.00
33 A;Georgie 100.00
34 thru 40. . . . . @100.00
Becomes:
CRIME CAN'T WIN
1950
41 Crime stories. 300.00
42 . . . . 175.00
43 GT,Horror story 200.00
4 thru 11 . . . . @150.00
12 Sept., 1953 . . . . 125.00

KRAZY KOMICS
Timely
[2nd Series], 1948
1 BW,HK,B:Eustice Hayseed . . . 600.00
2 BW,O:Powerhouse Pepper . . . 400.00

KRAZY KROW
Summer, 1945
1 B:Krazy Krow 250.00
2 . . . . 150.00
3 Winter, 1945-46 . . . . 150.00

KREE-SKRULL WAR
Sept.–Oct., 1983
1 & 2 JB,NA,reprints . . . . @5.00

KRULL
Nov.–Dec., 1983
1 Ph(c),BBI,movie adapt. 2.50
2 BBI,rep.,Marvel Super Spec. . . . 2.50

KULL THE CONQUEROR
[1st Series], June, 1971
1 MSe,RA,WW,A King Comes
   Riding,O:Kull 50.00
2 MSe,JSe,Shadow Kingdom. . . . 20.00
3 MSe,JSe,Death Dance of
   Thulsa Doom. 20.00
4 MSe,JSe,Night o/t Red Slayers. 20.00
5 MSe,JSe,Kingdom By the Sea . 20.00
6 MSe,JSe,Lurker Beneath
   the Sea 15.00
7 MSe,JSe,Delcardes'Cat,
   A:Thulsa Doom 15.00
8 MSe,JSe,Wolfshead 15.00
9 MSe,JSe,The Scorpion God . . . 15.00
10 MSe,Swords o/t White Queen . 15.00
11 MP,King Kull Must Die, O:Kull
   cont.,A:Thulsa Doom. 10.00
12 MP,SB,Moon of Blood,V:Thulsa
   Doom,B:SD,B.U.stories 10.00
13 MP,AM,Torches From Hell,
   V:Thulsa Doom 10.00
14 MP,JA,The Black Belfry,
   A:Thulsa Doom 10.00
15 MP,Wings o/t Night-Beast,
   E:SD,B.U.stories 10.00
16 EH,Tiger in the Moon,
   A:Thulsa Doom 12.00
17 AA,EH,Thing from Emerald
   Darkness 6.00
18 EH,AA,Keeper of Flame
   & Frost. 6.00
19 EH,AA,The Crystal Menace . . . 6.00
20 EH,AA,Hell Beneath Atlantis. . . 6.00
21 City of the Crawling Dead. 10.00

Kull the Conqueror #11
© Marvel Entertainment Group

22 Talons of the Devil-Birds...... 10.00
23 Demon Shade.............. 10.00
24 Screams in the Dark......... 9.00
25 A Lizard's Throne 9.00
26 Into Death's Dimension....... 9.00
27 The World Within 9.00
28 Creature and the Crown,
    A:Thulsa Doom,............. 9.00
29 To Sit the Topaz Throne,
    V:Thulsa Doom, final issue ... 9.00

[2nd Series], 1982

1 JB,Brule.................... 4.00
2 Misareenia 3.00

[3rd Series], 1983–85

1 JB,BWi,DG,Iraina............. 3.50
2 JB,Battle to the Death 3.00
3 JB......................... 3.00
4 JB......................... 3.00
5 JB 3.00
6 JB 3.00
7 JB,Masquerade Death 3.00
8 JB 3.00
9 JB 3.00
10 JB 3.00

KULL AND THE BARBARIANS
May, 1975

1 NA,GK,reprint Kull #1 .... 20.00
2 BBI,reprint,Dec., 1983........ 15.00
3 NA,HC,O:Red Sonja 15.00

LABRYNTH
1986–87

1 Movie adapt................. 3.00
2 and 3 .... @3.00

LAFF-A-LYMPICS
1978–79

1 F;Hanna Barbera 35.00
2 thru 5 .... @25.00
6 thru 13 .... @30.00

LANA
Aug., 1948

1 F:Lana Lane The Show Girl,
    A:Rusty,B:Millie 225.00
2 HK,Hey Look,A:Rusty 125.00
3 Show(c),B:Nellie 100.00
4 Ship(c) 100.00
5 Audition(c) 100.00
6 Stop sign(c) 100.00
7 Beach(c) 100.00
Becomes:

LITTLE LANA
1949

8 Little Lana(c) 100.00
9 Final Issue,March, 1950 ..... 100.00

LANCE BARNES: POST NUKE DICK
Epic, 1993

1 I:Lance Barnes............. 2.50
2 Cigarettes 2.50
3 Warring Mall Tribe 2.50
4 V:Ex-bankers,last issue 2.50

LAST AMERICAN
Epic, 1990–91

1 .... 3.50
2 .... 3.00
3 .... 2.50
4 Final issue.................. 2.25

THE LAST AVENGERS STORY
1995

1 PDd, Alterverse,Future world.... 6.00
2 PDd, Final fate,fully painted..... 6.00
TPB PDd,AOI, rep. Alterniverse
    story, 96pg................ 13.00

The Last Starfighter #3
© Marvel Entertainment Group

LAST STARFIGHTER, THE
Oct.–Dec., 1984

1 JG(c),BBI,Movie adapt......... 2.25
2 Movie adapt................. 2.25
3 BBI 2.25

LAWBREAKERS ALWAYS LOSE!
Spring, 1948–Oct., 1949

1 Partial Ph(c),Adam and Eve,
    HK,Giggles and Grins 400.00
2 FBI V:Fur Theives 250.00
3 .... 175.00
4 Asylum(c) 200.00
5 .... 200.00
6 Pawnbroker(c) 200.00
7 Crime at Midnight 350.00
8 Prison Break 150.00
9 Ph(c),He Prowled at Night ... 150.00
10 Phc(c),I Met My Murderer.... 150.00

LAWDOG
1993

1 B:CDi(s),FH,I:Lawdog 2.50
2 FH,V:Vocal-yokel Cultist 2.25
3 FH,Manical Nazis............. 2.25
4 FH,V:Zombies 2.25
5 FH 2.25
6 FH 2.25
7 FH,V:Zombies 2.25
8 FH,w/card 2.25
9 FH,w/card 2.25
10 last issue, w/card 2.25

LAWDOG & GRIMROD: TERROR AT THE CROSSROADS
1993

1 .... 3.50

LEGION OF MONSTERS
Sept., 1975
(black & white magazine)

1 NA(c),GM,I&O:Legion of
    Monsters,O:Manphibian 40.00

LEGION OF NIGHT
Oct., 1991

1 WPo/SW,A:Fin Fang Foom 5.50
2 WPo,V:Fin Fang Foom 5.50

LETHAL FOES OF SPIDER-MAN
1993

1 B:DFr(s),SMc,R:Stegron 3.00
2 SMc,A:Stegron.............. 3.00
3 SMc,V:Spider-Man............ 3.00
4 E:DFr(s),SMc,Last Issue 3.00

LIFE OF CAPTAIN MARVEL
Aug., 1985

1 rep.Iron Man #55,
    Capt.Marvel #25,26.......... 9.00
2 rep.Capt.Marvel#26-28 .... 6.50
3 rep.Capt.Marvel#28-30
    Marvel Feature #12.......... 6.00
4 rep.Marvel Feature #12,Capt.
    Marvel #31,32,Daredevil#105 .. 6.00
5 rep.Capt.Marvel #32-#34....... 6.00

LIFE OF CHRIST
1993

1 Birth of Christ............... 5.00
2 MW,The Easter Story......... 5.00

LIFE OF POPE JOHN-PAUL II
1983

1 JSt, Jan., 1983.............. 6.00
1a Special reprint 4.00

LIFE WITH MILLIE
See: DATE WITH MILLIE

LIGHT AND DARKNESS WAR
Epic, Oct., 1988

1 .... 4.00
2 .... 3.00
3 thru 6 Dec., 1989 .... @2.50

LINDA CARTER, STUDENT NURSE
Atlas, Sept., 1961

1 .... 75.00
2 thru 9, Jan., 1963 .... @50.00

LION KING

1 based on Movie.............. 2.75

LI'L KIDS
Aug., 1970–June, 1973

1 .... 90.00
2 thru 12 .... @60.00

LI'L PALS
Sept., 1972

1 .... 75.00
2 thru 5, May, 1973 .... @50.00

MARVEL

LITTLE ASPRIN
July, 1949
1 HK,A;Oscar 200.00
2 HK 125.00
3 Dec., 1949 . . . . 75.00

LITTLE LANA
See: LANA

LITTLE LENNY
June, 1949
1 . . . . 125.00
2 . . . . 75.00
3 November, 1949 . . . . 75.00

LITTLE LIZZIE
June, 1949
1 Roller Skating(c) 150.00
2 Soda(c) 75.00
3 Movies(c) 75.00
4 Lizzie(c) 75.00
5 Lizzie/Swing(c) April,1950 . . . . 75.00
[2nd Series], Sept., 1953
1 . . . . 75.00
2 . . . . 50.00
3 Jan., 1954 . . . . 50.00

LITTLE MERMAID, THE
1993
1 . . . . 3.50
2 Reception for Pacifica royalty . . . 2.50
3 TrR,Ariel joins fish club 2.50
4 . . . . 2.50
5 . . . . 2.50
6 TrR,Ariel decorates coral"tree" . . 2.50
7 TrR,Flogglefish banished 2.50
8 . . . . 2.50
9 Annual Sea Horse Tournament . 2.50
10 TrR,AnnualBlowfishTournament . 2.50
11 TrR,Sharkeena,King Triton 2.50
12 . . . . 2.50
13 Lobster Monster 2.50

LOGAN
1-shot HMe,48pg 6.00
1-shot Logan: Path of the
   Warrior (1996) 5.00
1-shot Logan: Shadow Society,
   HMe,TCk Early life of
   Wolverine (1996) 5.00

LOGAN'S RUN
Jan., 1977
1 GP,From Movie 15.00
2 GP,Cathedral Kill 7.00
3 GP,Lair of Laser Death 7.00
4 GP,Dread Sanctuary 7.00
5 GP,End Run 7.00
6 MZ,B.U.Thanos/Drax 25.00
7 TS,Cathedral Prime 7.00

LOKI
July, 2004
1 (of 4) 7.50
2 thru 4 . . . . @7.50

LONGSHOT
Sept., 1985
1 AAd,WPo(i),BA,I:Longshot 8.00
2 AAd,WPo(i),I:RicoshetRita 6.00
3 AAd,WPo(i),I:Mojo,Spiral 6.00
4 AAd,WPo(i),A:Spider-Man 6.00
5 AAd,WPo(i),A:Dr. Strange 6.00
6 AAd,WPo(i),A:Dr. Strange 6.00

TPB Reprints #1-#6 . . . . 16.95
1-shot, JMD,MZi,AW (1997) 4.00

LOOSE CANNONS
1 and 2 DAn . . . . @2.50
3 DAn 2.75

LORNA, THE JUNGLE GIRL
Atlas, 1953–57
1 Terrors of the Jungle,O:Lorna . 450.00
2 Headhunter's Strike
   I:Greg Knight 225.00
3 . . . . 200.00
4 . . . . 200.00
5 . . . . 200.00
6 RH(c),GT 150.00
7 RH(c) 150.00
8 Jungle Queen Strikes Again . 150.00
9 . . . . 150.00
10 White Fang 150.00
11 Death From the Skies 150.00
12 Day of Doom 125.00
13 thru 17 . . . . @125.00
18 AW(c) 150.00
19 thru 26 . . . . @100.00

LOVE ADVENTURES
Atlas, Oct., 1949
1 Ph(c) 200.00
2 BP,Ph(c),Tyrone Power/
   Gene Tierney 175.00
3 thru 12 . . . . @100.00
Becomes:

ACTUAL CONFESSIONS
1952
13 . . . . 65.00
14 Dec., 1952 . . . . 65.00

LOVE DRAMAS
Oct., 1949
1 Ph(c),JKa 200.00
2 Jan., 1950 . . . . 150.00

LOVE ROMANCES
See: IDEAL

LOVERS
See: ALL-SELECT COMICS

LOVE SECRETS
Oct., 1949
1 . . . . 175.00
2 Jan., 1950 . . . . 125.00

LUNATIK
1995
1 KG 2.25
2 V:The Avengers 2.25
3 conclusion 2.25

MACHINE MAN
April, 1978
1 JK,From 2001 . . . . 20.00
2 JK 10.00
3 JK,V:Ten-For,The Mean
   Machine 10.00
4 JK,V:Ten-For,Battle on A
   Busy Street 10.00
5 JK,V:Ten-For,Day of the
   Non-Hero 10.00
6 JK,V:Ten-For 10.00
7 JK,With A Nation Against Him . . 10.00

Machine Man #10
© Marvel Entertainment Group

8 JK,Escape:Impossible 10.00
9 JK,In Final Battle 10.00
10 SD,Birth of A Super-Hero 6.00
11 SD,V;Binary Bug 6.00
12 SD,Where walk the Gods 6.00
13 SD,Xanadu 6.00
14 SD,V:Machine Man 6.00
15 SD,A:Thing,Human Torch 6.00
16 SD,I:Baron Brimstone And the
   Satan Squad 6.00
17 SD,Madam Menace 6.00
18 A:Alpha Flight 20.00
19 I:Jack o'Lantern 20.00

MACHINE MAN
[Limited-Series]
Oct., 1984
1 HT,BWS,V:Baintronics 4.00
2 HT,BWS,C:Iron Man of 2020 . . . 4.00
3 HT,BWS,I:Iron Man of 2020 . . . . 4.00
4 HT,BWS,V:Iron Man of 2020 . . . 4.00
TPB rep.#1-4 . . . . 5.95

MACHINE MAN 2020
1994
1 rep. limited series #1–#2 . . . . . 2.25
2 rep. limited series #3–#4 . . . . . 2.25

MAD ABOUT MILLIE
April, 1969
1 . . . . 100.00
2 thru 3 . . . . @65.00
4 thru 10 . . . . @40.00
11 thru 16 . . . . @35.00
17 Dec., 1970 . . . . 35.00
Ann.#1 . . . . 40.00

MADBALLS
Star, Sept., 1986
1 Based on Toys 4.00
2 thru 9 . . . . @4.00
10 June, 1988 . . . . 4.00

MAD DOG
1 from Bob TV Show 2.50
2 V:Trans World Trust Corp 2.50
3 V:Cigarette Criminals 2.50
4 V:Dogs of War 2.50
5 thru 6 . . . . @2.50

MADE MEN
May, 1998
1-shot HMe gangster epic 6.00

MADROX
Sept., 2004
1 (of 5) PDd(s),F:Jamie Madrox . . 3.00
2 PDd(s) 3.00

MAGIK
Dec., 1983
1 JB,TP,F:Storm and Illyana 4.00
2 JB,TP,A:Belasco,Sym 3.00
3 TP,A:New Mutants,Belasco 3.00
4 TP,V:Belasco,A:Sym 3.00

MAGNETO
1993
0 JD,JBo,rep. origin stories. 6.00
0a Gold ed. 8.00
0b Platinum ed. 10.00

MAGNETO
1996
1 (of 4) PrM,KJo,JhB, Joseph. 2.50
2 PrM,KJo,JhB, Joseph's search
　for his past life 2.50
3 PrM,KJo,JhB 2.50
4 PrM,KJo,JhB, concl. 2.50
TPB 192-pg.. . . . . 20.00

MAGNETO:
DARK SEDUCTION
April, 2000
1 (of 4) FaN,X-Men: Revolution . . . 3.00
2 FaN,Scarlet Witch 3.00
3 FaN,RCz,V:Scarlet Witch 3.00
4 FaN,RCz,concl. 3.00

MAGNETO REX
March, 1999
1 (of 3) BPe,takes over Genosha . . 2.50
1a signed 20.00
2 BPe,V:Rogue 2.50
3 BPe,A:Rogue,Quicksilver 2.50
GN Magneto Ascendant,
　96-page rep. 4.00

MAN COMICS
Atlas, 1949–53
1 GT, Revenge 275.00
2 GT, Fury in his Fists 175.00
3 Mantrap 125.00
4 The Fallen Hero 125.00
5 Laugh,Fool,Laugh 125.00
6 Black Hate 125.00
7 The Killer 125.00
8 BEv,An Eye For an Eye 125.00
9 B:War Issues,Here Comes
　Sergeant Smith 100.00
10 Korean Communism 100.00
11 RH,Cannon Fodder 100.00
12 The Black Hate 100.00
13 GC,RH,Beach Head 100.00
14 GT,No Prisoners 110.00
15 . . . . 100.00
16 . . . . 65.00
17 RH. 65.00
18 thru 20 . . . . @65.00
21 GC. 65.00
22 BEv,BK,JSt 75.00
23 thru 26 . . . . @65.00
27 E:War Issues. 65.00
28 Where Mummies Prowl. 65.00

Man #9
© *Marvel Entertainment Group*

MANDRAKE
1995
1 fully painted series 3.25
2 V:Octon 3.25
3 final issue 3.25

MAN FROM ATLANTIS
Feb., 1978–Aug., 1978
1 TS,From TV Series,O:Mark
　Harris 20.00
2 FR,FS,The Bermuda Triangle
　Trap 12.00
3 FR,FS,Undersea Shadow 12.00
4 FR,FS,Beware the Killer
　Spores 12.00
5 FR,FS,The Ray of the
　Red Death 12.00
6 FR,FS,Bait for the Behemoth . . 12.00
7 FR,FS,Behold the Land
　Forgotten 12.00

MAN-THING
[1st Series] Jan., 1974
1 FB,JM,A:Howard the Duck 65.00
2 VM,ST,Hell Hath No Fury 25.00
3 VM,JA,I:Original Foolkiller 20.00
4 VM,JA,O&D:Foolkiller 17.00
5 MP,Night o/t Laughing Dead . . . 17.00
6 MP,V:Soul-Slayers,Drug Issue. . 17.00
7 MP,A Monster Stalks Swamp. . . 17.00
8 MP,Man Into Monster. 17.00
9 MP,Deathwatch 17.00
10 MP,Nobody Dies Forever 17.00
11 MP,Dance to the Murder 17.00
12 KJ,Death-Cry of a Dead Man . . 10.00
13 TS,V:Captain Fate 10.00
14 AA,V:Captain Fate 10.00
15 A Candle for Saint Cloud 10.00
16 JB,TP,Death of a Legend 10.00
17 JM,Book Burns in Citrusville. . . 10.00
18 JM,Chaos on the Campus 10.00
19 JM,FS,I:Scavenger 10.00
20 JM,A:Spider-Man,Daredevil,
　Shang-Chi,Thing 11.00
21 JM,O:Scavenger,Man Thing . . . 10.00
22 JM,C:Howard the Duck. 10.00
G-Size #1 MP,SD,JK,rep.TheGlob. . 5.00
G-Size #2 JB,KJ,The
　Monster Runs Wild 4.00
G-Size #3 AA,A World He
　Never Made. 4.00
G-Size #4 FS,EH,inc.Howard the
　Duck vs.Gorko. 4.00

Man-Thing Giant Size #1
© *Marvel Entertainment Group*

G-Size #5 DA,EH,inc.Howard the
　Duck vs.Vampire 6.00
[2nd Series] 1979–1981
1 JM,BWi. 11.00
2 BWi,JM,Himalayan Nightmare. . 10.00
3 BWi.JM,V:Snowman 10.00
4 BWi,DP,V:Mordo,A:Dr Strange . 10.00
5 DP,BWi,This Girl is Terrified. . . . 10.00
6 DP,BWi,Fraternity Rites 10.00
7 BWi,DP Return of Captain Fate. 10.00
8 BWi,DP,V:Captain Fate 10.00
9 BWi(c),Save the Life of My
　Own Child 10.00
10 BWi,DP,Swampfire 10.00
11 Final issue 10.00
[3rd Series] Oct., 1997
1 JMD,LSh, non-code 3.00
2 JMD,LSh, reunion with ex-wife,
　A:Dr. Strange 3.00
3 JMD,LSh, visit to Devil Slayer . . . 3.00
4 JMD,LSh, V:Devil-Slayer 3.00
5 JMD,LSh, new abilities revealed . 3.00
6 JMD,LSh, V:Cult of Entropy. 3.00
7 JMD,LSh, Muck Monster, Namor. 3.00
8 JMD,LSh, Muck Monster turned
　back into Ted Sallis 3.00
Storyline continues in Strange Tales

MAN-THING
July, 2004
1 (of 3) movie prequel. 3.00
2 movie prequel,pt.2 . . . . 3.00
3 movie prequel,pt.3 . . . . 3.00
TPB Whatever Knows Fear. 13.00

MARINES AT WAR
See: DEVIL-DOG DUGAN

MARINES IN ACTION
Atlas, June, 1955
1 B:Rock Murdock,Boot Camp
　Brady 125.00
2 thru 13 . . . . @100.00
14 Sept., 1957 . . . . 100.00

MARINES IN BATTLE
Atlas, Aug., 1954
1 RH,B:Iron Mike McGraw 250.00
2 . . . . 125.00
3 thru 6 . . . . @100.00

7 thru 17 . . . . @100.00
18 thru 22 . . . . @75.00
23 . . . . 100.00
24 . . . . 75.00
25 Sept., 1958 . . . . 100.00

MARK HAZZARD: MERC
Nov., 1986–Oct., 1987
1 GM,O:Mark Hazard 2.25
2 GM 2.25
3 M,Arab Terrorists 2.25
4 thru 8 GM . . . . @2.25
9 NKu/AKu 2.25
10 thru 12 . . . . @2.25
Ann.#1 D:Merc 2.25

MARSHALL LAW
Epic, 1987–89
1 . . . . 4.50
2 . . . . 3.00
3 thru 6 . . . . @2.50

MARVEL ACTION HOUR: FANTASTIC FOUR
1994–95
1 regular 2.25
1a bagged with insert print from
    animated series 3.00
2 thru 8 . . . . @2.25

MARVEL ACTION HOUR: IRON MAN
1994–95
1 regular 2.25
1a bagged with insert print from
    animated series 3.25
2 thru 8 . . . . @2.25

MARVEL ACTION UNIVERSE
TV Tie-in, Jan., 1989
1 Rep.Spider-Man & Friends 4.00

MARVEL ADVENTURES STARRING DAREDEVIL
Dec., 1975–Oct., 1976
1 Rep,Daredevil #22 . . . . 15.00
2 thru 6, Rep.,Daredevil . . . . @7.00

Marvel Action Hour: Iron Man #2
© Marvel Entertainment Group

MARVEL ADVENTURES
Feb., 1997
1 RMc,F:The Hulk 2.25
2 RMc,F:Spider-Man 2.25
3 RMc,F:Quicksilver & Scarlet
    Witch 2.25
4 RMc,BHr,F:Hulk,V:Brotherhood
    of Evil Mutants 2.25
5 RMc,BHr,F:Spider-Man, The
    X-Men 2.25
6 RMc,BHr,A:Spider-Man,Invisible
    Woman, Human Torch 2.25
7 RMc,F:Hulk,V:Tyrannus 2.25
8 RMc,V:Molto 2.25
9 RMc,F:Fantastic Four,
    Subterranean War, concl. 2.25
10 RMc,Sky-Rider vs. Gladiator . . . 2.25
11 RMc,F:Spider-Man,Sandman . . . 2.25
12 RMc,F:Fantastic Four,V:Frightful
    Four 2.25
13 AM,F:Spider-Man, Silver Surfer . 2.25
14 RMc,F:The Hulk,A:Dr. Strange,
    Juggernaut 2.25
15 RMc,F:X-Men,V:Beast's army . . . 2.25
16 RMc,F:Silver Surfer 2.25
17 RMc,F:Spider-Man, Iron Man . . . 2.25
18 RMc,F:Sentinel of Liberty 2.25
19 RMc,F:The Avengers 2.25
20 RMc,F:Iron Man 2.25

MARVEL AGE: FANTASTIC FOUR
April, 2004
1 V:Mole Man 2.25
2 V:Skrulls 2.25
3 V:Miracle Man 2.25
4 F:Namor,the Sub-Mariner 2.25
5 V:Doctor Doom 2.25
6 V:Doctor Doom 2.25
7 Invaders from Planet X 2.25
Digest #1 . . . . 6.00

HULK
Sept., 2004
1 . . . . 1.75
2 . . . . 1.75

MARY JANE
June, 2004
1 thru 4 . . . . @2.25
Digest #1 Circle of Friends 6.00

SENTINEL
2004
1 Salvage, digest 8.00
2 No Hero, digest 8.00

SPIDER-MAN
March, 2004
1 V:Vulture 2.25
2 V:Doc Ock 2.25
3 V:the Sandman 2.25
4 V:Doctor Doom 2.25
5 V:Lizard 2.25
6 V:Vulture 2.25
7 The Living Brain 2.25
8 Man Called Electro 2.25
9 The Enforcers 2.25
10 Return of Doctor Octopus 2.25
11 Unmasked Doctor Octopus 2.25
12 The Menace of Mysterio 2.25
13 Grotesque Green Goblin 2.25
14 Kraven the Hunter 2.25
Digest #1 thru #4 . . . . @6.00

SPIDER-MAN TEAM-UP
Sept., 2004
1 F:Fantastic Four 1.75
2 F:Captain America 1.75

MARVEL & DC PRESENTS
Nov., 1982
1 WS,TA,X-Men & Titans,A:Darkseid,
    Deathstroke(3rd App.), ... 25.00

MARVEL BOY
Dec., 1950
1 RH,O:Marvel Boy,Lost World 1,400.00
2 BEv,The Zero Hour 1,000.00
Becomes:

ASTONISHING
1951
3 BEv,Marvel Boy,V:Mr Death . 1,200.00
4 BEv,Stan Lee,The
    Screaming Tomb 900.00
5 BEv,Horro in the Caves of
    Doom 900.00
6 BEv,My Coffin is Waiting
    E:Marvel Boy 900.00
7 JR,JMn,Nightmare 400.00
8 RH,Behind the Wall 400.00
9 RH(c),The Little Black Box . . . 400.00
10 BEv,Walking Dead 400.00
11 BF,JSt.Mr Mordeau 350.00
12 GC,BEv,Horror Show 350.00
13 BK,MSy,Ghouls Gold 400.00
14 BK,The Long Jump Down . . . 400.00
15 BEv(c),Grounds for Death . . . 350.00
16 BEv(c),DAy,SSh,Don't Make
    a Ghoul of Yourself 350.00
17 Who Was the Wilmach
    Werewolf? 350.00
18 BEv(c),JR,Vampire at my
    Window 350.00
19 BK,Back From the Grave 350.00
20 GC,Mystery at Midnight 350.00
21 Manhunter 275.00
22 RH(c),Man Against Werewolf . 275.00
23 The Woman in Black 300.00
24 JR,The Stone Face 300.00
25 RC,I Married a Zombie 300.00
26 RH(c),I Died Too Often 275.00
27 . . . . 275.00
28 TLw,No Evidence 275.00
29 BEv(c),GC,Decapitation(c) . . . 275.00
30 Tentacled eyeball story 350.00
31 JMn 225.00
32 A Vampire Takes a Wife 225.00
33 SMo,JMn 225.00
34 JMn,Transformation 225.00
35 . . . . 225.00
36 Pithecanthrope Giant 225.00
37 BEv,TLw,Poor Pierre 225.00
38 The Man Who Didn't Belong . . 175.00
39 . . . . 175.00
40 . . . . 175.00
41 MD 175.00
42 TLw 175.00
43 BP,JR 175.00
44 RC,BP 190.00
45 BK 190.00
46 . . . . 190.00
47 BK,JO,BEv 190.00
48 BP 175.00
49 BEv 175.00
50 DCn 175.00
51 . . . . 175.00
52 GM 175.00
53 SD,JF,BEv 190.00
54 BEv 190.00
55 BEv 200.00
56 JMn,JK 175.00
57 JR 200.00
58 JF,JO 175.00
59 TSe,BEv 175.00
60 JF,BEv 175.00
61 GM,JO,JR,BEv 175.00
62 MD,BEv 175.00

63 BEv,August, 1957 . . . . 175.00

MARVEL BOY
June, 2000
1 (of 6) GMo,F:Noh-Varr. 4.00
2 GMo,V:Human Race 3.50
3 GMo,Hexus 3.50
4 GMo,Exterminatrix. 3.50
5 GMo,Oubliette 3.50
6 GMo,V:Dr. Midas,concl. 3.50
TPB rep.,144-page. 16.00

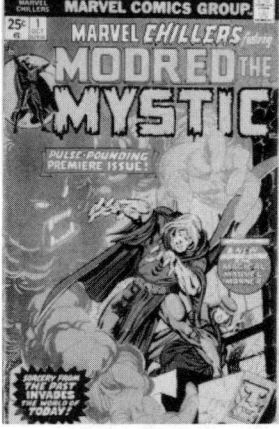

Marvel Chillers #1
© Marvel Entertainment Group

MARVEL CHILLERS
Oct., 1975
1 GK(c),I:Mordred the Mystic 20.00
2 E:Mordred 12.00
3 HC/BWr(c),B:Tigra,The Were
  Woman 22.00
4 V:Kraven The Hunter 12.00
5 V:Rat Pack,A:Red Wolf 12.00
6 RB(c),JBy,V:Red Wolf 12.00
7 JK(c),GT,V:Super Skrull
  E:Tigra,Oct., 1976 . . . . 12.00
GN MGu(s),LSh,F:The Hulk 10.00
GN LHa(s) F:Wolverine 10.00

MARVEL CHRISTMAS SPECIAL
1 DC/AAd/KJ/SB/RLm,A:Ghost Rider
  X-Men,Spider-Man. 2.25

MARVEL CLASSICS COMICS
1976–78
1 GK/DA(c),B:Reprints from
  Pendulum Illustrated Comics
  Dr.Jekyll & Mr. Hyde 25.00
2 GK(c),AN,Time Machine 15.00
3 GK/KJ(c) The Hunchback of
  Notre Dame 15.00
4 GK/DA(c),20,000 Leagues–
  Beneath the Sea by Verne . . . 15.00
5 GK(c),RN,Black Beauty 15.00
6 GK(c),Gullivers Travels 15.00
7 GK(c),Tom Sawyer 15.00
8 GK(c),AN,Moby Dick 15.00
9 GK(c),NR,Dracula 15.00
10 GK(c),Red Badge of Courage . 15.00
11 GK(c),Mysterious Island 12.00
12 GK/DA(c),AN,3 Musketeers . . . 12.00

13 GK(c),Last of the Mohicans . . . 12.00
14 GK(c),War of the Worlds. 12.00
15 GK(c),Treasure Island. 12.00
16 GK(c),Ivanhoe. 10.00
17 JB/ECh(c),The Count of
  Monte Cristo 10.00
18 ECh(c),The Odsyssey. 10.00
19 JB(c),Robinson Crusoe. 10.00
20 Frankenstein 10.00
21 GK(c),Master of the World 10.00
22 GK(c),Food of the Gods 10.00
23 Moonstone by Wilkie Collins. . . 10.00
24 GK/RN(c),She. 10.00
25 The Invisible Man by H.G.Wells 10.00
26 JB(c),The Illiad by Homer. 10.00
27 Kidnapped. 10.00
28 MGo(1st art) The Pit and
  the Pendulum 12.00
29 The Prisoner of Zenda 10.00
30 The Arabian Nights 10.00
31 The First Men in the Moon 10.00
32 GK(c),White Fang. 10.00
33 The Prince and the Pauper. . . . 10.00
34 AA,Robin Hood 10.00
35 FBe,Alice in Wonderland 10.00
36 A Christmas Carol. 10.00

MARVEL COLLECTORS ITEM CLASSICS
Feb., 1965
1 SD,JK,reprint FF #2. . . . . 150.00
2 SD,JK,reprint FF #3. . . . . 75.00
3 SD,JK,reprint FF #4. . . . . 65.00
4 SD,JK,reprint FF #7. . . . . 65.00
5 thru 10 SD,JK,rep.F.Four . . . @50.00
11 thru 22 SD,JK,rep.F.Four . . . @35.00
Becomes:

MARVEL'S GREATEST COMICS
1969–81
23 thru 34 SD,JK,rep.F.Four . . . @25.00
35 thru 37 JK,rep.F.Four . . . . . @15.00
38 thru 50 JK,rep.F.Four . . . . . @10.00
51 thru 75 JK,rep.F.Four . . . . . . @7.00
76 thru 96 rep.F.Four . . . . @6.00

MARVEL COMICS
Oct.-Nov., 1939
1 FP(c),BEv,CBu,O:Sub-Mariner
  I&B:The Angel,A:Human Torch,
  Ka-Zar,Jungle Terror,
  B:The Masked Raider . . 350,000.00
Becomes:

MARVEL MYSTERY COMICS
2 CSM(c),BEv,CBu,PGn,
  B:American, Ace,Human
  Torch,Sub-Mariner,Ka-Zar 40,000.00
3 ASh(c),BEv,CBu,PGn,
  E:American Ace 20,000.00
4 ASh(c),BEv,CBu,PGn,
  I&B:Electro,The Ferret,
  Mystery Detective. 18,000.00
5 ASh(c),BEv,CBu,PGn,
  Human Torch(c) 35,000.00
6 ASh(c),BEv,CBu,PGn,
  Angel(c) 11,000.00
7 ASh(c),BEv,CBu,PGn,
  Bondage(c) 11,000.00
8 ASh(c),BEv,CBu,PGn,Human
  TorchV:Sub-Mariner 16,000.00
9 ASh(c),BEv,CBu,PGn,Human
  Torch V:Sub-Mariner(c) . . 38,000.00
10 ASh(c),BEv,CBu,PGn,B:Terry
  Vance Boy Detective 12,000.00
11 ASh(c),BEv,CBu,PGn,
  Human Torch V:Nazis(c). . . 5,000.00

Marvel Mystery Comics #9
© Marvel Entertainment Group

12 ASh(c),BEv,CBu,
  PGn,Angel(c) 5,500.00
13 ASh(c),BEv,CBu,PGn,S&K,
  I&B:The Vision 7,500.00
14 ASh(c),BEv,CBu,PGn,S&K,
  Sub-Mariner V:Nazis 3,500.00
15 ASh(c),BEv,CBu,PGn,S&K,
  Sub-Mariner(c) 3,500.00
16 ASh(c),BEv,CBu,PGn,S&K,
  HumanTorch/NaziAirbase. . . 3,500.00
17 ASh(c),BEv,CBu,PGn,S&K
  Human Torch/Sub-Mariner 3,800.00
18 ASh(c),BEv,CBu,PGn,S&K,
  Human Torch & Toro(c) . . . 3,300.00
19 ASh(c),BEv,CBu,PGn,S&K,
  O:Toro,E:Electro 3,300.00
20 ASh(c),BEv,CBu,PGn,S&K,
  O:The Angel 3,300.00
21 ASh(c),BEv,CBu,PGn,S&K,
  I&B:The Patriot. 3,200.00
22 ASh(c),BEv,CBu,PGn,S&K,
  Toro/Bomb(c) 2,800.00
23 ASh(c),BEv,CBu,PGn,S&K,
  O:Vision,E:The Angel 2,800.00
24 ASh(c),BEv,CBu,S&K,
  Human Torch(c) 2,800.00
25 BEv,CBu,S&K,ASh Nazi(c) . 2,800.00
26 ASh(c),BEv,CBu,S&K,
  Sub-Mariner(c) 2,500.00
27 ASh(c),BEv,CBu,
  S&K,E:Ka-Zar. 2,500.00
28 ASh(c),BEv,CBu,S&K,Bondage
  (c),B:Jimmy Jupiter 2,500.00
29 ASh(c),BEv,CBu,Bondage(c) 2,500.00
30 BEv,CBu,Pearl Harbor(c) . . 2,500.00
31 BEv,CBu,Human Torch(c) . . 2,200.00
32 CBu,I:The Boboes 2,200.00
33 ASHc(c),CBu,Japanese(c) . . 2,200.00
34 ASh(c),CBu,V:Hitler 2,500.00
35 ASh(c),Beach Assault(c) . . . 2,200.00
36 ASh(c),Nazi Invasion of NY . 2,200.00
37 SSh(c),Nazi(c) 2,200.00
38 SSh(c),Battlefield(c). 2,200.00
39 ASh(c),Nazis/U.S(c). 2,200.00
40 ASh(c),Zeppelin(c) 2,200.00
41 ASh(c),Jap. Command(c) . . 2,000.00
42 ASh(c),Japanese Sub(c) . . . 2,000.00
43 ASh(c),Destroyed Bridge(c). 2,000.00
44 ASh(c),Nazi Super Plane(c). 2,000.00
45 ASh(c),Nazi(c) 2,000.00
46 ASh(c),Hitler Bondage(c). . . 2,000.00
47 ASh(c),Ruhr Valley Dam(c) . 2,000.00
48 ASh(c),E:Jimmy Jupiter,
  Vision,Allied Invasion(c) . . . 2,000.00

49 SSh(c),O:Miss America,
  Bondage(c) 2,500.00
50 ASh(c),Bondage(c),Miss
  Patriot 2,000.00
51 ASh(c),Nazi Torture(c) 1,800.00
52 ASh(c),Bondage(c). 1,800.00
53 ASh(c),Bondage(c). 1,800.00
54 ASh(c),Bondage(c). 1,800.00
55 ASh(c),Bondage(c). 1,800.00
56 ASh(c),Bondage(c). 1,800.00
57 ASh(c),Torture/Bondage(c) . 1,800.00
58 ASh(c),Torture(c). 1,800.00
59 ASh(c),Testing Room(c). . . . 1,800.00
60 ASh(c),Japanese Gun(c) . . 1,800.00
61 Torturer Chamber(c) 1,800.00
62 ASh(c),Violent(c) 1,800.00
63 ASh(c),Nazi High
  Command(c). 1,800.00
64 ASh(c),Last Nazi(c) 1,800.00
65 ASh(c),Bondage(c). 1,800.00
66 ASh(c),Last Japanese(c) . . . 1,800.00
67 ASh(c),Treasury raid(c) 1,600.00
68 ASh(c),Torture Chamber(c) . 1,600.00
69 ASh(c),Torture Chamber(c) . 1,600.00
70 Cops & Robbers(c) 1,600.00
71 ASh(c),Egyptian(c). 1,600.00
72 Police(c) 1,600.00
73 Werewolf Headlines(c). 1,600.00
74 ASh(c),Robbery(c),E:The
  Patriot. 1,600.00
75 Tavern(c),B:Young Allies . . . 1,600.00
76 ASh(c),Shoot-out(c),B:Miss
  America 1,600.00
77 Human Torch/Sub-
  Mariner(c) 1,600.00
78 Safe Robbery(c). 1,600.00
79 Super Villians(c),E:The
  Angel 1,500.00
80 I:Capt.America(in Marvel) . . 1,800.00
81 Mystery o/t Crimson Terror . 1,500.00
82 I:Sub-Mariner/Namora Team-up
  O:Namora,A:Capt.America. 3,800.00
83 The Photo Phantom,E;Young
  Allies 1,300.00
84 BEv,B:The Blonde Phantom 1,800.00
85 BEv,A:Blonde Phantom,
  E;Miss America. 1,400.00
86 BEv,Blonde Phantom ID
  Revealed,E:Bucky 1,300.00
87 BEv,I:Capt.America/Golden
  Girl Team-up. 1,500.00
88 BEv,I:Toro 1,300.00
89 BEv,I:Human Torch/Sun Girl
  Team-up 1,300.00
90 BEv,Giant of the Mountains 1,300.00
91 BEv,I:Venus,E:Blonde
  Phantom,Sub-Mariner 1,300.00
92 BEv,How the Human Torch was
  Born,D:Professor Horton,I:The
  Witness,A:Capt.America. . . 4,000.00
92a Marvel #33(c)rare,reps. . . 30,000.00
Becomes:

MARVEL TALES
Aug., 1949
93 The Ghoul Strikes 2,000.00
94 BEv,The Haunted Love 1,300.00
95 The Living Death. 900.00
96 MSy,The Monster Returns . . . 900.00
97 DRi,MSy,The Wooden
  Horror 1,100.00
98 BEv,BK,MSy,The Curse of
  the Black Cat. 900.00
99 DRi,The Secret of the Wax
  Museum. 900.00
100 The Eyes of Doom 900.00
101 The Man Who Died Twice . . 900.00
102 BW,A Witch Among Us . . . 1,300.00
103 RA,A Touch of Death 1,000.00
104 RH(c),BW,BEv,The Thing
  in the Mirror 1,300.00

105 RH(c),GC,JSt,The Spider. . 1,000.00
106 RH(c),BK,BEv,In The Dead of
  the Night 750.00
107 GC,OW,BK,The Thing in the
  Sewer 750.00
108 RH(c),BEv,JR,Horror in the
  Moonlight. 500.00
109 BEv(c),Sight for Sore Eyes. . 500.00
110 RH,SSh,A Coffin for Carlos . 500.00
111 BEv,Horror Under the Earth . 500.00
112 The House That Death Built . 500.00
113 RH,Terror Tale. 500.00
114 BEv(c),GT,JM,2 for Zombie. . 500.00
115 The Man With No Face. 500.00
116 JSt 500.00
117 BEv(c),GK,Terror in the
  North. 500.00
118 RH,DBr,GC,A World
  Goes Mad 500.00
119 RH,They Gave Him A Grave. 500.00
120 GC,Graveyard(c) 500.00
121 GC,Graveyard(c). 400.00
122 JKu,Missing One Body 400.00
123 No Way Out 400.00
124 He Waits at the Tombstone. . 400.00
125 JF,Horror House 400.00
126 DW,It Came From Nowhere . 375.00
127 BEv(c),GC,MD,Gone is the
  Gargoyle. 375.00
128 Emily,Flying Saucer(c) 375.00
129 You Can't Touch Bottom . . . 375.00
130 RH(c),JF,The Giant Killer . . 375.00
131 GC,BEv,Five Fingers 375.00
132 . . . . 250.00
133 . . . . 250.00
134 BK,JKu,Flying Saucer(c). . . 250.00
135 thru 143. . . . . @250.00
144 . . . . 265.00
145 . . . . 250.00
146 . . . . 200.00
147 . . . . 250.00
148 thru 151. . . . . @200.00
152 . . . . 225.00
153 . . . . 250.00
154 thru 158. . . . . @200.00
159 Aug., 1957. . . . . 225.00

MARVEL COMICS PRESENTS
Sept., 1988
1 WS(c),B:Wolverine(JB,KJ),Master
  of Kung Fu(TS),Man-Thing(TGr,DC)
  F:Silver Surfer(AM) 10.00
2 F:The Captain(AM) 5.00
3 JR2(c),F:The Thing(AM) 5.00
4 F:Thor(AM) 5.00
5 F:Daredevil(DT,MG). 5.00
6 F:Hulk 4.00
7 F:Submariner(SD) 4.00
8 CV(c),E:Master of Kung Fu,F:
  Iron Man(JS) 4.00
9 F:Cloak,El Aquila 4.00
10 E:Wolverine,B:Colossus(RL,CR),
  F:Machine Man(SD,DC) 4.00
11 F:Ant-Man(BL),Slag(RWi) 3.00
12 E:Man-Thing,F:Hercules(DH),
  Namorita(FS). 3.00
13 B:Black Panther(GC,TP),F:
  Shanna,Mr.Fantastic &
  Invisible Woman 3.00
14 F:Nomad(CP),Speedball(SD) . . . 3.00
15 F:Marvel Girl(DT,MG),Red
  Wolf(JS). 3.00
16 F:Ka-Zar(JM),Longshot(AA) 3.00
17 E:Colossus,B:Cyclops(RLm),
  F:Watcher(TS). 4.00
18 F:She-Hulk(JBy,BWi),Willie
  Lumpkin(JSt) 3.00
19 RLd(c)B:Dr.Strange(MBg),
  I:Damage Control(EC,AW) 3.00

20 E:Dr.Strange,F:Clea(RLm) 3.00
21 F:Thing,Paladin(RWi,DA) 3.00
22 F:Starfox(DC),Wolfsbane &
  Mirage 3.00
23 F:Falcon(DC),Wheels(RWi) 3.00
24 E:Cyclops,B:Havok(RB,JRu),
  F:Shamrock(DJ,DA) 3.00
25 F:Ursa Major,I:Nth Man. 4.00
26 B&I:Coldblood(PG),F:Hulk 2.50
27 F:American Eagle(RWi) 2.50
28 F:Triton(JS) 2.50
29 F:Quasar(PR) 2.50
30 F:Leir(TMo) 2.50
31 EL,E:Havok,B:Excalibur
  (EL,TA) 4.00
32 TM(c),F:Sunfire(DH,DC) 3.00
33 F:Namor(JLe) 4.00
34 F:Captain America(JsP) 3.00
35 E:Coldblood,F:Her(EL,AG) 4.00
36 BSz(c),F:Hellcat(JBr) 4.00
37 E:Bl.Panther,F:Devil-Slayer 3.00
38 E:Excalibur,B:Wonderman(JS),
  Wolverine(JB),F:Hulk(MR,DA). . 4.00
39 F:Hercules(BL),Spider-Man 3.50
40 F:Hercules(BL),Overmind(DH) . . 3.50
41 F:Daughters of the Dragon(DA),
  Union Jack(KD) 3.50
42 F:Iron Man(MBa),Siryn(LSn). . . . 3.50
43 F:Iron Man(MBa),Siryn(LSn). . . . 3.50
44 F:Puma(BWi),Dr.Strange 3.50
45 E:Wonderman,F:Hulk(HT),
  Shooting Star. 3.50
46 RLd(c),B:Devil-Slayer,F:Namor,
  Aquarian 3.50
47 JBy(c),E:Wolverine,F:Captain
  America,Arabian Knight(DP) . . . 3.50
48 B:Wolverine&Spider-Man(EL),
  F:Wasp,Storm&Dr.Doom 5.00
49 E:Devil-Slayer,F:Daredevil(RWi),
  Gladiator(DH) 4.50
50 E:Wolverine&Spider-Man,B:Comet
  Man(KJo),F:Captain Ultra(DJ),
  Silver Surfer(JkS) 4.50
51 B:Wolverine(RLd),F:Iron Man
  (MBr,DH),Le Peregrine 4.00
52 F:Rick Jones,Hulk(RWi,TMo) . . . 4.00
53 E:Wolverine,Comet Man,F:
  Silver Sable&Black Widow
  (RLd,BWi),B:Stingray. 4.00
54 B:Wolverine&Hulk(DR),
  Werewolf,F:Shroud(SD,BWi). . . 6.00
55 F:Collective Man(GLa) 6.00
56 E:Stingray,F:Speedball(SD) 6.00

Marvel Comics Presents #10
© Marvel Entertainment Group

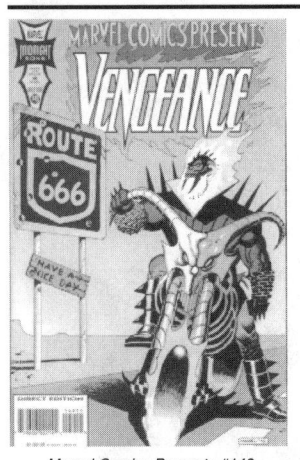

Marvel Comics Presents #149
© Marvel Entertainment Group

57 DK(c),B:Submariner(MC,MFm),
   Black Cat(JRu) 6.00
58 F:Iron Man(SD) 6.00
59 E:Submariner,Werewolf,
   F:Punisher 6.00
60 B:Poison,Scarlet Witch,
   F:Captain America(TL) 6.00
61 E:Wolverine&Hulk,
   F:Dr.Strange 6.00
62 F:Wolverine(PR),Deathlok(JG) . . 6.00
63 F:Wolverine(PR),E:Scarlet
   Witch,Thor(DH) 4.00
64 B:Wolverine&Ghost Rider(MT),
   Fantastic Four(TMo),F:Blade. . . 4.00
65 F:Starfox(ECh) 3.50
66 F:Volstagg 3.50
67 F:Poison,F:Spider-Man(MG). . . . 3.50
68 B:Shanna(PG),E:Fantastic Four
   F:Lockjaw(JA,AM) 3.50
69 B:Daredevil(DT),F:Silver Surfer . 3.50
70 F:BlackWidow&Darkstar(AM) . . . 3.50
71 E:Wolverine&Ghost Rider,F:
   Warlock(New Mutants)(SMc) . . . 3.50
72 B:Weapon X(BWS),E:Daredevil,
   F:Red Wolf(JS) 7.00
73 F:Black Knight(DC),
   Namor(JM) 5.00
74 F:Constrictor(SMc),Iceman &
   Human Torch(JSon,DA) 5.00
75 F:Meggan & Shadowcat,
   Dr.Doom(DC) 5.00
76 F:Death's Head(BHi,MFm),
   A:Woodgod(DC) 5.00
77 E:Shanna,B:Sgt.Fury&Dracula
   (TL,JRu),F:Namor 4.50
78 F:Iron Man(KSy),Hulk&Selene . . 4.50
79 E:Sgt.Fury&Dracula,F:Dr.Strange,
   Sunspot(JBy) 4.50
80 F:Daughters of the Dragon,Mister
   Fantastic(DJ),Captain America
   (SD,TA) 4.50
81 F:Captain America(SD,TA),
   Daredevil(MR,AW),Ant-Man . . . 4.00
82 B:Firestar(DT),F:Iron Man(SL),
   Power Man 4.00
83 F:Hawkeye,Hum.Torch(SD,EL) . 4.00
84 E:Weapon X 4.00
85 B:Wolverine(SK),Beast(RLd,JaL-
   1st Work),F:Speedball(RWi),
   I:Cyber 7.00
86 F:PaladinE:RLd on Beast 5.00
87 F:Firestar,F:Shroud(RWi) 5.00
88 F:Solo,Volcana(BWi) 5.00
89 F:Spitfire(JSn),Mojo(JMa) 5.00

90 B:Ghost Rider & Cable,F:
   Nightmare 4.50
91 F:Impossible Man 3.50
92 E:Wolverine,Beast,
   F:Northstar(JMa) 3.50
93 SK(c),B:Wolverine,Nova,
   F:Daredevil 3.00
94 F:Gabriel 3.00
95 SK(c),E:Wolverine,F:Hulk 3.00
96 B:Wolverine(TT),E:Nova,
   F:Speedball 3.00
97 F:Chameleon,Two-Gun Kid,
   E:Ghost Rider/Cable 3.00
98 E:Wolverine,F:Ghost Rider,
   Werewolf by Night 2.50
99 F:Wolverine,Ghost Rider,
   Mary Jane,Captain America. . . . 2.50
100 SK,F:Ghost Rider,Wolverine,
   Dr.Doom,Nightmare 3.00
101 SK(c),B:Ghost Rider&Doctor
   Strange,Young Gods,Wolverine
   &Nightcrawler,F:Bar With
   No Name 2.50
102 RL,GC,AW,F:Speedball 2.50
103 RL,GC,AW,F:Puck 2.50
104 RL,GC,AW,F:Lockheed 2.50
105 RL,GC,AW,F:Nightmare 2.50
106 RL,GC,AW,F:Gabriel,E:Ghost
   Rider&Dr.Strange 2.50
107 GC,AW,TS,B:Ghost Rider&
   Werewolf 2.50
108 GC,AW,TS,SMc,E:Wolverine&
   Nightcrawler,B:Thanos 2.50
109 SLi,TS,SMc,B:Wolverine&
   Typhoid Mary,E:Young Gods. . . 2.50
110 SLi,SMc,F:Nightcrawler. 2.50
111 SK(c),SLi,RWi,F:Dr.Strange,
   E:Thanos 2.50
112 SK(c),SLi,F:Pip,Wonder Man,
   E:Ghost Rider&Werewolf. 2.50
113 SK(c),SLi,B:Giant Man,
   Ghost Rider&Iron Fist 2.50
114 SK(c),SLi,F:Arabian Knight 2.50
115 SK(c),SLi,F:Cloak&Dagger 2.50
116 SK(c),SLi,E:Wolverine &
   Typhoid Mary 2.50
117 SK,PR,B:Wolverine&Venom,
   I:Ravage 2099 . . . . 4.00
118 SK,PB,RWi,E:Giant Man,
   I:Doom 2099 . . . . 3.00
119 SK,GC,B:Constrictor,E:Ghost
   Rider&Iron Fist,F:Wonder Man . 3.00
120 SK,GC,E:Constrictor,B:Ghost
   Rider/Cloak & Dagger,
   F:Spider-Man. 2.50
121 SK,GC,F:Mirage,Andromeda . . 2.50
122 SK(c),GK,E:Wolverine&Venom,
   Ghost Rider&Cloak&Dagger,F:
   Speedball&Rage,Two-Gun Kid . 2.50
123 SK(c),DJ,SLi,B:Wolverine&Lynx,
   Ghost Rider&Typhoid Mary,
   She-Hulk,F:Master Man 2.50
124 SK(c),DJ,MBa,SLi,F:Solo 2.50
125 SLi,SMc,DJ,B:Iron Fist 2.50
126 SLi,DJ,E:She-Hulk 2.50
127 SLi,DJ,DP,F:Speedball 2.50
128 SLi,DJ,RWi,F:American Eagle . 2.50
129 SLi,DJ,F:Ant Man 2.50
130 DJ,SLi,RWi,E:Wolverine&Lynx,
   Ghost Rider&Typhoid Mary,Iron
   Fist,F:American Eagle 2.50
131 MFm,B:Wolverine,Ghost Rider&
   Cage,Iron Fist&Sabretooth,
   F:Shadowcat 2.50
132 KM(c),F:Iron Man 2.50
133 F:Cloak & Dagger 2.50
134 SLi,F:Vance Astro 2.50
135 SLi,F:Daredevil 2.50
136 B:Gh.Rider&Masters of Silence,
   F:Iron Fist,Daredevil 2.50
137 F:Ant Man 2.50

138 B:Wolverine,Spellbound 2.50
139 F:Foreigner 2.50
140 F:Captain Universe 2.50
141 BCe(s),F:Iron Fist 2.50
142 E:Gh.Rider&Masters of Silence,
   F:Mr.Fantastic 2.50
143 Siege of Darkness,pt.#3,
   B:Werewolf,Scarlet Witch,
   E:Spellbound 2.50
144 Siege of Darkness,pt.#6,
   B:Morbius 2.50
145 Siege of Darkness,pt.#11 . . . . . 2.50
146 Siege of Darkness,pt.#14 . . . . . 2.50
147 B:Vengeance,F:Falcon,Masters of
   Silence,American Eagle 2.50
148 E:Vengeance,F:Capt.Universe,
   Black Panther 2.50
149 F:Daughter o/t Dragon,Namor,
   Vengeance,Starjammers 2.50
150 ANo(s),SLi,F:Typhoid Mary,DD,
   Vengeance,Wolverine 2.50
151 ANo(s),F:Typhoid Mary,DD,
   Vengeance. 2.50
152 CDi(s),PR,B:Vengeance,Wolverine,
   War Machine,Moon Knight 2.50
153 CDi(s),A:Vengeance,Wolverine,
   War Machine,Moon Knight 2.50
154 CDi(s),E:Vengeance,Wolverine,
   War Machine,Moon Knight 2.50
155 CDi(s),B:Vengeance,Wolverine,
   War Machine,Kymaera 2.50
156 B:Shang Chi,F:Destroyer 2.50
157 F:Nick Fury 2.50
158 AD,I:Clan Destine,E:Kymaera,
   Shang Chi,Vengeance. 2.50
159 B:Hawkeye, New Warriors,
   F:Fun,E:Vengeance. 2.50
160 B:Vengeance,Mace. 2.50
161 E:Hawkeye 2.50
162 B:Tigra,E:Mace 2.50
163 E:New Warriors 2.50
164 Tigra, Vengeance 2.50
165 Tigra, Vengeance 2.50
166 Turbo, Vengeance. 2.50
167 Turbo, Vengeance. 2.50
168 Thing, Vengeance. 2.50
169 Mandarin, Vengeance 2.50
170 Force, Vengeance. 2.50
171 Nick Fury. 2.50
172 Lunatik 2.50
173 . . . . 2.50
174 . . . . 2.50
175 . . . . 2.50
TPB Ghost Rider & Cable,rep. 3.95
TPB Save the Tyger, rep. 3.95

MARVEL COMICS
SUPER SPECIAL
[Magazine, 1977]
1 JB,WS,Kiss,Features &Photos 175.00
2 JB,Conan(1978) 20.00
3 WS,Close Encounters 15.00
4 GP,KJ,Beatles story 50.00
Becomes:

MARVEL SUPER SPECIAL
5 Kiss 1978 . . . . 175.00
6 GC,Jaws II 12.00
7 Does Not Exist
8 Battlestar Galactica(Tabloid) . . . 20.00
9 Conan 15.00
10 GC,Starlord 11.00
11 JB,RN,Weirdworld, ... 11.00
12 JB,Weirdworld, ... 11.00
13 JB,Weirdworld, ... 11.00
14 GC,Meteor,adapt. 11.00
15 Star Trek 11.00
15a Star Trek 12.00
16 AW,B:Movie Adapts,Empire
   Strikes Back 12.00
17 Xanadu 7.00

MARVEL

18 HC(c),JB,Raiders of the Lost
   Ark 7.00
19 HC,For Your Eyes Only 9.00
20 Dragonslayer 7.00
21 JB,Conan 7.00
22 JSo(c),AW,Bladerunner 9.00
23 Annie 9.00
24 Dark Crystal 9.00
25 Rock and Rule 9.00
26 Octopussy 8.00
27 AW,Return of the Jedi 9.00
28 PH(c),Krull 8.00
29 DSp,Tarzan of the Apes 8.00
30 Indiana Jones and the Temple
   of Doom 9.00
31 The Last Star Fighter 9.00
32 Muppets Take Manhattan 9.00
33 Buckaroo Banzai. 9.00
34 GM,Sheena. 9.00
35 JB,Conan The Destroyer 9.00
36 Dune 9.00
37 2010 . . . . 9.00
38 Red Sonja 9.00
39 Santa Claus 9.00
40 JB,Labrynth 9.00
41 Howard the Duck,Nov.,1986 . . . . 9.00

MARVEL DOUBLE FEATURE
Dec., 1973
1 JK,GC,B:Tales of Suspense
   Reprints,Capt.America,
   Iron-Man 18.00
2 JK,GC ,A:Nick Fury 12.00
3 JK,GC 12.00
4 JK,GC,Cosmic Cube 12.00
5 JK,GC,V:Red Skull 12.00
6 JK,GC,V:Adaptoid 12.00
7 JK,GC,V:Tumbler 12.00
8 JK,GC,V:Super Adaptoid 12.00
9 GC,V:Batroc 12.00
10 GC 12.00
11 GC,Capt.America Wanted 8.00
12 GC,V:Powerman,Swordsman . . 8.00
13 GC,A:Bucky 8.00
14 GC,V:Red Skull 8.00
15 GK,GC,V:Red Skull 8.00
16 GC,V:Assassin 8.00
17 JK,GC,V:Aim,Iron Man &
   Sub-Mariner #1 . . . . 8.00
18 JK,GC,V:Modok,Iron Man #1 . . . 8.00
19 JK,GC,E:Capt.America 8.00
20 JK(c) 7.00
21 Capt.America,Black Panther
   March, 1977 . . . . 7.00

MARVEL DOUBLE-SHOT
Nov., 2002
1 JJu(c),Hulk, Thor 3.00
2 JJu(c),Doom & Avengers 3.00
3 JJu(c),F:Mr. Fantastic 3.00
4 JJu(c),F:Iron Man. 3.00

MARVEL FANFARE
March, 1972
1 MG,TA,PS,F:Spider-Man,
   Daredevil,Angel. 7.00
2 MG,SM,FF,TVe,F:SpM,Ka-Zar . . 5.00
3 DC,F:X-Men 5.00
4 PS,TA,MG,F:X-Men,Deathlok . . . 5.00
5 MR,F:Dr.Strange 4.00
6 F:Spider-Man,Scarlet Witch 4.50
7 F:Hulk/Daredevil 3.00
8 CI,TA,GK,F:Dr.Strange 3.00
9 GM,F:Man Thing 3.00
10 GP,B:Black Widow 3.50
11 GP,D:M.Corcoran 3.50
12 GP,V:Snapdragon 3.50
13 GP,E:B.Widow,V:Snapdragon . . 3.50

14 F:Fantastic Four,Vision 2.75
15 BWS,F:Thing,Human Torch 3.00
16 DC,JSt,F:Skywolf 2.50
17 DC,JSt,F:Skywolf 2.50
18 FM,JRu,F:Captain America. 3.00
19 RL,F:Cloak and Dagger 2.50
20 JSn,F:Thing&Dr.Strange 3.00
21 JSn,F:Thing And Hulk 3.00
22 KSy,F:Iron Man. 2.50
23 KSy,F:Iron Man. 2.50
24 F:Weird World 3.00
25 F:Weird World 2.50
26 F:Weird World 2.50
27 F:Daredevil 2.50
28 KSy,F:Alpha Flight 2.50
29 JBy,F:Hulk. 3.00
30 BA,AW,F:Moon Knight 2.50
31 KGa,F:Capt.America,
   Yellow Claw 2.50
32 KGa,PS,F:Capt.America,
   Yellow Claw 2.50
33 JBr,F:X-Men 5.00
34 CV,F:Warriors Three 2.50
35 CV,F:Warriors Three 2.50
36 CV,F:Warriors Three 2.50
37 CV,F:Warriors Three 2.50
38 F:Captain America 2.50
39 JSon,F:Hawkeye,Moon Knight . . 2.50
40 DM,F:Angel,Storm,Mystique . . . 3.00
41 DGb,F:Dr.Strange 2.50
42 F:Spider-Man 3.00
43 F:Sub-Mariner,Human Torch. . . . 2.50
44 KSy,F:Iron Man vs.Dr.Doom . . . 2.50
45 All Pin-up Issue,WS,AAd,MZ,
   JOy,BSz,KJ,HC,PS,JBy. 3.00
46 F:Fantastic Four 2.50
47 MG,F:Spider-Man,Hulk 3.00
48 KGa,F:She-Hulk 2.50
49 F:Dr.Strange 2.50
50 JSon,JRu,F:Angel 3.00
51 JB,JA,GC,AW,F:Silver Surfer . . . 4.00
52 F:Fantastic Four 2.50
53 GC,AW,F:Bl.Knight,Dr.Strange . . 2.50
54 F:Black Knight,Wolverine 3.50
55 F:Powerpack,Wolverine 3.50
56 CI,DH,F:Shanna t/She-Devil 2.50
57 BBI,AM,F:Shanna,Cap.Marvel . . 2.50
58 BBI,F:Shanna,Vision/Sc.Witch . . 2.50
59 BBI,F:Shanna,Hellcat 2.50
60 PS,F:Daredevil,Capt.Marvel 2.50

MARVEL FANFARE
Second Series 1996
1 Captain America, Falcon 2.25
2 New Fantastic Four 2.25
3 BbB,F:Spider-Man, Ghost Rider, . 2.25
4 F:Longshot 2.25
5 F:Longshot. 2.25
6 F:Power Man & Iron Fist V:
   Sabretooth 2.25

MARVEL FEATURE
[1st Regular Series]
Dec., 1971
1 RA,BE,NA,I&O:Defenders &
   Omegatron. 225.00
2 BEv,F:The Defenders 100.00
3 BEv,F:The Defenders 75.00
4 F:Ant-Man 35.00
5 F:Ant-Man 20.00
6 F:Ant-Man 16.00
7 CR,F:Ant-Man 16.00
8 JSc,CR,F:Ant-Man,O:Wasp . . . 16.00
9 CR,F:Ant-Man 16.00
10 CR,F:Ant-Man 16.00
11 JSn,JSt,F:Thing & Hulk 65.00
12 JSn,JSt,F:Thing,Iron Man,
   Thanos,Blood Brothers 35.00

Marvel Feature 2nd Series #1
© *Marvel Entertainment Group*

[2nd Regular Series]
(All issues feature Red Sonja)
1 DG,The Temple of Abomination . 12.00
2 FT,Blood of the Hunter. 7.00
3 FT,Balek Lives 7.00
4 FT,Eyes of the Gorgon. 8.00
5 FT,The Bear God Walks 8.00
6 FT,C:Conan,Belit 8.00
7 FT,V:Conan,A:Belit,Conan#68 . . 12.00

MARVEL FRONTIER COMICS SPECIAL
1 All Frontier Characters 3.25
1994 . . . . 2.95

MARVEL FUMETTI BOOK
April, 1984
1 NA(c),Stan Lee, All photos 5.00

MARVEL GRAPHIC NOVEL
1982
1 JSn,D:Captain Marvel,A:Most
   Marvel Characters 30.00
1a 2nd printing 10.00
1b 3rd-5th printing 8.00
2 F:Elric,Dreaming City. 12.00
2a 2nd printing 7.00
3 JSn,F:Dreadstar. 15.00
3a 2nd-3rd printing 7.00
4 BMc,I:New Mutants,Cannonball
   Sunspot,Psyche,Wolfsbane. . . 22.00
4a 2nd printing 10.00
4b 3rd-4th printing 8.00
5 BA,F:X-Men. 20.00
5a 2nd printing 9.00
5b 3rd-5th printing 7.00
6 WS,F:Starslammers 10.00
6a 2nd printing 7.00
7 CR,F:Killraven 10.00
8 RWi,AG,F:Super Boxers 10.00
8a 2nd printing 7.00
9 DC,F:Futurians 12.00
9a 2nd printing 7.00
10 RV,F:Heartburst 10.00
10a 2nd printing 6.00
11 VM,F:Void Indigo 12.00
12 F:Dazzler the Movie 10.00
12a 2nd printing 6.00
13 MK,F:Starstruck 10.00
14 JG,F:SwordsofSwashbucklers . 10.00
15 CV,F:Raven Banner 10.00

MARVEL

16 GLa,F:Alladin Effect 10.00
17 MS,F:Living Monolith 10.00
18 JBy,F:She-Hulk 15.00
18 later printings 14.00
19 F:Conan 15.00
20 F:Greenberg the Vampire 10.00
21 JBo,F:Marada the She-wolf . . . 10.00
22 BWr,Hooky,F:Spider-Man 16.00
23 DGr,F:Dr.Strange 10.00
24 FM,BSz,F:Daredevil 15.00
25 F:Dracula 10.00
26 FC,TA,F:Alien Legion 15.00
27 BH,F:Avengers 15.00
28 JSe,F:Conan the Reaver 16.00
29 BWr,F:Thing & Hulk 10.00
30 F:A Sailor's Story 10.00
31 F:Wolf Pack 10.00
32 SA,F:Death of Groo 17.00
33 F:Thor 10.00
34 AW,F:Cloak & Dagger 10.00
35 MK/RH,F:The Shadow 18.00
36 F:Willow movie adaption 10.00
37 BL,F:Hercules 15.00
38 JB,F:Silver Surfer 20.00
39 F:Iron Man,Crash 14.50
40 JZ,F:The Punisher 12.00
41 F:Roger Rabbit 10.00
42 F:Conan of the Isles 15.00
43 EC,F:Ax. 12.00
44 BJ,F:Arena 10.00
45 JRy,F:Dr.Who 12.00
46 TD,F:Kull 10.00
47 GM,F:Dreamwalker. 10.00
48 F:Sailor's Storm II 10.00
49 MBd,F:Dr.Strange&Dr.Doom. . . 25.00
50 F:Spider-Man,Parallel Lives . . . 12.00
51 F:Punisher,Intruder 14.00
52 DSp,F:Roger Rabbit 12.00
53 PG,F:Conan 12.00
54 HC,F:Wolverine & Nick Fury. . . 20.00

MARVEL HALLOWEEN:
THE SUPERNATURALS
TOUR BOOK
Sept., 1999
1-shot, 16-page, cardstock cov 3.00

MARVEL HEROES
1 StL,FaN,Mega-Jam,48-pg. 3.00

MARVEL: HEROES
AND LEGENDS 1997
Aug., 1997
1-shot, Stan Lee, JR(c) 6.00

MARVEL HOLIDAY
SPECIAL
1 StG(s),PDd(s),SLo(s),RLm,PB, . . 3.25
1-shot MWa,KK. 2.95

MARVEL KIDS
1999
Fantastic Four: Franklin's
  Adventures 3.50
Incredible Hulk: Project Hide 3.50
Spider-Man Mysteries 3.50
X-Men: Mutant Search R.U.1 . . . . . 3.50

MARVEL KNIGHTS
May, 2000
1 JQ,JP,KJ 3.50
2A JQ,KJ,CDi,EB,V:Ulik 3.00
2B variant EB(c) 3.00
3 JQ,KJ,CDi,EB,V:Ulik 3.00
4 JQ,KJ,CDi,EB,Zaran 3.00
5 JQ,KJ,CDi,EB,DaddyWronglegs . 3.00

Marvel Holiday Special #1
© Marvel Entertainment Group

6 JQ,KJ,CDi,EB,MaximumSecurity. 3.00
7 JQ,KJ,CDi,EB,F:Dr.Strange 3.00
8 JQ,CDi,EB,V:Cloak 3.00
9 JQ,CDi,EB,Dagger vs. Cloak. . . . 3.00
10 JQ,CDi,EB,Punisher. 3.00
11 CDi,EB,Luke Cage, Power Man . 3.00
12 CDi,EB,A:Cloak. 3.00
13 CDi,EB,A:Black Widow,Dagger . 3.00
14 CDi,EB,one quits 3.00
15 CDi,EB,V:S.H.I.E.L.D. 3.00
GN Millennial Visions,TyH,48-pg. . . 4.00

MARVEL KNIGHTS
March, 2002
1 Punisher,Daredevil,Black Widow. 3.00
2 thru 6 . . . . @3.00

MARVEL KNIGHTS:
DOUBLE-SHOT
Oct., 2001
1 GEn,JQ,Daredevil & Punisher. . . 3.00
2 GEn,Nick Fury & Man-Thing 3.00
3 GF(c),Elektra & Cloak&Dagger . . 3.00
4 GeH,GF(c),Iron Fist 3.00
5 GeH,GF(c),Daredevil 3.00

MARVEL KNIGHTS 4
Feb., 2004
1 Wolf at the Door,pt.1 . . . . 3.00
2 thru 4 Wolf at the Door. . . . . . . @3.00
5 thru 7 The Pine Barrens. . . . . . @3.00
8 Frozen,pt.1 . . . . 3.00
9 Frozen,pt.2. . . . . 3.00
10 Stuff of Dreams,pt.1 . . . . 3.00
11 Stuff of Dreams,pt.2 . . . . 3.00
TPB Vol. 1: Wolf at the Door 17.00

MARVEL KNIGHTS
MAGAZINE
May, 2001
2 thru 7, 80-page, rep. . . . . @4.00

MARVEL KNIGHTS
SPIDER-MAN
April, 2004
1 TyD,Down Among the Dead,pt.1 . 3.00
2 TyD,Down Among the Dead,pt.2 . 3.00
3 TyD,Down Among the Dead,pt.3 . 3.00
4 TyD,Down Among the Dead,pt.4 . 3.00

5 Venomous,pt.1 . . . . 3.00
6 TyD,Venomous,pt.2 . . . . 3.00
7 TyD,Venomous,pt.3 . . . . 3.00
TPB Vol. 1: Down Among Dead
  Men 10.00
Digest Marvel Age, Vol. 1 . . . . 8.00

MARVEL KNIGHTS
TOUR BOOK
Aug., 1998
1-shot, cardstock cover 3.00

MARVEL KNIGHTS 2009
Sept., 2004
Spec. Daredevil #1 . . . . 3.00
Spec. Black Panther #1 . . . . 3.00
Spec. Inhumans #1 . . . . 3.00
Spec. Punisher #1 . . . . 3.00
Spec. Mutant #1 . . . . 3.00

MARVEL:
THE LOST GENERATION
Jan., 2000
12 (of 12) JBy,AM,Fireball, Flatiron,
  Cassandra, Oxbow, etx. 3.00
11 JBy,AM,F:Justice. 3.00
10 JBy,AM,O:Walkabout 3.00
9 JBy,AM,Effigy,Black Fox 3.00
8 JBy,AM,Nocturne 3.00
7 JBy,AM,Knight Templar 3.00
6 JBy,AM,First Line 3.00
5 JBy,AM,F:Thor 3.00
4 JBy,AM,Yankee Clipper 3.00
3 JBy,AM,Liberty Girl 3.00
2 JBy,AM,V:Yankee Clipper 3.00
1 JBy,AM,concl. 3.00

MARVEL MANGAVERSE
Jan., 2002
New Dawn #1 BDn 3.00
Avengers #1 . . . . 2.25
Fantastic Four #1 AWa 2.25
Ghost Rider #1 . . . . 2.25
Punisher #1 PDd(s) 2.25
Spider-Man #1 . . . . 2.25
X-Men #1 JMs 2.25
Eternal Twilight #1 BDn 3.00
TPB series rep. 224-pg.(2002) . . . 24.95
TPB Vol. 2 (2002) 13.00

MARVEL MANGAVERSE
April, 2002
1 BDn, F:Marvin Elwood. 3.00
2 BDn, Inhumans 2.25
3 BDn, V:Galactus 2.25
4 BDn, UN held hostage. 2.25
5 BDn 2.25
6 BDd, only Doom knows 2.25
TPB Vol. 3: Spider-Man 12.00
TPB Vol. 4: X-Men – Ronin 14.00

MARVEL MASTERPIECES
COLLECTION
1993
1 Joe Jusko Masterpiece Cards . . . 3.25
2 F:Wolverine,Thanos,Apocalypse . 3.00
3 F:Gambit,Venom,Hulk 3.00
4 F:Wolverine Vs. Sabretooth. 3.00

MARVEL MASTERPIECES
II COLLECTION
1994
1 thru 3 w/cards . . . . @3.00

MARVEL MINI-BOOKS
1966
(black & white)
1 F:Capt.America,Spider-Man,Hulk
  Thor,Sgt.Fury 75.00
2 F:Capt.America,Spider-Man,Hulk
  Thor,Sgt.Fury 75.00
3 F:Capt.America,Spider-Man,Hulk
  Thor,Sgt.Fury 75.00
4 thru 6 F:Capt.America,Spider-Man,
  Hulk,Thor,Sgt.Fury .... @75.00

MARVEL MOVIE PREMIERE
B&W Magazine, 1975
1 Land That Time Forgot 20.00

MARVEL MOVIE SHOWCASE FEATURING STAR WARS
Nov., 1982
1 Rep,Stars Wars #1-6 .... 5.00
2 Dec., 1982 .... 5.00

MARVEL MOVIE SPOTLIGHT FEATURING RAIDERS OF THE LOST ARK
Nov., 1982
1 Rep,Raiders of Lost Ark#1-3 ... 3.00

MARVEL MYSTERY COMICS
See: MARVEL COMICS

MARVEL MYSTERY COMICS
Oct., 1999
Spec. 80-pg.................. 4.00

MARVEL NO-PRIZE BOOK
Jan., 1983
1 MGo(c),Stan Lee as
  Dr.Doom(c) 4.00

MARVEL: PORTRAITS OF A UNIVERSE
1 Fully painted moments........ 3.00
2 Fully painted moments........ 3.00
3 F:Death of Elektra 3.00
4 final issue................... 3.00

MARVEL POSTER BOOK
June, 2001
Summer 2001, 64-page......... 3.50
Winter 2001, 64-page 3.50

MARVEL PREMIERE
April, 1972
1 GK,O:Warlock,Receives Soul Gem,
  Creation of Counter Earth 90.00
2 GK,JK,F:Warlock 35.00
3 BWS,F:Dr.Strange 70.00
4 FB,BWS,F:Dr.Strange 25.00
5 MP,CR,F:Dr.Strange,I:Sligguth . 20.00

6 MP,FB,F:Dr.Strange 15.00
7 MP,CR,F:Dr.Strange,I:Dagoth .. 15.00
8 JSn,F:Dr.Strange 15.00
9 NA,FB,F:Dr.Strange 15.00
10 FB,F:Dr.Strange,
  D:Ancient One............. 25.00
11 NA,FB,F:Dr.Strange,I:Shuma . 15.00
12 NA,FB,F:Dr.Strange 15.00
13 NA,FB,F:Dr.Strange 15.00
14 NA,FB,F:Dr.Strange 15.00
15 GK,DG,I&O:Iron Fist,pt.1 .. 100.00
16 DG,O:Iron Fist,pt.2,V:Scythe.. 35.00
17 DG,Citadel on the
  Edge of Vengeance........ 22.00
18 DG,V:Triple Irons........... 22.00
19 DG,A:Ninja 22.00
20 I:Misty Knight 22.00
21 V:Living Goddess 22.00
22 V:Ninja 22.00
23 PB,V:Warhawk 22.00
24 PB,V:Monstroid............. 22.00
25 1st JBy,AMc,E:Iron Fist....... 35.00
26 JK,GT,F:Hercules 8.00
27 F:Satana 10.00
28 F:Legion Of Monsters,A:Ghost
  Rider,Morbius,Werewolf...... 20.00
29 JK,I:Liberty Legion,
  O:Red Raven............... 6.00
30 JK,F:Liberty Legion.......... 6.00
31 JK,I:Woodgod 6.00
32 HC,F:Monark............... 5.00
33 HC,F:Solomon Kane......... 5.00
34 HC,F:Solomon Kane......... 5.00
35 I&O:Silver Age 3-D Man 5.00
36 F:3-D Man................. 5.00
37 F:3-D Man................. 5.00
38 AN,MP,I:Weird World 5.00
39 AM,I:Torpedo(1st solo) 5.00
40 AM,F:Torpedo 5.00
41 TS,F:Seeker 3000........... 5.00
42 F:Tigra.................... 5.00
43 F:Paladin.................. 5.00
44 KG,F:Jack of Hearts(1stSolo) ... 5.00
45 GP,F:Manwolf.............. 5.00
46 GP,F:Manwolf.............. 5.00
47 JBy,I:2nd Antman(Scott Lang) .. 6.00
48 JBy,F:2nd Antman.......... 5.00
49 F:The Falcon.............. 4.00
50 TS,TA,F:Alice Cooper 20.00
51 JBi,F:Black Panther,V:Klan 3.00
52 JBi,F:B.Panther,V:Klan 3.00
53 JBi,F:B.Panther,V:Klan 3.00
54 GD,TD,I:Hammer 3.00
55 JSt,F:Wonderman(1st solo) 4.00

Marvel Premier #54
© Marvel Entertainment Group

56 HC,TA,F:Dominic Fortune...... 3.00
57 WS(c),I:Dr.Who............. 5.00
58 TA(c),FM,F:Dr.Who.......... 3.00
59 F:Dr.Who.................. 3.00
60 WS(c),DGb,F:Dr.Who 3.00
61 TS,F:Starlord............... 3.00

MARVEL PRESENTS
Oct., 1975
1 BMc,F:Bloodstone.......... 15.00
2 BMc,O:Bloodstone........... 9.00
3 AM,B:Guardians/Galaxy 16.00
4 AM,I:Nikki 12.00
5 AM,Planet o/t Absurd 12.00
6 AM,V:Karanada 12.00
7 AM,Embrace the Void 12.00
8 AM,JB,JSt,reprint.S.Surfer#2 .. 15.00
9 AM,O:Starhawk 12.00
10 AM,O:Starhawk 12.00
11 AM,D:Starhawk's Children ... 12.00
12 AM,E:Guardians o/t Galaxy ... 12.00

MARVEL PREVIEW
Feb., 1975
(black & white magazine)
1 NA,AN,Man Gods From
  Beyond the Stars 20.00
2 GM(c),O:Punisher 125.00
3 GM(c),Blade the VampireSlayer 25.00
4 GM(c),I&O:Starlord 15.00
5 Sherlock Holmes 15.00
6 Sherlock Holmes 15.00
7 KG,Satana,A:Sword in the Star . 15.00
8 GM,MP,Legion of Monsters 25.00
9 Man-God,O:Starhawk 12.00
10 JSn,Thor the Mighty 25.00
11 JBy,I:Starlord 12.00
12 MK,Haunt of Horror.......... 10.00
13 JSn(c),Starhawk 10.00
14 JSn(c),Starhawk 10.00
15 MK(c),Starhawk........... 10.00
16 GC,Detectives............. 10.00
17 GK,Black Mask 6.00
18 GC,Starlord 6.00
19 Kull 6.00
20 HC,NA,GP,Bizarre Adventures .. 7.00
21 SD,Moonlight 7.00
22 JB,King Arthur............. 6.00
23 JB,GC,FM,Bizarre Adventures .. 7.00
24 Debut Paradox 6.00
Becomes:

BIZARRE ADVENTURES
1981
25 MG,TA,MR,Lethal Ladies 12.00
26 JB(c),King Kull 12.00
27 JB,AA,GP,Phoenix,A:Ice-Man.. 15.00
28 MG,TA,FM,NA,The Unlikely
  Heroes,Elektra............. 15.00
29 JB,WS,Horror 10.00
30 JB,Tomorrow 10.00
31 JBy,After the Violence Stops... 12.00
32 Gods 12.00
33 Ph(c),Horror 12.00
34 PS,Christmas Spec,Son of Santa
  Howard the Duck,Feb.,1983 .. 10.00

MARVEL PREVIEW
1993
Preview of 1993............... 4.00

MARVEL REMIX
Nov., 1998
1 (of 3) Fantastic Four 3.00
1a signed 20.00

2 Fantastic Four:Fireworks 3.00
3 Fantastic Four:Fireworks 3.00

MARVELS
1994
1 B:KBk(s),AxR,I:Phil Sheldon,
   A:G.A.Heroes,Human Torch Vs
   Namor 10.00
2 AxR,A:S.A.Avengers,FF,X-Men . . 8.00
3 AxR,FF vs Galactus 8.00
4 AxR,Final issue 8.00

MARVEL SAGA
Dec., 1985
1 JBy,Fantastic Four,Wolv. 3.00
2 Hulk 2.50
3 Spider-Man 3.00
4 X-Men 3.00
5 Thor 2.50
6 Fantastic Four 2.50
7 Avengers 2.50
8 X-Men 2.50
9 Angel 2.50
10 X-Men 2.50
11 X-Men 2.50
12 O:Capt. America 2.50
13 O:Daredevil,Elektra 2.50
14 O:Green Goblin 2.50
15 Avengers 2.50
16 Daredevil,X-Men 2.50
17 Ka-Zar,X-Men 2.50
18 Hawkeye-Quicksilver 2.50
19 SpM,Thor,Daredevil 2.50
20 Daredevil,Giant Man 2.50
21 FF,V:Frightful Four 2.50
22 Wedding 2.50
23 . . . . 2.50
24 . . . . 2.50
25 O:Silver Surfer,Dec.,1987 . . . . . 2.75

MARVEL SELECTS: FANTASTIC FOUR
Nov., 1999
1 (of 12) 2.75
2 rep. Vol. 1, #108, AD(c) 2.75
3 rep. Vol. 1, #109, AD(c) 2.75
4 rep. Vol. 1, #110, AD(c) 2.75
5 rep. Vol. 1, #111, AD(c) 2.75
6 rep. Vol. 1, #112, AD(c) 2.75

MARVEL SELECTS: SPIDER-MAN
Nov., 1999
1 (of 12) 2.75
2 rep. Amaz.Sp-M #101 . . . . 2.75
3 rep. Amaz.Sp-M #102 . . . . 2.75
4 rep. Amaz.Sp-M #103 . . . . 2.75
5 rep. Amaz.Sp-M #104 . . . . 2.75
6 rep. Amaz.Sp-M #105 . . . . 2.75

MARVEL: SHADOWS & LIGHT
B&W 1996
1-shot MGo,JPL,KJ,48-pg. 3.00

MARVEL 1602
Aug., 2003
1 (of 8) NGa(s),NKu 3.50
2 thru 7 NGa(s),NKu . . . . @3.50
8 NGa(s),NKu,48-pg. 4.00

MARVEL 65th ANNIVERSARY
Sept., 2004
Spec. F:Sub-Mariner,Human
   Torch,48-pg. 5.00

MARVEL SPECTACULAR
Aug., 1973–Nov., 1975
1 JK,rep Thor #128 . . . . 15.00
2 thru 10 JK,rep.Thor#129–#139 @7.00
11 thru 19 JK,rep Thor #140–#148 . . . . .
   @6.00

MARVEL SPOTLIGHT
[1st Regular Series] Nov., 1971
1 NA(c)WW,F:Red Wolf 55.00
2 MP,BEv,NA,I&O:Werewolf 225.00
3 MP,F:Werewolf 75.00
4 SD,MP,F:Werewolf 75.00
5 SD,MP,I&O:Ghost Rider 225.00
6 MP,TS,F:Ghost Rider 50.00
7 MP,TS,F:Ghost Rider 50.00
8 JM,MB,F:Ghost Rider 50.00
9 TA,F:Ghost Rider 45.00
10 SD,JM,F:Ghost Rider 45.00
11 SD,F:Ghost Rider 45.00
12 SD,2nd A:Son of Satan 45.00
13 F:Son of Satan 18.00
14 JM,F:Son of Satan,I:Ikthalon . . 18.00
15 JM, F:Son of Satan,
   I:Baphomet 15.00
16 JM,F:Son of Satan 15.00
17 JM,F:Son of Satan 15.00
18 F:Son of Satan, I:Allatou 15.00
19 F:Son of Satan 15.00
20 F:Son of Satan 15.00
21 F:Son of Satan 15.00
22 F:Son of Satan, Ghost Rider . . 18.00
23 F:Son of Satan 15.00
24 JM,F:Son of Satan 15.00
25 GT,F:Sinbad 15.00
26 F:The Scarecrow 12.00
27 F:The Sub-Mariner 22.00
28 F:Moon Knight (1st full solo) . . 35.00
29 F:Moon Knight 40.00
30 JSt,JB,F:Warriors Three 22.00
31 HC,JSn,F:Nick Fury 22.00
32 I:Spiderwoman, Jessica Drew . 22.00
33 F:Deathlok, I:Devilslayer 10.00

[2nd Regualar Series] 1979
1 PB,F:Captain Marvel 4.00
1a No`1' on Cover. 12.00
2 FM(c),F:Captain Marvel,A:Eon . . 3.00
3 PB,F:Captain Marvel 3.00
4 PB,F:Captain Marvel 3.00
5 FM(c),SD,F:Dragon Lord 3.00
6 F:Star Lord 3.00
7 FM(c),F:StarLord 3.00
8 FM,F:Captain Marvel 7.00
9 FM(c),SD,F:Captain Universe . . . 3.00
10 SD,F:Captain Universe 3.00
11 SD,F:Captain Universe 3.00

MARVEL SPOTLIGHT ON CAPTAIN AMERICA
1 thru 4, Captain America rep. . . @3.00

MARVEL SPOTLIGHT ON DR. STRANGE
1 thru 4, Dr. Strange, rep. . . . . . @3.00

MARVEL SPOTLIGHT ON SILVER SURFER
1 thru 4, Silver Surfer, rep. . . . . @3.00

MARVEL SUPER ACTION
Jan., 1976
1-shot TD,GE,FS,MP,HC,F:Punisher,
   Weirdworld,Dominic Fortune,
   I:Huntress(Mockingbird) 75.00

Marvel Super Action #11
© Marvel Entertainment Group

MARVEL SUPER ACTION
May, 1977–Nov., 1981
1 JK,reprint,Capt.America #100 . . 15.00
2 JK,reprint,Capt.America #101 . . 10.00
3 JK,reprint,Capt.America #102 . . 10.00
4 BEv,RH,reprint,Marvel Boy #1 . . 10.00
5 JK,reprint,Capt.America #103 . . 10.00
6 JK,reprint,Capt.America #104 . . . 8.00
7 JK,reprint,Capt.America #105 . . . 8.00
8 JK,reprint,Capt.America #106 . . . 8.00
9 JK,reprint,Capt.America #107 . . . 8.00
10 JK,reprint,Capt.America #108 . . . 8.00
11 JK,reprint,Capt.America #109 . . . 8.00
12 JSo,reprint,Capt.America #110 . . 8.00
13 JSo,reprint,Capt.America #111 . . 8.00
14 JB,reprint,Avengers #55 . . . . . . 8.00
15 JB,reprint,Avengers #56 . . . . . . 8.00
16 Reprint,Avengers,annual #2 . . . 5.00
17 Reprint,Avengers # 5.00
18 JB(c),reprint,Avengers #57 . . . . 5.00
19 JB(c),reprint,Avengers #58 . . . . 5.00
20 JB(c),reprint,Avengers #59 . . . . 5.00
21 Reprint,Avengers #60 . . . . 4.00
22 JB(c),reprint,Avengers #61 . . . . 4.00
23 Reprint,Avengers #63 . . . . 4.00
24 Reprint,Avengers #64 . . . . 4.00
25 Reprint,Avengers #65 . . . . 4.00
26 Reprint,Avengers #66 . . . . 4.00
27 BWS,Reprint,Avengers #67 . . . . 4.00
28 BWS,Reprint,Avengers #68 . . . . 4.00
29 Reprint,Avengers #69 . . . . 4.00
30 Reprint,Avengers #70 . . . . 4.00
31 Reprint,Avengers #71 . . . . 4.00
32 Reprint,Avengers #72 . . . . 4.00
33 Reprint,Avengers #73 . . . . 4.00
34 Reprint,Avengers #74 . . . . 4.00
35 JB(c),Reprint,Avengers #75 . . . . 4.00
36 JB(c),Reprint,Avengers #75 . . . . 4.00
37 JB(c),Reprint,Avengers #76 . . . . 4.00

MARVEL SUPERHEROES
Oct., 1966
1-shot Rep. D.D. #1, Avengers #2,
   Marvel Mystery #8 . . . . 175.00

All comics prices listed are for *Near Mint* condition.   **CVA Page 273**

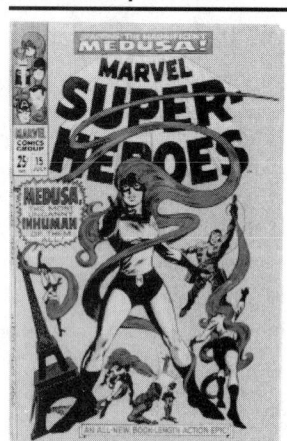

Marvel Super-Heroes #15
© Marvel Entertainment Group

MARVEL SUPER-HEROES
[1st Regular Series] 1967–71
(Prev.: Fantasy Masterpieces)

12 GC,I&O:Captain Marvel	200.00
13 GC,2nd A:Captain Marvel	100.00
14 F:Spider-Man	125.00
15 GC,F:Medusa	50.00
16 I:Phantom Eagle	50.00
17 O:Black Knight	50.00
18 GC,I:Guardians o/t Galaxy	65.00
19 F:Ka-Zar	30.00
20 F:Dr.Doom,Diablo	40.00
21 thru 31 reprints	@20.00
32 thru 55 rep. Hulk/Submariner from Tales to Astonish	@7.00
56 reprints Hulk #102	5.00
57 thru 105 reps.Hulk issues	@5.00

MARVEL SUPERHEROES
[2nd Regular Series] May, 1990

1 RLm,F:Hercules,Moon Knight, Magik,Bl.Panther,Speedball	4.00
2	3.50
3 F:Captain America,Hulk,Wasp	4.00
4 AD,F:SpM,N.Fury,D.D.,Speedball Wond.Man,Spitfire,Bl.Knight	3.50
5 F:Thor,Thing,Speedball, Dr.Strange	3.50
6 RB,SD,F:X-Men,Power Pack, Speedball,Sabra	3.00
7 RB,F:X-Men,Cloak & Dagger	2.75
8 F:X-Men,Iron Man,Namor	2.75
9 F:Avengers W.C,Thor,Iron Man	3.00
10 DH,F:Namor,Fantastic Four, Ms.Marvel#24	3.50
11 F:Namor,Ms.Marvel#25	3.00
12 F:Dr.Strange,Falcon,Iron Man	3.00
13 F:Iron Man	3.00
14 BMc,RWi,F:Iron Man, Speedball, Dr.Strange	3.00
15 KP,DH,F:Thor,Iron Man,Hulk	3.00
Holiday Spec.#1 AAd,DC,JRu,F:FF, X-Men,Spider-Man,Punisher	3.25
Holiday Spec.#2 AAd(c),SK,MGo, RLm,SLi,F:Hulk,Wolverine, Thanos,Spider-Man	3.25
Fall Spec.RB,A:X-Men,Shroud, Marvel Boy,Cloak & Dagger	3.00

MARVEL SUPERHEROES MEGAZINE

1 thru 6 rep.	@3.00

MARVEL SUPER SPECIAL
See: MARVEL COMICS

MARVEL SWIMSUIT
1992

1 Schwing Break	10.00

MARVEL TAILS
Nov., 1983

1 ST,Peter Porker	5.00

MARVEL TALES
1964

1 All reprints,O:Spider-Man	450.00
2 rep.Avengers #1,X-Men #1, Hulk #3	175.00
3 rep.Amaz.SpM.#6	75.00
4 rep.Amaz.SpM.#7	50.00
5 rep.Amaz.SpM.#8	50.00
6 rep.Amaz.SpM.#9	50.00
7 rep.Amaz.SpM.#10	50.00
8 rep.Amaz.SpM.#13	35.00
9 rep.Amaz.SpM.#14	35.00
10 rep.Amaz.SpM.#15	35.00
11 rep.Amaz.SpM.#16	35.00
12 rep.Amaz.SpM.#17	35.00
13 rep.Amaz.SpM.#18 rep.1950's Marvel Boy	35.00
14 rep.Amaz.SpM.#19, reps.Marvel Boy	25.00
15 rep.Amaz.SpM.#20, reps.Marvel Boy	25.00
16 rep.Amaz.SpM.#21, reps.Marvel Boy	25.00
17 thru 22 rep.Amaz.SpM. #22-#27	@25.00
23 thru 27 rep.Amaz.SpM. #30-#34	@25.00
28 rep.Amaz.SpM.#35&36	25.00
29 rep.Amaz.SpM.#39&40	25.00
30 rep.Amaz.SpM.#58&41	25.00
31 rep.Amaz.SpM.#42	25.00
32 rep.Amaz.SpM.#43&44	25.00
33 rep.Amaz.SpM.#45&47	25.00
34 rep.Amaz.SpM.#48	10.00
35 rep.Amaz.SpM.#49	10.00
36 thru 41 rep. Amaz.SpM#51-#56	@10.00
42 thru 53 rep. Amaz.SpM#59-#70	@10.00
54 thru 80 rep. Amaz.SpM#73-#99	@10.00
81 rep.Amaz.SpM.#103	10.00
82 rep.Amaz.SpM.#103-4	10.00
83 thru 97 rep. Amaz.SpM.#104-#118	@10.00
98 rep.Amaz.SpM.#121	10.00
99 rep.Amaz.SpM.#122	10.00
100 rep.Amaz.SpM.#123,BU:Two Gun Kid,Giant-Size	4.00
101 thru 105 rep.Amaz. SpM.#124-#128	@4.00
106 rep.Amaz.SpM.#129, (I:Punisher)	4.00
107 thur 110 rep.Amaz. SpM.#130-133	@4.00
111 Amaz.SpM#134,A:Punisher	4.00
112 Amaz.SpM#135,A:Punisher	4.00
113 thru 125 rep.Amaz.Spider Man #136-#148	@4.00
126 rep.Amaz.Spider-Man#149	4.00
127 rep.Amaz.Spider-Man#150	4.00
128 rep.Amaz.Spider-Man#151	4.00
129 thru 136 rep.Amaz.Spider Man #152-#159	@4.00
137 rep.Amaz.Fantasy#15	7.00
138 rep.Amaz.SpM.#1	7.00

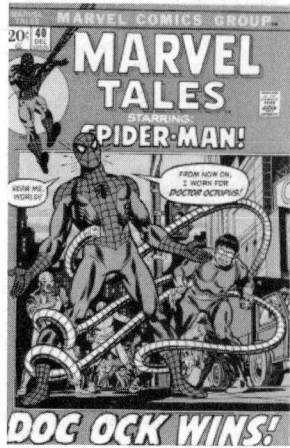

Marvel Tales #40
© Marvel Entertainment Group

139 thru 149 rep. AmazSpM#2-#12	@4.00
150 rep.AmazSpM Ann#1	4.00
151 rep.AmazSpM#13	4.00
152 rep.AmazSpM#14	4.00
153 thru 190 rep.AmazSpM#15-52	@2.50
191 rep. #96-98	2.50
192 rep. #121-122	2.50
193 thru 198 rep.Marv.Team Up#59-64	@2.50
199	2.50
200 rep. SpM Annual 14	2.50
201 thru 206 rep.Marv. Team Up#65-70	@2.50
207	2.50
208	2.50
209 MZ(c),rep.SpM#129,Punisher	3.00
210 MZ(c),rep.SpM#134	4.00
211 MZ(c),rep.SpM#135	4.00
212 MZ(c),rep.Giant-Size#4.	4.00
213 MZ(c),rep.Giant-Size#4.	4.00
214 MZ(c),rep.SpM#161	4.00
215 MZ(c),rep.SpM#162	3.00
216 MZ(c),rep.SpM#174	3.00
217 MZ(c),rep.SpM#175	3.00
218 MZ(c),rep.SpM#201	3.00
219 MZ(c),rep.SpM#202	3.00
220 MZ(c),rep.Spec.SpM #81	3.00
221 MZ(c),rep.Spec.SpM #82	3.00
222 MZ(c),rep.Spec.SpM #83	2.25
223 thru 227 TM(c),rep. SpM #88-92	@2.50
228 TM(c),rep.Spec.SpM#17	2.25
229 TM(c),rep.Spec.SpM#18	2.25
230 TM(c),rep.SpM #203	2.25
231 TM(c),rep.Team-Up#108	2.25
232 TM(c),rep.	2.25
233 thru 236 TM(c),rep. X-Men	@2.25
237 TM(c),rep.	2.25
238 TM(c),rep.	2.25
239 TM(c),rep.SpM,Beast	2.25
240 rep.SpM,Beast,MTU#90	2.25
241 rep.MTU#124	2.25
242 rep.MTU#89,Nightcrawler	2.25
243 rep.MTU#117,SpM,Wolverine	2.25
244 MR(c),rep.	2.25
245 MR(c),rep.	2.25
246 MR(c),rep.	2.25
247 MR(c),rep.MTU Annual #6	2.25
248 MR(c),rep.	2.25
249 MR(c),rep.MTU #14	2.25
250 MR(c),rep.MTU #100	2.25

251 rep.Amaz.SpM.#100 . . . . 2.25
252 rep.Amaz.SpM.#101 . . . . 3.50
253 rep.Amaz.SpM.#102 . . . . 3.00
254 rep.MTU #15,inc.2 Ghost
     Rider pin-ups by JaL 3.00
255 SK(c),rep.MTU #58,
     BU:Ghost Rider 2.25
256 rep. MTU 2.25
257 rep.Amaz.SpM.#238 . . . . 2.25
258 rep.Amaz.SpM.#239 . . . . 2.25
259 thru 261 rep.Amaz.SpM.#249
     thru #251 . . . . @2.25
262 rep Marvel Team-Up #53 . . . . . 2.25
263 rep Marvel Team-Up #54 . . . . . 2.25
264 rep.B:Amaz.SpM.Ann.#5 . . . . . 2.25
265 rep.E:Amaz.SpM.Ann.#5 . . . . . 2.25
266 thru 275 rep.Amaz.SpM#252
     thru #261 . . . . @2.25
276 rep.Amaz.SpM#263 . . . . 2.25
277 rep.Amaz.SpM#265 . . . . 2.25
278 thru 282 rep.Amaz.SpM #268
     thru #272 . . . . @2.25
283 rep.Amaz.SpM#273 . . . . 2.25
284 thru 287 rep.Amaz.SpM#275
     thru #278 . . . . @2.25
288 rep.Amaz.SpM#280 . . . . 2.25
289 rep.Amaz.SpM#281 . . . . 2.25
290 & 291 rep.Amaz.SpM 2.25

MARVEL TALES
See: MARVEL COMICS

MARVEL TEAM-UP
March, 1972
(Spider-Man in all,unless *)

1 RA,F:Hum.Torch,V:Sandman. . 200.00
2 RA,F:Hum.Torch,V:Sandman. . . 60.00
3 F:Human Torch,V:Morbius 75.00
4 GK,F:X-Men,A:Morbius 75.00
5 GK,F:Vision 25.00
6 GK,F:Thing,O:Puppet Master,
     V:Mad Thinker 25.00
7 RA,F:Thor 25.00
8 JM,F:The Cat 25.00
9 RA,F:Iron Man 25.00
10 JM,F:Human Torch 25.00
11 JM,F:The Inhumans 18.00
12 RA,F:Werewolf 30.00
13 GK,F:Captain America 25.00
14 GK,F:Sub-Mariner 18.00
15 RA,F:Ghostrider 30.00
16 GK,JM,F:Captain Marvel 18.00
17 GK,F:Mr.Fantastic,
     A:Capt.Marvel 18.00
18 *F:Hulk,Human Torch 18.00
19 SB,F:Ka-Zar 18.00
20 SB,F:Black Panther 17.00
21 SB,F:Dr.Strange 11.00
22 SB,F:Hawkeye 12.00
23 *F:Human Torch,Iceman,
     C:Spider-Man,X-Men 12.00
24 JM,F:Brother Voodoo 12.00
25 JM,F:Daredevil 12.00
26 *F:H.Torch,Thor,V:Lavamen . . . 12.00
27 JM,F:The Hulk 12.00
28 JM,F:Hercules 12.00
29 *F:Human Torch,Iron Man. 12.00
30 JM,F:The Falcon 12.00
31 JM,F:Iron Fist 12.00
32 *F:Hum.Torch,Son of Satan . . . 12.00
33 SB,F:Nighthawk 12.00
34 SB,F:Valkyrie 12.00
35 SB,*F:H.Torch,Dr.Strange 12.00
36 SB,F:Frankenstein 10.00
37 SB,F:Man-Wolf 10.00
38 SB,F:Beast 10.00
39 SB,F:H.Torch,I:Jean Dewolff. . . 10.00
40 SB,F:Sons of the Tiger 10.00
41 SB,F:Scarlet Witch 10.00

42 SB,F:Scarlet Witch,Vision 10.00
43 SB,F:Dr.Doom 10.00
44 SB,F:Moon Dragon 10.00
45 SB,F:Killraven 10.00
46 SB,F:Deathlok 8.00
47 F:The Thing 7.00
48 SB,F:Iron Man,I:Wraith 7.00
49 SB,F:Iron Man 7.00
50 SB,F:Dr.Strange 7.00
51 SB,F:Iron Man 7.00
52 SB,F:Captain America 7.00
53 1st JBy New X-Men,F:Hulk. . . . 35.00
54 JBy,F:Hulk,V:Woodgod 8.00
55 JBy,F:Warlock,I:Gardener 9.00
56 SB,F:Daredevil 8.00
57 SB,F:Black Widow 8.00
58 SB,F:Ghost Rider,V:Trapster . . . 8.00
59 JBy,F:Yellowjacket,V:Equinox . . 8.00
60 JBy,F:Wasp,V:Equinox 8.00
61 JBy,F:Human Torch. 8.00
62 JBy,F:Ms.Marvel 8.00
63 JBy,F:Iron Fist 8.00
64 JBy,F:Daughters o/t Dragon . . . 8.00
65 JBy,I:Captain Britain(U.S.)
     I:Arcade 7.50
66 JBy,F:Captain Britain 7.00
67 JBy,F:Tigra,V:Kraven 7.00
68 JBy,F:Man-Thing,I:D'Spayre . . . 7.00
69 JBy,F:Havok 7.00
70 JBy,F:Thor 7.00
71 F:The Falcon,V:Plantman 5.00
72 F:Iron Man 5.00
73 F:Daredevil 5.00
74 BH,F:Not ready for prime time
     players(Saturday Night Live) . . . 5.00
75 JBy,F:Power Man 6.00
76 HC,F:Dr.Strange 5.00
77 HC,F:Ms.Marvel 5.00
78 DP,F:Wonderman 5.00
79 JBy,TA,F:Red Sonja 6.00
80 SpM,F:Dr.Strange,Clea 5.00
81 F:Satana 5.00
82 SB,F:Black Widow 6.00
83 SB,F:Nick Fury 5.00
84 SB,F:Master of Kung Fu 5.00
85 SB,F:Bl.Widow,Nick Fury 5.00
86 BMc,F:Guardians o/t Galaxy . . . 4.00
87 GC,F:Black Panther 4.00
88 SB,F:Invisible Girl 4.00
89 RB,F:Nightcrawler 4.50
90 BMc,F:The Beast 4.00
91 F:Ghost Rider 4.00
92 Cl,F:Hawkeye,I:Mr.Fear IV 3.50
93 Cl,F:Werewolf
     I:Tatterdemalion (named) 4.00
94 MZ,F:Shroud 3.50
95 I:Mockingbird(Huntress) 4.00
96 F:Howard the Duck 3.50
97 *F:Hulk,Spider-Woman 3.50
98 F:Black Widow 3.50
99 F:Machine Man 3.50
100 FM,JBy,F:F.F.,I:Karma,
     BU:Storm & Bl.Panther 8.00
101 F:Nighthawk 3.00
102 F:Doc Samson,Rhino 3.00
103 F:Antman 3.00
104 *F:Hulk,Ka-zar. 3.00
105 *F:Powerman,Iron Fist,Hulk . . . 3.00
106 HT,F:Captain America 3.00
107 HT,F:She-Hulk 3.00
108 HT,F:Paladin 3.00
109 HT,F:Dazzler 3.00
110 HT,F:Iron Man 3.00
111 HT,F:Devil Slayer 3.00
112 HT,F:King Kull 3.00
113 HT,F:Quasar,V:Lightmaster. . . 3.00
114 HT,F:Falcon 3.00
115 HT,F:Thor 3.00
116 HT,F:Valkyrie 3.00
117 HT,F:Wolv,V:Prof Power 12.00
118 HT,F:Professor X. 4.00

119 KGa,F:Gargoyle 3.00
120 KGa,F:Dominic Fortune 3.00
121 KGa,F:Human Torch,I:Leap
     Frog(Frog Man) 3.00
122 KGa,F:Man-Thing 3.00
123 KGa,F:Daredevil 3.00
124 KGa,F:Beast 3.50
125 KGa,F:Tigra 3.00
126 BH,F:Hulk 3.00
127 KGa,F:Watcher,X-mass issue. . 3.00
128 Ph(c)KGa,F:Capt.America. 3.00
129 KGa,F:The Vision 3.00
130 KGa,F:The Scarlet Witch 3.00
131 KGa,F:Leap Frog 3.00
132 KGa,F:Mr.Fantastic 3.00
133 KGa,F:Fantastic Four 3.00
134 F:Jack of Hearts 3.00
135 F:Kitty Pryde 3.00
136 F:Wonder Man 3.00
137 *F:Aunt May & F.Richards 3.00
138 F:Sandman,I:New Enforcers. . . 3.00
139 F:Sandman,Nick Fury 3.00
140 F:Black Widow 3.00
141 SpM(2nd App Black Costume)
     F:Daredevil 12.00
142 F:Captain Marvel(2nd one) 3.00
143 F:Starfox 3.00
144 F:M.Knight,V:WhiteDragon . . . 3.00
145 F:Iron Man 3.00
146 F:Nomad 3.50
147 F:Human Torch 3.00
148 F:Thor 3.00
149 F:Cannonball. 3.50
150 F:X-Men,V:Juggernaut 5.50
Ann.#1 SB,F:New X-Men. 30.00
Ann.#2 F:The Hulk. 10.00
Ann.#3 F:Hulk,PowerMan 6.00
Ann.#4 F:Daredevil,Moon Knight. . . 5.00
Ann.#5 F:Thing,Scarlet Witch,
     Quasar,Dr.Strange. 5.00
Ann.#6 F:New Mutants,Cloak &
     Dagger(cont.New Mutants#22) . 5.00
Ann.#7 F:Alpha Flight 3.00

MARVEL TEAM-UP INDEX
See: OFFICIAL MARVEL
INDEX TO
MARVEL TEAM-UP

MARVEL TEAM-UP
1997
1 TPe,PO,AW, F:Spider-Man,
  Generation X 2.25
2 TPe,PO,AW, F:Spider-Man &
  Hercules 2.25
3 TPe,DaR,AW, F:Spider-Man &
  Sandman 2.25
4 TPe,DaR,F:Spider-Man &
  Man-Thing 2.25
5 TPe,DaR,F:Spider-Man &
  Mystery guest 2.25
6 TPe,F:Spider-Man & Sub-Mariner 2.25
7 MWn,TPe,F:Spider-Man & Blade 2.25
8 TPe,F:Sub-Mariner & Doctor
  Strange 2.25
9 TPe,F:Sub-Mariner & Captain
  America 2.25
10 TPe,AW,F:Sub Mariner & Thing . 2.25
11 TPe,AW,PO,F:Sub-Mariner & Iron
  Man, final issue 2.25

MARVEL
Treasury Edition
Sept., 1974
1 SD,Spider-Man,I:Contemplator . 75.00
2 JK,F:Fant.Four,Silver Surfer . . . 30.00
3 F:Thor 25.00
4 BWS,F:Conan 25.00
5 O:Hulk 25.00
6 GC,FB,SD,F:Dr.Strange. 25.00
7 JB,JK,F:The Avengers 25.00
8 F:X-Mass stories 25.00
9 F:Super-Hero Team-Up 25.00
10 F:Thor 25.00
11 F:Fantastic Four 20.00
12 F:Howard the Duck 20.00
13 F:X-Mas stories. 20.00
14 F:Spider-Man 22.00
15 BWS,F:Conan,Red Sonja 22.00
16 F:Defenders 20.00
17 F:The Hulk 20.00
18 F:Spider Man,X-Men. 25.00
19 F:Conan 22.00
20 F:Hulk 22.00
21 F:Fantastic Four 22.00
22 F:Spider-Man 25.00
23 F:Conan 22.00
24 F:The Hulk 22.00
25 F:Spider-Man,Hulk 22.00
26 GP,F:Hulk,Wolverine,Hercules . 25.00
27 HT,F:Hulk,Spider-Man. 22.00
28 JB,JSt,F:SpM/Superman. 50.00

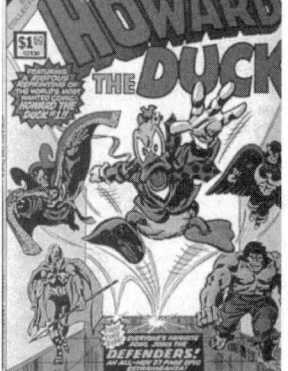
Marvel Treasury Edition #12
© Marvel Entertainment Group

MARVEL TREASURY OF OZ
(oversized) 1975
1 JB,movie adapt. 30.00

MARVEL TREASURY SPECIAL
Vol. I Spider-Man, 1974 . . . . 25.00
Vol. II Capt. America, 1976 . . . . . 30.00

MARVEL TRIPLE ACTION
Feb., 1972
1 Rep. 25.00
2 thru 5 rep. . . . . @15.00
6 thru 10 rep. . . . . @10.00
11 thru 47 rep. . . . . @5.00
G-Size#1 F:Avengers 7.00
G-Size#2 F:Avengers. 7.00

MARVEL TWO-IN-ONE
Jan., 1974
(Thing in all, unless *)
1 GK,F:Man-Thing 85.00
2 GK,JSt,F:Namor,Namorita 30.00
3 F:Daredevil 30.00
4 F:Capt.America,Namorita 20.00
5 F:Guardians of the Galaxy. . . . 22.00
6 F:Dr.Strange. 22.00
7 F:Valkyrie. 14.00
8 F:Ghost Rider 20.00
9 F:Thor 14.00
10 KJ,F:Black Widow. 14.00
11 F:Golem 10.00
12 F:Iron Man 10.00
13 F:Power Man 10.00
14 F:Son of Satan 11.00
15 F:Morbius 11.00
16 F:Ka-Zar 10.00
17 F:Spider-Man 10.00
18 F:Spider-Man 10.00
19 F:Tigra. 10.00
20 F:The Liberty Legion 10.00
21 F:Doc Savage 6.00
22 F:Thor,Human Torch 6.00
23 F:Thor,Human Torch 6.00
24 SB,F:Black Goliath 6.00
25 F:Iron Fist 6.00
26 F:Nick Fury 6.00
27 F:Deathlok. 6.00
28 F:Sub-Mariner 7.00
29 F:Master of Kung Fu 6.00
30 JB,F:Spiderwoman 10.00
31 F:Spiderwoman 7.00
32 F:Invisible girl 7.00
33 F:Modred the Mystic 7.00
34 F:Nighthawk,C:Deathlok 7.00
35 F:Skull the Slayer 7.00
36 F:Mr.Fantastic 7.00
37 F:Matt Murdock. 7.00
38 F:Daredevil 7.00
39 F:The Vision 7.00
40 F:Black Panther 7.00
41 F:Brother Voodoo 5.00
42 F:Captain America 5.00
43 JBy,F:Man-Thing. 6.00
44 GD,F:Hercules 4.00
45 GD,F:Captain Marvel 5.00
46 F:The Hulk 10.00
47 GD,F:Yancy Street Gang,
  I:Machinesmith 4.00
48 F:Jack of Hearts 4.00
49 GD,F:Dr.Strange. 4.00
50 JBy,JS,F:Thing & Thing 4.00
51 FM,BMc,F:Wonderman,Nick
  Fury, Ms.Marvel. 8.00
52 F:Moon Knight,I:Crossfire. 4.00
53 JBy,JS,F:Quasar,C:Deathlok . . . 4.00

54 JBy,JS,D:Deathlok,
  I:Grapplers. 11.00
55 JBy,JS,I:New Giant Man 4.00
56 GP,GD,F:Thundra 3.00
57 GP,GD,F:Wundarr. 3.00
58 GP,GD,I:Aquarian,A:Quasar . . . 3.00
59 F:Human Torch 3.00
60 GP,GD,F:Impossible Man,
  I:Impossible Woman 3.00
61 GD,F:Starhawk,I&O:Her 4.00
62 GD,F:Moondragon 4.00
63 GD,F:Warlock 4.00
64 DP,GD,F:Stingray,
  I:Serpent Squad 3.00
65 GP,GD,F:Triton 3.00
66 GD,F:Scarlet Witch,
  V:Arcade 3.00
67 F:Hyperion,Thundra 3.00
68 F:Angel,V:Arcade 3.00
69 GD,F:Guardians o/t Galaxy 3.00
70 F:The Inhumans 3.00
71 F:Mr.Fantastic,I:Deathurge,
  Maelstrom 3.00
72 F:Stingray 3.00
73 F:Quasar. 3.00
74 F:Puppet Master,Modred 3.00
75 F:The Avengers,O:Blastaar. . . . 4.00
76 F:Iceman,O:Ringmaster 3.00
77 F:Man-Thing 3.00
78 F:Wonder Man 3.00
79 F:Blue Diamond,I:Star Dancer . . 3.00
80 F:Ghost Rider 3.50
81 F:Sub-Mariner 2.50
82 F:Captain America 2.50
83 F:Sasquatch 3.50
84 F:Alpha Flight 3.50
85 F:Giant-Man 3.00
86 O:Sandman. 3.00
87 F:Ant-Man 3.00
88 F:She-Hulk 3.00
89 F:Human Torch 3.00
90 F:Spider-Man 4.00
91 V:Sphinx 3.00
92 F:Jocasta,V:Ultron. 3.00
93 F:Machine Man,D:Jocasta 3.00
94 F:Power Man,Iron Fist 3.00
95 F:Living Mummy 3.00
96 F:Sandman,C:Marvel Heroes . . . 3.00
97 F:Iron Man 3.00
98 F:Franklin Richards. 3.00
99 JBy(c),F:Rom 3.00
100 F:Ben Grimm 4.00
Ann.#1 SB,F:Liberty Legion. 7.00
Ann.#2 JSn,2nd D:Thanos,A:Spider
  Man,Avengers,Capt.Marvel,
  I:Lord Chaos,Master Order . . . 22.00
Ann.#3 F:Nova. 5.00
Ann.#4 F:Black Bolt. 4.00
Ann.#5 F:Hulk,V:Pluto 4.00
Ann.#6 I:American Eagle. 4.00
Ann.#7 I:Champion,A:Hulk,Thor,
  DocSamson,Colossus,Sasquatch,
  Wonder Man 4.00

MARVEL UNIVERSE: OFFICIAL HANDBOOK TO
Jan., 1983
1 Abomination-Avengers'
  Quintet. 7.50
2 BaronMordo-Collect.Man. 6.00
3 Collector-Dracula. 5.00
4 Dragon Man-Gypsy Moth 5.00
5 Hangman-Juggernaut 5.00
6 K-L. 4.00
7 Mandarin-Mystique 4.00
8 Na,oria-Pyro. 4.00
9 Quasar to She-Hulk. 4.00
10 Shiar-Sub-Mariner. 4.00
11 Subteraneans-Ursa Major. 4.00
12 Valkyrie-Zzzax. 4.00

Official Handbook of the Marvel
Universe #10 © Marvel Ent. Group

13 Book of the Dead 4.00
14 Book of the Dead 4.00
15 Weaponry 4.00

[2nd Series] 1985

1 Abomination-Batroc 5.00
2 Beast-Clea 4.00
3 Cloak & D.-Dr.Strange 4.00
4 Dr.Strange-Galactus 4.00
5 Gardener-Hulk 4.00
6 Human Torch-Ka-Zar 3.25
7 Kraven-Magneto 3.25
8 Magneto-Moleman 3.25
9 Moleman-Owl 3.25
10 . . . . 3.25
11 . . . . 3.00
12 S-T 3.00
13 . . . . 3.00
14 V-Z 3.00
15 . . . . 3.00
16 Book of the Dead 3.00
17 Handbook of the Dead,inc.
   JLe illus. 3.00
18 . . . . 3.00
19 . . . . 3.00
20 Inc.RLd illus. 3.00

Marvel Universe Update
1 thru 8 . . . . @3.00

Marvel Universe Packet
1 inc. Spider-Man 5.50
2 inc. Captain America 4.50
3 inc. Ghost Rider. 5.00
4 inc. Wolverine 4.50
5 inc. Punisher 4.25
6 inc. She-Hulk 4.00
7 inc. Daredevil 4.00
8 inc. Hulk 4.00
9 inc. Moon Knight 4.00
10 inc. Captain Britain 4.00
11 inc. Storm 4.00
12 inc. Silver Surfer 4.00
13 inc. Ice Man 4.50
14 inc. Thor 4.50
15 thru 22. . . . . @4.50
23 inc. Cage. 4.50
24 inc. Iron Fist 4.50
25 inc.Deadpool,Night Thrasher . . . 4.50
26 inc. Wonder Man. 5.00
27 inc.Beta Ray Bill,Pip 5.00
28 inc.X-Men 5.00
29 inc.Carnage. 5.00
30 thru 36. . . . . @5.00

MARVEL UNIVERSE
1996
1 Post Onslaught 3.25

MARVEL UNIVERSE
April, 1998
1 CPa(c),RSt,SEp,AW,F:Human
   Torch,Capt.Am.,Namor,48-pg. . . 3.00
2A JBy(c),RSt,SEp,AW,V:Hydra,
   Baron Strucker. 2.25
2B DGb(c). 2.25
3 RSt,SEp,AW,V:Hydra 2.25
4 RSt,MM, all-star jam cover,
   F:Monster Hunters. 2.25
5 MM,RSt,F:The Monster Hunters . 2.25
6 MM,RSt,F:Monster Hunters,pt.3 . 2.25
7 MM,RSt,F:Monster Hunters,pt.4 . 2.25
TPB Vol. 1: Thanos 18.00

MARVEL UNIVERSE: MILLENNIAL VISIONS
Dec., 2001
Spec.2001 48-page 4.00

MARVEL UNIVERSE: THE END
March, 2003
1 (of 6) JSn,AM. 2.25
2 JSn,AM 2.25
3 JSn,AM 3.00
4 JSn,AM 3.00
5 JSn,AM 3.00
6 JSn,AM 3.00

MARVEL VALENTINE'S SPECIAL
1997
1-shot MWa,TDF, 48-pg. 3.00

MARVEL VISIONARIES
July, 2002
TPB Gil Kane,256-pg. 30.00
TPB Jim Steranko, ... 15.00

MARVEL X-MEN COLLECTION
1994
1 thru 3 JL from the 1st series
   X-Men Cards . . . . @3.25

MARVELOUS ADVENTURES OF GUS BEEZER
April, 2003
Spec. F:Spider-Man 3.00
Spec. F:X-Men. 3.00
Spec. F:The Hulk. 3.00

MARVILLE
Sept., 2002
1 U-Decide 3.00
1b foil (c) 40-pg. 4.00
1c variant foil (c) 4.00
2 thru 6 . . . . @2.25
5a thru 6a MBr,variant (c) . . . . . . @2.25
7 . . . . 3.00
TPB Vol. 1 . . . . 13.00

MARVIN MOUSE
Atlas, Sept., 1957
1 BEv,F:Marvin Mouse 125.00

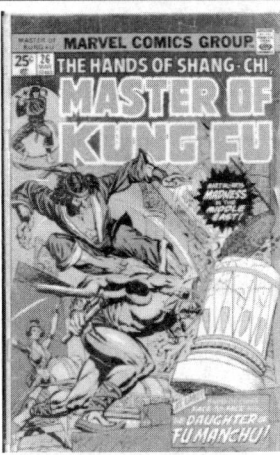

Master of Kung-Fu #26
© Marvel Entertainment Group

MASTER OF KUNG FU, SPECIAL MARVEL ED.
April, 1974
Prev: Special Marvel Edition
17 JSn,I:Black Jack Tarr 30.00
18 PG,1st Gulacy Art 15.00
19 PG,A:Man-Thing 18.00
20 GK(c),PG,AM,V:Samurai. 15.00
21 AM,Season of Vengeance..
   Moment of Death. 10.00
22 PG,DA,Death. 10.00
23 AM,KJ,River of Death 10.00
24 JSn,WS,AM,ST,Night of the
   Assassin 12.00
25 JSt(c),PG,ST,Fists Fury...
   Rites of Death 10.00
26 KP,ST,A:Daughter of
   Fu Manchu 10.00
27 SB,FS,A:Fu Manchu. 10.00
28 EH,ST,Death of a Spirit. 10.00
29 PG,V:Razor-Fist 10.00
30 PG,DA,Pit of Lions 10.00
31 GK&DA(c),PG,DA,Snowbuster . 10.00
32 GK&ME(c),SB,ME,Assault on an
   Angry Sea 10.00
33 PG,Messenger of Madness,
   I:Leiko Wu 10.00
34 PG,Captive in A Madman's
   Crown 10.00
35 PG,V:Death Hand 10.00
36 The Night of the Ninja's 10.00
37 V:Darkstrider & Warlords of
   the Web. 5.00
38 GK(c),PG,A:The Cat 5.00
39 GK(c),PG,A:The Cat 5.00
40 PG,The Murder Agency. 5.00
41 . . . . 5.00
42 GK(c),PG,TS,V:Shockwave 5.00
43 PG,V:Shockwave 5.00
44 SB(c),PG,V:Fu Manchu. 5.00
45 GK(c),PG,Death Seed. 5.00
46 PG,V:Sumo 5.00
47 PG,The Cold White
   Mantle of Death 5.00
48 PG,Bridge of a 1,000 Dooms . . . 5.00
49 PG,V:Shaka Kharn,The
   Demon Warrior 5.00
50 PG,V:Fu Manchu. 5.00
51 PG(c),To End...To Begin 5.00
52 Mayhem in Morocco 5.00
53 . . . . 5.00

MARVEL (vertical tab, right margin)

MARVEL

54 JSn(c),Death Wears Three
    Faces. 5.00
55 PG(c),The Ages of Death 5.00
56 V:The Black Ninja. 5.00
57 V:Red Baron 5.00
58 Behold the Final Mask 5.00
59 GK(c),B:Phoenix Gambit,
    Behold the Angel of Doom 5.00
60 A:Dr.Doom,Doom Came 5.00
61 V:Skull Crusher. 4.50
62 Coast of Death 4.50
63 GK&TA(c),Doom Wears
    Three Faces 4.50
64 PG(c),To Challenge a Dragon . . 4.50
65 V:Pavane 4.50
66 V:Kogar. 4.50
67 PG(c),Dark Encounters. 4.50
68 Final Combats,V:The Cat 4.50
69 . . . . 4.50
70 A:Black Jack Tarr,Murder
    Mansion. 4.50
71 PG(c),Ying & Yang (c) 4.50
72 V:Shockwave 4.50
73 RN(c),V:Behemoths 4.50
74 TA(c),A:Shockwave. 4.50
75 Where Monsters Dwell 4.50
76 GD,Battle on the Waterfront 4.00
77 GD,I:Zaran 4.00
78 GD,Moving Targets 4.00
79 GD,This Side of Death 4.00
80 GD,V:Leopard Men 4.00
81 GD,V:Leopard Men. 4.00
82 GD,Flight into Fear 4.00
83 GD, ... 4.00
84 GD,V:Fu Manchu 4.00
85 GD,V:Fu Manchu 4.00
86 GD,V:Fu Manchu 4.00
87 GD,V:Zaran, ... 4.00
88 GD,V:Fu Manchu 4.00
89 GD,D:Fu Manchu 4.00
90 MZ,Death in Chinatown 4.00
91 GD,Gang War,drugs 5.00
92 GD,Shadows of the Past 4.00
93 GD,Cult of Death 4.00
94 GD,V:Agent Synergon 4.00
95 GD,Raid 4.00
96 GD,I:Rufus Carter. 4.00
97 GD,V:Kung Fu's Dark Side. 4.00
98 GD,Fight to the Finish. 4.00
99 GD,Death Boat 4.00
100 GD,Doublesize 6.00
101 GD,Not Smoke,Nor Beads,
     Nor Blood 3.75
102 GD,Assassins,1st GD(p). 4.00
103 GD,V:Assassins 3.75
104 GD,Fight without Reason,
     C:Cerberus 3.75
105 GD,I:Razor Fist. 3.75
106 GD,C:Velcro 3.75
107 GD,A:Sata. 3.75
108 GD. 3.75
109 GD,Death is a Dark Agent 3.75
110 GD,Perilous Reign 3.75
111 GD. 3.75
112 GD(c),Commit and Destroy. . . . 3.75
113 GD(c),V:Panthers 3.75
114 Fantasy o/t Autumn Moon. 3.75
115 GD. 3.75
116 GD. 3.75
117 GD,Devil Deeds Done
     in Darkness 3.75
118 GD,D:Fu Manchu,double 4.50
119 GD. 3.75
120 GD,Dweller o/t Dark Stream . . . 3.75
121 Death in the City of Lights 3.00
122 . . . . 3.00
123 V:Ninjas. 3.00
124 . . . . 3.00
125 double-size 6.00
G-Size#1,CR,PG 20.00
G-Size#2 PG,V:Yellow Claw 3.00

G-Size#3 . . . . 3.00
G-Size#4 JK,V:Yellow Claw 3.00
Spec.#1 Bleeding Black. 3.00

MASTER OF KUNG FU: BLEEDING BLACK

1 V:ShadowHand, 1991 . . . . 3.00

MASTERS OF TERROR

July–Sept., 1975

1 GM(c),FB,BWS,JSn,NA 25.00
2 JSn(c),GK,VM, ... 20.00

MASTERS OF THE UNIVERSE

Star, May, 1986–March, 1988

1 I:Hordak 7.00
2 thru 11 . . . . @4.00
12 D:Skeletor 8.00
Movie #1 GT 2.00

MATT SLADE, GUNFIGHTER

Atlas, May, 1956

1 AW,AT,F:Matt Slade,Crimson
   Avenger 225.00
2 AW,A:Crimson Avenger 175.00
3 A:Crimson Avenger 150.00
4 A:Crimson Avenger 125.00
Becomes:

KID SLADE GUNFIGHTER

5 F:Kid Slade 125.00
6 . . . . 100.00
7 AW,Duel in the Night 110.00
8 July, 1957 . . . . 100.00

MAVERICK

1997

1 JGz,F:Christopher Nord/David
   North/Maverick, 48-pg. 3.50
2 JGz,A:Victor Creed and Logan . . 3.00
2a variant cover 3.00
3 JGz,V:Puck & Vindicator 3.00
4 JGz,A:Wolverine 3.00
5 JGz,A:The Blob 3.00
6 JGz,V:Sabretooth. 3.00
7 JGz,V:Sabretooth. 3.00
8 JGz,V:The Confessor 3.00
9 JGz,Maverick's secrets 3.00

Maverick #3
© Marvel Entertainment Group

10 JGz,V:Ivan the Terrible, Chris
   Bradley becomes Bolt 3.00
11 JGz,A:Darkstar,Vanguard,
   Ursa Major. 3.00
12 JGz, double sized last issue 3.50
1-shot LHa, V:Sabretooth,48-pg. . . . 2.95

MAXIMUM SECURITY

Oct., 2000

1 (of 3) KBk,JOy,x-over 3.00
2 KBk,JOy,x-over 3.00
3 KBk,JOy,x-over,concl. 3.00
Spec. Thor vs. Ego, 64-pg.,SL,JK . . 3.00
Spec. Dangerous Planet 3.00

MEKANIX

Oct., 2002

1 (of 6) CCI,F:Kitty Pryde 3.00
2 CCI,back in school. 3.00
3 CCI. 3.00
4 CCI. 3.00
5 CCI. 3.00
6 CCI, concl. 3.00

MELVIN THE MONSTER

Atlas, July, 1956

1 JMn 150.00
2 thru 6 . . . . @125.00
Becomes:

DEXTER THE DEMON

Sept., 1957

7 . . . . 75.00

MEMORIES

Epic

1 Space Adventures 2.50

MENACE

Atlas, May, 1953

1 RH,BEv,GT,One Head Too
   Many 900.00
2 RH,BEv,GT,JSt,Burton'sBlood . 650.00
3 BEv,RH,JR,The Werewolf 450.00
4 BEv,RH,The Four Armed Man. 450.00
5 BEv,RH,GC,GT,I&O:Zombie . 750.00
6 BEv,RH,JR,The Graymoor
   Ghost 450.00
7 JSt,RH,Fresh out of Flesh 350.00
8 RH,The Lizard Man 350.00
9 BEv,The Walking Dead 400.00
10 RH(c),Half Man,Half.... . . . . . 350.00
11 JKz,JR,Locked In,May, 1954 . 350.00

MEN IN ACTION

Atlas, April, 1952

1 Sweating it Out 200.00
2 US Infantry stories 100.00
3 RH 75.00
4 War stories 75.00
5 JMn,Squad Charge 75.00
6 War stories 75.00
7 RH(c),BK,No Risk Too Great . 100.00
8 JRo(c),They Strike By Night . . . 75.00
9 SSh(c),Rangers Strike Back . . . 75.00
Becomes:

BATTLE BRADY

10 SSh(c),F:Battle Brady 150.00
11 SSh(c). 100.00
12 SSh(c),Death to the Reds. 75.00
13 . . . . 75.00
14 Final Issue,June, 1953 . . . . . . 75.00

MEN IN BLACK

1 ANi, prequel to movie (1997). . . . 4.00
Spec. Movie Adaptation (1997) 4.00

MEN IN BLACK: RETRIBUTION
Aug., 1997
1 continuation from movie 4.00

MEN'S ADVENTURES
See: TRUE WESTERN

MEPHISTO vs. FOUR HEROES
April–July, 1987
1 JB,BWi,A:Fantastic Four 3.50
2 JB,BWi,A:X-Factor 3.00
3 JB,AM,A:X-Men 3.00
4 JB,BWi,A:Avengers 3.00

METEOR MAN
1993–94
1 R:Meteor Man 2.25
2 V:GhostStrike,Malefactor,Simon . 2.25
3 A:Spider-Man 2.25
4 A:Night Thrasher 2.25
5 Exocet 2.25
6 final issue 2.25

[TED McKEEVER'S} METROPOL
Epic, 1991–92
1 Ted McKeever 3.00
2 thru 12 . . . . @3.00

METROPOL A.D.
Epic, 1992
1 R:The Angels 3.50
2 V:Demons 3.50
3 V:Nuclear Arsenal 3.50

MICRONAUTS
[1st Series] Jan., 1979
1 MGo,JRu,O:Micronauts 5.00
2 MGo,JRu,Earth 3.00
3 MGo,JRu 3.00
4 MGo 3.00
5 MGo,V:Prometheus 3.00
6 MGo 3.00
7 MGo,A:Man Thing 3.00
8 MGo,BMc,I:Capt. Univ. 3.00
9 MGo,I:Cilicia 3.00
10 MGo 3.00
11 MGo 3.00
12 MGo 3.00
13 HC,F:Bug 3.00
14 HC,V:Wartstaff 3.00
15 HC,AM,A:Fantastic Four 3.00
16 HC,AM,A:Fantastic Four 3.00
17 HC,AM,A:Fantastic Four 3.00
18 HC,Haunted House Issue 3.00
19 PB,V:Odd John 3.00
20 PB,A:Antman 3.00
21 PB,I:Microverse 3.00
22 PB 3.00
23 PB,V:Molecule Man 3.00
24 MGo,V:Computrex 3.00
25 PB,A:Mentallo 3.00
26 PB,A:Baronkarza 3.00
27 PB,V:Hydra,A:Shield 3.00
28 PB,V:Hydra,A:Shield 3.00
29 PB,Doc Samson 3.00
30 PB,A:Shield 3.00
31 PB,A:Dr.Strange 3.00
32 PB,A:Dr.Strange 3.00
33 PB,A:Devil of Tropica 3.00
34 PB,A:Dr.Strange 3.00
35 O:Microverse 3.00

---

36 KG,Dr.Strange 3.00
37 KG,Nightcrawler 4.00
38 GK,1st direct 2.50
39 SD 2.50
40 GK,A:FF 2.50
41 GK,Dr.Doom 2.50
42 GK 2.50
43 . . . . 2.50
44 . . . . 2.50
45 Arcade 2.50
46 . . . . 2.50
47 . . . . 2.50
48 JG 2.75
49 JG,V:Baron Karza 2.50
50 JG,V:Baron Karza 2.50
51 JG 2.50
52 JG 2.50
53 JG,V:Untouchables 2.50
54 JG,V:Tribunal 2.50
55 JG,V:Karza World 2.50
56 JG,Kaliklak 2.50
57 JG,V:Baron Karza 2.50
58 JG,V:Baron Karza 2.50
59 JG,V:The Makers 2.50
Ann.#1,SD 2.50
#2 SD 2.50

[2nd Series] 1984
1 V:The Makers 2.50
2 AAd(c),V:The Makers 2.50
3 Huntarr'sEgg 2.50
4 V:The Makers 2.50
5 The Spiral Path 2.50
6 L:Bug 2.50
7 Acroyear 2.50
8 V:Scion 2.50
9 R:Devil 2.50
10 V:Enigma Force 2.50
11 V:Scion 2.50
12 V:Scion 2.50
13 V:Dark Armada 2.50
14 V:Keys of the Zodiac 2.50
15 O:Marionette 2.50
16 Secret Wars II 3.00
17 V:Scion 2.50
18 Acroyear 2.50
19 R:Baron Karza 2.50
20 Last Issue 2.50

MICRONAUTS
(Special Edition) Dec., 1983
1 MGo/JRu,rep. 3.00
2 MGo/JRu,rep. 3.00
3 Rep.MG/JRu 3.00
4 Rep.MG/JRu 3.00
5 Rep.MG/JRu,April, 1984 . . . . 3.00

MIDNIGHT MEN
Epic *Heavy Hitters*, 1993
1 HC,I:Midnight Men 3.00
2 HC,J:Barnett 2.25
3 HC,Pasternak is Midnight Man . . 2.25
4 HC,Last issue 2.25

MIDNIGHT SONS UNLIMITED
1993–95
1 JQ,JBi,MT(c),A:Midnight Sons . . . 4.25
2 BSz(c),F:Midnight Sons 4.25
3 JR2(c),JS,A:Spider-Man 4.25
4 Siege of Darkness #17,
    D:2nd Ghost Rider 4.25
5 DQ(s),F:Mordred,Vengeance,
    Morbius,Werewolf,Blaze,
    I:Wildpride 4.25
6 DQ(s),F:Dr.Strange 3.95
7 DQ(s),F:Man-Thing 3.95
8 . . . . 3.95
9 J:Mighty Destroyer 3.95

Midnight Sons Unlimited #3
© Marvel Entertainment Group

MIGHTY HEROES
Nov., 1997
1-shot SLo, Diaper Man, Rope Man,
Cuckoo Man, Tornado Man, Strong
Man, etc. 3.00

MIGHTY MARVEL WESTERN
Oct., 1968
1 JK,All reprints,B:Rawhide Kid
    Kid Colt,Two-Gun Kids 75.00
2 JK,DAy,Beware of the Barker
    Brothers 50.00
3 HT(c),JK,DAy,Walking Death . . 50.00
4 HT(c),DAy 50.00
5 HT(c),DAy,Ambush 50.00
6 HT(c),DAy Doom in the Desert . 50.00
7 DAy,V:MurderousMasquerader . 50.00
8 HT(c),DAy,Rustler's on the
    Range 50.00
9 JSe(c),JK,DAy,V:Dr Danger . . . 50.00
10 OW,DH,Cougar 50.00
11 V:The Enforcers 30.00
12 JK,V:Blackjack Bordon 40.00
13 V:Grizzly 40.00
14 JK.V:The Enforcers 40.00
15 Massacre at Medicine Bend . . . 40.00
16 JK,Mine of Death 40.00
17 Ambush at Blacksnake Mesa . . 25.00
18 Six-Gun Thunderer 25.00
19 Reprints cont. 25.00
20 same 25.00
21 same 20.00
22 . . . . 20.00
23 same 20.00
24 JDa,E:Kid Colt 20.00
25 B:Matt Slade 20.00
26 thru 31 Reprints . . . . @20.00
32 JK,AW,Ringo Kid #23 . . . . 15.00
33 thru 36 Reprints . . . . @15.00
37 JK,AW Two-Gun #51 . . . . 15.00
38 thru 45 Reprints . . . . @15.00
46 same,Sept., 1976 . . . . 15.00

[SABAN'S] MIGHTY MORPHIN POWER RANGERS
1 SLo,FaN,New ongoing series . . . 2.25
2 thru 7 . . . . @2.25
Photo Adaptation 2.95

MARVEL

[SABAN'S] MIGHTY MORPHIN POWER RANGERS: NINJA RANGERS/ VR TROOPERS

1 FaN,RLm,JP,flip book 2.25
2 JP,flip book. 2.25
3 thru 6 . . . . @2.25

MIGHTY MOUSE
[1st Series] Fall, 1946
1 Terytoons Presents. 1,600.00
2 . . . . 750.00
3 . . . . 500.00
4 Summer, 1947 . . . . 500.00

MIGHTY MOUSE
Oct., 1990
1 EC,Dark Mite Returns 3.00
2 EC,V:The Glove. 2.25
3 EC/JBr(c)Prince Say More 2.25
4 EC/GP(c)Alt.Universe #1. . . . . . . 2.25
5 EC,Alt.Universe #2 . . . . 2.25
6 Ferment',A:MacFurline 2.25
7 EC,V:Viral Worm 2.25
8 EC,BAT-BAT:Year One,
   O:Bug Wonder. 2.25
9 EC,BAT-BAT:Year One,
   V:Smoker. 2.25
10 Night o/t Rating Lunatics 2.25

MILLIE THE MODEL
Winter, 1945
1 O:Millie the Model,
   Bowling(c) 1,200.00
2 Totem Pole(c) 550.00
3 Anti-Noise(c) 350.00
4 Bathing Suit(c) 350.00
5 Blame it on Fame 350.00
6 Beauty and the Beast 350.00
7 Bathing Suit(c) 350.00
8 Fancy Dress(c),HK,Hey Look . 350.00
9 Paris(c),BW 400.00
10 Jewelry(c),HK,Hey Look 350.00
11 HK,Giggles and Grins 225.00
12 A;Rusty,Hedy Devine 160.00
13 A;Hedy Devine,HK,Hey Look . 175.00
14 HK,Hey Look. 175.00
15 HK,Hey Look. 150.00
16 HK,Hey Look. 150.00
17 thru 20. . . . . @165.00
21 thru 30. . . . . @125.00
31 thru 75. . . . . @125.00
76 thru 99. . . . . @60.00
100 . . . . 100.00
101 thru 126. . . . . @60.00
127 Millie/Clicker 65.00
128 A:Scarlet Mayfair. 45.00
129 The Truth about Agnes 45.00
130 thru 153. . . . . @45.00
154 B:New Millie 45.00
155 thru 206. . . . . @45.00
207 Dec., 1973 . . . . 45.00
Ann.#1 How Millie Became
   a Model 300.00
Ann.#2 Millies Guide to
   the world of Modeling 200.00
Ann.#3 Many Lives of Millie. 125.00
Ann.#4 Many Lives of Millie. 75.00

MISS AMERICA COMICS
1944
1 Miss America(c),pin-ups . . . 2,200.00

MISS AMERICA MAGAZINE
Nov., 1944—Nov., 1958
2 Ph(c),Miss America costume
   I;Patsy Walker,Buzz Baxter,
   Hedy Wolfe 1,700.00
3 Ph(c),A:Patsy Walker,Miss
   America 650.00
4 Ph(c),Betty Page,A:Patsy
   Walker,Miss America 650.00
5 Ph(c),A:Patsy Walker,Miss
   America. 650.00
6 Ph(c),A:Patsy Walker. 175.00
7 Patsy Walker stories 150.00
8 same 150.00
9 same 150.00
10 same 150.00
11 same 150.00
12 same. 150.00
13 thru 18. . . . . @150.00
21 . . . . 175.00
22 thru 93. . . . . @100.00

Miss Fury #1
© Marvel Entertainment Group

MISS FURY COMICS
Timely, Winter, 1942-43
1 Newspaper strip reprints,
   ASh(c) O:Miss Fury 5,500.00
2 V:Nazis(c) 2,500.00
3 Hitler/Nazi Flag(c) 2,000.00
4 ASh(c),Japanese(c) 1,500.00
5 ASh(c),Gangster(c) 1,300.00
6 Gangster(c). 1,200.00
7 Gangster(c) 1,100.00
8 Atom-Bomb Secrets(c)
   Winter, 1946 . . . . 1,100.00

MISSION: IMPOSSIBLE
May, 1996
1 RLd,MWn(s),Movie adapt. 3.00

MISTY
Star, Dec., 1985
1 F:Millie the Models Niece 3.50
2 thru 5 . . . . @3.50
6 May, 1986 . . . . 3.50

MITZI COMICS
Timely, Spring, 1948
1 HK:Hey Look,Giggles
   and Grins 300.00
Becomes:

MITZI'S BOYFRIEND
2 F:Chip,Mitzi/Chip(c) 150.00
3 Chips adventures 125.00
4 thru 7 same . . . . @125.00
Becomes:

MITZI'S ROMANCES
8 Mitzi/Chip(c) 125.00
9 . . . . 100.00
10 Dec., 1949 . . . . 100.00

MODELING WITH MILLIE
See: DATE WITH MILLIE

MOEBIUS
Epic, Oct., 1987
1 . . . . 12.00
2 . . . . 12.00
3 . . . . 15.00
4 . . . . 12.00
5 . . . . 12.00
6 1988 . . . . 12.00

MOEBIUS: FUSION
1 128-pg. Sketchbook. 20.00

MOLLY MANTON'S ROMANCES
Sept., 1949
1 Ph(c),Dare Not Marry 175.00
2 Ph(c),Romances of 150.00
Becomes:

ROMANTIC AFFAIRS
3 Ph(c) 125.00

MOMENT OF SILENCE
Dec., 2001
Spec. 9-11-01 tribute issue 3.50

MONSTER MENACE
1 thru 4 SD,rep. . . . . @3.00

MONSTER OF FRANKENSTEIN
Jan., 1973
1 MP,Frankenstein's Monster 65.00
2 MP,Bride of the Monster 40.00
3 MP,Revenge 40.00
4 MP,Monster's Death. 40.00
5 MP,The Monster Walks
   Among Us. 40.00
Becomes:

FRANKENSTEIN
1973–75
6 MP,Last of the Frankensteins . . 25.00
7 JB,The Fiend and the Fury 25.00
8 JB,A:Dracula 40.00
9 JB,A:Dracula 40.00
10 JB,Death Strikes Frankenstein . 20.00
11 Carnage at CastleFrankenstein 15.00
12 Frankenstein's Monster today. . 15.00
13 Undying Fiend. 15.00
14 Fury of the Night Creature 15.00
15 Trapped in a Nightmare 15.00
16 The Brute and the Berserker . . 15.00
17 Phoenix Aflame. 15.00
18 Children of the Damned 15.00

MONSTERS ON THE PROWL
See: CHAMBER OF DARKNESS

MONSTERS UNLEASHED
July, 1973
1 GM(c),GC,DW,B&W Mag 40.00
2 JB,FB,BEv,B:Frankenstein 35.00
3 NA(c),GK,GM,GT,B:Man-Thing 35.00
4 JB,GC,BK,I:Satana 25.00
5 JB 25.00
6 MP 25.00
7 AW 25.00
8 GP,NA 30.00
9 A:Wendigo 30.00
10 O:Tigra 30.00
11 FB(C),April, 1975 .... 30.00
Ann.#1 GK 30.00

MOON KNIGHT
[1st Regular Series] Nov., 1980
1 BSz,O:Moon Knight 5.00
2 BSz,V:Slasher 3.50
3 BSz,V:Midnight Man 3.50
4 BSz,V:Committee of 5 .... 3.50
5 BSz,V:Red Hunter 3.50
6 BSz,V:White Angels.......... 3.50
7 BSz,V:Moon Kings........... 3.50
8 BSz,V:Moon Kings, Drug...... 3.00
9 BSz,V:Midnight Man 3.00
10 BSz,V:Midnight Man 3.00
11 BSz,V:Creed (Angel Dust) ... 3.00
12 BSz,V:Morpheus............. 3.00
13 BSz,A:Daredevil & Jester 3.00
14 BSz,V:Stained Glass Scarlet ... 3.00
15 FM(c),BSz,1st Direct. 4.00
16 V:Blacksmith 3.00
17 BSz,V:Master Sniper. 3.00
18 BSz,V:Slayers Elite........... 3.00
19 BSz,V:Arsenal 3.00
20 BSz,V:Arsenal.............. 3.00
21 A:Bother Voodoo............. 2.50
22 BSz,V:Morpheus............. 2.50
23 BSz,V:Morpheus............. 2.50
24 BSz,V:Stained Glass Scarlet ... 2.50
25 BSz,Black Specter........... 2.50
26 KP,V:Cabbie Killer........... 2.50
27 A:Kingpin.................. 2.50
28 BSz,Spirits in the Sands 2.50
29 BSz,V:Werewolf 2.50
30 BSz,V:Werewolf 2.50
31 TA,V:Savage Studs........... 2.50
32 KN,Druid Walsh 2.50
33 KN,V:Druid Walsh 2.50
34 KN,Marc Spector............. 2.50
35 KN,X-Men,FF,V:The Fly
   DoubleSized 3.00

Moon Knight #36
© Marvel Entertainment Group

36 A:Dr.Strange 2.50
37 V:Zohar 2.50
38 V:Zohar.................... 2.50
[2nd Regular Series] 1985
1 O:Moon Knight,DoubleSize 2.50
2 Yucatan 2.50
3 V:Morpheus 2.50
4 A:Countess 2.50
5 V:Lt.Flint.................... 2.50
6 GI,LastIssue................. 2.50
[3rd Regular Series] 1989–94
1 V:Bushmaster............... 4.00
2 A:Spider-Man............... 3.00
3 V:Bushmaster 2.50
4 RH,A:Midnight,Black Cat 2.50
5 V:Midnight,BlackCat.......... 2.50
6 A:BrotherVoodoo 2.50
7 A:BrotherVoodoo 2.50
8 TP,A:Punisher,A of V 3.00
9 TP,A:Punisher,A of V 3.00
10 V:Killer Shrike,A of V. 2.00
11 TP,V:Arsenal 2.00
12 TP,V:Bushman,A:Arsenal 2.50
13 TP,V:Bushman 2.50
14 TP,V:Bushman 2.50
15 TP,Trial o/Marc Spector #1,A:
   Silv.Sable,Sandman,Paladin ... 3.00
16 TP,Trial o/Marc Spector #2,A:
   Silv.Sable,Sandman,Paladin ... 3.00
17 TP,Trial o/Marc Spector #3 .... 3.00
18 TP,Trial o/Marc Spector #4 .... 3.00
19 RLd(c),TP,SpM,Punisher. 3.00
20 TP,A:Spider-Man,Punisher 3.00
21 TP,Spider-Man,Punisher 3.00
22 I:Harbinger 2.50
23 Confrontation 2.50
24 A:Midnight................. 2.50
25 MBa,TP,A:Ghost Rider 3.00
26 BSz(c),TP,B:Scarlet Redemption
   V:Stained Glass Scarlet....... 2.50
27 TP,V:Stained Glass Scarlet..... 2.50
28 TP,V:Stained Glass Scarlet..... 2.50
29 TP,V:Stained Glass Scarlet..... 2.50
30 TP,V:Stained Glass Scarlet.... 2.50
31 TP,E:Scarlet Redemption,
   A:Hobgoblin 2.75
32 TP,V:Hobgoblin,SpM(in Black) .. 3.00
33 TP,V:Hobgoblin,A:Spider-Man. .. 3.00
34 V:Killer Shrike 2.50
35 TP,Return of Randall Spector
   Pt.1,A:Punisher 2.50
36 TP,A:Punisher,Randall 2.50
37 TP,A:Punisher,Randall 2.50
38 TP,A:Punisher,Randall 2.50
39 TP,N:Moon Knight,A:Dr.Doom .. 2.50
40 TP,V:Dr.Doom 2.50
41 TP,Infinity War,I:Moonshade 2.50
42 TP,Infinity War,V:Moonshade ... 2.50
43 TP(i),Infinity War 2.50
44 Inf.War,A:Dr.Strange.FF 2.50
45 V:Demogoblin 2.50
46 V:Demogoblin 2.50
47 Legacy Quest Scenario 2.50
48 I:Deadzone 2.50
49 V:Deadzone 2.50
50 A:Avengers,I:Hellbent,
   Die-cut(c).................. 3.50
51 A:Gambit,V:Hellbent 2.50
52 A:Gambit,Werewolf 2.50
53 Pang 2.50
54 .... 2.50
55 SPa,V:Sunstreak............. 6.00
56 SPa,V:Seth 6.00
57 SPa,Inf.Crusade 4.00
58 SPa(c),A:Hellbent 3.00
59 SPa(c),.................... 3.50
60 E:TKa(s),SPa,D:Moonknight.... 5.00
Spec.#1 ANi,A:Shang-Chi 2.50
1-shot Moon Knight: Divided We Fall
   DCw,V:Bushman (1992) 5.00

MOON KNIGHT
(Special Edition) Nov., 1983
1 BSz,reprints 2.50
2 BSz,reprints 2.50
3 BSz,reprints,Jan., 1984 .... 2.50

MOON KNIGHT
Nov., 1997–Feb., 1998
1 (of 4) DgM, Moon Knight returns. 2.50
1A signed by Tommy Lee Edwards
   (250 copies).............. 20.00
2 DgM,A:Scarlet 2.50
3 DgM,Resurrection War,V:Black
   Spectre 2.50
4 DgM,Resurrecton War, concl. ... 2.50

MOON KNIGHT
Dec., 1998
1 (of 4) DgM,MT,A:Marlene 3.00
2 DgM,MT 3.00
3 DgM,MT.................... 3.00
4 DgM,MT,concl............... 3.00

MOONSHADOW
Epic, May, 1985
1 JMu,O:Moonshadow 6.00
2 JMu,Into Space 4.00
3 JMu,The Looney Bin 4.00
4 JMu,Fights Ira 4.00
5 JMu,Prisoner 4.00
6 JMu,Hero of War 4.00
7 JMu,UnkshussFamily.......... 4.00
8 JMu,Social Outcast 4.00
9 JMu,Search For Ira 4.00
10 JMu,Internat.House of T....... 4.00
11 JMu,UnkshussFamily 4.00
12 JMu,UnkshussFamily,Feb.1987 . 4.00

MORBIUS
1992–95
1 V:Lilith,Lilin,A:Blaze,Gh.Rider,
   Rise o/t Midnight Sons #3,
   polybagged w/poster 3.00
2 V:Simon Stroud 2.50
3 A:Spider-Man 2.25
4 I:Dr.Paine,C:Spider-Man 2.25
5 V:Basilisk,(inc Superman tribute
   on letters page) 2.25
6 V:Basilisk 2.25
7 V:Vic Slaughter 2.25

Morbius #30
© Marvel Entertainment Group

MARVEL

8 V:Nightmare 2.25
9 V:Nightmare 2.25
10 Two Tales 2.25
11 A:Nightstalkers 2.25
12 Midnight Massacre#4 . . . . 2.50
13 R:Martine,A:Lilith 2.25
14 RoW,V:Nightmare,A:Werewolf . . 2.25
15 A:Ghost Rider,Werewolf 2.25
16 GWt(s),Siege of Darkness#5 . . . 2.25
17 GWt(s),Siege of Darkness#17 . . 2.25
18 GWt(s),A:Deathlok 2.25
19 GWt(s),A:Deathlok 2.25
20 GWt(s),I:Bloodthirst 2.25
21 B:Dance of the Hunter,A:SpM . . 2.25
22 A:Spider-Man 2.25
23 E:Dance of the Hunter,A:SpM . . 2.25
24 Return of the Dragon 2.25
25 RoW 2.50
26 . . . . 2.00
27 . . . . 2.00
28 A:Werewolf 2.00
29 . . . . 2.00
30 New Morbius 2.00
31 A:Mortine 2.00
32 Another Kill 2.00

MORBIUS REVISITED
1993
1 WMc,rep.Fear #20 . . . . 2.25
2 WMc,rep.Fear #28 . . . . 2.25
3 WMc,rep.Fear #29 . . . . 2.25
4 WMc,rep.Fear #30 . . . . 2.25
5 WMc,rep.Fear #31 . . . . 2.25

MORLOCKS
April, 2002
1 (of 4) SMa, outsiders 2.50
2 SMa,mutants stay hidden 2.50
3 SMa,where lurk the Morlocks . . . 2.50
4 SMa,concl 2.50

Mort The Dead Teenager #4
© Marvel Entertainment Group

MORT THE DEAD TEENAGER
1993–94
1 LHa(s),I:Mort 2.25
2 thru 4 LHa(s), ... @2.25

MOTHER TERESA
1984
1 Mother Teresa Story 5.00

MOTOR MOUTH & KILLPOWER
Marvel UK, 1992–93
1 GFr,A:Nick Fury,I:Motor
  Mouth,Killpower 2.50
2 GFr,A:Nick Fury, ... 2.25
3 GFr,V:Killpower,A:Punisher 2.25
4 GFr,A:Nick Fury,Warheads,
  Hell's Angel,O:Killpower 2.25
5 GFr,A:Excalibur,Archangel 2.25
6 GFr,A:Cable,Punisher 2.25
7 EP,A:Cable,Nick Fury 2.25
8 JFr,A:Cable,Nick Fury 2.25
9 JFr,A:Cable,N.Fury,V:Harpies . . 2.25
10 V:Red Sonja 2.25
11 V:Zachary Sorrow 2.25
12 A:Death's Head II 2.25
13 A:Death's Head II 2.25

MS. MARVEL
Jan., 1977
1 JB,O:Ms Marvel 15.00
2 JB,JSt,V:Scorpion 7.00
3 JB,JSt,V:Doomsday Man 7.00
4 JM,JSt,V:Destructor 7.00
5 JM,JSt,A:V:Vision 7.00
6 JM,JSt,V:Grotesk 7.00
7 JM,JSt,V:Modok 7.00
8 JM,JSt,GF(c),V:Grotesk 7.00
9 KP,JSt,I:Deathbird 8.00
10 JB,TP,V:Deathbird,Modok 6.00
11 V:Elementals 5.00
12 JSn(c),V:Hecate 5.00
13 Bedlam in Boston 5.00
14 CI,TA(c),V:Steeplejack 5.00
15 V:Tigershark 5.00
16 TA,V:Tigershark,A:Beast 12.00
17 TA,C:Mystique 10.00
18 I:Mystique,A;Avengers 20.00
19 A:Captain Marvel 5.00
20 V:Lethal Lizards,N:Ms.Marvel . 5.00
21 V:Lethal Lizards 5.00
22 TA,V:Deathbirds 5.00
23 The Woman who Fell to Earth
  April, 1979 . . . . 5.00

MUPPET BABIES
Star, Aug., 1984
1 thru 10 . . . . @2.25
11 thru 20 . . . . @2.25
21 thru 25 July, 1989 . . . . @2.25

MUPPETS TAKE MANHATTAN
1 movie adapt,November, 1984 . . . 3.00
2 movie adapt 3.00
3 movie adapt,Jan., 1985 . . . . 3.00

MUTANTS: THE AMAZING X-MEN
1 X-Men After Xavier 3.50
2 Exodus, Dazzler,V:Abyss 2.25
3 F:Bishop 2.25
4 V:Apocalypse 2.25

MUTANTS: THE ASTONISHING X-MEN
1 Uncanny X-Men 3.50
2 V:Holocaust 2.25
3 V:Abyss 2.25
4 V:Beast,Infinities 2.25

MUTANTS: GENERATION NEXT
1 Generation X Ax 3.50

2 Genetic Slave Pens 2.25
3 V:Sugar Man 2.25
4 V:Sugar Man 2.25

Mutant X #4
© Marvel Entertainment Group

MUTANT X
Aug., 1998
1 HMe,TR,F:Havok, 48-pg 3.00
2 HMe,TR,F:Havok 2.50
2a variant cover 2.50
3 HMe,TR,V:Pack 2.50
4 HMe,TR,V:Goblin Queen 2.50
5 HMe,F:Brute, Fallen 2.50
6 HMe,A:Mutant-X Spider-Man . . . 2.50
7 HMe,Trial of the Brute 2.50
8 HMe,V:Goblin Queen 2.50
9 HMe,V:Sentinels 2.50
10 HMe,V:The Six 2.50
11 HMe,Bloodstorm vs. Havok . . . 2.50
12 HMe,O:Goblin Queen,Havok,
  48-page 3.50
13 O:Bloodstorm 2.50
14 HMe,CNr,I:Cyclops 2.50
15 HMe,F:Havok 2.50
16 HMe 2.50
17 HMe,CNr,V:Cyclops 2.50
18 HMe,CNr,A:Punisher 2.50
19 HMe,A:Professor X 2.50
20 HMe,A:Havok 2.50
21 HMe,BS,Prof.X & Apocalypse . . 2.50
22 HMe,BS,Galactus 2.50
23 HMe,TL,Apocalypse 2.50
24 HMe,TL,Master Planner 2.50
25 HMe,TL,The Six,48-pg 3.50
26 HMe,TL,The Six,Bloodstorm . . . 2.50
27 HMe,TL,Dagger,Outcasts 2.50
28 HMe,TL,F:Wolverine 2.50
29 HMe,TL,F:Wolverine 2.50
30 HMe,RLm,F:Capt.America 2.50
31 HMe,RLm,F:Capt.America 2.50
32 HMe,RLm,48-page, final 3.00
GN Mutant X, rep.#1 & #2 . . . . 6.00
Ann.1999, 48-page 3.50
Ann.2000 HMe,secrets 3.50
Ann.2001 HMe,48-page 3.00

MUTANT X
Oct., 2001
1 HC,JHo, TV show tie-in 3.00
2 HC,JHo, ... 2.50
Spec.#1 48-pg.,photo(c) (2002) 3.50
Spec.Dangerous Discoveries (2002) 3.50

MARVEL

MUTANT X: FUTURE SHOCK
May, 2002
1 CCI,F:Shalimar,54-pg. 3.50

MUTATIS
Epic
1 I:Mutatis 2.50
2 O:Mutatis 2.50
3 A:Mutatis 2.50

MUTIES
Feb., 2002
1 (of 6) F:Jared 2.50
2 in Japan, I:Seiji 2.50
3 F:Riek Bukenya 2.50
4 . . . . 2.50
5 . . . . 2.50
6 concl 2.50

MY DIARY
Dec., 1949–March, 1950
1 Ph(c),The Man I Love 175.00
2 Ph(c),I Was Anybody's Girl . . . 150.00

MY LOVE
July, 1949
1 Ph(c),One Heart to Give 175.00
2 Ph(c),Hate in My Heart 125.00
3 Ph(c), ... 125.00
4 Ph(c),Betty Page, April,1950 . . 400.00

MY LOVE
Sept., 1969
1 Love story reprints 80.00
2 thru 9 . . . . @40.00
10 . . . . 50.00
11 thru 38 . . . . @30.00
39 March, 1976 . . . . 30.00

MY ROMANCE
Sept., 1948
1 Romance Stories 175.00
2 . . . . 125.00
3 . . . . 125.00
Becomes:

MY OWN ROMANCE
4 Romance Stories Continue . . . 175.00
5 thru 10 . . . . @100.00
11 thru 20 . . . . @100.00
21 thru 50 . . . . @75.00
51 thru 54 . . . . @60.00
55 ATh 75.00
56 thru 60 . . . . @60.00
61 thru 70 . . . . @50.00
71 AW 100.00
72 thru 76 . . . . @60.00
Becomes:

TEENAGE ROMANCE
77 Romance Stories Continue 50.00
78 thru 85 . . . . @50.00
86 March, 1962 . . . . 50.00

MYS-TECH WARS
Marvel UK, 1993
1 BHi,A:FF,X-Men,Avengers 2.25
2 A:FF,X-Men,X-Force 2.25
3 BHi,A:X-Men,X-Force 2.25
4 A:Death's Head II 2.25

MYSTERY TALES
Atlas, March, 1952
1 GC,Horror Strikes at
  Midnight 1,200.00

---

2 BK,BEv,OW,The Corpse
  is Mine 600.00
3 RH,GC,JM, Vampire Strikes . . 475.00
4 Funeral of Horror 475.00
5 Blackout at Midnight 475.00
6 A-Bomb Picture 475.00
7 JRo,The Ghost Hunter 475.00
8 BEv 475.00
9 BEv(c),the Man in the Morgue 475.00
10 BEV(c),GT,What Happened
  to Harry 475.00
11 BEv(c) 350.00
12 GT,MF 360.00
13 . . . . 350.00
14 BEv(c),GT 350.00
15 RH(c),EK 350.00
16 . . . . 350.00
17 RH(c). 350.00
18 AW,DAy,GC 360.00
19 . . . . 350.00
20 Electric Chair 350.00
21 JF,MF,BP,Decapitation 350.00
22 JF,MF 350.00
23 thru 27 . . . . @300.00
28 . . . . 250.00
29 thru 32 . . . . @275.00
33 BEv 250.00
34 . . . . 250.00
35 BEv,GC 250.00
36 . . . . 275.00
37 DW,BP,JR 250.00
38 BP 250.00
39 BK 275.00
40 JM 275.00
41 MD,BEv 250.00
42 JeR 250.00
41 GC 250.00
44 AW 250.00
45 SD 225.00
46 RC,SD,JP 225.00
47 DAy,BP 225.00
48 BEv 250.00
49 GM,AT,DAy 250.00
50 JO,AW,GM 225.00
51 DAy,JO 225.00
52 DAy 225.00
53 BEv 225.00
54 RC,Aug., 1957 . . . . 235.00

MYSTICAL TALES
Atlas, June, 1956
1 BEv,BP,JO,Say the Magical
  Words 600.00
2 BEv(c),JO,Black Blob 300.00
3 BEv(c),RC,Four Doors To 325.00
4 BEv(c).The Condemned 325.00
5 AW,Meeting at Midnight 350.00
6 BK,AT,He Hides in the Tower . 275.00
7 BEv,JF,JO,AT,FBe,The
  Haunted Tower 275.00
8 BK,SC, Stone Walls Can't
  Stop Him,Aug., 1957 . . . . . 275.00

MYSTIC COMICS
Timely, March, 1940
[1st Series]
1 ASh(c),O;The Blue Blaze,Dynamic
  Man,Flexo,B:Dakor the Magician
  A:Zephyr Jones,3X's,Deep Sea
  Demon,Bondage(c) 22,000.00
2 ASh(c),B:The Invisible Man
  Mastermind,Blue Blaze . . . 6,500.00
3 ASh(c),O:Hercules 4,500.00
4 ASh(c),O:Thin Man,Black Widow
  E:Hercules,Blue Blazes,Dynamic
  Man,Flexo,Invisible Man. . . 4,800.00
5 ASh(c)O:The Black Marvel,
  Blazing Skull,Super Slave
  Terror,Sub-Earth Man 4,500.00

Mystic Comics #6
© Marvel Entertainment Group

6 ASh(c),O:The Challenger,
  B:The Destroyer 5,500.00
7 S&K(c),B:The Witness,O:Davey
  and the Demon,E;The Black
  Widow,Hitler(c) 5,500.00
8 Bondage(c) 3,000.00
9 MSy,DRi,Hitler/Bondage(c) . 3,000.00
10 E:Challenger,Terror 3,000.00

[2nd Series] Oct., 1944
1 B:The Angel,Human Torch,
  Destroyer,Terry Vance,
  Tommy Tyme,Bondage(c) . 3,200.00
2 E:Human Torch,Terry
  Vance,Bondage(c) 1,600.00
3 E:The Angel,Tommy Tyme
  Bondage(c) 1,500.00
4 ASh(c),A:Young Allies
  Winter, 1944-45 . . . . 1,500.00

MYSTIC
[3rd Series] March, 1951
1 MSy,Strange Tree 1,300.00
2 MSy,Dark Dungeon 650.00
3 GC,Jaws of Creeping Death . . 575.00
4 BW,MSy,The Den of the
  Devil Bird 1,100.00
5 MSy,Face 400.00
6 BW,She Wouldn't Stay Dead 1,100.00
7 GC,Untold Horror waits
  in the Tomb 400.00
8 DAy(c),BEv,GK,A Monster
  Among Us 400.00
9 BEv 400.00
10 GC 400.00
11 JR,The Black Gloves 350.00
12 GC 350.00
13 In the Dark 350.00
14 The Corpse and I 350.00
15 GT,JR,House of Horror 350.00
16 A Scream in the Dark 350.00
17 BEv,Behold the Vampire 350.00
18 BEv(c),The Russian Devil. . . . 350.00
19 Swamp Girl 350.00
20 RH(c). 350.00
21 BEv(c),GC 275.00
22 RH(c). 275.00
23 RH(c),RA,RMn,Chilling Tales . 275.00
24 GK,RMn,How Many Times Can
  You Die 275.00
25 RH(c),RA,E.C.Swipe. 275.00
26 Severed Head(c). 275.00
27 Who Walks with a Zombie . . . 250.00
28 DW,RMn(c),Not Enough Dead 250.00

---

29 SMo,RMn(c),The Unseen 250.00
30 RH(c),DW 250.00
31 SC,JKz,RMn(c) 250.00
32 The Survivor 250.00
33 thru 36 .... @250.00
37 thru 51 .... @225.00
52 WW,RC 250.00
53 thru 57 .... @225.00
58 thru 60 .... @250.00
61 .... 225.00

MYSTIQUE
April, 2003
1 JLi(c),Drop Dead Gorgeous,pt.1 . 3.00
2 JLi(c),Drop Dead Gorgeous,pt.2 . 3.00
3 JLi(c),Drop Dead Gorgeous,pt.3 . 3.00
4 JLi(c),Drop Dead Gorgeous,pt.4 . 3.00
5 JLi(c),Drop Dead Gorgeous,pt.5 . 3.00
6 JLi(c),Drop Dead Gorgeous,pt.6 . 3.00
7 Tinker,Tailor,Mutant,Spy,pt.1 ... 3.00
8 Tinker,Tailor,Mutant,Spy,pt.2 ... 3.00
9 Tinker,Tailor,Mutant,Spy,pt.3 ... 3.00
10 Tinker,Tailor,Mutant,Spy,pt.4 .. 3.00
11 Maker's Mark,pt.1 .... 3.00
12 Maker's Mark,pt.2 .... 3.00
13 F:Shortpack. 3.00
14 Unnatural,pt.1 .... 3.00
15 Unnatural,pt.2 .... 3.00
16 Unnatural,pt.3 .... 3.00
17 Unnatural,pt.4 .... 3.00
18 Unnatural,pt.5 .... 3.00
19 Assassin's bullet 3.00
20 Quiet,pt.1 .... 3.00
TPB Dead Drop Gorgeous 20.00
TPB Vol. 2: Tinker Tailor 18.00

'NAM, THE
Dec., 1986
1 MGo,Vietnam War 3.00
1a 2nd printing 2.50
2 MGo,Dust Off. 2.50
3 MGo,Three Day Pass 2.25
4 MGo,TV newscrew 2.25
5 MGo,Top Sgt. 2.25
6 MGo,Monsoon 2.25
7 MGo,Cedar Falls 2.25
8 MGo,5th to the 1st. 2.25
9 MGo,Action Issue,Tunnel Rat ... 3.50
10 MGo,Saigon 2.25
11 MGo,Christmas 2.25
12 MGo,AgentOrange 2.25
13 MGo 2.25
14 .... 2.25
15 ReturningVets 2.25
16 .... 2.25
17 Vietcong 2.25
18 .... 2.25
19 .... 2.25
20 .... 2.25
21 .... 2.25
22 Thanksgiving. 2.25
23 XmasTruce of'67. .... 2.25
24 TetOffensive 2.25
25 TetOffensive-KheSanh 2.25
26 HomefrontIssue. 2.25
27 Candle in the Wind 2.25
28 Borderline. 2.25
29 PeaceTalks 2.25
30 TheBunker 2.25
31 Fire and Ice. 2.25
32 Nam in America 2.25
33 SpecialistDaniels. 2.25
34 OperationPhoenix. 2.25
35 Xmas-BobHope. 2.25
36 RacialTension 2.25
37 Colorblind 2.25
38 Minefields 2.25
39 .... 2.25
40 .... 2.25
41 ,A:Thor,Iron Man, Cap.Am 2.25

42 .... 2.25
43 .... 2.25
44 SDr 2.25
45 .... 2.25
46 .... 2.25
47 TD 2.25
48 TD 2.25
49 Donut Dolly #1 .... 2.25
50 HT,Donut Dolly #2 DoubSz..... 2.50
51 HT,Donut Dolly #3. .... 2.25
52 Frank Castle(Punisher)#1..... 3.00
52a 2nd printing. 2.25
53 Punisher #2. .... 2.50
54 Death of Joe Hallen #1....... 2.25
55 TD,Death of Joe Hallen #2 .... 2.25
56 TD,Death of Joe Hallen #3 .... 2.25
57 TD,Death of Joe Hallen #4 .... 2.25
58 TD,Death of Joe Hallen #5 .... 2.25
59 P.O.W. Story #1. .... 2.25
60 P.O.W. Story #2. .... 2.25
61 P.O.W. Story #3. .... 2.25
62 Speed & Ice,pt.1 .... 2.25
63 Speed & Ice,pt.2 .... 2.25
64 Speed & Ice,pt.3 .... 2.25
65 Speed & Ice,pt.4 .... 2.25
66 RH,Speed & Ice,pt.5 .... 2.25
67 A:Punisher. 2.25
68 A:Punisher. 2.25
69 A:Punisher. 2.25
70 Don Lomax writes........... 2.25
71 Vietnamese Point of View. 2.25
72 The trials of war 2.25
73 War on the Homefront 2.25
74 Seige at An Loc 2.25
75 My Lai Massacre. 2.50
76 R:Rob Little. 2.25
77 Stateside 2.25
78 .... 2.25
79 Beginning of the End#1 ..... 2.25
80 MGo(c),'68 Tet Offensive 2.25
81 MGo(c),TET Offensive ends.... 2.25
82 TET Offensive 2.25
83 thru 84 Last issue .... @2.25
TPB rep. #1–#4 (1999) 15.00

'NAM MAGAZINE, THE
(B&W) Aug., 1988–May, 1989
1 Reprints 3.00
2 thru 10 .... @2.50

NAMOR
April, 2003
1 MiS,manga. 2.25
2 MiS. 2.25
3 SvL. 2.25
4 SvL,F:Sandy 2.25
5 SvL,F:Sandy 2.25
6 SvL,Namor's choice. 2.25
7 PO 2.25
8 PO 2.25
9 PO,Namor and Sandy 3.00
10 PO,In Deep,pt.4 .... 3.00
11 JoB,In Deep,pt.5 .... 3.00
12 JoB,finale 3.00
TPB Vol. 1 Sea and Sand 13.00

NAMORA
Fall, 1948–Dec., 1948
1 BEv,DR 3,500.00
2 BEv,A:Sub-Mariner,Blonde
   Phantom 1,700.00
3 BEv,A:Sub-Mariner 1,900.00

NAMOR THE SUB-MARINER
April, 1990
1 JBy,BWi,I:Desmond
   & Phoebe Marrs 5.00

Namora #1
© Marvel Entertainment Group

2 JBy,BWi,V:Griffin 3.00
3 JBy,BWi,V:Griffin 3.00
4 JBy,A:Reed & Sue Richards,
   Tony Stark 3.00
5 JBy,A:FF,IronMan,C:Speedball .. 3.00
6 JBy,V:Sluj. 3.00
7 JBy,V:Sluj. 3.00
8 JBy,V:Headhunter,R:D.Rand 3.00
9 JBy,V:Headhunter 3.00
10 JBy,V:Master Man,Warrior
   Woman 2.50
11 JBy,V:Mast.Man,War.Woman ... 2.50
12 JBy,R:Invaders,Spitfire 2.50
13 JBy,Namor on Trial,A:Fantastic
   Four,Captain America,Thor 2.50
14 JBy,R:Lady Dorma,A:Ka-Zar
   Griffin 2.50
15 JBy,A:Iron Fist. 2.50
16 JBy,A:Punisher,V:Iron Fist 2.50
17 JBy,V:Super Skrull(Iron Fist). ... 2.50
18 JBy,V:SuperSkrull,A:Punisher... 2.50
19 JBy,V:Super Skrull,D:D.Marrs... 2.50
20 JBy,Search for Iron Fist,
   O:Namorita 2.50
21 JBy,Visit to K'un Lun 2.50
22 JBy,Fate of Iron Fist,
   C:Wolverine 2.50
23 JBy,BWi,Iron Fist Contd.,
   C:Wolverine 2.50
24 JBy,BWi,V:Wolverine 3.00
25 JBy,BWi,V:Master Man 2.50
26 JaL,BWi,Search For Namor 5.00
27 JaL,BWi,V:Namorita 4.00
28 JaL,BWi,A:Iron Fist. 3.00
29 JaL,BWi,After explosion 3.00
30 JaL,A:Doctor Doom 3.00
31 JaL,V:Doctor Doom. 3.00
32 JaL,V:Doctor Doom,
   Namor regains memory....... 3.00
33 JaL,V:Master Khan 2.50
34 JaL,R:Atlantis 2.50
35 JaL,V:Tiger Shark 2.50
36 JaL,I:Suma-Ket,A:Tiger Shark . 2.50
37 JaL,Blue Holo-Grafix,Altantean
   Civil War,N:Namor........... 2.75
38 JaL,O:Suma-Ket 2.50
39 A:Tigershark,V:Suma-Ket 2.50
40 V:Suma-Ket. 2.50
41 V:War Machine. 2.50
42 MCW,A:Stingray,V:Dorcas 2.50
43 MCW,V:Orka,Dorcas. 2.50
44 I:Albatross. 2.50
45 GI,A:Sunfire,V:Attuma. 2.50
46 GI, ... 2.50

47 GI,Starblast #2	2.50
48 GI,Starblast #9,A:FF	2.50
49 GI,A:Ms. Marrs	2.50
50 GI,Holo-grafx(c),A:FF	4.00
50a Newsstand Ed.	2.50
51 AaL, ...	2.50
52 GI,I:Sea Leopard	2.50
53 GI,V:Sea Leopard	2.50
54 GI,I:Llyron	2.50
55 GI,V:Llyron	2.50
56 GI,V:Llyron	2.50
57 A:Capt. America, V:Llyron	2.50
58	2.50
59 GI,V:Abomination	2.50
60 A:Morgan Le Fay	2.50
61 Atlantis Rising	2.50
62 V:Triton	2.50
Ann.#1 Subterran.Odyssey #3. . . .	3.00
Ann.#2 Return o/Defenders,pt.3 . .	4.00
Ann.#3 I:Assassin,A:Iron Fist,	
w/Trading card.	3.25
Ann.#4 V:Hydra	3.25

NAVY ACTION
Aug., 1954

1 BP,US Navy War Stories	225.00
2 TLn,Navy(c)	125.00
3 BEv	100.00
4 and 5 . . . . @	100.00
6 JH(c)	100.00
7 MD,JMn	100.00
8 JMn,GC.	100.00
9 thru 15 . . . . @	100.00
16 BEv(c).	100.00
17 MD,BEv(c).	100.00
18 Aug., 1957.	100.00

NAVY COMBAT
Atlas, June, 1955

1 DH,JMn(c),B:Torpedo Taylor . .	225.00
2 DH	125.00
3 DH,BEv	100.00
4 DH	100.00
5 DH	100.00
6 JMn,A:Battleship Burke	100.00
7 thru 10 . . . . @	100.00
11 MD,GC,JMn	100.00
12 RC.	125.00
13 GT.	100.00
14 AT,GT	100.00
15 GT	100.00
16	100.00
17 AW,AT,JMn	110.00
18	100.00
19	100.00
20 BEv,BP,AW,Oct., 1958	110.00

NAVY TALES
Atlas, Jan., 1957

1 BEv(c),BP,Torpedoes	175.00
2 AW,RC,JMn(c),One Hour	
to Live	175.00
3 JSe(c)	150.00
4 JSe(c),GC,JSt,RC,July, 1957 .	150.00

NELLIE THE NURSE
Atlas, 1945

1 Beach(c)	500.00
2 Nellie's Date(c)	250.00
3 Swimming Pool(c)	175.00
4 Roller Coaster(c)	175.00
5 Hospital(c),HK,Hey Look	175.00
6 Bedside Manner(c)	175.00
7 Comic book(c)A:Georgie	175.00
8 Hospital(c),A:Georgie	175.00
9 BW,Nellie/Swing(c)A:Millie . .	175.00
10 Bathing Suit(c),A:Millie	175.00
11 HK,Hey Look.	200.00

12 HK,Giggles `n' Grins.	175.00
13 HK.	125.00
14 HK.	150.00
15 HK.	150.00
16 HK.	150.00
17 HK.A:Annie Oakley	150.00
18 HK.	150.00
19	125.00
20	125.00
21	100.00
22	100.00
23	100.00
24	100.00
25	100.00
26	100.00
27	100.00
28 HK,Rusty Reprint	100.00
29 thru 35. . . . . @	75.00
36 Oct., 1952	75.00

NEW ADVENTURES OF CHOLLY & FLYTRAP
Epic

1	5.00
2	4.00
3	4.00

NEW ETERNALS: APOCALYPSE NOW
Dec., 1999

1-shot JoB,SHa,64-pg..	4.00

NEW MUTANTS, THE
March, 1983

1 BMc,MG,O:New Mutants	5.00
2 BMc,MG,V:Sentinels	4.00
3 BMc,MG,V:Brood Alien	3.50
4 SB,BMc,A:Peter Bristow	3.50
5 SB,BMc,A:Dark Rider	3.50
6 SB,AG,V:Viper	3.50
7 SB,BMc,V:Axe	3.50
8 SB,BMc,I:Amara Aquilla.	3.50
9 SB,TMd,I:Selene	3.50
10 SB,BMc,C:Magma	3.50
11 SB,TMd,I:Magma	3.50
12 SB,TMd,J:Magma	3.50
13 SB,TMd,I:Cypher(Doug Ramsey)	
A:Kitty Pryde,Lilandra	4.00
14 SB,TMd,J:Magik,A:X-Men.	3.00
15 SB,TMd,Mass.Academy	3.00
16 SB,TMd,V:Hellions,I:Warpath	
I:Jetstream.	4.00
17 SB,TMd,V:Hellions,A:Warpath . .	4.00
18 BSz,V:Demon Bear,I:New	
Warlock,Magus	5.00
19 BSz,V:Demon Bear.	3.00
20 BSz,V:Demon Bear.	3.00
21 BSz,O&J:Warlock,doub.sz	5.00
22 BSz,A:X-Men	3.50
23 BSz,Sunspot,Cloak & Dagger. . .	3.00
24 BSz,A:Cloak & Dagger	3.00
25 BSz,A:Cloak & Dagger	6.00
26 BSz,I:Legion(Prof.X's son)	7.00
27 BSz,V:Legion	4.00
28 BSz,O:Legion	4.00
29 BSz,V:Gladiators,I:Guido	
(Strong Guy)	3.00
30 BSz,A:Dazzler.	3.00
31 BSz,A:Shadowcat	3.00
32 SL,V:Karma.	3.00
33 SL,V:Karma.	3.00
34 SL,V:Amahl Farouk.	3.00
35 BSz,J:Magneto	3.00
36 BSz,A:Beyonder	3.00
37 BSz,D:New Mutants	3.00
38 BSz,A:Hellions	3.00
39 BSz,A:White Queen	3.00
40 JG,KB,V:Avengers.	3.00

41 JG,TA,Mirage	3.00
42 JG,KB,A:Dazzler.	3.00
43 SP,V:Empath,A:Warpath	3.00
44 JG,V:Legion.	5.00
45 JG,A:Larry Bodine.	3.00
46 JG,KB,Mutant Massacre	3.50
47 JG,KB,V:Magnus.	3.00
48 JG,CR,Future	3.00
49 VM,Future.	3.00
50 JG,V:Magus,R:Prof.X	4.00
51 KN,A:Star Jammers	3.00
52 RL,DGr,Limbo.	3.00
53 RL,TA,V:Hellions.	3.00
54 SB,TA,N:New Mutants	3.00
55 BBl,TA,V:Aliens.	3.00
56 JBr,TA,V:Hellions,A:Warpath. . .	3.00
57 BBl,TA,I&J:Bird-Boy	3.00
58 BBl,TA,Bird-Boy	3.00
59 BBl,TA,Fall of Mutants,	
V:Dr.Animus.	3.00
60 BBl,TA,F.of M.,D:Cypher.	2.50
61 BBl,TA,Fall of Mutants	2.50
62 JMu,A:Magma,Hellions	2.50
63 BHa,JRu,Magik	2.50
64 BBl,TA,R:Cypher.	2.50
65 BBl,TA,V:FreedomForce	2.50
66 BBl,TA,V:Forge	2.50
67 BBl,I:Gosamyr.	2.50
68 BBl,V:Gosamyr	2.50
69 BBl,AW,I:Spyder	2.50
70 TSh,AM,V:Spyder	2.50
71 BBl,AW,V:N'Astirh	2.50
72 BBl,A,Inferno.	2.50
73 BBl,W,A:Colossus.	3.00
74 BBl,W,A:X-Terminators	2.50
75 JBy,Mc,Black King,V:Magneto .	3.50
76 RB,TP,J:X-Terminators	2.50
77 RB,V:Mirage	2.50
78 RL,AW,V:FreedomForce	2.50
79 BBl,AW,V:Hela	2.50
80 BBl,AW,Asgard	2.50
81 LW,TSh,JRu,A:Hercules	2.50
82 BBl,AW,Asgard	2.50
83 BBl,Asgard	2.50
84 TSh,AM,A:QueenUla	2.50
85 RLd&TMc(c),BBl,V:Mirage	5.00
86 RLd,BWi,V:Vulture,C:Cable	6.00
87 RLd,BWi,I:Mutant Liberation	
Front,Cable	20.00
87a 2nd Printing.	2.00
88 RLd,2nd Cable,V:Freedom	
Force	7.50
89 RLd,V:Freedom Force	6.00
90 RLd,A:Caliban,V:Sabretooth. . . .	6.00

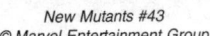

New Mutants #43
© Marvel Entertainment Group

91 RLd,A:Caliban,Masque,
 V:Sabretooth 6.00
92 RLd(c),BH,V:Skrulls 4.00
93 RLd,A:Wolverine,Sunfire,
 V:Mutant Liberation Front 6.00
94 RLd,A:Wolverine,Sunfire,
 V:Mutant Liberation Front 5.00
95 RLd,Extinction Agenda,V:Hodge
 A:X-Men,X-Factor,D:Warlock . . 5.00
95a 2nd printing(gold) 5.00
96 RLd,ATb,JRu,Extinction Agenda
 V:Hodge,A:X-Men,X-Factor . . . 5.00
97 E:LSi(s),RLd(c),JRu,Extinction
 Agenda,V:Hodge 5.00
98 FaN(s),RLd,I:Deadpool,Domino,
 Gideon,L:Rictor 9.00
99 FaN(s),RLd,I:Feral,Shatterstar,
 L:Sunspot,J:Warpath 5.00
100 FaN(s),RLd,J:Feral,Shatterstar,
 I:X-Force,V:Masque,Imperial
 Protectorate,A:MLF 6.00
100a 2nd Printing(Gold) 4.00
100b 3rd Printing(Silver) 3.50
Ann.#1 BMc,TP,L.Cheney 7.00
Ann.#2 AD,V:Mojo,I:Psylocke,Meggan
 (American App.) 10.00
Ann.#3 AD,PN,V:Impossible Man . . 4.00
Ann.#4 JBr,BMc,Evol.Wars 6.00
Ann.#5 RLd,JBg,MBa,KWi,Atlantis
 Attacks,A:Namorita,I:Surf 8.00
Ann.#6 RLd(c),Days o/Future Present
 V:FranklinRichards,(Pin-ups)... 6.00
Ann.#7 JRu,RLd,Kings of Pain,
 I:Piecemeal & Harness,
 Pin-ups X-Force. 5.00
Spec #1,AAd,TA,Asgard War. 6.00
Summer Spec.#1 BBl,Megapolis . . . 3.50
TPB New Mutants: Demon Bear . . . 8.95

NEW MUTANTS
Sept., 1997

1 (of 3) BRa,BCh,F:Cannonball,
 Moonstar, Wolfsbane,Karma &
 Sunspot 2.50
2 BRa,BCh,meeting with mutants
 of the past 2.50
3 BRa,BCh, will Magik return
 for good? 2.50

NEW MUTANTS
May, 2003

1 R:Original New Mutants. 2.50
2 F:Dani Moonstar 2.50
3 new student 2.50
4 F:Karma. 2.50
5 mutant teens 2.50
6 V:Reavers. 2.50
7 CBa(c),Ties That Bind,pt.1 . . . . 2.50
8 CBa(c),Ties That Bind,pt.2 . . . . 2.50
9 CBa(c),Ties That Bind,pt.3 . . . . 2.50
10 CBa(c),Ties That Bind,pt.4 . . . . 3.00
11 CBa(c),Ties That Bind,pt.5 . . . . 3.00
12 CBa(c),Ties That Bind,pt.6 . . . . 3.00
13 The More Things Change. 3.00
TPB Vol. 1 Back to School. 17.00

NEW WARRIORS
July, 1990

1 B:FaN(s),MBa,AW,V:Terrax,
 O:New Warriors. 5.00
1a Gold rep. 2.50
2 FaN(s),MBa,AW,I:Midnight's Fire,
 Silhouette. 3.50
3 MBa,LMa(i),V:Mad Thinker 3.50
4 MBa,LMa(i),I:Psionex 3.50
5 MBa,LMa(i),V:Star Thief,
 C:White Queen 3.50
6 MBa,LMa(i),V:StarThief,
 A:Inhumans 3.50

7 MBa,LMa(i),V:Bengal,
 C:Punisher. 3.50
8 MBa,LMa(i),V:Punisher,
 I:Force of Nature 3.50
9 MBa,LMa(i),V:Punisher,Bengal,
 Force of Nature 3.50
10 MBa,LMa(i),V:Hellions,White
 Queen,I:New Sphinx 3.50
11 MBa,LMa(i),V:Sphinx,
 B:Forever Yesterday 2.50
12 MBa,LMa(i),V:Sphinx 2.50
13 MBa,LMa(i),V:Sphinx,
 E:Forever Yesterday 2.50
14 MBa,LMa(i),A:Namor,
 Darkhawk. 2.50
15 MBa,LMa(i),V:Psionex,
 R:Terrax,N:Nova 2.50
16 MBa,LMa(i),A:Psionex,
 V:Terrax 2.50
17 MBa,LMa(i),A:Silver Surfer,Fant.
 Four,V:Terrax,I:Left Hand 2.50
18 MBa,LMa(i),O:Night Thrasher. . . 2.50
19 MBa,LMa(i),V:Gideon 2.50
20 MBa,LMa(i),V:Clan Yashida,
 Marvel Boy kills his father 2.50
21 MBa,LMa(i),I:Folding Circle 2.50
22 MBa,LMa(i),A:Darkhawk,Rage . . 2.50
23 MBa,LMa(i),V:Folding Circle. . . . 2.50
24 LMa(i),V:Folding Circle 2.50
25 MBa,LMa(i),Die-Cut(c),Marvel Boy
 found guilty of murder,D:Tai,
 O:Folding Circle. 2.50
26 DaR,LMa(i),V:Guardsmen 2.50
27 DaR,LMa(i),Inf.War,Speedball Vs.
 his doppelganger,N:Rage 2.50
28 DaR,LMa(i),I:Turbo,Cardinal. . . . 2.50
29 DaR,LMa(i),V:Trans-Sabal 2.50
30 DaR,LMa(i),V:Trans Sabal 2.50
31 DaR,LMa(i)A:Cannonball,Warpath,
 Magma,O&N:Firestar. 2.50
32 DaR,LMa(i),B:Forces of Darkness,
 Forces of Light,A:Spider-Man,
 Archangel,Dr.Strange 2.50
33 DaR,LMa(i),A:Cloak & Dagger,
 Turbo,Darkhawk. 2.50
34 DaR,LMa(i),A:Avengers,SpM,
 Thing,Torch,Darkhawk,
 C:Darkling 2.50
35 DaR,LMa(i),A:Turbo 2.50
36 DaR,LMa(i),A:Turbo 2.50
37 F:Marvel Boy,V:Wizard 2.50
38 DaR,LMa(i),D:Rage's granny,
 V:Poison Memories 2.50

New Warriors #56
© Marvel Entertainment Group

39 DaR,LMa(i),L:Namorita. 2.50
40 DaR,LMa(i),B:Starlost,
 V:Supernova 2.50
40a Newsstand Ed. 2.50
41 DaR,LMa(i),V:Supernova 2.50
42 DaR,LMa(i),E:Starlost,N:Nova,
 V:Supernova 2.50
43 DaR,LMa(i),N&I:Justice
 (Marvel Boy) 2.50
44 Ph(c),DaR,LMa(i),N&I:Kymaera
 (Namorita) 2.50
45 DaR,LMa(i),Child's Play#2,
 N:Silhouette,Speedball,
 V:Upstarts 2.50
46 DaR,LMa(i),Child's Play#4,
 V:Upstarts 2.50
47 DaR,LMa(i),Time&TimeAgain,pt.1,
 A:Sphinx,I:Powerpax 2.50
48 DaR,LMa(i),Time&TimeAgain,pt.4,
 J:Cloak&Dagger,Darkhawk,Turbo,
 Powerpax,Bandit 2.50
49 DaR,LMa(i),Time&TimeAgain,pt.8
 V:Sphinx 2.50
50 reg. (c) 2.25
50a Glow-in-the-dark(c),V:Sphinx . . 3.25
51 revamp 2.25
52 R:Psionex 2.25
53 V:Psionex 2.25
54 V:Speedball. 2.25
55 V:Soldiers of Misfortune 2.25
56 V:Soldiers 2.25
57 A:Namor 2.25
58 F:Sabra 2.25
59 F:Speedball. 2.25
60 Nova Omega,pt.2 . . . . 2.50
61 J:Scarlet Spider,Maximum
 Clonage prologue 2.25
62 F:Scarlet Spider,Maximum
 Clonage tie-in 2.25
63 F:Firestar. 2.25
64 I:Psionix 2.25
65 F:Scarlet Spider,V:Kymaera . . . 2.25
66 F:Speedball. 2.25
67 Nightmare in Scarlet,pt.2 . . . . . 2.25
68 Future Shock,pt.1 . . . . 2.25
69 . . . . 2.25
70 . . . . 2.25
71 Future Shock,pt.4 . . . . 2.25
Ann.#1 MBa,A:X-Force,V:Harness,
 Piecemeal,Kings of Pain #2 . . . 4.00
Ann.#2 Hero Killers #4,V:Sphinx . . 2.75
Ann.#3 LMa(i),E:Forces of Light,
 Forces of Darkness,I:Darkling
 w/card 3.25
Ann.#4 DaR(s),V:Psionex 3.25
TPB New Beginnings, rep.. . . . . . 13.00

NEW WARRIORS
Aug., 1999

1 F:Speedball,48-page 3.00
2A DaR 2.50
2B variant Steve Scott (c). 2.50
3 . . . . 2.50
4 . . . . 2.50
5 F:Generation X 2.50
6 F:Night Thrasher, Nova 2.50
7 F:Turbo 2.50
8 A:Iron Fist & Night Thrasher . . . 2.50
9 Iron Man #29 x-over 2.50
10 A:Hercules. 2.50

NEW X-MEN
See: X-MEN

NEW X-MEN
May, 2004

1 Choosing Sides,pt.1. . . . . 3.00
2 Choosing Sides,pt.2. . . . . 3.00

3 Choosing Sides,pt.3 . . . . 3.00
4 Choosing Sides,pt.4 . . . . 3.00
5 Choosing Sides,pt.5 . . . . 3.00
6 Choosing Sides,pt.6 . . . . 3.00

NFL SUPERPRO
1 . . . . 7.00
Spec.#1 reprints 2.50

[Regular Series] Oct., 1991
1 A:Spider-Man,I:Sanzionaire 2.50
2 V:Quickkick 2.50
3 I:Instant Replay 2.50
4 V:Sanction 2.50
5 A:Real NFL Player 2.50
6 Racism Iss.,recalled by Marvel . . 6.00
7 thru 11 . . . . @2.50
12 V:Nefarious forces of evil 2.50

NICK FURY, AGENT OF S.H.I.E.L.D.
[1st Regular Series] June, 1968
1 JSo/JSt,I:Scorpio 175.00
2 JSo,A:Centaurius 100.00
3 JSo,DA,V:Hell Hounds 100.00
4 FS,O:Nick Fury 100.00
5 JSo,V:Scorpio 125.00
6 FS,Doom must Fall 75.00
7 FS,V:S.H.I.E.L.D. 75.00
8 FS,Hate Monger 50.00
9 FS,Hate Monger 50.00
10 FS,JCr,Hate Monger 50.00
11 BS(c),FS,Hate Monger 50.00
12 BS 55.00
13 . . . . 50.00
14 . . . . 50.00
15 I:Bullseye 90.00
16 JK,rep 25.00
17 JK,rep 25.00
18 JK,rep 25.00

[Limited Series] 1983–94
1 JSo,rep 4.00
2 JSo,rep 3.50

[2nd Regular Series] 1989–93
1 BH,I:New Shield,V:Death's
   Head(not British hero) 3.00
2 KP,V:Death's Head 2.25
3 KP,V:Death's Head 2.25
4 KP,V:Death's Head 2.25
5 KP,V:Death's Head 2.25
6 KP,V:Death's Head 2.25
7 KP,Chaos Serpent #1 . . . . 2.25
8 KP,Chaos Serpent #2 . . . . 2.25
9 KP,Chaos Serpent #3 . . . . 2.25
10 KP,Chaos Serpent ends,
   A:Capt.America 2.25
11 D:Murdo MacKay 2.25
12 Hydra Affair #1 . . . . 2.25
13 Hydra Affair #2 . . . . 2.25
14 Hydra Affair #3 . . . . 2.25
15 Apogee of Disaster #1 . . . . 2.25
16 Apogee of Disaster #2 . . . . 2.25
17 Apogee of Disaster #3 . . . . 2.25
18 Apogee of Disaster #4 . . . . 2.25
19 Apogee of Disaster #5 . . . . 2.25
20 JG,A:Red Skull 2.50
21 JG,R:Baron Strucker 2.25
22 JG,A:Baron Strucker,R:Hydra . . . 2.25
23 JG,V:Hydra 2.25
24 A:Capt.Am,Thing,V:Mandarin . . 2.25
25 JG,Shield Vs. Hydra 2.25
26 JG,A:Baron Strucker,
   C:Wolverine 2.50
27 JG,V:Hydra,A:Wolverine 2.50
28 V:Hydra,A:Wolverine 2.50
29 V:Hydra,A:Wolverine 2.50
30 R:Leviathan,A:Deathlok 2.25
31 A:Deathlok,V:Leviathan 2.25
32 V:Leviathan 2.25
33 Super-Powered Agents 2.25

Nick Future Agent of S.H.I.E.L.D. #39
© Marvel Entertainment Group

34 A:Bridge(X-Force),V:Balance
   of Terror 2.25
35 A:Cage,V:Constrictor 2.25
36 . . . . 2.25
37 . . . . 2.25
38 Cold War of Nick Fury #1 . . . . . 2.25
39 Cold War of Nick Fury #2 . . . . . 2.25
40 Cold War of Nick Fury #3 . . . . . 2.25
41 Cold War of Nick Fury #4 . . . . . 2.25
42 I:Strike Force Shield 2.25
43 R:Clay Quatermain 2.25
44 A:Captain America 2.25
45 A:Bridge 2.25
46 V:Gideon,Hydra 2.25
47 V:Baron Strucker,last issue 2.25
TPB Death Duty V:Night Raven . . . 6.00
TPB Captain America 6.00
TPB Scorpion Connection 8.00
TPB JSo, 248-pg 20.00
TPB Scorpio 15.00

NICK FURY, VERSUS S.H.I.E.L.D.
June, 1988
1 JSo(c),D:Quartermail 6.00
2 BSz(c),Into The Depths 5.00
3 Uneasy Allies 4.00
4 V:Hydra 4.00
5 V:Hydra 4.00
6 V:Hydra, Dec., 1988 . . . . 4.00
TPB Reprints #1-#6 . . . . 16.00

NIGHTBREED
Epic, April, 1990
1 . . . . 4.00
2 . . . . 3.00
3 . . . . 2.50
4 . . . . 2.50
5 JG 2.50
6 BBI,Blasphemers,pt.1 . . . . 2.50
7 JG,Blasphemers,pt.2 . . . . 2.50
8 BBI,MM,Blasphemers,pt.3 . . . . . 2.50
9 BBI,Blasphemers,pt.4 . . . . 2.50
10 BBI,Blasphemers,pt.5 . . . . 2.50
11 South America,pt.1 . . . . 2.25
12 South America,pt.2 . . . . 2.25
13 Emissaries o/Algernon Kinder . . 2.25
14 Rawhead Rex Story 2.25
15 Rawhead Rex 2.25
16 Rawhead Rex 2.25
17 KN(i),V:Werewolves 2.25
18 V:Werewolves 2.25

19 V:Werewolves 2.25
20 Trapped in the Forest 2.25
21 V:Ozymandias 2.50
22 V:Ozymandias 2.50
23 F:Peloquin 2.50
24 Search for New Midian 2.50
25 Search for New Midian 2.50
Nightbreed:Genesis, Rep.#1-#4 . . 10.00

NIGHTCAT
1 DCw,I&O:Night Cat 4.50

NIGHTCRAWLER
Nov., 1985
1 DC,A:Bamfs 4.00
2 DC 3.50
3 DC,A:Other Dimensional X-Men . 3.50
4 DC,A:Lockheed,V:Dark Bamf . . . 3.50

NIGHTCRAWLER
Nov., 2001
1 (of 4) Passion Play 2.50
2 . . . . 2.50
3 . . . . 2.50
4 finale 2.50

NIGHTCRAWLER
Sept., 2004
1 DaR,Diabolique,pt.1 . . . . 3.00
2 DaR,Diabolique,pt.2 . . . . 3.00

NIGHTHAWK
July, 1998
1 (of 3) RCa,BWi,Nighthawk shake
   off coma 3.00
2 (of 3) RCa,BWi,V:Mephisto 3.00
3 RCa,BWi,conclusion 3.00

NIGHTMARE
1994
1 ANo 2.25
2 & 3 ANo . . . . @2.25

NIGHTMARE CIRCUS
1 video-game tie-in 2.50
2 video-game tie-in 2.50

NIGHTMARE ON ELM STREET
Oct., 1989
1 RB/TD/AA.,Movie adapt 3.00
2 AA,Movie adapt,Dec., 1989 . . . . 2.25

NIGHTMASK
Nov., 1986
1 O:Night Mask 2.50
2 V:Gnome 2.50
3 V:Mistress Twilight 2.50
4 EC,D:Mistress Twilight 2.50
5 EC,Nightmare 2.50
6 EC 2.50
7 EC 2.50
8 EC 2.50
9 . . . . 2.50
10 Lucian 2.50
11 . . . . 2.50
12 Oct., 1987 . . . . 2.50

NIGHT NURSE
Nov., 1972
1 The Making of a Nurse 175.00
2 Moment of Truth 125.00
3 . . . . 125.00
4 Final Issue,May, 1973 . . . . . . 125.00

MARVEL

NIGHT RIDER
Oct., 1974–Aug., 1975
1 Reprint Ghost Rider #1 . . . . . . 20.00
2 Reprint Ghost Rider #2 . . . . . . 12.00
3 Reprint Ghost Rider #3 . . . . . . 12.00
4 Reprint Ghost Rider #4 . . . . . . 12.00
5 Reprint Ghost Rider #5 . . . . . . 12.00
6 Reprint Ghost Rider #6 . . . . . . 12.00

NIGHTSIDE
Oct., 2001
1 (of 4) TDr,The OThers 3.00
2 TDr,The Others 3.00
3 TDr,Sydney Taine 3.00
4 TDr,Black Dragons. 3.00

NIGHTSTALKERS
1992–94
1 TP(i),Rise o/t Midnight Sons#5
  A:GR,J.Blaze,I:Meatmarket,
  polybagged w/poster 3.00
2 TP(i),V:Hydra 2.50
3 TP(i),V:Dead on Arrival 2.50
4 TP(i),V:Hydra 2.50
5 TP(i),A:Punisher 2.50
6 TP(i),A:Punisher 2.50
7 TP(i),A:Ghost Rider 2.50
8 Hannibal King vs Morbius 2.50
9 MPa,A:Morbius 2.50
10 Midnight Massacre#1,D:Johnny
  Blaze,Hannibal King 2.50
11 O:Blade 2.50
12 V:Vampires 2.50
13 V:Vampires 2.50
14 Wld,Siege of Darkness#1 . . . . . 2.50
15 Wld,Siege of Darkness#9 . . . . . 2.50
16 V:Dreadnought 2.50
17 F:Blade 2.50
18 D:Hannibal King,Frank Drake,
  last issue 2.50

NIGHT THRASHER
[Limited Series] 1992–93
1 B:FaN(s),DHv,N:Night Thrasher,
  V:Bengal 2.50
2 DHv,I:Tantrium 2.25
3 DHv,V:Gideon 2.25
4 E:FaN(s),DHv,A:Silhoutte 2.25
[Regular Series] 1993–95
1 B:FaN(s),MBa,JS,V:Poison
  Memories. 3.50
2 JS,V:Concrete Dragons 2.25
3 JS(c),I:Aardwolf,A:Folding Circle . 2.25
4 JS(c),V:Aardwolf,I:Air Force 2.25
5 JS,V:Air Force 2.25
6 Face Value,A:Rage 2.25
7 DdB,V:Bandit 2.25
8 DdB,V:Bandit 2.25
9 DdB,A:Tantrum 2.25
10 DdB,A:Iron Man,w/card. 2.25
11 DdB,Time & Time Again,pt.2. . . 2.25
12 DdB,Time & Time Again,pt.5. . . 2.25
13 Lost in the Shadows,pt.1 . . . . . 2.25
14 Lost in the Shadows,pt.2 . . . . . 2.25
15 Money Don't Buy,pt.1 . . . . 2.25
16 A:Prowler. 2.25
17 . . . . 2.25
18 . . . . 2.25
19 V:Tantrum 2.25
20 . . . . 2.25
21 Rage vs. Grind 2.25

NIGHTWATCH
1994–95
1 RLm,I:Salvo,Warforce Holo(c) . . . 3.00
1a Newsstand ed. 2.25
2 RLm,AM,I:Flashpoint 2.25

Nightwatch #11
© *Marvel Entertainment Group*

3 RLm,AM,V:Flashpoint 2.25
4 RLm,A:Warrent,V:Gauntlet 2.25
5 I:Sunstreak,A:Venom 2.25
6 V:Venom 2.25
7 I:Cardiaxe 2.25
8 V:Cardiaxe 2.25
9 origins 2.25
10 . . . . 2.25
11 . . . . 2.25
12 . . . . 2.25

NOCTURNE
1995
1 DAn, in London 2.25
2 DAn,O:Nocturne 2.25
3 Interview with Amy. 2.25
4 V:Dragon 2.25

NO ESCAPE
1994
1 & 2 Movie adaptation . . . . @2.25

NOMAD
[Limited Series] Nov., 1990
1 B:FaN(s),A:Capt.America 3.00
2 A:Capt.America 2.50
3 A:Capt.America 2.50
4 A:Capt.America, final issue,
  Feb., 1989. . . . . 2.50
[Regular Series] 1992–94
1 B:FaN(s),R:Nomad,[Gatetfold(c),
  map] 3.00
2 V:Road Kill Club. 2.50
3 V:U.S.Agent 2.25
4 DeadMan's Hand#2,V:Deadpool . 2.25
5 DeadMan's Hand#4,V:Punisher. . 2.25
6 DeadMan's Hand#8,A:Punisher,
  Daredevil 2.25
7 Infinity War,V:Gambit,
  Doppleganger 2.25
8 L.A.Riots 2.25
9 I:Ebbtide. 2.25
10 A:Red Wolf 2.25
11 in Albuquerque 2.25
12 In Texas 2.25
13 AIDS issue 2.25
14 Hidden in View 2.25
15 Hidden in View 2.25
16 A:Gambit. 2.25
17 Bucky Kidnapped 2.25
18 A:Captain America,Slug 2.25

19 FaN(s),Faustus Affair 2.25
20 A:Six Pack. 2.25
21 A:Man-Thing 2.25
22 American Dreamers#1,V:Zaran . 2.25
23 American Dreamers#2 . . . . 2.25
24 American Dreamers#3 . . . . 2.25
25 American Dreamers#4, finale . . . 2.25

NORTHSTAR
1994
1 SFr,DoC,V:Weapon:P.R.I.M.E. . . 2.25
2 SFr,DoC,V:Arcade 2.25
3 SFr,DoC,V:Arcade 2.25
4 SFr,DoC,final issue 2.25
N Presents James O'Barr 2.50

NOT BRAND ECHH
Aug., 1967
1 JK(c),BEv,Forbush Man(c) . . . 100.00
2 MSe,FrG,Spidey-Man,Gnat-Man
  & Rotten 50.00
3 MSe(C),TS,JK,FrG,O:Charlie
  America 50.00
4 GC,JTg,TS,Scaredevil,
  ECHHs-Men 50.00
5 JK,TS,GC,I&O:Forbush Man . . 50.00
6 MSe(c),GC,TS,W:Human Torch 50.00
7 MSe(c),JK,GC,TS,O:Fantastical
  Four,Stupor Man 50.00
8 MSe(c),GC,TS,C:Beatles 60.00
9 MSe,GC,TS,Bulk
  V:Sunk-Mariner 75.00
10 JK,TS,MSe,The Worst of... . . . 75.00
11 King Konk 75.00
12 MSe,Frankenstein,A:Revengers 75.00
13 GC,MSe,Stamp Out Trading
  Cards(c). 75.00

NOTHING CAN STOP THE JUGGERNAUT
1989
1 JR2,rep.SpM#229&#230 . . . . . . 4.00

NOVA
[1st Regular Series] Sept., 1976
1 B:MWn(s),JB,JSt,I&O:Nova 20.00
2 JB,JSt,I:Condor,Powerhouse . . . 10.00
3 JB,JSt,I:Diamondhead 10.00
4 SB,TP,A:Thor,I:Corruptor 10.00
5 SB,V:Earthshaker 7.00
6 SB,V:Condor,Powerhouse,
  Diamondhead,I:Sphinx 7.00
7 SB,War in Space,O:Sphinx 7.00
8 V:Megaman 7.00
9 V:Megaman 7.00
10 V:Condor,Powerhouse,
  Diamond-head Sphinx 7.00
11 V:Sphinx 8.00
12 A:Spider-Man 10.00
13 I:Crimebuster,A:Sandman. 6.00
14 A:Sandman 6.00
15 CI,C:Spider-Man, Hulk 6.00
16 CI,A:Yellow Claw. 6.00
17 A:Yellow Claw 6.00
18 A:Yellow Claw, Nick Fury 6.00
19 CI,TP,I:Blackout 6.00
20 What is Project X? 6.00
21 JB,BMc,JRu 6.00
22 CI,I:Comet. 6.00
23 CI,V:Dr.Sun 6.00
24 CI,I:New Champions,V:Sphinx . . 6.00
25 E:MWn(s),CI,A:Champions,
  V:Sphinx 6.00
[2nd Regular Series] 1994–95
1 B:FaN(s),ChM,V:Gladiator,Foil
  Embossed(c) 3.50
2 ChM,V:Tail Hook Rape 2.25

MARVEL

Nova, 2nd Series #9
© Marvel Entertainment Group

3 ChM,A:Spider-Man,Corruptor . . . 2.25
4 ChM,I:NovaO:O 2.25
5 ChM,R:Condor,w/card 2.25
6 ChM,Time & Time Again,pt.3. . . . 2.25
7 ChM,Time & Time Again,pt.6. . . . 2.25
8 ChM,I:Shatterforce. 2.25
9 ChM,V:Shatterforce 2.25
10 ChM,V:Diamondhead 2.25
11 ChM,V:Diamondhead 2.25
12 ChM,A:Inhumans 2.25
13 ChM,A:Inhumans 2.25
14 A:Condor. 2.25
15 V:Brethern of Zorr. 2.25
16 Countdown Conclusion. 2.25
17 Nova Loses Powers 2.25
18 Nova Omega,pt.1 . . . . 2.25

NOVA
March, 1999
1 EL,JoB,F:Rich Rider,48-page . . . 3.00
2 EL,JoB,A:Capt.America 2.25
2a variant JoB cover. 2.25
3 EL,JoB,A:Capt.America & Hulk . . 2.25
4 EL,JoB,A:Mr.Fantastic 2.25
5 EL,JoB,A:Spider-Man 2.25
6 EL,JoB,V:Sphinx 2.25
7 EL,JoB, final issue 2.25

Nth MAN
Aug., 1989
1 . . . . 2.25
2 thru 7 . . . . @2.25
8 DK 2.25
9 thru 16, finale, Sept., 1990. . . . @2.25

'NUFF SAID
Aug., 2002
TPB 240-pg., silent stories. 22.00

NYX
Oct., 2003
1 JQ,gutterpunks 10.00
2 JQ,self-preservation's price 7.00
3 JQ,Y-23 . . . . 28.00
4 JQ,F:Tatiana 5.00
5 JQ 5.00
6 JQ 3.00

OBNOXIO THE CLOWN
April, 1983
1 X-Men 3.50

OFFCASTES
Epic *Heavy Hitters,* 1993
1 MV,I:Offcastes 2.50
2 MV,V:Kaoro 2.25
3 MV,Last Issue 2.25

OFFICIAL HANDBOOK OF THE MARVEL UNIVERSE
Spec. Avengers 2004. . . . . 4.00
Spec. Daredevil 2004. . . . . 4.00
Spec. Hulk 2004. . . . . 4.00
Spec. Spider-Man 2004 . . . . 4.00
Spec. Wolverine 2004 . . . . 4.00
Spec. X-Men 2004 . . . . 4.00

OFFICIAL MARVEL INDEX:
1985–88
TO THE AMAZING SPIDER-MAN
Index 1 . . . . 3.00
Index 2 thru 9 . . . . @2.50
TO THE AVENGERS
Index 1 thru 7 . . . . @2.50
TO THE FANTASTIC FOUR
Index 1 thru 12. . . . . @2.25
TO MARVEL TEAM-UP
Index 1 thru 6 . . . . @2.25
TO THE X-MEN
Index 1 thru 7 . . . . @2.95
[Vol. 2] 1994
Index 1 thru 5 . . . . @2.25

OFFICIAL MARVEL TIMELINE
1-shot, 48-pg. 6.00

OFFICIAL TRUE CRIME CASES
Fall, 1947
24 (1)SSh(c),The Grinning Killer . 275.00
25 (2)She Made Me a Killer,HK. . 225.00
Becomes:

ALL-TRUE CRIME
26 SSh(c),The True Story of Wilbur
   Underhill 400.00
27 Electric Chair(c),Robert Mais . 300.00
28 Cops V:Gangsters(c) 125.00
29 Cops V:Gangsters(c) 125.00
30 He Picked a Murderous Mind   125.00
31 Hitchiking Thugs(c) 125.00
32 Jewel Thieves(c). 125.00
33 The True Story of Dinton
   Phillips 125.00
34 Case of the Killers Revenge. . 125.00
35 Ph(c),Date with Danger 125.00
36 Ph(c) 125.00
37 Ph(c),Story of Robert Marone. 125.00
38 Murder Weapon,Nick Maxim . 125.00
39 Story of Vince Vanderee 125.00
40 . . . . 125.00
41 Lou `Lucky' Raven 125.00
42 BK,Baby Face Nelson. 150.00
43 Doc Channing Paulson. 125.00
44 Murder in the Big House. 125.00
45 While the City Sleeps 125.00
46 . . . . 125.00
47 Gangster Terry Craig 125.00
48 GT,They Vanish By Night 125.00
49 BK,Squeeze Play 150.00

50 Shoot to Kill. 125.00
51 Panic in the Big House 125.00
52 Prison Break, Sept., 1952. . . . 125.00

OLYMPIANS
Epic, July, 1991
1 Spoof Series 4.00
2 Conclusion. 4.00

Omega the Unknown #3
© Marvel Entertainment Group

OMEGA THE UNKNOWN
March, 1976
1 JM,I:Omega 12.00
2 JM,A:Hulk 7.00
3 JM,A:Electro 7.00
4 JM,V:Yellow Claw 6.00
5 JM,V:The Wrench 6.00
6 JM,V:Blockbuster. 6.00
7 JM,V:Blockbuster. 6.00
8 JM,C:New Foolkiller,V:Nitro 7.00
9 JM,A:New Foolkiller,
   D:Blockbuster 10.00
10 JM,D:Omega the Unknown. . . . 5.00

ONE, THE
Epic, July, 1985
1 thru 5 . . . . @2.50
6 Feb., 1986 . . . . 2.50

100 GREATEST MARVELS
Sept., 2001
1 (of 5) weekly, 112-pages 8.00
2 thru 5 112-pages . . . . @8.00
5 Top 5 #5, 32-pages 4.00
4 Top 5 #4, 32-pages 4.00
3 Top 5 #3, 48-pages 4.00
2 Top 5 #2, 48-pages 4.00
1 Top 5 #1, 48-pages 4.00

101 WAYS TO END THE CLONE SAGA
1-shot (1997) 2.50

ONSLAUGHT
1996–97
Marvel Universe: AKu,SLo,MWd,
   Marvel Heroes vs. Onslaught . . 7.00
Marvel Universe: Gold edition . . . 15.00
X-Men: AKu,SLo,MWd (1996) 6.00
X-Men: Gold editon 15.00
Onslaught: Epilogue (1997) 3.00

MARVEL

TPB Book 1, rep. 13.00
TPB Book 2, rep. 10.00
TPB Book 3, rep. 10.00
TPB Book 4, rep. 10.00
TPB Book 5, rep. 10.00
TPB Book 6, rep. 13.00

ONYX OVERLORD
Epic, 1992–93
1 JBi,Sequel to Airtight Garage . . . 3.00
2 JBi,The Joule. 3.00
3 JBi,V:Overlord 3.00
4 V:Starbilliard. 3.00

OPEN SPACE
Dec., 1989–Aug., 1990
1 . . . . 6.00
2 thru 4 . . . . @5.25

ORDER, THE
Feb., 2002
1 (of 6) KBk,JDy,MHy,F:Hulk, Namor,
    Dr. Strange, & Silver Surfer. . . 2.25
2 KBk,JDy,MHy,A:Avengers 2.25
3 KBk,JDy,MHy,DPs,V:Avengers . . 2.25
4 KBk,JDy,DPs,Hulk,Nighthawk . . . 2.25
5 KBk,JDy,DPs,F:Nighthawk 2.25
6 KBk,JDy,DPs,V:everybody. 2.25

ORIGIN
Aug., 2001
1 (of 6) PJe,NKu,F:Wolverine. 3.50
2 PJe,NKu,JQ(c). 3.50
3 PJe,NKu,JQ(c). 3.50
4 PJe,NKu,JQ(c). 3.50
5 PJe,NKu,JQ(c), ... 3.50
6 PJe,NKu,final part 3.50
TPB JQ(c) 15.00

Original Ghost Rider #6
© Marvel Entertainment Group

ORIGINAL GHOST RIDER
1992–94
1 MT(c),rep. 2.25
2 thru 23 rep.. . . . . @2.25

ORIGINAL GHOST RIDER RIDES AGAIN
July, 1991
1 rep.GR#68+#69(O:JohnnyBlaze) 3.00

2 thru 7 rep.Ghost Rider. . . . . . @2.25

ORIGINS OF MARVEL COMICS
TPB StL,JK,SD rep., 260-pg. 25.00

OSBORN JOURNALS, THE
1997
1-shot KHt,F:Norman Osborn. 3.00

OUR LOVE
Sept., 1949
1 Ph(c),Guilt of Nancy Crane . . 175.00
2 Ph(c),My Kisses Were Cheap 125.00
Becomes:

TRUE SECRETS
3 Love Stories,continued 150.00
4 . . . . 75.00
5 . . . . 75.00
6 BEv 125.00
7 . . . . 75.00
8 . . . . 75.00
9 . . . . 75.00
10 . . . . 75.00
11 thru 21 . . . . @65.00
22 BEv 75.00
23 thru 39. . . . . @50.00
40 Sept., 1956 . . . . 50.00

OUR LOVE STORY
Oct., 1969
1 JB. 100.00
2 JB. 35.00
3 JB. 35.00
4 . . . . 35.00
5 JSo,JB 125.00
6 thru 13 . . . . @50.00
14 Gary Friedrich &Tarpe Mills . . . 55.00
15 thru 37. . . . . @30.00
38 Feb., 1976. . . . . 30.00

OUTLAW FIGHTERS
Atlas, Aug., 1954
1 GT,Western Tales 150.00
2 GT ,JMn(c). 100.00
3 . . . . 100.00
4 A;Patch Hawk 100.00
5 RH, Final Issue,April, 1955 . . . 100.00

OUTLAW KID
Atlas, Sept., 1954
1 SSh,DW,JMn(c),B&O:Outlaw Kid,
   A;Black Rider 350.00
2 DW,JMn(c),A:Black Rider 175.00
3 DW,AW,GWb,JMN(c) 175.00
4 DW(c),Death Rattle 150.00
5 JMn 150.00
6 JMn 150.00
7 JMn 150.00
8 AW,DW,JMn 150.00
9 . . . . 125.00
10 JSe 125.00
11 thru 17. . . . . @100.00
18 AW,JMn. 100.00
19 JSe,Sept., 1957 . . . . 100.00
[2nd series] Aug., 1970
1 JSe(c),DW,Jo,Showdown,rep . . 40.00
2 DW,One Kid Too Many 25.00
3 HT(c),DW,Six Gun Double
   Cross 25.00
4 DW 20.00
5 DW 20.00
6 DW 20.00
7 HT(c),DW,Treachery on
   the Trail 20.00
8 HT(c),DW,RC,Six Gun Pay Off . 30.00

9 JSe(c),DW,GWb,The Kids
   Last Stand 20.00
10 GK(c),DAy,NewO:Outlaw Kid . . 40.00
11 GK(c),Thunder Along the
   Big Iron 20.00
12 The Man Called Bounty Hawk . 20.00
13 The Last Rebel 20.00
14 The Kid Gunslingers of
   Calibre City 20.00
15 GK(c),V:Madman of Monster
   Mountain 20.00
16 The End of the Trail 20.00
17 thru 29. . . . . @20.00
30 Oct., 1975 . . . . 20.00

OVER THE EDGE AND UNDER A BUCK
1995–96
1 F:Daredevil vs. Mr. Fear 2.25
2 F:Doctor Strange 2.25
3 F:Hulk 2.25
4 in Cypress Hills 2.25
5 . . . . 2.25
6 F:Daredevil 2.25
7 Doc & Nightmare 2.25

PARADISE X: THE HERALDS
Oct., 2001
1 (of 3) AxR, Earth X trilogy 3.50
2 AxR,. 3.50
3 AxR,StP,concl. 3.50

PARADISE X
Feb., 2002
1 (of 13) AxR,Earth X trilogy. 3.50
2 AxR,DBw,F:Captain Mar-Vell. . . 3.50
3 AxR,DBw,King Britain,Medusa. . 3.00
4 AxR,DBw,nature of new Paradise 3.00
5 AxR,DBw 3.00
6 AxR,DBw,the new Death 3.00
7 AxR,DBw 3.00
8 AxR,DBw 3.00
9 AxR,DBw,O:Ghost Rider 3.00
10 AxR,DBw,F:Matt Murcock. 3.00
11 AxR,DBw,F:Harry Pym 3.00
12 AxR,DBw,concl.. . . . . 3.00
Spec.#0, AxR, prologue to series . . 3.50
Special A DBw 3.00
Special 1-shot, Earth X 3.00
GN Paradise X:Xen, 56-pg. 4.50
GN Devils AxR, 48-pg.. . . . . 4.50

PARADISE X/RAGNAROK
Jan., 2003
1 (of 2) AxR. 3.00
2 AxR 3.00

PARAGON
1 I:Paragon,Nightfire. 5.00

PATSY & HEDY
Atlas, Feb., 1952
1 AJ(c),B:Patsy Walker &
   Hedy Wolfe 250.00
2 Skating(c) 150.00
3 Boyfriend Trouble 125.00
4 Swimsuit(c) 125.00
5 Patsy's Date(c) 125.00
6 Swimsuit/Picnic(c) 125.00
7 Double-Date(c) 125.00
8 AJ(c),The Dance 125.00
9 . . . . 125.00
10 . . . . 125.00
11 thru 25 . . . . @100.00
26 thru 50. . . . . @60.00

51 thru 60 . . . . @50.00	
61 thru 109 . . . . @40.00	
110 Feb., 1967 . . . . 40.00	

PATSY & HER PALS
May, 1953

1 MWs(c),F:Patsy Walker 225.00	
2 MWs(c),Swimsuit(c) 125.00	
3 MWs(c),Classroom(c) 100.00	
4 MWs(c),Golfcourse(c) 100.00	
5 MWs(c).Patsy/Buzz(c) 9.00	
6 thru 10 . . . . @100.00	
11 thru 28 . . . . @75.00	
29 Aug., 1957 . . . . 75.00	

PATSY WALKER
1945–Dec., 1965

1 F:Patsy Walker Adventures . . 650.00	
2 Patsy/Car(c) 300.00	
3 Skating(c) 225.00	
4 Perfume(c) 225.00	
5 Archery Lesson, Eye Injury(c) 225.00	
6 Bus(c) 225.00	
7 Charity Drive(c) 225.00	
8 Organ Driver Monkey(c) 225.00	
9 Date(c) 225.00	
10 Skating(c),Wedding Bells,	
A:Millie 225.00	
11 Date with a Dream,A:Mitzi . . . 150.00	
12 Love in Bloom,Artist(c),	
A:Rusty 150.00	
13 Swimsuit(c),There Goes My	
Heart;HK,Hey Look 150.00	
14 An Affair of the Heart,	
HK,Hey Look 150.00	
15 Dance(c) 135.00	
16 Skating(c) 135.00	
17 Patsy's Diary(c),HK,Hey Look 150.00	
18 Autograph(c) 135.00	
19 HK,Hey Look 150.00	
20 HK,Hey Look 150.00	
21 HK,Hey Look 150.00	
22 HK,Hey Look 150.00	
23 . . . . 125.00	
24 . . . . 125.00	
25 HK,Rusty 175.00	
26 . . . . 125.00	
27 . . . . 125.00	
28 . . . . 125.00	
29 . . . . 125.00	
30 HK,Egghead Double 125.00	
31 . . . . 100.00	
32 thru 56 . . . . @75.00	
57 thru 58 AJ(c) . . . . @100.00	
59 thru 99 . . . . @60.00	
100 . . . . 55.00	
101 thru 124 . . . . @50.00	
Fashion Parade #1 . . . . 125.00	

PETER PARKER, THE SPECTACULAR SPIDER-MAN
Dec., 1976

1 SB,V:Tarantula 65.00	
2 SB,V:Kraven,Tarantula 25.00	
3 SB,I:Lightmaster 15.00	
4 SB,V:Vulture,Hitman 15.00	
5 SB,V:Hitman,Vulture 15.00	
6 SB,V:Morbius,rep.M.T.U.#3 . . . 16.00	
7 SB,V:Morbius,A:Human Torch . . 18.00	
8 SB,V:Morbius 17.00	
9 SB,I:White Tiger 15.00	
10 SB,A:White Tiger 12.00	
11 JM,V:Medusa 10.00	
12 SB,V:Brother Power 10.00	
13 SB,V:Brother Power 10.00	
14 SB,V:Brother Power 10.00	
15 SB,V:Brother Power 10.00	

16 SB,V:The Beetle 10.00	
17 SB,A:Angel & Iceman	
Champions disbanded 10.00	
18 SB,A:Angel & Iceman 10.00	
19 SB,V:The Enforcers 9.00	
20 SB,V:Lightmaster 9.00	
21 JM,V:Scorpion 9.00	
22 MZ,A:Moon Knight,V:Cyclone . . 9.00	
23 A:Moon Knight,V:Cyclone 9.00	
24 FS,A:Hypno-Hustler 8.00	
25 JM,FS,I:Carrion 9.00	
26 JM,A:Daredevil,V:Carrion 8.00	
27 DC,FM,I:Miller Daredevil,	
V:Carrion 30.00	
28 FM,A:Daredevil,V:Carrion . . . 22.00	
29 JM,FS,V:Carrion 7.00	
30 JM,FS,V:Carrion 7.00	
31 JM,FS,D:Carrion 7.00	
32 BL,JM,FS,V:Iguana 7.00	
33 JM,FS,O:Iguana 7.00	
34 JM,FS,V:Iguana,Lizard 7.00	
35 V:Mutant Mindworm 7.00	
36 JM,V:Swarm 7.00	
37 DC,MN,V:Swarm. 7.00	
38 SB,V:Morbius 7.00	

Peter Parker #12
© Marvel Entertainment Group

39 JM,JR2,V:Schizoid Man 8.00	
40 FS,V:Schizoid Man 8.00	
41 JM,V:Meteor Man,A:GiantMan . 7.00	
42 JM,A:Fant.Four,V:Frightful 4 . . . 7.00	
43 JBy(c),MZ,V:The Ringer,	
V:Belladonna 7.00	
44 JM,V:The Vulture 7.00	
45 MSe,V:The Vulture 7.00	
46 FM(c),MZ,V:Cobra 7.00	
47 MSe,A:Prowler II 7.00	
48 MSe,A:Prowler II 7.00	
49 MSe,I:Smuggler 7.00	
50 JR2,JM,V:Mysterio 7.00	
51 MSe&FM(c),V:Mysterio 7.00	
52 FM(c),D:White Tiger 7.00	
53 JM,FS,V:Terrible Tinkerer 7.00	
54 FM,WS,MSe,V:Silver Samurai . . 7.00	
55 LMc,JM,V:Nitro 7.00	
56 FM,JM,V:Jack-o-lantern 12.00	
57 JM,V:Will-o-the Wisp 6.00	
58 JBy,V:Ringer,A:Beetle 7.00	
59 JM,V:Beetle. 6.00	
60 JM&FM(c),O:Spider-Man,	
V:Beetle 7.00	
61 JM,V:Moonstone 5.00	
62 JM,V:Goldbug 5.00	
63 JM,V:Molten Man 5.00	
64 JM,I:Cloak & Dagger 12.00	

65 BH,JM,V:Kraven,Calypso 5.00	
66 JM,V:Electro 5.00	
67 AMb,V:Boomerang 5.00	
68 LMc,JM,V:Robot of Mendell	
Stromm 5.00	
69 AM,A:Cloak & Dagger. 6.00	
70 A:Cloak & Dagger 6.00	
71 JM,Gun Control issue 5.00	
72 AM,V:Dr.Octopus 5.00	
73 AM,JM,V:Dr.Octopus,A:Owl . . . 5.00	
74 AM,JM,V:Dr.Octopus,R:Bl.Cat . . 5.00	
75 AM,JM,V:Owl,Dr.Octopus 6.00	
76 AM,Black Cat on deathbed 5.00	
77 AM,V:Gladiator,Dr.Octopus 5.00	
78 AM,V:Dr.Octopus,C:Punisher . . . 5.00	
79 AM,V:Dr.Octopus,A:Punisher . . . 5.00	
80 AM,F:J.Jonah Jameson 5.00	
81 A:Punisher. 6.00	
82 A:Punisher. 6.00	
83 A:Punisher. 8.00	
84 AM,F:Black Cat 4.00	
85 AM,O:Hobgoblin powers	
(Ned Leeds) 10.00	
86 FH,V:Fly 4.00	
87 AM,Reveals I.D.to Black Cat . . . 4.00	
88 AM,V:Cobra,Mr.Hyde 4.00	
89 AM,Secret Wars,A:Kingpin 5.00	
90 AM,Secret Wars 6.00	
91 AM,V:Blob 4.00	
92 AM,I:Answer 4.00	
93 AM,V:Answer 4.00	
94 AM,A:Cloak & Dagger,V:	
Silver Mane 4.00	
95 AM,A:Cloak & Dagger,V:	
Silvermane 4.00	
96 AM,A:Cloak & Dagger,V:	
Silvermane 4.00	
97 HT,JM,A:Black Cat 4.00	
98 HT,JM,I:Spot 4.00	
99 HT,JM,V:Spot 4.00	
100 AM,V:Kingpin,C:Bl.Costume . . . 6.00	
101 JBy(c),AM,V:Killer Shrike 3.00	
102 JBy(c),AM,V:Backlash 3.00	
103 AM,V:Blaze;Not John Blaze . . . 3.00	
104 JBy(c),AM,V:Rocket Racer 3.00	
105 AM,A:Wasp 3.00	
106 AM,A:Wasp 3.00	
107 RB,D:Jean DeWolf,I:SinEater . . 4.00	
108 RB,A:Daredevil,V:Sin-Eater . . . 3.00	
109 RB,A:Daredevil,V:Sin-Eater . . . 3.00	
110 RB,A:Daredevil,V:Sin-Eater . . . 3.00	
111 RB,Secret Wars II 3.00	
112 RB,A:Santa Claus,Black Cat. . . 3.00	
113 RB,Burglars,A:Black Cat. 3.00	
114 BMc,V:Lock Picker 3.00	
115 BMc,A:Black Cat,Dr.Strange,	
I:Foreigner 4.00	
116 A:Dr.Strange, Foreigner,	
Black Cat, Sabretooth 5.00	
117 DT,C:Sabretooth,A:Foreigner,	
Black Cat,Dr.Strange 4.00	
118 MZ,D:Alexander,V:SHIELD . . . 3.00	
119 RB,BMc,V:Sabretooth,	
A:Foreigner,Black Cat 5.00	
120 KG. 3.00	
121 RB,BMc,V:Mauler 3.00	
122 V:Mauler 3.00	
123 V:Foreigner,Black Cat. 3.00	
124 V:Dr.Octopus. 3.00	
125 V:Wr.Crew,A:Spiderwoman 3.00	
126 JM,A:Sp.woman,V:Wrecker . . . 3.00	
127 AM,V:Lizard. 3.00	
128 C:DDevil,A:Bl.Cat,Foreigner . . 3.50	
129 A:Black Cat,V:Foreigner 3.00	
130 A:Hobgoblin. 6.00	
131 MZ,BMc,V:Kraven. 7.00	
132 MZ,BMc,V:Kraven. 7.00	
133 BSz(c),Mad Dog,pt.3 . . . . 3.00	
Ann.#1 RB,JM,V:Dr.Octopus 10.00	
Ann.#2 JM,I&O:Rapier. 7.00	
Ann.#3 JM,V:Manwolf 5.00	

Peter Parker King Size Ann. #3
© Marvel Entertainment Group

Ann.#4 AM,O:Aunt May,A:Bl.Cat . . . 5.00
Ann.#5 I:Ace,Joy Mercado 5.00
Ann.#6 V:Ace 4.50
Ann.#7 Honeymoon iss,A:Puma . . 4.50
Becomes:

SPECTACULAR
SPIDER-MAN

PETER PARKER:
SPIDER-MAN
Nov., 1998

1 JR2,HMe,SHa,A:new Spider-Man,
V:Ranger,48-page 3.00
1a signed 15.00
2 JR2,HMe,SHa,A:Thor 4.00
2a variant cover 4.00
3 HMe,JR2,SHa,A:Iceman,
V:Shadrac 3.00
4 HMe,JR2,SHa,V:Marrow 3.00
5 HMe,SHa,BS,JBy(c),F:Spider-
Woman,Aunt May, Black Cat. . . 3.00
6 HMe,SHa,RJ2,JBy(c),V:Kingpin . 3.00
7 JR2,HMe,SHa,Reality Bent 3.00
8 JR2,HMe,SHa,V:Bullseye 3.00
9 JR2,HMe,SHa,R:Venom 3.00
10 JR2,HMe,SHa,R:Carnage. 3.00
11 JR2,HMe,SHa,Eighth Day,pt.3
x-over. 3.00
12 JR2,HMe,SHa, 48-pg. 3.50
13 JR2,HMe 3.00
14 JR2,HMe,A:Hulk 3.50
15 JR2,HMe,x-over 3.50
16 JR2,HMe,V:Sinister Six. 3.00
17 JR2,HMe,SHa,V:Kraven 2.50
18 HMe,JR2,SHa,V:Green Goblin . 2.50
19 HMe,JR2,SHa,Mary Jane dies . . 2.50
20 PJe,MBu,DGr,Mary Jane dead. . 3.00
21 PJe,MBu,DGr,HumanTorch. . . . 2.50
22 PJe,MBu,DGr,FlintMarko 2.50
23 PJe,MBu,DGr,Type Face 2.50
24 PJe,MBu,DGr,Max.Security . . . 2.50
25 PJe,MBu,DGr,V:Green Goblin . 3.50
26 PJe,JoB,DGr,F:NYPD 2.50
27 PJe,MBu,DGr,F:NYPD 2.50
28 PJe,MBu,DGr, ... 2.50
29 PJe,CAd,DGr,x-over 7.00
30 PJe,MBu,HuR(c),I:Terminal . . . 7.00
31 PJe,MBu,HuR(c),I:Fusion 3.50
32 PJe,MBu,HuR(c),V:Fusion 2.50
33 PJe,MBu,HuR(c),ballpark 2.50
34 PJe,MBu,cleanse the city 2.50

35 PJe,MBu,Jamal. 2.50
36 PJe,MBu,private-eye. 2.50
37 PJe,slice-of-life 2.50
38 PJe,MBu,V:Mimes,'Nuff Said . . . 2.50
39 PJe,MBu,return of Dr. Octopus. . 2.50
40 PJe,MBu,Doc Octopus,pt.2 . . . . 2.50
41 PJe,MBu,Doc Octopus,pt.3 . . . . 2.50
42 Spring Break,pt.1 . . . . 2.50
43 Spring Break,pt.2 . . . . 2.50
44 PJe,HuR,R:Green Goblin 6.00
45 PJe,HuR,R:Green Goblin,pt.2 . . 4.00
46 PJe,HuR,R:Green Goblin,pt.3 . . 2.50
47 PJe,HuR,R:Green Goblin,pt.4 . . 2.50
48 PJe,MBu 2.50
49 PJe,MBu 2.50
50 PJe,MBu 4.00
51 pt.1 . . . . 2.50
52 pt.2 . . . . 2.50
53 pt.1 . . . . 2.50
54 pt.2 . . . . 2.50
55 pt.3 . . . . 2.50
56 SK,Reborn,pt.1,F:Sandman . . . 2.50
57 SK,Reborn,pt.2,F:Sandman . . . 2.50
Ann.1999,CCs, 48-pg. 4.00
Ann.2000 CCl,JoB,80-pg. 4.00
Ann.2001 South America, 28-pg. . . 3.50
Spec. Peter Parker, Spider-
Man 2000 . . . . 4.00
TPB Peter Parker:Spider-Man 14.95
TPB One Small Break, 160-pg. . . . 16.95
TPB Return of the Goblin 9.00
TPB Trials & Tribulations 12.00
TPB Vol. 5: Senseless Violence . . 15.00

PETER PORKER
Star, May, 1985

1 Parody 4.50
2 . . . . 3.00
3 . . . . 3.00
4 . . . . 3.00
5 V:Senior Simians 3.00
6 A Blitz in Time 3.00
7 . . . . 3.00
8 Kimono My House 3.00
9 Uncouth my Tooth 3.00
10 Lost Temple of the Golden
Retriever 3.00
11 Dog Dame Afternoon 3.00
12 The Gouda,Bad & Ugly. 3.00
13 Halloween issue 3.00
14 Heavy Metal Issue 3.00
15 . . . . 3.00
16 Porker Fried Rice,Final Issue . . . 3.00
17 Sept., 1987 . . . . 3.00

PETER, THE LITTLE PEST
Nov., 1969–May, 1970

1 F:Peter 75.00
2 Rep,Dexter & Melvin 50.00
3 Rep,Dexter & Melvin 50.00
4 Rep,Dexter & Melvin 50.00

PHANTOM

1 Lee Falk's Phantom. 4.00
2 V:General Babalar 4.00
3 final issue. 4.00

PHANTOM 2040

1 Based on cartoon 2.50
2 V:Alloy 2.50
3 MPa,V:Crime Syndicate. 2.50
4 Vision Quest 2.50

PHOENIX
(UNTOLD STORY)
April, 1984
1 JBy,O:Phoenix (R.Summers). . . 15.00

PILGRIM'S PROGRESS
1 adapts John Bunyans novel . . . 10.00

PINHEAD
1993–94

1 Red Foil(c),from Hellraiser. 3.00
2 DGC(s),V:Cenobites 2.50
3 DGC(s),V:Cenobites 2.50
4 DGC(s),V:Cenobites 2.50
5 DGC(s),Devil in Disguise 2.50
6 DGC(s), ... 2.50

PINHEAD VS.
MARSHALL LAW
1993

1 KON,In Hell 3.00
2 KON 3.00

PINOCCHIO & THE
EMPEROR OF THE NIGHT
March, 1988

1 Movie adapt. 3.00

PINT-SIZED X-BABIES:
MURDERAMA
June, 1998

1-shot, Mojo, Arcade, 48-pg. 3.00

PIRATES OF
DARK WATERS
Nov., 1991

1 based on T.V. series 2.00
2 Search for 13 Treasures 2.00
3 V:Albino Warriors,Konk 2.00
4 A:Monkey Birds 2.00
5 Tula Steals 1st Treasuer 2.00
6 thru 9 . . . . @2.00

PITT, THE
March, 1988

1 SB,SDr,A:Spitfire 4.00

PLANET OF THE APES
Aug., 1974–Feb., 1977
(black & white magazine)

1 MP 45.00
2 MP 25.00
3 . . . . 20.00
4 . . . . 20.00
5 . . . . 20.00
6 thru 10 . . . . @20.00
11 thru 20 . . . . @25.00
21 thru 29 . . . . @55.00

PLANET TERRY
Star, April, 1985

1 thru 11 . . . . @3.00
12 March, 1986 . . . . 3.00

PLASMER
Marvel UK, 1993–94

1 A:Captain America 3.50
2 A:Captain Britain,Black Knight . . . 2.25
3 A:Captain Britain 2.25
4 A:Captain Britain 2.25
5 thru 7 . . . . @2.00

PLASTIC FORKS
Epic, 1990

1 . . . . 6.00
2 thru 5 . . . . @5.50

MARVEL

POLICE ACADEMY
Nov., 1989
1 Based on TV Cartoon	2.25
2 thru 5	@2.25
6 Feb., 1990	2.25

POLICE ACTION
Jan., 1954
1 JF,GC,JMn(c),Riot Squad	225.00
2 JF,Over the Wall	150.00
3 JMn	125.00
4 DAy	125.00
5 DAy,JMn	125.00
6	125.00
7 BPNov., 1954	125.00

POLICE BADGE
See: SPY THRILLERS

POPPLES
Star, Dec., 1986
1 Based on Toys	3.00
2	3.00
3	3.00
4	3.00
5 Aug., 1987	3.00

POWDERED TOAST-MAN
Spec. F:Powder Toast-Man. 3.25

POWERHOUSE PEPPER COMICS
1943—Nov., 1948
1 BW,Movie Auditions(c)	2,500.00
2 BW,Dinner(c)	1,200.00
3 BW,Boxing Ring(c)	1,100.00
4 BW,Subway(c)	1,100.00
5 BW,Bankrobbers(c)	1,300.00

POWERLESS
June, 2004
1 (of 6)	3.00
2 thru 5	@3.00

POWER LINE
Epic, May, 1988
1 BMc(i)	2.25
2 Aw(i)	2.25
3 A:Dr Zero	2.25
4	2.25
5 thru 7 GM	@2.25
8 GM Sept., 1989	2.25

POWER MAN
Prev: Hero for Hire
Feb., 1974
17 GT,A:Iron Man	15.00
18 GT,V:Steeplejack	10.00
19 GT,V:Cottonmouth	10.00
20 GT,Heroin Story	10.00
21 V:Original Power Man	8.00
22 V:Stiletto & Discus	8.00
23 V:Security City	8.00
24 GT,I:BlackGoliath(BillFoster)	8.00
25 A:Circus of Crime	8.00
26 GT,V:Night Shocker	8.00
27 GP,AMc,V:Man Called X	8.00
28 V:Cockroach	8.00
29 V:Mr.Fish	8.00
30 RB,KJ,KP,I:Piranha	8.00
31 SB,NA(i),V:Piranha	8.00
32 JSt,FR,A:Wildfire	7.00
33 FR,A:Spear	7.00
34 FR,A:Spear,Mangler	7.00

Powerman #20
© Marvel Ent.Group

35 DA,A:Spear,Mangler	7.00
36 V:Chemistro	7.00
37 V:Chemistro	7.00
38 V:Chemistro	7.00
39 KJ,V:Chemistro,Baron	7.00
40 V:Baron	7.00
41 TP,V:Thunderbolt,Goldbug	7.00
42 V:Thunderbolt,Goldbug	7.00
43 AN,V:Mace	7.00
44 TP,A:Mace	7.00
45 JSn,A:Mace	7.00
46 GT,I:Zzzax(recreated)	7.00
47 BS,A:Zzzax	9.00
48 JBy,A:Iron Fist	12.00
49 JBy,A:Iron Fist	12.00

Becomes:

POWER MAN & IRON FIST
1978
50 JBy,I:Team-up with Iron Fist	11.00
51 MZ,Night on the Town	4.00
52 MZ,V:Death Machines	4.00
53 SB,O:Nightshade	4.00
54 TR,O:Iron Fist	4.00
55 Chaos at the Coliseum	4.00
56 Mayhem in the Museum	4.00
57 X-Men,V:Living Monolith	20.00
58 1st El Aguila(Drug)	4.00
59 BL(c),TVE,V:Big Apple Bomber	4.00
60 BL(c),V:Terrorists	4.00
61 BL(c),V:The Maggia	4.00
62 BL(c),KGa,V:Man Mountain D:Thunerbolt	4.00
63 BL(c),Cage Fights Fire	4.00
64 DGr&BL(c),V:Suetre,Muertre	4.00
65 BL(c),A:El Aquila,	4.00
66 FM(c),Sabretooth(2nd App.)	35.00
67 V:Bushmaster	4.00
68 FM(c),V:Athur Nagan	4.00
69 V:Soldier	4.00
70 FM(c)V:El Supremo	4.00
71 FM(c),I:Montenegro	4.00
72 FM(c),V:Chako	4.00
73 FM(c),V:Rom	4.00
74 FM(c),V:Ninja	4.00
75 KGa,O:IronFist	4.00
76 KGa,V:Warhawk	4.00
77 KGa,A:Daredevil	4.00
78 KGa,A:El Aguila,Sabretooth (Slasher)(3rd App.)	15.00
79 V:Dredlox	3.00
80 KJ(c),V:Montenegro	3.00
81 V:Black Tiger	3.00
82 V:Black Tiger	3.00
83 V:Warhawk	3.00
84 V:Constrictor,A:Sabertooth (4th App.)	12.00
85 KP,V:Mole Man	3.00
86 A:Moon Knight	3.00
87 A:Moon Kinght	3.00
88 V:Scimtar	3.00
89 V:Terrorists	3.00
90 V:Unus BS(c)	3.00
91 Paths and Angles	3.00
92 V:Hammeread,I:New Eel	3.00
93 A:Chemistro	3.00
94 V:Chemistro	3.00
95 Danny Rand	3.00
96 V,Chemistro	3.00
97 K'unlun,A:Fera	3.00
98 V:Shades & Commanche	3.00
99 R:Daught.of Dragon	3.00
100 O:K'unlun,DoubleSize	5.00
101 A:Karnak	3.00
102 V:Doombringer	3.00
103 O:Doombringer	3.00
104 V:Dr.Octopus,Lizard	3.00
105 F:Crime Buster	3.00
106 Luke Gets Shot	3.00
107 JBy(c),Terror issue	3.00
108 V:Inhuman Monster.	3.00
109 V:The Reaper	3.00
110 V:Nightshade,Eel	3.00
111 I:Captain Hero	3.00
112 JBy(c),V:Control7	3.00
113 JBy(c),A:Capt.Hero	3.00
114 JBy(c),V:Control7	3.00
115 JBy(c),V:Stanley	3.00
116 JBy(c),V:Stanley	3.00
117 R:K'unlun	3.00
118 A:Colleen Wing	3.00
119 A:Daught.of Dragon	3.00
120 V:Chiantang	3.00
121 Secret Wars II	3.00
122 V:Dragonkin	3.00
123 V:Race Killer	3.00
124 V:Yellowclaw	3.00
125 MBr,LastIssue;D:Iron Fist	5.00
G-Size#1 reprints	4.00
Ann.#1 Earth Shock	5.00

Power Pachyderms #1-
© Marvel Ent.Group

POWER PACHYDERMS
Sept., 1989
1 Elephant Superheroes 2.50

POWER PACK
Aug., 1984
1 JBr,BWi,I&O:Power Pack,
  I:Snarks 2.50
2 JBr,BWi,V:Snarks. 2.25
3 JBr,BWi,V:Snarks. 2.25
4 JBr,BWi,V:Snarks. 2.25
5 JBr,BWi,V:Bogeyman. 2.25
6 JBr,BWi,A:Spider-Man. 2.25
7 JBr,BWi,A:Cloak & Dagger 2.25
8 JBr,BWi,A:Cloak & Dagger 2.25
9 BA,BWi,A:Marrina. 2.25
10 BA,BWi,A:Marrina. 2.25
11 JBr,BWi,V:Morlocks. 2.25
12 JBr,BWi,A:X-Men,V:Morlocks . . . 3.00
13 BA,BWi,Baseball issue 2.25
14 JBr,BWi,V:Bogeyman 2.25
15 JBr,BWi,A:Beta Ray Bill 2.25
16 JBr,BWi,I&O:Kofi,J:Tattletale
  (Franklin Richards) 2.25
17 JBr,BWi,V:Snarks 2.25
18 BA,SW,Secret Wars II,
  V:Kurse 2.25
19 BA,SW,Doub.size,Wolverine. . . 4.00
20 BMc,A:NewMutants 2.25
21 BA,TA,C:Spider-Man. 2.25
22 JBg,BWi,V:Snarks. 2.25
23 JBg,BWi,V:Snarks,C:FF 2.25
24 JBg,BWi,V:Snarks,C:Cloak 2.25
25 JBg,BWi,A:FF,V:Snarks 2.25
26 JBg,BWi,A:Cloak & Dagger 2.25
27 JBg,AG,A:Wolverine,X-Factor,
  V:Sabretooth 5.00
28 A:Fantastic Four,Hercules. 2.25
29 JBg,DGr,A:SpM,V:Hobgoblin . . 2.50
30 VM,Crack 2.25
31 JBg,I:Trash 2.25
32 JBg,V:Trash 2.25
33 JBg,A:Sunspot,Warlock,
  C:Spider-Man. 2.25
34 TD,V:Madcap 2.25
35 JBg,A:X-Factor,D:Plague 2.25
36 JBg,V:Master Mold 2.25
37 SDr(i),I:Light-Tracker 2.25
38 SDr(i),V:Molecula 2.25
39 V:Bogeyman 2.25
40 A:New Mutants,V:Bogeyman . . . 2.25
41 SDr(i),V:The Gunrunners 2.25
42 JBg,SDr,Inferno,V:Bogeyman . . 2.25
43 JBg,SDr,AW,Inferno,
  V:Bogeyman 2.25
44 JBr,Inferno,A:New Mutants 2.25
45 JBr,End battle w/Bogeyman 2.25
46 WPo,A:Punisher,Dakota North . . 2.50
47 JBg,I:Bossko. 2.25
48 JBg,Toxic Waste #1 . . . . 2.25
49 JBg,JSh,Toxic Waste #2 . . . . 2.25
50 AW(i),V:Snarks 2.25
51 GM,I:Numinus. 2.25
52 AW(i),V:Snarks,A:Numinus. 2.25
53 EC,A of V,A:Typhoid Mary 2.25
54 JBg,V:Mad Thinker 2.25
55 DSp,V:Mysterio 2.25
56 TMo,A:Fant.Four,Nova 2.25
57 TMo,A:Nova,V:Star Stalker 2.25
58 TMo,A:Galactus,Mr.Fantastic . . . 2.25
59 TMo,V:Ringmaster 2.25
60 TMo,V:Puppetmaster 2.25
61 TMo,V:Red Ghost & Apes. 2.25
62 V:Red Ghost & Apes
  (last issue) 2.25
Holiday Spec.JBr,Small Changes . . 2.25

POWER PACK:
PEER PRESSURE
June, 2000
1 (of 4) TA,CDo. 3.00
2 TA,CDo,V:Snarks. 3.00
3 TA,CDo, ... 3.00

---

4 Ta,CDo,concl 3.00

POWERS
Marvel Icon, July, 2004
1 BMB,F:Deena Pilgrim 3.00
2 thru 5 BMB . . . . @3.00
TPB The Sellouts 20.00

PRINCE NAMOR,
THE SUB-MARINER
Sept., 1984
1 I:Dragonrider, Dara 3.00
2 I:Proteus 2.50
3 . . . . 2.50
4 Dec., 1984 . . . . 2.50

Prince Valiant #1
© *Marvel Entertainment Group*

PRINCE VALIANT
1994–95
1 JRy,CV,Thule, Camelot
  and the Misty Isles 4.00
2 JRy,CV. 4.00
3 JRy,CV. 4.00
4 JRy,CV, final issue. 4.00

PRIVATE EYE
Atlas, Jan., 1951
1 . . . . 250.00
2 . . . . 175.00
3 GT 175.00
4 . . . . 125.00
5 . . . . 125.00
6 JSt 125.00
7 . . . . 125.00
8 March, 1952. . . . . 125.00

PROFESSOR XAVIER
AND THE X-MEN
1995
1 1st Year Together. 3.00
2 V:The Vanisher 2.50
3 FaN,F:The Blob 2.50
4 V:Magneto & Brotherhood 2.50
5 . . . . 2.50
6 . . . . 2.50
7 FdS,Sub-Mariner 2.50
8 thru 12 . . . . @2.50
13 AHo,F:Juggernaut. 2.50
14 JGz,V:Juggernaut, ... 2.50

---

15 JGz,F:Quicksilver & Scarlet
  Witch 2.50
16 . . . . 2.50
17 JGz,V:Sentinels,F:Beast 2.50
18 JGz,X-Men vs. Sentinels,
  final issue 2.50

PROWLER, THE
1994
1 Creatures of the Night, pt.1 . . . . . 2.25
2 V:Nightcreeper, Creatures, pt.2 . . 2.25
3 Creatures of the Night, pt.3 . . . . . 2.25
4 V:Vulture, Creatures, pt.4 . . . . . . 2.25

PSI FORCE
Nov., 1986
1 MT,O:PSI Force 2.50
2 MT 2.50
3 MT,CIA 2.50
4 MT,J:Network 2.50
5 MT. 2.50
6 MT(c) 2.50
7 MT(c) 2.50
8 MT. 2.50
9 MT(c) 2.50
10 PSI Hawk 2.50
11 . . . . 2.50
12 MT(c) 2.50
13 . . . . 2.50
14 AW 2.50
15 . . . . 2.50
16 RLm 2.50
17 RLm 2.50
18 RLm 2.50
19 RLm 2.50
20 RLm,V:Medusa Web;Rodstvow . 2.50
21 RLm 2.50
22 RLm,A:Nightmask. 2.50
23 A:D.P.7 . . . . 2.50
24 thru 31 . . . . @2.50
32 June, 1989 . . . . 2.50
Ann.#1 . . . . 3.00

PSYCHONAUTS
Epic, 1993–94
1 thru 4 War in the Future. . . . . . @5.50

PSYLOCKE & ANGEL:
CRIMSON DAWN
1997
1 SvL,ATi,V:Obsideon 3.00
2 SvL,ATi, ... 3.00
3 BRa,SvL,ATi. 3.00
4 (of 4) BRa,SvL,ATi 3.00

PULSE, THE
Feb., 2004
1 BMB,MBa,Thin Air,pt.1. . . . . 5.00
2 BMB,MBa,Thin Air,pt.2,F:Vulture . 3.50
3 BMB,MBa,Thin Air,pt.3. . . . . 3.00
4 BMB,MBa,Thin Air,pt.4. . . . . 3.00
5 BMB,MBa,Thin Air,pt.5. . . . . 3.00

PUNISHER
[Limited Series] Jan., 1986
1 MZ,Circle of Blood,double size . 22.00
2 MZ,Back to the War. 15.00
3 MZ,V:The Right 10.00
4 MZ,V:The Right 10.00
5 V:Jigsaw,end Mini-Series. 10.00

[Regular Series] 1987–95
1 KJ,V:Wilfred Sobel,Drugs 12.00
2 KJ,V:General Trahn,Bolivia 6.00
3 KJ,V:Colonel Fryer. 5.00
4 KJ,I:The Rev,Microchip Jr. 5.00
5 KJ,V:The Rev. 5.00

Punisher #11
© Marvel Entertainment Group

6 DR,KN,V:The Rosettis 5.00
7 DR,V:Ahmad,D:Rose 5.00
8 WPo,SW(1st Punisher),
   V:Sigo & Roky 4.00
9 WPo,SW,D:MicrochipJr,V:Sigo . . 4.00
10 WPo,SW,A:Daredevil (x-over
   w/Daredevil #257) 7.00
11 WPo,SW,O:Punisher. 3.00
12 WPo,SW,V:Gary Saunders. 3.00
13 WPo,SW,V:Lydia Spoto 3.00
14 WPo,SW,I:McDowell,Brooks. . . . 3.00
15 WPo,SW,V:Kingpin 3.00
16 WPo,SW,V:Kingpin 3.00
17 WPo,SW,V:Kingpin 3.00
18 WPo,SW,V:Kingpin,C:X-Men . . . 3.00
19 LSn,In Australia. 2.50
20 WPo(c),In Las Vegas 2.50
21 EL,SW,Boxing Issue 2.50
22 EL,SW,I:Saracen. 2.50
23 EL,SW,V:Scully. 2.50
24 EL,SW,A:Shadowmasters. 2.50
25 EL,AW,A:Shadowmasters. 2.50
26 RH,Oper.Whistle Blower#1. . . . 2.50
27 RH,Oper.Whistle Blower#2. . . . 2.50
28 BR,A:Dr.Doom,A of Veng. 2.50
29 BR,A:Dr.Doom,A of Veng. 2.50
30 BR,V:Geltrate 2.50
31 BR,V:Bikers #1 . . . . 2.50
32 BR,V:Bikers #2 . . . . 2.50
33 BR,V:The Reavers 2.50
34 BR,V:The Reavers 2.50
35 BR,MF,Jigsaw Puzzle #1 . . . . . 2.50
36 MT,MF,Jigsaw Puzzle #2 . . . . . 2.50
37 MT,Jigsaw Puzzle #3 . . . . 2.50
38 BR,MF,Jigsaw Puzzle #4 . . . . . 2.50
39 JSh,Jigsaw Puzzle #5. . . . . 2.50
40 BR,JSh,Jigsaw Puzzle #6. . . . . 2.50
41 BR,TD,V:Terrorists 2.50
42 MT,V:Corrupt Mili. School 2.50
43 BR,Border Run 2.50
44 Flag Burner. 2.50
45 One Way Fare 2.50
46 HH,Cold Cache. 2.50
47 HH,Middle East #1 . . . . 2.50
48 HH,Mid.East #2,V:Saracen. . . . 2.50
49 HH,Punisher Hunted. 2.50
50 HH,MGo(c),I:Yo Yo Ng 2.50
51 Chinese Mafia. 2.50
52 Baby Snatchers 2.50
53 HH,in Prison 2.50
54 HH,in Prison 2.50
55 HH,in Prison 2.50
56 HH,in Prison 2.50

57 HH,in Prison 2.50
58 V:Kingpin's Gang,A:Micro. 2.50
59 MT(c),V:Kingpin 2.50
60 VM,AW,Black Punisher,
   A:Luke Cage 2.50
61 VM,A:Luke Cage. 2.50
62 VM,AW,A:Luke Cage 2.50
63 MT(c),VM,V:Thieves 2.50
64 Eurohit #1 . . . . 2.50
65 thru 70 Eurohit . . . . @ 2.50
71 AW(i) 2.50
72 AW(i) 2.50
73 AW(i),Police Action #1 . . . . 2.50
74 AW(i),Police Action #2 . . . . 2.50
75 AW(i),Police Action #3,foil(c),
   double size 3.00
76 LSn,in Hawaii 2.50
77 VM,Survive#1 . . . . 2.50
78 VM,Survive#2 . . . . 2.50
79 VM,Survive#3 . . . . 2.50
80 Goes to Church. 2.50
81 V:Crooked Cops 2.50
82 B:Firefight 2.50
83 Firefight#2 . . . . 2.50
84 E:Firefight 2.50
85 Suicide Run 2.25
86 Suicide Run#3,Foil(c), ... 2.25
87 Suicide Run#6 . . . . 2.25
88 LSh(c),Suicide Run#9. . . . . 2.25
89 . . . . 2.25
90 Hammered 2.25
91 Silk Noose. 2.25
92 Razor's Edge 2.25
93 Killing Streets 2.25
94 B:No Rules 2.25
95 No Rules 2.25
96 . . . . 2.25
97 CDi 2.25
98 . . . . 2.25
99 . . . . 2.25
100 New Punisher 4.00
100a Enhanced ed. 5.00
101 CC,Raid's Franks Tomb 2.25
102 A:Bullseye 2.25
103 Countdown 4. . . . . 2.25
104 CDi,Countdown 1, V:Kingpin,
   final issue 2.25
Ann.#1 MT,A:Eliminators,
   Evolutionary War. 4.00
Ann.#2 JLe,Atlantis Attacks #5,
   A:Moon Knight. 3.50
Ann.#3 LS,MT,Lifeform #1 . . . . 3.50
Ann.#4 Baron Strucker,pt.2
   (see D.D.Annual #7) 3.50
Ann.#5 System Bytes #1 . . . . 3.50
Ann.#6 I:Eradikator,w/card. 3.50
GNv 5.00
Summer Spec.#1 VM,MT. 3.50
Summer Spec.#2 SBs(c) 2.50
Summer Spec.#3 V:Carjackers 2.50
Summer Spec.#4. . . . . 3.25
Spec. Punisher/Batman,CDi,JR2,
   48-pg. (1994) 5.00
Spec.#1 Punisher/Daredevil, rep.
   Daredevil 6.00
Punisher:No Escape A:USAgent,
   Paladin (1990) 5.50
Punisher Movie Spec.BA (1989) . . . 6.00
GNv Punisher: The Prize (1990) . . 5.50
Punisher:Bloodlines DC 6.25
Punisher:Blood on the Moors 17.00
Punisher:G-Force. 5.25
Punisher:Origin of Mirco Chip #1,
   O:Mirco Chip 2.50
Punisher:Origin of Mirco Chip #2
   V:The Professor. 2.50
Classic Punisher rep early
   B&W magazines 7.00
Punisher:Back To School Spec.
   #1 JRy,short stories. 3.25
   #2 BSz. 3.00

Punisher 2nd Series #4
© Marvel Entertainment Group

Punisher:Die Hard in the Big
   Easy Mardi Gras 5.25
Holiday Spec.#1 V:Young
   Mob Capo 3.25
Holiday Spec #2. . . . . 3.00
Punisher:Ghosts of the Innocent#1
   TGr, V:Kingpin's Dead Men. . . . 6.00
Punisher:Ghosts of the Innocent#2
   TGr, V:Kingpin,Snake 6.00
TPB Punisher: Eye For An Eye . . . 10.00

[2nd Regular Series] 1995
1 JOs,TL,Clv,Punisher sent to
   the Electric Chair, foil(c) 3.00
2 JOs,TL,Clv,Crime family boss . . 2.50
3 JOs,TL,Clv,V:Hatchetman 2.50
4 JOs,TL,Clv,A:Daredevil,Jigsaw . 2.50
5 . . . . 2.50
6 . . . . 2.50
7 JOs,TL,Clv,V:Son of Nick Fury . . 2.50
8 . . . . 2.50
9 . . . . 2.50
10 . . . . 2.50
11 Onslaught saga. 2.50
12 A:X-Cutioner 3.00
13 JOs,TL, Working for S.H.I.E.L.D.?,
   A:X-Cutioner 2.50
14 . . . . 2.50
15 JOs,TL, X-Cutioner. 2.50
16 JOS,TL, concl.? 2.50
17 JOS,TL,A:Daredevil,Doc Samson,
   Spider-Man 2.50
18 JOS,TL,Frank Castle amnesia? . 2.50
19 JOS,TL,V:Taskmaster. 2.50
20 JOS,TL, fugitive Punisher. 2.50

PUNISHER
Sept., 1998
1 (of 4) BWr,JP,TSg,F:Frank
   Castle 3.00
2 BWr,JJu,JP,A:Hellstrom 3.00
3 BWr,JJu,TSg,JP,A:Gadriel 7.00
4 BWr,JJu,TSg,JP,Hell on Earth . . . 3.00

PUNISHER
Jan., 2000
1 (of 12) JP,GEn,SDi,R:Punisher . . 3.00
2A JP,GEn,SDi,V:Ma Gnucci 3.00
2B variant SDi(c). 3.00
3 GEn,JP,SDi,polybaged 7.00
4 GEn,JP,SDi,Gnuccis 3.00
5 GEn,JP,SDi,Mr.Payback 3.00
6 GEn,JP,SDi,Elite 3.00

7 GEn,SDi,Mr.Payback 3.00
8 GEn,JP,SDi,Gnuccis 3.00
9 GEn,JP,SDi,Russian 3.00
10 GEn,JP,SDi,Russian 3.00
11 GEn,JP,SDi,Russian 3.00
12 GEn,JP,SDi,concl. 3.00
Spec. Punisher/Painkiller Jane 3.50
GN Punisher Kills the Marvel
    Universe, 48-pg. GEn,DBw 6.00
TPB Welcome Back, Frank 25.00
TPB Circle of Blood 13.00

PUNISHER
June, 2001

1 GEn,JP,SDi,pt.1 . . . . 5.00
2A GEn,JP,SDi,pt.2 . . . . 3.00
2B variant SDi(c). 3.00
3 GEn,JP,SDi,Grand Nixon Island . 3.00
4 GEn,JP,SDi,Survivor 3.00
5 GEn,JP,SDi,V:Kriegkopf. 3.00
6 GEn,JP,Viet Nam 3.00
7 SDi,JP,'Nuff Said 3.00
8 TPe,Taxi Wars 3.00
9 TPe,Taxi Wars 3.00
10 TPe,Taxi Wars 3.00
11 TPe,Taxi Wars, Medallion 3.00
12 TPE,Taxi Wars, concl. 3.00
13 GeN,SDi, to South America . . . 3.00
14 GeN,SDi, in Columbia. 3.00
15 GeN,SDi,F:Wolverine 3.00
16 GeN,SDi,F:Wolverine 3.00
17 GeN,DaR,F:Wolverine 3.00
18 GeN,SDi,Northern Ireland. 3.00
19 GeN,SDi, ... 3.00
20 GEn,SDi,Brotherhood,pt.1 . . . . 3.00
21 GEn,SDi,Brotherhood,pt.2 . . . . 3.00
22 GEn,SDi 3.00
23 GEn,SDi,Giant Squid 3.00
24 GEn,TMd,Hidden,pt.1 . . . . 3.00
25 GEn,TMd,Hidden,pt.2 . . . . 3.00
26 GEn,TMd,Hidden,pt.3 . . . . 3.00
27 GEn,SDi,F:Elektra. 3.00
28 GEn,CK,Streets of Loredo,pt.1 . 3.00
29 GEn,CK,Streets of Loredo,pt.2 . 3.00
30 GEn,CK,Streets of Loredo,pt.3 . 3.00
31 GEn,CK,Streets of Loredo,pt.4 . 3.00
32 GEn,CK,Streets of Loredo,pt.5 . 3.00
33 GEn,JMC,Dunces,pt.1 . . . . 3.00
34 GEn,JMC,Dunces,pt.2 . . . . 3.00
35 GEn,JMC,Dunces,pt.3 . . . . 3.00
36 GEn,JMC,Dunces,pt.4 . . . . 3.00
37 GEn,JMC,Dunces,pt.5 . . . . 4.00
TPB Army of One, rep. 144-pg. . . . 16.00
TPB Vol. 3: Business as Usual . . . 15.00
TPB Vol. 4: Full Auto 18.00
TPB Vol. 5: Streets of Laredo 18.00
TPB Vol. 6: Confed. of Dunces . . . 15.00

PUNISHER
Max, 2004

1 GEn,In the Beginning,pt.1 . . . . . . 5.50
2 GEn,In the Beginning,pt.2 . . . . . . 3.50
3 GEn,In the Beginning,pt.3 . . . . . . 3.50
4 GEn,In the Beginning,pt.4 . . . . . . 3.50
5 GEn,In the Beginning,pt.5 . . . . . . 3.00
6 GEn,In the Beginning,pt.6 . . . . . . 3.00
7 GEn,Kitchen Irish,pt.1 . . . . 3.00
8 GEn,Kitchen Irish,pt.2 . . . . 3.00
9 GEn,Kitchen Irish,pt.3 . . . . 3.00
10 GEn,Kitchen Irish,pt.4. . . . . 3.00
11 GEn,Kitchen Irish,pt.5. . . . . 3.00
12 GEn,Kitchen Irish,pt.6. . . . . 3.00
TPB Born 14.00
Spec. Punisher: The End,RCo 5.00
TPB Vol. 1: In the Beginning 15.00

PUNISHER ARMORY
July, 1990

1 JLe(c). 3.00

2 JLe(c). 2.50
3 . . . . 2.50
4 thru 6 . . . . @2.50
7 thru 10 . . . . @2.50

PUNISHER/
CAPTAIN AMERICA:
BLOOD AND GLORY

1 thru 3 KJ,V:Drug Dealers. . . . . @6.25

CLASSIC PUNISHER

1 TDz 5.00

PUNISHER KILLS
THE MARVEL UNIVERSE
1995

1-shot Alterniverse 6.00

PUNISHER MAGAZINE
Oct., 1989

1 MZ,rep.,Punisher #1 . . . . 3.00
2 MZ,rep 2.50
3 thru 13 KJ,rep. . . . . @2.50
14 rep. PWJ #1&#2 . . . . 2.50
15 rep. PWJ. 2.50
16 rep.,1990 . . . . 2.50

PUNISHER
MEETS ARCHIE
1994

1 JB. 4.25
1a newsstand ed. 3.25

PUNISHER MOVIE COMIC
Nov., 1989

1 Movie adapt. 2.25
2 Movie adapt. 2.25
3 Movie adapt,Dec., 1989 . . . . . . 2.25

PUNISHER: THE MOVIE
March, 2004

1 (of 3) PO 3.00
2 and 3 PO . . . . @3.00
TPB 13.00

PUNISHER P.O.V.
July, 1991

1 BWr,Punisher/Nick Fury. 5.50
2 BWr,A:Nick Fury,Kingpin 5.50
3 BWr,V:Mutant Monster,
    A:Vampire Slayer. 5.50
4 BWr,A:Nick Fury 5.25

PUNISHER 2099
1993–95

1 TMo,Jake Gallows family
    Killed, foil(c). 2.50
2 TMo,I:Fearmaster,Kron,Multi
    Factor 2.25
3 TMo,V:Frightening Cult 2.25
4 TMo,V:Cyber Nostra 2.25
5 TMo,V:Cyber Nostra,Fearmaster. 2.25
6 TMo,V:Multi-Factor 2.25
7 TMo,Love and Bullets#1 . . . . . . 2.25
8 TMo,Love and Bullets#2 . . . . . . 2.25
9 TMo,Love and Bullets#3 . . . . . . 2.25
10 TMo,I:Jigsaw 2.25
11 TMo,V:Jigsaw 2.25
12 TMo,A:Spider-Man 2099 . . . . . 2.25
13 TMo,Fall of the Hammer#5. . . . 2.25
14 WSm, ... 2.25
15 TMo,V:Fearmaster,
    I:Public Enemy 2.25

Punisher 2099 #25
© Marvel Entertainment Group

16 TMo,V:Fearmaster,
    Public Enemy 2.25
17 TMo,V:Public Enemy 2.25
18 TMo,I:Goldheart 2.25
19 TMo,I:Vendetta 2.25
20 . . . . 2.25
21 . . . . 2.25
22 V:Hotwire 2.25
23 I:Synchron,V:Hotwire 2.25
24 V:Synchron 2.25
25 Enhanced cover 3.50
25a newsstand ed. 2.25
26 V:Techno-Shaman 2.25
27 R:Blue Max 2.25
Becomes:

PUNISHER 2099 A.D.

28 Minister of Punishment. 2.25
29 Minister of Punishment. 2.25
30 One Nation Under Doom 2.25
31 . . . . 2.25
32 Out of Ammo. 2.25
33 Counddown to final issue 2.25
34 final issue 2.25

PUNISHER
WAR JOURNAL
Nov., 1988

1 CP,JLe,O:Punisher 5.00
2 CP,JLe,A:Daredevil 4.00
3 CP,JLe,A:Daredevil 4.00
4 CP,JLeV:The Sniper. 4.00
5 CP,JLe,V:The Sniper 4.00
6 CP,JLe,A:Wolverine 4.00
7 CP,JLe,A:Wolverine 4.00
8 JLe,I:Shadowmasters 4.00
9 JLe,A:Black Widow 4.00
10 JLe,V:Sniper 4.00
11 JLe,Shock Treatment 3.50
12 JLe,AM,V:Bushwacker 3.50
13 JLe(c),V:Bushwacker 3.50
14 JLe(c),DR,RH,A:Spider-Man . . 3.50
15 JLe(c),DR,RH,A:Spider-Man. . . 3.50
16 MT(i),Texas Massacre 3.50
17 JLe,AM,Hawaii 3.00
18 JLe,AM,Kahuna,Hawaii. 3.00
19 JLe,AM,Traume in Paradise . . . 3.00
20 AM. 3.00
21 TSm,AM 3.00
22 TSm,AM,Ruins #1. . . . . 3.00
23 TSm,AM,Ruins #2. . . . . 3.00
24 . . . . 3.00
25 MT. 3.00

Punisher War Journal #14
© Marvel Entertainment Group

26 MT,A:Saracen 3.00
27 MT,A:Saracen 3.00
28 MT. 3.00
29 MT,A:Ghostrider 3.00
30 MT,A:Ghostrider 3.00
31 NKu,Kamchatkan
  Konspiracy#1. . . . . 3.00
32 Kamchatkan Konspiracy #2 . . . . 3.00
33 Kamchatkan Konspiracy #3 . . . . 3.00
34 V:Psycho. 3.00
35 Movie Stuntman 3.00
36 Radio Talk Show #1 . . . . 3.00
37 Radio Talk Show #2 . . . . 3.00
38 . . . . 3.00
39 DGr,V:Serial Killer. 3.00
40 MWg 3.00
41 Armageddon Express 3.00
42 Mob run-out 3.00
43 JR2(c) 3.00
44 Organ Donor Crimes. 3.00
45 Dead Man's Hand #3,V:Viper . . . 3.00
46 Dead Man's Hand #6,V:Chainsaw
  and the Praetorians. 3.00
47 Dead Man's Hand #7,A:Nomad,
  D,D,V:Hydra,Secret Empire. . . . 3.00
48 B:Payback. 3.00
49 JR2(c),V:Corrupt Cop 3.00
50 MT,V:Highjackers,I:Punisher
  2099. . . . . 3.00
51 E:Payback. 3.00
52 A:Ice(from The'Nam). 3.00
53 A:Ice(from the Nam) 3.00
54 Hyper#1 . . . . 3.00
55 Hyper#2 . . . . 3.00
56 Hyper#3 . . . . 3.00
57 A:Ghost Rider,Daredevil 3.00
58 A:Ghost Rider,Daredevil 3.00
59 F:Max the Dog 3.00
60 CDi(s),F:Max the Dog. 3.00
61 CDi(s),Suicide Run#1,Foil(c) . . . 3.00
62 CDi(s),Suicide Run#4 . . . . 2.50
63 CDi(s),Suicide Run#7 . . . . 2.50
64 CDi(s),Suicide Run#10 . . . . 3.00
64a Newsstand Ed. 2.50
65 B:Pariah 2.50
66 A:Captain America 2.50
67 Pariah#3 . . . . 2.50
68 A:Spider-Man 2.50
69 E:Pariah 2.50
70 . . . . 2.50
71 . . . . 2.50
72 V:Fake Punisher 2.50
73 E:Frank Castle 2.50

74 . . . . 2.50
75 MT(c). 3.00
76 First Entry 2.50
77 R:Stone COld 2.50
78 V:Payback,Heathen 2.50
79 Countdown 3. . . . . 2.50
80 Countdown 0, A:Nick Fury,
  V:Bullseye, final issue 2.50
TPB reprints #6,7. . . . . 4.95

PUNISHER WAR ZONE
1992

1 JR2,KJ,Punisher As Johnny Tower
  Die-Cut Bullet Hole(c) 3.00
2 JR2,KJ,Mafia Career 2.25
3 JR2,KJ,Punisher/Mafia,contd . . . 2.25
4 JR2,KJ,Cover gets Blown 2.25
5 JR2,KJ,A:Shotgun 2.25
6 JR2,KJ,A:Shotgun 2.25
7 JR2,V:Rapist in Central Park 2.25
8 JR2,V:Rapist in Central Park. . . . 2.25
9 JR2,V:Magnificent Seven 2.25
10 JR2,V:Magnificent Seven 2.25
11 JR2,MM,V:Magnificent Seven. . . 2.25
12 Punisher Married 2.25
13 Self-Realization. 2.25
14 Psychoville#3 . . . . 2.25
15 Psychoville#4 . . . . 2.25
16 Psychoville#5 . . . . 2.25
17 Industrial Esponiage 2.25
18 Jerico Syndrome#2. . . . . 2.25
19 Jerico Syndrome#3. . . . . 2.25
20 B:2 Mean 2 Die 2.25
21 2 Mean 2 Die#2 . . . . 2.25
22 A:Tyger Tyger 2.25
23 Suicide Run#2,Foil(c) 3.25
24 Suicide Run#5, ... 2.25
25 Suicide Run#8, ... 2.50
26 CDi(s),JB,Pirates 2.25
27 CDi(s),JB, ... 2.25
28 CDi(s),JB,Sweet Revenge 2.25
29 CDi(s),JB,The Swine 2.25
30 CDi(s),JB. 2.25
31 CDi(s),JB,River of Blood,pt.1 . . . 2.25
32 CDi(s),JB,River of Blood,pt.2 . . . 2.25
33 CDi(s),JB,River of Blood,pt.3 . . . 2.25
34 CDi(s),JB,River of Blood,pt.4 . . . 2.25
35 River of Blood,pt.5 . . . . 2.25
36 River of Blood,pt.6 . . . . 2.25
37 O:Max 2.25
38 Dark Judgment,pt.1 . . . . 2.25
39 Dark Judgment,pt.2 . . . . 2.25
40 In Court. 2.25
41 CDi,Countdown 2, final issue . . . 2.25
Ann.#1 Jb,MGo,(c),I:Phalanx,
  w/Trading card. 3.25
Ann.#2 CDi(s),DR 2.95
TPB CDi,JR2, rep. #1-#6. . . . . 16.00

PUNISHER: YEAR ONE
1994

1 O:Punisher. 2.50
2 thru 4 . . . . @2.50

PUSSYCAT
(B&W Magazine) Oct., 1968

1 BEv,BWa,WW 250.00

QUASAR
Oct., 1989

1 O:Quasar. 3.00
2 V:Deathurge,A:Eon 2.50
3 A:Human Torch,V:The Angler . . . 2.50
4 Acts of Vengeance,A:Aquarian . . 2.50
5 A of Veng,V:Absorbing Man. 2.50
6 V:Klaw,Living Laser,Venom,
  Red Ghost 3.00
7 MM,A:Cosmic SpM,V:Terminus . . 2.50

8 MM,A:New Mutants,BlueShield . . 2.25
9 MM,A:Modam 2.25
10 MM,A:Dr.Minerva 2.25
11 MM,A:Excalibur,A:Modred. 2.25
12 MM,A:Makhari,Blood Bros.. . . . . 2.25
13 JLe(c)MM,J.into Mystery #1 . . . . 2.25
14 TM(c)MM,J.into Mystery #2 . . . . 2.25
15 MM,Journey into Mystery #3 . . . 2.25
16 MM,Double sized 2.25
17 MM,Race,A:Makkari,Whizzer,
  Quicksilver,Capt.Marv,Super
  Sabre,Barry Allen Spoof 2.25
18 GCa,N:Quasar. 2.25
19 GCa,B:Cosmos in Collision,
  C:Thanos. 2.25
20 GCa,A:Fantastic Four. 2.25
21 GCa,V:Jack of Hearts. 2.25
22 GCa,D:Quasar,A:Ghost Rider. . . 2.25
23 GCa,A:Ghost Rider. 2.25
24 GCa,A:Thanos,Galactus,
  D:Maelstrom 2.25
25 GCa,A:Eternity & Infinity,N:Quasar,
  E:Cosmos Collision 2.25
26 GCa,Inf.Gauntlet,A:Thanos. 2.50
27 GCa,Infinity Gauntlet,I:Epoch . . . 2.25
28 GCa,A:Moondragon,Her,
  X-Men 2.25
29 GCa,A:Moondragon,Her 2.25
30 GCa,What If? tie-in 2.25
31 GCa,R:New Universe 2.25
32 GCa,Op.GalacticStorm,pt.3 . . . 2.25
33 GCa,Op.GalacticStorm,pt.10 . . . 2.25
34 GCa,Op.GalacticStorm,pt.17 . . . 2.25
35 GCa,Binary V:Her. 2.25
36 GCa,V:Soul Eater 2.25
37 GCa,V:Soul Eater 2.25
38 GCa,Inf.War,V:Warlock. 2.25
39 SLi,Inf.War,V:Deathurge 2.25
40 SLi,Inf.War,V:Deathurge 2.25
41 R:Marvel Boy 2.25
42 V:Blue Marvel 2.25
43 V:Blue Marvel 2.25
44 V:Quagmire. 2.25
45 V:Quagmire,Antibody 2.25
46 Neutron,Presence 2.25
47 1st Full Thunderstrike Story 2.25
48 A:Thunderstrike. 2.25
49 Kalya Vs. Kismet. 2.25
50 A:Man-Thing,Prism(c) 3.50
51 V:Angler,A:S.Supreme 2.25
52 V:Geometer. 2.25
53 . . . . 2.25
54 MGu(s),Starblast #2 . . . . 2.25

Quasar #52
© Marvel Entertainment Group

55 MGu(s),A:Stranger 2.25
56 MGu(s),Starblast #10 . . . . 2.25
57 MGu(s),A:Kismet. 2.25
58 . . . . 2.25
59 A:Thanos,Starfox. 2.25
60 final issue 2.25

QUEST
June, 2003
1 (of 6) Manga,F:Katherine West . . 2.50
2 Quest & Kaori 2.50

QUESTPROBE
Aug., 1984
1 JR,A:Hulk,I:Chief Examiner 3.00
2 AM,JM,A:Spider-Man 3.00
3 JSt,A:Thing & Torch 3.00

QUICKSILVER
Sept., 1997
1 CJ,TPe, V:Exodus, cont. from
   Excalibur #113. . . . . 3.00
2 TPe,CJ,A:Knights of Wundagore . 2.25
3 TPe,CJ,V:Arkon 2.25
4 TPe, Crystal returns. 2.25
5 TPe,V:Inhumans 2.25
6 TPe,Inhumands trilogy concl. . . . 2.25
7 JOs,F:The Black Knight. 2.25
8 JOs,F:Pietro,V:Pyro 2.25
9 JOs,Savage Land concl.,A:High
   Evolutionary. 2.25
10 JOS,Live Kree or Die, pt.3,
   x-over. 2.25
11 JOs,The Seige of Wundagore,
   pt.2 (of 5). 2.25
12 JOs,The Seige of Wundagore,
   pt.4 (of 5) 48-pg. 3.00
13 JOs,Seige of Wundagore,pt.5,
   final issue 2.25

QUICK-TRIGGER
WESTERN
See: WESTERN
THRILLERS

RAIDERS OF
THE LOST ARK
Sept., 1981
1 JB/KJ,movie adaption 3.00
2 JB/KJ, ... 3.00
3 JB/KJ,Nov.,1981 . . . . 3.00

RAMPAGING HULK, THE
May, 1998
1 RL,double size, savage Hulk era. 3.00
2A RL,DGr,I:Ravage. 2.25
2B JQ,JP,variant cover 2.25
3 RL,DGr,V:Ravage, concl. 2.25
4 DR,Trapped by an Avalanche . . . 2.25
5 RL,F:Fantastic Four. 2.25
6 RL,DGr,V:Puma. 2.25

RAVAGE 2099
1992–95
1 PR,I:Ravage 3.00
2 PR,V:Deathstryk 2.25
3 PR,V:Mutroids 2.25
4 PR,V:Mutroids 2.25
5 PR,Hellrock 2.25
6 PR,N:Ravage. 2.25
7 PR,New powers. 2.25
8 V:Deathstryke 2.25
9 PR,N:Ravage. 2.25
10 V:Alchemax. 2.25

Ravage 2099 #25
© *Marvel Entertainment Group*

11 A:Avatarr 2.25
12 Ravage Transforms 2.25
13 V:Fearmaster 2.25
14 V:Punisher 2099 . . . . 2.25
15 Fall of the Hammer #2 . . . . 2.25
16 I:Throwback 2.25
17 GtM,V:Throwback,O:X-11 . . . . . 2.25
18 GtM,w/card 2.25
19 GtM, ... 2.25
20 GtM,V:Hunter 2.25
21 Savage on the Loose 2.25
22 Exodus 2.25
23 Blind Justice 2.25
24 Unleashed. 2.25
25 Flame Bearer 2.25
25a Deluxe ed.. . . . . 3.00
26 V:Megastruck 2.25
27 V:Deathstryke 2.25
28 R:Hela 2.25
29 V:Deathstryke 2.25
30 King Ravage 2.25
Becomes:

RAVAGE 2099 A.D.
31 V:Doom. 2.25
32 One Nation Under Doom 2.25
33 Final issue. 2.25

RAWHIDE KID
Atlas, March, 1955—May, 1979
1 JMn,B:Rawhide Kid & Randy,
   A:Wyatt Earp 1,200.00
2 JMn,Shoot-out(c) 500.00
3 V:Hustler 350.00
4 Rh(c) 350.00
5 GC,JMn 350.00
6 JMn,Six-Gun Lesson 250.00
7 AW 250.00
8 . . . . 250.00
9 . . . . 250.00
10 thru 16 . . . . @225.00
17 JK,O:Rawhide Kid. 225.00
18 thru 20. . . . . @225.00
21 . . . . 225.00
22 . . . . 225.00
23 JK,O:Rawhide Kid Retold. . . . 300.00
24 thru 30 . . . . @200.00
31 JK,DAy,No Law in Mesa 200.00
32 JK,DAy,Beware of the
   Parker Brothers 200.00
33 JK(c),JDa,V:Jesse James. . . . 200.00
34 JDa,JK,V:Mister Lightning. . . . 200.00
35 JK(c),GC,JDa,I&D:The Raven 200.00

36 DAy,A Prisoner in
   Outlaw Town 125.00
37 JK(c),DAy,GC,V:The Rattler . . 125.00
38 DAy.V:The Red Raven 175.00
39 DAy 125.00
40 JK(c),DAy,A:Two Gun Kid . . . 125.00
41 JK(c),The Tyrant of
   Tombstone Valley 125.00
42 JK 125.00
43 JK 175.00
44 JK(c),V:The Masked Maverick 125.00
45 JK(c),O:Rawhide Kid Retold. . 165.00
46 JK(c),ATh 125.00
47 JK(c),The Riverboat Raiders . . 85.00
48 GC,V:Marko the Manhunter . . . 75.00
49 The Masquerader 75.00
50 A:Kid Colt,V:Masquerader 75.00
51 DAy,Trapped in the
   Valley of Doom 75.00
52 DAy,Revenge at
   Rustler's Roost 75.00
53 Guns of the Wild North 75.00
54 DH,BEv,The Last Showdown . . 75.00
55 . . . . 75.00
56 DH,JTgV:The Peacemaker. . . . 75.00
57 V:The Scorpion 75.00
58 DAy 75.00
59 V:Drako 75.00
60 DAy,HT,Massacre at Medicine
   Bend 75.00
61 DAy, TS,A:Wild Bill Hickok. . . . 60.00
62 Gun Town,V:Drako 60.00
63 Shootout at Mesa City 60.00
64 HT,Duel of the Desparadoes . . 60.00
65 JTg,HT,BE. 60.00
66 JTg,BEv,Death of a Gunfighter. 60.00
67 Hostage of Hungry Hills 60.00
68 JB,V:The Cougar 60.00
69 JTg,The Executioner. 60.00
70 JTg,The Night of the Betrayers. 40.00
71 JTg,The Last Warrior 40.00
72 JTg,The Menace of Mystery
   Valley. 40.00
73 JTg,The Manhunt 40.00
74 JTg,The Apaches Attack 40.00
75 JTg,The Man Who Killed
   The Kid 40.00
76 JTg,V:The Lynx 40.00
77 JTg,The Reckoning. 40.00
78 JTg 40.00
79 JTg,AW,The Legion of the Lost 40.00
80 Fall of a Hero 40.00
81 thru 85. . . . . @40.00
86 JK,DAy,O:Rawhide Kid retold . . 45.00
87 thru 89 . . . . @50.00
90 Kid Colt 55.00
91 . . . . 25.00
92 & 93 giants . . . . @30.00
94 thru 99 . . . . @40.00
100 O:Rawhide Kid retold 35.00
101 thru 124 . . . . @25.00
125 JDa 30.00
126 thru 151 . . . . @25.00

RAWHIDE KID
Aug., 1985
1 JSe,mini-series 6.00
2 thru 4 . . . . @5.00

RAWHIDE KID
Marvel Max, Feb., 2003
1 (of 5) JSe. 3.00
2 thru 5 JSe. . . . . @3.00
3 JSe. 3.00
4 JSe. 3.00
5 JSe,concl. 3.00
TPB 13.00

RAZORLINE FIRST CUT
1993
1 Intro Razorline 2.25

REAL EXPERIENCES
See: TESSIE THE TYPIST

RED RAVEN
See: HUMAN TORCH

Red Sonja #3
© Marvel Entertainment Group

RED SONJA
[1st Series] Jan., 1977
1 FT,O:Red Sonja,Blood of the
   Unicorn 15.00
2 FT,Demon of the Maze 8.00
3 FT,The Games of Gita 8.00
4 FT,The Lake of the Unknown . . . 8.00
5 FT,Master of the Bells 8.00
6 FT,The Singing Tower 8.00
7 FT,Throne of Blood 8.00
8 FT,Vengeance o/t Golden Circle . 8.00
9 FT,Chariot o/t Fire-Stallions 8.00
10 FT,Red Lace,pt.1 . . . . 8.00
11 FT,Red Lace,pt.2 . . . . 7.00
12 JB/JRu,Ashes & Emblems 7.00
13 JB/AM,Shall Skranos Fall 7.00
14 SB/AM,Evening on the Border . . 7.00
15 JB/TD,Tomb of 3 Dead Kings
   May, 1979 . . . . 7.00

[2nd Series] Feb., 1983
1 TD,GC, The Blood That Binds . . 4.00
2 GC, March,1983 . . . . 4.00

[3rd Series] Aug., 1983
1 . . . . 3.00
2 thru 13 . . . . @3.00
1 movie adaption, 1985 . . . . 2.50
2 movie adaption, 1985 . . . . 2.50

RED SONJA
1-shot Bros.Hildebrandt(c),48-pg. . . 3.00

RED WARRIOR
Atlas, Jan.–Dec., 1951
1 GT,Indian Tales 200.00
2 GT(c),The Trail of the Outcast 125.00
3 The Great Spirit Speaks 100.00
4 O:White Wing 100.00

5 . . . . 100.00
6 JMn(c) final issue. 100.00

RED WOLF
May, 1972–Sept., 1973
1 SSh(c),GK,JSe,F:Red Wolf
   & Lobo 35.00
2 GK(c),SSh,Day of the Dynamite
   Doom 20.00
3 SSh,War of the Wolf Brothers . 20.00
4 SSh,V:Man-Bear 20.00
5 GK(c),SSh 20.00
6 SSh,JA,V;Devil Rider 20.00
7 SSh,JA,Echoes from a Golden
   Grave 20.00
8 SSh,Hell on Wheels 20.00
9 DAy,To Die Again,O:Lobo 20.00

REN AND STIMPY SHOW
1992–96
1 Polybagged w/Air Fowlers,
   Ren(c) 5.00
1a Stimpy(c) 4.00
1b 2nd Printing 3.00
1c 3rd Printing 2.00
2 Frankenstimpy 3.00
2a 2nd Printing 2.00
3 Christmas issue 3.00
3a 2nd Printing 2.00
4 thru 12 . . . . @3.00
13 Halloween issue 2.50
14 Mars needs Vecro. 2.50
15 thru 24 . . . . @2.25
25 regular (c) 2.25
25a die-cut(c),A new addition 3.00
26 thru 42. . . . . @2.25
Spec.#1 . . . . 3.25
Spec.#2 . . . . 3.25
Spec.#3 Powder Toast Man 3.25
Spec.#4 . . . . 3.25
Spec.#5 Virtual Stupidity 3.25
Spec.#6 History of Music 3.25
Holiday Special 3.00
Spec. Radio Dazed & Confused . . 2.50
Spec. Around the World in a Daze . 3.00
TPB Running Joke,rep. 13.25
TPB Pick of the Litter. 13.25
TPB Tastes Like Chicken. 13.25
TPB Your Pals 12.95
TPB Seech Little Monkeys. 12.95

RETURN OF THE JEDI
1 AW,movie adapt. 3.00
2 AW,movie adapt. 3.00
3 AW,movie adapt. 3.00
4 AW,movie adapt. 3.00

REX HART
See: BLAZE CARSON

RICHIE RICH
1 Movie Adaptation 3.00

RINGO KID
[2nd Series] Jan., 1970
1 AW,Reprints 35.00
2 JSe,Man Trap 20.00
3 JR,Man from the Panhandle . . . 20.00
4 HT(c),The Golden Spur 20.00
5 JMn,Ambush 20.00
6 Capture or Death 20.00
7 HT(c),JSe,JA,Terrible Treasure
   of Vista Del Oro 20.00
8 The End of the Trail 20.00
9 JSe,Mystery of the Black
   Sunset 20.00
10 Bad day at Black Creek 20.00

11 Bullet for a Bandit 20.00
12 A Badge to Die For 30.00
13 DW,Hostage at Fort Cheyenne. 15.00
14 Showdown in the Silver
   Cartwheel 15.00
15 Fang,Claw, and Six-Gun. 15.00
16 Battle of Cattleman's Bank 15.00
17 Gundown at the Hacienda 15.00
18 . . . . 15.00
19 Thunder From the West 15.00
20 AW 15.00
21 thru 29. . . . . @15.00
30 Nov., 1973. . . . . 15.00

RINGO KID WESTERN
Atlas, Aug., 1954
1 JMn,JSt,O:Ringo Kid,
   B:Ringo Kid 350.00
2 JMn,I&O:Arab,A:Black Rider . 200.00
3 JMn 125.00
4 JMn 125.00
5 JMn 125.00
6 . . . . 125.00
7 . . . . 125.00
8 JSe 125.00
9 . . . . 100.00
10 JSe(c),AW 125.00
11 JSe(c) 100.00
12 JO 100.00
13 AW 125.00
14 thru 20. . . . . @100.00
21 Sept., 1957 . . . . 100.00

ROBOCOP
March, 1990
1 LS,I:Nixcops. 6.00
2 LS,V:Nixcops. 4.00
3 LS 3.00
4 LS 3.00
5 LS,WarzonePt1 . . . . 3.00
6 LS,WarzonePt2 . . . . 3.00
7 thru 10 LS . . . . @2.50
11 HT 2.50
12 thru 23. . . . . @2.50
Robocop Movie Adapt 4.95
Robocop II Movie Adapt. 4.95

ROBOCOP II
Aug., 1990
1 MBa,rep.Movie Adapt 2.50
2 and 3 MBa,rep.Movie adapt. . . @2.50

Rocko's Modern Life #1
© Marvel Entertainment Group

MARVEL

All comics prices listed are for *Near Mint* condition.

MARVEL

ROBOTIX
Feb., 1986
1 Based on toys 3.00

ROCKET RACCOON
May, 1985 — Aug., 1985
1 thru 4 MM. . . . . @3.00

ROCKO'S MODERN LIFE
1994
1 and 2 . . . . @2.25
3 and 4 . . . . @2.25

ROGUE
1995
1 Enhanced cover. 4.50
2 A:Gambit 4.00
3 Gamtit or Rogue? 3.00
4 final issue. 3.00

ROGUE
Aug., 2001
1 (of 4) AaL,RyE, ... 2.50
2 AaL,RyE. 2.50
3 AaL,RyE, leaves school. 2.50
4 AaL,RyE,JuB(c) 2.50

ROGUE
July, 2004
1 Going Rogue,pt.1. . . . . 3.00
2 Going Rogue,pt.2. . . . . 3.00
3 Going Rogue,pt.3. . . . . 3.00
4 Going Rogue,pt.4. . . . . 3.00

ROM
Dec., 1979
1 SB,I&O:Rom 10.00
2 FM(c),SB,V:Dire Wraiths 4.00
3 FM(c),SB,I:Firefall 4.00
4 SB,A:Firefall. 4.00
5 SB,A:Dr.Strange. 4.00
6 SB,V:Black Nebula 4.00
7 SB,V:Dark Nebula 4.00
8 SB,V:Dire Wraiths 4.00
9 SB,V:Serpentyne 4.00
10 SB,V:U.S.Air Force 4.00
11 SB,V:Dire Wraiths 4.00
12 SB,A:Jack O' Hearts 4.00
13 SB,V:Plunderer. 4.00
14 SB,V:Mad Thinker. 4.00
15 SB,W:Brandy and Dire Wraith . . 4.00
16 SB,V:Watchwraith 4.00
17 SB,A:X-Men 9.00
18 SB,A:X-Men 9.00
19 SB,JSt,C:X-Men 4.00
20 SB,JSt,A:Starshine 4.00
21 SB,JSt,A:Torpedo 4.00
22 SB,JSt,A:Torpedo 4.00
23 SB,JSt,A:Powerman,Iron Fist. . . 4.00
24 SB,JSt,A:Nova 6.00
25 SB,JSt,Double-Sized 6.00
26 SB,JSt,V:Galactus. 6.00
27 SB,JSt,V:Galactus. 6.00
28 SB,JSt,D:Starshine 3.00
29 SB,Down in the Mines 3.00
30 SB,JSt,A:Torpedo 3.00
31 SB,JSt,V:Evil Mutants,Rogue . . . 2.50
32 SB,JSt,V:Evil Mutants 2.50
33 SB,V:Sybil 2.50
34 SB,A:Sub-Mariner. 2.50
35 SB,A:Sub-Mariner. 2.50
36 SB,V:Scarecrow 2.50
37 SB,A:Starshine 2.50
38 SB,A:Master of Kung Fu. 2.50
39 SB,A:Master of Kung Fu. 2.50
40 SB,A:Torpedo 2.50

Rom #51
© Marvel Entertainment Group

41 SB,A:Dr.Strange 2.50
42 SB,A:Dr.Strange 2.50
43 SB,Rom Becomes Human 2.50
44 SB,A:Starshine,O:Gremlin 2.50
45 SB,V:Soviet Super Soldiers 2.50
46 SB,V:Direwraiths. 2.50
47 SB,New Look for Wraiths 2.50
48 SB,V:Dire Wraiths 2.50
49 SB,V:Dire Wraiths 2.50
50 SB,D:Torpedo,V:Skrulls 4.00
51 SB,F:Starshine 2.50
52 BSz(c),SB,V:Dire Wraiths 2.50
53 SB,BSz,V:Dire Wraiths 2.50
54 V:Dire Wraiths. 2.50
55 V:Dire Wraihs 2.50
56 A:Alpha Flight 3.00
57 A:Alpha Flight 3.00
58 JG(c),A:Antman 2.50
59 SD,BL,V:Microbe Menace. 2.50
60 SD,TP,V:Dire Wraiths 5.00
61 SD,V:Wraith-Realm. 2.50
62 SD,A:Forge 2.50
63 SD,V:Dire Wraiths. 2.50
64 SD,V:Dire Wraiths. 2.50
65 SD,A:X-Men,Avengers 2.50
66 SD,Rom leaves Earth. 2.50
67 SD,V:Scorpion 2.50
68 BSz(c)SD,Man & Machine 2.50
69 SD,V:Ego 2.50
70 SD. 2.50
71 SD,V:Raak 2.50
72 SD,Secret Wars II 2.50
73 SD,JSt. 2.50
74 SD,JBy,Code of Honor 2.50
75 SD,CR,Doublesize,last issue . . . 7.00
Ann.#1 PB,A:Stardust 3.00
Ann.#2 I:Knights of Galador. 3.00
Ann.#3 A:New Mutants 3.00
Ann.#4 V:Gladiator. 3.00

ROMANCE DIARY
Dec., 1949
1 . . . . 150.00
2 March, 1950 . . . . 125.00

ROMANCES OF THE WEST
Nov., 1949
1 Ph(c),Calamity Jane,
   Sam Bass 300.00
2 March, 1950 . . . . 175.00

ROMANCE TALES
Oct., 1949
(no #1 thru 6)
7 . . . . 150.00
8 . . . . 100.00
9 March, 1950 . . . . 100.00

ROMANTIC AFFAIRS
See: MOLLY MANTON'S ROMANCES

ROYAL ROY
Star, May, 1985
1 thru 5 . . . . @3.00
6 March, 1986 . . . . 3.00

RUGGED ACTION
Atlas, Dec., 1954
1 AyB,Man-Eater 150.00
2 JSe,DAy,JMn(c),Manta-Ray . . 100.00
3 DAy,JMn(c) 100.00
4 . . . . 100.00
Becomes:

STRANGE STORIES OF SUSPENSE
5 RH,JMn(c),Little Black Box . . . 500.00
6 BEv,The Illusion 300.00
7 JSe(c),BEv,Old John's House . 325.00
8 AW,BP,TYhumbs Down 325.00
9 BEv(c),Nightmare 350.00
10 RC,MME,AT 350.00
11 BEv(c) 225.00
12 AT 225.00
13 BEv,GM. 225.00
14 AW 250.00
15 BK 250.00
16 MF,BP, Aug., 1957 . . . . 250.00

RUINS
1995
1 Marvel's Alterverse 5.00
2 Fully painted, 32-pg. 5.00

RUNAWAYS
April, 2003
1 Pride & Joy, pt.1 . . . . 5.00
2 Pride & Joy, pt.2 . . . . 3.50
3 Pride & Joy, pt.3 . . . . 3.50
4 Pride & Joy, pt.4 . . . . 3.50
5 Pride & Joy, pt.5 . . . . 3.50
6 Pride & Joy, pt.6 . . . . 3.50
7 Teenage Wasteland,pt.1 . . . . 3.00
8 Teenage Wasteland,pt.2 . . . . 3.00
9 Teenage Wasteland,pt.3 . . . . 3.00
10 Teenage Wasteland,pt.4 . . . . . . 3.00
11 Lost & Found,pt.1 . . . . 3.00
12 Lost & Found,pt.2 . . . . 3.00
13 thru 17 The Good Die Young . @3.00
18 Season Finale. 3.00
TPB Runaways: Pride & Joy 15.00
Spec Runaways/Sentinel flip book . 4.00
Digest Marvel Age, Vol. 1 . . . . 8.00
Digest Vol. 2:Teenage Wasteland . . 8.00

RUSTY COMICS
See: KID KOMICS

SABRETOOTH
[Limited Series] 1993
1 B:LHa(s),MT,A:Wolverine 5.00
2 MT,A:Mystique,C:Wolverine. 4.00
3 MT,A:Mystique,Wolverine 4.00

4 E:LHa(s),MT,D:Birdy 4.00
TPB rep. #1–#4 . . . . 12.95

SABRETOOTH
Oct., 2004
1 (of 5) BS,F:Sasquatch 3.00
2 BS,F:Sasquatch 3.00

SABRETOOTH CLASSICS
1994–95
1 rep. Power Man/Iron Fist #66 . . . 4.00
2 rep. Power Man/Iron Fist #78 . . . 3.00
3 rep. Power Man/Iron Fist #84 . . . 3.00
4 rep. Spider-Man #116 . . . . 3.00
5 rep. Spider-Man #119 . . . . 3.00
6 reprints 3.00
7 reprints 3.00
8 reprints 3.00
9 reprints 3.00
10 Morlock Massacre 3.00
11 rep. Daredevil #238 . . . . 3.00
12 rep. V:Wolverine 3.00
13 rep. 3.00
14 A:Marauders 3.00
15 Mutant Massacre, rep.
　　Uncanny X-Men #221 . . . . 3.00

SABRETOOTH
Spec.#1 FaN, cont.from X-Men#48 . 4.95

SABRETOOTH
Oct., 1997
1-shot,F:Wildchild 2.50

SABRETOOTH
& MYSTIQUE
1 JGz,AOl, ... 2.50
2 thru 4 JGz,AOl . . . . @2.50

SABRETOOTH: MARY
SHELLEY OVERDRIVE
June, 2002
1 (of 4) F:Creed 3.00
2 TyH 3.00
3 . . . . 3.00
4 TyH 3.00

SACHS & VIOLENS
Epic, 1993–94
1 GP,PDd(s) 3.00
2 GP,PDd(s),V:Killer 2.50
3 GP,PDd(s),V:White Slavers 2.50
4 GP,PDd(s),D:Moloch 2.50

SAGA OF CRYSTAR
May, 1983
1 O:Crystar 5.00
2 A:Ika 4.00
3 A:Dr.Strange 4.00
4 . . . . 4.00
5 . . . . 4.00
6 A:Nightcrawler 4.00
7 I:Malachon 4.00
8 . . . . 4.00
9 . . . . 4.00
10 Chaos 4.00
11 Alpha Flight,Feb., 1985 . . . . 4.00

SAGA OF ORIGINAL
HUMAN TORCH
1 RB,O:Original Human Torch 3.00
2 RB,A:Toro 2.50
3 RB,V:Adolph Hitler 2.50
4 RB,Torch vs. Toro 2.50

ST. GEORGE
Epic, June, 1988
1 KJ,Shadow Line 2.25
2 KJ,I:Shrek 2.25
3 KJ 2.25
4 KJ 2.25
5 . . . . 2.25
6 . . . . 2.25
7 DSp 2.25
8 Oct., 1989 . . . . 2.25

SAINT SINNER
Razorline 1993–94
1 I:Phillip Fetter 2.75
2 thru 8 . . . . @2.25

SAM & MAX
GO TO THE MOON
1 Dirtbag Special,w/Nirvana Tape . . 4.00
[Regular Series]
1 MMi,AAd,F:Skull Boy 3.25
2 AAd,MMi 3.25
3 . . . . 3.25

SAMURAI CAT
Epic, 1991
1 I:MiaowaraTomokato 2.25
2 I:Con-Ed,V:Thpaghetti-Thoth 2.25
3 EmpireStateStrikesBack 2.25

SATANA
Nov., 1997
1 JaL,WEl,AOl,V:Doctor Strange,
　　non-code series 3.00
2 WEl,AOl,to the gates of Hell 3.00

SAVAGE SWORD
OF CONAN
Aug., 1974
(black & white magazine)
1 BWS,JB,NA,GK,O:Blackmark,
　　3rdA:Red Sonja,Boris(c) 135.00
2 NA(c),HC,GK,Black Colossus,
　　B.U.King Kull;B.U.Blackmark . 50.00
3 JB,BWS,GK,At The Mountain
　　of the Moon God;B.U.s:
　　Kull;Blackmark 30.00
4 JB,RCo,GK,Iron Shadows in the
　　Moon B.U.Blackmark,Boris(c) . 25.00
5 JB,Witch Shall be Born,Boris(c) 20.00
6 AN,Sleeper`Neath the Sands . . 20.00
7 JB,Citadel at the Center
　　of Time Boris(c) 20.00
8 inc.GK,Corsairs against Stygia . 20.00
9 Curse of the Cat-Goddess,
　　Boris(c),B.U.King Kull 20.00
10 JB,Sacred Serpent of Set
　　Boris(c) 20.00
11 JB,The Abode of the Damned . . 18.00
12 JB,Haunters of Castle Crimson
　　Boris(c) 18.00
13 GK,The Thing in the Temple,
　　B.U. Solomon Kane 18.00
14 NA,Shadow of Zamboula,
　　B.U.Solomon Kane 18.00
15 JB,Boris(c),Devil in Iron 18.00
16 JB,BWS,People of the Black
　　Circle,B.U.Bran Mak Morn . . . 18.00
17 JB,On to Yimsha!,
　　B.U.Bran Mak Morn 18.00
18 JB,The Battle of the Towers
　　B.U. Solomon Kane 18.00
19 JB,Vengeance in Vendhya
　　B.U. Solomon Kane 18.00
20 JB,The Slithering Shadow
　　B.U. Solomon Kane 15.00

Savage Sword of Conan #10
© Marvel Entertainment Group

21 JB,Horror in the Red Tower . . 15.00
22 JB,Pool o/t Black One
　　B.U. Solomon Kane 15.00
23 JB,FT,Torrent of Doom
　　B.U. Solomon Kane 15.00
24 JB,BWS,Tower of the
　　Elephant,B.U.Cimmeria 15.00
25 DG,SG,Jewels of Gwahlur,
　　B.U.Solomon Kane 15.00
26 JB/TD,Beyond the Black River,
　　B.U.Solomon Kane 15.00
27 JB/TD,Children of Jhebbal Sag 15.00
28 JB/AA,Blood of the Gods 15.00
29 ECh,FT,Child of Sorcery,
　　B.U. Red Sonja 15.00
30 FB,The Scarlet Citadel 15.00
31 JB/TD,The Flaming Knife,pt.1 . . 12.00
32 JB/TD,Ghouls of Yanaldar,pt.2 . 12.00
33 GC,Curse of the Monolith,
　　B.U.Solomon Kane 12.00
34 Cl/AA,MP,Lair o/t Ice Worm;B.U.
　　Solomon Kane,B.U.King Kull . . 12.00
35 ECh,Black Tears 12.00
36 JB,AA,Hawks over Shem 12.00
37 SB,Sons of the White Wolf
　　B.U. Solomon Kane 12.00
38 JB/TD,The Road of the Eagles . 12.00
39 SB/TD,The Legions of the Dead,
　　B.U.Solomon Kane concl. 12.00
40 JB/TD,A Dream of Blood 12.00
41 JB/TD,Quest for the Cobra Crown
　　A:Thoth-Amon,B.U.Sol.Kane . . 12.00
42 JB/TD,Devil-Tree of Gamburu,
　　A:Thoth-Amon,B.U.Sol.Kane . . 12.00
43 JB/TD,King Thoth-Amon,
　　B.U.King Kull 12.00
44 SB/TD,The Star of Khorala 12.00
45 JB/TD,The Gem in the Tower,
　　B.U. Red Sonja 12.00
46 EC/TD,Moon of Blood,
　　B.U. Hyborian Tale 12.00
47 GK/JB/JRu,Treasure of Tranicos
　　C:Thoth-Amon 12.00
48 JB/KJ,A Wind Blows from Stygia
　　C:Thoth-Amon 12.00
49 JB/TD,When Madness Wears the
　　Crown, B.U.Hyborian Tale 12.00
50 JB/TD,Swords Across the
　　Alimane 15.00
51 JB/TD,Satyrs' Blood 8.00
52 JB/TD,Conan the Liberator 8.00
53 JB,The Sorcerer and the Soul,
　　B.U. Solomon Kane 8.00
54 JB,The Stalker Amid the Sands,
　　B.U. Solomon Kane 8.00

55 JB,Black Lotus & Yellow Death	129 . . . . 6.00	195 JB/ECh,V:Yamatains,
B.U. King Kull 8.00	130 Reavers of the Steppes 6.00	Giant Tortoise 4.00
56 JB/TD,The Sword of Skelos 8.00	131 GI,Autumn of the Witch 6.00	196 JB/ECh,Treasure of the Stygian
57 JB/TD,Zamboula 8.00	132 ECh,Masters o/t Broadsword . . 6.00	Prince-Toth-Mekri,A:Valeria 4.00
58 JB/TD,KGa,For the Throne of	133 . . . . 6.00	197 RTs,JB,EC,Red Hand 4.00
Zamboula,B.U.OlgerdVladislav . 8.00	134 Conan the Pirate. 6.00	198 RTs,JB,EC,Red Hand 4.00
59 AA,ECh,City ofSkulls,B.U.Gault . 8.00	135 Conan the Pirate. 6.00	199 RTs,JB,EC,V:Black Zarona 4.00
60 JB,The Ivory Goddess 8.00	136 NKu,Stranded on DesertIsland . 6.00	200 RTs,JB,ECh,JJu(c),The Barbarian
61 JB,Wizard Fiend of Zingara 8.00	137 ECh,The Lost Legion 6.00	from Cross Plains 4.00
62 JB/ECh,Temple of the Tiger,	138 ECh,Clan o/t Lizard God. 6.00	201 RTs,MCW,return to Tarantia . . . 4.00
B.U. Solomon Kane. 8.00	139 ECh,A:Valeria 6.00	202 RTs,JB,ECh,Conan in the City
63 JB/ECh,TP/BMc,GK,Moat of Blood	140 ECh,The Ghost's Revenge. . . . 6.00	City of Magicians,pt.1 . . . . 4.00
I:Chane of the Elder Earth. 8.00	141 ECh. 6.00	203 RTs,JB,ECh,Conan in the City
64 JB/ECh,GK,Children of Rhan,	142 ECh,V:Warlord 6.00	City of Magicians,pt.2 . . . . 4.00
B.U. Chane 8.00	143 ECh. 6.00	204 RTs,JB,ECh,Conan in the City
65 GK,JB,Fangs of the Serpent,	144 ECh. 6.00	City of Magicians,pt.3 . . . . 4.00
B.U. Bront 8.00	145 ECh. 6.00	205 RTs,JB,ECh,Conan in the City
66 thru 80 . . . . @8.00	146 ECh. 6.00	City of Magicians,pt.4 . . . . 4.00
81 JB/ECh,Palace of Pleasure,	147 ECh. 6.00	206 RTs,JB,ECh,BLr(c),Conan in the
B.U. Bront 8.00	148 BMc. 6.00	City of Magicians,concl. 4.00
82 AA,BWS,Devil in the Dark.Pt.1	149 TGr,BMc,Conan Enslaved 6.00	207 RTs,JB,ECh,MK(c), Conan and
B.U.repConan#24,Swamp Gas . 8.00	150 ECh. 6.00	the Spider God, pt.1 . . . . 4.00
83 AA,MW,NA,ECh,Devil in the Dark	151 ECh. 6.00	208 RTs,JB,ECh, Conan and the
Pt.2,B.U. Red Sonja,Sol.Kane. . 8.00	152 ECh,Valley Beyond the Stars . . 6.00	Spider God, pt.2 . . . . 4.00
84 VM,Darksome Demon of	153 Blood on the Sand,Pt.1. . . . . . . 6.00	209 RTs,JB,Conan and the
Rabba Than. 8.00	154 Blood on the Sand,Pt.2. . . . . . . 6.00	Spider God,pt.3 . . . . 4.00
85 GK,Daughter of the God King. . 8.00	155 ECh,V:Vampires 6.00	210 RTs,Conan and the
86 GK,Revenge of the Sorcerer . . 8.00	156 V:Corinthian Army 6.00	Spider God,pt.4 . . . . 4.00
87 . . . . 8.00	157 V:Hyborians 6.00	211 RTs,Conan and the Gods of
88 JB,Isle of the Hunter 8.00	158 ECh,The Talisman-Gem 6.00	the Mountain,pt.1. . . . . 4.00
89 AA,MW,Gamesman of Asgalun,	159 Conan Enslaved 6.00	212 RTs,Conan and the Gods of
B.U. Rite of Blood 8.00	160 . . . . 6.00	the Mountain,pt.2. . . . . 4.00
90 JB,Devourer of Souls 8.00	161 V:Magician/Monsters 6.00	213 RTs,Conan and the Gods of
91 JB,VM,Forest of Friends,	162 AW,Horned God,B.U.Sol.Kane . 5.00	the Mountain,pt.3. . . . . 4.00
B.U. The Beast,The Chain 8.00	163 V:Picts. 5.00	214 RTs,Conan and the Gods of
92 JB,The Jeweled Bird. 8.00	164 Conan's Revenge 5.00	the Mountain,pt.4. . . . . 4.00
93 JB/ECh,WorldBeyond the Mists . 8.00	165 B.U. King Kull 5.00	215 RTs,JuB(c),Conan and the Gods
94 thru 101 . . . . @8.00	166 ECh,Conan in New World,Pt.1 . 5.00	of the Mountain,concl. 4.00
102 GD,B.U.Bran Mac Morn 6.00	167 ECh,Conan in New World,Pt.2 . 5.00	216 RTs,AA,Vengeance of Nitocris . 4.00
103 GD,White Tiger of Vendhya,	168 ECh,Conan in New	217 RTs,Conan theMercenary,pt.1 . 4.00
B.U. Bran Mac Morn 6.00	World,concl 5.00	218 RTs,Conan theMercenary,pt.2 . 4.00
104 . . . . 6.00	169 . . . . 5.00	219 RTs,A:Solomon Kane 4.00
105 . . . . 6.00	170 AW,A:Red Sonja,Valeria	220 RTs,V:Skull Out of Time 4.00
106 Feud of Blood 6.00	B.U. Solomon Kane. 5.00	221 RTs,C.L.Moore story adapt. . . . 4.00
107 thru 118 . . . . @6.00	171 TD,Conan Youth Story 5.00	222 RTs,The Haunter of the Towers
119 ECh,A:Conan's Sister 6.00	172 JS,JRu,Haunted Swamp,	B.U.JB,Conan Barbarian #1 . . . 4.00
120 Star of Thama-Zhu 6.00	B.U.King Kull,Valeria,	223 RTs,A:Tuzune Thune 4.00
121 . . . . 6.00	Red Sonja 5.00	224 RTs,JWk,The Dwellers Under the
122 . . . . 6.00	173 ECh,Under Siege 5.00	Tombs,adapt. B.U.V:Dinosaurs . 4.00
123 ECh,Secret of the GreatStone . 6.00	174 AA,Red Stones of	225 . . . . 4.00
124 ECh,Secret of the Stone 6.00	Rantha Karn 5.00	226 RTs,EN(c),The Four Ages
125 Altar of the Goat God 6.00	175 The Demonslayer Sword 5.00	of Conan, A:Red Sonja 4.00
126 The Mercenary 6.00	176 FH,TT,V:Wizard,B.U. Witch	227 RTs,JBu, besieged in a lost
127 Reunion in Scarlet,Return	Queen,Dagon,Ghouls 4.00	city, B.U. Kull,Red Sonja 4.00
of Valeria 6.00	177 LMc,TD,ECh,Conan the Prey,	228 RTs,AN,Conan in chains! 4.00
128 . . . . 6.00	B.U.King Conan,Red Sonja. . . . 4.00	229 RTs 4.00
	178 AA,The Dinosaur God. 4.00	
	179 ECh,A:Red Sonja,Valeria,	
	B.U.Conan 4.00	
	180 ECh,Sky-God Bardisattva,	
	B.U. King Kull 4.00	
	181 TD,Conan the Pagan God?,	
	B.U. Voodoo Tribe 4.00	
	182 RB/RT,V:Killer Ants 4.00	
	183 ECh,V:Kah-Tah-Dhen,	
	B.U.King Kull 4.00	
	184 AA,Return of Sennan 4.00	
	185 The Ring of Molub 4.00	
	186 AW,A:Thulsa Doom. 4.00	
	187 ECh,A:Conan's Brother? 4.00	
	188 V:Kharban the Sorcerer 4.00	
	189 A:Search Zukala for Gem 4.00	
	190 JB/TD,Skull on the Seas,pt.1 . . 4.00	
	191 JB/ECh,Skull on the Seas,pt.2	
	Thulsa Doom Vs.Thoth-Amon . . 4.00	
	192 JB/ECh,Skull on the Seas,pt.3	
	B.U. King Kull 4.00	
	193 JB/ECh,Skull on the Seas concl.	
	V:Thulsa Doom & Thoth-Amon . 4.00	
	194 JB/ECh,Wanted for Murder,	
	B.U. Li-Zya 4.00	

Savage Sword of Conan #23
© Marvel Entertainment Group

Savage Sword of Conan #232
© Marvel Entertainment Group

230 RTs, Acheron falls, Ring of
Tkrubu,pt.2, R:Kull. 4.00
231 RTs, V:Tuzoun Thune, B.U.
EM,Red Sonja. 4.00
232 RTs 4.00
233 A:Juma the Black, Kull 4.00
234 RTs,JBu, A:Nefartari;
A:Red Sonja, Zula 4.00
235 RTs,JBu,The Daughter of
Raktauanishi, final issue 4.00
Ann.#1 SB,BWS,inc.Beware the
Wrath of Anu,B.U. King
Kull Vs.Thulsa Doom. 4.00

SAVAGE TALES
May, 1971
(black & white magazine)
1 GM,BWS,JR,I&O:Man-Thing,
B:Conan,Femizons,A:Ka-Zar 225.00
2 GM,FB,BWS,AW,BWr,A:King
Kull rep,Creatures on
the Loose #10 . . . . 75.00
3 FB,BWS,AW,JSo 45.00
4 NA(c),E:Conan 40.00
5 JSn,JB,B:Brak the Barbarian . . 40.00
6 NA(c),JB,AW,B:Ka-Zar 25.00
7 GM,NA 20.00
8 JB,A:Shanna,E:Brak 20.00
9 MK,A:Shanna 20.00
10 RH,NA,AW,A:Shanna 20.00
11 RH 20.00
12 Summer, 1975 . . . . 20.00
Ann.#1 GM,GK,BWS,O:Ka-Zar . . . 20.00

SAVAGE TALES
Nov., 1985–March, 1987
(black & white magazine)
1 MGo,I:The `Nam 6.00
2 thru 9 MGo . . . . @4.00

SCARLET SPIDER
1995–96
1 HMe,GK,TP,VirtualMortality,pt.3 . 2.25
2 HMe,JR2,AW,CyberWar,pt.3 . . . 2.25
3 and 4 HMe . . . . @2.25

SCARLET SPIDER
UNLIMITED
1995
1 True Origin,64-pg. 4.50

SCARLET WITCH
1994
1 ALa(s),DAn(s),JH,I:Gargan,
C:Master Pandemonium 2.25
2 C:Avengers West Coast 2.25
3 A:Avengers West Coast. 2.25
4 V:Lore,last issue 2.25

SCOOBY-DOO
Oct., 1977
1 B:DynoMutt 35.00
2 thru 9 Feb., 1979 . . . . @25.00

SECRET DEFENDERS
1993–95
1 F:Dr.Strange(in all),Spider
Woman,Nomad,Darkhawk,
Wolverine,V:Macabre 3.25
2 F:Spider Woman,Nomad,Darkhawk,
Wolverine,V:Macabre 2.50
3 F:Spider Woman,Nomad,Darkhawk,
Wolverine,V:Macabre 2.25
4 F:Namorita,Punisher,
Sleepwalker,V:Roadkill 2.25

Secret Defenders #22
© Marvel Entertainment Group

5 F:Naromita,Punisher,
Sleepwalker, V:Roadkill. 2.25
6 F:Spider-Man,Scarlet Witch,Captain
America,V:Suicide Pack 2.25
7 F:Captain America,Scarlet Witch,
Spider-Man 2.25
8 F:Captain America,Scarlet Witch,
Spider-Man 2.25
9 F:War Machine,Thunderstrike,
Silver Surfer. 2.25
10 F:War Machine,Thunderstrike,
Silver Surfer. 2.25
11 TGb,F:Hulk,Nova,Northstar. . . . 2.25
12 RMz(s),TGb,F:Thanos 2.75
13 RMz(s),TGb,F:Thanos,Super Skrull,
Rhino,Nitro,Titanium Man 2.25
14 RMz(s),TGb,F:Thanos,Super Skrull,
Rhino,Nitro,Titanium Man,
A:Silver Surfer 2.25
15 F:Dr.Druid,Cage,Deadpool 2.25
16 F:Dr.Druid,Cage,Deadpool 2.25
17 F:Dr.Druid,Cage,Deadpool 2.25
18 F:Iron Fist,Giant Man 2.25
19 F:Dr.Druid,Cadaver,
Shadowoman. 2.25
20 V:Venom 2.25
21 V:Slaymaker 2.25
22 Final Defense,pt.1. . . . . 2.25
23 Final Defense,pt.2. . . . . 2.25
24 Final Defense,pt.3. . . . . 2.25
25 V:Dr.Druid 2.25

SECRET WAR
Feb., 2004
Book One BMB 4.00
Book One, Commemorative ed. . . . 6.00
Book Two BMB 5.00
Book Three BMB 4.00

SECRET WARS
May, 1984
1 MZ,A:X-Men,Fant.Four,Avengers,
Hulk,SpM in All,I:Beyonder 7.00
2 MZ,V:Magneto 6.00
3 MZ,I:Titania & Volcana. 6.00
4 BL,V:Molecule Man 6.00
5 BL,F:X-Men 6.00
6 MZ,V:Doctor Doom 6.00
7 MZ,I:New Spiderwoman. 7.00
8 MZ,I:Alien Black Costume
(for Spider-Man) 25.00
9 MZ,V:Galactus. 5.00

10 MZ,V:Dr.Doom 5.00
11 MZ,V:Dr.Doom. 5.00
12 MZ,Beyonder Vs. Dr.Doom. 7.00
TPB rep #1-#12. . . . . 19.95
TPB rep. 12 issues, 336-pg. 24.95

SECRET WARS II
July, 1985
1 AM,SL,A:X-Men,New Mutants . . . 5.00
2 AM,SL,A:Fantastic Four. 3.00
3 AM,SL,A:Daredevil. 3.00
4 AM,I:Kurse 3.00
5 AM,SL,I:Boom Boom 3.50
6 AM,SL,A:Mephisto 3.00
7 AM,SL,A:Thing. 3.00
8 AM,SL,A:Hulk. 3.00
9 AM,SL,A:Everyone,double-size . . 5.00

SECTAURS
June, 1985
1 Based on toys 3.00
2 . . . . 3.00
3 . . . . 3.00
4 . . . . 3.00
5 thru 10 1986. . . . . @3.00

SEEKER 3000
April, 1998
1 (of 4) DAn,IEd,sci-fi adventure,
48-pg. 3.00
2 DAn,IEd,encounter with aliens . . 3.00
3 DAn,IEd,V:Hkkkt,. 3.00
4 DAn,IEd,V:Hkkkt, concl.. . . . . . . 3.00

SEMPER FI
Dec., 1988
1 JSe. 2.50
2 JSe. 2.50
3 JSe. 2.50
4 JSe. 2.50
5 JSe. 2.50
6 . . . . 2.50
7 and 8 . . . . @2.50
9 Aug., 1989,final issue 2.50

SENSATIONAL
SPIDER-MAN
1 KM/TP/KJ,rep. (1989) 6.00

SENSATIONAL
SPIDER-MAN
Jan., 1996
0 DJu,KJ,Return of Spider-Man,pt.1
Lenticular cover. 6.00
1 DJu,KJ,Media Blizzard,pt.1,
V:New Mysterio 5.00
2 DJu,KJ,Return of Kaine,pt.2 . . . . 4.00
3 DJu,KJ,Web of Carnage,pt.1 . . . 4.00
4 DJu,KJ,Blood Brothers,pt.1 . . . . 4.00
5 DJu 4.00
6 DJu 3.00
7 TDz,A:Onslaught 3.00
8 TDz,The Looter 3.00
9 TDz,Onslaught tie-in 3.00
10 TDz,RCa,V:Swarm 3.00
11 TDz,Revelations, pt.2 . . . . 3.00
11A bagged with card, etc. 5.00
12 TDz,SwM, V:Trapster 3.00
13 TDz,RCa,A:Ka-Zar, Shanna . . . 3.00
14 TDz,RCa,Savage Land saga . . . 3.00
15 TDz,RCa,Savage Land saga . . . 3.00
16 TDz,RCa,R:Black Cat,
V:Prowler,Vulture 3.00
17 TDz,RCa,R:Black Cat,
Prowler,Vulture 3.00
18 TDz,RCa,V:Vulture 3.00

MARVEL

MARVEL

19 TDz,RCa,R:Living Monolith 2.50
20 TDz,RCa,Living Pharoah, concl.. 2.50
21 TDz,RCa,Techomancers........ 2.50
22 TDz,RCa,A:Doctor Strange..... 2.50
23 TDz,RCa,A:Doctor Strange..... 2.50
24 TDz,RCa,A:S.H.I.E.L.D., Looter . 3.00
25 TDz,RCa,Spider-Hunt,pt1 x-over 4.00
26 TDz,RCa,JoB,Identity Crisis
   prelude.................... 2.50
27 TDz,RCa,MeW,Identity Crisis,
   as Hornet V:Phaeton......... 2.50
28 TDz,RCa,as Hornet, V:Vulture . 2.50
29 TDz,RCa,V:Arcade, Black Cat . 2.50
30 TDz,A:Black Cat,V:Arcade 2.50
31 TDz,MeW,RCa,V:Rhino 2.50
32 TDz,JoB,The Gathering of the
   Five, pt.1 (of 5) 2.50
33 TDz,JoB,Gathering of
   the Five,pt.5................ 2.50
Minus 1 Spec.,TDz,RCa, flashback. 3.00
TPB In the Savage Land, rep...... 6.00
TPB Sensational Spider-Man '96
   seq. to Kraven's Last Hunt 3.00

SENTINEL
April, 2003
1 Salvage,pt.1................. 3.00
2 Salvage,pt.2................. 3.00
3 Salvage,pt.3................. 3.00
4 Salvage,pt.4................. 3.00
5 Salvage,pt.5................. 2.50
6 Salvage,pt.6................. 2.50
7 No Hero,pt.1 .... 2.50
8 No Hero,pt.2 .... 2.50
9 No Hero,pt.3 .... 2.50
10 Awakening,pt.1 .... 3.00
11 Awakening,pt.2 .... 3.00
12 Awakening,pt.3 .... 3.00
TPB Sentinel: Salvage, Vol. 1 .... 19.95
Digest Marvel Age, Vol. 1 .... 8.00

SENTRY
July, 2000
1 (of 5) PJe,JaL 3.00
2 PJe,JaL,Unicorn 3.00
3 PJe,JaL,Hulk,Spider-Man 3.00
4 PJe,JaL,Prof.X.............. 3.00
5 PJe,JaL,.................... 3.00
TPB The Sentry, JaL 24.95
Spec.#1 Sentry vs. The Void,
   JaL,PJe (2001) 3.00

SERGEANT BARNEY BARKER
Aug., 1956
1 JSe,Comedy 250.00
2 JSe,Army Inspection(c) 150.00
3 JSe,Tank(c) 150.00
Becomes:

G.I. TALES
4 JSe,At Grips with the Enemy .. 75.00
5 .... 60.00
6 JO,BP,GWb, July, 1957 ...... 55.00

SGT. FURY & HIS HOWLING COMMANDOS
May, 1963–Dec., 1981
1 Seven Against the Nazis ... 2,500.00
2 JK,Seven Doomed Men 600.00
3 JK,Midnight on Massacre
   Mountain 350.00
4 JK,V:Lord Ha-Ha,D:Junior
   Juniper 350.00
5 JK,V:Baron Strucker 350.00
6 JK,The Fangs of the Fox 200.00
7 JK,Fury Court Martial 200.00

8 JK,V:Dr Zemo,I:Percival
   Pinkerton 200.00
9 DAy,V:Hitler 200.00
10 DAy,On to Okinwawa,I:Capt.
   Savage 200.00
11 DAy,V:Capt.Flint 125.00
12 DAy,Howler deserts 125.00
13 DAy,JK,A;Capt.America 550.00
14 DAy,V:Baron Strucker 100.00
15 DAy,SD,Too Small to Fight
   Too Young to Die 100.00
16 DAy,In The Desert a Fortress
   Stands 100.00
17 DAy,While the Jungle Sleeps . 100.00
18 DAy,Killed in Action........ 100.00
19 DAy,An Eye for an Eye 100.00
20 DAy,V:the Blitz Squad 100.00
21 DAy,To Free a Hostage...... 75.00
22 DAy,V:Bull McGiveney 75.00
23 DAy,The Man who Failed 75.00
24 DAy,When the Howlers Hit
   the Home Front 75.00
25 DAy,Every Man my Enemy... 75.00
26 DAy,Dum Dum Does it the
   Hard Way. 75.00
27 DAy,O:Fury's Eyepatch...... 75.00
28 DAy,Not a Man Shall Remain
   Alive. 75.00
29 DAy,V:Baron Strucker 75.00
30 DAy,Incident in Italy 75.00
31 DAy,Into the Jaws of Death ... 50.00
32 DAy,A Traitor in Our Midst ... 50.00
33 DAy,The Grandeur That was
   Greece................. 50.00
34 DAy,O:Howling Commandoes . 50.00
35 DAy,Berlin Breakout,J:Eric
   Koenig................. 50.00
36 DAy,My Brother My Enemy.... 50.00
37 DAy,In the Desert to Die..... 50.00
38 This Ones For Dino 50.00
39 Into the Fortress of Fear..... 50.00
40 That France Might be Free ... 50.00
41 V:The Blitzers 50.00
42 Three Were AWOL 50.00
43 Scourge of the Sahara,A:Bob
   Hope,Glen Miller 50.00
44 JSe,The Howlers First Mission. 50.00
45 JSe,I:The War Lover......... 50.00
46 JSe,They Also Serve 50.00
47 Tea and Sabotage.......... 50.00
48 A:Blitz Squad 50.00
49 On to Tarawa 50.00
50 The Invasion Begins 50.00
51 The Assassin 50.00
52 Triumph at Treblinka........ 50.00

Sgt. Fury and His Howling Commandos #26 © Marvel Entertainment Group

53 To the Bastions of Bavaria 50.00
54 Izzy Shoots the Works 50.00
55 Cry of Battle, Kiss of Death ... 35.00
56 Gabriel Blow Your Horn 35.00
57 TS,The Informer 35.00
58 Second Front 35.00
59 D-Day for Dum Dum........ 35.00
60 Authorised Personnel Only ... 35.00
61 The Big Breakout 35.00
62 The Basic Training of Fury 35.00
63 V:Nazi Tanks.............. 35.00
64 The Peacemonger,A:Capt
   Savage 35.00
65 Eric Koenig,Traitor 35.00
66 Liberty Rides the Underground. 35.00
67 With a Little Help From My
   Friends................. 50.00
68 Welcome Home Soldier 35.00
69 While the City Sleeps 35.00
70 The Missouri Marauders 35.00
71 Burn,Bridge,Burn 35.00
72 Battle in the Sahara 35.00
73 Rampage on the
   Russian Front 35.00
74 Each Man Alone 35.00
75 The Deserter.............. 25.00
76 He Fought the Red Baron..... 25.00
77 A Traitor's Trap,A:Eric Koenig.. 25.00
78 Escape or Die 25.00
79 Death in the High Castle...... 25.00
80 To Free a Hostage 25.00
81 The All American........... 25.00
82 Howlers Hit The
   Home Front,rep 25.00
83 Dum DumV:Man-Mountain
   McCoy 25.00
84 The Devil's Disciple 25.00
85 Fury V:The Howlers 25.00
86 Germ Warfare 25.00
87 Dum Dum does it...rep 25.00
88 Save General Patton 25.00
89 O:Fury's eyepatch,rep. 25.00
90 The Chain That Binds 25.00
91 Not A Man...rep............ 25.00
92 Some Die Slowly, giant-sz..... 28.00
93 A Traitor...rep 20.00
94 GK(c),Who'll Stop the Bombs.. 20.00
95 7 Doomed Men, rep 20.00
96 GK(c),Dum-Dum Sees it
   Through 20.00
97 Till the Last Man Shall Fail 20.00
98 A:Deadly Dozen 20.00
99 Guerillas in Greece......... 20.00
100 When a Howler Falls 25.00
101 Pearl Harbor 18.00
102 Death For A Dollar 18.00
103 Berlin Breakout........... 18.00
104 The Tanks Are Coming 18.00
105 My Brother,My Enemy 18.00
106 Death on the Rhine........ 18.00
107 Death-Duel in the Desert 18.00
108 Slaughter From the Skies 18.00
109 This Ones For Dino,rep 18.00
110 JSe(c),The Reserve 18.00
111 V:Colonel Klaw 18.00
112 V:Baron Strucker 18.00
113 That France Might
   Be Free,rep............. 18.00
114 Jungle Bust Out 18.00
115 V:Baron Strucker 18.00
116 End of the Road 18.00
117 Blitz Over Britain 18.00
118 War Machine............. 18.00
118 War Machine............. 18.00
119 They Strike by Machine...... 18.00
120 Trapped in the Compound of
   Death 18.00
121 An Eye for an Eye......... 12.00
122 A;The Blitz Squad......... 12.00
123 To Free a Hostage 12.00
124 A:Bull McGiveney 12.00

All comics prices listed are for *Near Mint* condition.

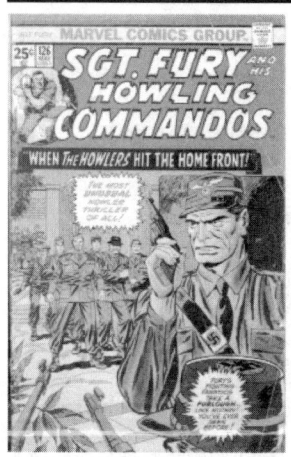

Sgt. Fury and his Howling Commandos #126 © Marvel EntertainmEnt Group

125 The Man Who Failed 12.00
126 When the Howlers Hit Home.. 12.00
127 Everyman My Enemy,rep 12.00
128 Dum Dum does it...rep 12.00
129 O:Fury's Eyepatch 12.00
130 A:Baron Strucker 12.00
131 Armageddon 12.00
132 Incident in Italy 12.00
133 thru 140. . . . . @12.00
141 thru 150. . . . . @12.00
151 thru 167. . . . . @12.00
Ann.#1 Korea #4,#5. . . . . 225.00
Ann.#2 This was D-Day. 75.00
Ann.#3 Vietnam 45.00
Ann.#4 Battle of the Bulge. 35.00
Ann.#5 Desert Fox. 25.00
Ann.#6 Blaze of Battle. 25.00
Ann.#7 Armageddon 25.00

SERGIO ARAGONES MASSACRES MARVEL
1996
1-shot Parody. 5.00

SEVEN BLOCK
Epic, 1990
1 . . . . 2.50

SHADOWMASTERS
Oct., 1989–Jan., 1990
1 RH 7.00
2 . . . . 5.00
3 . . . . 4.00
4 . . . . 4.00

SHADOWRIDERS
1993
1 I:Shadowriders,A:Cable,
   Ghost Rider. 3.00
2 A:Ghost Rider 2.50
3 A:Cable 2.50
4 A:Cable 2.50

SHADOWS & LIGHT
Dec., 1997
1 BSf,RMz,LWn,BWr,GeH,SD,B&W
   anthology series 3.00
2 JSn,LW,LSh,GK. 3.00
3 BL,JSn 3.00
4 three new tales 3.00

SHANG-CHI: MASTER OF KUNG FU
Marvel Max, Sept., 2002
1 (of 6) DgM,PG 3.00
2 DgM,PG,JP 3.00
3 thru 6 PG,JP. . . . . @3.00
TPB Vol. 1: Hellfire Apocalypse . . . 16.00

SHANNA, THE SHE-DEVIL
Dec., 1972–Aug., 1973
1 GT,F:Shanna 35.00
2 RA,The Dungeon of Doom . . . 25.00
3 RA,The Hour of the Bull 20.00
4 RA,Mandrill 20.00
5 JR(c),RA,V:Nekra 20.00

SHEENA
Dec., 1984–Feb., 1985
1 and 2 Movie adapt . . . . @3.00

SHE-HULK
[1st Regular Series] Feb., 1980
1 JB,BWi,I&O:She-Hulk 15.00
2 BWi,D:She-Hulk's best friend . . . 7.00
3 BWi,Wanted for Murder. 7.00
4 BWi,V:Her Father. 7.00
5 BWi,V:Silver Serpent 7.00
6 A:Iron Man 5.00
7 BWi,A:Manthing. 5.00
8 BWi,A:Manthing. 5.00
9 BWi,Identity Crisis 5.00
10 V:The Word. 5.00
11 BWi,V:Dr.Morbius. 5.00
12 V:Gemini 5.00
13 V:Man-Wolf 5.00
14 V:Hellcat 5.00
15 V:Lady Kills 5.00
16 She Hulk Goes Berserk 5.00
17 V:Man-Elephant 5.00
18 V:Grappler. 5.00
19 V:Her Father 5.00
20 A:Zapper 5.00
21 V:Seeker 5.00
22 V:Radius 5.00
23 V:Radius 5.00
24 V:Zapper. 5.00
25 Double-sized,last issue. 5.00

[2nd Regular Series] 1989–94
1 JBy,V:Ringmaster 4.00
2 JBy. 2.50

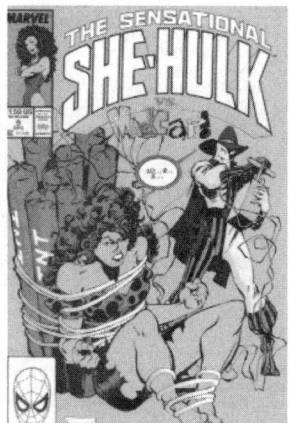

She-Hulk 2nd Series #9
© Marvel Entertainment Group

3 JBy,A:Spider-Man 2.50
4 JBy,I:Blond Phantom 3.00
5 JBy. 2.50
6 JBy,A:U.S.1,Razorback 2.50
7 JBy,A:U.S.1,Razorback 2.50
8 JBy,A:Saint Nicholas 2.50
9 AM(i) 2.50
10 AM(i) 2.50
11 . . . . 2.50
12 . . . . 2.50
13 SK(c) 2.50
14 MT(c),A:Howard the Duck 3.00
15 SK(c) 3.00
16 SK(c) 3.00
17 SK(c),V:Dr.Angst. 3.00
18 SK(c) 2.50
19 SK(c),V:Nosferata 2.50
20 SK(c),Darkham Asylum. 2.50
21 SK(c),V:Blonde Phantom 3.00
22 SK(c),V:Blonde Phantom,A:All
    Winners Squad 3.00
23 V:Blonde Phantom 3.00
24 V:Deaths'Head 4.00
25 A:Hercules,Thor 2.50
26 A:Excalibur 2.50
27 Cartoons in N.Y. 2.50
28 Game Hunter Stalks She-Hulk . . 2.50
29 A:Wolv.,Hulk,SpM,Venom 2.50
30 MZ(c),A:Silver Surfer,Thor
    Human Torch 2.25
31 JBy,V:Spragg the Living Hill 2.50
32 JBy,A:Moleman,V:Spragg 2.50
33 JBy,A:Moleman,V:Spragg 2.50
34 JBy,Returns to New York 2.50
35 JBy,V:X-Humed Men. 2.50
36 JBy,X-mas issue (#8 tie-in). 2.50
37 JBy,V:Living Eraser. 2.50
38 JBy,V:Mahkizmo 2.50
39 JBy,V:Mahkizmo 2.50
40 JBy,V:Spraggs,Xemnu 2.50
41 JBy,V:Xemnu. 2.50
42 JBy,V:USArcher 2.50
43 JBy,V:Xemnu. 2.50
44 JBy,R:Rocket Raccoon 2.50
45 JBy,A:Razorback. 2.50
46 JBy,A:Rocket Raccoon 2.50
47 JBy,V:D'Bari 2.50
48 JBy,A:Rocket Raccoon 2.50
49 V:Skrulls,D'Bari. 2.50
50 JBy,WS,TA,DGb,AH,HC,
    D:She-Hulk 4.00
51 TMo,V:Savage She-Hulk 2.50
52 D:She-Hulk,A:Thing,Mr.Fantastic,
    I:Rumbler,V:Titania 2.50
53 AH(c),A:Zapper 2.50
54 MGo(c),A:Wonder Man 2.50
55 V:Rumbler. 2.50
56 A:War Zone 2.50
57 A:Hulk 2.50
58 V:Electro 2.50
59 V:Various Villains 2.50
60 last issue 2.50
TPB rep. #1-#8 . . . . 12.95

SHE-HULK
March, 2004
1 F:Avengers 3.00
2 Class Action Comics 3.00
3 Dead Certain,F:The Thing 3.00
4 Web of Lies 3.00
5 The Big Picture,pt.1 . . . . 3.00
6 The Big Picture,pt.2. . . . . 3.00
7 Space Cases,pt.1. . . . . 3.00
8 Engagement Ring,pt.2 . . . . 3.00

SHE HULK: CEREMONY
1989
1 JBr/SDr 4.00
2 JBr/FS 4.00

MARVEL

SHIELD
Feb., 1973
1 JSo. 20.00
2 JSo. 15.00
3 JB,JSo,JK 15.00
4 JSo. 15.00
5 JSo,Oct., 1973 . . . . 15.00

Shogun Warriors #10
© Marvel Entertainment Group

SHOGUN WARRIORS
Feb., 1979
1 HT,DGr,F:Raydeen, Combatra,
   Dangard Ace 15.00
2 HT,DGr,V:Elementals of Evil . . . 10.00
3 AM(c),HT,DGr,V:Elementals
   of Evil. 10.00
4 HT,DGr,Menace of the
   Mech Monsters. 10.00
5 HT,DGr,Into The Lair
   of Demons 10.00
6 HT,ME 10.00
7 HT,ME 10.00
8 HT,ME 10.00
9 War Beneath The Waves. 10.00
10 Five Heads of Doom. 10.00
11 TA(c) 8.00
12 WS(c) 8.00
13 Demons on the Moon 8.00
14 V:Dr. Demonicus. 8.00
15 . . . . 8.00
16 . . . . 8.00
17 . . . . 8.00
18 . . . . 8.00
19 A:Fantastic Four 8.00
20 Sept., 1980 . . . . 8.00

SHROUD
Limited Series 1994
1 B:MiB(s),MCW,A:Spider-Man,
   V:Scorpion. 2.25
2 MCW . . . . @2.25

SILVERHAWKS
Aug., 1987
1 thru 5 . . . . @3.00
6 June, 1988 . . . . 3.00

SILVER SABLE
1992–95
1 Foil stamped(c),A:Sandman,
   Spider-Man. 3.00
2 I:Gattling 2.50

---

3 V:Gattling,Foreigner. 2.50
4 Infinity War,V:Doctor Doom 2.50
5 Infinity War,V:Doctor Doom 2.50
6 A:Deathlok 2.50
7 A:Deathlok 2.50
8 V:Hydra 2.50
9 O:Silver Sable 2.50
10 A:Punisher,Leviathan 2.50
11 Cyber Warriors,Hydra 2.25
12 V:Cyberwarriorss,R:Sandman . . 2.25
13 For Love Nor Money#3,
   A:Cage,Terror 2.25
14 For Love Nor Money#6,
   A:Cage,Terror 2.25
15 V:Viper,A:Captain America 2.25
16 SBt,Infinty Crusade. 2.25
17 Infinity Crusade. 2.25
18 A:Venom 2.25
19 Siege of Darkness x-over 2.25
20 GWt(s),StB,BU:Sandman,Fin . . 2.25
21 Gang War 2.25
22 . . . . 2.25
23 GWt(s),A:Deadpool,Daredevil,
   BU:Sandman 2.25
24 GWt(s),BU:Crippler,w/card 2.25
25 V:Hydra 2.50
26 F:Sandman 2.25
27 A:Code Blue 2.25
28 F:Chen 2.25
29 A:Wild Pack. 2.25
30 problems with law 2.25
31 V:terrorists. 2.25
32 A:The Foreigner 2.25
33 V:Hammerhead. 2.25
34 . . . . 2.25
35 Li'l Silvie Tale 2.25

SILVER SURFER
[1st Series] Aug., 1968
1 B:StL(s),JB,JSr,GC,O:Silver Surfer,
   O:Watcher,I:Shala Bal 700.00
2 JB,JSr,GC,A:Watcher 300.00
3 JB,JSr,GC,I:Mephisto 250.00
4 JB,A:Thor,low distribution
   scarce 650.00
5 JB,A:Fant.Four,V:Stranger. . . . 175.00
6 JB,FB,A:Watcher 175.00
7 JB,A:Watcher,I:Frankenstein's
   Monster 175.00
8 JB,DA,A:Mephisto,I:Ghost. . . . 150.00
9 JB,DA,A:Mephisto,A:Ghost . . . 150.00
10 JB,DA,South America 150.00
11 JB,DA 100.00
12 JB,DA,V:The Abomination . . . 100.00
13 JB,DA,V:Doomsday Man 100.00
14 JB,DA,A:Spider-Man. 125.00
15 JB,DA,A:Human Torch 100.00
16 JB,V:Mephisto 100.00
17 JB,V:Mephisto. 100.00
18 E:StL(s),JK,V:Inhumans 100.00

[2nd Regular Series] 1982
1 JBy,TP,Direct Only,V:Mephisto . 12.00

[3rd Regular Series] July, 1987
1 MR,JRu,A:Fantastic Four,
   Galactus,V:Champion 12.00
2 MR,A:Shalla Bal,V:Skrulls 6.00
3 MR,V:Collector & Runner 5.00
4 MR,JRu,A:Elders,I:Obliterator . . . 5.00
5 MR,JRu,V:Obliterator. 5.00
6 MR,JRu,O:Obliterator,A:Kree,
   Skrulls 5.00
7 MR,JRu,V:Supremor,Elders/
   Soul Gems. 5.00
8 MR,JRu,V:Supremor 5.00
9 MR,Elders Vs.Galactus 5.00
10 MR,A:Galactus,Eternity. 5.00
11 JSon,JRu,V:Reptyl 4.50
12 MR,JRu,V:Reptyl,A:Nova 4.50
13 JSon,DC,V:Ronan. 4.50
14 JSon,JRu,V:Skrull Surfer 4.50

---

15 RLm,JRu,A:Fantastic Four 6.00
16 RLm,Inbetweener possesses
   Soul Gem,A:Fantastic Four. . . . 4.00
17 RLm,A:Inbetweener,Galactus,
   Fantastic Four,D:Trader,
   Possessor,Astronomer 4.00
18 RLm,Galactus V:Inbetweener. . . 4.00
19 RLm,MR,V:Firelord 4.00
20 RLm,A:Superskrull,Galactus. . . . 4.00
21 MR,DC,V:Obliterator 4.00
22 RLm,V:Ego 4.00
23 RLm,V:Dragon 4.00
24 RLm,V:G.I.G.O. 4.00
25 RLm,V:Ronan,Kree Skrull War . . 4.00
26 RLm,V:Nenora 4.00
27 RLm,V:Stranger 4.00
28 RLm,D:Super Skrull,V:Reptyl . . . 4.00
29 RLm,V:Midnight Sun 4.00
30 RLm,V:Midnight Sun 4.00
31 RLm,O:Living Tribunal &
   Stranger (double size) 4.50
32 RF,JSt,A:Mephisto 4.00
33 Rlm,V:Impossible Man 4.00
34 RLm,(1stJSn),2nd R:Thanos . . . 5.00
35 RLm,A:Thanos,R:Drax 4.00
36 RLm,V:Impossible Man,A:Warlock
   Capt.Marvel,C:Thanos. 4.00
37 RLm,V:Drax,A:Mentor. 4.00
38 RLm,V:Thanos(continued in
   Thanos Quest). 4.00
39 JSh,V:Algol 3.00
40 RLm,V:Dynamo City 3.00
41 RLm,V:Dynamo City,A:Thanos . . 4.00
42 RLm,V:Dynamo City,A:Drax 3.00
43 RLm,V:DynamoCity 3.00
44 RLm,R:Thanos,Drax,
   O:Inf.Gems 4.00
45 RLm,Thanos vs. Mephisto 4.00
46 RLm,R:Warlock,A:Thanos 4.00
47 RLm,Warlock V:Drax,
   A:Thanos 4.00
48 RLm,A:Galactus,Thanos. 4.00
49 RLm,V:Thanos Monster 4.00
50 RLm,Silver Stamp(D.size),
   V:Thanos Monster 8.00
50a 2nd printing. 3.00
50b 3rd printing 3.00
51 RLm,Infinity Gauntlet x-over . . . 3.00
52 RLm,Infinity Gauntlet x-over . . . 3.00
53 RLm,Infinity Gauntlet x-over . . . 3.00
54 RLm,I.Gauntlet x-over,V:Rhino . . 3.00
55 RLm,I.Gauntlet x-over,Universe
   According to Thanos,pt.1 . . . . . 3.00
56 RLm,I.Gauntlet x-over,Universe
   According to Thanos,pt.2 . . . . . 3.00
57 RLm,Infinity Gauntlet x-over . . . 3.00
58 RLm(c),Infinity Gauntlet x-over,
   A:Hulk,Namor,Dr.Strange 3.00
59 RLm(c),TR,Infinity Gauntlet,
   Thanos V:Silver Surfer 3.00
60 RLm,V:Midnight Sun,
   A:Inhumans 2.50
61 RLm,I:Collection.Agency. 2.50
62 RLm,O:Collection Agency. 2.50
63 RLm,A:Captain Marvel 2.50
64 RLm,V:Dark Silver Surfer 2.50
65 RLm,R:Reptyl,I:Princess
   Alaisa 2.50
66 RLm,I:Avatar,Love & Hate 2.50
67 RLm(c),KWe,Inf.War,V:Galactus
   A:DrStrange 2.50
68 RLm(c),KWe,Inf.War,O:Nova . . . 2.50
69 RLm(c),KWe,Infinity War,
   A:Galactus 2.50
70 RLm(c),Herald War#1,I:Morg . . . 2.50
71 RLm(c),Herald War#2,V:Morg . . 2.50
72 RLm(c),Herald War#3,R:Nova . . 2.50
73 RLm,R:Airwalker 2.50
74 RLm,V:Terrax 2.50
75 RLm,E:Herald Ordeal,V:Morg,
   D:Nova. 3.00

Silver Surfer 3rd Series #85
© *Marvel Entertainment Group*

76 RLm,A:Jack of Hearts. 2.50
77 RLm,A:Jack of Hearts. 2.50
78 RLm,R:Morg,V:Nebula 2.50
79 RLm,V:Captain Atlas. 2.50
80 RLm,I:Ganymede,Terrax
   Vs.Morg. 2.50
81 RLm,O:Ganymedel:Tyrant 2.50
82 RLm,V:Tyrant,double sized. 2.50
83 Infinity Crusade. 2.50
84 RLm(c),Infinity Crusade. 2.50
85 RLm(c),Infinity Crusade 2.50
86 RLm(c), Blood & Thunder,pt.2
   V:Thor,A:Beta Ray Bill. 2.50
87 RLm(c),Blood & Thunder,pt.7 . . . 2.50
88 RLm(c),Blood & Thunder,pt.10 . . 2.50
89 RLm(c),CDo,C:Legacy 2.50
90 RLm(c),A:Legacy,C:Avatar 2.50
91 RLm 2.50
92 RLm,V:Avatar 2.50
93 V:Human Torch 2.50
94 A:Fantastic Four, Warlock. 2.50
95 SEa,A:Fantastic Four 2.50
96 A:Fantastic Four,Hulk 2.50
97 A:Fantastic Four,R:Nova. 2.50
98 R:Champion 2.50
99 A:Nova 2.50
100 V:Mephisto 2.50
100a enhanced ed. 5.00
101 RMz,JoP,A:Shalla Bal 2.25
102 V:Galactus 2.25
103 I:Death quad 2.25
104 Surfer Rampage 2.25
105 V:Super Skrull 2.25
106 A:Legacy,Morg 2.25
107 TGb,BAn,A:Galactus,Morg,
    Tyrant. 2.25
108 Galactus Vs. Tyrant 2.25
109 Morg has Ultimate Nulifier 2.25
110 JB,F:Nebula 2.25
111 GP,TGb,BAn,to Other Side
    of Galaxy 2.25
112 GP,TGb,BAn,. 2.25
113 GP,TGb,BAn,V:Blackbody. 2.25
114 . . . . 2.25
115 GP,TGb,BAn,Surfer in pieces . . 2.25
116 GP,TGb,BAn,Pieces cause
    trouble 2.25
117 . . . . 2.25
118 . . . . 2.25
119 . . . . 2.25
120 . . . . 2.25
121 A:Quasar, Beta Ray Bill 2.25
122 GP,SEa, returns to Marvel
    Universe 2.25

123 GP,RG. 2.25
124 GP,RG. 2.25
125 RG,V:Hulk, double size 3.50
126 JMD,RG,BWi,A:Dr. Strange . . . 2.25
127 JMD,RG,BWi,A:Alicia Masters . 2.25
128 JMD,RG,BWi,V:Puppet Master . 2.25
129 JMD,RG,BWi,back in time,
    late 1940s 2.25
130 JMD,CNr,BWi, trapped in past . 2.25
131 JMD,RG,BWi, ... 2.25
132 JMD,PaP,Puppet Master
    missing 2.25
133 JMD,MRy,PaP,V:PuppetMaster 2.25
134 JMD,TGm,MRy,Regains his
    memories, pt.1 (of 4). 2.25
135 JMD,TGm,MRy,Alicia summons
    Scrier. 2.25
136 JMD,TGm,MRy, ... 2.25
137 JMD,TGm,MRy,Mephisto v.
    Scrier. 2.25
138 JMD,RCz,MRy,A:The Thing,
    tie-in. 2.25
139 JMD,RCz,MRy,V:Gargoyle 2.25
140 JMD,JMu,on Zenn-La untouched
    by Galactus 2.25
141 JMD,JMu,A:Sama-D,Alicia
    Masters 2.25
142 JMD,JMu,Tenebrae,The Union,
    Cipher 2.25
143 JMD,DCw,Tenebrae,V:Psycho
    Man 2.25
Bi-Weekly Issues
144 JMD,JMu,V:Psycho-Man,
    A:Tenebrae 2.25
145 JMD,JMu,A:Psycho-Man,
    Tenebrae,Cypphyrr 2.25
146 TDF,DCw,V:Firelord 2.25
Minus 1 Spec., JMD,RG,BWi,
    flashback, first human contact. . 2.25
Spec. Silver Surfer: Dangerous Arti-
    facts,RMz, Galactus,Thanos
    (1996) 4.00
Spec. Silver Surfer: Inner Demons,
    rep. JMD,RGa,BWi (1998) . . . 3.00
Ann.#1 RLm,JSon,Evolution War . . 7.00
Ann.#2 RLm,Atlantis Attacks 5.00
Ann.#3 RLm,Lifeform #4 . . . . 4.00
Ann.#4 RLm,Korvac Quest #3,A:
    Guardians of Galaxy 3.00
Ann.#5 RLm,Ret.o/Defenders #3. . . 2.50
Ann.#6 RLm(c),I:Legacy,w/card. . . . 3.75
Ann.'97 1 JMD,VS,KJ,V:Scrier,
    48-pg. 2.25
Ann.'98 MPe,RBe,TDF,F:Thor 3.00
TPB Silver Surger, The Enslavers . . 17.00
TPB Homecoming,A:Moondragon . . 13.00
TPB Silver Surfer: Parable, rep. . . . 6.00
TPB Rebirth of Thanos, rep. 13.00
TPB StL,JK, new origin 13.00

SILVER SURFER
Epic, Dec., 1988
1 Moebius,V:Galactus 5.00
2 Moebius,V:Galactus. 5.00
Graphic Novel 15.00

SILVER SURFER
July, 2003
1 JJu(c),children disappear. 2.50
2 JaL(c),Denise Waters 2.50
3 Denise Waters 2.50
4 Communion,pt.4 . . . . 2.25
5 Communion,pt.5 . . . . 2.25
6 Communion,pt.6 . . . . 2.25
7 Revelation,pt.1. . . . . 3.00
8 Revelation,pt.2. . . . . 3.00
9 Revelation,pt.3. . . . . 3.00
10 Revelation,pt.4 . . . . 3.00
11 Revelation,pt.5 . . . . 3.00
12 Revelation,pt.6 . . . . 3.00

13 Revelation,pt.7 . . . . 3.00
14 Revelation,pt.8 . . . . 3.00
TPB Vol. 1: Communion 15.00

SILVER SURFER: LOFTIER THAN MORTALS
Aug., 1999
1 MFr,V:Dr. Doom. 2.50
2 MFr,V:Dr. Doom, concl. 2.50

SILVER SURFER/ SUPERMAN
Marvel/DC 1996
Spec. GP,RLm,TA, x-over 6.00

SILVER SURFER VS. DRACULA
1994
1 rep,MWn(s),GC,TP 2.50

SILVER SURFER/ WARLOCK: RESURRECTION
1993
1 JSn,V:Mephisto,Death 3.50
2 JSn,TA,V:Death 3.00
3 & 4 JSn,TA,V:Mephisto . . . . . . @3.00

SILVER SURFER/ WEAPON ZERO
Marvel/Top Cow 1997
1-shot Devil's Reign, pt.8 . . . . 4.00

SISTERHOOD OF STEEL
Epic, Dec., 1984
1 I:Sisterhood 4.00
2 thru 8 . . . . @3.00

SIX FROM SIRIUS
Epic, July, 1984
1 PG,limited series 3.00
2 thru 4 PG . . . . @2.25

SIX FROM SIRIUS II
Epic, Feb., 1986
1 PG 2.25

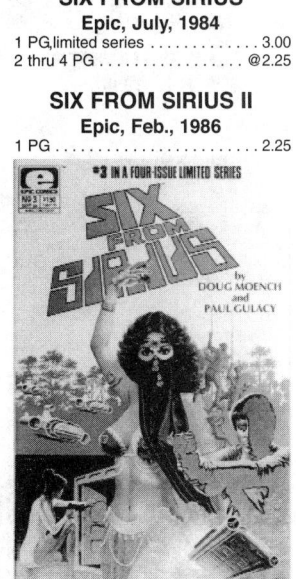

Six from Sirius #3
© *Marvel Entertainment Group*

SIX-GUN WESTERN
Atlas, Jan., 1957
1 JSe(c),RC,JR,Kid Yukon
  Gunslinger 225.00
2 SSh,AW,DAy,JO,His Guns
  Hang Low 150.00
3 AW,BP,DAy 150.00
4 JSe(c),JR,GWb 125.00

SKELETON WARRIORS
1995
1 based on cartoon 2.25
2 Legion of Light 2.25
3 V:Grimstar 2.25
4 Grimskull abandons Legion
  of Light 2.25

SKRULL KILL CREW
1995
1 I:Kill Crew 3.00
2 V:Hydra 3.00
3 V:Captain America 3.00
4 V:Fantastic Four 3.00
5 Conclusion 3.00

SKULL, THE SLAYER
Aug., 1975
1 GK(c),O:Skull the Slayer 15.00
2 GK(c),Man Against Gods 10.00
3 Trapped in the Tower
  of Time 10.00
4 Peril of the Pyramids,
  A:Black Knight 10.00
5 A:Black Knight 10.00
6 The Savage Sea 10.00
7 Dungeon of Blood 10.00
8 JK(c),Nov., 1976 . . . . 10.00

SLAPSTICK
1992–93
1 TA(i),I:Slapstick 2.25
2 TA(i),A:Spider-Man,V:Overkill . . . 2.25
3 V:Dr.Denton 2.25
4 A:GR,DD,FF,Cap.America 2.25

SLEDGE HAMMER
Feb., 1988
1 . . . . 5.00
2 March, 1988 . . . . 3.00

SLEEPWALKER
June, 1991
1 BBl,I:Rick Sheridan,C:8-Ball 3.00
2 BBl,V:8-Ball 2.25
3 BBl,A:Avengers,X-Men,X-Factor,
  FF,I:Cobweb,O:Sleepwalker . . . 2.25
4 RL,I:Bookworm 2.25
5 BBl,A:SpM,K.Pin,V:Ringleader . . 2.25
6 BBl,A:SpM,Inf.Gauntlet x-over . . . 2.25
7 BBl,Infinity Gauntlet x-over,
  V:Chain Gang 2.25
8 BBl,A:Deathlok 2.25
9 BBl,I:Lullabye 2.25
10 BBl,MM,I:Dream-Team 2.25
11 BBl,V:Ghost Rider 2.25
12 JQ,A:Nightmare 3.00
13 BBl,MM,I:Spectra 2.25
14 BBl,MM,V:Spectra 2.25
15 BBl,MM,I:Thought Police 2.25
16 BBl,MM,A:Mr.Fantastic,Thing . . . 2.25
17 BBl,A:Spider-Man,Darkhawk,
  V:Brotherhood o/Evil Mutants . . 2.25
18 JQ(c),Inf.War,A:Prof.X 2.25
19 V:Cobweb,w/pop out Halloween
  Mask 2.50
20 V:Chain Gang,Cobweb 2.25

21 V:Hobgoblin 2.25
22 V:Hobgoblin,8-Ball 2.25
23 V:Cobweb,Chain Gang 2.25
24 Mindfield#6 . . . . 2.25
25 O:Sleepwalker,Holo-grafx(c) 3.50
26 V:Mindspawn 2.25
27 A:Avengers 2.25
28 I:Psyko 2.25
29 DG,V:Psyko 2.25
30 V:Psyko 2.25
31 DG(ci),A:Spectra 2.25
32 V:Psyko 2.25
33 V:Mindspawn,Last issue 2.25
Holiday Spec.#1 JQ(c) 2.50

SLEEZE BROTHERS
Aug., 1989
1 Private Eyes 2.25
2 . . . . 2.25
3 . . . . 2.25
4 thru 6 . . . . @2.25

SLINGERS
Oct., 1998
1 Ccs,F:Ricochet, Hornet,
  Prodigy & Dusk, 48-page:
1a Ricochet edition 3.00
1b Hornet edition 3.00
1c Prodigy edition 3.00
1d Dusk edition 3.00
2 CCs,V:Maggia 2.50
2a variant cover 2.25
3 CCs,F:Prodigy 2.25
4 CCs,F:Prodigy 2.25
5 CCs,F:Black Marvel 2.25
6 CCs,Truth or Dare 2.25
7 CCs,V:The Griz 2.25
8 CCs,V:The Griz 2.25
9 CCs,A:Ricochet 2.25
10 CCs,Raising Hell'sChildren,pt.1 . 2.25
11 CCs,Raising Hell'sChildren,pt.2 . 2.25
12 CCs,Hell's Children,pt.3 final . . . 2.25

SMURFS
Dec., 1982
1 . . . . 10.00
2 . . . . 7.00
3 . . . . 7.00
Treasury Edition 30.00

SOLARMAN
Jan., 1989
1 JM 3.00
2 MZ/NR,A:Dr.Doom, May, 1990 . . 3.00

SOLDIER X
July, 2002
1 Cable's future, 40-pg. 3.00
2 . . . . 2.25
3 to Russia without love 2.25
4 Geo debuts 2.25
5 . . . . 2.25
6 . . . . 2.25
7 . . . . 2.25
8 Askani religion 2.25
9 V:Racist militia group 2.25
10 V:Racism 3.00
11 SEa,Dead Ends,pt.1 . . . . 3.00
12 SEa,Dead Ends,pt.2 . . . . 3.00

SOLO
[Limited Series] 1994
1 RoR,I:Cygnus 2.25
2 RoR,V:A.R.E.S. 2.25
3 RoR,V:Spidey 2.25
4 final issue 2.25

Solo Avengers #30
© Marvel Entertainment Group

SOLO AVENGERS
Dec., 1987
1 MBr,JRu,JLe,AW,Hawkeye;
  Mockingbird 4.00
2 MBr,JRu,KD,BMc,Hawkeye;
  Capt.Marvel 2.50
3 MBr,JRu,BH,SDr,Hawkeye;
  Moon Knight 2.50
4 RLm,JRu,PR,BL,Hawkeye;
  Black Knight 2.50
5 MBr,JRu,JRy,Hawkeye;
  Scarlet Witch 2.50
6 MBr,JRu,TGr,Hawkeye;Falcon . . 2.50
7 MBr,JG,BL,Hawkeye;Bl.Widow . . 2.50
8 MBr,Hawkeye;Dr.Pym 2.50
9 MBr,JBr,SDr,Hawkeye;Hellcat . . . 2.50
10 MBr,LW,Hawkeye;Dr.Druid 2.50
11 MBr,JG,BL,Hawkeye;Hercules . . 2.50
12 RLm,SDr,Hawkeye; New
  Yellow Jacket 2.50
13 RLm,JG,Hawkeye;WonderMan . . 2.50
14 AM,AD,JRu,Hawkeye;She-Hulk . 2.50
15 AM,Hawkeye;Wasp 2.50
16 AM,DP,JA,Hawkeye;
  Moondragon 2.50
17 AM,DH,DC,Hawkeye;
  Sub-Mariner 2.50
18 RW,DH,Hawkeye;Moondragon . . 2.50
19 RW,DH,Hawkeye,BlackPanther . . 2.50
20 RW,DH,Hawkeye;Moondragon . . 2.50
Becomes:

AVENGERS SPOTLIGHT

SOLOMON KANE
Sept., 1985
1 F:Solomon Kane 3.00
2 . . . . 3.00
3 BBl,Blades of the Brotherhood . . 3.00
4 MMi 3.00
5 Hills of the Dead 3.00
6 . . . . 3.00

SON OF SATAN
Dec., 1975–Feb., 1977
1 GK(c),JM,F:Daimon Hellstrom . . 32.00
2 Demon War,O:Possessor 20.00
3 . . . . 20.00
4 The Faces of Fear 15.00
5 V:Mind Star 15.00
6 A World Gone Mad 15.00

7 Mirror of Judgement 15.00
8 RH,To End in Nightmare 15.00

Soviet Super Soldiers #1
© Marvel Entertainment Group

SOVIET SUPER SOLDIERS
1 AMe,JS,I:Redmont 4 . . . . 2.25

SPACEKNIGHTS
Aug., 2000
1 (of 5) JSn,R:Spaceknights 3.00
2 JSn,Terminator. 3.00
3 JSn,Deathwings. 3.00
4 JSn,Wraith Knights 3.00
5 JSn,concl. 3.00

SPACEMAN
Atlas, Sept., 1953
1 BEv(c),F:Speed Carter and
   the Space Sentinals. 900.00
2 JMn,Trapped in Space. 600.00
3 BEv(c),JMn,V:Ice Monster. . . . 450.00
4 JMn, A-Bomb. 500.00
5 GT 450.00
6 JMn,Thing From Outer Space 450.00

SPACE SQUADRON
Atlas, June, 1951
1 AyB,F:Capt. Jet Dixon,Blast,
   Dawn,Revere,Rusty Blake . . 900.00
2 GT(c),. 750.00
3 Planet of Madness,GT. 600.00
4 . . . . 600.00
5 AyB 600.00
Becomes:

SPACE WORLDS
April, 1952
6 Midnight Horror 550.00

SPECIAL COLLECTOR'S EDITION
Dec., 1975
1 Kung-Fu,Iron Fist 10.00

SPECIAL MARVEL EDITION
Jan., 1971
1 JK,B:Thor,B:Reprints 45.00
2 JK,V:Absorbing Man 20.00
3 JK,While a Universe
   Trembles 20.00

4 JK,Hammer and the Holocaust,
   E:Thor 20.00
5 JSe(c),JK,DAy,B:Sgt. Fury 20.00
6 HT(c),DAy,Death Ray of
   Dr. Zemo 12.00
7 DAy,V:Baron Strucker 12.00
8 JSe(c),DAy,On To Okinawa 12.00
9 DAy,Crackdown-CaptainFlint . . . 12.00
10 DAy. 12.00
11 JK,DAy,A:Captain
   America & Bucky. 12.00
12 DAy,V:Baron Strucker 12.00
13 JK/DAy(c),DAy,SD,Too Small
   to Fight, Too Young To Die . . . 12.00
14 DAy,E:Reprints,Sgt. Fury 12.00
15 JSn,AM,I:Shang-Chi & Master of
   Kung Fu,I&O:Nayland Smith,
   Dr. Petrie 125.00
16 JSn,AM,I&O:Midnight 45.00
KingSz.Ann.#1 A:Iron Fist 18.00
Becomes:

MASTER OF KUNG FU

SPECTACULAR SCARLET SPIDER
1995
1 SB,BSz,Virtual Morality,pt.4. . . . 2.25
2 SB,BSz,CyberWar,pt.4. . . . . 2.25

SPECTACULAR SPIDER-MAN
(Magazine) July, 1968
1 JR,JM. 150.00
2 JR,JM,V:Green Goblin. 175.00

SPECTACULAR SPIDER-MAN
Dec., 1976
Prev: Peter Parker
134 SB,A:Sin-Eater,V:Electro 4.00
135 SB,A:Sin-Eater,V:Electro 3.00
136 SB,D:Sin-Eater,V:Electro 3.00
137 SB,I:Tarantula II 3.00
138 SB,A:Capt.A.,V:TarantulaII . . . 3.00
139 SB,O:Tombstone. 4.00
140 SB,A:Punisher,V:Tombstone. . . 3.50
141 SB,A:Punisher,V:Tombstone. . . 4.00
142 SB,A:Punisher,V:Tombstone. . . 4.00
143 SB,A:Punisher,D:Persuader,
   I:Lobo Brothers. 4.00
144 SB,V:Boomerang 3.00
145 SB,A:Boomerang 3.00
146 SB,R:Green Goblin 5.00
147 SB,V:Hobgoblin (Demonic
   Power) 10.00
148 SB,Inferno. 3.00
149 SB,V:Carrion II 5.00
150 SB,A:Tombstone,Trial
   J.Robertson 3.00
151 SB,V:Tombstone. 3.00
152 SB,O:Lobo Bros.,A:Punisher,
   Tombstone. 4.00
153 SB,V:Hammerhead,A:
   Tombstone. 3.00
154 SB,V:Lobo Bros.,Puma. 3.00
155 SB,V,Tombstone 3.00
156 SB,V:Banjo,A:Tombstone 3.00
157 SB,V:Shocker,Electro,
   A:Tombstone 3.00
158 SB,Super Spider Spec.,
   I:Cosmic Spider-Man 9.00
159 Cosmic Powers,V:Brothers
   Grimm 5.00
160 SB,A:Hydro Man,Shocker,
   Rhino,Dr.Doom 4.00

161 SB,V:Hobgoblin,Hammerhead,
   Tombstone. 3.00
162 SB,V:Hobgoblin,Carrion II. 3.00
163 SB,V:Hobgoblin,D:Carrion II . . . 3.00
164 SB,V:Beetle. 3.00
165 SB,SDr,D:Arranger,I:Knight
   & Fogg. 3.00
166 SB,O:Knight & Fogg 3.00
167 SB,D:Knight & Fogg 3.00
168 SB,A:Kingpin,Puma,
   Avengers 3.00
169 SB,I:Outlaws,A:R.Racer,
   Prowler,Puma,Sandman 3.00
170 SB,A:Avengers,Outlaws 3.00
171 SB,V:Puma 2.50
172 SB,V:Puma 2.50
173 SB,V:Puma 2.50
174 SB,A:Dr.Octopus. 2.50
175 SB,A:Dr.Octopus. 2.50
176 SB,I:Karona. 2.50
177 SB,V:Karona,A:Mr.Fantastic . . . 2.50
178 SB,B:Child Within,V:Green
   Goblin, A:Vermin 2.50
179 SB,V:Green Goblin,Vermin 2.50
180 SB,V:Green Goblin,Vermin 2.50
181 SB,V:Green Goblin 2.50
182 SB,V:Green Goblin 2.50
183 SB,V:Green Goblin 2.50
184 SB,E:Child Within,V:Green
   Goblin 2.50
185 SB,A:Frogman,White Rabbit. . . 2.50
186 SB,B:FuneralArrangements
   V:Vulture 2.50
187 SB,V:Vulture 2.50
188 SB,E:Funeral Arrangements
   V:Vulture 2.50
189 SB,30th Ann.,Hologram(c),
   V:Green Goblin 6.00
189a Gold 2nd printing 3.00
190 SB,V:Rhino,Harry Osborn. 2.50
191 SB,Eye of the Puma 2.50
192 SB,Eye of the Puma 2.50
193 SB,Eye of the Puma 2.50
194 SB,Death of Vermin#1 . . . . 2.50
195 SB,Death of Vermin#2 . . . . 4.00
195a Dirtbag Spec,w/Dirt#2 tape. . . 2.50
196 SB,Death of Vermin#3 . . . . 2.50
197 SB,A:X-Men,V:Prof.Power 2.50
198 SB,A:X-Men,V:Prof.Power 2.50
199 SB,A:X-Men,Green Goblin 2.50
200 SB,V:Green Goblin,D:Harry
   Osborn,Holografx(c) 4.00
201 SB,Total Carnage,V:Carnage,
   Shriek,A:Black Cat,Venom 2.50

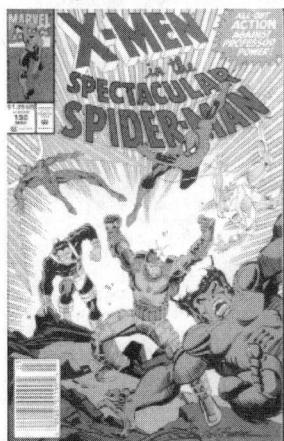

Spectacular Spider-Man #198
© Marvel Entertainment Group

Spectacular Spider-Man #263
© Marvel Entertainment Group

202 SB,Total Carnage#9,A:Venom,
    V:Carnage 2.50
203 SB,Maximum Carnage#13 . . . . 2.50
204 SB,A:Tombstone 2.50
205 StG(s),SB,V:Tombstone,
    A:Black Cat 2.50
206 SB,V:Tombstone 2.50
207 SB,A:The Shroud 2.50
208 SB,A:The Shroud 2.50
209 StB,SB,I:Dead Aim,
    BU:Black Cat 2.50
210 StB,SB,V:Dead Aim,
    BU:Black Cat 2.50
211 Pursuit#2,V:Tracer 2.50
212 . . . . 2.50
213 ANo(s),V:Typhiod Mary,w/cel . . 3.50
213a Newsstand Ed. 2.50
214 V:Bloody Mary. 2.50
215 V:Scorpion 2.50
216 V:Scorpion 2.50
217 V:Judas Traveller,clone 3.00
217a Foil(c),bonus stuff 5.00
218 V:Puma 2.50
219 Back from the Edge,pt.2 . . . . . 3.00
220 Web of Death,pt.3 . . . . 3.00
221 Web of Death,finale 3.00
222 The Price of Truth 2.50
223 Aftershocks,pt.4 . . . . 3.00
223a enhanced cover 3.00
224 The Mark of Kaine,pt.4 . . . . . . 2.50
225 SB,TDF,BSz,I:New Green
    Goblin, 48-pg. 3.00
225a 3-D HoloDisk Cover 5.00
226 SB,BSz,The Trial of Peter
    Parker,pt.4, identity revealed. . . 3.00
227 TDF,SB,BSz,Maximum
    Clonage,pt.5 . . . . 2.50
228 Timebomb,pt.1 . . . . 2.50
229 Greatest Responsibility,pt.3 . . . 3.00
229a Special cover 5.00
230 SB,Return of Spider-Man,pt.4 . . 2.50
231 SB,Return of Kaine,pt.1 . . . . . . 2.50
232 . . . . 2.50
233 SB,JP,Web of Carnage,pt.4 . . . 2.50
234 SB,Blood Brothers,pt.4 . . . . 2.50
235 . . . . 2.50
236 . . . . 2.50
237 V:Lizard 2.50
238 V:Lizard 2.50
239 V:Lizard 2.50
240 TDz,LRs,Book of Revelations,
    pt.1 (of 4) 3.00
241 Revelations epilogue 2.50
242 JMD,LRs,R:Chameleon,
    A:Kangaroo 2.50

243 JMD,LRs,R:Chameleon 2.50
244 JMD,LRs,V:Chameleon 2.50
245 JMD,LRs,V:Chameleon,
    A:Kangaroo 2.50
246 JMD,LRs,V:Kangaroo,Grizzly . . 2.50
247 JMD,LRs,F:JackO'Lantern,pt.1 . 2.50
248 JMD,LRs,DGr,F:Jack O'
    Lantern, pt.2 . . . . 2.50
249 JMD,LRs,DGr, Last Temptation
    of Flash Thompson 2.50
250 JR, V:Original Green Goblin,
    double gatefold cover 3.50
251 JMD,LRs,DGr,V:Kraven the
    Hunter 2.50
252 JMD,LRs,DGr,V:Norman
    Osborn. 2.50
253 JMD,LRs,DGr,V:Norman Osborn,
    Gibbon, Grizzly 2.50
254 JMD,LRs,DGr,V:Prof.Angst . . . 2.50
255 JMD,LRs,DGr,Spider-Hunt,pt.4
    x-over, double size 3.00
256 JMD,LRs,DGr,Identity Crisis
    prelude, A:Prodigy 2.50
257 JMD,LRs,DGr,Identity Crisis,
    as Prodigy, V:Conundrum 2.50
258 JMD,LRs,DGa,as Prodigy. 2.50
259 RSt,LRs,DGa,V:Hobgoblin 2.50
260 JR, RSt,LRs,DGa,Green Goblin
    vs. Hobgoblin. 2.50
261 RSt,LRs,AM,Goblins at the
    Gate,pt.3 . . . . 2.50
262 JBy, AM, LRs, The Gathering of
    the Five, pt.4 (of 5) x-over. 2.50
263 JBy,AM,LRs,The Final
    Chapter,pt.3 x-over 4.00
Ann.#8 MBa,RLm,TD,Evolutionary
    Wars,O:Gwen Stacy Clone 7.00
Ann.#9 DR,MG,DJu,MBa,Atlantis
    Attacks. 4.00
Ann.#10 SLi(c),RB,MM,TM,RA 6.00
Ann.#11 EL(c),RWi,Vib.Vendetta . . . 3.00
Ann.#12 Hero Killers#2,A:New
    Warriors,BU:Venom. 4.50
Ann.#13 I:Noctune,w/Card. 3.25
Ann.#14 V:Green Goblin 3.00
Super-Size Spec.#1 Planet of the
    Symbiotes,pt.4,64-pg.flip-book . 4.00
Minus 1 Spec., JMD,LRs,DGr,
    flashback, F:Flash Thompson . . 2.00
TPB rep. 80-pg. (2002) 13.00

SPECTACULAR
SPIDER-MAN
June, 2003

1 HuR,V:Venom,pt.1 . . . . 2.25
2 HuR,V:Venom,pt.2 . . . . 2.25
3 HuR,V:Venom,pt.3 . . . . 2.25
4 HuR,V:Venom,pt.4 . . . . 2.25
5 HuR,V:Venom,pt.5 . . . . 2.25
6 HuR,Countdown,pt.1,V:Doc Ock . 2.25
7 HuR,Countdown,pt.2 . . . . 2.25
8 HuR,Countdown,pt.3 . . . . 2.25
9 HuR,Countdown,pt.4 . . . . 2.25
10 HuR,Countdown,concl. 2.25
11 The Lizard's Tale,pt.1 . . . . 2.25
12 The Lizard's Tale,pt.2 . . . . 2.25
13 The Lizard's Tale,pt.3 . . . . 2.25
14 F:Morbius 2.25
15 F:Captain America 2.25
16 F:Captain America 2.25
17 Changes,pt.1. . . . . 2.25
18 Changes,pt.2. . . . . 2.25
19 Changes,pt.3. . . . . 2.25
20 Disassembled, tie-in,pt.4 . . . . . . 2.25
TPB Vol. 1: The Hunger. 12.00
TPB Vol. 2: Countdown 12.00
TPB Vol. 3: Here Be Monsters. . . . 11.00

SPEEDBALL
Sept., 1988

1 SD,JG,O:Speedball 2.50
2 SD,JG,V:Sticker,GraffitiGorillas . . 2.50
3 SD,V:Leaper Logan 2.50
4 SD,DA,Ghost Springdale High. . . 2.50
5 SD,V:Basher 2.50
6 SD,V:Bug-Eyed Voice 2.50
7 SD,V:Harlequin Hit Man. 2.50
8 SD,V:Bonehead Gang 2.50
9 SD,V:Nathan Boder 2.50
10 SD,V:Mutated Pigs,Killer
    Chickens, last issue. 2.50

Spellbound #3
© Marvel Entertainment Group

SPELLBOUND
Atlas, March, 1952

1 AyB(c),Step into my Coffin. . . . 900.00
2 BEv,RH,Horror Story,
    A:Edgar A. Poe 500.00
3 RH(c),OW 400.00
4 RH,Decapitation story 400.00
5 AyB,BEv,JM,Its in the Bag 400.00
6 AyB,BK,The Man Who Couldn't
    be Killed. 400.00
7 AyB,BEv,JMn,Don't Close
    the Door. 350.00
8 BEv(c),RH,JSt,DAy,
    The Operation 350.00
9 BEv(c),RH,The Death of
    Agatha Slurl. 350.00
10 AyB,BEv,RH,JMn(c),The Living
    Mummy 350.00
11 The Empty Coffin 275.00
12 RH,My Friend the Ghost 275.00
13 JM,AyB,The Dead Men. 275.00
14 BEv(c),RH,JMn,Close Shave . 275.00
15 AyB,CI,Get Out of my
    Graveyard 275.00
16 RH,BEv,JF,JSt,Behind
    the Door. 275.00
17 BEv(c),GC,BK,Goodbye
    Forever 275.00
18 BEv(c),JM 250.00
19 BEv(c),BP,Witch Doctor 250.00
20 RH(c),BP 250.00
21 RH(c). 225.00
22 . . . . 225.00
23 . . . . 225.00
24 JMn(c),JR 200.00
25 JO,AyB,Look into my Eyes . . . 200.00
26 JR,AyB,Things in the Box. 200.00
27 JMn,JR,AyB,Trap in the
    Mirage 200.00

28 BEv	200.00
29 JSe(c),SD	225.00
30 BEv(c)	200.00
31	200.00
32 BP,AyB,Almost Human	200.00
33 AT	200.00
34 June, 1957	200.00

SPELLBOUND
Jan., 1988
1 thru 5	2.50
6 double-size	3.00

SPIDER-GIRL
Aug., 1998
0 TDF,RF,BSz, cont. from What-If? #105, Peter & Mary Jane's daughter	5.00
1 TDF,PO,AW, F:Mayday Parker, V:Mr. Nobody	7.00
2 TDF,PO,AW,V:Crazy Eight & Darkdevil	4.00
2a variant cover	4.00
3 TDF,PO,AW,A:Fantastic Five	2.50
4 TDF,PO,AW,turning points	2.50
5 TDF,PO,AW,Ghosts of the Past	2.50
6 TDF,PO.AW,Majority Rules	2.50
7 TDF,PO.AW,Last Days of Spider-Man	2.50
8 TDF,PO,AW,A:Spider-Man, Uneasy Allies	2.50
8a autographed	20.00
9 TDF,PO,AW,Critical Choices	2.50
10 TDF,PO,AW,Incredible Journeys	2.50
11 TDF,PO.AW,V:Spider-Man	2.50
12 TDF,Po,AW,A:Darkdevil	2.50
13 TDF,Po,AW,Joins A-Next	2.50
14 TDF,PO,AW,Bloody Reunions x-over	2.50
15 TDF,PO,AW,A:Speedball	2.50
16 TDF,PO,AW	2.50
17 TDF,PO,AW,48-pg.	3.00
18 TDF,SB,RF,A:Buzz	2.50
19 TDF,AW,PO,V:A-Next foes	2.50
20 TDF,AW,PO,R:Green Goblin	2.50
21 TDF,AW,PO,V:Earthshaker	2.25
22 TDF,AW,PO,Darkdevil	2.25
23 TDF,AW,PO,Basketball	2.25
24 TDF,AW,PO,Dragonfist	2.25
25 TDF,AW,PO,Savage Six	3.50
26 TDF,AW,PO,Phil Urich	2.25
27 TDF,AW,PO,Parker/Osborn war concl.	2.25
28 TDF,AW,PO,V:Raptor	2.25
29 TDF,AW,PO,A:Nova	2.25
30 TDF,AW,PO,V:Avengers	2.25
31 TDF,AW,PO,V:Avengers	2.25
32 TDF,PO,Steel Spider	2.25
33 TDF,AW,PO,A:Spider-Man	2.25
34 TDF,AW,PO,A:Fant.Five	2.25
35 TDF,AW,PO,V:Canis	2.25
36 TDF,AW,PO,V:Canis	2.25
37 TDF,AW,PO,V:Green Goblin	2.25
38 TDF,AW,PO,V:Green Goblin	2.25
39 TDF,AW,PO,Green Goblin	2.25
40 TDF,AW,PO,Death in the family	2.25
41 TDF,AW,PO,V:Canis,'Nuff Said.	2.25
42 TDF,RF,mothers	2.25
43 TDF,AW,PO,original Spider-Man.	2.25
44 TDF,AW,PO,F:Ben Reilly	2.25
45 TDF,AW,PO,A:Big Brain,H.Torch	2.25
46 TDF,AW,PO,F:Fantastic Five	2.25
47 TDF,RF,V:Apox,+ Chapter 1	2.25
48 TDF,AW,PO,Spider-Man,Kaine.	2.25
49 TDF,AW,PO,V:Green Goblin	2.25
50 TDF,AW,PO,48-pg.	4.00
51 CJ	2.25
52 TDF,AW,RF	2.25
53 TDF,AW,PO	2.25
54 TDF,AW,PO,Serpent,pt.1	2.25

55 TDF,AW,PO,Serpent,pt.2	2.25
56 TDF,AW,PO,Serpent,pt.3	2.25
57 TDF,AW,PO,Serpent,pt.4	2.25
58 TDF,AW,PO,Serpent,pt.5	2.25
59 TDF,RF,Serpent,pt.6	3.00
60 TDF,RF,finale	3.00
61 TDF,RF,Marked for Death,pt.1	3.00
62 TDF,RF,Marked for Death,pt.2	3.00
63 TDF,RF,Marked for Death,pt.3	3.00
64 TDF,RF,Marked for Death,pt.4	3.00
65 TDF,RF,Marked for Death,pt.5	3.00
66 TDF,RF,Marked for Death,pt.6	3.00
67 TDF,RF,Monsters	3.00
68 TDF,RF,The Rules	3.00
69 TDF,RF,Truth,pt.1	3.00
70 TDF,RF,Truth,pt.2	3.00
71 TDF,RF,F:Doc Magus	3.00
72 TDF,RF,Whispers in the Night	3.00
73 TDF,RF,PO,F:Claw,the Cat	3.00
74 TDF,RF,PO,F:Claw,the Cat	3.00
75 TDF,RF,Team Spider	3.00
76 TDF,RF,Spider-Girl Must Die.	3.00
77 TDF,RF,Betrayed	3.00
78 TDF,RF,People Played by Games	3.00
79 RF,If this be my destiny	3.00
Ann.#1 TDF,PO,AW,A:Green Goblin	6.00
TPB rep. #1 & #2	10.00
TPB Spider-Girl,208-page	20.00
Digest Marvel Age, Vol. 1	8.00

SPIDER-GIRL PRESENTS: THE BUZZ
May, 2000
1 (of 3) TDF,RF,SB	3.00
2 TDF,RF,SB,A:Spider-Girl	3.00
3 TDF,RF,SB,Dr.Jade	3.00

SPIDER-GIRL PRESENTS: DARKDEVIL
Sept., 2000
1 (of 3) TDF,RF,AM,Kingpin	3.00
2 TDF,RF,AM,O:Darkdevil	3.00
3 TDF,RF,AM, concl	3.00

Spider-Man #57
© *Marvel Entertainment Group*

SPIDER-MAN
Aug., 1990
1 TM Purple Web(c),V:Lizard, A:Calypso,B:Torment	5.00
1a Silver Web(c)	6.00

1b Bag,Purple Web	9.00
1c Bag,Silver Web	20.00
1d 2nd print,Gold(c)	5.00
1e 2nd print Gold UPC(rare)	125.00
1f Platinum Ed.	100.00
2 TM,V:Lizard,A:Calypso	6.00
3 TM,V:Lizard,A:Calypso	6.00
4 TM,V:Lizard,A:Calypso	6.00
5 TM,V:Lizard,A:Calypso, E:Torment	6.00
6 TM,A:Ghost Rider,V:Hobgoblin	6.00
7 TM,A:Ghost Rider,V:Hobgoblin	6.00
8 TM,B:Perceptions,A:Wolverine I:Wendigo IV	6.00
9 TM,A:Wolverine,Wendigo	7.00
10 TM,RLd,SW,JLe(i),A:Wolv.	7.00
11 TM,A:Wolverine,Wendigo	7.00
12 TM,E:Perceptions,A:Wolv.	7.00
13 TM,V:Morbius,R:Black Cost.	6.00
14 TM,V:Morbius,A:Black Cost.	6.00
15 EL,A:Beast	5.00
16 TM,RLd,A:X-Force,V:Juggernaut, Black Tom,cont.in X-Force#4	6.00
17 RL,AW,A:Thanos,Death	4.00
18 EL,B:Return of the Sinister Six, A:Hulk	4.00
19 EL,A:Hulk,Deathlok	4.00
20 EL,A:Nova	4.00
21 EL,A:Hulk,Deathlok,Solo.	4.00
22 EL,A:Ghost Rider,Hulk	4.00
23 EL,E:Return of the Sinister Six, A:Hulk,G.Rider,Deathlok,FF.	4.00
24 Infinity War,V:Hobgoblin, Demogoblin	4.00
25 CMa,A:Excalibur,V:Arcade	4.00
26 RF,MBa,Hologram(c),30th Anniv. I:New Burglar.	5.00
27 MR,Handgun issue	3.00
28 MR,Handgun issue	3.00
29 CMa,Ret.to Mad Dog Ward#1	3.00
30 CMa,Ret.to Mad Dog Ward#2	3.00
31 CMa,Ret.to Mad Dog Ward#3	3.00
32 BMc,A:Punisher,V:Master of Vengeance	3.00
33 BMc,A:Punisher,V:Master of Vengeance	3.00
34 BMc,A:Punisher,V:Master of Vengeance	3.00
35 TL,Total Carnage#4,V:Carnage, Shriek,A:Venom,Black Cat	3.00
36 TL,Total Carnage#8,V:Carnage, A:Venom,Morbius	3.00
37 TL,Total Carnage#12, V:Carnage	3.00
38 thru 40 KJ,V:Electro	3.00
41 TKa(s),JaL,I:Platoon, A:Iron Fist	3.00
42 TKa(s),JaL,V:Platoon, A:Iron Fist	3.00
43 TKa(s),JaL,V:Platoon, A:Iron Fist	3.00
44 HMe(s),TL,V:Hobgoblin	3.00
45 HMe(s),TL,SHa,Pursuit#1, V:Chameleon	2.50
46 HMe(s),TL,V:Hobgoblin,w/cel	3.25
46a Newsstand Ed.	2.25
47 TL,SHa,V:Demogoblin	2.50
48 TL,SHa,V:Hobgoblin, D:Demogoblin	2.50
49 TL,SHa,I:Coldheart	2.50
50 TL,SHa,I:Grim Hunter,foil(c)	5.00
50a newsstand ed.	2.50
51 TL,SHa,Power,pt.3,foil(c)	4.00
51a newsstand ed.	2.50
52 TL,SHa,Spide-clone,V:Venom	2.50
53 TL,SHa,Clone,V:Venom	2.50
54 Web of Life,pt.3	3.00
55 Web of Life,finale	2.50
56 Smoke and Mirrors	2.50
57 Aftershocks,pt.1	2.50
57a enhanced cover	3.00

58 The Mark of Kaine,pt.3 . . . . 2.50
59 F:Travellor,Host. 2.50
60 TL,SHa,HMa,The Trial of
Peter Parker,pt.3. . . . . 2.50
61 TL,Maximum Clonage,pt.4 . . . . . 2.50
62 HMe,TL,Exiled,pt.3 . . . . 2.50
63 HMe,TL,Greatest
Responsibility,pt.2 . . . . 2.50
64 HMe,JR2,Return of
Spider-Man,pt.3 . . . . 2.50
65 HMe,JR2,AW,Media
Blizzard,pt.3. . . . . 2.50
66 HMe,JR2,Return of Kaine,pt.4 . . 2.50
67 HMe,JR2,Web of Carnage,pt.3. . 2.50
68 HMe,JR2,AW,Blood
Brothers,pt.3 . . . . 2.50
69 HMe,JR2,Blood Brothers
aftermath 2.50
70 HMe,JR2,A:Onslaught 3.00
71 HMe,JR2, ... 3.00
72 HMe,JR2,Onslaught saga. 3.00
73 HMe,JR2, ... 3.00
74 HMe,JR2,AW,A:Daredevil,
V:Fortunato 3.00
75 HMe,JR2,Revelations, pt.4 . . . . . 3.50
76 HMe,JR2,SHa,Post-Onslaught
world,I:Shoc. 2.50
77 HMe,JR2,SHa,V:Morbius 2.50
Becomes:

PETER PARKER, SPIDER-MAN
78 HMe,JR2,SHa,F:Mary Jane
Parker 2.50
79 HMe,JR2,SHa,V:Hydra,A:Captain
Arthur Stacy. 2.50
80 HMe,JR2,SHa,V:S.H.O.C. 2.50
81 HMe,JR2,SHa,V:Shang-Chi,pt.1. 2.50
82 HMe,JR2,SHa,Anti-Mutant
Movement 2.50
83 HMe,JR2,SHa,V:Morbius 2.50
85 HMe,JR2,SHa,V:Friends of
Humanity. 2.50
86 HMe,JR2,SHa,F:Jimmy Six,
Hammerhead. 2.50
87 HMe,JR2,SHa,A:Trapster &
Shocker. 2.50
88 HMe,JR2,SHa,Spider-Man is
Public Enemy #1 . . . . 2.50
89 HMe,JR2,SHa,Spider-Hunt,pt.3
x-over. 3.00
90 HMe,JR2,SHa,Identity Crisis
prelude. 2.50
91 HMe,JR2,SHa,Identity Crisis,
as Dusk 2.50
92 HMe,JR2,as Dusk, V:Trapster . . 2.50
93 HMe,JS,R:Ghost Rider 2.50
94 HMe,JR2,SHa,Who wasJoeyZ?. 2.50
95 HMe,JR2,SHa,Trapped in
elevator shaft. 2.50
96 HMe,JR2,SHa,The Gathering of
the Five (pt. 3 (of 5)x-over. 2.50
97 HMe,JR2,SHa,JBy(c),The Final
Chapter,pt.2 x-over 2.50
98 HMe,JR2,SHa,JBy(c),The Final
Chapter,pt.4 x-over 2.50
98a alternate JBy(c) (1:2) 2.50
Minus 1 Spec., HMe,JR2,SHa,
flashback, A:Stacys 2.50
Ann.'97 Simon Garth—Zombie . . . 3.50
Ann.'98 HMe, Spider-Man/Elektra,
V:The Silencer, 48-pg. 3.00
Spec. Chaos in Calgary 2.50
Spec. Double Trouble 2.50
Spec. Hit and Run, Canadian 2.50
Spec. Skating on Thin Ice 2.50
Spec. Trial of Venom,UNICEF 15.00
Spec.#1 Spider-Man (2000). 3.00
Spec. Spider-Man vs. Punisher . . . 3.00
Spec. Year in Review(1999)48-pg. . 3.00
Holiday Spec.'95 . . . . 3.00

Sup.Sz.Spec#1 Planet of the
Symbiotes, pt.2;
flipbook F:Scarlet Spider 4.00
Giant-Sized CCI,JBy 4.00
1-shot Spider-Man Startling Stories:
Megalomaniacal Spider-Man. . . 3.00
Spec.#1 Spider-Man/Daredevil 3.00
GN Fear Itself 13.00
GN Nothing Stops Juggernaut. . . . 4.00
GN Parallel Lives. 13.00
GN JMD,MZ,Soul of the Hunter. . . 6.00
GN Spider-Man: Made Men
HMe,gangster epic (1998). 6.00
GN Spider-Man ParallelLives(2002) 6.00
GN Sweet Charity,Scorpion,64-pg. . 5.00
TPB Assasination Plot 15.00
TPB Carnage. 7.00
TPB Cosmic Adventures 20.00
TPB Death of Gwen Stacy. 15.00
TPB Hooky. 7.00
TPB Identity Crisis 20.00
TPB Maximum Carnage 25.00
TPB Origin of the Hobgoblin 15.00
TPB Return of the Sinister Six. . . . 16.00
TPB Spider-Man: Revelations,JR2,
rep. +14 new pages (1997). . . 12.00
TPB Round Robin 16.00
TPB Saga of the Alien Costume . . 14.00
2nd printing 13.00
TPB Spider-Man vs. Venom 10.00
TPB Torment Rep.#1–#5 . . . . 13.00
TPB Venom Returns 13.00
TPB Very Best of Spider-Man 16.00
TPB The Wedding 13.00
TPB Invasion Spider Slayers. 16.00
TPB Clone Genesis 17.00
TPB V:Green Goblin 16.00
TPB Spider-Man'sGreatestVillains. 16.00
TPB Spider-Man vs. Doc Oc 18.00
TPB Kraven's Last Hunt (2001). . . 16.00
TPB Torment,128-page (2001) . . . 16.00
TPB Death of Gwen Stacy (2001). 15.00
TPB Visionaries: Todd McFarlane . 20.00
TPB Revenge of the Green Goblin 17.00
TPB Spider-Man: The Wedding. . . 16.00
TPB Kraven's Last Hunt 16.00
TPB Death of Gwen Stacy, rep. . . 13.00
TPB Legends (2003) 20.00
TPB Legends, Vol.3. . . . . 25.00
TPB Legends, Vol.4. . . . . 14.00
TPB Death of Captain Stacy 13.00
TPB Son of the Goblin 16.00

SPIDER-MAN ADVENTURES
1994–96
1 From animated series 2.25
1a foil (c). 3.00
2 Animated Adventures. 2.25
3 V:Spider-Slayer 2.25
4 Animated Adventures 2.25
5 V:Mysterio 2.25
6 V:Kraven 2.25
7 V:Doctor Octopus 2.25
8 O:Venom,pt.1. . . . . 2.25
9 O:Venom,pt.2. . . . . 2.25
10 V:Venom 2.25
11 V:Hobgoblin. 2.25
12 V:Hobgoblin 2.25
13 V:Chameleon 2.25
14 V:Doc Octopus 2.25
15 Doc Conners. 2.25
TPB Rep.#1–#5, 112-pg. 9.00

SPIDER-MAN & AMAZING FRIENDS
Dec., 1981
1 DSp,A:Iceman,I:Firestar. 10.00

Spider-Man Adventures #1
© Marvel Entertainment Group

SPIDER-MAN & WOLVERINE
June, 2003
1 (of 4) Stuff of Legends. 3.00
2 . . . . 3.00
3 . . . . 3.00
4 concl. 3.00

SPIDER-MAN/BADROCK
Marvel/Maximum Press 1997
1 x-over, pt.1. . . . . 3.00
2 x-over, pt. 2 . . . . 3.00

SPIDER-MAN/BATMAN
1995
1 JMD,MBa,MFm,V:Carnage,Joker 6.00

SPIDER-MAN/BLACK CAT: THE EVIL THAT MEN DO
June, 2002
1 (of 5) KSm,TyD 3.00
2 KSm,TyD 3.00
3 KSm,TyD 3.00
4 KSm,TyD,concl. 3.00
5 KSm,TyD,concl.,pt.2 . . . . 3.00

SPIDER-MAN: BLUE
May, 2002
1 (of 6) JLb,TSe,Green Goblin 5.00
2 JLb,TSe,Gwen Stacy,Rhino. 4.00
3 JLb,TSe,Gwen & Mary Jane 4.00
4 JLb,TSe,college years. 4.00
5 JLb,TSe, ... 4.00
6 JLb,TSe,concl. 4.00
TPB 15.00

SPIDER-MAN, CHAPTER 1
Oct., 1998
1 (of 13) JBy,formative years 2.50
1a signed 20.00
2 JBy,A:Fantastic Four 2.50
2a variant JBy cover. 5.00
2b signed, both covers 30.00
3 JBy,V:J.Jonah Jameson. 2.50
4 JBy,V:Dr.Octopus & Dr.Doom . . . 2.50
5 JBy,V:Lizard. 2.50
6 JBy,V:Electro 2.50
7 JBy,V:Mysterio 2.50

8 JBy,V:Green Goblin 2.50
9 JBy,V:Circus of Crime 2.50
10 JBy,V:Green Goblin 2.50
11 JBy,V:Giant-Man 2.50
12 JBy,V:Sandman, double size
  final issue 4.00
Spec.#0 JBy,O:Sandman,Vulture
  & Lizard 2.50

SPIDER-MAN CLASSICS
1993–94
1 rep.Amazing Fantasy#15 . . . . . . 2.50
2 thru 14 rep.Amaz.SpM . . . . . . @2.50
15 rep.Amaz.SpM#14,w/cel 3.25
15a Newsstand Ed. 2.50

SPIDER-MAN
COMICS MAGAZINE
Jan., 1987
1 . . . . 7.00
2 thru 13 . . . . @6.00

SPIDER-MAN:
DEAD MAN'S HAND
1997
1-shot, RSt,DaR,JeM,V:Carrion . . . 3.00

SPIDER-MAN:
DEATH & DESTINY
June, 2000
1 (of 3) LW,RCa,F:Gwen Stacy 3.00
2 LW,RCa,Doctor Octopus 3.00
3 LW,RCa,concl. 3.00
Spec.Death of Gwen Stacy,64-pg.
  rep. of Amaz.Sp-M #88–#90 . . . 3.50

SPIDER-MAN/
DOCTOR OCTOPUS:
OUT OF REACH
2004
1 (of 5) 3.00
2 thru 5 concl. . . . . @3.00
Digest. 8.00

SPIDER-MAN/DOCTOR
OCTOPUS: YEAR ONE
June, 2004
1 (of 5) First battle 3.00
2 thru 5 concl. . . . . @3.00

SPIDER-MAN:
THE FINAL ADVENTURE
1995–96
1 FaN,DaR,Clv,I:Tendril 3.00
2 FaN,DaR,JAl,V:Tendril 3.00
3 FaN,DaR,JAl,V:Tendril 3.00
4 FaN,DaR,JAl,V:Tendril,concl.. . . . 3.00

SPIDER-MAN:
FRIENDS AND ENEMIES
1995
1 V:Metahumes 2.00
2 A:Nova,Darkhawk,Speedball 2.00
3 V:Metahumes. 2.00
4 F:Metahumes. 2.00

SPIDER-MEN: FUNERAL
FOR AN OCTOPUS
1995
1 Doc Oc Dead. 2.50

2 A:Sinister Six 2.00
3 Final Issue 2.00

SPIDER-MAN/GEN13
Marvel/Wildstorm 1996
1-shot PDd,SI,CaS x-over 5.00

Spider-Man Hobgoblin Lives #3
© Marvel Entertainment Group

SPIDER-MAN:
HOBGOBLIN LIVES
1997
1 (of 3) RSt,RF,GP 2.50
2 RSt,RF,GP,Who was the original
  Hobgoblin? 2.50
3 RSt,RF,GP,Original identity
  revealed. 2.50
TPB RF(c), series rep. 15.00

SPIDER-MAN & THE
INCREDIBLE HULK
A.C.T.O.R./Marvel Epic, 2003
1-shot benefit issue 2.50

SPIDER-MAN:
GET KRAVEN
June, 2002
1 (of 7) F:Alyosha Kravinoff 3.00
2 wants to make a movie 2.25
3 JQ(c) 2.25
4 JQ(c) 2.25
5 JQ(c) 2.25
6 JQ(c) 2.25

SPIDER-MAN: LEGEND
OF THE SPIDER-CLAN
Marvel Mangaverse Oct., 2002
1 (of 3) 2.25
2 F:Manga Daredevil 2.25
3 F:Manga Green Govlin 2.25
4 . . . . 2.25
5 concl. 2.25

SPIDER-MAN: LIFELINE
Feb., 2001
1 (of 3) FaN,SR,BWi, ... 3.00
2 FaN,SR,BWi,V:Hammerhead . . . 3.00
3 FaN,SR,BWi,concl. 3.00

Spider-Man The Manga #20
© Marvel Entertainment Group

SPIDER-MAN:
THE MANGA
Black & White, Oct., 1997
Bi-weekly
1 imported, translated 4.00
2 thru 14 . . . . @3.00
15 V:Mysterio, double size. 4.00
16 thru 37 . . . . @3.00

SPIDER-MAN:
MAXIMUM CLONAGE
1995
Alpha Maximum Clonage,pt.1 . . . . . 5.50
Omega TL,Maximum Clonage,pt.6 . 4.95

SPIDER-MAN MEGAZINE
1994–95
1 thru 4 rep.. . . . . @3.00
5 Vision rep. 3.00
6 V:Thing & Torch, rep. 3.00

SPIDER-MAN: THE MOVIE
April, 2002
GN StL,AD,photo(c), 48-pg. 5.95
TPB movie + stories, 112-pg. 12.95

SPIDER-MAN 2:
THE MOVIE
June, 2004
1-shot 48-pg. 3.50
TPB The Movie 13.00

SPIDER-MAN:
MUTANT AGENDA
0 thru 2 Paste in Book . . . . @2.25
3 Paste in Book 2.25

SPIDER-MAN: THE
MYSTERIO MANIFESTO
Nov., 2000
1 (of 3) TDF,BMc,LW 3.00
2 TDF,BMc,LW 3.00
3 TDF,BMc,LW,concl. 3.00

SPIDER-MAN: POWER OF TERROR
1995
1 R:Silvermane,A:Deathlok. 2.25
2 V:Silvermane 2.25
3 New Scorpion 2.25
4 V:Silvermane 2.25

SPIDER-MAN/PUNISHER
Part 1 TL,A:Tombstone 3.00
Part 2 TL,A:Tombstone 3.00

SPIDER-MAN/PUNISHER/ SABERTOOTH: DESIGNER GENES
1 SMc,Foil(c). 9.50

SPIDER-MAN: QUALITY OF LIFE
May, 2002
1 (of 4) V:The Lizard, 40-pg. 3.00
2 the Yith. 3.00
3 V:The Lizard 3.00
4 concl 3.00
TPB series rep. 13.00

SPIDER-MAN: REDEMPTION
1996
1 thru 4 JMD,MZ,BMc, Mary Jane
   arrested for Murder . . . . @2.25

SPIDER-MAN: REVENGE OF THE GREEN GOBLIN
Aug., 2000
1 (of 3) RCa,LW,RSt,R:Norman
   Osborn. 3.00
2 LW,RSt,F:Norman Osborn 3.00
3 RSt,RF,PO, concl. 3.00

SPIDER-MAN SAGA
Nov., 1991
1 SLi(c),History from Amazing
   Fantasy #15-Amaz.SpM #100. . 3.25
2 SLi(c),Amaz.SpM #101-#175. . . . 3.25
3 Amaz.SpM #176-#238 . . . . 3.25
4 Amaz.SpM #239-#300 . . . . 3.25

SPIDER-MAN SUPER SIZE SPECIAL
1 Planet of the Symbiotes,pt.2 . . . . 3.95

SPIDER-MAN TEAM-UP
1995–96
1 MWa,KeL,V:Hellfire Club 3.00
2 thru 4 . . . . @3.00
5 SvG,DaR,JFr,F:Gambit,
   Howard the Duck. 3.00
6 JMD,LHa,F:Hulk & Doctor
   Strange 3.00
7 KBk,SB,F:Thunderbolts 3.00

SPIDER-MAN: THE ARACHNIS PROJECT
1984–95
1 Wld, beginnings. 2.25
2 Wld,V:Diggers 2.25
3 Wld,V:Jury 2.25
4 Wld,V:Life Foundation 2.25
5 Wld,V:Jury 2.25

SPIDER-MAN: THE CLONE JOURNALS
1-shot (1995) 2.25

SPIDER-MAN: THE JACKAL FILES
1 Files of the Jackal (1995) 2.25

SPIDER-MAN: THE LOST YEARS
1995
0 JMD,JR2,LSh,64-pg.,rep. 4.00
1 History of Kaine,Ben 3.00
2 JMD,JR2,KJ,Kaine & Ben 3.00
3 Ben vs. Kaine 3.00

SPIDER-MAN: THE PARKER YEARS
1995
1 JR2,JPi,F:The Real Clone. 2.50

SPIDER-MAN 2099
1992–96
1 RL,AW,I:Spider-Man 2099 . . . . . . 4.00
2 RL,AW,O:Spider-Man 2099 . . . . 3.00
3 RL,AW,V:Venture 2.50
4 RL,AW,I:Specialist,
   A:Doom 2099 . . . . 2.25
5 RL,AW,V:Specialist 2.25
6 RL,AW,I:New Vulture 2.25
7 RL,AW,Vulture of 2099 . . . . 2.25
8 RL,AW,V:New Vulture 2.25
9 KJo,V:Alchemax. 2.25
10 RL,AW,O:Wellvale Home 2.25
11 RL,AW,V:S.I.E.G.E. 2.25
12 RL,AW,w/poster 2.25
13 RL,AW,V:Thanatos 2.25
14 PDd(s),RL(c),TGb,Downtown . . 2.25
15 PDd(s),RL,I:Thor 2099,
   Heimdall 2099 . . . . 2.25
16 PDd(s),RL,Fall of the
   Hammer #1 . . . . 2.25
17 PDd(s),RL,V:Bloodsword 2.25
18 PDd(s),RLm,V:Lyla 2.25
19 PDd(s),RL,w/card 2.25
20 PDd(s),RL,Crash & Burn 2.25
21 V:Gangs 2.25
22 V:Gangs 2.25
23 RL,I:Risque 3.00

Spider-Man 2099 #42
© *Marvel Entertainment Group*

24 Kasey 2.25
25 A:Hulk 2099, dbl-size,foil(c) 4.00
25a Newsstand ed. 2.50
26 V:Headhunter, Travesty 2.25
27 V:Travesty. 2.25
28 V:Travesty. 2.25
29 V:Foragers 2.25
30 V:Flipside 2.25
31 I:Dash 2.25
Becomes:

SPIDER-MAN 2099 A.D.
32 I:Morgue 2.25
33 One Nation Under Doom 2.25
34 V:Alchemex. 2.25
35 . . . . 2.25
36a Spider-Man 2099(c) 2.25
36b Venom 2099(c) 2.25
37a Venom 2099 . . . . 2.25
37b variant cover 2.25
38 . . . . 2.25
39 A:Venom 2099 . . . . 2.25
40 V:Goblin 2099 . . . . 2.25
41 and 42. . . . . @2.25
43 V:Sub-Mariner 2099 . . . . 2.25
Ann.#1 PDd(s),RL 3.00
Spec.#1 I:3 new villains 4.00

SPIDER-MAN UNLIMITED
1993
1 RLm,Maximun Carnage #1,
   I:Shriek,R:Carnage 5.00
2 RLm,Maximum Carnage #14. . . . 4.50
3 RLm,O:Doctor Octopus 4.50
4 RLm,V:Mysrterio,Rhino 4.25
5 RLm,A:Human Torch,
   I:Steel Spider 4.25
6 RLm,A:Thunderstrike. 4.25
7 RLm,A:Clone 4.25
8 Tom Lyle. 4.25
9 The Mark of Kaine,pt.5 . . . . 4.25
10 SwM,Exiled,pt.4 . . . . 4.25
11 FaN,V:Black Cat 4.25
12 Blood Brother,tie-in 4.25
13 . . . . 3.25
14 JoB, an ally dies 3.25
15 TDF,JoB,F:Puma. 3.25
16 cont. from X-Force #64. . . . . . . 3.25
17 JoB, Revelations, sequel 3.25
18 TDF,JoB,F:Doctor Octopus. . . . 3.25
19 JoB,F:Lizard 3.25
20 JoB,A:Hannibal King, V:Lilith . . . 3.25
21 MD2,Frankenstein Monster Lives 3.25
22 MD2,V:The Scorpion. 3.25

SPIDER-MAN UNLIMITED
Nov., 1999
1 cartoon, tie-in. 3.50
2 thru 4 . . . . @2.25

SPIDER-MAN UNLIMITED
Jan., 2004
1 V:Slyde. 3.00
2 F:Mary Jane. 3.00
3 Preventive Medicine 3.00
4 true love. 3.00
5 hostage crisis. 3.00

SPIDER-MAN UNIVERSE
Jan., 2000
1 rep. 3 stories, 80-pg. 5.00
2 thru 6 rep. 3 stories, 80-pg. . . . @5.00
7 thru 9 rep. 3 stories, 80-pg . . . @4.00

SPIDER-MAN UNMASKED
1996
1-shot 64-pg. information source . . 6.00

SPIDER-MAN VS. DRACULA
1994
1 rep......................... 2.25

SPIDER-MAN VS. VENOM
1990
1 TM(c) 8.95

SPIDER-MAN: THE VENOM AGENDA
Nov., 1997
1-shot LHa,TL, J. Jonah Jameson,
V:Venom 3.00

SPIDER-MAN VS. WOLVERINE
1990
1 MBr,AW,D:Ned Leeds(the original
Hobgoblin),V:Charlie 25.00
1a reprint................... 5.00

SPIDER-MAN: WEB OF DOOM
1994
1 3-part series............... 2.25
2 Spidey falsely accused 2.25
3 conclusion 2.25

SPIDER-MAN & X-FACTOR: SHADOW GAMES
1 PB,I:Shadowforce 2.25
2 PB,V:Shadowforce........... 2.25
3 PB,V:Shadowforce, final issue... 2.25

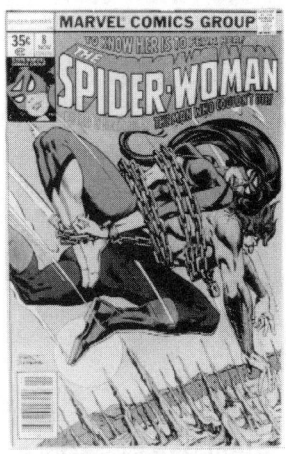

Spider-Woman #8
© Marvel Entertainment Group

SPIDER-WOMAN
April, 1978
1 CI,TD,O:Spider-Woman....... 25.00
2 CI,TD,I:Morgan LeFey........ 6.00
3 CI,TD,I:Brothers Grimm........ 6.00
4 CI,TD,V:Hangman 6.00
5 CI,TD,Nightmares 6.00
6 CI,A:Werewolf By Night........ 7.00
7 CI,SL,AG,V:Magnus........... 6.00
8 CI,AG,Man Who Would Not Die . 6.00

9 CI,AG,A:Needle,Magnus 6.00
10 CI,AG,I:Gypsy Moth 6.00
11 CI,AG,V:Brothers Grimm....... 6.00
12 CI,AG,V:Brothers Grimm....... 6.00
13 CI,AG,A:Shroud............. 6.00
14 BSz(c),CI,AG,A:Shroud....... 6.00
15 BSz(c),CI,AG,A:Shroud....... 6.00
16 BSz(c),CI,AG,V:Nekra........ 6.00
17 CI,Death Plunge 6.00
18 CI,A:Flesh 6.00
19 CI,A:Werewolf By Night,
V:Enforcer 7.00
20 FS,A:Spider-Man 7.00
21 FS,A:Bounty Hunter 6.00
22 FS,A:Killer Clown 6.00
23 TVE,V:The Gamesmen........ 6.00
24 TVE,V:The Gamesmen........ 6.00
25 SL,Two Spider-Women........ 6.00
26 JBy(c),SL,V:White Gardenia.... 6.00
27 BSz(c),JBi,A:Enforcer........ 6.00
28 BSz(c),SL,A:Enforcer,Spidey ... 7.00
29 JR2(c),ECh,FS,A:Enforcer,
Spider-Man 7.00
30 FM(c),SL,JM,I:Dr.Karl Malus.... 6.00
31 FM(c),SL,JM,A:Hornet 6.00
32 FM(c),SL,JM,A:Werewolf 6.00
33 SL,V:Yesterday's Villain 6.00
34 SL,AM,V:Hammer and Anvil 6.00
35 SL,AG,V:Angar the Screamer... 6.00
36 SL,Spider-Woman Shot 6.00
37 SL,TA,BWi,AM,FS,A:X-Men,I:
Siryn,V:Black Tom 8.00
38 SL,BWi,A:X-Men,Siryn 8.00
39 SL,BWi,Shadows 5.00
40 SL,BWi,V:The Flying Tiger 5.00
41 SL,BWi,V:Morgan LeFay 5.00
42 SL,BWi,V:Silver Samurai 5.00
43 SL,V:Silver Samurai 5.00
44 SL,V:Morgan LeFay 5.00
45 SL,Spider-Man Thief cover 5.00
46 SL,V:Mandroids,A:Kingpin 5.00
47 V:Daddy Longlegs............ 5.00
48 O:Gypsy Moth............... 5.00
49 A:Tigra.................... 5.00
50 PH(c),D:Spider-Woman 15.00

[Limited Series] 1993–94
1 V:Therak 2.25
2 O:Spider-Woman 2.25
3 V:Deathweb 2.25
4 V:Deathweb, last issue 2.25

SPIDER-WOMAN
May, 1999
1 JBy,BS,48-pg. 3.00
1a signed 20.00
2 BS,JBy,A:Dr. Octopus 2.00
2a variant JR2 cover............ 2.00
3 BS,JBy,V:Flesh & Bones 2.00
4 BS,JBy,V:Flesh & Bones 2.00
5 BS,JBy,I:Shadowcaster 2.00
6 BS,JBy,V:Shadowcaster 2.00
7 BS,JBy.................... 2.00
8 BS,JBy,A:Cluster,x-over........ 2.00
9 BS,JBy,A:Mattie.............. 2.00
10 BS,JBy,A:Rhino.............. 2.00
11 BS,JBy,V:Exomorph 2.00
12 BS,JBy,F:J.Jonah Jameson 2.25
13 BS,JBy,V:Werewolf 2.25
14 JBy,GN,BS(c),V:Nighteyes 2.25
15 JBy,BS,Itch & Scratch......... 2.25
16 JBy,BS,Flesh................ 2.25
17 JBy,BS,Flesh & Bones 2.25
18 JBy,BS,final issue 2.25

SPIDEY AND THE MINI MARVELS
April, 2003
Spec. Bullpen bits, 40-pg. 3.50

Spidey Super Stories #12
© Marvel Entertainment Group

SPIDEY SUPER STORIES
Oct., 1974
1 Younger reader's series in
association with the Electric
Company,O:Spider-Man 50.00
2 A:Kraven 30.00
3 A:Ringleader 20.00
4 A:Medusa 20.00
5 A:Shocker 20.00
6 A:Iceman 20.00
7 A:Lizard, Vanisher 20.00
8 A:Dr. Octopus 20.00
9 A:Dr. Doom 20.00
10 A:Green Goblin 20.00
11 A:Dr. Octopus 18.00
12 A:The Cat,V:The Owl 18.00
13 A:Falcon 18.00
14 A:Shanna 18.00
15 A:Storm 20.00
16 .... 18.00
17 A:Captain America 18.00
18 A:Kingpin................. 18.00
19 A:Silver Surfer,Dr. Doom...... 18.00
20 A:Human Torch,Invisible Girl .. 18.00
21 A:Dr. Octopus 16.00
22 A:Ms. Marvel,The Beetle...... 16.00
23 A:Green Goblin 16.00
24 A:Thundra 16.00
25 A:Dr. Doom 16.00
26 A:Sandman 16.00
27 A:Thor,Loki 16.00
28 A:Medusa 16.00
29 A:Kingpin................. 16.00
30 A:Kang 15.00
31 A:Moondragon,Dr. Doom 15.00
32 A:Spider-Woman,Dr. Octopus .. 15.00
33 .... 15.00
34 A:Sub-Mariner............. 15.00
35 .... 15.00
36 A:Lizard.................. 15.00
37 A:White Tiger 16.00
38 A:Fantastic Four 16.00
39 A:Hellcat,Thanos........... 18.00
40 A:Hawkeye 15.00
41 A:Nova,Dr. Octopus 15.00
42 A:Kingpin................. 15.00
43 A:Daredevil,Ringmaster 15.00
44 A:Vision 18.00
45 A:Silver Surfer,Dr. Doom...... 15.00
46 A:Mysterio................ 15.00
47 A:Spider-Woman,Stilt-Man 15.00

MARVEL

48 A:Green Goblin	15.00
49 Spidey for President	15.00
50 A:She-Hulk	15.00
51 and 52	@15.00
53 A:Dr. Doom	15.00
54 Attack of the Bird-Man	15.00
55 A:Kingpin	15.00
56 A:Captain Britain, Jack O'Lantern	15.00
57 March, 1982	15.00

SPITFIRE AND THE TROUBLESHOOTERS
Oct., 1986

1 HT/JSt	2.50
2 HT	2.50
3 HT,Macs Armor	2.50
4 TM/BMc(Early TM work)	3.50
5 HT/TD,A:Star Brand	2.50
6 HT,Trial	2.50
7 HT	2.50
8 HT,New Armor	2.50
9	2.50

Becomes:
CODE NAME: SPITFIRE

10 MR/TD	2.25
11 thru 13	@2.25

SPOOF
Oct., 1970

1 MSe	25.00
2 MSe,Brawl in the Family	15.00
3 MSe,Richard Nixon cover	15.00
4 MSe,Blechhula	15.00
5 MSe,May, 1973	20.00

SPORT STARS
Nov., 1949

1 The Life of Knute Rockne	600.00

Becomes:
SPORTS ACTION

2 BP(c),Life of George Gipp	550.00
3 BEv,Hack Wilson	300.00
4 Art Houtteman	250.00
5 Nile Kinnick	250.00
6 Warren Gun	250.00
7 Jim Konstanty	250.00
8 Ralph Kiner	275.00
9 Ed `Strangler' Lewis	250.00
10 JMn,The Yella-Belly	250.00
11 The Killers	250.00
12 BEv,Man Behind the Mask	250.00
13 BEv,Lew Andrews	260.00
14 MWs,Ken Roper,Sept.,1952	260.00

SPOTLIGHT
Sept., 1978

1 F:Huckleberry Hound,Yogi Bear	50.00
2 Quick Draw McGraw	35.00
3 The Jetsons	35.00
4 Magilla Gorilla, March, 1979	30.00

SPUMCO COMIC BOOK

1 I:Jimmy the Hapless Boy	7.00
2	7.00
3 64-pgs. of sick humor	7.00
4 More sick humor	7.00
TPB	24.95

SPY CASES
See: KID KOMICS

SPY FIGHTERS
March, 1951

1 GT	300.00

2 GT	150.00
3	125.00
4 thru 13	@125.00
14 thru 15 July, 1953	@135.00

SPYKE
Epic Heavy Hitters, 1993

1 MBn,BR,I:Spyke	2.75
2 MBn,BR,V:Conita	2.75
3 thru 4 MBn,BR	@2.00

SPY THRILLERS
Atlas, Nov., 1954

1 AyB(c),The Tickling Death	250.00
2 V:Communists	150.00
3	100.00
4	100.00

Becomes:
POLICE BADGE

5 Sept., 1955	125.00

Squadron Supreme #4
© Marvel Entertainment Group

SQUADRON SUPREME
Sept., 1985

1 BH,L:Nighthawk	5.00
2 BH,F:Nuke,A:Scarlet Centurion	4.00
3 BH,D:Nuke	4.00
4 BH,L:Archer	4.00
5 BH,L:Amphibian	4.00
6 PR,J:Institute of Evil	4.00
7 JB,JG,V:Hyperion	4.00
8 BH,V:Hyperion	4.00
9 BSz(c),PR,D:Tom Thumb	4.00
10 PR,V:Quagmire	4.00
11 PR,V:Redeemers	4.00
12 PR,D:Nighthawk,Foxfire, Black Archer	4.00
GN Death of a Universe	12.00
TPB 352 pages	15.00

STALKERS
Epic, 1990–91

1 MT	2.25
2 MT	2.25
3 MT	2.25
4 MT	2.25
5 MT	2.25
6 VM,MT	2.25
7 VM,MT	2.25
8 VM,MT	2.25
9 thru 12 VM	@2.25

STARBLAST
1994

1 MGu(s),HT,After the Starbrand	2.25
2 MGu(s),HT,After the Starbrand	2.25
3 MGu(s),HT,After the Starbrand	2.25
4 MGu(s),HT,final issue	2.25

STARBRAND
Oct., 1986

1 JR2,O:Starbrand	2.50
2 JR2/AW	2.50
3 JR2/AW	2.50
4 JR2/AW	2.50
5 JR2/AW	2.50
6 JR2/AW	2.50
7 JR2/AW	2.50
8 JR2/AW	2.50
9 KG/BWi,A:Nightmask	2.50
10	2.50
11 JR2,TP	2.50
12 JR2,TP,X-Men x-over	2.50
13 JR2,TP	2.50
14 JR2,TP	2.50
15	2.50
16	3.00
17 JBy,TP,New Starbrand	3.00
18 JBy,TP	3.00
19 JBy,TP	3.00
Ann.#1	3.00

STAR COMICS MAGAZINE
Dec., 1986 (digest size)

1 F:Heathcliff,Muppet Babies, Ewoks	2.25
2 thru 13 1988	@2.25

STARJAMMERS
1995–96

1 I:The Uncreated	3.00
2 thru 4	@3.00

STARJAMMERS
July, 2004

1 (of 6) Cadet & Corsairs,pt.1	3.00
2 Cadet and the Corsairs,pt.2	3.00
3 Cadet and the Corsairs,pt.3	3.00
4 Cadet and the Corsairs,pt.4	3.00
5 Cadet and the Corsairs,pt.5	3.00

STAR-LORD, SPECIAL EDITION
Feb., 1982

1 JBy reprints	6.00

STARLORD
Mini-Series 1996

1 (of 3) DLw	2.50
2 DLw	2.50
3 DLw,V:Damyish	2.50

STARLORD MEGAZINE

TPB CCI,JBy,TA, rep., 64-pg.	3.00

STAR MASTER

1 MGu,Cosmic Avengers assemble	2.25
2 MGu,World Engine saga	2.25
3 MGu,Cauldron of Conversion	2.25

STARRIORS
Aug., 1984

1	4.00
2 thru 4	@3.00

STARSTRUCK
March, 1985

1 MK 3.00
2 thru 8 MK, Feb., 1986 . . . . . . @3.00

STARTLING STORIES:
THE THING–NIGHT FALLS
ON YANCY ST.
May, 2003

1 (of 4) EDo(s),40-pg 3.50
2 EDo(s),40-pg. 3.50
3 EDo(s),40-pg. 3.50
4 EDo(s),concl. 3.50
Spec. Last Line of Defense 3.50

STARTLING STORIES:
THE INCORRIGIBLE HULK
Jan., 2004

1-shot 3.00

STAR TREK
April, 1980

1 DC,KJ,rep.1st movie adapt.. . . . 15.00
2 DC,KJ,rep.1st movie adapt. 8.00
3 DC,KJ,rep.1st movie adapt.. . . . . 8.00
4 DC,KJ,The Weirdest Voyage. . . . 8.00
5 DC,KJ,Dr.McCoy...Killer. 8.00
6 DC,KJ,A:Ambassador Phlu 8.00
7 MN,KJ,Kirk/Spock(c) 8.00
8 DC(p),F:Spock 8.00
9 DC,FS,Trapped in a Web of
   Ghostly Vengeance 8.00
10 KJ(i),Spock the Barbarian. 8.00
11 TP(i),Like A Woman Scorned . . . 8.00
12 TP(i),Trapped in a Starship
    Gone Mad 8.00
13 TP(i),A:Barbara McCoy. 8.00
14 LM,GD,We Are Dying,
    Egypt,Dying 8.00
15 GK,The Quality of Mercy 8.00
16 LM,There's no Space
    like Gnomes 8.00
17 EH,TP,The Long Nights Dawn . 15.00
18 A Thousand Deaths,last issue . 20.00

STAR TREK:
DEEP SPACE NINE
1996

1 HWe(s),TGb,AM,DS9 in the
   Gamma Quadrant,pt.1 (of 2) . . . 3.00
2 DS9 in Gamma Quadrant,pt.2 . . . 2.50
3 TGb,AM,pt.1 (of 2). 2.50
4 TGb,AM,pt.2 . . . . 2.50
5 AM,terrorist attack 2.50
6 HWe(s),TGb,AM,Shirn sentence
   Sisko to Death, Risk, pt.1 . . . . . 2.50
7 HWe(s),TGb,Risk, pt.2. . . . . 2.50
8 TGb,AM,V:Maquis & Romulans. . 2.50
9 TGb,AM,V:Maquis & Romulans,
   pt.2. . . . . 2.50
10 HWe,TGb, trapped in the
    holosuite 2.50
11thru 15 . . . . @2.50

STAR TREK:
EARLY VOYAGES
Dec., 1996

1 DAn,IEd,Captain Pike's crew,
   double size premier. 4.00
2 DAn,IEd,distress signal 2.50
3 DAn,IEd,on Rigel 7, prologue to
   "The Cage" 2.50
4 DAn,IEd, prologue to "The Cage" 2.50
5 DAn,IEd, V:Vulcans 2.50
6 DAn,IEd, Cloak & Dagger concl. . 2.50

Star Trek Deep Space Nine #9
© Marvel Entertainment Group

7 DAn,IEd, The wrath of Kaaj. 2.50
8 DAn,IEd,F:Dr. Boyce 2.50
9 DAn,IEd,F:Nano. 2.50
10 DAn,V:Chakuun, Tholians. 2.50
11 DAn,IEd,The Fallen, pt. 2 . . . . . 2.50
12 DAn,IEd,. 2.50
13 DAn,IEd,F:Yeoman Colt 2.50
14 DAn,IEd,Pike vs. Kirk 2.50
15 DAn,IEd,F:Yeoman Colt 2.50
16 . . . . 2.50
17 DAn,IEd, Pike & Kaaj 2.50

STAR TREK:
FIRST CONTACT

GN Movie adapt. 6.00

STAR TREK:
MIRROR, MIRROR
1996

1-shot continuation of famous
   classic episode 4.00

STAR TREK: THE NEXT
GENERATION—
RIKER SPECIAL
May, 1998

1-shot, DAn,IEd,Riker photo cover . 3.50

STAR TREK: THE NEXT
GENERATION/X-MEN:
SECOND CONTACT
March, 1998

1-shot, DAn,IEd,64-pg. 5.00
1-shot, variant CNr cover (1:5) 5.00

STAR TREK: OPERATION
ASSIMILATION

1-shot Borg story 3.00

STAR TREK:
STARFLEET ACADEMY
1996

1 Cadets vs. Gorns. 2.50
2 ALa, R&R in Australia 2.50
3 F:Decker 2.50
4 V:Klingon Bird-of-prey 2.50

5 V:Klingons 2.50
6 Funeral of Kamilah
   Goldstein,I:Edam Astrun 2.50
7 ALa,F:Edam Astrun,Nog 2.50
8 ALa, Return of Charlie X 2.50
9 ALa, on Talos, V:Jem'Hadar 2.50
10 ALa,F:Captain Pike, Jem'Hadar . 2.50
11 F:Christopher Pike 2.50
12 ALa, Telepathy War x-over 2.50
13 Parent's Day 2.50
14 T'Priell revealed, pt.1 (of 3) 2.50
15 T'Priell dead?, pt.2 . . . . 2.50
16 T'Priell Revealed, pt3 . . . . 2.50
17 Battle for T'Priell's Mind 2.50
18 Entirely in Klingon language. . . . 2.50
19 Pava vs. Kovold 2.50

STAR TREK:
TELEPATHY WAR
Sept., 1997

1-shot Telepathy War, pt.4
   x-over, 48-pg. 3.00

STAR TREK: UNLIMITED
1996

1 DAn,IEd,MBu,JeM,AW, Classic
   series & TNG. 5.00
2 DAn,IEd,MBu. 4.00
3 DAn,IEd,MBu. 4.00
4 DAn,IEd,MBu,AW, 2 tales 4.00
5 DAn,IEd,TMo,RoR,AW,ANi,48-pg.4.00
6 DAn, Telepathy War x-over 4.00
7 DAn,IEd,F:Q & Trelane 4.00
8 DAn,IEd,Day of Honor tie-in 4.00
9 DAn,IEd,V:Klingons 4.00
10 A Piece of the Action,
    conclusion of series. 4.00

STAR TREK:
THE UNTOLD VOYAGES
Jan., 1998

1 (of 5) Star Trek 2nd Five Year
   Mission 3.00
2 Spock, Savik, Dr. McCoy 3.00
3 F:McCoy, McCoy's Daughter . . . 3.00
4 F:Sulu 3.00
5 48-pg. finale. 3.50

STAR TREK: VOYAGER
1996

1 F:Neelix & Talaxians, pt.1 . . . . . . 3.00
2 F:Neelix & Talaxians, pt.2 . . . . . . 3.00
3 F:Neelix & Talaxians, pt.3 . . . . . . 3.00
4 HWe(s),Homeostasis, pt.1 . . . . . 3.00
5 HWe(s),Homeostasis, pt.2. . . . . . 3.00
6 HWe(s),Homeostasis, pt.3. . . . . . 3.00
7 Ancient Relic 3.00
8 Mysterious relic encountered. . . . 3.00
9 DAn,IEd,AM, rescue mission. . . . 3.00
10 The Borg are Back 3.00
11 Zoological Experiment 3.00
12 Zoological Experiment 3.00
13 Crew loses a member. 3.00
14 Distress Call 3.00
15 Tuvok Trapped 3.00

STAR TREK: VOYAGER:
SPLASHDOWN
Jan., 1998

1 (of 4) AM,Crash landing on
   water planet. 3.00
2 AM,The ship may sink 3.00
3 AM,adventure undersea. 3.00
4 AM,escape from sea creatures . . 3.00

MARVEL

STAR TREK/X-MEN
1-shot SLo,MS, 64-pg. 5.00
1a rep. of STAR TREK/X-MEN 5.00

STAR WARS
July, 1977
1 HC,30 Cent,movie adaption. . . . 65.00
1a HC,35 Cent(square Box). . . . 725.00
1b "Reprint". 7.50
2 HC,movie adaptation 30.00
2b "Reprint". 4.00
3 HC,movie adaptation 25.00
3b "Reprint". 4.00
4 HC,SL,movie adapt.(low dist.) . . 22.00
4b "Reprint". 4.00
5 HC,SL,movie adaptation 22.00
5b "Reprint". 3.00
6 HC,DSt,E:movie adaption 22.00
6b "Reprint". 3.00
7 HC,FS,F:Luke & Chewbacca. . . 20.00
8 HC,TD,Eight against a World . . 20.00
9 HC,TP,V:Cloud Riders 20.00
7b thru 9b "Reprint" . . . . @2.50
10 HC,TP,Behemoth From Below . 22.00
11 CI,TP,Fate of Luke Skywalker. . 20.00
12 TA,CI,Doomworld 20.00
13 TA,JBy,CI,Deadly Reunion 20.00
14 TA,CI 20.00
15 CI,V:Crimson Jack 20.00
16 WS,V:The Hunter 20.00
17 Crucible, low dist. 20.00
18 CI,Empire Strikes,low dist. . . . 20.00
19 CI,Ultimate Gamble,low dist . . . 20.00
20 CI,Death Game, scarce 20.00
21 TA,CI,Shadow of a Dark
    Lord(Scarce) 20.00
22 CI,Han Solo vs.Chewbacca . . . 15.00
23 CI,Flight Into Fury. 15.00
24 CI,Ben Kenobi Story 15.00
25 CI,Siege at Yavin 15.00
26 CI,Doom Mission 15.00
27 CI,V:The Hunter 15.00
28 CI,Cavern o/t Crawling Death. . 15.00
29 CI,Dark Encounter 15.00
30 CI,A Princess Alone 15.00
31 CI,Return to Tatooine 15.00
32 CI,The Jawa Express 15.00
33 CI,GD,V:Baron Tagge 15.00
34 CI,Thunder in the Stars. 15.00
35 CI,V:Darth Vader. 15.00
36 CI,V:Darth Vader. 15.00
37 CI,V:Darth Vader. 15.00
38 TA,MG,Riders in the Void 15.00
39 AW,B:Empire Strikes Back . . . 25.00
40 AW,Battleground Hoth. 25.00
41 AW,Imperial Pursuit. 25.00
42 AW,Bounty Hunters. 25.00
43 AW,Betrayal at Bespin 25.00
44 AW,E:Empire Strikes Back 25.00
45 CI,GD,Death Probe. 15.00
46 DI,TP,V:Dreamnaut Devourer . . 15.00
47 CI,GD,Droid World 15.00
48 CI,Leia vs.Darth Vader 15.00
49 SW,TP,The Last Jedi 15.00
50 WS,AW,TP,G-Size issue 15.00
51 WS,TP,Resurrection of Evil. . . . 12.00
52 WS,TP,D:Death Star II 12.00
53 CI,WS,Gift of Alderaan 12.00
54 CI,WS,Starfire Rising 12.00
55 thru 66 WS,TP . . . . @12.00
67 TP, The Darker 12.00
68 GD,TP,O:Boba Fett. 20.00
69 GD,TP,Death in City of Bone . . 20.00
70 A:Han Solo 20.00
71 A:Han Solo 20.00
72 Fool's Boontu 20.00
73 Secret of Planet Lansbane 20.00
74 thru 91 . . . . @20.00
92 BSz(c),The Dream 22.00
93 thru 97 . . . . @20.00

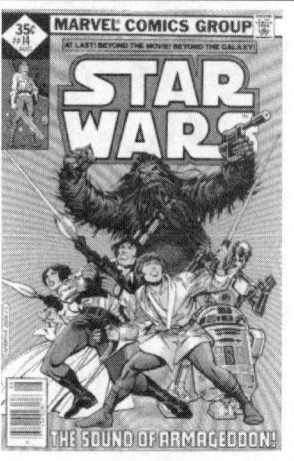

Star Wars #14
© *Marvel Entertainment Group*

98 AW,Supply & Demand 20.00
99 Touch of Goddess. 20.00
100 Painted(c),double-size 22.00
101 BSz, Far,Far Away 22.00
102 KRo's Back 15.00
103 thru 106 . . . . @15.00
107 WPo(i),last issue. 90.00
Ann.#1 WS(c),V:Winged Warlords 100.00
Ann.#2 RN 15.00
Ann.#3 RN,Darth Vader(c) 15.00

STEELGRIP STARKEY
Epic, July, 1986
1 . . . . 2.50
2 thru 5 . . . . @2.50
6 June, 1987 . . . . 2.50

STEELTOWN ROCKERS
April, 1990—Sept., 1990
1 SL 2.25
2 thru 6 SL . . . . @2.25

STOKER'S DRACULA
Oct., 2004
1 (of 4) RTs,DG 4.00

STORM
1 TyD,KIS,V:Candra 4.00
2 . . . . 4.00
3 . . . . 4.00
4 TyD,KIS, conclusion,foil cover . . . 4.00

STRANGE
Sept., 2004
1 MSz,BPe,O:Dr.Strange 3.50
2 MSz,BPe, ... 3.50

STRANGE COMBAT TALES
1 and 2 . . . . @2.75
3 Tiger by the Tail 2.50
4 Midnight Crusade. 2.50

STRANGE STORIES OF SUSPENSE
See: RUGGED ACTION

STRANGE TALES
[1st Regular Series] June, 1951
1 The Room. 4,000.00
2 Trapped In A Tomb 1,300.00
3 JMn,Man Who Never Was . . 1,000.00
4 BEv,Terror in the Morgue . . . 1,100.00
5 A Room Without A Door 1,000.00
6 RH(c),The Ugly Man 700.00
7 Who Stands Alone 700.00
8 BEv(c),Something in the Fog. . 700.00
9 Drink Deep Vampire 700.00
10 BK,Hidden Head. 800.00
11 BEv(c),GC,'O'Malley's Friend . 500.00
12 Graveyard At Midnight 500.00
13 BEv(c),Death Makes A Deal . . 500.00
14 GT,Horrible Herman 500.00
15 BK,Don't Look Down. 550.00
16 Decapitation cover 500.00
17 DBr,JRo,Death Feud. 500.00
18 Witch Hunt 500.00
19 RH(c),The Rag Doll 500.00
20 RH(c),GC,SMo,Lost World . . . 500.00
21 BEv 400.00
22 BK,JF 400.00
23 Strangest Tale in the World. . . 400.00
24 The Thing in the Coffin 400.00
25 . . . . 400.00
26 . . . . 400.00
27 JF,The Garden of Death 400.00
28 Come into my Coffin 400.00
29 Witch-Craft 400.00
30 The Thing in the Box 400.00
31 Man Who Played with Blocks . 400.00
32 . . . . 400.00
33 JMn(c),Step Lively Please . . . 400.00
34 Flesh and Blood 375.00
35 The Man in the Bottle 300.00
36 . . . . 300.00
37 Out of the Storm 300.00
38 . . . . 300.00
39 Karnoff's Plan 300.00
40 BEv,Man Who Caught
    a Mermaid 300.00
41 BEv,Riddle of the Skull 325.00
42 DW,BEv,JMn,Faceless One . . 325.00
43 JF,The Mysterious Machine . . 300.00
44 . . . . 300.00
45 JKa,Land of Vanishing Men . . 325.00
46 thru 57 . . . . @300.00
58 AW 300.00
59 BK. 300.00
60 . . . . 275.00
61 BK 300.00
62 . . . . 275.00
63 . . . . 300.00
64 AW 300.00
65 . . . . 275.00
66 . . . . 275.00
67 thru 78. . . . . @350.00
79 SD,JK,Dr.Strange Prototype . . 350.00
80 thru 83 SD,JK . . . . @250.00
84 SD,JK,Magneto Prototype . . . 250.00
85 SD,JK 250.00
86 SD,JK,I Created Mechano . . . 250.00
87 SD,JK,Return of Grogg. 250.00
88 SD,JK,Zzutak 250.00
89 SD,JK,Fin Fang Foom 700.00
90 SD,JK,Orrgo Unconquerable . 250.00
91 SD,JK,The Sacrifice 250.00
92 SD,JK,Thing That Waits 250.00
93 SD,JK,The Wax People 250.00
94 SD,JK,Pildorr the Plunderer . . 250.00
95 SD,JK,Two-Headed Thing . . . 250.00
96 SD,JK,I Dream of Doom 250.00
97 SD,JK,When A Planet Dies. . . 600.00
98 SD,JK,No Human Can
    Beat Me 250.00
99 SD,JK,Mister Morgan's
    Monster 250.00
100 SD,JK,I Was Trapped
    in the Crazy Maze 250.00

Strange Tales #115
© *Marvel Entertainment Group*

Strange Tales #163
© *Marvel Entertainment Group*

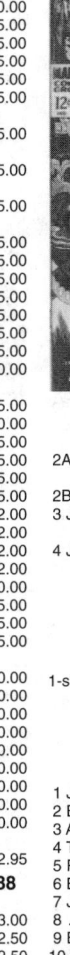

101 B:StL(s),SD,JK,
  B:Human Torch. 1,600.00
102 SD,JK,I:Wizard 500.00
103 SD,JK,I:Zemu 450.00
104 SD,JK,I:The Trapster 450.00
105 SD,JK,V:Wizard 450.00
106 SD,A:Fantastic Four 300.00
107 SD,V:Sub-Mariner. 375.00
108 SD,JK,A:FF,I:The Painter . . . 300.00
109 SD,JK,I:Sorcerer. 300.00
110 SD,I&B:Dr.Strange,
  Nightmare. 2,000.00
111 SD,I:Asbestos,BaronMordo. . 550.00
112 SD,I:The Eel 225.00
113 SD,I:Plant Man 225.00
114 SD,JK,A:Captain America . . . 650.00
115 SD,O:Dr.Strange 700.00
116 SD,V:Thing 200.00
117 SD,V:The Eel 150.00
118 SD,V:The Wizard 200.00
119 SD,C:Spider-Man 200.00
120 SD,1st Iceman/Torch T.U. . . . 225.00
121 SD,V:Plant Man 125.00
122 SD,V:Dr.Doom 100.00
123 SD,A:Thor,I:Beetle 125.00
124 SD,I:Zota 100.00
125 SD,V:Sub-Mariner. 125.00
126 SD,I:Dormammu,Clea. 100.00
127 SD,V:Dormammu 100.00
128 SD,I:Demon 100.00
129 SD,I:Tiboro 100.00
130 SD,C:Beatles 125.00
131 SD,I:Dr.Vega. 100.00
132 SD,I:Orini 100.00
133 SD,I:Shazana 100.00
134 SD,E:Torch,I:Merlin. 100.00
135 SD,JK,I:Shield & Hydra
  B:Nick Fury 250.00
136 SD,JK,V:Dormammu. 75.00
137 SD,JK,A:Ancient One 90.00
138 SD,JK,I:Eternity. 85.00
139 SD,JK,V:Dormammu. 85.00
140 SD,JK,V:Dormammu. 85.00
141 SD,JK,I:Fixer,Mentallo 85.00
142 SD,JK,I:THEM,V:Hydra. 85.00
143 SD,JK,V:Hydra 85.00
144 SD,JK,V:Druid,I:Jasper
  Sitwell 85.00
145 SD,JK,I:Mr.Rasputin 85.00
146 SD,JK,V:Dormammu,I:A.I.M. . 85.00
147 BEv,JK,F:Wong. 85.00
148 BEv,JK,O:Ancient One 100.00
149 BEv,JK,V:Kaluu. 75.00
150 BEv,JK,JB(1st Marvel Art)
  I:Baron Strucker,Umar. 75.00

151 JK,JSo(1st Marvel Art),
  I:Umar 100.00
152 BEv,JK,JSo,V:Umar 75.00
153 JK,JSo,MSe,V:Hydra 75.00
154 JSo,MSe,I:Dreadnought 75.00
155 JSo,MSe,A:L.B.Johnson. 75.00
156 JSo,MSe,I:Zom 75.00
157 JSo,MSe,A:Zom,C:Living
  Tribunal 75.00
158 JSo,MSe,A:Zom,I:Living
  Tribunal(full story) 75.00
159 JSo,MSe,O:Nick Fury,A:Capt.
  America,I:Val Fontaine 85.00
160 JSo,MSe,A:Captain America,
  I:Jimmy Woo. 75.00
161 JSo,I:Yellow Claw 75.00
162 JSo,DA,A:Captain America. . . 75.00
163 JSo,DA,V:Yellow Claw 65.00
164 JSo,DA,V:Yellow Claw 65.00
165 JSo,DA,V:Yellow Claw 65.00
166 DA,GT,JSo,A:AncientOne 65.00
167 JSo,DA,V:Doctor Doom 100.00
168 JSo,DA,E:Doctor Strange,Nick
  Fury,V:Yandroth 65.00
169 JSo,I&O:Brother Voodoo 20.00
170 JSo,O:Brother Voodoo 15.00
171 GC,V:Baron Samed 15.00
172 GC,DG,V:Dark Lord 15.00
173 GC,DG,I:Black Talon 15.00
174 JB,JM,O:Golem. 12.00
175 SD,R:Torr 12.00
176 F:Golem 12.00
177 FB,F:Golem. 12.00
178 JSn,B&O:Warlock,I:Magus . . . 40.00
179 JSn,I:Pip,I&D:Capt.Autolycus . 35.00
180 JSn,I:Gamora,Kray-tor 35.00
181 JSn,E:Warlock 35.00
182 SD,GK,rep. Str.Tales
  #123,124 . . . . 10.00
183 SD,rep.Str.Tales #130,131 . . . 10.00
184 SD,rep.Str.Tales #132,133 . . . 10.00
185 SD,rep.Str.Tales #134,135 . . . 10.00
186 SD,rep.Str.Tales #136,137 . . . 10.00
187 SD,rep.Str.Tales #138,139 . . . 10.00
188 SD,rep.Str.Tales #140,141 . . . 10.00
Ann.#1 V:Grottu,Diablo 800.00
Ann.#2 A:Spider-Man 1,200.00
Marvel Milestone rep. stories from
  #110–#111, #114–#115 (1995) . 2.95

[2nd Regular Series] 1987–88
1 BBI,CW,B:Cloak&Dagger,Dr.
  Strange,V:Lord of Light 3.00
2 BBI,CW,V:Lord of Light,Demon . . 2.50
3 BBI,AW,CW,A:Nightmare,Khat. . . 2.50
4 BBI,CW,V:Nightmare 2.50
5 BBI,V:Rodent,A:Defenders 2.50
6 BBI,BWi,V:Erlik Khan,
  A:Defenders. 2.50
7 V:Nightmare,A:Defenders 2.50
8 BBI,BWi,V:Kaluu 2.50
9 BBI,BWi,A:Dazzler,I:Mr.Jip,
  V:Kaluu 2.50
10 BBI,BWi,RCa,A:Black Cat,
  V:Mr.Jip,Kaluu 2.50
11 RCa,BWi,V:Mr.Jip,Kaluu 2.50
12 WPo,BWi,A:Punisher,V:Mr.Jip . . 2.50
13 JBr,BWi,RCa,Punisher,
  Power Pack 2.50
14 JBr,BWi,RCa,Punisher,P.Pack . . 2.50
15 RCa,BMc,A:Mayhem 2.50
16 RCa,BWi,V:Mr.Jip 2.50
17 RCa,BWi,V:Night 2.50
18 RCa,KN,A:X-Factor,V:Night 2.50
19 MMi(c),EL,TA,RCa,A:Thing. 2.50
TPB Fully painted 7.00

STRANGE TALES
June, 1998
1 JMD,PJe,LSh,Man-Thing, 64-pg. 5.00

2A JMD,PJe,LSh,Man-Thing,
  Werewolf, 64-pg. 5.00
2B variant cover 5.00
3 JMD,PJe,NA(c),Man-Thing,
  Werewolf, 64-pg. 5.00
4 JMD,PJe,LSh,F:Man-Thing
  final issue 5.00

STRANGE TALES:
DARK CORNERS
March, 1998
1-shot JEs, three stories, 48-pg. . . . 4.00

STRANGE TALES
OF THE UNUSUAL
Dec., 1955—Aug., 1957
1 JMn(c),BP,DH,JR,Man Lost . . . 600.00
2 BEv,Man Afraid 300.00
3 AW,The Invaders 325.00
4 The Long Wait 225.00
5 RC,SD,The Threat. 275.00
6 BEv 225.00
7 JK,JO 225.00
8 . . . . 225.00
9 BEv(c),BK 250.00
10 GM,AT. 225.00
11 BEv(c),Aug., 1957. . . . . 225.00

STRANGE WORLDS
Dec., 1958
1 JK,SD,Flying Saucer. 1,200.00
2 SD 650.00
3 JK 500.00
4 AW 450.00
5 SD 400.00

STRAWBERRY
SHORTCAKE
Star, June, 1985—April, 1986
1 . . . . 3.00
2 thru 7 . . . . @3.00

STRAY TOASTERS
Epic, Jan., 1988
1 BSz 5.00
2 BSz 4.50
3 and 4 BSz . . . . @4.00

STRIKEFORCE MORITURI
Dec., 1986
1 BA,SW,WPo(1st pencils-
  3 pages),I:Blackwatch 3.00
2 BA,SW,V:The Horde 2.50
3 BA,SW,V:The Horde 2.50
4 BA,SW,WPo,V:The Horde 2.50
5 BA,SW,V:The Horde 2.50
6 BA,SW,V:The Horde 2.50
7 BA,SW,V:The Horde 2.50
8 BA,SW,V:The Horde 2.50
9 BA,SW,V:The Horde 2.50
10 WPo(1st pencils-full story),
  SW,R:Black Watch,O:Horde . . . 3.00
11 BA,SW,V:The Horde 2.50
12 BA,SW,D:Jelene 2.50
13 BA,SW,Old vs. NewTeam 2.50
14 BA,AW,V:The Horde 2.50
15 BA,AW,V:The Horde 2.50
16 WPo,SW,V:The Horde 2.50
17 WPo(c),SW,V:The Horde 2.50
18 BA,SW,V:Hammersmith 2.50
19 BA,SW,V:THe Horde,D:Pilar . . 2.50
20 BA,SW,V:The Horde 2.50
21 MMi(c),TD(i),V:The Horde. 2.50
22 TD(i),V:The Horde. 2.50
23 MBa,VM,V:The Horde. 2.50
24 VM(i),V:Vax,V:The Horde 2.50
25 TD(i),V:The Horde. 3.00
26 MBa,VM,V:The Horde. 3.00
27 MBa,VM,O:Morituri Master 3.00
28 MBa,V:The Tiger. 3.00
29 MBa,V:Zakir Shastri 3.00
30 MBa,V:Andre Lamont,The Wind. 3.00
31 MBa(c),V:The Wind,last issue . . 3.00

STRONG GUY REBORN
Spec. TDz,ASm,ATi (1997) 3.00

STRYFE'S STRIKE FILE
1 LSn,NKu,GCa,BP,C:Siena
  Blaze,Holocaust (1993) 4.00
1a 2nd printing 2.25

SUB-MARINER
May, 1968
1 JB,O:Sub-Mariner 350.00
2 JB,A:Triton 150.00
3 JB,A:Triton 100.00
4 JB,V:Attuma 100.00
5 JB,I&O:Tiger Shark 100.00
6 JB,DA,V:Tiger Shark 125.00
7 JB,I:Ikthon 100.00
8 JB,V:Thing 100.00
9 MSe,DA,A:Lady Dorma 100.00
10 GC,DA,O:Lemuria 100.00
11 GC,V:Capt.Barracuda 50.00
12 MSe,I:Lyna 50.00
13 MSe,JS,A:Lady Dorma 50.00
14 MSe,V:Fake Human Torch 55.00
15 MSe,V:Dragon Man 50.00
16 MSe,I:Nekaret,Thakos 55.00
17 MSe,I:Stalker,Kormok 50.00
18 MSe,A:Triton 30.00
19 MSe,I:Stingray 30.00
20 JB,V:Dr.Doom 30.00
21 MSe,D:Lord Seth 30.00
22 MSe,A:Dr.Strange 30.00
23 MSe,I:Orka 30.00
24 JB,JM,V:Tiger Shark 30.00
25 SB,JM,O:Atlantis. 25.00
26 SB,A:Red Raven. 25.00
27 SB,I:Commander Kraken 25.00
28 SB,V:Brutivake 25.00
29 SB,V:Hercules 20.00
30 SB,A:Captain Marvel 22.00
31 SB,A:Triton 20.00
32 SB,JM,I&O:Llyra 22.00

Sub-Mariner #67
© *Marvel Entertainment Group*

33 SB,JM,I:Namora 25.00
34 SB,JM,AK,1st Defenders 100.00
35 SB,JM,A:Silver Surfer 100.00
36 BWr,SB,W:Lady Dorma 35.00
37 RA,D:Lady Dorma. 35.00
38 RA,JSe,O:Rec,I:Thakorr,Fen . . 35.00
39 RA,JM,V:Llyra. 35.00
40 GC,I:Turalla,A:Spidey 25.00
41 GT,V:Rock. 22.00
42 GT,JM,V:House Named Death . 22.00
43 GC,V:Tunal,king-sz. 30.00
44 MSe,JM,V:Human Torch 25.00
45 MSe,JM,V:Tiger Shark 25.00
46 GC,D:Namor's Father. 20.00
47 GC,A:Stingray,V:Dr.Doom. 20.00
48 GC,V:Dr.Doom 20.00
49 GC,V:Dr.Doom 20.00
50 BEv,I:Namorita 22.00
51 BEv,O:Namorita,C:Namora 20.00
52 GK,V:Sunfire 18.00
53 BEv,V:Sunfire 18.00
54 BEv,AW,V:Sunfire,I:Lorvex 18.00
55 BEv,V:Torg 18.00
56 DA,I:Coral 18.00
57 BEv,I:Venus 18.00
58 BEv,I:Tamara. 18.00
59 BEv,V:Tamara,A:Thor 25.00
60 BEv,V:Tamara 15.00
61 BEv,JM,V:Dr.Hydro 15.00
62 HC,JSt,I:Tales of Atlantis. 15.00
63 HC,JSt,V:Dr.Hydro,I:Arkus 15.00
64 HC,JSe,I:Maddox 15.00
65 DH,DP,V:She-Devil,inc.BEv
  Eulogy pin-up 15.00
66 DH,V:Orka,I:Raman 15.00
67 DH,A:FF,V:Triton,N:Namor
  I&O:Force 15.00
68 DH,O:Force. 15.00
69 GT,V:Spider-Man. 18.00
70 GT,I:Piranha 15.00
71 GT,V:Piranha. 15.00
72 DA,V:Slime/Thing. 15.00
Spec.#1 rep. Tales to Astonish
  #70-#73 . . . . 30.00
Spec.#2 rep. Tales to Astonish
  #74-#76 . . . . 25.00

[Limited Series]
1 RB,BMc,Namor's Birth. 2.50
2 RB,BMc,Namor Kills Humans . . . 2.25
3 RB,BMc,V:Surface Dwellers . . . 2.25
4 RB,BMc,V:Human Torch 2.25
5 RB,BMc,A:Invaders 2.25
6 RB,BMc,V:Destiny 2.25
7 RB,BMc,A:Fantastic Four 2.25

8 RB,BMc,A:Hulk,Avengers 2.25
9 RB,BMc,A:X-Men,Magneto 2.25
10 RB,BMc,V:Thing 2.25
11 RB,BMc,A:Namorita,Defenders . 2.25
12 RB,BMc,A:Dr.Doom,
  Alpha Flight 2.25

(SAGA OF THE) SUB-MARINER
[Mini-Series] Nov., 1988
1 RB,BMc,Namor's Birth. 3.00
2 RB,BMc,Namor Kills Humans . . . 3.00
3 RB,BMc,V:Surface Dwellers 3.00
4 RB,BMc,V:Human Torch 3.00
5 RB,BMc,A:Invaders 3.00
6 RB,BMc,V:Destiny 3.00
7 RB,BMc,A:Fantastic Four 3.00
8 RB,BMc,A:Hulk,Avengers 3.00
9 RB,BMc,A:X-Men,Magneto 3.50
10 RB,BMc,V:Thing 3.00
11 RB,BMc,A:Namorita,Defenders . 3.00
12 RB,BMc,A:Dr.Doom,Alp.Flight . . 3.00

SUB-MARINER COMICS
Timely, Spring, 1941
1 ASh(c),BEv,PGn,B:Sub-
  Mariner, The Angel 50,000.00
2 ASh(c),BEv,Nazi
  Submarine (c) 7,700.00
3 ASh(c),BEv,Churchill. 6,000.00
4 ASh(c),BEv,BW 4,500.00
5 . . . . 3,500.00
6 ASh(c) 3,000.00
7 . . . . 3,000.00
8 ASh(c) 3,000.00
9 ASh(c),BW,Flag(c) 3,000.00
10 ASh(c) 3,000.00
11 ASh(c) 3,000.00
12 ASh(c) 2,200.00
13 ASh(c) 2,200.00
14 ASh(c) 2,200.00
15 ASh(c) 2,200.00
16 ASh(c) 2,000.00
17 ASh(c) 2,000.00
18 ASh(c) 2,000.00
19 . . . . 2,000.00
20 ASh(c) 2,000.00
21 SSh(c),BEv,Last Angel. 1,500.00
22 SSh(c),BEv,A:Young Allies. . 1,500.00
23 SSh(c),BEv,Human Torch . . 1,500.00
24 MSy(c),BEv,A:Namora,
  bondage cover 1,500.00
25 MSy(c),HK,B:The Blonde
  Phantom, A:Namora,
  bondage(c) 1,800.00
26 BEv,A:Namora 1,300.00
27 DRi(c),BEv,A:Namora 1,300.00
28 DRi(c),BEv,A:Namora 1,300.00
29 BEv,A:Namora,Human Torch 1,300.00
30 DRi(c),BEv,Slaves Under
  the Sea 1,300.00
31 BEv,The Man Who Grew,
  A:Capt. America,E:Blonde
  Phantom 1,300.00
32 BEv,O:Sub-Mariner 2,100.00
33 BEv,O:Sub-Mariner,A:Human
  Torch,B:Namora 1,500.00
34 BEv,A:Human Torch,bondage
  cover. 1,000.00
35 BEv,A:Human Torch. 1,000.00
36 BEv,Hidden World 1,000.00
37 JMn(c),BEv 1,000.00
38 SSh(c),BEv,JMn,
  O:Sub-Mariner 1,100.00
39 JMn(c),BEv,Commie
  Frogman. 1,000.00
40 JMn(c),BEv,Secret Tunnel . . 1,000.00
41 JMn(c),BEv,A:Namora 1,000.00
42 BEv,Oct., 1955. . . . . 1,200.00

SUBURBAN JERSEY NINJA SHE-DEVILS
1 I:Ninja She-Devils 2.25

SUNFIRE & BIG HERO 6
July, 1998
1 (of 3) SLo,from Alpha Flight. 2.50
2 SLo,V:Everwraith 2.50
3 SLO,conclusion 2.50

SUPERNATURALS
Oct., 1998
1 (of 4) BnP,JBa(c),F:Brother Voodoo,
   V:Jack O'Lantern, with mask. . . 4.00
1a signed 30.00
2 BnP,JBa(c), with mask. 4.00
3 BnP,JBa(c), with mask. 4.00
4 BnP,JBa(c), with mask, concl. . . . 4.00

SUPERNATURAL THRILLERS
Dec., 1972
1 JSo(c),JSe,FrG,IT! 50.00
2 VM,DA,The Invisible Man 30.00
3 GK,The Valley of the Worm . . . 30.00
4 Dr. Jekyll and Mr. Hyde 30.00
5 RB,The Living Mummy 75.00
6 GT,JA,The Headless Horseman 40.00
7 VM,B:The Living Mummy,
   Back From The Tomb 40.00
8 VM,He Stalks Two Worlds 40.00
9 GK/AM(c),VM,DA,Pyramid of
   the Watery Doom 40.00
10 VM,A Choice of Dooms 40.00
11 VM,When Strikes the ASP 40.00
12 VM,KJ,The War That Shook
   the World 40.00
13 VM,DGr,The Tomb of the
   Stalking Dead 40.00
14 VM,AMc,All These Deadly
   Pawns 40.00
15 TS, E:The Living Mummy,Night
   of Armageddon, Oct.,1975 . . . 40.00

SUPER SOLDIERS
Marvel UK, 1993
1 I:Super Soldier,A:USAgent 2.75
2 A:USAgent 2.25
3 A:USAgent 2.25
4 A:USAgent,Avengers 2.25

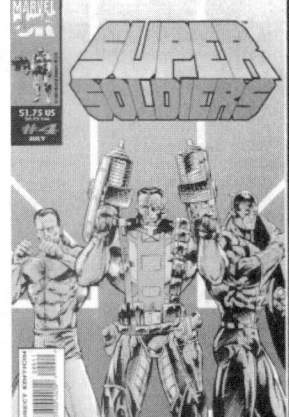

Super Soldiers #4
© Marvel Entertainment Group

5 A:Captain America,AWC 2.25
6 O:Super Soldiers 2.25
7 in Savage Land 2.25

SUPER-VILLAIN CLASSICS
May, 1983
1 O:Galactus 6.00

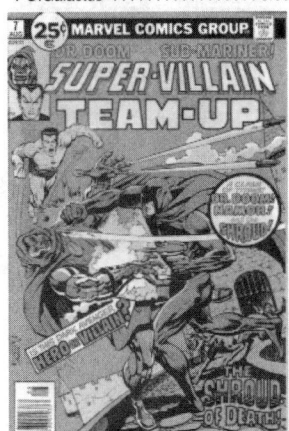

Super-Villain Team-Up #7
© Marvel Entertainment Group

SUPER-VILLAIN TEAM-UP
Aug., 1975
1 GT/BEv(c),B:Dr.Doom/Sub-
   Mariner,A:Attuma,Tiger Shark 40.00
2 SB,A:Tiger Shark, Attuma 15.00
3 EH(c),JA,V:Attuma. 15.00
4 HT,JM,Dr.Doom vs. Namor 15.00
5 RB/JSt(c),HT,DP,A:Fantastic
   Four,I:Shroud. 15.00
6 HT,JA,A:Shroud,Fantastic Four . 12.00
7 RB/KJ(c),HT,O:Shroud. 12.00
8 KG,V:Ringmaster 12.00
9 ST,A:Avengers,Iron Man 12.00
10 BH,DP,A:Capt.America,
   V:Attuma,Red Skull 12.00
11 DC/JSt(c),BH,DP,B:Dr. Doom,
   Red Skull,A:Capt. America . . . 12.00
12 DC/AM(c),BH,DP,Dr.Doom vs.
   Red Skull 12.00
13 KG,DP,Namor vs. Krang 12.00
14 JBy/TA(c),BH,DP,V:Magneto,
   x-over with Champions #15. . . 12.00
15 GT,ME,A:Red Skull 12.00
16 CI,A:Dr. Doom. 12.00
17 KP(c),Red Skull Vs.Hatemonger
   June, 1976. . . . . 12.00
G-Size#1 F:Namor, Dr.Doom. 12.00
G-Size#2 F:Namor, Dr.Doom. 12.00

SUPREME POWER
Marvel Max, July, 2003
1 MSz(s),GFr 7.00
1a special edition, JQ(c). 10.00
2 MSz(s),GFr 4.00
3 MSz(s),GFr 4.00
4 MSz(s),GFr,Whizzer,Nighthawk. . 3.00
5 MSz(s),GFr,F:The Blur. 3.00
6 MSz(s),GFr,Hyperion,Nighthawk . 3.00
7 MSz(s),GFr,pt.1 . . . . 3.00
8 MSz(s),GFr,pt.2 . . . . 3.00
9 MSz(s),GFr,Power Princess 3.00

10 thru 13 MSz(s),GF . . . . @3.00
TPB Vol. 1 Hyperion Project 15.00
TPB Vol. 2 . . . . 15.00

SUSPENSE
Atlas, Dec., 1949
1 BP,Ph(c),Sidney Greenstreet/
   Peter Lorne (Maltese Falcon) 800.00
2 Ph(c),Dennis O'Keefe/Gale
   Storm (Abandoned) 400.00
3 B:Horror stories,The Black
   Pit 450.00
4 Thing In Black 325.00
5 BEv,GT,RH,BK,DBr,
   Hangman's House 350.00
6 BEv,GT,PAM,RH,Madness
   of Scott Mannion 350.00
7 DBr,GT,DR,Murder. 325.00
8 GC,DRi,RH,Don't Open
   the Door. 325.00
9 GC,DRi,Back From The Dead. 325.00
10 JMn(c),WIP,RH,Trapped
   In Time. 325.00
11 MSy,The Suitcase 275.00
12 GT,Dark Road 275.00
13 JMn(c),Strange Man,
   bondage cover. 275.00
14 RH,Death And Doctor Parker . 400.00
15 JMn(c),OW,The Machine 275.00
16 OW,Horror Backstage. 275.00
17 Night Of Terror 275.00
18 BK,The Cozy Coffin 300.00
19 BEv,RH 275.00
20 . . . . 275.00
21 BEv(c) 275.00
22 BEv(c),BK,OW 275.00
23 BEv 275.00
24 RH,GT. 300.00
25 I Died At Midnight 350.00
26 BEv(c) 225.00
27 DBr 250.00
28 BEv 250.00
29 JMn,BF,JRo,April, 1953 . . . . . 250.00

SWORDS OF THE SWASHBUCKLERS
Epic, 1985–87
1 JG,Adult theme 3.00
2 thru 7 JG . . . . @2.50
8 thru 12, June, 1987 . . . . @2.50

TALE OF THE MARINES
See: DEVIL-DOG DUGAN

TALES OF ASGARD
Oct., 1968
1 . . . . 50.00
Vol.2 #1 Feb,1984. . . . . 4.00

TALES OF G.I. JOE
Jan., 1988
1 reprints,#1 . . . . 3.00
2 thru 7 reprints . . . . @2.50

TALES OF JUSTICE
See: JUSTICE COMICS

TALES OF THE AGE OF APOCALYPSE
1996
1-shot SLo,JoB,Age of Apocalypse
   stories 5.00
GN, rep. 6.00

TALES OF THE AGE OF APOCALYPSE: SINISTER BLOODLINE
Dec., 1997
GN JFM,SEp, 48-pg. bookshelf.... 6.00

TALES OF THE MARVELS: BLOCKBUSTER
Fully painted (1995)............. 6.00

TALES OF THE MARVELS: INNER DEMONS
Fully painted, 48-pg. (1996)...... 6.00

TALES OF THE MARVELS: WONDER YEARS
1 & 2 DAb (1995) .... @5.00

TALES OF SUSPENSE
Jan., 1959
1 DH(c),AW,The Unknown
  Emptiness.............. 2,600.00
2 SK,JH,Robot in Hiding.... 950.00
3 SD,JK,The Aliens Who
  Captured Earth 900.00
4 JK,AW,One Of Us
  Is A Martian 800.00
5 JF,Trapped in the Tunnel
  To Nowhere 500.00
6 JK(c),Howl in the Swamp ... 500.00
7 SD,JK,Molten Man-Thing 600.00
8 BEv,Monstro 500.00
9 JK(c),JF,Diablo............. 650.00
10 RH,I Brought Cyclops Back
  To Life 550.00
11 JK(c),I Created Sporr 425.00
12 RC,Gorkill The Living Demon. 425.00
13 Elektro................. 550.00
14 JK(c),I Created Colossus ... 550.00
15 JK/DAy(c),Behold...Goom... 450.00
16 JK/DAy(c),The Thing Called
  Metallo................. 550.00
17 JK/DAy(c),Goo Gam, Son
  of Goom................ 450.00
18 JK/DAy(c),Kraa the Inhuman . 450.00
19 JK,DAy,SD,The Green Thing . 450.00
20 JK,DAy,SD,Colossus Lives
  Again 450.00
21 JK/DAy(c),SD,This Is Klagg .. 325.00
22 JK/DAy(c),SD,Beware
  Of Bruttu 325.00
23 JK,DAy,SD,The Creature
  in the Black Bog 325.00
24 JK,DAy,SD,Insect Man 325.00
25 JK,DAy,SD,The Death of
  Monstrollo 325.00
26 JK,DAy,SD,The Thing That
  Crawled By Night.......... 300.00
27 JK,DAy,SD,When Oog Lives
  Again 300.00
28 JK,DAy,SD,Back From
  the Dead 300.00
29 JK,DAy,SD,DH,The Martian
  Who Stole A City 275.00
30 JK,DAy,SD,DH,The Haunted
  Roller Coaster 300.00
31 JK,DAy,SD,DH,The Monster
  in the Iron Mask. 325.00
32 JK,DAy,SD,DH,The Man in
  the Bee-Hive 500.00
33 JK,DAy,SD,DH,Chamber of
  Fear................... 275.00
34 JK,DAy,SD,DH,Inside The
  Blue Glass Bottle. 275.00
35 JK,DAy,SD,DH,The Challenge
  of Zarkorr. 350.00

Tales of Suspense #58
© Marvel Entertainment Group

36 SD,Meet Mr. Meek 275.00
37 DH,SD,Hagg............. 275.00
38 JDa,The Teenager Who Ruled
  the World................ 275.00
39 JK,O&I:Iron Man 8,500.00
40 JK,C:Iron Man 2,800.00
41 JK,A:Iron Man,V:Dr.Strange. 1,600.00
42 DH,SD,I:Red Pharoah 600.00
43 JK,DH,I:Kala,A:Iron Man..... 600.00
44 DH,SD,V:Mad Pharoah...... 600.00
45 DH,V:Jack Frost 600.00
46 DH,CR,I:Crimson Dynamo ... 550.00
47 SD,V:Melter............. 550.00
48 SD,N:Iron Man 650.00
49 SD,A:Angel.............. 900.00
50 DH,I:Mandarin........... 350.00
51 DH,I:Scarecrow.......... 300.00
52 DH,I:Black Widow 450.00
53 DH,O:Watcher........... 275.00
54 DH,V:Mandarin 200.00
55 DH,V:Mandarin 200.00
56 DH,I:Unicorn............ 200.00
57 DH,I&O:Hawkeye 450.00
58 DH,GT,B:Captain America ... 550.00
59 DH,1st S.A. Solo Captain
  America,I:Jarvis.......... 550.00
60 DH,JK,V:Assassins........ 300.00
61 DH,JK,V:Mandarin 150.00
62 DH,JK,O:Mandarin 150.00
63 JK,O:Captain America 400.00
64 DH,JK,A:Black Widow,
  Hawkeye 175.00
65 DH,JK,I:Red Skull 300.00
66 DH,JK,O:Red Skull........ 300.00
67 DH,JK,V:Adolph Hitler. 125.00
68 DH,JK,V:Red Skull 125.00
69 DH,JK,I:Titanium Man...... 125.00
70 DH,JK,GT,V:Titanium Man ... 125.00
71 DH,JK,WW,GT,V:TitaniumMan 100.00
72 DH,JK,GT,V:The Sleeper 100.00
73 JA,JK,GT,A:Black Knight 100.00
74 JA,JK,GT,V:The Sleeper..... 100.00
75 JA,JK,I:Batroc,Sharon Carter . 100.00
76 JA,JR,V:Mandarin 100.00
77 JA,JK,JR,V:Ultimo,I:Peggy
  Carter. 90.00
78 JA,GC,JK,V:Ultimo........ 90.00
79 JA,GC,JK,V:Red Skull,
  I:Cosmic Cube........... 125.00
80 JA,GC,JK,V:Red Skull 135.00
81 JA,GC,JK,V:Red Skull 90.00
82 GC,JK,V:The Adaptoid 90.00
83 GC,JK,V:The Adaptoid 90.00
84 GC,JK,V:Mandarin 90.00

85 GC,JK,V:Batroc............ 90.00
86 GC,JK,V:Mandarin 90.00
87 GC,V:Mole Man 90.00
88 GK,JK,GC,V:Power Man...... 90.00
89 GK,JK,GC,V:Red Skull 90.00
90 GK,JK,GC,V:Red Skull 90.00
91 GK,GC,JK,V:Crusher 90.00
92 GC,JK,A:Nick Fury 90.00
93 GC,JK,V:Titanium Man 90.00
94 GC,JK,I:Modok 90.00
95 GC,JK,V:Grey Gargoyle,
  IR:Captain America 90.00
96 GC,JK,V:Grey Gargoyle 90.00
97 GC,JK,I:Whiplash,
  A:Black Panther. 90.00
98 GC,JK,I:Whitney Frost
  A:Black Panther. 125.00
99 GC,JK,A:Black Panther 150.00
Marvel Milestone rep. #39 (1993) .. 3.00
Becomes:

CAPTAIN AMERICA

TALES OF THE ZOMBIE
Aug., 1973
(Black & White Magazine)
1 Reprint Menace #5,O:Zombie . 40.00
2 GC,GT 30.00
3 .... 30.00
4 Live and Let Die............. 30.00
5 BH 30.00
6 .... 30.00
7 thru 9 AA .... @30.00
10 March, 1975 .... 30.00

TALES TO ASTONISH
[1st Series] Jan., 1959
1 JDa,Ninth Wonder of the
  World 2,500.00
2 SD,Capture A Martian...... 1,000.00
3 SD,JK,The Giant From
  Outer Space 750.00
4 SD,JK,The Day The
  Martians Struck 750.00
5 SD,AW,The Things on
  Easter Island 800.00
6 SD,JK,Invasion of the
  Stone Men 600.00
7 SD,JK,The Thing on Bald
  Mountain 600.00
8 DAy,SD,JK,Mmmex, King of
  the Mummies............. 600.00
9 DAy,JK(c),SD,Droom, the
  Living Lizard 600.00
10 DAy,JK,SD,Titano 600.00
11 DAy,JK,SD,Monstrom, the Dweller
  in the Black Swamp........ 400.00
12 JK/DAy(c),SD,Gorgilla 400.00
13 JK,SD,Groot, the Monster
  From Planet X 400.00
14 JK,SD,Krang. 400.00
15 JK/DAy,The Blip 550.00
16 DAy,JK,SD,Thorr. 450.00
17 JK,SD,Vandoom 400.00
18 DAy,JK,SD,Gorgilla Strikes
  Again 400.00
19 DAy,JK,SD,Rommbu......... 400.00
20 JK,SD,X, The Thing
  That Lived 400.00
21 JK,SD,Trull the Inhuman..... 400.00
22 JK,SD,The Crawling
  Creature................ 300.00
23 JK,SD,Moomba is Here!..... 300.00
24 JK,SD,The Abominable
  Snowman................ 300.00
25 JK,SD,The Creature From
  Krogarr................. 300.00
26 JK,SD,Four-Armed Things ... 300.00
27 StL(s),SD,JK,I:Ant-Man 7,000.00
28 JK,SD,I Am the Gorilla Man .. 300.00

29 JK,SD,When the Space
  Beasts Attack. 300.00
30 JK,SD,Thing From the
  Hidden Swamp 300.00
31 JK,SD,The Mummy's Secret. . 300.00
32 JK,SD,Quicksand 300.00
33 JK,SD,Dead Storage. 300.00
34 JK,SD,Monster at Window . . . 300.00
35 StL(s),JK,SD, B:Ant-Man
  (2nd App.). 3,000.00
36 JK,SD,V:Comrade X 1,000.00
37 JK,SD,V:The Protector 700.00
38 JK,SD,Betrayed By the Ants. . 700.00
39 JK,DH,V:Scarlet Beetle. 700.00
40 JK,SD,DH,The Day Ant-Man
  Failed. 700.00
41 DH,St,SD,V:Kulla 500.00
42 DH,JSe,SD,Voice of Doom. . . 500.00
43 DH,SD,Master of Time 500.00
44 JK,SD,I&O:Wasp 750.00
45 DH,SD,V:Egghead 300.00
46 DH,SD,I:Cyclops(robot) 300.00
47 DH,SD,V:Trago 300.00
48 DH,SD,I:Porcupine 300.00
49 JK,DH,AM,Ant-Man Becomes
  Giant-Man 350.00
50 JK,SD,I&O:Human Top 225.00
51 JK,V:Human Top. 225.00
52 I&O:Black Knight 225.00
53 DH,V:Porcupine 225.00
54 DH,I:El Toro 200.00
55 V:Human Top. 200.00
56 V:The Magician. 200.00
57 A:Spider-Man 400.00
58 V:Colossus(not X-Men one) . 200.00
59 V:Hulk,Black Knight 500.00
60 SD,B:Hulk,Giant Man 300.00
61 SD,I:Glenn Talbot,
  V:Egghead. 150.00
62 I:Leader,N:Wasp 150.00
63 SD,O:Leader(1st full story) . . 150.00
64 SD,V:Leader 150.00
65 BP,DH,SD,N:Giant-Man,. 150.00
66 BP,JK,SD,V:Leader,
  Chameleon 150.00
67 BP,JK,SD,I:Kanga Khan 150.00
68 BP,JK,N:Human Top,V:Leader 150.00
69 BP,JK,V:Human Top,Leader,
  E:Giant-Man 150.00
70 GC,JK,B:Sub-Mariner/Hulk,I:
  Neptune. 175.00
71 GC,JK,V:Leader,I:Vashti 90.00
72 GC,JK,V:Leader 90.00
73 GC,JK,V:Leader,A:Watcher . . . 90.00

Tales To Astonish #23
© Marvel Entertainment Group

74 GC,JK,V:Leader,A:Watcher . . . 90.00
75 GC,JK,A:Watcher 90.00
76 GC,GK,JK,Atlantis 90.00
77 JK,V:Executioner 90.00
78 BEv,GC,JK,Prince and
  the Puppet. 90.00
79 BEv,GC,JK,Hulk vs.Hercules . . 90.00
80 BEv,GC,JK,Moleman vs.
  Tyrannus 90.00
81 BEv,GC,JK,I:Boomerang,Secret
  Empire,Moleman vs. Tyrannus 90.00
82 BEv,GC,JK,V:Iron Man 100.00
83 BEv,JK,V:Boomerang 90.00
84 BEv,GC,JK,Like a Beast at Bay 90.00
85 BEv,GC,JB,Missile &
  the Monster 90.00
86 BEv,JB,V:Warlord Krang. 90.00
87 BEv,JB,IR:Hulk. 90.00
88 BEv,GK,V:Boomerang. 90.00
89 BEv,GK,V:Stranger 90.00
90 JK,GK,BEv,I:Abomination 90.00
91 GK,BEv,DA,V:Abomination . . . 90.00
92 MSe,C:Silver Surfer x-over . . 100.00
93 MSe,Silver Surfer x-over. . . . 125.00
94 BEv,MSe,V:Dragorr,High
  Evolutionary. 90.00
95 BEv,MSe,V:High Evolutionary. . 90.00
96 MSe,Skull Island,High Evol. . . . 90.00
97 MSe,C:Ka-Zar,X-Men 100.00
98 DA,MSe,I:Legion of the Living
  Lightning,I:Seth 90.00
99 DA,MSe,V:Legion of the Living
  Lighting 90.00
100 MSe,DA,Hulk vs.Sub-Mariner 125.00
101 MSe,GC,V:Loki 125.00
Becomes:

INCREDIBLE HULK

TALES TO ASTONISH
[2nd Series] Dec., 1979
1 JB,rep.Sub-Mariner#1 . . . . 5.00
2 thru 14 JB,rep.Sub-Mariner . . . @3.00

TANGLED WEB
April, 2001
1 GEn,JMC,The Thousand. 3.00
2 GEn,JMC,The Thousand. 3.00
3 GEn,JMC,V:The Thousand 3.00
4 Severance Package. 3.00
5 PrM,DFg,Flowers for Rhino 3.00
6 PrM,DFg,Flowers/Rhino,pt.2 . . . 3.00
7 Gentlemen's Agreement 3.00
8 Gentlemen's Agreement 3.00
9 LW,Gentlemen's Agreement,pt.3 . 3.00
10 Impact on Kids 3.00
11 Open All Night, 48-pg. 3.50
12 I Was A Teenaged Frog-Man . . . 3.00
13 SeP,Double Shots. 3.00
14 The Last Shoot 3.00
15 The Collaborator 3.00
16 F:Tombstone, Kangaroo 3.00
17 Tombstone in jail. 3.00
18 TMK 3.00
19 F:Grizzly & Rhino 3.00
20 J.Jonah Jameson 3.00
21 . . . . 3.00
22 The System. 3.00
TPB Spider-Man: Tangled Web . . . 16.00
TPB Spider-Man: Tangled Web 2 . 15.00
TPB Spider-Man: Tangled Web 3 . 16.00

TARZAN
June, 1977
1 JB,Edgar Rice Burroughs Adapt.25.00
2 JB,O:Tarzan 18.00
3 JB,The Alter of the Flaming
  God,I:LA 18.00
4 JB,TD,V:Leopards 18.00

Tarzan #21
© Marvel Entertainment Group

5 JB,TD,Vengeance,A:LA 10.00
6 JB,TD,Rage of Tantor,A:LA 10.00
7 JB,TD,Tarzan Rescues The
  Moon 10.00
8 JB,Battle For The Jewel Of
  Opar. 10.00
9 JB,Histah, the Serpent. 10.00
10 JB,The Deadly Peril of
  Jane Clayton 10.00
11 JB 10.00
12 JB,Fangs of Death 10.00
13 JB,Lion-God 10.00
14 JB,The Fury of Fang and Claw. 10.00
15 JB,Sword of the Slaver. 10.00
16 JB,Death Rides the Jungle
  Winds. 10.00
17 JB,The Entrance to the
  Earths Core 10.00
18 JB,Corsairs of the Earth's Core 10.00
19 Pursuit. 10.00
20 Blood Bond 10.00
21 Dark and Bloody Sky 8.00
22 JM,RN,War In Pellucidar 8.00
23 To the Death 8.00
24 The Jungle Lord Returns 8.00
25 RB(c),V:Poachers 8.00
26 RB(c),Caged 8.00
27 RB(c),Chaos in the Caberet 8.00
28 A Savage Against A City 8.00
29 Oct., 1979 . . . . 8.00
Ann.#1 JB 7.00
Ann.#2 Drums of the
  Death-Dancers 7.00
Ann.#3 Ant-Men and the
  She-Devils. 7.00

TARZAN OF THE APES
July, 1984
1 (movie adapt.) 4.00
2 . . . . 4.00

TASKMASTER
Feb., 2002
1 (of 4) F:Iron Man 3.00
2 crime syndicates 3.00
3 syndicates catch on 3.00
4 concl. 3.00

TEAM AMERICA
June, 1982
1 O:Team America 2.50

MARVEL

2 V:Marauder	2.50
3 LMc,V:Mr.Mayhem	2.50
4 LMc,V:Arcade Assassins	2.50
5 A:Marauder	2.50
6 A:R.U. Ready	2.50
7 LMc,V:Emperor of Texas	2.50
8 DP,V:Hydra	2.50
9 A:Iron Man	2.50
10 V:Minister Ashe	2.50
11 A:Marauder,V:Ghost Rider	3.00
12 DP,Marauder unmasked, May, 1983	2.50

TEAM HELIX
1993
1 A:Wolverine	2.25
2 A:Wolverine	2.25

TEAM X/TEAM 7
1996
1-shot LHa,SEp,MRy	4.95

TEAM X 2000
Dec., 1998
1-shot, 48-page	3.50

TEEN COMICS
See: ALL WINNERS COMICS

TEENAGE ROMANCE
See: MY ROMANCE

TEK WORLD
See: WILLIAM SHATNER'S TEK WORLD

TERMINATOR 2
Sept., 1991
1 KJ,movie adaption	3.00
2 KJ,movie adaption	3.00
3 KJ,movie adaption	3.00
Terminator II (bookshelf format)	5.00
Terminator II (B&W mag. size)	2.25

TERRARISTS
Epic, 1993–94
1 thru 4 w/card	@2.50
5 thru 7	@2.50

TERROR INC.
1992–93
1 JZ,I:Hellfire	3.00
2 JZ,I:Bezeel,Hellfire	2.50
3 JZ,A:Hellfire	2.25
4 JZ,A:Hellfire,V:Barbados	2.25
5 JZ,V:Hellfire,A:Dr. Strange	2.25
6 JZ,MT,A:Punisher	2.25
7 JZ,V:Punisher	2.25
8 Christmas issue	2.25
9 JZ,V:Wolverine	2.25
10 V:Wolverine	2.25
11 A:Silver Sable,Cage	2.25
12 For Love Nor Money#4,A:Cage, Silver Sable	2.25
13 Inf.Crusade,A:Gh.Rider	2.25

TESSIE THE TYPIST
Timely, Summer, 1944
1 BW,Doc Rockblock	750.00
2 BW,Powerhouse Pepper	400.00
3 Football cover	150.00

Terrarists #3
© Marvel Entertainment Group

4 BW	300.00
5 BW	300.00
6 BW,HK,Hey Look	300.00
7 BW	300.00
8 BW	300.00
9 BW,HK,Powerhouse Pepper	325.00
10 BW,A:Rusty	325.00
11 BW,A:Rusty	325.00
12 BW,HK	325.00
13 BW,A:Millie The Model,Rusty	275.00
14 BW	275.00
15 HK,A:Millie,Rusty	275.00
16 HK	150.00
17 HK,A:Millie, Rusty	150.00
18 HK	150.00
19 Annie Oakley story	100.00
20	100.00
21 A:Lana, Millie	100.00
22	100.00
23	100.00

Becomes:

TINY TESSIE
24	100.00

Becomes:

REAL EXPERIENCES
25 Ph(c),Jan., 1950	100.00

TEXAS KID
Atlas, Jan., 1951
1 GT,JMn,O:Texas Kid	300.00
2 JMn	200.00
3 JMn,Man Who Didn't Exist	150.00
4 thru 9 JMn	@150.00
10 JMn,July, 1952	150.00

TEX DAWSON, GUNSLINGER
Jan., 1973
1 JSo(c)	35.00

Becomes:

GUNSLINGER
2	25.00
3 June, 1973	25.00

TEX MORGAN
Aug., 1948
1 Tex Morgan & Lobo	350.00
2 Boot Hill Welcome For A Bad Man	225.00
3 A:Arizona Annie	150.00

4 Trapped in the Outlaw's Den, A:Arizona Annie	125.00
5 Valley of Missing Cowboys	125.00
6 Never Say Murder, A:Tex Taylor	150.00
7 CCB,Ph(c),Captain Tootsie, A:Tex Taylor	200.00
8 Ph(c),Terror Of Rimrock Valley, A:Diablo	200.00
9 Ph(c),Death to Tex Taylor, Feb., 1950	200.00

TEX TAYLOR
Sept., 1948
1 Boot Hill Showdown	325.00
2 When Two-Gun Terror Rides the Range	175.00
3 Thundering Hooves and Blazing Guns	150.00
4 Ph(c),Draw or Die Cowpoke	200.00
5 Ph(c),The Juggler of Yellow Valley,A:Blaze Carson	200.00
6 Ph(c),Mystery of Howling Gap	200.00
7 Ph(c),Trapped in Time's Lost Land,A:Diablo	225.00
8 Ph(c),The Mystery of Devil-Tree Plateau,A:Diablo	225.00
9 Ph(c),Guns Along the Border, A:Nimo,March, 1950	225.00

THANOS
Oct., 2003
1 JSn	3.00
2 JSn,Galactus,Adam Warlock	3.00
3 JSn,F:Moondragon	3.00
4 JSn,Epiphany,pt.4	3.00
5 JSn,Epiphany,pt.5	3.00
6 JSn,concl.	3.00
7 KG,RLm	3.00
8 KG,RLm	3.00
9 KG,RLm	3.00
10 KG,RLm,V:The Maker	3.00
11 KG,RLm	3.00
12 KG,RLm	3.00
TPB The End, Vol.3	19.95
TPB Vol. 4: Epiphany	15.00
TPB Vol. 5: Samaritan	15.00

THANOS QUEST
1990
1 JSn,RLm,V:Elders, for Soul Gems	8.00
1a 2nd printing	4.00
2 JSn,RLm,O:SoulGems,I: Infinity Gauntlet cont.in Silver Surfer #44)	8.00
2a 2nd printing	4.00

THANOS QUEST
Jan., 2000
GN JSn,RLm,96-pg.	4.00

THING, THE
July, 1983
1 JBy,O:Thing	3.50
2 JBy,Woman from past	2.50
3 JBy,A:Inhumans	2.50
4 JBy,A:Lockjaw	2.50
5 JBy,A:Spider-Man,She-Hulk	2.50
6 JBy,V:Puppet Master	2.50
7 JBy,V:Goody Two Shoes	2.50
8 JBy,V:Egyptian Curse	2.50
9 JBy,F:Alicia Masters	2.50
10 JBy,Secret Wars	2.50
11 JBy,B:Rocky Grimm	2.50
12 JBy,F:Rocky Grimm	2.50
13 JBy,F:Rocky Grimm	2.50
14 F:Rocky Grimm	2.50

15 F:Rocky Grimm. 2.50	160 JK,I:Travrians 65.00
16 F:Rocky Grimm. 2.50	161 JK,Shall a God Prevail 65.00
17 F:Rocky Grimm. 2.50	162 JK,O:Galactus. 80.00
18 F:Rocky Grimm. 2.50	163 JK,I:Mutates,A:Pluto 50.00
19 F:Rocky Grimm. 2.50	164 JK,A:Pluto,V:Greek Gods . . . 50.00
20 F:Rocky Grimm. 2.50	165 JK,V:Him/Warlock 150.00
21 V:Ultron. 2.50	166 JK,V:Him/Warlock 125.00
22 V:Ultron. 2.50	167 JK,F:Sif 50.00
23 R:Thing to Earth,A:Fant. Four . . 2.50	168 JK,O:Galactus. 75.00
24 V:Rhino,A:Miracle Man 2.50	169 JK,O:Galactus. 75.00
25 V:Shamrock 2.50	170 JK,BEv,V:Thermal Man. 50.00
26 A:Vance Astro 2.50	171 JK,BEv,V:Wrecker. 50.00
27 I:Sharon Ventura. 2.50	172 JK,BEv,V:Ulik 50.00
28 A:Vance Astro 2.50	173 JK,BEv,V:Ulik,Ringmaster. . . . 50.00
29 A:Vance Astro 2.50	174 JK,BEv,V:Crypto-Man 50.00
30 Secret Wars II,A:Vance Astro . . 2.50	175 JK,Fall of Asgard,V:Surtur . . . 50.00
31 A:Vance Astro 2.50	176 JK,V:Surtur 50.00
32 A:Vance Astro 2.50	177 JK,I:Igon,V:Surtur 50.00
33 A:Vance Astro,I:New Grapplers . 2.50	178 JK,C:Silver Surfer 60.00
34 V:Titania,Sphinx 2.50	179 JK,MSe,C:Galactus. 50.00
35 I:New Ms.Marvel,Power Broker . 2.50	180 NA,JSi,V:Loki 60.00
36 Last Issue,A:She-Hulk 2.50	181 NA,JSi,V:Loki 60.00
	182 JB,V:Dr.Doom 45.00
[Mini-Series]	183 JB,V:Dr.Doom 45.00
1 rep.Marvel Two-in-One #50 . . . . . 2.50	184 JB,I:The Guardian. 45.00
2 rep Marvel Two-in-One,V:GR . . . 2.50	185 JB,JSt,V:Silent One. 45.00
3 rep Marvel Two-in-One #51 . . . . . 2.00	186 JB,JSt,V:Hela 45.00
4 rep Marvel Two-in-One #43 . . . . . 2.00	187 JB,JSt,V:Odin 45.00
	188 JB,JM,F:Odin 45.00
THING/SHE-HULK	189 JB,JSt,V:Hela 45.00
March, 1998	190 JB,I:Durok 45.00
1-shot TDz,V:Dragon Man, 48-pg . . 3.00	191 JB,JSt,V:Loki 45.00
1-shot The Long Night, 48-pg. 3.00	192 JB 45.00
	193 JB,SB,V:Silver Surfer 75.00
THING, THE: FREAKSHOW	194 JB,SB,V:Loki 40.00
June, 2002	195 JB,JR,V:Mangog 40.00
1 (of 4) ALa,grumpiest super-hero . 3.00	196 JB,NR,V:Kartag. 40.00
2 ALa,people are enthralled 3.00	197 JB,V:Mangog 40.00
3 ALa,ScK. 3.00	198 JB,V:Pluto 40.00
4 ALa,ScK,concl. 3.00	199 JB,V:Pluto,Hela. 40.00
	200 JB,Ragnarok 50.00
THOR, THE MIGHTY	201 JB,JM,Odin resurrected. 30.00
Prev: Journey Into Mystery	202 JB,V:Ego-Prime 30.00
March, 1966	203 JB,V:Ego-Prime 30.00
126 JK,V:Hercules 275.00	204 JB,JM,Demon from t/Depths. . 30.00
127 JK,I:Pluto,Volla 125.00	205 JB,V:Mephisto. 30.00
128 JK,V:Pluto,A:Hercules. 125.00	206 JB,V:Absorbing Man 25.00
129 JK,V:Pluto,I:Ares. 125.00	207 JB,V:Absorbing Man 25.00
130 JK,V:Pluto,A:Hercules. 125.00	208 JB,V:Mercurio 25.00
131 JK,I:Colonizers 125.00	209 JB,I:Druid 25.00
132 JK,A:Colonizers,I:Ego. 125.00	210 JB,DP,I:Ulla,V:Ulik. 25.00
133 JK,A:Colonizers,A:Ego 125.00	211 JB,DP,V:Ulik 25.00
134 JK,I:High Evolutionary,	212 JB,JSt,V:Sssthgar 25.00
Man-Beast 150.00	213 JB,DP,I:Gregor 25.00
135 JK,O:High Evolutionary. 100.00	214 SB,JM,V:Dark Nebula. 25.00
136 JK,F:Odin 100.00	215 JB,JM,J:Xorr 25.00
137 JK,I:Ulik. 100.00	216 JB,JM,V:4D-Man. 25.00
138 JK,V:Ulik,A:Sif. 100.00	217 JB,SB,I:Krista,V:Odin 25.00
139 JK,V:Ulik 100.00	218 JB,JM,A:Colonizers. 25.00
140 JK,V:Growing Man 100.00	219 JB,I:Protector 25.00
141 JK,V:Replicus 75.00	220 JB,V:Avalon. 25.00
142 JK,V:Super Skrull 75.00	221 JB,V:Olympus 25.00
143 JK,BEv,V:Talisman 75.00	222 JB,JSe,A:Hercules,V:Pluto . . . 25.00
144 JK,V:Talisman 75.00	223 JB,A:Hercules,V:Pluto. 25.00
145 JK,V:Ringmaster 75.00	224 JB,V:Destroyer 25.00
146 JK,O:Inhumans Part 1 . . . . . 100.00	225 JB,JSi,I:Fire Lord 30.00
147 JK,O:Inhumans Part 2 . . . . . 100.00	226 JB,A:Watcher,Galactus 20.00
148 JK,I:Wrecker,O:Black Bolt. . . 100.00	227 JB,JSi,V:Ego 20.00
149 JK,O:Black Bolt,Medusa. . . . 100.00	228 JB,JSi,A:Galactus,D:Ego 20.00
150 JK,A:Triton 100.00	229 JB,JSi,A:Hercules,I:Dweller . . 20.00
151 JK,V:Destroyer 90.00	230 JB,A:Hercules. 20.00
152 JK,V:Destroyer 90.00	231 JB,DG,V:Armak. 20.00
153 JK,F:Dr.Blake 90.00	232 JB,JSi,A:Firelord 20.00
154 JK,I:Mangog 90.00	233 JB,Asgard Invades Earth 20.00
155 JK,V:Mangog 90.00	234 JB,V:Loki. 20.00
156 JK,V:Mangog 90.00	235 JB,JSi,I:Possessor
157 JK,D:Mangog 90.00	(Kamo Tharnn) 20.00
158 JK,O:Don Blake Part 1 . . . . . 150.00	236 JB,JSi,V:Absorbing Man 20.00
159 JK,O:Don Blake Part 2 . . . . . . 90.00	237 JB,JSi,V:Ulik 20.00
	238 JB,JSi,V:Ulik 20.00
	239 JB,JSi,V:Ulik 20.00

Thor #233
© Marvel Entertainment Group

240 SB,KJ,V:Seth 20.00
241 JB,JGi,I:Geb 20.00
242 JB,JSi,V:Servitor. 20.00
243 JB,JSt,V:Servitor 20.00
244 JB,JSt,V:Servitor 20.00
245 JB,JSt,V:Servitor 20.00
246 JB,JSt,A:Firelord 20.00
247 JB,JSt,A:Firelord 20.00
248 JB,V:Storm Giant 20.00
249 JB,V:Odin 20.00
250 JB,D:Igron,V:Mangog 20.00
251 JB,A:Sif 15.00
252 JB,V:Ulik 15.00
253 JB,I:Trogg 15.00
254 JK,O:Dr.Blake rep. 15.00
255 Stone Men of Saturn rep. 15.00
256 JB,I:Sporr 15.00
257 JK,JB,I:Fee-Lon 15.00
258 JK,JB,V:Grey Gargoyle. 15.00
259 JB,A:Spider-Man. 15.00
260 WS,I:Doomsday Star 15.00
261 WS,I:Soul Survivors 15.00
262 WS,Odin Found,I:Odin Force . 15.00
263 WS,V:Loki 15.00
264 WS,V:Loki 15.00
265 WS,V:Destroyer 15.00
266 WS,Odin Quest. 15.00
267 WS,F:Odin 15.00
268 WS,V:Damocles 15.00
269 WS,V:Stilt-Man 15.00
270 WS,V:Blastaar. 15.00
271 Avengers,Iron Man x-over. . . . 15.00
272 JB,Day the Thunder Failed. . . 15.00
273 JB,V:Midgard Serpent. 15.00
274 JB,D:Balder,I:Hermod,Hoder . 15.00
275 JB,V:Loki,I:Sigyn. 15.00
276 JB,Trial of Loki 15.00
277 JB,V:Fake Thor. 15.00
278 JB,V:Fake Thor. 15.00
279 A:Pluto,V:Ulik 15.00
280 V:Hyperion 15.00
281 O:Space Phantom. 12.00
282 V:Immortus,I:Tempus 12.00
283 JB,V:Celestials 12.00
284 JB,V:Gammenon. 12.00
285 JB,R:Karkas 12.00
286 KP,KRo,D:Kro,I:Dragona. 12.00
287 KP,2nd App. & O:Forgotten
One(Hero) 12.00
288 KP,V:Forgotten One 12.00
289 KP,V:Destroyer 12.00
290 I:Red Bull(Toro Rojo) 12.00
291 KP,A:Eternals,Zeus. 12.00
292 KP,V:Odin 12.00
293 KP,Door to Mind's Eye 12.00

294 KP,O:Odin & Asgard,I:Frey . . . 12.00
295 KP,I:Fafnir,V:Storm Giants . . 12.00
296 KP,D:Siegmund. 12.00
297 KP,V:Sword of Siegfried 12.00
298 KP,V:Dragon(Fafnir) 12.00
299 KP,A:Valkyrie,I:Hagen 12.00
300 KP,giant,O:Odin & Destroyer,
     Rindgold Ring Quest ends,D:Uni-
     Mind,I:Mother Earth. 20.00
301 KP,O:Mother Earth,V:Apollo . . 12.00
302 KP,V:Locus 12.00
303 Whatever Gods There Be. . . . 12.00
304 KP,V:Wrecker 12.00
305 KP,R:Gabriel(Air Walker) 12.00
306 KP,O&V:Firelord,O:Air Walker. 12.00
307 KP,I:Dream Demon 12.00
308 KP,V:Snow Giants. 12.00
309 V:Bomnardiers 12.00
310 KP,V:Mephisto. 12.00
311 KP,GD,A:Valkyrie. 12.00
312 KP,V:Tyr 12.00
313 KP,Thor Trial 12.00
314 KP,A:Drax,Moondragon 12.00
315 KP,O:Bi-Beast 12.00
316 KP,A:Iron Man,Man Thing,
     V:Man-Beast 12.00
317 KP,V:Man-Beast 12.00
318 GK,V:Fafnir 12.00
319 KP,I&D:Zaniac. 12.00
320 KP,V:Rimthursar 12.00
321 I:Menagerie 12.00
322 V:Heimdall. 12.00
323 V:Death 12.00
324 V:Graviton 12.00
325 JM,O:Darkoth,V:Mephisto . . . 12.00
326 I:New Scarlet Scarab 12.00
327 V:Loki & Tyr. 12.00
328 I:Megatak 12.00
329 HT,V:Hrungnir 12.00
330 BH,I:Crusader. 12.00
331 Threshold of Death 12.00
332 V:Dracula 12.00
333 BH,V:Dracula 12.00
334 Quest For Rune Staff 12.00
335 V:Possessor 12.00
336 A:Captain Ultra 12.00
337 WS,I:Beta Ray Bill,A:Surtur . . 20.00
338 WS,O:Beta Ray Bill,I:Lorelei. . 18.00
339 WS,V:Beta Ray Bill. 12.00
340 WS,A:Beta Ray Bill 12.00
341 WS,V:Fafnir. 12.00
342 WS,V:Fafnir,I:Eilif 12.00
343 WS,V:Fafnir. 12.00
344 WS,Balder vs. Loki,I:Malekith. 12.00
345 WS,V:Malekith 12.00
346 WS,V:Malekith 12.00
347 WS,V:Malekith,I:Algrim
     (Kurse). 12.00
348 WS,V:Malekith 12.00
349 WS,R:Beta Ray Bill,O:Odin,
     I&O:Vili & Ve(Odin's brothers) . 12.00
350 WS,V:Surtur 12.00
351 WS,V:Surtur 12.00
352 WS,V:Surtur 12.00
353 WS,V:Surtur,D:Odin 8.00
354 WS,V:Hela 8.00
355 WS,SB,A:Thor's Great
     Grandfather 8.00
356 BL,BG,V:Hercules 8.00
357 WS,A:Beta Ray Bill. 8.00
358 WS,A:Beta Ray Bill 8.00
359 WS,V:Loki 8.00
360 WS,V:Hela 8.00
361 WS,V:Hela 8.00
362 WS,V:Hela 8.00
363 WS,Secret Wars II,V:Kurse. . . 8.00
364 WS,I:Thunder Frog 8.00
365 WS,A:Thunder Frog 8.00
366 WS,A:Thunder Frog 8.00
367 WS,D:Malekith,A:Kurse 8.00
368 WS,F:Balder t/Brave,Kurse. . . 8.00

369 WS,F:Balder the Brave. 8.00
370 JB,V:Loki. 8.00
371 SB,I:Justice Peace,V:Zaniac. . 8.00
372 SB,V:Justice Peace 8.00
373 SB,A:X-Factor,(Mut.Mass) . . . 10.00
374 WS,SB,A:X-Factor,(Mut.Mass)
     A:Sabretooth 12.00
375 WS,SB,N:Thor(Exoskeleton) . . 8.00
376 WS,SB,V:Absorbing Man 8.00
377 WS,SB,N:Thor,V:Ice Man 8.00
378 WS,SB,V:Frost Giants 8.00
379 WS,V:Midgard Serpent 8.00
380 WS,V:Midgard Serpent 8.00
381 WE,SB,A:Avengers. 8.00
382 WS,SB,V:Frost Giants,Loki. . . 10.00
383 BBr,Secret Wars story 8.00
384 RF,BBr,I:Future Thor(Dargo). . 12.00
385 EL,V:Hulk 8.00
386 RF,BBr,I:Leir 8.00
387 RF,BBr,V:Celestials. 8.00
388 RF,BBr,V:Celestials. 8.00
389 RF,BBr,V:Celestials. 8.00
390 RF,BBr,A:Avengers,V:Seth . . . 8.00
391 RF,BBr,I:Mongoose,Eric
     Masterson,A:Spider-Man. 12.00
392 RF,I:Quicksand 10.00
393 RF,BBr,V:Quicksand,A:DD . . . 10.00
394 RF,BBr,V:Earth Force 10.00
395 RF,V:Earth Force 10.00
396 RF,A:Black Knight. 10.00
397 RF,A:Loki. 10.00
398 RF,DH,R:Odin,V:Seth 10.00
399 RF,RT,R:Surtur,V:Seth 10.00
400 RF,JSt,CV,V:Surtur,Seth 12.00
401 V:Loki 7.00
402 RF,JSt,V:Quicksand 7.00
403 RF,JSt,V:Executioner 7.00
404 RF,JSt,TD,V:Annihilus. 7.00
405 RF,JSt,TD,V:Annihilus. 7.00
406 RF,JSt,TD,V:Wundagore. 7.00
407 RF,JSt,R:Hercules,High Evol. . . 7.00
408 RF,JSt,I:Eric Masterson/Thor,
     V:Mongoose 8.00
409 RF,JSt,V:Dr.Doom 7.00
410 RF,JSt,V:Dr.Doom,She-Hulk . . 7.00
411 RF,JSt,C:New Warriors
     V:Juggernaut,A of V 5.00
412 RF,JSt,I:New Warriors
     V:Juggernaut,A of V 6.00
413 RF,JSt,A:Dr.Strange 4.00
414 RF,JSt,V:Ulik 4.00
415 HT,O:Thor. 4.00
416 RF,JSt,A:Hercules. 4.00

Thor #338
© Marvel Entertainment Group

417 RF,JSt,A:High Evolutionary. . . . 4.00
418 RF,JSt,V:Wrecking Crew. 4.00
419 RF,JSt,B:Black Galaxy
     Saga,I:Stellaris. 4.00
420 RF,JSt,A:Avengers,V:Stellaris. . 4.00
421 RF,JSt,V:Stellaris. 4.00
422 RF,JSt,V:High Evol.,Nobilus . . 4.00
423 RF,JSt,A:High Evol.,Celestials
     Count Tagar. 4.00
424 RF,JSt,V:Celestials,E:Black
     Galaxy Saga 4.00
425 RF,AM,V:Surtur,Ymir. 4.00
426 RF,JSt,HT,O:Earth Force 4.00
427 RF,JSt,A:Excalibur 4.00
428 RF,JSt,A:Excalibur 4.00
429 RF,JSt,A:Ghost Rider 4.00
430 RF,AM,A:Mephisto,Gh.Rider. . 4.00
431 HT,AM,V:Ulik,Loki. 4.00
432 RF,D:Loki,Thor Banished,Eric
     Masterson becomes 2nd Thor. . 6.00
433 RF,V:Ulik 7.00
434 RF,AM,V:Warriors Three 5.00
435 RF,AM,V:Annihilus 5.00
436 RF,AM,V:Titania,Absorbing
     Man,A:Hercules. 5.00
437 RF,AM,V:Quasar. 5.00
438 RF,JSt,A:Future Thor(Drago) . . 5.00
439 RF,JSt,A:Drago 5.00
440 RF,AM,I:Thor Corps 6.00
441 RF,AM,Celestials vs.Ego 6.00
442 RF,AM,Don Blake,Beta Ray
     Bill,Mephisto 4.00
443 RF,AM,A:Dr.Strange,Silver
     Surfer,V:Mephisto 4.00
444 RF,AM,Special X-mas tale 4.00
445 AM,Galactic Storm,pt.7,
     V:Gladiator. 4.00
446 AM,Galactic Storm,pt.14,
     A:Avengers 4.00
447 RF,AM,V:Absorbing Man,
     A:Spider-Man. 4.00
448 RF,AM,V:Titania,A:SpM. 4.00
449 RF,AM,V:Ulik. 4.00
450 RF,AM,V:Heimdall,A:Code Blue
     Double-Sized,Gatefold(c),rep.
     Journey Into Mystery#87. . . . . 4.00
451 RF,AM,I:Bloodaxe 4.00
452 RF,AM,V:Bloodaxe 4.00
453 RF,AM,V:Mephisto 4.00
454 RF,AM,V:Mephisto,Loki,
     Karnilla. 4.00
455 AM(i),V:Loki,Karnilla,R:Odin,
     A:Dr.Strange 4.00
456 RF,AM,V:Bloodaxe 4.00
457 RF,AM,R:1st Thor 4.00
458 RF,AM,Thor vs. Eric 4.00
459 RF,AM,C&I:Thunderstrike(Eric
     Masterson). 3.00
460 I:New Valkyrie 3.00
461 V:Beta Ray Bill 3.00
462 A:New Valkyrie 3.00
463 Infinity Crusade 3.00
464 Infinity Crusade,V:Loki 3.00
465 Infinity Crusade. 3.00
466 Infinity Crusade. 3.00
467 Infinity Crusade. 3.00
468 RMz(s),Blood & Thunder#1 . . 3.00
469 RMz(s),Blood & Thunder#5 . . 3.00
470 MCW,Blood & Thunder#9. . . . 3.00
471 MCW,E:Blood & Thunder 3.00
472 B:RTs(s),MCW,I:Godling,C:High
     Evolutionary. 3.00
473 MCW,V:Godling,High Evolutionary,
     I&C:Karnivore(Man-Beast) 3.00
474 MCW,C:High Evolutionary 3.00
475 MCW,Foil(c),A:Donald Blake,
     N:Thor. 3.50
475a Newsstand ed. 3.00
476 V:Destroyer 3.00
477 V:Destroyer,A:Thunderstrike. . . 3.00
478 V:Norvell Thor. 3.00

MARVEL

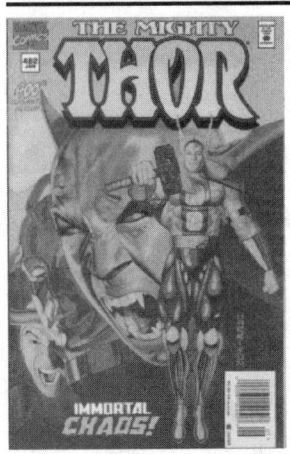

Thor #482
© *Marvel Entertainment Group*

Journey Into Mystery #510
© *Marvel Entertainment Group*

479 V:Norvell Thor 3.00
480 V:High Evolutionary 3.00
481 V:Grotesk 3.00
482 Don Blake construct 3.00
483 RTs,MCW,V:Loki 3.00
484 Badoy and Soul 3.00
485 V:The Thing 3.00
486 High Evolutionary,Godpack 3.00
487 V:Kurse 3.00
488 RTs,MCW,Kurse Saga concl. . . 3.00
489 RTs,V:Kurse,A:Hulk. 3.00
490 TDF,after Thunderstrike 3.00
491 N:Thor 7.50
492 Worldengine's Secrets 5.00
493 Worldengine trigers Ragnarok . 3.00
494 Worldengine saga conclusion . . 3.00
495 BML,Avengers:Timeslide 3.00
496 MD2,BML,A:Capt.America 3.00
497 MD2,BML,Thor Must Die 3.00
498 BML,V:Absorbing Man 3.00
499 MD2,BML 3.00
500 MD2,BML,double size,A:Dr.
  Strange 3.50
501 MD2,BML,I:Red Norvell 3.00
502 MD2,BML,Onslaught tie-in, A:Red
  Norvell, Jane Foster, Hela 3.00
Becomes:

JOURNEY INTO MYSTERY
[Third Series] Nov., 1996
503 TDF,MD2, The Lost Gods, New
  Norse gods? 2.50
504 TDF,Golden Realm in ruins,
  V:Ulik the Troll 2.50
505 TDF,MD2, V:Wrecker,
  A:Spider-Man 2.50
506 TDF,MD2, R:Heimdall 2.50
507 TDF,Odin kidnapped 2.50
508 TDF 2.50
509 TDF,Battle for the Future
  of Asgard 2.50
510 TDF,Return of Loki,A:Seth 2.50
511 TDF,EBe,Lost Gods reunited
  with Odin 2.50
512 EBe, Odin vs. Seth 2.50
513 TDF,SB,AM, Odin vs.
  Seth, concl. 2.50
514 BRa,VRu,F:Shang Chi, Master
  of Kung Fu 2.50
515 BRa,VRu,F:Shang Chi, Master
  of Kung Fu, pt.2 . . . . 2.50
516 BRa,VRu,F:Shang Chi, Master
  of Kung Fu, pt.3 . . . . 2.50
517 SLo,RGr,F:Black Widow 2.50

518 SLo,RGr,F:Black Widow 2.50
519 SLo,RGr,F:Black Widow, concl. 2.50
520 MWn,F:Hannibal King, pt.1 . . . . 2.50
521 MWn,F:Hannibal King, pt.2 . . . . 2.50
Ann.#2 JK,V:Destroyer 75.00
Ann.#3 JK,rep,Grey Gargoyle 30.00
Ann.#4 JK,rep,TheLivingPlanet. . . . 25.00
Ann.#5 JK,JB,Hercules,O:Odin . . . 25.00
Ann.#6 JK,JB,A:Guardians of the
  Galaxy,V:Korvac 25.00
Ann.#7 WS,Eternals. 20.00
Ann.#8 JB,V:Zeus 20.00
Ann.#9 LMc,Dormammu 20.00
Ann.#10 O:Chthon,Gaea,A:Pluto. . 15.00
Ann.#11 O:Odin 15.00
Ann.#12 BH,I:Vidar(Odin's son). . . 15.00
Ann.#13 JB,V:Mephisto 15.00
Ann.#14 AM,DH,Atlantis Attacks . . 7.00
Ann.#15 HT,Terminus Factor #3 . . . 5.00
Ann.#16 Korvac Quest,pt.2,
  Guardians of Galaxy 3.00
Ann.#17 Citizen Kang#2 . . . . 3.00
Ann.#18 TGr,I:The Flame,w/card. . . 3.50
Ann.#19 V:Flame 3.50
G-Size.#1 Battles,A:Hercules 14.00
TPB Alone Against the Celestials . . 6.00
TPB Ballad of Beta Ray Bill, rep. . . 9.00
Minus 1 Spec., TDF,EBe,flashback . 2.00
1-shot, Rough Cut, DJu,JR,original
  pencils, b&w 48-pg. 3.00

THOR
May, 1998
1 JR2,KJ,DJu,The hero returns,
  48-pg. 6.00
2A JR2,KJ,DJu,V:Destroyer,A:Hela,
  Marnot 3.50
2B JR2,KJ variant cover 3.50
3 DJu,JR2,KJ,A:Marnot,V:Sedna . . 3.00
4 DJu,JR2,KJ,A:Namor,Sedna 3.00
5 DJu,JR2,KJ,V:Charles Diamond . 3.00
6 DJu,JR2,KJ,V:Hercules 3.00
7 DJu,JR2,KJ,V:Zeus 3.00
8 DJu,JR2,KJ,PeterParker x-over. . . 3.00
9 DJu,JB,JOy,War on
  Asgard,prelude 3.00
10 DJu,JR2,KJ,War on Asgard,pt.1 . 3.00
11 DJu,JR2,KJ,War on Asgard,pt.2 . 3.00
12 DJu,JR2,KJ,War on
  Asgard,concl. 48-page 3.00
12a signed 20.00
13 DJu,JR2,KJ,A:Marnot 2.50
14 DJu,Hammer secret 2.50

15 DJu,KJ,JR2(c),A:Warriors 3 . . . . 2.50
16 DJu,KJ,JR2,A:Warriors 3 . . . . . . 2.50
17 DJu,KJ,JR2,Eighth
  Day,pt.1, x-over 2.50
18 DJu,KJ,JR2,V:Enrakt 2.50
19 DJu 2.50
20 DJu,V:Loki 2.50
21 DJu,JR2,KJ,R:Thanos 2.50
22 DJu,JR2,KJ,V:Thanos 2.50
23 DJu,JR2,DG,V:Thanos 2.50
24 DJu,JR2,DG,V:Thanos 2.50
25A DJu,JR2,DG,48-pg.,foil(c) 6.00
25B variant (c) 3.00
26 DJu,EL,KJ,V:AbsorbingMan . . . 2.25
27 DJu,EL,KJ,Dr.Jane Foster 2.25
28 DJu,EL,KJ,WarriorsThree 2.25
29 DJu,NKu,SHa,Jagrfelm. 2.25
30 DJu,NKu,SHa,MaxSecurity. . . . 2.25
31 DJu,NKu,SHa,V:Malekith 2.25
32 DJu,NKu,SHa,100-page 4.00
33 DJu,SI,I:new 2.25
34 DJu,NKu,SHa 2.25
35 DJu,NKu,SHa,V:Gladiator,
  48-page 3.50
36 DJu,R:Loki,A:Destroyer 2.25
37 DJu,JSn,AM,A:Watcher 2.25
38 DJu,SI,BWS(c),V:Destroyer 2.25
39 DJu,SI,BWS(c),V:Surtur 2.25
40 DJu,SI,V:Surtur 2.25
41 DJu,SI,V:Surtur,concl. 2.25
42 DJu,SI,Asgard,Midgard. 2.25
43 DJu,JoB,Thor:King of Asgard . . . 2.25
44 DJu,SI,Odin funeral,'Nuff Said . . 2.25
45 TR,new King in Asgard 2.25
46 DJu,SHa,TR,F:Thor-Girl 2.25
47 DJu,SHa,TR,Enchantress. 2.25
48 DJu,JoB,TP,V:Desak. 2.25
49 DJu,TR,SHa,V:Desak 2.25
50 DJu,TR,SHa,64-pg.. . . . . 6.00
51 DJu,TR,SHa,F:Spider-Man 2.25
52 DJu,TP 2.25
53 DJu 2.25
54 DJu,TR,SHa 2.25
55 DJu,TR,SHa 2.25
56 DJu,TR, ... 2.25
57 DJu,JoB 2.25
58 DJu,AD,Standoff,pt.1,x-over . . . 2.50
59 CPr(s) 2.50
60 DJu,JoB,Spiral,pt.1 . . . . 2.25
61 DJu,Spiral,pt.2 . . . . 2.25
62 DJu,Spiral,pt.3 . . . . 3.00
63 DJu,Spiral,pt.4 . . . . 3.00
64 DJu,Spiral,pt.5 . . . . 3.00
65 DJu,Spiral,pt.6 . . . . 3.00
66 DJu,Spiral,pt.7 . . . . 3.00
67 DJu,Spiral,concl. 3.00
68 DJu,SEa,The Reigning,prologue 3.00
69 DJu,SEa,The Reigning,pt.1 . . . . 3.00
70 DJu,SEa,The Reigning,pt.2 . . . . 3.00
71 DKi,SEa,The Reigning,pt.3 . . . . . 3.00
72 DJu,SEa,The Reigning,pt.4 . . . . 3.00
73 DJu,SEa,The Reigning,pt.5 . . . . 3.00
74 DJu,SEa,The Reigning,concl. . . . 3.00
75 DJu,SEa,Gods & Men,pt.1 . . . . . 3.00
76 DJu,SEa,Gods & Men,pt.2 . . . . . 3.00
77 DJu,SEa,Gods & Men,pt.3 . . . . . 3.00
78 DJu,SEa,Gods & Men,pt.4 . . . . . 3.00
79 DJu,SEa,Gods & Men,pt.5 . . . . . 3.00
80 F:The Avengers 10.00
81 F:The Avengers 7.00
82 Avengers Disassembled tie-in . . 5.00
83 Ragnarok,pt.3 . . . . 3.00
84 Ragnarok,pt.4 . . . . 3.00
85 Ragnarok,pt.5 . . . . 3.00
Ann.1999 DJu,KJ, 48-page 3.50
Ann.1999 signed 20.00
Ann.2000, 48-pg. 3.50
Ann.2001 TG,DJu,48-page 3.50
Spec.#1 Thor (2000) 2.25
Spec. rep.#1 & #2 . . . . 6.00
TPB The Dark Gods, 128-pg. 16.00

TPB Across All Worlds 17.00
TPB Thor Visionaries: Walt
     Simonson, 288-page 25.00
TPB The Death of Odin 13.00
TPB Lord of Asgard 16.00
TPB Vol. 2: Legends (2003) 25.00
TPB Vol. 3: Gods on Earth 22.00
TPB Vol. 4: Spiral (2003) 20.00
TPB Vol. 5: The Reigning 18.00
TPB Vol. 6: Gods & Men 14.00
TPB Visionaries MD2 . . . . 20.00

THOR CORPS
[Limited Series]
1 TDF(s),PO,V:Demonstaff 2.25
2 TDF(s),PO,A:Invaders 2.25
3 TDF(s),PO,A:Spider-Man 2099 . . 2.25
4 TDF(s),PO,last issue 2.25

THOR: GODSTORM
Sept., 2001
1 (of 3) KBk,SR 3.50
2 KBk,SR,V:Loki 3.50
3 KBk,SR,V:Loki,concl. 3.50

THOR: SON OF ASGARD
March, 2004
1 (of 6) The Warriors Teen,pt.1 . . . 3.00
2 The Warriors Teen,pt.2 . . . . 3.00
3 The Warriors Teen,pt.3 . . . . 3.00
4 The Warriors Teen,pt.4 . . . . 3.00
5 The Warriors Teen,pt.5 . . . . 3.00
6 The Warriors Teen,pt.6 . . . . 3.00
7 Enchanted,pt.1 . . . . 3.00
8 Enchanted,pt.2 . . . . 3.00
9 Enchanted,pt.3 . . . . 3.00
Digest #1 Warriors Teen 8.00

THOR: VIKINGS
Marvel Max, July, 2003
1 GEn(s),GF,Zombie Vikings 5.00
2 GEn(s),GF,F:Doctor Strange 4.00
3 GEn(s),GF 4.00
4 GEn(s),GF,back in time 4.00
5 GEn(s),GF,Zombie Vikings 4.00
TPB 14.00

THREE MUSKETEERS
1 thru 2 movie adapt. 2.25

THUNDERBOLTS
Feb., 1997
1 KBk,MBa,VRu,Post-onslaught new
   team:Citizen V, Meteorite, Techno,
   Songbird, Atlas & Mach-1 . . . . 10.00
1 rep. 3.00
2 KBk,MBa,VRu,V:Mad Thinker . . . 6.00
2a variant cover by MBa&VRu 6.00
2 rep. 4.50
3 KBk,MBa,VRu,Freedom's Plaza . 4.50
4 KBk,MBa,VRu,I:Jolt 4.50
5 KBk,MBa,VRu,V:Elements-Doom 4.50
6 KBk,MBa,VRu,V:Elements-Doom 4.50
7 KBk,MBa,VRu,F:Citizen V 4.00
8 KBk,MBa,VRu,Songbird alone. . . 4.00
9 KBk,MBa,VRu,Black Widow 4.00
10 KBk,MBa,VRu,Identy discovered 4.00
11 KBk,MBa,VRu,V:Citizen V 4.00
12 KBk,MBa,VRu,A:FF,Avengers . 10.00
13 KBk,MBa,SHa,on trial 3.00
14 KBk,MBa,VRu,V:Citizen V 3.00
15 KBk,MBa,VRu,V:S.H.I.E.L.D. . . 3.00
16 KBk,MBa,SHa,V:Lightningrods. . 3.00
17 KBk,MBa,SHa,V:Graviton 3.00
18 KBk,MBa,SHa,villains again? . . 3.00
19 KBk,MBa,SHa 3.00
20 KBk,MBa,SHa,V:Masters-Evil. . . 3.00

Thunderbolts #28
© Marvel Entertainment Group

21 KBk,MBa,SHa,F:Songbird 3.00
22 KBk,MBa,SHa,A:Hercules 3.00
23 KBk,MBa,SHa,V:U.S.Agent 3.00
24 KBk,MBa,SHa,R:Citizen V 3.00
25 KBk,MBa,SHa,48-page 3.50
25a signed 20.00
26 KBk,MBa,SHa,JoC,A:Mach-1 . . 2.50
27 KBk,MBa,SHa,A:Archangel 2.50
28 KBk,MBa,SHa,V:Graviton 2.50
29 KBk,MBa,SHa,V:Graviton 2.50
30 KBk,MBa,SHa,V:Graviton 2.50
31 KBk,MBa,SHa,R:Citizen V 2.50
32 KBk,MBa,SHa,V:Citizen V 2.50
33 KBk,MBa,SHa,F:Jolt 2.50
34 MBa,SHa. 2.50
35 FaN,MBa,SHa 2.50
36 FaN,MBa,SHa,V:Beetle 2.50
37 FaN,MBa,SHa,A:Hawkeye 2.50
38 FaN,MBa,SHa,V:Citizen V 2.50
39 FaN,MBa,SHa,100-pg. 3.00
40 FaN,MBa,SHa,V:Citizen V 2.25
41 FaN,MBa,Sandman 2.25
42 FaN,MBa,Avengers x-over 2.25
43 FaN,MBa,Avengers x-over 2.25
44 FaN,MBa,Avengers x-over 2.25
45 FaN,MBa,Maximum Security . . . 2.25
46 FaN,MBa,V:Scourge 2.25
47 FaN,MBa,A:Songbird 2.25
48 FaN,MBa,V:Scourge,pt.1 . . . . . 2.25
49 FaN,V:Scourge,face shown 2.25
50 FaN,MBa,48-page. 4.00
51 FaN,AV,rescue mission. 2.25
52 FaN,AV,V:Dr.Doom 2.25
53 FaN,AV,F:Charcoal 2.25
54 FaN,AV,F:Fixer 2.25
55 FaN,AV,V:Redeemers 2.25
56 FaN,AV,V:Graviton 2.25
57 FaN,AV,V:Graviton 2.25
58 FaN,AV,V:Graviton 2.25
59 FaN,MBa,AV,Songbird,'NuffSaid. 2.25
60 FaN,MBa,AV,Chain Gang 2.25
61 FaN,Heroes Return,pt.2 . . . . . . 2.25
62 FaN,Heroes Return,pt.3 . . . . . . 2.25
63 FaN,Hawkeye,Screaming Mimi . 2.25
64 FaN,F:Zemo 2.25
65 FaN,V:Masters of Evil 2.25
66 FaN,F:Baron Zemo,Jolt 2.25
67 FaN,F:Harrier, Hawkeye 2.25
68 FaN,F:Moonstone,PhantomEagle 2.25
69 FaN,AV 2.25
70 FaN, ... 2.25
71 FaN 2.25
72 FaN 2.25
73 Fan,AV 2.25

74 FaN 2.25
75 FaN,48-pg. 3.50
76 Fight club 2.25
77 JAr(s) 2.25
78 JAr(s) 3.00
79 JAr(s) 3.00
80 JAr(s),F:Spider-Man,pt.1 . . . . . 2.25
81 JAr(s),F:Spider-Man,pt.2 . . . . . 2.25
Ann. '97 KBk,MBa,TGu,GP,
    O:Thunderbolts, 48-pg. 3.00
Ann.2000 FaN,NBy, 48-pg. 3.50
Spec.#0 Wizard Nov., 1998 . . . . . . 5.00
Spec.First Strikes, rep.#1 & #2 . . . 5.00
Spec #1 Distant Rumblings KBk,
    SEp,Flashback,F:Citizen V 2.50
Spec.Life Sentences (2001) 3.50
TPB 176-pg., secret history 12.00
TPB Vol. 1: How to Lose 15.00

THUNDERCATS
Star, Dec., 1985
1 JM,TV tie-in 10.00
1a 2nd printing 7.00
2 JM,A:Berbils,V:Mumm-Ra 7.00
3 . . . . 7.00
4 JM,I:Lynxana 7.00
5 JM 7.00
6 JM 7.00
7 Return to Thundera 7.00
8 V:Monkiang 7.00
9 V:Pekmen 7.00
10 . . . . 7.00
11 I:The Molemen 5.00
12 The Protectors 5.00
13 EC/AW,V:Safari Joe 5.00
14 V:Snaf 5.00
15 JM,A:Spidera 5.00
16 Time Capsule 5.00
17 . . . . 5.00
18 EC/AW,Doom Gaze 5.00
19 . . . . 5.00
20 EC/AW 5.00
21 JM,A:Hercules Baby 5.00
22 I:Devious Duploids 5.00
23 V:Devious Duploids. 5.00
24 June, 1988 . . . . 5.00

THUNDERSTRIKE
1993–95
1 B:TDF(s),RF,Holografx(c),
    V:Bloodaxe,I:Car Jack 3.25
2 RF,V:Juggernaut 2.25
3 RF,I:Sangre 2.25
4 RF,A:Spider-Man,I:Pandora 2.25
5 RF,A:Spider-Man,V:Pandora . . . 2.25
6 RF,I:Blackwulf,Bristle,Schizo,Lord
    Lucian,A:SpM,Code:Blue,Stellaris,
    V:SHIELD,Pandora,C:Tantalus . 2.25
7 KP,V:Tantalus,D:Jackson 2.25
8 RF,I&V:Officer ZERO 2.25
9 RF,V:Bloodaxe 2.25
10 RF,A:Thor 2.25
11 RF,A:Wildstreak. 2.25
12 RF,A:Whyte Out 2.25
13 RF,Inferno 42 . . . . 2.25
13a Double Feature flip book
    with Code Blue #1 . . . . 2.50
14 RF, Inferno 42 . . . . 2.25
14a Double Feature flip book
    with Code Blue #2 . . . . 2.50
15 RF,V:Methisto 2.25
15a Double Feature flip book
    with Code Blue #3 . . . . 2.50
16 . . . . 2.25
17 V:Bloodaxe 2.25
18 V:New Villain 2.25
19 Shopping Network 2.25
20 A:Black Panther 2.25
21 A:War Machine,V:Loki. 2.25
22 TDF,AM,RF,Mystery of Bloodaxe
    blows open 2.25

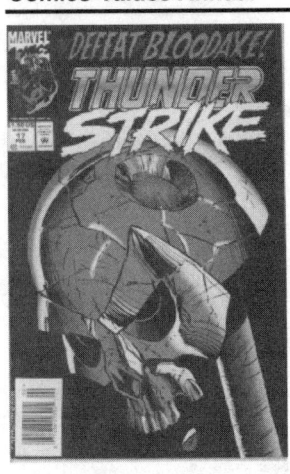

Thunderstrike #17
© Marvel Entertainment Group

23 TDF,A:Avengers 2.25
24 TDF,V:Bloodaxe, final issue 2.25

TIMELY PRESENTS: HUMAN TORCH COMICS
Aug., 1998
1-shot GN. 6.00

TIMESLIP COLLECTION
Sept., 1998
1-shot, 48-page 3.00

TIMESLIP: THE COMING OF THE AVENGERS
Aug., 1998
1-shot GN. 6.00

TIMESPIRITS
Epic, Jan., 1985
1 TY 3.00
2 . . . . 2.25
3 . . . . 2.25
4 AW 2.25
5 thru 8 . . . . @2.25

TIMESTRYKE
1 . . . . 2.25
2 . . . . 2.25

TINY TESSIE
See: TESSIE THE TYPIST

TOMB OF DARKNESS
See: BEWARE

TOMB OF DRACULA
April, 1972
1 GC,Night of the Vampire 300.00
2 GC,Who Stole My Coffin? 100.00
3 GC,TP,I:Rachel Van Helsing . . . 75.00
4 GC,TP,Bride of Dracula! 75.00
5 GC,TP,To Slay A Vampire 75.00
6 GC,TP,Monster of the Moors. . . 60.00
7 GC,TP,Child is Slayer of
   the Man 60.00
8 GC(p),The Hell-Crawlers 60.00
9 The Fire Cross. 60.00

10 GC,I:Blade Vampire Slayer. . . 175.00
11 GC,TP,Master of the Undead
   Strikes Again! 35.00
12 GC,TP,House that Screams . . . 35.00
13 GC,TP,O:Blade 75.00
14 GC,TP,Vampire has Risen
   from the Grave 35.00
15 GC,TP,Stay Dead 35.00
16 GC,TP,Back from the Grave . . . 35.00
17 GC,TP,A Vampire Rides This
   Train! 35.00
18 GC,TP,A:Werewolf By Night . . . 40.00
19 GC,TP,Snowbound in Hell 35.00
20 GC,TP,Manhunt For A Vampire. 35.00
21 GC,TP,A:Blade 30.00
22 GC,TP,V:Gorna 25.00
23 GC,TP,Shadow over Haunted
   Castle 25.00
24 GC,TP,I am your Death 30.00
25 GC,TP,Blood Stalkers of Count
   Dracula 30.00
26 GC,TP,A Vampire Stalks the
   Night. 25.00
27 GC,TP,..And the Moon Spews
   Death!. 25.00
28 GC,TP,Five came to Kill a
   Vampire 30.00
29 GC,TP,Vampire goes Mad? . . . 25.00
30 GC,TP,A:Blade 25.00
31 GC,TP,Child of Blood 25.00
32 GC,TP,The Vampire Walks
   Among Us. 25.00
33 GC,TP,Blood on My Hands. . . . 25.00
34 GC,TP,Bloody Showdown. 25.00
35 GC,TP,A:Brother Voodoo 25.00
36 GC,TP,Dracula in America 25.00
37 GC,TP,The Vampire Walks
   Among Us. 25.00
38 GC,TP,Bloodlust for a Dying
   Vampire 25.00
39 GC,TP,Final Death of Dracula . 25.00
40 GC,TP,Triumph of Dr.Sun 25.00
41 GC,TP,A:Blade 25.00
42 GC,TP,V:Dr.Sun 25.00
43 GC,TP,A:NewYear'sNightmare . 25.00
44 GC,TP,A:Dr.Strange 25.00
45 GC,TP,A:Hannibal King 25.00
46 GC,TP,W:Dracula & Domini . . . 20.00
47 GC,TP,Death-Bites 20.00
48 GC,TP,A:Hannibal King 20.00
49 GC,TP,A:Robin Hood,
   Frankenstein's Monster 20.00
50 GC,TP,A:Silver Surfer 30.00
51 GC,TP,A:Blade 15.00
52 GC,TP,V:Demon 15.00
53 GC,TP,A:Hannibal King,Blade . 15.00
54 GC,TP,Twas the Night Before
   Christmas 15.00
55 GC,TP,Requiem for a Vampire . 15.00
56 GC,TP,A:Harold H. Harold 15.00
57 GC,TP,The Forever Man. 15.00
58 GC,TP,A:Blade 30.00
59 GC,TP,The Last Traitor. 15.00
60 GC,TP,The Wrath of Dracula . . 15.00
61 GC,TP,Resurrection 15.00
62 GC,TP,What Lurks Beneath . . . 15.00
63 GC,TP,A:Janus 15.00
64 GC,TP,A:Satan 15.00
65 GC,TP,Where No Vampire
   Has Gone Before. 15.00
66 GC,TP,Marked for Death 15.00
67 GC,TP,A:Lilith 15.00
68 GC,TP,Dracula Turns Human . . 15.00
69 GC,TP,Cross of Fire 15.00
70 GC,TP,double size,last issue . . 25.00
Savage Return of Dracula. rep.
   Tomb of Dracula #1,#2 . . . . . . 2.50
Wedding of Dracula. rep.Tomb
   of Dracula #30,#45,#46. . . . . . 2.50
Requiem for Dracula. rep.Tomb
   of Dracula #69,#70 . . . . 2.50

Tomb of Dracula #25
© Marvel Entertainment Group

TOMB OF DRACULA
[Mini-Series] Nov., 1991
1 GC,AW,Day of Blood 6.00
2 GC,AW,Dracula in D.C. 5.50
3 GC,AW,A:Blade 5.50
4 GC,AW,D:Dracula 5.50

TOMB OF DRACULA
(B&W Mag.) Nov., 1979
1 . . . . 20.00
2 SD 15.00
3 FM 15.00
4 . . . . 12.00
5 . . . . 12.00
6 Sept., 1980 . . . . 12.00

TOMB OF DRACULA
2004
1 BSz(c) F:Blade. 3.00

TOMB OF DRACULA MEGAZINE
TPB Halloween, MWn,GC,TP 4.00

TOMORROW KNIGHTS
Epic, June, 1990
1 . . . . 2.25
2 thru 6 . . . . @2.25

TOP DOG
Star, April, 1985
1 . . . . 3.00
2 thru 14, June, 1987 . . . . @3.00

TOR
Epic *Heavy Hitters,* 1993
1 JKu,R:Tor,magazine format 6.25
2 JKu. 6.25
3 JKu,V:The Iduard Ring 6.25

TOUGH KID SQUAD COMICS
Timely, March, 1942
1 O:The Human Top,Tough Kid
   Squad,A:The Flying Flame,
   V:Doctor Klutch. 15,000.00

MARVEL

TOWER OF SHADOWS
Sept., 1969
1 JR(c),JSo,JCr,At The Stroke
  of Midnight 100.00
2 JR(c),DH,DA,NA,The Hungry
  One 50.00
3 GC,BWs,GT,Midnight in the
  Wax Museum. 50.00
4 DH,Within The Witching Circle . 40.00
5 DA,BWS,WW,Demon That
  Stalks Hollywood 50.00
6 WW,SD,Pray For the Man in
  the Rat-Hole 50.00
7 BWS,WW,Titano 50.00
8 WW,SD,Demons of
  Dragon-Henge. 50.00
9 BWr(c),TP,Lovecraft story 50.00
Becomes:

CREATURES ON THE LOOSE
March, 1971
10 BWr,A:King Kull 75.00
11 DAy,rep. Moomba is Here 25.00
12 JK,I Was Captured By Korilla . . 25.00
13 RC,The Creature
  From Krogarr 25.00
14 MSe,Dead Storage 25.00
15 SD,Spragg the Living Mountain 25.00
16 GK,BEv,GK,B&O:Gullivar Jones,
  Warrior of Mars. 20.00
17 GK,Slaves o/t Spider Swarm . . 20.00
18 RA,The Fury of Phra. 20.00
19 WB,JM,GK,Red Barbarian
  of Mars 20.00
20 GK(c),GM,SD,The Monster...
  And the Maiden 20.00
21 JSo(c),GM,Two Worlds To
  Win,E:Guilliver. 20.00
22 JSo(c),SD,VM,B:Thongor,
  Warrior of Lost Lemuria. 22.00
23 VM,The Man-Monster Strikes . . 12.00
24 VM,Attack of the Lizard-Hawks 12.00
25 VM,GK(c),Wizard of Lemuria . . 12.00
26 VM,Doom of the Serpent Gods 12.00
27 VM,SD,Demons Dwell in the
  Crypts of Yamath. 12.00
28 SD,The Hordes of Hell 12.00
29 GK(c),Day of the Dragon Wings,
  E:Thongor,Warrior of Lemuria . 12.00
30 B:Man-Wolf,Full Moon, Dark
  Fear. 25.00
31 GT,The Beast Within. 15.00
32 GT,V:Kraven the Hunter 15.00
33 GK(c),GP,The Name of the
  Game is Death 15.00
34 GP,Nightflight to Fear 12.00
35 GK(c),GP 12.00
36 GK(c),GP,Murder by Moonlight. 12.00
37 GP,Sept., 1975 . . . . 12.00

TOXIC AVENGER
March, 1991
1 VM(i),I&O:Toxic Avenger 2.25
2 VM(i) 2.25
3 VM(i),Night of Living H.bodies . . 2.25
4 Legend of Sludgeface 2.25
5 I:Biohazard. 2.25
6 V:Biohazard 2.25
7 Sewer of Souviaki 2.25
8 Sewer of Souviaki' conc. 2.25
9 Abducted by Aliens 2.25
10 Die,Yuppie Scum,pt.1 . . . . 2.25

TOXIC CRUSADERS
1992
1 F:Toxic Avengers & Crusaders . . 2.25
2 SK(c),V:Custard-Thing. 2.25
3 SK(c),V:Custard-Thing. 2.25

4 V:Giant Mutant Rats 2.25
5 V:Dr.Killemoff 2.25
6 V:Dr.Killemoff 2.25
7 F:Yvonne 2.25
8 V:Psycho 2.25

[2nd Series]
1 . . . . 2.25
2 . . . . 2.25

TRANSFORMERS
[1st Regular Series] Sept., 1984
1 FS,Toy Comic 20.00
2 FS,OptimusPrime V:Megatron . . 11.00
3 FS.A:Spider-Man 11.00
4 MT(c),FS 7.00
5 Transformers Dead? 7.00
6 Autobots vs.Decepticons 7.00
7 KB,V:Megatron. 7.00
8 KB,A:Dinobots 7.00
9 MM,A:Circuit Breaker. 7.00
10 Dawn of the Devastator 7.00
11 HT 6.00
12 HT,V:Shockwave. 6.00
13 DP,Return of Megatron 6.00
14 DP,V:Decepticons 6.00
15 DP 6.00
16 KN,A:Bumblebee 6.00
17 DP,I:New Transformers,pt.1 . . . 6.00
18 DP,I:New Transformers,pt.2 . . . 6.00
19 DP,I:Omega Supreme 6.00
20 HT,Skid vs.Ravage 6.00
21 DP,I:Aerialbots 6.00
22 DP,I:Stuntacons(Menasor) 6.00
23 DP,Return of Circuit Breaker . . 6.00
24 DP,D:Optimus Prime. 6.00
25 DP,Decpticons (full story) 6.00
26 DP 6.00
27 DP,V:Head Hunter. 6.00
28 DP 6.00
29 DP,I:Scraplets, Triplechangers . . 6.00
30 DP,V:Scraplets 6.00
31 DP,Humans vs. Decepticons . . . 6.00
32 DP,Autobots for Sale. 6.00
33 DP,Autobots vs.Decepticons. . . 6.00
34 V:Sky Lynx 6.00
35 JRy,I:U.K.version Transformers . 6.00
36 . . . . 6.00
37 . . . . 6.00
38 . . . . 6.00
39 . . . . 6.00
40 Autobots' New Leader. 6.00
41 . . . . 6.00
42 Return of Optimus Prime 6.00
43 Optimus Prime,Goldbug 6.00

Transformers #9
© *Marvel Entertainment Group*

44 FF,Return of Circuit Breaker 6.00
45 V:The Jammers. 6.00
46 I:New Transformers 6.00
47 B:Underbase saga,I:Seacons . . . 6.00
48 Optimus Prime/Megatron
  (past story). 6.00
49 Underbase saga cont. 6.00
50 E:Underbase saga,I:new
  characters 7.00
51 I:Pretender Decepticon Beasts. . 7.00
52 I:Mecannibles,pt.1 . . . . 7.00
53 Mecannibles,pt.2. . . . . 7.00
54 I:Micromasters 7.00
55 MG 7.00
56 Return of Megatron. 7.00
57 Optimus Prime vs.Scraponok . . . 7.00
58 V:Megatron 7.00
59 A:Megatron,D:Ratchet. 7.00
60 Battle on Cybertron. 10.00
61 O:Transformers. 10.00
62 B:Matrix Quest,pt.1 . . . . 10.00
63 . . . . 10.00
64 I:The Klud 10.00
65 GSr 17.00
66 E:Matrix Quest,pt.5 . . . . 17.00
67 V:Unicorn,also Alternative
  World 17.00
68 I:Neoknights 17.00
69 Fate of Ratchet & Megatron
  revealed. 17.00
70 Megatron/Ratchet fused
  together 17.00
71 Autobots Surrender to
  Decepticons. 20.00
72 Decepticon Civil War,
  I:Gravitron. 20.00
73 I:Unicron,A:Neoknights 20.00
74 A:Unicron & Brothers of Chaos. 20.00
75 V:Thunderwing & Dark Matrix. . 20.00
76 Aftermath of War. 20.00
77 Unholy Alliance 20.00
78 Galvatron vs.Megatron 28.00
79 Decepticons Invade Earth. 28.00
80 Return of Optimus Prime,final . 40.00

[2nd Regular Series]
1 Split Foil(c),A:Dinobots 3.00
2 A:G.I.Joe,Cobra 2.25
3 . . . . 2.25
4 MaG,V:Jhiaxus. 2.25
5 . . . . 2.25
6 V:Megatron 2.25
7 V:Darkwing. 2.25
8 V:Darkwing. 2.25
9 . . . . 2.25
10 Total War. 2.25
11 . . . . 2.25

TRANSFORMERS COMICS MAGAZINE
1986–88
1 Digest-size 2.25
2 thru 11 . . . . @2.25

TRANSFORMERS, THE MOVIE
Dec., 1986–Feb., 1987
1 thru 3 Animated movie adapt. . @2.25

TRANSFORMERS UNIVERSE
Dec., 1986
1 . . . . 3.00
2 . . . . 3.00
3 . . . . 3.00
4 March, 1987 . . . . 3.00

TRANSMUTATION OF IKE GARUDA
Epic, 1991
1 JSh,I:Ike Garuda 4.00
2 JSh,conclusion. 4.00

TROUBLE
Marvel Epic, June, 2003
1 MMr(s),Tyd,Teenage Romance . . 3.50
2 MMr(s),Tyd,photo (c) 3.00
3 MMr(s),Tyd,consequences 3.00
4 MMr(s),TyD,consequences 3.00
5 MMr(s),TyD,concl. 3.00
TPB 15.00

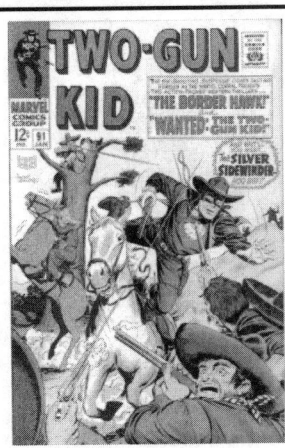

The Trouble With Girls #1
© Marvel Entertainment Group

TROUBLE WITH GIRLS: NIGHT OF THE LIZARD
Epic *Heavy Hitters*, 1993
1 BBI,AW,R:Lester Girls 2.75
2 BBI,AW,V:Lizard Lady 2.25
3 BBI,AW,V:Lizard Lady 2.25
4 BBI,AW,last issue. 2.25

TRUE COMPLETE MYSTERY
See: COMPLETE MYSTERY

TRUE SECRETS
See: OUR LOVE

TRUE WESTERN
Dec., 1949
1 Ph(c),Billy the Kid 200.00
2 Ph(c),Alan Ladd,Badmen vs.
   Lawmen 250.00
Becomes:

TRUE ADVENTURES
3 BP,MSy,Boss of Black Devil . . 200.00
Becomes:

MEN'S ADVENTURES
4 AvB,He Called me a Coward . 400.00
5 AvB,Brother Act 225.00
6 AvB,Heat of Battle 200.00
7 AvB,The Walking Death 200.00
8 AvB,RH,Journey Into Death . . 200.00
9 AvB,Bullets,Blades and Death 125.00

---

10 BEv,The Education of Thomas
   Dillon 125.00
11 Death of A Soldier 125.00
12 Firing Squad 125.00
13 RH(c),The Three Stripes. 125.00
14 GC,BEv,Steel Coffin 125.00
15 JMn(c). 125.00
16 . . . . 125.00
17 . . . . 125.00
18 . . . . 125.00
19 JRo 125.00
20 GC,RH(c) 125.00
21 BEv(c),JSt,The Eye of Man . . 225.00
22 BEv,JR,Mark of the Witch. . . . 225.00
23 BEv(c),RC,The Wrong Body. . 225.00
24 RH,JMn,GT,Torture Master. . . 225.00
25 SSh(c),Who Shrinks My Head 400.00
26 Midnight in the Morgue 225.00
27 BP,CBu(c),A:Capt.America,
   Human Torch,Sub-Mariner . 1,400.00
28 BEv,A:Capt.America,Human Torch,
   Sub-Mariner,July, 1954. . . . 1,300.00

TRUTH: RED WHITE BLACK
Nov., 2002
1 (of 7) untold Capt. America 3.50
2 thru 7 KB . . . . @3.50
GN Truth, Red White & Black 4.00
TPB Truth, Red, White & Black . . . 15.00

TRY-OUT WINNER BOOK
March, 1988
1 Spider-Man vs. Doc Octopus . . 15.00

TV STARS
Aug., 1978
1 A:Great Grape Ape 35.00
2 . . . . 25.00
3 ATh,DSt 30.00
4 A:Top Cat,Feb., 1979 . . . . 25.00

2-GUN KID
See: BILLY BUCKSKIN

TWO-GUN KID
Atlas, March, 1948–April, 1977
1 B:Two-Gun Kid,The Sheriff . 1,400.00
2 Killers of Outlaw City 600.00
3 RH,A:Annie Oakley 400.00
4 RH,A:Black Rider 400.00
5 RH 500.00
6 . . . . 400.00
7 RH,Brand of a Killer 400.00
8 The Secret of the Castle of
   Slaves 400.00
9 JSe,Trapped in Hidden Valley,
   A:Black Rider 400.00
10 JK(c),The Horrible Hermit
   of Hidden Mesa. 400.00
11 JMn(c),GT,A:Black Rider. . . . 250.00
12 JMn(c),GT,A:Black Rider . . . 250.00
13 thru 24. . . . . @225.00
25 AW,JMn. 225.00
26 DAy,JMn 150.00
27 DAy,JMn 150.00
28 JMn 150.00
29 . . . . 150.00
30 AW 150.00
31 thru 44. . . . . 125.00
45 JDa 100.00
46 JDa 100.00
47 JDa 100.00
48 . . . . 100.00
49 JMn 100.00
50 . . . . 100.00
51 AW 100.00

Two-Gun Kid #91
© Marvel Entertainment Group

52 thru 59. . . . . @100.00
60 DAy,New O:Two-Gun Kid . . . 125.00
61 JK,DAy,The Killer and The Kid . 90.00
62 JK,DAy,At the Mercy of Moose
   Morgan 90.00
63 DAy,The Guns of Wild Bill
   Taggert. 50.00
64 DAy,Trapped by Grizzly Gordon 50.00
65 DAy,Nothing Can Save Fort
   Henry. 50.00
66 DAy,Ringo's Raiders 50.00
67 DAy,The Fangs of the Fox 50.00
68 DAy,The Purple Phantom 50.00
69 DAy,Badman Called Goliath . . . 50.00
70 DAy,Hurricane 50.00
71 DAy,V:Jesse James 50.00
72 DAy,V:Geronimo 50.00
73 Guns of the Galloway Gang . . . 50.00
74 Dakota Thompson. 50.00
75 JK,Remember the Alamo 65.00
76 JK,Trapped on the Doom 65.00
77 JK,V:The Panther 65.00
78 V:Jesse James 45.00
79 The River Rats 45.00
80 V:The Billy Kid 45.00
81 The Hidden Gun 45.00
82 BEv,Here Comes the Conchos. 45.00
83 Durango,Two-Gun
   Kid Unmasked. 45.00
84 Gunslammer 45.00
85 Fury at Falcon Flats,
   A:Rawhide Kids. 45.00
86 V:Cole Younger. 45.00
87 OW,The Sidewinder and the
   Stallion. 45.00
88 thru 101 . . . . @40.00
102 thru 136. . . . . @30.00

TWO-GUN KID: SUNSET RIDERS
1995
1 FaN,R:Two-Gun Kid,64-pg. 7.00
2 FaN,concl. 64-pg. 7.00

TWO GUN WESTERN
See: CASEY–CRIME PHOTOGRAPHER

TWO-GUN WESTERN
See: BILLY BUCKSKIN

2001: A SPACE ODYSSEY
Oct., 1976
1 JK,FRg,Based on Movie 10.00

2001: A SPACE ODYSSEY
Dec., 1976—Sept., 1977
1 JK,Based on Movie 25.00
2 JK,Vira the She-Demon 15.00
3 JK,Marak the Merciless 15.00
4 JK,Wheels of Death 15.00
5 JK,Norton of New York 15.00
6 JK,Immortality ...Death 15.00
7 JK,The New Seed 15.00
8 JK,Capture of X-51,I&O:Mr.
Machine(Machine-Man) 20.00
9 JK,A:Mr Machine 15.00
10 Hotline to Hades,A:Mr Machine 15.00

2010
April, 1985
1 TP,movie adapt 2.25
2 TP,movie adapt,May, 1985 ... 2.25

2099 A.D.
1995
1 Chromium cover 4.00

2099 APOCALYPSE
1995
1 .... 5.00

2099 GENESIS
1996
1 Chromium Cover 4.00

2099: MANIFEST DESTINY
March, 1998
GN LKa,MMK,F:Miguel
O'Hara, 48-pg............. 6.00

2099 SPECIAL: THE WORLD OF DOOM
1995
1 The World of Doom 2.25

2099 UNLIMITED
1993—96
1 DT,I:Hulk 2099,A:Spider-Man 2099,
I:Mutagen................. 4.50
2 DT,F:Hulk 2099,Spider-Man 2099,
I:R-Gang 4.25
3 GJ(s),JJB,F:Hulk & SpM 2099... 4.25
4 PR(c),GJ(s),JJB,I:Metalscream
2099,Lachryma 2099....... 4.25
5 GJ(s),I:Vulx,F:Hazzrd 2099 ... 4.25
6 .... 4.25
Becomes:

2099 A.D. UNLIMITED
7 .... 4.25
8 F:Public Enemy 4.25
9 One Nation Under Doom....... 4.25
10 V:Chameleon 2099.......... 4.25
Spec. #1 The World of Doom 2.25

2099: WORLD OF TOMORROW
1996–97
1 .... 2.50
2 .... 2.50
3 MMk,MsM,ATi,F:Spider-Man,
X-Men 2.50
4 ATi,X-Men 2099 discover secret . 2.50
5 ATi 2.50

2099 World of Tomorrow #2
© Marvel Entertainment Group

6 PFe&ATi(c),Phalanx's final
assault.................. 2.50
7 Spider-Man 2099 searches for his
brother: Green Goblin 2.50
8 Phalanx invasion aftermath 2.50
9 Humanity vs. Lunatika 2.50

TYPHOID
1995–96
1 ANo,JVF,Painted series 4.00
2 ANo,JVF,Hunt for serial killer.... 4.00
3 ANo,JVF,sex,blood & videotapes. 4.00
4 ANo,JVF,conclusion 4.00

ULTIMATE ADVENTURES (OF HAWK-OWL & ZIPPY)
Sept., 2002
1 JQ designs,U-Decide.......... 2.25
2 DFg 2.25
3 DFg 2.25
4 DFg,Hawk-Owl & Zippy 2.25
5 DFg 3.00
6 DFg 3.00
TPB 13.00

ULTIMATE AGE OF APOCALYPSE
Rep. #1-#4 Age of Apocalypse stories:
Ultimate Amazing X-Men 9.00
Ultimate Astonishing X-Men...... 9.00
Ultimate Factor X 9.00
Ultimate Gambit and the X-Ternals . 9.00
Ultimate Generation Next 9.00
Ultimate Weapon X 9.00
Ultimate X-Calibre 9.00
Ultimate X-Man 9.00

ULTIMATE DAREDEVIL & ELEKTRA
Nov., 2002
1 (of 4) DaM, at Columbia U. 5.00
2 SvL,DaM 3.50
3 SvL,DaM 3.50
4 SvL,concl. 3.50
TPB Series rep............... 12.00

ULTIMATE ELEKTRA
Aug., 2004
1 (of 5) SvL,Devil's Due,pt.1...... 2.25

2 SvL,Devil's Due,pt.2 .... 2.25
3 SvL,Devil's Due,pt.3 .... 2.25

ULTIMATE FANTASTIC FOUR
Dec., 2003
1 BMB,AKu,The Fantastic,pt.1 ... 4.00
2 BMB,AKu,The Fantastic,pt.2 ... 3.50
3 BMB,AKu,The Fantastic,pt.3 ... 3.00
4 BMB,AKu,The Fantastic,pt.4 ... 3.00
5 BMB,AKu,The Fantastic,pt.5 ... 3.00
6 BMB,AKu,The Fantastic,pt.6 ... 3.00
7 WEI(s),SI,Doom,pt.1 .... 2.50
8 WEI(s),SI,Doom,pt.2 .... 2.50
9 WEI(s),SI,Doom,pt.3 .... 2.50
10 WEI(s),SI,Doom,pt.4 .... 2.50
11 WEI(s),SI,Doom,pt.5 .... 2.50
12 WEI(s),SI,Doom,pt.6 .... 2.50
TPB Vol. 1:The Fantastic....... 13.00

ULTIMATE MARVEL TEAM-UP
Feb., 2001
1 Spider-Man & Wolverine 5.00
2 Spider-Man & The Hulk 4.00
3 Spider-Man & The Hulk 4.00
4 Spider-Man & Iron Man 4.00
5 Spider-Man & Iron Man,MiA 4.00
6 Spider-Man & Punisher,BSz 3.50
7 Spider-Man & Daredevil,BSz.... 3.50
8 Spider-Man,Daredevil,Punisher.. 3.50
9 Spider-Man & Fantastic Four.... 3.50
10 Spider-Man & Man-Thing 3.50
11 BMB(s),Spider-Man & X-Men ... 3.50
12 Spider-Man & Dr. Strange...... 3.50
13 Spider-Man & Dr. Strange...... 3.50
14 Spider-Man & Black Widow 3.50
15 Spider-Man & Shang-Chi 3.50
16 Spider-Man & Shang-Chi 3.50
TPB Vol. 1 .... 15.00
TPB Vol. 2 .... 12.00
TPB Vol. 3 .... 13.00

ULTIMATE MARVEL MAGAZINE
May, 2001
5 thru 11, 80-page, rep........ @4.00

ULTIMATE NIGHTMARE
Aug., 2004
1 (of 5) Tunguska 2.25
2 WEI(s) 2.25
3 WEI(s) 2.25

ULTIMATES, THE
Jan., 2002
1 MMr,BHi,Nick Fury, heroes 6.00
2 MMr,BHi,Search for Cap.Am. ... 10.00
3 MMr,BHi,Cap.America lives..... 8.00
4 MMr,BHi,no one to fight........ 8.00
5 MMr,BHi, ... 8.00
6 MMr,BHi,celebrities 5.00
7 MMr,BHi,new additions 5.00
8 MMr,Quicksilver&ScarletWitch.. 3.00
9 MMr,BHi, ... 3.00
10 MMr,BHi,F:Hawkeye.......... 3.00
11 BHi,PNe 3.00
12 BHi,PNe 3.00
13 BHi,Chitauri,concl.48-pg. 3.50
Spec. Must Have rep. #1–#3..... 4.00
TPB Vol.1, 160-pg............ 15.00
TPB Vol.2: Homeland Security ... 18.00
Vol. 2
1 BHi....................... 3.00

ULTIMATE SIX
Sept., 2003
1 BMB,JQ,F:Villains 3.00
2 BMB,Sinister Six 3.00
3 BMB,Ultimate Spidey. 3.00
4 BMB,F:The Ultimates. 3.00
5 BMB,Spidey kidnapped 3.00
6 BMB,V:Sinister Six. 3.00
7 BMB,Green Goblin. 3.00

ULTIMATE SPIDER-MAN
Sept., 2000
1 BMB,JQ,MBa,ATi,A:Mary Jane
   48-pg.red card(c) 100.00
1A variant white (c) 150.00
1B Dynamic Forces (c) 65.00
2A BMB,MBa,ATi,Dr.Otto Octopus,
   car 50.00
2B Dynamic Forces JaL(c),
   Spider-Man swinging 35.00
3 BMB,ATi,MBa,A:Mary Jane 40.00
4 BMB,ATi,MBa,D:Uncle Ben 40.00
5 BMB,ATi,MBa,hand of fate,
   scarce 110.00
6 BMB,ATi,MBa,V:Green Goblin . . 50.00
7 BMB,ATi,MBa,V:Green Goblin . . 35.00
8 BMB,ATi,MBa,V:Shocker 20.00
9 BMB,ATi,MBa,V:Kingpin 15.00
10 BMB,ATi,MBa,V:Kingpin 10.00
11 BMB,ATi,MBa,V:Kingpin 10.00
12 BMB,ATi,MBa,V:Kingpin 10.00
13 BMB,ATi,MBa,Mary Jane 12.00
14 BMB,MBa,ATi,Doctor Octopus . 12.00
15 BMB,MBa,ATi,Doctor Octopus . . 9.00
16 BMB,MBa,ATi,F:Ock,Kraven. . . . 9.00
17 BMB,MBa,ATi,F:Justin Hammer . 8.00
18 BMB,MBa,ATi,Doc Oc kicks butt 8.00
19 BMB,MBa,ATi,Justin Hammer . . 8.00
20 BMB,MBa,ATi,Doc Oc,Kraven . . 8.00
21 BMB,MBa,ATi,vs. the press 8.00
22 BMB,MBa,ATi,R:Green Goblin
   + Chapter 1, 54-pg. 8.00
23 BMB,MBa,ATi,G.Goblin,G.Stacy . 8.00
24 BMB,MBa,ATi,Green Goblin deal 4.00
25 BMB,MBa,ATi 4.00
26 BMB,MBa,ATi,S.H.I.E.L.D. 3.00
27 BMB,MBa,ATi 3.00
28 BMB,MBa,ATi 3.00
29 BMB,MBa,ATi 3.00
30 BMB,MBa,ATi 3.00
31 BMB,MBa,ATi 3.00
32 BMB,MBa,ATi 3.00
33 BMB,MBa,ATi,V:Venom 10.00
34 BMB,MBa,ATi,V:Venom 8.00
35 BMB,MBa,ATi,V:Venom 8.00
36 BMB,MBa,ATi,V:Venom 5.00
37 BMB,MBa,ATi,V:Venom 5.00
38 BMB,MBa,ATi,V:Venom,concl. . . 5.00
39 BMB,MBa,ATi,F:Nick Fury 2.50
40 BMB,MBa,Irresponsible,pt.1 . . . 2.50
41 BMB,MBa,Irresponsible,pt.2 . . . 2.50
42 BMB,MBa,Irresponsible,pt.3 . . . 2.50
43 BMB,MBa,Irresponsible,pt.4 . . . 2.50
44 BMB,MBa,Irresponsible,pt.5 . . . 2.50
45 BMB,MBa,Irresponsible,pt.6 . . . 2.50
46 BMB,MBa,F:S.H.I.E.L.D.,40-pg . 3.00
47 BMB,MBa,Unfair,pt.1 . . . . 2.50
48 BMB,MBa,Unfair,pt.2 . . . . 2.25
49 BMB,MBa,Unfair,pt.3 . . . . 2.25
50 BMB,MBa,Claws,pt.1 . . . . 3.00
51 BMB,MBa,Claws,pt.2 . . . . 2.50
52 BMB,MBa,Claws,pt.3 . . . . 2.50
53 BMB,MBa,Claws,concl. 2.25
54 BMB,MBa,Goes Hollywood,pt.1 . 2.25
54a Arachnoman variant 12.00
55 BMB,MBa,Goes Hollywood,pt.2 . 2.25
56 BMB,MBa,Goes Hollywood,pt.3 . 2.25
57 BMB,MBa,Goes Hollywood,pt.4 . 2.25
58 BMB,MBa,Goes Hollywood,pt.5 . 2.25
59 BMB,MBa,Goes Hollywood,pt.6 . 2.25

60 BMB,MBa,Carnage,pt.1 . . . . . . 5.00
61 BMB,MBa,Carnage,pt.2 . . . . . . 3.50
62 BMB,MBa,Carnage,pt.3 . . . . . . 3.00
63 BMB,MBa,Carnage,pt.4 . . . . . . 2.25
64 BMB,MBa,Carnage,pt.5 . . . . . . 2.25
65 BMB,MBa,Carnage,pt.6 . . . . . . 2.25
66 BMB,MBa,Switcheroo,pt.1 . . . . 2.25
67 BMB,MBa,Switcheroo,pt.2 . . . . 2.25
Spec.1 Collected, rep.#1–#3 . . . . . 4.00
Spec.#1-#2-#3, 96-pg. 4.00
Spec.#1 all-star artists, 54-pg. 3.50
TPB Vol.3, 176-pg.. . . . . 18.00
TPB Vol 4, ... 15.00
TPB Power & Responsibility 15.00
TPB Vol. 5: Public Scutiny 12.00
TPB Vol. 6: Venom. 16.00
TPB Vol. 7: Irresponsible 13.00
TPB Vol. 8: Cats and Kings 18.00
TPB Vol. 9:Ultimate Six 18.00
TPB Vol.10:Hollywood 13.00
Spec. Must Have, rep. 4.00

ULTIMATE WAR
Marvel Dec. 2002
1 (of 4) CBa,X-Men vs. Ultimates . . 5.00
2 CBa 4.00
3 CBa 4.00
4 CBa,concl. 4.00

Ultimate X-Men #3
© Marvel Entertainment Group

ULTIMATE X-MEN
Dec., 2000
1 AKu,ATi,MMr,48-page, card (c) . 25.00
1A Dynamic Forces (c) 30.00
1B Preview 30.00
2 AKu,ATi,MMr,F:Wolverine 22.00
3 AKu,ATi,MMr,V:Magneto 15.00
4 AKu,ATi,MMr,V:Magneto 15.00
5 AKu,ATi,MMr,One traitor? 15.00
6 AKu,ATi,MMr,V:Magneto 15.00
7 AKu,ATi,MMr,Weapon X,pt.1 . . . 18.00
8 AKu,ATi,MMr,Weapon X,pt.2 . . . . 7.00
9 MMr,TR,SHa,Weapon X,pt.3 . . . . 7.00
10 MMr,TR,SHa,Weapon X,pt.4 . . . 7.00
11 MMr,AKu,ATi,Weapon X,pt.5. . . 4.00
12 MMr,AKu,Weapon X,pt.6 . . . . . 4.00
13 AKu(c),F:Gambit 5.00
14 AKu(c),F:Gambit,pt.2 . . . . 4.00
15 AKu,MMr,Xavier's teachings . . . 4.00
16 AKu,MMr,to Scotland 4.00
17 AKu,MMr,Proteus Saga,pt.2 . . . 4.00
18 AKu,MMr,World Tour. 4.00
19 AKu,MMr,World Tour,concl. 4.00
20 AKu,MMr,World Tour,epilogue. . . 3.75

21 MMr,DaM,Hellfire & Brimstone . . 3.75
22 MMr,DaM,Hellfire & Brimstone . . 3.75
23 MMr,DaM,Hellfire & Brimstone . . 3.75
24 MMr,DaM,Hellfire&Brimstone . . . 3.75
25 MMr,DaM,AKu(c), Hellfire &
   Brimstone, 48-pg. 5.00
26 MMr,AKu,Professor-X 5.00
27 MMr,AKu,V:Brotherhood 5.00
28 MMr,AKu,V:Brotherhood 5.00
29 MMr,AKu,Missing X-Man 5.00
30 MMr,AKu,Storm's gang 5.00
31 MMr,AKu,V:Magneto. 5.00
32 MMr,AKu,Ultimate fate 4.50
33 MMr,AKu,Return of the King. . . . 3.50
34 BMB,Blockbuster,pt.1 . . . . 6.00
35 BMB,Blockbuster,pt.2 . . . . 3.25
36 BMB,Blockbuster,pt.3 . . . . 3.25
37 BMB,Blockbuster,pt.4 . . . . 3.25
38 BMB,Blockbuster,pt.5 . . . . 3.25
39 BMB,Blockbuster,pt.6 . . . . 2.75
40 BMB,New Mutants,pt.1 . . . . 3.00
41 BMB,New Mutants,pt.2 . . . . 2.75
42 BMB,New Mutants,pt.3 . . . . 3.50
43 BMB,New Mutants,pt.4 . . . . 2.25
44 BMB,New Mutants,pt.5 . . . . 2.25
45 BMB,New Mutants,pt.6 . . . . 2.25
46 BPe,The Tempest,pt.1 . . . . 2.25
47 BPe,The Tempest,pt.2 . . . . 2.25
48 BPe,The Tempest,pt.3 . . . . 2.25
49 BPe,The Tempest,pt.4 . . . . 2.25
50 NKu,Cry Wolf,pt.1 . . . . 2.25
51 NKu,Cry Wolf,pt.2 . . . . 2.25
52 NKu,Cry Wolf,pt.3 . . . . 2.25
Spec. #1-#2-#3, 96-pg. 4.00
TPB rep.#1–#6, 160-pg. 14.95
TPB Ultimate X-Men, Weapon X . . 14.95
TPB Vol.3, World Tour 18.00
TPB Vol.4, Hellfire & Brimstone . . . 13.00
TPB Vol.5: Ultimate War 11.00
TPB Vol.6: Return of the King 17.00
TPB Vol. 7: Blockbuster. 13.00
TPB Vol. 8: New Mutants. 13.00
TPB Vol. 9: The Tempest 11.00
Spec. rep. Must Have #1–#3 . . . . . 4.00

ULTRAFORCE/AVENGERS
1 V:Loki,A:Malibu's Ultraforce 3.95

ULTRA GIRL
[Mini-series] 1996
1 BKs,I&O:Ultra Girl 2.25
2 & 3 BKs, ... @2.25

Ultragirl #1
© Marvel Entertainment Group

ULTRA X-MEN COLLECTION

1 Metallic(c), art from cards 3.00
2 thru 5 art from cards . . . . @3.00

ULTRA X-MEN III

Preview 3.00

ULTRON

June, 1999

1-shot Ultron Unleashed, rep. 3.50

UNCANNY ORIGINS

Sept., 1996

1 F:Cyclops. 2.25
2 F:Quicksilver 2.25
3 DHv,BAn,F:Archangel 2.25
4 F:Firelord 2.25
5 MHi,F:Hulk. 2.25
6 F:Beast 2.25
7 F:Venom 2.25
8 F:Nightcrawler 2.25
9 F:Storm 2.25
10 F:Black Cat 2.25
11 F:Luke Cage 2.25
12 F:Black Knight. 2.25
13 LWn,MCa,F:Doctor Strange 2.25
14 LWn,MCW,F:Iron Fist 2.25

UNCANNY TALES

Atlas, June, 1952

1 RH,While the City Sleeps . . 1,200.00
2 JMn,BEv 600.00
3 Escape to What 500.00
4 JMn,Nobody's Fool 500.00
5 Fear 500.00
6 He Lurks in the Shadows 550.00
7 BEv,Kill,Clown,Kill 550.00
8 JMn,Bring Back My Face. 450.00
9 BEv,RC,The Executioner. 450.00
10 JMn,RH(c),JR,The Man Who
   Came Back To Life 450.00
11 GC,The Man Who Changed . . 350.00
12 BP,BEv,Bertha Gets Buried . . 350.00
13 RH,Scared Out of His Skin . . 350.00
14 RH,TLw,Victims of Vonntor . . . 350.00
15 RA,JSt,The Man Who
   Saw Death. 350.00
16 JMn,GC,Zombie at Large 350.00
17 GC,TLw,I Live With Corpses . 350.00
18 JF,BP,Clock Face(c) 350.00
19 DBr,RKr,TLw,The Man Who
   Died Again. 350.00
20 DBr,Ted's Head 350.00
21 . . . . 300.00
22 DAy. 300.00
23 TLw 300.00
24 . . . . 300.00
25 MSy. 300.00
26 Spider-Man prototype story . . 400.00
27 RA,TLw 275.00
28 TLw 275.00
29 JMn 200.00
30 . . . . 200.00
31 . . . . 200.00
32 BEv 200.00
33 . . . . 200.00
34 BP 200.00
35 TLw,JMn 200.00
36 BP,BEv 200.00
37 MD 200.00
38 BP 200.00
39 BEv 200.00
40 . . . . 200.00
41 . . . . 200.00
42 MD 225.00
43 . . . . 200.00
44 . . . . 200.00

45 MD 200.00
46 GM 200.00
47 TSe 200.00
48 BEv 200.00
49 JO 200.00
50 JO 200.00
51 GM 225.00
52 GC. 200.00
53 JO,AT 200.00
54 . . . . 220.00
55 . . . . 200.00
56 Sept., 1957 . . . . 225.00

UNCANNY TALES FROM THE GRAVE

Dec., 1973 — Oct., 1975

1 RC,Room of no Return 30.00
2 DAy,Out of the Swamp 20.00
3 No Way Out 20.00
4 JR,SD,Vampire 20.00
5 GK,GT,Don't Go in the Cellar . 20.00
6 JR,SD,The Last Kkrul 20.00
7 RH,SD,Never Dance With a
   Vampire 20.00
8 SD,Escape Into Hell 20.00
9 JA,The Nightmare Men 20.00
10 SD,DH,Beware the Power of
   Khan 20.00
11 SD,JF,RH,Dead Don't Sleep . . 20.00
12 SD,Final Issue 20.00

UNCANNY X-MEN

See: X-MEN

UNKNOWN WORLDS OF SCIENCE FICTION

Jan., 1975

(Black & White Magazine)

1 AW,RKr,AT,FF,GC 25.00
2 FB,GP 20.00
3 GM,AN,GP,GC 20.00
4 . . . . 20.00
5 GM,NC,GC 20.00
6 FB,AN,GC,Nov., 1975 . . . . . . 20.00
Spec.#1 AN,NR,JB. 25.00

UNION JACK

Oct., 1998

1 (of 3) BRa,F:Joey Chapman 3.00
2 BRa,V:Baroness 3.00
3 BRa,conclusion 3.00
TPB 96-pg. (2002) 11.50

U.S.A. COMICS

Timely, Aug., 1941

1 S&K(c),BW,Bondage(c),The
   Defender(c). 20,000.00
2 S&K(c),BW,Capt.Terror(c). . . 6,000.00
3 S&K(c),Capt.Terror(c) 4,000.00
4 Major Liberty 3,500.00
5 Hitler(c),O:AmericanAvenger 3,800.00
6 ASh(c),Capt.America(c) 4,000.00
7 BW,O:Marvel Boy 3,800.00
8 Capt.America (c). 3,500.00
9 Bondage(c), Capt.America . . 3,500.00
10 SSh(c),Bondage(c), Capt.
   America 3,500.00
11 SSh(c),Bondage(c), Capt.
   America 2,000.00
12 ASh(c),Capt.America 2,000.00
13 ASh(c),Capt.America 2,000.00
14 AyB(c),Capt.America 1,500.00
15 Capt.America 1,500.00
16 ASh(c),Bondage(c),
   Capt.America 1,500.00
17 Bondage(c),Capt.America . . 1,500.00

U.S. 1 #2
© *Marvel Entertainment Group*

U.S. 1

May, 1983–Oct., 1984

1 AM(c),HT,Trucking Down the
   Highway 3.00
2 HT,Midnight 3.00
3 FS,ME,Rhyme of the Ancient
   Highwayman 3.00
4 FS,ME 3.00
5 FS,ME,Facing The Maze 3.00
6 FS,ME 3.00
7 FS,ME 3.00
8 FS,ME 3.00
9 FS,ME,Iron Mike-King of
   the Bike 3.00
10 thru 12 FS,ME. . . . . @3.00

U.S. AGENT

June–Dec., 1993

1 V:Scourge,O:U.S.Agent. 2.25
2 V:Scourge 2.25
3 V:Scourge 2.25
4 last issue 2.25

U.S. AGENT

May, 2001

1 (of 3) JOy,KK,Maximum Security. 3.00
2 JOy,KK, ... 3.00
3 JOy,KK,A:Capt.America. 3.00

U.S. WAR MACHINE

Marvel Max, Sept., 2001

1 (of 12) Weekly series,24-page. . . 2.25
2 thru 12 . . . . @2.25
TPB rep., 288-page 15.00

UNIVERSE X

July, 2000

0 AxR,DBw,48-pg. 4.00
1 (of 12) AxR,DBw,Capt.MarVell. . . 3.50
2 AxR,DBw, ... 3.50
3 AxR,DBw, ... 3.50
4 AxR,DBw,Cap.Am vs. Hydra . . . 3.50
5 AxR,DBw,Mar-Vell vs.Death . . . 3.50
6 AxR,DBw,Moonknight 3.50
7 AxR,DBw,Supreme Intelligence. . 3.50
8 AxR,DBw,Monster Generation. . . 3.50
9 AxR,DBw,Supreme Intelligence. . 3.50
10 AxR,DBw,V:Mephisto 3.50
11 AxR,DBw,A:Belasco 3.50
12 AxR,DBw,V:Absorbing Man 3.50

Spec."4",F:Fantastic Four 4.00
Spec. Spidey,AxR,JG,JR,48-page . . 4.00
Spec. Beasts,AxR,48-page 4.00
Spec. Omnibus,AxR. 4.00
Spec. Iron Men, 48-page 4.00
Spec. Universe X:X 48-page 4.00
TPB Vol.1 384-pg. 25.00
TPB Vol.2 336-pg. 30.00

UNTAMED
Epic *Heavy Hitters*, 1993
1 I:Griffen Palmer 2.75
2 V:Kosansui. 2.25
3 V:Kosansui. 2.25

Untold Legend of Captain Marvel #2
© Marvel Entertainment Group

UNTOLD LEGEND OF
CAPTAIN MARVEL, THE
1997
1 (of 3) Early days of Captain
   Marvel 2.50
2 Early days of Captain Marvel . . . 2.50
3 V:Kree 2.50

UNTOLD TALES
OF SPIDER-MAN
Sept., 1995 – Sept., 1997
1 F:Young Spider-Man 3.00
2 V:Batwing. 2.25
3 V:Sandman 2.25
4 V:J.Jonah Jameson 2.25
5 V:Vulture 2.25
6 A:Human Torch 2.25
7 . . . . 2.25
8 . . . . 2.25
9 A:Batwing,Lizard 2.25
10 KBk,PO,I:Commanda 2.25
11 KBk,PO, ... 2.25
12 KBk,PO, ... 2.25
13 KBk,PO, ... 2.25
14 KBk,PO, ... 2.25
15 KBk,PO,AV,Gordon's plan to
   control the Bugle 2.25
16 Re-I:Mary Jane Watson 2.25
17 KBk,PO,AV,V:Hawkeye. 2.25
18 KBk,PO,AV,A:Green Goblin,
   Headsman. 2.25
19 KBk,PO,AW,F:Doctor Octopus . 2.25
20 KBk,PO,AW,V:Vulture 2.25
21 KBk,PO,AW,V:Menace,A:Original
   X-Men 2.25

22 KBk,PO,AW,V:Scarecrow,. 2.25
23 KBk,PO,AW,V:Crime Master,
   A:Green Goblin 2.25
24 KBk,PO,BMc, Fate of Batwing . 2.25
25 LBl,PO,BMc, V:Green Goblin,
   final issue 2.25
Minus 1 Spec., RSt,JR, flashback,
   Peter's parents 2.25
Ann.'96 1 KBk,MiA,JSt,A date with
   Invisible Girl?. 2.25
Ann.'97 KBk,TL,A:everyone, 48-pg. 3.00
TPB rep. #1–#8 . . . . 17.00
one-shot GN KBk,SL,Encounter,
   A:Dr. Strange 48-pg. 6.00

US WAR MACHINE 2.0
June, 2003
1 (of 3) V:Iron Man 3.00
2 . . . . 3.00
3 concl. 3.00

VALKYRIE
1996
1-shot JMD 2.50

VAMPIRE TALES
Aug., 1973
(black & white magazine)
1 BEv,B:Morbius the Living
   Vampire 60.00
2 JSo,I:Satana 40.00
3 A:Satana 30.00
4 GK 30.00
5 GK,O:Morbius The Living
   Vampire 40.00
6 AA,I:Lilith 35.00
7 HC,PG 35.00
8 AA,A:Blade The Vampire
   Slayer 35.00
9 RH,AA 35.00
10 . . . . 35.00
11 June, 1975 . . . . 35.00
Ann.#1 . . . . 25.00

VAULT OF EVIL
Feb., 1973 – Nov., 1975
1 GK,B:1950's reps,Come
   Midnight,Come Monster 30.00
2 The Hour of the Witch 20.00
3 The Woman Who Wasn't 20.00

Vault of Evil #14
© Marvel Entertainment Group

4 Face that Follows 20.00
5 Ghost 20.00
6 GT,The Thing at the Window . . 20.00
7 Monsters 20.00
8 The Vampire is my Brother 20.00
9 Giant Killer 20.00
10 MD,The Lurkers in the Caves. . 20.00
11 JK,BEv,Two Feasts For
   a Vampire 20.00
12 Midnight in the
   Haunted Mansion 20.00
13 Hot as the Devil 20.00
14 SD,Midnight in the Haunted
   Manor 20.00
15 SD,Don't Shake Hands with
   the Devil 20.00
16 A Grave Honeymoon. 20.00
17 Grave Undertaking 20.00
18 The Deadly Edge 20.00
19 Vengeance of Ahman Ra 20.00
20 SD. 20.00
21 Victim of Valotorr. 20.00
22 SD. 20.00
23 Black Magician Lives Again . . . 20.00

VENOM
April, 2003
1 SK(c),Shiver,pt.1 . . . . 3.00
2 Shiver,pt.2 . . . . 2.50
3 SK(c),Shiver,pt.3 . . . . 2.50
4 SK(c),Shiver,pt.4 . . . . 2.50
5 SK(c),Shiver,pt.5 . . . . 2.50
6 . . . . 2.50
7 SK(c) 2.50
8 SK(c) Run,pt.3,F:Wolverine 3.00
9 SK(c) Run,pt.4 . . . . 3.00
10 Run,pt.5 . . . . 3.00
11 Patterns,pt.1 . . . . 3.00
12 Patterns,pt.2 . . . . 3.00
13 Patterns,pt.3 . . . . 3.00
14 Twist,pt.1. . . . . 3.00
15 Twist,pt.2. . . . . 3.00
16 Twist,pt.3. . . . . 3.00
17 Twist,pt.4. . . . . 3.00
18 Twist,pt.5. . . . . 3.00
TPB Shiver, Vol. 1 . . . . 14.00
TPB Vol. 2: Run 20.00

VENOM:
ALONG CAME A SPIDER
1996
1 LHA,GLz,V:New Spider-Man 3.00
2 LHa,JPi,V:New Spider-Man 3.00
3 . . . . 3.00
4 conclusion, 48-pg. 3.00

VENOM:
CARNAGE UNLEASHED
1995
1 Venom vs. Carnage 3.00
2 Venom vs. Carnage 3.00
3 No Spider-Help 3.00
4 JRu,Wld,LHa,cardstock(c) 3.00

VENOM:
THE ENEMY WITHIN
1994
1 BMc,Glow-in-the-dark(C),
   A:Demogoblin,Morbius 3.25
2 BMc,A:Demogoblin,Morbius . . . 3.25
3 BMc,V:Demogoblin,A:Morbius. . . 3.25

VENOM: FINALE
1997–98
1 (of 3) LHa, ... 3.00
2 & 3 LJa, ... @3.00

VENOM: FUNERAL PYRE
1993
1 TL,JRu,A:Punisher............ 3.50
2 TL,JRu,AM,V:Gangs 3.50
3 TL,JRu,Last issue 3.50

VENOM: THE HUNGER
1996
1 thru 4 LKa,TeH,V:Dr. Paine ... @2.25

VENOM: THE HUNTED
1996
1 LHa,3 part mini-series 3.00

VENOM: LETHAL PROTECTOR
1993
1 MBa,A:Spider-Man.holo-grafx(c) . 7.00
1a Gold Ed.................. 25.00
2 MBa,A:Spider-Man........... 3.50
3 MBa,Families of Venom's
  victims 3.50
4 RLm,A:Spider-Man,V:Life
  Foundation................. 3.50
5 RLm,V:Five Symbiotes,A:SpM... 3.50
6 RLm,V:Spider-Man........... 3.50
Super Size Spec.#1 Planet of
  the Symbiotes,pt.3.......... 4.00
Venom:Deathtrap:The Vault,RLm,
  A:Avengers,Freedom Force ... 7.00
TPB Lethal Protector RLm,DvM .. 16.00

VENOM: LICENSE TO KILL
1997
1 (of 3) LHa,KHt, sequel to Venom
  on trial 2.25
2 LHa,V:Dr. Yes 2.25
3 LHa,V:Dr. Yes 2.25

VENOM: THE MACE
1994
1 Embossed(c),CP(s),LSh,I:Mace . 3.25
2 CP(s),LSh,V:Mace........... 3.25
3 CP(s),LSh,V:Mace,final issue ... 3.25

VENOM: THE MADNESS
1993–94
1 B:ANi(s),KJo,V:Juggernaut 3.50
2 KJo,V:Juggernaut 3.25
3 E:ANi(s),KJo,V:Juggernaut 3.25

VENOM: NIGHTS OF VENGEANCE
1994
1 RLm,I:Stalkers,A:Vengeance.... 3.25
2 RLm,A:Vengeance,V:Stalkers ... 3.25
3 RLm,V:Stalkers 3.25
4 RLm,final issue 3.25

VENOM: ON TRIAL
Jan.–May, 1997
1 LHa,Tries to break out........ 2.25
2 LHa,Defended by Matt Murdock
  (Daredevil),A:Spider-Man 2.25
3 LHa,A:Spider-Man, Carnage,
  Daredevil................... 2.25

VENOM: SEED OF DARKNESS
1997
1 LKa,JFy,Flashback, early Eddie
  Brock 2.25

Venom Separation Anxiety #3
© Marvel Entertainment Group

VENOM: SEPARATION ANXIETY
1994–95
1 Embossed(c) 3.00
2 V:Symbiotes................. 3.00
3 .... 3.00
4 .... 3.00
TPB Rep.#1-#4 HMe,RoR,SDR.... 9.95

VENOM: SIGN OF THE BOSS
1997
1 (of 2) IV,TDr,V:Ghost Rider 2.25
2 (of 2) IV,TDr,conclusion 2.25

VENOM: SINNER TAKES ALL
1995
1 LHa,GLz,I:New Sin-Eater 3.00
2 V:Sineater 3.00
3 Wrong Man 3.00
4 LHa,GLz,V:Sin-Eater 3.00
5 LHa, finale 3.00

VENOM: TOOTH AND CLAW
1996–97
1 (of 3) LHa,JPi,AM, Dirtnap usurps
  Venom's body 2.25
2 LHa,JPi,AM,V:Wolverine 2.25
3 LHa,JPi,AM,V:Wolverine,
  Chimera................... 2.25

VENOM VS. CARNAGE
June, 2004
1 (of 4) 3.00
2 F:Black Cat 3.00
3 .... 3.00
4 F:Toxin..................... 3.00

VENUS
Atlas, Aug., 1948
1 B:Venus,Hedy Devine,HK,Hey
  Look 1,600.00
2 Venus(c) 1,000.00
3 Carnival(c) 750.00
4 Cupid(c).HK,Hey Look....... 750.00

5 Serenade(c) 750.00
6 Wrath of a Goddess,A:Loki ... 700.00
7 The Romance That Could
  Not Be 700.00
8 The Love Trap 700.00
9 Whom the Gods Destroy 700.00
10 JMn,B:Science Fiction/Horror,
  Trapped On the Moon 1,000.00
11 RH,The End of the World... 1,200.00
12 GC,The Lost World......... 650.00
13 BEv,King o/t Living Dead... 1,000.00
14 BEv,The Fountain of Death . 1,000.00
15 BEv,The Empty Grave..... 1,000.00
16 BEv,Where Gargoyles Dwell 1,000.00
17 BEv,Tower of Death,
  Bondage(c)............. 1,000.00
18 BEv,Terror in the Tunnel ... 1,000.00
19 BEv,PMo, Kiss Of Death ... 1,000.00

VERY BEST OF MARVEL COMICS
1-shot reps Marvel Artists
  Favorite Stories 13.00

VIDEO JACK
Nov., 1987
1 KGi,O:Video Jack 3.00
2 KGi........................ 2.50
3 KGi........................ 2.50
4 KGi........................ 2.50
5 KGi........................ 2.50
6 KGi,NA,BWr,AW 2.50

VISION, THE
1994–95
1 BHs,mini-series 2.25
2 BHs 2.25
3 BHs 2.25
4 BHs 2.25

VISION & SCARLET WITCH
[1st Series] Nov., 1982
1 RL,V:Halloween............. 3.00
2 RL,V:Isbisa,D:Whizzer....... 3.00
3 RL,A:Wonderman,V:GrimReaper 3.00
4 RL,A:Magneto,Inhumans....... 3.00
[2nd Series] 1985–86
1 V:Grim Reaper.............. 2.50
2 V:Lethal Legion,D:Grim Reaper.. 2.50
3 V:Salem's Seven 2.50
4 I:Glamor & Illusion 2.50
5 A:Glamor & Illusion 2.50
6 A:Magneto 2.50
7 V:Toad 2.50
8 A:Powerman 2.50
9 V:Enchantress 2.50
10 A:Inhumans................ 2.50
11 A:Spider-Man.............. 2.50
12 Birth of V&S's Child 2.50

VISIONARIES
Star, Nov., 1987
1 thru 5 .... @2.50
6 Sept., 1988 .... 2.50

VOID INDIGO
Epic, Nov., 1984
1 VM,Epic Comics 2.50
2 VM,Epic Comics,March, 1985 .. 2.50

WACKY DUCK
See: DOPEY DUCK

WALLY THE WIZARD
Star, April, 1985
1	4.00
2 thru 11	@4.00
12 March, 1986.	4.00

WAR, THE
1989
1 Sequel to The Draft & The Pit	4.00
2	4.00
3	4.00
4 1990.	4.00

WAR ACTION
Atlas, April, 1952
1 JMn,RH,War Stories, Six Dead Men	250.00
2 GT	125.00
3 Invasion in Korea	90.00
4 thru 10	@90.00
11	100.00
12	100.00
13 BK	100.00
14 Rangers Strike,June, 1953	90.00

WAR ADVENTURES
Atlas, Jan., 1952
1 GT,Battle Fatigue	200.00
2 The Story of a Slaughter	100.00
3 JRo	75.00
4 RH(c)	75.00
5 RH,Violent(c)	75.00
6 Stand or Die	75.00
7 JMn(c)	75.00
8 BK	100.00
9 RH(c)	75.00
10 JRo(c),Attack at Dawn	75.00
11 Red Trap	75.00
12	75.00
13 RH(c),The Commies Strike Feb., 1953	75.00

WAR COMBAT
Atlas, March, 1952
1 JMn,Death of Platoon Leader	175.00
2	100.00
3 JMn(c)	75.00
4 JMn(c)	75.00
5 The Red Hordes	75.00

Becomes:

COMBAT CASEY
6 BEv,Combat Casey cont	175.00
7	100.00
8 JMn(c)	90.00
9	75.00
10 RH(c).	125.00
11	60.00
12	60.00
13 thru 19	@125.00
20	60.00
21 thru 33	@55.00
34 July, 1957	55.00

WAR COMICS
Atlas, Dec., 1950
1 You Only Die Twice	300.00
2 Infantry's War	150.00
3	125.00
4 GC,The General Said Nuts	125.00
5	125.00
6 The Deadly Decision of General Kwang	125.00
7 RH,JMn	125.00
8 RH,No Survivors	125.00
9 RH,JMn	125.00
10	125.00
11 Flame thrower	135.00

12 thru 21	@100.00
22	100.00
23 thru 37	@75.00
38 JKu	80.00
39	75.00
40	75.00
41	75.00
42 JO	75.00
43 AT,MD	80.00
44	75.00
45	75.00
46 RC	85.00
47	75.00
48 MD,JO.	75.00
49 Sept., 1957	85.00

WARHEADS
Marvel UK, 1992–93
1 GEr,I:Warheads,A:Wolverine,	2.25
2 GEr,V:Nick Fury	2.25
3 DTy,A:Iron Man	2.25
4 SCy,A:X-Force	2.25
5 A:X-Force,C:Deaths'Head II	2.25
6 SCy,A:Death's Head II	2.25
7 SCy,A:Death's Head II,S.Surfer.	2.25
8 SCy,V:Mephisto	2.25
9 SCy,V:Mephisto	2.25
10 JCz,V:Mephisto	2.25
11 A:Death's Head II	2.25
12 V:Mechanix	2.25
13 Xenophiles Reptiles	2.25
14 last issue	2.25

WARHEADS: BLACK DAWN
1 A:Gh.Rider,Morbius	3.25
2 V:Dracula	2.25

WAR IS HELL
Jan., 1973—Oct., 1975
1 BP,B:reps.,Decision at Dawn	35.00
2 Anytime,Anyplace,War is Hell	20.00
3 Retreat or Die	20.00
4 Live Grenade	20.00
5 Trapped Platoon	20.00
6 We Die at Dawn	20.00
7 While the Jungle Sleeps,A:Sgt Fury	20.00
8 Killed in Action,A;Sgt Fury	20.00
9 B:Supernatural,War Stories	60.00
10 Death is a 30 Ton Tank	20.00
11 thru 15	@20.00

WARLOCK
[1st Regular Series] Aug., 1972
1 MGr,GK,I:Counter Earth, A:High Evolutionary	60.00
2 MGr,JB,TS,V:Man Beast	35.00
3 MGr,GK,TS,V:Apollo	35.00
4 MGr,JK,TS,V:Triax	20.00
5 MGr,GK,TS,V:Dr.Doom	20.00
6 MGr,TS(i),O:Brute	20.00
7 MGr,TS(i),V:Brute,D:Dr.Doom	20.00
8 MGr,TS(i),R:Man-Beast(cont. in Hulk #176)	20.00
9 MGr,JSn,1st`Rebirth'Thanos, O:Magnus,N:Warlock, I:In-Betweener	30.00
10 MGr,JSn,SL,O:Thanos,V:Magus, A:In-Betweener	35.00
11 MGr,JSn,SL,D:Magus,A:Thanos, In-Betweener	30.00
12 MGr,JSn,SL,O:Pip,V:Pro-Boscis A:Starfox	20.00
13 MGr,JSn,SL,I&O:Star-Thief.	20.00
14 MGr,JSn,SL,V:Star-Thief.	20.00
15 MGr,JSn,A:Thanos,V:Soul-Gem	30.00

Warlock #15
© Marvel Entertainment Group

[2nd Regular Series] 1992
1 JSn,rep.Strange Tales #178-180 Baxter Paper	5.00
2 JSn,rep.Strange Tales #180 & Warlock #9	4.00
3 JSn,rep.Warlock #10-#12	4.00
4 JSn,rep.Warlock #13-#15	4.00
5 JSn,rep.Warlock #15	4.00
6 JSn,rep.	4.00

WARLOCK
[Limited Series]
1 Rep.Warlock Series	3.50
2 thru 6 Rep.Warlock Series	@3.00

WARLOCK
Sept., 1998
1 (of 4) TL,RJn,R:Adam Warlock	3.00
2 TL,murderer revealed	3.00
3 TL,V:Drax.	3.00
4 TL,Concl.	3.00

WARLOCK
Aug., 1999
1 LSi,PFe,Marvel Tech	3.00
2 LSi,PFe,A:Iron Man	2.50
2a variant PFe cover	2.50
3 LSi,PFe,MMo,F:Psiren.	2.50
4 LSi,PFe,MMo,V:Mole Man	2.50
5 LSi,PFe,MMo	2.50
6 LSi,PFe,MMo,A:Kitty Pryde	2.50
7 LSi,PFe,MMo,R:Wolfsbane, Magus	2.50
8 LSi,PFe,MMo,V:Bastion.	2.50
9 LSi,PFe,MMo,F:Bastion.	2.50

WARLOCK
Sept., 2004
1 CAd,F:Adam Warlock	3.00
2 CAd	3.00

WARLOCK AND THE INFINITY WATCH
1992–95
1 AMe,Trial of the Gods(from Infinity Gauntlet)	3.00
2 AMe,I:Infinity Watch(Gamora,Pip, Moondragon,Drax & 1 other).	2.75
3 RL,TA,A:High Evolutionary, Nobilus,I:Omega	2.75

4 RL,TA,V:Omega 2.50
5 AMe,TA,V:Omega 2.50
6 AMe,V:Omega(Man-Beast) 2.50
7 TR,TA,V:Mole Man,A:Thanos . . . 2.50
8 TR,TA,Infinity War,A:Thanos . . . 2.25
9 AMe,TA,Inf.War,O:Gamora 2.25
10 AMe,Inf.War,Thanos vs
    Doppleganger 2.50
11 O:Pip,Gamora,Drax,M'dragon. . . 2.25
12 TR,Drax Vs.Hulk 2.25
13 TR,Drax vs Hulk 2.25
14 AMe,V:United Nations. 2.25
15 AMe,Magnus,Him 2.25
16 TGr,I:Count Abyss. 2.25
17 TGr,I:Maxam 2.25
18 AMe,Inf.Crusade,N:Pip 2.25
19 TGr,A:Hulk,Wolverine,Infinity
    Crusade. 2.25
20 AMe,Inf.Crusade. 2.25
21 V:Thor 2.25
22 AMe,Infinity Crusade. 2.25
23 JSn(s),TGb,Blood &
    Thunder#4 . . . . 2.25
24 JSn(s),TGb,V:Geirrodur 2.25
25 JSn(s),AMe,Die-Cut(c),Blood &
    Thunder #12 . . . . 3.50
26 A:Avengers 2.25
27 TGb,V:Avengers 2.25
28 TGb,V:Man-Beast 2.25
29 A:Maya 2.25
30 PO. 2.25
31 . . . . 2.25
32 Heart & Soul 2.25
33 V:Count Abyss 2.25
34 V:Count Abyss 2.25
35 V:Tyrannus 2.25
36 . . . . 2.25
37 A:Zaharius. 2.25
38 . . . . 2.25
39 V:Domitron 2.25
40 A:Thanos. 2.25
41 Monster Island 2.25
42 Warlock vs. Maxam, Atlantis
    Rising, final issue 2.25

WARLOCK CHRONICLES
1993–94
1 TR,F:Adam Warlock,holo-grafx(c),
    I:Darklore,Meer'lyn 3.25
2 TR,Infinity Crusade,Thanos revealed
    to have the Reality Gem 2.25
3 TR,A:Mephisto 2.25
4 TR,A:Magnus 2.25
5 TR(c),Inf.Crusade 2.25
6 TR,Blood & Thunder,pt.#3 . . . . . 2.25
7 TR,Blood & Thunder,pt.#7 . . . . . 2.25
8 TR,Blood & Thunder,pt.#11 . . . . 2.25
9 TR 2.25
10 TR 2.25
11 TR 2.25

WAR MACHINE
1994–96
1 GG,Foil Embossed(c),B:LKa&StB,
    O:War Machine,V:Cable,
    C:Deathlok. 3.25
1a Newstand Ed. 2.25
2 GG,V:Cable,Deathlok,w/card . . . 3.25
3 GG,V:Cable,Deathlok. 3.25
4 GG,C:Force Works. 3.25
5 GG,I:Deachtoll 3.25
6 GG,V:Deathtoll 3.25
7 GG,A:Hawkeye 3.25
8 reg ed. 3.25
8a neon(c),w/insert print 3.00
9 Hands of Mandarin,pt.2 . . . . 2.25
10 Hands of Mandarin,pt.5 . . . . 2.25
11 X-Mas Party 2.25
12 V:Terror Device 2.25
13 V:The Rush Team 2.25

War Machine #8
© Marvel Entertainment Group

14 A:Force Works 2.25
15 In The Past of WWII 2.25
16 DAn,A:Rick Fury,Cap.America . . 2.25
17 The Man Who Won WWII 2.25
18 DAn,N:War Machine 2.25
19 DAn,A:Hawkeye 2.25
20 DAn,The Crossing 2.25
21 DAn,The Crossing 2.25
22 DAn,V:Iron Man 2.25
23 DAn,Avengers:Timeslide. 2.25

WAR MAN
Epic, 1993
1 thru 2 CDi(s) 2.50

WEAPON X
1995
1 Wolverine After Xavier 4.00
2 Full Scale War 2.25
3 Jean Leaves 2.25
4 F:Gateway 2.25
TPB Rep.#1-#4 . . . . 9.00

WEAPON X
Aug., 2002
1-shot Wild Child #1, JWi 2.50
1-shot Sauron #1, JWi,KIK. 2.50
1-shot Kane #1, JWi 2.50
1-shot Marrow #1, JWi, ... 2.50
1-shot Agent Zero #1, JWi 2.50
1 . . . . 2.25
2 F:Marrow 2.25
3 . . . . 2.25
4 Hunt for Sabretooth 2.25
5 Evil plans,D.Maggot. 3.00
6 NRd,special mission 2.25
7 The Underground,pt.1 . . . . 2.25
8 The Underground,pt.2 . . . . 3.00
9 The Underground,pt.3 . . . . 3.00
10 The Underground,pt.4. . . . . 3.00
11 The Underground,pt.5. . . . . 3.00
12 The Underground,pt.6. . . . . 3.00
13 The Underground,concl. 3.00
14 R:Mr. Sinister 3.00
15 Defection,pt.1,F:X-Man 3.00
16 Defection,pt.2 . . . . 3.00
17 Defection,pt.3 . . . . 3.00
18 Defection,pt.4 . . . . 3.00
19 Countdown to Zero,pt.1 . . . . . . 3.00
20 Countdown to Zero,pt.2 . . . . . . 3.00
21 Countdown to Zero,pt.3 . . . . . . 3.00
22 Mutant feared 3.00

23 TMd,War of the Programs,pt.1 . . 3.00
24 TMd,War of the Programs,pt.2 . . 3.00
25 TMd,War of the Programs,pt.3 . . 3.00
26 TMd,Man and Superman,pt.1. . . 3.00
27 TMd,Man and Superman,pt.2. . . 3.00
28 TMd,Man and Superman,pt.3. . . 3.00
TPB Vol. 1 . . . . 22.00
TPB The Underground. 20.00

WEAVEWORLD
Epic, 1991–92
1 MM, Clive Barker adaptation 5.00
2 MM,Into the Weave 5.00
3 MM. 5.00

WEB OF
SCARLET SPIDER
1995–96
1 TDF,Virtual Mortality,pt.1 . . . . 2.00
2 TDF,CyberWar,pt.2 . . . . 2.00
3 Nightmare in Scarlet,pt.1 . . . . 2.00
4 Nightmare in Scarlet,pt.3 . . . . 2.00

WEB OF SPIDER-MAN
April, 1985
1 JM,V:New Costume 25.00
2 JM,V:Vulture 15.00
3 JM,V:Vulture 15.00
4 JM,JBy,V:Dr.Octopus 10.00
5 JM,JBy,V:Dr.Octopus 10.00
6 MZ,BL,JM,Secret Wars II. 10.00
7 SB,A:Hulk,V:Nightmare,
    C:Wolverine 10.00
8 V:Smithville Thunder 10.00
9 V:Smithville Thunder 10.00
10 JM,A:Dominic Fortune,
    V:Shocker 10.00
11 BMc,V:Thugs. 10.00
12 BMc,SB,V:Thugs. 10.00
13 BMc,V:J.JonahJameson 10.00
14 KB,V:Black Fox 10.00
15 V:Black Fox,I:Chance 7.00
16 MS,KB,V:Magma 7.00
17 MS,V:Magma 8.00
18 MS,KB,Where is Spider-Man? . . 7.00
19 MS,BMc,I:Solo,Humbug 7.00
20 MS,V:Terrorists 7.00
21 V:Fake Spider-Man 7.00
22 MS,V:Terrorists 7.00
23 V:Slyde 7.00
24 SB,V:Vulture,Hobgoblin 7.00
25 V:Aliens. 7.00
26 V:Thugs. 7.00
27 V:Headhunter 7.00
28 BL,V:Thugs 7.00
29 A:Wolverine,2nd App:New
    Hobgoblin 15.00
30 KB,O:Rose,C:Daredevil,Capt.
    America,Wolverine,Punisher . . 10.00
31 MZ,BMc,V:Kraven. 9.00
32 MZ,BMc,V:Kraven. 9.00
33 BSz(c),SL,V:Kingpin,Mad
    Dog Ward,pt.#1 . . . . 6.00
34 SB,A:Watcher 6.00
35 AS,V:Living Brain 6.00
36 AS,V:Phreak Out,I:Tombstone . . 7.00
37 V:Slasher 7.00
38 AS,A:Tombstone,V:Hobgoblin . . 7.00
39 AS,V:Looter(Meteor Man) 6.00
40 AS,V:Cult of Love 6.00
41 AS,V:Cult of Love 6.00
42 AS,V:Cult of Love 6.00
43 AS,V:Cult of Love 6.00
44 AS,V:Warzone,A:Hulk 5.00
45 AS,V:Vulture 5.00
46 A:Dr.Pym,V:Nekra 5.00
47 AS,V:Hobgoblin. 6.00
48 AS,O:New Hobgoblin's Demonic
    Power 15.00

MARVEL

Web of Spider-Man #103
© Marvel Entertainment Group

49 VM,V:Drugs. 5.00
50 AS,V:Chameleon(double size) . . 7.00
51 MBa,V:Chameleon,Lobo Bros. . . 5.00
52 FS,JR,O:J.Jonah Jameson
    V:Chameleon 5.00
53 MBa,V:Lobo Bros.,C:Punisher
    A:Chameleon. 5.00
54 AS,V:Chameleon,V:Lobo Bros. . 5.00
55 AS,V:Chameleon,Hammerhead,
    V:Lobo Bros. 5.00
56 AS,I&O:Skin Head,
    A:Rocket Racer. 5.00
57 AS,D:SkinHead,
    A:Rocket Racer. 5.00
58 AS,V:Grizzly 5.00
59 AS,Acts of Vengeance,V:Titania
    A:Puma,Cosmic Spider-Man . . . 7.00
60 AS,A of V,V:Goliath 5.00
61 AS,A of V,V:Dragon Man. 5.00
62 AS,V:Molten Man 3.00
63 AS,V:Mister Fear. 3.00
64 AS,V:Graviton,Titania,Trapster . 3.00
65 AS,V:Goliath,Trapster,Graviton . 3.00
66 AS,V:Tombstone,A:G.Goblin 3.00
67 AS,A:GreenGoblin,
    V:Tombstone 3.00
68 AS,A:GreenGoblin,
    V:Tombstone 3.00
69 AS,V:Hulk 4.00
70 AS,I:The Spider/Hulk. 4.00
71 A:Silver Sable 3.00
72 AM,A:Silver Sable 3.00
73 AS,A:Human Torch,
    Colossus,Namor 3.00
74 AS,I:Spark,V:Bora 3.00
75 AS,C:New Warriors. 3.00
76 AS,Spidey in Ice 3.00
77 AS,V:Firebrand,Inheritor 3.00
78 AS,A:Firebrand,Cloak&Dagger . . 3.00
79 AS,V:Silvermane. 3.00
80 AS,V:Silvermane. 3.00
81 I:Bloodshed. 3.00
82 V:Man Mountain Marko. 3.00
83 V:A.I.M. Supersuit. 3.00
84 AS,B:Name of the Rose 3.00
85 AS,Name of the Rose 3.00
86 AS,I:Demogoblin. 3.00
87 AS,I:Praetorian Guard. 3.00
88 AS,Name of the Rose 3.00
89 AS,E:Name of the Rose,
    I:Bloodrose 3.00
90 AS,30th Ann.,w/hologram,
    polybagged,V:Mysterio 3.50

90a Gold 2nd printing 3.00
91 AS,V:Whisper And Pulse 3.00
92 AS,V:Foreigner 3.00
93 AS,BMc,V:Hobgoblin,A:Moon
    Knight,Foreigner 3.00
94 AS,V:Hobgoblin,A:MoonKnight . . 3.00
95 AS,Spirits of Venom#1,A:Venom,
    J.Blaze,GR,V:Hag & Troll 3.00
96 AS,Spirits of Venom#3, A:G.R,
    J.Blaze,Venom,Hobgoblin 3.00
97 AS,I:Dr.Trench,V:Bloodrose 3.00
98 AS,V:Bloodrose,Foreigner 3.00
99 I:Night Watch,V:New Enforcer . . 3.00
100 AS,JRu,V:Enforcers,Bloodrose,
    Kingpin(Alfredo),I:Spider Armor,
    O:Night Watch,Holografx(c). . . . 4.00
101 AS,Total Carnage,V:Carnage,
    Shriek,A:Cloak and Dagger,
    Venom 3.00
102 Total Carnage#6,V:Carnage,
    A:Venom,Morbius 3.00
103 AS,Maximum Carnage#10,
    V:Carnage 3.00
104 AS,Infinity Crusade 2.50
105 AS,Infinity Crusade 2.50
106 AS,Infinity Crusade 2.75
107 AS,A:Sandman,Quicksand 2.50
108 B:TKa(s),AS,I:Sandstorm,
    BU:Cardiac 2.50
109 AS,V:Shocker,A:Night Thrasher,
    BU:D:Calypso 2.50
110 AS,I:Warrant,A:Lizard 2.50
111 AS,V:Warrant,Lizard 2.50
112 AS,Pursuit#3,V:Chameleon,
    w/card 2.50
113 AS,A:Gambit,Black Cat,w/cel . . 3.50
113a Newsstand Ed. 2.50
114 AS 2.50
115 AS,V:Facade 2.50
116 AS,V:Facade 2.50
117 Foil(c), flip book with
    Power & Responsibility #1 . . . . 5.00
117a Newsstand ed. 2.50
118 Spider-clone, V:Venom 3.00
119 Clone,V:Venom 3.00
119a bagged with Milestone rep.
    Amazing Sp-Man #150,checklist 8.00
120 Web of Life,pt.1. . . . . 2.50
121 Web of Life,pt.3. . . . . 2.50
122 Smoke and Mirrors,pt.1 . . . . . . 2.50
123 The Price of Truth,pt.2 . . . . 2.25
124 The Mark of Kaine,pt.1 . . . . . . 2.00
125 R:Gwen Stacy 3.00
125a 3-D Holodisk cover 4.25
126 The Trial of Peter Parker,pt.1 . . 2.25
127 Maximum Clonage,pt.2 . . . . . . 2.25
128 TDF,Exiled,pt.1 . . . . 2.50
129 Timebomb,pt.2 . . . . 3.00
Ann.#1 V:Future Max. 7.00
Ann.#2 AAd,MMi,A:Warlock. 10.00
Ann.#3 AS,DP,JRu,JM,BL 4.50
Ann.#4 AS,TM,RLm,Evolutionary
    Wars,A:Man Thing,V:Slug 5.00
Ann.#5 AS,SD,JS,Atlantis
    Attacks,A:Fantastic Four 4.00
Ann.#6 SD,JBr,SB,A:Punisher. . . . 4.50
Ann.#7 Vibranium Vendetta #3 . . . 3.50
Ann.#8 Hero Killers#3,A:New
    Warriors,BU:Venom,Black Cat . 3.50
Ann.#9 CMa,I:Cadre,w/card. 3.50
Ann.#10 V:Shriek. 4.00
Super Size Spec.#1 Planet of
    the Symbiotes,pt.5. . . . . 3.95

WEBSPINNERS:
TALES OF SPIDER-MAN
Nov., 1998

1 JMD,JR,MZi,A:Mysterio,seq.to
    Amaz.Sp-M#38, 48-page. 3.00
1a signed 7.00

2 JMD,JR,V:J.Jonah Jameson 2.50
2a variant SR cover 2.50
3 JMD,V:Mysterio, concl. 2.50
4 KG,ErS,seq.to Silver Surfer#18 . . 2.50
5 KG,ErS,A:Silver Surfer. 2.50
6 KG,ErS,F:Silver Surfer,
    Psycho-Man & Annihilus 2.50
7 BS,MPn,V:Sandman 2.50
8 BS,MPn,V:Sandman 2.50
9 V:Sandman 2.50
10 V:Chameleon, pt.1 . . . . 2.50
11 V:Chameleon, pt.2 . . . . 2.50
12 conclusion, 48-pg. 3.50
13 . . . . 2.50
14 HMe,BS,A:Carnage 2.50
15 V:Vulture 2.50
16 V:Vulture 2.50
17 TDF, black costume 2.50
18 TDF, Silversable 2.50

Weird Wondertales #20
© Marvel Entertainment Group

WEIRD WONDERTALES
Dec., 1973

1 B:Reprints 45.00
2 I Was Kidnapped by a Flying
    Saucer 25.00
3 BP,The Thing in the Bog 25.00
4 SD,SK,It Lurks Behind
    the Wall 25.00
5 SD 25.00
6 The Man Who Owned a Ghost . 25.00
7 BP,The Apes That Walked
    like Men. 25.00
8 JMn,Reap A Deadly Harvest . . 25.00
9 The Murder Mirror 25.00
10 SD,SK,Mister Morgan's
    Monster 25.00
11 SD,SK,Slaughter in
    Shrangri-La 20.00
12 SD,MD,The Stars Scream
    Murder 20.00
13 SD,The Totem Strikes. 20.00
14 Witching Circle 20.00
15 . . . . 20.00
16 GC,The Shark. 20.00
17 Creature From Krogarr 20.00
18 Krang 20.00
19 SD,A:Dr Druid 20.00
20 SD,MD,The Madness 20.00
21 SD,A:Dr Druid 20.00
22 The World Below,May, 1975 . . 20.00

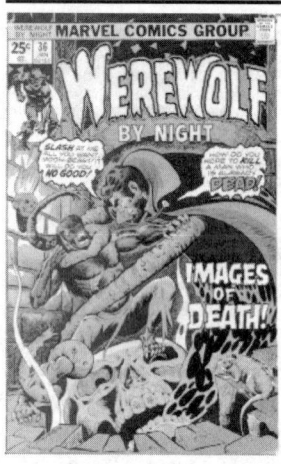

Werewolf by Night #36
© Marvel Entertainment Group

WEREWOLF BY NIGHT
Sept., 1972

1 MP(cont from Marvel Spotlight)
  FullMoonRise..WerewolfKill. . 200.00
2 MP,Like a Wild Beast at Bay . . . 75.00
3 MP,Mystery of the Mad Monk . . 50.00
4 MP,The Danger Game. 50.00
5 MP,A Life for a Death. 50.00
6 MP,Carnival of Fear. 40.00
7 MP,JM,Ritual of Blood 40.00
8 MP,Krogg,Lurker from Beyond . 40.00
9 TS,V:Tatterdemalion 40.00
10 TS,bondage cover 40.00
11 GK,TS,Full Moon..Fear Moon. . 30.00
12 GK,Cry Monster 30.00
13 MP,ManMonsterCalledTaboo . . 25.00
14 MP,Lo,the Monster Strikes 25.00
15 MP,(new)O:Werewolf,
  V:Dracula. 50.00
16 MP,TS,A:Hunchback of Notre
  Dame. 35.00
17 Behold the Behemoth. 35.00
18 War of the Werewolves. 35.00
19 V:Dracula 32.00
20 The Monster Breaks Free. 30.00
21 GK(c),To Cure a Werewolf 15.00
22 GK(c),Face of a Friend. 15.00
23 Silver Bullet for a Werewolf . . . 15.00
24 GK(c),V:The Brute 15.00
25 GK(c),Eclipse of Evil. 15.00
26 GK(c),A Crusade of Murder . . . 15.00
27 GK(c),Scourge o/t Soul-Beast . 15.00
28 GK(c),V:Dr.Glitternight 15.00
29 GK(c),V:Dr.Glitternight 15.00
30 GK(c),Red Slash across
  Midnight. 15.00
31 Death in White 15.00
32 I&O:Moon Knight 160.00
33 Were-Beast..Moon Knight
  A:Moon Knight(2nd App) 160.00
34 GK(c),TS,House of Evil..House
  of Death. 15.00
35 TS,JS,BWi,Jack Russell vs.
  Werewolf 15.00
36 Images of Death 15.00
37 BWr(c),BW,A:Moon Knight,
  Hangman,Dr.Glitternight 20.00
38 . . . . 22.00
39 V:Brother Voodoo 22.00
40 A:Brother Voodoo,V:Dr.
  Glitternight 15.00
41 V:Fire Eyes 15.00
42 A:IronMan,Birth of a Monster . . 15.00

43 Tri-Animal Lives,A:Iron Man . . . 15.00
G-Size#2,SD,A:Frankenstein
  Monster (reprint) 15.00
G-Size#3 GK(c),Transylvania . . 15.00
G-Size#4 GK(c),A:Morbius 15.00
G-Size#5 GK(c),Peril of
  Paingloss. 10.00

WEREWOLF BY NIGHT
Dec., 1997

1 PJe,F:Jack Russell returns 3.00
2 PJe,Search for wolf Amulet 3.00
3 PJe,Stuck between man & wolf. . 3.00
4 PJe,to the depths of hell 3.00
5 PJe, confronts demon 3.00
6 PJe, visit Underworld nightclub . . 3.00
Storyline continues in Strange Tales

WEST COAST AVENGERS
[Limited Series] Sept., 1984

1 BH,A:Shroud,J:Hawkeye,IronMan,
  WonderMan,Mockingbird,Tigra . 4.00
2 BH,V:Blank. 3.00
3 BH,V:Graviton 3.00
4 BH,V:Graviton 3.00

[Regular Series] 1985–89

1 AM,JSt,V:Lethal Legion 4.00
2 AM,JSt,V:Lethal Legion 3.00
3 AM,JSt,V:Kraven 3.00
4 AM,JSt,A:Firebird,Thing,I:Master
  Pandemonium 3.00
5 AM,JSt,A:Werewolf,Thing 3.00
6 AM,KB,A:Thing 3.00
7 AM,JSt,V:Ultron 3.00
8 AM,JSt,V:Rangers,A:Thing 3.00
9 AM,JSt,V:Master Pandemonium . 3.00
10 AM,JSt,V:Headlok,Griffen 3.00
11 AM,JSt,A:Nick Fury 2.50
12 AM,JSt,V:Graviton. 2.50
13 AM,JSt,V:Graviton. 2.50
14 AM,JSt,V:Pandemonium 2.50
15 AM,JSt,A:Hellcat 2.50
16 AM,JSt,V:Tiger Shark,
  Whirlwind. 2.50
17 AM,JSt,V:Dominus' Minions 2.50
18 AM,JSt,V:The Wild West. 2.50
19 AM,JSt,A:Two Gun Kid 2.50
20 AM,JSt,A:Rawhide Kid 2.50
21 AM,JSt,A:Dr.Pym,Moon Knight . . 2.50
22 AM,JSt,A:Fant.Four,Dr.Strange,
  Night Rider 2.50
23 AM,RT,A:Phantom Rider. 2.50
24 AM,V:Dominus 2.50
25 AM,V:Abomination 2.50
26 AM,V:Zodiac 2.50
27 AM,V:Zodiac 2.50
28 AM,V:Zodiac 2.50
29 AM,V:Taurus,A:Shroud 2.50
30 AM,C:Composite Avenger. 2.50
31 AM,V:Arkon. 2.50
32 AM,TD,V:Yetrigar,J:Wasp 2.50
33 AM,O:Ant-Man,Wasp;
  V:Madam X,El Toro 2.50
34 AM,V:Quicksilver,J:Vision &
  Scarlet Witch. 2.50
35 AM,V:Dr.Doom,Quicksilver 2.50
36 AM,V:The Voice 2.50
37 V:The Voice,A:Mantis 2.50
38 AM,TMo,V:Defiler 2.50
39 AM,V:Swordsman 2.50
40 AM,MGu,V:NightShift,
  A:Shroud 2.50
41 TMo,I:New Phantom Rider,
  L:Moon Knight 2.50
42 JBy,Visionquest#1,V:Ultron. . . . 2.75
43 JBy,Visionquest#2,. 2.50
44 JBy,Visionquest#3,J:USAgent . . 2.50
45 JBy,Visionquest#4,
  I:New Vision. 2.75

46 JBy,I:Great Lakes Avengers 2.50
Ann. #1 MBr,GI,V:Zodiak 2.75
Ann. #2 AM,A:SilverSurfer,V:Death,
  Collector,R:Grandmaster. 2.00
Ann. #3 AM,RLm,TD,Evolutionary
  Wars,R:Giant Man 3.50
Becomes:

AVENGERS WEST COAST

WESTERN GUNFIGHTERS
[2nd series] Aug., 1970

1 JK,JB,DAy,B:Ghost Rider
  A:Fort Rango,The Renegades
  Gunhawk 65.00
2 HT(c),DAy,JMn,O:Nightwind,
  V:Tarantula 35.00
3 DAy,MD,V:Hurricane, rep. 35.00
4 HT(c),DAy,TS,B:Gunhawk,
  Apache Kid,A:Renegades . . . 45.00
5 DAy,FrG,A:Renegades 35.00
6 HT(c),DAy,SSh,Death of
  Ghost Rider. 30.00
7 HT(c),DAy,SSh,O:Ghost Rider
  retold,E:Ghost Rider,Gunhawk 30.00
8 DAy,SSh,B:Black Rider,Outlaw
  Kid(rep) 25.00
9 DW,Revenge rides the Range. . 25.00
10 JK,JMn,O:Black Rider,B:Matt
  Slade,E:Outlaw Kid 25.00
11 JK,Duel at Dawn 25.00
12 JMn,O:Matt Slade 30.00
13 Save the Gold Coast Expires . . 25.00
14 JSo(c),Outlaw Town 25.00
15 E:Matt Slade,Showdown in
  Outlaw Canyon 25.00
16 B:Kid Colt,Shoot-out in Silver
  City 25.00
17 thru 20. . . . . @25.00
21 thru 24. . . . . @15.00
25 . . . . 15.00
26 F:Kid Colt,Gun-Slinger,
  Apache Kid 15.00
27 thru 32. . . . . @15.00
33 Nov., 1975. . . . . 15.00

WESTERN KID
[1st Series] Dec., 1954

1 JR,B:Western Kid,O:Western Kid
  (Tex Dawson) 250.00
2 JMn,JR,Western Adventure. . . 125.00
3 JMn(c),JR,Gunfight(c) 100.00
4 JMn(c),JR,The Badlands 100.00

Western Kid #3
© Marvel Entertainment Group

5 JR	100.00
6 JR	100.00
7 JR	100.00
8 JR	100.00
9 JR,AW	125.00
10 JR,AW,Man in the Middle	125.00
11 thru 16	@75.00
17 Aug., 1957	75.00

[2nd Series]

Dec., 1971–Aug., 1972

1 Reprints	35.00
2	20.00
3 AW	25.00
4	20.00
5	20.00

WESTERN OUTLAWS

Atlas, Feb., 1954—Aug., 1957

1 JMn(c),RH,BP,The Greenville Gallows,Hanging(c)	250.00
2	125.00
3 thru 10	@100.00
11 AW,MD	125.00
12 JMn	100.00
13 MB,JMn	125.00
14 AW	125.00
15 AT,GT	100.00
16 BP,JMn,JSe,AW	100.00
17 JMn,AW	100.00
18 JSe	90.00
19 JMn,JSe,RC	100.00
20 and 21 JSe	@90.00

WESTERN OUTLAWS & SHERIFFS
See: BEST WESTERN

WESTERN TALES OF BLACK RIDER
See: ALL WINNERS COMICS

WESTERN TEAM-UP

Nov., 1973

1 Rawhide Kid/Dakota Kid	50.00

WESTERN THRILLERS

Nov., 1954

1 JMn,Western tales	175.00
2	100.00
3	100.00
4	100.00

Becomes:

COWBOY ACTION

March, 1955–March, 1956

5 JMn(c),The Prairie Kid	150.00
6	100.00
7	100.00
9	100.00
10	100.00
11 MN,AW,The Manhunter	125.00

Becomes:

QUICK-TRIGGER WESTERN

May, 1956–Sept., 1957

12 Bill Larson Strikes	175.00
13 AW,The Man From Cheyenne	175.00
14 BEv,RH(c)	175.00
15 AT,RC	150.00
16 JK,JD	125.00
17 GT	125.00
18 GM	125.00
19 JSe	100.00

WESTERN WINNERS
See: ALL WINNERS COMICS

WHAT IF?

[1st Regular Series] Feb., 1977

1 Spider-Man joined Fant.Four	30.00
2 GK(c),Hulk had Banner brain	15.00
3 GK,KJ,F:Avengers	12.00
4 GK(c),F:Invaders	12.00
5 F:Captain America	12.00
6 F:Fantastic Four	12.00
7 GK(c),F:Spider-Man	10.00
8 GK(c),F:Daredevil	10.00
9 JK(c),F:Avengers of the '50s	10.00
10 JB,F:Thor	10.00
11 JK,F:FantasticFour	8.00
12 F:Hulk	8.00
13 JB,Conan Alive Today	8.00
14 F:Sgt. Fury	6.00
15 CI,F:Nova	6.00
16 F:Master of Kung Fu	6.00
17 CI,F:Ghost Rider	6.00
18 TS,F:Dr.Strange	5.00
19 PB,F:Spider-Man	6.00
20 F:Avengers	5.00
21 GC,F:Sub-Mariner	5.00
22 F:Dr.Doom	5.00
23 JB,F:Hulk	5.00
24 GK,RB,Gwen Stacy had lived	6.00
25 F:Thor,Avengers,O:Mentor	5.00
26 JBy(c),F:Captain America	5.00
27 FM(c),Phoenix hadn't died	20.00
28 FM,F:Daredevil,Ghost Rider.	15.00
29 MG(c),F:Avengers	6.00
30 RB,F:Spider-Man	10.00
31 Wolverine killed the Hulk	20.00
32 Avengers lost to Korvac	5.00
33 BL,Dazzler herald of Galactus	5.00
34 FM,FM,JBy,BSz:Humor issue	5.00
35 FM,Elektra had lived	6.00
36 JBy,Fant.Four had no powers	5.00
37 F:Thing,Beast,Silver Surfer	5.00
38 F:Daredevil,Captain America	5.00
39 Thor had fought Conan	5.00
40 F:Dr.Strange	5.00
41 F:Sub-Mariner	5.00
42 F:Fantastic Four	5.00
43 F:Conan	5.00
44 F:Captain America	5.00
45 F:Hulk,Berserk	5.00
46 Uncle Ben had lived	7.00
47 F:Thor,Loki	5.00
Spec.#1 F:Iron Man,Avengers	6.00
Best of What IF? rep.#1,#24, #27,#28	13.00

[2nd Regular Series]

1 RWi,MG,The Avengers had lost the Evolutionary War	5.00
2 GCa,Daredevil Killed Kingpin, A:Hobgoblin, The Rose	4.00
3 Capt.America Hadn't Given Up Costume,A:Avengers	3.50
4 MBa,Spider-Man kept Black Costume,A:Avengers,Hulk	4.50
5 Vision Destroyed Avengers, A:Wonder Man	3.50
6 RLm,X-Men Lost Inferno, A:Dr.Strange	6.00
7 RLd,Wolverine Joined Shield, A:Nick Fury,Black Widow	7.00
8 Iron Man Lost The Armor Wars, A:Ant Man	3.50
9 RB,New X-Men Died	6.00
10 MZ(c),BMc,Punisher's Family Didn't Die,A:Kingpin	3.00
11 TM(c),JV,SM,Fant.Four had the Same Powers,A:Nick Fury	3.50

What If Vol. 2 #1
© *Marvel Entertainment Group*

12 JV,X-Men Stayed in Asgard, A:Thor,Hela	5.00
13 JLe(c),Prof.X Became Juggernaut,A:X-Men	3.50
14 RLm(c),Capt.Marvel didn't die A:Silver Surfer	3.50
15 GCa,Fant.Four Lost Trial of Galactus,A:Gladiator	3.00
16 Wolverine Battled Conan, A:X-Men,Red Sonja	5.00
17 Kraven Killed Spider-Man, A:Daredevil,Captain America	3.00
18 LMc,Fant.Four fought Dr.Doom before they gained powers	3.00
19 RW,Vision took over Earth, A:Avengers,Dr.Doom	3.00
20 Spider-Man didn't marry Mary Jane,A:Venom,Kraven	3.00
21 Spider-Man married Black Cat, A:Vulture,Silver Sable	3.00
22 RLm,Silver Surfer didn't escape Earth,A:F.F,Mephisto,Thanos	4.00
23 New X-Men never existed, A:Eric the Red,Lilandra	3.00
24 Wolverine Became Lord of Vampires,A:Punisher	3.00
25 Marvel Heroes lost Atlantis Attacks,double size	3.50
26 LMc,Punisher Killed Daredevil, A:Spider-Man	3.00
27 Submariner Joined Fantastic Four,A:Dr. Doom	3.00
28 RW,Capt.America led Army of Super-Soldiers,A:Submariner	3.00
29 RW,Capt.America formed the Avengers	3.00
30 Inv.Woman's 2nd Child had lived,A:Fantastic Four	3.00
31 Spider-Man/Captain Universe Powers	3.00
32 Phoenix Rose Again,pt.1	3.00
33 Phoenix Rose Again,pt.2	3.00
34 Humor Issue	3.00
35 B:Time Quake,F.F. vs.Dr. Doom & Annihilus	3.00
36 Cosmic Avengers,V:Guardians of the Galaxy	3.00
37 X-Vampires,V:Dormammu	3.00
38 Thor was prisoner of Set	3.00
39 E:Time Quake,Watcher saved the Universe	3.00
40 Storm remained A thief?	3.00
41 JV,Avengers fought Galactus	3.00
42 KWe,Spidey kept extra arms	3.00

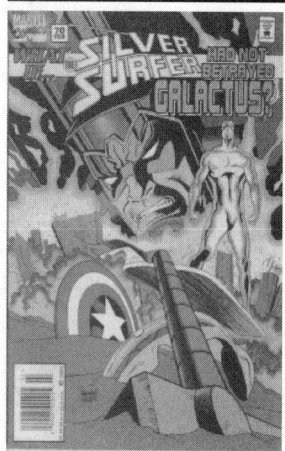

What If Vol. 2 #70
© Marvel Entertainment Group

43 Wolverine married Mariko 3.50
44 Punisher possessed by Venom . 3.00
45 Barbara Ketch became G.R. 3.00
46 Cable Killed Prof.X,Cyclops &
   Jean Grey 3.00
47 Magneto took over USA 3.00
48 Daredevil Saved Nuke 3.00
49 Silver Surfer had Inf.Gauntlet? . . 3.50
50 Hulk killed Wolverine 7.00
51 PCu,Punisher is Capt.America . . 3.00
52 BHi,Wolverine led Alpha Flight . . 3.50
53 F:Iron Man,Hulk 3.00
54 F:Death's Head 3.00
55 LKa(s),Avengers lose G.Storm . . 3.00
56 Avengers lose G.Storm#2 . . . . . 3.00
57 Punisher a member of SHIELD . . 3.00
58 Punisher kills SpM 3.00
59 Wolverine lead Alpha Flight 3.50
60 RoR,Scott & Jean's Wedding . . . 3.00
61 Spider-Man's Parents 3.00
62 Woverine vs Weapon X 3.50
63 F:War Machine,Iron Man 3.00
64 Iron Man sold out 3.00
65 Archangel fell from Grace 3.00
66 Rogue and Thor 3.00
67 Cap.America returns 3.00
68 Captain America story 3.00
69 Stryfe Killed X-Men 3.00
70 Silver Surfer 3.50
71 The Hulk 3.00
72 Parker Killed Burglar 3.00
73 Daredevil,Kingpin 3.00
74 Sinister Formed X-Men 3.00
75 Gen-X's Blink had lived 3.00
76 Flash Thompson Spider-Man . . . 3.00
77 Legion had killed Magneto 3.00
78 FF had stayed together 3.00
79 Storm had Phoenix's Power 3.00
80 KGa,Hulk was Cured 3.00
81 Age of Apocalypse didn't end . . . 3.00
82 WML,J.JonahJameson
   adopted Spider-Man 3.00
83 Daredevil 3.00
84 Shard 3.00
85 Magneto Ruled all mutants 3.00
86 Scarlet Spider vs. Spider-Man . . 3.00
87 Sabretooth 3.00
88 Spider-Man 3.00
89 Fantastic Four 3.00
90 Cyclops & Havok 3.00
91 F:Hulk, nice guy, Banner violent . 3.00
92 F:Cannonball,Husk 3.00
93 F:Wolverine 3.50

94 JGz,F:Juggernaut 3.00
95 IV,F:Ghost Rider 3.00
96 CWo,F:Quicksilver, ... 3.00
97 F:Black Knight 3.00
98 F:Nightcrawler & Rogue 3.00
99 F:Black Cat 3.00
100 IV,KJ,F:Gambit &
    Rogue, 48-pg. 3.50
101 ATi,F:Archangel 3.00
102 F:Daredevil's Dad 3.00
103 DaF,F:Captain America 3.00
104 F:Silver Surver,ImpossibleMan . 3.00
105 TDF,RF,F:Spider-Man and
    Mary Jane's Daughter 25.00
106 TDF,F:X-Men,Gambit
    sentenced to death 3.00
107 TDF,RF,BSz,F:Thor 3.00
108 TDF,F:The Avengers 3.00
109 TA,F:Fantastic Four 3.00
110 TDF,F:Wolverine 3.00
111 TDF,F:Wolverine 3.00
112 F:Ka-Zar 3.00
113 F:Iron Man, Dr. Strange, ... 3.00
114 F:Secret Wars, 32-page,
    final issue 3.50
Minus 1 Spec., AOI, flashback,
   F:Bishop 3.00
TPB Best of What If? 12.95

WHAT THE -?!
[Parodies]
Aug., 1988

1 . . . . 5.00
2 JBy,JOy,AW, ... 4.00
3 TM, ... 5.00
4 . . . . 3.00
5 EL,JLe,WPo,Wolverine 5.00
6 Wolverine,Punisher 3.00
7 . . . . 2.50
8 DK 2.50
9 . . . . 2.50
10 JBy,X-Men,Dr.Doom, Cap.
   America 2.50
11 DK, RLd(part) 2.50
12 Conan, F.F.,Wolverine 2.50
13 Silver Burper,F.F.,Wolverine . . . 2.50
14 Spittle-Man 2.50
15 Capt.Ultra,Wolverina 2.50
16 Ant Man,Watcher 2.50
17 Wulverean/Pulverizer,Hoagg/
   Spider-Ham,Sleep Gawker,F.F. . 2.50
18 . . . . 2.50
19 . . . . 2.50
20 Infinity Wart Crossover 2.50
21 Weapon XX,Toast Rider 2.50
22 F:Echs Farce 2.50
23 . . . . 2.50
24 Halloween issue 2.50
25 . . . . 2.50
26 Spider-Ham 2099 . . . . 2.50
Summer Spec. 2.50
Fall Spec. 2.50

WHERE CREATURES ROAM
July, 1970—Sept., 1971

1 JK,SD,DAy,B:Reprints
  The Brute That Walks 40.00
2 JK,SD,Midnight/Monster 25.00
3 JK,SD,DAy,Thorg 25.00
4 JK,SD,Vandoom 25.00
5 JK,SD,Gorgilla 25.00
6 JK,SD,Zog 25.00
7 SD 25.00
8 The Mummy's Secret,E:Reprints 25.00

WHERE MONSTERS DWELL
Jan., 1970

1 JK,SD,B:Reprints,Cyclops 40.00
2 JK,Sporr 25.00
3 JK,Grottu 25.00
4 . . . . 25.00
5 JK,Taboo 25.00
6 JK,Groot 25.00
7 JK,Rommbu 25.00
8 JK,SD,The Four-Armed Men . . 25.00
9 JK,Bumbu 25.00
10 JK,SD,Monster That Walks
   Like A Man 25.00
11 JK,Gruto 20.00
12 JK,GC,SD,Orogo,giant-size . . . 35.00
13 JK,The Thing That Crawl 20.00
14 JK,The Green Thing 20.00
15 JK,JSe,Kraa- The Inhuman . . . 20.00
16 JK,Beware the Son Of Goom . . 20.00
17 SD,The Hidden Vampires 20.00
18 SD,The Mask of Morghum 20.00
19 SD,The Insect Man 20.00
20 Klagg 20.00
21 Fin Fang Foom 20.00
22 Elektro 20.00
23 SD,The Monster Waits For Me . 20.00
24 SD,The Things on Easter Island 20.00
25 SD,The Ruler of the Earth 20.00
26 . . . . 20.00
27 . . . . 20.00
28 Droom,The Living Lizard 20.00
29 thru 37 Reprints . . . . @20.00
38 AW,reprints, Oct., 1975 . . . . . . 20.00

WHIP WILSON
See: BLAZE CARSON

WILD
Atlas, Feb., 1954

1 BEv,JMn,Charlie Chan
  Parody 300.00
2 BEv,RH,JMn,Witches(c) 175.00
3 CBu(c),BEv,RH,JMn, ... 150.00
4 GC,Didja Ever See a Cannon
  Brawl 150.00
5 RH,JMn,Aug., 1954 . . . . 150.00

WILD CARDS
Epic, Sept., 1990

1 JG 5.50
2 JG,V:Jokers 4.50
3 A:Turtle 4.50

WILDC.A.T.S/X-MEN: THE DARK AGE
Dec., 1997

1-shot MtB,WEI,V:Daemonites
  & Sentinels, 48-pg. 4.50
1a variant cover MGo 4.50

WILD THING
Marvel UK, 1993

1 A:Virtual Reality Venom and
  Carnage 3.00
2 A:VR Venom and Carnage 2.25
3 A:Shield 2.25
4 . . . . 2.25
5 Virtual Reality Gangs 2.25
6 Virtual Reality Villians 2.25
7 V:Trask 2.25
8 . . . . 2.25
9 . . . . 2.25
10 . . . . 2.25
11 . . . . 2.25

All comics prices listed are for *Near Mint* condition.

Wild Thing #2
© Marvel Entertainment Group

WILLIAM SHATNER'S TEK WORLD
1992–94

1 LS,Novel adapt.	2.25
2 LS,Novel adapt.cont.	2.25
3 LS,Novel adapt.cont.	2.25
4 LS,Novel adapt.cont.	2.25
5 LS,Novel adapt.concludes	2.25
6 LS,V:TekLords	2.25
7 E:The Angel	2.25
8	2.25
9	2.25
10	2.25
11 thru 17	@2.25
18	2.25
19 Sims of the Father#1	2.25
20 Sims of the Father#2	2.25
21 Who aren't in Heaven	2.25
22 Father and Guns	2.25
23 We'll be Right Back	2.25
24	2.25

WILLIE COMICS
See: IDEAL COMICS

WILLOW
Aug., 1988

1 Movie adapt.	3.00
2 Movie adapt.	3.00
3 Movie adapt,Oct., 1988.	3.00

WITCHES
June, 2004

1 MD2,F:Kale,Topaz,Satana	3.00
2 MD2,F:Kale,Topaz,Satana	3.00
3 MD2	3.00
4 MD2	3.00
TPB Vol. 1	10.00

WITNESS, THE
Sept., 1948

1	2,200.00

WOLFPACK
Aug., 1988

1 I:Wolfpack	10.00
2 thru 11	@2.50
12 July, 1988	2.50

WOLVERINE
[Limited Series] Sept., 1982

1 B:CCl(s),FM,JRu,A:Mariko, I:Shingen	75.00
2 FM,JRu,A:Mariko,I:Yukio	50.00
3 FM,JRu,A:Mariko,Yukio	50.00
4 B:CCl(s),FM,JRu,A:Mariko, D:Shingen	55.00

[Regular Series] 1988

1 JB,AW,V:Banipur	50.00
2 JB,KJ,V:Silver Samurai	25.00
3 JB,AW,V:Silver Samurai	17.00
4 JB,AW,I:Roughouse, Bloodsport	17.00
5 JB,AW,V:Roughouse, Bloodsport	17.00
6 JB,AW,V:Roughouse, Bloodsport	17.00
7 JB,A:Hulk	17.00
8 JB,A:Hulk	17.00
9 GC,Old Wolverine Story	17.00
10 JB,BSz,V:Sabretooth (1st battle)	35.00
11 JB,BSz,B:Gehenna Stone	10.00
12 JB,BSz,Gehenna Stone	10.00
13 JB,BSz,Gehenna Stone	10.00

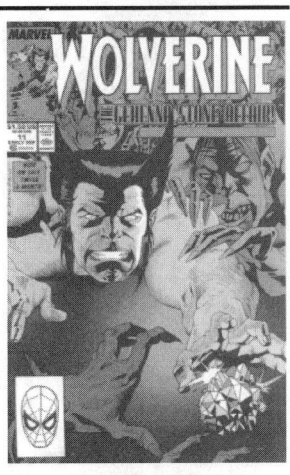

Wolverine #11
© Marvel Entertainment Group

14 JB,BSz,Gehenna Stone	10.00
15 JB,BSz,Gehenna Stone	10.00
16 JB,BSz,E:Gehenna Stone.	10.00
17 JBy,KJ,V:Roughouse	10.00
18 JBy,KJ,V:Roughouse	10.00
19 JBy,KJ,A of V,I:La Bandera.	10.00
20 JBy,KJ,A of V,V:Tigershark	7.00
21 JBy,KJ,V:Geist	7.00
22 JBy,KJ,V:Geist,Spore	7.00
23 JBy,KJ,V:Geist,Spore	7.00
24 GC,Snow Blind	6.00
25 JB,O:Wolverine(part)	6.00
26 KJ,Return to Japan	6.00
27 thru 30 Lazarus Project	6.00
31 MS,DGr,A:Prince o'Mandripoor	6.00
32 MS,DGr,V:Ninjas	6.00
33 MS,Wolverine in Japan	6.00
34 MS,DGr,Wolverine in Canada.	6.00
35 MS,DGr,A:Puck	6.00
36 MS,DGr,A:Puck,Lady D'strike	6.00
37 MS,DGr,V:Lady Deathstrike	6.00
38 MS,DGr,A:Storm,I:Elsie Dee.	6.00
39 MS,DGr,Wolverine Vs. Clone	6.00
40 MS,DGr,Wolverine Vs. Clone	6.00
41 MS,DGr,R:Sabretooth, A:Cable	8.00
41a 2nd printing	2.25
42 MS,DGr,A:Sabretooth,Cable	9.00
42a 2nd printing	2.50
43 MS,DGr,A:Sabretooth,C:Cable	7.00
44 LSn,DGr	6.00
45 MS,DGr,A:Sabretooth	7.00
46 MS,DGr,A:Sabretooth	7.00
47 V:Tracy	6.00
48 LHa(s),MS,DGr,B:Shiva Scenario	6.00
49 LHa(s),MS,DGr,	6.00
50 LHa(s),MS,DGr,A:X-Men,Nick Fury, I:Shiva,Slash-Die Cut(c)	8.00
51 MS,DGr,A:Mystique,X-Men.	5.00
52 MS,DGr,A:Mystique,V:Spiral.	5.00
53 MS,A:Mystique,V:Spiral,Mojo	5.00
54 A:Shatterstar	5.00
55 MS,V:Cylla,A:Gambit,Sunfire	5.00
56 MS,A:Gambit,Sunfire,V:Hand, Hydra	5.00
57 MS,D:Lady Mariko,A:Gambit	5.50
58 A:Terror	5.00
59 A:Terror	5.00
60 Sabretooth vs.Shiva, I:John Wraith	5.00
61 MT,History of Wolverine and Sabretooth,A:John Wraith	5.00

12	2.25
13	2.25

WILD THING
Aug., 1999

1 RLm,AM,LHa,F:Wolverine's daughter Rina	2.25
2A RLm,AM,LHa,Bloody Reunions	2.25
2B variant AW (c)	2.25
3 RLm,AM,LHa,A:Rina	2.25
4 RLm,AM,LHa	2.25
5 RLm,AM,LHa,V:Robot monster	2.25

WILD WEST
Spring, 1948

1 SSh(c),B:Two Gun Kids,Tex Taylor,Arizona Annie	400.00
2 SSh(c),CCb, Captain Tootsie.	250.00

Becomes:

WILD WESTERN

3 SSh(c),B:Tex Morgan,Two Gun Kid,Tex Taylor,Arizona Annie	350.00
4 Rh,SSh,CCB,Capt. Tootsie.	
A:Kid Colt,E:Arizona Annie	250.00
5 RH,CCB,Capt.Tootsie A;Black Rider,Blaze Carson	250.00
6 A:Blaze Carson,Kid Colt	200.00
7 Two-Gun Kid	200.00
8 RH	200.00
9 Ph(c),B:Black Rider, Tex Morgan	225.00
10 Ph(c), Black Rider	250.00
11 Black Rider	200.00
12 Black Rider	200.00
13 Black Rider	200.00
14 Prairie Kid,Black Rider	175.00
15 Black Rider	175.00
16 thru 18 Black Rider	@175.00
19 Black Rider	185.00
20 thru 29 Kid Colt	@150.00
30 JKa, Kid Colt	150.00
31 thru 40	@100.00
41 thru 47	@100.00
48 AW	125.00
49 thru 53	@100.00
54 AW	125.00
55 AW	125.00
56 and 57 Sept., 1957	@100.00

MARVEL

62 MT,A:Sabretooth,Silver Fox 5.00	
63 MT,V:Ferro,D:Silver Fox 5.00	
64 MPa,V:Ferro,Sabretooth 5.00	
65 MT,A:Professor X 5.00	
66 MT,A:X-Men 5.00	
67 MT,A:X-Men 5.00	
68 MT,V:Epsilon Red 5.00	
69 DT,A:Rogue,V:Sauron,tie-in to X-Men#300 .... 5.00	
70 DT,Sauron,A:Rogue,Jubilee 5.00	
71 DT,V:Sauron,Brain Child, A:Rogue, Jubilee 5.00	
72 DT,Sentinels 5.00	
73 DT,V:Sentinels 5.00	
74 ANi,V:Sentinels 5.00	
75 AKu,Hologram(c),Wolv.has Bone Claws,leaves X-Men ... 10.00	
76 DT(c),B:LHa(s),A:Deathstrike, Vindicator,C:Puck 5.00	
77 AKu,A:Vindicator,Puck,V:Lady Deathstrike 5.00	
78 AKu,V:Cylla,Bloodscream 5.00	
79 AKu,V:Cyber,I:Zoe Culloden 5.00	
80 IaC,V:Cyber, ... 5.00	
81 IaC,V:Cyber,A:Excalibur 5.00	
82 AKu,BMc,A:Yukio,Silver Samurai 5.00	
83 AKu,A:Alpha Flight 5.00	
84 A:Alpha Flight 5.00	
85 Phalanx Covenant, Final Sanction, V:Phalanx,holografx(c) 5.50	
85a newsstand ed. 5.00	
86 AKu,V:Bloodscream 3.00	
87 AKu,deluxe,V:Juggernaut 3.00	
87a newsstand ed. 3.00	
88 AKu,deluxe ed. 3.00	
88a newsstand ed. 3.00	
89 deluxe ed. 3.00	
89a newsstand ed. 2.00	
90 V:Sabretooth, deluxe ed. 4.00	
90a newsstand ed. 2.00	
91 LHa,Logan's future unravels. ... 3.00	
92 LHa,AKu,DGr,A:Sabretooth 3.00	
93 R:Cyber. 3.00	
94 Feral Wolverine. 3.00	
95 LHa,AKu,DGr,V:Dark Riders... 3.00	
96 LHa,Aku,DGr,Death of Cyber ... 3.00	
97 LHa,AKu,DGr,A:Genesis. 3.00	
98 LHa,AKu,F:Genesis 3.00	
99 .... 3.00	
100 LHa,AKu,DG,A:Elektra;double- size, Foil Hologram cover ... 12.00	
100a regular edition. 4.00	
101 LHa,AKu,A:Elektra 3.00	
102 LHa 3.00	
103 LHa,Elektra,A:Onslaught 3.00	
104 LHa,Gateway, Onslaught 3.00	
105 LHa,Gateway, Elektra 3.00	
106 LHa 3.00	
107 LHa,VS,prologue to Elektra#1 . 3.00	
108 LHa,back to Tokyo,A:Yukio.... 3.00	
109 LHa,DG, ... 3.00	
110 LHa,DG,Who's spying on Logan. 3.00	
111 LHa,DG,Logan moves to NYC . 3.00	
112 LHa,DG,Logan in NYC 3.00	
113 LHa,R:Ogun,A:Lady Deathstrike & Spiral 3.00	
114 LHa,back in costume,V:Cyborg Donald Pierce 3.00	
115 LHa,Zero Tolerance,V:Bastion . 3.00	
116 LHa,Zero Tolerance, ... 3.00	
117 LHa,Zero Tolerance, V:Prime Sentinels 3.00	
118 LHa,Zero Tolerance aftermath . 3.00	
119 WEI,Pt.1 (of 4). 3.00	
120 WEI,The White Ghost 3.00	
121 WEI,Not Yet Dead,pt.3 .... 3.00	
122 WEI,Not Yet Dead, pt.4 ...... 3.00	
123 TDF,DCw,R:Roughouse, Bloodscream 3.00	

124 TDF,DCw,A:Captain America, V:Rascal 3.00	
125 CCl,V:Viper,48-pg. 7.50	
125a Dynamic Forces (c). 6.50	
126 CCl,V:Sabretooth 3.50	
127 CCl,Sabretooth takes over 3.00	
128 CCl,V:Hydra, The Hand 3.00	
129 TDz,A:Wendigo. 3.00	
130 TDz,V:Viper. 3.00	
131 TDz,V:Viper. 3.00	
131a Uncensored. 12.00	
132 TDz,Halloween in SalemCenter 3.00	
133 EL,JMs,F:Warbird 3.00	
133a variant EL cover (1:4) 6.00	
134 EL,JMs,V:Big Apple heroes ... 3.00	
135 EL,JMs,Joins Starjammers 3.00	
136 EL,JMs,on prison planet 3.00	
137 EL,JMs,V:The Collector 3.00	
138 EL,JMs,Great Escape concl. .. 3.00	
139 EL,A:Cable 3.00	
140 EL,Xavier paranoid 3.00	
141 EL,Wolverine paranoid 3.00	
142 EL,R:Alpha Flight 3.00	
143 EL,A:Alpha Flight 3.00	
144 EL,A:Hercules,V:Leader 3.00	
145 EL,25th Anniv. 48-pg. 3.25	
145A Foil Stamped (c) 10.00	
146 EL 25.00	
147 FaN 5.00	
148 EL,Ages of Apocalypse,pt.3 ... 3.00	
149 EL,mutant no more? 3.00	
150 X-Men: Revolution 4.00	
150a variant (c) 7.00	
151 SSr,V:Lord Haan. 3.00	
152 SSr,Lord Haan, Gom 3.00	
153 SSr,Kia 3.00	
154 RLd,ErS,Deadpool 3.00	
155 RLd,Watchtower,Siryn 3.00	
156 RLd,IaC,F:Spider-Man 3.00	
157 RLd,IaC,F:Spider-Man 3.00	
158 RLd,IaC,V:Administrator 3.00	
159 SCh,V:Mr.X 3.00	
160 SCh,V:Lady Killers,Mr.X 3.00	
161 SCh,V:Mr.X 3.00	
162 SCh,A:Sabretooth 3.00	
163 SCh,F:Beast 3.00	
164 SCh,F:Beast 3.00	
165 SCh,NRd,trapped 3.50	
166 SCh,NRd,BWS,48-page 10.00	
167 DaF,NRd,BWS(c),V:Viper ... 2.50	
168 DaF,NRd,F:Patch 2.50	
169 DaF,NRd,Bloodsport,concl. ... 2.50	
170 SCh,NRd,Stay Alive,pt.1 ..... 2.50	

Wolverine #140
© Marvel Entertainment Group

171 SCh,NRd,V:Wendigo,'Nuff Said 2.50	
172 SCh,NRd,Stay Alive,pt.3 ...... 2.50	
173 SCh,NRd,in Las Vegas. 2.50	
174 SCh,NRd,Amiko & Yukio 2.50	
175 SCh,NRd,Omega Red,48-pg. .. 4.00	
176 SCh,NRd, ... 2.25	
177 SCh,DaF,Shadow Pulpit,pt.1 .. 2.25	
178 SCh,DaF,Shadow Pulpit,pt.2 .. 2.25	
179 SCh&MRd(c),R:Alpha Flight ... 2.25	
180 AKu(c) 2.25	
181 SCh, new direction 2.25	
182 SCh,TP 2.25	
183 SCh,, 48-pg. 3.50	
184 SCh,When Animals Attack ... 2.25	
185 SCh,When Animals Attack ... 2.25	
186 SCh,V:Punisher, Round 2. .... 3.00	
187 JMC 2.25	
188 pt.1 .... 2.25	
189 pt.2 .... 2.25	
Ann. '97 JOs,V:Volk 4.00	
Ann.1999 F:Deadpool, 48-pg. 4.00	
Ann.2000 48-page 4.00	
Ann.2001 48-page 3.50	
Spec. '95 LHa,F:Nightcrawler 4.00	
Spec.Minus 1, LHa,CNn, flashback, F:Weapon X. 2.25	
Spec.Global Jeapordy,PDd(s) 3.00	
Spec.Save the Tiger,rep. 3.00	
Spec.Winter Spec. MWa B&W. 3.00	
Spec.JungleAdventure,MMi,deluxe . 5.50	
1-shot Bloodlust,AD,V:Siberian Were-Creatures. 6.00	
GN Acts of Vengeance, rep. 7.00	
GN Black Rio, 48-page 6.00	
GN Bloody ChoicesJB,A:N.Fury .. 13.00	
GN Inner Fury,BSz,V:Nanotech Machines. 6.25	
GN Killing, KSW,JNR. 6.00	
GN Rahne of Terror, C:Cable 8.00	
GN Scorpio Rising, T.U.Fury 6.00	
GN Typhoid's Kiss,rep. 7.00	
GN Bloodhungry SK 7.00	
TPB Wolverine rep. Marvel Comics Presents #1-#10 .... 13.00	
TPB Triumphs & Tragedies 17.00	
TPB Not Dead Yet 15.00	
TPB Wolverine:Weapon X,BWS .. 16.00	
TPB Blood Debt, 112-page 13.00	
TPB Wolverine/Gambit: Victims. .. 13.00	
TPB Wolverine/Deadpool: WeaponX 22.00	
TPB The Best There Is 13.00	
TPB Legends, Vol. 3 .... 13.00	
TPB Legends, Vol. 4:Xisle 14.00	
TPB Snikt, Vol. 5 .... 14.00	

WOLVERINE
May, 2003

1 DaR,Brothers,pt.1, relaunch 3.50	
2 DaR,Brothers,pt.2 .... 2.25	
3 DaR,Brothers,pt.3 .... 2.25	
4 DaR,Brothers,pt.4 .... 2.25	
5 DaR,Brothers,pt.5 .... 2.25	
6 DaR,F:Nightcrawler 2.25	
7 Coyote Crossing,pt.1 .... 2.25	
8 Coyote Crossing,pt.2 .... 2.25	
9 Coyote Crossing,pt.3 .... 2.25	
10 Coyote Crossing,pt.4 .... 2.25	
11 Coyote Crossing,concl. 2.25	
12 Dreams 2.25	
13 DaR,Feral,pt.1. .... 2.25	
14 DaR,Feral,pt.2. .... 2.25	
15 DaR,Return of the Native,pt.3 .. 2.25	
16 DaR,Return of the Native,pt.4 .. 2.25	
17 DaR,Return of the Native,pt.5 .. 2.25	
18 DaR,Return of the Native,pt.6 .. 2.25	
19 DaR,Return of the Native,pt.7 .. 2.25	
20 JR2,Enemy of the State,pt.1 .... 2.25	
21 JR2,Enemy of the State,pt.2. ... 2.25	
TPB Vol. 1 The Brotherhood 13.00	

TPB Vol. 2 Coyote Crossing 12.00
TPB Vol. 3 Return of the Native . . 18.00
TPB Legends,Vol. 6 . . . . 20.00

*Wolverine & Punisher,
Damaging Evidence #2
© Marvel Entertainment Group*

WOLVERINE & PUNISHER: DAMAGING EVIDENCE
1993
1 B:CP(s),GEr,A:Kingpin 3.00
2 GEr,A:Kingpin,Sniper 3.00
3 GEr,Last issue 3.00

WOLVERINE/ CAPTAIN AMERICA
March, 2004
1 Alien technology stolen 3.00
2 thru 4 . . . . 3.00

WOLVERINE: DAYS OF FUTURE PAST
Oct., 1997
1 (of 3) JFM,JoB,JHo, Logan &
  Magneto in far future 2.50
2 JFM,JoB,JHo,with Jubilee 2.50
3 JFM,JoB,JHo,V:Council of the
  Chosen, concl 2.50

WOLVERINE: DOOMBRINGER
Nov., 1997
1-shot DgM,JP,F:Silver Samurai . . . 3.00

WOLVERINE/DOOP
May, 2003
1 (of 2) 3.00
2 . . . . 3.00

WOLVERINE ENCYCLOPEDIA
Vol. 1 AKu(c) 48-pg 8.50
Vol. 2 48-pg 6.50
Vol. 3 48-pg 6.50

WOLVERINE: THE END
Nov., 2003
1 (of 6) CCt 10.00

2 thru 3 CCt . . . . @5.00
4 thru 6 CCt . . . . @3.50

WOLVERINE/GAMBIT: VICTIMS
1995
1 Takes Place in London 3.00
2 Is Wolverine the Killer? 3.00
3 V:Mastermind 3.00
4 conclusion 3.00

WOLVERINE/HULK
Feb., 2002
1 (of 4) SK, and a girl named Po . . 3.50
2 SK,snowy wasteland 3.50
3 SK,ghostly little girl 3.50
4 SK,concl 3.50
TPB series rep. 10.00

WOLVERINE/NETSUKE
Sept., 2002
1 (of 4) GgP, Wolverine Samurai . . 3.00
2 GgP 4.00
3 GgP 4.00
4 GgP, concl 4.00

WOLVERINE/PUNISHER
March 2004
1 (of 5) LW 3.00
2 thru 5 LW . . . . @3.00
TPB Vol. 1 . . . . 14.00

WOLVERINE/PUNISHER: REVELATION
Apr. 1999
1 (of 4) TSg,PtL,Revelation 3.00
1a signed 30.00
2 TSg,PtL,V:Revelation 3.00
3 TSg,PtL,V:Revelation 3.00
4 TsG,PtL,V:Revelation,concl 3.00
TPB rep 14.95

WOLVERINE SAGA
Sept., 1989
1 RLd(c), ... 6.50
2 . . . . 5.50
3 . . . . 5.50
4 Dec., 1989 . . . . 5.50

WOLVERINE: SNIKT!
May, 2003
1 (of 5) 3.00
2 alien landscape 3.00
3 . . . . 3.00
4 V:Mandate aliens 3.00
5 Concl 3.00

WOLVERINE: X-ISLE
April, 2003
1 (of 5) A:Amiko 2.50
2 thru 5 . . . . @2.50

WONDER DUCK
Sept., 1949
1 Whale(c) 175.00
2 . . . . 125.00
3 March, 1950 . . . . 125.00

WONDERMAN
March, 1986
1 KGa,one-shot special 3.00

*Wonder Man #1
© Marvel Entertainment Group*

WONDER MAN
Sept., 1991
1 B:GJ(s),JJ,V:Goliath 2.50
2 JJ,A:West Coast Avengers 2.25
3 JJ,V:Abominatrix,I:Spider 2.25
4 JJ,I:Splice,A:Spider 2.25
5 JJ,A:Beast,V:Rampage 2.25
6 JJ,A:Beast,V:Rampage 2.25
7 JJ,Galactic Storm,pt.4,
  A:Hulk & Rich Jones 2.25
8 JJ,GalacticStorm,pt.11,A:Vision . . 2.25
9 JJ,GalacticStorm,pt.18,A:Vision . . 2.25
10 JJ,V:Khmer Rouge 2.25
11 V:Angkor 2.25
12 V:Angkor 2.25
13 Infinity War 2.25
14 Infinity War,V:Warlock 2.25
15 Inf.War,V:Doppleganger 2.25
16 JJ,I:Armed Response,
   A:Avengers West Coast 2.25
17 JJ,A:Avengers West Coast 2.25
18 V:Avengers West Coast 2.25
19 . . . . 2.25
20 V:Splice,Rampage 2.25
21 V:Splice,Rampage 2.25
22 JJ,V:Realm of Death 2.25
23 JJ,A:Grim Reaper,Mephisto 2.25
24 JJ,V:Grim Reaper,Goliath 2.25
25 JJ,N:Wonder Man,D:Grim Reaper,
   V:Mephisto 3.25
26 A:Hulk,C:Furor,Plan Master 2.25
27 A:Hulk 2.25
28 RoR,A:Spider-Man 2.25
29 RoR,A:Spider-Man 2.25
30 V:Hate Monger 2.25
31 . . . . 2.25
32 . . . . 2.25
33 . . . . 2.25
Spec.#1 (1985),KGa 3.00
Ann.#1 System Bytes #3 . . . . 2.25
Ann.#2 I:Hit-Maker,w/card 2.95

WORLD CHAMPIONSHIP WRESTLING
1 F:Lex Luger,Sting 2.25
2 . . . . 2.25
3 . . . . 2.25
4 Luger Vs El Gigante 2.25

MARVEL

5 Rick Rude Vs. Sting 2.25
6 F:Dangerous Alliance,R.Rude . . . 2.25
7 F:Steiner Brothers 2.25
8 F:Sting,Dangerous Alliance 2.25
9 Bunkhouse Brawl 2.25
10 Halloween Havoc 2.25
11 Sting vs Grapplers 2.25
12 F:Ron Simmons 2.25

WORLD OF FANTASY
Atlas, May, 1956

1 The Secret of the Mountain . . . 600.00
2 JMn,AW,Inside the Tunnel 400.00
3 DAy,SC, The Man in the Cave. 350.00
4 BEv(c),BP,JF,Back to the
    Lost City 250.00
5 BEv(c),BP,In the Swamp 250.00
6 BEv(c),BP,The Strange Wife
    of Henry Johnson 250.00
7 BEv(c),GM,Man in Grey 250.00
8 GM,JO,MF,The Secret of the
    Black Cloud 275.00
9 BEv,BK 250.00
10 . . . . 200.00
11 AT 200.00
12 BEv(c) 200.00
13 BEv,JO 200.00
14 JMn(c),GM,JO,CI,JM 200.00
15 JK(c) 200.00
16 AW,SD,JK 275.00
17 JK(c),SD 275.00
18 JK(c) 275.00
19 JK(c),SD,Aug., 1959 . . . . 275.00

WORLD OF MYSTERY
Atlas, 1956–57

1 BEv(c),AT,JO,The Long Wait . 600.00
2 BEv(c),The Man From
    Nowhere 225.00
3 SD,AT,JDa, The Bugs 300.00
4 SD(c),BP,What Happened in
    the Basement 300.00
5 JO,She Stands in Shadows . . 225.00
6 AW,SD,GC,Sinking Man 300.00
7 GC,JSe,Pick A Door 225.00

WORLD OF SUSPENSE
Atlas, April, 1956

1 JO,BEv,MO,JMn,A Stranger
    Among Us 500.00
2 SD,LC,JMN(c),When Walks
    the Scarecrow 300.00
3 AW,JMN(c),The Man Who
    Couldn't Be Touched 300.00
4 Something is in This House . . 225.00
5 BEv,DH,JO 225.00
6 BEv(c),BP 225.00
7 AW,The Face 300.00
8 Prisoner of the Ghost Ship . . 225.00

WORLDS UNKNOWN
May, 1973

1 GK,AT,The Coming of the
    Martians,Reprints 30.00
2 GK,TS,A Gun For A Dinosaur . . 20.00
3 The Day the Earth Stood
    Still 20.00
4 JB,Arena 20.00
5 DA,JM,Black Destroyer 20.00
6 GK(c),The Thing Called It 20.00
7 GT,The Golden Voyage of
    Sinbad,Part 1 . . . . 20.00
8 The Golden Voyage of
    Sinbad,Part 2, Aug., 1974 . . . 20.00

WYATT EARP
Atlas, Nov., 1955

1 JMn,F:Wyatt Earp 250.00

---

2 AW,Saloon(c) 150.00
3 JMn(c),The Showdown,
    A:Black Bart 125.00
4 Ph(c),Hugh O'Brian,JSe,
    India Sundown 125.00
5 Ph(c),Hugh O'Brian,DW,
    Gun Wild Fever 125.00
6 BEv(c) 125.00
7 AW 125.00
8 JMn,Wild Bill Hickok 125.00
9 and 10 . . . . @125.00
11 . . . . 125.00
12 AW,JMn 125.00
13 thru 20 . . . . @100.00
21 JDa(c) 100.00
22 thru 29 . . . . @75.00
30 AW,Reprints 25.00
31 thru 33 Reprints . . . . @20.00
34 June, 1973 . . . . 20.00

XAVIER INSTITUTE ALUMNI YEARBOOK

GN 48-pg. (1996) 5.95

X-CALIBRE
1995

1 Excaliber After Xavier 4.00
2 V:Callisto & Morlock Crew 3.00
3 D:Juggernaut 3.00
4 Secret Weapon 3.00
TPB Rep.#1–#4 . . . . 8.95

X-FACTOR
Feb., 1986

1 WS(c),JG,BL,JRu,I:X-Factor,
    Rusty 10.00
2 JG,BL,I:Tower 5.00
3 JG,BL,V:Tower 5.00
4 KP,JRu,V:Frenzy 5.00
5 JG,JRu,I:Alliance of Evil,
    C:Apocalypse 6.00
6 JG,BMc,I:Apocalypse 15.00
7 JG,JRu,V:Morlocks,I:Skids 5.00
8 MS,JRu,V:Freedom Force 5.00
9 JRu(i),V:Freedom Force
    (Mutant Massacre) 5.00
10 WS,BWi,V:Marauders(Mut.Mass),
    A:Sabretooth 6.00
11 WS,BWi,A:Thor(Mutant Mass) . . 5.00
12 MS,BWi,V:Vanisher 4.00
13 WS,DGr,V:Mastermold 4.00
14 WS,BWi,V:Mastermold 5.00
15 WS,BWi,D:Angel 5.00
16 DM,JRu,V:Masque 4.00
17 WS,BWi,I:Rictor 5.00
18 WS,BWi,V:Apocalypse 4.00
19 WS,BWi,V:Horsemen of
    Apocalypse 3.50
20 JBr,A:X-Terminators 3.50
21 WS,BWi,V:The Right 3.50
22 SB,BWi,V:The Right 3.50
23 WS,BWi,C:Archangel 8.00
24 WS,BWi,Fall of Mutants,
    I:Archangel 10.00
25 WS,BWi,Fall of Mutants 3.50
26 WS,BWi,Fall of Mutants,
    N:X-Factor 3.50
27 WS,BWi,Christmas Issue 3.50
28 WS,BWi,V:Ship 3.50
29 WS,BWi,V:Infectia 3.50
30 WS,BWi,V:Infectia,Free.Force . . 3.50
31 WS,BWi,V:Infectia,Free.Force . . 3.50
32 SLi,A:Avengers 3.50
33 WS,BWi,V:Tower & Frenzy,
    R:Furry Beast 3.50
34 WS,BWi,I:Nanny,
    Orphan Maker 3.50
35 JRu(i),WS(c),V:Nanny,
    Orphan Maker 3.50

X-Factor #50
© Marvel Entertainment Group

36 WS,BWi,Inferno,V:Nastirh 3.50
37 WS,BWi,Inferno,V:Gob.Queen . . 3.50
38 WS,AM,Inferno,A:X-Men,D:
    MadelynePryor(GoblinQueen) . . 3.50
39 WS,AM,Inferno,A:X-Men,
    V:Mr.Sinister 3.50
40 RLd,AM,O:Nanny,Orphan Maker
    1st Liefeld Marvel work 6.00
41 AAd,AM,I:Alchemy 3.50
42 AAd,AM,A:Alchemy 3.50
43 PS,AM,V:Celestials 3.50
44 PS,AM,V:Rejects 3.50
45 PS,AM,V:Rask 3.50
46 PS,AM,V:Rejects 3.50
47 KD,AM,V:Father 3.50
48 thru 49 PS,AM,V:Rejects 3.50
50 RLd&TM(c),RB,AM,A:Prof.X
    (double sized),BU:Apocalypse . 5.00
51 AM,V:Sabretooth,Caliban 4.00
52 RLd(c),AM,V:Sabretooth,
    Caliban 3.00
53 AM,V:Sabretooth,Caliban 3.00
54 MS,AM,A:Colossus,I:Crimson . . 3.00
55 MMi(c),CDo,AM,V:Mesmero . . . 3.00
56 AM,V:Crimson 3.00
57 NKu,V:Crimson 3.00
58 JBg,AM,V:Crimson 3.00
59 AM,V:Press Gang 3.00
60 JBg,AM,X-Tinction Agenda#3 . . . 4.00
60a 2nd printing(gold) 2.50
61 JBg,AM,X-Tinction Agenda#6 . . . 3.50
62 JBg,AM,JLe(c),E:X-Agenda 3.50
63 WPo,I:Cyberpunks 3.50
64 WPo,ATb,V:Cyberpunks 3.00
65 WPo,ATb,V:Apocalypse 3.00
66 WPo,ATb,I:Askani,
    V:Apocalypse 3.00
67 WPo,ATb,V:Apocalypse,I:Shinobi
    Shaw,D:Sebastian Shaw 3.00
68 WPo,ATb,JLe(c),V:Apocalypse,
    L:Nathan,(taken into future) 3.00
69 WPo,V:Shadow King 3.00
70 MMi(c),JRu,Last old team 3.00
71 LSn,AM,New Team 4.00
71a 2nd printing 2.50
72 LSn,AM,Who shot Madrox
    revealed 3.00
73 LSn,AM,Mob Chaos in D.C. 3.00
74 LSn,AM,I:Slab 3.00
75 LSn,AM,I:Nasty Boys(doub.sz) . . 3.50
76 LSn,AM,A:Hulk,Pantheon 3.25
77 LSn,AM,V:Mutant Lib. Front 3.25
78 LSn,AM,V:Mutant Lib. Front 3.25
79 LSn,AM,V:Helle's Belles 3.25

X-Factor #111
© Marvel Entertainment Group

80 LSn,AM,V:Helle's Belles,
   C:Cyber. 3.25
81 LSn,AM,V:Helle's Belles,Cyber. . 3.25
82 JQ(c),LSn,V:Brotherhood of Evil
   Mutants,I:X-iles 3.25
83 MPa,A:X-Force,X-iles 3.25
84 JaL,X-Cutioners Song #2,
   V:X-Force,A:X-Men 3.25
85 JaL,X-Cutioners Song #6,
   Wolv.& Bishop,V:Cable 3.25
86 JaL,AM,X-Cutioner's Song#10,
   A:X-Men,X-Force,V:Stryfe 3.25
87 JQ,X-Cutioners Song
   Aftermath. 3.00
88 JQ,AM,V:2nd Genegineer,
   I:Random. 4.00
89 JQ,V:Mutates,Genosha. 3.00
90 JQ,AM,Genosha vs. Aznia 3.00
91 AM,V:Armageddon 3.00
92 JQ,AM,V:Fabian Cortez,
   Acolytes,hologram(c). 6.00
93 Magneto Protocols 3.00
94 PR,J:Forge 3.00
95 B:JMD(s),AM,Polaris
   Vs. Random. 3.00
96 A:Random. 3.00
97 JD,I:Haven,A:Random 3.00
98 GLz,A:Haven,A:Random. 3.00
99 JD,A:Haven,Wolfsbane returns
   to human 3.00
100 JD,Red Foil(c),V:Haven,
   D:Madrox. 6.00
100a Newstand Ed. 3.00
101 JD,AM,Aftermath. 2.50
102 JD,AM,V:Crimson Commando,
   Avalanche 2.50
103 JD,AM,A:Malice 2.50
104 JD,AM,V:Malice,
   C:Mr. Sinister. 2.50
105 JD,AM,V:Malice 2.50
106 Phalanx Covenant,Life Signs
   Holografx(c). 3.50
106a newsstand ed 2.50
107 A:Strong Guy. 2.50
108 A:Mystique, deluxe ed. 2.50
108a newsstand ed.. . . . . 2.00
109 A:Mystique,V:Legion, deluxe. . . 2.50
109a newsstand ed. 2.25
110 Invasion. 2.50
110a deluxe ed. 2.25
111 Invasion. 2.50
111a deluxe ed. 2.25
112 AM,JFM,SEp,F:Guido,Havok . . 2.50
113 A:Mystique. 2.50

114 AM,Wild Child & Mystique. 2.50
115 F:Wild Child,Havok 2.50
116 F:Wild Child. 2.50
117 HMe,AM,F:Cyclops 2.50
118 HMe,AM,A:Random,Shard 2.50
119 HMe,AM,F:Sabretooth 2.50
120 A:Sabretooth 2.50
121 A:Sabretooth 2.50
122 HMe,SEp,AM,J:Sabretooth. . . . 2.50
123 A:Hound 2.50
124 A:Onslaught 3.50
125 Onslaught saga, double size . . 4.00
126 Beast vs. Dark Beast 2.50
127 Mystique 2.50
128 HMe,JMs,AM,Hound Program . 2.50
129 HMe,JMs,AM,Graydon Creed's
   campaign. 2.50
130 HMe,JMs,AM,Assassination of
   Graydon Creed 2.50
131 HMe,JMs,ATi,Havok strikes
   back. 2.50
132 HMe,JMs,ATi,Break away from
   government 2.50
133 HMe,JMs,ATi,A:Multiple Man &
   Strong Guy 2.50
134 HMe,JMs,Ati,Operation X-Factor
   Underground, cont. 2.50
135 HMe,JMs,Strong Guy awakes . 2.50
136 HMe,JMs,ATi, A:Sabretooth . . . 2.50
137 HMe,JMs,ATi, Final fate of
   Shard and Polaris 2.50
138 HMe,JMs,ATi,Sabertooth,
   V:Maberick. 2.50
139 HMe,ATi,Who killed Graydon
   Creed. 2.50
140 HMe,ATi,Who killed Graydon
   Creed, A:Mystique. 2.50
141 HMe,ATi,Shard's Plan. 2.50
142 ATi,F:Wild Child. 2.50
143 HMe,ATi,Havok vs.DarkBeast. . 2.50
144 HMe,ATi,V:Brotherhood,
   Dark Beast. 2.50
145 HMe,ATi,Havok vs. X.U.E. 2.50
146 HMe,ATi,Havok, Multiple
   Man,V:Polaris 2.50
147 HMe,Havok v. Mandroids 2.50
148 F:Shard 2.50
149 HMe,Polaris & Madrox rejoin . . 3.50
Spec #1 JG,Prisoner of Love 5.00
Ann.#1 BL,BBr,V:CrimsonDynamo . 5.00
Ann.#2 TGr,JRu,A:Inhumans. 4.00
Ann.#3 WS(c),AM,JRu,PC,TD,
   Evolutionary War 3.50
Ann.#4 JBy,WS,JRu,MBa,Atlantis
   Attacks,BU:Doom & Magneto . . 3.50
Ann.#5 JBg,AM,DR,GI,Days of Future
   Present,A:Fant.Four,V:Ahab. . . . 4.00
Ann.#6 Flesh Tears Saga,pt.4,
   A:X-Force, New Warriors 4.00
Ann #7 JQ,JRu,Shattershot,pt.3 . . . 4.00
Ann.#8 I:Charon,w/card 3.25
Ann.#9 JMD(s),MtB,V:Prof.Power,
   A:Prof.X,O:Haven 3.25
Minus 1 Spec., HMe,JMs,ATi,
   flashback,F:Havok 2.50
GN X-Men: Wrath of Apocalypse,
   rep.X-Factor#65-#68 . . . . 5.00

X-FACTOR
April, 2002

1 (of 4) When will it stop. 2.50
2 FBI agents 2.50
3 in San Francisco 2.50
4 Concl.. 2.50
TPB Vol. 1 . . . . 10.00

X-51
July, 1999

1 JQ&JP(c) Marvel Tech. 2.00
2 JoB,V:Brotherhood of Mutants. . . 2.00

2a variant cover 2.00
3 JoB,A:X.E.R.O. 2.00
4 JoB,A:Avengers. 2.00
5 JoB,V:Vision. 2.00
6 JoB. 2.00
7 JoB,A:Sebastian Shaw 2.00
8 JoB,F:X-Men 2.50
9 JoB, ... 2.50
10 JoB,F:Machine Man 2.50
11 JoB,F:Celestial 2.50
12 JoB,final issue. 2.50

X-FORCE
Aug., 1991

1 RLd,V:Stryfe,Mutant Liberation
   Front,bagged, white on black
   graphics with X-Force Card. . . . 4.00
1a with Shatterstar Card. 4.00
1b with Deadpool Card. 4.00
1c with Sunspot & Gideon Card . . . 4.00
1d with Cable Card. 5.00
1e Unbagged Copy. 2.75
1f 2nd Printing. 2.00
2 RLd,I:New Weapon X,V:
   Deadpool. 3.50
3 RLd,C:Spider-Man,
   V:Juggernaut,Black Tom 3.00
4 RLd,SpM/X-Force team-up,
   V:Juggernaut(cont.from SpM#16)
   Sideways format 3.00
5 RLd,A:Brotherhood Evil Mutants . 3.00
6 RLd,V:Bro'hood Evil Mutants. . . . 3.00
7 RLd,V:Bro'hood Evil Mutants. . . . 3.00
8 MMi,O:Cable(Part). 3.50
9 RLd,D:Sauron,Masque 3.00
10 MPa,V:Mutant Liberation Front. . 3.00
11 MPa,Deadpool Vs Domino 3.00
12 MPa,A:Weapon Prime,Gideon . . 2.50
13 MPa,V:Weapon Prime 2.50
14 TSr,V:Weapon Prime,Krule. 2.50
15 GCa,V:Krule,Deadpool 2.50
16 GCa,X-Cutioners Song #4,
   X-Factor V:X-Force 3.00
17 GCa,X-Cutioners Song#8,
   Apocalypse V:Stryfe 3.00
18 GCa,X-Cutioners Song#12,
   Cable vs Stryfe 3.00
19 GCa,X-Cutioners Song
   Aftermath,N:X-Force 2.50
20 GCa,O:Graymalkin 2.50
21 GCa,V:War Machine,SHIELD . . . 2.50
22 GCa,V:Externals 2.50
23 GCa,V:Saul,Gigeon,A:Six Pack . 2.50
24 GCa,A:Six Pack,A:Deadpool . . . 2.50

X-Force #27
© Marvel Entertainment Group

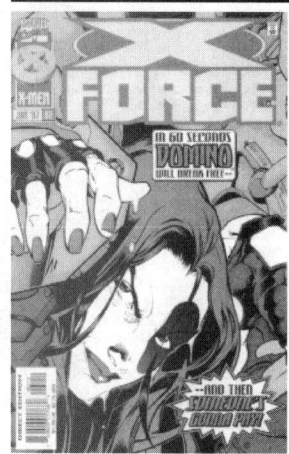

X-Force #62
© Marvel Entertainment Group

25 GCa,A:Mageneto,Exodus,
    R:Cable 5.00
26 GCa(c),MtB,I:Reignfire 2.50
27 GCa(c),MtB,V:Reignfire,MLF,
    I:Moonstar,Locus 2.50
28 MtB,V:Reignfire,MLF. 2.50
29 MtB,V:Arcade,C:X-Treme 2.50
30 TnD,V:Arcade,A:X-Treme 2.50
31 F:Siryn. 2.50
32 Child's Play#1,A:New Warriors. . 2.50
33 Child's Play#3,A:New Warriors,
    V:Upstarts 2.50
34 F:Rictor,Domino,Cable 3.00
35 TnD,R:Nimrod 2.50
36 TnD,V:Nimrod 2.50
37 PaP,I&D:Absalom 2.50
38 TaD,Life Signs,pt.2,
    I:Generation X, foil(c) 5.00
38a newsstand ed. 2.50
39 TaD 2.50
40 TaD, deluxe 2.50
40a newsstand ed. 2.50
41 TaD,O:feral,deluxe 2.50
41a newsstand ed. 2.25
42 Emma Frost, deluxe 2.50
42a newsstand ed. 2.25
43 Home is Where Heart 2.50
43a deluxe ed. 2.50
44 AdP,Prof.X,X-Mansion. 2.50
45 AdP,Caliban vs. Sabretooth 2.50
46 R:The Mimic 2.50
47 A:Deadpool 2.50
48 AdP,Siryn Takes Charge 2.50
49 ADp,MBu,Holocaust is here 2.50
50 AdP,MPn,F:Sebastian Shaw 3.00
50a prismatic foil cover 4.50
50b variant RLd(c) 6.00
51 AdP,MPn,V:Risque 2.50
52 A:Onslaught 3.50
53 . . . . 2.50
54 AdP, Can X-Force
    protect X-Ternals? 2.50
55 V:S.H.I.E.L.D. 2.50
56 Deadpool, A:Onslaught. 4.00
57 Onslaught saga. 2.50
58 Onslaught saga. 2.50
59 Longshot, with card. 2.50
60 JLb,,F:Shatterstar,A:Long Shot. . 2.50
61 JLb,R:Longshot,O:Shatterstar . . 2.50
62 JLb,F:Sunspot. 2.50
63 JFM,AdP,F:Risque,Cannonball . . 2.50
64 JFM,AdP,In Latveria, searching
    for Doctor Doom's weapons . . . 2.50

65 JFM,AdP,Warpath follows Risque
    to Florida 2.50
66 JFM,AdP,A:Risque,James
    Proudstar. 2.50
67 JFM,AdP,F:Warpath, Risque 2.50
68 JFM,AdP,Zero Tolerance. 2.50
69 JFM,AdP,Zero Tolerance
    aftermath 2.50
70 JFM,AdP,new direction starts . . . 2.50
71 JFM,AdP,new direction 2.50
72 JFM,AdP,on the road 2.50
73 JFM,AdP,in New Orleans 2.50
74 JFM,ASm,Skids is back 2.50
75 JFM,AdP,A:Reignfire,
    double size 3.00
76 JFM,AdP,F:Shatterstar 2.50
77 JFM,AdP,F:Sunfire & Meltdown . 2.50
78 JFM,AdP,Reignfire makes his
    move 2.50
79 JFM,AdP,O:Reignfire 2.50
80 JFM,AdP,V:Reignfire 2.50
81 JFM,AdP,trip to Hawaii,
    V:Lava Men, AdP Poster 2.50
82 JFM,V:Griffin, Damocles
    Foundation. 2.50
83 JFM,F:Cannonball. 2.50
84 JFM,V:Deviants. 2.50
85 JFM,Return of Skids 2.50
86 JFM,A:Hulk 2.50
87 JFM,V:new Hellions 2.50
88 JFM,V:new Hellions 2.50
89 JFM,prisoners of the Hellions . . . 2.50
90 JFM,Hellion War,concl. 2.50
91 JFM,home to San Francisco. . . . 2.50
92 JFM,F:Domino 2.50
93 JFM,Domino returns 2.50
94 JFM,destination Genosha. 2.50
95 JFM,F:Magneto. 2.50
96 JFM,A:Selene 2.50
97 JFM,V:Reignfire 2.50
98 . . . . 2.50
99 JFM,F:Dani Moonstar 2.50
100 JFM,Four Personas,48-pg. 3.00
101 new members,some gone 2.50
102 WPo,X-Men: Revolution 2.50
102a variant (c) 5.00
103 WPo,WEl,Games Without
    Frontiers,pt.2 . . . . 2.50
104 WPo,WEl,Games,pt.3 . . . . 2.50
105 WPo,WEl,Games,pt.4 . . . . 2.50
106 WEl,IEd,WPo,Murder
    Ballads,pt.1 . . . . 2.50
107 WEl,IEd,MurderBallads,pt.2 . . . 2.50
108 WEl,IEd,Ballads,pt.3 . . . . 2.50
109 WEl,IEd,Ballads,pt.4 . . . . 2.50
110 WEl,IEd,Rage War,pt.1 . . . . . . 2.50
111 WEl,IEd,Rage War,pt.2 . . . . . . 2.50
112 WEl,IEd,Rage War,pt.3 . . . . . . 2.50
113 WEl,IEd,Rage War,pt.4 . . . . . . 2.50
114 . . . . 2.50
115 IEd,final issue? 2.50
116 PrM,MiA,new team 5.00
117 PrM,MiA,new members. 5.00
118 PrM,MiA,F:U-Go Girl. 2.50
119 PrM,MiA,F:U-Go Girl. 2.50
120 PrM,MiA,A:Wolverine 2.50
121 PrM,MiA,I:Lacuna 2.50
122 PrM,MiA,F:Lacuna 2.50
123 PrM,MiA,'Nuff Said 2.50
124 PrM,Orphan & U-Go Girl 2.50
125 PrM,Anarchist, Doop. 2.50
126 PrM,MiA,one won't come home 2.50
127 PrM,MiA,who won't come home 2.50
128 PrM,MiA,body bag time 2.50
129 PrM,DFg,something
    even worse 2.50
Ann.#1 Shattershot,pt1 . . . . 3.00
Ann.#2 JaL,LSn,I:X-Treme,w/card. . 3.25
Ann.#3 . . . . 3.50
Ann.1998 X-Force/Champions. 6.00
Ann.1999 R:Shatterstar & Rictor . . . 3.50

Spec.#102 Rough cut edition. 3.00
Minus 1 Spec., JFM,AdP, flashback,
    F:John Proudstar. 2.50
TPB X-Force & Spider-Man:
    Sabotage, rep. 7.00
TPB New Beginnings. 13.00
TPB Vol.2 (2002) 20.00

X-FORCE
Aug., 2004
1 RLd,X-Men: Reload Wave 3.00
2 RLd,Cable completes team 3.00
3 RLd,Cable vs. Cannonball. 3.00
TPB Big Guns 16.00

X-FORCE MEGAZINE
TPB LSi,RLd, rep. New Mutants . . . 4.00

X-MAN
March, 1995
1 Cable after Xavier 5.00
2 Sinister's Plan 4.00
3 V:Domino 3.00
4 V:Sinister 3.00
5 Into this World 3.00
6 V:X-Men 2.50
7 Evil from Age of Apocalypse 2.50
8 Crossover Adventure 2.50
9 F:Nate's Past 2.50
10 Nate's Past 2.50
11 Young Nate seeks out X-Men . . . 2.50
12 F:Excalibur 2.50
13 . . . . 2.50
14 . . . . 2.50
15 JOs,X-Men/Cable war aftermath 3.00
16 Holocaust,A:Onslaught 2.50
17 Holocaust,Quicksilver,Scarlet
    Witch, A:Onslaught 2.50
18 Onslaught saga. 2.50
19 Onslaught saga. 2.50
20 . . . . 2.50
21 TKa,RCz,F:Nate 2.50
22 TKa,RCz,F:Threnody,A:Madelyne
    Pryor 2.50
23 TKa,RCz,F:Bishop 2.50
24 TKa,RCz,Spider-Man vs. Nate . . 2.50
25 TKa,RCz,Madelyne Pryor,
    double size 4.00
26 TKa,RCz,Nate limps to Muir
    Isle,A:Moira Mactaggert 2.50
27 TKa,RCz,Hellfire Club, concl. . . . 2.50

X-Man #53
© Marvel Entertainment Group

28 TKa,RCz,Dark Beast's offer 2.50
29 TKa,RCz,Back in New York,.... 2.50
30 TKa,RCz,F:Nate Grey.........2.50
31 RL,DGr,F:Nate Grey.........2.50
32 TKa,V:Jacknife 2.50
33 TKa,V:Jacknife 2.50
34 TKa,Secret of Nate's popularity .2.50
35 TKa,Terrorists Strike 2.50
36 TKa,V:Purple Man............2.50
37 TKa,Nate leaves N.Y.,
    A:Spider-Man..............2.50
38 TKa,A:Spider-Man, Gwen Stacy .2.50
39 TKa,AOl,Nate & Madeline Pryor .2.50
40 TKa,RPc,V:Great Beasts 2.50
41 TKa,RCz,Madelyne Pryor......2.50
42 TKa,RCz,hunted by leprechauns .2.50
43 TKa,RCz,Nate Grey–murderer?! .2.50
44 TKa,RCz,F:Nate Grey,Gauntlet .2.50
45 TKa,prelude to X-Man/Cable
    x-over...................2.50
46 TKa,Cable x-over 2.50
47 TKa,Blood Brothers,pt.3 ......2.50
48 LRs,V:Crusader.............2.50
49 LRs,TKa,F:Nate 2.50
50 TKa,LRs,War of the
    Mutants,pt.2, 48-page 3.50
51 TKa,LRs,V:Psi-Ops...........2.50
52 TKa,LRs,V:Psi-Ops...........2.50
53 TKa,Strange Relations,pt.1 .....2.50
54 TKa,Strange Relations,pt.2.....2.50
55 TKa,M'Kraan Crystal..........2.50
56 TKa,Nate in Greyville 2.50
57 TKa,V:Mysterio 2.50
58 TKa,V:Threnody 2.50
59 TKa.....................2.50
60 TKa, ...2.50
61 TKa, ...2.50
62 TKa,trapped 2.50
63 TKa,X-Men: Revolution.......2.25
63a variant(c)................2.25
64 WEl,No Direction Home,pt.2....2.25
65 WEl,No Direction Home,pt.3....2.25
66 WEl,No Direction Home,pt.4....2.25
67 WEl,Down the Spiral,pt.1 .....2.25
68 WEl,Down the Spiral,pt.2 .....2.25
69 WEl,Down the Spiral,pt.3 .....2.25
70 WEl,Down the Spiral,pt.4 .....2.25
71 AOl,StG,Fearful
    Symmetries,pt.1.............2.25
72 AOl,StG,Symmetries,pt.2 ......2.25
73 AOl,StG,Symmetries,pt.3 ......2.25
74 AOl,StG,Symmetries,pt.4 ......2.25
75 Anti-Man, final issue 3.00
Minus 1 Spec., TKa,RCz,
    flashback,O:Nate Grey 2.00
Spec.#1 X-Man '96 ....3.50
Ann. '97 RBe, Nate, Sugar Man,
    Dark Beast, Holocaust........3.00
Ann. '98 X-Man, The Hulk, Thanos,
    48-pg. 3.00
GNv X-Man,BRa,TyD, 48-pg. 6.00

X-MEN
Sept., 1963

1 JK,O:X-Men,I:Professor X,Beast
  Cyclops,Marvel Girl,Iceman
  Angel,Magneto 14,000.00
2 JK,I:Vanisher.............4,000.00
3 JK,I:Blob 1,500.00
4 JK,I:Quicksilver,Scarlet Witch
  Mastermind,Toad 2,000.00
5 JK,V:Broth. of Evil Mutants..1,500.00
6 JK,V:Sub-Mariner.........850.00
7 JK,V:Broth. of Evil Mutants,
  Blob 850.00
8 JK,I:Unus,1st Ice covered
  Iceman.................850.00
9 JK,A:Avengers,I:Lucifer......850.00
10 JK,I:Modern Ka-Zar 850.00
11 JK,I:Stranger 650.00

12 JK,O:Prof.X,I:Juggernaut... 1,000.00
13 JK,JSt,V:Juggernaut 500.00
14 JK,I:Sentinels 500.00
15 JK,O:Beast,V:Sentinels......500.00
16 JK,V:Mastermold,Sentinels...500.00
17 JK,V:Magneto 350.00
18 V:Magneto................350.00
19 I:Mimic..................350.00
20 V:Lucifer.................350.00
21 V:Lucifer,Dominus.........300.00
22 V:Maggia.................300.00
23 V:Maggia.................300.00
24 I:Locust(Prof.Hopper) 300.00
25 JK,I:El Tigre 300.00
26 V:El Tigre 275.00
27 C:Fant.Four,V:Puppet Master .275.00
28 I:Banshee 450.00
29 V:Super-Apaptoid..........300.00
30 JK,I:The Warlock...........175.00
31 JK,I:Cobalt Man 150.00
32 V:Juggernaut..............150.00
33 GK,A:Dr.Strange,Juggernaut .150.00
34 V:Tyrannus,Mole Man.......150.00
35 JK,A:Spider-Man,Banshee ...150.00
36 V:Mekano 150.00
37 DH,V:Blob,Unus 150.00
38 DH,A:Banshee,O:Cyclops....250.00
39 DH,GT,A:Banshee,V:Mutant
    Master,O:Cyclops 350.00
40 DH,GT,V:Frankenstein,
    O:Cyclops 250.00
41 DH,GT,I:Grotesk,O:Cyclops ..250.00
42 DH,GT,JB,V:Grotesk,
    O:Cyclops,D:Prof.X 135.00
43 GT,JB,V:Magneto,Quicksilver,
    Scarlet Witch,C:Avengers ...200.00
44 V:Magneto,Quicksilver,Sc.Witch,
    R:Red Raven,O:Iceman 175.00
45 PH,JB,V:Magneto,Quicksilver,
    Scarlet Witch,O:Iceman.....175.00
46 DH,V:Juggernaut,O:Iceman .125.00
47 DH,I:Maha Yogi...........125.00
48 DH,JR,V:Quasimodo........125.00
49 JSo,DH,C:Magneto,I:Polaris,
    Mesmero,O:Beast 125.00
50 JSo,V:Magneto,O:Beast 150.00
51 JSo,V:Magneto,Polaris,
    Erik the Red,O:Beast.......150.00
52 DH,MSe,JSt,O:Lorna Dane
    V:Magneto,O:Beast 125.00
53 1st BWS,O:Beast 125.00
54 BWS,DH,I:Havok,O:Angel ...125.00
55 BWS,DH,O:Havok,Angel 125.00
56 NA,V:LivingMonolith,O:Angel .125.00
57 NA,V:Sentinels,A:Havok 125.00
58 NA,A:Havoc,V:Sentinels.....175.00
59 NA,V:Sentinels,A:Havoc.....125.00
60 NA,I:Sauron 125.00
61 NA,V:Sauron..............125.00
62 NA,A:Ka-Zar,Sauron,Magneto 125.00
63 A:Ka-Zar,V:Magneto 110.00
64 DH,A:Havok,I:Sunfire 125.00
65 NA,MSe,A:Havok,Shield,
    Return of Prof.X...........125.00
66 SB,MSe,V:Hulk,A:Havok......125.00
67 rep.X-Men #12,#13.........100.00
68 rep.X-Men #14,#15.........100.00
69 rep.X-Men #16,#19.........100.00
70 rep.X-Men #17,#18.........100.00
71 rep.X-Men #20 ....100.00
72 rep.X-Men #21,#24.........100.00
73 thru 93 rep.X-Men #25-45... @75.00
94 GK(c),B:CCl(s),DC,BMc,B:2nd
    X-Men,V:Count Nefaria..1,500.00
95 GK(c),DC,V:Count Nefaria,
    Ani-Men,D:Thunderbird 300.00
96 DC,I:Moira McTaggert,
    Kierrok..................200.00
97 DC,V:Havok,Polaris,Eric
    the Red,I:Lilandra 200.00
98 DC,V:Sentinels,Stephen Lang 150.00

X-Men #91
© Marvel Entertainment Group

99 DC,V:Sentinels,S.Lang......150.00
100 DC,V:Stephen Lang 200.00
101 DC,I:Phoenix,Black Tom,
    A:Juggernaut.............200.00
102 DC,O:Storm,V:Juggernaut,
    Black Tom 125.00
103 DC,V:Juggernaut,Bl.Tom ...125.00
104 DC,V:Magneto,I:Star
    Jammers,A:Lilandra........100.00
105 DC,BL,V:Firelord...........90.00
106 DC,TS,V:Firelord...........90.00
107 DC,DGr,I:Imperial Guard,Star
    Jammers,Gladiator,Corsair ..100.00
108 JBy,TA,A:Star Jammers,
    C:Fantastic Four,Avengers...125.00
109 JBy,TA,I:Vindicator 110.00
110 TD,DC,V:Warhawk 75.00
111 JBy,TA,V:Mesmero,A:Beast,
    Magneto.................75.00
112 GP(c),JBy,TA,V:Magneto,
    A:Beast 75.00
113 JBy,TA,V:Magneto,A:Beast ...75.00
114 JBy,TA,A:Beast,R:Sauron 90.00
115 JBy,TA,V:Sauron,Garokk,
    A:Ka-Zar,I:Zaladane 75.00
116 JBy,TA,V:Sauron,Garokk,
    A:Ka-Zar 75.00
117 JBy,TA,O:Prof.X,I:Amahl
    Farouk (Shadow King)......70.00
118 JBy,I:Moses Magnum,A:Sunfire
    C:Iron Fist,I:Mariko 70.00
119 JBy,TA,V:Moses Magnum,
    A:Sunfire 70.00
120 JBy,TA,I:AlphaFlight (Shaman,
    Sasquatch,Northstar,Snowbird,
    Aurora)..................125.00
121 JBy,TA,V:Alpha Flight 100.00
122 JBy,TA,A:Juggernaut,Black
    Tom,Arcade,Power Man 70.00
123 JBy,TA,V:Arcade,A:SpM 60.00
124 JBy,TA,V:Arcade...........60.00
125 JBy,TA,A:Beast,Madrox the
    Multiple Man,Havok,Polaris..70.00
126 JBy,TA,I:Proteus,
    A:Havok,Madrox 70.00
127 JBy,TA,V:Proteus,A:Havok,
    Madrox..................70.00
128 GP(c),JBy,TA,V:Proteus,
    A:Havok,Madrox 70.00
129 JBy,TA,I:Shadow Cat,White
    Queen,C:Hellfire Club 110.00
130 JR2(c),JBy,TA,I:Dazzler
    V:White Queen 70.00
131 JBy,TA,V:White Queen,
    A:Dazzler................70.00

Uncanny X-Men #136
© Marvel Entertainment Group

132 JBy,TA,I:Hellfire Club,
  V:Mastermind 70.00
133 JBy,TA,V:Hellfire Club,
  Mastermind,F:Wolverine 70.00
134 JBy,TA,V:Hellfire Club,Master
  mind,I:Dark Phoenix,A:Beast . 70.00
135 JBy,TA,V:Dark Phoenix,
  Fant.Four,Silver Surfer 70.00
136 JBy,TA,V:Dark Phoenix,
  A:Beast 70.00
137 JBy,TA,D:Phoenix,V:Imperial
  Guard,A:Beast. 80.00
138 JBy,TA,History of X-Men,
  L:Cyclops,C:Shadow Cat 60.00
139 JBy,TA,A:Alpha Flight,R:Wendigo,
  N:Wolverine,J:Shadowcat 65.00
140 JBy,TA,V:Wendigo,A:Alpha
  Flight 60.00
141 JBy,TA,I:2nd Brotherhood of Evil
  Mutants,I:Rachel (Phoenix II) . 75.00
Becomes:

UNCANNY X-MEN

142 JBy,TA,V:Evil Mutants,
  A:Rachel (Phoenix II) 70.00
143 JBy,TA,V:N'Garai,I:Lee
  Forrester 50.00
144 BA,JRu,A:Man-Thing,
  O:Havok, V:D'Spayre. 20.00
145 DC,JRu,V:Arcade,A:DrDoom . 20.00
146 DC,JRu,V:Dr.Doom,Arcade . . 20.00
147 DC,JRu,V:Dr.Doom,Arcade . . 20.00
148 DC,JRu,I:Caliban,A:Dazzler
  Spiderwoman. 20.00
149 DC,JRu,A:Magneto. 20.00
150 DC,JRu,BWi,V:Magneto 22.00
151 JSh,BMc,JRu,V:Sentinels. . . . 20.00
152 BMc,JRu,V:White Queen 20.00
153 DC,JRu,I:Bamf 20.00
154 DC,JRu,BWi,I:Sidrian Hunters
  A:Corsair,O:Cyclops(part) 20.00
155 DC,BWi,V:Deathbird,I:Brood. . 20.00
156 DC,BWi,V:Death Bird,
  A:Tigra, Star Jammers. 20.00
157 DC,BWi,V:Deathbird 20.00
158 DC,BWi,2nd A:Rogue,
  Mystique 25.00
159 BSz,BWi,V:Dracula 20.00
160 BA,BWi,V:Belasco,I:Magik . . . 20.00
161 DC,BWi,I:Gabrielle Haller,
  O:Magneto,Professor X. 20.00
162 DC,BWi,V:Brood 20.00
163 DC,BWi,V:Brood 20.00
164 DC,BWi,V:Brood,I:Binary 18.00
165 PS,BWi,V:Brood 20.00

166 PS,BWi,V:Brood,A:Binary,
  I:Lockheed. 18.00
167 PS,BWi,V:Brood,A:N.Mutants . 22.00
168 PS,BWi,I:Madelyne Pryor 18.00
169 PS,BWi,I:Morlocks 18.00
170 PS,BWi,A:Angel,V:Morlocks . . 18.00
171 WS,BWi,J:Rogue,V:Binary . . . 26.00
172 PS,BWi,V:Viper,Silver
  Samurai, ... 20.00
173 PS,BWi,V:Viper,Silver
  Samurai, ... 18.00
174 PS,BWi,A:Mastermind 18.00
175 PS,JR2,BWi,W:Cyclops and
  Madelyne,V:Mastermind 20.00
176 JR2,BWi,I:Val Cooper. 12.00
177 JR2,JR,V:Brotherhood of
  Evil Mutants. 12.00
178 JR2,BWi,BBr,V:Brotherhood
  of Evil Mutants. 12.00
179 JR2,DGr,V:Morlocks 12.00
180 JR2,DGr,BWi,Secret Wars . . . 15.00
181 JR2,DGr,A:Sunfire 12.00
182 JR2,DGr,V:S.H.I.E.L.D. 12.00
183 JR2,DGr,V:Juggernaut 12.00
184 JR2,DGr,V:Selene,I:Forge . . . 16.00
185 JR2,DGr,V:Shield,U.S.
  Govt.,Storm loses powers 12.00
186 BWS,TA,Lifedeath,
  V:Dire Wraiths 14.00
187 JR2,DGr,V:Dire Wraiths 12.00
188 JR2,DGr,V:Dire Wraiths 12.00
189 JR2,SL,V:Selene,A:Magma . . 12.00
190 JR2,DGr,V:Kulan Gath,A:SpM,
  Avengers,New Mutants 12.00
191 JR2,DGr,A:Avengers,Spider-Man,
  New Mutants,I:Nimrod. 12.00
192 JR2,DGr,V:Magus. 12.00
193 JR2,DGr,V:Hellions,I:Firestar
  Warpath,20th Anniv. 20.00
194 JR2,DGr,SL,V:Nimrod. 12.00
195 BSz(c),JR2,DGr,A:Power
  Pack,V:Morlocks 12.00
196 JR2,DGr,V:Magneto 15.00
197 JR2,DGr,V:Arcade 12.00
198 BWS,F:Storm,Lifedeath II 12.00
199 JR2,DGr,I:Freedom Force,
  Rachel becomes 2nd Phoenix 12.00
200 JR2,DGr,A:Magneto,I:Fenris. . 20.00
201 RL,WPo(i),I:Nathan
  Christopher (Cyclops son). . . . 22.00
202 JR2,AW,Secret Wars II 12.00
203 JR2,AW,Secret Wars II 12.00
204 JBr,WPo,V:Arcade 12.00
205 BWS,A:Lady Deathstrike 22.00
206 JR2,DGr,V:Freedom Force. . . . 12.00
207 JR2,DGr,V:Selene. 12.00
208 JR2,DGr,V:Nimrod,
  A:Hellfire Club 12.00
209 JR2,CR,V:Nimrod,A:Spiral . . . 12.00
210 JR2,DGr,I:Marauders,
  (Mutant Massacre). 25.00
211 JR2,BBl,AW,V:Marauders,
  (Mutant Massacre). 25.00
212 RL,DGr,V:Sabretooth,
  (Mutant Massacre). 30.00
213 AD,V:Sabretooth (Mut.Mass) . 30.00
214 BWS,BWi,V:Malice,A:Dazzler. 12.00
215 AD,DGr,I:Stonewall,Super
  Sabre,Crimson Commando. . . 12.00
216 BWS(c),JG,DGr,V:Stonewall . . 12.00
217 WS(c),JG,SL,V:Juggernaut . . . 12.00
218 AAD(c),MS,DGr,V:Juggernaut 12.00
219 BBl,DGr,V:Marauders,Polaris
  becomes Malice,A:Sabertooth 12.00
220 MS,DGr,A:Naze 12.00
221 MS,DGr,I:Mr.Sinister,
  V:Marauders 24.00
222 MS,DGr,V:Marauders,Eye
  Killers,A:Sabertooth. 25.00
223 KGa,DGr,A:Freedom Force . . 12.00
224 MS,DGr,V:Adversary. 15.00

225 MS,DGr,Fall of Mutants
  I:1st US App Roma 16.00
226 MS,DGr,Fall of Mutants 16.00
227 MS,DGr,Fall of Mutants 16.00
228 RL,TA,A:OZ Chase 14.00
229 MS,DGr,I:Reavers,Gateway . . 14.00
230 RL,DGr,Xmas Issue 14.00
231 RL,DGr,V:Limbo 12.00
232 MS,DGr,V:Brood 12.00
233 MS,DGr,V:Brood 12.00
234 MS,JRu,V:Brood 15.00
235 RL,CR,V:Magistrates 12.00
236 MS,DGr,V:Magistrates 12.00
237 RL,TA,V:Magistrates 12.00
238 MS,DGr,V:Magistrates 12.00
239 MS,DGr,Inferno,A:Mr.Sinister . 12.00
240 MS,DGr,Inferno,V:Marauders . 15.00
241 MS,DGr,Inferno,O:Madeline
  Pryor,V:Marauders. 12.00
242 MS,DGr,Inferno,D:N'Astirh,
  A:X-Factor,Double-sized 12.00
243 MS,Inferno,A:X-Factor. 12.00
244 MS,DGr,I:Jubilee. 25.00
245 RLd,DGr,Invasion Parody. . . . 12.00
246 MS,DGr,V:Mastermold,
  A:Nimrod 12.00
247 MS,DGr,V:Mastermold 12.00
248 JLe(1st X-Men Art),DGr,
  V:Nanny & Orphan Maker 35.00
248a 2nd printing. 3.00
249 MS,DGr,C:Zaladane,
  V:Savage Land Mutates. 10.00
250 MS,SL,I:Zaladane. 10.00
251 MS,DGr,V:Reavers 10.00
252 JLe,BSz(c),RL,SW,V:Reavers 14.00
253 MS,SL,V:Amahl Farouk 10.00
254 JLe(c),MS,DGr,V:Reavers . . . 10.00
255 MS,DGr,V:Reavers,D:Destiny. 10.00
256 JLe,SW,Acts of Vengeance,
  V:Manderin,A:Psylocke. 20.00
257 JLe,JRu,AofV,V:Manderin. . . . 15.00
258 JLe,SW,AofV,V:Manderin 15.00
259 MS,DGr,V:Magistrates, ... 8.00
260 JLe(c),MS,DGr,A:Dazzler 8.00
261 JLe(c),MS,DGr,V:Hardcase &
  Harriers 8.00
262 KD,JRu,V:Masque,Morlocks. . . 8.00
263 JRu(i),O:Forge,V:Morlocks 8.00
264 JLe(c),MC,JRu,V:Magistrate. . . 8.00
265 JRu(i),V:Shadowking 8.00
266 NKu(c),MC,JRu,I:Gambit 50.00
267 JLe,WPo,SW,V:Shadowking. . 25.00
268 JLe,SW,A:Captain America,
  Black Widow,V:The Hand,
  Baron Strucker. 25.00

Uncanny X-Men #195
© Marvel Entertainment Group

269 JLe,ATi,Rogue V:Ms.Marvel . . 10.00
270 JLe,ATi,SW,X-Tinction Agenda
  #1, A:Cable,New Mutants 12.00
270a 2nd printing(Gold) 4.00
271 JLe,SW,X-Tinction Agenda
  #4,A:Cable,New Mutants 10.00
272 JLe,SW,X-Tinction Agenda
  #7,A:Cable,New Mutants 10.00
273 JLe,WPo,JBy,KJ,RL,MS,MGo,
  LSn,SW,A:Cable,N.Mutants . . 10.00
274 JLe,SW,V:Zaladane,A:Magneto,
  Nick Fury,Ka-Zar 10.00
275 JLe,SW,R:Professor X,A:Star
  Jammers,Imperial Guard. 12.00
275a 2nd Printing (Gold) 3.00
276 JLe,SW,V:Skrulls,Shi'ar 10.00
277 JLe,SW,V:Skrulls,Shi'ar 10.00
278 PS,Professor X Returns to
  Earth,V:Shadowking 8.00
279 NKu,SW,V:Shadowking 7.00
280 E:CCl(s),NKu,A:X-Factor,
  D:Shadowking,Prof.X Crippled . 7.00
281 WPo,ATi,new team (From X-Men
  #1),D:Pierce,Hellions,V:Sentinels,
  I:Trevor Fitzroy,Upstarts 10.00
281a 2nd printing,red(c). 3.00
282 WPo,ATi,V:Fitzroy,C:Bishop . . 15.00
282a 2nd printing,gold(c) of #281
  inside 3.00
283 WPo,ATi,I:Bishop,Malcolm,
  Randall 17.00
284 WPo,ATi,SOS from USSR. 5.00
285 WPo,I:Mikhail(Colossus'
  brother from Russia) 5.00
286 JLe,WPo,ATi,A:Mikhail 5.00
287 JR2,O:Bishop,
  D:Malcolm,Randall 6.00
288 NKu,BSz,A:Bishop 5.00
289 WPo,ATi,Forge proposes
  to Storm 5.00
290 WPo,SW,V:Cyberpunks,
  L:Forge 5.00
291 TR,V:Morlocks. 5.00
292 TR,V:Morlocks. 5.00
293 TR,D:Morlocks,Mikhail 5.00
294 BP,TA,X-Cutioner's Song#1,
  Stryfe shoots Prof X,A:X-Force,
  X-Factor,polybag.w/ProfX card . 5.00
295 BP,TA,X-Cutioners Song #5,
  V:Apocalypse. 5.00
296 BP,TA,X-Cutioners Song #9,
  A:X-Force,X-Factor,V:Stryfe . . . 5.00
297 BP,X-Cutioners Song
  Aftermath 5.00
298 BP,TA,V:Acolytes 5.00
299 BP,A:Forge,Acolytes,I:Graydon
  Creed (Sabretooth's son) 5.00
300 JR2,DGr,BP,V:Acolytes,A:Forge,
  Nightcrawler,Holografx(c) 12.00
301 JR2,DGr,I:Sienna Blaze,
  V:Fitzroy 5.00
302 JR2,V:Fitzroy 5.00
303 JR2,V:Upstarts,D:Illyana 6.00
304 JR2,JaL,PS,L:Colossus,
  V:Magneto,Holo-grafx(c) 8.00
305 JD,F:Rogue,Bishop. 5.00
306 JR2,V:Hodge. 5.00
307 JR2,Bloodties#4,A:Avengers,
  V:Exodus,Cortez 6.00
308 JR2,Scott & Jean announce
  impending marriage. 5.00
309 JR2,O:Professor X & Amelia . . 5.00
310 JR2,DG,A:Cable,V:X-Cutioner,
  w/card 5.00
311 JR2,DG,AV,V:Sabretooth,
  C:Phalanx 5.00
312 JMd,DG,A:Yukio,I:Phalanx,
  w/card 5.00
313 JMd,DG,V:Phalanx 5.00
314 LW,BSz,R:White Quen 5.00
315 F:Acolytes. 5.00

Uncanny X-Men #296
© Marvel Entertainment Group

316 V:Phalanx,I:M,Phalanx Covenant
  Generation Next,pt.1, holo(c) . . 5.00
316a newsstand ed. 3.00
317 JMd,V:Phalanx,prism(c) 5.00
317a newsstand ed. 3.00
318 JMd,L:Jubilee, deluxe 5.00
318a newsstand ed. 3.00
319 R:Legion, deluxe 5.00
319a newsstand ed. 3.00
320 deluxe ed. 5.00
320 newsstand ed. 3.00
321 R:Lilandra, deluxe ed. 5.00
321 newsstand ed. 5.00
322 SLo,TGu,Rogue,Iceman run from
  Gambit's Secret. 8.00
323 I:Onslaught 5.00
324 SLo,F:Cannonball 5.00
325 R:Colossus 7.00
326 SLo,JMd,F:Gambit,Sabretooth . 4.00
327 SLo,JMd,Magneto's Fate 4.00
328 SLo,JMd,Sabretooth freed 4.00
329 SLo,JMd,A:Doctor Strange 4.00
330 Dr.Strange. 4.00
331 White Queen. 4.00
332 SLo,JMd, cont from
  Wolverine #100 . . . . 4.00
333 SLo,JMd, Operation: Zero
  Tolerance, Onslaught saga 4.00
334 SLo,JMd, Onslaught saga 4.00
335 SLo,JMd, Onslaught saga 4.00
336 Apocalypse vs. Onslaught 4.00
337 Operation: Zero Tolerance 4.00
338 SLo,JMd,R:Angel 4.00
339 SLo,JMd,F:Cyclops, J.J.
  Jameson, Havok 4.00
340 SLo,JMd,F:Iceman 4.00
341 SLo,JMd,Rogue gets gift 4.00
342 SLo,JMd, Shi'ar Empire, pt.1 . . 5.00
342a Rogue cover 15.00
343 SLo,JMd, Shi'ar Empire, pt.2 . . 4.00
344 SLo,JMd, Shi'ar Empire, pt.3 . . 4.00
345 SLo,JMd, trip home, A:Akron . . 5.00
346 SLo,JMd,Zero Tolerance,
  A:Spider-Man. 4.00
347 SLo,JMd,Zero Tolerance. 4.00
348 SLo,JMd,at Magneto's base . . . 4.00
349 SLo,JMd,Maggot vs. Psylocke
  & Archangel. 4.00
350 SSe,JMd,Trial of Gambit,
  double-sized 4.00
350a Gambit (c) 10.00
351 SSe,JMd,Dr. Cecilia Reyes. . . . 3.00

352 SSe,EBe,Cyclops & Phoenix
  leave, Facade arrives 3.00
353 SSe,CBa,Rogues Anguish 3.00
354 SSe,CBa,F:Rogue 3.00
354a Jean Gray (c) 6.00
355 SSe,CBa, North & South
  pt.2 x-over 5.00
356 SSe,CBa, originals V:Phoenix . 3.00
357 SSe,Cyclops & Phoenix 3.00
358 SSe,CBa,Phoenix collapses . . . 3.00
359 SSe,CBa,Rogue 3.00
360A SSe,CBa, I:New X-Men, foil
  etched cover 5.00
360B regular cover 4.00
361 SSe,SSr,R:Gambit 3.50
362 SSe,CBa,Hunt for Xavier,pt.1 . . 3.50
363 SSe,CBa,Hunt for Xavier,pt.3 . . 3.50
364 SSe,Hunt for Xavier,pt.5 . . . . . 5.00
365 SSe,CBa,A:Professor X 3.00
366 AD,BPe,Magneto War,pt.1 . . . . 3.00
367 AD,Magneto War,pt.3 . . . . 3.00
368 AD,AKu,Requiem for an X-Man 3.00
368a signed 20.00
369 AD,AKu,V:Juggernaut. 3.00
370 AD,AKu,in the past 3.00
371 AD,AKu(c),Rage Against
  the Machine, pt.1 x-over 3.00
371a signed 20.00
372 AKu,AD,The Shattering,pt.1 . . . 3.00
373 AKu,AD,The Shattering,pt.2 . . . 3.00
374 AKu,AD,The Shattering. 3.00
375 AKu,AD,48-pg. 5.00
376 AKu,AD 5.00
377 AKu,AD,Apocalypse12,pt.5. . . . 5.00
378 AKu,AD,TTn,Ages of
  Apocalypse,pt.1,x-over 3.00
379 AKu,AD,TTn,mutants no more . 3.00
380 AD,TR,poly-bagged w/Genesis. 4.00
381 CCl,AKu,TTn,X-Men:
  Revolution 10.00
381a foil (c) 15.00
382 CCl,TTn,Shockwave Riders . . . 3.00
383 CCl,AKu,TTn,48-pg. 3.50
384 CCl,AKu,TTn,I:Killion 3.00
385 CCl,TR,Red Pirates 3.00
386 CCl,TR,Phoenix 3.00
387 CCl,TTn,Maximum Security . . . 3.00
388 CCl,SvL,Dream's End,pt.1 . . . . 5.00
389 CCl,SvL,F:Cecilia Reyes 3.00
390 CCl,SvL,Legacy Virus,
  D:Colossus 10.00
391 SLo,SvL,return 3.00
392 SLo,SvL,Eve of Destruction . . . 3.00
393 SLo,SvL,Eve of Destruction . . . 5.00
394 JoC,IaC,F:Warp Savant 5.00
395A JoC,IaC,Poptopia,pt.1 . . . . . . 3.00
395B variant BWS(c) 3.00
396 JoC, IaC,Poptopia,pt.2. . . . . . . 3.00
397 JoC,IaC,Poptopia,pt.3. . . . . 3.00
398 JoC,IaC,Poptopia,pt.4. . . . . 3.00
399 JoC,SHa,X-Ranch. 3.00
400 F:XStacy,48-page 5.00
401 JoC,RG,F:Banshee,'Nuff Said . 3.50
402 JoC,RG,vs.X-Corp. 2.50
403 JoC,AaL,DaM,X-Corp's secret . 2.50
404 JoC,RG,V:Multiple Men. 2.50
405 JoC,SeP,V:Banshee 2.50
406 JoC,AaL,X-Corps,concl. 2.50
407 JoC,SeP,Nightcrawler 2.50
408 JoC,SeP,V:Nightcrawler 2.50
409 JoC,SeP,V:Vanisher 2.50
410 RG,Hope 2.50
411 RG,Hope,pt.2. . . . . 2.50
412 RG,Hope,pt.3 . . . . 2.50
413 RG,Annie's Moving 2.50
414 Northstar Joins team. 2.50
415 SeP,F:Nightcrawler 2.50
416 KiA,F:Juggernaut 4.00
417 KiA,Dominant Species 3.00
418 KiA,Dominant Species 3.00
419 KiA,Archangel and Husk. 2.25

---

420 KiA,Dominant Species,concl. . . 2.25
421 RG,V:Alpha Flight,pt.1 . . . . 2.25
422 RG,V:Alpha Flight,pt.2,48-pg. . . 3.50
423 RG,Holy War,pt.1 . . . . 1.00
424 RG,Holy War,pt.2 . . . . 2.25
425 Sacred Vows,pt.1 . . . . 2.25
426 Sacred Vows,pt.2 . . . . 2.25
427 F:Jubilee, Angel, Husk 2.25
428 O:Nightcrawler,F:Mystique 2.25
429 Draco,pt.1 . . . . 2.25
430 Draco,pt.2 . . . . 2.25
431 Draco,pt.3 . . . . 2.25
432 Draco,pt.4 . . . . 2.25
433 Draco,pt.5 . . . . 2.25
434 Draco,pt.6 . . . . 2.25
435 Trial of the Juggernaut,pt.1 . . . . 2.25
436 Trial of the Juggernaut,pt.2 . . . . 2.25
437 She Lies With Angels,pt.1 . . . . . 2.50
438 She Lies With Angels,pt.2 . . . . . 2.25
439 She Lies With Angels,pt.3 . . . . . 2.25
440 She Lies With Angels,pt.4 . . . . . 2.25
441 She Lies With Angels,pt.5 . . . . . 2.25
442 Of Darkest Nights,pt.1 . . . . 2.25
443 Of Darkest Nights,pt.2 . . . . 2.25
444 The End of History,pt.1 . . . . 2.25
445 The End of History,pt.2 . . . . 2.25
446 The End of History,pt.3 . . . . 2.25
447 The End of History,pt.4 . . . . 2.25
448 CCl,Guess Who's Back,pt.1 . . . 2.25
449 CCl,Guess Who's Back,pt.2 . . . 2.25
450 CCl,AD,Cruelest Cut,pt.1 . . . . . 2.25
451 CCl,AD,Cruelest Cut,pt.2 . . . . . 2.25
Ann.#1 rep.#9,#11 . . . . 200.00
Ann.#2 rep.#22,#23 . . . . 100.00
Ann.#3 GK(c),GP,TA,A:Arkon 40.00
Ann.#4 JR2,BMc,A:Dr.Strange . . . 25.00
Ann.#5 BA,BMc,A:F.F. 20.00
Ann.#6 BSz,BWi,Dracula 20.00
Ann.#7 MGo,TMd,BWi,TA,BBr,
   BA,JRu,BBl,SL,AM,
   V:Impossible Man 15.00
Ann.#8 SL,Kitty's story 15.00
Ann.#9 AAd,AG,MMi,Asgard,V:Loki,
   Enchantress,A:New Mutants . . 20.00
Ann.#10 AAd,TA,V:Mojo,
   J:Longshot,A:New Mutants . . . 18.00
Ann.#11 AD,V:Horde,A:CaptBrit. . . . 7.00
Ann.#12 AAd,BWi,RLm,TD,Evol.
   War,V:Terminus,Savage Land . . 7.00
Ann.#13 MBa,JRu,Atlantis Attacks . 6.00
Ann.#14 AAd,DGr,BWi,AM,ATi,
   V:Ahab,A:X-Factor 10.00
Ann.#15,TR,JRu,MMi(c),Flesh Tears,
   Pt.3,A:X-Force,New Warriors . . 6.00

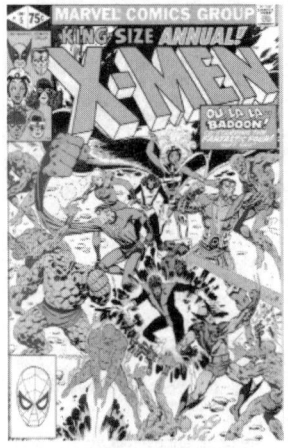

Ann.#16 JaL,JRu,Shattershot
   Part.2 . . . . 5.00
Ann.#17 JPe,MFm,I:X-Cutioner,
   D:Mastermind,w/card 5.00
Ann.#18 JR2,V:Caliban,
   BU:Bishop 4.00
Ann.1999 AD 3.50
Ann.2000 SLo,F:Professor X 3.50
Ann.2001 JoC,48-pg. 3.50
Marvel Milestone rep. #1 (1991) . . . 3.00
Marvel Milestone rep. #9 (1993) . . . 3.00
Marvel Milestone rep. #28 (1994) . . 3.00
G-Size #1,GK,DC,I:New X-Men
   (Colossus,Storm,Nightcrawler,
   Thunderbird,3rd A:Wolv.) . . 1,200.00
G-Size #2,rep.#57-59. . . . . 100.00
Marvel Milestone rep. Giant
   Size #1 (1991) 4.00
Spec.#1 X-Men: Earth Fall,
   rep. #232–#234 (1996) 3.00
Spec.#1 X-Men vs. Dracula, rep.
   X-Men Ann.#6 (1993) 2.00
GN X-Men: Days of Future Past
   rep. X-Men #141-142 . . . . 5.00
GN Pryde of the X-Men 11.00
GN God Loves,Man Kills,
   (1994) prestige 7.00
GN X-Men Firsts, I:Wolverine,Rogue,
   Gambit & Mr. Sinister, rep.
   Avengers Ann.#10, Uncanny
   X-Men 221,#266 & Incredible
   Hulk #181 (1996). 5.00
GN X-Men Rarities,F:Classic
   Stories (1995) 6.00
TPB Asgardian Wars 16.00
TPB Bloodties V:Exodus 16.00
TPB Coming of Bishop, rep.(1995) 13.00
TPB Dark Phoenix Saga 13.00
TPB Dark Phoenix, 192-pg.(2001). 20.00
TPB X-Men: Days of Future Present,
   MMi(c), rep. 15.00
TPB Fall of the Mutants, 272-pg. . . 25.00
TPB Fatal Attractions (1994) 18.00
TPB From the Ashes 17.00
TPB Greatest Battles 16.00
TPB X-Men: Poptopia (2001). 17.00
TPB X-Men: Inferno, 352-pg. 20.00
TPB X-Men Magazine,CCl,JLe,rep. . 4.00
TPB X-Men: Mutant Massacre,rep. 25.00
TPB Savage Land 10.00
TPB X-Cutioner's Song 25.00
TPB X-Tinction Agenda, rep. 20.00
X-Men Survival Guide to the
   Mansion, NKu(c) (1993) 7.00
TPB Vol. 1: Hope 13.00
TPB Vol. 2: Dominant Species. . . . 12.00
TPB Vol. 3: Holy War 11.00
TPB Vol. 4: The Draco (2004) 16.00
TPB Vol. 5: She Lies With Angels . 12.00
TPB Vol. 6: Bright New Mourning . 15.00

X-MEN
[2nd Regular Series] Oct., 1991

1A(c);Storm,Beast,B:CCl(s),JLe,SW
   I:Fabian Cortez,Acolytes,
   V:Magneto 4.00
1B(c);Colossus,Psylocke 5.00
1C(c);Cyclops,Wolverine 5.00
1D(c);Magneto 5.00
1E(c);Gatefold w/pin-ups 7.00
2 JLe,SW,V:Magneto Contd. 6.00
3 E:CCl(s),JLe,SW,V:Magneto . . . 6.00
4 JBy(s),JLe,SW,I:Omega Red,
   V:Hand. 8.00
5 B:SLo(s),JLe,SW,V:Hand,
   Omega Red,I:Maverick 6.00
6 JLe,SW,V:Omega Red, Hand,
   Sabretooth 6.00
7 JLe,SW,V:Omega Red,Hand,
   Sabretooth 6.00

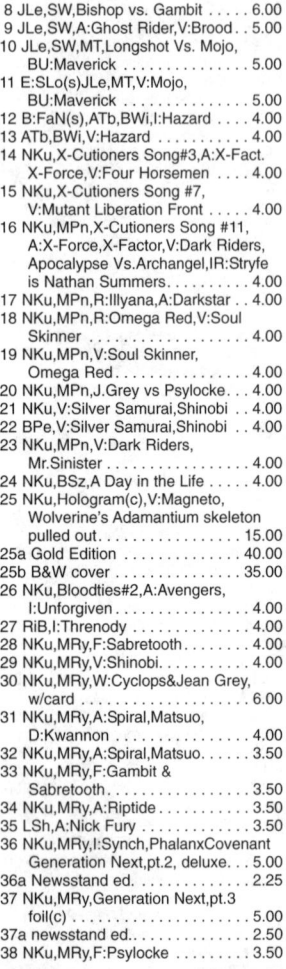

8 JLe,SW,Bishop vs. Gambit 6.00
9 JLe,SW,A:Ghost Rider,V:Brood . . 5.00
10 JLe,SW,MT,Longshot Vs. Mojo,
   BU:Maverick 5.00
11 E:SLo(s)JLe,MT,V:Mojo,
   BU:Maverick 5.00
12 B:FaN(s),ATb,BWi,I:Hazard 4.00
13 ATb,BWi,V:Hazard 4.00
14 NKu,X-Cutioners Song#3,A:X-Fact.
   X-Force,V:Four Horsemen 4.00
15 NKu,X-Cutioners Song #7,
   V:Mutant Liberation Front 4.00
16 NKu,MPn,X-Cutioners Song #11,
   A:X-Force,X-Factor,V:Dark Riders,
   Apocalypse Vs.Archangel,IR:Stryfe
   is Nathan Summers. 4.00
17 NKu,MPn,R:Illyana,A:Darkstar . . 4.00
18 NKu,MPn,R:Omega Red,V:Soul
   Skinner 4.00
19 NKu,MPn,V:Soul Skinner,
   Omega Red. 4.00
20 NKu,MPn,J.Grey vs Psylocke. . . 4.00
21 NKu,V:Silver Samurai,Shinobi . . 4.00
22 BPe,V:Silver Samurai,Shinobi . . 4.00
23 NKu,MPn,V:Dark Riders,
   Mr.Sinister. 4.00
24 NKu,BSz,A Day in the Life 4.00
25 NKu,Hologram(c),V:Magneto,
   Wolverine's Adamantium skeleton
   pulled out. 15.00
25a Gold Edition 40.00
25b B&W cover 35.00
26 NKu,Bloodties#2,A:Avengers,
   I:Unforgiven 4.00
27 RiB,I:Threnody 4.00
28 NKu,MRy,F:Sabretooth 4.00
29 NKu,MRy,V:Shinobi. 4.00
30 NKu,MRy,W:Cyclops&Jean Grey,
   w/card 6.00
31 NKu,MRy,A:Spiral,Matsuo,
   D:Kwannon 4.00
32 NKu,MRy,A:Spiral,Matsuo. 3.50
33 NKu,MRy,F:Gambit &
   Sabretooth. 3.50
34 NKu,MRy,A:Riptide 3.50
35 LSh,A:Nick Fury 3.50
36 NKu,MRy,I:Synch,PhalanxCovenant
   Generation Next,pt.2, deluxe. . . 5.00
36a Newsstand ed. 2.25
37 NKu,MRy,Generation Next,pt.3
   foil(c) 5.00
37a newsstand ed. 2.50
38 NKu,MRy,F:Psylocke 3.50

X-Men 2nd Series Ann. #2
© Marvel Entertainment Group

38a newsstand ed. 3.00
39 X-Treme, deluxe 3.50
39a newsstand ed. 3.00
40 deluxe 3.50
40a newsstand ed. 3.00
41 V:Legion, deluxe 3.50
41a newsstand ed. 3.00
42 PS,PaN,Mysterious Visitor 3.00
43 Rogue and Iceman 3.00
44 FaN,Mystery of Magneto 3.00
45 20th Anniv.pt.2 . . . . 5.00
46 FaN,Aku,V:Comcast 3.00
47 SLo,AKu,CaS,F:Dazzler 3.00
48 SLo,AKu,CaS,F:Sabretooth 3.00
49 SLo,AKu,Bishop wanted 3.00
50 Onslaught(c) 6.00
50a regular edition 5.00
51 MWa,Onslaught 5.00
52 MWa,AKu,CaS,V:Sinister 5.00
53 Onslaught saga. 7.00
54 Onslaught saga. 5.00
54a Foil cover 25.00
55 Onslaught saga. 3.50
56 Onslaught saga. 3.50
57 Operation: Zero Tolerance 3.50
58 SLo,NKu 3.50
59 . . . . 3.50
60 SLo,NKu,F:Ororo, V:Candra. . . . 3.50
61 SLo,CNn,F:Storm, V:Candra. . . . 3.50
62 SLo,CPa,F:Sebastian Shaw,
    Shang Chi 3.50
62A variant Storm/Wolverine(c) . . . 13.00
63 SLo,CPa,ATi,A:Sebastian Shaw,
    Inner Circle 3.00
64 SLo,CPa,ATi,V:Hellfire Club 3.00
65 SLo,CPa,ATi, No Exit prelude. . . 3.00
66 SLo,CPa,ATi, Zero Tolerance,
    A:Bastion 3.00
67 SLo,CPa,ATi Zero Tolerance,
    F:Iceman, Cecilia Reyes 3.00
68 SLo,CPa,ATi, Operation: Zero
    Tolerance 3.00
69 SLo,CPa, Operation: Zero
    Tolerance, concl. 3.50
70 ATi,Who will join X-Men?,
    double-sized 5.00
71 ATi,Cyclops banished 4.00
72 ATi,Professor Logan's School of
    Hard Knocks 3.00
73 ATi,Marrow visits Callisto 3.00
74 ATi,Terror in Morlock Tunnels . . . 3.00
75 ATi,V:N'Garai, double size 4.00

76 CCI,V:Sabretooth, 35th anniv
    kickoff 3.00
77 ATi,A:Black Panther,Maggott . . . 3.00
78 Return of Professor X 3.00
79 ATi,Cannonball must leave team 3.00
80A BPe, ATi, cont. from Uncanny
    X-Men #360, etched foil (c). . . . 7.50
80B regular cover 4.00
81 AKu,MFm,Search for Prof.X . . . 3.00
82 AKu,MFm,Hunt for Xavier. 3.00
83 AKu,MFm,Hunt for Xavier,pt.4 . . 3.00
84 AJu,Hunt for Xavier,concl. 3.50
85 AD,MFm,R:Magneto 3.00
85a signed 30.00
86 AD,MFm,Magneto War,pt.2,
    O:Joseph 3.50
87 AD,MFm,Magneto War,pt.4 . . . . 3.50
88 AD,MFm,R:Juggernaut 3.00
89 AD,MFm,In the past 3.00
90 AD,MFm,In the past,concl. 3.00
91 AD,AKu,Rage Against
    the Machine, pt.2 x-over 3.00
91a signed 30.00
92 AD,MFm,The Shattering x-over . 3.00
93 AD,MFm,The Shattering x-over . 3.00
94 AD,MFm,Shattering,x-over 4.00
95 AD,TR,A:Death, ... 3.00
96 AD 3.00
97 AD,MFm,Apocalypse12,pt.7 . . . 3.00
97a variant (c) 4.00
98 AD,MFm,Ages of Apocalypse . . 3.50
99 AD,BBh,mutants no more? 3.00
100 CCI,X-Men:Revolution,48-pg. . 4.00
100a variant covers 6.00
101 CCI,X-Men:Revolution 3.00
102 CCI,R:Wolverine 3.00
103 CCI,Wolverine v. Rogue 3.00
104 CCI,V:Killion 3.00
105 CCI,Archangel,Psylocke 3.00
106 CCI,Neo,Cecelia Reyes 3.50
107 CCI,Cadre K 4.00
108 CCI,Dream'sEnd,pt.4,x-over . . . 5.00
109 CCI,at X-Mansion, 100-page . . 4.00
110 SLo,F:Kitty Pryde 4.00
111 SLo,F:Trish Tilby 3.25
112 SLo,Eve of Destruction,pt.2 . . . 3.25
113 SLo,Eve of Destruction,pt.4 . . . 3.25
Becomes:

NEW X-MEN
114 GMo,E is for Extinction,pt.1 . . . 8.00
115A GMo,E for Extinction,pt.2 . . . . 6.00
115B variant BWS(c) 3.50
116 GMo,E for Extinction,pt.3 . . . . . 3.50
117 GMo,F:Beast. 3.50
118 GMo,GermFreeGeneration,pt.1 3.50
119 GMo,Germ Free Gen.,pt.2 . . . . 3.50
120 GMo,Germ Free Gen.,concl. . . . 3.50
121 GMo,Xavier's mind,'Nuff Said. . 3.00
122 GMo,Imperial,pt.1 . . . . 3.00
123 GMo,Imperial,pt.2 . . . . 2.50
124 GMo,Imperial,pt.3 . . . . 2.50
125 GMo,Imperial,pt.4 . . . . 2.50
126 GMo,Imperial,pt.5 . . . . 3.50
127 GMo,F:Xorn 3.00
128 GMo,Jean Grey, Emma Frost. . 3.00
129 GMo,Weapon XII 2.50
130 GMo 2.50
131 GMo,JPL,BSz 2.50
132 GMo,PJ,F:Storm 2.25
133 . . . . 2.25
134 GMo,NRd,no Magneto 2.25
135 GMo,Riot At Xavier's 2.25
136 GMo,Riot At Xavier's 2.25
137 GMo,Riot At Xavier's 2.25
138 GMo,Riot At Xavier's,concl. . . . 2.25
139 GMo,PJ,Murder at Mansion . . . 2.25
140 GMo,PJ,Murder at Mansion . . . 2.25
141 GMo,PJ,Murder at Mansion . . . 2.25
142 GMo,CBa,Weapon Plus,pt.1. . . 2.25
143 GMo,CBa,Weapon Plus,pt.2. . . 2.25
144 GMo,CBa,Weapon Plus,pt.3. . . 2.25

145 GMo,CBa,Weapon Plus,pt.4. . . 2.25
146 PJ,Planet X,pt.1 . . . . 2.25
147 PJ,Planet X,pt.2 . . . . 2.25
148 PJ,Planet X,pt.3 . . . . 2.25
149 PJ,Planet X,pt.4 . . . . 2.25
150 PJ,Planet X,finale,48-pg. 3.50
151 MS,Here Comes Tomorrow . . . 2.25
152 MS,Here Comes Tomorrow . . . 2.25
153 MS,Here Comes Tomorrow . . . 2.25
154 MS,Here Comes Tomorrow . . . 2.25
155 SvL,Bright New Mourning,pt.1 . 2.25
156 SvL,Bright New Mourning,pt.2 . 2.25
becomes:

X-MEN
157 SvL,Day of the Atom,pt.1 . . . . . 2.25
158 SvL,Day of the Atom,pt.2 . . . . . 2.25
159 SvL,Day of the Atom,pt.3 . . . . . 2.25
160 SvL,Day of the Atom,pt.4 . . . . . 2.25
161 SvL,Heroes & Villains,pt.1 . . . . 2.25
162 SvL,Heroes & Villains,pt.2 . . . . 2.25
163 SvL,Heroes & Villains,pt.3 . . . . 2.25
Ann.#1 JLe,Shattershot,pt.1,
    I:Mojo II 4.00
Ann.#2 I:Empyrean,w/card. 4.00
Ann.#3 F:Storm 4.00
Ann. Uncanny X-Men '97, V:Brother-
    hood, 48-pg. 3.50
Ann. '98 RMz, F:X-Men & Doctor
    Doom. 3.50
Ann. '98 X-Men/Fantastic Four, JoC,
    PaP, 48-pg. 3.50
Ann.1999 Rage Against the
    Machine, pt.3 x-over, 48-pg. . . . 3.50
Ann.2000 CCI,SHa,SEa,48-pg. . . . 4.00
Ann. 2001 GMo,Marvelscope 7.50
Uncanny X-Men'95 Spec. F:Husk . 4.00
Spec.X-Men'95, F:Mr.Sinister 5.00
Spec.X-Men'96 LHa, 64-pg., F:Gambit,
    Rogue, Magneto, Jubilee
    & Wolverine 4.00
Spec. X-Men'97,JFM,SEp,F:Gambit,
    Joesph & Phoenix 4.00
Minus 1 Spec., SLo,JMd,, flashback,
    discovery of mutants 2.00
Spec.#1 X-Men: Road to Onslaught
    (1996) 2.50
Spec. X-Men Universe: Past,
    Present and Future 3.00
Spec. X-Men:Year in Review 3.00
Spec.#1 X-Men (2000). 3.50
Spec. Millennial Visions 4.00
Spec.2001, Millennial Vision
    48-page 3.50
Spec. X-Men:Declassified,48-pg . . 3.50
Spec. Unearthed Archives
    Sketchbook 3.00
Spec. X-Men/Sentry, PJe,MT. 3.00
Spec. God Loves, Man Kills. 5.00
Spec. rep. Must Have #114–#116 . 4.00
Chrom.Classics GN,TKa,AD,MFm,
    Age of Apocalypse. 3.00
TPB Dark Phoenix Saga 16.00
TPB Dawn of the Age of
    Apocalypse, gold foil cover 9.00
TPB Twilight of the Age of
    Apocalypse, gold foil cover 9.00
TPB Legion Quest 9.00
TPB Magneto Returns 16.00
TPB Rise of Apocalypse 9.00
TPB Crossroads. 16.00
TPB Phoenix Rising. 15.00
TPB Road Trippin 20.00
TPB Zero Tolerance, 336-pg.. . . . . 25.00
TPB The Origin of Generation X . . 25.00
TPB X-Men: Vignettes 17.00
TPB Visionaries Joe Madureira . . . 18.00
TPB Visionaries Neal Adams. 25.00
TPB Jim Lee, 288-pg. (2002) 23.00
TPB Jim Lee (2002). 30.00
TPB Mutant Genesis (2002) 18.00
TPB Vol. 2, Imperial (2002) 20.00

TPB X-Men/Spider-Man: The Savage
    Land, rep. #1-#4, 80-pg. 10.00
TPB Vol. 3: New Worlds 15.00
TPB Vol. 4: Riot at Xaviers 12.00
TPB Vol. 5: Weapon Plus 15.00
TPB Evolution Vol. 2 . . . . 12.00
TPB X-Men Legends,Vol.1 . . . . . . 18.00
TPB X-Men Legends,Vol.2 . . . . . . 20.00
TPB X-Men Legends,Vol.3 . . . . . . 25.00
TPB Vol. 1: Day of the Atom 9.00
TPB Vol. 4: Legends 20.00
TPB Vol. 6: Planet X 13.00
TPB Vol. 7: Here Comes Tomorrow 11.00
TPB Days of Future Past 20.00

X-MEN ADVENTURES
[1st Season] 1992–94
1 V:Sentinals, Based on TV
    Cartoon 6.00
2 V:Sentinals,D:Morph 5.00
3 V:Magneto,A:Sabretooth 4.00
4 V:Magneto 4.00
5 V:Morlocks 4.00
6 V:Sabretooth 3.50
7 V:Cable,Genosha,Sentinels 3.00
8 A:Colossus,A:Juggernaut 3.00
9 I:Colussus(on cartoon),
    V:Juggernaut 3.00
10 A:Angel,V:Mystique 3.00
11 I:Archangel(on cartoon) 2.50
12 V:Horsemen of Apocalypse 2.50
13 RMc(s),I:Bishop(on cartoon) 2.50
14 V:Brotherhood of Evil Mutants . . 2.50
15 . . . . 2.50
TPB Vol.1 . . . . 5.00
TPB Vol.2 . . . . 5.00
TPB Vol.3 . . . . 6.00
TPB Vol.4 rep. Days of Future Past
    and Final Conflict. 7.00
[2nd Season] 1994–95
1 R:Morph,I:Mr. Sinister
    (on cartoon) 3.00
2 I:Nasty Boys (on cartoon) 2.50
3 I:Shadow King (on cartoon) 2.50
4 I:Omega Red (on cartoon) 2.50
5 I:Alpha Flight (on cartoon) 2.50
6 F:Gambit 2.50
7 A:Cable,Bishop,Apocalypse 2.50
8 A:Cable,Biship,Apocalypse 2.50
9 O:Rogue 2.50
10 . . . . 2.50
11 F:Mojo,Longshot 2.50
12 Reunions,pt.1 . . . . 2.50
13 Reunions,pt.1 . . . . 2.50
[3rd Season] 1995–96
1 Out of the Past,pt.1 . . . . 3.00
2 V:Spirit Drinker 2.50
3 Phoenix Saga,pt.1 . . . . 2.50
4 Phoenix Saga,pt.2 . . . . 2.50
5 Phoenix Saga,pt.3 . . . . 2.50
6 Phoenix Saga,pt.4 . . . . 2.50
7 Phoenix Saga,pt.5 . . . . 2.50
8 War in The Savage Land 2.50
9 F:Ka-Zar. 2.50
10 Dark Phoenix Saga,pt.1 . . . . . . 2.50
11 Dark Phoenix Saga,pt.2 . . . . . . 2.50
12 Dark Phoenix Saga,pt.3 . . . . . . 2.50
13 Dark Phoenix Saga,pt.4 . . . . . . 2.50

X-MEN: ALPHA
1994
1 Age of Apocalypse, double size. . 9.00
1a gold edition, 48pp 50.00

X-MEN/ALPHA FLIGHT
Jan., 1986
1 PS,BWi,V:Loki 5.00
2 PS,BWi,V:Loki 5.00

X-Men/Alpha Flight #1
© Marvel Entertainment Group

X-MEN/ALPHA FLIGHT: THE GIFT
Jan., 1998
1-shot CCI,PS, rep. of limited series 6.00

X-MEN/ ANIMATION SPECIAL
TV Screenplay Adapt 11.00

X-MEN ARCHIVES: CAPTAIN BRITAIN
1995
1 AMo,AD,Secret History 3.00
2 AMo,AD,F:Captain Britain 3.00
3 AMo,AD,Trial of Captain Britain . . 3.00
4 AMo,AD,Trial cont. 3.00
5 AD,AMo,F:Captain Britain 3.00
6 AMo,AD,Final Apocalypse? 3.00
7 AMo,AD,conclusion 3.00

X-MEN: ASKANI'SON
1 SLo,GeH,sequel to Adventures of
    Cyclops & Phoenix 3.00
2 SLo,GeH,A:Stryfe 3.00
3 SLo,GeH 3.00
4 SLo,GeH,conclusion 3.00
Books of Askani, portraits (1995). . . 3.00

X-MEN AT STATE FAIR
1 KGa,Dallas Times Herald 65.00

X-MEN: BLACK SUN
Sept., 2000
1 (of 5) CCI,New X-Men 3.00
2 CCI,Storm 3.00
3 CCI,RT,Banshee & Sunfire 3.00
4 CCI,LSi,Colossus&Nightcrawler . 3.00
5 CCI,Wolverine & Thunderbird . . . 3.00

X-MEN: CHILDREN OF THE ATOM
Jan., 2000
1 (of 6) JoC,SR,O:X-Men 5.00
2 JoC,SR,F:Professor X 3.00
3 JoC,SR 3.00
4 JoC,SR 3.00
5 JoC,SR, ... 3.00
6 JoC,SR,concl. 3.00

X-MEN CHRONICLES
1995
1 X-Men Unlimited AX 5.00
2 V:Abbatoir 5.00

X-MEN/CLANDESTINE
1996
1 & 2 AD,MFm,48-pg. . . . . @3.00

X-MEN CLASSICS
Dec., 1983
1 NA,rep. 7.00
2 NA,rep. 7.00
3 NA,rep. 7.00

CLASSIC X-MEN
Sept., 1986
1 AAd(c),JBo,New stories, rep.
    giant size X-Men 1 . . . . 9.00
2 rep.#94,JBo/AAd(c) 6.00
3 thru 9 rep#95-101,JBo/AAd(c) . @4.00
10 rep.#102,JBo/AAd(c),BU:Wolv. . . 8.00
11 rep.#103,JBo/BL(c), ... 3.00
12 rep.#104,JBo/AAd(c),BU:
    O:Magneto 7.00
13 thru 16 rep.,JBo/AAd(c) . . . . . @3.00
17 rep.#111,JBo/TA(c) 5.00
18 rep.#112,JBo/AAd(c) 4.00
19 rep.#113,JBo/AAd(c). 4.00
20 thru 22 rep.,JBo/AAd(c) . . . . . @3.00
23 thru 25 rep.,JBo/KGa(c) . . . . . @3.00
26 rep.#120,JBo/KGa(c). 4.00
27 thru 29 rep.,JBo/KD(c) . . . . . . @3.00
30 thru 35 rep.,JBo/SLi(c) . . . . . . @3.00
36 rep.#130,MBr/SLi(c) 3.00
37 rep.#131,RL/SLi(c) 3.00
38 rep.#132,KB/SLi(c) 3.00
39 rep.#133,2nd JLe X-Men/SLi(c) 11.00
40 thru 42 rep.,SLi(c) . . . . @3.00
43 rep.#137,JBy(c). 3.00
Becomes:

X-MEN CLASSICS
1990
44 rep.#138,KD/SLi(c) 3.00
45 thru 49 rep.#139-#145,SLi(c) . @3.00
50 thru 69 rep.#146-#165 . . . . . . @3.00
70 thru 105 rep.#166-#201 . . . . . @2.50
106 Phoenix vs. Beyonder. 2.50
107 F:Rogue 2.50
108 F:Nightcrawler. 2.50

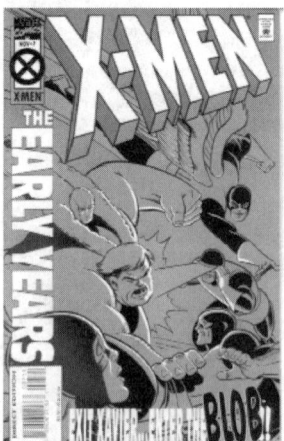
X-Men The Early Years #7
© Marvel Entertainment Group

109 Rep. Uncanny X-Men #205 . . . 2.50
110 Rep. Uncanny X-Men #206 . . . 2.50

X-MEN: EARLY YEARS
1 rep. X-Men (first series) #1 . . . . . 2.50
2 rep. X-Men (first series) #2 . . . . . 2.50
3 rep. X-Men (first series) #3 . . . . . 2.50
4 thru 16 rep. X-Men (first series)
   #4 to #16 . . . . @2.50
17 Rep. X-Men #17 & #18 . . . . 2.50

X-MEN: THE END
Aug., 2004
1 Dreamers and Demons,pt.1 . . . . 3.00
2 thru 4 Dreamers and Demons . @3.00

X-MEN EVOLUTION
Nov., 2001
1 cartoon series tie-in 2.25
2 F:Cyclops 2.25
3 F:Jean Grey 2.25
4 F:Nigntcrawler, Shadowcat,
   Spyke, Rogue 2.25
5 F:Mystique, Rogue 2.25
6 I:Mimic 2.25
7 new recruits, Beast 2.25
8 F:Angel, Storm 2.25
9 F:Professor X, Brotherhood 2.25
10 . . . . 2.25
TPB Vol.1, 96-pg 9.00
Digest 6.00

X-MEN FOREVER
Nov., 2000
1 (of 6) FaN,KM, ... 5.00
2 FaN,KM,displaced in time 4.00
3 FaN,KM, crucial points 4.00
4 FaN,KM,Toad 3.50
5 FaN,KM,Prosh 3.50
6 FaN,KM, concl. 3.50

X-MEN: HELLFIRE CLUB
Nov., 1999
1 (of 4) AKu,BRa,CAd. 3.00
2 AKu,BRa,CAd,O:Inner Circle 3.00
3 AKu,BRa,CAd,O:cont. 3.00
4 AKu,BRa,O:Concl. 3.00

X-MEN: THE HIDDEN YEARS
Oct., 1999
1 JBy,TP,Original team,48-pg. 4.00
2 JBy,TP 3.00
3 JBy,TP, ... 3.00
4 JBy,TP,Savage Land concl. 3.00
5 JBy,TP,A:Candy Southern 3.00
6 JBy,TP,F:Storm 3.00
7 JBy,TP,V:Deluge 3.00
8 JBy,TP,Fant.Four 3.00
9 JBy,TP,Phoenix 3.00
10 JBy,TP,Candy Southern 3.00
11 JBy,TP,Beast 3.00
12 JBy,TP,48-pg. 4.00
13 JBy,TP,Beast. 3.00
14 JBy,TP,Beast,Angel. 3.00
15 JBy,X-Mansion 3.00
16 JBy,return, to new conflicts 3.00
17 JBy,Kraven,Beast 3.00
18 JBy,Tad Carter,Lorna Dane. 3.00
19 JBy,TP,Lorna,Angel,Promise . . . 3.00
20 JBy,TP,Sub-Mariner,Magneto . . . 3.00
21 JBy,TP,Namor,Magneto 3.00
22 JBy,TP,X-Men & Fant.Four 3.00

X-MEN ICONS: CHAMBER
Aug., 2002
1 (of 4) NRd 3.50
2 NRd 3.00
3 NRd 3.00
4 NRd, concl 3.00

X-MEN INDEX
See: OFFICIAL MARVEL INDEX TO THE X-MEN

X-MEN: LIBERATORS
Sept., 1999
1 (of 4) PJ,F:Wolverine,Nightcrawler
   & Colossus 3.00
2 PJ,V:Russian army 3.00
3 PJ,V:Nikolas. 3.00
4 PJ,V:Omega Red 3.00

X-MEN: LOST TALES
1997
1 CCl,JBo,rep. from Classic X-Men 3.00
2 CCl,JBo,rep. from Classic X-Men 3.00

X-MEN: MAGIK
Oct., 2000
1 (of 4) DAn,ALa,LSh 3.00
2 DAn,ALa,LSh,V:Mephisto 3.00
3 DAn,ALa,LSh,F:Limbo 3.00
4 DAn,ALa,LSh,concl. 3.00

X-Men/Micronauts #1
© Marvel Entertainment Group

X-MEN/MICRONAUTS
Jan., 1984
1 JG,BWi,Limited Series 4.00
2 JG,BWi,KJo,V:Baron Karza 3.00
3 JG,BWi,V:Baron Karza. 3.00
4 JG,BWi,V:Baron Karza,Apr.1984 . 3.00

X-MEN: THE MAGNETO WAR
Jan., 1999
1-shot AD, Joseph vs. Magneto. . . . 3.00
1a signed 20.00

X-MEN: THE MANGA
Jan., 1998
1 b&w,translated,F:Jubilee 4.00
2 Jubilee joins, V:Sentinels. 3.00
3 Agent Gyrich strikes. 3.00
4 Beast captured, morph dead . . . 3.00
5 Magneto attempts to rescue
   Beast 3.00
6 Beast on trial, A:Sabretooth. 3.00
7 V:Magneto 3.00
8 V:Magneto 3.00
9 V:Morlocks 3.00
10 V:Morlocks, 40-pg. finale 3.00
11 Wolverine vs. Sabretooth 3.00
12 Wolverine vs. Sabretooth 3.00
13 F:Storm, Jubilee & Gambit 3.00
14 . . . . 3.00
15 . . . . 3.00
16 A:Colossus,V:Juggernaut,
   double-size 4.00
17 F:Cable & Angel 3.00
18 Angel becomes Archangel 3.00
19 Angel becomes Death. 3.00
20 Rogue vs. Apocalypse 3.00
21 V:Four Horsemen 3.00
22 V:Sentinels 3.00
23 RGr(c),F:Bishop 3.00
24 RGr(c),V:Nimrod. 3.00
25 Bishop vs. Gambit. 3.00
26 V:Brotherhood of Evil Mutants . . 3.00
27 Magneto Returns 3.00
28 V:Master Mold,A:Magneto 3.00
29 thru 32 . . . . @3.00

X-MEN: THE MOVIE
June, 2000
Magneto, photo(c) 6.00
Rogue, photo(c) 6.00
Wolverine, photo(c) 6.00
X-Men The Movie, photo(c) 6.00
TPB Beginnings, 144-pg. 15.00
TPB X-Men The Movie, 4 diff.
   photo(c)s . . . . @15.00

X-MEN OMEGA
1995
1 FaN,Slo,After Xavier, concl. 10.00
1a Gold ed. Chromium(c) 48-pg. . 50.00

X-MEN: PHOENIX
Oct., 1999
1 (of 3) JFM,F:Rachel Summers . . 3.00
2 JFM 3.00
3 JFM,concl. 3.00

X-MEN: PHOENIX
May, 2003
1 (of 3) Legacy of Fire 3.00
2 Sword of Limbo 3.00
3 Concl. 3.00

X-MEN PRIME
1995
1 SLo,FaN,BHi,major plotlines for
   all X books begin, chromium(c)10.00

X-MEN: PRYDE & WISDOM
1 WEI,TyD,KIS 3.00
2 & 3 WEI,TyD,KIS . . . . @3.00

MARVEL

MARVEL

X-MEN: RONIN
March, 2003
1 (of 5) manga mania 3.00
2 . . . . 3.00
3 . . . . 3.00
4 . . . . 3.00
5 . . . . 3.00

X-MEN: THE RISE OF APOCALYPSE
1 TKa,AdP, ancient history of
    X-Men 3.50
2 thru 4 TKa,AdP, ... @3.00
TPB 10.00

X-MEN: THE SEARCH FOR CYCLOPS
Oct., 2000
1A (of 4) TR,SHa, ... 3.00
1B variant AdP (c) 3.00
2A TR,SHa,Scott alive? 3.00
2B variant AdP(c) 3.00
3A TR,SHa, ... 3.00
3B variant AdP(c) 3.00
4A TR,SHa, concl. 3.00

X-MEN SPOTLIGHT ON STARJAMMERS
1990
1 DC,F:Starjammers,A:Prof.X 5.00
2 DC,F:Starjammers,A:Prof.X 5.00

X-MEN: TRUE FRIENDS
July, 1999
1 (of 3) CCI,RL,JP,F:Shadowcat . . . 3.00
2 CCI,RL,JP,A:Kitty Pryde 3.00
3 CCI,RL,JP,A:Wolverine,concl. . . . 3.00

X-MEN 2099
1993–96
1 B:JFM(s),RLm,JP,I:X-Men 2099 . 4.00
1a Gold Ed. 5.00
2 RLm,JP,V:Rat Pack 3.00
3 RLm,JP,D:Serpentina 3.00
4 RLm,JP,I:Theatre of Pain. 3.00
5 RLm,JP,Fall of the Hammer#3 . . . 3.00
6 RLm,JP,I:Freakshow 3.00
7 RLm,JP,V:Freakshow. 3.00
8 RLm(c),JS3,JP,N:Metalhead,
    I:2nd X-Men 2099 . . . . 3.00
9 RLm,JP,V:2nd X-Men 2099 . . . . . 3.00
10 RLm,JP,A:La Lunatica 3.00
11 RLm,JP,V:2nd X-Men 2099 . . . . 3.00
12 RLm,JP,A:Junkpile 3.00
13 RLm,JP 3.00
14 RLm,JP,R:Loki 3.00
15 RLm,JP,F:Loki,I:Haloween Jack . 3.00
16 . . . . 3.00
17 X'ian 3.00
18 Haloween Jack 3.00
19 Conclusion Halloween Jack 3.00
Becomes:

X-MEN 2099 A.D.
20 F:Bloodhawk 3.00
21 Doom Factor 3.00
22 One Nation Under Doom 3.00
23 V:Junkpile 3.00
24 . . . . 3.00
25 X-Men Reunited 3.00
25a variant cover 4.25
26 V:Graverobber 3.00
27 . . . . 3.00
28 X-Nation x-over. 3.00
29 X-Nation x-over. 3.00
30 . . . . 3.00

31 . . . . 3.00
32 V:Foolkiller 3.00
Spec.#1 Bros.Hildebrandt(c) 4.50
GN X-Men 2099: Oasis, rep., Greg
    Hildebrandt(c) 64-pg., (1998) . . 6.00

X-MEN 2: THE MOVIE
March, 2003
Prequel Wolverine, TMd 3.50
Prequel Nightcrawler 3.50
Spec. Movie Adapt., 48-pg. 3.50
TPB The Movie 13.00

X-MEN UNIVERSE
Oct., 1999
1 rep. July 99 stories, 80-pg. 5.00
2 thru 11 rep., 80-pg. . . . . @5.00
12 thru 17,rep., 80-pg. . . . . @4.00

X-MEN UNLIMITED
1993
1 CBa,BP,O:Siena Blaze 7.00
2 JD,O:Magneto 6.00
3 FaN(s),BSz(c),MMK,Sabretooth
    joins X-Men,A:Maverick. 7.00
4 SLo(s),RiB,O:Nightcrawler,Rogue,
    Mystique,IR:Mystique is
    Nightcrawler's mother 5.00
5 JFM(s),LSh,After Shi'ar/
    Kree War 4.50
6 JFM(s),PS,Sauron 4.50
7 JR2,HMe,O:Storm 4.50
8 Legacy Virus Victim 4.50
9 LHa,Wolverine & Psylocke 4.50
10 MWa,Dark Beast,Beast,
    double-size 8.00
11 Rogue & Magneto, double-size . 8.00
12 Onslaught x-over,A:Juggernaut . 3.00
13 GP,Binary gone berserk 3.00
14 TKa, Onslaught fallout 3.00
15 HMe,F:Wolverine, Iceman &
    Maverick 3.00
16 MvR,F:Banshee, White Queen,
    I:Primal 3.00
17 TKa,Wolverine vs. Sabretooth,
    minds are switched 4.00
18 TDF,V:Hydro Man 3.00
19 BRa,Nightcrawler v. Belasco . . 3.00
20 F:Generation X 3.00
21 TDz,Strong Guy returns 3.00
22 into Marrow's World 4.00

X-Men Unlimited #3
© *Marvel Entertainment Group*

23 F:Professor X 3.00
24 F:Wolverine & Cecilia Reyes . . . 3.00
25 BBh,48-pg. 3.00
26 BBh,Ages of Apocalypse,pt.4 . . 3.00
27 BBh,X-Men: Revolution 3.00
28 BBh,Russia 3.00
29 BBh,Maximum Security 3.00
30 BBh, ... 3.00
31 MGo(c) three stories 3.00
32 JIT(c) 3.00
33 MK(c),Sabretooth,Blob 3.00
34 Marvel Girl vs. Sabretooth 3.50
35 F:Emma Frost, Jubilee 3.50
36 three stories 3.50
37 multiple dimensions, 48-pg. . . . 3.50
38 DaR,F:Colossus 2.50
39 KIS,48-pg. 3.50
40 All evil issue, 48-pg. 3.50
41 I:MC Mystik,48-pg. 3.50
42 F:Prof. X, Jean Grey,48-pg. . . . 3.50
43 CCI,BSz 2.50
44 animal cruelty 2.50
45 V:Alpha Flight 2.50
46 SB,F:Wolverine 2.50
47 Return of Psylocke 2.50
48 Mystique returns 2.50
49 F:Nightcrawler. 2.50
50 PS,Japan connections 3.00

X-MEN UNLIMITED
March, 2004
1 TMd 3.00
2 F:Bishop. 3.00
3 F:Gambit 3.00
4 F:Juggernaut 3.00
5 F:Wolverine 3.00

X-MEN VS. AVENGERS
April, 1987
1 MS,JRu,V:Soviet SuperSoldiers . 5.00
2 MS,JRu,V:Sov.Super Soldiers . . 3.50
3 MS,JRu,V:Sov.Super Soldiers . . 3.50
4 KP,JRu,BMc,AW,AM,V:Magneto
    July, 1987 . . . . 3.50
TPB 13.00

X-MEN VS. THE BROOD
1996
1 and 2 Day of Wrath . . . . @3.00
TPB rep. 17.00

X-NATION 2099
1996
1 . . . . 4.00
2 . . . . 2.50
3 At Herod's Themepark 2.50

X.S.E.
Mini-Series 1996
1 (of 4) JOs,Bishop & Shard's
    secrets 2.25
2 JOs, How did Shard die. 2.25
3 JOs, How Shard died. 2.25
4 JOs, conclusion 2.25

X-STATIX
July, 2002
1 PrM,MiA,super-team, 40-pg. 3.00
2 PrM,MiA, ... 2.50
3 PrM,MiA 2.50
4 PrM, MiA, sex = death? 2.50
5 PrM,PPo 2.50
6 PrM,MiA,pt.1 . . . . 2.50
7 PrM,MiA 2.50
8 PrM,MiA,Orphan's New Love . . . 2.50
9 PrM,MiA, ... 2.50
10 PrM,Diaries of Edie Sawyer . . . 3.00

11 PrM,F:Latino 3.00	
12 PrM,If You Think I'm Sexy 3.00	
13 PrM,MiA,Di Another Day,pt.1 . . . 3.00	
14 PrM,MiA,Di Another Day,pt.2 . . . 3.00	
15 PrM,MiA,Di Another Day,pt.3 . . . 3.00	
16 PrM,MiA,Di Another Day,pt.4 . . . 3.00	
16 PrM,MiA,Back from Dead,pt.4 . . 3.00	
17 PrM,MiA,Back from Dead,pt.5 . . 3.00	
18 PrM,MiA,Back from Dead,pt.6 . . 3.00	
19 PrM,MiA,The Cure,pt.1 . . . . 3.00	
20 PrM,MiA,The Cure,pt.2 . . . . 3.00	
21 PrM,MiA,V:Avengers,pt.1 . . . . . 3.00	
22 PrM,MiA,V:Avengers,pt.2 . . . . . 3.00	
23 PrM,MiA,V:Avengers,pt.3 . . . . . 3.00	
24 PrM,MiA,V:Avengers,pt.4 . . . . . 3.00	
25 PrM,MiA,V:Avengers,pt.5 . . . . . 3.00	
26 PrM,MiA,finale. 3.00	
TPB Vol.1 . . . . 12.00	
TPB Vol.2:GoodGuys & BadGuys . 16.00	
TPB Vol.3:Back From the Dead. . . 20.00	

X-Terminators #4
© Marvel Entertainment Group

X-TERMINATORS
Oct., 1988 – Jan., 1989
1 JBg,AW,AM,I:N'astirh. 4.00
2 JBg,AM,V:N'astirh 3.50
3 JBg,AM,V:N'astirh 3.00
4 JBg,AM,A:New Mutants. 3.00

X-TREME X-MEN
June, 2001
1 CCI,SvL,Destiny,48-page. 4.50
2A CCI,SvL,Guardia,Vargas 3.50
2B variant CPa(c) 3.50
3 CCI,SvL,V:Vargas 3.00
4 CCI,SvL,V:Vargas 3.00
5 CCI,SvL,F:Gambit 3.00
6 CCI,SvL,F:Gambit,Rogue 3.00
7 CCI,SvL 3.00
8 CCI,SvL,concl.'Nuff Said 3.00
9 CCI,SvL,V:Lady Mastermind 3.00
10 CCI,SvL,Dimension X,pt.1 . . . . . 3.00
11 CCI,SvL,Dimension X,pt.2 . . . . . 3.00
12 CCI,SvL,V:Shaitan,Khan. 3.00
13 CCI,SvL,F:Gambit,Lifeguard. . . . 3.00
14 CCI,SvL,F:Storm, Sage. 3.00
15 CCI,SvL,F:Storm,Rogue 3.00
16 CCI,SvL,F:Rogue, Gambit 3.00
17 CCI,SvL 3.00
18 CCI,SvL,F:Jean Grey,Beast,

Nightcrawler. 3.00	
19 CCI,F:Jean Grey 3.00	
20 CCI,SvL,Scism,pt.1 . . . . 3.00	
21 CCI,SvL,Scism,pt.2 . . . . 3.00	
22 CCI,SvL,Scism,pt.3 . . . . 3.00	
23 CCI,SvL,Scism,pt.4 . . . . 3.00	
24 CCI,SvL,R:Cannonball 3.00	
25 CCI,SvL,God Loves,Man Kills2. . 3.00	
26 CCI,SvL,God Loves,Man Kills2. . 3.00	
27 CCI,SvL,God Loves,Man Kills2. . 3.00	
28 CCI,SvL,God Loves,Man Kills2. . 3.00	
29 CCI,SvL,God Loves,Man Kills2. . 3.00	
30 CCI,SvL,God Loves,Man Kills2. . 3.00	
31 CCI,SHa,Intifada,pt.1 . . . . 3.00	
32 CCI,SHa,Intifada,pt.2 . . . . 3.00	
33 CCI,SHa,Intifada,pt.3 . . . . 3.00	
34 CCI,SHa,Intifada,pt.4 . . . . 3.00	
35 CCI,SHa,Intifada,pt.5 . . . . 3.00	
36 Storm: The Arena,pt.1. . . . . 3.00	
37 Storm: The Arena,pt.2. . . . . 3.00	
38 Storm: The Arena,pt.3. . . . . 3.00	
39 Storm: The Arena,pt.4. . . . . 3.00	
40 CCI,Bogan,pt.1,Prisoner of Fire . 3.00	
41 CCI,Bogan,pt.2,Prisoner of Fire . 3.00	
42 CCI,Bogan,pt.3,Prisoner of Fire . 3.00	
43 CCI,Bogan,pt.4,Prisoner of Fire . 3.00	
44 CCI,Prisoner of Fire,pt.5 . . . . . . 3.00	
45 CCI,Prisoner of Fire,pt.6 . . . . . . 3.00	
46 CCI,finale 3.50	
Ann.2001 CCI,SvL,64-pg. 5.00	
TPB rep.#1-#4, 192-pg. (2002) . . . 19.00	
TPB Vol. 2: Invasion 20.00	
TPB Vol. 3: Schism 17.00	
TPB Vol. 4: Mekanix 17.00	
TPB Vol. 5: God Loves, Man Kills . 20.00	
TPB Vol. 6: Intifada 17.00	
TPB Vol. 7: Storm–The Arena 17.00	
TPB Vol. 8: Prisoner of Fire 20.00	

X-TREME X-MEN: SAVAGE LAND
July, 2001
1 (of 4) CCI,F:Rogue 3.50
2 CCI,Velociraptors & T-Rexes 3.00
3 CCI. 3.00
4 CCI,concl. 3.00
TPB 96-pg. 13.00

X-TREME X-MEN: X-POSE
Nov., 2002
1 (of 2) Ccl, two reporters 3.00
2 CCI,Forbidden Mutant Love. 3.00

X-UNIVERSE
1995
1 The Other Heroes 5.00
2 F:Ben Grimm,Tony Stark 5.00

YOGI BEAR
Nov., 1977
1 A:Flintstones 30.00
2 thru 9 March, 1979 . . . . @20.00

YOUNG ALLIES COMICS
Timely,
Summer, 1941 – Oct., 1946
1 S&K,Hitler(c),I&O:Young Allies
   1st meeting Capt. America &
   Human Torch,A:Red Skull 22,000.00
2 S&K,A;Capt.America,Human
   Torch. 5,500.00

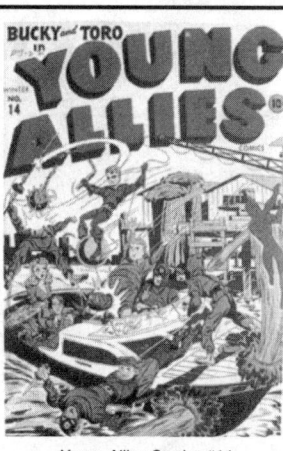

Young Allies Comics #14
© Marvel Entertainment Group

3 Remember Pearl Harbor(c) . 4,000.00
4 A;Capt. America,Torch,Red Skull
   ASh(c),Horror In Hollywood
   A:Capt.America,Torch. 5,500.00
5 ASh(c),Capt.America 2,500.00
6 ASh(c) 1,800.00
7 ASh(c) 1,800.00
8 ASh(c),WW2,Bondage 1,800.00
9 ASh(c),Axis leaders(c),
   B:Tommy Type,Hitler 2,000.00
10 ASh(c),O:Tommy Type. 1,800.00
11 ASh(c) 1,300.00
12 ASh(c),Decapitation 1,300.00
13 ASh(c) 1,300.00
14 . . . . 1,300.00
15 AxB,ASh(c). 1,300.00
16 ASh(c) 1,300.00
17 ASh(c) 1,300.00
18 ASh(c) 1,300.00
19 ASh(c),E:Tommy Type 1,300.00
20 . . . . 1,300.00

YOUNG HEARTS
Nov., 1949 – Feb., 1950
1 . . . . 150.00
2 Feb., 1950 . . . . 100.00

YOUNG MEN
See: COWBOY ROMANCES

YUPPIES FROM HELL
1989
1 Satire 3.00
2 . . . . 3.00
3 . . . . 3.00

ZORRO
Marvel UK, 1990
1 Don Diego 3.00
2 thru 12 . . . . @3.00

GOLDEN AGE

A-1 COMICS

Magazine Enterprises, 1944

N# F:Kerry Drake,BU:Johnny
Devildog & Streamer Kelly . . 200.00
1 A:Dotty Driple,Mr. EX,Bush
Berry and Lew Loyal 100.00
2 A:Texas Slim & Dirty Dalton,
The Corsair,Teddy Rich, Dotty
Dripple,Inca Dinca,Tommy Tinker
Little Mexico and Tugboat 75.00
3 same 75.00
4 same 75.00
5 same 75.00
6 same 75.00
7 same 75.00
8 same 75.00
9 Texas Slim Issue 90.00
10 Same characters as
issues #2–#8 . . . . 75.00
11 Teena 100.00
12 Teena 75.00
13 JCr,Guns of Fact and Fiction,
narcotics & junkies featured . 325.00
14 Tim Holt WesternAdventures . 950.00
15 Teena 75.00
16 Vacation Comics 50.00
17 Tim Holt #2, E:A-1 on cover . 450.00
18 Jimmy Durante, Ph(c) 550.00
19 Tim Holt #3 . . . . 300.00
20 Jimmy Durante Ph(c) 550.00
21 OW,Joan of Arc movie adapt.. 350.00
22 Dick Powell (1949) 300.00
23 Cowboys N' Indians #6 . . . . . 150.00
24 FF(c),LbC,Trail Colt #2 . . . . . 450.00
25 Fibber McGee & Molly (1949). 100.00
26 LbC, Trail Colt #2 . . . . 400.00
27 GhostRider#1,O:GhostRider 1,300.00
28 Christmas (Koko & Kola) 50.00
29 FF(c), Ghost Rider #2 . . . . . . 950.00
30 BP, Jet Powers #1 . . . . 425.00
31 FF,Ghost Rider#3,O:Ghost
Rider 950.00
32 AW,GE,Jet Powers #2 . . . . . 400.00
33 Muggsy Mouse #2 . . . . 75.00
34 FF(c),Ghost Rider #4 . . . . . . 950.00
35 AW,Jet Powers 425.00
36 Muggsy Mouse 125.00
37 FF(c),Ghost Rider 950.00
38 AW,WW,Jet Powers, Drugs . 450.00
39 Muggsy Mouse 50.00
40 Dogface Dooley 65.00
41 Cowboys 'N' Indians 85.00
42 BP,Best of the West 600.00
43 Dogface Dooley 45.00
44 Ghost Rider. 350.00
45 American Air Forces 75.00
46 Best of the West 300.00
47 FF,Thunda King of the
Congo. 1,900.00
48 Cowboys N' Indians 85.00
49 Dogface Dooley 45.00
50 BP,Danger Is Their Busines . . 150.00
51 Ghost Rider. 350.00
52 Best of the West 250.00
53 Dogface Dooley 45.00
54 BP,American Air Forces 75.00
55 BP,U.S. Marines 40.00
56 BP,Thunda King of the Congo 275.00
57 Ghost Rider, Drugs 350.00
58 American Air Forces 75.00
59 Best of the West 250.00
60 The U.S. Marines 65.00
61 Space Ace. 700.00
62 Starr Flagg–Undercover Girl . . 500.00

63 FF,Manhunt 475.00
64 Dogface Dooley 45.00
65 BP,American Air Forces 75.00
66 Best of the West 250.00
67 American Air Forces 75.00
68 U.S. Marines 40.00
69 Ghost Rider, Drugs 350.00
70 Best of the West 250.00
71 Ghost Rider, A:Frankenstein. . 325.00
72 U.S. Marines 40.00
73 BP,Thunda 200.00
74 BP,American Air Forces 75.00
75 Ghost Rider. 250.00
76 Best of the West 175.00
77 LbC,Grl,Manhunt 375.00
78 BP,Thunda 200.00
79 American Air Forces 75.00
80 Ghost Rider, Bondage(c) 250.00
81 Best of the West 125.00
82 BP,Cave Girl 600.00
83 BP,Thunda King of the Congo 175.00
84 Ghost Rider. 250.00
85 Best of the West 175.00
86 BP,Thunda King of the Congo 175.00
87 Best of the West 175.00
88 Bobby Benson's B-Bar-B 125.00
89 BP,Home Run,Stan Musial . . . 175.00
90 Red Hawk 150.00
91 BP,American Air Forces 75.00
92 Dream Book of Romance 125.00
93 BP,Great Western 225.00
94 FF,White Indian 275.00
95 BP,Muggsy Mouse 50.00
96 BP,Cave Girl 450.00
97 Best of the West 175.00
98 Starr Flagg–Undercover Girl . . 500.00
99 Muggsy Mouse 50.00
100 Badmen of the West 300.00
101 FF,White Indian. 275.00
101(a) BP(c),FG, Dream Book of
Romance, Marlon Brando . . . 225.00
103 BP,Best of the West 175.00
104 FF,White Indian. 275.00
105 Great Western 150.00
106 BP,Dream Book of Love 150.00
107 Hot Dog. 100.00
108 BP,BC,Red Fox. 250.00
109 BP,Dream Book of Romance 100.00

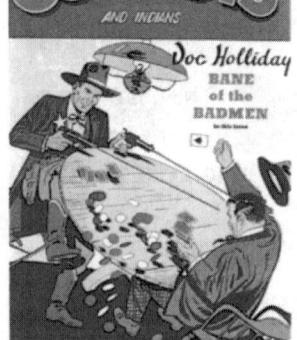

A-1 Comics #23
© Magazine Enterprises

110 Dream Book of Romance . . . 100.00
111 BP,I'm a Cop 180.00
112 Ghost Rider. 250.00
113 BP,Great Western 125.00
114 Dream Book of Love 125.00
115 Hot Dog. 80.00
116 BP,Cave Girl 400.00
117 White Indian 150.00
118 BP(c),Starr Flagg–
Undercover Girl 475.00
119 Straight Arrow's Fury. 180.00
120 Badmen of the West 200.00
121 Mysteries of the
Scotland Yard 200.00
122 Black Phantom 475.00
123 Dream Book of Love 100.00
124 Hot Dog. 75.00
125 BP,Cave Girl 400.00
126 BP,I'm a Cop 125.00
127 BP,Great Western 200.00
128 BP,I'm a Cop 150.00
129 The Avenger 500.00
130 BP,Strongman 275.00
131 BP,The Avenger 350.00
132 Strongman 225.00
133 BP,The Avenger 350.00
134 Strongman 225.00
135 White Indian 150.00
136 Hot Dog. 75.00
137 BP,Africa 300.00
138 BP,Avenger 350.00
139 BP,Strongman, 1955 . . . . 225.00

ABBIE AN' SLATS

United Features Syndicate,
March–Aug., 1948

1 RvB(c) 200.00
2 RvB(c) 175.00
3 RvB(c) 125.00
4 Aug., 1948 . . . . 125.00
N# 1940,Earlier Issue 450.00
N# 400.00

ABBOTT AND COSTELLO

St. John Publishing Co.,
Feb., 1948

1 PP(c), Waltz Time 750.00
2 Jungle Girl and Snake(c). 375.00
3 Outer Space (c) 250.00
4 MD, Circus (c) 225.00
5 MD,Bull Fighting (c) 225.00
6 MD,Harem (c) 225.00
7 MD,Opera (c) 225.00
8 MD,Pirates (c) 225.00
9 MD,Polar Bear (c) 225.00
10 MD,PP(c),Son of Sinbad tale . 275.00
11 MD. 175.00
12 PP(c), Movie issue 200.00
13 Fire fighters (c) 175.00
14 Bomb (c) 175.00
15 Bubble Bath (c). 175.00
16 thru 29 MD . . . . @150.00
30 thru 39 MD . . . . @100.00
40 MD,Sept., 1956. . . . . 100.00
3-D #1, Nov., 1953. . . . . 400.00

ACE COMICS

David McKay Publications,
April, 1937

1 JM, F:Katzenjammer Kids . . 4,500.00
2 JM, A:Blondie 1,200.00
3 JM, A:Believe It Or Not 875.00

All comics prices listed are for *Near Mint* condition.

4 JM, F:Katzenjammer Kids 850.00
5 JM, A:Believe It Or Not 850.00
6 JM, A:Blondie. 600.00
7 JM, A:Believe It Or Not 600.00
8 JM, A:Jungle Jim 600.00
9 JM, A:Blondie. 600.00
10 JM, F:Katzenjammer Kids. . . . 575.00
11 I:The Phantom series 1,100.00
12 A:Blondie, Jungle Jim 475.00
13 A:Ripley's Believe It Or Not . 450.00
14 A:Blondie, Jungle Jim 450.00
15 A:Blondie. 425.00
16 F:Katzenjammer Kids 425.00
17 A:Blondie. 425.00
18 A:Ripley's Believe It Or Not . . 425.00
19 F:Katzenjammer Kids 425.00
20 A:Jungle Jim 425.00
21 A:Blondie. 400.00
22 A:Jungle Jim 400.00
23 F:Katzenjammer Kids 400.00
24 A:Blondie. 400.00
25 . . . . 400.00
26 O:Prince Valiant. 1,400.00
27 thru 36. . . . . @400.00
37 Krazy Kat Ends. 300.00
38 thru 40. . . . . @275.00
41!s>thru 59. . . . . @225.00
60 thru 69. . . . . @200.00
70 thru 79. . . . . @150.00
80 thru 89. . . . . @150.00
90 thru 99. . . . . @125.00
100 . . . . 150.00
101 thru 109. . . . . @125.00
110 thru 119 . . . . @100.00
120 thru 143. . . . . @100.00
144 Phantom covers begin 125.00
145 thru 150. . . . . @100.00
151 Oct.–Nov., 1949 . . . . 125.00

ACES HIGH
E.C. Comics, March–April, 1955
1 GE(a&c),JDa,WW,BK 325.00
2 GE(a&c),JDa,WW,BK 200.00
3 GE(a&c),JDa,WW,BK 175.00
4 GE(a&c),JDa,WW,BK 175.00
5 GE(c),JDa,WW,BK,
  Nov.–Dec., 1955 . . . . 175.00

ADVENTURES INTO DARKNESS
Standard Publications, Aug., 1952
5 JK(c), ATh 500.00
6 GT, JK 325.00
7 JK(c) 325.00
8 ATh. 325.00
9 JK,ATh 325.00
10 JK,ATh,MSy 300.00
11 JK,ATh,MSy 300.00
12 JK,ATh,MYs 300.00
13 Cannibalism feature 350.00
14 . . . . 200.00

ADVENTURES INTO THE UNKNOWN!
American Comics Group, Fall 1948
1 FG, Haunted House (c). 3,000.00
2 Haunted Island (c) 1,000.00
3 AF, Sarcophagus (c) 1,000.00
4 Monsters (c). 500.00
5 Monsters (c). 500.00
6 Giant Hands (c) 400.00
7 Skeleton Pirate (c). 400.00
8 Horror. 400.00
9 Snow Monster 400.00
10 Red Bats. 400.00

Adventures Into the Unknown #39
© American Comics Group

11 Death Shadow 400.00
12 OW(c) 400.00
13 OW(c),Dinosaur 325.00
14 OW(c),Cave 325.00
15 Red Demons. 325.00
16 . . . . 325.00
17 OW(c),The Thing Type 400.00
18 OW(c),Wolves. 325.00
19 OW(c),Graveyard 325.00
20 OW(c),Graveyard 325.00
21 Bats and Dracula 275.00
22 Death 275.00
23 Bats. 275.00
24 . . . . 275.00
25 . . . . 275.00
26 . . . . 275.00
27 AW 350.00
28 thru 37. . . . . @275.00
38 A-Bomb 300.00
39 thru 49. . . . . @225.00
50 . . . . 225.00
51 Lazarus 450.00
52 Lazarus, 3-Dish. 425.00
53 thru 55. . . . . @425.00
56 Lazarus 425.00
57 . . . . 425.00
58 Lazarus 425.00
59 3-Dish 325.00
60 . . . . 175.00
61 . . . . 175.00
62 thru 69. . . . . @125.00
70 thru 79. . . . . @125.00
80 thru 90. . . . . @100.00
91 AW 125.00
92 thru 95. . . . . @75.00
96 AW 125.00
97 thru 99 . . . . @75.00
100 JB 90.00
101 thru 106. . . . . @75.00
107 AW 125.00
108 thru 115 . . . . @75.00
116 AW,AT 125.00
117 thru 127 . . . . @75.00
128 AW,Forbidden Worlds 75.00
129 thru 151 . . . . @75.00
152 JCr 75.00
153 A:Magic Agent. 75.00
154 O:Nemesis 90.00
155 Nemesis 60.00
156 A:Magic Agent. 60.00
157 thru 167. . . . . @65.00
168 JB,SD, Nemesis. 65.00
169 Nemesis vs. Hitler. 75.00
170 thru 174, Aug., 1967 . . . . . @60.00

ADVENTURES IN WONDERLAND
Lev Gleason Publications, April, 1955
1 . . . . 125.00
2 . . . . 75.00
3 . . . . 60.00
4 . . . . 60.00
5 Christmas. 75.00

ADVENTURES OF MIGHTY MOUSE
St. John Publishing Co., Nov., 1951
1 Mighty Mouse Adventures 350.00
2 Menace of the Deep 300.00
3 Storm Clouds of Mystery 200.00
4 Thought Control Machine 200.00
5 Jungle Peril 200.00
6 'The Vine of Destruction' 125.00
7 Space Ship(c) 125.00
8 Charging Alien(c). 125.00
9 Meteor(c) 100.00
10 'Revolt at the Zoo'. 100.00
11 Jungle(c) 100.00
12 A:Freezing Terror 100.00
13 A:Visitor from Outer Space . . 100.00
14 V:Cat. 100.00
15 . . . . 100.00
16 . . . . 100.00
17 . . . . 100.00
18 May, 1955 . . . . 100.00

AGGIE MACK
Four Star Comics/ Superior Comics, Jan., 1948
1 AF,HR(c),Johnny Prep 450.00
2 JK(c) 225.00
3 AF,JK(c) 225.00
4 AF, Johnny Prep 300.00
5 AF,JK(c). 225.00
6 AF,JK(c) 200.00
7 AF,Burt Lancaster on cover . . . 225.00
8 AF,JK(c), Aug., 1949 . . . . 200.00

BILL BARNES, AMERICA'S AIR ACE
Street and Smith Publications, July, 1940
1 (Bill Barnes Comics) 1,100.00
2 Second Battle Valley Forge . . . 600.00
3 A:Aviation Cadets 450.00
4 Shotdown(c). 450.00
5 A:Air Warden, Danny Hawk . . . 450.00
6 A:Danny Hawk,RocketRodney. 400.00
7 How to defeat the Japanese . . 400.00
8 Ghost Ship. 400.00
9 Flying Tigers, John Wayne . . . 425.00
10 I:Roane Waring. 400.00
11 Flying Tigers 400.00
12 War Workers. 400.00
Becomes:

AIR ACE
Jan., 1944
2-1 Invades Germany 500.00
2-2 Jungle Warfare 450.00
2-3 A:The Four Musketeers 200.00
2-4 A:Russell Swann. 200.00
2-5 A:The Four Musketeers 200.00
2-6 Raft(c). 200.00
2-7 BP, What's New In Science . 200.00
2-8 XP-59 . . . . 200.00
2-9 The Northrop P-61 . . . . 200.00
2-10 NCG-14 . . . . 200.00
2-11 Whip Lanch. 200.00

GOLDEN AGE

2-12 PP(c).	200.00
3-1	150.00
3-2 Atom and It's Future	150.00
3-3 Flying in the Future.	150.00
3-4 How Fast Can We Fly	150.00
3-5 REv(c).	150.00
3-6 V:Wolves.	150.00
3-7 BP(c), Vortex of Atom Bomb	300.00
3-8 BP,Feb.–March, 1947	175.00

AIRBOY
See: AIR FIGHTERS COMICS

Airfighters #10
© Hillman Periodicals

AIR FIGHTERS COMICS
Hillman Periodicals, Nov., 1941

1 I:Black Commander (only App)	3,000.00
2 O:Airboy A:Sky Wolf	5,000.00
3 O:Sky Wolf and Heap	2,500.00
4 A:Black Angel, Iron Ace	1,800.00
5 A:Sky Wolf and Iron Ace.	1,450.00
6 Airboy's Bird Plane	1,700.00
7 Airboy battles Kultur	1,600.00
8 A:Skinny McGinty	1,100.00
9 A:Black Prince, Hatchet Man	1,100.00
10 I:The Stinger	1,100.00
11 Kida(c)	1,100.00
12 A:Misery	1,100.00
2-1 A:Flying Dutchman	1,200.00
2-2 I:Valkyrie	1,450.00
2-3 Story Panels (c)	850.00
2-4 V:Japanese	850.00
2-5 Air Boy in Tokyo.	850.00
2-6 'Dance of Death'	850.00
2-7 A:Valkyrie	850.00
2-8 Airboy Battles Japanese	850.00
2-9 Airboy Battles Japanese	850.00
2-10 O:Skywolf	1,000.00

Becomes:

AIRBOY COMICS
Dec., 1945

2-11	1,000.00
2-12 A:Valkyrie	650.00
3-1	500.00
3-2	500.00
3-3 Never published	
3-4 I:The Heap	450.00
3-5 Airboy	375.00
3-6 A:Valykrie	375.00
3-7 AMc,Witch Hunt	375.00
3-8 A:Condor.	400.00
3-9 O:The Heap	425.00

3-10	350.00
3-11	350.00
3-12 Airboy missing	500.00
4-1 Elephant in chains (c).	425.00
4-2 I:Rackman	300.00
4-3 Airboy profits on name	300.00
4-4 S&K	350.00
4-5 S&K,The American Miracle	325.00
4-6 S&K,A:Heap and Flying Fool.	325.00
4-7 S&K	325.00
4-8 S&K,Girlfriend captured	325.00
4-9 S&K,Airboy in quick sand.	325.00
4-10 S&K,A:Valkyrie	325.00
4-11 S&K,A:Frenchy	325.00
4-12 FBe	350.00
5-1 LSt	225.00
5-2 I:Wild Horse of Calabra	225.00
5-3	225.00
5-4 Cl	225.00
5-5 Skull on cover.	225.00
5-6.	225.00
5-7.	225.00
5-8 Bondage (c)	225.00
5-9 Zoi,Row	225.00
5-10 A:Valykrie,O:The Heap	250.00
5-11 Airboy vs. The Rats.	225.00
5-12 BK,Rat Army captures Airboy	225.00
6-1	225.00
6-2.	225.00
6-3.	225.00
6-4 Airboy boxes.	275.00
6-5 A:The Ice People	225.00
6-6	225.00
6-7 Airboy vs. Chemical Giant	225.00
6-8 O:The Heap	235.00
6-9	225.00
6-10	225.00
6-11	225.00
6-12	225.00
7-1	200.00
7-2 BP.	200.00
7-3 BP.	200.00
7-4 I:Monsters of the Ice.	200.00
7-5 V:Monsters of the Ice	200.00
7-6	200.00
7-7 Mystery of the Sargasso Sea	200.00
7-8 A:Centaur	200.00
7-9 I:Men of the Starlight Robot.	200.00
7-10 O:The Heap	200.00
7-11	200.00
7-12 Airboy visits India	200.00
8-1 BP,A:Outcast and Polo Bandits.	200.00
8-2 BP,Suicide Dive (c).	200.00
8-3 BK, I:The Living Fuse	200.00
8-4 A:Death Merchants of the Air	210.00
8-5 A:Great Plane from Nowhere	200.00
8-6	200.00
8-7	200.00
8-8	200.00
8-9	200.00
8-10 A:Mystery Walkers	200.00
8-11	200.00
8-12	225.00
9-1	175.00
9-2 A:Valkyrie	150.00
9-3 A:Heap (c).	150.00
9-4 A:Water Beast, Frog Headed Riders	175.00
9-5 A:Heap vs.Man of Moonlight	150.00
9-6 Heap (c)	150.00
9-7 Heap (c)	150.00
9-8 Heap (c)	175.00
9-9	175.00
9-10 Space (c)	175.00
9-11	175.00
9-12 Heap (c)	175.00

10-1 Heap (c)	175.00
10-2 Ships on Space	150.00
10-3	175.00
10-4 May, 1953	175.00

AL CAPP'S DOG PATCH COMICS
Toby Press, June, 1949

1	300.00
2 A:Daisy.	200.00
3	175.00
4 Dec., 1949	175.00

AL CAPP'S SHMOO
Toby Press, July, 1949

1 100 Trillion Schmoos	425.00
2 Super Shmoo(c).	325.00
3	325.00
4	300.00
5 April, 1950	300.00

AL CAPP'S WOLF GAL
Toby Press, 1951

1 Pin-Up	400.00
2 1952.	375.00

ALL-FAMOUS CRIME
Star Publications, May, 1951

1 LbC(c) (8).	250.00
2 LbC(c) (9).	400.00
3 LbC(c) (10).	225.00
4 LbC(c) (4) Law Crime	200.00
5 LbC(c) (5).	200.00

Becomes:

ALL-FAMOUS POLICE CASES
Feb., 1952

6 LbC(c)	225.00
7 LbC(c)	200.00
8 LbC(c) Marijuana	200.00
9 LbC(c)	175.00
10 thru 15 LbC(c).	@175.00
16 Sept., 1954	175.00

ALL GOOD COMICS
R. W. Voight/Fox Publ./ St. John Publ.

1 1946.	300.00
N# 1949	900.00

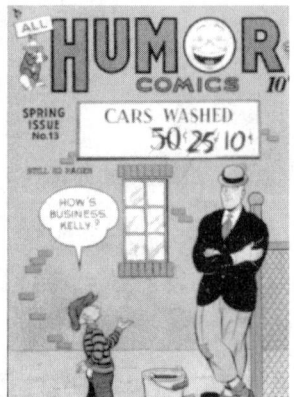

All-Humor Comics #13
© Quality Comics

ALL GREAT COMICS
See: DAGAR, DESERT HAWK

ALL HERO COMICS
Fawcett Publications, March, 1943
1 A:Capt. Marvel Jr.,Capt.
Midnight,Ibis, Golden Arrow
and Spy Smasher. 2,200.00

ALL HUMOR COMICS
Comic Favorites, Inc. (Quality Comics) Spring 1946
1 . . . . 250.00
2 PG Atomic Tot 125.00
3 I:Kelly Poole. 75.00
4 thru 7 . . . . @65.00
8 PG 65.00
9 . . . . 65.00
10 . . . . 65.00
11 thru 17 . . . . @55.00

ALL LOVE ROMANCES
See: SCREAM COMICS

ALL NEGRO COMICS
June,1947
1 . . . . 6,500.00

All-New Comics #10
© *Family Comics/Harvey Publications*

ALL-NEW COMICS
Family Comics (Harvey Publ.) Jan., 1943
1 A:Steve Case, Johnny Rebel
I:Detective Shane. 4,000.00
2 JKu,O:Scarlet Phantom 1,500.00
3 Nazi War 1,200.00
4 AdH 1,000.00
5 Flash Gordon 1,200.00
6 I:Boy Heroes and Red Blazer1,200.00
7 JKu,AS(c),A:Black Cat &
Zebra 1,200.00
8 JKu,A:Shock Gibson. 1,200.00
9 JKu,A:Black Cat 1,200.00
10 JKu,A:Zebra. 1,200.00
11 BP,A:Man in Black, Girl
Commandos. 1,200.00
12 JKu 900.00

13 Stuntman by S&K,
A:Green Hornet&(c) 1,100.00
14 BP,A:Green Hornet 850.00
15 Smaller size, Distributed
by Mail, March–April, 1947. 1,400.00

ALL TOP COMICS
William H. Wise Co., 1944
N# 132pgs.,A:Capt.
V,Red Robbins 375.00

ALL TOP COMICS
Fox Features Syndicate, Spring 1946
1 A:Cosmo Cat, Flash Rabbit . . . 300.00
2 . . . . 150.00
3 . . . . 100.00
4 . . . . 100.00
5 . . . . 100.00
6 . . . . 100.00
7 . . . . 100.00
7a 100.00
8 JKa(c),I:Blue Beetle 3,400.00
9 JKa(c),A:Rulah 1,800.00
10 JKa(c),A:Rulah. 1,900.00
11 A:Rulah,Blue Beetle 1,600.00
12 A:Rulah,Jo Jo,Blue Beetle . . 1,600.00
13 A:Rulah 1,600.00
14 A:Rulah,Blue Beetle 2,000.00
15 A:Rulah 1,600.00
16 A:Rulah,Blue Beetle 1,600.00
17 A:Rulah,Blue Beetle 1,600.00
18 A:Dagar,Jo Jo 1,000.00

Green Publ.
6 1957 Patoruzu the Indian 50.00
6 1958 Cosmo Cat. 50.00
6 1959 Atomic Mouse 50.00
6 1959 Little Eva 50.00
6 Supermouse (c) 50.00

ALLEY OOP
Argo Publications, Nov., 1955
1 . . . . 200.00
2 . . . . 150.00
3 March, 1956 . . . . 150.00

AMAZING ADVENTURE FUNNIES
Centaur Publ,. 1940
1 BEv,The Fantom of the Fair . 2,500.00
2 rep.After Fantoman. 1,500.00
Becomes:

FANTOMAN
Aug., 1940
2 The Fantom of the Fair. 1,700.00
3 . . . . 1,500.00
4 Red Blaze 1,500.00

AMAZING ADVENTURES
Ziff-Davis Publ., Co., 1950
1 MA,WW, Asteroid Witch 1,000.00
2 MA,Masters of Living Flame . . 500.00
3 Ma,The Evil Men Do 500.00
4 Invasion of the Love Robots . . 500.00
5 MA,Secret of the Crater-Men. . 500.00
6 BK,Man Who Killed a World . . 525.00

AMAZING GHOST STORIES
See: WEIRD HORRORS

AMAZING-MAN COMICS
Centaur Publications, Sept., 1939–Feb., 1942
5 BEv,O:Amazing Man. 24,000.00
6 BEv,FT,B:The Shark 5,000.00
7 BEv,I:Magician From Mars . . 3,200.00
8 BEv, Cat-Man as woman . . . 2,500.00
9 BEv,FT,A:Eternal Monster. . . 2,500.00
10 BEv,FT 1,800.00
11 BEv,I:Zardi 1,800.00
12 SG(c) 1,600.00
13 SG(c) 1,600.00
14 FT,B:Reef Kinkaid, Dr. Hypo 1,300.00
15 FT,A:Zardi 1,200.00
16 Mighty Man's powers
revealed 1,300.00
17 FT,A:Dr. Hypo 1,200.00
18 FT,BLb(a),SG(c). 1,200.00
19 FT,BLb(a),SG(c). 1,200.00
20 FT,BLb(a),SG(c). 1,200.00
21 FT,O:Dash Dartwell 1,300.00
22 A:Silver Streak, The Voice . . 1,600.00
23 I&O:Tommy the AmazingKid 1,100.00
24 B:King of Darkness,
Blue Lady 1,100.00
25 A:Meteor Marvin. 1,600.00
26 A:Meteor Marvin,ElectricRay 1,600.00

AMAZING MYSTERY FUNNIES
Centaur Publications, 1938
1 Skyrocket Steele in Year X . . 5,000.00
2 WE,Skyrocket Steele 2,500.00
3 . . . . 1,400.00
(#4) WE,bondage (c) 1,300.00
2-1(#5) 1,200.00
2-2(#6) Drug use. 1,100.00
2-3(#7) Air Sub DX 1,100.00
2-4(#8) Sand Hog 1,100.00
2-5(#9) 1,800.00
2-6(#10) 1,100.00
2-7(#11) Fantom of Fair, scarce 5,000.00
2-8(#12) Speed Centaur 1,900.00
2-9(#13) 1,100.00
2-10(#14) 1,100.00
2-11(#15)Robot(c). 1,100.00
2-12(#16) BW,I:Space Patrol . . 2,600.00
3-1(#17) I:Bullet 1,100.00
18 Fantom of Fair 1,100.00
19 BW,Space Patrol 1,300.00
20 . . . . 1,000.00
21 thru 24 BW,Space Patrol . @1,300.00

AMAZING WILLIE MAYS
Famous Funnies, 1954
1 Willie Mays(c) 1,100.00

AMERICAN LIBRARY
David McKay Publ., 1943
(#1) Thirty Seconds Over
Tokyo, movie adapt. 450.00
(#2) Guadalcanal Diary 350.00
3 Look to the Mountain 175.00
4 The Case of the Crooked
Candle (Perry Mason) 175.00
5 Duel in the Sun 175.00
6 Wingate's Raiders 175.00

AMERICA'S BEST COMICS
Nedor/Better/Standard Publications, Feb., 1942
1 B:Black Terror, Captain Future,
The Liberator,Doc Strange . 3,700.00
2 O:American Eagle. 1,500.00
3 B:Pyroman 1,100.00

4 A:Doc Strange, Jimmy Cole. . .	800.00
5 A:Lone Eagle, Capt. Future . . .	800.00
6 A:American Crusader.	750.00
7 A:Hitler,Hirohito	1,300.00
8 The Liberator ends	800.00
9 ASh(c),Fighting Yank	1,000.00
10 ASh(c),American Eagle.	700.00
11 ASh(c) Hirihito & Tojo(c). . . .	1,000.00
12 Red Cross (c)	700.00
13 Fighting Yank	700.00
14 Last American Eagle app	700.00
15 ASh(c),Fighting Yank	700.00
16 ASh(c),Fighting Yank	700.00
17 Doc Strange carries football .	700.00
18 Fighting Yank,Bondage(c). . . .	700.00
19 ASh(c),Fighting Yank	700.00
20 vs. the Black Market	700.00
21 Infinity (c)	700.00
22 A:Captain Future.	650.00
23 B:Miss Masque	750.00
24 Miss Masque,Bondage (c) . . .	750.00
25 A:Sea Eagle	500.00
26 A:The Phantom Detective. . . .	500.00
27 Pyroman,ASh(c)	500.00
28 A:Commando Cubs,	
Black Terror.	500.00
29 A:Doc Strange.	500.00
30 ASh(c).Xela.	500.00
31 ASh(c),Xela,July, 1949	500.00

AMERICA'S BIGGEST COMICS BOOK
William H. Wise, 1944

1 196 pgs. A:Grim Reaper, Zudo,	
Silver Knight, Thunderhoof,	
Jocko and Socko,Barnaby	
Beep,Commando Cubs.	500.00

AMERICA'S GREATEST COMICS
Fawcett Publications, Fall 1941

1 MRa(c),A:Capt. Marvel,	
Bulletman,Spy Smasher and	
Minute Man.	4,800.00
2 F:Capt. Marvel	2,000.00
3 F:Capt. Marvel	1,500.00
4 B:Commando Yank.	1,100.00
5 Capt.Marvel in 'Lost Lighting'	1,100.00
6 Capt.Marvel fires	
Machine Gun	1,000.00
7 A:Balbo the Boy Magician. . .	1,000.00
8 A:Capt.Marvel Jr.,Golden	
Arrow, Summer 1943	1,000.00

AMERICA IN ACTION
Dell Publishing Co., 1942

1	200.00

ANDY COMICS
See: SCREAM COMICS

ANGEL
Dell Publishing Co., Aug., 1954
(1) *see Dell Four Color #576*

2	40.00
3 thru 16	@25.00

ANIMAL ANTICS
Dell Publishing Co., 1946

1 B:Racoon Kids.	600.00
2	300.00
3 thru 10	@175.00
11 thru 23	@125.00

ANIMAL COMICS
Dell Publishing Co., 1942

1 WK,Pogo.	1,400.00
2 Uncle Wiggily(c),A:Pogo	700.00
3 Muggin's Mouse(c),A:Pogo . .	500.00
4 Uncle Wiggily(c).	350.00
5 Uncle Wiggily(c).	500.00
6 Uncle Wiggily	300.00
7 Uncle Wiggily	300.00
8 WK,Pogo	375.00
9 WK,War Bonds(c),A:Pogo . . .	400.00
10 WK,Pogo.	375.00
11 WK,Pogo.	225.00
12 WK,Pogo.	225.00
13 WK,Pogo.	225.00
14 WK,Pogo.	225.00
15 WK,Pogo.	225.00

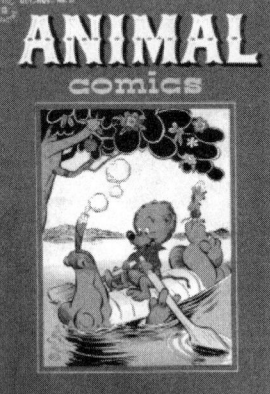

Animal Comics #17
© Dell Publishing Co.

16 Uncle Wiggily	150.00
17 WK,Pogo(c).	175.00
18 WK,Pogo(c).	175.00
19 WK,Pogo(c).	175.00
20 WK,Pogo.	150.00
21 WK,Pogo(c).	175.00
22 WK,Pogo.	125.00
23 WK,Pogo.	125.00
24 WK,Pogo(c).	135.00
25 WK,Pogo(c).	135.00
26 WK,Pogo(c).	135.00
27 thru 30 WK,Pogo(c)	@125.00

ANIMAL FABLES
E.C. Comics, July–Aug., 1946

1 B:Korky Kangaroo,Freddy Firefly	
Petey Pig & Danny Demon .	600.00
2 B:Aesop Fables	375.00
3	300.00
4	300.00
5 Firefly vs. Red Ants	300.00
6	300.00
7 O:Moon Girls,Nov.–Dec.1947 .	900.00

ANIMAL FAIR
Fawcett Publications, March, 1946

1 B:Captain Marvel Bunny,	
Sir Spot	325.00
2 A:Droopy, Colonel Walrus . .	175.00
3	125.00
4 A:Kid Gloves, Cub Reporter . .	125.00
5 thru 7	@125.00

8	100.00
9	100.00
10	100.00
11 Feb., 1947.	100.00

ANNIE OAKLEY & TAGG
Dell Publishing Co., 1953
(1) *see Dell Four Color #438*
(2) *see Dell Four Color #481*
(3) *see Dell Four Color #575*

4	250.00
5	200.00
6 thru 10	@150.00
11 thru 18	@125.00

ARCHIE COMICS
MLJ Magazines, Winter, 1942-43

1 I:Jughead & Veronica	22,000.00
2	4,500.00
3	3,500.00
4	1,800.00
5	1,800.00
6 Christmas issue	1,300.00
7 thru 10.	@1,400.00
11 thru 15	@900.00
16 thru 19.	@800.00

Archie Publications, 1946

20	850.00
21	550.00
22 thru 31.	@525.00
32 thru 42	@350.00
43 thru 50.	@225.00
51 A:Katy Keene	175.00
52 thru 64.	150.00
65 thru 70 A:Katy Keene	@150.00
71	100.00
72 thru 74 A:Katy Keene	@125.00
75 thru 99.	@75.00
100	100.00
101 thru 122.	@60.00
123 UFO,Vampire	50.00
124 thru 130.	@55.00
131 thru 145.	@35.00
146 thru 182.	@30.00
183 Caveman Archie	35.00
184	30.00
185 I:The Archies Band	40.00
186 thru 195	25.00
196 I:Cricket O'Dell	50.00
197 thru 200.	@30.00
201 thru 228.	@25.00
229 Lost Child	25.00
230 thru 260	15.00
261 thru 300.	@12.00

ARCHIE'S GIANT SERIES MAGAZINE
Archie Publications, 1954

1	1,700.00
2	1,000.00
3	700.00
4	650.00
5	650.00
6 thru 10	@500.00
11 thru 20	@300.00
21 thru 29	@175.00
30 thru 35	@125.00
136 thru 141	@125.00
142	125.00
143 thru 160	@75.00
161 thru 199	@50.00
200	45.00
201 thru 250	@25.00
251 thru 299	@15.00
300 thru 500.	@15.00

GOLDEN AGE

ARCHIE'S GIRLS
BETTY AND VERONICA
Archie Publications, 1950

1	2,500.00
2	1,200.00
3	650.00
4	600.00
5	600.00
6 thru 10	@500.00
11 thru 15	@400.00
16 thru 20	@350.00
21	275.00
22 thru 29	@250.00
30 thru 40	@200.00
41 thru 50	@175.00
51 thru 60	@125.00
61 thru 70	@110.00
71 thru 74	@100.00
75 Devil	200.00
76 thru 90	@75.00
91 thru 99	@65.00
100	75.00
101 thru 120	@50.00
121 thru 140	@35.00
141 thru 160	@30.00
161 thru 180	@25.00
181 thru 199	@25.00
200	28.00
201 thru 220	@15.00
221 thru 240	@18.00
241 thru 347	@15.00

ARCHIE'S JOKE
BOOK MAGAZINE
Archie Publications, 1953

1	1,200.00
2	650.00
3	500.00
15 thru 19	@300.00
20 thru 25	@175.00
26 thru 35	@150.00
36 thru 40	@125.00
41 1st NA art	300.00
42 & 43 TV Personalities	125.00
44 thru 48 NA	@150.00
49 thru 60	@60.00
61 thru 70	@35.00
71 thru 80	@30.00
81 thru 100	@30.00
101 thru 200	@20.00
201 thru 288	@15.00

ARCHIE'S MECHANICS
Archie Publications, 1954

1	1,200.00
2	650.00
3	500.00

ARCHIE'S PAL,
JUGHEAD
Archie Publications, 1949

1	2,000.00
2	1,000.00
3	600.00
4	550.00
5	550.00
6	400.00
7 thru 10	@325.00
11 thru 15	@250.00
16 thru 20	@175.00
21 thru 30	@125.00
31 thru 39	@100.00
40 thru 50	@100.00
51 thru 60	@65.00
61 thru 70	@65.00
71 thru 80	@45.00

81 thru 99	@40.00
100	40.00
101 thru 126	@30.00

Archie's Pals 'N' Gals #3
© Archie Publications

ARCHIE'S PALS
'N' GALS
Archie Publications, 1952–53

1	1,100.00
2	550.00
3	350.00
4	225.00
5	225.00
6	200.00
7	200.00
8 thru 10	@175.00
11 thru 15	@150.00
16 thru 20	@125.00
21 thru 30	@100.00
31 thru 40	@75.00
41 thru 50	@50.00
51 thru 60	@40.00
61 thru 70	@35.00
71 thru 80	@25.00
81 thru 99	@25.00
100	20.00
101 thru 120	@15.00
121 thru 160	@10.00
161 thru 224	@12.00

ARCHIE'S RIVAL
REGGIE
Archie Publications, 1950

1	1,100.00
2	500.00
3	375.00
4	350.00
5	350.00
6	275.00
7 thru 9	@250.00
10 thru 14 A: Katy Keen	@200.00
15	160.00
16 Aug., 1954	175.00

ARMY & NAVY COMICS
See: SUPERSNIPE
COMICS

ARROW, THE
Centaur Publications,
Oct., 1940–Oct., 1941

1 B:Arrow	4,500.00
2 BLB(c)	1,900.00
3 O:Dash Dartwell,Human Meteor, Rainbow, Bondage(c)	1,800.00

ATOMAN
Spark Publications, Feb., 1946

1 JRo,MMe,O:Atoman,A:Kid Crusaders	1,000.00
2 JRo,MMe	600.00

ATOMIC COMICS
Green Publishing Co.,
Jan., 1946

1 S&S,A:Radio Squad, Barry O'Neal	1,800.00
2 MB,A:Inspector Dayton, Kid Kane	900.00
3 MB,A:Zero Ghost Detective	600.00
4 JKa(c), July–Aug., 1946	600.00

ATOMIC COMICS
Daniels Publications,
1946 (Reprints)

1 A:Rocketman,Yankee Boy, Bondage (c),rep.	500.00

ATOMIC MOUSE
Capital Stories/
Charlton Comics,
March, 1953

1 AFa,O:Atomic Mouse	350.00
2 AFa,Ice Cream (c)	125.00
3 AFa,Genie and Magic Carpet (c)	100.00
4 AFa	100.00
5 AFa,A:Timmy the Timid Ghost	100.00
6 thru 10 Funny Animal	@75.00
11 thru 14 Funny Animal	@50.00
15 A:Happy the Marvel Bunny	60.00
16 Funny Animal,Giant	45.00
17 thru 30 Funny Animal	@35.00
31 thru 36 Funny Animal	@30.00
37 A:Atom the Cat	30.00
38 thru 40 Funny Animal	@25.00
41 thru 53 Funny Animal	@20.00
54 June, 1963	20.00

ATOMIC THUNDER
BOLT, THE
Regor Company, Feb., 1946

1 I:Atomic Thunderbolt, Mr. Murdo	900.00

AUTHENTIC
POLICE CASES
St. John Publ. Co., 1948

1 Hale the Magician	600.00
2 Lady Satan, Johnny Rebel	350.00
3 A:Avenger	600.00
4 Masked Black Jack	350.00
5 JCo	350.00
6 JCo,MB(c)	650.00
7 thru 10	@275.00
11 thru 15	@275.00
16 thru 23	@175.00
24 thru 28 Giants	@375.00
29 thru 38	@125.00

AVIATION AND MODEL BUILDING
See: TRUE AVIATION PICTURE STORIES

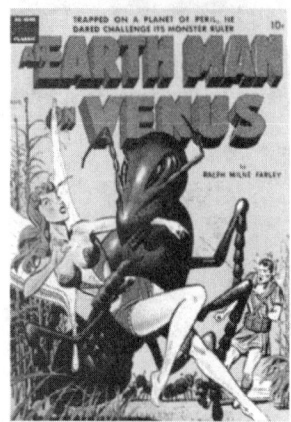

Avon One-Shot: An Earthman on Venus © Avon Periodicals

AVON ONE-SHOTS
Avon Periodicals, 1949-1953
{Listed in Alphabetical Order}
1 Atomic Spy Cases	400.00
N# WW,Attack on Planet Mars	1,100.00
1 Batchelor's Diary	450.00
1 Badmen of the West	450.00
N# Badmen of Tombstone	200.00
1 EK,Behind Prison Bars	375.00
2 Betty and Her Steady	125.00
N# EK,Blackhawk Indian Tomahawk War	225.00
1 EK,Blazing Sixguns	200.00
1 EK,Butch Cassidy	225.00
N# Chief Crazy Horse	235.00
N# FF,AW,EK,Chief Victorio's Apache Massacre	550.00
N# City of the Living Dead	600.00
1 Complete Romance	475.00
N# Custer's Last Fight	225.00
1 EK(c),Dalton Boys	225.00
N# GT(c),Davy Crockett	225.00
N# The Dead Who Walk	700.00
1 Diary of Horror,Bondage(c)	500.00
N# WW,Earth Man on Venus	1,800.00
1 Eerie, bondage (c)	1,000.00
1 EK,Escape from Devil's Island	500.00
N# EK,Fighting Daniel Boone	250.00
N# EK(c),For a Night of Love	375.00
1 WW,Flying Saucers	1,200.00
N# Flying Saucers	600.00
1 Going Steady with Betty	150.00
N# Hooded Menace	650.00
N# EK,King of the Badmen of Deadwood	175.00
1 King Solomon's Mines	500.00
N# EK(c),Kit Carson & the Blackfeet Warriors	100.00
N# EK,Last of the Comanches	200.00
N# EK,Masked Bandit	200.00
1 WW,Mask of Dr. Fu Manchu	1,300.00
N# EK,Night of Mystery	600.00
1 WW,JKu,Outlaws of the Wild West	400.00
1 JKu,Out of this World	1,000.00
N# EK,Pancho Villa	275.00
1 EK,Phantom Witch Doctor	600.00

1 Pixie Puzzle Rocket to Adventureland	150.00
1 EK,Prison Riot,drugs	375.00
N# EK,Red Mountain Featuring Quantrell's Raiders	350.00
N# Reform School Girl	2,000.00
1 Robotmen of the Lost Planet	1,500.00
N# JO,WW(c),Rocket to the Moon	1,500.00
N# JKu,Secret Diary of Eerie Adventures	2,500.00
1 EK,Sheriff Bob Dixon's Chuck Wagon	175.00
1 Sideshow	400.00
1 JKu,Sparkling Love	275.00
N# Speedy Rabbit	65.00
1 EK(c)Teddy Roosevelt & His Rough Riders	225.00
N# The Underworld Story	350.00
N# EK(c),The Unknown Man	350.00
1 EK,War Dogs of the U.S. Army	175.00
N# EK(c),White Chief of the Pawnee Indians	200.00
N# Women to Love	700.00

BABE
Prize/Headline Feature, June–July, 1948
1 BRo,A;Boddy Rogers	300.00
2 BRo,same	175.00
3 Bro,same	150.00
4 thru 9 BRo,same	@125.00

BABE RUTH SPORTS COMICS
Harvey Publications, April, 1949
1 BP	500.00
2 BP,Baseball	350.00
3 BP,Joe DiMaggio(c)	400.00
4 BP,Bob Feller(c)	325.00
5 BP,Football(c)	325.00
6 BP,Basketball(c)	325.00
7 BP	250.00
8 BP,Yogi Berra	325.00
9 BP,Stan Musial(c)	300.00
10	300.00
11 Feb., 1951	250.00

BANG-UP COMICS
Progressive Publ., 1941
1 CosmoMan, Lady Fairplay, O:Buzz Balmer	1,400.00
2 Buzz Balmer	750.00
3 Buzz Balmer	750.00

BANNER COMICS
Ace Magazines, Sept., 1941
3 B:Captain Courageous, Lone Warrior	1,500.00
4 JM(c),Flag(c)	900.00
5	850.00
Becomes:

CAPTAIN COURAGEOUS COMICS
March, 1942
6 I:The Sword	1,000.00

BARNYARD COMICS
Animated Cartoons, June, 1944
1 (fa)	225.00
2 (fa)	125.00
3 (fa)	75.00
4 (fa)	75.00
5 (fa)	75.00

6 thru 12 (fa)	@60.00
13 FF(ti)	85.00
14 FF(ti)	85.00
15 FF(ti)	85.00
16	60.00
17 FF(ti)	85.00
18 FF,FF(ti)	125.00
19 FF,FF(ti)	125.00
20 FF,FF(ti)	125.00
21 FF(ti)	60.00
22 FF,FF(ti)	125.00
23 FF(ti)	60.00
24 FF(ti)	125.00
25 FF,FF(ti)	125.00
26 FF(ti)	60.00
27 FF(ti)	60.00
28	40.00
29 FF(ti)	60.00
30 and 31	@30.00
Becomes:

DIZZY DUCK
32 Funny Animal	@75.00
33 thru 39	@40.00

BASEBALL COMICS
Will Eisner Productions, Spring, 1949
1 WE,A:Rube Rocky	1,000.00

BASEBALL HEROS
Fawcett Publications, 1952
N# Babe Ruth (c)	1,100.00

BASEBALL THRILLS
Ziff-Davis Publ. Co., 1951
10 Bob Feller Predicts Pennant Winners	600.00
2 BP, Yogi Berra story	400.00
3 EK, Joe DiMaggio story, Summer 1952	450.00

BATTLEFIELD ACTION
See: DYNAMITE

BEANY & CECIL
Dell Publishing Co., Jan., 1952
1	250.00
2	150.00
3	150.00
4	150.00
5	150.00

BEN BOWIE & HIS MOUNTAIN MEN
Dell Publishing Co., 1952
(1) *see Dell Four Color #443*
(2 thru 6) *see Dell Four Color*
7	125.00
8 thru 10	@60.00
11 I:Yellow Hair	75.00
12	40.00
13	40.00
14	40.00
15 thru 17	@40.00

BEST COMICS
Better Publications, Nov., 1939
1 B:Red Mask	1,200.00
2 A:Red Mask, Silly Willie	650.00
3 A:Red Mask	650.00
4 Cannibalism story, Feb., 1940	750.00

BEWARE
See: CAPTAIN SCIENCE

BIG CHIEF WAHOO
**Eastern Color Printing,
July, 1942**

1	500.00
2 BWa(c),Three Ring Circus	250.00
3 BWa(c)	200.00
4 BWa(c)	200.00
5 BWa(c),Wild West Rodeo	200.00
6 A:Minnie-Ha-Cha	150.00
7	125.00
8	100.00
9	100.00
10	125.00
11 thru 22	@100.00
23 1943	100.00

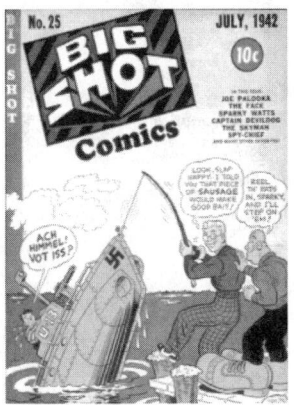

*Big Shot Comics #25
© Columbia Comics*

BIG SHOT COMICS
**Columbia Comics Group,
May, 1940**

1 MBi,OW,Skyman,B:The Face, Joe Palooka, Rocky Ryan	3,100.00
2 MBi,OW,Marvelo (c)	1,200.00
3 MBi,Skyman (c)	1,000.00
4 MBi,OW,Joe Palooka (c)	750.00
5 MBi,Joe Palooka (c)	650.00
6 MBi,Joe Palooka (c)	600.00
7 MBi,Elect Joe Palooka and Skyman	550.00
8 MBi,Joe Palooka and Skyman dress as Santa	550.00
9 MBi,Skyman	550.00
10 MBi,Skyman	550.00
11 MBi	500.00
12 MBi,OW	500.00
13 MBi,OW	500.00
14 MBi,OW,O:Sparky Watts	500.00
15 MBi,OW,O:The Cloak	600.00
16 MBi,OW	400.00
17 MBi(c),OW	400.00
18 MBi,OW	400.00
19 MBi,OW,The Face (c)	375.00
20 MBi,OW,OW(c),Skyman cov.	375.00
21 MBi,OW,A:Raja the Arabian Knight	350.00
22 MBi,OW,Joe Palooka (c).	350.00
23 MBi,OW,Sparky Watts (c)	300.00
24 MBi,OW,Uncle Sam (c)	500.00
25 MBi,OW,Hitler,Sparky Watts(c)	400.00
26 MBi,OW,Hitler,Devildog (c)	350.00
27 MBi,OW,Skyman (c)	350.00

28 MBi,OW,Hitler (c)	600.00
29 MBi,OW,I:Captain Yank	350.00
30 MBi,OW,Santa (c)	350.00
31 MBi,OW,Sparky Watts (c)	275.00
32 MBi,OW,B:Vic Jordan newspaper reps.	350.00
33 MBi,OW,Sparky Watts (c)	275.00
34 MBi,OW.	275.00
35 MBi,OW.	275.00
36 MBi,OW,Sparky Watts (c)	250.00
37 MBi,OW.	250.00
38 MBi,Uncle Slap Happy (c)	250.00
39 MBi,Uncle Slap Happy (c)	250.00
40 MBi,Joe Palooka Happy (c)	250.00
41 MBi,Joe Palooka.	225.00
42 MBi,Joe Palooka parachutes	225.00
43 MBi,V:Hitler.	350.00
44 MBi,Slap Happy (c).	225.00
45 MBi,Slap Happy (c).	225.00
46 MBi,Uncle Sam (c),V:Hitler	350.00
47 MBi,Uncle Slap Happy (c)	225.00
48 MBi	225.00
49 MBi	200.00
50 MBi,O:The Face	200.00
51 MBi	200.00
52 MBi,E:Vic Jordan (Hitler cov) newspaper reps.	275.00
53 MBi,Uncle Slap Happy (c)	175.00
54 MBi,Uncle Slap Happy (c)	175.00
55 MBi,Happy Easter (c)	175.00
56 MBi	175.00
57 MBi	175.00
58 MBi	175.00
59 MBi,Slap Happy	175.00
60 MBi,Joe Palooka.	175.00
61 MBi	150.00
62 MBi	150.00
63 MBi	150.00
64 MBi,Slap Happy	150.00
65 MBi,Slap Happy	150.00
66 MBi,Slap Happy	150.00
67 MBi	150.00
68 MBi,Joe Palooka.	150.00
69 MBi	150.00
70 MBi,OW,Joe Palooka (c)	150.00
71 MBi,OW.	155.00
72 MBi,OW.	155.00
73 MBi,OW,The Face (c)	155.00
74 MBi,OW.	155.00
75 MBi,OW,Polar Bear swim club (c).	155.00
76 thru 80 MBi,OW	@135.00
81 thru 84 MBi,OW	@135.00
85 MBi,OW,Dixie Dugan (c).	135.00
86 thru 95 MBi,OW	@125.00
96 MBi,OW,X-Mas (c)	125.00
97 thru 99 MBi,OW	@125.00
100 MBi,OW,Special issue.	150.00
101 thru 103 MBi,OW	@125.00
104 MBi, Aug., 1949	135.00

BIG-3
**Fox Features Syndicate,
Fall 1940**

1 B:BlueBeetle,Flame,Samson	3,000.00
2 A:BlueBeetle,Flame,Samson	1,200.00
3 same	900.00
4 same	800.00
5 same	800.00
6 E:Samson, bondage (c)	700.00
7 A:V-Man, Jan., 1942	700.00

BILL BARNES, AMERICA'S AIR ACE
See: AIR ACE

BILL BOYD WESTERN
Fawcett Publications, 1950

1 B:Bill Boyd, Midnite,Ph(c)	600.00
2 P(c)	300.00
3 B:Ph(c).	250.00
4	200.00
5	200.00
6	200.00
7	150.00
8	150.00
9	150.00
10	150.00
11	150.00
12	135.00
13	135.00
14	135.00
15 thru 21	@135.00
22 E:Ph(c)	135.00
23 June, 1952	150.00

BILL STERN'S SPORTS BOOK
**Approved Comics,
Spring-Summer, 1951**

1 Ewell Blackwell	250.00
2	200.00
2-2 EK Giant	250.00

BILLY THE KID ADVENTURE MAGAZINE
Toby Press, Oct., 1950

1 AW(a&c),FF(a&c)	375.00
2 Photo (c)	125.00
3 AW,FF	400.00
4	100.00
5	100.00
6 FF,Photo (c)	175.00
7 Photo (c)	100.00
8	100.00
9 HK Pot-Shot Pete	125.00
10	100.00
11	75.00
12	75.00
13 HK.	75.00
14 AW,FF	125.00
15 thru 21	@75.00
22 AW,FF	80.00
23 thru 29	@55.00
30 1955	65.00

BINGO COMICS
Howard Publications, 1945

1 LbC,Drug	500.00

BLACK CAT COMICS
**Harvey Publications
(Home Comics),
June–July, 1946**

1 JKu	950.00
2 JKu,JSm(c)	500.00
3 JSm(c)	350.00
4 B:Red Demon	350.00
5 S&K	475.00
6 S&K,A:Scarlet Arrow, O:Red Demon	475.00
7 S&K	475.00
8 S&K,B:Kerry Drake	400.00
9 S&K,O:Stuntman	475.00
10 JK,JSm	325.00
11	325.00
12 'Ghost Town Terror'.	325.00
13 thru 16 LEI	@300.00
17 A:Mary Worth, Invisible Scarlet	300.00
18 LEI.	300.00
19 LEI.	300.00

GOLDEN AGE

20 A:Invisible Scarlet	300.00
21 LEI	300.00
22 LEI thru 26	@300.00
27 X-Mas issue	275.00
28 I:Kit,A:Crimson Raider	275.00
29 Black Cat bondage (c)	260.00

Becomes:

BLACK CAT MYSTERY
Aug., 1951

30 RP,Black Cat(c)	375.00
31 RP	300.00
32 BP,RP,Bondage (c)	325.00
33 BP,RP,Electrocution (c)	300.00
34 BP,RP	250.00
35 BP,RP,OK, Atomic Storm	350.00
36 RP	325.00
37 RP	275.00
38 RP	275.00
39 RP	300.00
40 RP	275.00
41	275.00
42	275.00
43 BP	275.00
44 BP,HN,JkS,Oil Burning (c)	300.00
45 BP,HN,Classic (c)	500.00
46 BP,HN	275.00
47 BP,HN	275.00

Black Cat Mystery #48
© Harvey Publications

48 BP,HN	275.00
49 BP,HN	275.00
50 BP,Rotting Face	1,000.00
51 BP,HN,MMe	275.00
52 BP	175.00
53 BP	175.00

Becomes:

BLACK CAT WESTERN
Feb., 1955

54 A:Black Cat & Story	275.00
55 A:Black Cat	175.00
56 same	175.00

Becomes:

BLACK CAT MYSTIC
Sept., 1956

58 JK,Starts Comic Code	250.00
59 KB	225.00
60 JK	250.00
61 Colorama, HN	225.00
62	175.00
63 JK	200.00
64 JK	225.00
65 April, 1963	225.00

BLACK DIAMOND WESTERN
See: DESPERADO

UNCLE SAM QUARTERLY
Quality Comics Group,
Fall, 1941

1 BE,LF(c),JCo,O:Uncle Sam	5,500.00
2 LG(c),BE,Ray,Black Condor	1,800.00
3 GT(a&c)	1,400.00
4 GT,GF(c)	1,200.00
5 RC,GT	1,500.00
6 GT	1,200.00
7 Hitler, Tojo, Mussolini	1,500.00
8 GT	1,200.00

Becomes:

BLACKHAWK
Comic Magazines, Winter, 1944

9 Bait for a Death Trap	5,500.00
10 RC	1,800.00
11 RC	1,200.00
12 Flies to thrilling adventure	1,100.00
13 Blackhawk Stalks Danger	1,100.00
14 BWa	1,200.00
15 Patrols the Universe	1,100.00
16 RC,BWa,Huddles for Action.	1,000.00
17 BWa,Prepares for Action	1,000.00
18 RC(a&c),BWa,One for All and All for One	950.00
19 RC(a&c),BWa,Calls for Action	950.00
20 RC(a&c),BWa,Smashes Rugoth the ruthless God	950.00
21 BWa,Battles Destiny Written n Blood	650.00
22 RC(a&c),BWa,Fear battles Death and Destruction	650.00
23 RC(a&c),BWa,Batters Down Oppression	650.00
24 RC(a&c),BWa	650.00
25 RC(a&c),BWa,V:The Evil of Mung	650.00
26 RC(a&c),V:Menace of a Sunken World	600.00
27 BWa,Destroys a War-Mad Munitions Magnate	600.00
28 BWa,Defies Destruction in the Battle of the Test Tube	600.00
29 BWa,Tale of the Basilisk Supreme Chief	600.00
30 BWa,RC(a&c),The Menace of the Meteors	600.00
31 BWa,RC(a&c),JCo,Treachery among the Blackhawks	500.00
32 BWa,RC(a&c),A:Delya, Flying Fish	500.00
33 RC(a&c),BWa,A:The Mockers	500.00
34 BWa,A:Tana,Mavis	500.00
35 BWa,I:Atlo,Strongest Man on Earth	500.00
36 RC(a&c),BWa,V:Tarya	450.00
37 RC(a&c),BWa,V:Sari,The Rajah of Ramastan	450.00
38 BWa	450.00
39 RC(a&c),BWa,V:Lilith	450.00
40 RC(a&c),BWa,Valley of Yesterday	450.00
41 RC(a&c),BWa	400.00
42 RC(a&c),BWa,V:Iron Emperor	400.00
43 RC(a&c),BWa,Terror from the Catacombs	400.00
44 RC(a&c),BWa,The King of Winds	400.00
45 BWa,The Island of Death	400.00
46 RC(a&c),BWa,V:DeathPatrol	400.00
47 RC(a&c),BWa,War!	400.00
48 RC(a&c),BWa,A:Hawks of Horror,Port of Missing Ships	400.00

Blackhawk #13
© Comic Magazines

49 RC(a&c),BWa,A:Valkyrie, Waters of Terrible Peace	400.00
50 RC(a&c),BWa,I:Killer Shark, Flying Octopus	425.00
51 BWa,V:The Whip, Whip of Nonteton	400.00
52 RC(a&c),BWa,Traitor in the Ranks	400.00
53 RC(a&c),BWa,V:Golden Mummy	400.00
54 RC(a&c),BWa,V:Dr. Deroski, Circles of Suicide	400.00
55 RC(a&c),BWa,V:Rocketmen	400.00
56 RC(a&c),BWa,V:The Instructor, School for Sabotage	400.00
57 RC(a&c),BWa,Paralyzed City of Armored Men	400.00
58 RC(a&c),BWa,V:King Cobra, The Spider of Delanza	400.00
59 BWa,V:Sea Devil	400.00
60 RC(a&c),BWa,V:Dr. Mole and His Devils Squadron	400.00
61 V:John Smith, Stalin's Ambassador of Murder	325.00
62 V:General X, Return of Genghis Kahn	325.00
63 RC(a&c),The Flying Buzz-Saws	325.00
64 RC(a&c),V:Zoltan Korvas, Legion of the Damned	325.00
65 Olaf as a Prisoner in Dungeon of Fear	325.00
66 RC(a&c),V:The Red Executioner, Crawler	325.00
67 RC(a&c),V:Future Fuehrer	325.00
68 V:Killers of the Kremlin	300.00
69 V:King of the Iron Men, Conference of the Dictators	300.00
70 V:Killer Shark	300.00
71 V:Von Tepp, The Man Who could Defeat Blackhawk O:Blackhawk	350.00
72 V:Death Legion	300.00
73 V:Hangman,The Tyrannical Freaks	275.00
74 Plan of Death	275.00
75 V:The Mad Doctor Baroc, The Z Bomb Menace	275.00
76 The King of Blackhawk Island	275.00
77 V:The Fiendish Electronic Brain	275.00
78 V:The Killer Vulture, Phantom Raider	275.00
79 V:Herman Goering, The Human Bomb	275.00

80 V:Fang, the Merciless,
Dr. Death 275.00
81 A:Killer Shark, The Sea
Monsters of Killer Shark 275.00
82 V:Sabo Teur, the Ruthless
Commie Agent. 275.00
83 I:Hammmer & Sickle, V:Madam
Double Cross. 275.00
84 V:Death Eye,Dr. Genius,
The Dreaded Brain Beam . . . 275.00
85 V:The Fiendish Impersonator . 275.00
86 V:The Human Torpedoes 275.00
87 A:Red Agent Sovietta,V:Sea
Wolf, Le Sabre,Comics Code 225.00
88 V:Thunder the Indestructible,
The Phantom Sniper 225.00
89 V:The Super Communists. . . . 275.00
90 V:The Storm King, Villainess
who smashed the Blackhawk
team. 275.00
91 Treason in the Underground. . 275.00
92 V:The World Traitor. 275.00
93 V:Garg the Destroyer,
O:Blackhawk 250.00
94 V:Black Widow, Darkk the
Destroyer. 250.00
95 V:Madam Fury, Queen of the
Pirates 250.00
96 Doom in the Deep. 250.00
97 Revolt of the Slave Workers. . 250.00
98 Temple of Doom 250.00
99 The War That Never Ended . . 250.00
100 The Delphian Machine 275.00
101 Satan's Paymaster 225.00
102 The Doom Cloud 225.00
103 The Super Race 225.00
104 The Jet Menace 225.00
105 The Red Kamikaze Terror . . 225.00
106 The Flying Tank Platoon . . . 225.00
107 The Winged Menace 225.00
(Please see DC Listings)

BLACK HOOD
See: LAUGH COMICS

BLACK TERROR
Better Publications/
Standard, Winter, 1942-43
1 Bombing (c) 4,200.00
2 V:Arabs,Bondage(c) 1,600.00
3 V:Nazis,Bondage(c) 1,000.00
4 V:Sub Nazis. 875.00
5 V:Japanese 875.00
6 Air Battle 750.00
7 Air Battle,V:Japanese,
A:Ghost. 750.00
8 V:Nazis 750.00
9 V:Japanese,Bondage(c) 800.00
10 V:Nazis 750.00
11 thru 16. . . . . @700.00
17 Bondage(c) 750.00
18 ASh 600.00
19 ASh 600.00
20 ASh 600.00
21 ASh 700.00
22 FF,ASh 600.00
23 ASh 600.00
24 Bondga(c) 700.00
25 ASh 550.00
26 GT,ASh 550.00
27 MME,GT,ASh 550.00

BLAZING COMICS
Enwil Associates/Rural Home,
June, 1944
1 B:Green Turtle, Red Hawk,
Black Buccaneer 700.00
2 Green Turtle (c) 450.00

3 Green Turtle (c) 400.00
4 Green Turtle (c) 400.00
5 March, 1945 . . . . 400.00
5a Black Buccaneer(c),1955. . . . 250.00
6 Indian-Japanese(c), 1955 . . . . 250.00

BLONDIE COMICS
David McKay, Spring, 1947
1 . . . . 300.00
2 . . . . 150.00
3 . . . . 125.00
4 . . . . 125.00
5 . . . . 125.00
6 thru 10 . . . . @100.00
11 thru 15 . . . . @75.00

Harvey Publications
16 . . . . 100.00
17 thru 20. . . . . @75.00
21 thru 30. . . . . @50.00
31 thru 50. . . . . @40.00
51 thru 80. . . . . @35.00
81 thru 99. . . . . @35.00
100 . . . . 50.00
101 thru 124 . . . . @30.00
125 Giant 50.00
126 thru 135 . . . . @30.00
136 thru 140 . . . . @30.00
141 thru 163 . . . . @40.00

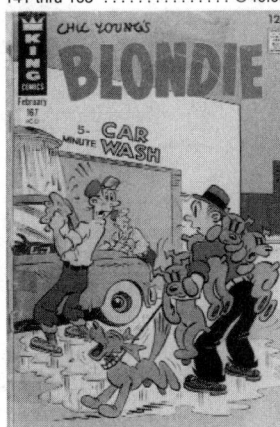
Blondie Comics #167
© King Publications

King Publications
164 thru 167. . . . . @25.00
168 thru 174. . . . . @15.00
Charlton Comics
175 thru 200. . . . . @15.00
201 thru 220. . . . . @15.00

BLUE BEETLE, THE
Fox Features Syndicate/
Holyoke Publ., Winter 1939
1 O:Blue Beetle,A:Master
Magician. 7,000.00
2 BP,Wonder World 2,200.00
3 JSm(c) 1,600.00
4 Mentions marijuana 1,200.00
5 GT,A:Zanzibar the Magician 1,000.00
6 B:Dynamite Thor,
O:Blue Beetle 1,000.00
7 A:Dynamo 900.00
8 E:Thor,A:Dynamo 900.00
9 BP(c),A:Black Bird,Gorilla 900.00
10 BP(c),A:BlackBird,bondage(c) 900.00
11 BP(c),A:Gladiator 750.00

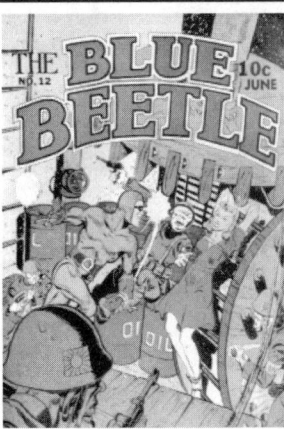
Blue Beetle #12
© Fox Features Syndicate

12 A:Black Fury 750.00
13 B:V-Man 900.00
14 JKu,I:Sparky 750.00
15 JKu 750.00
16 . . . . 600.00
17 AyB,A:Mimic 550.00
18 JKu,E:V-Man,A:Red Knight. . . 550.00
19 JKu,A:Dascomb Dinsmore . . . 600.00
20 I&O:The Flying Tiger
Squadron 650.00
21 . . . . 400.00
22 A:Ali-Baba. 400.00
23 A:Jimmy DooLittle 400.00
24 I:The Halo 400.00
25 . . . . 400.00
26 General Patton story. 425.00
27 A:Tamoa 400.00
28 . . . . 350.00
29 . . . . 350.00
30 L:Holyoke 350.00
31 F:Fox. 325.00
32 Hitler (c) 500.00
33 Fight for Freedom. 325.00
34 A:Black Terror,Menace of K-4 . 325.00
35 Threat From Saturn 325.00
36 The Runaway House 325.00
37 Inside the House. 325.00
38 Revolt of the Zombies. 325.00
39 . . . . 325.00
40 . . . . 325.00
41 A:O'Brine Twins 300.00
42 . . . . 300.00
43 . . . . 300.00
44 . . . . 300.00
45 . . . . 300.00
46 BP,A:Puppeteer. 350.00
47 JKa,V:Junior Crime Club . . . 1,700.00
48 JKa,A:Black Lace. 1,400.00
49 JKa. 1,400.00
50 JKa,The Ambitious Bride . . 1,400.00
51 JKa, Shady Lady 1,200.00
52 BP,JKa(c),Bondage (c) . . . 1,700.00
53 JKa,A:Jack "Legs"
Diamond,Bondage(c) 1,200.00
54 JKa,The Vanishing Nude . . . 1,800.00
55 JKa. 1,100.00
56 JKa,Tri-State Terror 1,100.00
57 JKa,The Feagle Bros. 1,100.00
58 . . . . 200.00
59 . . . . 200.00
60 Aug., 1960 . . . . 225.00

BLUE BEETLE
See: THING!, THE

Blue Bolt #20
© Star Publications

BLUE BOLT
Funnies, Inc./Novelty Press/
Premium Service Co, 1940

1 JSm,PG,O:Blue Bolt	5,000.00
2 JSm,S&K	2,500.00
3 S&K,A:Space Hawk	2,000.00
4 PG,S&K	1,800.00
5 BEv,B:Sub Zero	1,800.00
6 JK,JSm	1,600.00
7 S&K,BEv	1,600.00
8 S&K(c)	1,600.00
9	1,500.00
10 S&K(c)	1,500.00
11 BEv(c)	1,500.00
12	1,500.00
2-1 BEv(c),PG,O:Dick Cole & V:Simba	500.00
2-2 BEv(c),PG,O:Twister	400.00
2-3 PG,Cole vs Simba	300.00
2-4 BD	300.00
2-5 I:Freezum	300.00
2-6 O:Sgt.Spook, Dick Cole	250.00
2-7 BD,Lois Blake	225.00
2-8 BD	225.00
2-9 JW	225.00
2-10 JW	225.00
2-11 JW	225.00
2-12 E:Twister	225.00
3-1 A:115th Infantry	225.00
3-2 A:Phantom Sub	225.00
3-3	225.00
3-4 JW(c)	175.00
3-5 Jor	175.00
3-6 Jor	175.00
3-7 X-Mas (c)	175.00
3-8	175.00
3-9 A:Phantom Sub	175.00
3-10 DBa	175.00
3-11 April Fools (c)	175.00
3-12	175.00
4-1 Hitler,Tojo,Mussolini (c)	400.00
4-2 Liberty Bell (c)	135.00
4-3 What are You Doing for Your Country	135.00
4-4 I Fly for Vengence	135.00
4-5 TFH(c)	135.00
4-6 HcK	135.00
4-7 JWi(c)	135.00
4-8 E:Sub Zero	135.00
4-9	135.00
4-10	135.00
4-11	135.00
4-12	135.00
5-1 thru 5-12	@125.00

6-1	125.00
6-2 War Bonds (c)	125.00
6-3	125.00
6-4 Racist(c)	200.00
6-5 Soccer (c)	125.00
6-6 thru 6-12	@125.00
7-1 thru 7-12	@125.00
8-1 Baseball (c)	125.00
8-2 JHa	125.00
8-3 JHe	125.00
8-4 JHa	125.00
8-5 JHe	125.00
8-6 JDo	125.00
8-7 LbC(c)	250.00
8-8	125.00
8-9 AMc(c)	125.00
8-10	125.00
8-11 Basketball (c)	135.00
8-12	125.00
9-1 AMc,Baseball (c)	125.00
9-2 AMc	125.00
9-3	125.00
9-4 JHe	125.00
9-5 JHe	125.00
9-6 LbC(c),Football (c)	250.00
9-7 JHe	125.00
9-8 Hockey (c)	135.00
9-9 LbC(c),3-D effect	225.00
9-10	125.00
9-11	125.00
9-12	125.00
10-1 Baseball (c),3-D effect	135.00
10-2 3-D effect	135.00

Star Publications

102 LbC(c),Chameleon	450.00
103 LbC(c),same	400.00
104 LbC(c),same	400.00
105 LbC(c),O:Blue Bolt Space, Drug Story	700.00
106 S&K,LbC(c),A:Space Hawk	650.00
107 S&K,LbC(c),A:Space Hawk	650.00
108 S&K,LbC(c),A:Blue Bolt	650.00
109 BW,LbC(c)	650.00
110 B:Horror (c)s,A:Target	650.00
111 Weird Tales of Horror, A:Red Rocket	650.00
112 JyD,WiP	550.00
113 BW,JyD,A:Space Hawk	600.00
114 LbC(c),JyD	575.00
115 LbC(c),JyD,A:Sgt.Spook	600.00
116 LbC(c),JyD,A:Jungle Joe	600.00
117 LbC(c),A:Blue Bolt,Jo-Jo	600.00
118 WW,LbC(c),A:White Spirit	600.00
119 LbC(c)	600.00

Becomes:

GHOSTLY WEIRD STORIES
Star Publications, Sept., 1953

120 LbC,A:Jo-Jo	600.00
121 LbC,A:Jo-Jo	550.00
122 LbC,A:The Mask,Sci-Fi	600.00
123 LbC,A:Jo-Jo	500.00
124 LbC, Sept., 1954	500.00

BLUE CIRCLE COMICS
Enwil Associates/
Rural Home, June, 1944

1 B:Blue Circle,O:Steel Fist	350.00
2	250.00
3 Hitler parody (c)	300.00
4	200.00
5 E:Steel Fist,A:DriftwoodDavey	200.00
6	200.00

BLUE RIBBON COMICS
MLJ Magazines, Nov., 1939

1 JCo,B:Dan Hastings, Richy-Amazing Boy	5,500.00

2 JCo,B:Bob Phantom, Silver Fox	2,000.00
3 JCo,A:Phantom,Silver Fox	1,500.00
4 O:Fox,Ty Gor,B:Doc Strong, Hercules	1,600.00
5 Gattling Gun (c)	1,000.00
6 Amazing Boy Richy (c)	900.00
7 A:Fox (c),Corporal Collins V:Nazis	900.00
8 E:Hercules	900.00
9 O&I:Mr. Justice	4,000.00
10 Mr. Justice (c)	1,500.00
11 SCp(c)	1,500.00
12 E:Doc Strong	1,500.00
13 B:Inferno	1,500.00
14 A:Inferno	1,200.00
15 A:Inferno,E:Green Falcon	1,200.00
16 O:Captain Flag	2,500.00
17 Captain Flag V:Black Hand	1,200.00
18 Captain Flag-Black Hand	1,100.00
19 Captain Flag (c)	1,100.00
20 Captain Flag V:Nazis (c)	1,200.00
21 Captain Flag V:Death	1,100.00
22 Circus (c), March, 1942	1,100.00

BLUE RIBBON COMICS
St. John Publications, Feb., 1949

1 Heckle & Jeckle	100.00
2 MB(c),Diary Secrets	250.00
3 MB,MB(c),Heckle & Jeckle	100.00
4 Teen-age Diary Secrets	250.00
5 MB,Teen-age Diary Secrets	350.00
6 Dinky Duck	75.00

BO
Charlton Comics, June, 1955

1	75.00
2	75.00
3 Oct., 1955	75.00

BOB COLT
Fawcett Publications, Nov., 1950

1 B:Bob Colt,Buck Skin	500.00
2 Death Round Train	300.00
3 Mysterious Black Knight of the Prairie	225.00
4 Death Goes Downstream	225.00
5 The Mesa of Mystery	225.00
6 The Mysterious Visitors	225.00
7 Dragon of Disaster	200.00
8 Redman's Revenge	200.00
9 Hidden Hacienda	200.00
10 Fiend from Vulture Mountain	200.00

BOLD STORIES
Kirby Publishing Co., 1950

1 WW,Near nudity (c)	2,000.00
2 GI,Cobra's Kiss	1,500.00
3 WW,Orge of Paris	1,200.00
4 Case of the Winking Buddha	500.00
5 It Rhymes with Lust	500.00
6 Candid Tales, April, 1950	500.00

BOMBER COMICS
Elliot Publishing Co., 1944

1 B:Wonder Boy,Kismet, Eagle Evans	950.00
2 Wonder Boy(c) Hitler	750.00
3 Wonder Boy-Kismet (c)	500.00
4 Hitler,Tojo, Mussolini (c)	800.00

BOOK OF ALL COMICS
William H. Wise, 1945
1 A:Green Mask,Puppeteer 500.00

BOOK OF COMICS, THE
William H. Wise, 1945
N# A:Captain V 500.00

BOY COMICS
Comic House, Inc.
(Lev Gleason Publ.) April, 1942
3 O:Crimebuster,Bombshell,Young
　Robin, B:Yankee Longago,
　Swoop Storm 5,000.00
4 Hitler,Tojo,Mussolini (c) ... 2,000.00
5 Crimebuster saves day (c) . 1,500.00
6 O:Iron Jaw & Death of Son,
　B:Little Dynamite 4,000.00
7 Hitler,Tojo,Mussolini (c) ... 1,500.00
8 D:Iron Jaw 1,600.00
9 I:He-She 1,500.00
10 Iron Jaw returns.......... 1,800.00
11 Iron Jaw falls in love 1,200.00
12 Crimebuster V:Japanese 800.00
13 V:New,more terrible
　Iron Jaw................ 800.00
14 V:Iron Jaw................ 800.00
15 I:Rodent,D:Iron Jaw 1,000.00
16 Crimebuster V:Knight 500.00
17 Flag (c),Crimebuster
　V:Moth 500.00
18 Smashed car (c) 450.00
19 Express train (c) 450.00
20 Coffin (c) 450.00
21 Boxing (c) 300.00
22 Under Sea (c) 300.00
23 Golf (c) 300.00
24 County insane asylum (c).... 300.00
25 52 pgs.................. 300.00
26 68 pgs.................. 300.00
27 Express train (c) 325.00
28 E:Yankee Longago 325.00
29 Prison break (c) 325.00
30 O:Crimebuster,Murder (c) 400.00
31 68 pgs.................. 300.00
32 E:Young Robin Hood 300.00
33 .... 300.00
34 Suicide (c) & story 250.00
35 .... 225.00
36 .... 225.00
37 .... 225.00
38 .... 225.00

39 E:Little Dynamite.......... 225.00
40 .... 225.00
41 thru 50................. @200.00
51 thru 56................. @175.00
57 B:Dilly Duncan 200.00
58 .... 175.00
59 .... 175.00
60 Iron Jaw returns 200.00
61 O:Iron Jaw,Crimebuster 225.00
62 A:Iron Jaw............... 200.00
63 thru 70................. @150.00
71 E:Dilly Duncan 150.00
72 .... 150.00
73 .... 150.00
74 thru 79................. @150.00
80 I:Rocky X 100.00
81 thru 88................. @100.00
89 A:The Claw 120.00
90 same.................. 120.00
91 same.................. 120.00
92 same.................. 120.00
93 The Claw(c),A:Rocky X...... 120.00
94 .... 100.00
95 .... 100.00
96 .... 100.00
97 .... 100.00
98 A:Rocky X 100.00
99 .... 100.00
100 .... 125.00
101 .... 125.00
102 .... 125.00
103 thru 118............... @125.00
119 March, 1956 .... 125.00

BOY EXPLORERS
See: TERRY AND
THE PIRATES

BRENDA STARR
Four Star Comics Corp./
Superior Comics Ltd.,
Sept., 1947
13(1) 1,200.00
14(2) JKa,Bondage (c) 1,200.00
2-3 .... 1,000.00
2-4 JKa,Operating table (c).... 1,200.00
2-5 Swimsuit (c) 900.00
2-6 .... 900.00
2-7 .... 900.00
2-8 Cosmetic (c) 900.00
2-9 Giant Starr (c) 900.00
2-10 Wedding (c)............. 900.00
2-11 .... 900.00
2-12 .... 900.00

BRICK BRADFORD
Best Books
(Standard Comics)
July, 1949
5 .... 250.00
6 Robot (c) 400.00
7 AS 175.00
8 .... 175.00

BROADWAY ROMANCES
Quality Comics Group, 1950
1 PG,BWa(a&c)............. 425.00
2 BWa,Glittering Desire 300.00
3 BL,Stole My Love.......... 150.00
4 Enslaved by My Past........ 150.00
5 Flame of Passion,Sept.,1950 . 150.00

BRONCHO BILL
Visual Editions
(Standard Comics) Jan., 1948
5 .... 150.00

6 AS(c) 75.00
7 AS(c) 60.00
8 ASh 60.00
9 AS(c) 60.00
10 AS(c)................... 60.00
11 AS(c)................... 60.00
12 AS(c)................... 60.00
13 AS(c)................... 60.00
14 ASh 60.00
15 ASh 60.00
16 AS(c)................... 60.00

BRUCE GENTRY
Four Star Publ./
Visual Editions/
Superior, Jan., 1948
1 B:Ray Bailey reprints 650.00
2 Plane crash (c) 400.00
3 E:Ray Bailey reprints 350.00
4 Tiger attack (c) 300.00
5 .... 300.00
6 Help message (c) 300.00
7 .... 300.00
8 End of Marriage (c),July, 1949 300.00

BUCCANEERS
See: KID ETERNITY

BUCK JONES
Dell Publishing Co., 1950
1 Buck Jones & Horse Silver ... 200.00
2 .... 100.00
3 .... 75.00
4 .... 75.00
5 .... 75.00
6 .... 75.00
7 .... 75.00
8 .... 75.00

BUCK ROGERS
Eastern Color Printing,
Winter 1940
1 Partial Painted(c) 5,000.00
2 .... 2,000.00
3 Living Corpse from Crimson
　Coffin 1,500.00
4 One man army of greased
　lightning 1,400.00
5 Sky Roads 1,300.00
6 Sept., 1943 .... 1,300.00

All comics prices listed are for *Near Mint* condition.　　　　　**CVA Page 369**

Toby Press
100 Flying Saucers	350.00
101	300.00
9 MA	300.00

BUG MOVIES
Dell Publishing Co., 1931
1	400.00

BUGS BUNNY
DELL GIANT EDITIONS
Dell Publishing Co.
Christmas
1 Christmas Funnies (1950)	350.00
2 Christmas Funnies (1951)	300.00
3 Christmas Funnies (1952)	250.00
4 Christmas Funnies (1953)	200.00
5 Christmas Funnies (1954)	200.00
6 Christmas Party (1955)	175.00
7 Christmas Party (1956)	185.00
8 Christmas Funnies (1957)	185.00
9 Christmas Funnies (1958)	185.00
1 County Fair (1957)	200.00

Halloween
1 Halloween Parade (1953)	200.00
2 Halloween Parade (1954)	175.00
3 Trick 'N' Treat	
Halloween Fun (1955)	185.00
4 Trick 'N' Treat	
Halloween Fun (1956)	185.00

Vacation
1 Vacation Funnies (1951)	325.00
2 Vacation Funnies (1952)	275.00
3 Vacation Funnies (1953)	250.00
4 Vacation Funnies (1954)	200.00
5 Vacation Funnies (1955)	200.00
6 Vacation Funnies (1956)	175.00
7 Vacation Funnies (1957)	175.00
8 Vacation Funnies (1958)	175.00
9 Vacation Funnies (1959)	175.00

BUGS BUNNY
Dell Publishing Co., 1942
see Four Color for early years
28 thru 30	@85.00
31 thru 50	@60.00
51 thru 70	@40.00
71 thru 85	@35.00
86 Giant-Show Time	100.00
87 thru 100	@30.00
101 thru 120	@25.00
121 thru 140	@18.00
141 thru 190	@15.00
191 thru 245	@10.00

BULLETMAN
Fawcett Publications,
Summer, 1941
1 I:Bulletman & Bulletgirl	5,500.00
2 MRa(c)	2,200.00
3 MRa(c)	1,600.00
4 V:Headless Horror,	
Guillotine (c)	1,500.00
5 Riddle of Dr. Riddle	1,500.00
6 V:Japanese	1,100.00
7 V:Revenge Syndicate	1,100.00
8 V:Mr. Ego	1,100.00
9 V:Canine Criminals	1,100.00
10 I:Bullet Dog	1,200.00
11 V:Fiendish Fiddler	850.00
12	800.00
13	800.00
14 V:Death the Comedian	800.00
15 V:Professor D	800.00
16 VanishingElephant,Fall 1946	800.00

Buster Crabbe #7
© Famous Funnies

BUSTER CRABBE
Famous Funnies, Nov., 1951
1 The Arrow of Death	500.00
2 AW&GE(c)	550.00
3 AW&GE(c)	600.00
4 FF(c)	650.00
5 AW,FF(a&c)	1,500.00
6 Sharks (c)	225.00
7 FF	250.00
8 Gorilla (c)	225.00
9 FF	250.00
10	225.00
11 Snakes (c)	150.00
12 Sept., 1953	150.00

BUSTER CRABBE
Lev Gleason Pub., 1953
1 Ph(c)	250.00
2 ATh	225.00
3 ATh	225.00
4 F. Gordon(c)	225.00

BUZ SAWYER
Standard Comics, June, 1948
1	250.00
2 I:Sweeney	175.00
3	125.00
4	125.00
5 June, 1949	125.00

CALLING ALL BOYS
Parents Magazine Institute
Jan., 1946
1 Skiing	150.00
2 Roy Rogers Story	75.00
3 Peril Out Post	75.00
4 Model Airplane	75.00
5 Fishing	75.00
6 Swimming	75.00
7 Baseball	85.00
8 School	75.00
9 The Miracle Quarterback	75.00
10 Gary Cooper (c)	100.00
11 Rin-Tin-Tin (c)	75.00
12 Bob Hope (c)	150.00
13 Bing Crosby (c)	125.00
14 J. Edgar Hoover (c)	75.00
15 Tex Granger (c)	60.00
16	60.00
17 Tex Granger (c), May, 1948	60.00
Becomes:	

TEX GRANGER
June, 1948
18 Bandits of the Badlands	75.00
19 The Seven Secret Cities	65.00
20 Davey Crockett's Last Fight	55.00
21 Canyon Ambush	55.00
22 V:Hooded Terror	55.00
23 V:Billy the Kid	55.00
24 A:Hector, Sept., 1949	60.00

CALLING ALL GIRLS
Parent Magazine Press, Inc.,
Sept., 1941
1	175.00
2 Virginia Weidler (c)	100.00
3 Shirley Temple (c)	125.00
4 Darla Hood (c)	60.00
5 Gloria Hood (c)	60.00
6	60.00
7	60.00
8	60.00
9 Flag (c)	60.00
10	60.00
11 Gary Cooper as Lou Gerrig	75.00
12 thru 20	@50.00
21 thru 39	@40.00
40 Liz Taylor	175.00
41	40.00
42	40.00
43 Oct., 1945	40.00

CALLING ALL KIDS
Quality Comics, Inc.,
Dec./Jan., 1946
1 Funny Animal stories	125.00
2	60.00
3	45.00
4	45.00
5	45.00
6	45.00
7	45.00
8	45.00
9	45.00
10	45.00
11 thru 25	@40.00
26 Aug., 1949	40.00

CAMERA COMICS
U.S. Camera Publishing Corp.,
July–Sept., 1944
1 Airfighter,Grey Comet	250.00
2 How to Set Up a Darkroom	150.00
3 Linda Lens V:Nazi (c)	150.00
4 Linda Lens (c)	125.00
5 Diving (c)	125.00
6 Jim Lane (c)	125.00
7 Linda Lens (c)	125.00
8 Linda Lens (c)	125.00
9 Summer, 1946	125.00

CAMP COMICS
Dell Publishing Co., 1942
1 Ph(c),WK,A:Bugs Bunny	1,100.00
2 Ph(c),WK,A:Bugs Bunny	1,000.00
3 Ph(c),Wk	850.00

CAPTAIN AERO COMICS
Holyoke Publishing Co., 1941
1 B:Flag-Man&Solar,Master	
of Magic Captain Aero,	
Captain Stone	2,500.00
2 A:Pals of Freedom	1,200.00
3 JKu,B:Alias X,A:Pals of	
Freedom	1,200.00
4 JKu,O:Gargoyle,	
Parachute jump	1,200.00

5 JKu 1,000.00
6 JKu,Flagman,A:Miss Victory . . 900.00
7 Alias X 500.00
8 O:Red Cross,A:Miss Victory . . 500.00
9 A:Miss Victory,Alias X 425.00
10 A:Miss Victory,Red Cross 350.00
11 A:Miss Victory 300.00
12 A:Miss Victory 300.00
13 A:Miss Victory 300.00
14 A:Miss Victory 300.00
15 AS(c),A:Miss Liberty 300.00
16 AS(c),Leather Face. 275.00
17 LbC(c). 600.00
21 LbC(c). 600.00
22 LbC(c),I:Mighty Mite 600.00
23 LbC(c). 600.00
24 LbC(c) American Planes Dive
  Bomb Japan 900.00
25 LbC(c),Science Fiction(c) 550.00
26 LbC(c) 1,200.00

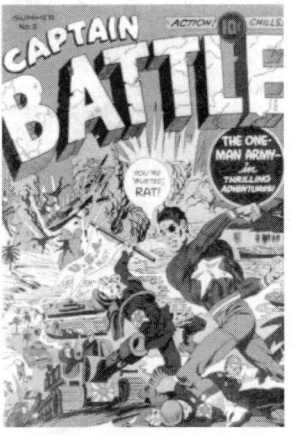

Captain Battle #5
© Magazine Press

CAPTAIN BATTLE
New Friday Publ./
Magazine Press, Summer, 1941
1 B:Captain Battle,O:Blackout 2,000.00
2 Pirate Ship (c) 1,200.00
3 Dungeon (c) 1,100.00
4 *.may not exist*
5 V:Japanese, Summer, 1943 . . 650.00

CAPTAIN BATTLE, Jr.
Comic House, Fall, 1943
1 Claw V:Ghost, A:Sniffer 1,800.00
2 Man who didn't believe
  in Ghosts 1,200.00

CAPTAIN COURAGEOUS
See: BANNER COMICS

CAPTAIN EASY
Standard Comics, 1939
N# Swash Buckler 1,500.00
10 . . . . 200.00
11 . . . . 150.00
12 . . . . 150.00
13 ASh(c). 150.00
14 . . . . 150.00
15 . . . . 150.00
16 ASh(c). 150.00
17 Sept., 1949 . . . . 150.00

CAPTAIN FEARLESS
COMICS
Helnit Publishing Co., 1941
1 O:Mr. Miracle,Alias X,Captain
  Fearless Citizen Smith,
  A:Miss Victory 1,200.00
2 A:Border Patrol, Sept.,1941. . . 750.00

CAPTAIN FLASH
Sterling Comics, Nov., 1954
1 O:Captain Flash 500.00
2 V:Black Knight 300.00
3 Beasts from 1,000,000 BC . . . 300.00
4 Flying Saucer Invasion 300.00

CAPTAIN FLEET
Approved Comics, Fall, 1952
1 Storm and Mutiny ...Typhoon . 175.00

CAPTAIN FLIGHT
COMICS
Four Star Publications,
March, 1944–Feb.-March, 1947
N# B:Captain Flight,Ace Reynolds
  Dashthe Avenger,Professor X 600.00
2 . . . . 300.00
3 . . . . 300.00
4 B:Rock Raymond Salutes
  America's Wartime Heroines . 300.00
5 Bondage (c),B:Red Rocket
  A:The Grenade 1,500.00
6 Girl tied at the stake 300.00
7 LbC(c),Dog Fight (c) 650.00
8 LbC(c),B:Yankee Girl,
  A:Torpedoman 650.00
9 LbC(c),Dog Fight (c) 650.00
10 LbC(c),Bondage (c) 650.00
11 LbC(c),Future(c). 1,500.00

CAPTAIN GALLANT
Charlton Comics, 1955
1 Ph(c),Buster Crabbe 125.00
2 . . . . 100.00
3 . . . . 100.00
4 Sept., 1956 . . . . 100.00

CAPTAIN JET
Four Star Publ., May, 1952
1 Factory bombing (c). 250.00
2 Parachute jump (c) 150.00
3 Tank bombing (c) 125.00
4 Parachute (c) 125.00
5 . . . . 125.00

CAPTAIN KIDD
See: ALL GREAT COMICS

CAPTAIN MARVEL
ADVENTURES
Fawcett Publications, 1941
N# JK, B:Captain Marvel &
  Sivana 45,000.00
2 GT,JK(c),Billy Batson (c). . . . 6,000.00
3 JK(c),Thunderbolt (c) 3,600.00
4 Shazam(c) 2,500.00
5 V:Nazis 2,000.00
6 Solomon, Hercules, Atlas, Zeus,
  Achilles & Mercury (c) 1,500.00
7 Ghost of the White Room. . . 1,500.00
8 Forward America. 1,500.00
9 A:Ibac the Monster, Nippo
  the Nipponese, Relm of
  the Subconscious. 1,500.00

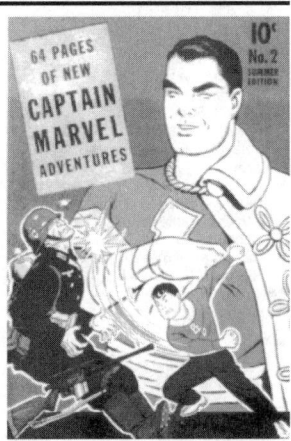

Captain Marvel Adventures #2
© Fawcett Publications

10 V:Japanese 1,500.00
11 V:Japanese and Nazis 1,200.00
12 Joins the Army 1,200.00
13 V:Diamond-Eyed Idol of
  Doom 1,200.00
14 Nippo meets his Nemesis . . 1,200.00
15 Big "Paste the Axis" contest. 1,200.00
16 Uncle Sam (c), Paste
  the Axis. 1,200.00
17 P(c), Paste the Axis. 1,100.00
18 P(c), O:Mary Marvel. 2,900.00
19 Mary Marvel & Santa (c) . . . 1,000.00
20 Mark of the Black
  Swastika 5,000.00
21 Hitler (c) 1,000.00
22 B:Mr. Mind serial,
  Shipyard Sabotage. 1,100.00
23 A:Steamboat 900.00
24 Minneapolis Mystery. 900.00
25 Sinister Faces (c) 900.00
26 Flag (c) 900.00
27 Joins Navy 750.00
28 Uncle Sam (c). 750.00
29 Battle at the China Wall 750.00
30 Modern Robinson Crusoe . . . 750.00
31 Fights his own Conscience. . . 750.00
32 V:Mole Men, Dallas. 750.00
33 Mt. Rushmore parody
  (c), Omaha 650.00
34 Oklahoma City 650.00
35 O:Radar the International
  Policeman, Indianapolis 600.00
36 Missing face contest,
  St. Louis. 600.00
37 V:Block Busting Bubbles,
  Cincinnati. 600.00
38 V:Chattanooga Ghost,
  Rock Garden City 600.00
39 V:Mr. Mind's Death Ray,
  Pittsburgh 600.00
40 V:Ghost of the Tower,Boston . 600.00
41 Runs for President, Dayton . . 500.00
42 Christmas special, St. Paul. . . 500.00
43 V:Mr. Mind,I:Uncle Marvel,
  Chicago 500.00
44 OtherWorlds,Washington,D.C. 500.00
45 V:Blood Bank Robbers 500.00
46 E: Mr. Mind Serial, Tall
  Stories of Jonah Joggins . . . 500.00
47 . . . . 450.00
48 Signs Autographs (c) 450.00
49 V: An Unknown Killer 450.00
50 Twisted Powers 450.00
51 Last of the Batsons. 400.00

GOLDEN AGE

GOLDEN AGE

52 O&I:Sivana Jr.,V:Giant
Earth Dreamer 400.00
53 Gets promoted 400.00
54 Marooned in the Future,
Kansas City 400.00
55 Endless String, Columbus . . . 400.00
56 Goes Crazy, Mobile 400.00
57 A:Haunted Girl, Rochester . . . 400.00
58 V:Sivana 400.00
59 . . . . 400.00
60 Man who made Earthquakes . 400.00
61 I&V: Oggar, the Worlds
Mightiest Immortal 425.00
62 The Great Harness Race 400.00
63 Stuntman 400.00
64 . . . . 400.00
65 V:Invaders from Outer Space . 400.00
66 Atomic War (c) 400.00
67 Hartford 350.00
68 Scenes from the Past,
Baltimore 350.00
69 Gets Knighted 350.00
70 Horror in the Box 350.00
71 Wheel of Death 350.00
72 . . . . 350.00
73 Becomes a Petrophile 350.00
74 Who is the 13th Guest 350.00
75 V:Astonishing Yeast Menace . 350.00
76 A:Atom Ambassador 350.00
77 The Secret Life 350.00
78 O:Mr. Tawny 375.00
79 O:Atom,A:World's Worst
Actor 400.00
80 Twice told story 800.00
81 A:Mr. Atom 300.00
82 A:Mr. Tawny 300.00
83 Indian Chief 300.00
84 V:Surrealist Imp 300.00
85 Freedom Train 350.00
86 A:Mr. Tawny 300.00
87 V:Electron Thief 300.00
88 Billy Batson's Boyhood 300.00
89 V:Sivana 300.00
90 A:Mr. Tawny 300.00
91 A:Chameleon Stone 300.00
92 The Land of Limbo 300.00
93 Book of all Knowledge 300.00
94 Battle of Electricity 300.00
95 The Great Ice Cap 300.00
96 V:Automatic Weapon 300.00
97 Wiped Out 300.00
98 United Worlds 300.00
99 Rain of Terror 300.00
100 V:Sivana,Plot against
the Universe 650.00
101 Invisibility Trap 275.00
102 Magic Mix-up 275.00
103 Ice Covered World of
1,000,000 AD 275.00
104 Mr. Tawny's Masquerade . . . 275.00
105 The Dog Catcher 275.00
106 V:Menace of the Moon 275.00
107 V:Space Hunter 275.00
108 V:Terrible Termites 275.00
109 The Invention Inventor 275.00
110 V:Sivana 275.00
111 The Eighth Sea 275.00
112 . . . . 275.00
113 Captain Marvel's Feud 275.00
114 V:The Ogre 275.00
115 . . . . 275.00
116 Flying Saucer 350.00
117 . . . . 275.00
118 V:Weird Water Man 275.00
119 . . . . 275.00
120 . . . . 275.00
121 . . . . 275.00
122 . . . . 275.00
123 . . . . 275.00
124 V:Discarded Instincts 275.00
125 V:Ancient Villain 275.00

126 thru 130 . . . . @275.00
131 . . . . 275.00
132 V:Flood 275.00
133 . . . . 275.00
134 . . . . 275.00
135 Perplexing Past Puzzle 275.00
136 . . . . 275.00
137 . . . . 275.00
138 V:Haunted Horror 325.00
139 . . . . 275.00
140 Hand of Horror 275.00
141 Horror 275.00
142 . . . . 275.00
143 Great Stone Face
on the Moon 275.00
144 thru 147 . . . . @275.00
148 V:The World 275.00
149 . . . . 275.00
150 Captains Marvel's Wedding,
Nov., 1953 . . . . 550.00

Captain Marvel Jr. #2
© Fawcett Publications

CAPTAIN MARVEL JR.
Fawcett Publications, 1942
1 MRa(c),O:Captain Marvel, Jr.,
A:Capt. Nazi 8,000.00
2 MRa(c),O:Capt.Nippon,
V:Capt. Nazi 2,800.00
3 MRa(c),Parade to
Excitement 1,800.00
4 MRa(c),V:Invisible Nazi 1,500.00
5 MRa(c),V:Capt. Nazi 1,400.00
6 MRa(c),Adventure of Sabbac 1,200.00
7 MRa(c),City under the Sea . 1,200.00
8 MRa(c),Dangerous Double . 1,200.00
9 MRa(c),Independence (c) . . 1,300.00
10 Hitler (c) 1,400.00
11 MRa(c) 1,000.00
12 MRa(c),Scuttles the Axis
Isle in the Sky 1,100.00
13 MRa(c),V:The Axis,Hitler,(c). 1,400.00
14 MRa(c),X-Mas (c), Santa wears
Capt. Marvel uniform 900.00
15 MRa(c),V:Capt. Nazi 1,000.00
16 MRa(c),A:Capt. Marvel,
Sivana, Pogo 850.00
17 MRa(c),Meets his Future self 850.00
18 MRa(c),V:Birds of Doom 850.00
19 MRa(c),A:Capt. Nazi &
Capt. Nippon 850.00
20 MRa(c),Goes on the Warpath 800.00
21 MRa(c),Buy War Stamps . . . 600.00
22 MRa(c),Rides World's oldest
steamboat 600.00

23 MRa(c) 600.00
24 MRa(c),V:Weather Man 600.00
25 MRa(c),Flag (c) 600.00
26 MRa(c),Happy New Year 600.00
27 MRa(c),Jungle Thrills 600.00
28 MRa(c),V:Sivana's Crumbling
Crimes 600.00
29 MRa(c),Blazes a Wilderness
Trail 600.00
30 MRa(c) 600.00
31 MRa(c) 400.00
32 Keeper of the Lonely Rock . . . 400.00
33 . . . . 400.00
34/35 I&O:Sivana Jr. 400.00
36 Underworld Tournament 400.00
37 FreddyFreeman'sNews-stand. 400.00
38 A:Arabian Knight 400.00
39 V:Sivana Jr., Headline
Stealer 400.00
40 Faces Grave Situation 400.00
41 I:The Acrobat 325.00
42 V:Sivana Jr. 325.00
43 V:Beasts on Broadway 325.00
44 Key to the Mystery 325.00
45 A:Icy Fingers 325.00
46 . . . . 325.00
47 V:Giant of the Beanstalk 325.00
48 Whale of a Fish Story 325.00
49 V:Dream Recorder 325.00
50 Wanted: Freddy Freeman . . . 325.00
51 The Island Riddle 300.00
52 A:Flying Postman 300.00
53 Atomic Bomb on the Loose. . . 325.00
54 V:Man with 100 Heads 300.00
55 Pyramid of Eternity 300.00
56 Blue Boy's Black Eye 300.00
57 MRa(c),Magic Ladder 300.00
58 Amazing Mirror Maze 300.00
59 MRa(c) 300.00
60 V:Space Menace 300.00
61 V:Himself 275.00
62 . . . . 275.00
63 V:Witch of Winter 275.00
64 thru 70 . . . . @275.00
71 thru 74 . . . . @275.00
75 V:Outlaw of Crooked Creek . . 275.00
76 thru 85 . . . . @275.00
86 Defenders of time 275.00
87 thru 89 . . . . @275.00
90 The Magic Trunk 225.00
91 thru 99 . . . . @225.00
100 V:Sivana Jr 275.00
101 thru 106 . . . . @225.00
107 The Horror Dimension 225.00
108 thru 118 . . . . @225.00
119 Condemned to Die, Electric
Chair, June, 1953 . . . . 225.00

CAPTAIN MIDNIGHT
Fawcett Publications, 1942
1 O:Captain Midnight,
Capt. Marvel (c) 5,000.00
2 Smashes Jap Juggernaut . . . 2,000.00
3 Battles the Phantom
Bomber 1,700.00
4 Grapples the Gremlins 1,500.00
5 Double Trouble in Tokyo . . . 1,500.00
6 Blasts the Black Mikado . . . 1,100.00
7 Newspaper headline (c) . . . 1,100.00
8 Flying Torpedoes
Berlin-Bound 1,000.00
9 MRa(c), Subs in Mississippi 1,000.00
10 MRa(c), Flag (c) 1,000.00
11 MRa(c), Murder in Mexico . . . 800.00
12 V:Sinister Angels 800.00
13 Non-stop Flight around
the World 800.00
14 V:King of the Villains 800.00
15 V:Kimberley Killer 800.00
16 Hitler's Fortress Breached . . . 800.00

All comics prices listed are for *Near Mint* condition.

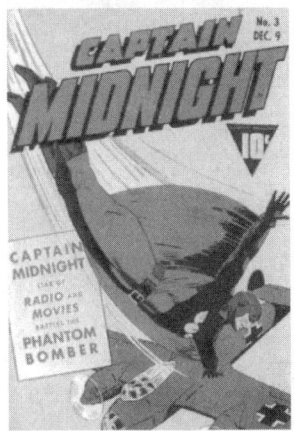

Captain Midnight #3
© Fawcett Publications

17 MRa(c), Hello Adolf. 750.00
18 Death from the Skies 750.00
19 Hour of Doom for the Axis . . . 750.00
20 Brain and Brawn against Axis 750.00
21 Trades with Japanese. 600.00
22 Plea for War Stamps. 600.00
23 Japanese Prison (c) 600.00
24 Rising Sun Flag (c). 600.00
25 Amusement Park Murder 600.00
26 Hotel of Horror 600.00
27 Death Knell for Tyranny 600.00
28 Gliderchuting to Glory. 600.00
29 Bomb over Nippon 600.00
30 . . . . 600.00
31 . . . . 450.00
32 . . . . 450.00
33 V:Shark. 450.00
34 thru 40. . . . . @450.00
41 thru 50. . . . . @350.00
51 thru 63. . . . . @350.00
64 V:XOG, Ruler of Saturn. 350.00
65 . . . . 350.00
66 V:XOG. 350.00
67 Fall, 1948 . . . . 350.00
Becomes:

SWEETHEARTS
Oct., 1948
68 Robert Mitchum 200.00
69 thru 110 . . . . @100.00
111 Ronald Reagan story 175.00
112 thru 118 . . . . @100.00
119 WW,Marilyn Monroe 600.00
120 Atomic Bomb story . . . . . . @125.00
121 Liz Taylor. 200.00
122 Marjuana,1954 . . . . 125.00

CAPTAIN SCIENCE
Youthful Magazines, 1950
1 WW,O:Captain Science,
   V:Monster God of Rogor . . 1,300.00
2 WW,V:Cat Men of Phoebus,
   Space Pirates 600.00
3 Ghosts from the Underworld   . 600.00
4 WW,Vampires 1,200.00
5 WW,V:Shark Pirates of
   Pisces. 1,200.00
6 WW,V:Invisible Tyrants,
   bondage (c) 700.00
7 WW,Bondage(c) Dec., 1951 . . 700.00
Becomes:

FANTASTIC
Feb., 1952
8 Isle of Madness 500.00
9 Octopus (c) 400.00
Becomes:

BEWARE
June, 1952
10 SHn,Doll of Death. 700.00
11 SHn,Horror Head 500.00
12 SHn,Body Snatchers 500.00
Becomes:

CHILLING TALES
Dec., 1952
13 MF,Screaming Skull 800.00
14 SHn,Smell of Death 500.00
15 SHn,Curse of the Tomb 600.00
16 HcK,Mark of the Beast
   Bondage(c) 450.00
17 MFc(c),Wandering Willie,
   Oct.,1953. . . . . 550.00

CAPTAIN STEVE SAVAGE
Avon Periodicals
[1st Series] 1950
N# WW 500.00
2 EK(c),The Death Gamble . . . 200.00
3 EK(c),Crash Landing in
   Manchuria 125.00
4 EK(c),V:Red Raiders from
   Siang-Po 100.00
5 EK(c),Rockets of Death 100.00
6 Operation Destruction 100.00
7 EK(c),Flight to Kill 100.00
8 EK(c),V:Red Mystery Jet 100.00
9 EK(c) 100.00
10 . . . . 100.00
11 EK(c) 110.00
12 WW 150.00
13 ThW 100.00
[2nd Series] Sept./Oct., 1954
5 . . . . 100.00
6 WW 125.00
7 thru 13 . . . . @75.00

CAPTAIN VIDEO
Fawcett Publications, 1951
1 GE,Ph(c) From TV series . . . 1,600.00
2 Time when Men could not
   Walk. 1,100.00
3 GE,Indestructible Antagonist 1,000.00
4 GE,School of Spies 1,000.00
5 GE,Missiles of Doom,
   photo (c) 1,000.00
6 GE,Island of Conquerors,
   Photo (c); Dec., 1951 . . . . . 1,000.00

CAPTAIN WIZARD
Rural Home, 1946
1 Impossible Man 400.00

CASPER, THE
FRIENDLY GHOST
St. John Publishing, 1949
1 O:Baby Huey 2,500.00
2 . . . . 1,100.00
3 . . . . 1,000.00
4 . . . . 800.00
5 . . . . 850.00
Harvey Publications
7 Baby Huey 600.00
8 thru 9 Baby Huey . . . . @300.00
10 I:Spooky 350.00
11 A:Spooky. 200.00

12 thru 18. . . . . @200.00
19 I:Nightmare 300.00
20 I:Wendy the Witch. 400.00
21 thru 30. . . . . @150.00
31 thru 40. . . . . @125.00
41 thru 50. . . . . @100.00
51 thru 60. . . . . @100.00
61 thru 69. . . . . @100.00
70 July, 1958 . . . . 100.00

CATMAN COMICS
Helnit Publ. Co./
Holyoke Publ. Co./
Continental Magazine, 1941
1 O:Deacon&Sidekick Mickey,
   Dr. Diamond & Ragman,A:Black
   Widow, B:Blaze Baylor. . . . 5,500.00
2 Ragman 2,000.00
3 B:Pied Piper 1,800.00
4 CQ 1,500.00
5 I&O: The Kitten 1,100.00
6 CQ 1,100.00
7 CQ 1,100.00
8 JKa, I:Volton 1,300.00
9 JKa 900.00
10 JKa,O:Blackout,
   B:Phantom Falcon. 900.00
11 JKa,DRi,BF,PzF 900.00
12 Volton 700.00
13 . . . . 1,200.00
14 CQ. 700.00
15 Rajah of Destruction 700.00
16 Bye-Bye Axis, Hitler. 1,100.00
17 Buy Bonds and Stamps 700.00
18 Buy Bonds and Stamps 700.00
19 CQ,Hitler,Tojo and
   Mussolini (c). 1,200.00
20 CQ,Hitler,Tojo and
   Mussolini (c) 1,200.00
21 CQ. 675.00
22 CQ. 675.00
23 CQ. 675.00
N# DRiV:Japanese,Bondage(c). . 700.00
N# V:Demon 675.00
N# LbC(c),A:Leather Face. 675.00
27 LbC(c),Flag (c),O:Kitten. . . 1,200.00
28 LbC(c),Horror (c) 1,200.00
29 LbC(c),BF,RP 1,200.00
30 LbC(c),BF,Bondage(c) 1,200.00
31 LbC(c) 1,200.00
32 LbC(c),RP,Aug., 1946 . . . . 1,200.00

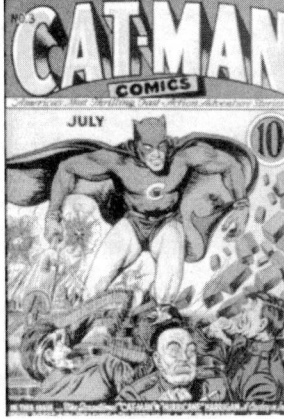

Cat Man Comics #3
© Continental Magazine

CHALLENGER, THE
Interfaith Publications, 1945
N# O:The Challenger Club 600.00
2 JKa 450.00
3 JKa 450.00
4 JKa,BF 450.00

CHAMBER OF CHILLS
**Harvey Publications/
Witches Tales, June, 1951**
21 (1) 650.00
22 (2) 350.00
23 (3) Eyes Ripped Out 350.00
24 (4) LE,Bondage (c) 400.00
5 LE,Shrunken Skull,
  Operation Monster......... 400.00
6 LE,Seven Skulls of Magondi . 350.00
7 LE,Pit of the Damned 350.00
8 LE,Formula for Death 375.00
9 LE,Bondage (c) 300.00
10 LE,Cave of Death 300.00
11 Curse of Morgan Kilgane ... 250.00
12 Swamp Monster 250.00
13 The Lost Race 325.00
14 LE,Down to Death. 300.00
15 LE,Nightmare of Doom..... 325.00
16 LE,Cycle of Horror 325.00
17 LE,Amnesia. 325.00
18 LE,Hair cut-Atom Bomb 350.00
19 LE,Happy Anniversary 300.00
20 Shock is Struck 300.00
21 LE,BP,RP,Decapitation 350.00
22 LE,Is Death the End? 325.00
23 LE,BP,RP,Heartline. 325.00
24 LE,BP,Bondage(c). 350.00
25 LE, ... 200.00
26 LE,HN,Captains Return 200.00
Becomes:

CHAMBER OF CLUES
Feb., 1955
27 BP,A:Kerry Drake 125.00
28 A:Kerry Drake 75.00

CHAMPION COMICS
Worth Publishing Co., 1939
2 B:Champ, Blazing Scarab, Neptina,
  Liberty Lads, Jingleman ... 2,500.00
3 .... 1,100.00
4 Bailout(c). 1,100.00
5 Jungleman(c) 1,100.00
6 MNe 1,100.00
7 MNe,Human Meteor 1,100.00
8 JK 2,000.00
9 JK,S&K. 2,000.00
10 JK,Bondage (c) 2,000.00
Becomes:

CHAMP COMICS
Oct. 1940
11 Human Meteor........... 1,200.00
12 Human Heteor 1,100.00
13 Dragon's Teeth.......... 1,000.00
14 Liberty Lads............ 1,000.00
15 RC,Liberty Lads......... 1,000.00
16 Liberty Lads 1,000.00
17 Liberty Lads............ 1,000.00
18 Liberty Lads 1,200.00
19 JSm,A:The Wasp........ 1,300.00
20 S&K,A:The Green Ghost ... 1,000.00
21 S&K................... 700.00
22 A:White Mask 750.00
23 Flag (c) 800.00
24 Hitler,Tojo & Mussolini...... 700.00
25 .... 700.00
26 thru 29................. @700.00

CHARLIE McCARTHY
Dell Publishing Co., 1947
1 Ph(c) 250.00
2 .... 125.00
3 .... 125.00
1 .... 125.00
2 .... 125.00
3 .... 125.00
4 .... 125.00
5 .... 125.00
6 .... 125.00
7 .... 125.00
8 .... 125.00
9 .... 125.00

CHIEF, THE
Dell Publishing Co., 1950
(1) *see Dell Four Color #290*
2 .... 100.00

CHILLING TALES
See: CAPTAIN SCIENCE

CHOICE COMICS
Great Comics, 1941
1 O:Secret Circle 2,200.00
2 .... 1,200.00
3 The Lost City 1,700.00

CHUCKLE THE GIGGLY BOOK OF COMIC ANIMALS
R. B. Leffing Well Co., 1944
1 .... 250.00

CINEMA COMICS HERALD
**Paramount/Universal/RKO/
20th Century Fox
Giveaways, 1941-43**
N# Mr. Bug Goes to Town 150.00
N# Bedtime Story 100.00
N# Lady for a Night,J.Wayne ... 200.00
N# Reap the Wild Wind 100.00
N# Thunderbirds 75.00
N# They All Kissed Me 75.00
N# Bombardier 90.00
N# Crash Dive 90.00
N# Arabian Nights............ 75.00

CIRCUS THE COMIC RIOT
Globe Syndicate, June, 1938
1 BKa,WE,BW 10,000.00
2 BKa,WE,BW 5,200.00
3 BKa, WE,BW, Aug., 1938 ... 4,500.00

CISCO KID, THE
Dell Publishing Co.
(1) *See Dell Four Color #292*
2 Jan., 1951 .... 200.00
3 thru 5 .... @175.00
6 thru 10 .... @150.00
11 thru 20 .... @125.00
21 thru 36 .... @100.00
37 thru 41 Ph(c)'s. .... @175.00

CLAIRE VOYANT
**Leader Publ./Visual Ed./
Pentagon Publ., 1946-47**
N# 900.00

2 JKa(c) 650.00
3 Case of the Kidnapped Bride . 800.00
4 Bondage (c) 650.00

CLOAK AND DAGGER
**Approved Comics
(Ziff-Davis), Fall, 1952**
1 NS(c),Al Kennedy of the Secret
  Service 350.00

Clue Comics #10
© Hillman Periodicals

CLUE COMICS
Hillman Periodicals, 1943
1 O:Boy King,Nightmare,Micro-Face,
  Twilight,Zippo........... 1,700.00
2 .... 1,000.00
3 Boy King V:The Crane...... 750.00
4 V:The Crane 600.00
5 V:The Crane 600.00
6 Hells Kitchen 375.00
7 V:Dr. Plasma,Torture(c) 375.00
8 RP,A:The Gold Mummy King . 350.00
9 I:Paris 350.00
10 O:Gun Master 350.00
11 A:Gun Master 350.00
12 O:Rackman. 350.00
2-1 S&K,O:Nightro,A:Iron Lady . 650.00
2-2 S&K,Bondage(c) 900.00
2-3 S&K 650.00
Becomes:

REAL CLUE CRIME STORIES
June, 1947
2-4 DBw,S&K,True Story of
  Ma Barker 650.00
2-5 S&K, Newface surgery(c) ... 500.00
2-6 S&K, Breakout (c) 500.00
2-7 S&K, Stick up (c) 500.00
2-8 Kidnapping (c) 125.00
2-9 DBa,Boxing fix (c) 125.00
2-10 DBa,Murder (c) 125.00
2-11 Attempted bankrobbery (c) . 125.00
2-12 Murder (c) 125.00
3-1 thru 3-12. .... @125.00
4-1 thru 4-12. .... @125.00
5-1 thru 5-12. .... @100.00
6-1 thru 6-12. .... @100.00
6-10 Bondage(c). 125.00
7-1 thru 7-12. .... @85.00
8-1 thru 8-5, May, 1953 .... @85.00

All comics prices listed are for *Near Mint* condition.

C-M-O COMICS
**Comic Corp. of America
(Centaur), May, 1942**
1 Invisible Terror 1,500.00
2 Super Ann 1,000.00

COCOMALT BIG BOOK OF COMICS
Harry A. Chesler, 1938
1 BoW,PGn,FG,JCo,(Give away)
  Little Nemo 3,000.00

COLOSSUS COMICS
**Sun Publications
March, 1940**
1 A:Colossus 8,000.00

COLUMBIA COMICS
William H. Wise Co., 1944
1 Joe Palooka,Charlie Chan . . . 350.00

COMICS, THE
**Dell Publishing Co.,
March, 1937**
1 I:Tom Mix & Arizona Kid 2,500.00
2 A:Tom Mix & Tom Beaty 1,200.00
3 A:Alley Oop 1,000.00
4 same 1,000.00
5 same 1,000.00
6 thru 11 same . . . . @1,000.00

COMICS ON PARADE
**United Features Syndicate,
April, 1938–Feb., 1955**
1 B:Tarzan,Captain and the Kids,
  Little Mary, Mixup,Abbie & Slats,
  Broncho Bill,Li'l Abner 5,000.00
2 Circus Parade of all 1,800.00
3 . . . . 1,300.00
4 On Rocket 1,000.00
5 All at the Store 1,000.00
6 All at Picnic 700.00
7 Li'l Abner(c) 700.00
8 same 700.00
9 same 700.00
10 same 700.00
11 same 600.00
12 same 600.00
13 same 600.00
14 Abbie n' Slats (c) 600.00
15 Li'l Abner(c) 600.00
16 Abbie n' Slats(c) 600.00
17 Tarzan,Abbie n' Slats(c) 650.00
18 Li'l Abner(c) 600.00
19 same 600.00
20 same 600.00
21 Li'l Abner(c) 500.00
22 Tail Spin Tommy(c) 500.00
23 Abbie n' Slats(c) 500.00
24 Tail Spin Tommy(c) 500.00
25 Li'l Abner(c) 500.00
26 Abbie n' Slats(c) 500.00
27 Li'l Abner(c) 500.00
28 Tail Spin Tommy(c) 500.00
29 Abbie n' Slats(c) 500.00
30 Li'l Abner(c) 300.00
31 The Captain & the Kids(c) . . . 200.00
32 Nancy and Fritzi Ritz(c) 175.00
33 Li'l Abner(c) 225.00
34 The Captain & the Kids(c) . . . 175.00
35 Nancy and Fritzi Ritz(c) 165.00
36 Li'l Abner(c) 225.00
37 The Captain & the Kids(c) . . . 175.00
38 Nancy and Fritzi Ritz(c) 150.00
39 Li'l Abner(c) 225.00

*Comics on Parade #9
© United Features Syndicate*

40 The Captain & the Kids(c) . . . 175.00
41 Nancy and Fritzi Ritz(c) 125.00
42 Li'l Abner(c) 225.00
43 The Captain & the Kids(c) . . . 175.00
44 Nancy and Fritzi Ritz(c) 125.00
45 Li'l Abner(c) 175.00
46 The Captain & the Kids(c) . . . 125.00
47 Nancy and Fritzi Ritz(c) 125.00
48 Li'l Abner(c) 175.00
49 The Captain & the Kids(c) . . . 125.00
50 Nancy and Fritzi Ritz(c) 125.00
51 Li'l Abner(c) 175.00
52 The Captain & the Kids(c) . . . 125.00
53 Nancy and Fritzi Ritz(c) 125.00
54 Li'l Abner(c) 175.00
55 Nancy and Fritzi Ritz(c) 125.00
56 The Captain & the Kids(c) . . . 125.00
57 Nancy and Fritzi Ritz(c) 125.00
58 Li'l Abner(c) 175.00
59 The Captain & the Kids(c) . . . 125.00
60 thru 76 Nancy &
  Fritzi Ritz(c) . . . . @100.00
77 Nancy & Sluggo(c) 75.00
78 thru 104 Nancy & Sluggo(c) . @75.00

COMPLETE BOOK OF COMICS AND FUNNIES
William H. Wise & Co., 1945
1 Wonderman-Magnet 500.00

COMPLETE BOOK OF TRUE CRIME COMICS
William H. Wise & Co., 1945
1 rep. Crime Does Not Pay . . . 1,500.00

CONFESSIONS OF LOVE
**Artful Publications,
April, 1950**
1 . . . . 300.00
2 July, 1950 . . . . 175.00

CONFESSIONS OF LOVE
Star Publications, July, 1952
11 AW,LbC(c)Intimate Secrets of
  Daring Romance 175.00
12 AW,LbC(c),I Couldn't Say No 175.00
13 AW,LbC(c),Heart Break 175.00
14 AW,LbC(c),My Fateful Love . 150.00
4 JyD,AW,LbC(c),The Longing
  Heart 150.00

5 AW,LbC(c),I Wanted Love 150.00
6 AW,LbC(c),My Jealous Heart. . 150.00
Becomes:

CONFESSIONS OF ROMANCE
Nov., 1953
7 LbC(c)Too Good 175.00
8 AW,LbC(c),I Lied About Love . 150.00
9 WW,AW,LbC(c),I Paid
  Love's Price 175.00
10 JyD,AW,LbC(c),My Heart Cries
  for Love 150.00
11 JyD,AW,LbC(c),Intimate
  Confessions, Nov., 1954 . . . . 150.00

CONFESSIONS OF LOVELORN
See: LOVELORN

CONQUEROR COMICS
**Albrecht Publications,
Winter, 1945**
1 . . . . 250.00

CONTACT COMICS
Aviation Press, July, 1944
N# LbC(c),B:Black Venus,
  Golden Eagle 700.00
2 LbC(c),Peace Jet 550.00
3 LbC(c),LbC,E:Flamingo 500.00
4 LbC(c),LbC 500.00
5 LbC(c),A:Phantom Flyer 550.00
6 LbC(c),HK 650.00
7 LbC(c),Flying Tigers 500.00
8 LbC(c),Peace Jet 500.00
9 LbC(c),LbC,A:Marine Flyers . . 500.00
10 LbC(c),A:Bombers of the AAF 500.00
11 LbC(c),HK,AF,Salutes Naval
  Aviation 600.00
12 LbC(c),A:Sky Rangers, Air Kids,
  May, 1946 . . . . 1,100.00

COO COO COMICS
**Nedor/Animated Cartoons
(Standard), Oct., 1942**
1 O&I:Super Mouse 350.00
2 . . . . 175.00
3 . . . . 100.00
4 . . . . 125.00
5 . . . . 125.00
6 . . . . 100.00
7 thru 10 . . . . @100.00
11 thru 33 . . . . @100.00
34 thru 40 FF illustration . . . . . @125.00
41 FF 225.00
42 FF 200.00
43 FF illustration 125.00
44 FF illustration 125.00
45 FF illustration 125.00
46 FF illustration 125.00
47 FF 175.00
48 FF illustration 125.00
49 FF illustration 125.00
50 FF illustration 125.00
51 thru 61 . . . . @100.00
62 April, 1952 . . . . 75.00

"COOKIE"
**Michel Publ./Regis Publ.
(American Comics Group)
April, 1946**
1 . . . . 250.00
2 . . . . 125.00
3 thru 5 . . . . @100.00
6 thru 20 . . . . @75.00

```
21 thru 30 . . . . . . . . . . . . . . . @50.00
31 thru 54 . . . . . . . . . . . . . . . @40.00
55 Aug., 1955. . . . . . . . . . . . . 40.00
```

COSMO CAT
Fox Features Syndicate, 1946
```
1 . . . . . . . . . . . . . . . . . . . . . . . 325.00
2 . . . . . . . . . . . . . . . . . . . . . . . 175.00
3 O:Cosmo Cat . . . . . . . . . . . . . 225.00
4 thru 10 . . . . . . . . . . . . . . . @100.00
```

COURAGE COMICS
J. Edward Slavin, 1945
```
1 . . . . . . . . . . . . . . . . . . . . . . . 150.00
2 Boxing (c). . . . . . . . . . . . . . . 150.00
77 Naval rescue, PT99 (c) . . . . . 150.00
```

COWBOY COMICS
See: STAR RANGER

COWBOYS 'N' INJUNS
Compix (M.E. Enterprises), 1946-47
```
1 Funny Animal Western . . . . . 150.00
2 thru 8 . . . . . . . . . . . . . . . . @100.00
```

COWBOY WESTERN COMICS/HEROES
See: YELLOWJACKET

COWGIRL ROMANCES
Fiction House Magazine, 1952
```
1 The Range of Singing Guns . . 450.00
2 The Lady of Lawless Range . . 225.00
3 Daughter of the
   Devil's Band. . . . . . . . . . . . . 200.00
4 Bride Wore Buckskin . . . . . . . 200.00
5 Taming of Lone-Star Lou . . . . 200.00
6 Rose of Mustang Mesa . . . . . 175.00
7 Nobody Loves a Gun Man. . . . 175.00
8 Wild Beauty . . . . . . . . . . . . . 175.00
9 Gun-Feud Sweethearts . . . . . 175.00
10 JKa,AW,No Girl of Stampede
    Valley. . . . . . . . . . . . . . . . . 375.00
11 Love is Where You Find It. . . . 175.00
12 Dec., 1952 . . . . . . . . . . . . . . 175.00
```

COW PUNCHER
Avon Periodicals/ Realistic Publ., Jan., 1947
```
1 JKu . . . . . . . . . . . . . . . . . . . . 500.00
2 JKu,JKa(c),Bondage (c) . . . . . 400.00
3 AU(c) . . . . . . . . . . . . . . . . . . . 350.00
4 . . . . . . . . . . . . . . . . . . . . . . . 350.00
5 . . . . . . . . . . . . . . . . . . . . . . . 350.00
6 WJo(c),Drug story . . . . . . . . . 400.00
7 . . . . . . . . . . . . . . . . . . . . . . . 350.00
1 JKu . . . . . . . . . . . . . . . . . . . . 350.00
```

CRACK COMICS
Comic Magazines (Quality Comics Group) May, 1940
```
1 LF,O:Black Condor,Madame
   Fatal, Red Torpedo, Rock
   Bradden, Space Legion,
   B:The Clock,Wizard Wells . 7,200.00
2 Black Condor (c) . . . . . . . . 3,200.00
3 The Clock (c) . . . . . . . . . . . 2,200.00
4 Black Condor (c) . . . . . . . . 2,000.00
5 LF,The Clock (c) . . . . . . . . 1,500.00
6 PG,Black Condor (c) . . . . . 1,400.00
7 Clock (c) . . . . . . . . . . . . . . 1,400.00
```

Crack Comics #18
© Quality Comics Group

```
8 Black Condor (c) . . . . . . . . 1,400.00
9 Clock (c) . . . . . . . . . . . . . . 1,400.00
10 Black Condor (c) . . . . . . . . 1,400.00
11 LF,PG,Clock (c) . . . . . . . . . 1,200.00
12 LF,PG,Black Condor (c) . . . 1,200.00
13 LF,PG,Clock (c) . . . . . . . . . 1,200.00
14 AMc,LF,PG,Clack Condor(c) 1,200.00
15 AMc,LF,PG,Clock (c) . . . . . 1,200.00
16 AMc,LF,PG,Black Condor(c) 1,200.00
17 FG,AMc,LF,PG,Clock (c) . . 1,200.00
18 AMc,LF,PG,Black Condor(c) 1,200.00
19 AMc,LF,PG,Clock (c) . . . . . 1,200.00
20 AMc,LF,PG,BlackCondor(c) 1,200.00
21 AMc,LF,PG,same. . . . . . . . . 900.00
22 LF,PG,same. . . . . . . . . . . . . 900.00
23 AMc,LF,PG,same. . . . . . . . . 900.00
24 AMc,LF,PG,same. . . . . . . . . 900.00
25 AMc,same . . . . . . . . . . . . . . 750.00
26 AMc,same . . . . . . . . . . . . . . 750.00
27 AMc,I&O:Captain Triumph . . 1,400.00
28 Captain Triumph (c) . . . . . . . 750.00
29 A:Spade the Ruthless . . . . . . 750.00
30 I:Biff . . . . . . . . . . . . . . . . . . 600.00
31 Helps Spade Dig His Own
    Grave. . . . . . . . . . . . . . . . . 350.00
32 Newspaper (c) . . . . . . . . . . . 350.00
33 V:Men of Darkness . . . . . . . . 350.00
34 . . . . . . . . . . . . . . . . . . . . . . 350.00
35 V:The Man Who Conquered
    Flame. . . . . . . . . . . . . . . . . 350.00
36 Good Neighbor Tour . . . . . . . 350.00
37 V:The Tyrant of Toar Valley. . . 350.00
38 Castle of Shadows . . . . . . . . 350.00
39 V:Crime over the City . . . . . . 350.00
40 Thrilling Murder Mystery . . . . 250.00
41 . . . . . . . . . . . . . . . . . . . . . . 250.00
42 All that Glitters is Not Gold . . 250.00
43 Smashes the Evil Spell of
    Silent . . . . . . . . . . . . . . . . . 250.00
44 V:Silver Tip . . . . . . . . . . . . . . 250.00
45 V:King-The Jack of all Trades. 250.00
46 V:Mr. Weary . . . . . . . . . . . . . 250.00
47 V:Hypnotic Eyes Khor. . . . . . 275.00
48 Murder in the Sky . . . . . . . . . 275.00
49 . . . . . . . . . . . . . . . . . . . . . . 275.00
50 A Key to Trouble . . . . . . . . . . 275.00
51 V:Werewolf . . . . . . . . . . . . . . 275.00
52 V:Porcupine . . . . . . . . . . . . . 275.00
53 V:Man Who Robbed the Dead 275.00
54 Shoulders the Troubles
    of the World. . . . . . . . . . . . . 275.00
55 Brain against Brawn . . . . . . . 275.00
56 Gossip leads to Murder . . . . . 275.00
57 V:Sitok–Green God of Evil . . . 275.00
58 V:Targets. . . . . . . . . . . . . . . . 200.00
```

```
59 A Cargo of Mystery . . . . . . . . 200.00
60 Trouble is no Picnic . . . . . . . . 200.00
61 V:Mr. Pointer-Finger of Fear . . 200.00
62 V:The Vanishing Vandals . . . . 200.00
Becomes:
```

CRACK WESTERN
Nov., 1949–May, 1951
```
63 PG, I&O:Two-Gun Lil, B:Frontier
   Marshal,Arizona Ames, . . . . . 250.00
64 RC,Arizona AmesV:Two-
   Legged Coyote . . . . . . . . . . 200.00
65 RC,Ames Tramples on
   Trouble . . . . . . . . . . . . . . . . . 200.00
66 Arizona Ames Arizona Raines,
   Tim Holt,Ph(c) . . . . . . . . . . . 150.00
67 RC, Ph(c),Randolph Scott . . . 200.00
68 Ph(c) . . . . . . . . . . . . . . . . . . 150.00
69 RC. . . . . . . . . . . . . . . . . . . . . 150.00
70 O&I:Whip and Diablo . . . . . . . 175.00
71 Bob Allen, Marshall,RC(c). . . . 200.00
72 RC,Tim Holt,Ph(c). . . . . . . . . 150.00
73 Tim Holt,Ph(c). . . . . . . . . . . . 100.00
74 RC(c). . . . . . . . . . . . . . . . . . . 150.00
75 RC(c). . . . . . . . . . . . . . . . . . . 150.00
76 RC(c),Stage Coach to
   Oblivion . . . . . . . . . . . . . . . . 150.00
77 RC(c),Comanche Terror . . . . 150.00
78 RC(c),Killers of Laurel Ridge . 150.00
79 RC(c),Fires of Revenge . . . . . 150.00
80 RC(c),Mexican Massacre . . . 150.00
81 RC(c),Secrets of Terror
   Canyon . . . . . . . . . . . . . . . . 150.00
82 The Killer with a Thousand
   Faces. . . . . . . . . . . . . . . . . . 100.00
83 Rattlesnake Pete's Revenge . 100.00
84 PG(c),Revolt at Broke Creek . 150.00
```

CRACKAJACK FUNNIES
Dell Publishing Co., June, 1938
```
1 AMc,A:Dan Dunn,The Nebbs,
   Don Winslow . . . . . . . . . . . 3,400.00
2 AMc,same . . . . . . . . . . . . . 1,300.00
3 AMc,same . . . . . . . . . . . . . . 950.00
4 AMc,same . . . . . . . . . . . . . . 650.00
5 AMc,Naked Women(c). . . . . . 750.00
6 AMc,same . . . . . . . . . . . . . . 550.00
7 AMc,same . . . . . . . . . . . . . . 550.00
8 AMc,same . . . . . . . . . . . . . . 550.00
9 AMc,A:Red Ryder . . . . . . . 2,300.00
10 AMc,A:Red Ryder . . . . . . . . 550.00
11 AMc,A:Red Ryder . . . . . . . . 500.00
12 AMc,A:Red Ryder . . . . . . . . 500.00
13 AMc,A:Red Ryder . . . . . . . . 500.00
14 AMc,A:Red Ryder . . . . . . . . 500.00
15 AMc,A:Tarzan . . . . . . . . . . . 550.00
16 AMc . . . . . . . . . . . . . . . . . . 400.00
17 AMc . . . . . . . . . . . . . . . . . . 400.00
18 AMc,A:Stratosphere Jim . . . . 400.00
19 AMc . . . . . . . . . . . . . . . . . . 400.00
20 AMc . . . . . . . . . . . . . . . . . . 400.00
21 AMc . . . . . . . . . . . . . . . . . . 400.00
22 AMc . . . . . . . . . . . . . . . . . . 400.00
23 AMc,A:Ellery Queen . . . . . . . 400.00
24 AMc . . . . . . . . . . . . . . . . . . 400.00
25 AMc,I:The Owl . . . . . . . . . 1,100.00
26 AMc . . . . . . . . . . . . . . . . . . 700.00
27 AMc . . . . . . . . . . . . . . . . . . 700.00
28 AMc,A:The Owl . . . . . . . . . . 700.00
29 AMc,A:Ellery Queen . . . . . . . 700.00
30 AMc,A:Tarzan . . . . . . . . . . . 700.00
31 AMc,A:Tarzan . . . . . . . . . . . 700.00
32 AMc,O:Owl Girl . . . . . . . . . . 750.00
33 AMc,A:Tarzan . . . . . . . . . . . 650.00
34 AMc,same . . . . . . . . . . . . . . 650.00
35 AMc,same . . . . . . . . . . . . . . 650.00
36 AMc,same . . . . . . . . . . . . . . 650.00
37 AMc . . . . . . . . . . . . . . . . . . 650.00
38 AMc . . . . . . . . . . . . . . . . . . 650.00
```

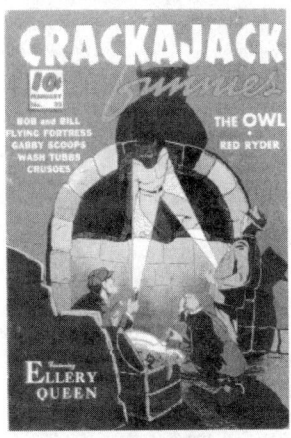

Crackajack Funnies #32
© Dell Pub. Co.

39 AMc,I:Andy Panada 750.00
40 AMc,A:Owl(c) 500.00
41 AMc. 500.00
42 AMc. 500.00
43 AMc,Terry & The Pirates,
    A:Owl(c). 450.00

CRASH COMICS
Tem Publishing Co.,
May, 1940
1 S&K,O:Strongman, B:Blue Streak,
    Perfect Human, Shangra . . 4,500.00
2 S&K 2,100.00
3 S&K 1,800.00
4 S&K,O&I:Catman 4,500.00
5 S&K, Nov., 1940 . . . . 1,800.00

CRIME AND
PUNISHMENT
Lev Gleason Publications,
April, 1948
1 CBi(c),Mr.Crime(c) 400.00
2 CBi(c). 200.00
3 CBi(c),BF 250.00
4 CBi(c),BF 150.00
5 CBi(c). 150.00
6 thru 10 CBi(c). . . . . @125.00
11 thru 15 CBi(c) . . . . @100.00
16 thru 27 CBi(c) . . . . @100.00
28 thru 38. . . . . @75.00
39 Drug issue. 125.00
40 thru 44 . . . . @75.00
45 Drug issue. 100.00
46 thru 58. . . . . @75.00
59 . . . . 350.00
60 thru 65. . . . . @75.00
66 ATh 450.00
67 Drug Storm 425.00
68 ATh(c) 350.00
69 Drug issue. 125.00
74 Aug., 1955. . . . . 75.00

CRIME DETECTIVE
COMICS
Hillman Publications,
March–April, 1948
1 BFc(c),A:Invisible 6 . . . . 350.00
2 Jewel Robbery (c) 150.00
3 Stolen cash (c). 125.00
4 Crime Boss Murder (c) 125.00
5 BK,Maestro (c). 125.00

6 AMc,Gorilla (c) 100.00
7 GMc,Wedding (c). 100.00
8 . . . . 100.00
9 Safe Robbery (c) (a classic) . . 425.00
10 . . . . 100.00
11 BP 100.00
12 BK 100.00
2-1 Bluebird captured 125.00
2-2 . . . . 100.00
2-3 . . . . 100.00
2-4 BK 110.00
2-5 . . . . 100.00
2-6 . . . . 100.00
2-7 BK,GMc 110.00
2-8 . . . . 100.00
2-9 . . . . 100.00
2-10 . . . . 100.00
2-11 . . . . 100.00
2-12 . . . . 100.00
3-1 Drug Story 100.00
3-2 thru 3-7 . . . . @100.00
3-8 May/June, 1953 . . . . 75.00

CRIME DOES NOT PAY
See: SILVER STREAK
COMICS

CRIME ILLUSTRATED
E.C. Comics, Nov.–Dec., 1955
1 Grl,RC,GE,JO 175.00
2 Grl,RC,JCr,JDa,JO 150.00

CRIME MUST STOP
Hillman Periodicals, Oct., 1952
1 BK. 1,000.00

CRIME MYSTERIES
Ribage Publishing Corp.,
May, 1952
1 Transvestism,Bondage(c) 750.00
2 A:Manhunter, Lance Storm,
    Drug. 500.00
3 FF-one page, A:Dr. Foo 400.00
4 A:Queenie Star, BondageStar . 700.00
5 Claws of the Green Girl 350.00
6 . . . . 350.00
7 Sons of Satan 350.00
8 Death Stalks the Crown,
    Bondage(c) 350.00
9 You are the Murderer 325.00
10 The Hoax of the Death 325.00
11 The Strangler. 325.00
12 Bondage(c). 350.00
13 AT,6 lives for one 400.00
14 Painted in Blood 325.00
15 Feast of the Dead,Acid Face . 500.00
Becomes:

SECRET MYSTERIES
Nov., 1954
16 Hiding Place,Horror 350.00
17 The Deadly Diamond,Horror. . 250.00
18 Horror 300.00
19 Horror,July, 1955. . . . . 300.00

INTERNATIONAL COMICS
E.C. Publ. Co., Spring, 1947
1 KS,I:Manhattan's Files 800.00
2 KS,A: Van Manhattan &
    Madelon 550.00
3 KS,same 475.00
4 KS,same 475.00
5 I:International Crime-Busting
    Patrol. 475.00
Becomes:

INTERNATIONAL
CRIME PATROL
Spring, 1948
6 A:Moon Girl & The Prince 800.00
Becomes:

CRIME PATROL
Summer, 1948
7 SMo,A:Capt. Crime Jr.,Field
    Marshall of Murder 1,000.00
8 JCr,State Prison (c) 800.00
9 AF,JCr,Bank Robbery 800.00
10 AF,JCr,Wanted:James Dore . . 800.00
11 AF,JCr 800.00
12 AF,Grl,JCr,Interrogation(c) . . . 800.00
13 AF,JCr 800.00
14 AF,JCr,Smugglers (c) 800.00
15 AF,JCr,Crypt of Terror 4,000.00
16 AF,JCr,Crypt of Terror 2,500.00
Becomes:

CRYPT OF TERROR
E.C. Comics, April, 1950
17 JCr(a&c),AF,'Werewolf
    Strikes Again' 4,200.00
18 JCr(a&c),AF,WW,HK
    'The Living Corpse' 2,500.00
19 JCr(a&c),AF,Grl,
    'Voodoo Drums' 2,400.00
Becomes:

TALES FROM
THE CRYPT
Oct., 1950
20 JCr(a&c),AF,Gl,JKa
    'Day of Death'. 1,800.00
21 AF(a&c),WW,HK,Gl,'Cooper
    Dies in the Electric Chair . 1,500.00
22 AF, JCr(c). 1,100.00
23 AF(a&c),JCr,JDa,Grl
    'Locked in a Mauseleum'. . . . 850.00
24 AF(c),WW,JDa,JCr,Grl
    'Danger...Quicksand' 850.00
25 AF(c),WW,JDa,JKa,Grl
    'Mataud Waxworks' 850.00
26 WW(c),JDa,Grl,
    'Scared Graveyard' 650.00
27 JKa, WW(c), Guillotine (c) . . . 650.00
28 AF(c),JDa,JKa,Grl,JO
    'Buried Alive' 650.00
29 JDa(a&c),JKa,Grl,JO
    'Coffin Burier'. 650.00
30 JDa(a&c),JO,JKa,Grl
    'Underwater Death' 650.00

Tales From the Crypt #32
© E.C. Comics

GOLDEN AGE

31 JDa(a&c),JKa,Grl,AW
 'Hand Chopper' 700.00
32 JDa(a&c),GE,Grl,'Woman
 Crushed by Elephant' 700.00
33 JDa(a&c),GE,JKa,Grl,'Lower
 Berth',O:Crypt Keeper 1,000.00
34 JDa(a&c),JKa,GE,Grl,'Jack the
 Ripper,'Ray Bradbury adapt. . 650.00
35 JDa(a&c),JKa,JO,Grl,
 'Werewolf' 700.00
36 JDa(a&c),JKa,GE,Grl, Ray
 Bradbury adaptation 700.00
37 JDa(c),JO,BE 700.00
38 JDa(c),BE,RC,Grl,'Axe Man' . 700.00
39 JDa(a&c),JKa,JO,Grl,'Children
 in the Graveyard' 700.00
40 JDa(a&c),GE,BK,Grl,
 'Underwater Monster' 600.00
41 JDa(a&c),JKa,GE,Grl,
 'Knife Thrower' 550.00
42 JDa(c),JO,Vampire (c) 550.00
43 JDa(c),JO,GE 550.00
44 JO,RC,Guillotine (c) 550.00
45 JDa(a&c),JKa,BK,GI,'Rat
 Takes Over His Life' 550.00
46 JDa(a&c),GE,JO,GI,Werewolf
 man being hunted,Feb.1955 . 675.00

CRIME REPORTER
St. John Publishing Co.,
Aug., 1948
1 Death Makes a Deadline 700.00
2 GT,MB(c),Matinee Murders . 1,000.00
3 GT,MB(c),Dec., 1948 . . . . . . 500.00

CRIMES BY WOMEN
Fox Features Syndicate,
June, 1948
1 Bonnie Parker 1,700.00
2 Vicious Female 900.00
3 Prison break (c) 800.00
4 Murder (c) 800.00
5 . . . . 800.00
6 Girl Fight (c) 850.00
7 . . . . 750.00
8 . . . . 750.00
9 . . . . 750.00
10 Girl Fight (c) 750.00
11 . . . . 750.00
12 . . . . 750.00
13 ACME jewelry robbery (c). . . . 750.00
14 Prison break (c) 750.00
15 Aug., 1951. . . . . 750.00

CRIME SMASHER
Fawcett Publications,
Summer, 1948
1 The Unlucky Rabbit's Foot . . . 600.00

CRIME SMASHERS
Ribage Publishing Corp.,
Oct., 1950
1 Girl Rape. 1,200.00
2 JKu,A:Sally the Sleuth, Dan
 Turner, Girl Friday, Rat Hale . 600.00
3 MFa 450.00
4 Zak(c) 450.00
5 WW 600.00
6 . . . . 350.00
7 Bondage (c),Drugs. 400.00
8 . . . . 350.00
9 Bondage (c) 400.00
10 . . . . 350.00
11 . . . . 350.00
12 FF, Eye Ingury. 400.00
13 . . . . 400.00
14 & 15. . . . . @350.00

CRIMES ON THE WATERFRONT
See: FAMOUS GANGSTERS

Crime SuspenStories #24
© E.C. Comics

CRIME SUSPENSTORIES
L.L. Publishing Co.
(E.C. Comics), Oct.–Nov., 1950
1a JCr,Grl 2,200.00
1 JCr,WW,Grl 1,600.00
2 JCr,JKa,Grl 900.00
3 JCr,WW,Grl,Poe Story 650.00
4 JCr,Gln,Grl,JDa 600.00
5 JCr,JKa,Grl,JDa. 600.00
6 JCr,JDa,Grl 500.00
7 JCr,Grl 500.00
8 JCr,Grl 500.00
9 JCr,Grl 500.00
10 JCr,Grl. 500.00
11 JCr,Grl. 400.00
12 JCr,Grl. 400.00
13 JCr,AW 450.00
14 JCr 400.00
15 JCr,Old Witch 400.00
16 JCr,AW 450.00
17 JCr,FF,AW, Ray Bradbury . . . 500.00
18 JCr,RC,BE. 425.00
19 JCr,RC,GE,AF(c) 425.00
20 RC,JCr, Hanging (c) 450.00
21 JCr 250.00
22 RC,JO,JCr(c),
 Severed head (c). 400.00
23 JKa,RC,GE 400.00
24 BK,RC,JO 250.00
25 JKa,(c),RC 250.00
26 JKa,(c),RC,JO. 250.00
27 JKa,(c),GE,Grl,March, 1955 . . 250.00

CRIMINALS ON THE RUN
Premium Group of Comics,
Aug., 1948
4-1 LbC(c) 375.00
4-2 LbC(c), A:Young King Cole . 300.00
4-3 LbC(c), Rip Roaring Action
 in Alps 300.00
4-4 LbC(c), Shark (c) 300.00
4-5 AMc 300.00
4-6 LbC,Dr. Doom 300.00
4-7 LbC 700.00

5-1 LbC 275.00
5-2 LbC 275.00
10 LbC 275.00
Becomes:

CRIME-FIGHTING DETECTIVE
April–May, 1950
11 LbC, Brodie Gang Captured . . 250.00
12 LbC(c), Jail Break Genius . . . 225.00
13 . . . . 200.00
14 LbC(c), A Night of Horror 250.00
15 LbC(c) 250.00
16 LbC(c), Wanton Murder 250.00
17 LbC(c), The Framer
 was Framed. 250.00
18 LbC(c), A Web of Evil 250.00
19 LbC(c), Lesson of the Law . . . 250.00
Becomes:

SHOCK DETECTIVE CASES
Sept., 1952
20 LbC(c), The Strangler 300.00
21 LbC(c), Death Ride. 300.00
Becomes:

SPOOK DETECTIVE CASES
Jan., 1953
22 Headless Horror 500.00
Becomes:

SPOOK SUSPENSE AND MYSTERY
23 LbC,Weird Picture of Murder . 350.00
24 LbC(c),Mummy's Case 400.00
25 LbC(c),Horror Beyond Door . 350.00
26 LbC(c),Face of Death . . . 350.00
27 LbC(c),Ship of the Dead. 350.00
28 LbC(c),JyD,Creeping Death . . 350.00
29 LbC(c),Solo for Death. 350.00
30 LbC(c),JyD,Nightmare,
 Oct.,1954. . . . . 350.00

CROWN COMICS
Golfing/McCombs Publ.,
Winter 1944
1 Edgar Allen Poe adapt. 500.00
2 MB,I:Mickey Magic 300.00
3 MB,Jungle adventure (c) 300.00
4 MB(c),A:Voodah. 350.00
5 MB(c),Jungle adventure (c) . 350.00
6 MB(c),Jungle adventure (c) . 350.00
7 JKa,AF,MB(c),Race Car (c) . 350.00
8 MB 300.00
9 . . . . 200.00
10 Plane crash (c),A:Voodah. . . . 200.00
11 LSt,A:Voodah 175.00
12 LSt,AF,Master Marvin 175.00
13 LSt,AF,A:Voodah 175.00
14 A:Voodah. 200.00
15 FBe,A:Voodah. 175.00
16 FBe,A:Voodah,Jungle
 adventure(c) 175.00
17 FBe,A:Voodah. 175.00
18 FBe,A:Voodah. 175.00
19 BP,A:Voodah,July, 1949 . . . . . 175.00

CRUSADER FROM MARS
Approved Publ.
(Ziff-Davis), Jan.–March, 1952
1 Mission Thru Space, Death in
 the Sai 1,100.00
2 Beachhead on Saturn's Ring,
 Bondage(c),Fall, 1952. . . . . . 750.00

All comics prices listed are for *Near Mint* condition.

CRYIN' LION, THE
William H. Wise Co.,
Fall, 1944
1 Funny Animal		200.00
2 A. Hitler		150.00
3 Spring, 1945		125.00

CRYPT OF TERROR
See: CRIME PATROL

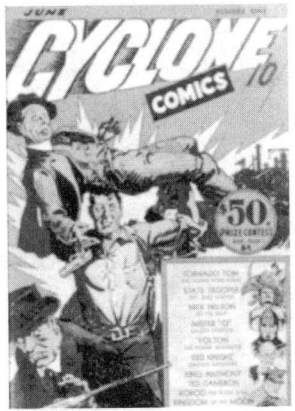

Cyclone Comics #1
© Bibara Publ. Co.

CYCLONE COMICS
Bibara Publ. Co., June, 1940
1 O:Tornado Tom		2,400.00
2		1,100.00
3		1,500.00
4 Voltron		900.00
5 A:Mr. Q,Oct., 1940		1,100.00

ALL GREAT COMICS
Fox Features Syndicate,
Oct., 1947
12 A:Brenda Starr		800.00
13 JKa,O:Dagar, Desert Hawk.		900.00
Becomes:		

DAGAR, DESERT HAWK
Feb., 1948
14 JKa,Monster of Mura		1,100.00
15 JKa,Curse of the Lost		
Pharaoh		650.00
16 JKa,Wretched Antmen		600.00
19 Pyramid of Doom		500.00
20		500.00
21 JKa(c),The Ghost of Fate		550.00
22		500.00
23 Bondage (c)		550.00
Becomes:		

CAPTAIN KIDD
June, 1949
24 Blackbeard the Pirate		200.00
25 Sorceress of the Deep		200.00
Becomes:		

MY SECRET STORY
Oct., 1949
26 He Wanted More Than Love.		200.00
27 My Husband Hated Me		125.00
28 I Become a Marked Women		125.00
29 My Forbidden Rapture,		
April, 1950		125.00

DAFFY
Dell Publishing Co.,
March, 1953
(1) *see Dell Four Color #457*		
(2) *see Dell Four Color #536*		
(3) *see Dell Four Color #615*		
4 thru 7		@75.00
8 thru 11		@50.00
12 thru 17		@45.00
Becomes:		

DAFFY DUCK
July, 1959
18		40.00
19		40.00
20		40.00
21 thru 30		@30.00

Gold Key, 1962
31 thru 40		@30.00
41 thru 59		@25.00
60 B&A:Road Runner		20.00
61 thru 90 same		@20.00
91 thru 127		@15.00

Whitman, 1980
128 thru 145		@12.00

DAGWOOD
Harvey Publications, 1950
1		250.00
2		125.00
3 thru 10		@100.00
11 thru 20		@75.00
21 thru 30		@60.00
31 thru 50		@50.00
51 thru 70		@40.00
71 thru 109		@30.00
110 thru 140		@30.00

DANGER AND
ADVENTURE
See: THIS MAGAZINE
IS HAUNTED

DANGER IS OUR
BUSINESS
Toby Press/
I.W. Enterprises, 1953
1 AW,FF,Men who Defy Death		
for a Living		550.00
2 Death Crowds the Cockpit		175.00
3 Killer Mountain		150.00
4		150.00
5 thru 9		@125.00
10 June, 1955		150.00

DAREDEVIL COMICS
Lev Gleason Publications,
July, 1941
1 Daredevil Battles Hitler, A:Silver		
Streak, Lance Hale, Dickey Dean,		
Cloud Curtis,V:The Claw,		
O:Hitler		20,000.00
2 I:The Pioneer, Champion of		
American,B:London,Pat		
Patriot,Pirate Prince		4,500.00
3 CBi(c),O:Thirteen		2,800.00
4 CBi(c),Death is the Refere		2,200.00
5 CBi(c),I:Sniffer&Jinx, Claw		
V:Ghost,Lottery of Doom		1,800.00
6 CBi(c)		1,500.00
7 CBi(c), What Ghastly Sight Lies		
within the Mysterious Trunk		1,400.00
8 V:Nazis (c), E:Nightro		1,300.00
9 V:Double		1,300.00

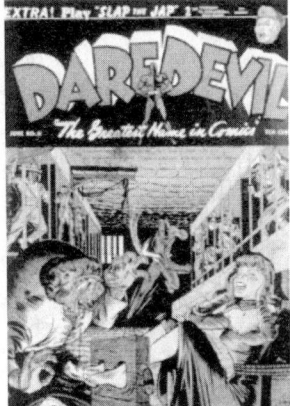

Daredevil Comics #11
© Lev Gleason

10 America will Remember		
Pearl Harbor		1,300.00
11 Bondage (c), E:Pat		
Patriot, London		1,500.00
12 BW,CBi(c), O:The Law		2,000.00
13 BW,I:Little Wise Guys		1,500.00
14 BW,CBi(c)		1,000.00
15 BW,CBi(c), D:Meatball		1,200.00
16 BW,CBi(c)		900.00
17 BW,CBi(c), Into the Valley		
of Death		900.00
18 BW,CBi(c), O:Daredevil,		
double length story		1,800.00
19 BW,CBi(c), Buried Alive		750.00
20 BW,CBi(c), Boxing (c)		750.00
21 CBi(c), Can Little Wise Guys		
Survive Blast of Dynamite?		1,300.00
22 CBi(c)		550.00
23 CBi(c), I:Pshyco		550.00
24 CBi(c), Punch and Judy		
Murders		550.00
25 CBi(c), baseball (c)		550.00
26 CBi(c)		500.00
27 CBi(c), Bondage (c)		550.00
28 CBi(c)		500.00
29 CBi(c)		500.00
30 CBi(c), Ann Hubbard White		
1922-1943		500.00
31 CBi(c), D:The Claw		1,200.00
32 V:Blackmarketeers		375.00
33 CBi(c)		375.00
34 CBi(c)		375.00
35 B:Two Daredevil stories		
every issue		400.00
36 CBi(c)		400.00
37 CBi(c)		400.00
38 CBi(c), O:Daredevil		600.00
39 CBi(c)		375.00
40 CBi(c)		375.00
41		375.00
42 thru 50 CBi(c)		@375.00
51 CBi(c)		250.00
52 CBi(c),Football (c)		275.00
53 thru 57		@250.00
58 Football (c)		275.00
59		250.00
60		250.00
61 thru 68		@250.00
69 E:Daredevil		250.00
70		150.00
71 thru 78		@100.00
79 B:Daredevil		150.00
80		135.00
81		100.00
82		100.00

83 thru 99 . . . . @100.00
100 . . . . 125.00
101 thru 133 . . . . @100.00
134 Sept., 1956 . . . . 100.00

DARING CONFESSIONS
See: YOUTHFUL HEART

DARING LOVE
See: YOUTHFUL ROMANCES

Dark Mysteries #24
© Merit Publications

DARK MYSTERIES
Merit Publications, June–July, 1951
1 WW(a&c), Curse of the
    Sea Witch 1,500.00
2 WW(a&c), Vampire Fangs
    of Doom 1,200.00
3 Terror of the Unwilling
    Witch 600.00
4 Corpse that Came Alive 600.00
5 Horror of the Ghostly Crew . . . 550.00
6 If the Noose Fits Wear It! 550.00
7 Terror of the Cards of Death . . 550.00
8 Terror of the Ghostly Trail 550.00
9 Witch's Feast at Dawn 550.00
10 Terror of the Burning Witch. . . 550.00
11 The River of Blood 500.00
12 Horror of the Talking Dead . . . 500.00
13 Terror of the Hungry Cats 500.00
14 Horror of the Fingers of Doom 550.00
15 Terror of the Vampires Teeth. . 450.00
16 Horror of the Walking Dead . . 450.00
17 Terror of the Mask of Death . . 450.00
18 Terror of the Burning Corpse . 450.00
19 The Rack of Terror 600.00
20 Burning Executioner 550.00
21 The Sinister Secret 350.00
22 The Hand of Destiny 350.00
23 The Mardenburg Curse. 250.00
24 Give A Man enough Rope,
    July, 1955 . . . . 250.00

DAVY CROCKETT
Avon Periodicals, 1951
1 . . . . 250.00

DEAD END CRIME STORIES
Kirby Publishing Co., April, 1949
N# BP 650.00

DEAD-EYE WESTERN COMICS
Hillman Periodicals Nov.–Dec., 1948
1 BK 250.00
2 . . . . 125.00
3 . . . . 100.00
4 thru 12 . . . . @75.00
2-1 . . . . 60.00
2-2 . . . . 60.00
2-3 . . . . 75.00
2-4 . . . . 75.00
2-5 thru 2-12 . . . . @60.00
3-1 . . . . 60.00

DEADWOOD GULCH
Dell Publishing Co., 1931
1 . . . . 450.00

DEAR BEATRICE FAIRFAX
Best Books (Standard Comics), Nov., 1950
5 . . . . 125.00
6 thru 9 . . . . @100.00

DEAR LONELY HEART
Artful Publications, March, 1951
1 . . . . 200.00
2 . . . . 100.00
3 MB,Jungle Girl 250.00
4 . . . . 100.00
5 thru 8 . . . . @80.00

DEAR LONELY HEARTS
Comic Media, Aug., 1953
1 Six Months to Live 125.00
2 Date Hungry, Price of Passion . 75.00
3 thru 8 . . . . @90.00

DEARLY BELOVED
Approved Comics (Ziff-Davis), Fall, 1952
1 Ph(c) 200.00

DEBBIE DEAN, CAREER GIRL
Civil Service Publishing, April, 1945
1 . . . . 165.00
2 . . . . 150.00

DELL GIANT EDITIONS
Dell Publishing Co., 1953-58
Abe Lincoln Life Story 150.00
Cadet Gray of West Point 150.00
Golden West Rodeo Treasury . . . 175.00
Life Stories of
    American Presidents 135.00
Lone Ranger Golden West 350.00
Lone Ranger Movie Story 750.00
Lone Ranger Western
    Treasury('53) 350.00
Lone Ranger Western
    Treasury('54) 450.00
Moses & Ten Commandments. . . 125.00
Nancy & Sluggo Travel Time 175.00
Pogo Parade 600.00
Raggedy Ann & Andy. 300.00
Santa Claus Funnies 175.00
Tarzan's Jungle Annual #1. . . . . . 300.00
Tarzan's Jungle Annual #2. . . . . . 200.00
Tarzan's Jungle Annual #3. . . . . . 175.00
Tarzan's Jungle Annual #4. . . . . . 175.00
Tarzan's Jungle Annual #5. . . . . . 175.00
Tarzan's Jungle Annual #6. . . . . . 175.00
Tarzan's Jungle Annual #7. . . . . . 175.00
Treasury of Dogs 150.00
Treasury of Horses 150.00
Universal Presents-Dracula-
    The Mummy & Other Stories. 450.00
Western Roundup #1. . . . . 500.00
Western Roundup #2. . . . . 300.00
Western Roundup #3. . . . . 250.00
Western Roundup #4 thru #5. . @225.00
Western Roundup #6 thru #10. @225.00
Western Roundup #11 thru #17 @200.00
Western Roundup #18. . . . . 200.00
Western Roundup #19 thru #25 . 180.00
Woody Woodpecker Back
    to School #1 . . . . 200.00
Woody Woodpecker Back
    to School #2 . . . . 175.00
Woody Woodpecker Back
    to School #3 . . . . 175.00
Woody Woodpecker Back
    to School #4 . . . . 175.00
Woody Woodpecker County
    Fair #5 . . . . 175.00
Woody Woodpecker Back
    to School #6 . . . . 200.00
Woody Woodpecker County
    Fair #2 . . . . 175.00
Also See: Bugs Bunny; Marge's Little Lulu; Tom and Jerry, and Walt Disney Dell Giant Editions

DELL GIANT COMICS
Dell Publishing Co., Sept., 1959
21 M.G.M. Tom & Jerry
    Picnic Time 225.00
22 W.Disney's Huey, Dewey & Louie
    Back to School (Oct 1959) . . 175.00
23 Marge's Little Lulu &
    Tubby Halloween Fun 225.00
24 Woody Woodpeckers
    Family Fun. 175.00
25 Tarzan's Jungle World. 200.00
26 W.Disney's Christmas
    Parade,CB. 450.00
27 W.Disney's Man in
    Space (1960). 200.00
28 Bugs Bunny's Winter Fun 200.00
29 Marge's Little Lulu &
    Tubby in Hawaii. 225.00
30 W.Disney's DisneylandU.S.A.. 175.00
31 Huckleberry Hound
    Summer Fun 250.00
32 Bugs Bunny Beach Party 150.00
33 W.Disney's Daisy Duck &
    Uncle Scrooge Picnic Time . . 175.00
34 Nancy&SluggoSummerCamp. 150.00
35 W.Disney's Huey, Dewey &
    Louie Back to School 225.00
36 Marge's Little Lulu & Witch
    Hazel Halloween Fun 225.00
37 Tarzan, King of the Jungle . . . 200.00
38 W.Disney's Uncle Donald and
    his Nephews Family Fun . . . 250.00
39 W.Disney's Merry Christmas. . 250.00
40 Woody Woodpecker
    Christmas Parade 125.00

GOLDEN AGE

41 Yogi Bear's Winter Sports.... 250.00
42 Marge's Little Lulu &
     Tubby in Australia 225.00
43 Mighty Mouse in OuterSpace . 400.00
44 Around the World with
     Huckleberry & His Friends .. 250.00
45 Nancy&SluggoSummerCamp. 125.00
46 Bugs Bunny Beach Party 125.00
47 W.Disney's Mickey and
     Donald in Vacationland 175.00
48 The Flintstones #1
     (Bedrock Bedlam) 400.00
49 W.Disney's Huey, Dewey &
     Louie Back to School 175.00
50 Marge's Little Lulu &
     Witch Hazel Trick 'N' Treat .. 225.00
51 Tarzan, King of the Jungle ... 150.00
52 W.Disney's Uncle Donald &
     his Nephews Dude Ranch .. 150.00
53 W.Disney's Donald Duck
     Merry Christmas 150.00
54 Woody Woodpecker
     Christmas Party.......... 150.00
55 W.Disney's Daisy Duck & Uncle
     Scrooge Show Boat (1961).. 175.00

DELL JUNIOR TREASURY
Dell Publishing Co.,
June, 1955

1 Alice in Wonderland........ 150.00
2 Aladdin.................. 125.00
3 Gulliver's Travels 100.00
4 Adventures of Mr. Frog 125.00
5 Wizard of Oz 125.00
6 Heidi................... 135.00
7 Santa & the Angel 135.00
8 Raggedy Ann............. 135.00
9 Clementina the Flying Pig 125.00
10 Adventures of Tom Sawyer... 125.00

DENNIS THE MENACE
Visual Editions/Literary Ent.
(Standard, Pines),
Aug., 1953

1 .... 800.00
2 .... 350.00
3 .... 200.00
4 .... 200.00
5 thru 10 .... @150.00
11 thru 20............... @125.00
21 thru 31............... @100.00

Hallden (Fawcett Publications)

32 thru 40............... @75.00
41 thru 50............... @60.00
51 thru 60............... @50.00
61 thru 70............... @40.00
71 thru 90............... @35.00
91 thru 140.............. @15.00
141 thru 166............. @12.00

DESPERADO
Lev Gleason Publications,
June, 1948

1 CBi(c) 175.00
2 CBi(c) 100.00
3 CBi(c) 125.00
4 CBi(c) 65.00
5 CBi(c) 65.00
6 CBi(c) 65.00
7 CBi(c) 65.00
8 CBi(c) 65.00
Becomes:

BLACK DIAMOND
WESTERN
March, 1949

9 CBi(c) 250.00
10 CBi(c) 125.00

---

11 CBi(c) 100.00
12 CBi(c) 100.00
13 CBi(c) 100.00
14 CBi(c) 100.00
15 CBi(c) 100.00
16 thru 28 BW,Big Bang Buster @125.00
29 thru 40................. @75.00
41 thru 50................. @50.00
51 thru 52 3-D Luse........... 175.00
53 thru 60................. @60.00

DETECTIVE EYE
Centaur Publications,
Nov., 1940

1 B:Air Man, The Eye Sees,
     A:Masked Marvel 2,900.00
2 O:Don Rance, Mysticape,
     Dec., 1940 .... 1,800.00

Detective Picture Stories #5
© Comics Magazine Co.

DETECTIVE
PICTURE STORIES
Comics Magazine Co.,
Dec., 1936

1 The Phantom Killer 5,000.00
2 .... 2,500.00
3 .... 1,500.00
4 WE, Muss Em Up........ 1,400.00
5 Trouble, April, 1937...... 1,700.00

DEVIL DOGS
Street and Smith, 1942
1 U.S. Marines 350.00

DEXTER COMICS
Dearfield Publications,
Summer, 1948–July, 1949
1 .... 125.00
2 .... 75.00
3 thru 5 .... @60.00

DIARY CONFESSIONS
See: TENDER ROMANCE

DIARY LOVES
Comic Magazines
(Quality Comics Group)
Sept., 1949
1 BWa Love Diary........... 200.00

---

2 BWa.................... 175.00
3 .... 75.00
4 RC 85.00
5 .... 60.00
6 .... 60.00
7 .... 60.00
8 BWa 125.00
9 BWa 125.00
10 BWa 125.00
11 .... 60.00
12 .... 60.00
13 .... 60.00
14 .... 60.00
15 BWa 125.00
16 BWa 125.00
17 .... 60.00
18 .... 60.00
19 .... 60.00
20 .... 60.00
21 BWa 100.00
22 thru 31................ @50.00
Becomes:

G.I. SWEETHEARTS
June, 1953
32 Love Under Fire 100.00
33 .... 75.00
34 .... 75.00
35 .... 75.00
36 Lend Lease Love Affair...... 75.00
37 thru 45................. @75.00
Becomes:

GIRLS IN LOVE
Sept., 1955
46 Somewhere I'll Find You...... 90.00
47 thru 56 .... @60.00
57 MB(a&c), Can Love Really
     Change Him, Dec., 1956.... 100.00

DIARY SECRETS
See: TEEN-AGE DIARY
SECRETS

DICK COLE
Curtis Publ./
Star Publications,
Dec.–Jan., 1949
1 LbC(a&c),CS,All sports(c) 400.00
2 LbC 200.00
3 LbC(a&c) 275.00
4 LbC(a&c),Rowing (c) 275.00
5 LbC(a&c) 275.00
6 LbC(a&c), Rodeo (c) 275.00
7 LbC(a&c) 200.00
8 LbC(a&c), Football (c) 200.00
9 LbC(a&c), Basketball (c) 200.00
10 Joe Louis 200.00
Becomes:

SPORTS THRILLS
Nov., 1950–Nov., 1951
11 Ted Williams & Ty Cobb 375.00
12 LbC, Joe DiMaggio & Phil
     Rizzuto, Boxing (c) 350.00
13 LbC(c),Basketball (c) 325.00
14 LbC(c),Baseball (c)........ 325.00
15 LbC(c),Baseball (c)........ 325.00

DICKIE DARE
Eastern Color Printing Co.,
1941–42
1 BEv(c),M.Caniff 800.00
2 .... 350.00
3 .... 350.00
4 H. Scorcery Smith 400.00

DICK TRACY MONTHLY

Dell Publishing Co., Jan., 1948

1 ChG,Dick Tracy & the Mad
  Doctor' 700.00
2 ChG,A:MarySteele,BorisArson 375.00
3 ChG,A:Spaldoni,Big Boy 375.00
4 ChG,A:Alderman Zeld 375.00
5 ChG,A:Spaldoni,Mrs.Spaldoni . . 350.00
6 ChG,'Steve the Tramp 350.00
7 ChG,A:Boris Arson,Mary
  Steele 350.00
8 ChG,A:Boris & Zora Arson . . . 350.00
9 ChG,A:Chief Yellowpony 350.00
10 ChG,A:Cutie Diamond. 350.00
11 ChG,A:Toby Townly,
  Bookie Joe. 275.00
12 ChG,A:Toby Townly,
  Bookie Joe. 275.00
13 ChG,A:Toby Townly, Blake . . . 300.00
14 ChG,A:Mayor Waite Wright. . . 250.00
15 ChG,A:Bowman Basil 250.00
16 ChG,A:Maw,'Muscle'
  & 'Cut' Famon 250.00
17 ChG,A:Jim Trailer,
  Mary Steele 250.00
18 ChG,A:Lips Manlis,
  Anthel Jones 250.00
19 I:Sparkle Plenty. 300.00
20 'Black Cat Mystery' 275.00
21 'Tracy Meets Number One'. . . 275.00
22 'Tracy and the Alibi Maker' . . . 225.00
23 'Dick Tracy Meets Jukebox' . . 225.00
24 'Dick Tracy and Bubbles' 225.00

Becomes:

DICK TRACY COMICS MONTHLY

Harvey, May, 1950

25 ChG,A:Flattop 300.00
26 ChG,A:Vitamin Flintheart. 200.00
27 ChG,'Flattop Escapes Prision' 200.00
28 ChG,'Case o/t Torture
  Chamber'. 200.00
29 ChG,A:Brow,Gravel Gertie . . . 250.00
30 ChG,'Blackmail Racket'. 200.00
31 ChG,A:Snowflake Falls 175.00
32 ChG,A:Shaky,Snowflake Falls 175.00
33 ChG,'Strange Case
  of Measles' 225.00
34 ChG,A:Measles,Paprika 200.00
35 ChG,'Case of Stolen $50,000'. 200.00
36 ChG,'Case of the
  Runaway Blonde' 225.00
37 ChG,'Case of Stolen Money'. . 200.00
38 ChG,A:Breathless Mahoney . . 200.00
39 ChG,A:Itchy,B.O.Pleanty. 200.00
40 ChG,'Case of Atomic Killer'. . . 200.00
41 ChG,Pt.1'Murder by Mail' 175.00
42 ChG,Pt.2'Murder by Mail' 175.00
43 ChG,'Case of the
  Underworld Brat' 175.00
44 ChG,'Case of the Mouthwash
  Murder' 175.00
45 ChG,'Case of the Evil Eyes' . . 175.00
46 ChG,'Case of the
  Camera Killers' 175.00
47 ChG,'Case of the
  Bloodthirsty Blonde'. 175.00
48 ChG,'Case of the
  Murderous Minstrel'. 175.00
49 ChG,Pt.1'Killer Who Returned
  From the Dead 175.00
50 ChG,Pt.2'Killer Who
  Returned from the Dead' . . . 175.00
51 ChG,'Case of the
  High Tension Hijackers'. 150.00

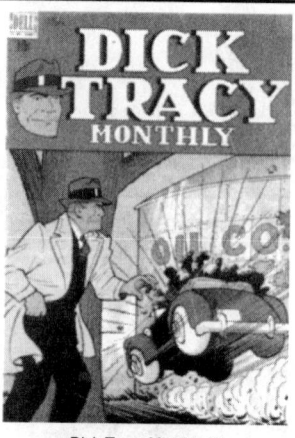

Dick Tracy Monthly #4
© *Dell Publishing Co.*

52 ChG,'Case of the
  Pipe-Stem Killer. 150.00
53 ChG,Pt.1'Dick Tracy Meets
  the Murderous Midget'. 150.00
54 ChG,Pt.2'Dick Tracy Meets
  the Murderous Midget'. 150.00
55 ChG,Pt.3'Dick Tracy Meets
  the Murderous Midget' 150.00
56 ChG,'Case of the
  Teleguard Terror' 150.00
57 ChG,Pt.1'Case of the
  Ice Cold Killer' 175.00
58 ChG,Pt.2'Case of the
  Ice Cold Killer' 150.00
59 ChG,Pt.1'Case of the
  Million Dollar Murder' 150.00
60 ChG,Pt.2'Case of the
  Million Dollar Murder' 150.00
61 ChG,'Case of the
  Murderers Mask' 150.00
62 ChG,Pt.1'Case of the
  White Rat Robbers' 150.00
63 ChG,Pt.2'Case of the
  White Rat Robbers' 150.00
64 ChG,Pt.1'Case of the
  Interrupted Honeymoon' 150.00
65 ChG,Pt.2'Case of the
  Interrupted Honeymoon' 150.00
66 ChG,Pt.1'Case of the
  Killer's Revenge' 150.00
67 ChG,Pt.2'Case of the
  Killer's Revenge' 150.00
68 ChG,Pt.1'Case o-t TV Terror' . 150.00
69 ChG,Pt.2'Case o-t TV Terror' . 150.00
70 ChG,Pt.3'Case o-t TV Terror' . 150.00
71 ChG,A:Mrs. Forchune,Opal. . . 135.00
72 ChG,A:Empty Wiliams,Bonny . 135.00
73 ChG,A:Bonny Braids. 135.00
74 ChG,A:Mr. & Mrs.
  Fortson Knox. 135.00
75 ChG,A:Crewy Lou, Sphinx . . . 135.00
76 ChG,A:Diet Smith,Brainerd . . . 135.00
77 ChG,A:Crewy Lou,
  Bonny Braids. 135.00
78 ChG,A:Spinner Records 135.00
79 ChG,A:Model Jones,
  Larry Jones 135.00
80 ChG,A:Tonsils,Dot View 135.00
81 ChG,A:Edward Moppet,Tonsils 135.00
82 ChG,A:Dot View,Mr. Crime . . . 135.00
83 ChG,A:RifleRuby,NewsuitNan. 135.00
84 ChG,A:Mr.Crime,NewsuitNan. . 135.00
85 ChG,A:NewsuitNan, Mrs.Lava 135.00
86 ChG,A:Mr. Crime,Odds Zonn . 135.00
87 ChG,A:Odds Zonn,Wingy 135.00

88 ChG,A:Odds Zonn,Wingy 135.00
89 ChG,Pt.1'Canhead' 135.00
90 ChG,Pt.2'Canhead' 135.00
91 ChG,Pt.3'Canhead' 135.00
92 ChG,Pt.4'Canhead' 135.00
93 ChG,Pt.5'Canhead' 135.00
94 ChG,Pt.6'Canhead' 135.00
95 ChG,A:Mrs. Green,Dewdrop . . 135.00
96 ChG,A:Dewdrop,Sticks 135.00
97 ChG,A:Dewdrop,Sticks 135.00
98 ChG,A:Open-Mind Monty,
  Sticks. 135.00
99 ChG,A:Open-Mind Monty,
  Sticks. 150.00
100 ChG,A:Half-Pint,Dewdrop . . . 175.00
101 ChG,A:Open-Mind Monty . . . 135.00
102 ChG,A:Rainbow Reiley,
  Wingy. 135.00
103 ChG,A:Happy,Rughead. 135.00
104 ChG,A:Rainbow Reiley,
  Happy 135.00
105 ChG,A:Happy,Rughead. 135.00
106 ChG,A:Fence,Corny,Happy. . 135.00
107 ChG,A:Rainbow Reiley 135.00
108 ChG,A:Rughead,Corny,
  Fence. 135.00
109 ChG,A:Rughead,Mimi,Herky. 135.00
110 ChG,A:Vitamin Flintheart. . . . 135.00
111 ChG,A:Shoulders,Roach 135.00
112 ChG,A:Brilliant,Diet Smith . . . 135.00
113 ChG,A:Snowflake Falls 135.00
114 ChG,A:'Sketch'Paree, ... 135.00
115 ChG,A:Rod & Nylon Hoze. . . 135.00
116 ChG,A:Empty Williams 135.00
117 ChG,A:Spinner Records 135.00
118 ChG,A:Sleet. 135.00
119 ChG,A:Coffyhead 135.00
120 ChG,'Case Against
  Mumbles Quartet' 135.00
121 ChG,'Case of the Wild Boys'. 135.00
122 ChG,'Case of the
  Poisoned Pellet'. 135.00
123 ChG,'Case of the Deadly
  Treasure Hunt'. 135.00
124 ChG,'Case of Oodles
  Hears Only Evil 135.00
125 ChG,'Case of the Desparate
  Widow' 135.00
126 ChG,'Case of Oodles'
  Hideout' 135.00
127 ChG,'Case Against
  Joe Period' 135.00
128 ChG,'Case Against Juvenile
  Delinquent'. 135.00
129 ChG,'Case of Son of Flattop' 135.00
130 ChG,'Case of Great
  Gang Roundup' 135.00
131 ChG,'Strange Case of
  Flattop's Conscience' 135.00
132 ChG,'Case of Flattop's
  Big Show' 135.00
133 ChG,'Dick Tracy Follows Trail
  of Jewel Thief Gang' 135.00
134 ChG,'Last Stand of
  Jewel Thieves' 135.00
135 ChG,'Case of the
  Rooftop Sniper' 135.00
136 ChG,'Mystery of the
  Iron Room'. 135.00
137 ChG,'Law Versus Dick Tracy' 135.00
138 ChG,'Mystery of Mary X'. . . . 135.00
139 ChG,'Yogee the Merciless' . . 135.00
140 ChG,'The Tunnel Trap' 135.00
141 ChG,'Case of Wormy &
  His Deadly Wagon. 135.00
142 ChG,'Case of the
  Killer's Revenge' 135.00
143 ChG,'Strange Case of
  Measles' 135.00
144 ChG,'Strange Case of
  Shoulders' 135.00

145 ChG,'Case of the Feindish
    Photo-graphers';April, 1961. . 135.00

DIME COMICS
Newsbook Publ. Corp., 1945
1 LbC,A:Silver Streak 900.00

DING DONG
**Compix
(Magazine Enterprises), 1947**
1 (fa) 300.00
2 (fa) 150.00
3 thru 5 (fa) . . . . @100.00

DINKY DUCK
**St. John Publ. Co./Pines,
Nov., 1951**
1 . . . . 150.00
2 . . . . 75.00
3 thru 10 . . . . @50.00
11 thru 15 . . . . @40.00
16 thru 18 . . . . @35.00
19 Summer, 1958 . . . . 35.00

DIXIE DUGAN
**Columbia Publ./
Publication Enterprises,
July, 1942**
1 Boxing (c),Joe Palooka 350.00
2 . . . . 200.00
3 . . . . 150.00
4 & 5 . . . . @100.00
6 thru 12 . . . . @75.00
13 1949 . . . . 75.00

DIZZY DAMES
**B&M Distribution Co.
(American Comics),
Sept.–Oct., 1952**
1 . . . . 200.00
2 . . . . 125.00
3 thru 6 July–Aug., 1953 . . . . @100.00

DIZZY DON COMICS
**Howard Publications/
Dizzy Dean Ent., 1943**
1 B&W interior 150.00
2 B&W Interior 100.00
3 B&W Interior 75.00
4 B&W Interior 75.00
5 thru 21 . . . . @75.00
22 Oct., 1946 . . . . 200.00
1a thru 3a . . . . @175.00

DIZZY DUCK
See: BARNYARD COMICS

DOC CARTER
V.D. COMICS
Health Publ. Inst., 1949
N# 250.00
N# 150.00

DOC SAVAGE COMICS
Street & Smith, May, 1940
1 B:Doc Savage, Capt. Fury, Danny
   Garrett, Mark Mallory, Whisperer,
   Capt. Death, Treasure
   Island, A: The Magician . . . 7,500.00
2 O:Ajax,The Sun Man,E:The
   Whisperer 2,500.00
3 Artic Ice Wastes 1,700.00

Doc Savage #5
© Street & Smith

4 E:Treasure Island, Saves
   U.S. Navy 1,400.00
5 O:Astron, the Crocodile
   Queen, Sacred Ruby 1,100.00
6 E: Capt. Fury, O:Red Falcon,
   Murderous Peace Clan 850.00
7 V:Zoombas 850.00
8 Finds the Long Lost Treasure . 850.00
9 Smashes Japan's Secret Oil
   Supply 850.00
10 O:Thunder Bolt, The Living
   Dead A:Lord Manhattan 850.00
11 V:Giants of Destruction 700.00
12 Saves Merchant Fleet from
   Complete Destruction 700.00
2-1 The Living Evil 700.00
2-2 V:Beggar King 700.00
2-3 . . . . 700.00
2-4 Fight to Death 700.00
2-5 Saves Panama Canal from
   Blood Raider 700.00
2-6 . . . . 700.00
2-7 V:Black Knight 700.00
2-8 Oct., 1943 . . . . 700.00

DR. ANTHONY KING
HOLLYWOOD LOVE
DOCTOR
Harvey, Publ., 1952
1 . . . . 150.00
2 . . . . 100.00
3 . . . . 100.00
4 BP,May, 1954 . . . . 100.00

DOLL MAN
**Comic Favorites
(Quality Comics Group),
Fall, 1941–Oct., 1953**
1 RC,B:Doll Man & Justine
   Wright 5,000.00
2 B:Dragon 1,800.00
3 Five stories 1,500.00
4 Dolls of Death, Wanted:
   The Doll Man 1,300.00
5 RC,Four stories 1,100.00
6 Buy War Stamps (c) 750.00
7 Four stories 750.00
8 BWa,Three stories,A:Torchy . 2,200.00
9 Torchy 750.00
10 RC,V:Murder Marionettes,
   Grim, The Good Sport 600.00

Doll Man #32
© Quality Comics Group

11 Shocks Crime Square in the
   Eye 600.00
12 Torchy 600.00
13 RC,Blows Crime Sky High . . . 600.00
14 Spotlight on Comics 600.00
15 Faces Danger 600.00
16 Torchy 550.00
17 Deals out Punishment for
   Crime 550.00
18 Redskins Scalp Crime 550.00
19 Fitted for a Cement Coffin . . . 550.00
20 Destroys the Black Heart of
   Nemo Black 550.00
21 Problem of a Poison Pistol . . . 500.00
22 V:Tom Thumb 500.00
23 V:Minstrel, musician
   of menace 500.00
24 V:Elixir of Youth 500.00
25 V:Thrawn, Lord of Lightning . . 500.00
26 V:Sultan of Satarr &
   Wonderous Runt 500.00
27 Space Conquest 500.00
28 V:The Flame 500.00
29 V:Queen MAB 500.00
30 V:Lord Damion 500.00
31 I:Elmo, the Wonder Dog 400.00
32 A:Jeb Rivers 400.00
33 & 34 . . . . @400.00
35 Prophet of Doom 400.00
36 Death Trap in the Deep 400.00
37 V:The Skull,B:Doll Girl,
   Bondage(c) 550.00
38 The Cult of Death 400.00
39 V:The Death Drug, Narcotics . 400.00
40 Giants of Crime 400.00
41 The Headless Horseman 250.00
42 Tale of the Mind Monster 250.00
43 The Thing that Kills 250.00
44 V:Radioactive Man 250.00
45 What was in the Doom Box? . . 250.00
46 Monster from Tomorrow 250.00
47 V:Mad Hypnotist 250.00

FAMOUS GANG,
BOOK OF COMICS
**Firestone Tire & Rubber Co.,
1942**
N# Porky Pig,Bugs Bunny 1,200.00
Becomes:

DONALD AND MICKEY
MERRY CHRISTMAS
N# (2),CB, 1943 . . . . 1,000.00
N# (3),CB, 1944 . . . . 900.00

All comics prices listed are for *Near Mint* condition.   **CVA Page 383**

N# (4),CB, 1945 . . . . 1,400.00
N# (5),CB, 1946 . . . . 1,000.00
N# (6),CB, 1947 . . . . 1,000.00
N# (7),CB, 1948 . . . . 1,000.00
N# (8),CB, 1949 . . . . 900.00

DONALD DUCK
Whitman
W.Disney's Donald Duck ('35) . 4,200.00
W.Disney's Donald Duck ('36) . 4,000.00
W.Disney's Donald Duck ('38) . 4,000.00

DONALD DUCK
GIVEAWAYS
Donald Duck Surprise Party (Icy
  Frost Ice Cream 1948)WK . 3,500.00
Donald Duck (Xmas Giveaway
  1944) 1,200.00
Donald Duck Tells About Kites
  (P.G.&E., Florida 1954) 3,500.00
Donald Duck Tells About Kites
  (S.C.Edison 1954) 3,000.00
Donald Duck and the Boys
  (Whitman 1948) 800.00
Donald Ducks Atom Bomb
  (Cherrios 1947) 800.00

(WALT DISNEY'S)
DONALD DUCK
Dell Publishing Co.,
Nov., 1952
(#1-#25) See *Dell Four Color*
26 CB;"Trick or Treat" (1952) 500.00
27 CB(c);"Flying Horse"('53) 200.00
28 CB(c); Robert the Robot 175.00
29 CB(c) 175.00
30 CB(c) 175.00
31 thru 39 . . . . @100.00
40 thru 44 . . . . @90.00
45 CB 225.00
46 CB; "Secret of Hondorica" . . . 300.00
47 thru 51 . . . . @100.00
52 CB; "Lost Peg-Leg Mine" 225.00
53 . . . . 100.00
54 CB; "Forbidden Valley" 250.00
55 thru 59 . . . . @90.00
60 CB; "Donald Duck & the
  Titanic Ants" 250.00
61 thru 67 . . . . @75.00
68 CB 175.00
69 thru 78 . . . . @75.00
79 CB (1 page) 100.00
80 . . . . 65.00
81 CB (1 page) 75.00
82 . . . . 65.00
83 . . . . 65.00
84 . . . . 65.00
See: Independent Color Listings

DON FORTUNE
MAGAZINE
Don Fortune Publ. Co.,
Aug., 1946
1 CCB 300.00
2 CCB 175.00
3 CCB,Bondage(c) 150.00
4 CCB 150.00
5 CCB 150.00
6 CCB, Jan., 1947 . . . . 150.00

DON NEWCOMBE
Fawcett Publications, 1950
1 Baseball Star 650.00

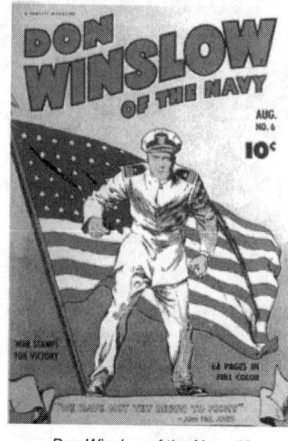

Don Winslow of the Navy #6
© Fawcett Publications

DON WINSLOW
OF THE NAVY
Fawcett Publ./
Charlton Comics, Feb., 1943
1 Captain Marvel (c) 1,600.00
2 Nips the Nipponese in
  the Solomons 750.00
3 Single-Handed invasion of
  the Philippines 500.00
4 Undermines the Nazis! 400.00
5 Stolen Battleship Mystery 400.00
6 War Stamps for Victory (c) . . . 400.00
7 Coast Guard 300.00
8 U.S. Marines 300.00
9 Fighting Marines 300.00
10 Fighting Seabees 300.00
11 . . . . 250.00
12 Tuned for Death 250.00
13 Hirohito's Hospitality 250.00
14 Catapults against the Axis . . . 250.00
15 Fighting Merchant Marine . . . 225.00
16 V:The Most Diabolical Villain
  of all Time 225.00
17 Buy War Stamps (c) 225.00
18 The First Underwater Convoy . 225.00
19 Bonape Excersion 225.00
20 The Nazi Prison Ship 225.00
21 Prisoner of the Nazis 175.00
22 Suicide Football 175.00
23 Peril on the High Seas 175.00
24 Adventures on the High Seas . 175.00
25 Shanghaied Red Cross Ship . 175.00
26 V:The Scorpion 175.00
27 Buy War Stamps 175.00
28 . . . . 175.00
29 Invitation to Trouble 175.00
30 . . . . 175.00
31 Man or Myth? 135.00
32 Return of the Renegade 135.00
33 Service Ribbons 135.00
34 Log Book 135.00
35 . . . . 135.00
36 . . . . 135.00
37 V: Sea Serpent 135.00
38 Climbs Mt. Everest 135.00
39 Scorpion's Death Ledger 135.00
40 Kick Off! 135.00
41 Rides the Skis! 125.00
42 Amazon Island 125.00
43 Ghastly Doll Murder Case . . . 125.00

44 The Scorpions Web 125.00
45 V:Highwaymen of the Seas . . 125.00
46 Renegades Jailbreak 125.00
47 The Artic Expedition 125.00
48 Maelstrom of the Deep 125.00
49 The Vanishing Ship! 125.00
50 V:The Snake 125.00
51 A:Singapore Sal 125.00
52 Ghost of the Fishing Ships . . . 125.00
53 . . . . 125.00
54 . . . . 125.00
55 . . . . 125.00
56 Far East 125.00
57 A:Singapore Sal 125.00
58 . . . . 125.00
59 . . . . 125.00
60 thru 63 . . . . @125.00
64 MB 125.00
65 Ph(c) 175.00
66 Ph(c) 175.00
67 Ph(c) 175.00
68 Ph(c) 175.00
69 Ph(c), Jaws of Destruction . . . 175.00
70 . . . . 125.00
71 . . . . 125.00
72 . . . . 125.00
73 Sept., 1955 . . . . 125.00

DOPEY DUCK
Non-Pareil Publ. Corp.,
Fall, 1945
1 A:Krazy Krow,Casper Cat 250.00
2 same 225.00
Becomes:

WACKY DUCK
Fall, 1946
3 . . . . 200.00
4 . . . . 175.00
5 . . . . 100.00
6 Summer, 1947 . . . . 100.00

DOROTHY LAMOUR
See: JUNGLE LIL

DOTTY DRIPPLE
Magazine Enterprises/
Harvey Publications, 1946
1 . . . . 100.00
2 . . . . 60.00
3 thru 10 . . . . @35.00
11 thru 20 . . . . @30.00
21 thru 23 . . . . @25.00
24 June, 1952 . . . . 25.00
Becomes:

HORACE &
DOTTY DRIPPLE
Aug., 1952
25 thru 42 . . . . @25.00
43 Oct., 1955 . . . . 25.00

DOUBLE COMICS
Elliot Publications
1 ('40),Masked Marvel 3,200.00
2 ('41),Tornado Tim 2,100.00
3 ('42) 1,600.00
4 ('43) 1,300.00
5 ('44) 1,300.00

DOUBLE UP
Elliot Publications, 1941
1 . . . . 1,100.00

All comics prices listed are for *Near Mint* condition.

DOWN WITH CRIME
Fawcett Publications,
Nov., 1951

1 A:Desarro	400.00
2 BP, A:Scanlon Gang	200.00
3 H-is for Heroin	150.00
4 BP, A:Desarro	135.00
5 No Jail Can Hold Me	150.00
6 The Puncture-Proof Assassin	135.00
7 The Payoff, Nov., 1952	135.00

DUDLEY
Prize Publications,
Nov.–Dec., 1952

1	175.00
2	125.00
3 March–April, 1950	100.00

DUMBO WEEKLY
The Walt Disney Co., 1942

1 Gas giveaways	950.00
2	300.00
3	300.00
4	300.00
5 thru 16	@300.00

DURANGO KID
Magazine Enterprises,
Oct.–Nov., 1949

1 FF, Charles Starrett photo (c) B:Durango Kid & Raider	1,000.00
2 FF, Charles Starrett Ph(c)	500.00
3 FF, Charles Starrett Ph(c)	450.00
4 FF, Charles Starrett Ph(c), Two-Timing Guns	400.00
5 FF, Charles Starrett Ph(c), Tracks Across the Trail	400.00
6 FF	250.00
7 FF,Atomic(c)	275.00
8 FF thru 10	@250.00
11 FF	175.00
12 FF	175.00
13 FF	175.00
14 thru 16 FF	@175.00
17 O:Durango Kid	225.00
18 FMe,DAy(c)	150.00
19 FMe,FG	125.00
20 FMe,FG	125.00
21 FMe,FG	125.00
22 FMe,FG	135.00
23 FMe,FG,I:Red Scorpion	135.00
24 thru 30 FMe,FG	@135.00
31 FMe,FG	135.00
32 thru 40 FG	@135.00
41 FG,Oct., 1941	135.00

DYNAMIC COMICS
Dynamic Publications
(Harry 'A' Chesler),
Oct., 1941

1 EK,O:Major Victory, Dynamic Man, Hale the Magician, A:Black Cobra	2,400.00
2 O:Dynamic Boy & Lady Satan,I:Green Knight, Lance Cooper	1,100.00
3 GT	950.00
8 Horror (c)	1,100.00
9 MRa,GT,B:Mr.E	1,000.00
10	750.00
11 GT	650.00
12 GT	600.00
13 GT	650.00
14	600.00
15 Sky Chief	600.00
16 GT,Bondage(c),Marijuana	850.00
17	900.00

Dynamic Comics #9
© Harry A Chesler

18 Ric	500.00
19 A:Dynamic Man	500.00
20 same,Nude Woman	1,000.00
21 same,Dinosaur(c)	500.00
22 same	500.00
23 A:Yankee Girl,1.0948	500.00

DYNAMITE
Comic Media/Allen Hardy Publ.,
May, 1953

1 DH(c),A:Danger#6	350.00
2	175.00
3 PAM(a&c),B:Johnny Dynamite,Drug	200.00
4 PAM(a&c),Prostitution	250.00
5 PAM(a&c)	150.00
6 PAM(a&c)	150.00
7 PAM(a&c)	150.00
8 PAM(a&c)	150.00
9 PAM(a&c)	150.00

Becomes:

JOHNNY DYNAMITE
Charlton Comics, June, 1955

10 PAM(c)	125.00
11	100.00
12	100.00

Becomes:

FOREIGN INTRIGUES
1956

13 A:Johnny Dynamite	90.00
14 same	60.00
15 same	60.00

Becomes:

BATTLEFIELD ACTION
Nov., 1957

16	70.00
17	40.00
18	40.00
19	40.00
20	40.00
21 thru 30	@30.00
31 thru 70	@15.00
71 thru 84 Oct., 1984	@12.00

EAGLE, THE
Fox Features Syndicate,
July, 1941

1 B:The Eagle,A:Rex Dexter of Mars	2,500.00
2 B:Spider Queen	1,200.00

3 B:Joe Spook	900.00
4 Jan., 1942	875.00

EAGLE, THE
Rural Home Publ.,
Feb.–March, 1945

1 LbC	650.00
2 LbC,April–May, 1945	350.00

EAT RIGHT
TO WORK AND WIN
Swift Co., 1942

N# Flash Gordon,Popeye	500.00

EDDIE STANKY
Fawcett Publications, 1951

N# New York Giants	450.00

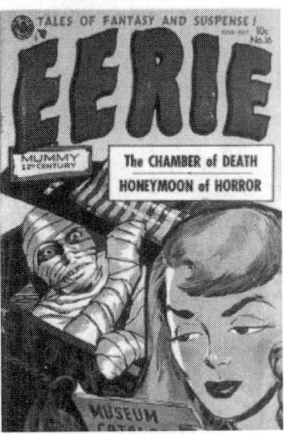

Eerie #16
© Avon Periodicals

EERIE
Avon Periodicals,
May–June, 1951–
Aug.–Sept., 1954

1 JKa,Horror from the Pit, Bondage(c)	5,500.00
2,WW(a&c), Chamber of Death	1,000.00
3 WW(a&c),JKa,JO Monster of the Storm	1,100.00
4 WW(c),Phantom of Reality	1,000.00
5 WW(c), Operation Horror	900.00
6 Devil Keeps a Date	450.00
7 WW(c),JKa,JO,Blood for the Vampire	700.00
8 EK, Song of the Undead	400.00
9 JKa, Hands of Death	400.00
10 Castle of Terror	400.00
11 Anatomical Monster	400.00
12 Dracula	500.00
13	400.00
14 Master of the Dead	400.00
15 Reprint #1	300.00
16 WW, Chamber of Death	300.00
17 WW(c),JO,JKa,	350.00

EERIE ADVENTURES
Approved Comics
(Ziff-Davis), Winter, 1951

1 BP,JKa,Bondage	500.00

EGBERT

**Arnold Publications/
Comic Magazine,
Spring, 1946**

1 I:Egbert & The Count	250.00
2	125.00
3	75.00
4	75.00
5	75.00
6	90.00
7	75.00
8	75.00
9	75.00
10	75.00
11 thru 17	@50.00
18 1950	50.00

EH!

**Charlton Comics,
Dec., 1953–Nov., 1954**

1 DAy(c),DG,Atomic Mouse	400.00
2 DAy(c)	250.00
3 DAy(c)	225.00
4 DAy(c),Sexual	250.00
5 DAy(c)	225.00
6 DAy(c),Sexual	250.00
7 DAy(c)	225.00

EL BOMBO COMICS

Frances M. McQueeny, 1945

1	125.00

ELLERY QUEEN

**Superior Comics,
May–Nov., 1949**

1 LbC(c),JKa,Horror	700.00
2	500.00
3 Drug issue	450.00
4 The Crooked Mile	500.00

ELLERY QUEEN

**Approved Comics
(Ziff-Davis),
Jan.–March, 1952**

1 NS(c),The Corpse the Killed	600.00
2 NS,Killer's Revenge,
Summer, 1952	500.00

ELSIE THE COW

**D.S. Publishing Co.,
Oct.–Nov., 1949**

1 P(c)	300.00
2 Bondage(c)	225.00
3 July–Aug., 1950	200.00

ENCHANTING LOVE

**Kirby Publishing Co.
Oct., 1949**

1 Branded Guilty, Ph(c)	150.00
2 Ph(c),BP	100.00
3 Ph(c),Utter Defeat was our
Victory; Jimmy Stewart	75.00
4 thru 6	@100.00

ETTA KETT

**Best Books, Inc.
(Standard Comics),
Dec., 1948**

11	100.00
12	75.00
13	75.00
14 Sept., 1949	75.00

ERNIE COMICS
See: SCREAM COMICS

*Exciting Comics #33
© Standard Comics*

EXCITING COMICS

**Better Publ./Visual Editions
(Standard Comics),
April, 1940**

1 O:Mask, Jim Hatfield,
Dan Williams	5,500.00
2 B:Sphinx	2,500.00
3 V;Robot	1,500.00
4 V:Sea Monster	1,000.00
5 V:Gargoyle	1,000.00
6	1,100.00
7 ASh(c)	800.00
8	800.00
9 O:Black Terror & Tim,
Bondage(c)	14,000.00
10 A:Black Terror	3,600.00
11 same	1,900.00
12 Bondage(c)	1,200.00
13 Bondage(c)	1,200.00
14 O:Sphinx	900.00
15 O:Liberator	850.00
16 Black Terror	750.00
17 same	750.00
18 same	750.00
19 same	750.00
20 E:Mask,Bondage(c)	700.00
21 A:Liberator	700.00
22 O:The Eaglet,B:American
Eagle	750.00
23 Black Terror	600.00
24 Black Terror	600.00
25 Bondage(c)	650.00
26 ASh(c)	600.00
27 ASh(c)	625.00
28 ASh(c),B:Crime Crusader	1,200.00
29 ASh(c)	800.00
30 ASh(c),Bondage(c)	900.00
31 ASh(c)	700.00
32 ASh(c)	700.00
33 ASh(c)	700.00
34 ASh(c)	700.00
35 ASh(c),E:Liberator	700.00
36 ASh(c)	700.00
37 ASh(c)	700.00
38 ASh(c)	700.00
39 ASh(c)O:Kara, Jungle
Princess	850.00
40 ASh(c)	900.00
41 ASh(c)	900.00

42 ASh(c),B:Scarab	950.00
43 ASh(c)	850.00
44 ASh(c)	850.00
45 ASh(c),V:Robot	850.00
46 ASh(c)	850.00
47 ASh(c)	850.00
48 ASh(c)	850.00
49 ASh(c),E:Kara &
American Eagle	850.00
50 ASh(c),E:American Eagle	850.00
51 ASh(c),B:Miss Masque	1,000.00
52 ASh(c),Miss Masque	750.00
53 ASh(c),Miss Masque	750.00
54 ASh(c),E:Miss Masque	750.00
55 ASh(c),O&B:Judy o/t Jungle	800.00
56 ASh(c)	750.00
57 ASh(c)	750.00
58 ASh(c)	750.00
59 ASh(c),FF,Bondage(c)	800.00
60 ASh(c),The Mystery Rider	750.00
61 ASh(c)	750.00
62 ASh(c)	750.00
63 ASh(c)	750.00
64 ASh(c)	750.00
65 ASh(c)	750.00
66	750.00
67 GT	750.00
68	750.00
69 Sept., 1949	750.00

EXCITING ROMANCES

Fawcett Publications, 1949

1 Ph(c)	150.00
2	100.00
3	100.00
4 Ph(c)	100.00
5 thru 14	@75.00

EXOTIC ROMANCE
See: TRUE WAR
ROMANCES

EXPLORER JOE

**Approved Comics
(Ziff-Davis), Winter, 1951**

1 NS,The Fire Opal
of Madagscar	150.00
2 BK, Oct.–Nov., 1952	165.00

EXPOSED

**D.S. Publishing Co.,
March–April, 1948**

1 Corpses Cash and Carry	275.00
2 Giggling Killer	350.00
3 One Bloody Night	150.00
4 JO,Deadly Dummy	150.00
5 Body on the Beach	150.00
6 Grl,The Secret in the Snow	450.00
7 The Gypsy Baron,
July–Aug., 1949	450.00

EXTRA COMICS

Magazine Enterprises, 1947

1	750.00

EXTRA!

**E.C. Comics,
March–April, 1955**

1 JCr,RC,JSe	300.00
2 JCr,RC,JSe	225.00
3 JCr,RC,JSe	225.00
4 JCr,RC,JSe	225.00
5 Nov.–Dec., 1955	225.00

GOLDEN AGE

FACE, THE

**Publication Enterprises
(Columbia Comics), 1942**
1 MBi(c),The Face 1,200.00
2 MBi(c) 750.00
Becomes:

TONY TRENT

1948
3 MBi,A:The Face 250.00
4 1949 . . . . 200.00

FAIRY TALE PARADE

Dell Publishing Co., 1942
1 WK,Giant 2,000.00
2 WK,Flying Horse 900.00
3 WK 600.00
4 WK 550.00
5 WK 550.00
6 WK 450.00
7 WK 450.00
8 WK 450.00
9 WK,Reluctant Dragon 450.00

FAMOUS COMICS

Zain-Eppy Publ.
N# Joe Palooka 600.00

FAMOUS CRIMES

**Fox Features Syndicate,
June, 1948**
1 Cold Blooded Killer 700.00
2 Near Nudity (c) 550.00
3 Crime Never Pays 650.00
4 . . . . 300.00
5 . . . . 300.00
6 . . . . 300.00
7 Drug issue 550.00
8 thru 19 . . . . @200.00
20 Aug., 1951 . . . . 200.00
51 1952 . . . . 125.00

FAMOUS FAIRY TALES

K.K. Publication Co., 1942
N# WK, Giveaway 500.00
N# WK, Giveaway 400.00
N# WK, Giveaway 400.00

FAMOUS FEATURE STORIES

Dell Publishing Co., 1938
1A:Tarzan, Terry and the Pirates
Dick Tracy,Smilin' Jack 1,000.00

FAMOUS FUNNIES

**Eastern Color Printing Co.,
1933**
N# A Carnival of Comics 13,000.00
N# Feb., 1934,
1st 10-cent comic 35,000.00
1 July, 1934 . . . . 25,000.00
2 . . . . 8,000.00
3 B:Buck Rogers 7,500.00
4 Football (c) 2,500.00
5 Christmas 2,200.00
6 . . . . 1,200.00
7 . . . . 1,200.00
8 . . . . 1,200.00
9 . . . . 1,200.00
10 . . . . 1,200.00
11 Four pages of Buck Rogers. 1,100.00
12 Four pages of Buck Rogers. 1,100.00
13 . . . . 1,000.00
14 . . . . 1,000.00

*Famous Funnies #89
© Eastern Color Printing*

15 Football (c) 1,000.00
16 . . . . 1,000.00
17 Christmas (c) 1,000.00
18 Four pages of Buck Rogers. 1,200.00
19 . . . . 900.00
20 . . . . 900.00
21 Baseball 700.00
22 Buck Rogers 750.00
23 . . . . 650.00
24 B: War on Crime 650.00
25 . . . . 650.00
26 . . . . 650.00
27 G-Men (c) 650.00
28 . . . . 650.00
29 Christmas 650.00
30 . . . . 650.00
31 . . . . 450.00
32 Phantom Magician 600.00
33 A:Baby Face Nelson &
John Dillinger 450.00
34 . . . . 450.00
35 Buck Rogers 550.00
36 . . . . 450.00
37 . . . . 450.00
38 Portrait,Buck Rogers 550.00
39 . . . . 450.00
40 . . . . 450.00
41 thru 50 . . . . @400.00
51 thru 57 . . . . @350.00
58 Baseball (c) 350.00
59 . . . . 350.00
60 . . . . 350.00
61 . . . . 300.00
62 . . . . 300.00
63 . . . . 300.00
64 . . . . 300.00
65 JK 300.00
66 . . . . 300.00
67 . . . . 300.00
68 JK 300.00
69 . . . . 300.00
70 . . . . 300.00
71 BEv 250.00
72 BEv,B:Speed Spaulding 250.00
73 BEv 250.00
74 BEv 250.00
75 BEv 250.00
76 BEv 250.00
77 BEv,Merry Christmas (c) 250.00
78 BEv 250.00
79 BEv 250.00
80 BEv,Buck Rogers 250.00
81 O:Invisible Scarlet O'Neil . . . 250.00
82 Buck Rogers (c) 250.00
83 Dickie Dare 175.00

84 Scotty Smith 175.00
85 Eagle Scout,Roy Rogers 175.00
86 Moon Monsters 175.00
87 Scarlet O'Neil 175.00
88 Dickie Dare 175.00
89 O:Fearless Flint 175.00
90 Bondage (c) 200.00
91 . . . . 175.00
92 . . . . 175.00
93 . . . . 175.00
94 War Bonds 200.00
95 Invisible Scarlet O'Neil 175.00
96 . . . . 175.00
97 War Bonds Promo 175.00
98 . . . . 175.00
99 . . . . 175.00
100 Anniversary issue 175.00
101 thru 110 . . . . @175.00
111 thru 130 . . . . @125.00
131 thru 150 . . . . @100.00
151 thru 162 . . . . @100.00
163 Valentine's Day (c) 100.00
164 . . . . 80.00
165 . . . . 80.00
166 . . . . 80.00
167 . . . . 80.00
168 . . . . 80.00
169 AW 125.00
170 AW 125.00
171 thru 190 . . . . @80.00
191 thru 203 . . . . @75.00
204 War (c) 85.00
205 thru 208 . . . . @75.00
209 FF(c),Buck Rogers 1,700.00
210 FF(c),Buck Rogers 1,700.00
211 FF(c),Buck Rogers 1,700.00
212 FF(c),Buck Rogers 1,700.00
213 FF(c),Buck Rogers 1,700.00
214 FF(c),Buck Rogers 1,700.00
215 FF(c),Buck Rogers 1,700.00
216 FF(c),Buck Rogers 1,700.00
217 . . . . 90.00
218 July, 1955 . . . . 90.00

FAMOUS GANG, BOOK OF COMICS

See: DONALD AND MICKEY MERRY CHRISTMAS

FAMOUS GANGSTERS

Avon Periodicals, 1951
1 Al Capone, Dillinger,
Luciano & Shultz 500.00
2 WW(c),Dillinger Machine-
Gun Killer 450.00
3 Lucky Luciano & Murder Inc. . . 450.00
Becomes:

CRIME ON THE WATERFRONT

May, 1952
4 Underworld Gangsters who
Control the Shipment of
Drugs! 400.00

FAMOUS STARS

Ziff-Davis Publ. Co., 1950
1 OW,Shelley Winter,Susan
Peters & Shirley Temple 400.00
2 BEv,Betty Hutton, Bing Crosby 300.00
3 OW,Judy Garland, Alan Ladd . 325.00
4 RC,Jolson, Bob Mitchum 300.00
5 BK,Elizabeth Taylor,
Esther Williams 400.00
6 Gene Kelly, Spring, 1952 . . . . 250.00

GOLDEN AGE

FAMOUS STORIES
Dell Publishing Co., 1942
1 Treasure Island 375.00
2 Tom Sawyer 350.00

FAMOUS WESTERN BADMEN
See: REDSKIN

FANTASTIC
See: CAPTAIN SCIENCE

Fantastic Comics #23
© Fox Features Syndicate

FANTASTIC COMICS
Fox Features Syndicate, 1939
1 LF(c),I&O:Samson,B:Star
  Dust, Super Wizard, Space
  Smith & Capt. Kid. 7,000.00
2 BP,LF(c),Samson destroyed the
  Battery & Routed the Foe. . 3,300.00
3 BP,LF(c),Slays the Iron
  Monster. 9,000.00
4 GT,LF(c),Demolishes the
  Closing Torture Walls 2,500.00
5 GT,LF(c),Crumbles the
  Mighty War Machine. 2,300.00
6 JSm(c),Bondage(c) 1,800.00
7 JSm(c) 1,800.00
8 GT,Destroys the Mask of
  Fire,Bondage(c) 1,300.00
9 Mighty Muscles saved the
  Drowning Girl 1,300.00
10 I&O:David. 1,300.00
11 Wrecks the Torture Machine
  to save his fellow American 1,100.00
12 Heaved the Huge Ship high
  into the Air 1,100.00
13 Samson(c) 1,100.00
14 Samson(c) 1,100.00
15 Samson(c) 1,100.00
16 E:Stardust 1,100.00
17 Samson(c) 1,100.00
18 I:Black Fury & Chuck. 1,100.00
19 Samson(c) 1,000.00
20 Samson(c) 1,000.00
21 B&I: The Banshee,Hitler(c) . 1,200.00
22 Hittler & Samson(c) 1,100.00
23 O:The Gladiator, Hitler (c)
  Nov., 1941 . . . . 1,200.00

FARGO KID
See: JUSTICE TRAPS OF THE GUILTY

FAST FICTION
**Seaboard Publ./
Famous Author Illustrated,
Oct., 1949**
1 Scarlet Pimpernel 500.00
2 HcK,Captain Blood 400.00
3 She 500.00
4 The 39 Steps 350.00
5 HcK,Beau Geste 350.00
Becomes:

STORIES BY FAMOUS AUTHORS ILLUSTRATED
Aug., 1950
1a Scarlet Pimpernel 400.00
2a Captain Blood 400.00
3a She 500.00
4a The 39 Steps 325.00
5a Beau Geste 300.00
6 HcK,MacBeth. 325.00
7 HcK,Window 275.00
8 HcK,Hamlet 300.00
9 Nicholas Nickleby 275.00
10 HcK,Romeo & Juliet 275.00
11 GS,Ben Hur. 290.00
12 GS,La Svengali. 275.00
13 HcK,Scaramouche 275.00

FAWCETT FUNNY ANIMALS
**Fawcett Publications,
Dec., 1942**
1 I:Hoppy the Marvel Bunny,
  Captain Marvel (c) 800.00
2 X-Mas Issue 400.00
3 Spirit of '43 . . . . 250.00
4 and 5 . . . . @250.00
6 Buy War Bonds and Stamps . . 175.00
7 . . . . 175.00
8 Flag (c). 175.00
9 and 10 . . . . @175.00
11 thru 20 . . . . @125.00
21 thru 30 . . . . @100.00
31 thru 40 . . . . @75.00
41 thru 83 . . . . @75.00

Charlton Comics
84 . . . . 75.00
85 thru 91 Feb., 1956. . . . . . . @50.00

FAWCETT MOVIE COMICS
Fawcett Publications, 1949
N# Dakota Lil 375.00
N#a Copper Canyon 300.00
N# Destination the Moon 1,100.00
N# Montana 300.00
N# Pioneer Marshal 300.00
N# Powder River Rustlers 450.00
N# Singing Guns 275.00
7 Gunmen of Abilene 325.00
8 King of the Bull Whip 425.00
9 BP,The Old Frontier 300.00
10 The Missourians 300.00
11 The Thundering Trail. 400.00
12 Rustlers on Horseback 325.00
13 Warpath. 250.00
14 Last Outpost,RonaldReagan . 550.00
15 The Man from Planet-X . . . 3,000.00
16 10 Tall Men 200.00
17 Rose Cimarron 150.00
18 The Brigand 175.00

19 Carbine Williams. 175.00
20 Ivanhoe, Dec., 1952 . . . . . . 300.00

FEATURE BOOKS
**David McKay Publications,
May, 1937**
N# Dick Tracy 10,000.00
N# Popeye 9,000.00
1 Zane Grey's King of the
  Royal Mounted 800.00
2 Popeye 1,200.00
3 Popeye and the "Jeep" 1,000.00
4 Dick Tracy 2,000.00
5 Popeye and his Poppa 1,000.00
6 Dick Tracy 1,200.00
7 Little Orphan Annie 1,400.00
8 Secret Agent X-9 . . . . 750.00
9 Tracy & the Famon Boys . . 1,200.00
10 Popeye & Susan 1,000.00
11 Annie Rooney 350.00
12 Blondie. 1,100.00
13 Inspector Wade. 325.00
14 Popeye in Wild Oats 1,200.00
15 Barney Baxter in the Air 500.00
16 Red Eagle. 400.00
17 Gang Busters 900.00
18 Mandrake the Magician 850.00
19 Mandrake 850.00
20 The Phantom 1,200.00
21 Lone Ranger 1,100.00
22 The Phantom 900.00
23 Mandrake in Teibe Castle. . . . 850.00

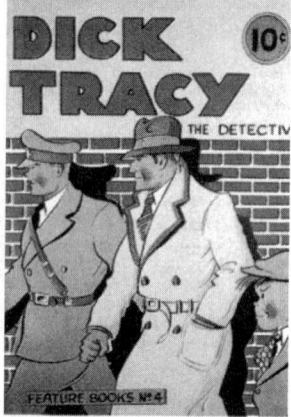

Feature Books #4
© David McKay Publications

24 Lone Ranger 1,100.00
25 Flash Gordon on the
  Planet Mongo 1,500.00
26 Prince Valiant. 1,300.00
27 Blondie 250.00
28 Blondie and Dagwood. 250.00
29 Blondie at the Home
  Sweet Home 250.00
30 Katzenjammer Kids 250.00
31 Blondie Keeps the Home
  Fires Burning. 250.00
32 Katzenjammer Kids. 200.00
33 Romance of Flying 200.00
34 Blondie Home is Our Castle . . 250.00
35 Katzenjammer Kids. 200.00
36 Blondie on the Home Front. . 225.00
37 Katzenjammer Kids. 250.00
38 Blondie the ModelHomemaker 225.00
39 The Phantom 700.00
40 Blondie 225.00

41 Katzenjammer Kids. 250.00
42 Blondie in Home-Spun Yarns . 225.00
43 Blondie Home-Cooked Scraps 225.00
44 Katzenjammer Kids in
   Monkey Business 250.00
45 Blondie in Home of the Free
   and the Brave 225.00
46 Mandrake in Fire World 500.00
47 Blondie in Eaten out of
   House and Home 225.00
48 The Maltese Falcon 1,200.00
49 Perry Mason - The Case of
   the Lucky Legs 350.00
50 The Shoplifters Shoe,
   P. Mason 350.00
51 Rip Kirby - Mystery of
   the Mangler 350.00
52 Mandrake in the Land of X . . . 450.00
53 Phantom in Safari Suspense . 500.00
54 Rip Kirby - Case of the
   Master Menace 425.00
55 Mandrake in 5-numbers
   Treasue Hunt 450.00
56 Phantom Destroys the
   Sky Band 500.00
57 Phantom in the Blue Gang,
   1948. . . . . 500.00

FEATURE FUNNIES
Harry A. Chesler Publ./
Comic Favorites, Oct., 1937
1 RuG(a&c),A:Joe Palooka,
   Mickey Finn, Bungles, Dixie
   Dugan, Big Top, Strange as
   It Seems, Off the Record . . 3,500.00
2 A: The Hawk 1,600.00
3 WE,Joe Palooka,The Clock . 1,200.00
4 RuG,WE,RuG(c),JoePalooka 1,200.00
5 WE, Joe Palooka drawing . . 1,200.00
6 WE, Joe Palooka (c) 1,200.00
7 WE,LLe, Gallant Knight story
   by Vernon Henkel 750.00
8 WE 700.00
9 WE, Joe Palooka story 1,000.00
10 WE,Micky Finn(c) 700.00
11 WE,LLe,The Bungles(c) 700.00
12 WE, Joe Palooka(c) 700.00
13 WE,LLe, World Series(c) 750.00
14 WE,Ned Brant(c). 525.00
15 WE,Joe Palooka(c). 550.00
16 Mickey Finn(c) 525.00
17 WE 525.00
18 Joe Palooka (c). 550.00
19 WE,LLe,Mickey Finn(c). 525.00
20 WE,LLe 525.00
Becomes:

FEATURE COMICS
Quality Comics Group,
June. 1939–May, 1950
21 Joe Palooka(c) 750.00
22 LLe(c),Mickey Finn(c) 500.00
23 B:Charlie Chan 550.00
24 AAr,Joe Palooka(c) 500.00
25 AAr,The Clock(c). 500.00
26 AAr,The Bundles(c). 500.00
27 WE,AAr,I:Doll Man. 6,500.00
28 LF,AAr,The Clock(c). 2,500.00
29 LF,AAr,The Clock(c). 1,400.00
30 LF,AAr,Doll Man(c) 1,400.00
31 LF,AAr,Mickey Finn(c) 1,700.00
32 PGv,LF,GFx,Doll Man(c) 900.00
33 PGv,LF,GFx,Bundles(c) 750.00
34 PGv,LF,GFx,Doll Man(c) 900.00
35 PGv,LF,GFx,Bundles(c) 750.00
36 PGv,LF,GFx,Doll Man(c) 900.00
37 PGv,LF,GFx,Bundles(c) 750.00
38 PGv,GFx,Doll Man(c) 650.00
39 PGv,GFx,Bundles(c) 650.00
40 PGv,GFx,WE(c),Doll Man(c) . 650.00

Feature Comics #36
© Quality Comics Group

41 PGv,GFx,WE(c),Bundles(c) . . 650.00
42 GFx,Doll Man(c) 500.00
43 RC,GFx,Bundles(c). 425.00
44 RC,GFx,Doll Man(c) 650.00
45 RC,GFx,Bundles(c). 400.00
46 RC,PGv,GFx,Doll Man(c) 600.00
47 RC,GFx,Bundles(c). 400.00
48 RC,GFx,Doll Man(c) 600.00
49 RC,GFx,Bundles(c). 400.00
50 RC,GFx,Doll Man(c) 600.00
51 RC,GFx,Bundles(c). 400.00
52 RC,GFx,Doll Man(c) 400.00
53 RC,GFx,Bundles(c). 325.00
54 RC,GFx,Doll Man(c) 400.00
55 RC,GFx,Bundles(c). 325.00
56 RC,GFx,Doll Man(c) 400.00
57 RC,GFx,Bundles(c). 325.00
58 RC,GFx,Doll Man (c) 400.00
59 RC,GFx,Mickey Finn(c) 325.00
60 RC,GFx,Doll Man(c) 400.00
61 RC,GFx,Bundles(c). 300.00
62 RC,GFx,Doll Man(c) 350.00
63 RC,GFx,Bundles(c). 300.00
64 BP,GFx,Doll Man(c) 350.00
65 BP,GFx(c),Bundles(c) 300.00
66 BP,GFx,Doll Man(c) 350.00
67 BP 300.00
68 BP,Doll Man vs.BeardedLady . 300.00
69 BP,GFx(c),Devil (c) 300.00
70 BP,Doll Man(c) 350.00
71 BP,GFx(c) 300.00
72 BP,Doll Man(c) 300.00
73 BP,GFx(c),Bundles(c) 250.00
74 Doll Man(c) 300.00
75 GFx(c) 250.00
76 GFx(c) 250.00
77 Doll Man (c) until #140 . . . . . 250.00
78 Knows no Fear but the
   Knife Does. 250.00
79 Little Luck God 250.00
80 . . . . 250.00
81 Wanted for Murder 200.00
82 V:Shawunkas the Shaman . . . 200.00
83 V:Mechanical Man 200.00
84 V:Masked Rider, Death
   Goes to the Rodeo 200.00
85 V:King of Beasts 200.00
86 Is He A Killer? 200.00
87 The Maze of Murder 200.00
88 V:The Phantom Killer 200.00
89 Crook's Goose 200.00
90 V:Whispering Corpse 200.00
91 V:The Undertaker 200.00
92 V:The Image 200.00
93 . . . . 200.00

94 V:The Undertaker 200.00
95 Flatten's the Peacock's Pride . 200.00
96 Doll Man Proves
   Justice is Blind. 200.00
97 V:Peacock 200.00
98 V:Master Diablo 200.00
99 On the Warpath Again! 200.00
100 Crushes the City of Crime . . 250.00
101 Land of the Midget Men!. . . . 150.00
102 The Angle 150.00
103 V:The Queen of Ants 150.00
104 V:The Botanist 150.00
105 Dream of Death 150.00
106 V:The Sword Fish 150.00
107 Hand of Horror!. 150.00
108 V:Cateye 150.00
109 V:The Brain 150.00
110 V:Fat Cat 150.00
111 V:The Undertaker 150.00
112 I:Mr. Curio & His Miniatures . 150.00
113 V:Highwayman 150.00
114 V:Tom Thumb 150.00
115 V:The Sphinx. 150.00
116 V:Elbows 150.00
117 Polka Dot on the Spot. 150.00
118 thru 144 . . . . @150.00

FEDERAL MEN COMICS
Gerard Publ. Co., 1942
2 S&S,Spanking 500.00

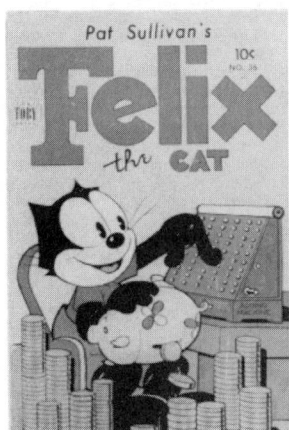

Felix the Cat #36
© Dell Publishing Co./Toby Press

FELIX THE CAT
Dell Publishing Co.,
Feb.–March, 1948
1 . . . . 450.00
2 . . . . 300.00
3 . . . . 200.00
4 . . . . 200.00
5 . . . . 200.00
6 . . . . 175.00
7 . . . . 175.00
8 . . . . 175.00
9 . . . . 175.00
10 . . . . 175.00
11 thru 19 . . . . @150.00

Toby Press
20 thru 30. . . . . @350.00
31 . . . . 150.00
32 . . . . 350.00
33 . . . . 350.00
34 & 35 . . . . 150.00
36 . . . . 300.00

GOLDEN AGE

37 Giant, Christmas(c)........ 750.00
38 thru 60................. @300.00
61 .... 275.00

Harvey

62 thru 80................. @75.00
81 thru 99................. @60.00
100 .... 75.00
101 thru 118............... @50.00
Spec., 100 pgs, 1952....... 350.00
Summer Ann., 100 pgs. 1953 ... 500.00
Winter Ann.,#2 100 pgs, 1954. .. 500.00

FERDINAND THE BULL
Dell Publishing Co., 1938

1 .... 250.00

FIGHT AGAINST CRIME
Story Comics May, 1951

1 Scorpion of Crime Inspector
   "Brains" Carroway 500.00
2 Ganglands Double Cross 300.00
3 Killer Dolan's Double Cross .. 250.00
4 Hopped Up Killers - The
   Con's Slaughter,Drug issue . 250.00
5 FF,Horror o-t Avenging Corpse 225.00
6 Terror of the Crazy Killer 200.00
7 .... 200.00
8 Killer with the Two-bladed
   Knife 175.00
9 Rats Die by Gas,Horror..... 450.00
10 Horror of the Con's Revenge . 450.00
11 Case of the Crazy Killer 450.00
12 Horror,Drug issue 500.00
13 The Bloodless Killer 450.00
14 Electric Chair (c).......... 500.00
15 .... 450.00
16 RA,Bondage(c)........... 500.00
17 Knife in Neck(c) 500.00
18 Attempted hanging (c)...... 500.00
19 Bondage(c)............... 500.00
20 Severed Head (c) 800.00
21 .... 375.00
Becomes:

FIGHT AGAINST
THE GUILTY
Dec., 1954

22 RA,Electric Chair 375.00
23 March, 1955 .... 250.00

FIGHT COMICS
Fight Comics Inc.
(Fiction House Magazines),
Jan., 1940

1 LF,GT,WE(c),O:Spy Fighter . 5,000.00
2 GT,WE(c),Joe Lewis 1,700.00
3 WE(c),GT,B:Rip Regan,
   The Powerman 1,400.00
4 GT,LF(c) 1,300.00
5 WE(c) 1,300.00
6 GT,BP(c) 750.00
7 GT,BP(c),Powerman-Blood
   Money 750.00
8 GT,Chip Collins-Lair of
   the Vulture 750.00
9 GT,Chip Collins-Prey of the
   War Eagle 750.00
10 GT,Wolves of the Yukon 750.00
11 .... 650.00
12 RA,Powerman-Monster of
   Madness 650.00
13 Shark Broodie-Legion
   of Satan................ 650.00
14 Shark Broodie-Lagoon
   of Death................ 650.00
15 Super-American-Hordes of
   the Secret Dicator 800.00
16 B:Capt.Fight,SwastikaPlague . 800.00

Fight Comics #14
© Fiction House Magazines

17 Super-American-Blaster of
   the Pig-Boat Pirates 750.00
18 Shark Broodie-Plague of
   the Yellow Devils 750.00
19 E:Capt. Fight.............. 750.00
20 .... 550.00
21 Rip Carson-Hell's Sky-Riders . 450.00
22 Rip Carson-Sky Devil's
   Mission 450.00
23 Rip Carson-Angels of
   Vengeance.............. 450.00
24 Baynonets for the Banzai
   Breed! Bondage(c) 400.00
25 Rip Carson-Samurai
   Showdown............. 400.00
26 Rip Carson-Fury of
   the Sky-Brigade.......... 400.00
27 War-Loot for the Mikado
   Bondage(c)............. 400.00
28 Rip Carson 400.00
29 Rip Carson-Charge of the
   Lost Region.............. 400.00
30 Rip Carson-Jeep-Raiders of
   the Torture Jungle 400.00
31 Gangway for the Gyrenes,
   Decapitation (c)........... 450.00
32 Vengeance of the Hun-
   Hunters,Bondage(c) 450.00
33 B:Tiger Girl 300.00
34 Bondage(c)............... 300.00
35 MB....................... 300.00
36 MB....................... 300.00
37 MB....................... 300.00
38 MB,Bondage(c)........... 325.00
39 MB,Senorita Rio-Slave Brand
   of the Spider Cult......... 300.00
40 MB,Bondage (c) 350.00
41 MB,Bondage (c) 350.00
42 MB....................... 300.00
43 MB,Senorita Rio-The Fire-Brides
   of the Lost Atlantis,
   Bondage(c) 325.00
44 MB,R:Capt. Fight 300.00
45 MB,Tonight Don Diablo Rides. 300.00
46 MB....................... 300.00
47 MB,SenoritaRio-Horror's
   Hacienda 300.00
48 MB....................... 300.00
49 MB,JKa,B:Tiger Girl(c) 300.00
50 MB....................... 300.00
51 MB,O:Tiger Girl........... 500.00
52 MB,Winged Demons of Doom 275.00
53 MB,Shadowland Shrine 275.00
54 MB,Flee the Cobra Fury..... 275.00

55 MB,Jungle Juggernaut 275.00
56 MB....................... 275.00
57 MB,Jewels of Jeopardy...... 275.00
58 MB....................... 275.00
59 MB,Vampires ofCrystalCavern 275.00
60 MB,Kraal of DeadlyDiamonds 275.00
61 MB,Seekers of the Sphinx,
   O:Tiger Girl 300.00
62 MB,Graveyard if the
   Tree Tribe 250.00
63 MB....................... 250.00
64 MB,DawnBeast from
   Karama-Zan! 250.00
65 Beware the Congo Girl..... 225.00
66 Man or Ape!.............. 225.00
67 Head-Hunters of Taboo Trek . 225.00
68 Fangs of Dr. Voodoo........ 225.00
69 Cage of the Congo Fury..... 225.00
70 Kraal of Traitor Tusks 225.00
71 Captives for the Golden
   Crocodile 225.00
72 Land of the Lost Safaris 225.00
73 War-Gods of the Jungle 225.00
74 Advengers of the Jungle..... 225.00
75 Perils of Momba-Kzar....... 225.00
76 Kraal of Zombi-Zaro 225.00
77 Slave-Queen of the Ape Man . 225.00
78 Great Congo Diamond
   Robbery................ 250.00
79 A:Space Rangers 275.00
80 .... 200.00
81 E:Tiger Girl(c) 200.00
82 RipCarson-CommandoStrike . 200.00
83 NobodyLoves a Minesweeper 200.00
84 Rip Carson-Suicide Patrol ... 200.00
85 .... 200.00
86 GE,Tigerman,Summer,1954 .. 225.00

FIGHTING AMERICAN
Headline Publications
(Prize), April–May, 1954

1 S&K,O:Fighting American &
   Speedboy 2,500.00
2 S&K(a&c) 1,200.00
3 S&K(a&c) 850.00
4 S&K(a&c) 850.00
5 S&K(a&c) 850.00
6 S&K(a&c),O:Fighting
   American 800.00
7 S&K(a&c), April–May, 1955 .. 700.00

FIGHTING DAVY
CROCKETT
See: KIT CARSON

FIGHTING INDIANS OF
THE WILD WEST
Avon Periodicals,
March, 1952

1 EK,EL,Geronimo, Crazy Horse,
   Chief Victorio 200.00
2 EK,Same, Nov., 1952 .... 150.00

FIGHTING
LEATHERNECKS
Toby Press, Feb., 1952

1 JkS,Duke's Diary 150.00
2 .... 125.00
3 .... 100.00
4 .... 100.00
5 .... 75.00
6 Dec., 1952 .... 75.00

FIGHTIN' TEXAN
See: TEXAN, THE

Fighting Yank #23
© Standard Comics

FIGHTING YANK

Nedor Publ./Better Publ.
(Standard Comics) Sept., 1942
1 B:Fighting Yank, A:Wonder Man,
   Mystico, Bondage (c) 3,800.00
2 JaB 1,500.00
3 . . . . 1,100.00
4 AS(c) 1,100.00
5 AS(c) 850.00
6 AS(c) 850.00
7 AS(c),A:Fighting Yank 800.00
8 AS(c) 800.00
9 AS(c) 800.00
10 AS(c). 800.00
11 AS(c), A:Grim Reaper, Nazis
   bomb Washington (c) 700.00
12 AS(c), Hirohito bondage (c) . . 700.00
13 AS(c). 650.00
14 AS(c). 650.00
15 AS(c). 650.00
16 AS(c). 650.00
17 AS(c). 650.00
18 AS(c), A:American Eagle . . 650.00
19 AS(c). 650.00
20 AS(c) 650.00
21 AS(c) A:Kara,Jungle
   Princess. 650.00
22 AS(c) A:Miss Masque-
   (c) story 700.00
23 AS(c) Klu Klux Klan
   parody (c) 900.00
24 A:Miss Masque 600.00
25 JRo,MMe,A:Cavalier. 750.00
26 JRo,MMe,A:Cavalier. 600.00
27 JRo,MMe,A:Cavalier. 600.00
28 JRo,MMe,AW,A:Cavalier 650.00
29 JRo,MMe,Aug., 1949 . . . . . . 650.00

FILM STAR ROMANCES

Star Publications, 1950
1 LbC(c), Rudy Valentino story . 650.00
2 Liz Taylor & Robert Taylor,
   photo (c) 700.00
3 May–June, 1950, photo(c). . . . 350.00

FIREHAIR COMICS

Flying Stories, Inc.
(Fiction House Magazine),
Winter, 1948–Spring, 1952
1 I:Firehair, Riders on the
   Pony Express 750.00
2 Bride of the Outlaw Guns 400.00

---

3 Kiss of the Six-Gun Siren! . . . 350.00
4 & 5 . . . . @350.00
6 . . . . 325.00
7 War Drums at Buffalo Bend . . 250.00
8 Raid on the Red Arrows 250.00
9 French Flags and Tomahawks 250.00
10 Slave Maiden of the Crees . . 250.00
11 Wolves of the Overland Trail. . 250.00

FLAME, THE

Fox Feature Syndicate,
Summer, 1940
1 LF,O:The Flame 5,000.00
2 GT,LF,Wing Turner 2,000.00
3 BP,Wonderworld 1,300.00
4 . . . . 1,200.00
5 GT 1,200.00
6 GT 1,200.00
7 A:The Yank 1,200.00
8 The Finger of the Frozen
   Death!, Jan., 1942 . . . . 1,200.00

FLAMING LOVE

Comic Magazines
(Quality Comics Group),
Dec., 1949
1 BWa,BWa(c),The Temptress
   I Feared in His Arms 500.00
2 Torrid Tales of Turbulent
   Passion 250.00
3 BWa,RC,My Heart's at Sea . . 300.00
4 One Women who made a
   Mockery of Love, Ph(c) 200.00
5 Bridge of Longing, Ph(c) 200.00
6 Men both Loved & Feared Me,
   Oct., 1950 . . . . 200.00

FLASH GORDON

Harvey Publications,
Oct., 1950
1 AR,Bondage(c) 450.00
2 AR 300.00
3 AR Bondage(c) 275.00
4 AR, April, 1951 . . . . 275.00

FLIP

Harvey Publications,
April, 1954
1 HN 275.00
2 HN,BP,June, 1954 . . . . 275.00

FLY BOY

Approved Comics
(Ziff-Davis) Spring, 1952
1 NS(c),Angels without Wings . . 300.00
2 NS(c),Flyboy's Flame-Out,
   Oct.–Nov., 1952 . . . . 200.00

THE FLYING A'S
RANGE RIDER

Dell Publishing Co.,
June–Aug., 1953
(1) = Dell Four Color #404
2 Ph(c) all 200.00
3 . . . . 150.00
4 . . . . 100.00
5 . . . . 100.00
6 . . . . 100.00
7 . . . . 100.00
8 . . . . 100.00
9 . . . . 100.00
10 . . . . 100.00
11 . . . . 75.00
12 . . . . 75.00
13 . . . . 75.00

---

14 . . . . 75.00
15 . . . . 75.00
16 . . . . 75.00
17 ATh 125.00
19 . . . . 75.00
20 . . . . 75.00
21 . . . . 75.00
22 . . . . 75.00
23 . . . . 75.00
24. . . . . 75.00

FOODINI

Continental Publications,
March, 1950
1 TV Puppet 275.00
2 Jingle Dingle 150.00
3 . . . . 100.00
4 Aug., 1950 . . . . 100.00

FOOTBALL THRILLS

Approved Comics
(Ziff-Davis),
Fall-Winter, 1952
1 BP,NS(c),Red Grange story . . 350.00
2 NS(c),Bronko Nagurski,
   Spring,1952 . . . . 250.00

FORBIDDEN LOVE

Comic Magazine
(Quality Comics Group),
March, 1950
1 RC,Ph(c),Heartbreak Road . 1,000.00
2 Ph(c),I loved a Gigolo 800.00
3 Kissless Bride 500.00
4 BWa,Brimstone Kisses,
   Sept., 1950 . . . . 500.00

FORBIDDEN WORLDS

American Comics Group,
July–Aug., 1951
1 AW,FF 2,200.00
2 . . . . 950.00
3 AW,WW,JD 1,000.00
4 Werewolf (c) 600.00
5 AW 750.00
6 AW,King Kong (c) 650.00
7 . . . . 400.00
8 . . . . 400.00
9 Atomic Bomb 450.00
10 JyD 375.00
11 The Mummy's Treasure 275.00
12 Chest of Death 275.00
13 Invasion from Hades. 275.00
14 Million-Year Monster. 275.00
15 The Vampire Cat. 275.00
16 The Doll 275.00
17 . . . . 275.00
18 The Mummy 275.00
19 Pirate and the Voodoo Queen 275.00
20 Terror Island 275.00
21 The Ant Master 225.00
22 The Cursed Casket. 225.00
23 Nightmare for Two 225.00
24 . . . . 225.00
25 Hallahan's Head 225.00
26 The Champ 225.00
27 SMo,The Thing with the
   Golden Hair 225.00
28 Portrait of Carlotta. 225.00
29 The Frogman 225.00
30 The Things on the Beach . . . 225.00
31 SMo,The Circle of the
   Doomed. 200.00
32 The Invasion of the
   Dead Things 200.00
33 . . . . 200.00
34 Atomic Bomb. 225.00

GOLDEN AGE (side tab)

35 Comics Code 200.00
36 thru 62 . . . . @150.00
63 AW 150.00
64 . . . . 100.00
65 . . . . 100.00
66 . . . . 100.00
67 . . . . 100.00
68 OW(c) 100.00
69 AW 100.00
70 . . . . 100.00
71 . . . . 100.00
72 . . . . 100.00
73 OW,I:Herbie 475.00
74 . . . . 100.00
75 JB 100.00
76 AW 125.00
77 . . . . 100.00
78 AW,OW(c) 125.00
79 thru 85 JB . . . . @100.00
86 Flying Saucer 110.00
87 . . . . 100.00
88 . . . . 100.00
89 . . . . 100.00
90 . . . . 100.00
91 . . . . 100.00
92 . . . . 100.00
93 . . . . 100.00
94 OW(c),A:Herbie 150.00
95 . . . . 75.00
96 AW 100.00
97 thru 115 . . . . @75.00
116 OW(c)A:Herbie 110.00
117 . . . . 75.00
118 . . . . 75.00
119 . . . . 75.00
120 thru 124 . . . . @75.00
125 I:O:Magic Man 100.00
126 A:Magic Man 60.00
127 same 60.00
128 same 60.00
129 same 60.00
130 same 60.00
131 same 60.00
132 same 60.00
133 I:O:Dragona 60.00
134 A:Magic Man 60.00
135 A:Magic Man 60.00
136 A:Nemesis 60.00
137 A:Magic Man 60.00
138 A:Magic Man 60.00
139 A:Magic Man 60.00
140 SD,A:Mark Midnight 75.00
141 thru 145 . . . . @50.00

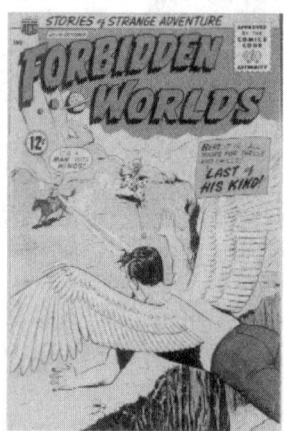

Forbidden Worlds #115
© American Comics Group

FOREIGN INTRIGUES
See: DYNAMITE

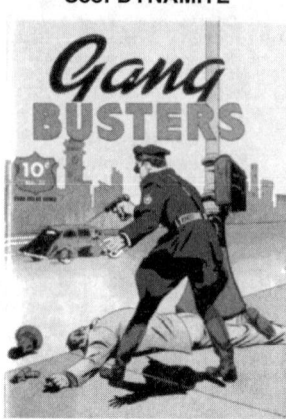

Four Color 1st Series #23
© Dell Publishing Co.

FOUR COLOR
Dell Publishing Co., 1939
N# Dick Tracy 10,000.00
N# Don Winslow of the Navy . 2,500.00
N# Myra North 1,300.00
4 Disney's Donald Duck
 (1940) 17,000.00
5 Smilin' Jack 1,000.00
6 Dick Tracy 2,300.00
7 Gang Busters 600.00
8 Dick Tracy 1,200.00
9 Terry and the Pirates 1,000.00
10 Smilin' Jack 900.00
11 Smitty 600.00
12 Little Orphan Annie 750.00
13 Walt Disney's Reluctant
 Dragon (1941) 2,500.00
14 Moon Mullins 600.00
15 Tillie the Toiler 600.00
16 W.Disney's Mickey Mouse Outwits
 the Phantom Blob (1941) . 17,000.00
17 W.Disney's Dumbo the Flying
 Elephant (1941) 3,500.00
18 Jiggs and Maggie 600.00
19 Barney Google and
 Snuffy Smith 600.00
20 Tiny Tim 500.00
21 Dick Tracy 1,000.00
22 Don Winslow 550.00
23 Gang Busters 500.00
24 Captain Easy 700.00
25 Popeye 1,200.00

[Second Series]
1 Little Joe 1,000.00
2 Harold Teen 500.00
3 Alley Oop 900.00
4 Smilin' Jack 700.00
5 Raggedy Ann and Andy 900.00
6 Smitty 350.00
7 Smokey Stover 500.00
8 Tillie the Toiler 400.00
9 Donald Duck finds Pirate
 Gold! 15,000.00
10 Flash Gordon 1,600.00
11 Wash Tubs 500.00
12 Bambi 1,000.00
13 Mr. District Attorney 500.00
14 Smilin' Jack 600.00
15 Felix the Cat 1,200.00
16 Porky Pig 1,500.00
17 Popeye 800.00

18 Little Orphan Annie's
 Junior Commandos 650.00
19 W.Disney's Thumper meets
 the Seven Dwarfs 900.00
20 Barney Baxter 500.00
21 Oswald the Rabbit 800.00
22 Tillie the Toiler 300.00
23 Raggedy Ann and Andy 600.00
24 Gang Busters 500.00
25 Andy Panda 900.00
26 Popeye 800.00
27 Mickey Mouse and the
 Seven Colored Terror 1,500.00
28 Wash Tubbs 375.00
29 CB,Donald Duck and the
 Mummy's Ring 10,000.00
30 Bambi's Children 900.00
31 Moon Mullins 300.00
32 Smitty 250.00
33 Bugs Bunny 1,800.00
34 Dick Tracy 700.00
35 Smokey Stover 275.00
36 Smilin' Jack 400.00
37 Bringing Up Father 350.00
38 Roy Rogers 4,000.00
39 Oswald the Rabbit 650.00
40 Barney Google and Snuffy
 Smith 375.00
41 WK,Mother Goose 375.00
42 Tiny Tim 300.00
43 Popeye 550.00
44 Terry and the Pirates 600.00
45 Raggedy Ann 550.00
46 Felix the Cat and the
 Haunted House 700.00
47 Gene Autry 750.00
48 CB,Porky Pig of the
 Mounties 1,600.00
49 W.Disney's Snow White and
 the Seven Dwarfs 1,000.00
50 WK,Fairy Tale Parade 450.00
51 Bugs Bunny Finds the
 Lost Treasure 600.00
52 Little Orphan Annie 500.00
53 Wash Tubbs 250.00
54 Andy Panda 500.00
55 Tillie the Toiler 250.00
56 Dick Tracy 600.00
57 Gene Autry 700.00
58 Smilin' Jack 400.00
59 WK,Mother Goose 350.00
60 Tiny Folks Funnies 275.00
61 Santa Claus Funnies 400.00
62 CB,Donald Duck in
 Frozen Gold 3,000.00
63 Roy Rogers-photo (c) 900.00
64 Smokey Stover 225.00
65 Smitty 225.00
66 Gene Autry 700.00
67 Oswald the Rabbit 300.00
68 WK,Mother Goose 300.00
69 WK,Fairy Tale Parade 400.00
70 Popeye and Wimpy 450.00
71 WK,Walt Disney's
 Three Caballeros 1,300.00
72 Raggedy Ann 450.00
73 The Grumps 250.00
74 Marge's Little Lulu 1,800.00
75 Gene Autry and the Wildcat . . 500.00
76 Little Orphan Annie 400.00
77 Felix the Cat 600.00
78 Porky Pig & the Bandit Twins . 400.00
79 Mickey Mouse in the Riddle
 of the Red Hat 1,800.00
80 Smilin' Jack 300.00
81 Moon Mullins 200.00
82 Lone Ranger 750.00
83 Gene Autry in Outlaw Trail . . . 500.00
84 Flash Gordon 750.00
85 Andy Panda and the
 Mad Dog Mystery 300.00

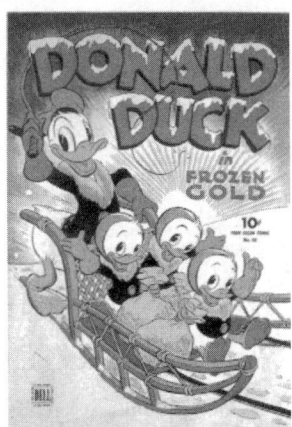

Four Color #62
© Dell Publishing Co.

86 Roy Rogers-photo (c) 600.00
87 WK,Fairy Tale Parade. 400.00
88 Bugs Bunny 375.00
89 Tillie the Toiler. 250.00
90 WK,Christmas with
    Mother Goose 300.00
91 WK,Santa Claus Funnies . . . 300.00
92 WK,W.Disney's Pinocchio. . . . 900.00
93 Gene Autry 500.00
94 Winnie Winkle 200.00
95 Roy Rogers,Ph(c) 600.00
96 Dick Tracy 500.00
97 Marge's Little Lulu. 900.00
98 Lone Ranger. 600.00
99 Smitty 200.00
100 Gene Autry Comics-photo(c) 500.00
101 Terry and the Pirates 500.00
102 WK,Oswald the Rabbit 250.00
103 WK,Easter with
    Mother Goose 300.00
104 WK,Fairy Tale Parade. 325.00
105 WK,Albert the Aligator 1,200.00
106 Tillie the Toiler. 200.00
107 Little Orphan Annie 350.00
108 Donald Duck in the
    Terror of the River 2,300.00
109 Roy Rogers Comics 500.00
110 Marge's Little Lulu 600.00
111 Captain Easy 250.00
112 Porky Pig's Adventure in
    Gopher Gulch 275.00
113 Popeye 250.00
114 WK,Fairy Tale Parade 325.00
115 Marge's Little Lulu. 550.00
116 Mickey Mouse and the
    House of Many Mysteries . . . 450.00
117 Roy Rogers Comics, Ph(c) . . 350.00
118 Lone Ranger. 500.00
119 Felix the Cat 550.00
120 Marge's Little Lulu 500.00
121 Fairy Tale Parade 225.00
122 Henry 250.00
123 Bugs Bunny's Dangerous
    Venture 275.00
124 Roy Rogers Comics,Ph(c) . . 350.00
125 Lone Ranger. 350.00
126 WK,Christmas with
    Mother Goose 250.00
127 Popeye 250.00
128 WK,Santa Claus Funnies . . . 250.00
129 W.Disney's Uncle Remus
    & his tales of Brer Rabbit . . . 500.00
130 Andy Panda 200.00
131 Marge's Little Lulu. 500.00

132 Tillie the Toiler. 200.00
133 Dick Tracy 350.00
134 Tarzan and the Devil Ogre. 1,100.00
135 Felix the Cat 400.00
136 Lone Ranger. 375.00
137 Roy Rogers Comics 375.00
138 Smitty 175.00
139 Marge's Little Lulu. 500.00
140 WK,Easter with
    Mother Goose 250.00
141 Mickey Mouse and the
    Submarine Pirates. 375.00
142 Bugs Bunny and the
    Haunted Mountain 250.00
143 Oswald the Rabbit & the
    Prehistoric Egg 175.00
144 Poy Rogers Comics,Ph(c) . . 350.00
145 Popeye 250.00
146 Marge's Little Lulu. 475.00
147 W.Disney's Donald Duck
    in Volcano Valley 1,600.00
148 WK,Albert the Aligator
    and Pogo Possum. 950.00
149 Smilin' Jack. 175.00
150 Tillie the Toiler 150.00
151 Lone Ranger. 325.00
152 Little Orphan Annie 250.00
153 Roy Rogers Comics 325.00
154 Andy Panda 200.00
155 Henry 175.00
156 Porky Pig and the Phantom . 200.00
157 W.Disney's Mickey Mouse
    and the Beanstalk 375.00
158 Marge's Little Lulu. 500.00
159 CB,W.Disney's Donald Duck
    in the Ghost of the Grotto. . 1,500.00
160 Roy Rogers Comics,Ph(c) . . 350.00
161 Tarzan & the Fires of Tohr . . 900.00
162 Felix the Cat 300.00
163 Dick Tracy 300.00
164 Bugs Bunny Finds the
    Frozen Kingdom 275.00
165 Marge's Little Lulu. 500.00
166 Roy Rogers Comics,Ph(c) . . 325.00
167 Lone Ranger. 325.00
168 Popeye 250.00
169 Woody Woodpecker,Drug . . . 275.00
170 W.Disney's Mickey Mouse
    on Spook's Island 350.00
171 Charlie McCarthy 450.00
172 WK,Christmas with
    Mother Goose 250.00
173 Flash Gordon 300.00
174 Winnie Winkle 150.00
175 WK,Santa Claus Funnies . . . 250.00
176 Tillie the Toiler. 150.00
177 Roy Rogers Comics,Ph(c) . . 325.00
178 CB,W.Disney's Donald
    Duck Christmas on Bear
    Mountain. 2,000.00
179 WK,Uncle Wiggily 275.00
180 Ozark the Ike 200.00
181 W.Disney's Mickey Mouse
    in Jungle Magic 325.00
182 Porky Pig in Never-
    Never Land 200.00
183 Oswald the Rabbit 175.00
184 Tillie the Toiler. 175.00
185 WK,Easter with
    Mother Goose 250.00
186 W.Disney's Bambi 300.00
187 Bugs Bunny and the
    Dreadful Bunny 200.00
188 Woody Woodpecker 200.00
189 W.Disney's Donald Duck in
    The Old Castle's Secret . . . 1,200.00
190 Flash Gordon 350.00
191 Porky Pig to the Rescue. . . . 200.00
192 WK,The Brownies. 250.00
193 Tom and Jerry 350.00

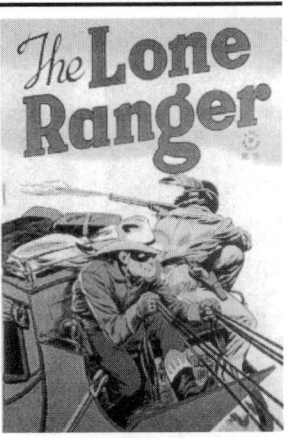

Four Color #151
© Dell Publishing Co.

194 W.Disney's Mickey Mouse
    in the World Under the Sea. . 325.00
195 Tillie the Toiler. 125.00
196 Charlie McCarthy in The
    Haunted Hide-Out 300.00
197 Spirit of the Border 200.00
198 Andy Panda 200.00
199 W.Disney's Donald Duck in
    Sheriff of Bullet Valley 1,400.00
200 Bugs Bunny, Super Sleuth . . 225.00
201 WK,Christmas with
    Mother Goose 200.00
202 Woody Woodpecker 150.00
203 CB,W.Disney's Donald Duck in
    The Golden Christmas Tree 1,100.00
204 Flash Gordon 250.00
205 WK,Santa Claus Funnies . . . 275.00
206 Little Orphan Funnies 200.00
207 King of the Royal Mounted . . 250.00
208 W.Disney's Brer Rabbit
    Does It Again. 200.00
209 Harold Teen 100.00
210 Tippe and Cap Stubbs 100.00
211 Little Beaver 150.00
212 Dr. Bobbs 75.00
213 Tillie the Toiler. 125.00
214 W.Disney's Mickey Mouse
    and his Sky Adventure 300.00
215 Sparkle Plenty. 200.00
216 Andy Panda and the
    Police Pup 150.00
217 Bugs Bunny in Court Jester . 200.00
218 W.Disney's 3 Little Pigs 225.00
219 Swee'pea 150.00
220 WK,Easter with
    Mother Goose 200.00
221 WK,Uncle Wiggly 175.00
222 West of the Pecos 125.00
223 CB,W.Disney's Donald Duck in
    Lost in the Andes 1,400.00
224 Little Iodine 200.00
225 Oswald the Rabbit 125.00
226 Porky Pig and Spoofy 175.00
227 W.Disney's Seven Dwarfs. . . 225.00
228 The Mark of Zorro 400.00
229 Smokey Stover 125.00
230 Sunset Press 125.00
231 W.Disney's Mickey Mouse
    and the Rajah's Treasure . . . 275.00
232 Woody Woodpecker 125.00
233 Bugs Bunny 200.00
234 W.Disney's Dumbo in Sky
    Voyage. 250.00
235 Tiny Tim 75.00
236 Heritage of the Desert 125.00

GOLDEN AGE

237 Tillie the Toiler 125.00
238 CB,W.Disney's Donald Duck
    in Voodoo Hoodoo 1,000.00
239 Adventure Bound 90.00
240 Andy Panda 125.00
241 Porky Pig 150.00
242 Tippie and Cap Stubbs 60.00
243 W.Disney's Thumper
    Follows His Nose 200.00
244 WK,The Brownies 175.00
245 Dick's Adventures in
    Dreamland 100.00
246 Thunder Mountain 75.00
247 Flash Gordon 250.00
248 W.Disney's Mickey Mouse
    and the Black Sorcerer 275.00
249 Woody Woodpecker 150.00
250 Bugs Bunny in
    Diamond Daze 200.00
251 Hubert at Camp Moonbeam . 100.00
252 W.Disney's Pinocchio 225.00
253 WK,Christmas with
    Mother Goose 225.00
254 WK,Santa Claus Funnies,
    A:Pogo 250.00
255 The Ranger 100.00
256 CB,W.Disney's Donald Duck in
    Luck of the North 750.00
257 Little Iodine 150.00
258 Andy Panda and the
    Ballon Race 150.00
259 Santa and the Angel 100.00
260 Porky Pig, Hero of the
    Wild West 150.00
261 W.Disney's Mickey Mouse
    and the Missing Key 250.00
262 Raggedy Ann and Andy 150.00
263 CB,W.Disney's Donald Duck in
    Land of the Totem Poles . . . 650.00
264 Woody Woodpecker in
    the Magic Lantern 150.00
265 King of the Royal Mountain . 150.00
266 Bugs Bunny on the Isle of
    Hercules 175.00
267 Little Beaver 100.00
268 W.Disney's Mickey Mouse's
    Surprise Visitor 250.00
269 Johnny Mack Brown,Ph(c) . . 400.00
270 Drift Fence 100.00
271 Porky Pig 150.00
272 W.Disney's Cinderella 200.00
273 Oswald the Rabbit 100.00
274 Bugs Bunny 150.00
275 CB,W.Disney's Donald Duck
    in Ancient Persia 700.00
276 Uncle Wiggly 150.00
277 PorkyPig in DesertAdventure 150.00
278 Bill Elliot Comics,Ph(c) 250.00
279 W.Disney's Mickey Mouse &
    Pluto Battle the Giant Ants . . 175.00
280 Andy Panda in the Isle
    of the Mechanical Men 150.00
281 Bugs Bunny in The Great
    Circus Mystery 175.00
282 CB,W.Disney's Donald Duck in
    The Pixilated Parrot 700.00
283 King of the Royal Mounted . . 150.00
284 Porky Pig in the Kingdom
    of Nowhere 150.00
285 Bozo the Clown 350.00
286 W.Disney's Mickey Mouse
    and the Uninvited Guest 200.00
287 Gene Autry's Champion in the
    Ghost of BlackMountain,Ph(c)200.00
288 Woody Woodpecker 150.00
289 BugsBunny in IndianTrouble. 175.00
290 The Chief 125.00
291 CB,W.Disney's Donald Duck in
    The Magic Hourglass 700.00
292 The Cisco Kid Comics 450.00
293 WK,The Brownies 175.00

294 Little Beaver 75.00
295 Porky Pig in President Pig . . 150.00
296 W.Disney's Mickey Mouse
    Private Eye for Hire 200.00
297 Andy Panda in The
    Haunted Inn 150.00
298 Bugs Bunny in Sheik
    for a Day 175.00
299 Buck Jones & the Iron Trail . 250.00
300 CB,W.Disney's Donald Duck in
    Big-Top Bedlam 700.00
301 The Mysterious Rider 100.00
302 Santa Claus Funnies 100.00
303 Porky Pig in The Land of
    the Monstrous Flies 125.00
304 W.Disney's Mickey Mouse
    in Tom-Tom Island 150.00
305 Woody Woodpecker 100.00
306 Raggedy Ann 100.00
307 Bugs Bunny in Lumber
    Jack Rabbit 150.00
308 CB,W.Disney's Donald Duck in
    Dangerous Disguise 600.00
309 Dollface and Her Gang 100.00
310 King of the Rotal Mounted . . 125.00
311 Porky Pig in Midget Horses
    of Hidden Valley 125.00
312 Tonto 200.00
313 W.Disney's Mickey Mouse in
    the Mystery of the Double-
    Cross Ranch 150.00
314 Ambush 75.00
315 Oswald Rabbit 100.00
316 Rex Allen,Ph(c) 250.00
317 Bugs Bunny in Hare Today
    Gone Tomorrow 150.00
318 CB,W.Disney's Donald Duck in
    No Such Varmint 600.00
319 Gene Autry's Champion 100.00
320 Uncle Wiggly 150.00
321 Little Scouts 75.00
322 Porky Pig in Roaring Rockies 100.00
323 Susie Q. Smith 75.00
324 I Met a Handsome Cowboy . 150.00
325 W.Disney's Mickey Mouse
    in the Haunted Castle 175.00
326 Andy Panda 75.00
327 Bugs Bunny and the
    Rajah's Treasure 150.00
328 CB,W.Disney's Donald Duck
    in Old California 650.00
329 Roy Roger's Trigger,Ph(c) . . 275.00
330 Porky Pig meets the
    Bristled Bruiser 100.00

Four Color #295
© Dell Publishing Co.

331 Disney's Alice in
    Wonderland 275.00
332 Little Beaver 75.00
333 Wilderness Trek 75.00
334 W.Disney's Mickey Mouse
    and Yukon Gold 200.00
335 Francis the Famous
    Talking Mule 200.00
336 Woody Woodpecker 100.00
337 The Brownies 100.00
338 Bugs Bunny and the
    Rocking Horse Thieves 200.00
339 W.Disney's Donald Duck
    and the Magic Fountain 200.00
340 King of the Royal Mountain . 150.00
341 W.Disney's Unbirthday Party
    with Alice in Wonderland 275.00
342 Porky Pig the Lucky
    Peppermint Mine 100.00
343 W.Disney's Mickey Mouse in
    Ruby Eye of Homar-Guy-Am 150.00
344 Sergeant Preston from
    Challenge of the Yukon 250.00
345 Andy Panda in Scotland Yard 100.00
346 Hideout 100.00
347 Bugs Bunny the Frigid Hare . 150.00
348 CB,W.Disney's Donald Duck
    The Crocodile Collector 350.00
349 Uncle Wiggly 125.00
350 Woody Woodpecker 100.00
351 Porky Pig and the Grand
    Canyon Giant 100.00
352 W.Disney's Mickey Mouse
    Mystery of Painted Valley . . . 150.00
353 CB(c),W.Disney'sDuckAlbum 200.00
354 Raggedy Ann & Andy 150.00
355 Bugs Bunny Hot-Rod Hair . . 150.00
356 CB(c),W.Disney's Donald
    Duck in Rags to Riches 325.00
357 Comeback 75.00
358 Andy Panada 100.00
359 Frosty the Snowman 150.00
360 Porky Pig in Tree Fortune . . . 75.00
361 Santa Claus Funnies 100.00
362 W.Disney's Mickey Mouse &
    the Smuggled Diamonds 150.00
363 King of the Royal Mounted . . 125.00
364 Woody Woodpecker 90.00
365 The Brownies 90.00
366 Bugs Bunny Uncle
    Buckskin Comes to Town . . . 150.00
367 CB,W.Disney's Donald Duck in
    A Christmas for Shacktown . . 700.00
368 Bob Clampett's
    Beany and Cecil 500.00
369 Lone Ranger's Famous
    Horse Hi-Yo Silver 175.00
370 Porky Pig in Trouble
    in the Big Trees 100.00
371 W.Disney's Mickey Mouse
    the Inca Idol Case 150.00
372 Riders of the Purple Sage . . . 75.00
373 Sergeant Preston 150.00
374 Woody Woodpecker 75.00
375 John Carter of Mars 450.00
376 Bugs Bunny 200.00
377 Susie Q. Smith 75.00
378 Tom Corbett, Space Cadet . . 325.00
379 W.Disney's Donald Duck in
    Southern Hospitality 175.00
380 Raggedy Ann & Andy 100.00
381 Marge's Tubby 350.00
382 W.Disney's Show White and
    the Seven Dwarfs 200.00
383 Andy Panada 75.00
384 King of the Royal Mounted . . 100.00
385 Porky Pig 75.00
386 CB,W.Disney's Uncle Scrooge
    in Only A Poor Old Man . . . 1,800.00
387 W.Disney's Mickey Mouse
    in High Tibet 150.00

GOLDEN AGE

388 Oswald the Rabbit 100.00
389 Andy Hardy Comics 75.00
390 Woody Woodpecker 75.00
391 Uncle Wiggly 125.00
392 Hi-Yo Silver 100.00
393 Bugs Bunny 150.00
394 CB(c),W.Disney's Donald Duck
   in Malayalaya 325.00
395 Forlorn River 75.00
396 Tales of the Texas Rangers,
   Ph(c) 200.00
397 Sergeant Preston o/t Yukon . 150.00
398 The Brownies 75.00
399 Porky Pig in the Lost
   Gold Mine 75.00
400 AMc,Tom Corbett 200.00
401 W.Disney's Mickey Mouse &
   Goofy's Mechanical Wizard. . 100.00
402 Mary Jane and Sniffles 100.00
403 W.Disney's Li'l Bad Wolf . . . 150.00
404 The Ranger Rider,Ph(c) 200.00
405 Woody Woodpecker 75.00
406 Tweety and Sylvester 125.00
407 Bugs Bunny, Foreign-
   Legion Hare. 125.00
408 CB,W.Disney's Donald Duck
   and the Golden Helmet 550.00
409 Andy Panda 75.00
410 Porky Pig in the
   Water Wizard. 75.00
411 W.Disney's Mickey Mouse
   and the Old Sea Dog. 100.00
412 Nevada 75.00
413 Disney's Robin Hood(movie),
   Ph(c) 200.00
414 Bob Clampett's Beany
   and Cecil 250.00
415 Rootie Kazootie 175.00
416 Woody Woodpecker 75.00
417 Double Trouble with Goober. . 75.00
418 Rusty Riley 75.00
419 Sergeant Preston 150.00
420 Bugs Bunny 125.00
421 AMc,Tom Corbett 175.00
422 CB,W.Disney's Donald Duck
   and the Gilded Man. 550.00
423 Rhubarb 100.00
424 Flash Gordon 175.00
425 Zorro 200.00
426 Porky Pig 75.00
427 W.Disney's Mickey Mouse &
   the Wonderful Whizzix. 100.00
428 Uncle Wiggily 100.00
429 W.Disney's Pluto in
   Why Dogs Leave Home 150.00
430 Marge's Tubby 200.00
431 Woody Woodpecker 100.00
432 Bugs Bunny and the
   Rabbit Olympics 125.00
433 Wildfire 75.00
434 Rin Tin Tin,Ph(c) 250.00
435 Frosty the Snowman. 100.00
436 The Brownies 75.00
437 John Carter of Mars 300.00
438 W.Disney's Annie
   Oakley (TV) 275.00
439 Little Hiawatha 100.00
440 Black Beauty 75.00
441 Fearless Fagan. 75.00
442 W.Disney's Peter Pan. 175.00
443 Ben Bowie and His
   Mountain Men 125.00
444 Marge's Tubby 200.00
445 Charlie McCarthy 100.00
446 Captain Hook and Peter Pan 150.00
447 Andy Hardy Comics 75.00
448 Beany and Cecil 275.00
449 Tappan's Burro 75.00
450 CB(c),W.Disney's Duck
   Album 150.00
451 Rusty Riley 65.00

452 Raggedy Ann and Andy 100.00
453 Susie Q. Smith 65.00
454 Krazy Kat Comics 65.00
455 Johnny Mack Brown Comics,
   Ph(c) 125.00
456 W.Disney's Uncle Scrooge
   Back to the Klondike 1,200.00
457 Daffy 150.00
458 Oswald the Rabbit 75.00
459 Rootie Kazootie 150.00
460 Buck Jones 175.00
461 Marge's Tubby 175.00
462 Little Scouts 50.00
463 Petunia 75.00
464 Bozo 150.00
465 Francis the Talking Mule. . . . 100.00
466 Rhubarb, the Millionaire Cat. . 75.00
467 Desert Gold. 75.00
468 W.Disney's Goofy 225.00
469 Beettle Bailey 175.00
470 Elmer Fudd 100.00
471 Double Trouble with Goober. . 40.00
472 Wild Bill Elliot,Ph(c). 75.00
473 W.Disney's Li'l Bad Wolf. 75.00
474 Mary Jane and Sniffles. 125.00
475 M.G.M.'s the Two
   Mouseketeers 125.00
476 Rin Tin Tin,Ph(c). 150.00
477 Bob Clampett's Beany and
   Cecil. 275.00
478 Charlie McCarthy 100.00
479 Queen o/t West Dale Evans . 400.00
480 Andy Hardy Comics 50.00
481 Annie Oakley and Tagg. 150.00
482 Brownies 75.00
483 Little Beaver 75.00
484 River Feud 75.00
485 The Little People. 125.00
486 Rusty Riley 75.00
487 Mowgli, the Jungle Book. . . . 100.00
488 John Carter of Mars 300.00
489 Tweety and Sylvester 100.00
490 Jungle Jim 125.00
491 EK,Silvertip 150.00
492 W.Disney's Duck Album 125.00
493 Johnny Mack Brown,Ph(c) . . 125.00
494 The Little King. 175.00
495 CB, W.Disney's Uncle
   Scrooge. 800.00
496 The Green Hornet. 450.00
497 Zorro, (Sword of). 225.00
498 Bugs Bunny's Album. 100.00
499 M.G.M.'s Spike and Tyke 90.00
500 Buck Jones 100.00
501 Francis the Famous
   Talking Mule 90.00
502 Rootie Kazootie 135.00
503 Uncle Wiggily 90.00
504 Krazy Kat 75.00
505 W.Disney's the Sword and
   the Rose (TV),Ph(c) 150.00
506 The Little Scouts 40.00
507 Oswald the Rabbit 75.00
508 Bozo 150.00
509 W.Disney's Pluto 100.00
510 Son of Black Beauty 60.00
511 EK,Outlaw Trail 75.00
512 Flash Gordon 125.00
513 Ben Bowie and His
   Mountain Men 60.00
514 Frosty the Snowman. 100.00
515 Andy Hardy 50.00
516 Double Trouble With Goober . 40.00
517 Walt Disney's Chip 'N' Dale . 200.00
518 Rivets 50.00
519 Steve Canyon 150.00
520 Wild Bill Elliot,Ph(c). 100.00
521 Beetle Bailey. 100.00
522 The Brownies 75.00
523 Rin Tin Tin,Ph(c) 150.00
524 Tweety and Sylvester 90.00

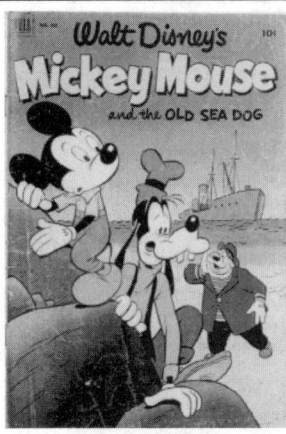

Four Color #411
© Dell Publishing Co.

525 Santa Claus Funnies 100.00
526 Napoleon. 50.00
527 Charlie McCarthy 100.00
528 Queen o/t West Dale Evans,
   Ph(c) 200.00
529 Little Beaver 75.00
530 Bob Clampett's Beany
   and Cecil 275.00
531 W.Disney's Duck Album 100.00
532 The Rustlers 60.00
533 Raggedy Ann and Andy 100.00
534 EK,Western Marshal. 125.00
535 I Love Lucy,Ph(c) 900.00
536 Daffy 100.00
537 Stormy, the Thoroughbred . . . 75.00
538 EK,The Mask of Zorro 250.00
539 Ben and Me 75.00
540 Knights of the Round Table,
   Ph(c) 150.00
541 Johnny Mack Brown,Ph(c) . . 125.00
542 Super Circus Featuring
   Mary Hartline. 125.00
543 Uncle Wiggly 100.00
544 W.Disney's Rob Roy(Movie),
   Ph(c) 150.00
545 The Wonderful Adventures
   of Pinocchio. 150.00
546 Buck Jones 100.00
547 Francis the Famous
   Talking Mule 90.00
548 Krazy Kat 75.00
549 Oswald the Rabbit 75.00
550 The Little Scouts 40.00
551 Bozo 150.00
552 Beetle Bailey. 100.00
553 Susie Q. Smith 50.00
554 Rusty Riley 60.00
555 Range War 60.00
556 Double Trouble with Goober. . 40.00
557 Ben Bowie and His
   Mountain Men 60.00
558 Elmer Fudd 75.00
559 I Love Lucy,Ph(c) 600.00
560 W.Disney's Duck Album 100.00
561 Mr. Magoo. 200.00
562 W.Disney's Goofy 150.00
563 Rhubarb, the Millionaire Cat. 100.00
564 W.Disney's Li'l Bad Wolf. . . . 100.00
565 Jungle Jim. 75.00
566 Son of Black Beauty 60.00
567 BF,Prince Valiant,Ph(c) 225.00
568 Gypsy Cat. 90.00
569 Priscilla's Pop 75.00
570 Bob Clampett's Beany
   and Cecil 275.00

All comics prices listed are for *Near Mint* condition. **CVA Page 395**

GOLDEN AGE

571 Charlie McCarthy 100.00	641 Steve Canyon 110.00	682 When Knighthood Was
572 EK,Silvertip 90.00	642 M.G.M.'s The Two	in Flower,Ph(c) 150.00
573 The Little People. 100.00	Mouseketeers 75.00	683 Hi and Lois 60.00
574 The Hand of Zorro 225.00	643 Wild Bill Elliott,Ph(c) 65.00	684 SB,Helen of Troy,Ph(c) 200.00
575 Annie and Oakley and Tagg,	644 Sir Walter Raleigh,Ph(c) . . . 125.00	685 Johnny Mack Brown,Ph(c) . . 150.00
Ph(c) 175.00	645 Johnny Mack Brown,Ph(c) . . 125.00	686 Duck Album. 100.00
576 Angel. 40.00	646 Dotty Dripple and Taffy 60.00	687 The Indian Fighter,Ph(c) 150.00
577 M.G.M.'s Spike and Tyke . . . 60.00	647 Bugs Bunny's Album. 100.00	688 SB,Alexander the Great,
578 Steve Canyon 90.00	648 Jace Pearson of the	Ph(c) 150.00
579 Francis the Talking Mule. 75.00	Texas Rangers,Ph(c). 100.00	689 Elmer Fudd 60.00
580 Six Gun Ranch 75.00	649 Duck Album. 100.00	690 The Conqueror,
581 Chip 'N' Dale. 100.00	650 BF,Prince Valiant 125.00	John Wayne Ph(c). 300.00
582 Mowgli, the Jungle Book. . . . 100.00	651 EK,King Colt 60.00	691 Dotty Dripple and Taffy 50.00
583 The Lost Wagon Train 75.00	652 Buck Jones 60.00	692 The Little People. 60.00
584 Johnny Mack Brown,Ph(c) . . 125.00	653 Smokey the Bear 200.00	693 W.Disney's Brer Rabbit
585 Bugs Bunny's Album. 100.00	654 Pluto 75.00	Song of the South 175.00
586 W.Disney's Duck Album 135.00	655 Francis the Famous	694 Super Circus,Ph(c) 125.00
587 The Little Scouts 50.00	Talking Mule 75.00	695 Little Beaver 60.00
588 MB,King Richard and the	656 Turok, Son of Stone 550.00	696 Krazy Kat 60.00
Crusaders,Ph(c) 175.00	657 Ben Bowie and His	697 Oswald the Rabbit 60.00
589 Buck Jones 100.00	Mountain Men 60.00	698 Francis the Famous
590 Hansel and Gretel. 125.00	658 Goofy 150.00	Talking Mule 60.00
591 EK,Western Marshal. 100.00	659 Daisy Duck's Diary 125.00	699 BA,Prince Valiant 150.00
592 Super Circus. 125.00	660 Little Beaver 65.00	700 Water Birds and the
593 Oswald the Rabbit 60.00	661 Frosty the Snowman. 100.00	Olympic Elk 100.00
594 Bozo 160.00	662 Zoo Parade. 100.00	701 Jimmy Cricket 150.00
595 Pluto 75.00	663 Winky Dink 150.00	702 The Goofy Success Story . . . 135.00
596 Turok, Son of Stone 1,000.00	664 W.Disney's Davy Crockett in	703 Scamp. 175.00
597 The Little King. 100.00	the Great Keelboat	704 Priscilla's Pop 60.00
598 Captain Davy Jones 90.00	Race (TV),Ph(c) 300.00	705 Brave Eagle,Ph(c). 125.00
599 Ben Bowie and His	665 The African Lion 100.00	706 Bongo and Lumpjaw. 100.00
Mountain Men 75.00	666 Santa Claus Funnies 100.00	707 Corky and White Shadow,
600 Daisy Duck's Diary 125.00	667 EK,Silvertip and the Stolen	Ph(c) 135.00
601 Frosty the Snowman. 100.00	Stallion 100.00	708 Smokey the Bear 100.00
602 Mr. Magoo and the Gerald	668 W.Disney's Dumbo 150.00	709 The Searchers,John
McBoing-Boing 225.00	668a W.Disney's Dumbo 125.00	Wayne Ph(c) 450.00
603 M.G.M.'s The Two	669 W.Disney's Robin Hood	710 Francis the Famous
Mouseketeers 90.00	(Movie),Ph(c) 100.00	Talking Mule 60.00
604 Shadow on the Trail 75.00	670 M.G.M.'s Mouse Musketeers . 75.00	711 M.G.M.'s Mouse Musketeers. . 50.00
605 The Brownies 75.00	671 W.Disney's Davey Crockett &	712 The Great Locomotive
606 Sir Lancelot. 150.00	the River Pirates(TV),Ph(c) . . 275.00	Chase, Ph(c) 135.00
607 Santa Claus Funnies 100.00	672 Quentin Durward,Ph(c). 125.00	713 The Animal World 60.00
608 EK,Silver Tip 75.00	673 Buffalo Bill Jr.,Ph(c) 125.00	714 W.Disney's Spin
609 The Littlest Outlaw,Ph(c). . . . 125.00	674 The Little Rascals 125.00	& Marty (TV) 250.00
610 Drum Beat,Ph(c) 175.00	675 EK,Steve Donovan,Ph(c) . . . 150.00	715 Timmy 60.00
611 W.Disney's Duck Album 100.00	676 Will-Yum!. 50.00	716 Man in Space 150.00
612 Little Beaver 65.00	677 Little King 100.00	717 Moby Dick,Ph(c) 150.00
613 EK,Western Marshal. 100.00	678 The Last Hunt,Ph(c) 150.00	718 Dotty Dripple and Taffy 50.00
614 W.Disney's 20,000 Leagues	679 Gunsmoke. 350.00	719 BF,Prince Valiant. 125.00
Under the Sea (Movie) 200.00	680 Out Our Way with the	720 Gunsmoke,Ph(c). 175.00
615 Daffy 100.00	Worry Wart 50.00	721 Captain Kangaroo,Ph(c) 300.00
616 To The Last Man. 75.00	681 Forever, Darling,Lucile	722 Johnny Mack Brown,Ph(c) . . 125.00
617 The Quest of Zorro 225.00	Ball Ph(c). 225.00	723 EK,Santiago 175.00
618 Johnny Mack Brown,Ph(c) . . 125.00		724 Bugs Bunny's Album. 75.00
619 Krazy Kat 65.00		725 Elmer Fudd 50.00
620 Mowgli, Jungle Book 90.00		726 Duck Album. 100.00
621 Francis the Famous		727 The Nature of Things 110.00
Talking Mule 65.00		728 M.G.M.'s Mouse Musketeers . 50.00
622 Beetle Bailey 100.00		729 Bob Son of Battle 60.00
623 Oswald the Rabbit 65.00		730 Smokey Stover 75.00
624 Treasure Island,Ph(c) 150.00		731 EK,Silvertip and The
625 Beaver Valley 125.00		Fighting Four 75.00
626 Ben Bowie and His		732 Zorro, (the Challenge of) . . . 250.00
Mountain Men 65.00		733 Buck Rogers 65.00
627 Goofy 150.00		734 Cheyenne,C.Walker Ph(c) . . 300.00
628 Elmer Fudd 65.00		735 Crusader Rabbit 550.00
629 Lady & The Tramp with Jock 150.00		736 Pluto 75.00
630 Priscilla's Pop 65.00		737 Steve Canyon 100.00
631 W.Disney's Davy Crockett		738 Westward Ho, the Wagons,
Indian Fighter (TV),Ph(c). . . . 350.00		Ph(c) 200.00
632 Fighting Caravans. 65.00		739 MD,Bounty Guns 75.00
633 The Little People. 65.00		740 Chilly Willy 100.00
634 Lady and the Tramp Album. . 100.00		741 The Fastest Gun Alive,Ph(c). 150.00
635 Bob Clampett's Beany		742 Buffalo Bill Jr.,Ph(c) 100.00
and Cecil 300.00		743 Daisy Duck's Diary 110.00
636 Chip 'N' Dale 100.00		744 Little Beaver 65.00
637 EK,Silvertip 75.00		745 Francis the Famous
638 M.G.M.'s Spike and Tyke . . . 50.00		Talking Mule 65.00
639 W.Disney's Davy Crockett		746 Dotty Dripple and Taffy 50.00
at the Alamo (TV),Ph(c). . . . 275.00	*Four Color #635*	747 Goofy 135.00
640 EK,Western Marshal 100.00	*© Dell Publishing Co.*	748 Frosty the Snowman. 100.00

Four Color #635
© Dell Publishing Co.

749 Secrets of Life,Ph(c) 100.00
750 The Great Cat 125.00
751 Our Miss Brooks,Ph(c) 150.00
752 Mandrake, the Magician 175.00
753 Walt Scott's Little People 75.00
754 Smokey the Bear 100.00
755 The Littlest Snowman 75.00
756 Santa Claus Funnies 100.00
757 The True Story of
     Jesse James,Ph(c) 175.00
758 Bear Country. 100.00
759 Circus Boy,Ph(c) 250.00
760 W.Disney's Hardy Boys(TV) . 250.00
761 Howdy Doody 250.00
762 SB,The Sharkfighters,Ph(c) . 150.00
763 GrandmaDuck'sFarmFriends 150.00
764 M.G.M.'s Mouse Musketeers . 50.00
765 Will-Yum!. 50.00
766 Buffalo Bill,Ph(c) 100.00
767 Spin and Marty 175.00
768 EK,Steve Donovan, Western
     Marshal,Ph(c) 125.00
769 Gunsmoke. 200.00
770 Brave Eagle,Ph(c) 65.00
771 MD,Brand of Empire 65.00
772 Cheyenne,C.Walker Ph(c) . . 150.00
773 The Brave One,Ph(c) 100.00
774 Hi and Lois 50.00
775 SB,Sir Lancelot and
     Brian,Ph(c). 175.00
776 Johnny Mack Brown,Ph(c) . . 125.00
777 Scamp. 135.00
778 The Little Rascals 100.00
779 Lee Hunter, Indian Fighter . . 100.00
780 Captain Kangaroo,Ph(c) 250.00
781 Fury,Ph(c) 150.00
782 Duck Album. 100.00
783 Elmer Fudd 50.00
784 Around the World in 80
     Days,Ph(c). 125.00
785 Circus Boys,Ph(c) 250.00
786 Cinderella 125.00
787 Little Hiawatha 100.00
788 BF,Prince Valiant. 125.00
789 EK,Silvertip-Valley Thieves. . 100.00
790 ATh,The Wings of Eagles,
     J.Wayne Ph(c) 300.00
791 The 77th Bengal Lancers,
     Ph(c) 150.00
792 Oswald the Rabbit 65.00
793 Morty Meekle 50.00
794 SB,The Count of Monte
     Cristo. 150.00
795 Jiminy Cricket 125.00
796 Ludwig Bemelman's
     Madeleine and Genevieve. . . . 60.00
797 Gunsmoke,Ph(c) 175.00
798 Buffalo Bill,Ph(c) 100.00
799 Priscilla's Pop 60.00
800 The Buccaneers,Ph(c) 150.00
801 Dotty Dripple and Taffy 50.00
802 Goofy 150.00
803 Cheyenne,C.Walker Ph(c) . . 150.00
804 Steve Canyon 100.00
805 Crusader Rabbit 450.00
806 Scamp. 125.00
807 MB,Savage Range 65.00
808 Spin and Marty,Ph(c) 175.00
809 The Little People. 75.00
810 Francis the Famous
     Talking Mule 65.00
811 Howdy Doody 200.00
812 The Big Land,A.Ladd Ph(c) . 200.00
813 Circus Boy,Ph(c) 225.00
814 Covered Wagon,A:Mickey
     Mouse 125.00
815 Dragoon Wells Massacre . . 150.00
816 Brave Eagle,Ph(c). 65.00
817 Little Beaver 65.00
818 Smokey the Bear 100.00
819 Mickey Mouse in Magicland . . 75.00

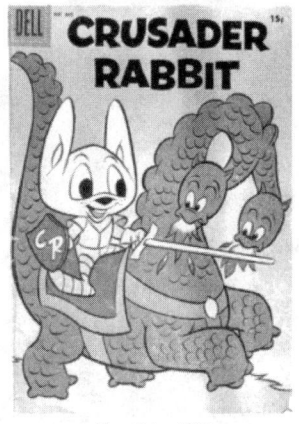

Four Color #805
© *Dell Publishing Co.*

820 The Oklahoman,Ph(c). 175.00
821 Wringle Wrangle,Ph(c) 150.00
822 ATh,W.Disney's Paul Revere's
     Ride (TV) 175.00
823 Timmy 50.00
824 The Pride and the Passion,
     Ph(c) 150.00
825 The Little Rascals 100.00
826 Spin and Marty and Annette,
     Ph(c) 400.00
827 Smokey Stover 90.00
828 Buffalo Bill, Jr,Ph(c). 90.00
829 Tales of the Pony Express,
     Ph(c) 90.00
830 The Hardy Boys,Ph(c) 175.00
831 No Sleep 'Til Dawn,Ph(c) . . . 125.00
832 Lolly and Pepper. 65.00
833 Scamp. 125.00
834 Johnny Mack Brown,Ph(c) . . 125.00
835 Silvertip- The Fake Rider 90.00
836 Man in Fight 135.00
837 All-American Athlete
     Cotton Woods 55.00
838 Bugs Bunny's Life
     Story Album 75.00
839 The Vigilantes 125.00
840 Duck Album 100.00
841 Elmer Fudd 50.00
842 The Nature of Things 100.00
843 The First Americans 150.00
844 Gunsmoke,Ph(c). 150.00
845 ATh,The Land Unknown 225.00
846 ATh,Gun Glory 175.00
847 Perri 90.00
848 Marauder's Moon 55.00
849 BF,Prince Valiant. 125.00
850 Buck Jones 60.00
851 The Story of Mankind,
     V.Price Ph(c) 135.00
852 Chilly Willy 65.00
853 Pluto 75.00
854 Hunchback of Notre Dame,
     Ph(c) 225.00
855 Broken Arrow,Ph(c) 100.00
856 Buffalo Bill, Jr.,Ph(c) 100.00
857 The Goofy Adventure Story . 150.00
858 Daisy Duck's Diary 90.00
859 Topper and Neil. 80.00
860 Wyatt Earp,Ph(c) 175.00
861 Frosty the Snowman. 75.00
862 Truth About Mother Goose . . 135.00
863 Francis the Famous
     Talking Mule 60.00
864 The Littlest Snowman 75.00
865 Andy Burnett,Ph(c) 175.00

866 Mars and Beyond 150.00
867 Santa Claus Funnies 100.00
868 The Little People. 90.00
869 Old Yeller,Ph(c) 110.00
870 Little Beaver 65.00
871 Curly Kayoe 50.00
872 Captain Kangaroo,Ph(c) 235.00
873 Grandma Duck's
     Farm Friends 90.00
874 Old Ironsides. 125.00
875 Trumpets West 60.00
876 Tales of Wells Fargo,Ph(c) . . 175.00
877 ATh,Frontier Doctor,Ph(c) . . . 175.00
878 Peanuts. 275.00
879 Brave Eagle,Ph(c). 60.00
880 MD,Steve Donovan,Ph(c) 75.00
881 The Captain and the Kids 60.00
882 ATh,W.DisneyPresentsZorro. 275.00
883 The Little Rascals 100.00
884 Hawkeye and the Last
     of the Mohicans,Ph(c) 135.00
885 Fury,Ph(c) 125.00
886 Bongo and Lumpjaw. 90.00
887 The Hardy Boys,Ph(c) 175.00
888 Elmer Fudd 50.00
889 ATh,W.Disney's Clint
     & Mac(TV),Ph(c) 225.00
890 Wyatt Earp,Ph(c) 135.00
891 Light in the Forest,
     C.Parker Ph(c). 135.00
892 Maverick,J.Garner Ph(c). . . . 450.00
893 Jim Bowie,Ph(c) 100.00
894 Oswald the Rabbit 60.00
895 Wagon Train,Ph(c) 200.00
896 Adventures of Tinker Bell . . . 150.00
897 Jiminy Cricket 125.00
898 EK,Silvertip 90.00
899 Goofy 100.00
900 BF,Prince Valiant 125.00
901 Little Hiawatha 90.00
902 Will-Yum!. 60.00
903 Dotty Dripple and Taffy 50.00
904 Lee Hunter, Indian Fighter . . . 60.00
905 W.Disney's Annette (TV),
     Ph(c) 500.00
906 Francis the Famous
     Talking Mule 60.00
907 Ath,Sugarfoot,Ph(c). 235.00
908 The Little People
     and the Giant. 75.00
909 Smitty 60.00
910 ATh,The Vikings,
     K.Douglas Ph(c) 150.00
911 The Gray Ghost,Ph(c). 150.00
912 Leave it to Beaver,Ph(c) 300.00
913 The Left-Handed Gun,
     Paul Newman Ph(c) 175.00
914 ATh,No Time for Sergeants,
     Ph(c) 175.00
915 Casey Jones,Ph(c) 100.00
916 Red Ryder Ranch Comics . . . 90.00
917 The Life of Riley,Ph(c) 225.00
918 Beep Beep, the Roadrunner. 200.00
919 Boots and Saddles,Ph(c) . . . 135.00
920 Ath,Zorro,Ph(c) 225.00
921 Wyatt Earp.Ph(c) 135.00
922 Johnny Mack Brown,Ph(c) . . 135.00
923 Timmy 50.00
924 Colt .45,Ph(c) 175.00
925 Last of the Fast Guns,Ph(c) . 135.00
926 Peter Pan 75.00
927 SB,Top Gun 60.00
928 Sea Hunt,L.Bridges Ph(c) . . 225.00
929 Brave Eagle,Ph(c). 60.00
930 Maverick,J. Garner Ph(c) . . . 200.00
931 Have Gun, Will Travel,Ph(c) . 250.00
932 Smokey the Bear 100.00
933 ATh,W.Disney's Zorro. 225.00
934 Restless Gun 225.00
935 King of the Royal Mounted . . . 65.00
936 The Little Rascals 100.00

937 Ruff and Ready. 225.00
938 Elmer Fudd 60.00
939 Steve Canyon 90.00
940 Lolly and Pepper 50.00
941 Pluto 60.00
942 Pony Express 90.00
943 White Wilderness 125.00
944 SB,7th Voyage of Sinbad . . . 250.00
945 Maverick,J.Garner Ph(c) . . . 250.00
946 The Big Country,Ph(c) 150.00
947 Broken Arrow,Ph(c) 90.00
948 Daisy Duck's Diary 90.00
949 High Adventure,Ph(c) 90.00
950 Frosty the Snowman 75.00
951 ATh,Lennon Sisters
　　Life Story,Ph(c) 250.00
952 Goofy 90.00
953 Francis the Famous
　　Talking Mule 60.00
954 Man in Space 135.00
955 Hi and Lois 50.00
956 Ricky Nelson,Ph(c) 350.00
957 Buffalo Bee 175.00
958 Santa Claus Funnies 90.00
959 Christmas Stories 75.00
960 ATh,W.Disney's Zorro 225.00
961 Jace Pearson's Tales of
　　Texas Rangers,Ph(c) 90.00
962 Maverick,J.Garner Ph(c) 200.00
963 Johnny Mack Brown,Ph(c) . . 125.00
964 The Hardy Boys,Ph(c) 175.00
965 GrandmaDuck'sFarmFriends . 90.00
966 Tonka,Ph(c) 150.00
967 Chilly Willy 60.00
968 Tales of Wells Fargo,Ph(c) . . 150.00
969 Peanuts 200.00
970 Lawman,Ph(c) 225.00
971 Wagon Train,Ph(c) 125.00
972 Tom Thumb 175.00
973 SleepingBeauty & the Prince 200.00
974 The Little Rascals 125.00
975 Fury,Ph(c) 125.00
976 ATh,W.Disney's Zorro,Ph(c) . 200.00
977 Elmer Fudd 50.00
978 Lolly and Pepper 50.00
979 Oswald the Rabbit 60.00
980 Maverick,J.Garner Ph(c) 200.00
981 Ruff and Ready 150.00
982 The New Adventures of
　　Tinker Bell 150.00
983 Have Gun, Will Travel,Ph(c) . 175.00
984 Sleeping Beauty's Fairy
　　Godmothers 165.00
985 Shaggy Dog,Ph(c) 150.00
986 Restless Gun,Ph(c) 150.00
987 Goofy 90.00
988 Little Hiawatha 90.00
989 Jimmy Cricket 125.00
990 Huckleberry Hound 235.00
991 Francis the Famous
　　Talking Mule 60.00
992 ATh,Sugarfoot,Ph(c) 200.00
993 Jim Bowie,Ph(c) 90.00
994 Sea HuntL.Bridges Ph(c) . . . 150.00
995 Donald Duck Album 125.00
996 Nevada 60.00
997 Walt Disney Presents,Ph(c) . 150.00
998 Ricky Nelson,Ph(c) 350.00
999 Leave It To Beaver,Ph(c) . . . 300.00
1000 The Gray Ghost,Ph(c). 150.00
1001 Lowell Thomas' High
　　Adventure,Ph(c). 90.00
1002 Buffalo Bee 125.00
1003 ATh,W.Disney's Zorro,Ph(c) 200.00
1004 Colt .45,Ph(c) 150.00
1005 Maverick,J.Garner Ph(c) . . . 200.00
1006 SB,Hercules 175.00
1007 John Paul Jones,Ph(c)　. . . 90.00
1008 Beep, Beep, the
　　Road Runner 90.00
1009 CB,The Rifleman,Ph(c)　. . . 450.00

1010 Grandma Duck's Farm
　　Friends 225.00
1011 Buckskin,Ph(c) 150.00
1012 Last Train from Gun
　　Hill,Ph(c) 155.00
1013 Bat Masterson,Ph(c) 225.00
1014 ATh,The Lennon Sisters,
　　Ph(c) 250.00
1015 Peanuts 200.00
1016 Smokey the Bear 75.00
1017 Chilly Willy 60.00
1018 Rio Bravo,J.Wayne Ph(c) . . 400.00
1019 Wagoon Train,Ph(c) 125.00
1020 Jungle 60.00
1021 Jace Pearson's Tales of
　　the Texas Rangers,Ph(c). 90.00
1022 Timmy 50.00
1023 Tales of Wells Fargo,Ph(c) . 150.00
1024 ATh,Darby O'Gill and
　　the Little People,Ph(c) 175.00
1025 CB,W.Disney's Vacation in
　　Disneyland 350.00
1026 Spin and Marty,Ph(c) 135.00
1027 The Texan,Ph(c) 150.00
1028 Rawhide,
　　Clint Eastwood Ph(c) 425.00
1029 Boots and Saddles,Ph(c) . . 100.00
1030 Spanky and Alfalfa, the
　　Little Rascals 100.00
1031 Fury,Ph(c) 125.00
1032 Elmer Fudd 50.00
1033 Steve Canyon,Ph(c) 90.00
1034 Nancy and Sluggo
　　Summer Camp 75.00
1035 Lawman,Ph(c). 135.00
1036 The Big Circus,Ph(c). 125.00
1037 Zorro,Ph(c) 275.00
1038 Ruff and Ready 150.00
1039 Pluto 75.00
1040 Quick Draw McGraw 250.00
1041 ATh,Sea Hunt,
　　L.Bridges Ph(c) 150.00
1042 The Three Chipmunks 125.00
1043 The Three Stooges,Ph(c) . . 400.00
1044 Have Gun,Will Travel,Ph(c) 165.00
1045 Restless Gun,Ph(c) 150.00
1046 Beep Beep, the
　　Road Runner 100.00
1047 CB,W.Disney's
　　GyroGearloose 300.00
1048 The Horse Soldiers
　　J.Wayne Ph(c) 250.00
1049 Don't Give Up the Ship
　　J.Lewis Ph(c) 150.00
1050 Huckleberry Hound 150.00

Four Color #938
© *Dell Publishing Co.*

1051 Donald in Mathmagic Land. 150.00
1052 RsM,Ben-Hur 175.00
1053 Goofy 90.00
1054 Huckleberry Hound
　　Winter Fun. 150.00
1055 CB,Daisy Duck's Diary 175.00
1056 Yellowstone Kelly,
　　C.Walker Ph(c) 120.00
1057 Mickey Mouse Album 65.00
1058 Colt .45,Ph(c) 175.00
1059 Sugarfoot 155.00
1060 Journey to the Center of the
　　Earth, P.Boone Ph(c) 225.00
1061 Buffalo Bill 125.00
1062 Christmas Stories 75.00
1063 Santa Claus Funnies 90.00
1064 Bugs Bunny's Merry
　　Christmas 90.00
1065 Frosty the Snowman 75.00
1066 ATh,77 Sunset Strip,Ph(c). . 225.00
1067 Yogi Bear 200.00
1068 Francis the Famous
　　Talking Mule 60.00
1069 ATh,The FBI Story,Ph(c) . . . 175.00
1070 Soloman and Sheba,Ph(c) . 160.00
1071 ATh,TheRealMcCoys,Ph(c). 175.00
1072 Blythe 90.00
1073 CB,Grandma Duck's Farm
　　Friends. 235.00
1074 Chilly Willy 60.00
1075 Tales of Wells Fargo,Ph(c) . 150.00
1076 MSy,The Rebel,Ph(c) 175.00
1077 SB,The Deputy,
　　H.Fonda Ph(c) 225.00
1078 The Three Stooges,Ph(c) . . 225.00
1079 The Little Rascals 100.00
1080 Fury,Ph(c) 125.00
1081 Elmer Fudd 50.00
1082 Spin and Marty 150.00
1083 Men into Space,Ph(c) 150.00
1084 Speedy Gonzales 90.00
1085 ATh,The Time Machine 300.00
1086 Lolly and Pepper. 50.00
1087 Peter Gunn,Ph(c) 175.00
1088 A Dog of Flanders,Ph(c) . . . 90.00
1089 Restless Gun,Ph(c). 150.00
1090 Francis the Famous
　　Talking Mule 60.00
1091 Jacky's Diary 90.00
1092 Toby Tyler,Ph(c) 125.00
1093 MacKenzie's Raiders,Ph(c) 125.00
1094 Goofy 90.00
1095 CB,W.Disney's
　　GyroGearloose 170.00
1096 The Texan,Ph(c) 150.00
1097 Rawhide,C.Eastwood Ph(c) 275.00
1098 Sugarfoot,Ph(c) 150.00
1099 CB(c),Donald Duck Album . 125.00
1100 W.Disney's Hercules
　　Life Story (TV),Ph(c) 400.00
1101 Robert Louis Stevenson's
　　Kidnapped,Ph(c) 125.00
1102 Wanted: Dead or Alive,
　　Ph(c) 225.00
1103 Leave It To Beaver,Ph(c). . . 275.00
1104 Yogi Bear Goes to College . 150.00
1105 ATh,Gale Storm,Ph(c) 225.00
1106 ATh,77 Sunset Strip,Ph(c). . 175.00
1107 Buckskin,Ph(c) 125.00
1108 The Troubleshooters,Ph(c) . 90.00
1109 This Is Your Life, Donald
　　Duck,O:Donald Duck 250.00
1110 Bonanza,Ph(c) 600.00
1111 Shotgun Slade 125.00
1112 Pixie and Dixie
　　and Mr. Jinks 150.00
1113 Tales of Wells Fargo,Ph(c) . 165.00
1114 Huckleberry Finn,Ph(c) 90.00
1115 Ricky Nelson,Ph(c) 275.00
1116 Boots and Saddles,Ph(c) . . 90.00
1117 Boy and the Pirate,Ph(c). . . 125.00

1118 Sword and the Dragon,Ph(c)135.00
1119 Smokey and the Bear
    Nature Stories 65.00
1120 Dinosaurus,Ph(c) 150.00
1121 RC,GE,HerculesUnchained 175.00
1122 Chilly Willy. 60.00
1123 Tombstone Territory,Ph(c) . . 175.00
1124 Whirlybirds,Ph(c). 165.00
1125 GK,RH,Laramie,Ph(c) 175.00
1126 Sundance,Ph(c) 125.00
1127 The Three Stooges,Ph(c) . . . 225.00
1128 Rocky and His Friends 600.00
1129 Pollyanna,H.Mills Ph(c). . . . 135.00
1130 SB,The Deputy,
    H.Fonda Ph(c) 175.00
1131 Elmer Fudd 50.00
1132 Space Mouse 75.00
1133 Fury,Ph(c) 125.00
1134 ATh,Real McCoys,Ph(c) . . . 175.00
1135 M.G.M.'s Mouse Musketeers. 90.00
1136 Jungle Cat,Ph(c) 120.00
1137 The Little Rascals 90.00
1138 The Rebel,Ph(c) 165.00
1139 SB,Spartacus,Ph(c). 225.00
1140 Donald Duck Album 125.00
1141 Huckleberry Hound for
    President 150.00
1142 Johnny Ringo,Ph(c) 135.00
1143 Pluto 60.00
1144 The Story of Ruth,Ph(c) . . . 150.00
1145 GK,The Lost World,Ph(c) . . 175.00
1146 Restless Gun,Ph(c). 135.00
1147 Sugarfoot,Ph(c). 150.00
1148 I aim at the Stars,Ph(c) 135.00
1149 Goofy. 90.00
1150 CB,Daisy Duck's Diary 175.00
1151 Mickey Mouse Album 60.00
1152 Rocky and His Friends 400.00
1153 Frosty the Snowman. 90.00
1154 Santa Claus Funnies. 175.00
1155 North to Alaska 275.00
1156 Walt Disney Swiss
    Family Robinson 135.00
1157 Master of the World. 90.00
1158 Three Worlds of Gulliver . . . 125.00
1159 ATh,77 Sunset Strip 170.00
1160 Rawhide 250.00
1161 CB,Grandma Duck's
    Farm Friends 225.00
1162 Yogi Bera joins the Marines 135.00
1163 Daniel Boone 90.00
1164 Wanted: Dead or Alive 175.00
1165 Ellery Queen 200.00
1166 Rocky and His Friends 375.00
1167 Tales of Wells Fargo,Ph(c) . 135.00
1168 The Detectives,
    R.Taylor Ph(c) 175.00
1169 New Adventures of
    Sherlock Holmes 275.00
1170 The Three Stooges,Ph(c) . . 225.00
1171 Elmer Fudd 50.00
1172 Fury,Ph(c) 125.00
1173 The Twilight Zone 375.00
1174 The Little Rascals 75.00
1175 M.G.M.'s Mouse Musketeers. 45.00
1176 Dondi,Ph(c) 75.00
1177 Chilly Willy. 60.00
1178 Ten Who Dared 135.00
1179 The Swamp Fox,
    L.Nielson Ph(c) 150.00
1180 The Danny Thomas Show . 275.00
1181 Texas John Slaughter,Ph(c) 135.00
1182 Donald Duck Album 75.00
1183 101 Dalmatians 175.00
1184 CB,W.Disney's
    Gyro Gearloose 165.00
1185 Sweetie Pie 75.00
1186 JDa,Yak Yak 145.00
1187 The Three Stooges,Ph(c) . . 200.00
1188 Atlantis the Lost
    Continent,Ph(c) 200.00

1189 Greyfriars Bobby,Ph(c) 135.00
1190 CB(c),Donald and
    the Wheel 135.00
1191 Leave It to Beaver,Ph(c) . . . 250.00
1192 Rocky Nelson,Ph(c) 265.00
1193 The Real McCoys,Ph(c) . . . 150.00
1194 Pepe,Ph(c) 50.00
1195 National Velvet,Ph(c) 125.00
1196 Pixie and Dixie
    and Mr. Jinks 90.00
1197 The Aquanauts,Ph(c) 135.00
1198 Donald in Mathmagic Land . 125.00
1199 Absent-Minded Professor,
    Ph(c) 150.00
1200 Hennessey,Ph(c) 125.00
1201 Goofy. 90.00
1202 Rawhide,C.Eastwood Ph(c) 275.00
1203 Pinocchio 90.00
1204 Scamp 65.00
1205 David & Goliath,Ph(c) 125.00
1206 Lolly and Pepper. 40.00
1207 MSy,The Rebel,Ph(c) 150.00
1208 Rocky and His Friends . . . 375.00
1209 Sugarfoot,Ph(c). 150.00
1210 The Parent Trap,
    H.Mills Ph(c) 175.00
1211 RsM,77 Sunset Strip,Ph(c) . 150.00
1212 Chilly Willy 60.00
1213 Mysterious Island,Ph(c) . . . 150.00
1214 Smokey the Bear 65.00
1215 Tales of Wells Fargo,Ph(c) . 135.00
1216 Whirlybirds,Ph(c). 135.00
1218 Fury,Ph(c) 125.00
1219 The Detectives,
    Robert Taylor Ph(c) 150.00
1220 Gunslinger,Ph(c) 150.00
1221 Bonanza,Ph(c) 300.00
1222 Elmer Fudd 50.00
1223 GK,Laramie,Ph(c) 125.00
1224 The Little Rascals 75.00
1225 The Deputy,H.Fonda Ph(c) . 175.00
1226 Nikki, Wild Dog of the North . 900.00
1227 Morgan the Pirate,Ph(c) . . . 135.00
1229 Thief of Bagdad,Ph(c). 125.00
1230 Voyage to the Bottom
    of the Sea,Ph(c) 200.00
1231 Danger Man,Ph(c) 200.00
1232 On the Double. 75.00
1233 Tammy Tell Me True 125.00
1234 The Phantom Planet. 135.00
1235 Mister Magoo 150.00
1236 King of Kings,Ph(c) 135.00
1237 ATh,The Untouchables,
    Ph(c) 375.00
1238 Deputy Dawg 200.00

Four Color #1013
© *Dell Publishing Co.*

1239 CB(c),Donald Duck Album . 125.00
1240 The Detectives,
    R.Taylor Ph(c) 150.00
1241 Sweetie Pies 50.00
1242 King Leonardo and
    His Short Subjects 225.00
1243 Ellery Queen 150.00
1244 Space Mouse 75.00
1245 New Adventures of
    Sherlock Holmes 250.00
1246 Mickey Mouse Album 60.00
1247 Daisy Duck's Diary 90.00
1248 Pluto 60.00
1249 The Danny Thomas Show,
    Ph(c) 275.00
1250 Four Horseman of the
    Apocalypse,Ph(c) 125.00
1251 Everything's Ducky 85.00
1252 The Andy Griffith Show,
    Ph(c) 600.00
1253 Spaceman. 135.00
1254 'Diver Dan' 90.00
1255 The Wonders of Aladdin . . . 125.00
1256 Kona, Monarch of
    Monster Isle 135.00
1257 Car 54, Where Are You?,
    Ph(c) 150.00
1258 GE,The Frogmen 135.00
1259 El Cid,Ph(c). 135.00
1260 The Horsemasters,Ph(c) . . . 225.00
1261 Rawhide,C.Eastwood Ph(c) 250.00
1262 The Rebel,Ph(c) 150.00
1263 RsM,77 Sunset Strip,Ph(c) . 150.00
1264 Pixie & Dixie & Mr.Jinks . . . 100.00
1265 The Real McCoys,Ph(c) . . . 150.00
1266 M.G.M.'s Spike and Tyke . . . 50.00
1267 CB,GyroGearloose 125.00
1268 Oswald the Rabbit 60.00
1269 Rawhide,C.Eastwood Ph(c) 250.00
1270 Bullwinkle and Rocky 350.00
1271 Yogi Bear Birthday Party. . . . 90.00
1272 Frosty the Snowman. 90.00
1273 Hans Brinker,Ph(c) 100.00
1274 Santa Claus Funnies 75.00
1275 Rocky and His Friends 375.00
1276 Dondi 45.00
1278 King Leonardo and
    His Short Subjects 225.00
1279 Grandma Duck's Farm
    Friends. 75.00
1280 Hennessey,Ph(c) 110.00
1281 Chilly Willy 60.00
1282 Babes in Toyland,Ph(c). . . . 225.00
1283 Bonanza,Ph(c) 300.00
1284 RH,Laramie,Ph(c). 125.00
1285 Leave It to Beaver,Ph(c) . . . 275.00
1286 The Untouchables,Ph(c). . . . 275.00
1287 Man from Wells Fargo,Ph(c) 100.00
1288 RC,GE,The Twilight Zone . . 225.00
1289 Ellery Queen 150.00
1290 M.G.M.'s Mouse
    Musketeers 45.00
1291 RsM,77 Sunset Strip,Ph(c) . 150.00
1293 Elmer Fudd 50.00
1294 Ripcord 125.00
1295 Mr. Ed, the Talking Horse,
    Ph(c) 225.00
1296 Fury,Ph(c) 125.00
1297 Spanky, Alfalfa and the
    Little Rascals 75.00
1298 The Hathaways,Ph(c) 75.00
1299 Deputy Dawg 200.00
1300 The Comancheros 275.00
1301 Adventures in Paradise 100.00
1302 JohnnyJason,TeenReporter . 50.00
1303 Lad: A Dog,Ph(c). 65.00
1304 Nellie the Nurse 125.00
1305 Mister Magoo 150.00
1306 Target: The Corruptors,
    Ph(c) 100.00
1307 Margie 90.00

1308 Tales of the Wizard of Oz . . 200.00
1309 BK,87th Precinct,Ph(c) 175.00
1310 Huck and Yogi Winter
     Sports 150.00
1311 Rocky and His Friends 375.00
1312 National Velvet,Ph(c) 60.00
1313 Moon Pilot.Ph(c) 135.00
1328 GE,The Underwater
     City,Ph(c) 125.00
1330 GK,Brain Boy 225.00
1332 Bachelor Father 135.00
1333 Short Ribs 90.00
1335 Aggie Mack 60.00
1336 On Stage 75.00
1337 Dr. Kildare,Ph(c) 150.00
1341 The Andy Griffith Show,
     Ph(c) 575.00
1348 JDa,Yak Yak 150.00
1349 Yogi Berra Visits the U.N. . . 175.00
1350 Commanche,Ph(c) 90.00
1354 Calvin and the Colonel 150.00

FOUR FAVORITES

**Ace Magazines,
Sept., 1941**

1 B:Vulcan, Lash Lighting, Magno
     the Magnetic Man, Raven,
     Flag (c),Hitler 2,200.00
2 A: Black Ace 800.00
3 E:Vulcan 650.00
4 E:Raven,B:Unknown Soldiers 575.00
5 B:Captain Courageous 575.00
6 A: The Flag, B: Mr. Risk 525.00
7 JM 500.00
8 . . . . 500.00
9 RP,HK 550.00
10 HK 650.00
11 HK,LbC,UnKnown Soldier. . . 750.00
12 LbC 425.00
13 LbC 350.00
14 Fer 350.00
15 Fer. 350.00
16 Bondage(c) 375.00
17 Magno Lighting 325.00
18 Magno Lighting 325.00
19 RP(a&c) 325.00
20 RP(a&c) 325.00
21 RP(a&c) 300.00
22 RP(c). 275.00
23 RP(c). 275.00
24 RP(c). 275.00
25 RP(c). 275.00
26 RP(c). 275.00
27 RP(c). 250.00
28 thru 29 . . . . @225.00
30 thru 32 . . . . @200.00

4MOST

**Novelty Publ./Star Publ.,
Winter 1941**

1 The Target, The Cadet 1,900.00
2 The Target 800.00
3 Dan'l Flannel, Flag(c) 550.00
4 Dr. Seuss (1pg.). 550.00
2-1 . . . . 200.00
2-2 . . . . 200.00
2-3 . . . . 200.00
2-4 Hitler,Tojo,Mussolini (c) 350.00
3-1 . . . . 150.00
3-2 . . . . 150.00
3-3 . . . . 150.00
3-4 . . . . 150.00
4-1 . . . . 125.00
4-2 Walter Johnson(c) 125.00
4-3 . . . . 125.00
4-4 . . . . 125.00
5-1 The Target, Football(c) 100.00
5-2 . . . . 100.00
5-3 . . . . 100.00

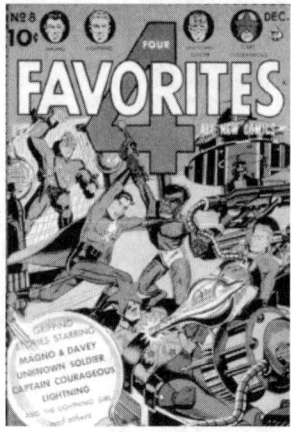

4 Favorites #8
© Novelty Publ.

5-4 Football(c) 100.00
6-1 Skiing(c) 100.00
6-2 LbC(c) 100.00
6-3 Tennis(c) 100.00
6-4 Football(c) 100.00
6-5 . . . . 250.00
7-1 Basketball(c) 100.00
7-2 LbC(c) 275.00
7-3 . . . . 125.00
7-4 LbC(c) 275.00
7-5 . . . . 125.00
7-6 LbC(c) 275.00
Becomes:

FOREMOST BOYS

Jan., 1949

8-1 . . . . 100.00
8-2 LbC(c),Surfing(c) 275.00
8-3 LbC(c) 275.00
8-4 LbC 200.00
8-5 LbC(c) 275.00
8-6 LbC 200.00
38 LbC(c), Johnny Weismuller. . 275.00
39 LbC(c), Johnny Weismuller. . 275.00
40 LbC(c), White Rider 275.00
Becomes:

THRILLING CRIME CASES

FRANKENSTEIN COMICS

**Crestwood Publications
(Prize Publ.),
Summer, 1945**

1 B:Frankenstein,DBr(a&c) . . . 1,500.00
2 DBr(a&c) 750.00
3 DBr(a&c) 500.00
4 DBr(a&c) 500.00
5 DBr(a&c) 500.00
6 DBr(a&c),S&K 425.00
7 DBr(a&c),S&K 425.00
8 DBr(a&c),S&K 425.00
9 DBr(a&c),S&K 425.00
10 DBr(a&c),S&K 425.00
11 DBr(a&c)A:Boris Karloff 350.00
12 DBr(a&c). 350.00
13 DBr(a&c). 350.00
14 DBr(a&c). 350.00
15 DBr(a&c). 350.00
16 DBr(a&c). 350.00
17 DBr(a&c). 350.00
18 DBr,B:Horror 500.00
19 DBr 300.00
3-4 DBr. 275.00
3-5 DBr. 275.00

3-6 DBr. 275.00
4-1 thru 4-6 DBr . . . . @275.00
5-1 thru 5-4 DBr . . . . @275.00
5-5 DBr, Oct.–Nov., 1954 . . . . . . 275.00

FRISKY FABLES

**Novelty Press/Premium Group,
Spring, 1945**

1 AFa 200.00
2 AFa 100.00
3 AFa 100.00
4 AFa 75.00
5 AFa 75.00
6 AFa 75.00
7 AFa,Flag (c) 80.00
2-1 AFa,Rainbow(c) 100.00
2-2 AFa 80.00
2-3 AFa 80.00
2-4 AFa 80.00
2-5 AFa 80.00
2-6 AFa 80.00
2-7 AFa 80.00
2-8 AFa,Halloween (c) 80.00
2-9 AFa,Thanksgiving(c) 75.00
2-10 AFa,Christman (c) 80.00
2-11 AFa. 80.00
2-12 AFa,Valentines Day (c) 75.00
3-1 AFa 75.00
3-2 AFa 75.00
3-3 AFa 80.00
3-4 AFa 75.00
3-5 AFa 75.00
3-6 AFa 75.00
3-7 AFa 75.00
3-8 AFa,Turkey (c) 75.00
3-9 AFa 75.00
3-10 AFa 75.00
3-11 AFa,1948(c) 75.00
3-12 AFa 75.00
4-1 thru 4-7 AFa . . . . @75.00
5-1 AFa 75.00
5-2 AFa 75.00
5-3 . . . . 75.00
5-4 Star Publications 75.00
39 LbC(c) 250.00
40 LbC(c), Christmas 250.00
41 LbC(c) 250.00
42 LbC(c) 250.00
43 LbC(c) 60.00
Becomes:

FRISKY ANIMALS

Star Publications Jan., 1951

44 LbC, Super Cat. 250.00
45 LbC 350.00
46 LbC,Baseball. 250.00
47 LbC 250.00
48 LbC 250.00
49 LbC 250.00
50 LbC 250.00
51 LbC(c) 250.00
52 LbC(c), Christmas 275.00
53 LbC(c) 250.00
54 LbC(c),Supercat(c) 250.00
55 LbC(c),same 250.00
56 LbC(c),same 250.00
57 LbC(c),same 250.00
58 LbC(c),same,July, 1954 . . . . . 250.00

FRITZI RITZ

**United Features Syndicate/
St. John Publications,
Fall, 1948**

N# Special issue 175.00
2 . . . . 100.00
3 . . . . 75.00
4 thru 7 . . . . @65.00
6 A:Abbie & Slats 70.00
8 thru 11 1958 . . . . @60.00

FROGMAN COMICS
Hillman Periodicals,
Jan.–Feb., 1952–May, 1953
1	150.00
2	90.00
3	90.00
4 MMe	65.00
5 BK,AT	75.00
6	50.00
7	50.00
8 thru 11	@50.00

FRONTIER ROMANCES
Avon Periodicals,
Nov.–Dec., 1949
1 She Learned to Ride and Shoot,
  and Kissing Came Natural .. 600.00
2 Bronc-Busters Sweetheart,
  Jan.–Feb., 1950 .... 450.00

FRONTLINE COMBAT
Tiny Tot Publications
(E.C. Comics), ,
July–Aug., 1951
1 HK(c),WW, JSe,JDa,Hanhung
  Changjn (c) 1,000.00
2 HK(c),WW,Tank Battle (c) 600.00
3 HK(c),WW,Naval Battleship
  fire (c) 400.00
4 HK(c),WW, Bazooka (c) 375.00
5 HK(c),JSe 325.00
6 HK(c),WW,JSe 275.00
7 HK(c),WW,JSe,Document of the
  Action at Iwo Jima 275.00
8 HK(c),WW,ATh 275.00
9 HK(c),WW,JSe,Civil War iss. . 275.00
10 GE,HK(c),WW,
  Crying Child (c) 300.00
11 GE 225.00
12 GE,Air Force issue 225.00
13 JSe,GE,WW(c),
  Bi-Planes (c) 225.00
14 JKu,GE,WW(c) 225.00
15 JSe,GE,WW(c), Jan., 1954 .. 225.00

FRONT PAGE
COMIC BOOK
Front Page Comics, 1945
1 JKu,BP,BF(c),I:Man in Black .. 500.00

New Funnies #94
© *Dell Publishing Co.*

FUGITIVES FROM
JUSTICE
St. John Publishing Co.,
Feb., 1952
1	250.00
2 MB, Killer Boomerang	275.00
3 GT	250.00
4	125.00
5 Bondage (c), Oct., 1952	150.00

FUNNIES, THE
(1ST SERIES)
Dell Publishing Co.,
1929-30
1 B:Foxy Grandpa, Sniffy..... 1,500.00
2 thru 21 .... @500.00
N#(22) 400.00
N#(23) thru (36) .... @400.00

FUNNIES, THE
(2ND SERIES)
Dell Publishing Co.,
Oct., 1936
1 Tailspin Tommy,Mutt & Jeff,
  Capt. Easy,D.Dixon 4,000.00
2 Scribbly 2,000.00
3 .... 1,200.00
4 Christmas issue 1,000.00
5 .... 1,000.00
6 thru 10 .... @750.00
11 thru 22 .... 650.00
23 thru 29 .... @550.00
30 B:John Carter of Mars 1,800.00
31 inc. Dick Tracy 1,100.00
32 .... 1,100.00
33 .... 1,100.00
34 .... 1,100.00
35 John Carter (c) 1,100.00
36 John Carter (c) 1,100.00
37 John Carter (c) 1,100.00
38 Rex King of the Deep (c) ... 1,100.00
39 Rex King (c) 1,100.00
40 John Carter (c) 1,100.00
41 Sky Ranger (c) 1,100.00
42 Rex King (c) 1,100.00
43 Rex King (c) 1,100.00
44 Rex King (c) 1,100.00
45 I&O:Phantasmo:Master of
  the World 1,200.00
46 Phantasmo (c) 700.00
47 Phantasmo (c) 650.00
48 Phantasmo (c) 650.00
49 Phantasmo (c) 650.00
50 Phantasmo (c) 650.00
51 Phantasmo (c) 650.00
52 Phantasmo (c) 600.00
53 Phantasmo (c) 600.00
54 Phantasmo (c) 600.00
55 Phantasmo (c) 600.00
56 Phantasmo (c) E:John Carter 600.00
57 I&O:Captain Midnight...... 4,800.00
58 Captain Midnight (c)...... 1,400.00
59 Captain Midnight (c)...... 1,400.00
60 Captain Midnight (c)...... 1,400.00
61 Captain Midnight (c)...... 1,200.00
62 Captain Midnight (c) 900.00
63 Captain Midnight (c) 900.00
64 B: Woody Woodpecker 1,550.00
Becomes:

NEW FUNNIES
Dell Publishing Co. July, 1942
65 Andy Panda, Ragady Ann &
  Andy, Peter Rabbit 1,300.00
66 same 500.00
67 Felix the Cat 500.00
68 .... 500.00

69 WK, The Brownies	500.00
70	500.00
71	350.00
72 WK	350.00
73	350.00
74	350.00
75 WK,Brownies	350.00
76 CB,Andy Panda, Woody	
Woodpecker	1,500.00
77 same	350.00
78 Andy Panda	350.00
79	250.00
80	250.00
81	250.00
82 WK,Brownies	265.00
83 WK,Brownies	265.00
84 WK,Brownies	265.00
85 WK,Brownies	265.00
86	200.00
87 Woody Woodpecker	175.00
88 same	175.00
89 same	175.00
90 same	175.00
91 thru 99	@125.00
100	135.00
101 thru 110	@100.00
111 thru 118	@100.00
119 Christmas	110.00
120 thru 142	@100.00
143 Christmas (c)	110.00
144 thru 149	@100.00
150 thru 154	@75.00
155 Christmas (c)	100.00
156 thru 167	@75.00
168 Christmas (c)	100.00
169 thru 181	@75.00
182 I&O:Knothead & Splinter	75.00
183 thru 200	@75.00
201 thru 240	@60.00
241 thru 288	@50.00

FUNNY BOOK
Funny Book Publ. Corp.,
(Parents Magazine) Dec., 1952
1 Alec, the Funny Bunny,
  Alice in Wonderland 150.00
2 Gulliver in Giant-Land 75.00
3 .... 60.00
4 Adventures of Robin Hood 50.00
5 .... 50.00
6 .... 50.00
7 .... 50.00
8 .... 50.00
9 .... 50.00

FUNNY FILMS
Best Syndicated Features
(American Comics Group),
Sept.–Oct., 1949
1 B:Puss An' Boots,
  Blunderbunny 225.00
2 .... 100.00
3 .... 65.00
4 .... 50.00
5 .... 50.00
6 .... 50.00
7 .... 50.00
8 .... 50.00
9 .... 50.00
10 .... 50.00
11 thru 20 .... @45.00
21 thru 28 .... @40.00
29 May–June, 1954 .... 40.00

FUNNY FUNNIES
Nedor Publ. Co.,
April, 1943
1 Funny Animals 225.00

COMICS MAGAZINE

**Comics Magazine/Centaur,
May, 1936**

1 S&S, Dr. Mystic.	15,000.00
2 S&S, Federal Agent	3,000.00
3	2,500.00
4	2,500.00
5	2,500.00

Becomes:

FUNNY PAGES

Nov., 1936

6 I:The Clock, 1st masked hero	3,000.00
7 WE	1,200.00
8 WE	1,200.00
9	1,200.00
10 WE	1,200.00
11	1,200.00
12	800.00
13 FG,BoW.	800.00
14 JCo,FG,BoW	800.00
15 JCo	800.00
16 JCo,FG	800.00
17 Centaur	1,200.00
18	800.00
19	800.00
20	800.00
21 B:The Arrow	4,400.00
22 BEv,GFx.	1,700.00
23	1,700.00
24 BKa,B.Wayne prototype.	1,900.00
25 JCo.	1,400.00
26	1,400.00
27	1,400.00
28	1,400.00
29 JCo,BoW	1,400.00
30 BoW,The Arrow(c)	3,000.00
31	1,500.00
32 JCo,BoW	1,500.00
33 JCo,BoW,The Arrow(c)	2,500.00
34 JCo,The Arrow(c).	3,000.00
35 BoW,The Arrow(c)	3,000.00
36 Mad Ming (c)	1,500.00
37 JCo,Mad Ming (c)	1,500.00
38 Mad Ming(c).	1,500.00
39 The Arrow(c)	2,400.00
40 BoW,The Arrow(c)	2,400.00
41 BoW,The Arrow(c)	2,400.00
42 BoW,The Arrow(c)	2,400.00

FUNNY PICTURE STORIES

**Comics Magazine/Centaur
Publ., Nov., 1936**

1 B:The Clock	4,500.00
2 The Spinner Talks	1,600.00
3 Tyrant Gold	1,000.00
4 WE,The Brothers Three	1,000.00
5 Timber Terror	1,000.00
6 War in Asia (c)	1,000.00
7 Racist Humor (c).	1,000.00

Vol 2

#1(10)	700.00
#2 (11) BoW.	700.00
#3 (12)BoW	600.00
#4 (13) Christmas (c).	700.00
#5 (14) BoW.	600.00
#6 (15) Centaur.	1,000.00
#7 (16)	550.00
#8 (17)	550.00
#9 (18)	550.00
#10 (19)	550.00
#11 (20)	550.00

Vol 3

#1	550.00
#2	550.00
#3	550.00

Becomes:

COMIC PAGES

July, 1939

4 BoW	800.00
5	600.00
6	600.00

FUNNYMAN

**Magazine Enterprises
of Canada, Dec., 1947**

1 S&K(a&c)	600.00
2 S&K(a&c)	325.00
3 S&K(a&c)	250.00
4 S&K(a&c)	250.00
5 S&K(a&c)	250.00
6 S&K(a&c), Aug., 1948	250.00

FUNNY TUNES

**Avon Periodicals,
July, 1953**

1 (fa),Space Mouse, Peter Rabbit Merry Mouse,Cicero the Cat	125.00
2 same	75.00
3 same	75.00

Becomes:

SPACE COMICS

**Avon Periodicals,
March–April, 1954**

4 (fa),F:Space Mouse	60.00
5 (fa),F:Space Mouse	50.00

FUTURE COMICS

**David McKay Publications,
June, 1940**

1 Lone Ranger,Phantom	3,500.00
2 Lone Ranger.	1,600.00
3 Lone Ranger.	1,400.00
4 Lone Ranger,Sept., 1940	1,300.00

FUTURE WORLD COMICS

**George W. Dougherty,
Summer, 1946**

1	400.00
2 Fall, 1946	350.00

GABBY HAYES WESTERN

Fawcett Publ., Nov., 1948

1 Ph(c)	650.00
2 Ph(c)	300.00
3 The Rage of the Purple Sage, Ph(c)	200.00
4 Ph(c)	200.00
5 Ph(c)	175.00
6 Ph(c)	175.00
7 Ph(c)	150.00
8 Ph(c)	150.00
9 Ph(c),V:The Kangaroo Crook	150.00
10 Ph(c)	150.00
11 Ph(c), Chariot Race	150.00
12 V:Beaver Ben, The Biting Bandit,Ph(c).	125.00
13 thru 15.	@125.00
16	110.00
17	110.00
18 thru 20.	@110.00
21 thru 50	@110.00

Charlton Comics

51 Charlton Issues Start	125.00
52 thru 59 Dec., 1954	@75.00

*Gangsters and Gun Molls #1
© Avon*

GANGSTERS AND GUN MOLLS

**Realistic Comics
(Avon), Sept., 1951**

1 WW,A:Big Jim Colosimo, Evelyn Ellis	600.00
2 JKa, A:Bonnie Parker, The Kissing Bandit	500.00
3 EK, A:Juanita Perez, Crimes Homicide Squad	400.00
4 A:Mara Hite, Elkins Boys, June, 1952	350.00

GANGSTERS CAN'T WIN

**D.S. Publishing Co.,
Feb.–March, 1948**

1 Shot Cop (c)	400.00
2 A:Eddie Bentz	200.00
3 Twin Trouble Trigger Man	175.00
4 Suicide on SoundStageSeven	225.00
5 Trail of Terror	175.00
6 Mystery at the Circus	175.00
7 Talisman Trail	150.00
8	150.00
9 Suprise at Buoy 13, June–July, 1949	150.00

GANG WORLD

**Literary Enterprises
(Standard Comics),
Oct., 1952**

5 Bondage	225.00
6 Mob Payoff, Jan., 1953	150.00

GASOLINE ALLEY

**Star Publications,
Oct., 1950**

1	250.00
2 LBc	275.00
3 LBc(c), April, 1950	250.00

GEM COMICS

Spotlight Publ. April, 1945

1 A:Steve Strong,Bondage(c)	600.00

GENE AUTRY COMICS

**Fawcett Publications,
Jan., 1942**

1 The Mark of Cloven Hoof	12,000.00

Gene Autry
© *Dell Publishing Co.*

2	2,200.00
3 Secret o/t Aztec Treasure	1,500.00
4	1,300.00
5 Mystery of Paint Rock Canyon	1,300.00
6 Outlaw Round-up	1,100.00
7 Border Bullets	1,100.00
8 Blazing Guns	1,100.00
9 Range Robbers	1,100.00
10 Fightin' Buckaroo, Danger's Trail, Sept., 1943	1,100.00
11	1,000.00
12	1,000.00

GENE AUTRY COMICS
Dell Publishing Co., May/June, 1946

1	700.00
2 Ph(c)	400.00
3 Ph(c)	300.00
4 Ph(c),I:Flap Jack	300.00
5 Ph(c), all.	300.00
6 thru 10	@250.00
11 thru 19	@250.00
20	235.00
21 thru 29	@175.00
30 thru 40, B:Giants	@150.00
41 thru 56 E:Giants	@125.00
57	125.00
58 Christmas (c)	110.00
59 thru 66	@100.00
67 thru 80, B:Giant	@110.00
81 thru 90, E:Giant	@80.00
91 thru 93	@75.00
94 Christmas (c)	80.00
95 thru 99	@75.00
100	100.00
101 thru 111	@60.00
112 thru 121	@60.00

GENE AUTRY'S CHAMPION
Dell Publishing Co., Aug., 1950

(1) *see Dell Four Color #287*
(2) *see Dell Four Color #319*

3	75.00
4 thru 19	@60.00

GEORGE PAL'S PUPPETOON'S
Fawcett Publications, Dec., 1945

1 Captain Marvel (c)	550.00
2	300.00
3	165.00
4 thru 17	@150.00
18 Dec., 1947	125.00

GERALD McBOING-BOING AND THE NEARSIGHTED MR. MAGOO
Dell Publishing Co., Aug.–Oct., 1952

1	225.00
2 thru 5	@175.00

GERONIMO
Avon Periodicals, 1950

1 Massacre at San Pedro Pass	200.00
2 EK(c), Murderous Battle at Kiskayah	125.00
3 EK(c)	125.00
4 EK(c),Apache Death Trap, Feb., 1952	110.00

GET LOST
Mikeross Publications, Feb.–March, 1954

1	350.00
2	225.00
3 June–July, 1954	200.00

GHOST
Fiction House Magazine, Winter, 1951–Summer, 1954

1 The Banshee Bells	900.00
2 I Woke In Terror	450.00
3 The Haunted Hand of X	350.00
4 Flee the Mad Furies	350.00
5 The Hex of Ruby Eye	350.00
6 The Sleepers in the Crypt	350.00
7 When Dead Rogues Ride	350.00
8 Curse of the Mist-Thing	350.00
9 It Crawls by Night,Bondage(c)	375.00
10 Halfway to Hades	350.00
11 GE, The Witch's Doll	350.00

Ghost Breakers #2
© *Street & Smith*

GHOST BREAKERS
Street & Smith, Sept., 1948

1 BP(a&c), A:Dr. Neff	500.00
2 BP(a&c), Breaks the Voodoo Hoodoo,Dec., 1948	400.00

GHOSTLY WEIRD STORIES
See: BLUE BOLT

GIANT BOY BOOK OF COMICS
Newsbook Publ. (Lev Gleason), 1945

1 A:Crime Buster & Young Robin Hood	1,200.00

GIANT COMICS EDITION
St. John Publ., 1948

1 Mighty Mouse	650.00
2 Abbie and Slats	325.00
3 Terry Toons	500.00
4 Crime Comics	750.00
5 MB, Police Case Book	750.00
6 MB(a&c), Western Picture Story	650.00
7 Mopsy	400.00
8 Adventures of Mighty Mouse	450.00
9 JKu,MB,Romance & Confession Stories,Ph(c)	750.00
10 Terry Toons	450.00
11 MB(a&c),JKu,Western Picture Stories	650.00
12 MB(a&c),Diary Secrets, Prostitute	1,500.00
13 MB,JKu, Romances	650.00
14 Mighty Mouse Album	450.00
15 MB(c),Romance	750.00
16 Little Audrey	450.00
N#, Mighty Mouse Album	450.00

GIANT COMICS EDITION
United Features Syndicate, 1945

1 A:Abbie & Slats, Jim Hardy, Ella Cinders,Iron Vic	500.00
2 Elmo, Jim Hardy, Abbie & Slats, 1945	350.00

G.I. COMBAT
Quality Comics Group, 1952

1 RC(c), Beyond the Call of Duty	900.00
2 RC(c), Operation Massacre	400.00
3 An Indestructible Marine	375.00
4 Bridge to Blood Hill	375.00
5 Hell Breaks loose on Suicide Hill	375.00
6 Beachhead Inferno	300.00
7 Fire Power Assault	250.00
8 RC(c),Death-trap Hill	250.00
9 Devil Riders	250.00
10 RC(c), Two-Ton Booby Trap	350.00
11 Hell's Heroes	225.00
12 Hand Grenade Hero	225.00
13 Commando Assault	225.00
14 Spear Head Assault	225.00
15 Vengeance Assault	225.00
16 Trapped Under Fire	200.00
17 Attack on Death Mountain	200.00
18 Red Battle Ground	200.00
19 Death on Helicopter Hill	200.00
20 Doomed Legion-Death Trap	200.00
21 Red Sneak Attack	175.00
22 Vengeance Raid	175.00

GOLDEN AGE

GOLDEN AGE

23 No Grandstand in Hell	175.00
24 Operation Steel	
Trap,Comics Code.	175.00
25 Charge of the CommieBrigade	175.00
26 Red Guerrilla Trap	175.00
27 Trapped Behind Commie	
Lines	175.00
28 Atomic Battleground	175.00
29 Patrol Ambush	175.00
30 Operation Booby Trap	175.00
31 Human Fly on Heartbreak Hill	175.00
32 Atomic Rocket Assault	200.00
33 Bridge to Oblivion	175.00
34 RC,Desperate Mission	200.00
35 Doom Patrol	175.00
36 Fire Power Assault	175.00
37 Attack at Dawn	175.00
38 Get That Tank	175.00
39 Mystery of No Man's Land	175.00
40 Maneuver Battleground	175.00
41 Trumpet of Doom	175.00
42 March of Doom	175.00
43 Operation Showdown	175.00

See DC Comics for 44-120

GIFT COMICS
Fawcett Publications,
March, 1942

1 A:Captain Marvel, Bulletman,	
Golden Arrow,Ibis, the	
Invincible, Spy Smasher	3,500.00
2	2,300.00
3	1,500.00
4 A:Marvel Family, 1949	1,000.00

GIGGLE COMICS
Creston Publ./
American Comics Group,
Oct., 1943

1 (fa)same.	350.00
2 KHu	150.00
3 KHu	125.00
4 KHu	100.00
5 KHu	100.00
6 KHu	75.00
7 KHu	75.00
8 KHu	75.00
9 I:Super Katt	85.00
10 KHu	60.00
11 thru 20 KHu	@50.00
21 thru 30 KHu	@50.00
31 thru 40 KHu	@40.00
41 thru 94 KHu	@45.00

Giggle Comics #39
© American Comics Group

95 A:Spencer Spook	40.00
96 KHu	40.00
97 KHu	40.00
98 KHu	40.00
99 KHu	40.00
100 and 101 March–April,1955	@40.00

G.I. JANE
Stanhall Publ.,
May, 1953

1	150.00
2 thru 6	@75.00
7 thru 9	@65.00
10 Dec., 1954	60.00

G.I. JOE
Ziff-Davis Publication Co.,
1950

10 NS(c),Red Devils of Korea,	
V:Seoul City Lou	175.00
11 NS(c),The Guerrilla's Lair	125.00
12 NS(c).	125.00
13 NS(c),Attack at Dawn	125.00
14 NS(c),Temple of Terror,	
A:Peanuts the Great	135.00
2-6 It's a Foot Soldiers Job,	
I:Frankie of the Pump	125.00
2-7 BP,NS(c),The Rout at	
Sugar Creek	125.00
8 BP,NS(c),Waldo'sSqueezeBox	125.00
9 NS(c),Dear John	125.00
10 NS(c),Joe Flies the Payroll	125.00
11 NS(c),For the Love of Benny	125.00
12 NS(c),Patch work Quilt	125.00
13 NS(c).	125.00
14 NS(c),The Wedding Ring	125.00
15 The Lacrosse Whoopee	125.00
16 Mamie's Mortar	125.00
17 A Time for Waiting.	125.00
18 Giant	275.00
19 Old Army Game..Buck Passer	90.00
20 General Confusion	90.00
21 Save 'Im for Brooklyn	90.00
22 Portrait of a Lady	90.00
23 Take Care of My Little Wagon	90.00
24 Operation 'Operation'	90.00
25 The Two-Leaf Clover	90.00
26 NS(c),Nobody Flies Alone	
Mud & Wings.	90.00
27 'Dear Son...Come Home'	90.00
28 They Alway's Come Back	
Bondage (c).	90.00
29 What a Picnic	75.00
30 NS(c),The One-Sleeved	
Kimono	75.00
31 NS(c),Get a Horse	60.00
32 thru 47	@60.00
48 Atom Bomb	75.00
49 thru 51 June, 1957	@60.00

GINGER
Close-Up Publ.
(Archie Publications),
Jan., 1951

1 GFs	150.00
2	100.00
3	75.00
4	75.00
5	60.00
6	60.00
7 thru 9	@100.00
10 A:Katy Keene,Summer,1954.	100.00

GIRLS IN LOVE
Fawcett Publications,
May, 1950

1	125.00

2 Ph(c),July, 1950	100.00

GIRLS IN LOVE
See: DIARY LOVES

G.I. SWEETHEARTS
See: DIARY LOVES

G.I. WAR BRIDES
Superior Publ. Ltd.,
April, 1954

1	100.00
2	50.00
3 thru 7	@40.00
8 June, 1955	40.00

GOING STEADY
See: TEEN-AGE
TEMPTATIONS

GOLDEN ARROW
Fawcett Publications,
Spring, 1942

1 B:Golden Arrow	1,100.00
2	550.00
3	400.00
4	375.00
5 Spring, 1947	375.00
6 BK	400.00
6a 1944 Well Known Comics	
(Giveaway)	450.00

GOLDEN LAD
Spark Publications,
July, 1945–June, 1946

1 MMe(a&c),A:Kid Wizards,	
Swift Arrow,B:Golden Ladd.	1,000.00
2 MMe(a&c)	450.00
3 MMe(a&c)	450.00
4 MMe(a&c), The Menace of	
the Minstrel	450.00
5 MMe(a&c),O:Golden Girl	450.00

GOLDEN WEST LOVE
Kirby Publishing Co.,
Sept.–Oct., 1949

1 BP,I Rode Heartbreak Hill,	
Ph(c)	250.00
2 BP	175.00
3 BP,Ph(c)	175.00
4 BP,April, 1950	175.00

GOLD MEDAL COMICS
Cambridge House, 1945

N# Captain Truth	350.00

GOOFY COMICS
Nedor Publ. Co./
Animated Cartoons
(Standard Comics),
June, 1943

1 (fa)	300.00
2	150.00
3 VP	125.00
4 VP	110.00
5 VP	110.00
6 thru 10 VP	@110.00
11 thru 15	@100.00
15 thru 19	@100.00
20 thru 35 FF	@125.00
36 thru 48	@75.00

All comics prices listed are for *Near Mint* condition.

GREAT AMERICAN COMICS PRESENTS– THE SECRET VOICE
4 Star Publ., 1944
1 Hitler,Secret Weapon. 400.00

GREAT COMICS
Novak Publ. Co., 1945
1 LbC(c) 500.00

GREAT COMICS
Great Comics Publications, Nov., 1941
1 I:The Great Zorro 1,700.00
2 Buck Johnson 850.00
3 The Lost City, Jan., 1942 . . . 3,500.00

GREAT LOVER ROMANCES
Toby Press, March, 1951
1 Jon Juan,A:Dr. King. 200.00
2 Hollywood Girl 100.00
3 Love in a Taxi 60.00
4 The Experimental Kiss 60.00
5 After the Honeymoon 60.00
6 HK,The Kid Sister Falls
   in Love 100.00
7 Man Crazy 60.00
8 Stand-in Boyfriend 60.00
9 The Cheat 60.00
10 Heart Breaker 60.00
11 . . . . 60.00
12 . . . . 60.00
13 Powerhouse of Deceit. 60.00
14 . . . . 60.00
15 Ph(c),Still Undecided,
   Liz Taylor 200.00
16 thru 21. . . . . @50.00
22 May, 1955. . . . . 50.00

GREEN GIANT COMICS
Pelican Publications, 1941
1 Black Arrow, Dr. Nerod
   O:Colossus. 17,000.00

GREEN HORNET COMICS
Helnit Publ. Co./ Family Comics (Harvey Publ.), Dec., 1940
1 B:Green Hornet,P(c) 7,500.00
2 . . . . 2,500.00
3 BWh(c) 1,900.00
4 BWh(c) 1,500.00
5 BWh(c) 1,500.00
6 . . . . 1,500.00
7 BP, O:Zebra, B:Robin
   Hood & Spirit of 76 . . . . . . 1,200.00
8 BP,Bondage (c). 1,000.00
9 BP,JK(c),Behind the (c) 1,200.00
10 BP 1,000.00
11 Who is Mr. Q? 1,000.00
12 BP,A:Mr.Q 1,000.00
13 Hitler (c) 1,100.00
14 BP,Spirit of 76-Twinkle
   Twins, Bondage(c). 800.00
15 ASh(c),Nazi Ghost Ship 800.00
16 BP,Prisoner of War 800.00
17 BP,ASh(c),Nazis' Last Stand. . 800.00
18 BP,ASh(c),Jap's Treacherous
   Plot,Bondage (c) 800.00
19 BP,ASh(c),Clash with the
   Rampaging Japs 800.00

20 BP,ASh(c),Tojo's
   Propaganda Hoax 800.00
21 BP,ASh(c),Unwelcome Cargo. 600.00
22 ASh(c),Rendezvous with
   Jap Saboteurs 600.00
23 BF,ASh(c),Jap's Diabolical
   Plot #B2978. . . . . 600.00
24 BF,Science Fiction (c). 650.00
25 thru 29. . . . . @600.00
30 BP,JKu 600.00
31 BP,JKu 650.00
32 BP,JKu 500.00
33 BP,JKu 500.00
34 BP,JKu 500.00
35 BP,JKu 500.00
36 BP,JKu,Bondage (c) 550.00
37 BP,JKu 500.00
38 BP,JKu 500.00
39 S&K. 650.00
40 thru 45. . . . . @400.00
46 Drug 425.00
47 Sept., 1949 . . . . 400.00

GREEN LAMA
Spark Publications/Prize Publ., Dec., 1944
1 I:Green Lama, Lt. Hercules
   & Boy Champions 1,700.00
2 MRa,Forward to Victory
   in 1945 . . . . 1,000.00
3 MRa,The Riddles of Toys 800.00
4 MRa,Dive Bombs Japan 775.00
5 MRa(a&c),Fights for
   the Four Freedoms 775.00
6 MRa,Smashes a Plot
   against America 775.00
7 MRa,Merry X-Mas 450.00
8 MRa,Smashes Toy Master
   of Crime, March, 1946. . . . . . 450.00

GREEN MASK, THE
Fox Features Syndicate, Summer, 1940
1 O:Green Mask & Domino . . 5,500.00
2 A:Zanzibar 1,900.00
3 BP 1,200.00
4 B:Navy Jones 900.00
5 . . . . 750.00
6 B:Nightbird,E:Navy Jones,
   Bondage (c) 600.00
7 B:Timothy Smith &
   The Tumbler 500.00

Green Mask #8
© *Fox Features Syndicate*

8 JSs 450.00
9 E:Nightbird, Death Wields
   a Scalpel! 475.00
10 . . . . 375.00
11 The Banshee of Dead
   Man's Hill. 375.00
2-1 Election of Skulls 300.00
2-2 Pigeons of Death 300.00
2-3 Wandering Gold Brick 250.00
2-4 Time on His Hands 250.00
2-5 JFe,SFd 300.00
2-6 Adventure of the Disappearing
   Trains, Oct.–Nov., 1946. . . . . 300.00

GUMPS, THE
Dell Publishing Co., 1945
1 . . . . 200.00
2 . . . . 175.00
3 . . . . 125.00
4 . . . . 125.00
5 . . . . 125.00

GUNS AGAINST GANGSTERS
Curtis Publ./Novelty Press, Sept.–Oct., 1948
1 LbC(a&c),B:Toni Gayle 500.00
2 LbC(a&c) 350.00
3 LbC(a&c) 300.00
4 LbC(a&c) 300.00
5 LbC(a&c) 300.00
6 LbC(a&c),Shark. 300.00
2-1 LbC(a&c),Sept.–Oct., 1949 . 300.00

GUNSMOKE
Western Comics, Inc., April–May, 1949
1 GRi(a&c),Gunsmoke & Masked
   Marvel,Bondage (c) 500.00
2 GRi(a&c) 350.00
3 GRi(a&c) 275.00
4 GRi(c),Bondage(c). 250.00
5 GRi(c) 250.00
6 . . . . 225.00
7 . . . . 125.00
8 . . . . 125.00
9 . . . . 125.00
10 . . . . 125.00
11 thru 15. . . . . @110.00
16 Jan., 1952. . . . . 110.00

HA HA COMICS
Creston Publ. (American Comics Group), Oct., 1943
1 Funny Animal, all 350.00
2 . . . . 175.00
3 . . . . 125.00
4 . . . . 125.00
5 . . . . 125.00
6 thru 10 . . . . @100.00
11 . . . . 75.00
12 thru 15 KHu. . . . . @75.00
16 thru 20 KHu. . . . . @75.00
21 thru 30 KHu. . . . . @60.00
31 thru 101. . . . . @50.00
102 Feb.–March, 1955 . . . . 50.00

MISTER RISK
Humor Publ., Oct., 1950
1 (7) B:Mr. Risk 100.00
2 . . . . 100.00
Becomes:

MEN AGAINST CRIME
Feb., 1951
3 A:Mr. Risk, Case of the Carnival
　Killer 125.00
4 Murder-And the Crowd Roars . 75.00
5 . . . . 75.00
6 . . . . 75.00
7 Get Them! 75.00
Becomes:

HAND OF FATE
Ace Magazines, Dec., 1951
8 . . . . 500.00
9 LC 275.00
10 LC 275.00
11 Genie(c) 225.00
12 . . . . 225.00
13 Hanging(c) 235.00
14 . . . . 235.00
15 . . . . 235.00
16 . . . . 225.00
17 . . . . 225.00
18 . . . . 225.00
19 Drug issue,Quicksand(c) 250.00
20 . . . . 225.00
21 Drug issue. 275.00
22 . . . . 225.00
23 Graveyard(c) 225.00
24 LC,Electric Chair. 350.00
25 Nov., 1954. . . . . 175.00
25a Dec., 1954 . . . . 225.00

HANGMAN COMICS
See: LAUGH COMICS

HAP HAZARD COMICS
A.A. Wyn/Red Seal Publ./
Readers Research,
Summer, 1944
1 Funny Teen 175.00
2 Dog Show 100.00
3 Sgr, ... 60.00
4 Sgr, ... 60.00
5 thru 10 Sgr, ... @60.00
11 thru 13 Sgr, ... @55.00
14 AF(c) 75.00
15 . . . . 55.00
16 thru 24. . . . . @55.00
Becomes:

REAL LOVE
April, 1949
25 Dangerous Dates 150.00
26 . . . . 100.00
27 LbC(c), Revenge Conquest . . 110.00
28 thru 40. . . . . @75.00
41 thru 66 . . . . @60.00
67 Comics code. 50.00
68 thru 76, Nov., 1956 . . . . @50.00

HAPPY COMICS
Nedor Publications/
Animated Cartoons,
Aug., 1943
1 Funny Animal in all 275.00
2 . . . . 150.00
3 . . . . 100.00
4 . . . . 100.00
5 thru 10 . . . . @100.00
11 thru 20 . . . . @75.00
21 thru 31 . . . . @75.00
32 FF 200.00
33 FF 300.00
34 thru 37 FF . . . . @100.00
38 thru 40. . . . . @50.00
Becomes:

HAPPY RABBIT
Standard Comics, Feb., 1951
41 Funny Animal in all 50.00
42 thru 50 . . . . @40.00
Becomes:

HARVEY COMIC HITS
Harvey Publications, Oct., 1951
51 Phantom 350.00
52 Steve Canyon's Air Power . . . 150.00
53 Mandrake 275.00
54 Tim Tyler's Tales of Jungle
　Terror 150.00
55 Love Stories of Mary Worth . . 100.00
56 Phantom, Bondage (c) 300.00
57 AR,Kidnap Racket 200.00
58 Girls in White 100.00
59 Tales of the Invisible 150.00
60 Paramount Animated Comics 500.00
61 Casper the Friendly Ghost . . . 550.00
62 Paramount Animated Comics,
　April, 1953 . . . . 175.00

HAPPY HOULIHANS
See: SADDLE JUSTICE

HAUNTED THRILLS
Four Star Publ.
(Ajax/Farrell), June, 1952
1 Ellery Queen 600.00
2 LbC,Ellery Queen 450.00
3 Drug Story 400.00
4 Ghouls Castle 350.00
5 Fatal Scapel 350.00
6 Pit of Horror 300.00
7 Trail to a Tomb 300.00
8 Vanishing Skull 300.00
9 Madness of Terror 300.00
10 . . . . 300.00
11 Nazi Concentration Camp. . . . 325.00
12 RWb 225.00
13 . . . . 225.00
14 RWb 250.00
15 The Devil Collects 225.00
16 . . . . 225.00
17 Mirror of Madness. 225.00
18 No Place to Go,
　Nov.–Dec., 1954 . . . . 250.00

HAUNT OF FEAR
Fables Publ. (E.C. Comics) ,
May–June, 1950
15 JCr(a&c),AF,WW 4,000.00
16 JCr(a&c),AF,WW 1,800.00
17 JCr(a&c),AF,WW,O:Crypt
　of Terror,Vault of Horror
　& Haunt of Fear 1,700.00
4 AF(c),WW,JDa 1,200.00
5 JCr(a&c),WW,JDa,Eye Injury. . 900.00
6 JCr(a&c),WW,JDa 650.00
7 JCr(a&c),WW,JDa 650.00
8 AF(c),JKa,JDa,
　Shrunken Head 650.00
9 AF(c),JCr,JDa 650.00
10 AF(c),Grl,JDa 600.00
11 JKa,Grl,JDa. 500.00
12 JCr,Grl,JDa. 500.00
13 Grl,JDa 500.00
14 Grl(a&c),JDa,O:Old Witch . . . 750.00
15 JDa 500.00
16 GRi(c),JDa,Ray Bradbury
　adaptation 500.00
17 JDa,Grl(c),Classic
　Ghastly (c) 500.00
18 JDa,Grl(c),JKa,Ray Bradbury
　adaptation 550.00
19 JDa,Guillotine (c),
　Bondage (c). 600.00

Haunt of Fear #13
© E.C. Comics

20 RC,JDa,Grl(a&c) 425.00
21 JDa,Grl(a&c). 325.00
22 JDa,Grl(a&c). 325.00
23 JDa,Grl(a&c). 325.00
22 JDa,Grl(a&c). 325.00
23 JDa,Grl(a&c). 325.00
24 JDa,Grl(a&c). 325.00
25 JDa,Grl(a&c). 325.00
26 RC,JDa,Grl(a&c). 350.00
27 JDa,Grl(a&c), Cannibalism. . . 325.00
28 Dec., 1954 . . . . 450.00

HAWK, THE
Approved Comics
(Ziff-Davis) ,
Winter, 1951
1 MA,The Law of the Colt,P(c) . 250.00
2 JKu,Iron Caravan of the
　Mojave, P(c) 125.00
3 Leverett's Last Stand,P(c) 110.00
4 Killer's Town,P(c) 100.00
5 . . . . 100.00
6 . . . . 100.00
7 . . . . 100.00
8 MB(c),Dry River Rampage . . . 135.00
9 MB(a&c),JKu 135.00
10 MB(c) 135.00
11 MB(c). 135.00
12 MB(a&c), May, 1955. . . . . 135.00

HEADLINE COMICS
American Boys Comics/
Headline Publ. (Prize Publ.),
Feb., 1943
1 B:Jr. Rangers. 650.00
2 JaB(a&c) 300.00
3 JaB(a&c) 250.00
4 . . . . 200.00
5 HcK 200.00
6 HcK 200.00
7 HcK,Jr. Rangers 200.00
8 HcK,Hitler (c) 700.00
9 HcK 200.00
10 HcK,Hitler story,Wizard(c). . . . 250.00
11 . . . . 175.00
12 HcK,Heroes of Yesterday 175.00
13 HcK,A:Blue Streak 175.00
14 HcK,A:Blue Streak 175.00
15 HcK,A:Blue Streak 175.00
16 HcK,O:Atomic Man 300.00
17 Atomic Man(c). 150.00
18 Atomic Man(c). 150.00

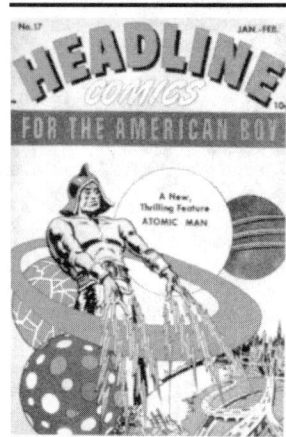

Headline Comics #17
© Prize Publications

19 S&K,Atomic Man(c)	350.00
20 Atomic Man(c)	150.00
21 E:Atomic Man	150.00
22 HcK	125.00
23 S&K(a&c),Valentines Day Massacre	325.00
24 S&K(a&c),You can't Forget a Killer	325.00
25 S&K(a&c),Crime Never Pays	325.00
26 S&K(a&c),Crime Never Pays	300.00
27 S&K(a&c),Crime Never Pays	300.00
28 S&K(a&c),Crime Never Pays	300.00
29 S&K(a&c),Crime Never Pays	300.00
30 S&K(a&c),Crime Never Pays	300.00
31 S&K(a&c),Crime Never Pays	300.00
32 S&K(a&c),Crime Never Pays	300.00
33 S&K(a&c),Police and FBI Heroes	300.00
34 S&K(a&c),same	300.00
35 S&K(a&c),same	300.00
36 S&K,same,Ph(c)	250.00
37 S&K,MvS,same,Ph(c)	275.00
38 S&K,same,Ph(c)	100.00
39 S&K,same,Ph(c)	100.00
40 S&K,Ph(c)Violent Crime	100.00
41 Ph(c),J.Edgar Hoover(c)	100.00
42 Ph(c)	75.00
43 Ph(c)	75.00
44 MMe,MvS,WE,S&K	150.00
45 JK	125.00
46	100.00
47	100.00
48	100.00
49 MMe	100.00
50	100.00
51 JK	90.00
52	100.00
53	100.00
54	100.00
55	100.00
56 S&K	150.00
57	50.00
58	50.00
59	50.00
60 MvS(c)	50.00
61 MMe,MvS(c)	50.00
62 MMe(a&c)	50.00
63 MMe(a&c)	50.00
64 MMe(a&c)	50.00
65 MMe(a&c)	50.00
66 MMe(a&c)	50.00
67 MMe(a&c)	50.00
68 MMe(a&c)	50.00
69 MMe(a&c)	50.00
70 MMe(a&c)	50.00
71 MMe(a&c)	50.00
72 MMe(a&c)	50.00
73 MMe(a&c)	50.00
74 MMe(a&c)	50.00
75 MMe(a&c)	50.00
76 MMe(a&c)	50.00
77 MMe(a&c),Oct., 1956	50.00

HEART THROBS

Comics Magazines (Quality), Aug., 1949

1 BWa(c),PG,Spoiled Brat	500.00
2 BWa(c),PG,Siren of the Tropics	300.00
3 PG	100.00
4 BWa(c),Greed Turned Me into a Scheming Vixen,Ph(c)	150.00
5 Ph(c)	75.00
6 BWa	150.00
7	75.00
8 BWa	150.00
9 I Hated Men,Ph(c)	125.00
10 BWa,My Secret Fears	135.00
11	70.00
12	70.00
13	70.00
14 BWa	70.00
15 My Right to Happiness,Ph(c)	125.00
16	60.00
17	60.00
18	60.00
19	60.00
20	60.00
21 BWa	100.00
22 BWa	90.00
23 BWa	90.00
24 thru 30	@60.00
31 thru 33	@60.00
34 thru 39	@60.00
40 BWa	90.00
41	60.00
42	50.00
43 thru 45	@60.00

(Please see DC listings)

HECKLE AND JECKLE

St. John Publ./Pines, Nov., 1951

1 Blue Ribbon Comics	300.00
2 Blue Ribbon Comics	125.00
3	100.00
4	75.00
5	75.00
6	75.00
7	70.00
8	65.00
9	65.00
10	65.00
11	60.00
12	60.00
13	60.00
14	60.00
15	60.00
16 thru 20	@50.00
21 thru 33	@45.00
34 June, 1959	45.00

HELLO PAL COMICS

Harvey Publications, Jan., 1943

1 B:Rocketman & Rocket Girl, Mickey Rooney (c), Ph(c) all	900.00
2 Charlie McCarthy (c)	750.00
3 Bob Hope (c), May, 1943	850.00

HENRY

Dell Publishing Co., Oct., 1946

1	150.00
2	75.00
3 thru 10	@60.00
11 thru 20	@50.00
21 thru 30	@40.00
31 thru 40	@35.00
41 thru 50	@25.00
51 thru 65	@20.00

HENRY ALDRICH COMICS

Dell Publishing Co., Aug.–Sept., 1950

1	125.00
2	75.00
3	60.00
4	60.00
5	60.00
6 thru 10	@50.00
11 thru 22	@40.00

HEROIC COMICS

Eastern Color Printing Co./ Famous Funnies Aug., 1940

1 BEv(a&c),O:Hydroman,Purple Zombie, B:Man of India	2,500.00
2 BEv(a&c),B:Hydroman (c)s.	1,000.00
3 BEv(a&c)	650.00
4 BEv(a&c)	650.00
5 BEv(a&c)	600.00
6 BEv(a&c)	550.00
7 BEv(a&c),O:Man O'Metal	600.00
8 BEv(a&c)	400.00
9 BEv	400.00
10 BEv	400.00
11 BEv,E:Hydroman (c)s	400.00
12 BEv,B&0:Music Master	425.00
13 BEv,RC,LF	400.00
14 BEv	425.00
15 BEv,I:Downbeat	425.00
16 BEv,CCB(c),A:Lieut Nininger, Major Heidger,Lieut Welch,B:P(c)	300.00
17 BEv,A:JohnJames Powers,Hewitt T.Wheless, Irving Strobing	300.00
18 HcK,BEv,Pass the Ammunition	300.00
19 HcK,BEv,A:Barney Ross	300.00
20 HcK,BEv	300.00
21 HcK,BEv	200.00

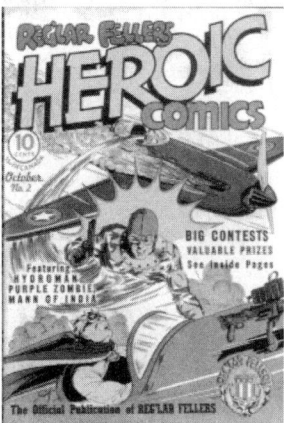

Heroic Comics #2
© Eastern Color Printing

All comics prices listed are for *Near Mint* condition.

GOLDEN AGE

22 HcK,BEv,Howard Gilmore. . . .	200.00
23 HcK,BEv	200.00
24 HcK,BEv	200.00
25 HcK,BEv	200.00
26 HcK,BEv	200.00
27 HcK,BEv	200.00
28 HcK,BEv,E:Man O'Metal.	200.00
29 HcK,BEv,E:Hydroman.	200.00
30 BEv	200.00
31 BEv,CCB,Capt. Tootsie	65.00
32 ATh,CCB,WWII(c),	
Capt. Tootsie	75.00
33 ATh, ...	85.00
34 WWII(c)	65.00
35 Ath,B:Rescue(c)	85.00
36 HcK,ATh	75.00
37 same	75.00
38 ATh	75.00
39 HcK,ATh	90.00
40 ATh,Boxing	90.00
41 Grl(c),ATh	90.00
42 ATh	90.00
43 ATh	65.00
44 HcK,ATh	65.00
45 HcK	65.00
46 HcK	65.00
47 HcK	65.00
48 HcK	75.00
49 HcK	65.00
50 HcK	65.00
51 HcK,ATh,AW	90.00
52 HcK,AW	75.00
53 HcK	75.00
54	75.00
55 ATh	75.00
56 ATh(c)	65.00
57 ATh(c)	65.00
58 ATh(c)	65.00
59 ATh(c)	65.00
60 ATh(c)	65.00
61 BEv(c)	60.00
62 BEv(c)	65.00
63 BEv(c)	65.00
64 GE,BEv(c)	65.00
65 HcK(c),FF,ATh,AW,GE	100.00
66 HcK(c),FF	70.00
67 HcK(c),FF,Korean War(c)	80.00
68 HcK(c),Korean War(c).	70.00
69 HcK(c),FF	100.00
70 HcK(c),FF,B:Korean War(c) . . .	70.00
71 HcK(c),FF	70.00
72 HcK(c),FF	100.00
73 HcK(c),FF	75.00
74 HcK(c).	60.00
75 HcK(c),FF	70.00
76 HcK,HcK(c).	50.00
77 same	50.00
78 same	50.00
79 same	50.00
80 same	50.00
81 FF,HcK(c)	60.00
82 FF,HcK(c)	60.00
83 FF,HcK(c)	60.00
84 HcK(c).	60.00
85 HcK(c).	60.00
86 FF,HcK(c)	75.00
87 FF,HcK(c)	75.00
88 HcK(c),E:Korean War (c)s	50.00
89 HcK(c).	50.00
90 HcK(c).	50.00
91 HcK(c).	50.00
92 HcK(c).	50.00
93 HcK(c).	50.00
94 HcK(c).	70.00
95 HcK(c).	50.00
96 HcK(c).	50.00
97 HcK(c),E:P(c),June, 1955	50.00

HICKORY
Comic Magazine
(Quality Comics Group),
Oct., 1949

1 ASa, ...	175.00
2 ASa, ...	100.00
3 ASa, ...	75.00
4 ASa, ...	75.00
5 ASa, ...	75.00
6 ASa,Aug., 1950	75.00

HI-HO COMICS
Four Star Publications, 1946

1 LbC(c)	450.00
2 LbC(c)	250.00
3 1946	220.00

HI-JINX
B & I Publ. Co. (American
Comics Group),
July–Aug., 1947

1 (fa) all.	250.00
2	175.00
3	100.00
4 thru 7	@75.00
N#	125.00

HI-LITE COMICS
E.R. Ross Publ. Fall, 1945

1	225.00

Hit Comics #38
© Quality Comics Group

HIT COMICS
Comics Magazine
(Quality Comics Group),
July, 1940

1 LF(c),O:Neon,Hercules,I:The	
Red Bee, B:Bob & Swab,	
Blaze Barton Strange	
Twins,X-5 Super Agent	
Casey Jones,Jack & Jill . . .	9,500.00
2 GT,LF(c),B:Old Witch	3,500.00
3 GT,LF(c),E:Casey Jones. . . .	3,200.00
4 GT,LF(c),B:Super Agent &	
Betty Bates,E:X-5	2,900.00
5 GT,LF(c),B:Red Bee (c)	8,000.00
6 GT,LF(c)	2,500.00
7 GT,LF(c),E:Red Bee (c)	2,500.00
8 GT,LF(c),B:Neon (c)	2,500.00
9 JCo,LF(c),E:Neon (c)	2,500.00
10 JCo,RC,LF(c),B:Hercules(c)	2,500.00

11 JCo,RC,LF(c),A:Hercules. . .	2,200.00
12 JCo,RC,LF(c),A:Hercules . .	2,200.00
13 JCo,RC,LF(c),A:Hercules . .	2,200.00
14 JCo,RC,LF(c),A:Hercules . .	2,200.00
15 JCo,RC,A:Hercules	1,500.00
16 JCo,RC,LF(c),A:Hercules . .	1,500.00
17 JCo,RC,LF(c),E:Hercules(c)	1,500.00
18 JCo,RC(a&c),O:Stormy	
Foster,B:Ghost of Flanders	1,600.00
19 JCo,RC(c),B:Stormy	
Foster(c)	1,300.00
20 JCo,RC(c),A:Stormy Foster .	1,400.00
21 JCo,RC(c)	1,350.00
22 JCo.	1,350.00
23 JCo,RC(a&c)	1,300.00
24 JCo,E:Stormy Foster (c) . . .	1,300.00
25 JCo,RP,O:Kid Eternity	2,500.00
26 JCo,RP,A:Black Hawk	1,400.00
27 JCo,RP,B:Kid Eternity (c)s . .	700.00
28 JCo,RP,A:Her Highness	700.00
29 JCo,RP	700.00
30 JCo,RP,HK,V:Julius Caesar	
and his Legion of Warriors . .	600.00
31 JCo,RP	600.00
32 JCo,RP,V:Merlin the Wizard .	350.00
33 JCo,RP	300.00
34 JCo,RP,E:Stormy Foster. . . .	300.00
35 JCo,Kid Eternity accused	
of Murder.	300.00
36 JCo,The Witch's Curse.	300.00
37 JCo,V:Mr. Silence	300.00
38 JCo	300.00
39 JCo,Runaway River Boat	300.00
40 PG,V:Monster from the Past .	300.00
41 PG,Did Kid Eternity Lose	
His Power?	250.00
42 PG,Kid Eternity Loses Killer	
Cronson.	250.00
43 JCo,PG,V:Modern Bluebeard .	250.00
44 JCo,PG,Trips up the Shoe . . .	250.00
45 JCo,PG,Pancho Villa against	
Don Pablo	250.00
46 JCo,V:Mr. Hardeel.	250.00
47 A Polished Diamond can be	
Rough on Rats	250.00
48 EhH,A Treasure Chest	
of Trouble	250.00
49 EhH,V:Monsters from	
the Mirror.	250.00
50 EhH,Heads for Trouble	250.00
51 EhH,Enters the Forgotten	
World	225.00
52 EhH,Heroes out of the Past . .	225.00
53 EhH,V:Mr. Puny	225.00
54 V:Ghost Town Killer.	225.00
55 V:The Brute.	225.00
56 V:Big Odds	225.00
57 Solves the Picture in	
a Frame	225.00
58 Destroys Oppression!	225.00
59 Battles Tomorrow's Crimes	
Today!	225.00
60 E:Kid Eternity (c)s,	
V:The Mummy	225.00
61 RC(a&c),I:Jeb Rivers	250.00
62 RC(c).	225.00
63 RC(c),A:Jeb Rivers	250.00
64 RC,A:Jeb Rivers	250.00
65 Bondage (c),RC,July, 1950. . .	275.00

HOLIDAY COMICS
Fawcett Publ., Nov., 1942

1 Captain Marvel (c)	2,100.00

HOLIDAY COMICS
Star Publ., Jan., 1951

1 LbC(c),(fa),Christmas (c).	400.00
2 LbC(c),Parade(c).	450.00
3 LbC(c),July 4th(c)	250.00

4 LbC(c),Vacation(c) 250.00
5 LbC(c),Christmas(c) 250.00
6 LbC(c),Birthday(c) 250.00
7 LbC(c) 225.00
8 LbC(c),Christmas(c) 250.00

HOLLYWOOD COMICS
New Age Publishers, Winter, 1944
1 (fa) 175.00

HOLLYWOOD CONFESSIONS
St. John Publ. Co., Oct., 1949
1 JKu(a&c) 350.00
2 JKu(a&c), Dec., 1949 . . . . 400.00

HOLLYWOOD DIARY
Comics Magazine (Quality Comics), Dec., 1949
1 . . . . 225.00
2 Photo (c) 150.00
3 Photo (c) 125.00
4 . . . . 125.00
5 Photo (c), Aug., 1950 . . . . 125.00

HOLLYWOOD FILM STORIES
Feature Publications, (Prize) April, 1950
1 June Allison,Ph(c) 250.00
2 Lizabeth Scott,Ph(c) 150.00
3 Barbara Stanwick,Ph(c) 150.00
4 Beth Hutton, Aug., 1950 . . . . . 150.00

HOLLYWOOD SECRETS
Comics Magazine (Quality Comics Group), Nov., 1949
1 BWa,BWa(c) 400.00
2 BWa,BWa(c),RC 250.00
3 Ph(c) 150.00
4 Ph(c),May, 1950 . . . . 150.00
5 Ph(c) 150.00
6 Ph(c) 150.00

HOLYOKE ONE-SHOT
Tem Publ. (Holyoke Publ. Co.), 1944
1 Grit Grady 175.00
2 Rusty Dugan 175.00
3 JK,Miss Victory,O:Cat Woman. 350.00
4 Mr. Miracle 150.00
5 U.S. Border Patrol 200.00
6 Capt. Fearless 150.00
7 Strong Man 200.00
8 Blue Streak 150.00
9 S&K, Citizen Smith 225.00
10 S&K, Capt. Stone 250.00

HONEYMOON ROMANCE
Artful Publications (Digest Size), April, 1950
1 . . . . 450.00
2 July, 1950 . . . . 425.00

HOODED HORSEMAN
See: OUT OF THE NIGHT

Hopalong Cassidy #40
© Fawcett Publications

HOPALONG CASSIDY
Fawcett Publications, Feb., 1943
1 B:Hopalong Cassidy & Topper,
  Captain Marvel (c) 7,000.00
2 . . . . 1,000.00
3 Blazing Trails 500.00
4 5-full length story 400.00
5 Death in the Saddle, Ph(c) . . . 350.00
6 . . . . 300.00
7 . . . . 300.00
8 Phantom Stage Coach 300.00
9 The Last Stockade 300.00
10 4-spine tingling adventures . . . 300.00
11 Desperate Jetters! Ph(c) 225.00
12 The Mysterious Message 225.00
13 The Human Target, Ph(c) 225.00
14 Land of the Lawless, Ph(c) . . . 225.00
15 Death holds the Reins, Ph(c) . 225.00
16 Webfoot's Revenge, Ph(c) . . . 225.00
17 The Hangman's Noose, Ph(c) 225.00
18 The Ghost of Dude Ranch,
   Ph(c) 225.00
19 A:William Boyd,Ph(c) 225.00
20 The Notorious Nellie Blaine!,
   B:P(c) 175.00
21 V:Arizona Kid 175.00
22 V:Arizona Kid 175.00
23 Hayride Horror 175.00
24 Twin River Giant 175.00
25 On the Trails of the Wild
   and Wooly West 175.00
26 thru 30 . . . . @150.00
31 52 pages 125.00
32 36 pages 125.00
33 52 pages 125.00
34 52 pages 125.00
35 52 pages 125.00
36 36 pages 100.00
37 thru 40, 52 pages . . . . @125.00
40 36 pages 125.00
41 E:P(c) 125.00
42 B:Ph(c) 125.00
43 . . . . 125.00
44 . . . . 100.00
45 . . . . 110.00
46 thru 51 . . . . @100.00
52 . . . . 90.00
53 . . . . 100.00
54 . . . . 100.00
55 . . . . 90.00
56 . . . . 100.00
57 thru 70 . . . . @100.00
71 thru 84 . . . . @75.00

85 E:Ph(c),Jan., 1954 . . . . 100.00
(See also: DC listings)

HOPPY THE MARVEL BUNNY
Fawcett Publications, Dec., 1945
1 A:Marvel Bunny 300.00
2 . . . . 150.00
3 . . . . 125.00
4 . . . . 125.00
5 . . . . 125.00
6 thru 14 . . . . @100.00
15 Sept., 1947 . . . . 100.00

HORRIFIC
Artful/Comic Media/ Harwell Publ./Mystery, Sept., 1952
1 Conductor in Flames(c) 650.00
2 Human Puppets(c) 350.00
3 DH(c),Bullet hole in
  head(c) 700.00
4 DH(c),head on a stick (c) 300.00
5 DH(c) 300.00
6 DH(c),Jack the Ripper 300.00
7 DH(c),Shrunken Skulls 300.00
8 DH(c),I:The Teller 350.00
9 DH(c),Claws of Horror, Wolves
  of Midnight 300.00
10 DH(c),The Teller-four
   eerie tales of Horror 300.00
11 DH(c),A:Gary Ghoul,Freddie,
   Demon,Victor Vampire
   Walter Werewolf 250.00
12 DH(c),A:Gary Ghoul,Freddie
   Demon,Victor Vampire,
   Walter Werewolf 250.00
13 DH(c),A:Gary Ghoul,Freddie
   Demom,Victor Vampire,
   Walter Werewolf 250.00
Becomes:

TERRIFIC COMICS
Dec., 1954
14 Eye Injury 700.00
15 . . . . 300.00
16 B:Wonderboy 300.00
Becomes:

WONDERBOY
Ajax/Farrell Publ., May, 1955
17 The Enemy's Enemy 600.00
18 Success is No Accident,
   July, 1955 . . . . 500.00

HORROR FROM THE TOMB
See: MYSTERIOUS STORIES

HORRORS, THE
Star Publications, Jan., 1953–April, 1954
11 LbC(c),JyD,of War 350.00
12 LbC(c),of War 350.00
13 LbC(c),of Mystery 300.00
14 LbC(c),of the Underworld 350.00
15 LbC(c),of the Underworld 350.00

HORSE FEATHER COMICS
Lev Gleason Publications, Nov., 1947
1 BW 225.00

GOLDEN AGE

2	100.00
3	75.00
4 Summer, 1948	75.00

HOT ROD AND SPEEDWAY COMICS
Hillman Periodicals Feb.–March, 1952

1	350.00
2 BK	250.00
3	125.00
4	125.00
5 April–May, 1953	125.00

HOT ROD COMICS
Fawcett Publications, Feb., 1952–53

N# BP,BP(c),F:Clint Curtis	400.00
2 BP,BP(c),Safety comes First	225.00
3 BP,BP(c),The Racing Game	150.00
4 BP,BP(c),Bonneville National Championships	150.00
5 BP,BP(c),	150.00
6 BP,BP(c),Race to Death	150.00

HOT ROD KING
Approved Comics (Ziff-Davis), Fall, 1952

1 P(c)	300.00

HOWDY DOODY
Dell Publishing Co., Jan., 1950

1 Ph(c)	1,600.00
2 Ph(c)	750.00
3 Ph(c)	350.00
4 Ph(c)	350.00
5 Ph(c)	350.00
6 P(c)	400.00
7	250.00
8	250.00
9	250.00
10	250.00
11	225.00
12	225.00
13 Christmas (c)	225.00
14 thru 20	@225.00
21 thru 38	@175.00

HOW STALIN HOPES WE WILL DESTROY AMERICA
Pictorial News, 1951

N# (Giveaway)	600.00

HUMBUG
Harvey Kurtzman, 1957

1 JDa,WW,WE,End of the World	350.00
2 JDa,WE,Radiator	150.00
3 JDa,WE	125.00
4 JDa,WE,Queen Victoria(c)	125.00
5 JDa,WE	125.00
6 JDa,WE	125.00
7 JDa,WE,Sputnik(c)	135.00
8 JDa,WE,Elvis/George Washington(c)	125.00
9 JDa,WE	125.00
10 JDa,Magazine	175.00
11 JDw,WE,HK,Magazine	150.00

HUMDINGER
Novelty Press/Premium Service, May–June, 1946

1 B:Jerkwater Line,Dink, Mickey Starlight	400.00
2	175.00
3	135.00
4	135.00
5	135.00
6	135.00
2-1	125.00
2-2 July–Aug., 1947	125.00

HUMPHREY COMICS
Harvey Publications, Oct., 1948

1 BP,Joe Palooka	150.00
2 BP	90.00
3 BP	75.00
4 BP,A:Boy Heroes	90.00
5 BP	60.00
6 BP	60.00
7 BP,A:Little Dot	60.00
8 BP,O:Humphrey	65.00
9 BP	50.00
10 BP	50.00
11 thru 21	@50.00
22 April, 1952	50.00

Hyper Mystery Comics #1
© Hyper Publications

HYPER MYSTERY COMICS
Hyper Publications, May, 1940

1 B:Hyper	2,700.00
2 June, 1940	1,500.00

IBIS, THE INVINCIBLE
Fawcett Publications, Jan., 1942–Spring, 1948

1 MRa(c),O:Ibis	2,700.00
2 Bondage (c)	1,400.00
3 BW	1,000.00
4 BW,A:Mystic Snake People	650.00
5 BW,Bondage (c),The Devil's Ibistick	700.00
6 BW, The Book of Evil.	700.00

IDEAL ROMANCE
See: TENDER ROMANCE

IF THE DEVIL WOULD TALK
Catechetical Guild, 1950

N# Rare	800.00
N#, 1958 Very Rare	600.00

ILLUSTRATED STORIES OF THE OPERA
B. Bailey Publ. Co., 1943

N# Faust	800.00
N# Aida	750.00
N# Carman	750.00
N# Rigoletto	750.00

I LOVED
See: ZOOT COMICS

I LOVE LUCY COMICS
Dell Publishing Co., 1954

(1) *see Dell Four Color #535*	
(2) *see Dell Four Color #559*	
3 Lucile Ball Ph(c) all	325.00
4	300.00
5	300.00
6 thru 10	@250.00
11 thru 20	@175.00
21 thru 35	@150.00

IMPACT
E.C. Comics, March–April, 1955

1 RC,GE,BK,Grl	250.00
2 RC,JDu,Grl,BK,JO	150.00
3 JO,RC,JDU,Grl,JKa,BK	125.00
4 RC,JO,JDa,GE,Grl,BK	125.00
5 Nov.–Dec., 1955	125.00

INCREDIBLE SCIENCE FANTASY
See: WEIRD SCIENCE

INCREDIBLE SCIENCE FICTION
E.C. Comics, July–Aug., 1955

30 JDa,BK,JO,WW	600.00
31 AW,WW,BK	550.00
32 AW,JDa,BK,JO	550.00
33 JDa,BK,JO,WW	550.00

INDIAN CHIEF
Dell Publishing Co., July–Sept., 1951

3 P(c) all	60.00
4	50.00
5	50.00
6 A:White Eagle	50.00
7	50.00
8	50.00
9	50.00
10	50.00
11	50.00
12 I:White Eagle	55.00
13 thru 29	@40.00
30 SB	45.00
31 thru 33 SB	@45.00

INDIAN FIGHTER
Youthful Magazines, May, 1950

1 Revenge of Chief Crazy Horse	150.00
2 Bondage (c)	100.00

3 . . . . 60.00
4 Cheyenne Warpath 60.00
5 . . . . 60.00
6 Davy Crockett in Death Stalks
   the Alamo 60.00
7 Tom Horn-Bloodshed at
   Massacre Valley 60.00
8 Tales of Wild Bill Hickory,
   Jan., 1952 . . . . 60.00

INDIANS
Wings Publ. Co.
(Fiction House), Spring, 1950
1 B:Long Bow, Manzar, White
   Indian & Orphan 350.00
2 B:Starlight 175.00
3 Longbow(c) 150.00
4 Longbow(c) 125.00
5 Manzar(c). 150.00
6 Captive of the Semecas 125.00
7 Longbow(c) 125.00
8 A:Long Bow 125.00
9 A:Long Bow 125.00
10 Manzar(c) 125.00
11 thru 16 . . . . @100.00
17 Spring, 1953,Longbow(c) 100.00

INDIANS ON
THE WARPATH
St. John Publ. Co., 1950
N# MB(c). 400.00

INFORMER, THE
Feature Television
Productions, April, 1954
1 MSy,The Greatest Social
   Menace of our Time! 150.00
2 MSy 100.00
3 MSy 75.00
4 MSy 75.00
5 Dec., 1954 . . . . 75.00

IN LOVE
Mainline, Aug., 1954
1 S&K,Bride of the Star 450.00
2 S&K,Marilyn's Men 250.00
3 S&K 250.00
4 S&K,Comics Code. 275.00
5 S&K(c) 125.00
6 . . . . 75.00
Becomes:

I LOVE YOU
Charlton Comics, Sept., 1955
7 JK(c),BP 125.00
8 . . . . 60.00
9 . . . . 60.00
10 . . . . 60.00
11 thru 16 . . . . @50.00
17 Giant 100.00
18 . . . . 50.00
19 . . . . 50.00
20 . . . . 50.00
21 thru 50. . . . . @35.00
51 thru 59. . . . . @25.00
60 Elvis 225.00
61 thru 100. . . . . @20.00
101 thru 130. . . . . @8.00

INTERNATIONAL COMICS
See: CRIME PATROL

INTERNATIONAL
CRIME PATROL
See: CRIME PATROL

INTIMATE
CONFESSIONS
Fawcett Publ./
Realistic Comics, 1951
1a P(c) all, Unmarried Bride . . 1,000.00
1 EK,EK(c),Days of Temptation...
   Nights of Desire 250.00
2 Doomed to Silence 250.00
3 EK(c), The Only Man For Me . 175.00
3a Robert Briffault 275.00
4 EK(c),Tormented Love 250.00
5 Her Secret Sin 250.00
6 Reckless Pick-up 250.00
7 A Love Like Ours,Spanking . . . 275.00
8 Fatal Woman, March, 1953 . . . 250.00

INTIMATE LOVE
Standard Magazines,
Jan., 1950
5 Wings on My Heart,Ph(c) 100.00
6 WE,JSe,Ph(c) 125.00
7 WE,JSe,Ph(c),I Toyed
   with Love 125.00
8 WE,JSe,Ph(c) 125.00
9 Ph(c) 50.00
10 Ph(c),My Hopeless Heart 50.00
11 . . . . 50.00
12 . . . . 50.00
13 thru 18. . . . . @50.00
19 ATh 75.00
20 . . . . 50.00
21 ATh 75.00
22 ATh 75.00
23 ATh 50.00
24 ATh 75.00
25 ATh 50.00
26 ATh 75.00
27 ATh 50.00
28 ATh,Aug., 1954 . . . . 50.00

INTIMATE SECRETS
OF ROMANCE
Star Publications,
Sept., 1953
1 LbC(c) 250.00
2 LbC(c) 225.00

INVISIBLE
SCARLET O'NEIL
Harvey Publications,
Dec., 1950
1 . . . . 175.00
2 . . . . 125.00
3 April, 1951 . . . . 125.00

IRON VIC
United Features Syndicate/
St. John Publ. Co., 1940
1-shot 400.00

IT REALLY HAPPENED
William H. Wise/
Visual Editions, 1945
1 Benjamin Franklin, Kit Carson 250.00
2 The Terrible Tiddlers 125.00
3 Maid of the Margiris 100.00
4 Chaplain Albert J. Hoffman . . . 100.00
5 AS(c),Monarchs of the Sea,Lou
   Gehrig, Amelia Earhart 200.00
6 AS(c),Ernie Pyle 100.00
7 FG,Teddy Roosevelt,Jefferson
   Davis,Story of the Helicopter. 100.00
8 FG,Man O' War,Roy Rogers . . 200.00

Iron Vic #1
© St. John Publ. Co.

9 AS(c),The Story of
   Old Ironsides 100.00
10 AS(c),Honus Wagner, The
   Story of Mark Twain. 150.00
11 AS(c),MB,Queen of the Spanish
   Main, Oct., 1947 . . . . 125.00

JACE PEARSON OF
THE TEXAS RANGERS
Dell Publishing Co.,
May, 1952
(1) *see Dell Four Color #396*
2 Ph(c),Joel McRae 100.00
3 Ph(c),Joel McRae 100.00
4 Ph(c),Joel McRae 100.00
5 Ph(c),Joel McRae 100.00
6 Ph(c),Joel McRae 100.00
7 Ph(c),Joel McRae 100.00
8 Ph(c),Joel McRae 100.00
9 Ph(c),Joel McRae 100.00
(10) *see Dell Four Color #648*
Becomes:

TALES OF JACE
PEARSON OF
THE TEXAS RANGERS
Feb., 1955
11 . . . . 75.00
12 . . . . 75.00
13 . . . . 75.00
14 . . . . 75.00
15 ATh 90.00
16 ATh 90.00
17 thru 20. . . . . @60.00

JACK ARMSTRONG
Parents' Institute,
Nov., 1947
1 Artic Mystery 600.00
2 Den of the Golden Dragon . . . 225.00
3 Lost Valley of Ice 175.00
4 Land of the Leopard Men 175.00
5 Fight against Racketeers of
   the Ring 175.00
6 . . . . 150.00
7 Baffling Mystery on the
   Diamond 150.00
8 . . . . 150.00
9 Mystery of the Midgets 150.00
10 Secret Cargo. 150.00

11 . . . . 150.00
12 Madman's Island, rare 175.00
13 Sept., 1949 . . . . 150.00

JACKIE GLEASON
St. John Publishing Co., Sept., 1955
1 Ph(c) 900.00
2 . . . . 550.00
3 . . . . 500.00
4 Dec., 1955 . . . . 500.00

JACKIE ROBINSON
Fawcett Publications, May, 1950
N# Ph(c) all issues. 1,350.00
2 . . . . 750.00
3 thru 5 . . . . @650.00
6 May, 1952 . . . . 600.00

JACK IN THE BOX
See: YELLOW JACKET
COMICS

JACKPOT COMICS
MLJ Magazines, Spring, 1941
1 CBi(c),B:Black Hood,Mr.Justice,
   Steel Sterling,Sgt.Boyle . . . 4,500.00
2 SCp(c), ... 2,000.00
3 Bondage (c) 1,500.00
4 First Archie 5,500.00
5 Hitler(c) 2,000.00
6 Son of the Skull v:Black
   Hood, Bondage(c) 1,400.00
7 Bondage (c) 1,400.00
8 Sal(c), ... 1,400.00
9 Sal(c), ... 1,400.00
Becomes:

JOLLY JINGLES
Summer, 1943
10 Super Duck,(fa). 450.00
11 Super Duck 225.00
12 Hitler parody (c),A:Woody
   Woodpecker 250.00
13 thru 15 Super Duck. . . . . . . @150.00
16 Dec., 1944 . . . . 150.00

JACK THE GIANT KILLER
Bimfort & Co., Aug.–Sept., 1953
1 HcK,HcK(c) 250.00

JAMBOREE
Round Publishing Co., Feb., 1946
1 . . . . 300.00
2 March, 1946 . . . . 175.00

JANE ARDEN
St. John Publ. Co., March, 1948
1 . . . . 200.00
2 June, 1948 . . . . 150.00

JEEP COMICS
R.B. Leffingwell & Co., Winter, 1944
1 B;Captain Power 700.00
2 . . . . 400.00
3 LbC(c),March–April, 1948 . . . . 600.00

JEFF JORDAN, U.S. AGENT
D.S. Publ. Co., Dec., 1947
1 . . . . 175.00

JESSE JAMES
Avon Periodicals/ Realistic Publ., Aug., 1950
1 JKu,The San Antonio Stage
   Robbery 200.00
2 JKu,The Daring Liberty Bank
   Robbery 150.00
3 JKu,The California Stagecoach
   Robberies 150.00
4 EK(c),Deadliest Deed! 75.00
5 JKu,WW,Great Prison Break . 150.00
6 JKu,Wanted Dead or Alive . . 150.00
7 JKu,Six-Gun Slaughter at
   San Romano! 125.00
8 EK,Daring Train Robbery! 100.00
9 EK 75.00
10 thru 14 {Do not exist}
15 EK 100.00
16 EK, Butch Cassidy 60.00
17 EK, Jessie James. 50.00
18 JKu 50.00
19 JKu 50.00
20 AW,FF,A:Chief Vic,Kit West . 150.00
21 EK, Two Jessie James 50.00
22 EK,Chuck Wagon 50.00
23 EK 50.00
24 EK,B:New McCarty 50.00
25 EK 50.00
26 EK 50.00
27 EK,E:New McCarty 50.00
28 Quantrells Raiders 50.00
29 Aug., 1956. . . . . 50.00

JEST
Harry 'A' Chesler, 1944
10 J. Rebel,Yankee Boy 200.00
11 1944,Little Nemo. 225.00

JET ACES
Real Adventure Publ. Co. (Fiction House), 1952
1 Set 'em up in MIG Alley 175.00
2 Kiss-Off for Moscow Molly . . . 100.00
3 Red Task Force Sighted 100.00
4 Death-Date at 40,000, 1953 . . 100.00

JET FIGHTERS
Standard Magazines, Nov., 1953
5 ATh,Korean War Stories 125.00
6 Circus Pilot 60.00
7 ATh, Iron Curtains for Ivan,
   March, 1953 . . . . 125.00

JETTA OF THE 21st CENTURY
Standard Comics, Dec., 1952
5 Teen Stories. 250.00
6 Robot (c) 150.00
7 April, 1953 . . . . 150.00

JIGGS AND MAGGIE
Best Books (Standard)/ Harvey Publ., June, 1949
11 . . . . 125.00
12 thru 21 . . . . @75.00
22 thru 25. . . . . @60.00

26 Part 3-D 150.00
27 Feb.–March, 1954. . . . . 60.00

JIM HARDY
Spotlight Publ., 1944
N# Dynamite Jim,Mirror Man . . . 500.00

JIM RAY'S AVIATION SKETCH BOOK
Vital Publishers, Feb., 1946
1 Radar, the Invisible eye 450.00
2 Gen.Hap Arnold, May, 1946 . . 300.00

Jingle Jangle Comics #6
© Eastern Color Printing

JINGLE JANGLE COMICS
Eastern Color Printing Co., Feb., 1942
1 B:Benny Bear,Pie Face Prince,
   Jingle Jangle Tales,Hortense 600.00
2 GCn 275.00
3 GCn 250.00
4 GCn,Pie Face (c). 250.00
5 GCn,B:Pie Face. 250.00
6 GCn, ... 175.00
7 . . . . 175.00
8 . . . . 175.00
9 . . . . 175.00
10 . . . . 175.00
11 thru 15 E:Pie Face . . . . @150.00
16 thru 20. . . . . @125.00
21 thru 25 . . . . @100.00
26 thru 30. . . . . @100.00
31 thru 41. . . . . @90.00
42 Dec., 1949 . . . . 90.00

JING PALS
Victory Publ. Corp., Feb., 1946
1 Johnny Rabbit 150.00
2 . . . . 75.00
3 . . . . 75.00
4 Aug., 1948 . . . . 75.00

JOE COLLEGE
Hillman Periodicals, Fall, 1949
1 BP,DPr. 125.00
2 BP, Winter, 1949 . . . . 100.00

JOE LOUIS
Fawcett Periodicals, Sept., 1950
1 Ph(c),Life Story 750.00
2 Ph(c),Nov., 1950 . . . . 500.00

JOE PALOOKA
Publication Enterprises (Columbia Comics Group) 1943
1 Lost in the Desert 1,200.00
2 Hitler (c) 750.00
3 KO's the Nazis! 450.00
4 Eiffel tower (c), 1944 . . . . . . 375.00

JOE PALOOKA
Harvey Publications, Nov., 1954–March, 1961
1 Joe Tells How he became
  World Champ 600.00
2 Skiing (c) 300.00
3 . . . . 175.00
4 Welcome Home Pals! 175.00
5 S&K,The Great Carnival
  Murder Mystery 250.00
6 Classic Joe Palooka (c) 175.00
7 BP,V:Grumpopski 175.00
8 BP,Mystery of the Ghost Ship . 150.00
9 Drooten Island Mystery 150.00
10 BP 150.00
11 . . . . 100.00
12 BP,Boxing Course 100.00
13 . . . . 110.00
14 BP,Palooka's Toughest Fight. . 110.00
15 BP,O:Humphrey 175.00
16 BP,A:Humphrey. 110.00
17 BP,I:Little Max,A:Humphrey . . 175.00
18 A:Little Max 110.00
19 BP,Freedom Train(c) 125.00
20 Punch Out(c) 110.00
21 . . . . 100.00
22 V:Assassin 100.00
23 Big Bathing Beauty Issue 100.00
24 . . . . 100.00
25 . . . . 100.00
26 BP,Big Prize Fight Robberies . 100.00
27 BP,Mystery of Bal
  Eagle Cabin,A:Little Max. . . . 100.00
28 BP,Fights out West, Babe
  Ruth. 100.00
29 BP,Joe Busts Crime
  Wide Open 100.00
30 BP,V:Hoodlums, Nude
  Painting 125.00
31 BP, Dizzy Dean 125.00
32 BP,Fight Palooka was sure
  to Lose. 70.00
33 BP,Joe finds Ann. 70.00
34 BP,How to Box like a Champ . . 70.00
35 BP,More Adventures of Little
  Max, Joe Louis 125.00
36 BP 70.00
37 BP,Joe as a Boy 70.00
38 BP 70.00
39 BP,Original Hillbillies with
  Big Leviticus 70.00
40 BP,Joe's Toughest Fight 70.00
41 BP,Humphrey's Grudge Fight . . 70.00
42 BP. 70.00
43 BP 70.00
44 BP,M:Ann Howe, Markies 75.00
45 BP 65.00
46 Champ of Champs 65.00
47 BreathtakingUnderwaterBattle . 65.00
48 BP,Exciting Indian Adventure . . 65.00
49 BP 65.00
50 BP,Bondage(c) 65.00
51 BP, Babe Ruth 65.00
52 BP,V:Balonki 65.00
53 BP. 65.00

54 V:Bad Man Trigger McGehee . . 65.00
55 . . . . 65.00
56 Foul Play on the High Seas . . . 65.00
57 Curtains for the Champ 65.00
58 V:The Man-Eating Swamp
  Terror. 65.00
59 The Enemy Attacks. 65.00
60 Joe Fights Escaped Convict . . 65.00
61 . . . . 60.00
62 S&K, Boy Explorers 90.00
63 . . . . 60.00
64 . . . . 60.00
65 . . . . 60.00
66 Drug 75.00
67 Drug 90.00
68. . . . . 60.00
69 Torture. 90.00
70 BP, Vs. "Gooks" 60.00
71 Bloody Bayonets 60.00
72 Tank 60.00
73 BP 60.00
74 thru 115 . . . . @60.00
116 thru 117 giants . . . . @100.00
118 Giant, Jack Dempsey . . . . @100.00
Giant 1 Body Building 100.00
Giant 2 Fights His Way Back. . . . 150.00
Giant 3 Visits Lost City. 80.00
Giant 4 All in Family. 100.00

JOE YANK
Visual Editions (Standard Comics), March, 1952
5 ATh,WE,Korean Jackpot! 100.00
6 Bacon and Bullets,
  G.I.Renegade 100.00
7 Two-Man War,A:Sgt. Glamour . 50.00
8 ATh(c),Miss Foxhole of 1952, . . 75.00
9 G.I.'s and Dolls,Colonel Blood . 50.00
10 A Good Way to Die,
  A:General Joe 50.00
11 . . . . 50.00
12 RA. 50.00
13 . . . . 50.00
14 . . . . 50.00
15 . . . . 50.00
16 July, 1954 . . . . 50.00

JOHN HIX SCRAPBOOK
Eastern Color Printing Co., 1937
1 Strange as It Seems 450.00
2 Strange as It Seems 350.00

JOHNNY DANGER
Toby Press, Aug., 1954
1 Ph(c),Private Detective 200.00

JOHNNY DYNAMITE
See: DYNAMITE

JOHNNY HAZARD
Best Books (Standard Comics), Aug., 1948
5 FR 225.00
6 FR,FR(c) 200.00
7 FR(c) 125.00
8 FR,FR(c), May, 1949 . . . . 125.00

JOHNNY LAW, SKY RANGER
Good Comics (Lev Gleason), April, 1955
1 . . . . 125.00

2 . . . . 75.00
3 . . . . 75.00
4 Nov., 1955 . . . . 75.00

JOHN WAYNE ADVENTURE COMICS
Toby Press, Winter, 1949
1 Ph(c),The Mysterious Valley
  of Violence 2,200.00
2 AW,FF,Ph(c) 1,000.00
3 AW,FF,Flying Sheriff 1,000.00
4 AW,FF,Double-Danger,Ph(c) 1,000.00
5 Volcano of Death,Ph(c) 650.00
6 AW,FF,Caravan of Doom,
  Ph(c) 800.00
7 AW,FF,Ph(c) 700.00
8 AW,FF,Duel of Death,Ph(c) . . 900.00
9 Ghost Guns,Ph(c) 500.00
10 Dangerous Journey,Ph(c) 450.00
11 Manhunt!,Ph(c) 450.00
12 HK,Joins the Marines,Ph(c) . . 450.00
13 V:Frank Stacy 400.00
14 Operation Peeping John. 400.00
15 Bridge Head 400.00
16 AW,FF,Golden Double-Cross . 400.00
17 Murderer's Music 400.00
18 AW,FF,Larson's Folly 475.00
19 . . . . 350.00
20 Whale (c) 350.00
21 . . . . 350.00
22 Flash Flood! 350.00
23 Death on Two Wheels 350.00
24 Desert 350.00
25 AW,FF,Hondo!,Ph(c) 475.00
26 Ph(c) 400.00
27 Ph(c) 400.00
28 Dead Man's Boots! 400.00
29 AW,FF,Ph(c),Crash in
  California Desert 450.00
30 The Wild One, Ph(c) 400.00
31 AW,FF,May, 1955 . . . . 450.00

JO-JO COMICS
Fox Features Syndicate, Spring, 1946
N# (fa) JoJo 200.00
2 (fa) Electro 100.00
3 (fa) 100.00
4 (fa) 100.00
5 (fa) 100.00
6 (fa) 100.00
7 B:Jo-Jo Congo King 1,200.00

Jo-Jo #5
© Fox Features Syndicate

GOLDEN AGE

8 (7)B:Tanee,V:The
  Giant Queen 900.00
9 (8)The Mountain of Skulls 750.00
10 (9)Death of the Fanged Lady . 750.00
11 (10) 750.00
12 (11)Bondage(c),
  Water Warriors. 625.00
13 (12) Jade Juggernaut 600.00
14 The Leopards of Learda 600.00
15 The Flaming Fiend 600.00
16 Golden Gorilla,bondage(c) . . . 600.00
17 Stark-Mad Thespian,
  bondage(c) 675.00
18 The Death Traveler. 600.00
19 Gladiator of Gore 600.00
20 . . . . 600.00
21 . . . . 600.00
22 . . . . 600.00
23 . . . . 600.00
24 . . . . 600.00
25 Bondage(c) 675.00
26 . . . . 600.00
27 . . . . 600.00
28 . . . . 600.00
29 July, 1949 . . . . 650.00

JOURNEY INTO FEAR
**Superior Publications,
May, 1951–Sept., 1954**

1 MB,Preview of Chaos. 1,000.00
2 Debt to the Devil 600.00
3 Midnight Prowler 500.00
4 Invisible Terror 500.00
5 Devil Cat 350.00
6 Partners in Blood 350.00
7 The Werewolf Lurks 350.00
8 Bells of the Damned 350.00
9 Masked Death 350.00
10 Gallery of the Dead. 350.00
11 Beast of Bedlam 300.00
12 No Rest for the Dead 300.00
13 Cult of the Dead 300.00
14 Jury of the Undead 300.00
15 Corpse in Make-up 350.00
16 Death by Invitation 300.00
17 Deadline for Death 300.00
18 Here's to Horror 300.00
19 This Body is Mine! 300.00
20 Masters of the Dead. 300.00
21 Horror in the Clock 300.00

JUDO JOE
**Jay-Jay Corp.,
Aug., 1952**

1 Drug. 125.00
2 . . . . 75.00
3 Drug, Dec., 1953 . . . . 85.00

JUDY CANOVA
**Fox Features Syndicate,
May, 1950–Sept., 1950**

23 (1)WW(a&c) 275.00
24 (2)WW(a&c) 250.00
3 JO,WW(a&c) 275.00

JUKE BOX
**Famous Funnies,
March, 1948**

1 ATh(c),Spike Jones 500.00
2 Dinah Shore,Transvestitism. . . 300.00
3 Vic Damone, Peggie Lee. 250.00
4 Jimmy Durante. 250.00
5 . . . . 250.00
6 Jan., 1949,Desi Arnaz 300.00

Jumbo Comics #10
© Fiction House

JUMBO COMICS
**Real Adventure Publ. Co.
(Fiction House),
Sept., 1938**

1 LF,BKa,JK,WE(a&c),B:Sheena
  Queen of the Jungle,The Hawk
  The Hunchback 30,000.00
2 LF,JK,WE,BKa,BP,
  O:Sheena 10,000.00
3 JK,WE(a&c),BP,LF,BKa 6,000.00
4 WE(a&c),MMe,LF,BKa,
  O:The Hawk 5,800.00
5 WE(a&c),BP,BKa 5,000.00
6 WE(a&c),BP,BKa 4,500.00
7 WE,BKa,BP 4,400.00
8 LF(c),BP,BKa,World of
  Tommorow 4,400.00
9 LF(c),BP 3,500.00
10 WE,LF(c),BKa,Regular size
  issues begin 2,500.00
11 LF(c),WE&BP,War of the
  Emerald Gas 2,000.00
12 WE(c),WE&BP,Hawk in Buccaneer
  Vengeance,Bondage(c) . . . 2,100.00
13 WE(c),BP,Sheena in The
  Thundering Herds. 2,000.00
14 WE(c),LF,BP,Hawk in Siege
  of Thunder Isle,B:Lightning 2,100.00
15 BP(a&c),Sheena(c) 1,100.00
16 BP(a&c),The Lightning
  Strikes Twice 1,500.00
17 BP(c), B:Sheena covers
  and lead stories 1,100.00
18 BP 1,100.00
19 BP(c),BKa,Warriors of
  the Bush 1,100.00
20 BP,BKa,Spoilers of the Wild. 1,100.00
21 BP,BKa,Prey of the
  Giant Killers. 800.00
22 BP,BKa,Victims of the
  Super-Ape,O:Hawk 900.00
23 BP,BKa,Swamp of the
  Green Terror 900.00
24 BP,BKa,Curse of the Black
  Venom 900.00
25 BP,BKa,Bait for the Beast. . . 800.00
26 BP,BKa,Tiger-Man Terror . . . 800.00
27 BP,BKa,Sabre-Tooth Terror. . 800.00
28 BKa,RWd,The Devil of
  the Congo 800.00
29 BKa,RWd,Elephant-Scourge . 800.00
30 BKa,RWd,Slashing Fangs . . . 800.00
31 BKa,RWd,Voodoo Treasure
  of Black Slave Lake. 750.00

32 BKa,RWd,AB,Captives of
  the Gorilla-Men 750.00
33 BKa,RWd,AB,Stampede
  Tusks. 750.00
34 BKa,RWd,AB,Claws of the
  Devil-Cat 750.00
35 BKa,RWd,AB,Hostage of the
  Devil Apes 750.00
36 BKa,RWd,AB,Voodoo Flames 750.00
37 BKa,RWd,AB,Congo Terror . . 750.00
38 BKa,RWd,ABDeath-Trap of
  the River Demons 750.00
39 BKa,RWd,AB,Cannibal Bait . . 750.00
40 BKa,RWd,AB,
  Assagai Poison 750.00
41 BKa,RWd,AB,Killer's Kraal,
  Bondage(c) 600.00
42 BKa,RWd,AB,Plague of
  Spotted Killers 600.00
43 BKa,RWd,AB,Beasts of the
  Devil Queen. 600.00
44 BKa,RWd,AB,Blood-Cult of
  K'Douma 600.00
45 BKa,RWd,AB,Fanged
  Keeper of the Fire-Gem 600.00
46 BKa,RWd,AB,Lair of the
  Armored Monsters. 600.00
47 BKa,RWd,AB,The Bantu
  Blood-Monster 600.00
48 BKa,RWd,AB,Red Meat for
  the Cat-Pack 600.00
49 BKa,RWd,AB,Empire of the
  Hairy Ones 600.00
50 BKa,RWd,AB,Eyrie of the
  Leopard Birds 600.00
51 BKa,RWd,AB,Monsters with
  Wings. 500.00
52 BKa,RWd,AB,Man-Eaters
  Paradise 500.00
53 RWd,AB,Slaves of the
  Blood Moon 500.00
54 RWd,AB,Congo Kill. 500.00
55 RWd,AB,Bait for the Silver
  King Cat. 500.00
56 RWd,AB,Sabre Monsters of
  the Aba-Zanzi,Bondage(c). . . 500.00
57 RWd,AB,Arena of Beasts . . . 500.00
58 RWd,AB,Sky-Atlas of the
  Thunder-Birds 500.00
59 RWd,AB,Kraal of Shrunken
  Heads 500.00
60 RWd,AB,Land of the
  Stalking Death 400.00
61 RWd,AB,King-Beast of
  the Masai. 400.00
62 RWd,AB,Valley of Golden
  Death 400.00
63 RWd,AB,The Dwarf Makers . 400.00
64 RWd,The Slave-Brand of Ibn
  Ben Satan,Male Bondage . . . 400.00
65 RWd,The Man-Eaters of
  Linpopo 400.00
66 RWd,Valley of Monsters 400.00
67 RWd,Land of Feathered Evil . 400.00
68 RWd,Spear of Blood Ju-Ju . . . 400.00
69 RWd,AB,MB,Slaves for the
  White Sheik 400.00
70 RWd,AB,MB,The Rogue
  Beast's Prey 400.00
71 RWd,AB,MB,The Serpent-
  God Speaks. 300.00
72 RWd,AB,MB,Curse of the
  Half-Dead 300.00
73 RWd,AB,MB,War Apes of
  the T'Kanis. 300.00
74 RWd,AB,MB,Drums of the
  Voodoo God 300.00
75 RWd,AB,MB,Terror Trail of
  the Devil's Horn. 300.00
76 RWd,AB,MB,Fire Gems of
  Skull Valley 300.00

Jumbo Comics #57
© Fiction House

77 RWd,AB,MB,Blood Dragons
   from Fire Valley 300.00
78 RWd,AB,MB,Veldt of the
   Vampire Apes 300.00
79 RWd,AB,MB,Dancing
   Skeletons 300.00
80 RWd,AB,MB,Banshee Cats . . 300.00
81 RWd,MB,AB,JKa,Heads for
   King' Hondo's Harem 250.00
82 RWd,MB,AB,JKa,Ghost Riders
   of the Golden Tuskers 250.00
83 RWd,MB,AB,JKa,Charge of
   the Condo Juggernauts 250.00
84 RWd,MB,AB,JKa,Valley of
   the Whispering Fangs 250.00
85 RWd,MB,AB,JKa,Red Tusks
   of Zulu-Za'an 250.00
86 RWd,MB,AB,JKa,Witch-Maiden
   of the Burning Blade 250.00
87 RWd,AB,MB,JKa,Sargasso of
   Lost Safaris 250.00
88 RWd,AB,MB,JKa,Kill-Quest
   of the Ju-Ju Tusks 250.00
89 RWd,AB,MB,JKa,Ghost Slaves
   of Bwana Rojo 250.00
90 RWd,AB,MB,JKa,Death Kraal
   of the Mastadons 250.00
91 RWd,AB,MB,JKa,Spoor of
   the Sabre-Horn Tiger 225.00
92 RWd,MB,JKa,Pied Piper
   of the Congo 225.00
93 RWd,MB,JKa,The Beasts
   that Dawn Begot 225.00
94 RWd,MB,JKa,Wheel of a
   Thousand Deaths 275.00
95 RWd,MB,JKa,Flame Dance
   of the Ju-Ju Witch 225.00
96 RWd,MB,JKa,Ghost Safari . . . 225.00
97 RWd,MB,JKa,Banshee Wail
   of the Undead,Bondage(c) . . 235.00
98 RWd,MB,JKa,Seekers of
   the Terror Fangs 235.00
99 RWd,MB,JKa,Shrine of
   the Seven Souls 235.00
100 RWd,MB,Slave Brand
   of Hassan Bey 275.00
101 RWd,MB,Quest of the
   Two-Face Ju Ju 235.00
102 RWd,MB,Viper Gods of
   Vengeance Veldt 235.00
103 RWd,MB,Blood for the
   Idol of Blades 235.00
104 RWd,MB,Valley of Eternal
   Sleep 235.00

105 RWd,MB,Man Cubs from
   Momba-Zu 300.00
106 RWd,MB,The River of
   No-Return 300.00
107 RWd,MB,Vandals of
   the Veldt 235.00
108 RWd,MB,The Orphan of
   Vengeance Vale 235.00
109 RWd,MB,The Pygmy's Hiss
   is Poison 235.00
110 RWd,MB,Death Guards the
   Congo Keep 235.00
111 RWd,MB,Beware of the
   Witch-Man's Brew 235.00
112 RWd,MB,The Blood-Mask
   from G'Shinis Grave 225.00
113 RWd,MB,The Mask's of
   Zombi-Zan 225.00
114 RWd,MB 225.00
115 RWd,MB,Svengali of
   the Apes 225.00
116 RWd,MB,The Vessel of
   Marbel Monsters 225.00
117 RWd,MB,Lair of the Half-
   Man King 225.00
118 RWd,MB,Quest of the
   Congo Dwarflings 225.00
119 RWd,MB,King Crocodile's
   Domain 225.00
120 RWd,MB,The Beast-Pack
   Howls the Moon 225.00
121 RWd,MB,The Kraal of
   Evil Ivory 225.00
122 RWd,MB,Castaways of
   the Congo 200.00
123 RWd,MB, ... 200.00
124 RWd,MB,The Voodoo Beasts
   of Changra-Lo 200.00
125 RWd,MB,JKa(c),The Beast-
   Pack Strikes at Dawn 200.00
126 RWd,MB,JKa(c),Lair of the
   Swamp Beast 200.00
127 RWd,MB,JKa(c),The Phantom
   of Lost Lagoon. 200.00
128 RWd,MB,JKa(c),Mad Mistress
   of the Congo-Tuskers 200.00
129 RWd,MB,JKa(c),Slaves of
   King Simbas Kraal 200.00
130 RWd,MB,JKa(c),Quest of
   the Pharaoh's Idol 200.00
131 RWd,JKa(c),Congo Giants
   at Bay 200.00
132 RWd,JKa(c),The Doom of
   the Devil's Gorge 200.00
133 RWd,JKa(c),Blaze the
   Pitfall Trail 200.00
134 RWd,JKa(c),Catacombs of
   the Jackal-Men 200.00
135 RWd,JKa(c),The 40 Thieves
   of Ankar-Lo 200.00
136 RWd,JKa(c),The Perils of
   Paradise Lost 200.00
137 RWd,JKa(c),The Kraal of
   Missing Men 200.00
138 RWd,JKa(c),The Panthers
   of Kajo-Kazar 200.00
139 RWd,JKa(c),Stampede of
   the Congo Lancers 200.00
140 RWd,JKa(c),The Moon
   Beasts from Vulture Valley . . 200.00
141 RWd,JKa(c),B:Long Bow . . . 225.00
142 RWd,JKa(c),Man-Eaters
   of N'Gamba 200.00
143 RWd,JKa(c),The Curse of
   the Cannibal Drum 200.00
144 RWd,JKa(c),The Secrets of
   Killers Cave 200.00
145 RWd,JKa(c),Killers of
   the Crypt 200.00
146 RWd,JKa(c),Sinbad of the
   Lost Lagoon. 200.00

147 RWd,JKa(c),The Wizard of
   Gorilla Glade 200.00
148 RWd,JKa(c),Derelict of
   the Slave King 200.00
149 RWd,JKa(c),Lash Lord of
   the Elephants 200.00
150 RWd,JKa(c),Queen of
   the Pharaoh's Idol 200.00
151 RWd,The Voodoo Claws
   of Doomsday Trek 200.00
152 RWd,Red Blades of Africa . . 200.00
153 RWd,Lost Legions of the Nile 200.00
154 RWd,The Track of the
   Black Devil 200.00
155 RWd,The Ghosts of
   Blow- Gun Trail 200.00
156 RWd,The Slave-Runners
   of Bambaru 200.00
157 RWd,Cave of the
   Golden Skull 200.00
158 RWd,Gun Trek to
   Panther Valley 200.00
159 RWd,A:Space Scout 175.00
160 RWd,Savage Cargo,
   E:Sheena covers 175.00
161 RWd,Dawns of the Pit 175.00
162 RWd,Hangman's Haunt 175.00
163 RWd,Cagliostro Cursed Thee 175.00
164 RWd,Death Bars the Door . . 175.00
165 RWd,Day off from a Corpse . 175.00
166 RWd,The Gallows Bird 175.00
167 RWd,Cult of the Clawmen,
   March, 1953 . . . . 175.00

JUNGLE COMICS
**Glen Kel Publ./Fiction House,
Jan., 1940**

1 HcK,DBr,LF(c),O:The White
   Panther,Kaanga,Tabu, B:The
   Jungle Boy,Camilla, all
   Kaanga covers & stories . . 7,000.00
2 HcK,DBr,WE(c),B:Fantomah 2,300.00
3 HcK,DBr,GT,The Crocodiles
   of Death River 1,900.00
4 HcK,DBr,Wambi in
   Thundering Herds 1,700.00
5 WE(c),GT,HcK,DBr,Empire
   of the Ape Men 1,900.00
6 WE(c),GT,DBr,HcK,Tigress
   of the Deep Jungle Swamp 1,200.00
7 BP(c),DBr,GT,HcK,Live
   Sacrifice,Bondage(c) 1,100.00
8 BP(c),GT,HcK,Safari into
   Shadowland 1,100.00

Jungle Comics #5
© Fiction House

All comics prices listed are for *Near Mint* condition.   **CVA Page 415**

GOLDEN AGE

9 GT,HcK,Captive of the
 Voodoo Master 1,100.00
10 GT,HcK,BP,Lair of the
 Renegade Killer 1,100.00
11 GT,HcK,V:Beasts of Africa's Ancient
 Primieval Swamp Land 750.00
12 GT,HcK,The Devil's
 Death-Trap 750.00
13 GT(c),GT,HcK,Stalker of
 the Beasts 800.00
14 HcK,Vengeance of the
 Gorilla Hordes 750.00
15 HcK,Terror of the Voodoo
 Cauldron 750.00
16 HcK,Caveman Killers 750.00
17 HcK,Valley of the Killer-Birds . 750.00
18 HcK,Trap of the Tawny
 Killer, Bondage(c) 800.00
19 HcK,Revolt of the Man-Apes . 750.00
20 HcK,One-offering to
 Ju-Ju Demon 750.00
21 HcK,Monster of the Dismal
 Swamp, Bondage(c) 600.00
22 HcK,Lair o/t Winged Fiend ... 550.00
23 HcK,Man-Eater Jaws 550.00
24 HcK,Battle of the Beasts..... 550.00
25 HcK,Kaghis the Blood God,
 Bondage(c) 600.00
26 HcK,Gorillas of the
 Witch-Queen 550.00
27 HcK,Spore o/t Gold-Raiders .. 550.00
28 HcK,Vengeance of the Flame
 God, Bondage(c) 600.00
29 HcK,Juggernaut of Doom 550.00
30 HcK,Claws o/t Black Terror .. 550.00
31 HcK,Land of Shrunken Skulls. 550.00
32 HcK,Curse of the King-Beast . 500.00
33 HcK,Scaly Guardians of
 Massacre Pool,Bondage(c) . . 500.00
34 HcK,Bait of the Spotted
 Fury,Bondage(c) 500.00
35 HcK,Stampede of the
 Slave-Masters 500.00
36 HcK,GT,The Flame-Death of
 Ju Ju Mountain 500.00
37 HcK,GT,Scaly Sentinel of
 Taboo Swamp 500.00
38 HcK,GT,Duel of the Congo
 Destroyers 500.00
39 HcK,Land of Laughing Bones. 500.00
40 HcK,Killer Plague 500.00
41 Hck,The King Ape
 Feeds at Dawn 400.00
42 Hck,RC,Master of the
 Moon-Beasts 425.00
43 HcK,The White Shiek 400.00
44 HcK,Monster of the
 Boiling Pool 400.00
45 HcK,The Bone-Grinders of
 B'Zambi, Bondage(c)....... 400.00
46 HcK,Blood Raiders of
 Tree Trail 400.00
47 HcK,GT,Monsters of the Man
 Pool, Bondage(c).......... 400.00
48 HcK,GT,Strangest Congo
 Adventure 350.00
49 HcK,GT,Lair of the King
 -Serpent. 350.00
50 HcK,GT,Juggernaut of
 the Bush 350.00
51 HcK,GT,The Golden Lion of
 Genghis Kahn 350.00
52 HcK,Feast for the River
 Devils, Bondage(c) 375.00
53 HcK,GT,Slaves for Horrors
 Harem 375.00
54 HcK,GT,Blood Bride of
 the Crocodile 350.00
55 HcK,GT,The Tree Devil..... 350.00
56 HcK,Bride for the
 Rainmaker Raj. 350.00

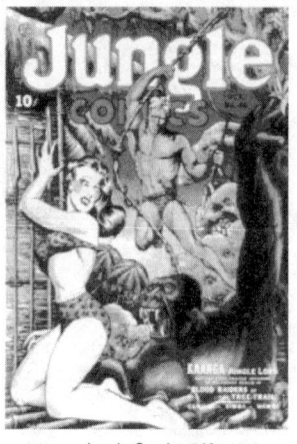

Jungle Comics #46
© *Fiction House*

57 HcK,Fire Gems of T'ulaki 350.00
58 HcK,Land of the
 Cannibal God 350.00
59 HcK,Dwellers of the Mist
 Bondage(c) 375.00
60 HcK,Bush Devil's Spoor 350.00
61 HcK,Curse of the Blood
 Madness 350.00
62 Bondage(c) 375.00
63 HcK,Fire-Birds for the
 Cliff Dwellers 300.00
64 Valley of the Ju-Ju Idols 300.00
65 Shrine of the Seven Ju Jus,
 Bondage(c) 325.00
66 Spoor of the Purple Skulls .. 300.00
67 Devil Beasts of the Golden
 Temple. 300.00
68 Satan's Safari 300.00
69 Brides for the Serpent King .. 300.00
70 Brides for the King Beast,
 Bondage(c) 325.00
71 Congo Prey,Bondage(c) 325.00
72 Blood-Brand o/t Veldt Cats ... 250.00
73 The Killer of M'omba Raj,
 Bondage(c) 275.00
74 AgF,GoldenJaws,Bondage(c) . 275.00
75 AgF,Congo Kill 250.00
76 AgF,Blood Thrist of the
 Golden Tusk 250.00
77 AgF,The Golden Gourds
 Shriek Blood,Bondage(c) ... 275.00
78 AgF,Bondage(c) 275.00
79 AgF,Death has a
 Thousand Fangs 250.00
80 AgF,Salome of the
 Devil-Cats Bondage(c) 275.00
81 AgF,Colossus of the Congo .. 250.00
82 AgF,Blood Jewels of the
 Fire-Bird. 250.00
83 AgF,Vampire Veldt,
 Bondage(c) 275.00
84 AgF,Blood Spoor of the
 Faceless Monster 250.00
85 AgF,Brides for the Man-Apes
 Bondage(c) 275.00
86 AgF,Firegems of L'hama
 Lost, Bondage(c)......... 275.00
87 AgF,Horror Kraal of the
 Legless One,Bondage(c).... 250.00
88 AgF,Beyond the Ju-Ju Mists .. 265.00
89 AgF,Blood-Moon over the
 Whispering Veldt 250.00
90 AgF,The Skulls for the
 Altar of Doom,Bondage(c) .. 265.00

91 AgF,Monsters from the Mist
 Lands, Bondage(c) 265.00
92 AgF,Vendetta of the
 Tree Tribes 250.00
93 AgF,Witch Queen of the
 Hairy Ones 250.00
94 AgF,Terror Raid of
 the Congo Caesar 250.00
95 Agf,Flame-Tongues of the
 Sky Gods................ 250.00
96 Agf,Phantom Guardians of the
 Enchanted Lake,Bondage(c). 250.00
97 AgF,Wizard of the Whirling
 Doom,Bondage(c) 275.00
98 AgF,Ten Tusks of Zulu Ivory . . 350.00
99 AgF,Cannibal Caravan,
 Bondage(c) 250.00
100 AgF,Hate has a
 Thousand Claws 250.00
101 AgF,The Blade of
 Buddha, Bondage(c) 250.00
102 AgF,Queen of the
 Amazon Lancers 225.00
103 AgF,The Phantoms of
 Lost Lagoon.............. 225.00
104 AgF 225.00
105 AgF,The Red Witch
 of Ubangi-Shan 225.00
106 AgF,Bondage(c) 250.00
107 Banshee Valley........... 250.00
108 HcK,Merchants of Murder... 250.00
109 HcK,Caravan of the
 Golden Bones 225.00
110 HcK,Raid of the Fire-Fangs . 225.00
111 HcK,The Trek of the
 Terror-Paws.............. 225.00
112 HcK,Morass of the
 Mammoths............... 225.00
113 HcK,Two-Tusked Terror 225.00
114 HcK,Mad Jackals Hunt
 by Night................. 225.00
115 HcK,Treasure Trove in
 Vulture Sky 225.00
116 HcK,The Banshees of
 Voodoo Veldt............. 225.00
117 HcK,The Fangs of the
 Hooded Scorpion. 225.00
118 HcK,The Muffled Drums
 of Doom................. 225.00
119 HcK,Fury of the Golden
 Doom................... 225.00
120 HcK,Killer King Domain 225.00
121 HcK,Wolves of the
 Desert Night 225.00
122 HcK,The Veldt of
 Phantom Fangs........... 225.00
123 HcK,The Ark of the
 Mist-Maids............... 225.00
124 HcK,The Trail of the
 Pharaoh's Eye............ 225.00
125 HcK,Skulls for Sale on
 Dismal River 225.00
126 HcK,Safari Sinister 250.00
127 HcK,Bondage(c) 200.00
128 HcK,Dawn-Men of the
 Congo 200.00
129 HcK,The Captives of
 Crocodile Swamp 200.00
130 HcK,Phantoms of the Congo 200.00
131 HcK,Treasure-Tomb of the
 Ape-King 200.00
132 HcK,Bondage(c) 225.00
133 HcK,Scourge of the Sudan
 Bondage(c) 225.00
134 HcK,The Black Avengers of
 Kaffir Pass 200.00
135 HcK 200.00
136 HcK,The Death Kraals
 of Kongola 200.00
137 BWg(c),HcK,The Safari of
 Golden Ghosts 200.00

138 BWg(c),HcK,Track of the
Black Terror Bondage(c) 200.00
139 BWg(c),HcK,Captain Kidd
of the Congo 200.00
140 BWg(c),HcK,The Monsters
of Kilmanjaro 200.00
141 BWg(c)HcK,The Death Hunt
of the Man Cubs 200.00
142 BWg(c),Hck,Sheba of the
Terror Claws,Bondage(c). ... 225.00
143 BWg(c)Hck,The Moon of
Devil Drums............. 225.00
144 BWg(c)Hck,Quest of the
Dragon's Claw 225.00
145 BWg(c)Hck,Spawn of the
Devil's Moon 225.00
146 BWg(c)Hck,Orphans of
the Congo 225.00
147 BWG(c),HcK,The Treasure
of Tembo Wanculu...... 225.00
148 BWg(c),HcK,Caged Beasts
of Plunder-Men,Bondage(c) . 225.00
149 BWg(c),HcK 175.00
150 BWg(c),HcK,Rhino Rampage,
Bondage(c) 225.00
151 BWg(c),HcK 175.00
152 BWg(c),HcK,The Rogue of
Kopje Kull 175.00
153 BWg(c),HcK,The Wild Men
of N'Gara.............. 175.00
154 BWg(c),HcK,The Fire Wizard 175.00
155 BWg(c),HcK,Swamp of
the Shrieking Dead 175.00
156 BWg(c),HcK 175.00
157 BWg(c),HcK 175.00
158 BWg(c),HcK,A:Sheena ... 175.00
159 BWg(c),HcK,The Blow-Gun
Kill 175.00
160 BWg,HcK,King Fang....... 175.00
161 BWg(c),HcK,The Barbarizi
Man-Eaters 175.00
162 BWg(c) 175.00
163 BWg(c),Jackals at the
Kill, Summer,1954 .... 175.00

JUNGLE JIM
**Best Books
(Standard Comics), Jan., 1949**
11 .... 100.00
12 Mystery Island......... 60.00
13 Flowers of Peril......... 60.00
14 .... 60.00
15 .... 60.00
16 .... 60.00
17 .... 60.00
18 .... 60.00
19 .... 60.00
20 1951 .... 60.00

JUNGLE JIM
Dell Publishing Co., Aug., 1953
(1) see Dell Four Color #490
(1) see Dell Four Color #565
3 P(c) all................. 60.00
4 .... 60.00
5 .... 60.00
6 .... 50.00
7 .... 50.00
8 thru 12 .... @50.00
13 'Mystery Island'.......... 50.00
14 'Flowers of Peril'.......... 50.00
15 thru 20............... @50.00

JUNGLE JO
**Hero Books
(Fox Features Syndicate),
March, 1950**
N# Congo King............. 550.00

1 WW,Mystery of Doc Jungle .. 600.00
2 Tangl 450.00
3 The Secret of Youth,
Sept., 1950 .... 450.00

JUNGLE LIL
Hero Books, April, 1950
1 Betrayer of the Kombe Dead.. 500.00
Becomes:
DOROTHY LAMOUR
**Fox Features Syndicate,
June 1950**
2 WW,Ph(c)The Lost Safari 500.00
3 WW,Ph(c), Aug., 1950 ...... 300.00

JUNGLE THRILLS
See: TERRORS OF
THE JUNGLE

JUNIE PROM
**Dearfield Publishing Co.
Winter, 1947**
1 Teenage Stories 150.00
2 .... 75.00
3 thru 5 .... @60.00
6 June, 1949 .... 60.00

JUNIOR COMICS
**Fox Features Syndicate,
Sept., 1947**
9 AF(a&c) ,Teenage Stories... 1,200.00
10 AF(a&c) 1,000.00
11 AF(a&c) 1,000.00
12 AF(a&c) 1,000.00
13 AF(a&c) 1,000.00
14 AF(a&c) 1,000.00
15 AF(a&c) 1,000.00
16 AF(a&c),July,1948 .... 1,000.00

JUNIOR HOOP COMICS
**Stanmor Publications,
Jan., 1952**
1 .... 100.00
2 .... 50.00
3 July, 1952 .... 50.00

JUSTICE TRAPS
THE GUILTY
**Headline Publications,
(Prize) Oct.–Nov., 1947**
2-1 S&K(a&c),Electric chair (c) . 800.00
2 S&K(a&c) 450.00
3 S&K(a&c) 400.00
4 S&K(a&c),True Confession
of a Girl Gangleader 400.00
5 S&K(a&c) 400.00
6 S&K(a&c) 400.00
7 S&K(a&c) 400.00
8 S&K(a&c) 400.00
9 S&K(a&c) 400.00
10 S&K(a&c) 400.00
11 S&K(a&c) 175.00
12 .... 100.00
13 .... 125.00
14 .... 100.00
15 .... 100.00
16 .... 100.00
17 .... 100.00
18 S&K(a&c) 100.00
19 S&K(a&c) 100.00
20 .... 90.00
21 S&K.................. 175.00

*Justice Traps the Guilty #60
© Headline Publications*

22 S&K(c)................. 175.00
23 S&K(c)................. 175.00
24 .... 75.00
25 .... 75.00
26 .... 75.00
27 S&K(c)................. 100.00
28 .... 75.00
29 .... 75.00
30 S&K.................. 125.00
31 thru 50............... @75.00
51 thru 54............... @60.00
55 .... 60.00
56 .... 60.00
57 .... 60.00
58 Drug 300.00
59 thru 92............... @50.00
Becomes:
FARGO KID
**Headline Publications
(Prize), June–July. 1958**
93 AW,JSe,O:Kid Fargo 175.00
94 JSe 125.00
95 June–July, 1958,JSe 125.00

KA'A'NGA COMICS
**Glen-Kel Publ.
(Fiction House),
Spring, 1949–Summer, 1954**
1 Phantoms of the Congo 700.00
2 V:The Jungle Octopus 350.00
3 .... 250.00
4 The Wizard Apes of
Inkosi-Khan 235.00
5 A:Camilla 225.00
6 Captive of the Devil Apes 175.00
7 GT,Beast-Men of Mombassa . 200.00
8 The Congo Kill-Cry 175.00
9 Tabu-Wizard............. 175.00
10 Stampede for Congo Gold ... 175.00
11 Claws of the Roaring Congo.. 125.00
12 Bondage(c) 150.00
13 Death Web of the Amazons .. 125.00
14 Slave Galley of the Lost
Nile Bondage(c)........... 150.00
15 Crocodile Moon,Bondage(c).. 150.00
16 Valley of Devil-Dwarfs,Sheena 150.00
17 Tembu of the Elephants 125.00
18 The Red Claw of Vengeance . 125.00
19 The Devil-Devil Trail 125.00
20 The Cult of the Killer Claws .. 125.00

All comics prices listed are for *Near Mint* condition.

KASCO COMICS
Kasco Grainfeed (Giveaway), 1945
1 BWo 200.00
2 1949,BWo 150.00

KATHY
Standard Comics, Sept., 1949
1 Teen-Age Stories 125.00
2 ASh 75.00
3 thru 6 . . . . @50.00
7 thru 17 . . . . @40.00

KATY KEENE
Archie Publications/Close-Up Radio Comics, 1949
1 BWo 1,300.00
2 BWo 700.00
3 BWo 500.00
4 BWo 500.00
5 BWo 450.00
6 BWo 400.00
7 BWo 400.00
8 thru 12 BWo . . . . @325.00
13 thru 20 BWo . . . . @300.00
21 thru 29 BWo . . . . @250.00
30 thru 38 BWo . . . . @235.00
39 thru 62 BWo . . . . @225.00
Ann.#1 . . . . 600.00
Ann.#2 thru #6 . . . . 350.00

KEEN DETECTIVE FUNNIES
Centaur Publications, July, 1938
1-8 B:The Clock, ... 3,000.00
1-9 WE 1,200.00
1-10 . . . . 1,100.00
1-11 Dean Denton 1,100.00
2-1 The Eye Sees. 900.00
2-2 JCo. 900.00
2-3 TNT. 900.00
2-4 Gabby Flynn 900.00
5 . . . . 1,000.00
6 . . . . 1,000.00
7 Masked Marvel 3,300.00
8 PGn,Gabby Flynn,Nudity
   Expanded 16 pages 1,200.00
9 Dean Denton 1,000.00
10 . . . . 1,000.00

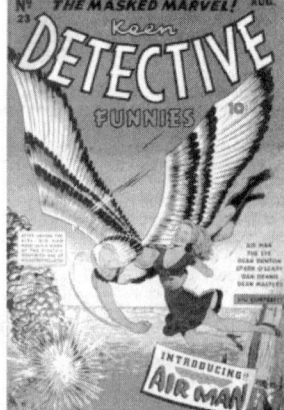

Keen Detective Funnies #23
© Centaur Publications

11 BEv,Sidekick 1,000.00
12 Masked Marvel(c) 1,200.00
3-1 Masked Marvel(c). 1,000.00
3-2 Masked Marvel(c). 1,000.00
3-3 BEv 1,000.00
16 BEv 1,000.00
17 JSm 1,000.00
18 The Eye Sees,Bondage(c). . 1,000.00
19 LFe 950.00
20 BEv,The Eye Sees. 1,400.00
21 Masked Marvel(c) 950.00
22 Masked Marvel(c) 950.00
23 B:Airman 1,300.00
24 Airman 1,400.00

KEEN KOMICS
Centaur Publications, May, 1939
1 Teenage Stories 1,300.00
2 PGn,JaB,CBu,Cut Carson . . . 800.00
3 JCo,Saddle Sniffl 800.00

KEEN TEENS
Life's Romances Publ./Leader/ Magazine Enterprises, 1945
N# P(c),Claire Voyant 450.00
N# Ph(c),Van Johnson 350.00
3 Ph(c), ... 125.00
4 Ph(c),Glenn Ford 150.00
5 Ph(c),Perry Como 150.00
6 . . . . 125.00

KEN MAYNARD WESTERN
Fawcett Publications, Sept., 1950–Feb., 1952
1 B:Ken Maynard & Tarzan (horse)
   The Outlaw Treasure Trail . . 800.00
2 Invasion of the Badmen 500.00
3 Pied Piper of the West 350.00
4 Outlaw Hoax 350.00
5 Mystery of Badman City 350.00
6 Redwood Robbery 350.00
7 Seven Wonders of the West . . 350.00
8 Mighty Mountain Menace 350.00

KEN SHANNON
Quality Comics Group, Oct., 1951–April, 1953
1 RC, Evil Eye of Count Ducrie . 500.00
2 RC, Cut Rate Corpses 350.00
3 RC, Corpse that Wouldn't
   Sleep 275.00
4 RC, Stone Hatchet Murder . . . 275.00
5 RC, Case of the Carney Killer 275.00
6 Weird Vampire Mob 275.00
7 RC,Ugliest Man in the World . 225.00
8 Chinatown Murders,Drug. . . . 250.00
9 RC, Necklace of Blood 200.00
10 RC, Shadow of the Chair . . . 200.00

KERRY DRAKE DETECTIVE CASES
Life's Romances/M.E., 1944
(1) *see N# A-1 Comics* 350.00
2 A:The Faceless Horror 200.00
3 . . . . 150.00
4 A:Squirrel, Dr. Zero, Caresse . 150.00
5 Bondage (c) 175.00
Harvey Publ., Jan., 1952
6 A:Stitches 125.00
7 A:Shuteye 135.00
8 Bondage (c) 150.00
9 Drug 200.00
10 BP,A:Meatball,Drug. 200.00

11 BP,I:Kid Gloves 100.00
12 BP 100.00
13 BP,A:Torso 90.00
14 BP,Bullseye Murder Syndicate . 90.00
15 BP,Fake Mystic Racket. 90.00
16 BP,A:Vixen 75.00
17 BP,Case of the $50,000
   Robbery. 75.00
18 BP,A:Vixen 75.00
19 BP,Case of the Dope
   Smugglers 90.00
20 BP,Secret Treasury Agent. . . . 75.00
21 BP,Murder on Record 75.00
22 BP,Death Rides the Air Waves . 75.00
23 BP,Blackmailer's Secret
   Weapon 75.00
24 Blackmailer's Trap 75.00
25 Pretty Boy Killer 75.00
26 . . . . 75.00
27 . . . . 75.00
28 BP 75.00
29 BP 75.00
30 Mystery Mine,Bondage(c) . . . 90.00
31 . . . . 60.00
32 . . . . 60.00
33 Aug., 1952. . . . . 60.00

KEWPIES
Will Eisner Publications, Spring, 1949
1 . . . . 600.00

KEY COMICS
Consolidated Magazines Jan., 1944
1 B:The Key, Will-O-The-Wisp . . 550.00
2 . . . . 300.00
3 . . . . 250.00
4 O:John Quincy,B:The Atom . . 275.00
5 HoK,Aug., 1946 . . . . 300.00

KID COWBOY
Approved Comics/ St. John Publ. Co., 1950
1 B:Lucy Belle & Red Feather . . 200.00
2 Six-Gun Justice 125.00
3 Shadow on Hangman's Bridge 100.00
4 Red Feather V:Eagle of Doom . 90.00
5 Killers on the Rampage 90.00
6 The Stovepipe Hat 90.00
7 Ghost Town of Twin Buttes . . . 90.00
8 Thundering Hoofs 90.00
9 Terror on the Salt Flats 90.00
10 Valley of Death 90.00
11 Vanished Herds,Bondage(c). . 100.00
12 . . . . 90.00
13 . . . . 90.00
14 1954 . . . . 90.00

KIDDIE KARNIVAL
Approved Comics, 1952
N# 450.00

KID ETERNITY
Comics Magazine, Spring, 1946
1 . . . . 1,300.00
2 . . . . 500.00
3 Follow Him Out of This World . 550.00
4 Great Heroes of the Past 350.00
5 Don't Kid with Crime 300.00
6 Busy Battling Crime 300.00
7 Protects the World 300.00
8 Fly to the Rescue 300.00
9 Swoop Down on Crime 300.00
10 Golden Touch from Mr. Midas. 300.00

11 Aid the Living by Calling
the Dead 250.00
12 Finds Death 250.00
13 Invades General Poschka. . . . 250.00
14 Battles Double 250.00
15 A: Master Man. 250.00
16 Balance Scales of Justice. . . . 225.00
17 A:Baron Roxx 225.00
18 A:Man with Two Faces 225.00
Becomes:

BUCCANEERS
Quality Comics Group, Jan., 1950
19 RC,Sword Fight(c) 700.00
20 RC,Treasure Chest 450.00
21 RC,Death Trap 500.00
22 A:Lady Dolores,Snuff,
Bondage(c) 350.00
23 RC,V:Treasure Hungry
Plunderers of the Sea 375.00
24 A:Adam Peril,Black Roger,
Eric Falcon 300.00
25 V:Clews 300.00
26 V:Admiral Blood 300.00
27 RC(a&c)May, 1951 . . . . 450.00

KID ZOO COMICS
Street & Smith, July, 1948
1 (fa) 325.00

KILLERS, THE
Magazine Enterprises, 1947
1 LbC(c),Thou Shall Not Kill . . 1,500.00
2 Grl,OW,Assassins Mad Slayers
of the East,Hanging(c),Drug1,300.00

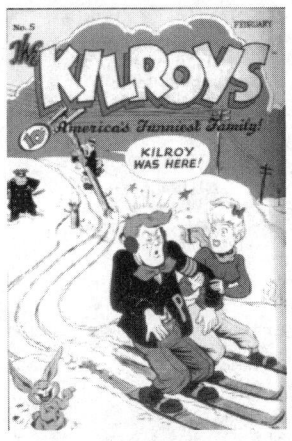

Kilroys #5
© B&L Publishing

KILROYS, THE
B&L Publishing Co./ American Comics, June–July, 1947
1 Three Girls in Love(c) 275.00
2 Flat Tire(c) 125.00
3 Right to Swear(c) 100.00
4 Kissing Booth(c) 100.00
5 Skiing(c) 100.00
6 Prom(c) 75.00
7 To School 75.00
8 . . . . 75.00
9 . . . . 75.00
10 B:Solid Jackson solo. 75.00
11 . . . . 60.00

12 Life Guard(c). 60.00
13 thru 21 . . . . @60.00
22 thru 30 . . . . @50.00
31 thru 40 . . . . @40.00
41 thru 47 . . . . @40.00
48 3-D effect 200.00
49 3-D effect 200.00
50 thru 54, July, 1954. . . . . @40.00

KING COMICS
David McKay Publications, April, 1936
(all have Popeye covers)
1 AR,EC,B:Popeye,Flash Gordon,B:
Henry,Mandrake 15,000.00
2 AR,EC,Flash Gordon 3,500.00
3 AR,EC,Flash Gordon 2,500.00
4 AR,EC,Flash Gordon 2,000.00
5 AR,EC,Flash Gordon 1,500.00
6 AR,EC,Flash Gordon 1,100.00
7 AR,EC,King Royal Mounties 1,050.00
8 AR,EC,Thanksgiving(c) 1,000.00
9 AR,EC,Christmas(c) 1,000.00
10 AR,EC,Flash Gordon 1,000.00
11 AR,EC,Flash Gordon 750.00
12 AR,EC,Flash Gordon 750.00
13 AR,EC,Flash Gordon 750.00
14 AR,EC,Flash Gordon 750.00
15 AR,EC,Flash Gordon 750.00
16 AR,EC,Flash Gordon 750.00
17 AR,EC,Flash Gordon 700.00
18 AR,EC,Flash Gordon 700.00
Covers say: "Starring Popeye"
19 AR,EC,Flash Gordon 700.00
20 AR,EC,Football(c) 700.00
21 AR,EC,Flash Gordon 600.00
22 AR,EC,Flash Gordon 600.00
23 AR,EC,Flash Gordon 600.00
24 AR,EC,Flash Gordon 600.00
25 AR,EC,Flash Gordon 550.00
26 AR,EC,Flash Gordon 550.00
27 AR,EC,Flash Gordon 550.00
28 AR,EC,Flash Gordon 550.00
29 AR,EC,Flash Gordon 550.00
30 AR,EC,Flash Gordon 550.00
31 AR,EC,Flash Gordon 550.00
32 AR,EC,Flash Gordon 550.00
33 AR,EC,Skiing(c) 550.00
34 AR,Ping Pong(c) 450.00
35 AR,Flash Gordon 450.00
36 AR,Flash Gordon 450.00
37 AR,Flash Gordon 450.00
38 AR,Flash Gordon 450.00
39 AR,Baseball(c) 450.00
40 AR,Flash Gordon 450.00
41 AR,Flash Gordon 400.00
42 AR,Flash Gordon 400.00
43 AR,Flash Gordon 400.00
44 AR,Popeye golf(c) 400.00
45 AR,Flash Gordon 400.00
46 AR,B:Little Lulu 400.00
47 AR,Flash Gordon 400.00
48 AR,Flash Gordon 400.00
49 AR,Weather Vane 400.00
50 AR,B:Love Ranger 400.00
51 AR,Flash Gordon 300.00
52 AR,Flash Gordon 300.00
53 AR,Flash Gordon 300.00
54 AR,Flash Gordon 300.00
55 AR,Magic Carpet. 300.00
56 AR,Flash Gordon 300.00
57 AR,Cows Over Moon(c) 300.00
58 AR,Flash Gordon 300.00
59 AR,Flash Gordon 300.00
60 AR,Flash Gordon 300.00
61 AR,B:Phantom,Baseball(c) . . . 300.00
62 AR,Flash Gordon 300.00
63 AR,Flash Gordon 200.00
64 AR,Flash Gordon 200.00
65 AR,Flash Gordon 200.00

66 AR,Flash Gordon 200.00
67 AR,Sweet Pea. 200.00
68 AR,Flash Gordon 200.00
69 AR,Flash Gordon 200.00
70 AR,Flash Gordon 200.00
71 AR,Flash Gordon 200.00
72 AR,Flash Gordon 200.00
73 AR,Flash Gordon 200.00
74 AR,Flash Gordon 200.00
75 AR,Flash Godron 200.00
76 AR,Flag(c). 200.00
77 AR,Flash Gordon 200.00
78 AR,Popeye,Olive Oil(c) 200.00
79 AR,Sweet Pea. 200.00
80 AR,Wimpy(c). 200.00
81 AR,B:Blondie(c). 200.00
82 thru 91 AR . . . . @150.00
92 thru 98 AR . . . . @150.00
99 AR,Olive Oil(c) 150.00
100 . . . . 200.00
101 thru 116 AR . . . . @175.00
117 O:Phantom 150.00
118 Flash Gordon 175.00
119 Flash Gordon 150.00
120 Wimpy(c). 125.00
121 thru 140 . . . . @125.00
141 Flash Gordon 125.00
142 Flash Gordon 125.00
143 Flash Gordon 125.00
144 Flash Gordon 125.00
145 Prince Valiant 100.00
146 Prince Valiant 100.00
147 Prince Valiant 100.00
148 thru 154. . . . . @75.00
155 E:Flash Gordon. 75.00
156 Baseball(c) 75.00
157 thru 159. . . . . @75.00

KING OF THE ROYAL MOUNTED
Dell Publishing Co., Dec., 1948–1958
(1) *see Dell Four Color #207*
(2) *see Dell Four Color #265*
(3) *see Dell Four Color #283*
(4) *see Dell Four Color #310*
(5) *see Dell Four Color #340*
(6) *see Dell Four Color #363*
(7) *see Dell Four Color #384*
8 Zane Grey adapt. 100.00
9 . . . . 75.00
10 . . . . 75.00
11 thru 28 . . . . @60.00

KIT CARSON
Avon Periodicals, 1950
N# EK(c) Indian Scout 150.00
2 EK(c),Kit Carson's Revenge,
Doom Trail. 100.00
3 EK(c),V:Comanche Raiders . . . 75.00
4 . . . . 75.00
5 EK(c),Trail of Doom 75.00
6 EK(c) 75.00
7 EK(c) 75.00
8 EK(c) 75.00
Becomes:

FIGHTING DAVY CROCKETT
Oct.–Nov, 1955
9 EK(c) 75.00

KOKO AND KOLA
Compix/Magazine Enterprises, Fall, 1946
1 (fa) 100.00
2 X-Mas Issue 75.00
3 . . . . 50.00

GOLDEN AGE

4 . . . . 50.00
5 . . . . 50.00
6 May, 1947 . . . . 50.00

KO KOMICS
Gerona Publications, Oct., 1945
1 . . . . 900.00

KRAZY KAT COMICS
Dell Publishing Co., May–June, 1951
1 . . . . 125.00
2 . . . . 75.00
3 . . . . 75.00
4 . . . . 75.00
5 . . . . 75.00

KRAZY LIFE
See: PHANTOM LADY

LABOR IS A PARTNER
Catechetical Guild Educational Society, 1949
1 . . . . 250.00

LAFFY-DAFFY COMICS
Rural Home Publ. Co., Feb., 1945
1 (fa) 100.00
2 . . . . 100.00

LANCE O'CASEY
Fawcett, 1946–47
1 High Seas Adventure
  from Whiz comics 400.00
2 thru 4 . . . . @250.00

LAND OF THE LOST
EC Comics, July–Aug., 1946–Spring 1948
1 Radio show adapt. 400.00
2 . . . . 275.00
3 thru 9 . . . . @225.00

LARGE FEATURE COMICS
Dell Publishing Co., 1939
1 Dick Tracy vs. the Blank 2,100.00
2 Terry and the Pirates 1,100.00
3 Heigh-Yo Silver!
  the Lone Ranger. 1,700.00
4 Dick Tracy gets his man 1,200.00
5 Tarzan of the Apes 2,000.00
6 Terry and the Pirates 1,200.00
7 Lone Ranger to the rescue. . . 1,600.00
8 Dick Tracy, Racket Buster . . 1,200.00
9 King of the Royal Mounted . . . 700.00
10 Gang Busters 800.00
11 Dick Tracy, Mad Doc Hump . 1,200.00
12 Smilin' Jack. 750.00
13 Dick Tracy and Scottie
  of Scotland Yard. 1,200.00
14 Smilin' Jack helps G-Men . . . 750.00
15 Dick Tracy and
  the kidnapped princes 1,200.00
16 Donald Duck, 1st Daisy. . . . 7,500.00
17 Gang Busters 600.00
18 Phantasmo The Master
  of the World 500.00
19 Walt Disney's Dumbo. 4,000.00
20 Donald Duck 8,000.00
21 Private Buck 150.00

22 Nuts and Jolts. 150.00
23 The Nebbs 200.00
24 Popeye in 'Thimble Theatre'. . 900.00

Large Feature #14
© Dell Publishing Co.

25 Smilin' Jack 700.00
26 Smitty 300.00
27 Terry and the Pirates 750.00
28 Grin and Bear It 100.00
29 Moon Mullins. 300.00
30 Tillie the Toiler. 275.00

[Series 2]
1 Peter Rabbit. 500.00
2 Winnie Winkle 250.00
3 Dick Tracy 1,000.00
4 Tiny Tim 300.00
5 Toots and Casper. 150.00
6 Terry and the Pirates 750.00
7 Pluto saves the Ship. 2,000.00
8 Bugs Bunny 2,000.00
9 Bringing Up Father 250.00
10 Popeye 650.00
11 Barney Google&SnuffySmith . 300.00
12 Private Buck 150.00
13 1001 Hours of Fun 200.00

LARRY DOBY, BASEBALL HERO
Fawcett Publications, 1950
1 Ph(c),BW 1,100.00

LARS OF MARS
Ziff-Davis Publishing Co., April–May, 1951
10 MA,'Terror from the Sky' . . 1,100.00
11 GC, The Terror Weapon 900.00

LASH LARUE WESTERN
Fawcett Publications, Summer, 1949
1 Ph(c),The Fatal Roundups . . 1,400.00
2 Ph(c),Perfect Hide Out 600.00
3 Ph(c),The Suspect. 500.00
4 Ph(c),Death on Stage 500.00
5 Ph(c),Rustler's Haven 500.00
6 Ph(c) 400.00
7 Ph(c),Shadow of the Noose. . 375.00
8 Ph(c),Double Deadline. 375.00
9 Ph(c),Generals Last Stand . . 375.00
10 Ph(c) 375.00
11 Ph(c) 300.00

12 thru 20 Ph(c) . . . . @250.00
21 thru 29 Ph(c) . . . . @200.00
30 thru 46 Ph(c) . . . . @175.00
46 Ph(c),Lost Chance 175.00

LASSIE
(& SEVERAL SPECIALISSUES) Dell Publishing Co., Oct.–Dec., 1950
1 Ph(c) all 225.00
2 . . . . 125.00
3 . . . . 75.00
4 . . . . 75.00
5 . . . . 75.00
6 . . . . 75.00
7 . . . . 75.00
8 . . . . 75.00
9 . . . . 75.00
10 . . . . 75.00
11 . . . . 60.00
12 Rocky Langford. 65.00
13 . . . . 60.00
14 . . . . 60.00
15 I:Timbu 65.00
16 . . . . 60.00
17 . . . . 60.00
18 . . . . 60.00
19 . . . . 60.00
20 MB. 75.00
21 MB. 75.00
22 MB. 75.00
23 thru 38. . . . . @55.00
39 I:Timmy 60.00
40 thru 62. . . . . @55.00
63 E:Timmy 50.00
64 thru 70. . . . . @40.00

LATEST COMICS
Spotlight Publ./ Palace Promotions, March, 1945
1 Funny Animal-Super Duper . . . 175.00
2 . . . . 150.00

SPECIAL COMICS
MLJ Magazines, Winter, 1941
1 O:Boy Buddies & Hangman,
  D:The Comet 4,000.00
Becomes:

HANGMAN COMICS
Spring, 1942
2 B:Hangman & Boy Buddies . 2,700.00
3 V:Nazis (c),Bondage(c) 1,800.00
4 V:Nazis (c) 1,500.00
5 Bondage (c) 1,500.00
6 . . . . 1,500.00
7 BF,Graveyard (c) 1,500.00
8 BF 1,500.00
Becomes:

BLACK HOOD
Winter, 1943–44
9 BF, Hang Man. 1,500.00
10 BF,A:Dusty, the Boy Detective 800.00
11 Here lies the Black Hood 600.00
12 . . . . 500.00
13 EK(c). 500.00
14 EK(c). 500.00
15 EK 500.00
16 EK(c). 500.00
17 Bondage (c) 550.00
18 . . . . 500.00
19 I.D. Revealed 700.00
Becomes:

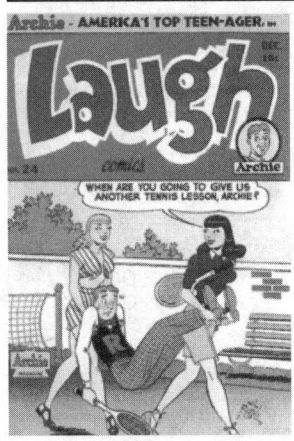

Laugh Comics #24
© Archie Comics

LAUGH COMICS
Archie Comics, Fall, 1946
20 BWo,B:Archie,Katy Keene . . .	850.00
21 BWo	400.00
22 BWo	400.00
23 Bwo.	400.00
24 BWo,JK,Pipsy	425.00
25 BWo	400.00
26 BWo	225.00
27 BWo	225.00
28 BWo	225.00
29 BWo	225.00
30 BWo	225.00
31 thru 40 BWo	@175.00
41 thru 50 BWo	@150.00
51 thru 60 BWo	@125.00
61 thru 80 BWo	@100.00
81 thru 99 BWo	@75.00
100 BWo	100.00
101 thru 126 BWo	@60.00
127 A:Jaguar	75.00
128 A:The Fly.	75.00
129 A:The Fly.	75.00
130 A:Jaguar	75.00
131 A:Jaguar	75.00
132 A:The Fly.	75.00
133 A:Jaguar	75.00
134 A:The Fly.	75.00
135 A:Jaguar	75.00
136 A:Fly Girl	75.00
137 A:Fly Girl	75.00
138 A:The Fly.	75.00
139 A:The Fly.	75.00
140 A:Jaguar	75.00
141 A:Jaguar	75.00
142 thru 144.	@75.00
145 A:Josie	45.00
146 thru 165.	@40.00
166 Beatles (c).	50.00
167 thru 220.	@30.00
221 thru 250.	@20.00
251 thru 300.	@20.00
301 thru 400.	@8.00

LAUGH COMIX
See: TOP-NOTCH COMICS

LAUREL AND HARDY
St. John Publishing Co., March, 1949
1	900.00
2	500.00

---

3	350.00
26 Rep #1	200.00
27 Rep #2	200.00
28 Rep #3	200.00

LAWBREAKERS
Law & Order Magazines (Charlton), March, 1951
1	500.00
2	250.00
3	200.00
4 Drug.	225.00
5	200.00
6 LM(c)	225.00
7 Drug.	250.00
8	200.00
9 StC(c).	200.00

Becomes:

LAWBREAKERS SUSPENSE STORIES
Jan., 1953
10 StC(c)	500.00
11 LM(c),Negligee(c).	1,300.00
12 LM(c).	275.00
13 DG(c)	275.00
14 DG(c),Sharks	275.00
15 DG(c),Acid in Face(c)	650.00

Becomes:

STRANGE SUSPENSE STORIES
Jan., 1954
16 DG(c)	400.00
17 DG(c)	300.00
18 SD,SD(c).	450.00
19 SD,SD(c),Electric Chair	600.00
20 SD,SD(c)	500.00
21 SD,SD(c).	300.00
22 SD,SD(c).	450.00

Becomes:

THIS IS SUSPENSE
Feb., 1955
23 WW; Comics Code	325.00
24 GE,DG(c)	175.00
25 DG(c)	150.00
26 DG(c)	50.00

Becomes:

STRANGE SUSPENSE STORIES
Oct., 1955
27	150.00
28	125.00
29	125.00
30	125.00
31 SD	250.00
32 SD	250.00
33 SD	250.00
34 SD	600.00
35 SD	250.00
36 SD	250.00
37 SD	250.00
38	125.00
39 SD	200.00
40 SD	225.00
41 SD	200.00
42	75.00
43	75.00
44	75.00
45	75.00
46	75.00
47 SD	225.00
48 SD	225.00
49	75.00
50 SD	225.00
51 SD	225.00
52 SD	225.00
53 SD.	225.00

---

54 thru 60.	@50.00
61 thru 74.	@40.00
75 SD,SD(c).	200.00
77 Oct 1965	75.00

LAWBREAKERS ALWAYS LOSE
Crime Bureau Stories, Spring, 1948
1 HK; FBI Reward Poster Photo.	500.00
2	200.00
3	150.00
4 AyB(c),Vampire	150.00
5 AyB(c)	150.00
6 Anti Wertham Edition	175.00
7 Drug.	350.00
8	150.00
9 Ph(c)	150.00
10 Ph(c), Oct., 1949.	150.00

LAW-CRIME
Essenkay Publications, April, 1948
1 LbC,LbC-(c);Raymond Hamilton Dies In The Chair	1,000.00
2 LbC,LbC-(c);Strangled Beauty Puzzles Police.	750.00
3 LbC,LbC-(c);Lipstick Slayer Sought; Aug., 1943	900.00

LEROY
Visual Editions (Standard Comics), Nov., 1949
1 FunniestTeenager of them All .	100.00
2	75.00
3 thru 6	@50.00

LET'S PRETEND
D.S. Publishing Company, May–June, 1950
1 From Radio Nursery Tales . . .	200.00
2	150.00
3 Nov., 1950	150.00

MISS LIBERTY
Burten Publishing, circa 1944
1 Reprints-Shield,Wizard	550.00

Becomes:

LIBERTY COMICS
Green Publishing, May, 1946
10 Reprints,Hangman	250.00
11 Wilbur in women's clothes . . .	225.00
12 Black Hood, Skull(c)	500.00
14 Patty of Airliner	150.00
15 Patty of Airliner	150.00

LIBERTY GUARDS
Chicago Mail Order (Comic Corp of America), Circa 1942
1 PG(c),Liberty Scouts	500.00

Becomes:

LIBERTY SCOUTS
June, 1941–Aug., 1941
PG(a&c)O:Fireman,Liberty Scouts	1,800.00
3 PG,PG(c),O:Sentinel.	1,200.00

LIFE STORY
Fawcett Publications, April, 1949
1 Ph(c)	150.00
2 Ph(c)	90.00

3 Ph(c)	75.00
4 Ph(c)	75.00
5 Ph(c)	75.00
6 Ph(c)	75.00
7 Ph(c)	60.00
8 Ph(c)	60.00
9 Ph(c)	60.00
10 Ph(c)	60.00
11	60.00
12	60.00
13 WW,Drug.	150.00
14 thru 21	@50.00
22 Drug	75.00
23 thru 35	@50.00
36 Drug	75.00
37 thru 42	@50.00
43 GE.	60.00
44	45.00
45 1952	45.00

LIFE WITH SNARKY PARKER
Fox Feature Syndicate, Aug., 1950

1	300.00

Sure Fire #3
© *Ace Magazines*

SURE-FIRE
Ace Magazines, 1940

1 O:Flash Lightning	2,200.00
2 Whiz Wilson	1,100.00
3 The Raven,Sept., 1940	800.00
3a Ace McCoy,Oct., 1940	800.00

Becomes:

LIGHTNING COMICS
Dec., 1940

4 Sure-Fire Stories	1,400.00
5 JM	900.00
6 JM,Dr. Nemesis	900.00

Vol. 2

1 JM	750.00
2 JM,Flash Lightning	750.00
3 JM	750.00
4 JM	750.00
5 JM	750.00
6 JM, bondage(c)	750.00

Vol. 3

1 I:Lightning Girl	750.00

LI'L ABNER
Harvey Publications, Dec., 1947

61 BP,BW,Sadie Hawkins Day	400.00
62	250.00
63	250.00
64	250.00
65 BP	250.00
66	200.00
67	200.00
68 FearlessFosdick V:Any Face	275.00
69	275.00
70	200.00

Toby Press

71	175.00
72	175.00
73	175.00
74	175.00
75 HK	200.00
76	175.00
77 HK	200.00
78 HK	200.00
79 HK	200.00
80	175.00
81	150.00
82	150.00
83 Baseball	175.00
84	150.00
85	150.00
86 HK	250.00
87	150.00
88	150.00
89	150.00
90	150.00
91 Rep. #77	165.00
92	150.00
93 Rep. #71	165.00
94	150.00
95 Fearless Fosdick	175.00
96 and 97 Jan., 1955	@150.00

LI'L GENIUS
Charlton Comics, 1955

1	125.00
2	60.00
3 thru 15	@50.00
16 Giants	75.00
17 Giants	75.00
18 Giants,100 pages	125.00
19 thru 40	@30.00
41 thru 54	@25.00
55 1965	25.00

LI'L PAN
Fox Features Syndicate, Dec.–Jan., 1946-47

6	100.00
7	75.00
8 April–May, 1947	75.00

LINDA
See: PHANTOM LADY

LITTLE AUDREY
St. John Publ. Co./ Harvey Comics, April, 1948

1	550.00
2	300.00
3 thru 6	@175.00
7 thru 10	@125.00
11 thru 20	@100.00
21 thru 24	@75.00
25 B:Harvey Comics	200.00
26 A: Casper	125.00
27 A: Casper	125.00
28 A: Casper	125.00

29 thru 31	@100.00
32 A: Casper	100.00
33 A: Casper	100.00
34 A: Casper	100.00
35 A: Casper	100.00
36 thru 53	@60.00

LITTLE BIT
Jubilee Publishing Company, March, 1949

1	100.00
2 June, 1949	75.00

LITTLE DOT
Harvey Publications, Sept., 1953

1 I: Richie Rich & Little Lotta	2,200.00
2	900.00
3	550.00
4	450.00
5 O:Dots on Little Dot's Dress	550.00
6 1st Richie Rich(c)	450.00
7	300.00
8	275.00
9	275.00
10	275.00
11 thru 20	@175.00
21 thru 30	@125.00
31 thru 39	@100.00
40 thru 50	@75.00
51 thru 60	@60.00
61 thru 70	@50.00
71 thru 80	@50.00
81 thru 100	@40.00
101 thru 130	@30.00
131 thru 140	@30.00
141 thru 145, 52 pages	@35.00
146 thru 163	@20.00

LITTLE EVA
St. John Publishing Co., May, 1952

1	175.00
2	100.00
3	75.00
4	75.00
5 thru 10	@60.00
11 thru 30	@60.00
31 Nov., 1956	60.00

LITTLE GIANT COMICS
Centaur Publications, July, 1938

1 PG, B&W with Color(c)	900.00
2 B&W with Color(c)	750.00
3 B&W with Color(c)	750.00
4 B&W with Color(c)	750.00

LITTLE GIANT DETECTIVE FUNNIES
Centaur Publications, Oct., 1938–Jan., 1939

1 B&W	1,000.00
2 B&W	750.00
3 B&W	750.00
4 WE	750.00

LITTLE GIANT MOVIE FUNNIES
Centaur Publications, Aug., 1938

1 Ed Wheelan-a	1,000.00
2 Ed Wheelan-a, Oct., 1938	750.00

LITTLE IKE
St. John Publishing Co.,
April, 1953
1 . . . . 100.00
2 . . . . 50.00
3 . . . . 40.00
4 Oct., 1953 . . . . 40.00

LITTLE IODINE
Dell Publishing Co.,
April, 1949
1 . . . . 150.00
2 . . . . 75.00
3 . . . . 75.00
4 . . . . 75.00
5 . . . . 75.00
6 thru 10 . . . . @50.00
11 thru 30 . . . . @40.00
31 thru 50 . . . . @30.00
51 thru 56 . . . . @30.00

LITTLE JACK FROST
Avon Periodicals, 1951
1 . . . . 100.00

LITTLE LULU
See: MARGE'S LITTLE
LULU

LITTLE MAX COMICS
Harvey Publications,
Oct., 1949
1 I: Little Dot,Joe Palooka(c) . . . 250.00
2 A: Little Dot,Joe Palooka(c) . . . 125.00
3 A: Little Dot,Joe Palooka(c) . . 100.00
4 . . . . 75.00
5 C: Little Dot 75.00
6 thru 10 . . . . @60.00
11 thru 22 . . . . @60.00
23 A: Little Dot 50.00
24 thru 37 . . . . @40.00
38 Rep. #20 . . . . 40.00
39 thru 72 . . . . @40.00
73 A: Richie Rich; Nov.'61 . . . . . . 40.00

LITTLE MISS MUFFET
Best Books
(Standard Comics),
Dec., 1948
11 Strip Reprints. 75.00
12 Strip Reprints 50.00
13 Strip Reprints; Mar.'49 . . . . . . 50.00

LITTLE MISS SUNBEAM COMICS
Magazine Enterprises,
June–July, 1950
1 . . . . 175.00
2 . . . . 100.00
3 . . . . 100.00
4 Dec.–Jan., 1951 . . . . 100.00

LITTLE ORPHAN ANNIE
Dell Publishing Co., 1941
1 . . . . 250.00
2 Orphan Annie and the Rescue 150.00
3 . . . . 150.00

LITTLE ROQUEFORT
St. John Publishing Co.,
June,1952
1 . . . . 100.00

2 . . . . 60.00
3 thru 9 . . . . @50.00

Pines
10 Summer 1958 . . . . 50.00

LITTLE SCOUTS
Dell Publishing Co.,
March, 1951
(1) see Dell Four Color #321
2 . . . . 40.00
3 . . . . 35.00
4 . . . . 35.00
5 . . . . 35.00
6 . . . . 35.00

LITTLEST SNOWMAN
Dell Publishing Co.,
Dec., 1956
1 . . . . 75.00

LIVING BIBLE, THE
Living Bible Corp.
Autumn, 1945
1 LbC-(c) Life of Paul 500.00
2 LbC-(c) Joseph &His Brethern. 400.00
3 LbC-(c) Chaplains At War 475.00

LONE EAGLE
Ajax/Farrell,
April–May, 1954
1 . . . . 150.00
2 . . . . 100.00
3 Bondage(c) 125.00
4 Oct.–Nov., 1954 . . . . 100.00

LONE RANGER
Dell Publishing Co.,
Jan.–Feb., 1948
1 B:Lone Ranger & Tonto
    B:Strip Reprint 1,100.00
2 . . . . 500.00
3 . . . . 350.00
4 . . . . 350.00
5 . . . . 350.00
6 . . . . 300.00
7 . . . . 300.00
8 O:Retold. 350.00
9 . . . . 300.00
10 . . . . 300.00

The Lone Ranger #5
© Dell Publishing Co.

11 B:Young Hawk. 200.00
12 thru 20. . . . . @200.00
21 . . . . 175.00
22 . . . . 175.00
23 O:Retold 225.00
24 thru 30 . . . . @175.00
31 (1st Mask Logo) 200.00
32 thru 36 . . . . @150.00
37 (E:Strip reprints) 150.00
38 thru 50 . . . . @125.00
51 thru 75 . . . . @125.00
76 thru 99 . . . . @100.00
100 . . . . 125.00
101 thru 111 . . . . @125.00
112 B:Clayton Moore Ph(c) 300.00
113 thru 117 . . . . @175.00
118 O:Lone Ranger & Tonto
    retold, Anniv. issue 375.00
119 thru 144 . . . . @175.00
145 final issue,May/July, 1962. . . 175.00

THE LONE RANGER'S COMPANION TONTO
Dell Publishing Co., Jan., 1951
(1) see Dell Four Color #312
2 P(c) all 200.00
3 . . . . 100.00
4 . . . . 75.00
5 . . . . 75.00
6 thru 10 . . . . @75.00
11 thru 20 . . . . @60.00
21 thru 25 . . . . @50.00
26 thru 33 . . . . @50.00

THE LONE RANGER'S FAMOUS HORSE HI-YO SILVER
Dell Publishing Co., Jan., 1952
(1) see Dell Four Color #369
(1) see Dell Four Color #392
3 P(c) all 75.00
4 . . . . 75.00
5 . . . . 75.00
6 thru 10 . . . . @75.00
11 thru 36 . . . . @60.00

LONE RIDER
Farrell (Superior
Comics), April, 1951
1 . . . . 350.00

The Lone Rider #3
© Superior Comics

All comics prices listed are for *Near Mint* condition.   **CVA Page 423**

GOLDEN AGE

GOLDEN AGE

2 I&O: Golden Arrow; 52 pgs. . . 200.00	13 Bugs/Porky(c) 650.00
3 . . . . 175.00	14 Bugs/Porky(c) 650.00
4 . . . . 175.00	15 Bugs/Porky X-Mas(c),F:WK
5 . . . . 175.00	Kandi the Cave 625.00
6 E: Golden Arrow 175.00	16 Bugs/Porky ice-skating(c) . . . 625.00
7 G.Arrow Becomes Swift Arrow 175.00	17 Bugs/Petunia Valentines(c). . . 625.00
8 O: Swift Arrow 200.00	18 Sgt.Bugs Marine(c) 625.00
9 thru 14 . . . . @100.00	19 Bugs/Painting(c) 625.00
15 O: Golden Arrow Rep. #2 . . . . 125.00	20 Bugs/Porky/ElmerWarBonds(c),
16 thru 19 . . . . @75.00	B:WK,Pat,Patsy&Pete 625.00
20 . . . . 75.00	21 Bugs/Porky 4th July(c) 625.00
21 3-D (c). 200.00	22 Porky(c). 625.00
22 . . . . 75.00	23 Bugs/Porky Fishing(c). 625.00
23 A: Apache Kid 75.00	24 Bugs/Porky Football(c) 625.00
24 . . . . 75.00	25 Bugs/Porky/Petunia Halloween
25 . . . . 75.00	(c),E:WK,Pat, Patsy & Pete. . 625.00
26 July, 1955 . . . . 75.00	26 Bugs Thanksgiving(c) 400.00
	27 Bugs/Porky New Years(c) 400.00
	28 Bugs/Porky Ice-Skating(c) . . . 400.00

LONG BOW
Real Adventures Publ.
(Fiction House), Winter, 1950

1 . . . . 200.00	29 Bugs Valentine(c) 400.00
2 . . . . 125.00	30 Bugs(c) 400.00
3 'Red Arrows Means War'. 125.00	31 Bugs(c). 375.00
4 'Trial of Tomahawk' 125.00	32 Bugs/Porky Hot Dogs(c) 375.00
5 . . . . 125.00	33 Bugs/Porky War Bonds(c) . . . 400.00
6 'Rattlesnake Raiders'. 100.00	34 Bugs/Porky Fishing(c). 375.00
7 . . . . 100.00	35 Bugs/Porky Swimming(c) 375.00
8 . . . . 100.00	36 Bugs/Porky(c) 375.00
9 Spring, 1953 . . . . 100.00	37 Bugs Halloween(c) 375.00
	38 Bugs Thanksgiving(c) 375.00
	39 Bugs X-Mas(c) 375.00

LOONEY TUNES AND
MERRIE MELODIES
Dell Publishing Co., 1941

1 B:&1st Comic App. Bugs Bunny	40 Bugs(c) 375.00
Daffy Duck,Elmer Fudd . . 17,000.00	41 Bugs Washington's
2 Bugs/Porky(c) 3,000.00	Birthday(c). 275.00
3 Bugs/Porky(c) B:WK,	42 Bugs Magician(c) 275.00
Kandi the Cave. 2,000.00	43 Bugs Dream(c). 275.00
4 Bugs/Porky(c),WK 2,000.00	44 Bugs/Porky(c) 275.00
5 Bugs/Porky(c),WK,	45 Bugs War Bonds(c). 275.00
A:Super Rabbit. 1,500.00	46 Bugs/Porky(c) 275.00
6 Bugs/Porky/Elmer(c),E:WK,	47 Bugs Beach(c) 250.00
Kandi the Cave. 1,400.00	48 Bugs/Porky Picnic(c). 250.00
7 Bugs/Porky(c) 900.00	49 Bugs(c) 250.00
8 Bugs/Porky swimming(c),F:WK,	50 Bugs(c). 250.00
Kandi the Cave. 1,200.00	51 thru 60. . . . . @200.00
9 Porky/Elmer car painted(c) . . . 900.00	61 thru 80. . . . . @150.00
10 Porky/Bugs/Elmer Parade(c) . 900.00	81 thru 86. . . . . @100.00
11 Bugs/Porky(c),F:WK,	87 Bugs X-Mas(c) 125.00
Kandi the Cave 900.00	88 thru 99. . . . . @100.00
12 Bugs/Porky rollerskating(c). . . 650.00	100 . . . . 125.00
	101 thru 110. . . . . @100.00
	111 thru 125. . . . . @90.00
	126 thru 150. . . . . @75.00
	151 thru 165. . . . . @60.00

Becomes:

LOONEY TUNES
Aug., 1955

166 thru 200. . . . . @60.00
201 thru 245. . . . . @55.00
246 final issue,Sept.1962 . . . . . . 60.00

LOST WORLD
Literacy Enterprises
(Standard Comics),
Oct., 1952

5 ATh, Alice in Terrorland 600.00
6 ATh 450.00

LOVE AND MARRIAGE
Superior Comics Ltd.,
March, 1952

1 . . . . 150.00
2 . . . . 100.00
3 . . . . 60.00
4 . . . . 60.00
5 . . . . 60.00
6 . . . . 60.00
7 . . . . 60.00
8 thru 15 . . . . @60.00
16 Sept., 1954 . . . . 60.00

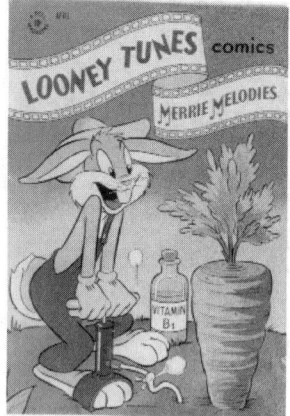

Looney Tunes and Merrie Melodies
© Dell PublishingCo.

Looney Tunes and Merrie Melodies
© Dell Publishing Co.

LOVE AT FIRST SIGHT
Periodical House
(Ace Magazines),
Oct., 1949

1 P(c) 150.00
2 P(c) 75.00
3 . . . . 65.00
4 P(c) 65.00
5 thru 10 . . . . @65.00
11 thru 33 . . . . @60.00
34 1st Edition Under Code 50.00
35 thru 41 . . . . @50.00
42 1956 . . . . 50.00

LOVE CONFESSIONS
Comics Magazine
(Quality Comics Group),
Oct., 1949

1 PG,BWa(c)& Some-a 350.00
2 PG,BWa(c) 200.00
3 . . . . 100.00
4 RC 125.00
5 BWa 150.00
6 Ph(c) 75.00
7 Ph(c) Van Johnson 75.00
8 BWa,Robert Mitchum 75.00
9 Ph(c)Jane Russell/Robert
    Mitchum 75.00
10 BWa 125.00
11 thru 18 Ph(c) . . . . @100.00
19 . . . . 100.00
20 BWa 100.00
21 . . . . 50.00
22 BWa 75.00
23 thru 28. . . . . @50.00
29 BWa 100.00
30 thru 38 . . . . @50.00
39 MB. 75.00
40 thru 42. . . . . @50.00
43 1st Edition Under Code 50.00
44 . . . . 50.00
45 BWa(a) 65.00
46 . . . . 50.00
47 BWa(c) 75.00
48 . . . . 50.00
49 MB. 75.00
50 thru 54 Dec., 1956 . . . . @50.00

LOVE DIARY
Our Publishing Co./Toytown,
July, 1949–Oct., 1955

1 BK,Ph(c) 250.00
2 BK,Ph(c) 150.00

3 BK,Ph(c) 150.00	
4 thru 9 Ph(c) . . . . @75.00	
10 BEv, Ph(c) 75.00	
11 thru 24 Ph(c) . . . . @60.00	
25 . . . . 50.00	
26 . . . . 50.00	
27 Ph(c) 60.00	
28 . . . . 50.00	
29 Ph(c) 50.00	
30 . . . . 50.00	
31 JB(c) 50.00	
32 thru 41 . . . . @50.00	
42 MB(c) 50.00	
43 thru 47 . . . . @50.00	
48 1st Edition Under Code 50.00	

LOVE DIARY
**Quality Comics Group,
Sept., 1949**

1 BWa(c) 400.00

LOVE LESSONS
**Harvey Publications,
Oct., 1949**

1 Silver(c) 150.00
2 BP 75.00
3 Ph(c) 60.00
4 . . . . 60.00
5 June, 1950 . . . . 60.00

LOVE LETTERS
**Comic Magazines
(Quality Comics Group),
Nov., 1949**

1 PG,BWa(c) 275.00
2 PG,BWa(c) 225.00
3 PG,Ph(c) 175.00
4 BWa,Ph(c) 225.00
5 Ph(c) 75.00
6 Ph(c) 75.00
7 Ph(c) 75.00
8 Ph(c) 75.00
9 Ph(c) of Robert Mitchum . . . 100.00
10 Ph(c) 75.00
11 BWa,Ph(c) Broadway
   Romances 100.00
12 Ph(c) 60.00
13 Ph(c) 60.00
14 Ph(c) 60.00
15 Ph(c) 60.00
16 Ph(c) of Anthony Quinn 125.00

*Love Letters #2
© Quality Comics Group*

17 BWa, Ph(c) of Jane Russell . . 125.00
18 thru 28 Ph(c) . . . . @60.00
29 . . . . 60.00
30 & 31 BWa . . . . @75.00
Becomes:

LOVE SECRETS
Aug., 1953

32 . . . . 125.00
33 . . . . 60.00
34 BWa 125.00
35 thru 39 . . . . @75.00
40 MB(c)1st Edition Under Code . 75.00
41 thru 48 . . . . @60.00
49 MB 75.00
50 MB 75.00
51 MB(c) 85.00
52 thru 56 . . . . @40.00

LOVELORN
**Best Syndicated/Michel Publ.
(American Comics Group),
Aug.–Sept., 1949**

1 . . . . 175.00
2 . . . . 100.00
3 thru 10 . . . . @75.00
11 thru 17 . . . . @60.00
18 2pgs. MD-a 60.00
19 . . . . 60.00
20 . . . . 60.00
21 Prostitution Story 75.00
22 thru 50 . . . . @60.00
51 July, 1954, 3-D 175.00
Becomes:

CONFESSIONS OF THE LOVELORN
Aug., 1954

52 3-D 350.00
53 . . . . 100.00
54 3-D 350.00
55 . . . . 100.00
56 Communist Story 125.00
57 Comics Code 60.00
58 thru 90 . . . . @60.00
91 AW 100.00
92 thru 105 . . . . @50.00
106 P(c) 50.00
107 P(c) 50.00
108 thru 114 . . . . @50.00

LOVE MEMORIES
**Fawcett Publications,
Autumn, 1949**

1 Ph(c) 175.00
2 Ph(c) 100.00
3 Ph(c) 100.00
4 Ph(c) 100.00

LOVE MYSTERY
**Fawcett Publications,
June, 1950**

1 GE, Ph(c) 250.00
2 GE, Ph(c) 200.00
3 GE & BP, Ph(c); Oct., 1950 . . . 200.00

LOVE PROBLEMS AND ADVICE ILLUSTRATED
**McCombs/Harvey Publications
Home Comics, June, 1949**

1 BP 175.00
2 BP 100.00
3 . . . . 75.00
4 . . . . 75.00
5 L. Elias(c) 60.00
6 . . . . 60.00
7 BP 60.00

8 BP 60.00
9 BP 60.00
10 BP 60.00
11 BP 50.00
12 BP 50.00
13 BP 50.00
14 BP 50.00
15 . . . . 45.00
16 . . . . 45.00
17 thru 23 BP . . . . @45.00
24 BP, Rape Scene 60.00
25 BP 45.00
26 . . . . 45.00
27 . . . . 45.00
28 BP 45.00
29 BP 45.00
30 . . . . 45.00
31 . . . . 45.00
32 Comics Code 40.00
33 BP 40.00
34 . . . . 40.00
35 . . . . 40.00
36 . . . . 40.00
37 . . . . 40.00
38 S&K (c) 40.00
39 . . . . 40.00
40 BP 40.00
41 BP 40.00
42 . . . . 40.00
43 . . . . 40.00
44 March, 1957 . . . . 40.00

LOVERS LANE
**Lev Gleason Publications,
Oct., 1949**

1 CBi (c),FG-a 125.00
2 P(c) 75.00
3 P(c) 60.00
4 P(c) 60.00
5 P(c) 60.00
6 GT,P(c), ... 60.00
7 P(c), ... 60.00
8 P(c), ... 60.00
9 P(c), ... 60.00
10 P(c) 60.00
11 thru 19 P(c) . . . . @50.00
20 Ph(c); FF 1 page Ad, ... 60.00
21 Ph(c) 45.00
22 Ph(c) 45.00
23 . . . . 45.00
24 . . . . 45.00
25 . . . . 45.00
26 Ph(c) 45.00
27 Ph(c) 45.00
28 Ph(c) 45.00
29 thru 38 . . . . @45.00
39 Story Narrated by
   Frank Sinatra 75.00
40 . . . . 45.00
41 June, 1954 . . . . 45.00

LOVE SCANDALS
**Comic Magazines
(Quality Comics Group),
Feb., 1950**

1 BW(a&c) 300.00
2 PG-a, Ph(c) 125.00
3 PG-a, Ph(c) 125.00
4 BWa(a&c) 18Pgs.; GFx-a 250.00
5 Ph(c), Oct., 1950 . . . . 125.00

LOVE STORIES OF MARY WORTH
**Harvey Publications,
Sept., 1949**

1 Newspaper Reprints 100.00
2 Newspaper Reprints 75.00
3 Newspaper Reprints 60.00

4 Newspaper Reprints, ... 60.00
5 May, 1950 . . . . 60.00

LUCKY COMICS
Consolidated Magazines,
Jan., 1944–Summer 1946
1 Lucky Star 250.00
2 Henry C. Kiefer(c) 150.00
3 . . . . 150.00
4 . . . . 150.00
5 Devil(c) 150.00

LUCKY DUCK
Standard Comics
(Literary Enterprises),
Jan.–Sept., 1953
5 IS(a&c) 125.00
6 IS(a&c) 100.00
7 IS(a&c) 100.00
8 IS(a&c) 100.00

LUCKY FIGHTS
IT THROUGH
Educational Comics, 1949
N# HK-a, V.D. Prevention 1,500.00

LUCKY "7" COMICS
Howard Publications, 1944
1 Bondage(c) Pioneer 500.00

LUCKY STAR
Nationwide Publications,
1950
1 JDa,B:52 pages western . . . 200.00
2 JDa 125.00
3 JDa 125.00
4 JDa 100.00
5 JDa 100.00
6 JDa 100.00
7 JDa 100.00
8 thru 13 . . . . @75.00
14 1955,E:52 pages western 75.00

LUCY, THE REAL
GONE GAL
St. John Publishing Co.,
June, 1953
1 Negligee Panels,Teenage 150.00
2 . . . . 100.00
3 MD-a 75.00
4 Feb., 1954 . . . . 75.00
Becomes:

MEET MISS PEPPER
April, 1954
5 JKu-a 225.00
6 JKu (a&c), June,1954 . . . . 175.00

MAD
E.C. Comics,
Oct.–Nov., 1952
1 JSe,HK(c),JDa,WW 10,000.00
2 JSe,JDa(c),JDa,WW. 3,000.00
3 JSe,HK(c),JDa,WW 2,700.00
4 JSe,HK(c),JDa-Flob Was
   A Slob,JDa,WW 2,700.00
5 JSe,BE(c).JDa,WW 3,000.00
6 JSe,HK(c),Jda,WW. 1,200.00
7 HK(c),JDa,WW 1,200.00
8 HK(c),JDa,WW 1,200.00
9 JSe,HK(c),JDa,WW 1,200.00
10 JSe,HK(c),JDa,WW 1,300.00
11 BW,BW(c),JDa,WW,Life(c). . 1,200.00
12 BK,JDa,WW 1,000.00

13 HK(c),JDa,WW,Red(c). 1,000.00
14 RH,HK(c),JDa,WW,
   Mona Lisa(c). 1,000.00
15 JDa,WW,Alice in
   Wonderland(c) 1,000.00
16 HK(c),JDa,WW,
   Newspaper(c) 1,000.00
17 BK,BW,JDa,WW 1,000.00
18 HK(c),JDa,WW. 1,000.00
19 JDa,WW,Racing Form(c) 900.00
20 JDa,WW,Composition(c). 900.00
21 JDa,WW,1st A.E.Neuman(c). . 900.00
22 BE,JDa,WW,Picasso(c) 900.00
23 Last Comic Format Edition,
   JDa,WW Think(c) 900.00
24 BK,WW, HK Logo & Border;
   1st Magazine Format 1,800.00
25 WW,AlJaffee Becomes Reg. 1,000.00
26 BK,WW,WW(c). 500.00
27 WWa,RH,JDa(c) 400.00
28 WW,BE(c),RH Back(c) 400.00
29 JKa,BW,WW,WW(c);
   1st Don Martin Artwork 400.00
30 BE,WW,RC; 1st A.E.
   Neuman(c) By Mingo 600.00
31 JDa,WW,BW,Mingo(c) 350.00
32 MD,JO 1st as reg.;Mingo(c);
   WW-Back(c) 350.00
33 WWa,Mingo(c);JO-Back(c) . . . 350.00
34 WWa,Mingo(c);1st Berg
   as Reg. 250.00
35 WW,RC,Mingo Wraparound(c) 225.00
36 WW,BW,Mingo(c),JO,MD . . . 200.00
37 WW,Mingo(c)JO,MD 200.00
38 WW,JO,MD 200.00
39 WW,JO,MD. 200.00
40 WW,BW,JO,MD 200.00
41 WW,JO,MD 150.00
42 WW,JO,MD 150.00
43 WW,JO,MD 150.00
44 WW,JO,MD 150.00
45 WW,JO,MD 150.00
46 JO,MD. 150.00
47 JO,MD. 150.00
48 JO,MD. 150.00
49 JO,MD. 150.00
50 JO,MD. 150.00
51 JO,MD. 125.00
52 JO,MD. 125.00
53 JO,MD. 125.00
54 JO,MD. 125.00
55 JO,MD. 125.00
56 JO,MD. 125.00
57 JO,MD. 125.00
58 JO,MD. 125.00
59 WW,JO,MD 150.00
60 JO,MD. 150.00
61 JO,MD. 100.00
62 JO,MD. 100.00
63 JO,MD. 100.00
64 JO,MD. 100.00
65 JO,MD. 100.00
66 JO,MD. 90.00
67 JO,MD. 90.00
68 Don Martin(c),JO,MD 90.00
69 JO,MD. 90.00
70 JO,MD. 90.00
71 JO,MD. 90.00
72 JO,MD. 90.00
73 JO,MD. 90.00
74 JO,MD. 90.00
75 Mingo(c),JO,MD 85.00
76 Mingo(c),SA,JO,MD 75.00
77 Mingo(c),SA,JO,MD 70.00
78 Mingo(c),SA,JO,MD 70.00
79 Mingo(c),SA,JO,MD 70.00
80 Mingo(c),SA,JO,MD 70.00
81 Mingo(c),SA,JO,MD 70.00
82 BW,Mingo(c),SA,JO,MD 70.00
83 Mingo(c),SA,JO,MD 70.00
84 Mingo(c),SA,JO,MD 70.00

85 Mingo(c)SA,JO,MD 70.00
86 Mingo(c);1st Fold-in Back(c),
   SA,JO,MD 75.00
87 Mingo(c),JO,MD 70.00
88 Mingo(c),JO,MD 70.00
89 WK,Mingo(c),JO,MD 75.00
90 Mingo(c); FF-Back(c),JO,MD . . 70.00
91 Mingo(c),JO,MD 60.00
92 Mingo(c),JO,MD 60.00
93 Mingo(c),JO,MD 60.00
94 Mingo(c),JO,MD 60.00
95 Mingo(c),JO,MD 60.00
96 Mingo(c),JO,MD 60.00
97 Mingo(c),JO,MD 60.00
98 Mingo(c),JO,MD 60.00
99 JDa,Mingo(c),JO,MD 70.00
100 Mingo(c),JO,MD 60.00
101 Infinity(c) by Mingo,JO,MD . . . 50.00
102 Mingo(c)JO,MD. 40.00
103 Mingo(c)JO,MD. 40.00
104 Mingo(c)JO,MD. 40.00
105 Mingo(c);Batman TV Spoof
   ,JO,MD 50.00
106 Mingo(c);FF-Back(c),JO,MD . . 50.00
107 Mingo(c),JO,MD 40.00
108 Mingo(c),JO,MD 40.00
109 Mingo(c),JO,MD 40.00
110 Mingo(c),JO,MD 40.00
111 Mingo(c),JO,MD 40.00
112 JO,MD 40.00
113 JO,MD 40.00
114 JO,MD 40.00
115 JO,MD 40.00
116 JO,MD 40.00
117 JO,MD 40.00
118 JO,MD 40.00
119 JO,MD 40.00
120 JO,MD 40.00
121 Beatles,JO,MD 40.00
122 MD & Mingo(c),JO,MD,
   Reagan 35.00
123 JO,MD 30.00
124 JO,MD 30.00
125 JO,MD 30.00
126 JO,MD 30.00
127 JO,MD 30.00
128 Last JO;MD. 30.00
129 MD 30.00
130 MD 30.00
131 MD 30.00
132 MD 30.00
133 MD 30.00
134 MD 30.00
135 JDa(c),MD. 35.00

136 MD	30.00
137 BW,MD	30.00
138 MD	30.00
139 JDa(c),MD.	30.00
140 thru 149 MD	@30.00
150	35.00
151 thru 153	@25.00
154 Mineo(c),MD	25.00
155 thru 159	@25.00
160 Mingo(c),JDa,AT	25.00
161	25.00
162 Mingo(c),MD,AT	25.00
163	25.00
164 Mingo,PaperMoon(c),AT, MD,SA	25.00
165 Don Martin(c),At,MD	25.00
166	25.00
167	25.00
168 Mingo(c),AT,MD	25.00
169 MD(c)	25.00
170	25.00
171 Mingo(c)	18.00
172 Mingo(c)	18.00
173 JDa(c)	18.00
174	18.00
175	18.00
176 MD(c)	18.00
177	18.00
178 JDa(c)	18.00
179	18.00
180 Jaws(c),SA,MD,JDA,AT	18.00
181 G.Washington(c),JDa	18.00
182	18.00
183 Mingo(c),AT,SA,MD.	18.00
184 Mingo(c),Md,AT.	18.00
185	18.00
186 Star Trek Spoof	25.00
187	18.00
188	25.00
189	18.00
190	18.00
191 Clark(c),JDa,MD,AT	18.00
192	18.00
193 Charlies Angels(c), Rickart,JDa,SA,MD	18.00
194 Rocky(c),Rickart,AT,MD	18.00
195	18.00
196 Star Wars Spoof, Rickart,AT,JDa	28.00
197	25.00
198 UPC(c),AT,MD.	18.00
199 Jaffee(c),AT,JDa,SA,MD	18.00
200 Rickart(c),Close Encounters	25.00
201 Rickart(c),Sat.Night Fever	18.00
202	18.00
203 Star Wars Spoof,Rickart(c)	15.00
204 Hulk TV Spoof,JawsII(c)	15.00
205 Rickart(c),Grease	15.00
206 Mingo,(c),AT,JDa.	15.00
207 Jones(c),Animal House(c)	15.00
208 Superman Movie Spoof, Rickart(c)	18.00
209 Mingo(c),AT,MD	15.00
210 Mingo,Lawn Mower,AT, JDa,MD	15.00
211 Mingo(c)	15.00
212 Jda(c),AT,MD	15.00
213 JDa(c),SA,AT,JDa	15.00
214	15.00
215 Jones(c),MD,AT,JDa	15.00
216	15.00
217 Jaffee(c),For Pres,AT,MD	15.00
218 Martin(c),AT,MD	15.00
219 thru 250	@15.00
251 thru 260	@10.00
261 thru 299	@8.00
300 thru 303	@10.00
304 thru 330	@6.00
331 thru 350	@5.00
350 thru 390	@4.00

MAD HATTER, THE
O.W. Comics, 1946

1 Freddy the Firefly	1,200.00
2 V:Humpty Dumpty	600.00

MAGIC COMICS
David McKay Publications, Aug.,1939–Nov.-Dec., 1949

1 Mandrake the Magician, Henry, Popeye,Blondie, Barney Baxter, Secret Agent X-9, Bunky, Henry on(c)	3,800.00
2 Henry on(c).	1,400.00
3 Henry on(c)	1,000.00
4 Henry on(c),Mandrake-Logo	850.00
5 Henry on(c),Mandrake-Logo	750.00
6 Henry on(c),Mandrake-Logo	525.00
7 Henry on(c),Mandrake-Logo	525.00
8 B:Inspector Wade,Tippie	500.00
9 Henry-Mandrake Interact(c)	500.00
10 Henry-Mandrake Interact(c)	500.00
11 Henry-Mandrake Interact(c)	425.00
12 Mandrake on(c).	425.00
13 Mandrake on(c).	425.00
14 Mandrake on(c).	425.00
15 Mandrake on(c).	425.00
16 Mandrake on(c).	425.00
17 B:Lone Ranger	500.00
18 Mandrake/Robot on(c)	400.00
19 Mandrake on(c)	500.00
20 Mandrake on(c)	400.00
21 Mandrake on(c)	300.00
22 Mandrake on(c)	300.00
23 Mandrake on(c)	300.00
24 Mandrake on(c).	300.00
25 B:Blondie, Mandrake in Logo for Duration.	300.00
26 Blondie (c).	275.00
27 Blondie(c); HighSchoolHeroes	275.00
28 Blondie(c); HighSchoolHeroes	275.00
29 Blondie(c); HighSchoolHeroes	275.00
30 Blondie (c)	275.00
31 Blondie(c);High School Sports Page	225.00
32 Blondie (c);Secret Agent X-9	225.00
33 C.Knight's-Romance of Flying	225.00
34 ClaytonKnight's-War in the Air	225.00
35 Blondie (c).	225.00
36 July'42; Patriotic-(c)	225.00
37 Blondie (c).	225.00
38 ClaytonKnight's-Flying Tigers	225.00
39 Blondie (c).	225.00
40 Jimmie Doolittle bombs Tokyo	225.00

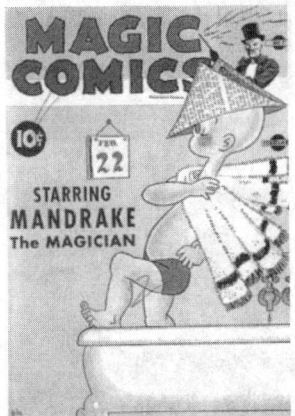

Magic Comics #7
© David McKay Publications

41 How German Became British Censor	200.00
42 Joe Musial's-Dollar-a-Dither	200.00
43 Clay Knight's-War in the Air	200.00
44 Flying Fortress in Action	200.00
45 Clayton Knight's-Gremlins	200.00
46 Adventures of Aladdin Jr.	200.00
47 Secret Agent X-9.	200.00
48 General Arnold U.S.A.F.	200.00
49 Joe Musial's-Dollar-a-Dither	200.00
50 The Lone Ranger	200.00
51 Joe Musial's-Dollar-a-Dither	150.00
52 C. Knights-Heroes on Wings	150.00
53 C. Knights-Heroes on Wings	150.00
54 High School Heroes	150.00
55 Blondie (c).	175.00
56 High School Heroes	150.00
57 Joe Musial's-Dollar-a-Dither	150.00
58 Private Breger Abroad	150.00
59	150.00
60	150.00
61 Joe Musial's-Dollar-a-Dither	125.00
62	125.00
63 B:Buz Sawyer, Naval Pilot	125.00
64 thru 70	@125.00
71 thru 80	@125.00
81 thru 90	@100.00
91 thru 99	@100.00
100	125.00
101 thru 108	@75.00
108 Flash Gordon	100.00
109 Flash Gordon	100.00
110 thru 113	@100.00
114 The Lone Ranger	100.00
115 thru 119	@100.00
120 Secret Agent X-9	120.00
121 Secret Agent X-9.	120.00
122 Secret Agent X-9.	120.00
123 Sec. Agent X-9	120.00

MAJOR HOOPLE COMICS
Nedor Publications, 1942

1 Mary Worth,Phantom Soldier; Buy War Bonds On(c)	500.00

MAJOR VICTORY COMICS
H. Clay Glover Svcs./ Harry A. Chestler, 1944

1 O:Major Victory,I:Spider Woman	850.00
2 A: Dynamic Boy	500.00
3 A: Rocket Boy	450.00

MAN HUNT!
Magazine Enterprises, 1953

1 LbC,FG,OW(c);B:Red Fox, Undercover Girl, Space Ace	650.00
2 LbC,FG,OW(c); Electrocution(c)	500.00
3 LbC,FG,OW,OW(c)	400.00
4 LbC,FG,OW,OW(c)	400.00
5 LbC,FG,OW,OW(c)	400.00
6 LbC,OW,OW(c)	375.00
7 LbC,OW; E:Space Ace	350.00
8 LbC,OW,FG(c);B:Trail Colt	350.00
9 LbC,OW	350.00
10 LbC,OW,OW(c),Gwl	350.00
11 LbC,FF,OW;B:The Duke, Scotland Yard	500.00
12 LbC,OW	300.00
13 LbC,FF,OW;Rep.Trail Colt #1	375.00
14 LbC,OW;Bondage, Hypo-(c);1953	375.00

MAN OF WAR
**Comic Corp. of America
(Centaur Publ.), Nov., 1941**
1 PG,PG(c);Flag(c);B:The Fire-
  Man,Man of War,The Sentinel,
  Liberty Guards,Vapoman . . 2,500.00
2 PG,PG(c);I: The Ferret 1,800.00

MAN O'MARS
**Fiction House/
I.W. Enterprises, 1953**
1 MA, Space Rangers 550.00
1 MA, Rep. Space Rangers 100.00

MARCH OF COMICS
**K.K. Publications/
Western Publ., 1946
(All were Giveaways)**
N# WK back(c),Goldilocks 325.00
N# WK,How Santa got His
  Red Suit 325.00
N# WK,Our Gang 450.00
N# CB,Donald Duck;
  'Maharajah Donald' 8,500.00
5 Andy Panda 200.00
6 WK,Fairy Tales 250.00
7 Oswald the Lucky Rabbit . . . 200.00
8 Mickey Mouse 600.00
9 Gloomey Bunny 125.00
10 Santa Claus 125.00
11 Santa Claus. 100.00
12 Santa's Toys 100.00
13 Santa's Suprise. 100.00
14 Santa's Kitchen 100.00
15 Hip-It-Ty Hop. 100.00
16 Woody Woodpecker 150.00
17 Roy Rogers. 275.00
18 Fairy Tales 125.00
19 Uncle Wiggily 100.00
20 CB,Donald Duck 5,000.00
21 Tom and Jerry 125.00
22 Andy Panda 100.00
23 Raggedy Ann and Andy 150.00
24 Felix the Cat; By
  Otto Messmer 250.00
25 Gene Autrey 250.00
26 Our Gang 275.00
27 Mickey Mouse. 450.00
28 Gene Autry 250.00
29 Easter 60.00
30 Santa 50.00
31 Santa. 50.00
32 Does Not Exist
33 A Christmas Carol. 50.00
34 Woody Woodpecker 125.00
35 Roy Rogers. 275.00
36 Felix the Cat 225.00
37 Popeye 150.00
38 Oswald the Lucky Rabbit 90.00
39 Gene Autry 250.00
40 Andy and Woody 90.00
41 CB,DonaldDuck,SouthSeas. 4,500.00
42 Porky Pig 100.00
43 Henry 75.00
44 Bugs Bunny 100.00
45 Mickey Mouse. 350.00
46 Tom and Jerry 100.00
47 Roy Rogers 250.00
48 Santa. 40.00
49 Santa. 40.00
50 Santa 40.00
51 Felix the Cat 175.00
52 Popeye 150.00
53 Oswald the Lucky Rabbit 75.00
54 Gene Autrey 250.00
55 Andy and Woody. 75.00
56 CB back(c),Donald Duck 350.00
57 Porky Pig 75.00
58 Henry 50.00

59 Bugs Bunny 90.00
60 Mickey Mouse 300.00
61 Tom and Jerry 75.00
62 Roy Rogers. 250.00
63 Santa. 40.00
64 Santa. 40.00
65 Jingle Bells 40.00
66 Popeye 125.00
67 Oswald the Lucky Rabbit 75.00
68 Roy Rogers. 225.00
69 Donald Duck 300.00
70 Tom and Jerry 60.00
71 Porky Pig 75.00
72 Krazy Kat 75.00
73 Roy Rogers. 200.00
74 Mickey Mouse. 300.00
75 Bugs Bunny 75.00
76 Andy and Woody. 65.00
77 Roy Rogers. 175.00
78 Gene Autrey; last regular
  sized issue. 175.00
79 Andy Panda,5"x7" format 50.00
80 Popeye 100.00
81 Oswald the Lucky Rabbit 35.00
82 Tarzan 200.00
83 Bugs Bunny 50.00
84 Henry 40.00
85 Woody Woodpecker 40.00
86 Roy Rogers. 150.00
87 Krazy Kat 65.00
88 Tom and Jerry 50.00
89 Porky Pig 40.00
90 Gene Autrey 125.00
91 Roy Rogers and Santa 150.00
92 Christmas w/Santa 35.00
93 Woody Woodpecker 35.00
94 Indian Chief. 100.00
95 Oswald the Lucky Rabbit 30.00
96 Popeye 90.00
97 Bugs Bunny 50.00
98 Tarzan,Lex Barker Ph(c). . . . 200.00
99 Porky Pig 30.00
100 Roy Rogers. 125.00
101 Henry 30.00
102 Tom Corbet,P(c) 150.00
103 Tom and Jerry. 30.00
104 Gene Autrey 100.00
105 Roy Rogers. 125.00
106 Santa's Helpers. 35.00
107 *Not Published*
108 Fun with Santa 35.00
109 Woody Woodpecker 35.00
110 Indian Chief 45.00
111 Oswald the Lucky Rabbit 30.00
112 Henry. 25.00
113 Porky Pig. 30.00

March of Comics #41
© *Walt Disney*

114 Tarzan,RsM. 175.00
115 Bugs Bunny. 50.00
116 Roy Rogers 125.00
117 Popeye 75.00
118 Flash Gordon, P(c) 150.00
119 Tom and Jerry 30.00
120 Gene Autrey 100.00
121 Roy Rogers 125.00
122 Santa's Suprise. 30.00
123 Santa's Christmas Book 30.00
124 Woody Woodpecker. 30.00
125 Tarzan, Lex Barker Ph(c) . . . 175.00
126 Oswald the Lucky Rabbit 30.00
127 Indian Chief 50.00
128 Tom and Jerry. 30.00
129 Henry 25.00
130 Porky Pig 30.00
131 Roy Rogers. 125.00
132 Bugs Bunny 35.00
133 Flash Gordon,Ph(c) 125.00
134 Popeye 75.00
135 Gene Autrey 100.00
136 Roy Rogers. 100.00
137 Gifts from Santa 20.00
138 Fun at Christmas 20.00
139 Woody Woodpecker 25.00
140 Indian Chief 50.00
141 Oswald the Lucky Rabbit 25.00
142 Flash Gordon 100.00
143 Porky Pig 25.00
144 RsM,Ph(c),Tarzan 150.00
145 Tom and Jerry. 25.00
146 Roy Rogers,Ph(c) 125.00
147 Henry 20.00
148 Popeye 60.00
149 Bugs Bunny 30.00
150 Gene Autrey 100.00
151 Roy Rogers. 100.00
152 The Night Before Christmas . . 20.00
153 Merry Christmas 25.00
154 Tom and Jerry 25.00
155 Tarzan,Ph(c) 150.00
156 Oswald the Lucky Rabbit 25.00
157 Popeye 50.00
158 Woody Woodpecker 25.00
159 Indian Chief. 50.00
160 Bugs Bunny 30.00
161 Roy Rogers 100.00
162 Henry 20.00
163 Rin Tin Tin 65.00
164 Porky Pig 25.00
165 The Lone Ranger 100.00
166 Santa & His Reindeer 20.00
167 Roy Rogers and Santa 100.00
168 Santa Claus' Workshop 20.00
169 Popeye 50.00
170 Indian Chief 50.00
171 Oswald the Lucky Rabbit 25.00
172 Tarzan 150.00
173 Tom and Jerry. 25.00
174 The Lone Ranger 100.00
175 Porky Pig 25.00
176 Roy Rogers 75.00
177 Woody Woodpecker 25.00
178 Henry 25.00
179 Bugs Bunny 25.00
180 Rin Tin Tin 75.00
181 Happy Holiday 20.00
182 Happi Tim 20.00
183 Welcome Santa. 20.00
184 Woody Woodpecker 20.00
185 Tarzan, Ph(c) 125.00
186 Oswald the Lucky Rabbit 20.00
187 Indian Chief. 40.00
188 Bugs Bunny 30.00
189 Henry 25.00
190 Tom and Jerry 22.00
191 Roy Rogers 75.00
192 Porky Pig 25.00
193 The Lone Ranger 100.00
194 Popeye 45.00

All comics prices listed are for *Near Mint* condition.

195 Rin Tin Tin 75.00
196 *Not Published*
197 Santa is Coming 25.00
198 Santa's Helper 25.00
199 Huckleberry Hound 75.00
200 Fury 40.00
201 Bugs Bunny 30.00
202 Space Explorer 75.00
203 Woody Woodpecker 20.00
204 Tarzan 100.00
205 Mighty Mouse 45.00
206 Roy Rogers,Ph(c) 75.00
207 Tom and Jerry 20.00
208 The Lone Ranger,Ph(c) 125.00
209 Porky Pig 20.00
210 Lassie 50.00
211 *Not Published*
212 Christmas Eve 20.00
213 Here Comes Santa 20.00
214 Huckleberry Hound 65.00
215 Hi Yo Silver 60.00
216 Rocky & His Friends 100.00
217 Lassie 45.00
218 Porky Pig 25.00
219 Journey to the Sun 50.00
220 Bugs Bunny 25.00
221 Roy and Dale,Ph(c) 75.00
222 Woody Woodpecker 20.00
223 Tarzan 100.00
224 Tom and Jerry 20.00
225 The Lone Ranger 75.00
226 Christmas Treasury 20.00
227 *Not Published*
228 Letters to Santa 20.00
229 The Flintstones 125.00
230 Lassie 40.00
231 Bugs Bunny 25.00
232 The Three Stooges 125.00
233 Bullwinkle 100.00
234 Smokey the Bear 30.00
235 Huckleberry Hound 50.00
236 Roy and Dale 75.00
237 Mighty Mouse 25.00
238 The Lone Ranger 75.00
239 Woody Woodpecker 20.00
240 Tarzan 100.00
241 Santa Around the World 16.00
242 Santa Toyland 16.00
243 The Flintstones 125.00
244 Mr.Ed,Ph(c) 50.00
245 Bugs Bunny 25.00
246 Popeye 35.00
247 Mighty Mouse 35.00
248 The Three Stooges 100.00
249 Woody Woodpecker 18.00
250 Roy and Dale 65.00
251 Little Lulu & Witch Hazel. . . . 135.00
252 P(c),Tarzan 80.00
253 Yogi Bear 60.00
254 Lassie 40.00
255 Santa's Christmas List 18.00
256 Christmas Party 18.00
257 Mighty Mouse 35.00
258 The Sword in the Stone
    (Disney Version) 75.00
259 Bugs Bunny 25.00
260 Mr. Ed 35.00
261 Woody Woodpecker 20.00
262 Tarzan 70.00
263 Donald Duck 90.00
264 Popeye 35.00
265 Yogi Bear 45.00
266 Lassie 35.00
267 Little Lulu 100.00
268 The Three Stooges 90.00
269 A Jolly Christmas 15.00
270 Santa's Little Helpers 15.00
271 The Flintstones 90.00
272 Tarzan 75.00
273 Bugs Bunny 25.00
274 Popeye 25.00

March of Comics #70
© M. G. M.

275 Little Lulu 90.00
276 The Jetsons 150.00
277 Daffy Duck 20.00
278 Lassie 35.00
279 Yogi Bear 45.00
280 Ph(c),The Three Stooges 90.00
281 Tom & Jerry 20.00
282 Mr. Ed 45.00
283 Santa's Visit 18.00
284 Christmas Parade 18.00
285 Astro Boy 350.00
286 Tarzan 55.00
287 Bugs Bunny 25.00
288 Daffy Duck 20.00
289 The Flintstones 90.00
290 Ph(c), Mr. Ed. 35.00
291 Yogi Bear 40.00
292 Ph(c), The Three Stooges. . . . 90.00
293 Little Lulu 75.00
294 Popeye 35.00
295 Tom & Jerry. 20.00
296 Lassie 30.00
297 Christmas Bells. 18.00
298 Santa's Sleigh 18.00
299 The Flintstones 90.00
300 Tarzan 60.00
301 Bugs Bunny 20.00
302 Ph(c), Laurel & Hardy 40.00
303 Daffy Duck 15.00
304 Ph(c), The Three Stooges. . . . 75.00
305 Tom & Jerry. 15.00
306 Ph(c), Daniel Boone 60.00
307 Little Lulu 60.00
308 Ph(c), Lassie. 30.00
309 Yogi Bear 35.00
310 Ph(c) of Clayton Moore;
    The Lone Ranger 125.00
311 Santa's Show 18.00
312 Christmas Album. 18.00
313 Daffy Duck 18.00
314 Laurel & Hardy 35.00
315 Bugs Bunny 20.00
316 The Three Stooges 60.00
317 The Flintstones 75.00
318 Tarzan 50.00
319 Yogi Bear 35.00
320 Space Family Robinson 135.00
321 Tom & Jerry. 18.00
322 The Lone Ranger 55.00
323 Little Lulu 35.00
324 Ph(c), Lassie. 30.00
325 Fun With Santa 18.00
326 Christmas Story 18.00
327 The Flintstones 75.00
328 Space Family Robinson 150.00

329 Bugs Bunny 20.00
330 The Jetsons 125.00
331 Daffy Duck 18.00
332 Tarzan 60.00
333 Tom & Jerry. 18.00
334 Lassie 25.00
335 Little Lulu 35.00
336 The Three Stooges 60.00
337 Yogi Bear 35.00
338 The Lone Ranger 60.00
339 *Not Published*
340 Here Comes Santa 18.00
341 The Flintstones 70.00
342 Tarzan 50.00
343 Bugs Bunny 25.00
344 Yogi Bear 28.00
345 Tom & Jerry. 18.00
346 Lassie 25.00
347 Daffy Duck 18.00
348 The Jetsons 80.00
349 Little Lulu 30.00
350 The Lone Ranger 40.00
351 Beep-Beep, The RoadRunner 25.00
352 Space Family Robinson 150.00
353 Beep-Beep, The RoadRunner 25.00
354 Tarzan 35.00
355 Little Lulu 30.00
356 Scooby Doo, Where Are You . 60.00
357 Daffy Duck & Porky Pig 18.00
358 Lassie 25.00
359 Baby Snoots 20.00
360 Ph(c), H.R. Pufnstuf 100.00
361 Tom & Jerry. 18.00
362 Smokey the Bear 20.00
363 Bugs Bunny & Yosemite Sam. 20.00
364 Ph(c), The Banana Splits 75.00
365 Tom & Jerry. 18.00
366 Tarzan 35.00
367 Bugs Bunny & Porky Pig 20.00
368 Scooby Doo 75.00
369 Little Lulu 25.00
370 Ph(c), Lassie. 25.00
371 Baby Snoots 18.00
372 Smokey The Bear. 20.00
373 The Three Stooges 60.00
374 Wacky Witch 15.00
375 Beep-Beep & Daffy Duck 18.00
376 The Pink Panther 25.00
377 Baby Snoots 15.00
378 Turok, Son of Stone 135.00
379 Heckle & Jeckle 15.00
380 Bugs Bunny & Yosemite Sam. 20.00
381 Lassie 18.00
382 Scooby Doo 75.00
383 Smokey the Bear 18.00
384 The Pink Panther 25.00
385 Little Lulu 20.00
386 Wacky Witch 20.00
387 Beep-Beep & Daffy Duck 15.00
388 Tom & Jerry 15.00
389 Little Lulu 25.00
390 The Pink Panther 25.00
391 Scooby Doo 60.00
392 Bugs Bunny & Yosemite Sam. 20.00
393 Heckle & Jeckle 15.00
394 Lassie 15.00
395 Woodsy the Owl 15.00
396 Baby Snoots 15.00
397 Beep-Beep & Daffy Duck 15.00
398 Wacky Witch 15.00
399 Turok, Son of Stone 125.00
400 Tom & Jerry. 15.00
401 Baby Snoots 15.00
402 Daffy Duck 15.00
403 Bugs Bunny 15.00
404 Space Family Robinson 100.00
405 Cracky. 10.00
406 Little Lulu 20.00
407 Smokey the Bear 10.00
408 Turok, Son of Stone 100.00
409 The Pink Panther 20.00

GOLDEN AGE

410 Wacky Witch	10.00
411 Lassie	15.00
412 New Terrytoons	8.00
413 Daffy Duck	8.00
414 Space Family Robinson	100.00
415 Bugs Bunny	15.00
416 The Road Runner	20.00
417 Little Lulu	20.00
418 The Pink Panther	20.00
419 Baby Snoots	8.00
420 Woody Woodpecker	8.00
421 Tweety & Sylvester	8.00
422 Wacky Witch	8.00
423 Little Monsters	8.00
424 Cracky	8.00
425 Daffy Duck	8.00
426 Underdog	50.00
427 Little Lulu	15.00
428 Bugs Bunny	10.00
429 The Pink Panther	11.00
430 The Road Runner	11.00
431 Baby Snoots	8.00
432 Lassie	9.00
433 Tweety & Sylvester	8.00
434 Wacky Witch	8.00
435 New Terrytoons	8.00
436 Cracky	8.00
437 Daffy Duck	8.00
438 Underdog	50.00
439 Little Lulu	15.00
440 Bugs Bunny	10.00
441 The Pink Panther	15.00
442 The Road Runner	7.00
443 Baby Snoots	7.00
444 Tom & Jerry	7.00
445 Tweety & Sylvester	7.00
446 Wacky Witch	7.00
447 Mighty Mouse	12.00
448 Cracky	8.00
449 The Pink Panther	8.00
450 Baby Snoots	8.00
451 Tom & Jerry	8.00
452 Bugs Bunny	8.00
453 Popeye	7.00
454 Woody Woodpecker	7.00
455 The Road Runner	8.00
456 Little Lulu	12.00
457 Tweety & Sylvester	7.00
458 Wacky Witch	7.00
459 Mighty Mouse	8.00
460 Daffy Duck	7.00
461 The Pink Panther	9.00
462 Baby Snoots	7.00
463 Tom & Jerry	7.00
464 Bugs Bunny	8.00
465 Popeye	7.00
466 Woody Woodpecker	7.00
467 Underdog	35.00
468 Little Lulu	7.00
469 Tweety & Sylvester	7.00
470 Wacky Witch	8.00
471 Mighty Mouse	8.00
472 Heckle & Jeckle	7.00
473 The Pink Panther	9.00
474 Baby Snoots	7.00
475 Little Lulu	7.00
476 Bugs Bunny	8.00
477 Popeye	7.00
478 Woody Woodpecker	7.00
479 Underdog	30.00
480 Tom & Jerry	10.00
481 Tweety & Sylvester	7.00
482 Wacky Witch	7.00
483 Mighty Mouse	8.00
484 Heckle & Jeckle	7.00
485 Baby Snoots	7.00
486 The Pink Panther	9.00
487 Bugs Bunny	8.00
488 April, 1982; Little Lulu	10.00

MARGE'S LITTLE LULU
Dell Publishing Co.

1 B:Lulu's Diary	1,000.00
2 I:Gloria,Miss Feeny	500.00
3	450.00
4	450.00
5	450.00
6	350.00
7 I:Annie,X-Mas (c)	350.00
8	350.00
9	350.00
10	350.00
11 thru 18	@300.00
19 I:Wilbur	300.00
20 I:Mr.McNabbem	300.00
21 thru 25	@250.00
26 rep.Four Color#110	250.00
27 thru 29	@250.00
30 Christmas (c)	250.00
31 thru 34	@225.00
35 B:Mumday Story	225.00
36 thru 38	@225.00
39 I:Witch Hazel	250.00
40 Halloween (c)	175.00
41	175.00
42 Christmas (c)	175.00
43 Skiing (c)	175.00
44 Valentines Day (c)	175.00
45 2nd A:Witch Hazel	175.00
46 thru 60	@175.00
61	150.00
62	150.00
63 I:Chubby	150.00
64 thru 67	@150.00
68 I:Professor Cleff	150.00
69 thru 77	@150.00
78 Christmas (c)	150.00
79	150.00
80	150.00
81 thru 89	@125.00
90 Christmas (c)	125.00
91 thru 99	@125.00
100	150.00
101 thru 122	@125.00
123 I:Fifi	110.00
124 thru 164	@100.00
165 giant sized	200.00
166 giant sized	200.00
167 thru 169	@75.00
170	35.00
171	35.00
172	40.00
173	35.00
174	35.00
175	40.00
176	40.00
177	35.00
178 thru 196	@35.00
197	35.00
198 thru 200	@40.00
201	25.00
202	30.00
203	25.00
204	30.00
205	30.00
206	25.00

MARMADUKE MOUSE
Quality Comics Group
(Arnold Publications), 1946

1 Funny Animal	175.00
2 Funny Animal	100.00
3 thru 8 Funny Animal	@75.00
9 Funny Animal	50.00
10 Funny Animal	50.00
11 thru 20 Funny Animal	@40.00
21 thru 30 Funny Animal	@30.00
31 thru 40 Funny Animal	@30.00
41 thru 50 Funny Animal	@30.00
51 thru 65 Funny Animal	@30.00

MARTIN KANE
Hero Books (Fox Features
Syndicate), June, 1950

1 WW,WW-(c)	350.00
2 WW,JO, Auguat, 1950	250.00

MARVEL FAMILY, THE
Fawcett Publications,
Dec., 1945–Jan., 1954

1 O:Captain Marvel,Captain Marvel Jr., Mary Marvel,Uncle Marvel; V:Black Adam	2,400.00
2 Uncle Marvel	1,100.00
3	750.00
4 The Witch's Tale	600.00
5 Civilization of a Prehistoric Race	550.00
6	500.00
7 The Rock of Eternity	450.00
8 The Marvel Family Round Table	450.00
9 V: The Last Vikings	450.00
10 V: The Sivana Family	450.00
11 V: The Well of Evil	350.00
12 V: The Iron Horseman	350.00
13	350.00
14 Captain Marvel Invalid	350.00
15 V: Mr. Triangle	325.00
16 World's Mightiest Quarrell	325.00
17	325.00
18	325.00
19 V: The Monster Menace	325.00
20 The Marvel Family Feud	325.00
21 V: The Trio of Terror	300.00
22 V: The Triple Threat	300.00
23 March of Independence (c)	325.00
24 V: The Fighting Xergos	300.00
25 Trial of the Marvel Family	300.00
26 V: Mr. Power	300.00
27 V: The Amoeba Men	300.00
28	300.00
29 V: The Monarch of Money	300.00
30 A:World's Greatest Magician	300.00
31 V:Sivana & The Great Hunger	250.00
32 The Marvel Family Goes Into Buisness	250.00
33 I: The Hermit Family	250.00
34 V: Sivana's Miniature Menace	250.00
35 V: The Berzerk Machines	250.00
36 V: The Invaders From Infinity	250.00
37 V: The Earth Changer	250.00
38 V: Sivana's Instinct Exterminator Gun	250.00

The Marvel Family #17
© *Fawcett Publications*

    All comics prices listed are for *Near Mint* condition.

39 The Legend of Atlantis 250.00
40 Seven Wonders of the
   Modern World 250.00
41 The Great Oxygen Theft. 250.00
42 V: The Endless Menace 200.00
43 . . . . 200.00
44 V: The Rust That Menaced
   the World. 200.00
45 The Hoax City. 200.00
46 The Day Civilization Vanished 200.00
47 V: The Interplanetary Thieves. 300.00
48 V: The Four Horsemen 200.00
49 ...Proves Human Hardness. . . 200.00
50 The Speech Scrambler
   Machine. 200.00
51 The Living Statues 210.00
52 The School of Witches 200.00
53 V: The Man Who Changed
   the World. 200.00
54 . . . . 200.00
55 . . . . 200.00
56 The World's Mightiest Project. 200.00
57 . . . . 200.00
58 The Triple Time Plot 200.00
59 . . . . 200.00
60 . . . . 200.00
61 . . . . 200.00
62 . . . . 200.00
63 V: The Pirate Planet 200.00
64 . . . . 200.00
65 . . . . 200.00
66 The Miracle Stone. 200.00
67 . . . . 200.00
68 . . . . 200.00
69 V: The Menace of Old Age . . . 200.00
70 V: The Crusade of Evil 200.00
71 . . . . 200.00
72 . . . . 200.00
73 . . . . 200.00
74 . . . . 200.00
75 The Great Space Struggle . . 200.00
76 . . . . 225.00
77 Anti-Communist. 275.00
78 V: The Red Vulture 200.00
79 Horror 175.00
80 . . . . 175.00
81 . . . . 175.00
82 . . . . 175.00
83 V: The Flying Skull 175.00
84 thru 87 . . . . @175.00
88 Jokes of Jeopardy. 175.00
89 And Then There Were None. . 175.00

MARVELS OF SCIENCE
Charlton Comics, 1946
1 1st Charlton Book; Atomic
   Bomb Story 275.00
2 . . . . 150.00
3 . . . . 150.00
4 President Truman(c); Jun.'6 . . 150.00

MARY MARVEL COMICS
Fawcett Publications/
Charlton Comics,
Dec., 1945
1 Intro: Mary Marvel. 2,700.00
2 . . . . 1,000.00
3 . . . . 750.00
4 On a Leave of Absence 700.00
5 Butterfly (c) Bullet Girl 500.00
6 A:Freckles,Teenager of
   Mischief 500.00
7 The Kingdom Undersea 500.00
8 Holiday Special Issue 500.00
9 Air Race (c) 450.00
10 A: Freckles 450.00
11 A: The Sad Dryads 300.00
12 Red Cross Appeal on(c) 300.00
13 Keep the Homefires Burning . 300.00

Mary Marvel #4
© Fawcet Publications

14 Meets Ghosts (c) 300.00
15 A: Freckles 300.00
16 The Jukebox Menace 275.00
17 Aunt Agatha's Adventures. . . . 275.00
18 . . . . 275.00
19 Witch (c) 275.00
20 . . . . 275.00
21 V: Dice Head. 225.00
22 The Silver Slippers 225.00
23 The Pendulum Strikes. 225.00
24 V: The Nightowl. 225.00
25 A: Freckles 225.00
26 A:Freckles dressed as Clown . 225.00
27 The Floating Oceanliner 225.00
28 Western, Sept., 1948 . . . . . . 225.00
Becomes:

MONTE HALE WESTERN
Oct., 1948
29 Ph(c),B:Monte Hale & His
   Horse Pardner. 650.00
30 Ph(c),B:Big Bow-Little
   Arrow; CCB,Captain Tootsie . 300.00
31 Ph(c),Giant 250.00
32 Ph(c),Giant 250.00
33 Ph(c),Giant 250.00
34 Ph(c),E:Big Bow-Little
   Arrow;B:Gabby Hayes,Giant . 250.00
35 Ph(c),Gabby Hayes, Giant . . . 250.00
36 Ph(c),Gabby Hayes, Giant . . . 250.00
37 Ph(c),Gabby Hayes 150.00
38 Ph(c),Gabby Hayes, Giant . . . 200.00
39 Ph(c);CCB, Captain Tootsie;
   Gabby Hayes, Giant 200.00
40 Ph(c),Gabby Hayes, Giant . . . 200.00
41 Ph(c),Gabby Hayes 150.00
42 Ph(c),Gabby Hayes, Giant . . . 175.00
43 Ph(c),Gabby Hayes, Giant . . . 175.00
44 Ph(c),Gabby Hayes, Giant . . . 175.00
45 Ph(c),Gabby Hayes 150.00
46 Ph(c),Gabby Hayes, Giant . . . 150.00
47 Ph(c),A:Big Bow-Little Arrow;
   Gabby Hayes, Giant 150.00
48 Ph(c),Gabby Hayes, Giant . . . 150.00
49 Ph(c),Gabby Hayes 150.00
50 Ph(c),Gabby Hayes, Giant . . . 150.00
51 Ph(c),Gabby Hayes, Giant . . . 135.00
52 Ph(c),Gabby Hayes, Giant . . . 135.00
53 Ph(c),A:Slim Pickens;
   Gabby Hayes. 125.00
54 Ph(c),Gabby Hayes, Giant . . . 135.00
55 Ph(c),Gabby Hayes, Giant . . . 135.00
56 Ph(c),Gabby Hayes, Giant . . . 125.00
57 Ph(c),Gabby Hayes 100.00
58 Ph(c),Gabby Hayes, Giant . . . 125.00

59 Ph(c),Gabby Hayes, Giant . . . 125.00
60 thru 79 Ph(c),Gabby Hayes @100.00
80 Ph(c),E: Gabby Hayes 100.00
81 Ph(c). 100.00
82 Final Ph(c) 125.00

Charlton Comics, Feb., 1955
83 R:G. Hayes Back B&W Ph(c) . 150.00
84 . . . . 100.00
85 . . . . 100.00
86 E: Gabby Hayes 100.00
87 . . . . 100.00
88 Jan., 1956. . . . . 100.00

MASK COMICS
Rural Home Publications,
Feb.–March, 1945
1 LbC,LbC-(c), Evil (c). 4,000.00
2 LbC-(c),A:Black Rider,The
   Collector The Boy Magician;
   Apr-May'45, Devil (c) 2,500.00

MASKED MARVEL
Centaur Publications,
Sept., 1940
1 I: The Masked Marvel 2,400.00
2 PG. 1,500.00
3 Dec., 1940 . . . . 1,400.00

MASKED RANGER
Premier Magazines,
April, 1954
1 FF,O&B: The Masked Ranger,
   Streak the Horse,The
   Crimson Avenger. 500.00
2 . . . . 175.00
3 . . . . 175.00
4 B: Jessie James,Billy the Kid,
   Wild Bill Hickok,
   Jim Bowie's Life Story 200.00
5 . . . . 200.00
6 . . . . 200.00
7 . . . . 200.00
8 . . . . 200.00
9 AT,E:All Features; A:Wyatt
   Earp Aug., 1955. . . . . 225.00

MASTER COMICS
Fawcett Publications,
March, 1940
1-6 Oversized,7-Normal Format
1 O:Master Man; B:The Devil's
   Dagger, El Carin-Master of
   Magic, Rick O'Say, Morton
   Murch, White Rajah, Shipwreck
   Roberts, Frontier Marshall,
   Mr. Clue, Streak Sloan . . . 12,000.00
2 Master Man (c) 3,000.00
3 Master Man (c) Bondage . . . 2,500.00
4 Master Man (c) 2,400.00
5 Master Man (c) 2,400.00
6 E: All Above Features 2,500.00
7 B:Bulletman,Zorro,The Mystery
   Man, Lee Granger, Jungle
   King,Buck Jones 4,000.00
8 B:The Red Gaucho,Captain
   Venture, Planet Princess . 2,000.00
9 Bulletman & Steam Roller . . 1,800.00
10 E: Lee Granger 1,800.00
11 O: Minute Man 3,500.00
12 Minute Man (c). 1,800.00
13 O:Bulletgirl; E:Red Gaucho . 2,600.00
14 B: The Companions Three. . 1,500.00
15 MRa, Bulletman & Girl (c) . . 1,500.00
16 MRa, Minute Man (c). 1,500.00
17 B:MRa on Bulletman 1,400.00
18 MRa, ... 1,400.00
19 MRa, Bulletman & Girl (c) . . 1,400.00

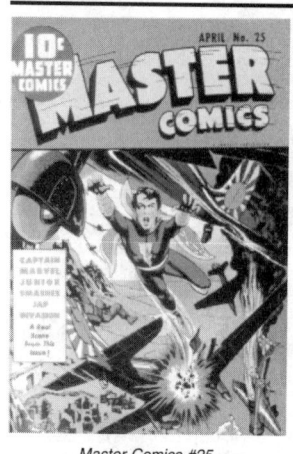

Master Comics #25
© Fawcett Publications

20 MRa,C:Cap.Marvel-
    Bulletman 1,400.00
21 MRa-(c),Capt. Marvel in
    Bulletman,I&O:CaptainNazi 7,500.00
22 MRa-(c),E:Mystery Man,Captain
    Venture; Bondage(c);Capt.
    Marvel Jr. X-Over In
    Bulletman; A:Capt. Nazi . . . 6,800.00
23 MRa(a&c),B:Capt. Marvel Jr.
    V:Capt. Nazi 4,000.00
24 MRa(a&c),Death By Radio . 1,400.00
25 MRa(a&c),The Jap Invasion 1,400.00
26 MRa(a&c),Capt. Marvel Jr.
    Avenges Pearl Harbor 1,300.00
27 MRa(a&c),V For Victory(c). . 1,300.00
28 MRa(a&c)Liberty Bell(c). . . . 1,300.00
29 MRa(a&c),Hitler &
    Hirohito(c). 1,500.00
30 MRa(a&c),Flag (c);Capt.
    Marvel Jr, V: Capt. Nazi . . 1,300.00
31 MRa(a&c),E:Companions
    Three,Capt.Marvel Jr,
    V:Mad Dr. Macabre 900.00
32 MRa(a&c),E: Buck Jones;
    CMJr Strikes Terror Castle . . 900.00
33 MRa(a&c),B:Balbo the Boy
    Magician,Hopalong Cassidy . 900.00
34 MRa(a&c),Capt.Marvel Jr
    V: Capt.Nazi 1,100.00
35 MRa(a&c),CMJr Defies
    the Flame 900.00
36 MRa(a&c),Statue Of
    Liberty(c) 900.00
37 MRa(a&c),CMJr Blasts
    the Nazi Raiders 800.00
38 MRa(a&c),CMJr V:the Japs . . 800.00
39 MRa(a&c),CMJr Blasts
    Nazi Slave Ship 800.00
40 MRa(a&c),Flag (c) 800.00
41 MRa(a&c),Bulletman,Bulletgirl,
    CMJr X-over In Minuteman . . 900.00
42 MRa(a&c),CMJr V: Hitler's
    Dream Soldier 500.00
43 MRa(c),CMJr Battles For
    Stalingrad. 500.00
44 MRa(c),CMJr In Crystal City
    of the Peculiar Penguins 500.00
45 MRa(c), ... 500.00
46 MRa(c) 500.00
47 MRa(c),A:Hitler; E: Balbo . . 550.00
48 MRa(c),I:Bulletboy;Capt.
    Marvel A: in Minuteman. 600.00
49 MRa(c),E: Hopalong Cassidy,
    Minuteman. 500.00

50 I&O: Radar,A:Capt. Marvel,
    B:Nyoka the Jungle Girl 500.00
51 MRa(c),CMJr V: Japanese . . . 300.00
52 MRa(c),CMJr & Radar Pitch
    War Stamps on (c). 300.00
53 CMJR V: Dr. Sivana 300.00
54 MRa(c),Capt.Marvel Jr
    Your Pin-Up Buddy 300.00
55 . . . . 300.00
56 MRa(c) 275.00
57 CMJr V: Dr. Sivana 275.00
58 MRa(a&c), ... 275.00
59 MRa(c),A:The Upside
    Downies. 300.00
60 MRa(c) 300.00
61 CMJr Meets Uncle Marvel . . . 300.00
62 Uncle Sam on (c) 300.00
63 W/ Radar (c) 250.00
64 W/ Radar (c) 250.00
65 . . . . 250.00
66 CMJr & Secret Of the Sphinx . 250.00
67 Knight (c) 250.00
68 CMJr in the Range of
    the Beasts 250.00
69 . . . . 250.00
70 . . . . 250.00
71 CMJr,V:Man in Metal Mask. . . 200.00
72 CMJr V: Sivana & The Whistle
    That Wouldn't Stop 200.00
73 CMJr V: The Ghost of Evil . . 200.00
74 CMJr & The Fountain of Age . 200.00
75 CMJr V: The Zombie Master. . 200.00
76 . . . . 200.00
77 Pirate Treasure (c) 200.00
78 CMJr in Death on the Scenic
    Railway 200.00
79 CMJr V: The Black Shroud . . . 200.00
80 CMJr-The Land of Backwards 200.00
81 CMJr & The Voyage 'Round
    the Horn. 175.00
82 CMJr,IN,Death at the
    Launching 175.00
83 . . . . 175.00
84 CMJr V: The Human Magnet . 175.00
85 CMJr-Crime on the Campus . . 175.00
86 CMJr & The City of Machines. 175.00
87 CMJr & The Root of Evil. 175.00
88 CMJr V: The Wreckers;
    B: Hopalong Cassidy. 175.00
89 . . . . 175.00
90 CMJr V: The Caveman 175.00
91 CMJr V: The Blockmen. 175.00
92 CMJr V: The Space Slavers . . 175.00
93 BK,CMJr,V:TheGrowingGiant. 175.00
94 E: Hopalong Cassidy 175.00
95 B: Tom Mix; CMJr Meets
    the Skyhawk 175.00
96 CMJr Meets the Worlds
    Mightiest Horse 175.00
97 CMJr Faces the Doubting
    Thomas 175.00
98 KKK Type 175.00
99 Witch (c) 175.00
100 CMJr V: The Ghost Ship. . . . 200.00
101 thru 105 . . . . @175.00
106 E: Bulletman 175.00
107 CMJr Faces the Disappearance
    of the Statue of Liberty 175.00
108 . . . . 175.00
109 . . . . 175.00
110 CMJr & The Hidden Death . . 175.00
111 thru 122 . . . . @175.00
123 CMJr V: The Flying
    Desperado. 175.00
124 . . . . 175.00
125 CMJr & The Bed of Mystery . 175.00
126 thru 131 . . . . @175.00
132 V: Migs 190.00
133 E: Tom Mix; April, 1953. . . . 200.00

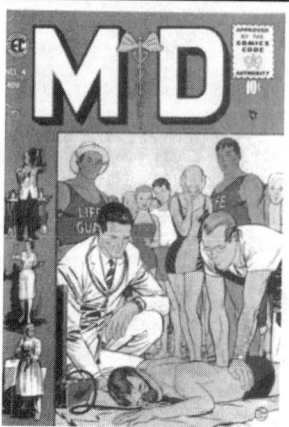

MD #4
© E.C. Publications

MD

E.C. Comics,
April, 1955–Jan., 1956
1 RC,GE,Grl,JO,JCr(c). 200.00
2 thru 5 RC,GE,Grl,JO,JCr(c). @150.00

MEDAL OF HONOR COMICS

Stafford Publication,
Spring, 1947
1 True Stories of Medal of Honor
    Recipants 125.00

MEET CORLISS ARCHER

Fox Features Syndicate,
March, 1948
1 AF,AF(c), Teenage 1,300.00
2 AF(c) 750.00
3 . . . . 600.00
Becomes:

MY LIFE

Sept., 1948
4 JKa,AF, ... 500.00
5 JKa, ... 250.00
6 JKa,AF, ... 275.00
7 WW,Watercolor & Ink Drawing
    on(c) 250.00
8 . . . . 125.00
9 . . . . 125.00
10 WW, July, 1950. . . . . 225.00

MEET MERTON

Toby Press, Dec., 1953
1 Dave Berg-a,Teen Stories 90.00
2 Dave Berg-a 50.00
3 Dave Berg-a 50.00
4 Dave Berg-a; June, 1954 . . . . . 50.00

MEET THE NEW POST GAZETTE SUNDAY FUNNIES

Pittsburg Post Gazette, 1949
N# One Shot Insert F: Several
    Syndicated Characters in Stories
    Exclusive to This Edition . . 7,000.00

MEL ALLEN
SPORTS COMICS
Visual Editions, 1949
1 GT 250.00
2 Lou Gehrig. 200.00

MEN AGAINST CRIME
See: HAND OF FATE

MERRY-GO-ROUND
COMICS
LaSalle/Croyden/
Rotary Litho., 1944
1 LaSalle Publications Edition . . 200.00
1a 1946, Croyden Edition 75.00
1b Sept-Oct.'47,Rotary Litho Ed. 100.00
2 . . . . 100.00

MERRY MOUSE
Avon Periodicals,
June, 1953
1 (fa),F. Carin (a&c) 100.00
2 (fa),F. Carin (a&c) 50.00
3 (fa),F. Carin (a&c) 50.00
4 (fa),F. Carin (a&c);Jan.'54 . . . . . 50.00

METEOR COMICS
Croyden Publications,
Nov., 1945
1 Captain Wizard & Baldy Bean . 500.00

MICKEY FINN
Eastern Color/
Columbia Comics Group, 1942
1 . . . . 350.00
2 . . . . 200.00
3 A: Charlie Chan 150.00
4 . . . . 100.00
5 thru 9 . . . . @75.00
10 thru 15. . . . . @50.00

(WALT DISNEY'S)
MICKEY MOUSE
Dell Publishing Co.,
Dec., 1952
#1-#27 Dell Four Color
28 . . . . 90.00
29 . . . . 75.00
30 . . . . 75.00
31 . . . . 75.00

Mickey Mouse Magazine Vol. 5, #4
© Western Publishing

32 thru 34. . . . . @75.00
35 thru 50. . . . . @60.00
51 thru 73. . . . . @50.00
74 . . . . 60.00
75 thru 99. . . . . @50.00
100 thru 105 rep. . . . . @60.00
106 thru 120. . . . . @50.00
121 thru 130. . . . . @30.00
131 thru 146. . . . . @30.00
147 rep,Phantom Fires 30.00
148 rep. 30.00
149 thru 158. . . . . @15.00
159 rep. 18.00
160 thru 170. . . . . @15.00
171 thru 199. . . . . @10.00
200 rep. 15.00
201 thru 218. . . . . @10.00
See: Color Comics section

MICKEY MOUSE
MAGAZINE
Kay Kamen
1 (1933) scarce 20,000.00
2 . . . . 3,000.00
3 thru 8. . . . . @2,500.00
9 . . . . 2,500.00

MICKEY MOUSE MAGAZINE
Kay Kamen
1 digest size (1933). 2,800.00
2 dairy give-away promo(1933) 1,200.00
3 dairy give-away promo(1934) 1,000.00
4 dairy give-away promo(1934) 1,000.00
5 dairy give-away promo(1934) 1,000.00
6 dairy give-away promo(1934) 1,000.00
7 dairy give-away promo(1934) 1,000.00
8 dairy give-away promo(1934) 1,000.00
9 dairy give-away promo(1934) 1,000.00
10 dairy give-awaypromo(1934) 1,000.00
11 dairy give-away promo(1934) 1,000.00
12 dairy give-awaypromo(1934) 1,000.00

Volume II
1 dairy give-away promo(1934) . 900.00
2 Christmas issue (1934) 900.00
3 dairy give-away promo(1935) . 900.00
4 dairy give-away promo(1935) . 900.00
5 1st Donald Duck as
  Sailor (1935). 2,000.00
6 dairy give-away promo(1935) . 900.00
7 dairy give-away promo(1935) . 900.00
8 dairy give-away promo(1935) . 900.00
9 dairy give-away promo(1935) . 900.00
10 dairy give-awaypromo(1935) . 900.00
11 dairy give-awaypromo(1935) . 900.00
12 dairy give-awaypromo(1935) . 900.00

MICKEY MOUSE MAGAZINE
K.K. Pub./Westen Pub.
1 (1935) 13¼"x10¼" 25,000.00
2 OM, new size 11-1/2x8-1/2. . 4,000.00
3 OM 2,000.00
4 OM 2,000.00
5 (1936) Donald Duck solo . . . 3,000.00
6 Donald Duck editor. 2,500.00
7 . . . . 2,000.00
8 Donald Duck solo 2,500.00
9 1st Minnie & Minnie 2,500.00
10 . . . . 2,000.00
11 Mickey & Pluto. 2,200.00
12 . . . . 2,000.00

Volume II
1 OM 1,500.00
2 OM 1,500.00
3 OM,Christmas issue, 100pg . 5,000.00
4 OM (1937) Roy Ranger
  adv.strip. 1,000.00
5 Ted True strip. 750.00
6 Mickey Mouse cut-outs 700.00
7 Mickey Mouse cut-outs 700.00
8 Mickey Mouse cut-outs 700.00

9 Mickey Mouse cut-outs 700.00
10 Full color 1,100.00
11 . . . . 700.00
12 Hiawatha. 700.00
13 . . . . 700.00

Volume III
2 Big Bad Wolf (c). 800.00
3 CB,First Snow White 2,500.00
4 CB,(1938) Snow White. 1,500.00
5 Snow White (c). 1,500.00
6 Snow White ends. 750.00
7 CB,7 Dwarfs Easter (c) 700.00
8 . . . . 600.00
9 CB,Dopey(c). 600.00
10 Goofy(c) 600.00
11 Mickey Mouse Sheriff 600.00
12 CB,A:Snow White 600.00

Volume IV
1 OM,Practile Pig & Brave
  Little Tailor 650.00
2 I:Huey,Louis & Dewey(c) . . . 1,000.00
3 Ferdinand the Bull 700.00
4 (1939),B:Spotty 600.00
5 Pluto solo. 700.00
7 Ugly Duckling. 650.00
7a Goofy & Wilber 650.00
8 Big Bad Wolf(c) 650.00
9 CB,The Pointer 650.00
10 CB,July 4th. 800.00
11 Slick, oversize. 650.00
12 CB,Donald's Penguin 700.00

Volume V
1 Black Pete 700.00
2 Goofy(c),I:Pinocchio 1,000.00
3 Pinocchio 1,100.00
4 (1940) 700.00
5 Jiminy Cricket(c) 700.00
6 Tugboat Mickey 700.00
7 Huey, Louis & Dewey(c) 700.00
8 Figaro & Cleo 700.00
9 Donald(c),J.Cricket 800.00
10 July 4th 800.00
11 Mickey's Tailor. 800.00
12 Change of comic format . . . 6,500.00
becomes:

WALT DISNEY COMICS
& STORIES

MICKEY MOUSE
Whitman
904 W.Disney's Mickey Mouse
  and his friends (1934) 1,500.00
948 Disney'sMickeyMouse('34) 1,500.00

MIDGET COMICS
St. John Publishing Co.,
Feb., 1950
1 MB(c),Fighting Indian Stories . 200.00
2 April, 1950;Tex West-Cowboy
  Marshall 100.00

MIGHTY ATOM, THE
See: PIXIES

MIGHTY MIDGET
COMICS
Samuel E. Lowe & Co., 1942-43
4"x5" Format
1 Bulletman. 300.00
2 Captain Marvel 300.00
3 Captain Marvel Jr. 300.00
4 Golden Arrow 250.00
5 Ibis the Invincible 300.00
6 Spy Smasher 300.00

7 Balbo, The Boy Magician 150.00
8 Bulletman 200.00
9 Commando Yank 150.00
10 Dr. Voltz, The Human
　　Generator 135.00
11 Lance O'Casey 135.00
12 Leatherneck the Marine 135.00
13 Minute Man 200.00
14 Mister Q 150.00
15 Mr. Scarlet & Pinky 135.00
16 Pat Wilson & His
　　Flying Fortress 125.00
17 Phantom Eagle 150.00
18 State Trooper Stops Crime ... 125.00
19 Tornado Tom 125.00

MIGHTY MOUSE
[1st Series], Fall, 1946
1 Terytoons Presents 1,700.00
2 .... 750.00
3 .... 500.00
4 Summer, 1947 .... 500.00
St. John Publishing, Aug., 1947
5 .... 500.00
6 thru 10 .... @250.00
11 thru 20 .... @150.00
21 thru 25 .... @125.00
26 thru 30 .... @100.00
31 thru 34 .... @75.00
35 Flying Saucer 125.00
36 .... 75.00
37 .... 75.00
38 thru 45 Giant 100 pgs .... @200.00
46 thru 66 .... @75.00
67 P(c), ... 75.00

Pines
68 thru 81 Funny Animal ..... @75.00
82 Infinity (c) 75.00
83 June, 1959 .... 75.00

MIGHTY MOUSE
ADVENTURE STORIES
St. John Publishing Co., 1953
N# 384 Pages,Rebound 600.00

MIKE BARNETT,
MAN AGAINST CRIME
Fawcett Publications,
Dec., 1951
1 The Mint of Dionysosi 250.00
2 Mystery of the Blue Madonna . 135.00
3 Revenge Holds the Torch 125.00
4 Special Delivery 125.00
5 Market For Morphine 150.00
6 Oct., 1952 .... 125.00

MILITARY COMICS
Comics Magazines
(Quality Comics Group),
Aug., 1941
1 JCo,CCu,FG,BP,WE(c),O:Blackhawk,
　Miss America, Death Patrol,
　Blue Tracer; B:X of the Under-
　ground, Yankee Eagle,Q-Boat,
　Shot & Shell, Archie Atkins,
　Loops & Banks 15,000.00
2 JCo,FG,BP,CCu,CCu(c),B:
　Secret War News 3,700.00
3 JCo,FG,BP,AMc,CCu,CCu(c),
　I&O:Chop Chop 3,000.00
4 FG,BP,AMc,CCu,CCu(c), .. 2,600.00
5 FG,BP,AMc,CCu,CCu(c),
　B: The Sniper 2,100.00
6 FG,BP,AMc,CCu,CCu(c) .. 1,500.00

Military Comics #1
© Quality Comics Group

7 FG,BP,AMc,CCu,CCu(c)
　E:Death Patrol 1,500.00
8 FG,BP,AMc,CCu,CCu(c) .. 1,500.00
9 FG,BP,AMc,CCu,CCu(c),
　B: The Phantom Clipper .. 1,500.00
10 FG,BP,CCu,AMc,WE(c) 1,600.00
11 FG,BP,CCu,AMc,
　WE(c),Flag(c) 1,400.00
12 FG,BP,AMc,RC(a&c) 1,500.00
13 FG,BP,AMc,RC(a&c),E:X of
　the Underground 1,400.00
14 FG,AMc,RC(a&c),B:Private
　Dogtag 1,400.00
15 FG,AMc,RC(a&c), ... 1,400.00
16 FG,AMc,RC(a&c),E:The Phantom
　Clipper,Blue Tracer 1,100.00
17 FG,AMc,RC(a&c),
　B:P.T. Boat 1,100.00
18 FG,AMc,RC(a&c), V:
　The Thunderer 1,100.00
19 FG,RC(a&c), V:King Cobra . 1,100.00
20 GFx,RC(a&c), Death Patrol 1,100.00
21 FG,GFx, ... 1,000.00
22 FG,GFx. 1,000.00
23 FG,GFx. 1,000.00
24 FG,GFx,V: Man-Heavy
　Glasses. 1,000.00
25 FG,GFx,V: Wang The Tiger . 1,000.00
26 FG,GFx,V: Skull 900.00
27 FG,JCo,R:The Death Patrol .. 900.00
28 FG,JCo, Dungeon of Doom .. 900.00
29 FG,JCo,V: Xanukhara 900.00
30 FG,JCo,BWa(a&c),B.Hwk
　V: Dr. Koro 900.00
31 FG,JCo,BWa,E:Death
　Patrol; I: Captain Hitsu 900.00
32 JCo,A: Captain Hitsu 800.00
33 W/ Civil War Veteran. 800.00
34 A: Eve Rice 800.00
35 Shipwreck Island. 800.00
36 Cult of the Wailing Tiger 800.00
37 Pass of Bloody Peace 800.00
38 B.Hwk Faces Bloody Death .. 800.00
39 A: Kwan Yin. 800.00
40 V: Ratru 750.00
41 W/ Chop Chop (c). 750.00
42 V: Jap Mata Hari 750.00
43 .... 750.00
Becomes:
MODERN COMICS
Nov., 1945
44 Duel of Honor 750.00
45 V: Sakyo the Madman 500.00

46 RC, Soldiers of Fortune 500.00
47 RC,PG,V:Count Hokoy 500.00
48 RC,PG,V:Pirates of Perool ... 500.00
49 RC,PG,I:Fear,Lady
　Adventuress. 500.00
50 RC,PG 500.00
51 RC,PG, Ancient City of Evil. .. 400.00
52 PG,BWa,V: The Vulture. 400.00
53 PG,BWa,B: Torchy 600.00
54 PG,RC,RC/CCu,BWa 400.00
55 PG,RC,RC/CCu,BWa 400.00
56 PG,RC/CCu,BWa 400.00
57 PG,RC,RC/CCu,BWa 400.00
58 PG,RC,RC/CCu,BWa,
　V:The Grabber. 400.00
59 PG,RC,RC/CCu,BWa 400.00
60 PG,RC/CCu,BWa,RC(c),
　V:Green Plague. 400.00
61 PG,RC/CCu,BWa,RC(c) 375.00
62 PG,RC/CCu,BWa,RC(c) 375.00
63 PG,RC/CCu,BWa,RC(c) 350.00
64 PG,RC/CCu,BWa,RC(c) 350.00
65 PG,RC/CCu,BWa,RC(c) 350.00
66 PG,RC/CCu,BWa 350.00
67 PG,RC/CCu,BWa,RC(c) 350.00
68 PG,RC/CCu,BWa,RC(c);
　I:Madame Butterfly 350.00
69 PG,RC/CCu,BWa,RC(c) 350.00
70 PG,RC/CCu,BWa,RC(c) 350.00
71 PG,RC/CCu,BWa,RC(c) 350.00
72 PG,RC/CCu,BWa,RC(c) 350.00
73 PG,RC/CCu,BWa,RC(c) 350.00
74 PG,RC/CCu,BWa,RC(c) 350.00
75 PG,RC/CCu,BWa,RC(c) 350.00
76 PG,RC/CCu,BWa,RC(c) 350.00
77 PG,RC/CCu,BWa,RC(c) 350.00
78 PG,RC/CCu,BWa,JCo,RC(c) . 400.00
79 PG,RC/CCu,BWa,JCo,RC(c) . 350.00
80 PG,RC/CCu,BWa,JCo,RC(c) . 375.00
81 PG,RC/CCu,BWa,JCo,RC(c) . 375.00
82 PG,RC/CCu,BWa,JCo,RC(c) . 350.00
83 PG,RC/CCu.BWa,JCo,RC(c);
　E: Private Dogtag 350.00
84 PG,RC/CCu,BWa,RC(c) 350.00
85 PG,RC/CCu,BWa,RC(c) 350.00
86 PG,RC/CCu,BWa,RC(c) 350.00
87 PG,RC/CCu,BWa,RC(c) 350.00
88 PG,RC/CCu,BWa,RC(c) 350.00
89 PG,RC/CCu,BWa,RC(c) 350.00
90 PG,RC/CCu,GFx,RC(c) 350.00
91 RC/CCu,GFx,RC(c) 350.00
92 RC/CCu,GFx,RC(c) 350.00
93 RC/CCu,GFx,RC(c) 350.00
94 RC/CCu,GFx,RC(c) 350.00
95 RC/CCu,GFx,RC(c) 350.00
96 RC/CCu,GFx,RC/CCu(c) 350.00
97 RC/CCu,GFx,RC/CCu(c) 350.00
98 RC/CCu,GFx,RC/CCu(c) 350.00
99 RC/CCu,GFx,JCo,RC/CCu(c). 350.00
100 GFx,JCo,RC/CCu(c) 375.00
101 GFx,JCo,RC/CCu(c) 350.00
102 GFx,JCo,WE,BWa,
　RC/CCu(c). 500.00

MILT GROSS FUNNIES
Milt Gross, Inc.,
Aug., 1947
1 Gag Oriented Caricature 225.00
2 Gag Oriented Caricature 150.00

MINUTE MAN
Fawcett Publications,
Summer, 1941
1 V: The Nazis 3,000.00
2 V: The Mongol Horde 2,000.00
3 V: The Black Poet;Spr'42 .. 2,000.00

Miracle Comics #3
© E.C. Comics

MIRACLE COMICS
**E.C. Comics,
Feb.,1940**
1 B:Sky Wizard,Master of Space,
Dash Dixon,Man of Might,Dusty
Doyle,Pinkie Parker, The Kid
Cop,K-7 Secret Agent,Scorpion
& Blandu,Jungle Queen . . 2,500.00
2 . . . . 1,400.00
3 B:Bill Colt,The Ghost Rider . 1,400.00
4 A:The Veiled Prophet,
Bullet Bob; Mar'41 . . . . . . 1,100.00

MISS CAIRO JONES
Croyden Publishers, 1944
1 BO,Rep. Newspaper Strip . . . 250.00

MR. ANTHONY'S
LOVE CLINIC
Hillman Periodicals, 1945
1 Ph(c) 150.00
2 . . . . 100.00
3 . . . . 75.00
4 . . . . 75.00
5 Ph(c),Apr/May'50 . . . . 75.00

MR. MUSCLES
See: THING, THE

MISTER MYSTERY
**Media Publ./SPM Publ./
Aragon Publ., Sept., 1951**
1 HK,RA,Horror 1,400.00
2 RA,RA(c) 800.00
3 RA(c) 800.00
4 Bondage(c) 900.00
5 Lingerie(c) 800.00
6 Bondage(c) 800.00
7 BW,Bondage(c);The Brain
Bats of Venus 1,700.00
8 Lingerie(c) 750.00
9 HN 750.00
10 . . . . 750.00
11 BW,Robot Woman 1,100.00
12 Flaming Object to Eye (c) . . 1,600.00
13 . . . . 525.00
14 . . . . 525.00
15 The Coffin & Medusa's Head . 500.00

16 Bondage(c) 500.00
17 Severed Heads 500.00
18 BW,Bondage(c) 850.00
19 Reprints 500.00

MISTER RISK
See: HAND OF FATE

MISTER UNIVERSE
**Mr. Publ./Media Publ./
Stanmore, July, 1951**
1 . . . . 250.00
2 RA(c);Jungle That time Forgot 150.00
3 Marijuana Story 150.00
4 Mr. Universe Goes to War 125.00
5 Mr. Universe Goes to War;
April, 1952 . . . . 125.00

MODERN COMICS
See: MILITARY COMICS

MODERN LOVE
**Tiny Tot Comics
(E.C. Comics),
June–July, 1949**
1 Grl,AF,Stolen Romance 900.00
2 Grl,JcR,AF(c),I Craved
Excitement 600.00
3 AF(c);Our Families Clashed . . 500.00
4 AF(c);I Was a B Girl, panties . 700.00
5 RP,AF(c);Saved From Shame 700.00
6 AF(c);The Love That
Might Have Been 700.00
7 Grl,WW,AF(c);They Won't Let
Me Love Him 500.00
8 Grl,AF(c);Aug-Sept'50 . . . . . . 550.00

MOE & SHMOE COMICS
**O.S. Publishing Co.,
Spring, 1948**
1 Gag Oriented Caricature 100.00
2 Gag Oriented Caricature 60.00

MOLLY O'DAY
**Avon Periodicals,
Feb., 1945**
1 GT;The Enchanted Dagger . . . 700.00

MONKEYSHINES COMICS
**Publ. Specialists/Ace/
Summer, 1944**
1 (fa),Several Short Features . . 125.00
2 (fa),Same Format Throughout
Entire Run 75.00
3 thru 16 Funny Animal . . . . . . @50.00
Ace
17 Funny Animal 70.00
18 thru 21 . . . . @50.00
Unity Publ.
22 (fa) 50.00
23 (fa) 50.00
24 (fa),AFa,AFa(c) 50.00
25 (fa) 50.00
26 (fa) 50.00
27 (fa),July, 1949 . . . . 50.00

MONSTER
Fiction House Magazines, 1953
1 Dr. Drew 750.00
2 . . . . 500.00

MONSTER CRIME
COMICS
**Hillman Periodicals,
Oct., 1952**
1 52 Pgs,15 Cent (c) Price . . . 1,400.00

MONTE HALL
WESTERN
See: MARY MARVEL
COMICS

MONTY HALL OF
THE U.S. MARINES
Toby Press, Aug., 1951
1 JkS,:Monty Hall,Pin-Up Pete;
(All Issues) 125.00
2 JkS 75.00
3 thru 5 JkS . . . . @50.00
6 JkS 50.00
7 JkS,The Fireball Express 50.00
8 JkS 50.00
9 JkS 50.00
10 The Vial of Death 50.00
11 Monju Island Prison Break 50.00

MOON GIRL AND
THE PRINCE
E.C. Comics, Autumn, 1947
1 JCr(c),O:Moon Girl 1,400.00
2 JCr(c),Battle of the Congo . . . 800.00
3 . . . . 750.00
4 V: A Vampire 750.00
5 1st E.C. Horror-Zombie
Terror 1,500.00
6 . . . . 700.00
7 O:Star;The Fient Who
Fights With Fire 700.00
8 True Crime Feature 700.00
Becomes:

A MOON, A GIRL
...ROMANCE
Sept.–Oct., 1949
9 AF,Grl,AF(c),C:Moon Girl;
Spanking Panels 1,000.00
10 AF,Grl,WW,AF(c),Suspicious
of His Intentions 800.00
11 AF,Grl,WW,AF(c),Hearts
Along the Ski Trail 800.00
12 AF,Grl,AF(c),
March–April, 1950 . . . . 1,100.00
Becomes:

WEIRD FANTASY

MOPSY
**St. John Publishing Co.,
Feb., 1948**
1 Paper Dolls Enclosed 200.00
2 . . . . 125.00
3 . . . . 100.00
4 Paper Dolls Enclosed 100.00
5 Paper Dolls Enclosed 100.00
6 Paper Dolls Enclosed 100.00
7 . . . . 75.00
8 Paper Dolls Enclosed;
Lingerie Panels 80.00
9 . . . . 75.00
10 . . . . 75.00
11 & 12 . . . . @75.00
13 Paper Dolls Enclosed 75.00
14 thru 18 . . . . @75.00
19 Lingerie(c);Paper
Dolls Enclosed 75.00

MORTIE
**Magazine Publishers,
Dec., 1952**
1 ...Mazie's Friend 75.00
2 .... 50.00
3 .... 45.00

MOTION PICTURE COMICS
**Fawcett Publications,
Nov., 1950**
101 Ph(c),Monte Hale's-
   Vanishing Westerner 350.00
102 Ph(c),Rocky Lane's-Code
   of the Silver Sage 325.00
103 Ph(c),Rocky Lane's-Covered
   Wagon Raid............... 325.00
104 BP,Ph(c),Rocky Lane's-
   Vigilante Hideout 325.00
105 BP,Ph(c),Audie Murphy's-
   Red Badge of Courage 400.00
106 Ph(c),George Montgomery's-
   The Texas Rangers........ 350.00
107 Ph(c),Rocky Lane's-Frisco
   Tornado 325.00
108 Ph(c),John Derek's-Mask
   of the Avenger............ 250.00
109 Ph(c),Rocky Lane's-Rough
   Rider of Durango.......... 325.00
110 GE,Ph(c), When Worlds
   Collide 1,400.00
111 Ph(c),Lash LaRue's-The
   Vanishing Outpost........ 400.00
112 Ph(c),Jay Silverheels'-
   Brave Warrior 200.00
113 KS,Ph(c),George Murphy's-
   Walk East on Beacon 150.00
114 Ph(c),George Montgomery's-
   Cripple Creek;Jan, 1953 .... 150.00

*Motion Pictures Funnies Weekly #1
© 1st Funnies, Inc.*

MOTION PICTURES FUNNIES WEEKLY
1st Funnies Incorporated, 1939
1 BEv,1st Sub-Mariner 30,000.00
2 Cover Only 1,500.00
3 Cover Only 1,500.00
4 Cover Only 1,500.00

MOVIE CLASSICS
**(NO #S) Dell Publishing Co.,
Jan., 1953**
1 Around the World Under
   the Sea 40.00
2 Bambi 50.00
3 Battle of the Buldge 50.00
4 Ph(c),Beach Blanket Bingo ... 125.00
5 Ph(c),Bon Voyage 45.00
6 Castilian 40.00
7 Cat 40.00
8 Cheyenne Autumn 80.00
9 Ph(c),Circus World,
   John Wayne (c) 150.00
10 Ph(c),Countdown,J.Caan(c) .. 45.00
11 Creature 125.00
12 Ph(c),David Ladd's Life Story . 125.00
13 Ph(c),Die Monster Die 75.00
14 Dirty Dozen.............. 65.00
15 Ph(c),Dr. Who & the Daleks .. 165.00
16 Dracula 100.00
17 El Dorado,J.WaynePh(c) 200.00
18 Ensign Pulver 40.00
19 Frankenstein 100.00
20 Ph(c),Great Race 65.00
21 B.LancasterPh(c) 75.00
22 Hatari 125.00
23 Horizontal Lieutenant 40.00
24 Ph(c) Mr. Limpet 50.00
25 Jack the Giant Killer 125.00
26 Ph(c),Jason & the Argonauts . 150.00
27 Lancelot & Guinevere....... 75.00
28 Lawrence 75.00
29 Lion of Sparta 50.00
30 Mad Monster Party 125.00
31 Magic Sword.............. 80.00
32 Ph(c),Masque of Red Death .. 100.00
33 Maya 55.00
34 McHale's Navy 65.00
35 Ph(c) Merrills' Marauders 40.00
36 Ph(c),Mouse on the Moon 50.00
37 Mummy................. 100.00
38 Music Man 40.00
39 Ph(c),Naked Prey 75.00
40 Ph(c),Night of the Grizzly 50.00
41 None but the Brave......... 75.00
42 Ph(c),Operation Bikini....... 40.00
43 Operation Cross Bold 40.00
44 Prince & the Pauper......... 50.00
45 Raven,V.Price(c) 90.00
46 Ring of Bright Water 45.00
47 Runaway................ 40.00
48 Ph(c),Santa Claus Conquers
   the Martians.............. 150.00
49 Ph(c),Six Black Horses....... 40.00
50 Sky Party 70.00
51 Smoky.................. 40.00
52 Ph(c),Sons of Katie Elder.... 200.00
53 GE,Tales of Terror.......... 75.00
54 Ph(c),3 Stooges-Hercules.... 150.00
55 Tomb of Legeia 75.00
56 Treasure Island 40.00
57 Twice Told Tales(V.Price) 100.00
58 Two on a Guillotine......... 55.00
59 Valley of Gwangi........... 150.00
60 War Gods of the Deep 45.00
61 War Wagon (John Wayne) ... 135.00
62 Who's Minding the Mint 40.00
63 Wolfman 100.00
64 Ph(c),Zulu 125.00
65 .... 40.00

MOVIE COMICS
**Fiction House Magazines,
Dec., 1946**
1 Big Town on(c) 700.00
2 MB,White Tie & Tails 500.00
3 MB,Andy Hardy Laugh Hit ... 500.00
4 MB,Slave Girl 650.00

MOVIE LOVE
**Famous Funnies Publications,
Feb., 1950**
1 Ph(c),Dick Powell(c) 175.00
2 Ph(c),Myrna Loy(c) 100.00
3 Ph(c),Cornell Wilde(c) 75.00
4 Ph(c),Paulette Goddard(c) 75.00
5 Ph(c),Joan Fontaine(c) 75.00
6 Ph(c),Ricardo Montalban(c) ... 75.00
7 Ph(c),Fred Astaire(c) 100.00
8 AW,FF,Ph(c),Corinne
   Calvert(c) 500.00
9 Ph(c),John Lund(c) 75.00
10 Ph(c),Mona Freeman(c) 550.00
11 Ph(c),James Mason(c) 100.00
12 Ph(c),Jerry Lewis &
   Dean Martin(c)........... 175.00
13 Ph(c),Ronald Reagan(c)..... 175.00
14 Ph(c),Janet Leigh,Gene Kelly .. 75.00
15 Ph(c), ... 75.00
16 Ph(c),Angela Lansbury 100.00
17 FF,Ph(c),Leslie Caron........ 75.00
18 Ph(c),Cornel Wilde 75.00
19 Ph(c),John Derek 75.00
20 Ph(c),Debbie Reynolds 100.00
21 Ph(c),Patricia Medina 75.00
22 Ph(c),John Payne 75.00

MOVIE THRILLERS
Magazine Enterprises 1949
1 Ph(c),Burt Lancaster's-
   Rope of Sand 375.00

MR. MUSCLES
See: THING!, THE

MUGGY-DOO, BOY CAT
**Stanhall Publications,
July, 1953**
1 .... 75.00
2 and 3 .... @50.00
4 Jan., 1954 .... 50.00

MURDER, INCORPORATED
**Fox Features Incorporated,
Jan., 1948–Aug., 1951**
1 For Adults Only-on(c) 750.00
2 For Adults Only-on(c);Male
   Bondage(c),Electrocution sty 500.00
3 Dutch Schultz-Beast of Evil .. 275.00
4 The Ray Hamilton Case,
   Lingerie(c) 275.00
5 thru 8 .... @275.00
9 Bathrobe (c) 275.00
9a Lingerie (c) 275.00
10 .... 250.00
11 .... 250.00
12 .... 250.00
13 .... 275.00
14 Bill Hale-King o/t Murderers .. 250.00
15 .... 250.00
16(5),Second Series 200.00
17(2)...................... 200.00
18(3), Bondage(c) w/Lingerie ... 225.00

MURDEROUS GANGSTERS
**Avon Periodicals/Realistic,
July, 1951**
1 WW,Pretty Boy Floyd,
   Leggs Diamond 550.00
2 WW,Baby Face Nelson,Mad
   Dog Esposito 350.00

3 P(c),Tony & Bud Fenner,
Jed Hawkins 300.00
4 EK(c),Murder By Needle-
Drug Story, June, 1952 . . . . . 300.00

MUTINY
**Aragon Magazines,
Oct., 1954**
1 AH(c),Stormy Tales of the
Seven Seas 200.00
2 AH(c) 150.00
3 Bondage(c),Feb., '55 . . . . 150.00

MY CONFESSIONS
See: WESTERN TRUE CRIME

MY DATE COMICS
**Hillman Periodicals,
July, 1944**
1 S&K,S&K (c), Teenage 400.00
2 S&K,DB,S&K(c) 300.00
3 S&K,DB,S&K(c) 300.00
4 S&K,DB,S&K(c) 300.00

MY DESIRE
**Fox Features Syndicate,
Oct., 1949**
1 Intimate Confessions 200.00
2 WW,They Called Me Wayward 125.00
3 I Hid My Lover 125.00
4 WW, April, 1950 . . . . 250.00

MY GREAT LOVE
**Fox Features Syndicate,
Oct., 1949–Apr., 1950**
1 Reunion In a Shack 175.00
2 My Crazy Dreams 100.00
3 He Was Ashamed of Me 100.00
4 My Two Wedding Rings 100.00

MY INTIMATE AFFAIR
**Fox Features Syndicate,
March, 1950**
1 I Sold My Love 175.00
2 I Married a Jailbird;May'50 . . . 100.00

MY LIFE
See: MEET CORLISS ARCHER

MY LOVE AFFAIR
**Fox Features Syndicate,
July, 1949**
1 Truck Driver's Sweetheart . . . 175.00
2 My Dreadful Secret 100.00
3 WW,I'll Make Him Marry Me . . 200.00
4 WW,They Called Me Wild 200.00
5 WW,Beauty Was My Bait 200.00
6 WW,The Man Downstairs 200.00

MY LOVE MEMORIES
See: WOMEN OUTLAWS

MY LOVE LIFE
See: TEGRA, JUNGLE EMPRESS

MY LOVE STORY
**Fox Features Syndicate,
Sept., 1949**
1 Men Gave Me Jewels 175.00
2 He Dared Me 100.00
3 WW,I Made Love a Plaything . 250.00
4 WW,I Tried to Be Good 250.00

MY PAST CONFESSIONS
See: WESTERN THRILLERS

MY PRIVATE LIFE
**Fox Features Syndicate,
Feb., 1950**
16 My Friendship Club Affair 150.00
17 My Guilty Kisses;April'50 . . . . 135.00

MY SECRET
**Superior Comics,
Aug., 1949**
1 True Love Stories 150.00
2 I Was Guilty of Being a
Cheating Wife 125.00
3 Was I His Second Love?; 125.00
Becomes:

OUR SECRET
Nov., 1949–June, 1950
4 JKa,She Loves Me,She Loves
Me Not. 200.00
5 . . . . 125.00
6 . . . . 125.00
7 How Do You Fall In Love? 135.00
8 His Kiss Tore At My Heart 125.00

MY SECRET AFFAIR
**Hero Books
(Fox Features Syndicate),
Dec., 1949**
1 WW,SHn,My Stormy
Love Affair 250.00
2 WW,I Loved a Weakling 200.00
3 WW, April, 1950 . . . . 235.00

MY SECRET LIFE
**Fox Features Syndicate,
July, 1949**
22 I Loved More Than Once 150.00
23 WW 200.00
24 Love Was a Habit 100.00
25 . . . . 100.00
Becomes:

ROMEO TUBBS
Dec., 1952
26 WW,That Lovable Teen-ager . 250.00

MY SECRET LOVE
See: PHANTOM LADY

MY SECRET MARRIAGE
**Superior Comics,
May, 1953**
1 I Was a Cheat 150.00
2 . . . . 75.00
3 We Couldn't Wait 60.00
4 . . . . 60.00
5 . . . . 60.00
6 . . . . 60.00
7 thru 23 . . . . @60.00
24 1956 . . . . 60.00

MY SECRET ROMANCE
**Hero Books
(Fox Features Syndicate),
Jan., 1950**
1 WW,They Called Me 'That'
Woman 150.00
2 WW,They Called Me Cheap . . 200.00

MYSTERIES WEIRD AND STRANGE
**Superior Comics/
Dynamic Publ., May, 1953**
1 The Stolen Brain 500.00
2 The Screaming Room,
Atomic Bomb 350.00
3 SD,The Avenging Corpse 300.00
4 SD,Ghost on the Gallows 300.00
5 SD,Horror a la Mode 300.00
6 SD,Howling Horror 300.00
7 SD,Demon in Disguise 200.00
8 SD,The Devil's Birthmark 200.00
9 SD 200.00
10 SD 300.00
11 SD 300.00

*Mysterious Adventures #5
© Story Comics*

MYSTERIOUS ADVENTURES
**Story Comics,
March, 1951**
1 Wild Terror of the
Vampire Flag 900.00
2 Terror of the Ghoul's Corpse . 450.00
3 Terror of the Witche's Curse . . 400.00
4 The Little Coffin That Grew . . . 400.00
5 LC,Curse of the Jungle,
Bondage(c) 450.00
6 LC,Ghostly Terror in the
Cave 400.00
7 LC,Terror of the Ghostly
Castle 500.00
8 Terror of the Flowers of Deat. . 650.00
9 The Ghostly Ghouls-
Extreme Violence 450.00
10 Extreme Violence 400.00
11 The Trap of Terror 450.00
12 SHn,Vultures of Death-
Extreme Violence 450.00
13 Extreme Violence 450.00
14 Horror of the Flame Thrower
Extreme Violence 450.00
15 DW,Ghoul Crazy 500.00

All comics prices listed are for *Near Mint* condition.   **CVA Page 437**

16 Chilling Tales of Horror 500.00
17 DW,Bride of the Dead. 500.00
18 Extreme Violence 500.00
19 The Coffin 500.00
20 Horror o/t Avenging Corpse . . 500.00
21 Mother Ghoul's Nursery
   Tales, Bondage (c) 500.00
22 RA,Insane 400.00
23 RA,Extreme Violence 400.00
24 KS, ... 350.00
25 KS,Aug., 1955. . . . . 350.00

HORROR FROM
THE TOMB
Premier Magazines,
Sept., 1954
1 AT,GWb,The Corpse Returns . 500.00
Becomes:
MYSTERIOUS STORIES
Dec., 1954–Jan., 1955
2 GWb(c),Eternal Life 600.00
3 GWb,The Witch Doctor 350.00
4 That's the Spirit 325.00
5 King Barbarossa 325.00
6 GWb,Strangers in the Night. . . 350.00
7 KS,The Pipes of Pan;Dec'55 . . 325.00

MYSTERIOUS TRAVELER
COMICS
Trans-World Publications,
Nov., 1948
1 BP,BP(c),Five Miles Down. . . . 700.00

MYSTERY COMICS
William H. Wise & Co., 1944
1 AS(c),B:Brad Spencer-Wonderman,
   King of Futeria,The Magnet, Zudo-
   Jungle Boy,Silver Knight. . . 1,500.00
2 AS(c),Bondage (c) 900.00
3 AS(c),Robot(c),LanceLewis,B . 800.00
4 AS(c),E:All Features,
   KKK Type(c) 800.00

MYSTERY MEN COMICS
Fox Features Syndicate,
Aug., 1939
1 GT,DBr,LF(c),Bondage(c);I:Blue
   Beetle,Green Mask,Rex Dexter
   of Mars,Zanzibar,Lt.Drake,D-13
   Secret Agent,Chen Chang,
   Wing Turner,Capt. Denny 15,000.00
2 GT,BP,DBr,LF(c),
   Rex Dexter (c) 5,000.00
3 LF(c) 6,000.00
4 LF(c),B:Captain Savage 3,500.00
5 GT,BP,LF(c),Green Mask (c) 3,500.00
6 GT,BP 3,000.00
7 GT,BP,Bondage(c),
   Blue Beetle(c). 3,500.00
8 GT,BP,LF(c),Bondage(c),
   Blue Beetle 3,200.00
9 GT,BP,DBr(c),B:The Moth . . . 1,500.00
10 GT,BP,JSm(c),A:Wing
   Turner; Bondage(c) 1,400.00
11 GT,BP,JSm(c),I:The Domino 1,400.00
12 GT,BP,JSm(c),BlueBeetle(c) 1,400.00
13 GT,I:The Lynx & Blackie . . . 1,000.00
14 GT,Male Bondage (c) 950.00
15 GT,Blue Beetle(c). 900.00
16 GT,Hypo(c),MaleBondage(c) . 950.00
17 GT,BP,Blue Beetle (c) 900.00
18 GT,Blue Beetle (c). 900.00
19 GT,I&B:Miss X 1,000.00
20 GT,DBr,Blue Beetle (c) 900.00
21 GT,E:Miss X 900.00
22 GT,CCu(c),Blue Beetle (c) . . . 900.00

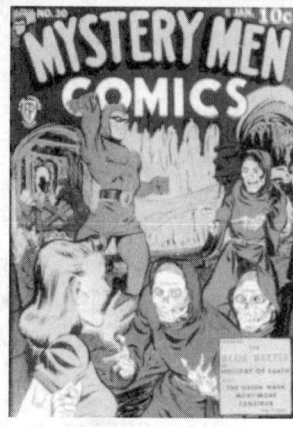

Mystery Men Comics #30
© Fox Features Syndicate

23 GT,Blue Beetle (c). 900.00
24 GT,BP,DBr, Blue Beetle (c) . . . 900.00
25 GT,Bondage(c);
   A:Private O'Hara 950.00
26 GT,Bondage(c);B:The Wraith . 950.00
27 GT,Bondage(c),BlueBeetle(c) . 950.00
28 GT,Bondage(c);Satan's
   Private Needlewoman. 950.00
29 GT,Bondage(c),Blue
   Beetle (c). 950.00
30 Holiday of Death 900.00
31 Bondage(c);Feb'42 . . . . 950.00

MY STORY
See: ZAGO, JUNGLE
PRINCE

NATIONAL COMICS
Comics Magazines
(Quality Comics Group),
July, 1940
1 GT,HcK,LF(c),B:Uncle Sam,Wonder
   Boy,Merlin the Magician,Cyclone,
   Kid Patrol,Sally O'Neil-Police-
   woman, Pen Miller,Prop
   Powers, Paul Bunyan . . . 8,000.00
2 WE,GT,HcK,LF&RC(c) 3,500.00
3 GT,HcK,WE&RC(c) 2,400.00
4 GT,HcK,LF&RC(c),E:Cyclone;
   Torpedo Islands of Death . . 1,900.00
5 GT,LF&RC(c),B:Quicksilver;
   O:Uncle Sam 2,500.00
6 GT,LF&RC(c) 1,800.00
7 GT,LF&RC(c) 2,900.00
8 GT,LF&RC(c) 1,800.00
9 JCo,LF&RC(c) 1,800.00
10 RC,JCo,LF&RC(c) 1,800.00
11 RC,JCo,LF&RC(c) 1,800.00
12 RC,JCo,LF&RC(c) 1,500.00
13 RC,JCo,LF,LF&RC(c). 1,400.00
14 RC,JCo,LF,PG,LF&RC(c). . 1,400.00
15 RC,JCo,LF,PG,LF&RC(c). . 1,400.00
16 RC,JCo,LF,PG,LF&RC(c). . 1,400.00
17 RC,JCo,LF,PG,LF&RC(c). . 1,000.00
18 JCo,LF,PG,LF&RC(c),
   Pearl Harbor. 1,700.00
19 JCo,LF,PG,RC(c),The Black
   Fog Mystery 1,000.00
20 JCo,LF,PG,LF&RC(c) 1,000.00
21 LF,JCo,PG,LF(c). 1,000.00
22 JCo,LF,PG,FG,GFx,LF(c),
   E:Jack & Jill,Pen Miller,
   Paul Bunyan. 1,000.00

23 JCo,PG,FG,GFx,AMc,LF
   & GFx(c),B:The Unknown,
   Destroyer 171 . . . . 1,100.00
24 JCo,PG,RC,AMc,FG,
   GFx,RC(c) 1,100.00
25 AMc,RC,JCo,PG,FG,
   GFx,RC(c) 750.00
26 AMc,Jco,RC,PG,RC(c),
   E:Prop Powers,WonderBoy. . 750.00
27 JCo,AMc 750.00
28 JCo,AMc 750.00
29 JCo,O:The Unknown;U.Sam
   V:Dr. Dirge. 775.00
30 JCo,RC(c) 750.00
31 JCo,RC(c) 600.00
32 JCo,RC(c) 600.00
33 JCo,GFx,RC(c),B:Chic Carter;
   U.Sam V:Boss Spring 600.00
34 JCo,GFx,U.Sam V:Big John
   Fales 600.00
35 JCo,GFx,E:Kid Patrol 500.00
36 JCo 500.00
37 JCo,FG,A:The Vagabond 500.00
38 JCo,FG,Boat of the Dead 500.00
39 JCo,FG,Hitler(c);U.Sam
   V:The Black Market. 600.00
40 JCo,FG,U.Sam V:The
   Syndicate of Crime 450.00
41 JCo,FG 450.00
42 JCo,FG,JCo(c),B:The Barker . 300.00
43 JCo,FG,JCo(c) 300.00
44 JCo,FG 300.00
45 JCo,FG,E:Merlin the Magician 300.00
46 JCo,JCo(c),Murder is no Joke 300.00
47 JCo,JCo(c),E:Chic Carter 300.00
48 JCo,O:The Whistler 300.00
49 JCo,JCo(c),A Corpse
   for a Cannonball 300.00
50 JCo,JCo(c),V:Rocks Myzer . . 300.00
51 JCo,BWa,JCo(c),
   A:Sally O'Neil 350.00
52 JCo,A Carnival of Laughs. . . . 250.00
53 PG,V:Scramolo 250.00
54 PG,V:Raz-Ma-Taz 250.00
55 JCo,AMc,V:The Hawk. 250.00
56 GFx,JCo,AMc,V:The Grifter . . 250.00
57 GFX,JCo,AMc,V:Witch Doctor 250.00
58 GFz,JCo,AMc,Talking Animals 250.00
59 GFx,JCo,AMc,V:The Birdman. 250.00
60 GFx,JCo,AMc,V:Big Ed Grew 250.00
61 GFx,AMc,Trouble Comes in
   Small Packages. 200.00
62 GFx,AMc,V:Crocodile Man . . . 200.00
63 GFx,AMc,V:Bearded Lady . . . 200.00
64 GFx,V:The Human Fly 200.00

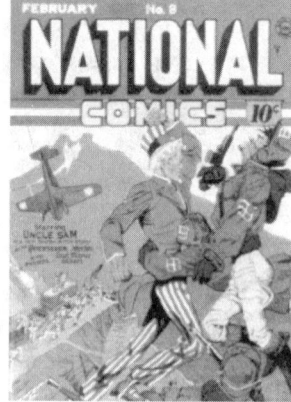

National Comics #8
© Quality Comics Group

65 GFx,GFx(c)V:The King 200.00
66 GFx,GFx(c)V:THe Man Who
    Hates the Circus 200.00
67 GFx,Gfx(c),A:Quicksilver;
    V:Ali Ben Riff Raff 200.00
68 GFx,GFx(c),V:Leo theLionMan 200.00
69 GFx,Gfx(c),A:Percy the
    Powerful. 200.00
70 GFx,GFx(c),Barker Tires
    of the Big Top 200.00
71 PG,GFx(c),V:SpellbinderSmith 200.00
72 PG,GFx(c),The Oldest Man
    in the World 200.00
73 PG,GFx(c),V:A CountrySlicker 200.00
74 PG,GFx(c),V:Snake Oil Sam. . 200.00
75 PG,GFx(c),Barker Breakes the
    Bank at Monte Marlo;Nov'49. 200.00

NEBBS, THE
Dell Publishing Co., 1941
1 rep. 150.00

NEGRO ROMANCE
**Fawcett Publications,
June, 1950**
1 GE,Ph(c), Love's Decoy 1,600.00
2 GE,Ph(c), A Tragic Vow 1,200.00
3 GE,Ph(c), My Love
    Betrayed Me 1,200.00
Charlton Comics
4 Rep.FawcettEd.#2;May,1955 1,000.00

NEW ROMANCES
**Standard Comics,
May, 1951**
5 Ph(c), The Blame I Bore 150.00
6 Ph(c), No Wife Was I 90.00
7 Ph(c), My Runaway Heart,
    Ray Miland 75.00
8 Ph(c) 75.00
9 Ph(c) 75.00
10 ATh,Ph(c) 100.00
11 ATh,Ph(c) of Elizabeth Taylor . 250.00
12 Ph(c) 75.00
13 Ph(c) 75.00
14 ATh,Ph(c) 100.00
15 Ph(c) 75.00
16 ATh,Ph(c) 100.00
17 Ath, ... 100.00
18 and 19 . . . . @75.00
20 GT, ... 75.00
21 April, 1954. . . . . 75.00

NICKEL COMICS
Dell Publishing Co., 1938
1 Bobby & Chip 1,000.00

NICKEL COMICS
**Fawcett Publications,
May, 1940**
1 JaB(c),O&I: Bulletman 6,000.00
2 JaB(c), ... 1,800.00
3 JaB(c), ... 1,400.00
4 JaB(c), B: Red Gaucho 1,300.00
5 CCB(c),Bondage(c) 1,300.00
6 and 7 CCB(c) . . . . @1,200.00
8 CCB(c),Aug. 23, 1940,
    World's Fair 1,300.00

NIGHTMARE
See: WEIRD HORRORS

NIGHTMARE
Ziff-Davis Publishing Co.
1 EK,GT,P(c),The Corpse That
    Wouldn't Stay Dead 750.00
2 EK,P(c),Vampire Mermaid . . . 500.00
St. John Publishing Co.
3 EK,P(c),The Quivering Brain . 400.00
4 P(c),1953 . . . . 350.00

NORTHWEST MOUNTIES
**Jubilee Publications/
St. John Publ. Co.,
Oct., 1948**
1 MB,BLb(c),Rose of the Yukon 600.00
2 MB,BLb(c),A:Ventrilo 500.00
3 MB, Bondage(c) 550.00
4 MB(c),A:Blue Monk,July'49 . 450.00

NURSERY RHYMES
Ziff-Davis Publishing Co., 1950
1 How John Came Clean 175.00
2 The Old Woman Who
    Lived in a Shoe 175.00

NUTS!
**Premere Comics Group,
March, 1954**
1 . . . . 350.00
2 . . . . 250.00
3 Mention of "Reefers" 275.00
4 . . . . 250.00
5 Captain Marvel Spoof;Nov.'54 250.00

NUTTY COMICS
**Fawcett Publications,
Winter, 1946**
1 (fa),F:Capt. Kid,Richard Richard,
    Joe Miller...Among others . . . 150.00

NUTTY LIFE
See: PHANTOM LADY

NYOKA THE
JUNGLE GIRL
**Fawcett Publications,
Winter, 1945**
1 Bondage(c);Partial Ph(c) of
    Kay Aldridge as Nyoka 750.00

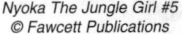

*Nyoka The Jungle Girl #5
© Fawcett Publications*

2 . . . . 400.00
3 . . . . 400.00
4 Bondage(c) 400.00
5 Barbacosi Madness;
    Bondage(c) 400.00
6 . . . . 275.00
7 North Pole Jungle;Bondage(c) 250.00
8 Bondage(c) 250.00
9 . . . . 225.00
10 . . . . 225.00
11 Danger! Death! in an
    Unexplored Jungle 225.00
12 . . . . 200.00
13 The Human Leopards 225.00
14 The Mad Witch Doctor;
    Bondage(c) 225.00
15 Sacred Goat of Kristan 200.00
16 BK,The Vultures of Kalahari . . 225.00
17 BK 225.00
18 BK,The Art of Murder 225.00
19 The Elephant Battle 225.00
20 Explosive Volcano Action . . . 225.00
21 . . . . 150.00
22 The Weird Monsters 150.00
23 Danger in Duplicate 150.00
24 The Human Jaguar;
    Bondage(c) 150.00
25 Hand Colored Ph(c) 135.00
26 A Jungle Stampede 135.00
27 Adventure Laden. 135.00
28 The Human Statues of
    the Jungle 135.00
29 Ph(c) 135.00
30 Ph(c) 135.00
31 thru 40 Ph(c) . . . . @125.00
41 thru 50 Ph(c) . . . . @135.00
51 thru 59 Ph(c) . . . . @75.00
60 Ph(c) 75.00
61 Ph(c),The Sacred Sword of
    the Jungle 75.00
62 & 63 Ph(c) . . . . @75.00
64 Ph(c), The Jungle Idol 75.00
65 Ph(c) 75.00
66 Ph(c) 75.00
67 Ph(c), The Sky Man 75.00
68 thru 74 Ph(c) . . . . @75.00
75 Ph(c), The Jungle Myth
    of Terror 75.00
76 Ph(c) 75.00
77 Ph(c),The Phantoms of the
    Elephant Graveyard;Jun'53. . . 75.00

OAKY DOAKS
**Eastern Color Printing Co.,
July, 1942**
1 Humor Oriented 450.00

OH, BROTHER!
**Stanhall Publications,
Jan., 1953**
1 Bill Williams-a 75.00
2 thru 5 . . . . @50.00

OK COMICS
**United Features Syndicate,
July, 1940**
1 B:Pal Peyton,Little Giant, Phantom
    Knight,Sunset Smith,Teller Twins,
    Don Ramon, Jerrry Sly,Kip Jaxon,
    Leatherneck,Ulysses 1,000.00
2 Oct., 1940 . . . . 1,100.00

100 PAGES OF COMICS
Dell Publishing Co., 1937
101 Alley Oop,OG,Wash Tubbs,
    Tom Mix,Dan Dunn. 2,000.00

GOLDEN AGE

ON THE AIR
NBC Network Comics, 1947
1 Giveaway, no cover 275.00

ON THE SPOT
Fawcett Publications,
Autumn, 1948
N# Bondage(c),PrettyBoyFloyd . . 450.00

OPERATION PERIL
American Comics Group
(Michel Publ.),
Oct.–Nov., 1950
1 LSt,OW,OW(c),B:TyphoonTyler,
  DannyDanger,TimeTravellers 450.00
2 OW,OW(c),War (c). 275.00
3 OW,OW(c),Horror 250.00
4 OW,OW(c), Flying Saucers . . . 250.00
5 OW,OW(c), Science Fiction . . . 250.00
6 OW, Tyr. Rex 250.00
7 OW,OW(c),Sabretooth. 250.00
8 OW,OW(c) 225.00
9 OW,OW(c) 225.00
10 OW,OW(c),science fiction . . . 225.00
11 OW,OW(c), War 225.00
12 OW,OW(c),E:Time Travellers . 225.00
13 OW,OW(c),War Stories. 150.00
14 OW,OW(c),War Stories. 150.00
15 OW,OW(c),War Stories. 150.00
16 OW,OW(c),April–May,1953,
   War Stories 150.00

Our Flag Comics #2
© Ace Magazines

OUR FLAG COMICS
Ace Magazines,
Aug., 1941–April, 1942
1 MA,JM,B:Capt.Victory,Unknown
  Soldier,The Three Cheers . 3,700.00
2 JM,JM(c),O:The Flag 1,500.00
3 Tank Battle (c). 1,200.00
4 MA 1,200.00
5 I:Mr. Risk, Male Bondage . . . 1,200.00

OUR GANG COMICS
Dell Publishing Co.,
Sept.–Oct., 1942
1 WK,Barney Bear, Tom &
  Jerry 1,500.00
2 WK. 750.00
3 WK,Benny Burro 500.00
4 WK. 500.00

Our Gang #4
© Dell Publishing Co.

5 WK. 500.00
6 WK. 750.00
7 WK. 350.00
8 WK,CB,Benny Burro 900.00
9 WK,CB,Benny Burro 850.00
10 WK,CB,Benny Burro. 600.00
11 WK,I:Benny Bear 850.00
12 thru 20 WK . . . . @400.00
21 thru 29 WK . . . . @300.00
30 WK,Christmas(c). 250.00
31 thru 34 WK . . . . @250.00
35 WK,CB 200.00
36 WK,CB 200.00
37 thru 40 WK . . . . @125.00
41 thru 50 WK . . . . @100.00
51 thru 56 WK . . . . @100.00
57 . . . . 75.00
58 Our Gang 75.00
59 Our Gang 75.00
Becomes:

TOM AND JERRY
July, 1949
60 . . . . 175.00
61 . . . . 125.00
62 . . . . 100.00
63 . . . . 100.00
64 . . . . 100.00
65 . . . . 100.00
66 Christmas (c) 120.00
67 thru 70. . . . . @100.00
71 thru 76. . . . . @90.00
77 Christmas (c) 100.00
78 thru 80. . . . . @90.00
81 thru 89. . . . . @75.00
90 Christmas (c) 90.00
91 thru 99. . . . . @75.00
100 . . . . 90.00
101 thru 120. . . . . @60.00
121 thru 150. . . . . @50.00
151 thru 212. . . . . @40.00

OUR SECRET
See: MY SECRET

OUTLAWS
D.S. Publishing Co.,
Feb.–March, 1948
1 HcK,Western Crime Stories . . 400.00
2 Grl,Doc Dawson's Dilema . . . 400.00
3 Cougar City Cleanup 175.00
4 JO,Death Stakes A Claim 200.00
5 RJ,RJ(c),Man Who Wanted

Mexico 175.00
6 AMc,RJ,RJ(c),The Ghosts of
  Crackerbox Hill 175.00
7 Grl,Dynamite For Boss Cavitt . 300.00
8 Grl,The Gun & the Pen 300.00
9 FF,Shoot to Kill;June–
  July, 1949 . . . . 600.00

WHITE RIDER AND SUPER HORSE
Star Publications,
Sept., 1950
1 LbC(c) 200.00
2 LbC(c) 125.00
3 LbC(c) 125.00
4 LbC(c) 125.00
5 LbC(c),Stampede of Hard
  Riding Thrills 150.00
6 LbC(c),Drums of the Sioux . . . 150.00
Becomes:

INDIAN WARRIORS
June, 1951
7 LbC(c),Winter on the Great
  Plains 225.00
8 LbC(c) 200.00
Becomes:

WESTERN CRIME CASES
Dec., 1951
9 LbC(c),The Card Sharp Killer . 250.00
Becomes:

OUTLAWS, THE
May, 1952
10 LbC(c),Federated Express . . . 250.00
11 LbC(c),Frontier Terror!!!. 200.00
12 LbC(c),Ruthless Killer!!! 200.00
13 LbC(c),The Grim Avengers. . . 200.00
14 AF,JKa,LbC(c),Trouble in
  Dark Canyon,April, 1954. . . . 200.00

OUT OF THE NIGHT
American Comics Group/
Best Synd. Feature,
Feb.–March, 1952
1 AW 900.00
2 AW 600.00
3 . . . . 350.00
4 AW 500.00
5 . . . . 350.00
6 The Ghoul's Revenge 350.00
7 . . . . 350.00
8 The Frozen Ghost 350.00
9 Death Has Wings,
  Science Fiction 350.00
10 Ship of Death 350.00
11 . . . . 275.00
12 Music for the Dead 275.00
13 HN,From the Bottom of
  the Well 275.00
14 Out of the Screen 275.00
15 The Little Furry Thing 250.00
16 Nightmare From the Past 250.00
17 The Terror of the Labyrinth . . . 250.00
Becomes:

HOODED HORSEMAN
Dec., 1954–Jan., 1955
18 B: The Hooded Horseman . . . 125.00
19 The Horseman's Strangest
  Adventure 175.00
20 OW,O:Johnny Injun. 125.00
21 OW,OW(c). 175.00
22 OW 125.00
23 . . . . 125.00
24 . . . . 125.00
25 . . . . 100.00

26 O&I:Cowboy Sahib 125.00
27 Jan.–Feb., 1953 . . . . 110.00

OUT OF THE SHADOWS
Visual Editions
(Standard Comics),
July, 1952–Aug., 1954
5 ATh,GT,The Shoremouth
　　Horror 750.00
6 ATh,JKz,Salesman of Death . . 500.00
7 JK,Plant of Death 350.00
8 Mask of Death 625.00
9 RC,Till Death Do Us Part 350.00
10 MS,We Vowed,Till Death
　　Do Us Part. 350.00
11 ATh,Fountain of Fear. 350.00
12 ATh,Hand of Death 500.00
13 MS,The Cannibal 350.00
14 ATh,The Werewolf. 350.00

OXYDOL-DREFT
Giveaways, 1950
The Set is More Valuable if the
Original Envelope is Present
1 L'il Abner 150.00
2 Daisy Mae 150.00
3 Shmoo 175.00
4 AW&FF(c),John Wayne 200.00
5 Archie 175.00
6 Terry Toons Comics 150.00

OZZIE AND BABS
Fawcett Publications,
Winter, 1946
1 Humor Oriented, Teenage 90.00
2 Humor Oriented 50.00
3 Humor Oriented 40.00
4 Humor Oriented 40.00
5 Humor Oriented 40.00
6 Humor Oriented 40.00
7 Humor Oriented 40.00
8 Humor Oriented 40.00
9 Humor Oriented 40.00
10 Humor Oriented 40.00
11 Humor Oriented 40.00
12 Humor Oriented 40.00
13 Humor Oriented;1949 . . . . . . 40.00

PAGEANT OF COMICS
St. John Publishing Co.,
Sept., 1947
1 Rep. Mopsy 100.00
2 Rep. Jane Arden,Crime
　　Reporter. 100.00

PANHANDLE PETE
AND JENNIFER
J. Charles Lave
Publishing Co., July, 1951
1 (fa) 100.00
2 (fa) 60.00
3 (fa),Nov.'51 . . . . 60.00

PANIC
Tiny Tot Publications
(E.C. Comics), March, 1954
"Humor in a Jugular Vein"
1 BE,JKa,JO,JDa,AF(c) 500.00
2 BE,JO,WW,JDa,A:Bomb 250.00
3 BE,JO,BW,WW,JDa,AF(c) . . . 200.00
4 BE,JO,WW,JDa,BW(c),
　　Infinity(c) 200.00
5 BE,JO,WW,JDa,AF(c) 150.00

6 BE,JO,WW,JDa,Blank (c) 150.00
7 BE,JO,WW,JDa 150.00
8 BE,JO,WW,JDa,Eye Chart (c) . 150.00
9 BE,JO,WW,JDa,Ph(c),
　　Confidential(c) 150.00
10 BE,JDa, Postal Package(c) . . 150.00
11 BE,WW,JDa,Wheaties parody
　　as Weedies (c) 150.00
12 BE,WW,JDa,JDa(c);
　　Dec.–Jan., 1955–56 . . . . . . 200.00

PARAMOUNT
ANIMATED COMICS
Family Publications
(Harvey Publ.), June, 1953
1 (fa),B:Baby Herman & Katnip,
　　Baby Huey,Buzzy the Crow . 275.00
2 (fa) 125.00
3 (fa) 100.00
4 (fa) 100.00
5 (fa) 100.00
6 (fa) 100.00
7 (fa), Baby Huey (c) 250.00
8 (fa), Baby Huey (c) 75.00
9 (fa), Infinity(c),Baby Huey (c). . 75.00
10 thru 21 (fa),Baby Huey(c) . . . @75.00
22 (fa), July, 1956, Baby Huey (c) . 75.00

PAROLE BREAKERS
Avon Periodicals/Realistic,
Dec., 1951–July, 1952
1 P(c),Hellen Willis,Gun
　　Crazed Gun Moll 550.00
2 JKu,P(c),Vinnie Sherwood,
　　The Racket King 400.00
3 EK(c),John "Slicer" Berry,
　　Hatchetman of Crime 350.00

PATCHES
Rural Home Publ./
Patches Publ.,
March–April, 1945
1 LbC(c),Imagination In Bed(c). . 500.00
2 Dance (c) 200.00
3 Rocking Horse (c) 150.00
4 Music Band (c). 150.00
5 LbC(c),A:Danny Kaye,Football 250.00
6 A: Jackie Kelk 150.00
7 A: Hopalong Cassidy 225.00
8 A: Smiley Burnettte 150.00
9 BK,A: Senator Claghorn 150.00
10 A: Jack Carson 150.00
11 A: Red Skeleton; Dec'47. . . . 200.00

PAWNEE BILL
Story Comics,
Feb.–July, 1951
1 A:Bat Masterson,Wyatt Earp,
　　Indian Massacre
　　at Devil's Gulch 125.00
2 Blood in Coffin Canyon 75.00
3 LC,O:Golden Warrior,Fiery
　　Arrows at Apache Pass 75.00

PAY-OFF
D.S. Publishing Co.,
July–Aug., 1948–
March–April, 1949
1 True Crime 1 & 2 . . . . 300.00
2 The Pennsylvania Blue-Beard 175.00
3 The Forgetful Forger 150.00
4 RJ(c),Lady and the Jewels . . . 150.00
5 The Beautiful Embezzeler 150.00

PEDRO
Fox Features Syndicate,
Jan., 1950
1 WW,WW(c),Humor Oriented . 250.00
2 Aug., 1950 . . . . 175.00

PENNY
Avon Publications, 1947
1 The Slickest Chick of 'em All . 125.00
2 . . . . 75.00
3 America's Teen-age Sweetheart 75.00
4 . . . . 75.00
5 . . . . 75.00
6 Perry Como Ph(c),Sept.–
　　Oct., 1949 . . . . 100.00

PEP COMICS
MJL Magazines/
Archie Publications,
Jan., 1940
1 IN,JCo,MMe,IN(c),I:Shield,
　　O:Comet,Queen of Diamonds,
　　B:The Rocket,Press Guardian,
　　Sergeant Boyle Chang,Bently
　　of Scotland Yard 15,000.00
2 CBi,JCo,IN,IN(c),O:Rocket . . 3,500.00
3 JCo,IN,IN(c),Shield (c) 2,500.00
4 Cbi,JCo,MMe,IN,IN(c),
　　C:Wizard(not Gareb) 2,000.00
5 Cbi,JCo,MMe,IN,IN(c),
　　C:Wizard. 2,000.00
6 IN,IN(c), Shield (c) 1,500.00
7 IN,IN(c),Bondage(c),Shield(c)1,500.00
8 JCo,IN, Shield (c) 1,500.00
9 IN, Shield (c). 1,500.00
10 IN,IN(c), Shield (c). 1,500.00
11 MMe,IN,IN(c),I:Dusty,
　　Boy Detective 1,600.00
12 IN,IN(c),O:Fireball
　　Bondage(c), E:Rocket,
　　Queen of Diamonds 1,800.00
13 IN,IN(c),Bondage(c). 1,200.00
14 IN,IN(c). 1,200.00
15 IN,Bondage(c) 1,200.00
16 IN,O:Madam Satan 2,000.00
17 IN,IN(c),O:Hangman,
　　D:Comet 4,800.00
18 IN,IN(c),Bondage(c) 1,200.00
19 IN 1,200.00
20 IN,IN(c),E:Fireball 1,200.00
21 IN,IN(c),Bondage(c),
　　E: Madam Satan. 1,200.00

Pep #16
© Archie Publications

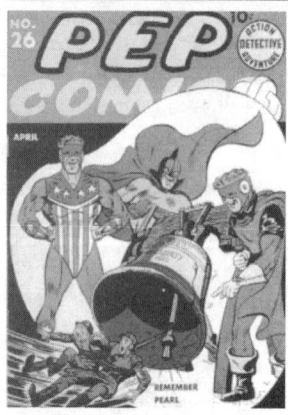

Pep Comics #26
© *Archie Publications*

22 IN,IN(c)I:Archie,
  Jughead, Betty 21,000.00
23 IN,IN(c). 2,200.00
24 IN,IN(c). 1,500.00
25 IN,IN(c). 1,500.00
26 IN,IN(c),I:Veronica 2,200.00
27 IN,IN(c),Bill of Rights (c) . . . 1,500.00
28 IN,IN(c), V:Capt. Swastika . . 1,500.00
29 ASH (c) 1,500.00
30 B:Capt.Commando 1,500.00
31 Bondage(c) 1,500.00
32 Bondage(c) 1,100.00
33 . . . . 1,100.00
34 Bondage(c) 1,100.00
35 . . . . 1,100.00
36 1st Archie(c). 2,500.00
37 Bondage(c) 750.00
38 ASH(c). 700.00
39 ASH(c), Human Shield 700.00
40 . . . . 700.00
41 2nd Archie; I:Jughead. 500.00
42 F:Archie & Jughead 500.00
43 F:Archie & Jughead 500.00
44 . . . . 500.00
45 . . . . 500.00
46 . . . . 500.00
47 E:Hangman,Infinity(c) 500.00
48 B:Black Hood 500.00
49 . . . . 500.00
50 . . . . 500.00
51 . . . . 350.00
52 B:Suzie 350.00
53 . . . . 350.00
54 E:Captain Commando 350.00
55 . . . . 350.00
56 thru 58 . . . . @300.00
59 E:Suzie 300.00
60 B:Katy Keene 300.00
61 . . . . 275.00
62 I L'il Jinx 275.00
63 . . . . 275.00
64 . . . . 275.00
65 E:Shield. 275.00
66 thru 71. . . . . @150.00
72 thru 80. . . . . @125.00
81 thru 90 . . . . @100.00
91 thru 99. . . . . @100.00
100 . . . . 150.00
101 thru 110 . . . . @100.00
111 thru 120 . . . . @75.00
121 thru 130 . . . . @60.00
131 thru 140. . . . . @50.00
141 thru 150. . . . . @40.00
151 thru 160,A:Super Heroes . . @40.00
161 thru 200. . . . . @35.00
201 thru 250. . . . . @20.00

251 thru 300 . . . . @20.00
301 thru 350 . . . . @20.00
351 thru 411 . . . . @10.00

PERFECT CRIME, THE
Cross Publications,
Oct., 1949

1 BP,DW 400.00
2 BP 200.00
3 . . . . 175.00
4 BP 175.00
5 DW 175.00
6 . . . . 175.00
7 B:Steve Duncan 175.00
8 Drug Story 200.00
9 . . . . 175.00
10 . . . . 175.00
11 Bondage (c) 200.00
12 . . . . 175.00
13 . . . . 175.00
14 Poisoning (c). 175.00
15 'The Most Terrible Menace',
  Drug. 200.00
16 . . . . 150.00
17 . . . . 150.00
18 Drug (c). 275.00
19 . . . . 150.00
20 thru 25. . . . . @125.00
26 Drug w/ Hypodermic (c) 250.00
27 . . . . 150.00
28 . . . . 150.00
29 . . . . 150.00
30 E:Steve Duncan, Rope
  Strangulation (c) 300.00
31 . . . . 125.00
32 . . . . 125.00
33 . . . . 125.00

PERFECT LOVE
Approved Comics(Ziff-Davis)/
St. John Publ. Co.,
Aug.–Sept., 1951

1 (10),P(c),Our Kiss was a
  Prelude to Love Adrift 250.00
2 . . . . 150.00
3 P(c) 100.00
4 . . . . 100.00
5 . . . . 100.00
6 . . . . 100.00
7 . . . . 100.00
8 EK 125.00
9 EK,P(c) 100.00
10 Ph(c), Dec '53. . . . . 100.00

PERSONAL LOVE
Famous Funnies, Jan., 1950

1 Ph(c) Are You in Love 225.00
2 Ph(c) Serenade for Suzette
  Mario Lanzo. 125.00
3 Ph(c) 100.00
4 Ph(c) 100.00
5 Ph(c) 100.00
6 Ph(c) Be Mine Forever 110.00
7 Ph(c) You'll Always Be
  Mine, Robert Walker 110.00
8 EK,Ph(c),Esther Williams &
  Howard Keel 125.00
9 EK,Ph(c),Debra Paget & Louis
  Jordan 125.00
10 Ph(c),Loretta Young
  Joseph Cotton 100.00
11 ATh, Ph(c),Gene Tierney &
  Glenn Ford 150.00
12 Ph(c) Jane Greer &
  William Lundigan 100.00
13 Ph(c) Debra Paget &
  Louis Jordan 100.00

14 Ph(c) Kirk Douglas &
  Patrice Wymore 110.00
15 Ph(c) Dale Robertson &
  Joanne Dru 75.00
16 Ph(c) Take Back Your Love . . 75.00
17 Ph(c) My Cruel Deception . . . 75.00
18 Ph(c) Gregory Peck &
  Susan Hayward 90.00
19 Ph(c) Anthony Quinn. 90.00
20 Ph(c) The Couple in the
  Next Apartment, Bob Wagner . 90.00
21 Ph(c) I'll Make You Care. 85.00
22 Ph(c) Doorway To Heartbreak . 85.00
23 Ph(c) SaveMe from that Man . 85.00
24 FF, Ph(c) Tyrone Power 500.00
25 FF, Ph(c) The Dark Light . . . 500.00
26 Ph(c) Love Needs A Break . . . 75.00
27 FF, Ph(c) Champ or Chump? . 500.00
28 FF, Ph(c) A Past to Forget . . 500.00
29 Ph(c) Charlton Heston 90.00
30 Ph(c) The Lady is Lost 75.00
31 Ph(c) Marlon Brando. 125.00
32 FF, Ph(c) The Torment,
  Kirk Douglas 700.00
33 Ph(c) June, 1955 . . . . 75.00

PETER COTTONTAIL
Key Publications,
Jan., 1954

1 No 3-D (fa) 100.00
1 Feb '54 3-D (fa) 250.00
2 Rep of 3-D #1,not in 3-D 50.00

PETER PAUL'S 4 IN 1
JUMBO COMIC BOOK
Capitol Stories, 1953

1 F: Racket Squad in Action,
  Space Adventures,Crime &
  Justice,Space Western 500.00

PETER PENNY AND HIS
MAGIC DOLLAR
American Bakers Assn., 1947

1 History from Colonial
  America to the 1950's 200.00
2 . . . . 125.00

PETER RABBIT
Avon Periodicals, 1947

1 H. Cady art 450.00
2 H. Cady art 275.00
3 H. Cady art 250.00
4 H. Cady art 250.00
5 H. Cady art 250.00
6 H. Cady art 250.00
7 thru 10 . . . . @60.00
11 . . . . 60.00

KRAZY LIFE
Fox Features Syndicate, 1945

1 (fa) 100.00
Becomes:

NUTTY LIFE
Summer, 1946

2 (fa) 75.00
Becomes:

WOTALIFE
Fox Features Synd./
Green Publ., Aug.–Sept., 1946

3 (fa)B:L'il Pan,Cosmo Cat 100.00
4 . . . . 75.00
5 thru 11 . . . . @60.00
12 July, 1947 . . . . 60.00
Becomes:

PHANTOM LADY
Fox Features Syndicate, Aug., 1947
13(#1) MB,MB(c) Knights of
the Crooked Cross 6,000.00
14(#2) MB,MB(c) Scoundrels
and Scandals 3,300.00
15 MB,MB(c) The Meanest
Crook In the World 3,200.00
16 MB,MB(c) Claa Peete The
Beautiful Beast, Negligee.. 3,200.00
17 MB.MB(c) The Soda Mint
Killer, Bondage (c) 8,000.00
18 MB,MB(c) The Case of
Irene Shroeder 2,500.00
19 MB,MB(c) The Case of
the Murderous Model 2,500.00
20 MB,MB(c) Ace of Spades... 2,000.00
21 MB,MB(c)............... 1,800.00
22 MB,JKa 1,800.00
23 MB,JKa Bondage (c) 2,000.00

Phantom Lady #16
© Fox Feature Syndicate

Becomes:
MY LOVE SECRET
June, 1949
24 JKa, My Love Was For Sale.. 200.00
25 Second Hand Love 125.00
26 WW I Wanted Both Men..... 250.00
27 I Was a Love Cheat 100.00
28 WW, I Gave Him Love 200.00
29............................ 100.00
30 Ph(c)..................... 100.00

LINDA
Ajax/Farrell, April–May, 1954
1 .... 175.00
2 Lingerie section 150.00
3 .... 100.00
4 Oct.–Nov.,1954 .... 100.00
Becomes:
PHANTOM LADY
Dec., 1954–Jan., 1955
5(1) MB 1,500.00
2 Last Pre-Code Edition 1,250.00
3 Comics Code 1,000.00
4 Red Rocket,June, 1955 .... 1,000.00

PHIL RIZZUTO
Fawcett Publications, 1951
Ph(c) The Sensational Story of
The American Leagues MVP 950.00

PICTORIAL CONFESSIONS
St. John Publishing Co., Sept., 1949
1 MB,MB(c),I Threw Away My Reputation on a Worthless Love .. 350.00
2 MB,Ph(c) I Tried to be a
Hollywood Glamour Girl 250.00
3 JKY,MB,MB(c),They Caught
Me Cheating 300.00
Becomes:
PICTORIAL ROMANCES
Jan., 1950
4 Ph(c) MB, Trapped By Kisses
I Couldn't Resist 350.00
5 MB,MB(c)................. 300.00
6 MB,MB(c) I Was Too Free
With Boys 250.00
7 MB,MB(c) 250.00
8 MB,MB(c) I Made a
Sinful Bargain 250.00
9 MB,MB(c) Dishonest Love.... 250.00
10 MB,MB(c) I Was The
Other Woman 200.00
11 MB,MB(c) The Worst
Mistake A Wife Can Make... 225.00
12 MB,MB(c) Love Urchin 200.00
13 MB,MB(c) Temptations of a
Hatcheck Girl............. 200.00
14 MB,MB(c) I Was A
Gamblers Wife............ 200.00
15 MB,MB(c) Wife Without
Pride or Principles 200.00
16 MB,MB(c) The Truth of My
Affair With a Farm Boy 200.00
17 MB,MB(c) True Confessions
of a Girl in Love........... 300.00
18 MB,MB(c) 300.00
20 MB,MB(c) 300.00
21 MB,MB(c) 175.00
22 MB,MB(c) 175.00
23 MB,MB(c) 175.00
24 MB,MB(c) March,1954 ...... 175.00

PICTORIAL LOVE STORIES
St. John Publishing Co., Oct., 1952
1 MB,MB(c) I Lost My Head, My
Heart and My Resistance ... 350.00

PICTURE NEWS
299 Lafayette Street Corp., Jan., 1946–Jan.-Feb., 1947
1 Will The Atom Blow The
World Apart 500.00
2 Meet America's 1st Girl Boxing
Expert,Atomic Bomb 250.00
3 Hollywood's June Allison Shows
You How to be Beautiful,
Atomic Bomb............. 200.00
4 Amazing Marine Who Became
King of 10,000 Voodoos,
Atomic Bomb............. 225.00
5 G.I.Babies,Hank Greenberg... 200.00
6 Joe Louis(c) 225.00
7 Lovely Lady, Englands
Future Queen 175.00
8 Champion of them All 175.00
9 Bikini Atom Bomb,
Joe DiMaggio 200.00
10 Dick Quick, Ace Reporter,
Atomic Bomb............. 200.00

PICTURE STORIES FROM SCIENCE
Educational Comics, Spring, 1947
1 Understanding Air and Water . 350.00
2 Fall '47 Amazing Discoveries
About Food & Health....... 300.00

PICTURE STORIES FROM WORLD HISTORY
E.C. Comics, Spring, 1947
1 Ancient World to the
Fall of Rome 350.00
2 Europes Struggle for
Civilization 300.00

PINHEAD AND FOODINI
Fawcett Publications, July, 1951–Jan., 1952
1 Ph(c) 350.00
2 Ph(c) 200.00
3 Ph(c) Too Many Pinheads 150.00
4 Foodini's Talking Camel...... 150.00

PIN-UP PETE
Minoan Magazine Publishers, 1952
1 Loves of a GI Casanova 250.00

PIONEER PICTURE STORIES
Street & Smith, Dec., 1941
1 Red Warriors in Blackface.... 350.00
2 Life Story Of Errol Flynn 200.00
3 Success Stories of Brain
Muscle in Action 150.00
4 Legless Ace & Boy Commando
Raid Occupied France 150.00
5 How to Tell Uniform and
Rank of Any Navy Man 150.00
6 General Jimmy Doolittle 150.00
7 Life Story of Admiral Halsey .. 165.00
8 Life Story of Timoshenko 150.00
9 Dec., '43,Man Who Conquered
The Wild Frozen North 150.00

PIRACY
E.C. Comics, Oct.–Nov., 1954
1 WW,JDa,AW,WW(c),RC,AT .. 400.00
2 RC,JDa(c),WW,AW,AT....... 250.00
3 RC,GE, RC(c),Grl 225.00
4 RC,GE,RC(c),Grl 200.00
5 RC,GE,BK(c),Grl 200.00
6 JDa,RC,GE,BK(c),Grl 200.00
7 Oct Nov GE(c),RC,GE,Grl ... 200.00

PIRATES COMICS
Hillman Periodicals, Feb., 1950
1 .... 300.00
2 .... 200.00
3 .... 175.00
4 Aug–Sept., 1950 .... 175.00

PIXIES, THE
Magazine Enterprises, Winter, 1946
1 Mighty Atom.............. 100.00
2 .... 50.00
3 .... 35.00
4 .... 35.00

5 . . . . 40.00
Becomes:

MIGHTY ATOM, THE
1949
6 . . . . 40.00

PLANET COMICS
**Love Romance Publ.
(Fiction House Magazines),
Jan., 1940–Winter, 1953**
1 AB,DBR,HCk, Planet Comics,
  WE&LF,O:Aura,B:Flint Baker,
  Red Comet,Spurt Hammond,
  Capt. Nelson Cole 17,000.00
2 HcK,LF(c) 6,500.00
3 WE(c),HcK 4,000.00
4 HcK,B:Gale Allan and
  the Girl Squad 3,500.00
5 BP,HcK 3,200.00
6 BP,HcK,BP(c),The Ray
  Pirates of Venus 3,400.00
7 BP,AB,HcK,BP(c) B:Buzz
  Crandall Planet Payson . . . 3,000.00
8 BP,AB HcK 3,000.00
9 BP,AB,GT,HcK,B:Don
  Granville Cosmo Corrigan . 3,000.00
10 BP,AB,GT HcK 3,000.00
11 HcK, B:Crash Parker 3,000.00
12 Dri,B:Star Fighter 3,000.00
13 Dri,B:Reef Ryan 2,000.00
14 Dri B:Norge Benson 2,000.00
15 B: Mars,God of War 3,900.00
16 Invasion From The Void . . . 1,800.00
17 Warrior Maid of Mercury . . . 1,800.00
18 Bondage(c) 2,000.00
19 Monsters of the Inner World 1,800.00
20 RP, Winged Man Eaters
  of the Exile Star 1,800.00
21 RP,B:Lost World
  Hunt Bowman. 2,000.00
22 Inferno on the Fifth Moon . . 1,800.00
23 GT,Lizard Tyrant of
  the Twilight World 1,700.00
24 GT,Grl Raiders From
  The Red Moon 1,700.00
25 Grl,B:Norge Benson 1,700.00
26 Grl,B:The Space Rangers
  Bondage(c) 1,800.00
27 Grl, The Fire Eaters of
  Asteroid Z 1,500.00
28 Grl, Bondage (c) 1,700.00
29 Grl,Dragon Raiders of Aztla. 1,500.00
30 GT,Grl City of Lost Souls . . . 1,500.00
31 Grl,Fire Priests of Orbit6X . . 1,200.00
32 Slaver's Planetoid 1,300.00
33 MA 1,200.00
34 MA,Bondage 1,200.00
35 MA B:Mysta of The Moon . . 1,100.00
36 MA Collosus of the
  Blood Moon 1,100.00
37 MA, Behemoths of the
  Purple Void 1,100.00
38 MA 1,000.00
39 MA.Death Webs Of Zenith 3 1,000.00
40 Chameleon Men from
  Galaxy 9 . . . . 1,000.00
41 MA,Aaf,New O: Auro
  Bondage (c) 1,050.00
42 MA,AaF,E:Gale Allan 1,000.00
43 MA,AaF Death Rays
  From the Sun. 1,000.00
44 MA,Bbl,B:Futura 1,000.00
45 Ma,Bbl,Her Evilness
  from Xanado. 1,000.00
46 MA,Bbl,GE The Mecho-Men
  From Mars 1,000.00
47 MA,Bbl,GE,The Great
  Green Spawn. 900.00
48 MA,GE 900.00

Planet Comics #40
© Fiction House Magazines

49 MA,GE, Werewolves From
  Hydra Hell 900.00
50 MA,GE,The Things of Xeves . 900.00
51 MA,GE, Mad Mute X-Adapts . 800.00
52 GE,Mystery of the Time
  Chamber 800.00
53 MB,GE,Bondage(c)
  Dwarflings From Oceania . . . 800.00
54 MB,GE,Robots From Inferno . 800.00
55 MB,GE,Giants of the
  Golden Atom 800.00
56 MB,GE,Grl 750.00
57 MB,GE,Grl 750.00
58 MB,GE,Grl 750.00
59 MB,GE,Grl,LSe 750.00
60 GE,Grl,Vassals of Volta 750.00
61 GE,Grl, The Brute in the
  Bubble 650.00
62 GE,Musta,Moon Goddess . . . 650.00
63 GE,Paradise or Inferno. 650.00
64 GE,Monkeys From the Blue . 650.00
65 The Lost World 650.00
66 The Plague of the
  Locust Men 650.00
67 The Nymphs of Neptune. . . . 650.00
68 Synthoids of the 9th Moon . . 650.00
69 The Mentalists of Mars 650.00
70 Cargo For Amazonia. 650.00
71 Sandhogs of Mars. 500.00
72 Last Ship to Paradise 500.00
73 The Martian Plague 500.00

PLASTIC MAN
**Comics Magazines
(Quality Comics Group),
Summer, 1943–Nov., 1956**
1 JCo(a&c)Game of Death . . . 6,000.00
2 JCo(a&c)The Gay Nineties
  Nightmare. 2,500.00
3 JCo(a&c). 1,600.00
4 JCo(a&c). 1,300.00
5 JCo(a&c). 1,200.00
6 JCo(a&c) 800.00
7 JCo(a&c) 800.00
8 JCo(a&c). 800.00
9 JCo(a&c). 800.00
10 JCo(a&c). 800.00
11 JCo(a&c) 700.00
12 JCo(a&c),V:Spadehead 700.00
13 JCo(a&c),V:Mr.Hazard 700.00
14 JCo(a&c),Words,Symbol
  of Crime 700.00
15 JCo(a&c),V:BeauBrummel . . . 700.00

16 JCo(a&c),Money
  Means Trouble. 700.00
17 JCo(a&c),A:The Last
  Man on Earth. 700.00
18 JCo(a&c),Goes Back
  to the Farm 700.00
19 JCo(a&c),V:Prehistoric
  Plunder 700.00
20 JCo(a&c),A:Sadly,Sadly 700.00
21 JCo(a&c),V:Crime Minded
  Mind Reader 600.00
22 JCo(a&c), Which Twin
  is the Phony. 600.00
23 JCo(a&c),The Fountain
  of Age 600.00
24 JCo(a&c),The Black Box
  of Terror 600.00
25 JCo(a&c),A:Angus
  MacWhangus 600.00
26 JCo(a&c),On the Wrong
  Side of the Law? 600.00
27 JCo(a&c),V:The Leader 600.00
28 JCo(a&c),V:Shasta 600.00
29 JCo(a&c),V:Tricky Toledo . . . 600.00
30 JCo(a&c),V:Weightless
  Wiggins 600.00
31 JCo(a&c),V:Raka the
  Witch Doctor 450.00
32 JCo(a&c),V:Mr.Fission 450.00
33 JCo(a&c),V:The Mad
  Professor 450.00
34 JCo(a&c),Smuggler'sHaven . . 450.00
35 JCo(a&c),V:The Hypnotist . . . 450.00
36 JCo(a&c),The Uranium
  Underground 450.00
37 JCo(a&c),V:Gigantic Ants 450.00
38 JCo(a&c),The Curse of
  Monk Mauley. 450.00
39 JCo(a&c),The Stairway
  to Madness 450.00
40 JCo(a&c),The Ghoul of
  Ghost Swamp 450.00
41 JCo(a&c),The Beast with
  the Bloody Claws. 350.00
42 JCo(a&c),The King of
  Thunderbolts 350.00
43 JCo(a&c),The Evil Terror . . . 350.00
44 JCo(a&c),The Magic Cup . . . 350.00
45 The Invisible Raiders 350.00
46 V:The Spider 350.00
47 The Fiend of a
  Thousand Faces 350.00
48 Killer Crossbones 350.00
49 JCo,The Weapon for Evil 350.00

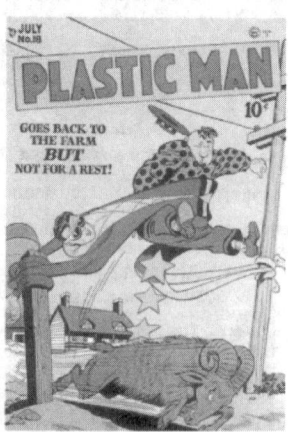

Plastic Man #18
© Quality Comics Group

---

50 V:Iron Fist 350.00
51 Incredible Sleep Weapon 300.00
52 V:Indestructible Wizard 350.00
53 V:Dazzia,Daughter of
   Darkness 350.00
54 V:Dr.Quomquat 350.00
55 The Man Below Zero 350.00
56 JCo, The Man Who Broke
   the Law of Gravity 350.00
57 The Chemist's Cauldron 350.00
58 JCo,The Amazing
   Duplicating Machine 350.00
59 JCo,V:The Super Spy 350.00
60 The Man in the Fiery
   Disguise 325.00
61 V:King of the Thunderbolts . . . 325.00
62 V:The Smokeweapon 325.00
63 V:Reflecto 325.00
64 The Invisible Raiders 325.00

POCAHONTAS

Pocahontas Fuel Co.,
Oct., 1941

N# 250.00
2 . . . . 225.00

POCKET COMICS

Harvey Publications,
Aug., 1941

1 100 pages,O:Black Cat,Spirit
   of '76,Red Blazer Phantom
   Sphinx & Zebra,B:Phantom
   Ranger,British Agent #99,
   Spin Hawkins,Satan 1,400.00
2 . . . . 900.00
3 . . . . 650.00
4 Jan.'42,All Features End 650.00

POGO POSSUM

Dell Publishing Co.

1 WK,A:Swamp Land Band 750.00
2 WK 600.00
3 WK 450.00
4 WK 450.00
5 WK 450.00
6 thru 10 WK . . . . @350.00
11 WK, Christmas (c) . . . . @375.00
12 thru 16 WK . . . . @300.00

POLICE COMICS

Comic Magazines
(Quality Comics Group),
Aug., 1941

1 JCo,WE.PGn,RC,FG,AB,
   GFx(a&c),B&O:Plastic Man
   The Human Bomb,#711,I&B,
   Chic Canter,The Firebrand
   Mouthpiece,Phantom Lady
   The Sword 11,000.00
2 JCo,PGn,WE,RC,FG,
   GFx(a&c) 5,000.00
3 JCo,PGn,WE,RC,FG,
   GFx(a&c) 3,000.00
4 JCo,GFx,PGn,WE,RC,FG,
   GFx&WEC(c) 2,600.00
5 JCo,PGn,WE,RC,FG,
   GFx(a&c) 2,500.00
6 JCo,PGn,WE,RC,FG,
   GFx(a&c) 2,200.00
7 JCo,PGn,WE,RC,FG,
   GFx(a&c) 2,200.00
8 JCo,PGn,WE,RC,FG,
   GFx(a&c),B&O:Manhunter 2,500.00
9 JCo,PGn,WE,RC,FG,
   GFx(a&c) 1,800.00
10 JCo,PGn,WE,RC,FG,
   GFx(a&c) 1,700.00

11 JCo,PGn,WE,RC,FG,GFx(a&c),
   B:Rep:Rep.Spirit Strips 3,000.00
12 JCo,GFX,PGn,WE,FG,AB,
   RC(c) I:Ebony 1,700.00
13 JCo,GFx,PGn,WE,FG,AB,RC(c)
   E:Firebrand,I:Woozy Winks 1,700.00
14 JCo,PGn,WE,Jku,GFX(a&c) 1,500.00
15 JCo,PGn,WE,Jku,GFX(a&c)
   E#711,B:Destiny 1,500.00
16 JCo,PGn,WE,JKu 1,500.00
17 PGn,WE,JKu,JCo(a&c) 1,500.00
18 PGn,WE,JCo(a&c) 1,500.00
19 PGn,WE,JCo(a&c) 1,500.00
20 PGn,WE,JCo(a&c),A:Jack
   Cole in Phantom Lady 1,500.00
21 PGn,WE,JCo(a&c) 1,100.00
22 PGn,WE,RP,JCo(a&c)
   The Eyes Have it 1,100.00
23 WE,RP,JCo(a&c),E:Phantom
   Lady 1,000.00
24 WE,HK,JCo(a&c),B:Flatfoot
   Burns 1,000.00
25 WE,HK,RP,JCo(a&c),The
   Bookstore Mysrery 1,000.00
26 WE,Hk,JCo(a&c)E:Flatfoot
   Burns 1,000.00
27 WE,JCo(a&c) 1,000.00
28 WE,JCo(a&c) 1,000.00
29 WE,JCo(a&c) 1,000.00
30 WE,JCo(a&c),A Slippery
   Racket 1,000.00
31 WE,JCo(a&c),Is Plastic
   Man Washed Up? 700.00
32 WE,JCo(a&c),Fiesta Turns
   Into a Fracas 700.00
33 JCo,WE 700.00
34 WE,JCo(a&c) 700.00
35 WE,JCo(a&c) 700.00
36 WE,JCo(a&c),Rest In Peace . 700.00
37 WE,PGn,JCo(a&c),Love
   Comes to Woozy 700.00
38 WE,PGn,JCo(a&c) 700.00
39 WE,PGn,JCo(a&c) 700.00
40 WE,PGn,JCo(a&c) 700.00
41 WE,PGn,JCo(a&c),E:Reps.
   of Spirit Strip 700.00
42 LF&WE,PGn,JCo(a&c),
   Woozy Cooks with Gas 650.00
43 LF&WE,PGn,JCo(a&c) 650.00
44 PGn,LF,JCo(a&c) 650.00
45 PGn,LF,JCo(a&c) 550.00
46 PGn,LF,JCo(a&c) 550.00
47 PGn,LF,JCo(a&c),V:Dr.Slicer . 550.00

Police Comics #83
© Quality Comics Group

48 PGn,LF,JCo(a&c),V:Big
   Beaver 550.00
49 PGn,LF,JCo(a&c),V:Thelma
   Twittle 550.00
50 PGn,LF,JCo(a&c) 550.00
51 PGn,LF,JCo(a&c),V:The
   Granite Lady 400.00
52 PGn,LF,JCo(a&c) 400.00
53 PGn,LF,JCo(a&c),V:Dr.Erudite 400.00
54 PGn,LF,JCo(a&c) 400.00
55 PGn,LF,JCo(a&c),V:The
   Sleepy Eyes 400.00
56 PGn,LF,JCo(a&c),V:The
   Yes Man. 400.00
57 PGn,LF,JCo(a&c),V:Mr.Misfit . 400.00
58 PGn,LF,JCo(a&c),E:The
   Human Bomb 400.00
59 PGn,LF,JCo(a&c),A:Mr.
   Happiness 400.00
60 PGn,LF,JCo(a&c) 375.00
61 PGn,LF,JCo(a&c) 375.00
62 PGn,LF,JCo(a&c) 375.00
63 PGn,LF,JCo(a&c),V:The Crab. 375.00
64 PGn,LF,HK,JCo(a&c) 375.00
65 PGn,LF,JCo(a&c) 375.00
66 PGn,LF,JCo(a&c) Love
   Can Mean Trouble. 375.00
67 LF,JCo(a&c),
   V:The Gag Man 375.00
68 LF,JCo(a&c) 375.00
69 LF,JCo(a&c),V:Strecho 375.00
70 LF,JCo(a&c) 375.00
71 LF,JCo(a&c) 300.00
72 LF,JCo(a&c),V:Mr.Cat 300.00
73 LF,JCo(a&c) 300.00
74 LF,JCo(a&c),V:Prof.Dimwit . 300.00
75 LF,JCo(a&c) 300.00
76 LF,JCo(a&c),V:Mr.Morbid . . . 300.00
77 LF,JCo(a&c),V:Skull Face
   & Eloc 300.00
78 LF,JCo(a&c),A Hot Time In
   Dreamland. 300.00
79 LF,JCo(a&c),V:Eaglebeak . . . 300.00
80 LF,JCo(a&c),V:Penetro 300.00
81 LF,JCo(a&c),V:A Gorilla 300.00
82 LF,JCo(a&c) 300.00
83 LF,JCo(a&c) 300.00
84 LF,JCo(a&c) 300.00
85 LF,JCo(a&c),V:Lucky 7 . . . . . 300.00
86 LF,JCo(a&c),V:The Baker 300.00
87 LF,JCo(a&c) 300.00
88 LF,JCo(a&c),V:The Seen 300.00
89 JCo(a&c),V:The Vanishers . . . 275.00
90 LF,JCo(a&c),V:Capt.Rivers . . . 275.00
91 JCo(a&c),The Forest Primeval 300.00
92 LF,JCo(a&c),V:Closets
   Kennedy 300.00
93 JCo(a&c),V:The Twinning
   Terror 275.00
94 JCo(a&c),WE 400.00
95 JCo(a&c),WE,V:Scowls 400.00
96 JCo(a&c),WE,V:Black Widow . 400.00
97 JCo(a&c),WE,V:The Mime . . . 400.00
98 JCo(a&c),WE 400.00
99 JCo(a&c),WE 400.00
100 JCo(a&c) 500.00
101 JCo(a&c) 500.00
102 JCo(a&c),E:Plastic Man 500.00
103 JCo,LF,B&I:Ken Shannon;
    Bondage(c) 325.00
104 The Handsome of Homocide 250.00
105 Invisible Hands of Murder. . . 250.00
106 Museum of Murder 250.00
107 Man with the ShrunkenHead 250.00
108 The Headless Horse Player . 250.00
109 LF,Bondage(c),Blood on the
    Chinese Fan 250.00
110 Murder with a Bang. 250.00
111 Diana, Homocidal Huntress . 250.00
112 RC,The Corpse on the
    Sidewalk 275.00

GOLDEN AGE

113 RC(a&c), The Dead Man
  with the Size 13 Shoe 275.00
114 The Terrifying Secret of
  the Black Bear. 250.00
115 Don't Let Them Kill Me 250.00
116 Stage Was Set For Murder . . 250.00
117 Bullet Riddled Bookkeeper . . 250.00
118 Case of the Absent Corpse. . 250.00
119 A Fast & Bloody Buck 250.00
120 Death & The Derelict 250.00
121 Curse of the Clawed Killer . . 250.00
122 The Lonely Hearts Killer 250.00
123 Death Came Screaming 250.00
124 Masin Murder 250.00
125 Bondage(c),The Killer of
  King Arthur's Court 275.00
126 Hit & Run Murders 250.00
127 Oct'53,Death Drivers 250.00

POLICE LINE-UP
Avon Periodicals/
Realistic Comics, Aug., 1951
1 WW,P(c). 500.00
2 P(c),Drugs 350.00
3 JKu,EK,P(c) 250.00
4 July, '52;EK 250.00

POLICE TRAP
Mainline, Sept., 1954
1 S&K(c) 350.00
2 S&K(c) 200.00
3 S&K(c) 200.00
4 S&K(c) 200.00
Charlton Comics, July, 1955
5 S&K,S&K(c) 300.00
6 S&K,S&K(c) 300.00
Becomes:

PUBLIC DEFENDER
IN ACTION
March, 1956
7 . . . . 100.00
8 thru 12, Oct., 1957 . . . . @75.00

POLLY PIGTAILS
Parents' Magazine Institute,
Jan., 1946
1 Ph(c) 125.00
2 Ph(c) 75.00
3 Ph(c) 50.00
4 Ph(c) 50.00
5 Ph(c) 50.00
6 Ph(c) 50.00
7 Ph(c) 40.00
8 . . . . 40.00
9 . . . . 40.00
10 . . . . 40.00
11 thru 22 . . . . @40.00
22 Ph(c) 40.00
23 Ph(c) 40.00
34 thru 43 . . . . @40.00

POPEYE
Dell Publishing Co., 1948
1 . . . . 450.00
2 . . . . 250.00
3 'Welcome to Ghost Island'. . . . 225.00
4 . . . . 225.00
5 . . . . 225.00
6 . . . . 225.00
7 . . . . 225.00
8 . . . . 225.00
9 . . . . 225.00
10 . . . . 225.00
11 . . . . 200.00
12 . . . . 200.00
13 . . . . 200.00

14 thru 20 . . . . @200.00
21 thru 30 . . . . @150.00
31 thru 40 . . . . @125.00
41 thru 45 . . . . @100.00
46 O:Swee' Pea 125.00
47 thru 50 . . . . @75.00
51 thru 60 . . . . @60.00
61 thru 65 . . . . @60.00

POPULAR COMICS
Dell Publishing Co.,
Feb., 1936
1 Dick Tracy, Little Orphan
  Annie 9,000.00
2 Terry Pirates 4,000.00
3 Terry,Annie,Dick Tracy 3,000.00
4 . . . . 2,000.00
5 B:Tom Mix 2,000.00
6 I:Scribbu 1,800.00
7 . . . . 1,500.00
8 Scribbu & Reg Fellers. 1,500.00
9 . . . . 1,500.00
10 Terry,Annie,Tracy 1,500.00
11 Terry,Annie,Tracy 1,000.00
12 Christmas(c). 1,000.00
13 Terry,Annie,Tracy 1,000.00
14 Terry,Annie,Tracy 1,000.00
15 Terry,Annie,Tracy 1,000.00
16 Terry,Annie,Tracy 1,000.00
17 Terry,Annie,Tracy 1,000.00
18 Terry,Annie,Tracy 1,000.00
19 Terry,Annie,Tracy 1,000.00
20 Terry,Annie,Tracy 1,000.00
21 Terry,Annie,Tracy 750.00
22 Terry,Annie,Tracy 750.00
23 Terry,Annie,Tracy 750.00
24 Terry,Annie,Tracy 750.00
25 Terry,Annie,Tracy 750.00
26 Terry,Annie,Tracy 750.00
27 E:Terry,Annie,Tracy. 750.00
28 A:Gene Autry. 550.00
29 . . . . 550.00
30 . . . . 550.00
31 A:Jim McCoy 550.00
32 A:Jim McCoy. 550.00
33 . . . . 550.00
34 . . . . 550.00
35 Christmas(c),Tex Ritter 550.00
36 . . . . 550.00
37 . . . . 550.00
38 B:Gang Busters 600.00
39 . . . . 550.00
40 . . . . 550.00
41 . . . . 550.00
42 . . . . 550.00
43 F:Gang Busters. 550.00
44 . . . . 400.00
45 Tarzan(c). 400.00
46 O:Martan the Marvel Man. . . . 500.00
47 F:Martan the Marvel Man. . . . 350.00
48 F:Martan the Marvel Man . . . 350.00
49 F:Martan the Marvel Man . . . 350.00
50 . . . . 350.00
51 B&O:Voice. 350.00
52 A:Voice 350.00
53 F:The Voice. 325.00
54 F:Gang Busters,A:Voice 325.00
55 F:Gang Busters. 350.00
56 F:Gang Busters. 325.00
57 F:The Marvel Man. 325.00
58 F:The Marvel Man. 325.00
59 F:The Marvel Man. 325.00
60 O:Prof. Supermind 350.00
61 Prof. Supermind & Son 275.00
62 Supermind & Son 275.00
63 B:Smilin' Jack 275.00
64 Smilin'Jack,Supermind 275.00
65 Professor Supermind 275.00
66 . . . . 275.00
67 Gasoline Alley. 275.00

Popular Comics #61
© Dell Publishing Co.

68 F:Smilin' Jack 275.00
69 F:Smilin' Jack 275.00
70 F:Smilin' Jack 275.00
71 F:Smilin' Jack 275.00
72 B:Owl,Terry & the Pirates . . . 500.00
73 F:Terry and the Pirates 300.00
74 F:Smilin' Jack 300.00
75 F:Smilin'Jack,A:Owl 300.00
76 Captain Midnight. 425.00
77 Captain Midnight. 425.00
78 Captain Midnight. 425.00
79 A:Owl. 300.00
80 F:Smilin' Jack,A:Owl 300.00
81 F: Terry&thePirates,A:Owl . . . 300.00
82 F:Smilin' Jack,A:Owl 300.00
83 F:Smilin' Jack,A:Owl 300.00
84 F:Smilin' Jack,A:Owl 300.00
85 F:ThreeLittleGremlins,A:Owl. . 300.00
86 F:Three Little Gremlins 200.00
87 F:Smilin' Jack 200.00
88 F:Smilin' Jack 200.00
89 F:Smokey Stover 200.00
90 F:Terry and the Pirates 200.00
91 F:Smokey Stover 200.00
92 F:Terry and the Pirates 200.00
93 F:Smilin' Jack 200.00
94 F:Terry and the Pirates 200.00
95 F:Smilin' Jack 200.00
96 F:Gang Busters. 200.00
97 F:Smilin' Jack. 200.00
98 F:Felix Cat 225.00
99 F:Bang Busters 200.00
100 . . . . 250.00
101 thru 141 . . . . @175.00
142 E:Terry & the Pirates. 125.00
143 . . . . 125.00
144 . . . . 125.00
145 F:Harold Teen 125.00

POPULAR ROMANCES
Better Publications
(Standard Comics), Dec., 1949
5 B:Ph(c) 125.00
6 Ph(c) 75.00
7 RP 75.00
8 Ph(c) 75.00
9 Ph(c) 75.00
10 WW 85.00
11 thru 16 . . . . @60.00
17 WE 75.00
18 thru 21 . . . . @75.00
22 thru 27 ATh,Ph(c) . . . . @100.00

SCHOOL DAY ROMANCES
Star Publications,
Nov.–Dec., 1949
1 LbC(c),Teen-Age 375.00
2 LbC(c) 350.00
3 LbC(c),Ph(c) 350.00
4 LbC(c),JyD,RonaldReagan . . . 400.00
Becomes:

POPULAR TEEN-AGERS
Sept., 1950
5 LbC(c),Toni Gay, Eve Adams . 400.00
6 LbC(c),Ginger Bunny,
   Midge Martin 350.00
7 LbC(c) 350.00
8 LbC(c) 350.00
9 LbC(c) 250.00
10 LbC(c) 225.00
11 LbC(c) 225.00
12 LbC(c) 225.00
13 LbC(c),JyD 225.00
14 LbC,WW,Spanking 300.00
15 LbC(c),JyD 225.00
16 . . . . 200.00
17 LbC(c),JyD 200.00
18 LbC(c) 200.00
19 LbC(c) 200.00
20 LbC(c),JyD 225.00
21 LbC(c),JyD 225.00
22 LbC(c) 200.00
23 LbC(c) 200.00

POWER COMICS
Holyoke/Narrative Publ., 1944
1 LbC(c) 2,000.00
2 B:Dr.Mephisto,Hitler(c) 2,100.00
3 LbC(c) 2,400.00
4 LbC(c) 2,000.00

PRIDE OF THE YANKEES
Magazine Enterprises, 1949
1 N#,OW,Ph(c),The Life
   of Lou Gehrig 1,100.00

PRISON BREAK
**Avon Periodicals/Realistic,
Sept., 1951**
1 WW(c),WW 550.00
2 WW(c),WW,JKu 400.00
3 JD,JO 300.00
4 EK 250.00
5 EK,CI 250.00

PRIZE COMICS
**Feature Publications
(Prize Publ.), March, 1940**
1 O&B:Power Nelson,Jupiter.
   B:Ted O'Neil,Jaxon of
   the Jungle,Bucky Brady,
   Storm Curtis, Rocket(c) . . . 3,200.00
2 B:The Owl 1,500.00
3 Power Nelson(c) 1,400.00
4 Power Nelson(c) 1,400.00
5 A:Dr.Dekkar. 1,200.00
6 A:Dr.Dekkar. 1,200.00
7 S&K,DBr,JK(c),O&B DR Frost,
   Frankenstein,B:GreenLama,
   Capt Gallant,Voodini
   Twist Turner 2,500.00
8 S&K,DBr 1,400.00
9 S&K,DBr,Black Owl(c) 1,300.00
10 DBr,Black Owl(c) 1,000.00
11 DBr,O:Bulldog Denny 900.00
12 DBr 900.00
13 DBR,O&B:Yank and
   Doodle,Bondage 1,000.00

14 DBr,Black Owl(c). 900.00
15 DBr,Black Owl(c). 900.00
16 DBr,JaB,B:Spike Mason 900.00
17 DBr,Black Owl(c). 900.00
18 DBr,Black Owl(c). 900.00
19 DBr,Yank&Doodle(c). 900.00
20 DBr,Yank&Doodle(c). 900.00
21 DBr,JaB(c),Yank&Doodle(c) . . 600.00
22 DBr,Yank&Doodle(c). 600.00
23 DBr,Uncle Sam(c) 600.00
24 DBr,Abe Lincoln(c) 600.00
25 DBr,JaB,Yank&Doodle(c) . . . 600.00
26 DBr,JaB,JaB(c),Liberty
   Bell(c) 600.00
27 DBr,Yank&Doodle(c) 400.00
28 DBr,Yank&Doodle(c) 350.00
29 DBr,JaB(c)Yank&Doodle(c). . 350.00
30 DBr,Yank&Doodle(c) 400.00
31 DBr,Yank&Doodle(c) 350.00
32 DBr,Yank&Doodle(c) 350.00
33 DBr,Bondage(c),Yank
   & Doodle 400.00
34 DBr,O:Airmale;New
   Black Owl 400.00

Prize Comics #44
© Prize Publications

35 DBr,B:Flying Fist & Bingo 300.00
36 DBr,Yank&Doodle(c) 300.00
37 DBr,I:Stampy,Hitler(c) 350.00
38 DBr,B.Owl,Yank&Doodle(c) . . 300.00
39 DBr,B.Owl,Yank&Doodle(c) . . 300.00
40 DBr,B.Owl,Yank&Doodle(c) . . 300.00
41 DBr,B.Owl,Yank&Doodle(c) . . 300.00
42 DBr,B.Owl,Yank&Doodle(c) . . 250.00
43 DBr,B.Owl,Yank&Doodle(c) . . 250.00
44 DBr, B&I:Boom Boom
   Brannigan 250.00
45 DBr 250.00
46 DBr 250.00
47 DBr 250.00
48 DBr,B:Prince Ra;Bondage(c) . 275.00
49 DBr,Boom Boom(c) 250.00
50 DBr,Frankenstein(c) 250.00
51 DBr 250.00
52 DBr, B:Sir Prize 250.00
53 DBr, The Man Who Could
   Read Features. 250.00
54 DBr 250.00
55 DBr,Yank&Doodle(c) 250.00
56 DBr,Boom Boom (c) 250.00
57 DBr,Santa Claus(c) 250.00
58 DBr,The Poisoned Punch 250.00
59 DBr,Boom Boom(c) 250.00
60 DBr, B:Sir Prise(c) 250.00
61 DBr,The Man wih the
   Fighting Feet 250.00

62 DBr,Hck(c),Yank&Doodle(c) . . 250.00
63 DBr,S&K,S&K(c),Boom
   Boom(c) 275.00
64 DBr,Blackowl Retires 200.00
65 DBr,DBr(c),Frankenstein. 200.00
66 DBr,DBr(c),Frankenstein. 200.00
67 DBr,B:Brothers in Crime 200.00
68 DBr,RP(c) 200.00
Becomes:

PRIZE COMICS WESTERN
April–May, 1948
69 ACa(c),B:Dusty Ballew 150.00
70 ACa(c) 125.00
71 ACa(c) 125.00
72 ACa(c),JSe 125.00
73 ACa(c) 125.00
74 ACa(c) 125.00
75 JSe,S&K(c),6-Gun Showdown
   at Rattlesnake Gulch 135.00
76 Ph(c),Randolph Scott 150.00
77 Ph(c),JSe,Streets of
   Laredo,movie. 135.00
78 Ph(c),JSe,HK,Bullet
   Code, movie 200.00
79 Ph(c),JSe,Stage to
   China, movie 200.00
80 Ph(c),Gunsmoke Justice. 150.00
81 Ph(c),The Man Who Shot
   Billy The Kid 150.00
82 Ph(c),MBi,JSe&BE,Death
   Draws a Circle. 150.00
83 JSe,S&K(c) 125.00
84 JSe 100.00
85 JSe,B:American Eagle 300.00
86 JSe 150.00
87 JSe&BE 150.00
88 JSe&BE. 150.00
89 JSe&BE. 150.00
90 JSe&Be 150.00
91 JSe&BE,JSe&BE(c) 150.00
92 JSe,JSe&BE(c) 150.00
93 JSe,JSe&BE(c), ... 150.00
94 JSe&BE,JSe&BE(c) 150.00
95 JSe,JSe&BE(c) 150.00
96 JSe,JSe&BE,JSe&BE(c). 150.00
97 JSe,JSe&BE,JSeBE(c) 150.00
98 JSe&BE,JSe&BE(c) 150.00
99 JSe&BE,JSe&BE(c) 150.00
100 JSe,JSe(c) 175.00
101 JSe 150.00
102 JSe 150.00
103 JSe 150.00
104 JSe 150.00
105 JSe 150.00
106 JSe 100.00
107 JSe 100.00
108 JSe 110.00
109 JSe&AW 125.00
110 JSe&BE. 125.00
111 JSe&BE 125.00
112 . . . . 100.00
113 AW&JSe 125.00
114 MMe,B:The Drifter. 100.00
115 MMe 100.00
116 MMe 100.00
117 MMe 100.00
118 MMe,E:The Drifter. 100.00
119 Nov/Dec'56 . . . . 100.00

PSYCHOANALYSIS
**E.C. Comics,
March–April, 1955**
1 JKa,JKa(c) 250.00
2 JKa,JKa(c) 200.00
3 JKa,JKa(c) 200.00
4 JKa,JKa(c) Sept.–Oct., 1955 . . 200.00

PUBLIC ENEMIES
D.S. Publishing Co., 1948
1 AMc 300.00
2 AMc 250.00
3 AMc 200.00
4 AMc 200.00
5 AMc 200.00
6 AMc 150.00
7 AMc,Eye Injury 200.00
8 . . . . 150.00
9 . . . . 150.00

PUNCH AND JUDY COMICS
Hillman Periodicals, 1944
1 (fa) 250.00
2 . . . . 150.00
3 . . . . 100.00
4 thru 12 . . . . @90.00
2-1 . . . . 75.00
2-2 JK. 250.00
2-3 . . . . 75.00
2-4 . . . . 75.00
2-5 . . . . 75.00
2-6 . . . . 75.00
2-7 . . . . 75.00
2-8 . . . . 75.00
2-9 . . . . 75.00
2-10 JK. 250.00
2-11 JK. 250.00
2-12 JK. 250.00
3-1 JK. 250.00
3-2 . . . . 200.00
3-3 . . . . 75.00
3-4 . . . . 75.00
3-5 . . . . 75.00
3-6 . . . . 75.00
3-7 . . . . 75.00
3-8 . . . . 75.00
3-9 . . . . 75.00

PUNCH COMICS
Harry 'A' Chesler, Dec., 1941
1 B:Mr.E,The Sky Chief,Hale
the Magician,Kitty Kelly . . . 1,700.00
2 A:Capt.Glory 1,100.00
3-8 Do Not Exist
9 B:Rocket Man & Rocket
girl,Master Ken 1,100.00
10 JCo,A:Sky Chief 900.00

Punch Comics #1
© Harry A Chesler

11 JCo,O:Master Key,A:Little
Nemo 900.00
12 A:Rocket Boy,Capt.Glory . . . 3,000.00
13 Ric(c). 900.00
14 GT 750.00
15 FSm(c) 750.00
16 . . . . 750.00
17 . . . . 750.00
18 FSm(c),Bondage(c),Drug. . . 1,000.00
19 FSm(c) 900.00
20 Women semi-nude(c) 1,400.00
21 Drug 750.00
22 I:Baxter,Little Nemo 350.00
23 A:Little Nemo 350.00

PUPPET COMICS
Dougherty, Co., Spring, 1946
1 Funny Animal 125.00
2 . . . . 125.00

PURPLE CLAW, THE
**Minoan Publishing Co./
Toby Press, Jan., 1953**
1 O:Purple Claw 400.00
2 and 3 . . . . @250.00

PUZZLE FUN COMICS
**George W. Dougherty Co.,
Spring, 1946**
1 PGn 275.00
2 . . . . 200.00

QUEEN OF THE WEST, DALE EVANS
**Dell Publishing Co.,
July, 1953**
(1) *see Dell Four Color #479*
(1) *see Dell Four Color #528*
3 ATh, Ph(c) all 125.00
4 ATh,RsM. 110.00
5 RsM 100.00
6 RsM 100.00
7 RsM 100.00
8 RsM 100.00
9 RsM 100.00
10 RsM 100.00
11 . . . . 75.00
12 RsM 85.00
13 RsM 85.00
14 RsM 85.00
15 RsM 85.00
16 RsM 85.00
17 RsM 85.00
18 RsM 85.00
19 . . . . 75.00
20 RsM 85.00
21 . . . . 75.00
22 RsM 85.00

RACKET SQUAD IN ACTION
**Capitol Stories/
Charlton Comics,
May–June, 1952**
1 Carnival(c) 350.00
2 . . . . 175.00
3 Roulette 175.00
4 FFr(c) 175.00
5 Just off the Boat 250.00
6 The Kidnap Racket 200.00
7 . . . . 150.00
8 . . . . 150.00
9 2 Fisted fix 150.00
10 Explosion Blast (c) 175.00
11 SD(a&c),Racing(c) 350.00

12 JoS,SD(c),Explosion(c). 750.00
13 JoS(c),The Notorious Modelling
Agency Racket,Acid 125.00
14 DG(c),Drug 175.00
15 Photo Extortion Racket. 125.00
16 thru 28 . . . . @125.00
29,March, 1958 . . . . 125.00

RAGGEDY ANN AND ANDY
Dell Publishing Co., 1942
1 Billy & Bonnie Bee. 500.00
2 . . . . 275.00
3 DNo,B:Egbert Elephant 275.00
4 DNo,WK 300.00
5 DNo 250.00
6 DNo 250.00
7 Little Black Sambo 275.00
8 . . . . 250.00
9 . . . . 250.00
10 . . . . 250.00
11 . . . . 200.00
12 . . . . 200.00
13 . . . . 200.00
14 . . . . 200.00
15 . . . . 200.00
16 thru 20 . . . . @200.00
21 Alice in Wonderland 225.00
22 thru 27 . . . . @150.00
28 WK 175.00
29 thru 39 . . . . @150.00

RALPH KINER HOME RUN KING
Fawcett Publications, 1950
1 N#, Life Story of the
Famous Pittsburgh Slugger. . 800.00

RAMAR OF THE JUNGLE
**Toby Press/
Charlton Comics, 1954**
1 Ph(c),TV Show. 250.00
2 Ph(c) 200.00
3 . . . . 200.00
4 . . . . 200.00
5 Sept '56 . . . . 200.00

RANGE ROMANCES
**Comics Magazines
(Quality Comics), Dec., 1949**
1 PGn(a&c) 300.00
2 RC(a&c) 350.00
3 RC,Ph(c) 275.00
4 RC,Ph(c) 250.00
5 RC,PGn,Ph(c) 250.00

RANGERS OF FREEDOM
**Flying Stories, Inc.
(Fiction House), Oct., 1941**
1 I:Ranger Girl & Rangers
of Freedom;V:Super-Brain . 4,000.00
2 V:Super -Brain 1,400.00
3 Bondage(c) The Headsman
of Hate 1,000.00
4 Hawaiian Inferno 800.00
5 RP,V:Super-Brain. 800.00
6 RP,Bondage(c);Bugles
of the Damned. 800.00
7 RP,Death to Tojo's Butchers . 600.00
Becomes:

RANGERS COMICS
Dec., 1942
8 RP,B:US Rangers 600.00

GOLDEN AGE

9 GT,BLb,Commando Steel
for Slant Eyes 600.00
10 BLb,Bondage (c) 650.00
11 Raiders of the
Purple Death 550.00
12 A:Commando Rangers 550.00
13 Grl,B:Commando Ranger 600.00
14 Grl,Bondage(c) 500.00
15 GT,Grl,Bondage(c) 500.00
16 Grl,GT;Burma Raid 550.00
17 GT,GT,Bondage(c),Raiders
of the Red Dawn 550.00
18 GT 550.00
19 GE,Blb,GT,Bondage(c) 450.00
20 GT 400.00
21 GT,Bondage(c) 450.00
22 GT,B&O:Firehair 400.00

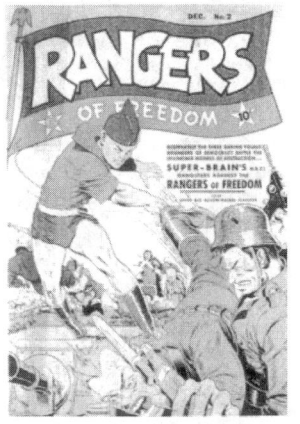

Rangers of Freedom #2
© Fiction House

23 GT,BLb,B:Kazanda 350.00
24 Bondage(c) 350.00
25 Bondage(c) 350.00
26 Angels From Hell 300.00
27 Bondage(c) 350.00
28 BLb,E:Kazanda;B&O Tiger
Man 350.00
29 Bondage(c) 350.00
30 BLb,B:Crusoe Island 375.00
31 BLb,Bondage(c) 300.00
32 BLb 275.00
33 BLb,Drug 275.00
34 BLb 275.00
35 BLB,Bondage(c) 300.00
36 BLb,MB 275.00
37 BLb,Mb 275.00
38 BLb,MB,GE,Bondage(c) 300.00
39 BLb,GE 275.00
40 BLb,GE,BLb(c) 275.00
41 BLb,GE, L:Werewolf Hunter . . 250.00
42 BLb,GE 225.00
43 BLb,GE 225.00
44 BLb,GE 225.00
45 BLb,GEl 225.00
46 BLb,GE 225.00
47 BLb,JGr, Dr. Drew 225.00
48 BLb,JGr, L:Glory Forces 225.00
49 BLb,JGr 225.00
50 BLb,JGr,Bondage(c) 250.00
51 BLb,JGr 225.00
52 BLb,JGr,Bondage(c) 250.00
53 BLb,JGr,Prisoners of
Devil Pass 225.00
54 JGr,When The Wild
Commanches Ride 225.00
55 JGr,Massacre Guns at
Pawnee Pass 225.00

56 JGr, Gun Smuggler of
Apache Mesa 225.00
57 JGr,Redskins to the
Rescue 200.00
58 JGr,Brides of the
Buffalo Men 200.00
59 JGr,Plunder Portage 200.00
60 JGr, Buzzards of
Bushwack Trail 200.00
61 BWh(c)Devil Smoke at
Apache Basin 150.00
62 BWh(c)B:Cowboy Bob 150.00
63 BWh(c) 150.00
64 BWh(c)B:Suicide Smith 150.00
65 BWh(c):Wolves of the
Overland Trail,Bondage(c) . . 165.00
66 BWh(c) 150.00
67 BWh(c)B:Space Rangers 150.00
68 BWh(c);Cargo for Coje 150.00
69 BWh(c);Great Red Death Ray 150.00

REAL CLUE
CRIME STORIES
See: CLUE COMICS

REAL FUNNIES
Nedor Publishing Co.,
Jan., 1943
1 (fa) 350.00
2 and 3 (fa) . . . . @200.00

REAL HEROES COMICS
Parents' Magazine Institiute,
Sept., 1941
1 HcK,Franklin Roosevelt 400.00
2 J, Edgar Hoover 200.00
3 General Wavell 150.00
4 Chiang Kai Shek, Churchill . . . 175.00
5 Stonewall Jackson 150.00
6 Lou Gehrig 250.00
7 Chennault and his
Flying Tigers 150.00
8 Admiral Nimitz 150.00
9 The Panda Man 125.00
10 Carl Akeley-Jungle
Adventurer 125.00
11 Wild Jack Howard 100.00
12 General Robert L
Eichelberger 100.00
13 HcK,Victory at Climback 100.00
14 Pete Gray 100.00
15 Alexander Mackenzie 100.00
16 Balto of Nome Oct '46 . . . . . . 100.00

REAL LIFE STORY
OF FESS PARKER
Dell Publishing Co., 1955
1 . . . . 125.00

REALISTIC ROMANCES
Avon Periodicals/
Realistic Comics,
July–Aug., 1951
1 EK,Ph(c) 250.00
2 Ph(c) 150.00
3 P(c) 125.00
4 P(c) 125.00
5 . . . . 125.00
6 EK 150.00
7 GE, Avon (c) 150.00
8 EK 110.00
9 thru 14 . . . . @100.00
15 . . . . 100.00
16 EK,Drug 125.00
17 EK 100.00

REAL LIFE COMICS
Visual Editions/Better/
Standard/Nedor, Sept., 1941
1 ASh(c),Lawrence of
Arabia,Uncle Sam(c) 750.00
2 ASh(c),Liberty(c) 300.00
3 Adolph Hitler(c) 1,200.00
4 ASh(c)Robert Fulton,
Charles DeGaulle, Old Glory. 200.00
5 ASh(c)Alexander the Great . . . 200.00
6 ASh(c)John Paul Jones,CDR . 175.00
7 ASh(c)Thomas Jefferson 175.00
8 Leonardo Da Vinci 175.00
9 US Coast Guard Issue 175.00
10 Sir Hubert Wilkens 175.00
11 Odyssey on a Raft 150.00
12 ImpossibleLeatherneck 150.00
13 ASh(c)The Eternal Yank 150.00
14 Sir Isaac Newton 150.00
15 William Tell 150.00
16 Marco Polo 150.00
17 Albert Einstein 175.00
18 Ponce De Leon 150.00
19 The Fighting Seabees 150.00
20 Joseph Pulitzer 150.00
21 Admiral Farragut 125.00
22 Thomas Paine 125.00
23 Pedro Menendez 125.00
24 Babe Ruth 250.00
25 Marcus Whitman 125.00
26 Benvenuto Cellini 125.00
27 A Bomb Story 175.00
28 Robert Blake 125.00
29 Daniel DeFoe, A Bomb 150.00
30 Baron Robert Clive 125.00
31 Anthony Wayne 125.00
32 Frank Sinatra 150.00
33 Frederick Douglas 125.00
34 Paul Revere,Jimmy Stewart . . 150.00
35 Rudyard Kipling 125.00
36 Story of the Automobile 125.00
37 Francis Manion, Motion
Picture, Bing Crosby 125.00
38 Richard Henry Dana 100.00
39 Samuel FB Morse 100.00
40 FG,ASh(c),Hans Christian
Anderson, Bob Feller 150.00
41 Abraham Lincoln,Jimmy Foxx. 125.00
42 Joseph Conrad,Fred Allen . . . 100.00
43 Louis Braille,O.W.Holmes 75.00
44 Citizens of Tomorrow 75.00
45 ASh(c),FrancoisVillon,
Olympics, Burl Ives 135.00
46 The Pony Express 135.00
47 ASh(c),Montezuma, Gershwin 125.00
48 . . . . 125.00
49 ASh(c),Gene Bearden,
Baseball 125.00
50 FF,ASh(c),Lewis & Clark 350.00
51 GE,ASh(c),Sam Houston 250.00
52 GE,FF,ASh(c),JSe&BE
Leif Erickson 375.00
53 GT,JSe&BE,Henry Wells &
William Fargo 150.00
54 GT,Alexander Graham Bell . . . 150.00
55 ASh(c),JSe&BE, The James
Brothers 150.00
56 JSe&BE 150.00
57 JSe&BE 150.00
58 JSe&BE,Jim Reaves 175.00
59 FF,JSe&BE,Battle Orphan
Sept '52 . . . . 150.00

REAL LOVE
See: HAP HAZARD
COMICS

GOLDEN AGE

GOLDEN AGE

REAL WEST ROMANCES

**Crestwoood Publishing Co./
Prize Publ., April–May, 1949**

1 S&K,Ph(c)	275.00
2 Ph(c),Spanking	150.00
3 JSe,BE,Ph(c)	150.00
4 S&K,JSe,BE,Ph(c)	250.00
5 S&K,MMe,JSe,Audie	
Murphy Ph(c)	225.00
6 S&K,JSe,BE,Ph(c)	150.00

RECORD BOOK OF FAMOUS POLICE CASES

St. John Publishing Co., 1949

1 N#,JKu,MB(c)	450.00

RED ARROW

**P.L. Publishing Co.,
May, 1951**

1 Bondage(c)	175.00
2	100.00
3 P(c)	100.00

RED BAND COMICS

**Enwil Associates,
Nov., 1944**

1 The Bogeyman	500.00
2 O:Bogeyman,same(c)as#1	350.00
3 A:Captain Wizard	300.00
4 May, '45,Repof#3,Same(c)	300.00

RED CIRCLE COMICS

**Enwil Associates
(Rural Home Public),
Jan., 1945**

1 B:Red Riot,The Prankster	500.00
2 LSt,A:The Judge	400.00
3 LSt(A&c)	250.00
4 LSt(a&c) covers of #4	
stapled over other comics	250.00

TRAIL BLAZERS

Street & Smith, Jan., 1942

1 Wright Brothers	400.00
2 Benjamin Franklin,Dodgers	400.00
3 Red Barber,Yankees	500.00
4 Famous War song	250.00

Becomes:

*Red Dragon #3
© Street & Smith*

RED DRAGON COMICS

Jan., 1943

5 JaB(c),B&O:Red Rover:	
B:Capt.Jack Comkmando	
Rex King&Jet,Minute Man	1,500.00
6 O:Red Dragon	3,000.00
7 The Curse of the	
Boneless Men	2,400.00
8 China V:Japan	1,000.00
9 The Reducing Ray,Jan '44	1,000.00

(2nd Series) Nov., 1947

1 B:Red Dragon	1,200.00
2 BP	900.00
3 BP,BP(c),I:Dr Neff	750.00
4 BP,BP(c)	1,000.00
5 & 6 BP,BP(c)	@550.00
7 BP,BP(c),May, 49.	550.00

RED MASK

See: TIM HOLT

RED RABBIT

**Dearfield/
J. Charles Lave Publ. Co.,
Jan., 1941**

1 (fa)	150.00
2	75.00
3 thru 10	@60.00
11 thru 22	@50.00

RED SEAL COMICS

See: SCOOP

REDSKIN

**Youthful Magazines,
Sept., 1950**

1 Redskin,Bondage(c)	200.00
2 Apache Dance of Death	125.00
3 Daniel Boone	100.00
4 Sitting Bull- Red Devil	
of the Black Hills	100.00
5	100.00
6 Geronimo- Terror of the	
Desert,Bondage	125.00
7 Firebrand of the Sioux	100.00
8	100.00
9	100.00
10 Dead Man's Magic	100.00
11	100.00
12 Quanah Parker,Bondage(c)	125.00

Becomes:

FAMOUS WESTERN BADMEN

Dec., 1952

13 Redskin- Last of the	
Comanches	150.00
14	100.00
15 The Dalton Boys Apr '52	100.00

REMEMBER PEARL HARBOR

Street & Smith, 1942

1 N# JaB,Battle of the	
Pacific,Uncle Sam(c)	600.00

RETURN OF THE OUTLAW

**Minoan Publishing Co.,
Feb., 1953**

1 Billy The Kid	125.00
2	60.00
3 thru 11	@50.00

REVEALING ROMANCES

**A.A. Wyn
(Ace Magazines), Sept., 1949**

1	135.00
2	75.00
3 thru 6	@60.00

REX ALLEN COMICS

**Dell Publishing Co.,
Feb., 1951**

(1) see Dell Four Color #316	
2 Ph(c) all	175.00
3 thru 10	@125.00
11 thru 23	@100.00
24 ATh	110.00
25 thru 31	@100.00

REX DEXTER OF MARS

**Fox Features Syndicate,
Autumn, 1940**

1 DBr,DBr(c) Battle ofKooba	2,800.00

RIBTICKLER

Fox Features Syndicate, 1945

1	200.00
2	100.00
3 Cosmo Cat	75.00
4 thru 6	@60.00
7 Cosmo Cat	60.00
8 thru 9	@60.00

RIN TIN TIN

**Dell Publishing Co.,
Nov., 1952**

(1) see Dell Four Color #434	
(1) see Dell Four Color #476	
(1) see Dell Four Color #523	
4 thru 10 Ph(c) all	@100.00
11 thru 20	@125.00

ROCKET COMICS

**Hillman Periodicals,
March, 1940**

1 O:Red Roberts;B:Rocket	
Riley,Phantom Ranger,Steel	
Shank,Buzzard Baynes,Lefty	
Larson,The Defender,Man	
with 1,000 Faces	3,500.00
2	1,500.00
3 May, '40 E:All Features	1,700.00

ROCKET KELLY

**Fox Features Syndicate,
Autumn, 1945–Oct., Nov., 1946**

N#	400.00
1	300.00
2 A:The Puppeteer	275.00
3 thru 6	@250.00

ROCKETMAN

**Ajax/Farrell Publications,
June, 1952**

1 Space Stories of the Future	500.00

ROCKET SHIP X

**Fox Features Syndicate,
Sept., 1951**

1	900.00
2 N# Variant of Original	500.00

All comics prices listed are for *Near Mint* condition.

Rocket Comics #1
© *Hillman Periodicals*

ROCKY LANE WESTERN
Fawcett/Charlton Comics, May, 1949

1 Ph(c)B:Rocky Lane,Slim Pickins	1,400.00
2 Ph(c)	600.00
3 Ph(c)	500.00
4 Ph(c)CCB,Rail Riders Rampage,F Capt Tootsie.	500.00
5 Ph(c)The Missing Stagecoaches	450.00
6 Ph(c)Ghost Town Showdown	300.00
7 Ph(c)The Border Revolt.	350.00
8 Ph(c)The Sunset Feud	350.00
9 Ph(c)Hermit of the Hills	350.00
10 Ph(c)Badman's Reward	300.00
11 Ph(c)Fool's Gold Fiasco	250.00
12 Ph(c),CCB,Coyote Breed F:Capt Tootsie,Giant	250.00
13 Ph(c),Giant	250.00
14 Ph(c)	200.00
15 Ph(c)B:Black Jacks Hitching Post,Giant	225.00
16 Ph(c),Giant	200.00
17 Ph(c),Giant	200.00
18 Ph(c)	225.00
19 Ph(c),Giant	235.00
20 Ph(c)The Rodeo Rustler E:Slim Pickens	235.00
21 Ph(c)B: Dee Dickens	200.00
22 Ph(c)	175.00
23 thru 30	@200.00
31 thru 40	@175.00
41 thru 55	@175.00
56 thru 87	@150.00

ROD CAMERON WESTERN
Fawcett Publications, Feb., 1950

1 Ph(c)	750.00
2 Ph(c)	350.00
3 Ph(c),Seven Cities of Cipiola	300.00
4 Ph(c),Rip-Roaring Wild West	250.00
5 Ph(c),Six Gun Sabotage	250.00
6 Ph(c),Medicine Bead Murders	250.00
7 Ph(c),Wagon Train Of Death	250.00
8 Ph(c),Bayou Badman	250.00
9 Ph(c),Rustlers Ruse	250.00
10 Ph(c),White Buffalo Trail	250.00
11 Ph(c),Lead Poison	225.00
12 thru 19 Ph(c)	@225.00
20 Phc(c),Great Army Hoax.	225.00

ROLY-POLY COMICS
Green Publishing Co., 1945

1 B:Red Rube&Steel Sterling	400.00
6 A:Blue Cycle	250.00
10 A:Red Rube	300.00
11	250.00
12 Black Hood	250.00
13	250.00
14 A:Black Hood, Decapitation	450.00
15 A:Steel Fist;1946	400.00

ROMANCE AND CONFESSION STORIES
St. John Publishing Co., 1949

1 MB(c),MB	500.00

ROMANTIC LOVE
Avon Periodicals/Realistic, Sept.–Oct., 1949

1 P(c)	275.00
2 P(c)	200.00
3 P(c)	200.00
4 Ph(c)	200.00
5 P(c)	200.00
6 Ph(c),Drug,Thrill Crazy	250.00
7 P(c)	200.00
8 P(c)	200.00
9 EK,P(c)	225.00
10 thru 11 P(c)	@225.00
12 EK	225.00
20	200.00
21	200.00
22 EK	200.00
23 EK	200.00

ROMANTIC MARRIAGE
Ziff-Davis/ St. John Publishing Co., Nov.–Dec., 1950

1 Ph(c),Selfish wife	250.00
2 P(c),Mother's Boy	150.00
3 P(c),Hen Peck House	135.00
4 P(c)	135.00
5 Ph(c)	135.00
6 Ph(c)	125.00
7 Ph(c)	125.00
8 P(c)	125.00
9 P(c)	125.00
10 P/PH(c)	250.00
11	125.00
12	125.00
13 Ph(c)	125.00
14 thru 20	@125.00
20 Ph(c)	125.00
21	125.00
22	125.00
23 MB	135.00
24	125.00

ROMANTIC PICTURE NOVELETTES
Magazine Enterprises, 1946

1 Mary Worth adventure	200.00

ROMANTIC SECRETS
Fawcett Publ./Charlton Comics, Sept., 1949

1 Ph(c)	200.00
2 MSy(c)	100.00
3 MSy(c)	100.00
4 GE	125.00
5 BP	90.00
6	75.00

7 BP	75.00
8	75.00
9 GE	80.00
10 BP	75.00
11	60.00
12 BP	75.00
13	60.00
14	60.00
15	60.00
16 BP,MSy	75.00
17 BP	75.00
18	60.00
19	60.00
20 BP,MBi	75.00
21	60.00
22	60.00
23	60.00
24 GE	75.00
25 MSy	60.00
26 BP,MSy	60.00
27 MSy	60.00
28	60.00
29 BP	60.00
30 thru 32	@60.00
33 MSy	60.00
34 BP	60.00
35	60.00
36 BP	60.00
37 BP	60.00
38 thru 52	@35.00

ROMANTIC STORY
Fawcett Publ./Charlton Comics, Nov., 1949

1 Ph(c)	200.00
2 Ph(c)	125.00
3 Ph(c)	100.00
4 Ph(c)	100.00
5 Ph(c)	100.00
6 Ph(c)	100.00
7 BP,Ph(c)	85.00
8 BP,Ph(c)	75.00
9 Ph(c)	75.00
10 Ph(c)	75.00
11 Ph(c)	75.00
12 Ph(c)	75.00
13 Ph(c)	75.00
14 Ph(c)	75.00
15 GE,Ph(c)	100.00
16 BP,Ph(c)	65.00
17 Ph(c)	60.00
18 Ph(c)	60.00
19 Ph(c)	60.00
20 BP,Ph(c)	60.00
22 ATh,Ph(c)	60.00

Charlton Comics

23	60.00
24 Ph(c)	50.00
25 thru 29	@50.00
30 BP	60.00
31 thru 39	@50.00

ROMANTIC WESTERN
Fawcett Publications, Winter, 1949

1 Ph(c)	300.00
2 Ph(c),AW,AMc	325.00
3 Ph(c)	250.00

ROMEO TUBBS
See: MY SECRET LIFE

ROUNDUP
D.S. Publishing Co., July–Aug., 1948

1 HcK	200.00
2 Drug	150.00

GOLDEN AGE

3 . . . . 125.00
4 . . . . 125.00
5 Male Bondage 135.00

ROY CAMPANELLA, BASEBALL HERO
Fawcett Publications, 1950
N# Ph(c),Life Story of the
  Battling Dodgers Catcher . . 1,000.00

ROY ROGERS COMICS
Dell Publishing Co.
1 photo (c) 1,500.00
2 . . . . 500.00
3 . . . . 350.00
4 . . . . 350.00
5 . . . . 350.00
6 thru 10 . . . . @250.00
11 thru 18 . . . . @225.00
19 Chuck Wagon Charlie 200.00
20 Trigger 200.00
21 thru 30 . . . . @200.00
31 thru 46 . . . . @150.00
47 thru 50 . . . . @125.00
51 thru 56 . . . . @110.00
57 Drug 125.00
58 Drug 135.00
59 thru 80 . . . . @110.00
81 thru 91 . . . . @80.00
Becomes:

ROY ROGERS AND TRIGGER
Aug., 1955
92 thru 99 . . . . @75.00
100 Trigger Returns 125.00
101 thru 118 . . . . @75.00
119 thru 125 ATn . . . . @150.00
126 thru 131 . . . . @90.00
132 Dale Evans 150.00
133 thru 144 RsM . . . . @110.00
145 . . . . 150.00

ROY ROGER'S TRIGGER
Dell Publishing Co., May, 1951
(1) see Dell Four Color #329
2 Ph(c) 250.00
3 P(c) 100.00
4 P(c) 100.00
5 P(c) 100.00
6 thru 17 P(c) . . . . @75.00

Roy Rogers and Trigger
© Dell Publishing Co.

RULAH, JUNGLE GODDESS
See: ZOOT COMICS

SAARI, THE JUNGLE GODDESS
P.L. Publishing Co., Nov., 1951
1 The Bantu Blood Curse 600.00

SABU, ELEPHANT BOY
Fox Features Syndicate, June, 1950
1(30) WW,Ph(c) 300.00
2 JKa,Ph(c),Aug.'50 . . . . 250.00

HAPPY HOULIHANS
Fables Publications (E.C. Comics), Autumn, 1947
1 O:Moon Girl 650.00
2 . . . . 350.00
Becomes:

SADDLE JUSTICE
Spring, 1948
3 HcK,JCr,AF 700.00
4 AF,JCr, Grl 600.00
5 AF,Grl,WI 500.00
6 AF,Grl 450.00
7 AF,Grl 450.00
8 AF,Grl,WI 500.00
Becomes:

SADDLE ROMANCES
Nov., 1949
9 Grl(c),Grl 600.00
10 AF(c),WW,Grl 550.00
11 AF(c),Grl 600.00

SAD SACK COMICS
Harvey Publications, Sept., 1949
1 I:Little Dot 750.00
2 Flying Fool 350.00
3 . . . . 200.00
4 thru 10 . . . . @150.00
11 thru 21 . . . . @100.00
22 Back in the Army Again,
  The Specialist 125.00
23 thru 50 . . . . @75.00
51 thru 100 . . . . @50.00
101 thru 150 . . . . @25.00
151 thru 200 . . . . @20.00
200 thru 287 . . . . @15.00
See also Other Pub. (Color)

SAINT, THE
Avon Periodicals, Aug., 1947
1 JKa,JKa(c),Bondage(c) 1,000.00
2 . . . . 500.00
3 Rolled Stocking Leg(c) 400.00
4 MB(c) Longerie 400.00
5 Spanking Panel 450.00
6 B:Miss Fury 550.00
7 P(c),Detective Cases(c) 350.00
8 P(c),Detective Cases(c) 300.00
9 EK(c),The Notorious
  Murder Mob 300.00
10 WW,P(c),V:The Communist
  Menace 350.00
11 P(c),Wanted For Robbery . . . 250.00
12 P(c),The Blowpipe Murders
  March, 1952 . . . . 250.00

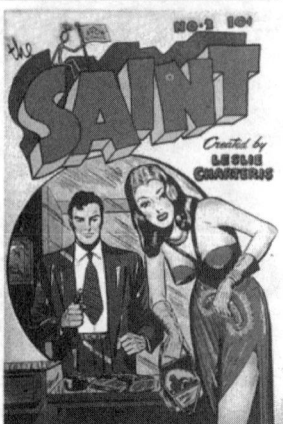
The Saint #2
© Avon Periodicals

SAM HILL PRIVATE EYE
Close-Up Publications, 1950
1 The Double Trouble Caper . . . 200.00
2 . . . . 150.00
3 . . . . 125.00
4 Negligee panels 150.00
5 thru 7 . . . . @100.00

SAMSON
Fox Features Syndicate, Autumn, 1940
1 BP,GT,A:Wing Turner 3,500.00
2 BP,A:Dr. Fung 1,400.00
3 JSh(c),A:Navy Jones 900.00
4 WE,B:Yarko 800.00
5 WE 750.00
6 WE,O:The Topper;Sept'41 . . . 750.00

SAMSON
Ajax Farrell Publ (Four Star), April, 1955
12 The Electric Curtain 350.00
13 Assignment Danger 300.00
14 The Red Raider;Aug'55 . . . . . 300.00

SANDS OF THE SOUTH PACIFIC
Toby Press, Jan., 1953
1 2-Fisted Romantic Adventure . 250.00

SCHOOL DAY ROMANCES
See: POPULAR TEEN-AGERS

SCIENCE COMICS
Fox Features Syndicate, Feb., 1940
1 GT,LF(c),O&B:Electro,Perisphere
  Payne,The Eagle,Navy Jones;
  B:Marga,Cosmic Carson,
  Dr. Doom; Bondage(c) . . . 6,000.00
2 GT,LF(c) 3,000.00
3 GT,LF(c),Dynamo 2,500.00
4 JK,Cosmic Carson 2,200.00
5 Giant Comiscope Offer
  Eagle(c) 1,300.00
6 Dynamop(c) 1,300.00

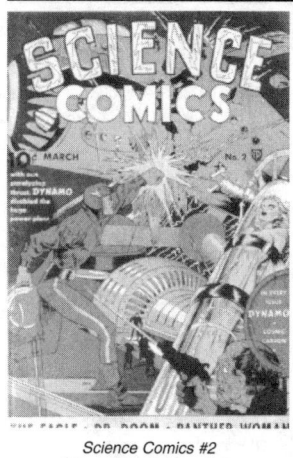

Science Comics #2
© Fox Features Syndicate

7 Bondage(c),Dynamo 1,300.00
8 Sept., 1940 Eagle(c). 1,200.00

SCIENCE COMICS
Humor Publications,
Jan., 1946
1 RP(c),Story of the A-Bomb . . . 250.00
2 RP(c),How Museum Pieces
  Are Assembled 100.00
3 AF,RP(c),How Underwater
  Tunnels Are Made 175.00
4 RP(c),Behind the Scenes at
  A TV Broadcast 75.00
5 The Story of the World's
  Bridges; Sept., 1946 . . . . 0.00

SCIENCE COMICS
Ziff-Davis Publ. Co.,
May, 1946
N# Used For A Mail Order
  Test Market 500.00

SCIENCE COMICS
Export Publication Enterprises,
March, 1951
1 How to resurrect a dead rat. . . 125.00

SCOOP COMICS
Harry 'A' Chesler Jr.,
Nov., 1941
1 I&B:Rocketman&Rocketgirl;B:Dan
  Hastings;O&B:Master Key . 1,800.00
2 A:Rocketboy,Eye Injury. 2,000.00
3 Partial rep. of #2 . . . . 900.00
4 thru 7 do not exist
8 1945 . . . . 600.00
Becomes:

SNAP
1944
N# Humorous 150.00
Becomes:

KOMIK PAGES
1944
1(10) JK,Duke of Darkness 350.00
Becomes:

BULLS-EYE
1944
11 Green Knight, Skull (c) 550.00

Becomes:
KAYO
1945
12 Green Knight. 200.00
Becomes:
CARNIVAL
1945
(13) Guardineer 225.00
Becomes:
RED SEAL COMICS
Harry 'A' Chesler, Jr./Superior,
Oct., 1945
14 GT,Bondage(c),Black Dwarf 1,000.00
15 GT,Torture. 650.00
16 GT. 800.00
17 GT,Lady Satan,Sky Chief 700.00
18 Lady Satan,Sky Chief 700.00
19 Lady Satan,Sky Chief 600.00
20 Lady Satan,Sky Chief 600.00
21 Lady Satan,Sky Chief 550.00
22 Rocketman 450.00

SCREAM COMICS
Humor Publ./Current Books
(Ace Magazines),
Autumn, 1944
1 . . . . 200.00
2 . . . . 100.00
3 . . . . 75.00
4 thru 15 . . . . @75.00
16 I:Lily Belle 80.00
17 . . . . 75.00
18 Drug 100.00
19 . . . . 75.00
Becomes:
ANDY COMICS
June, 1948
20 Teenage 75.00
21 . . . . 75.00
Becomes:
ERNIE COMICS
Sept., 1948
22 Teenage 75.00
23 thru 25 . . . . @40.00
Becomes:
ALL LOVE ROMANCES
May, 1949
26 Ernie 100.00
27 LbC 150.00
28 thru 32. . . . . @60.00

(Capt. Silvers Log of...)
SEA HOUND, THE
Avon Periodicals, 1945
N# The Esmerelda's Treasure . . 250.00
2 Adventures in Brazil 200.00
3 Louie the Llama 150.00
4 In Greed & Vengence;
  Jan-Feb, 1946 . . . . 150.00

SECRET LOVES
Comics Magazines
(Quality Comics),
Nov., 1949
1 BWa(c). 300.00
2 BWa(c),Lingerie(c). 250.00
3 RC 200.00
4 . . . . 150.00
5 Boom Town Babe 200.00
6 . . . . 150.00

SECRET MYSTERIES
See: CRIME MYSTERIES

SELECT DETECTIVE
D.S. Publishing Co.,
Aug.–Sept., 1948
1 MB,Exciting New Mystery
  Cases 350.00
2 MB,AMc,Dead Men. 200.00
3 Face in theFrame;Dec-Jan'48 . 175.00

SERGEANT PRESTON
OF THE YUKON
Dell Publishing Co., Aug., 1951
(1 thru 4) *see Dell Four Color #344;*
  #373, 397, 419
5 P(c) 75.00
6 Bondage, P(c) 125.00
7 thru 11 P(c) 75.00
12 P(c). 75.00
13 P(c),O:Sergeant Preston 100.00
14 thru 17 P(c) . . . . @75.00
18 Yukon King,P(c) 100.00
19 thru 29 Ph(c) . . . . @125.00

Seven Seas Comics #6
© Universal Phoenix

SEVEN SEAS COMICS
Universal Phoenix Features/
Leader Publ., April, 1946
1 MB,RWb(c),B:South Sea
  Girl, Captain Cutlass 1,200.00
2 MB,RWb(c) 1,000.00
3 MB,AF,MB(c) 900.00
4 MB,MB(c) 1,000.00
5 MB,MB(c),Hangman's Noose . 900.00
6 MB,MB(c);1947 . . . . 900.00

SHADOW COMICS
Street & Smith, March, 1940
1-1 P(c),B:Shadow,Doc Savage,
  Bill Barnes,Nick Carter,
  Frank Merriwell,Iron Munro 7,000.00
1-2 P(c),B: The Avenger 2,500.00
1-3 P(c),A: Norgill the
  Magician 2,000.00
1-4 P(c),B:The Three
  Musketeers. 1,500.00
1-5 P(c),E: Doc Savage 1,500.00
1-6 A: Captain Fury 1,200.00

All comics prices listed are for *Near Mint* condition.

1-7 O&B: The Wasp 1,300.00
1-8 A:Doc Savage 1,200.00
1-9 A:Norgill the Magician 1,200.00
1-10 O:Iron Ghost;B:The Dead
    End Kids 1,200.00
1-11 O:Hooded Wasp 1,200.00
1-12 Crime Does Not pay 1,100.00
2-1 . . . . 1,200.00
2-2 Shadow Becomes Invisible 1,700.00
2-3 O&B:supersnipe;
    F:Little Nemo 1,500.00
2-4 F:Little Nemo 900.00
2-5 V:The Ghost Faker 900.00
2-6 A:Blackstone the Magician . . 750.00
2-7 V:The White Dragon 750.00
2-8 A:Little Nemo 750.00
2-9 The Hand of Death 750.00
2-10 A:Beebo the WonderHorse . 750.00
2-11 V:Devil Kyoti 750.00
2-12 V:Devil Kyoti 700.00
3-1 JaB(c),V:Devil Kyoti 700.00
3-2 Red Skeleton Life Story 700.00
3-3 V:Monstrodamus 700.00
3-4 V:Monstrodamus 700.00
3-5 V:Monstrodamus 700.00
3-6 V:Devil's of the Deep 700.00
3-7 V: Monstrodamus 700.00
3-8 E: The Wasp 700.00
3-9 The Stolen Lighthouse 700.00
3-10 A:Doc Savage 700.00
3-11 P(c),V: Thade 700.00
3-12 V: Thade 700.00
4-1 Red Cross Appeal on (c) . . . 600.00
4-2 V:The Brain of Nippon 600.00
4-3 Little Men in Space 600.00
4-4 ...Mystifies Berlin 600.00
4-5 ...Brings Terror to Tokio 600.00
4-6 V:The Tarantula 600.00
4-7 Crypt of the Seven Skulls . . . 600.00
4-8 V:the Indigo Mob 600.00
4-9 Ghost Guarded Treasure
    of the Haunted Glen 600.00
4-10 V:The Hydra 600.00
4-11 V:The Seven Sinners 600.00
4-12 Club Curio 550.00
5-1 A:Flatty Foote 550.00
5-2 Bells of Doom 550.00
5-3 The Circle of Death 550.00
5-4 The Empty Safe Riddle 550.00
5-5 The Mighty Master Nomad . . 550.00
5-6 ...Fights Piracy Among
    the Golden Isles 550.00
5-7 V:The Talon 550.00
5-8 V:The Talon 550.00
5-9 V:The Talon 550.00
5-10 V:The Crime Master 550.00
5-11 The Clutch of the Talon 550.00
5-12 Most Dangerous Criminal . . 550.00
6-1 Double Z 500.00
6-2 Riddle of Prof.Mentalo 500.00
6-3 V:Judge Lawless 500.00
6-4 V:Dr. Zenith 500.00
6-5 . . . . 500.00
6-6 ...Invades the
    Crucible of Death 500.00
6-7 Four Panel (c) 500.00
6-8 Crime Among the Aztecs . . . 500.00
6-9 I:Shadow Jr. 550.00
6-10 Devil's Passage 500.00
6-11 The Black Pagoda 500.00
6-12 BP,BP(c),Atomic Bomb
    Secrets Stolen 550.00
7-1 The Yellow Band 550.00
7-2 A:Shadow Jr. 550.00
7-3 BP,BP(c),Crime Under
    the Border 700.00
7-4 BP,BP(c),One Tree Island,
    Atomic Bomb 750.00
7-5 A:Shadow Jr. 550.00

7-6 BP,BP(c),The Sacred Sword
    of Sanjorojo 700.00
7-7 Crime K.O. 550.00
7-8 ...Raids Crime Harbor 550.00
7-9 BP,BP(c),Kilroy Was Here . . 700.00
7-10 BP,BP(c),The Riddle of
    the Flying Saucer 800.00
7-11 BP,BP(c),Crime
    Doesn't Pay 700.00
7-12 BP,BP(c)Back From
    the Grave 700.00
8-1 BP,BP(c),Curse of the Cat . . 700.00
8-2 BP,BP(c),Decay,Vermin &
    Murder in the Bayou 700.00
8-3 BP,BP(c),The Spider Boy . . . 700.00
8-4 BP,BP(c),Death Rises
    Out of the Sea 700.00
8-5 BP,BP(c),Jekyll-
    Hyde Murders 700.00
8-6 Secret of Valhalla Hall 700.00
8-7 BP,BP(c),Shadow in Danger 700.00
8-8 BP,BP(c),...Solves a
    Twenty Year Old Crime . . . 700.00
8-9 BP,BP(c),3-D Effect(c) 700.00
8-10 BP,BP(c),Up&Down(c) 700.00
8-11 BP,BP(c). 700.00
8-12 BP,BP(c),Arabs,Boat(c) . . . 700.00
9-1 Airport(c) 700.00
9-2 BP,BP(c),Flying Cannon(c) . . 700.00
9-3 BP,BP(c),Shadow's Shadow . 700.00
9-4 BP,BP(c) 700.00
9-5 Death in the Stars;Aug'49 . . . 700.00

SHARP COMICS
H.C. Blackerby,
Winter, 1945

1 O:Planetarian(c) 550.00
2 O:The Pioneer 400.00

SHEENA, QUEEN OF
THE JUNGLE
Real Adventures
(Fiction House)
Spring, 1942–Winter, 1952

1 Blood Hunger 3,500.00
2 Black Orchid of Death 1,500.00
3 Harem Shackles 1,100.00
4 The Zebra Raiders 700.00
5 War of the Golden Apes 650.00
6 . . . . 625.00
7 They Claw By Night 600.00
8 The Congo Colossus 600.00

Sheena, Queen of the Jungle #1
© Fiction House

9 and 10 . . . . @550.00
11 Red Fangs of the Tree Tribe . . 550.00
12 . . . . 450.00
13 Veldt o/t Voo Doo Lions 450.00
14 The Hoo Doo Beasts of
    Mozambique 450.00
15 . . . . 450.00
16 Black Ivory 450.00
17 Great Congo Treasure Trek . . 450.00
18 Doom of the Elephant Drum . . 450.00

SHIELD-WIZARD
COMICS
MLJ Magazines,
Summer, 1940

1 IN,EA,O:Shield 7,000.00
2 O:Shield;I:Roy 3,000.00
3 Roy,Child Bondage(c) 2,000.00
4 Shield,Roy,Wizard 1,800.00
5 B:Dusty-Boy Dectective,Child
    Bondage 1,700.00
6 B:Roy the Super Boy,Child
    Bondage 1,500.00
7 Shield(c),Roy Bondage(c) . . 1,600.00
8 Bondage(c) 1,500.00
9 Shield/Roy(c) 1,200.00
10 Shield/Roy(c) 1,200.00
11 Shield/Roy(c) 1,200.00
12 Shield/Roy(c) 1,200.00
13 Bondage (c);Spring'44 . . . . 1,300.00

SHIP AHOY
Spotlight Publishers,
Nov., 1944

1 LbC(c) 250.00

SHOCK DETECTIVE
CASE(S)
See: CRIMINALS ON
THE RUN

SHOCK SUSPENSTORIES
Tiny Tot Comics
(E.C. Comics),
Feb.–March, 1952

1 JDa,JKa,AF(c),ElectricChair. 1,200.00
2 WW,JDa,Grl,JKa,WW(c) 750.00
3 WW,JDa,JKa,WW(c) 500.00
4 WW,JDa,JKa,WW(c) 500.00
5 WW,JDa,JKa,WW(c),Hanging . 550.00
6 WW,AF,JKa,WW(c),
    Bondage(c) 600.00
7 JKa,WW,GE,AF(c),Face
    Melting 600.00
8 JKa,AF,AW,GE,WW,AF(c) 500.00
9 JKa,AF,RC,WW,AF(c) 450.00
10 JKa,WW,RC,JKa(c),Drug . . . 450.00
11 JCr,JKa,WW,RC,JCr(c) 400.00
12 AF,JKa,WW,RC,AF(c)Drug(c) . 450.00
13 JKa,WW,FF,JKa(c) 600.00
14 JKa,WW,BK,WW(c) 400.00
15 JKa,WW,RC,JDa(c)
    Strangulation 350.00
16 GE,RC,JKa,GE(c),Rape 350.00
17 GE,RC,JKa,GE(c) 300.00
18 GE,RC,JKa,GE(c);Jan'55 . . . 300.00

SHOCKING MYSTERY
CASES
See: THRILLING CRIME
CASES

GOLDEN AGE

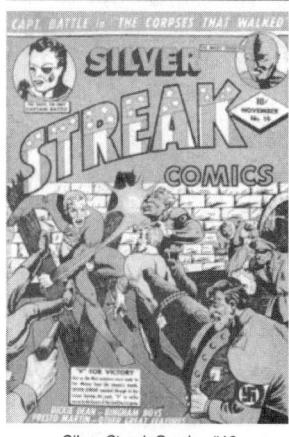

Silver Streak Comics #16
© Lev Gleason

SILVER STREAK COMICS

**Your Guide/New Friday/
Comic House/Newsbrook
Publications/Lev Gleason,
Dec., 1939**

1 JCo(a&c),I&B:The Claw,Red
  Reeves Capt.Fearless;B:Mr.Mid-
  night,Wasp;A:Spiritman . . 16,500.00
2 JSm,JCo,JSm(c) 6,000.00
3 JaB(c),I&O:Silver Streak;
  B:Dickie Dean,Lance Hale,
  Ace Powers,Bill Wayne,
  Planet Patrol 5,000.00
4 JCo,JaB(c)B:Sky Wolf;
  N:Silver Streak,I:Lance
  Hale's Sidekick-Jackie 2,500.00
5 JCo(a&c),Dickie Dean
  V:The Raging Flood 3,000.00
6 JCo,JaB,JCo(a&c),O&I:Daredevil
  [Blue & Yellow Costume];
  R:The Claw 21,000.00
7 JCo,N: Daredevil 15,000.00
8 JCo(a&c) 5,000.00
9 JCo,BoW(c) 3,000.00
10 BoW,BoW(c) 2,500.00
11 DRi(c) I:Mercury 2,000.00
12 DRi(c) 1,500.00
13 JaB,JaB(c),O:Thun-Dohr . . . 1,500.00
14 JaB,JaB(c),A:Nazi
  Skull Men 1,500.00
15 JaB,DBr,JaB(c),
  B:Bingham Boys 1,200.00
16 DBr,BoW(c),Hitler(c) 1,600.00
17 DBr,JaB(c),E:Daredevil 1,200.00
18 DBr,JaB(c),B:The Saint 1,100.00
19 DBr,EA 900.00
20 BW,BEv,EA 900.00
21 BW,BEv 900.00
Becomes:

CRIME DOES NOT PAY

June, 1942

22(23) CBi(c),The Mad Musician
  & Tunes of Doom 3,500.00
23 CBi(c),John Dillinger-One
  Man Underworld 1,900.00
24 CBi(c),The Mystery of the
  Indian Dick 1,500.00
25 CBi(c),Dutch Shultz-King
  of the Underworld 800.00
26 CBi(c),Lucky Luciano-The
  Deadliest of Crime Rats 800.00
27 CBi(c),Pretty Boy Floyd 800.00

28 CBi(c), ... 800.00
29 CBi(c),Two-Gun Crowley-The
  Bad Kid with the Itchy
  Trigger Finger 750.00
30 CBi(c),"Monk"Eastman
  V:Thompson's Mob 750.00
31 CBi(c) The Million Dollar
  Bank Robbery 500.00
32 CBi(c),Seniorita of Sin 500.00
33 CBi(c),Meat Cleaver Murder . . 550.00
34 CBi(c),Elevator Shaft 500.00
35 CBi(c),Case o/t MissingToe . . 500.00
36 CBi(c) 450.00
37 CBi(c) 400.00
38 CBi(c) 400.00
39 FG,CBi(c) 400.00
40 FG,CBi(c) 450.00
41 FG,RP,CBi(c),The Cocksure
  Counterfeiter 350.00
42 FG,RP,CBi(c) 350.00
43 FG,RP,CBi(c)Electrocution . . . 500.00
44 FG,CBi(c),The Most Shot
  At Gangster 250.00
45 FG,CBi(c) 250.00
46 FG,CBi(c),ChildKidnapping(c) . 300.00
47 FG,CBi(c),ElectricChair 400.00
48 FG,CBi(c) 250.00
49 FG,CBi(c) 250.00
50 FG,CBi(c) 250.00
51 FG,GT,CBi(c),1st Monthly Iss . . 225.00
52 FG,GT,CBi(c) 225.00
53 FG,CBi(c) 225.00
54 FG,CBi(c) 225.00
55 FG,CBi(c) 225.00
56 FG,GT,CBi(c) 225.00
57 FG,CBi(c) 225.00
58 FG,CBi(c) 225.00
59 FG,Cbi(c) 225.00
60 FG,CBi(c) 225.00
61 FG,GT,CBi(c) 225.00
62 FG,CBi(c),Bondage(c) 225.00
63 FG,GT,CBi(c) 200.00
64 FG,GT,CBi(c) 200.00
65 FG,CBi(c) 200.00
66 FG,GT,CBi(c) 200.00
67 FG,GT,CBi(c) 200.00
68 FG,CBi(c) 200.00
69 FG,CBi(c) 200.00
70 FG,Cbi(c) 200.00
71 FG,CBi(c) 150.00
72 FG,CBi(c) 150.00
73 FG,CBi(c) 150.00
74 FG,CBi(c) 150.00
75 FG,CBi(c) 150.00
76 FG,CBi(c) 150.00
77 FG,CBi(c),Electrified Safe 175.00
78 FG,CBi(c) 150.00
79 FG 150.00
80 FG 150.00
81 FG 150.00
82 FG 150.00
83 FG 150.00
84 FG 150.00
85 FG 150.00
86 FG 150.00
87 FG,P(c),The Rock-A-Bye
  Baby Murder 150.00
88 FG,P(c),Death Carries a Torch 150.00
89 FG,BF,BF P(c),The Escort
  Murder Case 150.00
90 FG,BF P(c),The Alhambra
  Club Murders 150.00
91 FG,AMc,BF P(c),Death
  Watches The Clock 150.00
92 BF,FG,BF P(c) 150.00
93 BF,FG,AMc,BF P(c) 150.00
94 BF,FG,BF P(c) 150.00
95 FG,AMc,BF P(c) 150.00
96 BF,FG,BF P(c),The Case of
  the Movie Star's Double 150.00
97 FG,BF P(c) 150.00

98 BF,FG,BF P(c),Bondage(c) . . . 150.00
99 BF,FG,BF P(c) 150.00
100 FG,BF,AMc,P(c),The Case
  of the Jittery Patient 150.00
101 FG,BF,AMc,P(c) 125.00
102 FG,BF,AMc,BF P(c) 125.00
103 FG,BF,AMc,BF P(c) 125.00
104 thru 110 FG . . . . @125.00
111 thru 120 . . . . @125.00
121 thru 140 . . . . @100.00
141 JKu 100.00
142 JKu,CBi(c) 100.00
143 JKu,Comic Code 100.00
144 I Helped Capture"Fat Face"
  George Klinerz 75.00
145 RP,Double Barrelled Menace . 75.00
146 BP,The Con & The Canary . . . 75.00
147 JKu,BP,A Long Shoe On the
  Highway;July, 1955 . . . . 125.00

SINGLE SERIES

**United Features Syndicate,
1938**

1 Captain & The Kids 1,200.00
2 Bronco Bill 650.00
3 Ella Cinders 500.00
4 Li'l Abner 1,000.00
5 Fritzi Ritz 300.00
6 Jim Hardy 500.00
7 Frankie Doodle 400.00
8 Peter Pat 400.00
9 Strange As it Seems 400.00
10 Little Mary Mixup 400.00
11 Mr. & Mrs. Beans 400.00
12 Joe Jinx 350.00
13 Looy Dot Dope 350.00
14 Billy Make Believe 350.00
15 How It Began 400.00
16 Illustrated Gags 250.00
17 Danny Dingle 300.00
18 Li'l Abner 800.00
19 Broncho Bill 550.00
20 Tarzan 1,500.00
21 Ella Cinders 400.00
22 Iron Vic 400.00
23 Tailspin Tommy 500.00
24 Alice In Wonderland 550.00
25 Abbie an' Slats 450.00
26 Little Mary Mixup 400.00
27 Jim Hardy 400.00
28 Ella Cinders & Abbie AN'
  Slats 1942 . . . . 400.00

SKELETON HAND

**American Comics Group,
Sept.–Oct., 1952**

1 . . . . 600.00
2 The Were-Serpent of Karnak . . 400.00
3 Waters of Doom 300.00
4 Black Dust 300.00
5 The Rise & Fall of the
  Bogey Man 300.00
6 July–Aug., 1953 . . . . 300.00

SKY BLAZERS

**Hawley Publications,
Sept., 1940**

1 Flying Aces,Sky Pirates 800.00
2 Nov., 1940 . . . . 600.00

SKYMAN

Columbia Comics Group, 1941

1 OW,OW(c),O:Skyman,Face . 1,600.00
2 OW,OW(c),Yankee Doodle . . . 800.00
3 OW,OW(c) 500.00
4 OW,OW(c),Statue of
  Liberty(c) 1948 . . . . 500.00

GOLDEN AGE

Skyman #3
© Columbia Comics Group

SKY PILOT
**Ziff-Davis Publishing Co.,
1950**
10 NS P(c),Lumber Pirates 175.00
11 Ns P(c),The 2,00 Foot Drop;
April–May, 1951 . . . . 150.00

SKY ROCKET
**Home Guide Publ.
(Harry 'A' Chesler), 1944**
1 Alias the Dragon,Skyrocket . . . 400.00

SKY SHERIFF
**D.S. Publishing,
Summer, 1948**
1 I:Breeze Lawson & the Prowl
Plane Patrol 150.00

SLAM BANG COMICS
**Fawcett Publications,
Jan., 1940**
1 B:Diamond Jack,Mark Swift,
Lee Granger,Jungle King . . 3,000.00
2 F:Jim Dolan Two-Fisted
Crime Buster 1,200.00
3 A: Eric the Talking Lion . . . 1,900.00
4 F: Hurricane Hansen-Sea
Adventurer 1,000.00
5 . . . . 1,000.00
6 I: Zoro the Mystery Man;
Bondage(c) 1,000.00
7 Bondage(c);Sept., 1940 . . . . 1,000.00

SLAPSTICK COMICS
**Comic Magazine
Distrib., Inc., 1945**
N# Humorous Parody 300.00
SLAVE GIRL COMICS
Avon Periodicals, Feb., 1949
1 . . . . 1,200.00
2 April, 1949 . . . . 900.00

SLICK CHICK COMICS
Leader Enterprises, Inc., 1947
1 Teen-Aged Humor 125.00
2 Teen-Aged Humor 100.00
3 1947 . . . . 100.00

SMASH COMICS
**Comics Magazine, Inc.
(Quality Comics Group),
Aug., 1939**
1 WE,O&B:Hugh Hazard, Bozo
the Robot,Black X, Invisible
Justice: B:Wings Wendall,
Chic Carter 4,500.00
2 WE,A:Lone Star Rider 1,500.00
3 WE,B:Captain Cook,JohnLaw 900.00
4 WE,PGn,B:Flash Fulton 850.00
5 WE,PGn,Bozo Robot 850.00
6 WE,PGn,GFx,Black X(c) 800.00
7 WE,PGn,GFx,Wings
Wendell(c) 750.00
8 WE,PGn,GFx,Bozo Robot 750.00
9 WE,PGn,GFx,Black X(c) 750.00
10 WE,PGn,GFx,Bozo robot(c) . . 750.00
11 WE,PGn,GFx,BP,Black X(c) . . 750.00
12 WE,PGn,GFx,BP,Bozo(c) 750.00
13 WE,PGn,GFx,AB,BP,B:Mango,
Purple Trio,BlackX(c). 750.00
14 BP,LF,AB,PGn,I:The Ray . . 4,000.00
15 BP,LF,AB,PGn,The Ram(c) . 1,700.00
16 BP,LF,AB,PGn,Bozo(c) 1,800.00
17 BP,LF,AB,PGn,JCo,
The Ram(c) 1,800.00
18 BP,LF,AB,JCo,PGn,
B&O:Midnight 2,200.00
19 BP,LF,AB,JCo,PGn,Bozo(c). 1,200.00
20 BP,LF,AB,JCo,PGn,
The Ram(c) 1,200.00
21 BP,LF,AB,JCo,PGn 1,200.00
22 BP,LF,AB,JCo,PGn,
B:The Jester 1,200.00
23 BP,AB,JCo,RC,PGn,
The Ram(c) 1,100.00
24 BP,AB,JCo,RC,PGn,A:Sword,
E:ChicCarter,
N:WingsWendall 1,100.00
25 AB,JCo,RC,PGn,O:Wildfire . 1,100.00
26 AB,JCo,RC,PGn,Bozo(c) . . 1,000.00
27 AB,JCo,RC,PGn,
The Ram(c) 1,000.00
28 AB,JCo,RC,PGn,
1st Midnight (c) 1,000.00
29 AB,JCo,Rc,PGn,B;
Midnight(c) 1,000.00
30 AB,JCo,PGn. 1,000.00
31 AB,JCo,PGn 750.00
32 AB,JCo,PGn 750.00
33 AB,JCo,PGn,O:Marksman . . . 800.00
34 AB,JCo,PGn 750.00
35 AB,JCo,RC,PGn 750.00
36 AB,JCo,RC,PGn,E:Midnight(c) 750.00
37 AB,JCo,RC,PGn,Doc Wacky
becomes Fastest Human
on Earth. 750.00
38 JCo,RC,PGn,B:YankeeEagle1,200.00
39 PGn,B:Midnight(c). 700.00
40 PGn,E:Ray 700.00
41 PGn. 500.00
42 PGn,B:Lady Luck 1,700.00
43 PGn,A:Lady Luck 600.00
44 PGn. 500.00
45 PGn,E:Midnight(c). 500.00
46 RC,Twelve Hours to Live . . . 500.00
47 Wanted Midnight,
Dead or Alive. 500.00
48 Midnight Meets the
Menace from Mars 500.00
49 PGn,FG,Mass of Muscle. . . . 500.00
50 I:Hyram the Hermit 500.00
51 A:Wild Bill Hiccup 300.00
52 PGn,FG,Did Ancient Rome Fall,
or was it Pushed? 350.00
53 Is ThereHonorAmongThieves. 300.00
54 A:Smear-Faced Schmaltz. . . . 350.00
55 Never Trouble Trouble until
Trouble Troubles You 350.00

Smash Comics#38
© Quality Comics Group

56 The Laughing Killer. 350.00
57 A Dummy that Turns Into
A Curse 350.00
58 . . . . 350.00
59 A Corpse that Comes Alive. . . 350.00
60 The Swooner & the Trush. . . . 350.00
61 . . . . 300.00
62 V:The Lorelet 300.00
63 PGn 300.00
64 PGn,In Search of King Zoris. . 300.00
65 PGn,V:Cyanide Cindy 300.00
66 Under Circle's Spell 300.00
67 A Living Clue. 300.00
68 JCo,Atomic Dice 300.00
69 JCo,V:Sir Nuts 300.00
70 . . . . 300.00
71 . . . . 250.00
72 JCo,Angela,the Beautiful
Bovine 250.00
73 . . . . 250.00
74 . . . . 250.00
75 The Revolution 250.00
76 Bowl Over Crime. 250.00
77 Who is Lilli Dilli? 250.00
78 JCo,Win Over Crime. 250.00
79 V:The Men From Mars 250.00
80 JCo,V:Big Hearted Bosco. . . . 250.00
81 V:Willie the Kid 250.00
82 V:Woodland Boy 250.00
83 JCo,Quizmaster 250.00
84 A Date With Father Time. 250.00
85 JCo,A Singing Swindle 250.00

SMASH HITS
SPORTS COMICS
**Essankay Publications,
Jan., 1949**
1 LbC,LbC(c) 350.00

SMILEY BURNETTE
WESTERN
**Fawcett Publications,
March, 1950**
1 Ph(c),B:Red Eagle 600.00
2 Ph(c) 400.00
3 Ph(c) 400.00
4 Ph(c) 400.00

SMILIN' JACK
Dell Publishing Co., 1948
1 . . . . 150.00

2 .... 100.00
3 thru 8 .... @75.00

SMITTY
Dell Publishing Co., 1948
1 .... 150.00
2 .... 75.00
3 .... 50.00
4 thru 7 .... @40.00

SNAPPY COMICS
**Cima Publications,
(Prize), 1945**
1 A:Animale 400.00

SNIFFY THE PUP
**Animated Cartoons
(Standard Comics), Nov., 1949**
5 FF,Funny Animal 100.00
6 thru 9 Funny Animal ...... @50.00
10 thru 17 Funny Animal ..... @40.00
18 Sept., 1953 .... 40.00

SOLDIER COMICS
**Fawcett Publications,
Jan., 1952**
1 Fighting Yanks on Flaming
　Battlefronts 150.00
2 Blazing Battles Exploding
　with Combat 100.00
3 .... 75.00
4 A Blow for Freedom 75.00
5 Only The Dead Are Free 75.00
6 Blood & Guts 60.00
7 The Phantom Sub 60.00
8 More Plasma! 60.00
9 Red Artillery 60.00
10 .... 60.00
11 Sept., 1953 .... 60.00

SOLDIERS OF FORTUNE
**Creston Publications
(American Comics Group),
Feb.–March, 1952**
1 OW(c),B:Ace Carter,
　Crossbones, Lance Larson . 300.00
2 OW(c) 175.00
3 OW(c) 125.00
4 .... 125.00
5 OW(c) 125.00

Space Adventures #3
© Charlton Comics

6 OW(c),OW,Bondage(c) 150.00
7 .... 125.00
8 OW thru 10............... @125.00
11 OW,Format Change to War ... 75.00
12 .... 75.00
13 OW,Feb.–March, 1953 .... 75.00

SON OF SINBAD
**St. John Publishing Co.,
Feb., 1950**
1 JKu,JKu(c),The Curse of the
　Caliph's Dancer 500.00

SPACE ACTION
**Junior Books
(Ace Magazines),
June, 1952–Oct., 1952**
1 Invaders from a Lost Galaxy 1,000.00
2 The Silicon Monster from
　Galaxy X 750.00
3 Attack on Ishtar 750.00

SPACE ADVENTURES
**Capitol Stories/
Charlton Comics,
July, 1952**
1 AFa&LM(c) 700.00
2 .... 325.00
3 DG(c) 250.00
4 DG(c) 250.00
5 StC(c) 250.00
6 StC(c),Two Worlds 225.00
7 DG(c),Transformation 250.00
8 DG(c),All For Love 225.00
9 DG(c) 225.00
10 SD,SD(c)................. 650.00
11 SD,JoS 750.00
12 SD(c) 800.00
13 A:Blue Beetle 250.00
14 A:Blue Beetle 250.00
15 Ph(c) of Rocky Jones 250.00
16 BKa,A:Rocky Jones 250.00
17 A:Rocky Jones 225.00
18 A:Rocky Jones 225.00
19 .... 200.00
20 First Trip to the Moon 350.00
21 War at Sea 200.00
22 Does Not Exist
23 SD,Space Trip to the Moon. .. 300.00
24 .... 225.00
25 Brontosaurus............. 225.00
26 SD,Flying Saucers 300.00
27 SD,Flying Saucers 300.00
28 Moon Trap............... 100.00
29 Captive From Space....... 100.00
30 Peril in the Sky 100.00
31 SD,SD(c),Enchanted Planet .. 250.00
32 SD,SD(c),Last Ship
　from Earth 250.00
33 Galactic Scourge,
　I&O:Captain Atom 650.00
34 SD,SD(c),A:Captain Atom.... 275.00
35 thru 40 SD,SD(c),
　A:Captain Atom .... @275.00
41 .... 75.00
42 SD,A:Captain Atom......... 75.00
43 .... 75.00
44 A:Mercury Man 75.00
45 A:Mercury Man 75.00
46 thru 58................. @75.00
59 Nov., 1964............... 75.00

SPACE BUSTERS
**Ziff-Davis Publishing Co.,
Spring, 1952**
1 BK,NS(c),Ph(c),Charge of
　the Battle Women 1,200.00

2 EK,BK,MA,NS(c),
　Bondage(c),Ph(c) 800.00
3 Autumn, 1952 .... 750.00

SPACE COMICS
See: FUNNY TUNES

SPACE DETECTIVE
**Avon Periodicals,
July, 1951**
1 WW,WW(c),Opium Smugglers
　of Venus 1,500.00
2 WW,WW(c),Batwomen of
　Mercury 1,200.00
3 EK(c),SeaNymphs ofNeptune 600.00
4 EK,Flame Women of Vulcan,
　Bondage(c) 650.00

SPACE MOUSE
**Avon Periodicals,
April, 1953**
1 Funny Animal 100.00
2 Funny Animal.............. 75.00
3 thru 5 Funny Animal ...... @50.00

SPACE PATROL
**Approved Comics
(Ziff-Davis),
Summer, 1952**
1 BK,NS,Ph(c), The Lady of
　Diamonds 1,400.00
2 BK,NS,Ph(c),Slave King of
　Pluto,Oct.–Nov., 1952 ..... 850.00

SPACE THRILLERS
Avon Periodicals, 1954
N# Contents May Vary....... 1,500.00

SPACE WESTERN
COMICS
See: YELLOWJACKET
COMICS

SPARKLER COMICS
**United Features Syndicate,
July, 1940**
1 Jim Handy 500.00
2 Frankie Doodle,Aug., 1940 ... 400.00

SPARKLER COMICS
**United Features Syndicate,
July, 1941**
1 BHg,O:Sparkman;B:Tarzan,Captain
　& the Kids,Ella Cinders,Danny
　Dingle,Dynamite Dunn, Nancy,
　Abbie an' Slats, Frankie
　Doodle,Broncho Bill 3,300.00
2 BHg, The Case of Poisoned
　Fruit 1,200.00
3 BHg 1,000.00
4 BHg,Case of Sparkman &
　the Firefly 1,000.00
5 BHg,Sparkman,Natch 800.00
6 BHg,Case o/t Bronze Bees .. 800.00
7 BHg,Case o/t Green Raiders . 800.00
8 BHg,V:River Fiddler 800.00
9 BHg,N:Sparkman 800.00
10 BHg,B:Hap Hopper,
　Sparkman's ID revealed 800.00
11 BHg,V:Japanese 600.00
12 BHg,Another N:Sparkman ... 600.00

13 BHg,Hap Hopper Rides
  For Freedom 600.00
14 BHg,BHg(c),Tarzan
  V:Yellow Killer 750.00
15 BHg 500.00
16 BHg,Sparkman V:Japanese . . 500.00
17 BHg,Nancy(c) 500.00
18 BHg,Sparkman in Crete 500.00
19 BHg,I&B:Race Riley,
  Commandos 500.00
20 BHg,Nancy(c) 500.00
21 BHg,Tarzan(c) 550.00
22 BHg,Tarzan(c) 400.00
23 BHg,Capt&Kids(c) 400.00
24 BHg,Nancy(c) 400.00
25 BHg,BHg(c),Tarzan(c) 550.00
26 BHg,Capt&Kids(c) 400.00
27 BHg,Nancy(c) 400.00
28 BHg,BHg(c),Tarzan(c) 550.00
29 BHg,Capt&Kids(c) 400.00
30 BHg,Nancy(c) 400.00
31 BHg,BHg(c),Tarzan(c) 550.00
32 BHg,Capt&Kids(c) 250.00
33 BHg,Nancy(c) 250.00
34 BHg,BHg(c),Tarzan(c) 550.00
35 BHg,Capt&Kids(c) 250.00
36 BHg,Nancy(c) 250.00
37 BHg,BHg(c),Tarzan(c) 550.00
38 BHg,Capt&Kids(c) 225.00
39 BHg,BHg(c),Tarzan(c) 550.00
40 BHg,Nancy(c) 225.00
41 BHg,Capt&Kids(c) 175.00
42 BHg,BHg,Tarzan(c) 350.00
43 BHg,Nancy(c) 175.00
44 BHg,Tarzan(c) 350.00
45 BHg,Capt&Kids(c) 175.00
46 BHg,Nancy(c) 175.00
47 BHg,Tarzan(c) 350.00
48 BHg,Nancy(c) 175.00
49 BHg,Capt&Kids(c) 175.00
50 BHg,BHg(c),Tarzan(c) 350.00
51 BHg,Capt&Kids(c) 175.00
52 BHg,Nancy(c) 175.00
53 BHg,BHg(c),Tarzan(c) 350.00
54 BHg,Capt&Kids(c) 150.00
55 BHg,Nancy(c) 150.00
56 BHg,Capt&Kids(c) 150.00
57 BHg,F:Li'l Abner 150.00
58 BHg,A:Fearless Fosdick 175.00
59 BHg,B:Li'l Abner 175.00
60 BHg,Nancy(c) 150.00
61 BHg,Capt&Kids(c) 150.00
62 BHg,Li'L Abner(c) 150.00
63 BHg,Capt&Kids(c) 150.00
64 BHg,Valentines (c) 150.00
65 BHg,Nancy(c) 150.00
66 BHg,Capt&Kids(c) 150.00
67 BHg,Nancy(c) 150.00
68 BHg 150.00
69 BHg,B:Nancy (c) 150.00
70 BHg 150.00
71 thru 80 BHg . . . . @100.00
81 BHg,E:Nancy(c) 100.00
82 BHg 100.00
83 BHg,Tarzan(c) 175.00
84 BHg 90.00
85 BHg,E:Li'l Abner 90.00
86 BHg 90.00
87 BHg,Nancy(c) 90.00
88 thru 96 BHg . . . . @90.00
97 BHg,O:Lady Ruggles 175.00
98 BHg 75.00
99 BHg,Nancy(c) 75.00
100 BHg,Nancy(c) 90.00
101 thru 107 BHg . . . . @60.00
108 & 109 BHg,ATh 100.00
110 BHg 60.00
111 BHg 60.00
112 BHg 60.00
113 BHg,ATh 100.00
114 thru 120 BHg . . . . @75.00

SPARKLING STARS
Holyoke Publishing Co., June, 1944
1 B:Hell's Angels,Ali Baba,FBI,
  Boxie Weaver,Petey & Pop . 250.00
2 Speed Spaulding 150.00
3 FBI 100.00
4 thru 12 . . . . @100.00
13 O&I:Jungo, The Man-Beast . . 110.00
14 thru 19 . . . . @100.00
20 I:Fangs the Wolfboy 100.00
21 thru 28 . . . . @100.00
29 Bondage(c) 110.00
30 thru 32 . . . . @75.00
33 March, 1948 . . . . 75.00

SPARKMAN
Frances M. McQueeny, 1944
1 O:Sparkman 375.00

SPARKY WATTS
Columbia Comics Group, 1942
1 A:Skyman,Hitler(c) 900.00
2 . . . . 350.00
3 . . . . 250.00
4 O:Skyman 250.00
5 A:Skyman 225.00
6 . . . . 100.00
7 . . . . 100.00
8 . . . . 150.00
9 . . . . 100.00
10 1949 . . . . 100.00

[STEVE SAUNDERS] SPECIAL AGENT
Parents Magazine/ Commended Comics, Dec., 1947
1 J. Edgar Hoover, Ph(c) 125.00
2 . . . . 75.00
3 thru 7 . . . . @60.00
8 Sept., 1949 . . . . 60.00

SPECIAL COMICS
See: LAUGH COMICS

SPECIAL EDITION COMICS
Fawcett Publications, Aug., 1940
1 CCB,CCB(c),F:Captain
  Marvel 14,000.00

SPEED COMICS
Brookwood/Speed Publ. Harvey Publications, Oct., 1939
1 BP,B&O:Shock Gibson,B:Spike
  Marlin,Biff Bannon 5,000.00
2 BP,B:Shock Gibson(c) 1,500.00
3 BP,GT 900.00
4 BP 750.00
5 BP,DBr 750.00
6 BP,GT 700.00
7 GT,JKu,Bondage, B:Mars
  Mason 700.00
8 JKu 650.00
9 JKu 650.00
10 JKu,E:Shock Gibson(c) 650.00
11 JKu,E:Mars Mason 650.00
12 B:The Wasp 750.00
13 I:Captain Freedom;B:Girls
  Commandos,Pat Parker 800.00
14 Pocket sized format-100pgs. . 900.00

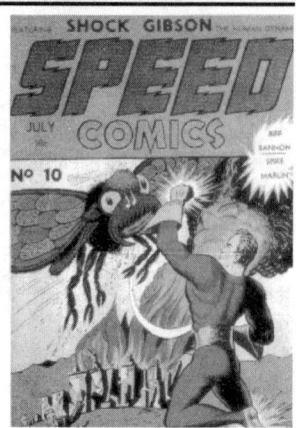

Speed Comics #10
© Harvey Publications

15 Pocket size 900.00
16 JKu,Pocket size 900.00
17 O:Black Cat 1,000.00
18 B:Capt.Freedom,Bondage(c) . 800.00
19 S&K 750.00
20 S&K 750.00
21 JKu(c),Hitler & Tojo 900.00
22 JKu(c) 750.00
23 JKu(c),O:Girl Commandos . . . 800.00
24 Hitler,Tojo & Mussilini(c) 750.00
25 . . . . 550.00
26 GT,Flag (c),Black Cat 550.00
27 GT,Black Cat 550.00
28 E:Capt Freedom 550.00
29 Case o/t Black Marketeers . . . 550.00
30 POW Death Chambers 550.00
31 ASh(c),Nazi Thrashing(c) . . . 850.00
32 ASh(c) 700.00
33 ASh(c) 700.00
34 ASh(c) 700.00
35 ASh(c),BlackCat'sDeathTrap . 725.00
36 ASh(c) 700.00
37 RP(c) 700.00
38 RP(c),War Bond Plea with Iwo
  Jima flag allusion(c) 700.00
39 RP(c),B:Capt Freedom(c) 500.00
40 RP(c) 500.00
41 RP(c) 500.00
42 JKu,RP(c) 500.00
43 JKu,E:Capt Freedom(c) 550.00
44 BP,JKu,Four Kids on a raft,
  Jan.–Feb., 1947 . . . . 600.00

SPEED SMITH THE HOT ROD KING
Ziff-Davis Publishing Co., Spring, 1952
1 INS,Ph(c),A:Roscoe
  the Rascal 250.00

SPIRIT, THE
Will Eisner (Weekly Coverless Comic Book), June, 1940
WE,O:SPirit 1,000.00
6/9/40 WE 600.00
6/16/40 WE,Black Queen . . . 300.00
6/23/40 WE,Mr Mystic 250.00
6/30/40 WE 250.00
7/7/40 WE,Black Queen 250.00
7/14/40 WE 200.00
7/21/40 WE 200.00
7/28/40 WE 200.00

GOLDEN AGE

8/4/40 WE	200.00
7/7/40-11/24/40,WE	165.00
11/10/40 WE,Black Queen	150.00
12/1/40 WE,Ellen	
Spanking(c)	225.00
12/8/40-12/29/40	125.00
1941 WE Each	125.00
3/16 WE I:Silk Satin	200.00
6/15 WE I Twilight	125.00
6/22 WE Hitler	125.00
1942 WE Each	100.00
2-1 Duchess	125.00
2-15	100.00
2-23	150.00
1943 WE Each,LF,WE scripts	50.00
1944 JCo,LF	30.00
1945 LF Each,	30.00
1946 WE Each	50.00
1/13 WE,O:The Spirit.	75.00
1/20 WE,Satin	75.00
3/17 WE,I:Nylon	75.00
4/21 WE,I:Mr.Carrion	85.00
7/7 WE,I:Dulcet Tone&Skinny	75.00
10/6 WE,I:F:Gell	100.00
1947 WE Each	50.00
7/13.,WE,Hansel &Gretel	70.00
7/20,WE,A:Bomb	75.00
9/28,WE,Flying Saucers	100.00
10/5,WE, Cinderella	70.00
12/7,WE,I:Power Puff	75.00
1948 WE Each	50.00
1/11,WE,Sparrow Fallon	60.00
1/25,WE,I:Last A Net	65.00
3/14,WE,A:Kretuama	60.00
4/4,WE,A:Wildrice	60.00
7/25,The Thing	100.00
8/22,Poe Tale,Horror	125.00
9/18, A:Lorelei	60.00
11/7,WE,A:Plaster of Paris	65.00
1949 WE Each	50.00
1/23 WE,I:Thorne	65.00
8/21 WE,I:Monica Veto	65.00
9/25 WE,A;Ice	65.00
12/4 WE,I:Flaxen	60.00
1950 WE Each	50.00
1/8 WE,I:Sand Saref	150.00
2/10, Horror Issue	60.00
1951 WE(Last WE 8/12/51)	@50.00
Non-Eisners	@25.00
1952 Non-Eisners	@25.00
7/27 WW,Denny Colt	500.00
8/3 WW,Moon	500.00
8/10 WW.Moon	500.00
8/17 WW,WE,Heart	400.00
8/24 WW,Rescue	400.00
8/31 WW,Last Man	400.00
9/7 WW,Man Moon	550.00
9/14 WE.	150.00
9/21 WE Space	350.00
9/28 WE Moon	400.00
10/5 WE Last Story	250.00

SPIRIT, THE
Quality Comics Group/ Vital Publ., 1944

N# Wanted Dead or Alive!	1,000.00
N# ...in Crime Doesn't Pay	600.00
N# ...In Murder Runs Wild	500.00
4 ...Flirts with Death	400.00
5 ...Wanted Dead or Alive	350.00
6 ...Gives You Triple Value	300.00
7 ...Rocks the Underworld	300.00
8	300.00
9 ...Throws Fear Into the Heart of Crime	300.00
10 ...Stalks Crime.	300.00
11 ...America's Greatest Crime Buster	250.00
12 WE(c),...The Famous Outlaw Who Smashes Crime	400.00

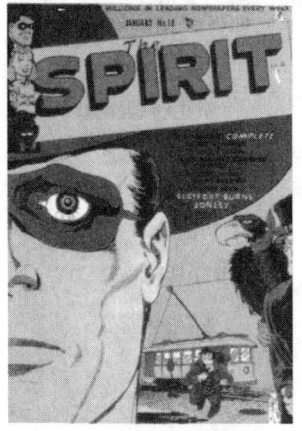

Spirit #19
© Quality Comics Group

13 WE(c),...and Ebony Cleans Out the Underworld;Bondage(c)	400.00
14 WE(c)	400.00
15 WE(c),Bank Robber at Large	400.00
16 WE(c),The Caase of the Uncanny Cat	400.00
17 WE(c),The Organ Grinding Bank Robber	400.00
18 WE,WE(c),'The Bucket of Blood	450.00
19 WE,WE(c),'The Man Who Murdered the Spirit'	450.00
20 WE,WE(c),'The Vortex'	450.00
21 WE,WE(c),'P'Gell of Paris'	450.00
22 WE(c),TheOctopus,Aug.1950	800.00

SPIRIT, THE
Fiction House Magazines, 1952

1 Curse of Claymore Castle	500.00
2 WE,WE(c),Who Says Crime Doesn't Pay	450.00
3 WE/JGr(c),League of Lions	400.00
4 WE,WE&JGr(c),Last Prowl of Mr. Mephisto;Bondage (c)	450.00
5 WE,WE(c),Ph(c)1954	450.00

SPIRITMAN
Will Eisner, 1944

1 3 Spirit Sections from 1944 Bound Together	250.00
2 LF, 2 Spirit Sections from 1944 Bound Together	200.00

SPITFIRE COMICS
Harvey Publ., Aug., 1941

1 MKd(c),100-pgs.,Pocket-size	1,000.00
2 100-pgs.,Pocket-size, Oct., 1941	950.00

SPOOK COMICS
Baily Publications, 1946

1 A:Mr. Lucifer	400.00

SPOOK DETECTIVE CASES
See: CRIMINALS ON THE RUN

SPOOKY
Harvey Publications, Nov., 1955

1 Funny Apparition	600.00
2 same	300.00
3 thru 10 same	@200.00
11 thru 20 same	@100.00
21 thru 30 same	@75.00
31 thru 40 same	@65.00
41 thru 70 same	@60.00
71 thru 90 same	@40.00
91 thru 120 same	@35.00
121 thru 130 same	@15.00
131 thru 161 same,Sept., 1980	@10.00

SPOOKY MYSTERIES
Your Guide Publishing Co., 1946

1 Rib-Tickling Horror	250.00

SPORT COMICS
See: TRUE SPORT PICTURE STORIES

SPORTS THRILLS
See: DICK COLE

SPOTLIGHT COMICS
Harry 'A' Chesler Jr. Publications, Nov., 1944

1 GT,GT(c),B:Veiled Avenger, Black Dwarf,Barry Kuda	900.00
2	750.00
3 1945,Eye Injury	800.00

SPUNKY
Standard Comics, April, 1949

1 FF,Adventures of a Junior Cowboy	125.00
2 FF	100.00
3	75.00
4	75.00
5	75.00
6	75.00
7 Nov., 1951	75.00

SPY AND COUNTER SPY
Best Syndicated Features (American Comics Group), Aug.–Sept., 1949

1 I&O:Jonathan Kent	350.00
2	200.00

Becomes:

SPY HUNTERS
Dec., 1949–Jan., 1950

3 Jonathan Kent	300.00
4 J.Kent.	150.00
5 J.Kent.	150.00
6 J.Kent.	150.00
7 OW(c),J.Kent.	150.00
8 OW(c),J.Kent.	150.00
9 OW(c),J.Kent	150.00
10 OW(c),J.Kent	150.00
11	125.00
12 OW(c),MD	125.00
13 and 14	@125.00
15 OW(c)	125.00
16 AW	175.00
17	100.00
18 War (c)	100.00

GOLDEN AGE

GOLDEN AGE

19 and 20 . . . . @100.00	
21 B:War Content 100.00	
22 . . . . 100.00	
23 Torture 250.00	
24 'BlackmailBrigade',July,1953 . 100.00	

SPY SMASHER
Fawcett Publications, Autumn, 1941
1 B;Spy Smasher 5,500.00
2 Mra(c) 2,500.00
3 Bondage (c) 1,500.00
4 . . . . 1,400.00
5 Mra,Mt. Rushmore(c) 1,400.00
6 MRa(a&c),V:The Sharks
  of Steel 1,200.00
7 Mra 1,200.00
8 AB 1,000.00
9 AB,Hitler,Tojo, Mussolini(c) . . 1,200.00
10 AB,Did Spy Smasher
  Kill Hitler? 1,200.00
11 AB,Feb., 1943 . . . . 1,000.00

SQUEEKS
Lev Gleason Publications, Oct., 1953
1 CBi(c),(fa) 75.00
2 CBi(c),(fa) 40.00
3 CBi(c),(fa) 35.00
4 (fa) 35.00
5 (fa),Jan., 1954 . . . . 35.00

STAMP COMICS
Youthful Magazines/Stamp Comics, Inc., Oct., 1951
1 HcK,Birth of Liberty 350.00
2 HcK,RP,Battle of White Plains 200.00
3 HcK,DW,RP,Iwo Jima 150.00
4 HcK,DW,RP 150.00
5 HcK,Von Hindenberg disaster . 175.00
6 HcK,The Immortal Chaplains. . 150.00
7 HcK,RKr,RP,B&O:Railroad . . . 250.00
Becomes:

THRILLING ADVENTURES IN STAMPS
Jan., 1953
8 HcK, 100 Pgs.. . . . . 1,000.00

STAR COMICS
Comic Magazines/Ultem Publ./Chesler Centaur Publications, Feb., 1937
1 B:Dan Hastings. 2,500.00
2 . . . . 1,100.00
3 . . . . 900.00
4 WMc(c) 900.00
5 WMc(c),A:Little Nemo 900.00
6 CBi(c),FG 850.00
7 FG 800.00
8 BoW,BoW(c),FG,A:Little
  Nemo,Horror 850.00
9 FG,CBi(c) 800.00
10 FG,CBi(c),BoW,A:Impyk. . . . 1,100.00
11 FG,BoW,JCo 850.00
12 FG,BoW,B:Riders of the
  Golden West 750.00
13 FG,BoW. 750.00
14 FG,GFx(c) 750.00
15 CBu,B:The Last Pirate 750.00
16 CBu,B:Phantom Rider 750.00
2-1 CBu,B:Phantom Rider(c) . . 800.00
2-2 CBu,A:Diana Deane 750.00
2-3 GFx(c),CBu 700.00
2-4 CBu 700.00

2-5 CBu 700.00
2-6 CBu,E:Phanton Rider 700.00
2-7 CBu,Aug., 1939 . . . . 700.00

STARLET O'HARA IN HOLLYWOOD
Standard Comics, Dec., 1948
1 The Terrific Tee-Age Comic . . . 275.00
2 Her Romantic Adventures in
  Movie land 150.00
3 and 4, Sept., 1949 . . . . . . @125.00

STAR RANGER
Comics Magazines/Ultem/Centaur Publ., Feb., 1937
1 FG,I:Western Comic 2,500.00
2 . . . . 1,300.00
3 FG 1,100.00
4 . . . . 1,100.00
5 . . . . 1,100.00
6 FG 1,000.00
7 FG 900.00
8 GFx,FG,PGn,BoW 900.00
9 GFx,FG,PGn,BoW 900.00
10 JCo,GFx,FG,PGn,BoW . . 1,300.00
11 . . . . 850.00
12 JCo(a&c),FG,PGn 850.00
Becomes:

COWBOY COMICS
July, 1938
13 FG,PGn 1,000.00
14 FG,PGn 900.00
Becomes:

STAR RANGER FUNNIES
Oct., 1938
15 WE,PGn 1,300.00
2-1(16) JCo(a&c) 1,000.00
2-2(17) PGn,JCo,A:Night Hawk. . 900.00
2-3(18) JCo,FG 750.00
2-4(19) A:Kit Carson 750.00
2-5(20) Oct., 1939 . . . . 750.00

STARS AND STRIPES COMICS
Comic Corp of America (Centaur Publications), May, 1941
2 PGn,PGn(c),'Called to Colors',
  The Shark,The Voice 3,000.00
3 PGn,PGn(c),O:Dr.Synthe . . . 1,700.00
4 PGn,PGn(c),I:The Stars
  & Stripes 1,500.00
5 . . . . 1,000.00
6(5), Dec., 1941 . . . . 1,000.00

STAR STUDDED
Cambridge House, 1945
N# 25 cents (c) price;128 pgs.;
  32 F:stories 400.00
N# The Cadet,Hoot Gibson,
  Blue Beetle 350.00

STARTLING COMICS
Better Publ./Nedor Publ., June, 1940
1 WE,LF,B&O:Captain Future,
  Mystico, Wonder Man;
  B:Masked Rider 3,500.00
2 Captain Future(c) 1,300.00
3 same 1,100.00

Stars and Stripes #2
© Centaur Publications

4 same 800.00
5 same 750.00
6 same 700.00
7 same 700.00
8 ASh(c),Captain Future 700.00
9 Bondage(c) 700.00
10 O:Fighting Yank 5,000.00
11 Fighting Yank(c) 1,500.00
12 Hitler,Mussolini,Tojo (c) 1,300.00
13 JBi 800.00
14 JBi. 800.00
15 Fighting Yank (c). 800.00
16 Bondage(c),O:FourComrades. 900.00
17 Fighting Yank (c),
  E:Masked Rider. 700.00
18 JBi,B&O:Pyroman 1,300.00
19 Pyroman(c) 600.00
20 Pyroman(c),B:Oracle 650.00
21 HcK,ASh(c)Bondage(c)O:Ape 750.00
22 HcK,ASh(c),Fighting Yank(c) . 600.00
23 HcK,BEv,ASh(c),Pyroman(c) . 600.00
24 HcK,BEv,ASh(c),Fighting
  Yank(c) 600.00
25 HcK,BEv,ASh(c),Pyroman(c) . 600.00
26 BEv,ASh(c),Fighting Yank(c). . 600.00
27 BEv,ASh(c),Pyroman(c) 600.00
28 BEv,ASh(c),Fighting Yank(c). . 600.00
29 BEv,ASh(c),Pyroman(c) 600.00
30 ASh(c),Fighting Yank(c) 600.00
31 ASh(c),Pyroman(c) 600.00
32 ASh(c),Fighting Yank(c) 600.00
33 ASh(c),Pyroman(c) 600.00
34 ASh(c),Fighting Yank(c),
  O:Scarab 600.00
35 ASh(c),Pyroman(c) 650.00
36 ASh(c),Fighting Yank(c) 500.00
37 ASh(c),Bondage (c) 500.00
38 ASh(c),Bondage(c) 500.00
39 ASh(c),Pyroman(c) 500.00
40 ASh(c),E:Captain Future. . . . 500.00
41 ASh(c),Pyroman(c) 500.00
42 ASh(c),Fighting Yank(c) 500.00
43 ASh(c),Pyroman(c),
  E:Pyroman. 500.00
44 Grl(c),Lance Lewis(c) 900.00
45 Grl(c),I:Tygra 900.00
46 Grl,Grl(c),Bondage(c) 1,300.00
47 ASh(c),Bondage(c) 800.00
48 ASh(c),Lance Lewis(c) 800.00
49 ASh(c),Bondage(c),
  E:Fighting Yank 5,000.00
50 ASh(c),Lance Lewis(c),
  Sea Eagle 800.00
51 ASh(c),Sea Eagle 800.00

Startling Comics #8
© *Nedor Publications*

52 ASh(c) 800.00
53 ASh(c),Sept., 1948 . . . . 800.00

STARTLING TERROR TALES
Star Publications, May, 1952
10 WW,LbC(c),The Story Starts 1,000.00
11 LbC(c),The Ghost Spider
    of Death 1,700.00
12 LbC(c),White Hand Horror . . . 350.00
13 JyD,LbC(c),Love From
    a Gorgor 375.00
14 LbC(c),Trapped by the
    Color of Blood 350.00
4 LbC(c),Crime at the Carnival . 300.00
5 LbC(c),The Gruesome
    Demon of Terror 300.00
6 LbC(c),Footprints of Death . . . 300.00
7 LbC(c),The Case of the
    Strange Murder 300.00
8 RP,LbC(c),Phantom Brigade . . 300.00
9 LbC(c),The Forbidden Tomb . . 275.00
10 LbC(c),The Horrible Entity . . . 325.00
11 RP,LbC(c),The Law Will
    Win, July, 1954 . . . . 300.00

STEVE CANYON COMICS
Harvey Publications, Feb., 1948–Dec., 1948
1 MC,BP,O:Steve Canyon. 275.00
2 MC,BP 175.00
3 MC,BP,Canyon's Crew 150.00
4 MC,BP,Chase of Death 150.00
5 MC,BP,A:Happy Easter 150.00
6 MC,BP,A:Madame Lynx. 165.00

STEVE ROPER
Famous Funnies, April, 1948
1 Reprints newspaper strips . . . 150.00
2 . . . . 75.00
3 . . . . 60.00
4 . . . . 60.00
5 Dec., 1948 . . . . 60.00

STORIES BY FAMOUS AUTHORS ILLUSTRATED
See: FAST FICTION

STORY OF HARRY S. TRUMAN, THE
Democratic National Committee, 1948
N# Giveaway-The Life of Our
    33rd President 200.00

STRAIGHT ARROW
Magazine Enterprises, Feb.–March, 1950
1 OW,B:Straight Arrow & his
    Horse Fury 600.00
2 BP,B&O:Red Hawk 275.00
3 BP,FF(c) 350.00
4 BP,Cave(c). 250.00
5 BP,StraightArrow'sGreatLeap . 250.00
6 BP 225.00
7 BP,The Railroad Invades
    Comanche Country 225.00
8 BP 225.00
9 BP 225.00
10 BP 225.00
11 BP,The Valley of Time 250.00
12 thru 19 BP . . . . @200.00
20 BP,Straight Arrow's
    Great War Shield. 225.00
21 BP,O:Fury 250.00
22 BP,FF(c) 275.00
23 BP 150.00
24 BP,The Dragons of Doom. . . . 200.00
25 BP, Secret Cave 150.00
26 BP,Red Hawk vs. Vikings 150.00
27 BP 125.00
28 BP,Red Hawk 125.00
29 thru 35 BP . . . . @125.00
36 BP Red Hawk, Drug 110.00
37 BP 110.00
38 BP 110.00
39 BP,The Canyon Beasts. 125.00
40 BP,Secret of the
    Spanish Specters. 125.00
41 BP. 100.00
42 BP 100.00
43 BP,I:Blaze 120.00
44 BP 100.00
45 BP 100.00

Straight Arrow #24
© *Magazine Enterprises*

46 thru 53 BP . . . . @100.00
54 BP,March, 1956 . . . . 100.00

STRANGE CONFESSIONS
Approved Publications (Ziff-Davis), Spring, 1952
1 EK,Ph(c) 650.00
2 Ph(c) 400.00
3 EK,Ph(c),Girls reformatory. . . . 400.00
4 Ph(c),Girls reformatory 400.00

STRANGE FANTASY
Farrell Publications/ Ajax Comics, Aug., 1952
(2)1 Jungle Princess. 600.00
2 Drug & Horror 500.00
3 The Dancing Ghost 500.00
4 Demon in the Dungeon,
    A:Rocketman. 500.00
5 Visiting Corpse 300.00
6 . . . . 300.00
7 A:Madam Satan 450.00
8 A:Black Cat 300.00
9 S&K,SD, Black Cat 400.00
10 . . . . 300.00
11 Fearful Things Can Happen
    in a Lonely Place. 400.00
12 The Undying Fiend 300.00
13 Terror in the Attic,
    Bondage(c) 400.00
14 Monster in the Building,
    Oct.–Nov., 1954. . . . . 300.00

UNKNOWN WORLD
Fawcett Publications, June, 1952
1 NS(c),Ph(c),Will You Venture
    to Meet the Unknown 600.00
Becomes:

STRANGE STORIES FROM ANOTHER WORLD
Aug., 1952
2 NS(c),Ph(c),Will You?
    Dare You 750.00
3 NS(c),Ph(c),The Dark Mirror . . 500.00
4 NS(c),Ph(c),Monsters of
    the Mind 500.00
5 NS(c),Ph(c),Dance of the
    Doomed Feb., 1953 . . . . 500.00

STRANGE SUSPENSE STORIES
Fawcett Publications, June, 1952
1 BP,MSy,MBi 1,000.00
2 MBi,GE 600.00
3 MBi,GE(c) 500.00
4 BP 500.00
5 MBi(c),Voodoo(c). 500.00
6 BEv 275.00
7 BEv 275.00
8 AW 275.00
9 . . . . 275.00
10 . . . . 350.00
11 . . . . 200.00
12 . . . . 200.00
13 . . . . 200.00
14 . . . . 250.00
15 AW,BEv(c). 250.00

Charlton Comics
16 . . . . 350.00
17 . . . . 300.00

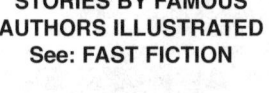

GOLDEN AGE

18 SD,SD(c)	500.00
19 SD,SD(c)	700.00
20 SD,SD(c)	500.00
21	250.00
22 SD(c)	450.00

Becomes:

THIS IS SUSPENSE!
Feb., 1955

23 WW	400.00
24	150.00
25	100.00
26	100.00

Becomes:

STRANGE SUSPENSE STORIES
Oct., 1955

27	200.00
28	150.00
29	150.00
30	150.00
31 SD(c)	300.00
32 SD	300.00
33 SD	300.00
34 SD,SD(c)	600.00
35 SD	300.00
36 SD,SD(c)	300.00
37 SD	375.00
38	300.00
39 SD	350.00
40 SD	300.00
41 SD	300.00
42	90.00
43	90.00
44	90.00
45 SD	250.00
46	90.00
47 SD	250.00
48 SD	250.00
49	90.00
50 SD	250.00
51 thru 53 SD	@150.00
54 thru 60	@75.00
61 thru 74	@50.00
75 Capt. Atom	250.00
76 Capt. Atom	100.00
77 Capt. Atom	100.00

STRANGE SUSPENSE STORIES
See: LAWBREAKERS

STRANGE TERRORS
St. John Publishing Co., June, 1952

1 The Ghost of Castle Karloff, Bondage(c)	700.00
2 UnshackledFlight intoNowhere	400.00
3 JKu,Ph(c),The Ghost Who Ruled Crazy Heights	500.00
4 JKu,Ph(c),Terror from the Tombs	700.00
5 JKu,Ph(c),No Escaping the Pool of Death	500.00
6 LC,PAM,Bondage(c),Giant	700.00
7 JKu,JKu(c),Cat's Death,Giant	750.00

STRANGE WORLD OF YOUR DREAMS
Prize Group, Aug., 1952

1 S&K(c),What Do They Mean– Messages Rec'd in Sleep	1,200.00
2 MMe,S&K(c),Why did I Dream That I Was Being Married to a Man without a Face?	700.00

3 S&K(c)	500.00
4 MMe,S&K(c),The Story of a Man Who Dreamed a Murder that Happened	450.00

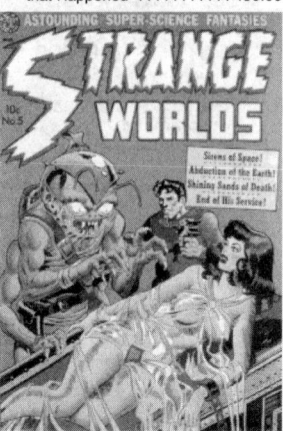
Strange Worlds #5
© Avon Periodicals

STRANGE WORLDS
Avon Periodicals, Nov., 1950

1 JKu,Spider God of Akka	1,500.00
2 WW,Dara of the Vikings	1,400.00
3 AW&FF,EK(c),WW,JO	2,700.00
4 JO,WW,WW(c),The Enchanted Dagger	1,600.00
5 WW,WW(c),JO,Bondage(c); Sirens of Space	900.00
6 EK,WW(c),JO,SC, Maid o/t Mist	600.00
7 EK, Sabotage on Space Station 1	500.00
8 JKu,EK,The Metal Murderer	500.00
9 The Radium Monsters	500.00
18 JKu	400.00
19 Astounding Super Science Fantasies	400.00
20 WW(c),Fighting War Stories	125.00
21 EK(c)	75.00
22 EK(c),Sept.–Oct., 1955	75.00

STRICTLY PRIVATE
Eastern Color Printing, July, 1942

1 You're in theArmyNow-Humor	275.00
2 F:Peter Plink, 1942	250.00

STUNTMAN COMICS
Harvey Publications, April–May, 1946

1 S&K,O:Stuntman	1,500.00
2 S&K,New Champ of Split- Second Action	900.00
3 S&K,Digest sized,Mail Order Only, B&W interior, Oct.–Nov., 1946	1,000.00

SUGAR BOWL COMICS
Famous Funnies, May, 1948

1 ATh,ATh(c),The Newest in Teen Age!	175.00
2	100.00
3 ATh	125.00

4	75.00
5 Jan., 1949	75.00

SUN FUN KOMIKS
Sun Publications, 1939

1 F:Spineless Sam the Sweetheart	400.00

SUNNY, AMERICA'S SWEETHEART
Fox Features Syndicate, Dec., 1947

11 AF,AF(c)	1,100.00
12 AF,AF(c)	750.00
13 AF,AF(c)	750.00
14 AF,AF(c)	750.00

SUNSET CARSON
Charlton Comics, Feb., 1951–Aug., 1951

1 Painted, Ph(c);Wyoming Mail	1,200.00
2 Kit Carson-Pioneer	800.00
3	700.00
4 Panhandle Trouble	700.00

SUPER BOOK OF COMICS
Western Publishing Co., 1943

N# Dick Tracy	500.00
1 Dick Tracy, Smuggling	500.00
1a Smilin' Jack	250.00
2 Smitty,Magic Morro	250.00
3 Capt. Midnight	500.00
3a Moon Mullins	200.00
4 Red Ryder,Magic Morro	250.00
4a Smitty	200.00
5 Don Winslow,Magic Morro	250.00
5a DonWinslow,StratosphereJim	250.00
5a Terry & the Pirates	300.00
6 Don Winslow	300.00
6a King of the Royal Mounties	300.00
7 Little Orphan Annie	200.00
7a Dick Tracy	400.00
8 Dick Tracy	300.00
8a Dan Dunn	200.00
9 Terry & the Pirates	300.00
10 Red Ryder, Magic Morro	225.00

SUPER-BOOK OF COMICS
Western Publishing Co., 1944

1 Dick Tracy (Omar)	250.00
1 Dick Tracy (Hancock)	175.00
2 Bugs Bunny (Omar)	75.00
2 Bugs Bunny (Hancock)	50.00
3 Terry & the Pirates (Omar)	125.00
3 Terry & the Pirates (Hancock)	100.00
4 Andy Panda (Omar)	75.00
4 Andy Panda (Hancock)	60.00
5 Smokey Stover (Omar)	75.00
5 Smokey Stover (Hancock)	60.00
6 Porky Pig (Omar)	75.00
6 Porky Pig (Hancock)	50.00
7 Smilin' Jack (Omar)	75.00
7 Smilin' Jack (Hancock)	75.00
8 Oswald the Rabbit (Omar)	75.00
8 Oswald the Rabbit (Hancock)	60.00
9 Alley Oop (Omar)	150.00
9 Alley Oop (Hancock)	135.00
10 Elmer Fudd (Omar)	75.00
10 Elmer Fudd (Hancock)	50.00
11 Little Orphan Annie (Omar)	75.00
11 Little Orphan Amnie (Hancock)	75.00
12 Woody Woodpecker (Omar)	75.00

12 WoodyWoodpecker(Hancock) .	50.00
13 Dick Tracy (Omar)..........	150.00
13 Dick Tracy (Hancock).......	125.00
14 Bugs Bunny (Omar)	75.00
14 Bugs Bunny (Hanock).......	50.00
15 Andy Panda (Omar)	60.00
15 Andy Panda (Hancock)......	50.00
16 Terry & the Pirates (Omar) .	150.00
16 Terry & the Pirates (Hancock).	125.00
17 Smokey Stover (Omar).......	75.00
17 Smokey Stover (Hancock)	60.00
18 Porky Pig (Omar)	60.00
18 Smokey Stover (Hancock)	35.00
19 Smilin' Jack (Omar)	75.00
N# Smilin' Jack (Hancock)......	60.00
20 Oswald the Rabbit (Omar) ...	35.00
N# Oswald the Rabbit (Hancock) .	20.00
21 Gasoline Alley (Omar).......	75.00
N# Gasoline Alley (Hancock)....	60.00
22 Elmer Fudd (Omar).........	50.00
N# Elmer Fudd (Hancock).......	40.00
23 Little Orphan Annie (Omar)....	75.00
N# Little Orphan Annie (Hancock).	60.00
24 Woody Woodpecker (Omar)...	50.00
N# WoodyWoodpecker(Hancock) .	40.00
25 Dick Tracy (Omar)..........	135.00
N# Dick Tracy (Hancock).......	125.00
26 Bugs Bunny (Omar)	50.00
N# Bugs Bunny (Hancock)	40.00
27 Andy Panda (Omar)	50.00
27 Andy Panda (Hancock).......	40.00
28 Terry & the Pirates (Omar) ...	150.00
28 Terry & the Pirates (Hancock).	125.00
29 Smokey Stover (Omar).......	50.00
29 Smokey Stover (Hancock)	40.00
30 Porky Pig (Omar)	50.00
30 Porky Pig (Hancock)........	40.00
N# Bugs Bunny (Hancock)	50.00

SUPER CIRCUS
**Cross Publishing Co.,
Jan., 1951**

1 Partial Ph(c)	75.00
2	60.00
3	50.00
4	50.00
5 1951	50.00

SUPER COMICS
**Dell Publishing Co.,
May, 1938**

1 Dick Tracy,Terry and the Pirates,Smilin'Jack,Smokey Stover,Orphan Annie,etc. . .	3,200.00
2	1,400.00
3	1,200.00
4	1,100.00
5 Gumps(c)	1,000.00
6	750.00
7 Smokey Stover(c)	750.00
8 Dick Tracy(c)	750.00
9	750.00
10 Dick Tracy(c).............	750.00
11	550.00
12	550.00
13	550.00
14	550.00
15	550.00
16 Terry & the Pirates	500.00
17 Dick Tracy(c).............	500.00
18	500.00
19	500.00
20 Smilin'Jack(c)	525.00
21 B:Magic Morro	400.00
22 Magic Morro(c)	450.00
23 all star(c)................	400.00
24 Dick Tracy(c).............	450.00
25 Magic Morro(c)	400.00
26	400.00

27 Magic Morro(c)	400.00
28 Jim Ellis(c)	450.00
29 Smilin'Jack(c)	400.00
30 inc.The Sea Hawk.........	450.00
31 Dick Tracy(c).............	350.00
32 Smilin' Jack(c)............	365.00
33 Jim Ellis(c)	350.00
34 Magic Morro(c)	350.00
35 thru 40 Dick Tracy(c).....	@350.00
41 B:Lightning Jim	300.00
42 thru 50 Dick Tracy(c).....	@300.00
51 thru 54 Dick Tracy(c).....	@250.00
55	250.00
56	250.00
57 Dick Tracy(c).............	250.00
58 Smitty(c)	250.00
59	250.00
60 Dick Tracy(c).............	275.00
61	235.00
62 Flag(c)...................	235.00
63 Dick Tracy(c).............	235.00
64 Smitty(c)	225.00
65 Dick Tracy(c).............	235.00
66 Dick Tracy(c).............	235.00
67 Christmas(c)	235.00
68 Dick Tracy(c).............	235.00
69 Dick Tracy(c).............	235.00
70 Dick Tracy(c).............	235.00
71 Dick Tracy(c).............	200.00
72 Dick Tracy(c).............	200.00
73 Smitty(c)	200.00
74 War Bond(c)	200.00
75 Dick Tracy(c).............	200.00
76 Dick Tracy(c).............	200.00
77 Dick Tracy(c).............	200.00
78 Smitty(c)	150.00
79 Dick Tracy(c).............	150.00
80 Smitty(c)	150.00
81 Dick Tracy(c).............	150.00
82 Dick Tracy(c).............	150.00
83 Smitty(c)	135.00
84 Dick Tracy(c).............	150.00
85 Smitty(c)	135.00
86 All on cover	150.00
87 All on cover..............	150.00
88 Dick Tracy(c).............	150.00
89 Smitty(c)	135.00
90 Dick Tracy(c).............	150.00
91 Smitty(c)	135.00
92 Dick Tracy(c).............	150.00
93 Dick Tracy(c).............	150.00
94 Dick Tracy(c).............	150.00
95 thru 99.................	@135.00
100	150.00
101 thru 115..............	@120.00

Super Comics #22
© Cross Publishing Co.

116 Smokey Stover(c)	100.00
117 Gasoline Alley(c).........	100.00
118 Smokey Stover(c)	100.00
119 Terry and the Pirates(c)....	110.00
120	100.00
121	100.00

SUPER-DOOPER COMICS
Able Manufacturing Co., 1946

1 A:Gangbuster	250.00
2	200.00
3 & 4	@150.00
5 A:Captain Freedom,Shock Gibson	150.00
6 & 7 same	@150.00
8 A:Shock Gibson, 1946	150.00

SUPER DUCK COMICS
**MLJ Magazines/Close-Up
(Archie Publ.), Autumn, 1944**

1 O:Super Duck, Hitler	750.00
2	300.00
3 I:Mr. Monster	250.00
4 & 5	@225.00
6 thru 10	@200.00
11 thru 20	@150.00
21 thru 40.................	@125.00
41 thru 60.................	@100.00
61 thru 94.................	@75.00

SUPER FUNNIES
**Superior Comics Publishers,
March, 1954**

1 Dopey Duck..............	500.00
2 Out of the Booby-Hatch	200.00

Becomes:

SUPER WESTERN FUNNIES
1954

3 F:Phantom Ranger	100.00
4 F:Phantom Ranger,Sept., 1954	100.00

SUPER MAGICIAN COMICS
Street & Smith, May, 1941

1 B:The Mysterious Blackstone .	800.00
2 V:Wild Tribes of Africa	500.00
3 V:Oriental Wizard	500.00
4 V:Quetzal Wizard,O:Transo...	475.00
5 A:The Moylan Sisters	475.00
6 JaB,JaB(c),The Eddie Cantor story	475.00
7 In the House of Skulls	500.00
8 A:Abbott & Costello	500.00
9 V:Duneen the Man-Ape	500.00
10 V:Pirates o/t Sargasso Sea...	500.00
11 JaB(c),V:Fire Wizards.......	500.00
12 V:Baal	500.00
2-1 A:The Shadow	500.00
2-2 In the Temple of the 10,000 Idols	250.00
2-3 Optical Illusion on (c)- turn Jap into Monkey	250.00
2-4 V:Cannibal Killers	250.00
2-5 V:The Pygmies of Lemuria .	250.00
2-6 V;Pirates & Indians	250.00
2-7 Can Blackstone Catch the Cannonball?	250.00
2-8 V:Marabout,B:Red Dragon . .	250.00
2-9	250.00
2-10 Pearl Dives Swallowed By Sea Demons	250.00
2-11 Blackstone Invades Pelican Islands	250.00

GOLDEN AGE

2-12 V:Bubbles of Death 250.00
3-1 . . . . 275.00
3-2 Bondage(c),Midsummers
 Eve 250.00
3-3 The Enchanted Garden . . . 250.00
3-4 Fabulous Aztec Treasure . . . 250.00
3-5 A:Buffalo Bill 250.00
3-6 Magic Tricks to Mystify . . . 250.00
3-7 V:Guy Fawkes 250.00
3-8 V:Hindu Spook Maker 250.00
3-9 . . . . 250.00
3-10 V:The Water Wizards 250.00
3-11 V:The Green Goliath 250.00
3-12 Lady in White 250.00
4-1 Cannibal of Crime 225.00
4-2 The Devil's Castle 225.00
4-3 V:Demons of Golden River . . 225.00
4-4 V:Dr. Zero 225.00
4-5 Bondage(c) 225.00
4-6 V:A Terror Gang 225.00
4-7 . . . . 225.00
4-8 Mystery of the
 Disappearing Horse 225.00
4-9 A Floating Light? 225.00
4-10 Levitation 225.00
4-11 Lost, Strange Land
 of Shangri 225.00
4-12 I:Nigel Elliman 225.00
5-1 V:Voodoo Wizards of the
 Everglades,Bondage (c) 225.00
5-2 Treasure of the Florida
 Keys; Bondage (c) 225.00
5-3 Elliman Battles Triple Crime . 225.00
5-4 Can A Human Being Really
 Become Invisible 225.00
5-5 Mystery of the Twin Pools . . 225.00
5-6 A:Houdini 225.00
5-7 F:Red Dragon 500.00
5-8 F:Red Dragon,
 Feb.–March, 1947 . . . . 500.00

SUPERMOUSE
Standard Comics/Pines,
Dec., 1948
1 FF,(fa) 350.00
2 FF,(fa) 150.00
3 FF,(fa) 135.00
4 FF,(fa) 135.00
5 FF,(fa) 135.00
6 FF,(fa) 135.00
7 thru 10 (fa) . . . . @75.00
11 thru 20 (fa) . . . . @60.00
21 thru 44 (fa) . . . . @45.00

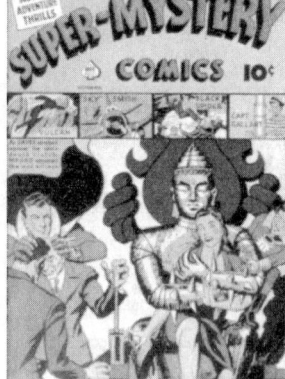

Super-Mystery Comics #4
© *Street & Smith*

45 (fa),Autumn, 1958 . . . . 45.00

SUPER-MYSTERY COMICS
Periodical House
(Ace Magazines), July, 1940
1 B:Magno,Vulcan,Q-13,Flint
 of the Mountes 4,000.00
2 Bondage (c) 1,300.00
3 JaB,B:Black Spider 1,000.00
4 O:Davy;A:Captain Gallant . . . 750.00
5 JaB,JM(c),I&B:The Clown . . . 750.00
6 JM,JM(c),V:The Clown 650.00
2-1 JM,JM(c),O:Buckskin,
 Bondage(c) 650.00
2-2 JM,JM(c),V:The Clown 600.00
2-3 JM,JM(c),V:The Clown 600.00
2-4 JM,JM(c),V:The Nazis 600.00
2-5 JM,JM(c),Bondage(c) 600.00
2-6 JM,JM(c),Bondage(c),
 'Foreign Correspondent' 600.00
3-1 B:Black Ace 600.00
3-2 A:Mr, Risk, Bondage(c) 600.00
3-3 HK,HK(c),I:Lancer;B:Dr.
 Nemesis, The Sword 650.00
3-4 HK 600.00
3-5 HK,LbC,A:Mr. Risk 600.00
3-6 HK,LbC,A:Paul Revere Jr. . . 600.00
4-1 HK,LbC,A:Twin Must Die . . . 550.00
4-2 A:Mr. Risk 375.00
4-3 Mango out to Kill Davey! . . . 375.00
4-4 Danger Laughs at Mr. Risk . . 375.00
4-5 A:Mr. Risk 375.00
4-6 RP,A:Mr. Risk 375.00
5-1 RP 375.00
5-2 RP,RP(c),The Riddle of the
 Swamp-Land Spirit 375.00
5-3 RP,RP(c),The Case of the
 Whispering Death 375.00
5-4 RP,RP(c) 375.00
5-5 RP,Harry the Hack 375.00
5-6 . . . . 375.00
6-1 . . . . 300.00
6-2 RP,A:Mr. Risk 300.00
6-3 Bondage (c) 300.00
6-4 E:Mango;A:Mr. Risk 300.00
6-5 Bondage(c) 300.00
6-6 A:Mr. Risk 300.00
7-1 . . . . 300.00
7-2 KBa(c) 300.00
7-3 Bondage(c) 300.00
7-4 . . . . 300.00
7-5 . . . . 300.00
7-6 . . . . 300.00
8-1 The Riddle of the Rowboat . . 275.00
8-2 Death Meets a Train 275.00
8-3 The Man Who Couldn't Die . 275.00
8-4 RP(c) 275.00
8-5 GT,MMe,Staged for Murder . 275.00
8-6 Unlucky Seven,July, 1949 . . 275.00

ARMY AND NAVY COMICS
Street & Smith, May, 1941
1 Hawaii is Calling You,Capt.
 Fury,Nick Carter. 750.00
2 Private Rock V;Hitler 600.00
3 The Fighting Fourth 600.00
4 The Fighting Irish 600.00
5 I:Super Snipe 700.00
Becomes:

SUPERSNIPE COMICS
Oct., 1942
6 A "Comic" With A Sense
 of Humor 1,300.00
7 A:Wacky, Rex King 700.00
8 Axis Powers & Satan(c),
 Hitler(c). 1,000.00

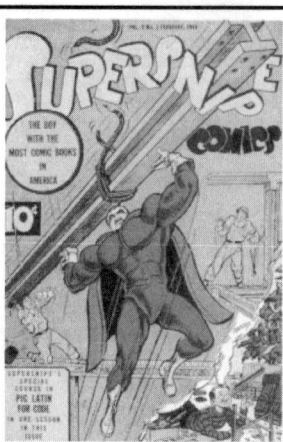

Supershipe Comics #13
© *Street & Smith*

9 Hitler Voodoo Doll (c) 1,100.00
10 Lighting (c) 700.00
11 A:Little Nemo. 700.00
12 Football(c). 700.00
2-1 B:Huck Finn 1,000.00
2-2 Battles Shark 550.00
2-3 Battles Dinosaur 500.00
2-4 Baseball(c). 500.00
2-5 Battles Dinosaur 500.00
2-6 A:Pochontas. 500.00
2-7 A:Wing Woo Woo 500.00
2-8 A:Huck Finn 500.00
2-9 Dotty Loves Trouble. 500.00
2-10 Assists Farm Labor
 Shortage 500.00
2-11 Dotty & the Jelly Beans . . . 500.00
2-12 Statue of Liberty. 500.00
3-1 Ice Skating(c). 400.00
3-2 V:Pirates(c) 400.00
3-3 Baseball(c). 400.00
3-4 Jungle(c) 400.00
3-5 Learn Piglatin. 400.00
3-6 Football Hero. 400.00
3-7 Saves Girl From Grisley 400.00
3-8 Rides a Wild Horse 400.00
3-9 Powers Santa's Sleigh. 400.00
3-10 Plays Basketball 400.00
3-11 Is A Baseball Pitcher 400.00
3-12 Flies with the Birds 400.00
4-1 Catches A Whale 300.00
4-2 Track & Field Athlete 300.00
4-3 Think Machine(c) 300.00
4-4 Alpine Skiier. 300.00
4-5 Becomes a Boxer 300.00
4-6 Race Car Driver. 300.00
4-7 Bomber(c) 300.00
4-8 Baseball Star 300.00
4-9 Football Hero. 300.00
4-10 Christmas(c) 300.00
4-11 Artic Adventure. 300.00
4-12 The Ghost Remover 300.00
5-1 Aug.–Sept., 1949 . . . . 300.00

SUPER SPY
Centaur Publications,
Oct.–Nov., 1940
1 O:Sparkler 1,500.00
2 A:Night Hawk, Drew Ghost, Tim
 Blain, S.S. Swanson the Inner
 Circle, Duke Collins, Gentlemen
 of Misfortune 900.00

SUPER WESTERN COMICS

Youthful Magazines, Aug., 1950
1 BP,BP,(c),B;Buffalo Bill,Wyatt
    Earp,CalamityJane,SamSlade 150.00
2 thru 4 March, 1951 ...... @100.00

SUPER WESTERN FUNNIES
See: SUPER FUNNIES

SUPERWORLD COMICS
**Komos Publications
(Hugo Gernsback), April, 1940**
1 FP,FP(c),B:MilitaryPowers,BuzzAllen
    Smarty Artie, Alibi Alige .. 10,000.00
2 FP,FP(c),A:Mario 6,000.00
3 FP,FP(c),V:Vest Wearing
    Giant Grasshoppers 4,000.00

SUSPENSE COMICS
**Et Es Go Mag. Inc.
(Continental Magazines),
Dec., 1945**
1 LbC, Bondage(c),B:Grey
    Mask 6,500.00
2 DRi,I:The Mask.......... 4,000.00
3 LbC,ASh(c),Bondage(c) ... 20,000.00
4 LbC,LbC(c),Bondage(c) ... 3,000.00
5 LbC,LbC(c) 3,000.00
6 LbC,LbC(c),The End of
    the Road 3,000.00
7 LbC,LbC(c) 2,500.00
8 LbC,LbC(c) 6,500.00
9 LbC,LbC(c) 2,500.00
10 RP,LbC,LbC(c)........... 2,500.00
11 RP,LbC,LbC(c),Satan(c).... 5,000.00
12 LbC,LbC(c),Dec., 1946 .... 2,500.00

SUSPENSE DETECTIVE
**Fawcett Publications,
June, 1952**
1 GE,MBi,MBi(c),Death Poised
    to Strike 650.00
2 GE,MSy 400.00
3 A Furtive Footstep 350.00
4 MBi,MSy,Bondage(c),A Blood
    Chilling Scream 350.00
5 MSy,MSy(c),MBi,A Hair-Trigger
    from Death, March, 1953 ... 350.00

SUZIE COMICS
See: TOP-NOTCH COMICS

SWEENEY
**Standard Comics,
June, 1949**
4 Buzz Sawyer's Pal 100.00
5 Sept., 1949 .... 80.00

SWEETHEART DIARY
**Fawcett,
Winter, 1949**
1 .... 200.00
2 .... 100.00
3 WW 250.00
4 WW 250.00
5 thru 10 .... @75.00
11 thru 14................. @50.00

SWEETHEART DIARY
**Charlton Comics,
Jan., 1953**
32 .... 60.00
33 thru 40................. @50.00
41 thru 65................. @30.00

SWEET HEART
See: CAPTAIN MIDNIGHT

SWEET LOVE
**Harvey Publications
(Home Comics), Sept., 1949**
1 Ph(c) 125.00
2 Ph(c) 75.00
3 BP 60.00
4 Ph(c) 50.00
5 BP,JKa,Ph(c) 100.00

SWEET SIXTEEN
**Parents' Magazine Group,
Aug.–Sept., 1946**
1 Van Johnson story 250.00
2 Alan Ladd story 200.00
3 Rip Taylor............... 150.00
4 Elizabeth Taylor ph(c) 250.00
5 Gregory Peck story (c). 150.00
6 Dick Haymes(c) 150.00
7 Ronald Reagan(c) & story.... 300.00
8 Shirley Jones(c)........... 125.00
9 William Holden(c). 125.00
10 James Stewart(c) 150.00
11 .... 125.00
12 Bob Cummings(c).......... 125.00
13 Robert Mitchum(c) 150.00

SWIFT ARROW
**Farrell Publications(Ajax),
Feb.–March, 1954**
1 Lone Rider's Redskin Brother 200.00
2 .... 125.00
3 .... 100.00
4 .... 100.00
5 Oct.–Nov., 1954 .... 100.00
(2nd Series) April, 1957
1 .... 100.00
2 B:Lone Rider 75.00
3 Sept., 1957 .... 60.00

TAFFY
**Orbit Publications/Rural Home/
Taffy Publications,
March–April, 1945**
1 LbC(c),(fa),Bondage(c) 800.00
2 LbC(c),(fa) 350.00
3 (fa) 150.00
4 (fa) 150.00
5 LbC(c),A:Van Johnson 250.00
6 A:Perry Como 150.00
7 A:Dave Clark 150.00
8 A:Glen Ford 150.00
9 A:Lon McCallister 150.00
10 A:John Hodiak. 150.00
11 A:Mickey Rooney 165.00
12 Feb., 1948............... 150.00

TAILSPIN
**Spotlight Publications,
Nov., 1944**
N# LbC(c),A:Firebird......... 350.00

TALES FROM THE CRYPT
See: CRIME PATROL

TALES FROM THE TOMB
See: DELL GIANTS

TALES OF HORROR
**Toby Press/Minoan Publ. Corp,
June, 1952–Oct., 1954**
1 Demons of the Underworld ... 500.00
2 What was the Thing in
    the Pool?,Torture......... 400.00
3 The Big Snake 300.00
4 The Curse of King Kala! 300.00
5 Hand of Fate 300.00
6 The Fiend of Flame 300.00
7 Beast From The Deep 300.00
8 The Snake that Held A
    City Captive 300.00
9 It Came From the Bottom
    of the World 350.00
10 The Serpent Strikes 300.00
11 Death Flower?............. 350.00
12 Guaranteed to Make Your
    Hair Stand on End,Torture... 350.00
13 Ghost with a Torch 350.00

TALES OF TERROR
Toby Press, 1952
1 Just A Bunch of Hokey
    Hogwash 300.00

*Tales of Terror Annual #3
© E.C. Comics*

TALES OF TERROR ANNUAL
E.C. Comics, 1951
N# AF.................... 6,000.00
2 AF..................... 3,000.00
3 .... 2,700.00

TALLY-HO COMICS
**Baily Publishing Co.,
Dec., 1944**
N# FF,A:Snowman 550.00

All comics prices listed are for *Near Mint* condition.

Target Comics Vol. 3 #10
© Star Publications

TARGET COMICS

**Funnnies Inc./Novelty Publ./
Premium Group/Curtis
Circulation Co./Star
Publications, Feb., 1940**

1 BEv,JCo,CBu,JSm;B,O&I:Manowar,
  White Streak,Bull's-Eye;B:City
  Editor,High Grass Twins,T-Men,
  Rip Rory,Fantastic Feature
  Films, Calling 2-R 7,500.00
2 BEv,JSm,JCo,CBu,White
  Streak(c) 4,000.00
3 BEv,JSm,JCo,CBu 2,500.00
4 JSm,JCo 2,500.00
5 CBu,BW,O:White Streak . . . 6,500.00
6 CBu,BW,White Streak(c) . . . 2,700.00
7 CBu,BW,BW(c),V:Planetoid
  Stories,Space Hawk(c) 7,500.00
8 CBu,BW,White Shark(c) 1,900.00
9 CBu,BW,White Shark(c) 1,900.00
10 CBu,BW,JK(c),The
   Target(c) 2,700.00
11 BW,The Target(c) 2,300.00
12 BW,same 2,000.00
2-1 BW,CBu 1,400.00
2-2 BW,BoW(c) 1,200.00
2-3 BW,BoW(c),The Target(c) . . . 800.00
2-4 BW,B:Cadet 800.00
2-5 BW,BoW(c),The Target(c) . . . 800.00
2-6 BW,The Target(c) 750.00
2-7 BW,The Cadet(c) 750.00
2-8 BW,same 750.00
2-9 BW,The Target(c) 750.00
2-10 BW,same 1,400.00
2-11 BW,The Cadet(c) 800.00
2-12 BW,same 800.00
3-1 BW,same 800.00
3-2 BW 800.00
3-3 BW,The Target(c) 800.00
3-4 BW,The Cadet(c) 800.00
3-5 BW 800.00
3-6 BW,War Bonds(c) 800.00
3-7 BW 800.00
3-8 BW,War Bonds(c) 800.00
3-9 BW 800.00
3-10 BW 800.00
3-11 . . . . 200.00
3-12 . . . . 200.00
4-1 JJo(c) 135.00
4-2 ERy(c) 135.00
4-3 AVi 135.00
4-4 . . . . 135.00
4-5 API(c),Statue of Liberty(c) . . . 150.00

4-6 BW 135.00
4-7 AVi 135.00
4-8,Christmas(c) 135.00
4-9 . . . . 135.00
4-10 . . . . 135.00
4-11 . . . . 135.00
4-12 . . . . 135.00
5-1 . . . . 125.00
5-2 The Target 125.00
5-3 Savings Checkers(c) 125.00
5-4 War Bonds Ph(c) 125.00
5-5 thru 5-12 . . . . @125.00
6-1 The Target(c) 125.00
6-2 . . . . 125.00
6-3 Red Cross(c) 125.00
6-4 . . . . 125.00
6-5 Savings Bonds(c) 150.00
6-6 The Target(c) 125.00
6-7 The Cadet(c) 125.00
6-8 AFa 125.00
6-9 The Target(c) 125.00
6-10 . . . . 125.00
6-11 . . . . 125.00
6-12 . . . . 125.00
7-1 . . . . 125.00
7-2 Bondage(c) 150.00
7-3 The Target(c) 125.00
7-4 DRi,The Cadet(c) 125.00
7-5 . . . . 125.00
7-6 DRi(c) 125.00
7-7 The Cadet(c) 125.00
7-8 DRi(c) 125.00
7-9 The Cadet(c) 125.00
7-10 DRi,DRi(c) 125.00
7-11 . . . . 125.00
7-12 JH(c) 125.00
8-1 . . . . 110.00
8-2 DRi,DRi(c),BK 110.00
8-3 DRi,The Cadet(c) 110.00
8-4 DRi,DRi(c) 110.00
8-5 DRi,The Cadet(c) 110.00
8-6 DRi,DRi(c) 110.00
8-7 BK,DRi,DRi(c) 110.00
8-8 DRi,The Cadet(c) 110.00
8-9 DRi,The Cadet(c) 110.00
8-10 DRi,KBa,LbC(c) 400.00
8-11 DRi,The Cadet 125.00
8-12 DRi,The Cadet 125.00
9-1 DRi,LbC(c) 400.00
9-2 DRi 125.00
9-3 DRi,Bondage(c),The Cadet(c) 150.00
9-4 DRi,LbC(c) 400.00
9-5 DRi,Baseball(c) 125.00
9-6 DRi,LbC(c) 400.00
9-7 DRi 125.00
9-8 DRi,LbC(c) 400.00
9-9 DRi,Football(c) 125.00
9-10 DRi,LbC(c) 400.00
9-11,The Cadet 125.00
9-12 LbC(c),Gems(c) 450.00
10-1,The Cadet 125.00
10-2 LbC(c) 400.00
10-3 LbC(c) 400.00
Becomes:

TARGET WESTERN ROMANCES

**Star Publications,
Oct.–Nov., 1949**

106 LbC(c),The Beauty Scar 500.00
107 LbC(c),The Brand Upon His
    Heart 450.00

TARZAN

**Dell Publishing Co.,
Jan.–Feb., 1948**

1 V:White Savages of Vari 1,900.00
2 Captives of Thunder Valley . . . 800.00
3 Dwarfs of Didona 600.00
4 The Lone Hunter 600.00

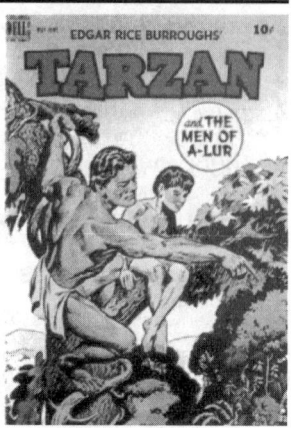

Tarzan #9
© Dell Publishing Co.

5 The Men of Greed 600.00
6 Outlaws of Pal-ul-Don 500.00
7 Valley of the Monsters 500.00
8 The White Pygmies 500.00
9 The Men of A-Lur 500.00
10 Treasure of the Bolgani 500.00
11 The Sable Lion 400.00
12 The Price of Peace 400.00
13 B:Lex Barker photo(c) 350.00
14 Lex Barker ph(c) 350.00
15 Lex Barker ph(c) 350.00
16 Lex Barker ph(c) 300.00
17 Lex Barker ph(c) 300.00
18 Lex Barker ph(c) 300.00
19 Lex Barker ph(c) 300.00
20 Lex Barker ph(c) 300.00
21 thru 24 Lex Barker ph(c) . . . @250.00
25 Brothers of the Spear 275.00
26 thru 54 E:L.Barker ph(c) . . . @225.00
55 thru 70 . . . . @150.00
71 thru 79 . . . . @100.00
80 thru 90 B:ScottGordonPh(c) . @75.00
91 thru 99 . . . . @65.00
100 . . . . 75.00
101 thru 110 E:S.GordonPh(c) . . @70.00
111 thru 120 . . . . @60.00
121 thru 131 . . . . @50.00

TEENA

Standard Comics, 1949
20 . . . . 60.00
21 . . . . 60.00
22 . . . . 60.00

TEEN-AGE DIARY SECRETS

**St. John Publishing Co.,
Oct., 1949**
6 MB,PH(c) 350.00
7 MB,PH(c) 300.00
8 MB,PH(c) 250.00
9 MB,PH(c) 300.00
Becomes:

DIARY SECRETS

Feb., 1952
10 MB 250.00
11 MB 200.00
12 thru 19 MB . . . . @150.00
20 MB,JKu 200.00
21 thru 28 MB . . . . @100.00
29 MB,Comics Code 100.00
30 MB 100.00

GOLDEN AGE

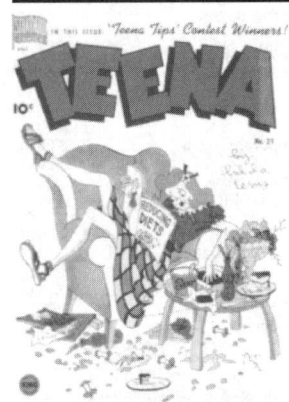

Teena #21
© *Standard Comics*

TEEN-AGE ROMANCES
St. John Publishing Co., Jan., 1949

1 MB(c),MB	500.00
2 MB(c),MB	300.00
3 MB(c),MB	350.00
4 Ph(c)	300.00
5 MB,Ph(c)	300.00
6 MB,Ph(c)	300.00
7 MB,Ph(c)	300.00
8 MB,Ph(c)	300.00
9 MB,MB(c),JKu	325.00
10 thru 27 MB,MB(c),JKu	@250.00
28 thru 30	@100.00
31 thru 34 MB(c)	@125.00
35 thru 42 MB(c),MB	@125.00
43 MB(c),MB,Comics Code	150.00
44 MB(c),MB	150.00
45 MB(c),MB	150.00

TEEN-AGE TEMPTATIONS
St. John Publishing Co., Oct., 1952

1 MB(c),MB	600.00
2 MB(c),MB	200.00
3 MB(c),MB	275.00
4 MB(c),MB	275.00
5 MB(c),MB	275.00
6 MB(c),MB	275.00
7 MB(c),MB	275.00
8 MB(c),MB,Drug	300.00
9 MB(c),MB	275.00

Becomes:

GOING STEADY
Dec., 1954

10 MB(c),MB	225.00
11 MB(c),MB	125.00
12 MB(c),MB	125.00
13 MB(c),MB	175.00
14 MB(c),MB	200.00

TEENIE WEENIES, THE
Ziff-Davis Publishing Co., 1951

10	250.00
11	250.00

TEEN LIFE
See: YOUNG LIFE

TEGRA, JUNGLE EMPRESS
See: ZEGRA, JUNGLE EMPRESS

TELEVISION COMICS
Animated Cartoons (Standard Comics), Feb., 1950

5 Humorous Format,I:Willie Nilly	100.00
6	75.00
7	75.00
8 May, 1950	75.00

TELEVISION PUPPET SHOW
Avon Periodicals, 1950

1 F:Sparky Smith,Spotty, Cheeta, Speedy	250.00
2 Nov., 1950	150.00

TELL IT TO THE MARINES
Toby Press, March, 1952

1 I:Spike & Pat	250.00
2 A:Madame Cobra	150.00
3 Spike & Bat on a Commando Raid!	100.00
4 Veil Dancing(c)	100.00
5	100.00
6 To Paris	75.00
7 Ph(c),The Chinese Bugle	75.00
8 Ph(c),V:Communists in South Korea	75.00
9 Ph(c)	75.00
10	75.00
11	75.00
12	75.00
13 John Wayne Ph(c)	150.00
14 Ph(c)	75.00
15 Ph(c),July, 1955	75.00

TENDER ROMANCE
Key Publications, Dec., 1953

1	200.00
2	125.00

Becomes:

IDEAL ROMANCE
April, 1954

3	100.00
4 thru 8	@60.00

Becomes:

DIARY CONFESSIONS
May, 1955

9	75.00
10	50.00

TERRIFIC COMICS
See: HORRIFIC

TERRIFIC COMICS
Et Es Go Mag. Inc./ Continental Magazines, Jan., 1944

1 LbC,DRi(c),F:Kid Terrific Drug	5,000.00
2 LcC,ASh(c),B:Boomerang, 'Comics' McCormic	3,500.00
3 LbC,LbC(c)	3,500.00
4 LbC,RP(c)	6,000.00

Terrific Comics #3
© *Continental Magazines*

5 LbC,BF,ASh(c),Bondage(c)	8,000.00
6 LbC,LbC(c),BF,Nov.,1944	3,200.00

TERROR ILLUSTRATED
E.C. Comics, Nov.–Dec., 1955

1 JCr,GE,Grl,JO,RC(c)	250.00
2 Spring, 1956	150.00

TERRIFYING TALES
Star Publications, Jan., 1953

11 LbC,LbC(c),'TyrantsofTerror'	700.00
12 LbC,LbC(c),'Bondage(c), 'Jungle Mystery'	600.00
13 LbC(c),Bondage(c),'The Death-Fire,Devil Head(c)	750.00
14 LbC(c),Bondage(c),'The Weird Idol'	550.00
15 LbC(c),'The Grim Secret', April, 1954	550.00

Becomes:

JUNGLE THRILLS
Star Publications, Feb., 1952

16 LbC(c),'Kingdom of Unseen Terror'	700.00

Becomes:

TERRORS OF THE JUNGLE
May, 1952

17 LbC(c),Bondage(c)	700.00
18 LbC(c),Strange Monsters	450.00
19 JyD,LbC(c),Bondage(c),The Golden Ghost Gorilla	400.00
20 JyD,LbC(c),The Creeping Scourge	400.00
21 LbC(c),Evil Eyes of Death!	450.00
4 JyD,LbC(c),Morass of Death	400.00
5 JyD,LbC(c),Bondage(c), Savage Train	425.00
6 JyD,LbC(c),Revolt of the Jungle Monsters	425.00
7 JyD,LbC(c)	450.00
8 JyD,LbC(c),Death's Grim Reflection	450.00
9 JyD,LbC(c),Doom to Evil-Doers	450.00
10 JyD,LbC(c),Black Magic, Sept., 1954	450.00

BOY EXPLORERS
1 S&K(c),S&K,The Cadet 1,000.00
2 S&K(c),S&K 1,400.00
Becomes:

TERRY AND THE PIRATES
April, 1947
3 S&K,MC(c),Terry and
Dragon Lady 500.00
4 S&K,MC(c),MC 300.00
5 S&K,MC(c),MC,BP,
Chop-Chop(c) 175.00
6 S&K,.MC(c),MC 175.00
7 S&K,MC(c),MC,BP 175.00
8 S&K,MC(c),MC,BP 175.00
9 S&K,MC(c),MC,BP 175.00
10 S&K,MC(c),MC,BP 175.00
11 S&K,MC(c),MC,BP,
A:Man in Black 150.00
12 S&K,MC(c),MC,BP 150.00
13 S&K,MC(c),MC,Belly Dancers 150.00
14 thru 20 S&K,MC(c),MC .... @125.00
21 thru 26 S&K,MC(c),MC .... @110.00
27 Charlton Comics 100.00
28 .... 100.00

TERRY-BEARS COMICS
**St. John Publishing Co.,
June, 1952**
1 .... 100.00
2 & 3 .... @50.00

TERRY-TOONS COMICS
**Select, Timely, Marvel,
St. Johns, 1942**
1 Paul Terry (fa) 2,500.00
2 .... 800.00
3 thru 6 .... @500.00
7 Hitler,Hirohito,Mussolini(c) ... 700.00
8 thru 20 .... @400.00
21 thru 37 .... @300.00
38 I&(c):Mighty Mouse 1,600.00
39 Mighty Mouse 500.00
40 thru 49 All Mighty Mouse .. @250.00
50 I:Heckle & Jeckle 600.00
51 thru 60 .... @150.00
61 thru 70 .... @125.00
71 thru 86 .... @125.00

TEXAN, THE
**St. John Publishing Co.,
Aug., 1948**
1 GT,F:Buckskin Belle,The Gay
Buckaroo,Mustang Jack 200.00
2 GT 125.00
3 BLb(c) 100.00
4 MB,MB(c) 200.00
5 MB,MB(c),Mystery Rustlers
of the Rio Grande 200.00
6 MB(c),Death Valley
Double-Cross 125.00
7 MB,MB(c),Comanche Justice
Strikes at Midnight 200.00
8 MB,MB(c),Scalp Hunters
Hide their Tracks 200.00
9 MB(c),Ghost Terror of
the Blackfeet 200.00
10 MB,MB(c),Treason Rides
the Warpath 125.00
11 MB,MB(c),Hawk Knife 200.00
12 MB 250.00
13 MB,Doublecross at Devil'sDen 200.00
14 MB,Ambush at Buffalo Trail .. 200.00
15 MB,Twirling Blades Tame
Treachery 200.00
Becomes:

FIGHTIN' TEXAN
Sept., 1952
16 GT,Wanted Dead or Alive ... 125.00
17 LC,LC(c);Killers Trail,
Dec., 1952 .... 100.00

TEX FARRELL
**D.S. Publishing Co.,
March–April, 1948**
1 Pride of the Wild West 175.00

TEX GRANGER
See: CALLING ALL BOYS

TEX RITTER WESTERN
**Fawcett Publications/
Charlton Comics,
Oct., 1950–May, 1959**
1 Ph(c),B:Tex Ritter, his Horse
White Flash, his dog Fury, and
his mom Nancy 900.00
2 Ph(c),Vanishing Varmints 400.00
3 Ph(c),Blazing Six-Guns 325.00
4 Ph(c),The Jaws of Terror 275.00
5 Ph(c),Bullet Trail 275.00
6 Ph(c),Killer Bait 250.00
7 Ph(c),Gunsmoke Revenge ... 225.00
8 Ph(c),Lawless Furnace Valley 225.00
9 Ph(c),The Spider's Web 225.00
10 Ph(c),The Ghost Town 225.00
11 Ph(c),Saddle Conquest 225.00
12 Ph(c),Prairie Inferno 175.00
13 Ph(c) 175.00
14 Ph(c) 175.00
15 Ph(c) 175.00
16 thru 19 Ph(c) .... @175.00
20 Ph(c),Stagecoach To Danger . 175.00
21 Ph(c), ... 200.00
22 Panic at Diamond B 150.00
23 A:Young Falcon 125.00
24 A:Young Falcon 125.00
25 A:Young Falcon 125.00
26 thru 38 .... @100.00
39 AW,AW(c) 100.00
40 thru 46 .... @100.00

THING!, THE
**Song Hits/Capitol Stories/
Charlton Comics, Feb., 1952**
1 Horror 1,300.00

The Thing! #3
© Charlton Comics

2 Crazy King(c) 750.00
3 .... 750.00
4 AFa(c),I Was A Zombie 625.00
5 LM(c),Severed Head(c) 650.00
6 .... 625.00
7 Fingenail to Eye(c). 900.00
8 .... 650.00
9 Severe cruelty 1,100.00
10 Devil(c) 625.00
11 SC,Cleaver, eye injury 850.00
12 SD,SD(c),Neck Blood
Sucking 1,200.00
13 SD,SD(c) 1,200.00
14 SD,SD(c) torture 1,200.00
15 SD,SD(c) 1,200.00
16 Eye Torture 550.00
17 BP,SD(c) 1,100.00
Becomes:

BLUE BEETLE
Feb., 1955
18 America's Fastest Moving
Crusader Against Crime 250.00
19 JKa,Lightning Fast 275.00
20 JKa 275.00
21 The Invincible 200.00
Becomes:

MR. MUSCLES
March, 1956
22 World's Most Perfect Man.... 100.00
23 Aug., 1956 .... 75.00

THIS IS SUSPENSE
See: LAWBREAKERS

THIS IS WAR
**Standard Comics,
July, 1952**
5 ATh,Show Them How To Die . 150.00
6 ATh,Make Him A Soldier 125.00
7 One Man For Himself 75.00
8 Miracle on Massacre Hill 75.00
9 ATh,May, 1953 .... 125.00

THIS IS SUSPENSE!
See: STRANGE
SUSPENSE STORIES

THIS MAGAZINE IS
HAUNTED
**Fawcett Publications/
Charlton Comics,
Oct., 1951**
1 MBi,F:Doctor Death 850.00
2 GE 650.00
3 MBi,Quest of the Vampire ... 400.00
4 BP,The Blind, The Doomed
and the Dead 400.00
5 BP,GE,The Slithering Horror
of Skontong Swamp! 650.00
6 Secret of the Walking Dead... 300.00
7 The Man Who Saw Too Much . 300.00
8 The House in the Web 300.00
9 The Witch of Tarlo 300.00
10 I Am Dr Death,
Severed Head(c) 500.00
11 BP,Touch of Death 300.00
12 BP 300.00
13 BP,Severed Head(c) 500.00
14 BP,Horrors of the Damned ... 300.00
15 DG(c) 250.00
16 SD(c) 500.00
17 SD,SD(c). 600.00
18 SD,SD(c). 500.00
19 SD(c). 450.00
20 SMz(c). 265.00

21 SD(c) 400.00
Becomes:

DANGER AND ADVENTURE
Feb., 1955

22 The Viking King,F:Ibis the
    Invincible 150.00
23 F:Nyoka the Jungle Girl
    Comics Code 125.00
24 DG&AA(c) 100.00
25 thru 27 . . . . @75.00
Becomes:

ROBIN HOOD AND HIS MERRY MEN
April, 1956

28 . . . . 100.00
29 thru 37 . . . . @75.00
38 SD,Aug., 1958 . . . . 150.00

3-D-ELL
Dell Publishing Co., 1953

1 Rootie Kazootie 500.00
2 Rootie Kazootie 450.00
3 Flunkey Louise 450.00

THREE RING COMICS
**Spotlight Publishers,
March, 1945**

1 Funny Animal 200.00

THREE STOOGES
**Jubilee Publ.,
Feb., 1949**

1 JKu,Infinity(c) 1,500.00
2 JKu,On the Set of the
    'The Gorilla Girl' 1,000.00

St. John Publishing Co.

1:JKu,'Bell Bent for
    Treasure, Sept., 1953 . . . . . 900.00
2 JKu 650.00
3 JKu,3D 650.00
4 JKu,Medical Mayhem 500.00
5 JKu,Shempador-Matador
    Supreme 500.00
6 JKu 500.00
7 JKu,Ocotber, 1954 . . . . 500.00

THRILLING COMICS
**Better Publ./Nedor/
Standard Comics,
Feb., 1940**

1 B&O:Doc Strange,B:Nickie
    Norton 4,000.00
2 B:Rio Kid,Woman in Red
    Pinocchio 1,800.00
3 B:Lone Eagle,The Ghost . . . 1,100.00
4 Dr Strange(c) 800.00
5 Bondage(c) 775.00
6 Dr Strange(c) 800.00
7 Dr Strange(c) 1,000.00
8 V:Pirates 750.00
9 ASh,Bondage(c) 750.00
10 V:Nazis 750.00
11 ASh(c),V:Nazis 700.00
12 ASh(c) 700.00
13 ASh(c),Bondage(c) 750.00
14 ASh(c) 700.00
15 ASh(c),V:Nazis 700.00
16 Bondage(c) 750.00
17 Dr Strange(c) 750.00
18 Dr Strange(c) 750.00
19 I&O:American Crusader 800.00
20 Bondage(c) 750.00
21 American Crusader(c) 600.00
22 Bondage(c) 625.00

Thrilling Comics #30
© Fawcett Publications

23 American Crusader 600.00
24 I:Mike in Doc Strange 600.00
25 DR Strange(c) 600.00
26 Dr Strange(c) 600.00
27 Bondage(c) 625.00
28 Bondage(c) 625.00
29 E:Rio Kid;Bondage(c) 625.00
30 Bondage(c) 625.00
31 Dr Strange(c) 550.00
32 Dr Strange(c) 550.00
33 Dr Strange(c) 550.00
34 Dr Strange(c) 550.00
35 Dr Strange 550.00
36 ASh(c),B:Commando 575.00
37 BO,ASh(c) 550.00
38 ASh(c) 550.00
39 ASh(c),E:American Crusader . 550.00
40 ASh(c) 550.00
41 ASh(c),F:American Crusader,
    Hitler 1,200.00
42 ASh(c) 450.00
43 ASh(c) 450.00
44 ASh(c),Hitler(c) 1,000.00
45 EK,ASh(c) 450.00
46 ASh(c) 450.00
47 ASh(c) 450.00
48 EK,ASh(c) 450.00
49 ASh(c) 450.00
50 ASh(c) 450.00
51 ASh(c) 450.00
52 ASh(c),E:Th Ghost;
    Peto-Bondage(c) 700.00
53 ASh(c),B:Phantom Detective . 450.00
54 ASh(c),Bondage(c) 450.00
55 ASh(c),E:Lone Eagle 400.00
56 ASh(c),B:Princess Pantha . . 650.00
57 ASh(c) 500.00
58 ASh(c) 500.00
59 ASh(c) 500.00
60 ASh(c) 500.00
61 ASh(c),GRi,A:Lone Eagle 500.00
62 ASh(c) 500.00
63 ASh(c),GT 500.00
64 ASh(c) 500.00
65 ASh(c),E:Commando Cubs,
    Phantom Detective 500.00
66 ASh(c) 500.00
67 FF,ASh(c) 600.00
68 FF,ASh(c) 600.00
69 FF,ASh(c) 600.00
70 FF,ASh(c) 600.00
71 FF,ASh(c) 600.00
72 FF,ASh(c),Sea Eagle 600.00
73 FF,ASh(c) 600.00

74 E:Princess Pantha;
    B:Buck Ranger 375.00
75 B:Western Front 200.00
76 Western 200.00
77 ASh(c) 200.00
78 Bondage(c) 225.00
79 BK 200.00
80 JSe,BE,April, 1951 . . . . 200.00

Thrilling Crime Cases #49
© Standard Comics

THRILLING CRIME CASES
**Star Publications,
June–July, 1950**

41 LbC(c),The Unknowns 350.00
42 LbC(c),The Gunmaster 325.00
43 LbC,LbC(c),The Chameleon . . 350.00
44 LbC(c),Sugar Bowl Murder . . 350.00
45 LbC(c),Maze of Murder 350.00
46 LbC,LbC(c),Modern
    Communications 300.00
47 LbC(c),The Careless Killer . . . 300.00
48 LbC(c),Road Black 300.00
49 LbC(c),The Poisoner 550.00
Becomes:

SHOCKING MYSTERY CASES
Sept., 1952–Oct., 1954

50 JyD,LbC(c),Dead Man's
    Revenge 550.00
51 JyD,LbC(c),A Murderer's
    Reward 350.00
52 LbC(c),The Carnival Killer . . . 350.00
53 LbC(c),The Long Shot of Evil . 350.00
54 LbC(c),Double-Cross of Death 350.00
55 LbC(c),Return from Death . . . 350.00
56 LbC(c),The Chase 375.00
57 LbC(c),Thrilling Cases 350.00
58 LbC(c),Killer at Large 350.00
59 LbC(c),Relentess Huntdown . . 350.00
60 LbC(c),Lesson of the Law 350.00

THRILLING ROMANCES
**Standard Comics,
Dec., 1949**

5 Ph(c) 150.00
6 Ph(c) 100.00
7 Ph(c),JSe,BE 125.00
8 Ph(c) 100.00
9 Ph(c),GT 125.00
10 Ph(c),JSe,BE 125.00
11 Ph(c),JSe,BE 125.00

12 Ph(c),WW 150.00
13 Ph(c),JSe 100.00
14 Ph(c),Danny Kaye. 75.00
15 Ph(c),Tony Martin,Ph(c) . . . 75.00
16 Ph(c). 75.00
17 Ph(c). 75.00
18 Ph(c). 75.00
19 Ph(c). 75.00
20 Ph(c). 75.00
21 Ph(c). 75.00
22 Ph(c),ATn 125.00
23 Ph(c),ATn 125.00
24 Ph(c),ATn3 . . . . 125.00
25 Ph(c),ATn 125.00

THRILLING TRUE STORY OF THE BASEBALL GIANTS
Fawcett Publications, 1952
N# Partial Ph(c),Famous Giants
  of the Past, Willie Mays . . . 1,000.00
2 Yankees Ph(c),Joe DiMaggio,
  Yogi Berra,Mickey Mantle,
  Casey Stengel 900.00

TICK TOCK TALES
Magazine Enterprises, Jan., 1946
1 (fa) Koko & Kola 150.00
2 (fa) Calender 100.00
3 thru 10 (fa) . . . . @75.00
11 thru 18 (fa) . . . . @60.00
19 (fa),Flag(c) 60.00
20 (fa). 60.00
21 (fa). 60.00
22 (fa). 60.00
23 (fa),Mugsy Mouse. 60.00
24 thru 33 (fa) . . . . @60.00
34 (fa), 1951 . . . . 60.00

TIM HOLT
Magazine Enterprises, Jan.–Feb., 1949
4 FBe,Ph(c). 900.00
5 FBe,Ph(c). 500.00
6 FBe,Ph(c),I:Calico Kid 400.00
7 FBe,Ph(c),Man-Killer Mustang 350.00
8 FBe,Ph(c) 350.00
9 FBe,DAy(c),TerribleTenderfoot 350.00
10 FBe,DAy(c),The Devil Horse . 350.00
11 FBe,DAy(c),O&I:Ghost Rider . 600.00
12 FBe,DAy(c),Battle at
  Bullock Gap. 150.00
13 FBe,DAy(c),Ph(c) 150.00
14 FBe,DAy(c),Ph(c),The
  Honest Bandits 150.00
15 FBe,DAy,Ph(c) 150.00
16 FBe,DAy,Ph(c) 150.00
17 FBe,DAy,Ph(c) 500.00
18 FBe,DAy,Ph(c) 140.00
19 FBe,DAy,They Dig By Night . . 125.00
20 FBe,DAy,O:Red Mask. 200.00
21 FBe,DAy,FF(c) 450.00
22 FBe,DAy 125.00
23 FF,FBe,DAy. 350.00
24 FBe,DAy,FBe(c) 125.00
25 FBe,DAy,FBe(c) 250.00
26 FBe,DAy,FBe(c) 125.00
27 FBe,DAy,FBe(c),V:Straw Man. 125.00
28 FBe,DAy,FBe(c),Ph(c) 125.00
29 FBe,DAy,FBe,Ph(c), ... 125.00
30 FBe,DAy,FBe(c),Lady Doom
  & The Death Wheel. 110.00
31 FBe,DAy,FBe(c) 110.00
32 FBe,DAy,FBe(c) 110.00
33 FBe,DAy,FBe(c) 110.00
34 FBe,DAy,FBe(c) 150.00

35 FBe,DAy,FBe(c) 150.00
36 FBe,DAy,FBe(c),Drugs 175.00
37 FBe,DAy,FBe(c) 150.00
38 FBe,DAy,FBe(c) 150.00
39 FBe,DAy,FBe(c),3D Effect . . 175.00
40 FBe,DAy,FBe(c) 175.00
41 FBe,DAy,FBe(c) 175.00
Becomes:

RED MASK
June–July, 1954
42 FBe,DAy,FBe(c),3D 250.00
43 FBe,DAy,FBe(c),3D 225.00
44 FBe,DAy,FBe(c),Death at
  Split Mesa,3D 225.00
45 FBe,DAy,FBe(c),V:False Red
  Mask 225.00
46 FBe,DAy,FBe(c) 225.00
47 FBe,DAy,FBe(c) 225.00
48 FBe,DAy,FBe(c),Comics Code 200.00
49 FBe,DAy,FBe(c) 200.00
50 FBe,DAy 200.00
51 FBe,DAy,The Magic of 'The
  Presto Kid' 200.00
52 FBe,DAy,O:Presto Kid 225.00
53 FBe,DAy 150.00
54 FBe,DAy,Sept., 1957 . . . . . . 225.00

TIM TYLER COWBOY
Standard Comics, Nov., 1948
11 . . . . 100.00
12 . . . . 75.00
13 The Doll Told the Secret 75.00
14 Danger at Devil's Acres 75.00
15 Secret Treasure 75.00
16 . . . . 75.00
17 . . . . 75.00
18 1950 . . . . 75.00

TINY TOTS COMICS
Dell Publishing Co., 1943
1 . . . . 500.00

TINY TOTS COMICS
E.C. Comics, March, 1946
N# Your First Comic Book
  B:Burton Geller(c) and art . . . 500.00
2 . . . . 275.00
3 Celebrate the 4th 225.00
4 Go Back to School 250.00
5 Celebrate the Winter 225.00
6 Do Their Spring Gardening . . . 225.00
7 On a Thrilling Ride 225.00
8 On a Summer Vacation 225.00
9 On a Plane Ride 225.00
10 Merry X-Mas Tiny Tots
  E:Burton Geller(c)and art . . . 225.00

TIP TOP COMICS
United Features,St. John, Dell, 1930
1 HF,Li'l Abner 10,000.00
2 HF. 2,600.00
3 HF,Tarzan(c) 2,400.00
4 HF,Li'l Abner(c) 1,500.00
5 HF,Capt&Kids(c) 1,000.00
6 HF 900.00
7 HF 900.00
8 HF,Li'l Abner(c) 900.00
9 HF,Tarzan(c) 1,200.00
10 HF,Li'l Abner(c) 900.00
11 HF,Tarzan(c) 850.00
12 HF,Li'l Abner 800.00
13 HF,Tarzan(c) 850.00
14 HF,Li'L Abner(c) 800.00
15 HF,Capt&kids(c) 800.00

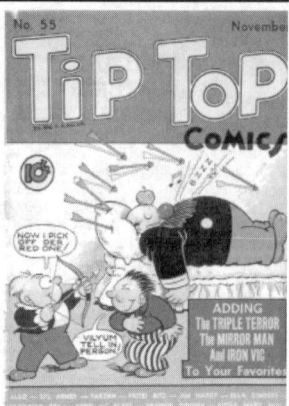

Tip Top #55
© Dell Publishing Co.

16 HF,Tarzan(c) 850.00
17 HF,Li'L Abner(c) 800.00
18 HF,Tarzan(c) 850.00
19 HF,Football(c) 750.00
20 HF,Capt&Kids(c) 750.00
21 HF,Tarzan(c) 750.00
22 HF,Li'l Abner(c) 500.00
23 HF,Capt&Kids(c) 500.00
24 HF,Tarzan(c) 750.00
25 HF,Capt&Kids(c) 500.00
26 HF,Li'L Abner(c) 500.00
27 HF,Tarzan(c) 750.00
28 HF,Li'l Abner(c) 500.00
29 HF,Capt&Kids(c) 500.00
30 HF,Tarzan(c) 750.00
31 HFCapt&Kids(c) 500.00
32 HF Tarzan(c). 700.00
33 HF,Tarzan(c) 750.00
34 HF,Capt&Kids(c) 750.00
35 HF. 450.00
36 HF,HK,Tarzan(c) 750.00
37 HF,Tarzan 750.00
38 HF 450.00
39 HF,Tarzan 700.00
40 HF 450.00
41 Tarzan(c) 750.00
42 . . . . 450.00
43 Tarzan(c) 400.00
44 HF 450.00
45 HF,Tarzan(c) 400.00
46 HF 450.00
47 HF,Tarzan(c) 400.00
48 HF 450.00
49 HF 450.00
50 HF,Tarzan(c) 400.00
51 . . . . 375.00
52 Tarzan(c) 450.00
53 . . . . 375.00
54 . . . . 475.00
55 . . . . 350.00
56 . . . . 350.00
57 BHg 400.00
58 . . . . 300.00
59 BHg 400.00
60 . . . . 300.00
61 and 62 BHg. . . . . @400.00
63 thru 90. . . . . @200.00
91 thru 99. . . . . @150.00
100. 175.00
101 thru 150. . . . . @125.00
151 thru 188. . . . . @100.00
189 thru 225. . . . . @75.00

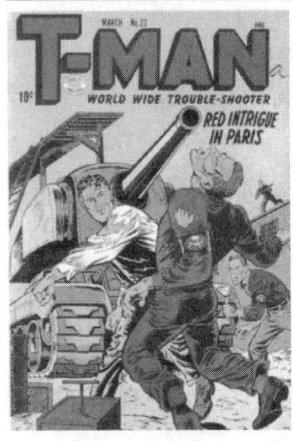

T-Man #21
© Quality Comics Group

T-MAN
Comics Magazines
(Quality Comics Group),
Sept., 1951

1 JCo,Pete Trask-the	
Treasury Man	500.00
2 RC(c),The Girl with Death	
in Her Hands	250.00
3 RC(a&c),Death Trap in Iran	250.00
4 RC(a&c),Panama Peril	250.00
5 RC(a&c),Violence in Venice	250.00
6 RC(c),The Man Who	
Could Be Hitler	225.00
7 RC(c),Mr. Murder & The	
Black Hand	225.00
8 RC(c),Red Ticket to Hell	225.00
9 RC(c),Trial By Terror	200.00
10	200.00
11 The Voice of Russia	175.00
12 Terror in Tokyo	175.00
13 Mind Assassins	175.00
14 Trouble in Bavaria, Hitler	200.00
15 The Traitor,Bondage(c)	175.00
16 Hunt For a Hatcheman	175.00
17 Red Triggerman	175.00
18 Death Rides the Rails	175.00
19 Death Ambush	175.00
20 The Fantastic H-Bomb Plot	200.00
21 The Return of Mussolini	150.00
22 Propaganda for Doom	165.00
23 Red Intrigue in Parid,H-Bomb	150.00
24 Red Sabotage	150.00
25 RC,The Ingenious Red Trap	150.00
26	125.00
27	125.00
28	125.00
29	125.00
30 thru 37	@125.00
38 Dec., 1956	125.00

TNT COMICS
Charles Publishing Co.,
Feb., 1946

1 FBI story,YellowJacket	400.00

TODAY'S BRIDES
Ajax/Farrell Publishing Co.,
Nov., 1955

1	75.00
2	50.00
3	50.00
4 Nov., 1956	50.00

TODAY'S ROMANCE
Standard Comics,
March, 1952

5 Ph(c)	100.00
6 ATh, Ph(c)	125.00
7 Ph(c)	75.00
8 Ph(c)	75.00

TOM AND JERRY
DELL GIANT EDITIONS
Dell Publishing Co.,
1952–58

Back to School	300.00
Picnic Time	250.00
Summer Fun 1	350.00
Summer Fun 2	200.00
Winter Carnival 1	500.00
Winter Carnival 2	350.00
Winter Fun 3	200.00
Winter Fun 4	175.00
Winter Fun 5	150.00
Winter Fun 6	150.00
Winter Fun 7	150.00

TOMB OF TERROR
Harvey Publications,
June, 1952

1 BP,The Thing From the	
Center of the Earth	550.00
2 RP,The Quagmire Beast	350.00
3 BP,RP,Caravan of the	
Doomed, Bondage(c)	350.00
4 RP,I'm Going to Kill You,	
Torture	300.00
5 RP	300.00
6 RP,Return From the Grave	300.00
7 RP,Shadow of Death	300.00
8 HN,The Hive	300.00
9 BP,HN,The Tunnel	300.00
10 BP,HN,The Trial	300.00
11 BP,HN,The Closet	300.00
12 BP,HN,Tale of Cain	325.00
13 BP,What Was Out There	400.00
14 BP,SC,End Result	400.00
15 BP,HN,Break-up, Exploding	
Head	750.00
16 BP,Going,Going,Gone	350.00
Becomes:	

THRILLS OF
TOMORROW
Oct., 1954

17 RP,BP,The World of Mr. Chatt	175.00
18 RP,BP,The Dead Awaken	150.00
19 S&K,S&K(c),A:Stuntman	450.00
20 S&K,S&K(c),A:Stuntman	400.00

TOM CORBETT
SPACE CADET
Dell Publishing Co.,
Jan., 1952

See also Dell Four Color

4 based on TV show	150.00
5	125.00
6	100.00
7	100.00
8	100.00
9	100.00
10 and 11	@100.00

TOM CORBETT
SPACE CADET
Prize Publications,
May–June, 1955

1 Robot(c)	400.00

Tom Corbett Space Cadet #2
© Prize Publications

2	300.00
3 Sept.–Oct., 1955	300.00

TOM MIX
Ralston-Purina Co.,
Sept., 1940

1 O:Tom Mix	4,500.00
2	1,500.00
3	800.00
4 thru 9	@750.00
Becomes:	

TOM MIX
COMMANDOS COMICS
Nov., 1942

10	700.00
11 Invisible Invaders	700.00
12 Terrible Talons Of Tokyo	700.00

TOM MIX WESTERN
Fawcett Publications,
Jan., 1948

1 Ph(c),Two-Fisted	
Adventures	1,500.00
2 Ph(c),Hair-Triggered Action	600.00
3 Ph(c),Double Barreled Action	500.00
4 Ph(c),Cowpunching	500.00
5 Ph(c),Two Gun Action	500.00
6 CCB,Most Famous Cowboy	350.00
7 CCB,A Tattoo of Thrills	350.00
8 EK,Ph(c),Gallant Guns	325.00
9 CCB,Song o/t Deadly Spurs	325.00
10 CCB,Crack Shot Western	325.00
11 CCB,EK(C),Triple Revenge	325.00
12 King of the Cowboys	250.00
13 Ph(c),Leather Burns	250.00
14 Ph(c),Brand of Death	250.00
15 Ph(c),Masked Treachery	250.00
16 Ph(c),Death Spurting Guns	250.00
17 Ph(c),Trail of Doom	250.00
18 Ph(c),Reign of Terror	225.00
19 Hand Colored Ph(c)	250.00
20 Ph(c),CCB,F:Capt Tootsie	225.00
21 Ph(c)	225.00
22 Ph(c),The Human Beast	225.00
23 Ph(c),Return of the Past	225.00
24 Hand Colored Ph(c),	
The Lawless City	225.00
25 Hand Colored Ph(c),	
The Signed Death Warrant	225.00
26 Hand Colored Ph(c),	
Dangerous Escape	225.00

27 Hand Colored Ph(c),
   Hero Without Glory 225.00
28 Ph(c),The Storm Kings 225.00
29 Hand Colored Ph(c),The
   Case of the Rustling Rose . . 225.00
30 Ph(c),Disappearance
   in the Hills 225.00
31 Ph(c) 175.00
32 Hand Colored Ph(c),
   Mystery of Tremble Mountain 175.00
33 . . . . 175.00
34 . . . . 175.00
35 Partial Ph(c),The Hanging
   at Hollow Creek. 175.00
36 Ph(c) 175.00
37 Ph(c) 175.00
38 Ph(c),36 pages 150.00
39 Ph(c) 175.00
40 Ph(c) 175.00
41 Ph(c) 175.00
42 Ph(c) 175.00
43 Ph(c) 150.00
44 Ph(c) 150.00
45 Partial Ph(c),The Secret
   Letter. 150.00
46 Ph(c) 150.00
47 Ph(c) 150.00
48 Ph(c) 150.00
49 Partial Ph(c),Blind Date
   With Death. 150.00
50 Ph(c) 150.00
51 Ph(c) 150.00
52 Ph(c) 150.00
53 Ph(c) 150.00
54 Ph(c) 150.00
55 Ph(c) 150.00
56 Partial Ph(c),Deadly Spurs . . . 150.00
57 Ph(c)5 . . . . 150.00
58 Ph(c) 150.00
59 Ph(c) 150.00
60 Ph(c) 150.00
61 Partial Ph(c),Lost in the
   Night,May, 1953. . . . . 175.00

TOMMY OF THE BIG TOP
**King Features/
Standard Comics, 1948**
10 Thrilling Circus Adventures . . . 100.00
11 . . . . 75.00
12 March, 1949 . . . . 75.00

TOM-TOM THE JUNGLE BOY
Magazine Enterprises, 1946
1 (fa) 125.00
2 (fa) 100.00
3 Winter 1947,(fa),X-mas issue . . 75.00
1 . . . . 75.00

TONTO
See: LONE RANGER'S COMPANION TONTO

TONY TRENT
See: FACE, THE

TOP FLIGHT COMICS
**Four Star/St. John Publ. Co.,
July, 1949**
1 . . . . 125.00
1 Hector the Inspector 75.00

TOP LOVE STORIES
**Star Publications,
May, 1951**
3 LbC(c) 300.00
4 LbC(c) 200.00
5 LbC(c) 200.00
6 LbC(c),WW 300.00
7 LbC(c) 250.00
8 LbC(c), WW Story 275.00
9 LbC(c) 250.00
10 thru 16 LbC(c) . . . . @250.00
17 LbC(c),WW 275.00
18 LbC(c). 250.00
19 LbC(c),JyD 250.00

*Top-Notch Comics #3
© MLJ Magazines*

TOP-NOTCH COMICS
**MLJ Magazines,
Dec., 1939**
1 JaB,JCo,B&O:The Wizard,
   B:Kandak,Swift of the Secret
   Service,The Westpointer,
   Mystic, Air Patrol,Scott
   Rand, Manhunter 9,000.00
2 JaB,JCo,B:Dick Storm,
   E:Mystic, B:Stacy Knight . . 3,500.00
3 JaB,JCo,EA(c),E:Swift of the
   Secret Service,Scott Rand 2,500.00
4 JCo,EA(c),MMe,O&I:Streak,
   Chandler 2,000.00
5 Ea(c),MMe,O&I:Galahad,
   B:Shanghai Sheridan 2,000.00
6 Ea(c),MMe,A:The Sheild . . . 1,500.00
7 Ea(c),MMe,N:The Wizard . . 2,000.00
8 E:Dick Sorm,B&O:Roy The1
   Super Boy,The Firefly 2,000.00
9 O&I:Black Hood,
   B:Fran Frazier 8,000.00
10 A:Black Hood 2,500.00
11 . . . . 1,400.00
12 . . . . 1,400.00
13 . . . . 1,400.00
14 Bondage(c) 1,400.00
15 MMe 1,400.00
16 . . . . 1,300.00
17 Bondage(c) 1,400.00
18 . . . . 1,300.00
19 Bondage(c) 1,300.00
20 . . . . 1,200.00
21 . . . . 1,000.00
22 . . . . 1,000.00
23 Bondage(c) 1,050.00
24 Black Hood Smashes
   Murder Ring 1,000.00

25 E:Bob Phantom 1,000.00
26 . . . . 1,000.00
27 E:The Firefly 1,000.00
28 B:Suzie,Pokey Okay,
   Gag Oriented 1,000.00
29 E:Kandak 1,000.00
30 . . . . 1,000.00
31 . . . . 500.00
32 . . . . 500.00
33 BWo,B:Dotty&Ditto 500.00
34 BWo 500.00
35 BWo 500.00
36 BWo 500.00
37 thru 40 BWo . . . . @500.00
41 . . . . 500.00
42 BWo 500.00
43 . . . . 500.00
44 EW:Black Hood,I:Suzie. 500.00
45 Suzie(c). 600.00
Becomes:

LAUGH COMIX
Summer, 1944
46 Suzie & Wilbur 250.00
47 Suzie & Wilbur 200.00
48 Suzie & Wilbur 200.00
Becomes:

SUZIE COMICS
Spring, 1945
49 B:Ginger 325.00
50 AFy(c) 200.00
51 AFy(c) 200.00
52 AFy(c) 200.00
53 AFy(c) 200.00
54 AFy(c) 250.00
55 AFy(c) 250.00
56 BWo,B:Katie Keene 150.00
57 thru 70 BWo . . . . @150.00
71 thru 79 BWo . . . . @100.00
80 thru 99 BWo . . . . @100.00
100 Aug., 1954, BWo. 100.00

TOPS
**Tops Mag. Inc.
(Lev Gleason), July, 1949**
1 RC&BLb,GT,DBa,CBi(c),I'll Buy
   That Girl,Our Explosive
   Children 1,500.00
2 FG,BF,CBi(c),RC&BLb 1,400.00

TOPS COMICS
**Consolidated Book Publishers,
1944**
2000 Don on the Farm. 300.00
2001 The Jack of Spades
   V:The Hawkman 200.00
2002 Rip Raiders 150.00
2003 Red Birch 50.00

TOP SECRET
**Hillman Publications,
Jan., 1952**
1 The Tricks of the Secret
   Agent Revealed 250.00

TOP SECRETS
Street & Smith, Nov., 1947
1 BP,BP(c),Of the Men Who
   Guard the U.S. Mail 400.00
2 BP,BP(c),True Story of Jim
   the Penman 350.00
3 BP,BP(c),Crime Solved by
   Mental Telepathy 300.00
4 Highway Pirates. 300.00
5 BP,BP(c),Can Music Kill 300.00
6 BP,BP(c),The Clue of the
   Forgotten Film 300.00

7 BP,BP(c),Train For Sale. 375.00
8 BP,BP(c) 300.00
9 BP,BP(c) 300.00
10 BP,BP(c),July–Aug., 1949. . . . 375.00

TOPS IN ADVENTURE

**Approved Comics
(Ziff-Davis),
Autumn, 1952**
1 BP,Crusaders From Mars 600.00

TOP SPOT COMICS

**Top Spot Publishing Co.,
1945**
1 The Duke Of Darkness 450.00

TOPSY-TURVY

**R.B. Leffingwell Publ.,
April, 1945**
1 I:Cookie 125.00

TOR

**St. John Publishing Co.,
Sept., 1953**
1 JKu,JKu(c),O;Tor,One Million
Years Ago 150.00
2 JKu,JKu(c),3-D Issue 100.00
3 JKu,JKu(c),ATh,historic Life . . 125.00
4 JKu,JKu(c),ATh 125.00
5 JKu,JKu(c),ATh,Oct., 1954 . . . 125.00

TORCHY

**Quality Comics Group,
Nov., 1949**
1 GFx,BWa(c),The Blonde
Bombshell 2,000.00
2 GFx,GFx(c),Beauty at
its' Best 900.00
3 GFx,GFx(c),You Can't
Beat Nature 900.00
4 GFx,GFx(c),The Girl to
Keep Your Eye On 1,100.00
5 BWa,GFx,BWa(c),At the
Masquerade Party 1,500.00
6 Sept., 1950,BWa,GFx,
BWa(c),The Libido Driven
Boy Scout 1,500.00

TORMENTED, THE

**Sterling Comics,
July, 1954**
1 Buried Alive 300.00
2 Sept., 1954,The Devils Circus 250.00

TOYLAND COMICS

**Fiction House Magazines,
Jan., 1947**
1 Wizard of the Moon 400.00
2 Buddy Bruin & Stu Rabbit 200.00
3 GT,The Candy Maker 250.00
4 July, 1947 . . . . 200.00

TOY TOWN COMICS

**Toytown Publ./Orbit Publ.,
Feb., 1945**
1 LbC,LbC(c)(fa) 500.00
2 LbC,(fa) 300.00
3 LbC,LbC(c),(fa) 250.00
4 LbC,(fa) 250.00
5 LbC,(fa) 250.00
6 LbC,(fa) 250.00
7 LbC,(fa),May, 1947 . . . . 250.00

*Torchy #4
© Quality Comics Group*

TRAIL BLAZERS
See: RED DRAGON
COMICS

TREASURE COMICS

Prize Comics Group, 1943
1 S&K,Reprints of Prize Comics
#7 through #11 . . . . 3,000.00

TREASURE COMICS

**American Boys Comics
(Prize Publications),
June–July, 1945**
1 HcK,B:PaulBunyan,MarcoPolo 500.00
2 HcK(a&c),B:Arabian Knight,
Gorilla King,Dr.Styx 250.00
3 HcK 175.00
4 HcK 175.00
5 HcK,JK, Marco Polo 300.00
6 BK,HcK(a&c) 250.00
7 FF,HcK(a&c),Capt.Kidd, Jr. . . . 500.00
8 HcK,FF 500.00
9 HcK,DBa 175.00
10 JK,DBa,JK(c) 400.00
11 BK,HcK,DBa,The Weird
Adventures of Mr. Bottle 250.00
12 DBa,DBa(c),Autumn, 1947 . . . 175.00

TREASURY OF COMICS

St. John Publishing Co., 1947
1 RvB,RvB(c),Abbie an' Slats . . 150.00
2 Jim Hardy 125.00
3 Bill Bimlin 125.00
4 RvB,RvB(c),Abbie an' Slats . . 125.00
5 Jim Hardy,Jan., 1948 . . . . 100.00

TRIPLE THREAT

**Gerona Publications,
Winter, 1945**
1 F:King O'Leary,The Duke of
Darkness,Beau Brummell . . . 350.00

TRUE AVIATION
PICTURE STORIES

**Parents' Institute/P.M.I.,
Aug., 1942**
1 How Jimmy Doolittle
Bombed Tokyo 200.00

2 Knight of the Air Mail 150.00
3 The Amazing One-Man
Air Force 125.00
4 Joe Foss America's No. 1
Air Force 125.00
5 Bombs over Germany 125.00
6 Flight Lt. Richard
Hillary R.A.F. 125.00
7 "Fatty" Chow China's
Sky Champ 125.00
8 Blitz over Burma 125.00
9 Off the Beam 125.00
10 "Pappy" Boyington 125.00
11 Ph(c) 125.00
12 . . . . 125.00
13 Ph(c),Flying Facts. 125.00
14 . . . . 125.00
15 True Aviation Adventures 125.00
Becomes:

AVIATION AND MODEL
BUILDING

Dec., 1946
16 . . . . 75.00
17 Feb., 1947. . . . . 100.00

TRUE COMICS

**True Comics/
Parents' Magazine Press,
April, 1941–Aug., 1950**
1 My Greatest Adventure-by
Lowell Thomas, Churchill . . . 450.00
2 BEv,The Story of the
Red Cross 200.00
3 Baseball Hall of Fame 225.00
4 Danger in the Artic 150.00
5 Father Duffy-the Fighting
Chaplain, Joe Louis. 165.00
6 The Capture of Aquinaldo 175.00
7 JKa,Wilderness Adventures of
George Washington 165.00
8 U.S. Army Wings 125.00
9 A Pig that Made History 125.00
10 Adrift on an Ice Pan 125.00
11 Gen. Douglas MacArthur. 110.00
12 Mackenzie-King of Canada. . . 110.00
13 The Real Robinson Crusoe. . . 110.00
14 Australia war base of
the South Pacific 110.00
15 The Story of West Point 125.00
16 How Jimmy Doolittle
Bombed Tokyo. 120.00
17 The Ghost of Captain Blig,
B.Feller 125.00
18 Battling Bill of the
Merchant Marine 135.00
19 Secret Message Codes. 110.00
20 The Story of India 100.00
21 Timoshenko the Blitz Buster . . 110.00
22 Gen, Bernard L. Montgomery . 100.00
23 The Story of Steel 100.00
24 Gen. Henri Giraud-Master
of Escape 100.00
25 Medicine's Miracle Men 100.00
26 Hero of the Bismarck Sea. . . . 100.00
27 Leathernecks have Landed. . . 110.00
28 The Story of Radar 100.00
29 The Fighting Seabees. 100.00
30 Dr. Norman Bethune-Blood
Bank Founder 100.00
31 Our Good Neighbor Bolivia,
Red Grange 110.00
32 Men against the Desert 75.00
33 Gen. Clark and his Fighting
5th 80.00
34 Angel of the Battlefield 75.00
35 Carlson's Marine Raiders 75.00
36 Canada's Sub-Busters 75.00
37 Commander of the Crocodile
Fleet. 75.00

GOLDEN AGE

GOLDEN AGE

38 Oregon Trailblazer 75.00
39 Saved by Sub, FBI 75.00
40 Sea Furies 75.00
41 Cavalcade of England. 50.00
42 Gen. Jaques Le Clerc-Hero
   of Paris 50.00
43 Unsinkable Ship 55.00
44 El Senor Goofy, Truman 50.00
45 Tokyo Express 50.00
46 The Magnificent Runt 50.00
47 Atoms Unleashed,
   Atomic Bomb. 125.00
48 Pirate Patriot. 50.00
49 Smiking Fists 50.00
50 Lumber Pirates 50.00
51 Exercise Musk-Ox. 50.00
52 King of the Buckaneers 50.00
53 Baseline Booby. 50.00
54 Santa Fe Sailor. 50.00
55 Sea Going Santa 50.00
56 End of a Terror 50.00
57 Newfangled Machines 50.00
58 Leonardo da Vinci-500 years
   too Soon, Houdini 50.00
59 Pursuit Pirates, Bob Hope 55.00
60 Emmett Kelly-The World's
   Funniest Clown 50.00
61 Peter Le Grand-
   Bold Buckaneer. 50.00
62 Sutter's Gold. 50.00
63 Outboard Outcome. 50.00
64 Man-Eater at Large. 50.00
65 The Story of Scotland Yard. . . . 50.00
66 Easy Guide to Football
   Formations, Will Rogers 55.00
67 The Changing Zebra. 50.00
68 Admiral Byrd 50.00
69 FBI Special Agent Steve
   Saunders, Jack Benny 55.00
70 The Case of the Seven
   Hunted Men. 50.00
71 Story of Joe DiMaggio 150.00
72 FBI,Jackie Robinson. 100.00
73 The 26 Mile Dash-Story of
   the Marathon, Walt Disney . . . 75.00
74 A Famous Coach's Special
   Football Tips, Amos & Andy . . 55.00
75 King of Reporters 55.00
76 Story of a Buried Treasure 55.00
77 France's Greatest Detective . . . 55.00
78 Cagliostro-Master Rogue 75.00
79 Ralph Bunche-Hero of Peace . . 55.00
80 Rocket Trip to the Moon 200.00
81 Red Grange 200.00
82 Marie Celeste Ship of
   Mystery 175.00
83 Bullfighter from Brooklyn. 175.00
84 King of the Buckaneers 175.00

TRUE CONFIDENCES
Fawcett Publications, Autumn, 1949
1 . . . . 200.00
2 and 3 . . . . @125.00
4 DP 125.00

TRUE CRIME COMICS
Magazine Village, Inc., May, 1947
2 JCo(c),James Kent-Crook,
   Murderer,Escaped Convict;
   Drug 2,000.00
3 JCo(a&c),Benny Dickson-
   Killer;Drug. 1,500.00
4 JCo(a&c),Little Jake-
   Big Shot 1,400.00
5 JCo(c),The Rat & the Blond
   Gun Moll;Drug 1,000.00
6 Joseph Metley-Swindler,

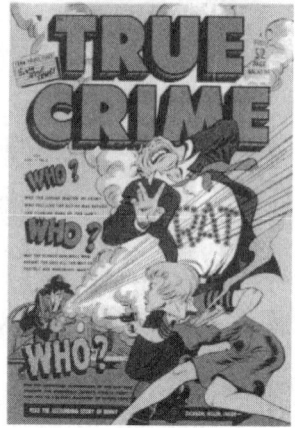

True Crime #3
© *Magazine Village*

Jailbird, Killer 800.00
2-1(7) ATh,WW,Ph(c),Phil
   Coppolla,Sept., 1949 . . . . 1,200.00

TRUE LIFE SECRETS
Romantic Love Stories/ Charlton Comics, March–April, 1951
1 Ph(c) 150.00
2 . . . . 75.00
3 thru 11 . . . . @60.00
12 Escort Girl 65.00
13 thru 20 . . . . @60.00
21 thru 25 . . . . @50.00
26 Comics Code 40.00
27 thru 29 . . . . @40.00

TRUE LIFE ROMANCES
Ajax/Farrell Publications, Dec., 1955
1 . . . . 125.00
2 . . . . 75.00
3 Aug., 1956 . . . . 75.00

TRUE LOVE PICTORIAL
St. John Publishing Co., 1952
1 Ph(c) 200.00
2 MB 250.00
3 MB(c),MB,JKu 400.00
4 MB(c),MB,JKu 400.00
5 MB(c),MB,JKu 400.00
6 MB(c) 200.00
7 MB(c) 200.00
8 MB(c) 150.00
9 MB(c) 150.00
10 MB(c),MB 150.00
11 MB(c),MB 150.00

TRUE MOVIE AND TELEVISION
Toby Press, Aug., 1950
1 Liz Taylor, Ph(c) 650.00
2 FF,Ph(c),John Wayne,
   L.Taylor 500.00
3 June Allyson,Ph(c) 350.00
4 Jane Powell,Ph(c),Jan.,1951 . . 200.00

SPORT COMICS
Street & Smith, Oct., 1940
1 F:Lou Gehrig 700.00
2 F:Gene Tunney 400.00
3 F:Phil Rizzuto 450.00
4 F:Frank Leahy 300.00
Becomes:

TRUE SPORT PICTURE STORIES
Feb., 1942–July-Aug., 1949
5 Joe DiMaggio 400.00
6 Billy Confidence 250.00
7 Mel Ott 275.00
8 Lou Ambers 250.00
9 Pete Reiser 250.00
10 Frankie Sinkwich. 250.00
11 Marty Serfo 250.00
12 JaB(c),Jack Dempsey. 265.00
2-1 JaB(c),Willie Pep 250.00
2-2 JaB(c) 250.00
2-3 JaB(c),Carl Hubbell 265.00
2-4 Advs. in Football & Battle . . . 275.00
2-5 Don Hutson 250.00
2-6 Dixie Walker. 275.00
2-7 Stan Musial 300.00
2-8 Famous Ring Champions
   of All Time 275.00
2-9 List of War Year Rookies . . . 300.00
2-10 Connie Mack 275.00
2-11 Winning Basketball Plays . . 250.00
2-12 Eddie Gottlieb 250.00
3-1 Bill Conn 250.00
3-2 Philadelphia Athletics 200.00
3-3 Leo Durocher 250.00
3-4 Rudy Dusek 200.00
3-5 Ernie Pyle 200.00
3-6 Bowling with Ned Day 200.00
3-7 Return of the Mighty (Home
   from War);Joe DiMaggio(c) . . 400.00
3-8 Conn V:Louis 300.00
3-9 Reuben Shark 200.00
3-10 BP,BP(c),Don "Dopey"
   Dillock 200.00
3-11 BP,BP(c),Death
   Scores a Touchdown. 200.00
3-12 Red Sox V:Senators 200.00
4-1 Spring Training in
   Full Spring 200.00
4-2 BP,BP(c),How to Pitch 'Em
   Where They Can't Hit 'Em . . 200.00
4-3 BP,BP(c),1947 Super Stars . 235.00
4-4 BP,BP(c),Get Ready for
   the Olympics 235.00
4-5 BP,BP,(c),Hugh Casey 200.00
4-6 BP,BP(c),Phantom Phil
   Hergesheimer 200.00
4-7 BP,BP(c),How to Bowl Better 200.00
4-8 Tips on the Big Fight 235.00
4-9 BP,BP(c),Bill McCahan 200.00
4-10 BP,BP(c),Great Football
   Plays 200.00
4-11 BP,BP(c),Football. 200.00
4-12 BP,BP(c),Basketball. 200.00
5-1 Satchel Paige 250.00
5-2 History of Boxing 200.00

TRUE SWEETHEART SECRETS
Fawcett Publications, May, 1950
1 Debbie Reynolds,Ph(c) 150.00
2 WW 250.00
3 BD 125.00
4 BD 125.00
5 BD 125.00
6 thru 11 . . . . @125.00

TRUE-TO-LIFE ROMANCES
Star Publications, Nov.–Dec., 1949

3 LbC(c),GlennFord/JanetLeigh	300.00
4 LbC(c)	200.00
5 LbC(c)	200.00
6 LbC(c)	200.00
7 LbC(c)	200.00
8 LbC(c)	200.00
9 LbC(c)	200.00
10 LbC(c)	200.00
11 LbC(c)	200.00
12 LbC(c)	200.00
13 LbC(c),JyD	200.00
14 LbC(c),JyD	200.00
15 LbC(c),WW,JyD	250.00
16 LbC(c),WW,JyD	250.00
17 LbC(c),JyD	175.00
18 LbC(c),JyD	175.00
19 LbC(c),JyD	175.00
20 LbC(c),JyD	175.00
21 LbC(c),JyD	175.00
22 LbC(c)	175.00
23 LbC(c)	175.00

TRUE WAR ROMANCES
Comic Magazines, Inc. (Quality Comics), Sept., 1952

1 Ph(c)	150.00
2	75.00
3 thru 10	@65.00
11 thru 20	@60.00
21 Comics Code	60.00

Becomes:

EXOTIC ROMANCES
Oct., 1955

22	125.00
23 thru 26	@60.00
27 MB	150.00
28 MB	125.00
29	60.00
30 MB	125.00
31 MB	150.00

TUROK, SON OF STONE
Dell Publishing Co., Dec., 1954

(1) see Dell Four Color #596	
(2) see Dell Four Color #656	
3 Cavemen	350.00
4 and 5	@300.00
6 & 7	@250.00
8 Dinosaur, Lost Valley	275.00
9 thru 16	@150.00
17 Prehistoric Pigmies	175.00
18 thru 29	@125.00
See Color Pub. section	

TWEETY AND SYLVESTER
Dell Publishing Co., June, 1952

(1) see Dell Four Color #406	
(2) see Dell Four Color #489	
(3) see Dell Four Color #524	
4 thru 20	@60.00
21 thru 37	@50.00

TWINKLE COMICS
Spotlight Publications, May, 1945

1 Humor Format	300.00

TWO-FISTED TALES
Fables Publications (E.C. Comics), Nov.–Dec., 1950–March, 1955

18 JCr,WW,JSe,HK(a&c)	1,500.00
19 JCr,WW,JSe,HK(a&c)	1,200.00
20 JDa,WW,JSe,HK(a&c)	750.00
21 JDa,WW,JSe,HK(a&c)	600.00
22 JDa,WW,JSe,HK(a&c)	600.00
23 JDa,WW,JSe,HK(a&c)	450.00
24 JDa,WW,JSe,HK(a&c)	400.00
25 JDa,WW,JSe,HK(a&c)	400.00
26 JDa,JSe,HK(c),Action at the Changing Reservoir	300.00
27 JDa,JSe,HK(c)	300.00
28 JDa,JSe,HK(c)	300.00
29 JDa,JSe,HK(c)	350.00
30 JSe,JDa(a&c)	350.00
31 JDa,JSe,HK(c),Civil War Story	300.00
32 JDa,JKu,WW(c)	300.00
33 JDa,JKu,WW(c),A-Bomb	325.00
34 JSe,JDa(a&c)	300.00
35 JSe,JDa(a&c),Civil War Story	300.00
36 JDa,JSe(a&c),A Difference of Opinion	250.00
37 JSe(a&c),Bugles & Battle Cries	250.00
38 JSe(a&c)	250.00
39 JSe(a&c)	250.00
40 JDa,JSe,GE(a&c)	300.00
41 JSe,GE,JDa(c)	250.00

UNCLE CHARLIE'S FABLES
Lev Gleason Publications, Jan., 1952

1 CBi(c),Ph(c)	200.00
2 BF,CBi(c),Ph(c)	125.00
3 CBi(c),Ph(c)	135.00
4 CBi(c),Ph(c)	135.00
5 CBi,Ph(c),Sept., 1952	135.00

UNCLE SAM
See: BLACKHAWK

UNCLE SCROOGE
Dell Publishing Co., March, 1952

(1) see Dell Four Color #386	
(2) see Dell Four Color #456	
(3) see Dell Four Color #495	
4 Gladstone Album #11	600.00
5 Gladstone Special	450.00
6	350.00
7 CB, Seven Cities of Cibola	325.00
8 thru 10	@300.00
11 thru 23	@275.00
24 Christmas issue	275.00
25 thru 30	@250.00
31 thru 39	@200.00
See Color Pub. section	

UNDERWORLD
D.S. Publishing Co., Feb.–March, 1948

1 SMo(c),Violence	600.00
2 SMo(c),Electrocution	600.00
3 AMc,AMc(c),The Ancient Club	500.00
4 Grl,The Beer Baron Murder	450.00
5 Grl,The Postal Clue	300.00
6 The Polka Dot Gang	250.00
7 Mono-The Master	250.00
8 The Double Tenth	250.00
9 Thrilling Stories of the Fight against Crime,June, 1953	250.00

UNDERWORLD CRIME
Fawcett Publications, June, 1952

1 The Crime Army	400.00
2 Jailbreak	250.00
3 Microscope Murder	200.00
4 Death on the Docks	200.00
5 River of Blood	200.00
6 The Sky Pirates	200.00
7 Bondage & Torture(c)	400.00
8	200.00
9 June, 1953	200.00

UNITED COMICS
United Features Syndicate, 1950

8 thru 26 Bushmiller(c), Fritzi Ritz	@60.00

UNITED STATES FIGHTING AIR FORCE
Superior Comics, Ltd., Sept., 1952

1 Coward's Courage	125.00
2 Clouds that Killed	60.00
3 Operation Decoy	50.00
4 thru 28	@50.00
29 Oct., 1959	50.00

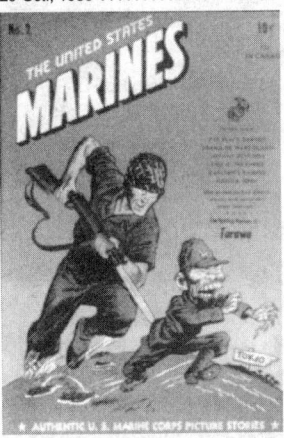

United States Marines #2
© E.C. Comics

UNITED STATES MARINES
Wm. H. Wise/Magazine Ent/ Toby Press, 1943

N# MBi,MBi(c),Hellcat out of Heaven	200.00
2 MBi,Drama of Wake Island, Tojo	450.00
3 A Leatherneck Flame Thrower, Tojo	350.00
4 MBi	125.00
5 BP	100.00
6 BP	100.00
7 BP	75.00
8 thru 10	@75.00
11 1952	75.00

GOLDEN AGE

UNKEPT PROMISE
Legion of Truth, 1949
1 Anti:Alcoholic Drinking 100.00

UNKNOWN WORLDS
See: STRANGE STORIES FROM ANOTHER WORLD

UNSEEN, THE
Visual Editions (Standard Comics), 1952
5 ATh,The Hungry Lodger 500.00
6 JKa,MSy,Bayou Vengeance . . 350.00
7 JKz,MSy,Time is the Killer . . . 350.00
8 JKz,MSy,The Vengance Vat . . 300.00
9 JKz,MSy,Your Grave is Ready 350.00
10 JKz,MSy 350.00
11 JKz,MSy 300.00
12 ATh,GT,Till Death Do Us Part . 350.00
13 . . . . 250.00
14 . . . . 250.00
15 ATh,The Curse of the
   Undead!, July, 1954. . . . . . . 350.00

UNTAMED LOVE
Comic Magazines (Quality Comics Group), Jan., 1950
1 BWa(c),PGn. 300.00
2 Ph(c) 175.00
3 PGn, Ph(c). 200.00
4 Ph(c) 175.00
5 PGn, Ph(c). 200.00

USA IS READY
Dell Publishing Co., 1941
1 Propaganda WWII 500.00

U.S. Jones #2
© Fox Features Syndicate

U.S. JONES
Fox Features Syndicate, Nov., 1941
1 Death Over the Airways 1,900.00
2 Nazi (c),Jan., 1942 . . . . 1,400.00

U.S. MARINES IN ACTION!
Avon Periodicals, Aug.–Dec., 1952
1 On Land,Sea & in the Air 100.00
2 The Killer Patrol 60.00
3 EK(c),Death Ridge. 65.00

U.S. TANK COMMANDOS
Avon Periodicals, June, 1952
1 EK(c),Fighting Daredevils
   of the USA 100.00
2 EK(c) 75.00
3 EK,EK(c),Robot Armanda 75.00
4 EK,EK(c),March, 1953 . . . . 75.00

VALOR
E.C. Comics, March, 1955
1 AW,AT,WW,WW(c),Grl,BK 400.00
2 AW(c),AW,WWGrl,BK 350.00
3 AW,RC,BK,JOc(c) 250.00
4 WW(c),RC,Grl,BK,JO 250.00
5 WW(c),WW,AW,GE,Grl,BK . . 225.00

VARIETY COMICS
Rural Home Publ./ Croyden Publ. Co., 1944
1 MvS,MvS(c),O:Capt, Valiant . . 300.00
2 MvS,MvS(c) 200.00
3 MvS,MvS(c) 150.00
4 . . . . 125.00
5 1946 . . . . 110.00

VAULT OF HORROR
See: WAR AGAINST CRIME

V...COMICS
Fox Features Syndicate, Jan., 1942
1 V:V-Man, Nazi(c) 1,800.00
2 The Horror of the
   Dungeons, March, 1942 . . 1,400.00

VERI BEST SURE SHOT COMICS
Holyoke Publishing Co., 1945
1 reprint Holyoke One-Shots . . . 500.00

VIC FLINT
St. John Publishing Co., Aug., 1948
1 ...Crime Buster 150.00
2 . . . . 125.00
3 . . . . 75.00
4 . . . . 75.00
5 April, 1949 . . . . 75.00

VIC JORDAN
Civil Service Publications, April, 1945
1 Escape From a Nazi Prison . . 150.00

VIC TORRY AND HIS FLYING SAUCER
Fawcett Publications, 1950
1 Ph(c),Revealed at Last. 1,000.00

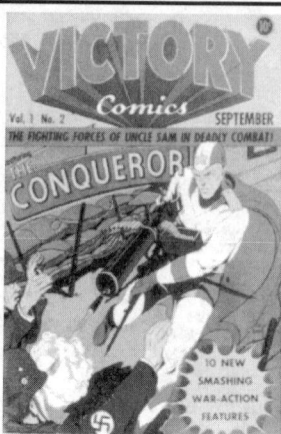

Victory Comics #2
© Hillman Periodicals

VICTORY COMICS
Hillman Periodicals, Aug., 1941
1 BEv,BEv(c),F:TheConqueror 4,200.00
2 BEv,BEv(c) 1,900.00
3 The Conqueror(c) 1,200.00
4 Dec., 1941 . . . . 1,100.00

VIC VERITY MAGAZINE
Vic Verity Publications, 1945
1 CCB,CCB(c),B:Vic Verity,Hot-
   Shot Galvan, Tom Travis . . . 250.00
2 CCB,CCB(c),Annual Classic
   Dance Recital 150.00
3 CCB 125.00
4 CCB,I:Boomer Young;The
   Bee-U-TiFul Weekend 125.00
5 CCB,Championship Baseball
   Game 125.00
6 CCB,High School Hero 125.00
7 CCB,CCB(c),F:Rocket Rex . . 125.00

VOODA
April, 1955
20 MB,MB(c),Echoes of
   an A-Bomb. 500.00
21 MB,MB(c),Trek of Danger. . . . 400.00
22 MB,MB(c),The Sun Blew
   Away, Aug., 1955. . . . . 400.00

VOODOO
Four Star Publ./Farrell/ Ajax Comics, May, 1952
1 MB,South Sea Girl. 800.00
2 MB 600.00
3 Face Stabbing 500.00
4 MB,Rendezvous 500.00
5 Ghoul For A Day,Nazi 350.00
6 The Weird Dead,
   Severed Head 400.00
7 Goodbye World 350.00
8 MB, Revenge 450.00
9 Will this thing Never Stew? . . 350.00
10 Land of Shadows & Screams . 350.00
11 Human Harvest 300.00
12 The Wazen Taper 300.00
13 Bondage(c),Caskets to
   Fit Everybody 325.00
14 Death Judges the
   Beauty Contest, Zombies . . . 300.00

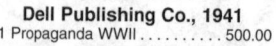

GOLDEN AGE

15 Loose their Heads, Opium . . . 325.00
16 Fog Was Her Shroud 300.00
17 Apes Laughter,Electric Chair . 325.00
18 Astounding Fantasy 300.00
19 MB,Bondage(c);
   Destination Congo. 450.00
Ann.#1 100-pg. 1,250.00
Becomes:

WACKY DUCK
See: DOPEY DUCK

WALT DISNEY'S
COMICS & STORIES
Dell Publishing Co.
N# 1943 dpt.store giveway 750.00
N# 1945 X-mas giveaway. 350.00

WALT DISNEY'S
COMICS & STORIES
Dell Publishing Co.,
Oct., 1940
1 (1940)FG,Donald Duck &
  Mickey Mouse 25,000.00
2 . . . . 9,000.00
3 . . . . 3,000.00
4 1st Huey, Dewey & Louie
  Christmas(c) 2,200.00
4a Promo issue 3,500.00
5 Goofy(c) 1,700.00
6 . . . . 1,500.00
7 . . . . 1,500.00
8 Clarabelle Cow(c) 1,500.00
9 . . . . 1,500.00
10 . . . . 1,500.00
11 2nd Huey,Louie,Dewey(c) . . 1,100.00
12 . . . . 1,200.00
13 . . . . 1,100.00
14 . . . . 1,100.00
15 3 Little Kittens 1,000.00
16 3 Little Pigs 1,000.00
17 The Ugly Ducklings 1,000.00
18 . . . . 850.00
19 . . . . 800.00
20 . . . . 800.00
21 . . . . 850.00
22 . . . . 750.00
23 . . . . 750.00
24 Flying Gauchito. 700.00
25 . . . . 700.00
26 . . . . 700.00
27 Jose Carioca. 700.00
28 . . . . 750.00
29 . . . . 700.00
30 . . . . 700.00
31 CB; Donald Duck 4,500.00
32 CB 1,900.00
33 CB 1,500.00
34 CB;WK; Gremlins. 1,200.00
35 CB;WK; Gremlins. 1,200.00
36 CB;WK; Gremlins 1,200.00
37 CB;WK; Gremlins 600.00
38 CB;WK; Gremlins 750.00
39 CB;WK; Gremlins, X-mas 750.00
40 CB;WK; Gremlins 750.00
41 CB;WK; Gremlins 650.00
42 CB. 600.00
43 CB,Seven Dwarfs 600.00
44 CB. 600.00
45 CB,Nazis in stories 600.00
46 CB,Nazis in stories 600.00
47 CB,Nazis in stories 600.00
48 CB,Nazis in stories 600.00
49 CB,Nazis in stories 600.00
50 CB,Nazis in stories 600.00
51 CB,Christmas 450.00
52 CB; Li'l Bad Wolf begins. 450.00

Walt Disney's Comics & Stories #102
© *Walt Disney*

53 CB. 450.00
54 CB. 450.00
55 CB. 450.00
56 CB. 450.00
57 CB. 450.00
58 CB. 450.00
59 CB. 450.00
60 CB. 450.00
61 CB; Dumbo 350.00
62 CB. 350.00
63 CB; Pinocchio 350.00
64 CB; Pinocchio, X-mas. 350.00
65 CB; Pluto. 350.00
66 CB. 350.00
67 CB. 350.00
68 CB, Mickey Mouse 350.00
69 CB. 350.00
70 CB. 350.00
71 CB. 300.00
72 CB. 300.00
73 CB. 300.00
74 CB. 300.00
75 CB; Brer Rabbit. 300.00
76 CB; Brer Rabbit, X-mas 300.00
77 CB; Brer Rabbit. 300.00
78 CB. 300.00
79 CB. 300.00
80 CB. 300.00
81 CB. 300.00
82 CB;Bongo,Googy 300.00
83 CB;Bongo 300.00
84 CB;Bongo 300.00
85 CB. 300.00
86 CB;Goofy & Agnes 300.00
87 CB;Goofy & Agnes 275.00
88 CB;Goofy & Agnes,
   I:Gladstone Gander 350.00
89 CB;Goofy&Agnes,Chip'n'Dale 275.00
90 CB;Goofy & Agnes 275.00
91 CB. 250.00
92 CB. 250.00
93 CB. 250.00
94 CB. 250.00
95 CB(c). 250.00
96 Little Toot 250.00
97 CB; Little Toot 250.00
98 CB; Uncle Scrooge 400.00
99 CB. 250.00
100 CB. 300.00
101 CB. 250.00
102 CB. 250.00
103 CB. 200.00
104 . . . . 200.00
105 CB. 250.00

106 CB. 250.00
107 CB, Donald super-powers . . 275.00
108 . . . . 200.00
109 . . . . 200.00
110 CB 250.00
111 CB 250.00
112 CB; drugs 275.00
113 CB 250.00
114 CB 250.00
115 . . . . 100.00
116 Dumbo. 100.00
117 . . . . 100.00
118 . . . . 100.00
119 . . . . 100.00
120 . . . . 100.00
121 Grandma Duck begins 100.00
122 . . . . 100.00
123 . . . . 100.00
124 CB,Christmas 150.00
125 CB;I:Junior Woodchucks . . . 200.00
126 CB. 125.00
127 CB. 125.00
128 CB. 125.00
129 CB. 125.00
130 CB. 125.00
131 CB. 125.00
132 CB A:Grandma Duck 125.00
133 CB. 125.00
134 I:The Beagle Boys 250.00
135 CB. 125.00
136 CB. 125.00
137 CB. 125.00
138 CB,Scrooge & Money 175.00
139 CB. 125.00
140 CB; I:Gyro Gearloose 250.00
141 CB. 100.00
142 CB. 100.00
143 CB; Little Hiawatha 100.00
144 CB; Little Hiawatha 100.00
145 CB; Little Hiawatha 100.00
146 CB; Little Hiawatha 100.00
147 CB; Little Hiawatha 100.00
148 CB; Little Hiawatha 100.00
149 CB; Little Hiawatha 100.00
150 CB; Little Hiawatha 100.00
151 CB; Little Hiawatha 100.00
152 thru 200 CB. . . . . @75.00
201 CB. 60.00
202 CB. 60.00
203 CB. 60.00
204 CB, Chip 'n' Dale & Scamp. . . 60.00
205 thru 240 CB. . . . . @60.00
241 CB; Dumbo x-over 50.00
242 CB. 50.00
243 CB. 50.00
244 CB. 50.00
245 CB. 50.00
246 CB. 50.00
247 thru 255 CB;GyroGearloose @50.00
256 thru 263 CB;Ludwig Von
   Drake & Gearloose . . . . . . @50.00
See: Independent Color Comics

WALT DISNEY
DELL GIANT EDITIONS
Dell Publishing Co.
1 CB,W.Disney'sXmas
  Parade('49) 1,200.00
2 CB,W.Disney'sXmas
  Parade('50). 1,000.00
3 W.Disney'sXmas Parade('51) . 300.00
4 W.Disney'sXmas Parade('52) . 250.00
5 W.Disney'sXmas Parade('53) . 250.00
6 W.Disney'sXmas Parade('54) . 250.00
7 W.Disney'sXmas Parade('55) . 250.00
8 CB,W.Disney'sXmas
  Parade('56) 500.00
9 CB,W.Disney'sXmas
  Parade('57) 500.00

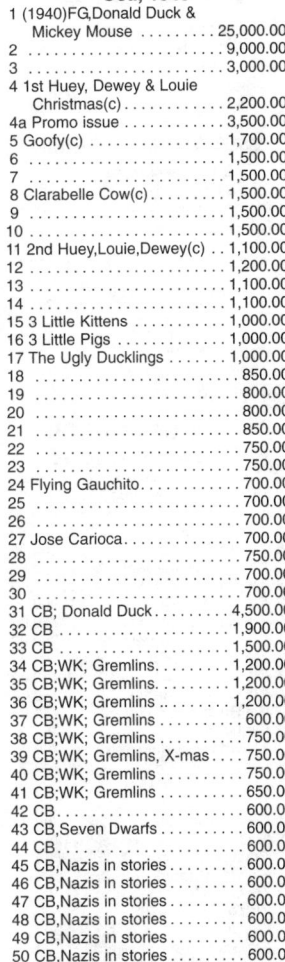

GOLDEN AGE

1 CB,W.Disney's Christmas in
 Disneyland (1957) 600.00
1 CB,W.Disney's Disneyland
 Birthday Party (1958) 600.00
1 W.Disney's Donald and Mickey
 in Disneyland (1958) 250.00
1 W.Disney's Donald Duck
 Beach Party (1954) 300.00
2 W.Disney's Donald Duck
 Beach Party (1955) 250.00
3 W.Disney's Donald Duck
 Beach Party (1956) 250.00
4 W.Disney's Donald Duck
 Beach Party (1957) 250.00
5 W.Disney's Donald Duck
 Beach Party (1958) 250.00
6 W.Disney's Donald Duck
 Beach Party (1959) 250.00
1 W.Disney's Donald Duck
 Fun Book (1954) 1,200.00
2 W.Disney's Donald Duck
 Fun Book (1954) 1,100.00
1 W.Disney's Donald Duck
 in Disneyland (1955) 275.00
1 W.Disney's Huey, Dewey
 and Louie (1958) 175.00
1 W.Disney's DavyCrockett('55) . 350.00
1 W.Disney's Lady and the
 Tramp (1955) 400.00
1 CB,W.Disney's Mickey Mouse
 Almanac (1957) 600.00
1 W.Disney's Mickey Mouse
 Birthday Party (1953) 700.00
1 W.Disney's Mickey Mouse
 Club Parade (1955) 600.00
1 W.Disney's Mickey Mouse
 in Fantasyland (1957) 275.00
1 W.Disney's Mickey Mouse
 in Frontierland (1956) 275.00
1 W.Disney's Summer Fun('58) . 275.00
2 CB,W.Disney'sSummer
 Fun('59) 275.00
1 W.Disney's Peter Pan
 Treasure Chest (1953) 2,200.00
1 Disney Silly Symphonies('52) . 600.00
2 Disney Silly Symphonies('53) . 500.00
3 Disney Silly Symphonies('54) . 450.00
4 Disney Silly Symphonies('54) . 450.00
5 Disney Silly Symphonies('55) . 400.00
6 Disney Silly Symphonies('56) . 400.00
7 Disney Silly Symphonies('57) . 400.00
8 Disney Silly Symphonies('58) . 400.00
9 Disney Silly Symphonies('59) . 400.00
1 Disney SleepingBeauty('59) . . 600.00
1 CB,W.Disney's Uncle Scrooge
 Goes to Disneyland (1957) . . 550.00
1 W.Disney's Vacation in
 Disneyland (1958) 250.00
1 CB,Disney's Vacation
 Parade('50) 1,700.00
2 Disney'sVacation Parade('51) . 600.00
3 Disney'sVacation Parade('52) . 300.00
4 Disney'sVacation Parade('53) . 300.00
5 Disney'sVacation Parade('54) . 300.00
6 Disney's Picnic Party (1955) . 250.00
7 Disney's Picnic Party (1956) . . 250.00
8 CB,Disney's Picnic
 Party (1957) 500.00

DELL JUNIOR TREASURY

1 W.Disney's Alice in Wonderland
 (1955) 150.00

WALT DISNEY
PRESENTS

**Dell Publishing Co.,
June–Aug., 1952**

1 Ph(c), Four Color. 125.00
2 Ph(c) 75.00

3 Ph(c) 75.00
4 Ph(c) 75.00
5 and 6 Ph(c) . . . . @75.00

WAMBI
JUNGLE BOY

**Fiction House Magazines,
Spring, 1942–Winter, 1952**

1 HcK,HcK(c),Vengence of
 the Beasts 1,200.00
2 HcK,HcK(c),Lair of the
 Killer Rajah 650.00
3 HcK,HcK(c) 500.00
4 HcK,HcK(c),The Valley of
 the Whispering Drums 250.00
5 HcK,HcK(c),SwamplandSafari. 250.00
6 Taming of the Tigress 225.00
7 Duel of the Congo Kings 225.00
8 AB(c),Friend of the Animals . . 225.00
9 Quest of the Devils Juju 225.00
10 Friend of the Animals 200.00
11 . . . . 200.00
12 Curse of the Jungle Jewels . . 200.00
13 New Adventures of Wambi . . . 175.00
14 . . . . 175.00
15 The Leopard Legions 175.00
16 . . . . 175.00
17 Beware Bwana! 175.00
18 Ogg the Great Bull Ape. 175.00

WANTED COMICS

**Toytown Comics/
Orbit Publications,
Sept.–Oct., 1947**

9 Victor Everhart. 250.00
10 Carlo Banone 150.00
11 Dwight Band 150.00
12 Ralph Roe. 165.00
13 James Spencer;Drug 175.00
14 John "Jiggs" Sullivan;Drug . . . 175.00
15 Harry Dunlap;Drug 125.00
16 Jack Parisi;Drug 135.00
17 Herber Ayers;Drug 135.00
18 Satan's Cigarettes;Drug 250.00
19 Jackson Stringer. 125.00
20 George Morgan. 125.00
21 BK,Paul Wilson. 135.00
22 Strong violence 135.00
23 George Elmo Wells. 80.00
24 BK,Bruce Cornett;Drug. 135.00
25 Henry Anger 80.00
26 John Wormly. 80.00
27 Death Always Knocks Twice. . . 80.00
28 Paul H. Payton 80.00
29 Hangmans Holiday 80.00
30 George Lee. 80.00
31 M Consolo. 80.00
32 William Davis 80.00
33 The Web of Davis 80.00
34 Dead End 80.00
35 Glen Roy Wright 125.00
36 SSh,SSh(c),Bernard Lee
 Thomas 75.00
37 SSh,SSh(c),Joseph M. Moore . 75.00
38 SSh,SSh(c). 75.00
39 The Horror Weed;Drug 175.00
40 . . . . 75.00
41 . . . . 75.00
42 . . . . 75.00
43 . . . . 75.00
44 . . . . 75.00
45 Killers on the Loose;Drug 125.00
46 Chalres Edward Crews. 75.00
47 . . . . 75.00
48 SSh,SSh(c) 75.00
49 . . . . 100.00
50 JB(c),Make Way for Murder . . 150.00

*The Vault of Horror #25
and the Tramp © Walt Disney*

51 JB(c),Dope Addict on a
 Holiday of Murder;Drug 135.00
52 The Cult of Killers;
 Classic Drug 135.00
53 April, 1953. . . . . 75.00

WAR AGAINST CRIME

**L.L. Publishing Co.
(E.C. Comics), Spring, 1948**

1 Grl, Stories from Police 1,000.00
2 Grl,Guilty of Murder 600.00
3 JCr(c) 600.00
4 AF,JCr(c) 500.00
5 JCr(c) 500.00
6 AF,JCr(c) 500.00
7 AF,JCr(c) 500.00
8 AF,JCr(c) 500.00
9 AF,JCr(c),The Kid 500.00
10 JCr(c),I:Vault Keeper 2,800.00
11 JCr(c) 1,600.00
Becomes:

VAULT OF HORROR

April–May, 1950–Jan., 1955

12 AF,JCr(a&c),Wax Museum. . 6,700.00
13 AF,WW,JCr(c),Grl,Drug . . . 1,500.00
14 AF,WW,JCr(c),Grl. 1,400.00
15 AF,JCr(a&c),Grl,JKa. 1,400.00
16 Grl,JKa,JCr(a&c). 900.00
17 JDa,Grl,JKa,JCr(a&c) 900.00
18 JDa,Grl,JKa,JCr(a&c) 800.00
19 JDa,Grl,JKa,JCr(a&c) 800.00
20 JDa,Grl,JKa,JCr(a&c) 750.00
21 JDa,Grl,JKa,JCr(a&c) 750.00
22 JDa,JKa,JCr(a&c) 750.00
23 JDa,Grl,JCr(a&c) 750.00
24 JDa,Grl,JO,JCr(a&c) 750.00
25 JDa,Grl,JKa,JCr(a&c) 750.00
26 JDa,Grl,JCr(a&c) 750.00
27 JDa,Grl,GE,JCr(a&c) 700.00
28 JDa,Grl,JCr(a&c) 700.00
29 JDa,Grl,JKa,JCr(a&c),
 Bradbury Adapt 700.00
30 JDa,Grl,JCr(a&c) 700.00
31 JDa,Grl,JCr(a&c),
 Bradbury Adapt 500.00
32 JDa,Grl,JCr(a&c) 500.00
33 JDa,Grl,RC,JCr(c). 500.00
34 JDa,Grl,RC,JCr(a&c) 500.00
35 JDa,Grl,JCr(a&c),X-mas 500.00
36 JDa,Grl,BK,JCr(a&c),Drug . . . 500.00

37 JDa,Grl,AW,JCr(a&c)
   Hanging. 500.00
38 JDa,Grl,BK,JCr(a&c). 500.00
39 GRi,BK,RC,JCr(a&c)
   Bondage(c) 500.00
40 Grl,BK,JO,JCr(a&c) 700.00

WAR BATTLES
Harvey Publications, Feb., 1952
1 BP,Devils of the Deep 175.00
2 BP,A Present From Benny . . . 100.00
3 BP 75.00
4 . . . . 75.00
5 . . . . 75.00
6 HN 75.00
7 BP 100.00
8 . . . . 75.00
9 Dec., 1953 . . . . 75.00

WAR BIRDS
Fiction House Magazines, 1952
1 Willie the Washout 175.00
2 Mystery MIGs of Kwanjamu . . 110.00
3 thru 6 . . . . @100.00
7 Winter, 1953,Across the
  Wild Yalu 100.00

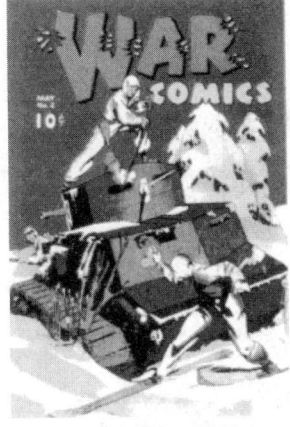

War Comics #2
© Dell Publishing Co.

WAR COMICS
Dell Publishing Co., May, 1940
1 AMc,Sky Hawk. 800.00
2 O:Greg Gildam. 450.00
3 . . . . 350.00
4 O:Night Devils 400.00

WAR HEROES
Dell Publishing Co., July–Sept., 1942
1 Gen. Douglas MacArthur (c) . . 350.00
2 . . . . 200.00
3 Pro-Soviet 150.00
4 A:Gremlins 250.00
5 . . . . 125.00
6 thru 11 . . . . @100.00

WAR HEROES
Ace Magazines, May, 1952
1 Always Comin' 125.00

2 LC,The Last Red Tank. 75.00
3 You Got it 60.00
4 A Red Patrol 60.00
5 Hustle it Up 60.00
6 LC,Hang on Pal 75.00
7 LC 75.00
8 LC, April, 1953 . . . . 75.00

WARPATH
Key Publications/ Stanmore, Nov., 1954
1 Red Men Raid 125.00
2 AH(c),Braves Battle 75.00
3 April, 1955 . . . . 75.00

WARRIOR COMICS
H.C. Blackerby, 1944
1 Ironman wing Brady. 300.00

WAR SHIPS
Dell Publishing Co., 1942
1 AMc 200.00

WAR STORIES
Dell Publishing Co., 1942
5 O:The Whistler. 300.00
6 A:Night Devils 250.00
7 A:Night Devils 250.00
8 A:Night Devils 250.00

WARTIME ROMANCES
St. John Publishing Co., July, 1951
1 MB(c),MB. 400.00
2 MB(c),MB. 300.00
3 MB(c),MB. 250.00
4 MB(c),MB. 250.00
5 MB(c),MB 225.00
6 MB(c),MB 250.00
7 MB(c),MB 225.00
8 MB(c),MB. 225.00
9 MB(c),MB 200.00
10 MB(c),MB 200.00
11 MB(c),MB 200.00
12 MB(c),MB 200.00
13 MB(c) 100.00
14 MB(c) 100.00
15 MB(c) 100.00
16 MB(c),MB 175.00
17 MB(c) 100.00
18 MB(c),MB 175.00

WAR VICTORY COMICS
U.S. Treasury/War Victory/ Harvey Publ., Summer, 1942
1 Savings Bond Promo with
  Top Syndicated Cartoonists,
  benefit USO 500.00
Becomes:

WAR VICTORY ADVENTURES
Summer, 1942
2 BP,2nd Front Comics 300.00
3 BP,F:Capt Cross of the
  Red Cross 250.00

WEB OF EVIL
Comic Magazines, Inc. (Quality Comics Group), Nov., 1952
1 Custodian of the Dead 750.00

Web of Evil #4
© Quality Comics Group

2 JCo,Hangmans Horror 500.00
3 JCo 500.00
4 JCo(a&c),Monsters of
  the Mist 500.00
5 JCo(a&c),The Man who Died
  Twice,Electric Chair(c). 600.00
6 JCo(a&c),Orgy of Death 500.00
7 JCo(a&c),The Strangling
  Hands 500.00
8 JCo,Flaming Vengeance 450.00
9 JCo,The Monster in Flesh . . . 450.00
10 JCo,Brain that Wouldn't Die . . 450.00
11 JCo,Buried Alive 450.00
12 Phantom Killer 300.00
13 Demon Inferno 300.00
14 RC(c),The Monster Genie. . . 300.00
15 Crypts of Horror 300.00
16 Hamlet of Horror 300.00
17 Terror in Chinatown, Drug. . . 325.00
18 Scared to Death,Acid Face. . . 300.00
19 Demon of the Pit. 275.00
20 Man Made Terror 275.00
21 Dec., 1954, Death's Ambush . 275.00

WEB OF MYSTERY
A.A. Wyn Publ. (Ace Magazines), Feb., 1951
1 MSy,Venom of the Vampires . 700.00
2 MSy,Legacy of the Accursed . 350.00
3 MSy,The Violin Curse 300.00
4 GC 300.00
5 . . . . 300.00
6 LC 300.00
7 MSy 300.00
8 LC,LC(c),MSy,The Haunt of
  Death Lake 300.00
9 LC,LC(c) 300.00
10 . . . . 300.00
11 MSy. 300.00
12 LC 275.00
13 LC,LC(c)Surealist 275.00
14 MSy. 275.00
15 . . . . 275.00
16 . . . . 275.00
17 LC,LC(c) 275.00
18 LC 275.00
19 LC 275.00
20 LC, Beyond. 275.00
21 MSy. 275.00
22 . . . . 275.00
23 . . . . 275.00
24 LC 275.00
25 LC 275.00

GOLDEN AGE

GOLDEN AGE

26 .... 275.00
27 LC, Beyond............. 275.00
28 RP,1st Issue under Comics
    Code Authority........... 200.00
29 MSy,Sept., 1955 .... 200.00

WEDDING BELLS
Quality Comics Group,
Feb., 1954

1 OW.................... 175.00
2 .... 100.00
3 .... 75.00
4 .... 75.00
5 .... 75.00
6 .... 75.00
7 .... 75.00
8 .... 75.00
9 Comics Code............. 75.00
10 BWa 150.00
11 .... 60.00
12 .... 60.00
13 .... 60.00
14 .... 60.00
15 MB(c) 75.00
16 MB(c),MB 125.00
17 .... 60.00
18 MB.................. 75.00
19 MB.................. 75.00

WEEKENDER, THE
Rucker Publishing Co.,
Sept., 1945

1-1 rep.(c), As Zip........... 175.00
1-2 thru -4 .... @175.00
2-1 rep.(c), As Dynamic 200.00
2-2 Jco,rep.(c), As Dynamic 175.00
2-3 WMc,Jan., 1946 .... 175.00

WEIRD ADVENTURES
P.L. Publishing,
May, 1951–Oct., 1951

1 MB,Missing Diamonds 700.00
2 Puppet Peril 600.00
3 Blood Vengeance.......... 500.00

WEIRD ADVENTURES
Approved Comics
(Ziff-Davis),
July–Aug., 1951

10 P(c),Seeker from Beyond 500.00

WEIRD CHILLS
Key Publications,
July, 1954

1 MBi(c),BW 1,100.00
2 Eye Torture(c) 1,000.00
3 Bondage(c),Nov., 1954 ..... 600.00

WEIRD COMICS
Fox Features Syndicate,
April, 1940

1 LF(c),Bondage(c),B:Birdman,
    Thor,Sorceress of Doom,
    BlastBennett,Typhon,Voodoo
    Man, Dr.Mortal 7,000.00
2 LF(c),Mummy(c) 3,000.00
3 JSm(c) 1,500.00
4 JSm(c) 1,500.00
5 Bondage(c),I:Dart,Ace;
    E:Thor 1,600.00
6 Dart & Ace(c) 1,400.00
7 Battle of Kooba 1,400.00
8 B:Panther Woman,Dynamo,
    The Eagle 1,400.00

Weird Comics #1
© Fox Features Syndicate

9 V:Pirates 1,000.00
10 A:Navy Jones............ 1,000.00
11 Dart & Ace(c).............. 800.00
12 Dart & Ace(c) 800.00
13 Dart & Ace(c) 800.00
14 The Rage(c) 800.00
15 Dart & Ace (c)............. 800.00
16 Flag,The Encore(c)......... 800.00
17 O:Black Rider 775.00
18 .... 750.00
19 .... 750.00
20 Jan., 1941,I'm The Master
    of Life and Death......... 950.00

WEIRD FANTASY
I.C. Publishing Co.
(E.C. Comics),
May–June, 1950

13(1)AF,HK,JKa,WW,AF(c),
    Roger Harvey's Brain 2,800.00
14(2)AF,HK,JKa,WW,AF(c),Cosmic
    Ray Brain Explosion...... 1,300.00
15(3)AF,HK,JKa,WW,AF(c),Your
    Destination is the Moon..... 900.00
16(4)AF,HK,JKa,WW,AF(c) 900.00
17(5)AF,HK,JKa,WW,AF(c),Not
    Made by Human Hands 750.00
6 AF,HK,JKa,WW,AF(c),Robot .. 750.00
7 AF,JKa,WW,AF(c) 700.00
8 AF,JKa,WW,AF(c) 700.00
9 AF,Jka,WW,JO,AF(c) 700.00
10 AF,Jka,WW,JO,AF(c) 800.00
11 AF,Jka,WW,JO,AF(c)....... 550.00
12 AF,Jka,WW,JO,AF(c) 550.00
13 AF,Jka,WW,JO,AF(c) 550.00
14 AF,JKa,WW,JO,AW&FF,AF(c). 800.00
15 AF,JKa,JO,AW&RKr,AF(c),
    Bondage(c) 550.00
16 AF,JKa,JO,AW&RKr,AF(c) ... 500.00
17 AF,JOP,JKa,AF(c),Bradbury . 500.00
18 AF,JO,JKa,AF(c),Bradbury ... 500.00
19 JO,JKa,JO(c),Bradbury...... 500.00
20 JO,JKa,FF,AF(c) 500.00
21 JO,JKa,AW&FF(c) 750.00
22 JO,JKa,JO(c),Nov.,1953 .... 400.00

WEIRD HORRORS
St. John Publishing Co.,
June, 1952

1 GT,Dungeon of the Doomed .. 750.00
2 Strangest Music Ever 400.00

3 PAM,Strange Fakir From
    the Orient, Drug 400.00
4 Murderers Knoll 350.00
5 Phantom Bowman 350.00
6 Monsters from Outer Space .. 600.00
7 LC,Deadly Double 700.00
8 JKu,JKu(c),Bloody Yesterday . 500.00
9 JKu,JKu(c),Map Of Doom 500.00
Becomes:

NIGHTMARE
Dec., 1953

10 JKu(c),The Murderer's Mask . 800.00
11 BK,Ph(c),Fangs of Death 600.00
12 JKu(c),The Forgotten Mask . 500.00
13 BP,Princess of the Sea...... 350.00
Becomes:

AMAZING GHOST
STORIES
Oct., 1954

14 EK,MB(c),Pit & Pendulum.... 400.00
15 BP,Weird Thrillers 300.00
16 Feb., 1955, EK,JKu........ 350.00

WEIRD MYSTERIES
Gilmore Publications,
Oct., 1952

1 BW(c) 1,100.00
2 BWi, Robot Woman 1,500.00
3 Severed Heads(c) 750.00
4 BW,Human headed ants(c) . 1,300.00
5 BW,Brains From Head(c) ... 1,500.00
6 Severed Head(c) 750.00
7 Used in "Seduction" 1,100.00
8 The One That Got Away 800.00
9 Epitaph,Cyclops, Violence.... 750.00
10 The Ruby 600.00
11 Voodoo Dolls............. 550.00
12 Sept., 1954 .... 550.00

WEIRD SCIENCE
E.C. Comics, 1950

1 AF(a&c),JKu,HK,WW 2,900.00
2 AF(a&c),JKu,HK,WW,Flying
    Saucers(c) 1,500.00
3 AF(a&c),JKu,HK 1,400.00
4 AF(a&c),JKu,HK 1,400.00
5 AF(a&c),JKu,HK,WW,
    Atomic Bomb(c).......... 850.00
6 AF(a&c),JKu,HK 750.00
7 AF(a&c),JKu,HK,Classic(c) .. 750.00
8 AF(a&c),JKu 750.00
9 WW(c),JKu,Classic(c) 750.00
10 WW(c),JKu,JO,Classic(c) 750.00
11 AF,JKu,Space war......... 600.00
12 WW(c),JKu,JO,Classic(c) 600.00
13 WW(c),JKu,JO,........... 600.00
14 WW(a&c),JO............. 700.00
15 WW(a&c),JO,GRi,AW,
    RKr,JKa 700.00
16 WW(a&c),JO,AW,RKr,JKa ... 700.00
17 WW(a&c),JO,AW,RKr,JKa ... 700.00
18 WW(a&c),JO,AW,RKr,
    JKa,Atomic Bomb 700.00
19 WW(a&c),JO,AW,
    FF,Horror(c)............ 750.00
20 WW(a&c),JO,AW,FF,JKa ... 750.00
21 WW(a&c),JO,AW,FF,JKa ... 750.00
22 WW(a&c),JO,AW,FF 750.00
Becomes:

WEIRD SCIENCE
FANTASY
March, 1954

23 WW(a&c),AW,BK 550.00
24 WW,AW,BK,Classic(c) 550.00
25 WW,AW,BK,Classic(c) 600.00

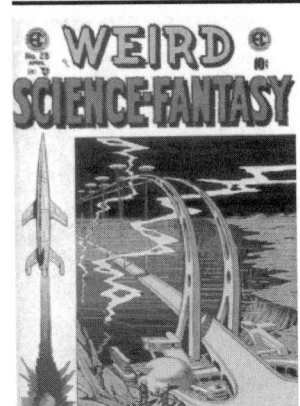

Weird Science-Fantasy #28
© E.C. Comics

26 AF(c),WW,RC,
   Flying Saucer(c) 500.00
27 WW(a&c),RC 450.00
28 AF(c),WW 600.00
29 AF(c),WW,Classic(c) 1,000.00
Becomes:

INCREDIBLE SCIENCE FANTASY
July–Aug., 1955
30 WW,JDa(c),BK,AW,RKr,JO . . 600.00
31 WW,JDa(c),BK,AW,RKr 750.00
32 JDa(c),BK,WW,JO 750.00
33 WW(c),BK,WW,JO 750.00

WEIRD TALES OF THE FUTURE
**S.P.M. Publ./
Aragon Publications,
March, 1952**
1 RA 1,400.00
2 BW,BW(c), Jumpin Jupiter . . 1,800.00
3 BW,BW(c) 1,800.00
4 BW,BW(c) 1,500.00
5 BW,BW(c),Jumpin' Jupiter
   Lingerie(c) 1,800.00
6 Bondage(c) 750.00
7 BW,Devil(c). 1,500.00
8 July–Aug., 1953 . . . . 1,000.00

WEIRD TERROR
**Allen Hardy Associates
(Comic Media), Sept., 1952**
1 RP,DH,DH(c),Dungeon of the
   Doomed;Hitler 750.00
2 HcK(c),PAM, Torture 600.00
3 PAM,DH,DH(c),Strange
   Violence. 600.00
4 PAM,DH,DH(c),Severed Head. 600.00
5 PAM,DH,RP,DH(c),Hanging(c). 550.00
6 DH,RP,DH(c),Step into
   My Parlour, Severed Head . . 550.00
7 DH,PAM,DH(c),Blood o/t Bats . 500.00
8 DH,RP,DH(c),Step into
   My Parlour, Severed Head . . 550.00
9 DH,PAM,DH(c),The Fleabite . . 450.00
10 DH,BP,RP,DH(c) 450.00
11 DH,DH(c),Satan's Love Call . . 500.00
12 DH,DH(c),King Whitey 450.00
13 DH,DH(c),Wings of Death,
   Severed Head, Sept. 1954 . . 450.00

WEIRD THRILLERS
**Approved Comics
(Ziff-Davis),
Sept.–Oct., 1951**
1 Ph(c),Monsters & The Model 1,200.00
2 AW,P(c),The Last Man 850.00
3 AW,P(c),Princess o/t Sea . . 1,100.00
4 AW,P(c),The Widows Lover. . . 800.00
5 BP,Oct., 1952,AW,P(c),
   Wings of Death 800.00

WESTERN ACTION THRILLERS
**Dell Publishing Co.,
April, 1937**
1 Buffalo Bill, Texas Kid. 1,200.00

WESTERN ADVENTURES COMICS
**A.A. Wyn, Inc.
(Ace Magazines), Oct., 1948**
N#(1)Injun Gun Bait 275.00
N#(2)Cross-Draw Kid 150.00
N#(3)Outlaw Mesa 150.00
4 Sheriff, Sal 125.00
5 . . . . 125.00
6 Rip Roaring Adventure 125.00
Becomes:

WESTERN LOVE TRAILS
Nov., 1949
7 . . . . 150.00
8 Maverick Love 125.00
9 March, 1950 . . . . 100.00

WESTERN BANDIT TRAILS
**St. John Publishing Co.,
Jan., 1949**
1 GT,MB(c), Blue Monk 300.00
2 GT,MB(c) 250.00
3 GT,MB,MB(c),Gingham Fury . 275.00

WESTERN CRIME-BUSTERS
**Trojan Magazines,
Sept., 1950–April, 1952**
1 Gunslingin' Galoots 400.00
2 K-Bar Kate 250.00
3 Wilma West 250.00
4 Bob Dale 250.00
5 Six-Gun Smith 250.00
6 WW 400.00
7 WW,Wells Fargo Robbery . . . 400.00
8 . . . . 250.00
9 WW,Lariat Lucy 400.00
10 WW,Tex Gordon 400.00

WESTERN CRIME CASES
See: WHITE RIDER

WESTERNER, THE
**Wanted Comics Group/
Toytown Publ.,
June, 1948**
14 F:Jack McCall 150.00
15 F:Bill Jamett 100.00
16 F:Tom McLowery 100.00
17 F:Black Bill Desmond 100.00
18 BK,F:Silver Dollar Dalton . . . 125.00
19 MMe,F:Jess Meeton 75.00

20 . . . . 75.00
21 BK,MMe 100.00
22 BK,MMe 100.00
23 BK,MMe 100.00
24 BK,MMe 100.00
25 O,I,B:Calamity Jane 100.00
26 BK,F:The Widowmaker. 150.00
27 BK 150.00
28 thru 31. . . . . @60.00
32 E:Calamity Jane 60.00
33 A:Quest. 60.00
34 . . . . 60.00
35 SSh(c). 60.00
36 . . . . 60.00
37 Lobo-Wolf Boy 60.00
38 . . . . 60.00
39 . . . . 60.00
40 SSh(c). 60.00
41 Dec., 1951 . . . . 60.00

WESTERN FIGHTERS
**Hillman Periodicals,
April–May, 1948**
1 S&K(c) 450.00
2 BF(c) 125.00
3 BF(c) 100.00
4 BK,BF 125.00
5 . . . . 75.00
6 . . . . 75.00
7 BK 125.00
8 . . . . 75.00
9 . . . . 75.00
10 BK. 125.00
11 AMC&FF 400.00
2-1 BK 125.00
2-2 BP 75.00
2-3 thru 2-12 . . . . @60.00
3-1 thru 3-11. . . . . @60.00
3-12 BK 125.00
4-1 . . . . 60.00
4-2 BK 100.00
4-3 BK 100.00
4-4 BK 100.00
4-5 BK 100.00
4-6 BK 100.00
4-7 March–April, 1953 . . . . 60.00

WESTERN FRONTIER
**P.L. Publishers
(Approved Comics),
May, 1951**
1 Flaming Vengeance. 125.00
2 . . . . 75.00
3 Death Rides the Iron Horse . . . 50.00
4 thru 6 . . . . @50.00
7 1952. 50.00

WESTERN HEARTS
**Standard Magazine, Inc.,
Dec., 1949**
1 JSe, Whip Wilson, Ph(c) 275.00
2 AW,FF, Palomino, Ph(c). 275.00
3 Rex Allen, Ph(c) 150.00
4 JSe,BE, Ph(c) 150.00
5 JSe,BE,Ray Milland, Ph(c) . . . 150.00
6 JSe,BE,Irene Dunn, Ph(c) 150.00
7 JSe,BE,Jock Mahoney Ph(c). . 150.00
8 Randolph Scott, Ph(c) 150.00
9 JSe,BE, Whip Wilson, Ph(c) . . 150.00
10 JSe,BE, Bill Williams,Ph(c). . . 150.00

WESTERN LOVE
**Feature Publications
(Prize Comics Group),
July–Aug., 1949**
1 S&K, Randolph Scott. 350.00

2 S&K, Whip Wilson 250.00
3 JSE,BE, Reno Brown 200.00
4 JSE,BE 200.00
5 JSE,BE, Dale Robertson 250.00

Western Picture Stories #1
© Comics Magazine Co.

WESTERN PICTURE STORIES

Comics Magazine Co., Feb., 1937–June, 1937

1 WE,Treachery Trail,
  1st Western 2,500.00
2 WE,Weapons of the West . . 1,500.00
3 WE,Dragon Pass 1,200.00
4 CavemanCowboy 1,200.00

WESTERN THRILLERS

Fox Features Syndicate, Aug., 1948

1 Velvet Rose 600.00
2 . . . . 250.00
3 GT,RH(c) 225.00
4 . . . . 250.00
5 Butch Cassidy 250.00
6 June, 1949 . . . . 225.00
Becomes:

MY PAST CONFESSIONS

Aug., 1949

7 . . . . 175.00
8 . . . . 100.00
9 . . . . 100.00
10 . . . . 100.00
11 WW 200.00
12 Crimes Inc. 75.00

WESTERN TRUE CRIME

Fox Features Syndicate, Aug., 1948

1 JKa, Zoot 14 . . . . 450.00
2 JKa, Violence. 300.00
3 JKa. 250.00
4 JCr 300.00
5 . . . . 200.00
6 . . . . 200.00
Becomes:

MY CONFESSION

Aug., 1949–Feb., 1950

7 WW 400.00
8 WW,My Tarnished Reputation 350.00
9 I:Tormented Men 150.00

---

10 I Am Damaged Goods 150.00

WHACK

St. John Publishing Co., Dec., 1953

1 Steve Crevice,Flush Jordan
  V:Bing(Crosby)The Merciful . 400.00
2 Bing Crosby(c) 200.00
3 F:Little Awful Fannie 200.00

WHAM COMICS

Centaur Publications, Nov., 1940

1 PG,The Sparkler & His
  Disappearing Suit 2,400.00
2 Dec., 1940,PG,PG(C),
  Men Turn into Icicles 1,500.00

WHIRLWIND COMICS

Nita Publications, June, 1940

1 F:The Cyclone 2,500.00
2 A:Scoops Hanlon,Cyclone(c) 1,500.00
3 Sept., 1940,A:Magic
  Mandarin,Cyclone(c) 1,400.00

WHITE PRINCESS OF THE JUNGLE

Avon Periodicals, July, 1951

1 EK(c),Terror Fangs 750.00
2 EK,EK(c),Jungle Vengeance . 500.00
3 EK,EK(c),The Blue Gorilla . . . 450.00
4 Fangs of the Swamp Beast . . 400.00
5 EK,Coils of the Tree Snake
  Nov., 1952 . . . . 400.00

WHIZ COMICS

Fawcett Publications, Feb., 1940

1 O:Captain Marvel,B:Spy
  Smasher,Golden Arrow,Dan
  Dare, Scoop Smith,Ibis
  the Invincible, Sivana . . . 90,000.00
2 . . . . 7,500.00
3 Make way for
  Captain Marvel 5,000.00
4 Captain Marvel
  Crashes Through 3,800.00
5 Captain Marvel
  Scores Again! 3,400.00
6 Circus of Death 2,400.00
7 B:Dr Voodoo,Squadron
  of Death 2,400.00
8 Saved by Captain Marvel! . . 2,400.00
9 MRa,Captain Marvel
  on the Job. 2,400.00
10 Battles the Winged Death . . 2,400.00
11 Hurray for Captain Marvel . 1,600.00
12 Captain Marvel rides
  the Engine of Doom 1,600.00
13 Worlds Most Powerful Man!. 1,600.00
14 Boomerangs the Torpedo . . 1,600.00
15 O:Sivana 1,800.00
16 Dr. Voodoo. 1,800.00
17 Knocks out a Tank 1,800.00
18 V:Spy Smasher 1,800.00
19 Crushes the Tiger Shark . . . 1,200.00
20 V:Sivana 1,200.00
21 O:Lt. Marvels 1,300.00
22 Mayan Temple 900.00
23 GT,A:Dr. Voodoo 900.00
24 . . . . 900.00
25 O&I:Captain Marvel Jr.,
  Stops the Turbine of Death. 8,500.00
26 . . . . 800.00

---

27 V:Death God of the Katonkas. 900.00
28 V:Mad Dervish of Ank-Har . . . 900.00
29 Three Lt. Marvels (c), Pan
  American Olympics 900.00
30 . . . . 800.00
31 Douglass MacArthur&Spy
  Smasher(c) 750.00
32 Spy Smasher(c) 750.00
33 Spy Smasher(c) 850.00
34 Three Lt. Marvels (c) 500.00
35 Capt. Marvel and the
  Three Fates. 700.00
36 Haunted Hallowe'en Hotel . . . 500.00
37 Return of the Trolls 500.00
38 Grand Steeplechase 500.00
39 A Nazi Utopia 500.00
40 A:Three Lt. Marvels, The
  Earth's 4 Corners 500.00
41 Captain Marvel 1,000 years
  from Now 400.00
42 Returns in Time Chair. 400.00
43 V:Sinister Spies,
  Spy Smasher(c) 400.00
44 Life Story of Captain Marvel . . 450.00
45 Cures His Critics 400.00
46 . . . . 400.00
47 Captain Marvel needs
  a Birthday 400.00
48 . . . . 400.00
49 Writes a Victory song 400.00
50 Captain Marvel's most
  embarrassing moment 400.00
51 Judges the Ugly-
  Beauty Contest 350.00
52 V:Sivana, Chooses
  His Birthday 350.00
53 Captain Marvel fights
  Billy Batson 350.00
54 Jack of all Trades 350.00
55 Family Tree 350.00
56 Tells what the Future Will Be . 350.00
57 A:Spy Smasher,Golden Arrow,
  Ibis 350.00
58 . . . . 350.00
59 V:Sivana's Twin. 350.00
60 Missing Person's Machine . . . 350.00
61 Gets a first name 325.00
62 Plays in a Band. 325.00
63 Great Indian Rope Trick 325.00
64 Suspected of Murder 325.00
65 Lamp of Diogenes 325.00
66 The Trial of Mr. Morris! 325.00
67 . . . . 325.00
68 Laugh Lotion, V:Sivana. 325.00
69 Mission to Mercury 325.00
70 Climbs the World's Mightiest
  Mountain 325.00
71 Strange Magician 275.00
72 V:The Man of the Future. 275.00
73 In Ogre Land. 275.00
74 Old Man River. 275.00
75 The City Olympics. 275.00
76 Spy Smasher become
  Crime Smasher 275.00
77 . . . . 275.00
78 Golden Arrow 275.00
79 . . . . 275.00
80 . . . . 275.00
81 . . . . 275.00
82 The Atomic Ship 275.00
83 Magic Locket. 275.00
84 . . . . 275.00
85 The Clock of San Lojardo . . . 275.00
86 V:Sinister Sivanas 275.00
87 The War on Olympia 275.00
88 The Wonderful Magic Carpet . 275.00
89 Webs of Crime 275.00
90 . . . . 275.00
91 Infinity (c) 275.00
92 . . . . 275.00

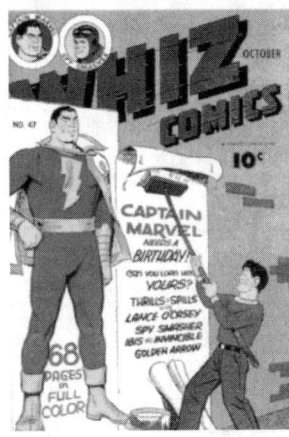

Whiz Comics #47
© Fawcett Publications

2 Diploma For Death 150.00
3 Dec.–Jan., 1949 . . . . 150.00

WHO IS NEXT?
Standard Comics,
Jan., 1953
5 ATh,RA,Don't Let Me Kill 250.00

WILD BILL ELLIOT
Dell Publishing Co.,
May, 1950
(1) see Dell Four Color #278
2 . . . . 125.00
3 thru 5 . . . . @100.00
6 thru 10 . . . . @100.00
(11-12) see Four Color #472, 520
13 thru 17. . . . . @70.00

WILD BILL HICKOK
AND JINGLES
See: YELLOWJACKET
COMICS

WILBUR COMICS
MLJ Magazines
(Archie Publications),
Summer, 1944
1 F:Wilbur Wilkin-America's Song
  of Fun 700.00
2 . . . . 350.00
3 . . . . 250.00
4 . . . . 200.00
5 I:Katy Keene 1,200.00
6 F:Katy Keene. 250.00
7 F:Katy Keene. 250.00
8 F:Katy Keene. 250.00
9 F:Katy Keene. 250.00
10 F:Katy Keene 250.00
11 thru 20 F:Katy Keene . . . . . @175.00
21 thru 30 F:Katy Keene . . . . . @125.00
31 thru 40 F:Katy Keene . . . . . @75.00
41 thru 56 F:Katy Keene . . . . . @60.00
57 thru 89. . . . . @60.00
90 Oct., 1965 . . . . 50.00

WILD BILL HICKOK
Avon Periodicals,
Sept.–Oct., 1949
1 GRI(c),Frontier Fighter. 275.00
2 Ph(c),Gambler's Guns 150.00
3 Ph(c),Great Stage Robbery . . 100.00
4 Ph(c),Guerilla Gunmen 100.00
5 Ph(c),Return of the Renegade 100.00
6 EK,EK(c),Along the Apache
  Trail 100.00
7 EK,EK(c)Outlaws of
  Hell's Bend 100.00
8 Ph(c),The Border Outlaws . . . 100.00
9 PH(c),Killers From Texas 100.00
10 Ph(c) 100.00
11 EK,EK(c),The Hell Riders . . . 100.00
12 EK,EK(c),The Lost Gold Mine 100.00
13 EK,EK(c),Bloody Canyon
  Massacre. 125.00
14 . . . . 125.00
15 . . . . 75.00
16 JKa,Bad Men of Deadwood . . 100.00
17 JKa 100.00
18 JKa,Kit West 80.00
19 thru 23 . . . . @75.00
24 EK,EK(c) 80.00
25 EK,EK(c) 80.00
26 EK,EK(c) 80.00
27 EK,EK(c) 80.00

93 Captain America become
  a Hobo?. 275.00
94 V:Sivana 275.00
95 Captain Marvel is grounded . . 275.00
96 The Battle Between Buildings. 275.00
97 Visits Mirage City 275.00
98 . . . . 275.00
99 V:Menace in the Mountains . . 275.00
100 Anniversary Issue 350.00
101 . . . . 275.00
102 A:Commando Yank 275.00
103 . . . . 275.00
104 Flag(c). 275.00
105 . . . . 275.00
106 A:Bulletman. 275.00
107 The Great Experiment 300.00
108 thru 114 . . . . @275.00
115 The Marine Invasion 275.00
116 . . . . 275.00
117 V:Sivana 275.00
118 . . . . 275.00
119 . . . . 275.00
120 . . . . 275.00
121 . . . . 275.00
122 V:Sivana 275.00
123. . . . . 275.00
124. . . . . 275.00
125 Olympic Games of the Gods 275.00
126 . . . . 275.00
127 . . . . 275.00
128 . . . . 275.00
129 . . . . 275.00
130 . . . . 275.00
131 The Television Trap. 275.00
132 thru 142. . . . . @275.00
143 Mystery of the Flying Studio . 275.00
144 V:The Disaster Master 275.00
145 . . . . 275.00
146 . . . . 275.00
147 . . . . 275.00
148 . . . . 275.00
149 . . . . 275.00
150 V:Bug Bombs 300.00
151 . . . . 300.00
152 . . . . 300.00
153 V:The Death Horror 400.00
154 Horror Tale, I:Dr.Death 400.00
155 V:Legend Horror,Dr.Death . . 425.00

WHODUNIT?
D.S. Publishing Co.,
Aug.–Sept., 1948
1 MB,Weeping Widow 300.00

28 EK,EK(c),May–June, 1956 . . . . 80.00

WILD BOY OF
THE CONGO
Approved(Ziff-Davis)/
St. John Publ. Co.,
Feb.–March, 1951
10(1)NS,PH(c),Bondage(c),The
  Gorilla God 275.00
11(2)NS,Ph(c),Star of the Jungle . 150.00
12(3)NS,Ph(c),Ice-Age Men. 150.00
4 NS.Ph(c),Tyrant of the Jungle 175.00
5 NS,Ph(c),The White Robe
  of Courage 125.00
6 NS,Ph(c) 125.00
7 MB,EK.Ph(c) 150.00
8 Ph(c),Man-Eater 125.00
9 Ph(c),Killer Leopard 125.00
10 . . . . 125.00
11 MB(c). 150.00
12 MB(c) 150.00
13 MB(c) 150.00
14 MB(c) 150.00
15 June, 1955 . . . . 100.00

WINGS COMICS
Wings Publ.
(Fiction House Magazines),
Sept., 1940
1 HcK,AB,GT,Ph(c),B:Skull Squad,
  Clipper Kirk,Suicide Smith,
  War Nurse,Phantom Falcons,
  GreasemonkeyGriffin,Parachute
  Patrol,Powder Burns 3,500.00
2 HCK,AB,GT,Bomber Patrol . . 1,500.00
3 HcK,AB,GT 850.00
4 HcK,AB,GT,B:Spitfire Ace . . . 850.00
5 HcK,AB,GT,Torpedo Patrol . . 850.00
6 HcK,AB,GT,Bombs for Berlin . 750.00
7 HcK,AB 750.00
8 HcK,AB,The Wings of Doom . 750.00
9 Sky-Wolf 700.00
10 The Upside Down 700.00
11 . . . . 650.00
12 Fury of the fire Boards 650.00
13 Coffin Slugs For The
  Luftwaffe 650.00
14 Stuka Buster 650.00
15 Boomerang Blitz 650.00
16 O:Capt.Wings 750.00
17 Skyway to Death. 600.00
18 Horsemen of the Sky 600.00
19 Nazi Spy Trap 600.00
20 The One Eyed Devil 600.00
21 Chute Troop Tornado 500.00
22 TNT for Tokyo 500.00
23 RP,Battling Eagles of Bataan . 500.00
24 RP,The Death of a Hero 500.00
25 RP,Suicide Squeeze 500.00
26 Tojo's Eagle Trap 500.00
27 Blb,Mile High Gauntlet 500.00
28 Blb,Tail Gun Tornado 500.00
29 Blb,Buzzards from Berlin . . . 500.00
30 Blb,Monsters of the
  Stratosphere 450.00
31 BLb,Sea Hawks away. 450.00
32 BLb,Sky Mammoth 450.00
33 BLb,Roll Call of the Yankee
  Eagles 450.00
34 BLb,So Sorry,Mr Tojo 450.00
35 BLb,RWb,Hell's Lightning. . . 450.00
36 RWb,The Crash-Master 450.00
37 RWb,Sneak Blitz. 450.00
38 RWb,Rescue Raid of the
  Yank Eagle 450.00
39 RWb,Sky Hell/Pigboat Patrol . 450.00
40 RWb,Luftwaffe Gamble. 450.00
41 RWb,.50 Caliber Justice 400.00

42 RWb,PanzerMeat forMosquito 400.00
43 RWb,Suicide Sentinels 400.00
44 RWb,Berlin Bombs Away 400.00
45 RWb,Hells Cargo 400.00
46 RWb,Sea-Hawk Patrol 400.00
47 RWb,Tojo's Tin Gibraltar 400.00
48 RWb 400.00
49 RWb,Rockets Away 400.00
50 RWb,Mission For a Madman . 400.00
51 RWb,Toll for a Typhoon 300.00
52 MB,Madam Marauder. 300.00
53 MB,Robot Death Over
      Manhattan 300.00
54 MB,Juggernauts of Death 300.00
55 MB. 300.00
56 MB,Sea Raiders Grave. 300.00
57 MB,Yankee Warbirds over
      Tokyo. 300.00
58 MB. 300.00
59 MB,Prey of the Night Hawks. . 300.00
60 MB,E:Skull Squad,
      Hell's Eyes. 300.00
61 MB,Raiders o/t Purple Dawn . 250.00
62 Twilight of the Gods 250.00
63 Hara Kiri Rides the Skyways . 250.00
64 Taps For Tokyo 250.00
65 AB,Warhawk for the Kill 250.00
66 AB,B:Ghost Patrol. 250.00
67 AB 250.00
68 AB,ClipperKirkBecomesPhantom
      Falcon;O:Phantom Falcon. . . 250.00
69 AB,O:cont,Phantom Falcon . . 250.00
70 AB,N:Phantom Falcon;
      O:Final Phantom Falcon 250.00
71 Ghost Patrol becomes
      Ghost Squadron 250.00
72 V:Capt. Kamikaze. 250.00
73 Hell & Stormoviks 250.00
74 BLb(c),Loot is What She
      Lived For 250.00
75 BLb(c),The Sky Hag 250.00
76 BLb(c),Temple of the Dead. . . 250.00
77 BLb(c),Sky Express to Hell . . 250.00
78 BLb(c),Loot Queen of
      Satan's Skyway 250.00
79 BLb(c),Buzzards of
      Plunder Sky. 250.00
80 BLb(c),Port of Missing Pilots . 250.00
81 BLb(c),Sky Trail of the
      Terror Tong 250.00
82 BLb(c),Bondage(c),Spider &
      The Fly Guy. 265.00
83 BLb(c),GE,Deep Six For
      Capt. Wings. 250.00
84 BLb(c),GE,Sky Sharks to
      the Kill 250.00
85 BLb(c),GE. 250.00
86 BLb(c),GE,Moon Raiders 250.00
87 BLb(c),GE. 250.00
88 BLb(c),GE,Madmans Mission . 250.00
89 BLb(c),GE,Bondage(c),
      Rockets Away 265.00
90 BLb(c),GE,Bondage(c),The
      Radar Rocketeers 265.00
91 BLb(c),GE,Bondage(c),V-9 for
      Vengeance. 265.00
92 BLb(c),GE,Death's red Rocket 250.00
93 BLb(c),GE,Kidnap Cargo 250.00
94 BLb(c),GE,Bondage(c),Ace
      of the A-Bomb Patrol. 265.00
95 BLb(c),GE,The Ace of
      the Assassins 250.00
96 BLb(c),GE. 250.00
97 BLb(c),GE,The Sky Octopus . 250.00
98 BLb(c),GE,The Witch Queen
      of Satan's Skyways 250.00
99 BLb(c),GE,The Spy Circus . . . 250.00
100 BLb(c),GE,King o/t Congo . . 265.00
101 BLb(c),GE,Trator of
      the Cockpit 250.00
102 BLb(c),GE,Doves of Doom . . 250.00

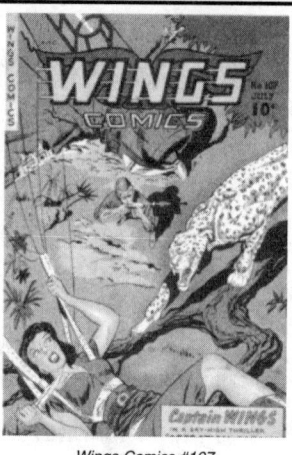

Wings Comics #107
© Fiction House

103 BLb(c),GE. 250.00
104 BLb(c),GE,Fireflies of Fury . . 250.00
105 BLb(c),GE. 250.00
106 BLb(c),GE,Six Aces & A
      Firing Squad 250.00
107 BLb(c),GE,Operation Satan . 250.00
108 BLb(c),GE,The Phantom
      of Berlin 250.00
109 GE,Vultures of
      Vengeance Sky 250.00
110 GE,The Red Ray Vortex 250.00
111 GE,E:Jane Martin 200.00
112 The Flight of the
      Silver Saucers 200.00
113 Suicide Skyways. 200.00
114 D-Day for Death Rays. 200.00
115 Ace of Space. 200.00
116 Jet Aces of Korea 200.00
117 Reap the Red Wind 200.00
118 Vengeance Flies Blind 200.00
119 The Whistling Death 200.00
120 Doomsday Mission 200.00
121 Ace of the Spyways 200.00
122 Last Kill Korea 200.00
123 The Cat & the Canaries 200.00
124 Summer, 1954, Death
      Below Zero 200.00

WINNIE WINKLE
**Dell Publishing Co.,
1941**
1 . . . . 125.00
2 . . . . 75.00
3 thru 7 . . . . @60.00

WITCHCRAFT
**Avon Periodicals,
March–April, 1952**
1 SC,JKu,Heritage of Horror . . . 900.00
2 SC,JKu,The Death Tattoo 700.00
3 EK,Better off Dead 500.00
4 Claws of the Cat,
      Boiling Humans 525.00
5 Ph(c),Where Zombies Walk . . 550.00
6 March, 1953 Mysteries of the
      Moaning Statue 500.00

WITCHES TALES
**Harvey Publications,
Jan., 1951**
1 RP,Bondage(c),Weird Yarns
      of Unseen Terror 700.00

2 RP,We Dare You 400.00
3 RP,Bondage(c)Forest of
      Skeletons. 300.00
4 BP 300.00
5 BP,Bondage(c),Share
      My Coffin 325.00
6 BP,Bondage(c),Servants of
      the Tomb 300.00
7 BP,Screaming City. 300.00
8 Bondage(c) 325.00
9 Fatal Steps. 300.00
10 BP,....,IT! 300.00
11 BP,Monster Maker. 250.00
12 Bondage(c);The Web
      of the Spider 275.00
13 The Torture Jar 250.00
14 Transformation 275.00
15 Drooling Zombie 250.00
16 Revenge of a Witch 250.00
17 Dimension IV 250.00
18 HN,Bird of Prey. 300.00
19 HN,The Pact. 300.00
20 HN,Kiss & Tell. 300.00
21 HN,The Invasion. 300.00
22 HN,A Day of Panic 300.00
23 HN,The Wig Maker 300.00
24 HN,The Undertaker. 325.00
25 What Happens at 8:30 PM?
      Severed Heads(c) 350.00
26 Up There. 210.00
27 The Thing That Grew 210.00
28 Demon Flies 210.00
Becomes:

WITCHES WESTERN TALES
Feb., 1955
29 S&K(a&c),F:Davy Crockett. . . 275.00
30 S&K(a&c) 300.00
Becomes:

WESTERN TALES
Oct., 1955
31 S&K(a&c),F:Davy Crockett . . . 250.00
32 S&K(a&c),F:Davy Crockett . . . 250.00
33 S&K(a&c),July–Sept.,1956 . . . 250.00

WITH THE MARINES ON THE BATTLEFRONTS OF THE WORLD
Toby Press, June, 1953
1 Flaming Soul, John
      Wayne, Ph(c) 325.00
2 Mar., 1954, Monty Hall, Ph(c) . 100.00

WITTY COMICS
**Irwin H. Rubin/Chicago Nite
Life News, 1945**
1 Pioneer, Jr. Patrol 325.00
2 1945. 150.00
3 thru 7 . . . . @125.00

WOMEN IN LOVE
**Fox Features Synd./
Hero Books/
Ziff-Davis, Aug., 1949**
1 . . . . 700.00

WOMEN OUTLAWS
**Fox Features Syndicate,
July, 1948**
1 . . . . 1,000.00
2 . . . . 800.00
3 . . . . 800.00
4 . . . . 700.00
5 thru 8 . . . . @550.00

GOLDEN AGE

Becomes:

MY LOVE MEMORIES
Nov., 1949

9	200.00
10	100.00
11	125.00
12 WW	150.00

WONDERBOY
See: HORRIFIC

WONDER COMICS
Great Publ./Nedor/ Better Publications, May, 1944

1 SSh(c),B:Grim Reaper, Spectro Hitler(c)	1,900.00
2 ASh(c),O:Grim Reaper,B:Super Sleuths,Grim Reaper(c)	1,000.00
3 ASh(c),Grim Reaper(c)	900.00
4 ASh(c),Grim Reaper(c)	850.00
5 ASh(c),Grim Reaper(c)	850.00
6 ASh(c),Grim Reaper(c)	750.00
7 ASh(c),Grim Reaper(c)	750.00
8 ASh(c),E:Super Sleuths, Spectro	750.00
9 ASh(c),B:Wonderman	750.00
10 ASh(c),Wonderman(c)	800.00
11 Grl(c),B:Dick Devins	850.00
12 Grl(c),Bondage(c)	850.00
13 ASh(c),Bondage(c)	850.00
14 ASh(c),Bondage(c) E:Dick Devins	850.00

Wonder Comics #6
© Better Publications

15 ASh(c),Bondage(c),B:Tara	1,000.00
16 ASh(c),A:Spectro, E:Grim Reaper	850.00
17 FF,ASh(c),A:Super Sleuth	900.00
18 ASh(c),B:Silver Knight	850.00
19 ASh(c),FF	850.00
20 FF,Oct., 1948	1,000.00

WONDERLAND COMICS
Feature Publications (Prize Comics Group), Summer, 1945

1 (fa),B:Alex in Wonderland	225.00
2	125.00
3 thru 8	@100.00
9 1947	100.00

WONDER COMICS
Fox Features Syndicate, May, 1939

1 BKa,WE,WE(c),B:Wonderman, DR.Kung,K-51	24,000.00
2 WE,BKa,LF(c),B:Yarko the Great,A:Spark Stevens	7,500.00

Becomes:

WONDERWORLD COMICS
July, 1939–Jan., 1942

3 WE,LF,BP,LF&WE,I:Flame	10,000.00
4 WE,LF,BP,LF(c)	5,000.00
5 WE,LF,BP,GT,LF(c),Flame	2,500.00
6 WE,LF,BP,GT,LF(c),Flame	2,400.00
7 WE,LF,BP,GT,LF(c),Flame	4,000.00
8 WE,LF,BP,GT,LF(c),Flame	3,400.00
9 WE,LF,BP,GT,LF(c),Flame	1,900.00
10 WE,LF,BP,LF(c),Flame	1,900.00
11 WE,LF,BP,LF(c),O:Flame	1,800.00
12 BP,LF(c),Bondage(c),Flame	1,600.00
13 E:Dr Fung,Flame	1,500.00
14 JoS,Bondage(c),Flame	1,600.00
15 JoS&LF(c),Flame	1,500.00
16 Flame(c)	1,200.00
17 Flame(c)	1,200.00
18 Flame(c)	1,200.00
19 Male Bondage(c),Flame	1,300.00
20 Flame(c)	1,200.00
21 O:Black Club &Lion,Flame	1,100.00
22 Flame(c)	950.00
23 Flame(c)	800.00
24 Flame(c)	800.00
25 A:Dr Fung,Flame	800.00
26 Flame(c)	800.00
27 Flame(c)	800.00
28 Bondage(c)I&O:US Jones, B:Lu-nar,Flame	1,200.00
29 Bondage(c),Flame	700.00
30 O:Flame(c),Flame	1,300.00
31 Bondage(c),Flame	700.00
32 Hitler(c),Flame	850.00
33 Male Bondage(c)	700.00

WORLD FAMOUS HEROES MAGAZINE
Comic Corp. of America (Centaur) Oct., 1941

1 BLb,Paul Revere	1,600.00
2 BLb,Andrew Jackson,V: Dickinson, Lou Gehrig	750.00
3 BLb,Juarez-Mexican patriot	600.00
4 BLb,Canadian Mounties	600.00

WORLD'S GREATEST STORIES
Jubilee Publications Jan., 1949

1 F:Alice in Wonderland	450.00
2 F:Pinocchio	400.00

WORLD WAR III
Ace Periodicals, March–May, 1953

1 Atomic Bomb (c)	1,000.00
2 The War That Will Never Happen	750.00

WOTALIFE COMICS
See: PHANTOM LADY

WOW COMICS
David McKay/Henle Publ., July, 1936–Nov., 1936

1 WE,DBr(c),Fu Manchu, Buck Jones	3,800.00
2 WE,Little King	2,800.00
3 WE,WE(c), Popeye	2,500.00
4 WE,BKa,AR,DBr(c),Popeye, Flash Gordon	3,000.00

WOW COMICS
Fawcett Publications, Winter, 1940

N#(1)S&K,CCB(c),B&O:Mr Scarlett; B:Atom Blake,Jim Dolan,Rick O'Shay,Bondage(c)	24,000.00
2 B:Hunchback	3,500.00
3 V:Mummy Ray Gun	1,800.00
4 O:Pinky	2,000.00
5 F:Pinky the Whiz Kid	1,000.00
6 O:Phantom Eagle; B:Commando Yank	1,000.00
7 Spearhead of Invasion	800.00
8 All Three Heroes	800.00
9 A:Capt Marvel,Capt MarvelJr. Shazam,B:Mary Marvel	1,800.00
10 The Sinister Secret of Hotel Hideaway	800.00
11	750.00
12 Rocketing adventures	750.00

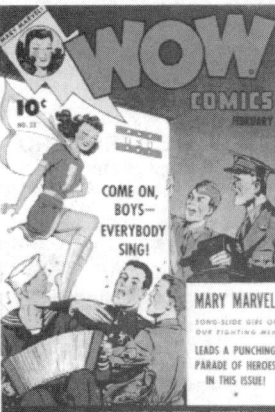

Wow Comics #22
© Fawcett Publications

13 Thrill Show	750.00
14 V:Mr Night	750.00
15 The Shazam Girl of America	700.00
16 Ride to the Moon	700.00
17 V:Mary Batson,Alter Ego Goes Berserk	700.00
18 I:Uncle Marvel,Infinity(c) V is For Victory	700.00
19 A Whirlwind Fantasy	700.00
20 Mary Marvel's Magic Carpet	700.00
21 Word That Shook the World	350.00
22 Come on Boys- Everybody Sing	350.00
23 Trapped by the Terror of the Future	350.00
24 Mary Marvel	350.00
25 Mary Marvel Crushes Crime	350.00
26 Smashing Star- Studded Stories	300.00
27 War Stamp Plea(c)	300.00
28 Pinky	300.00
29	300.00

GOLDEN AGE

30 In Mirror Land 300.00
31 Stars of Action 250.00
32 The Millinery Marauders 250.00
33 Mary Marvel(c) 250.00
34 A:Uncle Marvel 250.00
35 I:Freckles Marvel 250.00
36 Secret of the Buried City. 250.00
37 7th War loan plea 250.00
38 Pictures That Came to Life. . . 250.00
39 The Perilous Packages. 250.00
40 The Quarrel of the Gnomes . . 250.00
41 Hazardous Adventures 225.00
42 . . . . 225.00
43 Curtain Time 225.00
44 Volcanic Adventure 225.00
45 . . . . 225.00
46 . . . . 225.00
47 . . . . 225.00
48 . . . . 225.00
49 . . . . 225.00
50 Mary Marvel/Commando Yank 225.00
51 Command Yank 200.00
52 . . . . 200.00
53 Murder in the Tall Timbers . . . 200.00
54 Flaming Adventure 200.00
55 Earthquake!. 200.00
56 Sacred Pearls of Comatesh . . 200.00
57 . . . . 200.00
58 E:Mary Marvel;The Curse
    of the Keys 200.00
59 B:Ozzie the Hilarious
    Teenager 200.00
60 thru 64 . . . . @200.00
65 A:Tom Mix 200.00
66 A:Tom Mix 200.00
67 A:Tom Mix 200.00
68 A:Tom Mix 200.00
69 A:Tom Mix,Baseball 200.00
Becomes:

REAL WESTERN HERO
Sept., 1948

70 It's Round-up Time 400.00
71 CCB,P(c),A Rip
    Roaring Rodeo 250.00
72 w/Gabby Hayes 250.00
73 thru 75 . . . . @250.00
Becomes:

WESTERN HERO
March, 1949

76 Partial Ph(c)&P(c). 350.00
77 Partial Ph(c)&P(c). 200.00
78 Partial Ph(c)&P(c). 200.00
79 Partial Ph(c)&P(c),
    Shadow of Death. 175.00
80 Partial Ph(c)&P(c). 200.00
81 CCB,Partial Ph(c)&P(c),
    F:Tootsie 200.00
82 Partial Ph(c)&P(c),
    A:Hopalong Cassidy 200.00
83 Partial Ph(c)&P(c). 200.00
84 Ph(c) 175.00
85 Ph(c) 175.00
86 Ph(c),The Case of the
    Extra Buddy, giant 175.00
87 Ph(c),The Strange Lands 175.00
88 Ph(c),A:Senor Diablo 175.00
89 Ph(c),The Hypnotist 175.00
90 Ph(c),The Menace of
    the Cougar, giant. 150.00
91 Ph(c),Song of Death 150.00
92 Ph(c),The Fatal Hide-out,
    giant. 150.00
93 Ph(c),Treachery at
    Triple T, giant. 150.00
94 Ph(c),Bank Busters,giant 150.00
95 Ph(c),Rampaging River 150.00
96 Ph(c),Range Robbers,giant . . 150.00
97 Ph(c),Death on the
    Hook,giant 150.00

98 Ph(c),Web of Death,giant 150.00
99 Ph(c),The Hidden Evidence . . 150.00
100 Ph(c),A:Red Eagle,Giant . . . 150.00
101 Red Eagle, Ph(c) 150.00
102 thru 111 Ph(c) . . . . @150.00
112 Ph(c),March, 1952 . . . . 175.00

Yankee Comics #3
© *Charlton Comics*

YANKEE COMICS
Chesler Publications
(Harry A. Chesler),
Sept., 1941–March, 1942

1 F:Yankee Doodle Jones . . . 2,400.00
2 The Spirit of '41 . . . . 1,100.00
3 Yankee Doodle Jones 800.00
4 JCo,Yankee Doodle Jones . . . 800.00

YELLOWJACKET
COMICS
Levy Publ./Frank Comunale/
Charlton
Sept., 1944

1 O&B:Yellowjackets,B:Diana
    the Huntress 1,000.00
2 Rosita &The Filipino Kid 500.00
3 . . . . 450.00
4 Fall of the House of Usher. . . . 500.00
5 King of Beasts 500.00
6 . . . . 600.00
7 I:Diane Carter;The
    Lonely Guy 1,300.00
8 The Buzzing Bee Code 600.00
9 . . . . 550.00
10 Capt Grim V:The Salvage
    Pirates 600.00
Becomes:

JACK IN THE BOX
Feb., 1946

11 Funny Animal,Yellow Jacket . . 225.00
12 Funny Animal 100.00
13 BW,Funny Animal 225.00
14 thru 16 Funny Animal . . . . @125.00
Becomes:

COWBOY WESTERN
COMICS
July, 1948

17 Annie Oakley,Jesse James. . . 250.00
18 JO,JO(c) 200.00
19 JO,JO(c),Legends of Paul
    Bunyan 200.00
20 JO(c),Jesse James. 125.00

21 Annie Oakley VisitsDryGulch . 125.00
22 Story of the Texas Rangers . . 125.00
23 . . . . 125.00
24 Ph(c),F:James Craig. 125.00
25 Ph(c),F:Sunset Carson 125.00
26 Ph(c) 150.00
27 Ph(c),Sunset Carson movie . . 750.00
28 Ph(c),Sunset Carson movie . . 400.00
29 Ph(c),Sunset Carson movie . . 400.00
30 Ph(c),Sunset Carson movie . . 400.00
31 Ph(c) 100.00
32 thru 34 Ph(c) . . . . @100.00
35 thru 37 Sunset Carson . . . . @350.00
38 and 39 . . . . @100.00
Becomes:

SPACE WESTERN
COMICS
Charlton Comics, Oct., 1952

40 Spurs Jackson,V:The
    Saucer Men 1,100.00
41 StC(c),Space Vigilantes 750.00
42 StC(c),Aomic Bomb 900.00
43 StC(c),Battle of
    Spacemans Gulch 800.00
44 StC(c),The Madman of Mars . 750.00
45 StC(c),The Moon Bat,Hitler. . 775.00
Becomes:

COWBOY WESTERN
COMICS
Oct., 1953

46 . . . . 250.00
Becomes:

COWBOY WESTERN
HEROES
Dec., 1953

47 . . . . 100.00
48 . . . . 100.00
Becomes:

COWBOY WESTERN
May–June, 1954

49 . . . . 100.00
50 F:Jesse James 100.00
51 thru 57. . . . . @75.00
58, Wild Bill Hickok, giant 100.00
59 thru 66. . . . . @75.00
67 AW&AT 125.00
Becomes:

WILD BILL HICKOK
AND JINGLES
Aug., 1958

68 AW 125.00
69 AW 100.00
70 AW 75.00
71 thru 73. . . . . @60.00
74 1960 . . . . 60.00

YOGI BERRA
Fawcett, 1957

1 Ph(c) 1,000.00

YOUNG BRIDES
Feature Publications (Prize
Comics), Sept.–Oct., 1952

1 S&K,Ph(c) 400.00
2 S&K,Ph(c) 225.00
3 S&K,Ph(c) 200.00
4 S&K 200.00
5 S&K 200.00
6 S&K 200.00
2-1 S&K 175.00
2-2 S&K 100.00
2-3 S&K 175.00
2-4 S&K 175.00
2-5 S&K 175.00

2-6 S&K 175.00
2-7 S&K 175.00
2-8 S&K 75.00
2-9 S&K 75.00
2-10 S&K 175.00
2-11 S&K 175.00
2-12 S&K 175.00
3-1 . . . . 60.00
3-2 . . . . 60.00
3-3 . . . . 60.00
3-4 . . . . 60.00
3-5 . . . . 60.00
3-6 . . . . 60.00
4-1. . . . . 60.00
4-2 S&K 150.00
4-3. . . . . 60.00
4-4 S&K 150.00
4-5. . . . . 60.00

YOUNG EAGLE
Fawcett Publications/
Charlton Comics, Dec., 1950
1 Ph(c) 200.00
2 Ph(c),Mystery of Thunder
    Canyon 125.00
3 Ph(c),Death at Dawn 100.00
4 Ph(c) 100.00
5 Ph(c),The Golden Flood 100.00
6 Ph(c),The Nightmare Empire . . 100.00
7 Ph(c),Vigilante Veangeance . . 100.00
8 Ph(c),The Rogues Rodeo 100.00
9 Ph(c),The Great Railroad
    Swindle 100.00
10 June, 1952, Ph(c),Thunder Rides
    the Trail,O:Thunder 80.00

YOUNG KING COLE
Novelty Press/Premium
Svcs. Co., Autumn, 1945
1-1 Detective Toni Gayle 400.00
1-2 . . . . 200.00
1-3 . . . . 175.00
1-4 . . . . 175.00
2-1 . . . . 135.00
2-2 . . . . 135.00
2-3 . . . . 135.00
2-4 . . . . 135.00
2-5 . . . . 135.00
2-6 . . . . 135.00
2-7 . . . . 135.00
3-1 . . . . 125.00
3-2 LbC 200.00
3-3 The Killer With The Hat 125.00

Young King Cole #3-1
© Novelty Press

3-4 The Fierce Tiger 125.00
3-5 AMc 125.00
3-6 . . . . 135.00
3-7 LbC(c),Case of the
    Devil's Twin 250.00
3-8 . . . . 125.00
3-9 The Crime Fighting King 125.00
3-10 LbC(c) 225.00
3-11 LbC(c) 225.00
3-12 July, 1948,AMc(c) 120.00

YOUNG LIFE
New Age Publications,
Summer, 1945
1 Partial Ph(c),Louis Prima. . . . 175.00
2 Partial Ph(c),Frank Sinatra . . . 200.00
Becomes:

TEEN LIFE
Winter, 1945
3 Partial Ph(c),Croon without
    Tricks,June Allyson(c) 150.00
4 Partial Ph(c),Atom Smasher
    Blueprints,Duke Ellington(c) . 125.00
5 Partial Ph(c), Build Your Own
    Pocket Radio, Jackie
    Robinson(c) 150.00

YOUNG LOVE
Feature Publ.
(Prize Comics Group),
Feb.–March, 1949
1 S&K,S&K(c) 600.00
2 S&K,Ph(c) 300.00
3 S&K,JSe,BE,Ph(c) 250.00
4 S&K,Ph(c) 150.00
5 S&K,Ph(c) 150.00
2-1 S&K,Ph(c) 250.00
2-2 Ph(c) 135.00
2-3 Ph(c) 135.00
2-4 Ph(c) 135.00
2-5 Ph(c) 135.00
2-6 S&K(c) 200.00
2-7 S&K(c),S&K 200.00
2-8 S&K 200.00
2-9 S&K(c),S&K. 200.00
2-10 S&K(c),S&K 200.00
2-11 S&K(c),S&K 200.00
2-12 S&K(c),S&K 200.00
3-1 S&K(c),S&K 200.00
3-2 S&K(c),S&K. 200.00
3-3 S&K(c),S&K. 200.00
3-4 S&K(c),S&K. 200.00
3-5 Ph(c) 175.00
3-6 BP,Ph(c) 175.00
3-7 Ph(c) 175.00
3-8 Ph(c) 175.00
3-9 MMe,Ph(c) 175.00
3-10 Ph(c) 175.00
3-11 Ph(c) 175.00
3-12 Ph(c) 175.00
4-1 S&K 175.00
4-2 Ph(c) 150.00
4-3 Ph(c) 150.00
4-4 Ph(c) 150.00
4-5 Ph(c) 150.00
4-6 S&K,Ph(c) 150.00
4-7 thru 4-12 Ph(c). . . . . @125.00
5-1 thru 5-12 Ph(c). . . . . @75.00
6-1 thru 6-9 . . . . @60.00
6-10 thru 6-12 . . . . @60.00
7-1 thru 7-7 . . . . @50.00
7-8 thru 7-11 . . . . @50.00
7-12 thru 8-5 . . . . @50.00
8-6 thru 8-12 . . . . @60.00

YOUNG ROMANCE
COMICS
Feature Publ./Headline/
Prize Publ., Sept.–Oct., 1947
1 S&K(c),S&K. 650.00
2 S&K(c),S&K 350.00
3 S&K(c),S&K 300.00
4 S&K(c),S&K 300.00
5 S&K(c),S&K 300.00
6 S&K(c),S&K 300.00
2-1 S&K(c),S&K 275.00
2-2 S&K(c),S&K. 275.00
2-3 S&K(c),S&K 275.00
2-4 S&K(c),S&K 275.00
2-5 S&K(c),S&K 275.00
2-6 S&K(c),S&K 250.00
3-1 thru 3-12 S&K(c),S&K . . . . @250.00
4-1 thru 4-12 S&K . . . . @250.00
5-1 ATh,S&K 250.00
2 . . . . 250.00
3 . . . . 225.00
5-4 thru 5-12 S&K . . . . @225.00
6-1 thru 6-3. . . . . @100.00

YOUR UNITED STATES
Lloyd Jacquet Studios, 1946
1N# Teeming nation of Nations . 250.00

YOUTHFUL HEARTS
Youthful Magazines,
May, 1952
1 Frankie Lane(c) 350.00
2 Vic Damone 250.00
3 Johnnie Ray. 250.00
Becomes:

DARING CONFESSIONS
Nov., 1952
4 DW,Tony Curtis 175.00
5 Ray Anthony 125.00
6 DW. 135.00
7 . . . . 125.00
8 DW. 125.00

YOUTHFUL ROMANCES
Pix Parade/Ribage/
Trojan, Aug.–Sept., 1949
1 . . . . 300.00
2 Walter Johnson 200.00
3 Tex Beneke 150.00
4 . . . . 150.00
5 . . . . 150.00
6 . . . . 125.00
7 Tony Martin(c) 150.00
8 WW(c), Frank Sinatra 250.00
9 . . . . 125.00
10 Mel Torme. 135.00
11 . . . . 125.00
12 Tony Benett. 135.00
13 Richard Hays 125.00
14. . . . . 125.00
Becomes:

DARLING LOVE
Oct.–Nov., 1949
15 WD,Spike Jones, Ph(c). 125.00
16 Tony Bavaar, Ph(c) 125.00
17 DW,Ph(c). 125.00

ZAGO, JUNGLE PRINCE
Fox Features Syndicate,
Sept., 1948
1 A:Blue Beetle. 900.00
2 JKa. 750.00
3 JKa. 600.00
4 MB(c). 600.00
Becomes:

GOLDEN AGE

GOLDEN AGE

MY STORY
May, 1949
5 JKa,Too Young To Fall in Love 250.00
6 I Was A She-Wolf 125.00
7 I Lost My Reputation 125.00
8 My Words Condemned Me . . . 125.00
9 WW,Wayward Bride 225.00
10 WW,March, 1950,Second
Rate Girl 225.00
11 . . . . 125.00
12 Ph(c) 125.00

TEGRA, JUNGLE EMPRESS
Fox Features Syndicate
Aug., 1948
1 Blue Bettle,Rocket Kelly 750.00
Becomes:

ZEGRA, JUNGLE EMPRESS
Oct., 1948
2 JKa 750.00
3 . . . . 600.00
4 . . . . 600.00
5 . . . . 600.00
Becomes:

MY LOVE LIFE
June, 1949–Aug., 1950
6 I Put A Price Tag On Love . . . 175.00
7 An Old Man's Fancy 125.00
8 My Forbidden Affair 125.00
9 I Loved too Often 125.00
10 My Secret Torture 125.00
11 I Broke My Own Heart 125.00
12 I Was An Untamed Filly 125.00
13 I Can Never Marry You 100.00

ZIP COMICS
MLJ Magazines,
Feb., 1940–Summer, 1944
1 MMe,O&B:Kalathar,The Scarlet
Avenger,Steel Sterling,B:Mr
Satan,Nevada Jones,War Eagle
Captain Valor 7,500.00
2 MMe,CBi(c)B:Steel
Sterling(c) 3,000.00
3 MMe,CBi(a&c) 2,500.00
4 MMe,CBi(a&c) 2,000.00
5 MMe,CBi(a&c) 2,000.00
6 MMe,CBi(a&c) 1,700.00

7 MMe,CBi(a&c) 1,700.00
8 MMe,CBi(a&c),Bondage(c) . 1,700.00
9 CMMe,CBi(a&c),E:Kalathar,
Mr Satan;Bondage(c) 2,000.00
10 MMe,CBi(a&c),B:Inferno . . . 1,800.00
11 MMe,CBi(a&c) 1,500.00
12 MMe,CBi(a&c),Bondage(c) . 1,500.00
13 MMe,CBi(a&c),E:Inferno,
Bondage(c),Woman in
Electric Chair 1,600.00
14 MMe,CBi(a&c),Bondage(c) . 1,500.00
15 MMe,CBi(a&c),Bondage(c) . 1,600.00
16 MMe,CBi(a&c),Bondage(c) . 1,500.00
17 CBI(a&c),E:Scarlet
Avenger Bondage(c). 1,500.00
18 IN(c),B:Wilbur. 1,500.00
19 IN(c),Steel Sterling(c). 1,500.00
20 IN(c),O&I:Black Jack
Hitler(c). 2,400.00
21 IN(c),V:Nazis 1,200.00
22 IN(c) 1,200.00
23 IN(c),Flying Fortress 1,200.00
24 IN(c),China Town Exploit . . . 1,200.00
25 IN(c),E:Nevada Jones 1,200.00
26 IN(c),B:Black Witch,
E:Capt Valor 1,200.00
27 IN(c),I:Web,V:Japanese 2,000.00
28 IN(C),O:Web,Bondage(c). . . 1,600.00
29 Steel Sterling & Web. 750.00
30 V:Nazis 750.00
31 IN(c) 650.00
32 Nazi Skeleton, WWII. 800.00
33 Bondage(c) 700.00
34 I:Applejack;Bondage(c). 700.00
35 E:Zambini 650.00
36 I:Senor Banana. 650.00
37 . . . . 650.00
38 E:Web 650.00
39 O&B:Red Rube. 650.00
40 . . . . 550.00
41 . . . . 550.00
42 . . . . 550.00
43 . . . . 550.00
44 Red Rube 550.00
45 E:Wilbur. 550.00
46 Red Rube 550.00
47 Crooks Can't Win 550.00

ZIP-JET
St. John Publishing Co.,
Feb., 1953
1 Rocketman 1,000.00
2 April–May, 1953, Assassin
of the Airlanes 650.00

ZOOM COMICS
Carlton Publishing Co.,
Dec., 1945
N# O:Captain Milksop. 600.00

ZOOT COMICS
Fox Features Syndicate,
Spring, 1946
N#(1)(fa) 250.00
2 A:Jaguar(fa) 250.00
3 (fa) 150.00
4 (fa) 150.00
5 (fa) 125.00
6 (fa) 125.00
7 B:Rulah. 1,300.00
8 JKa(c),Fangs of Stone. 850.00
9 JKa(c),Fangs of Black Fury . . 850.00
10 JKa(c),Inferno Land 850.00
11 JKa,The Purple Plague,
Bondage(c) 900.00
12 JKa(c),The Thirsty Stone,
Bondage(c) 650.00
13 Bloody Moon. 650.00
14 Pearls of Pathos,Woman
Carried off by Bird 850.00
15 Death Dancers 650.00
16 . . . . 650.00
Becomes:

RULAH, JUNGLE GODDESS
Aug., 1948
17 JKa(c),Wolf Doctor. 1,300.00
18 JKa(c),Vampire Garden 900.00
19 JKa(c) 850.00
20 . . . . 850.00
21 JKa(c) 850.00
22 JKa(c) 850.00
23 . . . . 750.00
24 . . . . 650.00
25 . . . . 650.00
26 . . . . 650.00
27 . . . . 700.00
Becomes:

I LOVED
July, 1949–March, 1950
28 . . . . 150.00
29 thru 31. . . . . @100.00
32 My Poison Love 100.00

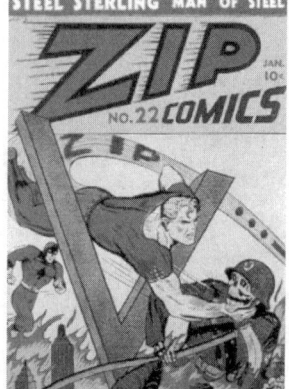

Zip Comics #22
© MLJ Magazines

Zoot #15
© Fox Features Syndicate

Rulah, Jungle Goddess #17
© Fox Features Syndicate

All comics prices listed are for *Near Mint* condition.

DARK HORSE

ABE SAPIEN:
DRUMS OF THE DEAD
Mar., 1998
1-shot Hellboy spin-off 3.00

ABYSS, THE
1989
1 & 2 MK,Movie Adaptation . . . . @2.50

ACCIDENT MAN
(B&W) 1993
1 I:Accident Man. 2.50
2 thru 3 . . . . @2.50

ADRENALYNN:
WEAPON OF WAR
Aug., 2001
TPB TnD 13.00

ADVENTURES OF
LUTHER ARKWRIGHT
DH/Valkyrie Press
(B&W) 1987–89
1 thru 9 . . . . @2.25
(B&W) 1990
1 thru 9 Rep. . . . . @2.25
TPB 15.00

ADVENTURES OF
THE MASK
1996
1 thru 12 by Michael Eury & Marc
 Campos, TV cartoon adapt. . . @2.50
Ash can (1995) 3.00

AGENTS OF LAW
Comics' Greatest World, 1995
1 KG, I:Law. 2.50
2 A:Barb Wire 2.50

RICARDO DELGADO

AGE OF
REPTILES
THE HUNT

Age of Reptiles, The Hunt #5
© Dark Horse Comics

3 KG,DLw,The Judgment Gate. . . . 2.50
4 Open Golden City 2.50
5 Who is the Mystery figure 2.50
6 V:Predator 2.50

AGE OF REPTILES
1993–94
1 DRd,Story on Dinosaurs 3.00
2 thru 4 DRd,Story on Dinosaurs @3.00
TPB Tribal Warfare 15.00

AGE OF REPTILES:
THE HUNT
1996
1 thru 5 by Ricardo Delgado. . . . @3.00
TPB The Hunt 18.00

AKIRA
TPB #1, 364-pg.,B&W 25.00
TPB #2, 304-pg.,B&W 25.00
TPB #3, 288-pg.,B&W 25.00
TPB #4, 400-pg.,B&W 28.00
TPB #5, 416-pg.,B&W 28.00
TPB #6, 440-pg.,B&W 30.00

AL CAPP'S LI'L ABNER:
THE FRAZETTA SUNDAYS
May, 2003
TPB Vol. 1 1954–55. . . . . 19.00
TPB Vol. 2 1956–57. . . . . 19.00
TPB Vol. 3 1958–59. . . . . 19.00
TPB Vol. 4 1960–61. . . . . 19.00

ALIEN RESURRECTION
Oct., 1997
1 (of 2) movie adaptation 2.50
2 DMc(c) 2.50

ALIENS
(B&W) 1988
1 Movie Sequel,R:Hicks,Newt . . . 20.00
1a 2nd printing 3.00
1b 3rd printing. 2.25
1c 4th printing. 2.25
2 Hicks raids Mental Hospital 8.00
2a 2nd printing 2.50
2a 3rd printing. 2.25
3 Realize Queen is on Earth 7.00
3a 2nd printing 2.25
4 Queen is freed, Newton on
 Aliens World 5.00
5 All out war on Aliens World 5.00
6 Hicks & Newt return to Earth. . . . 5.00
TPB rep.#1–#6 & DHP #24 . . . . . 11.00
TPB 2nd printing, DvD(c). 11.00

ALIENS (II)
[Mini-Series] 1989
1 DB,Hicks,Newt hijack ship. 5.00
1a 2nd Printing 3.00
2 DB,Crazed general trains aliens . 3.00
2a 2nd Printing 3.00
3 DB,HicksV:General Spears 3.00
3a 2nd Printing 2.50
4 DB,Heroes reclaim earth
 from aliens. 3.00

ALIENS
1-shot Earth Angel, JBy (1994) . . . 3.00

TPB rep. Earth Angel (1991) 15.00
1-shot Glass Corridor, DvL 3.00
1-shot Mondo Heat, I:Herk Mondo . 2.50
1-shot Mondo Pest (1995) 3.00
1-shot Purge, IEd,PhH. 3.00
1-shot Pig, CDi,FH. 3.00
1-shot Sacrifice, rep.Aliens UK
 (1993) 5.00
1-shot Salvation DGb,MMi,KN,
 F:Selkirk (1993). 5.00
1-shot Special 2.50
1-shot Stalker. 2.50
1-shot Wraith 3.00
GN Female War, remastered. 17.00
GN Genocide, remastered. 17.00
GN Labyrinth, remastered 18.00
GN Nightmare Asylum, remaster. . 17.00
GN Outbreak, remastered 18.00
GN Rogue, Remastered 17.00

ALIENS: ALCHEMY
Sept., 1997
1 (of 3) JAr,RCo 3.00
2 thru 3 . . . . @3.00

ALIENS: APOCALYPSE
— DESTROYING ANGELS
Jan., 1999
1 (of 4) MSh 3.00
2 thru 4 MSh . . . . @3.00
TPB 11.00
TPB Salvation and Sacrifice 13.00

ALIENS: BERSERKER
1995
1 I:Crew of the Nemesis 3.00
2 thru 4 . . . . @3.00

ALIENS:
COLONIAL MARINES
1993
1 I: Lt. Joseph Henry 4.00
2 I: Pvt. Carmen Vasquez. 3.00
3 thru 10 . . . . @3.00

ALIENS: EARTH WAR
1991
1 SK,JBo(c),Alien's War renewed . . 4.00
1a 2nd Printing 2.50
2 SK,JBo(c),To trap the Queen. . . . 4.00
3 SK,JBo(c) Stranded on
 Alien's planet. 3.00
4 SK,JBo(c),Resolution,final 5.00

ALIENS: GENOCIDE
1991
1 Aliens vs. Aliens 3.50
2 Alien Homeworld 3.00
3 Search for Alien Queen 3.00
4 Conclusion, inc. poster 3.00
TPB Genocide rep. #1–#4 . . . . 14.00

ALIENS: HIVE
1992
1 KJo,I:Stanislaw Mayakovsky 4.00
2 KJo,A:Norbert 3.50
3 KJo,A:Julie,Gill. 3.25
4 KJo,A:Stan,Final 3.00
TPB Hive rep. #1–#4 . . . . 14.00

DARK HORSE

All comics prices listed are for *Near Mint* condition.

ALIENS: HAVOC
1 (of 2) 'over 40 creators' 3.00
2 . . . . 3.00

ALIENS: KIDNAPPED
Dec., 1997–Feb., 1998
1 (of 3) 3.00
2 thru 3 . . . . @3.00
TPB Aliens:Kidnapped 10.00

ALIENS: LABYRINTH
1993
1 F:Captured Alien 3.00
2 thru 4 . . . . @3.00
TPB rep. #1–#4 . . . . 18.00
TPB remastered 18.00

ALIENS: MUSIC OF THE SPEARS
1994
1 I:Damon Eddington 3.00
2 thru 4TBd(c) . . . . @3.00

ALIENS: NEWT'S TALE
1992
1 How Newt Survived 5.50
2 JBo(c),Newt's point of view 5.50

ALIENS: ROGUE
1993
1 F:Mr.Kay 3.00
2 thru 4 V:Aliens . . . . @3.00
TPB Nel(c),rep.#1–#4 . . . . 15.00

ALIENS: STRONGHOLD
1994
1 DoM,JP 3.00
2 thru 4 DoM,JP . . . . @3.00
TPB 17.00

ALIENS: SURVIVAL
Feb.–Apr., 1998
1 (of 3) TyH(c) 3.00
2 thru 3 . . . . @3.00

ALIENS: TRIBES
TPB 12.00

Aliens vs. Predator, The Deadliest of the Species #11 © Dark Horse Comics

ALIENS/PREDATOR: DEADLIEST OF THE SPECIES
1993
1 B:CCl(s),JG,F:Caryn Delacroix . . 3.75
2 JG,V:Predator 3.00
3 JG,F:Caryn Delacroix 3.00
4 JG,V:Predator 3.00
5 JG,Roadtrip 3.00
6 JG,in Space Station 3.00
7 thru 9 JG,EB . . . . @3.00
10 CCl(s), Human Predators 3.00
11 CCl,EB,JBo(c),Delacroix vs.
   DeMatier 3.00
12 Caryn's Fate 3.00
TPB 30.00

ALIENS VS. PREDATOR
1996
0 PN,KS,Rep.DHP#34-36,(B&W) . . 9.00
1 Duel to the Death 9.00
1a 2nd Printing 3.00
2 Dr. Revna missing 5.00
3 Predators attack Aliens 5.00
4 CW,F:Machiko & Predator 5.00
TPB Rep.#1–#4 . . . . 20.00
TPB PN,KS,rep.DHP#34-36 . . . . . 20.00
TPB Thrill of the Hunt (2004) 7.00
Ann.#1 (1999) 5.00
1-shot Booty, rep. *Previews* 3.00

ALIENS VS. PREDATOR: DUEL
1995
1 Trap, JS 3.00
2 War 3.00

ALIENS VS. PREDATOR: ETERNAL
June, 1998
1 (of 4) IEd,GF(c) 3.00
2 thru 4 IEd,GF(c) . . . . @3.00
TPB 10.00

ALIENS VS. PREDATOR: WAR
1995
0 Prelude to New Series 3.00
1 RSd,MM,RCo(c) F:Machiko 3.00
2 thru 4 . . . . @3.00
TPB 20.00

ALIENS VS. PREDATOR: XENOGENESIS
Dec., 1999
1 (of 4) MvR 3.50
2 thru 4 MvR,trapped . . . . @3.50

ALIENS VS. PREDATOR VS. THE TERMINATOR
Apr., 2000
1 (of 4) MSh,MvR 3.50
2 MSh,MvR,V:Terminator-Alien
   hybrid 3.50
3 MSh,MvR,on Predator ship 3.50
4 MSh,MvR,concl. 3.50
TPB 96-pg. series rep. 12.00

ALIENS: XENOGENESIS
Aug., 1999
1 (of 4) 3.50
2 thru 4 DR . . . . @3.50

ALIEN 3
1992
1 thru 3 Movie Adaptation . . . . . . @3.00

AL WILLIAMSON: HIDDEN LANDS
(B&W) Nov., 2002
TPB AW,224-pg. 23.00

AMAZING ADVENTURES OF THE ESCAPIST, THE
Dec., 2003
1 Michael Chabon, 80-pg. 9.00
2 thru 4 . . . . @9.00
TPB Vol. 1 and Vol. 2 . . . . @18.00

AMAZING SCREW-ON HEAD, THE
May, 2002
1-shot MMi 3.00

AMERICAN, THE
(B&W) 1987
1 CW,'Chinese Boxes,'D:Gleason . 5.00
2 CW,'Nightmares 4.00
3 CW,Secrets of the American 4.00
4 CW,American vs.Kid America . . . 4.00
5 A:Kiki the Gorilla 4.00
6 Rashomon-like plot 3.50
7 Pornography business issue 3.50
8 Deals with violence issue 3.50
9 American Falls into a cult 3.50
Spec. (1990) 4.00

THE AMERICAN: LOST IN AMERICA
1992
1 CMa, American joins a cult 2.50
2 CMa, V:'Feel-Good' cult 2.50
3 CMa, 'Ape-Mask' cult 2.50
4 CMa, Final issue 2.50
ColorSpec.#1 . . . . 3.00

AMERICAN SPLENDOR
1993
1-shot Letterman by Harvey Pekar . 3.50
1-shot A Step Out of the Nest 3.50
1-shot On the Job 3.50
1-shot Comics Con, JZe 3.50
1-shot Music Comics 3.50
1-shot Odds & Ends 3.50
1-shot Transatlantic Comics 3.50
1-shot Terminal 3.50
1-shot Bedtime Stories 4.50
TPB (2002) 12.00

AMERICAN SPLENDOR: UNSUNG HERO
DH Maverick, Aug., 2002
1 (of 3) b&w 4.00
2 thru 3 . . . . @4.00

AMERICAN SPLENDOR WINDFALL
(B&W) 1995
1 Windfall Gained,pt.1 . . . . 4.25
2 Windfall Lost 4.25
1-shot Portrait of The Artist
   in his declining years 4.00

American Splendor, On the Job
© Dark Horse Comics

ANCIENT JOE
DH Maverick, Oct., 2001
1 (of 3) B&W 3.00
2 thru 3 . . . . @3.50
TPB 13.00

ANGEL
Oct., 1999
1 Buffy spin-off 3.00
2 thru 9 . . . . @3.00
10 TSg 3.00
11 TSg 3.00
12 TSg,MMi(c) 3.00
13 TSg,demonic rats 3.00
14 TSg,Little Girl Lost 3.00
15 TSg,Past Lives,Buffy x-over 4.00
16 TSg,Past Lives,Buffy x-over 4.00
17 The Cordelia Special. 3.00
1–17a newsstand photo(c) . . . . . @4.00
TPB Surrogates 10.00
TPB Earthly Possessions 10.00
TPB Hunting Ground 10.00
TPB Angel Autumnal 10.00
TPB The Hollower 10.00
TPB Strange Bedfellows, rep. 13.00

ANGEL
Sept., 2001
1 (of 4) 3.00
1a photo (c). 3.00
1b gold-foil (c) 13.00
1c gold-foil (c) signed 20.00
2 thru 4 . . . . @3.00
2a thru 4a photo (c) . . . . @3.00
TPB Long Night's Journey 13.00

ANOTHER CHANCE TO GET IT RIGHT
1995
1 B&W. 15.00
TPB AVs, GfD(c) 10.00
TPB 3rd printing (2002) 12.00

APPLESEED
(B&W–Manga)
TPB #1: Promethean Challenge . . 15.00
TPB #2: Prometheus Unbound . . . 15.00
TPB #3: Scales of Prometheus . . . 15.00
TPB #4: Promethean Balance 15.00

APPLESEED DATABOOK
(B&W–Manga) 1994
1 Flip Book, by Masamune Shirow. 5.00
1a 2nd printing 3.50
2 Flip Book 3.50
TPB Rep. #1–#2 (1995). 13.00

ARMY OF DARKNESS
1992
1 . . . . 20.00
2 thru 3 . . . . @15.00

ARZACH
1996
TPB by Moebius 7.00

A SMALL KILLING
GN by Alan Moore & Oscar Zarate 12.00

ASTRO BOY
(B&W) Mar., 2002
TPB Vol.1 224-pg.Osamu Tezuka . 10.00
TPB Vol.2 thru Vol. 23 . . . . @10.00

ATLAS
1994
1 BZ,I:Atlas 2.75
2 BZ,V:Sh'en Chui 2.75
3 BZ,V:Sh'en Chui 2.50
4 BZ, final issue 2.50

AUTOBIOGRAPHIX
Nov., 2003
TPB 15.00

BABE
Legend, 1994
1 JBy(a&s) 3.00
2 thru 4 JBy(a&s) . . . . @2.50

BABE 2
Legend, 1995
1 V:Shrewmanoid 2.50
2 A:Abe Sapien. 2.50

BACCHUS COLOR SPECIAL
1995
1 A:Thor 3.00
2 A:Abe Sapien. 2.50

BADGER: SHATTERED MIRROR
1994
1 R:Badger 3.00
2 thru 4 . . . . @3.00

BADGER: ZEN POP FUNNY ANIMAL VERSION
1 MBn,R:Badger (1994) 3.00
2 Ham. 3.00

BADLANDS
(B&W) 1991
1 I:Connie Bremen 3.50
2 Anne Peck, C.I.A. 3.00
3 Assassination Rumor. 2.50
4 Connie heads South 2.50
5 November 22, 1963, Dallas. 2.25
6 . . . . 2.25

BARB WIRE
Comics' Greatest World, 1994
1 Foil(c),I:Deathcard 3.00
2 DLw,I:Hurricane Max 3.00
3 V:Mace Blitzkrieg. 3.00
4 Ghost,pt.1 . . . . 3.00
5 Ghost,pt.2 . . . . 3.00
6 Hardhide, Ignition. 3.00
7 A:Motorhead 3.00
8 V:Ignition 3.00
9 A:Mecha, V:Ignition 3.00
Movie Spec. 4.00
TPB 9.00

Barb Wire: Ace of Spades #3
© Dark Horse Comics

BARB WIRE: ACE OF SPADES
1996
1 CW,TBd & DoM. 3.00
2 thru 4 CW,TBd & DoM. . . . . . . @3.00

BARRY WINDSOR-SMITH: STORYTELLER
Oct., 1996
TPBs 1 thru 9 9'x12½' . . . . @5.00

BASEBALL GREATS
1 Jimmy Piersall story. 3.25

BASIL WOLVERTON'S FANTASIC FABLES
(B&W) Oct., 1993
1 BW. 2.50
2 BW 2.50

BASIL WOLVERTON'S
GN Gateway to Horror (1988) 5.00
TPB In Space, 240-pg. (1999) . . . 17.00
GN Planet of Terror (1987) 5.00

BATMAN/ALIENS
DH/DC, Mar., 1997
1 (of 2) RMz,BWr 5.00
2 conclusion 5.00
TPB RMz,BWr 15.00

All comics prices listed are for *Near Mint* condition.

DARK HORSE

BATMAN/TARZAN: CLAWS OF THE CATWOMAN
1999
1 (of 4) RMz,DvD(c),V:Dent,x-over. 3.00
2 thru 4 RMz,DvD(c). . . . . @3.00
TPB 96-pg.,DvD(c). 11.00

BATTLE GODS: WARRIORS OF THE CHAAK
Apr., 2000
1 (of 9) by Francisco Ruiz
　Velasco 3.00
2 the Lucha Libre 3.00
3 F:Takan, El Charro. 3.00
4 another tournament 3.00
5 The Chaak begins 3.00
6 Deathmatch: Takan vs. Chilbacan 3.00
7 sleeping god awakens. 3.00
8 Hell breaks loose. 3.00
9 concl. 3.00
TPB 240-pg. 20.00

BERSERK
Oct., 2003
TPB Vol. 1 The Black Swordsman. 13.00
TPB Vol. 2 Guardians of Desire. . . 13.00
TPB Vol. 3 thru Vol. 5. . . . . @14.00

BETTIE PAGE COMICS
1996–97
1-shot, some nudity (1996) 4.00
1-shot Bettie Page Comics: Spicy
　Adventure, by Jim Silke (1997). 3.00
1 Queen of Hearts, movie adapt. . . 2.50
TPB Queen of Hearts 20.00

BETTIE PAGE: QUEEN OF THE NILE
Dec., 1999
1 (of 3) low-budget time machine . . 3.00
2 and 3 concl. . . . . @3.00
TPB, series rep. 13.00

BIG
1989
1 Movie Adaptation 2.25

BIG BLOWN BABY
(B&W) Aug., 1996
1 thru 4 by Bill Wray . . . . @3.00

BIG GUY AND RUSTY THE ROBOT BOY
1995
1 V:Monster. 5.00
2 V:Monster. 5.00
TPB FM & GfD. 15.00
TPB King Size 30.00

BIG HOAX
DH Venture 2001
TPB B&W 128-pg. 11.00

BILLI 99
(B&W) 1991
1 'Pray for us Sinners' 4.50
2 'Trespasses'. 4.00
3 'Daily Bread'. 4.00
TPB TSe,200-pg. B&W (2002) . . . 15.00

BIRD: THE TATTOO
Nov., 2001
TPB color, 48-pg. 15.00

BLACKBURNE COVENANT, THE
Apr., 2003
1 (of 4) FaN 3.00
2 thru 4 . . . . @3.00
TPB FaN 13.00

Black Cross: Dirty Work
© *Dark Horse Comics*

BLACK CROSS: DIRTY WORK
Apr., 1997
1-shot by Chris Warner 3.00

BLACK DRAGON, THE
(B&W) Apr., 1996
TPB C. Claremont & J. Bolton. . . . 18.00

BLACK MAGIC
(B&W) 1998
TPB 17.00

BLACK PEARL, THE
Sept., 1996
1 by Mark Hamill. 3.00
2 thru 5 . . . . @3.00
TPB by Mark Hamill. 17.00

BLADE OF THE IMMORTAL
(B&W–Manga) July, 1996
Conquest
1 by Hiroaki Samura 11.00
2 thru 4 pt. 2 thru pt.4 . . . . @6.00
Genius, Oct., 1996
5 & 6 . . . . @6.00
Fanatic, 1997
7 & 8 . . . . @6.00
Call of the Worm, Apr., 1997
9 thru 1148-pg. . . . . @6.00
TPB Cry of the Worm 13.00
Dreamsong, July, 1997
12 thru 18. . . . . @3.50
TPB Dreamsong 13.00
Rin's Bane, Mar., 1998

19 & 20 48-pg. . . . . @4.50
On Silent Wings, May, 1998
21 thru 25. . . . . @3.50
26 48-pg. 4.50
27 thru 28. . . . . @3.50
TPB Blood of a Thousand 13.00
TPB On Silent Wings. 15.00
TPB On Silent Wings II 15.00
Dark Shadows, Jan., 1999
29 thru 33 . . . . @3.50
TPB Dark Shadows 15.00
Food, June, 1999
34 48-pg. 4.50
Heart of Darkness
35 thru 42 . . . . @3.50
TPB Heart of Darkness 17.00
The Gathering
43 thru 57 . . . . @3.50
TPB The Gathering 16.00
TPB The Gathering, Vol.2 . . . . . . 16.00
Secrets
58 thru 61, pt.1 thru pt.4 . . . . . . @3.50
62 Stigmata 3.50
63 Husk 3.50
64 Skin,pt.1 . . . . 3.50
65 Skin,pt.2 . . . . 3.50
TPB Secrets, 232-pg. b&w 17.00
Beasts
66 thru 72 Beasta pt.1 thru pt. 7 . @3.50
Fall Frost, 2002
73 thru 78 pt.1 thru pt. 6 . . . . . . @3.50
79 The Wind and the Crane 3.50
80 Petals on the Wind 3.50
81 Shadows 3.50
82 Mourning Shadows. 3.50
83 Path of Shadows. 3.50
84 Thorns. 3.50
85 Mirror of the Soul,pt.1 . . . . 3.00
86 Mirror of the Soul,pt.2 . . . . 3.00
87 Mirror of the Soul,pt.3 . . . . 3.00
88 Light and Shadow. 3.00
89 Crossroads 3.00
90 Last Blood,pt.1 . . . . 3.00
91 Last Blood,pt.2 . . . . 3.00
92 Last Blood,pt.3 . . . . 3.00
93 Last Blood,pt.4 . . . . 3.00
94 Last Blood,pt.5 . . . . 3.00
TPB Fall Frost 17.00
TPB Vol. 13 Mirror of the Soul. . . . 18.00

BLAIR WHICH?
Dec., 1999
1-shot SA, Scary as heck 3.50

BLANCHE GOES TO NEW YORK
1 Turn of the Century N.Y. 3.00

BLAST CORPS
Sept., 1998
1-shot F:demolition experts 2.50

BLOOD TIES
Nov., 2000
GN 15.00

BLOOD WORLD
March 2003
1 (of 3) 3.00
2 . . . . 3.00

BLUE LILY
1993
1 thru 3 . . . . @4.00

BMWFILMS.COM
—THE HIRE
July, 2004
1 MWg,Scandal 3.00
2 Precious Cargo 3.00

BODY BAGS
Aug., 1996
1 (of 4) 3.00
2 and 3 . . . . @3.00
TPB 13.00

BOOK OF NIGHT
(B&W) 1987
1 CV 2.50
2 CV 2.25
TPB Children of the Stars 13.00

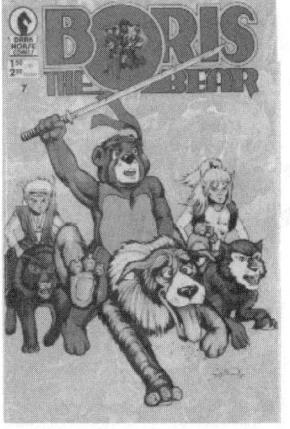

Boris the Bear #7
© Dark Horse Comics

BORIS THE BEAR
(B&W) 1986
1 V:Funny Animals 3.00
1a 2nd printing 2.25
2 V:Robots 2.25
3 V:Super Heroes 2.25
4 thru 7 . . . . @2.25
8 LargeSize. 2.50
9 thru 12 . . . . @2.25
See: B & W Pub. section
Color Classics 1987
1 thru 7 . . . . @2.25

B.P.R.D.
Mar., 2004
1 A Plague of Frogs 3.00
2 thru 5 A Plague of Frogs . . . . . @3.00

BRAVE
Mar., 1997
1 by Cully Hamner & Jason Martin. 3.00

BUBBLE GUM CRISIS:
GRAND MAL
(Manga) 1994
1 . . . . 2.75
2 and 3 . . . . @2.75
4 final issue. 2.50
TPB Rep.#1–#4 . . . . 15.00

BUFFY
THE VAMPIRE SLAYER
Sept., 1998
1 JoB,AAd(c) Wu-Tang Fang 10.00
1a 2nd printing 4.00
2 JoB, Halloween 6.00
3 JoB, Cold Turkey 6.00
4 White Christmas 6.00
5 Happy New Year 6.00
6 New Kid on the Block,pt.1 . . . . . . 6.00
7 JoB, New Kid on the Block,pt.2 . . 6.00
8 The Final Cut. 6.00
9 Hey, Good Looking,pt.1 . . . . 6.00
10 Hey, Good Looking,pt.2 . . . . 6.00
11 A Boy Named Sue. 6.00
12 A Nice Girl Like You 6.00
12a gold foil (c) 13.00
13 F:Cordelia Chase 5.00
14 Bad Blood,pt.5 . . . . 5.00
15 Bad Blood,pt.6 . . . . 5.00
16 Food Chain 5.00
17 Bad Blood,pt.7 . . . . 3.00
18 Mardi Gras 3.00
19 Bad Blood, concl. 3.00
20 Angel heads to L.A. 3.00
21 Blood of Carthage,pt.1 . . . . 3.00
22 Blood of Carthage,pt.2 . . . . 3.00
23 Blood of Carthage,pt.3 . . . . 3.00
24 Blood of Carthage,pt.4 . . . . 3.00
25 Blood of Carthage,concl. 3.00
26 Heart of the Slayer,pt.1 . . . . 3.00
27 Heart of the Slayer,pt.2 . . . . 3.00
28 revenge. 3.00
29 Past Lives,pt.2,Angel x-over. . . . 4.00
30 Past Lives,pt.4,Angel x-over . . . 4.00
31 Lost and Found. 4.00
32 hobo ghost 3.00
33 Demonic Entomology 3.00
34 Bug hunt, concl. 3.00
35 False Memories,pt.1 . . . . 3.00
36 False Memories,pt.2 . . . . 3.00
37 False Memories,pt.3 . . . . 3.00
38 False Memories,pt.4 . . . . 3.00
39 Night of a Thousand Vampires . . 3.00
40 JmP,Ugly Little Monsters,pt.1 . . 3.00
41 JmP,Ugly Little Monsters,pt.2 . . 3.00
42 JmP,Ugly Little Monsters,pt.3 . . 3.00
43 JmP,Death of Buffy,pt.1 . . . . 3.00
44 JmP,Death of Buffy,pt.2 . . . . 3.00
45 JmP,Death of Buffy,pt.3 . . . . 3.00
46 JmP,Withdrawal 3.00
47 Hellmouth to Mouth,pt.1 . . . . 3.00
48 Hellmouth to Mouth,pt.2 . . . . 3.00
49 Hellmouth to Mouth,pt.3 . . . . 3.00
50 Hellmouth to Mouth,pt.4 . . . . 3.50
51 SLo,FaN,Viva Las Buffy,pt.1 . . . 3.00
52 SLo,Viva Las Buffy, pt.2 . . . . 3.00
53 SLo,Viva Las Buffy, pt.3 . . . . 3.00
54 SLo,Viva Las Buffy, pt.4 . . . . 3.00
55 Dawn and Hoopy the Bear 3.00
56 Slayer, Interrupted,pt.1 . . . . 3.00
57 Slayer, Interrupted,pt.2 . . . . 3.00
58 Slayer, Interrupted,pt.3 . . . . 3.00
59 Slayer, Interrupted,pt.4 . . . . 3.00
60 FaN,A Stake to the Heart,pt.1. . . 3.00
61 FaN,A Stake to the Heart,pt.2. . . 3.00
62 FaN,A Stake to the Heart,pt.3. . . 3.00
63 FaN,A Stake to the Heart,pt.4. . . 3.00
2a–63a newsstand photo(c). . . . . @3.00
Ann. 1999, 64-pg. 5.00
Spec. 1-shot Spike and Dru 3.00
Spec. 1-shot Giles 3.00
　　Spec. 1-shot Giles, photo(c) . . . 3.00
Spec. 1-shot Jonathan. 3.00
　　Spec. 1-shotA photo (c). 3.00
Spec. 1-shot Lovers' Walk 3.00
　　Spec. 1-shotA photo (c). 3.00
Spec. 1-shot Spike & Dru—The
　　Queen of Hearts, photo (c) 3.00
Spec. 1-shot Spike & Dru—All'sFair 3.00

Spec. 1-shot Spike & Dru, ph(c) 3.00
Spec. 1-shot Willow & Tara 3.00
　　Spec. 1-shotA photo(c) 3.00
　　Spec. 1-shotB foil photo(c) . . . 10.00
Spec. 1-shotC foil photo(c) sgn 20.00
Spec. 1-shotD red foil 17.00
Spec.1-shot Lost & Found, FaN . . . 3.00
　　Spec.1-shotA photo (c) 3.00
Spec.1-shot Buffy the Vampire
　　Slayer/Angel: Reunion (2002) . . 3.00
　　Spec.1-shotA photo (c) 3.00
Spec.1-shot Tales of the Slayers
　　Broken Bottle of Djinn (2002) . . 3.50
　　Spec.1-shotA photo (c) 3.50
Spec. 1-shot Chaos Bleeds 3.00
　　Spec. Chaos Bleeds, photo(c). . 3.00
GN Ring of Fire, photo(c) 10.00
TPB The Dust Waltz 10.00
TPB The Remaining Sunlight 10.00
TPB Uninvited Guests 11.00
TPB The Origin 10.00
TPB Bad Blood 10.00
TPB Crash Test Demons,
　　rep.#9–#11. . . . . 10.00
TPB Pale Reflections, rep.#17–#19 10.00
TPB The Blood of Carthage. 11.00
TPB Spike and Dru 12.00
TPB Food Chain, 168-pg. 17.00
TPB Past Lives 10.00
TPB Autumnal 10.00
TPB Tales of the Slayer. 15.00
TPB Creatures of Habit (2002) . . . 18.00
TPB Out of the Woodwork (2002) . 13.00
TPB False Memories (2002) 13.00
TPB Ugly Little Monsters (2002) . . 13.00
TPB The Death of Buffy (2002) . . . 16.00
TPB Note From the Underground . 13.00
TPB Willow and Tara 10.00
TPB Viva Las Buffy 13.00
TPB Slayer, Interrupted 15.00
TPB A Stake to the Heart. 13.00

Buffy the Vampire Slayer: Angel #1
© Dark Horse Comics

BUFFY
THE VAMPIRE SLAYER:
ANGEL
May, 1999
1 (of 3) 3.00
2 & 3 . . . . @3.00
1a thru 3a newsstand, photo(c) . @3.00

BUFFY
THE VAMPIRE SLAYER:
HAUNTED
Dec., 2001
1 (of 4) deceased enemy's ghost . . 3.00
2 thru 4 . . . . @3.00
1a thru 4a photo (c) . . . . @3.00
TPB 96-pg. 13.00

BUFFY
THE VAMPIRE SLAYER:
THE ORIGIN
Feb., 1999
1 (of 3) DlB,JoB 3.00
2 & 3 . . . . @3.00
2a & 3a newsstand, photo(c) . . . @3.00
TPB rep. 10.00

BUFFY THE VAMPIRE
SLAYER: OZ
July, 2001
1 (of 3) 3.00
1a photo(c) 3.00
1b gold foil photo (c) 13.00
1c gold foil photo(c) signed. 25.00
1d fiery red foil photo(c) 17.00
2 . . . . 3.00
2a photo(c) 3.00
3 . . . . 3.00
3a photo(c) 3.00
TPB 80-pg. 10.00

BUFFY THE VAMPIRE
SLAYER: WILLOW AND
TARA — WILDERNESS
July, 2002
1 (of 2) 3.00
1a photo (c). 3.00
2 (of 2) 3.00
2a photo (c). 3.00

BY BIZARRE HANDS
(B&W) 1994
1 JLd(s). 2.50
2 JLd(s). 2.50
3 JLd(s). 2.50

CAIN
Nov., 2002
TPB 96-pg. B&W 10.00

CAL MCDONALD
MYSTERY
Jan., 2004
1-shot Love Me Tenderloin 3.00
1 thru 4 Last Train to Deadsville . @3.00
TPB Criminal Macabre. 15.00

CANNON GOD
EXAXXION
Manga, Nov., 2001
1 Stage 1, part 1 (of 8) 3.00
2 thru 8 Stage One,pt.2 thru pt.8 @3.00
9 Stage Two,pt.1 . . . . 3.00
10 Stage Two,pt.2 . . . . 3.50
11 Stage Two,pt.3 . . . . 3.50
13 thru 15. . . . . @3.50
16 thru 20 . . . . @3.00
TPB Stage One, rep., 208-pg. b&w 16.00
TPB Stage 2. . . . . 15.00
TPB Stage 3. . . . . 16.00

CARAVAN KIDD
(B&W–Manga) 1992
1 thru 10 by Johji Manabe . . . . . @2.50
[2nd Series] 1993
1 thru 10 F:Miam. . . . . @2.50
TPB Rep. #1–#10 . . . . 20.00
Holiday Spec. 2.50
Valentine's Day Spec. 2.50
[3rd Series] 1994
1 thru 8 . . . . @2.50
Christmas Special 2.50
TPB Vol. 2 . . . . 20.00
TPB Vol. 3 . . . . 20.00

CASTLE WAITING
2004
TPB Vol. 1 The Lucky Road 18.00

CATALYST: AGENTS
OF CHANGE
Comics' Greatest World, 1994
1 JPn(c),V:US Army 2.50
2 JPn(c),I:Grenade 2.50
3 JPn(c),Rebel vs. Titan 2.50
4 JPn(c),Titan vs. Grace. 2.50
5 JPn(c),V:Ape 2.50
6 and 7 . . . . @2.50

CHEVAL NOIR
(B&W) 1989
1 DSt(c). 4.00
2 thru 9 . . . . @3.50
10 80 pg. 4.50
11 80 pg. 4.50
12 MM(c) 4.50
13 thru 15. . . . . @4.50
16 thru 19 with 2-card strip . . . . @4.50
20 Great Power o/t Chninkel 4.50
21 Great Power o/t Chninkel 4.50
22 Great Power o/t Chninkel,concl. . 4.50
23 inc.'Rork','Forever War' concl. . . 4.50
24 In Dreams,pt.1 . . . . 4.50
25 In Dreams,pt.2 . . . . 4.50
26 In Dreams,pt.3 . . . . 4.50
27 I:The Man From Ciguri (Airtight
    Garage sequel) Dreams,pt.4 . . . 3.50
28 Ciguri cont. 3.50
29 Ciguri cont. 3.50
30 Ciguri,cont. 3.50
31 Angriest Dog in the World. 3.50
32 thru 40. . . . . @3.50
41 F:Demon. 3.50
42 F:Demon. 3.50
43 F:Demon. 3.50
44 F:Demon. 3.50
45 thru 47 . . . . @3.50
48 SwM(c). 3.50
49 F:Rork. 3.50
50 F:Rork. 3.50

CHOSEN
Dark Horse Dec., 2003
1 (of 3) MMr,PrG. 4.00
2 . . . . 3.00
3 . . . . 3.00
TPB 10.00

CHRONICLES OF CONAN
Sept., 2003
TPB Vol. 1 RTs,BWS reprints 16.00
TPB Vol. 2 Tower of the Elephant . 16.00
TPB Vol. 3 Monster of Monoliths. . 16.00
TPB Vol. 4 Red Nails. 16.00
TPB Vol. 5 Shadow in the Tomb . . 16.00
TPB Vol. 6 Curse of Golden Skull . 16.00

Chronowar #8
© Dark Horse Comics

CHRONOWAR
(B&W) Aug., 1996
1 (of 9) by Kazumasa Takayama . . 3.00
2 thru 9 . . . . @3.00

CLASSIC STAR WARS
1992
1 AW,newspaper strip reps. 6.00
2 thru 7 AW,newspaper reps. . . . @4.00
8 AW,newspaper reps. w/card 4.00
9 AW,newspaper reps. 3.50
10 AW,newspaper reps. 3.50
11 thru 19 AW,newspaper reps. . . @3.00
20 AW,newspaper strip reps., with
    trading card, final issue 4.00
TPB Vol. 1, In Deadly Pursuit . . . 16.00
TPB Vol. 1, rep. 2nd edition. 17.00
TPB Vol. 2, Rebel Storm 17.00
TPB Vol. 3, Escape to Hoth 17.00

CLASSIC STAR WARS:
A LONG TIME AGO
June, 2002
TPB Vol. 1 thru Vol. 3. . . . . @30.00
TPB Vol. 4 Screams in the Void . . 30.00
TPB Vol. 5 Fool's Bounty. 30.00
TPB Vol. 6 Wookiee World 30.00
TPB Vol. 7 Far, Far Away 30.00

CLASSIC STAR WARS:
A NEW HOPE
1994
1 AAd(c), rep. 4.25
2 AH(c), rep. 4.00
TPB Rep. #1–#2 . . . . 10.00

CLASSIC STAR WARS:
DEVILWORLDS
Aug., 1996
1 (of 2) by Alan Moore 2.50
2 . . . . 2.50

CLASSIC STAR WARS:
EARLY ADVENTURES
Aug., 1994–Apr., 1995
1 MiA(c), Gambler's World 3.00
2 RHo&MGr(c),Blackhole 2.50

3 EiS(c),Rebels of Vorzyd-5 . . . . . . 2.50
3 bagged with trading card DH2. . . 5.00
4 RHo(c),Tatooine 2.50
5 RHo(c),A:Lady Tarkin. 2.50
6 Weather Dominator 2.50
7 RHo(c),V:Darth Vader 2.50
8 KPI(c),X-Wing Secrets. 2.50
9 KPI(c),A:Boba Fett. 2.50
TPB RsM & AGw, AW(c) 20.00

CLASSIC STAR WARS: EMPIRE STRIKES BACK
1994
1 and 2 Movie Adaptation . . . . . . @4.00
TPB Rep.#1–#2 AW&CG(c). 10.00
TPB reprint, Hildebrandt(c) 10.00

Classic Star Wars Han Solo at Stars' End #1 © Dark Horse Comics

CLASSIC STAR WARS: HAN SOLO AT STAR'S END
Mar., 1997
1 thru 3 by Alfredo Alcala . . . . . . @3.00
TPB rep. AW(c) 7.00

CLASSIC STAR WARS: A LONG TIME AGO
(B&W) Mar., 1999
1 thru 6 rep. Marvel comics . . . . @6.00

CLASSIC STAR WARS: RETURN OF THE JEDI
1994
1 Movie Adaptation 4.00
2 Movie Adaptation 3.50
TPB Rep.#1–#2 . . . . 10.00
TPB rep. Hildebrandt(c) 10.00

CLASSIC STAR WARS: VANDELHELM MISSION
1995
1-shot F:Han Solo, Lando 4.00

CLONEZONE
(B&W) 1989
Spec #1 . . . . 2.25

CLOWNS, THE (PAGLIACCI)
Apr., 1998
1-shot B&W, CR. 3.00

CLUB 9
Feb., 2003
TPB B&W. 16.00
TPB Vol. 2 . . . . 16.00
TPB Vol. 3 . . . . 16.00

COLORS IN BLACK
Comics From Spike, 1995
1 B:Passion Play. 3.00
2 Images. 3.00
3 Back on the Bus 3.00
4 final issue. 3.00

COMIC BOOK
1 thru 4 9'x12' John Kricfalusi. . . @6.00

COMICS & STORIES
1996
1 (of 4) by Martin & Millionaire 3.00
2 thru 4 . . . . @3.00

COMICS' GREATEST WORLD
1993
(Arcadia)
1 B:MRi(s),FM(c),B:LW,B:O:Vortex,
  F:X,I:Seekers 3.00
1a B&W proof ed. (1,500 made). . . 9.00
1b Hologram(c), with cards. 7.00
2 JoP,I:Pit Bulls. 2.25
3 AH,I:Ghost 5.00
4 I:Monster 2.50
TPB Arcadia. 25.00
(Golden City)
1 B:BKs(s),JOy(c),I:Rebel,
  Amaz.Grace,V:WarMaker 2.50
1a Gold Ed. 5.00
2 I:Mecha 2.25
3 WS(c),I:Titan 2.25
4 E:BKs(s),GP(c),JD,I:Catalyst. . . 2.25
TPB Golden City 11.00
(Steel Harbor)
1 B:CW(s),PG,I:Barb Wire,
  V:Ignition 2.25
2 MMi(c),TNa,I:Machine 2.25
3 CW(a&s),I:Wolf Gang 2.25
4 E:CW(s),VGi,I:Motorhead 2.25
TPB Steel Harbor. 11.00
(Vortex)
1 B:RSd(s),LW,DoM,I:Division 13 . . 2.25
2 I:Hero Zero. 2.25
3 PC,I:King Tiger 2.25
4 B:RSd(s),E:MRi(s)BMc,E:LW,
  E:O:Vortex,C:Vortex 2.25
TPB Vortex. 11.00
Sourcebook 10.00

COMPLETELY PIP AND NORTON
DH Maverick, Sept., 2002
TPB 72-pg. 10.00

CONAN
Feb., 2004
1 KBk,CNr,JLi(c) from R.E.Howard 9.00
1a JSC(c) 2nd printing 5.00
1b CNr(c) 3rd printing 3.00
2 Frost Giant's Daughter 4.00

3 Asgard 3.00
4 Hyperborea 3.00
5 Breaks out of slavery 3.00
6 Rebel 3.00
7 Rebellion 3.00
8 Born on the Battlefield 3.00
9 KBk,CNr. 3.00
Spec. #1 Daughters of Midora 5.00
1-shot KBk,CNr,Conan the Legend
  prologue (2003) 0.25

CONCRETE
(B&W) 1987
1 PC,R:Concrete, A Stone among
  Stones 11.00
1a 2nd printing 3.00
2 PC,'Transatlantic Swim'. 7.00
3 PC 5.00
4 PC 4.00
5 PC,'An Armchair Stuffed with
  Dynamite'. 4.00
6 PC,Concrete works on farm 4.00
7 PC,Concrete grows horns 4.00
8 PC,Climbs Mount Everest 4.00
9 PC,Mount Everest,pt.2. . . . . 4.00
10 PC,last Issue. 4.00
TPB The Complete Concrete. 25.00
Spec. #1 Concrete ColorSpec.,PC
  (1989) 4.00
Spec. Concrete Celebrates Earth Day
  PC,Moebius (1990) 2.50
Spec. 1 A New Life, B&W rep.,
  O: Concrete (1989) 3.50
Spec. Concrete: Land & Sea,
  rep. #1 & #2 (1989) 3.25
Spec. Concrete: Odd Jobs,
  rep. #5 & #6 (1990) 3.50

CONCRETE: ECLECTICA
1993
1 PC,The Ugly Boy. 3.25
2 PC 3.25

CONCRETE: FRAGILE CREATURE
1991
1 PC,Rulers o/t Omniverse,pt.1 . . . 4.00
2 PC,Rulers o/t Omniverse,pt.2 . . . 3.00
3 PC,Rulers o/t Omniverse,pt.3 . . . 3.00
4 PC,Rulers o/t Omniverse,pt.3 . . . 3.00
TPB 16.00

Concrete: Killer Smile #1 © Dark Horse Comics

DARK HORSE

CONCRETE: KILLER SMILE
DH Legend, 1994
1 PC 3.50
2 thru 4 PC . . . . @3.00
TPB Rep.#1–#4 . . . . 17.00

CONCRETE: STRANGE ARMOR
Dec., 1997–Apr., 1998
1 (of 5) 3.00
2 thru 5 . . . . @3.00
TPB Strange Armor 17.00

CONCRETE: THINK LIKE A MOUNTAIN
(B&W) 1996
1 thru 6 PC,GfD(c) . . . . @3.00
TPB PC,GfD(c) 18.00

CORMAC MAC ART
July, 1989
1 Robert E. Howard adapt. 3.00
2 . . . . 3.00
3 . . . . 3.00

CORNY'S FETISH
April 1998
GN by Renee French, 64-pg. 5.00

COUTOO
(B&W)
1 Lt. Joe Kraft 3.50

CREEPY
(B&W) 1992
1 KD,TS,GC,SL,Horror 4.00
2 TS,CI,DC,Demonic Baby 4.00
3 JM,TS,JG,V:Killer Clown 4.00
4 TS,Final issue 4.00

CREATURE FROM THE BLACK LAGOON
1 Movie Adaptation 5.00

CRIMINAL MACABRE
May, 2003
1 (of 5) F:Cal McDonald 4.00
2 thru 5 . . . . @3.00

CRITICAL ERROR
1992
1 rep.Classic JBy story 2.75

[ANDREW VACHSS'] CROSS
1995
0 GfD(c),I:Cross,Rhino,Princess. . . 2.50
1 thru 7 . . . . @3.00

CROW, THE
June, 2004
TPB Flesh and Blood 10.00

CRUSH
DH Rocket Comics, Oct., 2003
1 . . . . 3.00
2 thru 4 . . . . @3.00
TPB 13.00

CUD COMICS
(B&W) 1996
1 thru 8 by Terry LaBan . . . . @3.00

THE CURSE OF DRACULA
July, 1998
1 (of 3) MWn,GC 3.00
2 thru 3 . . . . @3.00

DANGER UNLIMITED
DH Legend, 1994
1 JBy(a&s),KD,I:Danger Unlimited,
  B:BU:Torch of Liberty 2.50
2 JBy(a&s),KD,O:DangerUnlimited. 2.50
3 JBy(a&s),KD,O:Torch of Liberty. . 2.50
4 JBy(a&s),KD,Final Issue 2.50
TPB rep. #1–#4 . . . . 15.00

DARE DETECTIVES, THE
Oct., 2004
TPB Vol. 1 . . . . 6.00

DARK HORSE CLASSICS
(B&W) 1992
1 Last of the Mohicans 4.50
2 20,000 Leagues Under the Sea . 4.50

DARK HORSE CLASSICS: ALIENS VS. PREDATOR
Feb., 1997
1 thru 6 Rep. . . . . @3.00

DARK HORSE CLASSICS: GODZILLA, KING OF THE MONSTERS
July, 1998
1 RSd,SBi,now color. 3.00
2 rep. from 1995 . . . . 3.00
3 rep. from 1995 . . . . 3.00
4 rep. Godzilla #2, from 1995 . . . . . 3.00
5 & 6 . . . . @3.00

DARK HORSE CLASSICS: PREDATOR: JUNGLE TALES
1-shot Rep. 3.00

DARK HORSE CLASSICS: STAR WARS— DARK EMPIRE
1997
1 rep. by Tom Veitch,CK,DvD(c). . . 3.00
2 thru 6 rep., DvD(c) . . . . @3.00

DARK HORSE CLASSICS: TERROR OF GODZILLA
Aug., 1998
1 by Kazuhisa Iwata, AAd(c). 3.00
2 & 3 . . . . @3.00
4 rep. of 1988 B&W 3.00
5 & 6 AAd(c) . . . . @3.00

DARK HORSE COMICS
1992
1 RL,CW,F:Predator,Robocop,
  I:Renegade,Time Cop,(double
  gatefold cover). 4.00
2 RL,CW,F:Predator,Robocop,
  Renegade,Time Cop 3.00

3 CW,F:Robocop,Time Cop,Aliens,
  Indiana Jones 3.00
4 F:Predator,Aliens,Ind.Jones. 3.00
5 F:Predator,E:Aliens 3.00
6 F:Robocop,Predator, E:Indiana
  Jones 3.00
7 F:Robocop,Predator,B:StarWars . 6.00
8 B&I:X,Robocop 8.00
9 F:Robocop,E:Star Wars 4.00
10 E:X,B:Godzilla,Predator,
  James Bond 3.50
11 F:Godzilla,Predator,James
  Bond,B:Aliens 2.75
12 F:Predator. 2.75
13 F:Predator,B:Thing 2.75
14 MiB(s),B:The Mark 2.75
15 MiB(s),E:The Mark,B:Aliens . . . 2.75
16 B:Predator,E:Thing,Aliens. 2.75
17 B:Aliens,Star Wars:Droids. 2.75
18 E:Predator. 2.75
19 RL(c),B:X,E:Star Wars:Droids,
  Aliens. 2.75
20 B:Predator. 2.75
21 F:Mecha 2.75
22 B:Aliens, E:Mecha 2.75
23 B:The Machine 2.75
24 The Machine. 2.75
25 Final issue. 2.75

DARK HORSE DOWNUNDER
(B&W) 1994
1 F:Australian Writers 2.50
2 Australian Writers. 2.50
3 Australian Writers, finale 2.50

DARK HORSE MAVERICK
Ann.2000 48-pg. B&W 5.00
Ann.2001 48-pg. B&W 5.00

DARK HORSE MONSTERS
Feb., 1997
1-shot. 3.00

DARK HORSE PRESENTS
(B&W) 1986
1 PC,I:Concrete 15.00
1a 2nd printing 2.50

Dark Horse Monsters #1
© Dark Horse Comics

All comics prices listed are for *Near Mint* condition.

2 PC,Concrete	6.00
3 Boris theBear,Concrete	5.00
4 PC,Concrete	5.00
5 PC,Concrete	5.00
6 PC,Concrete	5.00
7 I:MONQ	5.00
8 PC,Concrete	5.00
9	5.00
10 PC,Concrete, I:Masque	10.00
11 Masque	6.00
12 PC,Concrete, Masque	5.00
13 Masque	5.00
14 PC,Concrete, Masque	5.00
15 Masque	5.00

Dark Horse Presents #14
© Dark Horse Comics

16 PC,Concrete, Masque	5.00
17	5.00
18 PC,Concrete, Mask.	5.00
19 Masque	5.00
20 double,Flaming Carrot	9.00
21 Masque	5.00
22 I:Duckman	5.00
23	5.00
24 PC,I:Aliens	20.00
25 thru 31	@3.00
32 A:Concrete	4.00
33	3.00
34 Aliens	4.00
35 Predator	4.00
36 Aliens vs.Predator	4.00
36a painted cover	5.00
37	3.00
38 A:Concrete	3.00
39	3.00
40 I:The Aerialist	3.00
41	3.00
42 Aliens	5.00
43 Aliens	4.00
44	3.00
45	3.00
46 Predator	4.00
47 Monkers	3.00
48 with 2-card strip	3.00
49 with 2-card strip	3.00
50 inc.'Heartbreakers', with 2-card strip	4.00
51 FM(c),inc.'Sin City'	4.00
52 FM,inc. 'Sin City'	4.00
53 FM,inc. 'Sin City'	4.00
54 FM,Sin City;JBy Preview of Next Men,pt.1	5.00
55 FM,Sin City;JBy Preview of Next Men (JBy),pt.2	6.00
56 FM,Sin City,JBy,Next MenPt.3 Aliens Genocide(prologue)	5.00

57 FM,SinCity;JBy Next Men,pt.4	5.00
58 FM,Sin City,Alien Fire	5.00
59 FM,Sin City,Alien Fire	5.00
60 FM,Sin City	5.00
61 FM,Sin City	5.00
62 FM,E:Sin City	5.00
63 Moe,Marie Dakar	3.00
64 MWg,R:The Aerialist	3.00
65 B:Accidental Death	3.00
66 PC,inc.Dr.Giggles	3.00
67 B:Predator story (lead in to 'Race War'),double size	4.50
68 F:Predator,Swimming Lessons (Nestrobber tie-in)	3.00
69 F:Predator	3.00
70 F:Alec	3.00
71 F:Madwoman	3.00
72 F:Eudaemon	3.00
73 F:Eudaemon	3.00
74 F:Eudaemon	3.00
75 F:Chairman	3.00
76 F:Hermes Vs.the Eye,Ball Kid	2.50
77 F:Hermes Vs.the Eye,Ball Kid	2.50
78 F:Hermes Vs.the Eye,Ball Kid	2.50
79 B:Shadow Empires Slaves	2.50
80 AAd,I:Monkey Man & O'Brien	5.00
81 B:Buoy	3.00
82 B:Just Folks	3.00
83 Last Impression	3.00
84 MBn,F:Nexus,E:Hermes Vs. the Eye Ball Kid	3.00
85 Winner Circle, Eighth Woman	3.00
86 Eighth Woman	3.00
87 F:Concrete	4.00
88 Hellboy	3.00
89 Hellboy	3.00
90 Hellboy	3.00
91 Blackheart, Baden	3.00
92 Too Much Coffee Man	6.00
93 Cud, Blackheart,Coffee Man	8.00
94 A:Eyeball Kid,Coffee Man	6.00
95 Too Much Coffee Man	7.00
96 Kabuli Kid	3.00
97 F:Kabuki Kid	3.00
98 Pot Full of Noodles	3.00
99 Anthology title	3.00
100–#1 Lance Blastoff	3.00
100–#2 Hellboy	3.00
100–#3 Concrete	3.00
100–#4 Black Cross.	3.00
100–#5 Pan Fried Girl	3.00
101 BW,F:Aliens	3.00
102 F:Mr. Painter	3.00
103 F:The Pink Tornado	3.00
104 F:The Pink Tornado	3.00
105 F:The Pink Tornado	3.00
106 F:Godzilla	3.00
107 F:Rusty Razorclam	3.00
108	3.00
109	3.00
110 F:Egg.	3.00
111 Ninth Gland	3.00
112 three stories, concl.	3.00
113 Trypto the Acid Dog	3.00
114 F:Star Slammers/Lance Blastoff	3.00
115 flip-book Dr. Spin/The Creep	3.00
116 Fat Dog Mendoza	3.00
117 F:Aliens	3.00
118 Monkeyman O'Brien	3.00
119 Trout	3.00
120 'One Last Job'.	3.00
121 F: Imago	3.00
122 'Lords of Misrule'.	3.00
123 F: Jack Zero	3.00
124 F:Predator	3.00
125 F:Nocturnals	3.00
126 flip book, 48-pg.	4.50
127 F:The Nocturnals	3.00
128 F:Dan & Larry	3.00
129 F:Hammer.	3.00
130 F:Wanted Man	3.00

131 F:Girl Crazy	3.00
132 flip book	3.00
133 F:Tarzan	3.00
134 F:The Dirty Pair	3.00
135 F:The Fall, concl.	3.00
136 The Ark	3.00
137 Predator	3.00
138 F:Terminators	3.00
139 F:Roachmill	3.00
140 F:Aliens	3.00
141 F:Buffy the Vampire Slayer	3.00
142 F:Lovecraftian tales	3.00
143 F:Tarzan tales	3.00
144 F:Vortex	3.00
145 F:Burglar Girls	3.00
146 F:Aliens vs. Predator	3.00
147 F:Ragnok	3.00
148	3.00
149 Wunderkind	3.00
150 F:Buffy, 48-pg.	4.50
151 F:Hellboy	3.00
152 It! The Beast from Twenty Billion Years Beyond Earth	3.00
153 Helm of Harxis	3.00
154 Iron Reich 3000, flip-book	3.00
155 Angel, flip-book	3.00
156 Witch's Son, flip-book	3.00

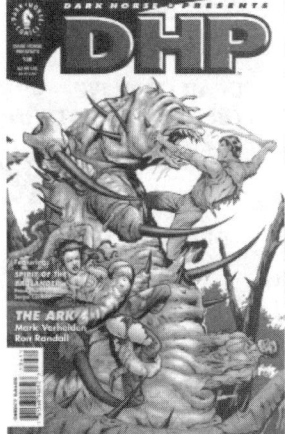

Dark Horse Presents #136
© Dark Horse Comics

157 F:Witch's Son, final issue	3.00
Fifth Anniv. Special DGi,PC, SBi,CW,MW,FM,Sin City, Aliens,Give Me Liberty	8.00
Ann. 1997 F:Body Bags.	5.00
Ann. 1998 F:Hellboy	5.00
Ann. 1999 DHP, JR.	5.00
Ann.2000 Girls Rule, 64-pg.	5.00
Milestone Ed.#1,rep.DHP#1	2.25
TPB rep.Sin City	6.00
TPB Best of DHP #1–#20	10.00
TPB Best of DHP #1–#20 2nd ed.	10.00
TPB Best of DHP #21–#30	9.00
TPB Best of DHP #31–#50	9.00
TPB Best of Dark Horse Presents Two	9.00
TPB Best of Dark Horse Presents Three	13.00

DARK HORSE PRESENTS: ALIENS

1 Rep.	5.00
1a Platinum Edition.	8.00

DARKNESS FALLS: THE TOOTH FAIRY— THE TRAGIC LIFE OF MATILDA DIXON
Jan., 2003
1-shot CAd 3.00

DEADFACE: DOING ISLANDS WITH BACCHUS
(B&W) 1991
1 rep. Bacchus apps. 3.00
2 rep. inc.'Book-Keeper of Atlantis . 3.00

DEADFACE: EARTH, WATER, AIR & FIRE
(B&W) 1992
1 Bacchus & Simpson in Sicily 2.50
2 A:Don Skylla 2.50
3 Mafia/Kabeirol-War prep 2.50
4 Last issue 2.50

DEAD IN THE WEST
(B&W) 1993
1 TT,Joe Landsdale adapt 5.00
2 TT,adapt 5.00
Spec. #1 TT(c) 4.00

DEAD OR ALIVE— A CYBERPUNK WESTERN
Apr., 1998
1 (of 4) by Tatjana and Alberto
   Ponticelli 2.50
2 thru 4 . . . . @2.50

DEADLINE USA
(B&W) 1991
1 rep. Deadline UK,Inc. Tank Girl
   Johnny Nemo 10.00
2 inc. Tank Girl,Johnny Nemo 10.00

DEAD TO RIGHTS
Oct., 2002
1-shot 64-pg. 6.00

DECADE OF DARK HORSE, A
1996
1 (of 4) inc. Star Wars, Nexus,
   Ghost 3.00
2 thru 4 . . . . @3.00

[RANDY BOWEN'S] DECAPITATOR
June, 1998
1 (of 4) GEr,DoM 3.00
2 GEr 3.00
3 MMi,KJo,AAI 3.00
4 MMi, conclusion 3.00

DEVIL CHEF
1994
1 I:Devil Chef 2.50

DEVIL'S FOOTPRINTS
March 2003
1 (of 4) 3.00
2 thru 4 . . . . @3.00
TPB 15.00

DIABLO: TALES OF SANCTUARY
Nov., 2001
1-shot 64-pg. 6.00

DIGIMON
June, 2000, Bi-weekly
1 . . . . 3.00
2 thru 6 . . . . @3.00
7 thru 12 ND(c) 3.00
TPB Digital Monsters 10.00

DIRTY PAIR
(B&W–Manga) 1999
TPB Book 3 A Plague of Angels . . 13.00
TPB Dangerous Acquaintances . . . 13.00
TPB Biohazards 13.00
1-shot Start the Violence, AWa(c) . . 3.00
1-shot Start the Violence, JPn(c) . . 3.00

DIRTY PAIR: FATAL BUT NOT SERIOUS
(Manga)1995
1 R:Kei,Yuri 3.00
2 V:Kevin Sleet,Yuri 3.00
3 Anti Yuri 3.00
4 V:Terrorists 3.00
5 conclusion 3.00

DIRTY PAIR: RUN FROM THE FUTURE
Jan., 2000
1 (of 4) AWa(c) 3.00
1a AH(c) 3.00
2 AWa(c) 3.00
2a BSf(c) 3.00
3 AWa(c) 3.00
3a Bruce Timm(c) 3.00
4 AWa(c) 3.00
4a HuR(c) 3.00
TPB series rep. 15.00

DIRTY PAIR: SIM HELL
(B&W–Manga) 1993
1 thru 4 by Adam Warren . . . . . . @3.25
TPB rep. #1–#4 . . . . 14.00

DIRTY PAIR: SIM HELL: REMASTERED
May, 2001
1 (of 4) full color, AWa 3.00
2 thru 4 AWa . . . . @3.00
TPB 3rd. ed. 15.00

DISNEY'S ATLANTIS THE LOST EMPIRE
June, 2001
GN 56-pg. color 7.00

DISNEY'S TARZAN
June, 1999
1 and 2 Animated movie adapt. . . @3.00

DIVISION 13
1 & 2 . . . . @2.50
3 A:Payback 2.50
4 Carnal Genesis 2.50

DOC SAVAGE: CURSE OF THE FIRE GOD
1 R:Man of Bronze 3.00

2 Exploding Plane 3.00
3 & 4 . . . . @3.00

DR. GIGGLES
1 Horror movie adapt 2.50
2 Movie adapt.contd 2.50

DR. ROBOT
Apr., 2000
1-shot, by Bernie E. Mireault 3.00

DOMINION
(B&W–Manga)
TPB 1 by Masamune Shirow 15.00
TPB 2nd printing 15.00
TPB 3rd edition 17.00

DOMINION: CONFLICT 1 — NO MORE NOISE
(B&W–Manga) 1996
1 thru 6 by Masamune Shirow . . @3.00
TPB series rep. 15.00

DOMINION SPECIAL: PHANTOM OF THE AUDIENCE
(B&W–Manga)
1-shot by Masamune Shirow 2.50

DOMU: A CHILD'S DREAMS
(B&W–Manga)
1 Psychic Warfare 6.00
2 Murders Continue 6.00
3 Psychic war conclusion 6.00
TPB by Katsuhiro Otomo 18.00
TPB 2nd edition 18.00

DRACULA
1 Movie Adaptation 5.00

DRAKUUN
(B&W) Feb., 1997
Rise of the Dragon Princess
1 (of 6) by Johji Manabe 3.00
2 thru 6 . . . . @3.00
TPB rep. 13.00

Drakuun #6
© Dark Horse Comics

The Revenge of Gustav (Aug., 1997)
7 (1 of 6) by Johji Manabe 3.00
8 thru 12 pt.2 thru pt.6 . . . . @3.00
TPB, rep. 15.00
Shadow of the Warlock (Feb., 1998)
13 (1 of 6) by Johji Manabe. 3.00
14 thru 18 pt.2 thru pt.6 . . . . @3.00
TPB rep. 15.00
The Hidden War (Sept., 1998)
19 (1 of 6) by Johji Manabe. 3.00
20 thru 24 pt.2 thru pt.6 . . . . @3.00
Flames of Empire (1999)
25 Flames of Empire (1 of 6). 3.00

DRAWING ON YOUR NIGHTMARES
Oct., 2003
1-shot Halloween 2003 Special 1 . . 4.00
1-shot Halloween Special 2 . . . . . 10.00

DYLAN DOG
(B&W) Bonelli Mar., 1999
1 (of 6) by Tiziano Di Sclavi & Angelo

Edgar Rice Burroughs' Tarzan #3
© Dark Horse Comics

Stano, MMi(c), 96-pg. 5.00
2 thru 6 . . . . @5.00
TPB Zed 96-pg. b&w 6.00

EDGAR RICE BURROUGHS' RETURN OF TARZAN
Apr., 1997
1 adapted by Thomas Yeates
    & John Totleben. 3.00
2 thru 3 . . . . @3.00

EDGAR RICE BURROUGHS' TARZAN
1996
Mugambi
1 Betrayed by 3 man-beasts 3.00
2 'Tarzan's Jungle Fury' 3.00
3 'Tarzan's Jungle Fury' 3.00
4 vs. the Tara virus 3.00
5 Cure to the Tara virus 3.00
6 . . . . 3.00
Tarzan and the Legion of Hate
7 pt.1. . . . . 3.00

8 pt.2. . . . . 3.00
9 pt.3. . . . . 3.00
10 pt.4, concl.. . . . . 3.00
Le Monstre, June, 1997
11 pt.1 . . . . 3.00
12 pt.2 Bernie Wrightson(c) 3.00
Modern Prometheus, Aug., 1997
13 pt.1 MK(c) in New York. 3.00
14 pt.2 MK(c) 3.00
Tooth and Nail, Oct., 1997
15 pt.1 MSh(c) 3.00
16 pt.2 . . . . 3.00
TPB adapts #11–#16 . . . . 17.00
Tarzan vs. the Moon Men
17 TT,AW,TY 3.00
18 TT,AW,TY 3.00
19 TT,AW,TY 3.00
20 TT,AW,TY 3.00
Primeval
21 MGr. 3.00
22 MGr. 3.00
23 MGr. 3.00
24 MGr. 3.00
TPB RsM,The Land That Time
    Forgot 13.00
TPB Tarzan of the Apes. 13.00
TPB The Jewls of Opar 11.00

EDGAR RICE BURROUGHS' TARZAN: CARSON OF VENUS
May, 1998
1 (of 4) by Darko Macan and
    Igor Kordey, F:Carson Napier . . 3.00
2 thru 4 novels adapt. . . . . @3.00
TPB Carson of Venus 13.00

EDGAR RICE BURROUGHS' TARZAN: THE LOST ADVENTURE
1995
1 Lost Manuscript 3.00
2 V:Gorgo the Buffalo 3.00
3 V:Bandits 3.00
4 V:Bandits 3.00

EDGAR RICE BURROUGHS' TARZAN: THE RIVERS OF BLOOD
Nov., 1999
1 . . . . 3.00
2 thru 8 . . . . @3.00

EDGAR RICE BURROUGHS' TARZAN— THE SAVAGE HEART
Apr., 1999
1 (of 4) MGr Jane is dead. 3.00
2 thru 4 . . . . @3.00

EGON
Jan.–Feb., 1998
1 and 2 . . . . @3.00

EIGHTH WONDER, THE
Nov., 1997
1-shot by P. Janes & K. Plunkett . . . 3.00

ELECTRIC FRANKENSTEIN
Jan., 2004
TPB 20.00

Elric: Stormbringer #7
© Dark Horse Comics

ELRIC: STORMBRINGER
DH/Topps, 1996
1 by Michael Moorcock & CR 3.00
2 thru 7 (of 7) . . . . @3.00
TPB rep. series 18.00

EL ZOMBO
April 2004
1 (of 3) 3.00
2 and 3 . . . . @3.00

ENEMY
1 MZ(c),StG(s),I:Enemy 2.75
2 MZ(c),StG(s),F:Heller. 2.75
3 MZ(c),StG(s),A:Heller 2.50
4 . . . . 2.50
5 final issue. 3.00
TPB 15.00

ENO AND PLUM
Sept., 1997
TPB 13.00

EUDAEMON, THE
1 Nel,I:New Eudaemon. 3.00
2 Nel,V:Mordare 2.75
3 Nel,V:Mordare 2.75

EVIL DEAD III: ARMY OF DARKNESS
1 JBo,Movie adaptation 4.00
2 JBo,Movie adaptation 3.50
3 JBo,Movie adaptation 3.00

EXOTICS, THE
TPB by Moebius 8.00

EYEBALL KID
(B&W)
1 I:Eyeball Kid. 2.25
2 V:Stygian Leech. 2.25
3 V:Telchines Brothers,last iss. . . . 2.25

FAT DOG MENDOZA
(B&W) 1992
1 I&O:Fat Dog Mendoza. 2.50

DARK HORSE

DARK HORSE (side tab)

FAX FROM SARAJEVO
Oct., 1996
GN JKu, 224 pg. 25.00

FEEDERS
Oct., 1999
1-shot MiA, prequel to Eyes
to Heaven 3.00

FELIX THE CAT'S GREATEST HITS
Sept., 2002
TPB 96-pg. 10.00

FIERCE
June, 2004
1 . . . . 3.00
2 thru 4 . . . . @3.00

F5 ORIGIN
1-shot, rep. 3.00

FLAMING CARROT
(B&W) 2001
Previous issues: see B&W section
18 . . . . 4.00
18a Ash-Can-Limited 4.00
19 . . . . 4.00
20 . . . . 4.00
21 . . . . 3.00
22 . . . . 3.00
23 . . . . 3.00
24 . . . . 4.00
25 F:TMNT,Mysterymen, with
2-card strip 3.00
26 A:TMNT. 3.00
27 TM(c),A:TMNT conclusion 3.00
28 . . . . 3.00
29 Man in the Moon,Iron City 3.00
30 V:Man in the Moon 3.00
31 A:Fat Fury 3.00
Ann. 1 by Bob Burden 5.00
TPB Man of Mystery, B&W 13.00
TPB The Wild Shall Wild Remain
rep. #4–#11 . . . . 18.00
TPB Flaming Carrot's Greatest Hits,
rep. #12–#18 . . . . 18.00
TPB Fortune Favors the Bold,
rep.#19–#24 . . . . 17.00

FLAXEN
1 Based on Model,w/poster 3.00

FLOATERS
(B&W) 1993–94
1 thru 6 From Spike Lee . . . . @2.50

FLOOD!
DH Maverick, 2002
TPB 160-pg. 15.00

FOOT SOLDIERS, THE
1 thru 4 by Jim Krueger 3.00
TPB 15.00
See also Image Comics

FORT: PROPHET OF THE UNEXPLAINED
June, 2002
1 (of 4) F:Charles Fort 3.00
2 thru 4 . . . . @3.00
TPB 96-pg. B&W 10.00

FRANKENSTEIN
1 Movie Adaptation 4.00

FRAY
2001
1 . . . . 8.00
1a 2nd printing 3.00
2 thru 3 . . . . @4.00
4 thru 5 . . . . @3.00
6 thru 8 . . . . @7.50

FREAKSHOW
1 JBo,DMc,KB, 'Wanda the Worm
Woman,' 'Lillie'. 10.00

FREAKS OF THE HEARTLAND
Jan., 2004
1 (of 6) horror 3.00
2 thru 5 . . . . @3.00

FUSED: THINK LIKE A MACHINE
Dec., 2003
1 Robotic Cy-Bot. 3.00
2 . . . . 3.00
3 . . . . 3.00
4 . . . . 3.00
TPB Canned Heat 13.00
TPB Think Like A Machine. 13.00

FUTURE WORLD
Sept., 2003
TPB Vol. 1 b&w,160-pg. 14.00
TPB Vol. 2 . . . . 14.00

GALACTIC
DH Rocket Comics Aug., 2003
1 . . . . 3.00
2 & 3 . . . . @3.00
TPB 10.00

GAMERA
Aug., 1996
1 (of 4) by Dave Chipps &
Mozart Couto. 3.00
2 thru 4 . . . . @3.00

Gamera #3
© Dark Horse Comics

GARY GIANNI'S MONSTERMEN
Aug., 1999
1-shot. 3.00

GHOST
Comics' Greatest World
Spec. AH(c) 4.00

GHOST
1995
1 by Eric Luke, R:Ghost 7.00
2 AH,MfM,Arcadia Nocturne,pt.2 . . 4.00
3 Arcadia Nocturn,pt.3 . . . . 4.00
4 . . . . 3.00
5 V:Predator 3.00
6 . . . . 3.00
7 Hell Night 3.00
8 thru 21 . . . . @3.00
22 The key is forever beyond
your reach 3.00
23 I: The Goblins 3.00
24 X is dead. 3.00
25 double size 4.00
26 Fairytale version 3.50
27 . . . . 3.50
28 CW(c),Painful Music,pt.1 . . . . . 3.50
29 CW(c),Painful Music,pt.2 . . . . . 3.50
30 CW(c),Painful Music,pt.3 . . . . . 3.50
31 CW(c),Painful Music,pt.4 . . . . . 3.50
32 A Pathless Land 3.50
33 Jade Cathedral,pt.1 . . . . 3.50
34 Jade Cathedral,pt.2 . . . . 3.50
35 Jade Cathedral,pt.3 . . . . 3.50
36 Jade Cathedral,pt.4 . . . . 3.50
Spec.#2 Immortal Coil 4.50
Spec.#3 Scary Monsters 4.50
TPB Ghost Stories 9.00
TPB Ghost: Nocturnes. 10.00
TPB Exhuming Elisa 18.00

GHOST
Sept., 1998
1 CW,O:Ghost. 3.00
2 CW,V:Dr.Trouvaille. 3.00
3 CW,V:Silhouette. 3.00
4 CW,The Devil Inside,O:pt.1 . . . . 3.00
5 CW,Stare at the Sun,O:pt.2 . . . . 3.00
6 CW,Stare at the Sun,O:pt.3 . . . . 3.00
7 CW,Shifter,pt.1,F:King Tiger 3.00
8 CW,Shifter,pt.2. . . . . 3.00
9 CW,Shifter,pt.3. . . . . 3.00
10 CW,Shifter,pt.4 . . . . 3.00
11 CW,back in Arcadia. 3.00
12 Red Shadows,pt.1 (of 4). 3.00
13 Red Shadows,pt.2 . . . . 3.00
14 Red Shadows,pt.3 . . . . 3.00
15 Red Shadows,pt.4 . . . . 3.00
16 When the Devil Daydreams,pt.1 . 3.00
17 When the Devil Daydreams,pt.2. 3.00
18 rogue agent. 3.00
19 Arcadia in chaos 3.00
20 F:Chris 3.00
21 F:Malcolm Greymater 3.00
22 final issue 3.00
TPB Black October 15.00
TPB Painful Music 10.00
TPB No World So Dark 15.00
Spec. Handbook #1 . . . . 3.00

GHOST/BATGIRL
Aug., 2000
1 (of 4) RBn,A:oracle 3.00
2 RBn,V:Two-Face 3.00
3 RBn,V:Carver, Greymater 3.00
4 RBn,concl 3.00
TPB 96-pg. 12.00

Ghost/Hellboy #1
#2 © Dark Horse Comics

GHOST/HELLBOY
1996
1 & 2 MMi 3.50
TPB Ghost Hellboy Collection,MMi . 5.00

GHOST AND
THE SHADOW
1995
Spec. 1-shot 3.00

GHOST IN THE SHELL
(Manga) 1995
1 Manga Style 25.00
2 Wetware Virus 20.00
3 Killer Robots 10.00
4 thru 8 . . . . @8.00
TPB by Masamune Shirow 25.00

GHOST IN THE SHELL 2:
MAN-MACHINE
INTERFACE
Oct., 2002
1 40-pg.by Masamune Shirow 4.00
2 32-pg. 3.50
3 thru 11 . . . . @3.50
Spec. #1 Holographic Edition 5.00

G.I. JOE
1995
1 by Mike Barr & Tatsuya Ishida . . . 3.00
2 thru 4 . . . . @3.00
Vol. 2 1996
1 . . . . 3.00
2 thru 4 . . . . @3.00

GIRL CRAZY
TPB by GHe, rep.#1–#3 . . . . 10.00

GIVE ME LIBERTY
1990
1 FM/DGb, Homes & Gardens 6.00
2 FM/DGb 5.00
3 and 4 FM/DGb . . . . @5.00
TPB 16.00
TPB Dell edition 16.00

GO BOY 7: HUMAN
ACTION MACHINE
DH Rocket Comics, July, 2003
1 TPe 3.00
2 thru 8 . . . . @3.00
TPB Vol. 1 Ready Set Go 13.00
TPB Vol. 2 The Human Factor 13.00

GODZILLA
(B&W) 1988
1 Japanese Manga 5.00
2 thru 6 . . . . @4.00
Spec #1 . . . . 2.25
TPB 2nd printing 18.00

GODZILLA
COLOR SPECIAL
1992
1 AAd,R:Godzilla,V:Gekido-Jin 3.50
1a rep (1998) 3.00
Spec.1 Godzilla vs. Barkley MBn(s),
    JBt,DvD (1993) 3.50

GODZILLA
1995
0 RSd,The King of Monsters
    is back! 4.00
1 R:Godzill 4.00
2 V:Cybersaur 4.00
3 I:Bagorah the Bat Creature 4.00
4 V:Bagorah,Cybersaur 4.00
5 V:U.S. Army 4.00
6 thru 14 . . . . @4.00
15 'Thunder Downunder' 4.00
16 'Thunder in the Past' 4.00
TPB Past, Present, Future 18.00
TPB Godzilla: Age of Monsters . . . 18.00
Spec.1 Godzilla vs. Hero Zero
    Tatsuya Ishida (1995) 2.50

GO GIRL!
Oct., 2002
TPB TrR 88-pg. b&w 12.00
TPB Vol. 1 The Time Team 6.00

GOON, THE
June, 2003
1 . . . . 6.00
2 . . . . 5.00
3 thru 9 . . . . @4.00
TPB Nothin' But Misery 16.00
TPB My Murderous Childhood 14.00
TPB Rough Stuff 13.00

GREEN LANTERN
VS. ALIENS
Aug., 2000
1 RMz,RL,F:Hal Jordan, x-over . . . 3.00
2 (of 4) RMz,RL,F:Kyle Rayner . . . 3.00
3 RMz,RL, without ring 3.00
4 RMz,RL, V:Alien Queen 3.00
TPB RMZ,RL 13.00

GRENDEL
TPB Past Prime,MWg 15.00
Spec.1 Grendel Cycle, Grendel
    History (1995) 6.00

GRENDEL: BLACK,
WHITE, AND RED
(B&W&R) Nov., 1998
1 (of 4) MWa, 48-pg. 5.00
2 thru 4 MWa, 48-pg. . . . . @4.00

TPB Black, White & Red, MWg . . . 19.00

GRENDEL CLASSICS
1995
1 Rep.#18–#19 Comico series 4.00
2 Rep. 4.00

GRENDEL: DEVIL BY
THE DEED
1993
1 MWg,RRa 4.00
1 representation (1997) 4.00
TPB Devil Tales 10.00

GRENDEL: DEVIL CHILD
June, 1999
1 (of 2) MWg 3.00
2 conclusion 3.00

GRENDEL:
THE DEVIL INSIDE
DH Maverick, Sept., 2001
1 (of 3) MWg 3.00
2 . . . . 3.00
3 concl. 3.00

GRENDEL:
DEVIL'S LEGACY
Aug., 1996
1 by Matt Wagner 3.00
2 thru 3 . . . . @3.00
TPB Devils and Deaths 17.00

Grendel: Devil's Legacy #2
© Dark Horse Comics

GRENDEL:
DEVIL'S LEGACY
DH/Maverick, Mar., 2000
1 (of 12) MWg, rep. from 1986 . . . . 3.00
2 thru 6 MWg . . . . @3.00
7 MWg,V:Tujiro XIV 3.00
8 MWg,back to N.Y. 3.00
9 MWg,F:Dominic Riley 3.00
10 MWg 3.00
11 MWg 3.00
12 MWg, concl. 3.00
TPB 328-pg. 30.00

DARK HORSE

GRENDEL: DEVIL'S REIGN
May, 2004
1 (of 7) MWg................3.50
2 thru 5 ....@3.50

GRENDEL:
GOD AND THE DEVIL
Jan., 2003
0 MWg,TSe..................3.50
1 MWg (of 10)...............3.50
2 thru 9 MWg ....@3.50
10 MWg, concl., 48-pg..........5.00
TPB The Devil Inside..........13.00

GRENDEL:
RED, WHITE, & BLACK
DH Maverick, Sept., 2002
1 (of 4) 48-pg. B&W...........5.00
2 MWg,KJo,DIB...............5.00
3.........................5.00
4 MWg.....................5.00

*Grendel Tales, The Devil's Apprentice
#1 © Dark Horse Comics*

GRENDEL TALES:
DEVIL'S APPRENTICE
Sept., 1997
1 (of 3) 3.00
2 thru 3 ....@3.00

GRENDEL TALES:
DEVILS AND DEATHS
1994
1.........................3.00
2.........................3.00
TPB rep. Devils and Deaths plus
   Devil's Choices 17.00

GRENDEL TALES:
DEVIL'S CHOICES
1995
1 F:Goran..................3.00
2 thru 4 ....@3.00

GRENDEL TALES:
FOUR DEVILS, ONE HELL
1 MWg(c),F:Four Grendels......3.50
2 MWg(c),F:Four Grendels......3.50

3 MWg(c),F:Four Grendels......3.50
4 MWg(c),F:Four Grendels......3.50
5 MWg(c),F:Four Grendels......3.50
6 MWg(c),last issue 3.25
TPB Rep. #1–#6 ....18.00

GRENDEL TALES:
HOMECOMING
1994
1 Babylon Crash..............3.00
2 Babylon Crash,pt. 2..........3.00
3 Too Dead To Die 3.00
TPB Homecoming..............8.00

GRENDEL TALES:
THE DEVIL IN
OUR MIDST
1994
1 MWg(c)..................3.50
2 MWg(c)..................3.25
3 thru 5 ....@3.00
TPB series rep................16.00

GRENDEL TALES:
THE DEVIL MAY CARE
1995
1 thru 6 mini-series...........3.00
TPB The Devil May Care (2002) . . 20.00

GRENDEL TALES:
THE DEVIL'S HAMMER
1994
1 MWg(a&s),I:Petrus Christus 3.50
2 MWg(a&s),A:P.Christus........3.25
3 MWg(a&s),last issue 3.25

GRENDEL: WAR CHILD
1992
1 MWg 4.00
2 thru 9 MWg 3.00
10 MWg, final issue, dbl.size......4.00
TPB 19.00
TPB War Child, 304-pg. (2002) . . . 25.00

GRIFTER AND THE MASK
Sept., 1996
1 by Seagle, Lima & Pimentel 2.50
2.........................2.50

GROO:
DEATH AND TAXES
DH Maverick, Dec., 2002
1 (of 4) SA 3.00
2 thru 4 ....@3.00
TPB series rep. 112-pg..........13.00

GUFF
Apr., 1998
1-shot by Sergio Aragones, flip
   book, with Meanie Babies
   card, B&W 2.25

GUNSMITH CATS
(B&W–Manga) 1995
1 I:Rally & Mini May 3.00
2 Revolver Freak 3.00
3.........................3.00
4 V:Bonnie and Clyde..........3.00
5 V:Bonnie and Clyde..........3.00
6 Hostage Situation 3.00
7 thru 10 (10 part series) 3.00

TPB Misfire rep. #7–#10 &
   Return of Gray #1–#3 ....13.00
TPB Misty's Run (2002).........15.00

GUNSMITH CATS:
BAD TRIP
(B&W) June, 1998
1 (of 6) by Kenichi Sonoda.......3.00
2 thru 4 ....@3.00
TPB Bad Trip 14.00

GUNSMITH CATS:
BEAN BANDIT
(B&W) June, 1998
1 (of 9) by Kenichi Sonoda.......3.00
2 thru 9 ....@3.00
TPB Bean Bandit, 224-pg........17.00

GUNSMITH CATS:
BONNIE & CLYDE
TPB by Kenichi Sonoda.........13.00

GUNSMITH CATS:
GOLDIE VS. MISTY
(B&W) Nov., 1997
1 (of 7) by Kenichi Sonoda.......3.00
2 thru 7 ....@3.00
TPB Goldie vs. Misty...........13.00

GUNSMITH CATS:
KIDNAPPED
Nov., 1999
1 (of 10) by Kenichi Sonoda......3.00
2 thru 10 ....@3.00
TPB Bad Trip 14.00

GUNSMITH CATS:
MISTER V
(B&W) Oct., 2000
1 (of 11) by Kenichi Sonoda......3.50
2 thru 11 ....@3.50
TPB Mister V, 224-pg...........19.00
TPB Kidnapped 17.00
Spec.......................3.00

GUNSMITH CATS:
SHADES OF GRAY
(B&W) May, 1997
1 (of 5) by Kenichi Sonoda.......3.00
2 thru 5 (of 5) ....@3.00

GUNSMITH CATS:
THE RETURN OF GRAY
(B&W) Aug., 1996
1 thru 7 by Kenichi Sonoda......@3.00
TPB rep. series 18.00

HAMMER OF GOD:
BUTCH
1994
1 MBn.....................2.50
2 and 3 MBn................@2.50

HAMMER OF
GOD: PENTATHLON
1994
1 MiB(s),NV 2.50

Hammer: Uncle Alex
Atlantis #1 © Dark Horse Comics

THE HAMMER:
UNCLE ALEX
Aug., 1998
1-shot KJo. 3.00

HAPPY BIRTHDAY
MARTHA WASHINGTON
1995
1 Frank Miller 3.00

HAPPY ENDINGS
DH Maverick, Sept., 2002
TPB 96-pg. B&W 10.00

HARD BOILED
1990
1 GfD 7.00
2 and 3 . . . . @6.00
TPB 15.00
TPB Big Damn Hard Boiled 30.00

HARD LOOKS
(B&W) 1992
1 thru 10 AVs Adaptations . . . . . . @2.50
Book One 15.00
TPB AVs 18.00
TPB 3rd printing 20.00

HARLAN ELLISON'S
DREAM CORRIDOR
1995
1 Various stories 3.00
2 Various stories 3.00
3 JBy, I Have No Mouth and I
    Must Scream & other stories. . . 3.00
4 thru 6 . . . . @3.00
Spec.#1 Various stories 5.00
TPB 19.00
Spec. Quarterly, vol. 1 . . . . 6.00
Spec. Quarterly, vol. 2 . . . . 6.00

HAUNTED MAN, THE
Mar., 2000
1 (of 3) GJ,MBg 3.00
2 GJ,MBg 3.00
3 . . . . 3.00

HEARTBREAKERS
1996
1 . . . . 3.00
2 thru 4 . . . . @3.00

HEART OF EMPIRE:
THE LEGACY OF
LUTHER ARKWRIGHT
Apr., 1999
1 (of 9) BT. 3.00
2 thru 5 . . . . @3.00
6 plot against royal family 3.50
7 countdown to cataclysm 3.50
8 . . . . 3.50
9 conclusion 3.00
TPB series rep. 30.00

HELL
DH Rocket Comics, July, 2003
1 BAu 3.00
2 thru 4 BAu . . . . @3.00
TPB Vol. 1 Hell and Gone 13.00

HELLBOY
Christmas Special (1997) MMi,
    48-pg. 4.00
Hellboy Junior Halloween Special . . 4.00
Hellboy Junior Lurid Easter Special . 4.00
TPB The Lost Army 15.00
TPB The Chained Coffin & Others 18.00
TPB The Right Hand of Doom,
    MMi 18.00
TPB The Bones of the Giants
    200-pg. 15.00
TPB Vol. 1 Seed of Destruction . . 18.00
TPB Vol. 2 Wake the Devil 18.00
TPB Vol. 3 Chained Coffin 18.00
TPB Vol. 4 Right Had of Doom . . 18.00
TPB Vol. 5 Conqueror Worm 18.00
TPB Art of Hellboy 30.00
TPB The Art of the Movie 25.00
1-shot The Corpse 0.25

HELLBOY:
ALMOST COLOSSUS
DH Legend, 1997
1 (of 2) MMi, sequel to *Wake the
    Devil*. 3.00
2 (of 2) 3.00

HELLBOY:
BOX FULL OF EVIL
Aug., 1999
1 (of 2) MMi 3.00
2 MMi, conclusion 3.00

HELLBOY:
CONQUEROR WORM
May, 2001
1 (of 4) MMi 3.00
2 thru 4 . . . . @3.00
TPB series rep. 144-pg. 18.00

HELLBOY JUNIOR
Jan., 2004
TPB 15.00

HELLBOY: SEEDS
OF DESTRUCTION
DH Legend
1 JBy,MMi,AAd,V:Vampire Frog,
    BU:Monkeyman & O'Brien 3.50

2 MMi(c),JBy,AAd,BU:Monkeyman
    & O'Brien 3.00
3 MMi(c),JBy,AAd,BU:Monkeyman
    & O'Brien 3.00
4 MMi(c),JBy,AAd,BU:Monkeyman
    & O'Brien 3.00
TPB Seed of Destruction 18.00

HELLBOY:
THE THIRD WISH
July, 2002
1 (of 2) MMi 3.00
2 . . . . 3.00

Hellboy: Wake the Devil #1
© Dark Horse Comics

HELLBOY:
WAKE THE DEVIL
DH Legend, 1996
1 (of 5) MMi 3.00
2 thru 5 . . . . @3.00
TPB Wake The Devil 18.00

HELLBOY: WEIRD TALES
Feb., 2003
1 FaN 3.00
2 thru 8 . . . . @3.00
TPB Weird Tales Vol. 1 . . . . 18.00
TPB Vol. 2 . . . . 18.00

HELLBOY JR.
October 1999
1 (of 2) MMi 3.00
2 . . . . 3.00

HELLHOUNDS
(B&W) 1994
1 I:Hellhounds 3.00
2 and 3 . . . . @3.00
Becomes:

HELLHOUNDS:
PANZER CORPS
3 thru 6 . . . . @3.00
TPB 15.00

HELLSING
2003
TPB Vol. 1 b&w 14.00
TPB Vol. 2 thru Vol. 5 . . . . @14.00

DARK HORSE

HERBIE
1992
1 JBy,reps.& new material 3.00
2 Reps.& new material 2.50

The Heretic #3
© Dark Horse Comics

HERETIC, THE
Nov., 1996
1 (of 4) by Rich DiLeonardo, Joe
   Phillips & Dexter Vines 3.00
2 thru 4 . . . . @3.00

HERMES VS. THE EYEBALL KID
1994
1 thru 3 Symphony of Blood 3.00

HERO ZERO
1994
1 First and last issue. 2.50

HIEROGLYPH
Nov., 1999
1 RdD,F:Francisco Chavez. 3.00
2 thru 4 RdD . . . . @3.00

THE HORROR OF COLLIER COUNTY
Oct., 1999
1 (of 5) Halloween special 3.00
2 thru 5 concl. . . . . @3.00
TPB 13.00

H.P.'S ROCK CITY
TPB by Moebius 8.00

HYPERSONIC
Nov., 1997
1 (of 4) DAn,GEr. 3.00
2 thru 4 . . . . @3.00

IGUANA, THE
DH Venture Feb., 2002
TPB 88-pg. 11.00

ILLEGAL ALIEN
June, 2003
TPB b&w 11.00

INDIANA JONES AND THE ARMS OF GOLD
1994
1 In South America 2.75
2 In South America 2.75
3 V:Incan Gods. 2.75
4 . . . . 2.50

INDIANA JONES AND THE FATE OF ATLANTIS
1991
1 DBa,Search for S.Hapgood with
   2-card strip 4.00
1a 2nd printing 3.00
2 DBa,Lost Dialogue of Plato with
   2-card strip 3.00
3 Map Room of Atlantis 3.00
4 Atlantis, Last issue. 3.00
TPB 14.00

INDIANA JONES AND THE GOLDEN FLEECE
1994
1 SnW. 2.75
2 SnW. 2.50

INDIANA JONES AND THE IRON PHOENIX
1994
1 . . . . 2.50
2 V:Nazis. 2.50
3 A:Nadia Kirov. 2.50
4 V:Undead. 2.50

INDIANA JONES AND THE SARGASSO PIRATES
1995
1 thru 4 . . . . @2.50

INDIANA JONES AND THE SHRINE OF THE SEA DEVIL
199
1 . . . . 2.50

INDIANA JONES AND THE SPEAR OF DESTINY
1995
1 I:Spear T/Pierced Christ 2.50
2 DSp, with Henry Jones 2.50
3 Search for the Shaft. 2.50

INDIANA JONES: THUNDER IN THE ORIENT
1993
1 DBa(a&s),in Tripoli. 2.75
2 DBa(a&s),Muzzad Ram. 2.75
3 DBa(a&s),V:Sgt.Itaki 2.75
4 DBa(a&s),In Hindu Kush 2.75
5 DBa(a&s),V:Japanese Army 2.75
6 DBa(a&s),last issue. 2.75

INSTANT PIANO
(B&W) 1994
1 Offbeat humor 4.00
2 . . . . 4.00
3 Various stories. 4.00
4 Devil Puppet 4.00

INTRON DEPOT
Nov., 1998
TPB Intron Depot. 40.00
TPB Intron Depot 2: Blades. 38.00

INTRON DEPOT
Feb., 2003
TPB Vol. 1 . . . . 45.00
TPB Vol. 2 Blades 45.00
TPB Vol. 3 Ballistics. 45.00

INVINCIBLE ED:
2003
1 The Beating of Ed 3.50
2 I'm Too Sexy 4.00
3 Lance Lundgrin Unleashes 3.00
4 The End 3.00
TPB 14.00

IRON EMPIRES
Dec., 2003
TPB Vol. 1 . . . . 18.00
TPB Vol. 2 Sheva's War 18.00

IRONHAND OF ALMURIC
(B&W) 1991
1 Robert E. Howard adaption 2.25
2 A:Cairn,V:Yagas. 2.25
3 V:Yasmeena,The Hive Queen . . . 2.25
4 Conclusion. 2.25
GN 11.00

JAMES BOND 007: QUASIMODO GAMBIT
1995
1 I:Maximillion Quasimodo 4.00
2 V:Fanatical Soldiers. 4.00
3 V:Steel 4.00

JAMES BOND 007: SERPENT'S TOOTH
1992
1 PG,DgM,V:Indigo 5.50
2 PG,DgM,V:Indigo 5.00
3 PG,DgM 5.25
TPB 16.00

JAMES BOND 007: SHATTERED HELIX
1994
1 V:Cerberus. 3.00
2 V:Cerberus. 3.00

JAMES BOND 007: A SILENT ARMAGEDDON
1993
1 V:Troy. 3.25
2 & 3 V:Omega . . . . @3.25

JOHN BOLTON'S STRANGE WINK
Mar., 1998
1 (of 3) 3.00
2 thru 3 . . . . @3.00

JOHNNY DYNAMITE
1994
1 . . . . 3.00
2 . . . . 3.00
3 V:Faust. 3.00
4 Last issue. 3.00

JOKER/MASK
May, 2000
1 (of 4) Batman x-over 3.00
2 Joker becomes Joker/Mask. . . . 3.00
3 A:Harley Quinn, Poison Ivy 3.00
4 three nuclear bombs, concl. 3.00
TPB 96-pg.. . . . . 12.00

JONNY DEMON
1994
1 SL(c),KBk,NV. 2.75
2 SL(c),KBk,NV. 2.75
2 SL(c),KBk,NV, final issue. 2.50

JOSS WHEDON'S FRAY
June, 2001
1 (of 8) 3.00
1a gold foil (c). 10.00
1b gold foil (c) signed 25.00
2 thru 8 . . . . @3.00
TPB Future Slayer. 20.00

JUDGE DREDD VS.
ALIENS: INCUBUS
Mar., 2003
1 (of 4) 3.00
2 thru 4 . . . . @3.00
TPB 104-pg.. . . . . 13.00

JUNIOR CARROT PATROL
(B&W) 1989
1 and 2 . . . . @2.50

KELLEY JONES'
THE HAMMER
Sept., 1997
1 (of 4) KJo, horror series. 3.00
2 thru 4 KJo, ... @3.00
TPB 13.00

KELLEY JONES'
THE HAMMER:
THE OUTSIDER
Feb., 1999
1 (of 3) KJo. 3.00
2 and 3 . . . . @3.00

KINGS OF THE NIGHT
1990
1 Robert E. Howard adapt. 2.25
2 end Mini-Series 2.25

KING TIGER/MOTORHEAD
1996
1 (of 2) by D.G. Chichester, Karl
  Waller & Eric Shanower 3.00
2 . . . . 3.00

KISS
July, 2002
1 JoC 4.00
2 thru 4 JoC . . . . @3.00
5 . . . . 3.00
6 . . . . 3.00

---

7 thru 10 SLo . . . . @3.00
11 . . . . 3.00
12 . . . . 3.00
13 MBn. 3.00
1a thru 13a photo (c) . . . . @3.00
TPB Rediscovery 11.00
TPB Return of the Phantom 10.00
TPB Men and Monsters. 13.00
TPB Vol. 4 Unholy War 13.00

KLING KLANG KLATCH
GN 12.00

KWAIDAN
Jan., 2004
TPB 15.00

Land of Nod #2
© Dark Horse Comics

LAND OF NOD
(B&W) July, 1997
1 (of 4) by Jay Stephens. 3.00
2 thru 4 . . . . @3.00
TPB Rockabye Book 14.00

LAST DAY IN VIETNAM
GN by Will Eisner. 11.00
GN rep.. 11.00

LAST TEMPTATION, THE
DH Maverick, Nov., 2000
TPB NGa,MZi,6'x9' 10.00

LAZARUS JACK
Sept., 2004
TPB 15.00

THE LEGEND OF
MOTHER SARAH
(B&W–Manga) 1995
1 I:Mother Sarah. 4.00
2 Sarah and Tsutsu. 4.00
3 Firing Squad 4.00
4 F:Toki 4.00
5 Yunnel Town 4.00
6 Kill or Be Killed 4.00
7 Firing Squad 4.00
8 Conclusion. 4.00
TPB The Tunnel Town 19.00

Legend of Mother Sarah: City of the
Angels #9 © Dark Horse Comics

THE LEGEND OF
MOTHER SARAH:
CITY OF THE ANGELS
(B&W–Manga) Oct., 1996
1 (of 9) by Katsuhiro Otomo and
  Takumi Nagayasu, 48-pg. 4.25
1 rep. (1997). 4.25
2 thru 4 . . . . 4.25
2 thru 4 rep. (1997). 4.25
5 Tsue a victim 4.25
6 Mother Teres questioned 4.25
7 put in front trenches. 4.25
8 Teres suicide run 4.25
9 concl., 32-pg. 3.25

THE LEGEND OF
MOTHER SARAH:
CITY OF THE CHILDREN
(B&W–Manga) 1996
1 thru 4 (7 part mini-series). . . . . @4.25

LITTLE ANNIE FANNY
1962–70
Oct., 2000
TPB cartoons from playboy 25.00
TPB Vol. 2 . . . . 25.00

LONE
DH Rocket Comics, Sept., 2003
1 . . . . 3.00
2 thru 6 . . . . @3.00
TPB 15.00

LONE GUNMEN, THE
June, 2001
1-shot 3.00
1-shot photo(c). 3.00
1-shot photo (c) lim ed. 7.00
1-shot photo (c) lim ed. signed . . . 20.00

LONE WOLF AND CUB
TPB Vol 1. . . . . 20.00
TPB Vol 2. . . . . 12.00
TPB Vol 3 Flute of the Fallen Tiger 12.00
TPB Vol.4 Shishogan Eyes 10.00
TPB Vol.5 Black Wind 10.00
TPB Vol.6 Lanterns For The Dead 10.00

DARK HORSE

All comics prices listed are for *Near Mint* condition.

TPB Vol.7 DragonCloud,WindTiger 10.00
TPB Vol.8 Chains of the Kurokuwa 10.00
TPB Vol.9 Shadows, Echoes..... 10.00
TPB Vol.10 Separate Paths...... 10.00
TPB Vol.11 Talisman of Hades ... 10.00
TPB Vol.12 Shattered Stones 10.00
TPB Vol.13 The Moon in the East,
　The Sun in the West 10.00
TPB Vol.14 Day of the Demons... 10.00
TPB Vol.15 Brothers of the Grass . 10.00
TPB Vol.16 Gateway Into Winter.. 10.00
TPB Vol.17 The Will of the Fang.. 10.00
TPB Vol.18 The Last Kurokuwa... 10.00
TPB Vol.19 Moon in Our Hearts . 10.00
TPB Vol.20 A Taste of Poison 10.00
TPB Vol.21 Fragrance of Death... 10.00
TPB Vol.22 Heaven and Earth.... 10.00
TPB Vol.23 Tears of Ice 10.00
TPB Vol.24 In These Small Hands 10.00
TPB Vol.25 Perhaps in Death 10.00
TPB Vol.26 Battle in the Dark 10.00
TPB Vol.27 Battle's Eve......... 10.00
TPB Vol.28 Falling Tree......... 10.00

LONE WOLF 2100
May, 2002
1 (of 4) War Spore 4.00
2 thru 4 War Spore .... @3.00
5 thru 11 .... @3.00
1-shot The Red File............ 3.00
TPB Shadows on Saplings 13.00
TPB Vol. 2 .... 15.00
TPB Vol. 3 Pattern Storm....... 13.00

LORDS OF MISRULE
(B&W) Jan., 1997
1 by DAn, PSj................. 3.00
2 thru 6 .... @3.00
TPB The Lords of Misrule 18.00

LOST IN SPACE
Apr., 1998
1 (of 3) sequel to film 3.00
2 thru 3 GEr(c) .... @3.00
TPB rep. series, GEr(c) 8.00

LOST WORLD
July, 2003
TPB b&w 18.00

THE LUCK IN THE HEAD
TPB 12.00

THE MACHINE
Comics Greatest World, 1994
1 (a) The Barb Wire spin 2.50
2 V:Salvage................... 2.50
3 Freak Show 2.50
4 I:Skion 2.50

MAC RAYBOY'S FLASH GORDON
Jan., 2003
TPB b&w 20.00
TPB Vol. 2 .... 20.00
TPB Vol. 3 .... 20.00
TPB Vol. 4 .... 20.00

MADMAN
DH Legend, 1994
1 MiA(s) 8.00
2 MiA(s) 6.00
3 MiA(s) 5.00
4 MiA(s),Muscleman........... 5.00
5 MiA(s),I:The Blast 4.00

Madman #14
© Dark Horse Comics

6 MiA(s),A:Big Guy, Big Brain-
　o-rama,pt.1 .... 12.00
7 MiA(s),FM,A:Big Guy, Big Brain-
　o-rama,pt.2 .... 6.00
8 MiA(s) 4.00
9 Micro Madman............... 4.00
10 .... 4.00
11 .... 4.00
Yearbook '95 TPB 18.00
Yearbook '96 TPB 18.00
Yearbook '95 new printing (2003) . 18.00
Apr., 1999
12 MiA 3.00
13 MiA 3.00
14 MiA 3.00
15 MiA 3.00
16 MiA 3.00
TPB Boogaloo 9.00
TPB The Exit of Dr. Boiffard 18.00
TPB Vol. 4 Heaven and Hell 18.00
G-Men From Hell (Aug., 2000)
17 Pt.1 MiA 3.00
18 Pt.2 MiA, Is Frank Einstein
　dead?.................... 3.00
19 Pt.3 MiA 3.00
20 Pt.4 MiA, V:Mr.Monstadt...... 3.00

MADMAN/THE JAM
July, 1998
1 (of 2) MiA................. 3.00
2 MiA...................... 3.00

MADWOMAN OF THE SACRED HEART, THE
(B&W)
TPB by Alex Jodorowsky & Moe .. 13.00

MAGIC: THE GATHERING
Mar., 1998
1 (of 4) MGr,Initiation 3.00
2 MGr, Legacy 3.00
3 MGr, Crucible............... 3.00
4 MGr, Destiny 3.00
TPB Gerrard's Quest 12.00

MAGNUS/NEXUS
DH/Valiant
1 MBn(s), SR 3.25
2 MBn(s), SR 3.25

MAN FROM THE CIGUIRI
TPB by Moebius 8.00

MARK, THE
1987–89
1 LSn, ... 2.50
2 LSn 2.50
3 LSn 2.50
4 thru 6.................. @2.50
[Second Series] 1993
1 MiB(s),in America,V:Archon..... 3.00
2 MiB(s),V:Archon............ 3.00
3 MiB(s),V:Archon,A:Pierce 3.00
4 MiB(s),last issue 3.00

MARSHALL LAW
GN Super Babylon, KON (1992) ... 5.00
TPB Blood Sweat and Fears
　(1998) 16.00
1-shot Marshall Law: Cape Fear ... 3.00

MARSHALL LAW: SECRET TRIBUNAL
1993
1 KON..................... 3.00
2 KON..................... 3.00

M.A.R.S. PATROL TOTAL WAR
Sept., 2004
TPB WW 13.00

MARGE'S LITTLE LULU
Nov., 2004
TPB Vol. 1 .... 10.00

MARTHA WASHINGTON GOES TO WAR
DH Legend, 1994
1 FM(s),DGb, V:Fat Boys Corp.... 3.25
2 FM(s),DGb, V:Fat Boys Corp.... 3.25
3 FM(s),DGb, V:Fat Boys Corp.... 3.25
4 FM(s),DGb, V:Fat Boys Corp.... 3.25
5 FM(s),DBb, final issue........ 3.25
TPB Rep.#1–#5 .... 18.00

MARTHA WASHINGTON SAVES THE WORLD
Dec., 1997
1 (of 3) FM,DGb 3.25
2 thru 3 .... @3.25
TPB rep.. .... 13.00

MARTHA WASHINGTON STRANDED IN SPACE
1995
1 .... 3.25

MARTIN MYSTRY
(B&W) DH/Bonelli, Mar., 1999
1 by Alfredo Castelli & Giancarlo
　Alessandrini, DGb(c) 92-pg. ... 5.00
2 thru 6 .... @5.00

MASAKAZU KATSURA'S SHADOW LADY
(B&W–Manga) Oct., 1998
Dangerous Love
1 (of 7) Masakazu Katsura 2.50
2 thru 7 .... @2.50

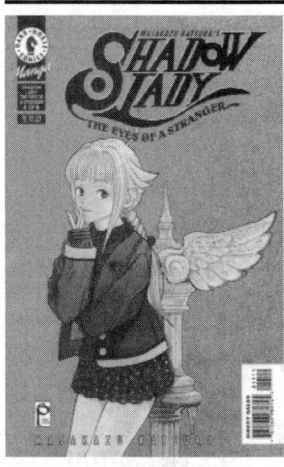

Masakazu Katsura's Shadow Lady #11
© Dark Horse Comics

The Eyes of a Stranger, May, 1999
8 thru 12, pt.1–pt.5 . . . . @2.50
The Awakening
13 thru 19, pt.1–pt.7 . . . . @2.50
Sudden Death
20 thru 24, pt.1–pt.5 . . . . @2.50
Spec.48-pg. final issue 4.00
TPB Dangerous Love 18.00
TPB The Awakening 16.00
TPB Sudden Death 15.00

MASK, THE
1991
0 'Who's Laughing Now' (B&W) . . . 6.00
1 I:Lt.Kellaway Mask 5.00
2 V:Rapaz & Walter 5.00
3 O:Mask 5.00
4 final issue 5.00
TPB 15.00

MASK, THE
1994
1 Movie Adaptation 3.00
2 Movie Adaptation 2.50

MASK , THE
[Mini-series] 1995
The Mask Strikes Back (1995)
1 Mask Strikes Back,pt.1 . . . . 2.50
2 Mask Strikes Back,pt.2 . . . . 2.50
3 Mask Strikes Back,pt.3 . . . . 2.50
4 DoM,Mask Strikes Back,pt.4 . . . . 2.50
5 Mask Strikes Back,pt.5 . . . . 2.50
TPB by John Arcudi, Doug Mahnke
& Keith Williams 15.00
The Hunt for Green October (1995)
6 Pt.1 . . . . 2.50
7 Pt.2 Kellaway vs. Ray Tuttle 2.50
8 Pt.3 F:Emily Tuttle 2.50
9 Pt.4 final issue 2.50
World Tour (1995)
10 Pt.1 . . . . 2.50
11 Pt.2 . . . . 2.50
12 Pt.3 . . . . 2.50
13 Pt.4 . . . . 2.50
Southern Discomfort (1996)
14 Pt.1 Mardi Gras time 2.50
15 Pt.2 . . . . 2.50
16 Pt.3 . . . . 2.50
17 Pt.4 . . . . 2.50

MASK/MARSHALL LAW
Feb., 1998
1 (of 2) by Pat Mills and Kevin
O'Neill 3.00
2 concl. 3.00

MASK RETURNS, THE
1992
1 inc.cut-out Mask. 5.00
2 Mask's crime spree 4.00
3 . . . . 4.00
4 . . . . 4.00
TPB by John Arcudi & Doug
Mahnke 15.00

The Mask: Toys in the Attic #4
© Dark Horse Comics

MASK: TOYS IN THE ATTIC
Aug., 1998
1 (of 4) 3.00
2 thru 4 . . . . @3.00

MASK, THE: VIRTUAL SURREALITY
1997
1-shot F: MMi,SA 3.00

MAXIMUM OVERLOAD
1 Masque (Mask) 12.00
2 thru 4 Mask . . . . @8.00

MAXIMUM OVERLOAD
1 thru 5 . . . . @4.00

MAYHEM
1989
1 F:The Mask, The Mark 5.00
2 thru 4 . . . . @4.00

MECHA
Comics Greatest World, 1995
1 color 3.00
2 color 3.00
3 thru 6 B&W. . . . . @3.00
Spec.(#1) CW(c),color 3.00

MEDAL OF HONOR
1994
1 Ace of Aces 2.50
2 . . . . 2.50
3 Andrew's Raid 2.50
4 Frank Miller(c) 2.50
5 final issue 2.50
Spec. #1 JKu (1994) 2.50

MEGATOKYO
Dec., 2003
TPB Vol. 1 . . . . 10.00
TPB Vol. 2 . . . . 10.00

METROPOLIS
Apr., 2003
TPB by Oxamu Tezuka, b&w 14.00

MEZZ GALACTIC TOUR 2494
1994
1 MBn,MV 2.50

MIKE MIGNOLA'S B.P.R.D.: HOLLOW EARTH
Jan., 2002
1 (of 3) 3.00
2 . . . . 3.00
3 . . . . 3.00
TPB 120-pg. 18.00
1-shot Something Under My Bed . . 3.00
1-shot The Soul of Venice 3.00
1-shot Dark Waters 3.00
1-shot Night Train 3.00
TPB Soul of Venice 18.00

MILKMAN MURDERS, THE
July, 2004
1 JoC,SvP 3.00
2 thru 4 JoC,SvP . . . . @3.00

THE MINOTAUR'S TALE
TPB by Al Davison 12.00

MR. MONSTER
(B&W) 1988
1 . . . . 3.50
2 . . . . 3.00
3 Alan Moore story 3.00
4 . . . . 3.00
5 I:Monster Boy 3.00
6 . . . . 3.00
7 . . . . 3.00
8 V:Vampires (giant size) 5.00

MONKEYMAN & O'BRIEN
DH Legend, 1996
1 by Arthur Adams 3.00
2 and 3 . . . . @3.00
Spec. 3.00
TPB 17.00

MONSTERS, INC.
Oct., 2001
1-shot 56-pg., Disney-Pixar 5.00

MORPHOS THE SHAPE CHANGER
July, 1996
1-shot BHg 5.00

All comics prices listed are for *Near Mint* condition.

DARK HORSE

MOTHER, COME HOME
Nov., 2003
TPB 15.00

MOTORHEAD
Comics Greatest World, 1995
1 V:Predator 2.50
2 Laughing Wolf Carnival 2.50
3 V:Jackboot 2.50
Spec.#1 JLe(c),V:Mace Blitzkrieg
   (1994) 4.00

[BOB BURDEN'S ORIGINAL] MYSTERYMEN
July, 1999
1 . . . . 3.00
2 The Amazing Disc Man 3.00
3 F:Screwball 3.00
4 All Villain Comics #1 . . . . 3.50

MYSTERY MEN
July, 1999
1 (of 2) Movie adapt.. . . . . 3.00
2 movie adaptation, concl. 3.00

MYST: THE BOOK OF THE BLACK SHIPS
Aug., 1997
1 (of 4) from CD-Rom game 3.00
2 thru 4 . . . . @3.00

NAIL, THE
June, 2004
1 (of 4) 3.00
2 thru 4 . . . . @3.00

NATHAN NEVER
(B&W) DH/Bonelli, Mar., 1999
1 (of 6) by Michele Medda & Nicola
   Mari, AAd(c) 102-pg. 5.00
2 thru 6 . . . . @5.00

NEVERMEN, THE
May, 2000
1 (of 4) GyD, V:Clockwork 3.00
2 GyD,V:Honshu 3.00
3 GyD,V:Clockwork 3.00
4 GyD,V:League of Crows 3.00
TPB 128-pg. 15.00

NEVERMEN, THE: STREETS OF BLOOD
Jan., 2003
1 (of 3) GyD 3.00
2 . . . . 3.00
3 concl. 3.00
TPB 10.00

NEW FRONTIER
(B&W) 1992
1 From series in Heavy Metal. 2.75
2 Who Killed Ruby Fields? 2.75
3 Conclusion 2.75

NEW TWO FISTED TALES: VOL II
1993
1 War stories. 5.00

Next Men #11
© *Dark Horse Comics*

[JOHN BYRNE'S] NEXT MEN
1992
0 Rep Next Men from Dark Horse
   Presents 6.00
1 JBy,'Breakout'inc.trading card
   certificate 6.00
1a 2nd Printing Blue 3.00
2 JBy,World View 4.00
3 JBy,A:Sathanis. 4.00
4 JBy,A:Sathanis. 4.00
5 JBy,A:Sathanis. 4.00
6 JBy,O:Senator Hilltop,
   Sathanis,Project Next Men 3.50
7 JBy,I:M-4,Next Men Powers
   explained 3.50
8 JBy,I:Omega Project,A:M-4 . . . . . 3.00
9 JBy,A:Omega Project,A:M-4 . . . . 3.00
10 JBy,V:OmegaProject,A:M-4 . . . . 3.00
11 JBy,V:OmegaProject,A:M-4 . . . . 3.00
12 JBy,V:Dr.Jorgenson. 3.00
13 JBy,Nathan vs Jack 3.00
14 JBy,I:Speedboy 3.00
15 JBy,in New York 3.00
16 JBy,Jasmine's Pregnant 3.00
17 FM(c),JBy,Arrested 3.00
18 JBy,On Trial 3.00
Next Men: Faith (1993)
19 Faith, pt.1 JBy(a&s),V:Dr.
   Trogg, Blue Dahila. 3.25
20 Faith, pt.2 JBy,(a&s),F:Jack 3.00
21 Faith,pt.3 MMi(c),JBy(a&s),
   I:Hellboy. 27.00
22 Faith,pt.4 JBy(a&s),Last issue . . 3.00
Next Men: Power (1994)
23 Power,pt.1, JBy(a&s) 2.75
24 Power,pt.2, JBy(a&s) 2.75
25 Power,pt.3, JBy(a&s) 2.75
26 Power,pt.4, JBY(a&s) concl. 2.50
Next Men: Lies (1994)
27 Lies,pt.1,JBy 2.50
28 Lies,pt.2,JBy 2.50
29 Lies,pt.3,JBy 2.50
30 Lies,pt.4, JBy 2.50
TPB rep.#1-6 . . . . 17.00
TPB Book 2, rep. #7–#12 . . . . . . 17.00
TPB Book 3, rep. #13–#18 . . . . . 17.00
TPB Book 4, rep. #19–#22 . . . . . 15.00
TPB Book 5, rep. #23–#26 . . . . . 15.00
TPB Book 6, rep. #27–#30 . . . . . 17.00

NEXUS: ALIEN JUSTICE
1992
1 . . . . 4.25
2 . . . . 4.25
3 . . . . 4.00
TPB series rep. (1996). 17.00

NEXUS: EXECUTIONER'S SONG
1996
1 (of 4) by Mike Baron, Steve
   Rude & Gary Martin 3.00
2 thru 4 . . . . @3.00

NEXUS: GOD CON
Apr., 1997
1 (of 2) by Mike Baron, Steve
   Rude & Gary Martin 3.00
2 . . . . 3.00

NEXUS: THE LIBERATOR
1992
1 'Waking Dreams' 3.00
2 Civil War,D:Gigo 3.00
3 Civil War contd. 3.00
4 Last issue. 3.00

NEXUS MEETS MADMAN
1996
1-shot. 3.00

NEXUS: NIGHTMARE IN BLUE
(B&W) July, 1997
1 (of 4) MBn,SR,GyM 3.00
2 thru 4 . . . . @3.00

NEXUS: THE ORIGIN
1995
1 SR,O:Nexus. 5.00

NEXUS: OUT OF THE VORTEX
1 R:Nexus. 3.00
2 Zolot & Nexus Together. 3.00
3 O:Vortex. 3.00

NEXUS: THE WAGES OF SIN
1995
1 The Client 3.00
2 V:Munson. 3.00
3 SR(c&a) Murders in New Eden . . 3.00

NIGHT BEFORE CHRISTMASK
1 Rick Geary. 10.00

NINA'S NEW AND IMPROVED ALL-TIME GREATEST
1994
1 Anthology: Nina Paley 2.50

NINTH GLAND, THE
(B&W) Mar., 1997
1-shot by Renee French 4.00

Nocturnals: Witching Hour
© Dark Horse Comics

NOCTURNALS: WITCHING HOUR
May, 1998
1-shot by Dan Brereton 5.00

NOSFERATU
(B&W) 1991
1 The Last Vampire. 4.00
2 . . . . 3.00

OH MY GODDESS!
(B&W–Manga) 1994
1 by Kosuke Fujishima. 5.00
2 & 3 . . . . @4.00
4 thru 6 . . . . @3.00
TPB 1-555-Goddess 13.00
TPB Vol.1 Wrong Number 14.00
TPB Vol.2 Leader of the Pack 14.00
TPB Vol.3 Final Exam 14.00
Part II, 1995
1 F:Keiichi. 4.00
2 thru 9. @3.00
TPB Sympathy for the Devil 13.00
Part III, 1996
1 Wishes are Granted. 3.00
2 Love Potion Number 9. . . . . 3.00
3 thru 5 . . . . @3.00
6 thru 11 Terrible Master Urd,
    pt.1 thru pt.6 . . . . @3.00
TPB Love Potion Number 9. . . . . . 13.00
TPB Terrible Master Urd 13.00
Part IV, 1996–97
1 Robot Wars 3.00
2 The Trials of Morisato,pt.1 . . . . . . 3.00
3 The Trials of Morisato,pt.2 . . . . . . 3.00
4 The Trials of Morisato,pt.3 . . . . . . 3.00
5 The Queen of Vengeance 3.00
6 Mara Strikes Back,pt.1,48-pg. . . . 4.00
7 Mara Strikes Back,pt.2. . . . . 3.00
8 Mara Strikes Back,pt.3. . . . . 3.00
Part V, 1997–98
1 The Forgotten Promise 3.00
2 The Lunch Box of Love 3.00
3 Meet Me by the Seashore, 48-pg. 4.00
4 You're So Bad, 48-pg. 4.00
5 Ninja Master,pt.1 . . . . 4.00
6 Ninja Master,pt.2, 48-pg. 4.00
7 Miss Keiichi,pt.1, 48-pg. 4.00
7 & 8 Miss Keiichi,pt.2 . . . . 3.00

9 It's Lonely at the Top 3.50
10 Fallen Angel, 48-pg. 4.00
11 Play the Game, 48-pg. 4.00
12 Sorrow, Fear Not. 4.00
Part VI, 1998–99
1 Devil in Miss Urd,pt.1, 40-pg. . . . 3.50
2 Devil in Miss Urd,pt.2. . . . . 3.00
3 Devil in Miss Urd,pt.3. . . . . 3.00
4 Devil in Miss Urd,pt.4. . . . . 3.00
5 Devil in Miss Urd,pt.5. . . . . 3.00
6 SuperUrd 3.00
Part VII, 1999
1 (of 8)The Fourth Goddess,pt.1 . . 3.00
2 The Fourth Goddess,pt.2. . . . . . . 3.00
3 The Fourth Goddess,pt.3. . . . . . . 3.00
4 The Fourth Goddess,pt.4,40-pg. . 3.50
5 The Fourth Goddess,pt.5,40-pg. . 3.50
TPB The Adventures of the
    Mini-Goddesses. 10.00
Part VIII, 1999
1 (of 2) Childhood's End,
    by Kosuke Fujishima 3.50
2 Childhood's End,pt.2 . . . . 3.50
3 The Queen and the Goddess . . . 3.50
4 Hail to the Chief,pt.1 . . . . 3.50
5 Hail to the Chief,pt.2 . . . . 3.50
6 Hail to the Chief,pt.3 . . . . 3.50
TPB Childhood's End 216-pg. 16.00
Part IX, 2000
1 Pretty in Scarlet 3.00
2 The Goddess's Apprentice. 3.00
3 Queen Sayoko,pt.1 . . . . 3.00
4 Queen Sayoko,pt.2 . . . . 3.50
5 Queen Sayoko,pt.3 (of 5) 3.00
6 Queen Sayoko,pt.4 . . . . 3.00
7 Queen Sayoko,pt.5 . . . . 3.50
TPB Ninja Master. 14.00
TPB Queen of Vengeance. 14.00
TPB Mara Strikes Back 15.00
TPB Miss Keiichi 17.00
TPB The Devil in Miss URD 15.00
TPB The Fourth Goddess 19.00
TPB Queen Sayoko, 240-pg. 17.00
PART X, Feb., 2001
1 The Secret of Speed 3.50
2 The Secret of Speed,concl. 3.00
3 one-shot. 3.50
4 Hand in Hand,pt.1 . . . . 3.50
5 Hand in Hand,pt.2 . . . . 3.50
PART XI, Aug., 2001
1 Banpei in Love,pt.1 (of 2) 3.50
2 Banpei in Love,pt.2 . . . . 3.50
3 Mystery Child,pt.1 (of 8) 3.00
4 Mystery Child,pt.2 . . . . 3.00
5 Mystery Child,pt.3 . . . . 3.00
6 Mystery Child,pt.4 . . . . 3.00
7 Mystery Child,pt.5 . . . . 3.50
8 Mystery Child,pt.6 . . . . 3.50
9 Mystery Child,pt.7 . . . . 3.00
10 Mystery Child,pt.8, 48-pg.. . . . . 4.00
TPB series rep. 19.00
PART XII, July, 2002
1 (of 3) Learning to Love,pt.1 . . . . . 3.50
2 Learning to Love,pt.2. . . . . 3.50
3 Learning to Love,pt.3. . . . . 3.50
Continuing series (Oct., 2002)
91 Traveler,pt.1 (of 5). 3.00
92 Traveler,pt.2 . . . . 3.00
93 Traveler, pt.3. . . . . 3.00
94 Traveler, pt.4. . . . . 3.00
95 Traveler, pt.5. . . . . 3.50
96 The Phantom Racer, pt.1 . . . . . . 3.00
97 The Phantom Racer, pt.2 . . . . . . 3.00
98 The Phantom Racer, pt.3 . . . . . . 3.00
99 The Phantom Racer, pt.4 . . . . . . 3.00
100 Dr. Moreau, pt.1 . . . . 3.00
101 Dr. Moreau, pt.2 . . . . 3.00
102 Dr. Moreau, pt.3 . . . . 3.00

Oh My Goddess, Vol. 7, #3
© Dark Horse Comics

103 Dr. Moreau, pt.4 . . . . 3.00
104 Dr. Moreau, pt.5 . . . . 3.50
105 Sora Unchained,pt.1 . . . . 3.00
106 thru 111 Sora,pt.2¬7 . . . . @3.00
112 Sora Unchained,pt.8, 48-pg. . . 4.00
TPB Hand in Hand. 18.00
TPB Traveler 18.00
TPB Vol. 18 Phantom Racer 18.00

OKTANE
1995
1 R:Oktane 2.50
2 V:God Zero 2.50
3 V:God Zero 2.50
4 conclusion 2.50

ONE BAD RAT
1 BT 3.00
2 thru 4 . . . . @3.00

ONE-TRICK RIP-OFF
1997
TPB by Paul Pope 13.00

ORION
(B&W–Manga) 1993
1 SF by Masamune Shirow 2.50
2 F:Yamata Empire. 3.00
3 thru 6 . . . . @3.00
TPB 16.00
TPB 3rd edition 20.00

OTIS GOES HOLLYWOOD
(B&W) Apr., 1997
1 (of 2) by Bob Fingerman 3.00
2 . . . . 3.00

OTTO PORFIRI:
Oct., 2001
TPB Drama on the Cliff 10.00
TPB Red Moon 88-pg. (2002) 10.00

OUT FOR BLOOD
(B&W) 1999
1 (of 4) GEr,F:Dan Sanger 3.00
2 The Wings; The Claws 3.00
3 . . . . 3.00
4 concl. 3.00

All comics prices listed are for *Near Mint* condition. ·

OUTLANDERS
(B&W–Manga) 1988

1	3.00
2	2.50
3 thru 7	@2.50
8 thru 20	@2.50
21 Operation Phoenix	2.50
22 thru 24	@2.50
25 thru 29 with 2-card strip	@2.50
30	2.50
31 Tetsua dying	2.50
32 D:The Emperor	2.50
33 Story finale	2.50
#0 The Key of Graciale	2.75
TPB Vol. 1 by Johji Manabe	14.00
TPB Vol. 1 2nd edition	14.00
TPB Vol. 2	14.00
TPB Vol. 2 2nd edition	14.00
TPB Vol. 3	14.00
TPB Vol. 4	13.00
TPB Vol. 5 thru Vol. 8	@15.00

OUTLANDERS: EPILOGUE
(B&W) 1994

1	2.75

OUTLAW 7
Aug., 2001

1 (of 4)	3.00
2 thru 4	@3.00

OUT OF THE VORTEX
Comics' Greatest World, 1993

1 B:JOs(s),V:Seekers	2.25
2 MMi(c),DaW,A:Seekers	2.25
3 WS(c),E:JOs(s),DaW,A:Seeker, C:Hero Zero.	2.25
4 DaW,A:Catalyst	2.25
5 V:Destroyers,A:Grace	2.25
6 V:Destroyers,A:Hero Zero	2.25
7 AAd(c),DaW,V:Destroyers, A:Mecha	2.25
8 DaW,A:Motorhead	2.25
9 DaW,V:Motorhead	2.25
10 MZ(c), A:Division 13	2.25
11 V:Reaver Swarm	2.50
12 Final issue.	2.50

OZ
by Eric Shanower

TPB The Blue Witch of Oz	10.00
TPB The Forgotten Forest of Oz	9.00
TPB The Ice King of Oz	9.00
TPB The Secret Island of Oz	9.00

PETE VON SHOLLY'S MORBID
Oct., 2003

TPB	15.00

PI: THE BOOK OF ANTS
Artisan Entertainment, 1998

1-shot, movie adapt.	3.00

PLANET OF THE APES: THE HUMAN WAR
June, 2001

1 (of 3) IEd,with trading card	3.00
1a photo (c).	3.00
2 IEd,JSC	3.00
2a photo (c).	3.00
3 IEd,JSC	3.00
3a photo (c).	3.00

PLANET OF THE APES
Sept., 2001

1 IEd,MWg	3.00
1a photo(c)	3.00
1b gold foil photo(c)	13.00
1c gold foil photo(c) signed.	30.00
2 IEd	3.00
2a photo(c)	3.00
3 IEd	3.00
3a photo(c)	3.00
4 DAn,IEd,Bloodlines,pt.1 (of 3)	3.00
4a photo (c).	3.00
5 DAn,IEd,Bloodlines,pt.2.	3.00
5a photo (c).	3.00
6 DAn,IEd,Bloodlines,pt.3.	3.00
6a photo (c).	3.00
TPB Vol. 1 80-pg.	10.00
TPB Vol. 2 Bloodlines	10.00

PLANET OF THE APES (MOVIE)

1-shot Movie adaptation	7.00
1-shotA Movie adapt, foil (c)	10.00
1-shotB Movie, foil(c) signed	30.00
TPB	10.00

POP GUN WAR
June, 2003

TPB b&w	14.00

PREDATOR
1989

1 CW,Mini Series	6.00
1a 2ndPrinting.	3.00
2 CW.	5.00
3 CW.	4.00
4 CW.	3.00
1 thru 4 later printings	@2.50

PREDATOR

1-shot Predator: Invaders from the Fourth Dimension (1994).	4.00
1-shot Predator Jungle Tales, Rite of Passage (1995)	3.00
1-shot Predator: Strange Roux (1995)	3.00
1-shot Predator: Captive (1998)	3.00
TPB Predator: Concrete Jungle.	15.00

Predator: Jungle Tales
© *Dark Horse Comics*

PREDATOR: BAD BLOOD
1993

1 CW,I:John Pulnick	3.00
2 CW,V:Predator.	3.00
3 CW,V:Predator,C.I.A.	3.00
4 Last issue.	3.00

PREDATOR: BIG GAME
1991

1 Corp.Nakai Meets Predator	3.50
2 Army Base Destroyed, with 2-card strip	3.50
3 Corp.Nakai Arrested, with 2-card strip	3.50
4 Nakai vs. Predator	3.50
TPB rep. #1–#4	14.00
TPB rep. #1–#4, 2nd edition	15.00

PREDATOR: BLOODY SANDS OF TIME
1992

1 DBa,CW,Predator in WWI	3.50
2 DBa,CW, WWII cont'd.	3.25

PREDATOR: COLD WAR
1991

1 Predator in Siberia	3.50
2 U.S. Elite Squad in Siberia	3.25
3 U.S. vs. USSR commandos	3.25
4 U.S. vs. USSR in Siberia.	3.00
TPB	14.00
TPB 2nd printing	14.00

PREDATOR: DARK RIVER
1996

1 thru 4 by Verheiden,RoR,RM.	@3.00

PREDATOR: HELL & HOT WATER
1997

1 thru 3 MSh, GC & GWt	@3.00
TPB rep.	10.00

PREDATOR: HELL COME A WALKIN'
Feb., 1998

1 (of 2) by Nancy Collins, Dean Ormston	3.00
2 concl.	3.00

PREDATOR: HOMEWORLD
Mar., 1999

1 (of 4)	3.00
2 thru 4	@3.00

PREDATOR: KINDRED
1996

1	3.00
2 thru 4	@3.00
TPB Predator: Kindred.	15.00

PREDATOR: NEMESIS
Dec., 1997

1 (of 2) TTg(c).	3.00
2	3.00

PREDATOR: PRIMAL
1997
1 (of 2) Kevin J. Anderson(s),
ScK,Low 3.00
2 (of 2) 3.00

PREDATOR: RACE WAR
1993
0 F:Serial Killer 3.00
1 V:Serial Killer 3.00
2 D:Serial Killer 3.00
3 in Prison 3.00
4 Last Issue 3.00
TPB Race War, series rep. 18.00

PREDATOR 2
1991
1 DBy, Movie Adapt,pt1 . . . . 3.50
2 MBr, Movie Adapt.,pt2 with
2-card strip 3.00

Predator:vs. Judge Dredd #2
© Dark Horse Comics

PREDATOR VS. JUDGE DREDD
Sept., 1997
1 (of 3) by John Wagner and
Enrique Alcatena 3.00
2 thru 3 . . . . @3.00
TPB Predator vs. Judge Dredd 9.00

PREDATOR VS. MAGNUS ROBOT FIGHTER
Valiant/Dark Horse 1992
1 LW,A:Tekla 3.00
1a Platinum Ed. 5.00
1b Gold Ed. 3.00
2 LW,Magnus Vs. Predator, with
2-card strip 3.00
TPB Rep. #1–#2 . . . . 8.00

PREDATOR: XENOGENESIS
Aug., 1999
1 (of 4) 3.00
2 IEd 3.00
3 IEd 3.00
4 . . . . 3.00

PRIMAL
1 Contd.from Primal:from the
Cradle to the Grave 3.00
2 A:TJ Cyrus 2.50
GN Primal From the Cradle
to the Grave. 10.00

PROPELLER MAN
1993
1 I:Propeller Man 3.00
2 O:Propeller Man,w/2 card strip . . 3.00
3 V:Manipulator. 3.00
4 V:State Police,w/2 card strip 3.00
5 V:Manipulator. 3.00
6 V:Thing, w/2 card strip. 3.00
7 . . . . 3.00
8 Last issue,w/2 card strip 3.00

PUBO
DH Maverick, Nov., 2002
1 (of 3) by Leland Purvis, B&W 3.50
2 . . . . 3.50
3 . . . . 3.50
TPB 96-pg. 10.00

PUMPKINHEAD: THE RITES OF EXORCISM
1992
1 Based on the movie. 2.50
2 thru 4 . . . . @2.50

RACE OF SCORPIONS
(B&W) 1990
Book 1 short stories 5.00
Book 2 . . . . 5.00

RACE OF SCORPIONS
(B&W) 1991
1 A:Argos,Dito,Alma,Ka 2.25
2 thru 4 . . . . @2.50

RACK & PAIN
1994
1 GCa(c),I:Rack,Pain 3.00
2 GCa(c),V:Web 3.00
3 GCa(c),V:Web 3.00
4 GCa(c),Final Issue. 3.00

Real Adventures of Jonny Quest #5
© Dark Horse Comics

RASCALS IN PARADISE
1994
1 I:Spicy Sanders 4.00
2 . . . . 4.00
3 last issue 4.00
TPB Rep.#1–#3 . . . . 17.00

REAL ADVENTURES OF JONNY QUEST, THE
Sept., 1996
1 . . . . 3.00
2 . . . . 3.00
3 thru 12 . . . . @3.00

REBEL SWORD
(B&W–Manga) 1994
1 by Yoshikazu Yashiko 2.50
2 . . . . 2.50
3 . . . . 2.50
4 V:Ruken 2.50
5 Choice of Jiro. 2.50
6 R:Ruken. 2.50

REDBLADE
1993
1 V:Demons 3.00
2 V:Tull 3.00
3 Last Issue 3.00

RED ROCKET 7
Aug., 1997
1 (of 7) MiA 4.00
2 thru 7 . . . . @4.00
TPB rep. series, 208 pg. 30.00

REID FLEMING/ FLAMING CARROT
(B&W) Jan., 2003
1-Shot Reid Fleming/Flaming
Carrot 4.00

REVEAL
Oct., 2002
1 64-pg. 7.00

RING OF ROSES
(B&W) 1991
1 Alternate world,1991 . . . . 2.50
2 Plague in London. 2.50
3 Plague cont.A:Secret Brother-
hood of the Rosy Cross. 2.50
4 Conclusion 2.50

R.I.P.D.
Nov., 1999
1 (of 4) F:Rest in Peace Dept. 3.00
2 thru 4 . . . . @3.00
TPB Rest in Peace Department . . 13.00

RING OF THE NIEBELUNG, THE:
DH Maverick, 2000
RHINEGOLD, Feb., 2000
1 (of 4) CR 3.00
2 CR 3.00
3 CR 3.00
4 CR, concl. 3.00
VALKYRIE Aug., 2000
1 (of 3) CR 3.00
2 CR 3.00
3 CR, concl. 3.00
SIEGFRIED, Dec., 2000
1 (of 3) CR 3.00

DARK HORSE

2 CR 3.00
3 CR, concl. 3.00
GOTTERDAMMERUNG June, 2001
1 (of 4) CR 3.00
2 . . . . 3.00
3 . . . . 3.00
4 finale, 64-pg. 6.00
TPB Vol. 1 Rhinegold & Valkyrie . . 22.00
TPB Vol. 2 Siegfried and Gotterdammerung, 224-pg.(2002). . . 22.00

RING, THE
Nov., 2003
TPB Vol. 1 . . . . 15.00
TPB Vol. 2 . . . . 14.00
TPB Vol. 3 . . . . 13.00
TPB Vol. 4 Birthday 13.00

RIO AT BAY
1992
1 F:Doug Wildey art 3.00
2 F:Doug Wildey art 3.00
TPB 7.00

RIPLEY'S
BELIEVE IT OR NOT
June, 2002
1 (of 4) Into Thin Air 3.00
2 Grim Reaping. 3.00
3 Human Wonders 3.00
4 Strange Invaders 3.00
TPB 10.00

ROACHMILL
(B&W) 1988
1 thru 8 . . . . @3.50
9 and 10 . . . . @2.25

ROBOCOP:
MORTAL COILS
1993
1 V:Gangs 2.75
2 V:Gangs. 2.75
3 V:Coffin,V:Gangs 2.75

ROBOCOP VERSUS
TERMINATOR
1992
1 FM(s),WS,w/Robocop cut-out . . . 3.50
2 FM(s),WS,w/Terminator cut-out. . 3.00
3 FM(s),WS,w/cut-out. 3.00
4 FM(s),WS,Conclusion 3.00

ROBOCOP:
PRIME SUSPECT
1992
1 Robocop framed 2.75
2 thru 4 V:ZED-309s . . . . @2.50
TPB series rep. 14.00

ROBOCOP: ROULETTE
1993
1 V:ED-309s 2.75
2 I:Philo Drut. 2.75
3 V:Stealthbot 2.75
4 last issue 2.75

ROBOCOP 3
1993
1 B:StG(s),Movie Adapt 2.75
2 V:Aliens,OCP 2.75
3 HNg,ANi(i) 2.75

ROCKETEER ADVENTURE
MAGAZINE
1988–95
1 and 2 . . . . @4.00
3 . . . . 3.00
TPB Cliff's New York Adventure
   by Dave Stevens 10.00

ROCKSTAR GAMES' ONI
Feb., 2001
1 video-game tie-in 3.00
1a gold foil (c) 7.00
2 . . . . 3.00
3 concl. 3.00

THE SAFEST PLACE
SC, SD 2.50

SAMURAI EXECUTIONER
June, 2004
TPB Vol. 1 . . . . 10.00
TPB Vol. 2 . . . . 10.00

Scatterbrain #3
© Dark Horse Comics

SCATTERBRAIN
June, 1998
1 (of 4) MMi 3.00
2 thru 4 . . . . @3.00

SCORPION KING, THE
Mar., 2002
1 (of 2) movie adapt. 3.00
1a photo (c). 3.00
2 (of 2) movie adapt. 3.00
2a photo (c). 3.00

SECRET OF
THE SALAMANDER
(B&W)
1 Jacquestardi, rep 3.00

SERAPHIC FEATHER
Nov., 2001
TPB 17.00
TPB Seeds of Chaos 18.00
TPB Target Zone 18.00
TPB Vol. 3 Dark Angel 18.00
TPB Vol. 5 War Crimes 18.00

SERGIO ARAGONES
ACTIONS SPEAK
Jan., 2001
1 (of 6) 3.00
2 thru 6 . . . . @3.00
TPB 160-pg.. . . . . 14.00

SERGIO ARAGONES'
BOOGEYMAN
(B&W) June, 1998
1 (of 4) 3.00
2 thru 4 . . . . @3.00
TPB, rep. 10.00

SERGIO ARAGONES'
DAY OF THE DEAD
Oct., 1998
1-shot 3.00

SERGIO ARAGONES'
GROO
Jan.–Apr., 1998
1 (of 4) 3.00
2 thru 4 . . . . @3.00
TPB The Most Intelligent Man
   in the World 10.00
TPB Houndbook. 10.00
TPB Inferno 10.00
TPB Jamboree. 10.00
TPB Library 10.00
TPB Kingdom. 10.00
TPB Groo Odyssey 13.00
TPB Mightier Than the Sword 14.00
TPB Groo Maiden 96-pg. 13.00
TPB The Groo Nursery 12.00

SERGIO ARAGONES'
GROO & RUFFERTO
Dec., 1998
1 (of 4) 3.00
2 thru 4 . . . . @3.00
TPB 10.00

SERGIO ARAGONES'
GROO: MIGHTIER THAN
THE SWORD
Jan., 2000
1 (of 4) SA 3.00
2 SA,V:Pipil Khan 3.00
3 SA,V:Relmihio 3.00
4 SA,concl. 3.00

SERGIO ARAGONES'
LOUDER THAN WORDS
(B&W) July–Dec., 1997
1 (of 6) SA 3.00
2 thru 6 . . . . @3.00
TPB rep. series 13.00

SERGIO STOMPS
STAR WARS
1-shot SA, parody 3.00

SEX WARRIORS
1 I:Dakini 2.50
2 V:Steroids. 2.50

SHADOW, THE
1994
1 MK 3.00
2 MK 3.00

The Shadow #2
© Dark Horse Comics

THE SHADOW AND DOC SAVAGE
1995
1 . . . . 3.50
2 The Shrieking Skeletons 3.50

THE SHADOW: HELL'S HEAT WAVE
1995
1 Racial War 3.00
2 MK,V:Ghost 3.00
3 Final issue 3.00

THE SHADOW: IN THE COILS OF LEVIATHAN
1993
1 MK,V:Monster 3.25
2 MK 3.25
3 MK,w/ GfD poster 3.25
4 MK,Final issue 3.25
TPB, reprints #1–#4. . . . . 14.00

THE SHADOW AND THE MYSTERIOUS 3
1994
1 Three stories 3.00

SHADOW EMPIRES: FAITH CONQURES
1994
1 CsM 3.00
2 thru 4 CsM . . . . @3.00

SHADOW STAR
Sept., 2001
TPB 16.00
TPB Darkness Visible 15.00
TPB Shadows of the Past 14.00
TPB Nothing But the Truth. 15.00
TPB Vol. 5 A Flower's Fragrance. . 16.00
TPB Vol. 6 What Can I Do For You 16.00

SHI: JUN-NEN
April 2004
1 BiT 3.00
2 thru 4 . . . . @3.00

SHINOBI
Nov., 2002
Spec.1-shot The Rise of Hotsuma. . 3.00

SHOCKROCKETS
July, 2004
TPB We Have Ignition 15.00

SHREK
Apr., 2003
1 (of 4) 3.00
2 . . . . 3.00
TPB 96-pg. 13.00

SIGNAL TO NOISE
Apr., 1999
TPB NGa,DMc 15.00

SILKE
Jan., 2001
1 TnD,F:Sandra Silke 3.00
1a variant(c) 3.00
2 TnD 3.00
3 TnD, The Hunt is on 3.00
4 TnD 3.00
4a variant(c) 3.00
TPB series rep. 96-pg. 13.00

SIN CITY:
DH-Legend
GN A Small Killing 14.00
GN Family Values (1997). 10.00
1-shot The Babe Wore Red (1994) . 3.50
1-shot The Babe Wore Red and
   other stories (1996) nudity 3.00
1-shot Lost Lonely, and Lethal,
   two-color 3.00
1-shot Sex and Violence 3.00
1-shot Silent Night (1995) 3.00
TPB, 10th Anniv. edition,
   with print & sketchbook 175.00

SIN CITY: A DAME TO KILL FOR
DH-Legend (B&W) 1993
1 FM(a&s),I:Dwight,Ava 6.00
2 FM(a&s),A:Ava 4.00
3 FM(a&s),D:Ava's Husband 4.00
1a thru 3a 2nd printings . . . . @3.00
4 thru 6 FM(a&s) . . . . @4.00
TPB rep. #1–#6, new pages 15.00

SIN CITY: HELL AND BACK
July, 1999
1 (of 9) FM 3.50
2 . . . . 3.50
3 . . . . 3.50
4 Five Foot Two, Eyes of Blue 3.50
5 . . . . 3.50
6 quest for Esther 3.50
7 . . . . 3.50
8 . . . . 3.50
9 56-pg. 5.00
TPB FM 25.00

SIN CITY: JUST ANOTHER SATURDAY NIGHT
DH/Wizard
1/2 (Wizard, 24-pg.) 7.00
1/2 rep., Dark Horse, new (c) 3.00

SIN CITY: THAT YELLOW BASTARD
(B&W) 1996
1 F.Miller 5.00
2 thru 6 . . . . @5.00

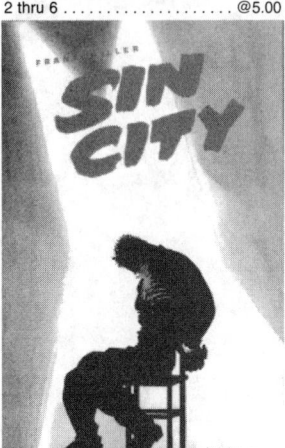

Sin City: That Yellow Bastard #3
© Dark Horse Comics

TPB by Frank Miller 15.00

SIN CITY: THE BIG FAT KILL
DH Legend, 1994
1 FM 5.00
2 FM 5.00
3 FM, Dump the Stiffs 5.00
4 FM, Town Without Pity 5.00
5 FM, final issue 5.00
TPB 15.00

SOCK MONKEY
(B&W) Sept., 1998
1 by Tony Millionaire 3.00
2 F:Uncle Gabby 3.00

VOLUME 2
1 and 2 . . . . @3.00

DH Maverick, Sept., 2002
Spec. #1 (of 2) 3.00
Spec. #2 . . . . 3.00
TPB Collected, Vol. 3ñ4 . . . . 13.00

SOLO
1996
1 and 2 . . . . @1.00

SPACE CIRCUS
DH Maverick, July, 2000
1 (of 4) SA 3.00
2 thru 4 SA . . . . @3.00

SPACEHAWK
(B&W) 1989
1 BW reps. 3.50
2 thru 5 BW . . . . @3.50

SPACE USAGI
[Vol. 3] 1996
1 thru 3 Stan Sakai . . . . @3.00
TPB 17.00

DARK HORSE

Species #1
© Dark Horse Comics

SPECIES
1995
1 Alien Human Hybrid 3.00
2 thru 4 SIL . . . . @3.00

SPECIES: HUMAN RACE
1996
1 PhH 3.00
2 . . . . 3.00
3 SBi 3.00
4 . . . . 3.00
TPB 12.00

SPIRIT OF WONDER
(B&W) 1996
1 thru 5 by Kenji Tsuruia . . . . . . @3.00
TPB 13.00

SPYBOY
Oct., 1999
1 PDd,F:Alex Fleming 3.00
2 PDd 3.00
3 PDd,F:Bombshell 3.00
4 PDd,F:Judge and Jury 3.00
5 PDd,V:Judge and Jury 3.00
6 PDd,V:Barbie Q 3.00
7 PDd,V:Madam Imadam 3.00
8 PDd,V:Madam Imadam 3.00
9 PDd,V:Madam Imadam
    & Barbie Q. 3.00
10 PDd,death-defying action 3.00
11 PDd,V:Slackjaw 3.00
12 PDd,V:Slackjaw 3.00
13 PDd 3.00
14 PDd,F:SpyGirl 3.00
15 PDd 3.00
15a variant TnD (c) 3.00
16 PDd 3.00
17 PDd 3.00
TPB Deadly Gourmet Affair, PDd . . 9.00
TPB Trial and Terror 10.00
TPB Bet Your Life 10.00
TPB Vol.4 Undercover, Underwear 10.00
TPB Vol.5 Spy-School Confidential 13.00
Spec. 1-shot 48-pg. 5.00

SPYBOY: FINAL EXAM
May, 2004
1 PDd 3.00
2 thru 4 . . . . @3.00

SPYBOY 13: THE M.A.N.G.A. AFFAIR
Apr., 2003
1 (of 3) PDd(s) 3.00
2 and 3 . . . . @3.00
TPB 10.00

SPYBOY/YOUNG JUSTICE
Feb., 2002
1 PDd, x-over 3.00
2 and 3 . . . . @3.00
TPB PDd(s) 10.00

STAN SHAW'S BEAUTY & THE BEAST
1 Based on the book 5.00

STARSHIP TROOPERS
Sept., 1997
1 (of 2) movie adaptation 3.00
2 movie adaptation, concl. 3.00
TPB rep., inc. Brute Creations,
    Insect Touch, & movie 152 pg. 15.00

STARSHIP TROOPERS: BRUTE CREATIONS
1997
1-shot RbC 3.00

STARSHIP TROOPERS: DOMINANT SPECIES
Aug., 1998
1 (of 4) 3.00
2 JoB,RyE 3.00
3 & 4 . . . . @3.00

STARSHIP TROOPERS: INSECT TOUCH
1997
1 by Warren Ellis & Paolo Parente . 3.00
2 and 3 (of 3) . . . . @3.00

STARSTRUCK: THE EXPANDING UNIVERSE
(B&W) 1990
1 Part 1 . . . . 3.00
2 Part 2, with 2-card strip 3.00

STAR WARS
Dec., 1998
1 F:Ki-Adi-Mundi 5.00
2 F:Ki-Adi-Mundi 4.00
3 F:Ki-Adi-Mundi 3.50
4 F:Sylvn 3.50
5 V:Ephant Mon 5.00
6 V:Jabba the Hutt 5.00
7 Outlander 3.00
8 A:Jabba the Hutt 3.00
9 A:Tusken Raiders 3.00
10 TT,RL,F:Ki-Adi-Mundi 3.00
11 TT,RL,F:Aurra Sing 3.00
12 TT 3.00
13 TT,TL,A'Sharad Hett 3.00
14 TT,TL,on Malastare 3.00
15 TT,TL,Podracing 3.00
16 TT,TL,V:Lannik terrorists 3.00
17 TT,TL,V:Red Iaro terrorists 3.00
18 TT,TL,Smugglers Moon 3.00
19 JOs,JD,Twilight,pt.1 . . . . 3.00
20 JOs,JD,Twilight,pt.2 . . . . 3.00
21 JOs,JD,Twilight,pt.3 . . . . 3.00
22 JOs,JD,Twilight,pt.4 . . . . 3.00

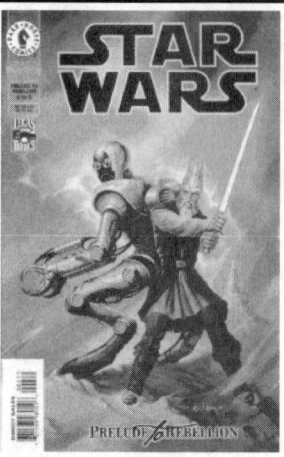

Star Wars #6
© Dark Horse Comics

23 Infinity's End,pt.1 . . . . 3.00
24 Infinity's End,pt.2 . . . . 3.00
25 Infinity's End,pt.3 . . . . 3.00
26 Infinity's End,pt.4 . . . . 3.00
27 Star Crash one-shot 3.00
28 Hunt for Aurra Sing,pt.1 . . . . . . 3.00
29 Hunt for Aurra Sing,pt.2 . . . . . . 3.00
30 Hunt for Aurra Sing,pt.3 . . . . . . 3.00
31 Hunt for Aurra Sing,pt.4 . . . . . . 3.00
32 Darkness,pt.1, JOs,JD 3.00
33 Darkness,pt.2, JOs,JD 3.00
34 Darkness,pt.3, JOs,JD 3.00
35 Darkness,pt.4, JOs,JD 3.00
36 Stark Hyperspace War,pt.1 . . . . 3.00
37 Stark Hyperspace War,pt.2 . . . . 3.00
38 Stark Hyperspace War,pt.3 . . . . 3.00
39 Stark Hyperspace War,pt.4 . . . . 3.00
40 The Devaronian Version,pt.1 . . . 3.00
41 The Devaronian Version,pt.2 . . . 3.00
42 Rite of Passage,pt.1 . . . . 3.00
43 Rite of Passage,pt.2 . . . . 3.00
44 Rite of Passage,pt.3 . . . . 3.00
45 Rite of Passage,pt.4 . . . . 3.00
46 Republic,pt.1 . . . . 3.00
47 Republic,pt.2 . . . . 3.00
48 Republic,pt.3 . . . . 3.00
49 Republic,pt.5 . . . . 3.00
50 Republic,pt.6, 64-page 6.00
51 Republic,pt.7 . . . . 3.00
52 Republic,pt.8 . . . . 3.00
53 Republic: Blast Radius 3.00
54 Republic 3.00
55 Republic:Battle of Jabiim,pt.1 . . 3.00
56 Republic:Battle of Jabiim,pt.2 . . 3.00
57 Republic:Battle of Jabiim,pt.3 . . 3.00
58 Republic:Battle of Jabiim,pt.4 . . 3.00
59 Republic: Enemy Lines 3.00
60 Republic 3.00
61 Republic 3.00
62 Republic 3.00
63 Republic 3.00
64 Republic 3.00
65 Mace Windu Unleashed,pt.1 . . . 3.00
66 Mace Windu Unleashed,pt.2 . . . 3.00
67 Clone army 3.00
68 Armor 3.00
69 Dreadnaughts of Rendili,pt.1 . . . 3.00
70 Dreadnaughts of Rendili,pt.2 . . . 3.00
TPB Prelude to Rebellion 15.00
TPB Darkness (2002) 13.00

DARK HORSE

STAR WARS: A NEW HOPE— SPECIAL EDITION
Jan.–Apr., 1997
1 EB, AW 6.00
2 thru 4 .... @5.00
TPB Rep. #1–#4 Hildebrandt(c)... 10.00
Spec. Edition boxed set 30.00

STAR WARS: A NEW HOPE
(B&W–Manga) July, 1998
1 (of 4) by Tamaki Hisao, 96-pg... 10.00
2 thru 4 .... @10.00

STAR WARS: A NEW HOPE—MANGA
Nov., 1999
1 (of 4) by Kia Asamiya,96-pg.... 10.00
2 thru 4, 88-pg. .... @10.00

STAR WARS: BATTLE OF THE BOUNTY HUNTERS
July, 1996
Pop-up Comic 18.00

STAR WARS: BOBA FETT—
1-shot Bounty on Bar-Kooda,
48-pg. 11.00
1-shot When the Fat Lady Swings.. 7.00
1-shot Murder Most Foul 7.00
1-shot Twin Engins of Destruction.. 6.00
1-shot Agent of Doom, CK........ 3.00
TPB Death, Lies & Treachery 13.00

STAR WARS: BOBA FETT— ENEMY OF THE EMPIRE
Jan., 1999
1 (of 4) V:Dark Lord of the Sith.... 3.00
2 thru 4 IG.................. @3.00
TPB rep., includes #1/2 .... 17.00

STAR WARS: BOUNTY HUNTERS
Aug., 1999
1-shot Aurra Sing, TT............ 3.00
1-shot Kir Kanos, MRi,RSd 3.00
1-shot Scoundrel's Wages,
F:Dengar, 4-LOM & Bossk 3.00
TPB Star Wars: Bounty Hunters.. 13.00

STAR WARS: CHEWBACCA
Jan., 2000
1 (of 4) various tales........... 4.00
1 gold foil (c)................. 13.00
2 thru 4 .... @3.50
TPB 13.00

STAR WARS: CLONE WARS
June, 2003
TPB Vol.1 Defense of Kamino 15.00
TPB Vol.2 Victories and Sacrifices 15.00
TPB Vol.3 Last Stand on Jabiim .. 13.00
TPB Vol.4 Light and Dark 17.00
TPB Vol.5 The Best Blades 15.00

Star Wars: Crimson Empire II #1
© *Dark Horse Comics*

STAR WARS: CLONE WARS ADVENTURES
2004
TPB Vol. 1 96-pg.............. 7.00
TPB Vol. 2 .... 7.00

STAR WARS: CRIMSON EMPIRE
Dec., 1997–May, 1998
1 PG,CR,DvD(c) 10.00
3 PG,CR,DvD(c) 8.00
3 thru 5 PG,CR,DvD(c) .... @5.00
TPB Crimson Empire 18.00

VOL II: COUNCIL OF BLOOD
1998
1 MRi,RSd,PG,DvD(c) 4.00
2 thru 6 RSd,PG,DvD(c) ...... @3.00
TPB Council of Blood.......... 18.00

STAR WARS: DARK EMPIRE
Dec., 1991
1 CK,Destiny of a Jedi 14.00
1a 2nd Printing 5.00
1b Gold Ed................. 15.00
2 CK,Destroyer of worlds, very
low print run............... 12.00
2a 2nd Printing 5.00
2b Gold Ed................. 15.00
3 CK,V:The Emperor 8.00
3a 2nd printing 4.00
3b Gold Ed................. 10.00
4 CK,V:The Emperor 5.00
4a Gold Ed................. 5.00
5 CK,V:The Emperor 5.00
5a Gold Ed................. 10.00
6 CK,V:Emperor,last issue 5.00
6a Gold Ed................. 9.00
Gold editions, foil logo set 50.00
Platinum editions, embossed set. 100.00
TPB Preview 32pg. 1.00
TPB rep.#1–#6............... 20.00
TPB CK & Tom Veitch 2nd ed. ... 18.00

STAR WARS DARK EMPIRE II
1994
1 2nd chapter 6.00
2 F:Boba Fett 5.00
3 V:Darksiders 5.00
4 Luke Vs. Darksiders 5.00
5 Creatures................. 5.00
6 CK,DvD(c), save the twins..... 5.00
Platinum editions, set.......... 50.00
TPB CK & Tom Veitch rep.#1–#6 . 18.00

STAR WARS: DARK FORCE RISING
May–Oct., 1997
1 thru 6 (of 6) MBn,TyD,KN .... @5.00
TPB series rep............... 18.00

STAR WARS: DARK FORCES
TPB Jedi Knight (Sept., 1998).... 15.00
TPB Rebel Agent (Mar., 1998).... 15.00
TPB Soldier for the Empire 15.00

STAR WARS: DARTH MAUL
Sept., 2000
1 (of 4) RMz,JD,Struzan(c)....... 3.00
1 photo (c)................. 5.00
2 Struzan(c),V:Black Sun 3.00
3 RMz,JD,Struzan(c)........... 3.00
4 RMz,JD,Struzan(c)........... 3.00
2 thru 4 photo(c) .... @3.00
TPB RMz,JD,Struzan(c)........ 13.00

STAR WARS: DROIDS
April–Sept., 1994
1 F:C-3PO,R2-D2 .... 5.00
2 V:Thieves................. 3.00
3 on the Hosk moon 3.00
4 .... 3.00
5 A meeting................. 3.00
6 final issue................ 3.00
Spec.#1 I:Olag Greck........... 3.00
TPB The Kalarba Adventures, rep. 18.00
[2nd Series] Apr., 1995
1 Deputized Droids............ 3.00
2 Marooned on Nar Shaddaa..... 3.00
3 C-3PO to the Rescue 3.00
4 .... 3.00
5 Caretaker virus 3.00
6 Revolution 3.00
7 & 8 .... @3.00
TPB Droids—Rebellion, rep. 18.00

STAR WARS: THE EMPIRE STRIKES BACK
TPB Hildebrandt(c) 10.00

STAR WARS: THE EMPIRE STRIKES BACK
(B&W–Manga) Dec., 1998
1 (of 4) by Toshiki Dudo, 96-pg.. . 10.00
2 thru 4 .... @10.00

STAR WARS: EMISSARIES TO MALASTARE
Aug., 2001
TPB TT,TL,JD 16.00

DARK HORSE

STAR WARS: EMPIRE
Sept., 2002

1	3.50
2	3.50
2 Betrayal	3.50
3 Betrayal	3.50
4	3.00
5 National Public Radio adapt.	3.00
6	3.00
7	3.00
8 Darklighter,pt.1	3.00
9 Darklighter,pt.2	3.00
10 Yavin Base,pt.1	3.00
11 Yavin Base,pt.2	3.00
12 Darklighter,pt.3	3.00
13 Darklighter,pt.4	3.00
14 Soldier's perspective	3.00
15	3.00
T16 To the Last Man,pt.1	3.00
17 To the Last Man,pt.2	3.00
18 To the Last Man,pt.3	3.00
19 To the Last Man,pt.3	3.00
20 Rebel base	3.00
21 Rebel base,pt.2	3.00
22 F:Deena Shan	3.00
23 F:BoShek	3.00
24 Idiot's Array,pt.1	3.00
25 Idiot's Array,pt.2	3.00
26	3.00
PB Vol. 1	13.00
TPB Vol. 2 Darklighter	18.00
TPB Vol. 3 Imperial Perspective	18.00

STAR WARS: EMPIRE'S END
Oct.–Nov., 1995

1 R:Emperor Palpatine	3.50
2 conclusion	3.50
TPB rep.	6.00

STAR WARS: EPISODE I THE PHANTOM MENACE
Apr., 1999

1 RdM,AW.	3.00
1a newsstand edition, photo (c)	3.00
2 RdM,AW.	3.00
2a newsstand edition, photo (c)	3.00
3 RdM,AW.	3.00
3a newsstand edition, photo (c)	3.00
4 RdM,AW.	3.00

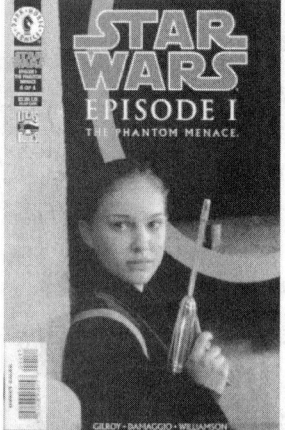

Star Wars: Episone I, The Phantom
Menace #4 © Dark Horse Comics

4a newsstand edition, photo (c)	3.00
GN Phantom Menace RdM,AW	13.00
Spec. Anakin Skywalker	3.00
Spec. Anakin Skywalker, newsstand	3.00
Spec. Obi-Wan Kenobi.	3.00
Spec. Obi-Wan Kenobi, newsstand	3.00
Spec. Queen Amidala	3.00
Spec. Qui-Gon Jinn	3.00
TPB	13.00
TPB Adventures, rep.	13.00

STAR WARS: EPISODE I THE PHANTOM MENACE—MANGA
Dec., 1999

1 (of 2) 88-pg.	10.00

STAR WARS EPISODE II—ATTACK OF THE CLONES
Apr., 2002

1 (of 4) 48-pg.	4.00
2 thru 4 48-pg.	@4.00
1A thru 4A photo (c)	@4.00
TPB 144-pg.	18.00

STAR WARS HANDBOOK
July, 1998

1 X-Wing Rogue Squadron	3.50
2 Crimson Empire	3.00
Dark Empire	3.00

STAR WARS: HEIR TO THE EMPIRE
Oct., 1995–Apr., 1996

1 I:Grand Admiral Thrawn	4.00
2 thru 6	@3.50
TPB from novel by Timothy Zahn	20.00

STAR WARS: THE HUNT FOR AURRA SING
July, 2002

TPB 96-pg. TT	13.00

STAR WARS: INFINITIES — A NEW HOPE
May, 2001

1 (of 4) CW,TyH,Luke's attack fails, Death Star survives	3.00
1a gold foil photo (c)	13.00
2 CW,TyH	3.00
3 CW,TyH	3.00
4 CW,TyH, concl.	3.00
TPB series rep. 96-pg.	13.00

STAR WARS: INFINITIES — THE EMPIRE STRIKES BACK
July, 2002

1 (of 4)	3.00
2 thru 4	@3.00
TPB	13.00

STAR WARS: INFINITIES — RETURN OF THE JEDI
Nov., 2003

1 (of 4)	3.00
2 thru 4	@3.00
TPB	13.00

STAR WARS: JABBA THE HUTT—
1995–1996

1-shot The Garr Suppoon Hit	3.00
1-shot Hunger of Princess Nampi	3.00
1-shot The Dynasty Trap	3.00
1-shot Betrayal.	3.00
1-shot The Jabba Tape	3.00

STAR WARS: JANGO FETT
Dec., 2001

TPB 64-pg..,RMz	6.00

STAR WARS: JANGO FETT—OPEN SEASONS
Apr., 2002

1 (of 4)	3.00
2 thru 4	@3.00
TPB 96-pg.	13.00

STAR WARS: JEDI
Feb., 2003

Spec. Mace Windu, JOs,JD,48-pg.	5.00
Spec. Shaak Ti, JOs,JD, 48-pg.	5.00
Spec. Aayla Secura, JOs,JD,48-pg.	5.00
Spec. Dooku,JOs,JD,48-pg.	5.00
Spec. Yoda, 48-pg.	5.00

Star Wars: Jedi Academy Leviathan #1
© Dark Horse Comics

STAR WARS: JEDI ACADEMY LEVIATHAN
Oct., 1998

1 (of 4) by Kevin J. Anderson	3.00
2 thru 4	@3.00
TPB	12.00

STAR WARS: JEDI COUNCIL — ACTS OF WAR
June, 2000

1 (of 4) RSd, V:Yinchorri	3.00
1b gold foil (c)	10.00
2 thru 4 RSd	@3.00
TPB 96-pg. rep	13.00

All comics prices listed are for *Near Mint* condition.

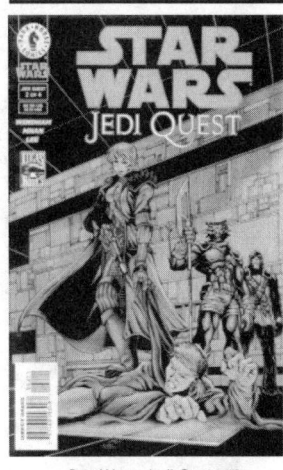

Star Wars: Jedi Quest #2
© Dark Horse Comics

STAR WARS: JEDI QUEST
Sept., 2001
1	3.00
1a ruby red foil	13.00
1b ruby red foil, signed	30.00
2 thru 4	@3.00

STAR WARS: JEDI VS. SITH
Apr., 2001
1 (of 6)	3.00
1a gold foil, lim.e.	10.00
2 V:Darth Bane	3.00
3 thru 6	@3.00
TPB 144-pg.	18.00

STAR WARS: THE LAST COMMAND
Nov., 1997–July, 1998
1 thru 6 MBn	@3.50
TPB, rep.	18.00

STAR WARS: MARA JADE— BY THE EMPEROR'S HAND
Aug., 1998
1 (of 6) by Timothy Zahn	5.00
2	4.00
3	4.00
4	4.00
5	4.00
6	4.00
TPB rep.	16.00

STAR WARS: OUTLANDER
Mar., 2001
TPB F:Ki-Adi-Mundi	13.00

STAR WARS: THE PROTOCOL OFFENSIVE
Sept., 1997
1-shot written by Anthony Daniels	5.00

STAR WARS: QUI-GON & OBI-WAN—LAST STAND ON ORD MANTELL
Jan., 2001
1	3.00
1a variant TnD (c)	3.00
1c gold foil (c)	15.00
2	3.00
3	3.00
1a thru 3a photo(c)	@3.00

STAR WARS: QUI-GON & OBI-WAN—THE AURORIENT EXPRESS
Feb., 2002
1 (of 2)	3.00
2	3.00

STAR WARS: RETURN OF THE JEDI—SPECIAL EDITION
TPB Hildebrandt(c)	10.00

STAR WARS: THE RETURN OF THE JEDI
(B&W–Manga) June, 1999
1 (of 4) Shin-ichi Hiromoto, 96-pg.	10.00
2 thru 4	@10.00

STAR WARS: THE RITE OF PASSAGE
Jan., 2004
TPB	13.00

STAR WARS: RIVER OF CHAOS
May–Nov., 1995
1 LSi,JBr,Emperor sends spies	3.00
2 Imperial in Allies Clothing	3.00
3	3.00
4 F:Ranulf	3.00

STAR WARS: SHADOWS OF THE EMPIRE
May, 1996
1 (of 6) by John Wagner, Kilian Plunkett & P. Craig Russell	3.50
2 thru 6	@3.50
TPB	18.00

STAR WARS: SHADOWS OF THE EMPIRE — EVOLUTION
Feb.–June, 1998
1 thru 5	@3.50
TPB Steve Perry(s)	15.00

STAR WARS: SHADOW STALKER
Nov., 1997
1-shot from Star Wars Galaxy Mag.	3.50

STAR WARS: SPLINTER OF THE MIND'S EYE
Dec., 1995–June, 1996
1 thru 4 A.D.Foster novel adapt.	@3.50
TPB	15.00

STAR WARS: STARFIGHTER— CROSSBONES
Jan., 2002
1 (of 3) F:Nym, pirate captain	3.00
2 from video game	3.00
3	3.00

STAR WARS: TAG & BINK ARE DEAD
Oct., 2001
1 (of 2)	3.00
2	3.00

STAR WARS TALES
Sept., 1999
1 various authors, 64-pg.	10.00
2 thru 4, 64-pg.	@6.00
5 F:Lando's Commandos	6.00
6 thru 9	@6.00
10 thru 21	@6.00
5a thru 19a photo(c)	@6.00
TPB Vol. 1	20.00
TPB Vol. 2	20.00
TPB Vol. 3	20.00
TPB Vol. 4	20.00

STAR WARS: TALES FROM MOS EISLEY
1-shot, from Star Wars Galaxy Mag. #2–#4	3.50

STAR WARS: TALES OFTHE JEDI
Oct., 1993
1 RV,I:Ulic Qel-Droma	6.00
2 RV,A:Ulic Qel-Droma	5.00
3 RV,D:Andur	5.00
4 RV,A:Jabba the Hut	4.00
5 RV,last issue	4.00
TPB	15.00
TPB 2nd printing	15.00
TPB Redemption, 112-pg.	15.00

STAR WARS: TALES OF THE JEDI: DARK LORDS OF THE SITH
Oct., 1994–Mar., 1995
1 Bagged with card	3.00
2	3.00
3 Krath Attack	3.00
4 F:Exar Kun	3.00
5 V:TehKrath	3.00
6 Final battle	3.00
TPB	18.00

STAR WARS: TALES OF THE JEDI: THE FREEDON NADD UPRISING
Aug.–Sept., 1997
1 and 2	@3.00
TPB series rep.	6.00

STAR WARS: TALES OF THE JEDI: THE SITH WAR
Aug., 1995–Jan., 1996
1 F:Exar Kun	3.00
2 F:Ulic Oel-Droma	3.00
3 F:Exar Kun	3.00
4 thru 6 (6 part mini-series)	@3.00
TPB	18.00

DARK HORSE

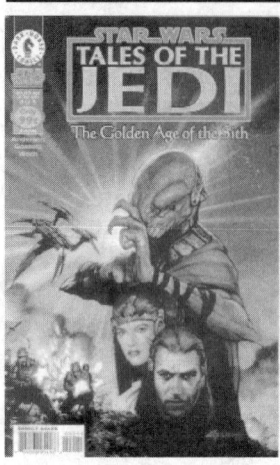

Star Wars: Tales of the Jedi–
The Golden Age of the Sith #2
© Dark Horse Comics

STAR WARS: TALES OF THE JEDI—THE FALL OF THE SITH EMPIRE
June–Oct., 1997
1 (of 5) 3.50
2 thru 5 . . . . @3.00

STAR WARS: TALES OF THE JEDI—THE GOLDEN AGE OF THE SITH
Oct., 1996–Feb., 1997
0 . . . . 2.25
1 thru 5 . . . . @3.50
TPB 17.00

STAR WARS: TALES OF THE JEDI— THE REDEMPTION OF ULIC QEL-DROMA
July, 1998
1 (of 5) by Kevin J. Anderson 3.50
2 thru 5 . . . . @3.50

STAR WARS: THE STARK HYPERSPACE WAR
Nov., 2003
TPB JOs. 13.00

STAR WARS: TWILIGHT
Nov., 2001
TPB JOs,JD 13.00

STAR WARS: UNDERWORLD—THE YAVIN VASSILIKA
Dec., 2000
1 (of 5) F:Han Solo 3.00
2 thru 5 . . . . @3.00
1a thru 5a photo (c) . . . . @3.00
TPB 120-pg. 15.00

STAR WARS: UNION
Nov., 1999
1 (of 4) by Stackpole 3.00
1a gold foil (c) 10.00
2 the wedding approaches 3.00
3 almost there 3.00
4 wedding day 3.00
TPB Luke & Mara Jade 13.00

STAR WARS: VADER'S QUEST
Feb., 1999
1 (of 4) DGb,AMK 3.00
2 thru 4 . . . . @3.00
TPB with poster 12.00

STAR WARS: A VALEN-TINE STORY
Feb., 2003
1-shot PC 3.50

STAR WARS: X-WING ROGUE SQUADRON
July, 1995
The Rebel Opposition
1 F:Wedge Antilles 5.00
2 . . . . 3.50
3 F:Tycho Clehu 3.50
4 F:Tycho Clehu 3.50
½ Wizard limited exclusive 6.00
The Phantom Affair
5 thru 8 . . . . @3.50
TPB rep. 13.00
Battleground Tatooine
9 thru 12 . . . . @3.50
TPB rep. 13.00
The Warrior Princess
13 thru 16 . . . . @3.50
TPB rep. 14.00
Requiem for a Rogue
17 thru 20 . . . . @3.50
TPB rep. 13.00
In the Empire's Service
21 thru 24 . . . . @3.50
TPB rep. 13.00
Making of Baron Fell
25 . . . . 5.00
Family Ties
26 thru 27 . . . . @3.50
Masquerade
28 thru 31 . . . . @3.50
TPB Masquerade, rep. 13.00
Mandatory Retirement
32 thru 35 . . . . @3.50
TPB Blood and Honor 13.00
TPB Mandatory Retirement 13.00

STAR WARS: ZAM WESELL
Feb., 2002
TPB RMz, 64-pg. 6.00

STRIP SEARCH
Dec., 2003
TPB 15.00

STEVE RUDE'S THE MOTH
Mar., 2004
1 . . . . 3.00
2 thru 4 . . . . @3.00
Spec. Double sized 5.00

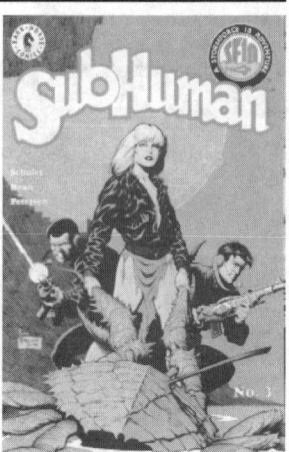

SubHuman #3
© Dark Horse Comics

SUBHUMAN
Nov., 1998
1 (of 4) MSh 3.00
2 thru 4 MSh . . . . @3.00

SUPERMAN/MADMAN HULLABALOO
June–Aug., 1997
1 (of 3) MiA 3.00
2 and 3 (of 3) . . . . @3.00

SUPERMAN/TARZAN: SONS OF THE JUNGLE
Oct., 2001
1 (of 3) CDi,HuR 3.00
2 CDi,HuR. 3.00
3 CDi,HuR(c) 3.00
TPB 80-pg. 10.00

SUPERMAN VS. ALIENS
DC/Dark Horse, 1995
1 DJu,KN 6.00
2 V:Queen Alien 5.00
TPB 15.00

SUPERMAN VS. ALIENS II
May, 2002
1 (of 4) CDi,JBg,KN, x-over 3.00
2 CDi,JBg,KN 3.00
3 CDi,JBg,KN 3.00
4 CDi,JBg,KN 3.00
TPB God War. 13.00

SUPERMAN VS. THE TERMINATOR: DEATH TO THE FUTURE
Dec., 1999
1 (of 4) AIG,StP,x-over. 3.00
2 AIG,StP,into the future 3.00
3 AIG,StP,A:Supergirl 3.00
4 AIG,StP,concl. 3.00
TPB AIG,StP,series rep. 11.00

SUPER MANGA BLAST
Mar., 2000
1 128-pg. 5.00

2 thru 6 128-pg.. . . . . @5.00
7 F:Oh My Goddess 5.00
8 F:Oh My Goddess 5.00
9 F:3x3 Eyes. 5.00
10 F:Seraphic Feather 5.00
11 F:Oh My Goddess. 5.00
12 F:Oh My Goddess. 5.00
13 F:Club 9 . . . . 5.00
14 F:Club 9 . . . . 5.00
15 F:Club 9, 50-pg. 6.00
16 F:3x3 Eyes 6.00
17 F:Club 9 . . . . 6.00
18 F:Club 9 . . . . 6.00
19 Seraphic Feather 6.00
20 What's Michael? 6.00
21 F:Club 9 . . . . 6.00
22 Club 9, 3x3 Eyes 6.00
23 Club 9, What's Michael?. 6.00
24 F:Seraphic Feather 6.00
25 F:Appleseed 6.00
26 F:Shadow Star 6.00
27 F:What's Michael? 6.00
28 thru 46. . . . . @6.00
TPB Vol.5 What's Michael's
   Favorite Spot 9.00

SYN
Rocket Comics Aug., 2003
1 KG 3.00
2 thru 5 . . . . @3.00
TPB 14.00

TALE OF ONE BAD RAT
1994
1 BT 3.00
2 thru 4 . . . . @3.00
TPB Rep.#1–#4 . . . . 15.00

TALES OF
ORDINARY MADNESS
(B&W)
1 JBo(c),Paranoid. 3.00
2 JBo(c),Mood 2.50
3 JBo(c),A Little Bit of Neurosis . . . 2.50

TALES OF THE VAMPIRES
Dec., 2003
1 Josh Whedon. 3.00
2 thru 5 . . . . @3.00
TPB 16.00

TALES TO OFFEND
July, 1997
1-shot by Frank Miller 3.00

TANK GIRL
(B&W) 1991
1 Rep. from U.K.Deadline Mag.
   with 2-card strip. 4.50
2 V:Indiana Potato Jones 4.00
3 On the Run 4.00
4 . . . . 4.00
TPB colorized. 15.00

[2nd Series] 1993
1 . . . . 3.50
2 thru 4 . . . . @3.00

TARZAN
TPB The Untamed 12.00

TARZAN/JOHN CARTER:
WARLORDS OF MARS
1996
1 (of 4) E.R.Burroughs adapt.. . . . 3.00

---

2 thru 4. . . . . @3.00

TARZAN VS. PREDATOR
AT THE EARTH'S CORE
1996
1 Tarzan vs. Predator 3.00
2 V:Predator 3.00
3 Tarzan on the Hunt 3.00
4 . . . . 3.00
TPB series rep. 13.00

TENTH, THE:
NIGHTWALKER
Apr., 2002
1 (of 4) TnD 3.00
2 thru 4 . . . . @3.00
1a thru 4a variant (c). . . . . @3.00
TPB No Sweets After Dark 10.00

TENTH, THE:
RESURRECTED
Apr., 2001
1 TnD 3.00
1a variant(c) 7.00
1b variant(c) signed 20.00
2 TnD 3.00
3 TnD 3.00
3a variant (c) 3.00
4 TnD 3.00
4a variant (c). 3.00
TPB Blackout, rep.#1–#5 . . . . 15.00

TERMINAL POINT
1993
1 . . . . 2.50
2 . . . . 2.50

TERMINATOR
1990
1 CW,Tempest 4.00
2 CW,Tempest 3.00
3 CW. 3.00
4 CW, conclusion 3.00

TERMINATOR
1-shot MW,3-D const(c2,
   pop-up inside (1991) 5.00
Spec. AIG,GyD,GeD(1998) 3.00

The Terminator #2
© Dark Horse Comics

TERMINATOR, THE
Sept., 1998
1 AIG,StP. 3.00
2 F:Sarah Connor. 3.00
3 F:Killerman. 3.00
4 F:D-800L & D-810X 3.00
TPB Death Valley. 15.00

TERMINATOR, THE:
THE DARK YEARS
Sept., 1999
1 (of 4) AIG,MvR,BWi 3.00
2 AIG,MvR,BWi,F:Jon Norden. 3.00
3 . . . . 3.00
4 AIG,MvR,concl.. . . . . 3.00

TERMINATOR:
END GAME
1992
1 JG,Final *Terminator* series. 3.00
2 JG,Cont.last Term.story 3.00
3 JG, Concl. 3.00
TPB Endgame 10.00

TERMINATOR:
ENEMY WITHIN
1991
1 cont. from Sec.Objectives 4.00
2 C890.L.threat contd. 3.00
3 Secrets of Cyberdyne 3.00
4 Conclusion 3.00
SC rep #1–#4. . . . . 14.00

TERMINATOR: HUNTERS
& KILLERS
1992
1 V:Russians. 3.00
2 V:Russians. 3.00
3 V:Russians. 3.00

TERMINATOR:
SECONDARY
OBJECTIVES
1991
1 cont. 1st DH mini-series 4.00
2 PG,A:New Female Terminator . . . 3.00
3 PG,Terminators in L.A.&Mexico . . 3.00
4 PG,Terminator vs Terminator 3.00

TERRITORY, THE
Jan., 1999
1 (of 4) JaD,DvL,F:Ishmael. 3.00
2 thru 4 . . . . @3.00

TEX AVERY'S DROOPY
1 Dr. Droopenstein 2.50
2 and 3 . . . . @2.50

TEX AVERY'S
SCREWBALL SQUIRREL
1 I:Screwball Squirrel 2.50
2 Cleaning House 2.50
3 School of Hard Rocks 2.50

THING, THE
1991
1 JHi, Movie adaptation 4.00
2 JHi, Movie adaptation 3.50

All comics prices listed are for *Near Mint* condition.

THING FROM ANOTHER WORLD: CLIMATE OF FEAR
1994
1 Argentinian Military Base
  (Bahiathetis) 2.75
2 Thing on Base 2.75
3 Thing/takeover 2.75
4 Conclusion 2.75
TPB 16.00

THING FROM ANOTHER WORLD: ETERNAL VOWS
1993
1 PG,I:Sgt. Rowan 2.75
2 PG 2.75
3 PG,in New Zealand 2.75
4 PG,Last issue. 2.75

THIRTEEN O'CLOCK
(B&W)
1 Mr.Murmer,from Deadline USA . . 3.00

3 X 3 EYES: CURSE OF THE GESU
(B&W–Manga) 1995
1 I:Pai,Yakumo 3.00
2 thru 5 . . . . @3.00
TPB Curse of the Gesu, by Yuzo
  Takada 13.00
TPB House of Demons 13.00
TPB 208-pg. 17.00
TPB Blood of the Sacred Demon . 14.00
TPB Summoning the Beast (2002) 15.00
TPB Key to the Sacred Land 14.00
TPB House of Demons, 2nd ed. . . 15.00
TPB Curse of the Gesu, 2nd ed. . . 15.00
TPB Shadow of the Kunlun 18.00
TPB Vol. 8 Descent of Mystic City . 19.00
TPB Vol. 9 . . . . 13.00

300
May, 1998
1 (of 5) FM & Lynn Varley. 3.00
2 F:Spartans 3.00
3 thru 5 . . . . @3.00

TIME COP
1994
1 Movie Adaptation 2.75
2 Movie Adaptation 2.50

TITAN
1994
Spec.#1 BS(c),I:Inhibitors 4.25

TITAN A.E.
May, 2000
1 (of 3) film prequel,pt.1 . . . . 3.00
2 thru 3 prequel,pt.2–pt.3 . . . . . . @3.00

TONGUE*LASH
Aug., 1996
1 by Randy and Jean-Marc
  Lofficier & Dave Taylor 3.00
2 . . . . 3.00

[VOL. II] 1999
1 (of 2) 3.00
2 . . . . 3.00

Tongue Lash, Vol. II, #2
© Dark Horse Comics

TONY DANIEL'S F5
May, 2002
TPB Color, 128-pg. 15.00

TONY MILLIONAIRE'S SOCK MONKEY
TPB 10.00

VOL. 3
1 & 2) . . . . @3.00
TPB A Children's Book. 10.00

TOO MUCH COFFEE MAN
(B&W) July, 1997
1-shot by Shannon Wheeler 3.00
TPB Guide for the Perplexed. . . . 11.00
TPB Parade of Tirade 13.00
TPB Amusing Musings. 13.00

TREKKER
(B&W) 1987
1 thru 4 . . . . @2.25
5 thru 7 . . . . @2.25
8 O:Trekker. 2.25
9 . . . . 2.25
Spec.#1 Sins of the Fathers 3.00

TRIGUN
Nov., 2003
TPB Vol. 1 b&w 15.00
TPB Vol. 2 . . . . 15.00
TPB Trigun Anime Manga 15.00

TRIGUN MAXIMUM
May, 2004
TPB Vol. 1 The Hero Returns 14.00
TPB Vol. 2 Death Blue 10.00
TPB Vol. 3 His Live as a 10.00

TRIPLE X
(B&W) 1994
TPB by Arnold & Jacob Pander . . . 25.00

TWO FACES OF TOMORROW, THE
(B&W–Manga) Aug., 1997
1 (of 13) from James P. Hogan
  novel, by Yukinobu Hoshino . . . 3.00

2 thru 4 . . . . @3.00
5 thru 13 . . . . @4.00

TWO FISTED TALES
Spec. WW,WiS. 5.00

2112
GN JBy,A:Next Men. 2.25
2nd Printing 5.00
TPB GNv, JBy,A:Next Men 10.00
2nd & 3rd printing 10.00

ULTRAMAN TIGA
Aug., 2003
1 (of 10) 4.00
2 thru 4 . . . . @4.00
5 thru 10 . . . . @4.00
TPB Vol. 1 . . . . 16.00

[ANDREW VACHSS'] UNDERGROUND
(B&W) 1993
1 AVs(s). 4.25
2 thru 5 AVs(s) . . . . @4.00

UNIVERSAL MONSTERS
1991
1 AAd,Creature From The
  Black Lagoon. 5.50
1 Dracula 5.50
1 Frankenstein 5.50
1 The Mummy. 5.50

USAGI YOJIMBO
(B&W) 1996
1 by Stan Sakai. 5.00
2 thru 9 . . . . @4.00
10 with Sergio Aragones 5.00
11 'The Lord of Owls'. 5.00
12 'Vampire Cat of the Geishu' . . . 3.00
13 thru 22 'Grasscutter,',pt.1
  thru pt. #10 . . . . @3.00
23 My Father's Sword 3.00
24 The Demon Flute 3.00
25 Momo-Usagi-Taro 3.00
26 The Hairpin Murders,pt.1 . . . . . 3.00
27 The Hairpin Murders,pt.2 . . . . . 3.00
28 Courtesan conspiracy,pt.1 . . . . 3.00
29 Courtesan conspiracy,pt.2 . . . . 3.00

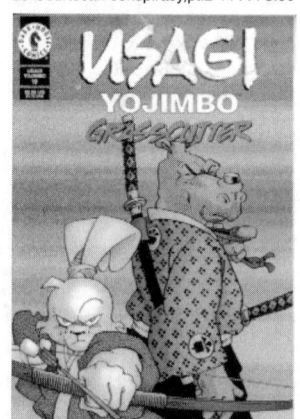

Usagi Yojimbo #19
© Dark Horse Comics

30 Inspector Ishida mystery 3.00
31 The Haunted Inn of Moon
   Shadow Hill 3.00
32 Two stories 3.00
33 . . . . 3.00
34 Demon Mask,pt.1 . . . . 3.00
35 Demon Mask,pt.2 . . . . 3.00
36 Demon Mask,pt.3 . . . . 3.00
37 F:Sasuke the Demon Queller . . . 3.00
38 Priest Sanshobo's temple 3.00
39 Grasscutter II,pt.1 . . . . 3.00
40 V:Captain Quark 3.00
41 V:Neko Ninja 3.00
42 Grasscutter II,pt.4 . . . . 3.00
43 Grasscutter II 3.00
44 Grasscutter II 3.00
45 Grasscutter II 3.00
46 wraparound(c),pt.1 . . . . 3.00
47 wraparound(c),pt.2 . . . . 3.00
48 . . . . 3.00
49 Three seasons 3.00
50 Usagi dead? 3.00
51 The Shrouded Moon 3.00
52 Kitsune's youth 3.00
53 hunt for four ronin 3.00
54 Lone Goat and Kid 3.00
55 Lord Yoshikawa is dying 3.00
56 Katsuichi vs. Nakamura Joji 3.00
57 Crows,pt.1, renegade ronin 3.00
58 Crows,pt.2 . . . . 3.00
59 Crows,pt.3 . . . . 3.00
60 duel at Kitanoji 3.00
61 F:Chizu 3.00
62 Cursed woods 3.00
63 SS, return of Kitsune 3.00
64 SS, Tomago 3.00
65 SS 3.00
66 SS,giant monsters,pt.1 . . . . 3.00
67 SS,giant monsters,pt.2 . . . . 3.00
68 SS,giant monsters,pt.3 . . . . 3.00
69 SS,Fathers and Sons,pt.1 . . . . . 3.00
70 SS,Fathers and Sons,pt.2 . . . . . 3.00
71 to 79 SS . . . . @3.00
TPB Vol. 18 Travels with Jotaro . . . 16.00
TPB Demon Mask 16.00
TPB Shades of Death, rep. of
   Mirage series 15.00
TPB Daisho, rep. Mirage 15.00
TPB The Brink of Life & Death . . . 15.00
TPB Seasons 15.00
TPB Grasscutter 17.00
TPB Grasscutter 17.00
TPB Grey Shadows 15.00
TPB Grasscutter II 16.00
TPB SS, Shrouded Moon, 184-pg. 16.00
TPB Duel at Kitanoji 17.00

USAGI YOJIMBO
1996
1 SS,color spec. 4.00
2 SS,color spec. 3.00
3 SS,color spec. 3.00
4 thru 6 . . . . @3.00

USAGI YOJIMBO
COLOR SPECIAL:
GREEN PERSIMMON
1-shot by Stan Sakai 3.00

VAMPIRELLA
(B&W)
1 'The Lion and the Lizard'Pt.1 . . . . 4.50
2 'The Lion and the Lizard'Pt.2 . . . . 4.00
3 'The Lion and the Lizard'Pt.3 . . . . 4.00
4 'The Lion and the Lizard'Pt.3 . . . . 4.00

VAN HELSING
May, 2004
1-shot Movie tie-in 3.00

VENUS WARS
(B&W–Manga) 1991
1 Aphrodia V:Ishtar, with
   2-card strip 3.00
2 I: Ken Seno 2.50
3 Aphrodia V:Ishtar 2.50
4 Seno Joins Hound Corps. 2.50
5 SenoV:Octopus Supertanks 2.50
6 Chaos in Aphrodia 2.50
7 All Out Ground War 2.50
8 Ishtar V:Aphrodia contd. 2.50
9 Ishtar V:Aphrodia contd. 2.50
10 Supertanks of Ishtar Advance . . 2.50
11 Aphrodia Captured 2.50
12 A:Miranda,48-pg. 2.75
13 Hound Brigade-Suicide Assault . 2.25
14 V:Army 2.50
15 . . . . 2.50
TPB Vol. 1 . . . . 14.00

VENUS WARS II
1992
1 V:Security Police 2.75
2 Political Unrest. 2.25
3 Conspiracy 2.25
4 A:Lupica 2.25
5 Love Hotel 2.25
6 Terran Consulate 2.25
7 Doublecross 2.25
8 D:Lupisa 3.00
9 A:Matthew 3.00
10 A:Mad Scientist 3.00
11 thru 15 V:Troopers . . . . @3.00

VERSION
(B&W–Manga)
1.1 by Hisashi Sakaguchi 2.50
1.2 thru 1.8 . . . . @2.50

VERSION II
(B&W–Manga)
1.1 by Hisashi Sakaguchi 2.50
1.2 thru 1.6 . . . . @2.50

VIDEO NOIRE
Sept., 2001
TPB 10.00

VIOLENT CASES
Oct., 2003
TPB NGa,DMc 15.00

VIRUS
1993
1 MP(c),F:The Wan Xuan & the
   crew of the Electra 3.00
2 MP(c),V:Captian Powell 3.00
3 MP(c),V:Virus 3.00
4 MP(c),Last issue 3.00
TPB rep.#1–#4. . . . . 17.00

VORTEX, THE
1 . . . . 2.25

WALTER:
CAMPAIGN OF TERROR
1 . . . . 2.50
2 and 3 . . . . @2.50

WARRIOR OF
WAVERLY STREET, THE
Nov., 1996
1 (of 2) by M.Coto & J. Stokes 3.00
1-shot Broodstorm 3.00

WARWORLD!
(B&W) 1989
1 . . . . 2.25

WHAT'S MICHAEL?
(B&W–Manga)
TPB by Makoto Kobayashi 6.00
TPB Living Together 6.00
TPB Off the Deep End 6.00
TPB A Hard Day's Life (2002) 9.00
TPB Show Time 9.00
TPB Fat Cat in the City 9.00

WHAT'S MICHAEL
July, 2002
TPB Vol. 9 The Ideal Cat 9.00

WHITE LIKE SHE
(B&W) 1994
1 by Bob Fingerman 3.00
2 thru 4 . . . . @3.00

WILL EISNER'S HAWKS
OF THE SEAS
July, 2003
TPB b&w 20.00

WILL TO POWER
Comics' Greatest World, 1994
1 BS, A:X 2.25
2 BS, A:X,Monster 2.25
3 BS, A:X 2.25
4 BS, In Steel Harbor 2.25
5 V:Wolfgang 2.25
6 V:Motorhead 2.25
7 JOy(c),V:Amazing Grace 2.25
8 V:Catalyst 2.25
9 Titan, Grace 2.25
10 Vortex alien, Grace 2.25

Will to Power #9
© Dark Horse Comics

DARK HORSE

11 Vortex alien, King Titan 2.25
12 Vortex alien 2.25

WITCHBLADE/ALIENS/ DARKNESS/PREDATOR: MINDHUNTER
Dec., 2000
1 (of 3) 3.00
2 . . . . 3.00
2a variant TnD (c) 3.00
3 concl 3.00
TPB 96-pg.. . . . . 13.00

WIZARD OF FOURTH STREET
(B&W) 1987
1 . . . . 2.25
2 thru 4 . . . . @2.25

WOLF & RED
1995
1 Looney Tunes 2.50
2 Watchdog Wolf 2.50
3 Red Hot Riding Hood 2.50

WOLVERTON IN SPACE
(B&W) Apr., 1997
TPB by Basil Wolverton 17.00

The World Below #3
© *Dark Horse Comics*

WORLD BELOW, THE
Mar., 1999
1 PC 2.50
2 thru 4 PC . . . . @2.50

WORLD BELOW II, THE
Dec., 1999
1 (of 4) PC 3.00
2 . . . . 3.00
3 PC,Deeper and Stranger 3.00
4 PC,Deeper and Stranger 3.00

X
Comics' Greatest World, 1994
1 B:StG(s),DoM,JP,I:X-Killer 3.00
2 DoM,JP,V:X-Killer. 2.50
3 DoM,JP,A:Pit Bulls 2.50
4 DoM,JP 2.50
5 DoM,JP,V:Chaos Riders 2.50
6 Cyberassassins 2.50
7 Alamout 2.50
8 A:Ghost 2.50
9 War for Arcadia 2.50
10 War for Arcadia 2.50
11 I:Coffin, War 2.50
12 V:Coffin, A:Monster 2.50
13 D:X 2.50
14 conclusion to War 2.50
15 JS,SiG,war survivors 2.50
16 V:Headhunter 2.50
17 . . . . 2.50
18 V:Predator 2.50
19 V:Challenge 2.50
20 thru 25 . . . . @2.50
Spec. #1 One Shot to the Head. . . 2.50

XENA: WARRIOR PRINCESS
Aug., 1999
1 . . . . 3.00
2 thru 9 . . . . @3.00
10 IEd,MD2,wayward viking 3.00
11 IEd,MD2,V:Lamia 3.00
12 IEd,MD2,Darkness Falls,concl.. . 3.00
13 IEd,MD2,F:Legion 3.00
14 conclusion 3.00
1 to 14 newsstand photo(c) . . . . . @3.00
TPB Slave 10.00
TPB The Warrior Way of Death . . . 10.00
TPB Blood and Shadows. 12.00

XXX
1 . . . . 4.00
2 V:Dr. Zemph. 4.00
3 . . . . 4.00
4 V:Rhine Lords 4.00
5 I:Klaar 4.00
6 Klaar captured 5.00
7 Revolution Consequences 5.00

XENOXOIC TALES
Apr., 2003
TPB Vol. 1 rep.. . . . . 15.00
TPB Vol. 2 rep.. . . . . 15.00

YOUNG CYNICS CLUB
(B&W) 1993
1 by Glenn Wong 2.50

THE YOUNG INDIANA JONES CHRONICLES
1992
1 DBa,FS,TV Movie Adapt 3.25
2 DBa,TV Movie Adapt 2.75
3 DBa,GM. 2.75
4 DBa,GM. 2.75
5 DBa,GM. 2.75
6 BBa,GM,WW1,French Army . . . 2.75
7 The Congo 2.75
8 Africa,A:A.Schweitzer 2.50
9 Vienna,Sophie-daughter of Arch-
    Duke Ferdinand 2.50
10 In Vienna continued 2.50
11 Far East 2.50
12 Fever Issue 2.50

YOU'RE UNDER ARREST!
(B&W–Manga) 1995–96
1 by Kosuke Fujishima 3.00
2 thru 8 . . . . @3.00
TPB rep.. . . . . 13.00

ZOMBIEWORLD:
1-shot Eat Your Heart Out, KJo . . . 3.00
1-shot Home for the Holidays 3.00

Zombieworld: Dead End #2
© *Dark Horse Comics*

ZOMBIEWORLD: DEAD END
Jan., 1998
1 (of 2) by Stephen Blue 3.00
2 . . . . 3.00

ZOMBIEWORLD: CHAMPION OF THE WORMS
Sept., 1997
1 (of 3) MMi 3.00
2 and 3 . . . . @3.00
Spec. Home for the Holidays 3.00
TPB 9.00

ZOMBIEWORLD: THE TREE OF DEATH
May, 1999
1 (of 4) by P. Mills & J.Deadstock. . 3.00
2 thru 4 . . . . @3.00

ZOMBIEWORLD: WINTER'S DREGS
May, 1998
1 (of 4) by Fingerman & Edwards. . 3.00
2 thru 4 . . . . @3.00

ZONE, THE
(B&W) 1990
1-shot 3.00

IMAGE

AARON STRIPS
(B&W) Apr., 1997
1 thru 4 rep. from Sunday comic
 strips, by Aaron Warner . . . . . @3.00

ACTION PLANET
(B&W) Sept., 1997
Prev. Action Planet Comics
3 . . . . 4.00

ADRENALYNN
Aug., 1999
1 F:Sabina Nikoli. 2.50
2 TnD,V:Russian monster androids 2.50
3 TnD,V:last 2 Monster-cyborgs . . . 2.50
4 TnD,the real Sabina. 2.50

ADVENTURES OF AARON
March, 1997
(B&W) by Aaron Warner
1 'Baby-sitter Gone Bad'. 3.00
2 'Thunder Thighs of the
 Terrordome' 3.00
3 'Baby-sitter Gone Bad,' concl. . . . 3.00
100 Super Special 3.00
Christmas Spectacular #1 . . . . 3.00

ADVENTURES OF BARRY WEEN, BOY GENIUS, THE
(B&W) March, 1999
1 (of 3) by Judd Winick. 3.00
2 Growing Pains 3.00
3 School 3.00

ADVENTURE STRIP DIGEST
(B&W) April, 1998
1 by Randy Reynaldo 3.00
2 F:Rob Hanes, detective 3.00

AGENTS, THE
April, 2003
1 (of 6) BDn, b&w 3.00
2 thru 6 . . . . @3.00

AGE OF BRONZE
(B&W) Nov., 1998
1 EiS,The Trojan War 3.00
2 EiS,Death of Paris 3.00
3 EiS,F:Herakles, Hektor 3.00
4 EiS,I:Helen. 3.00
5 EiS,Achilles disguised 3.00
6 EiS,Helen gone 3.50
7 EiS,Odysseus mad? 3.50
8 EiS,Achilles missing. 3.50
9 EiS,Will war start? 3.50
10 EiS,Sacrifice,pt.1. . . . . 3.50
11 EiS,Sacrifice,pt.2. . . . . 3.50
12 EiS,You're not the Trojans? 3.50
13 thru 18 EiS,Sacrifice,pt.4–pt.9 @3.50
19 EiS,Sacrifice,pt.10. . . . . 3.50
Spec.1-shot Behind the Scenes . . . 3.50
Spec.#1 EiS, House of Horror 3.00
Spec.#2 . . . . 3.00
TPB Vol.1 A Thousand Ships. 20.00

AGE OF HEROES, THE
Halloween, 1996
(B&W)
1 JHI & JRy. 3.00
2 JHI & JRy. 3.00
3 JHI & JRy,Luko,Trickster &
 Aerwyn try to steal treasure . . . 3.00
4 JHI & JRy,Drake, the blind
 swordsman returns 3.00
5 JHI & JRy,O:Conor One-Arm. . . . 3.00
Spec. #1 rep. #1 & #2 . . . . 5.00
Spec. #2 rep. #3 & #4 . . . . 7.00

AGE OF HEROES: WEX
(B&W) Aug., 1998
1 by JHI,Vurtex 3.00

AGENCY, THE
Top Cow, July, 2001
1 (of 6) PJe. 4.00
1a variant(c) 4.00
1b variant MS(c) 4.00
2 PJe. 2.50
3 PJe. 2.50
4 PJe,A Virtual Secret. 3.00
5 PJe,Virtual 3.00
6 PJe,concl. 48-pg. 5.00

Allegra #1 © WildStorm

ALLEGRA
WildStorm, 1996
1 ScC,SSe 2.50
2 thru 4 . . . . @2.50

ALLEY CAT
July, 1999
1 BNa,MHw,F:Alley Baggett 2.50
1a variant painted cover (1:4) 3.50
2 BNa,MHw,women murdered 2.50
3 photo(c) 2.50
3a variant JJu cover (1:4) 3.50
4 into darkness 2.50
5 The Martyr,pt.1. . . . . 3.00
6 The Martyr,pt.2. . . . . 3.00
7 The Martyr,pt.3. . . . . 2.50

Wizard World Spec.#1 . . . . 2.50
Lingerie Edition 5.00

ALLIANCE, THE
Shadowline, 1995
1 JV,I:The Alliance, A Call
 to Arms 2.50
2 JV,Team comes together 'Like
 Pieces of a Puzzle' 2.50
3 I:Slash C 2.50
4 . . . . 2.50
1a thru 4a variant covers . . . . . . @2.50

ALLIES, THE
Extreme, 1995
1 mini-series 2.50
2 thru 4 . . . . @2.50

ALONE IN THE DARK
July, 2002
GN 1-shot, 48-pg. 5.00

ALTERATION
Image, Feb., 2004
1 . . . . 3.00
1a variant (c) AAd 3.00
2 thru 4 . . . . @3.00
2a thru 4a variant (c)s . . . . @3.00

ALTERED IMAGE
April, 1998
1 JV,The Day Reality Went Wild. . . 2.50
2 JV,F:Everybody smooshed 2.50
3 JV,Middle Age Crisis, concl. 2.50
TPB F:everybody 10.00

AMANDA AND GUNN
(B&W) April, 1997
1 JeR, Montana 2036 . . . . 3.00
2 (of 4) JeR. 3.00
3 (of 4) JeR. 3.00
4 (of 4) JeR, conclusion 3.00

ANGELA
TMP, 1994–95
1 NGa(s),GCa,A:Spawn 15.00
2 NGa(s),GCa,Angela's trial 14.00
3 NGa(s),GCa,In Hell 12.00
Spec. Pirate Spawn(c) 32.00
Spec. Pirate Angela(c) (1995) 30.00
TPB Rep.#1–#3 . . . . 10.00

ANGELA/GLORY: RAGE OF ANGELS
TMP/Extreme, 1996
1 x-over begins 5.00

APHRODITE IX
Top Cow, Aug., 2000
1 by David Finch. 4.00
1a variant JBz(c). 4.00
1a signed 20.00
1b variant Michale Turner(c). 4.00
1c variant MS(c) 4.00
2 amnesia 3.50
3 conspiracy 3.50
0 with pin-up & poster. 3.00
4 Who is she? 48-pg. 5.50

IMAGE

Spec.1 Convention spec., signed . 20.00
Preview ed., signed 5.00
TPB 15.00

ARCANUM
Top Cow, March, 1997
[Mini-series]
1 BPe, from Medieval
   Spawn/Witchblade. 3.00
1a variant MS(s) (1:4). 2.50
2 BPe, Chi in Asylum 2.50
3 BPe, Ming Chang captive in
   Atlantis. 2.50
4 BPe,'The End?' 2.50
5 BPe,Royale's secret journal 2.50
6 BPe,Safe Haven? 2.50
7 BPe,Egypt 2.50

AREA 52
Jan., 2001
1 . . . . 3.00
2 The Gloves are off. 3.00
3 Out of the Frying Pan and
   into the Fire 3.00
4 Beginning of the End 3.00

ARIA
Avalon Nov., 1998
1 by Brian Holguin & Jay Anacleto . 3.00
1a variant cover 4.00
2 A:Mad Gwynnion 3.00
3 English Countryside. 3.00
4 V:Dark One 3.00
4a glow-in-the-dark(c). 15.00
5 London, 1966. . . . . 2.50
6 Subterranean Homesick Blues . . 2.50
7 Mad Gods and Irish Men. 2.50
Preview ed. F:Kildare. 3.00
Spec.#1 Blanc & Noir, sketchbook. . 3.00
Spec.#1 alternate cover. 7.00
Spec.#2 Blanc & Noir. 2.50
Sketchbook by Jay Anacleto 6.00
TPB The Magic of Aria. 14.00
Coll.Ed.#1, rep.#1–#2 . . . . 6.00

ARIA/ANGELA:
HEAVENLY CREATURES
Feb., 2000
1 (of 2) x-over. 5.00
1a variant JQ(c) (1:4) 3.00
1b variant J.G. Jones(c) (1:4) 4.00
1c variant Jay Anacleto(c) (1:4) . . . 3.00
1 B&W 3.00
2 x-over concl. 3.00
2a variant(c) 4.00
Museum edition 125.00

ARIA: THE SOUL MARKET
March, 2001
1 Legend continues 4.00
1a Museum edition 125.00
2 F:Robin Goodfellow. 3.00
3 A Dark Rider Approaches 3.00
4 Auction of imprisoned souls. 3.00
5 What price a soul?. 3.00
6 Mortality. 3.00
GN A Midwinter's Dream,40-pg. . . . 5.00
TPB 17.00

ARIA: A SUMMER SPELL
March, 2002
1 (of 2) London, summer 1967. . . . 3.00
2 Kildare is in love 3.00

ARIA: THE USES
OF ENCHANTMENT
Feb., 2003
1 (of 4) 3.00
2 thru 4 . . . . @3.00
TPB 17.00

ARKAGA
Sept., 1997
1 by Arnie Tang Jorgensen. 3.00
2 Desire for revenge. 3.00

ART OF ERIK LARSEN
1 Sketchbook 5.00

ART OF
HOMAGE STUDIOS
1 Various Pin-ups 5.00

ART OF JAY ANACLETO
Image
1-shot 48-pg. 6.00

ASCENSION
Top Cow, Sept., 1997
1 by David Finch,F:Angels 4.00
2 Andromeda fights alone. 3.00
3 reunited with Lucien. 3.00
4 . . . . 3.00
5 Gregorieff and Dayak Army 3.00
6 Voivodul returns, concl. 3.00
7 Andy's problems worsen 2.50
8 revenge on Dayaks & Mineans . . 2.50
9 Andy exiled 2.50
10 A:D. Gavin Taylor 2.50
11 A:D. Gavin Taylor 2.50
12 A:turning point. 2.50
13 A:Grigorieff, Petra 2.50
14 V:Marcus,A:Andromeda 2.50
15 Rowena's secrets 2.50
16 Petra joins Lucien 2.50
17 a schism 2.50
18 V:new entity 2.50
19 to Petra's Minean home 2.50
20 Resurrection,pt.1. . . . . 2.50
21 Resurrection,pt.2. . . . . 2.50
22 trapped 3.00
23 Andromeda's new outfit 3.00
Coll.Ed.#1, rep.#1–#2 . . . . 5.00
Coll.Ed.#2 . . . . 5.00

ASTOUNDING
SPACE THRILLS
April, 2000
1 Ken Kelly(c),Cydonian Contant . . 3.00
2 The Criminal Code. 3.00
3 Gordo:Earthling Prime,
   flip-book. 3.00
4 The Craving of Consumorr,
   flip-book 3.00
5 Attack of the Macrobes 3.00

ASTRO CITY
See: KURT BUSIEK'S
ASTRO CITY

ATHENA INC.
2002
1-shot Agents Roster,48-pg. 6.00
The Beginning, 48-pg. 6.00
1 reoffered 3.00
2 Gwen has a stalker 3.00
2a variant(c) 3.00

3 Gwen hearing voices. 3.00
3a variant(c) 3.00
4 Revelations 3.00
4a variant(c) 3.00
5 The Belly of the Beast 3.00
6 All Hell Breaks Loose. 3.00
5a– a variant (c) . . . . @3.00
TPB Vol. 1 Manhunter Project 20.00

ATOMIC TOYBOX
April, 1999
Odyssey Line
1 AaL,F:Ken Logan. 3.00
2 AaL,The Aliens are comming. . . . 3.00

AUTOMATION
Flypaper, 1998
1 Robots sent to Mars, and back . . 3.00
2 One goes mad. 3.00
3 Sherzad vs. Konak 3.00
TPB rep. #1–#3 . . . . 13.00

AVIGON
(B&W) Oct., 2000
Spec. 56-pg.. . . . . 6.00
GN 6.00

THE AWAKENING
(B&W) Oct., 1997
1 (of 4) by Stephen Blue. 3.00
2 thru 4 . . . . @3.00
TPB rep. #1–#4 . . . . 10.00

BACKLASH
WildStorm, 1994–97
1 Taboo, 2 diff. covers 4.00
1a variant edition, 2 covers. 3.00
2 Savage Dragon 2.50
3 V:Savage Dragon 2.50
4 SRf,A:Wetworks. 2.50
5 SRf,A:Dane 2.50
6 BBh,SRf,A:Wetworks. 2.50
7 BBh,SRf,V:Bounty Hunters 2.50
8 RMz,BBh,BWS(c),WildStorm
   Rising,pt.8,w/2 cards 2.50
8a Newsstand ed.. . . . . 2.25
9 F:Taboo,Dingo,V:Chasers 2.50
10 I:Crimson. 2.50
11 R:Bloodmoon 2.50

Backlash #11
© WildStorm

12 R:Taboo,Crimson's Costume . . . 3.00
13 Taboo to the Rescue. 2.50
14 A:Deathblow 2.50
15 F:Cyberjack. 2.50
16 F:Cole,Marc 2.50
17 F:Marc,Kink. 2.50
18 . . . . 2.50
19 Fire From Heaven,pt.2 . . . . 2.50
20 SRf,BBh,Fire From
  Heaven,pt.10 . . . . 2.50
21 SRf,BBh 2.50
22 SRf,BBh 2.50
23 SRf,BBh 2.50
24 SRf,BBh,return of Dingo 2.50
25 SRf,BBh,56-pg.. special 4.00
26 SRf,BBh,IR:Gramalkin 2.50
27 SRf,BBh 2.50
28 SRf,BBh,Backlash leads PSI
  team to Europe 2.50
29 SRf,BBh,Haroth raises the
  remnants of Atlantis. 2.50
30 SRf,BBh,Backlash confronts
  Kherubim lords 2.50
31 SRf,BBh,team returns to PSI . . . 2.50
32 SRf,BBh,earth-shattering
  final issue 2.50
TPB Backlash/Spider-Man, Webs &
  Whips, x-over. 5.00
TPB The Drahn War, rep.#27–#32 15.00

BACKLASH/SPIDER-MAN
WildStorm/Marvel, 1996
1 x-over,pt.1 . . . . 2.50
1a variant cover 3.00
2 x-over,pt.2 . . . . 2.50

BADGER
(B&W) May, 1997
1 MBn,'Betelgeuse' 3.00
2 MBn,'Beefalo don't like fences' . . 3.00
3 MBn,'Loose Eel'. 3.00
4 MBn,'Hot House' 3.00
5 MBn,Octopi in the hot tub 3.00
6 MBn,Prime Minister of
  Klactoveedesteen 3.00
7 MBn,Crime Comics 3.00
8 MBn,Root. 3.00
9 MBn 3.00
10 MBn,Tuesday Ruby 3.00
11 MBn,Watch the Skies 3.00
12 MBn,The Lady Cobras 3.00
13 MBn,Horse Police. 3.00
14 MBn,Badger Sells Out 3.00

BAD IDEAS
Image, Apr., 2004
1 (of 2) 48-pg. 6.00
2 48-pg. 6.00

BADROCK
Extreme, 1995
1a RLd(p),TM(c),A:Dragon 2.25
1b SPa(ic),A:Savage Dragon 2.25
1c DF(ic) 2.25
2 RLd,ErS(s),V:Girth,A:Savage
  Dragon, flip-book-Grifter/
  Badrock #2 . . . . 2.50
3 RLd,ErS,V:The Overlord 2.50
Ann.#1 I:Gunner, 48-pg. 3.00
Super-Spec. #1 A:Grifter & The
  Dragon. 2.50

BADROCK
AND COMPANY
Extreme, 1994–95
1 KG(s) 2.50
1a San Diego Comic Con ed. 3.00

Badrock and Company #4
© Extreme

2 RLd(c),Fuji 2.50
3 Overtkill,'Overt Operations' 2.50
4 TBm,MBm,TNu,A:Velocity 2.50
5 A:Grifter 2.50
6 Finale,A:ShadowHawk. 2.50

BALLISTIC
Top Cow, 1995
1 F:Wetworks 3.00
2 F:Wetworks,Jesters
  Transformation 3.00
3 F:Wetworks,final issue 3.00

BALLISTIC ACTION
Top Cow, 1996
1 MSi(c), pin-ups. 3.00

BALLISTIC IMAGERY
Top Cow, 1995
1 F:Hellcop,Heavy Space,
  Cyberforce,anthology 3.00

BALLISTIC/WOLVERINE
Top Cow/Marvel, 1996
1 Devil's Reign,pt.4,x-over 4.00

BANISHED KNIGHTS
Dec., 2001
1 vampire civil war 3.00
1A variant(c) 3.00
1B holofoil(c). 5.00
2 F:Greyson & Belmiro 3.00
TPB Vol. 1 Samurai Noir 13.00

BASTARD SAMURAI
April, 2002
1 (of 3) 3.00
2 F:Toshi 3.00
3 concl. 3.00

BATTLESTONE
Extreme, 1994
1 RLd,ErS,MMy,AV 2.50
1a variant cover 3.00
2 RLd,ErS,MMy,AV,I&D:Roarke,
  finale 2.50

BATTLE CHASERS
Cliffhanger, April, 1998
1 JMd, fantasy, team-up 9.00
1a Chromium ed. (5,000 made) . . 46.00
2 JMd,F:Gully 5.00
3 JMd,new ally 4.00
4 JMd,Red Monika 4.00
4a,b,c JMd variant covers. . . . . . . @3.00
5 JMd,V:Lord August,with 8-pg.
  Planetary #0 . . . . 3.00
6 JMd 3.00
6a variant AWa(c) 4.00
WildStorm/DC, Nov., 2000
7 JMd(c)(1:2) 3.00
7a variant JSC(c) (1:4) 4.00
7b variant HuR(c) (1:4) 7.00
8 JMd,V:Harvester 3.00
TPB Coll.Ed.#1, rep.#1 & #2 . . . . 6.00
TPB Coll.Ed #2 . . . . 6.00
TPB A Gathering of Heroes 15.00
Prelude #1, JMd, 16-pg. 10.00

BATTLE OF THE PLANETS
Top Cow, July, 2002
1 AxR 3.00
1a-c variant(c)s . . . . @3.00
1d convention(c) 3.00
1e holofoil edition 6.00
2 AxR,attack on earth begins 3.00
3 AxR,The Firey Phoenix 3.00
4 Zoltar 3.00
5 Spectra connected to suicides. . . 3.00
6 Under A Blood Red Sky,pt.1 . . . . 3.00
7 Under A Blood Red Sky,pt.2 . . . . 3.00
8 Under A Blood Red Sky,pt.3 . . . . 3.00
9 Under A Blood Red Sky,pt.4 . . . . 3.00
10 Aftermath. 3.00
11 Second Encounters. 3.00
12 concl., 48-pg. 5.00
1-shot flip-book Thundercats 5.00
1-shot Mark 3.00
1-shot Battle Book 5.00
1-shot Hell, 48-pg. 5.00
2 animation (c). . . . .
1/2 reprint. 3.00
TPB Destroy All Monsters 20.00
TPB Trial by Fire 8.00
TPB Blood Red Sky. 17.00
TPB Digest Trial by Fire. 10.00
TPB Digest Destroy All Monsters . 10.00

Battle Chasers #1
© Image

BATTLE OF THE PLANETS: MANGA
Image/Top Cow, Oct., 2003
1 . . . . 3.00
2 . . . . 3.00
3 finale 3.00

BATTLE OF THE PLANETS: PRINCESS
Image/Top Cow, 2004
1 (of 6) 3.00

BATTLE OF THE PLANETS: WITCHBLADE
Image/Top Cow, Jan., 2003
1 48-pg. 7.00

BEETLEBORGS
Extreme, Nov., 1996
1 from TV show 2.50

BERZERKERS
Extreme, 1995
1 F:Greylore,Hatchet,Psi-Storm,
  Cross,Wildmane,Youngblood#2 2.50
2 Into the Darkness 2.50
3 Slay Ride 2.50
4 final issue. 2.50

BIG BANG COMICS
Big Bang Studios, 1996
(B&W) Prev.: Caliber
1 F:Mighty Man. 2.25
2 Silver Age Shadowhawk 2.25
3 . . . . 2.25
4 . . . . 3.00
5 Top Secret Origins 3.00
6 Round Table of America and
  Knights of Justice meet, orig.
  mini-series #3 (color). 3.00
7 . . . . 3.00
8 F:Mister U.S. 3.00
9 I:Peter Chefren 3.00
10 F:Galahad. 3.00
11 Faulty Towers is destroying
  Midway City 3.00
12 F:The Savage Dragon 3.00
13 by Jeff Weigel, 40-pg.spec. . . . 3.00
14 RB,A:The Savage Dragon 3.00
15 SBi(c),F:Dr. Weird. 3.00
16 F:Thunder Girl. 3.00
17 . . . . 3.00
18 Savage Dragon on Trial 3.00
19 O:Beacon,Hummingbird 3.00
20 F:Knight Watchman,Blitz. 3.00
21 F:Shadow Lady. 3.00
22 The Bird-Man of Midway City . . . 3.00
23 Riddle of the Sphinx, sequel. . . . 3.00
24 History of Big Bang,Vol.1 . . . . . 4.00
25 Anniv. iss. 4.00
26 Murder by Microphone, concl. . . 3.00
27 History of Big Bang,Vol.2 . . . . . 4.00
28 Knight of the Living Dead,pt.1 . . 4.00
29 Knight of the Living Dead,pt.2 . . 4.00
30 F:Knight Watchman 4.00
31 F:Knight-Sprite 4.00
32 F:Pink Flamingo 4.00
33 Peril of Parallel Planets 4.00
34 To Save the Gods 4.00
35 Big Bang vs. 1963 . . . . 4.00
Giant Sz. Ann.#1 Ultiman. 5.00
TPB rep. 1994 mini-series 11.00
Summer Spec.b&w, 48-pg. (2003). . 5.00
1-shot Round Table of America 3.00

BIG BRUISERS
WildStorm, 1996
1 F:Maul,Impact,Badrock 3.50

BIG HAIR PRODUCTIONS
(B&W) Feb., 2000
1 by Andy Suriano,F:Astro-Bug . . . 3.50
2 . . . . 3.50

BLACK AND WHITE
Hack Studios, 1996
1 ATi,New heroes,'Beginnings' 2.25
2 ATi(p),apparent death 2.25
3 V:Chang. 2.25
Ashcan. 5.00

BLACK ANVIL
Top Cow, 1996
1 & 2. . . . . 2.50

BLACK FLAG
Extreme, 1994
1 B&W Preview. 3.00

BLACK FOREST, THE
Image, Mar., 2004
GN 10.00

BLACK OPS
WildStorm, 1996
1 . . . . 2.50
2 thru 5 . . . . @2.50
TPB, rep.#1–#5 . . . . 15.00

BLACK TIDE
Nov., 2001
1 . . . . 3.00
1a variant(c) 3.00
1b variant(c) 3.00
2 Balance of Power 3.50
3 One Man's Enemy 3.50
4 Deception, Secrets and Lies . . . 3.50

BLAIR WITCH: DARK TESTAMENTS
Oct., 2000
Spec. IEd,CAd 3.00

BLINDSIDE
Extreme, Aug., 1996
1 MMy & AV, F:Nucgaek Jeno 2.50
2 MMy & AV, Origin continues 2.50

BLISS ALLEY
(B&W) July, 1997
1 BML 3.00
2 BML,F:Wizard Walker 3.00
3 BML,Inky-Dinks 3.00

BLOKHEDZ
Nov., 2003
1 (of 4) 3.00
2 . . . . 3.00
Street Legends, 2004
3 thru 4 . . . . 3.00

BLOODHUNTER
Extreme, Nov., 1996
1 RV, Cabbot Stone rises from the
  slab 3.00

BLOOD LEGACY
Top Cow, April, 2000
1 MHw,The Story of Ryan. 2.50
1a variant Keu Cha(c). 2.50
1b variant Mike Turner(c) 2.50
2 MHw,F:Dr. Susan Ryerson 2.50
3 MHw. 2.50
4 MHw. 2.50
1-shot The Young Ones (2003) 4.00

Bloodpool #1
© *Extreme*

BLOODPOOL
Exteme, 1995
1 I:Seoul,Rubbe,Wylder,
  'Discharged'. 2.50
1a variant cover 2.50
2 The Hills Are Alive 2.50
3 Walk Like an Egyptian 2.50
4 final issue. 2.50
TPB Rep. #1-#4. . . . . 13.00
[Regular Series] 1996
1 thru 3 JDy. . . . . @2.50

BLOODSTREAM
Image, Jan., 2004
1 (of 4) 3.00
2 of 4. . . . . @3.00

BLOODSTRIKE
Extreme, 1993
1 A:Brigade,Rub the Blood(c)
  Blood Brother prelude,x-over . . 3.50
2 I:Lethal,V:Brigade,BloodBrothers,
  pt.2,B:BU:Knight 3.00
3 B:ErS(s),ATi(c),V:Coldsnap,Blood
  Brothers,pt.4,'Turning Point' . . . 3.00
4 ErS(s). 3.00
5 KG,I:Noble,A:Supreme. 3.00
6 KG(s),CAx,C&J:Chapel,'Inside
  Project:Born Again' 3.00
7 KG,RHe,A:Badrock,'Changing
  of the Guard' 3.00
8 RHe,A:Spawn,Sleeping & Waking 3.00
9 RHe,Extreme Prejudice,pt.3,
  I:Extreme Warrior,ATh,BU: Black
  & White 3.00
10 Extreme Prejudice,pt.7,
  V:Brigade, B:BU:Knight 3.00
25 I:Cabbot Bloodstrike 3.00
11 ErS(s),ATi(c),V:Coldsnap 3.00
12 ErS(s) 3.00

13 KG,A:Supreme,'BetterOffDead'. . 3.00
14 KG(s),CAx,C&J:Chapel. 3.00
15 KG,RHe,A:Badrock,War Games,
   pt.1,Extreme Sacrifice begins . . 3.00
16 KG,RHe,War Games,pt.3,Extreme
   Sacrifice ignites 3.00
17 KIA,V:The Horde. 3.00
18 ExtremeSacrifice,pt.3,x-over. . . . 3.00
19 V:The Horde 3.00
20 R:Deadlock New Order. 3.00
21 KA,V:Epiphany New Order 3.00
22 V:The Horde, last issue 3.00
25 see above, after #10
Ashcan 3.00

BLOODSTRIKE: ASSASSIN
Extreme, 1995
0 R:Battlestone 3.00
1 Debut new series 3.00
1a alternate cover 3.00
2 V:M.D.K. Assassins 3.00
3 V:Persuasion 3.00

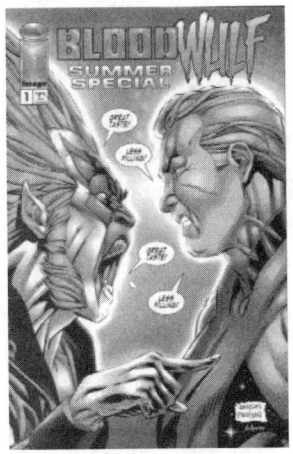

Bloow Wulf Summer Special #1
© Extreme

BLOODWULF
Extreme, 1995
1 RLd,R:Bloodwulf 2.50
1b Run OJ Run 2.50
1c Alternate cover 2.50
1d Alternate cover 2.50
2 A:Hot Blood 2.50
3 Slippery When Wet 2.50
4 Darkness Gnaws at my Soul,
   final issue 2.50
Summer Spec.#1 V:Supreme
   Freeferall (1995) 2.50

BLUE
Aug., 1999
1 Android teenager 2.50
2 by Greg Aronowitz 2.50
3 rescue mission 2.50

BLUNTMAN AND CHRONIC
Aug., 2001
GN MiA 15.00

BODYCOUNT
March, 1996
1 KEa,SBs 2.50
2 thru 4 KEa,SBs . . . . @2.50
TPB series rep. 18.00

BOHOS
Flypaper (B&W) 1998
1 by Maggie Whorf & B.Penaranda 3.00
2 F:teenage bohemians 3.00
3 concl. 3.00
TPB Bohos 13.00

BONE
(B&W) Dec., 1995
[Prev.: Cartoon Books]
21 thru 25 . . . . @3.00
26 The Turning 3.00
27 end of Dragonslayer storyline . . . 3.00
Bone Sourcebook 25

reprints with new covers
#1 thru #9 . . . . @3.00
10 rep. 'Great Cow Race' 3.00

Cartoon Books
11 Aftermath of the Great Cow
   Race 3.00
12 . . . . 3.00
13 Thar she blows 3.00
14 . . . . 3.00
15 Double or nothing 3.00
16 hiding from the Rat Creatures . . 3.00
17 with 5 new pages 3.00
18 Betrayed 3.00
19 'Three cheers for Dragon-slayer
   Phoney Bone' 3.00
20 Phoney Bone vs. Lucius 3.00

BOOF
TMP, 1994
1 . . . . 2.25
2 Meathook 2.25
3 Joyride 2.25
4 thru 6 . . . . @2.25

BOOF AND THE BRUISE CREW
TMP, 1994
1 . . . . 2.25
2 thru 5 . . . . @2.25
6 I:Mortar,O:Bruise Crew 2.25

BRASS
WildStorm, 1996
1 Rib,AWa,Folio Edition 3.50
2 Rib,AWa 2.50
3 Rib,AWa,concl. 2.50

BRIGADE
Extreme, 1993
[1st Series]
1 RLd(s),MMy,I:Brigade,Genocide . 3.50
1a Gold ed. 4.00
2 RLd(s),V:Genocide,w/coupon#4 . 4.00
2a w/o coupon 1.50
2b Gold ed. 4.00
3 I:Birds of Prey,V:Genocide 2.25
4 CyP,Youngblood#5 flip 2.25

[2nd Series]
0 RLd(s),ATi(c),JMs,NRd,I:Warcry,
   A:Emp,V:Youngblood 2.25
1 I:Boone,Hacker,V:Bloodstrike,
   Blood Brothers,pt.1 . . . . 2.75
1a Gold ed. 3.00
2 C:Coldsnap,Blood Brothers,pt.3 . 3.00

Brigade #4 © Extreme

3 ErS(s),GP(c),MMy,NRd(i),I:Roman
   V:Bloodstrike,Blood Brothers,
   pt.5 . . . . 2.25
4 Rip(s),MMy,RHe,Changes,
   BU:Lethal 2.25
5 Rip(s),MMy,It's A VeryDeepSea . . 2.25
6 Rip(s),MMy,I:Coral,Warlok,
   BU:Hackers Tale 2.25
7 Rip(s),MMy,V:Warlok 2.25
8 ErS(s),MMy,Extreme Prejudice,
   pt.2,BU:Black & White,pt.5 . . . 2.25
9 ErS(s),MMy,Extreme Prejudice
   pt.6,ATh,BU:Black & White . . . 2.25
25 ErS(s),MMy,D:Kayo,Coldsnap,
   Thermal 2.25
26 Images of Tomorrow 2.25
10 Extreme Prejudice 2.25
11 WildC.A.T.S. 2.50
12 Battlestone 2.50
13 Thermal 2.25
14 Teamate deaths 2.25
15 MWm,R:Roman Birds of Prey . . . 2.25
16 ExtremeSacrifice,pt.4,x-over . . . 2.50
17 MWn,I:New Team 2.50
18 I:The Shape New Order 2.50
19 MWn,F:Troll,Glory 2.50
20 MWn,alien cult saga,concl. 2.50
21 F:ShadowHawk 2.50
22 Supreme Apocalypse,pt.4 . . . . . . 2.50
23 . . . . 2.50
24 . . . . 2.50
25 & 26 see above
27 Extreme Babewatch 2.50
Sourcebook 3.00

BRIT
July, 2003
1-shot b&w, 48-pg. 5.00
1-shot Brit: Cold Death 5.00
1-shot Red,White,Black & Blue 5.00

BUGBOY
(B&W) June 1998
1-shot, by Mark Lewis, 48-pg. 4.00

BULLETPROOF MONK
Flypaper, Nov., 1998
1 in San Francisco 3.00
2 N.Y. Chinatown 3.00
3 conclusion 3.00
TPB 80-pg. 10.00
1-shot Tales of the B P M 3.00

IMAGE

BUNKER, THE
Apr., 2003
GN 96-pg. 10.00

BUTCHER KNIGHT
Top Cow, July, 2000
1 DT,F:Luther Washington 2.50
1a variant(c) MS (1:3) 2.50
1b variant(c) DT (1:3) 2.50
2 DT 2.50
3 DT,Blood & Gore 2.50
4 DT,concl. 3.00

CAPES
Sept., 2003
1 (of 3) 3.00
2 & 3 . . . . @3.00

CARVERS
Flypaper, Oct., 1998
1 F:five snowboarders 3.00
2 J:Crazy Jack 3.00
3 V:Evil Yeti 3.00
TPB rep. #1–#3 . . . . 10.00

CASEFILES:
SAM AND TWITCH
May, 2003
1 Have You Seen Me?,pt.1 . . . . 3.00
2 thru 6 Have You Seen
   Me?, pt.2 thru pt.6 . . . . @3.00
7 . . . . 3.00
7 Skeletons,pt.1 . . . . 3.00
8 Skeletons,pt.2 . . . . 3.00
9 Skeletons,pt.3 . . . . 3.00
10 Skeletons,pt.4 . . . . 3.00
11 Skeletons,pt.5 . . . . 3.00
12 Skeletons,pt.6 . . . . 3.00
13 Cops and Robbers 2.50
?13 Ancient Chinese Secret,pt.1 . . . 2.50
?14 Ancient Chinese Secret,pt.2 . . . 2.50
?15 Ancient Chinese Secret,pt.3 . . . 2.50
?16 Ancient Chinese Secret,pt.4 . . . 2.50
?17 Ancient Chinese Secret,pt.5 . . . 3.00

CASUAL HEROES
Motown, 1996
1 . . . . 2.50
2 thru 6 . . . . @2.50

Celestine2
© Extreme

CATHEDRAL CHILD
1998
GN by Lea Hernandez 10.00
GN 2nd printing 10.00

CELESTINE
Extreme, 1996
1 . . . . 2.50
2 . . . . 2.50

CHANNEL ZERO
(B&W) 1998
1 by Brian Wood 3.00
2 . . . . 3.00
3 gone global 3.00
4 Filter 3.00
5 Brink of Millennium crash 3.00
6 Sound system 3.00
TPB Collection 12.00

CHAPEL
Extreme, 1995
1 BWn,F:Chapel 3.50
2 V:Colonel Black 3.00
2a variant cover 2.50
[Regular Series]
1 BWn,F:Chapel 2.50
1a variant cover 2.50
2 V:Giger 2.50
3 V:Giger 2.50
4 Extreme Babewatch 2.50
5 Hell on Earth,pt.1 . . . . 2.50
6 Hell on Earth,pt.2 . . . . 2.50
7 Shadowhunt x-over,pt.2 . . . . 2.50

CHASING DOGMA
June, 2001
TPB DFg,120-pg. 13.00

CHASSIS
Nov., 1999
1 F:Chassis McBain 3.00
2 . . . . 3.00
2a variant Matt Busch(c) 3.00
3 Gizmotech Industries 3.00
4 . . . . 3.00
4a Collector's variant(c) 4.00
5 Slic's One Shot, flip-cover 3.00

CHILDHOOD'S END
(B&W) Oct., 1997
1 (of 5) JCf,community playground. 3.00

CHILLER
Dec., 1998
TPB JHl,F:Brian Marx 18.00

THE C.H.I.X.
THAT TIME FORGOT
Studiosaurus, Aug., 1998
1 F:Good Girl 3.00

CITY OF SILENCE
May, 2000
1 (of 3) WEl,GEr,F:Silencers 2.50
1a variant GEr,3-D(c)(1:4) 2.50
2 WEl,GEr 2.50
3 WEl,GEr 2.50
TPB 10.00

CLERKS
Image, July, 2001
TPB 11.00

CLOCK MAKER, THE
Jan., 2003
1 (of 12) 2.50
2 thru 7 . . . . @2.50
5 to 7 (of 12) cancelled
Spec. Act One (#1ñ#4) 5.00
Spec. Act Two (#5ñ#7) 5.00
Spec. Act Three 5.00

CLOCKWORK ANGELS
(B&W) March, 1999
GN seq. to Cathedral Child 10.00

CLOUDBURST
Image, June, 2004
GN 8.00

CLOUDFALL
Nov., 2003
1-shot b&w 48-pg. 5.00
1-shot Cloudfall: Loose Ends 5.00

CODE BLUE
(B&W) April, 1998
1 by Jimmie Robinson 3.00
2 F.I.T.E. creates havoc 3.00

CODENAME:
STYKE FORCE
Top Cow, 1994
1A MS(s),BPe,JRu(i). 3.50
1B Gold Embossed Cover 6.00
1C Blue Embossed Cover 9.00
2 MS(s),BPe,JRu(i) 2.50
3 MS(s),BPe,JRu(i) 2.50
4 MS(s),BPe,JRu(i) 2.50
5 MS(s),BPe,JRu(i) 2.50
6 MS(s),BPe,JRu(i) 2.25
7 MS(s),BPe,JRu(i) 2.25
8A Cyblade poster (Tucci) 4.00
8B Shi poster (Silvestri) 4.00
8C Tempest poster (Tan) 2.25
9 New Teamate 2.25
10 SvG, B:New Adventure 2.25
11 F:Bloodbow 2.25
12 F:Stryker 2.25
13 SvG(s),F:Strkyer 2.25
14 New Jobs 2.25
Spec.#0 O:Stryke Force 2.50
TPB rep. Death's Angel Saga 10.00

COMBAT
Jan., 1996
1 . . . . 2.50
2 . . . . 2.50

COMMON GROUNDS
Image/Top Cow, Jan., 2004
1 (of 6) DJu 4.00
2 DJu,SK 3.50
3 thru 6 DJu,SK . . . . @3.00

COMPLETE ALEX TOTH
ZORRO
(B&W) April, 1999
TPB Complete Alex Toth Zorro . . . 19.00

COSMIC RAY
June, 1999
1 by Stephen Blue 3.00
1a alternate cover (1:2) 3.00
2 F:Raymond Mann 3.00
3 F:Star Marshalls 3.00

COW, THE
Top Cow, April, 2000
1 Spring edition 3.00
2 Summer edition 3.00
3 Spring edition 2001 . . . . 3.00

CREECH, THE
TMP, Oct., 1997
1 GCa,DaM,F:Chirs Rafferty 2.50
2 GCa,DaM,F:Dennis Dross 2.50
TPB Race Against Death 10.00

[GREG CAPULLO'S ORIGINAL] CREECH
TMP, Aug., 2001
1 A Vision of Death 2.50
2 Awakenings 2.50
3 The Resurrection 2.50

CREECH, THE: OUT FOR BLOOD
Image, July, 2001
1 GCa,Out for Blood, Book 1 . . . . . 5.00
2 GCa,48-pg. 5.00
3 GCa,Killing Machine perfected . . 5.00

CREED: UTOPIATE
Jan., 2002
1 (of 4) TKn. 3.50
2 TKn,disorder in dreamworld 3.00
3 TKn,fantasy vs. reality 3.00
4 TKn,Death of Creed 3.00

CREEPS
Oct., 2001
1 (of 4) TMd 3.50
2 TMd,I:Gurgle,Chitter 3.00
3 TMd,Genesys Corporation 3.00
4 TMd,through their eyes 3.00

CRIMSON
Cliffhanger, May, 1998
1 BAu,HuR,F:Alex Elder, vampire
  'Dawn to Dusk' 5.00
1a variant AWa(c) 7.00
1b Chromium Edition 12.00
2 BAu,HuR,V:Jelly-Bats,
  'Unlife Story' 3.00

Crimson #1 © Image

2a variant AAd(c) 6.00
3 BAu,HuR,V:Rose,Payment
  in Blood 4.00
4 BAu,HuR,F:Red Hood,Children
  of Judas,pt.1 . . . . 3.50
5 BAu,HuR,A:Red Hood,Children
  of Judas,pt.2 . . . . 3.50
6 BAu,HuR,A:Red Hood,Children
  of Judas,pt.3 . . . . 3.50
7 BAu,HuR,Christmas day 3.00
½ Dynamic Forces exclusive 4.00

WildStorm/DC, 1999
8 thru 23 BAu,HuR . . . . @2.50
24 BAu,HuR, final issue 3.50
Spec.#1 Scarlet X: Blood on the
  Moon, BAu,HuR,one-shot 4.00
Spec. Crimson Sourcebook #1 . . . 3.00
TPB Crimson, rep.#1–#6 . . . . 13.00
TPB Heaven & Earth,rep#7–#12 . . 15.00
TPB Loyalty & Loss 13.00
TPB Earth Angel,rep.#13–#18 . . . . 15.00
TPB Redemption,160-pg. 15.00

CRIMSON PLAGUE
June, 2000
1 GP,64-pg. 3.00
2 GP,Sole Survivor 2.50
3 GP,Blood trail 2.50
4 GP,Plague hits home 2.50

CROW, THE
TMP, Feb., 1999
1 JMu,F:Eric Draven 3.00
1a variant TP cover (1:4) 3.00
2 JMu,hunt for killers 3.00
3 JMu,justice for killers 3.00
4 JMu,Line Between Devil's Teeth . 3.00
5 JMu,Skin of an Angel,pt.1 . . . . . 3.00
6 JMu,Skin of an Angel,pt.2 . . . . . 3.00
7 JMu,Touch of Evil,pt.1 . . . . 3.00
8 JMu,Touch of Evil,pt.2 . . . . 3.00
9 JMu,Wings and Black Feathers . 3.00
TPB Vol. 1 Vengeance 11.00
TPB Vol. 2 Evil Beyond Reach . . . 11.00
Crow Mag.#1, 56-pg. rep. 5.00
Crow Mag.#2 . . . . 5.00
Crow Mag.#3 . . . . 5.00

CRUSH, THE
Motown Jan., 1996
1 Mini-series 3.00
2 Let Me Light Your Fire 3.00
3 Million Dollar Smile 3.00
4 . . . . 3.00
5 The Hip Hop Slide 3.00

CRYPT
Extreme, 1995
1 A:Prophet 2.50
1a variant cover 2.50
2 A:Prophet 2.50

[JIM LEE'S] C-23
WildStorm, April, 1998
1 BCi,JMi,F:Corben Helix 2.50
2 JMi,TC(c),V:Angelans 2.50
3 JMi,TC(c),with game card 2.50
4 JMi,Corbin, banished 2.50
5 JMi,RCo(c),Queen Mother 2.50
5a variant JLe(c) (1:4) 2.50
6 JMi,RCo(c),V:Hyper Shock
  Troopers 2.50
7 JMi,RCo(c),Hail to the Queen . . . 2.50
8 JMi,RCo(c),Long Live the King . . 2.50

CURSED
Image/Top Cow, Sept., 2003
1 (of 4) It is Coming 3.00
2 The Walking Dead 3.00
3 The Nature of Curses 3.00
4 It is a Gift 3.00

CURSE OF THE SPAWN
TMP, Sept., 1996
1 DT,DaM,F:Daniel Lianso 6.00
1a B&W variant 20.00
2 DT,DaM,Dark Future,pt.2:
  Blood Lust 5.00
3 DT,DaM,Dark Future,pt.3:
  Corpse Candles 5.00
4 DT,DaM 4.00
5 DT,DaM,Sam & Twitch search
  for Gretchen Culver 3.00
6 DT,DaM,Sam & Twitch pursue
  Suture 3.00
7 DT,DaM,Suture is captured 3.00
8 DT,DaM,Suture escapes police
  custody 3.00
9 DT,DaM,Angela's secret origin . 5.00
10 DT,DaM,Angela, Spawn Slayer. 3.50
11 DT,DaM,Angela's story, concl. . 3.50
12 DT,DaM,Jessica Priest, movie
  photo(c) 3.50
13 DT,DaM 'Heart of Darkness' . . . 3.50
14 DT,DaM,Jessica, concl. 3.50
15 DT,DaM,Tempt an Angel,pt.1 . . 3.50
16 DT,DaM,Tempt an Angel,pt.2 . . 3.50
17 DT,DaM 3.50
18 DT,DaM,F:Tony Twist 3.50
19 DT,Curse & Tony Twist 3.50
20 DT,DaM,Monsters & Mythology . 3.50
21 DT,DaM,Zeus Must Die 3.50
22 DT,F:Ryan Hatchett 3.50
23 DT,TM,R:Overtkill 3.50
24 DT,TM,Pandemic 3.50
25 DT,TM,'Heart of Hell' 2.25
26 DT,TM,V:The Crocodile 2.25
27 DT,TM,F:Marc Simmons 2.25
28 DT,TM,V:Suture 2.25
29 DT,TM,A:Jonathan Edward
  Custer 2.25
TPB Vol. 1 Sacrifice the Soul 10.00
TPB Vol. 2 Blood & Sutures 10.00
TPB Vol. 3 Shades of Gray 10.00
TPB Vol. 4 Lost Values 10.00
TPB Vol. 5 Penumbra 10.00

Cyberforce #4 © Top Cow

IMAGE

All comics prices listed are for *Near Mint* condition.   **CVA Page 529**

CYBERFORCE
Top Cow, 1992–93
[Limited Series]

0 WS,O:Cyber Force	2.50
1 MS,I:Cyberforce,w/coupon#3	5.00
1a w/o coupon	3.00
2 MS,V:C.O.P.S.	3.50
3 MS	2.50
4 MS,V:C.O.P.S,BU:Codename Styke Force.	2.50
TPB Rep. mini-series.	13.00

[Regular Series] 1993

1 EcS(s),MS,SW.	2.50
1B Gold Foil Logo.	6.00
2 EcS(s),MS,SW,Killer Instinct #2,A:Warblade.	2.25
2B Silver Embossed Cover.	6.00
3 EcS(s),MS,SW,Killer Instinct #4, A:WildC.A.T.S.	2.25
3B Gold Embossed Cover	6.00
4 EcS(s),MS,Ballistic	2.50
5 EcS(s),MS	2.50
6 EcS(s),MS,Ballistic's Past	2.50
7 S.H.O.C.s.	2.50
8	2.50
9 A:Huntsman	2.50
10 A:Huntsman	2.50
10a Alternate Cover.	4.00
10b Silver Seal Oz-Con 500c	9.00
11	2.50
12 T.I.M.M.I.E. goes wild	2.50
13 EcS,MS,O:Cyberdata	2.50
14 EcS,MSl,V:T.I.M.M.I.E.	2.50
15 New Cyberdata Threat	2.50
16 O:Ripclaw	2.50
17 Regrouping	2.50
18 thru 24	@2.50
25	4.00
26 KWo	2.50
27 F:Ash.	2.50
27a variant JQ&JP(c) (1:4)	4.00

Top Cow, 1996

28 A:Gabriel	2.50
29	2.50
30 ScL,'Devil's Reign' tie-in	2.50
31 The team in conflict	2.50
32 Cyblade leads rejuvenated team	2.50
33 KWo, Cheleene in midst of civil war	2.50
34 KWo,Royal Blood,pt.3.	2.50
35 BTn,Royal Blood, concl.	2.50
Ashcan 1 (San Diego)	4.00
Ashcan 1 (signed)	6.00
Sourcebook 1.	2.50
Sourcebook 2 I:W.Zero	2.50
Ann.#1 O:Velocity	2.50
Ann.#2	3.00
TPB new art.	13.00
TPB EcS,MS,SW,Assault with a Deadly Woman	10.00

CYBERFORCE/ CODENAME STRYKEFORCE: OPPOSING FORCES
Sept., 1995

1 V:Dangerous Threat.	2.50
2 Team vs. Team.	2.50

CYBERFORCE ORIGINS
Top Cow, 1995

1 O:Cyblade	2.50
1B Gold Seal 1000c	6.00
2 O:Stryker	2.50
3 O:Impact	2.50
4 Misery	3.00

CYBERFORCE UNIVERSE SOURCEBOOK
Top Cow, 1994–95

1	2.50
2 MS,BTn	2.50

CYBERNARY
WildStorm, 1995–96

1 (of 5) mini-series	2.50
2 thru 5	@2.50

CYBERPUNX
Extreme, 1996

1 and 2	@3.00
3 RLe & Ching Lau,F:Drake	3.00

CYBLADE/SHI
1995

1 The Battle for Independents	3.00

CY-GOR
TMP, July, 1999

1 RV,I:Fatima,Frankie & Zevon.	2.50
2 RV,Fire in the Mind,pt.2.	2.50
3 RV,Needles and Pins.	2.50
4 RV, Exquisite Corpse.	2.50
5 RV	2.50
6 RV, the Terraplane.	2.50
7 RV,Young Doctor Acula	2.50

Damned #1 © Homage

DAMNED
Homage, June, 1997

1 (of 4) StG, MZ & DRo.	2.50
2 StG, MZ & DRo,F:Mick Thorne	2.50
3 StG, MZ & DRo	2.50
4 StG, MZ & DRo	2.50

DANGER GIRL
WildStorm/Cliffhanger 1998

1 JSC,AGo, 'Dangerously Yours,' 40-pg.	8.00
1a chromium edition, 40-pg.	55.00
1b Tour Edition	25.00
2 I:Johnny Barracuda,'Dangerous Liaisons'.	5.00
3 in Switzerland	4.00
3a variant AH(c)	5.00
3b variant TC(c)	5.00
4 I:Major Maxim	3.00

5 JSC,AGo	2.50
5a variant JMd(c)	9.00

WildStorm/DC, 1999

6 JSC,SW	2.50
6a variant JMd(c)	5.00
6b variant HuR(c)	4.00
7 JSC,SW,concl.,48-pg.	6.00
TPB Dangerous Coll.,Vol.1	6.00
TPB Dangerous Coll.,Vol.2,rep.2&3	6.00
J. Scott Campbell Danger Girl Sketchbook, 56-pg.	7.00

DARING ESCAPES
TMP, 1998

1 ANi,F:Harry Houdini.	3.00
2 ANi,search for Mystical Heart	2.50
3 A:Kimiel	2.50
4 conclusion	2.50

DARK ANGEL: PHOENIX RESURRECTION
May, 2000

1 by Kia Asamiya, color manga	3.00
2 thru 4	@3.00
1a thru 3a variant(c)	@3.00

Darkchyld #0
© Image/Homage

DARKCHYLDE
See: Maximum, 1996

1 Image reoffer	5.00
1C flip-book-Glory/Angel,Angels in Hell,pt.1, San Diego Con.	4.00
1D remastered, RLd(c)	6.00
2 Image reoffer	5.00
2a variant cover	3.00
2b remastered, with poster	2.50
3 Image reoffer	3.50
3a remastered, with poster	2.50

Image, 1997

4 RQu,Ariel & Kauldron's past	5.00
5 RQu,No one here gets out alive	4.00
TPB Rep. #1–#5	13.00

Homage, 1998

0 RQu,Ariel's back, Ariel's past.	2.50

DARKCHYLDE/GLORY
Extreme

1-shot, four variant covers, by RLd, RQu, JDy & PtL	3.00

IMAGE

DARKCHYLDE: THE DIARY
May, 1997
1-shot, RQu et al,diary excerpts ... 5.00

DARKCHYLDE: THE LEGACY
WildStorm, 1998
1 RQu,F:Ariel 2.50
2 RQu 2.50
WildStorm/DC, 1999
3 RQu,A:Silencer 2.50
4 RQu,Carnival of Fools 2.50
4a RQu,AAd(c), variant (c) 2.50
Summer Swimsuit Spectacular #1 .. 4.00
Spec.Dreams of the Darkchylde #0 . 2.50
TPB Darkchylde............. 20.00

DARKCHYLDE/ WITCHBLADE
Top Cow, July, 2000
1 RQu,Nightmare City......... 2.50

DARK CROSSINGS
Top Cow, May, 2000
Spec. #1 Dark Cloud Rising....... 6.00
Spec. #2 Dark Cloud Overhead.... 6.00

DARKER IMAGE
1993
1 BML,BCi(s),RLd,SK,JLe,I:Blood
  Wulf,Deathblow,Maxx 4.00
1a Gold logo(c)............... 8.00
1b White(c)................. 6.00
Ashcan 1 .... 4.00

DARKMINDS
1998
1 PtL,cyberpunk,detective 8.00
2 Neon Dragon.............. 5.00
2a variant cover 2.50
3 PtL,A:Neon Dragons 2.50
4 PtL,Paradox killer........... 2.50
5 PtL,Unlikely friends, enemies ... 3.00
6 PtL,Aurora Industries......... 3.00
7 PtL,V:Mamuro Hayabusa....... 3.00
8 Conclusion,1st story arc 2.50
½ PtL,Cyborg dreams.......... 2.50
TPB Collection #1 rep. #1–#3 .... 8.00
TPB Collection #2 rep. #4–#6 .... 8.00
TPB Collection #3 rep. #7 & #8.... 6.00
TPB Vol. I, rep.#1–#8........ 19.00
VOL. II Feb., 2000
1 JMd(c) one year later......... 2.50
1a variant PtL(c) 2.50
1b variant Omar Dogan(c) 2.50
2 Changing Faces............ 2.50
2a variant PtL(c) 2.50
2b variant Michael Turner(c)..... 2.50
2c variant(c)................ 2.50
3 PtL(c),F:Reiko Tetsunori 2.50
3a variant Omar Dogan(c) 2.50
3b variant JQ(c) 2.50
4 PtL,cyborg attack........... 2.50
5 PtL,The Prize.............. 2.50
6 PtL,9mm Answers 2.50
7 PtL,The Hunger 2.50
8 PtL,Born Again............. 2.50
9 PtL,A Million and One 2.50
10 PtL,concl................ 2.50
#0 The Bullet 2.50
#0a variant(c)............... 2.50
TPB Vol.1,Paradox, rep. 20.00
TPB Coming of Age 15.00

DARKMINDS: MACROPOLIS
Jan., 2002
1 (of 8) PtL 3.00
1a variant(c) 3.00
2 F:Tiny................... 3.00
2a variant PtL(c) 3.00

DARKNESS, THE
Top Cow, 1996
0 Preview edition,B&W 15.00
½ 15.00
½ variant cover 25.00
1/2 rep.+new story (2001),MS 3.00
1 GEn,MS,Coming of Age 16.00
1a Dark cover............... 10.00
1b Platinum cover............ 20.00
2 GEn,MS 8.00
3 GEn,MS,Jackie pursued by
  many foes 6.00
4 GEn,MS,Jackie explores
  Darkness power 6.00
5 GEn,MS,New York gangs on
  verge of all-out war 5.00
6 GEn,MS,F:JackieEstacado,concl. 4.00
7 MS 4.00
7a variant(c) 7.00
8 JBz,retribution 3.00
8a MS(c)(1:4)............... 5.00
9 Family Ties,pt.2,x-over 5.00
10 Family Ties,pt.3,x-over 6.00
11 GEn,MS,Hearts of Darkness ... 3.50
11a Chromium(c) 20.00
11b variant(c)............... 5.00
12 GEn,Hearts of Darkness...... 3.00
13 GEn,Hearts of Darkness 3.00
14 GEn,JBz,Hearts of Darkness .. 3.00
15 JBz,Spear of Destiny,pt.1 .... 3.00
16 JBz,Spear of Destiny,pt.2 .... 3.00
17 JBz,Spear of Destiny,pt.3 .... 3.00
18 JBz,aftermath 3.00
19 JBz,No Mercy,pt.1......... 2.50
20 JBz,No Mercy,pt.2......... 2.50
21 JBz,Wynnwood........... 2.50
22 JBz,Where is Jenny? 2.50
23 JBz,SLo,new characters...... 2.50
24 JBz,SLo,road trip to Vegas.... 2.50
25 JBz,SLo,48-pg............ 3.50
26 JBz,SLo,A:Joey Scarpaggio ... 2.50
27 SLo,FBI continues assault 2.50
28 Darkness/Witchblade,pt.4,x-over 2.50
29 SLo,High Noon,pt.1 .... 2.50
30 SLo,High Noon,pt.2 .... 2.50
31 SLo,High Noon,pt.3 .... 2.50
32 SLo,Dark Days Ahead 2.50
33 SLo,Capris Castagliano,pt.1 ... 2.50
34 SLo,Capris Castagliano,pt.2 ... 2.50
35 SLo,tour of his life......... 2.50
36 SLo,Ripclaw,pt.3........... 2.50
37 SLo,F:Robert Bearclaw....... 2.50
38 SLo,V:Conquistator......... 2.50
39 SLo,Jackie & Capris combine.. 2.50
40 DK,Darkness falls?......... 2.50
40a variant MS(c) 2.50
various foil (c)............. @9.00
Coll.Ed.#1,rep. #1–#2 .... 5.00
Coll.Ed.#2,rep. #3–#4, 56-pg. 5.00
Coll.Ed.#3,rep. #5–#6, 56-pg. 5.00
Coll.Ed.#3, with slipcase........ 10.00
Coll.Ed.#4,rep. #7–#8 .... 5.00
Slipcase and all 3 GNs 25.00
Signed Slipcase and all 3 GNs ... 50.00
Coll.Ed.#1,deluxe,rep.#1–#6 ..... 15.00
Coll.Ed.#5,rep.#11–#12 .... 6.00
Coll.Ed.#6,rep.#13–#14 .... 6.00
Spec. Infinity, SLo 3.50
Darkness/Witchblade,pt.3 x-over .. 4.00
Spec.#1, Dark Ages........... 5.00
TPB Vol.1 Spear of Destiny 13.00

Darkness #26 © Top Cow

TPB Vol.2 Heart of Darkness..... 15.00
TPB Vol. 2 #1............... 20.00
Spec. Vol. 2 #1 raw (no color) 3.00
TPB Darkness: Resurrection 15.00
1-shot Darkness/Hulk........... 3.00

DARKNESS
Top Cow, Nov., 2002
1 PJe,DK.................. 3.00
1a holofoil(c)............... 6.00
2 DK 3.00
2 Megacon edition 6.00
3 DK 3.00
4 Under Cover of Darkness 3.00
5 You Lose Some 3.00
6 As the World Turns 3.00
7 PJe,F:Ernie Palanco 3.00
7a alternate (c) 3.00
8 PJe,Law by Jackie Estacado.... 3.00
9 PJe,Search for Blue Goldfish ... 3.00
10 RMz,Hong Kong 3.00
11 RMz,Dragons and darklings ... 3.00
12 RMz,Army of assassins 3.00
13 RMz,Mystical Dragons 3.00
14 Streets Run Red,pt.1 .... 3.00
15 Streets Run Red,pt.2 .... 3.00
16 Streets Run Red,pt.3 .... 3.00
1-shot Wanted Dead 3.00

DARKNESS, THE/BATMAN
Top Cow, April, 1999
Spec. SLo,MS, x-over 6.00

DARK REALM
Oct., 2000
1 by Taeson Chang........... 3.00
2 S.F.P.D. in chaos 3.00
3 flip-book 3.00
4 Prophecy is fulfilled 3.00

DART
1996
1 thru 3 Jozef Szekeres .... @3.00

DAVID AND GOLIATH
Sept., 2003
1 .... 3.00
2 .... 3.00
3 .... 3.00

DAWN
March, 2002
TPB Return of the Goddess 13.00
Spec. Convention Sketchbook. 3.00
Spec. 2003 Convention Sketchbook 3.00

DAWN: THREE TIERS
June, 2003
1 thru 5 JLi . . . . @3.00

DEADLANDS
July, 1999
GN 1-shot role-play tie-in. 7.00

DEADLY DUO, THE
Highbrow, 1994–95
1 A:Kill-Cat 2.50
2 A:Pitt, O:Kid Avenger 2.50
3 A:Roman, O:Kill-Cat. 2.50

[Second Series] 1995
1 A:Spawn. 2.50
2 A:Savage Dragon. 2.50
3 A:Grunge, Gen13. . . . . 2.50
4 Movie Mayhem 2.50

Deathblow #0
© WildStorm

DEATHBLOW
WildStorm, 1993–96
1 JLe,MN,I:Cybernary. 3.00
2 JLe,BU:Cybernary. 2.50
3 JLe(a&s),BU:Cybernary. 3.00
4 JLe(s),TSe,BU:Cybernary 2.50
5 JLe(s),TSe,BU:Cybernary 2.50
5a different cover 5.00
6 Black Angel 2.25
7 . . . . 2.25
8 Black Angel 2.25
9 The Four Horsemen 2.25
10 Michael Cray, Sister Mary. 2.25
11 A:Four Horsemen 2.25
12 Final Battle 2.50
13 New Story Arc 2.50
14 A:Johnny Savoy 2.50
15 F:Michael Cray 2.50
16 TvS,BWS(c),WildStorm
   Rising,pt.6,w/2 cards. 2.50
16a Newsstand ed. 2.25
17 V:Gammorran Hunter Killers. . . . 2.50
18 F:Cybernary 2.50
19 F:Cybernary 2.50

20 A:Gen 13. . . . . 3.50
21 Brothers in Arms,pt.2,A:Gen13. . 3.50
22 Brothers in Arms,pt.3 . . . . 2.50
23 Brothers in Arms,pt.4 . . . . 2.50
24 Brothers in Arms,pt.5 . . . . 3.00
25 Brothers in Arms,pt.6 . . . . 2.50
26 Fire From Heaven prelude 2.50
27 Fire From Heaven,pt.8 . . . . 3.00
28 Fire From Heaven,finale,pt.3 . . 2.50
29 last issue. 2.50
0 JLe (1996) 3.00
Ashcan 1 . . . . 4.00
TPB Dark Angel Saga,rep.,216-pg. 30.00
TPB Sinners and Saints, rep. 20.00

DEATHBLOW/WOLVERINE
WildStorm, Sept., 1996
1 RiB, AWs,x-over, set in San
   Francisco's Chinatown 2.50
2 RiB, AWs,concl 2.50
TPB rep. series 9.00

DEATHMATE X-OVER
See: COLOR PUB.

DECEPTION, THE
(B&W) Flypaper, Jan., 1999
1 (of 3) F:Jordan Risk, magician . . 3.00
2 Framed for murder. 3.00
3 V:South American Drug Cartel . . 3.00

DEEP SLEEPER
Image, Aug., 2004
1 & 2 See B&W section
3 The Vacant. 3.00
4 conclusion 3.00
Omnibus rep.#1 & #2. . . . . 6.00

DEFCON 4
WildStorm, 1996
1 mini-series 2.50
2 thru 4 . . . . @2.50

DEFIANCE
Feb., 2002
1 The Messenger,pt.1 . . . . 3.00
2 thru 4 The Messenger,pt.2–pt.4 @3.00
5 thru 8 The Scabbard,pt.1–pt.4 . @3.00

DEITY
May, 1999
Coll.Ed. Vol. 1 . . . . 10.00
Coll.Ed. Vol. 2 . . . . 10.00

DEITY: REVELATIONS
June, 1999
1 F:Jamie 3.00
2 F:Joe Tripoli 3.00
3 A legend reborn 3.00
3a variant cover (1:10) 3.00

DEMONSLAYER
Nov., 1999
1 MMy. 3.00
2 Jaclyn begins her quest. 3.00
3 MMy, Michael & the Demon . . . 3.00
Shadow Edition,pt.1 B&W 5.00

VOL II
1 MMy,Into Hell,pt.1 . . . . 3.00
1a variant(c) (1:4) 3.00
2 MMy. 3.00
3 MMy, enter Ebon 3.00

DERRING RISK
June, 1999
1 Fantasy Adventure. 2.50
1a AWa variant(c) 2.50

Desperadoes #1 © Homage

DESPERADOS
Homage, Sept., 1997
1 by JMi & John Cassaday. 7.00
2 V:Leander Peik 3.00
2a 2nd printing 2.50
3 V:Leander Peik 3.00
4 V:Leander Peik, concl. 3.00
5 V:Gideon Brood,pt.1 . . . . 3.00
TPB A Moment's Sunlight,rep.
   #1–#5. 17.00

DESPERATE TIMES
(B&W) June, 1998
1 by Chris Eliopoulos 3.00
2 Strip joint 3.00
3 EL(c) 3.00
4 Christmas special 3.00
5 EL(c), sideways 3.00
6 . . . . 3.00
TPB 13.00

Image, Jan., 2004
0 . . . . 3.00
1 . . . . 3.00

DETECTIVES INC.
March, 1999
TPB Vol. 1 . . . . 15.00
TPB Vol. 2 A Terror of Dying 20.00

DEVASTATOR
(B&W) April, 1998
1 JHl and Greg Horn. 3.00
2 book 1,pt.2. . . . . 3.00
3 concl. to book 1 . . . . 3.00

DEVIL'S DUE STUDIOS
Mar., 2003
1-shot 2003 Preview 2.25

DIORAMAS, A LOVE STORY
Image, Apr., 2004
GN 13.00

DISCIPLES, THE
April, 2001
1 The new magic	3.00
2 Recruit Her or Kill Her	3.00
3 Viva Las Vegas	3.00
4 The Apples of Sodom	3.00

A DISTANT SOIL
(B&W) Highbrow, Aug., 1993
Prev: Aria Comics
15 CDo,Ascension,pt.3	3.00
16 CDo,A:Bast, Avatar	3.00
17 CDo,D'mer & Bast conflict	3.00
18 CDo,'Ascension' finale	3.00
19 CDo,'Spires of Heaven,'pt.1	3.00
20 CDo,Lord Merai's suicide	
weakens Hierachy	3.00
21 CDo,'Exile for D'mer?'	3.00
22 CDo,Avatar's secrets,32-pg.	3.00
23 CDo,three stories	3.00
24 CDo,malfunctioning spacesuit	3.00
25 CDo,NGa,Troll Bridge,48-pg.	4.00
26 CDo,B.U.:Red-Cloak by	
E.Kushner	3.00
27 CDo,B.U.:Liaden tale	3.00
28 CDo,B.U.:Liaden tale, concl.	3.00
29 CDo,B.U.:Delia Sherman story	3.00
30	4.00
31 Sometimes the good guys lose	4.00
32 F:Prince D'mer	4.00
33 Rebellion's final stand	4.00
34 CDo, 64-pg.	5.00
35 CDo, 32-pg.	4.00
36 CDo.	4.00
37 CDo.	4.00
Images of A Distant Soil.	3.00
Images of A Distant Soil, signed	35.00
GN The Gathering, rep.#1–#11	19.00
GN The Gathering, 2nd printing	20.00
TPB The Ascendant, rep.#13–#24.	19.00
TPB The Gathering	20.00
TPB Vol.3, The Aria	17.00

Divine Right #6 © WildStorm

DIVINE RIGHT:
THE ADVENTURES OF
MAX FARADAY
WildStorm, Sept., 1997
1 JLe,SW,Blaze of Glory.	7.00
1a variant cover	7.50
1b variant, signed	30.00
1c Voyager pollybaged pack.	6.00

1d Spanish edition	5.00
2 JLe,SW,Disco Inferno	5.00
2a variant(c)	5.00
3 JLe,SW,F:Christie Blaze,Enemies	
of the State	4.00
4 JLe,SW,F:Lynch,The Love	
Connection	2.50
4a variant(c)	4.00
5 JLe,SW,V:Dominique Faust,Party	
Crashers	3.00
6 JLe,SW,Truth or Consequences,	
Susanna Chaste located	3.00
7 JLe,SW,Into the Hollow Realm	3.00
8 JLe,SW,Tobru,V:Acheron.	3.00
8a variant SW(c).	3.00
Preview edition, JLe(c) (1997).	5.00
Coll.Ed.#1	6.00
Coll.Ed.#2	6.00

WildStorm/DC, 1999
9 JLe,SWi,Final Stand in	
Hollow Realm	3.00
10 JLe,SWi.	3.00
11 JLe,SWi,Divine Intervention	3.00
12 JLe,SWi,Divine Intervention	3.00
Coll.Ed.#3, rep.#5 & #6	6.00
TPB Book 1 JLe (2002)	18.00
TPB Book 2 JLe (2002)	18.00

DOCTOR CYBORG
Image, June, 2004
GN Outpatient	10.00

DODGE'S BULLETS
Image, Feb., 2004
GN B&W	10.00

DOLLZ
April, 2001
1 RGr,TSg.	3.00
1a-1c variant(c)s.	3.00
2 RGr	3.00
3 RGr	3.00

DOMINION
Jan., 2003
1 KG	3.00
2 thru 5 KG	@3.00

DOOM'S IV
Extreme, 1994
1 RL(s),MPa, I:Doom's IV.	2.50
1a variant(c),left side of art	2.50
1b variant(c),right side of art	2.50
2 Rld(s),MPa,MECH-MAX	2.50
2a variant (c).	2.50
3 Dr. Lychee, Brick	2.50
4 Dr. Lychee, Syber-idol	2.50
Sourcebook	2.50

DOUBLE IMAGE
Feb., 2001
1 The Bod, flip-book, Codeflesh	3.00
2 The Bod/Codeflesh	3.00
3 The Bod/Codeflesh	3.00
4 The Bod/Codeflesh	3.00
5 Trust in Me/Codeflesh	3.00

DRACULA VS. ZORRO
(B&W) Sept., 1998
1 DMG,RM	3.00
2 DMG,RM, conclusion	3.00

DRAGON, THE
March, 1995
1 rep. of Savage Dragon	2.25

2 thru 5 rep. of Savage Dragon	@2.25

THE DRAGON:
BLOOD AND GUTS
Highbrow, 1995
1 I:Grip	2.50
2 JPn,KIS	2.50
3 JPn,KIS	2.50
TPB series rep.	8.00

DROWNED, THE
Image, July, 2004
GN	10.00

DUNCAN'S KINGDOM
(B&W) Oct., 1999
1 by Gene Yang & Derek Kirk	3.00
2	3.00

DUSTY STAR
(B&W) April, 1997
0 sci-fi,western,adventure.	3.00
1 thru 3	@3.00

DV8
WildStorm, 1996
1 WEl(s),HuR,'Lust for Life'	4.00
1a JLe(c).	5.00
1b Kevin Nowlan(c).	4.00
2 WEl(s),HuR,Gen-active serial	
killers,'Some Weird Sin'.	3.00
3 WEl(s), Neighborhood Threat	3.00
4 WEl(s),HuR,Miss Drugstore.	3.00
5 Ivana sends DV8 to Japan	2.50
6 idle hands are the devil's tools	2.50
7 WEl(s),'Shades'.	2.50
8 HuR,Sublime, Evo & Frostbite	
abandoned,'Three'.	2.50
9 MHs,'Evolution'	2.50
10 MHs,'In Service to Nothing'	2.50
11 MHs,F:Copycat,'Facets'	2.50
12 MHs,F:Freestyle,V:Sen.Killory	2.50
13 MHs,'The Sad Tales of	
Senator Killory'	2.50
14 MHs,TR,New Horizon,TR(c),	
'Barely Legal'.	5.00
14a TC(c).	2.50
14b Voyager bagged pack.	3.50
15 MHs,F:Ivana Baiul,'Settling	
Accounts'.	2.50
16 MHs,V:Dominique Faust	
'Intersection'	2.50
17 MHs,Gen-Passive.	2.50
18 MHs,Team 7,A:Grifter,'Same as	
It Ever Was'.	2.50
19 MHs,First Mision,pt.1,'Larger	
Concerns'	2.50
20 MHs,First Mision,pt.2,'Lounging	
in the Ammo Dump'.	2.50
21 MHs,First Mision,pt.3,V:Anthrax	2.50
22 MHs,V:Copycat,'Choices'.	2.50
22a variant(c) JMd(1:4)	2.50
23 MHs,F:Threshold,'Gone to	
Ground'.	2.50
24 MHs,F:Sublime,'Slip Stream,'	
prologue.	2.50
25 MHs,Slipstream,pt.1	2.50
DV8 Rave,preview (1996)	3.00
Ann.#1 'Head Trips' (1998)	3.00

WildStorm/DC, 1999
26 MHs,TVs.	2.50
27 MHs,TVs,V:Gen-Actives	2.50
28 MHs,TVs,F:Evo.	2.50
29 MHs,TVs.	2.50
30 MHs,TVs,Things Fall Apart,pt.1	2.50
31 MHs,TVs,Things Fall Apart,pt.2	2.50
32 MHs,TVs,Things Fall Apart,pt.3	2.50

All comics prices listed are for *Near Mint* condition.

IMAGE

Ann.'99 Slipstream. 3.50
#0 40-pg. 3.00
TPB Neighborhood Threat (2002) . 15.00

DV8 vs. Black Ops #3
© WildStorm

DV8 VS. BLACK OPS
WildStorm, Oct., 1997
1 Techromis Design,pt.1 . . . . 3.00
2 Techromis Design,pt.2 . . . . 3.00
3 Techromis Design,pt.3 . . . . 3.00

ECHO
March, 2000
1 A Broken World 2.50
1a variant(c) 2.50
2 Sacrifices. 2.50
2a variant PtL(c) 2.50
3 Deadly new echo. 2.50
3a variant PtL(c) 2.50
4 PtL,Desperate Times. 2.50
5 PtL,Welcoming Party 2.50
6 Conspiracy Theory. 2.50
6a variant PtL(c) 2.50
7 Anarchy,pt.1 . . . . 2.50
8 A Life Worth Living. 3.00
#0 Thick as Thieves. 2.50
#0a variant(c). 2.50
#1 Holochrome edition. 7.00

ELECTROPOLIS
May, 2001
1 DMt, Infernal Machine,pt.1 . . . . . 3.00
2 DMt, Infernal Machine,pt.2 . . . . . 3.00
3 DMt, Heavy Meddle. 3.00
4 DMt, Infernal Machine,pt.4 . . . . . 3.00

ELEKTRA/CYBLADE
Top Cow/Marvel, 1997
1-shot 'Devil's Reign,'pt.7
  (of 8) x-over. 3.00

EMPIRE
May, 2000
1 MWa,BKi,F:Golgoth 5.00
2 MWa,BKi,F:Xanna 4.00
3 MWa,BKi,F:Lohkyn 4.00
4 MWa,BKi,Nature vs. nurture 4.00

ESPERS
April, 1997
(B&W) Vol. 3
1 JHl,A:Brian Marx,V:Architects . . . 3.00
1a 2nd printing 3.00
2 JHl 3.00
3 JHl,Black Magic. 3.00
4 JHl,Black Magic, concl. 3.00
5 JHl,two stories 3.00
6 JHl,F:Simon Ashley,Alan Black . . 3.00
7 JHl,Feel the Rapture 3.00
8 JHl, trip to Hong Kong 3.00
9 JHl,V:Architects 3.00
TPB Undertow, rep.Halloween
  Comics series 15.00
TPB Black Magic, rep.Vol.3,#1–4 . 15.00
TPB The Storm, rep. 16.00
TPB Interface, rep.2nd series 16.00

E.V.E. PROTOMECHA
Top Cow, Feb., 2000
1 . . . . 3.00
1a variant JMd(c) 3.00
1b variant David Finch(c) 3.00
2 Gunner Unleashed. 3.00
2a variant Michael Turner(c). 3.00
2b variant SPa(c) 3.00
3 thru 6 . . . . @3.00
TPB Vol.1 Sins of the Daughter. . . 18.00

[ADVENTURES OF] EVIL AND MALICE
June, 1999
1 by Jimmie Robinson 3.50
2 F:Max 2000 . . . . 3.50
3 V:Cold Heart & Le'Chef 3.50
4 final showdown 3.50
TPB F:Evelyn & Malinda 13.00

EVO
Top Cow
1 MS,Endgame,pt.3 x-over 3.00

EXPOSURE
July, 1999
1 F:Shawna & Lisa 2.50
2 Mirrors to the Soul 2.50
3 . . . . 2.50
2a & 3a alternate photo(c) (1:2) . @2.50
4 Spark-Spangled See-Through
  Girl. 2.50

Exposure #2 © Image

4a alternate photo(c) (1:2) 2.50
Prelude 16-pg 7.00
Prelude holo-foil. 15.00

EXTREME ANTHOLOGY
1 . . . . 2.50

EXTREME CHRISTMAS SPECIAL
Various artists, new work. 3.00

EXTREME DESTROYER
Extreme, 1996
1 prologue, x-over,bagged
  with card 2.50
2 epilogue, x-over 2.50

EXTREME HERO
1 . . . . 3.00

EXTREME PREJUDICE
Extreme, Nov., 1994
0 Prelude to X-over. 3.00

EXTREME SACRIFICE
Extreme, Jan., 1995
Prelude,x-over,pt.1, A:Everyone
  with trading card 2.50
Epiloque, x-over,pt.8, conclusion
  with trading card 2.50
TPB Rep. whole x-over series. . . . 17.00

EXTREME 3000
Prelude. 2.50

EXTREME TOUR BOOK
Tour Book 1992 . . . . 3.00
Tour Book 1994 . . . . 25.00

EXTREMELY YOUNGBLOOD
Extreme, Sept 1997
1 TBm&MBm(s) 3.50

EXTREME ZERO
0 RLd,CYp,ATi(i),I:Cybrid, Law &
  Order, Risk, Code 9, Lancers,
  Black Flag 3.00
0a Variant cover 3.00

FACTION PARADOX
Aug., 2003
1 War in Heaven. 3.00
2 . . . . 3.00

FALLING MAN
(B&W) Dec., 1997
1 (of 3) BMC,PhH. 3.00
2 Floyd vs. Duncan. 3.00
3 . . . . 3.00

FATHOM
Top Cow, 1998
1 by Michael Turner,F:Aspen 7.00
2 war beneath the waves 3.50
3 Life changed forever 3.50
4 Connection to water. 3.00
5 Aspen's connection to water 3.00
6 Admiral's plans revealed 3.00
7 Finale,pt.1 . . . . 3.00
8 Finale,pt.2 . . . . 3.00
9 Finale, conclusion, end 3.00

10 Fathom returns 3.00
11 Fathom returns,pt.2. . . . . 3.00
12 Tomb Raider & Witchblade
    x-over,pt.1 . . . . 3.00
12a variant(c). 5.00
13 x-over,pt.2 . . . . 3.00
13a variant(c) 5.00
14 Aspen & Vana, concl. 3.00
14a variant(c) 5.00
15 Killian's Blue Sun 2.50
15a variant(c) 5.00
16 Admiral's subterfuge discovered. 2.50
#0 rep. new Mike Turner(c) 2.50
1/2 . . . . 4.00
Spec. Swimsuit ed. 4.00
Fathom 2000 swimsuit calendar . . . 4.00
Fathom 2000 smimsuit Spec. 4.00
TPB Coll.Ed.#1, rep.#1 . . . . 6.00
TPB Coll.Ed.#2, rep.#2–#3 . . . . . . 6.00
TPB Coll.Ed.#3, rep.#4–#5 . . . . . . 6.00
TPB Coll.Ed.#4, rep.#6–#7 . . . . . . 6.00
TPB Coll.Ed.#5, rep.#8–#9 . . . . . . 6.00
TPB Vol. 1, rep. #1–#9 . . . . 25.00

FATHOM: KILLIAN'S TIDE
Top Cow, March, 2001
1 (of 4) 5.00
1a variant(c) 4.00
2 thru 4 . . . . @3.00

FEAR EFFECT
Top Cow, March, 2000
1-shot MHw, video game tie-in . . . 5.00

FEAR EFFECT SPECIAL: RETRO HELIX
Top Cow, March, 2001
1 . . . . 3.00

FEATHER
Aug., 2003
1 (of 6) 3.00
2 thru 4 . . . . @3.00
5 48-pg. 6.00

FELON
Top Cow, Oct., 2001
1 (of 4) 3.00
2 . . . . 3.00
3 concl. 3.00
4 I:Elizabeth Freeh 3.00

F5
April, 2000
1 TnD,48-pg. 3.00
2 TnD,life or death 2.50
3 TnD 2.50
4 TnD, betrayed 2.50
Preview Book, TnD,24-pg. 2.50

FIRE
(B&W) Dec., 1998
TPB International intelligence 10.00
TPB The Definitive Collection 10.00

FIREBREATHER
Jan 2003
1 (of 4) PhH(s) 3.00
2 thru 4 PhH(s) . . . . @3.00
TPB Vol. 1 . . . . 14.00

FIRE FROM HEAVEN
WildStorm, 1996
1 x-over,Chapter 1 . . . . 3.50

2 x-over,Finale 2 . . . . 2.50

FIRSTMAN
April, 1997
1 ASm,LukeHenry becomesApollo . 2.50

FLIGHT
Image, July, 2004
TPB 20.00

FOOT SOLDIERS, THE
(B&W) Sept., 1997
Prev.: Dark Horse
1 by Jim Krueger, Graveyard of
    Forgotten Heroes 3.00
2 Tragedy o/t Travesty Tapestry . . . 3.00
3 Arch enemies,pt.3 . . . . 3.00
4 'It's a Wicked World Afterall' 3.00
5 Loose Ends 3.00

FOREVER AMBER
(B&W) July, 1999
1 by Don Hudson 3.00
1a variant cover (1:2) 3.00
2 Lady fights back. 3.00
3 Amber sent to jail. 2.50
4 Amber's revenge, concl. 3.00

FORSAKEN
Image, Aug., 2004
1 Light of Other Days,pt.1. . . . . 3.00
2 Light of Other Days,pt.2. . . . . 3.00
3 Light of Other Days,pt.3. . . . . 3.00

40 OZ COLLECTED
Nov., 2003
TPB b&w 10.00

FRANKENSTEIN MOBSTER
Image, Oct., 2003
0 . . . . 3.00
0a variant (c). 3.00
1 MkW,Friday the 13th 3.00
2 MkW. 3.00
3 MkW,mystic control 3.00
4 MkW. 3.00
5 MkW,Blood debt. 3.00
6 Escape from police 3.00
1a thru 6a variant (c). . . . . @3.00

FREAK
Image, May, 2004
GN 7.00

FREAK FORCE
Highbrow, 1993–95
1 EL(s),KG 3.00
2 EL(s),KG 3.00
3 EL(s),KG 3.00
4 EL(s),KG,A:Vanguard. 3.00
5 EL(s),KG 3.00
6 EL(s),KG 3.00
7 EL(s),KG 3.00
8 EL(s),space ants 3.00
9 EL(s),Cyberforce 3.00
10 EL(s),Savage Dragon 3.00
11 EL(s),Invasion,pt.1 . . . . 3.00
12 EL(s),Invasion,pt.2 . . . . 3.00
13 EL(s),Invasion,pt.3 . . . . 3.00
14 EL(s),Team Defeated 3.00
15 EL(s),F:Barbaric 3.00
16 KG,EL(s),V:Chelsea Nirvana. . . 3.00
17 EL,KG,major plots converge . . . 3.00

Freak Force #7
© Highbrow

18 Final Issue 3.00
TPB 448-pg. 30.00

[Series Two] March, 1997
1 EL,Star joins team,V:The
    Frightening Force 3.00
2 EL,Dart quits team. 3.00
3 EL,'Lo there shall come..an
    ending' 3.00

FRIENDS OF MAXX
I Before E, April, 1996
1 thru 3 WML&SK . . . . @3.00

FUSED!
March, 2002
1 Canned Heat,pt.1 (of 4). 3.00
1a variant(c) 3.00
2 thru 4 Canned Heat,pt.2–pt.4 . @3.00

GALAXY-SIZE ASTOUNDING SPACE THIRLLS
March, 2001
1 Galaxy Size Showdown, 48-pg.
    flip-book. 5.00

GAMORRA SWIMSUIT SPECIAL
WildStorm, 1996
Spec.#1 . . . . 2.50

GAZILLION
Nov., 1998
1 HSm, Mars vs. Xof. 2.50
1a variant cover (1:4) 2.50

GEAR STATION, THE
March, 2000
1 DaF,Dominion of Souls 6.00
1a variant AxR(c) 2.50
1b variant PtL(c) 2.50
1c variant Michael Turner(c) 2.50
2 DaF,23rd Gear. 2.50
2a variant AAd(c) 2.50
3 DaF,Who is Fable 2.50
4 DaF,first showdown 2.50
5 DaF,Gear Station Prime. 2.50
6 DaF 2.50

IMAGE

GEEKSVILLE
(B&W) Mar., 2000
#0 by R.Koslowski & G.Sassaman . 3.00
1 Breaking into the Biz,pt.1 . . . . . . 3.00
2 Breaking into the Biz,pt.2 . . . . . . 3.00
3 Back to the Con 3.00
4 Breaking into the Biz 3.00
5 Dark Sky 3.00
6 End of 3 Geeks 3.00

GEMINAR
(B&W) June, 2000
1 . . . . 5.00
2 F:Captain Champion 5.00

GEN^{13}
WildStorm, 1994
0 Individual Hero Stories. 4.00
1 JLe(s),BCi(s),I:Fairchild,Grunge,
  Freefall,Burnout. 20.00
1a 2nd printing 4.00
2 JLe(s),BCi(s) 16.00
3 JLe(s),BCi(s),A:Pitt,'Payback' . . 10.00
4 JLe(s),BCi(s),'Free for All' 8.00
5 Final issue 5.00
5a WP variant cover 10.00
TPB Gen13 Coll.Ed. 13.00

[Regular Series] 1995
1a BCi(s),V:Mercenaries. 5.00
1b Common Cover 2 . . . . 8.00
1c Heavy Metal Gen. 8.00
1d Pulp Fiction Parody 10.00
1e Gen 13 Bunch 8.00
1f Lin-Gen-re. 10.00
1g Lil Gen 13 . . . . 8.00
1h Friendly Neighbor Grunge 8.00
1i Gen 13 Madison Ave 10.00
1j Gen-Et Jackson 8.00
1k Gen Dress Up cover 8.00
1l Verti-Gen. 8.00
1m Do It Yourself Cover 8.00
2 BCi,BWS(c),WildStorm Rising,
  pt.4, w/2 cards. 3.00
2a newstand ed. 2.25
3 BCi,'Magical Mystery Tour' 3.00
4 BCi,'Tourist Trap' 3.00
5 BCi,I:New Member,Family Feud . 3.00
6 BCi,JLe,I:The Deviants,
  'Roman Holiday' 3.00
7 BCi,JLe,European Vacation,pt.2
  'Veni, Vidi, Vici' 3.00
8 BCi,'Bewitched,Bothered
  and Bewildered'. 3.00
9 . . . . 3.00
10 Fire From Heaven,pt.3 . . . . 3.00
11 Fire From Heaven,pt.9 . . . . 3.00
12 F:Caitlin,her dad 3.00
13 A, B & C, each . . . . @3.00
14 'Higher Learning'. 3.00
15 Fraternity and Sorority rush 2.50
16. . . . . 2.50
17 BCi,JSC,AGo,battle royale in
  Tower of Luv,'Toy Soldiers' 2.50
18 BCi,JSC,AGo,V:Keepers,
  'Hello & Good-Byes' 2.50
19 BCi,JSC,AGo,Lynch & kids flee
  to Antarctica,'Bon Voyage'. . . . 2.50
20 BCi,JSC,AGo,'To Boldly Go' . . . 2.50
21 BCi,JSC,AGo,V:D'Rahn,'Lost
  in Space' 2.50
22 BCi,civil war,'Homecoming'. . . . 2.50
23 BCi,21st century 2.50
24 BCi,V:D'Rahn,'Judgment Day' . . 2.50
25 BCi,Homecoming,JsC(c). 3.50
25a TC(c),'Where Angels Fear
  to Tread' 3.50
25b Voyager bagged pack. 3.50

26 JAr,GFr,CaS,When Worlds
  Collide 2.50
27 JAr,GFr,CaS,'Search & Seizure'. 2.50
28 JAr,GFr,CaS,'Remote Control' . . 2.50
29 JAr,GFr,CaS,I:Tindalos,
  'A Firm Grip on Reality' 2.50
30 JAr,GFr,CaS,'Stranger Than
  Fiction'. 2.50
31 JAr,GFr,CaS,Roxy's Big Score,
  'Paradigm Shift'. 2.50
32 JAr,GFr,CaS,'Red Skies at
  Morning'. 2.50
33 JAr,GFr,CaS,aftermaths, 'Burning
  the Candle at Both Ends',
  with 8-page Planetary #0. . . . . 4.00

Gen^{13} #29 © WildStorm

34 JAr,GFr,CaS,AAd,A:Roxy
  & Sarah,'Overture'. 2.50
35 JAr,GFr,CaS,John Lynch resigns,
  'But You Can't Hide' 2.50
36 JAr,GFr,CaS,F:John Lynch,
  'That Was Then' 2.50
College Yearbook 1997, Superheroes
  at Large 2.50
Ann. #1 WEI,SDi,'London'sBrilliant' . 3.00
1-Shot Gen13:Unreal World (1996). 3.00
Gen13 3-D Special (1997). 5.00
3-D Spec. #1, (1997) 5.00
3-D Spec. #1, variant cover. 5.00
3-D Spec. #1, (1998) 5.00
TPB rep.1–#5 of original mini-
  series, 3rd printing. 13.00
TPB Lost in Paradise, rep. #3–#5 . 7.00
TPB EuropeanVacation,rep.#6–#7 . 7.00
TPB rep. #13 A, B & C. 7.00
TPB Ordinary Heroes 13.00
TPB WildStorm Archives, rep. mini-
  series, rep.#0–#13, covers, etc. . 13.00

WildStorm/DC, 1999
37 JAr,GFr,CaS,Reaper. 2.50
38 JAr,GFr,CaS,BU:Grunge. 2.50
38a variant cover 2.50
39 JAr,GFr,CaS,Genocide. 2.50
40 JAr,GFr,CaS,V:Reaper. 2.50
41 JAr,GFr,CaS 2.50
42 JoC(s),KM,pro wrestlers 2.50
43 AWa(s&c),F:Fairchild 2.50
44 AWa(s&c),A:Mr.Magestic 2.50
45 SLo,EBe,JSb,fashion show 2.50
46 SLo,EBe,JSb,MightyJoeGrunge. 2.50
47 SLo,EBe,JSb. 2.50
48 SLo,EBe,JSb. 2.50
49 SLo,EBe,JSb. 2.50
50 SLo,EBe,JSb,48-pg. 4.00

50a variant JLe,SW(c) (1:4). 4.00
51 SLo,breather 2.50
52 SLo,F:Caitlin Fairchild. 2.50
53 F:all Villains issue 2.50
54 SLo,EBe,SWi,F:Fairchild 2.50
55 EBe,Return to Pod 9,pt.2 . . . . . 2.50
56 EBe,Fairchild,pt.3 . . . . 2.50
57 BRa,EBe,Tokyo in danger. 2.50
58 BRa,EBe,mini-monster
  massacre. 2.50
59 BRa,EBe,V:Gaijin13 . . . . 2.50
60 AWa,Behind the Power. 2.50
61 AWa,Goin' back to Cali 2.50
62 AWa,fast food 2.50
63 AWa,EBe,sailboat outing 2.50
64 AWa,Superhuman Like You,pt.1 . 2.50
65 AWa,Superhuman Like You,pt.2 . 2.50
66 AWa,8 guest artists. 2.50
67 AWa,EBe,ColdAir on MyBehind . 2.50
68 AWa,Slave to Love,pt.1. . . . . . . 2.50
69 AWa,Slave to Love,pt.2. . . . . . . 2.50
70 AWa,F:Sara Rainmaker 2.50
71 AWa,Think Like A Gun,pt.1 . . . . 2.50
72 AWa,Think Like A Gun,pt.2 . . . . 2.50
73 AWa,Think Like A Gun,pt.3 . . . . 2.50
74 AWa,Think Like A Gun,pt.4 . . . . 2.50
75 AWa,How the Story Ends,pt.1. . . 2.50
76 AWa,How the Story Ends,pt.2. . . 2.50
77 AWa,Story Ends,pt.3, 40-pg. . . . 3.50
Annual'99 JAr(s) 3.50
Ann. 2000 #1, Devil's
  Night x-over,pt.1 . . . . 3.50
Spec. Wired 2.50
Spec.#1 3-D AAd 5.00
Spec.#1a variant(c) 5.00
Spec. Carny Folk 3.50
Spec. 1-shot Going West 2.50
GN Grunge Saves the World. 6.00
GN Bootleg: Grunge— The Movie. 10.00
GN Medicine Song, 48-pg. 6.00
GN Gen13/Fantastic Four 6.00
GN Science Friction, 48-pg. 6.00
GN London,New York,Hell 7.00
GN A Christmas Caper (2002). . . . 6.00
TPB Gen13 . . . . 13.00
TPB Interactive Plus 12.00
TPB Starting Over 15.00
TPB I Love New York. 10.00
TPB We'll Take Manhattan. 15.00
TPB Super-Human Like You 13.00

GEN^{13} BOOTLEG
WildStorm, Nov., 1996
1 MFm&AD,lost in the 'Linquist
  Fault,'pt.1. . . . . 3.00
1a signed 15.00
2 'Linquist Fault,'pt.2. . . . . 3.50
3 Gen13 Fairy Tale 3.50
4 WS&LSi,F:Valaria,'Little Girl
  Lost'. 3.50
5 F:Fairchild,'Timesick,'pt.1 . . . . . 3.50
6 F:Fairchild,'Timesick,'pt.2 . . . . . 3.50
7 'Renaissance Ruckus' 3.50
8 AWa,'Grunge's Movie,'pt.1. . . . . 4.00
9 AWa,'Grunge's Movie,'pt.2. . . . . 4.00
10 AWa,'Grunge's Movie,'pt.3 . . . . 4.00
11 AaL,WS,Chupacabra,pt.1 . . . . . 2.50
12 AaL,WS,Chupacabra,pt.2. . . . . 2.50
13 F:Grunge,'The Trickster' 2.50
14 JMi,JoP,GL,bad neighbors 2.50
15 KNo,V:Trance,'Hanging,'pt.1. . . 2.50
16 KNo,V:Trance,'Hanging,'pt.2. . . 2.50
17 'Virgil Chu's Reality'. 2.50
18 MFm,'A Day at the Beach' 2.50
19 BKs,JhB,Satyr. 2.50
20 CAd,F:John Lynch,'Numbskulls'. 2.50
Ann.#1 WEI,SDi, to NYC 3.00
TPB Grunge: The Movie,AWa 10.00
TPB Vol.1, rep.#1–#4. . . . . 12.00

GEN13: INTERACTIVE
WildStorm, Oct., 1997
1 vote via Internet 4.00
2 MHs,vote via Internet 3.00
3 MHs,conclusion 3.00
TPB Gen13 Interactive Plus, rep. . 12.00

GEN13/ GENERATION X
WildStorm, July, 1997
1 BCi&AAd,'Generation Gap' 3.00
1a variant JSC(c) 3.00
3-D edition, with glasses 5.00
3-Da variant cover, with glasses . . . 5.00

GEN13: MAGICAL DRAMA QUEEN ROXY
WildStorm, Oct., 1998
1 (of 3) AWa,Mall of Doom 4.00
2 AWa,V:Caitlin 4.00
3 AWa,dream sequence concl. 4.00

GEN13/THE MAXX
WildStorm, 1995
Spec.#1 BML,x-over 4.00

Gen13 Monkeyman and O'Brien #1
© WildStorm

GEN13/MONKEY MAN & O'BRIEN
WildStorm, June, 1998
1 (of 2) AAd 3.00
1a chromium edition 4.50
2 AAd,alternate universe, concl. . . . 3.00
2a variant AAd(c) 2.50

GEN13: ORDINARY HEROES
WildStorm, 1996
1 & 2 . . . . @3.00

GEN12
WildStorm, Feb., 1998
1 BCi,Team 7 tie-in,'The Legacy' . . 3.00
2 BCi,F:Morgan of I.O. 3.00
3 BCi,Dominique Faust 3.00

4 BCi,F:Miles Craven 3.00
5 BCi,Team 7 re-unites 3.00

GHOST SPY
Image, May, 2004
1 (of 6) 3.00
2 thru 5 . . . . @3.00

G.I. JOE
Sept., 2001
1 JSC(c) Reinstated,pt.1 . . . . 15.00
1a 2nd printing 5.00
2 Reinstated,pt.2 . . . . 6.00
3 JSC(c),Reinstated,pt.3 . . . . 5.00
4 JSC(c),Reinstated,pt.4 . . . . 5.00
5 F:Duke 3.50
6 Reckonings,pt.1 . . . . 3.00
7 Storm Shadow 3.00
8 Destro & Cobra Commander 3.00
9 Snake-eyes vs. Storm Shadow . . 3.00
10 Dreadnoks 3.00
11 Mob rule in Chicago 3.00
12 JBz(c),V:Android Trooper 3.00
13 JBz(c),V:Firefly 3.00
14 Cobra Suburbs Return 3.00
15 Reunion 3.00
16 missing child 3.00
17 kidnap Flint & Baroness 3.00
18 search for Flint & Baroness 3.00
19 . . . . 3.00
20 Storm Shadow 3.00
21 Snake-Eyes 3.00
22 Return of Serpentor,pt.1 . . . . . . 3.00
23 Return of Serpentor,pt.2 . . . . . . 3.00
24 Return of Serpentor,pt.3 . . . . . . 3.00
24a variant(c) 3.00
25 . . . . 3.00
25a variant (c) 3.00
Spec. M.I.A., rep. #1 & #2 . . . . . . 5.00
TPB Vol.1 Reinstated 15.00
TPB Vol. 2 Reckonings 13.00
TPB Vol. 3 Malfunction 13.00

Devil's Due 2004
26 thru 35 . . . . @3.00
TPB Vol. 4 Alliances 15.00
TPB Vol. 5 Return of Serpentor . . 13.00

G.I. JOE: BATTLE FILES
April, 2002
1 (of 3) G.I. Joe, 48-pg 6.00
2 F:Cobra 6.00
3 F:Vehicles and Tech 6.00
TPB 15.00

G.I. JOE FRONTLINE
Oct., 2002
1 LHa(s),DJu,BL,DvD(c) 3.00
2 DJu,BL,DvD(c) V:Destro 3.00
3 DJu,BL,DvD(c) V:Destro 3.00
4 DJu,BL,Silent Castle 3.00
5 Icebound 3.00
6 Icebound,pt.2 . . . . 3.00
7 Icebound,pt.3 . . . . 3.00
8 Icebound,pt.4 . . . . 3.00
9 Kansas City 3.00
10 . . . . 3.00
11 Chuckles 3.00
12 Chuckles 3.00
13 Chuckles 3.00
14 Chuckles 3.00
15 F:Stalker 3.00
16 Night Creepers 3.00
17 PJe,F:Beachhead 3.00
18 . . . . 3.00
18a variant (c) 3.00
16a–17a variant (c) . . . . @3.00
TPB Vol. 1 . . . . 13.00

Glory #3 © Extreme

G.I. JOE VS. TRANSFORMERS
June, 2003
1 . . . . 4.00
1a 2nd printing 3.00
2 thru 6 . . . . @3.00
1a–6a variant (c) . . . . @5.00

GLORY
Extreme, 1995
0 JDy 2.50
1 JDy,F:Glory 4.00
1a variant cover 4.00
2 JDy,V:Demon Father 3.00
3 JDy,A:Rumble & Vandal 2.50
4 Vandal vs. Demon Horde 2.50
4a JDy variant cover 3.00
5 Supreme Apocalypse,pt.3,
   F:Vandal 2.50
6 Drug Problem 2.50
7 F:Superpatriot 2.50
8 Extreme Babewatch 2.50
9 Extreme Destroyer,pt.5,
   x-over, bagged with card 2.50
10 . . . . 2.50
11 . . . . 2.50
12 JDy, EBe & JSb 3.50
13 JDy, EBe & JSb 2.50
14 JDy, EBe & JSb 2.50
15 JDy, EBe & JSb, Out for
    vengeance 2.50
TPB rep.#1-#4 . . . . 10.00
continued: see Color Comics section

GLORY/ANGELA ANGELS IN HELL
Extreme, 1996
1 . . . . 4.00

GLORY/AVENGELYNE
Extreme, 1996
1 V:B'lial,I:Faith 4.00
1a no chrome(c) 3.00

GLORY/AVENGELYNE: THE GODYSSEY
Extreme
1 RLd & JDy 3.00
1a photo(c) 4.00

GLORY/CELESTINE: DARK ANGEL
Extreme, Sept., 1996
1 (of 3) JDy,PtL,sequel to Rage of
   Angels, A:Maximage 2.50
2 JDy,PtL,'Doomsday+1'. 2.50
3 JDy,PtL, conclusion 2.50

GLORY & FRIENDS
Extreme, 1995
Bikini Fest #1 . . . . 2.50
Bikini Fest #2 . . . . 2.50
Lingerie Special #1 (1995). 3.00
Christmas Special #1 (1995) 2.50

GO GIRL!
Aug., 2000
1 TrR,F:Lindsay Goldman. 3.50
2 TrR,wonderful life?. 3.50
3 TrR,The Teacher from Hell 3.50
4 TrR,Vacation at dude ranch. 3.50
5 TrR,origin of powers 3.50

GOLDFISH
(B&W) 1998
TPB by Brian Michael Bendis 17.00
TPB 272-pg. Definitive Colleciton . 20.00

GRAY AREA, THE
Image, June, 2004
1 (of 3) JR2,KJ,48-pg. 6.00
2 JR2,KJ,32-pg. 4.00
3 JRw,KJ,48-pg. 6.00

GREASE MONKEY
March, 1998
1 TEl 3.00
2 TEl 3.00
3 TEl, The Calling; Rewards. 3.00

GRIFTER
WildStorm, 1995–96
1 BWS(c), WildStorm
   Rising,pt.5,w/2 cards 2.50
1a Newsstand ed. 2.25
2 V:Diabolik,pt.1 . . . . 3.00
3 V:Diabolik,pt.2 . . . . 3.00
4 R:Forgotten Hero. 3.00
5 Rampage of a Fallen Hero 3.00
6 V:Poerhouse 3.00
7 City of Angels,pt.1 . . . . 3.00
8 City of Angels,pt.2 . . . . 3.00
9 City of Angels,pt.3 . . . . 3.00
10 City of Angels,pt.4. . . . . 3.00

GRIFTER/BADROCK
Extreme, 1995
1 To Save Badrock's Mom 3.00
1a Variant cover 2.50
2 flip-book-Badrock #2 . . . . 3.00
3 double-size 3.50

GRIFTER-ONE SHOT
WildStorm, 1995
1 SS,DN 5.00

GRIFTER
WildStorm, 1996
1 StG. 4.00
2 StG,V:Joe the Dead 3.00
3 StG,captured by MadJackPower . 3.00
4 StG,vs. Condition Red 3.00
5 StG,Grifter meets his dad,
   F:Molly Ingram. 3.00

Grifter #13 © WildStorm

6 StG,A:Santini 3.00
7 StG,MtB,I:Charlatan 3.00
8 StG,MtB,Zealot
   disappears,V:Soldier 3.00
9 StG,Zealot captured?, secret
   history of Quiet Men 3.00
10 StG,Grifter & Soldier go to
   rescue Zealot. 3.00
11 StG, renegade former agent . . . 3.00
12 StG,'Who is Tanager?'. 3.00
13 StG,F:Condition Red,'Family
   Feud' 3.00
14 StG,V:Joe the Dead 3.00

GRIFTER/SHI
WildStorm, 1996
1 BCi,JLe,TC 3.00
2 BCi,JLe,TC 3.00

GROO
1994–95
1 SA 3.50
2 A:Arba, Dakarba 3.50
3 The Generals Hat 3.50
4 A Drink of Water. 3.50
5 SA,A Simple Invasion 3.50
6 SA,A Little Invention 3.50
7 The Plight of the Drazils 3.50
8 . . . . 3.50
9 I:Arfetto 3.50
10 The Sinkes 3.50
11 The Gamblers 3.50
12 . . . . 3.50

GRRL SCOUTS
Feb., 2003
1 (of 4) Work Sucks, b&w 3.00
2 thru 4 . . . . @3.00
TPB Vol. 1 . . . . 13.00
TPB Work Sucks 13.00

GUARDIAN ANGEL
May, 2002
1 (of 4) AWs,F:ChristianAngelos. . . 3.00
2 AWs,no place like home 3.00
3 AWs,Our onlyhope. 3.00
4 concl. 3.00

HAMMER OF THE GODS
Sept., 2002
TPB: Mortal Enemy, 176-pg. 19.00

HAMMER OF THE GODS: HAMMER HITS CHINA
Feb., 2003
1 thru 3 . . . . @3.00

HAWAIIAN DICK
Dec., 2002
1 thru 3 Hawaii in 1953 . . . . @3.00
TPB Vol. 1 Byrd of Paradise 15.00

HAWAIIAN DICK: THE LAST RESORT
Aug., 2004
1 (of 4) 3.00
2 & 3 . . . . @3.00

HAWKSHAWS
March, 2000
1 by Dietrich Smith 3.00
1a variant movie poster(c) 3.00
2 and 3 . . . . @3.00

HAZARD
WildStorm, 1996
1 JMi,RMr 3.00
2 JMi,RMr 3.00
3 JMi,RMr 3.00
4 JMi,RMr 3.00
5 JMi,RMr,Hazard finds Dr. D'Oro . 3.00
6 JMi,RMr 3.00
7 JMi,RMr,Hazard meets Prism . . . 3.00

HEADHUNTERS
(B&W) April, 1997
1 ChM,V:Army of Wrath 3.00
2 ChM,V:undead militia. 3.00
3 ChM,'Slaughterground' 3.00

HEARTBREAKERS
Superdigest, July 1998
1 B&W and color 104-pg. 10.00

HEARTBREAKERS VERSUS BIOVOC
Image
TPB 'Bust Out'. 10.00
TPB PGn 15.00

HEAVEN, LLC
Image, Mar., 2004
TPB 13.00

HEAVEN'S DEVILS
Sept., 2003
1 (of 4) 3.00
2 . . . . 3.00
3 . . . . 3.00
4 . . . . 3.00

HEAVEN'S WAR
Image
GN b&w, 120-pg. 13.00

HEDGE KNIGHT, THE
Aug., 2003
1 (of 6) MsM 5.00
1a variant (c) 12.00
2 . . . . 5.00
2a cardstock(c) 10.00
3 . . . . 4.00
3a holofoil (c) 6.00

Devils Due 2004
4 thru 6 . . . . @3.00
4a thru 6a variant holofoil (c)s . . @6.00
TPB 15.00

HEIRS OF ETERNITY
Apr., 2003
1 (of 5) 3.00
2 thru 5 . . . . @3.00

HELLCOP
Avalon, Oct., 1998
1 JoC,F:Virgil Hilts 2.50
2 JoC,It's a small underwold
  after all. 2.50
3 JoC,new circles of Hell 2.50
4 JoC,secrets of Hell revealed . . . 2.50
5 JoC,Hell & High Water. 2.50
5a variant cover 3.00

HELLHOLE
Top Cow, May, 1999
1 SLo,AdP,F:Michael Cabrini 2.50
2 SLo,AdP,The Devil's Candy. 2.50
3 SLo,AdP,power brokers 2.50

HELLHOUNDS
Aug., 2003
1 Hadean Gates 3.00
2 thru 5 . . . . @3.00
6 EL(c),F:Savage Dragon. 3.00
1a and 2a variant (c). . . . . @3.00
5a variant (c) 3.00

HELLSHOCK
1994
1 I:Hellshock. 3.50
2 Powers & Origin. 3.50
3 New foe 3.50
4 . . . . 3.50

HELLSHOCK
Jan., 1997
1 JaL,Something wrong with
  Daniel, 48-pg.. . . . . 3.00
2 JaL,Daniel learns to control
  powers. 2.50
3 JaL,Daniel free of madness. 2.50
4 JaL,Daniel searches for his
  mother, Jonakand plans escape
  from Hell 2.50
5 JaL,Jonakand and fallen angels
  tear hell apart 2.50
6 JaL,'The Milk of Paradise' 2.50
7 JaL,'A Mother's Story',
  double size 4.00
8 JaL,House of Torture 2.50

HELLSPAWN
TMP, July, 2000
1 The Clown,pt.1. . . . . 4.00
2 The Clown,pt.2. . . . . 3.00
3 Hate Me 3.00
4 Hate You 3.00
5 Selling Fear 3.00
6 Angels 5.00
7 The Group 2.50
8 The Suicide Gate. 2.50
9 Chains 2.50
10 Clash. 2.50
11 Conflicts of Interest 2.50
12 Monsters and Miracles 2.50
13 Heaven & Hell. 2.50
14 Light of Day. 2.50
15 Blinded 2.50
16 Hellworld,pt.4 . . . . 2.50

17 The Killing Hand,pt.1 . . . . 2.50
18 The Killing Hand,pt.2 . . . . 2.50
19 The Killing Hand,pt.3 . . . . 2.50
20 The Collection. 2.50
21 The Collection,pt.2 . . . . 2.50
22 Love Lost,pt.1 . . . . 3.00
23 Love Lost,pt.2 . . . . 2.50
24 In the Grip of Shadows. 2.50
25 Remember Me? 2.50

HOLY TERROR, THE
Aug., 2002
1 (of 4) PhH 3.00
2 thru 3 PhH . . . . @3.00

HOMAGE STUDIOS
April, 1993
Swimsuit Spec.#1 JLe,WPo, MS . . . 2.25

HONG ON THE RANGE
Matinee Entertainment/
Flypaper, Dec., 1997
1 (of 3) by William Wu & Jeff
  Lafferty. 2.50
2 in Washout. 2.50
3 Duke Goslin 2.50
TPB Hong on the Range 13.00

HOUDINI:
THE MAN FROM BEYOND
Image, Oct., 2004
TPB 17.00

HUMAN KIND
Image/Top Cow, Aug., 2004
1 TnD,F:Alia Sparrow 3.00
2 TnD 3.00
3 TnD,Roads to New Rome,pt.3. . . 3.00

IMAGE INTRODUCES:
Oct., 2001
1 Primate 3.00
1b variant AGo(c) 3.00
(2) Legend of Isis. 3.00
(3) The Believer 3.00
(4) Cryptopia 3.00
(5) Dog Soldiers. 3.00

IMAGE TWO-IN-ONE
(B&W) Mar., 2001
1 EL,48-pg. F:Herculian & Duncan. 3.00

IMAGE ZERO
1993
0 I:Troll,Deathtrap,Pin-ups,rep.
  Savage Dragon #4,O:Stryker,
  F:ShadowHawk 15.00

IMAGES OF
SHADOWHAWK
1993–94
1 KG,V:Trencher 2.25
2 thru 3 V:Trencher. 2.25

IMMORTAL TWO
May, 1997
(B&W) Half-Tone
1 MsM,F:Gaijin & Gabrielle. 2.50
2 MsM. 2.50
3 MsM. 2.50
4 MsM,V:Okami Red. 2.50
5 MsM,new drug epidemic 2.50
6 MsM,First Order, cont. 2.50

Immortal Two #1 © Image

7 MsM,vs. impossible odds 2.50
7 MsM,flip photo cover 2.50

INFERNO: HELLBOUND
Top Cow, Nov., 2001
1 MS,DT,Hell loose on Earth 2.50
1a-1f variant(c) . . . . @2.50
2 MS 2.50
3 MS 3.00
4 MS 2.50
#0 MS 16-pg., signed. 20.00

INTRIGUE
Aug., 1999
1 F:Kirk Best 2.50
1a variant cover (1:4) 2.50
2 on the run from the law 2.50
3 V:NYPD SWAT team 2.50
3a variant HuR cover (1:4) 2.50
4 . . . . 2.50
5 . . . . 3.00
5a variant Mike Wieringo(c) 3.00

INVINCIBLE
Jan., 2003
1 O:Mark Grayson 4.00
2 . . . . 3.50
3 quality time. 3.50
4 human bombs 3.50
5 It Came From Outer Space 3.50
6 . . . . 3.50
7 Guardians of the Globe 3.00
8 shperhero funeral. 3.00
9 Perfect Strangers,pt.1 . . . . 3.00
10 Perfect Strangers,pt.2 . . . . 3.50
11 Perfect Strangers,pt.3 . . . . 3.00
12 Perfect Strangers,pt.4 . . . . 3.00
13 Perfect Strangers,epilogue 3.00
14 Alien invaders return. 3.00
15 Aquaria 3.00
16 Immortal is back 3.00
17 High school graduation. 3.00
18 Space flight to Mars 3.00
TPB Vol. 1 Family Matters 13.00
TPB Vol. 2 Eight is Enough 13.00
TPB Vol. 3 Perfect Strangers. . . . 13.00

INVISIBLE 9
Flypaper, May, 1998
TPB 13.00

IRON WINGS
March, 2000
1 Legends of Iron Wings 2.50
1a variant Andy Park(c) 2.50
2 V:Amaxius 2.50
3 Nightmares 2.50

Jackie Chan's Spartan X #1
© Image

JACKIE CHAN'S SPARTAN X
(B&W) March, 1998
1 MGo,RM,Hell-Bent Hero for Hire. 3.00
2 MGo,to Russia. 3.00
3 MGo,V:Kenshi 3.00
4 MGo,RM, in Istanbul 3.00
5 MGo,RM, Mind of God. 3.00
5a MGo,RM, photo cover 3.00
6 MGo,RM, The Armor of Heaven . 3.00
6a MGo,RM, photo cover 3.00

JACK STAFF
Feb., 2003
1 Britain's Greatest hero. 3.00
2 thru 7 . . . . @3.00
TPB Vol. 1 . . . . 20.00
TPB Vol. 2 Soldiers 16.00

JADE WARRIORS
Aug., 1999
1 MD2,Destruction of Japan 2.50
2 MD2,V:Ramthar. 2.50
3 MD2,Blood of the Children 2.50
1a thru 3a photo(c) . . . . @2.50
3b movie poster style(c) 2.50

JINN
Jan., 2000
1 F:Karen Lane. 3.00
2 and 3 . . . . @3.00
1a thru 2a variant cover . . . . . . @3.00

JINX
(B&W) June, 1997
1 by Brian Michael Bendis 3.00
1a 2nd printing 3.00
2 F:Jinx, female bounty hunter . . . 3.00
3 thru 5 . . . . @4.00
Spec.#1 Buried Treasure. 4.00
Spec.#1 True Crime Confessions . . 4.00

TPB rep. prev. #1–#4 . . . . 10.00
TPB The Essential Collection 18.00
TPB 480-pg. 25.00

JINX: TORSO
(B&W) Aug., 1998
1 by Brian Michael Bendis, 48-pg. . 4.00
2 search continues 4.00
3 Torso Killer 4.00
4 breaking the law 4.00
5 48-pg. 5.00
6 conclusion, 48-pg. 5.00
Spec. #@%!! short stories 4.00

JOURNEYMAN
Aug., 1999
1 by Brandon McKinney 3.00
2 enemies become allies 3.00
3 V:Dragon King 3.00

J.U.D.G.E.
March, 2000
1 by Greg Horn,F:Victoria Grace . . 3.00
1a variant cover 3.00
2 V:John Lawson 3.00
3 Secret Rage,pt.3 . . . . 3.00

JUNKBOTZ ROTOGIN
Feb., 2003
1 . . . . 2.50

KABUKI
Sept., 1997
1 DMk,O:Kabuki 7.00
1a variant JSo(c). 7.00
2 DMk,O:Kabuki, pg.2. . . . . 5.00
3 DMk,surprise visitor 5.00
4 DMk,Akemi, romance 7.00
5 DMk,action. 4.00
6 DMk 3.00
7 DMk 3.00
7a DMk variant cover (1:2) 3.00
8 DMk 3.00
9 DMk, finale. 3.00
TPB Circle of Blood,rep. orig. series
     plus 'Fear the Reaper,' B&W . . 18.00
TPB Masks of the Noh. 11.00
TPB Masks of the Noh, 2nd pr. . . 13.00
TPB Images, part rep. #1, 48-pg. . . 5.00
TPB Dreams 10.00
     TPB Vol.2 Dreams. 13.00
TPB Vol.4 Skin Deep 10.00
     TPB Vol.4 Skin Deep, 2nd pr. . . 11.00
     TPB Vol.4 Skin Deep, rep. . . . 13.00
TPB Vol.5 Metamorphosis 25.00
TPB Vol. 6 Scarab 20.00
GN Reflections #1, 48-pg. 5.00
GN Reflections #1 signed 8.00
GN Reflections #2 art & stories . . . 5.00
GN Reflections,Vol.3 . . . . 5.00
GN Reflections,Vol.4 . . . . 5.00
Spec. 1-shot The Ghost Play 3.00
Spec. #2 Images, rep. #2 & #3 . . 6.00
Kabuki 1/2 Wizard Mail-in 3.00
Kabuki 1/2 signed 6.00

KABUKI AGENTS
(B&W) Aug., 1999
1 DMk,F:Scarab 4.00
1a JQ(c), DMk signed. 7.00
2 DMk,F:Scarab, Tiger Lily 3.00
3 DMk,F:Scarab, Tiger Lily 3.00
4 DMk,F:Scarab, Tiger Lily 3.00
5 thru 8 DMk . . . . @3.00
Artbook. 5.00
Kabuki Agents: Scarab #1 signed . . 6.00

KABUKI: THE ALCHEMY
Image, Jan., 2004
1 (of 6) DMk 3.00
2 DMk 3.00

KABUKI CLASSICS
Feb., 1999
1 Fear the Reaper, rep. 10.00
2 Dance of Death 3.00
3 Circle of Blood, act 1, 48-pg. . . . 6.00
4 Circle of Blood, act 2. . . . . 4.00
5 Circle of Blood, act 3 . . . . 3.00
6 Circle of Blood, act 4 . . . . 3.00
7 Circle of Blood, act 5 . . . . 3.00
8 Circle of Blood, conclusion 3.00
9 Masks of the Noh, Act 1 . . . . . . 3.00
10 Masks of the Noh, Act 2 . . . . . 3.00
11 Masks of the Noh, Act 3 . . . . . 3.00
12 Masks of the Noh, concl. 3.00
Kabuki Classics #1 signed. 7.00

KANE
Image, Jan., 2004
TPB Vol.1 From New Eden 12.00
TPB Vol.2 Rabbit Hunt. 13.00
TPB Vol.3 Histories 13.00

KARZA
Feb., 2003
1 Micronauts spin-off 3.00
2 thru 4 . . . . @3.00

KID SUPREME
Supreme 1996–97
1 & 2 . . . . 2.50
3 DaF,ErS 2.50
4 DaF,ErS,Party time 2.50
5 DaF,ErS,'Birds of a Feather' . . . 2.50
6 DaF,ErS,I: Sensational Spinner . 2.50
7 DaF,ErS,Everything falls apart. . . 2.50

KID TERRIFIC
(B&W) Nov., 1998
1 A:Snedak & Manny Stellar. 3.00

KILLER INSTINCT TOUR BOOK
1 All Homage Artist,I:Crusade. . . . 5.00
1a signed 45.00

KILLRAZOR SPECIAL
Aug., 1995
1 O:Killrazor 2.50

KIN
Top Cow, Feb., 2000
1 GFr,Neanderthal 3.00
2 GFr,F:McLoon 3.00
3 GFr,Alaska revenge. 3.00
4 GFr. 3.00
5 GFr,Born Free 3.00
6 GFr,40-pg.,The End?. 4.00
6a variant AAd(c) 4.00
1st 6 as set, signed GFr 25.00
TPB Descent of Man 18.00

KINDRED
WildStorm, 1994
1 JLe,BCi(s),BBh,I:Kindred. 5.00
2 JLe,BCi(s),BBh,V:Kindred 3.50
3 JLe,BCi(s),BBh,V:Kindred 3.00
3a WPo(c),Alternate(c) 6.00
4 JLe,BCi(s),BBh,V:Kindred 3.00
TPB rep. #1–#4 . . . . 10.00

'KINI
Flypaper, Feb., 1999
1 KK,BKs,F:Kim Walters 2.50

Kiss: The Psycho Circus #5
© Juke Box

KISS:
THE PSYCHO CIRCUS
TMP, July, 1997
1 SvG,AMe 8.00
2 AMe, unearthly origins 6.00
3 AMe, Judgment o/t Elementals . . 5.00
4 AMe,Smoke and Mirrors,pt.1 . . . . 4.00
5 AMe,Smoke and Mirrors,pt.2 . . . . 4.00
6 AMe,Smoke and Mirrors, concl . . 4.00
7 AMe,Creatures of the Night 3.00
8 AMe,Forever 3.00
9 AMe,Four Sides to Every Story . . 3.00
10 AMe,Destroyer,pt.1 . . . . 3.00
11 AMe,Destroyer,pt.2 . . . . 3.00
12 AMe,Destroyer,pt.3 (of 4) 3.00
13 AMe, Destroyer,pt.4 . . . . 3.00
14 AMe, in Feudal Japan 3.00
15 AMe, in Feudal Japan, choices . . 2.50
16 AMe, Ticket for Terror 2.50
17 AMe, World Without Heroes,pt.2 2.50
18 AMe, Sunburst Finish 2.50
19 Fate of the Psycho Circus 2.50
20 Mr. Makebelieve 2.50
21 Don't Talk to Strangers 2.50
22 Twin sisters 2.50
23 Tribunal of souls 2.50
24 Cat's Eye 2.50
25 . . . . 2.50
26 Nightingale's Song,pt.1 . . . . 2.50
27 Nightingale's Song,pt.2 . . . . 2.50
28 Perdition Blues 2.50
29 Shadow of the Moon,pt.1 . . . . . 2.50
30 Shadow of the Moon,pt.2 . . . . . 2.50
31 Sins of Omission 2.50
32 Gallery of God's Mistakes 2.50
33 Gallery of God's Mistakes,pt.2 . . 2.50
34 Far Corners of Night 2.50
TPB Vol. I, rep. #1–#6 . . . . 13.00
TPB Vol. II rep. #10–#13 . . . . 10.00
TPB Vol.3 Whispered Scream . . . 10.00
TPB Vol.4 Legends & Nightmares . 10.00
Kiss Mag.#5 rep. 5.00

KNIGHTMARE
Extreme, 1995
0 O:Knightmare 2.50

---

1 I:Knightmare MMy 2.50
2 I:Caine 2.50
3 RLd,AV,The New Order,
F:Detective Murtaugh 2.50
4 RLd,AV,MMy,I:Thrillkill 2.50
5 V:Thrillkill 2.50
6 Extreme Babewatch 2.50
7 . . . . 2.50
8 I:Acid 2.50

KNIGHTS OF
THE JAGUAR
Image/Top Cow, Jan., 2004
Spec. super limited 2.50

KNIGHTSTRIKE
Extreme, 1996
1 Extreme Destroyer,pt.6
x-over, bagged with card 2.50

KNIGHT WATCHMAN
(B&W) May, 1998
1 by Gary Carlson & Chris Ecker . . 3.00
2 thru 4 Graveyard Shift,pt.2–pt.3 @3.00

KORE
Apr., 2003
1 . . . . 3.00
1a variant (c) 3.00
2 thru 5 . . . . @3.00

KOSMIC KAT
July, 1999
Activity Book 3.00

KURT BUSIEK'S
ASTRO CITY
Juke Box, 1995–96
1 I:Samaritan,'In Dreams' 12.00
1a 2nd printing 2.25
2 I:Silver Agent,V:Shirak
the Devourer 10.00
3 F:Jack in the Box 10.00
4 I:Hanged Man,Safeguards 11.00
5 I:Crackerjack 12.00
6 O:Samaritan,F:Winged Victory . 14.00
TPB 20.00

[Vol. 2] Homage, 1996
½ F:Hanged Man (1996) 5.00
1 KBk(s),BA,Welcome to
Astro City 9.00
1a 2nd printing 8.00
1b 2nd printing 2.50
2 KBk(s),BA,O:First Family,
F:Astra, Everyday Life 7.00
2b 2nd printing 2.50
3 KBk(s),BA,Adventures in
Other Worlds 7.00
4 KBk,BA,Teenager seeks to
become teen sidekick,pt.1 (of 6) 6.00
5 Learning the Game 5.00
6 V: creatures of Shadow Hill 5.00
7 Aliens invade Astro City 4.00
8 The aliens are out there 4.00
9 Honor Guard vs. Aliens finale . . . 4.00
10 meet the junkman 4.00
11 Serpent's Teeth 4.00
12 F:Jack-In-The-Box 3.00
13 F:Looney Leo 3.00
14 F:Steeljack 3.00
15 F:supervillains 3.00
TPB Confession, rep.#4–#9 . . . . . 20.00
3-D #1 . . . . 5.00
TPB Life in the Big City 20.00
TPB Family Album 20.00

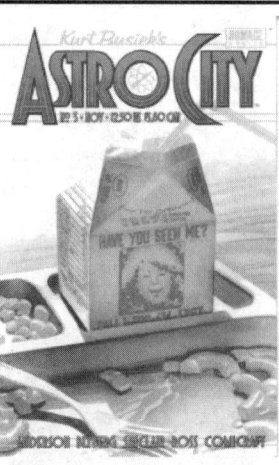

Kurt Busiek's Astro City, Vol. 2 #3
© Homage

Homage/DC, 1999
16 KBk(s), El Hombre 3.00
17 KBk(s), Mock Turtle 3.00
18 KBk(s), F:Steeljack 3.00
19 KBk(s), F:Steeljack 3.00
20 KBk(s) 3.00
21 KBk(s),F:Crackerjack 3.00
22 KBk(s),F:Samaritan 3.00
Spec.1/2 KBk(s) 3.00

LABMAN
1996
1 I:Labman 4.00
1a variant cover 4.00
2 & 3 . . . . @4.00

LADY PENDRAGON
Nov., 1998
1 MHw,Destiny's Embrace 2.50
1a remastered, new cover 2.50
1b Dynamic Forces variant cover . . 7.00
1c JeL(c) glow-in-the-dark 20.00
1d Tour Edition 5.00
2 MHw,Destiny's Embrace,pt.2 . . . . 3.00
3 MHw,Destiny's Embrace,pt.3 . . . . 3.00
3a variant cover (1:4) 2.50
0 MHw, Secrets & Origins 2.50
0a Eurosketch cover 10.00
Preview (Wizard, Chicago Comicon) 5.00
TPB Special, 64-pg. (2002) 8.00

LADY PENDRAGON:
DRAGON BLADE
April, 1999
1 MHw,Merlin trains Jennifer 2.50
1a variant cover (1:4) 2.50
1b Chrome Edition 5.00
2 MHw,F:Morgana 2.50
2a variant cover (1:4) 2.50
3 MHw,B.U.I:Alley Cat 3.00
4 MHw,Morgana returns 2.50
5 MHw,Spear of Destiny 2.50
6 MHw,Jennifer Drake resigns 2.50
7 MHw,Future Prophecy,pt.1 . . . . . 4.00
8 MHw,Future Prophecy,pt.2 . . . . . 2.50
9 MHw,Future Prophecy,pt.3 . . . . . 2.50
10 MHw,Messianic Lineage,pt.1 . . . 2.50
11 MHw,Messianic Lineage,pt.2 . . . 2.50
12 MHw,Messianic Lineage,pt.3 . . . 2.50
1a Glow-in-the-dark JaL(c) 2.50

IMAGE

Gallery Ed.#1 . . . . 3.00
Gallery Ed.#1a photo(c) 3.00

LADY PENDRAGON: MORE THAN MORTAL
May, 1999
1 MHw,Pendragon vs. Protector . . . 2.50
1a variant cover (1:4) 7.00
1b Gold foil(c) 7.00

Lady Supreme #1
© Extreme

LADY SUPREME
Extreme, 1996
1 TMr 2.50
2 TMr,Die & Let Die,pt.2 . . . . 2.50
3 TMr,V:Manassa 2.50
4 TMr,'Lady Supreme goes
   undercover' 2.50

LAST SHOT
Image, Aug., 2001
1 Foodchain,pt.1 . . . . 3.00
2 Metal in his Heart 3.00
3 Six String Noose 3.00
4 Angel of Death 3.00

LAST SHOT: FIRST DRAW
Image, May, 2001
1 First Draw Revolver 3.00

LAST STRAW MAN, THE
Image, Feb., 2004
1 (of 3) 4.00
2 40-pg. 4.00

LAZARUS CHURCHYARD: THE FINAL CUT
2000
Gn WEl 15.00

LEAVE IT TO CHANCE
Homage, 1996–98
1 JeR,PS,I:Chance Falconer 5.00
2 JeR,PS,Dragons are a Girl's
   Best Friend 5.00

Homage
3 JeR,PS,Chance and St. George
   race against time 5.00
4 JeR,PS. 3.00
5 JeR,PS,'Trick or Threat' 3.00
6 JeR,PS,Return of Cap'n Hitch . . . 3.00
7 JeR,PS,'And Not a Drop to Drink 3.00
8 JeR,PS,Phantom of the Mall 3.00
9 JeR,PS,Midnite Monster
   Madness 3.00
10 JeR,PS,'Destroy All Monsters' . . 3.00
11 JeR,PS,Dead Men Can't Skate . 3.00
12 JeR,PS,visits her friend Dash . . 3.00
13 JeR,PS,Reunion,48-pg. 5.00
TPB rep. #1–#4 . . . . 10.00
TPB Vol. II, rep. #5–#8 . . . . 13.00
TPB Trick or Threat 13.00

LEGACY
May, 2003
1 . . . . 3.00
2 thru 4 . . . . @3.00
4a variant (c) 3.00

LEGACY OF KAIN: DEFIANCE
Image, Jan., 2004
1-shot 3.00
1-shotA variant (c) 3.00

LEGEND OF ISIS
Feb., 2002
1 Origin of Isis 3.00

LEGEND OF SLEEPY HOLLOW, THE
Image, Oct., 2004
GN BHa 8.00

LEGEND OF SUPREME
Dec., 1994
1 KG(s),JJ,DPs,Revelations,pt.1 . . 2.50
2 Revelations,pt.2 . . . . 2.50
3 Conclusion 2.50

LETHAL
1996
1 & 2 . . . . @2.50

LEX TALIONIS: A JUNGLE TALE
Image, Jan., 2004
1-shot 48-pg. 6.00

LIBERTY MEADOWS
July, 2002
27 comic book convention 4.00
28 Ralph's Genetic Breakthrough . . 4.00
29 Brandy's Christmas Surprise . . . 4.00
30 Long Cold Winter,pt.1 . . . . 4.00
31 Long Cold Winter,pt.2 . . . . 4.00
32 The Cow is Back 3.50
33 Mad Cow, pt.2 . . . . 3.50
34 thru 37 . . . . @3.00
TPB Book #1 Eden, rep.#1-#9 . . . . 15.00
1-shot Sourcebook, 48-pg. 5.00
TPB Vol.1 Eden 20.00

LITTLE-GREYMAN
(B&W)
TPB by C. Scott Morse 7.00

LITTLE RED HOT: BOUND
Image, July, 2001
1 (of 3) by Dawn Brown 3.00
2 & 3 . . . . @3.00

LITTLE RED HOT: CHANE OF FOOLS
(B&W) Feb., 1999
1 (of 3) by Dawn Brown, F:Chane . 3.00
2 stranded in desert 3.00
3 Heaven vs. Hell 3.00
TPB The Foolish Collection, rep. . . 13.00

LOST ONES, THE
March, 2000
1 by Ken Penders 3.00
2 . . . . 3.00

LOVEBUNNY & MR. HELL
Feb., 2003
1-shot 3.00
1-shot Savage Love 3.00

LYNCH
WildStorm, June, 1997
1 TVs,'Terror in the Jungle' 2.50

MACE GRIFFIN: BOUNTY HUNTER
Image/Top Cow, Apr., 2003
1-shot 3.00

MAGDALENA
Top Cow, March, 2000
1 JBz,Darkness spin-off 4.00
1a variant MS(c) 4.00
1b variant Michael Turner(c) 4.00
2 JBz,secret revealed 2.50
3 JBz,Blood Divine,pt.3 . . . . 2.50
TPB JBz, 112-pg. 10.00
Preview, Magdalena/Blood
   Legacy, 22 pg.(2000) 3.00
1/2 Magdalena/Angelus, The Light
   and the Glory 3.00

MAGDALENA
Image/Top Cow, July, 2003
1 (of 4) 3.00
2 thru 4 . . . . @3.00
1a and 2a variant (c) . . . . @3.00
Spec. Con. Preview 2.50

MAGDALENA/ VAMPIRELLA
Image/Top Cow, June, 2003
1-shot 3.00
1-shotA variant (c) 1:4 . . . . 3.00

MAGE: THE HERO DEFINED
1997
1 MWg,F:Kevin Matchstick 5.00
2 MWg,Kirby Hero, V:harpies 4.00
3 MWg,Isis, Gretch 3.00
4 MWg,Isis, drug 3.00
5 MWg,into Canada 3.00
6 MWg,V:Dragonslayer 2.50
7 MWg 2.50
8 MWg,V:Red Caps 2.50

Mage: The Hero Defined, 3-D Special © Image

9 MWg,Sibling Trio 2.50
10 MWg,enchanted by a succubus . 2.50
11 MWg,Joe Phat, missing 2.50
12 MWg,Pale Incanter's Lair 2.50
13 MWg,What color is magic. 2.50
14 MWg,Man Mountain of???? 2.50
15 MWg, 48-pg. concl. 6.00
Spec. 3-D #1 (1998) 5.00
TPB Vol. 1 rep.. . . . . 10.00
TPB Vol. II, rep. #5–#8 . . . . 10.00
TPB Vol. 3, rep. #9–#12 . . . . 13.00
TPB Vol. 4, rep. #13–#15. . . . . . 15.00
Coll.Ed.Vol.1,rep.#1–#2 . . . . 6.00
Coll.Ed.Vol.2,rep.#3–#4 . . . . 6.00
Coll.Ed.Vol.3,rep.#5–#6 . . . . 6.00
Coll.Ed.Vol.4,rep.#7–#8 . . . . 5.00
Coll.Ed.Vol.5,rep.#9–#10 . . . . 5.00
Coll.Ed.Vol.6,rep.#11–#12 . . . . . . 5.00
Coll.Ed.Vol.7,rep.#13–#14 . . . . . . 5.50
Coll.Ed.Vol.8,rep.#15–#16 . . . . . . 5.00

MAN AGAINST TIME
Motown 1996
1 'Every Hero'. 2.50
2 . . . . 2.50
3 'Pro Patria Mori'. 2.50

MANIC
Image, Feb., 2004
1-shot 3.00

MARS ATTACKS
1996
1 KG,BSz(of 4) 2.50
2 thru 4 . . . . @2.50

MASK OF ZORRO, THE
July, 1998
1 (of 4) DMG,RoW,RM,MGo(c), . . . 3.00
2 DMG,RoW,RM,MGo(c) 3.00
3 DMG,RoW,MGo(c). 3.00
4 DMG,RoW,MGo concl. 3.00
4a photo cover 3.00

MASTERS OF THE UNIVERSE
2002
1 He-Man returns 3.00
1b variant JSC(c) 3.00

1b variant EN(c) 3.00
2 thru 4 . . . . @3.00
2a–4a variant (c). . . . . @3.00
Volume II
1 . . . . 3.00
2 thru 8 . . . . @3.00
1a–2a variant (c) . . . . @3.00
3a–4a holofoil (c) . . . . @6.00
1-shot Icons of Evil: Beast Man 5.00

MAXIMAGE
Extreme, 1995–96
1 RLe(c) 2.50
2 Extreme Destroyer,pt.2,
x-over, bagged with card 2.50
3 . . . . 2.50
4 A:Angela,Glory. 2.50
5 thru 8 . . . . @2.50
9 BML, Sex Slaves of Bomba
Island 2.50
10 BML, The King of Emotion is
back 2.50

The Maxx #22 © Image

MAXX, THE
1993
1/2 SK,from Wizard. 10.00
1 SK,I:The Maxx. 5.00
1a glow in the dark(c) 15.00
2 SK,V:Mr.Gone 4.00
3 SK,V:Mr.Gone 4.00
4 SK 4.00
5 SK 3.00
6 SK 3.00
7 SK,A:Pitt 3.50
8 SK,V:Pitt. 3.50
9 SK 3.00
10 SK 3.00
11 SK 2.50
12 SK 2.50
13 Maxx Wanders in Dreams 2.50
14 R:Julie 4.00
15 Julia's Pregnant 4.00
16 SK,Is Maxx in Danger?. 4.00
17 SK,Gardener Maxx 4.00
18 SK,'Beware The Hooley'. 2.50
19 SK,V:Hooley,'Last Fairy Tale' . . . 2.50
20 SK,Questions are answered. . . . 2.50
21 AM(s),SK. 2.50
22 SK,'Other Peoples' Crap' 2.50
23 SK,'Having to Believe' 2.50
24 SK 2.50
25 SK,'Lost and Found'. 2.50

26 SK 2.50
27 V:Iago the Killer Slug 2.50
28 Sara and Norberg look for Julie . 2.50
29 Sara and Gone defeat Iago the
Slug 2.50
30 Lil' Sara faces her fears 2.50
31 F:The Library girl. 2.50
32 F:The Library girl,pt.2 . . . . 2.50
33 Sara's back 2.50
34 Mark and Julia 2.50
35 who knows? 2.50
36 bumfuzzled 2.50
37 Megan's story concl 2.50
38 Mark,Julie,Larry,pt.1 (of 4) 2.50
Spec. Friends of Maxx,F:Dude
Japan. 3.00
The Maxx 3-D #1 . . . . 5.00
TPB Rep. #1-#5. . . . . 13.00
TPB Vol. 2 . . . . 13.00

MECHANIC, THE
Homage, Aug., 1998
GN JCh,JPe,time travel 6.00

MECH DESTROYER
Image, March, 2001
1 (of 4) Battle for Earth. 3.00
2 Face of the Enemy 3.00
3 rescue the captives 3.00
4 V:The Crimson Death 3.00

MEDIEVAL SPAWN/ WITCHBLADE
May, 1996
1 thru 3 . . . . @5.00
TPB series rep. 10.00

MEGADRAGON & TIGER
March, 1999
1 by Tony Wong, from Hong Kong . 3.00
2 F:Red Tiger 3.00
3 V:Single-Minded Arhat. 3.00
4 V:Fiery Lord 3.00
5 F:Gigi 3.00

MEGAHURTZ
(B&W) Aug., 1997
1 JPi,I:Megahurtz 3.00
2 JPi,visit to Wonderland 3.00
3 JPi,V:N-Filtraitors. 3.00
4 JPi,Liberaiders. 3.00

MEGATON MAN: BOMBSHELL
July, 1999
1 DSs,V:Unleash. 3.00

MEGATON MAN: HARDCOPY
Fiasco (B&W) Feb., 1999
1 by Don Simpson 3.00
2 with 6 new pages. 3.00

MESSENGER, THE
July, 2000
1-shot JOy, 48-pg. 6.00

MICRONAUTS
June, 2002
1 . . . . 3.00
2 thru 5 . . . . @3.00
6 Star Chamber,pt.1 . . . . 3.00
7 Star Chamber,pt.2 . . . . 3.00

Micronauts (cont.)

8 Invasion Earth,pt.1 . . . . 3.00
9 Invasion Earth,pt.2 . . . . 3.00
10 Invasion Earth,pt.3 . . . . 3.00
11 Invasion Earth,pt.4 . . . . 3.00
TPB Vol. 1 Rebellion 11.00
Spec. 2002 Con Special 3.00

MIDNIGHT NATION
Top Cow, Sept., 2000

1 MSz 5.00
1a variant GrF(c). 12.00
2 MSz,GrF, on the run 4.00
3 MSz,GrF, To Hell and inbetween . 4.00
4 MSz,GrF, V:Walkers. 4.00
5 MSz,GrF, Find your soul 4.00
6 MSz,GrF, Halfway 4.00
7 MSz,GrF, Change has begun . . . 4.00
8 MSz,GrF, Road gets worse 4.00
9 MSz,GrF, New York, New York . . 4.00
10 MSz,GrF, Soul's price 4.00
11 MSz,GrF, Still the Road to Hell . . 4.00
12 MSz,GrF, The End of the Road . 4.00
TPB series rep.288-pg. 30.00

MIKE GRELL'S
MAGGIE THE CAT
Jan., 1996

1 (of 4) Master Piece,pt.1 . . . . 2.50
2 Master Piece,pt.2. . . . . 2.50

MINISTRY OF SPACE
April, 2001

1 (of 3) WEI,CWn,World War II. . . . 3.00
2 WEI,CWn 3.00
3 WEI,CWn,concl. 3.00
Omnibus #1 & #2. . . . . 5.00
3 . . . . 3.00

MISERY SPECIAL
Dec., 1995

1 Cyberforce Origins 3.00

MISPLACED
May, 2003

1 . . . . 3.00
1a variant (c)s 3.00
2 & 3 . . . . @3.00

MONSTER FIGHTERS, INC.
April, 1999

1 Who you gonna call 3.00
2 Wake the dead 3.00
1-shot The Black Book 3.50

MONSTER FIGHTERS INC.:
THE GHOSTS OF
CHRISTMAS
Dec., 1999

1 The Fright Before Christmas 4.00

MONSTERMAN
(B&W) Sept., 1997

1 MM,from Action Planet 3.00
2 MM,Inhuman monsters 3.00
3 MM,King of Monsters 3.00
4 MM, conclusion 3.00

MORE THAN MORTAL/
LADY PENDRAGON
June, 1999

1 MHw,x-over 2.50
Prev. Edition 16-pg., B&W 5.00

MORE THAN MORTAL:
OTHERWORLDS
Liar Comics, July, 1999

1 F:Derdre & Morand 3.00
1a variant cover (1:2) 5.00
2 in Otherworld 3.00
2a variant cover (1:2) 4.00
3 Lady in white 3.00
3a variant Derdre cover (1:2) 3.00
4 Woman in white, concl. 3.00
5 Famine,pt.1 . . . . 3.00
6 Famine,pt.2 . . . . 3.00
7 Famine,pt.3 . . . . 3.00
Art Gallery #1. . . . . 3.50
TPB Vol. 1, rep. #1 & #2 . . . . 7.00
TPB Vol. 2 . . . . 7.00
TPB Vol. 3, Truths & Legends 6.00

MR. MONSTER
VS. GORZILLA
(2 color) July, 1998

1-shot, MGi 3.00

MR. MONSTER'S GAL
FRIDAY: KELLY
(B&W) Jan., 2000

1 MGi 3.50
2 MGi 3.50
3 MGi,AMo(s) 3.50

MR. RIGHT
Aug., 2001

1 TDF,RF,flip-book 3.00
2 TDF,RF,F:General Public 3.00

MOTH
July, 2003

1-shot 48-pg 6.00

M-REX
Nov., 1999

1 by Joe Kelly & Duncan Rouleau . 3.00
2 thru 5 . . . . @3.00
4a and 5a variant cover . . . . @3.00
#1 Limited Tour Edition 5.00
Preview, B&W, 16-pg. 5.00

MS. FORTUNE
(B&W) 1998

1 by Chris Marrinan 3.00
2 Carnage in the Caribbean 3.00
3 Doom at the Dawn of Time 3.00

MUTANT EARTH
May, 2002

1 (of 4) F:Trakk 3.00
2 F:Zeithian warlord, Gallowz 3.00
3 . . . . 3.00
4 concl. 3.00
1a thru 4a variant (c) . . . . @3.00
TPB Vol. 1 Trakk, sgn.& num. . . . 17.00

MYSTERY, INC.

Ashcan 1 . . . . 4.00

MYTHSTALKERS
Mar., 2003

1 The Labyrinth,pt.1 . . . . 3.00
2 The Labyrinth,pt.2 . . . . 3.00
3 The Labyrinth,pt.3 . . . . 3.00
4 The Labyrinth,pt.4 . . . . 3.00
5 London Nights 3.00
6 London Nights,pt.2. . . . . 3.00

7 Gangs of London 3.00
8 London Nights 3.00

MYTH WARRIORS
Image/Top Cow, Oct., 2004

GN 10.00

NAMELESS, THE
(B&W) May, 1997

1 PhH,I:The Nameless, protector of
Mexico City's lost children 3.00
2 thru 5 . . . . @3.00

NASH
July, 1999

1 MMy, by & starring Kevin Nash . 2.50
1a variant cover (1:2) 3.00
2 MMy, the end of Nash? 2.50
2a variant cover (1:2) 2.50
#1 Photo-Split edition 3.00
Preview edition MMy,F:Kevin Nash . 2.50
Preview ed.A variant cover (1:2) . . 2.50

NEON CYBER
July, 1999

1 F:Neon Dragons 2.50
1a variant cover (1:2) 2.50
1b glow-in-the-dark edition 7.00
2 gang alliance 2.50
2a variant cover (1:2) 2.50
3 Neon a suspect 2.50
4 who framed Neon? 2.50
5 . . . . 2.50
6 V:Mohawks 2.50
7 . . . . 2.50
8 conclusion of Vol. 1 . . . . 2.50

NEW ADVENTURES OF
ABRAHAM LINCOLN
Homage, Feb., 1998

TPB SMI, 144-pg.. . . . . 20.00

NEWFORCE
Extreme, 1996

1 Extreme Destroyer,pt.8
x-over, bagged with card 2.50
2 . . . . 2.50
3 . . . . 2.50
4 Team disbands 2.50

NEWMAN
Extreme, 1996

1 Extreme Destroyer,pt.3
x-over, bagged with card 2.50
2 . . . . 2.50
3 . . . . 2.50
4 Shadowhunt x-over,pt.5 . . . . 2.50

NEWMEN
Extreme, 1994

1 JMs 3.00
2 JMs,I:Girth 2.50
3 JMs,V:Girth,I:Ikonna 2.50
4 JMs,A:Ripclaw 2.50
5 JMs,Ripclaw,V:Ikonn 2.50
6 JMs 2.50
7 JMs 2.50
8 JMs,Team Youngblood 2.50
9 ErS(s),JMs,Kodiak Kidnapped . . 2.50
10 ExtremeSacrifice,pt.5,x-over . . . 2.50
11 F:Reign 2.50
12 R:Elemental 2.50
13 ErS,I:Bootleg 2.50
14 ErS,Dominion's Secret 2.50
15 I:Time Guild 2.50

IMAGE

16	2.50
16a variant cover	3.00
17 R:Girth.	2.50
18 F:Byrd	2.50
19 I:Bordda Khan,Shepherd	2.50
20 Extreme Babewatch	2.50
21 ErS,CSp,(1 of 5)	2.50
22 ErS,CSp, Who Needs the Newmen?	2.50
23 ErS,CSp,Who are the Newmen?	2.50

THE NEW ORDER HANDBOOK

Various artists ... 2.25

NEW SHADOWHAWK, THE
June, 1995

1 KBk,I:New ShadowHawk	3.00
2 KBk,V:Mutants	3.00
3 KBk,I:Trophy	3.00
4 KBk,V:Blowfish.	3.00
5 KBk,	3.00
6 KBk,	3.00
7 KBk,	3.00

NINE RINGS OF WU-TANG, THE
Nov., 1999

1 by Brian Haberlin	4.00
2	3.00
3 Bringers of Sleep	3.00
4 F:Mza	3.00
4a variant cover	3.00
5	3.00
#1 limited tour edition.	5.00
Preview, B&W, 16-pg.	5.00
TPB Book of Days	20.00

NINE RINGS OF WU-TANG, THE: FATIMA'S REVENGE
May, 2000

1 by Brian Haberlin ... 3.00

1963
April, 1993

1 Mystery Incorporated, AnM(s), RV,DGb	2.50
1a Gold ed.	4.00
1b Bronze ed.	3.00

1963 Book 5 © Image

2 No One Escapes...The Fury, RV,SBi,DGb,JV,I:The Fury.	2.25
3 Tales of the Uncanny, RV,SBi,I:U.S.A.	2.25
4 Tales From Beyond JV,SBi,I:N-Man, Johnny Beyond	2.25
5 Horus, Lord of Light, JV,SBi,I:Horus	2.25
6 Tomorrow Syndicate, JV,SBi,C:Shaft	2.25
Ashcan #1	3.00
Ashcan #2	2.50
Ashcan #4	2.00

NINE VOLT
Top Cow, 1997

1 ACh	3.00
1a Variant(c)	4.00
2 ACh	3.00
3 ACh,V:crazed junkie terrorists	2.50
4 ACh,V:Rev. Cyril Gibson	2.50

NOBLE CAUSES
Sept., 2001

1-shot First Impressions	3.00
1 two stories	3.00
2	3.00
2a variant RGr(c)	3.00
3 three's a crowd	3.00
3a variant Ccs(c).	3.00
4 In Sickness and in Health,pt.4	3.00
4a variant(c)	3.00
TPB In Sickness and in Health	13.00
1-shot Extended Family, 80-pg.	5.00

Image, July, 2004

1	3.50
1a & 2a variant(c)	@3.50
2 thru 4	@3.50

NOBLE CAUSES: DISTANT RELATIVES
July, 2003

1 (of 4)	3.00
2 thru 4	@3.00

NOBLE CAUSES: FAMILY SECRETS
Oct., 2002

1 (of 4) F:Liz Donnelly-Noble	3.50
1a variant(c)	3.00
2 spin control	3.00
2a variant(c)	3.00
3 guest stars galore	3.00
4	3.00
3a– variant(c).	@3.00
TPB Vol. 2 Family Secrets	13.00

NO HONOR
Top Cow, Feb., 2001

1 (of 4) F:Tanne Yojimbo.	5.00
2	5.00
3	2.50
4 concl.	2.50
Prev. 16-pg. B&W	5.00
TPB 96-pg.	13.00

NO HONOR: MAKYO
Top Cow, Nov., 2001

1 ... 4.00

NORMALMAN
Image, July, 2004

1-shot 20th Anniv. ... 3.00

NORMAL MAN/ MEGATON MAN SPECIAL

1 ... 2.50

NOWHERESVILLE
March, 2002

TPB MRc, 192-pg. b&w ... 15.00

NYC MECH
Image, Apr., 2004

1	3.00
2 thru 6	@3.00

OBERGEIST: RAGNAROK HIGHWAY
Top Cow/Minotaur 2001

1 TyH	3.00
2 TyH	3.00
3 TyH	3.00
4 TyH	3.00
5 TyH,Ambushed	3.00
6 TyH,His memory, Abyss's flame	3.00
TPB Directors' Cut	20.00

OBERGEIST: THE EMPTY LOCKET
Top Cow/Minotaur, 2002

1 TyH ... 3.00

OBJECTIVE FIVE
July, 2000

1 biological weapons	3.00
2 F:Lark, Alexis & DJ	3.00
3 Airborne Virus	3.00
4 Reunion	3.00
5 Hidden Enemies	3.00
6 in China	3.00
7 Origins	3.00

OPERATION KNIGHTSTRIKE
May, 1995

1 RHe,A:Chapel,Bravo,Battlestone	2.50
2 In Afganistan	2.50
3 final issue.	2.50

THE OTHERS
March, 1995

0 JV(s),From ShadowHawk	2.50
1 JV(s)V:Mongrel	2.50
2 JV,Mongrel takes weapons	2.50
3 War	2.50
4 O:Clone	2.50

OVERKILL
Top Cow, Oct., 2000

1 PJe,x-over,A:Aliens,Predator.	6.00
2 PJe,x-over,A:Aliens,Predator.	6.00

OXIDO
Sept., 2003

1 (of 6) LHa(s)	3.00
2 LHa(s)	3.00

PACT
1994

1 JV(s),WMc,I:Pact, C:Youngblood	2.25
2 JV(s),V:Youngblood	2.25
3 JV(s),V:Atrocity	2.25

IMAGE

PARADIGM
Sept., 2002
1 F:Chris Howells, 48-pg. b&w	3.50
2 40-pg. b&w.	3.50
3 40-pg. b&w.	3.50
4 40-pg.	3.50
5	3.00
6 All About the Community	3.00
7 40-pg.	3.00
8 Swirly Things	3.00
9 Real Swirly Things	3.00
10	3.00
11 40-pg.	3.50
12 40-pg.	3.50
TPB Vol. 1 Segue to an Interlude	14.00

PARLIAMENT OF JUSTICE, THE
Mar., 2003
1-shot b&w, 56-pg.	6.00

PARTS UNKNOWN: KILLING ATTRACTION
(B&W) April, 2000
1 Sci-Fi/UFO adventure	3.00

PARTS UNKNOWN: HOSTILE TAKEOVER
(B&W) June, 2000
1 by Beau Smith & Brad Gorby	3.00
2	3.00
3 & 4	@3.00

PATIENT ZERO
Image, Mar., 2004
1 (of 4) Eternity's Past,pt.1	3.00
2 thru 4 Eternity's Past,pt.2ñ4	@3.00

PHANTOM FORCE
Dec., 1993
1 RLd,JK,w/card	2.75
2 JK,V:Darkfire	2.25

See also Color Comics section

PHANTOM GUARD
WildStorm, Oct., 1997
1 by Sean Ruffner, Ryan Benjamin	3.00

Phantom Guard #3
© WildStorm

1a variant cover	3.00
1b Voyager bagged pack	3.50
2 Martian wasteland	3.00
3 Lowell Zerium Mines	3.00
4 'Target Locked'.	3.00
5 V:Vanox,	3.00
6 Countdown to Armageddon	3.00

PHANTOM JACK
Image, Mar., 2004
1 Roach Motel.	3.00
2 Back to Baghdad	3.00
3 Among the Enemy	3.00
4 Madison Blue, Who Are You	3.00
5 Sins of Saddam Hussein	3.00

PITT
Top Cow, 1993–95
1 DK,I:Pitt,Timmy	4.00
2 DK,V:Quagg.	3.00
3 DK,V:Zoyvod	4.00
4 DK,V:Zoyvod	3.00
5 DK	2.50
6 DK	2.50
7 DK	2.50
8 Ransom	2.50
9 DK,Artic Adventures.	2.50
Ashcan 1	3.00

POWER OF THE MARK
1 I:Ted Miller	2.50
2 V:The Fuse	2.50
3 TMB(s), The Mark	2.50
4 TMB,Mark's secrets revealed	2.50

POWER RANGERS ZEO
Extreme, Sept., 1997
1 thru 3 TBm&MBm(s),TNu,NRd	@2.50

POWER RANGERS ZEO YOUNGBLOOD
Extreme, Oct., 1997
1 thru 2 RLd,TBm,MBm	@3.00

POWERS
April, 2000
1 Who killed Retro Girl,pt.1	15.00
2 Who killed Retro Girl,pt.2.	20.00
3 Who killed Retro Girl,pt.3.	15.00
4	8.00
5 A murder solved.	8.00
6	8.00
7 WEI, Ride Along.	7.00
8 Role Play,pt.1	7.00
9 Role Play,pt.2.	7.00
10 Role Play,pt.3	7.00
11	5.00
12 Groupies	5.00
13 Groupies,pt.2	5.00
14 Groupies,pt.3	5.00
15 Supergroup,pt.1	5.00
16 Supergroup	5.00
17 incl. Bastard Samurai prequel	5.00
18 superhero wanted for murder	5.00
19 supergroup shocking concl.	5.00
20 supergroup explosive concl.	5.00
21 Anarchy,pt.1	3.50
22 Anarchy,pt.2	3.50
23 Anarchy,pt.3	3.50
24 Anarchy,pt.4	3.50
25 The Sellouts,pt.1	3.50
26 The Sellouts,pt.2.	3.50
27 The Sellouts,pt.3.	3.00
28 The Sellouts,pt.4.	3.00
29 The Sellouts,pt.5.	3.00
30 The Sellouts,pt.6.	3.00
31 Forever,pt.1.	3.00

Powers #9 © Image

32 Forever,pt.2.	3.00
33 Forever,pt.3.	3.00
34 Forever,pt.4.	3.00
35 Forever,pt.5.	3.00
36 Forever,pt.6.	3.00
37 Forever,pt.7.	3.00
Spec.-1 Coloring & Activity Book	2.25
1/2 Wizard story + new	3.00
Scriptbook 344-pg.	20.00
TPB Vol.1 Who Killed Retro Girl	20.00
TPB Vol.1 Who Killed Retro Girl	22.00
TPB Vol.1 readers addition	16.00
TPB Vol.2 Roleplay	14.00
TPB Vol.2 Roleplay, 2nd pr.	14.00
TPB Vol.3 Little Deaths	25.00
TPB Vol.4 Supergroup	20.00
TPB Vol.5 Anarchy	15.00
TPB Vol. 6 The Sellouts	20.00

VOLUME 2 (2004)
1 Legends,pt.1	3.00
2 Legends,pt.2	3.00
3 Legends,pt.3	3.00

PRIMAL INSTINCT
March, 2000
Preview	2.50

PRO, THE
July, 2002
GN 1-shot GEn,ACo,JP 56-pg.	8.00
Con. Ed. signed, numbered	25.00

PROPHET
Extreme, 1993–95
0 San Diego Comic-Con ed.	4.00
1 RLd(s)DPs,O:Prophet,I:Mary McCormick.	3.00
1a Gold ed.	4.00
2 RLd(s),DPs,C:Bloodstrike	2.50
3 RLd(s),DPs, V:Bloodstrike, I:Judas	2.50
4 RLd(s),DPs,I:Omen,A:Judas	2.50
4a SPa(c),Limited ed.	3.00
5 SPa,Supreme Apocalypse,pt.2	3.00
6 SPa	2.50
7 SPa War Games,pt.1	2.25
8 SPa War Games,pt.2.	2.50
9 SPa,Extreme Sacrifice Prelude	2.50
10 ExtremeSacrifice,pt.7,x-over.	2.50
Sourcebook	3.00
Ashcan #1	3.00
Ashcan #2	3.00

IMAGE

[Second Series] 1995

1 SPI, New Series.	3.50
2 SPI, New Direction.	2.50
2a variant cover	2.50
3 True Nature	2.50
4 The Dying Factor	2.50
5	2.50
6	2.50
7 CDi,SPa	2.50
8 & 9	@2.50
TPB	13.00
Ann.#1 Supreme Apocalypse	2.50
Spec.#1 Babewatch special (1995)	2.50

PROPHET/CHAPEL: SUPER SOLDIERS
May, 1996

1	2.50
1A variant(c) b&w	2.50
2	2.50

PROXIMITY EFFECT
Image/Top Cow, June, 2004

GN	10.00

PSCYTHE
Image, Sept., 2004

1 (of 2) MT	4.00
2 MT	4.00

PUFFED
July, 2003

1 (of 3)	3.00
2 & 3	@3.00

PVP
Mar., 2003

1 Player vs. Player	3.00
2 Lord of the Schwing	3.00
3 Lost and Found	3.00
4 V:Devilfish	3.00
5 Max Powers	3.00
6 Skull the Troll	3.00
7 Chilling events	3.00
8 Brent Sienna Dies	3.00
9 Skull in local Zoo	3.00
10 Skull hyper-intelligent	3.00
11 F:Savage Dragon	3.00
12 Halloween party	3.00
TPB Vol. 1 The Dork Ages	12.00
TPB Vol. 1 At Large	12.00
Spec. Replay #1, rep.#1 & #2	5.00

QUANTUM MECHANICS
Image, Oct., 2004

GN ATi,B&W, 48-pg.	7.00

Q-UNIT: REVENGE
Oct., 1999

1 KIA,BNa	3.00
1a variant cover (1:2)	3.00
2 KIA,BNa	3.00
2a variant cover (1:2)	3.00

RADISKULL AND DEVIL DOLL
Dec., 2002

1-shot b&w	2.50
1-shot Radiskull Hate Love	3.00

RADIX
Dec., 2001

1 mysterious new force	3.00

2 F:Val Fiores	3.00
3	3.00
4 mysterious object	3.00

RAGMOP
(B&W)

Vol.2 #1 by Rob Walton	3.00
Vol.2 #2	3.00

RAIL
June, 2001

GN DvD, 48-pg.	6.00

RANDY O'DONNEL IS THE MAN
Image, May, 2001

1 TDF,RLm,flip-book	3.00
2 TDF,RLm,The Chosen	3.00
3 TDF,RLm,Terror of the Warrior Toads	3.00
4 TDF,Merciless are the Malok	3.00

REALM OF THE CLAW
Oct., 2003

1 (of 6)	3.00
1a variant (c)	3.00
2	3.00
2a variant (c)	3.00

REAPER
Image, Mar., 2004

GN	7.00

RED STAR, THE
June, 2000

1 by Christian Gossett	8.00
2 Project: Antares	6.00
3 Fall of the Red Fleet	4.00
4 Marcus' mystic revelation	4.00
5 A worker's Tale.	4.00
6 War torn Nokgorka.	3.00
7 Nokgorka,pt.2	3.00
8 Nokgorka,pt.3	3.00
9 Marcus Antares is alive	3.00
9a variant(c)	3.00
Spec.#1 3-D Transformation	3.00
TPB Vol.1 Battle of Kar Dathra's Gate, 144-pg.	25.00

Regulators #1 © Image

REGULATORS
June, 1995

1 F:Blackjack,'Touch of Scandal'	2.50
2 F:Vortex	2.50
3 F:Arson	2.50
4 F:Scandal.	2.50

REPLACEMENT GOD AND OTHER STORIES, THE
(B&W) May, 1997

1 Knute vs. King Ursus.	3.00
2 by Zander Cannon.	3.00
3 thru 5	@3.00

RESIDENT EVIL
Wildstorm March, 1998

1 comic/game magazine 56-pg.	6.00
2 thru 4 comic/game mag. 56-pg.	@5.50
TPB Collection 1, series rep.	15.00

RETURN OF SHADOWHAWK, THE
Image, Sept., 2004

1-shot JV	3.00

REX MUNDI
Aug., 2002

0	4.00
1 Unexpected visitor	3.50
2 Puzzle in the Painting	3.50
3 The Archbiship and the Pimp	3.50
4 Shadows Beneath the City	3.00
5 Shadows Beneath the City	3.00
6 Secrets Revealed	3.00
7 Father of Wisdom	3.00
8 Suspicion grows.	3.00
9 National library.	3.00
10 Holy Grail	3.00
11 Treasure of the Temple	3.00
12 The Swan Knight	3.00
TPB Vol. 1 Guardian of Temple	15.00

RIDE, THE
Image, June, 2004

1 Wheels of Change,pt.1	3.00
2 Wheels of Change,pt.2	3.00
1a thru 2a signed	@15.00

RIDE, THE: 2 FOR THE ROAD
Image, Oct., 2004

1-shot Shotgun; Big Plans	3.00

RIPCLAW
Top Cow, 1995

1/2 Prelude to Series (Wizard)	3.00
1/2a Con versions.	7.00
1 A:Killjoy, I:Shadowblade.	3.00
2 Cyblade, Heatwave	2.50
3 EcS,BPe,AV,Alliance with S.H.O.C.s	2.50
4 conclusion	2.50
Spec.#1 I:Ripclaw's Brother	3.00

[1st Regular Series]

1 thru 5	@2.50

RIPTIDE
1995

1 O:Riptide	2.50
2 O:Riptide	2.50

IMAGE

RISING STARS
Top Cow, March, 1999
1 A celestial event	5.00
1a, b, & c variant covers	8.00
2 life & death of Peter Dawson	8.00
3 new special	8.00
4	8.00
5 To the netherworld	8.00
6 Things Fall Apart,pt.1	8.00
7 Things Fall Apart,pt.2	8.00
8 Things Fall Apart,pt.3	5.00
9 Act Two,pt.1	5.00
10 years later	3.50
11 Specials out of control	3.00
12 War for Chicago	3.00
12a Monstermart edition	10.00
12b Monstermart gold foil	17.00
12c Monstermart holofoil	25.00
13 Brothers	3.00
14 Patriot vs. Matthew Bright	3.00
15 The Secret	3.00
16 finale	3.00
17 campaign to change the world	3.00
18 will they change the world	3.00
19 MSz,government vs. Specials	3.00
20 MSz	3.00
21 MSz	3.00
22 Phoenix in Ascension,pt.1	3.00
1/2 rep	3.00
#0 rep. from Wizard	2.50
Preview MSz, 16-pg., B&W	5.00
Prelude	3.00
TPB Deluxe,rep.#1–#8	20.00
TPB Vol.2, rep.#9–#16	20.00
TPB Vol.3 Visitations	9.00

RISING STARS: BRIGHT
Image/Top Cow, Feb., 2003
1 (of 3)	3.00
2 Authority	3.00
3 Civilian Casualties	3.00

RISING STARS: UNTOUCHABLE
Image/Top Cow, Sept., 2003
1 Story of Laurel Darkhaven	3.00

ROB ZOMBIE'S SPOOK SHOW
Image, 2004
Int. Omnibus #1 48-pg	5.00
Int. Omnibus #2 48-pg	5.00

ROMP
Image, Dec., 2003
1-shot AdP	6.00

ROTOGIN: JUNKBOTZ
Apr., 2003
1 (of 8)	3.00
2 thru 4	@3.00
1a variant(c)	3.00

RUMBLE GIRLS
(B&W) April, 2000
1 (of 8) Silky Warrior Tansie	3.50
2	3.50
3 Sugar and Wax	3.50
4 Sapphire Bullets	3.50
5 It's Not Romantic	3.50
6 Boy, Girl, Boy Girl	3.50
7 The Life of My Time, concl.	4.00

RUN!
Image, Dec., 2003
1-shot MMr	3.00

SABRE
(B&W) 1998
TPB 20th Anniversary	13.00

SAFFIRE
April, 2000
1 MtB,SRf,F:Melanie,Lyssa, Priscilla	3.00
1a variant JMd(c)	3.00
1b Mat Broome blue foil(c)	11.50
1c Joe Mac blue foil(c)	13.00
2 MtB,SRf,V:The Kraken	3.00
2a randy green(c)	9.00
2b signed & number	11.00
3 MtB,SRf,Hades Gate	3.00

SAINT ANGEL
2000
Preview	3.00
1 KIA,BNa,40-pg.,flip-book	4.00
1a variant(c)	4.00
2 KIA,BNa,40-pg.,flip-book	4.00
3 KIA,BNa,40-pg.,flip-book	4.00
4 KIA,BNa,40-pg.,flip-book	4.00

Sam & Twitch #18 © Todd McFarlane

SAM & TWITCH
TMP, Aug., 1999
1 AMe,Spawn tie-in	2.75
2 AMe,The Udaku,pt.2	2.50
3 AMe,The Udaku,pt.3	2.50
4 AMe,The Udaku,pt.4	2.50
5 AMe,The Udaku,pt.5	2.50
6 AMe,The Udaku,pt.6	2.50
7 AMe,The Udaku,pt.7	2.50
8 AMe,The Udaku,pt.8	2.50
9 One Really Bad Day	2.50
10 Witch Hunter,pt.1	2.50
11 Witch Hunter,pt.2	2.50
12 Witch Hunter,pt.3	2.50
13 Witch Hunter,pt.4	2.50
14 Dumb Laws and Egg	2.50
15 Bounty Hunter Wars,pt.1	2.50
16 Bounty Hunter Wars,pt.2	2.50
17 Bounty Hunter Wars,pt.3	2.50
18 Bounty Hunter Wars,pt.4	2.50
19 Bounty Hunter Wars,pt.5	2.50
20 Jon Doe Affair,pt.1	2.50
21 Jon Doe Affair,pt.2	2.50
22 Jon Doe Affair,pt.3	2.50
23 Jon Doe Affair,pt.4	2.50
24 Jon Doe Affair,pt.5	2.50
25 Jon Doe Affair,pt.6	2.50
26 Jon Doe Affair,pt.7	2.50
27 Death Row Confessions	2.50
TPB Vol.1 Udaku, rep.#1-#8	22.00

SAMMY: A VERY SAMMY DAY
Image, May, 2004
GN	6.00

SAMMY: TOURIST TRAP
Feb., 2003
1 (of 4)	3.00
2	3.00
3 Fight! Fight! Fight!	3.00
4 concl	3.00

SAM STORIES: LEGS
Dec., 1999
1-shot SK, 24-pg	2.50

SAVAGE DRAGON
Highbrow, July, 1992
1 EL,I:Savage Dragon	3.00
2 EL,I:Superpatriot	3.50
3 EL,V:Bedrock,with coupon#6	3.00
3a EL,w/o coupon	3.00
Spec. Savage Dragon Versus Savage Megaton Man #1 EL,DSm	3.00
Gold ed.	12.00
TPB	10.00

[2nd Series] June, 1993
1 EL,I:Freaks	4.00
2 EL,V:Teen.Mutant Ninja Turtles, Flip book Vanguard #0	3.00
3 EL,A:Freaks	3.00
4 EL,A:Freaks	3.00
5 EL,Might Man flip book	3.00
6 EL,A:Freaks	3.00
7 EL,Overlord	3.00
8 EL,V:Cutthroat,Hellrazor	3.00
9 EL	3.00
10 EL	3.00
11 EL,A:Overlord	3.00
12 EL	3.00
13 EL,Mighty Man,Star,I:Widow (appeared after issue #20)	3.00
13a Larsen version of 13	3.00
14 Possessed,pt.1	3.00
15 Possessed,pt.2	3.00
16 Possessed,pt.3,V:Mace	3.00
17 V:Dragonslayer	3.50
18 R:The Fiend	3.00
19 V:The Fiend	3.00
20 Rematch with Overlord	3.00
21 V:Overlord	3.00
22 A:Teenage Mutant Turtles	3.00
23 Rapture vs. SheDragon	3.00
24 Gang War,pt.1	3.00
25 Gang War,pt.2 double size	4.00
26	3.00
27	3.00
28	3.00
29	3.00
30 EL,'Overlord Reborn'	3.00
31 'The Dragon is trapped in Hell'	3.00
32 Kill-Cat vs. Justice	3.00
33 fatherhood	3.00
34 F:Hellboy,pt.1	4.00
35 F:Hellboy,pt.2	4.00
36 Dragon & Star try to rescue Peter Klaptin	3.00
37 mutants struggle in ruins of	

IMAGE

Savage Dragon #28 © Erik Larsen

Chicago 3.00
38 Dragon vs. Cyberface 3.00
39 Dragon vs. Dung 3.00
40 'G-Man' 3.00
41 Wedding issue 3.00
42 V:Darklord 3.00
43 Stranded on another world 3.00
44 in flying saucer 3.00
45 . . . . 3.00
46 She-Dragon vs. Vicious Circle . . 3.00
47 A knight and a mummy 3.00
48 Unfinished Business,pt.1 . . . . . . 3.00
49 Unfinished Business,pt.2 . . . . . . 3.00
50 Unfinished Business,pt.3,
    some reps., 96-pg. 6.00
51 F:She-Dragon 3.00
52 F:She-Dragon,V:Hercules 3.00
53 EL,F:She Dragon 3.00
54 EL,V:imposter Dragon 3.00
55 EL,Dragon & She-Dragon 3.00
56 EL,Rita Medermade kidnapped . 3.00
57 EL,V:Overlord 3.00
58 EL,Dragon's Resurrection 3.00
59 EL,return of Savage Dragon . . . 3.00
60 EL,R:Devastator 3.00
61 EL,R:Rapture 3.00
62 EL,Savage Dragon married 3.00
63 EL,Dragon's honeymoon 3.00
64 EL,Overlord's secrets 3.00
65 EL,Possessed 3.00
66 EL,Dragon shrunk 3.00
67 EL,A:SuperPatriot 3.00
68 EL,V:PowerHouse 3.00
69 EL 3.00
70 EL, Hell on Earth 3.00
71 EL,End of the World,prequel . . . 3.00
72 EL,End of the World,prequel . . . 3.50
73 EL,End of the World,pt.1 . . . . . . 3.50
74 EL,End of the World,pt.2 . . . . . . 3.50
75 EL,End of the World,pt.3 . . . . . . 5.00
76 EL,Hell on Earth begins 3.50
77 EL,Wildstar Returns 3.50
77a Variant JOy(c) 3.50
78 EL,Mind-slaves of the
    Brain-Child 3.50
79 EL,Girl Trouble 3.50
80 EL,Lurkers beneath Lake Fear . . 3.50
81 EL,The Land Down Under 3.50
82 EL,The Bug Riders 3.50
83 EL,F:Madman 3.50
84 EL,F:Madman 3.50
85 EL,Peril in Pittsburgh 3.50
86 EL,Mighty Man returns 3.50

87 EL,Havoc in the Hidden City 3.50
88 EL,To Challenge the Gods 3.50
89 EL,Panic in Detroit 3.50
90 EL,Return to Chicago 3.50
91 EL,Rapture returns 3.50
92 EL,Reclaim the Earth,pt.1 . . . . . 3.50
93 EL,Reclaim the Earth,pt.2 . . . . . 3.50
94 EL,V:CyberFace 3.50
95 EL,V:Sebastian Khan,concl. 3.50
96 EL,V:The Creator 3.50
97 EL,F:She-Dragon 3.50
98 EL,return home 3.50
99 EL,Evil Twins 3.50
100 EL, Torn Between Two
    Worlds, 100-pg. 10.00
101 EL,F:son of Dragon 3.00
102 EL,V:Afterbirth 3.00
103 EL,Dragon & son 3.00
104 EL,secrets 3.00
105 EL,F:The Candyman 3.00
106 EL,Dragon as Santa 3.00
107 EL,flipcover Major Damage . . . 4.00
108 EL,Flying Shoes Incident 3.00
109 EL,Danger in Dimension X . . . 3.00
110 EL,Lost in Dimension X 3.00
111 EL,Mako the man-shark 3.00
112 EL,V:Octopus & OpenFace 3.00
113 EL,Vicious Circle 3.00
114 EL,Cutthroat 3.00
115 EL,concl.,80-pg. 7.00
116 I:Negate 3.00
117 EL,Powerless 3.00
118 EL,R:Arachnid 3.00
119 EL,Running Man,pt.1 . . . . 3.00
TPB A Talk With God 18.00
    TPB A Talk with God, 2nd pr. . . 20.00
TPB The Fallen, rep.#7–#11 . . . . . 13.00
TPB Possessed, rep.#12–#16 . . . . 13.00
TPB Archives #2, B&W,1982 rep. . . 3.00
TPB Archives #3, B&W,1984 rep. . . 3.00
TPB Archives #4, B&W,1986 rep. . . 3.00
TPB Revenge 14.00
TPB Greatest Team-ups 20.00
TPB Book 1 Baptism of Fire 15.00
    TPB Baptism of Fire (2002) . . . 15.00
TPB Gang War 17.00
TPB This Savage World 16.00
TPB Vol.9, Worlds at War 17.00
TPB Vol. 8 Terminated 16.00
TPB Vol. 10 Endgame 16.00
Spec. 1-shot Savage Dragon
    Companion,64-pg. 3.00
Spec. 1-shot Savage Dragon/
    Hellboy, collected ed. 6.00

SAVAGE DRAGON
DESTROYER DUCK
Nov., 1996
1 SvG,ChM,EL 4.00

SAVAGE DRAGON:
GOD WAR
Image, 2004
1 (of 4) 3.00
2 thru 4 . . . . @3.00

SAVAGE DRAGON, THE:
RED HORIZON
Comics Feb., 1997
1 MsM 3.00
2 MsM,Dragon in the ER,A:Freak
    Force 3.00
3 (of 3) MsM,Freak Force beaten . . 3.00

SAVAGE DRAGON:
MARSHAL LAW
(B&W) July, 1997
1 (of 2) PMs,KON,F:Marshal Law . . 3.00
2 PMs,KON, concl. 3.00

SAVAGE DRAGON:
SEX & VIOLENCE
July, 1997
1 (of 2) TBm,MBm 3.00
2 TBm,MBm,AH, concl. 3.00

SAVAGE DRAGONBERT:
FULL FRONTAL NERDITY
Oct., 2002
GN 80-pg. b&w 6.00

Savant Garde #1 © WildStorm

SAVANT GARDE
WildStorm, March, 1997
1 'A team without a rule book' 2.50
2 Between killer & killer cat 2.50
3 V: strange Tapestry 2.50
4 'Any super-villain can take
    over the world' 2.50
5 'The Final Showdown' 2.50
6 BKs,Guilty until proven innocent . 2.50
7 BKs,death of John Colt 2.50
Fan Edition #1, with Fan #22 . . . . . 3.00
Fan Edition #2, with Fan #23 . . . . . 3.00
Fan Edition #3, with Fan #24 . . . . . 3.00

SECTION ZERO
June, 2000
1 KK,TG,UFO's etc. 2.50
2 KK,TG,Sargasso sea 2.50
3 KK,TG,Curse of Sargasso 2.50
4 KK,TG,Ground Zero revealed . . . 2.50
5 KK,TG,Sargasso vs. Crust 3.00
6 KK,TG,Fire and Rain 3.00

SEI: DEATH & LEGEND
Nov., 2003
GN Manga 7.00

SEMANTIC LACE
June, 2003
GN b&w, 112-pg. 10.00

IMAGE

SHADOWHAWK

Shadowline, Aug., 1992

1 JV,I:ShadowHawk,Black Foil(c), Pin-up, with coupon#1	4.00
1a w/o coupon	2.25
2 JV,V:Arsenal,A:Spawn, I:Infiniti	3.00
3 JV,V:Arsenal,w/glow-in-the- dark(c)	3.50
4 V:Savage Dragon	2.50
TPB rep.#1-4	20.00
Ashcan #1	2.50
Ashcan #2	2.50
Ashcan #3	2.50
Ashcan #4	2.50

[2nd Series] 1993

1 JV,Die Cut(c)	2.50
1a Gold ed.	3.00
2 JV,ShadowHawk I.D.	2.50
2a Gold ed.	2.50
3 Poster(c),JV,w/Ash Can	2.50
TPB	20.00

[3rd Series] 1993

0 Zero issue	2.25
1 JV,CWf,V:Vortex,Hardedge, Red Foil(c)	2.50
1a Gold ed.	3.00
1b signed	6.00
2 JV,CWf,MA,I:Deadline, BU&I:US Male	2.50
3 JV(a&s),ShadowHawk has AIDS, V:Hardedge,Blackjak	2.25
4 JV(a&s),V:Hardedge	2.25

Note: #5 to #11 not used; #12 below
is the next issue, the 12th overall.

12 Monster Within,pt.1	2.25
13 Monster Within,pt.2	2.25
14 Monster Within,pt.3	2.50
15 Monster Within,pt.4	2.50
16 Monster Within,pt.5	2.50
17 Monster Within,pt.6	2.50
18 JV,D:ShadowHawk	2.50
Spec.#1	3.50
Gallery#1	2.25

SHADOWHAWK/ VAMPIRELLA

Feb., 1995

Book 2 V:Kaul	5.00

Book #1: see Vampi/ShadowHawk

SHADOWHUNT SPECIAL

Extreme, 1996

1 Shadowhunt x-over,pt.1	2.50

SHADOWS

Feb., 2003

1	3.00
2	3.00
3	3.00
4 b&w	3.00
5 b&w	3.00

SHAMAN'S TEARS

Creative Fire, 1993–96

0 MGr	2.50
1 MGr,I:Shaman,B:Origin	3.00
1a Siver Prism ed.	5.00
2 MGr,Poster(c)	2.50
3 MGr,V:Bar Sinister	2.50
4 MGr,V:Bar Sinister,E:Origin	2.25
5 MGr,R:Jon Sable	2.25
6 MGr,V:Jon Sable	2.25
7 MGr,V:Rabids	2.25
8 MGr,A:Sable	2.25
9 MGr,Becoming of Broadarrow	2.25
10 Becoming of Broadarrow,pt.2	2.50
11 Becoming of Broadarrow,pt.3	2.50

Shaman's Tears #9 © Creative Fire

12 Becoming of Broadarrow,pt.4	2.50
13 The Offspring,pt.1	2.50

SHANGRI-LA

Image, Jan., 2004

GN	8.00

SHARKY

1998

1 by Dave Elliott & Alex Horley	2.50
1a variant cover (5,000 made)	3.00
2 coma over	2.50
2a variant cover	3.00
3 R:Blazin' Glory	2.50
3a variant SBi(c)	2.50
4 tons of guest stars, concl.	2.50
4a variant DAy(c)	2.50

SHATTERED IMAGE

WildStorm, 1996

1 KBk,TnD,crossover	2.50
2 KBk	2.50
3 KBk	2.50
4 KBk,TnD,concl.	2.50

SHIDIMA

Jan., 2001

1 PtL, A Warlands saga	3.00
1a variant(c)	3.00
1b stormkote(c)	8.00
2 PtL	3.00
2a variant(c)	3.00
2b variant(c)	3.00
3 PtL	3.00
3a variant(c)	3.00
3b variant(c)	3.00
4	3.00
5	3.00
6	3.00
0 24-pg.	2.25
0 variant(c)	2.25

SHIP OF FOOLS

(B&W) Sept., 1997

0 Bryan J.L. Glass, Michael Avon Oeming	3.00
1 Death & Taxes,pt.1	3.00
2 Death & Taxes,pt.2	3.00
3 Death & Taxes,pt.3	3.00
4 Death & Taxes,pt.4	3.00
TPB rep. Caliber series	15.00

SHOCKROCKETS

April, 2000

1 (of 6) KBk,SI	2.50
2 KBk,SI,Command Decision	2.50
3 KBk,SI,The Triangle Trade	2.50
4 KBk,SI,Rocket Science	2.50
5 KBk,SI,sneak attack	2.50
6 KBk,SI,Final Battle,flip-book	2.50

SHUT UP & DIE

(B&W) 1998

1 JHI and Kevin Stokes	3.00
2 JHI,Angry White Man	3.00
3 JHI,Wife abducted	3.00
4 JHI	3.00
5 JHI,A:Earl Jackson	3.00

SIEGE

WildStorm, 1997

1 JPe,AV,Nothing you believe is real	2.50
2 JPe,AV,Omega goes to Hawaii for funeral	2.50
3 JPe,AV,Zontarian Crab Ships vs. Drop Ship	2.50
4 JPe,AV,Rescue of Omega Squad	2.50

SIGMA

WildStorm, 1996

1 BCi,Fire From Heaven prelude	2.50
2 BCi,Fire From Heaven,pt.6	2.50
3 BCi,Fire From Heaven,pt.14	2.50

SILENT SCREAMERS

Oct., 2000

1 Nosferatu, 40-pg.	5.00

SINKING

March, 1999

GN JHI	15.00

SIREN

(B&W) May, 1998

1 by J. Torres & Tim Levins	3.00
2 F:Zara Rush, private eye	3.00
3 cpmc;isopm	3.00
TPB rep. Shapes	10.00

SIX

Image, Aug., 2004

GN B&W,56-pg.	6.00

SKINNERS

TMP, July, 2000

1 MtB,JMd.	3.00
1a variant PtL(c)	3.00
1b variant Andy Park(c)	3.00
1c variant MtB 2-D	3.00
1d limited ed. Broom(c)	9.00
1e limited ed., signed	11.00
2 MtB,SRf	3.00
2a variant JBz(c)	3.00

SMALL GODS

Image, June, 2004

1 Killing Grin,pt.1	3.00
2 Killing Grin,pt.2	3.00
3 Killing Grin,pt.3	3.00
4 Killing Grin,pt.4	3.00

SOLAR LORD

March, 1999

1 by Khoo Fuk Lung	2.50

2 Nickson is Solar Lord 2.50
3 V:5 enemies 2.50
4 V:5 enemies 2.50
5 V:The Emperor of Darkness 2.50
6 O:Nickson 2.50
7 concl., book one 2.50

SOMETHING WICKED
Oct., 2003
1 (of 4) b&w 3.00
2 thru 4 Among the Living . . . . . . @3.00

SOUL OF A SAMURAI
Apr., 2003
1 (of 4) b&w, 48-pg 4.00
2 . . . . 4.00
3 48-pg 6.00
4 48-pg 6.00

SOUL REAVER:
LEGACY OF KAIN
Top Cow, June, 2000
1-shot MHw,video game tie-in 2.50

SOUL SAGA
Top Cow, 2000
1 SPa,F:Aries, Soulblade 5.00
1a variant(c) JMd (1:4) 5.00
1b variant Michael Turner(c) (1:4) . 5.00
2 SPa,death in the family 3.50
2a variant David Finch(c) 3.50
2b variant Pat Lee(c) 3.50
3 SPa, Khan Hordes 2.50
4 SPa, Dominion vs. Khan 2.50
5 SPa, F:Ares 2.50
Coll.Ed.Vol.1 . . . . 6.00

SOULWIND
(B&W) March, 1997
1 quest for Soulwind begins 3.00
2 Nick becomes 'Captain Crash' . . 3.00
3 Captain Crash & Poke pursue
　Soulwind info 3.00
4 concl. of story arc 3.00
5 The Day I Tried to Live,pt.1 . . . . . 3.00
6 The Day I Tried to Live,pt.2 . . . . . 3.00
7 The Day I Tried to Live,pt.3 . . . . . 3.00
8 The Day I Tried to Live,pt.4 . . . . . 3.00
TPB rep #1–#4 . . . . 10.00

SPARTAN:
WARRIOR SPIRIT
July, 1995
1 thru 4 . . . . @3.00

SPARTAN X
(B&W) Sept., 1998
1 MGo,RM,'Plague Train' 3.00
2 MGo,RM,'Plague Train,'pt.2 . . . . . 3.00
3 MGo,RM,'Plague Train,'pt.3 . . . . . 3.00

SPAWN
TMP, May, 1992
1 TM,I:Spawn,w/GP,DK pinups . . . 11.00
1a black & white 23.00
2 TM,V:The Violator 9.00
3 TM,V:The Violator 9.00
4 TM,V:The Violator,+coupon #2 . . 7.00
4a w/o coupon 3.00
5 TM,O:Billy Kincaid 7.00
6 TM,I:Overt-Kill 5.00
7 TM,V:Overt-Kill 5.00
8 TM,AMo(s),F:Billy Kincaid 5.00
9 NGa(s),TM,I:Angela 6.00

10 DS(s),TM,A:Cerebus 5.00
11 FM(s),TM, Home Story 4.00
12 TM,Chapel killed Spawn 4.00
13 TM,A:Youngblood 4.00
14 TM,A:The Violator 5.00
15 TM, Myths II 4.00
16 GCa,I:Anti-Spawn 5.00
17 GCa,V:Anti-Spawn 7.00
18 GCa,ATi,D:Anti-Spawn 9.00
19 & 20 see after #25
21 TM,The Hunt,pt.1 . . . . 9.00
22 TM,The Hunt,pt.2 . . . . 3.00
23 TM,The Hunt,pt.3 . . . . 3.00
24 TM,The Hunt,pt.4 . . . . 3.00

Spawn #11 © Todd McFarlane

25 Image X Book,MS,BTn 5.00
19 I:Houdini 5.00
20 J:Houdini 6.00
26 TM 4.00
27 I:The Curse 4.00
28 Faces Wanda 4.00
29 Returns From Angela 4.00
30 A:KKK 4.00
31 R:Redeemer 3.00
32 TM,GCa,New Costume 4.00
33 R:Violator 3.00
34 V:Violator 3.00
35 F:Sam & Twitch 3.00
36 Talks to Wanda 3.00
37 I:The Freak 3.00
38 . . . . 3.00
39 . . . . 3.00
40 V:Curse 3.00
41 V:Curse 3.00
42 thru 49 . . . . @3.00
50 48-pg 4.00
51 . . . . 3.00
52 . . . . 3.00
53 A:Malebolgia 3.00
54 return to New York, alliance
　with Terry Fitzgerald 3.00
55 plans to defeat Jason Wynn . . . 3.00
56 efforts to defeat Jason Wynn . . . 3.00
57 . . . . 3.00
58 sequel to Spawn #29 . . . . 3.00
59 . . . . 3.00
60 battle between Spawn and
　Clown cont. 3.00
61 battle with Clown concl. 3.00
62 Spawn is Al Simmons for 1 day . 3.00
63 Operation: Wynn fall,pt.1 . . . . . . 3.00
64 Wynn falls, bagged with toy
　catalog 2.50
65 recap issue 2.50

66 TM,GCa,lives of alley bums 2.50
67 TM,GCa,Sam and Twitch 2.50
68 TM,GCa,R:Freak 2.50
69 TM,GCa,F:Freak 2.50
70 TM,GCa 2.50
71 TM,GCa,Cold Blooded Truth . . . 2.50
72 TM,GCa,Haunting of the Heap . . 2.50
73 TM,GCa,R:The Heap 2.50
74 TM,GCa,pathway to misery 2.50
75 TM,GCa,Deadly Revelations . . . 2.50
76 TM,GCa,Granny Blake 2.50
77 TM,GCa,confronts 2.50
78 TM,GCa,DaM,'Sins of Excess' . . 2.50
79 TM,GCa,DaM,Killer in N.Y. 2.50
80 TM,GCa,DaM,F:Sam & Twitch . . 2.50
81 TM,GCa,DaM,Sins are reborn . . 2.50
82 TM,GCa,DaM,sea of self-doubt . 2.50
83 TM,GCa,V:Jason Wynn 2.50
84 TM,GCa,DaM,Helle's Belles 2.50
85 TM,GCa,DaM,Legend of
　Hellspawn 2.50
86 TM,GCa,DaM,V:Al Simmons . . . 2.50
87 TM,GCa,DaM,Al Simmons fate . 2.50
88 TM,GCa,DaM,Seasons of
　change 2.50
89 TM,GCa,DaM,secrets revealed . 2.50
90 TM,GCa,DaM,three stories 2.50
91 TM,GCa,DaM,Black Cat
　Bones,pt.1 . . . . 2.50
92 TM,GCa,DaM,Black Cat
　Bones,pt.2 . . . . 2.50
93 TM,GCa,DaM,Devil's Banquet . . 2.50
94 TM,GCa,DaM,Children's Hour . . 2.50
95 TM,GCa,DaM,Cracks in the
　Foundation 2.50
96 TM,GCa,DaM,Rules of
　Engagement 2.50
97 TM,GCa,DaM,Heaven's Folly . . . 2.50
98 TM,GCa,DaM,The Trouble
　with Angels 2.50
99 TM,GCa,DaM,Edge of Darkness 2.50
100A TM,GCa,DaM,TM(c)She dies 10.00
100B TM,GCa,DaM,FM(c) 5.00
100C TM,GCa,DaM,GCa(c) 5.00
100D TM,GCa,DaM,AshleyWood(c) 5.00
100E TM,GCa,DaM,MMi(c) 5.00
100F TM,GCa,DaM,AxR(c) 5.00
101 TM,AMe,DaM,The Speed
　of Night 2.50
102 TM,AMe,DaM,Remains 2.50
103 TM,AMe,DaM,A Town Called
　Malice 2.50
104 TM,Retribution Overdrive,pt.1 . . 2.50
105 TM,Retribution Overdrive,pt.2 . . 2.50
106 TM,The Kingdom,pt.1 . . . . 2.50
107 TM,The Kingdom,pt.2 . . . . 2.50
108 TM,The Kingdom,pt.3 . . . . 2.50
109 TM,Hour of Cleansing
　Approaches 2.50
110 TM,The Kingdom,pt.4 . . . . 2.50
111 TM,The Kingdom,pt.5 . . . . 2.50
112 TM,The Kingdom,pt.6 . . . . 2.50
113 TM,The Kingdom,pt.7 . . . . 2.50
114 TM,The Bridge,pt.1 . . . . 2.50
115 TM,The Bridge,pt.2 . . . . 2.50
116 TM,Consequences 2.50
117 TM,A Season in Hell 2.50
118 TM,A Season in Hell,pt.2 . . . . . 2.50
119 TM,A Season in Hell,pt.3 . . . . . 2.50
120 TM,A Season in Hell,pt.4 . . . . . 2.50
121 TM,The Devil His Due 2.50
122 TM,Salvation Road 2.50
123 TM,Freedom in Nothingness . . 2.50
124 TM,Through These Eyes 2.50
125 TM,Wake Up Dreaming,pt.1 . . . 2.50
126 TM,Wake Up Dreaming,pt.2 . . . 2.50
127 TM Loose Threads,pt.1 . . . . 2.50
128 TM,Loose Threads,pt.2 . . . . 2.50
129 TM,Loose Threads,pt.3 . . . . 2.50
130 TM,Loose Threads,pt.4 . . . . 3.00
131 TM,God is a Bullet,pt.1 . . . . 3.00

IMAGE

IMAGE

132 TM,God is a Bullet,pt.2 . . . . 2.50
133 TM,God is a Bullet,pt.3 . . . . 2.50
134 TM,God is a Bullet,pt.4 . . . . 2.50
135 TM,Mad Shadows,pt.1 . . . . 2.50
136 TM,Mad Shadows,pt.2 . . . . 2.50
137 TM,Mad Shadows,pt.3 . . . . 2.50
138 TM,Mad Shadows,pt.4 . . . . 2.50
139 TM,Asunder,pt.1 . . . . 2.50
140 TM,Asunder,pt.2 . . . . 2.50
140 TM,Asunder,pt.2 . . . . 2.50
138 TM,A Thousand Clowns,pt.5. . . 2.50
139 TM,Hellbound,pt.1. . . . . 2.50
?
141 TM,Asunder,pt.3 . . . . 2.50
142 TM,Asunder,pt.4 . . . . 2.50
143 TM,Errant,pt.1 . . . . 2.50
144 TM,Errant,pt.2 . . . . 2.50
145 TM,Errant,pt.3 . . . . 2.50
146 TM,Errant,pt.4 . . . . 2.50
147 TM,Scrawled,pt.1 . . . . 2.50
148 TM,Scrawled,pt.2 . . . . 2.50
149 TM,Scrawled,pt.3 . . . . 2.50
Ann.#1 Blood & Shadows, 64-pg. . . 5.00
GN Spawn Movie adapt. 5.00
TPB Capital Collection rep.#1-3
    limited to 1,200 copies 300.00
TPB TM,rep.#1–#5. . . . . 10.00
TPB Spawn III rep. #12–#15 . . . . . 10.00
TPB Spawn IV rep. #16–#20 . . . . . 10.00
TPB Spawn V rep.#21–#25 . . . . . . 10.00
TPB Spawn VI, rep.#26–#30 . . . . . 10.00
TPB Vol. VII Deadman's Touch . . . 10.00
TPB Vol. VIII Betrayal of Blood . . . 10.00
TPB Angela's Hunt. 10.00
TPB Vol.9 Urban Jungle 10.00
TPB Vol.10 Vengeance of
    the Dead 10.00
TPB Vol.11 Crossroads 10.00
TPB Vol.12 Immortality. 11.00
GN Spawn: Blood and Salvation . . 5.00
Fan Edition #1, with Fan #16. . . . . . 3.00
Fan Edition #1a variant cover 4.00
Fan Edition #1b gold logo,retailer . . 5.00
Fan Edition #2, with Fan #17. . . . . . 3.00
Fan Edition #2a variant cover 4.00
Fan Edition #2b gold logo,retailer . . 5.00
Fan Edition #2c platinum Foil logo . 5.00
Fan Edition #2, with Fan #18. . . . . . 3.00
Fan Edition #3a variant cover 4.00
Fan Edition #3b gold logo,retailer . . 5.00
1-shot Spawn: Simony, 64-pg. 8.00

SPAWN/BATMAN
Image/DC 1994
1 FM(s),TM 5.00

SPAWN BLOOD FEUD
June, 1995
1 V:Vampires. 4.00
2 . . . . 4.00
3 Hunted as a Vampire. 4.00
4 V:Heartless John 4.00

SPAWN BIBLE
TMP, Aug., 1996
1 TM,GCa 2.25
2 Book of the Dead, 56-pg. 5.00

SPAWN: THE DARK AGES
TMP, March, 1999
1 GF,LSh, from 12th century. 2.50
1a variant TM(c) (1:4) 7.00
2 LSh,A:Black Knight 2.50
3 LSh,A:Black Knight 2.50
4 LSh,Lord Covenant 2.50
5 LSh,Lord Covenant 2.50
6 LSh,Sister Immaculata. 2.50
7 LSh,Cogliostro 2.50

8 LSh,Acts of Contrition 2.50
9 LSh 2.50
10 LSh,F:Lord Covenant 2.50
11 LSh,Ghost on the Hill 2.50
12 LSh,The Faithful 2.50

Spawn, The Dark Ages #13
© Todd McFarlane

13 LSh,Blood and Glory. 2.50
14 LSh,The Innocent 2.50
15 LSh,New Beginnings 2.50
16 CWf,Heart of the HellSpawn. . . . 2.50
17 CWf,The Circle and the Worm . . 2.50
18 CWf,Crucified 2.50
19 CWf,Like Any Other Man 2.50
20 Voices in the Dark. 2.50
21 Sins of the Hellspawn 2.50
22 The Seedling. 2.50
23 The Beast 2.50
24 Bleed, Pagan, Bleed. 2.50
25 The Plague of Man 2.50
26 Lesion 2.50
27 Bubonic Nights 2.50
28 Stonehaven,pt.1 . . . . 2.50
29 Stonehaven,pt.2 . . . . 2.50
30 The Beast of the Wood. 2.50
31 Home to Roost 2.50

SPAWN THE IMPALER
TMP Oct., 1996
1 (of 3) MGr, fully painted 4.00
2 MGr 4.00
3 MGr 4.00

SPAWN: THE UNDEAD
TMP, May, 1999
1 PJe,DT,CWf,F:Spawn 2.25
2 PJe,DT,CWf,F:Travis Ward 2.25
3 PJe,DT,CWf,Heaven vs. Hell. . . . 2.25
4 PJe,DT,CWf,suicide cult 2.25
5 PJe,DT,CWf,The Wind That
    Shakes the Barley 2.25
6 PJe,DT,CWf 2.25
7 PJe,DT,CWf,Up the Down Stairs 2.25
8 PJe,DT,CWf,One Lunch to Live. . 2.25
9 PJe,DT,CWf,Waiting 2.25
10 PJe,DT,CWf,How to Win Friends
    and Influence People. 2.25
11 PJe,DT,CWf,Heaven and Hell
    and In Between 2.25

SPAWN/WILDC.A.T.S
Jan., 1996
1 AMo(s),Devilday, pt.1, x-over. . . . 3.50
2 AMo(s),Devilday,pt.2 . . . . 3.50

3 AMo(s),Devilday, pt.3 . . . . 3.50
4 AMo(s),Devilday, pt.4 . . . . 3.50

SPIRIT OF THE TAO
Top Cow, May, 1998
1 BTn,F:Lance & Jasmine 2.50
2 BTn,mission to destroy base 2.50
3 BTn,V:Jaikap Clan 2.50
4 BTn,F:Jasmine & Lance 2.50
5 BTn, Antidote to virus 2.50
6 BTn, Tao grows stronger 2.50
7 BTn, V:Menicus 2.50
8 BTn, A:Messiah 2.50
9 BTn, The Dragon is Loose 2.50
10 BTn, Jasmine out of control 2.50
11 BTn, Dragon ash race. 2.50
12 BTn, F:Disciple 2.50
13 BTn, friend or foe 2.50
14 BTn, must one die? 2.50
15 BTn,conclusion, 48-pg. 4.00

SPLITTING IMAGE
March, 1993
1 DsM,A:Marginal Seven 2.25
2 DsM,A:Marginal Seven 2.25

STAR
June, 1995
1 F:Star from Savage Dragon. 2.50
2 Buried Alive 2.50
3 A:Savage Dragon,Rapture. 2.50
4 A:Savage Dragon,Rapture. 2.50

STARCHILD: MYTHOPOLIS
(B&W) 1997
0 JOn, 'Prologue' 3.00
1 JOn, 'Pinehead' 3.00
2 JOn, 'Pinehead,'pt.2 . . . . 3.00
3 JOn, 'Pinehead,'pt.3 . . . . 3.00
4 JOn, 'Fisher King,'pt.1 . . . . 3.00
5 JOn, 'Fisher King,'pt.2 . . . . 3.00

STAY PUFFED
Image, Jan., 2004
1-shot 3.00
1-shot B variant (c) 3.00

STONE
Avalon Sept., 1998
2 WPo,V:Rook 2.50
3 WPo,A:Bann 2.50
4 WPo, conclusion 2.50
[VOL. II] Aug., 1999
1 WPo. 2.50
1a Chromium Edition 7.00
2 WPo, search for murderer 2.50
2 Stonechrome edition 15.00
3 WPo,Blood from a Stone 2.50
4 WPo,A Rose by Any Other Name 2.50
5 Wpo, series resumes 3.00

STORMWATCH
WildStorm, 1993
0 JSc(c),O:StormWatch,
    V:Terrorists,w/card 2.50
1 JLe(c&s),ScC,TvS(i),
    I:StormWatch 2.50
1a Gold ed. 4.00
2 JLe(c&s),ScC,TvS(i),I:Cannon,
    Winter,Fahrenheit,Regent . . . 2.50 3
JLe(c&s),ScC,TvS(i),V:Regent,
    I:Backlash 3.00
4 V:Daemonites 2.50
5 SRf(s),BBh,V:Daemonites 2.25

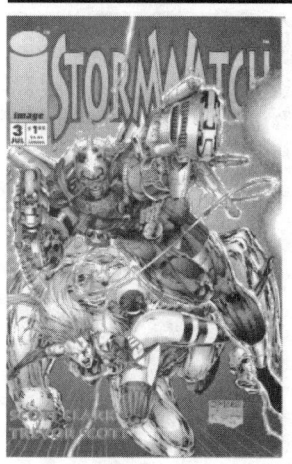

Stormwatch #3
© Wildstorm

6 BCi,ScC,TC,A:Mercs 2.25
7 BCi,ScC,TC,A:Mercs 2.50
8 BCi,ScC,TC,A:Mercs 2.50
9 BCi,I:Defile 2.50
10 V:Talos 2.50
10a variant(c) 5.00
11 RMz(s),the end? 2.50
12 RMz(s),V:Hellstrike,'Visions
    of Deathtrap' 2.50
13 V:M.A.D.-1 . . . . 2.50
14 Despot 2.50
15 Batallion, Flashpoint 2.50
16 V:Defile 2.50
17 D:Batallion 2.50
18 R:Argos 2.50
19 R:M.A.D.-1,L:Winter 2.50
20 F:Cannon,Winter,Bendix 2.50
21 V:Wildcats 2.50
22 RMz,BWS(c),WildStorm
    Rising,pt.9,w/2 cards 2.50
22a Newsstand ed. 2.25
23 RMz(s),R:Despot,Warguard 2.50
24 V:Despot 2.50
25 SSe,ScC,BCi,A:Spartan 2.75
25a 2nd printing 2.50
26 V:Despot 2.50
27 V:Despot,Rebuilding,'And in
    the End' 2.50
28 F:Blademaster,Swift,Flint,
    Comanche,New Adventures . . . 2.50
29 I:Prism,Reorganization 2.50
30 V:Heaven's Fist. 2.50
31 V:Middle Eastern Terrorists 2.50
32 . . . . 2.50
33 inc. Winters Journey 2.50
34 . . . . 2.50
35 Fire From Heaven,pt.5 . . . . 2.50
36 Fire From Heaven,pt.12 . . . . 2.50
37 Double size,F:Weatherman One,
    I:Rose Tatoo 8.00
38 WEI(s) 5.00
39 WEI(s) 5.00
40 WEI(s),virus. 5.00
41 WEI(s) 5.00
42 WEI(s),Weatherman discovers a
    conspiracy 5.00
43 WEI(s) 5.00
44 WEI(s),history of Jenny Sparks. . 5.00
45 WEI(s),Battalion visits
    his family 5.00
46 WEI(s),secrets and more
    secrets, prologue 5.00

47 WEI(s), JLe, SW, dangerous
    experiment gone awry 5.00
48 WEI(s),'Change or Die'pt.1 . . . . 5.00
49 WEI(s),'Change or Die'pt.2 . . . . 5.00
50 WEI(s),'Change or Die' concl.
    large size 8.00
Sourcebok JLe(s),DT 2.75
Spec.#1 RMz(s),DT 4.25
Spec.#2 F:Fleshpoint 2.50
Ashcan 1 . . . . 3.00
TPB Change the World 10.00
TPB A Finer World 15.00
TPB Change or Die 15.00
TPB Force of Nature 15.00
TPB Lightning Strikes 15.00

STORMWATCH
WildStorm, Oct., 1997
1 WEI,bacterial horror,'Strange
    Weather,'pt.1,'Hard Rain'. 5.00
1a Variant cover 5.00
1b Voyager bagged pack 5.00
2 WEI,Stormwatch Black team,
    'Strange Weather,'pt.2 . . . . 5.00
3 WEI,Black team,'Strange
    Weather,'pt.3,'A Storm Coming'. 5.00
4 WEI,A Finer World,pt.1 . . . . 5.00
5 WEI,A Finer World,pt.2 . . . . 5.00
6 WEI,A Finer World,pt.3 . . . . 5.00
7 WEI,Bleed,pt.1 . . . . 5.00
8 WEI,Bleed,pt.2 . . . . 5.00
9 WEI,Bleed,pt.3 . . . . 5.00
10 WEI,'No Reason'. 10.00
11 WEI,BHi,PNe,F:Jackson King,
    'No Direction Home' 10.00
TPB Change or Die 15.00
TPB Force of Nature,(DC) 15.00
TPB Final Orbit, 96-pg. (DC) 10.00

STRANGERS
Mar., 2003
1 (of 6) 3.00
2 In the Inwards of the Night 3.00
3 Caresses such as Snakes Give . 3.00
4 The Livid Daylights 3.00
5 Icy till the Evening 3.00
6 Icy till the Evening 3.00
2a–6a variant (c). 3.00

STRANGERS IN
PARADISE VOL. 3
Homage,1996
1 TMr. 5.00
2 TMr. 4.00

Homage,1996–97
3 TMr,David & Katchoo fight. 3.50
4 TMr,Katchoo makes startling
    discovery 3.50
5 TMr,Francine's college days 3.50
6 TMr,Katchoo searches for David . 3.50
7 TMr. 3.50
8 TMr,demons of the past 3.50

STREET FIGHTER
Sept., 2003
1 Round One! Fight! 5.00
2 . . . . 4.00
3 . . . . 4.00
4 Brothers 3.00
4a variant (c). 3.00
5 M.Bison 3.00
5a variant (c). 3.00
5b Power Cel Acetate (c) 5.00
6 The Beginning 3.00
6a variant (c). 4.00
6b Power Foil (c) 4.00
1a–3a variant (c) . . . . @5.00

STREETS
April, 1999
TPB Streets 17.00

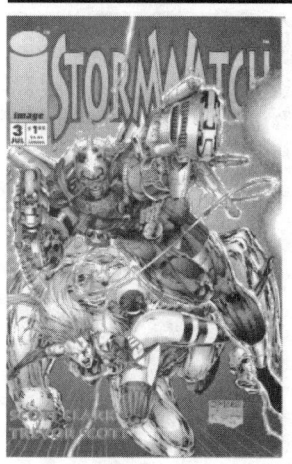

Strikeback #1
© Wildstorm

STRIKEBACK!
WildStorm, 1996
1 rep & new art 2.50
2 thru 5 . . . . @2.50

STRYKEFORCE
Image, Apr., 2004
1 (of 5) 3.00
2 thru 5 . . . . @3.00

STUPID COMICS
Sept., 2002
1-shot by Jim Mahfood,b&w 3.00
1-shot #2 . . . . 3.00

SUPER-PATRIOT
July, 1993
1 N:Super-Patriot 2.50
2 KN(i),O:Super-Patriot. 2.50
3 A:Youngblood 2.50
4 . . . . 2.50

SUPER-PATRIOT:
LIBERTY AND JUSTICE
June, 1995
1 R:Covenant 2.50
2 Tokyo 2.50
3 Tokyo gets Trashed 2.50
4 Final issue 2.50
TPB Liberty and Justice, 112-pg. . . 13.00

SUPERPATRIOT:
AMERICA'S FIGHTING
FORCE
July, 2002
1 (of 4) F:Johnny Armstrong 3.00
2 patriotic pandemonium 3.00
3 High Anxiety 3.00
4 The Final Battle, concl. 3.00

SUPERPATRIOT: WAR ON TERROR
Image, July, 2004
1 (of 4)	3.00
2 thru 4	@3.00

SUPERSTAR: AS SEEN ON TV
Jan., 2001
Spec. KBk,SI,48-pg.	6.00

SUPREME
Supreme, 1992
0 O:Supreme	2.50
1 B:RLd(s&i),BrM, V:Youngblood	3.00
1a Gold ed.	5.00
2 BrM,I:Heavy Mettle,Grizlock	3.00
3 BrM,I:Khrome.	3.00
4 BrM	3.00
5 BrM(a&s),Clv(i),I:Thor,V:Chrome.	2.50
6 BrM,Clv(i),I:Starguard, A:Thor,V:Chrome	3.00
7 Rip,ErS(s),SwM,A:Starguard, A:Thor	3.00
8 Rip(s),SwM,V:Thor.	3.00
9 Rip&KtH(s),BrM,Clv(i), V:Thor.	3.00
10 KrH(s),BrM,JRu(i), BU:I:Black & White	3.00
11 Extreme Prejudice,pt.4, I:Newmen	3.00
12 SPa(c),RLd(s),SwM	4.00
25 SPa(c),RLd(s),SwM,V:Simple Simon,Images of Tomorrow.	6.00
13 B:Supreme Madness	3.00
14 Supreme Madness,pt.2.	3.00
15 RLd(s)A:Spawn.	3.00
16 V:StormWatch	3.00
17 Supreme Madness,pt.5.	3.00
18 E:Supreme Madness	3.00
19 V:The Underworld	3.00
20 V:The Unterworld	3.00
21 God Wars	3.00
22 RLd,CNn,God Wars, V:Thor.	3.00
23 ExtremeSacrifice,pt.2,x-over.	3.00
24 Identity Questions	3.00
#25, see above, after #12	
26 F:Kid Supreme	3.00
27 Rising Son,I:Cortex.	3.00
28 Supreme Apocalypse:Prelude	3.00
29 Supreme Apocalypse,pt.1.	3.00
30 Supreme Apocalypse,pt.5.	3.00
31 V:Equinox	3.00
32 V:Cortex	3.00
33 Extreme Babewatch	3.00
34 She-Supreme	3.00
35 Extreme Destroyer,pt.7 x-over, bagged with card	3.00
36	3.00
37	3.00
38	3.00
39 AMo.	3.00
40 AMo.	3.00
41 AMo.	5.00
42 AMo,'Secret Origins'.	5.00
43 AMo,'Secrets of the Citadel Supreme'	3.00
44 See Color Comics section	
Ann.#1 TMB,CAd,KG,I:Vergessen	3.00
Ashcan #1	3.00
Ashcan #2	2.00

SUPREME: GLORY DAYS
Oct., 1994
1 Supreme in WWI	3.00
2 (of 2) BNa&KIA(s),DdW,GyM, A:Superpatriot	3.00

SWORD OF DAMOCLES
WildStorm, 1996
1 prelude to Fire From Heaven x-over.	2.50
2 Fire From Heaven,Finale,pt.2	2.50

SWORD OF DRACULA
Image, Oct., 2003
1	3.00
2 The Elders,pt.2	3.00
3 The Elders,pt.3	3.00
4 The Elders,pt.4	3.00
5 The Elders,pt.5	3.00
6 Concl.	3.00

SYLVIA FAUST
Image, Aug., 2004
1 (of 4)	3.00
2	3.00

SYPHONS
Image, Sept., 2004
TPB rep. Vol. 2, #1ñ#3	15.00

TALES FROM THE BULLY PULPIT
Image, Aug., 2004
1-shot 64-pg.	7.00

TALES OF THE DARKNESS
Top Cow, April, 1998
1 WPo,F:Jackie Estacado.	3.00
2 WPo,concl. first story.	3.00
3 Dungeon, Fire, and Sword,pt.1	3.00
4 Dungeon, Fire & Sword	3.00
5 in Dark Ages	3.00
6 futuristic story.	3.00
1/2	3.00

TALES OF THE REALM
Image, Aug., 2004
TPB	15.00

TALES OF TELLOS: MAIDEN VOYAGE
Image, March, 2001
1 48-pg.	4.00

TALES OF TELLOS
Image, Oct., 2004
1 (of 3) F:Dyn Jessa	3.50

TALES OF THE WITCHBLADE
Top Cow, 1996
1 TnD,F:Anne Bonney	9.00
1a TnD, variant cover (1:4)	12.00
1a signed, variant	20.00
2 TnD,F:Annabella	6.00
3 WEI,BTn,future	6.00
4 WEI,BTn,future,pt.2	5.00
5 RiB,past	5.00
6 RGr, time of Celts	3.00
7 in Ancient Egypt.	3.00
7a variant cover (1:4)	10.00
8 ancient Egypt,pt.2	3.00
9 ancient Egypt,pt.3	3.00
Coll.Ed.#1, rep. #1–#2.	5.00
Coll.Ed.#2, rep.#3–#4	6.00

Tales of the Witchblade #1
© Top Cow

TEAM 1: STORMWATCH
June, 1995
1 I:First StormWatch Team	2.50
2 V:Helspont,D:Think Tank	2.50

TEAM 1: WILDC.A.T.S
July, 1995
1 I:First Wildcats Team	2.50
2 B:Cabal	2.50

TEAM 7
WildStorm, 1994–95
1 New team.	4.00
2 New powers.	2.50
3 Members go insane.	2.50
4 final issue,V:A Nuke.	2.50
Ashcan.	2.25
TPB	10.00

TEAM 7 OBJECTIVE: HELL
May, 1995
1 CDi,CW,BWS(c),WildStorm Rising,Prologue,w/2 cards.	2.50
1a Newsstand ed.	2.25
2 Cambodia	2.50

TEAM 7: DEAD REACONING
Jan., 1996
1 CDi.	2.50
2 thru 4 CDi.	@2.50

TEAM YOUNGBLOOD
Extreme, 1993
1 B:ErS(s),ATi(c),CYp,NRD(i), I:Masada,Dutch,V:Giger	2.50
2 ATi(c),CYp,NRd(i),V:Giger	2.50
3 RLd(s),CYp,NRd(i),C:Spawn, V:Giger	2.50
4 ErS(s).	2.50
5 ErS(s),CNn,I:Lynx	2.50
6 ErS(s),N:Psi-Fire, BU:Black&White	2.50
7 ErS(s),CYp,ATh,Extreme Prejudice,pt.1,I:Quantum, BU:Black & White	2.50

Team Youngblood #16
© Extreme

Teenage Mutant Ninja #1
© Highbrow

8 ErS(s),CYp,ATh,Extreme Pre-
    judice,pt.5, V:Quantum,
    BU:Black & White 2.50
9 RLd 2.50
10 ErS(s),CYp,ATh. 2.50
11 RLd,ErS,Cyp. 2.50
12 RLd,ErS,Cyp. 2.50
13 ErS,Cyp. 2.50
14 RLd,ErS,Cya. 2.50
15 New Blood 2.50
16 RLd,ErS,TNu,I:New Sentinel,
    A:Bloodpool 2.50
17 ExtremeSacrifice,pt.6,x-over. . . . 2.50
18 MS, membership drive 2.50
19 R:Brahma 2.50
20 Contact,pt.1 1000 yr Badrock. . . 2.50
21 Contact,pt.2. . . . . 2.50
22 Shadowhunt x-over,pt.4 . . . . 2.50

TECH JACKET
2002
1 Origin issue 3.50
2 thru 8 . . . . @3.00
TPB Vol.1 Lost and Found. 13.00

TEENAGE MUTANT
NINJA TURTLES
(B&W) Highbrow,
June, 1996
1 . . . . 4.00
2 . . . . 3.00
3 . . . . 3.00
4 Donatello resurrected 3.00
5 FFo,Warlord Komodo uses
    Splinter as guinea pig 3.00
6 FFo 3.00
7 FFo,Raphael joins Foot Clan?. . . 3.00
8 FFo,Michelangelo tries to rescue
    Casey Jones' daughter 3.00
9 Enter: the Knight Watchman 3.00
10 'Enter: The Dragon'. 3.00
11 V:DeathWatch,A:Vanguard 3.00
12 F:Raph, Foot Gang warfare 3.00
13 Shredder is back! 3.00
14 Shredder vs. Splinter 3.00
15 F:Donatello 3.00
16 reunited with Splinter 3.00
17 F:Leonardo 3.00
18 UFO Sightings 3.00
19 F:Leatherhead. 3.00
20 F:Triceraton. 3.00

21 A:Pimiko 3.00
22 F:Lady Shredder 3.00
23 F:Lady Shredder. 3.00
TPB A New Beginning 10.00

TEKKEN FOREVER
Dec., 2001
1 (of 4) from Tekken 4 video game. 3.00
1a variant(c) 3.00
2 Iron Fist tournament 3.00

TELLOS
May, 1999
1 TDz, The Joining, part 1 . . . . . . 3.00
2 TDz, The Joining, part 2 . . . . . . 2.50
3 TDz, The Joining, part 3 . . . . . . 2.50
4 TDz,Hawke & Rikk. 2.50
4a variant JaL cover (1:4). 2.50
4b variant AAd cover (1:4) 2.50
4c variant RGr cover (1:4) 2.50
5 TDz,all-out battle 2.50
6 TDz,Aftermath 2.50
7 TDz,Darkness & Light 2.50
8 TDz,Tellos Joins Gorilla 2.50
8a variant Kia Asamiya(c). 2.50
8b variant HuR(c) 2.50
9 TDz,Jarek vs. Malesur. 2.50
10 TDz, concl. 3.00
Coll.Ed.#1 The Joining. 9.00
Prelude 16-pg 7.00
Prelude holo-foil. 15.00
GN Maiden Voyage 6.00
GN The Last Heist, 48-pg. 6.00
GN Sons & Moons, 48-pg. 6.00
TPB Vol.1 Reluctant Heroes 18.00
TPB Vol.2 Kindred Spirits. 18.00

TENTH, THE
Jan.,, 1997
1 BSt,TnD,Last stand against
    Hell on Earth 6.00
2 BSt,TnD,invasion of Darklon
    Corp. begins 5.00
3 BSt,TnD,Tenth & Espy team-up. . 4.00
4 BSt,TmD.confrontation with
    possible Armageddon 4.00
TPB rep.#1–#4. . . . . 11.00

[Regular Series] Aug., 1997
1 TnD,BSt,V:Blackspell. 5.00
2 TnD,BSt,V:Blackspell. 4.00
3 TnD,BSt,Gozza,Eve. 4.00

4 TnD,BSt,teleported to Japan 4.00
5 TnD,BSt 3.50
6 TnD,BSt,CollateralDamage,pt.1 . 3.50
7 TnD,BSt,CollateralDamage,pt.2. . 4.00
8 TnD,BSt,Dark Wind At
    Your Back 3.00
9 TnD,BSt,F:Adrenalynn. 3.00
10 TnD,pt.1 (of 3). 3.00
10a variant TnD(c). 3.00
11 TnD,Victor retains Tenth 3.00
11a variant cover 3.00
12 TnD,Black reign begins. 3.00
13 TnD,V:Rhazes Darkk 3.00
14 TnD,V:Rhazes Darkk 3.00
Coll.Ed.Vol.1 rep. #1–#2 . . . . 5.00
Spec.Configuration#1, sourcebook . 2.50
TPB rep.#1–#4. . . . . 12.00

TENTH, THE:
BLACK EMBRACE
Feb., 1999
1 TnD,SLo, V:Gozza. 4.00
1a variant cover (1:2) 12.00
2 TnD,SLo, F:Esperanza 2.50
3 TnD,SLo, F:Adrenalynn 2.50
4 TnD,SLo, conclusion 2.50

TENTH, THE:
EVIL'S CHILD
Sept., 1999
1 TnD, F:Gozza 3.00
1a variant cover (1:3) 3.00
1b variant cover (1:3) 3.00
2 TnD, F:Twisted 3 . . . . 2.50
3 TnD 2.50
4 TnD, someone dies 2.50
Spec.Ed.#1, rep.#0 & #1/2. . . . . . 3.00

10TH MUSE, THE
Nov., 2000
1 MWn,KeL 3.50
1a variant(c) 3.50
2 MWn,KeL,flip-book 3.50
2a variant(c) 3.50
2b photo(c) 3.50
3 MWn, critically wounded 3.50
3a variant(c) 3.50
3b photo(c) 3.50
4 MWn,Who is Medusa? 3.50
5 MWn,The Savage World 3.50
6 MWn,RCz,A:Serra 3.50
6 photo(c) 3.50
7 MWn,RCz,Maxwell Gideon 3.50
7a photo(c) 3.50
8 MWn,Assault on Olympus 3.50
8a photo(c) 3.50
9 MWn,San Francisco battle 3.50
9a photo(c) 3.50
10 MWn,RCr,I:The Odyssey 3.50
10a variant(c). 3.50
10b variant CBa(c). 3.50
11 RCr,The Endgame 3.50

TIMESEEKERS
Aug., 2003
1 . . . . 3.00

TINCAN MAN
Jan., 2000
1 F:Alex Darkstar 3.00
1a variant GfD(c) (1:4) 3.00
2 no mercy 3.00
3 . . . . 3.00
Preview Book, 24-pg 3.00

IMAGE

TOMB RAIDER
Top Cow, Nov., 1999
1 DJu,JSb 5.00
2 DJu,JSb,quest for Medusa Mask. 3.00
3 DJu,JSb,secret of Medusa Mask. 3.00
4 DJu,JSb,Medusa Mask found . . . 3.00
5 DJu,JSb,Ancient Futures 3.00
6 DJu,JSb,Death Dance 3.00
7 DJu,JSb,Dead Center,pt.1(of4) . . 3.00
8 DJu,JSb,Dead Center,pt.2 . . . . . 3.00
9 DJu,JSb,Death by Midnight 3.00
9a variant(c) 7.00
10 DJu,JSb,Eye of Creation 3.00
11 DJu,BTn 3.00
12 DJu,BTn 3.00
13 DJu,JSb,Honduras,pt.1 . . . . . . 3.00
14 DJu,JSb,Honduras,pt.2 . . . . . . 3.00
15 DJu,JSb,Without Limit 3.00
16 DJu,JSb,Pieces of Zero,pt.1 . . . 3.00
17 DJu,JSb,Pieces of Zero,pt.2 . . . 3.00
18 DJu,JSb,Pieces of Zero,pt.3 . . . 3.00
19 DJu,Pieces of Eight,pt.1 . . . . . . 3.00
20 DJu,Pieces of Zero,pt.4 . . . . . . 3.00
21 Hunt for Black Mandala 3.00
22 The Trap,pt.2 . . . . 3.00
23 Path of the Tiger,pt.3 . . . . 3.00
24 Isle of Hydra 3.00
25 Endgame,pt.1 . . . . 3.00
26 Abyss,pt.1 . . . . 3.00
27 Abyss,pt.2 . . . . 3.00
28 Abyss,pt.3, Tempting Fate 3.00
29 V:Lord Vymes 3.00
30 Strange Flesh, 48-pg. 5.00
31 Conquista 3.00
32 Angel of Darkness,pt.1 . . . . 3.00
33 Angel of Darkness,pt.2 . . . . 3.00
34 Angel of Darkness,pt.3 . . . . 3.00
35 Black Legion,pt.1 . . . . 3.00
36 Black Legion,pt.2 . . . . 3.00
37 Black Legion,pt.3 . . . . 3.00
38 Bloodstone,pt.1 . . . . 3.00
39 Bloodstone,pt.2 . . . . 3.00
40 Risen 3.00
41 Spirit Walker,pt.1 . . . . 3.00
42 Spirit Walker,pt.2 . . . . 3.00
43 Tower of Souls,pt.1 . . . . 3.00
44 Tower of Souls,pt.2 . . . . 3.00
45 Inner Demons 3.00
46 Gathering Storm,pt.1 . . . . 3.00
47 Gathering Storm,pt.2 . . . . 3.00
TPB Saga of the Medusa Mask . . . 13.00
TPB Vol.2 Mystic Artifacts 20.00
TPB Tomb Raider/Witchblade 13.00
GN The Greatest Treasure of All . . . 6.00
Spec. Gallery 3.00
Preview, B&W 16-pg. 2.50
0 Lara goes fishing 2.50
1/2 DJu, new(c). 3.00
TPB Vol.3 Chasing Shangri-La . . . 13.00
Spec. Tomb Raider vs. Darkness . . 3.00
1-shot The Greatest Pleasure of
  All, Prelude, DJu,JJu (2002) . . 5.00
1-shot Takeover 3.00
1-shot Epiphany 5.00
1-shot Arabian Nights 3.00

TOMB RAIDER:
JOURNEYS
Top Cow, Dec., 2001
1 (of 12) more Lara Croft 3.00
1A variant AH(c) 3.00
2 washed ashore in El Dorado 3.00
3 Sodom and Gomorrah 3.00
4 Deja vu. 3.00
5 Who's in your yearbook? 3.00
6 . . . . 3.00
7 Maori Dream-Spear 3.00
8 way to the Underworld 3.00
9 Akio 3.00

10 . . . . 3.00
11 . . . . 3.00
12 Settling Old Scores 3.00

TOMB RAIDER MAGAZINE
Top Cow, Feb., 2001
1 56-pg. 5.00
2 56-pg. 5.00

TOMB RAIDER/
WITCHBLADE
Top Cow, June, 2000
1/2 rep. 3.00

TOMB RAIDER/
WITCHBLADE REVISITED
Top Cow, Dec., 1998
1 Video game tie-in 3.00

TOM JUDGE:
END OF DAYS
Image/Top Cow, Dec., 2002
1 PJe,40-pg. 4.00
TPB The Rapture 20.00

TOMMYSAURUS REX
Image, Aug., 2004
TPB 112-pg. 12.00

TOOTH & CLAW
Aug., 1999
1 Reborn to rage 3.00
2 MPa 3.00
3 MPa,Retribution,concl. 3.00

TOP COW/BALLISTIC
Swimsuit Spec.#1 MS(c) (1995) . . . 4.00

TOP COW'S
CALIFORNIA CHRISTMAS
SPECTACULAR
Top Cow, 2001
Spec. Pin-ups. 3.00

TOP COW CLASSICS
Top Cow, 2000
Witchblade #1 B&W 3.00
The Darkness #1 B&W 3.00
Ascension #1 . . . . 3.00
Fathom #1 . . . . 3.00
Rising Stars #1 B&W 3.00
Cyberforce #1 B&W 3.00
Tomb Raider #1 B&W 3.00
Tomb Raider #1 B&W, signed 20.00
Aphrodite IX #1, B&W 3.00
Midnight Nation #1, B&W. 3.00
Witchblade #25, B&W 3.00
Magdalena #1 JBz,b&w 3.00
Tomb Raider/Wtchblace #1 . . . . . . 3.00
TPB Tomb Raider/Witchblade:
  Trouble Seekers 8.00
  Trouble Seekers 8.00
Battle of the Planets #1 . . . . 3.00
1-shot Book of Revelations (2003) . 4.00

TOP COW SECRETS
Jan., 1996
Winter Lingerie Spec. 3.00

TOTAL SELL OUT
Dec., 2003
TPB BMB 15.00

A TOUCH OF SILVER
(B&W) Jan., 1997
1 JV,'Birthday' 3.00
2 JV,'Dance' 3.00
3 JV,'Bullies' 3.00
4 JV,'Separation' 3.00
5 JV,inc. Tomorrow Syndicate vs.
  Round Table of America, 12-pg.
  color section 3.00
6 JV 'Choices' Aug., 1963. . . . . . . 3.00
TPB A Sociopath in Training 13.00

TRAKK: MONSTER
HUNTER
Sept., 2003
1 (of 6) 3.00
1a variant (c) 3.00
2 . . . . 3.00
2a variant (c) 3.00
2b variant SBs(c) 3.00
3 . . . . 3.00
3a variant SBS(c) 3.00

TREKKER
May, 1999
1 RoR, in New Gelaph 3.00

Trencher #2 © Image

TRENCHER
May, 1993
1 KG,I:Trencher 2.25
2 KG 2.25
3 KG,V:Supreme 2.25
4 KG,V:Elvis 2.25

TRIBE
March, 1993
1 TJn(s),LSn,I:The Tribe 2.50
1a Ivory(White) Editon 3.00
2 . . . . 2.25
Ashcan 1 . . . . 3.00

TROLL
Extreme, Dec., 1993
1 RLd(s),JMs,I:Evangeliste, V:Katellan
Command 2.50

Troll #1 ©
Extreme

2	2.50
Halloween Spec.#1	2.50
X-Mas Stocking Stuffer #1	3.00

TROLL: ONCE A HERO
Aug., 1994
1 Troll in WWII	2.50

TROUBLEMAN
Motown June, 1996
1 Charles Drost	2.50
2	2.50

TSUNAMI GIRL
Flypaper Jan., 1999
1 F:Michelle Vincent	3.00
2 Sorayama(c), A:Alan Poe	3.00
3 Sorayama(c), Surreal conspiracy	3.00

TUG & BUSTER
(B&W) June, 1998
1 MaH, humor, F:Stinkfinger	3.00

'21'
Top Cow, Feb., 1996
1 LWn,MDa	2.50
2 LWn,MDa	2.50
3 LWn,MDa	2.50
4 LWn,MDa,'Time Bomb,'pt.1	2.50
5 LWn,MDa,'Time Bomb,'pt.2	2.50
6 LWn,MDa,'Time Bomb,'pt.3 'Detonation'	2.50

ULTRA
Image, Aug., 2004
1 Seven Days,pt.1	3.00
2 Seven Days,pt.2	3.00
3 Seven Days,pt.3	3.00

UNBOUND
(B&W) Jan., 1998
1 by Joe Pruett & Michael Peters	3.00
2	3.00
3 F:Marta & Erik	3.00

UNION
WildStorm, Feb., 1995
0 O:Union	2.50
0a WPo(c)	5.00
1 MT,I:Union,A:StormWatch	2.75
2 MT	2.75
3 MT	2.75
4 MT,Good Intentions	2.75

Regular Series 1995
1 R:Union, Crusade	2.50
2 V:Crusade & Mnemo	2.50
3 A:Savage Dragon	2.50
4 JRo,BWS(c), WildStorm Rising,pt.3,w/2 cards	2.50
4a Newsstand ed.	2.25
5 V:Necros	2.50
6 V:Necros	2.50
7 Jill's Surprise	2.50
8 Regal Vengeance,pt.1	2.50
9 Regal Vengeance,pt.2	2.50
10 Regal Vengeance,pt.3	2.50
1-shot Final Vengeance, MHs, V:Regent (1997)	2.50

UNION
WildStorm, 1996
1 MHs,RBn,'Knight of Faith'	2.50
2 MHs,RBn	2.50
3 MHs,RBn	2.50

UNIVERSE
Top Cow, Aug., 2001
1 PJe,The Triad of Powers	2.50
1 variant foil(c)	12.00
2 PJe,Pilgrimage into the Inferno	2.50
3 PJe,Judge finds Hell	2.50
4 PJe,plan for mankind's fate	2.50
5 PJe,express train to hell	2.50
6 PJe,family held hostage	2.50
7 PJe,successor to the devil	2.50
8 PJe, Stairway to Heaven,48-pg.	5.00

VAGABOND
Aug., 2000
1 RBn,SRf,F:Sharon Armstrong	3.00
1a variant(c)	3.00
1b deluxe	9.00
1c signed	11.00
1d ruby red foil(c)	11.50
2 RBn,SRf	3.00

VAGRANT STORY
Top Cow, Sept., 2000
1 video game tie-in	3.00

VAMPIRE'S CHRISTMAS
GN JLi 48-pg.	6.00

VANGUARD
Highbrow, 1993–94
1 EL(s),BU:I:Vanguard	3.00
2 EL(s),Roxann	3.00
3 AMe	3.00
4 AMe	3.00
5 AMe,V:Aliens	3.00
6 V:Bank Robber	3.00
Spec. B&W 48-pg.	6.00

VANGUARD: STRANGE VISITORS
(B&W) 1996
1 (of 4) SEa,BAn,A:Amok,'Strange Visitors'	3.00
2 thru 4 SEa,BAn	@3.00

VELOCITY
Top Cow, 1995–95
1 V:Morphing Opponent	3.00
2 V:Charnel	3.00
3	3.00
4	3.00

VENTURE
Jan., 2003
1	3.00
2 thru 4	@3.00

VICTORY
May, 2003
1 thru 4	@3.00
1a–4a variant (c)	@3.00

Vol. 2 Aug., 2004
1 (of 4)	3.00
2	3.00
2a variant(c)	3.00

VIOLATOR
TMP, 1994
1 AMo(s),BS,I:Admonisher	5.00
2 AMo(s),BS	4.00
3 AMo(s),BS,last issue	4.00

Violator/Badrock #4
© Extreme

VIOLATOR/BADROCK
Extreme, 1995
1 AMo(s),RLe(c),A:Celestine,'Rocks and Hard Places,'pt.1	2.50
2 AMo(s),RLe(c),V:Celestine,'Mondo Inferno'	2.50
3 RLe(c),F:Dr. McAllister,'Where Angels Fear to Tread'	2.50
4 RLe(c),'Badrock's Bogus Journey,' final issue	2.50
TPB Rep.	10.00

VIOLENT MESSIAHS
June, 2000
1 F:Rankor Island	5.00
1a variant AMe(c) (1:4)	6.00
2	5.00
2a variant(c)	6.00
3 V:Citizen Pain	4.00
4 V:Jeremiah Parker	3.00
5 flip-book	3.00

All comics prices listed are for *Near Mint* condition.

6 Tonight The Door Opens	3.00
7 In the Final Stretch	3.00
8 North End Mansion	3.00
Spec. Genesis, 56-pg.	5.00
TPB Vol. 1 The Book of Job	25.00

VIOLENT MESSIAHS: LAMENTING PAIN
Sept., 2002

1 (of 4) F:Lt. Cheri Major	3.00
2 thru 4	@3.00
1a–4a variant (c)	@3.00

VISITATIONS
(B&W) 1997

GN by C. Stott Morse	7.00

VOGUE
Extreme, 1995–96

1 F:Vogue,I:Redbloods	2.50
2	2.50
3 conclusion	2.50

VOLTRON: DEFENDER OF THE UNIVERSE
May, 2003

0	3.00
1 Revelations,pt.1	3.00
1a variant (c)s	3.00
2 thru 5 Revelations,pt.2–pt.5	@3.00

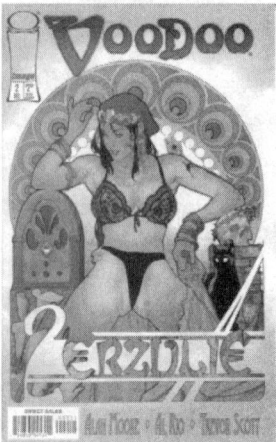

Voodoo #2 © WildStorm

VOODOO
WildStorm, Nov., 1997

1 AMo(s),WildStorm universe	2.50
2 AMo(s),in old New Orleans	2.50
3 AMo(s),Samedi	2.50
4 AMo(s), Christian Charles	2.50
TPB Voodoo Dancing in the Dark	10.00

WAHOO MORRIS
(B&W) Mar., 2000

1 Rock & Roll fantasy	3.00
2	3.00

WALKING DEAD
Oct., 2003

1	18.00
2 City of the Damned	22.00
3 Protection	12.00

4 Guns	11.00
5 Zombies	6.00
6 Grave Situations	5.00
7 Snowbound	5.00
8 Search for shelter	4.00
9 Zombie hell-hole	3.00
10 Safer shelter	3.00
11 All Good Things	3.00
12 Petty squabbles	3.00
13 CAd	3.00
TPB Vol. 1 Days Gone Bye	10.00
TPB Vol. 2 rep. #7ñ#12	13.00

WANTED
Image/Top Cow, Dec., 2003

1 (of 6) MMr	9.00
1a variant (c)s	9.00
1b Death Row edition	5.00
2 thru 5	@4.00
#1 Death Row edition,32-pg.	4.00
#2 Death Row edition,32-pg.	4.00
#3 Death Row edition,32-pg.	3.00
Spec. Wanted Dossier	3.00

WARBLADE: ENDANGERED SPECIES
WildStorm, 1995

1 I:Pillar	3.00
2 V:Ripclaw	2.50
3 I:Skinner	2.50
4 final issue	2.50

WARLANDS
Aug., 1999

1 by Pat Lee	2.50
1a, b & c variant covers	2.50
1d Armore Chrome edition	13.00
2 help from the Elves?	2.50
2a variant cover (1:2)	2.50
3 the Dataran invasion	2.50
3a variant cover (1:2)	2.50
4	2.50
5 trapped between enemies	2.50
6 enemies clash	3.00
7 the Dataran Horde	2.50
8	2.50
9 final battle begins	2.50
10 flip-book	3.00
11	2.50
12 concl.	2.50
Spec. Three stories	6.00
Chronicles Vol.1, rep.#1–#3	8.00
Chronicles Vol.2, rep.#4–#6	8.00
TPB Vol.1, 184-pg.	15.00

WARLANDS: AGE OF ICE
Image, July, 2001

1 Awakening	3.00
2 flip-book	3.00
3 thru 5	@3.00
1a and 2a variant covers	@3.00
Spec. #0 (2002)	3.00
Spec. #1/2 (2002)	3.00

WATERLOO SUNSET
Image, July, 2004

1 (of 4) B&W,56-pg.	7.00
2 Moving in High Places	7.00

WEAPON ZERO
Top Cow, 1995

T-Minus-4 WS	8.00
T-Minus-3 Alien Invasion	5.00
T-Minus-2 Formation of a Team	5.00
T-Minus-1 Alien Invasion	5.00

0 Whole Team Together	4.00
1	5.00
2	3.50
3	3.50
4 thru 9 WS,JBz	@3.00
10 WS,ScL,'Devil's Reign' tie-in.	3.00
11 WS,JBz,Weapon Zero & Lilith return to T'srii moonbase.	3.00
12 WS,JBz, What's wrong with Jamie.	3.00
13 WS,JBz,problems with Jamie	3.00
14 JBz,T'Srrii have returned	3.00
15 JBz,T'Srrii,concl.,48-pg.	3.50
Weapon Zero/Silver Surfer Spec. x-over (1997)	3.00

WEASEL GUY: ROADTRIP
(B&W) Aug., 1999

1 by Steve Buccellato	3.00
1a variant cover (1:4)	3.00
2 Peril in Pennsylvania	3.00
2a variant cover (1:4)	3.00
3 Don't Mess With Texas	3.00
3a variant cover (1:4)	3.00
4 48-pg, guest stars	5.00
4a variant KIA(c) (1:4).	5.00

WETWORKS
WildStorm, 1994

1 WPo,Rebirth	4.00
2 WPo,BCi,Brakken,Blood Queen	3.00
3 WPo,BCi,V:Vampire	3.00
4 WPo,BCi,Dozer	2.50
5 WPo,BCi,Pilgrim's Turn	2.50
6 WPo,BCi,Civil War	2.50
7 WPo,BCi,F:Pilgrim	2.50
8 WPo,SW,BWS(c), WildStorm Rising,pt.7,w/2 cards	2.50
8a Newsstand ed.	2.25
9 F:Jester,Pilgrim Dozer	2.50
10 R:Dozer to Action	2.50
11 Blood Queen Vs. Dane	2.50
12 V:Vampire Nation	2.50
13 WPo(c)	2.50
14	2.50
15	2.50
16 Fire From Heaven,pt.4	2.50
17 FTa,Fire From Heaven,pt.11	2.50
18 FTa	2.50
19 FTa	2.50
20 FTa	2.50
21 FTa	2.50

Wetworks #9 © WildStorm

22 FTa,Dave vs.Bloodqueen concl. . 2.50
23 FTa,Flattop & Crossbones,
V:Lady Feign 2.50
24 FTa 2.50
25 FTa,Can Pilgrim withstand the
beast that lurks within her,
double size 4.50
26 team parts ways with Armand
Waering 2.50
27 V:Craven, no rest for the weary . 2.50
28 Vampire tracked in Pacific
Northwest,A:Johnny Savoy 2.50
29 V:Soulbender,'Power Surge'. . . . 2.50
30 'Secret of the Siynn' 2.50
31 'Ashes to Ashes' 2.50
32 StG,PtL,V:Drakkar,'Sacrements
of Damnation,'pt.1 . . . . 2.50
32a Voyager pack, bagged with
Phantom Guard preview 3.50
33 StG,PtL,Sacraments,pt.2. . . . . . 2.50
34 StG,PtL,Sacraments,pt.3. . . . . . 2.50
35 StG,PtL,Sacraments,pt.4. . . . . . 2.50
36 StG,'Maximum Security' 2.50
37 StG,V:St.Crispin,'Diversionary
Tactics,'pt.1 . . . . 2.50
38 StG,'DiversionaryTactics,'pt.2 . . 2.50
39 StG,'Symbiote Seizure' 2.50
40 StG,'Drawn Swords' 2.50
41 StG,V:Stormwatch,'Drawn
Swords,' conclusion 2.50
42 StG,'Flash Back,'pt.1 . . . . 2.50
43 StG,'Flash Back,'conclusion 2.50
3-D Spec.#1 (1998) 5.00
Sourcebook #1 (1994) 2.50
Hero Ashcan 3.00
Promo Ashcans #1,#2,#3 . . . . . . @3.00
TPB Rebirth,rep. #1–#3 & preview 10.00

WETWORKS/VAMPIRELLA
WildStorm, 1997
1 JMi & GK, x-over 3.00

WHISKEY DICKEL,
INTERNATIONAL
COWGIRL
Aug., 2003
TPB b&w 120-pg. 13.00

WHIZ KIDS
Apr., 2003
1-shot b&w, 48-pg. 5.00

WICKED, THE
Dec., 1999
1 RMr,FTa,supernatural thriller 3.00
1a variant Jay Anacleto(c)(1:4) 3.00
2 thru 7 . . . . @3.00
3a & 4a variant covers . . . . @3.00
Special Medusa's Tale 4.00
TPB Vol. 1 Omnibus 20.00

WICKED WEST, THE
Image, Oct., 2004
GN 10.00

WILDC.A.T.S
WildStorm, 1992
1 B:BCi(s),JLe, SW(i), I:Wild-
C.A.T.S. 5.00
1a Gold ed. 10.00
1b Gold and Signed 10.00
2 JLe,SW(i),V:Master Gnome,
I:Wetworks, Prism foil(c),
with coupon #5 . . . . 4.00
2a w/o coupon 2.25
3 RLd(c),JLe,SW(i), V:Youngblood. 3.50

WildC.A.T.S. #31 © WildStorm

4 E:BCi(s),JLe,LSn,SW(i),w/card,
A:Youngblood,BU:Tribe 3.50
4a w/red card 5.00
5 BCi(s),JLe,SW,I:Misery 3.00
6 BCi(s),JLe,SW,Killer Instinct,
A:Misery,C:Ripclaw 3.00
7 BCi(s),JLe,SW, A:Cyberforce. . . . 3.00
8 BCi(s),JLe,SW 4.00
9 BCi(s),JLe,SW 3.50
10 CCi(s),JLe,SW,I:Huntsman 3.00
11 CCi(s),JLe,SW,V:Triad,
A:Huntsman 3.00
11a WPo(c) 5.00
12 JLe,CCi,A:Huntsman 3.00
13 JLe,CCi,A:Huntsman 3.00
14 X book. 3.00
15 F:Black Razors 3.00
16 Black Razors 3.00
17 A:StormWatch 3.00
18 R:Hightower 3.00
19 V:Hightower 3.00
20 TC,JeR,BWS(c),WildStorm
Rising,pt.2,w/2 cards 3.00
20a Newsstand ed. 3.00
21 Into Space Back Home 3.50
22 Space Adventures. 3.50
23 F:Mr. Majestic's Team 3.50
24 O:Maul 3.50
25 double sized 5.00
26 AMo. 3.50
27 AMo. 3.50
28 AMo. 3.50
29 AMo,Fire From Heaven,pt.7 . . . . 3.50
30 AMo,BKs,Fire From
Heaven,pt.13 . . . . 3.50
31 AMo,BKs,'Cats & Dogs' 3.50
32 AMo,BKs,'Catharsis' 3.50
33 AMo,BKs,'Belling the Cat' 3.50
34 AMo,MtB,New York seconds
away from nuclear disaster 3.50
35 AMo,MtB,BKs,V:Crusade 3.00
36 AMo,MtB,BKs,V:Crusade,
A:Union,pt.2 . . . . 3.00
37 BCi,JPe,MtB,WildC.A.T.s
team divided 3.00
38 BCi,JPe,MtB,Puritans debut . . . 3.00
39 BCi,JPe,MtB,'C.A.T. Fight' 3.00
40 BCi,JPe,MtB,MtB(c),'Fight
of Flight' 3.50
40a variant cover by TC 5.00
41 BCi,JPe,MtB,backwards in time . 3.00
42 BCi,JPe,MTb,in WWI 3.00
43 BCi,JPe,MTb,in ancient China . . 3.00
44 BCi,JPe,MTb,'Paradise Lost' . . . 3.00

45 BCi,JPe,MTb,'Circus Maximus' . 3.00
46 BCi,JPe,MTb,escape from
Rome. 3.00
47 BCi,JPe, MTb,time trip concl. . . . 3.00
47a variant JMd(c) 3.00
48 BCi,JPe,trapped in mothership . . 3.00
49 BCi,JPe,return to present 3.00
50 BCi,JPe,AMo,new
costumes,40-pg.(June, 1998) . . 4.00
TPB A Gathering of Eagles 10.00
Spec.#1 SrG(s),TC,SW,I:Destine,
Pin-ups 3.50
Spec.#2 . . . . 2.50
3-D #1 rep. #1 (1997) 5.00
3-Da variant cover 5.00
TPB rep. #1-4,w/0 . . . . 11.00
TPB Homecoming rep.#21–#27 . . 20.00
Ann.#1 JRo,LSn (1998) 3.00
TPB WildC.A.T.S/Cyberforce
Killer Instinct 17.00
TPB Gathering of Eagles 10.00
TPB Gang War,rep.#28–34 . . . . . . 17.00
TPB VOL. II Way of the Coda 13.00
Volume 2: See COLOR

WILDC.A.T.S
ADVENTURES
WildStorm, 1994
1 From animated TV series 3.00
2 Helspont,Troika 3.00
3 Caught in war 3.00
4 V:The President 3.00
5 I:Lonely 3.00
6 I:Majestics 3.00
7 . . . . 3.00
8 Betrayed 3.00
9 V:Black Razors 3.00
10 F:Voodoo. 3.00
Sourcebook (JS(c) 3.00

WILDC.A.T.S/ALIENS
WildStorm, 1998
1-shot WEI,CSp,KN 9.00
1-shotA, variant GK&KN(c)(1:4). . . 11.00

WILDC.A.T.S TRILOGY
June, 1993
1 BCi(s),JaL,V:Artemis 2.50
2 BCi(s),JaL,V:Artemis 2.25
3 BCi(s),JaL,V:Artemis 2.25

WILDC.A.T.S/X-MEN
WildStorm, Feb., 1997
1 (of 4) SLo,TC, giant Marvel/
Image x-over 5.00
1a alternate cover by JLe 5.00
2 & 4 see Marvel
TPB WildC.A.T.S/X-Men, rep. 18.50

WILDC.A.T.S/X-MEN
WildStorm/Marvel, 1997
Golden Age #1,SLo,TC 5.00
Golden Age #1a variant JLe(c) 5.00
3-D Golden Age #1, with glasses . . 5.00
3-D Golden Age #1, variant cover . . 5.00
Silver Age #1 SLo, JLe & SW,
x- over 4.50
Silver Age #1a NA&SW(c) 4.50
Silver Age #1b signed 20.00
Silver Age #1c signed, deluxe 30.00
3-D Silver Age #1, with glasses . . . 6.50
3-D Silver Age #1, NA(c) variant . . 6.50
Modern Age #1, JRo,AHu,MFm,
V:Hellfire Club 4.50
Modern Age #1a variant cover. 4.50
3-D Modern Age #1, with glasses . . 5.00
3-D Modern Age #1, variant cover . . 5.00

IMAGE

Wildcore #10 © WildStorm

WILDCORE
WildStorm, 1997–98

1 BBh,SRf,BBh(c), V:Drahn	2.50
1a variant TC(c)	2.50
1b Voyager bagged pack	3.00
2 BBh,SRf,Brawl joins	2.50
3 BBh,SRf,V:D'rahn	2.50
4 BBh,SRf,A:Majestic	2.50
5 BBh,SRf,Tapestry	2.50
6 BBh,SRf,Zealot missing	2.50
7 BBh,SRf,caught in fantasy world	2.50
8 RBn,SRf,V:Tapestry	2.50
9 RBn,SRf,Zealot's soul restored	2.50
10 RBn,SRf,Trans-dimensional trauma	2.50
GN Backlash & Taboo's African Vacation	6.00

WILDGUARD: CASTING CALL
Sept., 2003

1 (of 6) TNu	3.00
2 thru 6 TNu	@3.00
1a–6a variant (c)s	@3.00

WILDSTAR: SKY ZERO
March, 1993

1 JOy,AG,I:WildStar	2.50
1a Gold ed	5.00
2 JOy,AG	2.50
3 JOy,AG,V:Savage Dragon, D:WildStar	2.50
4 JOy,AG,Last Issue,Pin-ups	2.50
TPB WildStar Sky Zero (1994)	13.00

[Regular Series] Sept., 1995

1 R:WildStar	2.50
2 V:Mighty Man	2.50
3	2.50
Ashcan	2.25

WILDSTORM!
WildStorm, Aug., 1995

1 F:Spartan,Black Razors	2.50
2 F:Deathblow	2.50
3 F:Taboo,Spartan	2.50
4 F:Nautika,Sunburst	2.50
Winter Wonderfest Spec.#1	3.50
Spec.#1 Chamber of Horrors(1995)	3.50
Spec. Swimsuit Special '97	2.50

Spec. Ultimate Sports Official Program	2.50
Sketchbook	3.00
Spec. Halloween '97	2.50
GN Thunderbook #1	7.00
GN Summer Spec., 48-pg. (DC)	6.00

WILDSTORM ARCHIVES GENESIS
WildStorm, June, 1998

1 The #1 Collection, 238 pg	7.00

WILDSTORM RISING
WildStorm, May, 1995

1 JeR,BWS(c&a) WildStorm Rising, pt.1:Tricked by Defile,w/2 cards	2.50
1a Newsstand ed	2.25
2 RMz,BBo,BWS(c) WildStorm Rising,pt.10,w/2 cards	2.50
2a Newsstand ed	2.25
WildStorm Sourcebook #1	2.50
TPB Rep. Mini-series	17.00

WILDSTORM SPOTLIGHT
WildStorm, Feb., 1997

1 AMo,F:Majestic, at the end of time	2.50
2 StG,RMr,Loner returns	2.50
3 StG,RMr,Secret past of original Loner	2.50
4 F:Hellstrike,Stormwatch	2.50

WILDSTORM ULTIMATE SPORTS
WildStorm, 1997

Official Program #1	2.50

WILDSTORM UNIVERSE '97
WildStorm, Nov., 1997

Sourcebook #1 thru #3	@2.50

WITCHBLADE
Top Cow, 1995–96

1 I:Witchblade	35.00
1A Special retailer edition	35.00
1B Wizard Ace edition,acetate(c)	25.00
2	25.00
2 encore edition	7.00
3	20.00
4	15.00
5	14.00
6 thru 8	@10.00

Top Cow, 1996

9	9.00
9A variant cover	11.00
10 I:Darkness (Jackie Estacado)	12.00
10a variant Darkness cover (1:4)	16.00
11	6.00
12 Connection between Lisa, Microwave Murderer and Kenneth Irons	6.00
Witchblade 1/2 mail-in offer from Fan #8	4.00

Top Cow, 1997

13 Dannette Boucher's secret past	6.00
14 Sara searches for Microwave Murderer	5.00
15 'There is a war brewing...'	4.00
16 'Will Witchblade come between Sarah and Jake?'	4.00
17 New York City in shambles	4.00
18 Family Ties,pt.1,x-over	4.00
18a variant(c)	7.00
19 Family Ties,pt.4,x-over	4.00

20 Chief Siry, Ian Nottingham	3.00
21 another big surprise	3.00
22 F:Sara	3.00
22a special	12.00
23 F:Ian Nottingham	3.00
24 JPn,Sara learns truth	3.00
25 Save Jake's Life, 32 pg	3.50
26 'Grey'	3.00
27 A:Kenneth Irons	3.00
27a variant cover, all villains	9.00
28 A:Jackie Estacado	3.00
29 A:Kenneth Irons	3.00
30 Siry & Irons	3.00
31 How Sara's father died	3.00
32 answers and questions	3.00
33 F:Eric	3.00
34 F:Tommy Gallo	3.00
35 Sara gets who she wants	3.00
36 The Darkness,pt.1 x-over	3.00
37 V:wicked creatures	3.00
38 V:Demons of the Underworld	3.00
39 V:Demons of the Underworld	3.00
40 PJe,RV	3.00
41 PJe,RV,arsonist	3.00
41a variant chrome (c)	5.00
42 PJe,pez dispensers	3.00
43 PJe,Impossible Murders	2.50
44 PJe,Impossible Murders	2.50
45 PJe	2.50
46 PJe	2.50
47 PJe	2.50
48 PJe	2.50
49 PJe,Firestarter is back	2.50
49a gold logo	7.00
50 PJe,48-pg.	5.50
50a variant DK(c)	12.00
50b variant MS(c)	12.00
50c variant(c)	12.00
51 PJe,What is the Witchblade?	2.50
52 PJe,The Inferno is Coming	2.50
53 PJe	2.50
54 Ian Nottingham resurrected	2.50
55 Tora No Shi	2.50
55a Battle of the Planets(c)	7.00
55b Battle(c) signed	7.00
56 Nottingham vs. Tora No Shi	2.50
57 Sonatine,pt.4	2.50
58 Sara & Joe Siry	2.50
59 Jackie Estacado is dead?	2.50
60 Endgame,pt.2 x-over	3.00
61 Julie returns	3.00
61a sketch(c)	8.00
62 F:Magdalena	3.00
63 F:Magdalena	3.00
64 F:Magdalena	3.00
65 F:Magdalena,concl.	3.00
66	3.00
67 Mother's Meat	3.00
68 Road Trip,pt.1	3.00
69 Road Trip,pt.2	3.00
70 return from trip	3.00
71 V:Shine	3.00
72 Level 42	3.00
73 Level 42	3.00
74 Death Pool	3.00
75 Death Pool, concl.,46-pg.	5.00
75a variant (c)	5.00
76 Death Pool follow-up	3.00
77 F:Celestine	3.00
78 TnD(c)	3.00
79 TnD(c)	3.00
80 Witch Hunt,pt.1	3.00
Spec. 1 Movie edition, photo(c)	10.00
Spec. 1a Movie, foil(c)	17.00
Spec. 1b Movie, holofoil(c)	25.00
Coll.Ed.Vol.#1	5.00
Coll.Ed.Vol.#2	5.00
Coll.Ed.Vol.#3	5.00
Coll.Ed.Vol.#4, rep. #7 & #8	5.00
Coll.Ed.Vol.#5, rep. #9 & #10	5.00
Coll.Ed.Vol.#6, rep. #11 & #12	5.00

IMAGE

Coll.Ed.Vol.#7, rep. #13 & #14 .... 5.00
Coll.Ed.Vol.#8, rep. #15–#17...... 7.00
Delux Coll.Ed. rep.1–#8......... 25.00
Spec. Infinity SLo,AdP.......... 3.50
Spec.#40 Preview book, B&W..... 5.00
Spec.#1 rep.movie photo cover.... 2.50
Spec.Witchblade/Darkness,pt.2
   x-over, 48-pg. 4.00
Spec. Witchblade/Darkminds x-over 6.00
Gallery Edition #1 .... 3.00
TPB Collects Witchblade/Darkness
   Family Ties x-over......... 10.00
TPB Vol.3 Prevailing, deluxe.... 15.00
TPB Vol.3 Prevailing, deluxe.... 15.00
TPB Revelations, deluxe 25.00
TPB Revelations, deluxe 25.00
TPB Distinctions............. 15.00
Spec.1 Lady Death x-over....... 5.00
Spec. Tomb Raider 4.00
TPB Obakemono 10.00
1/2 24-pg................... 3.00
1-shot Nottingham, 48-pg...... 5.00
1-shot Witchblade Animated 3.00
TPB Vlood Relations 13.00
GN Witchblade/Darkminds:
   The Return of Paradox 7.00
1-shot Witchblade/Wolverine..... 3.00
1-shot Witchblade: Blood Oath ... 5.00

WITCHBLADE: DESTINY'S CHILD
Top Cow, April, 2000
1 (of 3) O:Witchblade,pt.1........ 3.00
2 O:Witchblade,pt.2 .... 3.00
3 O:Witchblade, concl. 3.00

WITCHFINDER, THE
Liar, Oct., 1999
1 by R. Lugibihl & S. Scott 3.00
1a variant cover (1:2) 3.00
2 .... 3.00
3 Concl...................... 3.00

WIZARDS TALE, THE
Homage, 1997
TPB KBk,DWe 20.00
TPB 2nd printing 20.00

WOLVERINE/ WITCHBLADE
Top Cow, Jan., 1997
1-shot 'Devil's Reign'pt.5 (of 8) 4.00

WONDERLAND
Image, Oct., 2004
GN 7.00

WORLD CLASS COMICS
Aug., 2002
1-shot, 40-pg. b&w............ 5.00

WYNONNA EARP
WildStorm, 1996–97
1 BSt,'Violent Territory' 2.50
2 BSt,The Law comes to San
   Diablo 2.50
3 BSt,desperate to stop Hemo
   from going nationwide....... 2.50
4 BSt,goes to New York,
   V:ancient evil 2.50
5 BSt,battle with Raduk–Eater
   of the Dead concl........... 2.50

Youngblood #8 © Extreme

YOUNGBLOOD
Extreme, April, 1992
0 RLd,O:Youngblood,w/coupon#7 . 3.00
0a without coupon............. 1.50
0b gold coupon............... 9.00
1 RLd,I:Youngblood (flipbook) 5.00
1a 2nd print.,gold border 2.50
1b RLD,Silent Edition 13.00
2 RLd,I:ShadowHawk 5.00
3 RLd,I:Supreme,Showdown 3.00
4 RLd,DK,A:Prophet,BU:Pitt..... 3.00
5 RLd,Flip book,w/Brigade #4 .... 2.50
6 RLd(a&s),J:Troll,Knight Sabre,
   2nd Die Hard, Proposal to Girl
   friend 3.50
7 Badrock, V:Overtkill 2.50
8 Chapel, V:Spawn 2.50
9 .... 2.50
9a variant cover 5.00
10 Bravo, Badrock, Troll 2.50
Yr.Bk.#1 CYp,I:Tyrax,Kaman..... 2.75
Ashcan #1 .... 8.00
Ashcan #2 .... 4.00
TPB rep. #1–#5 .... 17.00

[Volume 2] 1995
1 New Roster 2.50
2 The Program Continues 2.50
3 Extreme Babewatch.......... 2.50
4 Extreme Destroyer,pt.4
   x-over, bagged with card..... 2.50
5 .... 2.50
6 .... 2.50
7 Shadowhunt x-over,pt.3....... 2.50
8 ErS,RCz.................. 2.50
9 ErS,RCz.................. 2.50
10 ErS,RCz 2.50
TPB Baptism of Fire, F:Spawn 2.50
See Color Pub. section

YOUNGBLOOD BATTLEZONE
April, 1993
1 BrM 2.50
2 .... 3.00

YOUNGBLOOD STRIKEFILE
Extreme, 1993
1 JaL,RLd,I:Allies,A:Al Simmons
   (Spawn)I:Giger,Glory........ 3.00
1a Gold ed.................. 4.00
2 JaL,RLd,V:Super Patriot, Giger.. 3.00
2a Gold ed................. 3.50
3 RLd,JaL,DaM(i), A:Super Partiot . 3.00
4 I:Overtkill 3.00
5 .... 3.00
6 and 7 flip books .... @3.00
8 Shaft 3.00
9 Knight Sabre 3.00
10 RLd,TNu,I:Bloodpool,Task,
   Psilence,Wylder,Rubble....... 3.50
11 ExtremeSacrifice,pt.0,x-over
   O:Link Crypt 3.00
TPB rep.#1-#3,sketchbook 13.00
Ashcan 3.00

YOUNGBLOOD/X-FORCE
Extreme/Marvel, 1996
1-shot Mojo visits Image x-over ... 5.00
1-shot RLd variant cover 5.00

YOUNGBLOOD: YEAR ONE
1 KBk(s),RLd, the early years..... 2.50
2 KBk(s),RLd,V:Giger,Cybernet ... 2.50

ZEALOT
WildStorm, 1995
1 O:Zealot.................. 2.50
2 In Japan.................. 2.50
3 V:Prometheus 2.50

ZERO GIRL
WildStorm/Homage, 2000
1 thru 4 .... @3.00

ZORRO
(B&W) 1998
TPB #1 rep. classic Alex Toth 16.00
TPB #2 rep. classic Alex Toth 16.00
TPB The Lady Wears Red....... 13.00

ZORRO
(B&W) Sept., 2001
TPB The Dailies, 248-pg........ 19.00
TPB The Complete Alex Toth..... 19.00

ZORRO MANTANZAS
Sept., 1999
1 (of 4) DMG & Mike Mayhew 3.00
2 DMG,V:Machete.............. 3.00

ZORRO'S LADY RAWHIDE: OTHER PEOPLE'S BLOOD
(B&W) Feb., 1999
1 DMG,EM,JuB(c),cont. from Topps 3.00
2 DMG,EM,V:Scarlet Fever...... 3.00
3 DMG,EM,V:Ansel Plague....... 3.00
4 DMG,EM,V:Scarlet Fever...... 3.00
5 DMG,EM,Whiplash........... 3.00

ZORRO'S RENEGADES
Image, 1998
TPB Zorro's Renegades, B&W ... 15.00
TPB Vol. 2, Lady Rawhide....... 15.00

IMAGE

COLOR COMICS

ABADAZAD
Crossgen Comics, 2003
1 . . . . 3.00
2 thru 6 . . . . @3.00

ABBOTT AND COSTELLO
Charlton Comics, 1968–71
1 . . . . 125.00
2 thru 9 . . . . @75.00
10 thru 21 . . . . @50.00
22 . . . . 40.00

ACES HIGH
Gemstone, 1999
1 (of 5) EC Comics reprint 3.00
2 . . . . 3.00
3 . . . . 3.00
4 . . . . 3.00
5 . . . . 3.00
Annual rep. #1–#5 . . . . 13.50

ACME NOVELTY LIBRARY
Fantagraphics, 1994–98
1 thru 5 . . . . @4.50
6 thru 11 Jimmy Corrigan Meets
    His Dad, pt. 1 – pt. 6 (of 8) . . @4.50
12 Jimmy & Dad have lunch 5.00
13 Jimmy's Grandfather, 80-page . 11.00
14 F:Jimmy Corrigan 11.00
15 . . . . 10.00
1 thru 7, 2nd printings . . . . @4.00

A.D.A.M.
Toyman, 1998
1 . . . . 2.50
2 . . . . 2.50

ADAM-12
Gold Key, 1973–76
1 Photo(c), From TV show 100.00
2 thru 9 . . . . @50.00
10 . . . . 45.00

ADDAMS FAMILY
Gold Key, 1974–75
1 TV cartoon adapt. 150.00
2 . . . . 100.00
3 . . . . 75.00

ADLAI STEVENSON
Dell Publishing Co., 1966
1 Political Life Story 50.00

ADVENTURES OF
BARON MUNCHAUSEN
Now Comics, 1989
1 thru 4 movie adapt. series . . . . @2.50

ADVENTURES OF
FELIX THE CAT
Harvey, 1992
1 Short Stories 4.00

ADVENTURES OF
KUNG FU PIG
NINJA FLOUNDER
AND 4-D MONKEY
1 thru 6 . . . . @2.00
7 thru 10 . . . . @2.00

ADVENTURES OF
ROBIN HOOD
Gold Key, 1974–75
1 From Disney cartoon 25.00
2 thru 7 . . . . @15.00

Adventures of the Fly #14
© Archie Publications

ADVENTURES OF
THE FLY
Archie Publications/
Radio Comics, 1959–65
1 JSm/JK,O:Fly,I:SpiderSpry
    A:Lancelot Strong/Shield 800.00
2 JSm/JK,DAy,AW 475.00
3 Jack Davis Art, O:Fly 350.00
4 V:Dazzler NA panel 200.00
5 A:Spider Spry 125.00
6 V:Moon Men 125.00
7 A:Black Hood 150.00
8 A:Lancelot Strong/Shield 150.00
9 A:Lancelot Strong/Shield
    I:Cat Girl 125.00
10 A:Spider Spry 125.00
11 V:Rock Men. 75.00
12 V:Brute Invaders 75.00
13 I:Kim Brand 80.00
14 I:Fly-Girl(Kim Brand) 100.00
15 A:Spider 75.00
16 A:Fly-Girl 75.00
17 A:Fly-Girl 75.00
18 A:Fly-Girl 75.00
19 A:Fly-Girl 75.00
20 O:Fly-Girl. 80.00
21 A:Fly-Girl. 60.00
22 A:Fly-Girl. 60.00
23 A:Fly-Girl,Jaguar 60.00
24 A:Fly-Girl 60.00
25 A:Fly-Girl. 60.00

26 A:Fly-Girl,Black Hood 60.00
27 A:Fly-Girl,Black Hood 60.00
28 A:Black Hood 60.00
29 A:Fly-Girl,Black Hood 60.00
30 A:Fly-Girl,R:Comet 75.00
31 A:Black Hood, Shield, Comet . . 80.00
Becomes:

FLYMAN

ADVENTURES OF
THE JAGUAR
Archie Publications/
Radio Comics, 1961–63
1 I:Ralph Hardy/Jaguar. 300.00
2 10 cent cover. 150.00
3 Last 10 cent cover. 125.00
4 A:Cat-Girl 100.00
5 A:Cat-Girl 100.00
6 A:Cat-Girl 90.00
7 . . . . 75.00
8 . . . . 75.00
9 . . . . 75.00
10 . . . . 75.00
11 . . . . 75.00
12 A:Black Hood 75.00
13 A:Cat-Girl,A:Black Hood 75.00
14 A:Black Hood 75.00
15 V:Human Octopus,last issue . . 75.00

ADVENTURES OF
YOUNG DR. MASTERS
Archie Comics, 1964
1 . . . . 50.00
2 . . . . 25.00

ADVENTUROUS UNCLE
SCROOGE McDUCK
Gladstone, 1997
1 . . . . 3.00
2 Don Rosa, A Little Something
    Special 3.00
3 The Black Widow 3.00

AFTERMATH
Chaos! Comics, 2000
1 sequel to Armageddon. 3.00
1 premium. 10.00
Ashcan, Yellow. 10.00
Ashcan, Blue 25.00

AGAINST BLACKSHARD
Sirius Comics, 1986
1 3-D 3.00

AGENT: AMERICA
Awesome Entertainment, 1997
1 RLe 2.50
2 RLe,JSb,JLb,F:Supreme,
    V:Smash 2.50

AIRBOY
Eclipse, 1986–89
1 TT/TY,D:Golden Age Airboy
    O:New Airboy 6.00
2 TT/TY,I:Marisa,R:SkyWolf 5.00
3 A:The Heap 5.00
4 A:Misery. 5.00
5 DSt(c),R:Valkyrie 7.00

All comics prices listed are for *Near Mint* condition.

6 R:Iron Ace,I:Marlene 3.50
7 PG(c), ... 3.50
8 FH/TT(c) 3.50
9 R:Flying Fool, Riot, O'Hara
   Cocky, Judge & Turtle 3.00
10 I:Manic,D:Cocky, Judge & Turtle 3.00
11 O:Birdie 3.00
12 R:Flying Fool. 3.00
13 I:New Bald Eagle 3.00
14 A:Sky Wolf, Iron Ace 3.00
15 A:Ku Klux Klan 3.00
16 D:Manic,A:Ku Klux Klan 3.00
17 A:HarryS.Truman,Misery. 3.00
18 A:Gold.Age Black Angel 3.00
19 A:Gold.Age Rats 3.00
20 Rat storyline 3.00
21 I:Lester Mansfield, Artic
   Deathzone #1 . . . . 3.00
22 DSp,Artic Deathzone #2 . . . . . . 3.00
23 A:Gold.Age Black Angle, Artic
   Deathzone #3 . . . . 3.00
24 A: Heap 3.00
25 TY,I:Manure Man,A:Heap 3.00
26 R:Flying Dutchman 3.00
27 A:Iron Ace, Heap. 3.00
28 A:Heap 3.00
29 . . . . 3.00
30 A:Iron Ace; Sky Wolf story 3.00
31 A:Valkyrie; Sky Wolf story. 3.00
32 Hostage Virus, ... 3.00
33 DSp,SkyWolf sty,A:Sgt.Strike . . 3.00
34 DSp,A:La Lupina. 3.00
35 DSp,A:La Lupina, Sky Wolf 3.00
36 . . . . 3.00
37 DSp. 3.00
38 CI, Heap story. 3.00
39 CI, Heap story. 3.00
40 CI, Heap story. 3.00
41 V:Steel Fox, Golden Age rep.
   O:Valkyrie 3.00
42 A:Rackman 3.00
43 Sky Wolf sty, A:Flying Fool 3.00
44 A:Rackman 3.00
45 . . . . 3.00
46 EC,Airboy Diary #1 . . . . 3.00
47 EC,Airboy Diary #2 . . . . 3.00
48 EC,Airboy Diary #3 . . . . 3.00
49 EC,Airboy Diary #4 . . . . 3.00
50 AKu/NKu,double-size 4.00
Spec. Meets the Prowler 3.00
Spec. Mr. Monster 3.00
Spec. Vs Airmaidens 3.00

AIR FIGHTERS, SGT.
STRIKE SPECIAL
Eclipse, 1988
1 A:Airboy,Valkyrie 3.00

AIRMAIDENS SPECIAL
Eclipse Comics, 1987
1 A:Valkyrie. 3.00

AIRMAN
Malibu, 1993
1 I:Thresher 2.25

AIR WAR STORIES
Dell Publishing Co., 1964
1 . . . . 65.00
2 . . . . 50.00
3 thru 8 . . . . @40.00

AKEMI
Brainstorm Comics, 1997
1 . . . . 3.00

ALADDIN
Walt Disney
Prestige. Movie Adapt. 5.00

ALAN MOORE'S
AWESOME ADVENTURES
Awesome Entertainment, 1999
1 AMo 2.50
1a alternate AxR cover 7.00
2 F:Young Guns 3.00
Spec. Awesome Univ. Handbook. . . 3.00
Spec.A alternate AxR cover 3.00

ALAN MOORE'S GLORY
Comic Cavalcade, 2001
0 Park (c) 3.50
0a MHy (c) 3.50
0b Martin (c) 3.50
0c MMy (c) 3.50
0d white leather (c). 25.00
0e Lush Lands edition 6.00
0f Finch Prism Foil (c). 13.00
Avatar Press, 2001
Preview B&W 16-page. 3.00
Preview signed gold (c) 9.00
1 (of 4) JLi(c) 3.50
1a Finch (c). 3.50
1b Haley (c). 3.50
1c MMy(c). 3.50
1d Martin (c) 3.50
1e Wraparound (c) 3.50
1f Red velvet BPe (c) 25.00
1g Finch Prism Foil (c) 13.00
1h Andy Park (c). 6.00
1i SSh(c). 6.00
1j Royal Blue Edition 75.00
1k Defender (c). 6.00
2 AMo,MMy, Finch (c) 3.50
2a Park (c) 3.50
2b Haley (c) 3.50
2c Martin (c) 3.50
2d MMy (c) 3.50
2e Glory Freedom (c) 6.00
2f Hall painted (c) 6.00

ALARMING ADVENTURES
Harvey Publications, 1962–63
1 AW,RC,JSe 125.00
2 AW,BP,RC,JSe. 75.00
3 JSe 75.00

ALARMING TALES
Harvey Publications, 1957–58
1 JK,JK(c) 300.00
2 JK,JK(c) 225.00
3 JK. 175.00
4 JK,BP. 175.00
5 JK,AW 175.00
6 JK 175.00

ALBEDO, VOL. 3
Antarctic Press, 1994–95
Vol. 1 and II, See B&W
1 thru 4 Various Artists . . . . @3.00

ALBINO SPIDER
OF DAJETTE
Verotik, 1998
0 by Glenn Danzig
   & Wayne Robertson 3.00
0a alternate cover. 5.00
1 fan club cover 5.00

ALEISTER ARCANE
IDW Publishing, 2004
1 . . . . 4.00
2 thru 3 . . . . @4.00
TPB 18.00

ALIAS
Now Comics, 1990
1 . . . . 2.50
2 thru 5 . . . . @2.50

ALIAS: AGENT BRSITOW
Arcade Comics, 2003
0 RLd 3.00
0a photo (c). 3.00
0b Dlx. Foil photo (c) 10.00
0c Chromium (c) 15.00
0d sgn art (c) 50.00
1 . . . . 3.00
1a photo (c). 3.00
1b Dlx. Foil photo (c) 10.00

ALIAS: STORMFRONT
Now Comics
1 . . . . 2.50
2 . . . . 2.50

ALIEN ARENA
Atomeka, 2002
1 (of 2) 3.00
2 . . . . 3.00
1a thru 2a variant (c). . . . . @3.00

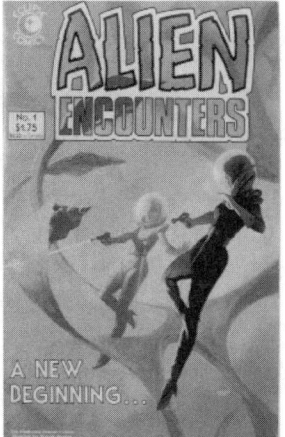

Alien Encounters #1 © Eclipse Comics

ALIEN ENCOUNTERS
Eclipse Comics, 1985–87
1 . . . . 5.00
2 . . . . 4.00
3 I Shot the Last Martian 4.00
4 JBo(c) 4.00
5 RCo,Night of the Monkey 4.00
6 Now You See It,Freefall. 4.00
7 . . . . 4.00
8 TY,Take One Capsule Every
   million Years,M.Monroe(c). 4.00
9 The Conquered 4.00
10 . . . . 4.00
11 TT,Old Soldiers 5.00
12 What A Relief,Eyes of
   the Sibyl. 5.00
13 GN,The Light at the End. 5.00

14 JRy,GN,TL,RT,Still born 5.00

ALIEN TERROR
Eclipse, 1986
3-D #1 Standard Procedure 3.00

Alien Worlds #5 © Pacific

ALIEN WORLDS
Pacific, 1982
1 AW,VM,NR 7.00
2 DSt 5.00
3 . . . . 4.00
4 DSt(i) 4.00
5 . . . . 4.00
6 . . . . 4.00
7 . . . . 4.00
3-D #1 AAd,DSt 7.00
Eclipse, 1985
8 AW 2.50
9 . . . . 2.50

[CAPTAIN JOHNER AND] ALIENS, THE
Gold Key, 1967
1 Rep. Magnus Robot Fighter . . . 50.00

ALISTER THE SLAYER
Midnight Press, 1995
1 I:Alister The Slayer 2.50
2 V:Lady Hate 2.50
3 JQ&JP(c) V:Subterranean
   Vampire Bikers 2.50

ALL AMERICAN SPORTS
Charlton, 1967
1 . . . . 40.00

ALL HALLOWS EVE
Innovation, 1991
1 . . . . 5.00

ALLEY OOP
Dell Publishing Co., 1962–63
1 . . . . 100.00
2 . . . . 75.00

ALLEY OOP ADVENTURES
Antarctic Press, 1998
1 . . . . 3.00
2 . . . . 3.00
3 I:Granny Green 3.00
TPB 11.00

ALLIES
Awesome Entertainment, 1999
1 RLe,AMo 2.50
1a alternate RLe cover 7.00

ALL NEW EXILES
Malibu Ultraverse, 1995–96
Infinity F:Juggernaut,Blaze 2.50
1 TKa,KeL,Beginning the Quest . . . 2.25
1a Computer painted cover (1:6) . . 2.50
1b signed edition 4.00
2 I:Hellblade, Phoenix flip issue . . . 2.25
3 TKa,KeL,Phoenix Resurrection . . 2.25
4 thru 11 . . . . @2.25

ALPHA KORPS
Diversity Comics, 1996
1 I:Alpha Korps 3.00
2 The Price of Freedom, pt.2 . . . . . 2.50
3 The Price of Freedom, pt.3 . . . . . 2.50
1 thru 3 signed . . . . @5.00
4 The Price of Freedom, pt.4 . . . . . 2.50

ALPHA WAVE
Darkline, 1987
1 . . . . 2.50

ALTER EGO
First, 1986
1 RTs, Ron Harris 2.50
2 thru 4 . . . . @2.50

ALVIN (& THE CHIPMUNKS)
Dell Publishing Co., 1962–73
1 . . . . 150.00
2 . . . . 100.00
3 . . . . 80.00
4 thru 10 . . . . @75.00
11 thru 20 . . . . @60.00
21 thru 28 . . . . @55.00
1 Alvin for President & his pals in
   Merry Christmas with Clyde
   Crashcup & Leonardo 60.00

AMAZING CHAN & THE CHAN CLAN
Gold Key, 1973
1 . . . . 50.00
2 . . . . 30.00
3 and 4 . . . . @25.00

AMAZING HEROES SWIMSUIT ANNUALS
Fantagraphics, 1990–93
1990 Spec. A:Dawn 25.00
1990 2nd printing 15.00
1991 A: Dawn 20.00
1992 A: Dawn 20.00
1993 A: Dawn 20.00

AMAZON, THE
Comico, 1989
1 . . . . 2.50

2 . . . . 2.50
3 end mini-series 2.50

AMELIA RULES!
Renaissance Press, 2001
1 by Jimmy Gownley 3.00
2 thru 11 . . . . @3.00
TPB Vol. 1 In with the Out Crowd . 15.00
TPB Orig. Art edition 60.00
TPB The Whole World's Crazy . . . 18.00

AMELIA RULES!: SUPERHEROES
Renaissance Press, 2003
1 thru 4 (of 6) . . . . @3.00

AMERICAN FLAGG
First, 1983–88
1 HC,I:American Flagg, Hard
   Times, pt.1 . . . . 6.00
2 HC,Hard Times,pt.2 . . . . 4.00
3 HC,Hard Times,pt.3 . . . . 4.00
4 HC,Southern Comfort,pt.1 . . . . . . 4.00
5 HC,Southern Comfort,pt.2 . . . . . . 4.00
6 HC,Southern Comfort,pt.3 . . . . . . 4.00
7 HC,State of the Union,pt.1 . . . . . . 4.00
8 HC,State of the Union,pt.2 . . . . . . 4.00
9 HC,State of the Union,pt.3 . . . . . . 4.00
10 HC,Solidarity-For Now,pt.1
   I:Luthor Ironheart 4.00
11 HC,Solidarity-For Now,pt.2 . . . . . 4.00
12 HC,Solidarity-For Now,pt.3 . . . . . 4.00
13 HC 4.00
14 PB 4.00
15 HC,American Flagg A Complete
   story,pt.1 . . . . 4.00
16 HC,Complete Story,pt.2 . . . . 4.00
17 HC,Complete Story,pt.3 . . . . 4.00
18 HC,Complete Story,pt.4 . . . . 4.00
19 HC,Bullets & Ballots, pt.1 . . . . . . 4.00
20 HC,LSn,Bullets & Ballots,pt.2 . . . 4.00
21 AMo,HC,LSn,Bull&Ballots,pt.3 . . 3.50
22 AMo,HC,LSn,Bull&Ballots,pt.4 . . 3.50
23 AMo,HC,LSn,England
   Swings, pt.1 . . . . 3.50
24 AMo,HC,England Swings,pt.2 . . . 3.50
25 AMo,HC,England Swings,pt.3 . . . 3.50
26 AMO,HC,England Swings,pt.4 . . . 3.50
27 AMo with Raul the Cat 3.50
28 BWg 3.50
29 JSon 3.50
30 JSon 3.50
31 JSon,O:Bob Violence 3.50
32 JSon,A:Bob Violence 3.50
33 A:Bob Violence 3.50
34 A:Bob Violence 3.50
35 A:Bob Violence 3.50
36 A:Bob Violence 3.50
37 A:Bob Violence 3.50
38 New Direction 3.50
39 JSon,A:Bob Violence 3.50
40 A:Bob Violence 3.50
41 . . . . 3.50
42 F:Luther Ironheart 3.50
43 . . . . 3.50
44 . . . . 3.50
45 . . . . 3.50
46 PS 3.50
47 PS 3.50
48 PS 3.50
49 . . . . 3.50
50 HC,last issue 3.50
Special #1 HC,I:Time2 . . . . 4.00
**See Also: Howard Chaykin's
American Flagg**

COLOR PUB.

AMERICOMICS
AC Comics, 1983
1 GP(c),O:Shade 5.00
2 . . . . 3.00
3 Blue Beetle 3.00
4 O:Dragonfly 3.00
5 and 6 . . . . @3.00
Spec.#1 Capt.Atom,BlueBeetle 3.00

AMERICA'S BEST COMICS
WildStorm/DC, 2000
Spec.#1 64-page 7.00
America's Best Comics Sketchbook 6.00
TPB 18.00

AMERICAN WOMAN
Antarctic Press, 1998
1 by Richard Stockton & Brian
   Denham 3.00
2 . . . . 3.00
2a deluxe 6.00

ANDROMEDA
Andromeda, 1995
1 I:Andromeda 2.50
2 Andromeda vs. Elite Force 2.50

ANGEL FIRE
Crusade Comics, 1997
1 BiT, from Shi #12, BiT(c) 3.00
1a with Roberto Flores cover 3.00
1b with photo cover 3.00
2 F:Shi 3.00
3 F:Shi, concl. 3.00

ANGEL OF DESTRUCTION
Malibu, 1996
1 . . . . 2.50

ANIMAL MYSTIC:
WATER WARS
Sirius, 1996
1 (of 6) DOe 4.00
2 thru 6 DOe . . . . @3.00
TPB rep. 20.00
TPB Klor. 10.00
GN Dark One's Animal
   Mystic Field Guide. 10.00

ANNE McCAFFREY'S
THE UNICORN GIRL
Big Entertainment, 1997
GN F:Acorna 22.00

ANNE RICE'S THE TALE
OF THE BODY THIEF
Sicilian Dragon, 1999
1 (of 12) 3.00
2 F:Lestat 3.00
3 thru 6 . . . . @3.00
7 F:Gretchen. 3.00
TPB 20.00
TPB Exclusive 20.00

ANT
Arcana Studios, 2004
1 . . . . 7.00
2 thru 4 . . . . @3.50

ANYTHING GOES
Fantagraphics, 1986
1 GK,FlamingCarot,Savage 4.00

2 S:AnM,JK,JSt,SK 3.50
3 DS,NA(c),A:Cerebus 3.50
4 . . . . 3.50
5 A:TMNTurtles. 5.00
6 . . . . 3.00

Ape Nation #4 © Adventure Comics

APE NATION
Adventure Comics, 1991
1 Aliens land on Planet of
   the Apes 3.00
2 General Ollo. 3.00
3 V:Gen.Ollo,Danada 2.50
4 D:Danada. 2.50

APOLLO SMILE
Eagle Wing, 1998
1 When the Levee Breaks 3.00
2 When the Levee Breaks, pt.2 . . . 3.00
3 When the Levee Breaks, pt.3 . . . 3.00

ARACHNAPHOBIA
Walt Disney, 1990
1 Movie Adapt 6.00
1a Newsstand 3.00

ARACHNID FOUNDATION
Quantum Comics, 1998
1 . . . . 3.00

ARAKNIS
Mushroom Comics, 1995–96
1 I:Araknis, Shades of Evil pt.1 . . . 3.50
2 Shades of Evil pt.2. . . . . 3.50
3 with pin-ups 2.50
4 . . . . 2.50

ARAKNIS
Mushroom Comics, 1996
0 Michael & Mario Ortiz 3.00
0 signed 4.00
1 . . . . 2.50
1 special edition 10.00
Mystic Comics
2 thru 6 . . . . @2.50

ARAKNIS: RETRIBUTION
Morning Star Productions, 1997
1 (of 4) by Michael & Mario Ortiz . . 2.50
1 signed 10.00

2 thru 4 . . . . @2.50

ARAKNIS:
SHADES OF EVIL
Morning Star Productions
1 thru 4 . . . . @2.50

ARCHANGELS: THE SAGA
Eternal Studios
1 I:Cameron 2.50
2 V:Demons 2.50
3 and 4 . . . . @2.75
5 and 6 . . . . @2.50
7 . . . . 3.50
8 . . . . 4.50

ARCHARD'S AGENTS
Crossgen Comics, 2002
1 CDi(s) spin-off from Ruse 3.50

ARCHER & ARMSTRONG
Valiant, 1992
0 JiS(s),BWS,BL,I&O:Archer,
   I:Armstrong,The Sec 3.00
0 Gold Ed. 5 . . . . 4.00
1 FM(c),B:JiS(s),BWS,BL,Unity #3,
   A:Eternal Warrior. 2.25
2 WS(c),E:JiS(s),BWS,BL,Unity
   #11,2nd A:Turok,A:X-O 2.25
3 B:BWS(a&s), BWi, V:Sect in
   Rome 2.25
4 BWS,BWi,V:Sect in Rome 2.25
5 BWS,BWi,I:Andromeda 2.25
6 BWS,BWi, A:Andromeda,
   V:Medoc 2.25
7 BWS,ANi,BWi,V:Sect in England. 2.25
8 BWS,as Eternal Warrior #8,
   Three Musketeers,I:Ivan 2.25
9 BCh,BWi,in Britain 2.25
10 BWS,A:Ivar 2.25
11 BWS,A:Solar,Ivar 2.25
12 BWS,V:The Avenger 2.25
13 B:MBn(s),RgM,In Los Angeles . . 2.25
14 In Los Angeles 2.25
15 E:MBn(s),In LasVegas, I:Duerst . 2.25
16 V:Sect 2.25
17 B:MBn(s),In Florida. 2.25
18 MV,in Heaven 2.25
19 MV,V:MircoboticCult,D:Duerst. . 2.25
20 MV,Chrismas Issue 2.25
21 MV,A:Shadowman,Master
   Darque. 2.25
22 MV,A:Shadowman,Master
   Darque,w/Valiant Era card. 2.25
23 MV, ... 2.25
24 MV, ... 2.25
25 MV,A:Eternal Warrior 2.25
26 Chaos Effect-Gamma #4, A:Ivar,
   Et. Warrior 2.25

ARCHIE
Archie Publications, 1981
1 thru 300 see Golden Age
301 thru 325. . . . . @6.50
326 Cheryl Blossom. 15.00
327 thru 335. . . . . @6.50
336 Michael Jackson 7.00
337 thru 400. . . . . @6.50
401 thru 429. . . . . @5.00
430 thru 529. . . . . @2.50
530 thru 552. . . . . @2.50
Archie's Christmas Stocking #4 . . . . 2.50
Archie's Christmas Stocking #5 . . . . 2.50
Archie's Christmas Stocking #6 . . . . 2.75
Archie's Christmas Stocking #7 . . . . 3.00
Archie's Spring Break Spec.1 . . . . . 2.50
Archie's Spring Break Spec.2 . . . . . 2.50

COLOR PUB.

Archie's Spring Break Spec.3 . . . . . 2.75
Archie's Spring Break Spec.4(1999) 2.75
Archie's Spring Break Spec.5(2000) 2.50
Archie's Vacation Spec.#4 . . . . 2.50
Archie's Vacation Spec.#5 . . . . 2.50
Archie's Vacation Spec.#6 . . . . 2.50
Archie's Vacation Spec.#7 . . . . 2.50
Archie's Vacation Spec.#8 . . . . 2.50

ARCHIE AND FRIENDS
Archie Publications, 1992—98
1 thru 10 . . . . @5.00
11 thru 14 . . . . @4.00
15 Babewatch 6.00
16 thru 19 . . . . @4.00
20 Archies Band 5.00
21 thru 48 . . . . @2.50
49 thru 56 Archie & Friends, Featuring
  Josie and the Pussy Cats . . . @2.50
57 thru 86 . . . . @2.50

Archie and Me #159
© Archie Publications

ARCHIE AND ME
Archie Publications, 1964–87
1 . . . . 250.00
2 . . . . 125.00
3 . . . . 75.00
4 . . . . 60.00
5 . . . . 60.00
6 thru 10 . . . . @50.00
11 thru 20 . . . . @25.00
21 thru 26 . . . . @30.00
27 Superheroes Groovymas 30.00
28 thru 100 . . . . @10.00
101 thru 162 . . . . @8.00

ARCHIE AS PUREHEART THE POWERFUL
Archie Publications, 1966–67
1 superhero parody 150.00
2 . . . . 100.00
3 thru 6 Captain Pureheart . . . . @75.00

ARCHIE AT RIVERDALE HIGH
Archie Publications, 1972
1 . . . . 100.00
2 . . . . 50.00
3 . . . . 35.00
4 . . . . 25.00
5 . . . . 25.00
6 thru 10 . . . . @22.00

11 thru 30 . . . . @15.00
31 thru 46 . . . . @11.00
47 in drag 7.00
48 thru 88 . . . . @6.00
89 & 90 Cheryl Blossmos Band . @15.00
91 . . . . 6.00
92 Cheryl Blossom 11.00
93 thru 95 . . . . @6.00
96 Cheryl Blossom 11.00
97 & 98 . . . . @6.00
99 Cheryl Blossom 11.00
100 thru 102 . . . . @5.00
103 Archie Dates Cheryl Blossom . 11.00
104 thru 113 . . . . @7.00

ARCHIE COMICS DIGEST
Archie Comics Digest, 1973
1 . . . . 125.00
2 . . . . 75.00
3 thru 5 . . . . @50.00
6 thru 10 . . . . 30.00
11 thru 32 . . . . @20.00
33 The Fly 25.00
34 thru 135 . . . . @6.00
136 Katy Keene 7.00
137 thru 204 . . . . @4.00

ARCHIE MEETS THE PUNISHER
Archie/Marvel, 1994
1-shot crossover, same contents
  as Punisher meets Archie 7.00

ARCHIE'S MADHOUSE
Archie Publications, 1959–69
1 . . . . 350.00
2 . . . . 175.00
3 thru 5 . . . . @125.00
6 thru 10 . . . . @100.00
11 thru 16 . . . . @75.00
17 thru 21 . . . . @50.00
22 I:Sabrina 350.00
23 thru 25 Sabrina . . . . @125.00
26 thru 28 . . . . @
29 thru 30 . . . . @30.00
31 thru 33 Sabrina . . . . @60.00
34 . . . . 25.00
35 B 35.00
36 Salem Cat & Sabrina 100.00
37 Sabrina 60.00
38 thru 66 . . . . 30.00

ARCHIE'S PAL JUGHEAD SEE: JUGHEAD

ARCHIE'S SUPERHERO MAGAZINE
Archie Publications, 1979
1 JSm/SK,Rept.Double of Capt.
  Strong #1,FLy,Black Hood 25.00
2 GM,NA/DG,AMc,I:'70's Black
  Hood, Superhero rept 30.00

ARCHIE'S TV LAUGH-OUT
Archie Publications, 1969–86
1 . . . . 125.00
2 giant 75.00
3 thru 6 giant . . . . @40.00
7 Josie 100.00
8 thru 22 . . . . @45.00
23 thru 41 . . . . @25.00
42 thru 80 . . . . @15.00
81 thru 90 . . . .
91 Cheryl Blossom & 22.00
92 thru 99 . . . . @12.00

100 Michael Jackson 20.00
101 thru 106 . . . . @12.00

ARCHIE 3000
Archie Publications, 1989–1991
1 thru 16 . . . . 2.00

ARCHIE'S WEIRD MYSTERIES
Archie Comics, 1999
1 from animated series 4.00
2 Shriek 3.00
3 thru 25 . . . . @3.00
Becomes

ARCHIE'S MYSTERIES
26 thru 34 . . . . @3.00

ARENA, THE
Alchemy, 1990
1 . . . . 2.50
1a signed, numbered, limited 3.00
2 . . . . 2.50

ARIANE & BLUEBEARD
Eclipse, 1988
Spec. CR 4.00

ARISTOKITTENS, THE
Gold Key, 1971–75
1 Disney 40.00
2 thru 9 . . . . @25.00

ARKANIUM
Dreamwave, 2002
1 triple gatefold cover 3.00
2 thru 6 . . . . @3.00

ARMAGEDDON
Chaos! Comics, 1999
1 (of 4) F:Lady Death, Evil Ernie . . 3.00
1a Premium edition 10.00
2 O:Chaos 3.00
3 . . . . 3.00
4 concl 3.00
TPB 13.00

ARMAGEDDON FACTOR
AC Comics, 1987
1 Sentinels of Justice 2.50
2 . . . . 2.50
3 (1990) 4.00

ARMOR
Continuity, 1985
1 TGr,NA,A:Silver Streak,
  silver logo 5.00
1a 2nd printing,red logo 3.00
2 TGr,NA(c) 3.00
3 TGr,NA(c) 3.00
4 TGr,NA(c) 3.00
5 BS,NA(c) 3.00
6 TVE,NA(c) 3.00
7 NA(c) 3.00
8 FS,NA(c) 3.00
9 FS,NA&KN(c) 3.00
10 FS,NA&KN(c) 3.00
11 SDr(i),KN(c) 3.00
12 KN(c) 3.00
13 NA(c),direct sales 3.00
14 KN(c), newsstand 3.00
[2nd Series]
1 V:Hellbender,Trading Card 3.00

[3rd Series, Deathwatch 2000]
1 Deathwatch 2000 pt.3,w/card . . . 4.00
2 Deathwatch 2000 pt.9,w/card . . . 3.00
3 Deathwatch 2000 pt.15,w/card . . 3.00
4 . . . . 3.00
5 Rise of Magic. 3.00
6 Rise of Magic. 3.00

ARMORED TROOPER VOTOMS
CPM Comics, 1996
1 TEI 3.00
2 TEI 3.00
3 TEI 3.00
4 TEI 3.00
GN Supreme Survivor 17.00

ARMORINES
Valiant, 1994
0 (from X-O #25),Card Stock (c),
  Diamond Distributors `Fall Fling'
  Retailer Meeting 2.50
0a Gold Ed. 3.00
1 JGz(s),JCf,B:White Death 2.25
2 JGz(s),JCf,E:White Death 2.25
3 JGz(s),JCf,V:Spider Aliens. 2.25
4 JCf, V: Spider Aliens 2.25
5 JCf, Chaos Effect-Delta #2,
  A:H.A.R.D. Corp 2.25
6 Spider Alien Mothership. 2.25
7 Rescue. 2.25
8 Rescue in Iraq 2.25
9 . . . . 2.25
10 Protect Fidel Castro 2.25
11 V: Spider Super Suit 2.25
12 F: Sirot 2.25
Yearbook I:Linoff 3.00

VOLUME 2
1 48-pg. 4.00
2 . . . . 4.00
3 and 4 . . . . @2.50

ARMY ATTACK
Charlton, 1964
1 SG 60.00
2 SG 40.00
3 SG 35.00
4 thru 47 . . . . @30.00

ARMY OF DARKNESS: ASHES 2 ASHES
Devil's Due Publishing, 2004
1 . . . . 3.00
2 thru 4 . . . . @3.00

ARMY WAR HEROES
Charlton, 1963–70
1 . . . . 60.00
2 . . . . 35.00
3 thru 21 . . . . @30.00
22 GS,O&I:Iron Corporal 35.00
23 thru 38. . . . . @20.00

ARROW
Malibu, 1992
1 V:Dr.Sheldon,A:Man O'War 2.25

ARROWSMITH
Wildstorm/DC, 2003
1 (of 6) KBk(s),CPa 3.00
2 KBk(s),mystical aviator 3.00
3 KBk(s) thru 6 . . . . @3.00
TPB So Smart in Fine Uniforms . . 15.00
Spec. Arrowsmith/Astro City 3.00

Arrow #1 © Malibu

ARTESIA
Sirius, 1999
1 (of 6) by Mark Smylie 3.00
1a limited edition. 10.00
2 thru 6 . . . . @3.00
Ann.#1 . . . . 3.50
Ann.#2 . . . . 4.00
TPB Vol. 1 . . . . 20.00

ARTESIA AFIELD
Sirius, 2000
1 (of 6) by Mark Smylie 3.00
1a Limited Ed. 6.00
2 thru 6 . . . . @3.00
Annual #3 Artesia. 5.00
TPB Vol. 3 Artesia Afire 25.00

ARTESIA AFIRE
Archaia Studios Press, 2003
1 (of 6) by Mark Smylie 4.00
2 thru 4 . . . . @4.00
TPB Vol. 1 . . . . 25.00
TPB Artesia Afield 25.00
Map Set Artesia: Know World 25.00

ASH
Event Comics, 1994
1 JQ,JP,Fire and Crossfire,pt.1. . . 12.00
1a David Finch/Batt(c) 3.00
1b omnichrome commemorative . 15.00
1c omnichrom signed & numbered 30.00
2 JQ,JP,Fire and Crossfire,pt.2. . . . 7.00
2a David Finch/Batt (c). 3.00
3 JQ,JP,Secret of Origin 4.50
4 I:Actor 3.00
5 I:New Character. 3.00
6 V:Gabriel 3.00
0 Red Laser ed., Current Ash (c) . 10.00
0 Red Laser ed., Future Ash (c) . . 10.00
TPB rep. #1–#5 . . . . 15.00
TPB Vol. 1, JQ,JP,sgn. lim. 35.00

ASH: CINDER AND SMOKE
Event Comics, 1997
1 MWa,BAu,HuR,JP 3.00
1a autographed virgin JQ cover . . 10.00
1b signed limited edition 12.00
2 HuR(c) 3.00
2 JQ(c) 3.00

3 (of 6) JQ&JP(c) 3.00
4 (of 6) JQ&JP(c) 3.00
5 (of 6) JQ&JP(c) 3.00
6 (of 6) JQ&JP(c) 3.00
3a thru 6a variant JP&HuR(c)s . . @3.00

ASH FILES, THE
Event Comics, 1997
1 JQ,JP. 3.00
1 signed, limited 20.00

ASH: FIRE AND CROSSFIRE
Event Comics, 1998
1 (of 5) JQ,JP 3.00
1a signed & numbered 25.00
2 . . . . 3.00

ASH: THE FIRE WITHIN
Event Comics
2 JQ,JP. 3.00
3 JQ,JP, Ash Rooftop cover 3.00
3a JQ,JP, Ash Firefighter cover . . . 3.00

ASH/22 BRIDES
Event Comics, 1996
1 FaN,HuR,JP. 3.00

ASPEN
Aspen 2003
1 Fathom. 5.00
1a variant (c). 20.00
2 Fathom. 3.50
2a San Diago 20.00
3 . . . . 3.00
3a Chicago 10.00
Aspen extended edition 6.00

ASSASSIN
Archangel Studios, 2003
1 (of 4) 3.00
1a variant (c). 3.00
2 . . . . 3.00

ASSASSIN, INC.
Solson
1 thru 4 . . . . @3.00

ASSASSIN SCHOOL
APC, 2003
1 . . . . 3.50
2 thru 5 . . . . @3.50
S.O.S.(Super one-shot) 6.00
TPB Vol. 1 . . . . 20.00

Vol. 2 (2004)
0 . . . . 3.00
1 thru 6 . . . . @3.50
TPB Vol. 2 . . . . 20.00

ASTER
Entity Comics, 1995
0 O:Aster the Celestial Knight 4.50
1 I:Celestial Knight 5.00
1b 2nd printing 3.00
2 . . . . 3.50
3 V:Tolmek 3.25
3a Variant cover 7.00
4 Final Issue 3.00
TPB Rep.#1–#4 + pin-up gallery . . 13.00

ASTER THE LAST CELESTIAL KNIGHT
Entity Comics, 1995
1 R:Aster Chromium Cover 3.00
1a Clear Chromium Edition 4.00
1b Holo Chrome Edition 5.00
2 World Defender 3.00

ASTRO BOY
Gold Key, 1965
1 I:Astro Boy 700.00

ASTRO BOY
Now
Prev. Original Astro Boy
18 . . . . 3.00
19 . . . . 3.00
20 . . . . 3.00

ASTRO CITY
Wildstorm/DC, 2004
Astro City Spec. (2004) 4.00
Spec. A Visitor's Guide (2004) 6.00

ASTRO CITY: LOCAL HEROES
Homage/DC, 2003
1 (of 5) KBk,BA. 3.00
2 thru 5 KBk,BA . . . . @3.00

ASYLUM
Pendragon, 1995
1 . . . . 3.00
2 . . . . 3.00
3 three stories. 3.00

ASYLUM
Maximum Press, 1995
1 Warchild, Beanworld, Avengelyne, Battlestar Galactica 3.00
2 I:Deathkiss. 3.00
3 . . . . 3.00
4 RLd,A:Cybrid 3.00
5 I:Black Seed. 3.00
6 R:Steve Austin & Jaime Sommers 3.00
7 RLe,F:Bloodwulf 3.00
8 RLd 3.00
9 RLd 3.00
10 . . . . 3.00
11 . . . . 3.00
12 MMy,F:Blindside 3.00
13 . . . . 3.00

ATLAS
Avatar Press, 2002
1 Gossett (c) 3.50
1b thru 1e variant (c)s. . . . . @3.50
2 Brooks (c) 3.50
2b variant (c). 3.50

ATOM ANT
Gold Key, 1966
1 . . . . 500.00

ATOM-AGE COMBAT
Fago Magazines, 1958–59
1 . . . . 300.00
2 . . . . 250.00
3 . . . . 225.00

ATOMIC RABBIT
Charlton Comics, 1955–58
1 . . . . 350.00
2 . . . . 150.00
3 thru 10 . . . . @100.00
11 . . . . 150.00
Becomes:

ATOMIC BUNNY
12 . . . . 150.00
13 thru 18. . . . . @75.00
19 Dec., 1959 . . . . 75.00

ATOMICS, THE
AAA Pop Comics, 1999
1 by Mike Allred 3.00
2 Zapman 3.00
3 Mutant Street Beatniks 3.00
4 refugees from the Innerverse . . . 3.00
5 The Light 3.00
6 The Physical 3.00
7 I:The Skunk 3.00
8 F:The Laser 3.00
9 taken hostage 3.00
10 . . . . 3.00
11 Heroes divided 3.00
12 with poster 3.50
13 World of Savage Dragon 3.50
14 World of Savage Dragon,pt.4 . . 3.50
15 World of Savage Dragon,pt.5 . . 3.50
16 World of Savage Dragon,pt.6 . . 3.50
King Size Giant 10.00
King-Size Spec. Lessons in Light Lava & Lasers 9.00
King-Size Spec. Jigsaw 10.00
King-Size Vol. 3 . . . . 9.00
King-Size Vol. 4, 80-page 9.00

Atomik Angels 3
© Crusade Entertainment

ATOMIK ANGELS
Crusade Entertainment, 1996
1 BiT 3.00
1 variant cover (1:25) 5.00
2 BiT 3.00
3 BiT 3.00
4 BiT, conclusion. 3.00

AUTHORITY, THE
WildStorm/DC, 1999
1 WEl(s),BHi,PNe 17.00
2 WEl(s),BHi,PNe,V:Kaizen Gamorra. 11.00
3 WEl(s),BHi,PNe,destruction. . . . 11.00

4 WEl(s),BHi,PNe,save L.A. 11.00
5 WEl(s),BHi,PNe,Swiftships,pt.1 . 11.00
6 WEl(s),BHi,PNe 7.00
7 WEl(s),BHi,PNe 7.00
8 WEl(s),BHi,PNe 7.00
9 WEl(s),BHi,PNe,OuterDark,pt.1. . 7.00
10 WEl(s),BHi,PNe,OuterDark,pt.2 . 7.00
11 WEl(s),BHi,PNe,OuterDark,pt.3 . 7.00
12 WEl(s),BHi,PNe,OuterDark,pt.4 . 7.00
13 MMr(s),TvS,Nativity,pt.1 . . . . . . 9.00
14 MMr(s),TvS,Nativity,pt.2 . . . . . . 6.00
15 MMr(s),TvS,Nativity,pt.3 . . . . . . 6.00
16 MMr(s),TvS,Nativity,pt.4 . . . . . . 6.00
17 MMr(s),TvS,Earth Inferno,pt.1 . . 6.00
18 MMr(s),TvS,Earth Inferno,pt.2 . . 6.00
19 MMr(s),TvS,Earth Inferno,pt.3 . . 6.00
20 MMr(s),TvS,Earth Inferno,pt.4 . . 6.00
21 JMC,All Tomorrow's Parties 6.00
22 MMr(s),TvS,Brave New World, pt.1 (of 4). 6.00
23 TPe(s),Brave-World,pt.2 . . . . . . 6.00
24 TPe(s),BU:Establishment,40-pg . 3.50
25 TPe(s),Re-Space 3.50
26 TPe(s),F:Old Authority 3.50
27 MMr(s),New World Order,pt.2 . . . 3.50
28 MMr(s),AAd,F:Seth 3.50
29 New World Order,pt.4 . . . . 3.50
Ann. 2000 #1, Devil's Night x-over, pt.2 . . . . 5.00
GN The Authority: Kev (2002) 5.00
GN Scorched Earth 5.00
TPB The Authority: Relentless. . . . 18.00
TPB Under New Management. 18.00
TPB Widescreen, 48-page. 6.00
TPB Earth Inferno (2002). 15.00
TPB Transfer of Power (2002). . . . 18.00
Volume 2
1 DT,F:Jack Hawksmoor, etc. 3.00
2 thru 13 DT . . . . @3.00
14 WPo,Jack Hawksmore origin . . . 3.00
Spec. #0, 40-pg.. . . . . 3.00
X-Mas Spec. The Authority/Lobo x-over, 48-pg. (2003). 5.00
TPB Harsh Realities 15.00

AUTHORITY, THE: MORE KEV
Wildstorm/DC, 2004
1 (of 4) GEn(s),GF 3.00
2 thru 4 GEn(s),GF . . . . @3.00

AUTHORITY, THE: REVOLUTION
Wildstorm/DC, 2004
1 . . . . 3.00

AUTOMATIC KAFKA
WildStorm/DC, 2002
1 JoC, Eye of the Storm 3.00
2 JoC,NPS agents 3.00
3 JoC,TV game show host 3.00
4 JoC, ... 3.00
5 JoC, ... 3.00
6 JoC, ... 3.00
7 JoC,who is Galaxia 3.00
8 JoC 3.00
9 JoC 3.00

AVENGEBLADE
Maximum Press, 1996
1 RLe 3.00
2 RLe 3.00

AVENGELYNE
Maximum Press, 1995
1 RLd,I:Avengelyne Dir ed. 12.00
1a Newstand Edition. 5.00

1b Holochrome Edition 15.00
1 gold edition 10.00
2 V:B'Lial. 4.00
3 I:Magogi. 4.00
3 variant cover, pin-up 5.00
TPB rep. #1–#3 . . . . 10.00

Regular Series, 1996
0 RLd,O:Avengelyne. 5.00
1 RLd,BNa,F:Devlin 4.00
1 variant photo cover 4.00
2 I:Darkchylde. 10.00
2a variant photo cover 12.00
3 . . . . 3.50
4 A:Cybrid 3.50
5 A:Cybrid, ... 3.50
6 RLd,F:Divinity 3.50
7 RLd,F:Divinity 3.50
8 RLd, ... 3.50
9 RLd, ... 3.50
10 BNa,The Possession, pt.1 . . . . 3.50
11 BNa,The Possession, pt.2 . . . . 3.50
12 BNa,The Possession, pt.3 . . . . 3.50
13 BNa,The Possession, pt.4 . . . . 3.50
14 A:Bloodwulf 3.50
15 A:Glory, Prophet 3.50
Swimsuit Edition. 3.50
Swimsuit book, American
    Entertainment exclusive 7.50

AVENGELYNE
Awesome Entertainment, 1999
Prelude 3.00
1 RLe,RNa 3.00
1a, b & c variant covers 3.00
2 RLe, ... 3.00
3 . . . . 3.00
Spec. Swimsuit, 1999 . . . . 3.50
Spec.#1-shot Demonslayer (2000) . 3.00
Spec.#1a Demonslayer variant (c) . 3.00
Spec.#1b Demonslayer variant (c) . 3.00
Spec.#1c Demonslayer variant (c). . 3.00

AVENGELYNE: ARMAGEDDON
Maximum Press, 1996–97
1 (of 3) RLd. 3.00
2 RLd, ... 3.00
3 BNa,ScC, finale 3.00

AVENGELYNE: BAD BLOOD
Avatar, 2000
1 Matt Haley (c) 3.50
1a Al Rio (c) 3.50
1b Tim Vigil (c) 3.50
1c prism foil (c) previews excl. . . . 13.00
1d Al Rio velvet (c) 20.00
1e leather (c). 25.00
1f platinum (c). 7.95
1g Ruby Red ed.. . . . . 20.00
1h Royal Blue edition 75.00
2 . . . . 3.50
2a Haley (c) 3.50
2b Moline (c). 3.50
Prelude Rick Lyon (c) 5.00
Prelude Al Rio (c) 5.00
Prelude Bikini (c) 6.00
Prelude prism foil(c) 16-page. 13.00
Prelude variant SSh(c). 6.00

AVENGELYNE BIBLE: REVELATIONS
Maximum Press
one-shot RLd, ... 3.50

AVENGELYNE: DARK DEPTHS
Avatar Press, 2001
1 (of 2) Rio(c) 3.50
1a MMy(c). 3.50
1b Martin (c) 3.50
1c blue velvet (c) 25.00
1d prism foil exclusive (c) 13.00
1e Heavenly Body edition. 6.00
1f Royal Blue (c). 75.00
2 (of 2) Rio(c) 3.50
2a MMy(c). 3.50
2b Lyon (c) 3.50
2c Blue leather (c) 25.00
1/2 Rio (c) 16-page 5.00
1/2 Lloyd painted (c) 5.00
1/2 Frillion (c). 5.00
1/2 Midnight Prayer (c) 6.00
1/2 Prism foil exclusive (c). 13.00

AVENGELYNE: DEADLY SINS
Maximum Press, 1996
1 RLd (c). 3.00
1 photo (c). 3.00
2 RLd(c) 3.00

AVENGELYNE: DRAGON REALM
Avatar Press, 2001
1/2 Rio (c) 5.00
1/2 Carrie Hall (c) 5.00
1/2 Lloyd (c) 5.00
1/2 Martin (c). 5.00
1/2 Dying Breath ed. 6.00
1/2 Prism foil ed. 13.00
1 (of 2) Rio(c) 3.50
1a Martin (c) 3.50
1b Vigil (c). 3.50
1c red leather (c) 25.00
1d bondage (c) 6.00
1e prism foil (c) 13.00
1f venomous edition 6.00
1g venomous emerald foil 14.00
1h Fearless edition 5.00
2 Rio(c) 3.50
2a Martin (c) 3.50
2b MMy (c) 3.50
2c Shaw (c). 3.50
2d Ron Adrian (c). 6.00

AVENGELYNE/GLORY
Maximum Press, 1995
1 V:B'Lial. 4.00
1a variant cover 5.00
Swimsuit Spec. #1 . . . . 3.00

AVENGELYNE/GLORY: THE GODYSSEY
Maximum Press, 1996
1 RLd,BNa 3.00
2 thru 5 RLd . . . . @3.00

AVENGELYNE/PANDORA
Avatar, 2000
Spec. x-over. 3.50
Spec.Preview exclusive 3.50
Spec.Preview Bikini ed. 6.00
Spec.McDaniel (c) 6.00
Spec.Previews exlusive Prism ed.. . 13.00
Spec.Red Velvet 25.00
Spec.Ruby Red edition 20.00
Spec.Royal Blue 75.00

AVENGELYNE/POWER
Maximum Press, 1995–96
1 RLd,V:Hollywood 3.00
1 variant cover 3.50
2 RLd(c) 3.00
3 . . . . 3.00
3a photo (c). 3.00

Avengelyne/Prophet #1
© Maximum Press

AVENGELYNE/PROPHET
Maximum Press, 1996
1 RLd,BNa,MD2 . . . . 3.00
Awesome Entertainment, 2000
Rage of Furies #1 RLe(c) 3.00
    #1a IaC(c) 3.00
    #1b Grant(c) 3.00
    #1c Walker Bros.(c). 3.00
    #1d Wizard world ed. 5.00
    #1e Wizard world, signed 10.00

AVENGELYNE: REVELATION
Avatar, 2000
1 Rio (c) 3.50
1a Haley (c) 3.50
1b Wraparound (c) 3.50
1c leather (c). 25.00
1d Matt Martin (c) 6.00
1e royal blue (c) 75.00
Previews prism foil (c) 13.00
Prelude Lyon (c). 6.00
Prelude platinum signed 11.00

AVENGELYNE: SERAPHACIDE
Avatar Press, 2001
1/2 Lyon (c). 5.00
1/2 Martin (c). 5.00
1/2 Rio (c) 5.00
1/2 Shaw (c) 5.00
1/2 Bound edition 6.00
1/2 Pax Romana (c) 6.00
1/2 Ron Adrian (c). 6.00
1 (of 2) Rio (c). 3.50
1a Hall (c) 3.50
1b Martin (c) 3.50
1c Lyon (c) 3.50
1d White Velvet (c) 25.00
1e Adam & Eve edition. 6.00
1f Hard Woman (c) 6.00
1g Bikini (c). 6.00

COLOR PUB.

AVENGELYNE/SHI
Avatar Press, 2001
1/2 RLd (c) 16-page 4.00
1/2a Rio (c) 4.00
1/2b MMy (c) 4.00
1/2c Martin (c) 4.00
1/2d Victory (c) 6.00
1/2e Sean Shaw, Cross cover 6.00
1 Finch (c) x-over 3.50
1a Martin (c) 3.50
1b Rio (c) 3.50
1c Shaw (c) 3.50
1d BTi wraparound (c) 3.50
1e Red Leather (c) 25.00
1f Prism foil (c) 13.00
1g Royal Blue edition 75.00
1h Waller (c) 6.00
1i Face off cover 6.00
1j ruby red edition 25.00

AVENGELYNE/SUPREMA
Awesome Entertainment, 2000
Rage of Furies #1 (2000) 4.00
  1a Wizard world ed. 5.00
  1b signed 10.00

AVENGELYNE/ WARRIOR NUN AREALA
Maximum Press, 1997
Spec. 3.00
Awesome Entertainment, 1997
Spec. #2 The Nazarene Affair 3.00

AVENGERS, THE
Gold Key, 1968
1 . . . . 400.00

AWESOME
Awesome Entertainment, 1997
Holiday Spec. #1 . . . . 2.50
Holiday Spec.'99 . . . . 5.00
Spring '99 Tourbook 5.00

AXA
Eclipse, 1987
1 Axa the Adopted 2.50
2 . . . . 2.50

AXEL PRESSBUTTON
Eclipse, 1984
1 BB(c),Origin 3.00
2 . . . . 3.00
3 thru 4 . . . . @3.00
Becomes:

PRESSBUTTON

AXIS ALPHA
Axis Comics, 1994
1 LSn,I:BEASTIES,Dethgrip,
  Shelter,W 3.00

AYA
Studio G, 2003
1 . . . . 3.00
2 thru 4 . . . . @3.00

AZTEC ACE
Eclipse, 1984
1 NR(i),I:AztecAce 3.50
2 NR(i) 3.50
3 thru 9 NR(i) . . . . @3.00
10 NR(i) 3.00
11 . . . . 3.50

---

12 thru 15 . . . . @2.50

Babes of Broadway #1
© Broadway

BABES OF BROADWAY
Broadway, 1996
1 . . . . 3.00

BABY HUEY, THE BABY GIANT
Harvey Publications, 1956–80
1 . . . . 800.00
2 . . . . 350.00
3 Anti-Pep Pills 250.00
4 . . . . 150.00
5 . . . . 150.00
6 thru 10 . . . . @100.00
11 thru 20 . . . . @75.00
21 thru 40 . . . . @50.00
41 thru 60 . . . . @35.00
61 thru 79 . . . . @30.00
80 . . . . 30.00
81 thru 95 giant size . . . . @35.00
96 Giant size 30.00
97 Giant size 30.00
98 . . . . 20.00
99 . . . . 15.00

BABY HUEY AND PAPA
Harvey Publications, 1962–68
1 . . . . 275.00
2 . . . . 125.00
3 . . . . 75.00
4 . . . . 75.00
5 . . . . 75.00
6 thru 10 . . . . @50.00
11 thru 20 . . . . @35.00
21 thru 33 . . . . @25.00

BABY HUEY DUCKLAND
Harvey Publications, 1962–66
1 . . . . 200.00
2 . . . . 100.00
3 . . . . 100.00
4 . . . . 100.00
5 . . . . 100.00
6 thru 10 . . . . @50.00
11 thru 20 . . . . @30.00
21 thru 33 . . . . @25.00

BACHELOR FATHER
Dell Publishing Co., 1962
1 . . . . 125.00
2 . . . . 100.00

BACK TO THE FUTURE
Harvey, 1991
1 Chicago 1927 . . . . 3.00
2 Cretaceous Period 3.00
3 World War I 3.00
4 Doc Retires 3.00

BAD BOY
Oni Press, 1997
GN Frank Miller & Simon Bisley . . . 5.00

BAD COMPANY
Quality, 1988
1 thru 19 . . . . @3.00

BAD EGGS
Acclaim, 1996
1 thru 4 BL,DP,That Dirty Yellow
  Mustard . . . . @3.00

BADGER
Capital, 1983
1 JBt,I:Badger,Ham,Daisy Yak,Yeti . 5.00
2 JBt,I:Riley,A:YakYeti 4.00
3 JBt,O:Badger,Ham 4.00
4 JBt,A'Ham 4.00
First, 1984–91
5 BR,DruidTree Pt1 . . . . 3.00
6 BR,DruidTree Pt2 . . . . 3.00
7 BR,I:Wonktendonk,Lord
  Weterlackus 3.00
8 BR,V:Demon 3.00
9 BR,I:Connie,WOatesCbra 3.00
10 BR,A:Wonktendonk, I:Hodag
  Meldrum 3.00
11 BR,V:Hodag,L.W'lackus 3.00
12 BR,V:Hodag,L.W'lackus 3.00
13 BR,A:L.W'lakus,Clonezone,
  Judah 3.00
14 BR,I:HerbNg 3.00
15 BR,I:Wombat,JMoranIbob 3.00
16 BR,A:Yak,Yeti 3.00
17 JBt,I:Lamont 3.50
18 BR,I:SpudsGroganA:Cbra 3.00
19 BR,I:Senator1,ClZone 3.00
20 BR,Billionaire'sPicnic 3.00
21 BR,I&O:Phantom 3.00
22 BR,I:Dr.Buick Riviera 3.00
23 I:BobDobb,A:Yeti 3.00
24 BR,A:Riley 3.00
25 BR,I:Killdozer 3.00
26 BR,I:RoachWranger 3.00
27 BR,O:RoachWranger 3.00
28 BR,A:Yeti 3.00
29 A:Clonezone,C:GrimJack 3.00
30 BR,I:Dorgan 3.00
31 BR,I:HopLingSung 3.00
32 BR,D:Dorgan,HopLingSng 3.00
33 RLm/AN,I:KidKang 3.00
34 RLm,I:Count Kohler 3.00
35 RLm,I:Count Kohler 3.00
36 RLm,V:Dire Wolf 3.00
37 AMe,A:Lamont 3.00
38 Animal Band 3.00
39 I:Buddy McBride 3.00
40 RLm,I:Sister Twyster 3.50
41 RLm,D:Sister Twyster 3.50
42 RLm,A:Paul Bunyan 3.50
43 RLm,V:Vampires 3.50
44 RLm,V:Vampires 3.50
45 RLm,V:Dr.Buick Riviera 3.50
46 RLm,V:Lort Weterlackus 3.50

47 RLm,Hmds.Sacr.Bloodl. 3.50
48 RLm,Hmds.Sacr.BloodlI 3.50
49 RLm,TRoof off Suckerl 3.50
50 RLm,TRoof off SuckerlI 5.00
51 RLm,V:Demon 3.00
52 TV,Tinku 4.00
53 TV,I:Shaza,Badass 4.00
54 TV,D:Shaza. 4.00
55 I:Morris Myer. 3.00
56 I:Dominance 3.00
57 A:KKang,V:L.W'lackus 3.00
58 A:Lamont,W'bat,V:SpudsJack. . . 3.00
59 Bad Art Issue 3.00
60 I:ChisumBros 3.00
61 V:ChismBros. 3.00
62 I:Shanks 3.00
63 V:Shanks. 3.00
64 A:Mavis Sykes 3.00
65 A:BruceLee 3.00
66 I:Joe Nappleseed 3.00
67 Babysitting 3.00
68 V:GiantFoot. 3.00
69 O:Mavis. 3.00
70 BR:Klaus(last monthly) 3.00
Graphic Nov.BR,I:Mazis
   Sykes,D:Hodag 10.00
Badger Bedlam 5.00

BADGER GOES BERSERK
First, 1989
1 I:Larry,Jessie 4.00
2 MZ,V:Larry,Jessie 3.50
3 JBt/MZ,V:Larry,Jessie 3.00
4 JBt/MZ,V:Larry,Jessie 3.00

BAD GIRLS
OF BLACKOUT
Blackout Comics, 1995
0 . . . . 3.50
1 I:Ms. Cyanide, Ice 3.50
Ann.#1 Hari Kari, Lady Vampre. . . . 3.50
Ann.#1 Commemorative ed. 10.00

BAD KITTY
Chaos! Comics, 2001
1 BnP 3.00
1a premium edition 10.00
2 . . . . 3.00
3 . . . . 3.00
Ashcan. 6.00
Script #1 . . . . 5.00
Script #1 premium 20.00

BAD KITTY:
MISCHIEF NIGHT
Chaos! Comics, 2001
1 . . . . 3.00
1a premium edition 13.00
1b super premium edition. 20.00

BAD KITTY: RELOADED
Chaos! Comics, 2001
1 . . . . 3.00
1a premium ed.. . . . . 10.00
2 F:Chastity. 3.00
3 . . . . 3.00
4 . . . . 4.00
2a thru 4a variant (c). . . . . @7.50

BADROCK/WOLVERINE
Awesome Entertainment, 1997
Spec. #1 JV,CYp,V:Sauron,48pg . . . 5.00

BAKER STREET
Caliber, 1989
1 . . . . 3.00
2 thru 10 . . . . @3.00
TPB Vol. 1 . . . . 15.00
TPB Vol. 2 . . . . 15.00

BALLAD OF HALO JONES
Quality, 1987
1 IG Alan Moore story. 2.50
1a IG rep. 2.50
2 thru 12 . . . . @2.50

BAMM-BAMM & PEBBLES
FLINTSTONE
Gold Key, 1964
1 . . . . 150.00

BANZAI GIRL
Sirius Entertainment, 2002
Preview book, lim. ed. 5.00
1 (of 4) by Jinky Coronado 3.00
2 thru 4 . . . . @3.00
2a thru 4a lim.,signed,ph(c) . . . @12.00
Ann. #1 . . . . 3.50
TPB Vol. 1 . . . . 15.00

The Barbarians #1
© Atlas

BARBARIANS, THE
Atlas, 1975
1 O: Andrax,F:Iron Jaw 30.00

BARBIE & KEN
Dell Publishing Co. 1962
1 . . . . 650.00
2 . . . . 500.00
3 . . . . 500.00
4 . . . . 500.00
5 . . . . 550.00

BARBIE TWINS
ADVENTURES, THE
Topps, 1995
1 I:Shane, Sia 3.00

BARBI TWINS
ADVENTURES
Studio Chikara, 1998
Color Spec. The Roswell Incident . . 4.00

BARNEY AND
BETTY RUBBLE
Charlton Comics, 1973–76
1 . . . . 75.00
2 . . . . 30.00
3 . . . . 30.00
4 . . . . 30.00
5 . . . . 30.00
6 thru 10 . . . . @25.00
11 thru 23 . . . . @20.00

BARRY M. GOLDWATER
Dell Publishing Co., 1965
1 . . . . 60.00

BAR SINISTER
Acclaim Windjammer, 1995
1 From Shaman's Tears 2.50
2 V:SWAT Team 2.50
3 F: Animus Prime 2.50
4 MGe,RHo,V:Jabbersnatch. 2.50

BART-MAN
Bongo, 1993
1 Foil(c),I:Bart-Man. 4.00
2 I:Penalizer 2.50
3 When Bongos Collide,pt.3,
   with card 2.50
4 Crime-Time,pt.1 . . . . 2.50
5 Bad Guys Strike Back 2.50

BART SIMPSON COMICS
Bongo Comics, 2000
1 . . . . 3.00
2 thru 9 . . . . @3.00
10 thru 20. . . . . @3.00
TPB Big Book of Bart Simpson . . . 12.00
TPB Big Bad Book of Bart Simpson . . . .
13.00
TPB Big Bratty Book of
   Bart Simpson. 13.00

BART SIMPSONS
TREEHOUSE OF HORROR
Bongo Comics, 1995
1 Bart People 3.00
2 thru 4 . . . . @3.00
5 48-pg. 3.50
6 and 7 64-page . . . . @.50
8 . . . . @3.50
9 thru 10 . . . . @5.00
1-shot Treehouse of Terror 2.50

BASEBALL
Kitchen Sink, 1991
1 WE (c) reprint of 1949 orig. 4.00
2 Ray Gotto (c), w/4 BB cards 3.00

BAT, THE
Adventure
1 R:The Bat,inspiration for Batman
   says Bob Kane 3.00

BATTLEBOOKS
Battlebooks Inc., 1999
all BTi(c)
Bubba-Busters Battlebook 5.00

Captain America Battlebook
  Blue print, signed edition 10.00
Colossus Battlebook 4.00
Daredevil Battlebook BTi(c) 4.00
Daredevil Battlebook JQ&JP(c) 4.00
Darkchylde A Battlebook 4.00
Darkchylde B Battlebook 4.00
The Darkness Battlebook 4.00
Dr. Doom Battlebook 4.00
Elektra Battlebook 4.00
  Blue print, signed edition 13.00
Elektra Battlebook, revised 4.00
Gambit Battlebook 4.00
Green Goblin Battlebook 4.00
Iron Man Battlebook
  Blue print, signed edition 13.00
  Blue print, signed edition 13.00
The Incredible Hulk Battlebook 4.00
  Blue print, signed edition 13.00
Magneto Battlebook 4.00
President Clinton Battlebook 5.00
Rogue Battlebook 4.00
  Blue print, signed edition 13.00
Sabretooth Battlebook 4.00
Shi: The Spirit of Benkei Battlebook 4.00
  Blue print, signed edition 10.00
Spider-Man Battlebook
  Blue print, signed edition 13.00
Storm Battlebook 4.00
The Thing Battlebook 4.00
Tomoe: Fan's of Fury Battlebook . . . 4.00
Vampirella Hell on Earth Battlebook 4.00
White Queen Battlebook 4.00
Witchblade Battlebook 4.00
Wolverine Battlebook 4.00
Wolverine with Bone Claws Battlebook
  Blue print, signed edition 13.00

BATTLE FORCE
Blackthorne, 1987
1 and 3 . . . . @3.00

BATTLE OF THE PLANETS
Gold Key, 1979
1 TV Cartoon 40.00
2 . . . . 25.00
3 . . . . 25.00
4 . . . . 25.00
5 . . . . 25.00
Whitman
6 . . . . 20.00
7 thru 10 . . . . @20.00

BATTLESTAR GALACTICA
Maximum Press, 1995
1 Finds Earth 3.00
2 Council of Twelve 3.00
3 R:Adama 3.00
4 Pyramid Secrets 3.00
TPB series rep. 13.00
Spec. Ed. Painted Book (1997) 3.00
Battlestar Galactica: The Compendium #1 rep. from Asylum 3.00

BATTLESTAR GALACTICA
Realm Press, 1997
1 by Chris Scalf 4.00
1a variant cover 3.00
2 Law of Volhad 3.00
3 Prison of Souls, pt.1 . . . . 3.00
3a alternate cover 3.00
4 Prison of Souls, pt.2 . . . . 3.00
5 . . . . 3.00
6 A Path of Darkness, pt.1 . . . . 3.00
7 A Path of Darkness, pt.2 . . . . 3.00
7a photo (c) 3.00

Battlestar Galactica #5
© *Realm Press*

7b signed and numbered 6.00
8 Centurion Prime 3.00
Spec.#1 20 Yahren Reunion 5.00
Spec.#1 No Memory of Earth 3.00
Spec.#1 CenturionPrime,Scott(c) . . 3.00
Spec.#1 CenturionPrime,Parsons(c) 3.00
Spec.#2 Centurion Prime 3.00
Spec. 1999 Tourbook 3.00
Spec. 1999 Tourbook con. ed. 7.00
Spec. 1999 Tourbook sign. 30.00
Spec. Gallery #1 . . . . 4.00
Tech Journal: The Galactica 4.00
Tech Journal: Ships of Fleet 4.00
Spec.No Man's Land 4.00
Spec.No Man's Land, deluxe 5.00
Cylon Dawn Spec. (2000) 4.00
Cylon Dawn Spec. deluxe 5.00
Darkest Night Spec. (2000) 4.00
Darkest Night Spec. variant (c) 5.00
Dire Prophecy Spec. (2000) 4.00
Dire Prophecy Spec. deluxe 5.00
Eve of Destruction Prelude(1999) . . 4.00
Spec.#1 Triad Triumph (2000) 4.00
Spec.#1a Triad Triumph,deluxe . . . 5.00
TPB New Beginnings, rep. #1–#4 . 14.00

BATTLESTAR GALACTICA APOLLO'S JOURNEY
Maximum Press, 1996
1 story by Richard Hatch 3.00
2 . . . . 2.50
3 . . . . 2.50

BATTLESTAR GALACTICA THE ENEMY WITHIN
Maximum Press, 1996
1 . . . . 3.00
2 . . . . 2.50
3 . . . . 2.50

BATTLESTAR GALACTICA JOURNEY'S END
Maximum Press, 1996
1 (of 4) RLd 3.00
2 RLd 3.00
3 RLd, the end of Galactica? 3.00
4 RLd, conclusion 3.00

BATTLESTAR GALACTICA SEARCH FOR SANCTUARY
Realm Press, 1998
1 (of 4) 3.00
2 Path of Darkness 3.00
3 tensions grow 3.00
4 . . . . 3.00

BATTLESTAR GALACTICA SEASON THREE
Real Press, 1999
1 . . . . 3.00
1a alternate JaL(c) 5.00
1b Cylon Attack (c) 5.00
1c Cylon Attack (c) signed 35.00
2 . . . . 3.00
2a alternate cover 5.00
2b pencil sketch cover 5.00
2c convention edition 5.00
3 Fire in the Sky 3.00
3a alternate cover 5.00
3b convention edition 5.00
4 Scott (c) 3.00
5 Busch (c) 3.00
6 . . . . 3.00
4a thru 6a variant(c) . . . . @3.00
7 . . . . 3.00
8 . . . . 3.00
7a & 8a deluxe . . . . @5.00
Spec. 80-page Juggernaut 9.00
Tour Book Sketch ed. 25.00

BATTLESTAR GALACTICA STARBUCK
Maximum Press, 1997
1 (of 3) RLd 3.00
2 RLd 3.00
3 RLd, the end of Galactica? 3.00

BATTLETECH
Blackthorne, 1987
1 . . . . 3.00
2 thru 6 . . . . @3.00
(Changed to Black & White)
1 3-D 3.00
2 3-D 3.00

BATTLETECH
Malibu, Feb. 1995
0 . . . . 3.00

BATTLETECH: FALLOUT
Malibu, Dec. 1994–Mar. 1995
1 3 tales, Based on FASA game . . . 3.00
1a gold foil limited edition 3.50
1b limited holographic editon 5.00
2 V:Clan Jade Falcon 3.00
3 R:Lea 3.00
4 Conclusion 3.00

BAY CITY JIVE
WildStorm/DC, 2001
1 (of 3) F:Sugah Rollins 3.00
1a variant (c) (1:4) 3.00
2 1976 streets of San Francisco . . . 3.00
3 Hell on Earth, concl. 3.00

BEAGLE BOYS, THE
Gold Key, 1964–79
1 . . . . 75.00
2 thru 5 . . . . @40.00
6 thru 10 . . . . @30.00

11 thru 20 . . . . @25.00
21 thru 47 . . . . @20.00

BEANIE THE MEANIE
Fargo Publications, 1958
1 thru 3 . . . . @40.00

B.E.A.S.T.I.E.S.
Axis Comics, 1994
1 JS(a&s),I:Beasties 2.50

THE BEATLES, LIFE STORY
Dell Publishing Co., 1964
1 . . . . 700.00

BEAUTIFUL KILLER
Black Bull Entertainment, 2001
1 JP(s) 5.00
1a variant (c). 4.00
2 JP(s) 4.00
3 JP(s) 4.00
Preview Edition, limited 5.00

BEAUTY AND THE BEAST
Innovation, 1993
1 From TV series 3.00
1a Deluxe 4.00
2 thru 7 . . . . @3.00

BEAUTY AND THE BEAST PORTRAIT OF LOVE
First, 1989–90
1 WP,TV tie in 12.00
2 . . . . 8.00
Book II:Night of Beauty 6.00

BEAUTY AND THE BEAST
Walt Disney, 1992
Movie adapt.(Prestige). 5.00
Movie adapt.(newsstand). 3.00
mini-series
1 Bewitched 3.00
2 Elsewhere 3.00
3 A:Catherine 3.00

BEDLAM!
Eclipse, 1985
1 SBi,RV,reprint horror 3.00
2 SBi,RV,reprint horror 3.00

BEETLE BAILEY
Harvey, 1992
1 F:Mort Walker's B.Bailey 4.00
2 Beetle builds a bridge 3.00
3 thru 12 . . . . 3.00

BEETLEJUICE
Harvey, 1991
1 EC,This is your lice 3.00
Holiday Special #1 . . . . 3.00

BEN CASEY
Dell Publishing Co., June-July, 1962
1 Ph(c) 100.00
2 Ph(c) 75.00
3 Ph(c) 50.00
4 Drug, Ph(c) 75.00
5 Ph(c) 50.00
6 thru 10 Ph(c) . . . . @50.00

BERNI WRIGHTSON MASTER OF THE MACABRE
Pacific
1 BWr 6.00
2 BWr 4.00
3 BWr 3.50
4 BWr 3.50
Eclipse, 1984
5 BWr 3.50

BEST FROM BOY'S LIFE
Gilberton Company, 1957
1 . . . . 150.00
2 . . . . 100.00
3 . . . . 60.00
4 LbC 110.00
5 . . . . 60.00

BEST OF BUGS BUNNY
Gold Key, 1966–68
1 Both Giants 100.00
2 . . . . 75.00

BEST OF DENNIS THE MENACE, THE
Hallden/Fawcett Publ., Summer, 1959–Spring, 1961
1 . . . . 125.00
2 thru 5 . . . . @75.00

BEST OF DONALD DUCK & UNCLE SCROOGE
Gold Key, 1964–67
1 . . . . 125.00
2 . . . . 100.00

BEST OF DONALD DUCK
Gold Key, 1965
1 . . . . 125.00

BETTA: TIME WARRIOR
Immortal Comics, 1997
1 (of 3)Beginnings's End,pt.1 . . . . 3.00
2 The Beginnings's End,pt.2 . . . . . . 3.00

BETTI COZMO
Antarctic Press, 1999
1 (of 3) 3.00
2 . . . . 3.00
3 Raygun For Hire 3.00

BETTY
Archie Publications, 1992
1 . . . . @6.00
2 thru 39 . . . . @4.00
40 thru 60 . . . . @4.00
61 thru 80 . . . . @3.00
81 thru 100 . . . . @3.00
101 thru 119 . . . . @3.00
120 thru 142 . . . . @3.00

BETTY AND ME
Archie Publications, 1965–92
1 . . . . 150.00
2 . . . . 75.00
3 O:Superteen 80.00
4 thru 8 Superteen . . . . @50.00
9 & 10 . . . . 40.00
11 thru 21 . . . . @30.00
22 Archie Band 30.00
23 thru 37 . . . . @25.00

Betty and Me #3
© Archie Publications

38 Sabrina 40.00
39 Josie & Sabrina. 35.00
40 Archie & Betty in Cabin. 25.00
41 . . . . 25.00
42 Betty Vamp 25.00
43 thru 55 . . . . @22.00
56 thru 200 . . . . @8.00

BETTY AND VERONICA
Archie Publications, 1987
1 . . . . 10.00
2 thru 10 . . . . @6.00
11 thru 50 . . . . @5.00
51 thru 104 . . . . @4.00
105 thru 119 . . . . @3.00
120 thru 141 . . . . @5.00
142 thru 160 . . . . @3.00
161 thru 181 . . . . @3.00
182 thru 203 . . . . @3.00
Summer Fun Special #5 . . . . 3.00
Summer Fun Special #6 . . . . 3.00
Summer Fun Special #7 . . . . 3.00
TPB Summer Fun Volume 1 . . . . . 11.00

BETTY & VERONICA SPECTACULAR
Archie Publications, 1992
1 thru 25 . . . . @3.00
26 thru 40 . . . . @3.00
41 thru 57 . . . . @3.00
58 thru 68 . . . . @3.00

BETTY BOOP'S SUNDAY BEST
Kitchen Sink, 1998
TPB Complete Color Comics,
1934–36, new printing 20.00

BEVERLY HILLBILLYS
Dell Publishing Co., April-June, 1963
1 Ph(c) 275.00
2 Ph(c) 150.00
3 Ph(c) 100.00
4 Ph(c) 50.00
5 thru 9 Ph(c) . . . . @100.00
10 . . . . 75.00
11 thru 14 Ph(c) . . . . @100.00
15 thru 21 Ph(c) . . . . @75.00

COLOR PUB.

BEWITCHED
**Dell Publishing Co.,
April-June, 1965**
1 Ph(c) 250.00
2 . . . . 150.00
3 thru 13 Ph(c) . . . . @100.00
14 . . . . 75.00

BEYOND THE GRAVE
Charlton Comics, 1975–84
1 SD,TS(c),P(c) 40.00
2 thru 5 . . . . @25.00
6 thru 17 . . . . @20.00

BIG BANG
Caliber Press, 1994
0 Whole Timeline inc. 3.00
1 . . . . 2.50
2 . . . . 2.50
3 . . . . 2.50
4 25 years after #3 . . . . 2.50

BIG VALLEY, THE
Dell Publishing Co., 1966
1 Ph(c) 75.00
2 thru 6 . . . . @50.00

BILL BLACK'S FUN COMICS
AC Comics
1 Cpt.Paragon,B&W 3.00
2 and 3 B&W . . . . @2.50
4 Color 2.50

BILL THE GALACTIC HERO
Topps, 1994
1 thru 3 Harry Harrison adapt. . . @5.00

BILLY THE KID
Charlton Publ. Co., 1957–83
9 . . . . 100.00
10 . . . . 60.00
11 O:Ghost Train 85.00
12 . . . . 60.00
13 AW,AT 75.00
14 . . . . 60.00
15 AW,O:Billy the Kid 75.00

Billy The Kid #62
© Charlton

16 AW 75.00
17 . . . . 60.00
18 . . . . 60.00
19 . . . . 60.00
20 JSe 75.00
21 JSe 75.00
22 JSe 75.00
23 JSe 75.00
24 JSe 75.00
25 JSe 75.00
26 JSe 75.00
27 . . . . 40.00
28 . . . . 40.00
29 . . . . 40.00
30 Masked Rider 50.00
31 thru 40 . . . . @30.00
41 thru 60 . . . . @25.00
61 thru 65 . . . . @20.00
66 Boundy Hunter 25.00
67 thru 87 . . . . @18.00
88 thru 153 . . . . @6.00

BIN4RY
APC, 2004
1 . . . . 3.50
2 thru 4 . . . . @3.50

BIONEERS
Mirage/Next, 1994
1 New Heroes 2.75
2 . . . . 2.75
3 All-out War 2.75

BIONIC WOMAN, THE
Charlton, 1977
1 Oct, 1977, TV show adapt. 30.00
2 thru 5 . . . . @20.00

BIONIX
Maximum Press, 1996
1 (of 3) RLd,F:Steve Austin &
   Jaime Sommers 3.00
2 RLd, ... 3.00

BIZARRE 3-D ZONE
Blackthorne, 1986
1 . . . . 3.00

BLACKBALL COMICS
Blackball Comics, 1994
1 KG,A:Trencher 3.25

[ORIGINAL] BLACK CAT
1 Reprints 3.00
2 MA(c) rep. 3.00
3 rep. 3.00

BLACK DIAMOND
AC Comics, 1983
1 Colt B..U. story 4.00
2 thru 5 PG(c) . . . . @3.00

BLACK ENCHANTRESS
Heroic Publishing
1 and 2 Date Rape issues . . . . . @3.00

BLACK FLAG
Maximum Press, 1995
1 Dan Fraga 3.00
2 I:New Character. 3.00
3 V:Network, I:Glitz. 3.00
4 V:Glitz, Network 3.00
5 I:Jammers 3.00
6 I:Alphabots 3.00

BLACK FURY
Charlton Comics, 1955
1 . . . . 75.00
2 . . . . 40.00
3 thru 15 . . . . @30.00
16 SD. 75.00
17 SD. 75.00
18 SD. 75.00
19 and 20 . . . . @20.00
21 thru 30 . . . . @15.00
31 thru 56 . . . . @15.00
57 March-April, 1966 . . . . 15.00

BLACK HOLE, THE
Whitman, 1980
1 & 2 movie adaptation . . . . @3.00
3 & 4 new stories . . . . @3.00

BLACK HOOD
Archie/Red Circle, 1983
1 ATh,GM,DW 4.00
2 ATh,DSp,A:Fox 3.00
3 ATh,GM 3.00

BLACK JACK
Charlton Comics, 1957–59
20 . . . . 90.00
21 . . . . 50.00
22 . . . . 75.00
23 AW,AT 75.00
24 SD 100.00
25 SD. 100.00
26 SD. 100.00
27 . . . . 50.00
28 SD. 100.00
29 . . . . 50.00
30 . . . . 50.00

BLACKJACK: BLOOD & HONOR
Dark Angel, 1997
1 by Alex Simmons,JoB, 1930s
   Adventure, Hildebrandts(c) 3.00
2 KeL, ... 3.00
3 Tim Cheng disappears. 3.00
4 . . . . 3.00

BLACK PHANTOM
AC Comics
1 F:Red Mask 3.00
2 F:Red Mask 3.00

BLACK RAVEN
Mad Monkey Press, 1996
1 Blueprints pt.1 . . . . 3.00
2 Blueprints pt.2 . . . . 3.00
3 V:Temple Assassins 3.00
4 Blueprints pt.4 . . . . 3.00
GN#1 Blueprints. 7.00
GN#2 Blueprints. 5.00

BLACK SEPTEMBER
Malibu Ultraverse, 1995
Infinity End of Black September . . . 3.00

BLACK SUN
WildStorm/DC, 2002
Eye of the Storm
1 (of 6) TvS,F:Maggie Sun 3.00
2 thru 6 TvS . . . . @3.00

BLACK TERROR
Eclipse, 1989–90
1	4.00
2	4.00
3	5.00

BLACK TIDE
Avatar Press, 2002
1A Park (c)	3.50
2 Miller (c)	3.50
3 Miller (c)	3.50
1a thru 3a variant (c)s	@3.50

Angel Gate Press
4 thru 8	@3.50
4a thru 8a variant (c)	3.50
9 thru 12	@3.00
9a thru 11a variant (c)s	@3.00
TPB Vol. 1 Awakening the Key	21.00
GN Vol. 1 Enter the Game	8.00

BLACK TIGER: LEGACY OF FURY
Beyond Time Comics, 2004
1 (of 4)	3.00
2 thru 4	@3.00

BLACK WEB
Inks Comics
1 thru 3 V:Seeker	@2.75

BLAST-OFF
Harvey Publications, 1965
1 JK,AW	100.00

BLAZING COMBAT
Warren Publishing Co., 1965–66
1 FF(c)	250.00
2 FF(c)	75.00
3 FF(c)	60.00
4 FF(c)	75.00

BLAZING SIX-GUNS
Skywald Comics, 1971
1 F: Red Mask, Sundance Kid	25.00
2 Jesse James	20.00

BLONDIE
See: Golden Age Section

BLOOD & ROSES
Sky Comics, 1993
1 I:Blood,Rose	3.00

BLOODBATH
Samson Comics
1 I:Alien,V:Starguile	3.00

BLOODCHILDE
Millennium, 1994
0 O:Bloodchilde	3.00
1 Neil Gaiman, Vampires	3.00
1 signed (lim. to 500)	5.00
2 Neil Gaiman, Vampires	3.00
3 Neil Gaiman, Vampires	3.00
4	3.00
5 Talk Show Host	3.00

BLOODFIRE
Lightning Comics, 1993
0 O:Bloodfire	3.00

1 JZy(s),JJn, red foil	5.00
1a Platinum foil Ed.	5.00
1b B&W Promo Ed. Silver ink	4.00
1c B&W Promo Ed. Gold ink	6.00
2 JZy(s),JJn,O:Bloodfire	4.00
3 JZy(s),JJn,I:Dreadwolf, Judgement Day,Overthrow	3.00
4 JZy(s),JJn,A:Dreadwolf,	3.00
5 JZy(s),JJn,I:Bloodstorm, w/card	3.00
6 SZ(s),TLw,V:Storman	3.00
7 SZ(s),TLw,A:Pres.Clinton	3.00
8 SZ(s),TLw,O:Prodigal	3.00
9 SZ(s),TLw,I:Prodigal (in Costume)	3.00
10 SZ(s),TLw,B:Rampage,I:Thorpe	3.00
11	3.00
12	3.00

BLOODFIRE/HELLINA
Lightning Comics, 1995
1 V:Slaughterhouse	3.00

BLOODLORE
Brave New Worlds
1 Dreamweavers	2.50
2 A Blow to the Crown	2.50

BLOODSCENT
Comico, 1988
1 GC	3.00

Bloodshot #6
© Valiant

BLOODSHOT
Valiant, 1992
0 KVH(a&s),DG(i),Chromium (c), O:Bloodshot,A:Eternal Warrior	3.00
0a Gold Ed.,w/Diamond `Fall Fling' logo	4.00
1 BWS(c),B:KVH(s),DP,BWi, V:Mafia, I:Carboni,1st Chromium(c)	2.50
2 DP,I:Durkins,V:Ax	2.50
3 DP,V:The Mob	2.50
4 DP,A:Eternal Warrior	2.25
5 DP,A:Eternal Warrior,Rai	2.25
6 DP,I:Ninjak (Not in Costume)	2.25
7 DP,JDx,A:Ninjak (1st appearance in costume)	2.25
8 DP,JDx,A:Geoff	2.25
9 DP,JDx,V:Slavery Ring	2.25
10 DP,JDx,V:Tunnel Rat	2.25
11 DP,JDx,V:Iwatsu	2.25

12 DP,JDx,Day Off	2.25
13 DP,JDx,V:Webnet	2.25
14 DP,JDx,V:Carboni	2.25
15 DP,JDx,V:Cinder	2.25
16 DP,JDx,w/Valiant Era Card	2.25
17 DP,JDx,A:H.A.R.D.Corps	2.25
18 DP,KVH,After the Missile	2.25
19 DP,KVH,I:Uzzi the Clown	2.25
20 DP,KVH, Chaos Effect-Gamma #1, V:Immortal Enemy	2.25
21 DP,V: Immortal Enemy, Ax	2.25
22 Immortal Enemy	2.25
23 Cinder	2.25
24 Geomancer, Immortal Enemy	2.25
25 V:Uzzi the Clown	2.25
26 V:Uzzi the Clown	2.25
27 Rampage Pt. 1	2.25
28 Rampage Pt. 2	2.25
29 Rampage Conc. A:Ninjak	2.25
30 V:Shape Shifter	2.25
31 Nanite Killer	2.25
32 KVH,SCh,V: Vampires	2.25
33 KVH,SCh,V: Vampires	2.25
34 NBy,KVH,new villains spawned	2.25
35 NBY,KVH,attempts to control	2.25
36 V:Voodoo Drug Dealer	2.25
37 V:Voodoo Drug Dealer	2.25
38 V:Rampage	2.25
39 V:Rampage	2.25
40 thru 51	@2.25
Yearbook #1 KVH,briefcase bomb	4.25
Yearbook 1995 Villagers	3.00
Spec.GN Last Stand	6.00

BLOODSHOT Series Two
Acclaim, 1997
1 LKa(s),SaV, Behold, a Pale Horseman	2.50
1a variant cover	3.00
2 LKa(s),SaV, Dead Man Walking	2.50
3 LKa(s),SaV, ChainsawMassacre	2.50
4 LKa(s),SaV Search for Identity	2.50
5 LKa(s),SaV V:Simon Oreck	2.50
6 LKa(s),SaV, Bloodwhispers	2.50
7 LKa(s),SaV, Bitter End.., pt.1	2.50
8 LKa(s),SaV, Bitter End.., pt.2	2.50
9 LKa(s),SaV, Suicide	2.50
10 LKa(s),SaV, Dreamland	2.50
11 LKa(s),SaV	2.50
12 LKa(s),SaV, Cat Scratch Fever	2.50
13 LKa(s),SaV in Russia	2.50
14 LKa(s),SaV to the Vatican	2.50
15 LKa(s),SaV DOA Headquarters	2.50
16 LKa(s),SaV final issue	2.50

BLOOD SWORD
Jademan, 1988
1	3.00
2	3.00
3 thru 5	@3.00
6 thru 9	@3.00
10 thru 21	@3.00
22 thru 45	@3.00
46 V:Cannibal	3.00
47 thru 53	@3.00

BLOOD SWORD DYNASTY
Jademan, 1989
1	3.00
2 thru 6	@2.75
7 thru 18 MB	@2.75
19 thru 40	@2.75

BLUE BEETLE
Charlton Comics, 1964
(1st Silver Age Series)
1 O:Dan Garrett/BlueBeetle	135.00
2	75.00

COLOR PUB.

Blue–Brian (continued)

3 V:Mr.Thunderbolt 80.00
4 V:Praying Mantis Man 75.00
5 V:Red Knight 75.00
(2nd S.A. Series), 1965
Previously: UNUSUAL TALES
50 V:Scorpion 75.00
51 V:Mentor 75.00
52 V:Magno 75.00
53 V:Praying Mantis Man. 75.00
54 V:Eye of Horus 75.00
Becomes:

GHOSTLY TALES
(3rd S.A. Series), 1967
1 SD,I:Question 75.00
2 SD,O:TedKord,D:DanGarrett . . . 40.00
3 SD,I:Madmen,A:Question 30.00
4 SD,A:Question 30.00
5 SD,VicSage(Question) app.
   in Blue Beetle Story 30.00

BLUE PHANTOM, THE
Dell Publishing Co., 1962
1 . . . . 65.00

BLUE RIBBON
Archie/Red Circle, 1983
1 JK,AV,O:Fly rep.. . . . . 7.00
2 TVe,Mr.Justice 6.00
3 EB/TD,O:Steel Sterling 6.00
4 . . . . 6.00
5 S&K,Shield rep. 6.00
6 DAy/TD,Fox 6.00
7 TD,Fox 6.00
8 NA,GM,Blackhood 7.00
9 thru 11 . . . . @6.00
12 SD,ThunderAgents 6.00
13 Thunderbunny. 6.00
14 Web & Jaguar. 6.00

BOLD ADVENTURE
Pacific, 1987
1 . . . . 3.00
2 . . . . 3.00
3 JSe. 3.00

BOLT & STARFORCE SIX
AC Comics, 1984
1 . . . . 2.00
Bolt Special #1 . . . . 2.00

Bram Stoker's Burial of the Rats #3
© Roger Corman's Comics

All comics prices listed are for *Near Mint* condition.

BOMBABY:
THE SCREEN GODDESS
Amaze Ink/Slave Labor Graphics, 2003
1 (of 4) 3.50
2 . . . . 3.50
3 and 4 . . . . @4.00

BOMBAST
Topps, 1993
1 V:Savage Dragon,Trading Card . 3.25

BONANZA
Dell Publishing Co., 1960
1 . . . . 300.00
2 . . . . 175.00
3 thru 10 . . . . @150.00
11 thru 20 . . . . @125.00
21 thru 37 . . . . @100.00

BORIS KARLOFF
TALES OF MYSTERY
Gold Key, 1963–80
1 (Thriller) 150.00
2 (Thriller) 100.00
3 thru 8 . . . . @60.00
9 WW 75.00
10 JO 50.00
11 AW,JO 60.00
12 AT,AMc,JO 50.00
13 & 14. . . . . @35.00
15 RC,GE. 35.00
16 thru 20 . . . . @35.00
21 JJ,Screaming Skull 75.00
22 thru 50. . . . . @25.00
51 thru 74. . . . . @20.00
75 thru 97. . . . . @15.00

BOZO
Innovation
1 1950's reprint stories 7.00

BOZO THE CLOWN
Blackthorne
1 3-D 3.00
2 3-D 3.00

BRADY BUNCH, THE
Dell Publishing Co., 1970
1 . . . . 175.00
2 . . . . 125.00

BRAIN BOY
Dell Publishing Co., April-June, 1962
1 . . . . 200.00
2 . . . . 150.00
3 . . . . 125.00
4 . . . . 125.00
5 . . . . 125.00
6 . . . . 125.00

BRAM STOKER'S
BURIAL OF THE RATS
Roger Corman's Comics, 1995
1 thru 3 film adaptation . . . . @2.50

BRASS
WildStorm/DC, 2000
1 (of 6) JAr,RiB 2.50
2 JAr,RiB. 2.50
3 JAr,RiB. 2.50
4 JAr,RiB. 2.50

5 JAr,RiB,war is over 2.50
6 JAr,RiB,concl. 2.50

BRATH
Crossgen Comics, 2003
Prequel CDi(s) 3.00
1 CDi(s). 3.50
2 thru 10 CDi(s). . . . . @3.00
11 thru 17 . . . . @3.00
TPB Brath Traveler 10.00

BRAVURA
Malibu, 1995
0 Preview book, mail-in 5.00

BREAK-THRU
Malibu Ultraverse, 1993–94
1 GJ(s),GP,AV(i),A:All Ultraverse
   Heroes 2.75
1a Foil Edition. 7.50
2 GJ(s),GP,AV(i),A:All Ultraverse
   Heroes 2.75

'BREED
Malibu Bravura
[Limited Series] 1994
1 JSn(a&s),Black (c),I:Stoner 3.00
2 JSn(a&s),I:Rachel 3.00
3 JSn(a&s),V:Rachel. 3.00
4 JSn(a&s),I:Stoner's Mom 3.00
5 JSn(a&s),V:Rachel. 3.00
6 JSn(a&s),final issue 3.00
TPB Book of Genesis, rep.#1-#6. . 13.00

'BREED II
Malibu Bravura
[Limited Series] 1994–95
1 JSn,The Book of Revelation 3.00
1a gold foil edition. 4.00
2 JSn,A:Rachel 3.00
3 JSn,V:Actual Demon 3.00
4 JSn,Language of Demons 3.00
5 JSn,R:Rachael 3.00
6 JSn,final issue 3.00

BREEDING GROUND
Samson Comics
1 I:Mazit, Zero 2.50

BRENDA LEE STORY, THE
Dell Publishing Co., 1962
1 . . . . 125.00

BRENDA STARR
REPORTER
Dell Publishing Co., 1963
1 . . . . 250.00

BRIAN BOLLAND'S
BLACK BOOK
Eclipse, 1985
1 BB 3.00

BRIAN PULIDO'S
BELLADONNA
Avatar Press, 2004
Preview 2.00
Preview variant (c)s 3.00
Convention Specials 3.00
1 . . . . 4.00
2 . . . . 4.00
1a-b thru 2a-b variant (c)s . . . . @4.00

BRIDES IN LOVE
Charlton Comics, 1956–65
1	100.00
2	60.00
3 thru 10	@40.00
11 thru 30	@35.00
31 thru 44	@25.00
45	20.00

BRIGADE
Awesome Entertainment
Vol II, 2000
1 A:Badrock	3.00

BRUCE LEE
Malibu, 1994
1 MBn(s), Stories of B.Lee	3.00
2 thru 6	@3.00

BRUTE, THE
Atlas, Feb.–July, 1975
1 thru 3	@25.00

BUCK ROGERS
Gold Key, 1964
1 P(c)	135.00
2 AMc,FBe,P(c),movie adapt	25.00
3 AMc,FBe,P(c),movie adapt	25.00
4 FBe,P(c).	25.00
5 AMc,P(c)	20.00
6 AMc,P(c)	20.00
Whitman	
7 thru 9 AMc,P(c)	@30.00
10 and 11 AMc,P(c)	@20.00
12 and 13 P(c)	@15.00
14 thru 16	@10.00

BUCK ROGERS
TSR, 1990–91
1 thru 3 O:Buck Rogers	@3.00
4 thru 6 Black Barney	@3.00
7 thru 10 The Martian Wars	@3.00

BUCKY O'HARE
Continuity, 1991
1 MGo	2.75
2 thru 5	@2.50

BUFFALO BILL JR.
Dell Publishing Co., 1956
1	125.00
2 thru 6	@75.00
7 thru 13	@60.00

BUGGED-OUT ADVENTURES OF RALFY ROACH
Bugged Out Comics
1 I: Ralfy Roach	3.00

BULLWINKLE
Gold Key, 1962
1 Bullwinkle & Rocky	250.00
2	150.00
3 thru 5	80.00
6 and 7, rep.	@75.00
8 thru 11	80.00
12 rep.	50.00
13 and 14	@60.00
15 thru 19	@50.00
20 thru 24, rep.	@25.00
25	35.00

BULLWINKLE
Charlton Comics, 1970
1	100.00

Becomes:

BULLWINKLE AND ROCKY
Charlton Comics, 1970–71
2 thru 7	@60.00

BULLWINKLE & ROCKY
Eclipse
3-D	25.00

BULLWINKLE FOR PRESIDENT
Blackthorne
1 3-D Special	3.00

BURKE'S LAW
Dell Publishing Co., 1964
1 from TV Show	75.00
2	50.00
3	50.00

Butch Cassidy #1
© Skywald

BUTCH CASSIDY
Skywald Comics, 1971
1	30.00
2 & 3	@20.00

CABBOT: BLOODHUNTER
Maximum Press, 1997
1 thru 4 RV	@2.50

CADILLACS & DINOSAURS
Kitchen Sink
1 Rep. from Xenozoic Tales in 3-D.	6.00
Topps, 1994	
BLOOD & BONES	
1 thru 3 rep. Xenozoic Tales, all covers	@3.00
MAN-EATER	
1 thru 3, all covers	3.00
THE WILD ONES	
1 thru 3, all covers	3.00

CAGES
Tundra
1 DMc	14.00
2 DMc	11.00
3 DMc	7.50
4 DMc	7.50
5 thru 7 DMc	5.00

CAIN
Harris, 1993
1 B:DQ(s),I:Cain,Frenzy	5.00
2 BSz(c),HBk,V:Mortatira	3.25

CAIN'S HUNDRED
Dell Publishing Co., May-July, 1962
1	45.00
2	30.00

CALIFORNIA RAISINS
Blackthorne, 1987
1 thru 4 3-D	@2.50
5 3-D,O:Calif.Raisins	2.50
6 thru 8 3-D	@2.50

CALVIN & THE COLONEL
Dell Publishing Co., April-June, 1962
1	150.00
2	100.00

CAP'N QUICK & FOOZLE
Eclipse, 1984–85
1	3.00
2 and 3	@3.00

CAPT. ELECTRON
Brick Computers Inc.
1	2.50
2	2.50

CAPTAIN ATOM
See: STRANGE SUSPENSE STORIES

CAPTAIN CANUCK
Comely Comix, 1975–81
1 I:Blue Fox.	25.00
2 I:Red Coat	20.00
3 I:Heather	20.00
4 thru 14	15.00
Summer Spec. #1	15.00

CAPTAIN CANUCK: UNHOLY WAR
Comely Comix, 2004
1 (of 3)	2.50
2	2.50

CAPTAIN GLORY
Topps, 1993
1 A:Bombast,Night Glider, Trading Card	3.25

CAPTAIN GRAVITY
Penny Farthing Press, 1998
1 by S.Vrattos & K. Martin	3.00
2 No one escapes Law of Gravity	3.00
3	3.00
4	3.00

TPB 20.00
Spec. One True Hero 3.00

CAPTAIN HARLOCK: FALL OF THE EMPIRE
Eternity, 1992
1 R:Captain Harlock 2.50
2 V:Tadashi 2.50
3 Bomb on the Arcadia 2.50
4 Final issue 2.50

CAPTAIN JOHNER & THE ALIENS
Valiant, 1995
1 Rep. Magnus Robot Fighter #1–7
(Gold Key 1963–64) 3.00

CAPTAIN MARVEL
M. F. Enterprises, 1966
1 . . . . 75.00
2 . . . . 50.00
3 Fights The Bat 40.00
4 . . . . 40.00
5 Captain Marvel Presents the
    Terrible Five 40.00

CAPTAIN NAUTICUS
Entity, 1994
1 V:Fathom 3.00
2 V:Fathom's Henchman 3.00
3 Surf's Up 3.00

CAPTAIN NICE
Gold Key, 1967
1 Ph(c) 100.00

CAPTAIN PARAGON
Americomics, 1983
1 thru 4 . . . . @3.00

CAPTAIN POWER
Continuity, 1988
1a NA,TVtie-in(direct sale) 3.00
1b NA,TVtie-in(newsstand) 3.00
2 NA 3.00

CAPTAIN STERN
Kitchen Sink Press
1 BWr,R:Captain Stern 5.25
2 BWr,Running Out of Time 5.00

CAPTAIN THUNDER AND BLUE BOLT
Hero Graphics
1 I:Capt.Thunder & Paul Fremont. . 2.50
2 Paul becomes Blue Bolt 2.50
3 O:Capt.Thunder 2.50
4 V:Iguana Boys 2.50
5 V:Ian Shriver, in Scotland 2.50
6 V:Krakatoa 2.50
7 V:Krakatoa 2.50
8 A:Sparkplug (from League
    of Champions) 2.50
9 A:Sparkplug 2.50
10 A:Sparkplug 2.50

CAPTAIN VENTURE & THE LAND BENEATH THE SEA
Gold Key, 1968
1 . . . . 75.00
2 . . . . 50.00

*Captain Victory and the Galactic
Rangers #9 © Pacific Comics*

CAPTAIN VICTORY AND THE GALACTIC RANGERS
Pacific, 1982
1 JK 3.00
2 JK 3.00
3 JK,BU:NA,I:Ms.Mystic 3.00
4 JK 3.00
5 JK 3.00
6 JK,SD 3.00
7 thru 13 JK . . . . @3.00
Spec.#1 JK 3.00

CAR 54, WHERE ARE YOU?
Dell Publishing Co., March-May, 1962
1 Ph(c) 150.00
2 thru 7 Ph(c) . . . . @75.00

CARCA JOU RENAISSANCE
1 and 2 . . . . @3.00

CARNOSAUR CARNAGE
Atomeka, 1993
TPB 5.00

CAROLINE KENNEDY
Charlton Comics, 1961
1 . . . . 150.00

CASEY JONES & RAPHAEL
Mirage, 1994
1 Family War. 2.75
2 Johnny Woo Woo 2.75
3 V:Johnny Woo Woo 2.75
4 9mm Raphael 2.75

CASPER & FRIENDS
Harvey, 1991
1 thru 4 . . . . @3.00
5 short stories, cont 3.00

CASPER & WENDY
Harvey, 1972–73
1 52-pg. giant 40.00

2 thru 5 . . . . @20.00
6 thru 8 . . . . @20.00

CASPER ENCHANTED TALES
Harvey, 1992
1 short stories 3.00

CASPER THE FRIENDLY GHOST, 1988
Blackthorne
1 3-D 3.00

CASPER GHOSTLAND
Harvey
1 short stories 3.00

CASPER'S GHOSTLAND
Harvey Publications, Winter, 1958-59
1 giant 300.00
2 . . . . 150.00
3 thru 10 . . . . 125.00
11 thru 20 . . . . @100.00
21 thru 40 . . . . @60.00
41 thru 61 . . . . @50.00
62 thru 77 . . . . @40.00
78 thru 97 . . . . @20.00
98 Dec., 1979 . . . . 20.00

CASPER THE FRIENDLY GHOST
Harvey, 1990–91
Prev: The Friendly Ghost Casper
254 thru 260 . . . . @3.00
[Second Series], 1991–94
1 thru 14 . . . . @3.00
15 thru 28 . . . . @3.00

CATSEYE
Awesome/Hyperwerks, 1999
0 KIA,BNa,O:Catseye 3.00

CAT TALES
Eternity
1 3-D F:Felix 2.50

CAULDRON
Real Comics, 1995
1 Movie Style Comic 3.00
1a Variat cover 3.00

CAVE GIRL
AC Comics
1 . . . . 3.00

CAVE KIDS
Gold Key, 1963
1 . . . . 125.00
2 . . . . 50.00
3 . . . . 50.00
4 . . . . 50.00
5 . . . . 50.00
6 . . . . 40.00
7 A:Pebbles & Bamm Bamm 45.00
8 thru 10 . . . . @35.00
11 thru 16 . . . . @35.00

COLOR PUB.

CAVEWOMAN
Avatar, 1999
Color Spec. 3.50
Color Spec. Fauna (c) 3.50
Color Spec. prism foil (c) 13.00
Color Spec. Royal Blue 75.00

CENTURY
Awesome Entertainment, 2000
1 RLe 3.00
1a Millennium edition 5.00
2 . . . . 3.00
2a Millennium edition 5.00
2b signed 13.00
3 . . . . 3.00

CHAINS OF CHAOS
Harris, 1994
1 Vampirella, Rook 5.00
2 V:Chaoschild 3.25
3 Final issue 3.25

CHAMPIONS
Eclipse, 1986–87
1 I:Flare,League of Champions
   Foxbat, Dr.Arcane 12.00
2 I:Dark Malice 12.00
3 I:Lady Arcane. 8.00
4 O:Dark Malice 12.00
5 O:Flare. 6.00
6 D:Giant Demonmaster. 6.00

[New Series]
Hero Graphics, 1987–88
1 EL,I:Madame Synn,Galloping
   Galooper 5.00
2 I:Fat Man, Black Enchantress . . . 2.25
3 I:Sparkplug&Icicle,O:Flare 2.25
4 I:Exo-Skeleton Man 2.25
5 A:Foxbat. 2.25
6 I:Mechanon, C:Foxbat 2.00
7 A:Mechanon,J:Sparkplug,Icicle . . 2.00
8 O:Foxbat 2.00
9 Flare #0 (Flare preview) 2.00
10 Olympus Saga #1 . . . . 2.00
11 Olympus Saga #2 . . . . 2.00
12 Olympus Saga #3 . . . . 2.00
Ann.#1 O:Giant & DarkMalice 2.75
Ann.#2 . . . . 4.00

CHAMPIONS CLASSIC
Hero Graphics
1 GP(c),Rep.1st champions series . 2.50

CHAOS! BIBLE
Chaos! Comics, 1995
1 Character Profiles 3.50

CHAOS! CHRONICLES–
THE HISTORY OF
A COSMOS
Chaos! Comics, 1999
Spec. 3.50
Spec. signed premium 15.00

CHAOS EFFECT
Valiant, 1994
Alpha DJ(c), BCh, JOy, A:All
   Valiant Characters 2.25
Alpha Red (c). 3.50
Omega DJ(c), BCh, JOy, A:All
   Valiant Characters 2.25
Omega Gold(c) 3.50
Epilogue pt.1 . . . . 3.00
Epilogue pt.2 . . . . 3.00

CHAOS! GALLERY
Chaos! Comics, 1997
1 . . . . 3.00

CHAOS!
NIGHTMARE THEATER
Chaos! Comics, 1997
1 (of 4) BWr(c) 2.50
2 BWr(c) 2.50
3 BWr(c) 2.50
4 BWr(c) 2.50

CHAOS QUARTERLY
Harris Comics, 1995
1 F:Lady Death 5.00
1a Premium Edition. 11.00
1b Signed,limited edition. 20.00

CHAPEL
Awesome Entertainment, 1997
1 BNa, from Spawn,Youngblood. . . 3.00

CHARLEMAGNE
Defiant, 1994
1 JiS(s),From Hero 3.00
2 JiS(s),I:Charles Smith 2.75
3 JiS(s),A:War Dancer 2.75
4 DGC(s),V:Dark Powers 2.75
5 Schism prequel 2.75
6 V:Wardancer 2.75
7 R:To Vietnam 2.75

CHARLIE CHAN
Dell Publishing Co., 1965
1 . . . . 75.00
2 . . . . 50.00

CHARLTON BULLSEYE
Charlton, 1981–82
1 Blue Beetle, I:Rocket Rabbit 3.50
2 Capt. Catnip; Nell the Horse 2.50
3 Grundar 2.50
4 Vanguards 2.50
5 Warhund 2.50
6 Thunder-bunny 2.50
7 Captain Atom 2.50
8 weird stories. 2.50
9 . . . . 2.50

Charlton Bullseye Vol. 2, #6
© Charlton Comics

10 . . . . 2.50
Spec. #1 . . . . 2.00
Spec. #2 Atomic Mouse 2.00

CHARLTON
SPORT LIBRARY
Charlton, 1970
1 Professional Football 50.00

CHASSIS
Millennium/Expand, 1995
1 I:Chassis McBain, Aero Run 3.00
1 2nd printing 3.00
1 chrome cover. 10.00
2 . . . . 3.00
2a with racing card 5.00
2b Amanda Conner cover. 3.00
2c Amanda Conner cover, signed. . 9.95
2d foil cover, signed 10.00
[Vol. 2] Hurricane Comics, 1998
0 by Joshua Dysart & Wm.O'Neill . 3.00
0a variant cover 3.00
1 . . . . 3.00
2 . . . . 3.00
3 . . . . 3.00

CHASTITY
Chaos! Comics, 2000
1/2 . . . . 3.00
1/2a premium ed., tattoo (c) 10.00
1/2b chromium edition 16.00
1/2 Ashcan 6.66
1 premium edition 10.00
Spec. #1 Reign of Terror (2000) . . . 3.00
Spec. #1 Reign of Terror, premium 10.00
Spec. #1 Love Bites (2001) 3.00
Spec. #1 Love Bites, premium ed.. 10.00
Ashcan Love Bites (2001) 6.00

CHASTITY: CRAZYTOWN
Chaos! Comics, 2002
Ashcan b&w. 6.00
1 (of 3) 3.00
1a premium edition 10.00
1b foil edition. 20.00
2 . . . . 3.00
3 . . . . 3.00
2a and 3a variant (c). . . . . @7.50

CHASTITY:
HEARTBREAKER
Chaos! Comics, 2002
1 . . . . 3.00
1a premium edition 10.00
1b super premium edition 20.00

CHASTITY LUST FOR LIFE
Chaos! Comics, 1999
1 (of 4) PNu 3.00
1a alternate cover. 7.00
1b alternate cover, signed 20.00
1c premium edition 10.00
2 V:Hemlock 3.00
3 . . . . 3.00

CHASTITY: RE-IMAGINED
Chaos! Comics, 2002
1 Gothic tale 3.00
1a premium edition 10.00
1b super premium edition 20.00
Ashcan re-imagined b&w. 6.00

COLOR PUB.

CHASTITY ROCKED
Chaos! Comics, 1998
1 (of 4) PNu 3.00
1a & 1b variant covers 3.00
2 V:Jade 3.00
3 V:Jade 3.00
4 conclusion 3.00
Chastity/Cremator Preview
Book, B&W 5.00

CHASTITY: SHATTERED
Chaos! Comics, 2001
1 BnP,LKa 3.00
1a premium edition 10.00
2 . . . . 3.00
3 . . . . 3.00
Ashcan 6.00

CHASTITY: THEATRE OF PAIN
Chaos! Comics, 1997
1 (of 3) BnP, ... 6.00
1a premium edition 15.00
2 . . . . 3.00
3 . . . . 3.00
3a premium edition 15.00
TPB rep.#1–#3, Sketchbook 10.00

CHEAP SHODDY ROBOT TOYS
Eclipse
1 A:Ronald Reagan 2.50

CHECKMATE
Gold Key, 1962
1 Ph(c) 100.00
2 Ph(c) 75.00

CHEMICAL MAN
1 . . . . 2.50

CHERYL BLOSSOM
Archie Comics, 1996
1 . . . . 2.50
2 thru 5 . . . . @2.50
6 thru 10 . . . . @2.50
11 thru 37 . . . . @2.50

CHERYL BLOSSOM GOES HOLLYWOOD
Archie Comics, 1996
1 (of 3) by Dan Parent &
Bill Golliher 3.50
2 and 3 . . . . @3.50

CHEYENNE
Dell Publishing Co., 1956
1 Ph(c) all 275.00
2 . . . . 150.00
3 . . . . 125.00
4 thru 12 . . . . @ 100.00
13 thru 25 . . . . @75.00

CHEYENNE KID
(see WILD FRONTIER)

CHI-CHIAN
Sirius, 1997
1 (of 6) by Voltaire 3.00
2 thru 6 . . . . @3.00

CHILD'S PLAY 2
Innovation
1 Movie Adapt Pt 1 . . . . 2.50
2 Adapt Pt 2 . . . . 2.50
3 Adapt Pt 3 . . . . 2.50

CHILD'S PLAY 3
Innovation
1 Movie Adapt Pt 1 . . . . 2.50
2 Movie Adapt Pt.2 . . . . 2.50

CHILD'S PLAY: THE SERIES
Innovation
1 Chucky's Back 2.50
2 Straight Jacket Blues 2.50
3 M.A.R.K.E.D. 2.50
4 Chucky in Toys 4 You 2.50
5 Chucky in Hollywood 2.50

CHILDREN OF FIRE
Fantagor
1 thru 3 RCo . . . . @4.00

Chilling Adventures in Sorcery as Told by Sabrina #2 © Archie Comics

CHILLING ADVENTURES IN SORCERY AS TOLD BY SABRINA
Archie, 1972–74
1 . . . . 65.00
2 . . . . 40.00
3 thru 5 . . . . @30.00

CHIMERA
Crossgen Comics, 2003
1 RMz,BPe 3.00
2 thru 4 . . . . @3.00
TPB 160-pg. 16.00

CHIP 'N DALE
Dell Publishing, 1955–66
4 . . . . 90.00
5 thru 10 . . . . 75.00
11 thru 30 . . . . @60.00
Gold Key, 1967
1 reprints 40.00
2 thru 10 . . . . 20.00
11 thru 20 . . . . 10.00
21 thru 83 . . . . @8.00

CHIP 'N DALE RESCUE RANGERS
Walt Disney, 1990
1 Rescue Rangers to the Rescue,
pt.1 . . . . 4.00
2 Rescue Rangers to the Rescue,
pt.2 . . . . 3.50
3 thru 7 . . . . @3.00
8 Coast to Coast Pt 1 . . . . 2.75
9 Coast to Coast Pt 2 . . . . 2.75
10 Coast to Coast Pt 3 . . . . 2.75
11 Coast to Coast Pt 4 . . . . 2.75
12 Showdown at Hoedown 2.75
13 Raining Cats & Dogs 2.75
14 Cobra Kadabra 2.75
15 I:Techno-Rats,WaspPatrol
Fearless Frogs Pt.1 . . . . 2.75
16 A:Techno-Rats,WaspPatrol,
Fearless Frogs Pt.2 . . . . 2.75
17 For the Love of Cheese 2.75
18 Ghastly Goat of Quiver
Moore, Pt.1 . . . . 2.75

CHOO CHOO CHARLIE
Gold Key, 1969
1 . . . . 150.00

CHOPPER: EARTH, WIND, AND FIRE
Fleetway
1 F:Chopper 3.00

CHOSEN, THE
Click Comics, 1995
1 I:The Chosen 2.50
2 I:Herman Cortez 2.50

CHRISTIAN
Maximum Press, 1996
1 and 2 (of 3) RLd . . . . @3.00

CHRISTMAS PARADE
Gladstone
1 GiantEdition 4.00
2 . . . . 3.50

CHRISTMAS SPIRIT, THE
Kitchen Sink
TPB Will Eisner art. 15.00

CHROMA-TICK SPECIAL EDITION
New England Press, 1992
1 Rep.Tick#1,new stories 4.00
2 Rep.Tick#2,new stories 5.00
3 thru 8 Reps.& new stories . . . . @3.50

CHROME
Hot Comics, 1986
1 Machine Man 3.50
2 thru 4 . . . . @3.00

CHROME WARRIORS IN A '59 CHEVY
Black Out Comics, 1998
0 . . . . 3.00
1 Rob Roman & Tommy Castillo . . 3.00

CHROMIUM MAN, THE
Triumphant Comics, 1994
0 Blue Logo. 6.00
0 Regular 2.50

1 I:Chromium Man,Mr.Death. 3.50
2 I:Prince Vandal. 3.00
3 I:Candi,Breaker,Coil. 2.50
4 JnR(s),AdP,Unleashed. 2.50
5 JnR(s),AdP,Unleashed. 2.50
6 JnR(s),Courier,pt.1. . . . . 2.50
7 JnR(s),Courier,pt.2. . . . . 2.50
8 JnR(s),Chromium finds peace . . . 2.50
9 V:Tarsak. 2.50
10 . . . . 2.50
11 Prince Vandal #8. . . . . 2.50
12 Prince Vandal #9. . . . . 2.50
13 V:Realm 2.50
14 A:Light. 2.50
15 . . . . 2.50

CHROMIUM MAN: VIOLENT PAST
Triumphant Comics
1 thru 4 JnR(s) . . . . @2.50

CHRONICLES OF CORUM
First, 1987–88
1 Michael Moorcock adapt.. . . . . . 3.00
2 thru 12 . . . . @2.50

CICERO'S CAT
Dell Publishing Co., 1959
1 . . . . 75.00
2 . . . . 60.00

CICI
Spilled Milk, 2002
1 (of 4) 3.00
2 thru 4 . . . . 2.50
Variant (c) . . . . @2.50

CIMMARON STRIP
Dell Publishing Co., 1968
1 . . . . 65.00

CISCO KID, THE
Moonstone, 2004
1 (of 3) 3.00
2 thru 3 . . . . @3.00

CITY KNIGHTS, THE
Windjammer 1995
1 I: Michael Walker. 2.50
2 thru 4 . . . . @2.50

CITY OF HEROES
Blue King Studios, 2004
1 . . . . 3.00
2 thru 6 . . . . @3.00

CITY KNIGHTS, THE
Windjammer, 1995
1 I:Michael Walker 2.50
2 I:Herald 2.50
3 & 4 V:Herald. . . . . @2.50

CITY PERILOUS
Broadway Comics
1 GI,Remember the Future,pt.1 . . . 3.00
2 GI,Remember the Future,pt.2 . . . 3.00
Becomes:

KNIGHTS ON BROADWAY
3 thru 5 GI. . . . . @3.00

CLASSICS ILLUSTRATED
See Also: CLASSICS ILLUSTRATED SECTION

CLASSICS ILLUSTRATED
First, 1990
1 GW,The Raven 5.00
2 RG,Great Expectations 5.00
3 KB,Thru the Looking Glass 5.00
4 BSz,Moby Dick 5.00
5 SG,TM,KE, Hamlet. 5.00
6 PCr,JT, Scarlet Letter. 5.00
7 DSp,Count of Monte Cristo 5.00
8 Dr.Jekyll & Mr.Hyde 5.00
9 MP,Tom Sawyer. 5.00
10 Call of the Wild 5.00
11 Rip Van Winkle 5.00
12 Dr. Moreau 5.00
13 Wuthering Heights 5.00
14 Fall of House of Usher 5.00
15 Gift of the Magi 5.00
16 A: Christmas Carol 5.00
17 Treasure Island. 5.00
18 The Devils Dictionary 5.00
19 The Secret Agent 5.00
20 The Invisible Man 5.00
21 Cyrano de Bergerac 5.00
22 The Jungle Book. 5.00
23 Swiss Family Robinson. 5.00
24 Rime of Ancient Mariner. 5.00
25 Ivanhoe 5.00
26 Aesop's Fables 5.00
27 The Jungle 5.00

CLASSICS ILLUSTRATED JUNIOR
Classics Illustrated Junior, 2003–2004
501 Show White & Seven Dwarfs . . 4.00
502 The Ugly Duckling. 4.00
503 Cinderella 4.00
512 Rumplestiltskin 4.00
514 Steadfast Tin Soldier. 4.00
515 Johnny Appleseed 4.00
519 Paul Bunyan 4.00
520 Thumbelina 4.00
530 The Golden Bird 4.00
535 The Wizard of Oz 4.00
536 The Chimney Sweep 4.00
539 The Enchanted Fish 4.00
540 Tinder Box. 4.00
546 The Elves and the Shoemaker . 4.00
563 The Wishing Well 4.00
564 Salt Mountain 4.00
565 THe Silly Princess. 4.00
570 Pearl Princess. 4.00

CLASSWAR
Com.X, 2001
1 . . . . 3.00
2 thru 3 . . . . @3.00
4 thru 6 . . . . @3.50
TPB Vol. 1 . . . . 13.00
1 Metal edition 50.00

CLAUS
Draco, 1997
1 by Bowden & Guichardon 3.00
2 thru 4 . . . . @3.25

CLIVE BARKER'S DREAD
Eclipse
Graphic Album 8.00

CLIVE BARKER'S TAPPING THE VEIN
Eclipse
1 . . . . 10.00
2 thru 5 . . . . @8.50

CLYDE CRASHCUP
Dell Publishing Co., 1963
1 . . . . 200.00
2 . . . . 175.00
3 thru 5 . . . . @160.00

COBALT 60
Innovation
1 reprints. 5.00

COBALT BLUE
Innovation, 1989
Spec.#1 . . . . 3.00
Spec.#2 . . . . 3.00
1 and 2 . . . . @3.00

Codename: Danger #2
© Lodestone

CODENAME: DANGER
Lodestone, 1985
1 RB/BMc,I:Makor. 3.50
2 KB,I:Capt.Energy 3.00
3 PS/RB 3.00
4 PG 3.00

CODE NAME: DOUBLE IMPACT
High Impact, 1997
1 RCI. 3.00
1 variant cover 10.00
1 signed holofoil cover 15.00

CODENAME: FIREARM
Malibu Ultraverse, 1995
0 I:New Firearm 3.00
1 F:Alec Swan. 3.00
2 Dual Identity. 3.00
3 F:Hitch and Lopez 3.00
4 F:Hitch and Lopez 3.00
5 Working Together. 3.00

CODENAME: STRIKEFORCE
Spectrum, 1984
1 .... 3.00

COLLECTOR'S DRACULA
Millennium
1 .... 4.25

COLOSSAL SHOW, THE
Gold Key, 1969
1 .... 75.00

COLOUR OF MAGIC
Innovation
1 Terry Pratchet novel adapt...... 3.00
2 The Sending of Eight.......... 3.00
3 Lure of the Worm............. 3.00
4 final issue.................. 3.00

COLT .45
Dell Publishing Co., 1958
1 Ph(c) all.................. 175.00
2 .... 135.00
3 .... 125.00
4 .... 125.00
5 .... 125.00
6 ATh....................... 150.00
7 .... 125.00
8 .... 125.00
9 .... 125.00

COLT SPECIAL
AC Comics, 1985
1 .... 3.00
2 .... 3.00
3 .... 3.00

COMBAT
Dell Publishing Co., 1961
1 SG 75.00
2 SG 50.00
3 SG 50.00
4 JFK cover, Story 2-D 60.00
5 SG 50.00
6 SG 35.00
7 SG 35.00
8 SG 35.00
9 SG 35.00
10 SG........................ 35.00
11 thru 27 SG.............. @30.00
28 thru 40 SG.............. @25.00

COMET, THE
Archie/Red Circle, 1983
1 AN,CI,O:Comet 3.00
2 AN,CI,D:Hangman............ 3.00

COMIC ALBUM
Dell Publishing Co., March-May, 1958
1 Donald Duck 150.00
2 Bugs Bunny 75.00
3 Donald Duck 100.00
4 Tom & Jerry 75.00
5 Woody Woodpecker......... 75.00
6 Bugs Bunny 75.00
7 Popeye.................... 85.00
8 Tom & Jerry 75.00
9 Woody Woodpecker......... 75.00
10 Bugs Bunny 75.00
11 Popeye................... 85.00
12 Tom & Jerry 60.00

13 Woody Woodpecker 60.00
14 Bugs Bunny 60.00
15 Popeye 75.00
16 Flintstones............... 125.00
17 Space Mouse 75.00
18 3 Stooges,Ph(c) 125.00

COMICO X-MAS SPECIAL
Comico, 1988
1 SR/AW/DSt(c) 3.00

COMIX INTERNATIONAL
Warren Magazines, 1974
1 .... 125.00
2 WW,BW 75.00
3 .... 40.00
4 RC 40.00
5 Spring, 1977 .... 40.00

CONCRETE JUNGLE: THE LEGEND OF THE BLACK LION
Acclaim, 1998
1 (of 6) CPr,JFy,F:Terry Smalls.... 2.50
2 CPr,JFy,Black Lion Order 2.50
3 CPr,JFy,The Man............. 2.50
4 CPr,JFy 2.50
5 CPr,JFy 2.50

CONSTRUCT
Mirage
1 I:Constructs 3.00
2 F:Sect.Eight, Armor 3.00
3 O:Constructs 3.00
4 Fist-O-God................. 3.00

CORBEN SPECIAL
Pacific
1 RCo 5.00

CORUM: THE BULL & THE SPEAR
First, 1989
1 thru 4 Michael Moorcock adapt.@2.50

COSMIC GUARD, THE
Devil's Due Publishing, 2004
1 JSn........................ 3.00
2 thru 3 JSn................. @3.00

COUGAR, THE
Atlas, April–July, 1975
1 .... 25.00
2 O:Cougar 25.00

COUNTDOWN
WildStorm/DC, 2000
1 (of 8) JMi,AaL 2.50
2 thru 6 JMi,AaL.............. @2.50
7 JMi,AaL,RyE,supercriminals 2.50
8 JMi,AAl,RyE,concl. 3.00

COUNTER-OPS
Antarctic Press, 2003
1 .... 4.00
2 thru 5 .... @4.00

COUNTER-STRIKE
Infinity Comics, 2000
1 (of 4) 2.50

1a premium chroma-foil (c)...... 12.00
2 thru 4 .... @2.50

COUP D'ETAT
Wildstorm/DC, 2004
1 (of 4) Sleeper, JLe 3.00
2 Stormwatch: Team Achilles 3.00
3 Wildcats Version 3.0 .... 3.00
4 The Authority, WPo 3.00
Spec. Afterword 3.00

COURTSHIP OF EDDIE'S FATHER
Dell Publishing Co., 1970
1 Ph(c)...................... 75.00
2 Ph(c) 60.00

Coven #1
© Awesome Entertainment

COVEN
Awesome Entertainment, 1997
1 IaC,JLb,JSb,V:The Pentad 8.00
1a variant covers 8.00
2 IaC,JLb,Who is Spellcaster? 5.00
3 IaC,JLb,V:The Pentad 5.00
4 IaC,JLb,Pentad, concl........ 4.00
5 IaC,JLb,..................... 4.00
5 gold foil cover 8.00
6 IaC,JLb,Mardi Gras madness ... 3.00
6 gold foil edition............. 8.00
7 IaC,JLb,V:Babylon............ 2.50
8 IaC,JLb,F:Thor, the God
    of Thunder................. 2.50
9 IaC,JLb,..................... 2.50
Coll.Ed. #1, rep. #1–#2,
    new IaC(c).................. 5.00
Fan Appreciation #1, rep. #1,
    new cover 2.50
Coven/Menace S.D.Con
    preview book............... 5.00
TPB The Gathering 17.00

VOL 2
1 IaC,JLb 2.50
1a, b & c variant covers 2.50
1d chrome edition............. 10.00
1e gold foil cover 8.00
2 IaC,JLb,V:Supreme 2.50
2a Lionheart (c)............... 8.00
2b signed 20.00
3 IaC,JLb, Long Flight Home 2.50
3 Ruby red edition 15.00
4 IaC,JLb 2.50
5 thru 7 .... @3.00

Coven Sourcebook #1 . . . . 3.00

COVEN 13
No Mercy Comics, 1997
1 by Rikki Rockett & Matt Busch . . 2.50
2 . . . . 2.50
3 . . . . 2.50
4 . . . . 2.50

COVEN/RE:GEX
Awesome Entertainment, 1999
1 (of 2) RLe,JLb,IaC 2.50
1a alternate IaC cover 7.00
2 JLb, conclusion 2.50

COVEN: DARK ORIGINS
Awesome Entertainment, 1999
1 . . . . 2.50
1a & b variant covers 2.50

COVEN: DARK SISTER
Avatar Press, 2001
1/2 Rio (c) 4.00
1/2 Shaw (c) 4.00
1/2 Martin (c) 4.00
1/2 Raptor attack (c) 5.00
1/2 Previews Raptor prism foil (c) . 13.00
1/2 Bad Vibes (c) 6.00
1 Park (c) 3.50
1a Rio (c) 3.50
1b Martin (c) 3.50
1c wraparound (c) 4.00
1d Blue leather (c) 25.00
1e Royal Blue edition, in case . . . 75.00
1f Haunting Vision edition 6.00
1g Prism foil edition 13.00
1h Embrace edition 6.00
1i Embrace edition, emerald (c) . . 14.00
2 Adrian (c) edition 6.00

COVEN: SPELLCASTER
Avatar Press, 2001
1/2 Bewitched edition 6.00
1/2 Bikini edition 6.00
1/2 Rio Royal Blue (c) 75.00
1 Finch (c) 3.50
1a Rio (c) 3.50
1b Martin (c) 3.50
1c Wraparound (c) 4.00
1d Leather 25.00
1e Finch Ruby Red(c) 25.00
1f Rio prism foil (c) 13.00
1g Royal Blue edition 75.00
2 Rio (c) 3.50
2a Shaw (c) 3.50
2b Martin (c) 3.50
2c Lyon (c) 3.50
Spec. #1 Free Spirit edition 5.96

COVEN: TOOTH & NAIL
Avatar Press, 2001
1 Adrian (c) 3.50
1a Rio (c) 3.50
1b Waller (c) 3.50
1c MMy(c) 3.50
1d Wraparound (c) 3.50
1e leather (c) 25.00
1f Royal Blue (c) 75.00
1g Bikini Edition (c) 6.00
1h Bad Ladies (c) 6.00
1i Prism exclusive (c) 13.00
1j Fantom (c) 6.00
1k Training Day (c) 6.00
1/2 Woman Scorned (c) 6.00
1/2a Prism Foil edition 13.00
1/2b Fantom edition 6.00
1/2c Adrian (c) 16-pg. 4.00

1/2d Waller (c) 4.00
1/2e MMy(c) 4.00
1/2f Martin (c) 4.00

COWBOY IN AFRICA
Gold Key, 1968
1 Chuck Conners,Ph(c) 75.00

CRACKED
Major Magazines, 1958
1 AW 225.00
2 . . . . 125.00
3 thru 6 . . . . @125.00
7 thru 10 . . . . @100.00
11 thru 20 . . . . @75.00
21 thru 30 . . . . @60.00
31 thru 36 . . . . @50.00
37 Beatles 50.00
38 thru 45 . . . . @40.00
46 Beatles 45.00
47 thru 50 . . . . @40.00
51 Beatles 45.00
52 Mysters 45.00
53 thru 56 . . . . @40.00
57 Rolling Stones 45.00
58 . . . . 40.00
59 Laurel & Hardy 45.00
60 & 61 . . . . @38.00
62 Beatles 42.00
63 thru 68 . . . . @38.00
69 Batman 40.00
70 Elvis 40.00
71 W.C. Fields 40.00
72 thru 99 . . . . @38.00
100 . . . . 50.00
101 thru 103 . . . . @25.00
104 Godfather 50.00
105 thru 114 . . . . @25.00
115 M.A.S.H. 30.00
116 thru 118 . . . . @25.00
119 Kung Fu 30.00
120 Six Million Dollar Man 30.00
121 American Grafiti 30.00
122 thru 130 . . . . @20.00
131 Godfather 25.00
132 Baretta 25.00
133 Space:1999 . . . . 28.00
134 Fonz 25.00
135 Bionic Woman 25.00
136 thru 145 . . . . @25.00
146 thru 148 Star Wars . . . . @35.00
149 Star Wars 30.00
150 thru 162 . . . . @20.00
163 Mork & Mindy, Alien 30.00
164 thru 174 . . . . @15.00
175 thru 200 . . . . @10.00
201 thru 252 . . . . @8.00
253 thru 300 . . . . @7.00
301 thru 348 . . . . @5.00

[THE INCREDIBLE] CRASH DUMMIES
Harvey, 1993
1 thru 3, from the toy series . . . . @2.50

CRAZYMAN
Continuity, 1992
[1st Series]
1 Embossed(c),NA/RT(i),
  O:Crazyman 6.00
2 NA/BB(c) 2.50
3 DBa,V:Terrorists 2.50
[2nd Series], 1993
1 Die Cut(c) 2.50
2 thru 3 . . . . 2.50
4 In Demon World 2.50

CREATURE
Antarctic Press, 1997
1 (of 2) by D.Walker&J.Maranto . . 3.00
2 concl. 3.00

CREED/TEENAGE MUTANT NINJA TURTLES
Lightning Comics, 1996
1 . . . . 3.00
1 variant cover 3.00

Creed: Cranial Disorder #1
© Lightning Comics

CREED: CRANIAL DISORDER
Lightning Comics, 1996
1 (of 3) 3.00
1a variant cover, *Previews*
  exclusive 3.00
1b Platinum edition 9.00
1c Platinum edition, autographed 16.00
2 . . . . 3.00
2a variant cover 3.00

CREMATOR: HELL'S GUARDIAN
Chaos! Comics, 1998
1 (of 5) LJi 3.00
2 . . . . 3.00
3 V:Asteroth 3.00
4 . . . . 3.00
5 . . . . 3.00

CRIME MACHINE
Skywald Publications, 1971
1 JK 75.00
2 AT 50.00

CRIME PATROL
Gemstone, 2000
1 rep. 2.50
2 rep. Fall 1948 . . . . 2.50
3 rep. Winter 1948 . . . . 2.50
4 rep. Feb. 1949 . . . . 2.50
5 rep. 2.50
6 rep. 2.50
7 rep. 2.50
8 rep. Oct. 1949 . . . . 2.50
9 rep. Dec. 1949 . . . . 2.50
10 rep. Feb. 1950 issue 2.50
`Annuals'

TPB Vol.#1 rep. #1–#5......... 13.50
TPB Vol.#2 rep. #6–#10......... 13.50

CRIME SUSPENSE STORIES
Russ Cochran, 1992
1 Rep. C.S.S. #1 (1950)........ 3.00
2 thru 7 Rep. C.S.S.......... @3.00
8 thru 15 Rep. .... @3.00

Gemstone, 1996
16 thru 27 EC comics reprint.... @3.00
Ann.#1, rep. #1–#5 .... 9.00
Ann.#2, rep. #6–#10 .... 9.00
Ann.#3, rep. #11–#15 .... 10.00
Ann.#4, rep. #16–#19 .... 10.50
Ann.#5, rep. #20–#23 .... 11.00
Ann.#6 rebinding #24–#27 ...... 11.00

CRIMSON NUN
Antarctic Press, 1997
1 (of 4) 3.00
2 .... 3.00
3 .... 3.00
4 concl 3.00

CRIMSON PLAGUE
Event Comics, 1997
1 GP,F:DiNA: Simmons 3.00
2 GP,....................... 3.00

Crossfire #1
© *Eclipse*

CROSSFIRE
Eclipse, 1984–86
1 DSp 3.00
2 thru 11 DSp .... @2.50
12 DSp,DSt(c),M.Monroe(c) & story 2.50
13 DSp....................... 2.50
14 DSp....................... 2.50
15 DSp,O:Crossfire 2.50
16 DSp,The Comedy Place 2.50
17 DSp,Comedy Place, Pt.2 ..... 2.50
See B&W

CROSSFIRE & RAINBOW
Eclipse, 1986
1 DSp,V:Marx Brothers......... 2.25
2 DSp,PG(c),V:Marx Brothers.... 2.25
3 DSp,HC(c),A:Witness 2.25

4 DSp,DSt(c),This Isn't Elvis...... 3.50

CROSSGEN CHRONICLES
Crossgen Comics, 2000
1 48-pg....................... 4.50
2 RMz,GP 4.00
2a 2nd printing 11.00
3 BKs,GP, 48-page 5.00
4 MWa,GP, 48-page 4.00
5 RMz,GP.................... 4.00
6 thru 8 .... @4.00

CROSSOVERS, THE
CG Entertainment, 2003
1 (of 6) Cross Currents 3.00
2 thru 11 .... @3.00
TPB Vol. 1 Cross Currents 10.00

CROSSROADS
First, 1988
1 Sable,Whisper.............. 4.00
2 Sable,Badger.............. 4.00
3 JSon,JAl,Badger/Luther Ironheart 4.00
4 Grimjack/Judah Macabee 4.00
5 LM,Grimjack/Dreadstar/Nexus... 4.00

CROUCHING TIGER, HIDDEN DRAGON
Comicson, 2002
GN #1 .... 14.00
GN #2 thru #8 .... @14.00

CROW, THE: CITY OF ANGELS
Kitchen Sink, 1996
1 thru 3 movie adaptation...... @3.00
1 thru 3 movie adaptation,
    photo covers .... @3.00
TPB The Crow, The Movie, new
    printing................. 19.00

CRUX
Crossgen Comics, 2001
1 MWa,SEp................... 7.00
2 MWa,SEp................... 5.00
3 thru 8 MWa,SEp........... @3.00
9 thru 20 .... @3.00
21 thru 33................... @3.00
TPB Vol. 1 .... 16.00
TPB Vol. 2 .... 16.00
TPB Vol. 3 Strangers in Atlantis.. 16.00
TPB Vol. 4 Chaos Reborn 16.00

CRYBABY
Event Comics, 1999
1 GrL,SLo................... 3.00
1a limited, signed 10.00

CRYING FREEMAN III
Viz, 1991
1 A:Dark Eyes,Oshu........... 6.00
2 A:Dark Eyes, V:Oshu......... 5.25
3 Freeman vs. Oshu........... 5.25
4 Freeman Defeated........... 5.25
5 Freeman clones, A:Nitta 5.25
6 V:Nitta 5.25
7 thru 9 .... @5.00

CRYING FREEMAN IV
Viz, 1992
1 B:The Pomegranate.......... 5.00
2 thru 7 .... @3.00
8 E:The Pomegranate.......... 3.00

[2nd Series]
1 The Festival................ 2.50

CRYPT OF DAWN
Sirius, 1996
1 JLi 6.00
2 JLi 4.00
3 thru 6 .... @3.00

CRYPTIC WRITINGS OF MEGADETH
Chaos! Comics, 1997
1 BnP 3.00
1a Tour Edition, leather........ 20.00
1b Tour Edition, deluxe 30.00
2 BnP 3.00
3 BnP 3.00
4 BnP 3.00
TPB 13.00

CSI: CRIME SCENE INVESTIGATION
IDW Publishing, 2003
1 (of 5) 5.00
1a photo(c) 8.00
2 thru 3 .... @5.00
4 thru 5 .... @4.00
GN Thicker Than Blood 7.00
GN Miami–Smoking Gun........ 7.00
GN Miami–Thou Shalt Not....... 7.00
GN Miami–Blood/Money 7.00
TPB Vol. 1 Serial 20.00

CSI: CRIME SCENE INVESTIGATION: BAD RAP
IDW Publishing, 2003
1 (of 5) 4.00
2 thru 5 .... @4.00
TPB 20.00

CSI: CRIME SCENE INVESTIGATION: DEMON HOUSE
IDW Publishing, 2004
1 (of 5) 4.00
2 thru 5 .... @4.00
TPB 20.00

CSI: CRIME SCENE INVESTIGATION: DOMINOS
IDW Publishing, 2004
1 .... 4.00
2 thru 3 .... @4.00

CURSE OF RUNE
Malibu Ultraverse, 1995
1A CU,Rune/Silver Surfer tie-in ... 2.50
1B CU, alternate cover.......... 2.50
2 COntrol of the Soul Gem...... 2.50
3 F:Marvel's Adam Warlock 2.50
4 N:Adam Warlock 2.50

CVO: COVERT VAMPIRIC OPERATIONS–ARTIFACT
IDW Publishing, 2003
1 .... 4.00
2 thru 3 .... @4.00
GN 6.00
TPB 20.00

1-shot Human Touch (2004) 4.00

CYBER CITY: PART ONE
CPM Comics, 1995
1 I:Oedo City. 3.00
2 Sengoku. 3.00

Part Two
1 Based on Animated Movie. 3.00

CYBERCRUSH: ROBOTS IN REVOLT
Fleetway/Quality
1 inc.Robo-Hunter,Ro-Busters 2.50
2 and 3 . . . . @2.50
4 and 5 V:Terraneks . . . . @2.50

CYBERFROG
Harris, 1995
0 O:Cyberfrog. 3.00
0 AAd(c), signed 20.00
0 Alternate AAd(c). 9.95
1 . . . . 2.50
2 thru 4 . . . . @3.00

CYBERFROG: RESERVOIR FROG
Harris, 1996
1 Preview Ashcan, signed
   & numbered 15.00
1 EL(c),V:the Swarm,
   Mr. Skorpeone 3.00
2 . . . . 3.00

CYBERHOOD
Entity Comics, 1995
1 R:Cyberhood 2.50
1a with PC Game 7.00

CYBERNARY 2.0
WildStorm/DC, 2001
1 (of 6) R:Yumiko Gamorra. 3.00
2 F:MechaMax 3.00
3 F:Toshiro 3.00
4 secret race of cyborgs 3.00
5 revolution or evolution 3.00
6 Kaizen Gamorra, concl. 3.00

CYBERPUNK
Innovation
1 . . . . 2.25
2 . . . . 2.25
Book 2,#1. . . . . 2.25
Book 2,#2. . . . . 2.25

CYBERPUNK: THE SERAPHIM FILES
Innovation, 1990
1 . . . . 2.50
2 . . . . 2.50

CYBERPUNX
Maximum Press, 1997
1 MHw, ... 2.50

CYBERRAD
Continuity, 1991
1 NA layouts,I:Cyberran 3.00
2 NA I/o. 2.50
3 NA I/o 2.50
4 NA I/o 2.50
5 NA I/o Glow in the Dark cov 5.00
6 NA I/o,Pullout poster 2.50

---

7 NA I/o,See-thru(c) 2.50
[2nd Series], 1992
1 Hologram cover 2.50
2 NA(c),The Disassembled Man. . . 2.50
[3rd Series]
1 Holo.(c),just say no 3.50
[4th Series], 1993 Deathwatch 2000]
1 Deathwatch 2000 pt.8,w/card . . . 2.50
2 Deathwatch 2000 pt. w/card 2.50

CYBRID
Maximum Press, 1995
1 F:Cybrid, I:The Clan 3.00

CYBRID
Maximum Press, 1997
0 RLd, 48pg 3.50
1 MsM,BNa. 3.00
2 MsM,BNa. 3.00

CYNDER
Immortelle Studios, 1996
1 thru 3: see B&W
Ann. #1 . . . . 3.00
Series II, 1997
1 A:Nira X 3.00

CYNDER/NIRA X
Immortelle Studios, 1996
1 x-over. 3.00
1 variant cover 3.00
1 gold edition 10.00

DAEMONSTORM
Caliber, 1997
1 TM(c),JMt. 4.00
1 signed 4.00

DAEMONSTORM: DEADWORLD
Caliber
one-shot 4.00

DAEMONSTORM: OZ
Caliber, 1997
1 . . . . 4.00

DAGAR THE INVINCIBLE
Gold Key, 1972–82
1 O:Daggar;I:Villians Olstellon
   & Scorpio. 35.00
2 . . . . 20.00
3 I:Graylon 15.00
4 . . . . 15.00
5 . . . . 15.00
6 1st Dark Gods story 12.00
7 thru 10 . . . . @12.00

11 thru 19 . . . . @10.00

DAI KAMIKAZE
Now, 1987–88
1 Speed Racer 7.00
1a 2nd printing 2.50
2 thru 12 . . . . @2.50

DAKTARI
Dell Publishing Co., 1967
1 Ph(c) 60.00
2 Ph(c) 40.00
3 Ph(c) 40.00

Dai Kamikaze #10
© Now

4 Ph(c) 40.00

DALGODA
Fantagraphics, 1984–86
1 . . . . 3.50
2 KN,I:Grinwood'Daughter 3.00
3 KN 2.50
4 thru 8 . . . . @2.25

DALKIEL: THE PROPHECY
Verotik, 1998
1-shot, prequel to Satanika 4.00

DANGER
Charlton Comics, 1955
12 . . . . 125.00
13 . . . . 100.00
14 . . . . 100.00
Becomes:

JIM BOWIE
15 . . . . 50.00
16 . . . . 40.00
17 . . . . 40.00
18 . . . . 40.00
19 April, 1957. . . . . 40.00

DANGER GIRL: KAMIKAZE
WildStorm/DC, 2000
1 (of 2) 3.00
1a variant(c) 3.00
2 concl. 3.00
GN Viva Las Danger 5.00
Spec. Danger Girl 3-D 5.00
Spec. Hawaiian Punch. 5.00

DANGER RANGER
Checker Comics, 1998
1 I:Kirby Jackson, BSz(c) 2.50
2 . . . . 2.50

DANIEL BOONE
Gold Key, 1965–69
1 . . . . 150.00
2 thru 5 . . . . @100.00
6 thru 14 . . . . @60.00
15 . . . . 50.00

DANNY BLAZE
Charlton Comics, 1955
1 . . . . 125.00
2 . . . . 90.00
Becomes:
NATURE BOY
3 JB,O:Blue Beetle 175.00
4 . . . . 125.00
5 Feb., 1957 . . . . 100.00

DARE
Fantagraphics
1 F:Dan Dare 2.75
2 F:Dan Dare 2.75
3 F:Dan Dare 2.50
4 F:Dan Dare 2.50

DARE THE IMPOSSIBLE
Fleetway/Quality
1 DGb,rep.Dan Dare from 2000AD 2.50
2 thru 14 DGb . . . . @2.50

DARK, THE
Continuum, 1990
1 LSn(c),MBr,V:Futura 4.00
2 LSn,Shot by Futura 3.00
3 MBr,Dark has amnesia 3.00
4 GT(c),MBr,O:The Dark. 3.00
Convention Book 1992 MBr,GP,
  MFm,MMi,VS,LSn,TV 5.00
Convention Book 1993 MBr,PC,
  ECh,BS,BWi,GP(c),Foil(c), ... 4.00
[2nd Series], 1994
1 Dark Regains Memory 3.00
1a Signed, Foil Cover 2.75
1 BS(c),Red Foil(c), ... 3.00
1a BS(c),newstand ed. 3.00
1b BS(c),Blue foil 3.00
2 War on Crime 2.75
3 Geoffery Stockton 2.50
3 BS(c),Foil(c), ... 3.00
4 I:First Monster 2.50
4 GP(c),Foil(c),w/cards 3.00
5 thru 9 . . . . @2.50

DARK ADVENTURES
Darkline
1 thru 3 . . . . @2.50

DARK CHYLDE
Maximum Press, 1996
1 RQu 10.00
1a Am.Entertainment edition. 15.00
1b variant cover 9.00
2 RQu 7.00
2 Variant cover 6.00
3 RQu 4.00
3 Variant cover 5.00
4 RQu 5.00
5 RQu,No One Here Gets Out
  Alive. 5.00
Spec. Dark Chylde/Avengelyne RLd,
  RQu,I:Witch Tower. 3.00
Spec. Dark Chylde/Glory RQu, . . . 3.00
Darkchylde Entertainment, 2001
0 remastered, RQu (2001) 3.00
Last Issue special (2002). 4.00
Last issue exclusive variant(c). . . . 4.00

DARKCHYLDE REDEMPTION
Darkchylde Entertainment, 2001
1 RQu 3.00

---

2 . . . . 3.00
3 . . . . 3.00

DARK DAYS
IDW Publishing, 2003
1 (of 6) 4.50
2 thru 6 . . . . @4.25
TPB 20.00

Dark Dominion #3
© Defiant

DARK DOMINION
Defiant, 1993–94
1 SD,I:Michael Alexander 3.25
2 LWn(s),SLi(i), ... 2.75
3 LWn(s),SLi(i), ... 2.75
4 LWn(s),B:Hoxhunt 3.00
5 LWn(s),I:Puritan,Judah 2.75
6 LWn(s),I:Lurk 2.75
7 LWn(s),V:Glimmer 2.75
8 LWn(s),V:Glimmer 2.50
9 LWn(s)V:Puritan 2.50
10 LWn(s),Schism Prequel 2.50
11 LWn(s), X-Over 2.50
12 LWn(s), V:Chasm 2.50

DARKHAM VALE
APC, 2003
1 (of 10) by Jack Lawrence 3.50
2 thru 9 . . . . @3.50
10 finale 4.00
Spec. #0 . . . . 3.00
TPB Vol. 1 . . . . 20.00
TPB Vol. 2 . . . . 20.00

DARKHAM VALE: THE DRACOU IMPERATIVE
APC, 2004
1 . . . . 3.50
2 thru 4 . . . . @3.50

DARKLON THE MYSTIC
Pacific, 1983
1 JSn 2.50

DARKMINDS: MACROPOLIS
Dreamwave, 2002
1 . . . . 3.00
2 thru 4 . . . . @3.00
3a variant Pat Lee (c) 3.00

TPB Vol. 1 . . . . 10.00
Vol. 2
1 thru 4 . . . . @3.00

DARK ONE'S THIRD EYE
Sirius, 1996
one-shot Vol. 1 DOe 5.00
Vol. 2 DOe 5.00

DARK SHADOWS
Gold Key, 1969
1 W/Poster,Ph(c). 425.00
2 Ph(c) 150.00
3 W/Poster,Ph(c). 225.00
4 thru 7,Ph(c) . . . . @125.00
8 thru 10 . . . . @100.00
11 thru 20 . . . . @75.00
21 thru 35 . . . . @60.00

DARK SHADOWS
Innovation, 1992
1 Based on 1990's TV series 3.50
2 O:Victoria Winters 2.50
3 Barnabus Imprisoned. 2.50
4 V: Redmond Swann. 2.75
[2nd Series]
1 A:Nathan 2.75
2 thru 4 . . . . 2.75
Dark Shadows:Resurrected 16.00

DARK SIDE
Maximum Press, 1997
1 RLd,RQu 3.00

DARKSHRINE
Antarctic Press, 1999
1 by Shelby Robertson 3.00
1a deluxe 6.00
2 16-page 2.50

DARK TOWN
Mad Monkey Press
1 (of 13) 4.00
2 thru 7 . . . . @4.00

DARKWING DUCK
Walt Disney, 1991
1 I:Darkwing Duck. 3.00
2 V:Taurus Bulba 3.00
3 Fowl Play 3.00
4 End o/t beginning,final issue . . . 3.00

DARKWOOD
Aircel
1 thru 5 . . . . @2.50

DARQUE PASSAGES
Acclaim, 1997
1 (of 4) sequal to Master Darque . . 2.50
1 signed edition. 4.00
2 . . . . 2.50
3 A:Pere Jean, Voodoo King. 2.50
4 conclusion 2.50

DAUGHTERS OF TIME
3-D Zone
1 I:Kris,Cori,Lhana 4.00

FRONTIER FIGHTER
Charlton Comics, 1955
1 JK,Davy Crocket-Buffalo Bill . . 250.00
2 JK. 150.00
Becomes:

DAVY CROCKETT
3 thru 7 JK. . . . . @150.00
8 Jan., 1957 JK. 100.00
Becomes:

KID MONTANA
9 . . . . 75.00
10 . . . . 60.00
11 . . . . 40.00
12 . . . . 40.00
13 AW 50.00
14 thru 20 . . . . @40.00
21 thru 35 . . . . @35.00
36 thru 49 . . . . @25.00
50 March, 1965 . . . . 25.00

DAWN
Sirius, 1995–97
? Wizard mail-in 10.00
? variant 25.00
1 JLi,R:Dawn 12.00
1a white trash edition 35.00
1b black light edition. 25.00
1c look sharp edition. 45.00
2 JLi, Trip to Hell. 7.00
2 variant cover 22.00
3 JLi 6.00
3 limited edition. 25.00
4 JLi,The Gauntlet 5.00
4a variant cover 15.00
5 JLi,Everybody Dies 4.00
5a variant cover 15.00
6 (of 6) JLi. 4.00
6a variant cover 12.00
TPB Lucifer's Halo. 20.00
TPB Tears of Dawn 18.00
10th Anniv. Spec. 3.00
10th Anniv. Spec, sgn,num. 5.00
Portable Dawn, art work 10.00

DAWN: PIN-UP GODDESS
Linsner.com, 2001
Spec. 3.00
Spec. Limited, signed. 12.00

DAWN: THE RETURN OF THE GODDESS
Sirius, 1999
1 (of 4) JLi. 3.00
1a limited, signed 25.00
2 A:Marinen. 3.00
3 . . . . 3.00
4 . . . . 3.00
2a thru 4a deluxe . . . . @20.00

DAZEY'S DIARY
Dell Publishing Co., 1962
1 . . . . 60.00

DEAD @ 17
Viper Comics, 2003
1 (of 4) 25.00
2 . . . . 22.00
3 . . . . 10.00
4 . . . . 7.00
Rough Cut #1. . . . . 4.00
TPB Vol. 1 . . . . 15.00
TPB Vol. 2 Blood of Saints 15.00

DEAD @ 17: BLOOD OF SAINTS
Viper Comics, 2004
1 (of 4) 4.00
2 thru 4 . . . . @3.00

DEAD BOYS: DEATH'S EMBRACE
London Night, 1996
1 EHr. 3.00
1 platinum edition 6.00

DEAD CLOWN
Malibu, 1996
1 I:Force America 2.50
2 I:Sadistic Six 2.50
3 TMs(s),last issue 2.50

DEADFORCE
Antarctic Press, 1999
1 (of 3) by Roy Burdine 3.00
2 . . . . 3.00
3 . . . . 3.00

DEAD KING
Chaos! Comics, 1997
1 (of 4) Burnt, pt.1, F:Homicide . . . 3.00
2 Burnt, pt.2 . . . . 3.00
3 Burnt, pt.3 . . . . 3.00
4 Burnt, pt.4, concl.. . . . . 3.00
TPB Dead King Burnt 13.00

DEADSIDE
Acclaim, 1998
1 (of 4) PJe, ... 2.50
2 thru 4 . . . . @2.50

DEAMON DREAMS
Pacific
1 . . . . 2.50
2 . . . . 2.50

DEAR NANCY PARKER
Gold Key, 1963
1 P(c) 35.00
2 P(c) 30.00

DEATHBLOW: BY BLOWS
WildStorm/DC, 1999
1 (of 3) AMo,JBa. 3.00
2 AMo,JBa 3.00

DEATHDEALER
Verotika, 1995
1 FF(c), I:Deathdealer. 15.00
2 thru 4 FF(c) . . . . @12.00

DEATHMASK
Future Comics, 2003
1 DvM,DG,BL 3.00
2 thru 9 . . . . @3.00
TPB 16.00

DEATHMATE
Valiant/Image, 1993
Preview (Advanced Comics) 2.25
Preview (Previews) 2.25
Preview (Comic Defense Fund). . . . 4.00
Prologue BL,JLe,RLd,Solar meets
    Void 3.25
Prologue Gold 4.00
Blue SCh, HSn, F:Solar, Magnus,
    Battlestone, Livewire, Stronghold,
    Impact, Striker, Harbinger, Brigade,
    Supreme 3.00
Blue Gold Ed.. . . . . 4.00
Yellow BCh,MLe,DP,F:Armstrong,
    H.A.R.D.C.A.T.S.,Ninjak,Zealot,
    Shadowman,Grifter,Ivar. 3.00

Yellow Gold Ed. 4.00
Black JLe,MS,F:Warblade,Ripclaw,
    Turok,X-O Manowar 4.00
Black Gold Ed. 6.00
Red RLd,JMs, ... 4.00
Red Gold Ed. 3.00
Epilogue 2.50
Epilogue Gold 3.00

DEATH OF HARI KARI
Blackout Comics, 1997
0 . . . . 3.00
0 super Sexy Kari Cover. 10.00
0 3-D super Sexy Kari Cover 15.00

Death of Lady Vampre #1
© *Blackout Comics*

DEATH OF LADY VAMPRE
Blackout Comics, 1995
1 V:Baraclaw. 3.00
1 Commemorative Issue. 10.00

DEATHRACE 2020
Cosmic Comics, 1995
1 Pat Mills, Tony Skinner 2.50
2 V:Spyda, Sawmill Jones 2.50
3 O:Frankenstein 2.50
4 Deathrace cont. 2.50
5 F:Death Racers, D:Alchoholic . . . 2.50
6 V:Indestructiman 2.50
7 Smallville Mall 2.50

DEATH RATTLE
Kitchen Sink, 1985–88
1 thru 7 . . . . @4.00
8 I:Xenozoic Tales. 9.00
9 thru 18 . . . . @3.00

DECOY
Penny Farthing Press, 1999
1 (of 4) 2.75
2 . . . . 2.75
3 . . . . 2.75
4 . . . . 2.75
TPB 16.00

DECOY: STORM OF THE CENTURY
Pennyfarthing Press, 2002
1 (of 4) 3.00
2 thru 4 . . . . @3.00

COLOR PUB.

DEFENDERS, THE
Dell Publishing Co., 1962
1 . . . . 60.00
2 . . . . 40.00

DEFIANT:
ORIGIN OF A UNIVERSE
Defiant, 1993
1 Giveaway 2.50

DEITY
Hyperwerks, 1997
0 . . . . 3.00
1 KIA 5.00
1a Director's Cut 3.00
2 thru 6 KIA . . . . @3.00
TPB rep. #1–#3 . . . . 8.00
TPB rep. #4–#6 . . . . 8.00

VOL II Awesome/Hyperwerks, 1998
1 KIA,BNa, F:Jamie 3.00
1a Limited edition 8.00
1b Silver Foil edition 13.00
1c Gold Edition 20.00
2 KIA,BNa, A:Diamond Diaz 3.00
3 KIA,BNa, The Soul Crusher 3.00
4 KIA,BNa, A:Ogden 3.00
5 KLa,BNa,V:Ma'Shiva 3.00
6 KIA,BNa 3.00

DEITY II: CATSEYE
Hyperwerks, 1998
1 KIA,BNa,F:Digby 3.00
2 KIA,BNa,A:II 3.00
3 KIA,BNa,F:Catseye 3.00
4 KIA,BNa,conclusion 3.00

DELIVERER
Zion Comics
1 thru 3 . . . . @2.50
4 F:Gabriel 2.50
5 V:Division 2.50

DEMON-HUNTER
Atlas, 1975
1 The Harvester of Eyes 15.00

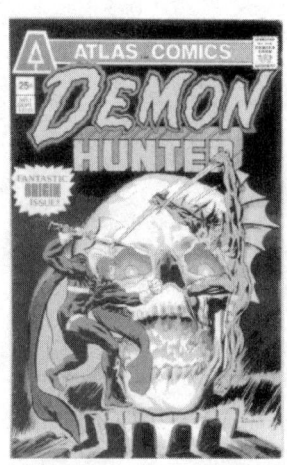
Demon Hunter #1 © Atlas

DEMONIC TOYS
Eternity, 1992
1 Based on 1992 movie 2.50
2 thru 4 . . . . @2.50

DEMONIQUE
London Night, 1996
0 Manga 3.00
1 EHr. 3.00
2 (of 2) 3.00

DEMONSLAYER
Avatar Press, 2001
0 16-page, signed 6.00
TPB Vol. 1 . . . . 20.00

DEMONSLAYER:
FUTURE SHOCK
Avatar Press, 2002
1/2 Eradicate Edition 6.00

DEMONSLAYER:
PATH OF TIME
Avatar, 2002
1 MMy 3.50
1a Medieval (c) 3.50
1b Ninja (c) 3.50
1c Western (c) 3.50
1d Matt Martin (c) 3.50
1e Serenity (c) 6.00
1f bondage (c) 6.00
1g Prism foil (c) 13.00
1/2 . . . . 4.00
1/2 Pirate (c) 4.00
1/2 Cave Girl (c) 4.00
1/2 Bikini (c) 4.00
1/2 Martin (c) 4.00

DEMONSLAYER:
PROPHECY
Avatar Press, 2001
1 MMy 3.50
1a Celtic (c) 3.50
1b Hell on Wheels (c) 3.50
1c Leather (c) 20.00
1d lace edition 6.00
1e Bad Omens (c) 6.00
1f Mouth of Evil edition 6.00
1g Prism foil (c) 13.00
1h Royal blue edition 75.00

DEMONSLAYER: RAVE
Avatar Press, 2001
Spec. 3.50
Spec. Bad Schoolgirl (c) 3.50
Spec. Silent Moment (c) 3.50
Rave in Style (c) 6.00
Rave Previews prism foil (c) 13.00

DEMONSLAYER: REBIRTH
Awesome Entertainment, 2000
1 . . . . 3.00

DEMONSLAYER:
VENGEANCE
Avatar Press, 2001
1 (of 2) MMy (c) 3.50
1a Park (c) 3.50
1b Wraparound (c) 4.00
1c Red Velvet (c) 20.00
1d prism foil (c) 13.00
1e fire (c). 6.00
1f ice (c) 6.00

1g Royal Blue edition 75.00
2 MMy, concl. 3.50
2a Bikini (c) 3.50
2b Jungle Girl (c) 3.50
2c Ruins edition 6.00

DEMONWARS:
EYE FOR AN EYE
Crossgen Comics, 2003
1 (of 5) 3.00
2 thru 5 . . . . @3.00
TPB 10.00

DEMONWARS:
TRIAL BY FIRE
Crossgen Comics, 2002
2 thru 5 . . . . @3.00
TPB Vol. 1 Trial by Fire 13.00

DEN
Fantagor
1 thru 10 RCo . . . . @2.00

DEN SAGA
Tundra/Fantagor
1 RCo,O:Den begins 5.00

DENNIS THE MENACE
Fawcett, 1960-61
Fun Book #1 . . . . 75.00
And his Pal Joey #1 . . . . 50.00
And his Dog Ruff #1 . . . . 50.00
Television Special #1 . . . . 60.00
Triple Feature #1 . . . . 60.00
Television Special #2 . . . . 35.00

DENNIS THE MENACE
AND HIS FRIENDS
[VARIOUS SUBTITLES]
Fawcett, 1969–1980
1 thru 10 rep. . . . . @35.00
11 thru 20 rep. . . . . @20.00
21 thru 46 rep. . . . . @15.00

DENNIS THE MENACE
GIANTS
[VARIOUS SUBTITLES]
Fawcett, 1955–69
N# Vacation Special 200.00
N# Christmas 175.00
2 thru 10 . . . . @150.00
11 thru 20 . . . . @100.00
21 thru 30 . . . . @50.00
31 thru 40 . . . . @30.00
41 thru 75 . . . . @25.00
Becomes:

DENNIS THE MENACE
BONUS MAGAZINE
[VARIOUS SUBTITLES]
Fawcett, 1970–79
76 thru 100 . . . . @20.00
101 thru 120 . . . . @15.00
121 thru 185 . . . . @10.00
186 thru 196 Big Bonus Series . . @8.00
Becomes:

DENNIS THE MENACE
Fawcett, 1979–80
#16 Fun Fest 5.00
#17 Fun Fest 5.00
#10 Big Bonus Series 5.00
#11 Big Bonus Series 5.00

DEPUTY DAWG
Gold Key, 1965
1 . . . . 200.00

DER VANDALE
Innervision, 1998
1 (of 3) 2.50
2 (of 3) 2.50
3 (of 3) 2.50
3 variant cover 2.50

DESERT STORM JOURNAL
Apple Comics, 1991
1 Hussein on (c) 2.75
1a Schwartzkopf on (c) 2.75
2 thru 8 . . . . @2.75

DESTROYER
Valiant, 1994
0 MM 41st Century 3.00

DESTROYER DUCK
Eclipse, 1982–84
1 JK,AA,SA,I:Groo 12.00
2 JK,AA,Starling 5.00
3 thru 7 JK. . . . . @5.00

DESTRUCTOR, THE
Atlas, 1975
1 thru 4 WW,SD . . . . @25.00

DETECTIVES, INC.
Eclipse, 1985
1 MR,rep.GraphicNovel 3.00
2 MR 2.50

[2nd Series]
1 GC,A Terror of Dying Dreams . . . 2.50
2 GC 2.25
3 GC,Cut to the Bone 2.25

DETONATOR
Chaos! Comics, 1994–95
1 I:Detonator 3.00
2 V:Messiah & Mindbender. 3.00

DEVIL KIDS STARRING HOT STUFF
Harvey Publications, 1962–81
1 . . . . 250.00
2 . . . . 125.00
3 thru 10 . . . . @100.00
11 thru 20 . . . . @60.00
21 thru 30 . . . . @40.00
31 thru 40 . . . . @30.00
41 thru 50 68 pgs. . . . . @30.00
51 thru 55 62 pgs. . . . . @25.00
56 thru 70 . . . . @20.00
71 thru 100 . . . . @15.00
101 thru 107 . . . . @10.00

DEVILMAN
Verotika, 1995
1 Go Nagi 3.00
1a San Diego Con Gatefold edition 5.00
2 F:Devilman 3.00
3 Through History 3.00
4 French Revolution 3.00
5 Custer's Last Stand 3.00

DEVIL MAY CRY
Dreamwave, 2004
1 . . . . 4.00
2 thru 4 . . . . @4.00
1a thru 4a variant (c)s . . . . @4.00

DEVLIN
Maximum Press, 1996
1 A:Avengelyne,3-part mini-series . 2.50
2 (of 3) RLd,BNa,A:Avengelyne . . . 2.50

DICK TRACY
Blackthorne, 1986
1 3-D 3.00

DICK TRACY: BIG CITY BLUES
1 Mini Series 4.00
2 Mini Series 6.00
3 Mini Series 6.00

DIGITAL GRAFFITI
APC, 2003
1 . . . . 3.50
2 thru 4 . . . . @3.50
TPB 17.00

Dino Island #1
© Mirage

DINO ISLAND
Mirage, 1993
1 thru 2 . . . . 2.75

DINOSAUR REX
Upshot/Fantagraphics, 1987
1 thru 3 by Jan Strand &
 Henry Mayo . . . . @2.00

DINOSAURS
Walt Disney
1 Citizen Robbie(From TV) 3.00

DINOSAURS ATTACK
Eclipse, 1991
1 HT,Based on Topps cards 3.50
2 and 3 HT,Based on cards . . . . @3.50

DINOSAURS FOR HIRE
Malibu
1 3-D rep. B&W 3.00
[2nd Series] 1993–94
1 B:TMs(s),A:Reese,Archie,
 Lorenzo 3.00
2 BU:Dinosaurs 2099 . . . . 2.50
3 A:Ex-Mutants 2.50
4 V:Poacher,Revenue. 2.50
5 . . . . 2.50
6 V:Samantha 2.50
7 V:Turret 2.50
8 Genesis #2, with Skycap 2.50
9 Genesis #5. . . . . 2.50
10 Flip(c) 2.50
11 V:Tiny Lorenzo 2.50
12 I:Manhatten Bob 2.50
13 I:Lil' Billy Frankenstein 2.50
14 final issue 2.50

DISNEY ADVENTURES
Walt Disney
1 . . . . 3.00
2 . . . . 3.00
3 thru 13 . . . . @3.00
14 thru 28 . . . . @3.00

DISNEY COLOSSAL COMICS COLLECTION
Walt Disney
1 inc.DuckTales, Chip'n'Dale 3.00
2 thru 9 . . . . @3.00

DISNEY COMICS IN 3-D
Walt Disney
1 . . . . 3.00

DISNEY COMICS SPEC: DONALD & SCROOGE
1 inc."Return to Xanadu" 9.00

DISNEYLAND BIRTHDAY PARTY
Gladstone, 1985
1 CB 15.00

DIVER DAN
Dell Publishing Co., Feb.-April, 1962
1 . . . . 75.00
2 . . . . 60.00

DIVINE INTERVENTION
WildStorm/DC, 1999
1 . . . . 3.00
Wildcats, pt.2, JLe,SLo,RiB 3.00
Gen13, pt.3, JLe,SLo,RiB. 3.00

DIVINE MADNESS
Dark Moon
1 Human Flesh Artist 2.50
2 . . . . 2.50
3 Ancient Cult 2.50

DNAGENTS
Eclipse, 1983–85
1 O:DNAgents 4.00
2 . . . . 3.00
3 thru 8 . . . . @2.50
9 DSp 2.50
10 thru 25 . . . . @2.50
See also: NEW DNAGENTS

All comics prices listed are for *Near Mint* condition.

DON BLUTH'S DRAGON'S LAIR
Crossgen Comics, 2003
1 (of 6) Singe's Revenge 3.00
2 thru 3 . . . . @3.00

DON BLUTH'S SPACE ACE
Crossgen Comics, 2003
1 (of 6) Defender of the Universe. . 3.00
2 thru 3 . . . . @3.00

DO YOU BELIEVE IN NIGHTMARES?
St. John Publishing Co., 1957–58
1 SD 650.00
2 DAy 400.00

DOBER-MAN
1 . . . . 2.50

DOC SAVAGE
Gold Key, 1966
1 . . . . 150.00

DOC SAVAGE
Millennium
1 V:Russians. 2.50

DOC SAVAGE, THE MAN OF BRONZE
Millennium
1 Monarch of Armageddon,pt.1 . . . 3.00
2 Monarch of Armageddon,pt.2 . . . 3.00
3 Monarch of Armageddon,pt.3 . . . 3.00
4 Monarch of Armageddon,pt.4 . . . 3.00

DOC SAVAGE: THE DEVIL'S THOUGHTS
Millennium
1 V:Hanoi Shan. 2.50
2 V:Hanoi Shan. 2.50
3 Final issue 2.50

DOC SAVAGE: DOOM DYNASTY
Millennium, 1991
1 and 2 . . . . @2.50

DOC SAVAGE: MANUAL OF BRONZE
Millennium
1 Fact File. 2.50

DOC SAVAGE: REPEL
Innovation
1 DvD(c) 2.50

DOCTOR BOOGIE
Media Arts
1 and 2 . . . . @2.25

DOCTOR CHAOS
Triumphant Comics, 1993
1 JnR(s),I:Doctor Chaos. 2.50
2 JnR(s),. 2.50
3 JnR(s),The Coming of
the Cry,pt.1,I:Cry 2.50

---

4 JnR(s),The Coming of
the Cry,pt.2,b:Ky'Li 2.50
5 JnR(s),E:Coming of the
Cry,pt.3,V:Cry 2.50
6 Recovery 2.50
7 w/coupon 2.50
8 w/coupon 2.50
9 V:Mirth 2.50
10 Co. X #3 . . . . 2.50
11 Co. X #4 . . . . 2.50
12 A:Charlotte 2.50

DR. KILDARE
Dell Publishing Co., April-June, 1962
1 . . . . 150.00
2 thru 9 . . . . @100.00

DOCTOR SOLAR MAN OF THE ATOM
Gold Key, 1962
1 BF,I:Dr. Solar 325.00
2 BF,I:Prof.Harbinger 125.00
3 BF,The Hidden Hands 80.00
4 BF,The Deadly Sea 80.00
5 BF,I:Dr.Solar in costume 90.00
6 FBe,I:Nuro 60.00
7 FBe,Vanishing Oceans 60.00
8 FBe,Thought Controller 60.00
9 FBe,Transivac The Energy
Consuming Computer 60.00
10 FBe,The Sun Giant. 60.00
11 FBe,V:Nuro 50.00
12 FBe,The Mystery of the
Vanishing Silver. 50.00
13 FBe,Meteor from 100 Mill.BC . . 50.00
14 FBe,Solar's Midas Touch 50.00
15 FBe O:Dr.Solar 60.00
16 FBe,V:Nuro 50.00
17 FBe,The Fatal Foe 50.00
18 FBe,The Mind Master 50.00
19 FBe,SolarV:Solar 50.00
20 AMc,Atomic Nightmares 50.00
21 AMc,Challenge from Outer
Space. 35.00
22 AMc,Nuro,I:King Cybernoid . . . 35.00
23 AMc,A:King Cybernoid 35.00
24 EC,The Deadly Trio 35.00
25 EC,The Lost Dimension 35.00
26 EC,When Dimensions Collide. . 35.00
27 (1969) The Ladder to Mars . . . 35.00
28 (1981),1-pg AMc,The Dome
of Mystery 25.00
29 DSp,FBe,Magnus 25.00
30 DSp,FBe,Magnus 25.00

DR. TOMORROW
Acclaim, 1997
1 (of 12) BL,Bart Simms finds
Angel Computer 2.50
2 BL,V:Teutonic Knight 2.50
3 BL,V:Teutonic Knight concl. 2.50
4 BL,V:Joe McCarthy 2.50
5 BL,V:J. Edgar Hoover 2.50
6 BL,DG,V:Mushroom Cloud. 2.50
7 BL,DG,A:Mushroom Cloud. 2.50
8 BL,GK,Vietnam 2.50
9 BL, ... 2.50
10 BL,SMc,on *Oprah*. 2.50
11 BL,the time capsule 2.50
12 BL,MBu(c),final issue 2.50

DOGHEAD
Tundra
1 Al Columbia,"Poster Child" 5.00

DOGS OF WAR
Defiant, 1994
1 F:Shooter,Ironhead 2.75
2 . . . . 2.50
3 Mouse Deserts. 2.50
4 Schism Prequel 2.50
5 X-over 2.50
6 Aftermath 2.50

DOLLMAN
Eternity, 1991
1 Movie adapt. sequel 2.50
2 V:Sprug & Braindead Gang 2.50
3 Toni Costa Kidnapped 2.50
4 . . . . 2.50

Donald Duck #203
© Disney

DONALD DUCK
Dell/Gold Key, 1962
85 thru 97. . . . . 60.00
98 rep. #46 CB 60.00
99 . . . . 50.00
100. . . . . 60.00
101 thru 111 . . . . @40.00
112 I:Moby Duck 50.00
113 thru 133 . . . . @35.00
134 CB rep. 35.00
135 CB rep. 35.00
136 thru 156. . . . . @25.00
157 CB rep. 25.00
158 thru 163. . . . . @25.00
164 CB rep. 25.00
165 thru 216. . . . . @20.00

Whitman
217. . . . . 20.00
218. . . . . 20.00
219 CB rep. 20.00
220 and 221 . . . . @40.00
222 scarce 250.00
223 thru 224 . . . . @50.00
225 thru 240. . . . . @20.00
241 thru 245 . . . . @25.00

Gladstone
246 CB,Gilded Man 25.00
247 CB. 20.00
248 CB,Forbidden Valley. 20.00
249 CB. 20.00
250 CB,Pirate Gold 20.00
251 CB,Donald's Best Xmas 15.00
252 CB,Trail o/t Unicorn 8.00
253 CB. 8.00
254 CB, in old Calif 9.00
255 CB. 8.00

---

256 CB,Volcano Valley 8.00
257 CB,Forest Fire 8.00
258 thru 260 CB. . . . . @8.00
261 thru 266 CB. . . . . @8.00
267 thru 277 CB. . . . . @8.00
278 CB 9.00
279 CB. 9.00
280 thru 298 CB rep. . . . . @6.00
299 Life Guard Daze 5.00
300 Donald's 300th Triumph' 48pg . 6.00
301 The Gold Finder 5.00
302 Monkey Business 5.00
303 The Cantankerous Cat 5.00
304 Donald Duck Rants
    about Ants 5.00
305 Mockingbird Ridge 5.00
306 Worst Class Mail. 5.00
307 Going to Sea. 5.00
308 Worst Class Mail. 5.00

DONALD DUCK ADVENTURES
Gladstone, 1987
1 CB,Jungle Hi-Jinks 8.00
2 CB,Dangerous Disquise 6.00
3 CB,Lost in the Andes. 6.00
4 CB,Frozen Gold. 6.00
5 CB,Rosa 6.00
6 CB 3.00
7 CB 3.00
8 CB,Rosa 6.00
9 CB 3.00
10 CB. 3.00
11 CB 3.00
12 CB,Rosa,Giant-size 6.00
13 CB,Rosa(c) 3.50
14 CB. 3.00
15 CB. 3.00
16 CB. 3.00
17 CB. 3.00
18 CB,No Such Varmint. 3.00
19 CB. 4.00
20 CB,Giant-size (1990) 4.00
21 CB,Rosa(c) (1993) 4.00
22 CB,The Pixilated Parrot 4.00
23 thru 30. . . . . @4.00
31 thru 40 . . . . @3.00
41 Bruce McDuck 3.00
42 The Saga of Sourdough Sam. . . 3.00
43 The Lost Charts of Columbus. . . 3.00
44 The Kitchy-Kaw Diamond 3.00
45 The Red Duck. 3.00
46. . . . . 3.00
47 CB,Trick or Treat. 3.00
48 The Saphead Factor 3.00

DONALD DUCK ADVENTURES
Walt Disney, 1990
1 Don Rosa, The Money Pit 6.00
2 CB 3.00
3 . . . . 3.00
4 CB 3.00
5 . . . . 3.00
6 . . . . 3.00
7 . . . . 3.00
8 . . . . 3.00
9 CB 3.00
10 Run-Down Runner 3.00
11 Whats for Lunch-Supper 3.00
12 Head of Rama Putra. 3.00
13 JustAHumble,BumblingDuck . . . 3.00
14 CB,Day Gladstone's Luck
    Ran Out. 4.00
15 A Tuft Luck Tale. 3.00
16 Magica's Missin'Magic 3.00
17 CB,Secret of Atlantis. 4.00
18 Crocodile Donald 3.00
19 Not So Silent Service 3.00

20 Ghost of Kamikaze Ridge. 3.00
21 CB,The Golden Christmas Tree . 4.00
22 The Master Landscapist 5.00
23 The Lost Peg Leg Mine 3.00
24 On Stolen Time 4.00
25 Sense of Humor 3.00
26 CB,Race to the South Seas 4.00
27 CB,Nap in Nature 4.00
28 Olympic Tryout 3.00
29 CB,rep.March of Comics#20. . . . 4.00
30 A:The Vikings 3.00
31 The Sobbing Serpent of Loch
    McDuck 3.00
32 It Was No Occident. 3.00
33 Crazy Christmas on Bear
    Mountain 3.00
34 Sup.Snooper Strikes Again. 4.00
35 CB rep. 4.00
36 CB rep. 4.00
37 CB rep. 3.00
38 CB rep. 4.00

Gemstone Publishing, 2003
TPB Vol. 1 . . . . 8.00
TPB Vol. 2 thru Vol. 8 . . . . @8.00

DONALD DUCK ALBUM
Dell Publishing Co., May-July, 1959
1 CB(c) 100.00
2 . . . . 75.00

DONALD DUCK AND FRIENDS
Gemstone Publishing, 2003
308 thru 321. . . . . @3.00

DONATELLO
Mirage
1 . . . . 10.00

DONNA MIA
Dark Fantasy Prod., 1995
1 I:Donna Mia 4.00
1a Deluxe Edition 5.00
1b signed & numbered (100 copies) . . .
9.00
2 . . . . 3.00

Doomsday +1 Vol. 2, #6
© Charlton Comics

DOOMSDAY + 1
Charlton, 1975–79
1 JBy,JBy(c) 25.00
2 JBy(c),P(c) 20.00
3 JBy,JBy(c),P(c) 15.00
4 JBy,JBy(c),P(c),I:Lok 15.00
5 and 6 JBy,JBy(c),P(c) . . . . . . @15.00
7 thru 12 JBy,JBy(c),rep . . . . . . @7.00

DOOMSDAY SQUAD
Fantagraphics, 1986
1 rep. JBy 3.00
2 rep. JBy 3.00
3 rep. SS,A:Usagi Yojimbo 3.00
4 thru 7, rep. JBy . . . . @3.00

DOUBLE DARE ADVENTURES
Harvey Publications, 1966
1 I:B-man,Glowing Gladiator,
    Magicmaster 100.00
2 AW/RC rep. A:B-Man,Glowing
    Gladiator, Magicmaster 75.00

DOUBLE IMPACT
High Impact Studios, 1995–96
1 RCI,I:China & Jazz, chrome(c) . . 7.00
1 holographic rainbow (c) with
    certificate 15.00
1 rainbow (c), no certificate 10.00
1 chromium variant (c) 8.00
2 RCI,V:Castillo. 3.00
2a signed, with certificate 4.00
3 China on cover 5.00
3a Jazzler on cover 3.00
3b Nikki on cover 3.00
3c Blondage 6.00
4 F:Mordred, The Rattler 3.00
4a Phoenix variant (c). 6.00
5 RCI 3.00
6 Buttshots 4.00
6a Jazz (c) 3.00
6a signed 6.00
7 I:Nikki Blade. 3.00
8 . . . . 3.00
8a variant (c). 4.00
Gold edition, Lingerie special. 3.00
Volume 2, 1996–97
0 RCI 3.00
1 RCI. 3.00
1a deluxe edition. 4.00
1b prism foil (c) 5.00
1c gold foil (c) 5.00
2 RCI. 3.00
3 . . . . 3.00
3a special edition RCI(c). 8.00

DOUBLE IMPACT: ALIVE
ABC Studios, 1999
1 RCI,F:China & Jazz 3.00
1a deluxe 8.00

DOUBLE IMPACT/ HELLINA
High Impact, 1996
1-shot RCI. 3.00

DOUBLE IMPACT/ LETHAL STRYKE: DOUBLE STRIKE
High Impact/London Night, 1996
1-shot RCI. 3.00

COLOR PUB.

DOUBLE IMPACT SUICIDE RUN
High Impact, 1997
1 RCI	3.00
1 gold edition	10.00
1 platinum edition	20.00
2	3.00
2a Suicide Cover	10.00

DOUBLE IMPACT: 2069
ABC Studios, 1999
1 RCI,Independent Day	3.00
1a premium edition	5.00
1b Sexy China ed.	5.00

DOUBLE LIFE OF PRIVATE STRONG
Archie Publications, 1959
1 JSm/JK,I:Lancelot Strong/ Shield, The Fly	850.00
2 JSm/JK,GT A:Fly	550.00

DRACULA
Dell Publishing Co., 1966
2 O:Dracula	50.00
3	35.00
4	35.00
6	30.00
7	25.00
8	25.00

DRACULA
Topps, 1992
1 MMi,Movie adaptation (trading cards in each issue)	5.00
1a Red Foil Logo	10.00
1b 2nd Print	3.00
2 MMi,Movie adapt.contd.	4.00
3 MMi,Movie adapt.contd.	4.00
4 MMi,Movie adapt.concludes	4.00
TPB Collected Album	14.00

DRACULA CHRONICLES
Topps
1 True Story of Dracula	2.50
2 RTs,rep. Vlad #2	2.50
3 RTs,rep. Vlad #3	2.50

DRACULA'S REVENGE
IDW Publishing, 2004
1	4.00
2	4.00

DRACULA VS. ZORRO
Topps, 1993
1 DMg(s),TY,Black(c),	3.25
2 DMg(s),TY,w/Zorro #0	3.00
TPB	6.00

DRACULA: VLAD THE IMPALER
Topps, 1993
1 EM,I:Vlad Dracua, w/cards	3.25
1a Red Foil	10.00
2 EM, w/cards	3.25

DRAGONCHIANG
Eclipse
1 TT	3.00

DRAGONFLIGHT
Eclipse, 1991
1 Anne McCaffrey adapt.	5.00
2 novel adapt	5.00
3 novel adapt	5.00

DRAGONFLY
AC Comics, 1985
1	3.50
2 and 3	@2.00
4 thru 8	@2.00

DRAGONLANCE: THE LEGEND OF HUMA
Devil's Due Publishing, 2004
1	3.00
1a variant (c)	3.00
2 thru 6	@3.00
TPB Vol. 1	15.00

Dragonring Vol. 2 #2 © Aircel

DRAGONRING
Aircel, 1987–88, Vol. 2
1	3.50
2 O:Dragonring	2.50
3 thru 15	@2.25
See also: B&W	

DRAKKON WARS, THE
Realm Press, 1997
0 by Richard Hatch & Chris Scalf	3.00
1	3.00

DREADSTAR
First, 1986–91
27 JSn,from Epic,traitor	3.00
28 JSn	3.00
29 JSn,V:Lord Papal	3.00
30 JSn,D:Lord Papal	3.00
31 JSn,I:The Power	3.00
32 JSn	3.00
33	3.00
34 LM/VM,A:Malchek	3.00
35 LM/VM	3.00
36 LM/VM	3.00
37 LM/VM,A:Last Laugh	3.00
38 LM/VM	3.00
39 AMc,Crossroads tie-in	3.00
40 LM/VM	3.00
41 AMe	3.00
42 JSn,AMe,B.U.Pawns begins	3.00

43 JSn,AMe,Pawns,pt.2	3.00
44 JSn,AMe,Pawns,pt.3	3.00
45 JSn,AMe,Pawns,pt.4	3.00
46 JSn,AMe,Pawns,pt.5	3.00
47 JSn,AMe,Pawns,pt.6	3.00
48 JSn,AMe,Pawns,pt.7	3.00
49 JSn,AMe,Pawns,pt.8	3.00
50 JSn,AMe,Pawns,pt.9 prestige	4.25
51 PDd,Woj,Pawns,pt.10, Paladox epic begins	4.00
52 AMe	4.00
53 AMe,Messing with Peoples Minds	4.00
54 JSn,AMe,Pawns ends	4.00
55 AMe,I:Iron Angel	4.00
56 AME,A:Iron Angel	4.00
57 A:Iron Angel	4.00
58 A:Iron Angel	4.00
59 A:Iron Angel	4.00
60 AMe,Paladox epic ends	4.00
61 AME,A:Iron Angel	4.00
62 O:Dreadstar,I:Youngscuz	4.00
63 AMe,A:Youngscuz	4.00
64 AMe,A:Youngscuz	4.00

DREADSTAR
Malibu Bravura, 1994–95
1 JSn(c),PDd(s),EC,I:New Dreadstar (Kalla),w/stamp	2.75
2 JSn(c),PDd(s),EC,w/stamp	2.50
3 JSn(c),PDd(s),EC,w/stamp	2.75
4 PDd,EC,Kalla's origin,w/stamp	2.50
5 PDd,F:Vanth,w/stamp	2.50
6 PDd,w/stamp	2.50

DREAMS OF THE DARKCHYLDE
Darkchylde Entertainment, 2000
1 RQu,BPe	3.00
2 thru 6	@3.00
4a Fear 2001 edition	6.00

DREDD RULES
Fleetway/Quality
1 SBs(c),JBy,Prev.unpubl. in USA	5.00
2 inc.Eldster Ninja Mud Wrestling Vigilantes	3.50
3 inc.That Sweet Stuff.	3.50
4 Our Man in Hondo City	3.50
5	3.25
6 BKi,DBw	3.25
7 "Banana City"	3.25
8 "Over the Top"	3.25
9 "Shooting Match"	3.25
10 SBs,inc.Mega-City primer	3.25
11 SBs,Legend/Johnny Biker	3.25
12 SBs,Rock on Tommy Who	3.25
13 BMy,The Ballad of Toad McFarlane	3.25
14 thru 15	@3.25
16 A:Russians	3.25
17 F:Young Giant	3.25
18 F:Jonny Cool	3.00
19 V:Hunter's Club	3.00

DRIFT MARLO
Dell Publishing Co., May-July, 1962
1	35.00
2	25.00

DRUNKEN FIST
Jademan, 1988
1	3.25
2	2.50
3 thru 9	@2.00

10 thru 53. . . . . @2.00

DUCKMAN
Topps, 1994
1 USA Cartoon 2.50
2 XXX Files. 2.50
3 I:King Chicken 2.50
4 V:Toys 2.50
5 F:Cornfed. 2.50
6 Star Trek Parody 2.50
7 rep. 1990 B&W 1st app., now
   in color. 2.50

DUCKMAN: THE MOB FROG SAGA
Topps, 1994
1 I:Mob Frog 2.50
2 D:Mob Frog 2.50
3 In the Name of the Duck 2.50

DUCK TALES
Gladstone, 1990
1 CB(r)I:LaunchpadMcQuck 7.00
2 CB(r) 4.00
3 . . . . 4.00
4 CB(r) 4.00
5 thru 11 . . . . @4.00
12 . . . . 5.00
13 . . . . 5.00

DUCK TALES
Walt Disney
1 . . . . 4.00
2 . . . . 3.00
3 thru 19 . . . . @3.00

DUDLEY DO-RIGHT
Charlton Comics, 1970–71
1 . . . . 150.00
2 thru 7 . . . . @125.00

DUEL MASTERS
Dreamwave, 2003
1 . . . . 3.00
1a variant (c)s. . . . . @3.00
2 thru 8 . . . . @3.00
Pocket Edition Vol. 2 . . . . 11.00

DUNC & LOO
Dell Publishing Co., 1961
1 . . . . 125.00
2 . . . . 100.00
3 thru 8 . . . . @75.00

DUNGEONS & DRAGONS: THE LOST CITY
Twenty First Century, 1999
1 (of 6) game tie-in 5.00
2 thru 6 . . . . @5.00

DUNGEONS & DRAGONS: AMBER CASTLE
Twenty First Century, 2000
1 (of 6) game tie-in 5.00

DUNGEONS & DRAGONS: TEMPEST'S GATE
Kenzer & Company, 2001
1 (of 4) Born of Fire 3.00
2 Forged in Tears 3.00
3 Tempered in Fellowship. 3.00
4 Sheathed in Justice 3.00

TPB 15.00

DUNGEONS AND DRAGONS: WHERE SHADOWS FALL
Kenzer & Company, 2003
1 (of 5) 3.50
2 thru 5 . . . . @3.50

DWIGHT D. EISENHOWER
Dell Publishing Co., 1969
1 . . . . 75.00

DYNAMO
Tower Comics, 1966
1 WW,MSy,RC,SD,I:Andor 150.00
2 WW,DA,GT,MSy,Weed solo
   story A:Iron Maiden 100.00
3 WW,GT,Weed solo story,
   A:Iron Maiden 100.00
4 WW,DA,A:Iron Maiden. 100.00

DYNAMO JOE
First, 1986–87
1 . . . . 3.00
2 . . . . 2.25
3 thru 14 . . . . @2.25
Spec.#1 . . . . 2.25

EARLY DAYS OF SOUTHERN KNIGHTS
Vol. 2 Graphic Novel 5.00

Earth 4 Vol. 2 #1
© Continuity

EARTH 4
Continuity, 1993
[1st Series, Deathwatch 2000]
1 Deathwatch 2000 Pt.6,w/card . . . 2.50
2 Deathwatch 2000 Pt.11,w/card . . 2.50
3 V:Hellbenders, w/card 2.50
[2nd Series]
1 WMc, ... 2.50
2 . . . . 2.50
3 . . . . 2.50

EAST MEETS WEST
Innovation
1 . . . . 2.50
2 . . . . 2.50

---

3 . . . . 2.50

EBONY WARRIOR
Africa Rising
1 I:Ebony Warrior 2.50

ECHO OF FUTUREPAST
Continuity, 1984–85
1 NA,MGo,I:Bucky O'Hare,
   Frankenstein 4.00
2 NA,MGo,A:Bucky O'Hare, Dracula,
Werewolf 3.50
3 NA,MGo,A:Bucky. 3.50
4 NA,MGo,A:Bucky. 3.50
5 NA,MGo,A:Drawla&Bucky 3.50
6 Ath,B:Torpedo 3.50
7 ATh. 3.50
8 Ath, ... 3.25
9 Ath,Last issue 3.25

ECLIPSE GRAPHIC NOVELS
Eclipse
1 Axa. 7.00
2 MR,I Am Coyote 7.00
3 DSt,Rocketeer 10.00
3a hard cover 40.00
4 Silver Heels 9.00
4a hard cover 40.00
5 Sisterhood of Steel 10.00
6 Zorro in Old Calif. 8.00

ECLIPSE MONTHLY
Eclipse, 1983–84
1 SD,DW,I:Static&Rio 2.50
2 GC,DW 2.50
3 thru 10 DW . . . . @2.50

EDGE
Malibu Bravura, 1994–95
1 GK,I:Edge 2.50
2 GK,STg,Gold Stamp 2.50
3 GK,The Ultimates 2.50
4 GK,V:Mr. Ultimate 2.50

EDGE
Crossgen Comics, 2002
TPB #1 224-page. 10.00
TPB #2 256-page. 10.00
TPB #3 272-page. 10.00
TPB #4 thru 8 . . . . @12.00
TPB #9 thru 13 192-page. . . . . . . @8.00
becomes:

VECTOR
TPB #14 . . . . 8.00

EDGE OF CHAOS
Pacific, 1983
1 GM. 2.50
2 GM. 2.50
3 GM. 2.50

EIGHT LEGGED FREAKS
WildStorm/DC, 2002
Spec. movie adapt. 64-pg. 7.00

87th PRECINCT
Dell Publishing Co., April-June, 1962
1 BK 175.00
2 . . . . 150.00

All comics prices listed are for *Near Mint* condition.

COLOR PUB.

EL CAZADOR
Crossgen Comics, 2003
1 CDi,SEp 3.00
2 thru 3 CDi,SEp . . . . @3.00
4 thru 8 . . . . @3.00
TPB Vol. 1 Collected edition 6.00
TPB Traveler edition, 208-pg. 13.00
Spec. #1 Bloody Ballad of
  Blackjack Tom 3.00

Elementals #14
© *Comico*

ELEMENTALS
Comico, 1984–88
1 BWg,I:Destroyers. 5.00
2 BWg 3.50
3 BWg 3.50
4 thru 12 BWg . . . . @3.00
13 thru 22 . . . . @3.00
23 thru 29 . . . . @3.00
Spec.#1 . . . . 3.00
Spec.#2 . . . . 3.00
[Second Series], 1989–94
1 . . . . 3.00
2 thru 4 . . . . @3.00
5 thru 28 . . . . @3.00
Spec.#1 Lingerie special 3.00
GN The Natural Order, rep. 10.00
GN Death & Resurrection 13.00
[Third Series], 1995
1 R:Elementals, polybagged with
  Chrysalis promo card 3.00
2 R:Original Monolith, polybagged
  with Chrysalis promo card. . . . 3.00
3A Destroy the Shadowspear 3.00
3B variant cover 3.00
4 Memoirs,pt.1 . . . . 3.00
5 Memoirs,pt.2 . . . . 3.00
GN Ghost of a Chance 6.00
Spec. Babes, photo multimedia
  bikini special 4.00
Spec. Hot Bikini Valentine 4.00
Spec. All New Summer Special 5.00
Spec.#1 Lingerie Metalite 4.00

ELEMENTALS:
HOW THE WAR WAS ONE
Comico, 1996
1 thru 4 . . . . @3.00

ELEMENTALS: THE
VAMPIRE'S REVENGE
Comico, 1996–97
1 thru 4 . . . . @3.00

ELEMENTALS VS.
THE CHARNEL PRIESTS
Comico, 1996
Spec. 1 (of 2) 3.00
2 . . . . 3.00

ELEVEN OR ONE
Sirius, 1995
1 JLi 5.00

ELFLORD
Aircel, 1986–88
Volume 1: *See B&W*
Volume II
1 . . . . 3.50
2 . . . . 3.00
3 thru 20 . . . . @3.00
21 double size 5.00
22 thru 24 . . . . @3.00
Spec.#1 . . . . 3.00
25 thru 32, see B&W

ELFQUEST
Warp Graphics, 1998
TPB 20th Anniv. Special. 9.00
TPB Scores, WPi, best of Elfquest
  stories 20.00

ELFQUEST: BLOOD OF
TEN CHIEFS
Warp Graphics, 1993–95
1 WP 3.00
2 WP 3.00
3 WP,B:Swift Spear pt. 1 . . . . 3.00
4 WP,B:Swift Spear pt. 2 . . . . 3.00
5 V:Dinosaurs 3.00
6 Snowbeast 3.00
7 . . . . 3.00
8 Spirit Quest 3.00
9 Shadow Shifter 3.00
10 Spheres pt. 1 . . . . 3.00
11 Spheres pt. 2 . . . . 3.00
12 . . . . 3.00
13 Forest 3.00
14 F:Mantricker 3.00
15 F:Bearclaw 3.00
16 Scar Vs. Bearclaw 3.00
17 F:Eldolil,Howl for Eldolil 3.00
18 F:Finder. 3.00
19 F:Cutter & Skywise 3.00
20 final issue 3.00

ELFQUEST:
HIDDEN YEARS
Warp Graphics
1 WP 3.00
2 WP, w/coupon promo. 3.00
3 WP, w/coupon promo.Cont.sty.
  previewed in Harbinger#11 . . . . 3.50
4 WP,w/coupon 3.00
5 WP,O:Skywise 3.00
6 WP,F:Timmain 3.00
7 F:Timmain 3.00
8 Daughter's Day 3.00
9 WP(s),Enemy Face 3.00
9 1/2 WP,JBy,Holiday Spec. 3.50
10 thru 14 WP . . . . @3.00
15 WP Wolfrider Tribe Splits 3.50
16 thru 18 WP 3.00

19 Mousehunt 3.00
20 F:Recognition 3.00
21 F:Teir, Messenger 3.00
22 F:Embu, Making a Point 3.00
23 Not Wolf And Teir 3.00
24 Magic Menace 3.00
25 *B&W* Wolfrider's Death 3.00
26 thru 29 *B&W* finale . . . . @3.00

ELFQUEST: JINK
Warp Graphics, 1994–96
1 Future 3.50
2 Future 3.00
3 Neverending Story 3.00
4 Neverending Story 3.00
5 V:True Sons, Hide and Seek 3.00
6 V:Truth Holder, Should Auld
  Acquaintance 3.00
7 F:Black Snakes 3.00
8 *B&W* V:Black Snakes 3.00
9 thru 12 . . . . 3.00

ELFQUEST:
NEW BLOOD
Warp Graphics, 1992–96
1 JBy,artists try Elfquest 5.00
2 Barry Blair story 3.50
3 thru 5 . . . . @3.00
6 thru 24 . . . . @3.00
25 Forevergreen pt. 13 . . . . 3.00
26 V:Humans 3.00
27 V:Door 3.00
28 I:Windkin, Triompe and Defeat . . 3.00
29 F:Windkin 3.00
30 V:Door 3.00
31 F:The Wanderer 3.00
32 *B&W* Sorrow's End 3.00
33 thru 35 *B&W* 3.00
Summer Spec.1993 . . . . 4.25

ELFQUEST: THE REBELS
Warp Graphics, 1994–96
1 Aliens, set several hundred
  years in future 3.00
2 Escape 3.00
3 He That Goes 3.00
4 Reasons 3.00
5 V:Skyward 3.00
6 F:Shimmer, The Edge 3.00
7 . . . . 3.00
8 Squatters & Defenders 3.00
9 *B&W* Brother vs. Brother 3.00
10 thru 12 . . . . @3.00

ELFQUEST: SHARDS
Warp Graphics, 1994–96
1 Division 3.50
2 thru 5 . . . . @3.00
6 F:Two-Edge 3.00
7 F:Shuma 3.00
8 WP,Turnabout,pt.1 . . . . 3.00
9 WP,Turnabout,pt.2,V:Djun 3.00
10 Revelations,pt.1 . . . . 3.00
11 V:Humans 3.00
12 *B&W* F:High One Timmain 3.00
13 thru 16 *B&W* finale 3.00

ELFQUEST:
WAVE DANCERS
Warp Graphics, 1993–96
1 Foil enhanced 3.50
2 thru 6 . . . . @3.00
Spec. #1 . . . . 3.00

All comics prices listed are for *Near Mint* condition.

ELIMINATOR COLOR SPECIAL
Eternity, 1991
1 DDo(c) set in the future 3.00

ELIMINATOR
Malibu Ultraverse, 1995
0 Man,DJa,MZ,Zothros tries to re-
  open passage to the Godwheel 3.00
1 MZ,Man,DRo, The Search for the
  Missing Infinity Gems,I:Siren . . . 3.00
1a Black Cover ed. 4.00
2 MZ 2.50
3 MZ, Infinity Gem tie-in,finale 2.50

ELRIC
Pacific, 1983–84
1 CR 4.00
2 CR 3.00
3 thru 6 CR . . . . @3.00

ELRIC
Topps, 1996
0 NGa,CPR, One Life, based on
  Michael Moorcock character . . . 3.00

ELRIC, BANE OF THE BLACK SWORD
First, 1988–89
1 Michael Moorcock adapt. 3.00
2 . . . . 3.00
3 thru 5 . . . . @3.00

ELRIC, SAILOR ON THE SEAS OF FATE
First, 1985–86
1 Michael Moorcock adapt. 4.00
2 . . . . 3.00
3 thru 7 . . . . @3.00

ELRIC–VANISHING TOWER
First, 1987–88
1 Michael Moorcock adapt. 3.00
2 thru 6 . . . . @3.00

ELRIC, WEIRD OF THE WHITE WOLF
First, 1986–87
1 Michael Moorcock adapt. 3.00
2 thru 5 . . . . @3.00
Graphic Novel CR 7.00

ELVEN
Malibu Ultraverse, 1994
0 Rep.,A:Prime, double size 3.00

Mini-Series 1994–95
1 A:Prime, Primevil 2.50
2 AaL,R:Maxi-Man 2.50
3 AaL,V:Duey, Primevil 2.50
4 AaL,F:Primevil 2.50

E-MAN
Charlton Comics, 1973–75
1 JSon,O:E-Man 35.00
2 SD 20.00
3 . . . . 20.00
4 SD 20.00
5 SD,Miss Liberty Belle 20.00
6 JBy,Rog 2000 . . . . 20.00
7 JBy,Rog 2000 . . . . 20.00

---

8 J:Nova 25.00
9 JBy,Rog 2000 . . . . 20.00
10 JBy,Rog 2000 . . . . 20.00

E-Man #1
© First

E-MAN
First, 1983
1 JSon,O:E-Man & Nova, A:Rog
  2000, 1 pg. JBy 3.00
2 JSon,I:F-Men (X-Men satire) 1-
  page Mike Mist 2.50
3 JSon, V:F-Men 2.50
4 JSon,Michael Mauser solo 2.50
5 JSon,I:Psychobabbler,A:Omaha,
  The Cat Dancer 2.50
6 JSon,O:E-Man,V:Feeder 2.50
7 JSon,V:Feeder 2.50
8 JSon,V:HotWax,A:CuteyBunny . . 2.50
9 JSon,I:Tyger Lili 2.50
10 JSon,O:Nova Kane pt.1 . . . . 2.50
11 JSon,O:Nova Kane pt.2 . . . . 2.50
12 JSon,A:Tyger Lili 2.50
13 JSon,V:Warp'sPrinceChaos 2.50
14 JSon,V:Randarr 2.50
15 JSon,V:Samuel Boar. 2.50
16 JSon,V:Samuel Boar. 2.50
17 JSon,Smeltquest satire. 2.50
18 JSon,Rosemary.& Time 2.50
19 JSon,Hoodoo Blues 2.50
20 JSon,A:Donald Duke 2.50
21 JSon,A:B-Team,(satire). 2.50
22 JSon,A:Teddy Q 2.50
23 JSon,A:TygerLili,B-Team. 2.50
24 JSon,O:Michael Mauser 2.50
25 JSon,last issue 2.50
Spec. #1 . . . . 2.75

E-MAN
Comico, 1989–90
1 JSon. 2.75
2 and 3 JSon. . . . . @2.50

E-MAN
Alpha Productions, 1993
1 JSon. 2.75

EMERGENCY
Charlton Comics, 1976
1 JSon(c),JBy 45.00
2 JSon. 25.00
3 Thru 4 . . . . 25.00

ENCHANTED: THE AWAKENING
Sirius, 1998
1 by Robert Chang 3.00
2 . . . . 3.00
3 conclusion 3.00

ENGIN
Samson Comics
1 I:The Mesh. 2.50

ENGINE
Shadow Planet, 2002
1 by Tim Tyler 3.50
1a signed sketch edition 10.00
2 thru 3 . . . . @3.00

ENSIGN O'TOOLE
Dell Publishing Co., 1962
1 . . . . 40.00
2 . . . . 30.00

EPSILON WAVE
Independent
1 . . . . 3.00
2 . . . . 2.50
3 . . . . 2.25
4 . . . . 2.25

Elite Comics
5 thru 10 . . . . @2.25

ESC.(ESCAPE)
Comico, 1996
1 SPr. 3.00
2 thru 4 SPr. . . . . @3.00
TPB SPr Rep. #1–#4 . . . . 15.00

ESC: NO EXIT
Comico, 1997
1 . . . . 3.00
1 medallion edition 10.00
2 . . . . 3.00

ESPERS
Eclipse, 1986
1 I:ESPers. 3.00
2 JBo(c),V:Terrorists 3.00
3 V:Terrorists. 3.00
4 Beirut 3.00
5 The Liquidators 3.00
6 V:Benito Giovanetti 3.00

ESPIONAGE
Dell Publishing Co., May–July, 1964
1 . . . . 50.00
2 . . . . 40.00

ESTABLISHMENT, THE
WildStorm/DC, 2001
1 IEd,CAd,F:Charlie Arrows 2.50
2 IEd,CAd 2.50
3 IEd,CAd 2.50
4 IEd,CAd 2.50
5 IEd,CAd 2.50
6 IEd,CAd 2.50
7 IEd,CAd 2.50
8 IEd,CAd, in Russia 2.50
9 IEd,CAd, demon-god embryos . . 2.50
10 IEd,CAd, Charlie Arrows. 2.50
11 IEd,CAd, DeadSpace 2.50
12 IEd,CAd, Moonbase Straker. . . . 2.50
13 IEd,CAd, final issue 2.50

ETERNAL WARRIOR
Valiant, 1992
1 FM(c),JDx,Unity #2,O:Eternal
  Warrior,Armstrong 3.00
1a Gold Ed. 4.00
1b Gold Foil Logo 5.00
2 WS(c),JDx,Unity #10,A:Solar,
  Harbinger,Eternal Warrior
  of 4001 . . . . 2.50
3 JDx,V:Armstrong,I:Astrea 2.50
4 JDx(i),I:Caldone, C:Bloodshot . . 2.50
5 JDx,I:Bloodshot,V:Iwatsu's Men . 2.50
6 BWS,JDx,V:Master Darque 2.50
7 BWS,V:Master Darque, D:Uncle
  Buck. 2.50
8 BWS,as Archer & Armstrong #8
  Three Musketeers,I:Ivar 2.50
9 MMo,JDx,B:Book of the
  Geomancer 2.50
10 JDx,E:Bk. o/t Geomancer. 2.50
11 B:KVH(s),JDx(i), V:Neo-Nazis. . 2.50
12 JDx(i),V:Caldone. 2.50
13 MMo,JDx(i),V:Caldone,
  A:Bloodshot 2.50
14 E:KVH(s),MMo,V:Caldone,
  A:Geoff 2.50
15 YG,A:Bloodshot,V:Tanaka 2.50
16 YG,A:Bloodshot. 2.50
17 A:Master Darque. 2.50
18 C:Doctor Mirage 2.50
19 KVH(s),TeH,A:Doctor Mirage . . 2.50
20 KVH(s),Access Denied 2.50
21 KVH(s),TeH,V:Dr. Steiner 2.50
22 V:Master Darque,w/Valiant Era
  Card. 2.50
23 KVH(s),TeH,Blind Fate 2.50
24 KVH(s),TeH,V:Immortal Enemy . 2.50
25 MBn(s),A:Archer,Armstrong . . . 2.50
26 Double(c), Chaos Effect-Gamma
  #4, A:Archer, Armstrong, Ivar . . 3.00
27 JOs(s) 2.25
28 War on Drugs 2.25
29 Immortal Enemy 2.25
30 Lt. Morgan. 2.25
31 JD,JOs 2.25
32 . . . . 2.25
33 Mortal Kin Pt.1 . . . . 2.25
34 Mortal Kin Pt.2 . . . . 2.25
35 Mortal Kin Finale. 2.50
36 Fenris League. 2.50
37 Youthful Tale 2.50
38 V:Niala, The Dead Queen. 2.50
39 JOs,JG,PG(c),V:body thieves . . 2.50
40 JOs,JG,PG(c),finds organ farm. . 2.50
41 War in Herznia 2.50
42 I: Brisbane. 2.50
43 V:Neo Nazi 2.50
44 V:Neo Nazi 2.50
45 R:Fenris Society 2.50
46 V:Fenris Society 2.50
47 Jihad 2.50
48 Immortal Life in Danger 2.50
49 JOs,JG,Hallucinations. 2.50
50 . . . . 2.50
Yearbook #1. . . . . 4.25
Yearbook #2. . . . . 4.00
Wings of Justice WWI 2.50
Quarterly
Time and Treachery. 4.00
Digital Alchemy 4.00
Spec. Blackworks AHo, ... 4.00

ETERNAL WARRIORS
Acclaim, 1997
Quarterly
Archer & Armstrong AHo 4.00
Mog AHo 4.00
The Immortal Enemy AHo 4.00

ETERNITY SMITH
Hero
1 . . . . 2.25
2 thru 10 . . . . @2.25
Heroic Publishing
1 Man Vs. Machine. 2.25
2 Man Vs. Machine. 2.25

EVA THE IMP
Red Top Comic/Decker, 1957
1 . . . . 35.00
2 . . . . 30.00

Evangeline #2
© Comico

EVANGELINE
Comico, 1984
1 Guns of Mars. 4.00
2 . . . . 3.00
Lodestone, 1986
1 . . . . 2.50
2 . . . . 2.50
First, 1988
1 . . . . 3.00
2 thru 9 . . . . @2.50
10 thru 12. . . . . @2.00

EVERQUEST
WildStorm/DC, 2001
GN The Ruins of Kunark, JLe 6.00
GN Transformation. 6.00

EVERYTHING'S ARCHIE
Archie Publications, 1969
1 Giant 125.00
2 Giant 75.00
3 thru 5 Giant . . . . @50.00
6 thru 10 Giant . . . . @35.00
11 thru 20. . . . . @25.00
21 thru 40. . . . . @15.00
41 thru 134. . . . . @10.00

EVIL ERNIE
See: B&W

EVIL ERNIE (THE SERIES)
Chaos! Comics, 1998
1 V:Purgatori. 3.00
2 Search for Chastity, A:Savior. . . . 3.00
3 V:Purgatori. 3.00

4 return to New Jersey 3.00
5 two beings 3.00
6 heart of America 3.00
7 Unholy Nights 3.00
8 Trauma,pt.1 . . . . 3.00
9 Trauma,pt.2 . . . . 3.00
10 Trauma,pt.3. . . . . 3.00

EVIL ERNIE: DEPRAVED
Chaos! Comics, 1999
1 (of 3) 4.00
1a premium edition 10.00
2 . . . . 3.00
3 . . . . 3.00

EVIL ERNIE: DESTROYER
Chaos! Comics, 1997
Prev.#1. 3.00
1 (of 9) BnP 3.00
2 BnP 3.00
3 to Atlanta 3.00
4 siege of Atlanta 3.00
5 . . . . 3.00
6 Nuclear launch codes 3.00
7 Nuclear attack 3.00
8 Nuclear attack continues 3.00
9 New forms of living dead, concl. . 3.00

EVIL ERNIE: REVENGE
Chaos! Comics, 1994–95
1 SHu,BnP,A:LadyDeath,glow(c) . . 7.00
1a limited, glow-in-the-dark (c) . . . 20.00
1a Commemorative edition. 15.00
2 SHu,BnP,Loses Smiley 6.00
3 SHu,BnP,V:Dr. Price 5.00
4 SHu,BnP,Final Issue 5.00
TPB Rep. #1-#4. . . . . 13.00
TPB Revenge #2, signed. 20.00

EVIL ERNIE:
STRAIGHT TO HELL
Chaos! Comics, 1995–96
1 Rampage in Hell, coffin(c) 4.00
1 limited, chromium edition. 17.00
2 Cremator 4.00
3 . . . . 4.00
3a Chastity (c). 20.00
4 and 5 . . . . @4.00
Ashcan. 1.50
Spec. 20.00

EVIL ERNIE:
THE RESURRECTION
Chaos! Comics, 1993–94
1 R:Evil Ernie 15.00
1a gold edition 35.00
2 Enhanced Cover 11.00
3 Massive Mayhem Lady Death
  poster. 11.00
4 final issue, extra pages 11.00
TPB Rep. #1-#4. . . . . 15.00
Ashcan Resurrection (2001) 20.00

EVIL ERNIE VS.
THE MOVIE MONSTERS
Chaos! Comics
1 one-shot 3.00
1 omega edition 5.00
1 premium edition, signed 15.00

EVIL ERNIE VS.
THE SUPER-HEROES
Chaos! Comics, 1995
1 one-shot 3.50

1a foil (c) 30.00
1b limited 10.00
Spec. #2 by Hart Fisher
   & Steve Butler 3.00
Spec. #2, Premium edition 10.00

EVIL ERNIE: WAR OF THE DEAD
Chaos! Comics, 1999
1 (of 3) 3.00
1a premium 10.00
2 . . . . 3.00
3 concl. 3.00

EVIL ERNIE'S BADDEST BATTLES
Chaos! Comics, 1996
1-shot, imaginary battles 3.00

EXECUTIONER
Innovation, 1993
1 Don Pendleton(s),F:Mack Bolan . 4.00
1a Collector's Gold Ed. 3.00
1b Tyvek cover 4.00
2 War against Mafia 2.75
3 War against Mafia,pt.3 . . . . 2.75

EXEMPLARS
1 and 2 . . . . @2.50

EXILES
Malibu Ultraverse, 1993
1 TMs(s),PaP,I:Exiles 4.00
1a w/out card 2.25
1b Gold hologram ed. 10.00
1c Ultra-limited 12.00
2 V:Kort 3.00
3 BWS,Mastodon,BU:Rune 4.00
4 V:Kort 3.00

EX MACHINA
Wildstorm/DC, 2004
1 F:Mitchell Hundred,40-pg. 3.00
2 thru 5 State of Emergency . . . . @3.00

EX-MUTANTS
Malibu, Nov. 1992–Apr. 1994
1 I&O:Ex-Mutants 2.25
2 V:El Motho,Beafcake,Brickhouse 2.25
3 A:Sliggo,Zygote 2.25
4 . . . . 2.25
5 Piper Kidnapped 2.25
6 A:Dr.Kildare 2.25
7 V:Dr.Kildare 2.25
8 O:Gelson 2.25
9 F:Dillion 2.25
10 F:Sluggtown 2.25
11 Man(s),Genesis#1,w/card 2.25
12 R0M(s),Genesis#4 . . . . 2.25
13 J:Gravestone,Arc 2.25
14 C:Eye 2.25
15 A:Arrow 2.50
16 A:Arrow,I:KillCorp 2.50
17 A:Arrow,V:KillCorp. 2.50
18 A:Arrow,V:KillCorp. 2.50

EXO-SQUAD
Topps, 1994
[Mini-Series]
0 . . . . 2.25
1 From Animated Series 2.50
2 F:Nara Burns 2.50
3 V:Neo-Sapiens 2.50

EXPLORERS
Explorer Press, 1995
1 I:Explorers 3.00
2 The Cellar 3.00

EXPOSURE SPECIAL
Avatar Press, 2000
1 . . . . 3.50
1a photo(c) 3.50

EXPOSURE: SECOND COMING
Avatar Press, 2000
1 (of 2) Angel (c) 40-page 5.00

EXTINCTIONERS
Vision Comics, 1998
1 by Shawntae Howard &
   Malcolm Earle 4.00
2 . . . . 4.00

EXTINCTION EVENT
Wildstorm/DC, 2003
1 (of 5) BBh,humans vs. dinos 2.50
2 thru 5 BBh . . . . @2.50

Extremes of Violet #1
© Blackout Comics

EXTREMES VIOLET
Blackout Comics, 1995
0 I:Violet 3.00
Becomes:

EXTREMES OF VIOLET
Blackout Comics, 1995
1 V:Drug Lords 3.00
2 A:Matt Chaney 3.00

EXTRA
Gemstone, 1999
1 (of 5) 2.50
2 . . . . 2.50
3 . . . . 2.50
4 . . . . 2.50
5 final issue 2.50
`Annuals'
TPB Vol. 1 . . . . 13.50

EYE OF THE STORM
Rival Productions
1 I:Killian, Recon, Finesse, Stray . . 3.00

2 Conspiracy 3.00
3 3-D Comic Background 3.00
4 F:Recon 3.00
5 Sinclair & Rott 3.00
Ann. 48-pg. 5.00

EZRA
Arcana Studio, 2004
1 . . . . 3.00
2 thru 3 . . . . @3.00

FADE FROM GRACE
Beckett Comics, 2004
1 . . . . 2.25
2 thru 3 . . . . @2.25

FALCON, THE
Aircel
Spec. #1 . . . . 2.25

FAMILY AFFAIR
Gold Key, 1970
1 W/Poster,Ph(c) 100.00
2 . . . . 50.00
3 Ph(c) 50.00
4 Ph(c) 50.00

FAMILY MATTER
Kitchen Sink, 1998
GN by Will Eisner 25.00

FAMOUS INDIAN TRIBES
Dell Publishing Co., 1962
1 . . . . 30.00
2 . . . . 15.00

FANG
Sirius
1 V:Vampires, I:Fang 4.00
2 5 . . . . 3.25
3 V:The Master 3.00

FANTASTIC VOYAGES OF SINBAD, THE
Gold Key, 1965
1 Ph(c) 75.00
2 June, 1967 . . . . 65.00

FANTASY FEATURES
AC Comics, 1987
1 . . . . 3.00
2 . . . . 3.00

FARO KORBIT
APC, 2003
1 (of 4) 3.50
2 thru 4 . . . . @3.50
TPB 17.00

FARSCAPE: WAR TORN
WildStorm/DC, 2001
1 (of 2) MWm, F:John Crichton . . . 5.00
2 MWm,48-page 5.00

FASHION IN ACTION
Eclipse
Summer Special #1 . . . . 2.25
Winter Special #1 . . . . 2.25

COLOR PUB.

FAT ALBERT
Gold Key, 1974–79

1	50.00
2	35.00
3 thru 10	@35.00
11 thru 29	@30.00

FATALE
Broadway, 1995

1 thru 6 JJo, Inherit the Earth, pt.5	@3.00
7 Fatale now Queen of the World.	3.00
8 Crown of Thorns, pt.2	3.00
9 Crown of Thorns, pt.3	3.00
TPB Inherit the Earth	15.00

FATE'S FIVE
Innervision, 1998

1 (of 4)	2.50
1 variant cover	2.50
2 (of 4)	2.50
3 (of 4)	2.50

FATHOM
Comico, 1987

1 thru 3 From Elementals	@2.50

[2nd Series], 1993

1 thru 3	@2.50

FATHOM: DAWN OF WAR
Aspen, 2003

0	2.50
1	3.00
2	3.00
Spec. Cannon Hawke #1	3.00

FATMAN, THE HUMAN FLYING SAUCER
Lightning Comics, 1967

1 CCB,O:Fatman & Tin Man	90.00
2 CCB	60.00
3 CCB,(Scarce)	65.00

FAUST: BOOK OF M
Avatar Press, 1999

1 (of 3) DQ,TV	4.00
1a (of 3) prism foil (c)	13.00
1b signed, leather cover	20.00
1c Royal Blue edition	75.00
2	4.00
3	4.00

FAZE ONE
AC Comics

1	2.50

FAZE ONE FAZERS
AC Comics

1	5.00
2	3.00
3 thru 6	@2.00

FEARBOOK
Eclipse

1 SBi,RV,A Dead Ringer	2.50

FELIX THE CAT
Harvey

1 thru 4	@4.00
5 thru 7	@3.00

FELIX THE CAT: THE MOVIE
Felix Comics, 1998

1-shot, issued a mere 10 years after movie	4.00

FELIX'S NEPHEWS INKY & DINKY
Harvey Publications, 1957

1	100.00
2 thru 7	@50.00

FEM 5
Entity, 1995

1 thru 4 five-part series	@3.00
1 signed & numbered	13.00

FEMFORCE
AC Comics

1 O:Femforce	11.00
2 A:Captain Paragon	5.00
3 Skin Game	5.00
4 Skin Game	5.00
5 Back in the Past	5.00
6 EL,Back in the Past	5.00
7 HB,O:Captain Paragon	5.00
8 V:Shade	5.00
9 V:Dr.Rivits	5.00
10 V:Dr.Rivits	5.00
11 D:Haunted Horsemen	4.00
12 V:Dr.Rivits	4.00
13 V:She-Cat	4.00
14 V:Alizarin Crimson	4.00
15 V:Alizarin Crimson	4.00
16 thru 56 See Black & White Pub.	
57 V:Goat God	3.00
58 I:New Sentinels	3.00
59 I:Paragon	3.00
60 V:Sentinels	3.00
61 V:Tara	3.00
62 V:Valkyra	3.00
63 I:Rayda	3.00
64 thru 67	@3.00
68 Spellbound	3.00
69 She-Cat Possessed	3.00
70 Island Out of Time	3.00
71	3.00
72 w/Sentinels of Justice	4.00
72a no extras	3.00
73 w/Compact Comic	4.00
73a Regular edition	3.00
74 Daughter of Darkness	4.00
74a Regular edition	3.00
75 Gorby Poster	5.00
75a Regular edition	3.00
76 Daughters pt. 3, polybagged with Compact Comic	4.00
76a no bag or comic	3.00
77 V:Sea Monster	3.00
78 V:Gorgana, bagged with comic.	5.00
78a no bag or comic	3.00
79 V:Iron Jaw, polybagged with Index	5.00
79a no bag or index	3.00
80 polybagged with Index	6.00
80a F:Mr. Brimstone, Rad	3.00
81 polybagged with Index	6.00
81a Valentines Day Spec.	3.00
82 polybagged with Index	6.00
82a F:Ms. Victory	3.00
83 F:Paragon	3.00
84 The Death of Joan Wayne polybagged with index #4B	6.00
84a no bag or index	3.00
85 Synn vs. Narett, polybagged with card	5.00
85a no bag or card	3.00

86 polybagged with index #5	5.00
86a unbagged, no suplements	3.00
87 Pandemonium in Paradise, polybagged with plate	10.00
87a unbagged, no plate	3.00
88 F:Garganta, polybagged with index #6	6.00
89 polybagged with index	6.00
90 polybagged with index	6.00
91 polybagged with index	6.00
92 polybagged with index	6.00
88a thru 92a unbagged, no index	@3.00
93 on see Black & White Pub.	
Spec.#1	2.50
Untold Origin Spec #1	5.00

Femforce: Up Close #6
© AC Comics

FEMFORCE: UP CLOSE
AC Comics, 1992–95

1 F:Stardust	4.00
2 F:Stardust	4.00
3	4.00
4	4.00
5 with Sticker	4.00
6 with Sticker	4.00
7 with Sticker	4.00
8 with Sticker	4.00
5a thru 8a Regular Edition	@3.00
9 thru 11	@3.00

FENRY
Raven Publications

1	7.00
1a Platinum Ed.	15.00

FERRET
Malibu, 1992

1 (From Protectors),DZ,V:Purple Dragon Tong,A:Iron Skull	2.25

[Regular Series] 1992–93

1 thru 3	2.50
4 V:Toxin	2.50
4a Newstand Ed.	2.25
5 SEr,Genesis	2.25
6 SEr,Genesis crossover	2.25
7 V:Airman	2.25
8 I:Posse	2.25
9 DZ,R:Iron Skull,I:Deathsong	2.25
10 DZ	2.25
11	2.25

FIGHT THE ENEMY
Tower Comics, 1966

1 BV,Lucky 7	60.00

2 AMc 40.00	
3 WW,AMc 40.00	

Fighting American #1
© Harvey

FIGHTING AMERICAN
Harvey, 1966
1 SK,Rep Fighting American
  from 1950's 75.00

FIGHTING AMERICAN
Awesome Entertainment
1 . . . . 8.00
1a variant (c) 4.00
1b Platinum (c) 15.00
2 . . . . 4.00
Coll.Ed.#1 rep.#1–#2 . . . . 5.00
Spec.#1 Fighting American: Cold War
  RLe,JLb 2.50

FIGHTING AMERICAN:
DOGS OF WAR
Awesome Entertainment, 1998
1 JSn,SPa,F:John Flagg 2.50
1a Tour Edition, RLe cover 5.00
1b Tour Edition, signed 12.00
2 JSn,SPa,other super-soldiers . . . 2.50
2a variant cover 2.50
3 A:Crimson Dragon 2.50
4 Who is No Name? 2.50
Spec.'98 Con preview,b&w,16-page 5.00

FIGHTING AMERICAN:
RULES OF THE GAME
Awesome Entertainment, 1997
1 JLb 3.00
2 JLb 2.50
3 JLb, Baby Buzz Bomber 2.50
TPB 13.00

FIREARM
Malibu Ultraverse, 1993–95
0 w/video,I:Duet 3.00
1 I:Firearm,Alec Swan 2.50
1 silver foil, limited edition 4.00
2 BWS,A:Hardcase,BU:Rune 2.75
3 V:Sportsmen 2.25
4 HC,Break-Thru x-over 2.25
5 O:Prime,I:Ellen 2.25
6 A:Prime 2.25
7 V:Killer 2.25
8 DIB(c) 2.25

9 at the Rose Bowl 2.25	
10 The Lodge 2.25	
11 Ultraverse Premier #5,BU:Prime. 3.50	
12 Rafferty Saga,pt.1 . . . . 2.25	
13 Rafferty Saga,pt.2 . . . . 2.25	
14 Swan 2.25	
15 Rafferty Saga,pt.3 . . . . 2.25	
16 Rafferty Saga,pt.4 . . . . 2.25	
17 Rafferty Saga,pt.5 . . . . 2.25	
18 JeR,HC(c),Rafferty Saga,finale . 2.50	

FIRST, THE
Crossgen Comics, 2000
1 BKs,BS 6.00
2 thru 13 BKs,BS . . . . @5.00
14 thru 25 . . . . @3.00
26 thru 36 . . . . @3.00
37 Atwaal returns 3.00
TPB Vol. 1 192-page 20.00
TPB Vol. 2 rep. #8–#13 . . . . 20.00
TPB Vol. 3 Sinister Motives 16.00
TPB Vol. 5 Liquid Alliances 16.00
TPB Vol. 6 Ragnarok 16.00

FIRST ADVENTURES
First
1 thru 5 . . . . @2.25

FIRST GRAPHIC
NOVELS
First 1984
1 JBi,Beowolf 8.00
1a 2nd Printing 7.00
2 TT,Time Beavers 10.00
3 HC,American Flag Hard Times . 12.00
4 Nexus,SR 10.00
5 Elric,CR 20.00
6 Enchanted Apples of Oz 6.00
7 Secret Island of Oz 10.00
8 HC,Time 2 . . . . 28.00
9 TMNT 20.00
10 TMNT II 18.00
11 Sailor on the Sea 15.00
12 HC,American Flagg 15.00
13 Ice King 10.00
14 TMNT III 14.00
15 Hex Breaker 10.00
16 Forgotten Forest 11.00
17 Mazinger 11.00
18 TMNT IV 13.00
19 O;Nexus 10.00
20 American Flagg 16.00

1st FOLIO
Pacific, 1984
1 Joe Kubert School 2.50

FIRST WAVE:
HEART OF A KILLER
Andromeda Entertainment, 2000
1 by Dan Parsons, TV tie-in 3.00
1a photo (c) 3.00
2 . . . . 4.00
2a photo (c) 4.00
2b signed 10.00
2c sketch edition 20.00
TPB Vol. 1 Heart of a Killer 9.00

FIRST WAVE:
IN THE BEGINNING
Andromeda Entertainment, 2001
1 . . . . 3.00
1a photo (c) 3.00

FIRST WAVE:
JORDAN RADCLIFFE
Andromeda Entertainment, 2001
1 painted (c) 3.00
1a photo (c) 3.00
1b limited foil (c) 10.00

FISH POLICE
Comico, 1987
Vol 2 #6 thru #15 rep. . . . . @2.50
Vol 2 #16 rep. 3.00
Vol 2 #17 rep.,AuA 3.00
1 Color Special (July 1987) 3.50

FIST OF
THE NORTH STAR
Gutsoon! Entertainment, 2003
TPB Vol.1 & 2 Master Edition . . @15.00
TPB Vol.3 thru 9 Master Edition. @18.00

FLAMEHEAD
JNCO Comics, 1998
1 I:Flamehead 2.25
2 thru 5 . . . . @2.25

FLARE
Hero Graphics
1 I:Darkon&Prof.Pomegranite 4.00
2 Blonde Bombshell,A:Galooper . . . 3.00
3 I:Sky Marshall 3.00
Ann.#1 . . . . 4.50

[2nd Series]
1 A:Galloping Galooper 3.00
2 A:Lady Arcane 3.00
3 I:Britannia 3.00
4 A:Indigo 2.50
5 R:Eternity Smith,O:Die Kriegerin . 4.00
6 I:Tigress 3.50
7 V:The Enemies 4.00
8 Morrigan Wars#4,A:Icicle Dragon 3.50
9 Morrigan Wars Pt.7 (B&W) 3.50

FLARE ADVENTURES
Hero Graphics, 1992
1 rep. 3.00
2 flipbook w/Champions Classics . . 3.00
3 flipbook w/Champions Classics . . 3.00
Becomes: B&W

FLASH GORDON
Gold Key, 1965
1 . . . . 75.00

FLASH GORDON
King, 1966–69
1 AW,DH,A:Mandrake 90.00
1a Comp. Army giveaway 60.00
2 FBe,A:Mandrake,R:Ming 50.00
3 RE,"Lost in the Land of
  The Lizardmen" 55.00
4 AW,B:Secret Agent X-9 . . . . . . 60.00
5 AW 60.00
6 RC,On the Lost Continent
  of Mongo 55.00
7 MR, rep. In the Human Forest . . 55.00
8 RC,JAp 55.00
9 AR,rep 60.00
10 AR,rep 60.00
11 RC 50.00

Charlton, 1969–70
12 RC 40.00
13 JJ 40.00
14 . . . . 30.00

15 .... 30.00
16 .... 30.00
17 Brick Bradford story 30.00
18 MK,Attack of the Locust Men .. 30.00

Gold Key, 1975

19 Flash returns to Mongo....... 15.00
20 thru 30.................... @10.00
31 thru 37 AW movie adapt .... @10.00

FLATLINE COMICS
Flatline Comics

1 Three stories River Prairie...... 2.50

FLAXEN: ALTER EGO
Caliber

1 V:Dark Flaxen 3.00

FLESH AND BONES
UpShot, 1986

1 Moore...................... 3.00
2 thru 4 Moore............... @3.00

FLINTSTONES
Harvey

1 .... 3.00
2 Romeo and Juliet............ 3.00

FLINTSTONES
Archie, 1995

1 thru 10 .... @3.50
2 thru 14 .... @3.00
15 Frankenstone's Monster 3.00
20 An Heir-Raising Tale 3.00
21 King Fred The Last 3.00
22 Something Gruesome This
   Way Comes............... 3.00

FLINTSTONES, THE
Dell Publishing Co., 1961
#1 see Dell Giant

2 .... 175.00
3 thru 6 .... @125.00

Gold Key

7 .... 125.00
8 A:Mr.& Mrs J. Evil Scientists .. 100.00
9 A:Mr.& Mrs.J. Evil Scientists .. 100.00
10 A:Mr.& Mrs.J. Evil Scientists .. 100.00
11 I:Pebbles................. 150.00
12 The Too-Old Cowhand 75.00
13 thru 15................... @75.00
16 I:Bamm-Bamm 135.00
17 thru 20 .... @75.00
21 thru 23................. @60.00
24 I:Gruesomes 75.00
25 thru 29.................. @65.00
30 Dude Ranch Roundup 65.00
31 Christmas(c)............... 65.00
32 .... 50.00
33 A:Dracula & Frankenstein.... 60.00
34 I:The Great Gazoo 125.00
35 .... 50.00
36 The Man Called Flintstone.... 50.00
37 thru 60.................. @50.00

FLINTSTONES, THE
Charlton Comics, 1970

1 .... 125.00
2 .... 60.00
3 thru 7 .... @40.00
8 Summer Vacation 75.00
9 .... 40.00
10 .... 40.00
11 thru 20.................. @35.00
21 thru 50.................. @30.00

FLINTSTONES IN 3-D
Blackthorne

1 thru 5 .... @3.00

FLIPPER
Gold Key, 1966

1 Ph(c) from TV series 100.00
2 and 3 Ph(c) .... @65.00

FLOOD RELIEF
Malibu Ultraverse, 1994

TPB Ultraverse Heroes 5.00

FLY IN MY EYE EXPOSED
Eclipse

1 JJo(c),"Our Visitor"........... 5.00

The Fly #3
© Archie/Red Circle

FLY, THE
Archie/Red Circle, 1983

1 JSn,A:Mr.Justice 6.00
2 thru 9 RB,SD .... @5.00

FLYING SAUCERS
Dell, 1967

1 .... 75.00
2 thru 5 .... @40.00

FLYMAN
Archie Publications
{Prev: Adventures of the Fly}

31 I:Shield (Bill Higgins), A:Comet,
   Black Hood 75.00
32 I:Mighty Crusaders 60.00
33 A:Mighty Crusaders, R:Hangman
   Wizard 60.00
34 MSy,A:Black Hood,Shield,Comet
   Shield back-up story begins .. 50.00
35 O:Black Hood 50.00
36 O:Web,A:Hangman in Shield
   strip 50.00
37 A:Shield................. 50.00
38 A:Web 45.00
39 A:Steel Sterling 45.00

FOES
Ram Comics

1 TheMaster's Game 2.25

---

2 TheMaster's Game #2........ 2.25

FOODANG
Aug. House

1 I:Foodang................. 2.25
1a Signed, Foil cover 2.50
2 I:Maude 2.50
3 V:Undead Clown Man 2.50
4 V:Executioner............... 2.50

FOOTSOLDIERS
Maximum Press, 1996

1 KJo,PhH,................... 3.00

FOOZLE
Eclipse, 1985

1 .... 2.50

FORBIDDEN PLANET
Innovation, 1992

1 Movie Adapt............... 2.50
2 Movie adapt.contd. 2.50
3 Movie adapt.contd. 2.50
4 Movie adapt.concl............ 2.50
GN rep.#1–#4 (1997)........... 9.00

FORCE OF THE BUDDHA'S PALM
Jademan

1 .... 3.00
2 .... 2.50
3 thru 10 .... @2.50
11 thru 24.................. @2.50
25 V:Maskman............... 2.50
26 V:Maskman............... 2.50
27 A:SmilingDemon............ 2.50
28 Maskman v 10 Demons 2.50
29 Giant Bat................. 2.50
30 .... 2.50
31 .... 2.50
32 White Crane Villa 2.50
33 Devilito defeats White Crane
   & Giant Bat 2.00
34 Samsun vs. Devilito 2.50
35 Samsun vs. Devilito 2.50
36 Samsun vs. Devilito 2.50
37 D:Galacial Moon............ 2.50
38 Persian Elders, Iron Boy....... 2.50
39 V:Mad Gen.,White Crane
   Iron Boy................. 2.50
40 D:Heaven & Earth Elders 2.50
41 thru 43................... @2.50
44 D:White Crane 3.00
45 V:Iron Boy 2.25
46 thru 48.................. @2.25
49 Iron Boy vs Sainted Jade 2.25
50 Iron Boy & The Holy Blaze 2.25
51 D:Aquarius 2.25
52 V:Son o/t Gemini Lord 2.25
53 Nine Continent's return to
   full powers............... 2.25

4-D MONKEY
Dr. Leung's, 1988–90

1 thru 11 .... @2.50

FOREVER WAR, THE
NBM

GN Vol. 1 Joe Haldeman adapt. ... 9.00
GN Vol. 2 Joe Haldeman adapt. ... 9.00
GN Vol. 3 Joe Haldeman adapt. ... 9.00

FORGE
Crossgen Comics, 2002

TPB #1 224-page............ 10.00

TPB #2 256-page............10.00
TPB #3 272-page............10.00
TPB #4 thru #8 ....@12.00
TPB #9 thru #16 192-page......@8.00

FOXFIRE
Malibu Ultraverse, 1996
1 From Phoenix Resurrection.....2.25
2 Fate of Mastodon revealed.....2.25
3 & 4......................@2.00

FRANK
Nemesis, 1994
1 thru 4 DGc(s),GgP.........@3.00
1a thru 4a variant(c).........@3.00

FRANK FRAZETTA FANTASY ILLUSTRATED
Frank Frazetta, 1998
1........................6.00
1a variant cover.............8.00
3........................6.00
3 Neil Gaiman signed &
  numbered..............25.00
3 Daniel signed & numbered....20.00
4 thru 9..................@6.00

FRANK FRAZETTA DEATH DEALER
Verotik, 1997
1 thru 4 by Glenn Danzig......@7.00

FRANK IN THE RIVER
Tundra
1 Avery/Jones style cartoons.....3.00

FRANK MERRIWELL AT YALE
Charlton Comics, 1955–56
1......................60.00
2 thru 4.................@40.00

FRANK MILLER'S ROBOCOP
Avatar Press/Pulsar Press, 2003
1........................3.50
1b robosteel (c)..............15.00
2 thru 9..................@3.50
1a thru 5a wraparound (c)......@4.00
6a thru 9a wraparound (c)......@3.50
2b Civic Duty edition...........4.00
4b Officer Lewis edition.........6.00
5b Sneak Attack (c).............6.00
6b breakdown edition (c)........6.00
Spec. Killing Machine............3.00
Spec. Killing Machine variant (c)...3.00

FRANKENSTEIN
Dell Publishing Co., 1964
1........................90.00
2........................50.00
3 and 4..................@40.00

FRANKENSTEIN
Caliber
Novel Adaptation..............3.00

FRANKENSTEIN
Topps, 1994
1 thru 4..................@3.00

FRANKENSTEIN
Malibu
1 thru 3 movie promo........@2.50

FRANKENSTEIN DRACULA WAR
Topps
1 Frank Vs. Drac............3.00
2 F:Saint Germaine............3.00
3 Frank Vs. Drac.............3.00

FREDDY
Dell Publishing Co., 1963
1........................35.00
2 and 3..................@20.00

FREDDY'S DEAD: THE FINAL NIGHTMARE
Innovation
1 Movie adaption, Pt.1.........3.00
2 Movie adaption, Pt.2.........3.00
GN Movie Adapt..............7.00
3-D Special.................2.50

Freex #8
© Malibu

FREEX
Malibu Ultraverse, 1993–95
1 I:Freex w/Ultraverse card......3.00
1a Ultra-Limited..............4.00
1b Full Hologram (c)............5.00
2 L:Valerie,I:Rush.............3.00
3 A:Rush...................3.00
4 GJ(s),DdW,BWS,BU:Rune.....2.75
5 GJ(s),V:Master of the Hunt.....2.50
6 GJ(s),BH,Break Thru x-over,
  A:Night Man..............2.25
7 BHr,MZ,O:Hardcase..........2.25
8 BHr,V:Lost Angel............2.25
9 BHr,A:Old Man..............2.25
10 BHr,V:Ms. Contrary.........2.25
11 BHr,E:Origins..............2.25
12 GJ,Ultraforce...............2.25
13 New look.................2.25
14 R:Boomboy...............2.25
15 Death of Teamate...........3.50
16 Prelude to Godwheel........2.25
17 A:Rune..................2.50
18 GJ,A:Contray, Cayman, Juice...2.50
Giant Size#1 A:Prime...........2.50

FREEMIND
Future Comics, 2003
5 and 6...................@3.50
7 thru 13..................@3.00
TPB Origin of Freemind.........17.00
TPB Vol. 2.................15.00

FRIDAY FOSTER
Dell Publishing Co., 1972
1........................45.00

FRIENDLY GHOST CASPER, THE
Harvey Publications, 1958
1........................500.00
2........................200.00
3 thru 10.................@125.00
11 thru 20................@100.00
21 thru 30.................@75.00
31 thru 50.................@60.00
51 thru 100................@40.00
101 thru 159...............@30.00
160 thru 163 52 pgs.........@20.00
164 thru 253...............@10.00
Becomes:

CASPER THE FRIENDLY GHOST

FRIGHT NIGHT
Now, 1988–90
1 thru 22.................@2.25

FRIGHT NIGHT 3-D
Now, 1992
1 Dracula,w/3-D Glasses........3.00
2........................3.00

FRIGHT NIGHT II
Now
Movie Adaptation..............4.00

FRISKY ANIMALS ON PARADE
Ajax-Farrell Publ., 1957
1 LbC(c)..................200.00
2........................125.00
3 LbC(c)..................175.00

FROGMEN, THE
Dell Publishing Co., 1962
1 GE,Ph(c)................125.00
2 GE,FF...................75.00
3 GE,FF...................75.00
4........................50.00
5 ATh....................60.00
6 thru 11.................@45.00

FROM HERE TO INSANITY
Charlton Comics, 1955
8........................200.00
9........................150.00
10 SD(c)..................250.00
11 JK....................250.00
12 JK....................250.00
3-1......................350.00

FRONTLINE COMBAT
EC Comics, 1995
1 thru 4 rep...............@3.00
Gemstone, 1996
5 thru 13 rep..............@3.00
14 WW(c)..................3.00

COLOR PUB.

15	3.00

Annuals'
TPB Vol. 1 rebinding of #1–#5 .... 11.00
TPB Vol. 2 rebinding of #6–#10 ... 13.00
TPB Vol. 3 rebinding of #11–#15 .. 13.50

F-TROOP
Dell Publishing Co., 1966
1 Ph(c) 150.00
2 thru 7 Ph(c) .... @75.00

FUN-IN
Gold Key, 1970–74
1 .... 100.00
2 thru 6 .... @50.00
7 thru 10 .... @40.00
11 thru 15 .... @40.00

FUNKY PHANTOM
Gold Key, 1972–75
1 .... 75.00
2 thru 5 .... @40.00
6 thru 13 .... @30.00

**FURRY NINJA HIGH
SCHOOL STRIKES BACK**
Shanda Fantasy Arts, 2003
1 (of 2) 5.00
2 .... 5.00

FUTURAMA COMICS
Bongo Comics, 2000
1 thru 6 .... @3.50
7 thru 10 .... @3.00
11 thru 15 .... @3.00
16 thru 19 .... @3.00
TPB Vol. 1 .... 13.00
TPB Vol. 2 .... 15.00
Spec. Futurama/Simpsons: Infinity
 Secret Crossover Crisis, pt.1 .. 2.50
Spec. Futurama/Simpsons Crossover
 Crisis, pt.2 .... 2.50

FUTURIANS
Lodestone, 1985
1 DC,I:Dr.Zeus 2.25
2 DC,I:MsMercury.......... 2.25
3 DC 2.25
Eternity Graphic Novel, DC, Rep.
 +new material 10.00

**GALACTICA: THE NEW
MILLENNIUM**
Realm Press, 1999
1 Battlestar Galactica 3.00
1 convention edition 5.00
1a signed 15.00
2 Busch (c) 3.00
2a Scalf (c) 3.00
2b convention edition 5.00
3 .... 3.00
3a 3.00
4 .... 3.00
4a deluxe 5.00
Spec. Fangs of the Beast 4.00
Spec. Fangs of the Beast,deluxe.. 5.00
Tour Book, Conv. Ed., signed 15.00
Spec.Search for Sanctuary 4.00

**GALL FORCE:
ETERNAL STORY**
CPM, 1995
1 F:Solnoids 3.00
2 V:Paranoid 3.00

3 .... 3.00
4 Implant Secrets 3.00

GALLANT MEN, THE
Gold Key, 1963
1 RsM 40.00

**GALLEGHER
BOY REPORTER**
Gold Key, 1965
1 .... 35.00

GARRISON
Zion Comics
1 I:Wage, Garrison 2.50

GARRISON'S GORRILLAS
Dell Publishing Co., 1968
1 Ph(c) 75.00
2 thru 5 Ph(c) .... @40.00

GASP!
American Comics Group
March, 1967
1 .... 60.00
2 thru 4, Aug. 1967 .... @35.00

GATE CRASHER
Black Bull Entertainment, 2000
1 (of 4) MWa,ACo,JP 2.50
1a variant (c)............ 5.00
2 MWa,ACo,JP 2.50
3 MWa,ACo,JP 2.50
3a variant JJu(c).......... 2.50
4 MWa,ACo,JP, concl. 2.50
4a variant JLi(c).......... 2.50

*Gate Crasher (Ring of Fire) #1
© Black Bull Entertainment*

GATE CRASHER
Black Bull Entertainment, 2000
1 MWa,JP,ACo,F:Alex Wagner 2.50
1a variant Wizard World (c) 5.00
2 MWa,JP,ACo,Blue Tonya, Otmar. 2.50
3 MWa,JP,ACo,F:Hazard 2.50
4 MWa,JP,ACo,ACo(c) 2.50
5 MWa,JP,ACo,AAd(c) 2.50
6 MWa,JP,ACo 2.50
2a thru 6a variant (c)s......... @2.50
TPB Ring of Fire, 104-page...... 13.00

G.E.I.
Cyberosia Publishing, 2004
1 .... 3.50
2 thru 3 .... @3.50

GEN-ACTIVE
WildStorm/DC, 2000
1 V:DV8,48-pg.quarterly 4.00
2 several stories 4.00
2a variant JPn (c) 4.00
3 BSz,JLe(c)............. 4.00
3a variant Lee Bermejo (c)...... 4.00
4 R:Wildcore 4.00
4a variant (c)............ 4.00
5 F:Sublime............. 4.00
5a variant (c) (1:2) 4.00
6 Freakville 4.00

GENE FUSION
Beckett Entertainment, 2003
1 Monsters on Parade,pt.1 ...... 3.00
2 Monsters on Parade,pt.2 ...... 3.00
3 Monsters on Parade,pt.3 ...... 3.00
4 Battle under the Big Tent 3.00

**GENE RODDENBERRY'S
LOST UNIVERSE**
Teckno-Comics, 1994
0 I:Sensua............. 2.50
1 Gene Roddenberry's 2.50
2 Grange Discovered 2.25
3 Secrets Revealed 2.25
4 F:Penultra 2.25
5 I:New Alien Race 2.25
6 Two Doctor Granges 2.25
7 F:Alaa Chi Tskare 2.25

**GENE RODDENBERRY'S
XANDER IN
LOST UNIVERSE**
Teckno-Comics, 1995
1 V:Black Ghost 3.00
2 V:Walker.............. 3.00
3 V:Lady Sensua 3.00
4 thru 7 .... @3.00
8 F:Lady Sensua 3.00
[Mini-Series], 1995
1 RoR,F:L.Nimoy's Primortals 3.00

GENESIS
Malibu, 1993
0 GP,w/Pog,F:Widowmaker,A:Arrow . . . 3.50
0a Gold Ed.............. 5.00

**GENSAGA:
ANCIENT WARRIOR**
Entity Comics, 1995
1 I:Gensaga 2.50
1a with Computer Games....... 2.50
2 V:Dinosaurs 2.50
3 V:Lord Abyss 2.50

GEN13
WildStorm/DC, 2002
1 CCI,Dylon & Ethan York....... 3.00
2 CCI,Herod strikes........... 3.00
3 CCI,Herod strikes........... 3.00
4 CCI,Hamza 3.00
5 CCI,V:Preston Kills 3.00
6 CCI,V:Purple Haze.......... 3.00
7 CCI,V:The Chrome 3.00
8 CCI,V:The Chrome 3.00

9 CCI,the alter or the morgue 3.00
10 CCI,October Surprise,pt.4 . . . . . . 3.00
11 CCI,Two Caitlins 3.00
12 CCI,G-Nome 3.00
13 CCI,G-Nome 3.00
14 CCI,F:Caitlin 3.00
15 CCI,V:The Clique 3.00
16 CCI,finale 3.00
Spec. #0 CCI,JP, preview. 0.13
TPB Meanwhile 18.00
TPB September Song 20.00
TPB October Surprises 20.00
TPB Ordinary Heroes 15.00
See also Image Comics section

GEN13
MOVIE ADAPTATION
WildStorm/DC, 2001
1 JMi, animated movie adapt 2.50

GENTLE BEN
Dell Publishing Co., 1968
1 Ph(c) 60.00
2 . . . . 40.00
3 thru 5 . . . . @35.00

GEOMANCER
Valiant, 1994
1 RgM, I:Geomancer 3.00
2 RgM, Eternal Warrior 2.25
3 RgM, Darque Elementals 2.25
4 RgM 2.25
5 Riot Gear pt. 1 . . . . 2.25
6 Riot Gear pt. 2 . . . . 2.25
7 F:Zorn 2.25
8 v:Zorn. 2.25

GEORGE A ROMERO'S
DAWN OF THE DEAD
IDW Publishing, 2004
1 . . . . 4.00
2 thru 3 . . . . @4.00
TPB 18.00

GEORGE OF THE JUNGLE
Gold Key, 1969
1 From animated TV show 200.00
2 . . . . 150.00

GE ROUGE
Verotik, 1997
1 by Glenn Danzig & Calvin Irving . 3.00
1 fan club cover (2000). 5.00
2 and 3 . . . . @3.00
Biz:GE Rouge #? SBs 3.00

GET SMART
Dell Publishing Co., 1966
1 Ph(c) all 175.00
2 SD 125.00
3 SD 100.00
4 thru 8 . . . . @85.00

[FILMATION'S]
GHOSTBUSTERS
First, 1987
1 thru 4 . . . . @3.00

GHOST BUSTERS II
Now, 1989
1 thru 3 Mini-series . . . . @3.00

GHOSTBUSTERS
88MPH Studios, 2004
1 . . . . 3.00
1a variant (c). 3.50
2 thru 3 . . . . @3.25

GHOSTBUSTERS: LEGION
88MPH Studios, 2004
1 (of 4) 5.00
1a 2nd printing 3.00
2 thru 4 . . . . @3.00
1a thru 4a variant (c)s . . . . @3.50

GHOST STORIES
Dell Publishing Co., 1962
1 . . . . 100.00
2 . . . . 45.00
3 thru 10 . . . . @40.00
11 . . . . 35.00
12 thru 19 . . . . @30.00
20 . . . . 35.00
21 thru 33 . . . . @30.00
34 rep 30.00
35 rep 35.00
36 rep 30.00
37 rep 30.00

Ghostly Tales #56
© Charlton

GHOSTLY TALES
Charlton, 1966
Previously: Blue Beetle
55 I&O Dr. Graves 75.00
56 thru 70 . . . . @40.00
71 thru 100 . . . . @30.00
101 thru 169 . . . . @25.00

GIANT COMICS
Charlton Comics Summer, 1957
1 A:Atomic Mouse,Hoppy 250.00
2 A:Atomic Mouse. 200.00
3 . . . . 200.00

GIDGET
Dell Publishing Co., 1966
1 Ph(c),Sally Field. 150.00
2 Ph(c),Sally Field. 100.00

GIFT, THE
First, 1990
Holiday Special 6.00

GIFT, THE
Overcast Comics, 2003
1 . . . . 6.00
2 . . . . 4.00
3 thru 5 . . . . @3.50
6 thru 7 . . . . @3.00

GIGANTOR
Antarctic Press, 2000
1 (of 12) BDn 2.50
2 V:Red Reich. 2.50
3 . . . . 2.50
4 Doppleganger,pt.1 . . . . 2.50
5 Doppleganger,pt.2 . . . . 2.50
6 Doppleganger,pt.3 . . . . 2.50
7 Rulers of the Sea 2.50
8 . . . . 2.50
9 Sting of the Spider 3.00
10 Sting of the Spider, pt.2 . . . . . . 3.00
11 Badge of Danger, pt.1 . . . . 3.00
12 Badge of Danger, pt.2, concl. . . . 3.00

G.I. JOE 3-D
Blackthorne, 1987
1 . . . . 3.00
2 thru 5 . . . . @2.50
Ann. #1. 2.50

G.I. JOE VS.
TRANSFORMERS
Devil's Due Publishing, 2004
Vol. II
1 . . . . 5.00
1a variant (c). 5.00
2 . . . . 3.00
2a variant (c). 3.00

G.I. JOE: FRONTLINE
Devil's Due Publishing, 2004
TPB Vol. 1 Icebound 13.00
TPB Vol. 2 History Repeating 10.00
TPB One-shots 16.00

G.I. JOE:
G.I. JOE REBORN
Devil's Due Publishing, 2004
Spec #1 . . . . 5.00
TPB G.I. Joe & Cobra Reborn 10.00

G.I. JOE:
MASTER & APPRENTICE
Devil's Due Publishing, 2004
1 . . . . 3.00
2 thru 4 . . . . @3.00

G.I. JOE: RELOADED
Devil's Due Publishing, 2004
1 . . . . 3.00
2 thru 8 . . . . @3.00
1-shot Cobra Reborn 5.00

GIL THORPE
Dell Publishing Co., 1963
1 . . . . 50.00

GINGER FOX
Comico, 1988
1 thru 4 . . . . @2.25

GIN-RYU
Believe In Yourself, 1995
1 F:Japanese Sword. 2.75

2 Identity Revealed. 2.75
3 . . . . 2.75
4 Manhunt For Gin-Ryu 2.75

G.I. R.A.M.B.O.T.
Wonder Color, 1987
1 thru 3 . . . . @2.25

G.I. ROBOT
Eternity
1 . . . . 2.25

GIRL FROM U.N.C.L.E.
Gold Key, 1967
1 The Fatal Accidents Affair 150.00
2 The Kid Commandos Caper . . 100.00
3 The Captain Kidd Affair 100.00
4 One-Way Tourist Affair. 100.00
5 The Harem-Scarem Affair 100.00

GIRL GENIUS
Studio Foglio, 2001
0 Secret Blueprints Preview B&W . 1.50
1 by Phil & Kaja Foglio 3.00
2 and 3 . . . . @3.00
4 40-page 4.00
5 . . . . 3.00
6 40-page (cancelled?) 4.00
7 40-page 4.00

GLOBAL FORCE
Silverline
1 thru 4 . . . . @2.25

GLOBAL FREQUENCY
WildStorm/DC, 2002
1 (of 12) WEI. 3.00
2 WEI,SDi 3.00
3 WEI,LSh 3.00
4 WEI,RMr 3.00
5 WEI,JMu 3.00
6 WEI, ... 3.00
7 WEI,Detonation 3.00
8 WEI,Miranda Zero disappears . . . 3.00
9 WEI,Cathedral Lung. 3.00
10 WEI,Superviolence 3.00
11 WEI,Aleph 3.00
12 WEI,concl. 3.00
TPB Planet Ablaze. 15.00

GLORY
Maximum Press, 1996
1–15 see Image
16 JDy 2.50
17 JDy 2.50
18 JDy 2.50
19 JDy,A:Demeter, Silverfall 2.50
20 JDy,A:Silverfall 2.50
21 JDy 2.50
22 JDy 2.50
23 A:Prophet 2.50
TPB Vol. 2, rep. 17.00
TPB Glory/Angela RLd,JDy 17.00
Awesome Entertainment, 1999
0 AMo 2.50
0a & b alternate covers. 2.50
0c Timeless Beauty MMy(c) 6.00
1 AMo & ATi 3.50
2 AMo & ATi 3.00

GLORY/CELESTINE: DARK ANGEL
Maximum Press, 1996
1 & 2 *See: Image*
3 (of 3) JDy. 2.50

GLORY/LIONHEART: RAGE OF FURIES
Awesome Entertainment, 2000
1 . . . . 3.00

G-MAN
Conquest Comics
1 I:Richard Glenn 2.50

GOAT, THE: H.A.E.D.U.S.
Acclaim, 1998
Spec. CPr,KG,F:Vincent Van Goat. . 4.00

GOBLIN LORD, THE
Goblin Studios, 1996
1 (of 6) sci-fi/fantasy 2.50
2 signed & numbered 10.00
3 . . . . 2.50
3a signed & numbered 10.00
4 thru 6 . . . . @2.50

Gods For Hire #2
© Hot Comics

GODS FOR HIRE
Hot Comics, 1986
1 thru 7 . . . . @2.25

GODWHEEL
Malibu Ultraverse, 1995
0 R:Argus to Godwheel 2.50
1 I:Primevil 2.50
2 Hardcase new costume 2.50
3 F:Lord Pumpkin 2.50
TPB Wheel of Thunder,rep.#0–#3 . 10.00

GO-GO
Charlton Comics, 1966
1 Miss Bikini Luv. 125.00
2 Beatles. 150.00
3 Blooperman 60.00
4 . . . . 60.00
5 . . . . 60.00
6 JAp,Petula Clark, Ph(c) 75.00
7 Beach Boys 65.00
8 JAp,Monkees, Ph(c) 75.00
9 Ph(c),Oct., 1967 . . . . 50.00

GOLD DIGGER
Antarctic Press, 1999
VOL 2
1 by Fred Perry, F:Gina Diggers. . . 2.50
2 . . . . 2.50
3 by Fred Perry. 2.50
4 tinted glass is magical 2.50
5 . . . . 2.50
6 ancient cauldrons. 2.50
7 Halls of the Extremely Dead 2.50
8 Gone Fishing 2.50
9 Fauntleroy..a God? 2.50
10 Arms Master of Jade. 2.50
11 Arms Master of Jade. 2.50
12 Arms Master of Jade. 3.00
13 Tournament of Arms 3.00
14 Tournament of Arms 3.00
15 . . . . 3.00
16 thru 26. . . . . @3.00
27 thru 37. . . . . @3.00
38 thru 42 . . . . @3.50
43 thru 57 . . . . @3.00
50a variant (c) 3.00
Ann. 2003 B&W 5.00
Ann. 2004 B&W 5.00
Swimsuit Spec. #1 . . . . 4.50
Spec. Swimsuit 2001 . . . . 4.50
Spec. Swimsuit 2002 . . . . 4.50
Spec. Swimsuit 2003 . . . . 4.50
Spec. Swimsuit 2004 . . . . 4.50
End of Summer Swimsuit (2002) . . 4.50
End of Summer Swimsuit (2003). . . 4.50
End of Summer Swimsuit (2004). . . 4.50
TPB Color series, Vol.1 . . . . 16.00
TPB Color Series, Vol.2. . . . . 16.00
TPB Pocket Manga #1. . . . . 13.00
TPB Pocket Manga #10. . . . . 13.00
TPB Pocket Manga #11. . . . . 13.00
TPB Pocket Manga #2. . . . . 10.00
TPB Pocket Manga #3. . . . . 10.00
GN Perfect Memory Vol. 2. . . . . . . 6.00
GN Perfect Memory Vol. 3 . . . . 6.00
GN Perfect Memory Vol. 4. . . . . . . 6.00
GN Pink Slip 10.00

GOLD DIGGER BETA
Antarctic Press, 1998
Spec. 0 by Ben Dunn, Special
  Origin Issue, 24pg 2.00
1A bu Fred Perry, John Pound (c) . 3.00
1B Jeff Henderson (c). 3.00
2 and 3 . . . . @3.00

GOLDEN COMICS DIGEST
Gold Key, 1969–76
1 Tom & Jerry,Woody Woodpecker,
  Bugs Bunny 75.00
2 Hanna-Barbera,TV Fun
  Favorites 100.00
3 Tom & Jerry, Woody
  Woodpecker 50.00
4 Tarzan 50.00
5 Tom & Jerry, Woody Woodpecker,
  Bugs Bunny 30.00
6 Bugs Bunny 30.00
7 Hanna-Barbera,TV Fun
  Favorites 75.00
8 Tom & Jerry, Woody Woodpecker,
  Bugs Bunny 25.00
9 Tarzan 60.00
10 Bugs Bunny 25.00
11 Hanna-Barbera,TV Fun
  Favorites 75.00
12 Tom & Jerry,Bugs Bunny 25.00
13 Tom & Jerry. 25.00
14 Bugs Bunny,Fun Packed
  Funnies 25.00

15 Tom & Jerry, Woody
   Woodpecker, Bugs Bunny 25.00
16 Woody Woodpecker 25.00
17 Bugs Bunny 25.00
18 Tom & Jerry, ... 25.00
19 Little Lulu 45.00
20 Woody Woodpecker 25.00
21 Bugs Bunny Showtime 25.00
22 Tom & Jerry Winter Wingding. . 25.00
23 Little Lulu & Tubby Fun Fling . . 40.00
24 Woody Woodpecker Fun
   Festival 22.00
25 Tom & Jerry. 22.00
26 Bugs Bunny Halloween Hulla-
   Boo-Loo,Dr. Spektor article . . . 22.00
27 Little Lulu & Tubby in Hawaii . . 45.00
28 Tom & Jerry. 22.00
29 Little Lulu & Tubby 45.00
30 Bugs Bunny Vacation Funnies . 22.00
31 Turk, Son of Stone 50.00
32 Woody Woodpecker
   SummerFun. 22.00
33 Little Lulu & Tubby Halloween
   Fun 45.00
34 Bugs Bunny Winter Funnies. . . 22.00
35 Tom & Jerry Snowtime Funtime 22.00
36 Little Lulu & Her Friends. 45.00
37 WoodyWoodpecker County Fair 22.00
38 The Pink Panther 22.00
39 Bugs Bunny Summer Fun 22.00
40 Little Lulu 45.00
41 Tom & Jerry Winter Carnival. . . 22.00
42 Bugs Bunny 22.00
43 Little Lulu in Paris 45.00
44 Woody Woodpecker Family Fun
   Festival 22.00
45 The Pink Panther 22.00
46 Little Lulu & Tubby 45.00
47 Bugs Bunny 22.00
48 The Lone Ranger 22.00

GOLDEN PICTURE STORY BOOK
Racine Press (Western), 1961
1 Huckleberry Hound 300.00
2 Yogi Bear 300.00
3 Babes In Toy Land 400.00
4 Walt Disney 375.00

GOMER PYLE
Gold Key, 1966
1 Ph(c) from TV show. 150.00
2 and 3 . . . . @100.00

GOOD GUYS
Defiant, 1993
1 JiS(s),I:Good Guys 3.75
2 JiS(s),V:Mulchmorg 3.25
3 V:Chasm 2.75
4 Seduction of the Innocent 3.25
5 I:Truc 3.00
6 A:Charlemagne 2.75
7 JiS(s),V:Scourge 2.50
8 thru 11 . . . . @2.50

GOOFY ADVENTURES
Walt Disney, 1990
1 Balboa de Goofy 3.00
2 . . . . 3.00
3 thru 9 . . . . @3.00
10 Samurai. 3.00
11 Goofis Khan 3.00
12 Arizona Goof, Pt. 1 . . . . 3.00
13 Arizona Goof, Pt. 2 . . . . 3.00
14 Goofylution 3.00
15 Super Goof Vs.Cold Ray 3.00
16 Sheerluck Holmes. 3.00
17 GC,TP,Tomb of Goofula 3.00

Goofy Adventures #2
© Walt Disney

GOON
Albatross 2002
1 . . . . 12.00
2 . . . . 8.00
3 thru 5 b&w . . . . @5.00
Spec. Color special 6.50

GOOP, THE
JNCO Comics, 1998
1 . . . . 2.50
2 thru 4 . . . . @2.50

GORGO
Charlton Comics, 1961–65
1 SD 325.00
2 SD,SD(c) 175.00
3 SD,SD(c) 150.00
4 SD(c) 100.00
5 thru 10 . . . . @100.00
11 . . . . 100.00
12 . . . . 75.00
13 thru 15 . . . . @75.00
16 SD. 75.00
17 thru 23 . . . . @60.00

GORGO'S REVENGE
Charlton Comics, 1962
1 . . . . 75.00
Becomes:

THE RETURN OF GORGO
2 . . . . 60.00
3 . . . . 60.00

G.O.T.H.
Verotik, 1995
1 thru 3 mini-series . . . . @3.00
TPB SBi, rep. of series 10.00

THE GOTHIC SCROLLS, DRAYVEN
Davdez Arts, 1997
1 16pg. 2.25
1a limited edition, new cover 3.00
2 and 3 . . . . @2.50
4 V:Lucifer. 2.50
GN 13.00

GRATEFUL DEAD COMIX
Kitchen Sink
1 TT,inc.DireWolf(large format) . . . 5.50
2 TT,inc.Jack Straw. 5.00
3 TT,inc. Sugaree 5.00
4 TT,inc. Sugaree 5.00
5 TT,Uncle John's Band 5.00
6 TT,Eagle Mall #1 . . . . 5.00

GRAVESTONE
Malibu, July 1993–Feb. 1994
1 D:Gravestone,V:Wisecrack 2.25
1a Newstand Ed. 2.25
2 A:Eternal Man, V:Night Plague . . 2.25
2a Newstand Ed. 2.25
3 Genesis Tie in,w/skycap 2.25
4 thru 9 . . . . @2.25

GREASE MONKEY
Kitchen Sink, 1997
1 by Tim Elred. 3.50
2 by Tim Elred. 3.50

GREAT AMERICAN WESTERN
AC Comics
1 . . . . 2.25
2 . . . . 3.00
3 . . . . 3.00
4 . . . . 3.50

GREAT EXPLOITS
Decker Publ./Red Top, 1957
91 BK. 75.00

GREEN HORNET, THE
Gold Key, 1967
1 Bruce Lee,Ph(c). 400.00
2 Ph(c) 350.00
3 Ph(c) 250.00

GREEN HORNET
Now, 1989
1 O:40's Green Hornet 7.00
1a 2nd Printing 4.00
2 O:60's Green Hornet 5.00
3 thru 5 . . . . @4.00
6 . . . . 3.00
7 BSz(c),I:New Kato 3.00
8 thru 12 . . . . @3.50
13 V:Ecoterrorists. 3.50
14 V:Ecoterrorists. 3.50
Spec.#1 . . . . 2.50
Spec.#2 . . . . 2.50
[2nd Series], 1991
1 V:Johnny Dollar Pt.1 . . . . 2.50
2 V:Johnny Dollar Pt.2 . . . . 2.50
3 V:Johnny Dollar Pt.3 . . . . 2.50
4 V:Ex-Con/Politician 2.50
5 V:Ex-Con/Politician 2.50
6 Arkansas Vigilante 2.50
7 thru 9 The Beast . . . . @2.50
10 Green Hornet-prey 2.50
11 F:Crimson Wasp 2.50
12 Crimson Wasp/Johnny Dollar
   Pt.1,polybagged w/Button 4.00
13 TD(i),Wasp/Dollar Pt.2 . . . . . . 2.50
14 TD(i),Wasp/Dollar Pt.3 . . . . . . 2.50
15 TD(i),Secondsight 2.50
16 A:Commissioner Hamilton 2.50
17 V:Gunslinger 2.50
18 V:Sister-Hood 2.50
19 V:Jewel Thief 2.50
20 F:Paul's Friend 2.50

21 V:Brick Arcade 2.50
22 V:Animal Testers, with
     Hologravure card. 4.00
23 with Hologravure card. 4.00
24 thru 25 Karate Wars . . . . . . @2.50
26 B:City under Siege 2.50
27 with Hologravure card. 2.50
28 V:Gangs 2.50
29 V:Gangs 2.50
30 thru 37. . . . . @2.50
38 R:Mei Li. 2.50
39 Crimson Wasp 4.50
40 . . . . 4.50
41 . . . . 2.50
42 Baby Killer. 2.50
43 Wedding Disasters 2.50
44 F:Amy Hamilton 2.50
45 Plane Hijacking. 2.50
46 Airport Terrorists 2.50
Ann.#1 The Blue & the Green 2.50
1993 Ann 3.00

Bonus Books
TPB rep. Now comics #1–#12,
     296pg. 10.00
TPB deluxe rep. Now comics
     #1–#12, 296pg. 20.00

GREEN HORNET: DARK TOMORROW
Now, 1993
1 thru 3 Hornet Vs Kato . . . . @3.00

GREEN HORNET: SOLITARY SENTINAL
Now, 1992
1 Strike Force 3.00
2 thru 3 . . . . @3.00

GREENHAVEN
Aircel
1 . . . . 3.00
2 . . . . 3.00
3 . . . . 3.00

GREEN PLANET
Charlton, 1962
1 DG 100.00

GRENDEL
Comico, 1986–91
1 MW 9.00
1a 2nd printing 2.00
2 MW 6.00
3 thru 6 MW . . . . @5.00
7 MW 5.00
8 thru 12 MW . . . . @5.00
13 KSy(c) MW 4.50
14 KSy(c) MW 3.00
15 KSy(c) MW 3.00
16 MW,Mage 6.00
17 thru 19 MW,Mage . . . . @5.00
20 thru 32 MW . . . . @3.00
33 MW,giant-size 3.50
34 thru 36 MW . . . . @3.00
37 MW 6.00
38 MW 9.00
39 MW,D:Grendel 10.00
40 MW,D:Orion Assante 30.00

GREYLORE
Sirius, 1985–86
1 thru 5 . . . . @2.25

GREYSHIRT: INDIGO SUNSET
WildStorm/DC, 2001
America's Best Comics
1 (of 6) RV 3.50
2 RV 3.50
3 RV 3.50
4 RV, Star of Indigo. 3.50
5 RV, Fanman. 3.50
6 RV, Black Jack Hawkins 3.50
TPB Indigo Sunset. 20.00

GRIMJACK
First, 1984–91
1 TT Teenage suicide story. 3.00
2 TT A:Munden's Bar 2.50
3 TT A:Munden's Bar 2.50
4 TT A:Munden's Bar 2.50
5 TT,JSon,A:Munden's Bar 2.50
6 TT,SR,A:Munden's Bar 2.50
7 TT,A:Munden's Bar 2.50

Grimjack #66
© First

8 TT,A:Munden's Bar 2.50
9 TT My Sins Remembered 2.50
10 TT,JOy,A:Munden's Bar 2.50
11 TT,A:Munden'sBar. 2.50
12 TT,A:Munden's Bar 2.50
13 TT,A:Munden'sBar 2.50
14 TT,A:Munden'sBar 2.50
15 TT,A:Munden'sBar 2.50
16 TT,A:Munden'sBar 2.50
17 TT,A:Munden'sBar 2.50
18 TT,A:Munden'sBar 2.50
19 TT,A:Munden'sBar 2.50
20 TT,A:Munden'sBar 2.50
21 TS,A:Munden's Bar. 2.50
22 A:Munden's Bar 2.50
23 TS,A:Munden's Bar. 2.50
24 PS,TT,rep.Starslayer10-11 . . . 2.50
25 TS,A:Munden's Bar. 2.50
26 1st color TMNTurtles. 10.00
27 TS,A:Munden's Bar. 2.25
28 TS,A:Munden's Bar. 2.25
29 A:Munden's Bar 2.25
30 A:Munden's Bar 2.25
31 A:Munden's Bar 2.25
32 A:Spook. 2.25
33 JSon,Munden'sBar
     Christmas Tale. 2.25
34 V:Spook. 2.25
35 A:Munden's Bar 2.25
36 3rd Anniv.IssueD:Grimjack 2.50

37 A:Munden's Bar 2.25
38 A:Munden's Bar 2.25
39 R.Grimjack 2.25
40 . . . . 2.25
41 Weeping Bride 2.25
42 Hardball. 2.25
43 Beneath the Surface. 2.25
44 Shadow Wars 2.25
45 Shadow Wars 2.25
46 Shadow Wars 2.25
47 Shadow Wars,A:EddyCurrent . . . 2.25
48 Shadow Wars 2.25
49 Shadow Wars 2.25
50 V:Dancer,ShadowWars ends . . . 2.25
51 Crossroads tie-in,
     A:Judah Macabee 2.25
52 . . . . 2.25
53 Time Story. 2.25
54 . . . . 2.50
55 FH 2.50
56 FH 2.50
57 FH 2.50
58 FH 2.50
59 FH 2.50
60 FH,Reunion Pt.1 . . . . 2.50
61 FH,Reunion Pt.2 . . . . 2.50
62 FH,Reunion Pt.3 . . . . 2.50
63 FH,A:Justice Drok. 2.50
64 FH,O:Multiverse 2.50
65 FH 2.50
66 FH(c),Demon Wars Pt.1 . . . . . 2.50
67 FH(c),Demon Wars Pt.2 . . . . . 2.50
68 Demon Wars Pt.3 . . . . 2.50
69 Demon Wars Pt.4 . . . . 2.50
70 FH,I:Youngblood 2.50
71 FH,A:Youngblood 2.50
72 . . . . 2.50
73 FH(c) 2.50
74 FH(c) 2.50
75 FH,TS,V:The Major. 2.50
76 FH,A:Youngblood 2.50
77 FH,A:Youngblood 2.50
78 . . . . 2.50
79 FH,Family Business #1. . . . . . . 2.50
80 FH,Family Business #2. . . . . . . 2.50
81 FH,Family Business #3. . . . . . . 2.50

GRIMJACK CASEFILE
First, 1990
1 thru 5 rep. . . . . @2.25

GRIMM'S GHOST STORIES
Gold Key/Whitman, 1972–82
1 . . . . 40.00
2 . . . . 25.00
3 . . . . 25.00
4 . . . . 25.00
5 AW 30.00
6 . . . . 15.00
7 . . . . 15.00
8 AW 20.00
9 . . . . 15.00
10 . . . . 15.00
11 thru 16 . . . . @12.00
17 RC. 15.00
18 thru 60 . . . . @10.00

GROO THE WANDERER
Pacific, 1982–84
1 SA,I:Sage,Taranto 25.00
2 SA,A:Sage. 15.00
3 SA,C:Taranto 15.00
4 SA,C:Sage. 15.00
5 SA,I:Ahax. 15.00
6 SA,I:Gratic 18.00
7 SA,I:Chakaal 18.00
8 SA,A:Chakaal 18.00

COLOR PUB.

Eclipse
Spec.#1 SA,O:Groo,rep Destroyer
Duck #1 . . . . 23.00

GROUP LARUE
Innovation, 1989
1 . . . . 2.25
2 . . . . 2.25
3 . . . . 2.25

GRUMPY OLD MONSTERS
IDW Publishing, 2003
1 (of 4) 2.25
2 thru 4 . . . . @4.00
TPB 14.00

GUILLOTIN
ABC, 1997
1 JQ(c) 3.00
1a RCl(c) 6.00
1b gold cover, polybagged with
    trading card 10.00
2 . . . . 3.00
2a Serpent (c) 6.00
2b Cold Series (c) 6.00

GULLIVER'S TRAVELS
Dell Publishing Co., 1965
1 . . . . 75.00
2 and 3 . . . . @50.00

GUMBY
Comico, 1987
1 AAd,Summer Fun Special 5.00
2 AAd,Winter Fun Special 3.50

GUMBY IN 3-D
Blackthorne
Spec.#1 . . . . 4.00
2 thru 7 . . . . @3.00

GUN FU: THE LOST CITY
Axiom, 2003
1 . . . . 3.50
1a variant (c) 6.00
2 . . . . 3.50
3 . . . . 3.50
2a thru 3a variant (c)s . . . . @3.50
Preview signed edition 3.00

GUNSMOKE
Dell Publishing Co., 1956
1 J.Arness Ph(c) all 300.00
2 . . . . 175.00
3 . . . . 175.00
4 . . . . 175.00
5 . . . . 175.00
6 . . . . 150.00
7 . . . . 150.00
8 . . . . 155.00
9 . . . . 155.00
10 AW,RC 165.00
11 . . . . 155.00
12 AW 165.00
13 thru 27 . . . . @125.00

GUY WITH A GUN: A ZOMBIE NIGHTMARE
Alpha Productions
1 V:Gracel, Zombies 3.00

HACK/SLASH
Devil's Due Publishing, 2004
1 . . . . 5.00
1-shot Girls Gone Dead 5.00
1-shot variant(c) 5.00

Hall of Fame #1
© J. C. Productions

HALL OF FAME
J.C. Productions
1 WW,GK,ThunderAgents 2.25
2 WW,GK,ThunderAgents 2.25
3 WW,Thunder Agents 2.25

HALLOWEEN
Chaos! Comics, 2000
1 premium glow-in-the-dark (c) . . . 13.00
1 chromium edition 16.00

HALLOWEEN: BEHIND THE MASK
Chaos! Comics, 2000
1 photo (c) 3.00

HALLOWEEN II: THE BLACKEST EYE
Chaos! Comics, 2001
Spec. 3.00
Spec. premium 10.00

HALLOWEEN III: THE DEVIL'S EYES
Chaos! Comics, 2001
Spec. 3.00
Spec. variant (c) 3.00
Spec. Previews exclusive 3.00

HALLOWEEN HORROR
Eclipse, 1987
1 . . . . 3.00

HALO: AN ANGEL'S STORY
Sirius, 1996
1 thru 3 by Chris Knowles . . . . . . @3.00
TPB rep. #1–#3 . . . . 13.00

HAMMER OF GOD
First
1 thru 4 . . . . @2.50
Deluxe #1 Sword of Justice Bk#1 . . 5.00
Deluxe #2 Sword of Justice Bk#2 . . 5.00

HAMSTER VICE
Blackthorne, 1985–87
1 thru 10 . . . . @2.50
3-D #1 . . . . 2.50

HAND OF FATE
Eclipse, 1988
1 I:Artemus Fate 2.25
2 F:Artemis & Alexis 2.25
3 Mystery & Suspense 2.25

HANDS OF THE DRAGON
Atlas, 1975
1 . . . . 18.00

HANNA-BARBERA ALL-STARS
Archie, 1995
1 thru 5 . . . . 3.00

HANNA-BARBERA BAND WAGON
Gold Key, 1962–63
1 . . . . 200.00
2 . . . . 150.00
3 . . . . 125.00

HANNA-BARBERA PARADE
Charlton Comics, 1971–72
1 . . . . 125.00
2 thru 10 . . . . @75.00

HANNA-BARBERA PRESENTS
Archie, 1995
1 thru 15 . . . . @3.00

HANNA-BARBERA SUPER TV HEROES
Gold Key, 1968
1 B:Birdman,Herculiods,Moby Dick,
Young Samson & Goliath 275.00
2 . . . . 200.00
3 thru 7 Oct. 1969 . . . . @175.00

HARBINGER
Valiant, 1992
0 DL,O:Sting,V:Harada, from TPB
    (Blue Bird Ed.) 2.25
0 from coupons 4.00
1 DL,JDx,I:Sting,Torque,
    Zeppelin,Flamingo,Kris 3.00
2 DL,JDx,V:Harbinger Foundation,
    I:Dr.Heyward 2.50
3 DL,JDx,I:Ax,Rexo, V:Spider
    Aliens 2.50
4 DL,JDx,V:Ax,I:Fort,
    Spikeman,Dog,Bazooka 2.50
5 DL,JDx,I:Puff,Thumper,
    A:Solar,V:Harada 2.50
6 DL,D:Torque,A:Solar,
    V:Harada,Eggbreakers 2.50
1a thru 6a w/o coupon . . . . @2.00
7 DL,Torque's Funeral 2.25

8 FM(c),DL,JDx,Unity#8,
  A:Magnus,Eternal Warrior 2.25
9 WS(c),DL,Unity #16,
  A:Magnus,Armstrong,Rai,
  Archer,Eternal Warrior 2.25
10 DL,I:H.A.R.D.Corps, Daryl,
  Shetiqua 2.25
11 DL,V:H.A.R.D.Corps 2.25
12 DL,F:Zeppelin,A:Elfquest 2.25
13 Flamingo Vs. Rock 2.25
14 A:Magnus(Dream Sequence),
  C:Stronghold 2.25
15 I:Livewire,Stronghold 2.25
16 A:Livewire,Stronghold 2.25
17 HSn,I:Simon 2.25
18 HSn,I:Screen 2.25
19 HSn,I:Caliph 2.25
20 HSn,V:Caliph 2.25
21 I:Pete's Father 2.25
22 HSn,A:Archer & Armstrong 2.25
23 HSn,B:Twilight of the
  Eighth Day. 2.25
24 HSn,V:Eggbreakers 2.25
25 HSn,V:Harada,E:Twlight of the
  Eighth Day. 2.50
26 SCh,AdW,I:Jolt,Amazon,
  Mircowave,Anvil,Sonix. 2.25
27 SCh,AdW,Chrismas issue. 2.25
28 SCh,AdW,O:Sonix,J:Tyger 2.25
29 SCh,AdW,A:Livewire,Stronghold,
  w/Valiant Era card 2.25
30 SCh,AdW,A:Livewire,Stronghold 2.25
31 SCh,AdW,V:H.A.R.D.Corps 2.25
32 SCh,AdW,A:Eternal Warrior 2.25
33 SCh, V:Dr. Eclipse 2.25
34 SCh,Chaos Effect-Delta#1, A:X-
  O, Dr. Eclipse 2.25
35 Zephyr. 2.25
36 Zephyr, Magnus 2.25
37 Magnus, Harada 2.25
38 A:Spikeman. 2.25
39 Zepplin vs. Harada 2.25
40 V:Harbinger. 2.25
41 V:Harbinger. 2.25
TPB w/#0,rep#1-4 . . . . 25.00
TPB 2nd Printing w/o #0 . . . . 10.00
TPB #2, Rep. 6-7,10-11 . . . . 10.00

HARBINGER FILES: HARADA
Valiant, 1994
1 BL,DC,O:Harada 2.75
2 Harada's ultimate weapon 2.50

HARDCASE
Malibu Ultraverse, 1993–95
1 I:Hardcase,D:The Squad 3.00
1a Ultra-Limited, silver foil 4.00
1b Full Hologram (c). 6.00
1c Platinum edition 3.50
2 w/Ultraverse card. 3.00
3 Hard decisions. 2.75
4 A:Strangers 2.75
5 BWS,V:Hardwire,BU:Rune 2.75
6 V:Hardwire 2.50
7 ScB,Break-Thru x-over,
  I:Nanotech,A:Solution 2.25
8 GP,O:Solitare 2.25
9 B:O:Choice,I:Turf 2.25
10 O:Choice. 2.25
11 ScB,V:Aladdin 2.25
12 AV,A:Choice 2.25
13 A:Choice 2.25
14 A:Choice 2.25
15 Hardwires, NIM-E 2.25
16 NIM-E 3.50
17 Prime,NIM-E 2.25
18 V:Nim-E, Battle Royale 2.25
19 Prelude to Godwheel 2.25

Hardcase #3
© Malibu

20 R:Rex Mindi 2.50
21 Mundiquest prelude 2.50
22 Mundiquest. 2.50
23 A:Loki 2.50
24 Mundiquest,pt.3 . . . . 2.50
25 Mundiquest,concl. 3.00
26 Time Gem Disaster. 3.00

H.A.R.D. CORPS
Valiant, 1992
1 JLe(c),DL,BL,V:Harbinger
  Foundation,I:Flatline,D:Maniac . 2.50
1a Gold Ed. 2.50
2 DL,BL,V:Harb.Foundation 2.50
3 DL,BL,J:Flatline 2.50
4 BL 2.50
5 BCh,BL(i),A:Bloodshot. 2.50
5a Comic Defense System Ed.. . . . 2.50
6 MLe,A:Spider Aliens 2.50
7 MLe,V:Spider Aliens, I:Hotshot . . 2.50
8 MLe,V:Harada,J:Hotshot 2.50
9 MLe,V:Harada,A:Turok 2.25
10 MLe,A:Turok,V:Dinosaurs 2.25
11 YG,I:Otherman 2.25
12 MLe,V:Otherman. 2.25
13 YG,D:Superstar. 2.25
14 DvM(s),YG,V:Edie Simkus 2.25
15 DvM(s),YG,V:Edie Simkus 2.25
16 DvM(s),YG, ... 2.25
17 DvM(s),RLe,V:Armorines 2.25
18 DvM(s),RLe,V:Armorines,
  w/Valiant Era card 2.25
19 RLe,A:Harada 2.25
20 RLe,V:Harbingers 2.25
21 RLe,New Direction 2.25
22 RLe,V:Midnight Earl 2.25
23 RLe,Chaos Effect-Delta #4,
  A:Armorines, X-O 2.25
24 Ironhead 2.25
25 Midnight Earl. 2.25
26 Heydrich, Omen 2.25
27 Heydrich shows evil 2.25
28 New Hardcorps 2.25
29 V:New Guard 2.25
30 Final Issue 2.25

HARDY BOYS, THE
Gold Key, 1970
1 . . . . 75.00
2 thru 4 . . . . @40.00

HARI KARI
Blackout Comics, 1995
0 I:Hari Kari. 3.00
1 . . . . 3.00
1a commemorative, variant(c) . . . 10.00
Specials & 1-shots
1 The Beginning, O:Kari (1996) . . . 3.00
1a The Beginning, commemorative,
  signed 10.00
1 Bloodshed (1996) 3.00
1a Bloodshed, deluxe, variant(c) . 10.00
1 Live & Untamed! (1996) 3.00
1 Rebirth (1996) 3.00
0 The Silence of Evil (1996). 3.00
0 The Silence of Evil, limited,
  foil stamped 13.00
? The Diary of Kari Sun (1997). . . . 3.00
? The Diary of Kari Sun, deluxe . . 10.00
0 Life or Death (1997) 3.00
0a Life or Death, super sexy
  parody edition 13.00
1 Passion & Death (1997) 3.00
1 Passion & Death, photo(c). 10.00
1 Possessed by Evil (1997) 3.00
1 Resurrection (1997). 3.00

HARLEM GLOBETROTTERS
Gold Key, 1972
1 . . . . 50.00
2 thru 12, Jan. 1975 . . . . @30.00

HARRIERS
Entity, 1995
1 I:Macedon Arsenal, Cardinal 3.00
1a with Video Game 7.00
2 . . . . 2.50
3 V:Kr'llyn 2.50

HARSH REALM
Harris, 1994
1 thru 6 JHi(s), ... @3.00
TPB 15.00

HARVEY HITS
Harvey Publications, 1957–67
1 The Phantom 400.00
2 Rags Rabbit 60.00
3 Richie Rich 2,000.00
4 Little Dot's Uncles 250.00
5 Stevie Mazie's Boy Friend 50.00
6 JK(c),BP,The Phantom 300.00
7 Wendy the Witch 400.00
8 Sad Sack's Army Life 100.00
9 Richie Rich's Golden Deeds . . 700.00
10 Little Lotta 175.00
11 Little Audrey Summer Fun . . . 150.00
12 The Phantom 250.00
13 Little Dot's Uncles 100.00
14 Herman & Katnip 50.00
15 The Phantom 250.00
16 Wendy the Witch. 200.00
17 Sad Sack's Army Life 75.00
18 Buzzy & the Crow. 50.00
19 Little Audrey 75.00
20 Casper & Spooky 100.00
21 Wendy the Witch. 100.00
22 Sad Sack's Army Life 75.00
23 Wendy the Witch. 100.00
24 Little Dot's Uncles 150.00
25 Herman & Katnip 50.00
26 The Phantom 200.00
27 Wendy the Good Little Witch . 125.00
28 Sad Sack's Army Life 50.00
29 Harvey-Toon 75.00
30 Wendy the Witch 125.00
31 Herman & Katnip 40.00

32 Sad Sack's Army Life	50.00
33 Wendy the Witch	100.00
34 Harvey-Toon	50.00
35 Funday Funnies	40.00
36 The Phantom	175.00
37 Casper & Nightmare	75.00
38 Harvey-Toon	50.00
39 Sad Sack's Army Life	50.00
40 Funday Funnies	35.00
41 Herman & Katnip	35.00
42 Harvey-Toon	40.00
43 Sad Sack's Army Life	40.00
44 The Phantom	175.00
45 Casper & Nightmare	75.00
46 Harvey-Toon	40.00
47 Sad Sack's Army Life	40.00
48 The Phantom	175.00
49 Stumbo the Giant	150.00
50 Harvey-Toon	30.00
51 Sad Sack's Army Life	30.00
52 Casper & Nightmare	65.00
53 Harvey-Toons	30.00
54 Stumbo the Giant	75.00
55 Sad Sack's Army Life	30.00
56 Casper & Nightmare	60.00
57 Stumbo the Giant	75.00
58 Sad Sack's Army Life	30.00
59 Casper & Nightmare	60.00
60 Stumbo the Giant	75.00
61 Sad Sack's Army Life	30.00
62 Casper & Nightmare	50.00
63 Stumbo the Giant	60.00
64 Sad Sack's Army Life	30.00
65 Casper & Nightmare	50.00
66 Stumbo the Giant	60.00
67 Sad Sack's Army Life	30.00
68 Casper & Nightmare	50.00
69 Stumbo the Giant	60.00
70 Sad Sack's Army Life	30.00
71 Casper & Nightmare	50.00
72 Stumbo the Giant	60.00
73 Little Sad Sack	30.00
74 Sad Sack's Muttsy	30.00
75 Casper & Nightmare	45.00
76 Little Sad Sack	30.00
77 Sad Sack's Muttsy	30.00
78 Stumbo the Giant	60.00
79 Little Sad Sack	30.00
80 Sad Sack's Muttsy	30.00
81 Little Sad Sack	30.00
82 Sad Sack's Muttsy	30.00
83 Little Sad Sack	30.00
84 Sad Sack's Muttsy	30.00
85 Gabby Gob	30.00
86 G.I. Juniors	30.00
87 Sad Sack's Muttsy	30.00
88 Stumbo the Giant	50.00
89 Sad Sack's Muttsy	25.00
90 Gabby Goo	25.00
91 G.I. Juniors	25.00
92 Sad Sack's Muttsy	25.00
93 Sadie Sack	25.00
94 Gabby Goo	25.00
95 G.I. Juniors	25.00
96 Sad Sack's Muttsy	25.00
97 Gabby Goo	25.00
98 G.I. Juniors	25.00
99 Sad Sack's Muttsy	25.00
100 Gabby Goo	25.00
101 G.I. Juniors	20.00
102 Sad Sack's Muttsy	20.00
103 Gabby Goo	20.00
104 G.I. Juniors	20.00
105 Sad Sack's Muttsy	20.00
106 Gabby Goo	20.00
107 G.I. Juniors	20.00
108 Sad Sack's Muttsy	20.00
109 Gabby Goo	20.00
110 G.I. Juniors	20.00
111 Sad Sack's Muttsy	20.00
112 G.I. Juniors	20.00
113 Sad Sack's Muttsy	20.00
114 G.I. Juniors	20.00
115 Sad Sack's Muttsy	20.00
116 G.I. Juniors	20.00
117 Sad Sack's Muttsy	20.00
118 G.I. Juniors	20.00
119 Sad Sack's Muttsy	20.00
120 G.I. Juniors	20.00
121 Sad Sack's Muttsy	20.00
122 G.I. Juniors	20.00

HATE
Fantagraphics, 1990
1 thru 15, see B&W

16 thru 29	@3.00
30 48pg	4.00
Ann.#1 48-page (2000)	4.00
Ann.#2 (2001)	4.00
Ann.#3 (2002)	4.00
Ann.#4 (2003)	5.00
TPB Vol.1 Hey, Buddy!, rep. #1–#5	13.00
TPB Vol.1 Hey, Buddy! signed	13.00
TPB Vol.2 Buddy the Dreamer, rep. #6–#10	13.00
TPB Vol.2 Buddy the Dreamer, sgn	13.00
TPB Vol.3 Fun with Buddy & Lisa	13.00
TPB Vol.4 Buddy Go Home	17.00
TPB Vol.4 Buddy Go Home! signed	17.00
TPB Vol.5 Buddy's Got Three Moms	17.00
TPB Vol.6 Buddy Bites the Bullet	17.00

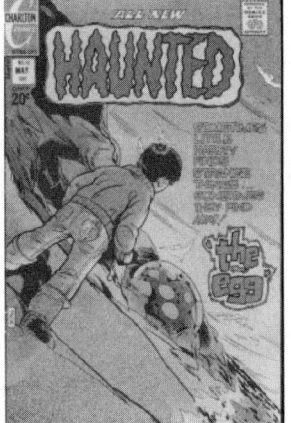

Haunted #12
© Charlton

HAUNTED
Charlton, 1971–84

1	65.00
2	30.00
3 thru 5	@30.00
6 thru 10	@25.00
11 thru 20	@20.00
21 thru 50	@15.00
51 thru 75	@10.00

HAUNTED, THE
Chaos! Comics, 2001

1 (of 4) PDd	3.00
1a variant Nat Jones (c)	3.00
1b premium ed.	10.00
2 PDd	3.00
2a variant Molenaar (c)	7.50
3 PDd	3.00
3a variant (c)	7.50
4	3.00
4a variant (c)	7.50
Ashcan, b&w	6.00

HAUNTED, THE: GRAY MATTERS
Chaos! Comics, 2002

1	3.00
1a premium edition	10.00

HAUNTED LOVE
Charlton, 1973–75

1	75.00
2	30.00
3 thru 5	@30.00
6 thru 11	@25.00

HAUNT OF FEAR
Gladstone, 1991

1 EC Rep. H of F #17,WS#28	3.00
2 EC Rep. H of F #5,WS #29	3.00

HAUNT OF FEAR
Russ Cochran, 1991

1 EC Rep. H of F #15	3.00
2 thru 5 EC Rep. H of F	@3.00

Second Series, 1992

1 EC Rep. H of F #14,WS#13	2.50
2 EC Rep. H of F #18,WF#14	2.50
3 EC Rep. H of F #19,WF#18	2.50
4 EC Rep. H of F #16,WF#15	2.50
5 EC Rep. H of F #5,WF#22	2.50
6 EC Rep. H of F	2.50
7 EC Rep. H of F	2.50
8 thru 15 Rep.	@2.50

Gemstone

16 thru 28 EC comics reprint	@2.50

`Annuals`

TPB Vol. 1 rebinding of #1–#5	9.00
TPB Vol. 2 rebinding of #6–#10	9.00
TPB Vol. 3 rebinding of #11–#15	9.00
TPB Vol. 4 rebinding of #16–#20	13.00
TPB Vol. 5 rebinding of #21–#25	13.50
TPB Vol. 6 rebinding of #26–#28	9.00

HAVE GUN, WILL TRAVEL
Dell Publishing Co., 1958

1 Richard Boone Ph(c) all	250.00
2	200.00
3	200.00
4 thru 14	@150.00

HAWKMOON, COUNT BRASS
First

1 Michael Moorcock adapt.	2.50
2 thru 4	@2.50

HAWKMOON JEWEL IN THE SKULL
First, 1986

1 Michael Moorcock adapt.	3.00
2 thru 4	@2.50

HAWKMOON, MAD GOD'S AMULET
First, 1987

1 Michael Moorcock adapt.	2.50
2 thru 4	@2.50

COLOR PUB.

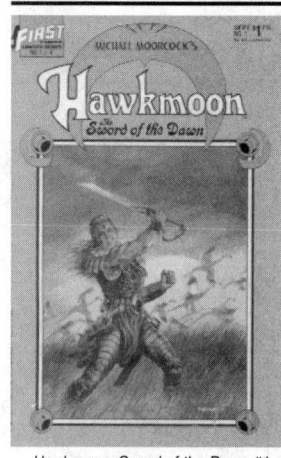

Hawkmoon, Sword of the Dawn #1
© First

HAWKMOON, SWORD OF THE DAWN
First, 1987
1 Michael Moorcock adapt 2.50
2 thru 4 . . . . @2.50

HAWKMOON, THE RUNESTAFF
First, 1988
1 Michael Moorcock adapt 2.50
2 thru 4 . . . . @2.50

HEADMAN
Innovation
1 . . . . 2.50
2 . . . . 2.50

HEARTSTOPPER
Millennium
1 V:Demons 3.00
2 V:Demons 3.00
3 F:Hellfire 3.00

HEAVY METAL MONSTERS
3-D-Zone, 1992
1 w/3-D glasses 4.00

HECTOR HEATHCOTE
Gold Key, 1964
1 . . . . 125.00

HEDG
Papyrus Media, 2002
1 by Patrick Sherman 3.00
1 signed 3.00
2 thru 4 . . . . @3.00
TPB Vol 1 . . . . 20.00

HELDEN
Caption Comics, 2001
1 (of 6) by Ralf Paul 3.00
2 thru 4 . . . . @3.00
5 . . . . 3.00
6 concl. 52-pg. 4.00

HELLINA
See Also B&W

HELLINA/ DOUBLE IMPACT
Lightning, 1996
1-shot JCy(c) 3.00
1-shot variant (c) 3.00

HELLINA: HEART OF THORNS
Lightning Comics, 1996
1 . . . . 3.00
1 autographed edition 10.00
2 . . . . 3.00
2 variant cover 3.00
2 platinum edition 6.00

HELLINA: HELLBORN
Lightning, 1997
1 . . . . 3.00
1 autographed edition 10.00

HELLINA/NIRA X: ANGEL OF DEATH
Lightning, 1996
1A cover A 3.00
1B cover B 3.00
1C Platinum cover 9.00
1D signed 9.00

HELLINA/NIRA X: CYBERANGEL
Lightning, 1996
1 autographed edition 10.00

HERBIE
American Comics Group April-May, 1964
1 . . . . 250.00
2 . . . . 125.00
3 . . . . 125.00
4 . . . . 125.00
5 A:Beatles,Dean Martin, Frank
    Sinatra 150.00
6 . . . . 100.00
7 . . . . 100.00
8 O:Fat Fury 130.00
9 . . . . 100.00
10 . . . . 100.00
11 . . . . 75.00
12 . . . . 75.00
13 . . . . 75.00
14 A:Nemesis,Magic Man 75.00
15 thru 22 . . . . @75.00
23 Feb., 1967. . . . . 75.00

HERCULES
Charlton Comics, 1967
1 . . . . 50.00
2 thru 7 . . . . @30.00
8 scarce 40.00
9 thru 13 Sept. 1969 . . . . @30.00

HERCULES: THE LEGENDARY JOURNEYS
Topps, 1996
1 & 2 . . . . @3.00
3 RTs,JBt,SeM,The Shaper,pt.1 . . . 5.00
3a Xena Ph(c) 15.00
4 RTs,JBt,SeM,The Shaper,pt.2 . . . 5.00
5 RTs,JBt,SeM,The Shaper,pt.3 . . . 5.00

HERE COMES THE BIG PEOPLE
Event Comics, 1997
1 ACo&JP(c) 3.00
1b JfD(c) 3.00
1c JQ&JP alternate (c) 10.00
1d JQ&JP alternate (c) signed . . . 30.00

HERO ALLIANCE
Wonder Color Comics, 1987
1 . . . . 2.50
Innovation, 1989–91
1 RLm,BS(c),R:HeroAlliance 6.00
2 RLm,BS(c),Victor vs.Rage 5.00
3 RLm,A:Stargrazers 4.00
4 . . . . 3.00
5 RLm(c) 2.50
6 BS(c),RLm pin-up 3.25
7 V:Magnetron 2.50
8 I:Vector 2.50
9 BS(c),V:Apostate 2.50
10 A:Sentry 2.50
11 . . . . 2.50
12 I:Bombshell 2.50
13 V:Bombshell 2.50
14 Kris Solo Story 2.50
15 JLA Parody Issue 2.50
16 V:Sepulchre 2.50
17 O:Victor,I&D:Misty 2.50
Annual #1 PS,BS,RLm 3.00
Spec.#1 Hero Alliance update 2.50
Spec.Hero Alliance & Justice Machine:
    Identity Crises 2.50

HERO ALLIANCE: THE END OF THE GOLDEN AGE
Pied Piper, 1986
1 Bart Sears/Ron Lim 20.00
1a signed 25.00
1b 2nd printing 2.50
2 . . . . 12.00
3 . . . . 3.00
Graphic Novel 10.00
Innovation, 1989
1 RLm 5.00
1A 2nd printing 2.50
2 RLm 4.00
3 RLm 3.00

HERO ALLIANCE QUARTERLY
Innovation
1 Hero Alliance stories 2.75
2 inc. Girl Happy 2.75
3 inc. Child Engagement 2.75
4 . . . . 2.75

HIGH CHAPPARAL
Gold Key, 1968
1 . . . . 75.00

HIGH ROADS
WildStorm/DC, 2002
Cliffhanger Productions
1 (of 6),SLo(s),F:Nick Highroad . . . 3.00
2 SLo(s),Paris 3.00
3 SLo(s),Nic Highroad 3.00
4 SLo(s),Iron Cross Brotherhood . . 3.00
5 SLo(s),Sloan,Bombridge 3.00
6 SLo(s),concl. 3.00
TPB 15.00

HIGH SCHOOL CONFIDENTIAL DIARY
Charlton Comics, 1960
1 . . . . 60.00
2 thru 11 . . . . @35.00
Becomes:
CONFIDENTIAL DIARY
12 . . . . 40.00
13 thru 17 March, 1963 . . . . . . @30.00

HIGH VOLTAGE
Blackout, 1996
O 3.00

HILLBILLY COMICS
Charlton Comics, 1955
1 . . . . 90.00
2 thru 4 July 1956 . . . . @50.00

HI-SCHOOL ROMANCE DATE BOOK
Harvey Publications, 1962
1 BP 75.00
2 . . . . 50.00
3 March, 1963 . . . . 50.00

HIS NAME IS ROG... ROG 2000
A Plus Comics
1 . . . . 2.25

HOBBIT, THE
Eclipse
1 . . . . 8.00
1a 2ndPrinting. 6.00
2 . . . . 7.00
2a 2ndPrinting. 5.00
3 . . . . 6.00

HOGAN'S HEROES
Dell Publishing Co., 1966
1 Ph(c) 125.00
2 Ph(c) 75.00
3 JD,Ph(c). 75.00
4 thru 8 Ph(c) . . . . @60.00
8 and 9 . . . . @60.00

HONEY WEST
Gold Key, 1966
1 . . . . 175.00

HONEYMOONERS
Lodestone, 1986
1 . . . . 4.00
5 Mag. 3.00
[2nd Series] Triad, 1987
1 They Know What They Like. 5.00
2 The Life You Save 4.00
3 X-mas special,inc.Art Carney
   interview 4.00
4 In the Pink 4.00
5 Bang, Zoom, To the Moon. 4.00
6 Everyone Needs a Hero inc.
   Will Eisner interview 4.00
7 . . . . 4.00
8 . . . . 4.00
9 Jack Davis(c) 5.00
10 thru 13. . . . . @4.00

HONG KONG
Blackout Comics, 1996
0 A:Hari Kari 3.00

---

0 limited commemorative edition . 10.00

HORSEMEN
Griot Enterprises, 2002
1 (of 3) 3.00
2 thru 3 . . . . @3.00
3.5 . . . . 3.00

HOT COMICS PREMIERE
Hot Comics
1 F:Thunderkill, Jacknife. 2.50

HOT ROD RACERS
Charlton Comics, 1964
1 . . . . 125.00
2 thru 5 . . . . @75.00
6 thru 15 July, 1967 . . . . @50.00

HOT STUFF, THE LITTLE DEVIL
Harvey Publications, 1957
1 . . . . 650.00
2 1st Stumbo the Giant 300.00
3 thru 5 . . . . @225.00
6 thru 10 . . . . @150.00
11 thru 20 . . . . @125.00
21 thru 40. . . . . @75.00
41 thru 60 . . . . @40.00
61 thru 100 . . . . @30.00
101 thru 105. . . . . @25.00
106 thru 112 52 pg Giants . . . . . @30.00
113 thru 139 . . . . @10.00
140 thru 177 . . . . @7.00

HOT STUFF SIZZLERS
Harvey Publications, 1960
1 B:68 pgs. 250.00
2 thru 5 . . . . @125.00
6 thru 10 . . . . @75.00
11 thru 20 . . . . @60.00
21 thru 30. . . . . @40.00
31 thru 44. . . . . @30.00
45 E:68 pgs 30.00
46 thru 50. . . . . @25.00
51 thru 59. . . . . @20.00

HOTSHOTS
1 thru 4 . . . . @2.50

HOTSPUR
Eclipse
1 RT(i),I:Josef Quist 3.00
2 RT(i),Amulet of Kothique Stolen . 3.00
3 RT(i),Curse of the SexGoddess . 3.00

HOWARD CHAYKIN'S AMERICAN FLAGG!
First
1 thru 9 . . . . @3.00
10 thru 12. . . . . @3.00

H.P.LOVECRAFT'S CTHULHU
Millennium
1 I:Miskatonic Project,V:Mi-Go . . . 3.00
2 Arkham, trading cards 3.00

H.R. PUFNSTUF
Gold Key, 1970
1 . . . . 300.00
2 & 3 . . . . @150.00
4 thru 8 . . . . @125.00

Howard Chaykin's American Flagg #3
© First

HUCK & YOGI JAMBOREE
Dell Publishing Co., March, 1961
1 . . . . 150.00

HUCKLEBERRY HOUND
Charlton, 1970
1 . . . . 75.00
2 thru 7 . . . . @40.00
3 Jan., 1972 . . . . 50.00

HUCKLEBERRY HOUND
Dell Publishing Co., May-July, 1959
1 . . . . 200.00
2 . . . . 150.00
3 thru 7 . . . . @125.00
8 thru 10 . . . . @100.00
11 thru 17. . . . . @75.00
Gold Key
18 Chuckleberry Tales 125.00
19 Chuckleberry Tales 100.00
20 Chuckleberry Tales 60.00
21 thru 30. . . . . @50.00
31 thru 43. . . . . @40.00

HUEY, DEWEY & LOUIE JUNIOR WOODCHUCKS
Gold Key, 1966
1 . . . . 85.00
2 thru 5 . . . . @50.00
6 thru 17 . . . . @40.00
18 . . . . 30.00
19 thru 25. . . . . @40.00
26 thru 30. . . . . @30.00
31 thru 57. . . . . @30.00
58 . . . . 25.00
59 . . . . 25.00
60 thru 80. . . . . @20.00
81 1984 . . . . 20.00

HYBRIDS
Continuity, 1993
0 Deathwatch 2000 prologue 5.00
1 Deathwatch 2000 pt.4,w/card . . . 3.00
2 Deathwatch 2000 pt.13,w/card . . 3.00
3 Deathwatch 2000 w/card. 3.00
4 A:Valeria. 3.00
5 O:Valeria 3.00

[2nd Series], 1994
1 Rise of Magic 3.00

HYBRIDS: ORIGIN
Continuity, 1993
1 thru 5 . . . . @3.00

HYDE-25
Harris, 1995
1 New Drug. 3.00

INU-YASHA ANI-MANGA
Viz Communications, 2004
TPB Vol. 1 . . . . 12.00
TPB Vol. 2 thru Vol. 5. . . . . @12.00

I DREAM OF JEANNIE
Dell Publishing Co., 1965
1 Ph(c),B.Eden 250.00
2 Ph(c),B.Eden 175.00

I SPY
Gold Key, 1966
1 Bill Cosby Ph(c) 350.00
2 Ph(c) 250.00
3 thru 4 AMc,Ph(c) . . . . @200.00
5 thru 6 Ph(c) Sept.1968. . . . . @200.00

I'M DICKENS – HE'S FENSTER
Dell Publishing Co., May-July, 1963
1 Ph(c) 75.00
2 Ph(c) 60.00

I-Bots #5
© Big Comics

I-BOTS
Big Comics, 1996
1 F:Lady Justice 2.50
2 thru 4 . . . . @2.25
5 StG(s),PB. 2.25
6 StG(s),PB. 2.25
7 PB,Rebirth,pt.1, triptych (c) 2.25
8 PB,Rebirth,pt.2, triptych (c) 2.25
9 PB,Rebirth,pt.3, Original I-Bots
return, triptych (c) 2.25

ICICLE
Hero Graphics
1 A:Flare,Lady Arcane,
V:Eraserhead. 5.00

IMP
Slave Labor, 1994
1 . . . . 2.50

IMPACT
Gemstone, 1999
1 EC Comic reprint 3.00
2 thru 5 . . . . @3.00
Annual #1 rep. #1–#5 . . . . 13.50

INCAL
Humanoids Publishing, 2001
1 . . . . 3.00
2 thru 6 . . . . @3.00
7 thru 13 . . . . 3.00
TPB Vol.1 Orphan of the City Shaft 18.00
TPB Vol.2 John Difool Detective . . 18.00
TPB Vol.3 The Epic Consipiracy . . 18.00

INMATES: PRISONERS OF SOCIETY
Delta Comics, 1997
1 (of 4) 3.00
2 thru 4 . . . . @3.00

INNER CIRCLE
Mushroom Comics, 1995
1.1 I:Point Blank 2.50
1.2 V:Deathcom 2.50
1.3 V:Deathcom 2.50
1.4 V:Deathcom 2.50

INNOCENTS
Radical Comics, 1995
1 I:Innocent. 2.50

INNOVATORS
Dark Moon, 1995
1 I:Innovator, LeoShan 2.50
2 O:Mr. Void 2.50
3 I:Quill 2.50

INSANE CLOWN POSSE
Chaos Comics, 1999
1 . . . . 3.00
1 premium edition 10.00
1 Jeckel Brothers premium ed. . . . 10.00
3 Raze the Desertz of Glass 3.00
3a variant (c). 10.00
Spec. The Amazing Jeckel Brothers 3.00
TPB Vol. 1 . . . . 9.00

INSANE CLOWN POSSE: DARK CARNIVAL
Chaos! Comics, 2002
1 . . . . 3.00
1a premium edition 10.00

INSANE CLOWN POSSE: MR. JOHNSON'S HEAD
Chaos Comics, 2002
Ashcan. 6.00
1 (of 2) 3.00
1a premium edition 10.00

INSANE CLOWN POSSE: THE PENDULUM
Chaos! Comics, 2000
1 polybagged with CD single 6.00
1a variant (c). 10.00
2 polybagged 6.00
3 polybagged 6.00
4 polybagged 6.00
5 Road Rage, polybagged 6.00
6 . . . . 6.00
7 Pendulum's Promise 6.00
8 Sport hunting, with CD-ROM 6.00
9 Glimpse of Crystal Death. 6.00
10 . . . . 6.00
11 with CD-ROM 6.00
12 . . . . 6.00
Spec. #1 Hallowicket 3.00
TPB Vol. 1 . . . . 9.00
TPB Vol. 2 . . . . 9.00

INTERVIEW WITH A VAMPIRE
Innovation, 1991
1 based on novel,preq.to Vampire
Chronicles 3.50
2 . . . . 3.00
3 Death & Betrayal 3.00
4 . . . . 3.00
5 D:Lestat 3.00
6 Transylvania Revelation. 3.00
7 Louis & Claudia in Paris 3.00
8 thru 10 . . . . @3.00
11 . . . . 3.00

INTERVIEW WITH A VAMPIRE
Innovation
1 based on novel, preq. to
Vampire Chronicles 3.50
2 . . . . 3.00
3 Death & Betrayal 3.00
4 . . . . 3.00
5 D:Lestat 3.00
6 Transylvania Revelation. 3.00
7 Louis & Claudia in Paris 3.00

INTIMATE
Charlton Comics, 1957
1 thru 3 . . . . @40.00
Becomes:

TEEN-AGE LOVE
4 . . . . 35.00
5 thru 9 . . . . @30.00
10 thru 35 . . . . @20.00
36 thru 96 . . . . @20.00

INTRUDER
TSR, 1990–91
1 thru 4 . . . . @3.00
5 thru 8 The Next Dimension . . . @3.00

INVADERS FROM HOME
Piranha Press, 1990
1 thru 6 . . . . @2.50

INVADERS, THE
Gold Key, 1967
1 Ph(c),DSp 175.00
2 Ph(c),DSp 125.00
3 Ph(c),DSp 125.00
4 Ph(c),DSp 125.00

COLOR PUB.

INVINCIBLE FOUR OF KUNG FU & NINJA
Dr. Leungs

1	3.00
2 and 3	@2.50
4	2.50
5 thru 11	@2.50

IO
Invictus Studios, 1994

1 I:IO	2.75
2	2.75
3 V:Major Damage	2.75

IRON HORSE
Dell Publishing Co., March, 1967

1	35.00
2	35.00

IRONJAW
Atlas, Jan.–July, 1975

1 NA(c),MSy	20.00
2 NA(c)	15.00
3	15.00
4 O:IronJaw	15.00

IRON MARSHAL
Jademan, 1990

1	2.50
2 thru 10	@2.25
11 thru 20	@2.25
21 thru 32	@2.25

IRREGULARS, THE: BATTLETECH Miniseries
Blackthorne

1	2.25
2	2.25
3 B&W	2.25

IRUKASHI

1	2.25

ISAAC ASIMOV'S I-BOTS
Tekno-Comix, 1995

1 I:I-Bots	2.25
2 O:I-Bots	2.25
3 V:Black OP	2.25

IT! TERROR FROM BEYOND SPACE
Millennium

1	2.50
2	2.50

IT'S ABOUT TIME
Gold Key, 1967

1 Ph(c)	65.00

ITCHY & SCRATCHY
Bongo Comics, 1993

1 DaC(s),	4.00
2 DaC(s),	3.50
3	3.50

IVANHOE
Dell Publishing Co., 1963

1	50.00

JACK
Med Systems Company

1 Anubis in the 90's	3.00
2 Modern Society	3.00

JACK HUNTER
Blackthorne, 1988

1	2.25
2	2.25
3	2.25

JACKIE CHAN'S SPARTAN X
Topps, 1997

1 The Armor of Heaven, pt.1	3.00
2 The Armor of Heaven, pt.2	3.00
3 (of 6)	3.00

JADE
Chaos! Comics, 2001

1	3.00
1a premium edition	10.00
2	3.00
3	3.00
4	3.00
4a variant	7.50
Preview book	2.00
Preview book, premium	6.00
Ashcan Jade #1	6.00

JADE: REDEMPTION
Chaos! Comics, 2001

1 (of 4)	3.00
1 premium edition	10.00
2	3.00
3	3.00
4	3.00
2a thru 4a variant (c)	@7.50
Ashcan	6.00

JADEMAN COLLECTION

1	4.50
2	3.00
3	2.50
4	2.50
5	2.50

JADEMAN KUNG FU SPECIAL

1 I:Oriental Heroes, Blood Sword, Drunken Fist	5.00

JADE WARRIORS: SLAVE OF THE DRAGON
Avatar Press, 2000

1 (of 3) MD2, 40-page	3.50
1a photo (c)	3.50
1b wraparound (c)	3.50
2 MD2	3.50
2a photo (c)	3.50

JAGUAR GOD
Verotika, 1995

1 Frazetta, I:Jaquar God	3.00
2 V:Yi-Cha	3.00
3 V:Yi-Cha	3.00
4 V:Yi-Cha	3.00
5 AOI	3.00
6 LSh,AOI	3.00
7 LSh,AOI	3.00
8 AOI	3.00
Spec.#1 Return to X'ibala,RCo	5.00
Spec. Jaguar God Illustrations	4.00
Spec. fan club edition	10.00

JAKE TRASH
Aircel

1 thru 3	@2.25

JALILA
Studio G, 2003

1	3.00
2 thru 4	@3.00

JAMES BOND 007
Eclipse, 1991

1 MGr,PerfectBound	5.50
2 MGr	5.00
3 MGr,end series	5.00
GN Licence to Kill, MGr l/o	8.00

JAMES BOND: GOLDENEYE
Topps, 1995

1 Movie adaptation	3.00
2 thru 3 Movie adaptation	@3.00

JAM SPECIAL
Comico

1	2.50

Jason Goes to Hell #3
© Topps

JASON GOES TO HELL
Topps, 1993

1 Movie adapt.,w/3 cards	3.25
2 Movie adapt.,w/3 cards	3.25
3 Movie adapt.,w/3 cards	3.25

JASON VS. LEATHERFACE
Topps, 1995

1 Jason Meets Leatherface	3.00
2 SBi(c) Leatherface's family	3.00
3 SBi(c),conclusion	3.00

JAVA
Committed Comics, 2004

1 (of 3)	3.00
2 thru 3	@3.00

JAVERTS
Firstlight, 1994
1 New Series 3.00
2 thru 5 Pieces of an Icon . . . . . . @3.00

JENNY SPARKS:
THE SECRET HISTORY
OF THE AUTHORITY
WildStorm/DC, 2000
1 (of 5) MMr,JMC 9.00
1a variant (c) (1:4) 4.00
2 MMr,JMC 3.00
3 MMr,JMC,O:Jack Hawksmoor . . . 3.00
4 MMr,JMC 3.00
5 MMr,JMC,conclusion 3.00
TPB 120-page, rep. 15.00

JET
WildStorm/DC, 2000
1 (of 4) DAn,ALa,F:Jodi Slayton . . . 2.50
2 DAn,ALa,Midnight to Midnight . . . 2.50
3 DAn,ALa,V:Timewaster 2.50
4 DAn,ALa,concl. 2.50

JET DREAM
Gold Key, 1968
1 . . . . 50.00

JETSONS, THE
Gold Key, 1963
1 . . . . 400.00
2 . . . . 200.00
3 thru 10 . . . . @150.00
11 thru 20 . . . . @125.00
21 thru 36 Oct. 1970 . . . . @100.00

JETSONS, THE
Charlton Comics, 1970
1 from Hanna-Barbera TV show. 125.00
2 . . . . 75.00
3 thru 10 . . . . @50.00
11 thru 20 Dec. 1973 . . . . @40.00

JETSONS, THE
Harvey Comics, 1991–92
1 thru 5 . . . . @3.00

JETSONS, THE
Archie, 1995
1 thru 17 . . . . @3.00

JEZEBELLE
WildStorm/DC, 2001
1 (of 6) F:Harper Harrison 2.50
1a variant(c) (1:2) 2.50
2 BRa(s) 2.50
3 BRa(s) F:Harper Harrison 2.50
4 BRa(s),Seance&Sensibility,pt.1 . . 2.50
5 BRa(s),Seance&Sensibility,pt.2 . . 2.50
6 BRa(s),concl. 2.50

JEZEBEL JADE
Comico, 1988
1 AKu,A:Race Bannon 3.00
2 AKu 3.00
3 AKu 3.00

JIGSAW
Harvey Publications, 1966
1 . . . . 45.00
2 . . . . 30.00

JIMBO
Bongo Comics
1 R:Jimbo 3.00
2 thru 4 . . . . @3.00

JIMMY CORRIGAN
Fantagraphics
1 Chris Ware 4.00

J. N. Williamson's Masques #1
© Innovation

J. N. WILLIAMSON'S
MASQUES
Innovation
1 TV,From horror anthology 5.00
2 Olivia(c) inc.Better Than One . . . 5.00

JOHN BOLTON,
HALLS OF HORROR
Eclipse
1 JBo 3.00
2 JBo 3.00

JOHN CARTER OF MARS
Gold Key, 1964
1 . . . . 100.00
2 & 3 . . . . @60.00

JOHN F. KENNEDY
LIFE STORY
(WITH 2 REPRINTS)
Dell Publishing Co., 1964
1 . . . . 75.00
2 . . . . 50.00
3 . . . . 50.00

JOHN JAKES
MULLKON EMPIRE
Tekno Comix, 1995
1 I:Mulkons 2.50
2 O:Mulkons 2.25
3 D:Company Man 2.25
4 Disposal Problems 2.25
5 F:Granny 2.25
6 Where's Karma 2.25

JOHN LAW
Eclipse, 1983
1 WE 2.25

JOHNNY GAMBIT
Hot
1 . . . . 2.25

JOHNNY JASON
TEEN REPORTER
Dell Publishing Co., 1962
1 . . . . 50.00
2 . . . . 40.00

JOHNNY NEMO
Eclipse, 1985–86
1 I:Johnny Nemo 2.50
2 . . . . 2.25
3 F:Sindy Shade 2.50

JOHN STEELE
SECRET AGENT
Gold Key, 1964
1 . . . . 125.00

JONNY QUEST
Gold Key, 1964
1 TV show 575.00

JONNY QUEST
Comico, 1986
1 DW,SR,A:Dr.Zin 6.00
2 WP/JSon,O:RaceBannon 4.00
3 DSt(c) 4.00
4 TY/AW,DSt(i) 3.50
5 DSt(c)A:JezebelJade 3.00
6 AKu 3.00
7 . . . . 3.00
8 KSy 3.00
9 MA 3.00
10 King Richard III 3.00
11 JSon,BSz(c) 3.00
12 DSp 3.00
12 DSp 3.00
13 CI 3.00
14 . . . . 3.00
15 thru 31 . . . . @3.00
Spec.#1 . . . . 3.00
Spec.#2 . . . . 3.00

JONNY QUEST
CLASSICS
Comico
1 DW 3.00
2 DW,O:Hadji 3.00
3 DW 3.00

JON SABLE
First, 1983
1 MGr,A:President 4.50
2 MGr,Alcohol Issue 3.50
3 MGr,O:Jon Sable 3.00
4 MGr,O:Jon Sable 3.00
5 MGr,O:Jon Sable 3.00
6 MGr,O:Jon Sable 3.00
7 MGr,The Target 2.50
8 MGr,Nuclear Energy 2.50
9 MGr,Nuclear Energy 2.50
10 MGr,Tripitych 2.50
11 MGr,I:Maggie 2.50
12 MGr,Vietnam 2.50
13 MGr,Vietnam 2.50
14 MGr,East Germany 2.50
15 MGr,Nicaragua 2.50
16 MGr,A:Maggie 2.50
17 MGr,1984 Olympics 2.50
18 MGr,1984 Olympics 2.50
19 MGr,The Widow 2.50

20 MGr,The Rookie	2.50
21 MGr,Africa	2.25
22 MGr,V:Sparrow	2.25
23 MGr,V:Sparrow	2.25
24 MGr,V:Sparrow	2.25
25 MGr,Shatter	3.00
26 MGr,Shatter	3.00
27 MGr,Shatter	3.00
28 MGr,Shatter	3.00
29 MGr,Shatter	3.00
30 MGr,Shatter	2.25
31 MGr,Nicaragua	2.25
32 MGr,Nicaragua	2.25
33 MGr,SA,Leprechauns	2.25
34 MGr,Indians	2.25
35 MGr,Indians	2.25
36 MGr,Africa	2.25
37 MGr,Africa	2.25
38 MGr,Africa	2.25
39 MGr,Africa	2.25
40 MGr,1st Case	2.25
41 MGr,1st Case	2.25
42 MGr,V:Sparrow	2.25
43 MGr,V:Sparrow	2.25
44 Hard Way	2.25
45 Hard Way II	2.25
46 MM,The Tower pt.1	2.25
47 MM,The Tower pt.2	2.25
48 MM,Prince Charles	2.25
49 MM,Prince Charles	2.25
50 A:Maggie the Cat	2.25
51 Jon Sable,babysitter pt.1	2.25
52 Jon Sable,babysitter pt.2	2.25
53 MGr.	2.25
54 Jacklight pt.1	2.25
55 Jacklight pt.2	2.25
56 Jacklight pt.3	2.25

JOSIE
Archie Publications, 1963

1	250.00
2	150.00
3	100.00
4	100.00
5	100.00
6 thru 10	@75.00
11 thru 20	@50.00
21 thru 30	@40.00
31 thru 40	@35.00
41 thru 54	@35.00
55 thru 74	@25.00
75 thru 105	@25.00
106 Oct., 1962	25.00

JUDGE COLT
Gold Key, 1969

1	35.00
2	20.00
3	20.00
4 Sept., 1970	20.00

JUDGE DREDD
Eagle, 1983

1 BB,I:Judge Death(in USA)	10.00
2 BB(c&a),The Oxygen Board	4.00
3 BB(c),Judge Dredd Lives	7.00
4 BB(c),V:Perps	7.00
5 BB(c),V:Perps	5.00
6 BB(c),V:Perps	5.00
7 BB(c),V:Perps	5.00
8 BB(c),V:Perps	5.00
9 BB(c),V:Perps	5.00
10 BB(c),V:Perps	5.00
11 BB(c)	4.00
12 BB(c)	4.00
13 BB(c), The Day the Law Died, pt.5	4.00
14 BB(c),Dredd vs. Dredd	4.00
15 BB(c)	4.00

Judge Dredd #2
© Eagle

16 BB(c)	4.00
17 BB(c)	4.00
18 BB(c)	4.00
19 BB(c)	4.00
20 BB(c)	4.00
21 BB(c)	4.00
22 BB(c),V:Perps	3.00
23 BB(c),V:Perps	3.00
24 BB(c),V:Perps	3.00
25 BB(c),V:Perps	3.00
26 BB(c),V:Perps	3.00
27 BB(c),V:Perps	3.00
28 A:Judge Anderson,V:Megaman	4.00
29 A:Monty, the guinea pig	3.00
30 V:Perps	3.00
31 Destiny's Angel, Pt. 1	3.00
32 Destiny's Angel, Pt. 2	3.00
33 V:League of Fatties	3.00
34 V:Executioner	3.00

JUDGE DREDD
Quality Press, 1986

1 Cry of the Werewolf Pt.1	6.00
2 Cry of the Werewolf Pt.2	5.00
3 Anti-smoking	4.00
4 Wreckers	4.00
5 Highwayman	4.00
6	3.00
7	3.00
8	3.00
9	3.00
10	3.00
11	3.00
12 Starborn Thing, Pt.1	3.00
13 Starborn Thing, Pt.2	3.00
14 BB, V:50 foot woman	3.00
15 City of the Damned Pt.1	3.00
16 City of the Damned Pt.2	3.00
17 City of the Damned conc.	3.00
18 V:Mean Machine Angel	3.00
19 Dredd Angel	3.00
20 V:Perps	3.00
21 V:Perps	3.00
22/23 Booby Trap	3.00
24 Junk food fiasco	3.00
25/26 V:Perps	3.00
27 V:Perps	3.00
28 Dredd Syndrome	3.00
29 V:Perps	3.00
30 V:Perps	3.00
31 Hunt Pudge Dempsey's killer	3.00
32 V:Mutated Sewer Alligator	3.00
33 V:Perps	3.00
34 V:Executioner	3.00

35 V:Shojan	3.00
36 V:Shojan	3.00
37 V:Perps	3.00
38 V:Perps	3.00
39 V:Perps	3.00
40 V:Perps	3.00
41 V:Perps	3.00
42 V:Perps	3.00
43 V:Perps	3.00
44 V:Perps	3.00
45 V:DNA Man	2.50
46 Genie lamp sty	2.50
47 V:Perps	2.50
48 Murder in Mega-City One	2.50
49 V:Perps	2.50
50 V:Perps	2.50
51 V:Perps	2.50
52 V:Perps	2.50
53 V:Perps	2.50
54 V:Perps	2.50
55 V:Perps	2.50
56 inc.JudgeDredd Postcards	2.50
57 V:Perps	2.50
58 V:370lb Maniac	2.50
59 V:Perps	2.50
60 Social Misfit	2.50
61 V:Perps	2.50

Becomes:

JUDGE DREDD CLASSICS

62	2.50
63 Mutants from the Radlands	2.50
64	2.50
65	2.50
66 Wit and wisdom of Dredd	2.50
67 V:Otto Sump	2.50
68 V:Otto Sump	2.50
69	2.50
70 Dinosaurs in Mega City 1	2.50
71	2.50
72 Pirates of the Black Atlantic	2.50
73	2.50
74	2.50
75	2.50
76 Diary of a Mad Citizen	3.00
TPB:Democracy Now	11.00
TPB:Rapture	13.00
Judge Dredd Special #1	2.50
GN Bad Science	8.00
GN Hall of Justice	8.00
GN Metal Fatigue	8.00

JUDGE DREDD
Titan, 2001

TPB The Emerald Isle	15.00
TPB Death Aid	15.00
TPB Goodnight Kiss (2002)	15.00
TPB Helter Skelter (2002)	15.00
TPB Justice One (2002)	15.00
TPB The Day the Law Died	20.00
TPB The Apocalypse War	25.00
TPB The Judge Child Quest	20.00
GN Muzak Killer (2002)	15.00
GN Innocents Abroad (2002)	15.00
GN Necropolis Book One	15.00
GN Necropolis Book Two	20.00
GN Cursed Earth	20.00
GN The Complete America	17.00
GN Judge Dredd vs. Judge Dredd	13.00

JUDGE DREDD: AMERICA
Fleetway

1 I:America	3.50

JUDGE DREDD: JUDGE CHILD QUEST
Eagle

1 thru 3	@3.00

COLOR PUB.

4 BB(c) 3.00
5 . . . . 3.00

JUDGE DREDD'S CRIME FILE
Eagle, 1984
1 Ron Smith, The Perp Runners . . 2.50
2 thru 6 . . . . @2.50

Quality (Prestige format)
1 A:Rogue Trooper 6.50
2 IG,V:Fatties, Energy Vampires &
   Super Fleas 6.00
3 Battles foes from dead A:Judge
   Anderson 6.00

JUDGE DREDD'S EARLY CASES
Eagle
1 Robot Wars, Pt.1 . . . . 4.00
2 Robot Wars, Pt.2 . . . . 3.00
3 V:Perps 3.00
4 IG, Judge Giant 3.00
5 V:Perps 3.00
6 V:Judge killing car Elvis. 3.00

JUDGE DREDD'S HARDCASE PAPERS
Fleetway/Quality
1 V:The Tarantula 7.50
2 Junkies & Psychos 6.50
3 Crime Call Vid. Show. 6.50
4 Real Coffee,A:Johnny Alpha 6.50

JUDGE DREDD: THE MEGAZINE
Fleetway/Quality, 1991
1 Midnite's Children Pt.1
   A:Chopper, Young Death. 5.50
2 Midnite's Children Pt.2. . . . . 5.00
3 . . . . 5.00
23 thru 34. . . . . @4.00
35 thru 43. . . . . @5.50
44 thru 45. . . . . @7.00

Egmont Fleetway Limited
46 thru 75 . . . . @7.00

JUDGE PARKER
Argo, Feb., 1956
1 . . . . 60.00
2 . . . . 50.00

JUDGMENT DAY
Lightning Comics, 1993
1 B:JZy(s),KIK,V:Razorr,Rift,
   Nightmare, red prism(c). 5.00
1a Gold Prism(c). 5.00
1b Purple Prism(c) 7.00
1c Misprint,Red Prism(c), Bloodfire
   Credits inside. 8.00
1d Misprint,Gold Prism(c), Bloodfire
   Credits inside. 8.00
1e Misprint,Green Prism(c),
   Bloodfire Credits inside 8.00
1f B&W promo ed. Gold ink 5.00
1g B&W promo ed. platinum ed. . . 7.00
2 TLw,I:War Party,BU:Perg,
   w/Perg card 4.00
3 ErP,O:X-Treme. 3.25
4 ErP,In Hell 3.25
5 TLw,In Hell. 3.25
6 TLw,I:Red Front,O:Salurio. 3.25
7 O:Safeguard 3.25
8 . . . . 3.00
9 . . . . 3.00

10 . . . . 3.00

JUDGMENT DAY
Maximum Press, 1997
Alpha AMo(s) 2.50
Alpha variant cover 2.50
Omega AMo(s). 2.50
Omega variant cover 2.50
Final Judgment AMo(s) 2.50
Final Judgment variant cover. 2.50

JUDOMASTER
Charlton Comics, 1966
(Special War Series #4)
   I:Judomaster 75.00
89 FMc,War stories begin 60.00
89 (90) FMc,A:Thunderbolt 50.00
91 FMc,DG,A:Sarge Steel 50.00
92 FMc,DG,A:Sarge Steel 50.00
93 FMc,DG,I:Tiger 50.00
94 FMc,DG,A:Sarge Steel 50.00
95 FMc,DG,A:Sarge Steel 40.00
96 FMc,DG,A:Sarge Steel 40.00
97 FMc,A:Sarge Steel 40.00
98 FMc,A:Sarge Steel 40.00

JUGHEAD
Archie Publications 1965–1987
127 thru 130. . . . . @35.00
131 thru 150. . . . . @30.00
151 thru 160. . . . . @15.00
161 thru 200. . . . . @12.00
201 thru 250. . . . . @10.00
251 thru 300. . . . . @8.00
301 thru 352. . . . . @5.00

Archie's Pal Jughead #46
© Archie Publications

JUGHEAD
Archie Publications [2nd Series], 1987
1 thru 45 . . . . @6.00
Becomes:

ARCHIE'S PAL JUGHEAD
June, 1993
46 thru 50. . . . . @3.50
51 thru 70 . . . . @2.50
71 thru 99. . . . . @2.50
100 A Storm Over Uniforms, x-over
   (Betty #57, Archie #467) 2.50

101 thru 122. . . . . @2.25
123 thru 125 . . . . @2.25
126 thru 133. . . . . @2.25
134 thru 147. . . . . @2.25
148 thru 161 . . . . @2.25

JUGHEAD AS CAPTAIN HERO
Archie Publications, 1966
1 . . . . 100.00
2 . . . . 65.00
3 thru 7 . . . . @50.00

JUGHEAD'S FANTASY
Archie Publications, 1960
1 . . . . 275.00
2 . . . . 200.00
3 . . . . 175.00

JUGHEAD'S JOKES
Archie Publications, 1967
1 . . . . 100.00
2 . . . . 75.00
3 thru 5 . . . . @40.00
6 thru 10 . . . . @35.00
11 thru 30 . . . . @25.00
31 thru 77. . . . . @10.00
78 Sept., 1982 . . . . 10.00

JUGHEAD WITH ARCHIE DIGEST
Archie Publications, March, 1974
1 . . . . 75.00
2 . . . . 50.00
3 thru 10 . . . . @35.00
11 thru 91 . . . . @20.00
92 thru 129. . . . . @15.00
130 thru 138. . . . . @10.00
139 thru 144. . . . . @10.00
145 thru 155. . . . . @7.00
156 thru 171. . . . . @5.00
172 thru 179. . . . . @5.00

JUNCTION 17
Antarctic Press, 2003
1 . . . . 3.50
2 thru 4 . . . . @3.00

JUNGLE ADVENTURES
Skywald, March–June, 1971
1 F:Zangar,Jo-Jo,Blue Gorilla. . . . 40.00
2 F:Sheena, Jo-Jo,Zangar 35.00
3 F:Zangar,Jo-Jo,White Princess . 35.00

JUNGLE BOOK, THE
NBM, 1997
TPB CR,Kipling adapt. 17.00

JUNGLE COMICS
Blackthorne, 1988
1 DSt(c). 3.00
2 . . . . 3.00
3 . . . . 3.00
See B&W

JUNGLE JIM
Charlton, 1969–70
22 . . . . 45.00
23 . . . . 25.00
24 . . . . 25.00
25 . . . . 25.00
26 . . . . 25.00
27 . . . . 35.00

28 . . . . 35.00

JUNGLE TALES OF TARZAN
Charlton Comics, 1964
1 . . . . 75.00
2 . . . . 50.00
3 . . . . 50.00
4 July, 1965 . . . . 50.00

JUNGLE WAR STORIES
Dell Publishing Co., 1962
1 P(c) all 50.00
2 thru 11 . . . . @35.00
Becomes:

GUERRILLA WAR
12 thru 14. . . . . @40.00

JUNIOR WOODCHUCKS
Walt Disney, 1991
1 CB,Bubbleweight Champ. 3.00
2 CB,Swamp of no Return 3.00
3 Rescue Run-Around 3.00
4 Cave Caper 3.00

Jurassic Park #1
© Topps

JURASSIC PARK
Topps, 1993
1 Movie Adapt.,w/card 5.00
1a Newsstand Ed. 4.00
2 Movie Adapt.,w/card 3.25
3 Movie Adapt.,w/card 3.25
4 Movie Adapt.,w/card 3.25
2a thru 4a Newsstand Ed.. . . . . . @2.75
Ann.#1 Death Lizards 4.00

JURASSIC PARK: ADVENTURES
Topps, 1994
1 thru 10 reprints titles . . . . @3.00

JURASSIC PARK: RAPTOR
Topps, 1993
1 SE w/Zorro #0 ashcan & cards. . . 3.25
2 w/3 cards 3.00

JURASSIC PARK: RAPTORS ATTACK
Topps, 1994
1 SEt(s), ... 2.75

2 SEt(s), ... 2.75
3 SEt(s), ... 2.75
4 SEt(s), ... 2.75

JURASSIC PARK: RAPTOR HIJACK
Topps
1 SEt(s), ... 2.50
2 SEt(s), ... 2.50
3 SEt(s), ... 2.50
4 SEt(s), ... 2.50

[JURASSIC PARK:] THE LOST WORLD
Topps, 1997
1 (of 4) movie adapt 3.00
2 thru 4 . . . . @3.00

JUST A PILGRIM
Black Bull Entertainment, 2001
1 GEn,MT(c) 6.00
1a variant (c) 12.00
2 GEn,GF(c) 4.00
3 GEn,KN(c), Bloody Baskets 4.00
4 GEn,BSz(c) Firestarter 4.00
5 GEn,JMC(c) 4.00
Preview Ed. 7.00
TPB GEn,MT(c) 13.00

JUST A PILGRIM: GARDEN OF EDEN
Black Bull Entertainment, 2002
1 GEn,JJu(c). 7.00
1a variant GF (c). 4.00
2 GEn,CE 4.00
3 GEn,CE 4.00
4 GEn,CE 4.00
Preview ed. limited. 7.00
TPB series rep. 13.00

JUSTICE MACHINE
Noble Comics, 1981–85
1 JBy(c) Mag size,B&W 30.00
2 MGu,Mag size,B&W 16.00
3 MGu,Mag size,B&W 10.00
4 MGu,Bluecobalt 8.00
5 MGu 7.00
Texas Comics
Ann.#1:BWG,I:Elementals,
   A: Thunder Agents. 5.00

JUSTICE MACHINE
[Featuring the Elementals]
Comico, 1986
1 thru 4 . . . . @2.50

JUSTICE MACHINE
Comico, 1987–89
1 MGu. 2.50
2 MGu. 2.25
3 thru 14 MGu . . . . @2.25
15 thru 27 MGu . . . . @2.25
28 MGu 2.25
29 MGu,IW. 2.25
Ann.#1 . . . . 2.50
SummerSpectacular 1 . . . . 2.75
MINI SERIES, 1990
1 thru 4 F:Elementals . . . . @2.25
Innovation, 1990
1 . . . . 2.25
2 thru 4 The Ragnarok Portfolio . @2.25
5 thru 7 Demon trilogy . . . . @2.25

JUSTICE MACHINE: CHIMERA CONSPIRACY
Millennium
1 AH,R&N:Justice Machine,
   wraparound cover 2.50

JUST MARRIED
Charlton Comics, 1958
1 . . . . 100.00
2 . . . . 60.00
3 thru 10 . . . . @40.00
11 thru 30 . . . . @25.00
31 thru 113 . . . . @20.00
114 Dec., 1976. . . . . 15.00

KABOOM
Awesome Entertainment, 1997
1 JLb,JMs, ... 5.00
1a variant (c)s 6.00
2 JLb,JMs, ... 3.00
3 JLb,JMs, ... 4.00
4 JLb,JMs,Kaboom the
   Barbarian,pt.1 (of 3) 2.50
5 JLb,JMs,Barbarian,pt.2 . . . . 2.50
6 JLb,JMs,Barbarian,pt.3 . . . . 2.50
VOL II
1 (of 3) 2.50
2 JLe,JLb,F:Kyra. 2.50
3 JLe,JLb, conclusion 2.50
Collected #1 & #2 . . . . 6.00

KABUKI
Caliber Press
1 Color Gallery,32 paintings 7.00
1-shot Color Special, inc.
   pin-up gallery 3.00
1-shot Fear the Reaper (1994). . . . 7.00

KABUKI: SKIN DEEP
Caliber, 1996
1 DMk 4.00
2 DMk(c) 3.50
2 AxR(c) 6.00
3 Origin issue 3.50
4 . . . . 3.50

KADE
Arcana Studios, 2003
1 . . . . 3.00
2 thru 4 . . . . @3.00

KAMIKAZE: 1946
Antarctic Press, 2000
1 Pickadon 3.00
2 Operation Olympic 3.00
3 Queens of the Seas. 3.00
4 Operation Coronet 3.00
5 Kaitens 3.00
6 Fortress Japan. 3.00

KAMIKAZE
Wildstorm/DC, 2003
1 (of 5) extreme sport 3.00
2 thru 6 . . . . @3.00

KATO OF THE GREEN HORNET
Now, 1991
1 BA,1st Kato solo story 2.50
2 BA,Kato in China contd. 2.50
3 Kato in China contd 2.50
4 Final Issue 2.50

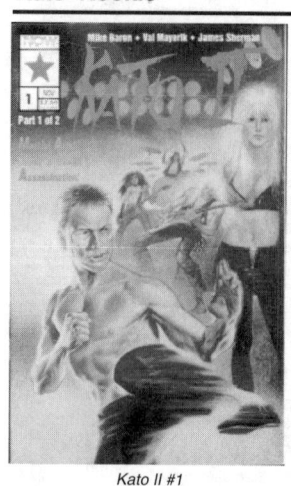

Kato II #1
© *Now*

KATO II
Now, 1992
1 VM,JSh,A:Karthage		2.50
2 VM,JSh,V:Karthage		2.50
3 VM,JSh,V:Karthage		2.50

KATY KEENE FASHION
BOOK MAGAZINE
Archie Publications, 1955
1 Woggon(a&c)		600.00
2		350.00
3 thru 10 not published		
11 thru 18		@250.00
19		200.00
20		200.00
21		200.00
22		200.00
23 Winter 1958-59		200.00

KATY KEENE
PINUP PARADE
Archie Publications, 1955
1		600.00
2		300.00
3		275.00
4		275.00
5		275.00
6		225.00
7		225.00
8		225.00
9		225.00
10 Woggon art		225.00
11 Story on comics		275.00
12		225.00
13		225.00
14		225.00
15 Sept., 1961		500.00

KELLY GREEN
Eclipse
1 SDr,O:Kelly Green		2.50
2 SDr,One,Two,Three		2.25
3 SDr,Million Dollar Hit		2.25
4 SDr,Rare		4.00

KELVIN MACE
Vortex
1		6.50
1a 2nd printing		2.25
2		4.00

KEN LASHLEY'S
LEGENDS
DHJ Comics, 2002
1 (of 6) by Ken Lashley		3.00
1a variant (c)		3.00
1b previews exclusive		5.00
2		3.00

KID DEATH & FLUFFY
Event Comics, 1997
Spec.#1 Halloween Spec. John Cebollero(c)		3.00
Spec.#1a Halloween Spec. JQ(c)		3.00

KILLER INSTINCT
Acclaim
1 thru 3		@2.50
Spec. Brothers by Art Holcomb		2.50

KILLER TALES
Eclipse, 1985
1 Tim Truman		3.00

KINDRED II
WildStorm/DC, 2002
1 (of 4) BBh		2.50
2 BBh		2.50
3 BBh,Backlash & Grifter		2.50
4 BBh,concl.		2.50

KING COMICS PRESENTS
King Comics
1 I:Rick Dees, Angel Lopez		2.25

KING LEONARDO AND
HIS SHORT SUBJECTS
Dell Publishing Co., 1961–62
1		225.00
2		150.00
3		175.00
4		150.00

KING LOUIE & MOWGLI
Gold Key, 1968
1		40.00

KING OF DIAMONDS
Dell Publishing Co., 1962
1 Ph(c)		50.00

KISS KISS BANG BANG
Crossgen, 2004
1		3.00
2 thru 7		@3.00

KIT KARTER
Dell Publishing Co., 1962
1		40.00

KNIGHTHAWK
Windjammer, 1995
1 NA(c&a),I:Knighthawk the Protector,V:Nemo		2.75
2 NA(c&a),Birth of Nemo		2.50
3 NA,V:Nemo		2.50
4 NA,V:Nemo		2.50
5 I:Cannon, Brick		2.50
6 V:Cannon, Brick		2.50

KNIGHTS OF THE
ROUND TABLE
Dell Publishing Co.,1963-64
1 P(c)		50.00

KNUCKLES
Archie Comics, 1997
1		2.25
2 thru 31		@2.25
32 thru 33		@2.25

KOLCHAK
THE NIGHT STALKER
Moonstone, 2002
GN		6.50
GN The Get of Belial		7.00
GN Fever Pitch		7.00
GN Lambs to the Slaughter		7.00
GN Pain Most Human		7.00
GN Pain Without Tears		7.00
TPB Vol. 1		18.00

KOLCHAK: TALES OF
THE NIGHT STALKER
Moonstone, 2003
1		3.50
2 thru 4		@3.50
GN Devil in the Details		7.00

KOL MANIQUE
RENAISSANCE
1		2.25
2		2.25

KOMAH
Anubis Press
1 Urban Decay Title		2.75

KOMBAT
Random Comics
1 (of 2) by Marcu Marshall & Pablo Villalobos		3.00
2 concl		3.00

KONA
Dell Publishing Co., 1962
1 P(c) all,SG		125.00
2 SG		60.00
3 SG		60.00
4 SG,B:Anak		60.00
5 thru 10 SG		@60.00
11 thru 21 SG		@50.00

KONGA
Charlton Comics, 1960–65
1 SD,DG(c), movie adapt.		350.00
2 DG(c)		175.00
3 SD		150.00
4 SD		150.00
5 SD		150.00
6 thru 15 SD		@100.00
16 thru 23		@75.00

KONGA'S REVENGE
Charlton Comics
2 Summer, 1962		100.00
3 SD,Fall, 1964		50.00
1 Dec., 1968		35.00

KOOKIE
Dell Publishing Co., 1962
1		150.00

2 . . . . 125.00

KORAK, SON OF TARZAN
Gold Key, 1964
1 . . . . 125.00
2 thru 11 . . . . @75.00
12 thru 21 . . . . @50.00
22 thru 30 . . . . @40.00
31 thru 40 . . . . @35.00
41 thru 44 . . . . @25.00
45 Jan., 1972 . . . . 25.00
Continued by DC

KRUSTY COMICS
Bongo Comics, 1995
1 Rise and Fall of Krustyland 2.50
2 Rise and Fall of Krustyland 2.50
3 Rise and Fall of Krustyland 2.50

KULL IN 3-D
Blackthorne
1 . . . . 2.50
2 . . . . 2.50
3 . . . . 2.50

LAD: A DOG
Dell Publishing Co., 1961
1 . . . . 60.00
2 . . . . 50.00

LADY ARCANE
Hero Graphics
1 A: Flare,BU:O:Giant 5.00
2 thru 3 . . . . @3.00

LADY DEATH
Chaos! Comics, 1994
1 BnP, A:Evil Ernie 15.00
1a signed gold foil 20.00
2 BnP 15.00
3 BnP 10.00
TPB Rep. #1-#3 . . . . 7.00
TPB The Reckoning 13.00
TPB The Reckoning, revised,
BnP,Shu 13.00
Specials & 1-shots
1 Swimsuit Edition 10.00
1a Velvet Edition 18.00

Lady Death Swimsuit Special #1
© Chaos! Comics

---

1 rep. with 8-page pin-up gallery . . 3.00
1 Lady Death in Lingerie,
various artists 5.00
1 Lady Death & the Women of
Chaos! Gallery, pin-ups (1996) . 2.25
1-shot Dragon Wars (1998) 3.00
1-shotA Dragon Wars, Premium Ed,
Sketchbook cover 15.00
1-shot Retribution (1998) 3.00
1-shotA Retribution (1998) variant
cover 3.00
1-shotB Retribution, premium ed. . 10.00

LADY DEATH
Chaos! Comics, 1998
? signed, limited 15.00
1 . . . . 3.00
1a signed, limited 10.00
2 R:Lady Demon 3.00
3 V:Levithia 3.00
4 V:Pagan 3.00
5 The Harrowing, pt.1 . . . . 3.00
6 V:Uriel 3.00
7 V:Moloch 3.00
8 time to sieze Hell 3.00
9 world scythe of the covenant 3.00
10 Goddess War,pt.2 x-over 3.00
11 V:Cremator 3.00
12 Unholy Nights 3.00
13 MD2,DQ,Inferno, pt.1 . . . . 3.00
13a signed 20.00
14 MD2,DQ,Inferno, pt.2 . . . . 3.00
15 MD2,DQ,Inferno, pt.3 . . . . 3.00
15a variant cover 6.00
16 MD2,DQ,Inferno, pt.4 . . . . 3.00
Swimsuit Spec.#1, signed 20.00

LADY DEATH
Chaos! Comics, 1999
1/2 Tribute Book 14.00
0 ashcan, yellow 10.00
0 ashcan, yellow, signed 20.00
0 ashcan, blue 25.00
1 (of 12) by Steve Hughes 3.00
1a signed 15.00
1b deluxe Steve Hughes (c) 16.00
Spec. Swimsuit 2001 #1 . . . . 3.00
Spec. Swimsuit 2001 #1 premium . 11.00
Vol. 1 Lady Death's Black Book . . 10.00
Vol. 1 Black Book,premium ed. . . . 15.00
Halloween Special Ashcan 6.00
Halloween Spec. Ashcan, premium 20.00
Halloween Spec. #1 . . . . 3.00
Halloween Spec. #1a premium ed. 10.00
Halloween Spec. #1b
super-premium edition 20.00
Halloween Spec. 1c foil edition . . . 20.00

LADY DEATH
Crossgen Code 6 Comics, 2003
1 thru 12 A Medieval Tale . . . . . . @3.00
GN Vol. 1 A Medieval Tale 10.00
Season Two, 2004
1 Spell Storm 3.00
2 thru 6 The Wild Hunt . . . . @3.00

LADY DEATH: ALIVE
Chaos! Comics, 2001
1 (of 4) 3.00
1a premium edition 12.00
2 . . . . 3.00
3 . . . . 3.00
4 concl. 3.00
4a variant Scott Lewis (c) 7.50
Ashcan 6.00

LADY DEATH/BAD KITTY
Chaos! Comics, 2001
1 . . . . 3.00
1a premium ed. 10.00
2 . . . . 3.00

LADY DEATH BEDLAM
Chaos! Comics, 2002
1 BAu 3.00
1a premium edition 10.00

LADY DEATH II: BETWEEN HEAVEN & HELL
Chaos! Comics, 1995
1 V:Purgatori 5.00
1a Limited Edition 5,000c 25.00
1b premium velvet cover, signed . 30.00
2 Lives As Hope 4.00
3 V:Purgatori 4.00
4 final issue 4.00
TPB 13.00

LADY DEATH/CHASTITY
Chaos! Comics, 2001
1 x-over 3.00
1a premium edition 10.00

LADY DEATH/CHASTITY/ BAD KITTY: UNITED
Chaos! Comics, 2002
1 . . . . 3.00
1a premium edition 10.00

LADY DEATH/THE CROW
Chaos! Comics, 2002
1 . . . . 3.00
1a premium edition 10.00
1b super premium edition 20.00
Script #1 . . . . 5.00
Script #1 premium edition 20.00
Ashcan 6.00
Ashcan, premium edition 20.00
Preview book b&w 2.00
Preview book, premium edition . . . 6.00

LADY DEATH: THE CRUCIBLE
Chaos! Comics, 1996
1 (of 6) BnP,SHu, ... 3.50
1 leather limited edition 15.00
2 BnP,SHu, ... 3.50
3 BnP,SHu, ... 3.50
4 BnP,SHu, ... 3.50
5 BnP,SHu, ... 3.50
6 BnP,SHu,V:Genocide,concl. 3.50
GN Collected ed. Vol. 1 . . . . 6.00
GN Collected ed. Vol. 2 . . . . 6.00
GN Collected ed. Vol. 3 . . . . 6.00
TPB rep.#1-#6 . . . . 20.00
Spec. Script 5.00
Spec. Script, premium ed. 20.00

LADY DEATH: DARK ALLIANCE
Chaos! Comics, 2002
Ashcan b&w 6.00
Ashcan premium edition 15.00
1 (of 5) F:everybody 3.00
1a premium edition 10.00
2 thru 5 . . . . @3.00
2a thru 5a Alternate cover (c) . . . @7.50

COLOR PUB.

COLOR PUB.

Lady Death The Crucible #4
© Chaos! Comics

LADY DEATH:
DARK MILLENNIUM
Chaos! Comics, 2000
1 (of 3) 3.00
1a premium edition 7.00
1a signed, limited 10.00
2 . . . . 3.00
3 . . . . 3.00
Preview Book B&W 5.00

LADY DEATH:
DEATH BECOMES HER
Chaos! Comics, 1997
0 follows the *Crucible*, leads to
   Wicked Ways. 3.00

LADY DEATH/EVIL ERNIE
Chaos! Comics, 2002
Ashcan 6.00
Ashcan premium edition 20.00
1 BnP, sequel to Dark Alliance 3.50
1a premium edition 10.00
1b super premium edition 20.00
1c foil edition 20.00

LADY DEATH:
THE GAUNTLET
Chaos! Comics, 2002
Ashcan b&w 6.00
1 (of 4) 3.00
1a premium edition 10.00
1b foil edition 20.00
2 . . . . 3.00
2a Variant JSC (c) 7.50

LADY DEATH:
THE GODDESS RETURNS
Chaos! Chomics, 2002
1 (of 2) JOs 3.00
1a premium edition 10.00
2 . . . . 3.00
2a variant (c). 7.50

LADY DEATH:
HEARTBREAKER
Chaos! Comics, 2002
1 . . . . 3.00

1a premium edition 10.00
1b super premium edition 20.00
1c foil (c) 20.00
1d MegaCon foil edition 25.00

LADY DEATH/JADE
Chaos! Comics, 2002
1 . . . . 3.00
1 premium edition 10.00

LADY DEATH:
JUDGMENT WAR
Chaos! Comics, 1999
Prelude 3.00
1 (of 3) 3.00
1a premium 10.00
2 . . . . 3.00
3 Hell is vanquished, concl. 3.00
Preview Book B&W 5.00

LADY DEATH:
LAST RITES
Chaos! Comics, 2001
1 (of 4) RCl(c) 3.00
1 premium ed. RCl(c) 15.00
2 . . . . 3.00
2 variant DkG(c) 7.50
3 . . . . 3.00
3a variant (c). 7.50
4 . . . . 3.00
4a variant (c). 7.50

LADY DEATH:
LOVE BITES
Chaos! Comics, 2001
1 . . . . 3.00
1 premium edition 10.00
Ashcan 6.00

LADY DEATH/
MEDIEVAL WITCHBLADE
Chaos! Comics, 2001
1 BAu,x-over 3.50
1a variant MS (c) (1:4) 3.50
1b premium edition 10.00
1c super premium 20.00
Preview book 2.00
Preview book, premium ed. 6.00
Ashcan 12-page, B&W 6.00

LADY DEATH:
MISCHIEF NIGHT
Chaos! Comics, 2001
1 . . . . 3.00
1a premium edition 13.00
1b super premium edition 20.00

LADY DEATH:
THE MOURNING
Chaos! Comics, 2002
Ashcan 6.00
1 (of 2) 3.00
1a premium edition 10.00
2 . . . . 3.00
2a variant (c). 7.50

LADY DEATH:
THE ODYSSEY
Chaos! Comics, 1996
Sneak Peek Preview 2.00
1 embossed cover 5.00
1 SHu(c) premium edition 15.00

2 . . . . 3.00
3 . . . . 3.00
4 . . . . 3.00
4a variant cover 15.00
Micro Premium Preview Book 15.00
TPB 10.00

LADY DEATH:
THE RAPTURE
Chaos! Comics, 1999
1 (of 4) BnP,V:Father Orbec 3.00
1a dynamic forces cover 7.00
1b dynamic forces, signed 15.00
1c premium edition 9.00
2 Heaven vs. Hell 3.00
3 V:Asteroth 3.00
4 BnP 3.00
Preview Book B&W 5.00
Collected ed. Vol. 1 . . . . 6.00
Collected ed. Vol. 2 . . . . 6.00

LADY DEATH:
RE-IMAGINED
Chaos! Comics, 2002
1 Spanish Inquisition 3.00
1a premium edition 10.00
1b super premium edition 20.00
Ashcan Re-imagined (b&w) 6.00

LADY DEATH:
RIVER OF FEAR
Chaos! Comics, 2001
1 . . . . 3.00
1a premium ed. 10.00

LADY DEATH:
TRIBULATION
Chaos! Comics, 2000
1 . . . . 3.00
1a premium edition, tattoo (c) 10.00
1b chromium (c) 16.00
1c chrome (c) signed 21.00
2 . . . . 3.00
3 . . . . 3.00
4 concl. 3.00
Ashcan B&W 6.66

LADY DEATH/
VAMPIRELLA:
DARK HEARTS
Chaos!/Harris, 1999
Spec. x-over, 40-page 3.50
Spec. Premium Edition 10.00

LADY DEATH
VS. PURGATORI
Chaos! Comics, 2000
1 gold foil 30.00
1 premium ed. 10.00

LADY DEATH
VS. VAMPIRELLA II
Chaos!/Harris, 2000
1 x-over 3.50
1a premium ed. 10.00
1b Gold foil ed. 30.00
1c Blue foil ed. 60.00

LADY DEMON
Chaos! Comics, 2000
1 (of 3) 3.00
1a premium ed. 10.00

COLOR PUB.

2	3.00
3 concl.	3.00
Preview book B&W	5.00

LADY PENDRAGON
Maximum Press, 1996
1 mini-series	2.50
2	2.50
3 (of 3) MD2	2.50

LADY RAWHIDE
Topps, 1995
1 All New Solo series	5.00
2 It Can't Happen Here,pt.2	3.50
3	3.00
4	3.00
5 conclusion	3.00
Spec.#1 Rep. Zorro #2-#3	6.50

LADY RAWHIDE
Topps, 1996
Mini-Series
1 DMG	4.00
1a DMG,signed, numbered	10.00
2 DMG	3.00
3 DMG	3.00
4 DMG, EM, Intimate Wounds	3.00
5 DMG, EM	3.00
6 DMG	3.00
7 DMG	3.00
TPB	11.00

LADY RAWHIDE:
OTHER PEOPLE'S BLOOD
Topps, 1996
Mini-Series
1 DMG,EM,A Slice of Breast.	3.00

LADY VAMPRE
Blackout, 1995
0 B&W	3.50
1	3.00

LANCELOT STRONG,
THE SHIELD
Red Circle, 1983
1 A:Steel Sterling	3.50
2 A:Steel Sterling	2.25
3 AN/EB,D:Lancelot Strong	2.25

LANDSALE & TRUMAN'S
DEAD FOLKS
Avatar Press, 2003
1	3.50
1a wraparound (c).	4.00
2 thru 3	@3.50
2a thru 3a wraparound (c).	@4.00
TPB	10.00

LARS OF MARS
Eclipse, 1987
1 3-D MA.	3.00

LASER ERASER &
PRESSBUTTON
Eclipse, 1985–87
1 GL,R:Laser Eraser.	2.50
2 GL	2.50
3 GL,CK,Tsultrine'.	2.50
4 MC,Death.	2.50
5 MC,JRy,Gates of Hell	2.50
6 Corsairs of Illunium	2.50

3-D#1 MC,GL(c),Triple Cross	2.50

LASH LARUE WESTERN
AC Comics
1	3.50
Annual	3.00

LAST OF THE
VIKING HEROES
Genesis West, 1987
1 JK.	4.00
2 JK.	3.50
3	3.50
4	3.50
5A sexy cover	4.00
5B mild cover	3.50
6	3.50
7 AA(c)	3.50
8	3.50
9 Great Battle of Nidhogger	3.50
10 Death Among the Heroes	3.50
Summer Spec.#1 FF,JK.	3.50
Summer Spec.#2	3.00
Summer Spec.#3,A:TMNT	2.50

Laugh #26
© *Archie Publications*

LAUGH
Archie, 1987–91
1	6.00
2 thru 10	@5.00
11 thru 29	@3.00

LAUREL AND HARDY
Dell Publishing Co., 1962
1	90.00
2	60.00
3	60.00
4	60.00

LAUREL & HARDY
Gold Key, 1967
1	75.00
2 Oct., 1967	60.00

LAWMAN
Dell Publishing Co., 1959
1 Ph(c) all	200.00
2	100.00
3 ATh	110.00
4	75.00
5	75.00

6	75.00
7	75.00
8 thru 11	@75.00

LAW AND ORDER
Maximum Press, 1995
1 MMy,D:Law,I:New Law, Order	2.50
2 V:Max Spur	2.50
3 V:Law's Murderer.	2.50

LAW OF DREDD
Quality
1 V:Perps	5.00
2 BB,Lunar Olympics	4.00
3 BB,V:Judge Death	3.00
4 V:Father Earth	3.00
5 Cursed Earth	3.00
6 V:Perps	3.00
7 V:Perps	3.00

Fleetway
8 Blockmania	3.00
9 BB,DGi,Framed for murders	3.00
10 BB,Day the Law Died Pt.1	2.50
11 BB,Day the Law Died Pt.2	2.50
12 BB,V:Judge Cal.	2.50
13 V:Judge Caligula.	2.50
14 BB, V:Perps	2.50
15 Under investigation	2.50
16 V:Alien Mercenary.	2.50
17 thru 24	@2.50
25 Ugly Clinic.	2.50
26 Judge Dredd & Gavel?	2.50
27 Cycles,Lunatics & Graffiti Guerillas	2.50
28 Cadet Training Mission	2.50
29 Guinea Pig that changed the world	2.50
30 Meka-City,V:Robot	2.50
31 Iso-Block 666	2.50
32 Missing Game Show Hosts	2.50
33 League of Fatties,final issue.	3.00

LAZARUS
CHURCHYARD
Tundra
1 From UK Blast anthology.	4.50
2 Goodnight Ladies.	4.50

LAZARUS: THE MANY
REINCARNATIONS
Lodestone Publishing, 2000
1 by Zak Hennessey	3.00
2	3.00
4 thru 7	@3.00

LEAGUE OF
CHAMPIONS
Hero Graphics, 1990
{Cont. from Champions #12}
1 Olympus Saga #4	3.00
2 Olympus Saga #5,O:Malice.	3.00
3 Olympus Saga ends	3.00

LEAGUE OF EXTRA-
ORDINARY GENTLEMEN
WildStorm/DC, 1999
America's Best Comics
1 (of 6) AMo(s),KON.	3.00
2 AMo(s),KON.	3.00
3 AMo(s),KON.	3.00
4 AMo(s),KON.	3.00
5 AMo(s),KON.	3.00
6 AMo(s),KON, concl.	3.00
GN Collected Edition	6.00

COLOR PUB.

Vol. II (July, 2002)
1 AMo(s),KON. 3.50
2 AMo(s),KON,Martian marauders . 3.50
3 AMo(s),KON,traitor 3.50
4 AMo(s),KON, ... 3.50
5 AMo(s),KON, one dies. 3.50
6 AMo(s),KON,finale. 3.50
TPB Book One. 15.00

LEATHERFACE
North Star
1 thru 3 . . . . @3.00

LEGACY
Majestic, 1993
0 platinum 10.00
1 I:Legacy 2.25
2 . . . . 2.25

LEGACY
Antarctic Press, 1999
1 by Fred Perry. 3.00
2 thru 5 . . . . @3.00

LEGEND OF CUSTER, THE
Dell Publishing Co., 1968
1 Ph(c) 35.00

LEGEND OF SLEEPY HOLLOW
Tundra
One shot.BHa,W.Irving adapt. 7.00

LEGEND OF THE ELFLORD
Davdez Arts, 1998
1 by Barry Blair & Colin Chan. . . . 3.00
2 . . . . 2.50
3 . . . . 3.00
4 . . . . 3.00
GN Vol. 1 112-page 12.00

LEGEND OF THE SAGE
Chaos! Comics, 2001
1 (of 4) F:Victoria Noble 3.00
1a premium edition 10.00
2 . . . . 3.00
2a variant (c). 7.50
3 . . . . 3.00
3a variant (c). 7.50
4 . . . . 3.00
4a variant (c). 7.50
Preview Book. 2.00
Preview Book, premium edition . . . 6.00

LEGENDS OF JESSE JAMES, THE
Gold Key, 1966
1 . . . . 40.00

LEGENDS OF LUXURA
Comic Cavalcade, 1998
Commemorative #1 by Kirk Lindo . . 6.00
Commemorative #1a deluxe 15.00

LEGENDS OF NASCAR
Vortex
1 HT,Bill Eliott ($1.50 cover Price)
  15,000 copies 10.00
1a ($2.00 cover price) 45,000
  copies 5.00
1b 3rd pr., 80,000 copies 4.00
2 Richard Petty. 4.00

3 Ken Schroder. 3.50
4 Bob Alison 3.00
5 Bill Elliott 3.00
6 Jr. Johnson 3.00
7 Sterling Marlin 3.00
8 Benny Parsons 3.00
9 Rusty Wallace 3.00
10 thru 14 . . . . @3.00

LEGENDS OF THE STARGRAZERS
Innovation, 1989
1 thru 5 . . . . @2.50

LEJENTIA
Opus
1 . . . . 2.50
2 . . . . 2.50

LEMONADE KID
AC Comics
1 . . . . 2.50

Leonard Nimoy's Primortals Vol. 2 #6
© Big Entertainment

LEONARD NIMOY'S PRIMORTALS
Teckno-Comics, 1994
1 I:Primortals. 5.50
2 Zeerus Reveals Himself 4.00
3 Contact 2.50
4 Message Deciphered. 2.25
5 Place & Time Announced 2.25
6 Zeerus Arrives on Earth. 2.25
7 Zeerus Recieved 2.25
8 Hyperspace Escape. 2.25
9 Pristar Lands on Earth. 2.25
10 V:U.S. Army. 2.25
11 V:U.S. Army. 2.25
12 V:Zeerus 2.25
13 thru 15. . . . . @2.25
Big Entertainment, 1996
0 SEa,MKb 2.25
1 . . . . 2.25
2 KWo,ANi 2.25
3 KWo,ANi 2.25
4 KWo,ANi 2.25
5 KWo,ANi 2.25
6 KWo,Scorched Earth, concl. 2.25
7 PB,KWo&ANi(c),Zeerus & Narab
  together again 2.25

LEONARDO
Mirage, 1986
1 TMNT Character. 5.00

LEOPARD
Millennium
1 I:Leopard 3.00
1a Gold Cover. 4.00
2 O:Leopard,V:Razor's Edge 3.00

LETHAL STRYKE
London Night Studios, 1995
1 F:Stryke 3.00
1a commemorative (1999) 6.00
2 O:Stryke 3.00
Ann. #1 EHr. 3.00
Ann. #1 platinum edition 10.00

LETHAL STRIKE/ DOUBLE IMPACT: LETHAL IMPACT
London Night, 1996
1 by Jude Millien. 3.00
1 limited 5.00

LIBERTY PROJECT, THE
Eclipse, 1987–88
1 I:Liberty Project 2.50
2 . . . . 2.25
3 V:Silver City Wranglers 2.25
4 . . . . 2.25
5 . . . . 2.25
6 F:Cimarron,Misery and Gin 2.25
7 I:Menace 2.25
8 V:Savage 2.25

LIDSVILLE
Gold Key, 1972
1 . . . . 75.00
2 . . . . 50.00
3 and 4 . . . . @50.00
5 Oct., 1973 . . . . 50.00

LIEUTENANT, THE
Dell Publishing Co., April–June, 1962
1 Ph(c) 50.00

LIFE & ADVENTURES OF SANTA CLAUS
Tundra
GN MP,L.Frank Baum adapt. 25.00

LIFE IN HELL
Blackthorne
1 3-D. 2.50

LIFE WITH ARCHIE
Archie Publications, 1958
1 . . . . 400.00
2 . . . . 200.00
3 . . . . 150.00
4 . . . . 150.00
5 . . . . 150.00
6 . . . . 100.00
7 . . . . 100.00
8 . . . . 100.00
9 . . . . 100.00
10 . . . . 100.00
11 thru 20. . . . . @75.00
21 thru 30. . . . . @60.00
31 thru 40. . . . . @50.00
41 . . . . 40.00

All comics prices listed are for *Near Mint* condition.

42 B:Pureheart	100.00
43	60.00
44	60.00
45 R.I.V.E.R.D.A.L.E.	100.00
46 O:Pureheart	75.00
47 thru 59	@50.00
60 thru 100	@40.00
101 thru 200	@15.00
201 thru 285	@10.00

The Light Fantastic #2
© Innovation

LIGHT FANTASTIC, THE
Innovation, 1992

1 Terry Pratchett adapt.	2.50
2 Adaptation continues	2.50
3 Adaptation continues	2.50
4 Adapt.conclusion	2.50

LIGHTNING COMICS PRESENTS
Lightning Comics, 1994

1 B&W Promo Ed.	3.50
1a B&W Promo Ed. Platinum	3.50
1b B&W Promo Ed. Gold	3.50

LILLITH: DEMON PRINCESS
Antarctic Press, 1996

1 (of 3) from Warrior Nun Areala	3.00
1a Commemorative Edition (1999)	6.00
2 and 3	@3.00

LIMBO CITY
Dreamwave, 2002

1 BAu,BBh	3.00
2 thru 3	@3.00

LINCOLN-16
Skarwood Productions, 1997

1 GI	3.00
2 GI	3.00
3 GI	3.00

LINDA LARK
Dell Publishing Co., 1961

1	40.00
2 thru 8	@25.00

LINUS, THE LIONHEARTED
Gold Key, 1965

1	150.00

LIONHEART
Awesome Entertainment, 1999

1 IaC,JLb, from *The Coven*	3.00
1 Wizard World exclusive	5.50
2 IaC,JLb	3.00
2a variant cover	3.00
2b variant IaC cover	7.00
3 concl	3.00

LIPPY THE LION AND HARDY HAR HAR
Gold Key, 1963

1	160.00

LISA COMICS
Bongo Comics, 1995

1 F:Lisa Simpson	3.00

LITA FORD
Rock-It Comix

1 JBa	4.00

LITTLE AMBROSE
Archie Publications, 1958

1	150.00

LITTLE ARCHIE
Archie Publications, 1956

1	1,000.00
2	400.00
3	250.00
4	250.00
5	250.00
6 thru 10	@200.00
11 thru 20	@150.00
21 thru 30	@100.00
31 thru 40	@75.00
41 thru 60	@75.00
61 thru 80	@50.00
81 thru 100	@15.00
101 thru 180	@10.00

LITTLE ARCHIE MYSTERY
Archie Publications, 1963

1	175.00
2 Oct., 1963	100.00

LITTLE AUDREY & MELVIN
Harvey Publications, 1962

1	150.00
2 thru 5	@75.00
6 thru 10	@60.00
11 thru 20	@50.00
21 thru 40	@20.00
41 thru 50	@20.00
51 thru 53 52 pgs Giant size	@20.00
54 thru 60	@25.00
61 Dec., 1973	20.00

LITTLE AUDREY TV FUNTIME
Harvey Publications, 1962

1 A:Richie Rich	150.00
2 same	100.00
3 same	75.00

4	75.00
5	75.00
6 thru 10	@50.00
11 thru 20	@35.00
21 thru 32	@25.00
33 Oct., 1971	25.00

LITTLE DOT DOTLAND
Harvey Publications, 1962

1	175.00
2	100.00
3	75.00
4	75.00
5	75.00
6 thru 10	@60.00
11 thru 20	@50.00
21 thru 50	@30.00
51 thru 60	@25.00
61 Dec., 1973	25.00

LITTLE DOT'S UNCLES & AUNTS
Harvey Enterprises, 1961

1	200.00
2	125.00
3	125.00
4	75.00
5	75.00
6 thru 10	@60.00
11 thru 20	@50.00
21 thru 40	@40.00
41 thru 51	@25.00
52 April, 1974	25.00

LITTLE LOTTA
Harvey Publications, 1955

1 B:Richie Rich and Little Lotta	550.00
2	250.00
3	150.00
4	125.00
5	125.00
6	100.00
7	100.00
8	100.00
9	100.00
10	100.00
11 thru 20	@75.00
21 thru 40	@50.00
41 thru 60	@40.00
61 thru 80	@30.00
81 thru 99	@25.00
100 thru 103 52 pgs	@20.00
104 thru 120	@20.00
121 May, 1976	20.00

LITTLE LOTTA FOODLAND
Harvey Publications, 1963

1 68 pgs	200.00
2	125.00
3	100.00
4	75.00
5	75.00
6 thru 10	@50.00
11 thru 20	@30.00
21 thru 26	@25.00
27	20.00
28	12.00
29 Oct., 1972	20.00

LITTLE MERMAID
Walt Disney, 1992

1 based on movie	3.00
2 Serpent Teen	3.00
3 Guppy Love	3.00
4	3.00

COLOR PUB.

LITTLE MONSTERS, THE
Gold Key, 1964
1	100.00
2	50.00
3 thru 10	@35.00
11 thru 20	@25.00
21 thru 43	@25.00
44 Feb., 1978	25.00

LITTLE MONSTERS
Now, 1990
1 thru 6	@2.25

LITTLE REDBIRDS
1	2.50
2	2.50
3	2.50
4	2.50

LITTLE SAD SACK
Harvey Publications, 1964
1 Richie Rich(c)	75.00
2	50.00
3	50.00
4	50.00
5	50.00
6 thru 19 Nov. 1967	@50.00

LITTLE STOOGES, THE
Gold Key, 1972
1	45.00
2	30.00
3	25.00
4	25.00
5	25.00
6 and 7 March, 1974	@25.00

LLOYD LLEWELLYN
Fantagraphics, 1987
Spec. #1	2.50

LOBO
Dell Publishing Co., 1965
1	40.00
2	30.00

LOCKE
Blackthorne
1 PO.Jones	2.25
2 TD	2.25
3 thru 5	@2.25

LONE RANGER, THE
Gold Key, 1964
1	100.00
2	50.00
3	40.00
4	40.00
5	40.00
6 thru 10	@30.00
11 thru 18	@30.00
19 thru 27	@20.00
28 March, 1977	20.00

LONE RANGER AND TONTO, THE
Topps, 1994
1 JLd,TT,RM,The Last Battle	2.50
2 JLd,TT,RM	2.50
3 JLd,TT,RM, O:Lone Ranger	2.50
4 JLd,TT,RM, It Crawls	2.50
TPB rep. #1–#4	10.00

Lookers Combo Special #1
© Avatar

LOOKERS
Avatar
Combo Spec. 16pg.	3.00
Combo Spec. Platinum	10.00

LORD PUMPKIN
Malibu, Oct. 1994
0 Sludge	2.50

LORE
IDW Publishing, 2003
1	6.00
2 thru 4	@4.00

LOST HEROES
Davdez Arts, 1998
0 by Rob Prior, lost SF heroes	3.00
1 thru 5	@3.00
6	3.00
GN 5/6 56-page	8.00

LOST IN SPACE
Innovation, 1991
{based on TV series}
1 O:Jupiter II Project	3.50
2 Cavern of IdyllicSummersLost	3.00
2a Special Edition	3.00
3 Do Not Go Gently into that Good Night,Bill Mumy script	3.00
4 People are Strange	3.00
5 The Perils of Penelope	3.00
6 thru 12	@3.00
Project Krell	3.00
Ann.#1 (1991)	3.00
Ann.#2 (1992)	3.00
1Spec.#1 & #2 rep. Seduction of the Innocent	@3.00
GN Strangers among Strangers	6.00
1-shot Project Robinson, follows story in issue #12 (1993)	2.50

Becomes:

LOST IN SPACE: VOYAGE TO THE BOTTOM OF THE SOUL
Innovation, 1993–94
13	3.00
14 thru 18	@3.00

LOST PLANET
Eclipse, 1987–88
1 BHa,I:Tyler FLynn	2.50
2 BHa,R:Amelia Earhart	2.25
3 BHa	2.25
4 BHa,Devil's Eye	2.25
5 BHa,A:Amelia Earhart	2.25
6	2.25

LOVECRAFT
Adventure Comics
1 The Lurking Fear adapt.	3.00
2 Beyond the Wall of Sleep	3.00
3 The Tomb	3.00
4 The Alchemist	3.00

LOVE DIARY
Charlton Comics, 1958
1	100.00
2	65.00
3	50.00
4	50.00
5	40.00
6	50.00
7 thru 10	@40.00
11 thru 15	@40.00
16 thru 20	@40.00
21 thru 40	@25.00
41 thru 101	@15.00
102 Dec., 1976	15.00

LOVE SHOWDOWN COLLECTION
Archie Comics, 1997
TPB x-over rep. Archie #429 (pt.1), Betty #19 (pt.2), Betty & Veronica #82, (pt.3), Veronica #39 (pt.4) Return of Cheryl Blossom	5.00

LUCIFER'S HAMMER
Innovation, 1993–94
1 thru 6 Larry Niven & Jerry Pournelle novel adaptation	@2.50

LUCY SHOW, THE
Gold Key, 1963
1 Ph(c)	225.00
2 Ph(c)	150.00
3 thru 5	@125.00

LUDWIG VON DRAKE
Dell Publishing Co., 1961
1	125.00
2 thru 4	@75.00

LUFTWAFFE 1946
Antarctic Press, 1998
1 color special, by Ted Namura	3.00

LUGER
Eclipse, 1986–87
1 TY,I:Luger,mini-series	2.25
2 TY	2.25
3 TY,BHa,V:Sharks	2.25

LUNATIC FRINGE
Innovation, 1989
1	2.25
2	2.25

LUXURA
Comic Cavalcade, 1998
Commemorative #1 by Kirk Lindo	6.00

All comics prices listed are for *Near Mint* condition.

Commemorative #1a deluxe 15.00

LUXURA COLLECTION
Brainstorm
Commemorative edition, red foil
cover, 48pg. 10.00

LYNCH MOB
Chaos! Comics, 1994
1 GCa(c), I:Mother Mayhem...... 3.00
2 Lynch Mob Loses............. 2.50
3 1994 Time Trip.............. 2.50
3a Gold cover 3.00
4 Mother Mayhem at UN 2.50

LYNDON B. JOHNSON
Dell Publishing Co., March, 1965
1 Ph(c) 50.00

M
Eclipse, 1990–91
1 thru 4 JMu .... @5.50

MACROSS
Comico
1 .... 35.00
Becomes:

ROBOTECH, THE MACROSS SAGA

MAD FOLLIES
E.C. Comics, 1963
(N#)........................ 400.00
2 1964...................... 300.00
3 1965...................... 200.00
4 1966...................... 225.00
5 1967...................... 150.00
6 1968...................... 125.00
7 1969...................... 125.00

MAD HOUSE
Red Circle, 1974–82
95 thru 97 Horror stories ..... @22.00
98 thru 130 Humor stories ..... @15.00
Annual #8 thru #11.......... @18.00

MADMAN
Tundra, 1992
1 .... 15.00
2 .... 12.00
3 .... 7.00
Oni Press, 2003
King-Size Super Special 7.00

MADMAN ADVENTURES
Tundra, 1992
1 R & N:Madman 9.00
2 .... 7.00
3 .... 7.00

MADMAN PICTURE EXHIBITION
AAA Pop Comics, 2002
1 (of 4) 4.00
2 thru 4 .... 4.00

MADRAVEN HALLOWEEN SPECIAL
Hamilton Comics, 1995
1 Song of the Silkies........... 3.00

MAD SPECIAL
E.C. Publications, Inc., 1970
1 .... 125.00
2 .... 90.00
3 .... 75.00
4 thru 8 .... @75.00
9 thru 13 .... @50.00
14 .... 40.00
15 .... 40.00
16 .... 35.00
17 .... 35.00
18 .... 32.00
19 thru 21................. @32.00
22 thru 31................. @25.00
32 .... 25.00
33 thru 58................. @15.00

Mage #15
© Comico

MAGE
Comico, 1984–86
1 MWg,I:Kevin Matchstick 25.00
2 MWg,I:Edsel 12.00
3 MWg,V:Umbra Sprite........ 10.00
4 MWg,V:Umbra Sprite........ 10.00
5 MWg,I:Sean (Spook) 10.00
6 MWg,Grendel begins........ 25.00
7 MWg,Grendel.............. 10.00
8 MWg,Grendel.............. 9.00
9 MWg,Grendel.............. 9.00
10 MWg,Grendel,Styx 9.00
11 MWg,Grendel,Styx 9.00
12 MWg,D:Sean,Grendel......... 9.00
13 MWg,D:Edsel,Grendel 8.00
14 MWg,Grendel,O:Kevin 8.00
15 MWg,D:Umbra Sprite 12.00

MAGEBOOK
Comico
1 rep. Mage #1-4 .... 9.00
2 rep. Mage #5-8 .... 9.00

MAGE KNIGHT: STOLEN DESTINY
IDW Publishing, 2002
1 (of 5) by TDz & D.Cabrera..... 3.50
2 thru 5 .... @3.50

MAGIC FLUTE
Eclipse, 1989
1 CR 5.00

MAGIC THE GATHERING: ANTIQUITIES WAR
Acclaim Armada, 1995
1 Based on the Antiquities Set 2.75
2 F:Urza, Mishra.............. 2.50
3 I:Tawnos, Ashod............. 2.50
4 The War Begins............. 2.50

MAGIC THE GATHERING: ARABIAN KNIGHTS
Acclaim Armada, 1995
1 Based on Rare Card set 2.75
2 V:Queen Nailah 2.50

MAGIC THE GATHERING: CONVOCATIONS
Acclaim Armada, 1995
1 Gallery of Art from Game....... 2.50

MAGIC THE GATHERING: FALLEN EMPIRES
[Mini-series]
Acclaim Armada
1 with pack of cards 2.75
2 F:Tymolin 2.50
TPB Rep. #1-#2............... 5.00

MAGIC THE GATHERING: HOMELANDS
Acclaim Armada, 1995
1 I:Feroz, Serra............... 6.00

MAGIC THE GATHERING: ICE AGE
Acclaim Armada, 1995
1 Dominaia, from card game 3.00
2 Ice Age Adventures 2.50
3 CV(c) Planeswalker battles 2.50
4 final issue................. 2.50
TPB Rep. #1-#2............... 5.00
TPB Rep. #3-#4............... 5.00

MAGIC THE GATHERING: SHADOW MAGE
Acclaim Armada, 1995
1 I:Jared 3.00
2 F:Hurloon the Minotaur 2.75
3 VMk(c&a),V:Juggernaut........ 2.50
4 Final issue 2.50
TPB Rep. #1-#2............... 5.00
TPB Rep. #3-#4............... 5.00

MAGIC THE GATHERING: THE URZA-MISHRA WAR
Acclaim Armada
1 & 2 with Ice Age II card 6.00

MAGIC THE GATHERING: WAYFARER
Acclaim Armada, 1995
1 R:Jared 2.75
2 I:New Land................. 2.50
3 R:Liana, Ravidel 2.50
4 I:Golthonor................. 2.50
5 .... 2.50

MAGIC THE GATHERING:
THE LEGENDS OF:
THE ELDER DRAGONS
1 & 2 . . . . @2.50
JEDIT OJANEN
1 & 2 . . . . @2.50
SHANDALAR
1 & 2 . . . . @2.50

[ON THE WORLD OF]
MAGIC THE GATHERING
GN Serra Angel + card 6.00
GN Legend of the Fallen Angel +
    card 6.00
GN Dakkon Blackblade + card 6.00

MAGILLA GORILLA
Gold Key, 1964
1 . . . . 175.00
2 thru 10 Dec. 1968 . . . . @125.00

MAGILLA GORILLA
Charlton Comics, 1970
1 . . . . 75.00
2 thru 5 . . . . @40.00

MAGIQUE
WildStorm/DC, 2000
Ann. 2000 #1, Devil's
    Night x-over, pt.4 . . . . 3.50

Magnus Robot Fighter #21
© Gold Key

MAGNUS:
ROBOT FIGHTER
Gold Key, 1963
1 RM,I:Magnus,Teeja,A-1,
    I&B:Capt.Johner&aliens 400.00
2 RM,I:Sen.Zeremiah Clane 175.00
3 RM,I:Xyrkol 175.00
4 RM,I:Mekamn,Elzy 100.00
5 RM,The Immortal One 100.00
6 RM,I:Talpa 90.00
7 RM,I:Malev-6,ViXyrkol 125.00
8 RM,I:Outsiders(Chet, Horio,
    Toun, Malf) 90.00
9 RM, I:Madmot 90.00
10 RM,Mysterious Octo-Rob 90.00
11 RM,I:Danae,Neo-Animals 75.00
12 RM,The Volcano Makers 75.00
13 RM,I:Dr Lazlo Noel 80.00

14 RM,The Monster Robs 75.00
15 RM,I:Mogul Radur 75.00
16 RM,I:Gophs 75.00
17 RM,I:Zypex 75.00
18 RM,I:V'ril Trent 75.00
19 RM,Fear Unlimited 75.00
20 RM,I:Bunda the Great 75.00
21 RM, Space Spectre 75.00
22 Rep. #1 . . . . 50.00
23 DSp,Mission Disaster 50.00
24 Pied Piper of North Am 50.00
25 The Micro Giants 50.00
26 The Venomous Vaper 50.00
27 Panic in Pacifica 50.00
28 Threats from the Depths 50.00
29 thru 46 rep. . . . . @20.00

MAGNUS:
ROBOT FIGHTER
Valiant, 1991
0 PCu,BL,Emancipator,w/ BWS
    card 6.00
0a PCu,BL,w/o card 3.00
1 ANi,BL,B:Steel Nation 4.00
2 ANi,BL,Steel Nation #2 . . . . 3.00
3 ANi,BL,Steel Nation #3 . . . . 3.00
4 ANi,BL,E:Steel Nation 3.00
5 DL,BL(i),I:Rai(#1),V:Slagger
    Flipbook format 3.00
6 DL,A:Solar,V:Grandmother
    A:Rai(#2) 2.50
7 DL,EC,V:Rai(#3) 2.50
8 DL,A:Rai(#4),Solar,X-O
    Armor.E:Flipbooks 2.50
1a thru 8a w/o coupon . . . . @2.00
9 EC,V:Xyrkol,E-7 . . . . 2.50
10 V:Xyrkol 2.50
11 V:Xyrkol 2.50
12 I:Turok,V:Dr. Noel,
    I:Asylum,40pgs 6.00
13 EC,Asylum Pt 1 . . . . 2.50
14 EC,Asylum Pt2 . . . . 2.50
15 FM(c),EC,Unity#4,I:Eternal
    Warrior of 4001, O:Unity 2.50
16 WS(c),EC,Unity#12,A:Solar,
    Archer,Armstrong,Harbinger, X-
    O,Rai,Eternal Warrior 2.50
17 JaB,V:Talpa 2.50
18 SD,R:Mekman,V:E-7 . . . . 2.50
19 SD,V:Mekmen 2.50
20 EC,Tale of Magnus' past 2.50
21 JaB,R:Malevaients, Grand-
    mother 3.00
21a Gold Ed. 4.00
22 JaB,D:Felina,V:Malevalents,
    Grandmother 2.50
23 V:Malevolents 2.50
24 V:Malevolents 2.50
25 N:Magnus,R:1-A,silver-foil(c) . . . 3.00
26 I:Young Wolves 2.50
27 V:Dr.Lazlo Noel 2.50
28 V:The Malevs 2.25
29 JCf,A:Eternal Warrior 2.25
30 JCf,V:The Malevs 2.25
31 JCf,V:The Malevs 2.25
32 JCf,Battle for South Am 2.25
33 B:JOs(s),JCf,A:Ivar 2.25
34 JCf,Captured 2.25
35 JCf,V:Mekman 2.25
36 JCf,w/Valiant Era Card 2.25
37 JCf,A:Starwatchers 2.25
38 JCf, ... 2.25
39 JCf,F:Torque 2.25
40 JCf,F:Torque, A:Rai. 2.25
41 JCf,Chaos Effect-Epsilon#4
    A:Solar, Psi-Lords,Rai 2.50
42 JCf, F:Torque,A:Takashi 2.25
43 JCf, F:Torque,Immortal E 2.25
44 JCf,F:Torque,Stagger 2.25
45 V:Immortal Enemy 2.25

46 V:Immortal Enemy 2.25
47 Cold Blooded,pt.1 . . . . 2.25
48 Cold Blooded,pt.2 . . . . 2.25
49 F:Slagger 2.25
50 V:Invisible Legion 2.25
51 KoK,RyR,Return of the
    Robots,pt.1 . . . . 2.25
52 KoK,RyR,Robots,pt.2 . . . . 2.25
53 KoK,RyR,Robots,pt.3 . . . . 2.25
54 KoK,RyR,Robots,pt.4 . . . . 2.25
55 KG,A:Rai 2.50
56 Magnus in Japan 2.50
57 . . . . 2.50
58 . . . . 2.50
59 V:Rai 2.50
60 R:The Malevs 2.50
61 Secrets of the Malevs 2.50
62 V:Leeja 2.50
63 R:Destroyer 2.50
64 Ultimatum, F:Destroyer 2.50
Yearbook #1 . . . . 4.00
TPB 1-4 . . . . 10.00

MAGNUS
(ROBOT FIGHTER)
Acclaim, 1997
1 Magnus back from the future 2.50
2 Tomorrow Never Knows 2.50
3 Tomorrow Never Knows 2.50
4 Tomorrow Never Knows 2.50
5 Tomorrow Never Knows 2.50
6 A:Janice Whitcraft 2.50
7 When Titans Clash 2.50
8 TPe,DdB,When Titans Clash 2.50
9 TPe,See Tirana and Die 2.50
10 TPe,The Memory 2.50
11 TPe,Where Angels Fear 2.50
12 TPe,Showdown 2.50
13 TPe, ... 2.50
14 TPe,Wild in the Streets 2.50
15 TPe,Magnus stands alone 2.50
16 TPe,Hart's Home 2.50
17 TPe,Invasive Procedures 2.50
18 TPe,Welcome to Salvation 2.50

MAJOR DAMAGE
Invictus Studios, 1994
1 I:Major Damage 2.25
2 V:Godkin 2.25
3 First Contact Conclusion 2.25

MALICE
Heroic Publishing
1 I:Queen of the Dead 2.25

MAN CALLED A-X
Malibu Bravura, 1994–95
[Limited Series]
0 1st Puzzle piece 3.00
1 MWn,SwM 3.00
1a Gold foil Edition 4.00
2 MWn,SwM,VLElectobot 3.00
3 MWn,SwM,Mercy Island 3.00
4 MWn, SwM,One Who Came
    Before 3.00
5 MWn,SwM,Climax 3.00

MANDRAKE
THE MAGICIAN
King Comics, 1966
1 . . . . 75.00
2 . . . . 50.00
3 . . . . 50.00
4 A:Girl Phantom 50.00
5 Cape Cod Caper 50.00
6 . . . . 50.00

COLOR PUB.

7 O:Lothar. 50.00
8 . . . . 60.00
9 A:Brick Bradford. 50.00
10 A:Rip Kirby 60.00

MAN FROM PLANET X
Planet X Prod.
1 . . . . 3.00

MAN FROM U.N.C.L.E.
Gold Key, 1965
1 The Explosive Affair. 250.00
2 The Forthur Cookie Affair 125.00
3 The Deadly Devices Affair 75.00
4 The Rip Van Solo Affair 75.00
5 Ten Little Uncles Affair 75.00
6 The Three Blind Mice Affair 75.00
7 The Pixilated Puzzle Affair
    I:Jet Dream (back-up begins) . 80.00
8 The Floating People Affair 75.00
9 Spirit of St.Louis Affair 75.00
10 The Trojan Horse Affair 75.00
11 Three-Story Giant Affair 60.00
12 Dead Man's Diary Affair 60.00
13 The Flying Clowns Affair 60.00
14 Great Brain Drain Affair 60.00
15 The Animal Agents Affair. 60.00
16 Instant Disaster Affair 60.00
17 The Deadly Visions Affair 60.00
18 The Alien Affair 60.00
19 Knight in Shining
    Armor Affair 60.00
20 Deep Freeze Affair 60.00
21 rep. #10 . . . . 55.00
22 rep. #7. . . . . 55.00

MAN FROM U.N.C.L.E.
Entertainment, 1987
1 thru 11 . . . . @3.00

MAN FROM U.N.C.L.E.
Millennium, 1993
1 The Birds of Prey Affair,pt.1 . . . 3.00
2 The Birds of Prey Affair,pt.2. . . . 3.00

MANGA SHI, 2000
Crusade Entertainment, 1997
1 (of 3) BiT, Final Jihad, flip-book
    Shi: Heaven and Earth 3.00
2 BiT, flip-book Tomoe:
    Unforgettable Fire preview 3.00
3 BiT, conclusion. 3.00

MAN IN BLACK
Harvey Publications, 1957
1 BP 200.00
2 BP 150.00
3 BP 150.00
4 BP, March, 1958 . . . . 150.00

MANIK
Millennium/Expand, 1995
1 I:Macedon, Arsenal,Cardinal 3.00

MANKIND
Chaos! Comics, 1999
1-shot StG. 3.00
1-shotA photo cover 3.00
1-shotB variant cover 7.00
1-shotC variant cover, signed. . . . 60.00

MAN OF THE ATOM
Valiant Heroes Special Project
Acclaim, 1997
Spec. 4.00
TPB The Rebirth of Solar 8.00

MAN OF WAR
Eclipse, 1987–88
1 thru 3 . . . . @2.25

Man of War #6
© *Malibu*

MAN OF WAR
Malibu, 1993–94
1 thru 3 V:Lift 2.50
1a thru 5a Newsstand Ed. 2.25
4 w/poster 2.50
5 V:Killinger. 2.50
6 KM,Genesis Crossover 2.50
7 DJu,Genesis Crossover. 2.50
8 TMs(s),A:Rocket Ranger. 2.25
9 thru 12 . . . . @2.25

MANTRA
Malibu Ultraverse, 1993–95
1 AV,I:Mantra,w/Ultraverse card . . . 3.00
1a Full Hologram (c). 10.00
1b Silver foil (c). 5.00
2 AV,V:Warstrike 3.00
3 AV,V:Kismet Deadly 3.00
4 BWS,Mantra's marriage,
    BU:Rune story 2.50
5 MiB(s),AV(i),V:Wiley Wolf 2.25
6 MiB(s),AV(i),Break Thru x-over . . 2.25
7 DJu,TA,A:Prime, O:Prototype . . 2.25
8 B:MiB(s),A:Warstrike 2.25
9 V:Iron Knight,Puppeteer 2.25
10 NBy(c),DaR,B:Archmage Quest,
    Flip/UltraversePremiere #2 . . . . 3.00
11 MiB(s),V:Boneyard 2.25
12 MiB(s),A:Strangers 2.25
13 Topaz, Boneyard. 2.25
14 Tradesmen, Boneyard 2.25
15 A:Prime,Doc Gross 2.25
16 A:Prime 2.25
17 A:Necromantra 2.25
18 Pregnancy. 2.25
19 MiB,Pregnancy 2.25
20 Aftermath of Godwheel. 2.25
21 TyD,MiB,Mantra goes bad 2.25
22 A:Marvel's Loki 2.25
23 I:Tremblor, A:Prime 2.25
24 V:Topaz. 2.25

Giant Sized#1 GP(c),I:Topaz 2.25
Ashcan #1 . . . . 2.25

MANTRA
Malibu Ultraverse, 1995–96
Infinity N:Mantra. 2.50
1 Mantra in all Female Body. 2.25
1a Computer Painted Cover. 2.25
2 Phoenix flip issue. 2.25
3 thru 7 . . . . @2.25

MANTRA: SPEAR OF DESTINY
Malibu Ultraverse, 1995
1 Search for Artifact 2.50
2 MiB,Eden vs. Aladdin. 2.50

MANY WORLDS OF TESLA STRONG, THE
Wildstorm/DC, 2003
1 through the dimensions 6.00

MARK OF CHARON
Grossgen Comics, 2003
1 (of 5) JoB. 3.00
2 thru 5 . . . . @3.00

MARK RAND'S SKY TECHNOLOGIES INC.
Red Mercenary, 1995
1 I:Jae,Elliot,Firnn 3.00

MARKSMAN, THE
Hero Graphics, 1988
1 O:Marksman, Pt.#1 . . . . 2.25
2 O:Marksman, Pt.#2 . . . . 2.25
3 O:Marksman ends.I:Basilisk 2.25
4 A:Flare 2.25
5 I:Radar,Sonar. 2.25
Ann. #1, A:Champions 2.25

MARRIED... WITH CHILDREN
Now, 1990
1 . . . . 4.00
1a 2nd printing 2.25
2 Ph(c) 3.00
3 . . . . 3.00
4 . . . . 2.50
5 Ph(c) 2.50
6 Ph(c) 2.25
7 . . . . 2.50

[2nd Series], 1991
1 Peg-Host of Radio Show 2.25
2 The Bundy Invention 2.25
3 Psychodad,(photo cover). 2.25
4 Mother-In-Law,(photo cover) 2.25
5 Bundy the Crusader. 2.25
6 Bundy J: The Order of the
    Mighty Warthog 2.25
7 Kelly the VJ 2.25
Spec. Ph(c) (1992). 2.25
Spec. Bud Bundy, Fanboy in
    Paradise 3.00
3-D Spec.(1993). 2.50

MARRIED WITH CHILDREN: DYSFUNCTIONAL FAMILY
Now
1 I:The Bundies. 2.50
2 TV Appearance 2.50

3 Morally Pure Bundys 2.50

MARRIED WITH CHILDREN: FLASHBACK SPECIAL
Now, 1993
1 Peg and Al's first date 2.25
2 and 3 . . . . @2.25

MARRIED WITH CHILDREN: KELLY BUNDY SPECIAL
Now, 1992
1 with poster 2.25
2 and 3 with poster . . . . @2.25

MARRIED... WITH CHILDREN: QUANTUM QUARTET
Now, 1993
1 thru 4 Fantastic Four parody . . @2.25
Fall 1994 Spec., flip book 2.25

MARRIED WITH CHILDREN 2099
Mirage, 1993
1 thru 3 Cable Parody . . . . @2.50

MARS
First, 1984
1 thru 12 . . . . @2.25

MARS ATTACKS
Topps, 1994
1 KG(s) 5.00
2 . . . . 4.00
3 thru 6 KG(s) . . . . @4.00
[Series 2], 1995
1 Counterstrike 3.50
2 Counterstrike,pt.2 . . . . 3.00
3 Counterstrike,pt.3 . . . . 3.00
4 Counterstrike,pt.4 Convictions. . . 3.00
5 Counterstrike concl. 3.00
6 Rescue of Janice Brown,pt.1. . . . 3.00
7 Rescue of Janice Brown,pt.2. . . . 3.00
8 . . . . 3.00
Spec. Baseball. 3.00

MARS ATTACKS HIGH SCHOOL
Topps, 1997
Spec. #1 (of 2) BSz(c) 3.00
Spec. #2. . . . . 3.00

MARS ATTACKS THE SAVAGE DRAGON
Topps, 1996
1 . . . . 3.00
2 thru 4 . . . . @3.00

MARVEL/ULTRAVERSE BATTLEZONES
Malibu Ultraverse, 1996
1 DPs(c),The Battle of the Heroes . 4.00

MARY WORTH
ARGO, 1956
1 . . . . 65.00

Masked Man #8
© Eclipse

MASKED MAN
Eclipse, 1985–88
1 . . . . 3.00
2 thru 10 . . . . @2.25

MASKS: TOO HOT FOR TV
Wildstorm/DC, 2003
Spec. 5.00

MASTER DARQUE
Acclaim, 1997
Spec. F:Brixton Sound, 48pg. 4.00

MASTERS OF THE UNIVERSE
Crossgen Comics, 2003
Spec. The Power of Fear. 3.00
1 Rise of the Snake Men 3.00
TPB Traveler #1 Shard of Darkness. . . . 10.00
Encyclopedia, Vol. 1 . . . . 3.00

MASTERS OF THE UNIVERSE
MVCreations, 2004
Vol. 3
1 . . . . 3.00
2 thru 6 . . . . @3.00
TPB Icons of Evil 19.00
TPB Vol. 2 . . . . 18.00
Season One Encyclopedia #4 . . . . 3.00
Season One Encyclopedia #5 . . . . 3.50
TPB Vol. 1 Revised Edition 13.00
TPB Vol. 2 . . . . 19.00

MASTERS OF THE UNIVERSE: ICONS OF EVIL
Crossgen Comics, 2003
Spec. Tri-Klops. 3.00
1 Mer-Man 5.00
1 Trapjaw 5.00

MASTERWORK SERIES
Seagate DC, 1983
1 FFrep.DC,Shining Knight. 4.00
2 FFrep.DC,Shining Knight. 4.00

3 BWr,Horror DC rep. 4.00

MATT BUSCH'S DARIA JONTAK
Realm Press, 2000
1 sexy sci-fi. 4.00
1a deluxe 5.00
2 . . . . 4.00
2a deluxe 5.00
Companion Book 3.00
Companion Book, deluxe. 4.00
Andromeda Entertainment/ PlanetMatt, 2001
Spec. Where Angels Fear to Tread . 4.00
Spec. deluxe 5.00

MAVERICK
Dell Publishing Co., 1958
1 Ph(c) Garner photos 400.00
2 Ph(c) 200.00
3 Ph(c) 200.00
4 Ph(c) 200.00
5 Ph(c) 200.00
6 thru 14 Ph(c) last Garner . . . @150.00
15 thru 19 Ph(c) R. Moore . . . . @125.00

MAVERICK MARSHALL
Charlton Comics, 1958
1 . . . . 50.00
2 thru 6 . . . . @35.00
7 May, 1960 . . . . 35.00

MAVERICKS
Dagger, 1994
1 PuD,RkL, I:Mavericks 3.00
2 PuD,RkL 3.00
3 thru 5 . . . . @3.00

MAXIMORTAL
King Hell/Tundra, 1992
1 RV,A:True-Man 4.50
2 Crack in the New World. 4.25
3 RV,Secret of the Manhattan Project revealed 4.25
4 . . . . 4.25
5 A:True Man 3.25
6 A:El Guano. 3.25

MAXIMUM FORCE
Atomeka, 2002
Spec. #1 SBs, ... 3.00

MAXX, THE
Wildstorm/DC, 2003
TPB Book One. 18.00
TPB Book Two. 18.00
TPB Book Three 18.00

MAYA
Gold Key, 1968
1 . . . . 35.00

MAZE AGENCY
Comico, 1988–91
1 O:Maze Agency 3.00
2 thru 6 . . . . @2.50
7 . . . . 2.75
8 thru 11 . . . . @2.50
12 . . . . 2.50
13 thru 15. . . . . @2.50
16 thru 23. . . . . @2.50
Spec. #1 . . . . 2.75

McHALE'S NAVY
Dell Publishing Co.
May-July, 1963
1 Ph(c) from TV show........ 100.00
2 Ph(c) 75.00
3 Ph(c) 75.00

McKEEVER & THE COLONEL
Dell Publishing Co., 1963
1 Ph(c) 100.00
2 Ph(c) 75.00
3 Ph(c) 75.00

M.D.
Gemstone, 1999
1 (of 5) New Direction.......... 3.00
2 .... 3.00
3 .... 3.00
4 .... 3.00
Annual #1.................... 13.50

M.D. GEIST
CPM, 1995
1 Cartoon Adaptation 3.00
2 J:Army 3.00
3 V:Final Terminator 3.00

M.D. GEIST: GROUND ZERO
CPM, 1996
1 thru 3 .... @3.00

MECHANICS
Fantagraphics
1 HB,rep.Love & Rockets........ 3.00
2 HB,rep.Love & Rockets........ 2.50
3 HB,rep.Love & Rockets........ 2.50

MEDIA STARR
Innovation, 1989
1 thru 3 .... @2.25

MEGACITY 909
Devil's Due/Studio ICE, 2004
1 .... 3.00
2 .... 3.00
1a thru 2a variant (c).......... @3.00

MEGADETH
Rock-it Comix
1 .... 4.25

MEGALITH
Continuity, 1990
1 MT........................ 6.00
2 MT........................ 4.00
3 MT, Painted issue 3.00
4 NA,TVE 3.00
5 NA,TVE 3.00
6 MN........................ 3.00
7 MN........................ 3.00
8 .... 3.00
9 SDr(i)..................... 3.00
10 .... 3.00
[2nd Series], 1993
Deathwatch, 2000
0 Deathwatch 2000 prologue 5.00
1 Deathwatch 2000 Pt.5,w/card ... 3.00
2 Deathwatch 2000 Pt.10,w/card .. 3.00
3 pt.16,Indestructible(c),w/card... 3.00
4 & 5 Rise of Magic........... @3.00

---

6 & 7 .... @3.00

MEGAMAN
Dreamwave, 2003
1 .... 3.00
1a holofoil (c) 6.00
2 thru 4 .... @3.00

MEGATON
Megaton, 1983
1 .... 4.00
Entity Comics, 1993
Holiday Spec. w/card........... 3.00

MEGATON EXPLOSION
1 RLd,AMe,I:Youngblood preview 25.00

Megaton Man #3
© Kitchen Sink

MEGATON MAN
Kitchen Sink, 1984
1 Don Simpson art,I:MegatonMan . 6.00
1a rep. B&W................. 3.00
2 .... 4.00
3 and 4 .... @3.00
5 .... 3.00
6 Border Worlds 3.00
7 Border Worlds 3.00
8 Border Worlds 3.00
9 Border Worlds 3.00
10 final issue, 1986 .... 3.00

MEK
DC/Homage, 2002
2 WEI 3.00
3 WEI, concl.................. 3.00

MELTING POT
Kitchen Sink, 1993
1 .... 4.00
2 and 3 .... @3.00
4 .... 3.50
TPB KEa,SBs, rep. 20.00

MELVIN MONSTER
Dell Publishing Co.1965
1 .... 175.00
2 thru 10 .... @125.00

[Katshuiro Otomo's]
MEMORIES
Epic, 1992
1 .... 2.50

MEN FROM EARTH
Future Fun
1 based on Matt Mason toy 6.50

MENACE
Awesome Entertainment, 1998
1 by Jada Pinkett & Don Fraga ... 2.50
1a signed 20.00
2 .... 2.50
3 .... 2.50

MERCENARY
NBM, 1998
TPB The Voyage 11.00
TPB The Black Globe 10.00
TPB The Fortress 10.00
TPB Giants, 48-pg............. 11.00
TPB Year 1000, 48-pg. 12.00
TPB Lost Civilization 11.00

MERCHANTS OF DEATH
Eclipse, 1988
1 King's Castle, The Hero........ 3.50
2 King's Castle,Soldiers of Fortune 3.50
3 Ransom, Soldier of Fortune..... 3.50
4 ATh(c),Ransom, Men o/t Legion . 3.50
5 Ransom,New York City Blues ... 3.50

MENDY AND THE GOLEM
The Golem Network, 2003
1 The Key 3.00
2 Blackout................... 3.00
3 .... 3.00
4 Meltdown 3.00
5 Beyond Control 3.00

MERIDIAN
Crossgen Comics, 2000
1 BKs 4.50
2 BKs 4.50
3 BKs 4.00
4 BKs 4.00
5 BKs 4.00
6 thru 11 BKs .... @3.50
12 thru 18 BKs............... @3.00
19 thru 30 BKs .... @3.00
31 thru 44 BKs............... @3.00
TPB rep #1–#7............... 20.00
TPB Vol. 2 192-pg............. 20.00
TPB Vol. 3 160-pg............. 16.00
TPB Vol. 4 .... 16.00
TPB Vol. 5 Minister of Cadador... 16.00
TPB Vol. 6 Changing Course..... 16.00
GN Meridian Traveler Vol.1 ..... 10.00
GN Meridian Traveler Vol.3 ..... 10.00
GN Meridian Traveler Vol.4 ..... 10.00

MERLIN REALM
Blackthorne, 1985
1 3-D....................... 2.50

METABARONS
Humanoids Publishing, 2000
1 .... 3.00
2 thru 9 .... @3.00
10 thru 17.................. @3.00
TPB Vol. 1 Path of the Warrior ... 15.00
TPB Vol. 2 Blood and Steel...... 15.00
TPB Vol. 3 Poet & Killer........ 12.00

All comics prices listed are for *Near Mint* condition.

TPB Vol. 4 Immaculate Conception 10.00
GN Alpha/Omega, 48-pg. 10.00

META 4
First 1990
1 IG. 4.50
2 IG. 2.50
3 IG/JSon,final monthly. 2.50

METALLICA
Rock-it Comix
1 . . . . 4.25

METALLIX
Future Comics, 2003
0 . . . . 3.50
4 thru 5 . . . . @3.50
6 thru 12 . . . . @3.00
TPB Vol. 1 . . . . 15.00
TPB Vol. 2 . . . . 17.00

METAL MILITIA
Entity Comics, 1995
1 I:Metal Militia 2.50
1a with Video Game 7.00
2 ICO 2.50
3 F:Detective Calahan 2.50
Ashcan 2.50

METAPHYSIQUE
Malibu Bravura, 1995
1 NBy,I:Metaphysique. 3.00
1a Gold foil edition 4.00
2 NBy,Mandelbrot malfunctions . . . 3.00
3 I:Harridas 3.00
4 D:Maj.Character,B:Superious . . . 3.00
5 V:Astral Kid 3.00
6 Apocalyptic Armageddon, finale . 3.00
Ashcan NBy,B&W 2.00

MICHAELANGELO
Mirage
1 TMNT Character 15.00

MICKEY & DONALD
Gladstone, 1988
1 1449 Firestone. 8.00
2 . . . . 4.00
3 Man of Tomorrow 3.00
4 thru 15 . . . . @3.00
16 giant-size. 3.00
17 . . . . 3.00
18 . . . . 4.00
Becomes:

DONALD AND MICKEY
19 thru 26 . . . . @3.00

MICKEY MANTLE COMICS
Magnum, 1991
1 JSt,Rise to Big Leagues 4.00

MICKEY MOUSE
Gladstone, 1986
219 FG,Seven Ghosts 20.00
220 FG,Seven Ghosts 10.00
221 FG,Seven Ghosts 10.00
222 FG,Editor in Grief 5.00
223 FG,Editor in Grief 4.00
224 FG,Crazy Crime Wave 4.00
225 FG,Crazy Crime Wave 4.00
226 FG,Captive Castaways 4.00
227 FG,Captive Castaways 4.00
228 FG,Captive Castaways 4.00
229 FG,Bat Bandit 4.00

230 FG,Bat Bandit 3.00
231 FG,Bobo the Elephant. 3.00
232 FG,Bobo the Elephant. 3.00
233 FG,Pirate Submarine 3.00
234 FG,Pirate Submarine 3.00
235 FG,Photo Racer 3.00
236 FG,Photo Racer 3.00
237 FG,Race for Riches. 3.00
238 FG,Race for Riches. 3.00
239 FG,Race for Riches. 3.00
240 FG,March of Comics 3.00
241 FG 4.00
242 FG 3.00
243 FG 3.00
244 FG,60th Anniv 5.00
245 FG,Giant Ants 4.00
246 FG 3.00
247 FG 3.00
248 FG 3.00
249 FG 5.00
250 FG 3.00
251 FG 3.00
252 FG 3.00
253 FG 3.00
254 FG 3.00
255 FG 4.00
256 FG 4.00

Mickey Mouse #1
© Walt Disney

MICKEY MOUSE
Walt Disney, 1990
1 The Phantom Gondolier 4.00
2 . . . . 3.50
3 V:Phantom Blot 3.00
4 . . . . 3.00
5 . . . . 3.00
6 . . . . 3.00
7 Phantom Blot 3.00
8 Phantom Blot 3.00
9 Fantasia 50th Anniversary 3.00
10 Sky Adventure. 3.00
11 When Mouston Freezes Over . . . 3.00
12 Hail & Farewell 3.00
13 What's Shakin' 3.00
14 Mouseton, Eagle-Landing 3.00
15 Lost Palace of Kashi 3.00
16 Scoundrels in Space 3.00
17 Sound of Blunder Pt.1 . . . . 3.00
18 Sound of Blunder Pt.2 . . . . 3.00
19 50th Ann. Fantasia Celebration
   Sorcerer's Apprentice adapt . . . 3.00

MICKEY MOUSE AND FRIENDS
Gemstone Publishing, 2003
257 thru 270 . . . . @3.25

MICKEY SPILLANE'S MIKE DANGER
Tekno Comix, 1995
1 I:Mike Danger 3.00
2 Underside of the City 2.50
3 Judicial System 2.50
4 Mike's First Job 2.50
5 Old New York. 2.50
6 Sin Syndicate Leader 2.50
7 thru 11 . . . . @2.50

Big Entertainment, 1996
1 . . . . 2.50
2 . . . . 2.50
3 MCn,PGr,TBe,EB. 2.50
4 . . . . 2.50
5 Time Heels. 2.50
6 TBe,Paradox Rule 2.50
7 TBe,Red Menace, pt.1 . . . . 2.50
8 TBe,Red Menace, pt.2 . . . . 2.50
9 TBe,Red Menace, pt.3 . . . . 2.50
10 TBe,Red Menace, concl. 2.50

MICROBOTS, THE
Gold Key, 1971
1 . . . . 30.00

MICRONAUTS
Devil's Due Publishing, 2004
1 . . . . 3.00
2 thru 4 . . . . @3.00

MIDNIGHT EYE: GOKU PRIVATE INVESTIGATOR
Viz
1 A.D. 2014: Tokyo city 5.25
2 V:Hakuryu,A:Yoko 5.00
3 A:Ryoko,Search for Ryu 5.00
4 Goku vs. Ryu. 5.00
5 Leilah Abducted 5.00
6 Lisa's I.D. discovered 5.00

MIGHTY COMICS
Archie, 1966
{Prev: Flyman}
40 A:Web 40.00
41 A:Shield, Black Hood 35.00
42 A:Black Hood 35.00
43 A:Shield, Black Hood,Web 35.00
44 A:Black Hood, Steel Sterling
   Shield. 35.00
45 Shield-Black Hood team-up
   O:Web 35.00
46 A:Steel Sterling, Black
   Hood, Web. 35.00
47 A:Black Hood & Mr.Justice . . . 35.00
48 A:Shield & Hangman. 35.00
49 Steel Sterling-Black Hood
   team-up, A:Fox 35.00

[ALL NEW ADVENTURES OF] THE MIGHTY CRUSADERS
Archie/Red Circle, 1965
[1st Series]
1 O:Shield (Joe Higgins & Bill
   Higgins) 90.00
2 MSy,O:Comet 60.00
3 O:Fly-Man 50.00

4 A:Fireball,Jaguar,Web,Fox,
  Blackjack Hangman & more
  Golden Age Archie Heroes . . . 55.00
5 I:Ultra-Men&TerrificThree. 50.00
6 V:Maestro,A:Steel Sterling 50.00
7 O:Fly-Girl,A:Steel Sterling 50.00

[2nd Series], 1983

1 RB,R:Joe Higgins & Lancelot
  Strong as the SHIELD, Mighty
  Crusaders, A:Mr.Midnight 7.00
2 RB,V:Brain Emperor & Eterno . . . 5.00
3 RB,I:Darkling 5.00
4 DAy,TD. 4.00
5 . . . . 4.00
6 DAy,TD,Shield 4.00
7 . . . . 4.00
8 . . . . 4.00
9 Trial of the Shield. 4.00
10 . . . . 4.00
11 DAy,D:Gold Age Black Hood, I:
   Riot Squad, series based on
   toy lines 5.00
12 DAy,I:She-Fox. 5.00
13 Last issue 5.00
TPB Origin of Super Team (2003) . 13.00

MIGHTY HERCULES, THE
Gold Key, 1963
1 . . . . 250.00
2 . . . . 225.00

MIGHTY MAGNOR, THE
Malibu, 1993
1 SA 2.25
2 thru 6 SA . . . . @2.25

MIGHTY MORPHIN POWER RANGERS
Hamilton, 1994–95
1 From TV Series 2.75
2 Switcheroo. 2.50
3 . . . . 2.25
4 F:White Ranger 2.25
5 F:Pink Ranger 2.25
6 V:Garganturon 2.25
TPB Re. #1-#6 photo (c) 10.00

[Series 2], 1995
1 Unstoppable Force 2.25
2 V:Mechanical Octopus. 2.25
3 . . . . 2.25
4 Lost Ranger. 2.25

[Series 3], 1995
1 O:Green Ranger 2.25
2 O:Green Ranger 2.25
3 I:New Megazords. 2.25

MIGHTY MOUSE
Spotlight, 1987
1 FMc,PC(c) 3.00
2 FMc,CS(c) 3.00
1 Holiday Special 3.00

MIGHTY MUTANIMALS
Archie Publications, 1991
[Mini-Series]
1 Cont.from TMNT Adventures#19,
  A:Raphael, Man Ray, Leather-
  head, Mondo Gecko,Deadman,
  Wingnut & Screwloose 2.25
2 V:Mr.Null,Malinga,Soul and Bean
  and the Malignoid Army. 2.25
3 Alien Invasion help off, Raphael
  returns to Earth 2.25
Spec.#1 rep. all #1-3 +SBi pin-ups . 3.00

MIGHTY MUTANIMALS
Archie, 1992
1 Quest for Jagwar's Mother 2.25
2 V:Snake Eyes 2.25
3 . . . . 2.25
4 Days of Future Past. 2.25
5 Into the Sun. 2.25
6 V:Null & 4 Horsemen Pt#2. . . . . 2.25
7 Jaws of Doom 2.25

Mighty Samson #19
© Gold Key

MIGHTY SAMSON
Gold Key, 1964–82
1 O:Mighty Samson 125.00
2 . . . . 75.00
3 . . . . 75.00
4 . . . . 75.00
5 . . . . 75.00
6 thru 10 . . . . @50.00
11 thru 20 . . . . @40.00
21 thru 32. . . . . @35.00

MIKE GRELL'S SABLE
First, 1990
1 thru 8 rep. . . . . @2.25
9 . . . . 2.25
10 Triptych 2.25

MIKE SHAYNE PRIVATE EYE
Dell Publishing Co., 1961-62
1 . . . . 50.00
2 . . . . 30.00
3 . . . . 30.00

MILLENNIUM INDEX
Independent Comics, 1988
1 . . . . 2.50
2 . . . . 2.50

MILTON THE MONSTER & FEARLESS FLY
Gold Key, 1966
1 . . . . 150.00

MIRACLEMAN
Eclipse, 1985–94
1 R:Miracleman. 15.00
2 AD,Moore,V:Kid Miracleman . . . 10.00
3 AD,Moore,V:Big Ben 10.00
4 AD,Moore,R:Dr.Gargunza 10.00
5 AD,Moore,O:Miracleman 10.00
6 Moore,V:Miracledog, D:Evelyn
  Cream 9.00
7 Moore,D:Dr.Gargunza 9.00
8 Moore. 9.00
9 RV,Moore,Birth of Miraclebaby . . 9.00
10 JRy,RV,Moore. 9.00
11 JTo,Moore,Book III,
   I:Miraclewoman. 9.00
12 thru 14 Moore . . . . @30.00
15 Moore 100.00
16 Moore 30.00
17 Golden Age. 20.00
18 . . . . 15.00
19 thru 22. . . . . @10.00
23 Silver Age 22.00
24 BWS(c),NGa(s), ... 15.00
25 . . . . 10.00
26 thru 28. . . . . @3.00
3-D Special #1 . . . . 3.00
Graphic Albums
TPB Book 1 A Dream of Flying . . . 25.00
TPB Book 2 The Red Kings
  Syndrome 25.00
TPB Book 3 Olympus 75.00
TPB Book 3 . . . . 25.00

MIRACLEMAN APOCRYPHA
Eclipse, 1991–92
1 inc. Rascal Prince 7.00
2 Miracleman, Family Stories 7.00
3 . . . . 7.00

MIRACLEMAN FAMILY
Eclipse, 1988
1 British Rep.,A:Kid Miracleman. . . 5.00
2 Alan Moore (s) 5.00

MIRACLE SQUAD, THE
Upshot/Fantagraphics, 1986
1 Hollywood 30's. 2.25
2 thru 4 . . . . @2.25

MISS FURY
Adventure Comics, 1991
1 O:Cat Suit 3.00
2 Miss Fury impersonator. 3.00
3 A:Three Miss Fury's. 3.00
4 conclusion 3.00

MISSION IMPOSSIBLE
Dell Publishing Co., 1967
1 Ph(c) 150.00
2 Ph(c) 125.00
3 Ph(c) 100.00
4 Ph(c) 100.00
5 Ph(c) 100.00

MISSIONS IN TIBET
Dimension Comics, 1995
1 I:New Series 2.50
2 F:Orlando,Ting,Alex. 2.50
3 Two Worlds Collide 2.50
4 V:Sada. 2.50

MISS PEACH
(& SPECIAL ISSUES)
Dell Publishing Co., 1963
1 . . . . 125.00

MR. AND MRS. J.
EVIL SCIENTIST
Gold Key, 1963
1 . . . . 125.00
2 . . . . 75.00
3 . . . . 75.00
4 . . . . 75.00

MR. MAJESTIC
WildStorm/DC, 1999
1 JoC,A:Desmond. 2.50
1a variant cover 3.00
2 JoC,time gone berserk 2.50
3 JoC,F:Maxine Manchester. 2.50
4 JoC,F:Junior Majestic 2.50
5 JoC 2.50
6 JoC,F:Desmond. 2.50
7 JoC,Universal Law,pt.1 . . . . 2.50
8 JoC,Universal Law,pt.2 . . . . 2.50
9 JoC,Universal Law,pt.3,
   final issue 2.50
TPB 15.00

MR. MONSTER
Eclipse, 1985–87
1 I:Mr. Monster 7.00
2 DSt(c). 5.00
3 V:Dr. NoZone 3.50
4 Trapped in Dimension X 3.00
5 V:Flesh-eating Amoebo 3.00
6 KG,SD,reprints 3.00
7 . . . . 3.00
8 V:Monster in the Atomic Telling
   Machine 3.00
9 V:Giant Clams 3.00
10 R:Dr.No Zone, 3-D 3.00

MR. MONSTER
ATTACKS
Tundra, 1992
1 DGb,SK,short stories 4.25
2 SK,short stories cont. 4.25
3 DGb,last issue 4.25

MR. MONSTER
SUPERDUPER SPECIAL
Eclipse, 1986–87
1 . . . . 3.00
2 . . . . 3.00
3 . . . . 3.00
4 . . . . 3.00
5 . . . . 3.00
6 . . . . 3.00
Hi-Voltage Super Science 4.00
3-D Spec. Hi-Octane Horror,JKu,
   Touch of Death reprint 5.00
Triple Treat 4.00

MR. MONSTER
TRUE CRIME
Eclipse, 1986
1 . . . . 3.00
2 . . . . 3.00
3-D Spec. #1 . . . . 3.00

MR. MUSCLES
Charlton Comics, 1956
22 . . . . 100.00

---

23 . . . . 75.00

MR. MYSTIC
Eclipse
1 . . . . 2.50
2 . . . . 2.50
3 . . . . 2.50

MR. T AND THE T FORCE
Now, 1993
1 NA,R:Mr.T,V:Street Gangs 2.50
1a Gold Ed. 10.00
2 NA,V:Demons 2.50
3 NBy,w/card. 2.50
4 NBy,In Urban America 2.50
5 thru 10, with card . . . . @2.50

MISTER X
Vortex, 1984
1 HB 7.00
2 HB 5.00
3 HB 3.50
4 HB 3.00
5 . . . . 3.00
6 thru 10 . . . . @3.00
11 thru 13 . . . . @3.00
14 . . . . 3.00

Mod Squad #1
© Dell Publishing Co.

MOD SQUAD
Dell Publishing Co., 1969–71
1 . . . . 125.00
2 . . . . 60.00
3 . . . . 60.00
4 thru 8 . . . . @60.00

MOD WHEELS
Gold Key, 1971–76
1 . . . . 50.00
2 thru 18 . . . . @30.00
19 . . . . 25.00

MONARCHY
WildStorm/DC, 2001
1 JMC,V:Young Authoritans 2.50
2 JMC,F:Union 2.50
3 JMC,Vox Populi,pt.1 . . . . 2.50
4 JMC,Vox Populi,pt.2 . . . . 2.50
5 JMC,Boy Who Talked to Spiders . 2.50
6 JMC,Making the Metropolitan . . . 2.50
7 JMC,Making the Metropolitan . . . 2.50

---

8 JMC,Making the Metropolitan . . . 2.50
9 JMC,Metropolitan epilog 2.50
10 JMC,V:Chimera. 2.50
11 JMC,V:Higher Power. 2.50
12 JMC,final issue 2.50
TPB Bullets over Babylon 13.00

MONKEE'S, THE
Dell Publishing Co., 1967
1 Ph(c) 175.00
2 Ph(c) 125.00
3 Ph(c) 125.00
4 Ph(c) 125.00
5 . . . . 100.00
6 Ph(c) 100.00
7 Ph(c) 100.00
8 and 9 . . . . @90.00
10 Ph(c) 100.00
11 thru 17 . . . . @75.00

MONOLITH
Comico, 1991
1 From Elementals 2.50
2 Seven Levels of Hell 2.50
3 Fugue and Variation 2.50
4 Fugue and Variation 2.50

MONROE'S, THE
Dell Publishing Co., 1967
1 Ph(c) 35.00

MONSTER CLUB
Autumn Press, 2003
1 . . . . 3.50
2 thru 4 . . . . @3.50
5 thru 11 . . . . @3.50
12 40-pg. 3.50
TPB Vol. 1 . . . . 20.00
TPB Vol. 2 . . . . 20.00
Vol. 2
0 . . . . 3.00
1 thru 5 . . . . @3.50
Preview ed. 3.00

MONSTER MASSACRE
Atomeka
1 SBs, DBr,DGb 8.50
1a Black Edition 35.00

MONSTERS, INC.
Tokyopop Press, 2002
GN Vol.1 Disney manga adaptation 8.00

MONSTER WORLD
WildStorm/DC, 2001
1 (of 4) SLo, ... 3.00
2 SLo, 5 young heroes 3.00
3 SLo, ... 3.00
4 SLo,concl. 3.00

MOONWALKER IN 3-D
Blackthorne
1 thru 3 . . . . @2.50

MORBID ANGEL
London Night, 1996
? Angel's Tear, signed. 10.00
1 Commemorative (1999) 10.00

MORBID ANGEL:
PENANCE
London Night, 1996
Revised Color Spec., double size . . 4.00

MORE THAN MORTAL
Liar Comics, 1997

1	3.00
1a 2nd printing	3.00
1b convention, sign, num	10.00
2 Derdre vs. the Host	3.00
2a variant painted cover	6.00
3 MS(c)	3.00
4 concl.	3.00
TPB rep. #1–#4	15.00

MORE THAN MORTAL: SAGAS
Liar Comics, 1998

1 by Sharon Scott & Romano Molenaar	3.00
1a variant Tim Vigil(c)	3.00
1b variant JLi(c)	10.00
2	3.00
3 conclusion	3.00

MORE THAN MORTAL: TRUTHS AND LEGENDS
Liar Comics, 1998

1 by Sharon Scott, Steve Firchow, Mark Prudeaux, O:Witchfinder	4.00
1a signed	10.00
2	3.00
3	3.00
4	3.00
5	3.00
5a variant cover (1:4)	3.00
6	3.00

Molock 2001 #3
© Atlas

MORLOCK 2001
Atlas, Feb.–July, 1975

1 thru 2 O:Morlock	@25.00
3 SD,BW,F:Midnight Men	35.00

MORRIGAN
Sirius, 1997

1 by Lorenzo Bartoli & Saverio Tenuta	3.00
2 and 3	@3.00
GN rep. #1–#3	10.00

MORTAL KOMBAT
Malibu, 1994

0 Four stories	3.00

1 Based on the Video Game	3.00
1a Foil Ed	4.00
1b with new material	3.00
2	3.00
3	3.00
4	3.00
5 I:Mortal Kombat II	3.00
6 Climax	3.00
Spec. #1 Tournament edition	4.00
Spec. #2 Tournament edition II	4.00
TPB rep. #1–#6	15.00

MORTAL KOMBAT: BARAKA
Malibu, 1995

1 V:Scorpion	3.00

MORTAL KOMBAT: BATTLEWAVE
Malibu, 1995

1 New series	3.00
2 Action, Action, Action	3.00
3 The Gathering	3.00
4 F:Goro	3.00
5 F:Scorpion	3.00
6 final issue	3.00

MORTAL KOMBAT: GORO, PRINCE OF PAIN
Malibu, 1994

1 Goro	3.00
1a Platinum Edition	6.25
2 Goro, V:Kombatant	3.00
3 Goro, V:God of Pain	3.00

MORTAL KOMBAT: KITANA & MILEENA
Malibu, 1995

1 Secrets of Outworld	3.00

MORTAL KOMBAT: KUNG LAO
Malibu, 1995

1 one-shot Battlewave tie-in	3.00

MORTAL KOMBAT: RAYDEN AND KANO
Malibu, 1995

1 J:Rayden Kano	3.00
1a Deluxe Edition	5.00
2 A:Reptile	3.00
3 Kano, conclusion	3.00

MORTAL KOMBAT: U.S. SPECIAL FORCES
Malibu, 1995

1 V:Black Dragon	3.50
2 V:Black Dragon	3.00

MOSTLY WANTED
WildStorm/DC, 2000

1 (of 4) SLo,F:Sister Crenn.	2.50
2 SLo(s),F:Andi Mooncrest	2.50
3 SLo(s),	2.50
4 SLo(s),conclusion	2.50

MOTORBIKE PUPPIES
Dark Zulu Lies, 1992

1 I:Motorbike Puppies	2.50

MOVIE COMICS
Gold Key/Whitman, 1962

Alice in Wonderland	50.00
Aristocats	125.00
Bambi 1	50.00
Bambi 2	40.00
Beneath the Planet of the Apes	150.00
Big Red	50.00
Blackbeard's Ghost	50.00
Buck Rogers Giant Movie Edition	40.00
Bullwhip Griffin	50.00
Captain Sinbad	100.00
Chitty, Chitty Bang Bang	100.00
Cinderella	50.00
Darby O'Gill & the Little People	75.00
Dumbo	50.00
Emil & the Detectives	45.00
Escapade in Florence	125.00
Fall of the Roman Empire	50.00
Fantastic Voyage	90.00
55 Days at Peking	50.00
Fighting Prince of Donegal	40.00
First Men of the Moon	50.00
Gay Purr-ee	75.00
Gnome Mobile	50.00
Goodbye, Mr. Chips	50.00
Happiest Millionaire	50.00
Hey There, It's Yogi Bear	125.00
Horse Without a Head	40.00
How the West Was Won	175.00
In Search of the Castaways	100.00
Jungle Book, The	125.00
Kidnapped	50.00
King Kong	50.00
King Kong N#	75.00
Lady and the Tramp	50.00
Lady and the Tramp 1	75.00
Lady and the Tramp 2	40.00
Legend of Lobo, The	35.00
Lt. Robin Crusoe	35.00
Lion, The	35.00
Lord Jim	40.00
Love Bug, The	40.00
Mary Poppins	75.00
Mary Poppins 1	100.00
McLintock	200.00
Merlin Jones as the Monkey's Uncle	100.00
Miracle of the White Stallions	40.00
Misadventures of Merlin Jones	100.00
Moon-Spinners, The	125.00
Mutiny on the Bounty	50.00
Nikki, Wild Dog of the North	35.00
Old Yeller	35.00
One Hundred & One Dalmatians	40.00
Peter Pan 1	50.00
Peter Pan 2	35.00
P.T. 109	75.00
Rio Conchos	80.00
Robin Hood	50.00
Shaggy Dog & the Absent-Minded Professor	75.00
Sleeping Beauty	125.00
Snow White & the Seven Dwarfs	50.00
Son of Flubber	50.00
Summer Magic	125.00
Swiss Family Robinson	40.00
Sword in the Stone	125.00
That Darn Cat	125.00
Those Magnificent Men in Their Flying Machines	50.00
Three Stooges in Orbit	175.00
Tiger Walks, A	60.00
Toby Tyler	50.00
Treasure Island	40.00
20,000 Leagues Under the Sea	45.00
Wonderful Adventures of Pinocchio	50.00
Wonderful World of Brothers Grimm	60.00
X, the Man with the X-Ray Eyes	125.00

COLOR PUB.

Yellow Submarine w/poster 450.00

MS. MYSTIC
Pacific
1 NA,Origin 7.00
2 NA,Origin,I:Urth 4 . . . . 6.00
Continuity, 1988
1 NA,Origin rep. 3.00
2 NA,Origin,I:Urth 4 rep 3.00
3 NA,New material 3.00
4 TSh 3.00
5 DT 3.00
6 . . . . 3.00
7 . . . . 3.00
8 CH/Sdr,B:Love Story 3.00
9 DB 3.00
9a Newsstand(c) 3.00
[3rd Series], 1993
1 O:Ms.Mystic 2.50
2 A:Hybrid 2.50
3 . . . . 2.50
4 . . . . 2.50
[4th Series, Deathwatch 2000]
1 Deathwatch 2000 pt.8,w/card . . 2.50
2 Deathwatch 2000 w/card 2.50
3 Indestructible cover, w/card 2.50

*Ms. Tree's Thrilling Detective
Cases #3 © Millennium*

MS. TREE'S THRILLING
DETECTIVE ADVENTURES
Eclipse, 1983
1 Miller pin up 5.00
2 . . . . 4.00
3 . . . . 4.00
Becomes:
MS. TREE
Eclipse, 1983
4 thru 6 . . . . @4.00
7 . . . . 4.00
8 . . . . 8.00
9 . . . . 4.00
Aardvark–Vanaheim, 1984
10 . . . . 4.00
Renegade
1 3-D 4.00

MS. VICTORY
GOLDEN ANNIVERSARY
AC Comics
1 Ms.Victory celebration 5.00

MS. VICTORY SPECIAL
AC Comics
1 . . . . 2.50

MUMMY ARCHIVES
Millennium, 1992
1.JM,Features,articles 2.50

MUMMY, OR RAMSES
THE DAMNED, THE
Millennium, 1992
1 Anne Rice Adapt. 5.00
2 JM,Mummy in Mayfair 3.75
3 JM 3.25
4 JM, To Egypt 3.00
5 JM,The Mummy's Hand 2.50
6 JM,20th Century Egypt 2.50
7 JM,More Ramses Past Revealed 2.50
8 JM,Hunt for Cleopatra 2.50
9 JM,Cleopatra's Wrath contd. 2.50
10 JM,Subterranian World 2.50
11 JM 2.50

MUMMY, THE:
VALLEY OF THE GODS
Chaos! Comics, 2001
1 (of 3) MWn,MtB, movie tie-in . . . 3.00
1a variant (c) 3.00
1b premium 10.00
2 . . . . 3.00
2a Scorpion King photo (c) 3.00
3 . . . . 3.00
3a Imhotep phoco (c) 3.00
Ashcan 6.00

MUNDEN'S BAR
ANNUAL
First, 1988
1 BB,JOy,JSn,SR 3.00

MUNSTERS, THE
Gold Key, 1965–68
1 . . . . 300.00
2 . . . . 150.00
3 thru 5 . . . . @135.00
6 thru 16 . . . . @125.00

MUPPET BABIES
Harvey, 1993
1 Return of Muppet Babies 2.50

MURCIELAGA/SHE-BAT
Studio G, 2001
1 by D.Gross & R.Lopez 3.00
2 thru 4 . . . . @3.00

MUTANT CHRONICLES—
GOLGOTHA
Valiant
1 thru 4 + game trading card . . . @3.00
TPB, Vol. 1 rep. Pt.#1–#4 . . . . . . 11.00

MUTANTS & MISFITS
Silverline
1 thru 4 . . . . @2.25

MY FAVORITE MARTIAN
Gold Key, 1964–66
1 . . . . 200.00
2 . . . . 125.00
3 thru 9 . . . . @100.00

MY LITTLE MARGIE
Charlton Comics, 1954–65
1 Ph(c) 400.00
2 Ph(c) 175.00
3 thru 8 . . . . @100.00
9 . . . . 90.00
10 . . . . 75.00
11 . . . . 65.00
12 . . . . 65.00
13 . . . . 65.00
14 thru 19 . . . . @50.00
20 Giant Size 125.00
21 thru 35 . . . . @50.00
36 thru 53 . . . . @40.00
54 Beatles (c). 225.00

MYSTERIES OF
UNEXPLORED WORLDS/
SON OF VULCAN
Charlton Comics, 1956
1 . . . . 400.00
2 . . . . 175.00
3 SD,SD(c) 300.00
4 SD,Forbidden Room 350.00
5 SD,SD(c) 350.00
6 SD 350.00
7 SD, giant 375.00
8 SD 325.00
9 SD 325.00
10 SD,SD(c) 325.00
11 SD,SD(c) 325.00
12 SD,Charm Bracelet 250.00
13 thru 18 . . . . @100.00
19 SD(c) 250.00
20 . . . . 100.00
21 thru 24 SD . . . . @250.00
25 . . . . 65.00
26 SD 250.00
27 thru 30 . . . . @60.00
31 thru 45 . . . . @50.00
46 I:Son ofVulcan,Dr.Kong(1965) . 60.00
47 V:King Midas 50.00
48 V:Captain Tuska 50.00
Becomes:
SON OF VULCAN
49 DC redesigns costume 45.00
50 V:Dr.Kong 45.00

MYSTERIOUS SUSPENSE
Charlton, 1968
1 SD,F:Question 125.00

MYSTERY COMICS
DIGEST
Gold Key, 1972–75
1 WW,Riley's Believe It Or Not . . . 60.00
2 WW,Boris Karloff 55.00
3 RC,GEv,Twilight Zone 50.00
4 Ripley's Believe It or Not 45.00
5 Boris Karloff 45.00
6 Twilight Zone 45.00
7 Believe It Or Not 45.00
8 RC,AW,Boris Karloff 45.00
9 Twilight Zone 45.00
10 thru 13 . . . . @45.00
14 1st Xorkon 45.00
15 thru 20 . . . . @45.00
21 thru 26 . . . . @30.00

MYSTIC
Crosgen Comics, 2000
1 RMz,BPe 6.00
2 RMz,BPe 5.00
3 RMz,BPe 4.00
4 RMz,BPe 3.25
5 RMz,BPe 3.25

6 thru 10 . . . . @3.25
11 . . . . 4.00
12 thru 30 . . . . @3.00
31 thru 43 . . . . @3.00
TPB Vol. 1 . . . . 20.00
TPB Vol. 2 . . . . 20.00
TPB Vol. 3 Siege of Scales 16.00
TPB Vol. 4 Out All Night. 16.00
TPB Vol. 5 Master Class 16.00
TPB Vol. 6 The Mathemagician. . . 16.00
TPB Mystic Traveler Vol. 2 . . . . . . 10.00

MYSTIC EDGE
Antarctic Press, 1998
1 by Ryan Kinnaird, F:Risa
  & Symattra. 3.00

NANCY & SLUGGO
Dell Publishing Co., 1957
146 B:Peanuts 80.00
147 Peanuts. 65.00
148 Peanuts. 65.00
149 Peanuts. 65.00
150 thru 161. . . . . @65.00
162 thru 165 . . . . @125.00
166 thru 176 A:OONA . . . . . . @125.00
177 thru 180 . . . . @65.00
181 thru 187 . . . . @65.00

NATIONAL VELVET
Dell Publishing Co., 1961
1 Ph(c) 125.00
2 Ph(c) 60.00

NEAT STUFF
Fantagraphics, 1986
1 . . . . 4.50
2 . . . . 3.00
3 thru 7 . . . . @2.50

NECROMANTRA/
LORD PUMPKIN
Malibu Ultraverse, 1995
1 A:Loki (from Marvel) 3.00
2 MiB,V:Godwheel, flipbook 3.00
3 O:Lord Pumpkin. 3.00
4 Infinity Gem tie-in. 3.00
4a variant cover 3.50

NECROPOLIS
Fleetway
1 SBs(c),CE,A:Dark Judges/
  Sisters Of Death 3.00
2 . . . . 3.00
3 thru 9 . . . . @3.00

NECROSCOPE
Malibu, 1992
1 Novel adapt., holo(c) 3.25
1a 2nd printing 3.00
2 thru 4 Adapt. cont. . . . . @3.00
Book II, Oct. 1994
1 thru 5 . . . . 3.00

NECROWAR
Dreamwave, 2003
1 . . . . 3.00
2 thru 4 . . . . @3.00

NEGATION
Crossgen Comics, 2001
1 MWa,PaP,F:Obregon Kaine. 3.00
2 MWa,PaP,Kaine's master-plan . . 3.00
3 MWa,PaP,F:Captain Fluxor 3.00

4 thru 12 PaP . . . . @3.00
13 thru 27 . . . . @3.00
Spec. #1 Negation: Lawbringer 3.00
Prequel MWa,PaP 3.00
TPB Vol. 1 Bohica 20.00
TPB Vol. 2 Baptism of Fire 16.00
TPB Vol. 3 Hounded 16.00

NEGATION WAR
Crossgen Comics, 2004
1 . . . . 3.00
2 thru 6 . . . . @3.00

NEGATIVE EXPOSURE
Humanoids Publishing, 2001
1 by Enrico Mirini 3.00
2 . . . . 3.00
3 thru 4 . . . . @3.00
TPB 19.00

NEIL GAIMAN'S
LADY JUSTICE
Tekno Comix (1995)
1 I:Lady Justice. 2.50
1a 6.00
2 V:Blood Pirate 2.50
3 V:Blood Pirate 2.50
4 New Story Arc 2.50
5 Street Gang War 2.50
6 Street Gang War 2.25
7 thru 11 . . . . @2.25
Big Entertainment, April, 1996
1 thru 4 . . . . @2.25
5 DIB(s) 2.25
6 DIB(s),Woman About Town, pt.1 . 2.25
7 DIB(s),Woman About Town, pt.2 . 2.25
8 DIB(s),Woman About Town, pt.3 . 2.25

NEIL GAIMAN'S
MR. HERO
THE NEWMATIC MAN
Tekno-Comics, 1994
1 I:Mr. Hero, Tecknophage 2.50
2 A:Tecknophage 2.25
3 I:Adam Kaine 2.25
4 I:New Body 2.25
5 Earthquake 2.25
6 I:New Character. 2.25
7 I:Deadbolt, Bloodboil 2.25
8 V:Avatar 2.25
9 in London 2.25
10 V:Demon 2.25
11 V:Monster 2.25
12 The Great Goward 2.25
13 thru 17 . . . . @2.25

NEIL GAIMAN'S
PHAGE
Tekno-Comics, 1996
1 . . . . 2.25

NEIL GAIMAN'S PHAGE:
SHADOW DEATH
Big Entertainment
1 thru 4 . . . . @2.25
5 O:Orlando Holmes,A:Lady
  Messalina 2.25
6 conclusion 2.25

NEIL GAIMAN'S
TECKNOPHAGE
Teckno-Comics, 1995
1 I:Kalighoul, Tom Vietch 2.25

*Neil Gaiman's Phage: Shadow Death
#4 © Big Entertainment*

1a Steel Edition. 4.00
2 F:Mayor of New Yorick. 2.25
3 Phange Building. 2.25
4 Horde eevils. 2.25
5 Middle Management 2.25
6 Escape from Phange 2.25
7 Mecca 2.25

NEIL GAIMAN'S
WHEEL OF WORLDS
Teckno-Comics, 1995
0 Deluxe Edition w/Posters. 3.00
0a I:Lady Justice. 2.50
1 . . . . 3.25

NEMESIS THE
WARLOCK
Eagle, 1984
1 . . . . 2.25
2 thru 8 . . . . @2.25

NEO DAWN
Committed Comics, 2004
1 (of 3) 3.00
2 thru 3 . . . . @3.00

NEOTOPIA
Antarctic Press, 2003
1 Princess for a Day 4.00
2 Philios to the Rescue. 4.00
3 thru 5 . . . . @4.00
Vol. 2
1 (of 6) 3.00
2 . . . . 3.00
3 . . . . 4.00
4 thru 5 . . . . @3.00
Vol. 3
1 thru 5 . . . . @3.00
Vol. 4
1 . . . . 3.00
2 thru 3 . . . . @3.00
TPB #1 thru #2 Pocket Manga. . @10.00

NEUTRAL WORLD
APC, 2003
1 . . . . 3.50
2 thru 4 . . . . @3.50

NEW ADVENTURES OF FELIX THE CAT
Felix Comics, Inc., 1992
1 New stories 2.25
2 The Magic Paint Brush 2.25

NEW ADVENTURES OF PINOCCHIO
Dell Publishing Co., 1962
1 . . . . 150.00
2 and 3 . . . . @125.00

NEW ADVENTURES OF SPEED RACER
Now
0 Premiere, 3-D cover 2.25
1 thru 11 . . . . @2.25

NEW AMERICA
Eclipse, 1987–88
1 A:Scout 2.25
2 A:Scout 2.25
3 A:Roman Catholic Pope 2.25
4 A:Scout 2.25

NEW BREED
Pied Piper
1 . . . . 2.75
2 . . . . 2.25

NEW DNAGENTS, THE
Eclipse, 1985–87
1 R:DNAgents 2.25
2 F:Tank 2.25
3 Repopulating the World 2.25
4 Major Catastrophe for Earth 2.25
5 Last Place on Earth 2.25
6 JOy(c),Postscript 2.25
7 V:Venimus 2.25
8 DSp,V:Venimus 2.25
9 V:Venimus,I:New Wave 2.25
10 I:New Airboy 2.25
11 Summer Fun Issue 2.25
12 V:Worm 2.25
13 EL,F:Tank 2.25
14 EL,Nudity,Grounded 2.25
15 thru 17 . . . . @2.25
3-D #1 . . . . 2.50

NEW JUSTICE MACHINE
Innovation, 1989
1 and 2 . . . . @2.25
2 . . . . 2.25

NEW KABOOM
Awesome Entertainment, 1999
1 RLe,JLb 2.50

NEWMEN
Maximum Press, 1997
1–22 see Image
23 ErS,CSp,AG,Anthem, pt.3 . . . . . . 2.50
24 ErS,CSp,AG,Anthem, pt.4 . . . . . . 2.50
25 ErS,CSp,AG,Anthem, pt.5 . . . . . . 2.50

NEW ORLEANS SAINTS
1 Playoff season(football team) . . . 6.00

NEW STATESMEN
Fleetway
1 . . . . 4.50
2 thru 5 . . . . @4.00

NEWSTRALIA
Innovation, 1989
1 and 2 . . . . @2.25
3 . . . . 2.25

NEW TERRYTOONS
Dell Publishing Co., 1960–61
1 . . . . 100.00
2 thru 8 . . . . @60.00
Gold Key, 1962
1 F:Heckle & Jeckle 150.00
2 . . . . 125.00
3 thru 10 . . . . @50.00
11 thru 20 . . . . @40.00
21 thru 30 . . . . @25.00
31 thru 40 . . . . @20.00
41 thru 54 . . . . @15.00

NEW WAVE, THE
Eclipse, 1986–87
1 Error Pages 2.25
1a Correction 2.25
2 . . . . 2.25
3 Space Station Called Hell 2.25
4 Birth of Megabyte 2.25
5 PG(c),O:Avalon 2.25
6 O:Megabyte 2.25
7 Avalon disappears 2.25
8 V:Heap,V:Druids 2.25
9 . . . . 2.25
10 V:Heap Team 2.25
11 . . . . 2.25
12 . . . . 2.25
13 V:Volunteers 2.25
14 1/3 issue 2.25

NEW WAVE vs. THE VOLUNTEERS
Eclipse, 1987
1 3-D,V:Volunteers 2.50
2 3-D,V:Volunteers 2.50

NEXT MAN
Comico, 1985
1 I&O:Next Man 2.50
2 . . . . 2.25
3 . . . . 2.25
4 . . . . 2.25
5 . . . . 2.25

The Next Man #4
© Comico

NEXT NEXUS
First, 1989
1 SR 2.25
2 SR 2.25
3 SR 2.25
4 SR 2.25

NEXUS
Capital, 1983
1 SR,I:Judah Maccabee 5.00
2 SR,Origin,V:Bellows 4.00
3 SR,Sundra Captive 4.00
4 SR,V:Ziggurat 4.00
5 SR,I'm Bored! 4.00
6 SR,A:Badger,TrialogueTrilogy#1 . 4.00
First
7 SR,A:Badger,TrialogueTrilogy#2 . 4.00
8 SR,A:Badger,TrialogueTrilogy#3 . 3.00
9 SR,Teen Angel 2.50
10 SR,BWg,Talking Heads 2.25
11 SR,V:Clausius 2.25
12 SR,V:The Old General 2.25
13 SR,Sundra Peale solo 2.25
14 SR,A:Clonezone,Hilariator 2.25
15 SR,A:Clonezone 2.25
16 SR,A:Clonezone 2.25
17 Judah vs. Jacque,the Anvil 2.25
18 SR,A:Clonezone 2.25
19 SR,A:Clonezone 2.25
20 SR,A:Clonezone 2.25
21 SR,A:Clonezone 2.25
22 KG,A:Badger 2.25
23 SR,A:Clonezone 2.25
24 SR,A:Clonezone 2.25
25 SR,A:Clonezone 2.25
26 SR,A:Clonezone 2.25
27 SR,A:Clonezone 2.25
28 MMi 2.25
29 A:Kreed & Sinclair 2.25
30 JL,C:Badger 2.50
31 Judah solo story 2.25
32 JG,Judah solo story 2.25
33 SR,A:Kreed & Sinclair 2.25
34 SR,Judah solo story 2.25
35 SR,Judah solo story 2.25
36 SR 2.25
37 PS 2.25
38 . . . . 2.25
39 SR, The Boom Search 2.25
40 SR 2.25
41 SR 2.25
42 SR,Bowl-Shaped world 2.25
43 PS 2.25
44 PS 2.25
45 SR,A:Badger Pt.1 . . . . 2.25
46 SR,A:Badger Pt.2 . . . . 2.25
47 SR,A:Badger Pt.3 . . . . 2.25
48 SR,A:Badger Pt.4 . . . . 2.25
49 PS,A:Badger Pt.5 . . . . 2.25
50 SF,double size,A:Badger Pt.6
    Crossroads tie-in 3.50
51 PS 2.25
52 PS 2.25
53 PS 2.25
54 PS 2.25
55 PS 2.25
56 . . . . 2.25
57 AH 2.25
58 Sr,I:Stanislaus Korivitsky
    as Nexus 2.25
59 SR 2.25
60 SR 2.25
61 . . . . 2.25
62 . . . . 2.25
63 V:Elvonic Order 2.25
64 V:Elvonic Order 2.25
65 V:Elvonic Order 2.25
66 V:Elvonic Order 2.25
67 V:Elvonic Order 2.25

68 LM. 2.25
69. . . . . 2.25
70. . . . . 2.25
71 V:Bad Brains. 2.25
72 V:Renegade heads 2.25
73 Horatio returns to Ylum. 2.25
74 Horatio vs. Stan 2.25
75 Horatio vs. Stan 2.25
76 . . . . 2.25
77 . . . . 2.25
78 O:Nexus,Nexus Files Pt#1 . . . . 2.25
79 Nexus Files Pt#2. . . . . 2.25
80 Nexus.Files Pt#3,last iss. 2.25

NEXUS LEGENDS
First, 1989
1 thru 13 rep.Nexus . . . . @2.25
14 rep.Nexus 2.25
15 rep.Nexus 2.25
16 rep.Nexus 2.25
17 rep.Nexus 2.25
18 rep.Nexus 2.25
19 rep.Nexus 2.25
20 SR,Sanctuary 2.25
21 thru 23 SR. . . . . @2.25

NICK HALIDAY
Argo, 1956
1 Strip reprints. 90.00

NICKI SHADOW
Relentless Comics, 1997
1 by Eric Burnham & Ted Naifeh . . 2.50
2 Killing Zone, pt.2 . . . . 2.50
3 Killing Zone, pt.3 . . . . 2.50
4 Killing Zone, concl. 2.50

Night Glider #1
© Topps

NIGHT GLIDER
Topps, 1993
1 V:Bombast,C:Captain Glory,
  Trading Card 3.25

NIGHTHUNTER
Empire Comics, 2001
1 (of 12) 3.75
2 thru 4 . . . . @3.75

NIGHTJAR
Avatar Press, 2004
1 (of 4) 3.50

2 thru 4 . . . . @3.50
1a and 4a wraparound (c)s. . . . @3.50

NIGHT MAN, THE
Malibu Ultraverse, 1993–95
1 I:Night Man,Deathmask 2.75
1a Silver foil (c). 4.00
2 GeH,V:Mangle 2.50
3 SEt,GeH,A:Freex,Mangle 2.50
4 HC,I:Scrapyard,O:Firearm 2.50
5 SEt(s). 2.50
6 thru 15 . . . . @2.50
16 I:Bloodfly. 3.50
17 D:Playland. 2.50
18 DZ,SEt,V:Bloodfly 2.50
19 DZ,SEt,V:Deathmask 2.50
20 DZ,V:Bloody fly 2.50
21 Identity Revealed 2.50
22 Infinity Gem tie-in,A:Loki. 2.50
23 R:Rhianon. 2.50
Ann.#1 V:Pilgrim, 64pg. 4.00

NIGHT MAN, THE
Malibu Ultraverse, 1995
Infinity Night Man vs. Night Man . . . 2.50
1 Discovers New powers 2.25
1a Computer Painted Cover. 2.25
2 phoenix flip issue 2.25
3 Phoenix Resurrection 2.25
4 final issue. 2.25

NIGHT MAN/GAMBIT
Malibu, 1996
1 thru 3 . . . . @2.50

NIGHTMARE
Innovation, 1989
1 AN 2.50

NIGHTMARE AND CASPER
Harvey Publications, 1963
1 . . . . 125.00
2 . . . . 65.00
3 . . . . 65.00
4 . . . . 65.00
5 . . . . 65.00
Becomes:

CASPER AND NIGHTMARE
6 B:68 pgs. 25.00
7 . . . . 15.00
8 . . . . 15.00
9 . . . . 15.00
10 . . . . 15.00
11 thru 20. . . . . @10.00
21 thru 30. . . . . @8.00
31 . . . . 8.00
32 E:68 pgs 8.00
33 thru 45. . . . . @7.00
46 Aug., 1974. . . . . 7.00

NIGHTMARE ON ELM STREET
Blackthorne, 1991
1 3-D. 2.50
2 3-D. 2.50
3 3-D. 2.50

NIGHTMARES ON ELM STREET
Innovation
1 Yours Truly, Freddy Krueger Pt.1 3.00
2 Yours Truly ,Freddy Krueger Pt.2 2.50

3 Loose Ends Pt.1,Return to
  Springwood 2.50
4 Loose Ends Pt 2 . . . . 2.50
5 . . . . 2.50
6 . . . . 2.50

NIGHTMARES
Eclipse, 1985
1 . . . . 2.50
2 . . . . 2.00

NIGHT MUSIC
Eclipse, 1984–88
1 . . . . 2.50
2 . . . . 2.50
3 CR, Jungle Bear 3.00
4 Pelias & Melisande 2.00
5 Pelias. 2.00
6 same as Salome #1
7 same as Red Dog #1
Graphic Novel 8.00

NIGHTS INTO DREAMS
Archie Comics, 1997
1 based on Sega game 2.00
2 thru 6 . . . . @2.00

NIGHTSHADE
No Mercy Comics, 1997
1 by Mark Williams 2.50
2 and 3 . . . . @2.50

NIGHT TRIBES
WildStorm/DC, 1999
1-shot Night Tribes unite 5.00

NIGHTVEIL
AC Comics, 1984
1 . . . . 3.50
2 . . . . 2.50
3 thru 7 . . . . @2.25
Spec.#1 . . . . 2.25

NIGHT WALKER
Fleetway
1 thru 2 rep.. . . . . @3.00

NIGHTWOLF
Entropy
1 . . . . 2.25
2 . . . . 2.25

9 LIVES OF FELIX
Harvey
1 thru 4 . . . . @2.25

NINJA BOY
WildStorm/DC, 2001
1 Ancient Japan, 40-pg. 3.50
2 . . . . 3.00
3 . . . . 3.00
4 . . . . 3.00
5 . . . . 3.00
6 Bishamon, God of War 3.00
TPB Faded Dreams 15.00

NINJA HIGH SCHOOL
Eternity, 1992
1 Reps.orig.N.H.S.in color 2.25
2 thru 13 reprints. . . . . @2.25

COLOR PUB.

Ninja High School #93
© Antarctic Press

NINJA HIGH SCHOOL
Antarctic Press, 2000
1 thru 74 see B&W
75	3.00
76 Quagmire gang	3.00
77	3.00
78 World Domination Tour	3.00
79 Dog Supreme	3.00
80 Jeremy Feeple is back	3.00
81 F:Diamond Diane	3.00
82 F:Quagmire Koalas	3.00
83 Time passes	3.00
84 Past, Present, Future	3.00
85 Time has past	3.00
86 Queen of the Conglomerate	3.00
87 Invaded by the Shallrams	3.00
88 Battle Chef battle	3.00
89 Sammie's secret	3.00
90 Earth's champion	3.00
91 The Toughest Contest	3.00
92 Round 2	3.00
93 Round 3	3.00
94 F:Red Ninja,V:Lendo Rivalsan	3.00
95 Ichi in a new place	3.00
96 Dash the Impede	3.00
97 F:Asrial, Jeremy	3.00
98 Asrial found	3.00
99 F:Lendo Rivalson dies	3.00
100 F:Asrial, Jeremy, & Ichi BDn(c) 48-pg.	5.00
100a Fred Perry (c)	5.00
100b Robert Dejesus (c)	5.00
100c Rod Espinosa (c)	5.00
101 thru 111	@3.50
112 thru 114	3.50
115 thru 121	@3.00
Yearbook 2001	4.00
Yearbook 2002	4.00
Yearbook 2003	5.00
Yearbook 2004	5.00
TPB Textbook Vol. 2, 600-pg.	50.00
Spec. Swimsuit special 2002	4.50
TPB Vol. Pocket Manga	10.00
TPB Vol. 2 Pocket Manga	10.00
TPB Vol. 3 Pocket Manga	10.00

NINJA HIGH SCHOOL VERSION 2
Antarctic Press, 1999
1 by Ben Dunn	7.00
2	5.00
3	4.00

4	3.00
5 thru 8	@2.50
9 Yumei strikes back	2.50
10	2.50
11 Time & space distorted	2.50
12 When Worlds Colide, last issue	2.50

NINJA HIGH SCHOOL FEATURING SPEED RACER
Eternity, 1993
1B	3.00
2B	3.00

NINJAK
Valiant, 1994
0: O:Ninjak, Pt. 1	2.50
00: O:Ninjak, Pt.2	2.50
1 B:MMo(s),JQ,JP,Chromium(c), I:Dr.Silk,Webnet	3.00
1a Gold Ed	4.00
2 JQ,JP,V:Dr.Silk,Webnet	2.50
3 JQ,JP,I:Seventh Dragon	2.25
4 MMo(a&s),V:Seventh Dragon, w/Valiant Era card	2.25
5 MMo(a&s),A:X-O Manowar	2.25
6 MMo(a&s),A:X-O Manowar, V:Dr.Silk,Webnet	2.25
7 MMo(a&s),I:Rhaman	2.25
8 MMo(a&s),Chaos Effect-Gamma #3, A:Madame Noir	2.25
9 Dogs of War	2.25
10 Cantebury Tale #1	2.25
11 Cantebury Tale #2	2.25
12	2.25
13 Mad Dogs and English	2.25
14 Cry Wolf pt. 1	2.25
15 Cry Wolf pt. 2	2.25
16 Plague Pt. 1	2.25
17 Plague Pt. 2	2.25
18 Computer Virus	2.25
19 DAn,ALa,MM,Breaking the Web,pt.1	2.25
20 DAn,ALa,MM,Breaking the Web,pt.2	2.25
21 DAn,ALa,MM,Breaking the Web,pt.3	2.25
22 Bitter Wind	2.25
23 w/o arsenal	2.25
24 Unusual sidekick	2.25
25	2.25
26	2.25
27 Diamond Smugglers	2.25
28 F:Sister Gabriela	2.25
Yearbook #1, Dr. Silk	4.00

NINJAK
Acclaim, 1996
1 KBk(s), Denny Meechum becomes Ninjak	2.50
2 KBk(s) video game spin-off	2.50
3 KBk(s) video game spin-off	2.50
4 KBk(s) video game spin-off	2.50
5 KBk(s) video game spin-off	2.50
6 KBk(s) The World's Finest	2.50
7 KBk(s) video game spin-off	2.50
8 KBk(s) video game spin-off	2.50
9 KBk(s) video game spin-off	2.50
10 KBk(s) F:Maria Barbella	2.50
11 KBk(s) Trial Continues	2.50
12 KBk(s) final issue	2.50

N.I.O.
Acclaim, 1998
1 (of 4) by Shon Bury & JPi	2.50
2	2.50
3	2.50

4 conclusion	2.50

NIRA X: ANIME
Entity Comics, 1997
1 BMs	3.00
1a deluxe, foil cover	3.50
2 BMs	3.00
2a deluxe, foil cover	3.50
Swimsuit #0	2.75
Swimsuit #0 Manga (c)	2.75

NIRA X: CYBERANGEL
Entity, 1994
1 From pages of Zen	3.00
1a 2nd printing	2.75
2 V:Parradox	2.50
3 In Hydro-Dams	2.50
4 final issue	2.50
4a with computer game	7.00
Ashcan	2.50
TPB Birth of an Angel	13.00
[Series 2], 1995
1 R:Nira X	3.75
1a Clear Chromium Edition	8.00
1b Holo-Chrome edition	10.00
2 Alien Invasion	2.50
3 Mecha New York	2.50
4 Final Issue	2.50
[Series 3], 1996
0	2.75
0a signed & numbered	8.00
1	2.50
1a gold edition, signed & numb.	5.00
2	2.50
3	3.00

NIRA X/CYNDER: ENDANGERED SPECIES
Entity Comics, 1996
1	3.00
1a gold ink enhanced, bagged	13.00

NOCTURNALS
Malibu Bravura, 1995
1 DIB,I:Nocturnals	3.00
1a Glow-in-the-Dark	4.00
2 DIB,I:Komodo, Mister Fane	3.00
3 DIB,F:Raccoon	3.00
4 DIB,I:The Old Wolf	3.00
5 Discovered by Police	3.00
6 DIB	3.00

NOCTURNALS: THE DARK FOREVER
Oni Press, 2001
1 by Dan Brereton	3.00
2	3.00
3	3.00
TPB The Dark Forever (2002)	10.00
TPB Unhallowed Eve (2002)	10.00
TPB Black Planet (1998)	20.00

NOID IN 3-D
Blackthorne
1 thru 3	@2.50

NOMAN
Tower Comics, 1966
1 GK,OW,WW,AW	125.00
2 OW,WW,A:Dynamo	75.00

NOOGIE KOOTCH: SECRET AGENT MAN
Hobo Comics
1 I:Noogie Kootch 2.75
2 F:Celutron CIty. 2.75

NO TIME FOR SERGEANTS
Dell Publishing Co., 1958
1 Ph(c) 175.00
2 Ph(c) 100.00
3 Ph(c) 75.00

NOVA HUNTER
Ryal Comics
1 thru 3 . . . . @2.50
4 Climax 2.50
5 Death and Betrayal 2.50

NUBIAN KNIGHT
Samson Comics
1 I:Shandai 2.50

NURSES, THE
Gold Key, April, 1963
1 . . . . 55.00
2 . . . . 35.00
3 . . . . 35.00

NYOKA, JUNGLE GIRL
Charlton Comics, 1955–57
14 . . . . 125.00
15 . . . . 100.00
16 . . . . 100.00
17 . . . . 100.00
18 . . . . 100.00
19 . . . . 100.00
20 . . . . 100.00
21 . . . . 100.00
22 . . . . 100.00

NYOKA, THE JUNGLE GIRL
AC Comics
1 and 2 . . . . @2.25

OBLIVION
Comico, 1995
1 R:The Elementals 2.50
2 I:Thunderboy, Lilith 2.50
3 I:Fen, Ferril 2.50
4 War 3.00
5 The Unholy Trilogy. 3.00

OCCULT FILES OF DR. SPEKTOR
Gold Key, April, 1973
1 I:Lakot 50.00
2 thru 5 . . . . @25.00
6 thru 10 . . . . @25.00
11 I:Spertor as Werewolf 25.00
12 and 13. . . . . @20.00
14 A:Dr. Solar. 35.00
15 thru 24 . . . . @15.00
Whitman
25 rep. 15.00

OCEAN
Wildstorm/DC, 2004
1 (of 6) WEl(s),CSp,KlS 3.00

ODYSSEY, THE
Avatar/TidalWave Studios, 2002
1A RCz (c) 3.50
1B MMy (c) 3.50
1C Parajullo (c). 3.50
1D Murphy (c). 3.50

O.G. WHIZ
Gold Key, 1971–79
1 . . . . 90.00
2 . . . . 50.00
3 thru 6 . . . . @40.00
7 thru 11 . . . . @30.00

OINK: BLOOD AND CIRCUS
Kitchen Sink, 1997
1 (of 4) by John Mueller 5.00
2 . . . . 5.00
3 . . . . 5.00
4 conclusion 5.00

OLYMPUS HEIGHTS
IDW Publishing, 2004
1 . . . . 4.00
2 thru 4 . . . . @4.00

O'MALLEY AND THE ALLEY CATS
Gold Key, 1971–74
1 . . . . 35.00
2 thru 9 . . . . @30.00

OMEGA 7
Omega 7
1 V:Exterminator X. 4.00
? by Alonzo L. Washington 4.00
0 . . . . 3.00

OMEGA SAGA, THE
Southpaw Publishing, 1998
0 by Mike Gerardo & Chris Navetta 3.00
1 Episode One, pt.1 . . . . 3.00
2 Episode One, pt.2 . . . . 3.00
Axess Comics
3 by Mike Gerardo, Heroes (c). . . . 3.00
3b Villains (c) 3.00

On a Pale Horse #5
© Innovation

OMEN, THE
Chaos! Comics, 1998
Preview Book, BnP 2.50
1 by PNu & Justiniano 3.00
2 . . . . 3.00
3 . . . . 3.00
4 . . . . 3.00
5 concl. 3.00
1-shot The Omen Vexed 3.00
TPB The Omen 13.00

ON A PALE HORSE
Innovation
1 Piers Anthony adapt 5.00
2 Magician,I:Kronos 5.00
3 . . . . 5.00
4 VV, ... 5.00
5 . . . . 5.00
6 . . . . 5.00

ONE-ARM SWORDSMAN
Dr. Leung's
1 . . . . 3.00
2 . . . . 3.00
3 . . . . 2.75
4 thru 11 . . . . @2.50

OPERATION: STORMBRINGER
Acclaim Special Event, 1997
Spec. F:Teutonic Knight. 4.00

ORBIT
Eclipse, 1990
1 DSt(c). 4.00
2 . . . . 4.00
3 . . . . 5.00

ORIENTAL HEROES
Jademan, 1988–92
1 by Tony Wong & MBn 2.50
2 . . . . 2.25
3 thru 13 . . . . @2.25
14 thru 27. . . . . @2.25
28 V:Skeleton Secretary 2.25
29 Barbarian vs.Lone Kwoon. 2.25
30 Barbarian vs.Lone Kwoon. 2.25
31 SkeletonSecretaryUprisng 2.25
32 Uprising Continues 2.25
33 Jupiter Kills His Brother 2.25
34 Skeleton Sec. Suicide. 2.25
35 Red Sect Vs. Global Cult 2.25
36 A:Tiger. 2.25
37 Old Supreme. 2.25
38 Tiger vs. 4 Hitmen. 2.25
39 D:Infinite White, V:Red Sect. . . . 2.25
40 The Golden Buddhha Temple. . . 2.25
41 thru 43. . . . . 2.00
44 SilverChime rescue 2.00
45 Global Cult Battle 2.25
46 thru 48. . . . . @2.25
49 F:GoldDragon/SilverChime. . . . 2.25
50 Return to Global Cult 2.25
51 Gang Of Three Vs.White Beau
    & Lone Kwoon-Tin. 2.25
52 Global Cult vs Red Sect 2.25
53 Global Cult vs.Red Sect 2.25

ORIGINAL ASTRO BOY
Now, 1987
1 KSy 3.00
2 thru 5 KSy . . . . @3.00
6 thru 17 KSy . . . . @3.00

COLOR PUB.

ORIGINAL CAPTAIN JOHNAR AND THE ALIENS
Valiant, 1995
1 Reprint from Magnus 3.00
2 Russ Manning rep. 3.00

ORIGINAL DICK TRACY
Gladestone, 1990
1 rep.V:Mrs.Pruneface 2.25
2 rep.V:Influence 2.25
3 rep.V:TheMole 2.25
4 rep.V:ItchyOliver 2.25
5 rep.V:Shoulders 2.25

ORIGINAL DR. SOLAR MAN OF THE ATOM
Valiant, 1995
1 Reprint 3.00
2 Reprints 3.00
3 Reprints 3.00

ORIGINAL E-MAN
First, 1985
{rep. Charlton stories}
1 JSon,O:E-Man & Nova 2.25
2 JSon,V:Battery,SamuelBoar 2.25
3 JSon,City in the Sand 2.25
4 JSon,A:Brain from Sirius 2.25
5 JSon,V:T.V. Man 2.25
6 JSon,I:Teddy Q 2.25
7 JSon,Vamfire 2.25

ORIGINAL MAGNUS ROBOT FIGHTER
Valiant, 1995
1 Reprint 3.00
2 Russ Manning Art 3.00
3 Russ Manning 3.00

ORIGINAL SHIELD
ABC
1 DAy/TD,O:Shield 2.25
2 DAy,O:Dusty 2.25
3 DAy 2.25
4 DAy 2.25

ORIGINAL TUROK, SON OF STONE
Valiant, 1995
1 Reprint 3.00
2 Alberto Gioletti art 3.00
3 Alberto Gioletti 3.00
4 Reprints 3.00

ORIGIN OF THE DEFIANT UNIVERSE
Defiant, 1994
1 O:Defiant Characters 2.25

ORIGINS
Malibu Ultraverse,
1 O:Ultraverse Heroes 2.25

OUTBREED 999
Blackout Comics, 1994
1 thru 4 . . . . @3.00
5 Search For Daige 3.00

Out Breed 999 #3
© Blackout Comics

OUTCAST SPECIAL
Valiant, 1995
1 R:The Outcast 2.50

OUTER LIMITS, THE
Dell Publishing Co., 1964
1 P(c) 200.00
2 P(c) 125.00
3 P(c) 125.00
4 P(c) 125.00
5 P(c) 125.00
6 P(c) 100.00
7 P(c) 100.00
8 P(c) 100.00
9 P(c) 100.00
10 P(c) 100.00
11 thru 18 P(c) . . . . @75.00

OUTLAWS OF THE WEST
Charlton Comics, 1956–80
11 . . . . 75.00
12 . . . . 50.00
13 . . . . 50.00
14 Giant 85.00
15 . . . . 40.00
16 . . . . 40.00
17 . . . . 40.00
18 SD 100.00
19 . . . . 40.00
20 . . . . 40.00
21 thru 30 . . . . @35.00
31 thru 50 . . . . @30.00
51 thru 70 . . . . @25.00
71 thru 88 . . . . @20.00

OUT OF THIS WORLD
Charlton Comics, 1956–59
1 . . . . 300.00
2 . . . . 125.00
3 SD 350.00
4 SD 350.00
5 SD 350.00
6 SD 350.00
7 SD,SD(c) 375.00
8 SD 300.00
9 SD 250.00
10 SD,Perfect Forcaster 250.00
11 SD 300.00
12 SD 250.00
13 thru 15 . . . . @125.00

---

16 . . . . 325.00

OUTPOSTS
Blackthorne, 1997
1 thru 6 . . . . @2.25

OUT THERE
WildStorm/DC, 2001
1 HuR, Cliffhanger 2.50
2 HuR, ... 2.50
3 HuR 2.50
4 HuR 2.50
5 HuR 2.50
6 HuR 2.50
7 HuR,Road to El Dorado,pt.1 . . . 2.50
8 HuR,Road to El Dorado,pt.2 . . . 2.50
9 HuR,Road to El Dorado,pt.3 . . . 2.50
10 HuR,Road to El Dorado,pt.4 . . . 3.00
11 HuR,Road to El Dorado,pt.5 . . . 3.00
12 HuR,Road to El Dorado,pt.6 . . . 3.00
13 HuR,The War in Hell,pt.1 . . . . . 3.00
14 HuR,The War in Hell,pt.2 . . . . . 3.00
15 HuR,Draedalus's Domain 3.00
16 HuR,Dreadrealm 3.00
17 HuR,all-silent issue 3.00
18 HuR,V:Draedalus 3.00
TPB The Evil Within, rep.#1-#6 . . 13.00

OWL, THE
Gold Key, April, 1967
1 . . . . 90.00
2 April, 1968 . . . . 65.00

OZZY OSBORNE
Rock-It Comix
1 w/guitar pick 4.00

PACIFIC PRESENTS
Pacific, 1992
1 DSt,Rocketeer,(3rd App.) 12.00
2 DSt,Rocketeer,(4th App.) 9.00
3 SD,I:Vanity 2.50
4 and 5 . . . . @2.50

P.A.C.
Artifacts Inc., 1993
1 I:P.A.C. 2.25

PAINKILLER JANE
Event Comics, 1997
1 JQ(c) 3.00
1 RL(c) 3.00
1 Red foil logo, signed 25.00
2 JQ&JP(c) 3.00
2 JP&RL(c) 3.00
3 JQ&JP(c) 3.00
3a JP&RL(c) 3.00
4 JQ&JP(c) A Too Bright Place
    For Dying 3.00
4a RL&JP(c) 3.00
5 JQ&JP(c) Purgatory
    Station—Next Stop Hell 3.00
5a RL&JP(c) 3.00
6 RL&JP(c) Blood Harvest 3.00
6a BSz&JP(c) 3.00
7 Jane in the Jungle,
    pt.1,BiT&JP(c) 3.00
7a RL&JP(c) 3.00
Spec.#0 O:Painkiller Jane,48-pg. . . 4.00
Spec.#0A signed 30.00
Spec. Painkiller Jane/Hellboy
    Ancient Laughter (1998) 3.00
Spec. Painkiller Jane/Hellboy,
    signed 20.00
Spec. Painkiller Jane/The Darkness,
    signed, limited edition, JQ(c) . . 30.00

PAINKILLER JANE/ DARKCHYLDE
Event Comics, 1998
1 BAu,RQu 3.00
1a signed & numbered 30.00
1b Omnichrome edition. 15.00
1c Omnichrome, signed 30.00
1d Dynamic Forces cover. 7.00

PAINKILLER JANE VS. THE DARKNESS: STRIPPER
Event Comics, 1997
1 GEn,JP,x-over, Amanda Connor
   cover 3.00
1a Greg & Tim Hildebrandt. 3.00
1b MS(c) 3.00
1c JQ(c) 3.00

PALADIN ALPHA
Firstlight
1 I:Paladin Alpha. 3.00
2 V:Hellfire Triger 3.00

PANDEMONIUM: DELIVERANCE
Chaos! Comics, 1998
1-shot by Jesse Leon McCann &
   Jack Jadson 3.00

PANIC
Gemstone, 1997
1 thru 12 EC Comics reprint . . . . @2.50
`Annuals'
TPB Vol. 1 rebinding #1–#4. . . . . . 10.50
TPB Vol. 2 rebinding #5–#8. . . . . . 11.00

PANTERA
Rock-it Comix, 1994
1 . . . . 4.00
1a Gold Ed. 20.00

PANTHA
Harris Comics, 1997
1 (of 2) MT 3.50
1 Marilyn Monroe MT alt.cov. 10.00
2 MT alternate (c) 10.00
2 photo (c). 10.00

PARA
Pennyfarthing Press, 2004
1 . . . . 3.00
2 thru 6 . . . . @3.00

PARADAX
Vortex, 1987
1 . . . . 2.25

PARADIGM
Gauntlet
1 A:Predator 3.00

PARADISE
Twenty First Century, 2000
1 thru 7 . . . . @3.00

PARAGON DARK APOCALYPSE
AC, 1993
1 thru 4, Fem Force crossover . . @3.00

PARANOIA
Adventure Comics, 1991
1 (based on video game) Clone1 . . 3.25
2 King-R-Thr-2 . . . . 3.00
3 R:Happy Jack,V:N3F 3.00
4 V:The Computer 3.00
5 V:The Computer 3.00
6 V:Lance-R-Lot,last issue 3.00

PARTRIDGE FAMILY, THE
Charlton Comics, 1971–73
1 . . . . 125.00
2 thru 4 . . . . @50.00
5 Summer Special 100.00
6 thru 21 . . . . @40.00

PASSOVER
Maximum Press, 1996
1 (of 2) BNa 3.00
2 BNa,A:Avengelyne. 3.00

PATH, THE
Crossgen Comics, 2002
1 . . . . 5.00
2 thru 4 . . . . @3.00
9 thru 23 . . . . @3.00
Prequel 48-pg. 5.00
TPB Vol. 1 Crisis of Faith. 20.00
TPB Vol. 2 Blood on Snow 16.00
TPB Vol. 3 Death and Dishonor. . . 16.00
TPB Traveler Vol. 2 Blood on Snow . . . .
10.00

PATHWAYS TO FANTASY
Pacific, 1984
1 BS,JJ art 3.00

PATRIOTS, THE
WildStorm/DC, 1999
1 BCi&JPe(s) 2.50
2 BCi&JPe(s) 2.50
3 BCi&JPe(s) 2.50
4 BCi&JPe(s) 2.50
5 BCi&JPe(s) 2.50
6 BCi&JPe(s) 2.50
7 BCi&JPe(s) 2.50
8 BCi&JPe(s),V:Stealthers 2.50
9 BCi&JPe(s) 2.50

Patriots #2
© *WildStorm*

10 JPe(s),final issue 2.50

PAT SAVAGE: WOMAN OF BRONZE
Millennium, 1992
1 F:Doc Savage's cousin 2.50

PEACEKEEPER
Future Comics, 2003
1 . . . . 3.00
2 thru 5 . . . . @3.00
TPB Vol. 1 . . . . 16.00

PEACEMAKER
Charlton, 1967
1 A:Fightin' 5 . . . . 5.00
2 A:Fightin' 5 . . . . 3.00
3 A:Fightin' 5 . . . . 3.00
4 O:Peacemaker,A:Fightin' 5 . . . . . 4.00
5 A:Fightin' 5 . . . . 2.50

PEANUTS
Dell Publishing Co., 1958
1 . . . . 250.00
2 . . . . 200.00
3 . . . . 150.00
4 . . . . 125.00
5 thru 13 . . . . @100.00

PEANUTS
Gold Key, 1963
1 . . . . 200.00
2 thru 4 . . . . @150.00

PEARL HARBOR
Antarctic Press, 2001
1 by Ted Nomura, Movie tie-in 4.00
2 movie tie-in, concl. 4.00
Spec. 60th Anniv. spec., 64-pg. . . . 13.00
Spec. 60th Anniv., Japanese (c) . . 13.00

PEBBLES & BAMM-BAMM
Charlton Comics, 1972–76
1 . . . . 75.00
2 thru 10 . . . . @35.00
11 thru 36 . . . . @30.00

PEBBLES FLINTSTONE
Gold Key, 1963
1 A Chip off the old block 150.00

PERG
Lightning Comics, 1993
1 Glow in the dark(c),JS(c),
   B:JZy(s),KIK,I:Perg 3.75
1a Platinum Ed. 5.00
1b Gold Ed. 7.00
1 gold edition, glow-in-the-dark
   flip cover 30.00
2 KIK,O:Perg. 3.25
2a Platinum Ed. 5.00
3 Flip Book (c), ... 3.25
3a Platinum Ed 5.00
4 TLw,I:Hellina 9.00
4a Platinum Ed 5.00
5 A:Hellina. 3.25
6 PIA,A:Hellina 3.25
7 . . . . 3.00
8 V:Police 3.00

PERRY MASON MYSTERY MAGAZINE
Dell Publishing Co., 1964
1 . . . . 75.00
2 Ray Burr Ph(c) 50.00

PETER PAN: RETURN TO NEVERNEVER LAND
Adventure
1 Peter in Mass. 2.50
2 V:Tiger Lily 2.50

PETER POTAMUS
Gold Key, 1965
1 . . . . 150.00

PETTICOAT JUNCTION
Dell Publishing Co., 1964
1 Ph(c) 125.00
2 Ph(c) 75.00
3 Ph(c) 75.00
4 . . . . 75.00
5 Ph(c) 75.00

PHANTOM, THE
Gold Key, 1962
1 RsM 250.00
2 B:King, Queen & Jack 150.00
3 . . . . 125.00
4 . . . . 125.00
5 . . . . 125.00
6 . . . . 125.00
7 The Super Apes 125.00
8 . . . . 125.00
9 . . . . 125.00
10 The Sleeping Giant 125.00
11 E:King,Queen and Jack 100.00
12 B:Track Hunter 100.00
13 . . . . 100.00
14 The Historian 100.00
15 . . . . 100.00
16 . . . . 100.00
17 Samaris. 100.00

King Comics, 1966
18 The Treasure of the Skull
    Cave;BU:Flash Gordon 100.00
19 The Astronaut & the Pirates . . . 75.00
20 A:GirlPhantom,E:FlashGordon . 75.00
21 BU:Mandrake 75.00
22 Secret of Magic Mountain 75.00
23 . . . . 75.00
24 A:Girl Phantom 75.00
25 . . . . 60.00
26 . . . . 60.00
27 . . . . 60.00
28 . . . . 60.00
29 *never published*

Charlton Comics, 1969–77
30 . . . . 40.00
31 JAp,Phantom of Shang-Ri-La . . 40.00
32 JAp,The Pharaoh Phantom . . . 40.00
33 The Jungle People 40.00
34 thru 39 . . . . @35.00
40 The Ritual 35.00
41 . . . . 25.00
42 . . . . 25.00
43 . . . . 25.00
44 To Right A Wrong 25.00
45 . . . . 25.00
46 I;Piranha 28.00
47 thru 72 . . . . @25.00
73 . . . . 20.00
74 . . . . 28.00

Phantom #4
© *Wolf Publishing*

PHANTOM
Wolf Publishing, 1992
1 Drug Runners 2.25
2 Mystery Child of the Sea 2.25
3 inc.feature pages on
    Phantom/Merchandise. 2.25
4 TV Jungle Crime Buster 2.25
5 Castle Vacula-Transylvania 2.25
6 The Old West 2.25
7 Sercet of Colussus 2.75
8 Temple of the Sun God 2.75

PHANTOM, THE
Moonstone, 2002
1 . . . . 3.50
2 thru 4 . . . . @3.50
GN #1 The Ghost Killer, 48-pg. . . . 6.00
GN #2 The Singh Web. 6.00
GN #3 The Treasures of Bangalla . . 7.00
GN #4 The Hunt. 7.00
GN #5 Valley of the Golden Men . . 7.00
TPB Vol. 1 Ghost Who Walks 17.00

PHANTOM BOLT, THE
Gold Key, 1964–66
1 A:Mr X 100.00
2 Super Goof 75.00
3 thru 7 . . . . @50.00

PHANTOM FORCE
Genesis West, 1994
Previously: Image
0 JK/JLe(c) 3.00
3 thru 10 . . . . @3.00

PHAZE
Eclipse, 1988
1 BSz(c),Takes place in future 2.25
2 PG(c),V:The Pentagon. 2.25
3 Schwieger Vs. Mammoth. 2.25

PHOENIX
Atlas, 1975
1 thru 4 . . . . @6.00

PHOENIX RESURRECTION
Malibu Ultraverse, 1995–96
0 Intro to Phoenix Resurrection . . . 2.25
Genesis, A:X-Men 4.00
Revelations, A:X-Men 4.00

Aftermath, A:X-Men 4.00

PINK PANTHER, THE
Gold Key, April, 1971
1 . . . . 75.00
2 thru 10 . . . . @35.00
11 thru 30 . . . . @25.00
31 thru 74 . . . . @15.00
75 thru 80 . . . . @25.00
81 thru 87 . . . . @20.00

PIRACY
Gemstone, 1998
1 EC comics reprint 2.50
2 thru 7 EC comics reprints . . . . @2.50
`Annuals'
TPB Vol. 1 rebinding #1–#4. . . . . 10.50
TPB Vol. 2 rebinding #5–#7. . . . . . 8.00

PIRATE CORP.
Eternity
1 thru 5 . . . . @2.25

P.I.'S, THE
First, 1985
1 JSon,Ms.Tree,M Mauser 2.25
2 JSon,Ms.Tree,M Mauser 2.25
3 JSon,Ms.Tree,M Mauser 2.25

PITT
Full Bleed Studios, 1996
1 thru 9, see Image
10 thru 14 DK. . . . . @2.50
14a variant cover 7.00
15 DK 2.50
16 DK, Ugly Americans, pt.1 . . . . . 2.50
17 DK, Ugly Americans, pt.2 . . . . . 2.50
18 DK, Ugly Americans, pt.3, concl. 2.50
19 by Brian Dawson. 3.00
20 DK, Urgral Thul. 2.50
TPB Vol. 1, rep. ? &#1–#4 . . . . . 11.00
TPB Vol. 2, rep. #5–#9 . . . . 12.00
Spec. In the Blood 2.50

PITT CREW
Full Bleed Studios, 1998
1 Monster 2.50
2 F:Rai-Kee. 2.50
3 Tyrants 2.50
4 The Slayer 2.50
5 . . . . 2.50

PITT: BIOGENESIS
Full Bleed Studios, 2000
1 (of 3) DK 2.50
2 DK 2.50

PLANETARY
WildStorm/DC, 1999
1 WEI 10.00
2 thru 12 WEI . . . . @5.00
13 WEI,secret history of
    Elijah Snow 4.00
14 WEI,The Four vs. Planetary . . . 4.00
15 WEI,in Australia. 4.00
16 WEI 4.00
17 WEI Elijah Snow's past 3.00
18 WEI,The Gun Club 3.00
19 WEI,Mystery in Space. 3.00
20 WEI,Mystery in Space,pt.2 . . . . 3.00
21 WEI 3.00
TPB All over the World 15.00
TPB The Fourth Man, 144-pg. . . . 15.00
TPB Planetary: Crossing Worlds . . 15.00
GN Planetary/The Authority 6.00

GN Planetery/JLA, Terra
  Occulta, JOy (2002) 6.00
GN WEI(s) Planetary/Batman
  Night on Earth x-over (2003). . . 6.00

PLAN 9 FROM
OUTER SPACE
Malibu
GNv Movie Adapt. 5.00

PLANESWALKER WAR
Acclaim, 1996
GN #1 Magic: The Gathering tie-in . 6.00

PLANET COMICS
Blackthorne, 1988
1 DSt(c). 3.00
2 thru 4 . . . . @3.00

PLANET OF VAMPIRES
Atlas, Feb.–July, 1975
1 NA(c),1st PB 25.00
2 NA(c) 25.00
3 RH 25.00

POGZ N SLAMMER
Blackout Comics, 1995
1 I:Pogz N Slammer 2.25
2 Contact Other Schools 2.25

POINT BLANK
WildStorm/DC, 2002
Eye of the Storm
1 (of 5) CWi, super-hero noir 3.00
2 CWi, ... 3.00
3 CWi,F:Jack Hawksmoor 3.00
4 CWi, ... 3.00
5 CWi,concl. 3.00
TPB 15.00

POISON ELVES
Sirius Entertainment, 1998
Color Special #1 by Drew Hayes . . . 3.00
Color Spec.#1 limited. 10.00

POIZON
London Night Studios, 1995
0 . . . . 3.00
0 signed gothchik edition 9.00
? O:Poizon 3.00
?a Commemorative (1999) 6.00
1 . . . . 3.00
1a signed 7.00
2 EHr 3.00

POIZON: CADILLACS
AND GREEN TOMATOES
London Night, 1997
2 . . . . 3.00
3 . . . . 3.00
6 deluxe 5.00

POIZON: DEMON HUNTER
London Night, 1998
1 . . . . 3.00
1 Green Death edition 15.00

POIZON: LOST CHILD
London Night Studios, 1996
0 . . . . 3.00
1 mini series 3.00
1 signed 9.00

1 Green Death edition 15.00
2 thru 3 . . . . @3.00

POKEMAN TALES:
Viz Communications, 1999
(Boardbooks)
1 Charmander Sees a Ghost 5.00
2 Pikachu's Day 5.00
3 Come Out, Squirtle! 5.00
4 Bulbasaur's Trouble. 5.00
5 . . . . 5.00
6 . . . . 5.00
7 . . . . 5.00
8 . . . . 5.00
9 Meet Mew 5.00
10 Snorlax's Snack 5.00
11 Jigglypuff's Magic Lullaby 5.00
12 Lapras Makes a Friend. 5.00
13 Eevee's Weather Report. 5.00
14 Diglett's Birthday Party 5.00
15 First Prize for Starmie 5.00
16 Seel to the Rescue 5.00
Gift Set Vol. 1. . . . . 20.00
Gift Set Vol. 2. . . . . 20.00
Movie Spec. 5.00

POKEMAN THE MOVIE
2000: REVELATION LUGIA
Viz Communications, 2000
1 . . . . 4.00
2 . . . . 4.00
3 . . . . 4.00
Spec. Pikachu's Rescue Adventure . 4.00
Art of Pokeman The Movie 2000 . . 10.00

POKEMAN:
THE FIRST MOVIE
Viz Communications, 1999
1 (of 4) Mewtwo Strikes Back 4.00
2 . . . . 4.00
3 . . . . 4.00
4 conclusion 4.00
Spec. Pikachu's Vacation. 4.00
Art of Pokeman: First Movie 9.00
TPB 16.00

POKEMON TV ANIMATION
Viz Comics, 2000
TPB Vol. 1 . . . . 11.00

POPEYE
Gold Key, 1962
1-65 See Golden Age Section
66 . . . . 100.00
67 . . . . 75.00
68 thru 80 . . . . @50.00
King Comics, 1966
81 thru 92 . . . . @40.00
Charlton, 1969
94 thru 99 . . . . @40.00
100 . . . . 50.00
101 thru 138. . . . . @25.00
Gold Key, 1978
139 thru 143 . . . . @15.00
144 50th Aniv. Spec. 18.00
155 . . . . @15.00
Whitman
156 thru 157 . . . . @15.00
158 thru 159 . . . . @25.00
162 thru 168 . . . . @15.00
169 thru 171 . . . . @20.00

Popeye #146
© Gold Key

POPEYE
Harvey Comics, 1993–94
1 thru 7 . . . . @2.25
Summer Spec.#1 . . . . 2.25

POPEYE SPECIAL
Ocean, 1987–88
1 . . . . 2.25
2 . . . . 2.25

POSSESSED, THE
Wildstorm/DC July, 2003
1 (of 6) LSh,demons. 3.00
2 thru 5 LSh,demon-infested. . . . @3.00
6 LSh,concl. 3.00
TPB series rep. 15.00

POWER & GLORY
Malibu Bravura, 1994
1A HC(a&s),I:American
  Powerhouse. 3.00
1B alternate cover. 3.00
1c Blue Foil (c) 5.00
1d w/seirgraph 5.00
1e Newsstand 3.00
2 HC(a&s), O:American
  Powerhouse. 2.75
3 HC(a&s). 2.50
4 HC(a&s). 2.50
Winter Special 3.00
TPB Series reprint, w/stamp 13.00

POWER FACTOR
Wonder Color Comics, 1986
1 . . . . 4.00
2 . . . . 3.00
3 . . . . 3.00

POWER FACTOR
Innovation, 1990
1 thru 4 . . . . @2.25

POWERKNIGHTS
Amara, 1995
P I:Powerknights. 2.25

POWER OF PRIME
Malibu Ultraverse, 1995
1 O:Prime Powers,Godwheel tie-in 2.50
2 V:Doc Gross, Godwheel tie-in . . . 2.50
3 F:Prime Phade. 2.50
4 F:Elven,Turbocharge 2.50

POWER RANGERS ZEO/YOUNGBLOOD
Maximum Press, 1997
1 TNu,NRd 3.00

POWERS THAT BE
Broadway Comics
Preview Editions, 1995
1 thru 3 B&W. . . . . @2.50
Regular Series, 1995
1 JiS,I:Fatale, Star Seed. 3.00
2 thru 4 . . . . @3.00
5 It's the End of the World As We
  Know It,pt.1 . . . . 3.00
6 End/World As We Know It,pt.2 . . 3.00
Becomes:

STAR SEED
7 End/World As We Know It,pt.3 . . 3.00
8 End/World As We Know It,pt.4 . . 3.00
9 End/World As We Know It,pt.5 . . 3.00
10 End/World As We Know It,pt.6. . 3.00
11 End/World As We Know It,pt.7... 3.00

PRESSBUTTON
Eclipse
(see Axel Pressbutton)
5 and 6 . . . . @2.25

PRIEST
Maximum Press, 1996
1 RLd, F:Michael O'Bannon 3.00
2 RLd,BNa, ... 3.00
3 RLd 3.00

PRIMAL RAGE
Sirius, 1996
1 TAr,from video game 3.00
1 foil cover, limited edition 3.00
2 TAr,DOe(c) 3.00

PRIME
Malibu Ultraverse, 1993–95
1 B:GJ(s),I:Prime 4.00
1a Ultra-Limited 5.00
1b Full Hologram (c). 5.00
2 V:Organism 8, with Ultraverse
  card 3.00
3 NBy,I:Prototype 3.00
4 NBy,V:Prototype. 3.00
5 NBy,BWS,I:Maxi-Man, BU:Rune . 3.00
6 NBy,A:Pres. Clinton 2.75
7 NBy,Break-Thru x-over 2.25
8 NBy,A:Mantra. 2.25
9 NBy,Atomic Lies. 2.25
10 NBy,A:Firearm,N:Prime. 2.25
11 NBy 2.25
12 NBy,(Ultraverse Premiere#3)
  I:Planet Class 3.50
13 NBy,V:Kutt,Planet Class 3.00
14 DaR,I:Voodoo Master 2.25
15 abused kids. 2.25
16 I:Turbo. 2.25
17 Atalon 2.25
18 Prime's new partner 2.25
19 Prime accused 2.25
20 GJ,LeS,A:Rafferty. 2.50
21 GJ,LeS,World without Prime. . . . 2.50
22 GJ,LeS,F:Primevil. 2.50

23 F:Prime's Mother 2.50
24 F:Prime's Mother 2.50
25 A:Chelsea Clinton. 2.50
26 True Powers 2.50
Ashcan (first) 7.00
Ashcan #1 BV(c),B&W. 2.00
Ann.#1 R:Doc Gross 4.00
TPB Rep. #1-#4. . . . . 10.00

Prime Vol. 2 #8 © Malibu

PRIME
Malibu Ultraverse, 1995–96
Infinty I:Spider-Prime 3.00
1 Spider-Prime vs. Lizard 2.25
1a Computer painted cover 2.25
2 Phoenix flip issue. 2.25
3 Phoenix Resurrection 2.25
4 . . . . 2.25
5 . . . . 2.25
6 Prime on Drugs,pt.1,F:Solitaire . . 2.25
7 F:Solitaire, pt.2. . . . . 2.25
8 F:Solitaire, pt.3. . . . . 2.25
9 and 10 . . . . @2.00
11 Absolute Power Corrupts?
  Absolutely!. 2.25
12 HuR,KG, pt.3 (of 3) 2.25
13 KG,Prime exposed, V:Colonel
  Rinaldo 2.25
14 KG, Return of Lord Pumpkin. . . 2.25
15 Return of Lord Pumpkin 2.25

PRIME/CAPTAIN AMERICA
Malibu Ultraverse, 1996
1 GJ,NBy 4.00

PRIME VS. HULK
Malibu
0 . . . . 10.00
0a signed premium edition 20.00

PRIMER
Comico, 1982–84
1 . . . . 15.00
2 I:Grendel 135.00
3 . . . . 10.00
4 C:Maxx. 10.00
5 I:Maxx 35.00
6 I:Evangelyne 15.00
[Volume 2], 1996
1 F:Lady Bathory 3.00

PRIMUS
Charlton Comics, 1972
1 . . . . 25.00
2 thru 5 . . . . @15.00
6 thru 7 . . . . @12.00

PRINCESS SALLY
Archie Comics, 1995
1 thru 3 Sonic tie-in. . . . . @3.00

PRINCE VANDAL
Triumphant
1 JnR(s),. 2.50
2 JnR(s),. 2.50
3 JnR(s),ShG,I:Claire,V:Nicket,
  Vandal goes to Boviden. 2.50
4 JnR(s),ShG,Game's End 2.50
5 JnR(s),ShG,The Sickness, the
  rat appears 2.50
6 JnR(s),ShG,B:Gothic 2.50

PRIORITY: WHITE HEAT
AC Comics, 1986
1 thru 2 miniseries. . . . . @2.25

PRIVATEERS
Vanguard Graphics
1 . . . . 2.25
2 . . . . 2.25

PROFESSIONAL: GOGOL 13
Viz
1 . . . . 5.00
2 and 3 . . . . @5.00

PROFESSOR OM
Innovation, 1990
1 I:Rock Warrior 2.50
2 Samurai Drama 2.50

PROJECT A-KO 0
Antarctic Press, 1994
0 digest size 5.00
Continued by Malibu

PROJECT A-KO 2
CPM, 1995
Previously Malibu
1 Space Saga. 3.00
2 Space Saga. 3.00
3 Queen Margarita 3.00

PROJECT A-KO: VERSUS THE UNIVERSE
CPM, 1995
1 Based on Animation. 3.00
2 strange magician 3.00
3 . . . . 3.00
4 (of 5) TEl 3.00

PROJECT A-KO
Malibu, 1994
1 thru 4 Based on anime movie . @3.00

PROTECTORS
Malibu, 1992–94
1 I:Protectors, inc. JBi poster
  (direct) 3.00
1a thru 12a Newsstand. . . . . . . @2.00
2 V:Mr.Monday,w/poster 2.50

3 V:Steel Army,w/poster 2.50
4 V:Steel Army 2.50
5 Die Cut(c),V:Mr.Monday 2.50
6 V:Mr.Monday 2.50
7 A:Thresher 2.50
8 V:Wisecrack 2.25
9 V:Wisecrack 2.50
10 I:Mantoka 2.50
11 A:Ms.Fury,V:Black Fury 2.50
12 A:Arrow 2.50
13 RAJ(s),Genesis#3. . . . . 2.25
14 RB(c),RAJ(s),Genesis#6. . . . . . 2.25
15 RAJ(s),J:Chalice 2.25
16 So Help Me God 2.25
17 L:Ferret 2.25
18 V:Regulators,BU:Mantako, R:Mr.
    Monday 2.25
19 A:Gravestone,Arc 2.50
20 V:Nowhere Man 2.50
Protectors Handbook 2.50

PROMETHEA
WildStorm/DC, 1999
America's Best Comics
1 AMo(s),F:Sophie Bangs,40-pg. . . 3.50
2 AMo(s),Judgment of Solomon . . . 3.00
3 AMo(s),Misty Magic Land 3.00
4 AMo(s),CV,JWi. 3.00
5 AMo(s),JWi,F:WW1 . . . . 3.00
6 AMo(s),JWi,F:Grace Brannagh . . 3.00
7 AMo(s),JWi,F:Sophie Bangs 3.00
8 AMo(s),JWi,V:Goetic demons . . . 3.00
9 AMo(s),JWi,The Temple. 3.00
10 AMo(s),JWi,Sex, Stars
    and Serpents 3.00
11 AMo(s),JWi,giant monster 3.00
12 AMo(s),JWi,flip-book. 3.00
13 AMo(s),JWi,. 3.00
14 AMo(s),JWi, Lunar Realm. 3.00
15 AMo(s),JWi,. 3.00
16 AMo(s),JWi,Five Swell Guys. . . . 3.00
17 AMo(s),JWi,Stacia vs. Hell 3.00
18 AMo(s),JWi,double demonic 3.00
19 AMo(s),JWi,Tree of Life 3.00
20 AMo(s),JWi,edge of existence . . 3.00
21 AMo(s),JWi,Binah 3.00
22 AMo(s),JWi,Jack Foust 3.00
23 AMo(s),JWi,40-pg. 3.50
24 AMo(s),JWi 3.00
25 AMo(s),JWi,A Higher Court. 3.00
26 AMo(s),JWi,Later 3.00
27 AMo(s),JWi,Tom Strong 3.00
28 AMo(s),JWi,Jack Faust 3.00
29 AMo(s),JWi 3.00
30 AMo(s),JWi,Painted Doll 3.00
31 AMo(s),JWi 3.00
TPB Promethea Book One 15.00
TPB Promethea Book Two 15.00
TPB Promethea Book Three 15.00

PROPHECY
Immortelle Studios, 1998
1 by Hawk, Lovalle, & Wong,
    F:Cynder & War Dragon 3.00
2 . . . . 3.00

PROPHECY OF
THE SOUL SORCERER
Arcane Comics, 1999
1 (of 4) by Eric Dean Seaton 3.00
2 . . . . 3.00
3 . . . . 3.00
3a variant (c). 3.00
4 . . . . 3.00
4a variant (c). 3.00
5 . . . . 3.00
5a variant (c). 3.00
6 Nighthawk vs. Morbid 3.00

6a variant (c). 3.00
7 . . . . 3.00
TPB Vol. 1 . . . . 11.00

PROPHET II
Awesome Entertainment, 1999
1 . . . . 3.00
1a holochrome wraparound (c). . . 15.00
TPB Timetrap. 13.00

PROPHET: LEGACY
Awesome Entertainment, 1999
1 RLe 3.00
2 . . . . 3.00
2a variant (c). 3.00
3 . . . . 3.00

PROPHET/CABLE
Maximum, 1997
1 (of 2) RLd x-over 3.50
2 RLd x-over,A:Domino, Kirby,
    Blaquesmith. 3.50

PROPHET OF DREAMS
Broken Tree Publications, 2002
1 (of 6) by Lawler & Vasquez 3.50
2 thru 6 . . . . @3.00

PROTOTYPE
Malibu Ultraverse, 1993–95
1 V:Ultra-Tech,w/card 2.50
1a Ultra-lim. silver foil(c) 5.00
1b Hologram 6.00
2 I:Backstabber. 2.50
3 LeS(s),DvA,JmP,BWS, V:Ultra-
    Tech,BU:Rune 2.50
4 TMs(s),V:Wrath 2.25
5 TMs(s),A:Strangers,Break-
    Thru x-over 2.25
6 TMs(s),Origins Month C:Arena . . 2.25
7 TMs(s),V:Arena 2.25
8 TMs(s),V:Arena 2.25
9 Prototype Unplugged. 2.25
10 TMs(s),V:Prototype 2.25
11 TMs(s),R:Glare 2.25
12 V:Ultratech 2.25
13 Ultraverse Premiere #6. . . . . . . 3.50
14 Jimmy Ruiz, new boss 2.25
15 Techuza, Donovan 2.25
16 New CEO for Terrordy 2.25

Prototype #9
© Malibu

17 Ranger Vs. Engine 2.25
18 Turf War 2.50
G-Size, Hostile Takeover 2.50
Spec.#0 LeS,JQ/JP(c) 2.50

PROTOTYPE: TURF WAR
Malibu Ultraverse,
1 LeS,V:Techuza. 2.50
2 LeS,F:Ranger,Arena 2.50
3 . . . . 2.50

PROWLER
Eclipse, 1987
1 I:Prowler. 2.25
2 GN,A:Original Prowler 2.25
3 GN 2.25
4 GN 2.25
5 GN, adaption of Vampire Bat. . . . 2.25
6 w/flexi-disk record 2.25

PROWLER IN
`WHITE ZOMBIE', THE
Eclipse, 1988
1 . . . . 2.25

PRUDENCE &
CAUTION
Defiant, 1994
1 CCl(s), ... 4.00
1a Spanish Version 3.25
2 CCl(s), ... 2.50
2a Spanish Version 2.50
3 CCl(s), ... 2.50
3a Spanish Version 2.50
4 CCl(s), ... 2.50
4a Spanish Version 2.50
5 CCl(s), ... 2.50
5a Spanish Version 2.50

PSI-LORDS: REIGN OF
THE STARWATCHERS
Valiant, 1994
1 MLe,DG,Chromium(c),Valiant
    Vision,V:Spider Aliens 3.00
2 MLe,DG,V:Spider Aliens 2.25
3 MLe,DG,Chaos Effect-Epsilon#2,
    A:Solar. 2.25
becomes:

PSI-LORDS
4 V:Ravenrok 2.25
5 V:Ravenrok 2.25
6 . . . . 2.25
7 Micro-Invasion 2.25
8 A:Solar the Destroyer 2.25
9 Frozen Harbingers 2.25
10 F:Ravenrok 2.25

PSYCHO
Innovation
1 Hitchcock movie adapt 2.50
2 continued 2.50
3 continued 2.50

PSYCHOANALYSIS
Gemstone, 1999
1 (of 4) 2.50
2 . . . . 2.50
3 . . . . 2.50
TPB Ann. #1. . . . . 11.00

PSYCHOBLAST
First, 1987
1 thru 9 . . . . @2.25

PUBLIC DEFENDER IN ACTION
Charlton Comics, 1957
7	125.00
8 and 9	@75.00
10 thru 12,	@75.00

PUDGE PIG
Charlton Comics, 1958
1	50.00
2	35.00

PUNCTURE
Com.X, 2001
1 (of 12) by R. Uttley & B.Oliver	3.00
2 thru 4	@3.00
3 thru 6	@4.00

PUNX
Windjammer, 1995
1 KG,I:Punx	2.50
2 KG,A:Harbinger	2.50
3 KG,F:P.M.S	2.50
4 KG,final issue	2.50
Spec.#1	2.50

PUNX REDUX
1 thru 4	@2.50

PUNX
Acclaim, 1997
One Shot Spec. F:Big Max	2.50

PUPPET MASTER
Eternity
1 Movie Adapt.Andre Toulon	2.50
2 Puppets Protecting Diary	2.50
3 R:Andre Toulon	2.50
4	2.50

PUPPET MASTER: CHILDREN OF THE PUPPET MASTER
Eternity
1 Killer Puppets on the loose	2.50
2 concl.	2.50

PURGATORI
Chaos! Comics, 1998
1 DQ from slave to Goddess?	3.00
2 Goddess War,pt.1, x-over	3.00
3 Goddess War, epilog	3.00
4 Unholy Nights	3.00
5 V:Karmilla	3.00
6	3.00
7 V:Dracula	3.00
1-shot prelude	3.00
1-shot signed, limited + print	15.00
Coll. Vol. 1	6.00
Coll. Vol. 2	6.00
Coll. Vol. 3	6.00
Coll. Vol. 4	6.00

PURGATORI
Chaos! Comics, 2000
1/2	3.00
1/2 premium edition, tattoo(c)	10.00
1/2 chromium (c)	15.00
1/2 chromium signed	21.00
1/2 Ashcan	7.00
0	3.00
0 premium edition	10.00
0 Ashcan	7.00

PURGATORI: DARKEST HOUR
Chaos! Comics, 2001
1	3.00
1a premium ed. RCl(c)	10.00
2	3.00
2a variant (c)	7.50

PURGATORI: THE DRACULA GAMBIT
Chaos! Comics, 1997
1 DQ & Brian LeBlanc	3.00
1a signed	20.00
1b premium	10.00
Sketchbook, b&w	3.50

PURGATORI: EMPIRE
Chaos! Comics, 2000
1 (of 3)	3.00
1a premium	10.00
1b Comic Legal Defense Fund ed.	10.00
2	3.00
3 concl.	3.00
Preview Book B&W	5.00

PURGATORI: GODDESS RISING
Chaos! Comics, 1999
1 (of 4) MD2	3.00
1a premium edition	10.00
2	3.00
3	3.00
4 conclusion	3.00
Preview Book B&W	5.00

PURGATORI: GOD HUNTER
Chaos! Comics, 2002
Ashcan b&w	6.00
1 (of 2)	3.00
1a premium edition	10.00
2	3.00
2a variant Rio & Broeker (c)	7.50

PURGATORI: GOD KILLER
Chaos! Comics, 2002
1 (of 2)	3.00
1a premium edition	10.00
2	3.00
2a variant (c)	7.50

PURGATORI: HEART-BREAKER
Chaos! Comics, 2002
1	3.00
1a premium edition	10.00
1b super premium edition	20.00
1c MegaCon foil edition	25.00

PURGATORI: LOVE BITES
Chaos! Comics, 2001
1	3.00
1 premium edition	10.00
Ashcan	6.00

PURGATORI: MISCHIEF NIGHT
Chaos! Comics, 2001
1	3.00
1a premium edition	13.00
1b super premium edition	20.00

PURGATORI: THE HUNTED
Chaos! Comics, 2001
1	3.00
1a premium edition	10.00
2	3.00
2a variant (c)	7.50
Ashcan	6.00

PURGATORI: RAVENOUS
Chaos! Comics, 2002
Ashcan b&w	6.00
1 (of 2)	3.00
1a premium edition	10.00

PURGATORI: RE-IMAGINED
Chaos! Comics, 2002
1 Salem witch trials	3.00
1a premium edition	10.00
1b super premium edition	20.00
Ashcan Purgatori re-imagined	6.00

PURGATORI: SANCTIFIED
Chaos! Comics, 2002
1 BnP	3.00
1 premium edition	10.00

PURGATORI: TRICK OR TREAT
Chaos! Comics, 2002
1	3.00
1a premium edition	10.00
1b super premium edition	20.00

PURGATORI: THE VAMPIRES MYTH
Chaos! Comics, 1996
1 (of 3)	4.00
1-shot limited chromium edition	20.00
2 BnP,JBa	3.00
3 BnP,JBa, final issue	3.00
TPB with CD	25.00
TPB	13.00
Micro Premium Preview Book	15.00

PURGATORI VS. CHASTITY
Chaos! Comics, 2000
1 Alpha ending	3.00
1a Omega ending	3.00
1b deluxe	12.00

PURGATORI VS. LADY DEATH
Chaos! Comics, 2000
1	3.00
1a premium edition	10.00
Ashcan B&W	7.00

PURGATORI VS. VAMPIRELLA
Chaos! Comics, 2000
1	3.00
1 premium	10.00

QUANTUM & WOODY
Acclaim, 1997
1 CPr(s),MBr Woodrow Van Chelton & Eric Henderson become unlikely superheros	4.00

1a Variant (c) 5.00
2 CPr(s),MBr,World's worst
   superhero team 3.00
3 CPr(s),MBr,Woody buys a goat. . 3.00
4 CPr(s),MBr. 3.00
5 CPr(s),MBr. 2.75
6 CPr(s),MBr. 2.75
7 CPr(s),MBr. 2.75
8 CPr(s),MBr,R:Warrant 2.75
9 CPr(s),DCw,Woody is dying 2.75
10 CPr(s),MBr,trapped in each
   other's bodies, Goat month. . . . 2.75
11 CPr(s),MBr,switched body
   delimma 2.50
12 CPr(s),MBr,switched bodies 2.50
13 CPr(s),MBr,back in own bodies . 2.50
14 CPr(s),MBr,Magnum Force,pt.1 . 2.50
15 CPr(s),MBr,Magnum Force,pt.2 . 2.50
16 CPr(s),MBr,Magnum Force,pt.3 . 2.50
17 CPr(s),MBr,Magnum Force,pt.4 . 2.50
32 Dr. Eclipse, pt.3. . . . . 2.50
18 thru 27 . . . . @2.50
TPB Director's Cut, rep.#1–#4. . . . . 8.00
TPB Kiss Your Ass Goodbye 8.00
TPB Holy S-word We're Cancelled . 8.00
TPB Magnum Force. 8.00

QUANTUM LEAP
Innovation, 1991
{based on TV series}
1 1968 Memphis 3.50
1a Special Edition 2.50
2 Ohio 1962,Freedom of
   the Press 3.00
3 1958, The $50,000 Quest 3.00
4 Small Miracles 2.50
5 . . . . 2.50
6 . . . . 2.50
7 Golf Pro,School Bus Driver 2.50
8 1958,Bank Robber. 2.50
9 NY 1969,Gay Rights 2.50
10 1960s' Stand-up Comic. 2.50
11 1959,Dr.(LSD experiments). 2.50
12 . . . . 2.50

QUANTUM LEAP
Acclaim, 1997
1 BML(s),Into the Void, pt.1 . . . . . . 2.50
2 BML(s),Into the Void, pt.2 . . . . . . 2.50
3 BML(s),Into the Void, pt.3 . . . . . . 2.50
Spec. The Leaper Before. 4.00

QUEEN OF THE
DAMNED
Innovation, 1991
1 Anne Rice Adapt.On the Road
   to the Vampire Lestat 3.50
2 Adapt. continued 2.50
3 The Devils Minion 2.50
4 Adapt.continued 2.50
5 Adapt.continued 2.50
6 Adapt.continued 2.50
7 Adapt.continued 2.50
8 Adapt.continued 2.50

QUICK-DRAW McGRAW
Charlton Comics, 1970–72
1 TV Animated Cartoon 75.00
2 . . . . 40.00
3 . . . . 40.00
4 thru 8 . . . . @40.00

Q-UNIT
Harris
1 I:Q-Unit,w/card. 3.25

RACE AGAINST TIME
Dark Ange., 1997
1 . . . . 2.50
2 . . . . 2.50

RACE FOR THE MOON
Harvey Publications, 1958
1 BP 175.00
2 JK,AW,JK/AW(c) 300.00
3 JK,AW,JK/AW(c) 350.00

RACER-X
Premiere
Spec.#1 . . . . 5.00
Now, 1988
1 thru 3 . . . . @2.50
4 thru 11 . . . . @2.25
[2nd Series], 1989
1 thru 10 . . . . @2.25

Racer-X #3
© WildStorm

RACER X
WildStorm/DC, 2000
1 (of 3) Rex Racer's secrets. 2.50
1a variant (c) (1:4) 2.50
2 racing thrills 2.50
3 conclusion 3.00

RACK & PAIN: KILLERS
Chaos! Comics, 1996
1 (of 4) JaL(c) 3.00
2 BnP,LJi,JaL(c) 3.00
3 (of 4) BnP,LJi, ... 3.00
4 BnP,LJi, final issue. 3.00

RADICAL DREAMER
Blackball, 1994
0 . . . . 2.25
1 thru 5 V:Jorge Futran. . . . . @2.50

RADIOACTIVE MAN
Bongo, 1993
1 I:Radioactive Man 4.00
1 80pg offered again. 3.25
88 V:Lava Man. 2.25
212 V:Hypno Head. 2.25
412 V:Dr. Crab, with trading card . . 2.25
679 with trading card 2.25

1000 Final issue. 2.25

RADIOACTIVE MAN
Bongo Comics, 2000
100 . . . . 2.50
136 . . . . 2.50
222 . . . . 2.50
4 . . . . 2.50
575 new Radioactive Man born. . . . 2.50
106 new Radioactive Man insane . . 2.50
7 . . . . 2.50
8 Official Movie Adaptation 3.00
Spec. Movie Adaptation 3.00

RAEL
Eclipse
Vol 1. . . . . 7.00

RAGAMUFFINS
Eclipse, 1985
1 . . . . 3.00

RAI
Valiant, 1991
0 DL,O:Bloodshot,I:2nd Rai,D:X-O,
   Archer,Shadowman,F:all Valiant
   heroes,bridges Valiant Universe
   1992-4001 . . . . 3.00
1 V:Grandmother 5.00
2 V:Icespike 2.50
3 V:Humanists,Makiko 3.00
4 V:Makiko,rarest Valiant 4.00
5 Rai leaves earth, C:Eternal
   Warrior. 2.50
6 FM(c),Unity#7,V:Pierce 2.50
7 WS(c),Unity#15,V:Pierce,
   D:Rai,A:Magnus 2.50
8 Epilogue of Unity in 4001 . . . . . . 2.50
Becomes:

RAI AND THE
FUTURE FORCE
Valiant, 1993
9 F:Rai,E.Warrior of 4001,Tekla,
   X-O Commander,Spylocke 2.50
9a Gold Ed. 3.00
10 Rai vs. Malev Emperor 2.25
11 SCh,V:Malevolents 2.25
12 V:Cyber Raiders 2.25
13 Spylocke Revealed 2.25
14 SCh,D:M'Ree 2.25
15 SCh,V:X-O 2.25
16 SCh,V:Malevs 2.25
17 . . . . 2.25
18 JOs(s),Spk,V:Malevs. 2.25
19 JCf,V:Malves. 2.25
20 JOs(s),DR,V:Malves,Spylocke
   realed to be Spider Alien. 2.25
21 DR,I:Starwatchers,b:Torque,
   w/Valiant Era card 2.25
22 DR,D:2nd Rai, A:Starwatchers . . 2.25
23 DR,A:Starwatchers,. 2.25
24 DR,in Tibet 2.25
25 DR,F:Spylocke 2.25
26 DR,Chaos Effect-Epsilon#3,
   A:Solar Magnus,Psi-Lords. 2.25
Becomes:

RAI
Valiant, 1994
27 Rising Son 2.25
28 V:Takashi 2.25
29 A:Rentaro Nakadai 2.25
30 Splocke 2.25
31 Bad Penny pt. 1 . . . . 2.25
32 Bad Penny pt. 2, F:Axscan 2.25
33 F:Spylocke, Rentaro 2.25
TPB #0–#4 . . . . 12.00

TPB Star System ed. 12.00

RAKAN
Studio G, 2003
1 . . . . 3.00
2 Den of Thieves 3.00
3 . . . . 3.00
4 . . . . 3.00

RALPH SNART ADVENTURES
Now
[Volumes 1 & 2]
see B&W
9 and 10, color 2.50
[Volume 3], 1988
1 . . . . 4.00
2 thru 10 . . . . @3.00
11 thru 21 . . . . @2.50
22 thru 26 . . . . @2.50
TPB 10.00
[Volume 4], 1992
1 thru 3, with 1 of 2 trading cards. . 2.50
[Volume 5], 1993
1 thru 5, with 1 of 2 trading cards. . 2.50
3-D Spec.#1 with 3-D glasses and
  12 trading cards. 3.50
TPB Let's Get Naked (2003) 25.00
TPB Vol. 2 Let's Be Good Citizens 25.00

RANDOM 5
Amara Inc., 1995
1 I:Random 5 . . . . 2.25

RANGO
Dell Publishing Co., 1967
1 Tim Conway Ph(c) 45.00

RANMA 1/2
Viz, 1992
1 I:Ranma 50.00
2 I:Upperclassmen Kuno 30.00
3 F:Upperclassmen Kuno 25.00
4 Confusion. 5.00
5 A:Ryoga 5.00
6 Ryoga plots revenge 9.00
7 Conclusion. 5.00
[Part 2], 1992
1 . . . . 8.00
2 . . . . 5.00
3 thru 7 . . . . @4.00
8 . . . . 5.00
9 . . . . 6.00
10 and 11 . . . . @3.00
continued, see B&W Pub.

RAPHAEL
Mirage, 1987
1 TMNTurtle characters 8.00

RARE BREED
Dark Moon Productions, 1995
1 V:Anarchy 2.50
2 V:Anarchy 2.50

RAT BASTARD
Crucial Comics, 1997
1 by The Huja Brothers. 2.25
2 thru 6 . . . . @2.25

RAT PATROL, THE
Dell Publishing Co., 1967
1 Ph(c) 125.00

---

2 . . . . 75.00
3 thru 6 Ph(c) . . . . @60.00

RAVEN
Renaissance Comics, 1993
1 I:Raven 2.50
2 V:Macallister 2.50
3 thru 5 . . . . @2.50
6 V:Nightmare Creatures 2.75

RAVEN HOUSE
Crossgen Comics, 2004
1 . . . . 3.00
2 . . . . 3.00

RAVENING
Avatar, 1998
1/2 Busch (c) F:Ravyn & Glyph . . . 3.00
1/2a Meadows(c) 3.00
1/2d Sketched Edition. 60.00
1/2e Blood Red Foil, signed 9.00

RAVENS AND RAINBOWS
Pacific, 1983
1 . . . . 2.25

Raver #3
© Malibu

RAVER
Malibu, 1993
1 Prism cover 3.00
1a Newsstand 2.25
2 . . . . 2.25
3 Walter Koenig(s) 2.25
4 and 5 . . . . @2.00

RAY BRADBURY CHRONICLES
Byron Press
1 short stories 10.00
2 short stories 10.00
3 short stories 10.00

RAY BRADBURY COMICS
Topps, 1993–94
1 thru 5 with Trading Card . . . . . @3.25
Spec.#1 The Illustrated Man 3.00
Spec. Trilogy of Terror 2.50
Spec. The Martian Chronicles 3.00

R.A.Z.E.
Firstlight
1 I:R.A.Z.E., Secret Weapon 3.00
2 V:Exterminators 3.00

RAZOR
London Night Studios, 1992
0 . . . . 9.00
0a 2nd printing (Fathom 1992) 4.00
0b reprint (1995) 3.00
1 I:Stryke (Fathom 1992) 9.00
1a second printing 3.00
2 J.O'Barr (c) 10.00
2a limited ed., red & blue 19.00
2b platinum ed. 20.00
3 Jim Balent (c). 7.00
3a with poster 15.00
4 . . . . 4.00
4a with poster 9.00
5 . . . . 7.00
5a platinum ed. 15.00
6 . . . . 5.00
7 . . . . 4.00
8 . . . . 3.00
9 . . . . 3.00
10 . . . . 3.00
11 & 12 B&W, Rituals,pt.1&2 . . . . @3.00
1/2 (1995). 5.00
Ann.#1 I:Shi (1993) 25.00
Ann.#2 O:Razor B&W (1994) 35.00
Becomes:

RAZOR UNCUT
See: B&W

RAZOR
Volume 2
London Knight, 1996
1 DQ, ... 3.00
1a holochrome edition 5.00
2 DQ 3.00
2a holochrome edition 4.00
3 thru 7 . . . . @3.00
Razor Analog Burn. 2.50

RAZOR AND SHI SPECIAL
London Night Studios, 1994
1 Rep. Razor Ann.#1 + new art . . . 5.00
1a platinum version 9.00

RAZOR ARCHIVES
London Night, 1997
1 & 2 see B&W
3 rep. Razor #10–12 . . . . 7.00

RAZOR BURN
London Night Studios, 1994
1 V:Styke. 3.00
1a signed 5.00
2 Searching for Styke 3.00
2a Platinum. 7.00
3 Stryke's War. 3.00
4 D:Razor, bagged 3.00
5 Epilogue. 3.00

RAZOR: CRY NO MORE
London Night Studios, 1995
1-shot 3.00
1a variant 4.00
1b Commemorative (1999). 6.00

RAZOR: HEX & VIOLENCE
EH! Productions, 2000
0 EHr. 3.00

RAZOR/MORBID ANGEL: SOUL SEARCH
London Night, 1996
1 (of 3)	3.00
1 platinum edition	5.00
1 Chromium edition	7.00
2	3.00
3	3.00

RAZOR/POISON/ AREALA WARRIOR NUN: LITTLE BAD ANGELS
London Night, 1999
Spec. x-over Raxor cover	4.00
Spec.A Poison cover	4.00
Spec.B Areala cover	4.00

RAZOR THE RAVENING
Avatar
1	3.50
1a Previews cover	3.50
1b Bondage cover	6.00

RAZOR'S EDGE, THE: WARBLADE
Wildstorm/DC, 2004
1 SBs	3.00

RAZOR: THE SUFFERING
London Night Studios, 1994
1	4.00
1a Director's cut	3.00
1b signed, limited	9.00
2	3.00
2a Director's cut	2.50
3 final chapter	3.00

RAZOR: TORTURE
London Night Studios, 1995
0 Razor back from dead	4.00
0a signed edition	7.00
1	3.00
1a Commemorative (1999)	6.00
2	3.00
3 EHr.	3.00
4	3.00
5 alt. cover, signed	4.00
6 alt. cover, signed	4.00

Razor Torture #6
© London Night Studios

7	3.00

RAZOR SWIMSUIT SPECIAL
London Night Studios, 1995
1 pin-ups	3.00
1a platinum version	7.00
1b commemorative edition	4.00

RAZOR/WARRIOR NUN AREALA: DARK MENACE
London Night, 1999
Spec. x-over	4.00
Spec.A x-over, variant cover	4.00

RAZOR/WARRIOR NUN AREALA: FAITH
London Night, 1996
1 by Jude Millien	3.00
1a variant cover	4.00

REAL GHOSTBUSTERS
Now, 1988
1 KSy(c)	4.50
2 thru 7	@2.50
8 thru 24	@2.00

[2nd Series], 1991
1 Halloween Special	2.25
Ann. 3-D w/glasses & pinups	3.00

REALITY CHECK
Sirius, 1996
1 by Tavicat	3.00
2 thru 8	@3.00
9 Nonesuch Nonsense, pt.1	3.00
10 Nonesuch Nonsense, pt.2	3.00
11 Nonesuch Nonsense, pt.3	3.00
12 Nonesuch Nonsense, pt.4	3.00
TPB Vol. 1	18.00
TPB Vol. 2, rep.#7–#12	18.00

REAL WAR STORIES
Eclipse, 1987–91
1 BB	3.00
1a 2nd printing	2.25
2	5.00

RE-ANIMATOR
Adventure Comics, 1991
1 movie adaption	3.00
2 movie adaption	3.00

RE-ANIMATOR
Adventure
1 Prequel to Orig movie	2.50

RE-ANIMATOR: DAWN OF THE RE-ANIMATOR
Adventure, 1992
1 Prequel to movie	2.50
2	2.50
3	2.50
4 V:Erich Metler	2.50

RE-ANIMATOR: TALES OF HERBERT WEST
Adventure Comics
1 H.P.Lovecraft stories	5.00

RED
DC Wildstorm July, 2003
America's Best Comics
1 (of 3) WEI,CHm	3.00
2 WEI,CHm	3.00
3 WEI,CHm	3.00
TPB Red/Tokyo Storm Warning	15.00

RED DOG
Eclipse, 1988
1 CR,Mowgli Jungle Book story	2.50

RED DRAGON
Comico, 1995
1 SBs,I:Red Dragon	2.50
2 How Soon is Nau?	3.00

REDEEMER, THE
Black Library, 2002
1	3.50
2 thru 4	@3.50

REDEEMERS
Antarctic Press, 1997
1 (of 5) by Herb Mallette & Patrick Blain	3.00
2	3.00

RED SONJA in 3-D
Blackthorne
1 thru 3	@2.50

RED SONJA
Cross Plains Comics, 1999
1 Death in Scarlet,pt.1	3.00
1a photo (c)	3.00
2 Death in Scarlet,pt.2	3.00
3 Death in Scarlet,pt.3	3.00

RED STAR, THE
Archangel Studios, 2002
Vol. 2
2	3.00
3 thru 6	@3.00
4	3.00
TPB Red Star Collected Edition	25.00
Annual #1 foil (c) signed	10.00
TPB Vol. 1 Battle of Kar Dathras Gate	25.00
TPB Vol. 2 Nokgorka	25.00
TPB Vol. 3 Prison of Souls	25.00

REESE'S PIECES
Eclipse, 1985
1 reprint from Web of Horror	2.25
2 reprint from Web of Horror	2.25

RE: GEX
Awesome Entertainment, 1998
0 RLe,	2.50
0a Red Foil variant	4.00
1 RLe,JLb	2.50
1a Platinum cover	7.00
1b Red Foil cover	12.00
1c Variant RL cover	4.00
1d prime	3.00
1e prime millennium ed.	5.00
2 RLe,JLb	2.50
2a prime	2.99
2b Millennium edition	5.00
3 RLe,A:The Coven,V:Youngblood	2.50
Con Spec. '98	5.00
Orlando Megacon ashcan	10.00

COLOR PUB.

Orlando Megacon ashcan, signed. 20.00

Arcade Comics, 2002
Ashcan #1, Museum Edition 60.00
Ashcan #1, Museum Ed., signed. . 80.00

REGGIE
Archie Publications, 1963–65
15 thru 18 . . . . @75.00
Becomes:

REGGIE AND ME
Archie Publications, 1966–80
19 . . . . 50.00
20 thru 23 . . . . @30.00
24 thru 40 . . . . @25.00
41 thru 50 . . . . @15.00
51 thru 99 . . . . @10.00
100 . . . . 15.00
101 thru 126 . . . . @8.00

REGGIE'S WISE GUY JOKES
Archie Publications, April, 1968
1 . . . . 60.00
2 . . . . 30.00
3 . . . . 30.00
4 . . . . 30.00
5 thru 15 Giants . . . . @30.00
16 thru 28 Giants . . . . @25.00
29 thru 40 . . . . @15.00
41 thru 60 . . . . @12.00
11 thru 59 . . . . @10.00
60 Jan., 1982 . . . . 10.00

REIVERS
Enigma
1 thru 3 Rock 'n' Roll . . . . @3.00

RELOAD
DC Homage, 2003
1 (of 3) WEI,JP 3.00
2 WEI,JP 3.00
3 WEI,JP, concl. 3.00
TPB Reload/Mek 15.00

REMAINS
IDW Publishing, 2004
1 . . . . 4.00
2 thru 5 . . . . @4.00

REPTILICUS
Charlton Comics, 1961
1 . . . . 300.00
2 . . . . 150.00
Becomes:

REPTISAURUS
1962
3 . . . . 125.00
4 . . . . 100.00
5 . . . . 100.00
6 . . . . 100.00
7 . . . . 100.00
8 Summer, 1963 . . . . 100.00

RESIDENT EVIL: FIRE & ICE
WildStorm/DC, 2000
1 (of 4) from videogame 2.50
2 . . . . 2.50
3 . . . . 2.50
4 concl. 2.50
TPB Codename Veronica, Vol. 1 . . 15.00
TPB Codename Veronica, Vol. 3 . . 15.00
TPB Code Veronica, Vol. 4 . . . . . . 15.00

RESISTANCE, THE
WildStorm/DC, 2002
1 JP(s),techno sci-fi 3.00
2 JP(s) 3.00
3 JP(s) 3.00
4 JP(s) 3.00
5 JP(s),V:Sampizi 3.00
6 JP(s),V:Sampizi & GCC 3.00
7 JP(s),F:Version Mary 3.00
8 JP(s),F:Version Mary 3.00

RETURN OF KONGA, THE
Charlton Comics, 1962
N# 100.00

RETURN OF MEGATON MAN
Kitchen Sink, 1988
1 Don Simpson art (1988) 2.25
2 Don Simpson art 2.25
3 Don Simpson art 2.25

RETURN TO JURASSIC PARK
Topps, 1995
1 R:Jurassic Park 3.00
2 V:Blosyn Team, Army. 3.00
3 The Hunted 3.00
4 Army. 3.00
5 Heirs to the Thunder,pt.1 . . . . . 3.00
6 Heirs to the Thunder,pt.2 . . . . . 3.00
7 Inquiring Minds,pt.1 . . . . 3.00
8 Photo Finish, concl. 3.00
9 Jurassic Jam issue 3.00

REVELATIONS
one-shot by Jim Krueger 4.00

REVENGE OF THE PROWLER
Eclipse, 1988
1 GN,R:Prowler. 2.25
2 GN,A:Fighting Devil Dogs with
  Flexi-Disk. 2.50
3 GN,A:Devil Dogs 2.25
4 GN,V:Pirahna. 2.25

REVENGERS
Continuity, 1985
1 NA,O:Megalith,I:Crazyman 4.00
2 NA,Megalith meets Armor & Silver
Streak,Origin Revengers#1 . . . . . . 2.50
3 NA/NR,Origin Revengers #2 . . . 2.50
4 NA,Origin Revengers #3 . . . . . . 2.50
5 NA,Origin Revengers #4 . . . . . . 2.50
6 I:Hybrids. 3.00
Spec. #1 F:Hybrids 5.00

RIBIT
Comico
1 FT,Mini-series 3.00
2 FT,Mini-series 3.00
3 FT,Mini-series 3.00
4 FT,Mini-series 3.00

RICHIE RICH
Harvey Publications, 1960–91
1 . . . . 2,700.00
2 . . . . 1,000.00
3 . . . . 600.00
4 . . . . 600.00
5 . . . . 600.00
6 . . . . 350.00
7 . . . . 350.00

8 Christmas(c) 350.00
9 . . . . 350.00
10 . . . . 350.00
11 thru 20 . . . . @225.00
21 thru 41 . . . . @150.00
42 Flying Saucer 150.00
43 thru 55 . . . . @125.00
56 Super Richie 120.00
57 . . . . 100.00
58 . . . . 100.00
59 Buck 125.00
60 thru 80 . . . . @100.00
81 thru 99 . . . . @40.00
100 Irona-Robot Maid 50.00
101 thru 111 . . . . @25.00
112 thru 116 52 pg Giants . . . . . @30.00
117 thru 120 . . . . @25.00
121 thru 136 . . . . @20.00
137 Mr. Cheepers 30.00
138 thru 160 . . . . @15.00
161 thru 180 . . . . @12.00
181 thru 236 . . . . @8.00
237 Money Monster 10.00
238 thru 254 . . . . @7.00

RICHIE RICH
Harvey, 1991
1 thru 15 . . . . @3.00
16 thru 28 . . . . @3.00

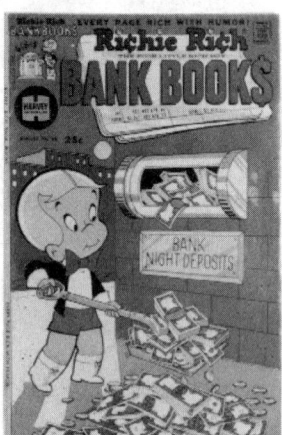
Richie Rich Bank Books #24
© Harvey Publications

RICHIE RICH BANK BOOKS
Harvey, 1972–82
1 . . . . 75.00
2 Money Monster 55.00
3 thru 5 . . . . @50.00
6 thru 10 . . . . @35.00
11 thru 20 . . . . @25.00
21 thru 30 . . . . @15.00
31 thru 40 . . . . @10.00
41 thru 59 . . . . @8.00

RICHIE RICH BILLIONS
Harvey, 1974–82
1 . . . . 50.00
2 thru 5 . . . . @30.00
6 thru 10 . . . . @25.00
11 thru 20 . . . . @15.00
21 thru 30 . . . . @10.00

COLOR PUB.

31 thru 48 . . . . @8.00

RICHIE RICH
DIAMONDS
Harvey, 1972–82

1	. . . . 75.00
2 thru 5	. . . . @35.00
6 thru 10	. . . . @30.00
11 thru 20	. . . . @25.00
21 thru 30	. . . . @12.00
31 thru 59	. . . . @10.00

RICHIE RICH
DOLLARS & CENTS
Harvey Publications, 1963–82

1	. . . . 225.00
2	. . . . 125.00
3 thru 5	. . . . @75.00
6 thru 10	. . . . @50.00
11 thru 24	. . . . @35.00
25 Nurse Jenny	. . . . 38.00
26 thru 30	. . . . @30.00
31 thru 43	. . . . @25.00
44 thru 60	. . . . @20.00
61 thru 70	. . . . @15.00
71 thru 99	. . . . @10.00
100 Anniversary	. . . . 12.00
102 thru 109	. . . . @10.00

RICHIE RICH
FORTUNES
Harvey, 1971–82

1	. . . . 75.00
2 thru 5	. . . . @50.00
6 thru 10	. . . . @40.00
11 Orion	. . . . 25.00
12 thru 20	. . . . @20.00
21 thru 30	. . . . @10.00
31 thru 63	. . . . @8.00

RICHIE RICH
GEMS
Harvey, 1974–82

1	. . . . 50.00
2 thru 5	. . . . @30.00
6 thru 10	. . . . @25.00
11 thru 20	. . . . @20.00
21 thru 30	. . . . @10.00
31 thru 35	. . . . @8.00
36 Orion	. . . . 10.00
37	. . . . 8.00
38 Stoneage Riches	. . . . 10.00
39 thru 43	. . . . @8.00

RICHIE RICH
JACKPOTS
Harvey, 1974–82

1	. . . . 75.00
2 thru 5	. . . . @50.00
6 thru 15	. . . . @30.00
16 Super Richie	. . . . 32.00
17 thru 20	. . . . @25.00
21 thru 30	. . . . @12.00
31 thru 58	. . . . @10.00

RICHIE RICH MILLIONS
Harvey Publications, 1961–82

1	. . . . 275.00
2	. . . . 175.00
3 thru 10	. . . . 150.00
11 thru 20	. . . . @100.00
21 thru 30	. . . . @75.00
31 Orion, giant	. . . . 40.00
32 thru 60	. . . . @30.00

Richie Rich Jackpots #29
© Harvey

61 thru 67	. . . . @25.00
68 Super Richie	. . . . 25.00
69 thru 74	. . . . @20.00
75 thru 94	. . . . @18.00
95 thru 113	. . . . @12.00

RICHIE RICH
MONEY WORLD
Harvey, 1972–82

1 Mayda Monny	. . . . 85.00
2 Super Richie	. . . . 60.00
3 thru 5	. . . . @50.00
6 thru 10	. . . . @35.00
11 thru 20	. . . . @18.00
21 thru 30	. . . . @10.00
31 thru 59	. . . . @8.00

RICHIE RICH
PROFITS
Harvey, 1974–82

1	. . . . 60.00
2 thru 5	. . . . @30.00
6 thru 10	. . . . @25.00
11 thru 20	. . . . @20.00
21 thru 30	. . . . @10.00
31 thru 47	. . . . @8.00

RICHIE RICH
RICHES
Harvey, 1972–82

1 Money Monster	. . . . 90.00
2 thru 5	. . . . @50.00
6 thru 10	. . . . @30.00
11 thru 16	. . . . @20.00
17 Super Richie	. . . . 22.00
18 thru 30	. . . . @15.00
31 thru 59	. . . . @10.00

RICHIE RICH
SUCCESS STORIES
Harvey Publications, 1964–82

1	. . . . 275.00
2 thru 5	. . . . @150.00
6 thru 10	. . . . @100.00
11 thru 26	. . . . @75.00
27 Penny Van Dough	. . . . 78.00
28 thru 43	. . . . @50.00
44 Super Richie	. . . . 35.00
45 thru 55	. . . . @35.00

56 thru 66	. . . . @20.00
67 thru 105	. . . . @15.00

RICHIE RICH
VAULT OF MYSTERY
Harvey, 1974–82

1	. . . . 50.00
2 thru 5	. . . . @30.00
6 thru 10	. . . . @15.00
11 thru 20	. . . . @10.00
21 thru 30	. . . . @10.00
31 thru 47	. . . . @10.00

RICHIE RICH
ZILLIONZ
Harvey, 1976–82

1	. . . . 35.00
2 thru 5	. . . . @20.00
6 thru 10	. . . . @15.00
11 thru 20	. . . . @10.00
21 thru 33	. . . . @8.00

RIFLEMAN, THE
Dell Publishing Co., 1959

1 Chuck Connors Ph(c) all	. . . . 350.00
2 Ph(c)	. . . . 200.00
3 ATh,Ph(c)	. . . . 175.00
4 Ph(c)	. . . . 165.00
5 Ph(c)	. . . . 165.00
6 ATh	. . . . 175.00
7 thru 10 Ph(c)	. . . . @150.00
11 thru 20	. . . . @125.00

RIOT GEAR
Triumphant, 1993

1 JnR(s),I:Riot Gear	. . . . 2.50
2 JnR(s),I:Rabin	. . . . 2.50
3 JnR(s),I:Surzar	. . . . 2.50
4 JnR(s),D:Captain Tich	. . . . 2.50
5 JnR(s),reactions	. . . . 2.50
6 JnR(s),Tich avenged	. . . . 2.50
7 JnR(s),Information Age	. . . . 2.50
8 JnR(s),	. . . . 2.50

RIOT GEAR:
VIOLENT PAST
Triumphant, 1994

1 and 2	. . . . @2.50

R.I.P.
TSR, 1990–91

1 thru 4	. . . . @3.00
5 thru 8 Brasher, Avenger of the Dead	. . . . @3.00

RIPFIRE
Malibu, 1995

0 Prequel to Ripfire Series	. . . . . . 2.50

RIPLEY'S BELIEVE IT
OR NOT!
Gold Key, 1967–80

4 Ph(c),AMc	. . . . 60.00
5 GE,JJ	. . . . 40.00
6 AMc	. . . . 40.00
7	. . . . 35.00
8	. . . . 40.00
9	. . . . 35.00
10 GE	. . . . 40.00
11	. . . . 30.00
12	. . . . 30.00
13	. . . . 30.00
14	. . . . 30.00
15 GE	. . . . 35.00

16	30.00
17	30.00
18	30.00
19	30.00
20	30.00
21 thru 30	@25.00
31 thru 38	@20.00
39 RC	20.00
40 thru 50	@18.00
51 thru 94	@15.00

RISE OF THE SNAKEMEN
Crossgen Comics 2003

1	3.00
2 thru 3	@3.00

RISK
Maximum Press, 1995

1 V:Furious	2.50

ROB
Awesome Entertainment, 1999

1 RLe	2.50

ROBERT E. HOWARD'S
Cross Plains Comics, 1999

GN Marchers of Valhalla	7.00
GN Wolfshead	7.00
GN Worms of the Earth	10.00

ROBIN HOOD
Eclipse, 1991

1 TT,Historically accurate series	2.75
2 and 3 TT	@2.75

ROBO DOJO
WildStorm/DC, 2002

1 (of 6) MWn, 40-pg.	3.50
2 MWn,	3.00
3 MWn,	3.00
4 MWn,Techno Council.	3.00
5 MWn,Robojin revolt	3.00
6 MWn,traitor revealed, concl.	3.00

ROBO HUNTER
Eagle

1	2.25
2 thru 5	@2.25

ROBOTECH
Antarctic Press, 1997

1 by Fred Perry & BDn	3.00
2	3.00
3	3.00
4 Rolling Thunder, pt.1	3.00
5 Rolling Thunder, pt.2	3.00
6 Rolling Thunder, pt.3	3.00
7 Rolling Thunder, pt.4	3.00
8 Variants, pt.1	3.00
9 Variants, pt.2	3.00
10 Variants, pt.3	3.00
11 Variants, pt.4	3.00
TPB Megastorm by Fred Perry & Ben Dunn	8.00
Spec.1-shot Robotech: Final Fire	3.00
Spec.1-shot Robotech: Class Reunion	3.00

ROBOTECH
Wildstorm/DC, 2002

0 JLe	2.50
1 (of 6) JLe	3.00
2	3.00
3	3.00
4	3.00

5	3.00
6 SeP, concl.	3.00
Spec. Robotech Sourcebook	3.00
TPB From the Stars	10.00

Robotech Genesis, The Legend of Zor
#6 © Eternity

ROBOTECH: GENESIS
THE LEGEND OF ZOR
Eternity

1 O:Robotech w/cards	3.00
1a Limited Edition,extra pages with cards #1 & #2.	6.00
2 thru 6, each with cards.	@2.50

ROBOTECH IN 3-D
Comico, 1985

1	2.50

ROBOTECH: INVASION
Wildstorm/DC, 2004

1 (of 5)	3.00
2 thru 5	@3.00

ROBOTECH:
LOVE AND WAR
Wildstorm/DC July, 2003

1 (of 6) Max and Miriya.	3.00
2 flight school	3.00
3 Max and Miriya meet	3.00
4 Max and Miriya fight	3.00
5 Dixon dead.	3.00
6 conclusion	3.00

ROBOTECH,
THE MACROSS SAGA
Comico, 1985–89
(formerly Macross)

2	5.00
3	4.00
4	3.50
5	3.50
6 J:Rick Hunter.	3.50
7 V:Zentraedi	3.00
8 A:Rick Hunter.	3.00
9 V:Zentraedi	3.00
10 Blind Game.	3.00
11 V:Zentraedi	3.00
12 V:Zentraedi	3.00
13 V:Zentraedi	3.00

14 Gloval's Reports	3.00
15 V:Zentraedi	3.00
16 V:Zentraedi	3.00
17 V:Zentraedi	3.00
18 D:Roy Fokker	3.00
19 V:Khyron	3.00
20 V:Zentraedi	3.00
21 A New Dawn	3.00
22 V:Zentraedi	3.00
23 Reckless	3.00
24 HB,V:Zentraedi	3.00
25 Wedding Bells.	3.00
26 The Messenger	3.00
27 Force of Arms	3.00
28 Reconstruction Blues	3.00
29 Robotech Masters.	3.00
30 Viva Miriya	3.00
31 Khyron's Revenge	3.00
32 Broken Heart.	3.00
33 A Rainy Night	3.00
34 Private Time	3.00
35 Season's Greetings	3.00
36 last issue.	3.00
Graphic Novel #1	6.00

ROBOTECH:
THE MACROSS SAGA
Wildstorm/DC, 2003

TPB Vol. 1	15.00
TPB Vol. 2	15.00
TPB Vol. 3	15.00
TPB Vol. 4	15.00

ROBOTECH MASTERS
Comico, 1985–88

1	4.00
2	3.00
3 Space Station Liberty.	3.00
4 V:Bioroids.	2.50
5 V:Flagship	2.50
6 Prelude to Battle	2.50
7 The Trap	2.50
8 F:Dana Sterling	2.50
9 Star Dust	2.50
10 V:Zor.	2.50
11 A:De Ja Vu	2.50
12 2OR.	2.50
13	2.50
14 Clone Chamber,V:Zor.	2.50
15 Love Song.	2.50
16 V:General Emerson	2.50
17 Mind Games	2.50
18 Dana in Wonderland.	2.50
19	2.50
20 A:Zor,Musica.	2.50
21 Final Nightmare	2.50
22 The Invid Connection	2.50
23 Catastrophe, final issue	2.50

ROBOTECH:
THE NEW GENERATION
Comico, 1985–88

1	4.00
2 The Lost City	3.00
3 V:Yellow Dancer.	3.00
4 A:Yellow Dancer.	3.00
5 SK(i),A:Yellow Dancer	3.00
6 F:Rook Bartley.	3.00
7 Paper Hero	3.00
8	3.00
9 KSy,The Genesis Pit	3.00
10 V:The Invid	3.00
11 F:Scott Bernard.	3.00
12 V:The Invid	3.00
13 V:The Invid	3.00
14 Annie's Wedding.	3.00
15 Seperate Ways	3.00
16 Metamorphosis	3.00

COLOR PUB.

17 Midnight Sun	3.00
18	3.00
19	3.00
20 Birthday Blues	3.00
21 Hired Gun	3.00
22 The Big Apple	3.00
23 Robotech Wars	3.00
24 Robotech Wars	3.00
25 V:Invid, last issue	3.00

ROBOTECH SPECIAL DANA'S STORY
Eclipse

1	5.00

ROBOTECH II: THE SENTINELS
Eternity

Swimsuit Spec.#1	3.00

ROB ZOMBIE'S SPOOKSHOW INTERNATIONAL
Crossgen Comics, 2003

1 (of 5)	3.50
2 thru 3	@3.00

MVCreations (2004)

4 thru 10	@3.00

ROCK 'N' ROLL
Revolutionary, 1990
Prev: Black & White

15 Poison	6.00
16 Van Halen	5.00
17 Madonna	6.00
18 AliceCooper	5.00
19 Public Enemy, 2 Live Crew	5.00
20 Queensryche	5.00
21 Prince	5.00
22 AC/DC	5.00
23 Living Color	5.00
24 Anthrax	5.00
25 Z.Z.Top	5.00
26 Doors	5.00
27 Doors	5.00
28 Ozzy Osbourne	6.00
29 The Cure	5.00
30	5.00
31 Vanilla Ice	5.00
32 Frank Zappa	5.00
33 Guns n' Roses	5.00
34 The Black Crowes	5.00
35 R.E.M.	5.00
36 Michael Jackson	5.00
37 Ice T	5.00
38 Rod Stewart	5.00
39 New Kids on the Block	5.00
40 N.W.A./Ice Cube	5.00
41 Paula Abdul	5.00
42 Metallica II	5.00
43 Guns `N' Roses	5.00
44 Scorpions	5.00
45 Greatful Dead	5.00
46 Grateful Dead	5.00
47 Grateful Dead	5.00
48 (now b/w),Queen	5.00
49 Rush	5.00
50 Bob Dylan Pt.1	5.00
51 Bob Dylan Pt.2	5.00
52 Bob Dylan Pt.3	5.00
53 Bruce Springsteen	5.00
54 U2 Pt.1	5.00
55 U2 Pt.2	5.00
56 David Bowie	5.00
57 thru 58	@4.00
59 Eric Clampton	5.00

60 thru 63	@4.00
64 San Francisco	4.00
65 Pink Floyd	4.00

ROCK 'N' ROLL HIGH SCHOOL
Cosmic Comics, 1995

1 Sequel to the movie	2.50

ROCKETEER
Walt Disney, 1991

1 DSt(c)RH,MovieAdaptation	7.00
Newsstand Version	3.25

ROCKETEER ADVENTURE MAGAZINE
Comico, 1988

1 DSt,MK,Rocketeer(6thApp.)	10.00
2 DSt,MK,Rocketeer(7thApp.)	8.00

ROCKETEER SPECIAL
Eclipse, 1984

1 DSt, Rocketeer(5th App.)	15.00

ROCKET MAN: KING OF THE ROCKET MEN
Innovation

1 thru 4 Adapts movie series	@2.50

ROCKET RANGER
Adventure Comics, 1991

1 (of 12) from computer game	3.00

ROCKMEEZ
Jzink Comics, 1992

1 I:Rockmeez,V:Pyrites	2.50
2 V:Pyrites,Silv.Embos.(c)	2.50

ROCKY HORROR PICTURE SHOW
Calibre/Tome, 1990

1	6.00
1a 2nd printing	3.25
2	3.50
3 The Conclusion	3.25
Rocky Horror Collection reps.	5.00

ROG 2000
Pacific, 1982

1 One-Shot, JBy	2.25

ROGER RABBIT
Walt Disney, 1990

1 I:Rick Flint, The Trouble with Toons	5.50
2	3.50
3	3.00
4	3.00
5	3.00
6 thru 9	@3.00
10 Tuned-in-toons	3.00
11 Who Framed Rick Flint	3.00
12 Somebunny to Love	3.00
13 Honey,I Stink with Kids	3.00
14 Who Fired Jessica Rabbit	3.00
15 The Great Toon Detective	3.00
16 See you later Aviator	3.00
17 Flying Saucers over Toontown	3.00
18 I Have Seen the Future	3.00

ROGER RABBIT'S TOONTOWN
Walt Disney, 1991

1 Baby Herman,Jessica stories	2.50
2 Pre-Hysterical Roger	2.50
3 Lumberjack of tomorrow	2.50
4 The Longest Daze	2.50

ROGUES
Dark Planet Productions, 2004

1	3.00
2 thru 5	@3.00
6	5.50

Rogue Trooper #4
© *Fleetway/Quality*

ROGUE TROOPER
Fleetway/Quality, 1986

1 thru 5	@2.25
6 thru 21	@2.25
22/23	2.25
24	2.25
25/26	2.25
27 thru 43	@2.25

ROGUE TROOPER: THE FINAL WARRIOR
Fleetway

1 RS,Golden Rebellion,pt 1	3.00
2 thru 3	@3.00
4 Saharan Ice-Belt War	3.00

ROLAND: DAYS OF WRATH
Terra Major, 1999

1 (of 4)	3.00
2 thru 4	@3.00
TPB	18.00

ROMAN HOLIDAYS, THE
Gold Key, 1973

1	65.00
2	40.00
3	40.00
4	40.00

ROOK, THE
Harris Comics, 1995

0 O:Rook	3.00
1 N:Rook	3.00

COLOR PUB.

2 I:Coffin 3.00
3 The Spider Obsidian 3.00

ROOM 222
Dell Publishing Co., 1970
1 . . . . 75.00
2 . . . . 50.00
3 Drug 60.00
4 Ph(c) 50.00

ROSE
Cartoon Books, 2000
1 (of 3) 48-pg. 6.00
2 JSi,CV,48-pg. 6.00
3 JSi,CV,48-pg., concl. 6.00
TPB 20.00

ROSWELL
Bongo Comics, 1996
1 by Bill Morrison,The Story
    of the Century 3.00
2 The Untold Story 3.00
3 The Untold Story, concl. 3.00
4 V:Mutato. 3.00
5 . . . . 3.00
6 time-traveling comic collector . . . 3.00
TPB Roswell Walks Among Us . . . 13.00

ROUTE 666
Crossgen Comics, 2002
1 . . . . 3.00
2 thru 5 . . . . @3.00
6 thru 24 . . . . @3.00
TPB Vol. 1 Highway of Horror 16.00
TPB Vol. 2 Three-Ring Circus 16.00
TPB Traveler Vol. 1 . . . . 10.00

ROY ROGERS
WESTERN CLASSICS
AC Comics
1 . . . . 3.00
2 . . . . 3.00
3 . . . . 3.00
4 . . . . 4.00

RUFF AND READY
Dell Publishing Co., 1958
1 . . . . 200.00
2 . . . . 150.00
3 . . . . 150.00
4 thru 12 . . . . @100.00

RUGRATS
COMIC ADVENTURES
New England Comics, 1999
VOL. 1
1 thru 10 . . . . @3.00
VOL. 2
1 thru 10 . . . . @3.00
VOL. 3
1 . . . . 3.00
2 thru 9 . . . . @3.00

RUN, BUDDY, RUN
Gold Key, 1967
1 . . . . 35.00

RUNE
Malibu Ultraverse, 1994–95
0 BWS(a&s) 4.00
1 BWS(a&s),from Ultraverse 2.50
1a Foil cover 4.00
2 CU(s),BWS,V:Aladdin 2.25

Rune #5
© Malibu

3 DaR,BWS,(Ultraverse Premiere
    #1), Flip book. 3.75
4 BWS,V:Twins 2.25
5 BWS. 2.25
6 BWS. 2.25
7 CU,JS 2.25
8 Rise of Gods,pt.2. . . . . 2.25
9 Prelude to Godwheel 2.25
G-Size #1. 2.50
TPB BWS(c&a),CU,The Awakening,
    rep.#1–#5 . . . . 13.00

RUNE
Malibu Ultraverse, 1995–96
Infinity V:Annihilus 2.50
1 A:Adam Warlock 2.25
1a Computer painted cover 2.25
2 Phoenix flip issue,A:Adam
    Warlock 2.25
3 Phoenix Resurrection 2.25
4 . . . . 2.25
5 . . . . 2.25
6 LKa,A:Warlock 2.25

RUNE:
HEARTS OF DARKNESS
Malibu Ultraverse, 1996
1 DgM(s),KHt,TBd, flip book. 2.25
2 DgM,KHt,TBd, flip book. 2.25
3 DgM,KHt,TBd, flip book. 2.25

RUNE/SILVER SURFER
Ultravrse 1995
1 BWS(c),A:Adam Warlock. 6.00
1a Lim. edition (5,000 made) 8.00
1b Standard ed.newsprint. 3.00

RUSE
Crossgen Comics, 2001
1 MWa. 8.00
2 MWa. 3.50
3 thru 14 . . . . @3.00
15 thru 27 . . . . @3.00
TPB Vol. 1 Enter the Detective . . . 16.00
TPB Vol. 3 Criminal Intent 16.00
Spec. Archard's Agents,
    Deadly Dare (2004) 3.00

RUST
Now, 1987
1 . . . . 4.00
2 . . . . 3.00
3 thru 11 . . . . @2.25
12 I:Terminator. 10.00
13 thru 15 . . . . @2.25
[Volume 2], 1989
1 thru 10 . . . . @2.25

RUST
Malibu
1 O:Rust 3.00
2 V:Marion Labs 3.00
3 I:Ashe Sapphire,5th Anniv. 3.00
4 I:Rustmobile. 3.00

RUULE: GANGLORDS
OF CHINATOWN
Beckett Entertainment, 2003
1 . . . . 6.00
2 thru 3 . . . . @6.00
4 thru 5 . . . . @3.00

RUULE: KISS & TELL
Beckett Entertainment, 2004
1 . . . . 3.00
2 thru 5 . . . . @3.00

SABLE
First, 1988–90
1 AIDS story 2.25
2 Sable in Iran 2.25
3 Pentathelon 2.25
4 . . . . 2.25
5 DCw,V:Tong Gangs 2.25
6 In Atlantic City 2.25
7 V:EnvironmentalTerrorists 2.25
8 In Argentina 2.25
9 In Kenya Pt.1 . . . . 2.25
10 In Kenya Pt.2 . . . . 2.25
11 Jon Sable bodyguard 2.25
12 In Cambodia Pt.1 . . . . 2.25
13 In Cambodia Pt.2 . . . . 2.25
14 Christmas story 2.25
15 A:Ted Koppel. 2.25
16 Sable as 'B.B.Flemm' rev. 2.25
17 Turning point issue 2.25
18 Richard Rockwell(i). 2.25
19 A:Maggie the Cat 2.25
20 A:Gary Adler 2.25
21 Richard Rockwell(i). 2.25
22 A:Eden Kendall 2.25
23 TV cover 2.25
24 TV cover 2.25
25 TV cover 2.25
26 TV cover 2.25
27 . . . . 2.25
28 last issue. 2.25

SABRE
Eclipse, 1982–85
1 PG 2.50
2 PG 3.00
3 thru 14 . . . . @2.25

SABRINA, THE
TEENAGE WITCH
Archie Publications, 1971–83
1 . . . . 225.00
2 Archie. 100.00
3 Archie. 75.00
4 . . . . 60.00
5 . . . . 60.00
6 thru 10 . . . . @60.00

11 thru 30	@50.00
31 thru 40	@25.00
41 thru 76	@20.00
77	25.00

SABRINA
THE TEENAGE WITCH
Archie Comics, 1996

one-shot photo cover	7.00
1 photo cover	5.00
2 Trouble in Time	5.00
3 photo cover	5.00
4 photo cover	5.00
5 Driver's License	5.00
6 Treasure Troubles	5.00
7 The Sculpture Switch	5.00
8 The Cable Girl, photo (c)	5.00
9 Farewell Feline	5.00
10 No Brain, No Pain	5.00
11 thru 17	@3.00
18 thru 33 photo (c)	@3.00

[Volume 2], 2000

1 thru 3 from animated series	@2.25
4 thru 13	@2.25
14 thru 62	@2.25
Halloween Spooktacular #1	2.25
Halloween Spooktacular #2	2.25
Holiday Spectacular #3	2.25

SAD SACK AND
THE SARGE
Harvey Publications, 1957–82

1	200.00
2	100.00
3 thru 10	@75.00
11 thru 20	@60.00
21 thru 40	@35.00
41 thru 50	@25.00
51 thru 90	@20.00
91 thru 96 52 pg Giants	@15.00
97 thru 155	@10.00

SAD SACK'S ARMY LIFE
Harvey Publications, 1963–76

1	125.00
2 thru 10	@50.00
11 thru 20	@30.00
21 thru 30	@25.00
31 thru 50	@18.00
51 thru 61	@15.00

SAD SACK'S
FUNNY FRIENDS
Harvey Publications, 1955–69

1	150.00
2 thru 10	@75.00
11 thru 20	@35.00
21 thru 30	@20.00
31 thru 40	@15.00
41 thru 75	@10.00

SAD SACK in 3-D
Blackthorne

1 and 2	@2.50

SAFETY-BELT MAN
ALL HELL
Sirius, 1996

1	3.00
2	3.00
3	3.00
4 Linsner back (c)	4.00
5	3.00

SAGA OF
THE METABARONS
Humanoids Publishing, 1999

1 (of 16) Sci-fi	3.00
2 thru 9	@3.00

SALOME
Eclipse, 1987

1 CR	2.25

SAM AND MAX, FREE-
LANCE POLICE SPECIAL
Comico, 1987–89

1	3.00

Sam Slade RoboHunter #20
© Quality

SAM SLADE
ROBOHUNTER
Quality, 1986–89

1	2.25
2 thru 10	@2.25
11 thru 21	@2.25
22/23	2.25
24	2.25
25/26	2.25
27 thru 33	@2.25

SAMSONS
Samsons Comics, 1995

1/2 Various Artists	2.50

SAMUREE
Windjammer, 1995

1 I:Samuree	2.50
2 V: The Dragon	2.50
3 V: The Dragon	2.50

SAMURAI
Eclipse

1	2.25
2	2.25
3 thru 5	@2.25

SAMURAI GUARD
Colburn Comics, 2000

1 by Kirk C. Abrigo	2.50
2	2.50

3	3.00
4 thru 6	@3.00

SAMUREE
Continuity, 1987

1 NA,A:Revengers	2.25
2 A:Revengers	2.25
3 NA,A:Revengers	2.25
4 A:Revengers	2.25
5 BSz(c),A:Revengers	2.25
6 A:Revengers	2.25
7	2.25
8 Drug story	2.25
9 Drug story	2.25

[2nd Series], 1993

1 thru 3 Rise of Magic	@2.50

SANDSCAPE
Dreamwave, 2003

1	3.00
2 thru 4	@3.00

SANTANA
Rock-it Comix, 1994

1 TT(c&s),TY	4.00

SARGE STEEL/
SECRET AGENT
Charlton, 1964–66

1 DG,I:SargeSteel & IvanChung	50.00
2 DG,I:Werner Von Hess	30.00
3 DG,V:Smiling Skull	30.00
4 DG,V:Lynx	30.00
5 FMc,V:Ivan Chung	30.00
6 FMc,A:Judomaster	40.00
7 DG	30.00
8 V:Talon	30.00
Becomes:	

SECRET AGENT

9 DG,A:The Lynx	40.00
10 DG,JAp,A:Tiffany Sinn	30.00

SATANIKA
Verotik, 1995

0	3.00
1 New ongoing series	4.00
2 Femininity	3.50
3 thru 5	@3.00
6 thru 10	@3.00
10a Wingbird variant cover	5.00
11 SBi,final issue	4.00
11a Jason Blood variant (c)	10.00
11b Superfest 99 limited	15.00
1-shot Satanika X (adult)	5.00
1-shot Satanika vs.Shilene	10.00

SATAN'S SIX
Topps, 1993

1 F:Satan's Six,w/3 cards	3.25
2 V:Kalazarr,w/3 cards	3.00
3 w/3 cards	3.00
4 w/3 cards	3.00

SATURDAY KNIGHTS
Hot

1	2.25
2 thru 4	@2.25

SAURAUS FAMILY
Blackthorne

1 3-D	2.25

SAURIANS: UNNATURAL SELECTION
Crossgen Comics, 2002
1 (of 2) 3.00
2 .... 3.00

SAVAGE COMBAT TALES
Atlas, Feb.–July, 1975
1 F:Sgt Strykers Death Squad ... 20.00
2 ATh,A:Warhawk 25.00
3 final issue................. 15.00

SAVAGE DRAGON/ TEENAGE MUTANT NINJA TURLTES CROSSOVER
Mirage, 1993
1 EL(s)...................... 3.00

SAVED BY THE BELL
Harvey, 1992
1 based on TV series 2.25
2 thru 5 .... @2.25

SCARLET CRUSH
Awesome Entertainment, 1998
1 by John Stinsman 2.50
2 .... 2.50
3 Icaria's decision 2.50
4 Nirasawa arrives 2.50

SCARY TALES
Charlton, 1975
1 .... 35.00
2 .... 15.00
3 SD,P(c) 15.00
4 TS,SD,P(c). 20.00
5 SD 20.00
6 .... 15.00
7 SD 18.00
8 SD 18.00
9 TS 20.00
10 .... 15.00
11 SD 18.00
12 .... 15.00
13 .... 12.00
14 .... 15.00
15 .... 15.00

Scary Tales #20
© Charlton Comics

16 .... 15.00
17 .... 12.00
18 .... 15.00
19 .... 15.00
20 .... 10.00
21 .... 15.00
22 .... 9.00
23 thru 28 .... @8.00
30 thru 37 .... @6.00
38 Mr. Jigsaw 9.00
39 SD 12.00
40 thru 46.................. @8.00

SCAVENGERS
Quality, 1988–89
1 thru 7 .... @2.25
8 thru 14 .... @2.25

SCAVENGERS
Triumphant Comics, 1993–94
0 Fso(c),JnR(s), ... 2.50
0a `Free Copy' 2.50
0b Red Logo 2.50
1 JnR(s),I:Scavengers,Ximos,
  C:Doctor Chaos. 2.50
1a 2nd Printing 2.50
2 JnR(s), ... 2.50
3 JnR(s),I:Lurok 2.50
4 JnR(s), ... 2.50
5 Fso(c),JnR(s),D:Jack Hanal. 2.50
6 JnR(s), ... 2.50
7 JnR(s),I:Zion 2.50
8 JnR(s),Nativity 2.50
9 JnR(s),The Challenge 2.50
10 JnR(s),Snowblind 2.50

SCHISM
Defiant
1 thru 4 Defiant's x-over....... @3.25

SCIENCE COMIC BOOK
Nature Publishing House, 1997
TPB Earth Adventures........... 9.00
TPB Car Adventure 9.00
TPB Volcano Adventures........ 9.00
TPB World of Dinosaurs 9.00
TPB Beyond the Star 9.00
TPB Weather Genie............ 9.00
TPB Rain Forest Adventure 9.00
TPB Wildlife Adventure 9.00

SCION
Crossgen Comics, 2000
1 RMz 5.00
2 RMz 5.00
3 RMz 4.50
4 & 5 .... 3.00
6 .... 4.00
7 thru 18 .... @3.00
19 thru 30 RMz .... @3.00
31 thru 44 RMz .... @3.00
TPB Vol. 1 rep. #1–#7 .... 20.00
TPB Vol. 2 .... 20.00
TPB Vol. 3 Divided Loyalties 16.00
TPB Vol. 4 Sanctuary. 16.00
TPB Vol. 5 The Far Kingdom..... 16.00
TPB Vol. 6 The Royal Wedding... 16.00
TPB Scion Traveler, Vol. 1 .... 10.00

SCI-TECH
WildStorm/DC, 1999
1 (of 4) BCi,Ebe,.............. 2.50
2 BCi,EBe, ... 2.50
3 BCi,EBe 2.50
4 BCi,EBe,concl.............. 2.50

SCOOBY DOO
Gold Key, 1970–75
1 .... 200.00
2 .... 125.00
3 .... 100.00
4 .... 100.00
5 .... 100.00
6 thru 20 .... @75.00
21 thru 30................. @50.00

SCOOBY DOO
Charlton Comics, 1975–76
1 .... 100.00
2 thru 5 .... @50.00
6 thru 11 .... @40.00

SCOOBY DOO
Archie, 1995
1 .... 6.00
2 thru 10 .... @5.00
11 thru 21 .... @4.00

SCORCHED EARTH
Tundra, 1991
1 Earth 2025,I:Dr.EliotGodwin 3.50
2 Hunt for Eliot 3.00
3 Mystical Transformation........ 3.00

SCORPION, THE
Atlas, 1975
1 HC, bondage cover 25.00
2 HC,BWi,MK 20.00
3 .... 15.00

SCORPION CORP.
Dagger, 1993
1 PuD,JRI,CH, ... 2.75
2 PuD,JRI,CH,V:Victor Kyner 2.75
3 PuD,BIH,V:Victor Kyner....... 2.75

SCORPIO ROSE
Eclipse, 1983
1 MR/TP,I:Dr.Orient............ 2.25
2 MR/TP 2.25

SCOUT
Eclipse, 1985–87
1 TT,I:Scout,Fash.In Action....... 6.00
2 TT,V:Buffalo Monster 3.00
3 TT,V:President Grail.......... 2.50
4 TT,V:President Grail......... 2.50
5 TT,Killin' Floor 2.50
6 TT,V:President Grail......... 2.50
7 TT,TY,Rosanna's Diary 2.50
8 TT,TY 2.50
9 TT,TY,A:Airboy............ 2.50
10 TT,TY,I:Proj.Mountain Fire 2.00
11 TT,FH,V:Rangers.......... 2.00
12 TT,FH,Me and the Devil 2.00
13 TT,FH,Monday:Eliminator 2.00
14 TT,FH,Monday:Eliminator 2.00
15 TT,FH,Monday:Eliminator 2.00
16 TT,3-D issue,F:Santana 3.00
17 TT,A:Beanworld........... 2.25
18 TT,FH,V:Lex Lucifer 2.25
19 TT,w/Record,V:Lex Lucifer 3.00
20 TT,A:Monday:Eliminator 2.25
21 TT,A:Monday:Eliminator 2.25
22 TT,A:Swords of Texas 2.25
23 TT,A:Swords of Texas........ 2.25
24 TT,last Issue 2.25

SCOUT: WAR SHAMAN
Eclipse, 1988–89
1 TT,R:Scout (now a father) 2.25

2 TT,I:Redwire............... 2.25
3 TT,V:Atuma Yuma 2.25
4 TT,Rollin' on the River 2.25
5 TT,Hopi Katchina dieties 2.25
6 TT,Scout vs. Rosa Winter 2.25
7 TT,R:Redwire.............. 2.25
8 TT,R:Beau LaDuke 2.25
9 TT,V:Doodyists............. 2.25
10 TT,TY,V:Redwire 2.25
11 TT,V:Redwire.............. 2.25
12 TT,V:Snow Leopards.......... 2.25
13 TT,F:Beau LaDuke 2.25
14 TT,V:Redwire.............. 2.25
15 TT,V:Redwire.............. 2.25
16 TT,Wall of Death,last issue 2.25

SEADRAGON
Elite, 1986–87
1 .... 3.00
1a 2nd printing 2.25
2 thru 8 .... @2.25

SEA HUNT
Dell Publishing Co., 1958
1 L.BridgesPh(c) all 200.00
2 .... 150.00
3 ATh....................... 165.00
4 RsM...................... 150.00
5 RsM...................... 150.00
6 RsM...................... 150.00
7 .... 125.00
8 RsM...................... 150.00
9 RsM...................... 150.00
10 RsM..................... 150.00
11 RsM..................... 150.00
12 .... 150.00
13 RsM..................... 150.00

SEAQUEST
Nemesis, 1994
1 HC(c),DGC,KP,AA,Based on
   TV Show 2.50

SEBASTIAN
Walt Disney
1 From Little Mermaid.......... 2.25
2 While da Crab's Away 2.25

SECOND LIFE
OF DR. MIRAGE, THE
Valiant, 1993
1 B:BL(s),BCh,V:Mast.Darque 2.50
1a Gold Ed................. 3.00
2 BCh,V:Master Darque 2.50
3 BCh 2.50
4 BCh,V:Bhrama.............. 2.50
5 BCh,A:Shadowman,V:Master
   Darque................. 2.50
6 BCh,V:Dr.Eclipse 2.50
7 BCh,V:Dr.Eclipse,w/card 2.50
8 BCh,.................... 2.50
9 BCh,A:Otherman 2.50
10 BCh,V:Otherman............ 2.50
11 BCh,Chaos Effect-Beta#2, ... 2.50
12 BCh..................... 2.25
13 BCh..................... 2.25
14 .... 2.25
15 Chaos Effect.............. 2.25
16 .... 2.25
17 .... 2.25
18 F:Deathsmith.............. 2.25
19 R:Walt Wiley 2.25

SECRET AGENT
Gold Key, 1966
1 .... 200.00

---

2 .... 150.00

SECRET CITY SAGA
Topps, 1993
0 JK...................... 3.25
0 Gold Ed.................. 15.00
0 Red 10.00
1 w/3 cards................. 3.25
2 w/3 cards................. 3.25
3 w/3 cards................. 3.25
4 w/3 cards................. 3.25

SECRET SKULL
IDW Publishing, 2004
1 .... 4.00
2 thru 3 .... @4.00

SECRETS OF THE
VALIANT UNIVERSE
Valiant, 1994
1 from Wizard 2.50
2 BH,Chaos Effect-Beta#4,A:Master
   Darque,Dr.Mirage,Max St.James,
   Dr. Eclipse 2.25

SECRET SQUIRREL
Gold Key, 1966
1 .... 165.00

Secret Weapons #4
© Valiant

SECRET WEAPONS
Valiant, 1993
1 JSP(a&s),BWi(i),I:Dr.Eclipse,
   A:Master Darque,A:Geoff,
   Livewire,Stronghold,Solar,X-O,
   Bloodshot,Shadowman 2.75
1a Gold Ed................. 4.00
2 JSP(a&s),V:Master Darque,
   Dr.Eclipse 2.25
3 JSP(a&s),V:Speedshots....... 2.25
4 JSP(a&s),V:Scatterbrain 2.25
5 JSP(a&s),A:Ninjak 2.25
6 JPS(s),JPh(pl),TeH, V:Spider
   Aliens.................. 2.25
7 JPS(s),V:Spider Aliens....... 2.25
8 JSP(a&pl),V:Harbingers....... 2.25
9 JSP(a&s),V:Webnet, w/Valiant
   Era card................ 2.25
10 JSP(a&s),V:Webnet 2.25
11 PGr,New Line-up............ 2.25
12 PGr,A:Bloodshot 2.25

---

13 PGr,Chaos Effect-Gamma#2 ... 2.25
14 PGr,F:Bloodshot 2.25
15 .... 2.25
16 .... 2.25
17 V:Dr. Silk................ 2.25
18 Gigo 2.25
19 A:Ninjak................. 2.25
20 Bloodshot Rampage Pt.2 ..... 2.25
21 Bloodshot Rampage Pt.4 ..... 2.25
22 I:Gestalt, Pyroclast......... 2.25
23 A:Bloodshot............... 2.25

SECRET WEAPONS:
PLAYING WITH FIRE
Valiant
1 & 2 .... @2.50

SEDUCTION OF
THE INNOCENT
Eclipse, 1985–86
1 ATh,Hanged by the Neck, reps... 3.00
2 .... 3.00
3 ATh,The Crushed Gardenia...... 3.00
4 ATh,NC,World's Apart 3.00
5 ATh,The Phantom Ship 3.00
6 ATh,RA,Hands of Don Jose..... 3.00
3-D #1 DSt(c)................. 5.00
3-D #2 ATh,MB,BWr,Man Who Was
   Always on Time............ 5.00

SEEKER
Sky Comics, 1995
1 JMt(s),I:Seeker 2.50

SENSEI
First, 1989
1 Mini-Series................. 2.75
2 .... 2.75
3 .... 2.75
4 .... 2.75

SENTINELS OF JUSTICE
AC Comics, 1990
1 Capt.Paragon............... 2.25
2 .... 2.25
3 EL art.................... 2.25
4 EL art.................... 2.25
5 .... 2.25
6 .... 2.25
7 .... 2.25

SENTRY: SPECIAL
Innovation, 1991
1 .... 2.75

SERAPHIM
Innovation, 1990
1 and 2 .... @2.50

SERINA
Antarctic, 1996
1 .... 3.00

SERPENTINA
Lightning, 1997
1 .... 3.00
1a variant cover 3.00

SEVEN SISTERS
Zephyr Comics, 1997
1 by Curley, Cruickshank & Garcia. 3.00
2 .... 3.00
3 .... 3.00

COLOR PUB.

4 . . . . 3.00

SEVENTH SHRINE, THE
Devil's Due Publishing, 2004
1 (of 2) R.Silverberg adapt. 6.00
2 . . . . 6.00

77 SUNSET STRIP
Dell Publishing Co., 1960
1 Ph(c) 150.00
2 Ph(c),RsM 165.00

SHADE SPECIAL
AC Comics, 1984
1 . . . . 2.25

SHADOW, THE
Archie Comics, 1964–65
1 . . . . 100.00
2 . . . . 75.00
3 . . . . 75.00
4 . . . . 75.00
5 . . . . 75.00
6 and 8 . . . . @50.00

SHADOW COMICS
1 Guardians of Justice &
    The O-Force 2.25

SHADOW MAN
Valiant, 1992
0 BH,TmR,Chromium (c),O:Maxim
    St.James,Shadowman. 3.00
0a Newstand ed.. . . . . 2.50
0b Gold Ed.. . . . . 4.00
1 DL,JRu,I&O:Shadowman. 5.00
2 DL,V:Serial Killer 3.00
3 V:Emil Sosa 3.00
4 DL,FM(c),Unity#6,A:Solar 2.50
5 DL,WS(c),Unity#14, A:Archer &
    Armstrong 2.50
6 SD,L:Lilora. 2.50
7 DL,V:Creature 2.50
8 JDx(i),I:Master Darque. 3.00
9 JDx(i),V:Darque's Minions 3.00
10 BH,I:Sandria 2.50
11 BH,N:Shadowman. 2.50
12 BH,V:Master Darque. 2.50
13 BH,V:Rev.Shadow Man 2.50
14 BH,JDx,V:Bikers 2.50
15 BH,JDx,V:JB,Fake Shadow
    Man,C:Turok 2.50
16 BH,JDx,I:Dr.Mirage, Carmen . . 3.00
17 BH,JDx,A:Archer & Armstrong . . 2.25
18 BH,JDx,A:Archer & Armstrong . . 2.25
19 BH,A:Aerosmith 2.25
20 BH,A:Master Darque,
    V:Shadowman's Father 2.25
21 BH,I:Maxim St.James (1895
    Shadowman) 2.25
22 V:Master Darque. 2.25
23 BH(a&s),A:Doctor Mirage,
    V:Master Darque 2.25
24 BH(a&s),V:H.A.T.E. 2.25
25 RgM,w/Valiant Era card 2.25
26 w/Valiant Era card. 2.50
27 BH,V:Drug Lord. 2.25
28 BH,A:Master Darque. 2.25
29 Chaos Effect-Beta#1,V:Master
    Darque. 2.25
30 R:Rotwak 2.25
31 thru 33. . . . . @2.25
34 Voodoo in Carribean. 2.25
35 A:Ishmael 2.25
36 F:Ishmael 2.25
37 A:X-O, V:Blister. 2.25
38 V:Ishmael, Blister 2.25

39 BH,TmR,Explores Powers 2.25
40 BH,TmR,I,Vampire! 2.25
41 A:Steve Massarsky 2.25
42 . . . . 2.25
43 V:Smilin Jack 2.25
TPB rep.#1-#3,#6. . . . . 10.00

SHADOWMAN
Acclaim, 1996
1 GEn(s),Deadside, pt.1 . . . . 2.50
2 GEn(s),Deadside, pt.2 . . . . 2.50
3 GEn(s),Deadside, pt.3 . . . . 2.50

ShadowMan Vol. 2, #16
© Acclaim

4 GEn(s),Deadside, pt.4 . . . . . 2.50
5 JaD,CAd,Nothing is True, pt.1 . . . 2.50
6 JaD,CAd,Nothing is True, pt.2 . . . 2.50
7 JaD,CAd,Nothing is True, pt.3 . . . 2.50
8 JaD,CAd,Nothing is True, pt.4 . . . 2.50
9 JaD,CAd,The Buzz, pt.1 . . . . . . 2.50
10 JaD,CAd,The Buzz, pt.2 . . . . . . 2.50
11 JaD,CAd,ClearBlueSkies,pt.1 . . 2.50
12 JaD,CAd,ClearBlueSkies,pt.2 . . 2.50
13 JaD,CAd,Hoodoo Bash,pt.1 . . . 2.50
14 JaD,CAd,Hoodoo Bash,pt.2 . . . 2.50
15 JaD,CAd,Hoodoo Bash,pt.3 . . . 2.50
16 Mask of Shadows ripped out . . . 2.50
17 Mask of Shadows, pt.2 . . . . 2.50
18 Claudine kidnapped? 2.50
19 pursuit of Mah 2.50
20 Deadside vortes 2.50

VOLUME 3 (1999)
1 DAn,ALa,48-page 4.00
2 . . . . 2.50
3 Flip-book 2.50
4 Flip-book 2.50
5 . . . . 2.50
6 . . . . 2.50
7 final issue 2.50

SHADOW OF THE TORTURER, THE
Innovation, 1991
1 thru 6 Gene Wolfe adapt.. . . . . @2.25

SHADOW RAVEN
Poc-It Comics, 1995
1 I:Shadow Raven 3.00

SHADOW REAVERS
Black Bull Entertainment, 2001
1 Nel,KM(c). 4.00
1a variant TDr(c). 12.00
2 Nel,GF(c). 3.00
2a variant TDr(c). 5.00
3 Nel 3.00
3a variant TDr(c). 5.00
4 Nel 3.00
4a variant limited master edition . . 5.00
5 Nel 3.00
5a variant limited master edition. . . 5.00
Preview Edition 3.00
Preview Edition, limited 5.00

SHADOW STATE
Preview Editions
1 and 2 B&W. . . . . @2.50
Broadway, 1995
1 thru 4 F:BloodS.C.R.E.A.M. . . . @2.50
5 JiS, Image Isn't Everything,
    concl. 2.50
6 Anger of Lovers, pt.1 . . . . 2.50
7 Anger of Lovers, pt.2 . . . . 3.00

SHAFT
Maximum Press, 1997
1 RLd 2.50

SHAIANA
Entity, 1995
1 R:Shaiana from Aster 3.75
1a clear chromium 8.00
1b Holochrome 10.00
2 Guardians of Earth 2.50

SHANGHAI BREEZE
1 . . . . 2.25

SHAOLIN
Black Tiger Press
1 I:Tiger. 3.00
2 I:Crane. 3.00

SHATTER
First, 1985–88
1 . . . . 3.00
2 . . . . 2.50
3 . . . . 2.50
4 thru 14 . . . . @2.25
Spec. #1 Computer Comic. 5.00
#1a 2nd Printing. 2.00

SHE-DEVILS ON WHEELS
Aircel
1 V:Man-Eaters. 3.00
2 V:Man-Eaters. 3.00
3 V:Man-Eaters. 3.00

SHEENA: QUEEN OF THE JUNGLE
London Night
0 by Gabriel Cain & Wilson 3.00
0a Zebra Edition 5.00
0b Leopard Edition 5.00
0c Alligator Edition 5.00

SHEENA: QUEEN OF THE JUNGLE: BOUND
London Night, 1998
1 (of 4) by Everette Hartsoe
    & Art Wetherell 3.00

All comics prices listed are for *Near Mint* condition.

1 ministry ed. 5.00
1 Leather retro edition 12.00

SHERIFF OF TOMBSTONE
Charlton Comics, 1958–61
1 AW,JSe 100.00
2 . . . . 50.00
3 thru 10 . . . . @40.00
11 thru 17 . . . . @35.00

SHIELD, THE: SPOTLIGHT
IDW Publishing, 2004
1 . . . . 4.00
2 thru 5 . . . . @4.00
TPB 20.00

Shi (The Way of the Warrior) #6
© Crusade Entertainment

SHI (THE WAY OF THE WARRIOR)
Crusade Comics, 1994–97
1 BiT,HMo,I:Shi 9.00
2 BiT 5.00
2a BiT, reissue, new cover 3.00
3 BiT 5.00
4 BiT 4.00
5 V:Arashi 3.00
5a variant cover 6.00
6 V:Tomoe 3.00
7 V:Nara Warriors 3.00
8 New costume 3.00
9 thru 11 . . . . @3.00
12 Way of the Warrior, concl, flip-
  book Angel Fire. 3.00
TPB Shi: Way of the Warrior 13.00
TPB Way of the Warrior, signed . . 15.00
TPB Vol. 1 revised rep.JuB(c) 15.00
TPB Vol. 2, rep. Shi #5–#8 . . . . . 15.00
TPB rep. Shi #9–#12 & Shi vs.
  Tomoe 18.00
Spec. #1 Shi/Cyblade,Battle of the
  Independents (1995) 4.00
Spec.#1a Shi/Cyblade,variant(c) . . 6.00
Ashcan #1, sign & num. (2000) . . . 10.00
Spec. #1 10th Anniv. Edition (2004). 3.00

SHI: THE SERIES
Crusade Entertainment, 1997
1 sequel to *Shi: Heaven and Earth*,
  F:Tomoe. 3.50

2 Unforgettable Fire, concl. 3.00
3 A Rock and a Hard Place, pt.1 . . 3.00
4 A Rock and a Hard Place, pt.2 . . 3.00
5 A Rock and a Hard Place, pt.3 . . 3.00
6 . . . . 3.00
7 Photographer's lucky picture . . . 3.00
8 V:Gemini Dawn twins 3.00
9 Bad Blood, pt.1 . . . . 3.00
9a variant BTi(c) 3.00
9b variant Ahn (c) 3.00
9c variant Kevin Lau (c) 3.00
10 Bad Blood, pt.2 . . . . 3.00
10a variant BTi(c) 3.00
10b variant Ahn (c) 3.00
10c variant Kevin Lau (c) 3.00
11 Bad Blood, pt.3 . . . . 3.00
12 The Dark Crusade, pt.1 (of 8) . . 3.00
13 The Dark Crusade, pt.2 (of 8) . . 3.00
14 The Dark Crusade, pt.3 (of 8) . . 3.00
15 The Dark Crusade, pt.4 (of 8) . . 3.00
16 The Dark Crusade, pt.5 (of 8) . . 3.00
1-shot The Essential Dark Crusade. 3.00
1-shot Shi:Five Year Celebration . . 5.00
1-shotA,B,C,&D variant covers . . . 5.00
#0 & Wolverine/Shi flip book 3.00
Spec. Shi/Vampirella,x-over(1997). . 3.00
Spec. Shi: Nightstalkers, VMk,
  F:T.C.B. (1997) 3.50
Spec. Shi: Masquerade (1997) . . . 3.50
Spec. Shi: Art of War Tour Book
  Wizard Chicago con (1998). . . . 6.00
G.I. Preview Edition (2001) 5.00
Spec. Through the Ashes (2001) . . 3.00
TPB Cover Gallery (2003) 30.00

SHI: AKAI
Crusade Entertainment, 2001
1 BTi, I:RAF Victoria Cross. 3.00
1 antiques edition 30.00
Ashcan, signed & numbered 10.00

SHI: BLACK WHITE & RED
Crusade Entertainment, 1998
1 Night of the Rat, pt.1 . . . . 3.00
2 Night of the Rat, pt.2 . . . . 3.00
Coll. Ed. rep. #1–#2. . . . . 7.00

SHI: EAST WIND RAIN
Crusade Entertainment, 1997
1 BiT,MSo, fully painted 3.50
2 BiT, concl. 3.50

SHI: HEAVEN AND EARTH
Crusade Entertainment, 1997
1 (of 3) BiT 3.00
1 variant cover 3.00
2 BiT 3.00
3 BiT 3.00
4 BiT 3.00
TPB rep. #1–#4 . . . . 16.00

SHI: HOT TARGET
Crusade Entertainment, 2003
1 . . . . 3.00

SHI: PANDORA'S BOX
Avatar Press, 2003
Preview Edition 16-pg. B&W 6.00
Preview BiT(c) 2.00
Preview prism foil (c) 13.00
1/2 prism foil (c) 13.00
1/2 royal blue (c) 75.00
1 BiT(c) 3.50
1a variant (c)s . . . . @3.50
1b prism foil (c) 13.00
1 royal blue edition 75.00

SHI: POISONED PARADISE
Avatar, 2002
Preview 16-pg., b&w 2.00
Preview, Ron Adrian (c) 6.00
Preview, prism foil edition 13.00
1 (of 2) BiT,Karl Waller,Martin(c). . . 3.50
1a BiT(c) 3.50
1b Waller (c) 3.50
1c Wraparound exclusive (c) 3.50
1d Angel of Death (c) 6.00
1e Angel of Death ruby foil (c) . . . 9.00
1f prism (c) 13.00
2 BiT(c) 3.50
2a-2c variant(c)s . . . . @3.50
1/2 Blossom (c) 6.00
1/2 variant (c)s . . . . @4.00

SHI: REKISHI
Crusade Entertainment, 1997
1 (of 2) BiT 3.00
2 BiT, conclusion. 3.00
Coll.Ed. Shi:Reshiki, sourcebook,
  MS(c). 5.00

SHI VS. TOMOE
Crusade, April, 1996
Spec. #1 BiT, double size 4.00
GN Unforgettable Fire, rep. 6.99

SHI-SENRYAKU
Crusade, 1995
1 BiT,R:Shi 3.00
1a variant cover 5.00
1 (of 3) 2nd edition 2.50
2 BiT,Arts of Warfare. 3.00
2 2nd edition 2.50
3 BiT 3.00
3 2nd edition 2.50
TPB Rep.#1-#2 . . . . 13.00
TPB 14.00

SHI: YEAR OF THE SERPENT
Crusade Entertainment, 2001
Spec. Tour Book, B&W 5.00

SHI – YEAR OF THE DRAGON
Crusade Entertainment, 2000
1 (of 3) BiT 3.00
1a variant (c). 3.00
1b signed & numbered 10.00
1c true colors ed. BiT 6.00
1d true colors ed. ruby red 30.00
2 Ana Tears (c) BiT 3.00
2a Death Incarnate (c) BiT 3.00
3 BTi, concl. 3.00
Ashcan, signed & numbered 10.00
Coll. Ed. Black,White,Red 7.00
GN #1 & #2 Black,White,Red 6.00
Poster Book 3.00
TPB Year of the Dragon (2002) . . . 10.00

SHOCK SUSPENSE STORIES
Russ Cochran Press, 1992
1 reps.horror stories 2.50
2 inc.Kickback. 2.50
3 thru 4 . . . . @2.50
5 thru 7 reps.horror stories . . . . . @2.50
8 reps.horror stories 2.50
Gemstone
18 EC comics reprint 2.50

COLOR PUB.

COLOR PUB.

Shock SuspenStories #1
© Russ Cochran

TPB Vol. 1 rebinding of #1–#5 . . . . . 9.00
TPB Vol. 2 rebinding of #5–#10 . . . 10.00
TPB Vol. 3 rebinding of #11–#15 . . . 9.00
TPB Vol. 4 rebinding of #16–#20 . . 10.00

SHOCK THE MONKEY
Millennium/Expand, 1995
1 Shock therapy 3.00

SHOGUNAUT
Firstlight
1 I:Shogunaut 3.00
2 V:Teckno Terror 3.00

SHOOTING STARS
1 . . . . 2.50

SHOTGUN MARY
Antarctic Press, 1995
1 I:Shotgun Mary 3.00
1a with CD Soundtrack 9.00
1b Red Foil cover 8.00
2 . . . . 3.00
Spec. Shooting Gallery 3.00
Spec. Deviltown 3.00
Spec. Deviltown, commem. (1999) . 6.00

SHOTGUN MARY
Antarctic Press, 1998
1 by Herb Mallette & Kelsey
  Shannon 3.00
2 Early Days, pt.2 . . . . 3.00
3 Early Days, pt.3 . . . . 3.00

SHOTGUN MARY:
BLOOD LORE
Antarctic Press, 1997
1 (of 4) by Herb Mallette
  & Neil Googe 3.00
2 . . . . 3.00
3 . . . . 3.00
4 concl. 3.00

SHOTGUN MARY:
SON OF THE BEAST,
DAUGHTER OF LIGHT
Antarctic Press, 1997
1 . . . . 3.00

SIEGEL & SHUSTER
Eclipse, 1984–85
1 . . . . 2.25
2 . . . . 2.25

SIGIL
Crossgen Comics, 2000
1 BKs 5.00
2 BKs 3.25
3 thru 5 BKs . . . . @3.50
6 thru 12 BKs . . . . @3.25
13 thru 18 MWa,SEa . . . . @3.00
19 thru 30 SEa . . . . @3.00
31 thru 43 CDi(s) . . . . @3.00
TPB Vol. 1 . . . . 20.00
TPB Vol. 2 . . . . 20.00
TPB Vol. 3 The Lizard God 16.00
TPB Vol. 4 Hostage Planet 16.00
TPB Vol. 5 Death Match 16.00

SILENT HILL:
DYING INSIDE
IDW Publishing, 2004
1 . . . . 5.00
2 thru 5 . . . . @4.50
TPB 20.00

SILENT MOBIUS
Viz, 1991–92
1 Katsumi 5.75
2 Katsumi vs. Spirit 5.25
3 Katsumi trapped within entity . . . 5.00
4 Nami vs. Dragon 5.00
5 Kiddy vs. Wire 5.00
6 Search for Wire 5.00
GN 15.00

SILENT MOBIUS II
Viz, 1991
1 AMP Officers vs. Entities cont . . . 5.00
2 Entities in Amp H.Q. 5.00
3 V:Entity 5.00
4 The Esper Weapon 5.00
5 Last issue 5.00

SILENT MOBIUS III
Viz, 1992
1 F:Lebia/computer network 2.75
2 Lebia/computer link cont 2.75
3 Lebia in danger 2.75
4 Return to Consciousness 2.75
5 Conclusion 2.75

SILKEN GHOST
Crossgen Comics, 2003
1 (of 5) CDi 3.00
2 thru 5 . . . . @3.00
Vol. 1 Silken Ghost Traveler 10.00

SILVERBACK
Comico, 1989–90
1 thru 3 . . . . @2.50

SILVER CROSS
Antarctic Press, 1997
1 (of 3) by Ben Dunn 3.00
2 . . . . 3.00

SILVERHEELS
Pacific, 1983–84
1 . . . . 2.25
2 and 3 . . . . @2.25

SILVER STAR
Pacific, 1983–84
1 JK 2.25
2 thru 6 JK . . . . @2.25

SILVER STAR
Topps, 1993
1 w/Cards 3.00

SILVER STORM
Silverline, 1998
1 . . . . 3.00
2 . . . . 2.50
3 . . . . 2.50
4 . . . . 2.50

SIMPSONS COMICS
Bongo Comics, 1993
1 Colossal Homer 8.00
2 A:Sideshow Bob 4.00
3 F:Bart 4.00
4 F:Bart 4.00
5 A:Itchy & Scratchy 4.00
6 F:Lisa 4.00
7 Circus in Town 4.00
8 Mr. Burns Voyage 4.00
9 Autobiographies 4.00
10 Tales of the Kwik-E-Mart 4.00
11 Ned Flanders Public Enemy 4.00
12 In the Blodome 4.00
13 F:Bart & Millhouse 4.00
14 Homer owns beer company 4.00
15 Waltons parody 4.00
16 thru 15 . . . . @4.00
26 Bart: action hero! 4.00
27 . . . . 4.00
28 Krusty the Clown, tax protest . . . 4.00
29 Captain Slamtastic 4.00
30 Montgomery Burns clones
  Smithers 4.00
31 Radioactive Homer 4.00
32 F:Lisa and her sax 4.00
33 Reality on the blink 4.00
34 C. Montgomery Burns
  International Games 4.00
35 20 kids 4.00
36 Three geeks computer company 4.00
37 Grampa Abe Simpson 4.00
38 chemically-engineered donuts . . 4.00
39 People vs. Homer Simpson
  and the Comic Book Guy 4.00
40 F:Krusty the Clown 4.00
41 Krusty Fun Factory 4.00
42 . . . . 4.00
43 Urban legends 4.00
44 substitute teachers 4.00
45 Santa's Little Helper 4.00
46 Sideshow Bob 4.00
47 30 years in the future 4.00
48 dating game 4.00
49 Lisa double feature 4.00
50 80-pg. 6.00
51 Thanksgiving 3.00
52 Worst Christmas Ever 3.00
53 The Beer Boys 3.00
54 Homer drives tank to work 3.00
55 Simpson's new pool 3.00
56 New king of Sweden 3.00
57 Bart turns tattletale 3.00
58 Mayor Quimby scandal 3.00
59 Boy band phenomenon 3.00
60 F:Waylon Smithers 3.00
61 Control of print media 3.00
62 Bible stories 3.00
63 Golf fever 3.00
64 Who dispenses justice 3.00
65 revolution in Bosqieverde 3.00
66 Set sail with Homer 3.00

All comics prices listed are for *Near Mint* condition.

COLOR PUB.

67 Lisa beautifies Springfield	3.00
68 Money to Burns	3.00
69 Merchants of Vengeance	3.00
70 The Iliad	3.00
71 F:Sideshow Cecil	3.00
72 Early retirement plan	3.00
73 collection give-away	3.00
74 Dr. the Clown	3.00
75 Untold tales	3.00
76 Shakespeare	3.00
77 Sideshow Bob	3.00
78 thru 85	@3.00
86	3.00
87 thru 88	@3.00
89 thru 99	@3.00
Spec. Simpsons Classics	4.00
TPB Rep.#1-#4	10.00
TPB Wing Ding, 120pg	12.00
TPB Simpsons Comics on Parade (1998)	12.00
TPB Simpsons Comics Big Bonanza	12.00
TPB Comics A Go-Go	12.00
TPB Comics Extravaganza	10.00
TPB Bartman Best of the Best	10.00
TPB Simpsons Comics Strike Back	11.00
TPB Comics Wing Ding	12.00
TPB Simpsons Unchained (2002)	15.00
TPB Madness	15.00
TPB Belly Buster (2004)	15.00
Comic Spectacular,Vol.1 Rep.	10.00
Comic Spectacular,Vol.2 Rep.	10.00

Simpsons Comics and Stories #1
© Bongo Comics

SIMPSONS COMICS & STORIES
Welch Publishing, 1993
1 with poster	4.00
1a without poster	2.50

Bongo Comics, 1998
1 F:Bartman, Itchy & Scratchy	3.00

SINGULARITY SEVEN
IDW Publishing, 2004
1	4.00
2 thru 4	@4.00

SINTHIA
Lightning, 1997
1A by Joseph Adam, Daughter of Lucifer	3.00
1B	3.00

1c Platinum Edition	10.00
1d Autographed Edition	10.00
2 Sisters of Darkness	3.00
2a variant cover	3.00
3 Wagner(c)	3.00
3a variant Abrams cover	3.00
3b deluxe variant cover	10.00
4 Wagner(c)	3.00
4a variant John Cleary cover	3.00

SIREN
Malibu Ultraverse, 1995
Infinity V:War Machine	2.50
1 V:War Machine	2.25
1a Computer painted cover	2.25
2 Phoenix flip issue	2.25
3 Phoenix Resurrection	2.25
Spec. #1 O:Siren	2.25

SISTERS OF MERCY
Maximum, 1995–96
1	2.50
1a variant(c)	2.50
2	2.50
3	2.50

No Mercy Comics
4	2.50
5	2.50
TPB rep. #1–#5	15.00

SISTERS OF MERCY: PARADISE LOST
London Night, 1997
1 by Ricki Rockett & Mark Williams	2.50
2	2.50
3	2.50
4	2.50

SISTERS OF MERCY: WHEN RAZORS CRY CRIMSON TEARS
No Mercy Comics, 1996
1	2.50

SIX MILLION DOLLAR MAN, THE
Charlton, 1976
1 JSon,Lee Majors Ph(c)	35.00
2 NA(c),JSon,Ph(c)	20.00
3 Ph(c) HC,NA	22.00
4 thru 9 Ph(c)	@20.00

666: MARK OF THE BEAST
Fleetway/Quality, 1986
1 I:Fludd, BU:Wolfie Smith	2.25
2 thru 18	@2.25

SIX STRING SAMURAI
Awesome Entertainment, 1998
1 RLe	3.00

SKATEMAN
Pacific, 1983
1 NA	2.25

SKY WOLF
Eclipse, 1988
1 V:Baron Von Tundra	2.25
2 TL,V:Baron Von Tundra	2.25
3 TL,cont. in Airboy #41	2.25

SLAINE THE BERSERKER
Quality, 1987–89
1 thru 14	@2.25
15/16	2.25
17	2.25
18/19	2.25
20	2.25

Becomes:

SLAINE THE KING
Quality, 1989
21 thru 26	@2.25

SLAINE
Fleetway
1 thru 4 SBs,From 2000 AD	@5.00

SLAINE THE HORNED GOD
Egmont Fleetway, 1998
1 (of 3) Pat Millagan & SBs, 68pg.	7.00
2 (of 3) Pat Millagan & SBs, 68pg.	7.00
3 68-pg., conclusion	7.00

SLEEPER
Wildstorm/DC, 2003
1 SeP,F:Holden Carver	3.00
2 SeP	3.00
3 SeP,O:Miss Misery	3.00
4 SeP,behind the curtain	3.00
5 SeP,F:Holden Carver	3.00
6 SeP,Holden's past	3.00
7 SeP,things get worse	3.00
8 SeP,Doppelganger	3.00
9 SeP,secret records	3.00
10 thru 12 SeP	@3.00
TPB Sleeper: Out in the Cold	18.00
TPB Sleeper: All False Moves	18.00

Season Two (2004)
1 (of 12) SeP	3.00
2 thru 5 SeP	@3.00

SLIDERS
Valiant, 1996
1 & 2	@2.50

SLIDERS: DARKEST HOUR
Acclaim
1 DGC,DG	2.50
2 DGC,DG	2.50
3 DGC,DG, Concl.	2.50
Spec. RgM, Montezuma IV rules the world	4.00
Spec. #2 Secrets	4.00
TPB from TV show	9.00

SLIDERS: ULTIMATUM
Valiant, 1996
1 & 2	@2.50

SLIMER
Now, 1989
1	2.50
2 thru 15	@2.50

Becomes:

SLIMER & REAL GHOSTBUSTERS
16 thru 18	@2.50

COLOR PUB.

SLUDGE
Malibu Ultraverse, 1993–94
1 BWS,I:Sludge,BU:I:Rune 2.75
1a Ultra-Limited 5.00
2 AaL,I:Bloodstorm 2.25
3 AaL,V:River Men 2.50
4 AaL,Origins Month, V:Alligator. . . 2.25
5 AaL,V:Garret Whale 2.25
6 AaL,A:Dragon Fang,Lord
   Pumpkin 2.25
7 V:Frank Hoag 2.25
8 AaL,V:Monsters 2.25
9 AaL,O:Sludge 2.25
10 AaL,O:Sludge 2.25
11 AaL,V:Bash Brothers 2.25
12 AaL,V:Prime, w/flip book
   w/Ultraverse Premiere #8 . . . . . 3.50
13 . . . . 2.25
Red X-Mas 2.50

SMAX
Wildstorm/DC, 2003
1 (of 5) AMo,F:Jeff Smax 3.00
2 AMo,O:Smax 3.00
3 AMo,funeral 3.00
4 . . . . 3.00
5 AMo,V:Morningbright 3.00

SMILEY
Chaos! Comics, 1998
1 the Psychotic Button 3.00
Spec. Smiley Anti-Holiday Spec. . . . 3.00
Spec. Smiley Psychotic Button's
   Spring Break Road Trip 3.00
Spec. Whacky Wrestling Spec. 3.00

SMOKE
**What's Next
Entertainment, 2000**
1 (of 12) by Ty Rawls 3.00
2 . . . . 3.25
3 . . . . 3.25
4 . . . . 3.00
5 . . . . 3.25
TPB Vol. 1 . . . . 20.00

SNAGGLEPUSS
Gold Key, 1962–63
1 . . . . 125.00
2 . . . . 100.00
3 . . . . 100.00
4 . . . . 100.00

SNAKE PLISSKEN
CHRONICLES
Crossgen Comics, 2003
1 . . . . 3.00
2 . . . . 3.00
3 . . . . 3.00

SNAK POSSE
HCom, 1994
1 . . . . 2.25
2 . . . . 2.25

SNOOPER AND
BLABBER DETECTIVES
Gold Key, 1962–63
1 . . . . 125.00
2 . . . . 100.00
3 . . . . 100.00

SNOW WHITE &
SEVEN DWARFS
GOLDEN ANNIVERSARY
Gladstone, 1987
1 w/poster & stickers 24.00

SOAP OPERA ROMANCES
Charlton, 1982–83
1 . . . . 40.00
2 thru 5 . . . . @30.00

SO DARK THE ROSE
CFD, 1995
1 Fully Painted 3.00

SOJOURN
Dreamer Comics, 1998
1 by Jim Somerville, Stranger
   & Stranger, pt.1 . . . . 3.00
2 Stranger & Stranger, pt.2 . . . . . . 3.00
3 Malice in Wonderland 3.00
4 A Game of Conscience, pt.1 . . . . 3.00
5 A Game of Conscience, pt.2 . . . . 2.25
6 A Game of Conscience, pt.3 . . . . 3.25
7 A Game of Conscience, pt.4 . . . . 3.25
8 The Hunt 3.25
9 The Hunt, pt.2 . . . . 3.25
10 The Hunt, Bloodied 3.25

SOJOURN
Crossgen Comics, 2001
1 RMz 7.00
2 thru 5 RMz . . . . @5.00
6 thru 17 RMz 3.00
18 thru 24 . . . . @3.00
25 IEd 2.50
26 thru 37 . . . . @3.00
Collected Ed. #1 . . . . 4.00
Prequel RMz 3.00
TPB Vol. 1 rep. #1–#6 . . . . 20.00
TPB Vol. 2 Dragon's Tale 16.00
TPB Traveler Vol. 2 Dragon's Tale. 10.00
TPB Vol. 3 The Warrior's Tale 16.00
TPB Vol. 4 The Thief's Tale 16.00
TPB Vol. 5 The Sorcerer's Tale . . . 16.00

SOJOURN/LADY DEATH
Crossgen Comics, 2004
1 (of 2) 3.00
2 . . . . 3.00

SOLAR: HELL ON EARTH
Acclaim, 1997
1 (of 4) CPr,DCw,Seleski twins
   have power of God 2.50
2 CPr,Goat Month prelude 2.50
3 CPr,RT,V:Jimmy Six 2.50
4 CPr, ... 2.50

SOLAR: MAN OF
THE ATOM
Valiant, 1991
1 BWS,DP,BL,B:2nd Death B:Alpha
   & Omega 4.00
2 BWS,DP,BL,V:Dr Solar 3.00
3 BWS,DP,BL,V:Harada I:Harbinger
   Foundation 3.00
4 BWS,DP,BL,E:2nd Death V:Dr
   Solar 2.50
5 BWS,EC,V:Alien Armada 2.50
6 BWS,DP,SDr, V:Alien Armada X-
   O Armor 2.50
7 BWS,DP,SDr, V:Alien Armada X-
   O Armor 2.50

Solar, Man of the Atom #28
© Valiant

8 BWS,V:Dragon of Bangkok 2.50
9 BWS,DP,SDr, V:Erica's Baby 2.50
10 BWS,DP,SDr,JDx,I:Eternal
   Warrior,E:Alpha&Omega 3.00
10a 2nd printing 2.25
11 SDr,A:Eternal Warrior, Prequel
   to Unity #0 . . . . 3.00
12 SDr,FM(c),Unity#9,O:Pierce,
   Albert 2.50
13 DP,SDr,WS(c),Unity #17,
   V:Pierce 2.50
14 DP,SDr,I:Bender (becomes
   Dr.Eclipse) 3.00
15 SD,V:Bender 3.00
16 Solar moves to California 2.50
17 SDr(i),V:X-O Manowar 2.50
18 SDr(i),A:X-Manowar 2.50
19 SDr(i),V:Videogame 2.50
20 SDr(i),Dawn of the Malevolence. 2.50
21 SDr(i),Master Darque 2.50
22 SDr(i),V:Master Darque,A:
   Bender(Dr.Eclipse) 2.50
23 SDr(i),JQ(c),V:Master
   Darque,I:Solar War God 2.50
24 SDr(i),A:Solar War God 2.50
25 V:Dr.Eclipse 2.25
26 Phil and Gayle on vaction 2.25
27 in Auristralia 2.25
28 A:Solar War God 2.25
29 KVH(s),JP(i),Valiant Vision,
   A:Solar War God 2.50
30 KVH(s),JP,V:Energy Parasite . . . 2.25
31 KVH(s),JP,Chrismas Issue 2.25
32 KVH(s),JP,Parent's Night 2.25
33 KVH(s),PGr,JP,B:Solar the
   Destroyer,w/Valiant Era card . . . 2.25
34 KVH(s),PGr,V:Spider Alien 2.25
35 KVH(s),PGr,JP,E:Solar the
   Destroyer,Valiant Vision 2.25
36 KVH(s),PGr,JP,B:Revenge times
   two,V:Doctor Eclipse, Ravenus. 2.25
37 PGr,JP,E:Revenge times two,
   V:Doctor Eclipse,Ravenus 2.25
38 PGr,JP,Chaos Effect-Epsilon#1 . 2.25
39 . . . . 2.25
40 . . . . 2.25
41 . . . . 2.25
42 Elements of Evil pt.1 . . . . 2.25
43 Elements of Evil pt.2 . . . . 2.25
44 I:New Character 2.25
45 Explores Powers 2.25
46 I:The Sentry 2.25
47 DJu,DG,Brave New World,pt.2 . . 2.25
48 DJu,DG,Brave New World,pt.3 . . 2.25

49 DJu,DG,Brave New World,pt.4 . . 2.25
50 DJu,DG,Brave New World,pt.5 . . 2.25
51 I:Aliens on the Moon. 2.25
52 Solar Saves Earth. 2.25
53 I:Marauder. 2.25
54 V:Marauder. 2.25
55 I:Black Star 2.25
56 V:Black Star 2.25
57 A:Armorines 2.25
58 I:Atman, The Inquisitor 2.25
59 and 60 KG. . . . . @2.25
TPB #0 JiS,BWS,BL,Alpha and
   Omega rep. from Solar #1–#10 10.00
TPB #1 JiS,BWS,GL,V:Doctor Solar
   rep. from Solar #1–#4 . . . . 10.00

SOLDIERS OF FREEDOM
Americomics, 1987
1 . . . . 2.25
2 . . . . 2.25

SOLITAIRE
Malibu Ultraverse, 1993–94
1 black baged edition with playing
   card: Ace of Clubs, Diamonds,
   Hearts or Spades. 2.75
1d Newsstand edition,no card 2.25
2 GJ(s),JJ,Break-Thru x-over,
   V:Moon Man 2.25
3 Origins Month, I:Monkey-Woman 2.25
4 O:Solitaire 2.25
5 JJ,V:Djinn. 2.25
6 JJ,V:Lone. 2.25
7 JJ,I:Double Edge 2.25
8 GJ,I:Degenerate 2.25
9 GJ,Degenerate Rafferty. 2.25
10 Hostile Takeover #2 . . . . 2.25
11 V:Djinn. 2.25
12 V:Anton Lowe 2.25

SOLOMON KANE
Blackthorne
1 3-D Special 2.50
2 3-D Special 2.50
1 thru 4 . . . . @2.50

SOLUS
Crossgen Comics, 2003
1 BKs,GP,RM,48-pg. 3.00
2 thru 10 . . . . @3.00
TPB Vol. 1 Genesis 16.00

SOLUTION
Malibu Ultraverse, 1993–95
0 DaR,O:Solution 4.00
1 DaR,I:Solution 2.50
1a foil cover 4.00
2 DaR,BWS,V:Rex Mundi,Quatro,
   BU:Rune 2.50
3 DaR,A:Hardcase,Choice 2.50
4 DaR,Break-Thru x-over,
   A:Hardcase,Choice 2.50
5 F:Dropkick 2.25
6 B:O:Solution. 2.25
7 KM,O:Solution 2.25
8 KM(c),E:O:Solution 2.25
9 F:Shadowmage 2.25
10 V:Vyr. 2.25
11 V:Vorlexx 2.25
12 JHi. 2.25
13 Hostile Takeover pt.3 . . . . 2.25
14 old foes 2.25
15 V:Casino 2.25
16 Flip/UltraverePremiere#10 . . . . 3.50
17 F:Casino, Dragons Claws. 2.50

SOMERSET HOLMES
Pacific, 1983–84
1 BA,AW,I:Cliff Hanger &
   Somerset Holmes 2.50
2 thru 4 BA,AW . . . . @2.50

Eclipse, 1984
5 BA,AW 2.50
6 BA 2.50

Sonic the Hedgehog #39
© Archie Publications

SONIC THE HEDGEHOG
Archie Publications, 1993
1 A:Mobius,V:Robotnik 20.00
2 . . . . 7.00
3 thru 6 . . . . @6.00
7 thru 10 . . . . @5.00
11 thru 30 . . . . @3.00
31 thru 39 . . . . @3.00
40 thru 54 . . . . @3.00
55 thru 78 . . . . @2.25
79 and 80 . . . . @2.25
81 thru 99 . . . . @2.25
100 . . . . 2.25
101 thru 116 . . . . @2.25
117 thru 142 . . . . @2.25
GN Sonic Firsts, rep.#0, #1/4
   ashcan,#3,#4,#13 . . . . 5.00
Sonic Live Spec.#1 . . . . 2.25

SONIC QUEST: THE DEATH EGG SAGA
Archie Comics, 1997
1 (of 3) by Mike Gallagher & MaG,
   cont. from Sonic the Hedgehog
   #41. . . . . 2.25
2 and 3 . . . . @2.25

SONIC THE HEDGEHOG PRESENTS KNUCKLES CHASTIC
Archie Comics, 1995
1 I:New Heroes. 2.25
Sonic Versus Knuckles Battle Royal
   Spec.#1 . . . . 2.25

SONIC THE HEDGEHOG PRESENTS TAILS
Archie Comics, 1995
1 F:Tails 2.25
2 F:Tails 2.25

SONIC'S FRIENDLY NEMESIS: KNUCKLES
Archie Comics, 1996
1 . . . . 2.25

SONIC SUPER SPECIAL
Archie Comics, 1997
1 Brave New World. 2.25
3 Sonic Firsts 2.25
4 The Return of the King 2.25
5 Sonic Kids 2.25
6 Expanded Sonic #50, 48pg 2.25
7 F:Shadowhawk, The Maxx,
   Savage Dragon 2.25
8 four stories, 48-pg. 2.25
9 R:Sonic Kids 2.25
10 Some Enchantra Evening. 2.25
11 . . . . 2.30
12 48-pg. 2.50
13 thru 15 . . . . @2.50

SON OF MUTANT WORLD
Fantagor, 1990
1 BA 2.25
2 . . . . 2.25

SOULCATCHER
Moonstone, 2004
1 (of 2) 3.50
2 . . . . 3.50

SOULFIRE
Aspen Entertainment, 2003
0 The Day the Magic Died 2.50
1 . . . . 3.00
1a previews exclusive (c) 4.00
2 thru 3 . . . . @3.00

SOULMAN
Quantum Comics, 1998
1 . . . . 3.00
2 . . . . 3.00
3 16-pg. 3.00
4 16-pg. 3.00
5 24-pg. 3.00

SOULQUEST
Innovation, 1989
1 BA 4.00

SOUPY SALES COMIC BOOK
Archie Publications, 1965
1 . . . . 135.00

SPACE ADVENTURES
Charlton, 1967–79, Volume 3
1 (#60) O&I:Paul Mann & The
   Saucers From the Future 75.00
2 thru 8 (1968–69) . . . . @40.00
9 thru 13 (1978–79) . . . . @15.00

SPACE: ABOVE AND BEYOND
Topps, 1995
1 thru 3 TV pilot adaptation. . . . . @3.00

COLOR PUB.

SPACE: ABOVE AND BEYOND— THE GAUNTLET
Topps, 1996
1 .... 3.00
2 (of 2) 3.00

SPACE ARK
AC Comics, 1985–87
1 .... 3.00
2 .... 2.25

SPACE FAMILY ROBINSON
Gold Key, 1962–69
1 DSp 400.00
2 .... 200.00
3 .... 125.00
4 .... 125.00
5 .... 125.00
6 B:Captain Venture 100.00
7 .... 100.00
8 .... 100.00
9 .... 100.00
10 .... 100.00
11 thru 20 .... @75.00
21 thru 36 .... @45.00

SPACE GHOST
Gold Key, 1967
1 .... 550.00

SPACE GHOST
Comico, 1987
1 SR,V:Robot Master 10.00

SPACE GIANTS, THE
Pyramid Comics, 1997
0 .... 2.25
0a deluxe 2.25
1 .... 2.25
3 by Jeff Newman 2.25

SPACE MAN
Dell Publishing Co., 1962–72
1 .... 125.00
2 .... 60.00
3 .... 60.00
4 .... 45.00
5 .... 45.00
6 .... 45.00
7 .... 45.00
8 .... 45.00
9 .... 45.00
10 .... 45.00

SPACE: 1999
Charlton, 1975–76
1 .... 25.00
2 JSon,Survival 22.00
3 JBy,Bring Them Back Alive 15.00
4 JBy 15.00
5 JBy 15.00
6 JBy 15.00
7 .... 15.00
8 B&W 15.00

SPACE: 1999
A Plus Comics
1 GM,JBy 2.50

SPACE USAGI
Mirage, 1993
1 thru 3 From TMNT .... @2.75

SPACE WAR
Charlton Comics, 1959
1 .... 200.00
2 .... 100.00
3 .... 90.00
4 SD,SD(c) 200.00
5 SD,SD(c) 200.00
6 SD 200.00
7 .... 75.00
8 SD,SD(c) 200.00
9 .... 75.00
10 SD,SD(c) 200.00
11 .... 75.00
12 .... 75.00
13 thru 15 .... @75.00
16 thru 27 .... @50.00
Becomes:

FIGHTIN' FIVE
28 SD,SD(c) 60.00
29 SD,SD(c) 60.00
30 SD,SD(c) 75.00
31 SD,SD(c) 75.00
32 .... 20.00
33 SD,SD(c) 75.00
34 Sd,SD(c) 75.00

SPECTER 7
Antarctic Press, 2002
1 (of 3) by Craig Babiar 5.00
2 and 3 .... @5.00

SPECTRUM COMICS PRESENTS
Spectrum, 1983
1 I:Survivors 3.50

SPECWAR
Peter Four Productions, 2002
1 .... 3.25
2 thru 5 .... @3.25
6 thru 8 .... @3.25

SPEED RACER
Now, 1987–90
1 .... 3.50
1a 2nd printing 2.50
2 thru 33 .... @2.50
34 thru 38 .... @2.50
Spec. #1 .... 2.50
#1 2nd printing 2.00
Spec. #2 .... 3.50
Classics, Vol #2 .... 4.00
Classics, Vol #3 .... 4.00
[2nd Series]
1 R:Speed Racer 2.50
2 .... 2.50
3 V:Giant Crab 2.50
4 .... 2.50
5 Racer-X 2.50
6 .... 2.50
7 .... 2.50

SPEED RACER
WildStorm/DC, 1999
1 Demon on Wheels 2.50
2 .... 2.50
3 concl 2.50
TPB Born to Race 10.00
TPB Original Manga 10.00

SPELLBINDERS
Quality, 1986–88
1 Nemesis the Warlock 2.25
2 thru 11 Nemesis the Warlock .. @2.25

S.P.I.C.E.
Awesome Entertainment, 1998
1 RLe,JLb,F:Kaboom 2.50

SPIDER
Eclipse, 1991
1 TT,Blood Dance 7.00
2 TT,Blood Mark 6.00
3 TT,The Spider Unmasked 5.50

Spider: Reigh on the Vampire King Book #3 © Eclipse

SPIDER: REIGN OF THE VAMPIRE KING
Eclipse, 1992
1 TT,I:Legion of Vermin 5.25
2 thru 4 TT .... @2.50

SPIDERFEMME
Personality
1 Rep. parody 2.50

SPIDER-MAN/BADROCK
Maximum Press, 1997
1 (of 2) DJu,MMy x-over 3.00
2 DJu,DaF x-over 3.00

SPIRAL PATH
Eclipse, 1986
1 V:Tairngir 2.25
2 V:King Artuk 2.25

SPIRIT
Harvey, 1966
1 WE,O:Spirit 100.00
2 WE,O:The Octopus 75.00

SPIRIT, THE
Kitchen Sink, 1983–92
1 WE(c) (1983) 5.25
2 WE(c) 4.25
3 WE(c) (1984) 4.00
4 WE(c) 4.00

5 WE(c) 3.00
6 WE(c) 3.00
7 WE(c) 3.00
8 thru 11 WE(c) (1985) . . . . @3.00
See: B&W Pub. section

SPIRIT, THE:
THE NEW ADVENTURES
Kitchen Sink, 1997
1 AMo,DGb 4.00
2 Eisner/Stout cover 3.50
2a Eisner/Schultz cover 3.50
3 AMo,Last Night I Dreamed of
   Dr. Cobra 3.50
4 Dr. Broca von Bitelbaum 3.50
5 Cursed Beauty 3.50
6 Swami Vashti Bubu 3.50
7 Central City 3.50
8 by Joe Lansdale 3.50
9 . . . . 3.50
10 CAd,BRa 3.50

SPIRIT OF THE AMAZON
NW Studios, 2002
1 . . . . 3.00
2 thru 7 . . . . @3.00

SPOOKY HAUNTED
HOUSE
Harvey Publications, 1972–75
1 . . . . 40.00
2 . . . . 30.00
3 thru 5 . . . . @30.00
6 thru 10 . . . . @25.00
11 thru 15 . . . . @20.00

SPOOKY SPOOKTOWN
Harvey Publications, 1966–76
1 B:Casper,Spooky,68 pgs 250.00
2 . . . . 150.00
3 . . . . 100.00
4 . . . . 100.00
5 . . . . 100.00
6 thru 10 . . . . @75.00
11 thru 20 . . . . @50.00
21 thru 30 . . . . @50.00
31 thru 39 E:68 pgs . . . . @40.00
40 thru 45 . . . . @30.00
46 thru 66 . . . . @20.00

SPOONER
Astonish Comics, 2004
1 . . . . 3.00
2 thru 4 . . . . @3.00
TPB 15.00

SPYMAN
Harvey, 1966
1 GT,JSo,1st prof work,
   I:Spyman 100.00
2 DAy,JSo,V:Cyclops 75.00
3 . . . . 60.00

SQUAD, THE
Malibu
0-A Hardcase's old team 2.50
0-B 2.50
0-C L.A.Riots 2.50

SQUALOR
First, 1989
1 . . . . 2.75
2 . . . . 2.75
3 . . . . 2.75

STAINLESS STEEL RAT
Eagle, 1986
1 Harry Harrison adapt. 2.25
2 thru 6 . . . . @2.25

STAR BLAZERS
Comico, 1989
1 . . . . 3.00
2 . . . . 3.00
3 . . . . 3.00
4 . . . . 3.00

[2nd Series]
1 . . . . 3.00
2 . . . . 3.00
3 thru 5 . . . . @3.00

STARBLAZERS
Argo Press, 1995
0 Battleship Yamato 3.00
1 F:Dereck Wildstar 3.00
2 After the Comet War 3.00
3 . . . . 3.00
4 TEI 3.00
5 thru 12 . . . . @3.00

STARFORCE SIX
SPECIAL
AC Comics, 1984
1 . . . . 2.25

Stargate #4
© Entity Comics

STARGATE
Entity Comics, 1996
1 . . . . 3.00
2 . . . . 3.00
3 . . . . 3.00
4 . . . . 3.00
4a deluxe limited edition 3.50

STARGATE:
DOOMSDAY WORLD
Entity Comics, 1996
1 new crew explores 2nd StarGate 3.00
1 prism-foil edition 3.50
2 . . . . 3.00
3 . . . . 3.00
3 deluxe 3.50

STARGATE SG–1
Avatar, 2003
Convention Spec. 3.00
Convention Spec. Photo (c) 4.00
Spec. First Prime Edition 6.00
Prism foil (c) con special 13.00
Convention Spec. 2004 . . . . 3.00
Convention Spec. 2004, ph(c) 4.00

STARGATE SG-1:
ARIS BOCH
Avatar, 2004
1 . . . . 3.00
1a photo (c) 3.00
1b wraparound (c) 3.00

STARGATE SG-1:
FALL OF ROME
Avatar, 2004
Prequel 3.00
Prequel wraparound (c) 3.00
Prequel photo(c) 3.00
1 . . . . 4.00
2 thru 3 . . . . @4.00
1a thru 3a photo (c)s . . . . @4.00
1b thru 3b wraparound (c)s . . . . @4.00

STARGATE SG-1: P.O.W.
Avatar, 2004
1 . . . . 3.50
1a wraparound (c) 3.50
1b photo (c) 3.50
1c Teal'c photo (c) 6.00
2 . . . . 3.50
2a wraparound (c) 3.50
2b photo (c) 3.50
3 . . . . 3.50
3a wraparound (c) 3.50
3b photo (c) 3.50

STARGODS
Antarctic Press, 1998
1 by Zachary, Clark & Beaty 3.00
1a deluxe 6.00
2 The Golden Bow 3.00
2a deluxe, with poster 6.00
Spec. Stargods Visions 3.00

STARK RAVEN
Hardline Studios, 2000
1 The Screaming Rain,pt.1 . . . . 3.00
2 The Screaming Rain,pt.2 . . . . 3.00
3 . . . . 3.00
Endless Horizons, 2000
4 . . . . 3.00
5 . . . . 3.00
6 Ken Kelly (c) 3.00
7 . . . . 3.00
8 . . . . 3.00

STAR MASTERS
AC Comics, 1994
1 . . . . 2.25

STAR REACH CLASSICS
Eclipse, 1984
1 JSn,NA(r) 2.25
2 AN 2.25
3 HC 2.25
4 FB(r) 2.25
5 . . . . 2.25
6 . . . . 2.25

COLOR PUB.

STAR SEED
See: POWERS THAT BE

STAR SLAMMERS
Malibu Bravura, 1994
1 WS(a&s) 2.75
2 WS(a&s),F:Meredith 2.75
3 WS(a&s) 2.50
4 WS(a&s) 2.50
5 WS,Rojas Choice. 2.50

STARSLAYER
Pacific, 1982–83
1 MGr,O:Starslayer 4.00
2 MGr,DSt,I:Rocketeer 10.00
3 DSt,MGr,A:Rocketeer(2ndApp.). . 6.00
4 MGr,Baraka Kuhr. 2.25
5 MGr,SA,A:Groo 7.00
6 MGr.conclusion story 2.25
First, 1983–85
7 MGr layouts 2.25
8 MGr layouts, MG 2.25
9 MGr layouts, MG 2.25
10 TT,MG,I:Grimjack 4.00
11 TT,MG,A:Grimjack. 2.25
12 TT,MG,A:Grimjack. 2.25
13 TT,MG,A:Grimjack. 2.25
14 TT,A:Grimjack 2.25
15 TT,A:Grimjack 2.25
16 TT,A:Grimjack 2.25
17 TT,A:Grimjack 2.25
18 TT,Grimjack x-over 2.25
19 TT,TS,A:Black Flame 2.25
20 TT,TS,A:Black Flame 2.25
21 TT,TS,A:Black Flame 2.25
22 TT,TS,A:Black Flame 2.25
23 TT,TS,A:Black Flame 2.25
24 TT,TS,A:Black Flame 2.25
25 TS,A:Black Flame 2.25
26 TS,Black Flame full story 2.25
27 A:Black Flame. 2.25
28 A:Black Flame. 2.25
29 TS,A:Black Flame 2.25
30 TS,A:Black Flame 2.25
31 2nd Anniversary Issue 2.25
32 TS,A:Black Flame 2.25
33 TS,A:Black Flame 2.25
34 last issue. 2.25
Graphic Novel 10.00

STARSLAYER DIRECTORS CUT
Windjammer, 1995
1 R:Starslayer, Mike Grell. 2.50
2 I:New Star Slayer. 2.50
3 Jolly Rodger. 2.50
4 V:Battle Droids. 2.50
5 I:Baraka Kuhi 2.50
6 V:Valkyrie. 2.50
7 MGr(c&a),Can Torin destroy? . . . 2.50
8 MGr(c&a),JAI, Can Torin live with
his deeds?,final issue 2.50

STAR TREK
Gold Key, 1967–79
1 Planet of No Return 750.00
2 Devil's Isle of Space 500.00
3 Invasion of City Builders 250.00
4 Peril of Planet Quick Change . 250.00
5 Ghost Planet 250.00
6 When Planets Collide 210.00
7 Voodoo Planet 225.00
8 Youth Trap 200.00
9 Legacy of Lazarus 200.00
10 Sceptre of the Sun 175.00
11 Brain Shockers 175.00

12 Flight of the Buccaneer. 150.00
13 Dark Traveler 150.00
14 Enterprise Mutiny 150.00
15 Museum a/t End of Time. 150.00
16 Day of the Inquisitors 150.00
17 Cosmic Cavemen 150.00
18 The Hijacked Planet 150.00
19 The Haunted Asteroid. 150.00
20 A World Gone Mad 150.00
21 The Mummies of Heitus VII . . 100.00
22 Siege in Superspace. 100.00
23 Child's Play. 100.00
24 The Trial of Capt. Kirk. 100.00
25 Dwarf Planet 100.00
26 The Perfect Dream 100.00
27 Ice Journey 100.00
28 The Mimicking Menace. 100.00
29 rep. Star Trek #1. . . . . 100.00
30 Death of a Star 75.00
31 The Final Truth.. . . . . 75.00
32 The Animal People 75.00
33 The Choice 75.00
34 The Psychocrystals. 75.00

Star Trek #29
© Gold Key

35 rep. Star Trek #4 . . . . 75.00
36 A Bomb in Time. 75.00
37 rep. Star Trek #5. . . . . 60.00
38 One of our Captains
is Missing. 60.00
39 Prophet of Peace 60.00
40 AMc,Furlough to Fury, A:
Barbara McCoy 60.00
41 AMc,The Evictors 60.00
42 World Against Time. 60.00
43 World Beneath the Waves 60.00
44 Prince Traitor 60.00
45 rep. Star Trek #7. . . . . 60.00
46 Mr. Oracle. 60.00
47 AMc,This Tree Bears Bitter
Fruit 60.00
48 AMc,Murder on Enterprise . . . 60.00
49 AMc,A Warp in Space 60.00
50 AMc,The Planet of No Life . . . 60.00
51 AMc,DestinationAnnihilation6 . . 50.00
52 AMc,And A Child Shall
Lead Them 50.00
53 AMc,What Fools..Mortals Be . . 50.00
54 AMc,Sport of Knaves 50.00
55 AMc,A World Against Itself 50.00
56 AMc,No Time Like The Past,
A:Guardian of Forever. 50.00
57 AMc,Spore of the Devil 50.00
58 AMc,Brain Damaged Planet . . . 50.00
59 AMc,To Err is Vulcan. 50.00

60 AMc,The Empire Man 50.00
61 AMc,Operation Con Game 50.00
Checker Book, 2004
TPB Vol. 1 rep. Gold Key. 23.00
TPB Vol. 2 rep. Gold Key. 23.00

STAR TREK
WildStorm/DC, April, 2001
TPB Other Realities, 192-pg. 15.00

STAR TREK: ALL OF ME
WildStorm/DC, 2000
1-shot AaL,RyE 6.00

STAR TREK: DEEP SPACE NINE
Malibu, 1993
1 Direct ed. 3.25
1a Photo(c). 3.00
1b Gold foil 5.00
2 w/skycap 3.50
3 Murder on DS9 . . . . 2.75
4 MiB(s),F:Bashir,Dax. 2.75
5 MiB(s),V:Slaves 2.75
6 MiB(s),Three Stories 2.75
7 F:Kira 2.75
8 B:Requiem 2.75
9 E:Requiem. 2.75
10 Descendants. 2.50
11 A Short Fuse 2.75
12 Baby on Board 2.50
13 Problems with Odo 2.75
14 on Bejor 2.75
15 mythologic dilemma 2.75
16 Shangheid. 2.50
17 Voyager preview 2.50
18 V:Gwyn 2.50
19 Wormhole Mystery 2.50
20 Sisko Injured. 2.50
21 Smugglers attack DS9 . . . . . . 2.50
22 Commander Quark 2.50
23 Secret of the Lost Orb,pt.1 . . . 2.50
24 Secret of the Lost Orb,pt.2 . . . 2.50
25 Secret of the Lost Orb,pt.3 . . . 2.50
26 Mudd's Pets, pt.1 . . . . 2.50
27 Mudd's Pets, pt.2 . . . . 2.50
28 F:Ensign Ro 2.50
29 F:Thomas Riker,Tuvok 2.50
30 F:Thomas Riker 2.50
31 thru 32. . . . . @2.50
Ann.#1 Looking Glass 4.00
Spec. #1 Collision Course 3.50
Spec. #0 Terok Nor 3.00

STAR TREK: DEEP SPACE NINE CELEBRITY SERIES: BLOOD AND HONOR
Malibu, 1995
1 Mark Lenard(s) 3.00
2 Rules of Diplomacy 3.00

STAR TREK: DEEP SPACE NINE: LIGHTSTORM
Malibu, 1994
1 Direct ed. 3.50
1a Silver foil 8.00

STAR TREK: DEEP SPACE NINE: HEARTS AND MINDS
Malibu, 1994
1 . . . . 3.00

2 . . . . 2.50
3 Into the Abyss,X-over preview. . . 2.50
4 final issue. 2.50

STAR TREK: DEEP SPACE NINE: THE MAQUIS
Malibu, 1995
1 Federation Renegades 2.50
1a Newsstand, photo(c) 2.50
2 Garack 2.50
3 F:Quark, Bashir 2.50

STAR TREK: DEEP SPACE NINE/ THE NEXT GENERATION
Malibu, 1994
1 Prophet & Losses, pt.2 . . . . 2.50
2 Prophet & Losses, pt.4 . . . . 2.50

STAR TREK: DIVIDED WE FALL
WildStorm/DC, 2001
1 (of 4) TNG & DS9 x-over. 3.00
2 . . . . 3.00
3 . . . . 3.00
4 concl. 3.00

STAR TREK: ENTER THE WOLVES
WildStorm/DC, 2001
1-shot, 48-pg. 6.00

STAR TREK SPECIAL
WildStorm/DC, 2000
GN #1 64-pg. 7.00

STAR TREK: DEEP SPACE NINE — N-VECTOR
WildStorm/DC, 2000
1 (of 4),F:Kira 2.50
2 sabotage 2.50
3 N-Vector viroid 2.50
4 F:Quark,concl. 2.50

STAR TREK: THE NEXT GENERATION
WildStorm/DC, 2000
GN Embrace the Wolf, 48-pg. 6.00
TPB Enemy Unseen, 224-pg. 18.00
TPB The Gorn Crisis (2002) 18.00
TPB Forgiveness (2002) 18.00

STAR TREK: NEW FRONTIER — TIME MANAGEMENT
WildStorm/DC, 2001
GN PDd, novel adapt. 6.00

STAR TREK: THE NEXT GENERATION — THE KILLING SHADOWS
WildStorm/DC, 2000
1 (of 4) V:Bodai Shin, assassin . . 2.25
2 V:Bodai Shin 2.25
3 V:Bodai Shin 2.25
4 concl. 2.50

STAR TREK: THE NEXT GENERATION — PERCHANCE TO DREAM
WildStorm/DC, 1999
1 (of 4) 2.50
2 . . . . 2.50
3 . . . . 2.50
4 conclusion 2.50

STAR TREK: VOYAGER
WildStorm/DC, 2000
Spec. Elite Force 6.00
Spec. Avalon Rising 6.00
TPB Encounters with the Unknown 20.00

STAR TREK: VOYAGER
Malibu
A V:Maquis. 2.75
Aa Newsstand, photo(c) 2.50
B conclusion. 2.75
Ba Newsstand, photo(c) 2.50

STAR TREK: VOYAGER — PLANET KILLER
WildStorm/DC, 2001
1 (of 3) F:Kirk,Janeway. 3.00
2 Doomsday Machine. 3.00
3 concl. 3.00

STAR WARS IN 3-D
Blackthorne, 1987
1 thru 7 . . . . @2.50

STARWATCHERS
Valiant
1 MLe,DG,Chromium(c),Valiant
  Vision, ... 3.50

STARWOLVES: JUPITER RUN
1 . . . . 2.25

S.T.A.T.
Majestic, 1993
1 FdS(s),PhH,I:S.T.A.T.. . . . . 2.50

STATIC-X
Chaos! Comics, 2002
1 by BnP, with CD-Rom 6.00
1a photo (c) with CD-Rom 6.00
1b collector's edition 20.00
Vol. 2
1 with CD-Rom 6.00
1a collector's edition 20.00

STEALTH SQUAD
Petra Comics, 1993
1 I:Stealth Squad 2.50

STEAMPUNK
WildStorm/DC Cliffhanger, 2000
1 CBa 2.50
1 chromium edition . . . .
2 CBa,V:Absinthe 2.50
3 CBa,F:Cole Blaquesmith 2.50
4 CBa,CBa(c) 2.50
4a variant JSC (c) (1:4) 2.50
4b variant JMd (c) (1:4) 2.50
4c variant HuR (c) (1:4) 2.50
5 CBa,V:Abbey Monsters 2.50
6 Mechanica Sundown,pt.1 . . . . . . 2.50
7 Mechanica Sundown,pt.2 . . . . . . 2.50

8 Mechanica Sundown,pt.3 . . . . . . 2.50
9 Mambutu X, pt.1 . . . . 2.50
10 Mambutu X, pt.2. . . . . 2.50
11 CBa, Stonehenge secret. 2.50
12 CBa, 40-pg. final issue 3.50
TPB Drama Obscura 15.00
TPB Manimatron 15.00

Steed And Mrs. Peel #2
© Eclipse

STEED & MRS. PEEL
Eclipse, 1990
1 IG,The Golden Game. 5.00
2 IG,The Golden Game. 5.00
3 IG,The Golden Game. 5.00

STEEL CLAW
Quality, 1986
1 H:Ken Bulmer 2.25
2 . . . . 2.25
3 . . . . 2.25
4 . . . . 2.25

STEEL STERLING
Archie Publications, 1984 (formerly LANCELOT STRONG)
4 EB 2.25
5 EB 2.25
6 EB 2.25
7 EB 2.25

STEVE CANYON 3-D
Kitchen Sink, 1986
Milton Caniff & Peter Poplaski(c),
  w/glasses (1985) 2.25

STEVE ZODIAC & THE FIREBALL XL-5
Gold Key, 1964
1 . . . . 150.00

STING OF THE GREEN HORNET
Now, 1992
1 Polybagged w/trading card 2.75
2 inc.Full color poster 2.75
3 inc.Full color poster 2.75

STINGER
1 . . . . 2.25

COLOR PUB.

STITCH
Samsons Comics
1 I:Stitch 2.50

STONE COLD STEVE AUSTIN
Chaos! Comics, 1999
1 (of 4) Whoop Ass personified . . . 3.00
1a photo (c) 3.00
1b Premium 9.99
2 . . . . 3.00
2a photo (c) 3.00
3 . . . . 3.00
3a photo (c) 3.00
4 . . . . 3.00
4a photo (c) 3.00
TPB Vol. 1 . . . . 13.00

STORMQUEST
Caliber, 1994
1 I:Stormquest 2.25
2 Time Stone 2.25
3 BU:Seeker 2.25
4 F:Shalimar 2.25
5 Reunion 2.25
6 V:Samuroids 2.25

STORM RIDERS
Comicsone.com, 2001
GN #1 by Wing Shing Ma, 178-pg. 10.00
GN #2 127-pg. 10.00
GN #3 thru #5, 120-pg. . . . . @12.00
GN #6 thru #8, 120-pg. . . . . @14.00
GN #9 thru #12 . . . . @14.00

Part 2 (2003) Invading Sun
TPB Vol. 1 . . . . 10.00
TPB Vol. 2 thru Vol. 6. . . . . @10.00

STORMWATCH: TEAM ACHILLES
WildStorm/DC, 2002
Eye of the Storm
1 WPo,SW,new team 3.00
2 WPo,SW,extremists vs. U.N. 3.00
3 WPo,SW,military action 3.00
4 WPo,SW,hunt for Ivana Baiul . . . 3.00
5 WPo,F:The Authority 3.00
6 WPo,F:The Authority 3.00
7 MT,V:Ivana Baiul 3.00
8 F:Jukko Hamalainen 3.00
9 WPo,V:super-human 3.00
10 WPo 3.00
11 WPo 3.00
12 WPo,funeral 3.00
13 BSz,The Suiciders 3.00
14 WPo,Citizen Soldier 3.00
15 The Suiciders 3.00
16 V:Citizen Soldier 3.00
17 V:Citizen Soldier 3.00
18 O:Citizen Soldier 3.00
19 Citizen Soldier,concl. 3.00
20 . . . . 3.00
21 . . . . 3.00
22 Hallibastard 3.00
23 Baron Chaos 3.00
24 Project Entry Universe 3.00
TPB Vol. 1 . . . . 15.00
TPB Vol. 2 . . . . 15.00

STORY OF THE TAO
Comicsone, 2002
TPB #1 thru #5 . . . . @14.00
TPB #6 . . . . @15.00
TPB #7 thru #9 . . . . @15.00

STRANGE DAYS
Eclipse, 1984–85
1 . . . . 3.50
2 . . . . 2.50
3 . . . . 2.50

Strangers #15
© Malibu

STRANGERS, THE
Malibu Ultraverse, 1993–95
1 I:Strangers 3.00
1a Ultra-Limited 4.00
1b Full Hologram (c) 5.00
2 A:J.D.Hunt,w/Ultraverse card . . . 3.00
3 I:TNTNT 2.50
4 A:Hardcase 2.50
5 BWS,BU:Rune 2.50
6 J:Yrial,I:Deathwish 2.25
7 Break-Thru x-over 2.25
8 RHo,ANi,O:Solution 2.25
9 AV(i),I:Ulta Pirates 2.25
10 AV(i),V:Bastinado 2.25
11 in Alderson Disk 2.25
12 O:Yrial 2.25
13 (Ultraverse Premiere#4) 3.50
14 . . . . 2.25
15 Zip-Zap, Yrail 2.25
16 Ultras, Teknight 2.25
17 Rafferty 2.25
18 Ultra Pirates 2.25
19 V:Pilgrim 2.25
20 Stranger Destroyed 2.25
21 A:Rex Mundi 2.50
22 SEt,V:Guy Hunt 2.50
23 SEt,RHo,V:Taboo 2.50
24 RHo,SEt,V:Taboo 2.50
25 V:Godwheel Aliens 2.50
26 RHo,SEt,V:Aladdin 2.50
Ann.#1 Death 4.00
TPB rep. #1-#4 . . . . 10.00
Ashcan 1 (signed) 8.00
Ashcan 1 (unsigned) 8.00

STRANGE SUSPENSE STORIES/ CAPTAIN ATOM
Charlton Comics, 1965
75 SD,O:CaptainAtom,1960Rep.. 175.00
76 SD, Capt.Atom,1960Rep. 100.00
77 SD, Capt.Atom,1960Rep. 100.00
Becomes:

CAPTAIN ATOM
Charlton Comics, 1965–67
78 SD, new stories begin. 125.00
79 SD,I:Dr.Spectro 90.00
80 SD 90.00
81 SD,V:Dr.Spectro 90.00
82 SD,I:Nightshade,Ghost 90.00
83 SD,I:Ted Kord/Blue Beetle 75.00
84 SD,N:Captain Atom 75.00
85 SD,A:Blue Beetle,I:Punch & Jewelee 75.00
86 SD,A:Ghost, Blue Beetle 75.00
87 SD,JAp,A:Nightshade 75.00
88 SD/FMc,JAp,A:Nightshade 75.00
89 SD/FMc,JAp,A:Nightshade, Ghost, last issue Dec.,1967 . . 75.00

STRAW MEN
Innovation
1 & 2 . . . . @2.25

STREET FIGHTER
Ocean, 1986–87
1 thru 3 . . . . @2.25

STREET FIGHTER
Malibu
1 thru 3 Based on Video Game . @3.00

STREET FIGHTER
Devil's Due/UDON, 2004
7 . . . . 4.50
7a variant (c) 4.50
8 thru 11 . . . . @3.00
8a thru 11a variant (c)s . . . . @3.00
TPB Vol. 1 . . . . 10.00
TPB Eternal Challenge 34.00

STREET SHARKS
Archie Comics, 1995
1 & 2 Based on Cartoons . . . . . . @2.25

STRIKE!
Eclipse, 1988
1 TL,RT,I&O:New Strike 2.25
2 TL,RT 2.25
3 TL,RT 2.25
4 TL,RT,V:Renegade CIA Agents . . 2.25
5 TL,RT,V:Alien Bugs 2.25
6 TL,RT,Legacy of the Lost 2.25
Spec. #1 Strike vs. Sgt. Strike TL,RT,The Man 2.25

STRIKEBACK
Malibu Bravura, 1994–95
1 . . . . 3.00
2 . . . . 3.00
3 V:Doberman 3.00
4 V:Dragonryder Island 3.00
Spec.#1 KM,JRu,V:Dragon 3.50

STRIKER
Viz
1 thru 2 . . . . @2.75

STRIKEFORCE AMERICA
Comico, 1995
1 ScC,SK(c),I:StrikeforceAmerica. . 2.50
2 V:Superior-prisoner 3.00
3 Breakout, pt.2 . . . . 3.00

[Volume 2], 1995
1 ScC,polybagged with Chrysalis promo card 3.00

All comics prices listed are for *Near Mint* condition.

COLOR PUB.

STRONG MAN
AC Comics
1 . . . . 3.00

STRONTIUM DOG
[Mini Series]
Eagle, 1985
1 thru 4 . . . . @2.25

[Regular Series]
Quality, 1988
Story line continued from 2000 A.D.
7 thru 14 . . . . @2.25
15/16 . . . . 2.25
17 . . . . 2.25
18/19 . . . . 2.25
20 thru 29 . . . . @2.25
Spec.#1 . . . . 2.25

[2nd Series], 1997
1 thru 6 . . . . @2.25

STRYKE
London Night Studios, 1995
0 I:Stryke 5.00
1 . . . . 4.00

STUMBO THE GIANT
Blackthorne
1 3-D 2.50

STUMBO TINYTOWN
Harvey Publications, 1963–66
1 . . . . 225.00
2 . . . . 150.00
3 . . . . 100.00
4 . . . . 100.00
5 . . . . 100.00
6 thru 13 . . . . @75.00

STUPID HEROES
Next, 1994
1 PeL(s),w/ 2 card-strip 2.75
2 . . . . 2.75
3 F:Cinder 2.75

STURM THE TROOPER
1 . . . . 2.25
2 . . . . 2.25
3 . . . . 2.25

SUBSPECIES
Eternity, 1991
1 Movie Adaptation 3.00
2 Movie Adaptation 2.50
3 Movie Adaptation 2.50
4 Movie Adaptation 2.50

SUN GLASSES AFTER DARK
Verotik, 1995
1 . . . . 3.00
2 and 3 . . . . @3.00
4 thru 6 . . . . @4.00
6 fan club cover 5.00
? prequel, San Diego Con ed. 3.00

SUN-RUNNERS
Pacific, 1984
1 . . . . 2.50
2 . . . . 2.50
3 . . . . 2.50

Eclipse, 1984–86
4 thru 7 . . . . @2.50
Summer Special #1 . . . . 2.50

SUNSET CARSON
AC Comics
1 Based on Cowboy Star 5.00

SUPERBABES: FEMFORCE
AC Comics
1 Various Artists 5.00

SUPER CAR
Gold Key, 1962–63
1 . . . . 350.00
2 . . . . 200.00
3 . . . . 200.00
4 . . . . 225.00

SUPERCOPS
Now, 1990
1 thru 4 . . . . @2.25

SUPER COPS, THE
Red Circle, 1974
1 . . . . 3.00

SUPER GOOF
Gold Key, 1965–82
1 . . . . 60.00
2 thru 10 . . . . @30.00
11 thru 20 . . . . @25.00
21 thru 30 . . . . @20.00
31 thru 74 . . . . @15.00

SUPER HEROES VERSUS SUPERVILLIANS
Archie Publications, 1966
1 A:Flyman,Black Hood,The Web,
The Shield 80.00

SUPERHUMAN SAMURAI SYBER SQUAD
Hamilton Comics, 1995
0 Based on TV Show 3.00

SUPER MARIO BROS.
Valiant, 1991
1 thru 6 . . . . @2.25
Spec. #1 . . . . 2.25

SUPERNAUT
Anarchy, 1997
1 (of 3) 3.00
1 gold logo 6.00
2 by Rob Hand, Hand of Doom . . . 3.00
2a gold logo 6.00

SUPREME
Maximum Press, 1997
#1–#43 see Image
44 AMo, JoB, A:Glory 3.00
45 AMo, JoB, A:Glory 3.00
46 AMo,Suprema 3.00
47 AMo 3.00
48 AMo 2.50
49 AMo 2.50
50 double size 4.00
51 . . . . 3.50
52A AMo, Book 1 . . . . 3.50
52B AMo, Book 2, continuation 3.50
53 AMo,CSp,AG,V:Omniman 3.00
54 AMo,CSp,AG,Ballad of Judy
Jordan 3.00
55 AMo,CSp,AG,Silence At
Gettysburg 3.00
56 AMo,CSp,AG,Reflections,pt.1 . . . 3.00
57 AMo,CSp,AG,Reflections,pt.2 . . . 3.00
58 AMo,CSp,AG,A World of
His Own 3.00
59 AMo,CSp,AG,Professor Night of
the Prism World 3.00
60 AMo,CSp,AG,F:Radar in Puppy
Love 3.00
61 AMo,CSp,AG,Meet Mr. Meteor . . 3.00
Coll.Ed.#1, rep.#1–#2 . . . . 5.00
Coll.Ed.#2, rep. 5.00
Coll.Ed.#3 rep. #45–#46, AMo 5.00
Classic Col.Ed.#1,rep.#1&#2 . . . . . 6.00
Classic Col.Ed.#2,rep.#43&#44 . . . . 6.00
TPB Secret Origins, rep. 17.00
TPB Supreme Madness 15.00
TPB rep. #41–#46, AMo 15.00

SUPREME: THE RETURN
Awesome Entertainment, 1999
1 AMo,CSp,AG 3.00
1a variant AxR cover 7.00
2 AMo,JSn, ... 3.00
3 thru 8 . . . . @3.00

Surge #3
© Eclipse

SURGE
Eclipse, 1984
1 A:DNAgents 3.00
2 A:DNAgents 3.00
3 A:DNAgents 3.00
4 A:DNAgents 3.00

SURVIVORS
Spectrum
1 Mag. size 5.00
2 . . . . 3.50
3 The Old One 2.50
4 . . . . 2.50

SURVIVORS
Fantagraphics
1 thru 3 . . . . @2.50

SUSPIRA: THE GREAT WORKING
Chaos! Comics, 1997
1 (of 4) PNa 3.00
2 PNa 3.00

3 PNa 3.00
4 PNa 3.00

SWORD OF VALOR
A Plus Comics
1 . . . . 2.50
2 . . . . 2.50
3 . . . . 2.50
4 . . . . 2.50

SWORDS OF TEXAS
Eclipse, 1987
1 FH,New America 2.25
2 FH,V:Baja Badlands 2.25
3 FH,TY(c),V:Dogs of Danger. 2.25
4 FH,V:Samurai Master 2.25

SYMBOLS OF JUSTICE
High Impact Studios, 1995
1 I:Granger,Justice,Rayven 3.00
2 V:Devil's Brigade 3.00

SYPHONS
Now, 1988
1 . . . . 2.50
2 thru 7 . . . . @2.50

SYPHONS: COUNTDOWN
Now, 1994
1 F:Brigade 3.00
2 Led By Cross. 3.00
3 Blown Cover 3.00
1995 Ann. Doomsday Device 3.00

SYPHONS: THE STARGATE STRATAGEM
Now, 1994
1 thru 3 . . . . @3.00

TALES CALCULATED TO DRIVE YOU BATS
Archie Publications, 1961–62
1 . . . . 200.00
2 . . . . 100.00
3 thru 6 . . . . @75.00

TALES FROM THE CRYPT
Gladstone, 1990–91
1 E.C.rep.AW/FF,GS. 5.00
2 rep.. . . . . 4.00
3 rep. 3.50
4 rep.. . . . . 3.00
5 rep.TFTC #45 . . . . 3.00
6 rep.TFTC #42 . . . . 3.00

TALES FROM THE CRYPT
Russ Cochran Publ, 1992
1 rep. TFTC #31,CSS#12. . . . . . . 3.00
2 rep. TFTC #34,CSS#15. . . . . . . 3.00
3 rep. TFTC, CSS. 3.00
4 rep. TFTC #43,CSS#18. . . . . . . 3.00
5 rep. TFTC,CSS#23 . . . . 3.00

[2nd Series]
1 rep.horror stories 3.00
2 inc.The Maestro's Hand. 3.00
3 thru 6 . . . . @3.00
7 thru 8 . . . . @3.00

Gemstone, 1996
16 thru 30 EC comics reprint. . . . @3.00
`Annuals'

TPB Vol. 1 rebinding of #1–#5. . . . 9.00
TPB Vol. 2 rebinding of #5–#10. . . . 9.00
TPB Vol. 3 rebinding of #11–#15. . . . 9.00
TPB Vol. 4 rebinding of #16–#20. . 13.00
TPB Vol. 5 rebinding of #21–#24. . . 14.00

Tales of Evil #3
© Atlas Comics

TALES OF EVIL
Atlas Comics, 1975
1 Werewolf 25.00
2 Bog Beast 20.00
3 Man-Monster 20.00

TALES OF TERROR
Eclipse, 1985–87
1 . . . . 3.00
2 Claustrophobia' 3.00
3 GM,Eyes in the Darkness 3.00
4 TT,TY,JBo(c),The Slasher 3.00
5 Back Forty,Shoe Button Eyes . . . 3.00
6 Good Neighbors. 3.00
7 SBi,JBo,SK(i),Video. 3.00
8 HB,Revenant,Food for
   Thought 3.00
9 . . . . 3.00
10 . . . . 3.00
11 TT,JBo(c),Black Cullen 3.00
12 JBo,FH,Last of the Vampires . . . 3.00
13 . . . . 3.00

TALES OF THE GREEN BERET
Dell Publishing Co., 1967
1 SG 50.00
2 thru 4 . . . . @40.00
5 . . . . 40.00

TALES OF THE GREEN HORNET
Now, 1990
1 NA(c),O:Green Hornet Pt.1 . . . . 3.00
2 O:Green Hornet Pt.2 . . . . 2.50
3 Gun Metal Green 2.50
4 Targets. 2.50

TALES OF THE MYSTERIOUS TRAVELER
Charlton Comics, 1956
1 DG. 600.00
2 SD 500.00

3 SD,SD(c) 425.00
4 SD,SD(c) 500.00
5 SD,SD(c) 500.00
6 SD,SD(c) 500.00
7 SD 450.00
8 SD 450.00
9 SD 450.00
10 SD,SD(c) 475.00
11 SD,SD(c) 475.00
12 . . . . 200.00
13 . . . . 225.00
14 (1985) 20.00
15 (1985) 20.00

TALES OF THE REALM
Crossgen Comics, 2003
1 (of 6) 3.00
2 . . . . 3.00

TALES OF THE SUN RUNNERS
Sirius Comics, 1986
1 . . . . 2.25
2 and 3 . . . . @2.25

TALESPIN
Walt Disney, 1991 (Reg.-Series)
1 Sky-Raker, Pt.1 . . . . 2.50
2 Sky-Raker, Pt.2 . . . . 2.50
3 Idiots Abroad 2.50
4 Contractual Desperation 2.50
5 The Oldman & the Sea Duck. . . . 2.50
6 F'reeze a Jolly Good Fellow 2.50

TALESPIN
Walt Disney, 1991 [Mini-Series]
1 Take-off Pt.1. . . . . 3.00
2 Take-off Pt 2. . . . . 3.00
3 Take-off Pt 3,Khan Job 3.00
4 Take-off pt 4 . . . . 3.00

TALEWEAVER
WildStorm/DC, 2001
1 (of 6) 40-pg.. . . . . 3.50
2 . . . . 3.00
2a variant (c). 3.00
3 . . . . 3.00
4 . . . . 3.00
5 . . . . 3.00
6 . . . . 3.00

TANK GIRL
Titan, 2002
TPB Vol. 1 128-pg.. . . . . 17.00
TPB Vol. 2 . . . . 17.00
TPB Vol. 3 . . . . 15.00

TAOLAND
Severe Reality Productions
4 1st full color issue 6.00
5 48pg. 6.00

TAOLAND ADVENTURES
Antarctic Press, 1999
1 by Jeff Amano 3.00
2 . . . . 3.00

TARGET AIRBOY
Eclipse, 1988
1 SK,A:Clint 2.25

TARGITT
Atlas, 1975
1 thru 3 . . . . @6.00

TAROT WITCH OF THE BLACK ROSE
Broadsword Comics, 2000
1 JBa(c) 3.00
2 . . . . 3.00
3 . . . . 3.00
4 . . . . 3.00
5 JBa. 3.00
6 Goulish Intentions 3.00
7 Return of the Dark Witch,pt.1 . . . 3.00
8 Return of the Dark Witch,pt.2 . . . 3.00
9 Return of the Dark Witch,pt.3 . . . 3.00
2a thru 16a signed . . . . @10.00
1b, 4b, 6b, 8b deluxe . . . . . . @20.00
7b double-deluxe edition. 25.00
9b thru 23b deluxe . . . . @20.00
10 Quest for the Black Rose Sword 3.00
11 Black Rose Sword,pt.2 . . . . 3.00
12 . . . . 3.00
13 . . . . 3.00
13b previews exlusive (c) 15.00
14 . . . . 3.00
15 . . . . 3.00
16 . . . . 3.00
17 Cold Spell 3.00
18 Diary of a Witch 3.00
19 Mists of Darkness, pt.1 . . . . 3.00
19a photo (c) 10.00
20 Mists of Darkness, pt.2 . . . . 3.00
21 Mists of Darkness, pt.3 . . . . 3.00
22 Mists of Darkness, pt.4 . . . . 3.00
23 Ghouls Gone Wild 3.00
24 Ghouls Gone Wild,pt.2 . . . . 3.00
25 thru 28 . . . . @3.00
24a thru 28a deluxe . . . . @20.00
TPB Vol. 1 . . . . 25.00
TPB Vol. 1 deluxe 35.00
TPB Vol. 2 . . . . 25.00

TARZAN OF THE APES
Gold Key, 1962–72
prev. Dell (see Golden Age)
132 . . . . 65.00
133 . . . . 50.00
134 . . . . 50.00
135 . . . . 55.00
136 . . . . 50.00

Tarzan of the Apes #193
© Gold Key

137 . . . . 50.00
138 . . . . 50.00
139 I:Korak. 55.00
140 thru 154 . . . . @50.00
155 O:Tarzan 60.00
156 thru 161 . . . . @40.00
162 TV photo (c) 50.00
163 . . . . 40.00
164 . . . . 40.00
165 TV photo (c) 50.00
166 . . . . 40.00
167 . . . . 40.00
168 TV photo (c) 50.00
169 A:Leopard Girl. 40.00
170 . . . . 40.00
171 TV photo (c) 60.00
172 thru 177 . . . . @30.00
178 O:Tarzan, rep. #155 . . . . 30.00
179 thru 191 . . . . @30.00
192 Tarzan and the Foreign Legion
    adaptation 30.00
193 thru 199 . . . . @30.00
200 . . . . 40.00
201 thru 205 . . . . @30.00
206 last issue 30.00
Continued by DC; see also Marvel

TARZAN IN COLOR
NBM, 1997
TPB Vol. 1, 1931–1933, by
    Hal Foster 25.00
TPB Vol. 2, 1933–1935, by
    Hal Foster 25.00
TPB Vol. 3, 1935–1937, by
    Hal Foster 25.00

TARZAN: THE BECKONING
Malibu, 1992
1 TY,I:The Spider Man 2.75
2 TY,Going back to Africa 2.50
3 thru 6 . . . . 2.50

TARZAN THE WARRIOR
Malibu, 1992
1 SBs(c),O:Tarzan 3.50
2 . . . . 2.75
3 . . . . 2.75
4 Wom'cha's Ship 2.75
5 . . . . 2.75

TARZAN: LOVE, LIES, AND THE LOST CITY
Malibu, 1992
1 MWg&WS(s),Short Stories 4.00
2 The lost city of Opar 2.50
3 Final issue 2.50

TASK FORCE ALPHA
Alpha Productions
1 Forged in Fire 3.50

TASMANIAN DEVIL & HIS TASTY FRIENDS
Gold Key, 1962
1 . . . . 225.00

TASTEE-FREEZ COMICS
Harvey Comics, 1957
1 Little Dot. 60.00
2 Rags Rabbit. 30.00
3 Casper 40.00
4 Sad Sack 30.00
5 Mazie 30.00
6 Dick Tracy 50.00

TEAM ANARCHY
Anarchy, 1993
1 I:Team Anarchy 2.75
2 thru 3 . . . . 2.75
4 PuD,MaS,I:Primal 2.75

TEAM YANKEE
First, 1989
1 Harold Coyle novel adapt. 2.25
2 thru 6 . . . . @2.25
Trade Paperback 13.00

T.E.C.H. BOYZ HYPERACTIVE
Dynasty Comics
1 I:T.E.C.H. Boyz 3.00
2 Man vs. Nature 3.00

TEEN-AGE CONFIDENTIAL CONFESSIONS
Charlton Comics, 1960–64
1 . . . . 50.00
2 thru 5 . . . . @35.00
6 thru 10 . . . . @30.00
11 thru 22 . . . . @25.00

TEENAGE HOTRODDERS
Charlton Comics, April, 1963
1 . . . . 75.00
2 thru 5 . . . . @40.00
6 thru 10 . . . . @38.00
11 thru 23 . . . . @35.00
24 . . . . 35.00
Becomes:

TOP ELIMINATOR
25 thru 29 . . . . @30.00
Becomes:

DRAG 'N' WHEELS
30 . . . . 60.00
31 thru 39 . . . . 40.00
40 thru 50 Scot Jackson 35.00
51 thru 59 May, 1973 . . . . 25.00

TEENAGE MUTANT NINJA TURTLES
First
1 . . . . 6.00
2 . . . . 4.50
Graphic Novel 17.00

TEENAGE MUTANT NINJA TURTLES
Archie, 1988
(From T.V. Series)
1 O:TMNT,April O'Neil,Shredder
    Krang 6.00
2 V:Shredder,O:Bebop &
    Rocksteady 4.00
3 V:Shredder & Krang. 3.00

TEENAGE MUTANT NINJA TURTLES
Mirage, 1993
1 A:Casey Jones. 3.00
2 JmL(a&s) 3.00
3 thru 8 . . . . @2.75
9 V:Baxter Bot. 2.75
10 Mr. Braunze 2.75
11 V:Raphael 2.75
12 V:Darpa. 2.75
13 J:Triceraton. 2.75

COLOR PUB.

TEENAGE MUTANT NINJA TURTLES ADVENTURES
Archie, 1988 [2nd Series]
1 Shredder,Bebop,Rocksteady
  return to earth 5.00
2 I:Baxter Stockman 3.00
3 Three Fragments #1 . . . . 3.00
4 Three Fragments #2 . . . . 2.50
5 Original adventures begin,
  I:Man Ray 2.50
6 I:Leatherhead,Mary Bones 2.50
7 I:Cuddley the Cowlick; Inter-
  Galactic wrestling issue 2.50
8 I:Wingnut & Screwloose 2.50
9 I:Chameleon 2.50
10 I:Scumbug, Wyrm 2.50
11 I:Rat King & Sons of Silence;
  Krang returns to earth 2.50
12 Final Conflict #1, A:Leatherhead
  Wingnut,Screwloose,Trap,
  I:Malinga 2.50
13 Final Conflict #2 . . . . 2.50
14 Turtles go to Brazil;I:Jagwar
  Dreadman 2.50
15 I:Mr. Null 2.50
16 I&D:Bubbla,the Glubbab 2.50
17 Cap'n Mossback 2.50
18 'Man Who Sold World' 2.50
19 I: Mighty Mutanimals 2.50
20 V:Supersoldier,War.Dragon. . . . 2.50
21 V:Vid Vicious. 2.50
22 GC,Donatello captured 2.50
23 V:Krang,I:Slash,Belly Bomb . . . 2.50
24 V:Krang 2.50
25 . . . . 2.50
26 I:T'Pau & Keeper 2.50
27 I:Nevermore,Nocturno&Hallocat . 2.50
28 Turtle go to Spain, I:Nindar &
  Chein Klan. 2.50
29 Warrior Dragon captured 2.50
30 TMNT/Fox Mutant Ninjara
  team-up 2.50
31 TMNT/Ninjara team-up cont 2.50
32 A:Sumo Wrestler Tatoo 2.50
33 The Karma of Katmandu 2.50
34 Search For Charlie Llama. 2.50
35 . . . . 2.50
36 V:Shredder 2.50
37 V:Shredder 2.50
38 V:Null & 4 Horsemen Pt.1. . . . . 2.50
39 V:Null & 4 Horseman Pt.3. . . . . 2.50
40 thru 70. . . . . @2.50
1990 Movie adapt(direct). 5.50
1990 Movie adapt(newsstand). . . . 2.50
1991 TMNT meet Archie 2.50
1991 Movie Adapt II. 2.50
Spec.#2 Ghost of 13 Mile Island . . 2.50
Spec.#3 Night of the Monsterex . . 2.50
TMNT Mutant Universe Sourcebook 2.00

TEENAGE MUTANT NINJA TURTLES ANIMATED
Dreamwave, 2003
1 . . . . 3.00
2 thru 9 . . . . @3.00
TPB Vol. 1 . . . . 10.00

TEENAGE MUTANT NINJA TURTLES/ FLAMING CARROT
Mirage/Dark Horse, 1993
1 JmL 3.00
2 thru 3 JmL 3.00
4 JmL 3.00

TMNT PRESENTS:
Archie, 1993
APRIL O'NEIL
1 A:Chien Khan,Vid Vicious 2.25
2 V:White Ninja,A:V.Vicious 2.25
3 V:Vhien Khan,concl. 2.25
Spec. April O'Neil, May East Saga . 2.25

DONATELLO AND LEATHERHEAD
1 thru 2 . . . . @2.25

MERDUDE VS. RAY FILLET
1 thru 3 . . . . @2.25

TMNT: THE MALTESE TURTLE
Mirage
Spec. F:Raphael Detective 3.00

TMNT: YEAR OF THE TURTLE
Archie Comics, 1995
1 All New Era 2.25

[JACK KIRBY'S] TEENAGENTS
Topps
[Mini-Series]
1 WS,AH,w/3 cards. 3.00
2 NV,w/3 cards 3.00
3 NV,w/3 cards 3.00
4 NV,w/3 leftover? cards. 3.00

TEEN CONFESSIONS
Charlton Comics, 1959–76
1 . . . . 125.00
2 . . . . 60.00
3 . . . . 35.00
4 . . . . 35.00
5 . . . . 35.00
6 . . . . 35.00
7 . . . . 35.00
8 . . . . 35.00
9 . . . . 35.00
10 . . . . 35.00
11 thru 30 . . . . @30.00
31 Beatles cover. 125.00
32 thru 36 . . . . @25.00
37 Beatles cover,Fan Club story . 175.00
38 thru 97 . . . . @20.00

TEEN SECRET DIARY
Charlton Comics, 1959–61
1 . . . . 65.00
2 . . . . 40.00
3 . . . . 35.00
4 . . . . 35.00
5 . . . . 35.00
6 . . . . 35.00
7 . . . . 35.00
8 . . . . 35.00
9 . . . . 35.00
10 . . . . 35.00
11 . . . . 35.00

TEKKEN 2
Knightstone, 1997
1 (of 4) Tekken Saga, pt.3 . . . . . . 3.00
2 . . . . 3.00
2a photo cover 3.00
3 . . . . 3.00
3a photo cover 3.00

Teeken Saga #1
© Knightstone

TEKKEN SAGA
Knightstone, 1997
1 . . . . 4.00
2 . . . . 3.00
3 . . . . 3.00
4 Paul vs. Kazuya. 3.00
5 Paul a prisoner 3.00
Nightstone Unlimited & Tekken ?. . . 3.00

TENSE SUSPENSE
Fargo Publications, 1958–59
1 . . . . 100.00
2 . . . . 75.00

10TH MUSE
Avatar/Tidal Wave Studios, 2002
1A MWn,RCz, Andy Park (c) 3.50
1B CBa(c). 3.50
1C RCz(c). 3.50
1D Mark Brooks (c). 3.50
1E Valdez (c) 3.50
2 RCz(c) 3.50
2a Caldwell (c) 3.50
2b Rousseau (c) 3.50
2 RCz(c) 3.50
2a Green (c) 3.50
2b Grant (c). 3.50
TPB Vol. 1 . . . . 14.00
TPB Vol. 1 photo (c) 14.00
Angel Gate, 2003
TPB Vol. 1 Maze of the Minotaur. . . 8.00
TPB Vol. 2 Round Two 15.00

TERMINATOR, THE
Now, 1988–89
1 . . . . 10.00
2 . . . . 5.00
3 . . . . 4.00
4 thru 11 . . . . @3.50
12 I:JohnConnor($1.75,cov,dbl.sz) . 3.50
13 thru 17 . . . . @3.50
Spec. #1 . . . . 3.50

TERMINATOR
I-Books, 2003
TPB The Burning Earth 18.00
TPB Rewired (2004) 18.00

All comics prices listed are for *Near Mint* condition.

COLOR PUB.

TERMINATOR:
ALL MY FUTURES PAST
Now, 1990
1 Painted Art 3.00
2 Painted Art 3.00

TERMINATOR:
THE BURNING EARTH
Now, 1990
1 . . . . 18.00
2 . . . . 12.00
3 . . . . 10.00
4 . . . . 10.00
5 . . . . 10.00

TERMINATOR 2:
CYBERNETIC DAWN
Malibu, 1995–96
1 thru 4 . . . . @2.50
0 flip-book/T2 Nuclear Twilight 2.50

TERMINATOR 2:
NUCLEAR TWILIGHT
Malibu, 1995–96
1 thru 4 . . . . @2.50
0 flip-book, see above

TERMINATOR 3
Beckett Entertainment, 2003
1 Before the Rise 6.00
2 Before the Rise 6.00
3 Eyes of the Rise 6.00
4 Eyes of the Rise 6.00
5 Fragmented 6.00
6 Fragmented 6.00

TERRAFORMERS
Wonder Comics, 1987
1 . . . . 2.25
2 thru 4 . . . . @2.25

TERRANAUTS
Fantasy General, 1986
1 . . . . 2.25
2 . . . . 2.25

TERRA OBSCURA
Wildstorm/DC June, 2003
America's Best Comics
1 (of 6) AMo(s) 3.00
2 AMo(s),F:Grant Halford 3.00
3 thru 5 AMo(s) . . . . @3.00
6 AMo(s),concl.,40-pg. 4.00
TPB 15.00
Vol. 2, 2004
1 AMo(s) 3.00
2 AMo(s) 3.00
3 . . . . 3.00

TEXAS RANGERS
IN ACTION
Charlton Comics, 1956–70
5 . . . . 80.00
6 . . . . 50.00
7 . . . . 50.00
8 SD 100.00
9 . . . . 50.00
10 . . . . 50.00
11 AW 100.00
12 . . . . 35.00
13 AW 75.00
14 thru 20 . . . . @35.00

---

21 thru 30 . . . . @30.00
31 thru 59 . . . . @25.00
60 B:Riley's Rangers 28.00
61 thru 79 . . . . @15.00

THAT WILKIN BOY
Archie Publications, 1969
1 . . . . 50.00
2 thru 10 . . . . @30.00
11 thru 20 . . . . @20.00
21 thru 26 E:Giant size . . . . . . @15.00
27 thru 52 . . . . @15.00

THESPIAN
Dark Moon, 1995
1 I:Thespian 2.50
2 V:Lemming 2.50
3 Lord of Manhattan 2.50

THING: COLD FEAR
1 R:Thing 3.00
2 . . . . 3.00

THIRD WORLD WAR
Fleetway, 1990–91
1 HamburgerLady 2.50
2 . . . . 2.50
3 The Killing Yields 2.50
4 . . . . 2.50
5 . . . . 2.50
6 . . . . 2.50

13: ASSASSIN
TSR, 1990–91
1 thru 4 from game . . . . @3.00
5 thru 8 The Search for
Maggie Darr . . . . @3.00

THOSE ANNOYING
POST BROTHERS
Vortex
1 . . . . 3.00
2 thru 5 . . . . @2.25
6 thru 18 . . . . @2.25
See also B&W listings

3-D ZONE PRESENTS
Renegade, 1987–89
1 L.B.Cole(c) 2.25
2 . . . . 2.25
3 . . . . 2.25
4 . . . . 2.25
5 . . . . 2.25
12 3-D Presidents 2.50
13 Flash Gordon 2.50
14 Tyranostar 2.50
15 Tyranostar 2.50
16 SpaceVixen 2.50

3 LITTLE KITTENS
Broadsword Comics, 2002
1 JBa, Purrr-fect weapons 3.00
2 Puss N Bullets 3.00
3 Purrr-Fect Weapons 3.00
1a thru 3a deluxe . . . . @20.00
1b thru 3b signed . . . . @10.00

THREE STOOGES
Dell Publishing Co., 1959
6 Ph(c),B:Prof. Putter 175.00
7 Ph(c) 175.00
8 Ph(c) 175.00
9 Ph(c) 175.00

Three Stooges #28
© Gold Key

Gold Key, 1962
10 Ph(c) 175.00
11 Ph(c) 150.00
12 Ph(c) 150.00
13 Ph(c) 150.00
14 Ph(c) 150.00
15 Ph(c) Go Around the World . . . 175.00
16 Ph(c),E:Prof. Putter 150.00
17 Ph(c),B:Little Monsters 150.00
18 Ph(c) 150.00
19 Ph(c) 150.00
20 Ph(c) 150.00
21 Ph(c) 150.00
22 Ph(c),Movie Scenes 150.00
23 thru 30 Ph(c) . . . . @125.00
31 thru 50 Ph(c) . . . . @100.00
51 . . . . 100.00
52 thru 55 Ph(c) . . . . @100.00

THREE STOOGES 3-D
Eclipse, 1991
1 thru 3 reprints from 1953 . . . . . @2.50
4 reprints from 1953 . . . . 3.50

THRILLING SCIENCE
TALES
AC Comics, 1989
1 . . . . 3.50

THRILLOGY
Pacific, 1984
1 . . . . 2.25

THRILL-O-RAMA
Harvey Publications, 1965–66
1 A:Man in Black(Fate),DW,AW . . 75.00
2 AW,A:Pirana,I:Clawfang,
The Barbarian 50.00
3 A:Pirana, Fate 40.00

30 DAYS OF NIGHT
IDW Publishing, 2002
1 by S.Niles & B.Templesmith . . . 60.00
1a 2nd printing 7.00
2 . . . . 27.00
3 . . . . 7.00
TPB 18.00
Spec. Bloodsucker Tales (2004) . . . 4.00
Annual 2004 . . . . 5.00

COLOR PUB.

---

30 DAYS OF NIGHT: RETURN TO BARROW
IDW Publishing, 2004
```
1 . . . . . . . . . . . . . . . . . . . . . . . . 4.00
2 thru 6 . . . . . . . . . . . . . . . . . . . @4.00
```

THUNDER AGENTS
Tower, 1965–69
```
1 WW,RC,GK,MSy,GT,I:Thunder
   Agents,IronMaiden,Warlord . . 300.00
2 WW,MSy,D:Egghead . . . . . . . . 150.00
3 WW,DA,MSy,V:Warlords . . . . 125.00
4 WW,MSy,RC,I:Lightning . . . . 125.00
5 WW,RC,GK,MSy . . . . . . . . . . 125.00
6 WW,SD,MSy,I:Warp Wizard . . 100.00
7 WW,MSy,SD,D:Menthor . . . . 100.00
8 WW,MSy,GT,DA,I:Raven . . . . 100.00
9 OW,WW,MSy,A:Andor . . . . . . 100.00
10 WW,MSy,OW,A:Andor . . . . . 100.00
11 WW,DA,MSy . . . . . . . . . . . . . 75.00
12 SD,WW,MSy . . . . . . . . . . . . . 75.00
13 WW,OW,A:Undersea Agent . . . 75.00
14 SD,WW,GK,N:Raven,A:Andor . 75.00
15 WW,OW,GT,A:Andor . . . . . . . . 65.00
16 SD,GK,A:Andor . . . . . . . . . . . 65.00
17 WW,OW,GT . . . . . . . . . . . . . . 65.00
18 SD,OW,RC . . . . . . . . . . . . . . 50.00
19 GT,I:Ghost . . . . . . . . . . . . . . . 50.00
20 WW,RC,MSy,all reprints . . . . . 50.00
```

T.H.U.N.D.E.R. AGENTS
J.C. Productions, 1983
```
1 MA,Centerfold . . . . . . . . . . . . . 5.00
2 I:Vulcan . . . . . . . . . . . . . . . . . . 5.00
```

T.H.U.N.D.E.R. AGENTS
Maximum, 1995
```
1 and 2 . . . . . . . . . . . . . . . . . . . @3.00
```

THUNDERBOLT
Charlton Comics, 1966–67
```
1 PAM,O:Thuderbolt . . . . . . . . . . 50.00
Prev: Son of Vulcan
51 PAM,V:Evila . . . . . . . . . . . . . 35.00
52 PAM,V:Gore the Monster . . . . 25.00
53 PAM,V:The Tong . . . . . . . . . . . 25.00
54 PAM,I:Sentinels . . . . . . . . . . . 25.00
55 PAM,V:Sentinels . . . . . . . . . . 25.00
56 PAM,A:Sentinels . . . . . . . . . . 25.00
57 A:Sentinels . . . . . . . . . . . . . . 25.00
58 PAM,A:Sentinels . . . . . . . . . . 25.00
59 PAM,A:Sentinels . . . . . . . . . . 25.00
60 PAM,JAp,I:Prankster . . . . . . . 30.00
```

THUNDERCATS
WildStorm/DC, 2002
```
0 JSC, preview issue . . . . . . . . . . 5.00
1a (of 5) King Lion-O . . . . . . . . . . 5.00
1b variant AAd (c) . . . . . . . . . . . . 3.50
2a V:Mumm-ra . . . . . . . . . . . . . . 3.00
2b variant JLe(c) . . . . . . . . . . . . . 3.00
3 F:Lion-O . . . . . . . . . . . . . . . . . 3.00
3a variant JMd(c) . . . . . . . . . . . . 3.00
4 F:New Thundera . . . . . . . . . . . 3.00
5 concl. . . . . . . . . . . . . . . . . . . . 3.00
GN Thundercats/Battle
   of the Planets . . . . . . . . . . . . 5.00
TPB Reclaiming Thundera . . . . . . 13.00
Sourcebook . . . . . . . . . . . . . . . . . 3.00
```

THUNDERCATS: DOGS OF WAR
Wildstorm/DC June, 2003
```
1 (of 5) 10 years in future . . . . . . . 3.00
2 New Thundera . . . . . . . . . . . . . 3.00
```

```
3 thru 5 BBh,AV . . . . . . . . . . . . @3.00
TPB . . . . . . . . . . . . . . . . . . . . . 15.00
```

THUNDERCATS: ENEMY'S PRIDE
Wildstorm/DC June, 2004
```
1 Cat vs. Cat . . . . . . . . . . . . . . . . 3.00
2 thru 5 . . . . . . . . . . . . . . . . . . . @3.00
```

THUNDERCATS: HAMMERHAND'S REVENGE
Wildstorm/DC, 2003
```
1 (of 5) . . . . . . . . . . . . . . . . . . . . 3.00
2 F:Lion-O . . . . . . . . . . . . . . . . . 3.00
3 . . . . . . . . . . . . . . . . . . . . . . . . 3.00
4 (two covers) . . . . . . . . . . . . . . . 3.00
5 (two covers) . . . . . . . . . . . . . . . 3.00
TPB . . . . . . . . . . . . . . . . . . . . . 15.00
Spec. Superman/Thundercats . . . . 6.00
```

THUNDERCATS: ORIGINS
Wildstorm/DC, 2003
```
Spec. Heroes & Villains,pt.1 . . . . . 3.50
Spec. Villains & Heroes,pt.1 . . . . . 3.50
```

THUNDERCATS: THE RETURN
Wildstorm/DC, 2003
```
1 (of 5) EBe,F:Lion-O . . . . . . . . . . 3.00
2 EBe,V:Mumm-Ra . . . . . . . . . . . 3.00
3 EBe . . . . . . . . . . . . . . . . . . . . . 3.00
4 EBe,Wilykat . . . . . . . . . . . . . . . 3.00
5 EBe, concl. . . . . . . . . . . . . . . . . 3.00
TPB Series rep. . . . . . . . . . . . . . 13.00
```

TICK, THE
New England Comics, 2001
```
1 all new, all color . . . . . . . . . . . . 4.00
1a variant (c) . . . . . . . . . . . . . . . . 4.00
2 thru 5 . . . . . . . . . . . . . . . . . . . @4.00
6 return of Proto-Tick . . . . . . . . . . 4.00
TPB The Naked City, 2nd pr. . . . . 16.00
TPB Circus Maximus Giant ed. . . . 15.00
Spec. Big Halloween 2000 . . . . . . 3.50
Spec. Big Halloween 2001 . . . . . . 4.00
Spec. Introducing the Tick (2002) . . 4.00
Spec. Circus Maximus Update . . . . 4.00
```

TICK & ARTIE
New England Comics, 2002
```
1 . . . . . . . . . . . . . . . . . . . . . . . . 3.50
2 BEd(c) . . . . . . . . . . . . . . . . . . . 3.50
```

TICK, THE: BIG XMAS TRILOGY
New England Comics, 2002
```
1 . . . . . . . . . . . . . . . . . . . . . . . . 4.00
2 thru 3 . . . . . . . . . . . . . . . . . . . @4.00
```

TICK'S INCREDIBLE INTERNET COMIC, THE
New England Comics, 2001
```
1 . . . . . . . . . . . . . . . . . . . . . . . . 4.00
```

TIGER GIRL
Gold Key, 1968
```
1 . . . . . . . . . . . . . . . . . . . . . . . 50.00
```

Tiger-Man #1
© Atlas Comics

TIGER-MAN
Atlas, 1975
```
1 thru 3 . . . . . . . . . . . . . . . . . . @15.00
```

TIGERS OF TERRA
Antarctic Press, 2000
Vol. 3
```
1 (of 4) War Against the Sun . . . . . 3.00
2 Night of the Amazons . . . . . . . . 3.00
3 . . . . . . . . . . . . . . . . . . . . . . . . 3.00
4 Planet of War . . . . . . . . . . . . . . 3.00
```

TIME TUNNEL, THE
Gold Key, 1967
```
1 from TV show . . . . . . . . . . . . . 125.00
2 . . . . . . . . . . . . . . . . . . . . . . . 75.00
```

TIME TWISTERS
Quality, 1987–89
```
1 Alan Moore ser. . . . . . . . . . . . . 2.25
2 Alan Moore ser. . . . . . . . . . . . . 2.25
3 Alan Moore ser. . . . . . . . . . . . . 2.25
4 Alan Moore ser. . . . . . . . . . . . . 2.25
5 . . . . . . . . . . . . . . . . . . . . . . . . 2.25
6 Alan Moore ser. . . . . . . . . . . . . 2.25
7 Alan Moore ser. . . . . . . . . . . . . 2.25
8 thru 21 . . . . . . . . . . . . . . . . . . @2.25
```

TIME 2
```
1 Graphic Novel . . . . . . . . . . . . . . 8.00
```

TIMEWALKER
Valiant, 1994
```
0 BH,DP,O:3 Immortals . . . . . . . . 3.00
1 DP, BH . . . . . . . . . . . . . . . . . . 2.50
2 DP,BH . . . . . . . . . . . . . . . . . . . 2.50
3 DP BH . . . . . . . . . . . . . . . . . . . 2.50
4 Ten Commandments . . . . . . . . . 2.50
5 DP,BH . . . . . . . . . . . . . . . . . . . 2.50
6 Harbinger Wars Pt.1 . . . . . . . . . 2.50
7 Harbinger Wars Pt.2 . . . . . . . . . 2.50
8 Harbinger Wars Pt.3 . . . . . . . . . 2.50
9 V:Jahk rt. . . . . . . . . . . . . . . . . . 2.50
10 Last God of Dura-Europus,pt.1
   time: 260 A.D. . . . . . . . . . . . . . 2.50
11 Last God of Dura-Europus,pt.2 . . 2.50
12 3RW,DP,Ashes to Ashes,pt.1 . . . 2.50
13 3RW,DP,Ashes to Ashes,pt.2 . . . 2.50
14 Meets Mozart . . . . . . . . . . . . . 2.50
15 26th Century . . . . . . . . . . . . . . 2.50
```

Yearbook F:Harada 3.00
TPB F:Archer & Armstrong 10.00

TIME WARRIOR
Blazing Comics, 1993
1 . . . . 2.50

TIPPY'S FRIENDS
GO-GO & ANIMAL
Tower Comics, 1966–69
1 . . . . 100.00
2 . . . . 65.00
3 . . . . 65.00
4 . . . . 65.00
5 . . . . 65.00
6 . . . . 65.00
7 . . . . 65.00
8 Beatles on cover & back 125.00
9 thru 15 . . . . @50.00

TIPPY TEEN
Tower Comics, 1965–70
1 . . . . 100.00
2 thru 27 . . . . @60.00

TOHUBOHU
New Breed Comics, 1999
1 . . . . 3.25
2 thru 5 . . . . @3.00
6 A Serpent in the Garden 3.25

TO DIE FOR
1 3-D 2.50

TOKYO STORM WARNING
Wildstorm/DC June, 2003
1 (of 3) giant robots 3.00
2 WEl 3.00
3 WEl 3.00

TOM & JERRY
Harvey, 1991–94
1 . . . . 2.50
2 thru 18 . . . . @2.00

TOM MIX WESTERN
AC Comics, 1988
1 . . . . 3.00

TOM TERRIFIC!
Pines Comics
Summer, 1957
1 . . . . 250.00
2 . . . . 175.00
3 . . . . 175.00
4 . . . . 175.00
5 . . . . 175.00
6 Fall, 1958 . . . . 175.00

TOMMI-GUNN
London Night, 1997
0 . . . . 3.00
? 3.00
1 signed 15.00
1a, chromium, elite edition 20.00
2 . . . . 3.00
3 . . . . 3.00

TOMMI-GUNN:
KILLER'S LUST
London Night, 1997
1 . . . . 3.00

1 Japanese Chromium edition . . . 12.00
2 . . . . 3.00

TOMOE
Crusade Entertainment, 1996
0 BiT, ... 3.00
1 BiT,Fan Appreciation Edition . . . 3.00
2 . . . . 3.00
TPB rep 14.00

TOMOE/WITCHBLADE:
FIRE SERMON
Crusade Entertainment, 1996
1 . . . . 5.00
1a Gold foil 10.00

TOMOE:
UNFORGETTABLE FIRE
Crusade Entertainment, 1997
1 (of 3) 3.00

TOMORROW STORIES
WildStorm/DC, 1999
America's Best Comics
1 AMo,AxR(c) anthology 4.00
1a AxR(c),variant cover 3.50
2 AMo(s),KN,RV,JBa 3.00
3 AMo(s),KN,RV,JBa 3.00
4 AMo(s),KN,RV,JBa 3.00
5 AMo(s),KN,RV,JBa 3.00
6 AMo(s),RV,JBa 3.00
7 AMo(s),RV,JBa 3.00
8 AMo(s),RV,JBa 3.00
9 AMo(s),RV,JBa 3.00
10 AMo(s),RV,JBa,Jack B. Quick. . . 3.00
11 AMo(s),RV,JBa,AAd,F:Cobweb . . 3.00
12 AMo(s),RV,JBa, x-over 3.00

TOM STRONG
WildStorm/DC, 1999
America's Best Comics
1 AMo(s),CSp,40-pg. 4.00
2 AMo(s),CSp,Millennium City 3.00
3 AMo(s),CSp,Millennium City 3.00
4 AMo,CSp,AAd,Berlin in WW2 . . . 3.00
5 AMo,JOy,CSp,Memories of
   Pangea 3.00
6 AMo,CSp,DGb, Dead
   Man's Hand 3.00
7 AMo,CSp,GFr. 3.00
8 AMo,CSp,Lost Mesa 3.00
9 AMo,CSp, ... 3.00
10 AMo,CSp,F:Warren Strong 3.00
11 AMo,CSp,F:Tom Strange 3.00
12 AMo,CSp,F:Tom Strange,pt.2 . . . 3.00
13 AMo,CSp,Warren Strong 3.00
14 AMo,CSp,Space Family Strong . . 3.00
15 AMo,CSp, Val Var Garm 3.00
16 AMo(s),CSp,KIS,Modular Man . . 3.00
17 AMo(s),CSp,KIS,Weird Rider . . . 3.00
18 AMo(s),CSp,KIS,Weird Rider . . . 3.00
19 AMo(s),CSp,KIS 3.00
20 AMo(s),CSp,KIS,JOy,pt.1 . . . . . . 3.00
21 AMo(s),CSp,KIS,JOy,pt.2 . . . . . . 3.00
22 AMo(s),CSp,KIS,JOy,pt.3 . . . . . . 3.00
23 CSp,KIS,rescue mission 3.00
24 CSp,KIS, ... 3.00
25 JPL,F:Strongmen of America . . . 3.00
26 MSh(s),PFe 3.00
27 SwM 3.00
28 . . . . 3.00
29 DFg 3.00
TPB Book One, 208-pg 15.00
TPB Book Two, 192-pg 15.00

TOM STRONG'S
TERRIFIC TALES
WildStorm/DC, 2001
America's Best Comics
1 AMo,AAd 3.50
2 AMo,AAd 3.00
3 AMo,AAd,JOy 3.00
4 AMo(s),AAd,Jonni Future 3.00
5 AMo(s),SA,AAd(c) 3.00
6 AMo(s),JOy,AAd 3.00
7 AMo(s),AAd 3.00
8 AMo(s),AAd, young Tom 3.00
9 AMo(s),three stories 3.00
10 AMo(s),three stories 3.00
11 AMo(s), ... 3.00

TOOL AND DIE
Samson Comics
1 Autographed 5.00
1a Blue Edition 10.00

Top Cat #20
© Charlton Comics

TOP CAT
Charlton Comics, 1970–73
1 . . . . 100.00
2 thru 10 . . . . @50.00
11 thru 20 . . . . @30.00

TOP TEN
WildStorm/DC, 1999
America's Best Comics
1 AMo(s),GeH,40-pg. 3.50
2 AMo(s),GeH 3.00
3 thru 9 AMo(s),GeH . . . . @3.00
10 AMo(s),GeH,killer revealed 3.00
11 AMo(s),GeH,aftermath 3.00
12 AMo(s),GeH,season finale 3.00
TPB AMo(s),GeH 15.00
TPB Top 10 Book Two 15.00

TOR IN 3-D
Eclipse, 1986
1 JKu 3.00
1a B&W limited 100 sign 5.00
2 JKu 3.00

TORI-SHI-KITA
Relative Burn
1 Hunter Prey 2.50

TORMENTRESS: MISTRESS OF HELL
Blackout Comics, 1977
0 . . . . 3.00

TOTAL ECLIPSE
Eclipse, 1988–89
1 BHa,BSz(c),A:Airboy,Skywolf . . . 4.00
2 BHa,BSz(c),A:New Wave, Liberty
  Project 4.00
3 BHa,BSz(c),A:Scout,Ms.Tree . . . 4.00
4 BHa,BSz(c),A:Miracleman,
  Prowler 4.00
5 BHa,BSz(c),A:Miracleman, Aztec
  Ace 4.00

TOTAL ECLIPSE, THE SERAPHIM OBJECTIVE
Eclipse, 1988
1 tie-in Total Eclipse #2 . . . . 2.25

Total War #2
© Gold Key

TOTAL WAR
Gold Key, 1965
1 WW 100.00
2 WW 100.00
Becomes:

M.A.R.S. PATROL
3 WW 100.00
4 thru 10 . . . . @60.00

TOY BOY
Continuity, 1986–91
1 NA.I&O:Toy Boy,A:Megalith 3.00
2 TVE 3.00
3 TVE 3.00
4 TVE 3.00
5 TVE 3.00
6 TVE 3.00
7 MG 3.00

TRANCERS: THE ADVEN-TURES OF JACK DETH
Eternity
1 I:Jack Deth. 2.50
2 A:Whistler, final issue. 2.50

TRANSFORMERS
1 Robotics. 2.25

2 . . . . 2.25
3 . . . . 2.50

TRANSFORMERS
Titan, 2001
GN Vol. 1 All Fall Down 20.00
GN Vol. 2 End of the Road 20.00
GN Vol. 3 Primal Scream. 20.00
GN Vol. 4 Matrix Quest 20.00
GN Vol. 4 Matrix Quest exclusive(c). . . .
  25.00
GN Vol. 5 Target 2006 . . . . 20.00
GN Vol. 6 Dark Design 20.00
GN Vol. 7 Fallen Angel 20.00
GN Beginnings. 17.00
GN Showdown. 20.00
GN City of Fear 20.00
GN Space Pirates 17.00
GN New Order. 17.00
GN Cybertron Redux 17.00
GN Time Wars 20.00
TPB Dinobot Hunt 20.00
TPB Breakdown. 20.00
TPB Prey 20.00
TPB Treason 20.00
TPB Trial by Fire 20.00

TRANSFORMERS: ARMADA
Dreamwave, 2002
1 . . . . 4.00
2 thru 5 . . . . @3.00
6 thru 17 . . . . @3.00
18 thru 28 Energon . . . . @3.00
TPB Vol. 1 . . . . 14.00
TPB Vol. 2 . . . . 16.00
TPB Vol. 3 Worlds Collide 21.00
Spec. Summer Special #1 . . . . . . 5.00

TRANSFORMERS: GENERATION ONE
Dreamwave, 2002
1 . . . . 7.00
1a exclusive holofoil (c) 20.00
2 thru 6 . . . . @3.00
5a thru 6a variant (c). . . . . @3.00
7 thru 10 . . . . @3.00
0 . . . . 3.00
TPB Vol. 1 Prime Directive 18.00
TPB Vol. 2 War and Peace 18.00
Preview book, exclusive (c) 4.00
TPB rep. #1–#6 . . . . 18.00
TPB Profile Book One 13.00
TPB Profile Book Two 13.00
TPB Transformers Genesis
  Art Book. 29.45
Vol. 2
1 (of 6) 3.50
1a chrome edition 6.00
2 thru 6 . . . . @3.00
GN More than meets the Eye, guide 5.25
GN More than meets the Eye #3. . . 5.25

TRANSFORMERS/G.I. JOE
Dreamwave, 2003
1 . . . . 3.00
1a holofoil (c) 6.00
2 thru 6 . . . . @3.00
TPB 18.00
1-shot Divided Front 3.00

TRANSFORMERS: MICROMASTERS
Dreamwave, 2004
1 (of 4) 3.00
2 thru 3 . . . . @3.00

TRANSFORMERS: MORE THAN MEETS THE EYE
Dreamwave, 2003
1 (of 8) 5.25
2 thru 7 . . . . @5.25
8 final issue. 6.00
TPB 25.00
Vol. 2 Transformers Armada
1 thru 3 More than meets the Eye. . . . .
  @5.00

TRANSFORMERS: THE WAR WITHIN
Dreamwave, 2002
1 . . . . 3.00
2 thru 6 . . . . @3.00
TPB Vol. 1 . . . . 16.00
Vol. 2 The Dark Ages
1 . . . . 3.00
2 . . . . 3.00
3 thru 6 . . . . @3.00
TPB The Dark Ages. 18.00
Vol. 3 The Age of Wrath
1 . . . . 3.00
2 . . . . 3.00

TRANSFORMERS in 3-D
Blackthorne
1 thru 5 . . . . @2.50

TRAVEL OF JAMIE McPHEETERS, THE
Gold Key, 1963
1 Kurt Russell 50.00

TRAVELLER
Maximum Press, 1996
1 (of 3) RLd,MHw,. 3.00

TRIAL BY FIRE
Crossgen Comics, 2002
1 (of 5) 3.00

TRIBE
Axis Comics, 1993–94
1 see Image Comics section
2 TJn(s),LSn,V:Alex 2.25
3 TJn(s),LSn, ... 2.25
Good Comics, 1996
0 TJn,LSn 3.00
1 TJn,LSn,Choice and
  Responsibility 3.00
2 TJn,LSn,Choice and
  Responsibility 3.00

TRIBULATION FORCE
Tyndale House, 2002
GN Vol. #1 . . . . 6.00
GN Vol. #2 thru Vol. 5 . . . . @6.00

TRINITY ANGELS
Acclaim, 1997
1 KM,DPs, Maria, Gianna &
  Theresa Barbella become Trinity
  Angels 2.50
2 KM,DPs, V:The 99. . . . . 2.50
3 KM,DPs, looking for a little head. 2.50
4 KM,DPs, V:Flaming Queen 2.50
5 KM, New costumes 2.50
6 KM, in Las Vegas. 2.50
7 KM, in Las Vegas. 2.50
8 KM, A Woman Scorned 2.50

9 KM, A:Rumblin' Guys 2.50
10 KM, Mad Cow 2.50
11 KM, ... 2.50
12 KM, Final issue 2.50

TROLL LORDS
Comico, 1989–90
Spec. #1 . . . . 2.50
1 . . . . 2.50
2 thru 4 . . . . @2.50

TRON: DEREZZED
88MPH Studios, 2004
1 (of 4) 3.00
2 thru 3 . . . . @3.00
1a thru 3a variant (c)s . . . . @3.50

TROUBLEMAKERS
Acclaim, 1996
1 FaN(s) 2.50
2 FaN(s) go back in time 2.50
3 FaN(s) Jane has a big problem . . 2.50
4 FaN(s) Can Blur prevent parents
    divorce? 2.50
5 FaN(s) A:Ninjak 2.50
6 FaN(s) in outer space 2.50
7 FaN(s) I:The Rabble Rousers . . . 2.50
8 FaN(s) Rabble Rousers,pt.2 . . . . 2.50
9 FaN(s) F:Christine 2.50
10 FaN(s) F:Zach 2.50
11 FaN(s) F:Calamity Jane 2.50
12 FaN(s) a Troublemaker dead . . . 2.50
13 FaN(s) F:XL 2.50
14 FaN(s) 2.50
15 FaN(s) Is Parker alive? 2.50
16 FaN(s) Andrew Chase 2.50
17 FaN(s) V:Turnabout 2.50
18 FaN(s) Jacinda Monroe 2.50
19 FaN(s) V:Rabblerousers 2.50

TROUBLE WITH GIRLS
Comico, 1987–88
1 . . . . 3.00
2 . . . . 2.50
3 . . . . 2.50
4 . . . . 2.50

TRUE LOVE
Eclipse, 1986
1 ATh,NC,DSt(c),reprints 3.00
2 ATh,NC,BA(c),reprints 3.00

TRUE ROMANCE
Pyramid Comics, 1997
1 . . . . 2.50
1a deluxe 3.00
2 . . . . 2.50
3 . . . . 2.50
4 . . . . 2.50

TUFF GHOSTS
STARRING SPOOKY
Harvey Publications, 1962–72
1 . . . . 200.00
2 thru 5 . . . . @125.00
6 thru 10 . . . . @75.00
11 thru 20 . . . . @60.00
21 thru 30 . . . . @40.00
31 thru 39 . . . . @30.00
40 thru 42 52 pg. Giants . . . . . . @35.00
43 . . . . 35.00

TUROK
Acclaim, 1998
1 FaN 3-D cover 2.50

2 FaN,A:Armorines 2.50
3 FaN,Lazarus Concordance 2.50
4 FaN, real President? 2.50
TPB Dinosaur Hunter, FaN 10.00

TUROK: CHILD OF BLOOD
Acclaim, 1997
1-shot FaN, 48pg 4.00

TUROK:
COMIC BOOK MAGAZINE
Acclaim, 1998
Seeds of Evil 5.00
Adon's Curse 5.00
Turok/Shadowman 5.00

Turok: Dinosaur Hunter #20
© Valiant

TUROK: DINOSAUR
HUNTER
Valiant, 1993
1 BS,Chromium(c),O:Turok
    retold,V:Monark 3.00
1a Gold Ed 4.00
2 BS,V:Monark 2.75
3 BCh,V:Monark 2.75
4 TT(s),RgM,O:Turok 2.75
5 TT(s),RgM,V:Dinosaurs 2.75
6 TT(s),RgM,V:Longhunter 2.75
7 TT(a&s),B:People o/t Spider . . . 2.75
8 TT(a&s),V:T-Rex 2.75
9 TT(a&s),E:People o/t Spider . . . 2.75
10 MBn,RgM,A:Bile 2.75
11 MBn,RgM,V:Chun Yee,w/card . . 2.75
12 MBn,RgM,V:Dinosaur 2.75
13 B:TT(c&s),RgM, ... 2.75
14 V:Dino-Pirate 2.50
15 RgM,V:Dino-Pirate 2.25
16 Chaos Effect-Beta#3, V:Evil
    Shaman 2.75
17 V:C.I.A. 2.50
18 V:Bionosaurs 2.50
19 A:Manowar 2.50
20 Chichak 2.50
21 Ripsaw 2.50
22 . . . . 2.50
23 A:Longhunter 2.50
24 R:To The Lost Land 2.50
25 I:Warrior of Mother God 2.50
26 V:Overlord 2.50
27 TT,RgM,Lost Land,pt.4 . . . . 2.50
28 MBn,DEA hunts rogue T-Rex . . 2.50
29 SFu,Manhunt,pt.1 . . . . 2.50

30 SFu,Manhunt,pt.2 . . . . 2.50
31 F:Darwin Challenger 2.50
32 V:Special Effects 2.50
33 V:Aliens 2.50
34 V:Alien Ooze 2.50
35 Early Years 2.50
36 Confronts Past 2.50
37 V:Nazi Women 2.50
38 V:Bigfoot 2.50
39 TT,Shainer Silver 2.50
40 A:Longhunter 2.50
41 Church of the Poison Mind 2.50
42 Church of the Poison Mind 2.50
43 thru 47 . . . . @2.50
Yearbook #1 MBn(s),DC, N&V:Mon
    Ark 4.25
Yearbook 1995 MGr,The Hunted . . 3.00
Spec. Tales of the Lost Land 4.00
TPB FaN 112pgs.rep. game 10.00

TUROK QUARTERLY—
REDPATH
Acclaim, 1997
March 1997, FaN(s),Spring Break
    in the Lost Land 4.00
June 1997, FaN(s), Killer loose in
    Oklahoma City 4.00

TUROK/SHADOWMAN
Acclaim, 1999
1-shot 4.00

TUROK 3:
SHADOW OF OBLIVION
Acclaim, 2000
Spec. 48-page 5.00

TUROK/SHAMAN'S TEARS
Valiant, 1995
1 MGr,Ghost Dance Pt. 1 . . . . 2.50
2 MGr,JAl,White Buffalo
    kidnapped,V:Bar Sinister 2.50
3 V:Supremeists/Circle Sea 2.50

TUROK: SON OF STONE
Gold Key, 1962
1 thru 29 see Golden Age
30 . . . . 125.00
31 Drug 135.00
32 thru 40 . . . . @90.00
41 thru 50 . . . . @75.00
51 thru 60 . . . . @60.00
61 thru 75 . . . . @50.00
76 thru 91 . . . . @40.00

Whitman
92 thru 130 . . . . @40.00
Giant #1 . . . . 150.00

TUROK: THE HUNTED
Valiant
1 & 2 . . . . 2.50

TUROK/TIMEWALKER
Acclaim, 1997
1 of 2 FaN(s),Seventh Sabbath . . 2.50
2 of 2 FaN(s),Seventh Sabbath . . 2.50

TURTLE SOUP
Millennium, 1991
1 Book 1, short stories 2.50
2 thru 4 . . . . @2.50

COLOR PUB.

TV CASPER & COMPANY
Harvey Publications, 1963–74
1 B:68 pg. Giants 200.00
2 . . . . 100.00
3 . . . . 100.00
4 . . . . 100.00
5 . . . . 100.00
6 . . . . 75.00
7 . . . . 75.00
8 . . . . 75.00
9 . . . . 75.00
10 . . . . 75.00
11 thru 20 . . . . @50.00
21 thru 31 E:68 pg. Giants . . . . @35.00
32 thru 46 . . . . @30.00

TWEETY AND SYLVESTER
Gold Key, 1963–84
1 . . . . 75.00
2 thru 10 . . . . @40.00
11 thru 30 . . . . @25.00
31 thru 121 . . . . @10.00

21 DOWN
WildStorm/DC, 2002
1 JP,JJu(c),F:Preston Kills 3.00
2 JP,JJu(c),Herod 3.00
3 JP,JJu(c),Bear Mountain 3.00
4 JP,JJu(c) 3.00
5 JP,JJu(c) 3.00
6 JP,JJu(c),The Conduit 3.00
7 JP,JJu(c),secret of Herod 3.00
8 JP,Roadside Attractions,pt.1 . . . 3.00
9 JP,Roadside Attractions,pt.2 . . . 3.00
10 JP,Roadside Attractions,pt.3 . . . 3.00
11 JP,Roadside Attractions,pt.4 . . . 3.00
12 JP,Roadside Attractions,concl. . . 3.00
TPB rep. #1 thru #7 . . . . 20.00

22 BRIDES
Event, 1996
1 . . . . 3.00
2 . . . . 3.00
2a variant (c). 4.00
3 . . . . 3.00
3a variant (c). 4.00
4 . . . . 3.00

TWILIGHT AVENGER
Elite, 1986
1 thru 4 . . . . @2.25

TWILIGHT MAN
First, 1989
1 Mini-Series. 2.75
2 Mini-Series. 2.75
3 Mini-Series. 2.75
4 Mini-Series. 2.75

TWILIGHT X-TRA
Antarctic Press, 1999
1 (of 3) by Joe Wright. 2.50
2 . . . . 2.50
3 conclusion 2.50

TWILIGHT ZONE, THE
Gold Key, 1962
See also: Four Color #1173 & #1288
1 RC,FF,GE,P(c) all 200.00
2 . . . . 125.00
3 ATh,MSy 100.00
4 ATh. 100.00
5 . . . . 90.00

6 . . . . 90.00
7 . . . . 90.00
8 . . . . 90.00
9 ATh. 100.00
10 . . . . 75.00
11 . . . . 75.00
12 AW 75.00
13 AW,RC,FBe,AMc. 75.00
14 RC,JO,RC,AT 75.00
15 RC,JO. 75.00
16 . . . . 50.00
17 . . . . 50.00
18 . . . . 50.00
19 JO 50.00
20 . . . . 45.00
21 RC. 45.00
22 JO 45.00
23 JO 45.00
24 . . . . 40.00
25 GE,RC,ATh. 40.00
26 RC,GE. 40.00
27 GE 40.00
28 . . . . 30.00
29 . . . . 30.00
30 . . . . 30.00
31 . . . . 30.00
32 GE 35.00
33 . . . . 30.00
34 . . . . 30.00
35 . . . . 30.00
36 . . . . 30.00
37 . . . . 30.00
38 . . . . 30.00
39 WMc 30.00
40 . . . . 25.00
41 . . . . 25.00
42 . . . . 25.00
43 RC. 30.00
44 . . . . 25.00
45 . . . . 25.00
46 . . . . 25.00
47 . . . . 25.00
48 . . . . 25.00
49 . . . . 25.00
50 FBe,WS. 25.00
51 AW 30.00
52 . . . . 22.00
53 . . . . 22.00
54 . . . . 22.00
55 . . . . 22.00
56 . . . . 22.00
57 FBe 22.00
58 . . . . 22.00
59 FBe,AMc. 25.00
60 thru 70 . . . . @20.00
71 rep. 15.00
72 . . . . 20.00
73 rep. 15.00
74 . . . . 20.00
75 . . . . 20.00
76 . . . . 20.00
77 FBe 20.00
78 FBe,AMc,The Missing Mirage. 225.00
79 rep. 15.00
80 FBe,AMc. 22.00
81 . . . . 20.00
82 AMc. 25.00
83 FBe,WS. 25.00
84 FBe,AMc. 25.00
85 . . . . 20.00
86 rep. 15.00
87 thru 91 . . . . @20.00

TWILIGHT ZONE
Now, 1990
1 NA,BSz(c) 8.00
1a 2nd printing Prestige +Harlan
  Ellison story. 6.00
[Volume 2]
#1 The Big Dry (direct) 3.00

#1a Newsstand. 2.50
2 Blind Alley 2.50
3 Extraterrestrial 2.50
4 The Mysterious Biker. 2.50
5 Queen of the Void 2.50
6 Insecticide 2.50
7 The Outcasts,Ghost Horse 2.50
8 Colonists on Alcor 2.50
9 Dirty Lyle's House of Fun
  (3-D Holo) 3.00
10 Stairway to Heaven,Key
  to Paradise 2.50
11 TD(i),Partial Recall 2.50
3-D Spec. 2.50
Ann. #1. 2.75
[Volume 3]
1 thru 2 . . . . @2.50

Twisted Tales #6
© Pacific Comics

TWISTED TALES
Pacific, 1982–84
1 RCo. Infected. 5.00
2 thru 8 . . . . @4.00
Eclipse
9 . . . . 4.00
10 GM,BWr 5.50

TWISTED TALES OF BRUCE JONES
Eclipse, 1982–84
1 . . . . 2.50
2 . . . . 2.50
3 . . . . 2.50
4 . . . . 2.50

TWISTER
Harris
1 inc.Special newspaper/poster,
  and trading cards. 3.00

TWO FISTED TALES
Russ Cochran, 1992
1 JSe,HK,WW,JCr,reps. 2.50
2 Reps inc.War Story 2.50
3 rep.. . . . . 2.50
4 thru 6 rep.. . . . . @2.50
7 thru 8 rep.. . . . . @2.50
Gemstone
17 thru 24 EC comics reprints . . . @2.50
`Annuals'

TPB Vol.#4 reprint #16–#20......	13.00
TPB Vol. 2 rebinding of #5–#10..	10.00
TPB Vol. 3 rebinding of #11–#15..	11.00
TPB Vol. 4 rebinding	11.00
TPB Vol. 5 rebinding	11.00

2000 A.D. MONTHLY
Eagle, 1985
1 A:JudgeDredd 4.00
2 A:JudgeDredd 3.00
3 A:JudgeDredd 2.50
4 A:JudgeDredd 2.50
5 .... 2.50
6 .... 2.50

[2nd Series]
1 thru 4 .... @2.25

Quality
5 thru 27 .... @2.25
28/29 .... 2.25
30 .... 2.25
31/32 .... 2.25
33 thru 37 .... @2.25
Becomes:

2000 A.D. SHOWCASE
38 thru 54................ @2.25
TPB: Killing Time 13.00

TWO-STEP
Wildstorm/DC Oct. 2003
1 (of 3) WEI(s),ACo,JP 3.00
2 WEI(s),ACo,JP.............. 3.00
3 WEI(s),ACo,JP,concl.......... 3.00

2 TO THE CHEST
Dark Planet Productions, 2004
1 .... 3.00
2 thru 5 .... @3.00
TPB 13.00

TZU THE REAPER
Murim Studios, 1997
1 by Gary Cohn & C.S. Chun..... 3.00
2 .... 3.00
3 .... 3.00
4 .... 3.00
5 .... 3.00

TZU: SPIRITS OF DEATH
Murim Studios, 1997
1 .... 3.00

UFO FLYING SAUCERS
Gold Key, 1968
1 .... 65.00
2 .... 30.00
3 thru 13 .... @25.00
Becomes:

UFO & OUTER SPACE
Gold Key, 1978
14 thru 25................ @15.00

ULTIMATE SPORTS FORCE PRESENTS:
Ultimate Sports Entertainment 2004
1 Hardwood Heroes 4.00
1 The Guardians.............. 4.00
1 The Zone.................. 4.00
1 Air and Space 4.00

ULTRAFORCE
Malibu Ultraverse, 1994–95
1 Prime, Prototype 2.50

2	2.25
3	2.25
4	2.25
5 V:Atalon	2.25
6 V:Atalon	2.50
7 CU,GP(c),F:Ghoul	2.50
8 MWn,CV,GP,F:Black Knight	2.50
9 A:Marvel's Black Knight	2.50
10	2.50
Spec.#0	2.50

Ultraforce #3
© Malibu

ULTRAFORCE
Malibu Ultraverse, 1995–96
Infinity Fant. Ultraforce Four 2.50
1 George Perez cover 2.25
1a Computer painted cover 2.25
2 Phoenix flip issue,I:Lament 2.25
3 .... 2.25
4 .... 2.25
5 .... 2.25
6 Smoke and Bone,pt.2 .... 2.25
7 .... 2.25
8 .... 2.25
9 .... 2.25
10 A:Sersi,Eliminator 2.25
11 .... 2.25
12 MD2,LWn, cont. from All-New
    Exiles #12 .... 2.25
13 LWn,MD2,new UltraForce lineup 2.25
14 LWn,MD2,Hardcase returns 2.25
15 LWn,MD2,Hardcase returns 2.25

ULTRAFORCE/AVENGERS
Malibu Ultraverse, Aug. 1995
1 GP 4.00

ULTRAFORCE/ SPIDER-MAN
Malibu Ultraverse, 1996
1 .... 4.00

ULTRAMAN
Nemesis, 1994
1 EC,O:Ultraman 2.50
2 .... 2.50
3 .... 2.50
4 V:Blue Ultraman............. 2.50

ULTRAMAN
Harvey/Ultracomics, 1993
1 with 1 of 3 cards 2.50
2 with 1 of 3 cards & virgin cover.. 2.50
3 with 1 of 3 cards & virgin cover.. 2.50

ULTRAVERSE DOUBLE FEATURE
Malibu Ultraverse, 1995
1 F:Prime, Solitaire............ 4.00

ULTRAVERSE FUTURE SHOCK
Malibu Ultraverse, 1996
1 one-shot,MPc,alternate futures .. 2.50

ULTRAVERSE ORIGINS
Malibu Ultraverse, 1994
1 O:Ultraverse Heroes 2.25
1a Silver foil cover 12.50

ULTRAVERSE UNLIMITED
Malibu Ultraverse, 1996
1 F:Warlock................. 2.25
2 LWn,KWe, A:All-New Exiles,
    V:Maxis 2.25

ULTRAVERSE: YEAR ZERO: THE DEATH OF THE SQUAD
Malibu Ultraverse, 1995
0-A Hardcase's old team 2.50
0-B 2.50
0-C L.A. Riots................ 2.50
1 JHI,A:Squad, Mantra 3.00
2 JHI,DaR(c) prequel to Prime#1 .. 3.00
3 Cont. Year Zero Story 3.00
4 I:NM-E 3.00

ULTRAVERSE: YEAR ONE
Malibu Ultraverse, 1995
1 Handbook, double size 5.00
2 Prime.................... 2.25

ULTRAVERSE: YEAR TWO
Malibu Ultraverse, 1996
1 Marvel/Ultraverse/Info 5.00

UNCLE SCROOGE
Dell/Gold Key, 1962
40 CB,X-Mas 175.00
41 .... 150.00
42 .... 150.00
43 CB..................... 150.00
44 CB..................... 150.00
45 CB..................... 150.00
46 Lost Beneath the Sea....... 150.00
47 CB..................... 150.00
48 CB..................... 150.00
49 CB,Loony Lunar Gold Rush... 150.00
50 CB,Rug Riders in the Sky.... 150.00
51 CB,How Green Was my
    Lettuce................. 135.00
52 CB,Great Wig Mystery 135.00
53 CB,Interplanetary Postman... 135.00
54 CB,Billion-Dollar Safari! 135.00
55 CB,McDuck of Arabia 135.00
56 CB,Mystery of the Ghost
    Town Railroad 135.00
57 CB,Swamp of No Return 135.00
58 CB,Giant Robot Robbers 135.00
59 CB,North of the Yukon 135.00
60 CB,Phantom of Notre Duck .. 135.00

COLOR PUB.

61 CB,So Far and No Safari 125.00
62 CB,Queen of the Wild
    Dog Pack. 125.00
63 CB,House of Haunts! 125.00
64 CB,Treasure of Marco Polo! . . 175.00
65 CB,Micro-Ducks from
    OuterSpace 125.00
66 CB,Heedless Horseman 125.00
67 CB rep. 125.00
68 CB,Hall of the Mermaid
    Queen!. 125.00
69 CB,Cattle King! 125.00
70 CB,The Doom Diamond!. 125.00
71 CB. 125.00
72 CB rep. 125.00
73 CB rep. 125.00
74 thru 110 . . . . @75.00
111 thru 148 . . . . @40.00
149. . . . . 35.00
150 thru 168. . . . . @35.00
169 thru 173. . . . . @35.00

Whitman, 1980
174 thru 176. . . . . @35.00
177 and 178. . . . . @40.00
179 Rare 600.00
180 thru 182 . . . . @60.00
183 thru 195 . . . . @25.00
196 and 197 . . . . @30.00
1981 thru 209. . . . . @35.00

Gladstone, 1986
210 CB,Beagle Boys 20.00
211 CB,Prize of Pizzaro 18.00
212 CB,city-golden roofs 18.00
213 CB,city-golden roofs 18.00
214 CB. 18.00
215 CB, a cold bargain 18.00
216 CB. 18.00
217 CB,7 cities of Cibola 18.00
218 CB. 18.00
219 Don Rosa,Son of Sun 30.00
220 CB,Don Rosa 10.00
221 CB,A:BeagleBoys 4.00
222 CB,Mysterious Island 4.00
223 CB. 4.00
224 CB,Rosa,Cash Flow 7.00
225 CB. 4.00
226 CB,Rosa 5.00
227 CB,Rosa 5.00
228 CB. 4.00
229 CB. 4.00
230 CB. 5.00
231 CB,Rosa(c) 4.00
232 CB. 4.00
233 CB. 4.00
234 CB. 4.00
235 Rosa 7.00
236 CB. 4.00
237 CB. 4.00
238 CB. 4.00
239 CB. 4.00
240 CB. 4.00
241 CB,giant 7.00
242 CB,giant 7.00

Walt Disney, 1990
243 CB,Pie in the Sky 4.00
244 . . . . 3.50
245 . . . . 3.50
246 . . . . 3.50
247 . . . . 3.50
248 . . . . 3.50
249 . . . . 3.50
250 CB. 5.00
251 . . . . 3.00
252 No Room For Human Error . . . 3.00
253 Fab.Philosophers Stone 3.00
254 The Filling Station 3.00
255 The Flying Dutchman 3.00
256 CB,Status Seeker 3.00
257 Coffee,Louie or Me 3.00
258 CB,Swamp of no return 3.00

259 The only way to Go. 3.00
260 The Waves Above, The
    Gold Below 3.00
261 Rosa,Return to Zanadu, Pt.1 . . 6.00
262 Rosa,Return to Zanadu, Pt.2 . . 6.00
263 Rosa,Treasure Under Glass. . . 6.00
264 Snobs Club 3.00
265 CB,Ten Cent Valentine 3.00
266 The Money Ocean,Pt.1 . . . . . . 3.00
267 The Money Ocean,Pt 2. . . . . . 3.00
268 CB,Rosa,Island in the Sky . . . 3.00
269 The Flowers 3.00
270 V:Magica DeSpell 3.00
271 The Secret o/t Stone. 3.00
272 Canute The Brute's Battle Axe . 3.00
273 CB,Uncle Scrooge-Ghost 3.25
274 CB,Hall of the Mermaid Queen. 3.25
275 CB,Rosa,Christmas Cheers,inc.
    D.Rosa centerspread 3.25
276 Rosa, thru 277 . . . . @7.00
278 thru 280. . . . . @3.00

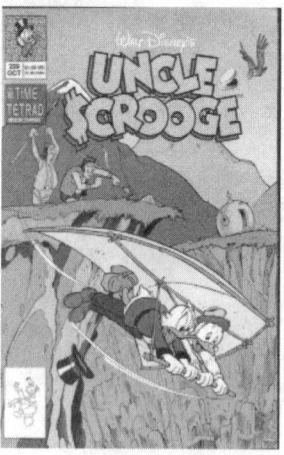

Uncle Scrooge #259
© Walt Disney

Gladstone, 1993
281 Rosa 7.00
282 thru 284. . . . . @3.00
285 Rosa, Life & Times 11.00
286 thru 293 Rosa, Life & Times . @6.00
294 thru 299. . . . . @3.00
300 Rosa & Barks 5.00
301 Statuesque Spendthrifts 3.00
302. . . . . 3.00
303 Rocks to Riches 3.00
304 My Private Eye 3.00
305 Vigilante of Pizen Bluff 3.00
306. . . . . 3.00
307 Temper Temper. 3.00
308 Revenge of the Witch 3.00
Prestige format, 64pg.
309 Whadalottajargon 8.00
310 The Sign of the Triple
    Distelfink 8.00
311 The Last Lord of Eldorado . . . 8.00
312 The Hands of Zeus. 8.00
313 The Fantastic River Race 8.00
314 . . . . 8.00
315 The Flying Scot, pt.1. . . . . 8.00
316 The Flying Scot, pt.2. . . . . 8.00
317 Pawns of the Lamp Garou . . . 8.00
318 Cowboy Captain of Cutty Sark . 8.00
319 The Horse Radish Story 8.00
320 The Mysterious Stone Ray . . . 8.00
321 The Giant Robot Robbers . . . 8.00

322 Secret of the Lost
    Dutchman's Mine. 8.00

UNCLE SCROOGE
Gemstone Publishing, 2003
319 thru 335. . . . . @7.00

UNCLE SCROOGE ADVENTURES
Gladstone, 1987
1 CB,McDuck of Arabia 9.00
2 translated from Danish 5.00
3 translated from Danish 5.00
4 CB 5.00
5 Rosa 5.00
6 CB 3.50
7 CB 3.00
8 CB 3.00
9 Rosa 3.50
10 CB. 3.00
11 CB 3.00
12 CB. 3.00
13 CB. 3.00
14 Rosa 3.50
15 CB. 3.00
16 CB. 3.00
17 CB. 3.00
18 CB. 3.00
19 CB,Rosa(c) 3.50
20 CB,giant 6.00
21 CB,giant 6.00
22 Rosa(c) 6.00
23 CB,giant 4.00
24 thru 26. . . . . @2.50
27 Rosa,O:Jr. Woodchuck 4.00
28 giant 4.00
29 . . . . 2.50
30 giant 5.00
31 thru 32. . . . . @3.00
33 Barks. 5.00
34 thru 40. . . . . @3.00
41 . . . . 2.50
42 The Dragon's Amulet 2.50
43 Queen of the Wild Dog Pack . . . 2.50
44 . . . . 2.50
45 Secret of the Duckburg Triangle. 2.50
46 The Tides Turn 2.50
47 The Menehune Mystery 2.50
48 The Tenth Avatar. 2.50
49 Dead-Eye Duck. 2.50
50 CB,The Secret of Atlantis 3.00
51. . . . . 2.50
52 The Black Diamond 2.50
53 Secret of the Incas 2.50
54 Secret of the Incas, pt.2 . . . . . . 2.50

UNCLE SCROOGE ADVENTURES
Gladstone, 1997–98
Don Rosa Specials
Spec.#1 (of 4). 11.00
Spec.#2 thru #4 . . . . @10.00
Van Horn Specials
Spec.#1 . . . . 10.00
Spec.#2 . . . . 10.00
Spec.#3 . . . . 10.00
Spec.#4 . . . . 10.00

UNCLE SCROOGE ADVENTURES IN COLOR
Gladstone, 1987–98
Carl Barks reprints
1 thru 32 . . . . @10.00
33 thru 35. . . . . @11.00
36 32pg. 9.00
37 thru 53. . . . . @10.00

COLOR PUB.

54 Hall of the Mermaid Queen. . . . 10.00
55 The Doom Diamond 10.00
56 two adventures 10.00

UNCLE SCROOGE & DONALD DUCK
Gold Key, 1965
1 rep.. . . . . 125.00

UNCLE SCROOGE AND DONALD DUCK
Gladstone, 1997
1 . . . . 2.50
2 Christmas stories. 2.50
3 Back to Long Ago 2.50
TPB Vol. 1 . . . . 10.00
TPB Vol. 2 . . . . 10.00
TPB Vol. 3 . . . . 10.00
TPB Vol. 4 . . . . 10.00

UNCLE SCROOGE GOES TO DISNEYLAND
Gladstone, 1985
1 CB,etc. 100pp 13.00

UNDEAD, THE
Chaos! Comics Black Label,, 2001
Ashcan 6.00
Ashcan, premium edition 20.00
1 zombie wasteland 5.00
1a previews exclusive (c) 5.00
1b signed edition. 15.00
1c premium edition 10.00
1d super-premium edition. 20.00
1e foil (c). 20.00

UNDERDOG
Charlton, 1970
1 Planet Zot 125.00
2 Simon Sez/The Molemen 75.00
3 Whisler's Father. 75.00
4 The Witch of Pycoon 75.00
5 The Snowmen 75.00
6 The Big Shrink. 75.00
7 The Marbleheads. 75.00
8 The Phoney Booths. 75.00
9 Tin Man Alley 75.00
10 Be My Valentine (Jan., 1972) . . 75.00

UNDERDOG
Gold Key, 1975
1 The Big Boom 100.00
2 The Sock Singer Caper. 50.00
3 The Ice Cream Scream 50.00
4 . . . . 50.00
5 . . . . 50.00
6 Head in a Cloud. 50.00
7 The Cosmic Canine 50.00
8 . . . . 50.00
9 . . . . 50.00
10 Bouble Trouble Gum. 50.00
11 The Private Life of
    Shoeshine Boy 35.00
12 The Deadly Fist of Fingers 35.00
13 . . . . 35.00
14 Shrink Shrank Shrunk. 35.00
15 Polluter Palooka 35.00
16 The Soda Jerk 35.00
17 Flee For Your Life 35.00
18 Rain Rain Go Away...Okay 35.00
19 Journey To the Center of
    the Earth 35.00
20 The Six Million Dollar Dog 35.00
21 Smell of Success 40.00

22 Antlers Away 40.00
23 Wedding Bells In Outer Space
    (Feb.,1979) 40.00

UNDERDOG
Spotlight, 1987
1 FMc,PC(c),The Eredicator. 3.50
2 FMc,CS(c), Prisoner of Love/
    The Return of Fearo 3.50

UNDERDOG IN 3-D
Blackthorne
1 Wanted Dead or Alive 2.50

UNDERSEA AGENT
Tower, 1966–97
1 F:Davy Jones,UnderseaAgent. 135.00
2 thru 4 . . . . @100.00
5 O&I:Merman 100.00
6 GK,WW(c) 100.00

Undertaker #3
© Chaos! Comics

UNDERTAKER
Chaos! Comics, 1999
Preview BSt, WWF character 2.50
Preview, photo (c). 2.50
1 Prophecy of the Dead 3.00
1a photo cover 3.00
1b premium edition 10.00
1c Death Chrome cover 15.00
1d Death Chrome cover, signed. . 20.00
2 V:Embalmer & Paul Bearer 3.00
3 O:Undertaker 3.00
4 Kane 3.00
5 Jezebel 3.00
6 thru 12 . . . . @3.00
2a thru 12a photo covers . . . . . . @3.00
Halloween Spec. 3.00
Halloween Spec. photo(c) 3.00
TPB Prophecy of the Dead,
    rep.#1–#4 . . . . 13.00
TPB Vol.2 rep.#5–#8 . . . . 13.00

UNDERWORLD: RED IN TOOTH AND CLAW
IDW Publishing, 2004
1 . . . . 4.00
2 thru 3 . . . . @4.00

UNEARTHLY SPECTACULARS
Harvey, 1965
1 DW,AT,I:Tiger Boy 75.00
2 WW,AW,GK,I:Earthman,Miracles,
    Inc. A:Clawfang,TigerBoy . . . 75.00
3 RC,AW,JO,A:Miracles,Inc. 60.00

U.N. FORCE
Gauntlet Comics, 1995
0 BDC(s). 3.00
1 B:BDC(s),I:U.N.Force 3.00
2 O:Indigo 3.00
3 . . . . 3.00
4 A:Predator 3.00
5 B:Critical Mass. 3.00

U.N. FORCE FILES
Gauntlet Comics
1 KP(c),F:Hunter Seeker, Lotus . . . 3.00

UNION OF JUSTICE
Quantum Comics, 1998
1 by David Watkins & Steve Kurth . 3.00
2 . . . . 3.00
3 A:Golden Age Union 3.00

UNITY
Valiant, 1992
0 BWS,BL,Chapter#1,A:All Valiant
    Heroes,V:Erica Pierce 3.00
0a Red ed.,w/red logo 4.00
1 BWS,BL,Chapter#18,A:All Valiant
    Heroes,D:Erica Pierce. 3.00
1a Gold logo 4.00
1b Platinum. 4.00
TPB Previews Exclusive,Vol.I
    Chap.#1-9 . . . . 8.00
TPB Previews Exclusive,Vol.II
    Chap.#10-18 . . . . 3.00
TPB #1 rep Chapters #1-4. . . . . 11.00
TPB #2 rep Chapters #5-9. . . . . 10.00
TPB #3 rep Chapters #10-14. . . . 10.00

UNITY 2000
Acclaim, 1999
1 (of 6) 2.50
2 . . . . 2.50
3 . . . . 2.50
4 . . . . 2.50
5 . . . . 2.50

UNIT ZERO: MARQUIS FILES
Marquis Models, 2004
1 . . . . 4.00
2 thru 4 . . . . 4.00

UNIVERSAL SOLDIER
Now, 1992
1 Based on Movie,Holo.(c) 2.75
2 Luc & Ronnie on the run
    from UniSols 2.50
2a Photo cover 2.50
3 Photo(c) 2.50

UNKNOWN WORLDS OF FRANK BRUNNER
Eclipse, 1985
1 and 2 FB . . . . @2.50

COLOR PUB.

UNLEASHED!
Triumphant
0 JnR(s),I:Skyfire 2.50
1 JnR(s), ... 2.50

UNLV
1 Championship season (basketball based on college team) 3.00

UNTAMED LOVE
Fantagraphics, 1987
1 FF 2.25

UNTOLD TALES OF
Chaos! Comics, 2000
Purgatori #1 . . . . 3.00
Purgatori #1 premium ed. 13.00
Chastity #1 . . . . 3.00
Chastity premium #1 . . . . 13.00
Lady Death #1 . . . . 3.00
Lady Death #1 premium 13.00
Lady Death #1 chromium ed. 16.00

UNUSUAL TALES
Charlton Comics, 1955–65
1 . . . . 325.00
2 . . . . 175.00
3 thru 5 . . . . @125.00
6 SD,SD(c) 225.00
7 SD,SD(c) 300.00
8 SD,SD(c) 300.00
9 SD,SD(c) 325.00
10 SD,SD(c). 350.00
11 SD 325.00
12 SD 225.00
13 . . . . 100.00
14 SD 200.00
15 SD,SD(c). 250.00
16 thru 20 . . . . @100.00
21 . . . . 75.00
22 SD 150.00
23 . . . . 75.00
24 . . . . 75.00
25 SD 150.00
26 SD 150.00
27 SD 150.00
28 . . . . 75.00
29 SD 150.00
30 thru 49 . . . . @65.00

URI-ON
1 and 2 . . . . @2.25

URTH 4
Continuity, 1990
1 TVE,NA(c) 2.25
2 TVE,NA 2.25
3 TVE,NA 2.25
4 NA,Last issue. 2.25

USAGI YOJIMBO
Mirage, 1993
1 A:TMNT 6.00
2 . . . . 5.00
3 . . . . 5.00
4 thru 16 . . . . @5.00
17 . . . . 8.00

VALERIA, THE SHE BAT
Continuity, 1993
1 NA,I:Valeria 10.00
2 thru 4 . . . . [NOT RELEASED]
5 Rise of Magic. 2.50

VALERIA, THE SHE-BAT
Windjammer, 1995
1 (of 2) NA,Valeria & 'Rilla 2.50
2 (of 2) NA,BSz, final issue 2.50

VALHALLA
Antarctic Press, 1999
1 BDn set in 1939. . . . . 3.00

VALIANT ERA
Valiant
TPB rep.Magnus #12,Shadowman #8, Solar #10-11,Eternal Warrior#4-5 . . . . 14.00

VALIANT READER: GUIDE TO THE VALIANT UNIVERSE
Acclaim
1 O:Valiant Universe. 2.25

VALIANT VISION STARTER KIT
Valiant
1 w/3-D Glasses 3.00
2 F:Starwatchers 3.00

VALKYRIE
Eclipse, 1988
1 PG,I:Steelfox,C:Airboy, Sky Wolf . 3.00
2 PG,O:New Black Angel 2.50
3 PG 2.50

[2nd Series]
1 BA,V:Eurasian Slavers 2.25
2 BA,V:Cowgirl 2.25
3 BA,V:Cowgirl 2.25

VALLEY OF THE DINOSAURS
Charlton, 1975
1 Hanna-Barbera TV adapt. 30.00
2 thru 11 . . . . @20.00

VALOR
Gemstone, 1998
1 EC comics reprint 2.50
2 . . . . 2.50
3 AW, The Cloak of Command 2.50
4 WW(c) 2.50
5 final issue. 3.50
Annual
TPB Vol. 1 rebinding of series 13.50

VAMPEROTICA
Brainstorm, 1996
1–16 see B&W
17 . . . . 3.00
17a signed 5.00
17 Holochrome cover. 40.00
18 Blood of the Damned (color). . . . 3.00
18a signed 5.00
19 Hunter's Blood 3.00
19a deluxe 3.00
20 Vampire Quest 3.00
21 hunting & feeding 3.00
22 . . . . 3.00
TPB Red Reign, rep. 13.00

VAMPEROTICA LINGERIE
Comic Cavalcade, 1998
Commemorative #1 by Kirk Lindo . . 6.00
Commemorative #1a deluxe 15.00

Vampi #3
© Harris Comics

VAMPI
Harris Comics, 2000
1/2 24-pg.. . . . . 10.00
1/2 variant edition 20.00
1 Switchblade Kiss,pt.1. . . . . 3.00
1c signed & numbered 20.00
1d gold foil 30.00
1e convention special, B&W 10.00
1g limited holochrome edition. . . . 25.00
1g royal blue edition 60.00
1h Platinum edition 20.00
1i limited edition 10.00
2 Switchblade Kiss,pt.2. . . . . 8.00
1b thru 2b limited chrome (c) . . @15.00
2c limited holochrome edition . . . 25.00
3 Switchblade Kiss,pt.3. . . . . 5.00
4 Dark Angel Rising,pt.1 . . . . 3.00
5 Dark Angel Rising,pt.2. . . . . 3.00
6 Dark Angel Rising,pt.3. . . . . 3.50
7 Underworld, pt.1 (of 3). 3.00
8 Underworld, pt.2 . . . . 3.00
9 Underworld, pt.3 . . . . 3.00
1a thru 9a deluxe . . . . @10.00
Ashcan Vampi Dark Angel Rising platinum leather limited B&W . 15.00
Ashcan Vampi Underworld preview. 6.00
Ashcan Tainted Love 6.00
Vampi #1 preview 3.00
TPB Vol. 1, rep. #1–#3 . . . . 20.00

Anarchy Studios, 2001
10 . . . . 3.00
10b convention ed. 10.00
10c convention ed., signed 20.00
11 . . . . 3.00
12 . . . . 3.00
12b holo-fx chrome ed. 15.00
12c gold-fx chrome 25.00
13 . . . . 3.00
14 framed, I:Xenocyde. 3.00
15 V:Xenocyde. 3.00
16 saved by Xenocide 3.00
17 Ultimatrix, pt.2. . . . . 3.00
18 Ultimatrix, pt.3. . . . . 3.00
19 Serpent's Kiss, pt.1. . . . . 3.00
20 Serpent's Kiss, pt.2. . . . . 3.00
21 Serpent's Kiss, pt.3. . . . . 3.00
22 Serpent's Kiss, pt.4. . . . . 3.00
23 Fallout, pt.1 . . . . 3.00
24 Fallout, pt.2. . . . . 3.00
25 . . . . 3.00
10a thru 16a deluxe . . . . @10.00
14a thru 25a limited . . . . @10.00
Sketchbook platinum leather 15.00

All comics prices listed are for *Near Mint* condition.

Ashcan Vampi:End Game 6.00
Ashcan Vampi #19–#21 . . . . 6.00
Ashcan Ultimatrix Leather Gold . . . 15.00
Ashcan Vampi: Anarchy in the USA
   giant-sized, limited (2001) 6.00
TPB Vol. 1 Switchblade Kiss/
   Dark Angel Rising 15.00
TPB Underworld Tainted Love 15.00

VAMPI (DIGITAL)
Harris Comics, 2001
1 digital art 3.00
1a limited ed. 10.00
Preview edition, digital 3.00
Ashcan, Underworld gold leather. . 15.00

VAMPI VICIOUS
Anarchy Studios, 2003
Prototype Convention edition. 10.00
1 . . . . 3.00
1a variant (c). 3.00
1 royal blue edition 40.00
1 gold foil edition. 30.00
2 thru 3 . . . . @3.00
2a thru 3a variant (c) 3.00

VAMPI VICIOUS CIRCLE
Anarchy Studios, 2004
Ashcan Vicious Circle 6.00
1 . . . . 3.00
2 thru 3 . . . . @3.00
1a thru 3a variant (c). . . . . @10.00

VAMPI VS. XIN
Anarchy Studios, 2004
1 . . . . 3.00
2 . . . . 3.00
1a thru 2a limited . . . . @10.00

VAMPIRE LESTAT
Innovation, 1990–91
1 Anne Rice Adapt. 20.00
1a 2nd printing 4.00
1b 3rd printing 2.50
2 . . . . 9.00
2a 2nd printing 4.00
2b 3rd printing 2.50
3 . . . . 5.00
3a 2nd printing 2.50
4 . . . . 5.00
4a 2nd printing 2.50
5 . . . . 5.00
6 . . . . 5.00
7 . . . . 5.00
8 . . . . 5.00
9 scarce 8.00
9a 2nd Printing 3.00
10 . . . . 5.00
11 Those Who Must Be Kept. 4.00
12 conclusion 4.00
Vampire Companion #1 . . . . 4.00
Vampire Companion #2 (preview
   Interview With The Vampire . . . 3.00
Vampire Companion #3 . . . . 3.00
GN rep.#1-#12 (Innovation) 25.00
GN rep.#1-#12 (Ballantine) 25.00

VAMPIRELLA
Warren Publishing Co., 1969–83
1 NA,FF(c),I:Vampirella 650.00
2 B:Amazonia 225.00
3 Very scarce 550.00
4 . . . . 150.00
5 FF(c) 165.00
6 . . . . 150.00
7 FF(c) 175.00

8 B:horror 150.00
9 BWS,BV(c),WW. 160.00
10 No Vampirella,WW 75.00
11 TS,FF(c)O&I Pendragon. 125.00
12 WW 125.00
13 . . . . 100.00
14 . . . . 100.00
15 . . . . 100.00
16 . . . . 100.00
17 B:Tomb of the Gods 100.00
18 . . . . 100.00
19 WW,1973 Annual 125.00
20 thru 25 . . . . @100.00
26 . . . . @75.00
27 1974 Annual 90.00
28 thru 30 . . . . @75.00
31 FF(c) 90.00
32 thru 36 . . . . @50.00
37 1975 Annual 60.00
38 . . . . 50.00
39 . . . . 50.00
40 . . . . 50.00
41 thru 45 . . . . @40.00
46 O:Vampirella 50.00
47 thru 99 . . . . @40.00
100 Double Size 100.00
101 thru 110 . . . . @60.00
111 Giant Edition 75.00
112 . . . . 60.00

VAMPIRELLA
Harris, 1992
0 Dracula Wars 5.00
0a Blue version 22.00
1 V:Forces of Chaos, w/coupon for
   DSt poster 20.00
1a 2nd printing 5.00
2 AH(c) 18.00
3 A:Dracula 7.00
4 A:Dracula 6.00
5 . . . . 6.00
Spec. #1 Vampirella/Shadowhawk:
   Creatures of the Night (1995) . . 5.50

Harris Comics, 1996
0 gold foil signed & numbered . . . 22.00
1 Commemorative Edition 3.00
1a Commemorative Edition,
   sgn & num. 10.00
25th Anniv. Spec., FF(c). 6.00
25th Anniv. Spec., lim. 7.00
Spec. Death of Vampirella,
   memorial, chromium cover . . . 20.00
Spec. 1-shot Vampirella/Cain,
   flipbook, 72-pg. (1996) 7.00
Spec. Vampirella Pin-up (1995) . . . 3.50

VAMPIRELLA
Harris Comics, 1997
1 Ascending Evil, pt.1 . . . . 3.00
1a ultra-violent cover 3.00
1b JaL(c). 10.00
2 Ascending Evil, pt.2 . . . . 3.00
2a JaL(c). 10.00
3 Ascending Evil, pt.3 . . . . 3.00
3a JaL(c). 10.00
4 Holy War, pt.1 . . . . 3.00
4a Crimson ed., Joe Linsner (c) . . . 3.00
5 Holy War, pt.2 . . . . 3.00
6 Holy War, pt.3 . . . . 3.00
7 Queen's Gambit, pt.1 . . . . 3.00
7a chromium Edition 11.00
8 Queen's Gambit, pt.2 . . . . 3.00
9 Queen's Gambit, pt.3, concl. 3.00
10 Hell on Earth, pt.1, V:Nyx 3.00
10a variant JaL cover 10.00
11 Hell on Earth, pt.2 . . . . 3.00

12 Hell on Earth, pt.3,
   New costume. 3.00

Vampirella #12
© Harris Comics

12a variant cover, new costume . . . 3.00
12b chromium cover 11.00
13 World's End,pt.1 . . . . 3.00
13b Pantha cover. 10.00
14 World's End,pt.2 . . . . 3.00
15 World's End,pt.3 . . . . 3.00
13a thru 15a variant (c)s . . . . @3.00
16 Pantha #1 . . . . 3.00
17 Pantha #2 . . . . 3.00
16b limited photo ed. 10.00
16a thru 17a Phantha photo(c)s . @3.00
18 Rebirth, pt.1,JaL(c) 3.00
19 Rebirth, pt.2, ... 3.00
20 Rebirth, pt.3 . . . . 3.00
21 Dangerous Games,pt.1 . . . . 3.00
21c Millennium ed. 20.00
22 Dangerous Games,pt.2 . . . . 3.00
22a Dorian (c) 10.00
16c thru 22c Julie Strain (c)s . . @10.00
23 Vampirella/Lady Death:
   The Revenge, pt.1 . . . . 3.00
23a limited ed. 10.00
21b thru 23b limited chrome ed. @15.00
24 Hell's Angels, Vampirella (c) . . . 3.00
24a Pantha (c) 3.00
25 Hells Angels, vol.2 . . . . 3.00
25a alternate (c). 3.00
25b Monte Moore (c) 15.00
26 The End #1 . . . . 3.00
26a alternate (c). 10.00
26b platinum ed. 20.00
Ashcan, Ascending Evil, b&w, 16pg. 1.50
Ashcan, Ascending Evil, b&w,
   signed, limited 25.00
Ashcan, Queen's Gambit,B&W . . . 6.00
Ashcan, Queen's Gambit,signed . . 25.00
Ashcan World's End, B&W,16pg. . . 6.00
Ashcan Rebirth preview,B&W,16-pg 6.00
Vampirella/Lady Death Limited
   Preview Ashcan, B&W. 6.00
Vampirella, Queen's Gambit #1
   special edition, alternate (c) . . 10.00
   Chromium Edition 11.00
Spec.#0 A:Lady Death,B.U.:Pantha. 3.00
Spec.#0a Pantha(c) 3.00
Spec.#0b Vampirella(c) 10.00
Spec.#0c Vampirella(c), signed . . 30.00
Spec.#0d Pantha(c) 10.00
Spec. Vampirella/Dracula: The
   Centennial, A:Pantha,16pg. . . . 2.00
Spec. Vampirella/Dracula: The
   Centennial, 48pg. (1997) 5.00
Spec.#1 Dangerous Games,
   holochrome (2001) 15.00

TPB Ascending Evil 7.50
Ann.Ed.#2 Rebirth 10.00
Ann.Ed.#3 Rebirth,Bruce Timm(c) . 10.00
Julie Strain Special. 4.00
Julie Strain Special variant(c) 10.00
Julie Strain Spec. chrome (c) 15.00
Julie Strain Spec. holochrome(c) . . 25.00

VAMPIRELLA
Harris Comics, 2001
0 Gold edition 20.00
1 Nowheresville, Mayhew (c) 3.00
1a JSC (c). 3.00
1b Anacleto (c) 3.00
1c JaL (c) 3.00
1d commemorative ed. B&W, FF(c) 5.00
1e Chicago convention edition . . . 10.00
1f Chicago convention, limited . . . 20.00
1g photo edition, limited 10.00
1h gold edition 30.00
1i holographic chrome (c) 15.00
1j royal blue edition. 60.00
1k gold-fx chrome (c) 25.00
1l Ascending evil gold (c) 20.00
2 thru 4 . . . . @3.00
4c holo FX chrome (c) 15.00
4d gold-fx chrome 30.00
2a thru 22a limited . . . . @10.00
2b thru 22b photo (c) . . . . @10.00
5 thru 22 . . . . @3.00
7c thru 10c limited Pantha
  MT(c). . . . . @10.00
7d Pantha holo fx MC(c). 15.00
Ashcan #1 giant-size 6.00
Ashcan #4–#6 giant-size, 16-pg. . . 6.00
Preview #7–#9 16-pg. 3.00
Ashcan #7–#9 giant-size,16-pg. . . . 6.00
Ashcan #11–#13 . . . . 6.00
Ashcan #11–#13 leather 15.00
1-shot Vampirella Genesis (2001) . . 3.00
1-shot Vampirella Genesis,
  variant 10.00
TPB Nowheresville. 13.00
TPB Vol. 1 Crimson Chronicles . . . 20.00
TPB Vol. 2 Crimson Chronicles . . . 20.00
TPB Vol. 2 Fear of Mirrors 15.00
Spec. Model Search. 10.00
Spec. Halloween 2004 . . . . 5.00

VAMPIRELLA:
BLOOD LUST
Harris, 1997
1 (of 2) JeR & JJu. 5.00
2 JJu(c) 5.00
Book 1, JJu(c) Virgin edition 11.00
Book 2, JJu(c) Virgin edition 11.00

VAMPIRELLA CLASSIC
Harris Comics, 1995
1 Dark Angel 3.50
2 V:Demogorgon. 3.25
3 V:Were Beast. 3.25
4 R:Papa Voodoo 3.25
5 . . . . 3.00

VAMPIRELLA:
CROSSOVERS
Harris, 1996–98
1-shot Vampirella vs.
  Eudaemon (1996) 10.00
1-shot StG,SSh,Vampirella/
  Wetworks, image x-over (1997) 3.00
1-shotA Vamp/Wetworks,
  SS&KN(c) 10.00
1-shot Vampirella/Shi (1997) 3.00
1-shotA Vamp/Shi, Chromium ed. . . 7.00
1-shot Vamp/Shi, penciled(c). . . . 10.00

Vampirella/Shi 1-shot
© *Harris Comics*

Ashcan #1, Vamp/Shi, 16pg 3.00
1-shot Vampirella/Painkiller
  Jane, foil JQ(c) (1998). 3.50
1-shotA Vampirella/Painkiller
  Jane, alternate RL&JP(c) 10.00
1 Crossover art gallery 3.00
1a Art gallery, chromium ed. 10.00
1b Art gallery, holochrome(c) 20.00

VAMPIRELLA: DEATH
AND DESTRUCTION
Harris
1 limited preview ashcan 4.00
1a The Dying of the Light 3.00
1b signed & numbered 3.00
1c satin edition 25.00
1d Lim. Ed., Mark Beachum (c) . . 10.00
2 The Nature of the Beast 3.00
3 TSg,ACo,JP,JJu(c),Mistress
  Nyx kills Vampi 3.00
TPB 15.00

VAMPIRELLA/
LADY DEATH
Harris/Chaos!, 1999
1 x-over 3.50
1a Valentine ed. 10.00
1b signed and numbered 20.00
1c gold edition. 30.00
1d penciled edition 10.00
Spec.#1 TheEnd,chrome(c)(2000). 15.00
Spec.#1a The End,holochrome(c) . 25.00
Spec.#1 Revenge, chrome(c)(2000). . . .
  15.00
Spec.#1a Revenge,holochrome(c) 25.00

VAMPIRELLA LIVES
Harris, 1996–97
1 Linen Edition 7.00
1a Censored Photo cover edition . . 8.00
2 Vengeance edition 3.00
2a alternate edition, AH(c) 10.00
3 WEl(s),ACo,JP,Graveyard edition,
  JSC(c) 3.00
2b thru 3b Model photo edition . . @3.00
TPB Vampirella Lives (2002) 13.00

VAMPIRELLA
OF DRAKULON
Harris Comics, 1996
1 V:assassin 3.00
1a alternate MiB(c) 10.00
2 Dracula returns 3.00
3 thru 5 . . . . @3.00

VAMPIRELLA:
SAD WINGS OF DESTINY
Harris, 1996
1 DQ(s),JJu(c) 4.00
1 signed & numbered (#1,500). . . . 5.00
Gold Emblem Seal Edition. 4.00

VAMPIRELLA STRIKES
Harris Comics, 1995
1 The Prize,pt.1 . . . . 3.00
1a limited, signed & numbered 10.00
1b full moon background 3.50
2 V:Dante Corp.,A:Passion. 3.00
3 V:subway stalker 3.00
4 IEd,RN, Soul Food. 3.00
5 DQ,RN,F:Eudaemon 3.00
5 signed & numbered, (200) 10.00
6 . . . . 3.00
6 signed, alternate cover 10.00
6 signed & numbered 12.00
7 silver special flip book 3.00
Ann. #1 new cover. 10.00

VAMPIRELLA
VS. HEMORRHAGE
Harris, 1997
1 IEd,MIB 3.50
1 signed & numbered 12.00
1 Linen edition, signed & numb. . . 25.00
1 MIB alternate cover 10.00
2 IEd,MIB 3.50
3 (of 3) IEd,MIB. 3.50

VAMPIRELLA VS. PANTHA
Harris, 1997
Showcase #1 preview   2.00
1 MMr,MT, MT(c) Vampirella vs.
  Pantha 3.50
1 MMr,MT, MT(c) Pantha vs.
  Vampirella 3.50
1a MMr,MT, MT(c). 10.00

VAMPIRELLA/
WITCHBLADE
Harris Comics, 2003
1 . . . . 3.00
1a variant (c). 10.00
Spec. Union of the Damned. 3.00
Spec. Variant (c) 10.00

VAMPIRE
THE MASQUERADE
Moonstone, 2001
1-shot Toreador. 6.00
1-shot Nosferatu (2002) 7.00
1-shot Beckett. 7.00
1-shot Ventrue 7.00
1-shot Calebros 6.00
1-shot Giovanni. 5.50
1-shot Assamite 5.50
1-shot Lasombra. 5.50
1-shot Isabel 5.00
1-shot Lucita. 5.00
TPB Vol. 1 . . . . 17.00
TPB Vol. 2 . . . . 21.00
TPB Vol. 3 Five Undead 21.00

VAMPRESS LUXURA, THE
Brainstorm, 1996
1	3.00
1a gold edition	10.00
2	3.00
2a gold foil	10.00

VANDALA
Chaos! Comics, 2000
1	3.00
1 premium	9.99

VANDALA II
Chaos! Comics, 2001
1 PDa,EBe	3.00
1a premium ed. Matt Hughes (c)	10.00

VANGUARD ILLUSTRATED
Pacific, 1983
1	3.00
2 DSt(c)	3.00
3 thru 5 SR	@3.00
6 GI	3.00
7 GE,I:Mr.Monster	6.00

VANITY
Pacific, 1984
1 and 2	@2.25

VARICK: CHRONICLES OF THE DARK PRINCE
Q Comics, 1999
1 by Nick Marcari & Major Fareed	2.25
2 32-pg	2.25
3 thru 6	@2.25

VAULT OF HORROR
Gladstone, 1990–91
1 Rep.GS,WW	5.00
2 Rep.VoH #27 & HoF #18	3.00
3 Rep.VoH #13 & HoF #22	3.00
4 Rep.VoH #23 & HoF #13	3.00
5 Rep.VoH #19 & HoF #5	3.00
6 Rep.VoH #32 & WF #6	3.00
7 Rep.VoH #26 & WS #7	3.00

VAULT OF HORROR
Russ Cochran Publ., 1991–92
1 Rep.VoH #28 & WS #18	4.00
2 Rep.VoH #33 & WS #20	3.00
3 Rep.VoH #26 & WS #7	3.00
4 Rep.VoH #35 & WS #15	3.00
4 Rep.VoH #18 & WS #11	3.00
5 Rep.VoH #18 & WS #11	3.00

2nd Series
1 thru 7 Rep.VoH	@3.00
8	3.00

Gemstone
17 thru 29 EC comics reprints	@3.00

‘Annuals’
TPB Vol. 1 rebinding of #1–#5	9.00
TPB Vol. 2 rebinding of #6–#10	9.00
TPB Vol. 3 rebinding of #11–#15	11.00
TPB Vol. 4 rebinding of #16–#20	13.00
TPB Vol. 5 rebinding #21–#25	13.50
TPB Vol. 6 reginding of #26–#29	11.00

VECTOR
Now, 1986
1	2.50
2 thru 5	@2.50

VEGAS KNIGHTS
Pioneer, 1989
1	2.25
2	2.25
3	2.25

VENGEANCE OF VAMPIRELLA
Harris, 1994
1 Hemmorhage	6.00
1a Gold Edition	9.00
1 gold edition, signed, numbered	15.00
2 Dervish	3.00
3 On the Hunt	3.00
4 Teenage Vampires	3.00
5 Teenage Vampires	3.00
6	3.00
7	3.00
8 bagged w/card	3.00
9	3.00
10 Bad Jack Rising	3.00
11 Pits of Hell, w/card	3.00
12 V:Passion	3.00
13 V:Passion	3.00
14 Prelude to the Walk,pt.2	3.00
15 The Mystery Walk,pt.1	3.25
16 The Mystery Walk,pt.2	3.25
17 The Mystery Walk,pt.3	3.25
18 The Mystery Walk,pt.4	3.00
19 The Mystery Walk,pt.5	3.00
20 Mystery Walk epilog	3.00
14a thru 19a Buzz	@5.00
21 thru 24	@3.00
25 The End	3.00
25 variant cover, signed & numbered	8.00
25 signed & numbered (2,500)	8.00
25 gold edition, signed & numb.	20.00
25 alternate cover, signed by Jae Lee & numbered (#1,500)	15.00
Mini-comic gold foil, signed	20.00
TPB 1-3 Bloodshed	7.00

VENTURE
AC Comics, 1986
1	2.25
2 thru 4	@2.25

Veronica #37
© *Archie Publications*

VERONICA
Archie Publications, April, 1989
1	@7.00
2 thru 10	@5.00
11 thru 38	@4.00
39 Love Show Dolon	6.00
40 thru 50	@4.00
51 thru 71	@3.50
72 thru 93	@3.00
94 thru 97	@2.50
98 thru 120	@2.50
121 thru 133	@2.50
134 thru 156	@2.25

VEROTIKA
Verotika, 1995
1 thru 3 Jae Lee, Frazetta	@3.00
4 thru 9	@3.00
1-shot Rogues Gallery of Villians (1998)	4.00

VEROTIK ILLUSTRATED
Verotik, 1997
1 48pg	7.00
2	7.00
3	7.00
3a alternate cover	7.00
3 variant cover	10.00

VESPER
Acetylene Comics, 2001
Preview B&W	3.00
1 Girls Night Out	2.50
1a JOb (c)	2.50
2	2.50
2a variant Wizardworld 2001(c)	5.00
3 The Word for the Day	2.50
3a variant HbK(c)	2.50
4	2.50
5 Soul Harvest	2.50
6	2.50
6a variant (c)	2.50
7 Return of Gruel	3.00

VESPERS
Mars Media Group, 1995
1 Tony Caputo	2.50
2 I:Dark Side	2.50

VIC FLINT
Argo Publ., 1956
1	90.00
2	75.00

VICKI
Atlas, 1975
1 Rep	50.00
2 thru 4	@40.00

VICTORIAN
Penny Farthing Press, 1999
1	3.00
2 thru 5	@3.00
6 thru 13	@3.00
14 thru 17	@3.00
18 thru 24	@3.00
TPB Vol. 2 Self-Immolation	20.00
TPB Act 3: Self Estrangement	20.00

VILLAINS & VIGILANTES
Eclipse, 1986–87
1 A:Crusaders,Shadowman	2.25
2 A:Condor	2.25
3 V:Crushers	2.25
4 V:Crushers	2.25

COLOR PUB.

COLOR PUB.

VINTAGE MAGNUS ROBOT FIGHTER
Valiant
1 rep. Gold Key Magnus #22
.... (which is #1)
5.00
2 rep. Gold Key Magnus #3 ..... 4.50
3 rep. Gold Key Magnus #13 .... 3.50
4 rep. Gold Key Magnus #15 .... 3.50

VIOLENT CASES
Tundra
1 20's Chicago 11.00

VIOLENT MESSIAHS
Hurricane 1997
1 .... 7.00

VIP
TV Comics, 2000
1 (of 3) 3.00
2 .... 3.00
3 .... 3.00
1a thru 3a photo (c) .... @3.00
TPB Collected Edition 9.00
Preview Edition 6.00

VIRGINIAN, THE
Gold Key, 1963
1 .... 75.00

VIRTEX
Oktomica Entertainment, 1998
0 16-pg.. .... 2.50
1 V:Ripnun 2.50
2 V:Ripnun 2.50
3 alternate endings 2.50
4 Night of the Ninjella,pt.1 .... 2.50
5 Night of the Ninjella,pt.2 .... 3.00
6 All My Sins Remembered 3.00

VIRTUA FIGHTER
Malibu, 1995
1 New Video Game Comic 3.00

VISITOR
Valiant, 1994
1 New Series 2.50
2 F:The Harbinger............. 2.50
3 The Bomb 2.50
4 V:F/X Specialists 2.50
5 R:Harbinger 2.50
6 KVH,BS(c),V:Men in Black 2.50
7 KVH,BS(c),V:Men in Black,pt.2 .. 2.50
8 KVH,V:Harbinger identity...... 2.50
9 KVH,A:Harbinger,Flamingo 2.50
10 Weather Problems 2.50
11 V:Cannibals................ 2.50
12 V:Harada, Men in Black 2.50
13 Visitor is the Future Harbinger .. 2.50

VISITOR VS. VALIANT
Valiant, 1994
1 V:Solar..................... 3.00
2 .... 3.00

VOLTRON
Solson, 1985
1 TV tie-in 3.50
2 .... 3.50
3 .... 3.50

VOLTRON: DEFENDER OF THE UNIVERSE
Devil's Due/UDON, 2004
Vol 2
1 .... 3.00
2 thru 10 .... @3.00
TPB Voltron Revelations 12.00

VORTEX
Vortex, 1982–88
1 Peter Hsu art 9.00
2 Mister X on cover........... 6.00
3 .... 4.00
4 .... 4.00
5 .... 3.00
6 thru 8 .... @3.00
9 thru 13 .... @2.00

Vortex #1
© Comico

VORTEX
Comico, 1991
1 SBt,from Elementals 2.50
2 SBt, ... 2.50

VORTEX: THE SECOND COMING
Entity, 1996
1 (of 6) 3.00
1a variant cover 3.00
2 .... 3.00

VOYAGE TO THE DEEP
Dell Publishing Co., 1962
1 P(c) 75.00
2 P(c) 50.00
3 P(c) 50.00
4 P(c) 50.00

WACKY ADVENTURES OF CRACKY
Gold Key, 1972–75
1 .... 25.00
2 thru 11 .... @15.00
12 .... 12.00

WACKY WITCH
Gold Key, 1971–75
1 .... 50.00
2 .... 25.00
3 thru 20 .... @20.00
21 .... 15.00

WAGON TRAIN
Gold Key, 1964
1 .... 100.00
2 .... 75.00
3 .... 75.00
4 .... 75.00

WAKE THE DEAD
IDW Publishing, 2003
1 (of 5) 4.00
2 .... 4.00
3 thru 5 .... @4.00
TPB Let Sleeping Dead Lie 20.00

WALLY
Gold Key, 1962–63
1 .... 50.00
2 .... 35.00
3 .... 35.00
4 .... 35.00

WALLY WOOD'S THUNDER AGENTS
Delux, 1984–86
1 GP,KG,DC,SD,I:New Menth..... 6.00
2 GP,KG,DC,SD,The Raven 5.00
3 KG,DC,SD 5.00
4 GP,KG,RB,DA 5.00
5 JOy,KG,A:CodenamDangr..... 5.00

WALT DISNEY ANNUALS
Walt Disney's Autumn Adventure... 4.00
Walt Disney's Holiday Parade #1 . 3.50
Walt Disney's Spring Fever 3.50
Walt Disney's Summer Fun 3.50
Walt Disney's Holiday Parade #2 . 3.50

WALT DISNEY'S AUTUMN ADVENTURE
1 Rep. CB................... 4.00

WALT DISNEY'S CHRISTMAS PARADE
Gemstone Publishing, 2003
1 .... 9.00

WALT DISNEY'S COMICS AND STORIES
Dell/Gold Key, 1962
264 CB,Von Drake & Gearloose .. 60.00
265 CB,Von Drake & Gearloose .. 60.00
266 CB,Von Drake & Gearloose .. 60.00
267 CB,Von Drake & Gearloose .. 60.00
268 CB,Von Drake & Gearloose .. 60.00
269 CB,Von Drake & Gearloose .. 60.00
270 CB,Von Drake & Gearloose .. 60.00
271 CB,Von Drake & Gearloose .. 60.00
272 CB,Von Drake & Gearloose .. 60.00
273 CB,Von Drake & Gearloose .. 60.00
274 CB,Von Drake & Gearloose .. 60.00
275 CB. 55.00
276 CB. 55.00
277 CB. 55.00
278 CB. 55.00
279 CB. 55.00

All comics prices listed are for *Near Mint* condition.

280 CB 55.00	506 . . . . 20.00	557 . . . . 5.00
281 CB 55.00	507 CB rep. 22.00	558 Donald's Fix-it Shop 5.00
282 CB 55.00	508 CB rep. 22.00	559 Bugs 5.00
283 CB 55.00	509 CB rep. 22.00	560 CB,April Fools Story 5.00
284 . . . . 30.00	510 CB rep. 22.00	561 CB,Donald the Flipist 5.00
285 . . . . 30.00	**Gladstone, 1986**	562 CB,3DirtyLittleDucks 5.00
286 CB 35.00	511 translation of Dutch 30.00	563 CB,Donald Camping 5.00
287 . . . . 30.00	512 translation of Dutch. 25.00	564 CB,Dirk the Dinosaur 5.00
288 CB 35.00	513 translation of Dutch. 25.00	565 CB,DonaldDuck,TruantOfficer. . 5.00
289 CB 35.00	514 translation of Dutch 11.00	566 CB,Will O' the Wisp 5.00
290 . . . . 30.00	515 translation of Dutch 11.00	567 CB,Turkey Shoot. 5.00
291 CB 35.00	516 translation of Dutch 11.00	568 CB,AChristmas Eve Story. 5.00
292 CB 35.00	517 translation of Dutch. 6.00	569 CB, New Years Resolutions . . . 5.00
293 CB; Grandma Duck's Farm	518 translation of Dutch. 6.00	570 CB,Donald the Mailman
Friends 35.00	519 CB,Donald Duck 6.00	+Poster 5.00
294 CB 35.00	520 translation of Dutch, Rosa . . . 11.00	571 CB,Atom Bomb. 8.00
295 . . . . 30.00	521 Walt Kelly 6.00	572 CB,April Fools. 5.00
296 . . . . 30.00	522 CB,WK,nephews. 6.00	573 TV Quiz Show. 5.00
297 CB; Gyro Gearloose 35.00	523 Rosa,Donald Duck 15.00	574 Pinnochio,64pgs 6.00
298 CB; Daisy Duck's Dairy 35.00	524 Rosa,Donald Duck 15.00	575 Olympic Torch Bearer, Li'l
299 CB rep. 35.00	525 translation of Dutch. 15.00	Bad Wolf,64 pgs. 6.00
300 CB rep. 35.00	526 Rosa,Donald Duck 10.00	576 giant 6.00
301 CB rep. 35.00	527 CB 6.00	577 A:Truant Officers,64 pgs. 6.00
302 CB rep. 35.00	528 Rosa,Donald Duck 15.00	578 CB,Old Quacky Manor 5.00
303 CB rep. 35.00	529 CB 6.00	579 CB,Turkey Hunt 5.00
304 CB rep. 35.00		580 CB,The Wise Little Red Hen,
305 CB rep. Gyro Gearloose 35.00		64 pg.-Sunday page format. . . . 5.50
306 CB rep. 35.00		581 CB,Duck Lake. 5.00
307 CB rep. 35.00		582 giant 5.50
308 CB 35.00		583 giant 5.50
309 CB 35.00		584 . . . . 5.50
310 CB 35.00		585 CB, giant. 5.50
311 CB 35.00		**Gladstone, 1993**
312 CB 35.00		586 . . . . 5.00
313 thru 327 . . . . @25.00		587 thru 599 . . . . @5.00
328 CB rep. 30.00		600 CB 6.00
329 . . . . 25.00		601 thru 605 prestige format . . . . @7.00
330 . . . . 25.00		606 Winging It 7.00
331 . . . . 25.00		607 Number 401 . . . . 7.00
332 . . . . 25.00		608 Sleepless in Duckburg 7.00
333 . . . . 25.00		609 . . . . 7.00
334 . . . . 25.00		610 Treasures Untold 7.00
335 CB rep. 30.00		611 Romance at a Glance 7.00
336 . . . . 25.00		612 The Sod Couple 7.00
337 . . . . 25.00		613 Another Fine Mess 7.00
338 . . . . 25.00		614 Airheads 7.00
339 . . . . 25.00		615 Backyard Battlers 7.00
340 . . . . 25.00		616 . . . . 7.00
341 . . . . 25.00		617 Tree's A Crowd 7.00
342 thru 350 CB rep. . . . . @25.00		618 A Dolt from the Blue 7.00
351 thru 361 CB rep. with poster @50.00		619 Queen of the Ant Farm. 7.00
351a thru 361a. without poster . @25.00		620 Caught in the Cold Rush 7.00
361 thru 400 CB rep. . . . . @35.00		621 Room and Bored. 7.00
401 thru 409 CB rep. . . . . @22.00		622 . . . . 7.00
410 CB rep. Annette Funichello. . . 22.00		623 All Quacked Up. 7.00
411 thru 429 CB rep. . . . . @22.00		624 Their Loaded Forebear. 7.00
430 . . . . 15.00		625 Mummery's the Word 7.00
431 CB rep. 20.00		626 A Real Gone Guy 7.00
432 CB rep. 20.00		627 To Bee or Not to Bee 7.00
433 . . . . 15.00		628 Officer for a Day 7.00
434 CB rep. 20.00		629 The Ghost Train 7.00
435 CB rep. 20.00		630 two Donald Duck stories. 7.00
436 CB rep. 20.00		631 Music Hath Charms 7.00
437 . . . . 15.00		632 A Day in a Duck's Life. 7.00
438 . . . . 15.00		633 All Donald issue 7.00
439 CB rep. 16.00		634 The Runaway Train. 7.00
440 CB rep. 16.00		635 Volcano Valley 7.00
441 . . . . 15.00		636 Mission to Codfish Cove. 7.00
442 CB rep. 16.00		637 Pizen Springs Dude Ranch. . . 7.00
443 CB rep. 16.00		
444 . . . . 15.00		**WALT DISNEY'S**
445 . . . . 15.00	**Walt Disney, 1990**	**COMICS AND STORIES**
446 thru 465 CB rep. . . . . @16.00	548 CB,WK,Home is the Hero. . . . 12.00	**Gemstone Publishing, 2003**
466 . . . . 16.00	549 CB, ... 5.00	634 thru 650 . . . . @7.00
467 thru 473 CB rep. . . . . @16.00	550 CB,prev.unpub.story! 8.00	Spec. Walt Disney's Vacation
Whitman, 1980	551 . . . . 5.00	Parade. 9.00
474 thru 478 CB rep. . . . . @20.00	552 . . . . 5.00	
479 CB 50.00	553 . . . . 5.00	
480 CB Rare 150.00	554 . . . . 5.00	
481 thru 484 . . . . @50.00	555 . . . . 5.00	
485 thru 505 . . . . @25.00	556 . . . . 5.00	

Special 48 page issue 50¢

WALT DISNEY'S comics and stories

Donald Duck is out to win a Rocket Race around the world

MICKEY DISCOVERS GOOFY HAS TALENTED EARS

Tinker Bell meets THE GROUNCHED WITCH

PLUS: LUDWIG VON DRAKE LI'L BAD WOLF • BRER RABBIT

Walt Disney's Comics and Stories
#446 © Gold Key

530 Rosa,Donald Duck 7.00
531 WK(c),Rosa,CB. 7.00
532 CB 6.00
533 CB 6.00
534 CB 6.00
535 CB 6.00
536 CB 6.00
537 CB 6.00
538 CB 6.00
539 CB 6.00
540 CB new art 6.00
541 double-size,WK(c). 6.00
542 CB 7.00
543 CB,WK(c) 6.00
544 CB,WK(c) 6.00
545 CB 6.00
546 CB,WK,giant 7.00
547 CB,WK,Rosa,giant 15.00

WALT DISNEY COMICS DIGEST
Gold Key, 1968–76
[All done by Carl Barks]

1 Rep,Uncle Scrooge	125.00
2 CB,ATh	75.00
3 CB,ATh	75.00
4 CB,ATh	75.00
5 CB,Daisy Duck	125.00
6 thru 13 CB,ATh	@60.00
14 ATh	35.00
15 ATh	35.00
16 ATh,rep.Donald Duck #26	60.00
17 CB,ATh	45.00
18 CB,ATh	45.00
19 CB,ATh	45.00
20 CB,ATh	45.00
21 CB,ATh	35.00
22 CB,ATh	35.00
23 CB,ATh	35.00
24 CB,ATh,Zorro	35.00
25 thru 31 CB,ATh	@35.00
32 ATh	30.00
33 ATh	35.00
34 ATh,rep.Four Color #318	35.00
35 ATh	35.00
36 ATh	35.00
37 ATh	35.00
38 ATh,rep.Disneyland#1	35.00
39 ATh	35.00
40 ATh,FG	30.00
41 ATh	25.00
42 CB	30.00
43 CB	30.00
44 Rep. Four Color #29 & others	75.00
45	25.00
46 CB	25.00
47	25.00
48	25.00
49	25.00
50 CB	25.00
51 rep.Four Color #71	35.00
52 CB	25.00
53	25.00
54	25.00
55	25.00
56 CB,rep. Uncle Scrooge #32	30.00
57 CB	25.00

WALT DISNEY SHOWCASE
Gold Key, 1970–80

1 Boatniks (photo cover)	40.00
2 Moby Duck	30.00
3 Bongo & Lumpjaw	25.00
4 Pluto	25.00
5 $1,000,000 Duck (photo cover)	30.00
6 Bedknobs & Broomsticks	25.00
7 Pluto	25.00
8 Daisy & Donald	25.00
9 101 Dalmatians rep.	35.00
10 Napoleon & Samantha	30.00
11 Moby Duck rep.	20.00
12 Dumbo rep.	25.00
13 Pluto rep.	25.00
14 World's Greatest Athlete	30.00
15 3 Little Pigs rep.	25.00
16 Aristocats rep.	30.00
17 Mary Poppins rep.	30.00
18 Gyro Gearloose rep.	40.00
19 That Darn Cat rep.	35.00
20 Pluto rep.	25.00
21 Li'l Bad Wolf & 3 Little Pigs	20.00
22 Unbirthday Party rep.	30.00
23 Pluto rep.	25.00
24 Herbie Rides Again rep.	25.00
25 Old Yeller rep.	25.00
26 Lt. Robin Crusoe USN rep.	25.00

27 Island at the Top of the World	30.00
28 Brer Rabbit, Bucky Bug rep.	25.00
29 Escape to Witch Mountain	30.00
30 Magica De Spell rep.	45.00
31 Bambi rep.	25.00
32 Spin & Marty rep.	25.00
33 Pluto rep.	20.00
34 Paul Revere's Ride rep.	20.00
35 Goofy rep.	20.00
36 Peter Pan rep.	20.00
37 Tinker Bell & Jiminy Cricket rep.	20.00
38 Mickey & the Sleuth, Pt. 1	20.00
39 Mickey & the Sleuth, Pt. 2	20.00
40 The Rescuers	20.00
41 Herbie Goes to Monte Carlo	20.00
42 Mickey & the Sleuth	20.00
43 Pete's Dragon	25.00
44 Return From Witch Mountain & In Search of the Castaways	25.00
45 The Jungle Book rep.	25.00
46 The Cat From Outer Space	20.00
47 Mickey Mouse Surprise Party	20.00
48 The Wonderful Adventures of Pinocchio	20.00
49 North Avenue Irregulars; Zorro	20.00
50 Bedknobs & Broomsticks rep.	20.00
51 101 Dalmatians	20.00
52 Unidentified Flying Oddball	20.00
53 The Scarecrow	20.00
54 The Black Hole	20.00

WALT DISNEY COMICS IN COLOR
Gladstone, 1998

TPB Vol. 1	10.00
TPB Vol. 2	10.00
TPB Vol. 3	10.00
TPB Vol. 4	10.00

WALT KELLY'S CHRISTMAS CLASSICS
Eclipse, 1987

1	3.00

WALT KELLY'S SPRINGTIME TALES
Eclipse, 1988

1	3.00

WAR AGAINST CRIME
Gemstone, 2000

1 rep.	2.50
2 rep. Summer 1942	2.50
3 rep. Fall 1948	2.50
4 rep. Winter 1948	2.50
5 rep. Feb. 1949	2.50
6 rep. June 1949	2.50
7 rep.	2.50
8 rep. Aug. 1949	2.50
9 rep. Oct. 1949	2.50
10 rep. Dec. 1949 issue	2.50
11 rep. Feb. 1950 issue	2.50

`Annuals'
TPB Vol. 1 rep. #1–#5	13.50
TPB Vol. 2 rep. #6–#11	16.00

WARCAT SPECIAL
Entity Press, 1995

1 I:Warcat	3.00

WARCHILD
Maximum Press, 1995

1 I:Sword, Stone	3.50
2 I:Morganna Lefay	3.00
3 V: The Black Knight	2.50

4 Rescue Merlyn	2.50

[2nd Series]
1	2.50

WAR DANCER
Defiant, 1994

1 B:JiS(s),I:Ahrq Tsolmec	2.75
2 I:Massakur	2.75
3 V:Massakur	2.75
4 JiS(s),A:Nudge	3.25

WARHAWKS
TSR, 1990–91

1 thru 6 from game	@3.00
7 thru 10 The Battle of Britain	@3.00

WARHAWKS 2050
TSR

1 Pt.1	3.00

WAR HEROES
Charlton Comics, 1963–67

1	50.00
2 J.F.Kennedy	45.00
3 thru 10	@25.00
11 thru 26	@20.00
27 Devils Brigade	30.00

WARLASH
CFD, 1995

1 Project Hardfire	3.00

WARMASTER

1 and 2	@4.00

WARP
First, 1983

1 FB,JSon,I:Lord Cumulus & Prince Chaos, play adapt pt.1	2.50
2 FB,SD,play adapt pt.2	2.25
3 FB,SD,play adapt pt.3	2.25
4 FB,SD,I:Xander,play pt.4	2.25
5 FB, play adapt pt.5	2.25
6 FB/MG, play adapt pt.6	2.25
7 FB/MG, play adapt pt.7	2.25
8 FB/MG,BWg,play adapt pt.8	2.25
9 FB/MG,BWg,play adapt conc.	2.25
10 JBi/MG,BWg, Second Saga, I:Outrider	2.25

Warp #3
© First

11 JBi/MG,A:Outrider 2.25
12 JBi/MG,A:Outrider 2.25
13 JBi/MG,A:Outrider 2.25
14 JBi/MG,A:Outrider 2.25
15 JBi/MG/BWg 2.25
16 BWg/MG,A:Outrider 2.25
17 JBi/MG,A:Outrider 2.25
18 JBi/MG,A:Outrider&Sargon 2.25
19 MG,last issue 2.25
Spec. #1 HC,O:Chaos 2.25
Spec. #2 MS/MG,V:Ylem 2.25
Spec. #3 . . . . 2.25

WARRIOR BUGS, THE
Artcoda Productions, 2002
1 . . . . 3.00
2 thru 5 . . . . @3.00

WARRIOR NUN AREALA
Antartic Press, 1995
1 V:Lilith 4.00
1a limited edition. 8.00
2 V:Lilith 3.00
3 V:Hellmaster 3.00
3 silver edition. 12.00
TPB Rep.#1-#3 . . . . 10.00

BOOK II: RITUALS, 1996
1 Land of Rising Sun 3.00
1 Red edition. 9.00
1 signed 10.00
2 I:Cheetah 3.00
3 Iraq, 1989. . . . . 3.00
4 . . . . 3.00
5 Rituals,pt.5. . . . . 3.00
6 . . . . 3.00
Spec. Warrior Nun Portraits 4.00
Spec. Warrior Nun Portraits
  Commemorative Edition (1999). 6.00
TPB Rituals 16.00

BOOK III, 1997
1 The Hammer & the Holocaust . . . 3.00
2 Hammer & the Holocaust,pt.2 . . . 3.00
3 Hammer & the Holocaust,pt.3 . . . 3.00
4 Holy Man, Holy Terror,pt.1 . . . . . 3.00
5 Holy Man, Holy Terror,pt.2 . . . . . 3.00
6 by Barry Lyga & Ben Dunn 3.00
TPB Vol. 1 . . . . 10.00
TPB Vol. 1 reprint. 10.00
Spec. Warrior Nun Areala/Glory
  by Ben Dunn 3.00
Spec. poster edition 6.00
Spec. Warrior Nun Areala vs. Razor,
  BDn,JWf x-over 4.00
Spec.Warrior Nun Areala vs. Razor
  commemorative (1999) 6.00
Spec.Warrior Nun Areala/Avengelyne
  comm. edition (1999). 6.00

VOL 3
1 F:Sister Shannon Masters 2.50
2 . . . . 2.50
3 . . . . 2.50
4 Antichrist arrives 2.50
5 . . . . 2.50
6 Crimson Nun 2.50
7 V:Ruprecht Marsh 2.50
8 V:Mr.Zhu 2.50
9 in the Vatican 2.50
10 V:Nebelhexa 2.50
11 A:Demoness Lillith 2.50
12 F:Lillith. 3.50
13 V:Julius Salvius. 3.00
14 Rebirth, pt.2 . . . . 3.00
15 Rebirth, pt.3 . . . . 3.00
16 Rebirth, pt.4 . . . . 3.00
17 Seven Deadly Sins, pt.1 . . . . . . 3.00
18 Seven Deadly Sins, pt.2 . . . . . . 3.00
19 Seven Deadly Sins, pt.3 . . . . . . 3.00
Ann.2000 b&W. 4.00

Warrior Nun Book 3, #6
© Antarctic Press

WARRIOR NUN AREALA:
SCORPIO ROSE
Antarctic Press, 1996
1 SEt & BDn 3.00
1a commemorative (1999) 6.00
2 thru 4 (of 4) . . . . @3.00

WARRIOR NUN DEI:
AFTERTIME
Antarctic Press, 1997
1 (of 3) by Patrick Thornton 3.00
1 Commemorative edition (1999) . . 6.00
2 . . . . 3.00
3 . . . . 3.00

WARRIOR NUN: FRENZY
Antarctic Press, 1998
1 (of 2) by Miki Horvatic
  & Esad T. Ribic 3.00
2 . . . . 3.00

WARRIOR NUN:
NO JUSTICE
Antarctic Press, 2002
1 F:Areala,V:The Judge 4.00

WARRIOR NUN:
RESURRECTION
Antarctic Press, 1998
1 by Ben Dunn 3.00
1a deluxe 6.00
2 quest for lost God Armor 3.00
3 . . . . 3.00

WARRIORS OF PLASM
Defiant, 1993–95
1 JiS(s),DL,A:Lorca. 3.25
2 JiS(s),DL,Sedition Agenda. 3.25
3 JiS(s),DL,Sedition Agenda. 3.25
4 JiS(s),DL,Sedition Agenda. 3.25
5 JiS(s),B:The Demons of
  Darkedge. 2.75
6 JiS(s),The Demons of
  Darkedge,pt.2 . . . . 2.75
7 JiS(s),DL,. 2.75
8 JiS(s),DL,40-pg. 3.00
9 JiS(s),LWn(s),DL,40-pg. 3.00
10 DL, ... 2.50

GN Home for the Holidays. 6.00

WARRIOR'S WAY
Bench Press Studios, 1998
1 . . . . 3.00
2 thru 7 . . . . @3.00

WARSTRIKE
Malibu Ultraverse, 1994–95
1 HNg,TA,in South America 2.25
2 HNg,TA,Gatefold(c) 2.25
3 in Brazil 2.25
4 HNg,TA,V:Blind Faith. 2.25
5 . . . . 2.25
6 Rafferty 2.25
7 Origin 2.25

WARSTRIKE:
PRELUDE TO GODWHEEL
Malibu Ultraverse, 1994
1 Blind Faith/Lord Pumpkin 2.25

WART AND THE
WIZARD
Gold Key, 1964
1 . . . . 60.00

WATCH, THE:
CASUS BELLI
Phosphorescent Comics, 2004
1 . . . . 3.25
2 thru 3 . . . . @3.25

WATERDOGS
Roaring Studio, 2002
1 (of 3) 3.00
2 thru 3 . . . . @3.00

WATERWORLD
Acclaim, 1997
1 of 4 V:Leviathan. 2.50
2 of 4 Children of Leviathan 2.50
3 of 4 KoK. 2.50
4 of 4 KoK Children of Leviathan . . 2.50

WAVE WARRIORS
Astroboys
1 . . . . 2.25
2 . . . . 2.25

WAXWORK in 3-D
Blackthorne
1 . . . . 2.50

WAYFARERS
Eternity
1 . . . . 2.25
2 . . . . 2.25

WAY OF THE RAT
Crossgen Comics, 2002
1 CDi 4.00
2 thru 7 CDi. . . . . @3.00
8 thru 24 CDi. . . . . @3.00
GN Traveler Vol. 1 Walls of
  Zhumar 10.00
TPB Vol. 1 The Walls of Zhumar . . 16.00
TPB Vol. 2 The Dragon's Wake . . . 16.00

WEAPONS OF THE GODS
Comicsone.com, 2002
TPB Vol. 1 by Tony Wong	14.00
TPB Vol. 2 thru Vol. 7	@14.00
TPB Vol. 8 thru Vol.10	@15.00

WEAPON ZERO
See: Image

WEASEL GUY
WITCHBLADE
Hyperwerks, 1998
1-shot by Steve Succellato	3.00
1a variant Jeff Matsuda(c)	5.00
1b variant Karl Altstoeter(c)	8.00

WEB-MAN
Argosy
1 flip book with Time Warrior	2.50

WEB OF HORROR
Major Magazines, 1969
1 JJ(c),Ph(c),BWr	125.00
2 JJ(c),Ph(c),BWr	100.00
3 BWr,April, 1970	100.00

WEDDING OF POPEYE AND OLIVE, THE
Ocean Comics, 1999
1 PDa,	2.75
1a signed, numbered	16.00
Spec. Sketch edition	40.00

Weird Fantasy #1
© Russ Cochran

WEIRD FANTASY
Russ Cochran, 1992
1 Reps	3.50
2 Reps.inc.The Black Arts	3.00
3 thru 4 rep.	@3.00
5 thru 7 rep.	3.00
8	3.00

Gemstone
9 thru 22 EC comics reprint	@3.00

`Annuals'
TPB Vol. #1 rebinding of #1–#5.	10.00
TPB Vol. #2 rebinding of #6–#10.	11.00
TPB Vol. #3 rebinding of #11–#14.	10.00
TPB Vol. #4 rebinding of #15–#18.	11.00

TPB Vol. #5 rebinding of #19–#22.	12.00

WEIRD SCIENCE
Gladstone, 1990–91
1 Rep. #22 + Fantasy #1	4.00
2 Rep. #16 + Fantasy #17	3.50
3 Rep. #9 + Fantasy #14	3.50
4 Rep. #27 + Fantasy #11	3.00

Russ Cochran/Gemstone, 1992
1 thru 21 EC comics reprint	@3.00

`Annuals'
TPB Vol. #1 rebinding of #1–#5.	9.00
TPB Vol. #2 rebinding of #6–#10.	10.00
TPB Vol. #3 rebinding of #11–#15.	9.00
TPB Vol. #4 rebinding of #16–#18.	10.00
TPB Vol. #5 rebinding of #19–#22.	10.50

WEIRD SCIENCE–FANTASY
Russ Cochran/Gemstone, 1992
1 Rep. W.S.F. #23 (1954)	3.50
2 Rep. Flying Saucer Invasion	3.00
3 Rep.	3.00
4 thru 6 Rep.	@3.00
7 rep #29.	3.00
8	3.00

Gemstone
`Annuals'
TPB Vol. #1 rebinding of #1–#5.	9.00
TPB Vol. #2 rebinding of #6–#10.	13.00

WEIRD SUSPENSE
Atlas, Feb.–July, 1975
1 thru 3 F:Tarantula	@25.00

WEIRD TALES ILLUSTRATED
Millennium, 1992
1 KJo,JBo,PCr,short stories	5.00

WENDY
Blackthorne
1 3-D	2.50

WENDY, THE GOOD LITTLE WITCH
Harvey Publications, 1960–76
1 Wendy & Casper	400.00
2	200.00
3	150.00
4	150.00
5	150.00
6	100.00
7	100.00
8	100.00
9	100.00
10	100.00
11 thru 20	@75.00
21 thru 30	@50.00
31 thru 50	@35.00
51 thru 64	@25.00
65 O:Wendy	35.00
66 thru 69	@25.00
70 thru 74 52 pg Giants	@30.00
75 thru 93	@20.00

WENDY WITCH WORLD
Harvey Publications, 1961–74
1	200.00
2	125.00
3	125.00
4	125.00
5	125.00
6	75.00

7	75.00
8	75.00
9	75.00
10	75.00
11 thru 20	@60.00
21 thru 30	@45.00
31 thru 39	@35.00
40 thru 50	@25.00
51 thru 53	@20.00

WEREWOLF
Blackthorne
1 3-D	3.50

Western Action #1
© Atlas

WESTERN ACTION
Atlas, 1975
1 F:Kid Cody,Comanche Kid	25.00

WESTWYND
Westwynd, 1995
1 I:Sable,Shiva,Outcast,Tojo.	2.50

WHAM
1	2.25

WHISPER
Capital, 1983–84
1 MG(c)	8.00
2	6.00

First
1	2.50
2 thru 10	@2.25
11 thru 19	@2.25
20 O:Whisper	2.25
21 thru 26	@2.25
27 Ghost Dance #2	2.25
28 Ghost Dance #3	2.25
29 thru 37	@2.25
Spec. #1	4.00

WHITE FANG
Walt Disney, 1990
1 Movie Adapt.	6.00

WHITE TRASH
Tundra
1 I:Elvis & Dean	4.00
2 Trip to Las Vegas contd.	4.00

3 V:Purple Heart Brigade 4.00

WHODUNNIT
Eclipse, 1986–87
1 DSp,A:Jay Endicott 2.25
2 DSp,Who Slew Kangaroo? 2.25
3 DSp,Who Offed Henry Croft 2.25

WIDOW MADE IN BRITAIN
N Studio
1 I:Widow 2.75
2 F:Widow 2.75
3 Rampage 2.75
4 In Jail 2.75

WIDOW METAL GYPSIES
London Night Studios, 1995
1 I:Emma Drew 3.00
2 Father Love 3.00
3 Final issue 3.00

WILD ANIMALS
Pacific, 1982
1 . . . . 2.25

WILD BILL PECOS
AC Comics, 1989
1 . . . . 3.50

WILDCATS
WildStorm/DC, 1999
Previously from Image
VOLUME 2
1 SLo,TC, ... 2.50
1a variant cover 2.50
1b variant cover 2.50
1c variant cover 2.50
1d variant cover 2.50
1e variant cover 2.50
2 SLo,TC 2.50
3 SLo,TC,F:Grifter 2.50
4 SLo,TC, ... 2.50
5 SLo,BHi,PNe, ... 2.50
6 SLo, ... 2.50
7 SLo,R:Pike 2.50
8 JoC(s),SeP,TC(c) 2.50
8a variant JLe&SW(c) (1:4) 2.50
9 JoC(s),SeP,TC(c),Las Vegas . . . 2.50
10 JoC(s),SeP,TC(c),Las Vegas . . . 2.50
11 JoC(s),SeP,TC(c),R:Ladytron . . 2.50
12 JoC(s),SeP,TC(c),go west 2.50
13 JoC(s),SeP,F:Void 2.50
14 JoC(s),SeP,Serial Boxes,pt.1 . . . 2.50
15 JoC(s),SeP,Serial Boxes,pt.2 . . . 2.50
16 JoC,SeP,Serial Boxes,pt.3 . . . . . 2.50
17 JoC,SeP,Serial Boxes,pt.4 . . . . . 2.50
18 JoC,SeP,Serial Boxes,pt.5 . . . . . 2.50
19 JoC,SeP,Serial Boxes,pt.6 . . . . . 2.50
20 JoC,SDi,F:Grifter, Maul 2.50
21 JoC,SDi,F:Grifter, Maul, pt.2 . . . 2.50
22 JoC,SeP,R:Grifter 2.50
23 JoC,SeP,F:Grifter 2.50
23a variant WPo(c) (1:4) 2.50
24 JoC,SeP,F:Voodoo 2.50
25 JoC,SeP, 40-pg. 3.50
26 JoC,SeP, control of Halo 2.50
27 JoC,SeP,Grifter vs. Zealot 2.50
28, JoC,SeP,Voodoo,final issue . . . 2.50
Spec. WildC.A.T.s: Mosaic 4.00
Ann. 2000 #1, Devil's
   Night x-over, pt.3 . . . . 3.50
GN Ladytron 6.00
TPB WildC.A.T.S.: Compendium . . 10.00
TPB WildC.A.T.S.: Homecoming . . 20.00
TPB Gang War 17.00
TPB Homecoming 20.00

TPB Vicious Circles 15.00
TPB Serial Boxes, 144-pg. 15.00
TPB Street Smart 15.00
TPB Battery Park 18.00
TPB Wildcats/Cyberforce:
   Killer Instinct (2004) 15.00

WILDCATS VERSION 3.0
Wildcats/DC, 2002
Eye of the Storm
1 JoC,old and new team members. 3.00
2 JoC,Jack Marlowe,Halo corp 3.00
3 JoC 3.00
4 JoC, ... 3.00
5 JoC 3.00
6 JoC 3.00
7 JoC,I:Beef Boys 3.00
8 JoC,BU:The Authority,pt.3 . . . . . 3.00
9 JoC,new Grifter 3.00
10 JoC,new Grifter 3.00
11 JoC,Lights Out in Garfield 3.00
12 JoC,Jack Marlowe 3.00
13 JoC,Mister Wax 3.00
14 JoC,Halo Corp 3.00
15 JoC,Car of tomorrow 3.00
16 JoC,new assassin 3.00
17 JoC,SeP 3.00
18 JoC 3.00
19 JoC(s) 3.00
20 JoC(s),new team 3.00
21 JoC(s),Grifter's team 3.00
22 JoC(s),Coda War One 3.00
23 JoC(s),Coda War One 3.00
24 JoC(s),final issue 3.00
TPB Brand Building 15.00
TPB Full Disclosure 15.00

WILDFIRE
Zion Comics
1 thru 3 V:Mr. Reeves . . . . @2.25
4 Lord D'Rune 2.25

WILD FRONTIER
Charlton Comics, 1955
1 Davy Crockett 125.00
2 same 75.00
3 same 75.00
4 same 75.00
5 same 75.00
6 same 75.00
7 O:Cheyenne Kid 75.00
Becomes:

CHEYENNE KID
8 . . . . 75.00
9 . . . . 40.00
10 AW,AT,SD(c) 100.00
11 Giant,Geronimo 100.00
12 AW,AT 100.00
13 AW,AT 75.00
14 AW 75.00
15 . . . . 40.00
16 . . . . 40.00
17 . . . . 40.00
18 . . . . 40.00
19 . . . . 40.00
20 JSe 50.00
21 JSe 50.00
22 JSe 50.00
23 . . . . 20.00
24 JSe 40.00
25 JSe 40.00
26 JSe 35.00
27 . . . . 30.00
28 . . . . 30.00
29 . . . . 30.00
30 JSe 35.00
31 thru 59 . . . . @20.00
60 thru 98 . . . . @20.00

99 Nov., 1973 . . . . 20.00

WILD TIMES
WildStorm/DC, 1999
Deathblow 2.50
DV8 . . . . 2.50
Gen13 . . . . 2.50
Grifter 2.50
Wetworks 2.50

WILD WEST C.O.W.-
BOYS OF MOO MESA
Archie, 1992–93
1 Based on TV cartoon 2.25
2 Cody kidnapped 2.25
3 Law of the Year Parade,
   last issue 2.25
(Regular series)
1 Valley o/t Thunder Lizard 2.25
2 Plains, Trains & Dirty Deals 2.25

Wild Western Action #2
© Skywald

WILD WESTERN ACTION
Skywald, 1971
1 thru 3 . . . . @30.00

WILD WILD WEST
Gold Key, 1966–69
1 TV show tie-in 200.00
2 . . . . 150.00
3 . . . . 125.00
4 . . . . 125.00
5 . . . . 125.00
6 . . . . 125.00
7 . . . . 125.00

WILD WILD WEST
Millennium, 1990–91
1 . . . . 3.00
2 thru 4 . . . . @3.00

WILL EISNER'S
3-D CLASSICS
Kitchen Sink, 1985
WE art, w/glasses (1985) 2.25

WIN A PRIZE COMICS
Charlton Comics, 1955
1 S&K,Edgar Allen adapt...... 900.00
2 S&K..................... 650.00
Becomes:

TIMMY THE
TIMID GHOST
3 .... 75.00
4 .... 40.00
5 .... 40.00
6 .... 30.00
7 .... 30.00
8 .... 30.00
9 .... 30.00
10 .... 30.00
11 .... 75.00
12 .... 75.00
13 thru 20................. @30.00
21 thru 44................. @25.00
45 1966 .... 25.00

WINDRAGE
1 and 2 .... @2.25

WINTERWORLD
Eclipse, 1987–88
1 JZ,I:Scully, Wynn........... 2.25
2 JZ,V:Slave Farmers.......... 2.25
3 JZ,V:Slave Farmers.......... 2.25

WIREHEADS
Fleetway
1 .... 3.00

WISP
Oktomica Entertainment, 1999
1 All Along the Watchtower,pt.1 ... 2.50
2 All Along the Watchtower,pt.2 ... 2.50
3 All Along the Watchtower,pt.3 ... 3.00
4 The Acheron Protocol 3.00

WITCHBLADE
SEE: IMAGE

WITCHING HOUR, THE
Millennium/Comico, 1992
1 Anne Rice adaptation 2.50
2 thru 5 .... @2.50

WOOD BOY, THE
Devil's Due Publishing, 2004
1 (of 2) 3.00
2 .... 3.00

WOODY WOODPECKER
Harvey, 1991–93
1 thru 5 .... @2.25

WORLD OF ARCHIE
Archie, 1994
1 thru 21 .... @2.25

WORLD OF WOOD
Eclipse, 1986–87
1 WW 2.25
2 WW,DSt(i) 2.25
3 WW 2.25
4 WW 2.25

WORLD WAR II: 1946
Antarctic Press, 1999
1 by Ted Nomura 4.00
2 Born to Die............... 4.00
3 Battle for Moscow 4.00
4 Flying Tigers 4.00
5 .... 4.00
6 The Hunley vs. the Potsdam 4.00
7 The Yamato 4.00
8 Tuskegee Airmen.......... 4.00
9 Firestorm 4.00
10 Destination: Space 4.00
11 Night Witches 4.00
12 Korea 4.00
Ann. 2000 b&w 4.00

Wrath #1
© *Malibu*

WRATH
Malibu Ultraverse, 1994–95
1 B:MiB(s),DvA,JmP,C:Mantra 2.25
1a Silver foil................. 3.00
2 DvA,JmP,V:Hellion........... 2.25
3 DvA,JmP,V:Radicals, I:Slayer ... 2.25
4 DvA,JmP,V:Freex............ 2.25
5 DvA,JmP,V:Freex............ 2.25
6 DvA,JmP 2.25
7 DvA,JmP,I:Pierce,Ogre, Doc
   Virtual 2.25
8 .... 2.25
9 A:Prime 2.25
G-Size #1.................... 2.50

WULF THE BARBARIAN
Atlas, 1975
1 O:Wulf 15.00
2 NA,I:Berithe The Swordsman .. 12.00
3 & 4 .... @8.00

WWF BATTLEMANIA
Valiant
1 WWF Action 2.50
2 thru 5 .... @2.50

WYATT EARP
Dell Publishing Co., 1957
1 RsM 175.00
2 RsM 150.00
3 RsM 135.00
4 .... 125.00
5 Ph(c) 125.00
6 .... 125.00

7 .... 125.00
8 .... 125.00
9 .... 125.00
10 .... 125.00
11 .... 100.00
12 RsM..................... 100.00
13 AT 100.00

WYNONNA EARP: HOME
ON THE STRANGE
IDW Publishing, 2003
1 .... 4.00
2 thru 3 .... @4.00

XANADU
Eclipse, 1988
1 .... 2.25

XENYA
Sanctuary Press, 1994
1 Hildebrandt Brothers 4.00
2 .... 3.25
3 .... 3.25
4 conclusion, Homecoming....... 3.00

XENA:
WARRIOR PRINCESS
Topps, 1997
1 RTs,Revenge of the Gorgons,
   pt.1.................... 5.00
1a photo (c)................ 8.00
2 (of 2) rescue of Gabrielle....... 4.00
TPB 10.00

[VOL 2]
0 AaL Temple of the Dragon God .. 3.00
1 (of 3) Joxer, Warrior Prince, pt.1 . 5.00
1a deluxe 8.00
2 Joxer, Warrior Prince, pt.2...... 4.00
2a photo (c)................. 4.00
TPB rep. #0–#2 .... 10.00

XENA:
WARRIOR PRINCESS:
BLOOD LINES
Topps, 1997
1 (of 3) ALo................ 3.00
1a photo (c)................ 3.00
2 (of 3) ALo................ 3.00
2a photo (c)................ 3.00

XENA:
WARRIOR PRINCESS:
CALLISTO
Topps, 1997
1 (of 3) RTs,................ 3.00
1a photo (c)................ 3.00
2 (of 3) RTs,................ 3.00
2a photo (c)................ 3.00
3 (of 3) RTs,................ 3.00
3a photo (c)................ 3.00

XENA:
WARRIOR PRINCESS:
ORPHEUS
Topps, 1998
1 (of 3) 3.00
2 (of 3) 3.00
3 (of 3) 3.00
1a thru 3a photo (c)s......... @3.00

XENA: WARRIOR PRINCESS: THE ORIGINAL OLYMPICS
Topps, 1998

1 (of 3)	3.00
1a photo cover	3.00
2 F:Hercules	3.00
2a photo cover	3.00
3	3.00
3a photo cover	3.00

XENA: WARRIOR PRINCESS: THE WEDDING OF XENA & HERCULES
Topps, 1998

1-shot	3.00
1-shot photo (c)	3.00

XENA, WARRIOR PRINCESS: THE WRATH OF HERA
Topps, 1998

1 (of 2)	3.00
1a photo cover edition	3.00
2 conclusion	3.00
2a photo cover edition	3.00

XENA: WARRIOR PRINCESS: XENA AND THE DRAGON'S TEETH
Topps, 1997

1 (of 3) RTs,	3.00
1a photo (c)	3.00
2 (of 3) RTs,	3.00
2a photo (c)	3.00
3 (of 3) RTs,	3.00
3a photo (c)	3.00

XENO MEN
Blackthorne

1	2.25

XENOTECH
Mirage, 1993–94

1 I:Xenotech	2.75
2	2.75
3 w/2 card strip	2.75

X-FILES
Topps, 1994–97

1 From Fox TV Series	40.00
1a Newstand	30.00
2 Aliens Killing Witnesses	25.00
3 The Return	22.00
4 Firebird,pt.1	15.00
5 Firebird,pt.2	10.00
6 Firebird,pt.3	8.00
7 Trepanning Opera	7.00
8 Silent Cities of the Mind,pt.1	6.00
9 Silent Cities of the Mind,pt.2	5.00
10 Feeling of Unreality,pt.1	5.00
11 Fealing of Unreality,pt.2	5.00
12 Fealing of Unreality,pt.3	5.00
13 A Boy and His Saucer	5.00
14	4.00
15 Home of the Brave	4.00
16 Home of the Brave,pt.2	3.50
17 DgM,CAd	3.50
18 thru 21	@3.50

X-Files #3
© *Topps Comics*

22 JRz,CAd,The Kanishibari	3.00
23 JRz,CAd,Donor	3.00
24 JRz,Silver Lining	3.00
25 JRz,CAd,Remote Control,pt.1	3.00
26 JRz,CAd,Remote Control,pt.2	3.00
27 JRz,CAd,Remote Control,pt.3	3.00
28 JRz,Be Prepared, pt.1, V:Windigo	3.00
29 JRz,Be Prepared, pt.2	3.00
30 JRz,Surrounded, pt.1	3.00
31 JRz,Surrounded, pt.2 (of 2)	3.00
32	3.00
33 widows on San Francisco	3.00
33 variant photo (c)	3.00
34 Project HAARP	3.00
35 Near Death Experience	3.00
36 Near Death Experience, pt.2	3.00
37 JRz,The Face of Extinction	3.00
38 JRz,	3.00
39 JRz, Widow's Peak	3.00
40 Devil's Advocate	3.00
40a photo cover	3.00
41 Severed	3.00
41a photo cover	3.00
Ann.#1 Hollow Eve	5.00
Ann.#2 E.L.F.S.	4.50
Spec.#1 Rep. #1-#3	6.00
Spec.#2 Rep. #4-#6 Firebird	5.00
Spec.#3 Rep. #7-#9	5.00
Spec.#4 Rep.	5.00
TPB Vol. 2	20.00
GN Afterflight	6.00
GN Official Movie Adapt. (1998)	6.00

X-FILES DIGEST
Topps, 1995

1 All New Series, 96pg.	4.00
2 and 3	4.00

X-FILES, THE: GROUND ZERO
Topps, 1997

1 (of 4) based on novel	3.00
2 thru 4	@3.00

X-FILES, THE: SEASON ONE
Topps, 1997

1 RTs,JVF(c) Deep Throat	5.00
Deep Throat, variant (c)	7.50
2 RTs,JVF(c) Squeeze	4.00
Squeeze, RTs, JVF(c)	5.00
3 RTs,SSc,Conduit	4.00

Conduit, RTs	5.00
4 RTs,The Jersey Devil	4.00
5 RTs,Shadows	4.00
Shadows JVF(c)	5.00
6 Fire	4.00
Fire	5.00
7 RTs,JVF,Ice	4.00
Ice	5.00
8 RTs,Space	4.00
Space JVF(c)	5.00
Spec. Pilot Episode RTs,JVF new JVF(c)	5.00
Beyond the Sea JVF(c)	5.00

XIMOS: VIOLENT PAST
Triumphant, 1994

1 JnR(s)	2.50
2 JnR(s)	2.50

XIN
Anarchy Studios, 2002

Alpha Preview edition	2.50
Alpha Preview, collector's ed.	10.00
Ashcan limited edition	6.00
Ashcan gold foil leather	15.00
1 Legend of the Monkey King	3.00
1a variant JMd(c)	3.00
1b Royal blue edition	30.00
1c gold foil edition	30.00
1d holo foil fx edition	10.00
2 thru 3	@3.00
2a thru 3a variant limited (c)	@10.00
TPB Legend of the Monkey King	13.00

XIN: JOURNEY OF THE MONKEY KING
Anarchy Studios, 2003

1	3.00
1a variant (c)	3.00
2 thru 3	@3.00
2a thru 3a variant (c)	3.00
1b thru 3b limited edition	@10.00
TPB Journey of the Monkey King	13.00

X-O MANOWAR
Valiant, 1992

0 JQ,O:Aric,1st Full Chromium(c)	3.00
0a Gold Ed.	3.50
1 BL,BWS,I:Aric,Ken	4.00
2 BL(i),V:Lydia,Wolf-Class Armor	3.00
3 I:X-Caliber,A:Solar	3.00
4 MM,A:Harbinger,C:Shadowman (Jack Boniface)	3.00
5 BWS(c),V:AX	3.00
5a w/Pink logo	3.00
6 SD,V:Ax(X-O Armor)	3.00
7 FM(c),Unity#5,V:Pierce	2.75
8 WS(c),Unity#13,V:Pierce	2.75
9 Aric in Italy,408 A.D.	2.75
10 N:X-O Armor	2.75
11 V:Spider Aliens	2.50
12 A:Solar	2.50
13 V:Solar	2.50
14 BS,A:Turok,I:Randy Cartier	3.00
15 BS,A:Turok	2.50
15a Red Ed.	3.00
16 V:The Mob	2.50
17 BL	2.50
18 JCf,V:CIA,A:Randy,I:Paul	2.50
19 JCf,V:US Government	2.50
20 A:Toyo Harada	2.50
21 V:Ax	2.50
22 Aria in S.America	2.50
23 Aria in S.America	2.50
24 Aria comes back	2.50
25 JCf,JGz,PaK,I:Armories, BU:Armories#0	3.00
26 JGz(s),RLv,F:Ken	2.50

X-O Manowar, Series 2, #2
© Acclaim

27 JGz,RLe,A:Turok,Geomancer,
   Stronghold,Livewire 2.50
28 JGz,RLe,D:X-O,V:Spider
   Aliens,w/Valiant Era card. 2.75
29 JGz,RLe,A:Turok,V:SpiderAliens 2.50
30 JGz,RLe,A:Solar. 2.50
31 JGz,RLe,. 2.50
32 JGz,RLe,at Orb,Inc. 2.25
33 JGz,RLe,Chaos Effect-Delta#3,
   A:Armorines,H.A.R.D. Corps . . 2.25
34 thru 36 . . . . @2.25
37 Wolfbridge Affair pt.1 . . . . 2.25
38 Wolfbridge Affair pt.2 . . . . 2.25
39 Wolfbridge Affair pt.3 . . . . 2.25
40 Wolfbridge Affair pt.4 . . . . 2.25
41 Aftermath. 2.25
42 A:Shadowman Surprise 2.25
43 Chastity's Boys 2.25
44 Bart Sears New Direction 2.50
45 RMz,V:Crescendo. 2.50
46 RMz,V:Crescendo. 2.50
47 RMz,V:Crescendo. 2.50
48 RMz,BS,A:Turok 2.50
49 RMz,loses control of armor. 2.50
50-X R:Paul, I:Alloy 2.50
50-O V:Alloy. 2.50
51 V:Lummox. 2.50
52 V:A Blast From the Past 2.50
53 Returns To Space 2.50
54 I:New Aliens 2.50
55 V:Aliens. 2.50
56 V:Aliens. 2.50
57 I:Gamin 2.50
58 I:Volt 2.50
59 thru 67 . . . . @2.50
TPB rep.#1-4,w/X-O Manual 11.00

X-O MANOWAR
Series Two, Acclaim, 1997
1 Rand Banion v. R.A.G.E. 2.50
2 v. R.A.G.E. 2.50
3 . . . . 2.50
4 R.A.G.E. is back. 2.50
5 Donovan Wylie vs. Internaut 2.50
6 Internaut controls X-O suit. 2.50
7 SEa, Donovan wears his armor. . 2.50
8 SEa, V:Basilisk 2.50
9 SEa, A: new Hard Corps 2.50
10 SEa, R:Bravado 2.50
11 BAu,MWa,SEa,alien creators . . . 2.50
12 BAu,MWa,SEa,O:armor 2.50
13 BAu,SEa,V:Alien creators. 2.50
14 BAu,SEa,V:Aliens of Unity 2.50

---

15 BAu,SEa,out of armor. 2.50
16 BAu,SEa, ... 2.50
17 DMD,SEa,civil war 2.50
18 DMD,SEa,Rand Banion 2.50
19 DMD,SEa,V:Master Blaster 2.50
20 DMD,trapped in a sleep-state. . . 2.50
TPB MWa,BAu rep. #1–#4 . . . . . . 10.00

YAKKY DOODLE
& CHOPPER
Gold Key, 1962
1 . . . . 125.00

YEAH!
Homage/DC, 1999
1 GHe 3.00

YIN FEI
Leung's Publications, 1988–90
5 . . . . 2.25
6 thru 11 . . . . @2.25

YOGI BEAR
Dell, 1962
#1 thru #6, See Dell Four Color
7 thru 9 . . . . 100.00
Gold Key
10 . . . . 135.00
11 Jellystone Follies. 125.00
12 . . . . 75.00
13 Surprise Party 125.00
14 thru 19. . . . . @75.00
20 thru 29 . . . . @40.00
30 thru 42 . . . . @35.00

YOGI BEAR
Charlton Comics, 1970–76
1 . . . . 60.00
2 thru 10 . . . . @35.00
11 thru 35 . . . . 30.00

YOGI BEAR
Archie Comics, 1997
1 . . . . 2.25

YOSEMITE SAM
Gold Key/Whitman, 1970–84
1 . . . . 60.00

Yosemite Sam #5
© Gold Key

---

2 thru 10 . . . . @35.00
11 thru 40 . . . . @25.00
41 thru 81. . . . . @20.00

YOUNGBLOOD
Maximum Press/Extreme
Volume 2, 1996
Vol. 1 & Vol. 2 #1–#10, see Image
11 RLd,RCz,. 2.50
12 Rle, V:Lord Dredd,A:New
   Man,double size 3.50
13 RLd,RCz,F:Die-Hard. 2.50
14 RLd,RCz, ... 2.50
Super Spec.#1 ErS,CSp,AG 3.00
TPB Youngblood, rep. orig.
   Youngblood #1–#5. . . . . 17.00
TPB Baptism of Fire rep.
   Youngblood #6–#8, #10 & Team
   Youngblood #9–#11. . . . . 17.00

YOUNGBLOOD
Awesome Entertainment, 1998
1 AMo,SSr. 2.50
1a variant covers, 7 different. . . . @2.50
1b foil logo 6.00
1c plus custom illustration 72.00
2 AMo,SSr,Baptism of Fire 2.50
3 AMo,SSr,V:Professor Night 2.50
4 AMo,SSr,Young Guns 2.50
5 AMo,SSr,Young Guns 2.50
TPB rep.#1–#10 orig. series 15.00
1-shot, Youngblood/X-Force
   x-over,48pg. (1998) 5.00

YOUNGBLOOD:
BLOODSPORT
Arcade Comics, 2002
1 MMr,RLd, RLd(c) 5.00
1a variant Quietly (c) 6.00
1b variant Park (c) 4.00
1c Foil ed. 10.00
1d Foil ed., signed 20.00
1e convention sketch ed. 50.00
1f San Diego con lim. ed. 10.00
1g San Diego con lim. signed. . . . 20.00
1h ltd (c) 20.00
2 MMr,RLd, RLd(c) 3.00
2a variant Quietly (c) 3.00
2b variant Park (c) 3.00
2c Foil ed. 10.00
2d Foil ed., signed 20.00

YOUNGBLOOD CLASSICS
Image/Extreme, 1996
1 RLd,ErS,series rewritten &
   redrawn, new cover. 2.25
2 RLd,ErS 2.25
3 RLd,ErS 2.25

YOUNGBLOOD GENESIS
Awesome Entertainment, 2000
1 . . . . 4.00
1a signature edition 9.00
Arcade Comics, 2004
2 . . . . 4.00
2a RLd(c) 9.00

ZAANAN
Mainstream Comics
1 The Collection,I:Zaanan. 2.50

ZAK RAVEN, ESQ.
Avatar/Tidalwave Studios, 2002
1A Cha (c). 3.50
1B Arlem (c) 3.50

COLOR PUB.

1C Miller (c) 3.50
1D Murphy (c). 3.50

ZEIN GHOSTS OF HELIOPOLIS
Studio G, 2003

1 . . . . 3.00
2 thru 4 . . . . @3.00

ZEN
Zen Comics, 2003

0 . . . . 3.00
1 . . . . 3.00
2 thru 4 . . . . @3.00
TPB Vol. 1 Return of the
  Alien Hero 15.00

ZENDRA
Pennyfarthing Press, 2001
Volume 2

1 (of 6) Windmills of the World 3.00
2 All the Flesh Inherits 3.00
3 thru 5 . . . . @3.00
6 . . . . 3.00
TPB Vol. 1 . . . . 18.00
TPB Vol. 2 Heart of Fire. 25.00

ZEN INTERGALACTIC NINJA
Archie, 1992

1 Rumble in the Rain Forest
prequel,inc.poster 3.00
2 Rumble in Rain Forest #1 . . . . . 3.00
3 Rumble in Rain Forest #2 . . . . . 3.00

Entity Comics, 1994

0 Chromium (c),JaL(c) 4.00
1 Joe Orbeta. 3.00
1a Platinum Edition. 20.00
2 Deluxe Edition w/card 5.00
3 V:Rawhead 3.00
4 thru 7 . . . . @3.25
GN A Fire Upon The Earth. 13.00

[2nd Series]

1 Joe Orbeta. 5.00
2 . . . . 5.00
3 thru 5 . . . . @2.50

Zen Comics, 1998
Commemorative Ed. #1 . . . . 6.00

ZEN INTERGALACTIC NINJA
Studio Chikara, 1999

1 . . . . 4.00
1 variant (c). 10.00
2 . . . . 4.00
3 . . . . 4.00

ZEN/NIRA X: HELLSPACE
Zen Comics

1 . . . . 3.00

ZEN: NOVELLA
Eternity Comics

1 thru 8 . . . . @3.00

ZEN SPECIALS
Eternity

Spring#1 V:Lord Contaminous 2.50
April Fools#1 parody issue 2.50
Color Spec.#0 . . . . 3.50

ZEN: WARRIOR
Eternity Comics, 1994

1 vicious video game 3.00

ZENDRA
Pennyfarthing Press, 2001

1 (of 6) 3.00
2 thru 6 . . . . @3.00

ZENITH PHASE I
Fleetway

1 thru 3 . . . . @2.25

ZENITH PHASE II
Fleetway

1 thru 2 . . . . @2.25

ZERO GIRL: FULL CIRCLE
DC/Homage, 2002

2 SK 3.00
3 SK 3.00
4 SK 3.00
5 SK, concl.. . . . . 3.00
TPB Full Circle. 18.00

ZERO PATROL
Continuity, 1984–90

1 EM,NA,O&I:Megalith 4.00
2 EM,NA 4.00
3 EM,NA,I:Shaman. 3.00
4 EM,NA 3.00
5 EM 3.00
6 thru 8 EM . . . . @3.00

ZERO TOLERANCE
First, 1990–91

1 TV 3.50
2 TV 3.00
3 TV 3.00
4 TV 3.00

ZOONIVERSE
Eclipse, 1986–87

1 I:Kren Patrol,wrap-around(c) 2.25
2 . . . . 2.25
3 . . . . 2.25
4 V:Wedge City. 2.25
5 Spak vs. Agent Ty-rote. 2.25
6 last issue 2.25

ZORRO
Dell Publ. Co., 1959–61

1 thru 8, see Dell 4-Color
8 . . . . 125.00
9 . . . . 150.00
10 . . . . 125.00
11 . . . . 125.00
12 ATh 150.00
13 . . . . 110.00
14 . . . . 110.00
15 . . . . 110.00

ZORRO
Gold Key, 1966–68

1 ATh,Rep. 125.00
2 Rep. 75.00
3 Rep. 75.00
4 Rep. 75.00
5 Rep. 75.00
6 Rep. 75.00
7 Rep. 75.00
8 Rep. 75.00

9 ATh,Rep. 75.00

ZORRO
Topps, Nov., 1993

0 BSf(c),DMG(s), came bagged
  with Jurassic Park Raptor #1 and
  Teenagents #4. . . . . 4.00
1 DMG(s),V:Machete 3.00
2 DMG(s) 5.00
3 DMG(s) I:Lady Rawhide 12.00
4 MGr(c),DMG(s),V:Moonstalker . . 3.00
5 MGr,DMG(s),V:Moonstalker. 3.00
6 A:Lady Rawhide. 8.00
7 A:Lady Rawhide 7.00
8 MGr(c),DMG(s) 3.00
9 A:Lady Rawhide. 4.00
10 A:Lady Rawhide 4.50
11 A:Lady Rawhide 8.00

ZOT!
Eclipse, 1984–85

1 by Scott McCloud 7.00
2 . . . . 4.00
3 Art and Soul. 4.00
4 Assault on Castle Dekko 3.00

Zot #6
© Eclipse

5 Sirius Business 3.00
6 It's always darkest. 3.00
7 Common Ground. 3.00
8 Through the Door 3.00
9 Gorilla Warfare. 3.00
10 T.K.O. The Final Round 3.00
10a B&W 6.00
10b 2nd printing. 3.00
Original Zot! Book 1 . . . . 10.00
Book One TPB. 25.00
(Changed to B & W)

ZOT!
Kitchen Sink

Book One TPB. 25.00

All comics prices listed are for *Near Mint* condition.

B&W COMICS

A1
Atomeka Press, 1989–92
1 BWs,A:Flaming Carrot,Mr.X. . . . 10.00
2 BWs 9.75
3 . . . . 9.75
4 . . . . 6.00
5 . . . . 7.00
6a 5.00

AARDWOLF
Aardwolf, 1994
1 DC,GM(c). 3.00
1a Certificate ed. signed. 12.00
2 World Toughest Milkman 3.00
3 R.Block(s),O:Aardwolf 3.00

AARON STRIPS
Amazing Aaron Prod., 1999
1 thru 4, see Image
5 thru 9 . . . . @3.00
10 48-pg. 4.00

A.B.C. Warriors #6
© *Fleetway/Quality*

A.B.C. WARRIORS
Fleetway/Quality, 1990
1 thru 8 . . . . @2.25
Titan, 2002
TPB Vol. 1 The Mek-nificent Seven 20.00
TPB Vol. 2 Black Hole 20.00

ABSOLUTE ZERO
Antarctic Press, 1995
1 . . . . 3.00
2 Rooftop,Athena 3.00
3 Stan Sakai 3.50
4 3-D Man and Kirby. 3.00
5 & 6 Super Powers . . . . @3.00

AC ANNUAL
Aircel, 1990
1 . . . . 4.00
2 Based on 1940's heroes 5.00
3 F:GoldenAge Heroes. 3.50
4 F:Sentinels of Justice 4.00

ACE COMICS PRESENTS
Ace, 1987
1 thru 7 . . . . @2.25

ACE McCOY
ACG Comics, 1999
1 FF 3.00
2 FF, SD 3.00
3 & 4 FF . . . . @3.00
TPB Collected ed. FF,rep.5 issues 13.00

ACES
Eclipse, 1988
1 thru 5, mag. size . . . . @3.00

ACG'S AMAZING COMICS
ACG Comics, 2000
1 (of 4) F:Dragon Lady 3.00
2 thru 5 . . . . @3.00

ACHILLES STORM
Brainstorm, 1997
1 by Sandra Chang. 3.00

ACHILLES STORM: DARK SECRET
Brainstorm, 1997
1 by Sandra Chang. 3.00
2 . . . . 3.00
2a luxury edition 5.00

ACME
Fandom House, 1985–89
1 thru 9 . . . . @2.25

ACOLYTE CHRONICLES
Azure Press, 1995
1 I:Korath 3.00
2 V:Korath 3.00

A COP CALLED TRACY
ACG Comics, 1998
1 by Chester Gould. 3.00
2 thru 9 . . . . @3.00
9a deluxe 3.00
10 thru 18. . . . . @3.00
19 thru 24 giant-size,64-pg. . . . . @6.00
Ann.#1 . . . . 3.00

ACTION GIRL COMICS
Slave Labor Graphics, 1994
1 thru 7 . . . . @3.00
1 thru 7, later printings . . . . @2.75
8 thru 12 . . . . @3.00
13 Halloween issue 3.00
14 F:Elizabeth Lavin 3.00
15 . . . . 3.00
16 GoGo Gang,pt.1 . . . . 2.75
17 GoGo Gang,pt.2 . . . . 2.75
18 Blue Monday. 3.00
19 Halloween 3.00

ADAM AND EVE A.D.
Bam, 1985–87
1 . . . . 3.00
2 thru 10 . . . . @2.25

ADDAM OMEGA
Antarctic Press, 1997
1 (of 4) by Bill Hughes 3.00
2 thru 4 . . . . @3.00

ADOLESCENT RADIOACTIVE BLACK-BELT HAMSTERS
Eclipse, 1986
1 I:Bruce,Chuck,Jackie,Clint. 2.50
1a 2nd printing 2.25
2 A parody of a parody 2.25
3 I:Bad Gerbil 2.25
4 A:Heap (3-D),Abusement Park . . 2.25
5 Abusement Park #2 . . . . 2.25
6 SK,Abusement Park #3 . . . . 2.25
7 SK,V:Toe-Jam Monsters 2.25
8 SK 2.25
9 All-Jam last issue. 2.25
[2nd Series]
Parody Press
1 . . . . 2.50
2 Hamsters Go Hollywood 2.50

ADVENTURERS
Aircel/Adventure, 1986
0 Origin Issue 2.50
1 with Skeleton 7.00
1a Revised cover 5.00
1b 2nd printing 2.50
2 thru 6 Peter Hsu (c) . . . . @2.50
7 thru 9 . . . . @2.25

ADVENTURERS BOOK II
Adventure Publ., 1987
0 O:Man Gods 2.25
1 . . . . 2.25
2 thru 9 . . . . @2.25

ADVENTURERS BOOK III
Adventure Publ., 1989
1A Lim.(c)Ian McCaig 2.25
1B Reg.(c)Mitch Foust 2.25
2 thru 6 . . . . @2.25

ADVENTURES INTO THE UNKNOWN
A Plus Comics, 1990
1 AW,WW, rep. classic horror 3.00
2 AW 3.00
3 AW 3.00
Halloween Spec. reps. Charlton &
   American Comics GroupHorror . 2.50
ACG Comics, 1997
1 FF,AW, Charlton comics reprint . . 3.00

ADVENTURES OF BARRY WEEN BOY GENIUS
Oni Press, 2000
1 (of 6) by Judd Winick. 3.00
2 Monkey Tales,pt.2 . . . . 3.00
3 Monkey Tales,pt.3 . . . . 3.00
4 Monkey Tales,pt.4 . . . . 3.00
5 Monkey Tales,pt.5 . . . . 3.00
6 Monkey Tales,pt.6 . . . . 3.00
TPB Vol. 1 thru Vol. 4. . . . . @9.00

ADVENTURES OF CHRISSY CLAWS, THE
Heroic, 1991
1 thru 2 . . . . @3.25

ADVENTURES OF CHUK THE BARBARIC
White Wolf, 1987
1 & 2 . . . . @2.25

ADVENTURES OF LIBERAL MAN, THE
Political Comics, 1996
1 by Marcus Pierce & Pete Garcia . 3.00
2 V:Right Wing talk show hosts . . . 3.00
3 Contract with America,'pt.2 . . . . . 3.00
4 Terminate with Extreme
  Prejudice,'pt.2 . . . . 3.00
5 Extreme Prejudice,pt.3 . . . . 3.00
6 . . . . 3.00
7 1996 Election issue 3.00
9 . . . . 3.00
10 The Last Boy Scouts,pt.2 . . . . . . 3.00
Sharkbait Press, 1999
TPB Final Mission 15.00

ADVENTURES OF LUTHER ARKWRIGHT
Valkyrie Press, 1987–89
1 thru 9 . . . . @2.25
See Also: Dark Horse section

ADVENTURES OF THE AEROBIC DUO
Lost Cause Productions
1 thru 3 . . . . @2.25
4 Gopher Quest 2.25
5 V:Stupid Guy 2.25

ADVENTURES OF THEOWN
Pyramid, 1986
1 thru 3, Limited series . . . . @2.25

AESOP'S FABLES
Fantagraphics, 1991
1 Selection of Fables 2.25
2 Selection of Fables 2.25
3 inc. Boy who cried wolf 2.25

AETOS
Hall of Heroes, 1997
1 by Dan Parsons 2.50
1 variant cover 4.00
2 . . . . 2.50

AETOS THE EAGLE
Ground Zero, 1997
1 (of 3) by Dan Parsons 3.00
2 . . . . 3.00
3 concl. 3.00

AETOS 2: CHILDREN OF THE GRAVES
Orphan Underground, 1995
1 A:Nightmare 2.50

AGENT UNKNOWN
Renegade, 1987
1 thru 3 . . . . @2.25

Agent Unknown #1
© Renegade

AGE OF HEROES, THE
Halloween Comics, 1996
1 JHI 3.50
1A signed 7.00
2 JHI 3.50
2A signed 7.00

AGONY ACRES
AA2 Entertainment, 1995
1 thru 3 . . . . @2.50
4 and 5 . . . . @3.00

AIRFIGHTERS CLASSICS
Eclipse, 1987
1 O:Airboy,rep.Air Fighters#2 . . . . . 4.00
2 rep.Old Airboy appearances 4.00
3 thru 6 . . . . @4.00

AIRWAVES
Caliber, 1990
1 Radio Security 2.50
2 A:Paisley,Ganja 2.50
3 Formation of Rebel Alliance. 2.50
4 Big Annie,pt. 1 . . . . 2.50
5 Big Annie,pt 2 . . . . 2.50

AKIKO
Sirius, 1996
1 MCi, Akiko on the Planet Smoo. . 6.00
2 MCi 4.00
3 thru 17 MCi . . . . @3.00
18 Alia Rellapor, concl. 3.00
19 new story,pt.1 . . . . 3.00
20 F:Mr. Beeba 3.00
21 On the Road 3.00
22 . . . . 3.00
23 space station Fognon-6 . . . . 3.00
24 escape spaceship 3.00
25 Done in One, 32pg. 3.00
26 reunited on planet Smoo 3.00
27 MCi,Bornstone's Elixir,pt.2 . . . . . 3.00
28 MCi,Bornstone's Elixir,pt.3 . . . . . 3.00
29 MCi,Bornstone's Elixir,pt.4 . . . . . 3.00
30 MCi,Bornstone's Elixir,pt.5 . . . . . 3.00
31 MCi,Bornstone's Elixir, concl. . . . 3.00
32 MCi,On Planet Earth,pt.1 . . . . . . 3.00
33 MCi,On Planet Earth,pt.2 . . . . . . 3.00
34 MCi,On Planet Earth,pt.3 . . . . . . 3.00
35 Moonshopping,pt.1 . . . . 3.00
36 Moonshopping,pt.2 . . . . 3.00

37 Moonshopping,pt.3 . . . . 3.00
38 Moonshopping,pt.4 . . . . 3.00
39 Big Bag of This and That 3.00
40 Battle of Boach's Keep,pt.1 . . . . 3.00
41 Battle of Boach's Keep,pt.2 . . . . 3.00
42 Battle of Boach's Keep,pt.3 . . . . 3.00
43 Battle of Boach's Keep,pt.4 . . . . 3.00
44 Battle of Boach's Keep,pt.5 . . . . 3.00
45 Battle of Boach's Keep,pt.6 . . . . 3.00
46 Battle of Boach's Keep,pt.7 . . . . 3.00
47 Battle of Boach's Keep,pt.8 . . . . 3.00
48 Akiko on Planet Earth,pt.1 . . . . . 3.00
49 Akiko on Planet Earth,pt.2 . . . . . 3.00
50 40-pg. 3.50
51 . . . . 3.00
52 . . . . 3.00
Spec. Akiko on the Planet Smoo . . 3.50
TPB Vol. 1 rep. #1–#6 . . . . 15.00
TPB Vol. 2 rep. #8–#13 . . . . 12.00
TPB Vol. 3 rep. #14–#18 . . . . 12.00
TPB Vol. 4 rep. #19–#24 . . . . 15.00
TPB Vol. 5 . . . . 13.00
TPB Vol. 6 . . . . 15.00
TPB Vol. 7 . . . . 15.00
TPB Vol. 1 Flights of Fancy 15.00
GN Akiko on the Planet Smoo. . . . 15.00
GN Pocket-Sized Vol. 1 . . . . 12.00
GN Pocket-Sized Vol. 2 . . . . 10.00
GN Pocket-Sized Vol. 3 . . . . 10.00

ALAN MOORE'S THE COURTYARD
Avatar Press, 2003
1 . . . . 3.50
2 . . . . 3.50
1a thru 2a wraparound (c). . . . . . @4.00
TPB 6.95
TPB The Courtyard, companion . . . 9.95

ALAN MOORE'S YUGGOTH CULTURES
Avatar Press, 2003
1 thru 3 . . . . @3.50
1 thru 3a wraparound (c) 4.00
Necrocomicon ashcan, 16-pg. 4.95

ALBEDO
Thoughts & Images, 1985–89
0 white cover, yellow drawing table
  Blade Runner 35.00
0a white(c) 15.00
0b blue(c),1st ptg 12.00
0c blue(c),2nd ptg 10.00
0d blue(c),3rd ptg 5.00
0e Photo(c),4th ptg.,inc. extra
  pages 3.00
1 SS,I:Nilson Groundthumper,
  dull red cover. 10.00
1a bright red cover 6.00
2 SS,I:Usagi Yojimbo 15.00
3 SS,Erma, Usagi 5.00
4 SS,Usagi 6.00
5 Nelson Groundthumper 5.00
6 Erma, High Orbit 4.00
7 . . . . 2.25
8 Erna Feldna 2.25
9 High Orbit,Harvest Venture 2.25
10 thru 14 . . . . @2.25

ALBEDO VOL. II
Antarctic Press, 1991–93
1 New Erma Story. 3.00
2 E.D.F. HQ. 3.00
3 Birth of Erma's Child 3.00
4 Non action issue 3.00
5 The Outworlds 3.00
6 War preparations 3.00

7 Ekosiak in Anarchy 3.00
8 EDF High Command 3.00
Spec. Color 3.00

VOL. III
1 . . . . 3.50

ALIEN FIRE
Kitchen Sink Press, 1987
1 Eric Vincent art 3.50
2 Eric Vincent art 2.50
3 Eric Vincent art 2.25

ALIEN NATION:
A BREED APART
Adventure Comics, 1990
1 Friar Kaddish 3.00
2 Friar Kaddish 2.50
3 The `Vampires' Busted 2.50
4 Final Issue 2.50

ALIEN NATION:
THE FIRSTCOMERS
Adventure Comics, 1991
1 New Mini-series 2.50
2 Assassin. 2.50
3 Search for Saucer 2.50
4 Final Issue 2.50

ALIEN NATION:
THE PUBLIC ENEMY
Adventure Comics, 1991
1 `Before the Fall' 2.50
2 Earth & Wehlnistrata 2.50
3 Killer on the Loose. 2.50

ALIEN NATION:
THE SKIN TRADE
Adventure Comics, 1991
1 `Case of the Missing Milksop' . . . 2.50
2 `To Live And Die in L.A' 2.50
3 A:Dr. Jekyll. 2.50
4 D.Methoraphan Exposed 2.50

ALIEN NATION:
THE SPARTANS
Adventure Comics, 1990
1 JT/DPo,Yellow wrap. 4.00
1a JT/DPo,Green wrap 4.00
1b JT/DPo,Pink wrap 4.00
1c JT/DPo,blue wrap 4.00
1d LTD collectors edition 7.00
2 JT,A:Ruth Lawrence. 2.50
3 JT/SM,Spartans 2.50
4 JT/SM,conclusion 2.50

ALISON DARE,
LITTLE MISS
ADVENTURES
Oni Press, 2001
1 (of 3) 3.00
TPB 9.00

Vol. 2
1 (of 2) Heart of the Maiden 3.00
2 Heart of the Maiden. 3.00
1-shot 48-pg. (2000) 4.50

ALL-NEW TENCHI MUYO
Viz Communications, 2002
Part 1
1 (of 5) by Hitoshi Okuda 3.00
2 thru 5 . . . . @3.00

Part 2
1 (of 5) 3.00
2 thru 5 . . . . @3.00
TPB Vol. 1 Alien Nation 9.00
TPB Vol. 2 Doom Time 9.00
TPB Vol. 3 Dark Washu. 9.00
TPB Vol. 4 Girls Get Busy 9.00
TPB Vol. 5 Point and Shoot. 9.00

ALL-PRO SPORTS
All Pro Sports
1 Unauthorized Bio-Bo Jackson . . . 2.50
2 Unauthorized Bio-Joe Montana . . 2.50

ALLURA AND
THE CYBERANGELS
Avatar Press, 1998
Spec.#1 by Bill Maus 4.00

ALLY
Ally Winsor Productions, 1995
1 I&O: Ally. 3.00
2 and 3 . . . . @3.00

ALTERNATE HEROES
Prelude Graphics, 1986
1 and 2 . . . . @2.25

Amazing Comics Premiers #2
© Amazing Comics

AMAZING COMICS
PREMIERES
Amazing, 1987
1 thru 9 . . . . @2.25

AMAZON WOMAN
Fantaco, 1994
1 . . . . 3.00
2 . . . . 3.00

VOL. 2 (1996)
1 thru 4 . . . . @3.00
Christmas Spec. 5.00
Beach Party 6.00
Amazing Colossal Amazon
  Woman #1 . . . . 8.00
Amazing Colossal Amazon Album. 13.00
Jungle Annual #1 . . . . 6.00
Jungle Album 10.00
TPB Amazon Woman: The Art of
  Tom Simonton 10.00
TPB Amazon Woman, deluxe 20.00

Spec. Invaders of Terror (1996). . . . 6.00
TPB Book One by Tom Simonton . 15.00
TPB Book Two The Curse of the
  Amazon 15.00
1-shot Attack of the Amazon Girls,
  cont. nudity 5.00

AMAZONS GONZANGAS:
BAD GIRLS
OF THE JUNGLE
Academy Comics, 1995
0 Rites of passage,JWt. 3.50

AMERICAN SPLENDOR
Harvey Bekar, 1976–90
1 thru 15 . . . . @3.25

Tundra, 1991
16 . . . . 4.00

AMERICAN WOMAN
Antarctic Press, 1998
1 by B.Denham & R.Stockton 3.00

AMERICA'S GREATEST
COMICS
AC Comics, 2002
1 F:Phantom Lady, golden-age rep. 7.00
2 F:Mysta on the Moon. 7.00
3 F:Spy Smasher 7.00
4 F:Yarko, Master Magician 7.00
5 F: Captain Science 7.00
6 thru 10 . . . . @7.00

AMERIMAGNA
Ironcat, 2002
Vol. 1
TPB #1 . . . . 8.00
TPB #2 thru #3 . . . . @8.00

I.C. Entertainment, 2003
TPB #4 thru #12. . . . . @8.00

AMUSING STORIES
Blackthorne
1 thru 3 . . . . @2.25

ANATOMIC BOMBS
Brainstorm, 1998
1 Angelissa, by Mike James 3.00
1a Bad Tabitha, by Mike James . . 3.00
1b Bad Tabitha, photo cover edition 4.00

ANGEL GIRL
Angel Entertainment, 1997
0 by David Campiti & Al Rio 3.00
1 by D.Campiti & R.Fraga. 3.00
1 deluxe 6.00
Spec. #1 Angels Illustrated Swimsuit
  Special 5.00
1-shot Against All Evil 3.00
1-shot Before the Wings 3.00
1-shot Demonworld, by Ellis Bell &
  Mark Kuettner 3.00
1-shot Doomsday, by Ellis Bell &
  Mark Kuettner 3.00

ANGEL GIRL:
HEAVEN SENT
Angel Entertainment, 1997
0 by David Campiti & Al Rio 3.00
1 . . . . 3.00

ANGEL OF DEATH
Innovation
1 thru 4 . . . . @2.25

ANGELS 750
Antarctic Press 2004
1 (of 9) 3.00
2 thru 5 . . . . @3.00

ANIMAL MYSTIC
Cry For Dawn/Sirus, 1993–95
1 DOe 32.00
1a variant, signed 47.00
1b 2nd printing, new (c) 7.00
2 I:Klor 30.00
2a 2nd printing, new (c) 6.00
3 . . . . 12.00
3a 2nd printing 5.00
4 last issue 4.00
4a special 15.00
TPB DOe 15.00

ANIMAL MYSTIC: KLOR
Sirius, 1999
1 thru 3 DOe . . . . @3.00

ANIMERICA
Viz Comics
1 F:Bubble Gum Crisis 3.00
2 F:Bubble Gum Crisis 3.00
3 F:Bubble Gum Crisis 3.00

ANIMERICA
Viz Communications, 2000
Vol. 8
11 & 12. @5.00
Vol. 9, 2001
1 thru 10 . . . . @5.00
11/12 . . . . 5.00
Vol. 10, 2001
1 thru 12 . . . . @5.00
TPB Best of Animerica 2003 . . . . . 13.00
Vol. 11 Jan., 2003
1 thru 12 . . . . @5.00
Vol. 12 Jan., 2004
1 thru 11 . . . . @5.00

ANIMERICA EXTRA
Viz Communications, 1998
1 & 2 . . . . @5.00
VOL. 2, 1998
1 thru 11 . . . . @5.00
VOL. 3, 1999
1 thru 12 . . . . @5.00
VOL. 4, 2000
1 thru 12 . . . . @5.00
Vol. 5, 2001
1 thru 12 . . . . @5.00
Vol. 6
1 thru 12 . . . . @5.00
Vol. 7 Jan 2004
1 thru 11 . . . . @5.00

ANTARES CIRCLE
Antarctic Press
1 . . . . 2.25
2 . . . . 2.25

ANUBIS
Unicorn Books
1 I:Anubis 2.50

2 F:Anubis. 2.50
3 . . . . 2.50
Didactic Chocolate Press
3 by Scott Berwanger 2.75
4 thru 6 . . . . @2.75
Adventure Comics
7 `Sandy's Plight' 2.75
8 . . . . 3.00

A-OK
Antarctic Press, 1993
1 Ninja H.S. spin-off series 2.50
2 F:Paul,Moniko,James 2.50
3 Confrontation 2.50
4 . . . . 2.50

APATHY KAT
Entity, 1995
1 . . . . 2.75
1 signed, numbered 10.00
1 2nd printing 2.75
2 . . . . 2.75
2 2nd printing 2.75
3 & 4 . . . . 2.75
TPB Kollection #1 . . . . 8.00

APE CITY
Adventure Comics
1 Monkey Business. 3.00
2 thru 4 . . . . @2.50

APPARITION, THE
Caliber, 1995
1 thru 4 . . . . @3.00
5 `Black Clouds' 3.00

APPLESEED
Eclipse, 1988
1 MSh,rep. Japanese comic 9.00
2 MSh,arrival in Olympus City 6.00
3 MSh,Olympus City politics. 5.00
4 MSh,V:Director. 5.00
5 MSh,Deunan vs. Chiffon 5.00
Book Two, 1989
1 MSh,AAd(c),Olympus City 4.00
2 MSh,AAd(c),Hitomi vs.EswatUnit . 4.00
3 MSh,AAd(c),Deunan vs.Gaia. . . . 4.00
4 MSh,AAd(c),V:Robot Spiders . . . 4.00
5 MSh,AAd(c),Hitome vs.Gaia 4.00
Book Three, 1989
1 MSh,Brigreos vs.Biodroid 5.00
2 MSh,V:Cuban Navy 4.00
3 MSh,`Benandanti' 4.00
4 MSh,V:Renegade biodroid. 4.00
5 MSh 4.00
Book Four, 1990
1 MSh,V:Munma Terrorists 3.50
2 MSh,V:Drug-crazed Munma 3.50
3 MSh,V:Munma Drug Addicts 3.50
4 MSh,Deunan vs. Pani 3.50

AQUA KNIGHT
Viz Communications, 2000
1 (of 6) by Yukito Kishiro 3.50
2 thru 6 . . . . @3.50
PART 2
1 (of 5) 3.50
2 thru 5 . . . . @3.50
PART 3, 2001
1 thru 5 . . . . @3.50
TPB Vol. 1 . . . . 17.00
TPB Vol. 2 . . . . 17.00
TPB Vol. 3 . . . . 17.00

AQUARIUM
CPM Manga, 2000
1 by Tomoko Taniguchi 3.00
2 thru 6 . . . . @3.00

Aramis #2
© Comics Interview

ARAMIS WEEKLY
Comics Interview
1 mini-series 2.25
2 & 3 . . . . @2.25

AREA 88
Eclipse, 1987
1 I:Shin Kazama 3.00
1a 2nd printing 2.25
2 Dangerous Mission 2.25
2a 2nd printing 2.25
3 O:Shin,Paris '78. . . . . 2.25
4 thru 8 . . . . @2.25
9 thru 36 . . . . @2.25
Viz Communications, 1988
37 thru 42 . . . . @2.25

AREALA, ANGEL OF WAR
Antarctic Press, 1998
1 F:Warrior Nun Areala, color 3.00
2 color 3.00
3 b&w 3.00
4 b&w, conclusion. 3.00

ARGONAUTS
Eternity
1 thru 5 . . . . @2.25

ARIK KHAN
A Plus Comics
1 I:Arik Khan. 2.50
2 . . . . 2.50
ACG Comics, 1998
1 by Frank Reyes, heroic fantasy . 3.00

ARISTOCRATIC X-TRA-TERRESTRIAL TIME-TRAVELING THIEVES
Fictioneer Books, 1987
1 V:IRS 2.25
2 V:Realty 2.25
3 V:MDM 2.25
4 thru 12 . . . . @2.25

ARIZONA:
A SIMPLE HORROR
London Night/EH Prod., 1998
1 (of 3) by Joe Kennedy &
　Jerry Beck 3.00
2 double sized. 3.00
3 . . . . 3.00
1-shot Wild at Heart, signed
　alternate cover. 10.00

A.R.M. #3
© Adventure Comics

A.R.M.
Adventure Comics, 1990
1 Larry Niven adapt. Death by
　Ecstasy,pt.1 . . . . 2.50
2 Death by Ecstasy,pt.2 . . . . 2.50
3 Death by Ecstasy,pt.3 . . . . 2.50

ARMAGEDDON PATROL
Alchemy Texts, 1999
Spec. The Shot 3.00
1 (of 2) Cherries 3.00
2 Cherries 3.00
Spec. Maiden America (2002) 3.00
Spec. Fatal Mistakes 3.00
Spec. Life and Death 3.50
Spec. First Mission #1 . . . . 3.50
Spec. First Mission #2 . . . . 3.50
Spec. First Mission #3 . . . . 3.50

ARMED & DANGEROUS
Valiant, 1995
1 thru 4 . . . . @3.00
Spec.#1 . . . . 3.00

ARMED & DANGEROUS
Acclaim, 1996
1 BH,Hell's Slaughterhouse, pt.1 . . 3.00
2 BH,Hell's Slaughterhouse, pt.2 . . 3.00
3 BH,Hell's Slaughterhouse, pt.3 . . 3.00
4 BH,Hell's Slaughterhouse, pt.4 . . 3.00

ARMED & DANGEROUS
No. 2
Acclaim, 1996
1 BH,When Irish Eyes are
　Dying, pt.1 . . . . 3.00
2 BH,When Irish Eyes, pt.2 . . . . . . 3.00
3 BH,When Irish Eyes, pt.3 . . . . . . 3.00
4 BH,When Irish Eyes, pt.4 . . . . . . 3.00

ARROW SPOTLIGHT
Arrow Comics, 1998–99
Advendures of Simone & Ajax 3.00
Allison Chains 3.00
Descendants of Toshin. 3.00
Max Velocity, by Jack Snider 3.00
Red Vengeance, by Chris Kemple . . 3.00
Talonback 3.00

ARSENIC LULLABY
A Silent Comics, 1999
Spec. May '99 . . . . 2.50
Spec. July '99. . . . . 2.50
Spec. Sept.'99 . . . . 2.50
Spec. Jan. 2000. . . . . 2.50
8 thru 15 . . . . @2.50
Sept. 2001 . . . . 2.50
Nov. 2001. . . . . 2.65
Christmas 2001 . . . . 2.65
Spec. Christmas Special 2.50
Spec. Halloween Special 2.75
TPB The Devil Your Neighbor 13.00
TPB Arsenic Lullaby, Year Two . . . 13.00
Volume 2, 2002
1 by Douglas Paszkiewicz 2.50
2 . . . . 2.65
3 . . . . 2.65
4 . . . . 2.75
TPB Vol. 1 Damned Laughter 13.00
TPB The Devil's hat Trick 19.00
AAA Milwaukee Publishing 2002
Lost issue, signed 4.00
AAA Milwaukee Publishing
15 thru 16 . . . . @2.65
17 . . . . 2.70
18 . . . . 2.85

ASHEN VICTOR
Viz Communications, 1998
1 (of 4) by Yukito Kishiro 3.00
2 thru 4 concl. . . . . @3.00
TPB 15.00

ASHES
Caliber, 1990–91
1 thru 6 . . . . @2.50

ASHLEY DUST
Knight Press, 1995
1 thru 3 . . . . @2.50
4 V:Allister Crowley. 2.50
5 Metaphysical Adventure. 2.50

ASRIAL VS. CHEETAH
Antarctic Press, 1995–96
1 & 2 Ninja High School Gold
　Digger x-over . . . . @3.00

ASSASSINATE HITLER!
New England Comics, 2001
1 (of 3) by Ron Ledwell 3.75
2 thru 3 . . . . @3.75

ASSASSINETTE
Pocket Change Comics, 1994
1 thru 4 . . . . @2.50
5 V:Nemesis 2.50
6 The Second Coming,pt.2 . . . . 2.50
7 The Second Coming,pt.3 . . . . 2.50
8 V:Crazy Actor. 2.50
9 . . . . 2.50
10 final issue. 2.50
Spec. Assassinette Returns 2.50
Spec. Assassinette Violated 2.50
Deluxe Assassinette Violated 4.25

ASSASSINETTE:
HARDCORE 1995
Pocket Change Comics
1 By Shadow Slasher Team 2.50
2 V:Bolero 2.50

AS TOLD BY...
NDP Comics 2004
1 Rapunzel 2.95
2 Sleeping Beauty. 2.95

ASSEMBLY
Antarctic Press, 2003
1 (of 4) 3.00
2 thru 4 . . . . @3.50
TPB Pocket Manga 10.00

ASTOUNDING
SPACE THRILLS
Day One Comics, 1998
1 by Steve Conley, The Codex
　Reckoning,pt.1. . . . . 3.00
2 Bros. Hildebrandt (c) 3.00
3 Aspects of Iron. 3.00
4 The Robot Murders 3.00
5 Gordo returns. 3.00

ASTOUNDING SPACE
THRILLS: BLOOP
Day One Comics 2004
1 . . . . 2.95
2 . . . . 2.95

ASTRA
CPM Manga, 2001
1 . . . . 3.00
1a variant JBa (c) 3.00
1b variant JBa(c) signed. 30.00
2 thru 5 . . . . @3.00
6 thru 8 . . . . @3.00
TPB Jerry Robinson's Astra 16.00

ASTRONAUTS
IN TROUBLE:
LIVE FROM THE MOON
Gun Dog Comics, 1999
1 (of 5) 3.00
2 thru 5 . . . . @3.00
AIT Comics, 1999
Spec.#1 Cool Ed's 3.00
Spec.#1 CAd, One Shot, One Beer. 8.00

ASTRONAUTS IN
TROUBLE: SPACE:, 1959
AIT/Planetlar, 2000
1 (of 3) by Larry Young, CAd 3.00
2 . . . . 3.00
3 . . . . 3.00
TPB 72-pg. 8.00
TPB Astronauts in Trouble 17.00

ATHENA
A.M. Works
7 thru 14 by Dean Hsieh . . . . @3.00
TPB Vol. 1 . . . . 15.00
TPB Vol. 2 . . . . 16.00

ATOMIC CITY TALES
Kitchen Sink, 1996
1 thru 4 by Jay Stephens . . . . . . @3.50
TPB Vol. 1 Go Power. 13.00

TPB Vol. 1 signed & numbered . . . 21.00

Oni Press, 2002

TPB Vol. 1 Go Power. 13.00
TPB Vol. 2 Doc Phantom. 13.00

ATOMIC COMICS

1 . . . . 2.25

Becomes:

MARK I

ATOMIC MAN

Blackthorne, 1986

1 . . . . 3.00
2 & 3 . . . . @2.25

ATOMIC MOUSE

A Plus Comics, 1990

1 A:Atomic Bunny 2.50

ATOMIC OVERDRIVE

Caliber

1 by Dave Darrigo & PGr 3.00
2 & 3 . . . . @3.00

A TRAVELLER'S TALE

Antarctic Press

1 I:Goshin the Traveller 2.50
2 . . . . 2.50

ATTACK OF THE MUTANT MONSTERS

A Plus Comics

1 SD,rep.Gorgo(Kegor). 2.50

AUGUST

Arrow Comics, 1998

1 thru 4 . . . . @3.00

AUTUMN

Caliber Press, 1995

1 I:James Turell 3.00
GN 7"x10" 13.00

AVALON

Harrier, 1987

1 thru 3 . . . . @2.25

Avalon #3
© Harrier

AVANT GUARD

Day 1 Comics, 1994

1 thru 4 F:Feedback . . . . @2.50

AVATARS

Avatar Press, 1998

1 (of 2) by Gregory & Holaso 4.00
2 F:Pandora & Atlas 3.50

AV IN 3D

Aardvark–Vanaheim, 1984

1 Color,A:Flaming Carrot 6.00

AVELON

Kenzer & Company, 1998

1 . . . . 3.00
2 thru 5 . . . . @3.00
6 thru 11 Legacy of Thrain . . . . . @3.00
11 & 12 Heir to Legend . . . . @3.00

AVENUE X

Innovation

1 Based on NY radio drama 2.50

Purple Spiral

3 signed & numbered 3.00

AWAKENING COMICS

Awakening Comics, 1997

1 by Steve Peters 3.50
2 . . . . 3.50
3 . . . . 3.00
4 . . . . 3.00

Awakening Comics, 1999

1 by Steve Peters 3.50
Spec. Millennium Bug Fever 3.00

AWESOME COMICS

1 thru 3 . . . . @2.25

AXED FILES, THE

Entity Comics, 1995

1 X-Files Parody 2.50
1 3rd printing, parody 2.75

B-MOVIE PRESENTS

B-Movie Comics, 1986

1 . . . . 2.25
2 . . . . 2.25
3 Tasma, Queen of the Jungle 2.25
4 . . . . 2.25

BABES OF AREA 51

Blatant Comics, 1997

1 . . . . 3.00

BABY ANGEL X

Brainstorm, 1996

1 . . . . 3.00
2 . . . . 3.00
3 gold edition 5.00
3a signed edition. 10.00

BABY ANGEL X: SCORCHED EARTH

Brainstorm, 1997

1 by Scott Harrison 3.00
2 . . . . 3.00

BABYLON CRUSH

Boneyard Press, 1995

1 I:Babylon Crush 3.00

---

2 V:A Gang 3.00
3 V:Mafiaso Brothers 3.00
4 & 5 . . . . @3.00

CFD

6 & 7 . . . . @4.00

Boneyard, 1998

1-shot Buddha, F:Lesbian dominatrix
    vigilante 5.00
Spec. Babylon Bondage Christmas . 3.00
Spec. Girlfriends. 3.00
Spec. The Last Shepherd 3.00

BAD APPLES

High Impact, 1997

1 . . . . 3.00
1 Bad Candies cover 10.00
2 . . . . 3.00
2 deluxe 15.00
3 by Billy Patton 3.00

ABC Studios, 1999

VOL 2

1 RCI. 3.00
1a deluxe variant 8.00
2 . . . . 3.00

VOL 3

1 by Greg Narvasa 3.00
1a gold manga 10.00

BAD APPLES: HIGH EXPECTATIONS

ABC Studios, 1999

1 . . . . 3.00
1a Beach Fun (c) 8.00
2 . . . . 3.00
2a deluxe 8.00

BAKER STREET

(Prev. color)
Caliber, 1989

3 . . . . 3.25
4 . . . . 2.25
5 & 6 Children of the Night . . . . . @2.25
7 thru 10 Children of the Night . . @2.50

BAKER STREET: GRAPHITTI

Caliber

1 `Elementary, My Dear'. 2.50

BALANCE OF POWER

MU Press, 1990–91

1 thru 4 . . . . @2.50

BALLAD OF UTOPIA

Black Daze, 2000

1 by B.Buchanan & M.Hoffman . . . 3.00
2 thru 5 . . . . @3.00
TPB Vol. 1 . . . . 9.00

Antimatter/Hoffman International, 2003

7 thru 8 . . . . @3.00

BANDY MAN, THE

Caliber, 1996

1 SPr,CAd 3.00
2 SPr,CAd,JIT 3.00
3 SPr,CAd,JIT, conclusion. 3.00

BANANA FISH

Viz Communications, 1998

TPB by Akimi Yoshida 16.00
TPB Vol. 2 . . . . 16.00

B & W PUB.

TPB Vol. 3 . . . . 16.00
TPB Vol. 4 . . . . 16.00
TPB Vol. 5 . . . . 16.00
TPB Vol. 6 . . . . 16.00
TPB Vol. 7 . . . . 16.00

BAOH
Viz, 1990
1 thru 8 . . . . @3.00
GN V:Juda Laboratory 15.00

BARABBAS
Slave Labor, 1986
1 . . . . 4.50
2 thru 4 . . . . @2.25

BARBARIANS
ACG Comics
1 by Jeff Jones, Mike Kaluta,
   Wayne Howard 3.00
2 WW 3.00

BARBARIC TALES
Pyramid
1 . . . . 3.00
2 and 3 . . . . @2.25

BASEBALL SUPERSTARS
Revolutionary, 1991–93
1 Nolan Ryan 2.50
2 Bo Jackson 2.50
3 Ken Griffey Jr. 2.50
4 Pete Rose 2.50
5 Rickey Henderson 2.50
6 Jose Canseco 2.50
7 Cal Ripkin Jr. 2.50
8 Carlton Fisk 2.50
9 George Brett 2.50
10 Darryl Strawberry 2.50
11 Frank Thomas 2.50
12 Ryne Sandberg (color) 2.75
13 Kirby Puckett (color) 2.75
14 Roberto & Sandy Alomar (color). 2.75
15 Roger Clemens (color) 2.75
16 Mark McGuire 3.00
17 Avery & Glavin 3.00
18 Dennis Eckersley 3.00
19 Dave Winfield 3.00
20 Jim Abbott 3.00

BASTARD!!
Viz Communications, 2001
1 thru 2 Wizard . . . . @4.00
3 thru 5 Ninja . . . . @4.00
6 thru 8 Fighter . . . . @4.00
9 thru 10 Vampire . . . . @4.00
11 thru 12 Empress . . . . @4.00
13 thru 15 Empress . . . . @4.00
TPB Vol. 1 thru Vol. 3 . . . . @15.00
TPB Vol. 4 thru Vol. 5 . . . . @13.00

BATTLE ANGEL ALITA
Viz, 1992
1 I:Daisuka,Alita 8.00
2 Alita becomes warrior 6.00
3 A:Daiuke,V:Cyborg. 4.00
4 Alita/Cyborg,A:Makaku 4.00
5 The Bounty Hunters' Bar 4.00
6 Confrontation 4.00
7 Underground Sewers,A:Fang . . . 3.00
8 & 9 . . . . @2.75
Part Two, 1993
1 V:Zapan 3.00
2 V:Zapan 3.00
3 F:Ido. 2.75
4 thru 7 V:Zapan . . . . @2.75

TPB Killing Angel 16.00
Part Three, 1993
1 thru 5 . . . . @2.75
6 . . . . 5.00
7 thru 13 . . . . @2.75
Part Four, 1994
1 thru 7 . . . . @2.75
Part Five, 1995
1 thru 6 . . . . @2.75
7 . . . . 3.00
Part Six, 1995–96
1 thru 8 YuK . . . . @3.00
TPB Angel of Chaos 16.00
Part Seven, 1996
1 thru 8 YuK . . . . @3.00

Battle Angel Alita, Part Eight #5
© *Viz Communications*

Part Eight, 1997
1 thru 9 YuK . . . . @3.00
TPB Vol. 2 Tears of an Agnel. 16.00
TPB Vol. 4 Angel of Victory 16.00
TPB Vol. 5 . . . . 16.00
TPB Vol. 6 Angel of Death 16.00
TPB Vol. 7 Angel of Chaos 16.00
TPB Vol. 8 Fallen Angel 16.00
TPB Vol. 9 Angel's Ascension 17.00

BATTLE ANGEL ALITA: LAST ORDER
Viz Communicatons, 2002
Part 1
1 by Yukito Kishiro 3.00
2 thru 6 . . . . @3.00
GN Vol. 1 . . . . 10.00
GN Vol. 2 thru 5 . . . . @10.00
TPB Vol. 3 Killing Angel 16.00
TPB Vol. 5 Angle of Redemption . . 16.00

BATTLE ARMOR
Eternity, 1988
1 thru 4 . . . . @2.00

BATTLE BEASTS
Blackthorne, 1988
1 thru 4 . . . . @2.25

BATTLE GIRLZ
Antarctic Press, 2002
1 by Rod Espinosa 3.00
2 thru 6 . . . . @3.00

BATTLEGROUND EARTH
Best Comics, 1996
1 . . . . 2.50
2 . . . . 2.50
3 `Destiny Quest: The Vengeance'
   concl. 2.50
4 V:Conjura. 2.50
5 `The Pit of Black Death'. 2.50

BATTLE POPE
Funk-O-Tron, 2000
1 . . . . 3.00
2 thru 4 . . . . @3.00
Spec.#1 Shorts. 5.00
Spec.#2 Shorts. 5.00
Spec.#3 Shorts. 3.00
Spec.#1 Christmas Popetacular . . . 5.00
TPB Vol. 1 . . . . 13.00
TPB Vol. 2 . . . . 13.00
TPB Saint Michael (2001) 13.00

BATTLE POPE MAYHEM
Funk-O-Tron, 2001
1 (of 2) 3.00
2 . . . . 3.00

BATTLE POPE PRESENTS: SAINT MICHAEL
Funk-O-Tron, 2001
1 (of 3) 3.00
2 & 3 . . . . @3.00

BATTLE POPE: WRATH OF GOD
Funk-O-Tron, 2002
1 (of 3) by R.Kirkman & T.Moore . . 3.50
2 thru 3 . . . . @3.50

BATTLESTAR BLACK & WHITE
Realm Press, 2000
1-shot Battlestar Galactica. 2.99

BATTLETECH
Blackthorne, 1987
(Prev. Color)
7 thru 12 . . . . @2.25
Ann.#1 . . . . 4.50

BATTRON
NEC
1 WWII story 2.75
2 WWII contd. 2.75

BEAR
Amaze Ink/SLG, 2003
1 by Jamie Smart 2.95
2 thru 6 . . . . @2.95
TPB Vol. 1 Immortal. 14.95

BEAST WARRIOR OF SHAOLIN
Pied Piper, 1987
1 thru 5 . . . . @2.25

THE BEATLES EXPERIENCE
Revolutionary, 1991
1 Beatles 1960's 3.00

2 Beatles 1964-1966. . . . . 2.50
3 . . . . 2.50
4 Abbey Road, Let it be 2.50
5 The Solo Years 2.50
6 Paul McCartney & Wings. 2.50
7 The Murder of John Lennon 2.50
8 To 1992, final issue 2.50

BECK AND CAUL
Gauntlet, 1994
1 I:Beck and Caul 3.00
2 thru 6 . . . . @3.00
Ann.#1 A Single Step. 3.50

BENZINE
Antarctic Press, 2000
1 manga, by Ben Dunn. 5.00
2 thru 7 . . . . @5.00

BERLIN
Drawn & Quarterly, 1999
1 by Jason Lutes 3.00
2 thru 8 . . . . @3.00
9 thru 11 . . . . @3.50
TPB Book One. 16.00

BERZERKER
Gauntlet (Caliber), 1993
1 thru 6 . . . . @3.00

BEST OF THE WEST
AC Comics, 1998
1 F:Durango Kid 5.00
2 F:The Haunted Horseman. 5.00
3 F:The Haunted Horseman. 5.00
4 F:Roy Rogers, 44-pg. 6.00
5 F:Durango Kid 6.00
6 F:Durango Kid 6.00
7 F:Monte Hale. 6.00
8 . . . . 6.00
9 F:Sunset Carson 6.00
10 F:Durango Kid. 6.00
11 F:Black Diamond. 6.00
12 F:Latigo Kid. 6.00
13 F:The Durango Kid 6.00
14 F:Haunted Horseman 6.00
15 F:Roy Rogers 6.00
16 O:The Whip. 6.00
17 F:Lone Ranger 6.00
18 F:Black Bull. 6.00
19 F:Rocky Lane 6.00
20 F:Durango Kid. 6.00
21 F:Masked Marvel 6.00
22 F:Ken Maynard 6.00
23 F:Freaks of Fear. 6.00
24 F:Redmask, Black Phantom 6.00
25 FF(c),F:Haunted horsemen 6.00
26 F:Lazo Kid, Lemonade Kid 6.00
27 F:Roy Rogers 6.00
28 F:Red Mask 6.00
29 F:Jim Bowie 6.00
30 F:The Durango Kid 6.00
31 F:Haunted Horseman 6.00
32 F:Haunted Horseman 6.00
33 F:Zorro 7.00
34 Roy Rogers. 7.00
35 The Haunted Horseman 7.00
36 Gene Autry 7.00
37 Origins Issue. 7.00
38 Durango Kid 7.00
39 Roy Rogers. 6.95
40 Redmask. 6.95
41 The Haunted Horseman 6.95
42 Black Diamond 5.95
43 The Haunted Horseman 6.95
44 The Hooded Horseman 6.95
45 The Haunted Horsean 6.95

BETHANY THE VAMPFIRE
Brainstorm, 1997
0 O:Bethany 3.00
1 by Holly Galightly. 3.00
1a luxury edition 5.00
2 & 3 . . . . @3.00

BETTIE PAGE THE '50s RAGE
Illustration Studio, 2001
1 revised edition, Steve Woron. . . . 3.25
2 all pin-up layout 3.25
2 tame cover. 3.25
Ann.#1 revised. 3.25

BEYOND MARS
Blackthorne
1 thru 5 . . . . @2.25

BIGGER
Free Lunch Comics, 1998
Spec.#1 . . . . 3.50
1 (of 4) The Devil's Concubine 3.00
2 Devil's Concubine,pt.2 . . . . 3.00
3 Devil's Concubine,pt.3 . . . . 3.00
4 Devil's Concubine,pt.4 . . . . 3.00

BIG NUMBERS
Mad Love
1 BSz,AMo(s) 6.00
2 BSz,AMo(s) 5.50

BIG O, THE
Viz Communications, 2002
Part 1
1 (of 5) by Hitoshi Ariga 3.50
2 thru 5 . . . . @3.50
Part 2
1 (of 4) by Hitoshi Ariga 3.50
2 thru 4 . . . . 3.50
Part 3
1 (of 4) by Hitoshi Ariga 3.50
2 thru 4 . . . . @3.50
TPB Vol. 1 . . . . 16.00
Part 4
1 (of 4) by Hitoshi Ariga 3.50
2 thru 4 . . . . @3.50
TPB Vol. 2 thru Vol. 6. . . . . @10.00

Bill the Bull: Burnt Cain
© Boneyard

BILL THE BULL: BURNT CAIN
Boneyard, 1992
1 I:Bill the Bull 3.00
2 & 3 For Hire . . . . @3.00

BILL THE BULL: ONE SHOT, ONE BOURBON, ONE BEER
Boneyard, 1994
1 . . . . 3.00
2 . . . . 3.00

BILLY DOGMA
Millennium, 1997
1 by Dean Haspiel 3.00
1a signed print edition 5.00
2 . . . . 3.00
3 . . . . 3.00
4 They Found A Sawed-Off in
   My Afro 3.00

BILLY NGUYEN PRIVATE EYE
Caliber, 1990
1 . . . . 2.25
1a 2nd printing 2.25
2 thru 6 . . . . @2.25

BIO-BOOSTER ARMOR GUYVER
Viz Communications
Part One, 1993
1 by Yoshiki Takaya 4.00
2 thru 12 . . . . @3.00
TPB Vol. 1 rep.Part One,#1–#6 . . 16.00
TPB Vol. 2 Revenge of Chronos . . 16.00
Part Two, 1994–95
1 F:Sho 2.75
2 thru 7 . . . . @2.75
TPB Vol. 3 Dark Masters 16.00
Part Three, 1995
1 Sho Unconscious. 2.75
2 thru 7 . . . . @2.75
TPB Vol. 4 Escape From Chronos. 16.00
Part Four, 1995–96
1 thru 7 . . . . @3.00
TPB Vol. 5 Guyver Reborn 16.00
Part Five, 1996
1 thru 7 . . . . @3.00
TPB Vol. 6 Heart of Chronos 16.00
Part Six, 1996–97
1 thru 6 by Yoshiki Takaya . . . . . @3.00
TPB Vol. 7 Armageddon 16.00

BIRTHDAY BOY, THE
Beetlebomb Books, 1997
1 by Jason Lethcoe 3.00
2 . . . . 3.00
3 . . . . 3.00
4 16-pg. 3.00
VOL 2
1 16-pg. 3.00
TPB 56 pg. 8.00

BIZARRE HEROES
Kitchen Sink, 1990
1 DSs, parody 2.50
Fiasco Comics
1 DSs, reprint 3.00

All comics prices listed are for *Near Mint* condition.

[Original] BLACK CAT
Recollections, 1991
4 rep.. . . . . 2.25
5 A:Ted Parrish 2.25
6 50th Anniv. Issue 2.25
7 rep.. . . . . 2.25

BLACK AND WHITE
Viz Communications, 1999
1 (of 5) by Taiyo Matsumoto 3.25
2 thru 5 . . . . @3.25
TPB Vol. 1 216-pg.. . . . . 16.00
TPB Vol. 2 208-pg.. . . . . 16.00
TPB Vol. 3 208-pg.. . . . . 16.00

BLACKENED
Enigma
1 V:Killing Machine 3.00
2 V:Killing Machine 3.00
3 Flaming Altar 3.00

BLACK HOLE
Kitchen Sink, 1995
1 by Charles Burns 3.50
1 new printing 4.50
2 . . . . 3.50
3 . . . . 3.50
3 2nd printing 4.50
Fantagraphics Books, 2000
5 by Charles Burns 4.00
6 . . . . 4.50
7 . . . . 4.50
8 . . . . 4.50
9 . . . . 4.50

BLACK JACK
Viz Communications, 1996
GN by Osamu Tezuka 16.00
GN Vol 2 Two-Fisted Surgeon. . . . 16.00
Spec. Operation Down Under 3.50
Spec. Under the Knife 3.25

BLACK KISS
Vortex, 1988
1 HC,Adult 7.00
1a 2nd printing 4.00
1b 3rd printing. 2.25
2 HC 6.00
2a 2nd printing 3.00
3 HC 5.00
4 HC 4.00
5 & 6 HC . . . . @2.25
7 thru 12 HC . . . . @2.25

BLACKMASK
Eastern Comics, 1988
1 thru 6 . . . . @2.25

BLACK MIST
Caliber Core, 1998
1 by James Pruett & Mike Perkins,
   Blood of Kali,pt.1 . . . . 3.00
1a variant MV(c) 3.00
1b variant Jordan Raskin(c) 3.00
1c variant GyD(c) 3.00
1d premium edition, signed 10.00
2 thru 5 Blood of Kali,pt.2–pt.5 . . @3.00
Spec. Dawn of Armageddon, Blood
   of Kali,pt.6 & pt.7, 48-pg.. . . . . . 4.00

BLACK SCORPION
Special Studio, 1991
1 Knight of Justice 2.75
2 A Game for Old Men 2.75
3 Blackmailer's Auction. 2.75

BLACKTHORNE 3 in 1
Blackthorne, 1987
1 & 2 . . . . @2.25

BLACK ZEPPELIN
Renegade, 1985
1 GD 2.50
2 thru 6 GD . . . . @2.25

BLADE OF SHURIKEN
Eternity, 1987
1 thru 8 . . . . @2.25

BLAIR WITCH PROJECT
Oni Press, 1999
Spec. Movie adapt. 3.00

BLAIR WITCH CHRONICLES
Oni Press, 2000
1 (of 4) by Jen Van Meter
   & Guy Davis 3.00
2 thru 4 . . . . @3.00
TPB Rep.. . . . . 16.00

BLIND FEAR
Eternity
1 thru 4 . . . . @2.25

BLONDE AVENGER
Blonde Avenger Comics, 1998
25 flip-book, Full Metal Corset. . . . 4.00
27 Full Metal Corset,pt.2 . . . . 4.00
Spec. Short Blonde Girl with
   the Two Big Boobs 4.00

BLONDE AVENGER: DANGEROUS CONCLUSIONS
Brainstorm, 1997
1 V:Victor Von Fuchs 3.00
1a photo deluxe cover 4.00
2 . . . . 3.00
2a photo deluxe cover 4.00

BLOOD & ROSES ADVENTURES
Knight Press, 1995
1 F:Time Agents 3.00
2 F:Time Agents 3.00
3 Search for Time Agents 3.00
4 Time Adventures 3.00
TPB Vol. 1 . . . . 13.00
TPB Art of Blood & Roses 15.00

BLOOD 'N' GUTS
Aircel, 1990
1 thru 3 . . . . @2.50

BLOODBROTHERS
Eternity
1 thru 4 . . . . @2.25

BLOOD IS THE HARVEST
Eclipse, 1992
1 I:Nikita,Milo 4.50
2 V:M'Raud D:Nikita? 2.50
3 Milo captured. 2.50
4 F:Nikita/Milo 2.50

BLOOD JUNKIES
Eternity, 1991
1 Vampires on Capitol Hill 2.50
2 final issue. 2.50

BLOODLETTING
Fantaco
1 A Shilling for a Redcoat 3.00
2 . . . . 3.00
3 Flee 3.00
4 thru 10 (of 11) by Chynna
   Clugston. . . . . @4.00

Blood of Dracula #18
© Apple

BLOOD OF DRACULA
Apple, 1987–90
1 thru 7 . . . . @3.00
8 thru 14 . . . . @3.00
15 with Record & Mask 4.00
16 . . . . 5.00
17 thru 20 . . . . @4.50

BLOOD OF THE INNOCENT
Warp Graphics, 1986
1 thru 4 . . . . @2.50

BLOODSHED
Damage, 1993
1 Little Brother 3.00
1a Commemorative issue. 4.00
1b Encore edition, gold foil(c). 3.50
2 Little Brother 3.00
3 O:Bloodshed 3.00
3 `The Wastelands,' cont. 3.50
4 The City 3.50
5 the end is near. 3.50
6 . . . . 3.50
7 Lies, concl.. . . . . 3.50
`M' 3.50
`M' deluxe 5.00
Spec. Lunatics Fringe 3.50
Spec. Lies Epilogue, final issue. . . . 3.50
Spec. Chris Mass #1 . . . . 3.50
Spec. Requiem 3.50

BLOODTHIRSTY PIRATE TALES
Black Swan Press, 1995
1 . . . . 2.50

2	2.50
3	2.50
4 'Blockade of Charleston Harbor'	2.50
5 'The Queen Anne's Revenge'	2.50
6 Blackhand's Party	2.50
7 Battle of Ocracoke Inlet	3.00
8 final issue	3.00

BLOODWING
Eternity, 1988
1 thru 5	@2.25

BLOODY SCHOOL
Curtis Comics, 2002
Vol. 1 Manga
1 by S.Yang & K. Yoo	3.00
2 thru 5	@3.00

BLUDGEON
Aardwolf, 1997
1 by JPi & David Chylsetk	3.00
2 'Alise in Wonderland'	3.00
3 'Seeing Red'	3.00

BLUE BULLETEER
AC Comics, 1989
1	2.25

BLUE MONDAY:
ABSOLUTE BEGINNERS
Oni Press, 2000
1 (of 4)	3.00
2 thru 4	@3.00
Spec. Nobody's Fool	3.00
Spec. Lovecats (2002)	3.00
Spec. Dead Man's Party (2002)	3.00

BLUE MONDAY:
THE KIDS ARE ALRIGHT
Oni Press, 2000
1 by Chynna Clugston-Major	3.00
2	3.00
3 concl.	3.00

BLUE MONDAY:
PAINTED MOON
Oni Press 2004
1 (of 4)	3.00
2 thru 4	@3.00

BOGIE MAN: CHINATOON
Atomeka
1 I:Francis Claine	3.00
2 F:Bogie Man	3.00
3 thru 4 F:Bogie Man	3.00

BOGIE MAN:
MANHATTEN PROJECT
Apocalypse
1-shot D.Quale Assassination Plot	4.00

BONAFIDE
Bonafide Productions
1 F:Doxie 'th Mutt	3.50
2 F:Doxie 'th Mutt	3.50
3 F:Doxie 'th Mutt	3.50

BONE
Cartoon Books, 1991
1 by Jeff Smith,I:Bone	80.00
1a 2nd printing	10.00

1b 3rd Printing	8.00
2 JSi,I:Thorn	45.00
2a 2nd printing	7.00
3 JSi	35.00
3a 2nd printing	5.00
4 JSi	22.00
5 JSi,I	20.00
6 JSi	20.00
7 JSi	15.00
8 JSi,The Great Cow Race,pt.1	9.00
9 JSi,The Great Cow Race,pt.2	8.00
1c thru 9a later printings	@3.00
10 JSi,The Great Cow Race,pt.3	8.00
11 JSi	4.00
12 JSi	4.00
13 JSi	8.00
14 thru 20 JSi,	@4.00
21 thru 27, see Image	
21 thru 27 reprints	@3.00

Bone #13
© Cartoon Books

28 JSi,'Rockjaw: Master of the Eastern Border'	3.00
29 JSi	3.00
30 JSi	3.00
31 JSi	3.00
32 JSi,Bartleby the Rat Creature Cub saga, concl.	3.00
33 JSi,Phoney's fate	3.00
34 JSi,Kingdok Slayer	3.00
35 JSi,Return of Gran'ma Ben	3.00
36 JSi,Return of Rockjaw	3.00
37 JSi,Extravaganza Issue	3.00
38 JSi,48-pg.	5.00
39 JSi,Ghost Circles	3.00
40 JSi,wrap-around cover	3.00
41 JSi,Deep in enemy territory	3.00
42 JSi,	3.00
43 JSi,sacred wall	3.00
44 JSi,rooftop eatery	3.00
45 JSi,Inner Circle of Power	3.00
46 JSi,Rat Creature Army	3.00
47 JSi,Making money	3.00
48 JSi,Surrender or Die	3.00
49 JSi,The usurper Tarsil	3.00
50 JSi,War, Rat Creatures	3.00
51 JSi,Casualties	3.00
52 thru 53	@3.00
54 This Mortal Coil	3.00
55 Final issue	2.95
Spec.10th Anniv. Ed.with PVC fig.	6.00
TPB Bone Reader	10.00
TPB rep.#1-#4	14.00
TPB Vol. 1 Rep.#1-#6	13.00
TPB Vol. 2 Rep.#7-#12	13.00

TPB Vol. 3 Eyes of the Storm	17.00
TPB Vol. 4 Dragonslayer	17.00
TPB Vol. 5 Rock Jaw	15.00
TPB Vol. 6 Old Man's Cave	18.00
TPB Vol. 7 Ghost Circles	25.00
TPB Vol. 8 Treasure Hunters	16.00
TPB Vol. 9 Crown of Horns	16.95
TPB One Volume Edition, 1,300-pg.	40.00

BONESHAKER
Caliber Press
1 Suicidal Wrestler	3.50

BONEYARD
NBM Books, 2001
1 by Richard Moore	3.00
2 thru 4	@3.00
5 thru 15	@3.00
Spec. Swimsuit Issue	3.00
TPB Vol. 1	13.00
TPB Vol. 2	11.00
TPB Vol. 3	9.95

BOOK, THE
DreamSmith Studios, 1998
1 epic fantasy 72pg.	3.50
2	3.50
3 thru 7	@4.00
Ashcan Preview, 24-pg.	5.00
Ashcan Preview, GP(c)	10.00
Handbook, 32-pg.	2.25

BOOK OF BALLADS
AND SAGAS
Green Man Press, 1995
1 False Knight in the Road	3.00
2 thru 4	3.00
5	3.50

BOOK OF THE TAROT
Caliber Tome Press, 1998
1 History/Development o/t Tarot	4.00
1a 64pg.	5.00
1b signed	5.00

BOOKS OF LORE
Peregrine
Spec.#1 fantasy anthology	3.00
Spec.#2	3.00
Spec.#3	3.00
1-shot Shattered Lives	3.00

BOOKS OF LORE:
THE KAYNIN GAMBIT
Peregrine, 1998
0 by Kevin Tucker & David Napoliello	3.00
1 (of 4)	3.00
1a Xavier (c)	3.00
2 thru 4	@3.00

BOOKS OF LORE:
THE SHAPE OF EVIL
Peregrine Entertainment, 1999
1 (of 2)	3.00
2	3.00

BOOKS OF LORE:
THE STORYTELLER
Peregrine Entertainment, 2000
1 (of 3) by K.Tucker & P.Xavier	3.00
2 & 3	@3.00

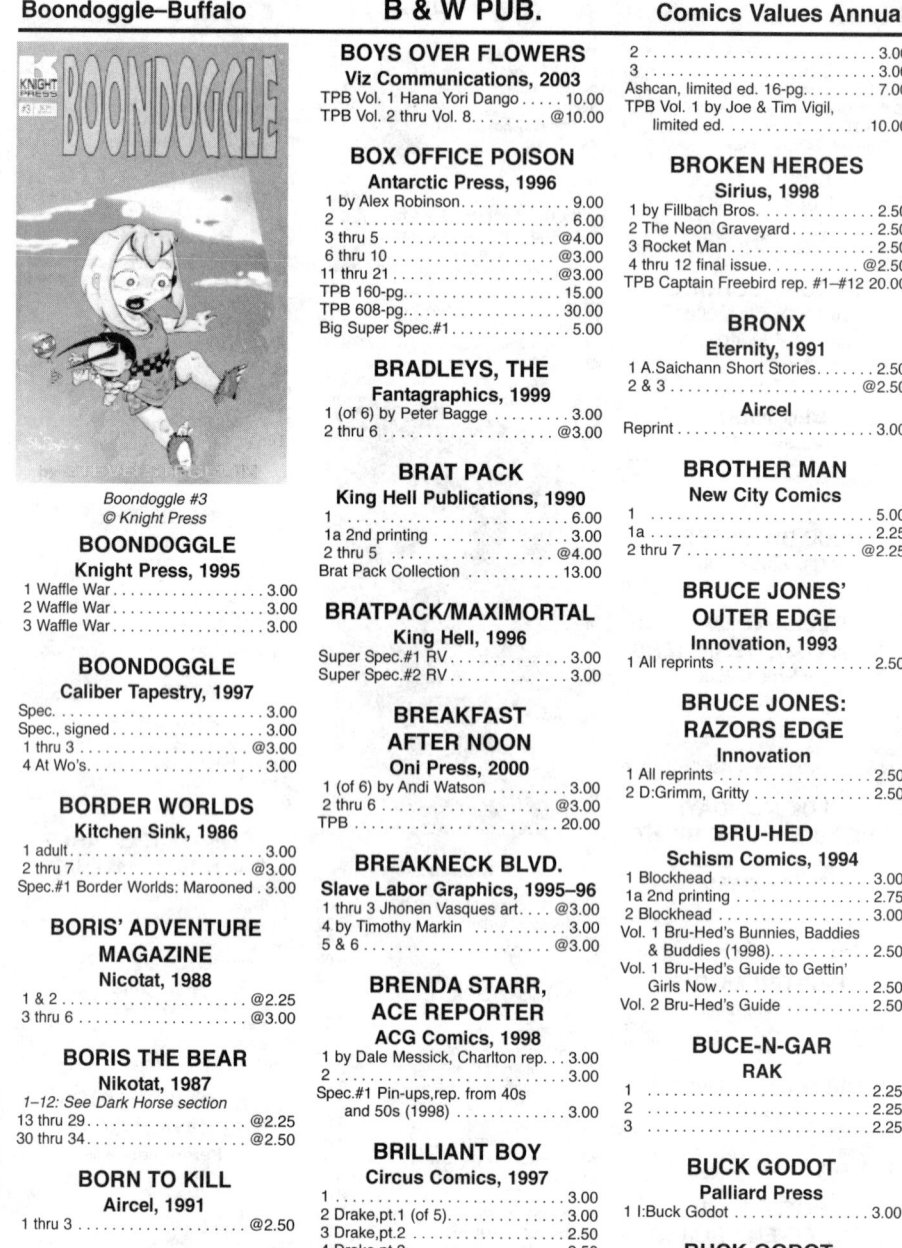

Boondoggle #3
© Knight Press

BOONDOGGLE
Knight Press, 1995
1 Waffle War 3.00
2 Waffle War 3.00
3 Waffle War 3.00

BOONDOGGLE
Caliber Tapestry, 1997
Spec. 3.00
Spec., signed 3.00
1 thru 3 . . . . @3.00
4 At Wo's. 3.00

BORDER WORLDS
Kitchen Sink, 1986
1 adult 3.00
2 thru 7 . . . . @3.00
Spec.#1 Border Worlds: Marooned . 3.00

BORIS' ADVENTURE MAGAZINE
Nicotat, 1988
1 & 2 . . . . @2.25
3 thru 6 . . . . @3.00

BORIS THE BEAR
Nikotat, 1987
1–12: See Dark Horse section
13 thru 29 . . . . @2.25
30 thru 34 . . . . @2.50

BORN TO KILL
Aircel, 1991
1 thru 3 . . . . @2.50

BOSTON BOMBERS
Caliber
1 . . . . 2.25
2 . . . . 2.50
Spec.#1 . . . . 4.00
Note: other issues are flip-books with:
Oz #17; The Searchers #5; Raven
Chronicles #12; & LegendLore #6

BOUNTY
Caliber, 1991
1 `Bounty,"Navarro,'pt.1 . . . . 2.50
2 & 3`Bounty,"Navarro,'pt.2–pt3 @2.50

BOYS OVER FLOWERS
Viz Communications, 2003
TPB Vol. 1 Hana Yori Dango 10.00
TPB Vol. 2 thru Vol. 8. . . . . @10.00

BOX OFFICE POISON
Antarctic Press, 1996
1 by Alex Robinson. 9.00
2 . . . . 6.00
3 thru 5 . . . . @4.00
6 thru 10 . . . . @3.00
11 thru 21 . . . . @3.00
TPB 160-pg. 15.00
TPB 608-pg. 30.00
Big Super Spec.#1 . . . . 5.00

BRADLEYS, THE
Fantagraphics, 1999
1 (of 6) by Peter Bagge 3.00
2 thru 6 . . . . @3.00

BRAT PACK
King Hell Publications, 1990
1 . . . . 6.00
1a 2nd printing 3.00
2 thru 5 . . . . @4.00
Brat Pack Collection 13.00

BRATPACK/MAXIMORTAL
King Hell, 1996
Super Spec.#1 RV 3.00
Super Spec.#2 RV 3.00

BREAKFAST AFTER NOON
Oni Press, 2000
1 (of 6) by Andi Watson 3.00
2 thru 6 . . . . @3.00
TPB 20.00

BREAKNECK BLVD.
Slave Labor Graphics, 1995–96
1 thru 3 Jhonen Vasques art. . . . @3.00
4 by Timothy Markin 3.00
5 & 6 . . . . @3.00

BRENDA STARR, ACE REPORTER
ACG Comics, 1998
1 by Dale Messick, Charlton rep. . . 3.00
2 . . . . 3.00
Spec.#1 Pin-ups,rep. from 40s
and 50s (1998) 3.00

BRILLIANT BOY
Circus Comics, 1997
1 . . . . 3.00
2 Drake,pt.1 (of 5). 3.00
3 Drake,pt.2 . . . . 2.50
4 Drake,pt.3 . . . . 2.50
5 Drake,pt.4 . . . . 2.50
6 Drake,pt.5 . . . . 2.50
7 & 8 The Great Thunder,pt.1–2 . 2.50

BROID
Eternity, 1990
1 thru 4. . . . . @2.25

BROKEN HALO: IS THERE NOTHING SACRED
Broken Halos Comics, 1998
1 by Donald J. Vigil & Tim Vigil. . . 3.00

2 . . . . 3.00
3 . . . . 3.00
Ashcan, limited ed. 16-pg. 7.00
TPB Vol. 1 by Joe & Tim Vigil,
limited ed. 10.00

BROKEN HEROES
Sirius, 1998
1 by Fillbach Bros. 2.50
2 The Neon Graveyard 2.50
3 Rocket Man 2.50
4 thru 12 final issue . . . . @2.50
TPB Captain Freebird rep. #1–#12 20.00

BRONX
Eternity, 1991
1 A.Saichann Short Stories. 2.50
2 & 3 . . . . @2.50

Aircel
Reprint 3.00

BROTHER MAN
New City Comics
1 . . . . 5.00
1a 2.25
2 thru 7 . . . . @2.25

BRUCE JONES' OUTER EDGE
Innovation, 1993
1 All reprints 2.50

BRUCE JONES: RAZORS EDGE
Innovation
1 All reprints 2.50
2 D:Grimm, Gritty 2.50

BRU-HED
Schism Comics, 1994
1 Blockhead 3.00
1a 2nd printing 2.75
2 Blockhead 3.00
Vol. 1 Bru-Hed's Bunnies, Baddies
& Buddies (1998). 2.50
Vol. 1 Bru-Hed's Guide to Gettin'
Girls Now 2.50
Vol. 2 Bru-Hed's Guide 2.50

BUCE-N-GAR
RAK
1 . . . . 2.25
2 . . . . 2.25
3 . . . . 2.25

BUCK GODOT
Palliard Press
1 I:Buck Godot 3.00

BUCK GODOT: ZAP GUN FOR HIRE
Studio Foglio, 1993
1 thru 6 . . . . @3.00
7 by Phil Foglio & Barb Kaalberg . . 3.00
8 finale 3.50
TPB Gallimaufry Vol. 1. . . . . 12.50
TPB Gallimaufry Vol. 2. . . . . 15.00

BUFFALO WINGS
Antarctic Press, 1993
1 & 2 . . . . @2.50

B & W PUB.

BUG
Planet X Productions, 1997
1 . . . . 2.25
2 . . . . 2.25

B.U.G.G.S
Acetylene Comics, 2001
1 . . . . 2.50
1a variant San Diego Con (c) 3.00
2 . . . . 2.50
3 . . . . 2.50
3a variant (c). 2.50
4 . . . . 2.50
5 . . . . 2.50

BULLET CROW
Eclipse, 1987
1 & 2 Fowl of Fortune . . . . @2.50

BULWARK
Millennium, 1995
1 I:Bulwark 3.00
2 O:Bulwark 3.00

BUREAU OF MANA INVESTIGATION
Radio Comix, 2002
1 by C.Hanson & E.Garcia 3.00
2 thru 5 . . . . @3.00

BURGLAR BILL
Dancing Elephant Press, 2003
1 (of 6) by Paul Grist 2.95
2 thru 3 . . . . @2.95
4 thru 5 . . . . @2.95

BURNING BLUE, THE
Crusade Entertainment, 2001
1 BTi 3.00
1a computer gen (c) 3.00

BUSHIDO
Eternity, 1988
1 thru 6 . . . . @2.25

BUZZ
Kitchen Sink
1 Mark Landman (c) (1990) 3.00
2 Mark Landman (c) 3.00
3 Mark Landman (c) (1991) 3.00

BUZZARD
Cat Head Comics, 1990–95
1 thru 9 . . . . @2.75
10 thru 20 . . . . @3.50

CABLE TV
Parody Press
1 Cable Satire 2.50

CADILLACS AND DINOSAURS
Kitchen Sink, 1992
3-D comic 4.00

CALIBER CORE
Caliber, 1998
0 48pg 3.00
1 Gestalt cover 3.00
1a Rain People cover 3.00
1b Spiral cover 3.00

2 F:Al-Haquat 3.00

CALIBER DOUBLE FEATURE
Caliber, 2000
1 48-pg 4.00
2 . . . . 4.00
3 . . . . 4.00

CALIBER FOCUS
Caliber, 2000
1 48-pg 4.00
2 thru 4 . . . . @4.00

CALIBER PRESENTS
Caliber, 1989
1 TV,I:Crow 60.00
2 Deadworld 10.00
3 Realm 4.00
4 Baker Street 4.00
5 TV,Heart of Darkness, Fugitive . . 3.50
6 TV,Heart of Darkness, Fugitive . . 3.50
7 TV,Heart of Darkness,
  Dragonfeast 3.50
8 TV,Cuda,Fugitive 3.50
9 Baker Street,Sting Inc 3.50
10 Fugitive, The Edge 3.50
11 Ashes,Random Thoughts 3.50
12 Fugitive,Random Thoughts 3.50
13 Random Thoughts,Synergist 3.50
14 Random Thoughts,Fugitive 3.50
15 Fringe, F:The Crow 4.00
16 Fugitive, The Verdict 3.50
17 Deadworld, The Verdict 3.50
18 Orlak,The Verdict 3.50
19 Taken Under,Go-Man 3.50
20 The Verdict,Go-Man 3.50
21 The Verdict,Go-Man 3.50
22 The Verdict,Go-Man 3.50
23 Go-Man,Heat Seeker 3.50
24 Heat Seeker,MacktheKnife 3.50
Christmas Spec. A:Crow,Deadworld
  Realm,Baker Street 10.00
Summer Spec. inc. the Silencers,
  Swords of Shar-Pei (preludes) . 4.00
1-Shot 2.50
1-shot Hybrid 2.50

CALIBER SPOTLIGHT
Caliber, 1995
1 F:Kabuki,Oz 3.00

CALIBRATIONS
Caliber, 1996
1 WEI,MCy,`Atmospherics,'pt.1 . . . 3.00
2 WEI,MCy,`Atmospherics,'pt.2 . . . 3.00
3 WEI,MCy,`Atmospherics,'pt.3 . . . 3.00
4 WEI,MCy,`Atmospherics,'pt.4 . . . 3.00
5 WEI,MCy,`Atmospherics,' concl. . 3.00

CALIFORNIA GIRLS
Eclipse, 1987
1 thru 8 . . . . @2.25

CALIGARI 2050
Monster
1 Gothic Horror 2.25
2 &3 Gothic Horror . . . . @2.25

CALL ME PRINCESS
CPM Manga, 1999
1 by Tomoko Taniguchi 3.00
1a variant cover 3.00
2 thru 6 . . . . @3.00
TPB Vol. 1 . . . . 16.00

CAMELOT ETERNAL
Caliber, 1990
1 . . . . 3.00
2 . . . . 2.50
3 . . . . 2.50
4 Launcelot & Guinevere 2.50
5 Mordred Escapes 2.50
6 MorganLeFay returns from dead. 2.50
7 Revenge of Morgan 2.50
8 Launcelot flees Camelot 2.50

Canton Kid #1
© Millennium

CANTON KID
Millennium, 1997
1 . . . . 2.50

CAPTAIN CANUCK REBORN
Semple Comics, 1995–96
1 thru 3 by Richard Comely . . . . @2.50

CAPT. CONFEDERACY
Steel Dragon, 1985–88
1 adult 6.00
2 . . . . 2.50
3 . . . . 2.25
4 . . . . 2.25
4a 2.25
5 thru 12 . . . . @2.25

CAPT. ELECTRON
Brick Computers Inc., 1986
1 . . . . 2.50
2 . . . . 2.25

CAPTAIN HARLOCK
Eternity
1 BDn 3.00
1a 2nd printing 2.50
2 . . . . 2.50
3 . . . . 2.50
4 thru 13 . . . . @2.25
Christmas special 2.50
Spec.#1 The Machine People 2.50

CAPTAIN HARLOCK DEATHSHADOW RISING
Eternity, 1991
1 . . . . 2.75
2 . . . . 2.50
3 . . . . 2.25

B & W PUB.

B & W PUB.

4 Harlock/Nevich Truce. 2.25
5 Reunited with Arcadia Crew 2.25
6 . . . . 3.00

[ADVENTURES OF]
CAPTAIN JACK
Fantagraphics, 1986
1 . . . . 4.00
2 & 3 . . . . @2.50
4 thru 12 . . . . @2.25

CAPTAIN KOALA
Koala Comics, 1997
1 . . . . 3.00
2 thru 7 . . . . @2.50

CAPTAIN STERNN:
RUNNING OUT OF TIME
Kitchen Sink, 1993
1 BWr(c) (1993) 6.00
2 BWr(c) 6.00
3 BWr(c) (1994) 6.00
4 BWr(c) 6.00

CAPTAIN THUNDER
AND BLUE BOLT
Hero Graphics, 1987
1 New stories 3.50
2 Hard Targets 3.50

CARDCAPTOR SAKURA
Mixx Entertainment, 1999
1 by Clamp 3.00
2 thru 6 . . . . @3.00
TPB Pocket Mixx, Vol. 1 thru 5 . @10.00

Tokyopop.Com, 2000
7 thru 25 . . . . @3.00
26 thru 34 . . . . @3.00
GN Vol. 1 Passages. 10.00
GN Vol. 2 Master of the Clow 10.00
GN Vol. 3 thru Vol. 6 . . . . @10.00

CARTOON HISTORY OF
THE UNIVERSE
Rip Off Press
1 Gonick art 2.50
2 Sticks & Stones 2.50
3 River Realms 2.50
4 Old Testament 2.50
5 Brains & Bronze. 2.50
6 These Athenians 2.50
7 All about Athens. 2.50

CASES OF
SHERLOCK HOLMES
Renegade, 1986
1 thru 18 . . . . @2.25
19 . . . . 2.25

CASTLE IN THE SKY
Viz Communications, 2003
GN Vol. 1 . . . . 10.00
GN Vol. 2 thru Vol. 4 . . . . @10.00

CASTLE WAITING
Olio, 1997
1 by Linda Medley 10.00
1a 2nd printing 3.00
2 . . . . 5.00
2a 2nd printing 3.00
3 Labors of Love. 3.00
4 birth of Lady Jain's baby 3.00

5 . . . . 3.00
6 City Mouse, Country Mouse,pt.1 . 3.00
7 City Mouse, Country Mouse,pt.2 . 3.00
Spec. The Curse of Brambly
   Hedge (1996) 3.00
Spec. Curse of Brambly Hedge,
   revised 1998, 96-pg. 9.00
TPB Vol. 1 Lucky Road 17.00

VOL. 2, 2000
1 by Linda Medley 3.00
2 Solicitine,pt.1 . . . . 3.00
3 thru 7 . . . . @3.00
#13 (Vol. 2, #6) 3.00
#14 (Vol. 2, #7) 3.00
#15 thru #16 . . . . @3.00
TPB Vol. 1 Lucky Road 18.00
TPB Vol. 2 Solicitine 18.00
GN The Curse of Brambly Hedge . . 9.00

Cat & Mouse #7
© Aircel

CAT & MOUSE
Aircel, 1989–92
1 . . . . 4.00
2 . . . . 3.00
3 thru 8 . . . . @2.25
9 Cat Reveals Identity 2.25
10 Tooth & Nail 2.25
11 Tooth & Nail. 2.25
12 Tooth & Nail, Demon. 2.25
13 `Good Times, Bad Times'. 2.25
14 Mouse Alone 2.25
15 Champion ID revealed 2.25
16 Jerry Critically Ill 2.25
17 Kunoichi vs. Tooth. 2.25
18 Search for Organ Donor 2.25
Graphic Novel 10.00

CAT CLAW
Eternity, 1990
1 O:Cat Claw 2.75
1a 2nd printing 2.50
2 thru 9 . . . . @2.50

CATFIGHT
Lightning Comics, 1996
1 V:Prince Nightmare 4.00
1a Gold Edition 6.00
Spec.#1 Dream Warrior,
   V:The Slasher 2.75
Spec.#1 Dream intoAction,A:Creed . 3.00
Spec.#1a signed and numbered . . . 8.00

Spec.#1 Escape From Limbo 2.75
Spec.#1a variant cover (1996). . . . 2.75
Spec.#1b platinum cover 6.00
Spec.#1d variant nude cover. 8.00
Spec.#1 Sweet Revenge (1997) . . . 3.00
Spec.#1a variant cover 3.00

CAT-MAN RETRO COMIC
AC Comics
0 by Bill Black & Mark Heike 6.00
1 thru 3 . . . . @6.00
Ashcan #1 I:Catman & Kitten . . . 6.00

CAVEWOMAN
Basement/Caliber, 1994–95
1 . . . . 70.00
1a by Budd Root 2nd printing. . . . 4.00
1b 3rd printing, new cover 3.00
2 . . . . 40.00
2a 2nd printing 3.00
2 3rd printing, new cover 3.00
3 . . . . 35.00
4 . . . . 35.00
5 Cavewoman vs. Klyde,
   Round Two 25.00
6 . . . . 25.00

CAVEWOMAN
Basement Comics 2002
1-shot Movie special edition 8.95
1-shot movie oscar-gold edition. . . . 9.95
1-shot Summer Spec. My Kylde
   has Fleas (2004) 3.50
1-shot Prehistoric Pin-ups #4. . . . . 3.50

CAVEWOMAN
INTERVENTION
Basement Comics, 2000
1 by Devon Massey 3.00
1a variant Budd Root (c). 9.00
1b gold foil alternate (c) 12.50
2 . . . . 3.00
2a variant (c). 9.00
2b Purple foil (c) 12.50
Spec. Klyde & Meriem 1-shot 3.00
Spec. Klyde & Meriem, KDM(c). . . . 9.00
Spec. Klyde & Meriem green foil . . 10.00
Spec. Klyde & Meriem, Beauty,
   Blizzard & the Beast 9.00
Spec. Beauty, Blizzard, gold foil . . 12.50
Spec. Prehistoric Pin-ups 4.50
Spec. Prehistoric Pin-ups gold foil . 12.50
Spec. Prehistoric Pin-ups, Book 2 . 4.50
Spec. Prehistoric Pin-ups 2,lim. . . . 9.00
Spec. Prehistoric Pin-ups 2,
   gold foil 11.50
Spec. Prehistoric Pin-ups 3 . . . . . . 4.50
Spec. Prehistoric Pin-Ups 3 Spec. . 9.00
Cavewoman Cover Gallery, 48-pg. . 4.50
Cavewoman Cover Gallery spec. . . 9.00
1-shot He Said, She Said 3.50
1-shot He Said, She Said special . . 9.00
1-shot Cavewoman The Movie 3.25

CAVEWOMAN:
JUNGLE TALES
Basement Comics, 2000
1 by Budd Root 3.00
1a Frank Cho (c). 11.00
2 . . . . 3.00
2a spec. edition. 9.00

All comics prices listed are for *Near Mint* condition.

CAVEWOMAN: MERIEM'S GALLERY
Basement Comics, 2001
1	3.50
1a Spec. lim. ed.	9.00
1b Gold foil edition	11.50
2 pin-up book	3.50
2a Special edition	9.00
2b gold special edition	11.50
3	3.00
3a	9.00

CAVEWOMAN: MISSING LINK
Basement Comics, 1997
1 (of 4)	3.00
2 thru 4	@3.00
TPB 96-pg.	20.00
TPB 2nd printing	10.00

CAVEWOMAN: ODYSSEY
Caliber, 1999
1 (of 5)	3.00
2 thru 4	@3.00

Basement Comics, 2000
1a front row seat (c) by Budd Root	9.00
1b foil (c)	12.50
2a variant (c)	6.00
2b jungle green foil (c)	12.50
1-shot spec.	3.00
1-shot spec. variant (c)	9.00
1-shot spec. foil (c)	12.50

CAVEWOMAN: PANGAEAN SEA
Basement Comics, 1999
0 Origin issue	3.00
0 variant AAd (c)	9.00
0 special Root (c)	10.00
0 green foil (c)	11.50
0 alternate gold foil (c)	11.50
1 by Bud Root	5.00
1a variant Massey (c)	9.00
1b Root Sea Blue Foil (c)	12.50
1c Cho Sea Blue Foil (c)	12.50
2	3.00
2 Blue Foil (c)	11.50
3	3.25
3 silver foil (c)	11.50
4	3.25
4b red foil edition	11.50
5	3.25
5 red foil edition	11.50
6	3.25
6b red foil (c)	10.00
7	3.25
8	3.25
2a thru 8a special edition (c)	@9.00
Spec. #1 Prehistoric Pin-ups	4.50
Prologue	3.00

CAVEWOMAN: RAIN
Caliber, 1996
1 by Budd Root	7.00
1a 2nd printing	3.00
2	5.00
2a 2nd printing	3.00
3	4.00
3a 2nd edition, new cover	3.00
4	4.00
4a 2nd edition, new cover	3.00
5	3.50
5 2nd edition, new cover	3.00
6 thru 8	@3.00

CAVEWOMEN: RAPTOR
Basement Comics, 2002
1 (of 2)	3.25
1a special edition	9.00
1b red foil edition	11.50
2	3.25
2a special edition	9.00
2b Purple foil (c)	11.50

CECIL KUNKLE
Darkline Comics, 1987
1	2.25

CELESTIAL MECHANICS
Innovation, 1990
1 thru 3	@2.25

CELESTIAL ZONE
Asiapac Books, 2000
1 by Wee Tian Beng	9.00
2 thru 8	@9.00
9 152-pg.	9.00
11 Fantasy on Moonlit Lotus	9.00
12 THe Battle of Maling	9.00
13 Assault on Mt. Dream-Cloud	10.00
14 An Onerous Battle	10.00
15 Capturing Mt. Dream-Cloud	10.00
16 Chi Xue & Xuan Hua injured	10.00

TCZ Studio, 2002
17 thru 25 152-pg.	@10.00

Vol. 2
1	10.00
2 thru 16	@9.50

CEMENT SHOOZ
Horse Feathers, 1991
1 with color pin-up	2.50

CEREBUS
Aardvark–Vanaheim, 1977
0	3.00
0a Gold Ed.	10.00
1 B:DS(s&a),I:Cerebus	325.00
1a Counterfeit	50.00
2 DS,V:Succubus	90.00
3 DS,I:Red Sophia	125.00
4 DS,I:Elrod	75.00
5 DS,A:The Pigts	60.00
6 DS,I:Jaka	60.00
7 DS,R:Elrod	45.00
8 DS,A:Conniptins	45.00
9 DS,I&V:K'cor	45.00
10 DS,R:Red Sophia	45.00
11 DS,I:The Cockroach	30.00
12 DS,R:Elrod	30.00
13 DS,I:Necross	25.00
14 DS,V:Shadow Crawler	25.00
15 DS,V: Shadow Crawler	25.00
16 DS, at the Masque	20.00
17 DS,`Champion'	20.00
18 DS,Fluroc	20.00
19 DS,I:Perce & Greet-a	20.00
20 DS,Mind Game	20.00
21 DS,A:CaptCockroach,rare	40.00
22 DS,D:Elrod	20.00
23 thru 29 DS	@10.00
30 DS,Debts	15.00
31 DS,Chasing Cootie	15.00
32 DS	8.00
33 DS,Friction	5.00
34 thru 50 DS	@6.00
51 DS,(scarce)	12.00
52 DS	5.00
53 DS,C:Wolveroach	7.00
54 DS,I:Wolveroach	9.00
55 DS,A:Wolveroach	8.00

Cerebus #47
© Aardvark–Vanaheim

56 DS,A:Wolveroach	8.00
57 DS	5.00
58 DS	5.00
59 DS,Memories,pt.V	5.00
60 DS,more vignettes	5.00
61 DS,A:Flaming Carrot.	6.00
62 DS,A:Flaming Carrot.	6.00
63 thru 66 DS	@5.00
67 thru 70 DS	@5.00
71 thru 81 DS	@4.00
82 thru 100 DS	@3.50
101 thru 125 DS	@3.00
126 thru 130 DS	@2.50
131 thru 146 DS	@4.00
147 Neil Gaiman, DS	6.00
148 thru 150 DS	@3.00
151 DS,B:Mothers & Daughters, Book 1: Flight,pt.1	4.00
152 thru 155 DS,Flight,pt.2–pt.5	@4.00
151a thru 53a 2nd printings	@2.50
156 thru 160 DS,Flight,pt.6–pt.10	@3.00
161 DS,Flight,pt.11, Bone story	15.00
162 DS,E:M&D,Bk.1:Flight pt.12	3.00
163 DS, Book 2: Women,pt.1	2.75
164 thru 174 Women,pt.2–12.	@3.00
175 thru 186 Reads,pt.1–12	@3.00
187 DS, Book 4:Minds,pt.1	3.00
188 thru 199 Minds,pt.2–13	@3.00
200	3.50
201 thru 219 Guys,pt.1 to pt.19	@3.00
220 thru 231 Rick'sStory,pt.1–12	@3.00
232 thru 265 GoingHome,pt.1–34	@2.50
266 thru 296 LatterDays,pt.1– pt.31	@2.50
297 Latter Days, pt.32	2.25
298 Latter Days, pt.33	2.25
299 Latter Days, pt.34	2.25
300 Latter Days, pt.35, finale.	2.25
Spec.#1 Cerebus Companion	4.00
Spec. Following Cerebus #2	3.95

TPBs
Vol.1 Cerebus, rep.#1–#25	25.00
Vol.2 High Society, rep.#26–#50	25.00
Vol.3 Church&StateI,rep.#52–#85	30.00
Vol.4 Church&StateII,rep.#86–#111	30.00
Vol.5 Jaka'sStory,rep.#114–#136.	25.00
Vol.6 Melmoth, rep.#139–#150	17.00
Vol.7, Flight, rep.#151–#162	17.00
Vol.8 Women, rep.#163–#174	17.00
Vol.9 Reads, rep.#175–#186	17.00
Vol.9 Reads, 2nd printing.	15.00
Vol.9 Reads, signed & numb.	28.00
Vol.10 Minds, rep.#187–#199.	16.00
Vol.11 Guys rep.#201–#219	30.00
Vol.11, 2nd printing	20.00

Vol.12 Rick's Story 17.00
Vol.12 signed 25.00
Vol.13 Going Home, 420-pg. 25.00
Vol.13 deluxe 37.00
Vol.14 Form & Void 25.00
Vol.14a deluxe 37.00
Vol.15 Latter Days 30.00
Vol.15 signed 40.00
Vol.16 . . . . 20.00

CEREBUS
CHURCH & STATE
Aardvark–Vanaheim, 1991
1 DS rep #51 . . . . 2.50
2 thru 30 DS rep #52–#80 . . . . . @2.50

CEREBUS HIGH SOCIETY
Aardvark–Vanaheim, 1990
1 thru 14 DS (biweekly) . . . . @2.50
15 thru 24 DS rep. . . . . @2.50
25 DS rep. #50, final 2.50

CEREBUS JAM
Aardvark–Vanaheim, 1985
1 MA,BHa,TA,WE,A:Spirit. 15.00

CEREBUS REPRINTS
Aardvark–Vanaheim
1A thru 28A DS rep . . . . @2.50
See also: Church & State
See also: Swords of Cerebus

CERES,
CELESTIAL LEGEND
Viz Communications, 2001
1 thru 6 . . . . @3.00
TPB Vol. 1 Aya. 16.00
Part 2
1 thru 6 . . . . @3.00
Part 3
1 (of 4) 3.50
2 thru 4 . . . . @3.50
Part 4
1 (of 4) by Yu Watase. 3.50
2 thru 4 . . . . @3.50
Part 5
1 . . . . 3.50
TPB Vol. 1 Ayuhi 16.00
TPB Vol. 2 Yuhi 16.00
TPB Vol. 3 Suzumi. 16.00
TPB Vol. 4 thru Vol. 9 . . . . @10.00

CHAINSAW VIGILANTE
New England Press
1 Tick Spinoff 3.25
2 & 3 . . . . @2.75

CHAMPION OF KITARA:
DUM DUM & DRAGONS
MU Press, 1992
1 Dragons Secret 3.00
2 Dragons Secret 3.00
3 Dragons Secret 3.00

CHANGE COMMANDER
GOKU II
Antarctic Press, 1996
1 (of 4) by Ippongi Bang. 3.00
2 . . . . 3.00
3 . . . . 3.00
TPB Vol 1, Change Commander
  Goku, rep. #1–#5. . . . . 13.00

CHARLIE CHAN
Eternity, 1989
1 thru 4 . . . . @2.25
5 and 6 . . . . @2.25

CHARM SCHOOL
Amaze Ink/Slave Labor
Graphics, 2000
1 by Elizabeth Watasin 3.00
2 . . . . 3.00
4 Vampire Dragster Dean. 3.00
5 Vampire Dragster Dean. 3.00
6 fight to the death 3.00
7 thru 9 . . . . 3.00
10 . . . . 10.00
TPB Vol. 1 Magical Witch
  Girl Bunny 12.00

CHASER PLATOON
Aircel, 1990–91
1 Interstellar War 2.25
2 Ambush 2.25
3 New Weapon 2.25
4 Saringer Battle Robot 2.25
5 Behind Enemy Lines 2.25
6 Operation Youthtest. 2.25

CHESTY SANCHEZ
Antarctic Press, 1995
1 & 2 . . . . @3.00
Giant Size Spec. #1 (1999) 6.00

CHIBI-POP MANGA
Chibi-Pop (1998)
2 thru 6 64-pg.. . . . . @4.00
VOL 2
1 72-pg.. . . . . 4.00
2 thru 6 . . . . @4.00

CHINA & JAZZ
ABC Comics, 1999
1 RCI. 3.00
VOL. 2
1 (of 3) RCI 3.00
2 RCI. 3.00
Spec. Raising Hell 5.00

CHINA & JAZZ
CODE NAME
DOUBLE IMPACT
High Impact, 1996
1 . . . . 3.00
2 . . . . 3.00

CHINA & JAZZ:
TRIGGER HAPPY
ABC Comics, 1998
1 (of 4) by Clayton Henry 3.00
1a Jazz Bikini cover 4.00
1b China Bikini cover 4.00
1c gold variant cover 6.00
2 . . . . 3.00
2a Playtoy edition 6.00
2b Mercenary edition 6.00
2c Gold edition 6.00
Spec. Trigger Happy Special 3.00
Spec.A manga cover 8.00
Spec. China & Jazz 3.00

CHINA & JAZZ:
SUPERSTARS
ABC Studios, 1999
1 (of 3) 3.00
Spec. China Platinum 3.00

CHIRALITY
CPM Manga Comics, 1997
6 by Satoshi Urushihara, SS(c) . . . 3.00
7 final battle for Shiori's life 3.00
8 thru 18 . . . . @3.00
Spec. Gallery, pin-up book. 4.00
GN Book One rep. #1–#4 . . . . . . 10.00
GN Book Two rep. #4–#8 . . . . . . 10.00
TPB Book Three rep. #8–#12 . . . . 16.00
TPB Book Four, rep. #13–#18. . . . 16.00

CHIRALITY:
TO THE PROMISED LAND
CPM Comics, 1997
1 by Satoshi Urushihara. 3.00
2 thru 4 . . . . @3.00

CHIRON
Annurel Studio Graphics
1 . . . . 2.50
1a 2nd printing 2.50
2 Transported to Doran. 2.50
3 Transported to Doran. 2.50
3a Gold Edition 4.00

CIRCLE WEAVE, THE
Indigo Bean Productions, 1995
1 Apprentice to a God. 2.25
2 Apprentice to a God,pt.2 . . . . . . 2.25
3 Apprentice to a God,pt.3 . . . . . . 2.25
4 Apprentice to a God,pt.4 . . . . . . 2.25
5 Apprentice to a God,pt.5 . . . . . . 2.50

CLAN APIS
Active Synapse, 1998
1 (of 5) by Jay Hosler, F:Bees . . . 3.00
2 F:Nyuki, Zambur 3.00
3 . . . . 3.00
4 . . . . 3.00
5 conclusion 3.00
TPB 160-pg.. . . . . 15.00

CLANDE, INC.
Domain Publishing
1 I:Sam Davidson, Jeremy Clande. 3.00
2 V:Dias 3.00

CLERKS:
THE COMIC BOOK
Oni Press, 1998
1 KSm & Jim Mahfood 12.00
1a 2nd printing 4.00
Spec. The Lost Scene 5.00
Holiday Special 5.00
TPB 11.00

CLIFFHANGER COMICS
AC Comics
1 rep. 2.50
2 rep.. . . . . 2.50

CLINT THE HAMSTER
Eclipse
1 . . . . 2.50
2 . . . . 2.50

COBRA
Viz, 1990–91
1 thru 6 . . . . @3.00
7 . . . . 3.25
8 V:SnowHawks 3.25
9 Zados. 3.25
10 thru 12. . . . . @3.25

COFFIN
Oni Press, 2000
1 . . . . 3.00
2 thru 4 . . . . @3.00
TPB 112-pg. 12.00

COLD BLOODED
CHAMELEON
COMMANDOS
Blackthorne, 1986
1 . . . . 2.25
2 thru 7 . . . . @2.25

COLD EDEN
Legacy, 1995
1 Last City on Earth 2.35
2 V:Mutant Hunting Pack 2.35
3 D6 Tower 2.35

COLE BLACK
Hartberg
1 . . . . 15.00
2 . . . . 10.00
3 . . . . 10.00
4 . . . . 10.00
5 . . . . 12.00
Vol. 2
1 . . . . 3.50
2 & 3 . . . . @2.25

COLONEL KILGORE
Special Studios
1 WWII stories 2.50
2 Command Performance. 2.50

COLT
K-Z Comics
1 . . . . 4.00
2 pin-up by Laird. 6.00
2 pin-up by Henbeck. 2.25
3 thru 5 . . . . @2.25

COMIC BOOK HEAVEN
Amaze Ink/Slave Labor
Graphics, 2001
Vol. 2
1 . . . . 2.25
2 thru 5 . . . . @2.25
6 thru 9 . . . . @2.25

COMICS EXPRESS
Eclipse, 1989
1 thru 4 . . . . @3.00
5 thru 11 . . . . @4.00

COMING OF APHRODITE
Hero Graphics
1 Aphrodite/modern day 4.00

COMMAND REVIEW
Thoughts & Images, 1986
1 rep. Albedo #1-4 . . . . 6.00
2 rep. Albedo #5-8 . . . . 4.00
3 rep. Albedo #9-13 . . . . 4.00

CONDOM-MAN
Aaaahh!! Comics
1 I:Condom Man 3.50
2 F:Condom Man 3.50
3 V:Alien Army 3.50
4 Brother bought back to life 3.50
5 O:Condom-Man (Chris Swafford) 3.50

CONQUEROR
Harrier, 1984–86
1 . . . . 3.50
2 thru 4 . . . . @2.25
5 thru 9 . . . . @2.25

CONSPIRACY COMICS
Revolutionary, 1991
1 Marilyn Monroe. 2.50
2 Who Killed JFK 2.50
3 Who Killed RFK 2.50

CONSTELLATION
GRAPHICS
STG
1 thru 4 . . . . @2.25

CONSTRUCT
Caliber New Worlds, 1996
1 (of 6) PJe,LDu, sci-fi,48pg. 4.00
2 PJe,LDu. 3.00
3 PJe,LDu. 3.00
4 PJe,LDu. 3.00
5 PJe,LDu. 3.00
6 PJe,LDu, conclusion 3.00

CORRECTOR YUI
Tokyopop Press, 2001
1 48-pg. 3.00
2 . . . . 3.00
3 . . . . 3.00
4 . . . . 3.00

CORTO MALTESE:
BALLAD OF
THE SALT SEA
NBM, 1997
1 by Hugo Pratt. 3.00
1 a 2nd printing 3.00
2 by Hugo Pratt. 3.00
3 Escondida 3.00
4 . . . . 3.00
5 . . . . 3.00
6 . . . . 3.00
7 final issue 3.00
TPB by Hugo Pratt, `In Siberia' . . . 11.00
TPB `Fable of Venice' 11.00
TPB `Banana Conga' 9.00
TPB `Voodoo for the President'. . . . 9.00
TPB `Midwinter's Morning' 9.00
TPB `In Africa' 9.00

COSMIC HEROES
Eternity, 1988
1 Buck Rogers rep. 2.50
2 thru 6 Buck Rogers rep. . . . . . . @2.25
7 thru 9 Buck Rogers rep. . . . . . . @2.25
10 . . . . 3.50
11 . . . . 4.00

COUNTER PARTS
Tundra, 1993
1 thru 3 . . . . @3.00

Cosmic Heroes #7
© Eternity

COURTNEY CRUMRIN &
THE COVEN OF MYSTICS
Oni Press, 2003
1 (of 4) by Ted Naifeh. 3.00
2 thru 4 . . . . @3.00
TPB Vol. 1 . . . . 12.00
TPB The Night Things 12.00

COURTNEY CRUMRIN IN
THE TWILIGHT KINGDOM
Oni Press, 2003
1 (of 4) 3.00
2 thru 4 . . . . @3.00
TPB 12.00

COVENTRY
Fantagraphics, 1996
1 BWg, `The Frogs of God' 4.00
2 BWg, `Thirteen Dead Guys
   Named Bob' 4.00
3 BWg. 4.00
4 . . . . 4.00

COWBOY BEBOP
Tokyopop Press, 2002
1 (of 4) by Yukata Nanten. 3.00
2 . . . . 3.00
3 . . . . 3.00
4 . . . . 3.00
Spec. Complete Anime Guide #1. . 13.00
Spec. Complete Anime
   Guide #2–#6 . . . . @13.00

CRAY BABY
ADVENTURES, THE
Electric Milk, 1997
1 by Art Baltazar 3.00
TV Comics, 1997
1 2nd printing 3.00
2 . . . . 3.00
4 Captain Camel 3.00
5 . . . . 3.00
Advent.Spec.San Diego Con
   lim. ed. 5.00
TPB Vol. 1 rep. #1–#5 . . . . 15.00

B & W PUB.

CRAY BABY ADVENTURES: WRATH OF THE PEDDIDLERS
TV Comics, 1998
1 (of 3) by Art Baltazar 3.00
2 . . . . 3.00
3 concl. 3.00

CREED
Hall of Heroes, 1994
1 TKn,I:Mark Farley 25.00
1A Wizard Ace edition rep. 20.00
2 TKn,Camping. 35.00
TPB The Void, Collected ed. 6.00
TPB Deluxe 10.00

CREED
Lightning Comics, 1995
1-shot TKn retelling of #1&#2 . . . . . 2.75
See also: Color

CREED/TEENAGE MUTANT NINJA TURTLES
Lightning Comics, 1996
1 TKn(c) 3.00
2 TKn(c) 3.00
1 Gold Collector's Edition 6.00
1 Platinum Edition. 10.00

CREED: CRANIAL DISORDER
Lightning Comics, 1996
1 . . . . 4.00
1A Previews variant cover 3.00
1B Platinum Edition 6.00
1C signed platinum edition 8.00
2 . . . . 3.00
2b variant cover 3.00
3 . . . . 3.00
3b variant cover 3.00
3c limited edition 10.00

CREED: THE GOOD SHIP & THE NEW JOURNEY HOME
Lightning Comics, 1998
1 . . . . 3.00
1a variant cover 3.00
1b limited edition. 10.00

CREED: MECHANICAL EVOLUTION
Gearbox Press, 2000
1 (of 2) 3.00
1a variant (c). 3.00
1b signed 10.00
2 . . . . 3.00

CREED: USE YOUR DELUSION
Avatar Press, 1998
1 (of 2) by Trent Kaniuga 3.00
1 white leather 30.00
2 . . . . 3.00
2 deluxe 5.00
GN rep. #1–#2 . . . . 4.00

CRIME BUSTER
AC Comics
0 from FemForce 3.00
1 Rep. From Boys Illustrated 4.00

CRIMEBUSTER
ACG Comics, 2000
1 (of 3) F:Dick Tracy 3.00
2 & 3 . . . . @3.00

CRIME CLASSICS
Eternity, 1988
1 thru 11 rep. Shadow comic
  strip . . . . @2.25
12 . . . . 2.25

CRIMSON DREAMS
Crimson
1 thru 11 . . . . @2.25

CRITTERS
Fantagraphics Books, 1986–90
1 SS,Usagi Yojimbo,Cutey 7.00
2 Captain Jack,Birthright. 6.00
3 SS,Usagi Yojimbo,Gnuff 5.00
4 Gnuff,Birthright. 5.00
5 Birthright 5.00
6 SS,Usagi Yojimbo,Birthright. . . . 5.00
7 SS,Usagi Yojimbo,Jack Bunny . . 5.00
8 SK,Animal Graffiti,Lizards 5.00
9 Animal Graffiti 5.00
10 SS,Usagi Yojimbo 5.00
11 SS,Usagi Yojimbo, ... 3.00
12 Birthright II 2.50
13 Birthright II,Gnuff. 2.50
14 SS,Usagi Yojimbo,BirthrightII . . 3.00
15 Birthright II,CareBears 2.50
16 SS,Groundthumper,Gnuff 2.50
17 Birthright II,Lionheart 2.50
18 Dragon's 2.50
19 Gnuff,Dragon's 2.50
20 Gnuff 2.50
21 Gnuff 2.50
22 Watchdogs,Gnuff 2.50
23 Flexi-Disc,X-Mas Issue 4.00
24 Angst,Lizards,Gnuff. 2.50
25 Lionheart,SBi,Gnuff. 2.50
26 Angst,Gnuff 2.50
27 SS,Ground Thumper. 2.50
28 Blue Beagle,Lionheart 2.50
29 Lionheart,Gnuff 2.50
30 Radical Dog,Gnuff 2.50
31 SBi,Gnuffs,Lizards 2.50
32 Lizards,Big Sneeze 2.50
33 Gnuff,Angst,Big Sneeze 2.50
34 Blue Beagle vs. Robohop. 2.50
35 Lionheart,Fission Chicken 2.50
36 Blue Beagle,Fission Chicken . . . 2.50
37 Fission Chicken 2.50
38 SS,double size,Usagi Yojimbo . . 4.00
39 Fission Chicken 2.50
40 Gnuff 2.50
41 Duck'Bill Platypus 2.50
42 Glass Onion 2.50
43 Lionheart. 2.50
44 Watchdogs 2.50
45 Ambrose the Frog. 2.50
46 Lionheart. 2.50
47 Birthright 2.50
48 Birthright 2.50
49 Birthright 2.50
50 SS,Neil the Horse, UsagiYojimbo 5.00
Spec.1 Albedo,rep+new 10pgStory . 2.50

CROSSFIRE
Eclipse, 1987
Prev. Color
18 thru 26 DSp. . . . . @2.25

CROW, THE
Caliber, 1989
1 . . . . 40.00

1a 2nd Printing 5.00
1b 3rd Printing 5.00
2 . . . . 25.00
2a 2nd Printing 4.00
2b 3rd Printing 4.00
3 . . . . 20.00
3a 2nd Printing 4.00
4 . . . . 20.00

The Crow Trade Paperback
© Kitchen Sink

Tundra, 1992
1 reps. Crow #1, #2 . . . . 15.00
2 . . . . 8.00
3 . . . . 10.00
TPB 20.00

CROW, THE
Kitchen Sink, 1996
TPB Flesh & Blood Collection 11.00
TPB The Crow Collection,
  7th printing 224pg 16.00

CROW, THE: DEAD TIME
Kitchen Sink, 1996
1 . . . . 5.00
2 . . . . 4.00
3 . . . . 3.00
TPB Collection rep. 11.00

CROW, THE: DEMON IN DISGUISE
Kitchen Sink, 1997
1 (of 4) by John J. Miller &
  Dean Ormston. 3.00
2 . . . . 3.00
3 . . . . 3.00

CROW, THE: FLESH AND BLOOD
Kitchen Sink, 1996
1 thru 3 . . . . @3.00
TPB rep. 96-pg. 11.00

CROW, THE: WAKING NIGHTMARES
Kitchen Sink, 1997
1 PhH 3.00
2 thru 4 PhH . . . . @3.00

CROW, THE:
WILD JUSTICE, 1996
Kitchen Sink
1 thru 3 . . . . @3.00

CROW/RAZOR:
KILL THE PAIN
London Night, 1998
1 (of 3) JOb,EHr, ... 3.00
1b EHr & Jerry Beck, Director's
   Cut, 40pg. 5.00
1c black leather, signed
   & numbered. 30.00
1d Ministry of Night (c) 5.00
1e Ministry (c) signed 15.00
1f black leather, red foil logos. . . . 20.00
2 . . . . 3.00
2a Ministry of Night (c) 5.00
2b Leather edition. 10.00
3 . . . . 3.00
3a Ministry of Night (c) 5.00
4 . . . . 3.00
4a Ministry of Night (c) 6.00
4b Leather edition. 15.00
4c Leather edition, signed 15.00
Spec. Finale 3.00
Spec. Finale, Ministry (c) 5.00
0 . . . . 3.00
0a Ministry (c). 5.00
0b Red Velvet Elite 20.00
1-shotA Tour Book, cover A 5.00
1-shotB Tour Book, cover B 5.00
1-shotC Tour Book, cover C 5.00
1-shotD Tour Book, ministry edition. 5.00
1-shotE Tour Book, limited black
   leather 15.00
1-shotF Tour Book, signed. 18.00

Crow of the Bear Clan #2
© Blackthorne

Spec. Nocturnal Masque 48-pg. . . . 6.00
TPB Kill The Pain, 150-pg. 16.00
EH! Productions, 1999
Spec. The Lost Chapter 5.00
Spec. The Lost Chapter,
   Elite Fan Ed. 6.00

CROW OF
THE BEAR CLAN
Blackthorne, 1986
1 . . . . 2.25
2 thru 6 . . . . @2.25

CRUSADERS
Guild, 1982
1 Southern Knights, Mag. size . . . 10.00

CRUSHER JOE
Ironcat, 1999
1 by Haruka Takachiho 3.00
2 thru 6 . . . . @3.00
TPB 16.00

CRY FOR DAWN
Cry For Dawn, 1989–90
1 . . . . 90.00
1a 2nd Printing 35.00
1b 3rd Printing 25.00
2 . . . . 40.00
2a 2nd Printing 10.00
3 . . . . 30.00
4 . . . . 20.00
5 . . . . 20.00
6 . . . . 20.00
7 Corporate Ladder,Rock A
   Bye Baby. 15.00
8 Decay,This is the Enemy. 15.00
9 . . . . 15.00
1-shot Subtle Violents,F:Ryder 3.00

CRYING FREEMAN
Viz, 1989
1 . . . . 4.00
2 . . . . 3.50
3 thru 5 . . . . @3.50
6 thru 8 . . . . @3.00

CRYING FREEMAN II
Viz, 1990–91
1 . . . . 4.00
2 . . . . 3.50
3 . . . . 3.50
4 thru 6 . . . . @3.00
7 V:Bugnug 3.00
8 Emu & The Samurai Sword. 3.00
9 Final Issue 3.00

CRYING FREEMAN III
Viz, 1991
1 thru 10 . . . . @4.00

CRYING FREEMAN IV
Viz, 1992
1 thru 3 . . . . @4.00
4 thru 8 . . . . @2.75

CRY FREEMAN V
Viz, 1993
1 Return to Japan 4.00
2 A:Tateoka-assassin 4.00
3 . . . . 4.00
4 A:Bagwana. 4.00
5 V:Tsunaike 4.00
6 V:Aido Family. 4.00
7 V:Tsunaike 4.00
GN:Taste of Revenge 15.00

CRYPT OF DAWN
Sirius, 1996
1 JLi(c) 6.00
1 variant cover 10.00
2 JLi(c) 4.00
3 . . . . 3.00
4 JLi(c) 3.00
5 JLi(c) 3.00
6 Vanguard of Comics 3.00

CRYSTAL BREEZE
High Impact, 1996
1 thru 3 . . . . @3.00
Spec.#1 Crystal Breeze Unleashed. 3.00
Spec.#1 Crystal Breeze Revenge . . 3.00
Spec.#1a gold edition cover 10.00

CUDA
Rebel Studios
1 I:Cuda,Zora,V:Shanga Bai 2.25
CUDA B.C. (Rebel Studios) signed 13.00
Avatar Press, 1998
1 (of 4) by Tim & Joe Vigil 3.50
1b Leather cover. 20.00
1c signed 15.00
1d Royal Blue edition 60.00
2 . . . . 3.50
3 . . . . 3.50
4 . . . . 3.50
1 thru 4 gore (c) . . . . @6.00
0 80-pg. 8.00
0a Gore (c) 9.00
0c prism foil (c) 13.00
0d Royal blue 75.00
TPB Vol. 1, 160-pg. 20.00

CUTEY BUNNY
Army Surplus Comix, 1982
1 . . . . 8.00
2 thru 4 . . . . @4.00
Eclipse, 1985
5 X-Men, Batman parody 3.00

CUTIE HONEY
Ironcat, 1997
1 crime fighting android 3.00
2 . . . . 3.00
3 Wonderful Mask. 3.00
4 thru 6 . . . . @3.00
VOL 2, 1998
CUTIE HONEY '90
1 Sorayama cover. 3.00
2 thru 6 . . . . @3.00

CYBER 7
Eclipse, 1989
1 . . . . 2.50
2 thru 5 . . . . @2.25
Book 2: Rockland, 1990
1 thru 7 . . . . @2.25
8 thru 10 . . . . @2.50

CYBERFROG
Hall of Heroes, 1994
1 I:Cyberfrog. 5.00
1a 2nd printing 2.50
2 V:Ben Riley 4.00
2a 2nd printing 2.50

CYBERFROG
Harris, 1997
1 3rd Anniv. Special 3.00
1a Walt Simonson(c) 6.00
1b signed & numbered 10.00
2 . . . . 3.50
2a variant cover 4.00
3 . . . . 3.50
4 . . . . 3.50
4a signed 10.00
Ashcan Cyberfrog: Amphibionix. . . 6.00
Spec. Cyberfrog Amphibionix(2001) 3.00

CYBERFROG VS CREED
Harris, 1997
1 . . . . 3.50

Cyclops #1
© Comics Interview

1 Creed vs. Cyberfrog, alternate
   edition 10.00

CYBERZONE
Jet Black Grafiks, 1994
1 thru 8 Never-never Land . . . . . @2.50

CYCLOPS
Comics Interview, 1988
1 Mini-series, BSz. 2.50
2 . . . . 2.50
3 . . . . 2.50

CYCLOPS
Blackthorne
1 Mini-series 2.50
2 . . . . 2.50
3 . . . . 2.50

CYGNUS X-1
Twisted Pearl Press
1 V:Yag'Nost 2.50
2 F:Rex and Bounty Hunters . . . 2.50

CYNDER
Immortelle Studios, 1995
1 I:Cynder. 5.00
2 . . . . 3.00
3 conclusion 2.50
Second Series, 1996
1 thru 3 . . . . 3.00

CYNDER/HELLINA
Immortelle Studios, 1996
Spec. 1 x-over 3.00

DAEMONIFUGE:
THE SCREAMING CAGE
Black Library, 2002
1 by Kev Walker 2.50
2 and 3 . . . . @2.50

DAIKAZU
Ground Zero
1 . . . . 5.00
2 . . . . 3.00
3 . . . . 3.00
1a thru 3a 2nd Printings . . . . . . @2.25
4 thru 7 . . . . @2.25
8 . . . . 2.25

DA'KOTA
Millennium, 1997
1 by Pavlet & Petersen. 3.00
1 signed 5.00
1 foil edition. 10.00
2 . . . . 3.00
2 foil edition. 5.00
3 foil deluxe edition. 7.00
3 . . . . 3.00
3a variant cover 3.00
Spec.#1 Orig.Art Edition 10.00

DAMONSTREIK
Imperial Comics
1 I:Damonstreik. 2.25
2 V:Sonix. 2.25
3 V:Sonix. 2.25
4 J:Ohm 2.25
5 V:Drakkus 2.25

DANCE TIL TOMORROW
Viz Communications, 1998
TPB Vol. 1 by Naoki Yamanoto . . 16.00
TPB Vol. 2 thru Vol. 5. . . . . . . @16.00
TPB Vol. 6 thru Vol. 7. . . . . . . @13.00

DANGEROUS TIMES
Evolution
1 MK 2.50
2 MA(c) 2.25
2a 2nd printing 2.25
3 MR(c) 2.25
3a 2nd printing 2.25
4 GP(c) 2.25

DAN TURNER
HOLLYWOOD DETECTIVE
Eternity, 1991
1 `Darkstar of Death' 2.50
Spec.#1 Dan Turner, Homicide
   Hunch, Dan Turner Framed . . . 2.50
Spec.#1 Dan Turner, The Star
   Chamber, Death of Folly
   Hempstead 2.50

DARK ANGEL
Boneyard, 1991
1 by Hart Fisher 2.25
2 . . . . 2.25

DARK ANGEL
Boneyard, 1997
1 by H.Fisher & J.Helkowski. 2.25
2 . . . . 2.25
3 by Hart Fisher & John Cassaday. 2.25
4 The Quiet Demon 2.25
Spec.#1 Dark Angel/Bill the Bull,
   48-pg. (1998). 5.00
Spec. 1999. . . . . 5.00
GN Last Decade Dead Century . . 16.00
GN deluxe 20.00

DARK ANGEL
CPM Manga, 1999
1 by Kia Asamiya 3.00

2 thru 9 . . . . @3.00
10 thru 31 . . . . @3.00
TPB Vol. 1 rep. #1–#5 . . . . 16.00
TPB Vol. 2 . . . . 16.00
TPB Vol. 3 . . . . 16.00

DARK ASSASSIN
Silverwolf, 1987
1 thru 3 . . . . @2.25
Vol. 2
1 thru 5 . . . . @2.25

DARK CITY ANGEL
Freak Pit Productions
1 I:Lt.Michelle Constello 3.50
2 . . . . 3.50
3 Sex Doll is Prime Suspect 3.50

DARK FANTASIES
Dark Fantasy, 1994–97
0 Donna Mia foil (c) 8.00
0 Destiny Angel foil (c) 7.50
1 Jli (c) 9.00
1a test print Jli (c) 12.00
1 2nd printing 4.00
1 signed & numbered 8.00
2 Kevin J. Taylor Girl (c) 4.00
2a foil stamped 3.00
3 JOb Crow (c) 4.00
3a foil stamped 3.50
4 . . . . 4.00
4a foil stamped 3.50
5 . . . . 4.00
5a foil stamped 3.50
6 Angel Destiny. 4.00
6a foil stamped 3.50
7 . . . . 4.00
7a foil stamped 3.50
8 . . . . 4.00
8 Blue cover 3.50
8 Red cover 3.50
8 deluxe foil-enhanced 4.00
9 Destiny Angel (c) 3.50
9a Destiny Angel, red foil (c) 4.00
9b Horror (c) 3.50
9c Horror, red foil (c). 4.00
10 . . . . 3.50
10a red foil (c) 4.00
Spec.#1 Summers Eve Pin-up. . . . 3.00
Spec.#1 foil-stamped 3.50

DARK FRINGE
Brainstorm, 1996
1 . . . . 3.00

DARK FRINGE:
SPIRITS OF THE DEAD
Brainstorm, 1997
1 by Eman Torre & John Kisse 3.00
2 concl. 3.00

DARK ISLAND
Davdez Arts, 1998
1 by Barry Blair & Colin Chan. 2.50
2 thru 4 . . . . @2.50

DARKLIGHT: PRELUDE
Sirius, 2000
1 (of 3) by Teri Sue Wood. 3.00
2 . . . . 3.00
3 concl 3.00

DARK LORD
RAK
1 thru 3 . . . . @2.25

DARK MANGA
London Night
1 Featuring Demonique 5.00

DARK MUSE
Dark Muse Productions
1 with mini-comic 3.50
1a with mini-comic 5.00
2 . . . . 4.00
3 F:Coffin Joe 4.00

DARK OZ
Arrow Comics, 1997
1 (of 5) by Griffith, Kerr & Bryan. . . 2.75
2 thru 5 . . . . @2.75
Spec. Bill Bryan's Oz Collection . . . 3.00

DARK REGIONS
White Wolf, 1987
1 . . . . 2.50

Dark Visions #2
© *Pyramid*

2 . . . . 2.50
3 Scarce 3.00
4 and 5 . . . . @2.25

DARK STAR
Rebel
1 I:Ran 2.25
2 thru 3 . . . . @2.25

DARK VISIONS
Pyramid, 1987
1 I:Wasteland Man 2.25
2 thru 4 . . . . @2.25

DARK WOLF
Eternity, 1988
1 and 2 . . . . @2.25
Volume 2
1 thru 14 . . . . @2.25
Ann. #1. 2.25

DARQUE RAZOR
London Night, 1996
? by Dan Membeila & Albert Holaso,
    Dark Birth 2.25
? necro-embossed edition 10.00
1 thru 3 . . . . @3.00

DAYS OF DARKNESS
Apple
1 From Pearl Harbor
    to Midway. 2.75
2 Pearl Harbor Attack,cont 2.75
3 Japanese Juggernaut 2.75
4 Bataan Peninsula. 2.75
GN 15.00

DEADBEATS
Claypool Comics, 1993
1 thru 13 . . . . @2.50
14 New Ways to Dream. 2.50
15 thru 25. . . . . @2.50
26 by Richard Howell & Ricardo
    Villagran, The Southland
    Family Saga 2.50
27 Christine transformed into
    Predator. 2.50
28. . . . . 2.50
29 forbidden antiquities 2.50
30 V:Dracula 2.50
31 Reconstructing Deadbeats 2.50
32 New generation of Deadbeats . . 2.50
33 Quiet Night in Fear City 2.50
34 Dagger of Deliverance 2.50
35 Deadbeats of Danger Street. . . . 2.50
36 By His Majesty's Request. 2.50
37 Carnival of Goals 2.50
38 HorrorFest begins. 2.50
39 HorrorFest. 2.50
40 HorrorFest. 2.50
41 Guys Night Out. 2.50
42 Dark Dealings 2.50
43 Dodging the Bullet 2.50
44 Town for Sale 2.50
45 thru 50. . . . . @2.50
51 thru 68. . . . . @2.50
TPB Rep. #1–#6 . . . . 13.00
TPB Vol. 2 Tangy Treats, 160-pg. . 13.00

DEADKILLER
Caliber
1 Rep Deadworld 19 thru 21 . . . . . 3.00

DEADTIME STORIES
New Comics, 1987
1 AAd,WS 2.25

DEADWORLD
Arrow, 1986
1 Arrow Pyb 5.00
2 . . . . 4.00
3 V:King Zombie 3.50
4 V:King Zombie 3.50
5 Team Rests 3.50
6 V:King Zombie 3.50
7 F:KZ & Deake, Graphic(c) 3.50
8 V:Living Corpse, Graphic(c). 2.50
9 V:Sadistic Punks, Graphic(c). . . . 2.50
10 V:King Zombie, Graphic(c) 2.50
7a thru 10a Tame cover . . . . @2.25
11 V:King Zombie, Graphic(c) 3.00
12 I:Percy, Graphic(c) 3.00
13 V:King Zombie, Graphic(c) 3.00
14 V:Voodoo Cult,Graphic(c) 3.00
15 Zombie stories,Graphic(c) 3.00
11a thru 15a Tame cover . . . . . . @2.50
16 V:`Civilized' Community 2.50
17 V:King Zombie 2.50
18 V:King Zombie 2.50
19 V:Grakken. 2.50
20 V:King Zombie 2.50
21 Dead Killer 2.50
22 L:Dan & Joey 2.50
23 V:King Zombie 2.50
24 . . . . 2.50

25 (R:Vince Locke) 2.50
26. . . . . 2.50
Caliber
1 thru 11 . . . . @3.00
12 thru 15 Death Call. . . . . @3.00
Spec. Deadworld Archives, rep. . . . 2.50
Spec. Bits & Pieces, rep.
    Caliber Presents #2&#8 . . . . . . 2.25
Spec. To Kill A King,R:Deadkiller . . . 3.00

DEATH ANGEL
Lightning, 1997
1 by J. Cleary & Anderson 3.00
1 variant cover 3.00
1 limited edition A 10.00
1 limited edition B 10.00

DEATHDREAMS OF DRACULA
Apple
1 Selection of short stories 2.50
2 short stories. 2.50
3 Inc. Rep. BWr,`Breathless' 2.50
4 short stories. 2.50

DEATH HUNT
Eternity
1 & 2 . . . . @2.25

DEATHMARK
Lightning Comics, 1994
1 O:War Party. 2.75

DEATH OF ANGEL GIRL
Angel Entertainment, 1997
1 by E.Bell & C.Forrest,F:Michelle . 3.00

DEATH OF BLOODFIRE
Lightning
1 . . . . 3.00
1a variant cover 3.00

DEATH RATTLE
Kitchen Sink, 1995
(Prev. Color)
1 thru 3 . . . . @3.50
4 . . . . 3.00
5 . . . . 2.50
6 Steve Bissette(c) 2.25
7 Ed Gein 2.25
8 I:Xenozoic Tales. 10.00
9 BW,rep. 2.25
10 AW,rep. 2.25
11 thru 15. . . . . @2.25
16 BW,Spacehawk 2.25
17 Rand Holmes(c) 2.25
18 FMc. 2.25

DEATH'S HEAD
Crystal
1 thru 3 . . . . @2.25

DEATHWORLD
Adventure Comics, 1990
1 Harry Harrison adapt. 2.50
2 thru 4 . . . . @2.50
BOOK II, 1991
1 Harry Harrison adapt. 2.50
2 thru 4 . . . . @2.50
BOOK III, 1991
1 H.Harrison adapt.,colonization. . . 2.50
2 Attack on the Lowlands 2.50
3 Attack on the Lowlands contd. . . . 2.50

4 last issue 2.50

DEE VEE
Dee Vee, 1997
1 ECa, F:Alex 3.00
2 ECa 3.00
3 ECa 3.00
4 thru 14 . . . . @3.00
Spec. #1 Life is Cheap. 3.00

DEEP SLEEPER
Oni Press 2004
1 (of 4) 3.50
2 thru 4 . . . . @3.50

DEFENSELESS DEAD
Adventure Comics, 1991
1 Larry Niven adapt. A:Gil 2.50
2 A:Organlegger 2.50
3 A:Organlegger 2.50

DELTA TENN
Entertainment, 1987
1 thru 11 . . . . @2.25

DEMO
AIT/Planet Lar, 2003
1 . . . . 4.00
2 thru 11 . . . . @3.00

DEMON BABY
SQP/666 Comics, 1997
1 by Rich Larson, seq. to Hell
  on Heels 3.00
2 & 3 . . . . @3.00
1a thru 3a deluxe . . . . @10.00
GN Hell on Heels 10.00
GN Hell on Heels, deluxe 20.00

DEMON BITCH
Forbidden, 1997–98
1-shot 3.00
Spec.#1 Demon Bitch vs.
  Angel Girl. 3.00
Spec.#1 Demon Bitch: Devilspawn, by
  Angela Benoit & Nirut Chaswan 3.00
Spec.#1 Demon Bitch: Hellslave,
  Free on Earth cover 3.00
Spec.#1 Demon Bitch: Tales of
  the Damned 3.00

DEMONGATE
Sirius, 1996–97
1 thru 12 by Bao Lin Hum &
  Colin Chan. . . . . @2.50

DEMON GUN
Crusade Entertainment, 1996
1 thru 3 GCh,KtH . . . . @3.00

DEMON HUNTER
Aircel, 1989
1 thru 4 . . . . @2.25

DEMON HUNTER
Davdez Arts, 1998
1 by Barry Blair & Colin Chan 2.50
2 F:Hunter Gordon 2.50
3 . . . . 2.50

DEMONIQUE
London Night, 1997
? by SKy Owens, A:Anvil 3.00

1 by Membeila & Owens. 3.00
2 F:Viper 3.00
3 Mayhem. 3.00
4 Final issue 3.00

DEMONIQUE: ANGEL OF NIGHT
London Night, 1997
1 (of 3) by Skylar Owens 3.00
2 . . . . 3.00
3 final issue. 3.00

DEMONSLAYER: LORDS OF NIGHT
Avatar Press, 2003
1/2 Fire Edition. 6.00
1/2 Ice Edition. 6.00
1/2 Attitude Edition. 6.00
Preview 2.25
Preview variant (c)s. 6.00
1 . . . . 3.50
1a variant (c)s. 3.50
1b wraparound (c). 4.00

DEMON'S TAILS
Adventure
1 . . . . 2.50
2 A:Champion. 2.50
3 V:Champion 2.50
4 V:Champion 2.50

DEMON WARRIOR
Eastern, 1987
1 thru 12 . . . . @2.25
13 and 14 . . . . @2.25

DENIZENS OF DEEP CITY
Jabberwocky, 1988
1 thru 8 . . . . @2.25

DERRECK WAYNE'S STRAPPED
Gothic Images
1 Confrontational Factor 2.25
2 Confrontational Factor 2.25

Descending Angels #1
© Millennium

DESCENDING ANGELS
Millennium, 1995
1 I:3 Angels. 2.25
2 F:Jim Johnson 3.00
3 F:Jim Johnson 3.00

DESERT PEACH
Thoughts & Images, 1988
1 thru 4 . . . . @2.25

DESTINY ANGEL
Dark Fantasy, 1996
1 (of 3) 4.00
1 2nd printing 4.00
1a deluxe 4.50
2 `Sunless Garden'. 3.50
2a foil cover 4.00
2b photo cover 4.00

DESTROY
Eclipse, 1986
1 Large Size 5.00
2 Small Size,3-D 5.00

DETECTIVE, THE
Caliber, 1998
1 by Gerard Goffaux 3.00
2 . . . . 3.00
3 Clutches of the Past 3.00

DEVIL JACK
Doom Theatre, 1995
1 I:Devil Jack 3.00
1a Directors Cut 3.00
2 V:Belegosi 3.00
3 . . . . 3.00

DEVIL'S WORKSHOP
Blue Comet Press, 1995
1 Iron Cupcakes 3.00

DIABOLIK
Scorpion Productions, 1999
VOL. 1
1 Terror Aboard The Karima 6.00
2 Fight Against Time 6.00
3 Crumbs for the Scum. 6.00
4 Family with no morals 6.00
5 & 6 . . . . @6.00
VOL. 2
1 Target: Diabolik 6.00
2 One Crazy Love. 6.00
3 . . . . 6.00
4 Interrupted Game. 6.00

DICK DANGER
Olsen Comics, 1998
1 by W.W. Olsen 3.00
2 F:Red Olga 3.00
3 The Angel Murder 3.00
4 Is Hitler Still Alive? 3.00
5 Nikita, The Cat Girl 3.00

DICKS
Caliber, 1997
1 (of 4),GEn,JMC, ... 3.00
2 thru 4 GEn,JMC . . . . @3.00
TPB GEn,JMC 13.00

DICK TRACY
Tony Raiola, 2003
GN Purple Cross Gang 9.50
GN Large Feature reprint #3–#6 . . @9.50

GN Scottie of Scotland Yard 9.50
GN Kidnapped Princes 9.50
GN Family Affair. 9.50

DICK TRACY
CRIMEBUSTER
ACG Comics, 1998
1 by M.A.Collins & D.Locher 3.00
2 thru 9 . . . . @3.00
TPB rep. (2001) 20.00

DICK TRACY DETECTIVE
ACG Comics, 1999
1 (of 4) by Chester Gould 3.00
2 thru 4 . . . . @3.00

DICK TRACY MAGAZINE
1 V:Little Face Finnyo. 4.00

DICK TRACY
Blackthorne, 1984–89
1 thru 12 . . . . @6.50
13 thru 25 . . . . @7.50
Becomes:

DICK TRACY
MONTHLY/WEEKLY
Blackthorne, 1988
1 thru 25 monthly . . . . @3.00
26 thru 108 weekly . . . . @4.00
Unprinted Stories #3 . . . . 3.00
1 3-D Special 3.00
Spec. #1. 3.00
Spec. #2. 3.00
Spec. #3. 3.00

DICK TRACY:
THE EARLY YEARS
Blackthorne, 1987
1 thru 3, 78-pg. . . . . @7.50
4 thru 6 . . . . @3.50
7 and 8 . . . . @4.00

DICK TRACY
UNPRINTED STORIES
Blackthorne, 1987
1 thru 4 . . . . @3.00

DICTATORS
Antarctic Press 2004
Hitler #1 (of 4) 3.00
Hitler #2 thru #4 . . . . @3.00
Saddam Hussein #1 . . . . 3.95
Saddam Hussein #2 . . . . 3.95

DIGITAL DRAGON
Peregrine Entertainment, 1999
1 by Bryan Heyboer 3.00
2 thru 4 . . . . @3.00

DIM-WITTED DARRYL
Slave Labor Graphics, 1998
1 by Michael Bresnahan. 3.00
2 thru 5 . . . . @3.00

DINOSAURS FOR HIRE
Eternity, 1988
1 . . . . 3.00
1a Rep. 2.25
2 thru 9 . . . . @2.25
Fall Classic #1 . . . . 2.25

Malibu, 1993
#1 3-D special 3.50

DIRTY PAIR
Eclipse, 1988
1 . . . . 9.00
2 . . . . 7.00
3 . . . . 6.00
4 end mini-series 6.00
Vol. 2, 1989
1 thru 5 . . . . @5.00
Vol. 3, 1990
1 thru 5 . . . . @5.00

DIRTY PAIR:
SIM EARTH
Eclipse
1 thru 4 . . . . @4.00

DISCIPLES
Caliber Core, 1998
1 Climate of fear. 3.00
2 . . . . 3.00

A DISTANT SOIL
Warp Graphics, 1983
1 A:Panda Khan 10.00
2 . . . . 5.00
3 . . . . 4.00
4 . . . . 3.00
5 thru 9. . . . . @3.00
Aria Press, 1991
1 F:Seasons of Spring 6.00
1a-2nd to 4th printing 2.50
2 Seasons of Spring,pt.2 . . . . 5.00
3 . . . . 3.00
4 . . . . 3.00
5 thru 8 . . . . @3.00
9 thru 11 Knights of the Angel. . . @3.00
12 thru 14 . . . . @3.00
GN Knights of the Angel, deluxe . . 16.00
GN Immigrant Song rep.#1–#3 . . . 7.00
See Image Comics

DITKO'S WORLD: STATIC
Renegade
1 thru 3 SD . . . . @2.25

DOCTOR
Ironcat, 1997
1 (of 5) by Bang Ippongi 3.00
2 . . . . 3.00
4 . . . . 3.00
5 Pay Back in the City of
     Santa La Paz 3.00
6 final issue 3.00

DR. GORPON
Eternity, 1991
1 I:Dr.Gorpon,V:Demon 2.25
2 A:Doofus,V:ChocolateBunny 2.50
3 D:Dr.Gorpon. 2.50

DR. RADIUM
Silverline
1 . . . . 3.00
2 . . . . 2.25
3 and 4 . . . . @2.25

DR. RADIUM:
MAN OF SCIENCE
Slave Labor, 1992
1 And Baby makes 2, BU: Dr.
     Radiums' Grim Future 2.50

DOC WEIRD'S
THRILL BOOK
1 AW. 2.25
2 & 3 . . . . @2.25

DOCTOR WEIRD
Caliber Press, 1994
1 V:Charnogg 2.50
2 V:Charnogg 2.50

Dogs O' War #3
© Crusade

DR. WONDER
Old Town Publishing, 1996
1 thur 5 . . . . @3.00

DODEKAIN
Antarctic Press, 1994
1 and 2 by Masayuki Fujihara. . . @3.00
3 Rampage Vs. Zogerians 3.00
4 V:Zogerians 3.00
5 F:Takuma. 3.00
6 Dan vs. Takuma. 2.75
7 V:Okizon 2.75
8 V:Okizon 3.00

DOGAROO
Blackthorne, 1988
1 . . . . 2.25

DOGS O'WAR, THE
**Crusade Entertainment,
1996–97**
1 thru 3 (of 3) . . . . @3.00

DOGWITCH
Sirius Entertainment 2002
1 . . . . 3.50
1a signature plate edition 12.00
2 thru 13 . . . . @3.00

TPB Vol. 2 Twisted. 15.00

DOLLS
Sirius, 1998
1-shot science fiction 3.00

Donna Mia #2
© Avatar

DOMINION
Eclipse Manga, 1990
1 . . . . 3.00
2 thru 6 . . . . @2.25

DOMINO CHANCE
Chance, 1982
1 1,000 printed 10.00
1a 2nd printing 3.50
2 thru 6 . . . . @3.00
7 I:Gizmo 7.00
8 A:Gizmo 11.00
9 . . . . 2.50

[2nd Series]
1 . . . . 3.00
2 and 3 . . . . @2.25

DONATELLO
Mirage, 1986
1-shot A:TMNTurtles. 12.00

DONNA MIA
Avatar Press, 1997
0 by Tevlin Utz 3.00
0b leather cover 15.00
0c signed 8.00
1 . . . . 4.00
1a signed 8.00
1b Royal Blue edition 50.00
2 . . . . 4.00
2a deluxe 4.50
3 (of 3) 3.00
3a deluxe 8.00
Giant Size #1 . . . .
Giant Size #1 leather cover 15.00
Giant Size #1 signed 8.00
Giant Size #2 . . . . 4.00
Giant Size #2 Deluxe 10.00
TPB rep. #0–#3 & G-Size #1&#2. 16.00
Spec. Infinity 3.00
Spec.#1 Pin-up (1997) 3.00

DON SIMPSON'S BIZARRE HEROES
Fiasco Comics, 1990
0 thru 7 . . . . 3.00
8 V:Darkcease 3.00
9 R:Yan Man 3.00
10 F:Mainstreamers 3.00
11 Search for Megaton Man 3.00
12 . . . . 3.00
13 House of Megaton Man 3.00
14 Cec Vs. Dark Cease 3.00
TPB Apocalypse Affiliation 13.00

DOOMSDAY + 1
ACG Comics, 1998
1 by JBn rep. Charlton 3.00
2 A Faceless Foe 3.00
3 . . . . 3.00
4 The Hidden Enemy 3.00
5 Rule of Fear. 3.00
6 . . . . 3.00
7 NA(c), final issue 3.00

DORK
Amaze Ink/Slave Labor Graphics, 1993–2001
1 EDo 3.00
2 EDo 3.00
3 EDo 3.00
1 thru 3 2nd printings . . . . @3.00
4 thru 7 . . . . @3.00
8 . . . . 3.50
9 . . . . 3.00
TPB Vol. 1 Who's Laughing Now. . 12.00
TPB Vol. 2 Circling the Drain 14.00

DORK TOWER
Corsair Publishing, 1998
1 by John Kovalic 3.00
2 thru 8 . . . . @3.50

Dork Storm, 2000
9 Angry Young Fan 3.00
10 Road Rules 3.00
11 World of Dorkness 3.00
12 . . . . 3.00
13 . . . . 3.00
14 Gilly, Warrior Princess 3.00
15 . . . . 3.00
16 Trader of the Last Orc. 3.00
17 Halloween in Mud Bay 3.00
17 At the Big Con. 3.00
18 Understanding Games 3.00
19 Junk Food Issue 3.00
20 Featuring Gilly. 3.00
21 20th Century Boy 3.00
22 Daily Carson 3.00
23 Dork Tower Frag 3.00
24 . . . . 3.00
25 . . . . 4.00
26 thru 30 . . . . @3.00
Spec. Lord of the Rings 3.00
Swimsuit Special #1 . . . . 3.00
Best of Dork Tower #1 . . . . 2.25
TPB Vol. 1 Dork Covenant. 16.00
TPB Vol. 2 Dork Shadows 16.00
TPB Vol. 3 Heart of Dorkness 16.00
TPB Dork Tower. 16.00
TPB Vol. 5 Understanding Gamers 16.00
TPB Vol. 6 1d6 Degrees of
    Spearation 16.00
1-shot Wizkids Special. 3.00
TPB Vol. 7 Dork Side of the Goon. 16.00

DOUBLE EDGE DOUBLE
Double Edge
1 thru 3 . . . . 3.50
4 Heroes Inc. Rep.#1-#2 . . . . 3.00

DOUBLE IMPACT
High Impact Studios, 1995–96
1 I: China & Jazz 5.00
1a Chromium (c) variant, signed . . 6.00
1b Rainbow (c) w/certificate 15.00
1c Rainbow (c) w/o certificate. . . . 10.00
2 Castilo's Crime. 3.00
2b silver version 10.00
2c signed, w/certificate 5.00
3 . . . . 5.00
3a Bondage (c) 15.00
4 . . . . 5.00
4a Phoenix (c). 15.00
5 . . . . 5.00
6 China cover 3.00
6a Jazz cover 3.00
6b signed China or Jazz(c). 15.00
6c bondage(c). 10.00
7 & 8 . . . . @3.00
8a variant 8.00

2nd Series, 1996–97
0 . . . . 3.00
1 . . . . 3.00
1a chromium (c) 4.00
1b Chromium variant edition 15.00
1c Christmas (c) 10.00
2 . . . . 3.00
2a Sweedish Erotica(c). 10.00
Spec.#1 Double Impact/Lethal Strike:
    Double Strike, x-over. 3.00
Spec.#1 Double Impact/Nikki Blade:
    Hard Core x-over (1997) 3.00
    Platinum variant RCI(c) 10.00
    Gold Metal variant RCI(c) 20.00
Spec.#1 Raising Hell, RCI,RkB 3.00

ABC Comics, 1998
1 encore 3.00
1a encore, Chicago cover. 6.00
1b encore, San Diego nude cover . 6.00
Spec. Double Impact/Luxura (1998) 3.00
Spec. Vampeurotica edition. 6.00
Bikini Spec. 3.00
Christmas Spec. 3.00
Christmas Spec., gold foil 10.00
Coll.#1 . . . . 3.00
Coll.#1a x-mas. 8.00
Spring Spec.#1. . . . . 3.00
Spring Spec.#1a manga cover. 8.00
Summer Bikini Spec. 1999 . . . . 3.00
Gallery Collection #1 . . . . 5.00
Lingerie Special 3.00

DOUBLE IMPACT ALIVE
ABC Comics, 1999
1 (of 3) Double Impact Alive 2000 . 3.00
1a Double Impact Alive 2000,
    gold foil ed. 8.00
1b Red Leather. 15.00
2 RCI. 3.00
2a Manga cover 8.00
2c silver embossed foil 10.00

DOUBLE IMPACT: ASSASSINS FOR HIRE
High Impact, 1997
1 RCI,RkB 3.00
2 . . . . 3.00

ABC Comics, 1998
1 . . . . 3.00

DOUBLE IMPACT: FROM THE ASHES
ABC Comics, 1998
1 (of 2) RCI 3.00
2 RCI. 3.00
2A variant cover A. 6.00

DOUBLE IMPACT: HOT SHOTS
ABC Studios, 1999
1 RCI 3.00
2 . . . . 3.00

DOUBLE IMPACT MERCS
ABC Comics, 1999
1 (of 3) RCI 3.00
1a deluxe 8.00
2 RCI 3.00
2a deluxe 10.00

DOUBLE IMPACT: ONE STEP BEYOND
ABC Comics, 1998
1 (of 2) RCI 3.00
1a Leather cover 20.00

DOUBLE IMPACT RAW
ABC Comics, 1997
1 (of 3) RCI, adult 3.00
1b Star photo (c) 10.00
1A Wraparound cover A 6.00
1B Wraparound cover B 6.00
2 . . . . 3.00
3 concl. 3.00
3A Variant cover A 6.00
VOL. 2
1 (of 3) adult material 3.00

DOUBLE IMPACT/RAZOR
ABC Studios, 1999
1 (of 3) 3.25
1b Previews exclusive 8.00
1c Manga alt.(c) 8.00
2 . . . . 3.25

DOUBLE IMPACT SUICIDE RUN
ABC Comics, 1998
1 (of 2) RCI 3.00
1b Leather cover 15.00
2 adult material 3.00
Collected edition 3.00
Collected, gold foil 10.00

DOUBLE IMPACT 2069
ABC Comics, 1999
1 Virgin Encore Edition 3.00
1a Deluxe Erotica edition 8.00
Christmas Spec 3.00
Christmas Spec. Previews (c) 8.00

DOUBLE IMPACT X
ABC Comics, 2000
1 . . . . 6.00
1a alternate (c) 6.00
2 . . . . 6.00
2 deluxe, vinyl (c) 20.00
Intro 20.00

DRACULA
Eternity
1 . . . . 3.75
1a 2nd printing 2.50
2 thru 4 . . . . @2.50

DRACULA IN HELL
Apple
1 O:Dracula 2.50
2 O:Dracula contd 2.50

DRACULA: SUICIDE CLUB
Adventure, 1992
1 I:Suicide Club in UK 2.50
2 Dracula/Suicide Club cont. 2.50
3 Club raid,A:Insp.Harrison 2.50
4 Vision of Miss Fortune 2.50

DRACULA: THE LADY IN THE TOMB
Eternity
1 . . . . 2.50

DRACULA'S COZY COFFIN
Draculina Publishing, 1995
1 thru 4 Halloween issue . . . . . . @3.00

DRAGON ARMS
Antarctic Press 2002
1 48-pg 5.00
2 thru 6 . . . . @3.50
Pocket Manga TPB Vol. 1 . . . . . . 10.00

DRAGON ARMS: CHAOS BLADE
Antarctic Press, 2004
1 (of 6) 3.00
2 thru 6 . . . . @3.00

DRAGONBALL
Viz Communications, 1998
1 (of 12) by Akira Toriyama 8.00
2 thru 4 . . . . @5.00
5 thru 12 . . . . @3.00
TPB Vol. 1 . . . . 15.00
TPB Vol. 2 rep. #7–#12 . . . . 15.00
PART TWO, 1999
1 (of 15) by Akira Toriyama 5.00
2 thru 4 . . . . @4.00
5 thru 15 . . . . @3.00
TPB Vol. 3 rep.Vol.2 #3–#8 . . . . . . 15.00
TPB Vol. 4 rep.Vol.2 #7–#13 . . . . . 15.00
PART THREE, 2000
1 (of 14) by Akira Toriyama 3.00
2 thru 5 . . . . @3.00
8 thru 14 . . . . @3.00
PART FOUR, 2001
1 thru 4 (of 10) . . . . @3.00
5 thru 10 . . . . @3.00
PART FIVE, 2002
1 (of 7) 3.00
2 thru 6 . . . . @3.00
7 . . . . 3.00
Part 6
1 . . . . 3.50
2 . . . . 3.50
TPB Vol. 11 thru Vol. 16 . . . . . . @8.00
TPB Vol. 1 thru 7 2nd print . . . . . @8.00

DRAGONBALL Z
Viz Communications, 1998
1 (of 9) by Akira Toriyama 13.00
2 thru 9 . . . . @5.00
TPB Vol. 1 . . . . 15.00
TPB Vol. 2 . . . . 15.00
PART TWO (1998)
1 (of 14) by Akira Toriyama 4.00

2 thru 9 . . . . @3.50
10 thru 14 . . . . @3.50
TPB Vol. 3 . . . . 15.00
TPB Vol. 4 . . . . 15.00
PART THREE (1999)
1 (of 10) by Akira Toriyama 3.50
2 thru 10 . . . . @3.00
TPB Vol. 5, Part 3, #1–#6 . . . . . . 13.00
TPB Vol. 6, Part 3, #7–#11 . . . . . 13.00
PART 4 (2000)
1 thru 13 (of 15) . . . . @3.00
PART 5 (2001)
1 (of 12) 3.00
2 thru 10 . . . . @3.00
TPB Vol. 7 thru Vol. 10 . . . . . . @13.00
TPB Vol. 11 thru Vol. 17 . . . . . . @8.00
TPB Vol. 1 thru Vol. 7 2nd print . . @8.00

DRAGONFORCE
Aircel, 1988
1 DK 6.00
2 thru 7 DK . . . . @4.00
8 thru 12 . . . . @4.00
13 . . . . 2.25

DRAGONFORCE CHRONICLES
Aircel, 1988
Vol. 1 thru Vol. 5 rep. . . . . @3.00

DRAGON KNIGHTS
Tokyopop Press, 2001
1 by Mineko Ohkami 3.00
2 thru 6 . . . . @3.00

Dragontok Saga #12
© Hanthercraft

DRAGONMIST
Raised Brow Publications
1 I:Dragonmist 2.75
2 F:Assassin 2.75

DRAGON OF THE VALKYR
Rak
1 . . . . 2.25
2 thru 4 . . . . @2.25

DRAGON QUEST
Silverwolf
1 TV	15.00
2 TV	7.50
3 TV	6.50

DRAGONRING
[1st Series]
1 B.Blair,rare	110.00

Aircel, 1986
1	3.50
2	2.25
3 thru 6	@2.25

See Also Color Comics

DRAGONROK SAGA
Hanthercraft
1 thru 12	@2.50

DRAGON WARS
Ironcat, 1998
1 by Ryukihei	3.00
2 thru 11	@3.00
TPB Vol. 1	18.00

DRAGON WEEKLY
1 Southern Knights	2.25
2 and 3	@2.25

DREAD OF NIGHT
Hamilton
1 Horror story collection	4.00
2 Json, inc.`Genocide'	4.00

DREAM ANGEL
AND ANGEL GIRL
Angel Entertainment, 1998
1	3.00

DREAM ANGEL:
THE QUANTUM DREAMER
Angel Entertainment, 1997
1 by Mort Castle & Adriana Melo	3.00
2	3.00

DREAM ANGEL:
WORLD WITHOUT END
Angel Entertainment, 1998
1 Dream world cover	3.00

DREAMERY
Eclipse, 1986
1 thru 13	@2.25

DREAMGIRL
Angel Entertainment, 1996
0 by David Campitti & Al Rio	3.00
1	3.00
1 deluxe	6.00
1 Manga cover	5.00

DREAMLANDS
Caliber New Worlds, 1996
1	3.00
2 flip book with Boston Bombers #3	3.00

DREAMTIME
Blind Rat, 1995
1 Young Deserter	3.00
2 Gypsy Trouble	2.50

DREAMWALKER
Caliber Tapestry, 1997
1 thru 4	@3.00
5 by Jenni Gregory, 2nd story arc.	3.00
6 2nd story arc, concl.	3.00

Drifters #1
© Infinity Graphics

DREAMWALKER:
CAROUSEL
Avatar, 1998
0	3.00
1 by Jenni Gregory	3.00
2 conclusion	3.00

DREAMWALKER:
SUMMER RAIN
Avatar, 1999
1 by Jenni Gregory	3.00

DREAMWALKER:
AUTUMN LEAVES
Avatar, 1999
1 by Jenni Gregory	3.00
2 conclusion	3.00

DREAMWOLVES
Dramenon Studios, 1994
1	3.00
2	3.00
3 F:Desiree	3.00
4 V:Venefica	3.00
5 V:Venefica	3.00
6 R:Carnifax	3.00
7	3.00
8 F:Wendy Bascum	3.00

DRIFTERS
Infinity Graphics, 1986
1	2.25

DRYWALL AND OSWALD
SHOW, THE
Fireman Press, 1998
1 by Mandy Carter,Trent Kaniuga	3.00

DUNGEONEERS
Silverwolf, 1986
1 thru 8	@2.25

DUNGEONS & DRAGONS:
BLACK & WHITE
Kenzer & Company, 2002
1 (of 8) by J.Limke & R.Pereira	3.00
2 thru 6	@3.00

DUNGEONS & DRAGONS
IN SHADOW OF DRAGONS
Kenzer & Company, 2001
1 (of 8) The Last of My Father	3.00
2 thru 4	@3.00
5 thru 8	@3.00

DWELLING, THE
Chaos! Comics/Black Label
Graphics, 2002
Ashcan	6.00
1 BnP	5.00
1a premium edition	10.00
1b super premium edition	20.00
1c signed edition	15.00
Spec. #1 script edition	5.00
Spec. #1 premium script edition	20.00

EAGLE
Crystal, 1986
1	3.00
1a signed & limited	5.00
2 thru 5	@2.75
6 thru 11	@2.50
12	2.50
13 thru 17	@2.50

Apple, 1988
18 thru 26	@2.25

EAGLE
Viz Communications, 2000
1 (of 14) The Candidate,112-pg.	7.00
2 Scandal	7.00
3 The Vice-President	7.00
4 New Hampshire	7.00
5 On the Battlefield	7.00
6 King of New York	7.00
7 Pandora's Box	7.00
8 The Debate	7.00
9 Passion	7.00
10 Gone to Texas	7.00
11 Super Tuesday	7.00
12 Suspicion	7.00
13 Illegitimate child	7.00
14 Confession	7.00
15 The Nomination	7.00
16 The General	7.00
17 Coming Home	7.00
18 Frame Up	7.00
19 Fires in the Plain	7.00
20 Someone You Can Trust	7.00
21 End of the Trail	7.00
22 Father & Son	7.00
TPB Vol. 1 424-pg.	20.00
TPB Vol. 2	20.00
TPB Vol. 3 416-pg.	20.00
TPB Vol. 4 512-pg.	23.00

EAGLE: DARK MIRROR
Comic Zone
1 A:Eagle, inc reps	2.75
2 In Japan, V:Lord Kagami	2.75
3	3.00
4	3.00

EAGLES DARE
Aager Comics, 1994
1 thru 4 . . . . 2.25
5 V:Dragon 2.25

EARTH LORE: LEGEND OF BEK LARSON
Eternity
1 . . . . 2.25

EARTH LORE: REIGN OF DRAGON LORD
1 . . . . 2.25
2 . . . . 2.25

EARTH WAR
Newcomers Publishing, 1995
1 and 2 from Newcomers Illus. 3.00

EARTH: YEAR ZERO
Eclipse
1 thru 4 . . . . @2.25

EAT-MAN
Viz Communications, 1997
1 (of 6) by Akihito Yoshitami 3.00
2 thru 6 . . . . @3.00
Vol.1 Full Course Meal,rep.Pt.1 . . . 16.00
PART TWO, 1998
1 (of 5) by Akihito Yoshitami 3.00
2 (of 5) 3.50
3 thru 5 . . . . @3.25
TPB Vol. 2 Second Course 16.00

EB'NN THE RAVEN
Now
1 . . . . 5.00
2 . . . . 3.00
3 . . . . 2.50
4 . . . . 2.25
5 thru 9 . . . . @2.25

EBONIX-FILES, THE
Blatant Comics, 1998
1A TV parody, cover A 4.00
1B TV parody, cover B 4.00

EDDIE CAMPELL'S BACCHUS
Eddie Campell Comics, 1995
1 V:Telchines. 7.00
1 2nd printing 3.00
2 thru 10 V:Telchines 4.00
11 thru 26 ECa . . . . @3.00
27 thru 37 ECa. . . . . @3.00
38 thru 46. . . . . @3.00
47 thru 56. . . . . @3.00
57 thru 60 . . . . @3.00
GN Collected Bacchus, Vol. 1 . . . . 10.00
GN Collected Bacchus, Vol. 2 . . . . 10.00
GN Collected Bacchus, Vol. 3,
   Doing the Islands. 18.00
GN Collected Bacchus, Vol. 4,
   One Man Show 8.50
GN Collected Bacchus, Vol. 5
   Earth, Air, Water & Fire 10.00
GN Collected Bacchus, Vol. 6
   1001 Nights of Bacchus 10.00
GN Collected Bacchus, Vol. 9,
   King Bacchus 13.00
TPB 1001 Nights of Bacchus. 13.50
TPB King Bacchus. 14.00

EDDY CURRENT
Mad Dog, 1987
1 thru 12 . . . . @2.25

EDGAR ALLAN POE
Eternity, 1988
1 Black Cat 2.50
2 Pit & Pendulum 2.25
3 Masque of the Red Death 2.25
4 Murder in the Rue Morgue 2.25
5 Tell Tale Heart 2.25

EDGE
1 . . . . 3.00
Vol 2 #1 thru #3 . . . . @3.00
Vol 2 #4 thru #6 . . . . @2.25

EIGHTBALL
Fantagraphics, 1989
1 . . . . 13.00
2 . . . . 8.00
3 . . . . 7.00
4 . . . . 6.00
1a thru 4a later printings . . . . @3.00
5 thru 8 . . . . @6.00
9 thru 10 . . . . @4.00
11 A:Ghost World. 4.00
12 F:Ghost World. 4.00
13 thru 17. . . . . @4.00
18 . . . . 4.00
19 . . . . 4.00
20 . . . . 5.00
21 48-pg. 5.00
22 . . . . 7.00
23 . . . . 7.00
TPB Orgy Bound, rep. #7–#14 . . . 15.00
TPB Lout Rampage 15.00
TPB Pussey. 9.00
TPB Velvet glove cast in iron. 17.00
TPB Caricature 17.00

ELECTRIC GIRL
Mighty Gremlin, 1998
1 . . . . 3.50
2 thru 9 . . . . @3.00
AIT/Planet Lar, 2002
10 by Mike Brennan. 3.00
TPB Vol. 1 . . . . 10.00
TPB Vol. 2 152-pg.. . . . . 14.00

ELFLORD
Aircel, 1986
1 I:Hawk 5.00
1a 2nd printing 3.50
2 . . . . 3.00
2a 2nd printing 2.25
3 V:Doran 3.00
4 V:Doran 3.00
5 V:Doran 2.25
6 V:Nendo 2.25
Compilation Book. 5.00
(Vol 2), #1 to #24, see Color
25 thru 31 . . . . @2.25
32 . . . . 2.50

ELFLORD
[3rd Series]
Nightwynd
1 . . . . 2.50
2 thru 4 . . . . @2.50

ELFLORD
Warp Graphics, 1997
1 (of 4) by Barry Blair & Colin Chan 3.00
2 . . . . 3.00

3 . . . . 3.00
4 . . . . 3.00

ELFLORD: ALL THE LONELY PLACES
Warp Graphics, 1997
1 (of 4)Barry Blair & Colin Chan. . . 3.00
Becomes:

HAWK AND WINDBLADE: ALL THE LONELY

Elfquest #2
© Warp Graphics

PLACES
2 (of 2) 3.00

ELFLORD CHRONICLES
Aircel, 1990
1 (of 12) thru 8 rep B.Blair . . . . . @2.50

ELFLORD CUTS LOOSE
Warp Graphics, 1997
1 by Barry Blair and Colin Chan . . . 3.00
2 F:Hawk Erik-san 3.00
3 . . . . 3.00
4 all out attack 3.00
5 north to safety 3.00
6 homeward 3.00
7 back to Greenhaven 3.00
8 Greenhaven Siege. 3.00
9 Felines, Nothing More Than
   Felines. 3.00

ELFLORD: HAWK
China Winds, 1998
1-shot by Barry Blair and
   Colin Chan. 3.50

ELFLORE: THE HIGH SEAS
Raw Comics
4 by Barry Blair (500 copies) 5.00

ELFQUEST
Warp Graphics, 1979–85
1 WP 30.00
1a WP,2nd printing 10.00
1b WP,3rd printing 5.00
1c WP,4th printing (1989) 4.00

2 WP	15.00
2a WP,2nd printing	4.00
3 WP	12.00
3a WP,2nd printing	4.00
4 WP	12.00
4a WP,2nd printing	4.00
5 WP	12.00
5a WP,2nd printing	4.00
6 WP	12.00
6a WP,2nd printing	4.00
7 WP	10.00
8 WP	10.00
9 WP	10.00
2a thru 9a WP,later printings	@3.00
10 thru 15	@5.00
16 WP,I:DistantSoil	8.00
17 thru 21 WP	@5.00
TPB Gatherum	20.00

ELFQUEST
Warp Graphics, 1996

4 thru 14 ed. RPi	@5.00
15	5.50
16 What if Cutter never became chief	5.50
17 F:Fire-Eye	5.50
18 Dreamtime, concl.	5.50
19 Wolfrider begins	5.50
20	5.50
21 20th anniv.	5.50
22 F:Wolfrider	5.00
23 F:WaveDancers	5.00
24 F:Wolfrider	5.00
25 F:Wolfrider	5.00
26 Wild Hunt	5.00
27	5.00
28 F:Ember & Teir	5.00
29 three new stories	5.00
30 new stories	5.00
31 new stories	5.00
32 Wild Hunt,pt.1, 24-pg.	3.50
33 Wild Hunt,pt.2	3.50
34 Wild Hunt,pt.3	3.50
35 Wild Hunt,pt.4	3.50
Spec.#1 Worldpool,pt.1 (1997)	3.50
Spec.#2 Worldpool,pt.2 (1997)	3.50

READERS COLLECTIONS

TPB Vol.1 Fire & Flight	12.00
TPB Vol.2 The Forbidden Grove	12.00
TPB Vol.3 Captives of Blue Mountain	12.00
TPB Vol.4 Quest's End	12.00
TPB Vol.5 Siege at Blue Mountain	12.00
TPB Vol.6 Secret of Two-Edge	12.00
TPB Vol.7 Cry From Beyond	12.00
TPB Vol.8 Kings of the Broken Wheel	12.00
TPB Vol.8A Dreamtime	12.00
TPB Vol.8B In All But Blood	17.00
TPB Vol.9 Rogue's Curse	14.00
TPB Vol.9A Wolfrider	13.00
TPB Vol.9B Blood of Ten Chiefs	14.00
TPB Vol.9C Kahvi	14.00
TPB Vol.11A Huntress	12.00
TPB Vol.11B Ascent	13.00
TPB Vol.11C Shadowstalker	13.00
TPB Vol.12 Ascent	13.00
TPB Vol.12A Reunion	13.00
TPB Vol.13A Rebels	12.00
TPB Vol.13B Junk	12.00
TPB Vol.14 JINK	12.00
TPB Vol.14A Skyward Shadow	12.00
TPB Vol.14B Mindcoil	12.00
TPB Vol.15 Forevergreen	13.00
TPB Vol.15A Dreams End	13.00
TPB Vol.15B Phoenix	14.00
TPB Vol.16 Wave Dancers	12.00
TPB Vol.'?' Worldpool	13.00
TPB The Rebels, 176-pg.	12.00
GN Shards	14.00

GN Legacy (Hidden Years #16–#22)	12.00
GN A Gift of Her Own	17.00
TPB Wolfrider's Guide, revised	17.00
Spec. Metamorphosis, WP, RPi (1996)	3.00
Spec. Elfquest: Wolfrider	3.00
Summer Spec. 2001 Recognition	3.00
Summer Spec. 2001 Wolfshadow	4.00

ELFQUEST: KAHVI
Warp Graphics, 1995

1 thru 6 I:Kahvi	@2.25

ELFQUEST: KINGS OF THE BROKEN WHEEL
Warp Graphics, 1990–92

1 WP	2.25
2 thru 9 WP	@2.25

ELFQUEST: SEIGE AT BLUE MOUNTAIN
Warp Graphics/Apple Comics, 1987–88

1 WP,JSo	9.00
1a 2nd printing	3.00
2 WP	6.00
2a 2nd printing	3.00
3 WP	5.00
3a 2nd printing	2.25
4 thru 8 WP	@5.00

Elfquest, Mistress of the Dark #59
© *Claypool Comics*

ELFQUEST: TWO SPEAR
Warp Graphics, 1995

1 thru 3 (of 5) Two-Spears past	@2.25

ELFQUEST: WORLDPOOL
Warp Graphics, 1997

Spec.#1 (of 2)	3.00
Spec.#2 (of 2)	3.00

ELFTREK
Dimension, 1986

1 Elfquest's Star Trek parody	2.25
2	2.25

ELF WARRIOR
Adventure, 1987

1	3.00
2	2.50
3 thru 5	@2.25

EL HAZARD: THE MAGNIFICENT WORLD
Viz Communications, 2000

1 by Hidetomo Tsubura	3.00
2	3.00
3 thru 5	@3.00

Part 2, 2001

1 thru 5	@3.00

Part 3, 2001

1 thru 5 (of 6)	@3.00
6	3.00
TPB Vol. 1	16.00
TPB Vol. 2	16.00
TPB Vol. 3	16.00

ELIMINATOR
Eternity

1 `Drugs in the Future'	2.50
2	2.50

ELVIRA, MISTRESS OF THE DARK
Claypool Comics, 1993

1	7.00
2 thru 35	@4.00
36 thru 74 photo covers	@3.50
75 Mistress of the Jungle,pt.1	3.50
76 Mistress of the Jungle,pt.2	3.50
77 Rome on the Range	3.50
78 thru 90 photo covers	@3.50
91 thru 103	@3.00
104 thru 127	@3.00
128 thru 128	@2.50
TPB Elvira, Mistress of the Dark	13.00
TPB Vol. 2 Double Delights	13.00

ELVIRA
Eclipse

1 Rosalind Wyck	2.50

EMBRACE
London Night, 1996

1 NC17 edition, EHr, signed	10.00

EMBRACE: HUNGER OF THE FLESH
London Night, 1997

1 DQ,last of the original vampire race	3.00
1a DQ,deluxe	6.00
1b signed by Kevin West	15.00
2 DQ	3.00
2a DQ,deluxe	6.00
3 by Dan Membiela & Kevin West, concl.	3.00

EMERALDAS
Eternity, 1990

1 thru 4	@2.25

EMMA DAVENPORT
Lohamn Hill Press, 1995

1 I:Emma Davenport	2.75
2	2.75
3 O:Hammerin Jim	2.75
4 Cookie Woofer War	2.75

EMPIRE
Eternity, 1988
1 thru 4 . . . . @2.25

EMPTY ZONE
Sirius, 1998
1 by Jason Alexander 3.00
1a limited edition 5.00
2 . . . . 2.50
3 . . . . 2.50
4 . . . . 2.50
TPB 12.00
TPB Vol. 2 . . . . 17.00

VOL. 2 TRANSMISSIONS, 1999
1 by Jason Alexander 3.00
2 thru 7 . . . . @3.00
8 History Lessions,pt.1 . . . . 3.00

EMPTY ZONE: CONVERSATIONS WITH THE DEAD
Sirius Entertainment, 2002
1 (of 5) by Jason Alexander 3.00
2 thru 3 . . . . @3.00

ENCHANTED
Sirius, 1997
1 (of 3) by Robert Chang 3.00
2 . . . . 3.00
3 concl. 3.00

ENCHANTED VALLEY
Blackthorne
1 . . . . 2.25
2 . . . . 2.25

ENCHANTER
Eclipse, 1987
1 thru 3 . . . . @2.50

ENCHANTER: APOCALYPSE WIND NOVELLA
Entity
1 Foil Enhanced Cover 3.00

ENFORCERS
Dark Visions Publishing, 1995
0 From Anthology Title 2.50

ENNIS AND MCCREA'S BIGGER DICKS
Avatar Press, 2002
1 (of 4) GEn,JMC,F:Dougie & Ivor . 5.00
1a Guaranteed to Offend cover . . . 5.00
2 thru 4 . . . . @5.00
2a thru 4a offensive (c) . . . . @5.00

ENNIS AND MCCREA'S DICKS 2
Avatar Press, 2002
1 (of 4) 3.50
2 thru 4 . . . . @3.50
1a thru 4a offensive (c) . . . . @4.00
X-Mas Spec. #1 . . . . 3.50
X-Man Spec. #1 offensive (c) 4.00

ENTITY
Avatar
? Nira X cover 6.00

? Snowman cover 11.00
? Nira X silver cover 11.00
? Snowman silver cover 16.00

ENTROPY TALES
Entropy
1 . . . . 2.25
2 Domino Chance 2.25
3 thru 5 . . . . @2.25

EPSILON WAVE
Elite
1 . . . . 3.00
2 . . . . 2.25

Escape Velocity #2
© Escape Velocity Press

3 thru 5 . . . . @2.25

EQUINE THE UNCIVILIZED
GraphXpress
1 . . . . 4.00
2 . . . . 2.50
3 thru 6 . . . . @2.25

EQUINOX CHRONICLES
Innovation, 1991
1 I:Team Equinox, Black Avatar . . . 2.25
2 Black Avatar Plans US conquest. 2.25

ERADICATORS
Greater Mercury, 1990–91
1 RLm (1st Work) 5.00
1a 2nd printing 2.25
2 . . . . 2.50
3 Vigil 2.25
4 thru 8 . . . . @2.25

ERIC PRESTON IS THE FLAME
B-Movie Comics, 1987
1 Son of G.A.Flame 2.25

ESCAPE TO THE STARS
Visionary
1 thru 7 . . . . @2.25

[2nd Series]
1 . . . . 2.25
2 . . . . 2.25

ESCAPE VELOCITY
Escape Velocity Press, 1986
1 and 2 . . . . @2.25

ESMERALDAS
Eternity
1 thru 4 . . . . 2.25

ESP
Curtis Comics, 2002
Vol. 1 Manga
1 by Jihoon Park & Takyoung Lee . 3.00
2 thru 5 . . . . @3.00

Vol. 2
1 . . . . 3.00

ESPERS
Halloween Comics, 1996
1 JHI, R:ESPers 3.00
1 JHI,signed 3.00
2 JHI,signed 3.00
3 JHI,. 3.00
3 JHI,signed 3.00
4 thru 6 JHI, conclusion . . . . @3.00

Volume 2
1 `Undertow' 3.00
2 . . . . 3.00

ESP ULTRA
Komics, Inc., 1999
TPB Vol. 1 . . . . 9.00
TPB Vol. 2 thru Vol. 7 . . . . @9.00

ETERNITY TRIPLE ACTION
Malibu B&W
1 F:Gazonga 2.25
2 F:Gigantor 2.50

EVENT PRESENTS THE ASH UNIVERSE
Event Comics, 1998
1-shot JQ,JP, 48pg 3.00

EVERETTE HARTSOE'S RAZOR
EH! Productions, 2000
1 . . . . 3.50
1a Ruby Foil 5.00
2 . . . . 4.00

EVIL ERNIE
Eternity, 1991–92
1 SHu,BnP,I&O:Evil Ernie,
  Lady Death 50.00
1a Spec. 1992 reprint, 16 extra
  pages. 30.00
2 Death & Revival of Ernie,
  A:Lady Death, 1st (c) 30.00
3 Psycho Plague, A:Lady Death . . 28.00
4 A:Lady Death 22.00
5 A:Lady Death 20.00
TPB rep #1-5 . . . . 11.00

EVIL ERNIE
Chaos! Comics
1 thru 5 reprints . . . . @3.00
Spec. Youth Gone Wild, die-cut
  cover, Director's cut. 5.00
TPB Youth Gone Wild 10.00

B & W PUB.

Chaos! Comics, 1996
1 encore presentation 3.00
2 thru 5 encore presentation 3.00
TPB Revenge 13.00
Preview Book Depraved 5.00
Pieces of Me Script 5.00

EVIL ERNIE: THE HORROR
Chaos! Comics, 2002
Ashcan b&w 6.00
1 BnP 4.50
1a premium edition 10.00
1b signed edition 15.00
1c super-premium edition 20.00
Spec. Script edition 5.00
Spec. Script Edition, premium 20.00

EVIL ERNIE: MANHATTAN DEATH TRIP
Chaos! Comics, 2002
1 BnP 3.50
1a premium edition 10.00
1b super-premium edition 20.00
Spec. #1 script 5.00
Spec. #1 script, premium edition . . 20.00

EVIL ERNIE RETURNS
Chaos! Comics, 2001
1 BnP 4.00
1a premium edition 13.00
1b super premium edition 20.00
1c signed ed 15.00
Ashcan 6.00
Script #1 . . . . 5.00
Script #1 premium edition 20.00

EVIL ERNIE: YOUTH GONE WILD
Chaos! Comics, 2001
Script 25.00
Script, signed 35.00

EVIL EYE
Fantagraphics, 1998
1 by Richard Sala 3.00
2 Glass Scorpion,pt.2 . . . . 3.00
3 thru 7 . . . . @3.00
8 thru 11 . . . . @3.50
12 . . . . 4.00

Ex-Mutants: The Shattered Earth Chronicles #12 © Eternity

EXCEL SAGA
Viz Communications, 2003
GN Vol. 1 . . . . 10.00
GN Vol. 2 thru Vol. 9 . . . . @10.00

EXIT
Caliber, 1995
1 I:New series 3.00
2 thru 4 `The Traitors,'pt.2–pt.4 . . . 3.00
Epilogue 3.00
GN rep. 320-pg 20.00
GN rep. 160-pg 15.00

EX-MUTANTS
Amazing Comics, 1986
1 AC/RLm 5.00
1a 2nd printing 2.25
2 and 3 . . . . @3.00
EC
4 and 5 . . . . @2.25
6 PP 2.25
7 . . . . 2.25
8 . . . . 2.25
Ann. #1 . . . . 2.25
Pin-Up Spec. #1 . . . . 2.25

EX-MUTANTS: THE SHATTERED EARTH CHRONICLES
Eternity, 1988
1 thru 3 . . . . @2.25
4 RLd(c) 2.75
5 RLd(c) 2.75
6 thru 14 . . . . @2.25
Winter Special #1 . . . . 2.25

EXPLORERS
Caliber Tapestry, 1997
1 . . . . 3.00
2 . . . . 3.00
3 `Nahuatl' 3.00
4 `The Sky is Falling' 3.00

EXTINCTIONERS
Shanda Fantasy Arts
VOL 2, 1999
1 . . . . 3.00
2 thru 7 . . . . @3.00
8 . . . . 3.00
9 . . . . 3.00
10 thru 14 48-pg . . . . @5.00
Spec. #2 Tales of the Endangered . . 5.00

EXTREMELY SILLY
Antarctic Press
1 . . . . 4.00
Vol. II, 1996
1 . . . . 2.25
2 . . . . 2.25

EYE OF MONGOMBO
Fantagraphics Books, 1990–91
1 . . . . 3.00
2 thru 7 . . . . @2.25

FAITH
Lightning Comics, 1997
1 (of 2) 3.00
1a variant cover 3.00
1b Limited, cover A 10.00
1c Limited, cover B 10.00
1d signed & numbered 10.00
1 encore edition 3.00

1a encore, cover B 3.00
1b deluxe encore edition, cover A 10.00
1c deluxe encore edition, cover B 10.00

FANG: TESTAMENT
Sirius, 1997
1 by Kevin J. Taylor 2.50
2 . . . . 2.50
3 . . . . 2.50
4 (of 4) 2.50
TPB 12.00

FANGS OF THE WIDOW
London Night Studios, 1995
1 O:The Widow 3.00
1a platinum edition 5.00
2 Body Count 3.00
3 Emma Revealed 3.00
4 and 5 . . . . @3.00
Ground Zero, 1995
7 thru 9 `Metal Gypsies,'pt.#1–#3 @3.00
10 thru 13 rep. Widow: Bound by
 Blood #1–#4 + additional
 material 3.50
14 `Search and Destroy'pt.1 . . . . . 3.00
15 `Search and Destroy'pt.2 . . . . . 3.00
Ann. #1 Search and Destroy 6.00

FANTASCI
Warp Graphics-Apple, 1986
1 . . . . 2.50
2 and 3 . . . . @2.25
4 . . . . 4.00
5 thru 8 . . . . @2.25
9 `Apple Turnover' 2.25

FANTASTIC ADVENTURES
1 thru 5 . . . . @2.25

FANTASTIC FABLES
Silver Wolf, 1987
1 and 2 . . . . @2.25

FANTASTIC PANIC
Antarctic, 1993–94
1 thru 8 Ganbear . . . . @2.75
Vol. 2, 1995
1 thru 4 . . . . @2.75
4 thru 9 . . . . @3.00
10 concl 3.50

FANTASTIC STORIES
Basement Comics, 2001
1 F:Grakoom, the Forgotten God . . 3.00
1a special edition 9.00
2 Lost Women of the Moon 3.00
2a special edition 9.00
3 . . . . 3.00
3a special edition 9.00

FANTASTIC WORLDS
Flashback Comics, 1995
1 Space Opera 3.00
2 F:Attu, Captain Courage 3.00

FANTASY QUARTERLY
Independent, 1976
1 1978 1st Elfquest 65.00

FART WARS: SPECIAL EDITION
Entity Comics, 1997
1 Star Wars trilogy parody,A:Nira X 2.75

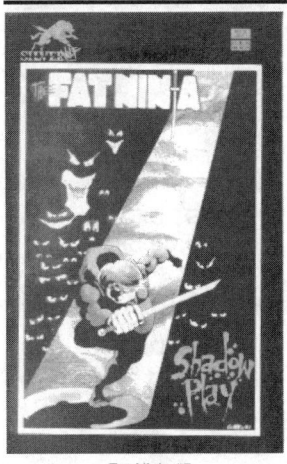

Fat Ninja #5
© Silver Wolf Comics

1a Empire Attacks Back cover 2.75
1b Return of the One-Eye cover... 2.75

FAR WEST
Antarctic Press, 1998
1 (of 4) by Richard Moore........ 3.00
2 thru 4 .... @3.00
VOL. 2
1 (of 4) 2.99
2 .... 2.50

FASTLANE ILLUSTRATED
Fastlane Studios, 1994
1 Super Powers & Hot Rods 2.50
2 & 3 .... @2.50

FATALIS
Caliber Core, 1998
1 by Mark Chadbourn
  & Vince Danks.............. 3.00
1a signed & numbered 7.00
2 .... 3.00

FAT NINJA
Silver Wolf Comics, 1985–86
1 .... 2.50
2 Vigil 2.50
3 thru 8 .... @2.25

FAUST
Northstar, 1985
1 Vigil 25.00
1a Vigil,2nd Printing 5.00
1b Vigil,3rd Printing. 2.25
1c Tour Edition 25.00
2 Vigil 15.00
2a Vigil,2nd Printing 3.00
2b Vigil,3rd Printing. 2.50
3 Vigil 10.00
3a Vigil,2nd Printing 2.50
4 Vigil 5.00
5 Vigil 5.00
6 Vigil 5.00
Rebel Studios
7 Vigil 5.00
8 TV 3.50
9 TV,Love of the Damned....... 3.50
10 E:DQ(s),TV,Love o/t Damned... 3.50

VOL. II
1 TV,Love of the Damned....... 2.50

FAUST/777: THE WRATH
Avatar Press, 1998
0 by David Quinn & Tim Vigil,
  Darkness in Collision x-over ... 3.00
0a wrap...................... 4.00
0b leather cover 20.00
0c Royal Blue edition 60.00
0d Platinum edition 16.00
1 (of 4) 3.50
2 Darkness in Collision,pt.3 ..... 3.50
3 .... 3.50
4 .... 3.50
Faust Hornbook 5.00
TPB 112-pg.................. 17.00

FAUST: SINGHA'S TALONS
Avatar, 2000
1/2 .... 3.50
1/2 wraparound (c)............. 4.00
1/2 Beachum (c) 6.00
1/2 prism foil 13.00
1/2 royal blue edition 75.00
1/2 Blood Curse 5.00
1 (of 4) 4.00
1a wraparound (c)............. 4.50
1c red foil leather 25.00
1d prism foil 13.00
1 commemorative............. 6.00
2 .... 4.00
2a previews exclusive.......... 4.50
3 .... 4.00
3a previews exclusive.......... 4.50
4 .... 4.00
4a previews exclusive.......... 4.50
Preview Book 6.00

FELIX THE CAT
Felix Comics, 1997
1 inc. Felix's Cafe 2.25
2 Crusin' for a Brusin'.......... 2.25
3 Ah Choo................... 2.25
4 inc. Spaced Out 2.25
5 Holiday/Winter issue 2.25
6 The Felix Force 2.25
7 A Rash of Trash 2.25
8 Halloween 2.25
Cat-A-Strophic Wrestling Spec.#1 .. 2.25
Felix Summer Splash #1 .... 2.50

FELIX THE CAT TRUE CRIME STORIES
Felix Comics, 2000
1 .... 2.50
Spec.#1 Blockbuster movie
  bonanza.................. 2.50
Spec. Felix Jurassic Jamboree 2.50
Spec. Felix Magic Bag of Tricks ... 2.50
Spec. Felix Laff-A-Palooza 2.50
1-shot Felix's Totally Wacky News.. 2.50
TPB Comic Adventures of Felix... 12.95
1-shot Halloween Spectacular #13 . 2.50
1-shot House of 1000 Ha Ha's 2.50

FELIX THE CAT'S TV EXTRAVAGANZA
Felix Comics, 2002
1 .... 2.50

FEM FANTASTIQUE
AC Comics, 1988
1 .... 2.25

FEM FORCE
AC Comics, 1987
1 thru 15 See Color
16 I:Thunder Fox 3.00
17 F:She-Cat,Ms.Victory, giant 3.00
18 double size 3.00
19 .... 3.00
20 V:RipJaw, Black Commando ... 3.00
21 V:Dr.Pretorius 3.00
22 V:Dr.Pretorius 3.00
23 V:Rad 3.00
24 A:Teen Femforce........... 3.00
25 V:Madame Boa 3.00
26 V:Black Shroud............ 3.00
27 V:Black Shroud............ 3.00
28 A:Arsenio Hall 3.00
29 V:Black Shroud............ 3.00
30 V:Garganta 3.00
31 I:Kronon Captain Paragon 3.00
32 V:Garganta 3.00
33 Personal Lives of team....... 3.00
34 V:Black Shroud............ 3.00
35 V:Black Shroud............ 3.00
36 giant,V:Dragonfly,Shade...... 3.00
37 A:Blue Bulleteer,She-Cat 3.00
38 V:Lady Luger.............. 3.00
39 F:She-Cat 3.00
40 V:Sehkmet 3.00
41 V:Captain Paragon 3.00
42 V:Alizarin Crimson 3.00
43 V:Glamazons of Galaxy G ... 3.00
44 V:Lady Luger,F:Garganta 5.00
45 Nightveil Rescued.......... 3.00
46 V:Lady Luger. 3.00
47 V:Alizarin Crimson 3.00
48 .... 3.00
49 I:New Msw.Victory......... 3.00
50 Ms.Victory Vs.Rad,flexi-disc ... 3.00
51 .... 3.00
52 V:Claw & Clawites 3.00
53 I:Bulldog Deni,V:(Dick
  Briefer's)Frightenstein........ 3.00
54 The Orb of Bliss 3.00
55 R:Nightveil................ 3.00
56 V:Alizarin Crimson 3.00
57 thru 92 See Color
93 `Shattered Memories,'pt.2 ..... 3.00
93a deluxe 6.00
94 `Shattered Memories,'pt.3 ..... 3.00
94a deluxe 6.00
95 .... 3.00
95a deluxe 6.00
96 .... 3.00
96a deluxe 6.00
97 .... 3.00
98 deluxe 6.00
98 .... 3.00
98 deluxe 6.00
99 .... 3.00
99 deluxe 6.00
100 Anniv. issue, with poster...... 8.00
100A signed, with poster 12.00
100B no poster, not signed 4.00

THE YESTERDAY SYNDROME
101 Pt.1 .... 5.00
102 Pt.2 .... 5.00
103 Pt.3 .... 5.00

RETURN FROM THE ASHES
104 pt.1 Firebeam, 44pg 5.00
105 pt.2 .... 5.00
106 pt.3 concl. 5.00

DARKGODS: RAMPAGE
107 Darkgods: Rampage,pt.1 ..... 5.00
108 Darkgods: Rampage,pt.2 ..... 5.00
109 Darkgods: Rampage,pt.3 ..... 6.00
110 thru 117 .... @6.00
118 44-pg. 7.00
118a spec. edition, 60-pg. 10.00
119 The Missing Mask.......... 7.00

B & W PUB.

120 Superbabes,pt.1	7.00
121 Superbabes,pt.2	7.00
121a Femme Noir (c)	10.00
122 Superbabes,pt.3	7.00
122a spec. editions, variant(c)	@10.00
123	7.00
124	7.00
125 Firebeam Rising	7.00
126 Totally Absorbed	7.00
127 No Return	7.00
128 Halloween Special	7.00
129 Shorty	7.00
Spec.#1 FemForce Timelines, O:Femforce (1995)	3.00
Spec.#1 FemForce:Frightbook, Horror tales by Briefer, Ayers, Powell	3.00
Spec.#2 (2001)	6.00
Spec.#1 Femforce:Uncut (2001)	10.00
Untold Origin of FemForce	5.00
GN The Capricorn Chronicles	12.50
GN FemForce: Timestorm	10.00
GN, FemForce: Timestorm, deluxe	15.00
TPB Origins	13.00
TPB Origins, signed	14.00
TPB Sisters in Sin, lim. ed.	22.00
Secret Files of Femforce, deluxe	5.00
Pulp Fiction Portfolio #2	18.00
Spec. #1 Femforce vs. The Claw	7.00
Spec. #1 Rampaging She-Cat	7.00
1-shot Claws of the She-Cat	4.95
Features #1: Giantess	6.95

FEMFORCE SPECIAL
AC Comics, 1999

1 Femforce Special: Rayda– The Cyberian Connection	3.00
1a Variant cover	3.00
1b Variant cover, signed	10.00
2	3.00
3 conclusion	4.00

FEVER, THE
Dark Vision Publishing

1 O:The Fever	2.50
2 Fever's Father	2.50

FIFTIES TERROR
Eternity, 1988

1 thru 6	@2.25

FIGHTING YANK
AC Comics, 2001

1 by Hack Koilby	6.00
2	6.00
3 Cave Girl	6.00
4	6.00
5 Three Chambers of Horror	6.00

FINAL CYCLE
Sirius

Graphic Novel	4.00
1 thru 4	@2.25

FINDER
Lightspeed Comics, 1996

1 thru 5 by Carla Speed McNeil	@3.00
6 thru 19	@3.00
20 thru 24	@3.00
25 thru 35	@3.00
TPB Vol. 1 Sin Eater	16.00
TPB Vol. 2 Sin-Eater	20.00
TPB Vol. 3 King of the Cats	14.00
TPB Vol. 4 Talisman	14.00
TPB Vol. 5 Dream Sequence	21.00
TPB Vol. 6 Mystery Date	17.95

FINDER FOOTNOTES
Lightspeed Press

1 thru 4	@6.00

FIRE TEAM
Aircel, 1990

1 thru 3 by Don Lomax	@2.50
4 V:Vietnamese Gangs	2.50
5 Cam in Vietnam	2.50
6	2.50

FIRST WAVE
Andromeda Entertainment, 2001

1 Patriot or Traitor	3.00
1a signed	10.00
GN Through Alien Eyes	8.00

FIRST WAVE: DOUBLE VISION
Andromeda Entertainment, 2001

1 (of 2)	3.00
1a photo (c)	3.00

FIRST WAVE: GENESIS OF A GENIUS
Andromeda Entertainment, 2001

Spec. painted (c)	3.00

Fist of the North Star Vol. 2 #7
© Viz Communications

Spec. photo (c)	3.00

FISH POLICE
Fishwrap Productions, 1985

1 1st printing	7.00
1a 2nd printing	3.00

Becomes:

INSPECTOR GILL OF THE FISH POLICE

2	5.00
3 thru 11	@4.00

[Vol 2]
Comico Publ., 1987

5 thru 12	@3.50
13 thru 17 **see Color issues**	

Apple Publ.

18 thru 24	@2.50

FISH SHTICKS
Apple, 1991

1 and 2 Fish Police	@2.75
3 and 4	@2.50

FIST OF GOD
Eternity, 1988

1 thru 4	@2.25

FIST OF THE BLUE SKY
Gutsoon! Entertainment, 2003

TPB Vol. 1	10.00
TPB Vol. 2 thru Vol. 3	@10.00

FIST OF THE NORTH STAR
Viz Select, 1996

1 thru 3	@3.25
4	2.25
5	3.25
6	3.00
7	3.00
TPB Vol. 2 Night of the Jackal, rep.	17.00

Part Three

1 thru 5 by Buronson & Tetsuo Hara	@3.00

Part Four, 1996

1 thru 7	@3.00
TPB Volume 2: Southern Cross	17.00

FLAG FIGHTERS
Ironcat, 1997

1 by Masaomi Kanzaki	3.00
2 Student Flagger,pt.1	3.00
3 Student Flagger,pt.2	3.00
4 Student Flagger,pt.3	3.00
5	3.00
6 Death Window	3.00
7 F:Murasame	3.00

FLAMING CARROT
Aardvark–Vanaheim, 1984

1 1981 Killian Barracks	50.00
1a 1984	25.00
2	25.00
3	20.00
4 thru 6	@15.00

Renegade

7	12.00
8	10.00
9	8.00
10	8.00
11	6.00
12	6.00
13 thru 15	@5.00
15a variant without cover price	8.00
16 and 17	@5.00

See: Dark Horse

FLARE
Hero Graphics

1 thru 8	@4.00
9 F:Sparkplug	4.00
10 thru 12	3.00

FLARE ADVENTURES
Hero Graphics, 1988

1 Rep 1st issue Flare	2.25

Becomes:

FLARE ADVENTURES/ CHAMPIONS CLASSICS

2 thru 15	@4.00

FLARE VS. TIGRESS
Hero Graphics
1 and 2 . . . . @3.50

FORBIDDEN KINGDOM
1 thru 11 . . . . @2.25

FORBIDDEN VAMPIRE TALES
Forbidden, 1997
0 . . . . 3.00
1 sexy vampire 3.00
2 thru 7 . . . . @3.00
Spec.#1 Vault of Innocents 3.00

FORBIDDEN WORLDS
ACG, 1996
1 SD,JAp,rep. 2.50

FORCE SEVEN
Lone Star Press, 1999
1 . . . . 3.00
2 thru 7 . . . . @3.00

FORCE 10
Crow Comics
0 Ash Can Preview 75
1 I:Force 10. . . . . 2.50
2 Children of the Revolution,pt#2 . . 2.50
3 Against all Odds. 2.50

FORETERNITY
Antarctic Press, 1997
1 by Rod Espinoza 3.00
2 . . . . 3.00
3 . . . . 3.00

FOREVER WARRIORS
Aardwolf, 1996
1 (of 3) RTs,RB 3.00
2 RTs,RB 3.00
3 RTs,RB, concl. 3.00

FOREVER WARRIORS
CFD, 1997
1 RB,RTs 3.00
2 RB,RTs,KN. 3.00
3 RB,RTs, finale 3.00

FORTY WINKS
Oddjobs Limited, 1997
1 (of 4) by Sneed & Peters 3.00
2 Everything Right is Wrong Again. 3.00
3 Where Your Eyes Don't Go 3.00
4 There Might be Giants 3.00
Peregrine Entertainment, 1998
Christmas Spec. 3.00
TV Party Spec. 3.00
Spec.#1 Buzzboy (2000) 3.00

FORTY WINKS: MR. HORRIBLE
Peregrine Entertainment, 2000
1 . . . . 3.00
2 . . . . 3.00

FORTY WINKS: THE FABLED PIRATE QUEEN OF THE SOUTH CHINA SEA
Peregrine Entertainment, 1999
1 by Vincent Sneed & Martinez . . . 3.00
2 . . . . 3.00
3 . . . . 3.00

FOUR KUNOICHI: ENTER THE SINJA
Lightning Comics, 1997
1 . . . . 3.00

FOX COMICS
1 Spec. 3.00
25 . . . . 3.00
26 . . . . 3.50

FRANK
Fantagraphics
1 JWo 3.00
2 JWo 4.00
3 . . . . 4.00
4 . . . . 4.00
GN rep. from various sources 15.00
TPB Vol. 1, signed 15.00
Vol. 2 partial color 17.00

FRANKENSTEIN
Eternity
1 . . . . 2.25
2 . . . . 2.25
3 . . . . 2.25

FRANKIES FRIGHTMARES
1 Celebrates Frank 60th Anniv. . . . 2.25

FRANK THE UNICORN
Fish Warp
1 thru 7 . . . . @2.25

FREAK-OUT ON INFANT EARTHS
Blackthorne, 1987
1 Don Chin 2.25
2 Don Chin 2.25

FREAKS
Monster Comics
1 Movie adapt. 2.50
2 Movie adapt.cont. 2.50
3 thru 4 Movie adapt. . . . . @2.50

FRED THE POSSESSED FLOWER
Happy Predator, 1998
1 The Plant Behind the Scenes . . . 3.00
2 . . . . 3.00
3 Interview with a Demon 3.00
4 The People vs. Hell 3.00
5 . . . . 3.00
6 The Origin of Fred 3.00

FRENCH ICE
Renegade Press, 1987
1 thru 15 . . . . @2.25

FRIENDS
Renegade, 1987
1 thru 5 . . . . @2.25

FRIGHT
Eternity
1 thru 13 . . . . @2.25

FRINGE
Caliber
1 thru 7 . . . . @2.50

FROM BEYOND
Studio Insidio
1 Short stories-horror 2.25
2 inc.Clara Mutilares. 2.50
3 inc.The Experiment 2.50
4 inc.Positive Feedback 2.50

FROM HELL
Tundra, 1991
1 . . . . 20.00
1a 2nd printing 10.00
2 . . . . 12.00

Kitchen Sink Volume Three
1 AMo,ECa 10.00
2 AMo,ECa 7.00
2a 2nd printing 6.00
3 . . . . 7.00
3a 2nd printing 6.00
4 . . . . 7.00
4 new printing 5.00
5 . . . . 7.00
5 new printing 5.00

Fugitoid 1-shot
© Mirage

6 . . . . 7.00
7 . . . . 7.00
8 . . . . 7.00
8 AMo,ECa,new printing 5.00
9 AMo,ECa 7.00
9 new printing 5.00
10 AMo,ECa. 7.00
10 new printing 5.00
Spec. Dance of the Gull Catchers . . 5.00

FROM THE DARKNESS
Adventure Comics, 1990
1 JBa. 25.00
2 . . . . 30.00
3 and 4 . . . . @12.00

The Furies #3
© Carbon-Based

FROM THE DARKNESS II
BLOOD VOWS
Cry For Dawn
1 R:Ray Thorn,Desnoires	12.00
2 V:Desnoires	8.00
3	8.00

FROM THE VOID
1 1st B.Blair,1982	75.00

FROST:
THE DYING BREED
Caliber
1 thru 3 Vietnam Flashbacks	@3.00

F–III BANDIT
Antarctic Press, 1995
1 F:Akira, Yoohoo	3.00
2 F:Yukio	3.00
3 F:Were-Women	3.00
4	3.00
5 Romeo & Juliet story	3.00
6 thru 8	@3.00

FUGITOID
Mirage
1-shot TMNT Tie-in	8.00

FULL METAL FICTION
London Night, 1997
1 EHr	4.00
1a Nun with a Gun edition	10.00
1b dark room edition cover	4.00
2	4.00
2a signed	10.00
3 `Hellborne' concl.	4.00
4 thru 8	@4.00

FURIES
Carbon-Based, 1996
1 thru 6	@2.75

FURRLOUGH
Antarctic Press, 1991
1 Funny Animal Military stories.	3.00
2 thru 10	@2.50
11 thru 20	@2.75
21 thru 33	@2.75

34	3.00
35 48pg	4.00
36 thru 40	@3.00
41 thru 51	@3.00
Best of Furlough, Vol.1	5.00
Best of Furlough, Vol.2	5.00

Radio Comix
52 thru 75	@3.00
76 thru 99	@3.00
100 80-pg.	6.00
101	3.00
102	3.00
103 thru 139	@3.00
140 thru 142	@3.50
Furrlough's Finest Vol. 1	6.00
Furrlough Presents Sex Kitten #1	5.00

FURRY NINJA
HIGH SCHOOL
Shanda Fantasy Arts, 2002
1 (of 2) x-over (self) parody	5.00
2 x-over, concl.	5.00

FURY
Aircel
1 thru 3	@2.25

FURY OF HELLINA, THE
Lightning Comics, 1995
1 V:Luciver	3.50
1a limited & signed	8.00
1b platinum	8.00

FUSHIGI YUGI
Viz Communications, 1999
TPB by Yu Watase.	16.00
TPB Vol. 2 Oracle	16.00
TPB Vol. 3 Disciple	16.00
TPB Vol. 5 Rival.	16.00
TPB Vol. 6 Summoner.	16.00
TPB Vol. 7 Castaway.	16.00
TPB Vol. 8	10.00
TPB Vol. 9 The Mysterious Play	10.00
TPB Vol. 10 thru Vol. 12	@10.00
TPB The Art of Fushigi Yugi	23.00

FUSION
Eclipse, 1987
1	2.50
2 thru 17	@2.25

FUTABA-KUN CHANGE
Ironcat, 1998
1 by Hiroshi Aro	3.00
2 thru 6	@3.00
GN Vol. 1	16.00

VOL. 2
1	3.00
2 thru 6	@3.00

VOL. 3, 1999
1	3.00
2 thru 6	@3.00
TPB Vol. 3	16.00

VOL. 4, 2000
1	3.00
2 thru 6	@3.00

VOL. 5, 2000
1 by Hiroshi Aro	3.00
2 thru 6	@3.00

VOL. 6, 2001
1	3.00
2 thru 6	@3.00
TPB Vol. 4	16.00
TPB Vol. 5 rep..	16.00

VOL. 7, 2001
1	3.00
2 thru 6	@3.00

VOL. 8
1 thru 6	@3.00
TPB Vol. 5	16.00
TPB Vol. 7	16.00
TPB Vol. 8	16.00

FUTURAMA
Slave Labor, 1989
1 thru 4	@2.50

FUTURETECH
Mushroom Comics, 1995
1 Automotive Hi-Tech	3.50
2 Cyber Trucks	3.50

FUTURIANS
Aardwolf, 1995
0 DC R:Futurians, sequel to Lodestone color series	3.00
0 second printing, DC	3.00

GAIJIN
Caliber, 1990
1-shot, 64pg.	3.50
1 thru 3	@2.25

GALAXION
Helikon, 1997
1 by Tara Jenkins, science fiction.	2.75
2	2.75
3	2.75
4 Choices	2.75
5	2.75
6 Communication	2.75
7 Song of Hiawatha	2.75
8 Persuasion.	2.75
9 Deal with the Devil.	2.75
10	2.75
11	2.75
Spec. #1, 16pg.	2.00
GN Vol. 1	16.00
Spec. Flip Book Galaxion & Amy Unbound	2.75

GALAXY EXPRESS
Viz Communications, 1998
TPB Vol. 1 232-pg..	17.00
TPB Vol. 2	17.00
TPB Vol. 3	17.00
TPB Vol. 4	17.00
TPB Vol. 5	19.00

GATEKEEPER
GK Publishing, 1987
1	2.50
2 and 3	@3.00

GATES OF THE NIGHT
Jademan
1 thru 4	@3.50

GEAR
Fireman Press, 1998
1 (of 6) by Douglas TenNaple	3.00
2 thru 6	@3.00
TPB	15.00

GEISHA
Oni Press, 1998
1 (of 4) by Andi Watson	3.00
2	3.00

3 . . . . 3.00
4 . . . . 3.00
TPB by Andi Watson 10.00

GEMS OF THE SAMURAI
Newcomers Publishing
1 I:Master Samurai 3.00

GENERIC COMIC BOOK
Comics Conspiracy, 2001
1 thru 4 . . . . @2.25
5 . . . . 2.25
5a Hyper Fanboy variant edition. . . 6.00
6 thru 13 . . . . @2.25
TPB 9.00

GENOCYBER
Viz, 1993
1 I:Genocyber 2.75
2 thru 5 . . . . @2.75

GEOBREEDERS
CPM Manga, 1999
1 by Akhiro Ito 3.00
2 thru 10 . . . . @3.00
11 thru 36 . . . . @3.00
TPB Vol. 1 . . . . 16.00
TPB Vol. 2 rep. #8–#14 . . . . 16.00
TPB Vol. 3 . . . . 16.00
TPB Vol. 4 Unfriendly Skies. 16.00
TPB #5 Big Trouble at Tokyo
  Tower. 16.00

GERIATRIC GANGRENE
JUJITSU GERBILS
Planet X Productions
1 . . . . 2.50
2 . . . . 2.25

GHOSTS OF DRACULA
Eternity
1 A:Dracula & Houdini 2.50
2 A:Sherlock Holmes 2.50
3 A:Houdini 2.50
4 Count Dracula's Castle 2.50
5 Houdini, Van Helsing, Dracula
  team-up 2.50

GI GOVERNMENT ISSUED
Paranoid Press, 1994
1 thru 7 F:Mac, Jack . . . . @2.25

GIANT SHANDA ANIMAL
Shanda Fantasy Arts, 1998
1 . . . . 5.00
2 . . . . 5.00
3 . . . . 5.00
4 . . . . 4.50
5 . . . . 5.00
6 48-pg. 5.00
7 & 8 . . . . @5.00

GIDEON HAWK
Big Shot Comics, 1995
1 I:Gideon Hawk, Max 9471 . . . . . . 2.25
2 The Jewel of Shamboli,pt.2 . . . . . 2.25
3 The Jewel of Shamboli,pt.3 . . . . . 2.25
2 The Jewel of Shamboli,pt.4 . . . . . 2.50
3 The Jewel of Shamboli,pt.5 . . . . . 2.50

GIGANTOR
Antarctic Press, 2000
1 (of 12) by Ben Dunn 3.00

2 thru 8 . . . . @3.00

GIRL GENIUS
Studio Foglio, 2001
1 thru 5 . . . . @3.00
Airship Entertainment, 2002
6 thru 10 . . . . @4.00
11 thru 13 . . . . @4.00
TPB Vol. 1 Phil Foglio, 96-pg. 10.00
TPB Vol. 2 . . . . 20.00

GIRLS OF NINJA
HIGH SCHOOL, 1997
Antarctic Press
Spec. 4.00
Spec. 1998 cover A 3.00
Spec. 1998 cover B 3.00
Spec. 1999 . . . . 3.00

GIZMO
Chance, 1986
1 . . . . 7.50

GIZMO
Mirage, 1987
1 . . . . 5.50
2 . . . . 3.00
3 . . . . 2.50
4 thru 7 . . . . @2.50

GIZMO & THE FUGITOID
Mirage, 1989
1 and 2 . . . . @2.25

GLOOM COOKIE
Slave Labor Graphics, 1999
1 by Serena Valentino
  & Ted Naifeh 3.00
2 . . . . 3.00
3 . . . . 3.00
4 . . . . 3.00
5 . . . . 3.00
6 Sebastian's Search 3.00
7 thru 9 . . . . @3.00
10 thru 21 . . . . @3.00
TPB Vol. 1 200-pg. 18.00
TPB Vol. 2 192-pg. 17.00
TPB Vol. 3 . . . . 15.95
Color Spec. A Monster's Christmas . 4.00

GNATRAT
Prelude
1 . . . . 5.00
2 Early Years. 2.25

GNATRAT: THE MOVIE
Innovation
1 . . . . 2.25

GOBBLEDYGOOK
Mirage, 1986
1 1st series, Rare 200.00
2 1st series, Rare 150.00
1 TMNT series reprint. 5.00

GOJIN
Antarctic Press, 1995
1 F:Terran Defense Force. 3.00
2 F:Terran Defense Force. 3.00
3 V:Alien Monster 3.00
4 Aliens Bone 3.00
5 thru 8 . . . . @3.00

Gold Digger #36
© Antarctic Press

GOLD DIGGER
Antarctic Press, 1992
[Limited Series]
1 Geena & Cheetah in Peru 8.00
2 Adventures contd. 6.00
3 Adventures contd 6.00
4 Adventures contd 5.00
GN Rep. #1–#4 + new material . . . 10.00
[Volume 2], 1993
1 by Fred Perry 10.00
2 Fred Perry 8.00
3 Fred Perry 8.00
4 Fred Perry 6.00
5 misnumbered as #0 . . . . 5.00
6 thru 8 by Fred Perry . . . . @4.00
9 and 10 by Fred Perry . . . . @3.50
11 thru 27 by Fred Perry . . . . . . @3.00
28 and 29 by Fred Perry . . . . . . @2.75
30 thru 39 . . . . @3.00
40 Wedding day. 3.00
41 Gold Digger Beta 3.00
42 . . . . 3.00
43 Beta Phase phenomenon 3.00
44 Beta tool 3.00
45 F:Priestess Tanya 3.00
46 Agent M. 3.00
47 Old Dirty Bastard 3.00
48 . . . . 3.00
49 The Library of Time. 3.00
50 . . . . 3.00
50a deluxe 6.00
Ann. 1995, 48-pg. 4.00
Ann. 1996. . . . . 4.00
Ann. 1997. . . . . 4.00
Ann. 1998. . . . . 4.00
Ann. 2000 b&w 4.00
Ann. 2001 . . . . 4.00
Ann. 2002 B&W 4.00
Best of Gold Digger Ann. Vol. 1. . . 3.00
Collected Gold Digger,Vol.1 . . . . . 10.00
Collected Gold Digger,Vol.2 . . . . . 10.00

Collected Gold Digger,Vol.3 . . . . . 10.00
Collected Gold Digger,Vol.4 . . . . . 10.00
Collected Gold Digger,Vol.5 . . . . . 10.00
Collected Gold Digger,Vol.6 . . . . . 11.00
Collected Gold Digger,Vol.7 . . . . . 11.00
Collected Gold Digger,Vol.8 . . . . . 11.00
Collected Gold Digger,Vol.9 . . . . . 13.00
Magazine Spec. #1 . . . . 3.00

GOLD DIGGER/ NINJA HIGH SCHOOL
Antarctic Press, 1998
Spec. Asrial vs. Cheetah Compilation,
x-over rep. 5.00
Spec. Science Fair Compilation,
x-over rep. 5.00
TPB Time Warp 16.00

GOLD DIGGER: EDGE GUARD
Radio Comix, 2000
1 (of 4) by John Barrett. 3.00
2 thru 6 . . . . @3.00
7 finale 3.00

GOLDEN AGE GREATS
AC Comics, 1995
Vol.#1 thru #6 40s and 50s . . . . @10.00
Vol. 7 Best of the West 10.00
Vol. 8 F:Phantom Lady, Miss Victory . . . 10.00
Vol. 9 Fabulous Femmes of Fiction
House 10.00
Vol. 11 Roy Rogers & The Silver
Screen Cowboys. 12.00
Vol. 12 Thrilling Science Fiction. . . 10.00
Vol. 13 . . . . 10.00
Vol. 14 The Comic Book Jungle . . 12.00

GOLDEN-AGE MEN OF MYSTERY
AC Comics
5 . . . . 7.00
7 . . . . 6.00
8 . . . . 6.00
9 . . . . 6.00
10 Masked comic book
heroes, 52 pg. 7.00
11 rep. Cat-Man comics. 7.00
12 Espionage, WE 7.00
13 F:Daredevil vs. The Claw 7.00
14 F:Commando Yank 7.00
15 F:Captain 3-D 7.00
16 F:Mr. Scarlet, Airboy 7.00
17 F:Stuntman 7.00
18 . . . . 7.00
19 Space edition 7.00
19a spec. ed. 68-pg. 11.00
20 F:Phantom Lady 7.00
21 Fawcett superheroes 7.00
22 Manhunter. 7.00
23 Skyman. 7.00
24 Captain Flash 7.00
25 . . . . 7.00
26 Emerald. 7.00
27 The Fog Robbers 7.00
Becomes:

MEN OF MYSTERY
AC Comics, 2000
28 F:Black Terror,Miss Masque 7.00
29 The Lynx, Wildfire. 7.00
30 War Years 7.00
31 Speed and Space 7.00
32 Phantom Lady. 7.00
33 Red white and blue. 7.00
34 Halloween Issue 7.00
35 F:Spy Smasher 7.00
36 F:Captain Flash 7.00
37 F:Cat-Man and Kitten 7.00
38 Spy Smasher vs. Iron Mask 7.00
39 Spy Smasher, Airboy 7.00
40 The Black Terror 7.00
41 Bulletman 7.00
42 Blue Bolt 7.00
43 The Flame. 7.00

44 Cat-Man and Bulletman 7.00
45 thru 50. . . . . @7.00
Coll. Ed. #7 . . . . 20.00
Digest Spec. #1 . . . . 16.00
Spotlight Spec. #1 . . . . 15.00

GOLDEN WARRIOR
Industrial Design, 1997
1 by Eric Bansen & RB 3.00
2 and 3 . . . . @3.00

GOLDEN WARRIOR ICZER ONE
Antarctic, 1994
1 thru 5 . . . . @3.00

GOLDWYN 3-D
Blackthorne
1 . . . . 2.25

GO-MAN
Caliber
1 thru 4 . . . . @2.25
Graphic Novel `N' 10.00

GOOD GIRL COMICS
AC
1 F:Tara Fremont 4.00

GOOD GIRLS
Fantagraphics, 1987
1 adult. 2.25
2 thru 4 . . . . @2.25

GOON, THE
Avatar Press, 1999
1 by Eric Powell 30.00
2 . . . . 25.00
3 . . . . 25.00

GORE SHRIEK
Fantaco
1 . . . . 2.50
2 and 3 . . . . @2.25
4 +Mars Attacks 3.00
5 . . . . 3.00
6 . . . . 3.50
Vol 2 #1 . . . . 2.50

GOTHESS: DARK ECSTASY
SCC Entertainment, 1997
1 (of 3) 3.00
2 . . . . 3.00
3 . . . . 3.00

GRACKLE, THE
Acclaim, 1996
1 MBn,PG,Double Cross, pt.1. . . . 3.00
2 MBn,PG,Double Cross, pt.2. . . . 3.00
3 MBn,PG,Double Cross, pt.3. . . . 3.00
4 MBn,PG,Double Cross, pt.4. . . . 3.00

GRAPHIC CLASSICS
Eureka Productions, 2001
TPB Vol. 1 Edgar Allan Poe. 8.00
TPB Vol. 2 Arthur Conan Doyle. . . 10.00
TPB Vol. 3 H.G. Wells 10.00
TPB Vol. 4 H.P. Lovecraft 10.00
TPB Vol. 5 Jack London 10.00
TPB Vol. 6 Ambrose Bierce 10.00
TPB Vol. 7 Bram Stoker. 10.00

TPB Vol. 9 Robert Louis Stevenson 9.95
TPB Vol. 10 Horror Classics 9.95

GRAPHIC STORY MONTHLY
Fantagraphics
1 thru 7 . . . . @3.00

GRAPHIQUE MUSIQUE
Slave Labor, 1989–90
1 . . . . 35.00
2 . . . . 30.00
3 . . . . 25.00

GRAVEDIGGERS
Acclaim, 1996
1 (of 4) 3.00
2 thru 4 . . . . @3.00

GRAVE TALES
Hamilton, 1991
1 JSon,GM, mag. size 8.00
2 JSon,GM,short stories. 6.00
3 JSon,GM, inc.`Stake Out' 6.00

GREAT DETECTIVE STARRING SHERLOCK HOLMES
ACG Comics, 1999
1 by Otto Lagoni. 3.00
2 thru 5 . . . . @3.00

Grendel #3
© Comico

GREEN BERETS
ACG, 2000
1 JKu. 3.00
2 thru 7 JKu, Robin Moore . . . . . @3.00
TPB Limited Signed. 25.00

GREENLEAF IN EXILE
Cat's Paw Comics, 1998
1 by Doug Anderson. 3.00
2 thru 7 . . . . @3.00

GREMLIN TROUBLE
Anti-Ballistic Pixelation
1 & 2 Airstrike on Gremlin Home @3.00

B & W PUB.

1 new printing	3.00
3 thru 5	@3.00
6 `Fun with Electricity'.	3.00
7 `Cypher in Fairyland'	3.00
8	3.00
9 F:Candy Tsai	3.00
10 The Tuberians are coming	3.00
11 V:X-the-Unmentionable	3.00
12 preemptive strike on Site X	3.00
13 Gremlin-Goblin war	3.00
14	3.00
15 Battle of 5 Armies	3.00
16	3.00
17 kidnapped to Fairyland	3.00
18	3.00
19 The Sky Stone	3.00
20 Ring Fortress	3.00
21 A-Girls	3.00
22 Gremlin Guild	3.00
23 escape from Mordovania	3.00
24 thru 30	@3.00
TPB Vol.1 rep.#1–#6	15.00
TPB Vol.2 rep.#7–#12	13.00
TPB Vol.3 rep.#13–#18	13.00
TPB Vol.4 rep. #19–#25.	13.00
TPB Vol.5 rep. #26–#30.	15.00
Spec. #1 Super Special	3.00
Super Special Final (2004)	3.25

GRENDEL
Comico, 1983

1 MW,O:Hunter Rose, rare	90.00
2 MW,O:Argent, rare.	75.00
3 MW,rare	70.00

GREY
Viz Select, 1989

Book 1	5.00
Book 2 scarce	5.50
Book 3	3.00
Book 4	3.00
Book 5	3.00
Book 6 thru Book 9	@2.50

Guerrilla Groundhog #1 #1
© Eclipse

GREYMATTER
Alaffinity Studios, 1993

1 thru 14 by Marcus Harwell	@3.00

GRIFFIN, THE
Slave Labor, 1988

1	2.25
1a 2nd printing	2.25
2 thru 4	@2.25

5	2.25

Amaze Ink, 1997

1 by DVa & Phil Allora	3.00
2 by DVa & Paul Way	3.00

GRIPS
Silver Wolf, 1986

1 Vigil	15.00
2 Vigil	12.00
3 Vigil	9.00
4 Vigil	8.00
Vol 1 #1 rep	2.50

Volume 2

1	2.50
2	2.50
3 thru 8	@2.25
9 thru 12	@2.50

GROUND ZERO
Eternity

1 Science Fiction mini-series	2.50
2 Alien Invasion Aftermath	2.50

GRRL SCOUTS
Oni Press, 1999

1 (of 4) by Jim Mahfood	3.00
2 thru 4	@3.00
TPB	12.00

Amazing Aaron, 1999

1 Aaron Warner.	3.00
2	3.00

GUERRILLA GROUNDHOG
Eclipse, 1987

1	2.25
2	2.25

GUILLOTIN
High Impact, 1997

Preview JQ,RCI	5.00

ABC Studios, 1999

Spec. Ed.	3.00
Spec. Ed. Serpent Ed.	8.00

GUILLOTINE
Silver Wolf

1 and 2	@2.25

GUN CRISIS
Ironcat, 1998

1 (of 3) by Masoami Kanzaki	3.00
2 & 3	@3.00

GUNDAM WING
Mixx Entertainment, 2000

1	5.00
2 thru 4	@4.00
TPB Pocket Mixx, Vol.1	10.00
TPB Pocket Mixx, Vol.2	10.00
TPB Pocket Mixx, Vol.3	10.00

Tokyopop.Com, 2000

5 thru 12	@3.00
TPB Vol. 1 Blue Destiny Mixx	13.00
TPB Gundam Technical Manual #1	13.00
TPB Gundam Technical Manual #2 thru #6	@13.00

GUNDAM WING: BATTLEFIELD OF PACIFISTS
Tokyopop Press, 2001

1 48-pg.	3.00

2 thru 5	@3.00
TPB Vol. 1	10.00

GUNDAM WING: ENDLESS WALTZ
Tokyopop Press, 2002

1 (of 5)	3.00
2 thru 4	@3.00
TPB 184-pg.	10.00

GUNDAM WING: G-UNIT
Tokyopop Press, 2002

1 (of 12)	3.00
2	3.00

GUNDAM WING: THE LAST OUTPOST
Tokyopop Press, 2002

1 (of 12)	3.00
2 thru 4	@3.00
TPB Vol. 1 (of 3)	10.00
TPB Vol. 2 thru Vol. 3.	@10.00

GUNDAM: THE ORIGIN
Viz Communications, 2002

GN #1 by Yoshikazu Yasuhiko.	8.00
GN #2 thru #12	@8.00

GUNFIGHTERS IN HELL
Broken Halos, 1999

GN by Tim & Joe Vigil	20.00
GN leather(c), signed & numbered	35.00
TPB Original Sin	8.00
TPB Original Sin, variant (c)	10.00
TPB Original Sin, special ed.	12.00
TPB Leather Hell	20.00
TPB Leather Hell, signed.	30.00

GUNFIGHTERS IN HELL: ORIGINAL SIN
Broken Halos, 2001

1	4.00
1a variant (c).	6.00
1 limited edition 16-pg.	7.00
2 24-pg.	4.00
2a cardstock (c)	4.50
2b limited edition.	6.00

GUN FURY
Aircel, 1989

1 thru 10	@2.25

GUN FURY RETURNS
Aircel, 1990

1	3.00
2	3.00
3 V:The Yes Men	2.25
4	2.25

GUNNER
Gun Dog Comics, 1999

1 by Eric Yonge.	3.00
2 thru 7	@3.00

GUNS OF SHAR-PEI
Caliber

1 The Good,the Bad & the Deadly	3.00
2 & 3	@3.00

GUTWALLOW
Numbskull Press, 1998

1 by Dan Berger	3.00

B & W PUB.

2 thru 7 The Gingerbread Man . . @3.00

GUTWALLOW
Digital Webbing 2002
1 (of 3) 3.00
2 Fury of the Furry 3.00
3 concl. 3.00
TPB Fury of the Furry 13.00

GYRE
Abaculus, 1997
1 by Martin Shipp & Marc Laming . 3.00
2 . . . . 3.00
3 Soul Keeper, pt. 3.00
4 . . . . 3.00
5 . . . . 3.00
6 . . . . 3.00
Spec. Edition 56-pg.. . . . . 4.50

HADES
Domain Publishing, 1995
1 F:Civil War Officer 3.00

HALL OF HEROES
Hall of Heroes, 1993
1 I:Dead Bolt. 12.00
2 and 3 . . . . @4.50
Ashcan, 8-pg.. . . . . 6.00
Halloween Horror Special 2.50
Halloween Horror Special '98 . . . . . 2.50

HALL OF HEROES PRESENTS
Hall of Heroes, 1996–97
0 by Doug Brammer & Matt Roach,
  `Slingers' by Matt Martin 2.50
1 . . . . 2.50
1a signed & numbered 4.00
2 `The Last Days' 2.50
3 `The Power of the Golem' 2.50
4 F:Turaxx the Trobbit. 2.50
5 . . . . 2.50

HALLOWIENERS
Mirage
1 . . . . 2.25
2 . . . . 2.25

HALO BROTHERS
Fantagraphics
Special #1 . . . . 2.25

HAMMER GIRL
Brainstorm, 1996
1 dinosaur, sci-fi adventure. 3.00
2 . . . . 3.00
2a deluxe 5.00

HAMSTER VICE
Blackthorne, 1986
1 . . . . 3.50
2 . . . . 2.50
3 thru 11 . . . . @2.25
New Series
Eternity, 1989
1 and 2 . . . . @2.25

HANGED MAN
Caliber, 1998
1 (of 2) by AIG & Arthur Ranson. . . 3.00
2 (of 2) 3.00
TPB 6.00

HARD GORE
Komics, Inc., 2000
TPB Vol. 1 . . . . 9.85
TPB Vol. 2 thru Vol. 7. . . . . @9.85

HARD ROCK COMICS
Revolutionary, 1992
1 Metallica-The Early Years 6.00
2 Motley Crew. 4.00
3 Jane's Addiction. 3.50
4 Nirvana 4.00
5 Kiss 9.00
5a 2nd printing 5.00
6 Def Leppard II 3.00
7 Red Hot Chili Peppers. 3.00
8 Pearl Jam. 3.00
9 Queen II. 3.00
10 Birth of Punk 3.00
11 Pantera 3.00
12 Hendrix 3.00
13 Dead Kennedys 3.00
14 Van Halen II 2.50
15 Megadeath 2.50
16 Joan Jett 2.50
17 Not printed
18 Queensryche. 2.50
19 Tesla 2.50
20 The Sweet. 2.50

HARI KARI
Blackout, 1995
1 . . . . 3.00
1a platinum. 8.00
1-shot Possessed by Evil(1997) . . . 3.00
1-shot Hari Kari Goes Hollywood
  (1997) 3.00
  Deluxe 15.00
Spec #1 Sexy Summer Rampage,
  gallery issue (1997). 3.00
  Deluxe, super sexy cover 10.00
1-shot Cry of Darkness (1998) 3.00
  Variant photo ultra sexy ed.. . . 10.00
1-shot The Last Stand (1998) 3.00
  Ultra sexy edition. 10.00
  Deluxe 15.00

HARI KARI MANGA
Blackout Comics, 1998
Spec. 0 Sex, Thugs & Rock 'n' Roll 3.00
1-shot Manga Adventures (1997) . . 3.00
1-shot Deadly Exposure, by Rob
  Roman & Nigel Tully 3.00
  Deluxe 15.00
1-shot Deadtime Stories, by Rob
  Roman & Nigel Tully 3.00
  Deluxe edition 15.00
1-shot Manga To Die For. 3.00
  Deluxe 15.00
1-shot Running From Poison. 3.00

HARPY: PRIZE OF THE OVERLORD
Ground Zero, 1996
1 (of 6) 3.00
2 thru 6 . . . . @3.00
1-shot Harpy Preview, prequel. 3.00
Peregrine, 1998
TPB rep. #1–#6 . . . . 15.00
Spec. Harpy Pin-up Book 3.00

HARTE OF HARKNESS
Eternity
1 I:Dennis Harte,Vampire
  private-eye. 2.50
2 V:Satan's Blitz St.Gang 2.50
3 Jack Grissom/Vampire. 2.50

4 V:Jack Grissom, conc. 2.50

HARVY FLIP BOOK
Blackthorne
1 . . . . 2.25
2 . . . . 2.25
3 . . . . 2.25

HATE
Fantagraphics, 1990
1 . . . . 15.00
2 . . . . 12.00
3 . . . . 9.00
4 . . . . 8.00
5 . . . . 8.00
6 . . . . 8.00
7 . . . . 7.00
8 thru 10 . . . . @6.00

Hellina X-mas in Hell
© Lightning Comics

11 and 12 . . . . @5.00
1a to 12a reprints . . . . @2.50
13 thru 15. . . . . @4.00
Hate Jamboree, 64-pg. 4.00
See Color

HAVOC, INC.
Radio Comix, 1998
1 by Mark Barnard & Terrie Smith . 3.00
2 thru 9 . . . . @3.00
10 . . . . 3.50
TPB Vol. 1 128-pg. 13.00

HEAD, THE
1 Old Airboy (1966). 2.25

HEAVEN SENT
Antarctic Press 2004
1 BDn 3.00
2 thru 5 . . . . @3.00

HEAVY METAL MONSTERS
Revolutionary, 1992
1 `Up in Flames' 2.25

HE IS JUST A RAT
Exclaim Bound Comics, 1995
1 & 2 V:Jimmy and Billy Bob 2.75

HELLGIRL
Knight Press, 1995
1 I:Jazzmine Grayce 3.00
1-shot Demonseed II, Bob Hickey &
Bill Nichols (1997) 3.00
1-shot Demonsong, Bob Hickey &
Bill Nichols (1997) 3.00
1-shot Purgatory (1997) 3.00

HELLINA
Lightning Comics, 1994
1-shot I&O:Hellina 5.00
Commemorative 10.00
1996 rep. gold 5.00
Spec. Hellina: Genesis with poster
(1996) 3.00
Platinum edition 4.00
Spec. Hellina: In the Flesh (1997)
two diff. mild covers . . . . @3.00
Spec. Hellina: Naked Desire (1997) 3.00
Cover B 3.00
Signed, ... 3.00
Spec. Hellina: Taking Back the Night
(1995) V:Michael Naynar 3.00
Spec. Hellina: Wicket Ways (1995)
A:Perg 2.75
Encore editions 3.00
Encore variant (c) 3.00
Spec. Hellina: X-Mas in Hell (1996)
two different covers . . . . @3.00
Platinum edition 5.00
Spec. Hellina: The Relic 3.00
Variant cover 3.00
Spec. 1997 Pin-up 3.50
1997 Pin-up, cover B 3.50
X-Over Hellina/Catfight (1995)
V:Prince of Sommia 2.75
Gold 4.00
Encore edition, mild covers,
2 different . . . . @3.00
X-Over Hellina/Cynder (1997) covA 3.00
Cover B 3.00
Spec Hellina #1 Skybolt Toyz
lim. ed. (1997) 2.25
TPB rep. Hellina appearances 9.00
TPB rep. one-shots 13.00

HELLINA
Avatar Press, 2003
0 . . . . 3.50
0a variant (c) 3.50
0b wraparound (c) 4.00
0c Hard Ruler Edition 6.00
0d Prism foil edition 13.00

HELLINA: HEART OF THORNS
Lightning Comics, 1996
1 (of 2) 3.00
1b autographed 5.00
2 . . . . 2.75
2a variant cover 2.75
2b platinum edition 6.00

HELLINA: HELL'S ANGEL
Lightning Comics, 1996
1 . . . . 2.75
1a platinum edition 8.00
1a platinum edition, signed 10.00
1c nude platinum edition 15.00
2 . . . . 2.75
2a platinum edition 8.00
1 encore edition, cover A 3.00
1a encore edition, cover B 3.00
1b deluxe encore edition, cover A . 5.00
1c deluxe encore edition, cover B . 5.00

HELLINA: KISS OF DEATH
Lightning Comics, 1995
1-shot A:Perg 4.00
1-shot gold edition 10.00
1-shot Encore editions 3.00
Lightning, 1997
1A 3.00
1B variant cover 3.00
1 encore, signed & numbered 5.00

HELLINA: SEDUCTION
Avatar Press, 2003
1/2 Carnage Edition 6.00
1/2 Statuesque Edition 6.00
Preview 2.25
Preview variant (c) 6.00
Preview Bad Girl edition 6.00
1 . . . . 3.50
1a wraparound (c) 4.00

HELLINA VS PANDORA
Avatar Press, 2003
0 16-pg 2.50
0a variant (c)s . . . . @4.00
1 (of 3) 3.50
2 thru 3 . . . . @3.50
1a thru 3a variant (c)s . . . . @3.50
Preview 2.25
Preview variant (c) 6.00

HELSING
Caliber Core, 1998
1W by Gary Reed & Low,
Wozniak(c) 3.00
1L Loudon (c) 3.00
1 variant cover 9.00
1 premium, signed 10.00
2 . . . . 3.00
3 . . . . 3.00
4 Secrets and Lies 3.00
Spec. Dawn of Armageddon, Secrets
& Lies, concl. 48-pg. 4.00

HELTER SKELTER
Antarctic Press, 1997
0 by Mike Harris & Duc Tran 3.00
1 (of 4) 3.00
2 thru 6 . . . . @3.00

HEPCATS
Double Diamond, 1989
1 . . . . 15.00
2 . . . . 12.00
3 Snow Blind 12.00
4 thru 9 . . . . @9.00
10 thru 13 . . . . @3.50
14 Chapter 12 . . . . 3.00
15 Snowblind Chp. 13 . . . . 2.75
Antarctic Press, 1996
1 by Martin Wagner 3.00
2 'Trial by Intimacy' 3.00
3 Snowblind,pt.1 . . . . 3.00
4 Snowblind,pt.2 . . . . 3.00
5 Snowblind,pt.3 . . . . 3.00
6 Snowblind,pt.4 . . . . 3.00
7 Snowblind,pt.5 Intrusion 3.00
8 Snowblind,pt.6 Super Heroes . . . 3.00
9 Snowblind,pt.7 Kevin & Kathryn . 3.00
10 Snowblind,pt.8 Exorcism,
Prelude 3.00
11 Snowblind,pt.10 Exorcism(a) . . 3.00
12 Snowblind,pt.10 Exorcism(b) . . 3.00
13 Snowbling,pt.11 It's a Garden
of Eden... . . . . 3.50
TPB Collected Hepcats 15.00

HERCULES
A Plus Comics
1 Hercules Saga 2.50

HERCULES PROJECT
Monster Comics, 1991
1 Origin issue,V:Mutants 2.25

HEROBEAR AND THE KID
Astonish Comics, 2000
1 . . . . 15.00
1a 2nd printing 3.50
2 . . . . 12.00
2a 2nd printing 3.50
3 . . . . 3.50
4 . . . . 3.50
5 Belief 3.50
TPB Vol. 1 The Inheritance 18.00

HEROBEAR AND THE KID: SAVING TIME
Astonish Comics 2004
1 (of 3) partial color 3.50

Hero Sandwich #1
© Slave Labor Graphics

HEROES
Blackbird, 1987
1 . . . . 5.00
2 . . . . 3.00
3 . . . . 2.25
4 comic size 2.25
5 thru 7 . . . . @2.25

HEROES ANONYMOUS
Bongo Comics, 2003
1 (of 6) 3.00
2 thru 5 . . . . @3.00

HEROES FROM WORDSMITH
Special Studios
1 WWI,F:Hunter Hawke 2.50

HEROES INCORPORATED
Double Edge Publishing
1 I:Heroes, Inc. 3.00
2 Betrayal 3.00

B & W PUB.

HEROIC TALES
Lone Star Press, 1997
1 by Robb Phipps & Bill Williams	2.50
2 Steel of a Soldier's Heart,pt.2	2.50
3 Steel of a Soldier's Heart,pt.3	2.50
4	2.50
5	2.50
6 The Belles of Freedom, prequel	2.50
7 The Children of Atlas,pt.1	2.50
8 by B.Williams & J.Parker, I:Atlas	2.50

HEROINES, INC.
Avatar
1 thru 5	@2.25

HERO SANDWICH
Slave Labor, 1987
1 thru 4	@2.25
5 thru 8	@2.25
9	2.25
Graphic Novel	8.00

HEY MISTER
Insomnia Comics, 1997
1	2.50
2	2.50

Top Shelf
3 by Pete Sickman-Garner	3.00
4	3.00
Spec. Behind the Green Door	3.00
Spec. The Trouble With Jesus	3.00
Spec. Eyes on the Prize	3.00
Spec. Dial "M" for Mister	3.50
TPB After School Special	5.00
TPB Celebrity Roast 144-pg	10.00

HIGH CALIBER
Caliber, 1997
1 64pg.	4.00
1 signed edition.	4.00
2 64pg.	4.00
3 48pg.	4.00
4	4.00

HIGH SCHOOL AGENT
Sun Comics, 1992
1 I:Kosuke Kanamori	2.50
2 Treasure Hunt at North Pole	2.50
3 and 4	@2.50

HIGH SHINING BRASS
Apple
1 thru 4	@2.75

HIGH SOCIETY
Aardvark–Vanaheim
1 DS,Cerebus	25.00

HIGHWAY 13
Amaze Ink/Slave Labor Graphics, 2000
1 thru 11 by Les McClaine	@3.00

HILLY ROSE'S SPACE ADVENTURES
Astro Comics, 1995
1 confronts Steeltrap.	6.00
1 2nd & 3rd pr. by B.C. Boyer	3.00
2	5.00
2 2nd & 3rd printing	3.00
3	3.50
3 2nd printing	3.00
4 thru 9	@3.00

TPB Vol.1 Rocket Reporter	13.00

HINO HORROR
DH Publishing 2004
GN Vol. 1 The Red Snake	10.00
GN Vol. 2 The Bug Boy	10.00
GN Vol. 3 thru Vol. 16	@10.00

HIT THE BEACH
Antarctic, 1993
1	3.00
1a deluxe edition.	5.00
2 & 3	@3.00
Spec. funny animal	3.00
Spec. 32 pg	3.00
Spec. deluxe	4.00
Spec. deluxe poster edition	5.00
Spec. 48-pg., 1999.	4.00
Spec. (#7) 48-pg., 2000	4.00
Ann. 2001.	4.00
Ann. 2002.	4.00
1-shot Hit the Beach 2003	5.00
1-shot Hit the Beach 2004	5.00

HITOMI AND HER GIRL COMMANDOS
Antarctic Press, 1992
1 Shadowhunter,from Ninja HS	2.50
2 Synaptic Transducer	2.50
3 Shadowhunter in S.America	2.50
4 V:Mr.Akuma,last issue	2.50

[Series II]
1 thru 10	@2.75

HOLLYWOOD'S GOLDEN ERA, 1930S
A-List Comics, 1999
1 (of 3)	3.00
2	3.00
3	3.00

HOLO BROTHERS, THE
Monster Comics, 1991
1 thru 10	@2.25

Fantagraphics
Spec.#1	2.25
TPB The Curse of the Bloated Toad	5.00

HOLY KNIGHT
Pocket Change Comics
1 thru 3	@2.50
4 V:His Past	2.50
5 V:Souljoiner	2.50
6 V:Demon Priest	2.50
7 Silent Scream,pt.2	2.50
8 `Dragon Quest,'pt.1	2.50
9 `Dragon Quest,'pt.2	2.50
10 `Dragon Quest,'pt.3	2.50
11 `Dragon Quest,'pt.4.	2.50

HONK
Fantagraphics, 1986
1 Don Martin	2.75
2	2.75
3	2.75

HONOR AMONG THIEVES
Gateway Graphics, 1987
1 and 2	@2.25

HOON
Eenieweenie Comics, 1995
1 I:Hoon	2.50

Horobi Part 1 #2
© Antarctic Press

2 Calazone Disaster	2.50
3 Reality Check.	2.50
4 thru 8	@2.50

HOON, THE
Caliber Tapestry, 1996
1	3.00
2 & 3	@3.00

HOPELESS SAVAGES
Oni Press, 2001
1	3.00
2 thru 4	@3.00
TPB Vol. 1	14.00
TPB Vol. 2 Ground Zero	12.00

HOPELESS SAVAGES: GROUND ZERO
Oni Press, 2002
1 (of 4)	3.00
2 thru 4	@3.00

HOROBI
Viz, 1990
1	4.00
2 thru 8	@3.75

Book 2, 1990–91
1 by Yoshihisa Tagami	3.50
2 D:Okado,Shoko Kidnapped	4.25
3 Madoka Attacks Zen	4.25
4 D:Abbess Mitsuko	4.25
5 Catharsis!.	4.25
6 Shuichi Vs. Zen	4.25
7 Shuichi vs. Zen, conc.	4.25

HORROR IN THE DARK
Fantagor
1 RCo,Inc.Blood Birth	2.25
2 RCo,Inc.Bath of Blood	2.25
3 RCo	2.25
4 RCo,Inc.Tales of the Black Diamond	2.25

HORROR SHOW
Caliber
1 GD,1977-80 reprint horror	3.50

HOT GIMMICK
Viz Communications, 2003
GN Vol. 1 . . . . 10.00
GN Vol. 2 thru Vol. 7 . . . . @10.00

HOUSE OF FRIGHTENSTEIN
AC Comics
1 . . . . 3.00

HOUSE OF HORROR
AC Comics
1 . . . . 2.50

HOWL
Eternity
1 & 2 . . . . @2.25

HOW TO DRAW TEENAGE MUTANT NINJA TURTLES
Solson
1 Lighter cover 10.00
1a Dark cover 5.00

H.P. LOVECRAFT'S THE CALL OF CTHULHU AND OTHERS
Cross Plains Comics, 1999
1-shot RTs,EM 6.00

H.P. LOVECRAFT'S THE DREAM-QUEST OF UNKNOWN KADATH
Mock Man Press, 1997
1 (of 5) by Jason Thompson 3.00
1 2nd printing 3.00
2 thru 5 . . . . @3.00

H.P. LOVECRAFT'S THE RETURN OF CTHULHU
Cross Plains Comics, 2000
1-shot RTs & EM 6.00

HSU AND CHAN
Amaze Ink/SLG, 2003
1 thru 5 . . . . @2.95
6 thru 7 . . . . @2.95
TPB Vol. 1 . . . . 13.95

HUGO
Fantagraphics, 1985
1 . . . . 4.00
2 thru 4 . . . . @2.25

HUMAN GARGOYLES
Eternity, 1988
Book one 2.25
Book two 2.25
Book three 2.25
Book four 2.25

HUNT AND THE HUNTED, THE
Newcomers Publishing
1 I:Aramis Thiron 3.00
2 V:Werewolves 3.00
3 Rio De Janero 3.00
4 F:Aramis Thiron 3.00

I Am Legend #2
© Eclipse

HURRICANE GIRLS
Antarctic Press, 1995
1 & 2 Tale of Dinon . . . . @3.50
3 thru 7 seven part series . . . . . . @3.00

HUZZAH
1 I:Albedo'sErmaFelna 50.00

HY-BREED
Division Publishing
1 thru 3 F:Cen Intel . . . . @2.25
4 thru 9 . . . . @2.50

HYPER DOLLS
Ironcat Manga, 1998
1 by Shinpei Itoh, F:Miyu & Maika . 3.00
2 thru 6 . . . . @3.00

VOL 2
1 . . . . 3.00
2 thru 6 . . . . @3.00

VOL 3
1 . . . . 3.00
2 thru 6 . . . . @3.00

VOL 4, 2000
1 . . . . 3.00
2 thru 6 . . . . @3.00

VOL 5, 2000
1 . . . . 3.00
2 thru 6 . . . . @3.00
TPB Vol. 1 . . . . 16.00
TPB Vol. 3 thru Vol. 5 . . . . @16.00

I.F.S. ZONE
1 thru 6 . . . . @2.25

I AM LEGEND
Eclipse, 1991
1 Novel adapt. aka Omega Man . . . 6.00
2 thru 3 68-pg. . . . . @6.00

ICARUS
Aircel, 1987
1 thru 9 . . . . @2.25

ICON DEVIL
Spider
1 by Neil Hanson 2.25

2 . . . . 2.25

2nd Series
1 thru 5 . . . . @2.25

I DREAM OF JEANNIE
Airwave Comics, 2002
1 JJu(c) 3.00
1 special edition 6.00
2 . . . . 3.00
2a variant photo (c). 3.00
3 . . . . 3.00
Preview Book #1 . . . . 7.00
Spec. Trick-or-Treats Annual #1 . . . 3.50
Spec.#1 Wishbook (2001) 3.00
Spec.#1 Wishbook, photo (c). 3.00
Spec. Spring Spectacular. 3.50
Spec. Spring Spectacular, photo(c) . 3.50

I HUNT MONSTERS
Antarctic Press 2004
1 . . . . 3.00
2 thru 8 . . . . @3.00
Pocket Manga TPB Vol. 1 . . . . 10.00

ILIAD
Amaze Ink, 1997
1 by Darren Brady & Alex Ogle . . . 3.00
2 thru 7 . . . . @3.00

ILIAD II
MicMac
1 . . . . 3.00
1a 2nd cover variation 3.00
2 . . . . 2.25
3 . . . . 2.25
4 . . . . 2.25

ILLUMINATUS
Rip Off, 1990
1 . . . . 2.25
2 . . . . 2.50
3 . . . . 2.50

INDUSTRIACIDE
Broken Tree Publications, 2002
1 (of 6) by Sean Dietrich. 3.00
2 thru 6 . . . . @3.00

INFERNO
Caliber Press, 1995
1 I:City of Inferno 3.00
2 Search for Identity 3.00
3 V:Malateste 3.00
4 by MCy and Michael Gaydos . . . 3.00
5 . . . . 3.00

INTERZONE
Brainstorm Comics
1 w/4 cards 2.50
2 w/4 cards 2.50

INTO THE STORM
Curtis Comics, 2002
Vol. 1 Manga
1 by Jihoon Park & Takyoung Lee . 3.00
2 thru 4 . . . . @3.00
Vol. 2
1 . . . . 3.00

INU YASHA
Viz Communications, 1997
1 thru 5 (of 10) by Rumiko
   Takahashi. . . . . @3.00

PART TWO:
A FEUDAL FAIRY TALE
Viz Communications, 1998
1 (of 9) by Rumiko Takahashi 3.00
2 thru 7 . . . . @3.00
8 thru 15 (of 15) . . . . @3.25
TPB 16.00
TPB Vol. 2 . . . . 16.00
PART THREE, 1999
1 (of 7) thru 7 . . . . @3.25
TPB Vol. 3 . . . . 16.00
PART FOUR, 1999
1 (of 7) by Rumiko Takahashi 3.25
2 thru 7 . . . . @3.25
TPB Vol. 4 . . . . 16.00
PART FIVE, 2000
1 (of 11) by Rumiko Takahashi 3.00
2 thru 11 . . . . @3.00
TPB Vol. 5 . . . . 16.00
TPB Vol. 6 . . . . 16.00
PART SIX, 2001
1 (of 15) 3.00
2 thru 7 . . . . @3.00
8 thru 15 . . . . @3.00
PART SEVEN, 2002
1 (of 8) by Rumiko Takahashi 3.00
2 thru 7 . . . . @3.00
TPB Vol.8 rep. Vol.4 #6–Vol5 #3 . . 16.00
TPB Vol.9 . . . . 16.00
TPB Vol.10 thru 12 . . . . @16.00
TPB Vol.13 thru Vol. 15 . . . . @9.00
TPB Vol.16 thru Vol. 19 . . . . @9.00
TPB Art of Inu-Yasha, color 23.00
Visual Manga Vol. 1 . . . . 9.95
Visual Manga Vol. 2 . . . . 11.95

Jackaroo #1
© Eternity

INVADERS FROM MARS
Eternity, 1990
1 . . . . 2.50
2 . . . . 2.50
3 . . . . 2.50
BOOK II, 1991
1 Sequel to '50's SF classic 2.50
2 Pact of Tsukus/Humans 2.50
3 Last issue. 2.50

INVASION '55
Apple, 1990
1 . . . . 2.25
2 . . . . 2.25
3 . . . . 2.25

INVISIBLE PEOPLE
Kitchen Sink
1 WE,I:Peacus Pleatnik 3.00
2 WE,The Power. 3.00
3 WE,Final issue. 3.00

ISLAND
Tokyopop Press, 2001
1 48-pg. 3.00
2 . . . . 3.00
3 . . . . 3.00
4 . . . . 3.00

ISMET
Canis
1 Cartoon Dog 8.00
2 . . . . 5.00
3 Rare 5.00
4 . . . . 5.00

IT'S SCIENCE
WITH DR. RADIUM
Slave Labor, 1986
1 thru 9 . . . . @2.25
Spec #1 . . . . 3.00

JACKAROO
Eternity, 1990
1 GCh 2.25
2 GCh 2.25
3 GCh 2.25

JACK HUNTER
Blackthorne, 1987
1 . . . . 3.50
2 . . . . 3.50
3 . . . . 3.50

JACK OF NINES
1 . . . . 2.25
2 thru 4 . . . . @2.25
5 . . . . 2.25

JACK STAFF
Dancing Elephant Press, 2000
1 by Paul Grist 3.00
2 thru 4 . . . . @3.00
5 . . . . 3.00
6 . . . . 3.00
7 . . . . 3.00
8 36-pg. 4.50
9 thru 12 . . . . @3.00
TPB Vol. 1 Yesterday's heroes . . . 16.00

JACK THE LANTERN
Castle Rain Entertainment 2002
0a signed and numbered 7.95
1 thru 3 . . . . @3.00
4 The quest. 3.00
5 The quest. 3.50
TPB 17.95

JACK THE RIPPER
Eternity
1 thru 4 . . . . @2.25

JAM, THE
Slave Labor, 1989
1 . . . . 3.00
2 thru 5 . . . . @3.00
Dark Horse, 1993
6 thru 8 . . . . 3.00
Caliber, 1995
9 . . . . 3.00
9 signed edition. 3.00
10 It's a Kafka Thing 3.00
11 thru 14 . . . . @3.00
15 `The Kinetic,'pt.3 . . . . 3.00

JAMES O'BARR
ORIGINAL SINS
ACG Comics, 2000
1 . . . . 3.00
2 . . . . 3.00

JAMES O'BARR
TASTY BITES
ACG Comics, 1999
1 . . . . 3.00
1a signed 10.00

JANE'S WORLD
Girl Twirl, 2003
1 by Paige Braddock 3.00
2 thru 12 . . . . @3.00
13 thru 15 56-pg. . . . . @6.00
TPB Vol. 1 . . . . 15.00
TPB Vol. 2 . . . . 15.00

JASON AND THE
ARGONAUTS
Caliber
1 thru 5 . . . . @2.50

JAY & SILENT BOB
Oni Press, 1998
1 (of 4) by Kevin Smith & Duncan
   Fregedo 5.00
1a Ph(c) 7.00
1b 2nd printing 3.00
2 thru 4 . . . . @4.00
TPB rep. #1–#4 . . . . 12.00

JAZZ
High Impact, 1996
1 . . . . 3.00
1 Gold variant edition RCI(c) 10.00
2 . . . . 3.00
2a deluxe edition. 10.00
3 . . . . 3.00
3a variant (c). 10.00

JAZZ THE SERIES
ABC Comics, 1999
1 RCI(c). 3.00
1a DOe(c). 3.00
2 . . . . 3.00

JAZZ: SOLITAIRE
ABC Comics, 1998
1 (of 4) by Jose Varese 3.00
1a photo cover 6.00
2 . . . . 3.00
2a Variant Exotika (c) 6.00
2b Variant Naughty (c) 6.00
3 . . . . 3.00
Collected Ed. 5.00

JAZZ: SUPERSTAR
ABC Comics, 1998
1 (of 3) by Jose Varese 3.00
1a JQ cover 6.00

JAZZ AGE CHRONICLES
Caliber, 1990
1 thru 6 . . . . @2.25
7 . . . . 2.50

JCP FEATURES
J.C. Productions, 1982
1 1st MT;S&K,NA/DG rep.
A:T.H.U.N.D.E.R.Agents,
TheFly, Black Hood Mag.Size . 11.00

JENNY FINN
Oni Press, 1999
1 (of 4) by MMi & Troy Nixey 3.00
2 MMi 3.00
3 MMi 3.00
4 MMi, concl.. . . . . 4.00

JEREMIAH
Fantagraphics, 1982–83
GN #1.. 35.00
GN #2.. 32.00

JEREMIAH: BIRDS OF PREY
Adventure Comics, 1991
1 I: Jeremiah,A:Kurdy 4.00
2 conclusion 4.00

JEREMIAH: EYES LIKE BURNING COALS
Adventure Comics, 1991
1 & 2 fourth series. . . . . @4.00

JEREMIAH: FIST FULL OF SAND
Adventure Comics
1 A:Captain Kenney 4.00
2 conclusion 4.00

JEREMIAH: THE HEIRS
Adventure Comics, 1991
1 Nathanial Bancroft estate 4.00
2 conclusion 4.00

JERRY IGERS FAMOUS FEATURES
Blackthorne
1 . . . . 3.00
2 thru 4 . . . . @2.25
Pacific
5 thru 8 . . . . @2.25

JETCAT CLUBHOUSE
Oni Press, 2001
1 by Jay Stephens 3.25
2 thru 4 . . . . @3.25
5 . . . . 3.25
TPB by Jay Stephens (2002) 11.00

JIM
Fantagraphics, 1987–90
1 . . . . 15.00
2 . . . . 12.00
3 and 4 . . . . @8.00

Second Series, 1994
1 . . . . 4.00
1a 2nd printing 3.00
2 . . . . 3.50
2a 2nd printing 3.00
3 thru 5 . . . . @3.00

JINGLE BELLE
Oni Press, 1999
1 (of 2) by PDi. 3.00
2 PDi. 3.00
All-Star Holiday Hullabaloo 5.00
1-shot Jingle Belle Jubilee. 3.00
1-shot The Mighty Elves 3.00
TPB Jingle Belle's Cool Yule 14.00
1-shot Winter Wingding 3.00
TPB Naughty & Nice (2000) 9.50

J. O'BARR's THE CROW
Kitchen Sink, 1998
0 F:Eric Draven, 48-pg. 3.50
1 . . . . 3.50
2 Demon in Disguise 3.50

JOE PSYCHO & MOO FROG
Goblin Studios, 1996
1 Fanatics Edition 2.50
1 Fanatics signed and numbered
    Edition 10.00
2 . . . . 2.50
2 signed & numbered 10.00
3 . . . . 2.50
4 . . . . 2.50
4B San Diego Con cover 5.00
5 . . . . 2.50
Spec. Psychosis Abnormalis 2.50

JOE R. LANSDALE'S BY BIZARRE HANDS
Avatar Press 2004
1 . . . . 3.50
2 thru 6 . . . . 3.50
1a thru 6a wraparound (c)s. . . . . @3.50

JOE R. LANSDALE'S THE DRIVE-IN
Avatar Press, 2003
1 (of 4) 3.50
2 thru 4 . . . . @3.50
1a thru 4a wraparound (c). . . . . . @4.00

JOE SINN
Caliber
1 I:Joe Sinn,Nikki 3.00
2 . . . . 3.00

JOHNNY ATOMIC
Eternity
1 I:Johnny A.Tomick 2.50
2 Project X-contingency plan 2.50
3 . . . . 2.50

JOHNNY COMET
ACG Comics, 1999
1 . . . . 3.00
2 . . . . 3.00
3 FF, rep.. . . . . 3.00
4 FF, rep.. . . . . 3.00
5 FF, rep.. . . . . 3.00

JOHNNY DARK
Double Edge
1 V:Biker Gang 3.00

JOHNNY RAYGUN
Jetpack Press, 2003
1 . . . . 2.95
2 thru 3 . . . . @2.95
Spec. Quarterly #1. . . . . 2.95

JOHNNY THE HOMICIDAL MANIAC
Slave Labor, 1996
1 by Jhonen Vasquez 15.00
1 3rd printing. 4.00
1 signed, limited 9.00
2 . . . . 8.00
2 3rd printing. 3.00
3 . . . . 7.00
3 3rd printing. 3.00
4 . . . . 5.00
4 2nd & 3rd printing 3.00
5 . . . . 4.00
5 2nd printing 3.00
6 . . . . 3.00
7 . . . . 3.00
TPB 20.00
TPB Director's Cut. 20.00

JOURNEY
Aardvark–Vanaheim, 1983
1 . . . . 7.00
2 . . . . 6.00
3 . . . . 5.00
4 . . . . 3.00
5 thru 7 . . . . @3.00
8 thru 14 . . . . @2.50
Fantagraphics, 1985
15 . . . . 2.50
16 thru 28 . . . . @2.25

JR. JACKALOPE
1 orange cover,1981. . . . . 8.00
1a Yellow cover,1981 . . . . 12.00
2 . . . . 8.00

JUDGE DREDD
Hamlyn, 2001
TPB Doomsday for Mega-City One 25.00
TPB Doomsday for Dredd 20.00
TPB Wilderlands, 216-pg. 30.00
GN Judge Dredd: Pit 16.00
GN Judge Dredd: Fetish 10.00
Titan, 2001
TPB Judge Dredd: The Emerald
    Isle. 15.00
TPB Judge Dredd: Death Aid 15.00

JULIE'S JOURNEY/ GRAVITY
Paper Live Studios, 1998
1 by David Keye 2.50
2 thru 6 . . . . @2.50

JULINE
Tokyopop Press, 2000
TPB Pocket Mixx, Vol. 1 . . . . 10.00
TPB Pocket Mixx, Vol. 2 . . . . 13.00
TPB Pocket Mixx, Vol. 3 . . . . 15.00
TPB Pocket Mixx, Vol. 4 . . . . 13.00
TPB Pocket Mixx, Vol. 5 . . . . 13.00

B & W PUB.

JUNGLE COMICS
Blackthorne, 1988
4 thru 6 . . . . @2.25

JUNGLE COMICS
A-List Comics, 1997
1 reprint of golden age 3.00
2 thru 6 . . . . @3.00
TPB Book of Jungle Comics
  Covers, 1940–54. . . . . 8.00

JUNGLE FANTASY
Avatar Press, 2002
Preview 2.25
Preview, Fauna (c) 2.25
Preview, Wild (c) 6.00
1 . . . . 3.50
1b wraparound (c). 4.00
2 . . . . 3.50
3 . . . . 3.50
3b Back to the Hunt Edition 6.00
4 . . . . 3.50
4b volcanic edition 5.95
1a thru 4a variant (c)s. . . . . @3.50
5 . . . . 3.50
5a wraparound (c). 3.50
1/2 Winged Death Edition 6.00

JUNGLE GIRLS
AC Comics, 1989–93
1 incGold.Age reps. 3.00
2 . . . . 3.00
3 Greed,A:Tara 3.00
4 CaveGirl. 3.00
5 Camilla. 3.00
6 TigerGirl. 3.00
7 CaveGirl. 3.00
8 Sheena Queen o/t Jungle 3.00
9 Wild Girl,Tiger Girl,Sheena 3.00
10 F:Tara,Cave Girl,Nyoka 3.00
11 F:Sheena,Tiger Girl,Nyoka 3.00
12 F:Sheena,Camilla,Tig.Girl. 3.00
13 F:Tara, Tiger Girl. 3.00

JUNIOR
Fantagraphics, 2000
1 (of 5) by Peter Bogge 3.00
2 thru 5 . . . . @3.00

JUPITER
Sandberg Publishing, 1999
1 by Jason Sandberg 3.00
2 thru 10 . . . . @3.00

JURASSIC JANE
London Night, 1997
1 by Sky Owens, F:Tira, elf
  princess of Atlantis 3.00
2 Sky Owens. 3.00
3 Sky Owens. 3.00
4 EHr, Sky Owens 3.00
5 by Preston Owens. 3.00
6 by Sky Owens 3.00
7 by Sky Owens 3.00
Coll. Ed. 5.00

JUSTICE
Newcomers Publishing, 1995
1 I:Judiciary Urban Strike Team . . . 3.00

JUSTY
Viz Communications, 1988
1 thru 9 . . . . @2.25

KABUKI:
CIRCLE OF BLOOD
Caliber Press, 1995
1 R:Kabuki 6.00
2 Kabuki Goes Rogue 5.00
3 V:Noh Agents. 5.00

Kansas Thunder #1
© Red Menace

4 V:Noh Agents. 3.50
5 V:Kai 3.00
6 . . . . 3.00
TPB Rep.#1-#6 . . . . 17.00
TPB deluxe, signed, etc. 25.00
TPB Compilation 8.00

KABUKI:
DANCE OF DEATH
London Night Studios, 1995
1 1st Full series 8.00

KABUKI:
MASKS OF THE NOH
Caliber, 1996
1A JQ(c) 3.00
1B Mays/Mack(c) 3.00
1C Buzz(c) 3.00
2 . . . . 3.00
3 DMk 3.00
4 epilog 3.00

KAFKA
Renegade, 1987
1 thru 6 . . . . @2.25
The Execution Spec. 2.25

KAMUI
Eclipse, 1987
1 Sanpei Shirato Art 4.00
1a 2nd printing 2.50
2 Mystery of Hanbie 3.00
2a 2nd printing 2.25
3 V:Ichijiro 2.25
3a 2nd printing 2.25
4 thru 15 . . . . @2.25
16 thru 19. . . . . @2.25
20 thru 37. . . . . @2.25

KANE
Dancing Elephant
14 thru 17 by Paul Grist. . . . . . . @3.50

18 thru 22. . . . . @3.50
23 thru 33. . . . . @3.00
TPB Book 1: rep. #1–#4 . . . . 12.00
TPB Book 2: Rabbit Hunt 12.50
TPB Book 3: Histories 12.50
TPB Book 4: Thrity Ninth. 20.00
TPB #5 Untouchable Rico Costas. 13.00

KANSAS THUNDER
Red Menace, 1997
1 . . . . 3.00

KAOS MOON
Caliber, 1996
1 by DdB. 3.50
1a 2nd edition 3.00
2 . . . . 3.50
2a 2nd edition, new cover. 3.00
3 . . . . 3.50
4 Anubian Nights, Chapter 2. . . . . 5.00
GN Full Circle, rep #1–#2 . . . . 6.00

KAPTAIN KEEN
Vortex, 1986
1 thru 3 . . . . @2.25
4 and 5 . . . . @2.25
6 and 7 . . . . @2.25

KATMANDU
Antarctic Press, 1993
1 thru 3 . . . . @2.75
4 & 5 Woman of Honor. 2.75
6 F:Laska 2.75
Med Systems
7 and 8 . . . . @2.25
Vision Comics, 1996
9 `When Warriors Die,'pt.3(of 3). . . 2.25
10 `The Curse of the Blood,'pt.1 . . 2.50
11 `The Curse of the Blood,'pt.2 . . 2.50
12 `The Curse of the Blood,' concl . 3.00
13 `The Search For Magic,'pt.1 . . . 3.00
Shanda Fantasy Arts
14 `The Search For Magic,'pt.2 . . . 3.00
15 `The Search For Magic,'pt.3 . . . 3.00
16 `Ceremonies,'pt.1 (of 3) 3.00
17 `Ceremonies,'pt.2 . . . . 3.00
18 `Ceremonies,'pt.3 . . . . 3.00
19 `Peace Keeper,'pt.1 . . . . 3.00
20 `Peace Keeper,'pt.2 . . . . 3.00
21 `Peace Keeper,'pt.3 . . . . 3.00
22 . . . . 3.00
23 and 24 . . . . @3.00
25 thru 31 48-pg. . . . . @5.00
Ann. #1 48-pg. 5.00
Ann. #2 . . . . 5.00
Ann. #3. . . . . 5.00
Ann. #4 . . . . 5.00

KAZAN
Comicsone.com, 2001
TPB Vol.1 188-pg. by Gaku Miyao 10.00
TPB Vol.2 187-pg. 10.00
TPB Vol.3 188-pg. 10.00
TPB Vol.4 188-pg. 10.00
TPB Vol.5 188-pg. 10.00
TPB Vol.6 202-pg. 10.00
TPB Vol.7 202-pg. 10.00

KEIF LLAMA
Fantagraphics
1 thru 6 . . . . @2.25

KELLEY BELLE, POLICE DETECTIVE
Newcomers Publishing
1 Debut issue	3.00
2 Case of the Jeweled Scarab	3.00
3 Case o/t Jeweled Scarab,pt.2	3.00
TPB #1	9.00

KID CANNIBAL
Eternity, 1991
1 I:Kid Cannibal	2.50
2 Hunt for Kid Cannibal	2.50
3 A:Janice	2.50
4 final issue	2.50

KIKU SAN
Aircel, 1988
1 thru 6	@2.25

KILLBOX
Antarctic Press, 2002
1	5.00
2 thru 3	@5.00

King Kong #1
© Monster Comics

KILLING STROKE
Eternity, 1991
1 British horror tales	2.50
2 inc.`Blood calls to Blood'	2.50
3 and 4	@2.50

KILROY
Caliber Core, 1998
1C by Joe Pruett & Feliciano Zecchin, John Cassaday(c)	3.00
1P JoP (c)	3.00
1a premium edition	10.00
2	3.00
3	3.00
4 O:Kilroy	3.00
Spec. Dawn of Armageddon, x-over, 48-pg.	4.00
Spec.#1 The Origin	5.00
Spec.#2 The Origin,pt.2	5.00
TPB Kilroy is Here: Pride, Prejudice & Persecution	7.00

KILROY IS HERE
Caliber Press, 1995
1 Kilroy Rescues Infant	3.00
2 Reflections,pt.2	3.00
3 Reflections,pt.3	3.00
4 Lincoln Memorial	3.00
5 thru 8	@3.00
9 and 10	@3.00
11 WEI,RPc,`Screen'	3.00
12 Khymer Rouge	3.00
Spec. Kilroy: Daemonstorm (1997)	3.00

KIMBER, PRINCE OF FELONS
Antarctic Press, 1992
1 I:Kimber	2.50
2 V:Lord Tyrex	2.50

KINDERGOTH
Bloodfire 2004
1	2.95
2 thru 4	@2.95

KINGDOM OF THE WICKED
Caliber, 1996
1 IEd	3.00
2 IEd	3.00
3 IEd	3.00
4 IEd	3.00
TPB rep. #1–#4	13.00

KING KONG
Monster Comics, 1991
1 thru 6	@2.50

KINGS IN DISGUISE
Kitchen Sink, 1988
1 thru 5	@2.25
6 end Mini-series	2.25

KING ZOMBIE
Caliber, 1998
1L by Tom Sniegoski & Jacen Burroughs, VcL(c)	3.00
1M Meadows (c)	3.00
2	3.00
3	3.00

KIRBY KING OF THE SERIALS
Blackthorne, 1989
1	2.25
2	2.25
3	2.25
4	2.25

KISSING CHAOS
Oni Press, 2001
1 (of 8) by Arthur Dela Cruz	2.50
2 16-pg.	2.50
3 16-pg.	2.50
4	3.00
5 16-pg.	2.50
6 16-pg.	2.50
7 16-pg.	2.50
8 24-pg.	2.50
TPB Vol. 1	18.00

KISSING CHAOS: NONSTOP BEAUTY
Oni Press, 2002
3 thru 4	@3.00
TPB Vol. 2	12.00
1-shot 1000 Words	3.00
1-shot Nine Lives	3.00

KITZ 'N' KATZ
Phantasy
1	3.50

Eclipse
2	2.25
3	2.25
4 and 5	@2.25

KLOWN SHOCK
North Star
1 Horror Stories	2.75

KNEWTS OF THE ROUND TABLE
Pan Entertainment, 1998
1	2.50
2 thru 6	@2.50

KNIGHTMARE
Antarctic Press, 1994
1	2.75
2	2.75
3 Wedding Knight,pt.1	2.75
4 Wedding Knight,pt.2	2.75
5 F:Dream Shadow	2.75
6 V:Razorblast	2.75

KNIGHT MASTERS
1 thru 7	@2.25

KNIGHTS OF THE DINNER TABLE
Alderac Group, 1994
1	50.00
2	30.00
3	20.00

Kenzer & Company, 1997
4 Have Dice Will Travel	15.00
5 Master of the Game	15.00
6 on the high seas	10.00
7 Lord of Steam	10.00
8 A:magic cow	5.00
9 To Dice for Sister Sara	5.00
16 thru 18	@5.00
19 thru 49	@3.00
50 double-size	5.00
51 thru 69	@3.00
70 thru 96	@4.00

TPB Vol. 1 thru Vol. 9 Bundle of Trouble	@10.00
TPB Vol. 10 Bundle of Trouble	12.00
TPB Tales From the Vault	10.00
TPB Tales From the Vault, Vol.2	10.00
TPB Tales From the Vault, Vol.3	13.00
TPB Tales From the Vault, Vol.4	10.00
TPB Fuzzy Knights	10.00
Spec. Black Hands Gaming Society	3.00
Spec. Origins 2003	3.00
Spec #2 Black Hands Gaming	3.00
Spec. Origins 2004	3.00

B & W PUB.

KNIGHTS OF THE DINNER TABLE: EVERKNIGHTS
Kenzer & Company, 2002
1 . . . . 3.00
2 thru 14 . . . . @3.00
Spec. Vs. King Arthur (2004) 3.00

KNIGHTS OF THE DINNER TABLE/FAANS
Six-Handed Press, 1999
X-over Spec. 3.00

KNIGHTS OF THE DINNER TABLE: HACKMASTERS
Kenzer & Company, 2000
1 . . . . 3.00
2 thru 8 . . . . @3.00
9 and 11 . . . . @3.00
11 . . . . 3.00
Becomes:

KNIGHTS OF THE DINNER TABLE: HACKMASTERS OF EVERKNIGHT
11 thru 15 . . . . @3.00
TPB Vol. 1 Ultimate Hackmasters . 14.00

KNIGHTS OF THE DINNER TABLE ILLUSTRATED
Kenzer & Company, 2000
1 . . . . 3.00
2 thru 8 . . . . @3.00
9 thru 39 . . . . @3.00
Travelers Special #1 . . . . 3.00
TPB Vol. 1 Overkill. 14.00

KNIGHTS OF THE DINNER TABLE MINI-SERIES
Kenzer & Company, 2003
Vol. 1
1 (of 3) 3.00
2 thru 3 . . . . @3.00
1a thru 3a variant (c) . . . . @3.00

KNIGHT WATCHMAN
Caliber Press, 1994
1 Graveyard Shift,pt. 1 . . . . 3.00
2 Graveyard Shift,pt. 2 . . . . 3.00

KODOCHA: SANA'S STAGE
Tokyopop Press, 2002
1 (of 5) by Miho Obana 3.00
2 . . . . 3.00
3 thru 5 . . . . @3.00

KOMODO & THE DEFIANTS
Victory
1 thru 6 . . . . @2.25

KORVUS
Human Monster Press, 1997
1 by Mick Fernette 3.00
2 . . . . 3.00
Arrow Comics, 1998
3 . . . . 3.00
VOL 2
1 . . . . 3.00
2 . . . . 3.00

KUNG FU WARRIORS
(Prev. ROBOWARRIORS)
CFW
12 . . . . 2.25
13 thru 19 . . . . @2.25

Lady Vampire #0
© Blackout

KUNOICHI
Lightning Comics, 1996
1 2 diff. mild covers. 3.00
1 platinum edition. 6.00
1 autographed edition 10.00

KYRA
Elsewhere, 1989
1 thru 5 by Robin Ator . . . . @2.25
TPB rep #1–#5 + pin-ups. 7.00

L33T: COMICS FOR GAMERS
Keenspot Entertainment, 2002
1 . . . . 5.00
2 thru 4 . . . . @5.00
5 24-pg. 3.00
6 thru 11 . . . . @5.00

LABOR FORCE
Blackthorne, 1986
1 thru 4 . . . . @2.25
5 thru 8 . . . . @2.25

LA COSA NOSTROID
Fireman Press, 1997
1 by Don Harmon & Rob Schrab . . 3.00
2 by Don Harmon & Edvis 3.00
3 . . . . 3.00
4 . . . . 3.00
5 . . . . 3.00
6 x-over madness 3.00
7 . . . . 3.00
8 . . . . 3.00
9 . . . . 3.00
10 final issue of Volume 1 . . . . 3.00

LACUNAE
CFD Productions, 1995
1 thru 4 F:Monkey Boys 2.50
5 thru 10 . . . . @2.50
11 HMo 2.50
12 HMo 2.50

LADIES OF LONDON NIGHT
London Night, 1997
Fall Special. 5.00
Winter Special 5.00
   Winter Wonderland Edition 7.00
Spring 98 Special 5.00
Spotlight: Devon Michaels 4.00

LADY ARCANE
Heroic Publishing
1 thru 4 . . . . @3.50

LADY VAMPRE
Blackout Comics, 1996
0 (1995) 2.75
1 flip-book 3.00
0 Immortal No More (1998) 3.00
Spec.#1 In the Flesh (1996) 3.00
Spec.#1a photo sexy cover 10.00

LADY VAMPRE RETURNS
Blackout Comics, 1998
1 by Rob Roman & Kirk Manley . . . 3.00
1a Deluxe edition 15.00

LAFFIN GAS
Blackthorne, 1986
1 . . . . 2.50
2 thru 12 . . . . @2.25

LANCE STANTON WAYWARD WARRIOR
1 and 2 . . . . @2.25

LANDER
Mermaid Producions
1 Power of the Dollar,pt.1 . . . . 2.25
2 Power of the Dollar,pt.2 . . . . 2.25
3 Power of the Dollar,pt.3 . . . . 2.25
Vol. 2
1 'By Whose Authority,'pt.1 . . . . . . 2.75
2 'By Whose Authority,'pt.2 . . . . . . 2.75

LAND OF OZ
Arrow Comics, 1998
1 by Gary Bishop & Bill Bryan 3.00
2 thru 6 . . . . @3.00

LAST DITCH
Edge Press
1 CCa(s),THa, ... 2.50

LAST GENERATION
Black Tie Studios, 1987
1 . . . . 5.00
2 . . . . 4.00
3 . . . . 2.25
4 . . . . 2.25
5 . . . . 2.25
Book One Rep. 7.00

LATEX ALICE
Basement Comics, 2003
0 . . . . 3.00
0a special edition 9.00
1 Blonde Ambition. 3.00
1a Blonde Ambition, special 9.00
Spec. Papercuts 3.00
Spec. #1 Paper Cuts 9.00
Bikini Bash Gallery #1 spec. 9.00

B & W PUB.

B & W PUB.

All comics prices listed are for *Near Mint* condition.

LEAGUE OF CHAMPIONS
Hero Comics, 1990
(cont. from Innovation L.of C. #3)
1 GP,F:Sparkplug,Icestar	3.50
2 GP(i),F:Marksman,Flare,Icicle	3.50
3	3.50
4 F:Sparkplug,League.	3.50
5 Morrigan Wars,pt.#1	3.50
6 Morrigan Wars,pt.#3	3.50
7 Morrigan Wars,pt.#6	3.50
8 Morrigan Wars Conclusion	3.50
9 A:Gargoyle.	3.50
10 A:Rose	3.50
11 thru 12.	4.00
13 V:Malice	4.00
14 V:Olympians	4.00
15 V:Olympians	3.00

LE FEMME VAMPRIQUE
Brainstorm, 1997
1	3.50

LEGENDLORE
Caliber New Worlds
1 JMt signed	3.00
3 JMt.	3.00
4 JMt	3.00
5 JMt.	3.00
6 flip book w/Boston Bombers #4	3.00
7 JMt.	3.00
8 JMt.	3.00
TPB Tainted Soul, rep. #1–#4	13.00
TPB In Misery's Shadow, Rep. #5–#7	10.00

LEGENDLORE: REALM WARS
Caliber New Worlds
1 by Joe Martin & Philip Xavier, Fawn cover by Xavier	3.00
1a Falla cover by Boller	3.00
1b signed	3.00
2	3.00
3	3.00
4 concl.	3.00

LEGENDLORE: WRATH OF THE DRAGON
Caliber Fantasy, 1998
1 by JMt & Philip Xavier	3.00
1 variant Philip Xavier(c).	3.00
2	3.00
3	3.00
4	3.00
5 Prisoner set free	3.00
Spec. Handbook	4.00
1-shot Legendlore: Slave of Fate by JMt & Philip Xavier	3.00
1-shot The Wind Spirits, 48-pg.	4.00
Giant Size Spec. 48-pg.	4.00

LEGENDS FROM DARKWOOD
Antarctic Press, 2003
1 thru 3	@3.50
4	3.00
TPB Vol. 1	10.00

LEGENDS OF CAMELOT
Caliber Fantasy, 1999
Excalibur	3.00
Quest For Honor	3.00
Merlin	3.00
The Enchanted Lady	3.00
Sir Balin & The Dolorous Stroke	3.00

LEGEND OF LEMNEAR
CPM Manga, 1997
1	3.00
2 thru 18	@3.00

Lensman Galactic Patrol #1
© Eternity

TPB Vol. 1 thru Vol. 3	@16.00

LEGEND OF THE EIGHT DRAGON GODS
Komics, Inc., 2000
GN Vol. 1	10.00
GN Vol. 2 thru Vol. 6	@10.00

LEGENDS OF LUXURA
Brainstorm, 1996
1 platinum edition	5.00
2 gold edition	5.00
3	3.00
TPB #1	13.00

LEGION ANTHOLOGY
Limelight, 1997
1 four stories	3.00
2	3.00
3 F:Binary Angel	3.00
4	3.00
5 Binary Angel.	3.00

LEGION X-I
Greater Mercury
1 McKinney.	5.00
2 McKinney,rare	15.00
Volume 2, 1989
1 thru 4	@2.25

LEGION X-2
Vol 2 #1	2.25
Vol 2 #2	2.25
Vol 2 #3	2.25
Vol 2 #4	2.25

LENORE
Slave Labor, 1998
1 by Roman Dirge.	3.00
2 thru 11	@3.00
TPB	12.00
TPB Vol. 2 Wedgies!	14.00

LENSMAN
Eternity, 1990
1 E.E.`Doc' Smith adapt.	2.25
2	2.25
3	2.25
4	2.25
5 On Radelix.	2.25
6	2.25
Collectors Spec #1, 56 pgs.	4.00
TPB Birth of a Lensman, rep.	6.00
TPB Secret of the Lens, rep.	6.00

LENSMAN: GALACTIC PATROL
Eternity, 1990
1 thru 7 E.E. `Doc' Smith adapt.	@2.25

LENSMAN: WAR OF THE GALAXIES
Eternity, 1990
1 thru 7	@2.25

LEONARDO
Mirage, 1986
1-shot TMNTurtles	13.00

LETHAL LADIES OF BRAINSTORM
Brainstorm, 1997
1 F:Luxura, Vampfire, etc.	3.00
1 luxury edition	5.00

LETHAL STRIKE ARCHIVES
London Night, 1997
1 rep. Razor #7, #10 & Uncut #19–#21.	3.00
TPB Lethal Strike (1998)	13.00

LETHAL STRIKE: SHADOW VIPER
London Night, 1998
1 (of 2) from Razor: Torture #4.	3.00
1 leather	15.00

LETHARGIC LAD ADVENTURES
Crusade Entertainment, 1997
1 by Greg Hyland	3.00
2	3.00
Becomes:	

LETHARGIC LAD
TV Comics, 1997
3 by Greg Hyland	3.00
4	3.00
5	3.00
TPB Big Book of Lethargic Lad	16.00
Lethargic Comics
6 by Greg Hyland	3.00
7 thru 14	@3.00

LEVEL X
Caliber, 1997
1	3.00
2 32pg.	3.00
3 48pg.	4.00

B & W PUB.

LEVEL X:
THE NEXT REALITY
Caliber, 1997
1 (of 2) by Dan Harbison & Randy
 Buccini, 64pg. 4.00
2 48pg. 4.00

LIBBY ELLIS
Eternity, 1988
1 thru 4 . . . . @2.25

LIBERATOR
Eternity
1 thru 6 . . . . @2.25

LIBERTY FROM HELL
Radio Comics, 2003
1 . . . . 3.00
2 thru 6 . . . . @3.00

LIBERTY MEADOWS
Insight Studios, 1999
1 by Frank Cho 26.00
2 . . . . 18.00
3 . . . . 10.00
4 thru 10 . . . . @8.00
11 thru 20 . . . . @6.00
21 thru 23. . . . . @5.00
24 Virtual Reality Adventure 5.00
25 Pool Party 5.00
26 Fossil Dinosaurs 5.00
Spec. Wedding Album 5.00

L.I.F.E. BRIGADE
Blue Comet
1 A:Dr. Death 2.25
1a 2nd printing 2.25
2 . . . . 2.25

LIFE OF A FETUS
Slave Labor, 1999
1 by Andy Ristaino 3.00
2 thru 7 . . . . @3.00

LIFEQUEST
Caliber, 1997
1 by Matt Vanderpol 3.00
2 thru 6 . . . . @3.00

LITTLE GLOOMY
**Amaze Ink/Slave Labor
Graphics, 1999**
1 by Landry Walker & Eric Jones . . 3.00
2 thru 6 . . . . @3.00
Halloween Spec. 3.50
TPB Vol. 1 . . . . 13.00

LITTLE ORPHAN ANNIE
Tony Raiola, 2001
TPB Man of Mystery 9.50
TPB Pro and the Con 9.50
TPB Little Worker 9.50
TPB The Dreamer 9.50
TPB Rich Man, Poor Man 9.50

LITTLE WHITE MOUSE
(THE SERIES)
Caliber, 1998
1 by Paul Sizer 3.00
2 Fever Dreams 3.00
3 Filthy Jake 3.00
4 . . . . 3.00

LITTLE WHITE MOUSE:
ENTROPY DREAMING
Blue Line Pro Comics, 2001
1 by Paul Sizer 3.00
2 Nuts and Bolts 3.00
3 . . . . 3.00
4 concl. 3.00

Logan's Run #3
© Adventure Comics

LITTLE WHITE MOUSE:
OPEN SPACE
Blue Line Pro Comics, 2002
1 (of 4) by Paul Sizer 3.00
2 thru 4 . . . . @3.00
TPB Vol. 3 . . . . 15.00

LIVINGSTONE MOUNTAIN
Adventure Comics, 1991
1 I:Scat,Dragon Rax 2.50
2 Scat & Rax Create Monsters 2.50
3 Rax rescue attempt 2.50
4 Final issue 2.50

LLOYD LLEWELLYN
Fantagraphics, 1986
1 Mag Size 4.00
2 thru 6 Mag Size . . . . @2.25
7 Regular Size 2.25

LOCO VS. PULVERINE
Eclipse, 1992
1 Parody 2.50

LODOSS WAR:
CHRONICLES OF THE
HEROIC KNIGHT
CPM Manga, 2000
1 by Ryo Mizuno & M. Natsumoto . 3.00
2 thru 19 . . . . @3.00
TPB Vol. 1 . . . . 16.00
TPB Vol. 2 thru Vol. 6. . . . . @16.00

LODOSS WAR:
DEELIT'S TALE
CPM Manga, 2001
1 by R. Mizuno & S. Yoneyama . . . 3.00

1a signed & numbered 15.00
2 thru 4 . . . . @3.00
5 thru 8 . . . . @3.00
TPB Vol. 1 Choices 16.00
TPB Vol. 2 Forest of No Return. . . 16.00

LODOSS WAR:
THE GREY WITCH
CPM Manga, 1998
1 by Ryo Mizuno & Yoshihiko Ochi. 3.00
2 by Ryo Mizuno & Akikiro Yamada 3.00
3 thru 10 . . . . @3.00
11 thru 22 . . . . @3.00
TPB Vol. 2 . . . . 16.00
TPB Vol. 3 . . . . 16.00

LODOSS WAR:
THE LADY OF PHARIS
CPM Manga, 1999
1 by Ryo Mizuno & Akihiro Yamada 3.00
2 thru 7 . . . . @3.00
TPB Vol. 1 208-pg. 16.00

LOGAN'S RUN
Adventure Comics, 1990
1 thru 6 Novel adapt. . . . . @2.50

LOGAN'S WORLD
Adventure Comics, 1991
1 Seq. to Logan's Run 2.50
2 thru 6 . . . . @2.50

LONER
Fleetway
1 Pt.1 (of 7). 2.25
2 thru 6 Pt.2 thru Pt.6 . . . . @2.25

LONE WOLF & CUB
First, 1987–91
1 FM(c) 7.00
1a 2nd printing 2.50
1b 3rd printing. 2.25
2 . . . . 4.00
2a 2nd printing 2.25
3 . . . . 4.00
4 thru 10 . . . . @4.00
11 thru 17. . . . . @3.00
18 thru 25. . . . . @3.00
26 thru 36. . . . . @3.00
37 and 38 . . . . @4.00
39 120-pg. 6.00
40 . . . . 3.25
41 MP(c), 60-pg. 4.00
42 thru 45 MP(c) . . . . @3.25

LOOKERS
Avatar Press, 1997
1 . . . . 3.00
1 deluxe 5.00
1 signed 12.00
2 . . . . 3.00
2 Deluxe cover 8.00
Spec. #1 . . . . 3.00
Spec. #1 signed 8.00
Spec. Allure of the Serpent (1999) . 3.50
Spec. Slaves of Anubis (1998). 3.50

LORD OF THE DEAD
Conquest
1 R.E.Howard adapt. 3.00

LORELEI
Power Comics, 1996
2 `Building the Perfect Beast,'pt.7 . 2.50

Love and Rockets #44
© Fantagraphics

3 `Building the Perfect Beast,'pt.8 . 2.50

Vol.2

0 2nd printing 2.50
1 . . . . 2.50
1a deluxe 4.00
1b signed 8.00

LORI LOVECRAFT
Caliber, 1997
1 MV, 48pg 4.00
1a signed 4.00
1-shot The Dark Lady (1997) 3.00
1-shot Repression (1998) 3.00
Spec. The Big Comeback (1998). . . 3.00

AV Publications, 2000
TPB Vol. 1 160-pg.. . . . . 12.00

LOST, THE
Caliber, 1996
1 . . . . 3.00
1a special ed. 7.00
1b signed 3.00
2 thru 4 . . . . @3.00

LOST CONTINENT
Eclipse, 1990
1 thru 5, Manga. . . . . @3.50

LOST STORIES
Creative Frontiers, 1998
1 . . . . 3.00
2 . . . . 3.00
3 . . . . 3.00
4 The Big Horn Bruhaha 3.00
5 Strike Force O'Shea,pt.1 . . . . 3.00
6 Strike Force O'Shea,pt.2 . . . . 3.00
7 Gnome for a Day 3.00
8 A Vampire Too Far 3.00
9 The Undertroll Saga,pt.1 . . . . 3.00

LOST WORLD, THE
Millennium, 1996
1 & 2 Arthur Conan Doyle adapt. @3.00

LOTHAR
Powerhouse Graphics
1 I:Lothar,Galactic Bounty Hunter. . 2.50
2 I:Nightcap. 2.50

LOUIS RIEL
Drawn & Quarterly, 1999
1 (of 10) by Chester Brown 3.00

---

2 thru 5 . . . . @3.00
6 thru 10 . . . . @3.00

LOVE AND ROCKETS
Fantagraphics Books, 1982–96
1 HB,B&W cover, adult 30.00
1a HB,Color cover 20.00
1b 2nd printing 4.00
2 HB 10.00
3 HB 6.00
4 HB 6.00
5 HB 6.00
6 HB 5.00
7 HB 6.00
8 HB 6.00
9 HB 5.00
10 HB. 5.00
11 thru 21 HB . . . . @3.00
22 thru 39 HB . . . . @3.00
40 thru 50 . . . . @3.00
Bonanza rep. 3.00
TPB Vol 9 Flies on the Ceiling,
    2nd printing 17.00
TPB Vol 10 . . . . 12.00
TPB Vol 11 . . . . 15.00
TPB Vol 12 . . . . 17.00
TPB Vol 14 Luba Conquers the
    World 15.00
TPB Vol 15 . . . . 15.00

Vol. 2, 2001
1 GHe,JHr, ... 4.00
1a 2nd printing 4.00
2 thru 9 . . . . @4.00
10 . . . . 5.95
11 . . . . 4.50

LOVE FIGHTS
Oni Press, 2003
1 . . . . 3.00
2 thru 4 . . . . @3.00
5 . . . . 6.00
6 thru 12 . . . . @3.00
TPB Vol. 1 . . . . 14.95

LOVE HINA
Tokyopop Press, 2002
1 (of 4) by Ken Akamatsu 3.00
2 thru 4 . . . . @3.00

LOVE IN TIGHTS
Amaze Ink, 1998
1 . . . . 3.00
Spec. Valentine's Day Special 3.00
Spec. Spring Fling 3.00
Anniv. #1 . . . . 3.00
6 . . . . 3.00
7 . . . . 3.00

LOVELY PRUDENCE
Millennium, 1997
1 by Maze 3.00
2 . . . . 3.00
3 Nightmares of Breeding 3.00
#M 24-pg. 2.25
#M 24-pg., signed 3.00
Spec. Swimsuit Special 3.00
Christmas Misery Spec.#1 . . . . 3.00

LUBA
Fantagraphics, 1998
1 by Gilbert Hernandez 3.00
2 thru 5 . . . . @3.00
6 thru 9 . . . . @3.50
TPB Luba in America (2001) 20.00

LUBA'S COMICS
& STORIES
Fantagraphics, 2000
1 by Gilbert Hernandez 3.00
2 GHe 3.50
3 GHe, Ofelia 3.50
4 GHe, The Light of Venus 3.50
5 GHe, Lovers and Hector 3.50
6 GHe 3.50

LUFTWAFFE 1946
[Mini-Series]
Antarctic Press, 1996
1 . . . . 5.00
2 thru 4 . . . . @4.00
TPB Vol.1, rep.mini-series #1–#4 . 11.00
Antarctic Press, 1997
1 by Ted Namura & BDn. 3.00
2 Luftsturm,pt.2 . . . . 3.00
3 Luftsturm,pt.3 . . . . 3.00
4 Luftsturm,pt.4 . . . . 3.00
5 new weapons. 3.00
6 Projekt Saucer,pt.1 . . . . 3.00
7 Projekt Saucer,pt.2 . . . . 3.00
8 Projekt Saucer,pt.3 . . . . 3.00
9 Projekt Saucer,pt.4 . . . . 3.00
10 Projekt Saucer,pt.5 . . . . 3.00
11 Projekt Saucer, epilogue 3.00
12 Richthofen's Flying Circus,pt.1 . 3.00
13 Richthofen's Flying Circus,pt.2 . 3.00
14 Jagdeschwader,pt.2 . . . . 3.00
15 Jagdeschwader,pt.3 . . . . 3.00
16 Jagdeschwader,pt.4 . . . . 3.00
17 Jagdeschwader,pt.5 . . . . 3.00
18 Schweinfurt. 3.00
Tech Manual Vol. 1 . . . . 4.00
Tech Manual Vol. 2 . . . . 4.00
Tech Manual Vol. 3 Rocket Fighters 3.99
Tech Manual Vol. 4 Amerika
    Bombers 3.99
Tech Manual Vol. 5 Wonder
    Weapons 3.99
Tech. Manual Vol. 6 . . . . 6.00
Spec.#1 Triebflugel 3.00
Spec.#1 World War II: 1946. . . . . . 4.00
Ann. #1 prototype artwork 3.00
TPB Vol.2, rep. #1–#5 . . . . 11.00
TPB Vol. 3, rep. 11.00
TPB Vol. 4, rep. #13–#18 . . . . . . 15.00
TPB 600-pg.. . . . . 50.00
New Volume (2002)
1 Tigers of the Luftwaffe 6.00
2 thru 18 . . . . @6.00
Pocket Manga Vol. 1 . . . . 10.00
Pocket Manga Vol. 2 thru Vol. 4. @10.00
Annual #2. 4.95
TPB Technical Manual 22.00

LUM*URUSEI YATSURA
Viz Communications
1 Art by Rumiko Takahashi 3.00
2 . . . . 3.00
3 . . . . 3.00
4 . . . . 3.00
5 . . . . 3.25
6 thru 8 . . . . @3.00

LUNAR DONUT
Cosmic Lunchbox Comics,
1996
1 thru 4 by Parham & Tucker . . . @3.00
Lunar Donut
5 . . . . 3.00
6 Powdered Sugar 3.00

LUXURA
Brainstorm, 1996
Convention Book 2 . . . . 3.00
Ann.#1 48pg (1998). 4.00
Pin-up mag. Luxura: The Good, The
  Bad and the Beautiful (1999) . . 4.00
Spec.1 Luxura & Vampfire, x-over
  by Fauve (1997) 3.00
Luxura Leather, Platinum edition . . . 5.00
Luxura Leather, Signed edition 8.00

LUXURA/BABY ANGEL X
Brainstorm, 1996
Spec. x-over. 3.00
Spec. deluxe 5.00
Luxury edition. 8.00
Deluxe luxury edition 12.00

LUXURA/WIDOW:
BLOOD LUST
Brainstorm
Omega x-over pt.2 concl.. . . . . 3.00
Omega Fusion cover 5.00
Luxury edition. 8.00
Deluxe luxury edition 12.00
See: Widow/Luxura for pt.1

LYNX: AN ELFLORD TALE
Peregrin, 1999
1 by Barry Blair 3.00
2 by Barry Blair & Colin Chan. 3.00
3 & 4 . . . . @3.00

M.A.C.H. 1
Fleetway
1 I:John Probe-Secret Agent 2.25
2 thru 9 . . . . @2.25

MACKENZIE QUEEN
Matrix, 1985
1 thru 5 . . . . @3.75

MACROSS II
Viz Comics, 1992
1 Macross Saga sequel 2.75
2 A:Ishtar. 2.75
3 F:Reporter Hibiki,Ishtar 2.75
4 V:Feff,The Marduk 2.75
5 . . . . 2.75
6 . . . . 2.75
7 Sylvie Confesses. 2.75
8 F:Ishtar. 2.75
9 V:Marduk Fleet 2.75
10. . . . . 2.75

MACROSS II: THE
MICRON CONSPIRACY
Viz, 1994
1 Manga 2.75

MAD DOGS
Eclipse, 1992
1 I:Mad Dogs(Cops) 2.50
2 V:Chinatown Hood 2.50
3 . . . . 2.50

MADMAN
Oni Press, 2002
TPB Madman Adventures (2002) . 15.00
TPB The Odyity Odyssey,
  10th Anniv. (2002) 16.00

MAD RACCOONS
MU Press, 1991
1 thru 7 by Cathy Hill, Angst of
  an Artist . . . . @3.00

Mai, The Psychic Girl #7
© Eclipse

MAELSTROM
Aircel, 1987
1 thru 13 . . . . @2.25

MAGGOTS
Hamilton, 1991
1 JSon, mag size 4.00
2 JSon, mag size 4.00
3 GM/JSon,inc.`Some Kinda
  Beautiful' 4.00

MAGICAL MATES
Antarctic Press, 1995
1 & 2 Manga, by Mio Odagi . . . . @3.00
3 thru 8 (of 8) . . . . @3.00

MAGICAL POKEMON
JOURNEY
Viz Communications, 2000
1 How Do You Do, Pikachu 5.00
2 Cooking with Jigglypuff 5.00
3 Pokemon Holiday. 5.00
4 Fun at the Beach 5.00
TPB Vol. 1 Party with Pikachu. . . 14.00

PART 2, 2000
1 thru 4 . . . . @5.00

PART 3, 2000
1 thru 4 . . . . @5.00
TPB Vol.3 Wal Comes Crashing
  Down 14.00

PART 4, 2001
1 thru 4 Love Potion Pursuit . . . . @5.00
TPB Vol.4 Friends & Family. 14.00

PART 5, 2001
1 thru 4 . . . . @5.00
TPB Vol.5 Going Coconuts 14.00

PART 6, 2001
1 (of 4) 5.00
2 thru 4 . . . . @5.00
TPB Vol.6 Gold & Silver. 14.00

PART 7, 2002
1 . . . . 5.00
2 thru 4 . . . . @5.00
TPB Vol.7 From the Heart 14.00

MAGIC PRIEST
Antarctic Press, 1998
1 (of 3) by B.Lyga & N.Googe . . . 3.00
2 . . . . 3.00

MAGIC WHISTLE
Alternative Press
Vol 2
1 by Sam Henderson 3.00
2 thru 8 . . . . @3.00
9 96-pg. 11.95

MAGUS
Caliber Core, 1998
1L by Gary Reed & Craig Brasfield,
  VcL(c) 3.00
1D GyD(c). 3.00
1 premium edition, signed 10.00
2 Magus secrets 3.00
3 Lilith & Beezlebub 3.00
1-shot Magus: The Forever King. . . 3.00
Spec. Dawn of Armageddon,
  x-over, 48-pg. 3.00

MAI, THE PSYCHIC GIRL
Eclipse, 1987
1 I:Mai,Alliance of 13 Sages 3.75
1a 2nd printing 2.50
2 V:Wisdom Alliance 2.50
2a 2nd printing 2.50
3 V:Kaeida,I:Ojii-San. 2.50
4 . . . . 2.50
5 thru 19 . . . . @2.50
20 thru 28 . . . . @2.50

MAID ATTACK
**White Lightning Productions,
2003**
1 (of 4) 4.00
2 thru 4 . . . . @4.00

MAISON IKKOKU
Viz Comics, 1993
1 thru 7 Manga 3.00

[Part Two]
1 thru 6 . . . . 3.00

[Part Three]
1 thru 6 . . . . 3.00

[Part Four]
1 thru 6 F:Kyoko 3.00
7 thru 10 . . . . @3.00

[Part Six], 1996
1 thru 11 by Rumiko Takahashi. . @3.50

[Part Seven], 1997
1 thru 8 by Rumiko Takahashi . . @3.25
9 thru 10 . . . . @3.50

[Part Eight], 1998
1 (of 8) 3.25
2 . . . . 3.50
3 thru 8 . . . . @3.25

[Part Nine], 1999
1 (of 10) 3.25
2 thru 10 . . . . @3.25
TPB Vol. 2 Family Affairs 10.00
TPB Vol. 3 . . . . 10.00
TPB Vol. 4 Good Housekeeping . . 16.00
TPB Vol. 5 Empty Nest 16.00
TPB Vol. 6 Bedside Manners. 16.00
TPB Vol. 7 Intensive Care 16.00

TPB Vol. 8 Domestic Dispute 17.00
TPB Vol. 10 Dogged Pursuit 18.00
TPB Vol. 11 Student Affairs 17.00
TPB Vol. 12 The Hounds of War . . 17.00
TPB Vol. 14 Welcome Home 17.00

MANDRAKE
1 . . . . 4.00
2 . . . . 4.00
3 . . . . 4.00
Ultimate Mandrake. 15.00

MANDRAKE MONTHLY
1 . . . . 4.00
2 . . . . 4.00
3 . . . . 5.00
4 . . . . 5.00
5 . . . . 5.00
6 . . . . 7.00
Special #1 . . . . 7.00

MAN-EATING COW
New England Comics, 1992
1 Spin-off from the Tick. 3.25
2 O:Mr.Krinkles,A:Lt.Valentine . . . 2.75
3 Final issue 2.75

Man of Rust #1B
© Blackthorne

Bonanza #1, 128pg (1996) 5.00
Bonanza #2, 100pg.. . . . . 5.00

MAN-ELF
3 A:Jerry Cornelius 2.25

MAN FROM U.N.C.L.E.
Entertainment Publ., 1987
1 `Number One with a Bullet Affair . 3.50
2 `Number One with a Bullet Affair . 3.00
3 `The E-I-E-I-O Affair' 3.00
4 `The E-I-E-I-O Affair,' concl. 3.00
5 `The Wasp Affair' 3.00
6 `Lost City of THRUSH Affair'. . . . 3.00
7 `The Wildwater Affair' 3.00
8 `The Wilder West Affair' 3.00
9 `The Canhadian Lightning Affair'. 3.00
10 `The Turncoat Affair' 3.00
11 `Craters of the Moon Affair'. 3.00

MANGA EX
Antarctic Press, 2001
1 thru 5 . . . . @7.00
6 . . . . 7.00

MANGAPHILE
Radio Comix, 1999
1 thru 5 . . . . @3.00
6 thru 11 . . . . @3.00
12 48-pg. 4.00
13 48-pg. 4.00
14 thru 21 48-pg. 4.00
22 thru 25. . . . . @5.00

MANGA VIZION
Viz Communications
Vol. 1, 1995
1 thru 10 Ogre Slayer . . . . @5.00
Vol. 2, 1996
1 thru 12 . . . . @5.00
Vol. 3, 1997
1 thru 8 . . . . @5.00
Vol. 4
1 thru 8 . . . . @5.00

MANGAZINE
Antarctic Press, 1985
1 newsprint cover 15.00
1a reprint. 3.00
2 . . . . 9.00
3 . . . . 8.00
4 . . . . 8.00
5 . . . . 8.00
New Series
1 . . . . 3.00
2 . . . . 3.00
3 . . . . 2.25
4 . . . . 2.25
5 thru 7 . . . . @2.25
8 thru 13 . . . . @2.25
14 New Format 3.00
15 thru 44. . . . . @3.00
VOL. 3, 1999
1 thru 15 . . . . @9.00
16 thru 27 140+-pg. . . . . @9.00
28 thru 39. . . . . @9.00
40 thru 59 . . . . @10.00

MANIMAL
Renegade, 1986
1 EC,rep.. 2.25

MAN OF RUST
Blackthorne, 1986
1 Cover A 2.25
1 Cover B 2.25

MANSLAUGHTER
Brainstorm, 1996
1 . . . . 3.00
1a gold foil edition. 5.00

MANTUS FILES
Eternity
1 Sidney Williams novel adapt 2.50
2 Vampiric Figures 2.50
3 Securas' Mansion 2.50
4 A:Securas 2.50

MARCANE
Eclipse
1 Book 1,JMu 6.00

MARK I
(Prev.: Atomic Comics)
2 . . . . 2.25

MARK MILLAR'S THE UNFUNNIES
Avatar, 2003
1 thru 3 . . . . @3.50
1a Platinum (c) 6.00
1a thru 3a offensive (c) . . . . @3.50

MARMALADE BOY
Tokyopop Press, 2001
1 (of 5) by Wataru Yoshizumi 3.00
2 thru 5 . . . . 3.00

MARQUIS, THE
Caliber, 1997
1 GyD 3.00
1 spec. double gatefold cover. 6.00
2 Marquis cover by Vincent Locke . 3.00
2a Marquis view of world GyD(c) . . 3.00
3 . . . . 3.00
Spec. The Marquis, Gallery of
Hell, GyD 4.00
Spec. The Marquis: Les Preludes,
GyD prelude edition (1996). . . . 3.00
Spec.A Les Preludes, signed. 3.00

MARQUIS, THE: DANSE MACABRE
Oni Press, 2000
1 (of 5) by Guy Davis 3.00
2 . . . . 3.00
3 thru 5 . . . . @3.00
TPB 19.00

MARTIAN SUCCESSOR NADESICO
CPM Manga, 1999
1 by Kia Asamiya 3.00
2 . . . . 3.00
3 . . . . 3.00
4 thru 15 . . . . @3.00
16 thru 26 . . . . @3.00
TPB Vol. 1 . . . . 16.00
TPB Book 2 176-pg. 16.00
TPB Book 3 176-pg. 16.00
TPB Book 4 208-pg. 16.00

MASKED WARRIOR X
Antarctic Press, 1996
1 (of 6) by Masayuki Fujihara 3.50
2 . . . . 3.00
3 The Girls of Olympus,' pt.2 . . . . . 3.00
4 `Protect the Silver Fortress'. 3.00

MASQUERADE
Eclipse
1 . . . . 2.25
2 . . . . 2.25
3 . . . . 2.25

MATAAK
K-Blamm, 1995
1 I:Mataak 2.50
2 Spirit of Peace 2.50

MATT CHAMPION
Metro
1 EC 2.25
2 EC 2.25

MAVIS
Exhibit A, 1998
1 BLs, F:Wolff & Byrd's secretary . 3.00
2 . . . . 3.00

B & W PUB.

MAXION
CPM, 1999
1 by Takeshi Takebayashi.	3.00
2 thru 11	@3.00
12 thru 24	@3.00
25	3.00
26	3.00
TPB Book 1	16.00
TPB Book 2	16.00
TPB Book 3 Waves of Misfortune	16.00
TPB Book 4 Maniac Obsessions	16.00

MAX OF THE REGULATORS
Atlantic
1	4.00
2	3.50
3	3.50
4	3.50

MAXWELL MOUSE FOLLIES
Renegade, 1986
1 Large format (1981)	4.00
1a Comic Size(1986)	3.00
2 thru 6	@2.25

MAYHEM
1 Mask(c)	9.00
2 thru 6	@8.00

MAZE AGENCY
Caliber, 1997
1 The Death of Justice Girl reprint series	3.00
1a signed	3.00
2 and 3	@3.00
2a and 3a variant AH(c)s	@3.00

MEASLES
Fantagraphics, 1998
1 by Gilbert Hernandez.	3.00
2 thru 8	@3.00

MEAT CAKE
Fantagraphics, 1995
1 thru 4	@2.50
5 thru 8	@3.00
9 thru 13	@4.00

MECHANOIDS
Caliber, 1991
1	2.50
2 thru 5	@3.50

MECHARIDER: THE REGULAR SERIES
Castle
1 thru 3 F:Winter	3.00
Spec.#1 Limited Edition	3.00

MEDABOTS
Viz Communications, 2002
Part 1
1 (of 4) by Rin Horuma	2.75
2 thru 4	@2.75
Part 2
1 (of 4) New Challenges	2.75
2 thru 4	@2.75
Part 3
1 (of 4)	2.75
2 thru 4	@2.75

Part 4
1 by Horumarin	2.75
2 thru 4	2.75
TPB Vol. 1 A Boy and His 'Bot.	10.00
TPB Vol. 2 Let's Get Ready to Robattle	10.00
TPB Vol. 3 The Medaforce	10.00
TPB Vol. 4 Finale	10.00

MEGATON
Megaton, 1983
1 JG(c),EL(1stProWork),GD,MG, A:Ultragirl,Vanguard	9.00
2 EL,JG(pin-up),A:Vanguard.	8.00
3 MG,AMe,JG,EL,I:Savage Dragon.	13.00
4 AMe,EL,2nd A:Savage Dragon (inc.EL profile)	9.00
5 AMe,RLd(inside front cover)	3.00
6 AMe,JG(inside back cover), EL(Back cover)	3.00
7 AMe	3.00
8 RLd,I:Youngblood(Preview)	18.00

Merlin #2
© Adventure Comics

MEGATON MAN MEETS THE UNCATEGORIZABLE X-THEMS
Jabberwocky, 1989
1	2.25

MEGATON MAN VS. FORBIDDEN FRANKENSTEIN
Fiasco Comics, 1996
1 by Don Simpson & Anton Drek	3.00

MELISSA MOORE: BODYGUARD
Draculina Publishing, 1995
1 thru 3 V:Machine Gun Eddie	@3.00

MEMORY MAN
Emergency Stop Press, 1995
1 thru 2 Some of the Space Man	3.00

MEN IN BLACK
Aircel, 1991
1 by Lowell Cunningham & Sandy

Carruthers, basis of Movie	35.00
2	20.00
3 F:Jay, Arbiter Doran	20.00
[Book II], 1991
1	15.00
2 thru 3	@8.00

MEN IN BLACK: THE ROBORG INCIDENT
Castle
1 thru 3	@3.00

MERCEDES
Angus Publishing, 1995
8 thru 15 by Mike Friedland & Grant Fuhst	@3.00
TPB Vol. 2	11.00
TPB Vol. 3, rep. The Wicked from #11–#15.	11.00
VOL. 4
1 thru 4	@3.00
VOL. 5, 1997
1	3.00
2	3.00
3	3.00
Spec. Senseless Acts of Beauty (1998)	3.00

MERCHANTS OF DEATH
Eclipse, 1988
1 thru 5	@2.25

MERCY
Avatar Press, 1997
0 O:Mercy	3.00
0b leather cover	30.00
1 (of 2) by Bill Maus	3.00
1 leather cover	25.00
1 signed	10.00

MERLIN
Adventure Comics, 1990
1 BMC,Merlin's Visions.	2.50
2 V:Warlord Carados	2.50
3	2.50
4 Ninevah	2.50
5 D:Hagus.	2.50
6 Final Issue	2.50
[2nd Series]
1 Journey of Rhiannon & Tryon	2.50
2 Conclusion	2.50

MERMAID'S GAZE
Viz Comics, 1995
1 thru 3 V:Shingo	2.75
4 final issue	2.75
TPB	16.00

METACOPS
Monster Comics, 1991
1 and 2	@2.25

METAL GUARDIAN FAUST
Viz Communications, 1997
1 by Tetsuo Ueyama	@3.00
2 thru 8	@3.00
TPB Vol. 1	17.00

METROPOLIS
Caliber, 1997
0 movie adaptation, series prequel,48pg	4.00
1 The Last Fredersen, pt.1	3.00

All comics prices listed are for *Near Mint* condition.

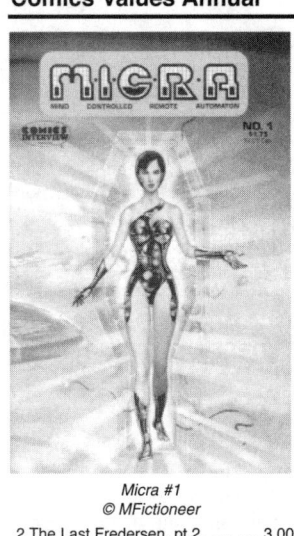

Micra #1
© MFictioneer

2 The Last Fredersen, pt.2 . . . . . . 3.00
3 The Last Fredersen, pt.3 . . . . . . 3.00

METAPHYSIQUE
Eclipse
1 NB,Short Stories 2.50
2 NB,Short Stories 2.50

MIAMI MICE
Rip Off Press, 1986
1 1st printing 3.00
1a 2nd printing 2.25
3 . . . . 2.25
4 Record,A:TMNT 3.00

MICHELANGELO
Mirage, 1986
1 TMNT 17.00
1a 2nd Printing 4.50

MICRA
Fictioneer, 1986
1 . . . . 4.00
2 . . . . 3.00
3 . . . . 3.00
4 thru 8 . . . . @2.25

MIDNIGHT
Blackthorne
1 thru 4 . . . . @2.25

MIDNIGHT MOVER
Oni Press, 2003
1 (of 4) 2.95
2 thru 4 . . . . @2.95
TPB 11.95

MIDNIGHT PANTHER
CPM Comics, 1997
1 Manga, translated 3.00
2 . . . . 3.00
3 . . . . 3.00
4 . . . . 3.00
5 . . . . 3.00
6 Den of Scoundrels 3.00
7 The Sleeping Town 3.00
8 to Reincarnation City 3.00
9 O:Midnight Panthers 3.00
10 . . . . 3.00

11 . . . . 3.00
12 . . . . 3.00
TPB Sex, Death and Rock 'n' Roll.
  rep #1–#6 . . . . 16.00
TPB Book 2: Feline Fanatics,
  rep.#7–#12 . . . . 16.00
Spec. Breaking Up is Hard to Do . . . 3.00

MIDNIGHT PANTHER: FEUDAL FANTASY
CPM Manga, 1998
1 by Yu Asagiri 3.00
2 thru 5 . . . . @3.00
TPB Book 4: Feudal Fantasy 16.00

MIDNIGHT PANTHER: SCHOOL DAZE
CPM Comics, 1998
1 (of 5) by Yu Asagiri 3.00
2 thru 5 . . . . @3.00
TPB Book 3: School Daze 16.00

MIDNITE SKULKER
Target, 1986
1 thru 7 . . . . @2.25

MIGHTY GUY
C&T, 1987
1 thru 6 . . . . @2.25
Summer Fun Spec #1 . . . . 2.50

MIGHTY MITES
Eternity, 1986
1 I:X-Mites 2.25
2 & 3 . . . . @2.25

MIGHTY MOUSE ADVENTURE MAGAZINE
Spotlight, 1987
1 . . . . 5.00

MIGHTY TINY
Antarctic
1 thru 4 . . . . @2.25
5 . . . . 2.50
Mouse Marines Collection rep. 7.50

MIKE HOFFMAN'S LOST WORLDS OF FANTASY AND SCI-FI
Antimater/Hoffman Int., 2003
1 . . . . 3.00
1 spec. edition 9.00
2 thru 10 . . . . @3.00
3a thru 4a special edition 9.00
7a special edition 8.95
TPB Best of Lost Worlds 9.95
Basement comics
8 . . . . 9.00
10 special ed. 8.00

MIKE HOFFMAN'S MONSTERS AND MAIDENS
Antimater/Hoffman International, 2003
1 . . . . 3.50
2 . . . . 3.00

MIKE HOFFMAN'S TIGRESS
Black Daze, 2000
1 by Mike Hoffman 3.00
Antimater/Hoffman Int., 2003
TPB Vol. 1 Journey to Caldathrea . 10.00
Spec. Cover Gallery Spec 9.00

MILK & CHEESE
Slave Labor, 1991–97
1 EDo, Milk Products gone bad . . 55.00
1a 2nd thru 7th printing 3.50
2 . . . . 32.00
2a 2nd thru 4th printing 10.00
3 . . . . 22.00
3a 2nd thru 4th printing 10.00
4 . . . . 15.00
4a 2nd & 3rd printing 3.00
5 . . . . 15.00
5a 2nd & 3rd printing 3.00
6 . . . . 10.00
6a 2nd printing 2.75
Other #1 . . . . 2.75
Third #1 . . . . 2.75
Fourth #1 . . . . 2.75
First #2 . . . . 2.75
Six Six Six #1 . . . . 2.75
Six Six Six 2nd printing, EDo 2.75
Latest Thing 3.00
TPB Fun with Milk & Cheese, rep.
  1st 4 issues 12.00

MILLENNIUM 2.5: THE BUCK ROGERS SAGA
ACG Comics, 2000
1 by Dick Calkin 3.00
2 thru 4 . . . . @3.00

MILTON CANIFF'S TERRY & THE PIRATES
ACG Comics, 1999
1 by Milton Caniff 3.00
2 . . . . 3.00
3 . . . . 3.00
4 . . . . 3.00
TPB Spec. (2001) 13.00

MINIMUM WAGE
Fantagraphics, 1995
Vol. 1, new printing 11.00
Vol. 2, 1995
1 thru 4 . . . . @3.00
5 by Bob Fingerman 3.00
6 . . . . 3.00
7 . . . . 3.00
8 . . . . 3.00
9 Artsy Fartsy 3.00
10 . . . . 3.00
TPB Vol. 2, rep. #1–#5 . . . . 13.00

MIRACLE GIRLS
Tokyopop Press, 2000
1 . . . . 3.00
2 . . . . 3.00
3 thru 14 . . . . @3.00
15 thru 17 . . . . @3.00
18 thru 23 . . . . @3.00

MIRACLE SQUAD BLOOD & DUST
Apple, 1989
1 thru 3 . . . . @2.25

MISTER BLANK
Amaze Ink, 1997
0 by Chris Hicks 2.25
0a 2nd printing 2.25
1 F:Sam Smith 3.00
2 thru 14 . . . . @3.00
TPB rep. #1–#14, 360-pg. 30.00

MISTER X
Vortex, Vol 2, 1989–90
1 thru 11 . . . . @2.25

MITES
Continuum
1 . . . . 2.50
1a 2.25
2 thru 4 . . . . @2.25

MOBILE POLICE
PATLABOR
Viz Communications, 1997
1 (of 12) by Masami Yuki 3.00
PART TWO, 1998
1 by Masami Yuki 3.00
2 thru 6 . . . . @3.00
TPB Vol. 1 . . . . 16.00
TPB Vol. 2 Basic Training 16.00

MOBILE SUIT
GUNDAM 0079
Viz Communications, 1999
1 (of 8) by Kazhisa Kondo 3.00
2 thru 7 . . . . @3.00
PART TWO, 1999
1 (of 5) 3.00
2 thru 5 . . . . @3.00
TPB Vol. 1 . . . . 16.00
TPB Vol. 1 2nd edition 10.00
TPB Vol. 2 . . . . 16.00
TPB Vol. 2 2nd edition 10.00
TPB Vol. 3 thru 9 . . . . @10.00

MOBILE SUIT GUNDAM
WING: BLIND TARGET
Viz Communications, 2001
1 thru 4 . . . . @3.00
TPB 13.00

MOBILE SUIT GUNDAM
WING: EPISODE ZERO
Viz Communications, 2001
1 thru 8 . . . . @3.00
TPB Art of Mobile Suit
  Gundam Wing 20.00
TPB (2002) 17.00

MOBILE SUIT GUNDAM
WING: GROUND ZERO
Viz Communications, 2000
1 (of 4) by Reku Fuyynagi 3.00
2 thru 4 . . . . @3.00
TPB 144-pg. 15.00

MODERN PULP
Special Studio
1 Rep.from January Midnight 2.75

MOEBIUS COMICS
Caliber, 1996
1 Moe 3.00
2 Moe 3.00

Monsters From Outer Space #2
© Adventure

3 Moe 3.00
4 Moe,MP 3.00
5 Moe,SL 3.00
6 Moe 3.00

MOGOBI DESERT RATS
Midnight Comics, 1991
1 I&O:Desert Rats 'Waste of the
  World' 2.25

MONNGA
Daikaiyu Enterprises, 1995
1 & 2 Titanic Omega 4.00

MONOGRAPHS
Coppervale, 1997
1 by James Owen 3.00
2 Bob Phantom 3.00
3 Sidekick Wanted—Benefits
  Available 3.00
4 thru 6 . . . . 3.00

MONSTER BOY
Monster Comics
1 A:Monster Boy 2.25

MONSTER POSSE
Malibu Adventure, 1992
1 I:Monster Posse 2.50
2 I:P.O.N.E,Wack Mack Dwac's
  sister,D-Vicious 2.50
3 . . . . 2.50

MONSTERS ATTACK
Globe
1 GM,JSe 2.25
2 GC 2.25
3 ATh,GC 2.25

MONSTERS FROM
OUTER SPACE
Adventure, 1992
1 thru 3 . . . . @2.50

MOONSTONE MONSTERS
Moonstone Books, 2003
1-shot Sea Creatures 2.95
1-shot Vampire Vixens 2.95

1-shot Ghosts 2.95
1-shot Witches 2.95
1-shot Demons 2.95
TPB Vol. 1 . . . . 16.95

MOONSTONE NOIR
Moonstone 2002
GN The Hat Squad 5.50
GN Jack Hagee, Private Eye 5.50
GN The Mysterious Traveler 5.50
GN The Lone Wolf, Vol. #1 . . . . . . 4.95
GN Johnny Dollar 4.95
GN Mysterious Traveler Returns . . . 4.95
GN Bulldog Drummond 4.95

MORBID ANGEL:
DESPERATE ANGELS
London Night, 1998
0 EHr, & Jude Millien 3.00
0A Powell(c) 5.00
0B Powell(c) 5.00

MORBID ANGEL:
PENANCE
London Night Studios, 1995
1 I:Brandon Watts 4.00

MORBID ANGEL:
TO HELL AND BACK
London Night, 1996
1 (of 3) EHr, ... 4.00
2 and 3 . . . . @3.00

MORNING GLORY
Radio Comix, 1998
1 by Loran Gayton & Michael Vega 3.00
2 thru 6 . . . . @3.00

MORTAL COIL
Mermaid
1 thru 3 . . . . @2.25
4 F:Red-Line,Gift 2.25
5 Pin-Up Issue 2.25

MORTOL COILS
Red Eye Press, 2003
1 . . . . 2.50
2 . . . . 3.50
3 . . . . 2.50
TPB Vol. 1 . . . . 16.95

MORTAR MAN
Marshall Comics, 1993
1 I:Mortar Man 2.25
2 thru 3 . . . . @2.25

MOSAIC
Oktober Black Press
1 F:Halo,Daeva 2.25
2 "Gun Metal Gray" 2.50
3 . . . . 2.50
4 Elf(c) 2.50
5 Wisps 2.50

MOSAIC
Sirius, 1999
1 by Kyle Hotz 3.00
2 thru 5 conclusion . . . . @3.00
TPB 15.00

B & W PUB.

MOUNTAIN WORLD
Newcomers Press, 1995
1 I:Jeremiah Rainshadow 3.00

MR. BEAT ADVENTURES
Moordam Comics, 1997
1 . . . . 3.00
1 deluxe 5.00
Spec. House of Burning Jazz Love . 3.00
Spec. deluxe 5.00
Two-Fisted Atomic Action
   Super Spec. 3.00
Two-Fisted Atomic Action
   Super Spec., deluxe 10.00
Two-Fisted Atomic Action
   Super Spec., mega deluxe . . . 20.00
Spec. Mr. Beat: Superstar 3.00
Spec. Mr. Beat: Superstar, deluxe . 10.00
Ann.#1 Babes and Bongos 3.00

MR. FIXITT
Apple, 1989
1 and 2 . . . . @2.25

MR. KEEN: TRACER OF LOST PERSONS
Moonstone, 2003
1 (of 3) 2.95
2 . . . . 2.95
3 . . . . 2.95
TPB 10.95

MR. MOTO
Moonstone, 2003
1 (of 3) Welcome Back, Mr. Moto . . 2.95
2 thru 3 . . . . @2.95

MR. MYSTIC
Eclipse
1 Will Eisner 2.50

MR. NIGHTMARE'S WONDERFUL WORLD
Moonstone, 1995
1 thru 3 Dreams So Real,
   pt.1–pt.3 . . . . @3.00

MS. CHRIST
Draculina Publishing, 1995
1 I:Ms. Christ. 3.00

MS. TREE
Aardvark–Vanaheim, 1984
1-10 see Other Pub. (color)
11 thru 18 . . . . @2.25
Renegade, 1985
19 thru 49 . . . . @2.25
50 . . . . 4.50
1 3-D Classic 3.00

MUMMY, THE
Monster Comics
1 A:Dr.Clarke,Prof.Belmore. 2.25
2 Mummy's Curse. 2.25
3 A:Carloph. 2.25
4 V:Carloph, conc. 2.25

MUMMY'S CURSE
Aircel, 1990
1 thru 4 B.Blair . . . . @2.25

MUNSTERS, THE
TV Comics, 1998
1 photo (c). 3.00
1a variant (c). 8.00
2 Beverly Owen(c) 3.00
2 Pat Priest (c) 3.00
2 Pat Priest (c) signed 20.00
3 . . . . 3.00
3a Celebrity autograph edition . . . 23.00
4 . . . . 3.00
4a variant photo (c) 3.00
4b variant (c) celebrity autograph
   edition 23.00
5 Herman photo (c). 3.00
5 Grandpa photo (c) 3.00
Spec. Comic Con edition 10.00
Celebrity Autograph Edition: Butch
   Patrick 23.00
TPB Vol 1, rep. #1–#4 . . . . 11.00
Spec.#1 Herman/Grandpa (c) 3.00
Spec.#1a Grandpa (c) 3.00
Halloween Spec. Munsters 1313 . . 3.00
Golden Age Adventure Spec.A(c) . . 3.00
Golden Age Adventure Spec.B(c) . . 3.00

MUNSTERS CLASSICS
TV Comics
0 The Fregosi Emerald 3.00
0 variant (c). 8.00

MURCIELAGA: SHE-BAT
Hero Graphics, 1993
1 Daerick Gross reps. 2.25
2 Reps. contd 3.00

MURDER
Renegade, 1986
1 SD 2.25
2 CI(c). 2.25
3 SD 2.25
[2nd series]
1 . . . . 2.25

MURDER CAN BE FUN
Slave Labor, 1996
1 thru 6 . . . . @3.00
2 2nd printing 3.00
7 . . . . 3.00
8 . . . . 3.00
9 Seedy Side of Sex 3.00
10 We Love Sports 3.00
11 . . . . 3.00
12 Amusement Park Terror 3.00

MURDER ME DEAD
El Capitan Books, 2000
1 (of 8) by David Lapham 3.00
2 . . . . 3.00
3 thru 8 . . . . @3.00
9 64-pg. 5.00
TPB 20.00

MUTANT ZONE
Aircel, 1991
1 Future story 2.50
2 F.B.I. Drone Exterminators 2.50
3 conclusion 2.50

MYSTERY MAN
Slave Labor, 1988
1 thru 5 . . . . @2.25

MYTH ADVENTURES
Warp Graphics, 1984
1 Mag size 2.25
2 thru 4 . . . . @2.25
5 Comic size 2.25
6 thru 11 . . . . @2.25
12 . . . . 2.25

MYTH CONCEPTIONS
Apple, 1987
1 . . . . 2.25
2 . . . . 2.25
3 thru 8 . . . . @2.25

MYTHOGRAPHY
Bardic Press, 1966
1 F:Poison Elves. 5.00
2 fantasy stories 5.00

Negative Burn #13
© Caliber

3 fantasy stories, inc. Elfquest 5.00
4 . . . . 4.50
5 72-pg. 4.50
6 F:Anubis Squadron 72pg. 4.00
7 80-pg. 4.50
8 72-pg. 4.50

MYTHOS
Wonder Comix, 1987
1 and 2 . . . . @2.25

NANTUCKET BROWN ROASTERS
House of Usher, 2003
1 (of 2) 2.00
2 . . . . 2.00
GN Second Law of Thermodynamics . . .
7.50
1-shot The Lady of Shadows. 2.50

NATURE OF THE BEAST
Caliber
1 thru 3 `The Beast' . . . . @3.00

NAUGHTY BITS
Fantagraphics, 1996
20 . . . . 3.00
21 I:Bitchy Butch 3.00
22 . . . . 3.00
23 O:Bitchy Butch 3.00

B & W PUB.

24 .... 3.00
25 by Roberta Gregory 3.00
26 thru 38 .... @3.00
39 .... 3.50
TPB Vol. 4: Bitchy's School Daze . 10.00
TPB Vol. 5: Bitchy Butch 10.00
TPB Work & Play with Bitchy Bitch 10.00
TPB A Bitch is Born, sgn 10.00
TPB Vol.6 Burn, Bitchy, Burn..... 10.00

NAUSICAA OF THE VALLEY OF WIND
Viz Select, 1988

Book One.......................... 4.50
Book Two.......................... 5.50
Book Three........................ 4.00
Book Four.......................... 3.00
Book Five.......................... 2.50
Book Six........................... 3.00
Book Seven........................ 3.00

[Part 2]
#1 thru #4.................... @3.00

[Part 3]
#1 thru #3 .... @3.00
TPB Vol. 4 .... 18.00

NAZRAT
Imperial, 1986

1 .... 2.50
2 thru 6 .... @2.25

NECROSCOPE
Caliber, 1997

1 Brian Lumley adapt........... 3.00
1 signed 3.00
2 .... 3.00
3 .... 3.00
4 .... 3.00

NEGATIVE BURN
Caliber, 1993

1 I:Matrix 7, Flaming Carrot 5.00
2 .... 3.50
3 Bone preview.................. 12.00
4 thru 12 various stories .... @3.25
13 Strangers in Paradise 10.00
14 thru 18 various stories...... @3.50
19 Flaming Carrot 5.00
20 In the Park 4.00
21 Trollords 4.00
22 Father the Dryad............. 4.00
23 I:The Creep.................... 4.00
24 The Factor 4.00
25 The Factor 4.00
26 Very Vicki 4.00
27 Nancy Kate 4.00
28 Favorite Song 4.00
29 thru 33........................ 4.00
34 Kaos Moon 6.00
35 thru 38 .... @4.00
39 'Iron Empires,' pt. 4 .... 4.00
40 'Suzi Romaine'............... 4.00
41 'Iron Empires,' cont. 4.00
42 .... 4.00
43 'Iron Empires,' concl. 4.00
44 'Skeleton Key'................ 4.00
45 'Divine Winds'................ 4.00
46 'A Bullet For Me'............. 4.00
47 .... 4.00
48 special 80-pg. issue 5.00
49 special 80-pg. issue 5.00
50 96-pg., final issue 7.00
TPB Best of Year One 10.00
TPB Best of Year Two 10.00

NEIL THE HORSE
Aardvark–Vanaheim, 1983

1 Art:Arn Sara 5.00
1a 2nd printing 2.25
2 .... 3.00
3 .... 4.00
4 .... 3.00
5 Video Warriors................ 2.50
6 Video Warriors................ 2.50
7 Video Warriors................ 2.50
8 Outer Space................... 2.50
9 Conan 2.50
10 .... 2.50

Renegade, 1985

11 Fred Astair................... 2.25
12 .... 2.25
13 .... 2.25
14 Special 3.00
15 .... 2.25

NEMESIS THE WARLOCK
Fleetway, 1989

1 thru 16 .... @2.25

NEON GENESIS EVANGELION
Viz Communication, 1997

1 (of 6) by Gainax & Yoshiyuki Sadamoto 3.25
1 special collectors edition 3.00
2 thru 6 .... @3.00
2 thru 6 special collectors ed.... @3.00
TPB Vol. 1 .... 16.50
TPB Vol. 1 special collectors ed... 16.50

BOOK TWO, 1998
1 (of 5) by Yoshiyuki Sadamoto ... 3.00
1 special collectors edition 3.00
2 thru 5 .... @3.00
2 thru 5 special collectors ed.... @3.00
TPB Book 2 .... 16.00
TPB Book 2, collector ed...... 16.00

BOOK THREE, 1998
1 thru 6 by Yoshiyuki Sadamoto . @3.00
1a thru 6a Collectors edition.... @3.00
GN Vol. 3 Evangelion........... 16.00
GN Vol. 3 Evangelion, coll. ed. ... 16.00

BOOK FOUR, 1999
1 thru 7 by Yoshiyuki Sadamoto . @3.00
1a thru 7a special collectors ed.. @3.00

BOOK FIVE, 2000
1 .... 3.00
1a collectors ed................. 3.00
2 thru 7 .... @3.00
2a thru 7a deluxe .... @3.00
TPB Book 5 .... 16.00
TPB Collect. Ed 16.00

BOOK SIX, 2001
1 thru 4 .... @3.50
1a thru 4a coll. ed. .... @3.50
TPB Vol. 6 .... 16.00
TPB Vol. 6 collector ed....... 16.00

BOOK SEVEN
1 (of 7) 3.50
2 thru 5 .... @3.00
6 .... 3.50
2a thru 5a collector's edition.... @3.00
6a collector's edition .... @3.50
TPB Vol. 7 .... 16.00
TPB Vol. 7 collector ed....... 16.00
TPB Vol. 8 .... 9.95

NEON– THE FUTURE WARRIOR
Komics, Inc., 2000

TPB Vol. 1 .... 12.85

New Humans #2
© Pied Piper

TPB Vol. 2 .... 12.85
TPB Vol. 3 .... 12.85
TPB Vol. 4 187-pg............. 12.85
TPB Vol. 5 183-pg............. 12.85
TPB Vol. 6 186-pg............. 12.85
TPB Vol. 7 185-pg............. 12.85
TPB Vol. 8 185-pg............. 12.85
TPB Vol. 9 185-pg., final 12.85

NERVOUS REX
Blackthorne, 1985

1 .... 3.00
1a 2nd printing 2.25
2 .... 3.00
3 .... 3.00
4 .... 2.50
5 thru 10 .... @2.25
GraphicNovel.................... 3.50

NEW ADVENTURES OF TERRY & THE PIRATES
ACG Comics, 1998

1 by Bros. Hildebrandt 3.00
2 thru 7 .... @3.00

NEWCOMERS ILLUSTRATED
Newcomers Publishing

1 thru 5 various artists......... @3.00
6 Science Fiction 3.00
7 thru 8 .... @3.00
9 Shocking Machines 3.00
10 .... 3.00
11 Hitman....................... 3.00
12 final issue 3.00

NEW ERADICATORS

Vol 2 #1 NewBeginnings 2.25
Vol 2 #2 NewBeginnings 2.25
Vol 2 #3 NewFriends 2.25

NEW FRONTIERS

1 CS(c) 3.00
1a 2nd Printing 2.25

NEW FRONTIERS
Evolution

1 A:Action Master, Green Ghost... 2.25
2 .... 2.25

NEW HERO COMICS
Pierce
1 and 2 . . . . @2.25

NEW HORIZONS
Shanda Fantasy Arts, 1997
1 . . . . 5.00
2 thru 5 . . . . @4.50
6 thru 15 . . . . @5.00

NEW HUMANS
Pied Piper, 1987
1 and 2 . . . . @2.25

NEW HUMANS
Eternity, 1987
1 . . . . 2.25
2 thru 15 . . . . @2.25
Ann. #1. . . . . 3.00

Nexus #2
© Capitol Comics

NEW HUMANS
1 Shattered Earth Chronicles 2.25

NEW LOVE
Fantagraphics, 1996
1 GHe, Love & Rockets tie-in 3.00
2 thru 3 GHe . . . . @3.00
4 thru 6 GHe . . . . @3.00

NEW PULP
ADVENTURES SPECIAL
Dunewadd Comics
1 I:Kawala. 2.50

NEW REALITY
1 thru 6 . . . . @2.25

NEWSTRALIA
Innovation, 1989
(Prev. Color)
4 . . . . 2.25
5 . . . . 2.25

NEW TRIUMPH
Matrix Graphics, 1985
1 F:Northguard 3.00
1a 2nd printing 2.25
2 thru 4 . . . . @2.25

NEW VAMPIRE MIYU
Ironcat, 1997
1 by Narumi Kakinouchi 3.00
2 thru 6 . . . . @3.00
7 The Past Lies Beyond a Door,
  finale 3.00
GN rep. #1–#7. . . . . 18.00
VOL. 2, 1998
1 by Narumi Kakinouchi 3.00
2 thru 6 . . . . @3.00
VOL. 3, 1998
1 . . . . 3.00
2 thru 7 . . . . @3.00
VOL. 4, 1999
1 by Narumi Kakinouchi 3.00
2 thru 6 . . . . @3.00
VOL. 5
1 . . . . 3.00
2 thru 7 . . . . @3.00
GN Vol. 4, The Return of Miyu . . . 18.00
GN Vol. 5, Wrath of Miyu 18.00

NEW WORLD DISORDER
Millennium, 1995
1 I:King Skin Gang 3.00

NEW WORLD ORDER
Blazer Studios, 1993
1 thru 8 . . . . @2.50

NEW YORK CITY
OUTLAWS
Outlaw
1 thru 5 . . . . @2.50

NEW YORK, YEAR ZERO
Eclipse, 1988
1 thru 4 . . . . @2.25

NEXUS
Capital, 1981
1 SR,I:Nexus,large size 12.00
2 SR,Mag size 8.00
3 SR,Mag size 5.00

NIGHT
Amaze Ink, 1995
0 V:The Prince 2.25

NIGHT ANGEL
Substance Comics, 1995
1 I:Night Angel 3.00

NIGHT CRY
CFD Productions, 1995
1 Evil Ernie & Razor story 8.00
1 signed 9.00
2 . . . . 6.00
3 . . . . 5.00
4 . . . . 4.00
4a platinum (c) 6.00
5 . . . . 4.00
6 . . . . 2.75
6a signed 8.00

NIGHT LIFE
Caliber
1 thru 7 . . . . @2.25

NIGHT MASTER
Silver Wolf, 1987
1 Vigil 5.50
2 Vigil 2.50
3 . . . . 2.25

NIGHT OF THE
LIVING DEAD
Fantaco
0 prelude 2.25
1 based on cult classic movie. 5.00
2 Movie adapt,continued. 5.00
3 Movie adapt,conclusion 5.00
5 . . . . 6.00
TPB Official Complete story, rep... 25.00
TPB London, Clive Barker's story . 15.00

NIGHT'S CHILDREN
Fantaco
1 . . . . 3.50
2 . . . . 3.50
3 . . . . 3.50
4 . . . . 3.50

NIGHT'S CHILDREN
Millennium, 1995
1 The Ripper, Klaus Wulfe 4.00
Spec. High Noon (1996) 3.00
Spec. The Churchyard (1997) 3.25

NIGHT'S CHILDREN:
THE VAMPIRE
Millennium, 1995
1 F:Klaus Wulfe 3.00
2 F:Klaus Wulfe 3.00

NIGHT STREETS
Arrow, 1986
1 . . . . 2.50
2 thru 4 . . . . @2.25

NIGHTVISION
London Night, 1996
1 DQ,KHt, All About Eve. 3.00
1 signed 13.00
1a erotica edition 10.00

NIGHT WARRIORS:
DARKSTALKERS'
REVENGE
Viz Communications, 1998
1 (of 6) by Run Ishida 3.00
2 . . . . 3.25
3 thru 6 . . . . @3.00
TPB 16.00

NIGHT ZERO
Fleetway
1 thru 4 . . . . @2.25

NIKKI BLADE
High Impact, 1997
0 . . . . 3.00
0a deluxe adult cover 10.00
0b gold edition variant cover. 15.00
Spec.#0 Nikki Blade: Forever Nikki
  (1997) MIB(c). 3.00
  Deluxe RCI(c) 10.00
ABC Comics, 1998
Spec. Nikki Blade: Blades of Death
  (1998) by RCI & Clayton Henry. 3.00
  Puzzle variant A cover. 6.00

B & W PUB.

Puzzle variant B cover	6.00
Puzzle variant C cover	6.00
Spec. Nikki Blade: Revenge	3.00

NIMROD, THE
Fantagraphics, 1998

1 by Lewis Trondheim	3.00
2 thru 4	@3.00
5	4.00
6	3.50
7	4.00

NINJA
Eternity

1	3.00
2 thru 6	@2.25
7 thru 13	@2.25

NINJA ELITE
Adventure, 1987

1 thru 5	@2.25
6 thru 8	@2.25

NINJA FUNNIES
Eternity

1 and 2	@2.25
3 thru 5	@2.25

NINJA HIGH SCHOOL
Antarctic, 1987

1	15.00
2 thru 4	@11.00

Eternity, 1988

5 thru 22	@3.00
23 Zardon Assassin	2.50
24	2.50
25 Return of the Zetramen	2.50
26 Stanley the Demon	2.50
27 Return of the Zetramen	2.50
28 Threat of the super computer	2.50
29 V:Super Computer	2.50
30 I:Akaru	2.50
31 Jeremy V:Akaru	2.50
32 thru 34 V:Giant Monsters Pt.1 thru Pt. 3	@2.50
35 thru 43	@2.50
44 Combat Cheerleaders	2.75
45 Cheerleader Competition	2.75
46 Monsters From Space	2.75
47	2.75
48 F:Jeremy Feeple	2.75
49 thru 51	@3.00
52 thru 57 Time Warp, pt.4–pt.8	@3.00
58 Zardon ambassador, BU:BDn	3.00
59 Akaru overwhelmed	3.00
60 to the Himalayas	3.00
61 ancient Himalayan temple	3.00
62 Hillbilly girl	3.00
63 F:Tetsuo Rivalsan	3.00
64 Jeremy Feeple: Saboteur?	3.00
65 Quagmire Trial of the Century	3.00
66	3.00
67 F:Eolata	3.00
68 F:Akaru & Asrial	3.00
69 Guri-Guri Island	3.00
70 Mad Bomber in Space	2.50
71 traitor in secret police	3.00
72	2.50
73	2.50
74 Girl Scouts	2.50
Special #1	3.00
Special #2	3.00
Special #3	3.00
Special #3 1/2	2.25
Ann. 1989	3.00
Ann.#3	4.00
TPB Vol. 1 rep. #1–3	12.00

TPB Vol. 1, new edition	15.00
TPB Vol. 2 rep. #4–7	12.00
TPB Vol. 3 rep. #8–11	9.00
TPB Vol. 3, rep. #8–#11	11.00
TPB Vol. 4 rep. #12–15	8.00
TPB Vol. 4, rep. #12–#15	11.00
TPB Vol. 5 rep. #16–18	8.00
TPB Vol. 6 rep. #19–21	8.00
TPB Vol. 7 rep. #22–24	8.00
TPB Vol. 7, rep. #22–#24 The Ides of May	11.00
TPB Vol. 8 rep. #25–27	8.00
TPB Vol. 9 rep. #28–31	11.00
TPB Vol. 9, rep. #28–#31 Long Distance Bottle	11.00
TPB Vol. 10 rep. #32–35	11.00
TPB Vol. 11 rep. #36–39	11.00
TPB Vol. 11, rep. #36–#39 Shades of Grey	11.00
TPB Vol. 12	11.00
TPB Vol. 15 three stories	8.00
Yearbook 1994	4.00
Yearbook 1995	4.00
Yearbook 1996	4.00
Yearbook 1997, cover A	4.00
Yearbook 1997, cover B	4.00
Yearbook 1998, cover A	3.00
Yearbook 1998, cover B	3.00
Spec. Girls of Ninja High School (1997)	4.00
Spec. Girls of Ninja High School 1998 cover A	3.00
1998 cover B	3.00
Spec. 1999	3.00
Spotlight #4 Rod Espinosa	3.00
Summer Spec.#1	3.00

Antarctic Press, 2000

Swimsuit Spec. 2000	4.50
Swimsuit Spec. 2001	4.50
TPB Vol. 1, signed	20.00
TPB Textbook Vol. 1 600-pg	50.00

NINJA HIGH SCHOOL GIRLS
Antarctic Press

0	2.75
1 and 2 rep	@2.75
3 thru 5 rep	@4.00
Yearbook	4.00

NINJA HIGH SCHOOL PERFECT MEMORY
Antarctic Press, 1993

1 thru 2, 96pg	@5.00

NINJA HIGH SCHOOL SMALL BODIES
Antarctic Press

1 "Monopolize"	2.50
2 Omegadon Cannon	2.75
3 Omegadon Cannon	2.75
3a deluxe	4.50
4 Omegadon Cannon	2.75
5 Wrong Order	2.75
6 Chicken Rage	3.00
7	3.00

NIRA X: CYBERANGEL
Entity Comics, 1996

1	5.00
1a deluxe	8.00
2 BMs	4.00
3 and 4 BMs	@3.00
4a with PC Game	8.00
Ann.#1 BMs flip-cover	2.75

2nd Mini Series, 1995

1	4.00

1a 2nd printing	2.50
2 thru 4	@2.50

3rd Mini Series, 1995–96

1	2.50
1a Gold(c)	5.00
2	2.50
3	3.00

Regular Series

1	2.75
1a with game	7.00
2 thru 4	@2.75
4a with game	7.00
Spec. Nira X:Headwave, encore special toy edition	2.50
Encore special toy edition, signed & numbered	13.00
Spec. Nira X:Memoirs (1997) BMs	2.75
Deluxe	3.50

NIRA X/HELLINA: HEAVEN & HELL
Entity Comics

1 San Diego Con edition, BMs	5.00
1a foil	3.00

NIRA X: EXODUS
Avatar, 1997

0 (of 2) BMs	3.00
0a Leather cover	20.00
0b signed	10.00
1 (of 2)	3.00
1a leather cover	18.00
1b signed	9.00
2	3.00
Spec. Shoot First	3.00
Spec. Summer Splash	5.00

NIRA X: HISTORY
Avatar Press, 1999

1 (of 2) by Bill Maus	3.50
2	3.50

NIRA X: SOUL SKURGE
Entity, 1996

1 (of 3) BMs, A:Vortex	2.75
2 BMs	2.75
3	2.75

NOBODY
Oni Press, 1998
1 (of 4) 3.00
2 thru 4 . . . . @3.00
TPB Sacrifices 12.00
AIT/Planetlar, 2000
TPB 13.00

NODWICK
Henchman Publishing, 2000
1 by Aaron Williams 3.00
2 & 3 . . . . @3.00
Dork Storm, 2000
1 by Aaron Williams 3.00
5 . . . . 3.00
6 thru 11 . . . . @3.00
12 thru 26 . . . . @3.00
TPB Vol. 1 thru Vol. 4 . . . . @16.00

NO GUTS, NO GLORY
Fantaco
1-shot, K.Eastman's 1st solo
    work since TMNT 3.00

NOMADS OF ANTIQUITY
1 thru 6 . . . . @2.25

NO NEED FOR TENCHI
Viz Comics
PART ONE
1 thru 7 (of 7) . . . . @3.00
PART TWO, 1996
1 thru 7 by Hitoshi Okuda . . . . . . @3.00
TPB Sword Play 16.00
PART THREE, 1997
1 (of 6) by Hitoshi Okuda 3.00
2 . . . . 3.00
3 thru 6 . . . . @3.00
TPB Magical Girl Pretty Sammy . . 16.00
PART FOUR, 1997
1 (of 6) by Hitoshi Okuda 3.00
2 thru 6 . . . . @3.00
TPB Vol.4 Samurai Space Opera . 16.00
PART FIVE, 1998
1 (of 6) 3.00
2 thru 6 . . . . @3.00
TPB Vol.5 Unreal Genius. 16.00
PART SIX, 1998
1 (of 6) 3.00
2 thru 6 . . . . @3.00
TPB Vol.6 Dream a Little Scheme. 16.00
PART SEVEN, 1999
1 (of 6) 3.00
2 thru 6 . . . . @3.00
TPB Vol.7 Tenchi in Love. 16.00
PART EIGHT, 1999
1 (of 5) by Hitoshi Okuda 3.25
2 thru 5 . . . . @3.00
TPB Vol.8 Chef of Iron. 16.00
PART NINE
1 (of 6) by Hitoshi Okuda 3.00
2 thru 6 . . . . @3.00
TPB Vol.9 Quest for More Money . 16.00
PART TEN, 2000
1 (of 7) 3.00
2 thru 7 . . . . @3.00
TPB Vol.10 Mother Planet 16.00
PART ELEVEN, 2001
1 thru 4 . . . . @3.50
TPB Vol.11 Ayeka's Heart 16.00
PART TWELVE, 2001
1 thru 4 (of 6) . . . . @3.50
5 thru 6 . . . . @3.00

TPB Vol.12 . . . . 16.00

NORM, THE
The Norm Comics, 2003
1 . . . . 4.95
2 thru 5 . . . . @4.95
1-shot The 12 Steps to Marriage . . . 4.95

NORMAL MAN
Aardvark–Vanaheim, 1984
1 . . . . 4.00
2 thru 9 . . . . @3.00
Renegade
10 thru 19 . . . . @2.25

NOSFERATU: PLAGUE OF TERROR
Millennium
1 I:Orlock 2.50
2 19th Century India,A:Sir W.
    Longsword. 2.50
3 WWI/WWII to Viet Nam 2.50
4 O:Orlock,V:Longsword,conc. . . . 2.50

NOVA GIRLS
MN Design, 1998
1 The Immortality Quest, pt.1 . . . . 2.25
1a JJu (c) 3.00
1b photo (c) 4.00
1 variant Starship Discover #0(c) . . 4.00
1 variant Phazer #0 cover. 4.00
2 The Immortality Quest, pt.2 . . . . 2.25
2a deluxe 3.00
3 The Immortality Quest, pt.3 . . . . 2.25
3a deluxe 3.00
Space 34–24–34 Gold Seal 10th
    Anniv. Edition. 75.00

NOWHERESVILLE
Caliber, 1996
1 thru 3 by MRc . . . . @3.00
Spec. The History of Cool 3.00

NYOKA THE JUNGLE GIRL
AC Comics
3 . . . . 2.25
4 . . . . 2.25
5 . . . . 2.50

OCTOBRIANA
Revolution Comics
0 16pg. 2.00
1 `The Octobriana Files,'pt.1 . . . . 3.00
2 `The Octobriana Files,'pt.2 . . . . 3.00
3 `The Octobriana Files,'pt.3 . . . . 3.00
4 `The Octobriana Files,'pt.4 . . . . 3.00
5 `The Octobriana Files,'pt.5 . . . . 3.00
Alchemy Texts, 2001
Spec. 30th Anniv. Spec. 3.00

ODD JOB
Amaze Ink/Slave Labor Graphics, 2000
1 by Ian Smith & Tyson Smith 3.00
2 thru 8 . . . . @3.00
TPB Vol. 1 . . . . 20.00

OFFERINGS
Cry For Dawn
1 Sword & Sorcery stories 7.00
2 and 3 . . . . @6.00

THE OFFICIAL Modesty BLAISE by PETER O'DONNELL and JIM HOLDAWAY

international intrigue and danger

Official Modesty Blaise #1
© Pioneer

OFFICIAL BUZ SAWYER
Pioneer, 1988
1 . . . . 2.25
2 . . . . 2.25
3 . . . . 2.25
4 . . . . 2.25
5 . . . . 2.25
6 . . . . 2.25

OFFICIAL HOW TO DRAW G.I. JOE
Blackthorne, 1987
1 thru 5 . . . . @2.25

OFFICIAL HOW TO DRAW ROBOTECH
Blackthorne, 1987
1 thru 11 . . . . @2.25
12 . . . . 3.00
13 thru 16. . . . . @2.25

OFFICIAL HOW TO DRAW TRANSFORMERS
Blackthorne, 1987
1 thru 7 . . . . @2.25

OFFICIAL JOHNNY HAZARD
Pioneer, 1988
1 thru 3 . . . . @2.25
4 . . . . 2.25
5 . . . . 2.25

OFFICIAL JUNGLE JIM
Pioneer, 1988
1 thru 5 AR,rep. . . . . @2.25
6 AR,rep. 2.25
7 thru 10 AR,rep. . . . . @2.25
11 thru 20 AR,rep. . . . . @2.50
Ann.#1 . . . . 2.25
Giant Size 4.00

OFFICIAL MANDRAKE
Pioneer, 1988
1 thru 5 . . . . @2.25
6 . . . . 2.25
7 thru 10 . . . . @2.25

11	2.50
12	2.25
13 thru 17	@2.50
Ann. #1	4.00
King Size #1	4.00
Giant Size #1	4.00

OFFICIAL MODESTY BLAISE
Pioneer, 1988

1 thru 4	@2.25
5	2.25
6 thru 14	@2.25
Ann. #1	4.00

Omen #2
© North Star

King Size #1	4.00

OFFICIAL PRINCE VALIANT
Pioneer, 1988

1 Hal Foster,rep	2.25
2 Hal Foster,rep	2.25
3 Hal Foster,rep	2.25
4 Hal Foster,rep	2.25
5 Hal Foster,rep	2.25
6 Hal Foster,rep	2.25
7	2.25
8 thru 14	@2.25
15 thru 24	@2.50
Ann. #1	4.00
King Size #1	4.00

OFFICIAL RIP KIRBY
Pioneer, 1988

1 thru 3 AR	@2.25
4 AR	2.25
5 and 6 AR	@2.25

OFFICIAL SECRET AGENT
Pioneer, 1988

1 thru 5 AW rep	@2.25
6 AW	2.25
7 thru 9 AW	@2.25

OF MIND AND SOUL
Rage Comics, 1997

0	3.00
1	2.50
2	2.50

3	2.25
Spec. Standing on a Beach	2.50
Spec. Soul'd Out`	3.00
Spec. A Day in Hell	3.00
Spec. 1-shot	2.25

OHM'S LAW
Imperial Comics

1 thru 2	@2.25
3 V:Men in Black	2.25
4 A:Damonstriek	2.25
5 F:Tryst	2.25

OH MY GOTH!
Sirius/Dog Star, 1998

1 by Voltaire	3.00
2 thru 4	@3.00
TPB	13.00

OH MY GOTH: HUMANS SUCK!
Sirius Entertainment, 2000

1 (of 3)	3.00
1 deluxe	5.00
2 and 3	@3.00

OKTOBERFEST
Now & Then

1 (1976) Dave Sim	20.00

OMEGA
North Star

1 1st pr by Rebel,rare	50.00
1a Vigil(Yellow Cov.)	15.00
2	2.25

OMEGA ELITE
Blackthorne

1	2.25
2	2.25

OMEN
North Star, 1987

1	8.00
1a 2nd printing	2.25
2 thru 4	@3.50

OMICRON
Pyramid, 1987

1 and 2	@2.25
3	2.50

OMNI MEN
Blackthorne, 1989

1 & 2	@2.25

ONE-POUND GOSPEL
Viz Communications, 1996

1	3.50
2	3.50
3 & 4	@3.00
TPB rep.	17.00
ROUND TWO, 1997
1 thru 8 by Rumiko Takahashi	@3.00
TPB Vol. 1	16.96
TPB Vol. 2 Hungry For Victory	16.00
TPB Vol. 3 Knuckle Sandwich	16.00
PART 7
1 (of 13) by Rumiko Takahashi	3.00

ONE SHOT WESTERN
Calibur
1-shot F:Savage Sisters, Tornpath Outlaw	2.50

ONI DOUBLE FEATURE
Oni Press, 1997
1 F:Jay & Silent Bob	12.00
1a 2nd printing	3.00
2 F:Car Crash on the 405	3.50
3 F:Troy Nixey	3.50
4 F:A River in Egypt	3.50
5 F:Fan Girl From Hell	4.00
6 inc. NGa Only the End of the World, pt.1	3.00
7 inc. NGa Only the End of the World, pt.2	3.00
8 inc. NGa Only the End of the World, pt.3	3.00
9 thru 10	@3.00
11 Usagi Yojimbo	3.50
12 Bluntman & Chronic	7.00
13	3.00

ONIGAMI
Antarctic Press, 1998
1 (of 3) by Michael Lacombe, sequel to Winter Jade storyline from Warrior Nun: Black and White	3.00
2	3.00
3 concl.	3.00

OPEN SEASON
Renegade, 1987
1 thru 7	@2.25

OPTIC NERVE
Adrian Tomine, 1990
1 thru 5, mini-comic	12.00
6	7.00
7	5.00
8	3.00
9	4.00

OPTIC NERVE
Drawn & Quarterly, 1995
1 Summer Job	9.00
1a 2nd printing	6.00
2	5.00
3 and 4	@5.00
5 thru 8	@4.00
TPB 32 Stories	10.00

ORACLE PRESENTS
Oracle, 1986
1 thru 4	@2.25

ORBIT
Eclipse, 1990
1 and 2	@5.00
3	5.00

ORIGINAL TOM CORBETT
Eternity, 1990
1 thru 10 rep. newspaper strips	@3.00

ORIGINS OF REID FLEMING, WORLD'S TOUGHEST MILKMAN
Deep Sea Comics, 1998
1 by David Boswell	3.00

ORLAK: FLESH & STEEL
Caliber
1 1991 A.D. 2.50

ORLAK REDUX
Caliber, 1991
1 rep. Caliber Presents, 64-pg. . . . 4.00

OUTLAW OVERDRIVE
Blue Comet Press
1 Red Edition I:Deathrow 3.00
1a Black Edition 3.00
1b Blue Edition 3.00

OZ
Imperial Comics, 1996
1 Land of Oz Gone Mad. 9.00
2 Land of Oz Gone Mad. 7.00
3 Land of Oz Gone Mad. 6.00
4 Tin Woodsmen. 6.00
5 F:Pumkinhead 6.00
6 Emerald City 6.00
7 V:Bane Wolves 4.00
8 V:Nome Hordes 4.00
9 Freedom Fighters Vs. Heroes . . . 4.00
10 thru 15. . . . . @4.00
16 . . . . 3.50
Spec.#1 . . . . 6.00
Spec. Scarecrow #1. . . . . 3.00
Spec. Lion #1. . . . . 3.00
Spec. Tin Man #1. . . . . 3.00
Spec. Freedom Fighters #1 . . . . . . 3.00
TPB Rep. #1-#4. . . . . 15.00

Caliber `New Worlds'
17 by Ralph Griffith, Stuart Kerr &
    Tim Holtrop 3.50
18 thru 20. . . . . @3.00
21 `Witches War' pt.1 (of 5). 3.00
22 . . . . 3.00
GN Heroes of Oz 15.00

OZ: ROMANCE IN RAGS
Caliber, 1996
1 thru 3 Bill Bryan . . . . @3.00

OZ SQUAD
Patchwork Press, 1992
1 . . . . 4.00
2 thru 8 . . . . @3.00

Pandora #2
© Avatar Press

OZ: STRAW AND SORCERY
Caliber `New Worlds', 1997
1 thru 3 . . . . @3.00

PAKKINS' LAND
Caliber Tapestry, 1996
1 . . . . 6.00
1a signed edition. 3.00
1a second edition, new cover. . . . 3.00
2 . . . . 4.00
2a second edition, new cover. . . . 3.00
3 . . . . 4.00
3 2nd edition, new cover. 3.00
4 thru 6 . . . . @3.00
GN Book One: Paul's Adventure . . 10.00

Pakkins Presents, 2000
TPB Vol.1 Paul's Adventure. 16.00
TPB Vol.2 Quest For Kings 16.00
TPB Vol.3 Forgotten Dreams. . . . 16.00
TPV Vol.4 Tavitah. 17.00

PAKKINS' LAND: FORGOTTEN DREAMS
Caliber, 1998
1 by Gary & Rhoda Shipman 3.00
2 thru 5 . . . . @3.00

PAKKINS' LAND: QUEST FOR KINGS
Caliber, 1997
1G by Gary & Rhoda Shipman,
    Shipman(c) 3.00
1J by Gary & Rhoda Shipman,
    JSi(c). 3.00
2 . . . . 3.00
3 Rahsha's city 3.00
4 . . . . 3.00
5 . . . . 3.00

PALANTINE
Gryphon Rampant, 1995
1 thru 5 V:Master of Basilisk. 2.50

PALOOKA-VILLE
Drawn & Quarterly
1 third printing. 3.00
1 10th Anniv. Ed. 3.75
10 by Seth 3.75
11 Clyde Fans, pt.2 . . . . 3.75
12 Clyde Fans, pt.3 . . . . 3.75
13 Clyde Fans 3.75
14 . . . . 3.75
15 . . . . 3.75
16 . . . . 4.75
TPB Its a Good Life If You
    Don't Weaken 13.00

PANDA KHAN
1 thru 4 . . . . @2.25

PANDEMONIUM
Curtis Comics, 2002
Vol. 1 Manga
1 by Jaeongtae Lee 3.00
2 thru 5 . . . . @3.00
Vol. 2
1 . . . . 3.00

PANDORA
Brainstorm, 1996
1 (of 2) 3.00

PANDORA
Avatar Press, 1997
0 . . . . 3.00
1 signed 12.00
2 (of 2) 3.00
2 deluxe 9.00
X-over Pandora/Ranzor:Devil Inside
    (1998) signed 12.00
    Haley (c) 5.00
X-over Pandora/Razor (1999) . . . 3.50
    Leather cover, signed 15.00
    Expanded Edition 5.00
X-over Pandora/Shotgun Mary:
    Demon Nation (1998) 3.00
    Deluxe 5.00
    Leather 20.00
    Royal Blue edition 50.00
X-over Pandora/Widow (1997) . . . 4.00
    Leather cover 15.00
Spec. Arachnophobia. 3.50
Spec. Pandora Special (1997) . . . 3.00
    Leather cover 15.00
    Avatar convention (c) ed. 15.00
Spec. Pandora Pin-up (1997) 3.00
    Signed 15.00
Spec. Nudes (1997). 3.50
GN Love and War (2003). 6.00

PANDORA'S CHEST
Avatar Press, 1999
1 (of 3) 2.75

PANDORA: DEMONOGRAPHY
Avatar Press, 1997
1 . . . . 3.00
2 (of 3) 3.00
3 (of 3) 3.00

PANDORA DEVILS ADVOCATE
Avatar Press, 1999
1 (of 3) 3.50
1a Previews exclusive foil (c) 13.00
2 . . . . 3.50
3 . . . . 3.50

PANDORA: PANDEMONIUM
Avatar Press, 1997
1 Pandora goes to Hell. 3.00
1 leather cover 25.00
1 signed 10.00
2 (of 3) 3.00

PANTHEON
Lone Star Press, 1998
1 (of 12) 3.00
2 Welcome to the Machine. 3.00
3 V:Death Boy. 3.00
4 F:Tangeroa. 3.00
5 Under Pressure 3.00
6 All-villain issue 3.00
7 . . . . @3.00
10 thru 12. . . . . @3.00
13 . . . . 5.00
Spec. Ancient History (1999) 3.50

PAPER CUTS
1 E Starzer-1982. . . . . 15.00
2 and 3 . . . . @2.50

PARTICLE DREAMS
Fantagraphics, 1986
1 . . . . 3.00
2 thru 6 . . . . @2.25

PARTNERS IN PANDEMONIUM
Caliber
1 Hell on Earth 2.50
2 Sheldon & Murphy are mortal . . . 2.50
3 A:Abra Cadaver 2.50

PARTS OF A HOLE
Caliber, 1991
1 Short Stories 2.50

PARTS UNKNOWN
Eclipse, 1992
1 I:Spurr,V:Aliens 2.50
2 Aliens on Earth cont. 2.50

PARTS UNKNOWN: DARK INTENTIONS
Knight Press, 1995
0 . . . . 3.00
1 I:Prelude to limited Series 3.00
2 V:Luggnar 3.00
3 V:Luggnar 3.00
4 . . . . 3.00
1-shot, Handbook, The Roswell
  Agenda 3.00
Super-Ann. #1 . . . . 4.00

PATRICK THE WOLF BOY
Blindwolf Studios, 2000
1 by Art Baltazar & Franco 3.00
Halloween Special 3.00
Next Halloween Special 3.00
Valentine's Day Special 3.00
Christmas Spec. 3.00
Mother's Day Special 3.00
Summer Spec. 3.00
Superhero Spec.(2002) 3.00
Sci-Fi Special (2002) 3.00
Another Halloween Special (2002) . 3.00
Spec. This Year's Halloween Spec. . 3.00
Spec. Grimm Reaper Super Spec. . 3.00
Spec. Wedding Special 3.00
Spec. After School Special. 3.00
Rock-n-Roll spec. 3.00
Father's Day spec. 3.00
Spec. Vol. 1 & Vol. 2 collection . . . 15.00
Spec. Vol. 3 & Vol. 4 collection . . . 15.00
TPB Vol. 1 . . . . 10.00
TPB Vol. 2 . . . . 10.00

PATTY CAKE
Caliber Tapestry, 1996
1 by Scott Roberts 3.00
2 . . . . 3.00
3 . . . . 3.00
4 . . . . 3.00
Christmas special. 4.00

PATTY-CAKE & FRIENDS
Slave Labor, 1997
1 by Scott Roberts 3.00
2 thru 15 . . . . @3.00
Halloween Spec. 4.00
VOL. 2, 2000
1 by Scott Roberts, 48-pg. 5.00
2 thru 4 48-pg. . . . . @5.00
5 thru 12 . . . . @5.00
TPB Sugar & Spice..Mostly Spice . 14.00

TPB Vol. 2 And Everything Nice . . 14.00
TPB Vol. 3 Love is All Around 14.00

PAUL THE SAMURAI
New England Comics, 1991
1 thru 3 . . . . @2.75
Bonanza #2 100pg. 5.00
GN Collected 9.00

PENDULUM
Adventure, 1993
1 Big Hand,Little Hand 2.50
2 The Immortality Formula 2.50
3 . . . . 2.50

PENNY CENTURY
Fantagraphics, 1997
1 by Jaime Hernandez 3.00
2 thru 7 . . . . @3.00

PENTACLE: THE SIGN OF THE FIVE
Eternity, 1991
1 . . . . 2.25
2 Det.Sandler,H.Smitts 2.25
3 Det.Sandler becomes New
  Warlock 2.25
4 5 warlocks Vs. Kaji 2.50

PETE THE P.O.'D POSTAL WORKER
Sharkbait Press, 1998
1 by Marcus Pierce & Pete

Pixy Junket #6
© Viz Communications

Garcia, Route 666 . . . . 3.00
2 prison mail 3.00
3 To Aliens with Love 3.00
4 Special Delivery to
  Conad the Alien. 3.00
5 England Vacation. 3.00
6 Benedict Postman 3.00
7 Postman on Elm Street 3.00
8 Postman on Elm Street 3.00
9 Pete Meets Jerry Ringer 3.00
10 Y2K Express. 3.00
11 Postal Wars. 3.00
12 . . . . 3.00
X-mas Spec.#1 . . . . 3.50
Spec. War Journal 3.00

TPB Pete Unplugged 13.00

PHANTOM
1 thru 3 . . . . @6.00
4 and 5 . . . . @7.00

PHANTOM, THE
Tony Raiola, 2000
TPB Diamond Hunters 9.50
TPB The Little Toma 9.50
TPB Sea Horse 9.50
TPB Game of Alvar 9.50
TPB Diana Aviatrix. 9.50
TPB Phantom's Treasure. 9.50

PHANTOM OF FEAR CITY
Claypool, 1994–95
1 thru 12 . . . . 2.50

PHANTOM OF THE OPERA
Eternity
1 . . . . 2.25

PHASE ONE
Victory, 1986
1 . . . . 3.00
2 . . . . 2.25
3 thru 5 . . . . @2.25

PHIGMENTS
Amazing, 1987
1 . . . . 5.00
2 . . . . 2.25
3 . . . . 2.25

PHONEY PAGES
Renegade
1 and 2 . . . . @2.25

PINEAPPLE ARMY
Viz Communications, 1988
1 thru 10 . . . . @2.25

PINK FLOYD EXPERIENCE
Revolutionary, 1991
1 based on rock group 2.50
2 Dark Side of the Moon. 2.50
3 Dark Side of the Moon, Wish you
  were here 2.50
4 The Wall. 2.50
5 A Momentary lapse of reason . . 2.50

PIRATE CORPS!
Eternity, 1987
6 and 7 . . . . @2.25
Spec. #1 . . . . 2.25

PIRANHA! IS LOOSE
Special Studio
1 Drug Runners,F:Piranha 3.00
2 Expedition into Terror. 3.00

PIXY JUNKET
Viz, 1993
1 thru 6 . . . . @2.75

P.J. WARLOCK
Eclipse, 1986
1 thru 3 . . . . @2.25

PLANET COMICS
Blackthorne, 1988
(Prev. Color)
4 and 5 . . . . @2.25

PLANET COMICS
A-List Comics, 1997
1 by L.Hampton & R.Leonardo 2.50
2 rep. from 1940 . . . . 3.00
3 . . . . 3.00
5 . . . . 3.00
6 . . . . 3.00
TPB Book of Planet Comics
  Covers, 1949–54 . . . . 8.00

PLANET COMICS
ACG Comics, 2000
1 WW, rep. 7.00
2 64-pg. 6.00

PLANET OF THE APES
Adventure Comics, 1990
1 WD,collect.ed. 6.00
1 2 covers 4.00
1a 2nd printing 2.50
1b 3rd printing 2.25
2 . . . . 3.00
3 . . . . 3.00
4 . . . . 3.00
5 D:Alexander? 3.00
6 Welcome to Ape City 3.00
7 . . . . 3.00
8 Christmas Story 2.75
9 Swamp Ape Village 2.75
10 Swamp Apes in Forbidden City . 2.75
11 Ape War continues 2.75
12 W:Alexander & Coure 2.75
13 Planet of Apes/Alien Nation/ Ape
   City x-over 2.75
14 Countdown to Zero Pt.1 . . . . . . 2.75
15 Countdown to Zero Pt.2 . . . . . . 2.75
16 Countdown to Zero Pt.3 . . . . . . 2.75
17 Countdown to Zero Pt.4 . . . . . . 2.75
18 Ape City (after Ape Nation mini-
   series 2.75
19 1991 `Conquest..' tie-in. 2.75
20 Return of the Ape Riders 2.75
21 The Terror Beneath,Pt.1 . . . . . . 2.75
22 The Terror Beneath,Pt.2 . . . . . . 2.75
23 The Terror Beneath,Pt.3 . . . . . . 2.75
Ann #1,`Day on Planet o/t Apes' . . 3.50
Lim.Ed. #1 . . . . 5.00

PLANET OF THE APES: BLOOD OF THE APES
Adventure Comics, 1991
1 A:Tonus the Butcher 3.00
2 Valia/Taylorite Connection 2.75
3 Ape Army in Phis 2.75
4 . . . . 2.75

PLANET OF THE APES: FORBIDDEN ZONE
Adventure
1 Battle for the Planet of the Apes
  & Planet of the Apes tie-in. 2.75
2 A:Juilus 2.75

PLANET OF THE APES: SINS OF THE FATHER
Adventure Comics, 1992
1 Conquest Tie-in 2.75

Poison Elves #11
© Sirius

PLANET OF THE APES URCHAKS' FOLLY
Adventure Comics, 1991
1 . . . . 3.00
2 thru 4 . . . . @2.75

PLANET 29
Caliber
1 A Future Snarl Tale 2.50
2 A:Biff,Squakman 2.50

PLANET-X
Eternity, 1991
1 three horror stories 2.50

PLAN 9 FROM OUTER SPACE
Eternity, 1991
1 . . . . 2.50
2 and 3 . . . . @2.25

PLASTIC LITTLE
CPM Comics, 1997
1 (of 5) Manga, by Satoshi
  Urushihara R:Captain Tita 3.00
2 F:Joshua Balboa 3.00
3 . . . . 3.00
4 . . . . 3.00
5 concl. 3.00
TPB Captain's Log, rep. #1—#5 . . 16.00

PLASTRON CAFE
Mirage, 1992
1 RV,inc.North by Downeast. 2.25
2 thru 4 . . . . @2.25

PLEASE SAVE MY EARTH
Viz Communications, 2003
GN Vol. 1 . . . . 10.00
GN Vol. 2 thru Vol. 7 . . . . @10.00

POE
Cheese Comics, 1996
1 by Jason Asala, reoffer 3.00
2 . . . . 3.00
3 `The System of Doctor Tarr and
  Professor Fether'. 3.00

4 thru 6 . . . . @3.00

Sirius/Dog Star
TPB Vol. 1 . . . . 15.00

VOL 2, 1997
1 by Jason Asala 3.00
2 House of Usher, pt.1 (of 4) 3.00
3 House of Usher, pt.2 . . . . 3.00
4 House of Usher, pt.3 . . . . 3.00
5 House of Usher, pt.4 . . . . 3.00
6 . . . . 3.00
7 . . . . 3.00
8 Small Town 3.00
9 Small Town, pt.2 . . . . 3.00
10 Small Town, pt.3 . . . . 3.00
11 Gold & Lead, pt.1 . . . . 3.00
12 Gold and Lead, pt.2 . . . . 3.00
13 F:Pluto the cat. 3.00
14 A:Mad Meg Mayflower 3.00
15 Airship 3.00
16 path of next demon. 3.00
17 22 one-page stories 3.00
18 Airship 3.00
19 thru 24 Balloon Hoax . . . . @3.00

POINT BLANK
Acme/Eclipse, 1989
1 thru 5 . . . . @3.00

POISON ELVES
Mulehide Graphics, 1993–95
Previously: I, Lusipher
8 DHa(c&a) 12.00
9 DHa 10.00
10 DHa 10.00
11 DHa, comic size 10.00
12 DHa 10.00
13 DHa 15.00
14 and 15 DHa . . . . @15.00
15a 2nd printing 6.00
16 and 17 DHa . . . . @7.00
17a 2nd printing 6.00
18 DHa 7.00
19 DHa 7.00
20 DHa 7.00

2nd Series, Sirius, 1995–97
1 F:Lusipher 6.00
2 V:Assassins Guild 4.00
3 Sanctuary, pt.3. . . . . 4.00
4 Sanctuary, pt.4 . . . . 4.00
5 Sanctuary, pt.5 . . . . 4.00
6 I:Lester Gran 4.00
7 thru 24 . . . . @4.00
25 DHa. 3.00
26 DHa. 3.00
27 DHa. 3.00
28 DHa,F:Lusiphur. 3.00
29 DHa, ... 3.00
30 DHa,F:Vido 3.00
31 DHa 3.00
32 DHa, Cassandra is dead 3.00
33 DHa, temporary truce 3.00
34 DHa, Lusiphur's feminine side . . 3.00
35 DHa, Purple Marauder
   reappears 3.00
36 DHa, Lusiphur tracked down . . . 3.00
37 DHa, questionable help 3.00
38 DHa. 3.00
39 DHa. 3.00
40 DHa, Sanctuary, concl. 3.00
41 DHa, on to Amrahly'nn 3.00
42 DHa, Just in Town
   for the Night,pt.1 . . . . 3.00
43 DHa, Town for the Night, pt.2 . . . 3.00
44 DHa, Town for the Night, pt.3 . . . 3.00
45 DHa, Petunia 3.00
46 DHa, High Price of
   Unemployment 2.50
47 The Fairy and the Imp 2.50

48 South for the Winter,pt.1 . . . . . . 2.50
49 South for the Winter,pt.2 . . . . . . 2.50
50 South for the Winter,pt.3 . . . . . . 3.00
51 South for the Winter,pt.4 . . . . . . 3.00
52 South for the Winter,pt.5 . . . . . . 3.00
53 South for the Winter,pt.6 . . . . . . 3.00
54 South for the Winter,pt.7 . . . . . . 3.00
55 thru 60 . . . . @3.00
61 by The Fillbach Brothers. 3.00
62 thru 68 . . . . @3.00
69 thru 81 . . . . @3.00
TPB Vol. 1 Requiem for an Elf. . . . 15.00
TPB Vol. 2 Traumatic Dogs 15.00
TPB Vol. 3 Desert of the Third Sin 15.00
TPB Vol. 4 Patrons, 48pg 5.00
TPB Vol. 5 rep. 272-pg. 15.00
TPB Vol. 6 rep. 280-pg. 15.00
TPB Vol. 7 . . . . 20.00
TPB Vol. 8 . . . . 16.00
TPB Vol. 9 Baptism by Fire 20.00
TPB The Muleskinner Years 35.00
TPB Lusipher & Lirilith (2001) 12.00
TPB Parintachin 9.00
Spec. Poison Elves Companion. . . . 3.50
Sketchbook 3.00
Sketchbook, limited 13.00

POISON ELVES:
HYENA
Sirius Entertainment, 2004
1 (of 4) 2.95
2 . . . . 2.95

POISON ELVES:
LUSIPHER & LIRILITH
Sirius Entertainment, 2001
1 (of 4) by Drew Hayes 3.00
1a limited ed. 10.00
2 . . . . 3.00
2a delux 10.00
3 . . . . 3.00
3a limited 6.50
4 . . . . 3.00
4a limited 6.50

POISON ELVES:
PARINTACHIN
Sirius Entertainment, 2001
1 (of 3) 3.00
2 . . . . 3.00
3 . . . . 3.00

POIZON: DEMON HUNTER
London Night, 1998
1 . . . . 3.00
2 . . . . 3.00
3 . . . . 3.00
4 double sized finale. 3.00

POKEMON ADVENTURES
Viz Communications, 1999
1 (of 5) Mysterious Mew 6.00
2 Wanted: Pikachu 6.00
3 The Snorlax Stop 6.00
4 . . . . 6.00
5 The Ghastly Ghosts 6.00

PART TWO, 2000
1 (of 6) Team Rocket Returns 3.00
2 The Hunt for Eevee 3.00
3 The Nidoking Safari 3.00
4 Mission: Magmar 3.00
5 The Dangerous Dragonite 3.00
6 The Mythical Moltres 3.00

PART THREE, 2000
1 . . . . 3.00

2 thru 7 . . . . @3.00

PART FOUR, 2001
Spec. 5.00

PART FIVE, 2001
1 thru 5 . . . . @5.00

PART SIX
1 (of 4) 5.00
2 thru 4 . . . . @5.00

PART SEVEN
1 (of 5) 5.00
2 thru 5 . . . . @5.00
TPB Pokemon: The Movie 2000 . . 16.00
TPB Art of Pokemon Third Movie . 13.00
TPB Vol. 1 Wanted: Pikachu 15.00
TPB Vol. 2 Legendary Pokemon . . 15.00
TPB Vol. 3 Saffron City Siege 14.00
TPB Vol. 4 Trainer in Yellow 14.00
TPB Vol. 5 Making Waves 14.00
TPB Vol. 6 The Cave Campaign . . 14.00
TPB Vol. 7 Pokemon Elite 14.00

POKEMON: ELECTRIC
PIKACHU BOOGALOO
Viz Communications, 1999
1 (of 4) by Toshihiro Ono, 48-pg. . . 3.50
2 . . . . 3.00
3 . . . . 3.00
4 finale 3.00
TPB 13.00

POKEMON:
THE ELECTRIC
TALE OF PIKACHU
Viz Communications, 1998
1 (of 4) by Toshihiro Ono 12.00
1a 2nd printing 4.00
2 . . . . 7.00
2a 2nd printing 4.00
3 . . . . 4.00
4 . . . . 4.00
GN The Electric Tale of Pikachu . . 13.00

POKEMON: PIKACHU
SHOCKS BACK
Viz Communications, 1999
1 (of 4) by Toshihiro Ono 3.25
2 thru 4 . . . . @3.25

POKEMON:
SURF'S UP PIKACHU
Viz Communications, 1999
1 (of 4) thru 3 . . . . @3.00
4 . . . . 3.50
TPB Vol. 3 . . . . 13.00

POKEMON TALES
Viz Communications, 2001
Prev. Color
17 Mewtwos Watching You 5.00
18 Magnemites Mission 5.00
19 Don't Laugh Charizard 5.00
20 Onix Underground 5.00
Gold and Silver Board Books
Vol. 1 Chikorita. 5.50
Vol. 2 Cyndaquil. 5.50
Vol. 3 Totodile 5.50
Vol. 4 Muddy Pichi 5.50
Vol. 5 Wobuffet Watches Clouds . . . 5.50
Vol. 6 Swinub's Nose 5.50
Vol. 7 Wake Up Lugia 5.50
Vol. 8 Look Out Hondour 5.50
Vol. 9 Corsola's Brave New World. . 5.50

POKEWOMON: GOTTA
SHAG 'EM ALL!
Blatant Comics, 1999
1 by Mike Rosenzweig 3.00

Primer #1
© Comico

POOT
Fantagraphics, 1997
1 by Walt Holcombe 3.00
2 Swollen Holler, pt.2 . . . . 3.00
3 sex issue 3.00
4 final issue, 40-pg. 4.00

POPCORN
Discovery, 1993
1 . . . . 4.00

POP PARODY
Studio Chikara, 1999
Big Fat Sci-Fi Spec.:Stawars 3.00
Pokymon–World Domination 3.00
Dixxi Chix vs. Spice Galz. 3.00
The Blair Snitch Project 4.00

PORTIA PRINZ
OF THE GLAMAZONS
Eclipse, 1986
1 thru 6 . . . . @2.25

POST BROTHERS
Rip Off Press
15 thru 18 . . . . @2.25
19 and 20 . . . . @2.50

POWER COMICS
Power Comics, 1977
1 Smart-Early Aardvark. 15.00
1a 2nd printing 7.00
2 I:Cobalt Blue 10.00
3 and 4 . . . . @8.00
5 . . . . 8.00

POWER COMICS
Eclipse, 1988
1 BB,DGb,Powerbolt. 2.50
2 BB,DGb 2.50
3 BB,DGb 2.50

PPV
Antarctic Press, 2002
1 by Tom Root & Jerzy Drozd. 3.00
2 thru 3 . . . . @3.00

PREMIERE
Diversity Comics, 1995
1 F:Kolmec The Savage 2.75

PRETEEN DIRTY GENE KUNG FU KANGAROOS
Blackthorne, 1986
1 and 2 . . . . @2.25

PREY
Monster Comics
1 I:Prey,A:Andrina 2.25
2 V:Andrina. 2.25
3 conclusion 2.25

PRICE, THE
1 Dreadstar mag. size 20.00

PRIMITIVES
Spartive Studios, 1995
1 thru 3 On the Moon . . . . @2.50

PRIME CUTS
Fantagraphics
1 adult. 3.50
2 thru 6 . . . . @3.50
7 thru 12 . . . . @4.00

PRIMER
Comico, 1982
1 . . . . 10.00
2 MW,I:Grendel. 100.00
3 . . . . 9.00
4 . . . . 8.00
5 SK(1st work),I:Maxx. 30.00
6 IN,Evangeline 14.00

PRIME SLIME TALES
Mirage, 1986
1 . . . . 5.00
2 . . . . 2.50
3 thru 6 . . . . @2.25

PRINCE VALIANT
1 thru 4 . . . . @5.00
Spec #1 . . . . 7.00

PRINCE VALIANT MONTHLY
Pioneer
1 thru 6 . . . . @4.00
6 . . . . 5.00
7 . . . . 5.00
8 . . . . 5.00
9 . . . . 7.00

PRINCESS PRINCE
CPM Manga, 2000
1 . . . . 3.00
1a Leah Hernandez (c). 3.00
2 thru 14 . . . . @3.00
15 . . . . 3.00
16 . . . . 3.00

PRIVATE BEACH
Amaze Ink/Slave Labor

Puma Blues #6
© Aardvark Vanaheim

Graphics, 2001
1 by David Hahn. 3.00
2 . . . . 3.00
3 . . . . 3.00
4 . . . . 3.00
5 thru 8 . . . . @3.00
TPB Vol. 1 Fun & Perils. 13.00
TPB Vol. 2 Secret Messages. . . . 14.00

PRIVATE EYES
Eternity, 1988
1 Saint rep. 2.25
2 . . . . 2.25
3 . . . . 2.25
4 . . . . 2.25
5 . . . . 2.25

PROJECT ARMS
Viz Communications, 2002
4 thru 6 . . . . @3.25
TPB Vol. 1 Awakenings 10.00
TPB Vol. 2 Egrigori 10.00
TPB Vol. 3 Secrets of the Past . . . 10.00
TPB Vol. 4 thru Vol. 6. . . . . @10.00

PROTHEUS
Caliber, 1986
1 . . . . 2.50
2 . . . . 2.50

PS238
Dork Storm Press, 2002
1 thru 5 . . . . @3.00
6 thru 8 . . . . @3.00
TPB Vol. 1 . . . . 16.00

PSI–JUDGE ANDERSON
Fleetway, 1989
1 thru 15 . . . . @2.25

PULP
Viz Communications, 1997
1 Manga anthology magazine 6.00
2 thru 5 . . . . @6.00
VOL. TWO
1 thru 12 . . . . @6.00
VOL. THREE
1 thru 11 . . . . @6.00

VOL. FOUR
1 . . . . 6.00
2 thru 12 . . . . @6.00
VOL. FIVE, 2000
1 . . . . 6.00
2 thru 12 . . . . @6.00
VOL SIX
1 thru 8 . . . . @6.00

PULP FICTION
A-List Comics, 1997
1 thru 2 rep. of golden age . . . . @2.50
3 . . . . 3.00
4 . . . . 3.00
5 . . . . 3.00
6 . . . . 3.00
7 . . . . 3.00
Spec. Art of Pulp Fiction 3.00

PUMA BLUES
Aardvark–Vanaheim, 1986
1 10,000 printed 4.00
1a 2nd printing 2.25
2 . . . . 3.00
3 thru 19 . . . . @2.50
20 Special 2.50
Mirage
21 thru 24. . . . . @2.25
25 . . . . 2.50
26 thru 28. . . . . @2.25

PVP
Dork Storm Press, 2001
1 by Scott Kurtz 3.00
2 . . . . 3.00
3 . . . . 3.00
4 . . . . 3.00
5 thru 8 . . . . @3.00
Collected ed. #1 Hat Trick 3.00
TPB Vol. 1 Striptease. 16.00

QUACK!
Star Reach, 1976
1 Duckaneer 11.00
1a 2nd printing 4.00
2 Newton the Rabbit Wonder 8.00
3 Dave Sim,The Beavers 8.00
4 Dave Sim. 8.00
5 Dave Sim. 8.00
6 . . . . 8.00

QUAGMIRE USA
Antarctic Press, 2004
1 . . . . 3.00
2 thru 5 . . . . @3.00

QUANTUM MECHANICS
Avatar, 1999
1 (of 2) by Barry Gregory &
Jacen Burrows. 3.50
1a wraparound cover 4.00
2 conclusion 3.50
2a wraparound cover 4.00

QUANTUM: ROCK OF AGES
Dreamchilde Press, 2003
1 (of 12) 3.00
2 thru 4 . . . . @3.00
TPB Vol. 1 . . . . 15.00

QUEEN & COUNTRY
Oni Press, 2001
1 by Greg Rucka & Steve Rolston 20.00

B & W PUB.

2	20.00
3 thru 5	@5.00
6 thru 24	@3.00
25	6.00
26 thru 28	@3.00
TPB Vol. 1	12.00
TPB Vol. 2 Morning Star	10.00
TPB Vol. 3 Crystal Ball	15.00
TPB Vol. 4 Operation Blackwall	9.00
TPB Vol. 5 Operation: Stormfront	14.95
TPB Vol. 6 Operation: Dandelion	11.95

QUEEN & COUNTRY: DECLASSIFIED
Oni Press, 2002

1 (of 3)	3.00
2	3.00
3	3.00
TPB Vol. 1	9.00

QUEST FOR DREAMS LOST
Literacy Vol. of Chicago, 1987

1-shot inc. TMNTurtles	2.25

QUEST PRESENTS
Quest, 1983

1 JD	2.25
2 JD	2.25
3 JD	2.25

QUICKEN FORBIDDEN
Cryptic Press, 1998

1	3.00
2	3.00
3	3.00
4	3.00
5	3.00
6 Trial Separation,pt.1	3.00
7 Trial Separation,pt.2	3.00
8 Trial Separation, concl.	3.00
9 Anxiety Disorder, pt.1	3.00
10 Anxiety Disorder, pt.2	3.00
11 thru 12	@3.00
TPB 152-pg.	15.00

RABID MONKEY
D.B.I. Comics, 1997

1 thru 4 by Joel Steudler	@2.25
5 thru 7	@2.25
8 thru 13	@2.50
#1–#5 Autographed pack	12.00

Dreamriders Workshop, 1998
Vol. 2

1	3.00

RADICAL DREAMER
Mark's Giant Economy Sized Comics, 1995–96

1 thru 3 F:Max Wrighter	@3.00
4 is Max the Devil?	3.00

VOL 2, 1998

1 (of 6) by Mark Wheatley, sci-fi	3.00

RAGMOP
Planet Lucy Press, 1995
See Image also

1 by Rob Walton, 3rd. printing	3.00
2 thru 8 reoffer	@2.75
8	2.75
9	2.75
10	2.75

VOL 2, 1997

3 by Rob Walton	3.00
4 O-ring saga, pt. 2 (of 3)	3.00

RAGNAROK
Sun Comics

1 I:Ragnarok Guy,Honey	2.50
2 The Melder Foundation	2.50
3 Guy/Honey mission contd.	2.50
4 I:Big Gossage	2.50

RAGNAROK
Tokyopop Press, 2002

1 (of 4) by Myung Jin Lee	3.00
2 thru 4	@3.00

RAIJIN COMICS
Gutsoon! Entertainment, 2002

1 manga	5.00
2 thru 36	@5.00
37 thru 44	@6.00
45	10.00
46	6.00

RAIKA
Sun Comics

1 thru 12	@2.50

RAISING HELL
ABC Comics, 1997

1	3.00
1a gold series, 2 extra pages	3.00
2 RCI,F:China & Jazz	3.00
3 conclusion, A:Wild Things	3.00
3 Baby Cheeks edition	10.00
3 Baby Cheeks Gold Edition	15.00

RALPH SNART
Now, 1986

1	5.00
2	4.00
3	4.00

[Volume 2] 1986

1	3.00
2 thru 8	@2.25
Trade Paperback	3.00

RAMBO
Blackthorne, 1988

1 thru 5	@2.25

RAMBO III
Blackthorne

1	2.25

RAMM
Megaton Comics, 1987

1 and 2	@2.25

RANMA 1/2
Viz, 1993
Parts 1 & 2, see color

PART 3, 1993–94

1 thru 13	@3.00

PART 4, 1995

1 thru 11	@3.00

PART 5, 1996

1 thru 9	@3.00
10 thru 12	@3.00

PART 6, 1996

1 thru 8 (of 14)	@3.00
9 thru 14	@3.00

TPB Vol. 6	16.00
TPB Vol. 7	16.00
TPB Vol. 8	16.00
TPB Vol. 9	16.00
TPB Vol. 10 rep. Part Six, 1st half	16.00
TPB Vol. 11 rep. Part Six, 2nd half	16.00

PART 7, 1998

1 (of 14)	3.00
2 thru 14	@3.00
TPB Vol. 12	16.00
TPB Vol. 13	16.00

PART 8, 1999

1 (of 13) thru 5	@3.00
6 thru 13	@3.00
TPB Vol. 14	16.00

The Ravening #0
© Avatar Press

TPB Vol. 15	17.00
TPB Vol. 16	16.00

PART 9, 2000

1 (of 11)	3.00
2 thru 11	@3.00
TPB Vol. 17 rep. Vol.9, #1–#6	16.00
TPB Vol. 18 rep. Vol.9, #6–#11	16.00

PART 10, 2001

1 (of 11)	3.00
2 thru 8	@3.00
9 thru 11	@3.00

PART 11, 2002

1 (of 11)	3.00
2 thru 11	3.00
TPB Vol. 19	16.00
TPB Vol. 20	16.00
TPB Art of Ranma 1/2	25.00

Part 12 (March, 2003)

1	3.00
TPB Vol. 21	16.00
TPB Vol. 22 thru Vol. 28	@10.00

RAPHAEL
Mirage, 1985

1 TMNT	17.50
1a 2nd printing	7.50

RAPTUS
High Impact

1	3.00
1 2nd printing, new cover	3.00
2	3.00
3	3.00

B & W PUB.

Razor Shi Special
© *London Night Studios*

RAPTUS:
DEAD OF NIGHT
High Impact

1	3.00
2	3.00
3	3.00

RAT FINK
World of Fandom

1	2.50
2 & 3	@2.50

RAVAGER
Kosmic Comic, 1997

0 Ashcan	2.25
1 The First Coming	3.55
2	3.55
3	3.55
4 by Kirk Patrick & Babak Homayoun	3.55
5	3.55
6 by Kirk Patrick & Romel Cruz	3.55

RAVEN
Ariel Press, 2003

1	2.25
2 thru 6	@2.25
7 thru 10	@2.00

RAVEN CHRONICLES
Caliber Press, 1995

1	3.00
1a Special Edition	6.00
2 Landing Zone	3.00
3 The Rain People	3.00
4 The Healer	3.00
5 thru 9	@3.00

Caliber `New Worlds'

10 by Scott Andrews, Laurence Campbell & Tim Perkins	3.00
11 `The Ghost of Alanzo Mann'	3.00
12 `The Compensators' flip book with Boston Bombers #1	3.00
13 48pg, bagged with back issue	4.00
14	3.00
15	3.00
16 inc. Black Mist	3.00
Spec. Heart of the Dragon	3.00
GN 192pg rep	17.00

RAVENING, THE
Avatar Press, 1997

0 Trevlin Utz (c)	4.00
0 Matt Martin (c)	4.00
0 Matt Haley (c)	4.00
0 leather cover	25.00
0 signed	15.00
1	3.00
1 leather cover	25.00
1 Avatar con cover edition	15.00
2 (of 2)	3.00
Spec. Secrets of the Ravening	2.75

RAW CITY
Dramenon Studios

1 I:Dya,Gino	3.00
2 V:Crucifier	3.00
3 The Siren's Past	3.00

RAW MEDIA MAGS.
Rebel

1 TV,SK,short stories	5.00

RAZOR
London Night, 1992

6 signed	20.00
10 signed	15.00
TPB The Suffering, rep. #1–#3	13.00
GN Let Us Prey, rep. of Razor/Wild Child, 80pg	5.00
X-over Razor/Embrace: The Spawning (1997)	3.00
Carmen Electra photo (c)	3.00
Carmen Electra photo embossed (c), signed	19.00
Spec. Razor: Switchblade Symphony, Tour Book, limited black leather	15.00

RAZOR ANALOG BURN
London Night Studios, 1999

1 by Lee Duhig	2.50
2	2.50

RAZOR: ARCHIVES
London Night, 1997

1 EHr, rep #1–#4	5.00
1a signed	12.00
2 EHr, rep #5–#8	5.00
3 EHr, rep #9–#15	5.00
4 EHr, rep #16–#17	5.00

RAZOR:
BLEEDING HEART
Avatar Press, 2001

1 Fillion (c)	3.50
1a Martin (c)	3.50
1b Wraparound (c)	5.00
1c Adult (c)	6.00
1d Worship (c)	6.00

RAZOR/DARK ANGEL:
THE FINAL NAIL
Boneyard/London Night

1 X-over (Boneyard Press)	4.00
2 X-over concl.(London Night)	3.00

RAZOR:
THE DARKEST NIGHT
London Night, 1998

1	5.00
1a white velvet	20.00

2 velvet edition	10.00

EH! Productions, 1999

1	5.00
1a Velvet Edition, signed	25.00
2	5.00
3	5.00
3a Fan ed	6.00

RAZOR: THE FURIES
Avatar, 2000

1 48-pg	5.00
1a Previews Exclusive	5.00

RAZOR: GOTHIC
London Night, 1998

1 (of 4) by EHr and Scott Wilson	3.00
1 leather	12.00
2 EHr	3.00
2a Graphic/violent cover	6.00
2b Gothic/leather cover	15.00

EH! Productions

3	3.00
3a Elite Fan ed	5.00
4	3.00
4a Elite Fan ed	5.00
Spec. Gotherotica	5.00

RAZOR: TILL I
BLEED DAYLIGHT
Avatar, 2000

1 (of 2) Tim Vigil (c)	3.50
1a wraparound (c)	4.00
1b Vampire Razor (c)	5.00
1c adult (c)	6.00
1d prism foil	13.00
1e expanded edition	5.00
2	3.50
2a wraparound (c)	4.00
2b adult (c)	6.00
2c expanded edition, 56-pg	5.00

RAZOR: TORTURE
London Night, 1995

0 chromium signed	4.00
1 platinum signed	3.00

RAZOR UNCUT
London Night Studios, 1995
Prev. RAZOR (Ind. Color)

13	3.00
14 V:Child Killer	3.00
15 Questions About Father	3.00
16 Nicole's Life,pt.1	3.00
17 Nicole's Life,pt.2	3.00
18	3.00
19 thru 21 Kiss from a Rose	@3.00
22 thru 24	@3.00
25 mild cover I:Knyfe	3.00
25b signed	13.00
26	3.00
27 A:Sade, pt.1	3.00
28 A:Sade, pt.2	3.00
29	3.00
30	3.00
31 `Strength by Numbers'	3.00
32 double sized	3.50
33 `Let Us Prey,' pt.2	3.00
34 `Let Us Prey,' pt.4 (of 4)	3.00
35 Let the battle begin	3.00
36 all-out war for Queen City	3.00
37 `After the Fall' pt.1	3.00
38 `After the Fall,' pt.2	3.00
39 `Money For Hire'	3.00
40 `Father's Bane,' pt.1	3.00
41 `Father's Bane,' pt.2	3.00
42 `Father's Bane,' pt.3	3.00

43 `Father's Bane,' pt.4 . . . . 3.00
44 Razor finds abandoned child . . . 3.00
45 An American Tragedy, pt.1 (of 5) 3.00
45a commemmorative edition, EHr . 5.00
46 An American Tragedy, pt.2 . . . . . 3.00
47 An American Tragedy, pt.3 . . . . . 3.00
48 An American Tragedy, pt.4 . . . . . 3.00
49 An American Tragedy, pt.5 . . . . . 3.00
50 back in Asylum, Tony Daniel (c) . 3.00
50a Michael Bair (c). 5.00
50b Stephen Sandoval (c) 5.00
50c Blood Red Velvet EHr (c) 25.00
Spec. Deep Cuts (1997) 5th Anniv.
    rep. #6,#13–#15, 80 pg 5.00

EH! Productions, 1999
51 . . . . 3.00

RAZORGUTS
Monster Comics, 1992
1 thru 4 . . . . 2.25

RAZOR'S EDGE
London Night, 1999
0 Razor/Stryke (c). 5.00
0b Night Vixen (c) 5.00
1 . . . . 5.00
1a Arizona (c) 5.00
2 Razorblaze (c) 5.00
2a Battle Girl (c) 6.00
2b Nightvixen (c). 5.00
3 . . . . 5.00
3a Nightvixen (c). 5.00
4 . . . . 5.00
4a (c) 5.00
5 . . . . 5.00
5a Stryke (c) 5.00

EH! Productions, 1999
6 48-pg.. . . . . 5.00
7 . . . . 5.00
8 . . . . 5.00
9 . . . . 5.00

REACTOMAN
B-Movie Comics
1 . . . . 2.25
1a signed,numbered. 2.75
2 thru 4 . . . . @2.25
collection 5.00

REAGAN'S RAIDERS
Solson
1 thru 6 . . . . @2.50

REALM
Arrow, 1986
1 Fantasy 6.00
2 . . . . 4.00
3 . . . . 3.00
4 TV,Deadworld 21.00
5 I:L.Kazan 2.25
6 thru 13 . . . . @2.25

Caliber Press, 1990
14 thru 18. . . . . @2.25
19 . . . . 2.50

REAL STUFF
Fantagraphic, 1990
1 thru 12 . . . . 2.50

REAPER
Newcomers Publishing
1 V:The Chinde. 3.00
2 . . . . 3.00
3 conclusion 3.00

Reid Fleming, World's Thoughest
Milkman #2 © Eclipse

REBELLION
Daikaiyu Enterprises, 1995
1 I:Rebellion 2.50

RECORD OF THE
LODOSS WAR
CPM Manga, 2000
TPB Book 1 The Grey Witch 16.00
TPB Book 2 The Grey Witch 16.00
TPB The Lady of Pharis 16.00
TPB Welcome to Lodoss Island . . 16.00
TPB Vol.2 Welcome Lodoss Island 16.00

RED DIARY
Caliber, 1998
1 (of 4) F:Marilyn, JFK, Hoover,
    CIA. 4.00
1a deluxe 7.00
2 . . . . 4.00
3 (of 4) 4.00
1 (signed) 4.00
4 . . . . 4.00

RED FOX
Harrier, 1986
1 scarce 6.00
1a 2nd printing 2.50
2 rare 5.00
3 . . . . 3.00
4 I:White Fox. 3.00
5 I:Red Snail. 3.00
6 . . . . 2.25
7 Wbolton 2.25
8 . . . . 2.25
9 Demosblurth 2.25

RED & STUMPY
Parody Press
1 Ren & Stimpy parody. 3.00

REDMOON
Comicsone.com, 2001
GN #1 196-pg. by Mina Hwang . . . 12.00
GN #2 196-pg. 12.00
GN #3 196-pg. 12.00
GN #4 200-pg. 12.00
GN #5 206-pg. 12.00
GN #6 208-pg. 12.00

RE:GEX: BLACK & WHITE
Awesome Entertainment, 1999
1 RLe,JLb 3.00

REHD
Antarctic Press, 2003
0 . . . . 2.50
1 thru 2 . . . . @3.00
3 . . . . 3.00

REID FLEMING, WORLD'S
TOUGHEST MILKMAN
Blackbird-Eclipse, 1986
1 David Boswell,I:Reid Fleming . . . 5.00
1a 2nd printing 3.00
1b 3rd–5th printing . . . . @2.50

Volume 2, 1986
#1 Rogues to Riches Pt.1 . . . . 5.00
#2 Rogues to Riches Pt.2 (1987) . . 3.00
#2a Later printings 2.50
#3 Rogues to Riches Pt.3 (1988) . . 3.00
#3a Later printings 2.50
#4 Rogues to Riches Pt.4 (1989) . . 3.00
#5 Rogues to Riches Pt.5 (1990) . . 2.50

Deep-Sea Comics, 1987
3 `Rogue to Riches,' pt.2,4th pr . . 3.00
4 `Rogue to Riches,' pt.3,3rd pr . . 3.00
5 `Rogue to Riches,' pt.4,2nd pr . . 3.00
6 `Rogue to Riches,' pt.5,2nd pr . . 3.00
7 `Another Dawn,'Pt.1 . . . . 3.00
8 `Another Dawn,'Pt.2. . . . . 3.00
9 `Another Dawn,'Pt.3. . . . . 3.00
TPB Rogue to Riches rep. 14.00
Spec#1 Origins (1998). 3.00

REIVERS
Enigma
1 thru 2 Ch'tocc in Space 3.00

RENEGADES OF JUSTICE
Blue Masque
1 I:Monarch,Bloodshadow 2.50
2 Madfire. 2.50
3 Television Chronicles. 2.50
4 R:Karen Styles. 2.50

RENFIELD
Caliber, 1994
1 thru 3 . . . . @3.00
GN Conclusion of series 9.00

REPENTANCE
Advantage Graphics, 1995
1 I:Repentance 2.25

REPLACEMENT GOD
Amaze Ink, 1995
1 Child in The Land of Man 6.00
1a 2nd & 3rd printing 3.00
2 Eye of Knute 4.00
3 & 4 `Bravery' . . . . @3.50
5 thru 7 . . . . @3.00
8 Fairie, book one, concl. 3.00
TPB rep. #1–#8 . . . . 20.00

REPLACEMENT GOD
& OTHER STORIES
Handicraft Guild, 1998
Previously published by Image
6 by Zander Cannon, 80pg. 7.00

RETALIATOR
Eclipse
1 I&O:Retaliator 2.50
2 O:Retaliator cont.. . . . . 2.50
3 thru 5 . . . . @2.50

RETIEF
Adventure, 1987–88
1 thru 6 Keith Laumer adapt. . . . @2.25
[Vol. 2], 1989–90
1 thru 6 . . . . @2.25
Spec.#1 Retief:Garbage Invasion . . 2.50
Spec.#1 Retief:The Giant Killer,
   V:Giant Dinosaur (1991) . . . 2.50
Spec.#1 Grime & Punishment,
   Planet Slunch (1991). 2.50

RETIEF OF THE CDT
Adventure, 1990
1 Keith Laumer Novel Adapt. 2.25
2 thru 6 . . . . @2.25

RETIEF AND
THE WARLORDS
Adventure Comics
1 Keith Laumer Novel Adapt. 2.50
2 Haterakans 2.50
3 Retief Arrested for Treason 2.50
4 Final Battle (last issue) 2.50

RETIEF: DIPLOMATIC
IMMUNITY
Adventure Comics, 1991
1 Groaci Invasion. 2.50
2 Groaci story cont. 2.50

RETRO-DEAD
Blazer Unlimited, 1995
1 Dimensional Rift. 3.00
2 by Dan Reed 3.00

RETROGRADE
Eternity
1 thru 4 . . . . @2.25

RETURN OF
HAPPY THE CLOWN
Caliber Press
1 & 2 V:Oni 3.00

RETURN OF LUM
URUSEI* YATSURA, THE
Viz Comics, 1994
1 thru 6 . . . . @3.00
TPB #1 . . . . 16.00
PART TWO, 1995
1 thru 13 . . . . @3.00
TPB Trouble Times Ten, rep.,pt#2 . 16.00
PART THREE, 1996
1 thru 11 by Rumiko Takahashi. . @3.00
TPB Creature Features 16.00
PART FOUR, 1997
1 thru 11 by Rumiko Takahashi. . @3.00
TPB Vol. 5 Feudal Furor 16.00
TPB Vol. 6 Creature Features 16.00
TPB Vol. 7 For Better or Curse . . . 16.00
TPB Vol. 8 Ran Attacks 16.00

RETURN OF THE SKYMAN
Ace Comics, 1987
1 SD 2.25

REVOLVER
Renegade, 1985
1 SD 2.25
2 thru 12 . . . . @2.25
Ann. #1. 2.25

REVOLVING DOORS
Blackthorne, 1986
1 . . . . 2.25
2 & 3 . . . . @2.25
Graphic Novel 4.00

RHEINTOCHTER
Antarctic Press, 1998
1 by Y.Paquette & M.Lacombe 3.00
2 (of 2) concl. 3.00

RHUDIPRRT
PRINCE OF FUR
MU Press, 1990–91
1 thru 6 . . . . @2.25
7 thru 12 . . . . @3.00

RICK RAYGUN
1 . . . . 2.25
2 thru 8 . . . . @2.25

RIO KID
Eternity
1 I:Rio Kid 2.50
2 V:Blow Torch Killer. 2.50
3 . . . . 2.50

RIOT
Viz, 1995
1 F:Riot,Axel 2.75
2 & 3 . . . . 2.75
4 final issue. 2.75
TPB Rep. 16.00

RIOT ACT TWO
Viz Comics, 1996
1 thru 7 . . . . @3.00
TPB rep.. . . . . 16.00

Robotech Invid War #15
© Eternity

RIP IN TIME
Fantagor, 1986
1 RCo,Limited series 3.00
2 RCo 2.25
3 RCo 2.25
4 RCo 2.25
5 RCo,Last 2.25

ROACHMILL
Blackthorne, 1986
1 . . . . 5.00
2 . . . . 3.00
3 . . . . 3.00
4 . . . . 3.00
See: Dark Horse

ROBERT E. HOWARD'S
Cross Plains Comics, 1999
1-shot Horror, 64-pg. 6.00
TPB Kull. 20.00
1-shot Black Stone. 4.00

ROBIN HOOD
Eternity, 1989
1 thru 4 . . . . @2.25

ROBO DEFENSE TEAM
MECHA RIDER
Castle Comics
1 I:RDT Mecha Rider 3.00
2 Identity of Outlaw. 3.00

ROBOTECH
Eternity
1-shot Untold Stories 2.50
Academy Comics, 1995–96
0 Robotech Information 2.50
Spec. Robotech: Macross Tempest
   F:Roy Fokker, Tempest (1995) . 3.00
Spec. Robotech: Mech Angel,
   I:Mech Angel (1995) 3.00
Spec. Robotech: The Misfits, from
   Southern Cross transferred to
   Africa 3.00
Spec. #1 & #2 Robotech The Movie,
   Benny R. Powell & Chi . . . . @3.00
Spec. Robotech Romance. 3.00
Spec. Robotech: Sentinels Star Runners
   Carpenter's Journey (1996) . . . 3.00
GN The Threadbard Heart. 10.00
Antarctic Press, 1998
Ann. #1. 3.00
Spec.#1 Robotech: Escape (1998) . 3.00

ROBOTECH:
ACADEMY BLUES
Academy Comics
0 Classroom Blues 3.50
1 F:Lisa 3.00
2 Bomb at the Academy 3.00
3 Roy's Drinking Buddy 3.00

ROBOTECH: AFTERMATH
Academy Comics
1 thru 10 R:Bruce Lewis . . . . @3.00
11 Zentradi Traitor 3.00
12 and 13. . . . . @3.00

ROBOTECH: CLONE
Academy Comics
1 Dialect of Duality 3.00
2 V:Monte Yarrow 3.00
3 Ressurection 3.00

B & W PUB.

4 Ressurection 3.00
5 F:Bibi Ava. 3.00

ROBOTECH: COVERT OPS
Antarctic Press, 1998
1 (of 2) by Greg Lane 3.00
2 . . . . 3.00

ROBOTECH: INVID WAR
Eternity, 1993
1 No Man's Land 2.50
2 V:Defoliators 2.50
3 V:The Invid,Reflex Point 2.50
4 V:The Invid. 2.50
5 Moonbase Aluce II 2.50
6 Moonbase-Zentraedi plot. 2.50
7 Zentraedi plot contd. 2.50
8 A:Lancer. 2.50
9 A:Johnathan Wolfe. 2.50
10 . . . . 2.50
11 F:Rand 2.50
12 thru 15. . . . . 2.50

ROBOTECH: INVID WAR AFTERMATH
Eternity
1 thru 6 F:Rand. 2.75

ROBOTECH: MORDECAI
Academy Comics
1 . . . . 3.00
2 Annie meets her clone 3.00

ROBOTECH: RETURN TO MACROSS
Eternity, 1993
1 thru 12 . . . . @2.50
Academy Comics
13 thru 17 Roy Fokker . . . . @2.75
18 F:The Faithful 2.75
19 F:Lisa 2.75
20 F:Lisa 2.75
21 V:Killer Robot 3.00
22 War of the Believers 3.00
23 War of the Believers,pt.2 . . . . . 3.00
24 War of the Believers,pt.3 . . . . . 3.00
25 War of the Believers,pt.4 . . . . . 3.00
26 thru 30. . . . . @3.00
31 What is the Federalist Plan?. . . 3.00
32 thru 34 . . . . @3.00
35 Typhoon threatens Macross
  Island. 3.00
36 . . . . 3.00
37 round up of Federalist Agents. . . 3.00

ROBOTECH: SENTINELS: RUBICON
Antarctic Press, 1998
1 (of 7) 3.00
2 Shadows of the Past 3.00

ROBOTECH II THE SENTINELS
Eternity, 1988
1 . . . . 3.00
2 & 3 . . . . @2.50
1a thru 3a 2nd printings . . . . . . @2.25
4 thru 16 . . . . @2.50
Book 2, 1990
1 thru 12 . . . . @2.25
13 thru 20. . . . . @2.25
Wedding Special #1 (1989) 2.25

Wedding Special #2. . . . . 2.25
Robotech II Handbook. 2.50
Book Three
1 thru 8 V:Invid 2.50

Rocket Ranger #3
© Adventure

Book Four
Academy Comics, 1995
1 by Jason Waltrip 3.00
2 thru 4 F:Tesla. . . . . @2.75
5 JWp,JWt,interior of Haydon IV . . 3.00
6 thru 8 . . . . @3.00
9 JWp,JWt,Breetai, Wolf & Vince
  return to Tirol 3.00
10 JWp,JWt,Ark Angel attacked by
  The Black Death Destroyers . . . 3.00
11 JWp,JWt,Tirol, Wolff, Vince &
  Breetai on trial for treason. 3.00
12 JWp,JWt,Dr. Lang exposes
  General Edwards' evil designs . 3.00
13 F:Tesla 2.75
14 V:Invid. 2.75
15 . . . . 2.75
16 . . . . 2.75
17 V:Invid Mechas 2.75
18 F:"HIN" 3.00
19 V:Invid. 3.00
20 Final Aplp. Invid Regiss 3.00
21 Predator and Prey. 3.00
22 A Clockwork Planet. 3.00
Halloween Special JWp,JWt, ... 3.00

ROBOTECH II: THE SENTINELS: CYBERPIRATES
Eternity, 1991
1 The Hard Wired Coffin. 2.25
2 thru 4 . . . . @2.25

ROBOTECH II: THE SENTINELS: THE MALCONTENT UPRISING
Eternity
1 thru 12 . . . . @2.25

ROBOTECH: VERMILION
Antarctic Press, 1997
1 (of 4) by Duc Tran 3.00
2 Why did Hiro die? 3.00
3 . . . . 3.00
4 . . . . 3.00

ROBOTECH: WARRIORS
Academy Comics, 1995
1 F:Breetai 3.00
2 F:Mirya. 3.00
3 F:Mirya. 3.00
GN The Terror Maker. 10.00

ROBOTECH: WINGS OF GIBRALTAR
Antarctic Press, 1998
1 (of 2) by Lee Duhig 3.00
2 . . . . 3.00

ROBO WARRIORS
CFW
1 thru 11 . . . . @2.25
Becomes:
KUNG FU WARRIORS

ROCK 'N' ROLL COMICS
Revolutionary, 1989
1 Guns & Roses 10.00
1a 2nd printing 3.50
1b 3rd printing. 3.00
1c 4th-7th printing. 3.00
2 Metalica 11.00
2a 2nd printing 3.00
2b 3rd-5th printing. 3.00
3 Bon Jovi. 9.00
4 Motley Crue 5.00
5 Def Leppard 5.00
6 Rolling Stones 8.00
6a 2nd-4th printing 3.00
7 The Who 5.00
7a 2nd-3rd printing 3.00
9 Kiss 15.00
9a 2nd-3rd Printing 5.00
10 Warrant/Whitesnake 6.00
10a 2nd Printing. 3.00
11 Aerosmith 5.00
12 New Kids on Block 5.00
12a 2nd Printing. 2.25
13 LedZeppelin 6.00
14 Sex Pistols 5.00
See Independent Color

ROCKET RANGERS
Adventure, 1992
1 . . . . 3.00
2 . . . . 3.00
3 . . . . 3.00

ROCKIN' ROLLIN' MINER ANTS
Fate Comics, 1992
1 As seen in TMNT #40 . . . . 2.25
1a Gold Variant copy 7.50
2 Elephant Hunting, A:Scorn,
  Blister 2.25
3 V:Scorn, Inc.,K.Eastman Ant
  pin-up. 2.25
4 Animal Experiments,V:Loboto . . . 2.25

Sailor Moon #8
© *Mixx Entertainment*

ROLLING STONES: THE SIXTIES
Personality
1 Regular Version 3.00
1a Deluxe Version,w/cards 7.00

ROOTER
Custom Comics of America, 1996–97
1 Sweatin' Bullets 3.00
2 Big Bad Beaver 3.00
3 The Big Izzy 3.00
4 Da Voodoo Blues 3.00
5 . . . . 3.00
6 Blues Power 3.00
Ann. #1, 120pg 15.00
VOL 2, 1998
1 by Kelly Campbell 3.00
2 . . . . 3.00
3 Hot Rocks Mojo 3.00

ROSE
Hero Graphics, 1993
1 From The Champions 3.50
2 A:Huntsman 3.50
3 thru 5 . . . . @3.00

ROSE AND GUNN
London Night, 1996
1 . . . . 3.00
1b signed 10.00
2 . . . . 3.00
3 . . . . 3.00

ROSE AND GUNN: RECKONING
London Night
1 (of 2) 3.00

ROSE 'N' GUNN
Bishop Pres, 1995
1 Deadly Duo 5.00
2 V:Marilyn Monroe 3.00
3 Presidential Affairs 3.00
4 Without Each Other 3.00
5 V:Red 3.00
6 & 7 . . . . @3.00
Creator's Choice Rep. #1 . . . . 3.00

Creator's Choice Rep. #2 . . . . 3.00
Creator's Choice Rep. #3 . . . . 3.00

ROVERS
Eternity
1 thru 7 . . . . @2.25

RUBES REVIVED
Fish Warp
1 thru 3 . . . . @2.25

RUK BUD WEBSTER
Fish Warp
1 thru 3 . . . . @2.25

SADE
Bishop Press, 1995
0 B:Adventures of Sade 3.00
1 . . . . 3.00
1a variant 6.00
2 . . . . 3.00

SADE SPECIAL
Bishop Press
1 V:Razor 5.00
1a signed 7.00

SADE
London Night, 1996
1 . . . . 3.00
2 thru 5 . . . . @3.00

SADE/ROSE AND GUNN
London Night, 1996
1 Confederate Mist 3.00

SADE: TESTAMENTS OF PAIN
London Night, 1997
1 (of 2) 3.00

SAGA OF THE MAN-ELF
Trident, 1989
1 thru 5 . . . . @2.25

SAGE
Fantaco, 1995
1 O:Sage 5.00

SAILOR MOON
Mixx Entertainment, 1998
1 by Naoko Tekeuchi 20.00
2 thru 5 . . . . @12.00
6 thru 11 . . . . @5.00
12 thru 20 . . . . @5.00
Pocket #1 (of 18) 192-pg. 10.00
Pocket #2 rep. 10.00
Pocket #3 rep. 10.00
Pocket #4 rep. 10.00
Pocket #5 rep. #11–#13 . . . . 10.00
Pocket #6 rep. #14–#17 . . . . 10.00
Scout Guide: Sailor Mars: Fire . . . 13.00
Scout Guide: Sailor Venus: Love . . 13.00
Scout Guide: Sailor Jupiter:
   Thunder 13.00
Novel A Scout is Born 5.00
Novel The Power of Love 5.00
Novel 3: Mercury Rising 5.00
Tokyopop.Com, 2000
21 thru 25 . . . . @3.00
26 thru 35 . . . . @3.00
Pocket Mixx Vol. 7 thru 11 . . . . @10.00

Pocket Mixx Stars, Vol.1 thru 3 . @10.00
TPB Scout Guide-Meet Sailor
   Moon: Crystal 13.00
TPB Scout Guide-Meet Sailor
   Mercury: Ice 13.00
TPB Scout Guide-Meet Sailor
   Jupiter: Thunder 13.00

SAILOR MOON SUPER S
Mixx Entertainment, 1999
1 (of 18) 192-pg. 10.00
2 thru 4 Pocket Mixx . . . . @10.00

SAINT
Kick Ass Comics
1 & 2 V:Cerran 2.50

SAINT GERMAINE
Caliber `Core', 1997
0 O:St. Germaine 4.00
1 VcL, two immortals, St. Germain
   cover 3.00
1 Lilith cover 3.00
2 VcL 3.00
3 VcL 3.00
3a signed 3.00
4 VcL 3.00
5 The Kilroy Mandate, VcL(c) 3.00
5a Meyer (c) 3.00
6 Kilroy Mandate 3.00
8 Ghost Dance 3.00
8 The Man in the Iron Mask 3.00
10 The Tragedy of Falstaff 3.00
11 by Gary Reed & James Lyle . . . 3.00
GN Shadows Fall, rep. #1–#4 . . . . 15.00
Spec. Casanova's Lament, 48-pg . . 4.00
Spec. Restoration, VcL 4.00

SAINT GERMAINE: PRIOR ECHOES
Caliber `Core', 1998
1 (of 4) by Gary Reed 3.00
2 . . . . 3.00
3 . . . . 3.00

SAINT TAIL
Tokyopop Press, 2000
1 . . . . 3.00
2 thru 13 . . . . @3.00
14 thru 16 . . . . @3.00
17 thru 20 . . . . @3.00
TPB Pocket Vol. 1 thru Vol. 7 . . . @10.00

SAMURAI (1st series)
1 . . . . 50.00
2 . . . . 25.00
3 . . . . 25.00
4 . . . . 25.00
5 . . . . 25.00

SAMURAI
Aircel, 1985
1 rare 6.00
1a 2nd printing 3.00
1b 3rd printing 2.25
2 . . . . 5.00
2a 2nd printing 2.50
3 . . . . 3.00
4 . . . . 3.00
5 thru 12 . . . . @2.25
13 DK (1st art) 4.00
14 thru 16 DK . . . . @4.00
17 thru 23 . . . . @2.25
[3rd series], 1988
#1 thru 3 . . . . @2.25

B & W PUB.

B & W PUB.

#4 thru 7 . . . . @2.25
Compilation Book 5.00

SAMURAI
Warp Graphics, 1997
1 by Barry Blair & Colin Chan. 3.00
2 . . . . 3.00
3 . . . . 3.00
4 . . . . 3.00

SAMURAI FUNNIES
Solson
1 thru 3 . . . . @2.25

SAMURAI PENGUIN
Solson, 1986
1 . . . . 3.00
2 I:Dr.Radium 2.25
3 . . . . 2.25
4 . . . . 2.25
5 FC 2.25
6 color 2.25
7 . . . . 2.25
8 . . . . 2.25
9 . . . . 2.25

SAMURAI 7
Gauntlet Comics
1 I: Samurai 7 . . . . 2.50

SAMURAI, SON OF DEATH
Eclipse
1 . . . . 4.00
1a 2nd printing 4.00

SANCTUARY
Viz Communications, 1993
1 World of Yakuza. 5.00
2 thru 4 . . . . @5.00
5 thru 9 . . . . @5.00
[Part Two], 1994
1 thru 9 . . . . @5.00
[Part Three], 1994–95
1 thru 8 . . . . @3.50
[Part Four], 1995–96
1 thru 7 . . . . @3.50
[Part Five], 1996
7 thru 13 by Sho Fumimura &
  Ryoichi Ikegami . . . . @3.50
GN rep. ? of part 4 & ? part 5 . . . . 17.00
GN Vol. 5 . . . . 18.00
GN Vol. 6 . . . . 18.00
GN Vol. 9 . . . . 17.00

SANTA CLAWS
Eternity
1 `Deck the Mall with Blood
  and Corpses'. 3.00

SAPPHIRE
Ariel Press, 1996
1 by Vince Danks 3.00
6 . . . . 3.00
7 . . . . 3.00
8 . . . . 3.00
9 . . . . 3.00

SARAI
Comicsone.com, 2001
Vol. 1
TPB #1 by Masahiro Shibata. 10.00
TPB #2 thru #4 186-pg. 10.00

GN #6 200-pg. 10.00
GN #7 188-pg. 10.00
GN #8 200-pg. 10.00

SAVAGE HENRY
Vortex, 1987
1 thru 13 . . . . @2.25
Rip Off Press, 1991
14 thru 15. . . . . @2.25
16 thru 24. . . . . @2.50

SAVAGE HENRY: POWERCHORDS
Aeon, 2004
1 (of 3) 2.95
2 and 3 . . . . @2.95
Spec. Puppet Trap 2.95

Scud: Disposable Assassin #4
© Fireman Press

SCARLET IN GASLIGHT
Eternity, 1988
1 A:SherlockHolmes 4.00
2 . . . . 3.00
3 & 4 . . . . @2.50

SCARLET SCORPION/ DARKSIDE
AC Comics, 1995
1 & 2 Flipbooks 3.50

SCARLET THUNDER
Amaze Ink, 1995
1 thru 3 . . . . @2.50

SCARY GODMOTHER
Sirius Entertainment, 2001
1 by Jill Thompson 3.00
2 thru 6 concl. . . . . @3.00
TPB Wild About Harry 10.00
TPB Ghouls Out For Summer 15.00
TPB Spooktacular Stories 10.00
GN Vol. 1 Storybook 10.00
GN Vol. 2 The Revenge of Jimmy . 10.00
GN The Mystery Date Storybook. . 10.00

SCARY GODMOTHER: BLOODY VALENTINE
Sirius Entertainment, 1998
1 . . . . 4.00
1a signed and numbered 10.00
Holiday Spooktacular 3.00

SCARY GODMOTHER: WILD ABOUT HARRY
Sirius Entertainment, 2000
1 (of 3) by Jill Thompson 3.00
2 . . . . 3.00
3 concl. 3.00

SCIMIDAR
Eternity
1 . . . . 4.00
1a 2nd Printing 2.50
2 and 3 . . . . @3.00
4 HotCover 3.50
4A MildCover 3.00

SCOOTER GIRL
Oni Press, 2003
1 (of 6) 3.00
2 thru 6 . . . . @3.00
TPB 14.95

SCORN
SCC Entertainment, 1996
Lingerie Spec. 3.00
Lingerie Spec. deluxe 10.00
Super Spec.#1 rep. Deadly
  Rebellion, Headwave, Fabric
  of the Mind. 5.00
X-over Scorn/Ardy: Alien Influence
  (1997) by Rob Potchak & Timothy
  Johnson 4.00
  Bill Maus (c). 4.00
  Deluxe gold 10.00
X-over Scorn/Dracula: The Vampire's
  Blood (1997) 4.00
  Dracula cover 4.00
  Scorn cover 4.00
Spec.#1A Scorn; Dead or Alive
  (1997) Mike Morales(c) 4.00
  Andrea Seri(c) 4.00
Spec.# Scorn:Deadly Rebellion . . 4.00
  Birthday Suit cover 10.00
  Celebrity photo cover 10.00
Spec.#1 Scorb: Fractured (1997)
  Fear cover 4.00
  Rage cover 4.00
Spec: Scorn: Heatwave (1997) by
  Chris Crosby & Mike Morales . . 4.00
Spec. Scorn: Hostage 4.00
Spec. Scorn: Naked Truth (1997) . . 4.00

SCRATCH
Outside, 1986
1 . . . . 3.00
2 thru 4 . . . . @2.25

SCREAMING ANGELS
Antarctic Press, 2004
1 (of 3) 3.50
2 thru 3 . . . . @3.50

SCRIMIDAR
CFD Productions, 1995
1 I:Bloody Mary 2.75

All comics prices listed are for *Near Mint* condition.

SCUD: DISPOSABLE ASSASSIN
Fireman Press, 1994

```
1 I:Scud.....................10.00
1a 3rd printing.................3.50
2...........................7.00
3...........................5.00
4 thru 6 F:Scud.............@5.00
7 Lupine Thoughts.............4.00
8 Scud Looks for His Arm.......4.00
9 Scud Looks for His Arm.......4.00
10 thru 16 by Rob Schrab......@3.00
17...........................3.00
18...........................3.00
19...........................3.00
20 Horse series, concl..........3.00
TPB Rep.#1-#4...............13.00
TPB Programmed for Damage,
   rep.#5–#9................15.00
TPB Solid Gold Bomb..........18.00
TPB Yellow Horseman (2001)....15.00
```

SCUD: TALES FROM THE VENDING MACHINE
Fireman Press, 1998

```
1...........................2.50
2...........................2.50
3...........................2.50
4...........................2.50
5...........................2.50
```

SEAMONSTERS & SUPERHEROES
Amaze Ink/SLG, 2003

```
1 (of 3)....................3.00
2 thru 6...................@3.00
```

SEARCHERS
Caliber `New Worlds', 1996

```
1A Red cover, signed...........3.00
1B Blue cover, signed..........3.00
3...........................3.00
4...........................3.00
5 flip book with Boston Bombers ..3.00
```

SEARCHERS: APOSTLE OF MERCY
Caliber, 1997

```
1 (of 2).....................4.00
2...........................4.00
```

Vol 2?

```
1...........................3.00
2...........................3.00
3 (of 3) 48pg................4.00
```

SECRET FILES
Angel Entertainment, 1996

```
0 gold edition................7.00
0 commemorative edition.......3.00
1...........................3.00
1 spooky silver foil edition.......6.00
2...........................3.00
2 deluxe....................6.00
Spec. Secret Files vs. Vampire Girls:
   The Vampire Effece (1997)...3.00
Pin-up Book Secret Files: Erotic
   Experiments (1997)..........3.00
Spec.#1 Secret Files: F.B.I.
   Conspiracy (1997)F:Sabrina
   & Susanna Sorenson........3.00
```

SECRET FILES: THE STRANGE CASE
Angel Entertainment, 1996

```
0 by David Campitti & Al Rio.....3.00
1 by David Campitti & Al Rio.....3.00
```

SECRET MESSAGES
NBM Books, 2001

```
1 Abductions, pt.1.............3.00
2 Abductions, pt.2.............3.00
3 Abductions, pt.3.............3.00
4 Abductions, pt.4.............3.00
5 Abductions, pt.5.............3.00
```

SECTION 8
Noir Press, 1995

```
1 Anthology series............2.50
2 thru 6...................@2.50
7 `Retribution,' pt.1..........2.50
8 `Retribution,' pt.2..........2.50
9...........................2.50
10 `Chance'..................2.50
```

SEEKER
Caliber `Core', 1998

```
1M by Gary Reed & Chris
   Massarotto, Meadows(c).....3.00
1W David Williams(c)..........3.00
1a variant Greg Louden (c)......3.00
1 premium, signed...........10.00
2...........................3.00
3...........................3.00
4...........................3.00
5 Gestalt vs. LeAnn Heywood ...3.00
Spec. Dawn of Armageddon,
   x-over, 48-pg..............4.00
```

SENTINEL
Harrier, 1986

```
1...........................2.25
2 thru 4...................@2.25
```

SERAPHIN
Newcomers Press, 1995

```
1 I:Roy Torres................3.00
```

SERENITY ROSE
Amaze Ink/SLG, 2003

```
1...........................3.00
2 thru 5...................@3.00
```

7 GUYS OF JUSTICE, THE
False Idol Studios, 2000

```
1 Jerque Imperitive,pt.1........2.25
2 Jerque Imperitive,pt.2........2.25
3 Jerque Imperitive,pt.3........2.25
4 thru 11..................@2.25
12 thru 16.................@2.25
```

777: THE WRATH
Avatar Press, 1998

```
1 (of 3) by David Quinn & Tim Vigil 3.00
1a wraparound cover...........3.50
1c leather cover..............6.00
1d royal blue foil logo........75.00
1e signed...................15.00
1f foil platinum edition........17.00
2...........................3.00
3 concl.....................3.00
TPB 777:The Wrath/
   Faust Fearbook...........16.00
```

SEVENTH SYSTEM, THE
Sirius Entertainment, 1997

```
1 (of 6) by Roel...............3.00
```

Shatterpoint #3
© Eternity

```
2 thru 6...................@3.00
```

SFA SPOTLIGHT
Shanda Fantasy Arts, 1999

```
4 Tales of the Morphing Period....4.50
5 Zebra, by Carl Gafford........4.50
6 Women in Fur 1999..........5.00
7 Tales From Supermegatopia....5.00
8 Women in Fur 2000..........5.00
9 Knight & Mouse.............5.00
10 Atomic Mouse..............5.00
11 Plush Beauties.............5.00
12 Courageous Man Adventures...5.00
13 Women in Fur 2001.........5.00
14 Fission Chicken............5.00
15 Women in Fur 2002.........5.00
16 Star Quack................5.00
```

SF SHORT STORIES
Webb Graphics, 1991

```
1...........................2.50
2...........................2.50
```

SHADES OF BLUE
AMP Comics, 2001

```
1...........................2.50
2 thru 4...................@2.50
5 Silence, pt.3...............2.50
6 F:Heidi, Marcus.............2.50
7 Winter, pt.1................3.00
8 Winter, pt.2................3.00
9 Winter, pt.3................3.00
10..........................3.00
```

SHADES OF BLUE
Digital Webbing, 2003

```
1 thru 5...................@3.00
TPB Vol. 1.................12.00
```

SHADES OF GRAY COMICS AND STORIES
Caliber Tapestry, 1996

```
1...........................3.00
2...........................3.00
3...........................3.00
```

4 . . . . 3.00
Super Summer Spec. rep. 4.00

SHADOW CROSS
Darkside Comics, 1995
1 I:Shadow Cross 5.00
2 thru 7 . . . . @2.50

SHADOWGEAR
Antarctic Press, 1999
1 by Locke 3.00
2 . . . . 3.00
3 conclusion 3.00

SHADOWALKER
Aircel
1 thru 4 . . . . @2.25

SHADOW SLASHER
Pocket Change Comics, 1994
1 I:Shadow Slasher. 2.50
2 V:Riplash 2.50
3 F:Matt Baker 2.50
4 Evolution 2.50
5 F:Riplash 2.50
6 Next Victim. 2.50
7 What Can Kill Him 2.50
8 . . . . 2.50
9 final issue. 2.50

SHANDA [THE PANDA]
Mu, 1992
1 . . . . 2.50
Antarctic Press, 1993
1 thru 11 . . . . @2.75
12 thru 14. . . . . @3.00
Med Systems
15 and 16 . . . . @2.25
Vision Comics, 1996
17 by Mike Curtis & Michelle Light . 2.25
18 `Rocky Horror Picture Show' . . . 2.25
19 `Shine on Me, Cajun Moon' 2.50
20 falling in love. 2.50
22 Bright Eyes 3.00
Shanda Fantasy, 1999
23 Sweet Young Things. 3.00
24 graduation night 3.00
25 48-pg. 5.00
26 thru 30. . . . . @3.00
31 thru 33. . . . . @3.00
34 48-pg. 5.00
35 thru 42. . . . . @5.00

SHANGHAIED
Eternity
1 & 2 . . . . @2.25
3 & 4 . . . . @2.25

SHARDS
Acension Comics, 1994
1 I:Silver, Raptor, RIpple. 2.50
2 F:Anomoly 2.50

SHATTERED EARTH
Eternity, 1988–89
1 thru 9 . . . . @2.25

SHATTERPOINT
Eternity, 1990
1 thru 4 Broid miniseries . . . . @2.25

Shi, The Way of the Warrior #1
Comm Edition © Crusade

SHEBA
Sirius Dogstar, 1997
VOL 2
1 by Walter S. Crane IV 2.50
2 . . . . 2.50
3 . . . . 2.50
4 . . . . 2.50
Sick Mind Press
5 . . . . 3.00
6 . . . . 3.00
7 . . . . 3.00
TPB Vol. 2 (2000) 16.00
TPB Vol. 3 (2004) 18.00
Shanda Fantasy Arts, 2001
Vol. 3
1 by Walter Crane IV 5.00
2 thru 4 . . . . @5.00

SHE-CAT
AC Comics, 1989
1 thru 4 . . . . @2.50

SHE-DEVILS ON WHEELS
Aircel, 1992
1 thru 3 by Bill Marimon 3.00

SHERLOCK HOLMES
Eternity, 1988
1 thru 22 . . . . @2.25

SHERLOCK HOLMES
Caliber/Tome Press, 1997
1-shot Dr. Jekyll and Mr. Holmes by
    Steve Jones & Seppo Makinen . 3.00
1-shot Return of the Devil 4.00
1-shot Return of the Devil, signed . . 4.00
GN Adventure of the Opera Ghost . 7.00
TPB Case of Blind Fear. 13.00
TPB Scarlet in Gaslight 13.00
TPB Sussex Vampire. 13.00

SHERLOCK HOLMES CASEBOOK
Eternity
1 and 2 . . . . @2.25

SHERLOCK HOLMES: CHRONICLES OF CRIME AND MYSTERY
Northstar
1 `The Speckled Band' 2.25

SHERLOCK HOLMES: HOUND OF THE BASKERVILLES
Caliber/Tome Press, 1997
1 (of 3) by Martin Powell & PO. . . . 3.00

SHERLOCK HOLMES: MARK OF THE BEAST
Caliber/Tome Press, 1997
1 (of 3) by Martin Powell
    & Seppo Makinen 3.00
2 . . . . 3.00
GN 13.00

SHERLOCK HOLMES MYSTERIES
Moonstone, 1997
1-shot by Joe Gentile & Richard
    Gulick. 3.00
1-shot Sherlock Holmes and the
    Clown Prince of London (2001). 3.00
TPB Vol. 1 . . . . 19.00
TPB Vol. 2 . . . . 15.00

SHERLOCK HOLMES OF THE '30's
Eternity
1 thru 7 strip rep.. . . . . @3.00

SHERLOCK HOLMES READER
Caliber `Tome Press', 1998
1 Curse of the Beast. 4.00
2 The Loch Ness Horror 4.00
3 The Loch Ness Horror. 4.00
4 The Loch Ness Horror 4.00
5 . . . . 4.00

SHERLOCK HOLMES: RETURN OF THE DEVIL
Adventure, 1992
1 V:Moriarty. 2.50
2 V:Moriarty. 2.50

SHERLOCK JUNIOR
Eternity
1 Rep.NewspaperStrips 2.25
2 Rep.NewspaperStrips 2.25
3 Rep.NewspaperStrips 2.25

SHI
Crusade, 1999
0 rough cut edition 5.00
0 ashcan, signed. 10.00
Spec.#1 Black,White & Red. 3.00
Spec. San Diego (Con) Art of War
    Tour Book 1998 . . . . 10.00
Spec. Lim. Ed. Shi/Daredevil
    Banzai 14.00
Spec.#1 Kaidan, macabre 3.00
Spec.#1 Kaidan, signed & numb. . 20.00
Spec. Shi/First Wave, Voices
    of the Dead x-over (2001) 3.00
Spec. Shi/FirstWave,variant BiT(c) . 3.00

Spec. Shi/FirstWave,signed 10.00
Spec. First Wave/Shi, Voices of
   the Dead, pt.2 x-over (2001) . . . 3.00
Spec. FirstWave/Shi,variant BiT(c) . 3.00
Coll. Ed. Heaven & Earth,
   Yin & Yang,96-pg. 6.00
Year of the Dragon preview book . . 3.00
Year of the Dragon tour book 5.00
Year of the Dragon tour Wizard 5.00
Year of the Dragon tour San Diego . 5.00
Umadoshi Tour Book, 2002 . . . . . . 5.00
Umadoshi, Tour Book, sketch (c) . . . 5.00
Umadoshi Tour Book, Pittsburgh . . . 5.00

SHI: THE ILLUSTRATED WARRIOR
Crusade Entertainment, 2002
1 (of 7) BiT 3.00
2 BiT thru 7 . . . . @3.00

Silent Mobius, Love and Chaos #1
© Viz Communications

SHI: SEMPO
Avatar, 2003
1/2 Prism Foil Edition 13.00
1/2 Royal Blue Edition 75.00
1/2 Prism Foil (c) 13.00
Preview edition 2.25
Preview variant (c) 6.00
Preview wraparound (c) 6.00
Preview prism foil (c) 13.00
1 . . . . 3.50
1a variant (c) 3.50
2 . . . . 3.50
2a variant (c) 3.50
2b wraparound (c) 4.00

SHIP OF FOOLS
Caliber, 1996
1 signed edition 3.00
2 `Dante's Compass' 3.00
3 The Great Escape begins 3.00
4 MiA 3.00
5 MiA 3.00
Spec. #1, Bon Voyage, Go to Hell,
   Mama Hades 4.00
TPB sci-fi action/adventure 12.00
continued: See Image Comics

SHOCK THE MONKEY
Millennium
1 & 2 Entering the Psychotic Mind . 4.00

SHONEN JUMP
Viz Communications, 2002
1 thru 8 . . . . @5.00
Vol. 2
1 thru 12 . . . . @5.00
Vol. 3
1 thru 8 . . . . @5.00

SHOUJO
Antarctic Press, 2003
1 . . . . 5.95
2 thru 3 . . . . @5.95
4 . . . . 5.95
Pocket Manga #1 . . . . 10.00

SHRED
CFW
1 thru 10 . . . . @2.25

SHRIEK
Fantaco
1 . . . . 5.00
2 . . . . 5.00
3 . . . . 8.00

SHURIKEN
Victory, 1986
1 Reggi Byers 5.00
1a 2nd printing 2.25
2 . . . . 3.00
3 . . . . 2.25
4 . . . . 2.25
5 thru 13 . . . . @2.25
Graphic Nov. Reggie Byers 8.00

SHURIKEN
Eternity, 1991
1 Shuriken vs. Slate 2.50
2 Neutralizer, Meguomo 2.50
3 R:Slate 2.50
4 Morgan's Bodyguard Serrate 2.50
5 Slate as Shuriken & Megumo . . . 2.50
6 Hunt for Bionauts, final issue . . . 2.50

SHURIKEN: COLD STEEL
Eternity, 1989
1 . . . . 2.25
2 . . . . 2.25
3 thru 6 . . . . @2.25

SHURIKEN TEAM-UP
ETernity, 1989
1 thru 3 . . . . @2.25

SIEGEL & SHUSTER
Eclipse, 1984
1 . . . . 2.25
2 . . . . 2.25

SILBUSTER
Antarctic Press, 1994
1 thru 10 . . . . @3.50
11 I:Kizuki Sister 3.50
12 thru 14 . . . . @3.50
15 . . . . 4.00
16 thru 19 . . . . @3.50
TPB Rep. #1-#4 . . . . 11.00
TPB Vol.2 . . . . 11.00

SILENT INVASION
Renegade, 1986
1 . . . . 4.00
2 thru 12, final issue . . . . @3.00
Combined Ed. #1 & #2 . . . . 17.00

SILENT INVASION
Caliber
4 Red Shadows, pt.1 . . . . 3.00
5 Red Shadows, pt.2 . . . . 3.00

SILENT INVASION: ABDUCTIONS
Caliber, 1998
1 by Larry Hancock & Michael
   Cherkos 3.00

SILENT MOBIUS
Viz Communications
Part 1 thru Part 4: See Color
TPB by Kia Asamiya 17.00
TPB Vol. 2 . . . . 17.00
TPB Vol. 3 . . . . 17.00
TPB Vol. 4 Into the Labyrinth 17.00
TPB Vol. 5 . . . . 17.00
TPB Vol. 6 Catastrophe 16.00
TPB Vol. 7 . . . . 17.00
TPB Vol. 8 Adventures 16.00
TPB Vol. 9 Turnabout 16.00
Part 5 INTO THE LABYRINTH, 1999
1 (of 6) by Kia Asamiya 3.00
2 thru 4 . . . . @3.00
5 & 6 . . . . @3.25
Part 6 KARMA, 1999
1 (of 7) by Kia Asamiya 3.25
2 thru 7 . . . . @3.25
Part 7 CATASTROPHE, 2000
1 (of 6) by Kia Asamiya 3.00
2 thru 6 . . . . @3.00
Part 8 LOVE & CHAOS, 2000
1 thru 7 . . . . @3.00
Part 9 ADVENTURERS, 2001
1 thru 6 (of 6) . . . . @3.00
Part 10 TURNABOUT, 2002
1 (of 6) by Kia Asamiya 3.00
2 thru 6 . . . . @3.00
Part 11 BLOOD, 2002
1 (of 5) by Kia Asamiya 3.00
2 thru 5 . . . . @3.00
TPB Vol. 10 Blood 13.00
Part 12 HELL, 2003
1 thru 3 . . . . @3.00
TPB Vol. 11 Hell 13.00
TPB Vol. 12 That's All Folks 13.00

SILENT RAPTURE
Brainstorm, 1996
1 Jacob Grimm vs. Six Devils
   of Twilight 3.00
1a Vicious variant edition 5.00
Avatar Press, 1997
2 by Jude Millien 3.00
2a deluxe (c) 10.00

SILLY DADDY
Joe Chiappetta, 1995
1 . . . . 3.50
2 thru 5 . . . . 3.00
6 thru 10 . . . . @2.75
11 thru 18 . . . . @2.75
TPB The Long Goodbye 8.00
TPB A Death in the Family 9.00

SILVER STORM
Aircel, 1990
1 thru 4 . . . . @2.25

SIMON/KIRBY READER
1 . . . . 2.25

SINBAD
Adventure, 1989
1 . . . . 2.25
2 . . . . 2.25
3 . . . . 2.25
4 . . . . 2.25

SINBAD: HOUSE OF GOD
Adventure Comics, 1991
1 Caliph's Wife Kidnapped 2.50
2 Magical Genie 2.50
3 Escape From Madhi 2.50
4 A:Genie 2.50

SINNAMON
Catfish Comics, 1995
1 remastered. 2.75
1a remastered deluxe. 3.75
6 thru 8 . . . . @2.75

Mythic Comics
9 `Ashes to Ashes—The Pyre-Anna
   Saga,' pt.2 . . . . 2.75
10 `Twas Beauty Bashed
   The Beast'. 2.75
11 . . . . 2.75
12 M.G.Delaney (c) 2.75
12 Poliwko (c) 2.75
Archives #1 . . . . 2.75

SISTER ARMAGEDDON
Dramenon Studios
1 & 2 Nun with a Gun . . . . @2.50
3 Mother Superior. 2.50
4 V:Apoligon 3.00

SKELETON KEY
Amaze Ink, 1995
1 1 I:Skeleton Key 4.00
1 2nd printing 3.00
2 F:Tansin 3.00
3 V:Japanese Burglar. 3.00
4 V:Closet Monster 3.00
5 thru 10 . . . . @3.00
11 . . . . 3.00
12 . . . . 3.00
14 by Andi Watson. 3.00
15 `The Celestial Calendar' 3.00
16 thru 30. . . . . @3.00
Spec. 5.00
TPB Vol. 1, Threshold rep.#1–#6 . 12.00
TPB Vol.2 Celestial Calendar,
   rep.#7–#18 . . . . 20.00
TPB Vol. 3, rep. #19–#24 . . . . . . 13.00
TPB Vol. 4, Cats & Dogs, rep.
   #25–#30. . . . . 13.00
Spec.Skeleton Key/Sugar Kat 3.00

VOL 2
1 (of 4) 3.00
2 . . . . 3.00
3 . . . . 3.00
4 conclusion 3.00

SKIN 13
Entity/Parody, 1995
1/2a Grungie/Spider-Man 2.50
1/2b Heavy Metal 2.50
1/2c Gen-Et Jackson 2.50

SKULL MAN
Tokyopop Press, 2000
1 (of 5) 3.00
2 thru 5 . . . . @3.00

SKUNK, THE
Entity Comics, 1997
#Uno 2.75
5 BMs 2.75
6 BMs 2.75
Collection #1 rep. #1–#3 . . . . 5.00
Collection #1a signed & numbered 10.00
Collection #2 rep. #4–#6 . . . . 5.00

SKUNK/FOODANG
FOODANG/SKUNK
Entity Comics
Spec. 1 BMs, BMs(c) 2.75
Spec. 1a BMs, Mike Duggan(c). . . . 2.75

SKYNN & BONES: DEADLY ANGELS
Brainstorm, 1996
1 . . . . 3.00

SKYNN & BONES: FLESH FOR FANTASY
Brainstorm, 1997
1 erotic missions. 3.00
2 erotic missions. 3.00
Spec. #1 Dare to Bare 3.00

SLACK
Legacy Comics
1 Slacker Anthology 2.50
2 Loser 2.50

SLACKER COMICS
Slave Labor, 1994
1 thru 15 by Doug Slack . . . . @3.00
16 . . . . 3.00
17 . . . . 3.00
18 . . . . 3.00
19 . . . . 3.00
TPB Randy Sells Out, rep.#1–#4 . 12.00

SLAUGHTERHOUSE
Caliber
1 Bizarre medical Operations 3.00
2 House of Death 3.00
3 House of Death 3.00
4 Dead Killer vs. Mosaic. 3.00

SLAUGHTERMAN
Comico, 1983
1 . . . . 2.25
2 . . . . 2.25

SLAYERS
CPM Manga, 1998
1 by Hajime Kanzaka & Rui
   Araizumi. 3.00
2 thru 6 . . . . @3.00
TPB Book 1: Medieval Mayham . . 16.00
Spec. #1 F:Lina Inverse 3.00
Spec. #2 thru #6. . . . . 3.00
TPB Vol. 1 Touch of Evil (2001). . . 16.00
TPB Vol. 2 Notorious 16.00
TPB Vol. 3 Lesser of Two Evils . . . 16.00
TPB Vol. 4 Spellbound. 16.00
GN Vol. 1 Slayers Return 10.00
GN City of Lost Souls 10.00
GN Lina The Teenage Sorceress . 10.00

Sold-Out #1
© Fantaco

SLAYERS: SUPER– EXPLOSIVE DEMON STORY
CPM Manga, 2001
1 by H. Kanzaka & S. Yoshinaka . . 3.00
2 . . . . 3.00
3 thru 6 . . . . @3.00
TPB Book 1 Legend of Darkness . 16.00
TPB Book 2 Legacy of the
   Dragon God. 16.00

SMILE
Tokyopop Press, 2000
Vol. 3
1 magazine 3.00
2 thru 12 magazine . . . . @5.00

Vol. 4
1 magazine 5.00
2 thru 4 . . . . @5.00
5 thru 6 . . . . @6.00
7 . . . . 5.00

SMITH BROWN JONES
Kiwi Studios, 1997
1 thru 5 . . . . @3.00
TPB Calm, Cook, and Collected . . 13.00

SMITH BROWN JONES: ALIEN ACCOUNTANT
Slave Labor, 1998
1 by Jon Hastings 3.00
2 . . . . 3.00
3 . . . . 3.00
4 . . . . 3.00
Spec.#1 Halloween Special 3.00
Spec. Convention Mayhem 6.00

SNOWMAN
Hall of Heroes, 1996
1 . . . . 15.00
1a variant (c). 20.00
1 3rd printing 2.75
1 San Diego Con. ed. 5.00
2 . . . . 8.00
2a 2nd printing 2.75
2b variant (c). 9.00
3 . . . . 6.00
3a variant (c). 7.00

SNOWMAN
Avatar Press, 1997
0 by Matt Martin, O:Snowman 3.00
0a Frozen Fear extra-bloody 5.00
0b Leather cover. 25.00
0c signed 10.00
Spec.#1 Snowman 1944 . . . . 4.00
Spec.#1 Snowman 1944, deluxe . . . 5.00
Spec.#1 Snowman 1944, signed . . 10.00
1-shot Flurries, Glynn (c). 5.00
1-shotA Flurries, Snowman (c) 5.00
TPB Snowman rep. 128-pg. 14.00

SNOWMAN:
DEAD & DYING
Avatar Press, 1997
1 (of 3) by Matt Martin 3.00
1 deluxe 5.00
1 signed 10.00
2 . . . . 3.00
2 deluxe 5.00
3 by Matt Martin 3.00
3 Frozen Fear. 5.00
3 White Velvet. 25.00

SNOWMAN:
HORROR SHOW
Avatar Press, 1998
1 by Matt Martin 3.00
1a Frozen Fear (c) 5.00
1b Leather cover. 25.00
1 deluxe 5.00

SNOWMAN: 1994
Entity, 1996
1 flip cover #0, by Matt Martin,
O:Snowman. 3.00
1 signed, numbered 7.00
3 . . . . 2.75
3 deluxe, variant, foil cover. 3.50
4 . . . . 2.75
4 deluxe, variant, foil cover. 3.50

SNOWMAN2
Avatar Press, 1997
1 (of 2) Snowman vs. Snowman . . 3.00
1a Face-off cover 5.00
1b Leather cover. 25.00
1c Royal Blue edition 50.00
2 concl. 3.00
2a Sudden Death variant cover . . . 5.00

SOB: SPECIAL
OPERATIONS BRANCH
Promethean Studios, 1994
1 I:SOB. 2.50

SOCKETEER
Kardia
Rocketeer parody. 2.25

SOLD OUT
Fantaco, 1986
1 & 2 . . . . @2.25

SOLO EX-MUTANTS
Eternity
1 thru 6 . . . . @2.25

SOMETHING DIFFERENT
Wooga Central, 1991
1 . . . . 2.50
2 . . . . 2.50

US $1.50   CAN $2.25

TEN-BUCK COMICS

SPACE BEAVER

BOOK ONE

Space Beaver Book 1
© Ten-Buck Comics

SONAMBULO: SLEEP
OF THE JUST
Ninth Circle Studios, 1999
1 (of 3) by Rafael Navarro 3.00
2 . . . . 3.00
3 (of 3) 3.00
TPB Sleep of the Just 15.00
Spec. Strange Tales (2000) 4.00
Spec. Ghost of a Chance (2002) . . . 5.00

SONG OF THE CID
Calibre/Tome
1 Story of El Cid 3.00
2 Story of El Cid concl. 3.00

SONG OF THE SIRENS
Millennium
Earth 3.00
Earth, signed print edition 7.00
Fire. 3.00
Fire, signed print edition 10.00
Wind. 3.00
Wind collectors edition. 5.00
Wind with trading card 5.00
Secrets, Lies, & Videotape Pin-Up
Special. 3.00
Secrets, Lies, & Videotape Pin-Up
Special, foil logo 6.00
Secrets, Lies, & Videotape Pin-Up
Special, deluxe 10.00

SOUL
Samson Comics
1 thru 3 F:Sabbeth . . . . @2.50

SOULFIRE
Aircel
1 mini-series 2.25
2 . . . . 2.25
3 . . . . 2.25

SOULSEARCHERS
AND CO.
Claypool, 1993–98
1 thru 10 Peter David(s) . . . . @5.00
11 thru 20. . . . . @3.00
21 thru 24. . . . . @3.00
25 ACo&SL(c) 2.50
26 O:Soulsearchers, pt.1. . . . . 2.50

27 O:Soulsearchers, pt.2. . . . . 2.50
28 O:Soulsearchers, pt.3. . . . . 2.50
29 O:Soulsearchers, pt.4. . . . . 2.50
30 thru 68 . . . . @2.50
TPB 13.00

SOUTHERN KNIGHTS
Guild, 1983
1 See Crusaders
2 . . . . 7.00
3 and 4 . . . . @5.00
5 thru 7 . . . . @4.00

Fictioneer, 1985
8 thru 11 . . . . @3.00
12 thru 33. . . . . @3.00
34 . . . . 3.00
35 The Morrigan Wars Pt.#2 . . . . . 3.50
36 Morrigan Wars Pt.#5. . . . . 3.50
37 Hell in a Handbasket 3.00
Ann. #1. . . . . 2.50
DreadHalloweenSpec #1 . . . . 2.25
Primer #1 . . . . 2.25

SOUTHERN SQUADRON
Aircel, 1990
1 thru 4 . . . . @2.25

Eternity
1 I:SQUAD 2.50
2 . . . . 2.25
3 . . . . 2.25
4 . . . . 2.25

SOUTHERN SQUADRON
FREEDOM OF INFO. ACT.
Aircel, 1992
1 F.F.#1 Parody/Tribute cov. 2.50
2 A:Waitangi Rangers. 2.50
3 . . . . 2.50

SPACE ARK
Apple, 1986
1 & 2 see color
3 . . . . 2.25
4 . . . . 2.25
5 . . . . 2.25

SPACE BEAVER
Ten-Buck Comics, 1986
1 . . . . 2.50
2 . . . . 2.25
3 O&I:Stinger 2.25
4 A:Stinger 2.25
5 . . . . 2.25
6 O:Rodent 2.25
7 thru 12 . . . . @2.25

SPACED
Anthony Smith Publ., 1988
1 I:Zip; 800 printed 40.00
2 . . . . 25.00
3 I:Dark Teddy. 15.00
4 . . . . 15.00
5 and 6 . . . . @5.00
7 and 8 . . . . @2.25

Eclipse
9 . . . . 2.25
10 . . . . 2.25
11 thru 13. . . . . @2.25

SPACE PATROL
Adventure, 1992
1 thru 3 . . . . 2.50

B & W PUB.

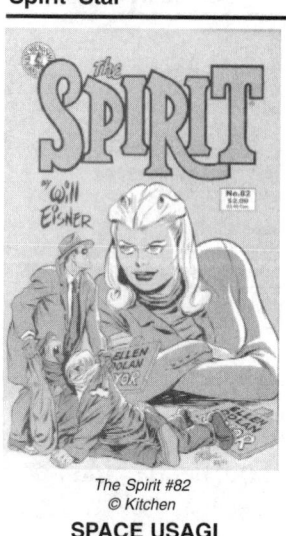

The Spirit #82
© Kitchen

SPACE USAGI
Mirage Studios, 1992
1 Stan Sakai,Future Usagi 3.00
2 Stan Sakai,Future Usagi 3.00
3 Stan Sakai.Future Usagi 3.00

SPACE WOLF
Antarctic Press
1 From Albedo,by Dan Flahive 2.50

SPANDEX TIGHTS
Lost Cause Prod.
Vol. 1, 1994
1 thru 6 . . . . @2.50
Vol. 2, 1997
1 . . . . 2.50
2 prelude to Space Opera. 3.00
6 . . . . 3.00
Spec. Vs. Mighty Awful Sour
  Rangers, signed 3.00

SPANDEX TIGHTS
PRESENTS:
SPACE OPERA
Lost Cause Productions, 1997
Part 1 by Bryan J.L. Glass & Bob
  Dix, parody 3.00
Part 1, signed, Star Wars parody. . . 3.00
Part 2 'Star Bored,' pt.2 . . . . 3.00
Part 3 . . . . 3.00

SPANDEX TIGHTS
PRESENTS:
THE GIRLS OF '95
Lost Cause Productions
1 The Good, Bad and Deadly,
  signed (1997) 4.00

SPANDEX TIGHTS
PRESENTS:
WIN A DREAM DATE
WITH SPANDEX-GIRL
Lost Cause Productions
1 (of 3) (1998). 3.00
2 . . . . 3.00
3 . . . . 3.00

SPANDEX TIGHTS:
THE LOST ISSUES
Lost Cause Productions
1 (of 4) 3.00
2 . . . . 3.00
3 . . . . 3.00
4 concl. 3.00

SPANK THE MONKEY
Arrow Comics, 1999
1 by Randy Zimmerman 3.00
2 thru 6 . . . . @3.00
Skip Month Spec.#1. . . . . 3.00

SPANK THE MONKEY ON
THE COMIC MARKET
Arrow Comics, 2000
1 (of 3) by Randy Zimmerman 3.25
2 and 3 . . . . @3.25

SPARKPLUG
Hero Graphics
1 From League of Champions 3.00

SPARKPLUG SPECIAL
Heroic Publishing
1 V:Overman. 2.50

SPARROW
Millennium, 1995
1 I:Sparrow 3.00
2 . . . . 3.00
3 Valley of Fire 2.50

SPEED RACER CLASSICS
Now, 1998
1 . . . . 3.00
1a 2nd Printing 2.25

SPENCER SPOOK
A.C.E. Comics
1 and 2 . . . . @2.25
3 thru 8 . . . . @2.25

SPICY TALES
Eternity, 1998
1 thru 13 . . . . @2.25
14 thru 20. . . . . @2.25
Special #2 . . . . 2.25

SPIDER KISS
1 Harlan Ellison. 4.00

SPINELESS MAN
Parody Press, 1992
1 Spider-Man 2099 spoof 2.50

SPIRIT, THE
Kitchen Sink, 1986
Note: #1 to #11 are in color
12 thru 86 WE,rep (1986–92) . . . @3.00
GN The Spirit Casebook 17.00
TPB Vol.2 All About P'Gell. 19.00
GN The Spirit Jam, 50 artists in
  48-pg. (1998) 6.00

SPIRIT, THE:
THE ORIGIN YEARS
Kitchen Sink, 1997
1 F:The Origin of the Spirit 3.00
2 F:The Black Queen's Army 3.00

3 F:Palyachi,The Killer Clown. 3.00
4 F:The Return of the Orang 3.00
5 WE. 3.00
6 WE,Kiss of Death 3.00
7 F:The Kidnapping of Ebony. 3.00
8 F:Christmas Spirit of 1940 . . . . . 3.00
9 WE 3.00
10 F:The Substitute Spirits. 3.00

SPIRITED AWAY
Viz Communications, 2002
TPB Vol. 2 thru Vol. 5 . . . . . . @10.00
TPB Picture Book (color). 20.00
TPB Art of Spirited Away 35.00

SPIRITS
Mindwalker, 1995
1 thru 3 Silver City 3.00
4 Caleb Escapes Zeus 3.00

SPITTIN' IMAGE
Eclipse, 1992
1 Marvel & Image parody 2.50

SPONGEBOB
SQUAREPANTS
Tokyopop Press, 2003
GN Vol. 1 Krusty Krap Adventures . 8.00
GN Vol. 2 Friends Forever. 8.00
GN Vol. 3 thru Vol. 5 . . . . @8.00

SQUEE
Slave Labor, 1997
1 by Jhonen Vasquez 5.00
1a 2nd printing 3.00
2 . . . . 3.00
3 . . . . 3.00
4 . . . . 3.00
TPB 16.00

STAIN
Fathom Press, 1998
1 Byler (c). 3.00
1a Vigil (c). 3.00
1b limited edition. 8.00
2 . . . . 3.00
2a Vigil (c). 3.00
3 . . . . 3.00
3a Vigil (c). 3.00
4 . . . . 3.00
4a Vigil (c). 3.00
5 King cover 3.00
5a Ang cover. 3.00
6 . . . . 3.00
7 . . . . 3.00

STAINLESS STEEL
ARMIDILLO
Antarctic Press, 1995
1 I:Saisni, Tania Badan. 3.00
2 V:Mirage. 3.00
3 V:Mirage. 3.00
4 Spirit of Gaia 3.00
5 V:Giant. 3.00
6 finale 3.00

STAR BLEECH
THE GENERATION GAP
Parody Press
1 Parody 4.00

STARCHILD
Taliesin Press, 1992–97
0 . . . . 15.00
1 . . . . 20.00
1a 2nd printing 4.00
2 . . . . 18.00
2a 2nd printing 4.00
3 . . . . 8.00
4 . . . . 6.00
5 thru 13 . . . . @5.00
14 . . . . 3.00
Coppervale
TPB Coll. Ed. Awakenings, rep.
#1–#12. . . . . 5.00
Essential Starchild, Book 3 . . . . . . 7.00
Essential Starchild, Book 4 . . . . . . 7.00
Essential Starchild, Book 5 . . . . . . 7.00

STARCHILD: CROSSROADS
Coppervale, 1995
1 thru 4, reoffer, by James Owen @3.00
TPB Coll. Ed.112-pg. 12.00
Conoisseurs Edition. 100.00

STARGATE: THE NEW ADVENTURES COLLECTION
Entity, 1997
1 rep. Underworld; One Nation
   Under Ra. 6.00
1a photo cover 5.00

STARGATE: ONE NATION UNDER RA
Entity, 1997
1 . . . . 3.00
1a deluxe 3.50

STARGATE: REBELLION
Entity, 1997
1 (of 3) from novel, sequel to movi13.00
1 deluxe 3.50
2 . . . . 3.00
2 deluxe 3.50
3 (of 3) 3.00
3 foil cover 3.50
GN rep. 80-pg. 8.00
GN photo (c) 8.00

STARGATE: UNDERWORLD
Entity, 1997
1 . . . . 3.00
1a deluxe 3.50

STAR HAWKS
ACG Comics, 2000
1 by Ron Goulart & Gil Kane 3.00
2 . . . . 3.00
3 . . . . 3.00

STARK: FUTURE
Aircel, 1986
1 . . . . 2.50
2 thru 7 . . . . @2.25
8 . . . . 2.25
9 thru 14 . . . . @2.25

STARLIGHT AGENCY
Antarctic Press, 1991
1 I:Starlight Agency. 2.25

2 Anderson Kidnapped 2.25
3 . . . . 2.25

STAR RANGERS
Adventure, 1987
1 thru 3 . . . . @3.00
4 . . . . 2.25
BOOK II
1 . . . . 2.25
2 . . . . 2.25

STAR REACH
Taliesin Press, 1974
1 HC,I:CodyStarbuck 15.00
2 DG,JSn,NA(c) 6.00
3 FB 6.00
4 HC,HC(c) 6.00
5 JSon,HC(c) 6.00
6 GD,Elric 6.00
7 DS 6.00
8 CR,KSy 6.00
9 KSy 6.00
10 KSy 6.00
11 GD. 6.00
12 MN,SL. 10.00
13 SL,KSy 10.00
14 . . . . 10.00
15 . . . . 10.00
16 thru 18. . . . . @9.00

STAR WESTERN
ACG Comics, 2000
1 . . . . 6.00
2 John Wayne. 6.00
3 Clint Eastwood. 6.00
4 Clayton Moore 6.00
5 F:Tonto 6.00
6 F:Fess Parker 6.00
7 F:Masked Riders of the Plains . . 6.00
8 James Arness-Matt Dillon(c) 6.00
9 Sam Elliott photo (c) 6.00
10 Chuck "Rifleman" Connors 6.00
11 John Hart 6.00
12 Davy Crockett, Daniel Boone . . . 6.00
13 Gabby Hayes 6.00
TPB Compendium, #1–#4 . . . . . . 20.00

STATIC
1 SD 2.25
2 SD 2.25
3 SD 2.25

STEALTH FORCE
Malibu, 1987
1 thru 7 . . . . @2.25
Eternity, 1988
8 . . . . 2.25

STEALTH SQUAD
Petra Comics, 1993
0 O:Stealth Squad 2.50
1 I:Stealth Squad 2.50
2 I:New Member 2.50
Volume II
1 F:Solar Blade 2.50
2 American Ranger Vs.Jericho. . . . 2.50

STEAM DETECTIVES
Viz Communications, 1999
TPB by Kia Asamiya 16.00
TPB Vol. 2 . . . . 16.00
TPB Vol. 3 thru Vol. 7. . . . . @16.00

STEELE DESTINES
Nightscapes
1 & 2 I:One Eyed Stranger 3.00

Strangers in Paradise #10
© Abstract Studios

3 Kidnapped by Aliens 3.00

STEVE CANYON
Kitchen Sink
1 thru 14 by Doug Allen . . . . @5.00
3-D Spec. #1 (1986) 6.00

STEVE DITKO'S STRANGE AVENGING TALES
Fantagraphics, 1997
1 SD 3.00
2 SD 3.00

STEVE GRANT'S MORTAL SOULS
Avatar Press, 2002
1 . . . . 3.50
2 . . . . 3.50
3 . . . . 3.50
1a thru 3a wraparound (c)s. . . . . @4.00

STEVE GRANT'S MY FLESH IS COOL
Avatar Press, 2003
1 . . . . 3.50
2 . . . . 3.50
3 . . . . 3.50
1a thru 3a wraparound (c)s. . . . . @3.50

STEVEN
Kitchen Sink
1 . . . . 4.00
1a 2ndPrinting. 3.00
2 . . . . 4.00
3 . . . . 3.00
4 and 5 . . . . @3.50
TPB The Best of Steven by Doug
   Allen (1998). 13.00

STICKBOY
Revolutionary
1 . . . . 2.25
2 thru 5 . . . . @2.50

All comics prices listed are for *Near Mint* condition.   **CVA Page 773**

STIG'S INFERNO
Vortex, 1985
1	5.00
2	3.50
3	3.00
4	3.00
5	2.25

Eclipse
6	2.25
7	2.25

STINZ
Fantagraphics, 1989
1	4.00
2	4.00
3	4.00
4	4.00

[2nd series]
Brave New Words, 1990
1 thru 3 . . . . 2.50

STORMBRINGER
Taliesin Press
1 thru 3 . . . . @2.25

STORMWATCHER
Eclipse, 1989
1 thru 4 . . . . @2.25

STRAIN
Viz Communications, 1998
GN Vol. 1	17.00
TPB Vol. 2	16.00
TPB Vol. 3	16.00
TPB Vol. 4	17.00
TPB Vol. 5	17.00

STRANGE BEHAVIOR
Twilite Tone Press
1 LSn,MBr,Short Stories 3.00

STRANGE BREW
Aardvark–Vanaheim
1 . . . . 5.00

Strata #2
© Renegade

STRANGEHAVEN
Abiogenesis Press, 1995
1 Surrealistic Comic	3.00
2 Secret Brotherhood	3.00
3 thru 10 by Gary S. Millidge	@3.00
11 thru 16	@3.00
TPB Arcadia, rep. #1–#6	15.00
TPB Brotherhood, rep.#7–#12	15.00

STRANGE SPORTS STORIES
Adventure, 1992
1 w/2 card strip	2.50
2 The Pick-Up Game, w/cards	2.50
3 Spinning Wheels,w/cards	2.50
4 thru 6 w/cards	@2.50

STRANGE WEATHER LATELY
Metaphrog, 1997
1	3.50
2 thru 4	@3.50
5 thru 10	@3.00
TPB Vol. 1 rep. #1–#5	10.00
TPB Vol. 2	10.00

STRANGERS IN PARADISE
Antarctic Press, 1993–94
1 by Terry Moore,I:Katchoo	65.00
1a 2nd printing	15.00
1b 3rd printing	5.00
2	45.00
3	35.00

Abstract Studio, 1994
1 TMr, Gold Logo edition	15.00
1a 2nd printing	6.00
2 and 3, Gold Logo edition	@10.00
4	6.00
5 R:Mrs. Parker.	6.00
6	5.00
7 Darcey Uses Francine	5.00
8 thru 13 TMr	@4.00

VOL. 2
1 TMr, Gold Logo edition, I Dream of You.	3.00
2 thru 13 gold logo	@3.00
TPB I Dream of You.	17.00

VOL III, 1997
1 thru 8 See Image
9 TMr,Detective Walsh returns	4.00
10	4.00
11	3.00
12	3.00
13 High School, pt.1 (of 3).	3.00
14 High School, pt.2	10.00
15 High School, pt.3	3.00
16A Francine/Katchoo Princess Warrior (c)	22.00
16B Tambi Princess Warrior (c)	25.00
17	3.00
18 Francine & Datchoo	3.00
19 Lifesize nude of Francine	3.00
20 Night at the Opera	3.00
21 All not well in paradise	3.00
22 The Big Rift	3.00
23 Katchoo moves out.	3.00
24 steamy affairs	3.00
25 All Beach, All the Time	3.00
26	3.00
27 at odds with the Big Six	3.00
28 thru 35	@3.00
36 Katchoo vs. Veronica	3.00
37 return to Tennessee	3.00
38 from rags to ritches	3.00
39 Good news and bad news	3.00

40 Engaged to right brother?	3.00
41 Expelled from college	3.00
42 Slumber Party	3.00
43 Tropic Of Desire	3.00
44 Marooned	3.00
45 Francine and Katchoo.	3.00
46 Molly & Poo, Borderline Lover	3.00
47 Francine pregnant.	3.00
48 Casey's Story	3.00
49 Molly & Poo.	3.00
50 Celebrate #50	3.00
51	3.00
52 Francine & Katchoo	3.00
53 My Maiden Voyage	3.00
54 Girl Trouble, pt.1	3.00
55 Girl Trouble, pt.2	3.00
56 Girl Trouble, pt.3	3.00
57 Blue Bird of Happiness.	3.00
58 thru 69	@3.00
TPB Vol.4 Love Me Tender	13.00
TPB Vol.5 Immortal Enemies, rep. #6–#12.	13.00
TPB Vol. 6 High School	9.00
TPB Vol. 8 My Other Life	15.00
TPB Vol. 9 Child of Rage.	16.00
TPB Vol. 10 Tropic of Desire	13.00
TPB Vol. 11 Brave New World.	9.00
TPB Vol. 12 Field of GOld	13.00
TPB Vol. 13 Flower to Flame.	16.00
TPB Vol. 14 David's Story	9.00
Pocket TPB Vol. 1	18.00
Pocket TPB Vol. 2	18.00
Spec. Sourcebook	3.00
Spec. #93268 Songs & Lyrics	2.75

STRANGELOVE
Entity Comics, 1995
1 I:Strangelove	2.50
2 V:Hyper Bullies	2.50
3 I:Bogie	2.50

STRANGE WORLDS
Eternity
1	4.00
2 thru 4	@4.00

STRATA
Renegade, 1986
1	3.00
2	2.50
3	2.25
4	2.25
5	2.25
6	2.25

STRAW MEN
All American, 1989
1 thru 5	@2.25
6 thru 8	@2.25

STRAY BULLETS
El Capitan, 1995
1	15.00
1a 2nd & 3rd printing	4.00
2	8.00
2a 2nd printing	3.50
3	7.00
4	7.00
5 Dysfunctional Family	4.00
6 F:Amy Racecar	4.00
7 Virginias Freedom	4.00
8 DL,`Lucky to Have Her'	3.00
9 DL,`26 Guys Named Nick'.	3.00
10 DL,`Here Comes the Circus'.	3.00
11 DL,`How to Cheer Up Your Best Friend'.	3.00
12 DL, People Will be Hurt	3.00
13 DL `Selling Candy'	3.00

14 DL,The Killers arrive,48pg	3.50
15 Sex and Violence	3.00
16	3.00
17 While Ricky Fish Was Sleeping	3.00
18 Sex and Violence, pt.2	3.00
19 Young and sexy	3.00
20 Motel	3.00
21	3.00
22 40-pg.	3.50
23 thru 30	@3.50
31 thru 34	@3.00
35 thru 36	@3.50
TPB Vol. 1 Innocence of Nihilism	12.00
TPB Vol. 2	12.00
TPB Vol. 3	12.00
TPB Vol. 4 rep. #13–#16	12.00
TPB Vol. 5 rep. #17–#20	12.00
TPB Vol. 6	15.00
TPB Vol. 7	15.00
TPB Vol. 8	15.00

STREET ANGEL
Amaze Ink/SLG, 2004

1	2.95
2 thru 3	@2.95

STREET FIGHTER
Ocean Comics, 1986

1 thru 4 limited series	@2.25

STREET HEROES 2005
Eternity, 1989

1 thru 3	@2.25

STREET MUSIC
Fantagraphics

1	2.75
2	2.75
3	3.00
4	3.00
5	2.50
6	4.00

STREET POET RAY
Fantagraphics, 1989

1	2.50
2	2.25
3	3.00
4	3.00

STREET WOLF
Blackthorne, 1986

1 limited series	2.25
2 and 3	@2.25
Graphic Novel	7.00

STRIKER: SECRET OF THE BERSERKER
Viz

1 & 2 V:The Berserker	@2.75
3 F:Yu and Maia	2.75

STRIKER: THE ARMORED WARRIOR
Viz

1 Overture	2.75
2 V:Child Esper	2.75
3 Professor taken hostage	2.75
GN Vol.1 The Armored Warrior	17.00
GN Vol.2 Forest of No Return	16.00

STUPID, STUPID RAT TAILS:THE ADVENTURES OF BIG JOHNSON BONE
Cartoon Books, 1999

1 I:Big Johnson Bone,FrontierHero	3.00
2	3.00
TPB	10.00

STYGMATA
Entity, 1994

0	3.00
1 V:The Rodent	3.00
2 thru 3	@3.00
Yearbook #1 (1995)	3.00
TPB Dragon Prophet	7.00

SUBTLE VIOLENTS
CFD Productions, 1991

1 Linsner (c&a)	25.00
1a San Diego Con	80.00

SUGAR BUZZ
Slave Labor, 1998

1 by I.Carney & W. Phoenix	3.00
2	3.00

System Seven #2
© Arrow

3	3.00
4	3.00
5	3.00
6 F:Ultra Spacers	3.00
7 I:Precious & Percival	3.00
8 thru 10	@3.00

SUGAR RAY FINHEAD
Wolf Press, 1992

1 I&O Sugar Ray Finhead	2.50
2 I:Bessie & Big-Foot Benny the Pit Bull Man	3.00
3 thru 7 Mardi Gras	@3.00
9 & 10	@3.00

SULTRY TEENAGE SUPER-FOXES
Solson, 1987

1 thru 4 RB,Woj.	@2.25

SUPERMODELS IN THE RAINFOREST
Sirius, 1998

1 (of 3)	3.00
2 and 3	@3.00

SUPERSWINE
Caliber

1 Parody, I:Superswine	2.50

SURVIVALIST CHRONICLES
Survival Art

1	6.50
2	6.50
3 I:Bessie & Big Foot Benny	2.25

SURROGATE SAVIOR
Hot Brazer Comic Pub.

1 I:Ralph	2.50
2 Baggage	2.50

SWAN
Little Idylls, 1995

1 thru 3 Ghost of Lord Kaaren	@3.00
4 V:Slake	3.00

SWEET CHILDE BATTLE BOOK
Advantage Graphics, 1995

1 I:Tasha Radcliffe	2.50

SWEET CHILDE: LOST CONFESSIONS
Anarchy Bridgeworks, 1997

1 F:Tasha Radcliffe	3.00

SWEET LUCY
Brainstorm Comics

1 with 4 cards	2.50
2	2.50

SWERVE
Amaze Ink, 1995

1 thru 3 by Kyle Hunter	@2.25

SWIFTSURE
Harrier Comics, 1985

1	2.25
2	2.25
3 thru 8	@2.25
9	9.00
9a 2nd printing	2.25
10	2.25
11	2.25

SWITCH B.L.A.Z.E. MANGA
London Night, 1999

0	3.50
? Con special	5.00
? Con special, Japanese (c)	6.00
1	3.50
1a Elite fan ed.	6.00
1b Anime cell ed.	20.00

SWORD OF VALOR
A Plus Comics

1 JAp,rep.Thane of Bagarth	2.50
2 JAp/MK rep	2.50

SWORDS AND SCIENCE
Pyramid
1 thru 3 . . . . @2.25

SWORDS OF CEREBUS
Aardvark–Vanaheim
1 rep. Cerebus 1-4 . . . . 15.00
1a reprint editions 10.00
2 rep. Cerebus 5-8 . . . . 12.00
2a reprint editions 8.00
3 rep. Cerebus 9-12 . . . . 12.00
3a reprint editions 8.00
4 rep. Cerebus 13-16 . . . . 12.00
4a reprint editions 8.00
5 rep. Cerebus 17-20 . . . . 12.00
5a reprint editions 8.00
6 rep. Cerebus 21-25 . . . . 12.00
6a reprint editions 8.00

Tales Too Terrible to Tell #3
© New England Comics

SWORDS OF SHAR-PAI
Caliber, 1991
1 Mutant Ninja Dog 2.50
2 Shar-Pei 2.50
3 Final issue 2.50

SWORDS OF VALORS: ROBIN HOOD
A Plus Comics
1 rep. of Charlton comics 2.50
2 thru 4 . . . . @2.50

SYSTEM SEVEN
Arrow, 1987
1 thru 4 . . . . @2.25

TAKEN UNDER COMPENDIUM
Caliber
1 rep. Cal Presents #19-#22 . . . . . 3.00

TALES FROM THE ANIVERSE
Arrow
1 7,400 printed 9.00
2 . . . . 4.00

---

3 10,000 printed 2.50
4 . . . . 2.50

[2nd series]
Massive Comics Group
1 thru 3 . . . . @2.25

TALES FROM THE BOG
Aberation Press, 1995
1 thru 4 by Marcus Lusk . . . . . . @3.00
1a thru 4a Director's cut . . . . . . @4.00
5 thru 7 . . . . @4.00
1a Director's Cut, 32pg. 3.00
2a Director's Cut, 32pg. 4.00
3a Director's Cut, 48pg. 4.00
4a Director's Cut, 40pg. 4.00
8 . . . . 3.00

TALES FROM THE EDGE
Vanguard, 1993
5 . . . . 3.00
5a signed 6.00
6 . . . . 3.00
7 . . . . 3.00
7a signed 6.00
8 . . . . 3.00
8a signed 6.00
9 . . . . 3.00
10 . . . . 3.00
10a signed 6.00
11 F:Sacred Monkeys 3.00
12 spec.F:Steranko 4.00
12a signed, limited 15.00
13 F:Steranko 3.00
14 . . . . 3.00
15 Sienkiewicz special 4.00
Spec. Nightstand Chillers Benefit
   Edition 5.00
Spec. Nightstand Chillers, signed . 10.00
Spec. Sienkiewicz Special 10.00

TALES FROM THE HEART
Entropy, 1988–94
1 thru 5 . . . . @2.25
6 . . . . 2.25
7 . . . . 2.25

TALES OF THE BEANWORLD
Eclipse, 1985
1 . . . . 10.00
2 . . . . 4.00
3 . . . . 2.50
4 I:Beanish 2.25
5 thru 20 . . . . @2.25
21 . . . . 3.00

TALES OF THE FEHNRIK
Antarctic Press, 1995
1 I:Lady Zeista 3.00

TALES OF THE JACKALOPE
Blackthorne, 1986
1 . . . . 4.00
2 . . . . 3.00
3 and 4 . . . . @2.50
5 thru 9 . . . . @2.25

TALES OF THE NINJA WARRIORS
CFW
1 thru 14 . . . . @2.25
15 thru 19 . . . . @2.25

TALES OF THE PLAGUE
Eclipse
1 RCo 4.00

TALES OF THE SUNRUNNERS
Sirius, 1986
Vol. 2
1 thru 3 . . . . @2.50
Christmas Spec. 2.50

TALES OF THE TEENAGE MUTANT NINJA TURTLES
Mirage, 1987
1 . . . . 8.00
1B 2nd printing 3.00
2 . . . . 8.00
3 . . . . 5.00
4 . . . . 5.00
5 . . . . 5.00
6 thru 9 . . . . @4.00

Mirage Studios, 2004
1 . . . . 2.95
2 thru 5 . . . . @2.95

TALES TOO TERRIBLE TO TELL
New England Comics, 1991
1 thru 6 Pre-code horror stories . @3.50

TALL TAILS
Vision Comics, 1998
1 Earth Shaking 3.00
1a Anime Blast cover 3.00
1b Spell Warrior cover 3.00
1c signed 5.00
2 Fire Quest, Pt.1 . . . . 3.00
3 Fire Quest, Pt.2 . . . . 3.00
4 Pain and Compromises,pt.1 . . . 3.00
5 . . . . 3.00
6 Trail Blazing, pt.1 . . . . 3.00
7 Trail Blazing, pt.2 . . . . 3.00
8 When It Almost Happened 3.00
GN Vol. 1 . . . . 9.00

TANTALIZING STORIES
Tundra, 1992
1 F:Frank & Montgomery Wart . . . 2.25
2 Frank & Mont.stories cont. 2.25

TAOLAND
Sunitek
1 V:The Crocodile Warlord 2.25
2 & 3 I:New Enemy . . . . @3.25

TASK FORCE ALPHA
Academy Comics
1 I:Task Force Alpha 3.50

TEAM NIPPON
Aircel
1 thru 7 by Barry Blair . . . . @2.25

TECHNOPHILIA
Brainstorm Comics
1 with 4 cards 2.50

TEENAGE MUTANT NINJA TURTLES*
Mirage Studios, 1981
***Counterfeits Exist - Beware**
1 I:Turtles	200.00
1a 2nd printing	25.00
1b 3rd printing	20.00
1c 4th printing	12.00
1d 5th printing	4.00
2	50.00
2a 2nd printing	12.00
2b 3rd printing	4.00
3	30.00
3a 2nd printing	3.50
3b Special printing,rare	50.00
4	20.00
4a 2nd printing	3.50
5 A:Fugitoid	8.00
5a 2nd printing	3.50
6 A:Fugitoid	7.00
6a 2nd printing	2.50
7 A:Fugitoid	8.00
7a 2nd printing	2.50
8 A:Cerebus	9.00
9	7.00
10 V:Shredder	7.00
11 A:Casey Jones	6.00
12 thru 18	@6.00
19 Return to NY	4.00
20 Return to NY	4.00
21 Return to NY,D:Shredder	4.00
22 thru 32	@4.00
33 color, Corben	3.50
34 Toytle Anxiety	3.50
35 Souls Withering	3.50
36 Souls Wake	3.50
37 Twilight of the Rings	3.50
38 Spaced Out Pt.1, A:President Bush	3.50
39 Spaced Out Pt.2	3.50
40 Spaced Out concl.,I:Rockin' Rollin' Miner Ants (B.U. story)	2.50
41 Turtle Dreams issue	2.50
42 Juliets Revenge	2.50
43 Halls of Lost Legends	2.50
44 V:Ninjas	2.50
45 A:Leatherhead	2.50
46 V:Samurai Dinosaur	2.50
47 Space Usagi	2.50
48 Shades of Grey Part 1	2.50
49 Shades of Grey Part 2	2.50
50 Eastman/Laird,new direction, inc.TM,EL,WS pin-ups	3.00
51 City at War #2	2.50
52 City at War #3	2.50
53 City at War #4	2.50
54 City at War #5	2.50
55 thru 65	@2.50
1990 Movie adaptation	6.50
Spec. The Haunted Pizza	2.50

Volume 2
1 thru 8	@2.75
9 V:Baxter Bot	2.75
10 Mr. Braunze	2.75
11 F:Raphael	2.75
12 V:DARPA	2.75
13 J:Triceraton	2.75

Vol. 4, 2001
1 PLa & Jim Lawson	3.00
2 thru 18 PLa	@3.00

TMNT TRAINING MANUAL
1	5.00
2 thru 5	@3.00

TEMPEST COMICS PRESENTS
Academy Comics
1 I:Steeple, Nemesis	2.50

10TH MUSE/ DEMONSLAYER
Avatar Press, 2002
Preview, 16-pg.	2.25
1 MMy(c)	3.50
1a Matt Martin (c)	3.50
1b SSh(c)	3.50
1c Karl Waller (c)	3.50
1d wraparound (c)	3.50
1e Red Leather (c)	25.00
1f prism foil edition	13.00
1g Aftermath (c)	6.00
1h Art Nouveau (c)	6.00
1/2 MMy bikini (c)	6.00
1/2 Conflict edition	6.00
1/2 Catfight (c)	6.00

TERROR ON THE PLANET OF THE APES
Adventure Comics, 1991
1 MP,collectors edition	2.50
2 MP, the Forbidden Zone	2.50
3	2.50

TERRY AND THE PIRATES
ACG Comics, 1998
1 by Georges Wunder, Charlton reprint	3.00
2	3.00
3	3.00

TERRY & THE PIRATES
Tony Raiola, 2001
Feature Comics #6, 1938 reprint	8.00
Feature Comics #2 1937 reprint	8.00
Feature Comics #28 1938 reprint	8.00
Raven Evermore 1941 reprint	8.00

TERRY MOORE'S PARADISE, TOO
Abstract Studio, 2000
1	3.00
2	3.00
3	3.00
4	3.00
5 thru 14	@3.00
TPB Vol. 1 Drunk Ducks	16.00
TPB Vol. 2 Checking for Weirdos	16.00

TEX BENSON
Metro Comics
1 thru 4	@2.25

39 SCREAMS
Thunder Baas
1 thru 6	@2.25

THEY WERE 11
Viz
1 Galactic University	2.75
2 The Accident	2.75
3 Virus	2.75
4 V:Virus	2.75

THIEVES AND KINGS
I Box, 1994–97
1 F:Ruebel The Intrepid	8.00

1a 2nd printing	2.50
2	6.00
2a 2nd printing	2.50
3	5.00
3a 2nd printing	2.50
4	4.00
5	4.00
6 V:Shadow Lady	4.00
7 V:Shadow Lady	3.00
8 thru 18 by Mark Oakley	@3.00
19 thru 24	@2.50
25 thru 36	@2.50
37 thru 39	@2.50
40 thru 46	@3.00
TPB Vol. 1: The Red Book, rep.#1–#6	12.00
TPB Vol. 1: 2nd printing	13.50

Threshold #2
© Avatar

TPB Vol. 2: The Green Book	14.00
TPB Vol. 2: 2nd printing	16.50
TPB Vol. 3: The Blue Book	16.50
TPB Vol. 4: Shadow Book	16.50

THORR SUERD OR SWORD OF THOR
Vincent
1	3.00
1a 2nd printing	2.25
2	2.25
3	2.25

THOSE ANNOYING POST BROS.
1 thru 18 see Color
Becomes:

POST BROTHERS
Rip Off, 1991–94
19 thru 38	@2.25
Becomes:

THOSE ANNOYING POST BROS.
Vortex, 1994
39 thru 45	@2.50
46 thru 56	@3.00
57 Russ working on chaos wave	3.00
58 Fearsome chaos wave	3.00
59 Recondite Silicates	3.00
60	3.00
61 Assassinate JFK's ghost	3.00
62 Post Digestion 64pg.	6.00

B & W PUB.

63 . . . . 6.00
GN Distrub the Neighbors 10.00
Ann. #3 Before the Flood, 56pg. . . . 5.00
TPB Das Loot 15.00

THREAT
Fantagraphics, 1985
1 . . . . 5.00
2 . . . . 3.00
3 and 4 . . . . @2.25
5 thru 10 . . . . @2.25

3 X 3 EYES
Innovation
1 Labyrinth of the Demons
   Eye,Pt.1 . . . . 2.25
2 Demons Eye, Pt.2 . . . . 2.25
3 Demons Eye, Pt.3 . . . . 2.25
4 Demons Eye, Pt.4 . . . . 2.25
5 Demons Eye, concl.. . . . . 2.25

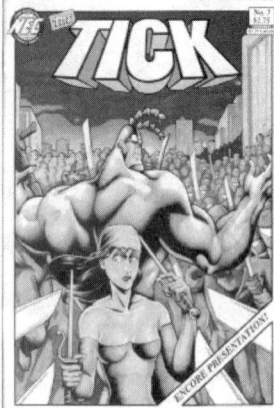

Tick #3 (4th printing)
© New England Comics

THREE GEEKS, THE
3 Finger Prints, 1997
1 by Rich Koslowski, Going
   to the Con, pt.1 . . . . 9.00
2 Going to the Con, pt.2 . . . . 6.00
3 Going to the Con, pt.3 (of 3) 3.00
4 . . . . 4.00
5 five more geeks 2.50
6 F:Allen 2.50
7 . . . . 2.50
8 48-pg. 4.00
9 24-pg. 2.50
10 Happy Birthday Allen 2.50
10a variant cover 3.50
11 Happy Birthday Allen, pt.2 . . . . . 2.50
TPB 9.00

THREE ROCKETEERS
Eclipse
1 JK,AW,rep. 2.25
2 JK,AW,rep. 2.25

THREE STRIKES
Oni Press, 2003
1 (of 5) 3.00
2 thru 5 . . . . @3.00
TPB 15.00

THRESHOLD
Sleeping Giant, 1996
1 . . . . 2.50
2 . . . . 2.50

[2nd Series], 1997
1 . . . . 2.50
2 . . . . 2.50
3 . . . . 2.50

Avatar Press, 1998
1 Snowman cover. 4.50
1a Tales of the Cyberangels cover. 4.50
1b Furies cover. 4.50
1c Fuzzie Dice cover 4.50
2 Snowman cover. 5.00
3 Ravening (c) 5.00
4 Donna Mia (c) 5.00
5 Black Reign (c) 5.00
6 Luna cover 5.00
7 Darkness in Collision,
   Cavewoman(c) 5.00
8 Vigil/Cuda (c). 5.00
9 August (c). 5.00
2a thru 9a variant (c)s. . . . . @5.00
10 Calico (c). 5.00
11 Scythe (c) 5.00
12 Snowman (c). 5.00
13 Snowman (c). 5.00
14 Kaos Moon (c) 5.00
15 Luna (c). 5.00
16 Scythe (c) 5.00
17 Cimmerian (c) 5.00
18 Nightvision (c) 5.00
19 Pandora (c). 5.00
20 Kaos Moon (c) 5.00
21 Jungle Girl (c) 5.00
22 . . . . 5.00
23 Ravening (c) 5.00
24 Faust: Singha's Talons 5.00
25 Dark Blue (c). 5.00
26 Dark Blue (c). 5.00
27 Dark blue (c). 5.00
28 Dark blue (c). 5.00
29 Dark Blue (c). 5.00
30 Dark Blue (c). 5.00
10a thru 30a variant (c)s . . . . . . @5.00
31 Luna (c). 5.00
32 Ravening (c) 5.00
33 Pandora (c). 5.00
34 Pandora (c). 5.00
35 Pandora (c). 5.00
36 Pandora (c). 5.00
37 Pandora (c). 5.00
38 Pandora (c). 5.00
39 Razor (c). 5.00
40 Lookers (c) 5.00
41 Razor (c). 5.00
42 Razor (c). 5.00
43 Razor (c). 5.00
43 Razor (c). 5.00
45 Demonslayer (c) 5.00
46 Demonslayer (c) 5.00
47 Pandora (c). 5.00
31a thru 47a variant (c)s . . . . . . @5.00
48 Pandora (c). 5.00
49 Pandora (c). 5.00
48a thru 49a connecting (c). 6.00
50 64-pg. 9.00
50 connecting (c)s 9.00
50a variant (c)s . . . . @9.00
51 . . . . 5.00
51b Pandora Western edition 6.00
52 . . . . 5.00
51a and 52a variant (c)s . . . . . . @5.00
TPB Razor X, 48-pg. 7.00
TPB Razor X, Vol. 2. . . . . 7.00

THRESHOLD OF REALITY
Maintech, 1986
1 5,000 printed 2.50

2 thru 4 . . . . @2.25

THUNDERBIRD
Newcomers Publishing
1 & 2 2 Stories . . . . @3.00
3 . . . . 3.00
4 I:Mercer 3.00
5 R:Raven. 3.00
6 & 7 . . . . @3.00
8 final issue. 3.50
Ann.#1 The Great Escape. 3.50

THUNDER BUNNY
Mirage, 1985
1 O:Thunder Bunny 2.50
2 VO:Dr.Fog 2.25
3 I:GoldenMan 2.25
4 V:Keeper 2.25
5 I:Moon Mess 2.25
6 V:Mr.Endall. 2.25
7 VI:Dr.Fog 2.25
8 . . . . 2.25
9 VS:Gen. Agents 2.25
10 thru 12. . . . . @2.25

THUNDER MACE
Rak, 1986
1 Proto type-blue & red very
   rare:1,000 printed 15.00
1a four color cover 3.00
2 thru 5 . . . . @2.25
6 . . . . 2.25
7 . . . . 2.25
Graphic Novel, rep.1-4. . . . . 5.00

TICK
New England Comics, 1988
1 BEd 45.00
1a 2nd printing 10.00
1b 3rd printing. 8.00
1c 4th printing. 5.00
2 BEd 50.00
2a 2nd printing 10.00
2b 3rd printing 4.00
2c 4th printing 2.50
3 BEd 10.00
3a 2nd printing 3.00
4 BEd 8.00
4a 2nd printing 3.00
5 BEd 8.00
6 BEd 7.00
7 BEd,A:Chairface Chippendale. . . 7.00
8 BEd 7.00
8a Spec.No Logo edition 12.00
9 BEd,A:Chainsaw Vigilante,
   Red Eye. 5.00
10 BEd. 5.00
11 thru 12 BEd . . . . @4.00
9 thru 12, new printings . . . . @3.00
Spec. Ed. #1, I:Tick 25.00
Spec. Ed. #2, 2nd App. Tick 20.00
Spec. #1 Reprise edition 6.00
TPB Omnibus #1 rep. #1–#6. . . . . 18.00
TPB Omnibus #2 BEd,fifth printing 15.00
TPB Omnibus #3 BEd 11.00
TPB Omnibus #4 BEd 11.00
The Tick Big Yule Log Special 1998 3.50
The Tick Big Yule Log Special 1999 3.50
Tick's Big Yule Log Special 2001. . . 3.50
Big Giant Summer Special #1, The
   Sidekicks are Revolting. 3.50
Big Summer Annual #1 . . . . 3.50
Tick's Big Red-N-Green X-mas 4.00
TPB Tick Bonanza #3 . . . . 5.00
TPB Tick Bonanza #4 . . . . 5.00
Spec.#1 Back to School. 3.50
Big Halloween Special #1 . . . . 3.50
Massive Summer Double Spectacle

Photo-Cover set of 2 . . . . 8.00
13 Pseudo-Tick, not by Edlund 3.50
Big Year 2000 Spectacle 3.50
Big Romantic Adventure #1, 2nd ed. 3.50
Big Tax Time Terror #1. . . . . 3.50
Big Mother's Day Spec. #1 . . . . . . 3.50
Big Halloween Special 2000 . . . . . 3.50
Big Father's Day Special 3.50
Big Cruise Ship Vacation Spec.#1 . 3.50
Massive Summer Double Spec.#1 . 3.50
Massive Summer Double Spec.#2 . 3.50

TICK AND ARTHUR, THE
New England Comics, 1999
1 by Sean Wang & Mike Baker . . . 3.50
2 Return of the Thorn,pt.2 . . . . . . 3.50
3 Return of the Thorn,pt.3 . . . . . . 3.50
4 Tick & Arthur meet Flea & Doyle . 3.50
5 Flea & Doyle superheroes?. 3.50
6 Chainsaw Vigilantes 3.50
TPB Bonanza #1 rep. #1–#3 . . . . . 5.50
TPB Bonanza #2 rep. #4–#6 . . . . . 5.50

TICK, THE:
BIG BLUE DESTINY
New England Comics, 1997
1 by Eli Stone, Keen edition 3.00
1 Wicked Keen edition 5.00
2A cover A. 3.00
3B cover B 3.00
3 . . . . 3.50
4 . . . . 3.50
5 The Chrysalis Crisis. 3.50

TICK CIRCUS MAXIMUS
New England Comics, 2000
1 (of 4) by Sean Wang 3.50
2 . . . . 3.50
3 . . . . 3.50
4 concl. 3.50
Spec.#1 Circus Maximus
Redux (2001). 3.50

TICK: GIANT CIRCUS
OF THE MIGHTY
New England Press, 1992
1 A-O. 3.00
2 P-Z. 3.00
3 . . . . 3.00

TICK, THE: GOLDEN AGE
New England Comics, 2002
1 Entertaining cover 5.00
1a Classic cover 5.00
2 extremely creepy cover 5.00
2a Ferociously heroic cover 5.00
3 Bleeding Heart (c) 5.00
3a Criminally Maniacal (c) 5.00
TPB Golden Age giant edition 13.00

TICK, THE:
HEROES OF THE CITY
New England Comics, 1999
1 three stories. 3.50
2 . . . . 3.50
3 . . . . 3.50
4 . . . . 3.50
5 . . . . 3.50
6 . . . . 3.50
TPB Bonanza #1 rep. #1–#3 . . . . . 5.50
TPB Bonanza #2 rep. #4–#6 . . . . . 5.50

TICK: KARMA TORNADO
New England Press, 1993
1 . . . . 4.00

Time Jump War #2
© Apple

1 2nd printing 3.00
2 . . . . 3.50
2 2nd printing 3.00
3 thru 9 . . . . @3.50
3 thru 9 2nd printings . . . . @3.00
TPB #1 second edition. 14.00
TPB Bonanza Edition, Vol.2. . . . . . 5.00
TPB Bonanza Edition, Vol.3. . . . . . 5.00

TICK, THE: LUNY BIN
New England Comics, 1998
1 (of 3) by Eli Stone, Back to
the Luny Bin 3.50
2 To the Rescue 3.50
3 Six Eyes in Tears. 3.50
Preview Special, 32pg 2.25
TPB Luny Bin Trilogy 120-pg. 5.00

TICK OMNIBUS
New England Press
1 1 to 6 Rep. 15.00

TICK'S BACK, THE
New England Comics, 1997
0 by Eli Stone, V:Toy DeForce 3.00

TIGERS OF
THE LUFTWAFTE
Antarctic Press, 2001
1 48-pg. 6.00
2 48-pg. 6.00
3 48-pg. 6.00
4 Wild Angels, 48-pg. 6.00
5 Black Devil, 48-pg. 6.00
6 Black Devil, pt.2. . . . . 6.00
7 April Fools phoney issue 6.00
8 Fighter General 6.00
9 Adolf Galland 6.00
10 final issue 6.00

TIGERS OF TERRA
Mind-Visions, 1992
1 6,000 printed 4.50
1a Signed & Num. 14.00
2 . . . . 2.25
2a Signed & Num. 11.00
5 thru 7 . . . . @3.50
8 thru 10 . . . . @3.75

Antarctic, 1993
11 and 12 . . . . @4.00
[Vol. 2], 1993
0 thru 14 . . . . @2.75
15 Totenkopf Police,pt.2. . . . . 2.75
16 Battleship Arizona,pt.3 . . . . 2.75
17 thru 22. . . . . @3.00
23 `Trouble with Tigers' pt.3 . . . . . 3.00
24 48pg 10th Anniv. 4.00
25 `Battle for Terra' pt.1 . . . . 3.00
TPB Book Two 10.00
TPB Book Three 10.00
TPB Book Four 10.00

TIGER-X
Eternity, 1988
Special #1 . . . . 2.50
Spec. #1a 2nd printing. 2.25
1 thru 3 . . . . @2.25
Book II, 1989
1 thru 4 . . . . @2.25

TIGRESS
Hero Graphics, 1992
1 Tigress vs. Flare 4.00
2 . . . . 3.00
3 A:Lady Arcane 3.00
4 inc. B.U. Mudpie 4.00
5 . . . . 4.00
6 . . . . 4.00

TIGRESS
Basement Comics, 1998
1 by Budd Root and Mike Hoffman 3.00
2 concl. 3.00
1-shot Mike Hoffman special 9.00
1-shot green foil edition 12.50
1-shot gold foil edition 12.50

TIGRESS TALES
Amryl Entertainment, 2001
1 by Mike Hoffman 3.00
2 Slave Planet. 3.00
Basement Comics, 2001
1a spec. edition. 9.00
2 Special Edition 9.00
2 Blue foil (c). 12.50
3a Special ed. 9.00
3b special edition, purple foil 11.50
4 . . . . 3.00
4a Special ed. 9.00
4b special edition, gold foil 11.50
5 . . . . 3.00
5a Special ed. 9.00
Pin-Up book (2001) 3.50
Pin-Up Book, special edition 9.00

TIGRESS: THE
HIDDEN LANDS
Basement Comics, 2002
1 by Mike Hoffman 3.50

TIME DRIFTERS
Innovation, 1990
1 . . . . 2.25
2 . . . . 2.25
3 . . . . 2.25

TIME GATES
Double Edge
1 SF series,The Egg #1 . . . . 2.25
2 The Egg #2 . . . . 2.25
3 Spirit of the Dragon #1. . . . . 2.25
4 Spirit of the Dragon #2. . . . . 2.25

4a Var.cover 2.25

TIME JUMP WAR
Apple
1 thru 3 . . . . @2.25

TIME MACHINE
Eternity, 1990
1 thru 3 H.G. Wells adapt. . . . . . . @2.50

TIME TRAVELER AI
CPM Manga, 1999
1 by Ai Ijima &
  Takeshi Takebayashi 3.00
2 thru 13 . . . . @3.00
14 thru 21 . . . . @3.00
TPB Book One, rep.. . . . . 16.00
TPB Sexy Pirates. 16.00
TPB Vol. 2 Sexy Pirates 16.00
TPB Vol. 3 Sexy Ninja Girl. 16.00

TIME WARRIORS
Fantasy General, 1986
1 rep.Alpha Track #1 . . . . 2.25
1a Bi-Weekly. 2.25
2 . . . . 2.25
3 . . . . 2.25

TIM VIGIL'S WEBWITCH
Avatar Press, 2002
Preview, 16-pg. 2.25
Preview, Temptress (c) 6.00
Preview, Serenity (c) 6.00
Preview, prism foil exclusive(c) . . . 13.00
Preview Cave of Evil edition 6.00
1 (of 3) Finch(c) 3.50
2 Vigil(c) 3.50
3 Adrian (c). 3.50
1a thru 3a variant(c) . . . . @3.50
1b thru 3b wraparound (c)s. . . . . @4.00
Webwitch Companion 5.00
Webwitch Companion Waller (c) . . . 5.00
Webwitch Companion Martin (c) . . . 5.00
TPB 11.00

TITANESS
Draculina Publishing, 1995
1 I:Titaness,Tomboy 3.00

TO BE ANNOUNCED
Strawberry Jam, 1986
1 thru 6 . . . . @2.25

TOMB TALES
Cryptic Entertainment, 1997
1 . . . . 3.00
2 . . . . 3.00
3 . . . . 3.00
4 A Rare Gem. 3.00
5 . . . . 3.00
6 The Flame Game. 3.00
7 Invasion of the Shoddy Snatchers 3.00

TOM CORBETT SPACE CADET
Eternity, 1990
1 . . . . 2.25
2 . . . . 2.25
3 . . . . 2.25
4 . . . . 2.25

TOM CORBETT II
Eternity, 1990
1 . . . . 2.25

2 . . . . 2.25
3 . . . . 2.25
4 . . . . 2.25

TOMMI GUNN: KILLERS LUST
London Night, 1997
1 . . . . 3.00
1 photo cover 6.00
Ann. #1. . . . . 3.00

TOM MIX HOLIDAY ALBUM
Amazing Comics
1 . . . . 3.50

TOM MIX WESTERN
AC Comics, 1988
1 . . . . 2.50
2 . . . . 2.50

TOMMY & THE MONSTERS
New Comics
1 thru 3 . . . . @2.25

TOMORROW MAN
Antarctic, 1993
1 R:Tommorrow Man 3.00
Spec.#1 48-pg.. . . . . 4.00

TOMORROW MAN
Antarctic Press, 2000
1 Requiem for Nepton,pt.1 . . . . . . 5.00
2 Requiem for Nepton,pt.2 . . . . . . 3.00
3 Requiem for Nepton,pt.3 . . . . . . 3.00

TONY DIGEROLAMO'S JERSEY DEVIL
South Jersey Rebellion
1 by Tony DiGerolamo 3.00
2 . . . . 3.00
3 . . . . 2.25
4 . . . . 3.00
5 Robin Hood of the Pines,pt.1 . . . 2.25
6 Robin Hood of the Pines,pt.2 . . . 3.00

TONY DIGEROLAMO'S THE TRAVELERS
Kenzer & Company, 2000
1 thru 3 . . . . @2.25
7 . . . . 3.00
8 Vlad Tepes in Romania 3.00
9 Arcimedes & Time Machine. 3.00
10 Strange storm 3.00
11 Wrath of the Imprechaun 3.00
12 thru 20. . . . . @3.00
Wingnut Comics, 2003
21 thru 25. . . . . @3.00
TPB Vol. 1 Keg O' Fun 12.00

TONY DIGEROLAMO'S THE FIX
South Jersey Rebellion, 2001
1 (of 4) 2.50
2 thru 4 . . . . @2.50

TOO MUCH COFFEE MAN
Adhesive Comics, 1994
1 F:Too Much Coffee Man 16.00
1a 2nd printing 4.00

2 Wheeler (s&a) 8.00
3 Wheeler (s&a) 6.00

Trouble With Girls #15
© Eternity

4 In love 6.00
5 thru 7 . . . . @4.00
8 thru 10 . . . . @3.00
Mag. #11 64-pg.. . . . . 5.00
Mag. #12 . . . . 5.00
Mag. #13 thru #21 . . . . @5.00

TOO MUCH HOPELESS SAVAGES
Oni Press, 2003
1 (of 4) 3.00
2 thru 3 . . . . @3.00

TORG
Adventure
1 Based on Role Playing Game . . . 2.50
2 thru 3 Based on Game. . . . . . . @2.50

TOR JOHNSON: HOLLYWOOD STAR
Monster Comics
1 Biographical story 2.50

TORRID AFFAIRS
Eternity, 1988
1 . . . . 2.25
2 . . . . 2.25
3 thru 5, 60-pg. . . . . @3.00

TOTALLY ALIEN
Trigon
1 . . . . 15.00
2 . . . . 10.00
3 . . . . 8.00

TOUCH OF DEATH
Brain Scan Studios, 2003
0 . . . . 2.50
1 thru 3 . . . . @2.50

TOUGH GUYS AND WILD WOMEN
Eternity, 1989
1 . . . . 2.25

B & W PUB.

2 . . . . 2.25

TRACKER
Blackthorne, 1988
1 . . . . 2.25
2 thru 4 . . . . @2.25

TRAILER PARK OF TERROR
Imperium Comics, 2003
1 . . . . 3.00
2 thru 8 . . . . @3.00
5a variant (c). 3.00
Color Spec. 4.00
Color Spec. variant(c) 4.00
Spec. Halloween Special 4.00

TRANSFORMERS ARMADA CINEMANGA
Tokyopop Press, 2003
GN Vol. 1 (of 3) 8.00
GN Vol. 2 . . . . 8.00
GN Vol. 3 . . . . 8.00

TRANSFORMERS: ENERGON
Tokyopop Press 2004
GN Vol. 1 Cine-manga. 8.00
GN Vol. 2 thru Vol. 3 . . . . 8.00

TRANSIT
Vortex, 1987
1 . . . . 2.25
2 thru 6 . . . . @2.25

TRICKSTER KING MONKEY
Eastern
1 thru 5 . . . . @2.25

TRIDENT
Trident, 1989
1 thru 7 . . . . @3.50
8 . . . . 4.50

TRIUMVERATE
Mermaid Productions
1 I:Trimverate 2.25
2 & 3 Team captured. . . . . @2.25
4 V:Ord,Ael 2.25

TROLLORDS
Tru Studios, 1986
1 1st printing. 5.00
1a 2nd printing 2.25
2 . . . . 3.00
3 . . . . 2.25
4 thru 15 . . . . @2.25
#1 special. 2.25

TROLLORDS
Apple Comics, 1989–90
1 thru 6 . . . . @2.50

TROLLORDS
Caliber Tapestry, 1996
1 and 2 . . . . @3.00

Twisted Tantrums of the Purple Snit
#2 © Blackthorne

TROLLORDS: DEATH & KISSES
Apple Comics, 1989
1 . . . . 2.25
2 thru 5 . . . . @2.25

TROUBLE SHOOTERS
Nightwolf, 1995
1 I:Trouble Shooters 2.50
2 V:Ifrit,Djin,Ghul. 2.50
3 V:Morgath 2.50

TROUBLE WITH GIRLS
Eternity, 1989–91
1 . . . . 3.00
2 . . . . 2.50
3 thru 14 . . . . @2.25
15 thru 21. . . . . @2.25
22 Lester's Origin. 2.25
Ann. #1 . . . . 3.00
Graphic Novel 8.00
Graphic Novel #2. . . . . 8.00
Xmas special 'World of Girls' 3.00
NEW SERIES
1 thru 4 see color
5 thru 11 . . . . @2.25

TROUBLE WITH TIGERS
Antarctic Press, 1992
1 Ninja High School/Tigers x-over . 2.25
2 . . . . 2.25

TRUE CRIME
Eclipse
1 thru 2 . . . . @3.00

TRUE STORY, SWEAR TO GOD
Clib's Boy Comics, 2001
5 thru 6 . . . . @2.95
7 thru 11 . . . . @2.95
AIT/Planet Lar, 2004
TPB 9.95

TRUFAN ADVENTURES THEATRE
Paragraphics, 1986
1 . . . . 7.00
2 3-D issue 5.00

TUPELO
Amaze Ink/SLG, 2003
1 . . . . 3.00
2 thru 4 . . . . @3.00
TPB 18.00

TURTLE SOUP
Mirage, 1985
1 A:TMNTurtles. 6.00

TURTLES TEACH KARATE
Solson
1 . . . . 4.00
2 . . . . 3.50

TUXEDO GIN
Viz Communications, 2003
TPB Vol. 1 . . . . 10.00
TPB Vol. 2 thru Vol. 8. . . . . @10.00

TV WESTERN
AC Comics, 2001
1 F:Jock Mahoney, Range Rider . . 6.00
Becomes:

WESTERN MOVIE HERO
AC Comics, 2001
2 F:Monte Hale. 6.00
3 F:John Wayne 6.00
4 F:Rex Allen 7.00

TWILIGHT AVENGER
Eternity, 1988
1 thru 18 . . . . @2.25
Miracle Studios
Spec. Twilight Avenger Super
  Summer Special 2.75

TWILIGHT X
Antarctic Press, 2002
Pocket Manga #1. . . . . 15.00
Pocket Manga #2 thru #4. . . . . . @10.00

TWILIGHT-X: INTERLUDE
Antarctic Press, 1992
1 thru 3 by Joseph Wright. . . . . . @2.50
Vol. 2, 1993
1 thru 5 . . . . @2.50

TWILIGHT-X QUARTERLY
Antarctic Press, 1994
1 thru 3 by Joseph Wright. . . . . . @3.00
4 Celebration 3.00

TWILIGHT X: STORM
Antarctic Press, 2003
1 . . . . 3.50
2 thru 6 . . . . @3.50
7 thru 8 . . . . @3.00
Pocket Manga #1. . . . . 10.00

TWIST
Kitchen Sink, 1988
1 . . . . 2.25
2 and 3 . . . . @2.25

TWISTED TANTRUMS OF THE PURPLE SNIT
Blackthorne, 1986
1	2.50
2	2.25

2001 NIGHTS
Viz, 1990–91
1 by Yukinobu Hoshino	5.00
2	4.00
3 thru 5	@3.75
6 thru 10	@4.25

TYRANNY REX
Fleetway
GN reps. from 2000A.D.	8.00

ULTIMATE STRIKE
London Night, 1996
1	2.25
1 holochrome edition	15.00
2	2.25
3	2.25
4	2.25
5	2.25
6 sequel to Strike #0	2.25
7 by Kevin Hill, `Strike: Year One' concl.	2.25
8 Year One,	2.25
9 Year One, cont.	2.25
10	2.25
11	2.25
12	2.25

ULTRA KLUTZ
Onward Comics
1	2.50
2 thru 18	@2.25
19 thru 24	@2.25
25 thru 30	@2.25
31	3.00

Bad Habit
TBP Book One, rep. #1–#23	30.00

UNCANNY MAN-FROG
Mad Dog
1 and 2	@2.25

UNCENSORED MOUSE
Eternity, 1989
1 Mickey Mouse	10.00
2 Mickey Mouse	11.00

UNFORGIVEN, THE
Trinity Comics Ministries
Mission of Tranquility
1 thru 6 V:Dormian Grath	@2.25
7 I:Faith	2.25

UNICORN ISLE
Genesis West, 1986
1	2.50
2	2.25
3	2.25

Apple, 1987
4 thru 6	@2.25

UNLEASHED
Caliber Press
1 F:Carson Davis	3.00
2 V:North Harbor Crime	3.00

UNSUPERVISED EXISTENCE
Fantagraphics
1	2.25
2 and 3	@2.50

UNTOLD TALES OF EVIL ERNIE
Chaos! Comics, 2000
Pieces of Me #1	3.50
Black Death premium #1	13.00
Evil Ernie:chromium #1	16.00
Relentless 1 BnP (2002)	5.00
Relentless 1a premium ed.	10.00
Relentless 1b Super premium ed.	20.00
Relentless 1c signed ed.	15.00
Relentless, Script	5.00
Relentless Script, premium ed.	20.00

UNTOUCHABLES
1 thru 20	@2.25

UNTOUCHABLES
Caliber, 1997
1K by Joe Pruett & John Kissee, MK(c)	3.00
1S Showman (c)	3.00
2	3.00
3 MK (c)	3.00
4 MK (c)	3.00
Spec. High Society Killer (1998)	4.00

USAGI YOJIMBO
Fantagraphics, 1987
1 SS	11.00
1a 2nd printing	5.00
2 SS,Samurai	8.00
3 SS,Samurai,A:Croakers	6.00
4 SS	5.00
5 thru 7 SS	@5.00
8 SS,A Mother's Love	5.00
8a 2nd printing	3.00
9 SS	5.00
10 SS,A:Turtles	5.00
10a 2nd printing	3.00
11 thru 18 SS	@4.00
19 SS,Frost & Fire,A:Nelson Groundthumper	4.00
20 thru 21 SS	@4.00
22 SS,A:Panda Khan	4.00
23 SS,V:Ninja Bats	4.00
24 SS	4.00
25 SS,A:Lionheart	4.00
26 SS,Gambling	4.00
27 SS	4.00
28 thru 31 SS,Circles pt.1–4	@4.00
32	4.00
33 SS,Ritual Murder	4.00
34 thru 37	@4.00
Spec.#1 SS,SummerSpec, C:Groo	45.00
TPB Vol 4, rep.	17.00
TPB Vol 6, rep., new printing	13.00
TPB Vol 7, Gen's Story	17.00

Radio Comix
Vol. 1 The Art of Usagi Yojimbo	4.00

VAGABOND
Viz Communications, 2001
Part 1
1 (of 8) by Takehiko Inoue	5.00
2 thru 16	@5.00
TPB Vol. 1 thru Vol. 4	@13.00
TPB Vol. 5 thru Vol. 16	@10.00

VALENTINO
Renegade, 1985
1	2.25
2 and 3	@2.25

VAMPEROTICA
Brainstorm Comics, 1994
1 I:Luxura	8.00
1a 2nd & 3rd printing	3.00
2	6.00
2 2nd printing	3.00
3	4.00
4 I:Blood Hunter	4.00
5 Deadshot	4.00
6 Deadshot	4.00
7 Baptism	4.00
8 Pains,Peepers	4.00
9 thru 11	@4.00
12 thru 16	@3.00
17 thru 22 see: color	
20 signed	5.00
23	3.00
23 encore edition	3.00
24	3.00
25	3.00
26	3.00
27	3.00
28 A:China & Jazz	3.00
29 mild cover	3.00
30 Legends of Luxura x-over, concl.	3.00
31 V:Red Militia	3.00
32	3.00
33 by Kirk Lindo	3.00
34 V:Pontius Vanthor	3.00
34a luxury edition	5.00
35	3.00
36 I:Countess Vladimira	3.00
36a photo cover edition	4.00
37	3.00
37a statue cover	3.00
38	3.00
39 Death From Above, pt.1	3.00
40 Death From Above, pt.2	3.00
41	3.00
42 Hostile Seduction	3.00
43 Harvest	3.00
44 F:Luxura	3.00
45 The Kindred Kill	3.00
45b photo cover	4.00
46 Murder Most Foul	3.00
47 Camelot	3.00
48 Reflections Over Blood	3.00
49 Love's Story	3.00
50 final issue, 48-pg.	5.00

Vampirella Silver Anniversary Collection #3 © Harris

50b commemorative edition, Julie Strain photo (c)	7.00
50c commem. signed.	10.00
Commemorative Edition.	3.00
Lingerie Special #1	3.00
Spec. Lingerie, encore edition	3.00
Spec. Lingerie, deluxe	4.00
Spec. Swimsuit, encore edition	3.00
Gallery #1.	5.00
Gallery #2.	5.00
Bondage Spec. #1	3.00
Bondage Spec. #1, manga	4.00
Ann. #1 Encore	3.00
Spec.#2 Dare to Bare	3.00
Spec.#4 Encore Edition, new(c)	3.00
Spec.#5 Encore Edition	3.00
Spec.#1 Vamperotica Presents: Countess Vladimira (1998)	3.00
Vamperotica Collector Vol. 1	4.00
Pin-Up #1 (2000)	3.00
Spec. Blood of Japan.	3.00
1-shot Blond Goddess (2003)	3.00
1-shot Dark Fantasy	3.00
1-shot Bondage Gallery	3.00
Spec. #1 Voluptuous Vamps (2004)	3.00
GN Blood of the Impaler	8.00
GN Deadly Vixens	8.00
TPB Drop Dead Dangerous (2004).	8.00

VAMPEROTICA: DARK FICTION
Vamperotica Ent., 2001

1 F:Vampress Luxura	3.00
1a adult (c)	4.00
1b premium edition	5.00
2	3.00
3	3.00
4	3.00
TPB Vamperotica Maximum Excitement (2001)	8.00
TPB Vamperotica Slave to Love (2000)	8.00

VAMPEROTICA: DIVIDE & CONQUER
Brainstorm, 1999

1 V:The Juicious Edicts	3.00
1b Commemorative #1	5.00
1c Commemorative #1 deluxe	7.00
2 conclusion	3.00

VAMPEROTICA ILLUSTRATED
Brainstorm

1 F:Vampress Luxura	3.00
1b premium ed.	5.00
1c premium signed	6.00
2	3.00
3	3.00
4	3.00
5	3.00
6	3.00

VAMPEROTICA LUST FOR LUXURA
Vamperotica, 2002

1 by Kirk Lindo	3.00
1a premium edition	5.00
2	3.00
3	3.00
1c Sketch cover edition	4.00
3a photo(c)	5.00

VAMPEROTICA MANGA
Brainstorm, 1998

1	3.00
2	3.00

VAMPEROTICA'S PIN-UP ILLUSTRATED
Vamperotica, 2004

1	5.00
2 thru 3	@5.00

VAMPEROTICA TALES
Brainstorm, 1998

1	3.00
2 thru 5	@3.00

VAMPEROTICA: TALES FROM THE BLOODVAULT
Vamperotica Ent., 2000

Mag. #1	5.00
Mag. #1b premium ed.	7.00

VAMPEROTICA: WHEN DARKNESS FALLS
Vamperotica Ent., 2002

1	3.00
1b premium edition	5.00
2	3.00
3	3.00
TPB Dark Ages, series rep.	8.00

VAMPFIRE
Brainstorm, 1996

1	3.00
1b commemorative photo cover	10.00
2	3.00
2b signed	5.00
2d Remastered	3.00
2e signed	10.00
2f deluxe with litho	20.00
3 remastered.	4.00
3a signed	10.00
3b deluxe	20.00
Pin-Up Spec.	3.00
Pin-Up Spec. deluxe	4.00
Tour Book #1	3.00

VAMPFIRE: EROTIC ECHO
Brainstorm, 1997

1 by Fauve	3.00
1b photo cover	3.00
2	3.00
2b photo cover	3.00

VAMPFIRE: NECROMANTIQUE
Brainstorm, 1997

1 by Holly Golightly.	3.00
1b luxury edition, virgin cover.	5.00
1c luxury edition, signed	15.00
1d regular, signed	8.00
2 by Fauve	3.00

VAMPIRE BITES
Brainstorm, 1995

1	3.00
2	3.00

VAMPIRE CONFESSIONS
Brainstorm, 1998

1	3.00

Vampirella: Morning in America #3
© Harris

VAMPIRE DAHLIA, THE
Ironcat, 2001

1 (of 6) by Narumi Kakinouchi	3.00
2 thru 6	@3.00
TPB Vol. 1 Death is a Kiss	17.00

VAMPIRE GIRLS: CALIFORNIA 1969
Angel Entertainment, 1996

1 blood red foil deluxe edition.	6.00
2	3.00
2 deluxe	6.00
TPB	5.00

VAMPIRE GIRLS: NEW YORK 1979
Angel Entertainment, 1996

0	3.00
0 gold edition	8.00
1	3.00

VAMPIRE GIRLS: BUBBLEGUM & BLOOD
Angel Entertainment, 1996

1	3.00
1 deluxe edition.	6.00
2	3.00
2 deluxe edition.	6.00

VAMPIRE GIRLS EROTIQUE
Angel Entertainment, 1996

1	3.00
2	3.00
3	3.00
4	3.00
5	3.00
6	3.00
7 Bloodsucker cover.	3.00
Spec. Gravedigger (1996) by Alexandra Scott & Bill Wylie	3.00
Spec. Paris 1968 (1997) by Alexandra Scott & Dean Burnett	3.00
Spec. Titanic 1912 (1998) by Alexandra Scott & Dean Burnett	3.00

VAMPIRE GIRLS EROTIQUE: GRAVEDIGGER
Angel Entertainment, 1996
1 by Alexandra Scott & Bill Wylie . . 3.00

VAMPIRE GIRLS VS. ANGEL GIRL
Angel Entertainment, 1997
1 . . . . 3.00

VAMPIRELLA
Harris
1 DC,SL,Summer Nights,48pg. . . . 4.00
Pantha Ashcan, 16-pg. 6.00
Dangerous Games Preview Ashcan 6.00
Hell on Earth, Leather Ashcan. . . . 15.00
Hell on Earth, Leather Ashcan,
  signed 30.00
30th Ann. Spec. Julie
  Strain photo (c) 10.00
Painkiller Jane preview Ashcan 6.00
Spec.#1 Vampirella vs. Hemorrhage,
  Limited Preview Ashcan 5.00
Vampirella/Lady Death Ashcan
  16-pg., Rematch 6.00
Vampirella/Lady Death Ashcan
  16-pg., Finale 6.00
Vampirella/Lady Death Ashcan
  16-pg., Revenge, platinum . . . 20.00
Vampirella 2999 A.D.
  Manga Ashcan. 8.00
Vampirella 2999 A.D. Manga
  Ashcan, leather edition 15.00
Vampirella 3000 A.D.
  Manga Ashcan. 8.00
Vampirella 3000 A.D.Manga
  Ashcan, leather edition 15.00

VAMPIRELLA
Harris Comics, 2002
#1 magazine reprint from 1969. . . 30.00
#1 royal blue foil (c) 60.00
#1 platinum foil (c) 20.00
TPB Vampirella and the Blood Red
  Queen of Hearts, rep. from Warren
  Vampirella, 96pg 10.00

VAMPIRELLA
Silver Anniversary Collection
Harris, 1996
0 Vampirella of Darkulon, EM. 3.00
1 good girl edition. 2.50
1a bad girl edition. 2.50
2 good girl edition. 2.50
2a bad girl edition. 2.50
3 good girl edition. 2.50
3a bad girl edition. 2.50
4 Silkie(c) 2.50
4a MBc(c). 2.50

VAMPIRELLA COMICS MAGAZINE
Harris Comics, 2003
1 . . . . 4.00
1a photo (c). 10.00
1b Frankenstein Mobster (c). 10.00
1c JP(c). 10.00
2 thru 7 . . . . @4.00
2a thru 7a photo (c)s. . . . . @10.00

Vengeance of the Aztecs #2
© Caliber

VAMPIRELLA: MORNING IN AMERICA
Harris/Dark Horse, 1991–92
Book 1 thru 4 . . . . @7.00
Book 2 thru 4 . . . . @5.00
TPB 25.00

VAMPIRELLA NOVELLA
Anarchy Studios/
Harris Comics, 2004
1 Deadly Sins 3.95
1a limited 9.95

VAMPIRELLA RETRO
Harris, 1998
1 (of 3) rep. Warren stories. 2.50
2 (of 3) rep. Warren stories. 2.50
3 (of 3) rep. Warren stories. 2.50

VAMPIRELLA: LEGENDARY TALES
Harris Comics, 2000
1 . . . . 3.00
1a deluxe 10.00
1b Julie Strain photo (c) 10.00
2 . . . . 3.00
2a variant (c). 10.00
2b Julie Strain photo (c) 10.00

VAMPIRE MIYU
Antarctica Press, 1996
1 I:Vampire Princess Miyu 3.00
2 thru 5 . . . . @4.00
6 48pg. 5.00

VAMPIRE PRINCESS MIYU
Ironcat, 2000
1 by Narumi Kakinouchi 3.00
2 thru 4 . . . . @3.00
TPB Vol. 1 (2001) 18.00
TPB Vol. 2 thru Vol. 3. . . . . @18.00
TPB Vol. 4 . . . . 18.00
TPB Vol. 5 Intrusions 16.00
TPB Vol. 6 . . . . 16.00
TPB Vol. 7 Vortex. 16.00
TPB Vol. 8 . . . . 13.00
Artbook (color) 25.00

VAMPIRE PRINCESSS YUI
Ironcat, 2000
Vol. 1
1 . . . . 3.00
2 thru 6 . . . . @3.00
Vol. 2
1 . . . . 3.00
2 thru 6 . . . . @3.00

VAMPIRE YUI
Ironcat, 2000
Vol. 3
1 . . . . 3.00
2 thru 4 . . . . @3.00
5 thru 6 . . . . @3.00
Vol. 4 (2002)
1 thru 7 . . . . @3.00
Vol. 5
1 . . . . 3.00
2 thru 7 . . . . @3.00
TPB Vol. 1 . . . . 18.00
TPB Vol. 2 . . . . 18.00
TPB Vol. 3 . . . . 18.00
TPB Vol. 4 . . . . 16.00
TPB Vol. 5 . . . . 16.00

VAMPIRE'S TATTOO
London Night, 1997
1 (of 2) by Art Wetherell 3.00
2 . . . . 3.00
3 . . . . 3.00

VAMPIRE VERSES, THE
CFD Productions, 1995
1 thru 3 . . . . @3.00

VAMPIRE ZONE, THE
Brainstorm, 1998
1 . . . . 3.00

VAMPORNRELLA
Forbidden, 1997
1 parody 3.00

VAMPYRES
Eternity, 1988
1 thru 4 . . . . @2.25

VAPOR LOCH
Sky Comics, 1994
1 . . . . 2.50

VENGEANCE OF DREADWOLF
Lightning Comics
1 O:Dreadwolf. 2.75

VENGEANCE OF THE AZTECS
Caliber, 1993
1 . . . . 2.50
2 . . . . 2.50

VERDICT
Eternity, 1988
1 thru 4 . . . . @2.25

VEROTIKA
Verotika, 1995–97
1 Magical Times 12.00

2 . . . . 7.00
3 . . . . 5.00
4 thru 6 . . . . @4.00
7 thru 15 . . . . @3.00

VERY VICKY
Meet Danny Ocean, 1993
1 . . . . 3.50
1a 2nd printing 3.00
2 thru 8 . . . . @2.50
Spec. Calling All Hillbillies 2.50

VIC & BLOOD
Renegade, 1987
1 and 2 RCo,Ellison . . . . @2.25

VICKY VALENTINE
Renegade, 1985
1 thru 4 . . . . @2.25

VICTIM
Silver Wolf, 1987
1 & 2 . . . . @2.25

VICTIMS
Eternity, 1988
1 thru 5 . . . . @2.25

VIDEO CLASSICS
Eternity
1 Mighty Mouse 3.50
2 Mighty Mouse 3.50

VIDEO GIRL AI
Viz Communications, 1999
TPB by Masakazu Katsura 16.00
TPB Vol. 2 Mix Down 16.00
TPB Vol. 3 Recall 16.00
TPB Vol. 4 Offline 16.00
TPB Vol. 5 . . . . 16.00
TPB Vol. 6 Cutting Room 13.00
TPB Vol. 7 . . . . 13.00
TPB Vol. 8 . . . . 10.00
TPB Vol. 9 . . . . 10.00

VIETNAM JOURNAL
Apple Comics, 1987
1 . . . . 5.00
1a 2nd printing 3.00
2 . . . . 3.00
3 thru 5 . . . . @3.00
6 thru 13 . . . . @3.00
14 thru 16 . . . . @3.00

VIGIL
Duality Press, 1997
Baby Steps 3.00
Dirt, by A.Laudermilk & M.Iverson . . 3.00
Slash and Burn, Bloodline story . . 3.00
The Vegas Shuffle, Bloodline story . 3.00
Desertion 3.00
Outreach 3.00
Penetration 3.00
Daddy's Little Girl, final issue 3.00
TPB Vol. 1, rep. #1–#5 . . . . 20.00

VIGIL: DESERT FOXES
Millennium, 1995
1 & 2 F:Grace Kimble . . . . @4.00

VIGIL: ERUPTION
Millennium, 1996
1 (of 2) vampire hunters 4.00

2 (of 2) 4.00

Wandering Star #17
© Sirius

VIGIL: FALL
FROM GRACE
Innovation, 1992
1 'State of Grace' 2.75
2 The Graceland Hunt 2.50

VIGIL: SCATTER SHOTS
Duality Press, 1997
1 by A.Laudermilk & M.Iverson 4.00
2 . . . . 4.00

VINSON WATSON'S RAGE
Trinity Visuals
1 I:Rena Helen 3.00

VINSON WATSON'S
SWEET CHILDE
Advantage Graphics
Vol. 2
1 F:Spyder 2.25

VIRGIN: SLUMBER
Entity, 1997
1 BMs 2.75
1 deluxe 3.50

VIRGIN: SURROUNDED
Entity, 1997
1 BMs 2.75
1 deluxe 3.50

VIRGIN: TILL DEATH
DO US PART
Entity, 1997
1 BMs 2.75
1 deluxe 3.50

VISIONS
Vision Publication, 1979–83
1 I:Flaming Carrot 50.00
2 Flaming Carrot 30.00
3 Flaming Carrot 15.00

4 Flaming Carrot 25.00

VISUAL ASSAULT
OMNIBUS
Visual Assault Comics, 1995
1 thru 4 O:Dimensioner . . . . @3.00

VIXEN
Meteor Comics
1 & 2 Battle of the Vixens . . . . . . @3.00

VORTEX
Hall of Heroes, 1993
1 . . . . 15.00
1a commemorative 5.00
2 . . . . 10.00
3 thru 5 . . . . @3.50
6 V:The Reverend 3.00

War of the Worlds #3
© Caliber

VORTEX SPECIAL:
CYBERSIN
Avatar Press, 1997
1 by Matt Martin & Bil Maus 3.00
1b velvet cover 15.00
1c signed 10.00
1d Snowman spec. (c) 5.00

VORTEX: DR. KILBOURN
Entity, 1997
1 by Matt Martin 3.00
1a deluxe 3.50

VORTEX: INTO THE DARK
Entity, 1997
1 . . . . 3.00
1 deluxe 3.50

VOX
Apple, 1989
1 JBy(c) 2.25
2 and 3 . . . . @2.25
4 and 5 . . . . @2.25

All comics prices listed are for *Near Mint* condition.

WABBIT WAMPAGE
Amazing Comics, 1987
1 .... 2.25

WAFFEN SS
New England Comics, 2000
1 by Ron Ledwell 3.50
2 thru 7 .... @3.50

WAITING PLACE, THE
Slave Labor, 1997
5 .... 3.00
6 .... 3.00
Vol. 2, 2000
1 .... 3.00
2 .... 3.00
3 A Sporting Chance............ 3.00
4 I Care....................... 3.00
5 The Road Home 3.00
6 .... 3.00
7 .... 3.00
8 Under a Frozen Sky........... 3.00
9 Intrusions, pt.1............. 3.00
10 Intrusions, pt.2 .... 3.00
11 Intrusions, pt.3 .... 3.00
TPB Vol. 1 .... 16.00
TPB Vol. 2 thru Vol. 3 .... @16.00

WALKING DEAD
Aircel
1 thru 4 .... @2.25
Zombie Spec. 1 .... 2.25

WALK THROUGH OCTOBER
Caliber
1 I:Mr. Balloon............... 3.00
2 .... 3.00
3 All Hallow's Eve............. 3.00

WALT THE WILDCAT
Motion Comics, 1995
1 I:Walt the Wildcat........... 2.50

WANDERING STAR
Pen & Ink, 1993
1 I:Casandra Andrews 12.00
1a 2nd & 3rd printing 3.00
2 .... 8.00
3 .... 5.00
4 .... 4.00
5 .... 4.00
6 thru 11 .... @3.00
Sirius, 1995–97
12 thru 20 TWo .... @2.50
21 TWo, final issue 2.50
TPB Vol. 1 rep. #1–#7 .... 15.00
TPB Vol. 2 .... 15.00
TPB Vol. 3 168-pg.. .... 15.00

WANDERLUST
Antarctic Press, 2000
1 (of 3) by Bryant Shiu 2.50
2 .... 2.50
3 conclusion 2.50

WARCAT
Alliance Comics
1 thru 7 A:Ebonia .... @2.50

WARD: A BULLET SERIES
Liar Comics
1 Foresight,pt.1.............. 2.50

2 Foresight,pt.2.............. 2.50
3 Foresight,pt.3.............. 2.50

WARLOCK 5
Aircel, 1986
1 .... 6.00
2 .... 5.00
3 .... 6.00
4 .... 5.00
5 .... 5.00
6 thru 11 .... @4.00
12 .... 3.50
13 .... 3.50
14 thru 16................... @3.00
17 .... 3.00
18 .... 3.00
19 thru 22.................. @3.00
Book 2 #1 thru #7........... @3.00

WARLOCK 5
Sirius, 1997
1 (of 4) by Barry Blair & Colin Chan 2.50
2 .... 2.50
3 .... 2.50
4 finale 2.50

WARLOCKS
Aircel, 1988
1 thru 3 .... @2.25
4 thru 12 .... @2.25
Spec #1 Rep................... 2.25

WAR OF THE WORLDS
Eternity
1 TV tie-in 2.50
2 thru 6..................... @2.50

WAR OF THE WORLDS, THE
Caliber `New Worlds', 1996
1 from H.G. Wells 3.00
1a signed 3.00
2 war for Kansas City 3.00
3 Haven & The Hellweed 3.00
4 .... 3.00
5 .... 3.00
TPB rep. #1–#5 .... 15.00

WAR OF THE WORLDS: THE MEMPHIS FRONT
Arrow Comics, 1998
1 (of 5) by Randy Zimmerman
  & Richard Gulick 3.00
2 thru 5 .... @3.00
Spec.#1 signed & numbered 3.00

WARREN ELLIS' ATMOSPHERICS
Avatar Press, 2002
GN 6.00

WARREN ELLIS' BAD SIGNAL
Avatar Press, 2002
GN 7.00
GN Vol. 2 .... 7.00

WARREN ELLIS' BAD WORLD
Avatar Press, 2001
1 (of 3) 3.50
2 .... 3.50

3 .... 3.50
1a thru 3a wraparound (c)...... @4.00
TPB series rep. 11.00

WARREN ELLIS' DARK BLUE
Avatar Press, 2000
GN 72-pg. 9.00
TPB Scriptbook 7.00

WARREN ELLIS' SCARS
Avatar Press, 2002
Sampler 0.75
1 (of 6) 3.50
2 thru 6 .... @3.50
1a–6a wraparound (c)....... 4.00
TPB 18.00

WARREN ELLIS' STRANGE KILLINGS
Avatar Press, 2002
1 (of 3) WEI.................. 3.50
1a wraparound (c)............. 4.00
2 .... 3.50
2a wraparound (c)............. 4.00
3 .... 3.50
3a wraparound (c)............. 3.50
TPB 10.00

WARREN ELLIS' STRANGE KILLINGS: THE BODY ORCHARD
Avatar Press, 2002
1 (of 6) WEI.................. 3.50
2 thru 6 WEI .... @3.50
1a thru 6a wraparound (c)...... @4.00
TPB Body Orchard............. 17.00

WARREN ELLIS' STRANGE KILLINGS: NECROMANCER
Avatar Press, 2004
1 .... 3.50
2 thru 6 .... @3.50
1a thru 6a wraparound (c)s..... @3.50

Werewolf #2
© Blackthorne

WARREN ELLIS' STRANGE KILLINGS: STRONG MEDICINE
Avatar Press, 2003
1 . . . . 3.50
2 thru 3 . . . . @3.50
1a thru 3a wraparound (c). . . . . @4.00
TPB Strong Medicine. 10.00

WARREN ELLIS' STRANGE KISS
Avatar Press, 1999
1 . . . . 3.00
1a 4.00
1b signed 30.00
2 . . . . 2.25
2a wraparound (c). 4.00
3 . . . . 3.00
3a wraparound (c). 4.00
TPB 9.00

WARREN ELLIS' STRANGER KISSES
Avatar Press, 2000
1 (of 3) 3.00
1a leather signed 25.00
2 . . . . 3.00
3 . . . . 3.00
1a thru 3a wraparound (c). . . . . @4.00
TPB series rep. 10.00

WARRIOR NUN AREALA: BOOKS OF PERIL
Antarctic Press, 2001
1 (of 4) 3.00
2 The Book of Sharate 3.00
3 Book of Xitan 3.00
4 Devil's Deal 3.00
5 Scepter of the Crescent Moon. . . 3.00
6 Scepter of the Crescent Moon. . . 3.00
7 Scepter of the Crescent Moon. . . 3.00
8 The Good Son, pt.1 . . . . 3.00
9 The Good Son, pt.2 . . . . 3.00
10 The Good Son, pt.3 . . . . 3.00
11 Dissension, pt.1 . . . . 3.00
12 Dissension, pt.2 . . . . 3.00
13 Dissension, pt.3 . . . . 3.00
14 Curse of Looming Plague,pt.1 . . 3.50
15 Curse of Looming Plague,pt.2 . . 3.50
16 Curse of Looming Plague,pt.3 . . 3.50
17 Soul Reaper 3.50
18 Soul Reaper, pt.2 . . . . 3.50
19 Soul Reaper, pt.3 . . . . 3.50
20 thru 22 . . . . @3.50
Spec. Swimsuit Special (2002) 4.00

WARRIOR NUN AREALA: DANGEROUS GAME
Antarctic Press, 2001
1 (of 3) 3.00
2 . . . . 3.00
3 . . . . 3.00

WARRIOR NUN AREALA: GHOSTS OF THE PAST
Antarctic Press, 2001
1 (of 4) 3.00
2 thru 4 . . . . @3.00

White Devil #6
© Eternity

WARRIOR NUN AREALA/RAZOR: DARK PROPHECY
London Night, 1999
1 16-pg. 2.50
2 16-pg. 2.50
Antarctic Press
3 . . . . 2.50
4 . . . . 2.50

WARRIOR NUN AREALA: THE MANGA
Antarctic Press, 2000
1-shot 3.00

WARRIOR NUN BRIGANTIA
Antarctic Press, 2000
1 V:Fata Morgana 3.00
2 Sister Anna 3.00
3 . . . . 3.00

WARRIOR NUN: BLACK AND WHITE
Antarctic Press, 1997
1 . . . . 3.00
2 . . . . 3.00
3 . . . . 3.00
4 Winter Jade, pt.1 F:Ninja Nun . . . 3.00
5 Winter Jade, pt.2 . . . . 3.00
6 Winter Jade, pt.3 . . . . 3.00
7 . . . . 3.00
8 . . . . 3.00
9 Return of the Redeemers 3.00
10 Return of Lillith 3.00
11 The Redeemers, cont. 3.00
12 The Redeemers, cont. 3.00
13 I:Sister Trinity 3.00
14 Redeemers saga again. 3.00
15 F:Sister Trinity. 3.00
16 F:Sister Trinity. 3.00
17 Showdown 3.00
18 Reaction 3.00
19 Carnivale. 3.00
20 Twilight Earth 3.00
21 Lost Souls of Blue
   Moon Mountain 2.50
Spec. Warrior Nun Areala/Razor:

Revenge 3.00
Spec.A Revenge, deluxe 6.00

WARRIORS
1 . . . . 2.50
2 thru 7 . . . . @2.25

WARZONE
Entity, 1995
1 I:Bella & Supra. 3.00
2 F:Bladeback, Alloy, Granite 3.00
3 F:Bladeback. 3.00

WEATHER WOMAN
CPM Manga, 2000
1 signed & limited 20.00
4 thru 8 . . . . @3.00

WEBWITCH
Avatar Press, 1997
0 by Raff Ienco 3.00
1 (of 2) signed. 10.00
1 (of 2) 3.00
2 (of 2) 3.00
Boxed Set, all rare editions 35.00

WEBWITCH: PRELUDE TO WAR
Avatar Press, 1998
1 by Raff Jenco. 3.00
1b Leather cover. 30.00

WEBWITCH: WAR
Avatar Press, 1998
1 (of 2) by Bill Maus 3.00
1b Leather cover. 30.00
2 conclusion 3.00

WEDDING PEACH
Viz Communications, 2003
TPB Vol. 1 . . . . 10.00
TPB Vol. 2 thru Vol. 5. . . . . @10.00
TPB Young Love 10.00

WEIRDFALL
Antarctic Press, 1995
1 I:Weirdfall. 2.75
2 O:Weirdfall. 2.75
3 . . . . 2.75

WEIRDSVILLE
Blindwolf Studios, 1997
1 . . . . 3.50
1 2nd printing 3.00
2 . . . . 3.50
2 2nd printing 3.00
3 . . . . 3.50
3 2nd printing 3.00
4 . . . . 3.50
5 . . . . 3.00
6 The Usual Weirdoes, concl. 3.00
7 . . . . 3.00
8 An American Werewolf in
   Weirdsville, pt.1 (of 2) 3.00
9 An American Werewolf in
   Weirdsville, pt.2. . . . . 3.00
10 . . . . 3.00

WEIRDSVILLE/CRYBABY: HEY YOU TWO
Blindwolf Studios, 1999
1 . . . . 3.00

WEREWOLF
Blackthorne, 1988–89
1 TV tie-in 2.25
2 thru 7 . . . . @2.25

WHAT IS THE FACE?
A.C.E. Comics, 1986
1 SD/FMc,I:New Face. 2.25
2 SD/FMc 2.25
3 SD 2.25

WHISPERS & SHADOWS
Oasis
1 8 1/2 x 11. . . . . 2.25
1a Regular size. 2.25
2 8 1/2 x 11. . . . . 2.25
3 8 1/2 x 11. . . . . 2.25
4 thru 9 . . . . @2.25

WHITE DEVIL
Eternity, 1991
1 thru 6 adult. . . . . @2.50

WHITE ORCHID, THE
Atlantis
1 (of 6) 3.00
2 . . . . 3.00
3 . . . . 3.00
4 . . . . 3.50
5 `Death Trap,' pt.1 . . . . 3.00
6 The Price of Vengeance 3.50

WHITEOUT
Oni Press, 1998
1 (of 4) by Greg Rucka &
 Steve Leiber 3.00
2 . . . . 3.00
3 . . . . 3.00
4 conclusion 3.00
TPB 128-pg. 11.00

WHITEOUT: MELT
Oni Press, 1999
1 (of 4) by Greg Rucka
 & Steve Lieber. 3.00
2 . . . . 3.00
3 . . . . 3.00
4 concl. 3.00
TPB 12.00

WHITE RAVEN
Visionary Publications
1 Government Intrigue 3.00
2 . . . . 3.00
3 Mystery Man Gets Wheels 3.00
4 Facility 3.00
5 V:Douglas 3.00
6 . . . . 3.00
7 . . . . 3.00

WHITLEY STRIEBER'S BEYOND COMMUNION
Caliber, 1997
1 UFO Odyssey 3.00
1 signed 3.00
1 special edition, signed
 by Strieber 7.00
1a 2nd printing 3.00
2 . . . . 3.00
3 . . . . 3.00
4 . . . . 3.00

WICKED
Millennium, 1994
1 thru 4 . . . . @2.50

WICKED: THE RECKONING
Millennium
1 R:Wicked 3.00
2 F:Rachel Blackstone 3.00

WIDOW
Ground Zero, 1996
Cinegraphic Spec.#1: Daughter
 of Darkness 4.00

Wizards of Last Resort #1
© *Blackthorne*

WIDOW/LUXURA: BLOOD LUST
Ground Zero, 1996
Alpha x-over, pt.1 . . . . 3.50
see Luxura/Widow for pt. 2

WIDOW: BOUND BY BLOOD
Ground Zero, 1996
1 thru 5 by Mike Wolfer. . . . . . . @3.50

WIDOW: PROGENY
Ground Zero, 1997
1 by Mike Wolfer & Karl Moline . . . 3.00
2 (of 3) 3.00
3 concl. 3.00

WIDOW: THE COMPLETE WORKS
Ground Zero, 1996
Vol.1 Flesh and Blood 11.00
Vol.1 deluxe 17.00
Vol.2 Kill Me Again. 11.00
Vol.2 deluxe 17.00
Vol.3 Metal Gypsies 11.00
Vol.3 deluxe 17.00

WIDOW
Avatar Press, 1997
0 by Mike Wolfer 4.00
0b Black leather cover 25.00
0 signed 10.00

WIDOW: THE ORIGIN
Avatar Press, 1997
1 (of 3) by Mike Wolfer 4.00
1a leather cover 25.00
2 (of 3) 3.00

WILD, THE
1 and 2 . . . . @2.25
3 thru 7 . . . . @2.25

WILDFLOWER: DARK EUPHORIA
Neko Press, 2004
1 . . . . 3.00
2 . . . . 3.00
1a thru 2a variant (c)s. . . . . . . @4.00

WILDFLOWER
Sirius/Dog Star, 1998
1 by Billy Martinez 2.50
2 thru 6 . . . . @2.50

Neko Press, 2002
TPB Vol.1 Beginnings, rep.
 from 1997 . . . . 15.00

WILDFLOWER: TRIBAL SCREAMS
Neko Press, 2002
1 Martinez (c) 3.00
1a Dark One (c) 5.00
2 thru 4 . . . . @3.00
Spec. Wildflower Y2K, 16-pg. 10.00

WILD KNIGHTS
Eternity, 1988
1 thru 10 . . . . @2.25
Shattered Earth Chron. #1. . . . . . 2.25

WILDLIFE
Antarctic, 1993
1 thru 12 . . . . @2.75

WILDMAN
Miller
1 and 2 . . . . @2.25
3 thru 6 . . . . @2.25

WILD 7
Comicsone.com, 2001
GN #1 by Mikiya Mochizuki, 200-pg. . . . 10.00
GN #2 185-pg. 10.00
GN #3 257-pg. 10.00
GN #4 256-pg. 10.00
GN #5 200-pg. 10.00
GN #6 200-pg. 10.00
GN #7 185-pg. 10.00

WILD THINGZ
ABC Comics, 1998
0 RCI & Armando Huerta 3.00
0a painted cover. 6.00
0b Fan edition 6.00
0c Summer edition 6.00
0d Leather cover, original art 55.00
1 (of 2) RCI 3.00
1b Leather cover. 30.00

All comics prices listed are for *Near Mint* condition.

Xenon #2
© Eclipse

1c virgin cover. 3.00
1d gold cover 6.00
1e Platinum cover. 6.00

WILLOW
Angel Entertainment, 1996
0 commemorative edition 3.00
1 . . . . 3.00
1 black magic foil edition 6.00
2 . . . . 3.00
2 gold edition 8.00
2 nude platinum cover 15.00

WIND BLADE
1 Elford 1st Blair. 40.00

WINGS
A-List Comics, 1997
1 rep. of golden age 2.50
2 . . . . 3.00
3 . . . . 3.00
4 . . . . 3.00
5 . . . . 3.00

WINDRAVEN
Hero Graphics/Blue Comet
1 The Healing,(see Rough Raiders) 3.00

WITCH
Amaze Ink/Slave Labor
Graphics, 2001
1 by Lorna Miller. 3.00
2 . . . . 3.00
3 thru 4 . . . . @3.00
TPB Vol. 1 . . . . 12.00

WIZARD OF TIME
David House, 1986
1 . . . . 2.25
1a 2nd printing(blue). 2.25
2 and 3 . . . . @2.25

WIZARDS OF THE
LAST RESORT
Blackthorne, 1987
1 . . . . 2.50

WOLFF & BYRD,
COUNSELORS OF
THE MACABRE
Exhibit A, 1994
1 . . . . 6.00
2 thru 4 . . . . @3.50
5 thru 11 . . . . @2.50
12 thru 16 BLs . . . . @2.50
17 thru 23. . . . . @2.50
TPB Casefiles Vol. I rep. #1–#4,
      3rd printing 10.00
TPB Casefiles Vol. 2 rep.#5–#8. . . 10.00
TPB Casefiles Vol.III rep.#9–#12. . 11.00
TPB Casefiles Vol.IV rep.#13–#16. 11.00

Xenozoic Tales #3
© Kitchen Sink

TPB Supernatural Law. 8.00
TPB Supernatural Law rep. 8.00
TPB Fright Court rep.. . . . . 10.00
Spec.#1 Greatest Writs (1997) BLs . 3.00
Spec. #1 Secretary Mavis (1998) . . 3.00
Spec. #2 Secretary Mavis (1999) . . 3.00
Becomes:
SUPERNATURAL LAW
Exhibit A Press, 2000
24 . . . . 2.50
25 The end of 1999 . . . . 2.50
26 Black Market Souls. 2.50
27 Creatures of the Night,
      with lawyers. 2.50
28 While the City Doesn't Sleep . . . 2.50
29 thru 31 . . . . @2.50
32 . . . . 3.00
33 thru 35. . . . . @2.50
36 thru 40 . . . . @3.00
Spec. #101 10th anniversary. 3.50
TPB Sonofawitch, rep. 15.00

WORDSMITH
Renegade, 1985
1 . . . . 3.00
2 thru 6 . . . . @2.25
7 thru 12 . . . . @2.25
Series 2, Caliber, 1996
1 thru 6 . . . . @3.00

WORLD HARDBALL
LEAGUE
Titus Press, 1994
1 F:Big Bat 3.00
2 F:Big Bat 3.00
3 Mount Evrest 3.00
4 Juan Hernandez 3.00

WORLD OF ROBOTECH
Academy Comics, 1995
GN Tales of Planets. 13.00

WORLD OF WOOD
Eclipse, 1986
1 thru 4 see color
5 Flying Saucers. 2.25

WORLDS OF FANTASY
Newcomers Publishing, 1995
1 The Jenn Chronicles 3.00

WORLDS OF
H.P. LOVECRAFT
Caliber Tome Press, 1997
1-shot The Alchemist 3.00
1-shot The Tomb. 3.00
1-shot The Lurking Fear 3.00
1-shot Beyond the Walls of Sleep . 3.00

WORLD WAR 2
New England Comics, 2001
3 Eastern Front, pt.2. . . . . 3.50
4 Falaise Pocket 3.50
5 D-Day. 3.50
6 Tarawa 3.50
7 Afrika Korps 3.50
8 Midway. 3.50

WORLD WAR 2:
STALINGRAD
New England Comics, 2000
1 by Ron Ledwell 3.50
2 . . . . 3.50

WOUNDED MAN
Comicsone.com, 2001
GN #1 400-pg. by R. Ikegami 15.00
GN #2 400-pg. 15.00
GN #3 448-pg. 15.00
GN #4 thru #9 200-pg. . . . . @10.00

WRETCH, THE
Caliber, 1996
1 PhH 3.00
2 PhH 3.00
Amaze Ink, 1997
3 PhH 3.00
4 PhH 3.00
5 PhH & Jim Woodyard. 3.00
6 PhH & Bruce McCorkindale 3.00
7 PhH 3.00

WU WEI
Animus, 1995
1 `Debaser'. 2.50
2 Blind Whisper. 2.50
3 . . . . 2.50
4 . . . . 2.50
5 `Testament' pt.5 . . . . 2.50
6 by Oscar Stern. 2.50
7 Explicador 3.00
8 Dead Skin 3.00

Zen Intergalactic Ninja Starquest #3
© Entity

9 Apotheosis or Bang You're Dead. 3.00

WW2
New England Comics, 2003
1-shot Snipers 4.00
1-shot War in the Air 4.00
1-shot Mercenaries 4.00
1-shot U-Boats. 4.00
1-shot Hitler's Special Forces 3.95
1-shot Last Ditch Stand at Berlin. . . 3.95
1-shot Hitler's Paratroopers
 The Assult on Crete. 3.95
1-shot Tobruk. 3.95

WYRD: THE RELUCTANT WARRIOR
Amaze Ink, 1999
1 (of 6) JSn. 3.00
2 . . . . 3.00
3 Telemarketing Horrors 3.00
4 Maxi-Man 3.00
5 . . . . 3.00
6 . . . . 3.00
TPB JSn, 132-pg. 17.00

XANADU
Thoughts & Images, 1988
1 thru 5 . . . . @2.25

XENON
Eclipse, 1987
1 . . . . 3.00
2 thru 23 . . . . @2.25

XENO'S ARROW
Cup O' Tea Studios, 1999
1 by Greg Beettam 2.50
2 thru 10 . . . . @2.50
Radio Comix, 2001
Book 2
1 (of 6) 3.00
2 and 3 . . . . @3.00
4 and 5 . . . . @3.00

XENOZOIC TALES
Kitchen Sink, 1986
1 by Mark Schultz 10.00
1a Reprint 2.50
2 . . . . 5.00
2a Reprint 2.50
3 . . . . 7.00
4 . . . . 6.00
5 thru 7 . . . . @4.00
8 thru 13 . . . . @3.00
14 MSh. 3.00

X-BABES VS. JUSTICE BABES
Personality
1 Spoof/parody 3.00

X-CONS
Parody Press
1 X-Men satire,flip cover. 2.50

X-FARCE
Eclipse, 1992
One-Shot X-Force parody 3.00

X-FLIES BUG HUNT
Twist and Shout, 1997
1 Vampires 3.00
2 Monsters 3.00
3 Aliens 3.00
4 The Truth 3.00
Conspiracy. 3.00
Spec. #1 Flies in Black 3.00

XIOLA
Zion Comics
1 thru 3 F:Kantasia . . . . @2.25
4 Visitor. 2.25

XMEN
1 Parody 2.25

X-1999
Viz
1 I:Kamir Shiro 2.75
2 thru 5 F:Princess Hitane . . . . . @2.75
6 Battle for X-1999 . . . . 2.75
TPB Vol. 3 Serenade 16.00
TPB Vol. 4 Intermezzo 16.00
TPB Vol. 6 Duet. 16.00
TPB Vol. 7 Rhapsody. 16.00
TPB Vol. 8 Crescendo (2002) 16.00
TPB Vol. 9 Requiem 16.00
TPB Vol. 10 thru Vol. 16. . . . . . . @10.00

X-THIEVES
1 . . . . 3.00
2 . . . . 2.25
3 . . . . 2.25

YAHOO
Fantagraphics, 1988
1 thru 4 . . . . @2.25

YAKUZA
Eternity, 1987
1 thru 5 . . . . @2.25

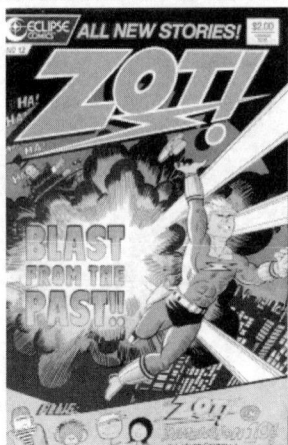

Zot #12
© Fantagraphics

YAWN
Parody Press
1 Spawn parody 2.50
Enigma
1 Spawn parody rep.?. 2.75

YELLOW CABALLERO
Viz Communications, 2001
1 thru 4 Pikachu's New Partner . @3.00

YOUNG DRACULA: PRAYER OF THE VAMPIRE
Boneyard Press, 1997
1 (of 5) sequel to Young Dracula:
 Diary of a Vampire. 3.00
2 Empire of Madness, pt.2 . . . . . . 3.00
3 Children of Madness 3.00
4 Madness Prime 3.00
5 V:Cartiphilus. 4.00

YOUNG MASTERS
New Comics, 1987
1 thru 10 . . . . @2.25

YU-GI-OH!
Viz Communications, 2003
TPB Vol. 1 The Millennium Puzzle . 8.00
TPB Vol. 2 thru Vol. 3. . . . . @8.00
TPB Vol. 4 thru Vol. 6. . . . . @18.00

YUGGOTH CREATURES
Avatar Press, 2004
1 . . . . 4.00
2 thru 3 . . . . @4.00
1a thru 3a wraparound (c). . . . . . @4.00

YUYU HAKUSHO
Viz Communications, 2003
TPB Vol. 1 Goodbye Material World 8.00
TPB Vol. 2 Lonesome Ghosts 8.00
TPB Vol. 3 thru Vol. 5. . . . . @8.00

Classics Illustrated

[Issued As Classic Comics]
001-THE THREE MUSKETEERS
By Alexandre Dumas

10/41 (—-) MKd(a&c),
  Original,10¢ (c) Price 6,800.00
05/43 (10) MKd(a&c),
  No(c)Price; rep 400.00
11/43 (15) MKd(a&c),Long
  Island Independent Ed; 300.00
6/44 (18/20) MKd(a&c),
  Sunrise Times Edition;rep . . . 200.00
7/44 (21) MKd(a&c),Richmond
  Courier Edition;rep 175.00
6/46 (28) MKd(a&c);rep 150.00
4/47 (36) MKd(a&c),
  New CILogo;rep 75.00
6/49 (60) MKd(a&c),CI Logo;rep . . 50.00
10/49 (64) MKd(a&c),CI Logo;rep . 50.00
12/50 (78) MKd(a&c),15¢(c)
  Price; CI Logo;rep 30.00
03/52 (93) MKd(a&c),
  CI Logo;rep 30.00
11/53 (114) CI Logo;rep 25.00
09/56 (134) MKd(a&c),New
  P(c),CI Logo,64 pgs;rep 30.00
03/58 (143) MKd(a&c),P(c),
  CI Logo,64 pgs;rep 25.00
05/59 (150) GE&RC New Art,
  P(c),CILogo;rep 30.00
03/61 (149) GE&RC,P(c),
  CI Logo;rep 18.00
62-63 (167) GE&RC,P(c),
  CI Logo;rep 18.00
04/64 (167) GE&RC,P(c),
  CI Logo;rep 18.00
01/65 (167) GE&RC,P(c),
  CI Logo;rep 18.00
03/66 (167) GE&RC,P(c),
  CI Logo;rep 18.00
11/67 (166) GE&RC,P(c),
  CI Logo;rep 18.00
Sp/69 (166) GE&RC,P(c),25¢(c)
  Price,CILogo, Rigid(c);rep 18.00

CI #1, The Three Musketeers
© Gilberton Publications

Sp/71 (169) GE&RC,P(c),
  CI Logo,Rigid(c);rep 18.00

002-IVANHOE
By Sir Walter Scott

1941 (—-) EA,MKd(c),Original . 3,000.00
05/43 (1) EA,MKd(c),word "Presents"
  Removed From(c);rep 375.00
11/43 (15) EA,MKd(c),Long Island
  Independent Edition;rep 250.00
06/44 (18/20) EA,MKd(c),Sunrise
  Times Edition;rep. 200.00
07/44 (21) EA,MKd(c),Richmond
  Courier Edition;rep 175.00
06/46 (28) EA,MKd(c),rep 150.00
07/47 (36) EA,MKd(c),New
  CI Logo; rep. 100.00
06/49 (60) EA,MKd(c),CI Logo;rep 50.00
10/49 (64) EA,MKd(c),CI Logo;rep 40.00
12/50 (78) EA,MKd(c),15¢(c)
  Price; CI Logo;rep 30.00
11/51 (89) EA,MKd(c),CI Logo;rep 25.00
04/53 (106) EA,MKd(c),CI
  Logo;rep 20.00
07/54 (121) EA,MKd(c),CI
  Logo;rep 30.00
01/57 (136) NN New Art,New
  P(c),CI Logo;rep 30.00
01/58 (142) NN,P(c),CI Logo;rep . . 18.00
11/59 (153) NN,P(c),CI Logo;rep . . 18.00
03/61 (149) NN,P(c),CI Logo;rep . . 18.00
62/63 (167) NN,P(c),CI Logo;rep . . 15.00
05/64 (167) NN,P(c),CI Logo;rep . . 15.00
01/65 (167) NN,P(c),CI Logo;rep . . 15.00
03/66 (167) NN,P(c),CI Logo;rep . . 15.00
09/67 (166) NN,P(c),CI Logo;rep . . 15.00
1968 (166) NN,P(c),CI Logo;rep . . 15.00
Wr/69 (169) NN,P(c),CI
  Logo Rigid(c);rep 15.00
Wr/71 (169) NN,P(c),CI
  Logo,Rigid(c);rep 15.00

003-THE COUNT OF MONTE CRISTO
By Alexandre Dumas

03/42 (—-) ASm(a&c),Orig. 2,000.00
05/43 (10) ASm(a&c);rep 300.00
11/43 (15) ASm(a&c),Long Island
  Independent Edition;rep 250.00
06/44 (18/20) ASm(a&c),
  Sunrise Times Edition;rep . . . 225.00
06/44 (20) ASm(a&c),Sunrise
  Times Edition;rep. 200.00
07/44 (21) ASm(a&c),Richmond
  Courier Edition;rep 175.00
06/46 (28) ASm(a&c);rep 150.00
04/47 (36) ASm(a&c),New
  CI Logo; rep. 100.00
06/49 (60) ASm(a&c),CI
  Logo;rep 60.00
08/49 (62) ASm(a&c),CI
  Logo;rep 75.00
05/50 (71) ASm(a&c),CI
  Logo;rep 50.00
09/51 (87) ASm(a&c),15¢(c)
  Price, CI Logo;rep 30.00
11/53 (113) ASm(a&c),
  CI Logo; rep. 25.00
11/56 (—-) LC New Art,New
  P(c), CI Logo;rep 25.00
03/58 (135) LC,P(c),CI Logo;rep . . 30.00
11/59 (153) LC,P(c),CI Logo;rep . . 18.00

03/61 (161) LC,P(c),CI Logo;rep . . 18.00
62/63 (167) LC,P(c),CI Logo;rep . . 15.00
07/64 (167) LC,P(c),CI Logo;rep . . 15.00
07/65 (167) LC,P(c),CI Logo;rep . . 15.00
07/66 (167) LC,P(c),CI Logo;rep . . 15.00
1968 (166) LC,P(c),25¢(c)
  Price, CI Logo;rep 15.00
Wn/69 (169) LC,P(c),CI Logo,
  Rigid(c);rep 15.00

004-THE LAST OF THE MOHICANS
By James Fenimore Cooper

08/42 (—-) RR(a&c),Original . . 1,500.00
06/43 (12) RR(a&c),Price
  Balloon Deleted;rep. 300.00
11/43 (15) RR(a&c),Long Island
  Independent Edition;rep 250.00
06/44 (20) RR(a&c),Long Island
  Independent Edition;rep 225.00
07/44 (21) RR(a&c),Queens
  Home News Edition;rep. 200.00
06/46 (28) RR(a&c);rep 150.00
04/47 (36) RR(a&c),New
  CI Logo; rep. 100.00
06/49 (60) RR(a&c),CI Logo;rep . . 50.00
10/49 (64) RR(a&c),CI Logo;rep . . 35.00
12/50 (78) RR(a&c),15¢(c)
  Price,CI Logo rep 35.00
11/51 (89) RR(a&c),CI Logo;rep . . 30.00
03/54 (117) RR(a&c),CI Logo;rep . 28.00
11/56 (135) RR,New P(c),
  CI Logo; rep. 28.00
11/57 (141) RR,P(c),CI Logo;rep . . 30.00
05/59 (150) JSe&StA New Art;
  P(c), CI Logo;rep. 35.00
03/61 (161) JSe&StA,P(c),CI
  Logo; rep 15.00
62/63 (167) JSe&StA,P(c),CI
  Logo; rep 15.00
06/64 (167) JSe&StA,P(c),CI
  Logo; rep 15.00
08/65 (167) JSe&StA,P(c),CI
  Logo; rep 15.00
08/66 (167) JSe&StA,P(c),CI
  Logo; rep 15.00

CI #4, The Last of the Mohicans
© Gilberton Publications

All comics prices listed are for *Near Mint* condition.

1967 **(166)** JSe&StA,P(c),25¢(c)
Price, CI Logo;rep 15.00
Sp/69 **(169)** JSe&StA,P(c),CI
Logo, Rigid(c);rep 15.00

005-MOBY DICK
By Herman Melville
09/42 **(—-)** LZ(a&c),Original . . . 2,100.00
05/43 **(10)** LZ(a&c),Conray Products
Edition, No(c)Price;rep 350.00
11/43 **(15)** LZ(a&c),Long Island
Independent Edition;rep 275.00
06/44 **(18/20)** LZ(a&c),Sunrise
Times Edition;rep. 250.00
07/44 **(20)** LZ(a&c),Sunrise
Times Edition;rep. 225.00
07/44 **(21)** LZ(a&c),Sunrise
Times Edition;rep. 200.00
06/46 **(28)** LZ(a&c);rep. 150.00
04/47 **(36)** LZ(a&c),New CI
Logo;rep 100.00
06/49 **(60)** LZ(a&c),CI Logo;rep. . . 50.00
08/49 **(62)** LZ(a&c),CI Logo;rep. . . 55.00
05/50 **(71)** LZ(a&c),CI Logo;rep. . . 40.00
09/51 **(87)** LZ(a&c),15¢(c)
Price, CI Logo;rep 30.00
04/54 **(118)** LZ(a&c),CI Logo;rep . . 25.00
03/56 **(131)** NN New Art,New
P(c), CI Logo;rep 35.00
05/57 **(138)** NN,P(c),CI Logo;rep. . 18.00
01/59 **(148)** NN,P(c),CI Logo;rep. . 18.00
09/60 **(158)** NN,P(c),CI Logo;rep. . 18.00
62/63 **(167)** NN,P(c),CI Logo;rep. . 18.00
06/64 **(167)** NN,P(c),CI Logo;rep. . 18.00
07/65 **(167)** NN,P(c),CI Logo;rep. . 18.00
03/66 **(167)** NN,P(c),CI Logo;rep. . 18.00
09/67 **(166)** NN,P(c),CI Logo;rep. . 18.00
Wn/69 **(166)** NN,P(c),25¢(c) Price,
CI Logo, Rigid(c);rep 25.00
Wn/71 **(169)** NN,P(c),CI Logo;rep . 20.00

006-A TALE OF TWO CITIES
By Charles Dickens
11/42 **(—-)** StM(a&c),Original . . 1,500.00
09/43 **(14)** StM(a&c),No(c)
Price; rep 300.00
03/44 **(18)** StM(a&c),Long Island
Independent Edition;rep 275.00
06/44 **(20)** StM(a&c),Sunrise
Times Edition;rep. 235.00
06/46 **(28)** StM(a&c);rep 150.00
09/48 **(51)** StM(a&c),New CI
Logo; rep 75.00
10/49 **(64)** StM(a&c),CI
Logo;rep 40.00
12/50 **(78)** StM(a&c),15¢(c)
Price, CI Logo; rep 30.00
11/51 **(89)** StM(a&c),CI Logo;rep. . 30.00
03/54 **(117)** StM(a&c),CI
Logo;rep 25.00
05/56 **(132)** JO New Art,New
P(c), CI Logo;rep. 35.00
09/57 **(140)** JO,P(c),CI Logo;rep . . 15.00
11/57 **(147)** JO,P(c),CI Logo;rep . . 15.00
09/59 **(152)** JO,P(c),CI Logo;rep 250.00
11/59 **(153)** JO,P(c),CI Logo;rep. . 18.00
03/61 **(149)** JO,P(c),CI Logo;rep. . 18.00
62/63 **(167)** JO,P(c),CI Logo;rep. . 15.00
06/64 **(167)** JO,P(c),CI Logo;rep. . 15.00
08/65 **(167)** JO,P(c),CI Logo;rep. . 15.00
05/67 **(166)** JO,P(c),CI Logo;rep. . 15.00
Fl/68 **(166)** JO,NN New P(c),
25¢(c)Price,CI Logo;rep 25.00
Sr/70 **(169)** JO,NN P(c),CI
Logo, Rigid(c);rep 20.00

007-ROBIN HOOD
By Howard Pyle
12/42 **(—-)** LZ(a&c),Original . . 1,400.00
06/43 **(12)** LZ(a&c),P.D.C.
on(c) Deleted;rep. 300.00
03/44 **(18)** LZ(a&c),Long Island
Independent Edition;rep 225.00
06/44 **(20)** LZ(a&c),Nassau
Bulletin Edition;rep 250.00
10/44 **(22)** LZ(a&c),Queens
City Times Edition;rep 225.00
06/46 **(28)** LZ(a&c),rep 150.00
09/48 **(51)** LZ(a&c),New CI
Logo;rep 75.00
06/49 **(60)** LZ(a&c),CI Logo;rep. . 35.00
10/49 **(64)** LZ(a&c),CI Logo;rep. . 32.00
12/50 **(78)** LZ(a&c),CI Logo;rep. . 32.00
07/52 **(97)** LZ(a&c),CI Logo;rep. . 30.00
03/53 **(106)** LZ(a&c),CI Logo;rep. . 30.00
07/54 **(121)** LZ(a&c),CI Logo;rep. . 30.00
11/55 **(129)** LZ,New P(c),
CI Logo;rep 35.00
01/57 **(136)** JkS New Art,P(c);rep . 30.00
03/58 **(143)** JkS,P(c),CI Logo;rep . 18.00
11/59 **(153)** JkS,P(c),CI Logo;rep . 15.00
10/61 **(164)** JkS,P(c),CI Logo;rep . 15.00
62/63 **(167)** JkS,P(c),CI Logo;rep . 15.00
06/64 **(167)** JkS,P(c),CI Logo;rep . 20.00
05/65 **(167)** JkS,P(c),CI Logo;rep . 15.00
07/66 **(167)** JkS,P(c),CI Logo;rep . 15.00
12/67 **(166)** JkS,P(c),CI Logo;rep . 20.00
Sr/69 **(169)** JkS,P(c),CI
Logo, Rigid(c);rep 15.00

008-ARABIAN KNIGHTS
By Antoine Galland
03/43 **(—-)** LCh(a&c),Original . . 2,200.00
09/43 **(14)** LCh(a&c);rep 700.00
01/44 **(17)** LCh(a&c),Long Island
Independent Edition;rep 750.00
06/44 **(20)** LCh(a&c),Nassau
Bulletin Edition,64 pgs;rep. . . 600.00
06/46 **(28)** LCh(a&c);rep 400.00
09/48 **(51)** LCh(a&c),New CI
Logo; rep 400.00
10/49 **(64)** LCh(a&c),CI
Logo;rep 300.00
12/50 **(78)** LCh(a&c),CI
Logo;rep 250.00
10/61 **(164)** ChB New Art,P(c),
CI Logo;rep 225.00

009-LES MISERABLES
By Victor Hugo
03/43 **(—-)** RLv(a&c),Original . . 1,300.00
09/43 **(14)** RLv(a&c);rep 300.00
03/44 **(18)** RLv(a&c),Nassau
Bulletin Edition;rep 275.00
06/44 **(20)** RLv(a&c),Richmond
Courier Edition;rep 250.00
06/46 **(28)** RLv(a&c);rep 200.00
09/48 **(51)** RLv(a&c),New CI
Logo; rep 100.00
05/50 **(71)** RLv(a&c),CI
Logo;rep 75.00
09/51 **(87)** RLv(a&c),CI Logo,
15¢(c)Price;rep 60.00
03/61 **(161)** NN New Art,GMc
New P(c), CI Logo;rep. 60.00
09/63 **(167)** NN,GMc P(c),CI
Logo; rep 35.00
12/65 **(167)** NN,GMc P(c),CI
Logo; rep 35.00
1968 **(166)** NN,GMc P(c),25¢(c)
Price, CI Logo;rep 35.00

010-ROBINSON CRUSOE
By Daniel Defoe
04/43 **(—-)** StM(a&c),Original . . 1,100.00
09/43 **(14)** StM(a&c);rep 350.00
03/44 **(18)** StM(a&c),Nassau Bulletin
Ed.,'Bill of Rights'Pge.64;rep. 300.00
06/44 **(20)** StM(a&c),Queens
Home News Edition;rep. 250.00
??/45 **(23)** StM(a&c);rep 150.00
06/46 **(28)** StM(a&c);rep 150.00
09/48 **(51)** StM(a&c),New CI
Logo; rep 75.00
10/49 **(64)** StM(a&c),CI Logo;rep. . 50.00
12/50 **(78)** StM(a&c),15¢(c)
Price, CI Logo;rep 35.00
07/52 **(97)** StM(a&c),CI Logo;rep. . 32.00
12/53 **(114)** StM(a&c),CI
Logo;rep 30.00
01/56 **(130)** StM,New P(c),CI
Logo; rep 32.00
09/57 **(140)** SmC New Art,P(c),
CI Logo; rep. 32.00
11/59 **(153)** SmC,P(c),CI Logo;rep 15.00
10/61 **(164)** SmC,P(c),CI Logo;rep 15.00
62/63 **(167)** SmC,P(c),CI Logo;rep 18.00
07/64 **(167)** SmC,P(c),CI Logo;rep 20.00
05/65 **(167)** SmC,P(c),CI Logo;rep 15.00
06/66 **(167)** SmC,P(c),CI Logo;rep 18.00
Fl/68 **(166)** SmC,P(c),CI Logo,
25¢(c)Price;rep 18.00
1968 **(166)** SmC,P(c),CI Logo,No
Twin Circle Ad;rep 15.00
Sr/70 **(169)** SmC,P(c),CI Logo,
Rigid(c);rep 15.00

011-DON QUIXOTE
By Miguel de Cervantes Saavedra
05/43 **(—)** LZ(a&c),Original . . . 1,200.00
03/44 **(18)** LZ(a&c),Nassau
Bulletin Edition;rep 300.00
07/44 **(21)** LZ(a&c),Queens
Home News Edition;rep. 250.00
06/46 **(28)** LZ(a&c);rep 150.00
08/53 **(110)** LZ,TO New P(c),New
CI Logo;rep 50.00
05/60 **(156)** LZ,TO P(c),Pages
Reduced to 48,CI Logo;rep. . . 30.00
1962 **(165)** LZ,TO P(c),CI Logo;rep 20.00
01/64 **(167)** LZ,TO P(c),CI
Logo;rep 20.00
11/65 **(167)** LZ,TO P(c),CI
Logo;rep 20.00

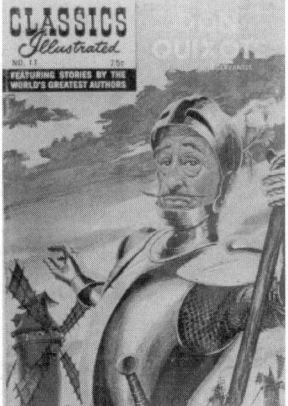

CI #11, Robin Hood
© Gilberton Publications

1968 **(166)** LZ,TO P(c),CI Logo,
25¢(c)Price;rep 40.00

012-RIP VAN WINKLE & THE HEADLESS HORSEMAN
By Washington Irving
06/43 **(— —)** RLv(a&c),Original. 1,200.00
11/43 **(15)** RLv(a&c),Long Island
Independent Edition;rep 275.00
06/44 **(20)** RLv(a&c),Long Island
Independent Edition;rep 250.00
10/44 **(22)** RLv(a&c),Queens
City Times Edition;rep 225.00
06/46 **(28)** RLv(a&c);rep 150.00
06/49 **(60)** RLv(a&c),New CI
Logo;rep 75.00
08/49 **(62)** RLv(a&c),CI
Logo;rep 45.00
05/50 **(71)** RLv(a&c),CI
Logo;rep 35.00
11/51 **(89)** RLv(a&c),15¢(c)
Price, CI Logo;rep 30.00
04/54 **(118)** RLv(a&c),CI
Logo;rep 32.00
05/56 **(132)** RLv,New P(c),
CI Logo; rep 35.00
05/59 **(150)** NN New Art;P(c),
CI Logo; rep 35.00
09/60 **(158)** NN,P(c),CI Logo;rep. . 20.00
62/63 **(167)** NN,P(c),CI Logo;rep. . 20.00
12/63 **(167)** NN,P(c),CI Logo;rep. . 20.00
04/65 **(167)** NN,P(c),CI Logo;rep. . 22.00
04/66 **(167)** NN,P(c),CI Logo;rep. . 20.00
1969 **(166)** NN,P(c),CI Logo,
25¢(c)Price,Rigid(c);rep. 26.00
Sr/70 **(169)** NN,P(c),CI Logo,
Rigid(c);rep 25.00

013-DR. JEKYLL AND MR.HYDE
By Robert Louis Stevenson
08/43 **(--)** AdH(a&c),Original. . 1,600.00
11/43 **(15)** AdH(a&c),Long Island
Independent Edition;rep 400.00
06/44 **(20)** AdH(a&c),Long Island
Independent Edition;rep 275.00
06/46 **(28)** AdH(a&c),No(c)
Price; rep 225.00
06/49 **(60)** AdH,HcK New(c),New CI
Logo,Pgs.reduced to 48;rep . . 75.00
08/49 **(62)** AdH,HcK(c),CI
Logo;rep 45.00
05/50 **(71)** AdH,HcK(c),CI
Logo;rep 40.00
09/51 **(87)** AdH,HcK(c),Erroneous
Return of Original Date,
CI Logo;rep 40.00
10/53 **(112)** LC New Art,New
P(c), CI Logo;rep 40.00
11/59 **(153)** LC,P(c),CI Logo;rep . . 20.00
03/61 **(161)** LC,P(c),CI Logo;rep . . 20.00
62/63 **(167)** LC,P(c),CI Logo;rep . . 20.00
08/64 **(167)** LC,P(c),CI Logo;rep . . 20.00
11/65 **(167)** LC,P(c),CI Logo;rep . . 20.00
1968 **(166)** LC,P(c),CI Logo,
25¢(c)Price;rep 22.00
Wr/69 **(169)** LC,P(c),CI Logo,
Rigid(c);rep 20.00

014-WESTWARD HO!
By Charles Kingsley
09/43 **(--)** ASm(a&c),Orig. 2,500.00
11/43 **(15)** ASm(a&c),Long Island
Independent Edition;rep 750.00
07/44 **(21)** ASm(a&c);rep 650.00
06/46 **(28)** ASm(a&c),No(c)

Price; rep 450.00
11/48 **(53)** ASm(a&c),Pages reduced
to 48, New CI Logo;rep 400.00

015-UNCLE TOM'S CABIN
By Harriet Beecher Stowe
11/43 **(—-)** RLv(a&c),Original . . 1,000.00
11/43 **(15)** RLv(a&c),Blank
Price Circle, Long Island
Independent Ed.;rep 300.00
07/44 **(21)** RLv(a&c),Nassau
Bulletin Edition;rep 250.00
06/46 **(28)** RLv(a&c),No(c)
Price; rep 200.00
11/48 **(53)** RLv(a&c),Pages Reduced
to 48, New CI Logo;rep 75.00
05/50 **(71)** RLv(a&c),CI Logo;rep. . 45.00
11/51 **(89)** RLv(a&c),15¢(c)
Price, CI Logo;rep 45.00
03/54 **(117)** RLv,New P(c),CI
Logo, Lettering Changes;rep. . 32.00
09/55 **(128)** RLv,P(c),"Picture
Progress"Promotion,CI
Logo;rep 22.00
03/57 **(137)** RLv,P(c),CI Logo;rep . 15.00
09/58 **(146)** RLv,P(c),CI Logo;rep . 15.00
01/60 **(154)** RLv,P(c),CI Logo;rep . 15.00
03/61 **(161)** RLv,P(c),CI Logo;rep . 17.00
62/63 **(167)** RLv,P(c),CI Logo;rep . 15.00
06/64 **(167)** RLv,P(c),CI Logo;rep . 15.00
05/65 **(167)** RLv,P(c),CI Logo;rep . 15.00
05/67 **(166)** RLv,P(c),CI Logo;rep . 15.00
Wr/69 **(166)** RLv,P(c),CI
Logo, Rigid(c);rep 26.00
Sr/70 **(169)** RLv,P(c),CI
Logo, Rigid(c);rep 25.00

016-GULLIVER'S TRAVELS
By Johnathan Swift
12/43 **(— —)** LCh(a&c),Original. 1,000.00
06/44 **(18/20)** LCh(a&c),Queen's
Home News Edition,No(c)Price;
rep 275.00
10/44 **(22)** LCh(a&c),Queen's
Home News Editon;rep 225.00
06/46 **(28)** LCh(a&c);rep 150.00
06/49 **(60)** LCh(a&c),Pgs. Reduced
To 48, New CI Logo;rep 75.00
08/49 **(62)** LCh(a&c),CI Logo;rep . 45.00
10/49 **(64)** LCh(a&c),CI Logo;rep . 45.00
12/50 **(78)** LCh(a&c),15¢(c)
Price, CI Logo;rep 35.00
11/51 **(89)** LCh(a&c),CI Logo;rep. . 30.00
03/60 **(155)** LCh,New P(c),CI
Logo; rep 35.00
1962 **(165)** LCh,P(c),CI Logo;rep . 20.00
05/64 **(167)** LCh,P(c),CI Logo;rep . 20.00
11/65 **(167)** LCh,P(c),CI Logo;rep . 20.00
1968 **(166)** LCh,P(c),CI Logo,
25¢(c)Price;rep 20.00
Wr/69 **(169)** LCh,P(c),CI
Logo, Rigid(c);rep 20.00

017-THE DEERSLAYER
By James Fenimore Cooper
01/44 **(— —)** LZ(a&c),Original . . . 900.00
03/44 **(18)** LZ(a&c),No(c)Price;
rep 275.00
10/44 **(22)** LZ(a&c),Queen's
City Times Edition;rep 200.00
06/46 **(28)** LZ(a&c);rep 150.00
06/49 **(60)** LZ(a&c),Pgs. Reduced
to 48,New CI Logo;rep 75.00
10/49 **(64)** LZ(a&c),CI Logo;rep. . . 35.00
07/51 **(85)** LZ(a&c),15¢(c)
Price, CI Logo;rep 30.00
04/54 **(118)** LZ(a&c),CI Logo;rep. . 28.00
05/56 **(132)** LZ(a&c),CI Logo;rep. . 25.00
11/66 **(167)** LZ(a&c),CI Logo;rep. . 25.00

CC #17, The Deerslayer
© *Gilberton Publications*

1968 **(166)** LZ,StA New P(c),CI
Logo, 25¢(c)Price;rep 35.00

Sg/71 **(169)** LZ,StA P(c),CI Logo,
Rigid(c), Letters From Parents
and Educators;rep 25.00

018-THE HUNCHBACK OF NOTRE DAME
By Victor Hugo
03/44 **(—-)** ASm(a&c),Original
Gilberton Edition 1,200.00
03/44 **(—-)** ASm(a&c),Original
Island Publications Edition . 1,000.00
06/44 **(18/20)** ASm(a&c),Queens
Home News Edition;rep. 300.00
10/44 **(22)** ASm(a&c),Queens
City Times Edition;rep 250.00
06/46 **(28)** ASm(a&c);rep 225.00
06/49 **(60)** ASm,HcK New(c)8 Pgs.
Deleted, New CI Logo;rep. . . . 75.00
08/49 **(62)** ASm,HcK(c),CI
Logo;rep 40.00
12/50 **(78)** ASm,HcK(c),15¢(c)
Price; CI Logo;rep 35.00
11/51 **(89)** ASm,HcK(c),CI
Logo;rep 32.00
04/54 **(118)** ASm,HcK(c),CI
Logo;rep 35.00
09/57 **(140)** ASm,New P(c),CI
Logo; rep 32.00
09/58 **(146)** ASm,P(c),CI Logo;rep 32.00
09/60 **(158)** GE&RC New Art,GMc
New P(c),CI Logo;rep 20.00
1962 **(165)** GE&RC,GMc P(c),CI
Logo; rep 20.00
09/63 **(167)** GE&RC,GMc P(c),CI
Logo; rep 20.00
10/64 **(167)** GE&RC,GMc P(c),CI
Logo; rep 20.00
04/66 **(167)** GE&RC,GMc P(c),CI
Logo; rep 20.00
1968 **(166)** GE&RC,GMc P(c),CI
Logo, 25¢(c)Price;rep 20.00
Sr/70 **(169)** GE&RC,GMc P(c),CI
Logo, Rigid(c);rep 20.00

019-HUCKLEBERRY FINN
By Mark Twain
04/44 **(—-)** LZ(a&c),Original
Gilberton Edition 750.00
04/44 **(—-)** LZ(a&c),Original Island
Publications Company Ed. . . 800.00

03/44 **(18)** LZ(a&c),Nassau
    Bulletin Editon;rep 300.00
10/44 **(22)** LZ(a&c),Queens City
    Times Edition;rep. 250.00
06/46 **(28)** LZ(a&c);rep 200.00
06/49 **(60)** LZ(a&c),New CI Logo,
    Pgs.Reduced to 48;rep 75.00
08/49 **(62)** LZ(a&c),CI Logo;rep. . . 40.00
12/50 **(78)** LZ(a&c),CI Logo;rep. . . 35.00
11/51 **(89)** LZ(a&c),CI Logo;rep. . . 30.00
03/54 **(117)** LZ(a&c),CI Logo;rep . . 30.00
03/56 **(131)** FrG New Art,New
    P(c), CI Logo; rep 30.00
09/57 **(140)** FrG,P(c),CI Logo;rep . 20.00
05/59 **(150)** FrG,P(c),CI Logo;rep . 20.00
09/60 **(158)** FrG,P(c),CI Logo;rep . 20.00
1962 **(165)** FrG,P(c),CI Logo;rep . . 20.00
62/63 **(167)** FrG,P(c),CI Logo;rep . 20.00
06/64 **(167)** FrG,P(c),CI Logo;rep . 20.00
06/65 **(167)** FrG,P(c),CI Logo;rep . 20.00
10/65 **(167)** FrG,P(c),CI Logo;rep . 20.00
09/67 **(166)** FrG,P(c),CI Logo;rep . 20.00
Wr/69 **(166)** FrG,P(c),CI Logo,
    25¢(c)Price, Rigid(c);rep 20.00
Sr/70 **(169)** FrG,P(c),CI Logo,
    Rigid(c);rep 20.00

020-THE CORSICAN BROTHERS
By Alexandre Dumas

06/44 **(—-)** ASm(a&c),Original
    Gilberton Edition 650.00
06/44 **(—-)** ASm(a&c),Original
    Courier Edition. 550.00
06/44 **(—-)** ASm(a&c),Original Long
    Island Independent Edition . . 550.00
10/44 **(22)** ASm(a&c),Queens
    City Times Edition;rep 275.00
06/46 **(28)** ASm(a&c);rep. 250.00
06/49 **(60)** ASm(a&c),No(c)Price,
    New CI Logo,Pgs. Reduced
    to 48;rep 225.00
08/49 **(62)** ASm(a&c),CI
    Logo;rep 165.00
12/50 **(78)** ASm(a&c),15¢(c)
    Price, CI Logo;rep 150.00
07/52 **(97)** ASm(a&c),CI
    Logo;rep 135.00

021-FAMOUS MYSTERIES
By Sir Arthur Conan Doyle
Guy de Maupassant
& Edgar Allan Poe

07/44 **(—-)** AdH,LZ,ASm(a&c),
    Original Gilberton Edition . . 1,300.00
07/44 **(—-)** AdH,LZ,ASm(a&c),
    Original Island Publications
    Edition; No Date or Indicia 1,350.00
07/44 **(—-)** AdH,LZ,ASm(a&c),
    Original Richmond Courier
    Edition. 1,100.00
10/44 **(22)** AdH,LZ,ASm(a&c),
    Nassau Bulletin Edition;rep . . 450.00
09/46 **(30)** AdH,LZ,ASm(a&c);
    rep. 350.00
08/49 **(62)** AdH,LZ,ASm(a&c),
    New CI Logo;rep 300.00
04/50 **(70)** AdH,LZ,ASm(a&c),
    CI Logo;rep 275.00
07/51 **(85)** AdH,LZ,ASm(a&c),
    15¢(c) Price,CI Logo;rep 250.00
12/53 **(114)** ASm,AdH,LZ,New
    P(c), CI Logo;rep. 250.00

022-THE PATHFINDER
By James Fenimore Cooper

10/44 **(—-)** LZ(a&c),Original
    Gilberton Edition 600.00

10/44 **(—-)** LZ(a&c),Original
    Island Publications Edition; . . 450.00
10/44 **(—-)** LZ(a&c),Original
    Queens County Times Edition450.00
09/46 **(30)** LZ(a&c),No(c)
    Price;rep 150.00
06/49 **(60)** LZ(a&c),New CI Logo,
    Pgs.Reduced To 48;rep. 50.00
08/49 **(62)** LZ(a&c),CI Logo;rep. . . 45.00
04/50 **(70)** LZ(a&c),CI Logo;rep. . . 35.00
07/51 **(85)** LZ(a&c),15¢(c)
    Price, CI Logo;rep 32.00
04/54 **(118)** LZ(a&c),CI Logo;rep. . 30.00
05/56 **(132)** LZ(a&c),CI Logo;rep. . 30.00
09/58 **(146)** LZ(a&c),CI Logo;rep. . 35.00
11/63 **(167)** LZ,NN New P(c),CI
    Logo; rep 30.00
12/65 **(167)** LZ,NN P(c),CI
    Logo;rep 30.00
08/67 **(166)** LZ,NN P(c),CI
    Logo;rep 30.00

023-OLIVER TWIST
By Charles Dickens
(First Classic produced by the Iger shop)

07/45 **(—-)** AdH(a&c),Original . . . 600.00
09/46 **(30)** AdH(a&c),Price
    Circle is Blank;rep 400.00
06/49 **(60)** AdH(a&c),Pgs. Reduced
    To 48, New CI Logo;rep 50.00
08/49 **(62)** AdH(a&c),CI
    Logo;rep 45.00
05/50 **(71)** AdH(a&c),CI
    Logo;rep 35.00
07/51 **(85)** AdH(a&c),15¢(c)
    Price CI Logo;rep 32.00
04/52 **(94)** AdH(a&c),CI
    Logo;rep 32.00
04/54 **(118)** AdH(a&c),CI
    Logo;rep 30.00
01/57 **(136)** AdH,New P(c),CI
    Logo; rep 30.00
05/59 **(150)** AdH,P(c),CI Logo;rep . 25.00
1961 **(164)** AdH,P(c),CI Logo;rep . 25.00
10/61 **(164)** GE&RC New Art,P(c),
    CI Logo;rep 35.00
62/63 **(167)** GE&RC,P(c),CI
    Logo; rep 15.00
08/64 **(167)** GE&RC,P(c),CI
    Logo; rep 15.00
12/65 **(167)** GE&RC,P(c),
    CI Logo;rep 15.00

CI #24, A Connecticut Yankee in King Arthur's Court © Gilberton Publications

1968 **(166)** GE&RC,P(c),CI
    Logo, 25¢(c)Price;rep 15.00
Wr/69 **(169)** GE&RC,P(c),CI
    Logo, Rigid(c);rep 15.00

024-A CONNECTICUT YANKEE IN KING ARTHUR'S COURT
By Mark Twain

09/45 **(—-)** JH(a&c),Original 450.00
09/46 **(30)** JH(a&c),Price Circle
    Blank;rep 150.00
06/49 **(60)** JH(a&c),8 Pages
    Deleted,New CI Logo;rep 50.00
08/49 **(62)** JH(a&c),CI Logo;rep. . . 45.00
05/50 **(71)** JH(a&c),CI Logo;rep. . . 35.00
09/51 **(87)** JH(a&c),15¢(c) Price
    CI Logo;rep 30.00
07/54 **(121)** JH(a&c),CI Logo;rep. . 30.00
09/57 **(140)** JkS New Art,New
    P(c),CI Logo; rep. 35.00
11/59 **(153)** JkS,P(c),CI Logo;rep . 18.00
1961 **(164)** JkS,P(c),CI Logo;rep. . 15.00
62/63 **(167)** JkS,P(c),CI Logo;rep . 15.00
07/64 **(167)** JkS,P(c),CI Logo;rep . 15.00
06/66 **(167)** JkS,P(c),CI Logo;rep . 15.00
1968 **(166)** JkS,P(c),CI logo,
    25¢(c)Price;rep 15.00
Sg/71 **(169)** JkS,P(c),CI Logo,
    Rigid(c);rep 15.00

025-TWO YEARS BEFORE THE MAST
By Richard Henry Dana Jr.

10/45 **(—-)** RWb,DvH,Original; . . 450.00
09/46 **(30)** RWb,DvH,Price Circle
    Blank;rep 150.00
06/49 **(60)** RWb,DvH,8 Pages
    Deleted,New CI Logo;rep 50.00
08/49 **(62)** RWb,DvH,CI Logo;rep . 45.00
05/50 **(71)** RWb,DvH,CI Logo;rep . 35.00
07/51 **(85)** RWb,DvH,15¢(c) Price
    CI Logo;rep 30.00
12/53 **(114)** RWb,DvH,CI Logo;rep 28.00
05/60 **(156)** RWb,DvH,New P(c),
    CI Logo, 3 Pgs. Replaced
    By Fillers;rep 32.00
12/63 **(167)** RWb,DvH,P(c),CI
    Logo; rep 15.00
12/65 **(167)** RWb,DvH,P(c),CI
    Logo; rep 15.00
09/67 **(166)** RWb,DvH,P(c),CI
    Logo; rep 15.00
Wr/69 **(169)** RWb,DvH,25¢(c)
    Price, CI Logo,Rigid(c);rep . . . 15.00

026-FRANKENSTEIN
By Mary Wollstonecraft Shelley

12/45 **(—-)** RWb&ABr(a&c),
    Original 1,400.00
09/46 **(30)** RWb&ABr(a&c),
    Price Circle Blank;rep 350.00
06/49 **(60)** RWb&ABr(a&c),
    New CI Logo;rep 175.00
08/49 **(62)** RWb&ABr(a&c),
    CI Logo;rep 165.00
05/50 **(71)** RWb&ABr(a&c),
    CI Logo;rep 75.00
04/51 **(82)** RWb&ABr(a&c),
    15¢(c) Price,CI Logo;rep 65.00
03/54 **(117)** RWb&ABr(a&c),
    CI Logo;rep 30.00
09/58 **(146)** RWb&ABr,NS
    New P(c), CI Logo; rep 35.00
11/59 **(153)** RWb&ABr,NS
    P(c),CI Logo; rep. 50.00
01/61 **(160)** RWb&ABr,NS
    P(c),CI Logo; rep. 16.00

165 **(1962)** RWb&ABr,NS P(c),
CI Logo; rep 16.00
62/63 **(167)** RWb&ABr,NS P(c),
CI Logo; rep 15.00
06/64 **(167)** RWb&ABr,NS P(c),
CI logo; rep 15.00
06/65 **(167)** RWb&ABr,NS P(c),
CI Logo; rep 15.00
10/65 **(167)** RWb&ABr,NS P(c),
CI Logo; rep 15.00
09/67 **(166)** RWb&ABr,NS P(c),
CI Logo; rep 15.00
Fl/69 **(169)** RWb&ABr,NS P(c),25¢(c)
Price,CI Logo,Rigid(c);rep 15.00
Sg/71 **(169)** RWb&ABr,NS P(c),
CI Logo, Rigid(c);rep 15.00

027-THE ADVENTURES
MARCO POLO
By Marco Polo & Donn Byrne
04/46 **(— —)** HFI(a&c);Original. . . 500.00
09/46 **(30)** HFI(a&c);rep 150.00
04/50 **(70)** HFI(a&c),8 Pages Deleted,
No(c) Price,New CI Logo;rep . 45.00
09/51 **(87)** HFI(a&c),15¢(c)
Price,CI Logo;rep 30.00
03/54 **(117)** HFI(a&c),CILogo;rep. . 25.00
01/60 **(154)** HFI,New P(c),CI
Logo;rep 25.00
1962 **(165)** HFI,P(c),CI Logo;rep . . 15.00
04/64 **(167)** HFI,P(c),CI Logo;rep . 15.00
06/66 **(167)** HFI,P(c),CI Logo;rep . 15.00
Sg/69 **(169)** HFI,P(c),CI Logo,
25¢(c)Price,Rigid(c);rep 15.00

028-MICHAEL STROGOFF
By Jules Verne
06/46 **(— —)** AdH(a&c),Original . . . 500.00
09/48 **(51)** AdH(a&c),8 Pages
Deleted,New CI Logo;rep . . . 150.00
01/54 **(115)** AdH,New P(c),CI
Logo; rep 45.00
03/60 **(155)** AdH,P(c),CI Logo;rep . 18.00
11/63 **(167)** AdH,P(c),CI Logo;rep . 18.00
07/66 **(167)** AdH,P(c),CI Logo;rep . 18.00
Sr/69 **(169)**AdH,NN,NewP(c),25¢(c)
Price, CI Logo,Rigid(c);rep . . . 28.00

029-THE PRINCE
AND THE PAUPER
By Mark Twain
07/46 **(— —)** AdH(a&c),Original . . . 750.00
06/49 **(60)** AdH,New HcK(c),New CI
Logo,8 Pages Deleted;rep. . . . 70.00
08/49 **(62)** AdH,HcK(c),CILogo;rep 50.00
05/50 **(71)** AdH,HcK(c),CILogo;rep 35.00
03/52 **(93)** AdH,HcK(c),CILogo;rep 32.00
12/53 **(114)** AdH,HcK(c),CI
Logo;rep 30.00
09/55 **(128)** AdH,New P(c),CI
Logo; rep 30.00
05/57 **(138)** AdH,P(c),CI Logo;rep. 18.00
05/59 **(150)** AdH,P(c),CI Logo;rep. 18.00
1961 **(164)** AdH,P(c),CI Logo;rep . 18.00
62/63 **(167)** AdH,P(c),CI Logo;rep . 18.00
07/64 **(167)** AdH,P(c),CI Logo;rep . 18.00
11/65 **(167)** AdH,P(c),CI Logo;rep . 18.00
1968 **(166)** AdH,P(c),CI Logo,
25¢(c)Price;rep 18.00
Sr/70 **(169)** AdH,P(c),CI Logo,
Rigid(c);rep 18.00

030-THE MOONSTONE
By William Wilkie Collins
09/46 **(— —)** DRi(a&c),Original. . . . 500.00
06/49 **(60)** DRi(a&c),8 Pages
Deleted,New CI Logo;rep 90.00

04/50 **(70)** DRi(a&c),CI Logo;rep . . 65.00
03/60 **(155)** DRi,LbC New P(c),
CI Logo;rep 90.00
1962 **(165)** DRi,LbC P(c),CI Logo;
rep 35.00
01/64 **(167)** DRi,LbC P(c),CI Logo;
rep 28.00
09/65 **(167)** DRi,LbC P(c),CI Logo;
rep 20.00
1968 **(166)** DRi,LbC P(c),CI Logo,
25¢(c)Price;rep 18.00

CI #31, The Black Arrow
© Gilberton Publications

031-THE BLACK ARROW
By Robert Louis Stevenson
10/46 **(— -)** AdH(a&c),Original . . . 400.00
09/48 **(51)** AdH(a&c),8 Pages
Deleted,New CI Logo;rep 50.00
10/49 **(64)** AdH(a&c),CI
Logo;rep 35.00
09/51 **(87)** AdH(a&c),15¢(c)
Price;CI Logo;rep 30.00
06/53 **(108)** AdH(a&c),CI
Logo;rep 28.00
03/55 **(125)** AdH(a&c),CI
Logo;rep 27.00
03/56 **(131)** AdH,New P(c),CI
Logo; rep 22.00
09/57 **(140)** AdH,P(c),CI Logo;rep . 20.00
01/59 **(148)** AdH,P(c),CI Logo;rep . 20.00
03/61 **(161)** AdH,P(c),CI Logo;rep . 20.00
62/63 **(167)** AdH,P(c),CI Logo;rep . 20.00
07/64 **(167)** AdH,P(c),CI logo;rep . 20.00
11/65 **(167)** AdH,P(c),CI Logo;rep . 20.00
1968 **(166)** AdH,P(c),CI Logo,
25¢(c)Price;rep 20.00

032-LORNA DOONE
By Richard Doddridge
Blackmore
12/46 **(— -)** MB(a&c),Original 475.00
10/49 **(53/64)** MB(a&c),8 Pages
Deleted,New CI Logo;rep 90.00
07/51 **(85)** MB(a&c),15¢(c)
Price, CI Logo;rep 65.00
04/54 **(118)** MB(a&c),CI Logo;rep . 35.00
05/57 **(138)** MB,New P(c); Old(c)
Becomes New Splash Pge.,CI
Logo;rep 35.00
05/59 **(150)** MB,P(c),CI Logo;rep. . 20.00
1962 **(165)** MB,P(c),CI Logo;rep . . 20.00
01/64 **(167)** MB,P(c),CI Logo;rep. . 22.00
11/65 **(167)** MB,P(c),CI Logo;rep. . 22.00

1968 **(166)** MB,New P(c),
CI Logo;rep 35.00

033-THE ADVENTURES
OF SHERLOCK HOLMES
By Sir Arthur Conan Doyle
01/47 **(— -)** LZ,HcK(c),Original . 1,600.00
11/48 **(53)** LZ,HcK(c),"A Study in Scarlet"
Deleted,New CI Logo;rep . . . 600.00
05/50 **(71)** LZ,HcK(c),CI Logo;rep 500.00
11/51 **(89)** LZ,HcK(c),15¢(c)
Price,CI Logo;rep 400.00

034-MYSTERIOUS ISLAND
By Jules Verne
Last Classic Comic
02/47 **(— -)** RWb&DvH,Original . . 500.00
06/49 **(60)** RWb&DvH,8 Pages
Deleted,New CI Logo;rep 65.00
08/49 **(62)** RWb&DvH,CI Logo;rep 45.00
05/50 **(71)** RWb&DvH,CI Logo;rep 65.00
12/50 **(78)** RWb&DvH,15¢(c) Price,
CI Logo;rep 35.00
02/52 **(92)** RWb&DvH,CI Logo;rep 35.00
03/54 **(117)** RWb&DvH,CI Logo;
rep 35.00
09/57 **(140)** RWb&DvH,New P(c),
CI Logo;rep 35.00
05/60 **(156)** RWb&DvH,P(c),CI
Logo;rep 20.00
10/63 **(167)** RWb&DvH,P(c),CI
Logo;rep 20.00
05/64 **(167)** RWb&DvH,P(c),CI
Logo;rep 20.00
06/66 **(167)** RWb&DvH,P(c),CI
logo;rep 20.00
1968 **(166)** RWb&DvH,P(c),CI Logo,
25¢(c)Price;rep 20.00

035-LAST DAYS
OF POMPEII
By Lord Edward Bulwer Lytton
First Classics Illustrated
03/47 **(— -)** HcK(a&c),Original . . . 500.00
03/61 **(161)** JK,New P(c),
15¢(c)Price;rep 65.00
01/64 **(167)** JK,P(c);rep 30.00
07/66 **(167)** JK,P(c);rep 30.00
Sg/70 **(169)** JK,P(c),25¢(c)
Price, Rigid(c);rep 30.00

036-TYPEE
By Herman Melville
04/47 **(— -)** EzW(a&c),Original. . . 275.00
10/49 **(64)** EzW(a&c),No(c)price,
8 pages deleted;rep. 90.00
03/60 **(155)** EzW,GMc New
P(c);rep 35.00
09/63 **(167)** EzW,GMc P(c);rep . . 25.00
07/65 **(167)** EzW,GMc P(c);rep . . 25.00
Sr/69 **(169)** EzW,GMc P(c),25¢(c)
Price, Rigid(c);rep 25.00

037-THE PIONEERS
By James Fenimore Cooper
05/47 **(37)** RP(a&c),Original 250.00
08/49 **(62)** RP(a&c),8 Pages
Deleted;rep 45.00
04/50 **(70)** RP(a&c);rep 35.00
02/52 **(92)** RP(a&c),15¢(c)price;
rep 35.00
04/54 **(118)** RP(a&c);rep 30.00
03/56 **(131)** RP(a&c);rep 30.00
05/56 **(132)** RP(a&c);rep 30.00
11/59 **(153)** RP(a&c);rep 25.00
05/64 **(167)** RP(a&c);rep 25.00

All comics prices listed are for *Near Mint* condition.

06/66 **(167)** RP(a&c);rep 25.00
1968 **(166)** RP,TO New P(c),
   25¢(c)Price;rep 35.00

038-ADVENTURES
OF CELLINI
By Benvenuto Cellini
06/47 **(—-)** AgF(a&c),Original . . . 350.00
1961 **(164)** NN New Art,New P(c);
  rep 35.00
12/63 **(167)** NN,P(c);rep 25.00
07/66 **(167)** NN,P(c);rep 25.00
Sg/70 **(169)** NN,P(c),25¢(c)
  Price, Rigid(c);rep 28.00

039-JANE EYRE
By Charlotte Bronte
07/47 **(—-)** HyG(a&c),Original . . . 350.00
06/49 **(60)** HyG(a&c),No(c)Price,
  8 pages deleted;rep 50.00
08/49 **(62)** HyG(a&c);rep 45.00
05/50 **(71)** HyG(a&c);rep 35.00
02/52 **(92)** HyG(a&c),15¢(c)
  Price; rep 32.00
04/54 **(118)** HyG(a&c);rep 32.00
01/58 **(142)** HyG,New P(c);rep. . . . 32.00
01/60 **(154)** HyG,NN No(c)rep 32.00
1962 **(165)** HjK New Art,P(c);rep . . 32.00
12/63 **(167)** HjK,P(c);rep 32.00
04/65 **(167)** HjK,P(c);rep 32.00
08/66 **(167)** HjK,P(c);rep 32.00
1968 **(166)** HjK,NN New P(c);rep . 75.00

040-MYSTERIES
(The Pit & the Pendulum,
The Adventures of Hans Pfall,
Fall of the House of Usher)
By Edgar Allan Poe
08/47 **(—-)** AgF,HyG,HcK(a&c),
  Original 800.00
08/49 **(62)** AgF,HyG,HcK(a&c),
  8 Pages deleted;rep 350.00
09/50 **(75)** AgF,HyG,
  HcK(a&c);rep 300.00
02/52 **(92)** AgF,HyG,HcK(a&c)
  15¢(c) Price;rep 250.00

041-TWENTY YEARS
AFTER
By Alexandre Dumas
09/47 **(—-)** RBu(a&c),Original . . . 600.00
08/49 **(62)** RBu,HcK New(c),No(c)
  Price, 8 Pages deleted;rep . . . 65.00
12/50 **(78)** RBu,HcK(c),15¢(c)
  Price; rep 45.00
05/60 **(156)** RBu,DgR New P(c);
  rep 35.00
12/63 **(167)** RBu,DgR P(c);rep . . . 50.00
11/66 **(167)** RBu,DgR P(c);rep. . . . 50.00
Sg/70 **(169)** RBu,DgR P(c),25¢(c)
  Price, Rigid(c);rep 50.00

042-SWISS FAMILY
ROBINSON
By Johann Wyss
10/47 **(42)** HcK(a&c),Original. . . . 275.00
08/49 **(62)** HcK(a&c),No(c)price,
  8 Pages Deleted,Not Every Issue
  Has 'Gift Box' Ad;rep 75.00
09/50 **(75)** HcK(a&c);rep 35.00
03/52 **(93)** HcK(a&c);rep 32.00
03/54 **(117)** HcK(a&c);rep 30.00
03/56 **(131)** HcK,New P(c);rep. . . . 28.00
03/57 **(137)** HcK,P(c);rep. 28.00
11/57 **(141)** HcK,P(c);rep. 28.00
09/59 **(152)** NN New art,P(c);rep. . 28.00

09/60 **(158)** NN,P(c);rep 25.00
12/63 **(165)** NN,P(c);rep 30.00
12/63 **(167)** NN,P(c);rep 15.00
04/65 **(167)** NN,P(c);rep 15.00
05/66 **(167)** NN,P(c);rep 15.00
11/67 **(166)** NN,P(c);rep. 15.00
Sg/69 **(169)** NN,P(c);rep 15.00

043-GREAT
EXPECTATIONS
By Charles Dickens
11/47 **(—-)** HcK(a&c),Original. . . 1,400.00
08/49 **(62)** HcK(a&c),No(c)price;
  8 pages deleted;rep. 850.00

044-MYSTERIES
OF PARIS
By Eugene Sue
12/47 **(44)** HcK(a&c),Original. . . . 900.00
08/47 **(62)** HcK(a&c),No(c)Price,
  8 Pages Deleted,Not Every Issue
  Has 'Gift Box' Ad;rep 350.00
12/50 **(78)** HcK(a&c),15¢(c)
  Price; rep 300.00

045-TOM BROWN'S
SCHOOL DAYS
By Thomas Hughes
01/48 **(44)** HFl(a&c),Original,
  1st 48 Pge. Issue 200.00
10/49 **(64)** HFl(a&c),No(c)
  Price;rep 60.00
03/61 **(161)** JTg New Art,GMc
  New P(c);rep 30.00
02/64 **(167)** JTg,GMc P(c);rep. . . . 20.00
08/66 **(167)** JTg,GMc P(c);rep. . . . 20.00
1968 **(166)** JTg,GMc P(c),
  25¢(c)Price;rep 20.00

046-KIDNAPPED
By Robert Louis Stevenson
04/48 **(47)** RWb(a&c),Original . . . 165.00
08/49 **(62)** RWb(a&c),Red Circle
  Either Blank or With 10¢;rep . . 90.00
12/50 **(78)** RWb(a&c),15¢(c)
  Price; rep 35.00
09/51 **(87)** RWb(a&c);rep. 32.00
04/54 **(118)** RWb(a&c);rep. 30.00
03/56 **(131)** RWb,New P(c);rep . . . 30.00
09/57 **(140)** RWb,P(c);rep 18.00
05/59 **(150)** RWb,P(c);rep 18.00
05/60 **(156)** RWb,P(c);rep 18.00
1961 **(164)** RWb,P(c),Reduced Pge.
  Wdth;rep 18.00
62/63 **(167)** RWb,P(c);rep 18.00
03/64 **(167)** RWb,P(c);rep 18.00
06/65 **(167)** RWb,P(c);rep 18.00
12/65 **(167)** RWb,P(c);rep 18.00
09/67 **(167)** RWb,P(c);rep 18.00
Wr/69 **(166)** RWb,P(c),25¢(c)
  Price, Rigid(c);rep 18.00
Sr/70 **(169)** RWb,P(c),Rigid(c);rep. 18.00

047-TWENTY
THOUSAND LEAGUES
UNDER THE SEA
By Jules Verne
05/58 **(47)** HcK(a&c),Original. . . . 180.00
10/49 **(64)** HcK(a&c),No(c)
  Price; rep 45.00
12/50 **(78)** HcK(a&c),15¢(c)
  Price; rep 35.00
04/52 **(94)** HcK(a&c);rep 35.00
04/54 **(118)** HcK(a&c);rep 30.00
09/55 **(128)** HcK,New P(c);rep. . . . 30.00

07/56 **(133)** HcK,P(c);rep. 25.00
09/57 **(140)** HcK,P(c);rep. 18.00
01/59 **(148)** HcK,P(c);rep. 18.00
05/60 **(156)** HcK,P(c);rep. 18.00
62/63 **(165)** HcK,P(c);rep. 18.00
05/48 **(167)** HcK,P(c);rep. 18.00
03/64 **(167)** HcK,P(c);rep. 18.00
08/65 **(167)** HcK,P(c);rep. 18.00
10/66 **(167)** HcK,P(c);rep. 18.00
1968 **(166)** HcK,NN New P(c),
  25¢(c)Price;rep 25.00
Sg/70 **(169)** HcK,NN P(c),
  Rigid(c);rep 25.00

048-DAVID
COPPERFIELD
By Charles Dickens
06/48 **(47)** HcK(a&c),Original. . . . 175.00
10/49 **(64)** HcK(a&c),Price Circle
  Replaced By Image of Boy
  Reading;rep 45.00
09/51 **(87)** HcK(a&c),15¢(c)
  Price; rep 35.00
07/54 **(121)** HcK,New P(c);rep. . . . 30.00
10/56 **(130)** HcK,P(c);rep. 18.00
09/57 **(140)** HcK,P(c);rep. 18.00
01/59 **(148)** HcK,P(c);rep. 18.00
05/60 **(156)** HcK,P(c);rep. 18.00
62/63 **(167)** HcK,P(c);rep. 18.00
04/64 **(167)** HcK,P(c);rep. 18.00
06/65 **(167)** HcK,P(c);rep. 18.00
05/67 **(166)** HcK,P(c);rep. 18.00
R/67 **(166)** HcK,P(c);rep. 25.00
Sg/69 **(166)** HcK,P(c),25¢(c)
  Price, Rigid(c);rep 18.00
Wr/69 **(169)** HcK,P(c),Rigid(c);rep. 18.00

049-ALICE IN
WONDERLAND
By Lewis Carroll
07/48 **(47)** AB(a&c),Original. 250.00
10/49 **(64)** AB(a&c),No(c)Price;
  rep 60.00
07/51 **(85)** AB(a&c),15¢(c)Price;
  rep 50.00
03/60 **(155)** AB,New P(c);rep. 50.00
1962 **(165)** AB,P(c);rep 35.00
03/64 **(167)** AB,P(c);rep 30.00
06/66 **(167)** AB,P(c);rep 30.00
Fl/68 **(166)** AB,TO New P(c),25¢(c)
  Price, New Soft(c);rep 50.00
Fl/68 **(166)** AB,P(c),Both Soft &
  Rigid(c)s;rep 100.00

050-ADVENTURES OF
TOM SAWYER
By Mark Twain
08/48 **(51)** ARu(a&c),Original. . . . 200.00
09/48 **(51)** ARu(a&c),Original. . . . 225.00
10/49 **(64)** ARu(a&c),No(c)
  Price; rep 35.00
12/50 **(78)** ARu(a&c),15¢(c)
  Price; rep 30.00
04/52 **(94)** ARu(a&c);rep 30.00
12/53 **(114)** ARu(a&c);rep 30.00
03/54 **(117)** ARu(a&c);rep 25.00
05/56 **(132)** ARu(a&c);rep 25.00
09/57 **(140)** ARu,New P(c);rep. . . . 22.00
05/59 **(150)** ARu,P(c);rep. 25.00
10/61 **(164)** New Art,P(c);rep. 15.00
62/63 **(167)** P(c);rep. 15.00
01/65 **(167)** P(c);rep. 15.00
05/66 **(167)** P(c);rep. 15.00
12/67 **(166)** P(c);rep. 15.00
Fl/69 **(169)** P(c),25¢(c) Price,
  Rigid(c);rep 15.00
Wr/71 **(169)** P(c);rep 15.00

051-THE SPY

By James Fenimore Cooper
09/48 **(51)** AdH(a&c),Original,
   Maroon(c) 175.00
09/48 **(51)** AdH(a&c),Original,
   Violet(c) 165.00
11/51 **(89)** AdH(a&c),15¢(c)
   Price; rep 35.00
07/54 **(121)** AdH(a&c);rep 30.00
07/57 **(139)** AdH,New P(c);rep. . . . 30.00
05/60 **(156)** AdH,P(c);rep 18.00
11/63 **(167)** AdH,P(c);rep 18.00
07/66 **(167)** AdH,P(c);rep 18.00
Wr/69 **(166)** AdH,P(c),25¢(c)Price,
   Both Soft & Rigid(c)s;rep. . . . 35.00

052-THE HOUSE OF SEVEN GABLES

By Nathaniel Hawthorne
10/48 **(53)** HyG(a&c),Original . . . 175.00
11/51 **(89)** HyG(a&c),15¢(c)
   Price; rep 35.00
07/54 **(121)** HyG(a&c);rep 30.00
01/58 **(142)** GWb New Art,New
   P(c); rep. 35.00
05/60 **(156)** GWb,P(c);rep 18.00
1962 **(165)** GWb,P(c);rep 18.00
05/64 **(167)** GWb,P(c);rep 18.00
03/66 **(167)** GWb,P(c);rep 18.00
1968 **(166)** GWb,P(c),25¢(c)
   Price;rep 18.00
Sg/70 **(169)** GWb,P(c),Rigid(c);rep 18.00

053-A CHRISTMAS CAROL

By Charles Dickens
11/48 **(53)** HcK(a&c),Original. . . . 250.00

054-MAN IN THE IRON MASK

By Alexandre Dumas
12/48 **(55)** AgF,HcK(c),Original . . 165.00
03/52 **(93)** AgF,HcK(c),15¢(c)
   Price; rep 45.00
09/53 **(111)** AgF,HcK(c);rep 60.00
01/58 **(142)** KBa New Art,New
   P(c); rep. 35.00
01/60 **(154)** KBa,P(c);rep. 18.00
1962 **(165)** KBa,P(c);rep 18.00
05/64 **(167)** KBa,P(c);rep. 18.00
04/66 **(167)** KBa,P(c);rep. 18.00
Wr/69 **(166)** KBa,P(c),25¢(c)
   Price, Rigid(c);rep 18.00

055-SILAS MARINER

By George Eliot
01/49 **(55)** AdH,HcK(c),Original . . 165.00
09/50 **(75)** AdH,HcK(c),Price Circle
   Blank,'Coming next'Ad(not
   usually in reps.);rep 45.00
07/52 **(97)** AdH,HcK(c);rep 32.00
07/54 **(121)** AdH,New P(c);rep. . . . 30.00
01/56 **(130)** AdH,P(c);rep. 18.00
09/57 **(140)** AdH,P(c);rep. 18.00
01/60 **(154)** AdH,P(c);rep. 18.00
1962 **(165)** AdH,P(c);rep. 18.00
05/64 **(167)** AdH,P(c);rep. 18.00
06/65 **(167)** AdH,P(c);rep. 18.00
05/67 **(166)** AdH,P(c);rep. 18.00
Wr/69 **(166)** AdH,P(c),25¢(c) Price,
   Rigid(c);rep,Soft & Stiff 35.00

056-THE TOILERS OF THE SEA

By Victor Hugo
02/49 **(55)** AgF(a&c),Original 275.00
01/62 **(165)** AT New Art,New
   P(c); rep. 60.00
03/64 **(167)** AT,P(c);rep. 35.00
10/66 **(167)** AT,P(c);rep. 35.00

057-THE SONG OF HIAWATHA

By Henry Wadsworth Longfellow
03/49 **(55)** AB(a&c),Original. 165.00
09/50 **(75)** AB(a&c),No(c)price,'
   Coming Next'Ad(not usually
   found in reps.);rep 50.00
04/52 **(94)** AB(a&c),15¢(c)
   Price;rep 35.00
04/54 **(118)** AB(a&c);rep 32.00
09/56 **(134)** AB,New P(c);rep 30.00
07/57 **(139)** AB,P(c);rep. 18.00
01/60 **(154)** AB,P(c);rep. 18.00
62/63 **(167)** AB,P(c),Erroneosly
   Has Original Date;rep 18.00
09/64 **(167)** AB,P(c);rep. 18.00
10/65 **(167)** AB,P(c);rep. 18.00
Fl/68 **(166)** AB,P(c),25¢(c)Price;
   rep 18.00

CI #58 The Prairie
© Gilberton Publications

058-THE PRAIRIE

By James Fenimore Cooper
04/49 **(60)** RP(a&c),Original 165.00
08/49 **(62)** RP(a&c);rep 75.00
12/50 **(78)** RP(a&c),15¢(c) Price
   In Double Circle;rep. 35.00
12/53 **(114)** RP(a&c);rep 30.00
03/56 **(131)** RP(a&c);rep 30.00
05/56 **(132)** RP(a&c);rep 30.00
09/58 **(146)** RP,New P(c);rep. 30.00
03/60 **(155)** RP,P(c);rep. 20.00
05/64 **(167)** RP,P(c);rep. 18.00
04/66 **(167)** RP,P(c);rep. 18.00
Sr/69 **(169)** RP,P(c),25¢(c)
   Price; Rigid(c);rep 18.00

059-WUTHERING HEIGHTS

By Emily Bronte
05/49 **(60)** HcK(a&c),Original. . . . 225.00
07/51 **(85)** HcK(a&c),15¢(c)

Price; rep. 50.00
05/60 **(156)** HcK,GB New P(c);rep 35.00
01/64 **(167)** HcK,GB P(c);rep. 25.00
10/66 **(167)** HcK,GB P(c);rep. 25.00
Sr/69 **(169)** HcK,GBP(c),25¢(c)
   Price, Rigid(c);rep 22.00

060-BLACK BEAUTY

By Anna Sewell
06/49 **(62)** AgF(a&c),Original. . . . 165.00
08/49 **(62)** AgF(a&c);rep 225.00
07/51 **(85)** AgF(a&c),15¢(c) Price;
   rep 40.00
09/60 **(158)** LbC&NN&StA New
   Art, LbC New P(c);rep 35.00
02/64 **(167)** LbC&NN&StA,LbC
   P(c); rep. 30.00
03/66 **(167)** LbC&NN&StA,LbC
   P(c); rep. 30.00
03/66 **(167)** LbC&NN&StA,LbC
   P(c), 'Open Book'Blank;rep. . . 30.00
1968 **(166)** LbC&NN&StA,AIM New
   P(c) 25¢(c) Price;rep 75.00

061-THE WOMAN IN WHITE

By William Wilke Collins
07/49 **(62)** AB(a&c),Original,
   Maroon & Violet(c)s. 175.00
05/60 **(156)** AB,DgR New P(c);rep 40.00
01/64 **(167)** AB,DgR P(c);rep. 30.00
1968 **(166)** AB,DgR P(c),
   25¢(c)Price;rep 30.00

062-WESTERN STORIES

(The Luck of Roaring Camp & The Outcasts of Poker Flat)
By Bret Harte
08/49 **(62)** HcK(a&c),Original. . . . 165.00
11/51 **(89)** HcK(a&c),15¢(c)
   Price; rep. 40.00
07/54 **(121)** HcK(a&c);rep 32.00
03/57 **(137)** HcK,New P(c);rep. . . . 30.00
09/59 **(152)** HcK,P(c);rep. 20.00
10/63 **(167)** HcK,P(c);rep. 20.00
06/64 **(167)** HcK,P(c);rep. 18.00
11/66 **(167)** HcK,P(c);rep. 18.00
1968 **(166)** HcK,TO New P(c),
   25¢ Price;rep 30.00

063-THE MAN WITHOUT A COUNTRY

By Edward Everett Hale
09/49 **(62)** HcK(a&c),Original. . . . 165.00
12/50 **(78)** HcK(a&c),15¢(c)Price
   In Double Circles;rep. 40.00
05/60 **(156)** HcK,GMc New P(c);
   rep 35.00
01/62 **(165)** AT New Art,GMc P(c),
   Added Text Pages;rep. 32.00
03/64 **(167)** AT,GMc P(c);rep 18.00
08/66 **(167)** AT,GMc P(c);rep 18.00

Sr/69 **(169)** AT,GMc P(c),25¢(c)
   Price, Rigid(c);rep 18.00

064-TREASURE ISLAND

By Robert Louis Stevenson
10/49 **(62)** AB(a&c),Original. 165.00
04/51 **(82)** AB(a&c),15¢(c)
   Price;rep 40.00
03/54 **(117)** AB(a&c);rep 32.00
03/56 **(131)** AB,New P(c);rep. 30.00
05/57 **(138)** AB,P(c);rep. 18.00
09/58 **(146)** AB,P(c);rep. 18.00
09/60 **(158)** AB,P(c);rep. 18.00

Classics Illus.

1962 **(165)** AB,P(c);rep 18.00
62/63 **(167)** AB,P(c);rep 18.00
06/64 **(167)** AB,P(c);rep 18.00
12/65 **(167)** AB,P(c);rep 18.00
10/67 **(166)** AB,P(c);rep 22.00
10/67 **(166)** AB,P(c),GRIT Ad
   Stapled In Book;rep 100.00
Sg/69 **(169)** AB,P(c),25¢(c)
   Price, Rigid(c);rep 18.00

065-BENJAMIN FRANKLIN
By Benjamin Franklin
11/49 **(64)** AB,RtH,GS(Iger Shop),
   HcK(c),Original 165.00
03/56 **(131)** AB,RtH,GS(Iger Shop),
   New P(c) ;rep 35.00
01/60 **(154)** AB,RtH,GS(Iger Shop),
   P(c);rep 20.00
02/64 **(167)** AB,RtH,GS(Iger Shop),
   P(c);rep 18.00
04/66 **(167)** AB,RtH,GS(Iger Shop),
   P(c);rep 18.00
Fl/69 **(169)** AB,RtH,GS(Iger Shop),
   P(c), 25¢(c)Price,Rigid(c);rep . 20.00

066-THE CLOISTER
AND THE HEARTH
By Charles Reade
12/49 **(67)** HcK(a&c),Original. . . . 350.00

067-THE SCOTTISH
CHIEFS
By Jane Porter
01/50 **(67)** AB(a&c),Original. 165.00
07/51 **(85)** AB(a&c),15¢(c)
   Price;rep 40.00
04/54 **(118)** AB(a&c);rep 35.00
01/57 **(136)** AB,New P(c);rep. 32.00
01/60 **(154)** AB,P(c);rep. 20.00
11/63 **(167)** AB,P(c);rep. 25.00
08/65 **(167)** AB,P(c);rep. 20.00

Cl #68, Julius Caesar
© Gilberton Publications

068-JULIUS CEASAR
By William Shakespeare
02/50 **(70)** HcK(a&c),Original. . . . 150.00
07/51 **(85)** HcK(a&c),15¢(c)
   Price; rep. 40.00
06/53 **(108)** HcK(a&c);rep 32.00
05/60 **(156)** HcK,LbC New P(c);rep35.00

1962 **(165)** GE&RC New Art,
   LbC P(c);rep 35.00
02/64 **(167)** GE&RC,LbC P(c);rep . 18.00
10/65 **(167)** GE&RC,LbC P(c),Tarzan
   Books Inside(c);rep 18.00
1967 **(166)** GE&RC,LbC P(c);rep . 18.00
Wr/69 **(169)** GE&RC,LbC P(c),
   Rigid(c);rep 18.00

069-AROUND THE
WORLD IN 80 DAYS
By Jules Verne
03/50 **(70)** HcK(a&c),Original. . . . 150.00
09/51 **(87)** HcK(a&c),15¢(c)
   Price; rep 45.00
03/55 **(125)** HcK(a&c);rep 32.00
01/57 **(136)** HcK,New P(c);rep. . . . 32.00
09/58 **(146)** HcK,P(c);rep. 20.00
09/59 **(152)** HcK,P(c);rep. 20.00
1961 **(164)** HcK,P(c);rep 20.00
62/63 **(167)** HcK,P(c);rep. 18.00
07/64 **(167)** HcK,P(c);rep. 18.00
11/65 **(167)** HcK,P(c);rep. 18.00
07/67 **(166)** HcK,P(c);rep. 18.00
Sg/69 **(169)** HcK,P(c),25¢(c)
   Price, Rigid(c);rep 18.00

070-THE PILOT
By James Fenimore Cooper
04/50 **(71)** AB(a&c),Original. 125.00
10/50 **(75)** AB(a&c),15¢(c)
   Price;rep 45.00
02/52 **(92)** AB(a&c);rep 32.00
03/55 **(125)** AB(a&c);rep 35.00
05/60 **(156)** AB,GMc New P(c);rep 30.00
02/64 **(167)** AB,GMc P(c);rep 30.00
05/66 **(167)** AB,GMc P(c);rep 28.00

071-THE MAN WHO
LAUGHS
By Victor Hugo
05/50 **(71)** AB(a&c),Original. 250.00
01/62 **(165)** NN,NN New P(c);rep 125.00
04/64 **(167)** NN,NN P(c);rep 100.00

072-THE OREGON TRAIL
By Francis Parkman
06/50 **(73)** HcK(a&c),Original. . . . 150.00
11/51 **(89)** HcK(a&c),15¢(c)
   Price; rep. 40.00
07/54 **(121)** HcK(a&c);rep 32.00
03/56 **(131)** HcK,New P(c);rep. . . . 30.00
09/57 **(140)** HcK,P(c);rep. 20.00
05/59 **(150)** HcK,P(c);rep. 18.00
01/61 **(164)** HcK,P(c);rep. 18.00
62/63 **(167)** HcK,P(c);rep. 18.00
08/64 **(167)** HcK,P(c);rep. 18.00
10/65 **(167)** HcK,P(c);rep. 18.00
1968 **(166)** HcK,P(c),25¢(c)Price;
   rep 18.00

073-THE BLACK TULIP
By Alexandre Dumas
07/50 **(75)** AB(a&c),Original. 450.00

074-MR. MIDSHIPMAN
EASY
By Captain Frederick Marryat
08/50 **(75)** BbL,Original 450.00

075-THE LADY OF
THE LAKE
By Sir Walter Scott
09/50 **(75)** HcK(a&c),Original. . . . 125.00

07/51 **(85)** HcK(a&c),15¢(c)
   Price; rep 40.00
04/54 **(118)** HcK(a&c);rep 35.00
07/57 **(139)** HcK,New P(c);rep. . . . 35.00
01/60 **(154)** HcK,P(c);rep. 18.00
1962 **(165)** HcK,P(c);rep. 18.00
04/64 **(167)** HcK,P(c);rep. 18.00
05/66 **(167)** HcK,P(c);rep. 18.00
Sg/69 **(169)** HcK,P(c),25¢(c)
   Price, Rigid(c);rep 18.00

076-THE PRISONER
OF ZENDA
By Anthony Hope Hawkins
10/50 **(75)** HcK(a&c),Original. . . . 125.00
07/51 **(85)** HcK(a&c),15¢(c) Price;
   rep 40.00
09/53 **(111)** HcK(a&c),rep 35.00
09/55 **(128)** HcK,New P(c);rep. . . . 35.00
09/59 **(152)** HcK,P(c);rep. 20.00
1962 **(165)** HcK,P(c);rep 18.00
04/64 **(167)** HcK,P(c);rep. 18.00
09/66 **(167)** HcK,P(c);rep. 18.00
Fl/69 **(169)** HcK,P(c),25¢(c) Price,
   Rigid(c);rep 18.00

077-THE ILLIAD
By Homer
11/50 **(78)** AB(a&c),Original 135.00
09/51 **(87)** AB(a&c),15¢(c)
   Price;rep 40.00
07/54 **(121)** AB(a&c);rep 35.00
07/57 **(139)** AB,New P(c);rep. 35.00
05/59 **(150)** AB,P(c);rep. 20.00
1962 **(165)** AB,P(c);rep 18.00
10/63 **(167)** AB,P(c);rep 18.00
07/64 **(167)** AB,P(c);rep. 18.00
05/66 **(167)** AB,P(c);rep. 18.00
1968 **(166)** AB,P(c),25¢(c)
   Price;rep 18.00

078-JOAN OF ARC
By Frederick Shiller
12/50 **(78)** HcK(a&c),Original. . . . 125.00
09/51 **(87)** HcK(a&c),15¢(c)
   Price; rep 40.00
11/53 **(113)** HcK(a&c);rep 35.00
09/55 **(128)** HcK,New P(c);rep. . . . 35.00
09/57 **(140)** HcK,P(c);rep. 20.00
05/59 **(150)** HcK,P(c);rep. 20.00
11/60 **(159)** HcK,P(c);rep. 18.00
62/63 **(167)** HcK,P(c);rep. 18.00
12/63 **(167)** HcK,P(c);rep. 18.00
06/65 **(167)** HcK,P(c);rep. 18.00
06/67 **(166)** HcK,P(c);rep. 18.00
Wr/69 **(166)** HcK,To New P(c),
   25¢(c)Price, Rigid(c);rep 35.00

079-CYRANO DE
BERGERAC
By Edmond Rostand
01/51 **(78)** AB(a&c),Original,Movie
   Promo Inside Front(c) 125.00
07/51 **(85)** AB(a&c),15¢(c)
   Price;rep 40.00
04/54 **(118)** AB(a&c);rep 35.00
07/56 **(133)** AB,New P(c);rep. 35.00
05/60 **(156)** AB,P(c);rep. 30.00
08/64 **(167)** AB,P(c);rep 30.00

080-WHITE FANG
By Jack London
(Last Line Drawn (c)
02/51 **(79)** AB(a&c),Original. 125.00
09/51 **(87)** AB(a&c);rep 40.00
03/55 **(125)** AB(a&c);rep 35.00
05/56 **(132)** AB,New P(c);rep. 35.00

07/51 **(85)** HcK(a&c),15¢(c)
   Price; rep 40.00
04/54 **(118)** HcK(a&c);rep 35.00
07/57 **(139)** HcK,New P(c);rep. . . . 35.00
01/60 **(154)** HcK,P(c);rep. 18.00
1962 **(165)** HcK,P(c);rep. 18.00
04/64 **(167)** HcK,P(c);rep. 18.00
05/66 **(167)** HcK,P(c);rep. 18.00
Sg/69 **(169)** HcK,P(c),25¢(c)
   Price, Rigid(c);rep 18.00

09/57 **(140)** AB,P(c);rep 20.00
11/59 **(153)** AB,P(c);rep 20.00
62/63 **(167)** AB,P(c);rep 18.00
09/64 **(167)** AB,P(c);rep 18.00
07/65 **(167)** AB,P(c);rep 18.00
06/67 **(166)** AB,P(c);rep 18.00
Fl/69 **(169)** AB,P(c),25¢(c)
   Price, Rigid(c);rep 18.00

CI #81, The Odyssey
© Gilberton Publications

081-THE ODYSSEY
By Homer
(P(c)s From Now on)
03/51 **(82)** HyG,AB P(c),Original . 125.00
08/64 **(167)** HyG,AB P(c);rep 30.00
10/66 **(167)** HyG,AB P(c);rep 30.00
Sg/69 **(169)** HyG,TyT New P(c),
   Rigid(c);rep 35.00

082-THE MASTER OF BALLANTRAE
By Robert Louis Stevenson
04/51 **(82)** LDr,AB P(c),Original . . 80.00
08/64 **(167)** LDr,AB P(c);rep 30.00
Fl/68 **(166)** LDr,Syk New P(c),
   Rigid(c);rep 35.00

083-THE JUNGLE BOOK
By Rudyard Kipling
05/51 **(85)** WmB&AB,AB P(c),
   Original 80.00
08/53 **(110)** WmB&AB,AB P(c);rep 20.00
03/55 **(125)** WmB&AB,AB P(c);rep 20.00
05/56 **(134)** WmB&AB,AB P(c);rep 20.00
01/58 **(142)** WmB&AB,AB P(c);rep 20.00
05/59 **(150)** WmB&AB,AB P(c);rep 18.00
11/60 **(159)** WmB&AB,AB P(c);rep 18.00
62/63 **(167)** WmB&AB,AB P(c);rep 18.00
03/65 **(167)** WmB&AB,AB P(c);rep 18.00
11/65 **(167)** WmB&AB,AB P(c);rep 18.00
05/66 **(167)** WmB&AB,AB P(c);rep 18.00
1968 **(166)** NN Art,NN New P(c),
   Rigid(c);rep 35.00

084-THE GOLD BUG & OTHER STORIES
(Inc. The Telltale Heart & The Cask of Amontillado)
By Edgar Allan Poe
06/51 **(85)** AB,RP,JLv,AB P(c),
   Original 165.00

07/64 **(167)** AB,RP,JLv,AB
   P(c);rep 125.00

085-THE SEA WOLF
By Jack London
08/51 **(85)** AB,AB P(c),Original . . . 75.00
07/54 **(121)** AB,AB P(c);rep 20.00
05/56 **(132)** AB,AB P(c);rep 20.00
11/57 **(141)** AB,AB P(c);rep 20.00
03/61 **(161)** AB,AB P(c);rep 18.00
02/64 **(167)** AB,AB P(c);rep 18.00
11/65 **(167)** AB,AB P(c);rep 18.00
Fl/69 **(169)** AB,AB P(c),25¢(c)
   Price, Rigid(c);rep 18.00

086-UNDER TWO FLAGS
By Oiuda
08/51 **(87)** MDb,AB P(c),Original . . 75.00
03/54 **(117)** MDb,AB P(c);rep 25.00
07/57 **(139)** MDb,AB P(c);rep 20.00
09/60 **(158)** MDb,AB P(c);rep 20.00
02/64 **(167)** MDb,AB P(c);rep 18.00
08/66 **(167)** MDb,AB P(c);rep 18.00
Sr/69 **(169)** MDb,AB P(c),25¢(c)
   Price, Rigid(c);rep 18.00

087-A MIDSUMMER NIGHTS DREAM
By William Shakespeare
09/51 **(87)** AB,AB P(c),Original . . . 75.00
03/61 **(161)** AB,AB P(c);rep 20.00
04/64 **(167)** AB,AB P(c);rep 18.00
05/66 **(167)** AB,AB P(c);rep 18.00
Sr/69 **(169)** AB,AB P(c),25¢(c)
   Price; rep 18.00

088-MEN OF IRON
By Howard Pyle
10/51 **(89)** HD,LDr,GS,Original . . . 75.00
01/60 **(154)** HD,LDr,GS,P(c);rep . . 20.00
01/64 **(167)** HD,LDr,GS,P(c);rep . . 18.00
1968 **(166)** HD,LDr,GS,P(c),
   25¢(c)Price;rep 18.00

089-CRIME AND PUNISHMENT
By Fedor Dostoevsky
11/51 **(89)** RP,AB P(c),Original . . . 75.00
09/59 **(152)** RP,AB P(c);rep 25.00
04/64 **(167)** RP,AB P(c);rep 18.00
05/66 **(167)** RP,AB P(c);rep 18.00
Fl/69 **(169)** RP,AB P(c),25¢(c)
   Price, Rigid(c);rep 18.00

090-GREEN MANSIONS
By William Henry Hudson
12/51 **(89)** AB,AB P(c),Original . . . 75.00
01/59 **(148)** AB,New LbC P(c);rep . 30.00
1962 **(165)** AB,LbC P(c);rep 18.00
04/64 **(167)** AB,LbC P(c);rep 18.00
09/66 **(167)** AB,LbC P(c);rep 18.00
Sr/69 **(169)** AB,LbC P(c),25¢(c)
   Price, Rigid(c);rep 18.00

091-THE CALL OF THE WILD
By Jack London
01/52 **(92)** MDb,P(c),Original 75.00
10/53 **(112)** MDb,P(c);rep 20.00
03/55 **(125)** MDb,P(c),'PictureProgress'
   Onn. Back(c);rep 20.00
09/56 **(134)** MDb,P(c);rep 20.00
03/58 **(143)** MDb,P(c);rep 18.00
1962 **(165)** MDb,P(c);rep 18.00
1962 **(167)** MDb,P(c);rep 18.00

04/65 **(167)** MDb,P(c);rep 18.00
03/66 **(167)** MDb,P(c);rep 18.00
03/66 **(167)** MDb,P(c),Record
   Edition;rep 18.00
11/67 **(166)** MDb,P(c);rep 18.00
Sg/70 **(169)** MDb,P(c),25¢(c)
   Price, Rigid(c);rep 18.00

092-THE COURTSHIP OF MILES STANDISH
By Henry Wadsworth Longfellow
02/52 **(92)** AB,AB P(c),Original . . . 75.00
1962 **(165)** AB,AB P(c);rep 20.00
03/64 **(167)** AB,AB P(c);rep 20.00
05/67 **(166)** AB,AB P(c);rep 20.00
Wr/69 **(169)** AB,AB P(c),25¢(c)
   Price, Rigid(c);rep 20.00

093-PUDD'NHEAD WILSON
By Mark Twain
03/52 **(94)** HcK,HcK P(c),Original . 75.00
1962 **(165)** HcK,GMc New P(c);rep 25.00
03/64 **(167)** HcK,GMc P(c);rep . . . 20.00
1968 **(166)** HcK,GMc P(c),25¢(c)
   Price, Soft(c);rep 20.00

094-DAVID BALFOUR
By Robert Louis Stevenson
04/52 **(94)** RP,P(c),Original 75.00
05/64 **(167)** RP,P(c);rep 25.00
1968 **(166)** RP,P(c),25¢(c)Price;rep 25.00

095-ALL QUIET ON THE WESTERN FRONT
By Erich Maria Remarque
05/52 **(96)** MDb,P(c),Original 165.00
05/52 **(99)** MDb,P(c),Original 85.00
10/64 **(167)** MDb,P(c);rep 35.00
11/66 **(167)** MDb,P(c);rep 35.00

096-DANIEL BOONE
By John Bakeless
06/52 **(97)** AB,P(c),Original 75.00
03/54 **(117)** AB,P(c);rep 20.00
09/55 **(128)** AB,P(c);rep 20.00
05/56 **(132)** AB,P(c);rep 20.00
——— **(134)** AB,P(c),'Story of
   Jesus'on Back(c);rep 20.00
09/60 **(158)** AB,P(c);rep 20.00
01/64 **(167)** AB,P(c);rep 18.00
05/65 **(167)** AB,P(c);rep 18.00
11/66 **(167)** AB,P(c);rep 18.00
Wr/69 **(166)** AB,P(c),25¢(c)
   Price, Rigid(c);rep 25.00

097-KING SOLOMON'S MINES
By H. Rider Haggard
07/52 **(96)** HcK,P(c),Original 75.00
04/54 **(118)** HcK,P(c);rep 20.00
03/56 **(131)** HcK,P(c);rep 20.00
09/51 **(141)** HcK,P(c);rep 20.00
09/60 **(158)** HcK,P(c);rep 18.00
02/64 **(167)** HcK,P(c);rep 18.00
09/65 **(167)** HcK,P(c);rep 18.00
Sr/69 **(169)** HcK,P(c),25¢(c)
   Price; Rigid(c);rep 20.00

098-THE RED BADGE OF COURAGE
By Stephen Crane
08/52 **(98)** MDb,GS,P(c),Original . . 75.00

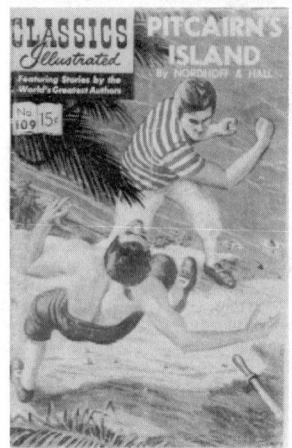

CI #109, Pitcairn's Island
© Gilberton Publications

04/54 **(118)** MDb,GS,P(c);rep 20.00
05/56 **(132)** MDb,GS,P(c);rep 20.00
01/58 **(142)** MDb,GS,P(c);rep 20.00
09/59 **(152)** MDb,GS,P(c);rep 20.00
03/61 **(161)** MDb,GS,P(c);rep 20.00
62/63 **(167)** MDb,GS,P(c),Erronously
   Has Original Date;rep 20.00
09/64 **(167)** MDb,GS,P(c);rep 20.00
10/65 **(167)** MDb,GS,P(c);rep 20.00
1968 **(166)** MDb,GS,P(c),25¢(c)
   Price, Rigid(c);rep 30.00

099-HAMLET
By William Shakespeare
09/52 **(98)** AB,P(c),Original 75.00
07/54 **(121)** AB,P(c);rep 20.00
11/57 **(141)** AB,P(c);rep 20.00
09/60 **(158)** AB,P(c);rep 18.00
62/63 **(167)** AB,P(c),Erroneously
   Has Original Date;rep 18.00
07/65 **(167)** AB,P(c);rep 18.00
04/67 **(166)** AB,P(c);rep 18.00
Sg/69 **(169)** AB,EdM New P(c),
   25¢(c)Price, Rigid(c);rep 30.00

100-MUTINY ON
THE BOUNTY
By Charrles Nordhoff
10/52 **(100)** MsW,HcK P(c),Orig... 75.00
03/54 **(117)** MsW,HcK P(c);rep ... 20.00
05/56 **(132)** MsW,HcK P(c);rep ... 20.00
01/58 **(142)** MsW,HcK P(c);rep ... 20.00
03/60 **(155)** MsW,HcK P(c);rep ... 18.00
62/63 **(167)** MsW,HcK P(c),Erroneously
   Has Original Date;rep 18.00
05/64 **(167)** MsW,HcK P(c);rep ... 18.00
03/66 **(167)** MsW,HcK P(c),N#
   or Price;rep 20.00
Sg/70 **(169)** MsW,HcK P(c),
   Rigid(c); rep 18.00

101-WILLIAM TELL
By Frederick Schiller
11/52 **(101)** MDb,HcK P(c),Orig.. 75.00
04/54 **(118)** MDb,HcK P(c);rep ... 20.00
11/57 **(141)** MDb,HcK P(c);rep ... 20.00
09/60 **(158)** MDb,HcK P(c);rep ... 18.00
62/63 **(167)** MDb,HcK P(c),Erroneously
   Has Original Date;rep 18.00
11/64 **(167)** MDb,HcK P(c);rep ... 18.00
04/67 **(166)** MDb,HcK P(c);rep ... 18.00

Wr/69 **(169)** MDb,HcK P(c)25¢(c)
   Price, Rigid(c);rep 18.00

102-THE WHITE
COMPANY
By Sir Arthur Conan Doyle
12/52 **(101)** AB,P(c),Original 125.00
1962 **(165)** AB,P(c);rep 35.00
04/64 **(167)** AB,P(c);rep 35.00

103-MEN AGAINST
THE SEA
By Charles Nordhoff
01/53 **(104)** RP,HcK P(c),Original . 75.00
12/53 **(114)** RP,HcK P(c);rep 30.00
03/56 **(131)** RP,New P(c);rep 35.00
03/59 **(149)** RP,P(c);rep 30.00
09/60 **(158)** RP,P(c);rep 38.00
03/64 **(167)** RP,P(c);rep 25.00

104-BRING 'EM BACK
ALIVE
By Frank Buck & Edward
Anthony
02/53 **(105)** HcK,HcK P(c)Original. 75.00
04/54 **(118)** HcK,HcK P(c);rep 20.00
07/56 **(133)** HcK,HcK P(c);rep 20.00
05/59 **(150)** HcK,HcK P(c);rep..... 18.00
09/60 **(158)** HcK,HcK P(c);rep 18.00
10/63 **(167)** HcK,HcK P(c);rep..... 18.00
09/65 **(167)** HcK,HcK P(c);rep..... 18.00
Wr/69 **(169)** HcK,HcK P(c),25¢(c)
   Price, Rigid(c);rep 18.00

105-FROM THE EARTH
TO THE MOON
By Jules Verne
03/53 **(106)** AB,P(c),Original 65.00
04/54 **(118)** AB,P(c);rep 20.00
03/56 **(132)** AB,P(c);rep 20.00
11/57 **(141)** AB,P(c);rep 20.00
09/58 **(146)** AB,P(c);rep 20.00
05/60 **(156)** AB,P(c);rep 20.00
62/63 **(167)** AB,P(c),Erroneously
   Has Original Date;rep 18.00
05/64 **(167)** AB,P(c);rep 18.00
05/65 **(167)** AB,P(c);rep 18.00
10/67 **(166)** AB,P(c);rep 18.00
Sr/69 **(169)** AB,P(c),25¢(c)
   Price, Rigid(c);rep 18.00
Sg/71 **(169)** AB,P(c);rep.......... 18.00

106-BUFFALO BILL
By William F. Cody
04/53 **(107)** MDb,P(c),Original.... 60.00
04/54 **(118)** MDb,P(c);rep 20.00
03/56 **(132)** MDb,P(c);rep 20.00
01/58 **(142)** MDb,P(c);rep 20.00
03/61 **(161)** MDb,P(c);rep 18.00
03/64 **(167)** MDb,P(c);rep 18.00
07/67 **(166)** MDb,P(c);rep 18.00
Fl/69 **(169)** MDb,P(c),Rigid(c);rep . 18.00

107-KING OF THE
KHYBER RIFLES
By Talbot Mundy
05/53 **(108)** SMz,P(c),Original 60.00
04/54 **(118)** SMz,P(c);rep........ 20.00
09/58 **(146)** SMz,P(c);rep 20.00
09/60 **(158)** SMz,P(c);rep 18.00
62/63 **(167)** SMz,P(c),Erroreously
   Has Original Date;rep 18.00
62/63 **(167)** SMz,P(c);rep 18.00
10/66 **(167)** SMz,P(c);rep 18.00

108-KNIGHTS OF THE
ROUND TABLE
By Howard Pyle?
06/53 **(108)** AB,P(c),Original 65.00
06/53 **(109)** AB,P(c),Original 70.00
03/54 **(117)** AB,P(c);rep 20.00
11/59 **(153)** AB,P(c);rep 18.00
1962 **(165)** AB,P(c);rep 18.00
04/64 **(167)** AB,P(c);rep 18.00
04/67 **(166)** AB,P(c);rep 18.00

109-PITCAIRN'S ISLAND
By Charles Nordhoff
07/53 **(110)** RP,P(c),Original 65.00
1962 **(165)** RP,P(c);rep 20.00
03/64 **(167)** RP,P(c);rep 20.00
06/67 **(166)** RP,P(c);rep 20.00

110-A STUDY IN
SCARLET
By Sir Arthur Conan Doyle
08/53 **(111)** SMz,P(c),Original ... 150.00
1962 **(165)** SMz,P(c);rep 100.00

111-THE TALISMAN
By Sir Walter Scott
09/53 **(112)** HcK,HcK P(c),Original 75.00
1962 **(165)** HcK,HcK P(c);rep 20.00
05/64 **(167)** HcK,HcK P(c);rep.... 20.00
Fl/68 **(166)** HcK,HcK P(c),
   25¢(c)Price;rep 20.00

112-ADVENTURES OF
KIT CARSON
By John S. C. Abbott
10/53 **(113)** RP,P(c),Original 65.00
11/55 **(129)** RP,P(c);rep.......... 20.00
11/57 **(141)** RP,P(c);rep 20.00
09/59 **(152)** RP,P(c);rep.......... 18.00
03/61 **(161)** RP,P(c);rep 18.00
62/63 **(167)** RP,P(c);rep 18.00
02/65 **(167)** RP,P(c);rep 18.00
05/66 **(167)** RP,P(c);rep 18.00
Wr/69 **(166)** RP,EdM New P(c),
   25¢(c)Price, Rigid(c);rep 25.00

113-THE FORTY-FIVE
GUARDSMEN
By Alexandre Dumas
11/53 **(114)** MDb,P(c),Original ... 100.00
07/67 **(166)** MDb,P(c);rep 50.00

114-THE RED ROVER
By James Fenimore Cooper
12/53 **(115)** PrC,JP P(c),Original . 100.00
07/67 **(166)** PrC,JP P(c);rep 50.00

115-HOW I FOUND
LIVINGSTONE
By Sir Henry Stanley
01/54 **(116)** SF&ST,P(c),Original . 120.00
01/67 **(167)** SF&ST,P(c);rep 60.00

116-THE BOTTLE IMP
By Robert Louis Stevenson
02/54 **(117)** LC,P(c),Original 120.00
01/67 **(167)** LC,P(c);rep......... 60.00

Classics Illus.

117-CAPTAINS COURAGEOUS
By Rudyard Kipling
03/54 **(118)** PrC,P(c),Original . . . 125.00
02/67 **(167)** PrC,P(c);rep 32.00
Fl/69 **(169)** PrC,P(c),25¢(c)
Price, Rigid(c);rep 30.00

118-ROB ROY
By Sir Walter Scott
04/54 **(119)** RP,WlP,P(c),Original . 120.00
02/67 **(167)** RP,WlP,P(c);rep 60.00

119-SOLDERS OF FORTUNE
By Richard Harding Davis
05/54 **(120)** KS,P(c),Original 90.00
03/67 **(166)** KS,P(c);rep. 32.00
Sg/70 **(169)** KS,P(c),25¢(c)
Price, Rigid(c);rep 30.00

120-THE HURRICANE
By Charles Nordhoff
1954 **(121)** LC,LC P(c),Original . . . 90.00
03/67 **(166)** LC,LC P(c);rep 45.00

121-WILD BILL HICKOK
Author Unknown
07/54 **(122)** MI,ST,P(c),Original . . . 60.00
05/56 **(132)** MI,ST,P(c);rep 20.00
11/57 **(141)** MI,ST,P(c);rep. 20.00
01/60 **(154)** MI,ST,P(c);rep 20.00
62/63 **(167)** MI,ST,P(c);rep 18.00
08/64 **(167)** MI,ST,P(c);rep 18.00
04/67 **(166)** MI,ST,P(c);rep 18.00
Wr/69 **(169)** MI,ST,P(c),Rigid
(c);rep 18.00

122-THE MUTINEERS
By Charles Boardman Hawes
09/54 **(123)** PrC,P(c),Original 75.00
01/57 **(136)** PrC,P(c);rep 20.00
09/58 **(146)** PrC,P(c);rep 20.00
09/60 **(158)** PrC,P(c);rep 18.00
11/63 **(167)** PrC,P(c);rep 18.00
03/65 **(167)** PrC,P(c);rep 18.00
08/67 **(166)** PrC,P(c);rep 18.00

123-FANG AND CLAW
By Frank Buck
11/54 **(124)** LnS,P(c),Original 75.00
07/56 **(133)** LnS,P(c);rep 20.00
03/58 **(143)** LnS,P(c);rep 20.00
01/60 **(154)** LnS,P(c);rep 18.00
62/63 **(167)** LnS,P(c),Erroneously
Has Original Date;rep 18.00
09/65 **(167)** LnS,P(c);rep 18.00

124-THE WAR OF THE WORLDS
By H. G. Wells
01/55 **(125)** LC,LC P(c),Original . 100.00
03/56 **(131)** LC,LC P(c);rep 20.00
11/57 **(141)** LC,LC P(c);rep 20.00
01/59 **(148)** LC,LC P(c);rep 20.00
05/60 **(156)** LC,LC P(c);rep 25.00
1962 **(165)** LC,LC P(c);rep 20.00
62/63 **(167)** LC,LC P(c);rep 20.00
11/64 **(167)** LC,LC P(c);rep 20.00
11/65 **(167)** LC,LC P(c);rep 20.00
1968 **(166)** LC,LC P(c),25¢(c)
Price; rep 20.00

Sr/70 **(169)** LC,LC P(c),Rigid
(c);rep 20.00

125-THE OX BOW INCIDENT
By Walter Van Tilberg Clark
03/55 **(—-)** NN,P(c),Original 65.00
03/58 **(143)** NN,P(c);rep 20.00
09/59 **(152)** NN,P(c);rep 20.00
03/61 **(149)** NN,P(c);rep 20.00
62/63 **(167)** NN,P(c);rep. 18.00
11/64 **(167)** NN,P(c);rep. 18.00
04/67 **(166)** NN,P(c);rep 18.00
r/69 **(169)** NN,P(c),25¢(c)
Price, Rigid(c);rep 18.00

126-THE DOWNFALL
By Emile Zola
05/55 **(—-)** LC,LC P(c),Original,'
Picture Progress'Replaces
Reorder List. 75.00
08/64 **(167)** LC,LC P(c);rep 25.00
1968 **(166)** LC,LC P(c),25¢(c)
Price;rep 25.00

127-THE KING OF THE MOUNTAINS
By Edmond About
07/55 **(128)** NN,P(c),Original 75.00
06/64 **(167)** NN,P(c);rep 22.00
Fl/68 **(166)** NN,P(c),25¢(c)
Price;rep 22.00

128-MACBETH
By William Shakespeare
09/55 **(128)** AB,P(c),Original 75.00
03/58 **(143)** AB,P(c);rep 20.00
09/60 **(158)** AB,P(c);rep 20.00
62/63 **(167)** AB,P(c);rep 18.00
06/64 **(167)** AB,P(c);rep 18.00
04/67 **(166)** AB,P(c);rep 18.00
1968 **(166)** AB,P(c),25¢(c)
Price;rep 18.00
Sg/70 **(169)** AB,P(c),Rigid(c);rep . . 18.00

129-DAVY CROCKETT
Author Unknown
11/55 **(129)** LC,P(c),Original 150.00
09/66 **(167)** LC,P(c);rep 100.00

130-CAESAR'S CONQUESTS
By Julius Caesar
01/56 **(130)** JO,P(c),Original 75.00
01/58 **(142)** JO,P(c);rep. 20.00
09/59 **(152)** JO,P(c);rep 20.00
03/61 **(149)** JO,P(c);rep 20.00
62/63 **(167)** JO,P(c);rep. 18.00
10/64 **(167)** JO,P(c);rep. 18.00
04/66 **(167)** JO,P(c);rep. 18.00

131-THE COVERED WAGON
By Emerson Hough
03/56 **(131)** NN,P(c),Original 75.00
03/58 **(143)** NN,P(c);rep 20.00
09/59 **(152)** NN,P(c);rep 20.00
09/60 **(158)** NN,P(c);rep 20.00
62/63 **(167)** NN,P(c);rep 18.00
11/64 **(167)** NN,P(c);rep 18.00
04/66 **(167)** NN,P(c);rep 18.00
Wr/69 **(169)** NN,P(c),25¢(c)
Price, Rigid(c);rep 18.00

132-THE DARK FRIGATE
By Charles Boardman Hawes
05/56 **(132)** EW&RWb,P(c),Orig. . 75.00
05/59 **(150)** EW&RWb,P(c);rep . . . 20.00
01/64 **(167)** EW&RWb,P(c);rep . . . 20.00
05/67 **(166)** EW&RWb,P(c);rep . . . 20.00

133-THE TIME MACHINE
By H. G. Wells
07/56 **(132)** LC,P(c),Original 90.00
01/58 **(142)** LC,P(c);rep. 20.00
09/59 **(152)** LC,P(c);rep 20.00
09/60 **(158)** LC,P(c);rep 20.00
62/63 **(167)** LC,P(c);rep 25.00
06/64 **(167)** LC,P(c);rep 25.00
03/66 **(167)** LC,P(c);rep 20.00
03/66 **(167)** LC,P(c),N# Or Price;
rep 20.00
12/67 **(166)** LC,P(c);rep 20.00
Wr/71 **(169)** LC,P(c),25¢(c)
Price, Rigid(c);rep 20.00

134-ROMEO AND JULIET
By William Shakespeare
09/56 **(134)** GE,P(c),Original 75.00
03/61 **(161)** GE,P(c);rep 20.00
09/63 **(167)** GE,P(c);rep 18.00
05/65 **(167)** GE,P(c);rep 18.00
06/67 **(166)** GE,P(c);rep 18.00
Wr/69 **(166)** GE,EdM New P(c),
25¢(c)Price, Rigid(c);rep 32.00

135-WATERLOO
By Emile Erckmann & Alexandre Chatrian
11/56 **(135)** Grl,AB P(c),Original . . 75.00
11/59 **(153)** Grl,AB P(c);rep. 20.00
62/63 **(167)** Grl,AB P(c);rep. 18.00
09/64 **(167)** Grl,AB P(c);rep. 18.00
1968 **(166)** Grl,AB P(c),25¢(c)
Price; rep. 18.00

136-LORD JIM
By Joseph Conrad
01/57 **(136)** GE,P(c),Original 75.00
62/63 **(165)** GE,P(c);rep 18.00
03/64 **(167)** GE,P(c);rep 18.00
09/66 **(167)** GE,P(c);rep 18.00
Sr/69 **(169)** GE,P(c),25¢(c)
Price, Rigid(c);rep 18.00

137-THE LITTLE SAVAGE
By Captain Frederick Marryat
03/57 **(136)** GE,P(c),Original 75.00
01/59 **(148)** GE,P(c);rep 20.00
05/60 **(156)** GE,P(c);rep 20.00
62/63 **(167)** GE,P(c);rep 18.00
10/64 **(167)** GE,P(c);rep 18.00
08/67 **(166)** GE,P(c);rep 18.00
Sg/70 **(169)** GE,P(c),25¢(c)
Price, Rigid(c);rep 18.00

138-A JOURNEY TO THE CENTER OF THE EARTH
By Jules Verne
05/57 **(136)** NN,P(c),Original 100.00
09/58 **(146)** NN,P(c);rep 20.00
05/60 **(156)** NN,P(c);rep 20.00
09/60 **(158)** NN,P(c);rep 20.00
62/63 **(167)** NN,P(c);rep 18.00
06/64 **(167)** NN,P(c);rep 20.00
04/66 **(167)** NN,P(c);rep 20.00
1968 **(166)** NN,P(c),25¢(c)
Price;rep 18.00

All comics prices listed are for *Near Mint* condition.

139-IN THE REIGN OF TERROR
By George Alfred Henty
07/57 **(139)** GE,P(c),Original 65.00
01/60 **(154)** GE,P(c);rep 20.00
62/63 **(167)** GE,P(c),Erroneously
Has Original Date;rep 18.00
07/64 **(167)** GE,P(c);rep 20.00
1968 **(166)** GE,P(c),25¢(c)
Price;rep 18.00

140-ON JUNGLE TRAILS
By Frank Buck
09/57 **(140)** NN,P(c),Original 65.00
05/59 **(150)** NN,P(c);rep 20.00
01/61 **(160)** NN,P(c);rep 20.00
09/63 **(167)** NN,P(c);rep 18.00
09/65 **(167)** NN,P(c);rep 18.00

141-CASTLE DANGEROUS
By Sir Walter Scott
11/57 **(141)** StC,P(c),Original 85.00
09/59 **(152)** STC,P(c);rep 20.00
62/63 **(167)** StC,P(c);rep 18.00
07/67 **(166)** StC,P(c);rep 18.00

142-ABRAHAM LINCOLN
By Benjamin Thomas
01/58 **(142)** NN,P(c),Original 75.00
01/60 **(154)** NN,P(c);rep 20.00
09/60 **(158)** NN,P(c);rep 20.00
10/63 **(167)** NN,P(c);rep 18.00
07/65 **(167)** NN,P(c);rep 18.00
11/67 **(166)** NN,P(c);rep 18.00
Fl/69 **(169)** NN,P(c),25¢(c) Price,
Rigid(c);rep 18.00

143-KIM
By Rudyard Kipling
03/58 **(143)** JO,P(c)Original 65.00
62/63 **(165)** JO,P(c);rep 18.00
11/63 **(167)** JO,P(c);rep 18.00
08/65 **(167)** JO,P(c);rep 18.00
Wr/69 **(169)** JO,P(c),25¢(c) Price,
Rigid(c);rep 18.00

144-THE FIRST MEN IN THE MOON
By H. G. Wells
05/58 **(143)** GWb,AW,AT,RKr,
GMC P(c), Original 90.00
11/59 **(153)** GWb,AW,AT,RKr,
GMC, P(c); rep 20.00
03/61 **(161)** GWb,AW,AT,RKr,
GMC, P(c); rep 18.00
62/63 **(167)** GWb,AW,AT,RKr,
GMC, P(c); rep 18.00
12/65 **(167)** GWb,AW,AT,RKr,
GMC, P(c); rep 18.00
Fl/68 **(166)** GWb,AW,AT,RKr,GMC
P(c),25¢(c) Price,Rigid(c);rep . 18.00
Wr/69 **(169)** GWb,AW,AT,RKr,GMC
P(c), Rigid(c);rep 28.00

145-THE CRISIS
by Winston Churchill
07/58 **(143)** GE,P(c),Original 75.00
05/60 **(156)** GE,P(c);rep 20.00
10/63 **(167)** GE,P(c);rep 18.00
03/65 **(167)** GE,P(c);rep 18.00
1968 **(166)** GE,P(c),25¢(c)
Price;rep 18.00

146-WITH FIRE AND SWORD
By Henryk Sienkiewicz
09/58 **(143)** GWb,P(c),Original . . . 75.00
05/60 **(156)** GWb,P(c);rep 25.00
11/63 **(167)** GWb,P(c);rep 20.00
03/65 **(167)** GWb,P(c);rep 20.00

147-BEN-HUR
By Lew Wallace
11/58 **(147)** JO,P(c),Original 60.00
11/59 **(153)** JO,P(c);rep 65.00
09/60 **(158)** JO,P(c);rep 20.00
62/63 **(167)** JO,P(c),Has the
Original Date;rep 20.00
—— **(167)** JO,P(c);rep 18.00
02/65 **(167)** JO,P(c);rep 18.00
09/66 **(167)** JO,P(c);rep 18.00
Fl/68 **(166)** JO,P(c),25¢(c)Price,
Both Rigid & Soft (c)s;rep 50.00

148-THE BUCKANEER
By Lyle Saxon
01/59 **(148)** GE&RJ,NS P(c),orig. . 65.00
—— **(568)** GE&RJ,NS P(c),Juniors
List Only;rep 20.00
62/63 **(167)** GE&RJ,NS P(c);rep . . 20.00
09/65 **(167)** GE&RJ,NS P(c);rep . . 20.00
Sr/69 **(169)** GE&RJ,NS P(c),25¢(c)
Price, Rigid(c);rep 20.00

CI #149, Off on a Comet
© Gilberton Publications

149-OFF ON A COMET
By Jules Verne
03/59 **(149)** GMc,P(c),Original 75.00
03/60 **(155)** GMc,P(c);rep 20.00
03/61 **(149)** GMc,P(c);rep 20.00
12/63 **(167)** GMc,P(c);rep 18.00
02/65 **(167)** GMc,P(c);rep 18.00
10/66 **(167)** GMc,P(c);rep 18.00
Fl/68 **(166)** GMc,EdM New P(c),
25¢(c)Price;rep 30.00

150-THE VIRGINIAN
By Owen Winster
05/59 **(150)** NN,DrG P(c),Original . 90.00
1961 **(164)** NN,DrG P(c);rep 30.00
62/63 **(167)** NN,DrG P(c);rep. 35.00
12/65 **(167)** NN,DrG P(c);rep. 30.00

151-WON BY THE SWORD
By George Alfred Henty
07/59 **(150)** JTg,P(c),Original 75.00
1961 **(164)** JTg,P(c);rep. 25.00
10/63 **(167)** JTg,P(c);rep. 25.00
1963 **(167)** JTg,P(c);rep. 25.00
07/67 **(166)** JTg,P(c);rep. 25.00

152-WILD ANIMALS I HAVE KNOWN
By Ernest Thompson Seton
09/59 **(152)** LbC,LbC P(c),Original 85.00
03/61 **(149)** LbC,LbC P(c),P(c);rep 20.00
09/63 **(167)** LbC,LbC P(c);rep 18.00
08/65 **(167)** LbC,LbC P(c);rep 18.00
fl/69 **(169)** LbC,LbC P(c),25¢(c)
Price, Rigid(c);rep 18.00

153-THE INVISIBLE MAN
By H. G. Wells
11/59 **(153)** NN,GB P(c),Original . 100.00
03/61 **(149)** NN,GB P(c);rep 20.00
62/63 **(167)** NN,GB P(c);rep 18.00
02/65 **(167)** NN,GB P(c);rep 18.00
09/66 **(167)** NN,GB P(c);rep 18.00
Wr/69 **(166)** NN,GB P(c),25¢(c)
Price, Rigid(c);rep 18.00
Sg/71 **(169)** NN,GB P(c),Rigid(c),
Words Spelling'Invisible Man'
Are' Solid'Not'Invisible';rep . . . 18.00

154-THE CONSPIRACY OF PONTIAC
By Francis Parkman
01/60 **(154)** GMc,GMc P(c),
Original 75.00
11/63 **(167)** GMc,GMc P(c);rep . . 30.00
07/64 **(167)** GMc,GMc P(c);rep . . 30.00
12/67 **(166)** GMc,GMc P(c);rep . . 30.00

155-THE LION OF THE NORTH
By George Alfred Henty
03/60 **(154)** NN,GMc P(c),Original. 75.00
01/64 **(167)** NN,GMc P(c);rep . . . 25.00
1967 **(166)** NN,GMc P(c),25¢(c)
Price; rep 20.00

156-THE CONQUEST OF MEXICO
By Bernal Diaz Del Castillo
05/60 **(156)** BPr,BPr P(c),Original . 75.00
01/64 **(167)** BPr,BPr P(c);rep. 20.00
08/67 **(166)** BPr,BPr P(c);rep. 20.00
Sg/70 **(169)** BPr,BPr P(c),25¢(c)
Price; Rigid(c);rep 18.00

157-LIVES OF THE HUNTED
By Ernest Thompson Seton
07/60 **(156)** NN,LbC P(c),Original . 90.00
02/64 **(167)** NN,LbC P(c);rep. 28.00
10/67 **(166)** NN,LbC P(c);rep. 28.00

158-THE CONSPIRATORS
By Alexandre Dumas
09/60 **(156)** GMc,GMc P(c),
Original 90.00
07/64 **(167)** GMc,GMc P(c);rep . . 28.00
10/67 **(166)** GMc,GMc P(c);rep . . 28.00

159-THE OCTOPUS
By Frank Norris
11/60 **(159)** GM&GE,LbC P(c),
Original 90.00
02/64 **(167)** GM&GE,LbC P(c);rep. 28.00
166 **(1967)** GM&GE,LbC P(c),25¢(c)
Price;rep 28.00

160-THE FOOD OF THE GODS
By H.G. Wells
01/61 **(159)** TyT,GMc P(c),Original 85.00
01/61 **(160)** TyT,GMc P(c),Original;
Same Except For the HRN# . . 60.00
01/64 **(167)** TyT,GMc P(c);rep 28.00
06/67 **(166)** TyT,GMc P(c);rep 28.00

161-CLEOPATRA
By H. Rider Haggard
03/61 **(161)** NN,Pch P(c),Original . 75.00
01/64 **(167)** NN,Pch P(c);rep 30.00
08/67 **(166)** NN,Pch P(c);rep 30.00

162-ROBUR THE CONQUEROR
By Jules Verne
05/61 **(162)** GM&DPn,CJ P(c),
Original 80.00
07/64 **(167)** GM&DPn,CJ P(c);rep. 28.00
08/67 **(166)** GM&DPn,CJ P(c);rep. 28.00

163-MASTER OF THE WORLD
By Jules Verne
07/61 **(163)** GM,P(c),Original. 80.00
01/65 **(167)** GM,P(c);rep 28.00
1968 **(166)** GM,P(c),25¢(c)
Price;rep 28.00

164-THE COSSACK CHIEF
By Nicolai Gogol
1961 **(164)** SyM,P(c),Original 80.00
04/65 **(167)** SyM,P(c);rep 28.00
Fl/68 **(166)** SyM,P(c),25¢(c)
Price;rep 28.00

165-THE QUEEN'S NECKLACE
by Alexandre Dumas
01/62 **(164)** GM,P(c),Original. 80.00
04/65 **(167)** GM,P(c);rep 28.00
Fl/68 **(166)** GM,P(c),25¢(c)
Price;rep 28.00

166-TIGERS AND TRAITORS
By Jules Verne
05/62 **(165)** NN,P(c),Original 125.00
02/64 **(167)** NN,P(c);rep 40.00
11/66 **(167)** NN,P(c);rep. 40.00

167-FAUST
By Johann Wolfgang von Goethe
08/62 **(165)** NN,NN P(c),Original. 200.00
02/64 **(167)** NN,NN P(c);rep 75.00
06/67 **(166)** NN,NN P(c);rep 75.00

168-IN FREEDOM'S CAUSE
By George Alfred Henty
Wr/69 **(169)** GE&RC,P(c),
Original, Rigid (c). 225.00

169-NEGRO AMERICANS THE EARLY YEARS
AUTHOR UNKNOWN
Sg/69 **(166)** NN,NN P(c),
Original, Rigid(c) 200.00
Sg/69 **(169)** NN,NN P(c),
Rigid; rep 100.00

CLASSICS ILLUSTRATED GIANTS
An Illustrated Library of Great
Adventure Stories -(reps. of
Issues 6,7,8,10) 2,000.00
An Illustrated Library of Exciting
Mystery Stories -(reps. of
Issues 30,21,40,13) 2,100.00
An Illustrated Library of Great
Indian Stories -(reps. of
Issues 4,17,22,37) 2,000.00

CLASSICS ILLUSTRATED JUNIOR
Oct., 1953–Spring., 1971
501-Snow White and the
Seven Dwarfs 125.00
502-The Ugly Duckling 75.00
503-Cinderella 50.00
504-The Pied Piper 45.00
505-The Sleeping Beauty 45.00
506-The Three Little Pigs 45.00
507-Jack and the Beanstalk 45.00
508-Goldilocks & the Three Bears. 45.00
509-Beauty and the Beast 45.00
510-Little Red Riding Hood 45.00
511-Puss-N-Boots 45.00
512-Rumpelstiltskin 45.00
513-Pinocchio 55.00
514-The Steadfast Tin Soldier . . . 75.00
515-Johnny Appleseed 50.00
516-Aladdin and His Lamp 40.00
517-The Emperor's New Clothes . 40.00
518-The Golden Goose 40.00
519-Paul Bunyan 40.00
520-Thumbelina 50.00
521-King of the Golden River 45.00
522-The Nightingale. 35.00
523-The Gallant Tailor 35.00
524-The Wild Swans 35.00
525-The Little Mermaid 40.00
526-The Frog Prince 40.00
527-The Golden-Haired Giant . . . 40.00
528-The Penny Prince 35.00
529-The Magic Servants 35.00
530-The Golden Bird 35.00
531-Rapunzel. 40.00
532-The Dancing Princesses. . . . 35.00
533-The Magic Fountain 35.00
534-The Golden Touch 35.00
535-The Wizard of Oz 75.00
536-The Chimney Sweep 40.00
537-The Three Fairies 35.00
538-Silly Hans 35.00
539-The Enchanted Fish 50.00
540-The Tinder-Box. 50.00
541-Snow White and Rose Red . . 35.00
542-The Donkey's Tail 35.00
543-The House in the Woods 32.00
544-The Golden Fleece 55.00
545-The Glass Mountain 42.00
546-The Elves and the Shoemaker 35.00
547-The Wishing Table 35.00
548-The Magic Pitcher. 30.00
549-Simple Kate 30.00
550-The Singing Donkey 30.00
551-The Queen Bee 30.00
552-The Three Little Dwarfs 40.00
553-King Thrushbeard 30.00
554-The Enchanted Deer 30.00
555-The Three Golden Apples. . . 30.00
556-The Elf Mound 30.00
557-Silly Willy. 50.00
558-The Magic Dish,LbC(c). 50.00
559-The Japanese Lantern,LbC(c) 60.00
560-The Doll Princess,LbC(c) . . . 60.00
561-Hans Humdrum,LbC(c). 40.00
562-The Enchanted Pony,LbC(c) . 60.00
563-The Wishing Well,LbC(c) . . . 40.00
564-The Salt Mountain,LbC(c). . . 40.00
565-The Silly Princess,LbC(c) . . . 40.00
566-Clumsy Hans,LbC(c). 40.00
567-The Bearskin Soldier,LbC(c). . 40.00
568-The Happy Hedgehog,LbC(c). 40.00
569-The Three Giants 40.00
570-The Pearl Princess 40.00
571-How Fire Came to the Indians 55.00
572-The Drummer Boy 55.00
573-The Crystal Ball 55.00
574-Brightboots 50.00
575-The Fearless Prince 50.00
576-The Princess Who Saw
Everything 65.00
577-The Runaway Dumpling 75.00

CLASSICS ILLLUSTRATED SPECIAL ISSUE
Dec., 1955–July, 1962
N# United Nations 400.00
129-The Story of Jesus,Jesus on
mountain(c) 125.00
129a-Three Camels(c). 135.00
129b-Mountain(c),HRN to 161 . . 100.00
129c-Mountain(c) (1968) 75.00
132A-The Story of America 90.00
135A-The Ten Commandments. . 80.00
138A-Adventures in Science 75.00
138Aa-HRN to 149 . . . . 50.00
138Ab-rep.,12/61 . . . . 60.00
141A-GE,The Rough Rider 75.00
144A-RC,GE,Blazing the Trails . . 80.00
147A-RC,GE,Crossing the Rockies 75.00
150A-Grl,Royal Canadian Police. . 75.00
153A-GE,Men, Guns, & Cattle. . . 75.00
156A-GE,GM,The Atomic Age . . 75.00
159A-GE,GM,Rockets, Jets and
Missiles 75.00
162A-RC,GE,War Between
the States 165.00
165A-RC/GE,JK,Grl,To the Stars. 100.00
166A-RC-GE,JK,Grl,World War II 125.00
167A-RC/GE,JK,Prehistoric
World 125.00
167Aa-HRN to 167. . . . . 110.00

Classics Illus.

UNDERGROUND

AMAZING DOPE TALES
Greg Shaw
1 Untrimmed black and white pages,
   out of order;artist unknown . . 110.00
2 Trimmed and proper pages 95.00

AMERICAN SPLENDOR
Harvey Pekar, May, 1976
1 B:Harvey Pekar Stories,
   HP,RCr,GDu,GBu 25.00
2 HP,RCr,GDu,GBu 10.00
3 HP,RCr,GDu,GBu 10.00
4 HP,RCr,GDu,GBu 8.00
5 HP,RCr,GDu,GBu 8.00
6 HP,RCr,GDu,GBu,GSh 7.00
7 HP,GSh,GDu,GBu 5.00
8 HP,GSh,GDu,GBu 3.00
9 and 10 HP,GSh,GDu,GBu . . . . @3.00
11 . . . . 3.00
12 . . . . 4.50
13 thru 19 . . . . @3.50
20 E:Harvey Pekar Stories 4.00

ANTHOLOGY OF SLOW DEATH
Wingnut Press/Last Gasp
1 140 pgs, RCr,RCo, GiS, DSh,
   Harlan Ellison VB,RTu 37.00

APEX TREASURY OF UNDERGROUND COMICS, THE
Links Books Inc., Oct., 1974
1 . . . . 40.00

APEX TREASURY OF UNDERGROUND COMICS –BEST OF BIJOU FUNNIES
Quick Fox, 1981
1 Paperback,comix,various artists 21.00

ARCADE THE COMICS REVUE
Print Mint Inc. Spring, 1975
1 ASp,BG,RCr,SRo,SCW 25.00
2 ASp,BG,RCr,SRo 15.00
3 ASp,BG,RCr,RW,SCW 10.00
4 ASp,BG,RCr,WBu,RW, SCW . . . 10.00
5 thru 7 ASp,BG,SRo,RW,SCW . @7.50

BABYFAT
Comix World/Clay Geerdes, 1978
1 B:8pg news parodies, one page
   comix by various artists 4.50
2 thru 9 same . . . . @3.00
10 thru 26 same . . . . @2.00

BATTLE OF THE TITANS
University of Illinois SF Society, 1972
1 Sci-Fi;VB,JGa 50.00

BEST BUY COMICS
Last Gasp Eco-Funnies
1 Rep Whole Earth Review;RCr. . . 3.50

BEST OF BIJOU FUNNIES, THE
Links Books Inc., 1975
1 164 pgs,paperback 250.00

BEST OF RIP-OFF PRESS
Rip Off Press Inc., 1973
1 132 pgs paperback,SCW,
   RCr,SRo,RW 25.00
2 100 pgs,GS,FT 27.50
3 100 pgs,FS 10.75
4 132 pgs,GiS,DSh 13.00

BIG ASS
Rip Off Press, 1969–71
1 28 pgs,RCr. 80.00
2 RCr 50.00

BIJOU FUNNIES
Bijou Publishing Empire, 1968
1 B:JLy,editor;RCr,GS SW 300.00
2 RCr,GS,SW 125.00
3 RCr,SWi,JsG 80.00
4 SWi,JsG 45.00
5 SWi,JsG 50.00
6 E:JLy,editor,SWi,RCr,JsG 40.00
7 and 8 . . . . @40.00

BINKY BROWN MEETS THE HOLY VIRGIN MARY
Last Gasp Eco-Funnies, March, 1972
N# Autobiography about Growing up
   w/a Catholic Neurosis,JsG . . . 25.00
2nd Printing:only text in
   bottom left panel 12.00

Bizarre Sex #10
© Kitchen Sink

BIZARRE SEX
Kitchen Sink Komix, May, 1972
1 B:DKi,editor,various
   artists 30.00
2 . . . . 25.00
3 . . . . 20.00
4 thru 6 . . . . @15.00
7 . . . . 6.00
8 . . . . 5.00
9 Omaha the Cat Dancer,RW 25.00
10 inc.Omaha the Cat
   Dancer,RW 20.00

BLACK LAUGHTER
Black Laughter Pub. Co, Nov,. 1972
1 James Dixon art 64.00

BLOOD FROM A STONE (GUIDE TO TAX REFORM)
New York Public Interest Research Group Inc., 1977
1 Tax reform proposals 8.50

BOBBY LONDON RETROSPECTIVE AND ART PORTFOLIO
Cartoonist Representatives
1 . . . . 19.50

BOBMAN AND TEDDY
Parrallax Comic Books Inc., 1966
1 RFK & Ted Kennedy's struggle to
   control Democratic party 60.00

BODE'S CARTOON CONCERT
Dell, Sept., 1973
1 132 pgs; VB 27.50

BOGEYMAN COMICS
San Fransisco Comic Book Co., 1969
1 Horror,RHa. 65.00
2 Horror,RHa. 50.00
The Company & Sons
3 . . . . 35.00

BUFFALO RAG/THE DEAD CONCERT COMIX
Kenny Laramey, Dec., 1973
1 Alice in Wonderland parody 60.00

CAPTAIN GUTS
The Print Mint,1969
1 Super patriotV:Counter
   culture 30.00
2 V:Black Panthers 20.00
3 V:Dope Smugglers 20.00

CAPTAIN STICKY
Captain Sticky, 1974–75
1 Super lawyer V:SocialInjustice . 20.00

All comics prices listed are for *Near Mint* condition.

CARTOON HISTORY OF THE UNIVERSE
Rip Off Press, Sept., 1978
1 Evolution of Everything;
    B:Larry Gonick 8.00
2 Sticks and Stones 8.00
3 River Realms-Sumer & Egypt . . 8.00
4 Part of the Old Testament 5.00
5 Brains and Bronze 5.00
6 Who are these Athenians 5.00

CASCADE COMIX MONTHLY
Everyman Studios, March, 1978
1 Interviews,articles about
    comix & comix artists 6.50
2 and 3 same . . . . @6.50
4 thru 11 . . . . @3.00
12 thru 23 . . . . @2.25

CHECKERED DEMON
Last Gasp, July, 1977
1 SCW 15.00
2 SCW 8.50
3 SCW 6.50

CHEECH WIZARD
Office of Student Publications, Syracuse U, 1967
n/n VB 150.00

Cherry Collection TPB #2
© Kitchen Sink

CHERRY
Kitchen Sink
1 by Larry Welz 10.00
2 . . . . 7.00
3 thru 5 . . . . @5.00
6 thru 10 . . . . @4.00
11 thru 15 . . . . @4.00
TPB Cherry Collection #1 . . . . . . 15.00
TPB Cherry Collection #2 . . . . . . 15.00
TPB Cherry Collection #3 . . . . . . 13.00
Cherry's Jubilee #1 thru #4 . . . . . @3.00

CHICAGO MIRROR
Jay Lynch/Mirror Publishing Empire, Autumn, 1967
1 B:Bijou Funnies 50.00
2 same 40.00

---

3 same 125.00

COLLECTED CHEECH WIZARD, THE
Company & Sons, 1972
n/n VB 60.00

COLLECTED TRASHMAN #1, THE
Fat City & The Red Mountain Tribe Productions
n/n SRo 32.50

COMICS & COMIX
Oct., 1975
1 . . . . 15.00

COMIX BOOK
Magazine Management Co. Oct., 1974
1 Compilation for newsstand
    distribution 20.00
2 and 3 . . . . @10.00
Kitchen Sink Enterprises
4 . . . . 20.00
5 . . . . 10.00

COMIX COLLECTOR, THE
Archival Press Inc., Dec., 1979
1 Fanzine 5.00
2 & 3 Fanzine . . . . @4.00

COMMIES FROM MARS
Kitchen Sink, March, 1973
1 TB 40.00
Last Gasp
2 thru 5 TB . . . . @15.00

COMPLETE FRITZ THE CAT
Belier Press 1978
n/n RCr,SRo,DSh 65.00

CONSPIRACY CAPERS
The Conspiracy, 1969
1 Benefit Legal Defense of the
    Chicago-8 . . . . 100.00

DAN O'NEIL'S COMICS & STORIES
Company & Sons, Vol.1
1 B:Dan O'Neill 50.00
2 & 3 . . . . @30.00
1971 Vol. 2
1 . . . . 6.50
2 and E:Dan O'Neill . . . . @4.50

DAS KAMPF
Vaughn Bode, May, 1963
N# 100 Loose pgs. 750.00
2nd Printing 52pgs.-produced by
    W.Bachner & Bagginer,1977 . . 20.00

DEADBONE EROTICA
Bantam Books Inc., April, 1971
n/n 132 pgs VB 50.00

DEADCENTER CLEAVAGE
April, 1971
1 14 pgs 50.00

DEATH RATTLE
Kitchen Sink, June, 1972
1 RCo,TB 25.00
2 TB 20.00
3 TB 16.00

DESPAIR
The Print Mint, 1969
1 RCr 50.00

DIRTY DUCK BOOK, THE
Company & Sons, March, 1972
1 Bobby London 30.00

DISNEY RAPES THE 1st AMENDMENT
Dan O'Neil, 1974
1 Benefit Air Pirates V:Disney
    Law suit; Dan O'Neill 15.00

DOPE COMIX
Kitchen Sink, Feb., 1978
1 Drugs comix;various artists 10.00
2 same 7.00
3 & 4 LSD issue . . . . @5.00
5 Omaha the Cat Dancer, RW . . . 10.00

DOPIN DAN
Last Gasp Eco-Funnies, April, 1972
1 TR 15.00
2 and 3 TR . . . . @10.00
4 Todays Army,TR. 7.50

DR. ATOMIC
Last Gasp Eco-Funnies, Sept., 1972
1 B:Larry S. Todd 15.00
2 and 3 . . . . @12.00
4 . . . . 10.00
5 E:Larry S. Todd 6.00

DR. ATOMIC'S MARIJUANA MULTIPLIER
Kistone Press, 1974
1 How to grow great pot 10.00

DRAWINGS BY S. CLAY WILSON
San Francisco Graphics
1 28 pgs 200.00

DYING DOLPHIN
The Print Mint ,1970
n/n 20.00

EBON
San Francisco Comic Book Company
1 Comix version; RCr 30.00
1 Tabloid version 20.00

EL PERFECTO COMICS
The Print Mint, 1973
N# Benefit Timothy Leary 30.00
2nd Printing-1975 . . . . 4.00

Underground

ETERNAL TRUTH
Sunday Funnies Comic Corp
1 Christian Comix 25.00

EVERMUCH WAVE
Atlantis Distributors
1 Nunzio the Narc; Adventures
    of God 60.00

The Fabulous Furry Freak Brothers #9
© Rip Off Press

FABULOUS FURRY FREAK BROTHERS, THE
COLLECTED ADVENTURES OF
Rip Off Press, #1 Feb., 1971
1 GiS 90.00
FURTHER ADVENTURES OF
Rip Off Press, #2
1 GiS,DSh 60.00
A YEAR PASSES LIKE NOTHING WITH
Rip Off Press #3
1 GiS. 25.00
BROTHER CAN YOU SPARE $.75 FOR
Rip Off Press #4
1 GiS,DSh 20.00
FABULOUS FURRY FREAK BROTHERS, THE
Rip Off Press #5
1 GiS,DSh 15.00
SIX SNAPPY SOCKERS FROM THE ARCHIVES OF
Rip Off Press #6
1 GiS 10.00

FANTAGOR
1970
1 (Corben), fanzine. 125.00
1a (Last Gasp) 22.00
2 & 3 . . . . @25.00
4 . . . . 35.00

THE ADVENTURES OF FAT FREDDY'S CAT,
Rip Off Press, Feb., 1977
1 . . . . 20.00
2 . . . . 10.00

---

3 . . . . 12.00
4 . . . . 8.00
5 & 6 . . . . @8.00

FEDS 'N' HEADS
Gilbert Shelton/Print Mint, 1968
N# I:Fabulous Furry Freak Bros.;
    Has no `Print Mint' Address
    24 pgs. 400.00
2nd printing, 28 pgs. 60.00
3rd printing, May, 1969 . . . . 50.00
4th printing, Says `Forth
    Printing' 25.00
5th-12th printings . . . . @8.00
13th printing 6.50
14th printing 4.75

FELCH
Keith Green
1 RW,SCW,RCr. 45.00

FEVER PITCH
Kitchen Sink Enterprises, July, 1976
1 RCo 25.00
Jabberwocky Graphix
2 250 signed & numbered 20.00
3 400 signed & numbered 18.00
4 . . . . 10.00

50'S FUNNIES
Kitchen Sink Enterprises, 1980
1 Larry Shell, editor,various
    artists 10.00

FLAMING CARROT
Kilian Barracks Free Press, 1981
1 Bob Budden,various artists 15.00

FLASH THEATRE
Oogle Productions, 1970
1 44 pgs 50.00

FLESHAPOIDS FROM EARTH
Popular Culture, Dec., 1974
1 36 pgs 40.00

THE COMPLETE FOO!
Bijou Publishing, Sept., 1980
1 RCr, Charles Crumb, r:Crumb
    brothers fanzines 50.00

FRITZ BUGS OUT
Ballentine Books, 1972
n/n RCr. 70.00

FRITZ THE CAT
Ballentine Books, 1969
n/n RCr. 125.00

FRITZ THE NO-GOOD
Ballentine Books, 1972
n/n RCr. 60.00

FRITZ: SECRET AGENT FOR THE CIA
Ballentine Books, 1972
n/n RCr. 60.00

FUNNY AMINALS
Apex Novelties/Don Donahue, 1972
1 RCr 65.00

GAY COMIX
Kitchen Sink Sept., 1981
1 36 pgs 7.50
2 36 pgs 5.00

GEN OF HIROSHIMA
Educomics/Leonard Rifas, Jan., 1980
1 Antiwar comix by Hiroshima
    survivor Keiji Nakawaza 9.50
2 same 6.50

GHOST MOTHER COMICS
John "Mad" Peck, 1969
1 SCw,JsG 55.00

GIMMEABREAK COMIX
Rhuta Press, Feb., 1971
2 48 pgs, #0 & #1 were advertised,but .
may not have been printed 125.00

GIRLS & BOYS
Lynda J. Barry, 1980
1 B:12 pgs with every other page
    blank, all Barry art 10.00
2 thru 10 same . . . . @6.50
11 thru 20 same . . . . @4.50
20 thru 25 same . . . . @3.50

GOD NOSE
Jack Jackson/ Rip Off Press, 1964
N# 42 pgs. 125.00
2nd printing,Pinkish(c);44p 60.00
3rd printing,Blue Border(c) 30.00
4th printing,Red Border(c) 15.00

GOTHIC BLIMP WORKS LTD.
East Village Other/ Peter Leggieri, 1969
1 VB,Editor,various artists. 200.00
2 same 145.00
3 KDe,editor 135.00
4 KDe,editor 130.00
5 thru 7 KDe,editor . . . . @125.00
8 various artists. 185.00

GREASER COMICS
Half-Ass Press, Sept., 1971
1 28 pgs, George DiCaprio 25.00
Rip Off Press, July, 1972
2 George DiCaprio 15.00

GRIM WIT
Last Gasp, 1972
1 RCo 40.00
2 RCo 30.00

HAROLD HEAD, THE COLLECTED ADVENTURES OF
Georgia Straight, 1972
1 . . . . 50.00
2 . . . . 15.00

HARRY CHESS THAT MAN FROM A.U.N.T.I.E.
The Uncensored Adventures, Trojan Book Service, 1966
N# 1st Comix By & For Gay
  Community 135.00

HEAR THE SOUND OF MY FEET WALKING....
Glide Urban Center, 1969
1 Dan O'Neill, 128 pgs. 70.00

HISTORY OF UNDERGROUND COMIX
Straight Arrow Books, 1974
1 Book by Mark James Estren about
  Underground Comix 40.00

HOMEGROWN FUNNIES
Kitchen Sink, 1971
1 RCr 60.00

HONKYTONK SUE, THE QUEEN OF COUNTRY SWING
Bob Boze Bell, Feb., 1979
1 BBB 15.00
2 & 3 BBB . . . . @10.00

IKE LIVES
Warm Neck Funnies, 1973
1 20 pgs,Mark Fisher 15.00

INSECT FEAR
Last Gasp, 1970
1 SRo,GiS,RHa,JsG 75.00
Print Mint, 1970–72
2 . . . . 30.00
3 . . . . 20.00

IT AIN'T ME BABE
Last Gasp Eco-Funnies, July. 1970
n/n First all women comix
  Womens Liberation theme . . . 40.00

JAPANESE MONSTER
Carol Lay, July, 1979
1 8pgs, Carol Lay 10.00

JESUS LOVES YOU
Zondervan Books/Craig Yoe, 1972
1 Christian, RCr 35.00

THE NEW ADVENTURES OF JESUS
Rip Off Press, Nov., 1971
1 44 pgs, FSt 50.00

JIZ
Apex Novelty, 1969
1 36 pgs; RCr, SRo, VMo, SCW; hand
  trimmed and unevenly stapled 60.00

JUNKWAFFEL
The Print Mint, 1971
1 VB 35.00
2 and 3 VB . . . . @30.00
4 VB,JJ 25.00

KANNED KORN KOMIX
Canned Heat Fan Club, 1969
1 20pgs 15.00

KAPTAIN AMERIKA KOMIX
Brief Candle Comix, March 1970
1 anti U.S. involvement in Laos . . . 35.00

KING BEE
Apex/Don Donahue & Kerry Clark, 1969
1 RCr,SCW 140.00

KURTZMAN COMIX
Kitchen Sink, Sept., 1976
1 HK,RCr,GiS,DKi,WE 30.00

LAUGH IN THE DARK
Last Gasp
n/n KDe,RHa,SRo,SCW 20.00

LENNY OF LAVEDO
Sunbury Productions/Print Mint, 1965
N# Green(c);1st Joel Beck-a . . . 550.00
2nd printing, Orange(c) 400.00
3rd printing, White(c) 200.00

THE MACHINES
Office of Student Publications Syracuse University, 1967
1 VB 135.00

THE MAN
Office of Student Publications Syracuse University, 1966
1 VB 165.00

MAGGOTZINE
Charles Schneider, May, 1981
1 Various Artists,conceptual
  maggot stuff 10.00

MANTICORE
Joe Kubert School of Cartooning & Graphic Arts Inc., Autumn, 1976
1 Fanzine,various artists 10.00

MEAN BITCH THRILLS
The Print Mint, 1971
1 SRO 15.00

MICKEY RAT
Los Angeles Comic Book Co., May, 1972
1 Robert Armstrong 35.00
2 same 35.00
3 same 15.00

MOM'S HOMEMADE COMICS
Kitchen Sink, June, 1969
1 DKi, RCr 130.00
The Print Mint
2 DKi 40.00
Kitchen Sink Enterprises
3 DKi,RCr 30.00

MONDAY FUNNIES, THE
Monday Funnies, 1977
1 8pgs,various artists 6.50
2 16pgs,various artists 9.00
3 16pgs,various artists 6.50
4 16pgs,various artists 5.50

MONDAY FUNNIES, THE
Passtime Publ., July–Aug., 1980
1 thru 8 Marc L.Reed . . . . @8.00

MOONCHILD COMICS
Nicola Cuti, 1968
0 Nicola Cuti 35.00
2 Nicola Cuti 35.00
3 Nicola Cuti 35.00

MOONDOG
The Print Mint, March, 1970
1 All George Metzer 20.00
2 same 15.00
3 and 4 same . . . . @10.00

MORE ADVENTURES OF FAT FREDDY'S CAT
Rip Off Press, Jan., 1981
1 GiS 14.00

MOTOR CITY COMICS
Rip Off Press, April, 1969
1 RCr 180.00
2 RCr 140.00

Mr. Natural No. 3
© Kitchen Sink

Underground

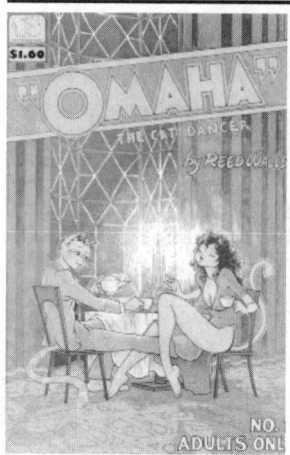

Omaha, The Cat Dancer #1
© Reed Waller

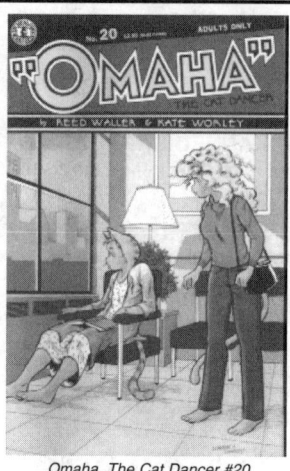

Omaha, The Cat Dancer #20
© Reed Waller

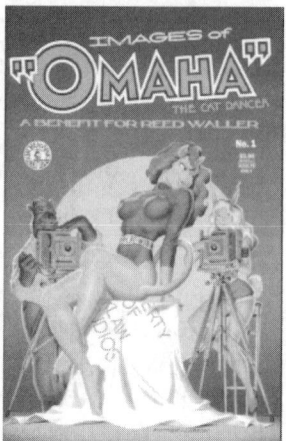

Images of Omaha #1
© Reed Waller

MOUSE LIBERATION FRONT
COMMUNIQUE #2, August, 1979
1 SRo, SCW, VMo,DKi; Disney's sues
Dan O'Neil's Air Pirates 15.00

MR. NATURAL
San Fransisco Comic Book Co., August, 1970
1 RCr 130.00
2 RCr 70.00
Kitchen Sink
3 RCr, (B&W) 35.00

NARD 'N' PAT, JAYZEY LYNCH'S
Cartoonists Cooperative Press, March, 1974
1 Jay Lynch. 15.00
2 Jay Lynch. 10.00
Kitchen Sink Press, 1972
3 . . . . 15.00

NEVERWHERE
Ariel Inc., Feb., 1978
1 RCo 25.00

NICKEL LIBRARY
Gary Arlington
1 1 pg heavy stock colored
  paper, Reed Crandall 5.00
2 Kim Deitch 2.25
3 Harrison Cady 2.25
4 Frank Frazetta 4.00
5 Will Eisner 4.00
6 Justin Green 2.25
7 C.C. Beck 4.00
8 Wally Wood 4.00
9 Winsor McCay 2.25
10 Jim Osborne 2.25
11 Don Towlley. 2.25
12 Frank Frazetta 4.00
13 Will Eisner 4.00
14 Bill Griffith 2.25
15 George Herriman 2.25
16 Cliff Sterrett 2.25
17 George Herriman 2.25
18 Rory Hayes & Simon Deitch . . . 2.25

19 Disney Studios 2.25
20 Alex Toth 2.25
21 Will Eisner 2.25
22 Jack Davis 3.00
23 Alex Toth 2.25
24 Michele Brand 2.25
25 Roger Brand 2.25
26 Arnold Roth 2.25
27 Murphy Anderson 2.25
28 Wally Wood 3.00
29 Jack Kirby 4.00
30 Harvey Kurtzman 3.00
31 Jay Kinney 2.25
32 Bill Plimpton 2.25
33 . . . . 2.25
34 Charles Dallas 2.25
35 thru 39 . . . . @2.25
40 Bill Edwards 2.25
41 Larry S. Todd 2.25
42 Charles Dallas 2.25
43 Jim Osborne 2.25
43 1/2 Larry S. Todd 2.25
44 Jack Jackson 2.25
45 Rick Griffin 2.25
46 Justin Green 2.25
47 and 48 Larry S. Todd. . . . . . . @2.25
49 Charles Dallas 2.25
50 Robert Crumb 3.00
51 Wally Wood 3.00
52 Charles Dallas 3.00
53 and 54 Larry S. Todd. . . . . . . @2.25
55 Charles Dallas 2.25
56 Jim Chase. 2.25
57 Charles Dallas 2.25
58 Larry S. Todd 2.25
59 Dave Geiser 2.25
60 Charles Dallas 2.25

ODD WORLD OF RICHARD CORBEN
Warren Publishing, 1977
1 84pgs paperback 20.00

O.K. COMICS
Kitchen Sink, June, 1972
1 and 2 Bruce Walthers . . . . . . @10.00

O.K. COMICS
O.K. Comic Company, 1972
1 Tabloid with comix, articles,
  reviews, nudie cuties photos . . 30.00

2 thru 18 . . . . @20.00

OMAHA THE CAT DANCER
Steel Dragon Press, 1984
1 RW,F:Omaha, Shelly, Chuck . . . 15.00
Kitchen Sink, 1986
1 RW. 10.00
2 RW 8.00
3 thru 5 . . . . @7.00
6 thru 10 . . . . @6.00
11 thru 20 . . . . @5.00
Spec.#0, 25th Anniv. Classic 15.00
Images of Omaha, RW benefit 8.00
Images No. 2 . . . . 7.00
TPB Collected Omaha #1, rep. . . . 15.00
TPB Collected Omaha #2, rep. . . . 13.00
TPB Collected Omaha #3, rep. . . . 13.00
TPB Collected Omaha #4, rep. . . . 13.00
TPB Collected Omaha #5, rep. . . . 13.00
Vol. 2, Fantagraphics, 1994
1 . . . . 5.00
2 . . . . 5.00

ORACLE COMIX
Thru Black Holes Comix Productions, Oct., 1980
1 and 2 Michael Roden. . . . . . . @5.00

PENGUINS IN BONDAGE
Sorcerer Studio/ Wayne Gibson, July, 1981
1 8pgs,Wayne Gibson 4.00

PHANTOM LADY
Randy Crawford, June, 1978
1 Sex funnies 5.00

PHUCKED UP FUNNIES
Suny Binghamton, 1969
1 ASp;insert bound in yearbook . 400.00

PINK FLOYD, THE
October, 1974
1 sold at concerts 35.00

PLASTIC MAN
Randy Crawford, May, 1977
1 Sex funnies,RandyCrawford . . . 10.00

PORK
Co-op Press, May, 1974
1 SCW 15.00

PORTFOLIO OF UNDERGROUND ART
Schanes & Schanes, 1980
1 SRo,SCW,VMo,RW and many others
13 loose sheets in folder, 32pg
book, 1200 signed & numb. . . 75.00

POWERMAN AND POWER MOWER SAFETY
Frank Burgmeir, Co.
Outdoor Power Equipment
1 VB; educational comic about power
mower safety 185.00

PROMETHIAN ENTERPRISES
Promethian Enterprises
Memorial Day, 1969
1 B:Jim Vadeboncuor editor 75.00
2 same 60.00
3 thru 5 . . . . @25.00

PURE ART QUARTERLY
John A. Adams, July, 1976
1 16pgs, All John A.Adams. 10.00
2 thru 5 same . . . . @10.00
6 thru 10 same . . . . @8.00
11 thru 14 same . . . . @6.00

QUAGMIRE COMICS
Kitchen Sink, Summer, 1970
1 DKi,Peter Poplaski 15.00

RAW
Raw Books, 1980
1 36pgs,10pgs insert 310.00
2 36pgs,20pgs insert 185.00
3 52pgs,16pgs insert 155.00
4 44pgs,32pgs insert,Flexi
disk record 125.00

R. CRUMB'S COMICS AND STORIES
Rip Off Press, 1969
1 RCr 125.00

RAWARARAWAR
Rip Off Press, 1969
1 GSh. 60.00

RED SONJA & CONAN "HOT AND DRY"
Randy Crawford, May, 1977
1 Sex funnies,Randy Crawford. . . . 7.00

REID FLEMING WORLD'S TOUGHEST MILKMAN
David E. Boswell, Dec., 1980
1 . . . . 6.00

RIP OFF COMIX
Rip Off Press, April, 1977
1 GiS,FSt,JsG,DSh 20.00
2 thru 5 GiS,FSt . . . . @12.00
6 thru 10 . . . . @6.00

ROWLF
Rip Off Press, July, 1971
1 RCo 55.00

RUBBER DUCK TALES
The Print Mint, March, 1971
1 Michael J Becker 20.00
2 Michael J Becker 15.00

S. CLAY WILSON TWENTY DRAWINGS
Abington Book
Shop Inc., 1967
N# (a),Cowboy(c) 500.00
  (b),Pirate(c) 475.00
  (c),Motorcyclist(c) 475.00
  (d),Demon(c) 475.00
  (e),Deluxe with all 4
  variations on same(c) with
  Gold Embossed Lettering . 675.00

SAN FRANCISCO COMIC BOOK
San Francisco Comic
Book Co., Jan.-Feb., 1970
1 . . . . 120.00
2 . . . . 25.00
3 . . . . 20.00
4 thru 6 . . . . @15.00

SAVAGE HUMOR
The Print Mint, 1973
1 . . . . 10.00

SAY WHAT?
Loring Park Shelter
Community Cartooning
Workshop, April, 1979
1 B:Charles T. Smith,editor,
various artists 10.00
2 thru 6 same . . . . @8.00

SCHIZOPHRENIA, CHEECH WIZARD
Last Gasp Eco-Funnies,
Jan., 1974
1 VB 30.00

SEX AND AFFECTION
C.P. Family Publishers, 1974
1 Sex Education for Children 10.00

SHORT ORDER COMIX
Head Press/Family Fun, 1973
1 50 cents,36pgs. 10.00
2 75 cents,44pgs 5.00

SKULL COMICS
Last Gasp, March, 1970
1 Horror,RHa 50.00
2 GiS,DSh,RCo 30.00
3 SRo,DSh,RCo 20.00
4 DSh,Lovecraft issue 20.00
5 SRo,RCo,Lovecraft issue 20.00
6 RCo,Herman Hesse 20.00

Slow Death #5 #3
© Last Gasp Funnies

SLOW DEATH FUNNIES
Last Gasp, April 1970
1 Ecological Awarness & Red
Border on (c) 50.00
2nd-4th Printings White
Border(c) 10.00
2 Silver(c);1st edition' 34 pgs . . . 100.00
2b Non Silver(c);Says 1st
Edition, 34 pgs. 20.00
2nd Amorphia Ad on pg 34 . . . . . . 6.75
3rd Yellow Skull on (c) 7.00
4th `Mind Candy For the Masses'
Ad on pg. 34 . . . . 7.00
5th $1.00(c) price 3.50
3 thru 5 . . . . @12.00
6 thru 10 . . . . @4.50

SMILE
Kitchen Sink, Summer, 1970
1 Jim Mitchell 15.00
2 Jim Mitchell 12.00
3 Jim Mitchell 11.00

Skull #6
© Last Gasp Funnies

Underground

All comics prices listed are for *Near Mint* condition.

SNARF
Kitchen Sink, Feb., 1972
1 DKi,editor,various artists 27.00
2 thru 5 same . . . . @15.00
6 thru 9 same . . . . @6.50

SNATCH COMICS
Apex Novelties, 1968
1 RCr,SCW 320.00
2 RCr,SCW 160.00
3 RCr,SCW,RW 80.00

SNATCH SAMPLER
Keith Green, 1979
n/n RCr,SCw,RW,RHa 35.00

SPACE INVADERS COMICS, DON CHIN'S
Comix World/Clay Geerdes, April, 1972
1 8pgs 8.00

SPASM!
Last Gasp Eco-Funnies, April, 1973
1 JJ 15.00

STONED PICTURE PARADE
San Francisco Comic Book Co., 1975
1 RCr,SRo,SCW,WE 25.00

SUBVERT COMICS
Rip Off Press, Nov., 1970
1 SRo 25.00
2 SRo 20.00
3 SRo 12.00

TALES OF SEX & DEATH
Print Mint, 1971
1 JsG,KDe.RHa,SRo 35.00
2 JsG,KDe.RHa,SRo 20.00

THRILLING MURDER COMICS
San Francisco Comic Book Co., 1971
1 SCW,KDe,RCr,SRo,Jim
Arlington,editor 32.00

2 (TWO)
Keith Green, Feb., 1975
1 SCW 10.00

VAMPIRELLA
Randy Crawford, June, 1978
1 Sex Funnies 7.00

VAUGHN BODE THE PORTFOLIO
Northern Comfort Com., 1976
1 VB,16pgs 125.00

VAUGHN BODE PORTFOLIO #1
Vaughn Bode Productions, 1978
1 VB,10 pgs 35.00

VAUGHN BODE'S CHEECH WIZARD, THE COLLECTED ADVENTURES OF THE CARTOON MESSIAH
Northern Comfort Com., 1976
1 VB,88pgs 55.00

VAUGHN BODE'S DEADBONE, THE FIRST TESTAMENT OF CHEECH WIZARD
Northern Comfort Com., 1975
1 VB 65.00

VIETNAM
N# 20pgs. Role of Blacks in
the War,TG Lewis 125.00

WEIRDO
Last Gasp Eco-Funnies, March, 1981
1 thru 3 RCr . . . . @12.00

WEIRDO, THE
Rodney Schroeter, Oct., 1977
1 B:Rodney Schroezer,1pg 6.00
2 88pgs 6.00
3 44pgs 6.00

WIMMEN'S COMIX
Last Gasp Eco-Funnies, Nov., 1972
1 All women artists&comix 15.00
2 thru 3 same . . . . @12.00
4 thru 7 same . . . . @8.00

WONDER WART-HOG AND THE NURDS OF NOVEMBER
Rip Off Press, Sept., 1980
1 GiS 20.00

WONDER WART-HOG, CAPTAIN CRUD & OTHER SUPER STUFF
Fawcett Publications, 1967
1 GiS,VB 25.00

YELLOW DOG
The Print Mint, May, 1968
1 4pgs,RCr 45.00
2 and 3 8pgs,RCr . . . . @30.00
4 8pgs,RCr,SCW 30.00
5 8pgs,RCr,SCW,KDe 30.00
6 thru 12 . . . . @25.00
13/14 52pgs RCr,Jay Lynch 12.00
15 Don Scheneker,editor 59.00

Zap #4 © Apex Novelties

16 . . . . 55.00
17 thru 24 . . . . @15.00

YOUNG AND LUSTLESS
San Francisco Comic Book Co., 1972
1 BG 20.00

YOUNG LUST
Company & Sons, Oct., 1970
1 BG,ASp 30.00
2 BG 15.00
3 BG,JsG,RCr,ASp 15.00
4 KDe,BG,SRo 10.50
5 BG,SRo 7.50
6 SRo,KDe 5.50

YOW
Last Gasp, April, 1978
1 BG 5.75
2 BG 4.75
Becomes:

ZIPPY
3 BG 6.50

ZAP COMIX
Apex Novelties, Oct., 1967
0 RCr 360.00
1 RCr 350.00
2 RCr,SCW 135.00
3 RCr,SCW,VMo,SRo 60.00
4 VMo,RW,RCr,SCW.SRo,GiS . . . 60.00
5 RW,GiS,RCr,SCW,SRo 50.00
6 RW,GiS,RCr,SCW,SRo 30.00
7 RW,GiS,RCr,SCW,SRo 20.00
8 RW,GiS,RCr,SCW,SRo 15.00
9 RW,GiS,RCr,SCW,SRo 20.00

CVA GRADING GUIDE

Grading comics is an objective art. This grading guide outlines the many conditions you should look for when purchasing comics, from the highest grade and top condition to the lowest collectible grade and condition. Your own comics will fall into one of these categories. A more complete description and our comments on comics grades can be found inside. We would like to point out, however, that no reader or advertiser is required to follow this or any other standard. All prices in Comics Values Annual are for comics in Near Mint condition. Happy collecting!

Mint: Perfect, pristine, devoid of any trace of wear or printing or handling flaws. Covers must be fully lustrous with sharply pointed corners. No color fading. Must be well centered. Many "rack" comics are not "Mint" even when new.

Near Mint: Almost perfect with virtually no wear. No significant printing flaws. Covers must be essentially lustrous with sharp corners. Spine is as tight as new. In older comics, minimal color fading is acceptable, as is slight aging of the paper. Most price guides, including CVA, quote prices in this grade.

Very Fine: Well preserved, still pleasing in appearance. Small signs of wear, most particularly around the staples. Most luster is readily visible. Corners may no longer be sharp, but are not rounded. Typical of a comic read only a few times and then properly stored.

Fine: Clean, presentable, with noticeable signs of wear. Some white may show through enamel around staples, and moderate rounding of corners. No tape or writing damage. Book still lies flat.

Very Good: A well worn reading copy with some minor damage such as creasing, small tears or cover flaking. Some discoloration may be evident, with obvious wear around the staples. Little luster remains, and some rolling of the spine may be seen when comic is laid flat on the table.

Good: A fully intact comic with very heavy wear. Tears, cover creases and flaking, and rolled spine will all be evident. No tape repairs present. Only very scarce or valuable issues are collected in this state.

The adjoining price table shows the prices for the other collectible grades which correspond to any "near mint" price given in this book.

Mint	Near Mint	Very Fine	Fine	Very Good
$6,000	$5,000	$3,500	$2,000	$1,000
4,800	4,000	2,800	1,600	800
3,600	3,000	2,100	1,200	600
2,400	2,000	1,400	800	400
1,800	1,500	1,050	600	300
1,200	1,000	700	400	200
1,080	900	630	360	180
960	800	560	320	160
900	750	525	300	150
840	700	490	280	140
780	650	455	260	130
720	600	420	240	120
660	550	385	220	110
600	500	350	200	100
570	475	332	190	95
540	450	315	180	90
510	425	297	170	85
480	400	280	160	80
450	375	262	150	75
420	350	245	140	70
390	325	227	130	65
360	300	210	120	60
330	275	192	110	55
300	250	175	100	50
270	225	157	90	45
240	200	140	80	40
210	175	122	70	35
180	150	105	60	30
150	125	87	50	25
120	100	70	40	20
114	95	66	38	19
108	90	63	36	18
102	85	59	32	17
96	80	56	32	16
90	75	52	30	15
84	70	49	28	14
78	65	45	26	13
72	60	42	24	12
66	55	38	22	11
60	50	35	2	10
54	45	31	18	9
48	40	28	16	8
42	35	24	14	7
36	30	21	12	6
30	25	17	10	5
24	20	14	8	4
22	18	12	7	4
21	17	11	7	4
18	15	10	6	3
17	14	9	5	3
16	13	9	5	3
15	12	8	5	2
14	11	7	4	2
12	10	7	4	2
11	9	6	4	2
10	8	5	3	1
9	7	5	3	1
7	6	4	3	1
6	5	4	2	1
5	4	3	2	0
4	3	2	1	0
3	2	2	0	0
2	1	0	0	0